time in 872. Of a prestigious family of which two Popes (Stephen IV and Sergius II) had originated, Adrian became cardinal of San Marco, Florence, in 842 and on 14 December 867 was elected Pope. He was chosen to fulfil this office as a compromise between two clerical groups: those in favour of and those against the conservation and implementation of Pope **Nicholas** I's policies. Adrian's gentle nature and advancing age meant that he would present few problems to either party. As he strove to enforce Nicholas' policies, papal power diminished and his pontificate was fraught with tensions. He was involved in serious disputes with **Anastasius the Librarian** and several German princes. These remained largely unsolved until his death. As Pope he tried to claim jurisdiction in the Balkans, but failed partly because of Adrian's decision to back **Cyril** and **Methodius**' mission to the Slavs. This eventually led to the Photian schism. Adrian died November–December 872 a wearied man,

Adrian III   Pope and saint, date of birth unknown (Rome), died near Modena, Italy, some time in 885. Lasting only sixteen months, he was Pope 17 May 884 – c. September 885. During this time Adrian implemented the policies of Pope **John III** rather than those of his predecessor, **Marinus I**. An exceptionally severe character, he is known to have had an official of the Lateran palace blinded and administered a dreadful punishment to a certain woman named Mary. Adrian met his death while on his way to Germany, where he was to speak to Emperor **Charles III** regarding a possible successor (Charles had no legitimate heir). Adrian's veneration was officially approved in 1891; feast day 8 July.

Adrian IV   Pope, born Nicholas Breakspear, Abbott's Langley, Herefordshire, England, some time between 1110 and 1120, died 1159. Famed for being the one and only Englishman to become Pope, Adrian was of a poor family. Though information regarding his father is scarce, he is believed to have abandoned his family to enter a monastery. Though Adrian wanted to join him, his father seemingly forbade it. Eventually Adrian went to France and here he was accepted to enter the Augustinian community of St Rufo. He became this community's abbot in 1135. On a trip to Rome, Pope **Eugene III** urged him to stay on as cardinal of Albano (c.1150). Between 1152 and 1154 he acted as papal envoy to Norway and Sweden and successfully resolved a turbulent ecclesiastical situation there. Following the death of **Anastasius IV** (4 December 1154), he was appointed bishop of Rome. His pontificate was fraught with problems and there were great conflicts between the Church and State. **Frederick I Barbarossa** was at the centre of these and after a cardinal was injured in Rome on Palm Sunday 1155, Adrian placed the city under an interdict. At a meeting between Barbarossa and Adrian (11 June 1155) Barbarossa reluctantly agree to recognize and submit to the pontiff's supreme authority. Despite his being made Roman Emperor, the city was again subjected to another battle. In the midst of his great efforts to quell the ecclesiastical-political problems surrounding him, Adrian died on 1 September 1159.

Adrian V   Pope, born Ottobono Fieschi in Genoa, Italy, 1205, died 1276 at the basilica of St Francis, Viterbo, Italy. A nephew of **Innocent IV**, Adrian was elected to the Papacy following his uncle's death. His appointment is remarkable since, at the time, he was not even an ordained priest. Prior to this though, he had successfully undertaken several ecclesiastical appointments: at Rheims, Notre-Dame, Parma and St Adrian. His tactful and diplomatic character was confirmed especially on his trip to England in 1265, where he resolved a dispute between King Henry III and his noblemen. He also asserted Roman jurisdiction over the Church in England. He was buried at the basilica of St Francis.

Adrian VI   Pope and church reformer, born Adrian Florensz Dedal at Utrecht, 2 March 1459, died 1523. After reading and teaching theology at the Louvain, he became university chancellor in 1497. A learned and devout man by nature, he was employed by Margaret of Burgundy in 1515 whose son he instructed. Adrian's pontificate ran from 9 January 1522 to 14 September 1523. To his own surprise, he was elected bishop of Rome after the death of **Leo X**. He had not foreseen this possibilty and though he felt ill-prepared for it, accepted the office as part of God's plan. A foreigner to Rome, his pontificate faced immediate problems; not only were **Francis I** of France and Emperor **Charles V** at war, but Rome had to try and cope with the Lutheran revolt. Adrian was the first Pope to contemplate and foster reform within the Church. Because of this, he faced hostility and misunderstanding on all sides. By the time he faced death, Adrian was a tired and lonely man who – despite almost single-handed efforts – was unable to bring unity to the Church, so leaving it open for attack from the Turks.

Adrian of Castello   Cardinal, born at Corneto in 1458, died in 1521. On his way to Scotland as Pope **Innocent VIII**'s representative in settling a dispute betweeen James III and his noblemen, Adrian stopped off at England (1488). Immediately he won the king's respect and was appointed his delegate in Rome. Also given the privilege of collecting Peter's Pence, he returned to England in 1489 to fulfil this duty. Adrian's ecclesiastical career escalated rapidly as in 1502 he was made bishop of Hereford and the following May was appointed cardinal by **Alexander VI**. In addition, he also held the post of diplomat to Henry VII and secretary of the pontiff's treasury. Subsequent to Alexander VI's death, Adrian became much involved in politics; this incited the anger of Julius II so much that Adrian moved to Venice and Trent in 1509. He was present at **Leo X**'s election (1513), but was later discovered as having a part in Cardinal Alfonso Petrucci's plan to poison him. Though he sought and received pardon from Leo, Adrian moved back to Venice. As a result of his involvement in the plans to kill the Pope, **Henry VIII** stripped him of his Peter's Pence privilege and on 5 July 1518 he was also demoted from being cardinal and bishop of Bath, England. Following Leo's death, Adrian would appear to have been assassinated while on his way to Rome in 1521.

Adrianus   Antiochene exegete, date of birth unknown, died 530. All that can be said with any great certainty regarding this figure is that he was of Syrian origins and spoke and wrote Greek fluently. Nothing else at all is known about him. If we take him to be the same person as the one to whom St **Nilus** (died *c.*430) wrote several letters, Adrianus was a monk and priest. He authored one influential work, renowned for being the first extant book to bear the title: 'Introduction to Holy Scripture'. This work is very precise and its text and content evinces the influence that the likes of **Theodore of Mopsuestia** and **Theodoret** of Cyrrhus had on his exegesis. **Photius** (820–89) deemed it 'useful for beginners' and Adrianus' name is present in a list of exegetes drawn up by **Cassiodurus**.

Adso of Montier-en-Der (Azo, Asso)   Benedictine writer and scholar, born at Jura, France, 925, died at sea, 992; also known as Azo, Asso and Hermericus. Influential in his own time, Adso was friends with **Abbo of Fleury**, Gerbert (later Pope **Sylvester II**) and **Adalbero of Rheims**. Originally a monk at Luxeuil, he went on to teach at Saint-Evre. He was abbot of two commmunities: firstly at Montier-en-Der (*c.*960) and then at Saint-Benigne (Dijon). Adso was a prolific hagiographer and writer, producing his famous *De Antichristo* and works on the lives of Sts **Frodobert**, Mansuetus, Basolus, Bercharius and Waldebert. Adso died while on a voyage to the Holy Land. He is buried at Cyclades.

Aduarte, Diego Francisco   Dominican bishop, missionary and writer, born at Zaragoza, Spain, 1569, died 1636 at Nueva Segovia. After taking his vows in 1587, Diego set off for the Philippines already ordained. His exceptional missionary spirit took him to Manila, Cambodia, Canton and Malacca. He did go to Cochin China, but there he faced many difficulties, which rendered vain his missionary efforts. He was deeply convinced of the need for missionary activity in the Far East and between 1603 and 1607 made two trips to Spain to bring back more missionaries with him. A devout and wise man, Diego was appointed bishop of Nueva Segovia in 1632, an office which he fulfilled with characteristic generosity and fairness. His main written work is *Historia de la Provincia del Santo Rosario de la Orden de Predicatores en Filipinas, Japon y China*. This two-volume work has been reprinted on several occasions. The coffin holding Diego's dead body was buried in very damp earth but, despite this, his body was later discovered completely intact.

Aelfric Grammaticus   Abbot of Eynsham and writer, born 950, died 1020. An exceptional scholar and writer, Aelfric received much of his education under **Ethelwold**, bishop of Winchester, and concerned himself with the moral and intellectual formation of diocesan priests. Ethelwold clearly held his pupil in high regard since he entrusted him with the abbotship of two communities; at Cerne (987) and at the newly founded Eynsham Monastery (c.1005). Aelfric did much of his writing at Cerne. From his works he emerges as a fervent Latinist and great observor of his time and culture. His works are, therefore, a source of important historical information. He was particularly popular among the Reformers for his translation of parts of the Old Testamant into English and for openly condemning the doctrine of Transubstantiation. A gifted writer, Aelfric was also asked to compose letters for the bishop of Sherborne and the archbishop of York.

Aelfric of Canterbury Saint and archbishop, date of birth unknown, died 16 November 1005. Originally a monk of Abingdon, Aelfric became abbot of St Alban's and bishop of Ramsbury and Wilton (c.990). Success in his ecclesiastical endeavours can be presumed since on Easter Sunday 995 he received his appointment as bishop of Canterbury and in 997 he received the pallium of **Gregory V**. Either Sigeric (Aelfric's predecessor) or Aelfric himself were responsible for removing diocesan clergy from Canterbury Cathedral in favour of monks. Aelfric was buried at Abingdon, but some time after 1067 his remains were transferred to St John's, Canterbury. His will is extant and there are references to him in various documents and chronicles of his time.

Aelfryth Saint, date of birth unknown, died Croyland 834. A hermit and virgin, Aelfryth (also known as Elfrieda, Etheldreda, Etheldritha) was one of King **Offa** of Mercia's daughters. It is commonly believed that she was to be married to St **Ethelbert**, King of East Anglia. He, under King Offa's orders, was killed c.790. Aelfryth took to the solitary life and led a life of prayer at Crowland Monastery. She outlived her father by some 38 years and is sometimes mistaken for her sister Aelfreda who was tragically assassinated. Feast day 2 August.

Aelred (Ailred) Saint, English abbot, spiritual writer and historian, born the son of a Saxon priest in Hexham, England in 1109, and died on 12 January 1166. He lived at the court of King **David I**, son of St **Margaret of Scotland**, joined the Cistercians at the recently founded abbey of Rievaulx, Yorkshire, in about 1133 and took charge of the newly founded abbey of Revesby, Lincolnshire, in 1143. He became abbot of Rievaulx in 1147, in which capacity he not only had charge of some 300 monks in the abbey but was head of all the Cistercian abbots in England and had to travel to visit them. He attended the general chapter of his Order in France and was present at the translation of the relics of **Edward the Confessor** in Westminster Abbey in 1163. He wrote a life of David of Scotland and of Edward. He also left many, very eloquently written sermons, very similar in style and spirit to those of **Bernard of Clairvaux**, at whose invitation he wrote his *Speculum Caritatis*. He suffered much physical pain in his own life and showed a devotion to the suffering humanity of Christ. His *De Spirituali Amicitia*, following Cicero's work, is a detailed discussion on friendship.

Aeonius of Arles Saint and bishop, date of birth unknown, died 500. Appointed bishop and metropolitan of the Diocese of Arles on 23 August 494, Aeonius kept this position for six years. On 29 September 500 he was, at his own request, succeeded by **Caesarius of Arles**. Whilst Aeonius was bishop he defined the diocese's boundary with Vienne and asserted its superiority. A great enthusiast of the monastic movement, Aeonius founded Chalon-sur-Saône with Caesarius and did much to help the spread of monasticism in France. Among his correspondents were Popes **Anastasius II** and **Symmachus** and also Ruricius I of Limoges. Feast day 18 August.

Aertnys, Jozef Theologian of the Congregation of the Divine Redeemer, born at Eindhoven, Holland, 15 January 1828, died at Wittem, Holland, 30 June 1915. Also known as Josef Aertinijs, he occupied the post of professor of moral theology at Wittem from 1860 to 1898 and simultaneously acted as theological consultant to bishops and priests of his diocese on canonical and moral matters. An exceptional theologian and scholar in his own right, Jozef wrote various works; one of which – *Compendium liturgiae sacrae* – is currently on its seventeenth reprint. In addition to publishing many articles on the moral issues of his day in various journals, Jozef was also a founder of the Neder-landse Katholiche Stemmen.

Afanasiev, Nicholas   Orthodox priest and theologian, born Odessa, Russia, 4 September 1893, died Paris, 4 December 1966. Emigrating from Russia in 1920, he taught at the Orthodox Theological Institute of St Sergius in Paris from 1930 until his death. His works have been very influential, especially in the field of ecclesiology. His book *The Lord's Supper* (1952) is a classic argument for a eucharistic ecclesiology. He also wrote on the Petrine ministry and was an indirect influence on the theology of Vatican II and, even more, on the contemporary Greek theologian Bishop John Zizioulas.

Affre, Denis Auguste   Archbishop of Paris, born 28 September 1793 at Saint-Rome-de-Tara, Paris, died at Paris, 27 June 1848. After receiving his education at the seminary of Saint-Sulpice, Paris, Denis was ordained 16 May 1818 and joined the Sulpicians. In 1819, he occupied the chair of professor of theology at Paris University, but already in 1820 an upsurge of Gallicanism impelled him to return to the diocese. He became chaplain to an orphanage and also worked on the periodical *La France chrétienne*. His ecclesiastical career escalated in this period as from 1822 to 1834 he went on from being Lucon diocesan vicar general to becoming the honorary vicar general of Paris. On 27 May 1840 he became the archbishop of Paris. Whilst occupying this position, he met with conflicts from religious congregations, but was nonetheless successful in founding a school for advanced studies of an ecclesiastical nature. A great defender of the freedom of intellectual and academic thought, he found himself in direct opposition to Louis-Philippe's government. After receiving a severe bullet wound in the rebellion of June 1848, Denis died leaving a legacy of intellectual works and fine pastoral letters.

Afonso I (Mvemba Nzinga)   King of Kongo, born c.1455 and baptized 4 June 1491, died 1543. He became king in 1506 after defeating his pagan brother in a battle inspired by a vision of St James. His Christian commitment was apparent in his attempts to improve his country educationally, religiously and medically. He relied on the Portu-guese to help him but their aid was half-hearted. Afonso tried to limit Portuguese slave trading and was almost killed by traders as a result. His frequent plea for priests often went unheard and so he encouraged lay teachers to evangelise. His son Henry was the first Roman Catholic bishop in sub-Saharan Africa.

Afra   Saint and martyr, date of birth unknown, died a martyr of the Diocletian persecution in 302. Patron of Augsburg Diocese, legend has it that she was originally a prostitute who repented and converted to Christianity. This fact is disputed though, since there is no historical information to back it up. The issue is further confused by the fact that on the Augsburg calendars she is said to be a virgin. Her life, *Conversio s Afrae*, was largely fictional and in later Passio she is said to have been martyred alongside SS Jovita and Faustinus. While the circumstances and date of her martyrdom are disputed, we can be sure that she did die a martyr's death. In 565 Venantius **Fortunatus** went to her grave and veneration of her is evident in the ancient manuscripts: *Vita s martini* and *Martryrol-ogium Hieronymianum*, the former being written by Fortunatus. A woman's body in a stone coffin found in the fifteenth century at St Afra's Church was placed under the saint's altar. Feast day 5 August.

Agagianian, Gregory Peter   Cardinal and patriarch to Catholic Armenians, born 18 September 1895 at Akhaltsikhe, Russian Georgia, died 16 May 1971, in Rome. An exceptionally intelligent and receptive child, Gregory left home at eleven to be taught at the Urbanian University, Rome. Here he became a Doctor of Philosophy, theology and canon law. Following his ordination in 1917, he taught at Rome for two years before dedicating himself to pastoral work among Armenian Catholics in Georgia. Returning to Rome, he was elected rector to the Pontifical Armenian College in 1932. He took up his position as patriarch of Catholic Armenia and Cilicia in 1937 and in 1946 Pope **Pius XII** appointed him cardinal. In the 1950s he occupied various roles on pontifical commissions, becoming so prominent a figure that many believed him a likely non-Italian successor to Popes Pius XII and **John XXIII**. Due to demanding responsibilities he had with the Holy See and since being made head of the Congregation for the Evangelization of Peoples, Gregory resigned as patriarch. During Vatican Council II, he was part of the commission that compiled *Ad Gentes* (a missionary decree). Gregory was an extraordinary example of Christian life and was tireless in his duties to the Holy See and his Armenian flock.

Agapetus I Pope and saint, born Rome, date of birth unknown, died Constantinople 22 April 536. Agapetus was of a noble family, his father being Gordianus, a priest assassinated in 502. Agapetus' great love of the intellectual life led him to erect a Christian university in Rome. His pontificate ran from 13 May 535 to 22 April 536 and as soon as he was appointed he had **Dioscorus** anathematized. A firm supporter of Chalcedonian faith, he would not allow penitent Arians to rise to clerical office, even against the wishes of Emperor **Justinian**. He was also responsible for approving Pope **John II**'s document stating that the Theopaschite formula was orthodox, himself adding that laypersons were not to be allowed to preach. Agapetus was especially popular in the East and was involved in anathematizing many Monophysites. A great advocate of orthodoxy, he died in Constantinople and on 20 September 536 his remains were brought to St Peter's Basilica, Rome.

Agapetus II Pope, born Rome, date of birth unknown, died 955. The successor of **Marinus II**, his pontificate dated from 10 May 946 to December 955. He was appointed as Pope by **Alberic II**, prince and ruler of Rome (*c.*905–54). Little of Agapetus' life is known. As pontiff he yielded political as well as ecclesiastical power and was particularly concerned with the promotion of monastic reform. It was Agapetus who granted Cluny its particular position and enlisted monks from Metz to come to St Paul's-without-the-walls in order that the correct order be restored. The restoration of the Roman Empire that occurred in 962 also owed some of its success to Agapetus. It was he who had granted **Otto I**'s brother Bruno the authority to form and define sees of the empire. Though a man of great intelligence and diplomatic prowess, his weakness was evinced at Alberic II's death. On his deathbed Alberic had summoned all the noblemen and clergy of Rome to himself, forcing them to swear that Octavian –

his bastard son – would become Pope on Agapetus' death. Agapetus consented to this and on 31 August 954, Octavian became prince of Rome and then, following Agapetus' death, its pontiff as **John XII**. Agapetus was buried at St John Lateran, Rome.

Agapios of Hierapolis Melkite bishop of Hierapolis in Osrhoene (Manbij, north-east Syria). His Arabic name was Mahbub ibn Qustantin and he was a contemporary of **Eutychius of Alexandria** (877–940); he died after 941. He composed in Arabic a universal history from the creation of the world to his own time, entitled *The Book of the Title* (Kitab al-Unwan). Although the original work ended in 941, in its surviving form it extends only to 776, or 777, the second year of the caliphate of Al-Mahdi. The history relies, uncritically, on much apocryphal and popular legend in its treatment of ancient Christianity, but he also uses the *Church History* of **Eusebius of Caesarea**, which he cites. For later ecclesiastical and profane history, he uses Syrian sources such as the Greek *World Chronicle* of the Maronite Theophilos of Edessa (died 785), to explain the downfall of the dynasty of the Umayyads and the rise of the Abbasids. The history preserves fragments of otherwise lost works, of which the most important are his list of the Eastern metropolitans, and his references to the famous text of Papias of Hierapolis of Phrygia, concerning the four Gospels. In turn, the work of Agapios was a source for the *Chronicle* of Michael I, the Syrian.

Agapitus *see* Felicissimus and Agapitus

Agassiz, Jean Louis Rudolphe Swiss naturalist and geologist, born Motier, 28 May 1807, died Cambridge, Massachusetts, 12 December 1873. The son of cultured Protestant parents, his father a parson, he was brought up in simplicity and poverty. He studied medicine and natural history, especially botany, at Zurich, Heidelberg and Munich. He was led into ichthyological pursuits through the classification of freshwater fish in Brazil by J. B. Spix and C. F. P. von Martius. Agassiz followed their research with his own into the history of fishes in Lake Neuchatel, and a prospectus of a *History of the Freshwater Fishes of Central Europe* in 1830. He was professor of natural history at Neuchatel in 1832. The foundation of his world fame was laid with his five-volume *Recherches sur les poissons fossiles* (1833–44). He was assisted in further research by the British Association, awarded, in 1836, the Wollaston medal for fossil ichthyology, and elected to the Royal Society in 1838. He also published *Nomenclator Zoologicus*, a classified list, with references, of all names employed in zoology for genera and groups. Appointed professor of zoology and geology at Harvard University, 1846. Published four-volume *Contributions to the Natural History of the United States* (1857–62). Despite his extensive knowledge of natural history, it is remarkable that Agassiz steadily rejected the doctrine of evolution from first to last, and affirmed his belief in independent creations.

Agatha   Saint, virgin and martyr, patroness of Catania, in Sicily. Died in the Decian persecution (possibly in 250). According to legend, she was sent to a brothel to induce her to renounce her faith. She was tortured by rods, rack and fire; her breasts were cut off, but she was miraculously healed by a vision of St Peter; she died of new cruelties the next day. Her cult spread throughout the Church. Her name is in the first eucharistic prayer, and in all the martyrologies, both Greek and Latin. She is credited with preserving Catania from successive eruptions of Mount Etna. She is the patroness of wet-nurses, bell-founders and jewellers. In art, her emblem is usually a dish on which her severed breasts repose, and a knife, or shears, in the other. Palermo and Catania both claim to be her birthplace. Feast day 5 Feburary.

Agatho   Saint, Pope, born Palermo, Sicily, *c*.577, elected 27 June 678, died 10 January 681. He had been a monk, and spoke Greek as well as Latin. His election to the Papacy was speedily ratified by the imperial exarch at Ravenna; he supported the Sixth General Council convened by **Constantine IV** Pogonatus in 680 against the Monothelites, at which was asserted, in explicit agreement with Agatho's letters, the orthodox doctrine of two wills and operations in Christ. His short reign was thus important for the abandonment of Monothelitism by the Byzantine government and the resultant reopening of amicable relations between the Holy See and Constantinople. He upheld Bishop **Wilfrid** of York's appeal to Rome against the unexpected division by **Theodore**, archbishop of Canterbury,

of his see, and restored him to York. He also furthered the spread of the Roman liturgy in England. He was a kindly man, loved by all for his cheerful good humour, and generous to his clergy even though he was desperately short of funds. Buried in St Peter's, he came to be venerated in the Eastern as well as the Western Church. Feast day 10 January.

Agazzari, Agostino   Born Siena, 2 December 1578, died there 10 April 1640. Composer of baroque church music and madrigals, and a theorist of renown. He was maestro di capella at the German College in Rome, 1602, and at the Roman Seminary in 1606. He is thought to have been maestro at Siena cathedral from *c*.1630 until his death. His treatise *Del sonare sopra il basso* (1607) was influential in how to accompany an ensemble from an unfingered bass. His treatise *La musica ecclesiastica* (1638) discusses decrees of the Council of Trent. In his own sacred compositions he employed baroque techniques of monody and the *concertato* style. He is seen as a transition figure, however, who drew on the Roman conservative tradition and its *stile antico* techniques. In addition to religious music he composed an early opera, the pastoral drama *Eumelio*, performed at the Rome Seminary in 1606. General books of sacred music and secular madrigals survive.

Agil (Agile, Aile, Aygul)   Saint, abbot and missionary, born Franche-Comte, *c*.583, died Rebais *c*.650. Received in infancy the blessing of St **Columbanus** after which he became, in 590, an oblate at Luxeuil Abbey. He remained there and accompanied St **Eustace**, successor to St **Columbanus**, to Bavaria in 612. He was designated bishop of Langres in 628, but must have refused the dignity since no record of the election remains. He became first abbot of Rebais, and was consecrated in the presence of Dagobert I at Clichy in 636, at which time the king granted the abbey a charter of immunity conceding the privilege of following the rule of St **Benedict** and of St **Columbanus** in the manner of Luxeuil, i.e. the compromise rule practised by St Walderbert since 629. Miracles operated by Agile are recounted by the monks in two volumes in the eleventh and twelfth centuries, in the second of which is mentioned a fountain whose waters healed the sick. Agile was buried at St Peter's church, Rebais, and a grave with water fountain was erected there in the thirteenth century. Feast day 30 August.

Agilulf of Cologne Saint, bishop of Cologne, died c.750. He became bishop of Cologne after 745, supported the reforms of St **Boniface** and attended the Frankish synod of 747. The cultus of St Agilulf flourished after 1062 when Archbishop **Anno II** of Cologne translated the relics from the abbey of Malmedy to St Maria ad Gradus in Cologne, where they remained until their removal to the cathedral in 1846. The *Passio sancti Agilolfi*, composed before 1062, indicates that he was a simple monk and martyred by the Neustrians at Ambleve (Amel) on 31 March 716. However, there has been some confusion with others named Agilulf. He may have been wrongly identified with the martyr Agilulf (died March 716), and with the Benedictine monk Agilulf, said to have been abbot of Stavelot-Malmedy and bishop of Cologne after 745. Written accounts in the *Passio sancti Agilolfi*, and the *Miracula sancti Qurini*, written at Malmedy late in the eleventh century, contain references which do not correct the inaccuracies of identity. Feast day 9 July.

Agnelli, Giuseppe Italian Jesuit writer of catechetical and devotional works, born Naples, 1 April 1621, died Rome, 8 September 1706. He entered the Society in 1637 and was successively professor of moral theology and rector of several Jesuit colleges, including Montepulciano, Macerata and Ancona, where he was also consultor of the Inquisition of the March of Ancona. His principal writing, *Il Catechismo Annuale* (Macerata, 1657), is an adaptation for parish priests containing an explanation of the Gospel for every Sunday of the year. He also wrote four commentaries on the Exercises of St **Ignatius** and a ten-day retreat for Jesuits about to make profession, as well as a collection of meditations for a triduum and sermons for Advent and Lent. He passed the last thirty years of his life at the Society's house in Rome, where he died.

Agnellus of Pisa Blessed, founder of the English Franciscan province, born at Pisa, c.1194, died at Oxford, 3 March 1232. He was received into the Friars Minor at Pisa by St **Francis** himself, who sent him to Paris c.1217 to found a convent. Though still a deacon, Francis despatched him to England in 1224. He established friaries at Canterbury and Oxford and was ordained priest before 1229 at the urging of his superior. The friars were received everywhere with enthusiasm and **Matthew Paris** says that Agnellus was on familiar terms with the king, Henry III, who built churches for them and granted them land in aid of their foundation at Oxford. There he engaged **Robert Grosseteste** to teach, which helped Oxford to rise to a position equal to that of Paris as a centre of learning. He was politically influential in the conflict between Henry and the Earl Marshal. His cultus was confirmed by **Leo XIII** in 1892 and his feast is celebrated by the English Franciscans on 10 September. Feast day 13 March.

Agnes Saint, virgin and martyr, died c.302. One of the most celebrated Roman martyrs at the end of the persecution of Diocletian. Her name figured already in the *Deposito Martyrium* of 354. The basilica erected in her honour in the via Nomentana c.350 is counted among the Constantinian foundations and was embellished or restored by successive popes. Pope **Damasus** had engraved for her in c.385 an inscription, of which the original marble is still extant. St **Ambrose** and the poet Prudentius both sang her praises. Her name occurs in the first eucharistic prayer, and, as a special patroness of chastity, she is one of the most popular of saints. Early legends of her martyrdom vary considerably, and nothing certain can be deduced as to the manner of her death. We do know, however, that she was a young girl of twelve or thirteen when decapitated, after refusing marriage and resisting all attempts to make her lose her virginity. Her head, brought to the Lateran in the ninth century, is preserved in the Sancta Sanctorum of the pontifical palace. In art she is represented with a lamb, and the archiepiscopal pallium is made from the wool of two lambs, blessed each year in her basilica, on her feast. Feast day 21 February.

Agnes of Assisi Saint, Poor Clare abbess, born Assisi, 1197, and died there 27 August 1253. Younger sister of St **Clare**, whom she joined, aged sixteen, at the Benedictine convent of San Angelo di Panzo, and where she heroically resisted family opposition. St **Francis** gave Agnes the habit, as she desired, and sent her and Clare to San Damiano. When the Benedictines of Montecelli at Florence asked to become Poor Clares, Francis sent her to them as abbess, c.1219. From there she opened houses at Padua, Venice and Mantua. Agnes firmly upheld her sister in her long struggle for the privilege of complete poverty. She returned to San Damiano in 1253, where she witnessed the death of Clare, dying herself three months later. She was buried there until 1260, when her body was translated, with Clare's, to the new church of Santa Chiara at Assisi. Her iconography sometimes includes the Christ child of whom she is said to have had a vision. Feast day 16 November.

Agnes of Bohemia   Blessed, Poor Clare abbess, born Prague, 1205, died Prague, 2 March 1282. Of royal blood, descendant of **Wenceslas** the Holy ('Good King Wenceslas'), daughter of Ottokar, King of Bohemia, and Constantia of Hungary (St **Elizabeth of Hungary** was her first cousin). She was educated by Cistercian nuns at Trebnitz in Silesia. She was betrothed as a child, but resisted strongly and, with help from **Gregory IX**, was able subsequently to appeal against the marriages proposed for her to, among others, Henry III of England and Emperor **Frederick II** of Austria. Having established her right to freedom, Agnes consecrated herself and her possessions wholly to God. She built a convent in Prague for the Friars Minor, she endowed a great hospital for the poor staffed by the Brothers of the Cross and a convent for Poor Clares; she herself received the veil in 1236. Gregory IX induced her, with great difficulty, to become abbess and she obtained the same concession as St **Clare** to embrace absolute poverty. Four letters from St Clare to Agnes as well as personal articles are extant and reserved as sacred relics. Her cultus was confirmed by **Pius IX** and is general throughout Bohemia and Moravia. Feast day 2 March.

Agnes of Poitiers   Saint, abbess. She died c.588. She was brought up as the adopted daughter of St **Radegunda** whom she followed into her monastery, where the foundress designated her first abbess, and where she was consecrated in that office by St Germain of Paris in 561. Around 570, she accompanied Radegunda to Arles to study, before adopting the rule of St **Caesarius**. In 573, Radegunda, seeking from several bishops confirmation of her institution, insisted that authority should rest with Agnes alone. She was replaced in 589 following on a revolt by some of the nuns. Her saintly character is commemorated by the poet Venantius **Fortunatus**, who called her his 'sister', and who was also a correspondent of her mother. Agnes died shortly after Radegunda and her relics are preserved in the church of St Radegunda, a place of popular pilgrimage. Feast day 13 May in Poitier.

Agnesi, Maria Gaetana   Mathematician, linguist and philosopher, born Milan, 16 May 1718, died Milan, 9 January 1799. One of 23 children in a cultured family, she had mastered eight languages before her thirteenth year; two years later she declaimed before a circle of some of the most learned men in Bologna a series of theses on the most abstruse philosophical questions, records of which were published in 1738. Being of a retiring disposition, however, Maria found these displays uncongenial and, from her twentieth year, lived in a retirement almost conventual, avoiding all society and devoting herself entirely to the study of mathematics. She published in 1748 *Le Instituzione Analitiche*, a precise summary of the mathematical knowledge of the time, which was translated into French by d'Autelmy at Paris in 1755, and into English by John Colson at Cambridge in 1801. Mme Agnesi also wrote a commentary on the *Traité analytique des sections coniques* of the Marquis de l'Hôpital, which was highly praised, but not published. She was appointed by Pope **Benedict XIV** to the chair of mathematics and natural philosophy at Bologna in 1750. She joined the austere order of the Hospice Trivulzio, a home for aged and sick poor at Milan, and there ended her days.

Agobard of Lyons   Archbishop and reformer, born Spain, 769, died Lyons, 6 June 840. Consecrated coadjutor to Leidrad in 813, he succeeded to the see in 816. Little is known of his early life. He pursued the same rigorous policy as his predecessor, who had been one of **Charlemagne**'s most active agents in the reformation of the Church. His opposition to the schemes of the empress Judith, and his support for **Lothair I** and Pippin against their father **Louis I**, led to his deposition at the Council of Thionville and to his exile in Italy in 835. His position was given to his opponent, **Amalarius of Metz**, but he was reconciled to Louis and reinstated in 837. Agobard was a versatile scholar whose works were marked by much originality. He attacked the excessive veneration of images, trial by ordeal, belief in witchcraft and 'the absurd opinion of the vulgar concerning hail and thunder', that it was due to magic. His theological writings include a treatise against the Adoptianist heresy of Felix of Urgel, and *De insolentia Judaeorum*, against the Jews. Agobard was one of the greatest prelates of his day; he played an important role in the Carolingian Renaissance and, though ignored during the Middle Ages, his works were rediscovered in 1605. He was revered as a saint in Lyons and, though his cult is disputed, his life does not lack grandeur. Feast day 6 June.

Agostini, Paolo Italian composer of the colossal baroque; born Vallerano, *c.*1593, died Rome, 3 October 1629. Studied under his father-in-law, G. B. Nanino, as we learn from the dedication in the third and fourth books of his Masses; he in turn taught Francesco **Foggia**, who became his son-in-law. Agostini succeeded Ugolini as maestro di capella at St Peter's from February 1626, until his death. His musical compositions, numerous and of great merit, include Masses, psalms, magnificats and motets and a specially admired *Agnus Dei* for eight voices. Most of his works are preserved in the Vatican and Corsini libraries.

Agreda, María Fernández Coronel Poor Clare and abbess, known in religion as Sor Maria de Jesus, born at Agreda, on the borders of Navarre and Aragon, 2 April 1602, died there, 24 May 1665. Her family was much influenced by the ecstatic piety of Spain in that age. From childhood she was favoured by ecstasies and visions, and made a vow of chastity at eight years; her apparent lack of intelligence was piously accounted for by extreme humility. When she was fifteen the whole family entered religion and she established a Franciscan nunnery, with her mother and sister, in the family house at Agreda. Maria became abbess at the age of 25, and remained in office for life except for a period of three years. She was much esteemed by Philip IV with whom she corresponded, the letters

being invaluable as illustrations for the second part of his reign. She was the author of a controversial work called *Mystical City of God*, an extraordinary book full of apocryphal history, visions and scholasticism, which aroused considerable opposition in the Sorbonne, particularly the chapter on the Immaculate Conception, although it is said that the translator misunderstood the Spanish text in many places. The Inquisition took notice of her, condemned the book and placed it on the Index in 1681, but a condemnatory decree was suspended later in the year, following a request from the king. The work was eventually approved in 1729.

Agricius of Trier Saint, bishop, died in 329. He probably succeeded St Paternus as bishop of Trier. He is known to have taken part in the Council of Arles in 314, with the exorcist Felix. According to an anonymous *Life of St Maximinus*, Agricius was his master and, on the advice of an angel, designated him as his successor in 329, which date seems to mark the end of his life. An eleventh-century legend makes him Patriarch of Antioch prior to his transfer to Trier at the request of the Empress **Helena**, who made him a gift of several relics of the Passion, including the so-called 'Holy Tunic of Trier' and the bones of St Matthias, which she was said to have recovered from the Holy Land. However this and other such stories about his life away from Trier would appear to be apocryphal. Feast day 13 January.

Agricola, Alexander Franco-Flemish composer, born Flanders *c.*1446, died Valladolid, 1506. His career was spent in the service of French and Italian royalty and aristocracy, mostly the latter, at Milan, Florence and with the Aragonese court at Naples; and briefly at Cambrai and on several occasions for the French royal chapel. During a visit to Spain with the court of Philip the Handsome, Duke of Burgundy and King of Castile, he died, apparently of the plague. He wrote Masses and motets, and other liturgical items, which, in terms of both quality and quantity, have been ranked on a level with those of **Compère** and **Brumel**. His songs and instrumental pieces were widely known. Lively, syncopated and decorative melodic lines were a feature of much of his work.

Agricola, Georgius (Georg Bauer) Physician,

scholar, contemporary of **Erasmus**, born Glauchan, Saxony, 24 March 1490, died Chemnitz, 21 November 1555. He studied the humanities and theology at Leipzig, where he obtained a bachelor of arts degree in classics, and taught Latin and Greek at Zwickau until 1520; he took a medical degree at Ferrara in 1526. In Italy he met Erasmus and they became lifelong friends. He settled as a physician at Joachimsthal in the Bohemian Erz mountains, an important mining centre. His pharmacological interests prompted him to undertake a thorough study of metallurgy, whence his famous *Bermannus sive de re metallica* (1530). A manuscript of this dialogue was sent to Erasmus who appreciated its value and originality and suggested that it be published. He was appointed town physician in Chemnitz in 1531, where he prospered from investments in various mines and smelters. He was a loyal Catholic and, even though all of Chemnitz had gone over to the Lutheran creed with the advent of the Reformation, he was elected mayor for the years 1546–7, 1551 and 1553. Agricola pursued his scholarly work and with Erasmus' support published, through the Froben Press in Basle, *De mensemis et ponderibus* (1533); *De ortu et causis subterraneorum* (1546) and, his crowning achievement, *De re metallica* (1556). Agricola also published medical works, amongst which *De peste* (1544) had a certain success. He was buried in Zeitz, seven miles from Chemnitz, because of the theological feeling against him there.

Agricola, Rudolphus Frisius (Roelof Huysman) Dutch scholar, humanist and educator, contemporary of **Erasmus**. He was born at Baflo, near Groningen, 17 February 1444, the natural son of Hendrick Vries, abbot of the Benedictine house at Selwert. He studied at Groningen, Erfurt, Cologne and Louvain, where he graduated as master of arts. He perfected his Latin style, especially in poetry, at Pavia and Ferrara, and achieved proficiency in Greek. He was appointed professor at Heidelberg and for three years delivered lectures there and at Worms on the literature of Greece and Rome. Agricola belonged to the second generation of German humanists who prepared the way for Erasmus and other critics, who are full of his praises. He moved to Ferrara, where he was organist in the court of the Duke Ercole d'Este, and translated many works from Greek into Latin,

once even being credited with Erasmus' translations of Euripides. He returned to Germany in 1479 and, at Dillingen, completed his most important work *De inventione dialectica*, an influential study of the proper place of logic in rhetorical studies. He returned to Groningen as town secretary (*scriba et orator*), but was not content with his position. After much delay, he joined Johan von Dalberg, bishop of Worms, at Heidelberg in 1484. Here he lectured, learnt Hebrew and wrote *De formando studio* (1484), a defence of humanistic studies. He accompanied Dalberg to Rome for an audience with **Innocent VIII**. On the return journey Agricola fell ill; he died at Heidelberg, 27 October 1485 of the quartian fever and, as Erasmus recalled in the colloquy *Exequiae seraphicae*, was buried in the Franciscan habit.

Agrippa von Nettesheim, Heinrich Cornelius German writer, soldier, physician and, by common reputation, a magician; contemporary of **Erasmus**, born at Cologne, 14 September 1486, died Grenoble, 21 February 1535. Details of his early life are somewhat obscure, but he appears to have obtained a knowledge of eight languages, was educated at Cologne, Paris (law, medicine, theology) and at Pavia. In 1509, he taught theology at Dole and Cologne; he was syndic (town orator) at Metz; physician at Geneva, Freiburg and Lyons; archivist and historiographer to **Charles V**. He was openly interested in theosophy and magic, and in an important work, *De occulta philosophia*, defended magic by which men may come to a knowledge of nature and of God; and it contains Agrippa's idea of the universe with its three worlds, or spheres. In his other major work, which circulated in manuscript for many years, *De incertitudine et vantitate scientiarum atque declamatio* (1530), he emphasizes the tension between human knowledge and the word of God. Agrippa denounces the accretions which had grown around the simple doctrines of Christianity, and wishes for a return to the primitive belief of the early Church. The furore created by the *De vanitate* and its attacks on scholastic theology forced Agrippa to flee to Cologne. From there he travelled to Bonn and finally back to Lyons, where he was not favourably received. He died in poverty at Grenoble. He had married three times and fathered seven children; his last marriage ended in divorce. Although Erasmus was not interested in magic and the occult, Agrippa was from an early age his admirer and shared both in his desire for a Christianity founded on the Bible and on the Fathers of the Church, and in his dislike of scholastic theologians. Though charged with heresy and inclining toward Luther, Agrippa refused to abandon his Catholic faith.

Aguado, Pedro de   Spanish chronicler of the conquest of Venezuela and Colombia, born at Castile in 1538 and died, probably at Bogotá, c.1609. He took the Franciscan habit when very young. In 1560, he accompanied to America, with several other friars minor, the conquistador Quesada, and became the first provincial of his order at Santa-Fe de Bogotá in New Grenada. As provincial he went to Spain in 1573, where he was granted permission to publish his chronicle *Recopilacion Historial*, the first history written of the country; it was not however published until 1906, when a partial version of the first part was published in Bogotá. In 1913 and 1915, the second part was published in Caracas and the entire work under its original title in 1956. The manuscript, dedicated to Philip II, is preserved in two large volumes in the Royal Academy of History in Madrid.

Aguesseau, Henri François d'   Chancellor of France, born Limoges, 27 November 1668, died Paris, 5 February 1751. He had a solid literary, moral and religious upbringing, and studied the law under Dornat, whose ideas inspired his juridical writings and his legislative work. He was early initiated into affairs by his father, Henri, the intendant of Limousin, Guyenne and Languedoc, and in 1685 was called to Paris as councillor of state. François was brought up on religious principles deeply tinged with Jansenism. He was appointed, at 21, one of the three advocates-general to the parliament of Paris, and became the first great master of forensic eloquence in France. In 1700, he was appointed procurator-general and gained the greatest popularity by his defence of the rights of the Gallican Church in the Quietist troubles and in those connected with the Papal Bull, *Unigenitus*, in which matter he opposed the king, **Louis XIV**, refusing its registration. His disgrace was only averted by the king's death. He was made chancellor by the regent, Orléans, in 1717. An able magistrate, he did not, however, possess the political

qualities necessary for the major social reforms required, and he was exiled to Fresnes in 1717. Recalled by Law in 1720, he surprised by approving the registration of the Bull by the Grand Council; exiled again to Fresnes in 1722, for having battled with Law and embarrassed Jean Domat, he turned to religious and philosophical writing. However, he received the great seals of the office of chancellor in 1737 and became, upon the death of cardinal **Andre-Hercule Fleury** in 1743, the most important person in parliament, adding to his office of chancellor, the presidency, in the absence of the king, of the Council of Finance and that of Reports. He resigned in 1750 for reasons of health. He was a man of considerable dignity of character who refrained from politics and whose most lasting contribution was to the project of **Charles-Joachim Colbert** to revise and reform the whole corpus of legislation into one structure. He based himself on the work of Dornat, and his correspondence was considerable on all matters concerning ordinances, testaments, the Code Louis and on Privy Council procedures. However, he made no reforms, and accomplished no really definitive work.

Aguiar y Seixas, Francisco   Bishop of Michoacan, and archbishop of Mexico (1682–9), born at Betanzos in Gallicia (date unknown), died in Mexico City, 1698. He was admitted to the court of Audrade y Sotomayor, archbishop of St James of Compostella, and then as a student at the college of Fonseca, where he was later professor of philosophy; he was also a member of the faculty of the University of Salamanca. He was proposed as bishop of Michoacan as 'priest, doctor of theology'. His prudence and virtue were known to Pope **Innocent XI**, who sent him to Manila to resolve a dispute about jurisdictions. He set about his duties in Mexico with zeal and charity, devoting himself to all the needs of his diocese: building churches, convents, a mental hospital for deranged women, a seminary, schools and a college. In the face of calamities which desolated his diocese – plague and famine – he showed great piety, abnegation and love for the suffering. In 1692, the people of Mexico City revolted against the governor, burnt his palace and were determined on all-out war. Mgr Aguiar was able to restore calm and bring peace to the troubled land. He was a model prelate and father of his people. He was reburied in the cathedral 22 years after his death. His virtue was such that he was popularly proposed for the honour of beatification and the documentation attesting to this is conserved in the archives of the archbishop's palace.

Aguilar, Nicolás Secular priest and revolutionist, born at Tonacatepeque, El Salvador, 15 December 1741, died San Salvador, 12 September 1818. He studied under the Jesuits in Guatemala and was ordained in 1767. He became pastor, in a competition, of San Salvador. In 1811, he directed an uprising against the unpopular governor Don Antonio Gutierrez Ulloa. The insurrection failed through bad planning; he subsequently, from the pulpit, urged the populace to be obedient to the captive king, Ferdinand VII. He performed his duties as pastor conscientiously until his death, but he was inconsistent, sometimes haranguing the crowds to rise up in arms, other times trying to subdue them, preaching love of neighbour and pardon of one's enemies. He directed a new uprising in 1814, but that also failed. He was very bitter during his last years because of the treatment of his brothers, exemplary priests and patriots, one of whom was deported and the other, who was blind, imprisoned.

Aiblinger, Johann Kaspar German church composer, scholar and conductor, born 23 February 1779 at Wasserburg, Bavaria, died Munich, 6 May 1867. He studied first at the monastery of Tegernsee and at the university at Landshut (1800). He travelled and studied at Bergamo, under Richard Mayr, and at Milan, and co-founded the Odeon Institute in Venice. Recalled to Munich in 1819, he became kapellmeister of the Italian Opera there, and when that theatre closed, he was named director of the court chapel. He returned to Italy in 1833 to collect ancient and church music, now in the Munich State Library. Other than an unsuccessful opera, Rodrigo and Ximene in 1821 (based on Le Cid), and three ballets, he composed only religious music, in almost every medium, which was highly appreciated. His compositions, however, were thought to be unequal, sometimes too dry and, without transition, suddenly too sentimental. He was much regarded by church musicians of his time for the welding of Renaissance and contemporary techniques.

Aichinger, Gregor German priest, organist and baroque composer, born at Regensburg in 1564, died 1 January 1628, at Augsburg. Born a Protestant, he entered Ingolstadt University, then under strong Jesuit influence, in 1578. He turned to music and was taken up by the Fugger family (the international bankers), who sent him to Italy where he studied the Venetian style under Giovanni **Gabrieli**. He converted to Roman Catholicism and returned to Germany in 1588, holding various musical positions and benefices in churches in Augsburg; visited Perugia, Venice and Rome, 1598–1601, and took holy orders in 1600. His religious choral works are among the finest of his time; he was one of the first Germans to use the basso continuo, a baroque innovation. His music is distinguished by harmonic richness without excessive chromatic effect, and his compositions generally are a mastery of vocal scoring, structure and tonal texture. He died of the plague while a priest at St Gertrude, leaving a library which showed a wide range of interests in geography, philosophy, history and botany, as well as music and religion.

Aidan of Lindisfarne Saint, monk of Iona and first bishop of Lindisfarne, born Ireland, died at Bamborough, 651. At the request of St **Oswald**, king of Northumbria, he was sent to revive the missionary work of **Paulinus** who had failed to transform 'the rude character and indocile disposition of the English'. Consecrated bishop in 635, Oswald bestowed on him the episcopal seat of the isle of Lindisfarne (Holy Island) in the North Sea, accessible to the shore at low tide, facing the royal residence at Bamborough. The Christian practices taught by Aidan were those of the Celtic Church, and his see was referred to as the English Iona. He carefully educated a group of twelve English boys to be the future leaders of their people, among them St **Chad**. According to **Bede**, almost the sole source of knowledge about the saint, Aidan's asceticism and gentleness won rapid success for his mission, exhibiting such apostolic activity and having such great influence as to be referred to as the apostle of Northumbria. Feast day 31 August.

Aiguani, Michele (Auguani, Augriani), Commonly known as **Michael of Bologna** Carmelite theologian, born Bologna, c.1320, died Bologna, 16 November 1400. He studied Scripture and theology at Paris, taught theology at Bologna and was among the most highly regarded of early Carmelite schoolmen. Michael was elected provincial of his own province of Bologna, vicar-general of the Order in 1380, prior-general in 1381 until 1386, when **Urban VI** removed him from office, probably because his loyalty to the Pope was in doubt, but he was exonerated by **Boniface IX**, who made him vicar-general of Bologna in 1395. Many of his manuscripts are extant, amongst which are his chief works: *Lectura Sententiarum* (Milan, 1510), *Lectura super Psalterio* (1524).

Aigulf of Lerins (Aygulphe) Saint, abbot of Lerins, born at Blois, c.630, died c.674. At the age of 20 he joined the recently founded Benedictine abbey of Fleury-sur-Loire (St Benoît-sur-Loire). Abbot Mummolus is reported to have sent him, in 652, to Monte Cassino, ravaged by the Lombards, to bring back the remains of St **Benedict**. Having benefited from a miraculous indication as to the whereabouts of Benedict and his sister **Scholastica**, Aigulf and his companions took charge of the bodies and returned quickly to France, with their precious cargo, to avoid soldiers sent by the Pope to apprehend them. The monks at Fleury are said to have kept the body of Benedict while pilgrims from Mano took that of Scholastica to their diocese. The authenticity of these events has always been highly controversial and there is no reference whatever to them in the *Life* of Aigulf, said to be by a contemporary at Fleury, Adrevald, but probably anonymous, nor in other writings of the period, and they are considered by many a legend. Aigulf was made abbot of Lerins in 671, and his strict reform of the rule led to his abduction and martyrdom on Capri. Feast day 3 September.

Aikenhead, Mary Foundress of the Irish Sisters of Charity, born at Cork, 19 January 1787, died at Dublin, 22 July 1858. Brought up in the Church of England, she became a Catholic at the age of sixteen and, at the instigation of Archbishop **Murray**, entered a convent at York, where she made a novitiate of three years, taking the name Sister Mary Augustine, though always known to the world as Mrs Aikenhead. She then made her profession and returned to Dublin where she opened the first convent of the Sisters of Charity, in North William Street. She was chosen superior general of the new congregation, canonically established in 1816. Despite poor health and chronic spinal trouble, which confined her to bed for the last 27 years of her life, Mrs Aikenhead succeeded in establishing ten houses, including St Vincent's Hospital, the first Catholic hospital in Ireland. Since her death, the congregation has spread to England, the USA, Australia and Africa. The cause of her beatification was introduced at Rome in 1921.

Ailred *see* **Aelred**.

Aimeric of Angoulême French Latin poet and metrist, born at Gastinaux, date unknown, died c.1090. He was educated at Senlis. His *Ars lectoria*, written in 1086, proposed rules to ensure the correct use of quantity and accent in the liturgy, and other forms of spoken Latin, and therein revealed his extensive knowledge of ancient literature, even of such little-known poets as Luxorius in the sixth century.

Aimeric of Piacenza (de Plaiseice) Twelfth Dominican master-general, born in Lombardy, date unknown, died at Bologna, 1327. He entered the Dominican Order at Bologna in 1267, studied at Milan and spent 24 years teaching philosophy and theology at Bologna. He was especially active in the organization of studies in the Order. During his mastership the Order could count more than 150 bishops and over 50 illustrious masters or professors. He is best known, however, for his role in the trial of the Templars under **Clement V**. The Pope ordered Aimeric to proceed against the Templars in Castile and Leon, but the Inquisition, not having found them guilty, dispensed with torture. Their report displeased the Pope who blamed Aimeric and his colleagues for not having applied torture. Aimeric believed that the Order's exemption allowed him to dispense with torture, apparently unaware that Clement had expressly ordered it in a Bull. Clement, however, summoned the Council of Vienne to judge the Templars and convoked Aimeric and the other generals of Orders. Aimeric refused to attend the Council, and resigned his office rather than take part in the process against the Templars.

Aimeric of Santa Maria Nuova   cardinal-deacon of Santa Maria Nuova, born in Burgundy, date unknown, died 28 May 1141. He was made a cardinal by Pope **Callixtus II** in 1120 and Chancellor of the Roman Church from 1123 until his death. He was a friend of eminent monastic reformers such as **Bernard of Clairvaux**, **Guigo I** and **Peter the Venerable**. He played an important, though controversial role in the ecclesiastical politics of the time. He was a powerful chancellor to **Honorius II** and when he died in 1130, Aimeric, with a minority of cardinals from Italy and France sympathetic to the newer reform tendencies, hastily buried him in a temporary grave and clandestinely elected Gregorio Papareschi as **Innocent II**, enthroning him at daybreak in the Lateran. When the news got abroad, the majority of cardinals – old Gregorians from Rome and south Italy, for the most part – refused to accept the coup and elected the following morning in San Marco Pierleoni as Anacletus II. Both elections were irregular, but both were consecrated on 23 February, Innocent in Aimeric's titular church of Santa Maria Nuova. The result was an eight-year schism.

Aimerich, Mateo   A learned philologist and historian of Latin literature, born at Bordil, Spain, February 1715, died at Ferrara in 1799. He entered the Society of Jesus at eighteen and, having completed his studies, taught philosophy and theology in several Jesuit colleges. He was subsequently rector of Barcelona, and chancellor of the University of Gandia. He was at Madrid when Charles III expelled the Jesuits from Spain (1767). He left without murmur and found refuge at Ferrara, where he spent his remaining years. In exile he composed the works which ensured for him a distinguished place among the philologists and critics of the eighteenth century. It is remarkable that the public library was his only help, and his infirmities often prevented him from attending there. He was most erudite, wrote much, in elegant and pure Latin, treatises in philosophy and ascetics, biographies and funeral orations. His reputation was made with *Novum lexicon historicum et criticum antiquae romanae literaturae* (Bassano, 1787).

Ainsworth, Henry   Christian Hebraist and founding Congregationalist, born Swanton Morley, Norfolk, March 1570, died Amsterdam, 1622/3. He went into exile in Holland *c.*1592 and became teacher of the English Separatist Church in Amsterdam under the pastorship of Francis Johnson with whom he co-authored *A Confession of Faith of the People called Brownists* (1596). He wrote works justifying his Separatist position, published polemical works against the Church of England, Anabaptists, Presbyterians, the Roman Catholic Church and the Family of Love. He is best known for his *Annotations on the Psalms* (1612) and *The Pentateuch* (1616–19). The latter shows extensive knowledge of rabbinical tradition and contains the earliest direct translations into English of Maimonides' *Commentary on the Talmud*.

Aistulf (Aistulph)   King of the Lombards, died 756. He succeeded his brother **Rachis** in 749, and set about the conquest of all Italy. He took the Exarchate of Ravenna from the Greeks in 751, and either took, or threatened, a number of towns formerly part of the Byzantine Exarchate, but currently claimed by the Papacy. He was about to seize the Patrimony of St Peter when Pope **Stephen II** appealed for aid to Pepin the Short, king of the Franks. The Lombards were defeated, but not overthrown, and Aistulf recovered to besiege Rome itself, provoking a second defeat by Pepin. The land in dispute between the Lombards and Papacy was conferred by Pepin on the Pope. It is probable that Aistulf contemplated yet another try at conquest, but a fall from his horse while hunting ended his life before he had time to renew his warlike enterprises.

Alacocque, Marguerite Marie   Saint, contemplative nun of the Visitation Order, born Lauthecourt, France, 22 July 1647, died Paray-le-Monial, 17 October 1690. The fifth of seven children, she seems to have been of a morbid and unhealthy temperament, and the subject of a paralytic seizure. Having been cured of this, as she believed, by the intercession of the Holy Virgin, she vowed to devote her life to her service. In 1671 she entered the Visitation Convent at Paray-le-Monial and was professed in November 1672. The appalling austerities to which she was allowed to subject herself affected her health, and she succeeded in reducing herself to such a state of ecstatic suffering that she believed herself to be undergoing in her own person the Passion of the Lord. Her reward was several revelations of the Sacred Heart, the first in December 1673 and the final one eighteen months later. The form of a devotion was revealed to her, the chief features being Holy Communion on the first Friday of the month, a Holy Hour on Thursdays and a festival in honour of the Sacred Heart. Her visions were at first treated with contempt by her superiors, who regarded them as delusions. It was not until ten years later, in 1685, that the festival was first celebrated at Paray, and not until after the death of Marguerite that the cult of the Sacred Heart, fostered by the Jesuits and the subject of violent controversies within the Church, spread throughout France and Christendom. Marguerite was beatified by **Pius IX** in 1864 and canonized by **Benedict XV** in 1920. Feast day 17 October.

Alamanni, Cosmo Italian philosopher, theologian and commentator on the works of St **Thomas Aquinas**, born Milan, 30 August 1559, died there, 14 May (or July) 1634. He entered the Jesuit novitiate at Novellara in 1575, studied theology at the Roman College under **Suárez** and Vasquez, and taught literature, philosophy and theology at the Brera College, Milan. Illness interrupted his career after seventeen years and in 1606 he became the bishop's theologian at the Pavia curia. Among his numerous publications, Alamanni completed his *Summa totius philosophiae e divi Thomae Aquinatis doctrina* (Pavia, 1618–23), which was very influential in the revival of Thomism in the twentieth century as a clear and accurate exposition of the great saint's teaching.

Alan de la Roche (Alanus de Rupe) Blessed, OP, born in Brittany *c.*1428, died Zwolle, Holland, 18 September 1475. He early entered the Order of Preachers at Dinan in the Diocese of St-Malo. He studied at St Jacques in Paris, distinguishing himself in philosophy and theology. He taught at Paris, Lille, Douai, Ghent and Rostock, where, in 1473, he was made master of sacred theology. He saw it as his special mission to preach and re-establish devotion to the rosary, which he did with success throughout northern France, Flanders and The Netherlands. At his death Alan left numerous writings, but most of them were published in an edition of the seventeenth century (*Beatus Alanus de Rupe, redivivus*, Fribourg, 1619). His writings have occasioned much controversy among scholars. Echard, the renowned and erudite Dominican, judged him fairly in recognizing his great devotion to the Holy Virgin, as being most zealous for souls, as a teacher whose visions and revelations, or rather parables, brought excellent results, but all of which cannot be regarded as having added anything to history. The title of Blessed, traditionally attributed to Alan, has not been officially ratified by the Church.

Alan of Lille Monk, poet, preacher, theologian and eclectic philosopher, born at Lille in 1128, died Cîteaux, 1202–3. He studied at Chartres and Paris, where he taught, and at Montpellier. He took part in the Third Council of the Lateran and battled against the Catharist heresy. He entered the monastery of Cîteaux, where he died. Alan is one of the great figures of the twelfth century. He attained extraordinary celebrity in his day as a teacher and a learned man. He was called Universal Doctor, Alan the Great, etc. He did not leave a coherent and complete philosophical system; his theology is characterized by a variety of rationalism tinged with mysticism in a style which consists in the effort to prove that all religious truths, even the mysteries of faith, flow out of principles that are self-evident to the human reason unaided by revelation. The *Ars fidei catholicae*, an attempt to confute non-Christians on rational grounds alone, which until recently was attributed to him, has been shown to be the work of Nicholas of Amiens. The principal elements of his philosophy are Platonism, Aristotelianism and Pythagoreanism. He esteemed Plato as the philosopher; Aristotle he regarded merely as a subtle logician. As a writer, Alain exhibited an unusual combination of poetic imaginativeness and dialectical precision. He is counted among the medieval writers who influenced **Dante**.

Alan of Tewkesbury Benedictine abbot and writer, died 1202. **Gervase of Canterbury**, a contemporary chronicler, states that Alan was English by race, not of Norman or any immigrant extraction. On his return from Benevento in 1174, where he had been a canon, he entered the Benedictine monastery at Canterbury, becoming prior when Herlewin resigned in 1179. He made an enemy of Henry II in supporting **Thomas Becket**, in obtaining the privilege of collecting Peter's Pence, and in objecting to the choice of **Baldwin** as archbishop of Canterbury. The latter transferred him to Tewkesbury, where he could less effectively oppose Henry's encroachments on the rights of the Church, and where he became abbot in 1186. Alan was throughout his life acquainted with the politico-ecclesiastical controversies of the time, and well qualified to write a life of his friend St Thomas, and to petition Henry concerning the translation of the saint's remains. There is doubt as to the genuineness of other works traditionally ascribed to him.

Alan of Walsingham   Monk, reputedly an architect of Ely, died at Ely, c.1364. He became sub-prior, sacristan and prior (1341) at Ely. He has been spoken of as architect of the Lady Chapel (now Trinity Church) attached to the cathedral, Prior Cranden's Chapel, the new sacristy and the cathedral's octagonal central dome, erected after the Norman tower fell in 1322, taking with it the choir and other attached portions of the structure. The result of the fourteenth-century additions was not only beautiful, but also highly original work, and some doubt has been cast on the architectural role of Alan, even if the idea to build was his. Alan was twice elected bishop of Ely by the monastic chapter and twice put aside by Rome, in favour of Thomas Lisle in 1344, and Simon Langham in 1361.

Alanus Anglicus   Of Welsh origin, he was a leading medieval canonist and one of the principal professors at Bologna in the decade preceding the Fourth Lateran Council (1215). His date and place of birth and death are unknown. It is thought that both he and his fellow countryman, **Gilbertus Anglicus**, may have ended their days as Dominicans. Tancred refers to him in the preface of his apparatus to the *Compilatio tertia antiqua* simply as an English professor in the schools of Bologna. Certainly his collection of decretals suggests English affiliations, and he may have studied or taught law in England before the Bologna period, or had some connection with John of Tynmouth and his associates in the English schools.

Alban   Saint, martyr, third century. A non-Christian, possibly a soldier, living in Britain under Roman rule, he sheltered a priest who was escaping persecution. Impressed by his guest's faith, Alban was baptized before helping the priest to escape by exchanging clothes with him. He was arrested in this disguise and, when his true identity was discovered, condemned to death in place of the priest. His courage so impressed his executioner that he also declared himself a Christian and asked to be put to death. The story is told in **Bede**'s *History of the English Church*. Feast day 20 June.

Albani, Alessandro   Cardinal, born at Urbino, 19 October 1692, died in Rome, 11 December 1779. Member of the distinguished family of Urbino, of whom the most influential was Pope **Clement XI** (1700–21); nephew, through his father, of Clement. He was created cardinal by **Innocent XIII** (1721), having distinguished himself in the papal diplomatic service. He was primarily a scholar, even though involved in the political life of the curia, and was director of the Vatican Library after 1761. He was a patron of the arts, and the foremost collectors of antiques were among his friends. His building of the Villa Albani in Rome brought him much renown, not least for his valuable collection of Greek and Roman sculpture.

Albani, Annibale   Cardinal, papal diplomat, brother of Alessandro, born at Urbino, 15 August 1682, died in Rome, 21 September 1751. Nephew, through his father, of **Clement XI**, whose first works he published in several volumes. His name was also attached to the edition of the Menologue of the Emperor Basil II (1727). He was created cardinal in 1711 by his uncle and appointed bishop of Sabina in 1730. Annibale was a most active diplomat in the Vatican service during Clement's reign, as, successively, nuncio in Vienna, Dresden and Frankfurt. He was influential in the elections of both **Innocent XIII** and **Benedict XIV**. He bequeathed his valuable library, gallery of paintings, and a collection of coins and antiques to the Vatican collection.

Albani, Giovanni Francesco   Cardinal, a third

nephew of **Clement XI**, born at Rome, 26 February 1727, died Rome, September 1803. He was cardinal-bishop of Ostia. Like his brothers, Alessandro and Annibale, he was very close to the papal curia where he was a spokesman for the Austrians. Toward the end of his career, he was dean of the Sacred College of Cardinals and particularly influential in the election of **Pius VII**.

Albani, Giuseppe Cardinal, born at Rome, 26 February 1750, died Rome, 1834. He was the nephew of Giovanni Francesco and thus a grand-nephew of **Clement XI**. He was created cardinal in 1801, following some years of service as nuncio in Vienna. He was Secretary of State to **Pius VIII**.

Albar Born *c*.800 at Cordoba, died *c*.861, place unknown. Studied under the Abbot Esperaindeo at Saint-Zoile. His friend, the martyr **Eulogius**, made himself the champion of intransigence in Cordoban Christianity in the last years of Abder-Rahman II (822–52), and under Muhammad I (852–86). He himself did not take holy orders, but married. He was a landowner, probably of the nobility, and worked by his pen to support the faith of his compatriots. If one relies on his correspondence, he fell under a sentence of excommunication because of his Semi-Pelagian tendencies, but submitted himself to the penance exacted. His *Indiculus Luminosus* (854) was the first book of a work of apologetics directed against the critics of the martyrs of Cordoba, and contains one of the earliest known polemics against Islam. He left eleven letters to diverse correspondents: his relative **John of Seville**; Abbot Esperaindeo; the apostate Bodo, who went over to Judaism, taking the name Eleazar (840); Bishop Saul, his ordinary. He also left some 600 lines of rather bad descriptive verse of this period in Cordoba.

Alberdingk Thijm, Josephus Albertus Dutch poet and pioneer of Catholic emancipation, born Amsterdam, 13 August 1820, died Amsterdam, 17 March 1889. From a middle-class business-oriented family, he grew up a militant Catholic with wide intellectual and aesthetic interests. Against the mediocrity and narrow-mindedness of many fellow Catholics he defended the necessity of good theatre, and friendship with non-Catholic authors to whose periodicals he contributed essays

and poetry. He equally deplored a growing agnostic materialism of the age, following, in this respect, his master Willem Bilderdijk, Holland's first romantic poet and a Protestant, for whom sentiment should form the basis of religion. His friend, E. J. Potgieter (1808–75), called him the Catholic romantic, and encouraged him to elevate Catholic culture. Having considered as pagan and heretical Holland's golden age of the seventeenth century, he now began to understand its greatness, especially of Vondel, Holland's greatest poet, the study of whose works was taken up by Catholic scholars. He saw in the Middle Ages support for his ideals of Catholic unity and harmony. He was active in the field of art, especially architecture, and in one of his best essays, *De heilige Linie* (1875), he discusses the symbolism of church architecture. In 1876 he was appointed professor of art history at the Academy of Arts in Amsterdam.

Albergati, Niccolò Blessed, cardinal and bishop of Bologna, born at Bologna, 1357, died at Siena, 14 May 1443. Entered the Carthusian Order in 1394, having begun to study for the law. He became superior of several houses and, in 1417, the clergy and citizens of Bologna chose him for their bishop, which only the express command of his superiors could induce him to accept. He continued to follow the rule of his Order, was zealous for the reform of regular and secular clergy, and a great patron of learned men, among whom was Aeneas Sylvius, afterwards **Pius II**. **Martin V** and his successors charged him with important diplomatic missions, thrice to France and thrice to Lombardy, between 1422 and 1435. He was made a cardinal in 1426, attended the Council of Basle in 1432, 1434 and 1436, as legate of **Eugenius IV**, and also opened the Council of Ferrara, where, and at Florence, he had much to do with the reconciliation of the Greeks. The Pope held him in the highest esteem; consulted him in most things, made him Grand Plenipotentiary, and visited him when he was ill. Though not formally canonized, he has long been popularly venerated as Blessed. He was a great patron of learning. Feast day 3 March.

Alberic I of Spoleto Duke, Count of Camerino and Tuscany, date of birth unknown, died *c*.925.

He was a Lombard adventurer, married Marioza, daughter of Theophylactus and Theodora, and thus into the family that exercised effective power in Rome during the early tenth century. In *c.*915, he distinguished himself as a member of the alliance which, under the leadership of Pope **John X**, defeated the Saracens at the Garigliano River and drove them out of Italy.

Alberic II of Spoleto Roman senator, born *c.*905, died 954. Probably the natural son of **Alberic I** and **Marozia**. In 932, on the occasion of his mother's third marriage, to Hugh of Provence, Alberic led an uprising, expelled Hugh and imprisoned both Marioza and Pope **John XI**, his half-brother. Alberic was able to exert such power due to the opposition within Rome to Hugh. Liutprand of Cremona called Alberic's government 'monarchia', but Alberic adopted the unusual title 'princeps', as leader of the Roman nobility, usurping the imperial prerogative by placing his name with the Pope's on his coinage. Roman politics were unusually peaceful during Alberic's rule from 932 to his death, during which time he replaced the popes as temporal ruler. On Alberic's invitation, **Leo VII** and **Odo of Cluny** co-operated in a restoration of Roman monasteries, following the expulsion of the Saracens. Alberic's influence appears to have weakened under Stephen VIII, since Hugh of Provence was able to visit Rome in 941, and his influence over individual popes thereafter varied. Before his death in 954, Alberic arranged for the election of his illegitimate son, Octavian, to the Papacy, as **John XII**.

Alberic of Monte Cassino Rhetorician, author, monk, perhaps a native of Trier, born 1020, died 1105. He was a major figure in the revival of classical culture in southern Italy that spread from the monastery at Monte Cassino, which he entered as an adult, *c.*1060, during the time of Abbot Desiderius. His interests were diverse. He is the author of the earliest medieval treatise on letter-writing, *Ars dictaminis*, an influential three-book work on metrics, rhythm, grammar and letter composition. His Latin style influenced the work of his students, among whom was Pope **Gelasius II**. He opposed the heresy of **Berengarius of Tours**, defended the measures of **Gregory VII**, and composed several theological and scientific works.

Most of his writings, among them his letters to **Peter Damian** on the controversy of Berengarius, and on the investiture struggle, are lost.

Alberic of Ostia Benedictine monk, cardinal-bishop of Ostia, papal legate, born Beauvais, *c.*1080, died Verdun, 1148. He entered the monastery at Cluny, became its sub-prior, and later prior of St Martin-des-Champs, but was recalled to Cluny by Peter the Venerable to aid in the restoration of discipline there. In 1131 he was abbot of Vezelay and, in 1138, made cardinal-bishop of Ostia by **Innocent II**, who sent him as papal legate to England. His main business was to visit the chief monastic and episcopal centres of England and Scotland, to hold a council in which the recent Gregorian Reform decrees might be applied, and to supervise the election of the archbishop of Canterbury; **Theobald**, the former abbot of Bec was elected. He returned to Rome where he participated in the Second Lateran Council. Having been sent in 1147 to combat the Henrician heretics in Toulouse, St **Bernard of Clairvaux**, in a letter written to the bishops of the district, calls Alberic 'The venerable bishop of Ostia, a man who has done great things in Israel, through whom Christ has often given victory to his Church.' His last years were spent as legate in southern France, where he opposed the Albigenses, **Eon of Stella**, and the followers of **Henry of Lausanne**, and co-operated with St Bernard in promoting the Second Crusade.

Alberic of Rosate Italian jurist, born Rosciate, near Bergamo, 1290, died Bergamo, September 1360. His family had been judges and notaries and he studied law in Padua under Oldradus da Ponte and Riccardo Malombra. On his return to Bergamo in the second decade of 1300 to practise law, he became a principal exponent of the Italian juridical school of commentators and promoted the first real lexicographic attempt in the juridical field. In 1331 and 1333, he reformed the statutes of the city of Bergamo and was ambassador for Bergamo and the Visconti family to the Pope in Avignon on several occasions between 1335 and 1340. His *Quaestiones statutorum* is a fundamental work in statutory legislation, and perhaps the first doctrinal treatise on private international law. He wrote commentaries on various parts of

Justinian's Digest and Code. His contemporaries and posterity described him as 'summus practicus'. His *Dictionarium iuris*, reprinted several times, is the first ample lexicon of civil and canon law.

Alberic of Utrecht Saint, Benedictine monk, bishop of Utrecht, died Utrecht, 784. Nephew of an earlier bishop of Utrecht, St **Gregory**, the successor of St **Boniface**. He was a friend of intellectual leaders of the Carolingian Renaissance, such as **Alcuin** and **Ludger** of Münster. He was consecrated bishop in 780 at Cologne. As bishop of Utrecht he reorganized the cathedral school, dividing the teaching under four masters. Alberic participated in the mission to convert the pagan Frisians, directing Ludger's activity there. His relics are preserved at Susteren. Feast day in the Diocese of Roermond is 14 November; in Utrecht 4 March.

Alberoni, Giulio Spanish-Italian statesman, cardinal, born Fiorenzuola, Piacenza, 31 May 1664, died Piacenza, 27 June 1752. Educated by the Jesuits and the Barnabites, Alberoni acted as agent of the Duke of Parma in Madrid, and successfully negotiated the marriage of Philip V to Elizabeth Farnese of Parma in 1714. He became prime minister to the Spanish Crown in 1716, and sought to restore Spain's prestige in Italy, to which end he ordered Spanish troops to invade Sicily and Sardinia, in 1719. The Quadruple Alliance reconquered the islands, accused Alberoni of treason and expelled him from Spain. **Innocent XIII** ultimately cleared him of the charge and made him bishop of Malaga in 1725.

Albers, William American philanthropist, born Cincinnati, Ohio, 23 May 1880, died there, 6 June 1954. Albers became president of the Kroger Grocery and Baking Company, and presided over a huge expansion in merchandising from 185 to over 5500 stores; he founded Albers Super Markets Inc. in 1933, and opened 67 supermarkets in Ohio and Kentucky. Active in cultural and educational associations, he directed the Catholic Youth Organization and the National Council of Catholic Men; acted as trustee of the Catholic University of America and a member of the lay advisory board of Xavier University in Cincinnati. His philanthropic activities were rewarded with Knight Commander of the Order of St Gregory, and the annual citation of the National Council of Christians and Jews in 1954.

Albert the Great (Albertus Magnus) Saint, Dominican philosopher, theologian and scientist. Born Lauingen, near Ulm, *c.*1200, died Cologne, 15 November 1280. Known also as Albertus Magnus or Albert of Cologne, he was born into a noble family and attended the University of Padua, which is where he joined the Order, despite opposition of his family who tried to remove him by force, in 1222. By 1228 he was teaching in Cologne, and then taught at a number of German houses and held one of the Dominican chairs of theology at Paris, in 1245–48, before being sent back to Cologne where he became the teacher of St **Thomas Aquinas**, and a proponent of Aristotelianism. Always keen on the natural sciences, he went out of his way to observe natural phenomena, and combined this with proficiency in all branches of philosophy and theology. Albert commented on almost the whole corpus of Aristotle presented in the Latin translations and notes of Averroes, and other Arabic commentators, including the *Liber de Causis*, which Albert believed to be the crown of peripatetic philosophy. His own scientific observations allowed him considerably to expand on Aristotle's *Naturalia*; he also wrote on mathematics, and several biblical commentaries. His principal theological works are a commentary in three volumes on the *Books of the Sentences*, of **Peter Lombard**, and the *Summa Theologiae* in two volumes; his contemporaries bestowed on him the honourable surnames 'The Great' and 'Doctor Universalis'. In 1254 he became prior provincial of Germany, and in 1260, at the express instruction of Pope **Alexander IV**, he became bishop of Regensburg in an unsuccessful effort to restore order in that diocese. He resigned after two years and returned to Cologne. In 1274 he went to the Council of Lyons, and in 1277 he went to Paris to defend the teachings of his former pupil Thomas Aquinas. In 1278 his memory suddenly failed him in the middle of a lecture, and he suffered from an increasing loss of memory. Canonized and declared a Doctor of the Church by **Pius XI** in 1931, **Pius XII** proclaimed him patron of natural scientists in 1941. Feast day 15 November.

Albornoz, Gil Álvarez de Spanish cardinal, born

Cuenca, c.1295, died near Viterbo, Italy, 23 August 1367. Albornoz succeeded his uncle in the see of Toledo in 1338, by favour of King Alfonso XI; he crusaded against the Moors in Andalusia and helped to unify Castile with the *Ordenamiento of Alcalá* of 1348. In 1353 **Innocent VI** sent him as a legate into Italy to prepare the Papal States for the return of the Popes, and during the next fourteen years he brought one petty tyrant after another to recognize the Popes as overlords, culminating in the return of **Urban V** to Rome in 1367. His constitution, *Constitutiones Aegidianae* (1357), governed the Papal States until 1816.

Albright, Jacob American evangelical preacher, born at Fox Mountain, Pennsylvania, 1 May 1759, died Pottstown, 18 May 1808. The son of immigrants from the German Palatinate, Albright was confirmed into the local Lutheran Church. He became a Methodist in 1791, and preached in German to settlers in neighbouring states; he received ordination as a minister from his congregation. Because language separated them from mainstream Methodism, Albright organized his followers into the Newly Formed Methodist Conference in 1807, and became their first bishop. They were not accepted by other bishops and in 1813, having declared themselves an Evangelical Association, and later the Evangelical Church, severed their nominal ties with Methodism.

Albright, William Foxwell American archaeologist, born Coquimbo, Chile, 24 May 1891, died Baltimore, Maryland, 19 September 1971. The son of missionary parents, Albright received a doctorate from the Oriental Seminary of Johns Hopkins University, and became director of the American Schools of Oriental Research in Jerusalem in 1921–36, during which time he completed major excavations in the area, recounted in *The Excavations of Tell Beit Mirsim*, and other treatises. He also wrote *From the Stone Age to Christianity*, outlining his philosophical, historical and theological positions. Albright made an important contribution to biblical and Near Eastern scholarship in a career of 60 years, during which he influenced many modern Scripture scholars.

Alcuin Anglo-Saxon contributor to the Carolingian Renaissance, born York, c.735, died Tours, 19 May 804. He was educated in the episcopal school at York and succeeded Aelbert in its headship in 767, when Aelbert became archbishop. On a journey to Rome in 780, he met **Charlemagne** at Parma, who persuaded him to join his court in 781, where he systematized the educational programme, his principal subjects of academic concern being **Boethius**, **Augustine** and the grammarians; France became his residence until his death. His extant literary works include a quantity of biblical exegesis; a major work on the Trinity; treatises directed against the Adoptionism of Felix of Urgel, whom he opposed in person at the Council of Aachen; moral and philosophical writings; the *Lives* of SS **Willibrord** and **Martin of Tours**; manuals of grammar, rhetoric, dialectic, orthography and mathematics. He wrote numerous poems and letters (311 are extant), above all to Charlemagne; they are a mine of information as to the literary, political and social conditions of the time, and the most reliable authority for the history of humanism in the Carolingian age.

Aldhelm Saint, Anglo-Saxon writer, born Wessex, c.640; died Doulting, Somerset, 709. Related to Ine, King of Wessex, and educated at the church school of Canterbury, Aldhelm became bishop of Sherborne (705), and bequeathed to the Church a mixed Roman and Celtic tradition. Much of his Latin writing has survived: *De Virginitate*, a study of saints of the Bible and the early Church; *Carmina ecclesiastica*, a collection of religious poems; *De metris et enigmatibus ac pedum regulis*, a treatise on grammar. Held in high repute as a poet, and esteemed by St Bede, Aldhem's learning and piety inspired many scholars, including William of Malmesbury. Feast day 25 May.

Aldobrandini, Cinzio Passeri Born Sinigaglia, 1551, died Rome, 1 January 1610, of a celebrated Florentine family, active in Vatican affairs in the sixteenth and seventeenth centuries. One of three nephews of **Clement VIII** who became prominent.

Aldobrandini, Gian Francesco Born Rome, 1545 died Varadin, 1601. Made general of the papal armies, he distinguished himself in a crusade against the Turks, and died in battle in Hungary. One of three nephews of **Clement VIII** who became prominent.

Aldobrandini, Giovanni   Born Florence, 1525, died Rome, 17 September 1573. **Paul V** made him bishop of Imola and cardinal in 1570. He figured prominently in forming the league of Spain and Venice in the Crusade of Lepanto, and in controlling the policy of granting indulgences.

Aldobrandini, Ippolito   Born Fano, 1536, died Rome, 5 March 1605. He became Pope **Clement VIII**, from 1592. A man of high principles, he ensured the representation of all shades of interest in the curia, and limited the dominance of Spanish influence. He supported the Catholic League against Henry of Navarre, but received him anyway into the Church; he was largely responsible for the Treaty of Vervins of 1598, which brought peace between France and Spain. He had to abandon hope of converting **James I** of England.

Aldobrandini, Ippolito   Younger son of Gian, born Rome, 1592, died Rome, 22 July 1638. Long a simple domestic prelate, **Gregory XV** made him a cardinal in 1621, and appointed him to high office, including as legate to Ferrara under **Urban VIII**, but he concerned himself little with his duties, preferring to manage family affairs. The male line ended with his death; his niece Olympia, granddaughter of Gian Francesco, married Paolo Borghese, becoming a princess and duchess of Rossano.

Aldobrandini, Pietro   Died 1587, a distinguished jurist who succeeded his father as fiscal advocate in 1556.

Aldobrandini, Pietro   Born Rome, 1571, died there, 21 February 1621. Brother of Cinzio. Both were made cardinals in 1593, and shared the office of secretary of state. Although favoured by **Clement VIII**, Cinzio had to give way to Pietro, who became second only to the Pope himself; he handled intricate political affairs and had Clement's confidence. He received the annexation of the Duchy of Ferrara to the Papal States in 1598; cultivated harmony with **Henry IV of France** and secured peace between France and Savoy in 1600. One of three nephews of Clement who became prominent.

Aldobrandini, Silvestro   Eldest son of **Gian Francesco**, jurist, born Florence, 24 November 1499, died Rome, 7 June 1558. He played an active part in the revolution which expelled the Medicis from Florence. He went to Rome in 1531 and began his relationship with the papal court. **Paul III** appointed him to various offices; under **Paul IV**, he rose and gained considerable influence, becoming first secretary to the Pope in 1556. He had one daughter and five sons.

Aldobrandini, Silvestro   Eldest son of Gian Francesco, born Rome, 1587, died Rome, 4 January 1612. **Clement VIII** made him a cardinal at the age of sixteen in 1603, at the instigation of his uncle, Cardinal Pietro. He took part in the conclave of **Paul V** in 1605, but was little more than a pawn in the hands of his protector.

Aldobrandini, Tommaso   Died 1572, was secretary of briefs under **Paul IV**.

Aldred   *see* **Ealdred of York**

Aleandro, Girolamo   Italian cardinal-bishop, humanist, born Motta, 13 February 1480, died Rome, 1 February 1542. He studied at Padua and taught at Venice, where he became friends with **Erasmus**, who suggested that he seek his fortune in Paris, where he gave lectures in Greek and oriental languages, becoming rector of the University in 1513. He played an important part in the history of the Reformation, when **Leo X** sent him to represent the Church at the Diet of Worms in 1520, and to implement the Bull, *Exsurge Domine*, excommunicating Martin **Luther**. Aleandro, however, did not appreciate the complexities of the problem: he vigorously denounced Luther in his Ash Wednesday sermon, refused to let him explain himself, and demanded his condemnation without trial. In this he did not succeed, but helped the Diet to formulate its edict against Luther. His relations with Erasmus, warm before Worms, became bitterly hostile afterwards, when Aleandro blamed him, unjustly, for the errors of Luther. It was not an open quarrel, but Erasmus rejected all efforts at reconciliation and lumped Aleandro, together with other sometime friends, in a wholesale rejection of all things Italian. Aleandro was never in doubt as to Luther's popularity in Germany, nor as to the pressing need for disciplinary reform in the Church, and he died discouraged by the size of the growing crisis that he had not been able to avert. He became archbishop of Brindisi in 1524, and a cardinal in 1538.

Alemany, Joseph Sadoc Spanish Dominican missionary, archbishop, born Vich, 13 July 1814, died Valencia, 14 April 1888. He joined the Order of Preachers in 1829, and went to the USA in 1840, to serve the Dominican foundations in Ohio, Kentucky and Tennesee. Named American provincial, he became bishop of Monterey in 1850, with jurisdiction over all of California, Nevada and Utah. The Mexican government protested his control over Lower California, which was Mexican territory, and withheld payments to the 'Pious Fund', an important source of revenue. Despite a shortage of priests and churches, he made some progress in evangelization, and became archbishop of San Francisco in 1853. He attended Vatican I, as a member of the 24-man commission to explore the teaching on papal infallibility. His archdiocese grew rapidly and after three decades he retired to the parish of Nuestra Señora de la Pilar, until his death.

Alen, John (Alan, Allen) Chancellor of Ireland, and last pre-Reformation archbishop of Dublin, born Cottenshall, Norfolk, 1476, died Artane, Ireland, 28 July 1534. A graduate of Cambridge, ordained in 1499, he studied canon law at Rome. He served as commissary to Cardinal **Wolsey**, and played his part as minister of the royal supremacy in the subjection of the clergy and dissolution of the monasteries, in 1524. Consecrated archbishop of Dublin in 1529, and chancellor of Ireland, he untiringly pursued the rights of his see, of which he produced a full description, *Reportorium Viride*, in 1532. His earlier association with Wolsey counted against him, and he earned the hatred of the Irish House of Kildare, so that when it was rumoured, falsely, that Gerald Fitzgerald, the ninth Earl, then imprisoned in the Tower, had been put to death, he was murdered by two retainers of the Earl's son.

Aleni, Giulio Italian Jesuit missionary to China, born Brescia, 1582, died Fuchow, China, 3 August 1649. He entered the Society in 1600, went to the Chinese mission in 1610, and spent three years waiting at Macao teaching mathematics, during which time he published his observation of a lunar eclipse there, in 1612. Finally admitted to China in 1613, he remained in Kiang-si and Fukien provinces for nearly 30 years, converting some 20,000 Chinese before being expelled in 1638; he returned the following year for a further decade. He adopted Chinese dress and manners, wrote some 50 volumes in Chinese and became, after Matteo **Ricci**, their most famous Italian missionary, and 'Confucius of the West', to Chinese scholars.

Alerding, Herman Joseph German church historian in the USA, born Ibbenbueren, Westphalia, 13 April 1845, died Fort Wayne, Indiana, 6 December 1924. He went to America with his parents as an infant; entered St Gabriel Seminary, Indiana, studied further in Kentucky; ordained in 1868, he did pastoral work in Indiana until 1874, and transferred to Indianapolis. Consecrated bishop of Fort Wayne in 1900, he advanced the parochial school system and secondary education among a growing population of foreign-born Catholics in the steel mills of northern Indiana. His *History of the Catholic Church in the Diocese of Vincennes* (1883), the first general history of the Church in Indiana, contained a vast amount of information. In 1907 he published *Diocese of Fort Wayne*.

Alès, Adhémar d' French Jesuit theologian and patrologist, born Orléans, 2 December 1861, died Paris, 24 February 1938. He entered the Society in 1880, and taught philosophy, Greek and Latin literature for twelve years, from 1896. When Patrick Bainvel inaugurated La Bibliothèque de Théologie historique, he called on Ales, and they published detailed theological studies on **Tertullian**, **Hippolytus**, the Edict of Callistus, St **Cyprian** and **Novatian**. These works attracted the attention of historians for their precise and sure erudition, and of theologians for their soundness of judgement. He became dean of the faculty of theology in the Institute Catholique de Paris, in 1925. During this period his principal work was the *Dictionnaire apologetique de la Foi catholique*, which he directed for fifteen years.

Alexander Saint, patriarch of Alexandria from 312, born *c*.250; died Alexandria, 18 April 328. He vigorously attacked Arianism and convened a synod of all Egyptian bishops, which condemned and excommunicated **Arius** in 321. Arius received support from **Eusebius**, bishop of Caesarea and **Eusebius of Nicomedia**, but Alexander defended his action, adhering to the doctrine of **Origen** and inisting on the natural, eternal generation of the Son and on his perfect likeness to the Father. He allied himself with **Hosius** of Cordoba and, together with his deacon, St **Athanasius**, attended the Council of Nicea in 325, where the term *homoousias* was included in the Nicene Creed. The Council determined that Melitius, who had founded a schismatic church with clergy of his own ordination, would be allowed to remain a bishop, though subordinated to Alexander, but this arrangement broke down when Athanasius succeeded him. Alexander is also venerated as a saint in the Coptic Church on 22 April, and in the Greek Church on 29 May. Feast day 26 February.

Alexander I Saint, Pope *c.*109–*c.*116, birth and death dates unknown. Early accounts have him succeeding **Evaristus** as fifth in line from St Peter, but later convention reckoned him as sixth Pope. According to **Eusebius** his reign lasted ten years, but this is uncertain. The *Liber Pontificalis* reports him as being a Roman, the son of a man also called Alexander, and attributes to him, with transparent anachronism, the insertion of the 'Qui Pridie', the narrative of the Last Supper, into the canon of the Mass. The Roman tradition that he died a martyr, decapitated on the via Nomentana, apparently confused him with an actual martyr bearing the same name, whose tomb was discovered in 1855. **Irenaeus** knows of no martyrdoms of Roman bishops before Telesphorus, and the story of Alexander's martyrdom is most unlikely. Virtually nothing is reliably known about him, other than that he held a leading position in the Roman Church, and his constitutional position as leader of the community remains obscure. Feast day 3 May.

Alexander I Emperor of Russia, born St Petersburg, 12 December 1777, died Tagaurog, 19 November 1825. The son of Tsar Paul I and Sophia Dorothea of Württemburg, he initiated important internal reforms, following the assassination of his father, which, though idealistically conceived, were largely impractical and unsuccessful in execution. His other major effort arose out of his involvement in the Napoleonic wars from which, at the Congress of Vienna, Russia emerged as the leading power in Europe. Though he supported the Orthodox Church and the Synod of Russian Churches, he normally dealt justly with the Latin Churches, and established diplomatic relations with the Vatican in 1801. He founded the Roman Catholic Ecclesiastical College, without the approval of the Holy See, which regulated the affairs of the Latin Church in Russia. He obtained from **Pius VII** authority for the presence of the Jesuits, but expelled them from St Petersburg in 1815, and from the empire in 1820. He guaranteed freedom of worship and education to the Jews in 1804. Alexander was the moving force behind the Holy Alliance, with Prussia and Austria, to promote religion, peace and justice, guided by the Commandments, which provided, at least outwardly, an aura of rectitude to the Congress of Vienna in 1815. Alexander maintained peaceful relations with the Holy See until his death, when it was thought that he had been contemplating reunion.

Alexander II Pope, born Anselm of Baggio, near Milan, *c.*1000, elected 30 September 1061 died Rome, 21 April 1073. He favoured the Patarenes, an extreme reforming movement supported by Rome, and strongly opposed the simoniacal practices that kept ecclesiastical benefices in the hands of unworthy clerics. He became bishop of Lucca in 1057, and Pope in 1061, with the help of Hildebrand (**Gregory VII**), but without the support of **Henry IV**, who had an antipope, **Honorius II**, elected at a Basel synod. The schism was officially ended by the Synod of Mantua in 1064, but not definitively until Honorius' death in 1072. Unsuccessful in his efforts to heal the rift between East and West, the conquest of Muslim territory in Italy and Spain by his allies prepared the way for the first Crusades. Alexander intervened to defend the Jews in southern France and Spain in 1263, and renewed the prohibition of **Gregory I** against their maltreatment. He blessed **William I**'s invasion of England in 1066, and two of his legates presided over a great council of the British Church at Winchester in 1070. He acquired considerable stature as Pope and moderate reformer, and his qualities have become more widely appreciated in modern times.

Alexander III Pope, born Orlando Bandinelli, at Siena, c.1105, elected 7 September 1159, died Città Castellana, 30 August 1181. A prominent canon lawyer in the school of Bologna, a cardinal in 1150, chancellor of the Roman Church, 1153 and, as legate under **Eugenius III** and **Adrian IV**, he strongly influenced papal policy in European politics, and succeeded Adrian IV in 1159. Victor IV, an antipope, supported by **Frederick I Barbarossa**, immediately opposed him, and the schism lasted seventeen years, during which time Alexander lived in France. He became involved in the controversy over **Thomas Becket**, and though embarrassed, as a subtle diplomatist, by the impetuous archbishop, he nevertheles imposed a penance upon **Henry II** for Becket's murder. At the Third Lateran Council in 1179, over which he presided, the right of electing a Pope was vested in a two-thirds majority of cardinals. He strongly encouraged the scholastic revival of the twelfth century; he sent missionaries to Scandinavia, and legates to France to check the growing influence of Albigensian doctrines. For the last two years of his pontificate he was driven out of Rome by a popular uprising against him.

Alexander IV Pope, born Rinaldo, count of Segni, c.1195, elected 12 December 1254, died Viterbo, 25 May 1261. A nephew of **Gregory IX**, Rinaldo had been made a cardinal-deacon in 1227 and cardinal-bishop of Ostia in 1231. He had played little part in the government of the Church, being preoccupied by the problems of the Franciscans, whose protector he was. He was elected in Naples, and was immediately concerned with issues in Southern Italy and Sicily. He was not politically adept, but was more successful with problems internal to the Church, reopening discussions with the Byzantines over reunion of the churches, and encouraging the friars in their conflicts with the secular clergy. He failed to establish himself in Rome, and governed the Church from Viterbo.

Alexander V Antipope, born Pietro Philargia in Crete (then under Venice) to a poor family, and orphaned when young, elected 26 June 1409, died Bologna 3 May 1410. He was brought up by the Franciscans and joined the Order. He studied at Padua, Norwich and Oxford, then taught in Russia, Bohemia, Poland, Paris and Pavia where he was professor of theology at the time of his appointment to the bishopric of Piacenza. He went as bishop to Vicenza two years later, and to Novara the year after that, finally becoming archbishop of Milan in 1402. He was made a cardinal in 1405, and legate for Lombardy, but was discontented by the failure to end the Great Schism. He took a lead in calling the Council of Pisa in an attempt to end the Schism, and was himself elected. The two other claimants, however, retained some, though diminished, support. He dispatched Baldassare Cossa, the future antipope **John XXIII**, to capture Rome, which he did, and a group of Romans came to Bologna to submit to Alexander, but he died there unexpectedly.

Alexander VI Pope 1492–1503, born Rodrigo Borgia at Valencia, c.1431, died Rome, 18 August 1503. A nephew of **Calixtus III**, who made him a cardinal in 1456, and chancellor of the Roman Church the following year. He secured his own election to the Papacy largely through bribery, not unexpected in a family riddled with nepotism and favouratism, of whom nearly 20 kin or familiars were cardinals during his lifetime. A powerful clan, the Borgias tended to extremes of villainy and holiness, Alexander's uncle being personally austere, and his great-grandson, **Francis Borgia**, became general of the Jesuits, and was canonized. Alexander led a dissipated life, both as cardinal and Pope, and through his numerous illegitimate children, his blood now flows in many of the princely families of Europe. A capable administrator and a patron of the arts (**Michelangelo** created the 'Pietà' for him), he encouraged the recitation of the Angelus, maintained a policy of tolerance towards the Jews, despite pressure to do otherwise, and prosecuted **Savonarola** for schism and heresy. He promoted the evangelization of Greenland, supported Portuguese missionary work and worked for peace between Portugal and Castile in the Far East and the Americas, as well as encouraging the spread of the Gospel. Despite his positive contributions in many areas of the Church's apostolate, any overall judgement of him and his pontificate will probably always be negative, even though the calumnies of his enemies have often been exaggerated.

Alexander VII Pope 1655–67, born Fabio Chigi, Siena, 13 February 1599, died Rome, 22 May 1667.

Named papal nuncio at Cologne in 1639 for thirteen years, and representative at the Peace Conference of Münster, he refused to negotiate with heretics, and protested vehemently against provisions in the treaties he considered injurious to Catholicism. Elected on the death of **Innocent X**, in a stormy conclave that lasted 80 days, his position as Pope was weak and he failed to establish good relations with Cardinal **Mazarin**, who had opposed his election, and had the support of **Louis XIV** of France. On the other hand, relations with Venice were more friendly; he persuaded the city to permit the return of the Jesuits in 1656, and lent it support against the Turks. As a theologian, Alexander had strong anti-Jansenist views, as did his predecessor, and when Antoine **Arnauld**, the great Jansenist leader, proposed that, while the *Five Propositions* were indeed wrong and one could accept the Pope's condemnation of them, they were not to be found in Cornelius Jansen's *Augustinus*, Alexander made this subterfuge impossible in a Bull saying that the *Five Propositions* were in fact contained in *Augustinus*, and condemned them in the sense Jansen had meant them. A great patron of the arts, he commissioned **Bernini** to enclose the piazza of St Peter's within the great colonnade.

Alexander VIII Pope 1689–91, born Pietrio Vito Ottaboni, Venice, 22 April 1610, died Rome, 1 February 1691. Descended from a noble Venetian family, he entered the curial service and, named judge of the Rota (1643–53), became famous for his judicial decisions. A trusted collaborator of **Innocent XI**, who made Ottaboni a cardinal in 1652, Grand Inquisitor of Rome and Secretary of the Holy Office. A complete contrast to his severe predecessor when elected to the Papacy, but a jealous guardian of the faith, he condemned two laxist propositions current among Jesuits, one denying the necessity of an explicit act of love for God after the attainment of reason, the other admitting the notion of 'philosophic sin', i.e. a sin involving no offence to God because committed without knowledge or thought of him. He condemned in 1690 31 Jansenist propositions concerning penance, the Virgin, baptism and the Church's authority; also the *Four Gallican Propositions* (1682). He punished with life imprisonment the surviving followers of the Spanish

Quietist Miguel de **Molinos**; effected a reconciliation with **Louis XIV** who, in 1690, gave back Avignon and Venaissin, taken from **Alexander VII**. His reign was notable for generous aid to Venice in the Turkish wars; for extravagance in dispensing papal monies and offices, and nepotism; and for his patronage of the Vatican Library.

Alexander,   Archibald American Presbyterian theologian, born Lexington, Vermont, 17 April 1772, died Princeton, NJ, 22 October 1851. He studied at Washington College, Chestertown, and, ordained in 1794, served as president of Hampden-Sydney College, the first Presbyterian college in Virginia. In 1807 he went to Philadelphia and, as moderator of the general assembly, persuaded Presbyterians of the need for a theological seminary, which he duly founded in 1812, becoming its first professor and remaining there until his death. One of the principal Old School theologians, he based his courses on Turretini and other Calvinist theologians, and opposed the New School in his *Thoughts on Religious Experience* (1841), and in the columns of the *Biblical Repertory*, which he founded in 1825. His *Brief Outline of the Evidences of the Christian Religion* (1825) was widely adopted as a standard apologetical work. He had much influence in advocating foreign missions, and in the American Colonization Society.

Alexander, Cecil Frances, née Humphreys Writer, born Ballydean House, Redcross, Co. Wicklow, Ireland, 1818, died Londonderry, 12 October 1895. She was the daughter of Major John Humphreys, and published poems and hymns for little children, which achieved over 100 editions. She married the Reverend William Alexander, who became bishop of Derry and Raphoe, and later archbishop of Armagh and primate of all Ireland. Mrs Alexander's most popular hymn is *All Things Bright and Beautiful*. Originally stanza three ran: 'The rich man in his castle/ The poor man at his gate/ God made them high or lowly/ and ordered his estate', but this is usually omitted in later printings.

Alexander Nevsky Saint, Grand Duke of Vladimir and Kiev, born 30 May 1220, died 19 November 1263. Son of Grand Duke Yaroslav II, who made him Prince of Novgorod in 1228, Alexander recognized the impossibility of resisting the conquest of Russia by the Mongol armies of Batu Khan, who overran the south and a great part of the eastern country. He ensured the protection of his people by remaining a loyal vassal of the Mongol empire, and the Great Khan appointed him Grand Duke and thus primal Prince of Russia. He is venerated as a saint in the Russian Church. Feast days 23 November and 30 August.

Alexander of Hales   English Franciscan theologian, born Halesowen, Shropshire, c.1185, died Paris, 21 August 1245. He studied arts and theology at Paris, is an important figure in the flowering of thirteenth-century theology, the first master at Paris to lecture on the *Sentences* of Peter Lombard, rather than on Scripture. In 1236 he joined the Franciscans, and kept his chair at Paris, henceforth filled by a Franciscan. Alexander quoted freely from Aristotle, by then available in translation, but read him in an Augustinian light, adapting fragmentary texts to the teaching of St **Augustine**. He thus failed to achieve a synthesis of the new theology with traditional theology. His authentic works show a fidelity to the tradition of Augustine, to **Boethius** and to the Master of St-Victor. He is regarded as the founder of the Franciscan school of theology, but the *Summa theologica*, which goes under his name, was only begun by him, and added to for the next 70 years by others of his Order, which accounts for the variable quality of the work, but illustrates the thought of the thirteenth-century Franciscan school of theology at the University of Paris.

Alexander of Jerusalem   Saint, bishop and martyr, died Caesarea, Palestine, c.250. One of the great bishops of the early Church, and a pupil of **Origen**. Bishop of a see in Cappadocia in c.200, imprisoned c.204 in the Severan persecution, he became bishop of Jerusalem in 222, and founded the library later used by **Eusebius of Caesarea** in preparing his great history of the early Church. When Origen was condemned by the bishop of Alexandria, he took refuge at Jerusalem, where Alexander ordained him, and appointed him to teach Scripture and theology in the diocese. Alexander died in prison at Caesarea during the persecution of Decius. Feast day 18 March.

Alexandra, Mother (Princess Eleana of Romania)

Orthodox monastic founder, born Bran Castle, Romania, 5 January 1909, died Youngstown, Ohio, 21 January 1991. She was the sister of King Carol of Romania and was married to a Habsburg archduke, but in later life became a nun and in 1964 founded a flourishing convent in the USA under Archbishop **Valerian**. She wrote many popular books on Orthodox doctrine and spirituality in addition to her autobiography (in English) *I Live Again* (1952).

Alexis I (Simansky) of Moscow   Born Moscow 27 October 1877, died 17 April 1970. He was consecrated bishop 1913. After the revolution he was closely associated with Metropolitan **Sergius** (Stragorodsky) in coming to a modus vivendi with the Soviet regime in 1927. At the outbreak of the Second World War he was one of the very few bishops still at liberty. After the death of Sergius in 1944 he was unanimously elected patriarch by the 41 bishops permitted to assemble. Consistently loyal to the Soviet government he also tried to preserve the Church, as far as he felt able, in the very oppressive Krushchev years.

Alexis (Toth)   Orthodox saint, priest and missionary, born Szepes, Hungary (now Slovakia) 18 March 1854, died Pennsylvania, USA, 7 May 1909. Son of a Greek Catholic (Uniate) priest he was ordained and emigrated to America to care for the many Carpatho-Russians there. Rejected by the local Catholic bishop he eventually united himself and his parish to the Russian Orthodox bishop in San Francisco. Thus began the mass return of the Uniates to Orthodoxy, involving about 30,000 people. He worked tirelessly among his poor immigrants and was a great temperance promoter. He was canonized by the Orthodox in America on 30 May 1994. Feast day 7 May.

Alexius I Comnenos   Byzantine emperor, 1081–1118, born c.1057, died Constantinople, 15 August 1118. Son of John Comnenos, and brother of Isaac I, with whom he revolted against Nicephoros in 1081, sacked Constantinople and seized the throne with support of the military aristocracy, especially the Dukai, to whom he was linked in marriage by Irene Dukaina. A difficult situation faced the empire and, by his brilliant diplomatic and military manoeuvres, he averted disaster by making a treaty with Suleiman, ruler of the Seljuk Turks, overcame the Norman Robert Guiscard and crushed the Patzinaks, Turkic nomads. However, the concessions he made, both domestic and foreign, to obtain the support needed, greatly weakened the empire, and he had to negotiate with **Gregory VII** and **Urban II** for aid to fight the Turks, which brought on the Crusades, not what Alexius had intended. He could not prevent the creation of independent Crusader states in Syria and Palestine, nor was the question of reunion between the Eastern and Western Churches settled. Despite a firm policy at home and strong action against the dualist Bogomil heresy, he did not recreate a really effective central authority, and the apparent success of his able rule was only a façade concealing deep-seated separatism. **Zonaras** judged him harshly, but his daughter, **Anna Comnenos**, eulogized him.

Alexius the Studite   Patriarch of Constantinople, 1025–43, born, date and place unknown, died Constantinople, 20 February 1043. Abbot of the monastery of Studies (hence Studites), and appointed patriarch, without the necessary canonical formalities, by Emperor **Basil II**, on his deathbed. The importance of his patriarchate lies in his administrative policies, beginning in 1026, with the anathema of any revolt against the *basileus*, and recorded in numerous edicts, synods and disciplinary laws. He tried to protect the independence of the clergy by stressing that no clergyman or monk could be judged by a civil authority and, in 1027, he condemned the practice of *charistirion*, by which monasteries were given over to private use. He concerned himself extensively with the doctrines of the Monophysites and the Messalians, and with Byzantine marriage laws, though he was weak in not opposing the second and third marriages of Empress Zoe, daughter of Constantine VIII, which were against canon law and the tradition of his monastery. In 1034, he founded a monastery of the Dormition devoted to the Blessed Virgin.

Alfieri, Pietro   Composer and scholar, born Rome, 29 June 1801, died there, 12 June 1863. He contributed greatly to the mid-nineteenth-century revival of interest in Palestrina, the subject of a biography by S. Baini (1828), and his *Raccolta di musica sacra* (1841–6) contained many important works of the master. However, because he believed that every new work must aspire to be like Palestrina, his own compositions comprising Masses, motets, Marian hymns, settings of litanies and much more, are relatively undistinguished.

Alfonso X   King of Castile and León, 1252–84, born Toledo 1221, died Seville, 1284. His reputation as a scholar and patron of the arts outshines his unfortunate political career. During his reign, Spanish culture and literature reached one of its high water marks, and he became known as El Sabio (the Wise). He sponsored valuable translations such as *Las siete partidas*, a legal work embodying the first educational code of its kind in Europe; he established schools in Seville, Murcia and Toledo, and three chairs of civil and canon law at Salamanca. His *Cantigas de Sancta Maria* consists of 420 lyrics concerning miracles of the Blessed Virgin. His schools were open to Christians, Muslims and Jews for cultivating the arts and sciences. He sought, without success, the title Emperor of the Holy Roman Empire, and suffered from enemies without, and disloyalty within, his own family.

Alfonso de Castro   Spanish theologian, born Zamora, 1495, died Brussels, 3 February 1558. He became a Franciscan at Salamanca in 1511, held a chair of theology there for 30 years and is the author of several works: *Adversus omnes haereses lib. XIV* (Paris, 1534), which catalogues and refutes heresies from the time of the Apostles to the sixteenth century; and the most noted, *De potestate legis poenalis* (1550), one of the first works of its kind dealing with punishment and penal justice. Indeed, his skill in the knowledge of penal law earned him renown as 'princeps paenalistarum'. He was active in discussions on original sin and the Canon of Sacred Scripture at the Council of Trent; participated in the controversy (1530) on the validity of **Henry VIII**'s marriage to **Catherine of Aragon**, and wrote a treatise on the subject. Named archbishop of Compostella in 1557, he died before he could be consecrated.

Alfonso of Madrid   Spanish Franciscan spiritual writer, born Madrid c.1475; died after 1521. A gifted writer and a popular spiritual director in aristocratic circles, he wrote a treatise on spiritual perfection, *Espejo de illustres personas* (1542), especially for the wealthy and noble; and *Memorial de la vida de JC*, meditations on the life of Jesus, for wealthy women. His masterpiece, *Arte para servir a Dios* (1521), one of the first works on asceticism written in the vernacular, is ranked among the great spiritual treatises by both **Teresa of Avila** and **Francis de Sales**. The book has three parts: principles of the Christian life, intellect and will; the establishment and ordering of prayer and virtue, and the control of natural dispositions; charity, God's mercy, love of neighbour based on the love of God and three degrees of the spiritual life. Reprinted many times, the Dominicans at Louvain translated it into Latin, and it had much influence in the Catholic Reform.

Alford, Michael (Griffin, 'John Flood')   English Jesuit, born in London in 1587, died of fever at St-Omer, 11 August 1652. Joined the Jesuits in Louvain in 1607 and studied philosophy in Seville and theology in Louvain. After his ordination he was sent to look after the English in Naples, and between 1615 and 1620 he was in Rome. He was rector of the Jesuit College in Ghent for the next eight years, was sent to England and was immediately arrested. He was freed and served secretly in England for over thirty years, based in Combe in Hereford where he had a large library at his disposal. He is the author of *Annales Ecclesiastici et Civiles Britannorum, Saxonum et Anglorum* and probably of the *Britannia Illustrata*.

Alfred of Sareshel (Alfredus Anglicus)   English scientist, early thirteenth century. A scholar and intermediary between Arabic and Western knowledge, who reinforced thirteenth-century science with new texts from antiquity, especially those of Aristotle, whose *Parva naturalia*, and *De anima*, he glossed; and of Avicenna, of whose *On Meteors*, he translated the appendix, and *Liber de congelatis*, used by Roger **Bacon**, among others. His scientific interests produced *De mortu cordis*, dedicated to Alexander Neckham, and cites principally Aristotle, but also the physiological writings of **Galen**, **Costa ben Luca**, Avicenna and Hippocrates, postulating the heart as the basic organ and domicile of life. Alfred's scientific researches helped to focus attention on physiology and medicine.

Alfred the Great   King of Wessex from 871, born Wantage, 849, died Winchester, 26 October 899. The son of King Aethelwulf, and Osburh, he defeated the Danes in 878 and 885, and united the English, which contributed materially to the maintenance of Christianity in England. Alfred is chiefly remembered in church history for the care he brought to ecclesiastical reform and a revival of learning. A man of deep piety and considerable learning, he gathered about him scholars from England, Wales and the Continent. With them he developed an educational plan for clergy and laity based on translations of the most popular Latin works of the time, of which he himself is largely responsible for *Pastoral Care* by **Gregory I** the Great, the *Consolation of Philosophy* of **Boethius**, the *Soliloquies* of St **Augustine**, and the first 50 psalms of the Psalter. These and other works mark the beginnings of English prose through which Alfred hoped to give to his people an education at once practical and liberal, and so to rebuild the once flourishing Christian civilization ruined by the Danish invasions. He promoted the interests of the Church, founded monastic communities at Shaftesbury and Athelney. He is remembered as having done his utmost for the education of his clergy and monks and, in his own life, as the model of a Christian king. Feast day 26 October.

Alipius   Saint, born Tagaste, Africa (Algeria), c.360, died after 429. A close friend of St **Augustine**, they were students together, he of law, and both deviated into Manichaeism in Carthage. He joined Augustine at Rome in 384, and went with him to Milan where they were baptized by **Ambrose** that year. He afterwards participated in the dialogues organized by Augustine at Cassiciacum, and followed him back to Africa in 388, where they lived a quasi-monastic community at Hippo; after three years he was ordained a priest. On a pilgrimage to the Holy Land, c.393, he met **Jerome** and helped to foster a relationship between him and Augustine. In 394 he was elected bishop of Tagaste where he remained for the rest of his life, taking part in the same councils as Augustine, and in struggles against the Pelagians and the Donatists. He long served as Augustine's assistant in his public activities, who called him old in 429; Alipius does not seem to have survived long after that. Feast day 15 August.

Allamano, Giuseppe Italian founder of missionary congregations, born Castel d'Asti, 21 January 1851, died Turin, 16 February 1926. A nephew of St Joseph **Cafasso**, he had the spiritual guidance of St John **Bosco** while a student, and was ordained in 1873. He became rector of the Santuario della Consolata in Turin in 1850, and famous as a confessor and preacher. He founded, in 1901, the Institute of the Consolata Foreign Missions, and its companion, the Missionary Sisters of the Consolata, in 1910; he sent missionaries to Kenya, Mozambique, Ethiopia and Tanzania. A decree for his beatification was issued in 1960.

Allard, Paul French archaeologist and historian, born Rouen, 15 September 1841, died Senneville-sur-Fécamp, December 1916. While on a journey through Europe, 1861–8, studying art and social conditions, he met in Rome G. B. de **Rossi**, who introduced him to the catacombs and to the study of Christian antiquity. His career thereafter combined historical studies with an interest in the Christian social apostolate. He admired Henri **Lacordaire**, Albert de Broglie and Alexis de Toqueville, and was influenced to write articles and monographs on social problems. He founded l'Union Catholique de la Seine-inférieure, and participated in four Catholic international scientific conferences in France between 1888 and 1897. He turned his attention to a study of the Acts of the Martyrs, intending to preserve the essence of the narratives through archaeological discoveries. He produced *Histoire des persecutions*, and *Dix lectures sur les martyrs*, which gave new impetus to the scientific study of the evidence. He was a perceptive and rigorous scholar, and director, from 1904, of *Revue des questions historiques*, helping to further its reputation for excellence.

Allegranza, Joseph Dominican theologian and archaeologist, born Milan 1713, died there 1785. He received the Dominican habit in Brescia in 1731, taught for a time and then studied in Rome for a doctorate, which he received in 1743. He undertook archaeological research in southern France, Italy and Malta. From 1755 he lived in Milan, and undertook the cataloguing of the Petusati library. He wrote a number of archaeological and historical works.

Allegri, Gregorio Italian composer and priest, born 1582, died Rome 7 February 1652. He first worked at the cathedral of Fermo and became a singer in the papal choir, composing much church music. His compositions were the unique preserve of the Vatican Choir, an early example of copyright. His nine-part *Miserere* was sung every year in the Sistine Chapel in Holy Week. **Mozart** as a young man is famous for having heard Allegri's *Miserere* there and copied it down from memory.

Allen, Asa Alonso Evangelist and healer, born Sulphur Rock, Arkansas, 1911, died (of liver sclerosis) San Francisco, 1970. Licensed by the Assemblies of God, in 1951 he established his ministry in Dallas. However, following an arrest for drunken driving he surrendered his credentials and started his Miracle Revival Fellowship. In 1958 he opened his Miracle Revival Training Centre for pastors in Arizona. Allen's message included financial blessing, and as well as his *Miracle Magazine* (from 1954), he produced books including *God's Guarantee to Heal You* (1950), *Power to Get Wealth* (1963) and *God's Guarantee to Bless and Prosper You Financially* (1968).

Allen, Frances Margaret American religious and nurse, born Sunderland, Vermont, 13 November 1784, died Montreal, Quebec, 10 December 1819. Daughter of Ethan Allen, hero of the American Revolution and averse to religion, she grew up in a period of religious revival fuelled in part by reaction to her father's deistic work, *Reason: The Only Oracle of Man* (1784), and asked to attend the school of the Sisters of Notre Dame in Montreal, where she became a Catholic. In 1809 she entered the nursing order of the Sisters of Hotel-Dieu de St Joseph, pronounced vows in 1811, and devoted herself to pharmacy. She died at Hotel-Dieu, having brought converts to the Church during the war of 1812, when it became a military hospital. Frances is remembered in Vermont by a hospital erected in 1894 on a plot that once formed part of her father's farm there, which the Sister Hospitallers of Hotel-Dieu were asked to manage.

Allen, Horace Newton Pioneer Protestant missionary in Korea, born New England, 1858, died 11 December 1932, Toledo, Ohio. In 1883 he was appointed as a medical missionary to China by the

Board of Foreign Missions of the Presbyterian Church in the USA. In 1884 he and his wife Frances relocated to Korea. His medical work brought connections with the royal family and in 1887 he accompanied the first Korean legation to Washington. He encouraged American business interests in Korea and in 1890 became secretary to the American legation in Seoul. By 1897 he was US minister and consul general. He strove to preserve Korean sovereignty, but failed to convince President Roosevelt that Korea did not belong to Japan. He was recalled in 1905 and practised medicine in Toledo. His writings, including *Korean Tales* (1889), introduced Korean literature to the English-speaking world.

Allen, Hugh (Sir)   Organist, composer and teacher, born Reading, 23 December 1869, died Oxford, 20 February 1946. He was educated at Cambridge, held various posts as an organist and teacher, notably director of the Royal College of Music and professor, and helped to compile the BBC Hymn Book which appeared after his death.

Allen, Roland   Mission strategist, born Bristol, England, 29 December 1868, died Kenya, 9 June 1947. Educated at Oxford and Leeds, he became an Anglican priest in 1893 and in 1895 went to North China with the Society for the Propagation of the Gospel. He survived the Boxer siege and following furlough and marriage returned briefly to China. He resigned from parish ministry in 1907 and worked in association with the Survey Application Trust and World Dominion Press. His classic *Missionary Methods: St Paul's or Ours?* and other writings argued for independent indigenous churches. He influenced Pentecostal missions and a new generation of missionaries from the 1960s.

Allen, William   English cardinal, born Rossall, Lancashire, 1532, died Rome, 16 October 1594. A fellow of Oriel College, Oxford, he went to Louvain in 1565, because of his opposition to the Elizabethan Settlement, and established a college at Douai for the training of priests for England, believing that the English were still Catholic at heart, and that Protestantism was a passing phase. Douai became the most important centre for English Catholics, and he founded English colleges at Rome, and Valladolid (1589). From the press at Douai came a stream of Catholic propaganda, and the Douai Version of the Bible. Philip II obtained from Sixtus V a cardinal's hat for Allen in 1584, but his support for Philip's invasion in 1588 incurred the hostility of many English Catholics. He ended his days at the English College, Rome.

Allies, Thomas William   Theologian, born Midsomer Norton, Somersetshire, 12 February 1813, died London, 17 June 1903. A fellow of Wadham College, Oxford, and vicar of Launton, near Bicester, he became closely associated with leaders of the Oxford Movement, especially G. B. Pusey, and having begun to doubt the Anglican position while travelling abroad in 1845–7, he converted to Catholicism in 1850. His learning was wide and in later years he became a prominent apologist for Roman Catholicism in his lectures and writings, which include *The See of Peter* (1850), and *The Formation of Christendom*. Cardinal **Wiseman** appointed him secretary of the Catholic Poor Schools Committee, where he rendered distinguished service until 1890. John Henry **Newman** offered him the chair of modern history in the Catholic University of Ireland, but this did not materialize.

Allo, Ernest Bernard   French Dominican scriptural scholar, born Quintin, 3 February 1873, died Paris, 19 January 1945. He went to Mosul, Iraq, in 1900, to teach theology in the Chaldean Seminary, and in 1903, to the École Biblique in Jerusalem. In 1905 he went to the University of Fribourg, where he spent his teaching career, and published commentaries on the Apocalypse and on the Epistles to the Corinthians, regarded as representative of the modern scientific exegetical approach. He attempted to show that the Gospel transcended other mystery religions, publishing *Plaies d'Europe et baumes de Gange* (1931), a study of Hinduism. Allo won international renown in the fields of biblical exegesis and comparative religion.

Allouez, Claude Jean   French Jesuit missionary, born St Didier-en-Forez, 6 June 1622, died near Niles, Michigan, 27 August 1689. Studied at Toulouse, joined the Society of Jesus, and went to Canada in 1658, where he spent seven years ministering to settlers in the area around Trois Rivieres; then in the Great Lakes area of Wisconsin,

Michigan and Ontario, which enclosed Lakes Huron, Superior, Erie and Michigan, preaching to the many Indian tribes and baptizing thousands. He wrote a prayer book in Illinois and French, establishing missions in Lake Nipigon and Georgian Bay, and wrote *Récit d'un 3e voyage fait aux Illinois* (1679). He is honoured in the USA, especially in Wisconsin, where there is a monument to him erected in 1899, at De Pere, centre of his missionary activity.

Almain, Jacques Theologian, born Sens, *c.*1480; died Paris, 1515. He taught first at Paris, then at Navarre, where he received a doctorate and taught theology until his death, expounding, as was then the custom, the 'Books of Sentences'. He became prominent through his efforts to refute Thomas de Vio's (Cardinal **Cajetan**) defence, *De comparatione auctoritatis papae et concilii*, of the superiority of the Pope, to a general council of bishops. Almain set forth his position in *De auctoritate ecclesiae et conciliorum generalium adversus Thomam de Vio* (1512), invoking Matthew 18:17 to argue that bishops gathered in a general council have divine power to judge all the faithful, including the Pope, because the latter is a member of the Church; that they have the right to impose their will upon him and even to depose him; that the Pope is superior to bishops individually, but inferior to them gathered in a council.

Almond, John Saint, English martyr, born Allerton, near Liverpool, *c.*1577, died Tyburn, 5 December 1612. He studied in Ireland, and at the English College, Rome. He went on the English mission in 1602, was imprisoned in 1608, but worked again in Staffordshire, around 1609. Again arrested in 1612, and brought before John King, bishop of London, for interrogation, he exercised his usual ingenuity and cleverness of speech to confound his questioners who, though continuing to hope for a recantation, were always beaten in argument. Although no proof could be brought against him, he refused to take the oath of allegiance in the form proposed to him, was judged guilty and executed at Tyburn the same year. His last words on the scaffold were: 'In manus tuas Domine . . .'. Feast day 5 December.

Alopen Pioneer missionary to China. A Syriac-speaking Nestorian from Persia who travelled over the Silk Route to be welcomed on the borders of China in 635. The story of his founding of churches and monasteries in China in a window of religious toleration under the second Tang Emperor, T'ai-Tsung, is recorded on the Nestorian monument erected near Xian in 781 and rediscovered in 1623. The Church was free from significant association with foreign political forces, but it accommodated to Buddhism, and remained overdependent on long and fragile lines of communication. Nestorianism had faded in China by 900 but reappeared in the Western Chinese Empire among the Mongols (1260–1368). Alopen's work remains highly significant for Mongol and Chinese Christianity.

Aloysius Gonzaga Saint, Spanish Jesuit, patron of youth, born Castiglione, 9 March 1568, died Rome, 21 June 1591. Of noble descent, and destined for a military career, he made a vow of virginity at the age of seven; at twelve, he became devoted to the Eucharist after receiving his First Communion from Charles **Borromeo**; at thirteen, influenced by reading **Louis of Granada**, he practised mental prayer as much as five hours a day, while also studying philosophy at Alcala. He renounced his inheritance in favour of a younger brother in 1585, entered the Society of Jesus, despite his father's objections, and studied at the Roman College, under the spirtitual direction of St Robert **Bellarmine**. Humble and obedient as a novice, he laboured among the sick and was himself a victim of the plague among the stricken of Rome. Feast day 21 June.

Alphanus of Salerno Italian scholar and archbishop, born Salerno, *c.*1015, died there, 9 October 1085. He taught at the University of Salerno before becoming a monk, with Desiderius, later Pope **Victor III**, at Monte Cassino, then a centre of humanistic learning. His reputation rests essentially in the field of medicine, but also as a theologian and hagiographer. Alphanus is important in the politics and development of Christian humanism in the eleventh century. In an ode addressed to Hildebrand, the future **Gregory VII**, he called on the Papacy to crush with spiritual weapons the forces of barbarism that opposed the Church.

Alphege of Canterbury Saint, English archbishop and martyr, born 954, died Greenwich, 19 April 1012. (Also known as Elphege, Godwine.) He left the monastery at Deerhurst, or possibly Glastonbury, to become an anchorite near Bath, and later abbot, until St **Dunstan** called him to succeed **Ethelwold** at Winchester in 984; translated to Canterbury, he went to Rome in 1006 for his pallium. Five years later the Danes sacked Canterbury and held him ransom, which at first he agreed to pay, but his captors murdered him during a drunken feast, when he refused to ransom himself at the expense of his poor tenants. In later years **Lanfranc** wished to remove his name from the English calendar, but St **Anselm** felt that to die for justice and charity was tantamount to martyrdom. Feast day 19 April.

Alphonsus Liguori Saint, Italian founder of the Redemptorists, Doctor of the Church, born Marianella, 27 September 1696, died Pagani, near Salerno, 1 August 1787. Of an ancient Neapolitan family, he founded in Naples an association of mission preachers, approved by Benedict XIV in 1749 as the Congregation of the Holy Redeemer; elected superior-general for life, and bishop of Sant' Agata dei Goti in 1762. He resigned his see in 1775 on the plea of ill-health and retired to Nocera, but lived another twelve years, a period taken up in much controversy arising from the affairs of his Congregation.

He dedicated himself to the devotion and working for the morality of the Church. He sought to commend the Gospel to a sceptical age by methods which totally engaged his gifts of delicate sensibility, intelligence, tenacity of will and a strong sense of the practical. He preached simply and to the heart, believing that the largely Jansenist influence on the rigorism of the sacrament of penance repelled rather than reconciled the sinful. It is as a moral theologian that he is chiefly celebrated, and his *Theologia Moralis* (1753–5), for the use of religious and priests engaged in pastoral work, especially the confessional, stresses the search for the will of God in all circumstances. Alphonsus developed a system known as 'Equiprobabilism', an effort to keep a golden mean, in contradistinction to the Jesuits, between Probabiliorism, with its Jansenist severity, and Probabilism, especially in its lax exaggerations. Many of the manuals of moral theology used in seminaries throughout the world either belong to his school or are strongly marked by his influence, and the practical direction traced by him has been substantially adopted by the Church. 'St Alphonsus was more than a great personage of history,' says Arquillière in *Histoire illustrée de l'Église*, 'he is a symbol and a very significant one.' Feast day 1 August.

Alphonsus Rodríguez *see* **Rodríguez, Alphonsus**

Altamirano, Diego Francisco de Spanish Jesuit missionary, born Madrid, 26 October 1625, died Lima, 22 December 1715. He joined the Society of Jesus, lived for some ten years in the Philippines and as professor of theology at the University of Cordoba del Tucuman, Argentina. A missionary to the Chaco, he founded the reduction of St **Francis Xavier**; he served as provincial of Paraguay from 1677 to 1681, procurator for Madrid and Rome, 1683, visitor to the Nuevo Reino, visitor and provincial of Peru and rector of the College of Lima. An outstanding religious superior, he strongly advocated Jesuit rights in their relationship with the crown and the bishops. As missionary he wrote a catechism in the Mocobi tongue, and supervised the establishment of missions as far south as the Strait of Magellan. He supported the reductionist policy of military protection for missions, and their protection against incursions of the Paulistas and other Indian tribes.

Altaner, Berthold German Catholic historian and patristic scholar, born St Annaberg, Silesia, 10 September 1885, died Bad Kissinger, Bavaria, 30 January 1964. Ordained in 1910, he taught church history at Breslau and, in 1929, was appointed professor of patrology, ancient church history and Christian archaeology there. The first theologian to be deprived of his university position by the Nazis, in 1933, he held a post at Breslau Cathedral until expelled by the Gestapo in 1945, when he fled to Bavaria. Appointed to the chair of patrology and liturgy at Würzburg after the war, he remained there until his retirement in 1950. His early works deal with the history of the Dominican Order, and he is best known for his one-volume *Patrologie: Leben, Schriften und Lehre du Kirchenvater* (1938, 17 editions and 6 languages), a standard work of reference dealing with the influence of Eastern theology on Western writers, especially St **Augustine**.

Altenstaig, Johannes German humanist, educator and theologian, born Mindelheim, Bavaria, *c.*1480, died there, *c.*1525. He studied poetry and rhetoric under Heinrich Bebel at Tübingen, taught Latin at Mindelheim, became a friend of Johann **Eck**, and other humanist theologians, with whom he conducted an intensive cultural exchange aimed at restoring classical purity to the debased Latin language of the day. He opposed the Reformation but, like Bebel, was critical of ecclesiastical abuses, and inveighed against them in *Kommentar zum Bebels Triumphus Verens* (1515).

Altmann of Passau Saint, German bishop and great reformer, born Westphalia, *c.*1015, died Zeiselmauer, near Vienna, 8 August 1091. He became canon and teacher at Paderborn, provost at Aachen, chaplain to Empress Agnes, and bishop of Passau in 1065. Concerned for the spiritual well-being of his clergy, he imposed the Rule of St **Augustine** in several churches, and founded Augustinian houses at Rothenbuch and Reichersberg. With some courage he vigorously supported papal decrees against married priests in 1094, and was the first to announce Emperor **Henry IV**'s excommunication in Germany, in 1076. Exiled from his diocese by the imperial party in 1077, he fled to Rome, but continued his pastoral and political duties, in spite of Henry's persecution, under the protection of Margrave **Leopold II**, until his death. His cult has been permitted in the Dioceses of Passau, Linz and Sankt Polten, since the late nineteenth century.

Alva, Duke of (Fernando Álvarez de Toledo) Spanish soldier and statesman, born Avila, 29 October 1508, died Tomar, near Lisbon, 12 December 1582. At seventeen he joined the campaign that drove the French from Spain, and after service against the Turks in Hungary and North Africa, he commanded Charles V's armies against German Protestants with much success. In 1555, Alva became commander in Italy with orders to halt French expansion in the peninsula; he presided over the break-up of the Franco-papal alliance, and Spanish supremacy in Italy, under Philip II. Alva is best known for his rule of the Spanish Netherlands. He arrived in Brussels with 10,000 men in 1567 to succeed the regent, **Margaret of Parma**, whose rule had been mild and conciliatory, with a programme of hard 'Castilianization', a reign of terror in which the Spaniards attempted forcibly to uproot the now firmly entrenched Protestantism of the northern provinces. Alva eschewed the support of the Catholics and, instead, alienated them with harshness, severity and higher taxes. His Council of Troubles (dubbed Council of Blood by Netherlanders) executed hundreds of rebels, nobles and burghers. The alienated Catholics united with the Protestants against Alva, and his repressions finally ended with his defeat at Alkmaar in 1573. Alva returned to Spain in 1573, but Philip called on Alva again in 1580 to lead the army against Portugal, winning, in a masterly campaign, a crushing victory at Alcantara; Spain then ruled Portugal until 1640.

Alva y Astorga, Pedro de Spanish Franciscan, born 1602 died 1667. A lecturer in theology, he belonged to the Franciscan Province of the Twelve Apostles of Peru. He is noted for his writings on the Immaculate Conception, one of the outstanding figures in seventeenth-century debates on the subject and, with **Duns Scotus**, credited with development of belief in the great mystery. Procurator-general of the Franciscans in Rome and, using his own press in the Low Countries, he published his copious, related theological writings, the most important of which is the *Armentarium Seraphicum pro tuendo Immaculatae Conceptionis titulo* (1648). He also contributed to the history of his Order with his *Bullarium*, in 10 vols, of which the 'Indiculus', is well known.

Alvarado, Francisco de Spanish/Mexican missionary, born Mexico, *c.*1560, died Teposculula, March 1603. He joined the Dominicans in 1574, and became a missionary among the Mixtec Indians; he learnt the language and wrote a lexicon in Mixtec, *Vocabulario Misteco*, based on the works of other missionaries, with corrections and amplification from his own experience. These vocabularies and grammars were of great importance in the training of Indian missionaries.

Alvare, Paul *see* **Albar**

Alvares, Francisco Portuguese missionary priest, born, date unknown, died Rome(?), *c.*1540. Appointed chaplain to the first royal embassy to Ethiopia, he left Lisbon for Massawa, via Goa, in 1517, arriving there in 1520. The Portuguese started their return journey six years later, accompanied by David II's ambassador to Portugal, and his commission to Alvares was to convey to the Holy See his pledge of loyalty, which he did, after a forced delay of five years, to **Clement VII** at Bologna. Alvares wrote a monumental description of Christian Ethiopia, 'Verdadera informacam das Terras do Preste Joam'; a version, published in 1540 and translated into several European languages, contained accurate information that supplemented what Damião de **Góis** had made available at second hand, and is highly regarded in Ethiopia today. When, in 1533, Alvares finally rendered David's obedience to Clement, news of it was rapidly circulated and caused a great stir, but nothing came of it and an opportunity for formal reunion was missed. The manuscript of his great treatise remained unpublished and is lost, but the 1540 version reveals a great mind, tolerant and critical, Portuguese and ecumenical.

Álvarez, Baltasar Spanish Jesuit spiritual writer, born Cernera del Rio Alhama, 1533, died Belmonte, 25 July 1580. He entered the Society at Alcala in 1555, became rector of Salamanca, Medina del Campo and Villagarcia, and provincial of Toledo; for six years he acted as confessor to St **Teresa of Avila**. His dedication to contemplation, in relation to the apostolic work of the Jesuits, being considered incompatible with the spirit of the Society, the provincial, Juan Suarez, and the visitor, Diego Avellaneda, condemned it. Their opposition stemmed mainly from the disfavour with which the Society of the time viewed the tendency to encourage contemplation at the expense of the apostolic ministry, their principal objective. Luis de **La Puente**, SJ, wrote a popular biography, and drew attention to Alvarez' commentaries on the rules for novices, retreat sermons and treatises on the prayer of silence, which expressed the intensity of his personal spiritual experience.

Álvarez, Diego Spanish Dominican theologian, bishop, born Medina del Rio Secco, date unknown, died Trani, 1631. He entered the Order at Medina, taught theology at Burgos, Palencia and Valladolid. He became involved in controversy with the Jesuits on the issue of grace and free will, and went to Rome, with Tomás de **Lemos**, to defend the Thomist school in the 'Congregatio de auxiliis' debates ordered by the Pope in an effort to resolve the dispute. Named bishop of Trani in 1606, he remained there until his death. Most of his published works are concerned with efficacious grace and freedom, and were edited several times in the seventeenth century. He also published his courses on theology, on the third part of the Summa Theologiae of St **Thomas Aquinas**, and on the second *Disputationes theologicae in primam secundae S. Thomae* (Trani, 1617). Many texts and documents remain unedited in the archives of the Order, at Rome.

Álvarez of Cordoba Blessed, Portuguese Dominican preacher and reformer, born Cordoba, 1360, died there, 19 February 1430. He preached throughout Andalusia and in Italy; swung Castile against the antipope Pedro de Luna (**Benedict XIII**). He acted as confessor and counsellor to Queen Catherine and King John II, and retired to Cordoba in 1423, where he founded the Scala Coeli Priory. He developed a great devotion to the Passion of Christ during a pilgrimage to Palestine in 1405, and this moved him to erect in the priory gardens tableaux of the Passion that were forerunners of the Way of the Cross. Feast day 19 February.

Álvarez de Paz, Diego Spanish Jesuit spiritual writer, born Toledo, 1560, died Potosi, 17 January 1620. He entered the Society at Alcala and went to Peru in 1589 as professor of philosophy and theology; in 1616 he was provincial, and remained there until he died. His works are contained in three large volumes and treat respectively of perfection; the overcoming of sin, vices, passions and the practice of virtues, especially humility; the search for peace through prayer. Though profuse, the trilogy is notable for its depth, precision, clarity and dogmatic reliability. Álvarez was influenced by the work of P. Cordeses, SJ, on prayer, and was the first Jesuit to make a detailed study of infused contemplation.

Alzate, José Antonio Mexican philosopher, journalist and scientist, born Mexico City, November 1737, died there, 2 February 1799. Of humble origins, his family provided for his early education, and a 'Capellania' enabled him to study philosophy and theology at the University of Mexico. The strong influences of Diderot, Condorcet and the Enlightenment fed his curiosity about physical and natural science, and he became very critical of Spanish policy, which inhibited investigation and development of scientific research. He participated in the reform of scientific education in Mexico, and in the founding of the Royal School of Mines, in 1792. He edited collections of scientific and technological information for popular publications such as *Gacitas de literatura de Mexico*, in which are described machines and instruments, and inventions useful in agriculture, mining and industry. He himself made experiments with electricity, and recorded his meteorological observations, particularly of the *aurora borealis* of 1789. Included in his natural scientific observations are investigations of Indian ruins on which he wrote archaeological reports. He received honours from a number of scientific academies in his lifetime.

Alzog, Johann Baptist German theologian and historian, born Ohlau, Silesia, 29 June 1808, died Freiburg, 1 March 1878. Ordained at Cologne, he became professor of ecclesiastical history at Posen, Hildesheim and Freiburg from 1853, until his death. A voluminous writer of sound theological sense and scientific method in research, he is known for *History of the Church* (1841), and for *Handbuch der Patrologie* (1866), a model of exactness, conciseness of doctrinal exposition and bibliography. Although overtaken by more recent scholarship, these works rendered great service at the time they were published. Alzog also published in German other important books, and edited the *Oratio apologetica de fuga sera* of St **Gregory of Nazianzus**. **Pius IX** invited him to take part in the preparatory work for the First Vatican Council.

Alzon, Emmanuel d' French founder of religious congregations, born Vigau, 30 August 1810, died Nimes, 21 November 1880. Of an aristocratic family, he studied at Montpellier and Rome, and became vicar-general of Nîmes, a post he occupied for 45 years. In 1845 he founded the congregations of the Augustinians of the Assumption (Assumptionists), whose superior-general he remained in his lifetime, and, in 1865, the Oblate Sisters of the Assumption. As well as concerning himself with his Order, he campaigned against the State's monopoly of higher education and, at the insistence of **Montalembert**, was appointed member of the Higher Council of Public Instruction (1850). He took the lead in opening a school of higher education in the College of the Assumption; pushed for the creation of Catholic normal schools; requested, in 1852, bishops and religious superiors to establish a French seminary at Rome. He attended Vatican I as theologian to Bishop Claude Plantier, and worked hard for the definition of papal infallibity. A strong spiritual director, his letters to Mother Marie Eugenie de Jesus, foundress of the Congregation of the Assumption, are notable for their literary and spiritual excellence. The cause for his beatification was introduced in 1935.

Amadeus VIII of Savoy (Felix V, Antipope), born Chambery, 4 September 1383, died Ripaille, 7 January 1451. The Council of Basel, having deposed **Eugenius IV**, elected Amadeus Pope, irregularly, it being carried out by only one cardinal and 32 nominated electors, which he accepted even though he had retired to the convent he had founded at Ripaille on Lake Geneva. However, he received little support – the great powers held aloof, or were hostile. His relations with the Council deteriorated, and he abdicated in 1449, the last antipope, to be succeeded by the Roman **Nicholas V** who, generously, made him a cardinal-bishop, gave him a substantial pension and appointed him papal vicar and legate in Savoy and adjacent dioceses.

Amadeus IX of Savoy Blessed, duke of Savoy, born Thonen, 1 February 1435, died Vercelli, Italy, 30 March 1472. The husband of Yolanda, daughter of **Charles VII** of France, he succeeded to the throne in 1456. Austere and devout, generous to the poor, he readily forgave his enemies; an able and wise administrator, but tolerant of troublemakers, he showed great forbearance and forgiveness toward his adversaries, the Sforzas, and some of his many brothers, which appears to have encouraged strife. He suffered from epilepsy, which eventually wore him down, and he relinquished authority to his wife. Feast day 30 March.

Amadeus of Lausanne Saint, French Cistercian abbot of Hautecombe and bishop of Lausanne, born Chateau de Chatte, Dauphine, 21 January 1110, died Lausanne, 27 August 1159. He quit his noble rank for the anonymity of the cloister in 1125, but his abbot, St **Bernard of Clairvaux**, urged him to undertake positions of leadership as counsellor to the counts of Savoy and envoy to the papal court. As bishop he practised the monastic ideals of personal piety and devotion to communal peace. He was the author of eight homilies in honour of the Blessed Virgin, the seventh of which was cited twice in the 1950 dogmatic declaration of the Assumption by **Pius XII**. **Pius X** confirmed his cult. Feast day 28 January.

Amalarius of Metz Liturgical scholar, born area of Metz, *c*.775, died Metz, *c*.850. He studied under **Alcuin** and became a prominent figure in the Carolingian Renaissance. He has been identified with another Amalarius, archbishop of Trier, 809–813, but this has been questioned by some scholars, though not disproved. He did, however, administer the see of Lyons, in 835, after the deposition of its archbishop, **Agobard**, but was removed in his turn in 838, because of his untraditional and even heretical theology. His principal treatise, *De ecclesiasticis officiis*, is partly an attempt to fuse Roman and Gallican ceremonial practices, and became the most influential liturgical book of the early Middle Ages in the West; it remains a fundamental source for the history of liturgy.

Amalberga Saint. The lives of two saints of this name, one seventh century and the other eighth century, have become intertwined in history and legend to the point where they are indistinguishable. It seems, however, that the first, a widow, became the wife of Count Witger and had two daughters, **Gudula**, patroness of Brussels, and Remilde, and a son, **Emebert**, later to become bishop of Cambrai. After the birth of Gudula, the parents entered religion and Amalberga, having received the veil from St **Aubert**, entered the convent at Maubeuge, where she died *c*.690, and her body was transferred to the Benedictine abbey at Lobbes, where Witger had become a monk. The

second Amalberga was born in the Ardennes (Belgium), and introduced to a holy life by St Landrade, abbess of Bilsen, possibly sent there by St **Willibrord**; she led a pious life at a retreat in Flanders, which she owned, and where she died in *c*.772. Her relics were translated to the church of St Pierre in Ghent in 1073. It has been said that her beauty was such that Pepin III wished her to marry his son **Charlemagne**, but that she escaped his attentions by taking the veil, but not his brutality, amongst which was a broken arm sustained while fending him off. However this is one among several romantic and complicated anachronisms. Feast day 10 July.

Amalric of Bene (Amaury) Twelfth-century theologian and heretic, born Bene, near Chartres, mid-twelfth century, died Paris, *c*.1206. He studied at Paris in the last years of the twelfth century, and, soon among the masters, he taught liberal arts, then theology and Scripture. He conceived the idea, unfortunate for him, to undertake an explication of Aristotle's *Metaphysics*, recently translated into Latin from Arabic, according to which all beings issue from primary matter, which itself possesses neither form nor figure, but is possessed of continual motion. Amalric, already full of the doctrines of John Scotus **Eriugena**, who, in the ninth century, saw the universe in God, the soul of the universe, came to conceive a pure pantheism in which, essentially, God and matter are one and the same simple being; he outlined this in *Physion, Traite des choses naturelles*, which **Innocent III** condemned in a Bull in 1204, and Amalric, obliged to retract his doctrine, died of sorrow soon after. Shortly after that, some clerics and laymen calling themselves Amalricians were discovered in Paris teaching pantheism, proclaiming the age of the incarnation of the Holy Spirit in every man, and that those so deified were, like Christ, incapable of sinning. A synod in Paris in 1210, and Lateran Council IV in 1215, condemned Amalric's teaching.

Amandus Saint, apostle of Flanders, born south of Nantes, Aquitaine, *c*.584; died Elnon, 6 February, after 675. He played an important role in the history of the Church, but his life is not well known, partly because of legendary aspects which have been introduced, and an absence of chronology and precision in biographical accounts; also because of confusion with other saints with more or less similar names, such as Alanus of Lavaur. His itinerant existence does not facilitate matters; essentially a missionary going from country to country, he stopped only to found church or monastery, returning to the search for other souls to be gained for Christ. Consecrated bishop in 628, he began active misssionary work in Flanders and Carinthia; in 633 he founded two monasteries at Ghent under the patronage of St Peter, and later a large monastery at Elnone near Tournai, of which he was abbot in his last years. He is said to have been bishop of Tongres, Maastricht, from 649 to 652, which is referred to in a letter of 649 from Martin I, dissuading him from resigning his see. His *Testament* survives, and his life is otherwise known from a *Vita prima*, assigned to the late eighth century. Feast day 6 February.

Amann, Emile French theologian and historian, born Pont-à-Mousson, 4 June 1880, died Strasburg, 10 January 1948. He studied at Nancy, and at l'Institut Catholique de Paris, where he obtained a doctorate in theology. In 1910, with other scholars at the Institut, he inaugurated a collection of apocryphal NT writings, *Apocryphes du Nouveau Testament*, in which he edited 'Protoévangile de Jacques', and added *Actes de Paul et ses lettres apocryphes* (1913), and *Actes de Pierre* (1920). He became director of *Dictionnaire de théologie catholique* in 1922, to which project Amann himself contributed over 100 articles, and edited nearly 20 vols. He joined the faculty of theology at Strasburg as professor of ancient church history in 1919.

Amat, Thaddeus Spanish missionary in California, born Barcelona, 31 December 1811, died Los Angeles, 12 May 1878. Ordained in the Congregation of the Missions (Vincentians) in Barcelona, in 1837, he went to the USA in 1835, and did missionary work in Louisiana, then in Missouri; in 1848, he became superior of St Charles Seminary, Philadelphia, and in 1853, second bishop of Monterey, with residence at Los Angeles. His diocese grew rapidly, his Spanish and American cultural upbringing being of great effect in its administration, and he held several synods to cope with the problems this expansion generated. He

attended Vatican Council I, where he participated actively in discussions on the constitutions: 'On Catholic Faith', and 'On Primacy'. He is buried in St Vibiana Cathedral, whose cornerstone he had laid.

Amatus of Nusco Saint, Italian bishop and abbot, born Nusco, *c.*1104, died 13 August 1193. There are two versions of his life, the later of which appears the more reliable, and, according to which, he issued of noble parents, entered the religious life and became a Benedictine. He founded Fontignano Abbey, near Orvieto, in 1142, and was made bishop of Nusco in 1154. A zealous and popular bishop, a generous benefactor of religious houses, he is said to have worked many miracles before and after his death. Feast day 31 August.

Ambrose Saint, born Trier, *c.*340, of a distinguished family (his father had been Praetorian Prefect of Gaul), died Milan, 4 April 397. He studied in Rome and became consul of Liguria and Aemilia, administered from Milan. He became bishop of Milan in 373 or 374, elected by the people of the city although he was not yet a baptized Christian. He was an outstanding preacher, a staunch opponent of Arianism, and a powerful influence on the Roman emperors who lived in Milan. He wrote *De Sacramentis*, and a study of ethics, with particular reference to the clergy, entitled *De Officiis Ministorum*. He is sometimes known as the founder of Latin hymnody. His name is given to a specific liturgy and thereby to a set of chants. He is one of the four ancient doctors of the Western Church. The hymn *Aeterna Christi Munera* has been ascribed to St Ambrose. Feast day 7 December.

Ambrose of Cahors Saint, French bishop, date of birth unknown, died near Bourges, *c.*770. He lived around the middle of the eighth century, and was named bishop of Cahors, under Pepin III, the Short. It seems that despite his works of charity, the faithful hated and calumnied him, so he gave up his see and lived in a cave for three years near the river Lot. He went to Rome on pilgrimage and died on the return journey. There is an abbey built over his grave, which went to the Canons Regular of St Augustine around 1550. Feast day 16 October.

Ambrose of Massa Venerable, Italian Franciscan, born Massa Maritima, Tuscany, died Orvieto, 17 April 1240. A parish priest in the Tuscan Maremma, when led to reform his life by the preaching of Moricus, an early companion of St **Francis**, he joined the Franciscans in 1225. For the last fifteen years of his life he devoted himself to penance and works of charity. Many miracles were performed at his tomb in the church of St Francis, Orvieto, and a petition submitted for his canonization is still open, but the Franciscans honour him with the title of blessed.

Ambrose of Optina (Ambrosy Grenkov) Saint and elder of the Russian Orthodox Church, born Tambov province, 23 November 1812, died Optina, 10 October 1891. He entered the monastery of Optina in 1842 and in 1860 he became the main staretz (elder). He was visited by vast numbers for spiritual and even practical assistance. **Dostoevsky** and **Tolstoy** both revered him. For much of his life he received visitors from 9am until 11pm each day. Feast day 10 October.

Ambrose Traversari Blessed, Italian monk and early Christian humanist, born Portico, 16 September 1386, died Fontebuono, 17 November 1439. In 1400 he entered the Camaldolese Cenobitic monastery of St Mary of the Angels at Florence, than which, during the Quattrocento, there were few intellectual and spiritual centres more open or active, Ambrose being one of its more endearing figures. Of a modest family, a model of discipline and work, he had an excellent knowledge of Greek, and translated numerous works of the Greek Fathers, notably SS **John Chrysostom** (his preferred author), **Basil** and **Athanasius**. A renowned professor and of a comprehensive charity, he established relations with the greatest names of the age, and Florentine humanists such as Niccoli, Strozzi and Cosimo de Medici visited him to discuss classical and patristic literature, philosophy and theology. **Eugene IV**, who regarded him highly, named him general of his Order in 1431, and supported his movement for reform. He represented Eugenius at the Council of Basel, defended the primacy of the Papacy, and opposed all schism in the Church. At Ferrara and Florence, in 1438, he negotiated with Byzantine representatives in discussions leading to reunion. Feast day 17 November.

Ambrosius Catharinus (Lancelot Politi), Italian Dominican theologian and archbishop, born Siena, c.1484, died Naples, 8 November 1553. A doctor of civil and canon law, he joined the Dominicans in 1517, because of **Savonarola**'s preaching, and engaged in anti-Lutheran polemics. He incurred some disfavour in the Order because of his defence of the doctrine of the Immaculate Conception. He published several works on current theological problems, e.g. predestination, where his position foreshadowed that of **Luis de Molina**; justification, purgatory, veneration of the saints, all of which persuaded **Pallavicino** that Ambrosius 'was second to none among his contemporaries in contest with heretics'. He attended the Council of Trent (1545–7) as papal theologian, and the conciliar fathers petitioned for him to be named bishop of Muion in 1546, and later archbishop of Conza. His many and original works, often on uncharted areas of theology, contained flaws, such as on the value of the words 'Hoc est corpus meum', which he held to be secondary to the preceding epiclesis, 'Quam oblationem . . .', of the Roman Mass. He influenced the juridico-moral explanation of the transmission of original sin; his works emphasize the 'magisterium' of the Church and a return to the Scriptures and the teaching of the Fathers.

Amelry, Francis Belgian Carmelite, spiritual writer and mystic, born, c.1498, died Ieper, c.1552. Prior of the Carmel at Ieper, he is known to have written some ten spiritual works, in which love and its mystical experience is the dominant theme. Two of his treatises, *What the Love of God Can Do*, and *The Loving Soul*, rank among the classics of spiritual literature in the Low Countries; the first is a handbook of the spiritual life, while the second, his masterpiece, is a systematic and logical presentation of the stages of love, in seven steps, describing its progressively enveloping nature. His mystical doctrine, sound theologically, is much influenced by personal experience.

Amerbach, Bonifacius Born at Basel, 11 October 1495, died there, 24 April 1562. Youngest son of Johann **Amerbach**, he had a humanist education in Latin and Greek, met **Erasmus** around 1516, and became his close friend and legal heir. Bonifacius took a very critical attitude to the Reformation, reminiscent of Erasmus' own. He supported the reforms demanded by **Luther**, but withdrew his allegiance when Erasmus was attacked, and moved towards a conciliatory attitude between the Swiss and Lutheran conceptions of the Eucharist, becoming converted to a moderate Protestantism. He lent his support to that current which made of Basel a centre of 'Erasmian' inspiration and humanistic culture for nearly half a century, the main feature of which was religious and philosophical toleration.

Amerbach, Johann Editor, printer and bookseller. Born Amerbach, Franconia, c.1443, died Basel, 25 December 1513. Studied at Paris with Johann Heynlin von Stein, and took up residence in Basel in 1475. His printing shop prospered rapidly, and he collaborated with Heynlin von Stein, who persuaded him to edit the collected works of the Church Fathers, and fostered his connection with the Carthusian monastery, whose library contained manuscripts going back to the Council of Basel. Amerbach's edition of St **Jerome** was so far advanced at the time of his death that Johann **Froben**, assisted by **Erasmus**, was able to publish it in 1516. Johann died while working on his greatest enterprise, the publication of the collected works of the four Doctors of the Church: **Ambrose**, **Jerome**, **Gregory** and **Augustine**.

Amerbach, Veit German humanist scholar, born Wembling, 1503, died Ingolstadt, 13 September 1557. He studied at Wittemberg from 1522, and taught there from 1530. He bacame disaffected with his colleagues, and concluded that the patristic writings did not support **Luther**'s doctrine of justification by faith alone. He took up the arguments of Johann **Eck**, who, until the controversy on indulgences broke out, had himself been on good terms with Luther, but contributed largely to procuring his excommunication in the Bull *Exsurge Domine* (1520). Amerbach also favoured Eck's defence for the primacy of the papal position in *De primatu Petri adversum Lutherum*. In November 1543, he converted to Catholicism, and became a professor of philosophy and rhetoric at Ingolstadt, where Eck was professor of theology. He never wrote against Protestantism; most of his

many writings deal with classical authors, i.e. Cicero, Ovid and Chrysostom.

Amette, Léon Adolphe French cardinal, born Douville (Eure), 6 September 1850, died Antony (Seine), 29 August 1920. Born into modest family circumstanes, he studied at St Sulpice, worked in Evreux, and was consecrated bishop of Bayeux, 1899, archbishop of Paris, 1908, and cardinal, 1911. The law of 1905 separating Church and State had created tensions between the civil and ecclesiastical authorities, and he actively sought, in a peaceful way, to prepare a reconciliation between the two. In the Great War, he participated in relief efforts, and often acted as an intermediary between the French government and the Holy See. Throughout his episcopate he effectively championed free elementary education, the establishment of parish committees, the cause of labour and collective bargaining. He built 50 churches and chapels.

Amiot, Jean Joseph Marie French missionary to China, born Toulon, 8 February 1718, died Peking, 8 October 1793. He entered the Society of Jesus and went in 1750 to Peking, where he won the confidence of the Emperor Kien-lung, and spent the remainder of his life. A prolific writer on Chinese and Tartar art and history, the Manchus esteemed him for his many talents, linguistic and scientific, as an astronomer and mathematician. His *Dictionnaire tartare–mantchou–francais* (1789) is a work of great value, the language having been previously quite unknown in Europe. His studies of Asian peoples, treatises on Confucius and Chinese history, on warfare and on music were highly prized. His other writings are to be found in *Mémoires concernant l'histoire, les sciences et les arts des Chinois* (1776–91). Eminently fitted to make good use of the advantages which his situation afforded, Amiot's works did more than had ever been done before to make known to the Western world the thought and life of the Far East.

Ammanati, Bartolomeo Italian mannerist sculptor and architect, born Settignano, 1511, died Florence, 1592. He trained under Baccio Bandinelli in Florence and Jacopo Sansovino in Venice, closely imitated the style of **Michelangelo**, and collaborated with Vasari and Vignola on projects in Rome during the reign of **Julius III** (1550–5). Chief architect in Florence to Cosimo di **Medici**, Ammanati created an addition to the Pitti Palace acclaimed as one of his most celebrated works. He also built in 1569 the beautiful bridge over the River Arno, known as Ponte della Trinità – a great success. Another of his important works is the colossal *Neptune of the Fountain* in Piazza della Signoria. He worked on the Jesuit church of San Giovamino in 1579, until his health and eyesight began to fail in his final years.

Ammanati de' Piccolomini, Jacopo   Italian humanist, cardinal, patron of the arts, born Villa Basilica, near Lucca, 8 March 1422, died San Lorenzo, 10 September 1479. From a poor family, he owed his advancement to classical studies, becoming private secretary to Cardinal Domenico **Capranica**, in 1450. Appointed secretary of briefs to **Calixtus III** and **Pius II**, who valued him highly and adopted him into the Piccolomini family, he made him a citizen of Siena, bishop of Pavia in 1460, and cardinal the following year. He disagreed with Pius, however, who imprisoned him on a charge of conspiracy, but transferred him to Lucca in 1470, and named him papal legate to Umbria. A Christian humanist, he stood out as a conscientious ecclesiastic.

Ammonius, Andreas (Ammonio, Andrea)   Italian humanist and author, born Lucca, 1478, died London, 16 August 1517. A member of one of the oldest families of Lucca, and later given the Hellenized name of Ammonio. He studied and taught at Bologna and travelled to England, *c.*1504, probably with Silvestro Gigli, the Luccanese bishop of Worcester, sent to England in 1505 to give Henry VII tokens of the esteem of **Julius II**. By 1511 he had become Latin secretary to **Henry VIII**, was prependary in the cathedral of St Stephen, Westminster, in 1512, and went to France the same year with the English army at the Battle of the Spurs. A close friend of Desiderius **Erasmus** and Thomas **More**, he assisted the former in his quest for financial security and freedom from the bonds of his religious order, the Canons of St Augustine. In 1515 **Leo X** appointed him sub-collector of papal taxes in England, but this position he enjoyed only briefly, dying suddenly of the 'sweating sickness', before the age of 40. Ammonio's small literary output contained a volume of Latin poetry and a panegyric of Henry. Erasmus wrote a poem to Ammonio in 1511, partly to thank him for a gift of excellent wine.

Amort, Eusebius   German philosopher and theologian, born Bibermuhle, Bavaria, 15 November 1692, died Polling, 5 February 1775. Educated by the Jesuits, he became a Canon Regular of the Lateran. A prolific writer on religious subjects: some 70 volumes on philosophy, apologetics, theology, history, devotional works, of which the best known are four folios on *Theology, eclectic, moral and scholastic* (1752), admired by **Benedict XIV**. He took a middle way between rigorism and laxism in the controversy on 'probabilism', and co-founded 'equibrobabilism', in as much as St **Alphonsus Liguori** appealed to his authority in defence of the moral system. Although very critical of the revelations in the *Mystical City of God* of Maria **Agreda** in 1744, and even though his views on private revelation, generally, were valuable, he had an imperfect understanding of Maria's Spanish text, and this marred the relevance of them to the Agredan revelations. He also made a significant contribution in defending the claim, against that of the Benedictine Jean Serson, that **Thomas à Kempis** was indeed the author of *The Imitation of Christ*.

Amphilochius of Iconium   Bishop, born Caesarea, *c.*340, died after 394. A cousin of St **Gregory of Nazianzus** and a friend of St **Basil**, he became bishop of Iconium in 373, having retired from public life in 370, after a decade of teaching law. As metropolitan of Lycaonia, he supported the cause of orthodoxy and played an important role at the Council of Constantinople I, in 381. He presided at the Council of Side, in 390, which condemned the Messalians, and he campaigned against puritanical and extremist cults. Among his extant works are a synodal letter in defence of the Holy Spirit issued after a council at Iconium in 376, a poem 'Iambi ad Seleucum', preserved among the works of St Gregory of Nazianzus. He earned great esteem as a source of patristic teaching in the fifth century.

Amsdorf, Nikolaus von   Lutheran theologian and bishop, born Torgau, 3 December 1483, died

Eisenach, 14 May 1565. He studied and taught at Wittenberg in 1511–24, became a close friend and disciple of Martin **Luther**, assisted him in translating the Bible, and later supervised the Jena edition (1555–8) of Luther's works. He accompanied Luther to the Disputations at Leipzig in 1519, and to the Diet of Worms in 1521. Luther and the Elector of Saxony named him bishop of Maumburg in 1541, but the Imperialists expelled him during the Schmalkaldic War of 1547. Held responsible for Luther's renewed dispute with **Erasmus**, he later quarrelled with Philipp **Melanchthon**, urging the high Lutheran party to separate from him; he fought ceaselessly for Luther's teaching, and maintained not only the uselessness but also the actual harmfulness of good works to salvation, a one-sided interpretation of Luther criticized in the Formula of Concord. He held unswervingly to a conservative Lutheran position in theology, and helped to found the Univerity of Jena, a Lutheran stronghold.

Amyot, Jacques French humanist and bishop, born Melun, 30 October 1513; died Auxerre, 6 February 1593. He studied at the College de France, taught Greek and Latin at Bourges, and received from **Francis I** the Premonstratensian abbey of Bellozane-en-Bray. One of the four great prose stylists of sixteenth-century France, his literary work consists mostly of translations which, though free and containing errors, became very popular and influenced moral thought and literary style for many years. His oeuvre includes *Histoire aethiopique d'Heliodorus* (1547), *Sept livres des histoires de Diodore Sicilien* (1554), *Amours pastorales de Daphnis et Chloe* (1559), and Plutarch's *Lives* and *Morals*, the translation of which by Sir Thomas North in 1579, **Shakespeare** used. Appointed bishop of Auxerre in 1570, he suffered constant attack during his last years by the Holy League, particularly for his participation in the Estates of Blois in 1589.

Amyraut, Moïse French Calvinist theologian, born Bourgueil, Touraine, September 1596, died Saumur, 8 January 1664. He studied theology at Saumur under John **Cameron**, whose doctrine of divine election he developed and defended as a theory of predestination called, after him, Amyraldism. A man of courtly manners, he moved with ease among eminent persons and was on occasion consulted by **Richelieu** and **Mazarin**. A prolific and influential writer, his 'hypothetic universalism', on divine election, is elaborated in *Echantillon de la doctrine de Calvin sur la prédestination* (1634). In an era of sharp conflict, Amyraut's works were notably pacific and moderate.

Anacletus (Cletus) Saint, bishop of Rome, *c*.79 – *c*.91. His name is correctly Anencletus, a Greek adjective meaning 'blameless', and is probably to be identified with 'Cletus', a shortened form of the full name. He followed St **Linus** (the successor of St Peter), but preceded St **Clement I** of Rome, and is commemorated as Cletus in the canon of the Mass. Nothing further is known of him, and while his existence and leading position need not be doubted, the fact that the monarchical episcopate had not yet emerged at Rome makes it impossible to form any clear conception of his role.

Anacletus II, Antipope *see* **Pierleoni, Petrus Leonis**

Anastasia Saint, martyr. Apparently martyred during the persecution of Diocletian at Sirmium in Pannonia, her relics were translated to Constantinople by St **Gennadius** in the fifth century, and interred in the church of the Anastasis, founded by St **Gregory of Nazianzus**. Her cult spread, perhaps through the agency of Byzantine officials, to the ancient church in Rome near the Circus Maximus, known as the *Titulus Anastasiae*, the basilica referred to in the sixth century as a title church. Thus, though originally unconnected with Rome, she is mentioned in the canon of the Mass and in the second Mass of Christmas, indicating her cult there. Feast day 25 December.

Anastasius Patriarch of Constantinople, 730–54, died Constantinople, January. Probably of Syrian origin, and originally a disciple and 'synkellos' of Patriarch **Germanus I**. When the latter was dismissed for opposing Emperor **Leo III**'s iconoclasm, Anastasius, who had changed sides and now supported the policy, became patriarch. He issued a document (*libelloi*) against the veneration of icons, and sent it to Pope **Gregory II**, in defence of the iconoclastic position; Gregory excommunicated Anastasius as a heretic and pretender. Politically an opportunist, Anastasius modified his strong iconoclastic policies to win the favour of the usurper to the throne, Artabasdus (741), and denounced **Constantine V**, alleging that the emperor had stated to the patriarch that Christ had been an ordinary man and not the Son of God. When Constantine regained the throne, he ordered that Anastasius be flogged and ignominiously paraded naked on a donkey in the Hippodrome, though he retained him on the patriarchal throne, demanding his renewed support of iconoclasm as the price of retaining it. This did nothing for the declining reputation of the patriarchate.

Anastasius   Saint, bishop of Grau, born, date unknown, died 12 November *c.*1036. A disciple of **Adalbert**, bishop of Prague, he became abbot of his newly founded monasteries at Brevnov, near Prague, in 993, and then in Poland. He later went as apostle to the Magyars, at the request of King Stephen I of Hungary, and became Hungary's first prelate, abbot of St Stephen's foundation at Pannonkalma, and later archbishop of Esztergom. He spent himself with great zeal in the evangelization of the Magyars, and his possible German origin, as well as his presence at German synods, is witness to the close links between Germany and the Christianization of Hungary under Duke Geza and Stephen I. Feast day 12 November.

Anastasius I   Saint, Pope from 399, date of birth unknown, died Rome, 19 December 401. A Roman by birth, he plunged immediately on his election into the controversy over **Origen** and his writings, particularly a whitewashing translation of his *First Principles* by **Rufinus of Aquileia**, which had greatly offended **Jerome** in Bethlehem, and his influential circle of friends in Rome. Though Origen's was only a name to Anastasius, and he had little grasp of the issues at stake, he condemned a number of Origen's doctrines on the strength of a letter, received in 400 from Theophilus, the powerful patriarch of Alexandria, dwelling on the evils caused by Origen's works, and reporting their recent condemnation in Egypt. Rufinus then defended his translation and his own theological position, and Anastasius, though sceptical about the motive behind Rufinus' notorious translation, left him to God's judgement. Anastasius thereby earned the praise of Jerome and Paulinus of Nola

for his blameless life and apostolic solicitude. In other matters, Anastasius did not commend himself to the African bishops who, because of a shortage of clergy, wanted a relaxation of the ban on Donatist clergy returning to the Church; Anastasius told them to continue the struggle against Donatism, advice the Africans tactfully ignored. Feast day 19 December.

Anastasius I   Byzantine emperor from 491, born Epidammus, Albania, 431, died Constantinople, 9 July 518. Nicknamed *Dikoros* (with two pupils), because his eyes were of different colours. At heart a Monophysite, he married Emperor **Zeno**'s widow, Ariadne, who selected him as emperor, but he had to sign a profession of faith in the doctrine of Chalcedon before Patriarch Euphemius would crown him. An able administrator, he did much to reorganize the internal administration, e.g. reform of the fiscal apparatus and coinage, distribution of state property in favour of royal estates; and controlled public spending, which made for a healthy treasury at his death. He tried to impose the Monophysite Trisagion on the Eastern bishops, but this brought strong reactions in Constantinople and, in 496, he deposed Euphemius on charges that stemmed from his intransigent support of Chalcedon. His relations with Theodoric the Great were hostile; the Popes condemned the Acacian Schism and tried to establish their jurisdiction over the northern Balkans. Anastasius, despite the failure of his religious policy, proved to be one of the more able and remarkable Byzantine emperors. He is sometimes held to be the emperor portrayed in the Barberini ivory in Rome.

Anastasius I   Saint, Patriarch of Antioch from 559, born in Palestine, died at Antioch, *c.*599. A monk of Sinai and *Apokisianios* of Alexandria before his election to the see of Antioch, he suffered banishment to Jerusalem for his strenuous opposition to **Justinian I**'s edict on 'Aphthartodocetism'. St **Gregory the Great** befriended him and requested Emperor Maurice to restore him to his see. As a neo-Chalcedonian, Anastasius strongly defended Orthodoxy, and staunchly defended the creed of Chalcedon, though he attempted to close the gap with the Monophysites. His works greatly influenced later Greek theologians, e.g. **Maximus the Confessor**, and **John Damascene**. Five important treatises on christological and trinitarian questions have survived in Latin translations, in addition to a compendium of Christian doctrine in Greek. Feast day 21 April.

Anastasius II Pope from 496, died Rome, 19 November 498. A Roman and the son of a priest named Peter, his election reflected dissatisfaction with the hard-line attitude of **Felix III** and **Gelasius I** to the Acacian Schism (484–519). He sent legates to Constantinople exhorting Emperor **Anastasius** to help in bringing the Alexandrian Church back to Chalcedonian orthodoxy, making it evident that he wanted peace and would make concessions, such as recognizing the baptisms and ordinations performed by Acacians. The emperor refused, however, hoping the Pope would eventually accept the *Henoticon*, a superficially innocuous statement which made concessions to Monophytism. Anastasius' efforts at reconciliation were misunderstood and created dismay among the Roman clergy, some of whom renounced communion with him, and a schism threatened. At the height of the crisis, Anastasius suddenly died and with him possibly the last hope of reunion of East and West, on the basis of an orthodox interpretation of the *Henoticon*. Anastasius' name is not found in any martyrologies, and there is no evidence of devotion paid to him. Medieval tradition has it that, seen as a traitor to the Holy See, who wished to restore the heretic **Acacius**, and this led **Dante** to consign Anastasius to the sixth circle of hell in his Inferno. He is in fact buried in the portico of St Peter's, and his epitaph in elegiacs survives.

Anastasius II Saint, Patriarch of Antioch from 599. He died *c*.609. He succeeded **Anastasius I** at Antioch, and **Gregory the Great's** letter acknowledging him as patriarch and accepting his profession of faith has survived. He translated Gregory's *Liber regulae pastoralis* into Greek. He met his death during an insurrection of the Jews against the Emperor Phocas, who had attempted to convert them by force. **Baronius** inserted his name into the Roman martyrology. Feast day 21 December.

Anastasius III Pope from 911, born Rome, died there, *c*.August 913. A Roman by birth, son of Lucian, esteemed for his rectitude of life, little is

known of his earlier career, or of his election and brief reign. He succeeded **Sergius III**, and ruled in a time of turmoil when Rome was dominated by Theophylact, consul and senator, and his ambitious, energetic wife, Theodora the Elder; this powerful and unscrupulous family effectively controlled the Papacy. It is unlikely that, in such circumstances, the mild and unassertive Anastasius exercised any independent initiative. In 912 he received a letter from **Nicholas I** Mysticus, patriarch of Constantinople, deploring Rome's attitude in approving Emperor **Leo VI**'s fourth marriage in 906; no response is extant, but Nicholas cannot have found it satisfactory, for he proceeded to remove the Pope's name from the diptychs, i.e. the names of the living and departed publicly prayed for at Mass, and a gulf yawned between Rome and Constantinople.

Anastasius IV Pope from 1153, born Rome, died there, 3 December 1154. Nothing is known of his career until **Paschal II** appointed him cardinal-priest, *c*.1112. In 1126 he became cardinal-bishop of Santa Sabina and, in 1130, actively supported **Innocent II** in a divided election, proving himself a determined partisan, and an opponent of **Anacletus II**. Elected Pope on the day of **Eugenius III**'s death, and enthroned in the Lateran, in marked contrast to Eugenius and **Adrian IV**, he resided undisturbed in Rome. A very old man, he had much experience in curial business and had proved his abilities as vicar of the Holy See in testing times. In matters of policy, he showed conciliation, and was criticized for being weak. He restored St William Fitzherbert, who had been deposed by Eugenius as archbishop of York, and thus closed a dispute over his appointment, which had raged through four pontificates. Through the efforts of Nicholas Breakspear (**Adrian IV**), Anastasius' legate in Scandinavia, both Norway and Sweden began paying Peter's Pence. He is buried in the Lateran in the porphyry sarcophagus of St Helena.

Anastasius Sinaita Byzantine church saint and abbot, died *c*.700. A Palestinian monk and abbot of St Catherine's Monastery on Mount Sinai. A champion of orthodoxy against all forms of heresy, he became known as the New Moses, and attacked, as early as 640, the Egyptian and Syrian Monophysites at Alexandria, against whom his most important treatise, the *Hodegos*, i.e. *Guide*, is primarily directed. He also published an allegorical exegesis of the *Hexaemeron*, in twelve books, as well as a collection of 154 *Questions and Answers* on various theological themes, which is in substance the work of Anastasius, but in its present form shows signs of later additions. Feast day 21 April.

Anastasius the Librarian (Bibliothecarius)   Scholar, born, probably Rome, *c*.810–17, died there *c*.878. An enigmatic personality and, by his own account, the nephew of Arsenius, the influential bishop of Orte, and educated by Greek monks, he became papal librarian. Learned, often troublesome and very influential, he played an important role in formulating papal letters, especially those dealing with the Byzantine Church, indeed, regarded as ninth-century Europe's leading expert on Byzantium and the best Greek scholar of his age. In 855 the imperial party proclaimed him antipope against **Benedict III**, but he was disowned by his supporters a month later, being too rash and undisciplined. Subsequently rehabilitated, **Nicholas I** gave him the abbacy of Santa Maria in Trastevere, while later Popes made him their librarian (*Bibliothecus Romanae ecclesiae*). He attended the Ecumenical Council of 869, and translated its Acts into Latin; he also translated the Acts of the Seventh Council of 787. Among his writings are *Chronographia tripartita*, composed out of extracts from the Byzantine chronicles of Patriarch **Nicephorus I**, **George Syncellus** and Theophanes the Confessor; and several works on dogmatic theology.

Anastassy (Gribanovsky)   Metropolitan, Russian Orthodox émigré leader, born Tambov, Russia, 6 August 1873, died New York, 21 May 1965. He was consecrated bishop in 1906, was friend and adviser to Grand Duchess **Elizabeth** and took a prominent part in the local Church Council of 1917 which restored the patriarchate. After the revolution he helped to found the Russian Orthodox Church Abroad (ROCA) and represented it in Jerusalem in 1924–35. Elected metropolitan in 1936 he lead the ROCA through the difficult war years, eventually moving its headquarters to New York in 1950. Author of works on the monastic life and memoirs of the Grand Duchess Elizabeth and other Russian martyrs.

Anatolius of Constantinople   Patriarch, born Alexandria, *c*.400, died Constantinople, 3 July 458. A disciple of St **Cyril**, who sent him to Constantinople, he succeeded the deposed **Flavian** as bishop. Pope **Leo I** challenged his good faith, and demanded that he rehabilitate the bishops deposed at Ephesus in 449, explicitly condemn **Eutyches** and **Nestorius**, and subscribe to Leo's *Tome to Flavian*. On the accession of **Marcian** and Pulcheria as emperors in 450, Anatolius accepted Leo's terms and exhumed the body of Flavian for burial in the church of the Holy Apostles. He seems to have encouraged Marcian to summon the Council of Chalcedon in 451, and helped to convince the Illyrian and Egyptian bishops of the orthodoxy of the *Tome to Flavian*; he played a part in formulating the Definition of Chalcedon. He also promoted the famous Canon 28 of the Council, which declared the see of Constantinople second after Rome, but this led to acrimony; in general, however, he and Leo co-operated in pursuing an anti-Monophysite policy.

Anatolius of Laodicea   Saint, bishop, born at Alexandria, died there, *c*.282. He founded a school of Aristotelian philosophy, and achieved the honour of a seat in the senate. Consecrated coadjutor bishop by Theotecnus, bishop of Caesarea, he became bishop of Laodicea, in 268, on his way to the Synod at Antioch to deal with **Paul of Samosata**. A man of great learning, **Eusebius** and St **Jerome** held him in high esteem. His writings were few, but include a treatise on the date of Easter, based on the nineteen-year cycle still in use, and a work in ten books on the **Elements of Arithmetic**. Feast day 30 July.

Anchieta, José de   Portuguese missionary and linguist, born San Cristobal de la Laguna, Tenerife, 19 March 1534, died Reritiba (Anchieta), 9 June 1597. Related to the family of **Ignatius of Loyola**, he studied at Coimbra, entered the Society of Jesus in 1551, and went to the missions in Brazil two years later to work among the Puru and Guarani Indians. He learnt Tupi, the language of the coast, wrote grammars and dictionaries as well as catechetical and pastoral manuals, and became provincial of Brazil (1577–87). During 44 years as a missionary, Anchieta is remembered for his apostolic work, his lofty ideals and a reputation, unsubstantiated, for heroic deeds. He is reputed to have suppressed cannibalism, and to have protected the chastity of Christian Indian women against the lust of pagan barbarians. Famed for many extraordinary deeds, no one has been so readily termed a saint and Father of Christianity in colonial Brazil, indeed, the bishop of Bahia gave him the name 'Apostle of Brazil' in the eulogy at his funeral.

Anderson, Henry James American mathematician and astronomer, born New York, 6 February 1799, died Lahore, India, 19 October 1875. He studied at Columbia University and the College of Physicians and Surgeons, graduating in 1823. After the death abroad of his wife in 1843, he joined a government expedition to the Holy Land, which published his report, *Geological Reconnaissance of Part of the Holy Land*, in 1848. He became a Roman Catholic while abroad and actively promoted Catholicism after his return to the USA, serving in many lay posts, including that of president of the Society of St Vincent de Paul. He retained his interest in astronomy, journeying to Australia in 1874 to observe Venus in transit, and died while exploring the Himalayas.

Anderson, Lars (Lamentius, Lorenz Andreae) Swedish theologian and reformer, born Strangnas, *c.*1480, died there, 29 April 1552. After study at Rostock, Leipzig and Greifswald, he became a canon at Strangnas and secretary to Bishop Mattias. He converted to Lutheranism under the influence of Olaus **Petri**, and when Gustavus Vasa was chosen king, Anderson became his chancellor in 1523, helping Olaus Petri to introduce the Reformation into Sweden. They worked for a breach with Rome and for a Swedish national church, fully establishing the Reformation at the Council of Oerebo in 1529. However, he opposed Vasa's attempt to transform the Swedish Church in the direction of Presbyterianism, for which the king sentenced him to death, but commuted the penalty to a heavy fine and deprived him of office, after which he lived out his days in retirement. He wrote a theological treatise on 'Faith and Good Works'.

Anderton, Lawrence English Jesuit writer and controversialist, born Lostock(?), Lancashire, *c.*1575/6, died there, 17 April 1643. He was educated at Christ's College, Cambridge, where he was admired for his brilliance and ready eloquence. He seems to have taken Protestant orders, but as he was 'much addicted to reading books of controversy, he could not reconcile some difficulties he met with concerning the origin and doctrines of the Reformation', and this speedily ended in his conversion to the Catholic Church. In 1604 he published his first notable work against the English Protestants called the *Protestant's Apologie*, issued no doubt from the Anderton press, later seized by the government. He then went to Rome and entered the Society of Jesus at the age of 28, becoming 'one of the most distinguished ornaments of the English Province'. He remained on the continent for several years teaching in various colleges, and published *Liturgy of the Mass*, and the *Life of Luther*. He returned to England and was Superior of the Lancashire district in 1621; in 1624 he was sent to London, remained there until 1641 and returned to Lancashire, where he died.

Anderton, Roger English Catholic writer and controversialist. Born Lostock(?), Lancashire; died 1640(?). The fourth son of Christopher Anderton of Lostock and cousin of Lawrence **Anderton**. He inherited Birchley Hall near Preston, *c.*1615, and was probably the patron of a secret press set up and supported by the Anderton family, who were numerous at the time, with probably more than one member of the family connected with it. It was discovered and seized by the government in 1621. Several of the books printed at this press were issued under the pseudonym 'John Brerely, Priest', who has sometimes been identified with Lawrence Anderton, though the evidence is not conclusive. At any rate, Gee, in his *Foot out of the Snare* (1624), states that 'there was a printing-house in Lancashire suppressed about some three years since, where all Brerely's works, with many other Popish pamphlets, were printed'.

Andia y Varela, Ignacio Chilean priest and artist, born Santiago, 2 February 1757, died there, 13 August 1822. His early career was spent in colonial administration where he was secretary to the captain general, and administrator of the tobacco regime. He was a skilled draughtsman and his inspection tours of the country with Governor O'Higgins, enabled him to produce a valuable map of Chile as well as illustrations of meetings with Indians at Lonquilmo. Having to provide for a large family of eighteen children, he sought commissions outside the official administration and was invited to do the monumental Escudo de España for the Palacios de la Moneda built by his brother-in-law, Joaquin Toesca; also plans for the Casa Fundicion and the Tremulo Funebre of Carlo III, considered a masterwork. Most of his works have been lost, but the artistic copy of the MSS, *La Venida des Mesias en Gloria y Majestad*, by the Jesuit theologian Manuel **Lacunza** remains as proof of his talent. He was received into the Church at the age of 62 and became a priest in San Felipe where he built the so-called Gallery of the Monk, still preserved.

Andrade, Antonio de Missionary, explorer of Tibet, born Oleiros, Portugal, 1580, died Goa, 19 March 1634. A priest of the Society of Jesus, he went to India in 1596, and for four years was the chief Jesuit missionary in the Indies, becoming rector of the college at Goa and, in 1621, superior of the Mogul mission at Agra. Having learned of Christian communities in the north, he crossed the Himalayas in 1624, and succeeded after almost incredible hardships in penetrating into Tibet and, having been kindly received by the head lama of the country, in establishing, with six other Jesuits, a mission at Chaparangue. He was recalled to Goa to become superior of the Indies and died, perhaps from poison, for the faith. The mission at Chaparangue was destroyed during a revolt by hostile lamas in 1631. The Christian community had numbered about 400 souls. Andrada gave, in letters to his superiors and others, a graphic and accurate account of his discoveries and labours. These have been published in Spanish and French, and incorporated in the works of P. J. Darde, SJ, *Histoire de ce qui s'est passé au royaume du Tibet* (Paris, 1629).

Andrade y Pastor, Manuel Surgeon, born Mexico City, 1809, died there, 1848. He qualified in 1831, and spent some years in the Hôtel-Dieu in Paris where he was most impressed with the efficiency and dedication of the Sisters of Charity. Returning to Mexico in 1838, he published a report on their work in hospitals, and the rules of the Order, as well as reports on the medical organization in France. He was named professor of surgery in the Establecimiento de Ciencias Medicas. With the aid of the Contessa de la Cortona, he obtained permission in 1843 to bring eleven Sisters of Charity to Mexico City. When the Americans invaded Mexico in 1847, the Surgeon General of the USA warmly praised Andrade for his work as Director of the Hôpital de Jesus. He died from a bullet wound received during the campaign. He had founded the Mexican Academy of Medicine in 1836, to which, as both secretary and vice-president, he presented learned and outstanding papers.

Andre, Bernard Poet laureate of England and historiographer, born Toulouse, *c*.1450, died London, after 1521. He was a doctor of civil and canon law, but his fame was as a poet and humanist. He went to England, *c*.1485, was introduced to the Court where Henry VII appointed him poet laureate and tutor to Prince Arthur, and he probably had a share in the education of **Henry VIII**. He was also a tutor at Oxford, and seems to have been blind, being frequently referred to in official records as 'the blind poet'. His writings are mostly in Latin and his *Historia Henrici Septimi*, edited by James Gardiner in 1858, is typical of his other works as having value chiefly as a source of contemporary information.

Andrea del Sarto Painter, born Florence, 17 July 1486, died Florence, 29 September 1530. Known as 'del Sarto' because his father was a tailor, he was apprenticed to Piero di Cosimo, but also influenced by Fra **Bartolommeo**, **Leonardo da Vinci**, **Michelangelo** and **Raphael**, and numbered Pontormo and Rosso Fiorentino among his pupils. Apart from a period as **Francis I**'s court painter in 1418–19, he was based in his native city and filled the void left when many of the other Florentine masters were employed in Rome and elsewhere. His output included frescoes and altarpieces, the latter including the *Madonna of the Harpies* (Florence, Uffizi, 1517).

Andreas Capellanus (Andre le Chapelin) Author of the treatise *De amore*. Dates, places of birth and death unknown. He is believed to have served as chaplain to the French court – hence his surname

– in the twelfth century, and is known only from his own work, written about 1186, in the rubrics of which is an indirect reference to his position as chaplain of the king of France. Nothing certain is known of his life, but he may have been chaplain of La Comtesse Marie de Champagne in 1185–7, and it is not impossible that he was later chaplain of Pope **Innocent IV**. His famous treatise, *Liber de arte honeste amandi et de reprobatione inhonesti amoris* (3 vols) is a work of first importance for knowledge of the ideas, manners and morals of his time; the first treats of how one acquires love, the second, how one conserves it, the third, how one ought to reject it. The first two volumes appear as a manual of seduction containing sample dialogues between men and women, and 31 rules of love, and the amatory judgements of various noble ladies. The third book contradicts the first two and contains traditional anti-feminist arguments on why love should be avoided. There are manuscripts in the Vatican, at the Bibliothèque Nationale in Paris and in the Ambrosian Library, Milan, dating from the thirteenth, fourteenth and fifteenth centuries. It was translated into English (*Art of Courtly Love*) by J. J. Parry in 1941.

Andrelini, Publio Fausto Renaissance humanist and poet, born Forli, Italy, *c*.1461, died Paris, 25 February 1518. At the age of 22 he was crowned poet laureate at Rome, and settled in Paris in 1488. His arrival there was badly viewed by other Italian writers who had made reputations in Paris, notably Girolamo **Balbi**, whom Andrelini treated as a plagiarist and who, in turn, accused the latter of heresy, obliging him to seek refuge at Poitiers and Toulouse. Andrelini was authorized to teach *belles-lettres* at the University of Paris, and in 1489 he published a libellous letter against Balbi (a copy of which he sent to **Erasmus**, who praised him when he was alive, and criticized him after his death), who was ultimately obliged to leave Paris. As court poet from 1492, he composed many occasional pieces, e.g. on the death of **Charles VIII**, the captivity of Ludovic Sforza, a panegyric of Queen Anne of Bretagne, who pensioned him. He has been described as the characteristic humanist – presumptuous and mediocre, totally lacking in originality – but he was much admired by his contemporaries and knew how to be well viewed by people of influence. He obtained a canonry in

Bayeux, even though he was reproached for an irregular life of little worth. His was a vulgar spirit, of whom it is said that he gave to humanism a gross and unchristian direction.

Andrew Abellon Blessed, Dominican teacher, reformer and artist, born St-Maximin-la-Sainte-Baume, *c*.1375, died Aix, 15 May 1450. He joined the Dominicans at an early age and taught philosophy and theology in various priories until 1408, when he was sent to Montpellier where he became master of theology, despite his course having been interrupted by the plague, during which he ministered to the population. In October 1419, Andrew was named prior of the monastery in his native village, where he applied three principal directives: to restore the traditional discipline, to assure the resources necessary for the life of the religious and to rebuild and complete the cloister buildings. In 1432 he was sent to Arles to restore discipline there, and then to Aix, as prior, in 1438. He spent several years in Marseilles, and was appointed prior at Aix-en-Provence, but refused the office, going instead as a simple religious. He fell ill there and died among his brothers in religion. He used his artistic talents to teach the eternal truths by painting. **Leo XIII** raised him to the altar in 1902. Feast day 17 May.

Andrew Caccioli Blessed, Franciscan preacher, early companion of St Francis, born Spello, near Assisi, 1194, died Spello, 3 June 1254. His surname is unusual since the use of surnames was not common at the time, and not in the case of mendicants. He received the habit from St Francis himself and was among the first, if not the first priest, to join the group (*inter quos fuit primus sacerdos*). Francis commissioned Andrew to preach, and he was present at Francis' death in 1226. Like many of the saint's early companions, Andrew interpreted the Rule strictly, even rigidly, and for this he was twice imprisoned under the administration of **Elias of Cortona**; released by **Gregory IX**, the first time on the intercesssion of **Anthony of Padua**, and on the second, by **John of Parma**. He attended the general chapter held at Soria in 1233. His remains lie in the chapel of St Andrew the Apostle in Spello, and his cult was confirmed by **Clement XII** in 1738. Feast day 3 June.

Andrew Corsini Saint, confessor, bishop of Fiesole, born Florence, 30 November 1302, died Fiesole, 6 January 1373. Repenting his misspent youth, he joined the Carmelite Order, c.1317. He studied at the University of Paris, 1329; was named provincial of the Order in Tuscany, 1348. He was active in this office during the plague, and in rebuilding the hard-hit religious communities to restore their spiritual fervour and monastic discipline. Consecrated bishop of Fiesole in 1360, he was a wise and able administrator, sought everywhere as a peacemaker; at Bologna he made peace between the nobility and the people. Miracles multiplied at his death. He is represented holding a cross, with a wolf and lamb at his feet, floating above a battlefield on a cloud. He was canonized in 1609. Feast day 4 February.

Andrew de Comitibus Blessed, Italian Franciscan brother, born Anagni, c.1240, died convent of San Lorenzo al Piglio, 1 February 1302. Of the noble family of the Conti, he was a close relative of Popes **Innocent III**, **Gregory IX**, **Alexander IV** and **Boniface VIII**. He was known for his humility and holiness of life, and this led him to refuse the dignity of the cardinalate preferred by Boniface, although some chronicles suggest that, indeed, he was created cardinal but renounced the office. In any event, he lived the life of a simple friar. He is said to have been the author of a treatise *De partu Beatae Mariae Virginis*, not extant. Andrew was famous for miracles even during his lifetime, and Boniface is recorded as having said that he would have canonized Andrew had he died during the former's reign. He is buried in the church of San Lorenzo and was beatified by **Innocent XIII** in 1724. Feast day 17 February.

Andrew Dotti Blessed, Servite preacher, born San Sepolcro, Tuscany, 1256, died Vallucola, 31 August 1315. Of noble parentage, he entered the Servite Order in 1278 at Florence, where Alexius **Falconieri**, one of the seven founders, was superior. He progressed rapidly in religious virtue and occupied various positions of honour in the Order. He joined a group of hermits at Vallucola, and united them with the Servites in 1294. His zeal in preaching and in penance had extraordinary results throughout Italy. After the death of Alexius Falconieri, he returned to the hermitage at Vallucola,

where he led a life of charity, mortification and contemplation. Visions were attributed to him, and he worked many duly authenticated miracles. Feast day 31 August.

Andrew Franchi Blessed, Italian preacher and bishop, born Pistoia, 1335, died there 26 May 1401. He was of the noble family Franchi-Boccagni, became a Dominican, c.1351, and earned a doctorate in theology at Rome. He was prior at Pistoia, Orvieto and twice at Lucca, between 1370 and 1375, and distinguished himself as a preacher, teacher and spiritual director. Noted for his austerity, Andrew was devoted to Christ Crucified, the Madonna and Infant, and the Magi. He was made bishop of Pistoia, c.1380, but resigned his see in 1400, having lived as a religious; he preached, spent his income on the poor and on pious causes, converted many sinners and healed factional strife. His body, buried in San Domenico, Pistoia, was found incorrupt in 1911. His cult was approved by **Benedict XV** in 1921, and by **Pius XI** in 1922. Feast day 30 May.

Andrew of Crete Saint, confessor, born Damascus, c.660, died Erissos, 4 July 740. He was a monk in Jerusalem in 678, became a deacon in Constantinople c.685, and head of a refuge for orphans and the aged. He became archbishop of Gortyna in Crete in 692. He subscribed to the repudiation of 'two wills' in Christ, defined at Constantinople III; in 713 he retracted, explaining his doctrine in a metrical confession, and participated in the quarrels over iconoclasm. He was remarkable as an orator. He was the author of many scriptural discourses, but is principally interesting as the inventor of the 'Greek Canon', a form of hymnology previously unknown, which earned him respect as one of the principal hymnographers of the Oriental Church. Feast day 4 July.

Andrew of Fiesole Saint, archdeacon of Fiesole, near Florence, born in Scotland, or Ireland, died c.876/7. A tradition has it that Andrew accompanied St Donatus to Fiesole on his return from Rome, just when the local bishop's see was vacant and the local people were assembled in prayer for a new and worthy replacement. There was much ringing of bells and lighting of candles, considered miraculous by the assembly, who inferred that

Donatus was to be their new bishop. He ordained Andrew as his archdeacon. Andrew is reported to have restored the church of San Martino di Mensola at Fiesole, where his relics were reportedly found in 1285, and where they are still venerated. However, this story of Andrew apparently only came to light long after Donatus, and there is some doubt that he existed at all. Feast day 22 August.

Andrew of Longjumeau (Lonjumeau, Lonjumel, etc.) French Dominican, explorer and diplomatist, born Longjumeau, early thirteenth century, died France, *c.*1270. In 1239 he brought a relic of the Crown of Thorns from Constantinople to Paris, where **Louis IX** built, next to his palace of La Cité, the magnificent chapel, Sainte Chapelle, to house it. He accompanied friar **Ascellino**, sent by **Innocent IV** in 1247 to the Mongols, to negotiate the return of the Nestorian Churches to unity with Rome. While on the Crusades with King Louis (1248–54), he went as ambassador to the Great Khan Kuyuk at Karakorum to investigate his reported conversion to the faith (1249–51). When he arrived at the Mongol court, he found Kuyuk Khan dead, poisoned, as Andrew supposed. Andrew's report to King Louis at Caesarea, in Palestine, attested to Mongol Christianity, but his mission was judged a failure due to the Mongols' treating his gifts to the dead Khan as evidence of submission. In Tunis in 1256, he worked for the conversion of the Sultan, but shortly thereafter returned to France, where he died.

Andrew of Peschiera Blessed, Dominican preacher, born Peschiera, Lake Garda, 1400, died Morbegno, Switzerland, 18 January 1485. Of Greek origin, Andrew Grego became a Dominican at Brescia and was sent to Florence for his studies. He was attracted especially to the life of obedience. His career was spent in the evangelization of Vatellina and neighbouring districts, where heresy and general moral deterioration meant that he was not well received. He none the less preached tirelessly and won many converts by his words and, during 45 years, by his humble and austere way of life and his great charity for the poor. He assisted in the foundation of two Dominican houses, and at times acted as inquisitor at Como. His cult began immediately at his death, and was confirmed in 1800 by **Pius VII**. Feast day 19 Jamuary.

Andrew of Rinn Blessed, martyr (alleged), born 16 November 1459, died Rinn, near Innsbruck, 12 July 1462. When his father died, his mother entrusted him to his uncle's care. At the age of three his mother found his body hanging from a tree in a nearby wood. The uncle claimed he had sold the child to Jews returning from a fair, who, he said, cruelly put him to death through hatred of the faith. There is no extant evidence of a juridical investigation. His cult spread through northern Tyrol. He was beatified by **Benedict XIV** in 1752, but was refused canonization. Feast day 12 July.

Andrew of Saint-Victor Abbot and biblical exegete, born England, *c.*1110, died Wigmore Abbey, Herefordshire, 19 October 1175. He entered the monastery of Saint-Victor, Paris, *c.*1130, and studied under **Hugh** of Saint-Victor, whom he later succeeded as Scripture teacher. He was first abbot of the Victorine Abbey at Wigmore. He went back to to Saint-Victor after a few years but, between 1161 and 1163, he returned to Wigmore where he died. He wrote commentaries on the Octateuch, the Prophets, Proverbs and Ecclesiasticus. Using Jewish sources, he concentrated on the literal sense of Scripture to an extent not found elsewhere in the Middle Ages, and was responsible for sending later exegetes to the original Hebrew.

Andrew of Strumi Blessed, Italian abbot and church reformer, born Parma, early eleventh century, died Parma, 10 March 1097. He was a disciple of Arialdo, a deacon of the church in Milan, who battled against abuses, attacking especially married priests and those in concubinage, numerous in north Italy. Arialdo was tortured and massacred in 1066 by partisans of the simoniacal Archbishop Guido of Velate, who favoured the abuses; at great personal risk, Andrew recovered Arialdo's body. Andrew entered the Vallambrosans around 1069 and became abbot of Strumi, *c.*1085, when they replaced the Benedictines there. Andrew wrote a life of Arialdo and also one of **John Gualbert**, founder of the Vallambrosans. His relics were enshrined in the church of San Fedele at Strumi in the thirteenth century. Feast day 10 March.

Andrewe, Richard English cleric, dean of York, born Adderbury, died York, 1477. Educated at

Winchester and New College, Oxford; doctor of civil law, 1432, practised as a canon lawyer, and became chancellor of Archbishop Henry **Chichele**. He was first warden of Chichele's new college of All Souls in 1438, and a king's secretary, 1443–55. He served in the negotiations for **Henry VI**'s marriage, and was rewarded with preferment to York, though imposed by king and Pope on a reluctant chapter, from 1452 to 1477. His political career ended with the fall of Henry VI, but he acted as vicar-general of the archbishop of York.

Andrewes, Lancelot Bishop, scholar and poet, born Barking, Essex, near London 1555, died at Southwark, London, 27 September 1626. He was educated at Pembroke Hall, Cambridge, where he became master in 1589, the same year he became vicar of St Giles, Cripplegate, London, where his eloquent preaching first attracted attention. He successively became dean of Westminster in 1603; and bishop of Chichester 1605, Ely 1609 and Winchester 1619. He attended the Hampton Court Conference of 1604 and subsequently helped to prepare the Authorized Version of the Bible. In the wake of the Gunpowder Plot he engaged in controversy with the Jesuit cardinal Robert **Bellarmine**. His own theology was, however, rather Catholic in tone, and it contributed to the distinctively Anglican voice in Christian thought. He is regarded as a saint in certain parts of the Anglican communion. Feast day either 25 or 26 September.

Andrews, Charles F. Anglican friend of the poor, friend of Gandhi, born in Birmingham, England, 12 February 1871, died in India, 4 April 1940. Studied and then taught at Cambridge, became an Anglican and was later ordained priest. In 1904 he went to teach at St Stephen's College in India, and went to live at Shantinaketan, Rabindrath Tagore's ashram. A few years later he met Mohandas Gandhi in South Africa and they became lifelong friends in the struggle there, and later in India, for justice for the poor and dispossessed. Andrews nursed Gandhi when he was on his great hunger strike. Feeling that his orders were a barrier to the ministry of simply bearing prophetic witness to Christ through his actions, to which he felt called, Andrews ceased his active ministry – though he remained a member of the Anglican communion. He travelled to Fiji, the South Pacific and Africa to minister to the Indian indentured workers and played a large part in having this system abolished.

Andrieu, Michel French Oratorian, and liturgical scholar, born Millau, 28 May 1886, died Strasburg, 2 October 1956. He was a member of the Catholic theological faculty at Strasburg, and dedicated his critical scholarship to the study, for more than 30 years, of ordinals and pontificals, to which he brought an exacting scientific method aware that, once restored, the liturgy of the past would be a vital source of theology. His monumental essays on Roman liturgy were published in *Revue des sciences religieuses*, and in two great collections of his works *Ordines Romani* (5 vols, Louvain 1931–6), and *Pontifical Romain* (5 vols, Vatican City, 1938–63).

Andronicus II Palaeologus Eastern Roman emperor, the son of Michael VIII Palaeologus whom he succeeded in 1282, born at Constantinople, 1256, died there, 24 May 1332. His father had adopted a conciliatory policy toward Rome, but Andronicus deposed **John XI** Beccus and restored the deposed anti-union Patriarch of Constantinople, **Joseph**, on whose death in March 1283 he imposed Gregory of Cyprus in the patriarchate, forcing his mother, Theodora, to renounce communion with Rome. Andronicus' administration was marked by internal religious quarrels and political misadventure. On the death of Gregory in 1289, he installed **Athanasius I**, but he abdicated in 1293. In 1295 the emperor attempted an alliance with the Serbs, but this failed and he restored Athanasius in 1304–10, then deposed Niphon of Cyzicus in 1315, for simony, replacing him with **John XIII** Glycas in 1315–19, then Gerasimus 1320–1, then with Isaac the Monk 1323. He allowed the fleet of ships to fall into decay, and the empire was thus more vulnerable to the exacting demands of Venice and Genoa. The Turks under Osman, who had conquered nearly the whole of Bythnia, were defeated by Roger di Flor, but he proved to be no less an enemy to the imperial power. From 1320 onward, Andronicus was engaged in war with his grandson, **Andronicus III**.

Andronicus III Palaeologus Eastern Roman emperor, grandson of **Andronicus II**, son of

Michael VIII, born Constantinople, 1296, died there, June 1341. His conduct as a youth was so violent that, after the death of his father in 1320, his grandfather resolved to deprive him of his right to the Crown. Andronicus rebelled and his grandfather was compelled to accept him as a colleague in 1325. The quarrel broke out again and the emperor was forced to abdicate in 1328 in favour of Andronicus. During the latter's reign, he was engaged in constant war, chiefly with the Turks, against whom he sought the assistance of Pope **Benedict XII**, promising him to join a crusade. Having sent envoys to Avignon for aid, the matter of church reunion was inevitably raised, but Latin hatred for the Greeks, rather than dogmatic differences, was cited as the obstacle and the question of an ecumenical council was raised. Andronicus annexed large regions in Thessaly and Epirus, but they were lost before his death to the rising power of Serbia under Stephen Dusan.

Aneiros, Leon Federico Archbishop of Buenos Aires, born Buenos Aires, 28 August 1828, died there, 4 September 1894. He was educated at San Ignacio College and received doctorates in theology and civil and canon law. He was a delegate for the province of Buenos Aires and secretary of bishop Escalada. A zealous man, he strove somewhat ineffectually to combat secularism, which was gaining ground, by promoting education and the Catholic press. He founded, in 1853, *La Religion*, and in 1855, *El Orden*, both directed by Felix Frias, but they ceased publication in 1861. He facilitated the establishment of colleges at San José and El Salvador. His problems were compounded by the difficulty in taking clerics from abroad, one of whom, a Spanish priest, tried to set fire to the archiepiscopal curia, and did indeed burn El Salvador College. During a persecution of the Church in 1883–4, he endorsed the brave action of Catholic legates in upholding Christian interests, but did little himself. He was a holy man, but rather short-sighted and not very energetic.

Anerio, Felice Baroque composer, born Rome, *c.*1560; died there, 27 September 1614. The older brother of Giovanni Francesco **Anerio**, they were great Roman masters of sixteenth-century polyphony. Felice studied under G. M. **Nanino** and succeeded **Palestrina** as composer to the papal choir

in 1594, as well as being named director of music at the English College. He composed four books of madrigals, and several Masses and motets of his are printed in Proske's *Musica Divina*, and other modern anthologies. His style follows the principles of balance and clarity that are the hallmarks of Palestrina's music, and they are considered for the most part worthy of Palestrina himself. The twelve-part Stabat Mater in the seventh volume of Palestrina's complete works has, by some authorities, been ascribed to Felice. Towards the end of his career, he worked with Soriano in the revision of plainchant.

Anerio, Giovanni Francesco Baroque composer, born Rome, *c.*1567, died Poland, June 1630. Younger brother of Felice. He sang at St Peter's from 1575 to 1579, and subsequently was director of music at the Lateran, and at the court of Sigismund XI of Poland, before holding the post of maestro at the Jesuit church of Santa Maria dei Monti, from 1613 to 1620. Some of his numerous compositions have been attributed to his older brother, which is excusable, since they both adhered to the Palestrinian technique, though employing newly developed methods of baroque expression. That he/they were 'among the first of Italians to use the quaver and its subdivisions', as it has sometimes been said, is not, however, correct; quavers were commonly used quite early in the sixteenth century, and semiquavers appear in a madrigal published in 1544. For Giovanni as for Felice, sixteenth-century music was their 'mother-language', as it were, and they wrote pure polyphony because they understood it and loved it. Giovanni took holy orders in 1616, aged 49. He died on the way from Poland to Italy and was buried at Graz, Austria.

Anfredus Gonteri (Alfredus, Aufredus, Gaufredus) Franciscan theologian, born *c.*1270 in Brittany, died *c.*1330. He studied at Paris 1302–4, where he was a follower of **Duns Scotus**, whom he called 'my master'. He was involved in an appeal against Pope **Boniface VIII**, when the latter was in dispute with Philip the Fair. He became a master of theology in 1325, and was considered by his contemporaries as an able theologian, one of whom, Vaurmilion, referred to him as 'an outstanding disciple of Scotus'. Anfredus wrote commentaries on the *Sentences* at both Barcelona and Paris in 1322 and 1325; only Book 2 of the first has been identified, while Books 1–3 of his Paris commentaries are extant. There is also his *Quaestio de paupertate Christi*, written at Barcelona, *c*.1322, but his other works have not been found. He holds the honorific title *Doctor providus*.

Ange de Joyeuse *see* Joyeuse, Henri Duc de

Angela Maria of the Immaculate Conception Venerable, abbess, Trinitarian reformer, born at Cantalapiedra, Diocese of Salamanca, 1 March 1649, died El Toboso (Toledo), 13 April 1690. She entered the Discalced Carmelites, against the opposition of her devout and prosperous family, at the age of 21, but left before her profession. She then entered the Order of the Holy Trinity at Medina del Campo, Valladolid, where she was professed. In 1681, her desire for a more austere way of life was realized when she founded, with some young companions, a Trinitarian convent under a reformed rule, approved by **Innocent XI** as Trinitarians of the Primitive Observance. She was gifted with a high degree of intelligence and knowledge; her theological learning astounded the theologians of her time; she was favoured with discernment of souls and had extraordinary administrative ability. She published in 1691 an autobiography, *Vida de la Venerable Madre Sor Angela de la Concepcion*, which went through several editions until the beginning of this century; and, in the same year, *Riego espiritual para nuevas plantas*, a treatise on perfection by way of meditation and contemplation. She is represented kneeling and being offered the scapular of the Order of the Holy Trinity, while the Holy Spirit, as a dove, hovers over her head.

Angela of Foligno Blessed, penitent and mystical writer, born Foligno, *c*.1248, died there, 4 January 1309. She was married and lived a worldly, even sinful, life until nearly 40 years of age. She suddenly converted, for reasons unknown, and established a community at Foligno of the Third Order of St Francis. She desired an austere life of chastity away from the world, but as this could not be fulfilled as a wife and mother, she is reported to have prayed for the death of her family. Her *Book of Visions and Instructions* records the history of her conversion and, in a penetrating analysis, Angela traces the 'twenty steps of penitence' which brought her to the threshold of the mystical life. Through this experience, she wrote, she felt 'a divine sweetness in my soul', and she then began a sequence of seven steps into the mystical life proper, i.e. intellectual revelations, an increase of grace, an awareness of the presence of God, entering in spirit into the side of Christ, revelation of the divine union and love accompanied by profound ecstacies, the night of the spirit and divine vision. Angela's doctrine has been praised as being in the authentic Franciscan tradition with its stress on poverty and its passionate love of the crucified Christ. She is represented being invited by Our Lord to receive Holy Communion; and chaining the devil. Her relics are in the church of St Francis, Foligno. She was beatified in 1693. Feast day 4 January.

Angelico, Fra Florentine painter of the early Renaissance, born Vicchio, Tuscany, 1387, died Rome, 18 February 1455. His baptismal name was Guido, hence 'Guido da Vicchio', as he is also known. At 20, he entered the Dominican monastery at Fiesole and took vows in 1408. The artist Lorenzo Monaco may have contributed to his training, and the influence of the Sienese school is discernible in his work. According to Vasari, the first paintings, probably in fresco, were in the 'Cortisa' of Florence, but these no longer exist. His earliest extant works are at Cortona, whither he was sent during his novitiate. He is known as the representative, beyond all other men, of pietistic painting. 'His visages have an air of rapt suavity, devotional fervency and bearing esoteric consciousness, which is intensely attractive to some minds, and realize beyond rivalry a particular ideal – that of ecclesiastical saintliness and detachment from secular fret and turmoil' (W. M. Rosetti). Angelico was much in demand during the last decade of his life. In 1445, Pope **Eugenius IV** summoned him to work on the frescoes of the Blessed Sacrament chapel in the Vatican. In 1447 he began the *Last Judgement* in the San Brixio Chapel, Orvieto. **Nicholas V** got him to paint scenes from the lives of SS Stephen and Laurence in the Nicholas Chapel, where he demonstrated his command of the contemporary interest in light and shade, perspective and foreshortening. He is buried in Santa Maria sopra Minerva.

Angelina Saint, princess and despot of Serbia, born fifteenth century, died Frusha Gora, Yugoslavia, c.1510. A daughter, or relative, of Ivan Tornoievic, prince of the independent state of Zeta, she married Stephen Branovic, who became Despot of Serbia in 1458, on the death of his brother. Her husband died in 1477 and, after the death of Vanuk, who succeeded him, Angelina herself assumed the title of Despot, ruled the Zetans 1497–9, and repulsed the Turks to preserve Zetan independence. She was a devout woman, became a heroine to the Serbians, to whom she was known as the mother and Queen of Montenegro. She is still venerated for her piety and patriotism in Yugoslavia, and commemorated there in folk poems and songs. She is buried in the monastery of Krusedol in the Frusha Gora mountains. Feast day 30 June.

Angelina of Marsciano (Angelina of Corbara and of Foligno) Blessed, foundress of the Franciscan Third Order Regular for women, born 1377, died Foligno, 14 July 1435. She was the daughter of Jacques Angioballi, Count of Marsciano, near Orvieto, and Anne Corbara. She was forced to marry Jean de Thermis, Count of Civitella, at the age of fifteen. It was agreed with him that she would conserve her virginity and dedicate herself to works of charity and piety. After his death two years later, she took the habit of the Third Order of St Francis and, with some other young girls, converted her household in the Abruzzi into a kind of religious community. Persecuted by her family and by King Ladislaus, who accused her of sorcery and heresy for encouraging young girls to a life of virginity, she was finally banished from the kingdom. Following a visit to Assisi, she founded at Foligno in 1397 the convent of St Anne, according to the Franciscan Rule, followed by other foundations in Italy. **Martin V** assembled the sixteen houses existing in 1450 into one congregation, making Angelina superior-general of what became the Third Order Regular for women. After a life of action and ecstasy, she died in the odour of sanctity. Her body was found incorrupt in 1492 and **Leo XII** approved her cult in 1825. Feast day 21 July.

Angelo Carletti di Chivasso Blessed, moral theologian and canonist, born Chivasso, 1411, died Cuneo, Piedmont, 1495. Of a wealthy and distinguished family, he obtained a doctorate in civil and canon law, gave up worldly pursuits at the age of 30, and became a Franciscan of the Cismontane Observance. He was four times chosen vicar-general of his Order. He was appointed apostolic nuncio by **Sixtus IV** to preach a holy war against the invading Turks at Otranto, and by **Innocent VIII** to prevent the spread of the Waldensian heresy. Angelo's reputation as a moralist rests chiefly on his *Cases of Conscience*, a famous dictionary of moral theology, originally printed at Venice by himself in 1486, and many times reprinted. **Luther** detested the work and consigned it to the flames at Wittenburg in 1520, along with the bull of his excommunication, and the *Summa Theologiae* of St **Thomas Aquinas**.

Angelo of Acri Blessed, Capuchin preacher, born Luke Anthony Falcone, Acri, 19 October 1669, died there, 30 October 1739. Of poor parents in southern Italy, he was successful, on his third attempt, in joining the Capuchin Order in 1690. He won fame in southern Italy for his preaching at home missions and at forty hours devotions, talks which were simple and void of all ornate rhetoric. He was elected provincial for the province of Cosenze in 1717, and founded a convent of Capuchinesses in 1725, for whom he wrote a book of prayers on Christ's sufferings. He was beatified by **Leo XII** in 1825, and the cause for his canonization is still active. Feast day 31 October.

Angelram French abbot and scholar, born Saint-Riquier, Somme, c.975, died 9 December 1045. From a knightly family at Ponthieu, Angelram (also Ingelram, Angalram) joined the Benedictines at the abbey of Saint-Riquier, c.1884, and studied there, and at Chartres under **Fulbert**. In 1016 or 1020, he accompanied King Robert the Pious to Rome and, at the insistence of the latter, became abbot of Saint-Riquier in 1022, on the death of Ingelard, until his own death. He was a skilled administrator and worked for the restoration of the cloisters, an increase in the goods of the abbey, reorganization of the library and the copying of manuscripts. He was also a scholar of note, distinguishing himself in music, grammar and dialectic, earning the surname 'The Wise'. He composed a poem *Vita Richarie*, which survives, but his histories in verse of St Vincent and others have been lost. He has at times been given the title saint, but there is no cult.

Angelus de Scarpetis Blessed, born Borgo San Sepolcro, Umbria, date unknown, died there, *c*.1306. He became a missionary, taking the Augustinian habit, *c*.1254, and is supposed to have been sent to England, where he preached and built many monasteries, but the source for this tradition has not been ascertained. He was notable for his humility, innocence, his spirit of poverty and apostolic zeal. He was beatified 24 July 1921. Feast day 1 October.

Angelus Silesius German mystic and poet of the baroque period, born Breslau, December 1624, died there, 9 July 1677. He was born Johannes Scheffler, and brought up a Lutheran, his father being a Protestant landowner, who had emigrated from Poland for religious reasons. He studied philosophy and medicine and was appointed physician to the duke of Württemberg. Reacting against the religious intolerance of the court chaplain, Johannes resigned his post in 1652, and became a Catholic in 1653, taking the name Angelus Silesius. He returned to Breslau and entered the Franciscans, was ordained in 1661 and became co-adjutor to Sebastian **Rostock**, prince-bishop of Breslau. He died at St Mathias Monastery, Breslau. Angelus had admired the writings of a Silesian mystic, Jakob **Böhme**, 'the Cobbler of Gorlitz', and in 1657 he published a collection of *Reimspuche*, or rhymed distichs, embodying a strange, mystical pantheism drawn mainly from the writings of Böhme and his followers. Silesius delighted especially in the subtle paradoxes of mysticism. He held the essence of God to be love; God, he said, can love nothing inferior to himself; but he cannot be an object of love to himself without going out, so to speak, of himself, without manifesting his infinity in a finite form; in other words, by becoming man. God and man are therefore essentially one. Angelus' theme was not so much the ascent of the soul to God, but rather God's descent to the soul. 'I know that God cannot live a moment without me; if I perish, he must needs give up the ghost.' Whereas the uneducated Böhme saw his

way through intuition and poetic talent, Angelus' ambiguously expressed quest was considered pantheistic, but has appealed to romantics and moderns, like Rainer Maria **Rilke**, who see in his epigrams a new variety of Christian mysticism. His musical poems (1657) reveal the zealous convert who, in the spirit of the Song of Songs, wants to testify to his love for Jesus. Some of these songs have become favourites in both Protestant and Catholic churches.

Angilbert Saint, poet and courtier, abbot, born *c*.750, died 18 February 814. Of a Frankish family, he was an early, and remained always, friend of **Charlemagne**; a figure in the Carolingian Renaissance, a student of **Alcuin** and tutor to young Pepin the Short, made king of Italy in 781. Angilbert was a member of the court and the Palatine Academy under the name of Homer, being held in great esteem as a poet. Angilbert had not received holy orders, but was none the less chaplain and counsellor to the king. Against the advice of his friend Alcuin, he led a worldly life and had, with Bertha, daughter of Charles, two sons out of wedlock. Angilbert was appointed, in 781, lay abbot of Saint-Riquier, which he restored; he took part in three embassies to Rome between 792 and 796, taking the *Livres carolins* to **Adrian I** in 794, and was present at Charlemagne's coronation in 800. He was touched by the spirit of monastic life and his last years were spent in edifying penance. Though he may have risen to higher orders, it is not sure that he was ever ordained. He died within a month of Charlemagne. He left various writings: poems of which the metre and grammar are not always correct, letters and treatises which do give an interesting insight into life at Charlemagne's court. His cult is a popular and traditional one, that has not been solemnized. Feast day 18 February.

Angilramnus of Metz Canonist, abbot of Sens, bishop of Metz, date of birth unknown, died Metz, 791. He was perhaps the nephew of St **Chrodegang**, bishop of Metz. His life is known with certainty only from his accession to the see of Metz, 25 September 786. In 784, he succeeded abbot Fulrad as chaplain at **Charlemagne**'s court. His historical importance derives almost accidentally from his being named author of the *Capitula*

Angilramni, a part of the psuedo-Isidorian decretals. The collection contains 71 capitularies concerned mostly with the prosecution of clerics, especially bishops, which was sent by Pope **Adrian I**, it is said, to Angilramnus, and subsequently by him to **Adrian II** as a defence of his own administration at Metz. He died during one of the campaigns of Charlemagne against the Avars. Angilramnus' somewhat anomalous place in history is preserved due to the unresolved debate as to the true condition of the alleged evils in his episcopal administration.

Angles, Higini Catalan priest and musicologist, born Maspujols, Spain, 1 January 1888, died Rome, 8 December 1969. He studied musicology with F. Pedrell and was appointed head of the music section of the Biblioteca de Catalunya, Barcelona, 1917. He worked with W. Gurlitt and F. Ludwig in Germany, and was named professor of music history at the Barcelona Conservatory in 1927, and at the University, 1933; director of the Instituo Español de Musicologia in 1943; and president of the Pontifical Institute of Sacred Music, Rome, 1947, a post he held until his death. His great interest was the music of Spain, especially that of the Middle Ages and Renaissance, such as the *Las Huelgas* codex, the edition of the *Cantigas* of **Alfonso X**, his greatest work, and the *Cancionero musical de Palacios*, the collected works of **Cabanilles**. His numerous articles on the interpretation to be given to medieval secular modod) and his arguments for a theory of mixed rhythmic modes, based on the evidence of the notation of the *Cantigas*, as well as their relationship to Spanish folk music, have appeared in *Die Musik in Geschichte und Gegenwart* and various journals.

Anglin, Francis Alexander Chief justice of Canada, born St John, New Brunswick, 2 April 1865, died Ottawa, 2 March 1933. Educated at St Mary's College, Montreal, and Ontario Law School. He practised law in Toronto; was made king's counsel in 1902; appointed judge of the High Court of Ontario, 1904, and to the Supreme Court of Canada, 1909, serving as chief justice from 1924 to 1933. Appointed imperial privy counsellor, 1925, and a knight commander of the Order of St Gregory the Great. He was among the most able

judges of the Canadian bench and a strong Catholic layman.

Anglin, Timothy Warren Statesman and journalist, born Clonakilty, County Cork, 31 August 1822, died Toronto, 4 May 1896. He emigrated to St John, New Brunswick, in 1849, where he founded the *Morning Freeman*. He opposed, as being too drastic and unworkable, measures prohibiting the manufacture and sale of alcoholic beverages. He was the first Catholic returned to Parliament from the city and county of St John, and became speaker of the House of Commons, 1874–7. He fought the anti-separate school legislation of New Brunswick, and forced a compromise allowing Catholics to have their own schools and teachers to give religious instruction before and after school hours. From 1879 to 1882, he was a prominent member of the Liberal opposition under Edward Blake. In 1883, he moved to Toronto, joining the editorial staff of the *Toronto Globe*, and editor of the *Tribune*, a Catholic weekly. He was the father of Francis Alexander **Anglin**, Chief Justice of Canada, and Margaret Mary, the New York stage actress.

Anianus and Marinus Saints, hermits of the seventh century. Anianus, deacon, and Marinus, a bishop, established a hermitage at Wilparting in the Bavarian Alps. Of either Irish or West Frankish origin, their life was first noticed by bishop Arbeo of Freising in the eighth century, and attested by two manuscripts of the twelfth and fifteenth centuries. They were martyred by a band of Vandals, or Wends, and their cult, which is still active, derives historical support from a twelfth-century sacramentary of Emperor **Henry II**, the patron of Rott; a dispute between Rott and Wilparting as to the whereabouts of the relics was settled in favour of Wilparting in the eighteenth century. Feast day 15 November.

Anianus of Chartres Saint, bishop. He was fifth bishop of Chartres in the early years of the fifth century, according to medieval accounts, but no source earlier than the eleventh century mentions him. The church bearing his name and in which his relics are preserved was twice burned, in 1136 and 1262. His feast is kept on the date on which the relics were returned to the church on the first reconstruction. Feast day 7 December.

Anianus of Orléans Saint, bishop, born Vienne, died Orléans, c.453. Sidonius Apollinaris, in a letter to Bishop Prosper of Orléans, confirmed that his city was preserved, by intercession of Anianus, from devastation by the Huns under Attila in 451. **Gregory of Tours** concurred in this a century later, giving a detailed and picturesque account, according to which Anianus seems to have mobilized the citizens to defend the city, and requested assistance from the Roman general Aetius. His relics are contained in the church bearing his name in Orléans. The congregation of the Sisters of St Anianus, a teaching and nursing congregation, was approved in 1852. Feast day 17 November.

Anicetus Saint, Pope and martyr, died 168. The *Liber Pontificalis* says Anicetus was from Emesa in Syria, that he was a martyr and that he was the eleventh Pope. According to **Eusebius**, he ruled eleven years, placing his death in 168, the eighth year of Marcus Aurelius. Following on his accession, St **Polycarp** came to Rome from Smyrna to urge the Pope to adopt the practice of the churches in Asia Minor of observing Easter on the 14th of the Jewish month Nisan, the Quartodeciman date (the Passover). Although Rome did not observe at the time a special Easter festival, Anicetus pleaded that he felt bound by his predecessors' custom of celebrating the Lord's resurrection every Sunday. The discussion remained friendly, Anicetus invited Polycarp to preside at Mass, but Rome and the East continued their separate practices, the Roman date for the Easter festival not being fixed until the Council of Nicea in 325. The tradition that he died a martyr lacks confirmation. It was probably Anicetus, not **Anacletus**, who built a sepulchral monument to St Peter on Vatican Hill that was familiar to visitors c.200, and which was revealed by recent excavations. Feast day 17 April.

Animucia, Giovanni Italian musical composer of the Renaissance, born Florence, c.1500; died Rome, 25 March 1571. He composed madrigals which revealed the influence of Corteccia and were Florentine in both style and spirit. He was appointed maestro di capella at St Peter's in 1555, and retained the position until his death, when he was succeeded by **Palestrina**, his friend and probably his pupil. At the request of St Philip **Neri**, he composed a number of *laudi*, or hymns of praise,

in two collections, 1563 and 1570. These have given him an accidental prominence in musical history, since their performance in Philip's oratory eventually gave rise to an early form of oratorio. Philip admired Animucia so warmly that he declared he had seen the soul of his friend fly upward toward heaven. Animucia strove to conform to the general aims laid down by the Council of Trent, and stated in the preface to a collection of Masses (1567), that he had striven to embellish the texts with melody 'which did not obscure the meaning of the words'. The manuscripts of many of Animucia's compositions are still preserved in the Vatican Library.

Anna Comnena Byzantine princess, first woman historian, born Constantinople, 1 December 1083, died c.1154. She was the daughter of Emperor **Alexius I Comnenus** and Irene Ducas. She was her father's favourite, and was carefully trained in the study of poetry, science and Greek philosophy. She was intriguing and ambitious, ready to go to any lengths to gratify her longing for power. Her childhood betrothal to her cousin Constantine, whose father Michael VII shared the imperial office with Alexius, ended with the deposition of Michael, his own death and the accession of Alexius' son, John. Having married a young nobleman Nicephorous Bryennius, she united with her mother, Irene, in a vain attempt to prevail upon her father to disinherit John and give the crown to Nicephorous. She then conspired to depose her mother after his accession; and when her husband refused to join the enterprise, she exclaimed that 'nature had mistaken their sexes, for he ought to have been the woman'. She was banished with her mother to a convent where she wrote the *Alexiad*, a history, in Greek, of her father's life and reign (1081–1118). It is more a family panegyric than a scientific history, both her affection and vanity being prominent. Despite its weaknesses, however, the *Alexiad* remains the best source for Alexius' reign. Anna was a determined opponent of the Latin Church and an enthusiastic admirer of the Byzantine Empire, regarding all foreigners as barbarians; she saw the crusades as a danger both political and religious.

Annabilis Saint, French priest of Auvergne, born Riom, c.397, died 1 November c.475. In the sixth century **Gregory of Tours** attested to his virtue and power, and witnessed Annabilis' power over serpents at the saint's tomb. A procession of his relics is traditionally celebrated each year in a church dedicated to him at Riom, in 1120, where he served as parish priest. Feast day 11 June.

Anne of Denmark   Queen of **James I** of England, and VI of Scotland, daughter of Frederick II of Denmark and Norway, born Skanderborg, Jutland, 12 December 1574, died Hampton Court Palace, 2 March 1619. She was sought in marriage to James VI as a means of settling, in Scotland's favour, its claims to the Orkney and Shetland Islands. Brought up a Lutheran and fond of pleasure, she showed no liking for Scottish Calvinism, and soon incurred rebukes on account of her religion. The absence of Lutheran services seems to have led to her inclination to Roman Catholicism, and she attended Mass with the king's connivance. She was claimed as a convert by the Jesuits at Holyroodhouse Palace, through the good offices of Robert **Abercromby**, SJ, in 1600. James used her conversion in negotiations with **Clement VIII** for recognition of his right to the throne of England at **Elizabeth I**'s death in March 1603.

At her coronation with James in July 1603, Anne caused a sensation by refusing to take the sacrament according to the Anglican rite. It is known that during her reign (1603–19), a Jesuit was her chaplain, and the English Jesuit provincial visited her secretly on a number of occasions. Her courage in refusing Anglican Communion at her coronation raised the hopes of Catholic England. She is buried in Westminster Abbey. She was generally regretted as intelligent and tactful, a faithful wife, a devoted mother and a staunch friend. At her death, attended by the archbishop of Canterbury and the bishop of London, she seemed to deny her Catholicism with a renunciation of 'the mediation of all saints and her own merits'. This position has recently been accepted by Philip **Caraman**, SJ, who felt she was 'persuaded against her true conviction'.

Anne of Jesus   Venerable, Discalced Carmelite, born Medina del Campo, Leon, 25 November 1545, died Brussels, 4 March 1621. Of a prominent Spanish family, she rejected marriage, because of a vow of chastity, and sought admission to the

reformed Carmel at Salamanca; she was professed in October, 1571. She aided St **Teresa of Avila** to found convents in Andalusia, 1575, where she was prioress for three years, and in Granada, 1581. After Teresa's death, she became prioress in Madrid, edited Teresa's works and wrote her biography. At the invitation of Cardinal Pierre de Benille, she and Blessed **Anne of St Bartholomew** and four other nuns founded the reformed Carmelite houses at Paris, Pointoise and Brussels (1604–7). She returned to Spain and approved of foundations at Cracow, Galicia and Antwerp. She translated Teresa's works into Latin and Flemish.

Anne of St Bartholomew   Blessed, Spanish Discalced Carmelite, born Almendral, near Avila, 1 October 1549, died Antwerp, 7 June 1626. Though from the lowly peasantry, Anne Garcia was very advanced in the way of prayer. She entered the Carmelite convent of St Joseph at Avila as a lay sister, the first to be received under the Reform, and was professed in 1572. Very faithful to St **Teresa**, whom she served personally night and day, she accompanied her on her travels and held her in her arms as she was dying. She was much in demand in the Spanish Carmels as the inheritor of the Teresian tradition, and in this capacity accompanied **Anne of Jesus** to France, there to establish the Carmelite reform. In 1605, she replaced Anne of Jesus as prioress at Paris, and shared with her an inflexible desire to submit only to the authority of the Discalced Carmelites. In 1612, she founded the Carmel at Antwerp and there, having been a witness for Teresa in the cause of her canonization, she died. She left various works: an autobiography, and other works of spiritual value, which were all the more remarkable in that Anne could not write when she entered the Carmel, and only learnt to do so on the order of Teresa. She was beatified on 6 May 1917. Feast day 7 June.

Annibale, Giuseppe d'   Italian cardinal, canonist and moral theologian, born Borbonna (Aquila), 22 September 1815, died Riveti, 18 July 1892. One of the best moral theologians of the nineteenth century, he taught at the seminary, Borbonna, was vicar-general, and became in 1881 titular bishop of Caristo and assessor of the Holy Office. He was created cardinal by **Leo XIII** in 1889, and was prefect of the Sacred Congregation of Indulgences.

Leo said of him at his elevation that he was 'illustrious by his integrity, his modesty and the richness of his doctrine'. His compendium of moral theology, *Summula theologiae mordis* (3 vols, Milan, 1881–2), presents very precise and dense formulae, not without some obscurity at times; the notes are much longer than the text and provide ample bibliographic, historical and canonical indications, all of which make for a complete and excellent exposition of moral theology, widely used at the end of the nineteenth century and beginning of the twentieth.

Annius, Johannes (Giovanni Nanni) Italian Dominican humanist, historian, archaeologist, contemporary of **Erasmus**, born Viterbo, *c.*1432, died Rome, 13 November 1502. He studied at Florence and had an active career in Viterbo as an astrologer and teacher. Around 1490, he began to forge documentation that attributed to ancient Viterbo an historical role of great importance, which fantasies greatly impressed **Alexander VI**, when he came there in 1493, who made him 'Master of the Sacred Palace' in 1499. He was notorious for *Antiquitates* (Rome, Silber, 1498), a much reprinted work which included forged texts of ancient near-eastern Greek and Roman historians, whose names were known though their works were lost, along with prolix commentaries by Annius himself, showing that the forged texts contradicted – and therefore discredited – the extant pagan historians of Greece and Rome. Several of Annius' Italian contemporaries saw through the fraud, but Erasmus did not, and he used Annius' invented material when he discussed the genealogy of Jesus given in Luke 3. Erasmus had not much regard for Annius, declaring himself 'not really satisfied with what I have collected out of Annius, who as a scholar, I suspect, is rash and pompous, and, in any case, is a Dominican'. He none the less retained the Annian material in the editions of his *Annotationes*.

Anno of Cologne (Hanno, Anno II) Saint, archbishop of Cologne, born Swabia, *c.*1010, died Abbey of Siegburg, 4 December 1075. Belonged to a noble Swabian family and educated at Bambury. He became confessor to **Henry III**, who appointed him to Cologne, and chancellor of the Empire in 1056. He was prominent in the government of Germany and led the party which, in 1063, seized **Henry IV**, still a minor, deprived his mother, the Empress Agnes, of power, and made himself guardian and regent of the boy. Anno settled, in 1064, the dispute between the antipope Cadalus, bishop of Parma, and **Alexander II**, declaring the latter to be the rightful Pope at a synod held at Mantua in May 1064. Returning to Germany he found that **Adalbert** of Bremen had usurped his place of power, and he was dismissed by Henry who disliked him because of his severe discipline. He returned to power in 1066, however, on the fall of Adalbert, put down a rising against his authority in Cologne in 1074, and retired to the monastery of Seigburg, where he died; he was canonized in 1183 by Pope **Lucius III**. He was a founder of monasteries and a builder of churches, advocated clerical celibacy and was a strict disciplinarian. He was a man of great energy and ability, whose action in recognizing Alexander II was of the utmost consequence for Henry IV, and for Germany. Feast day 4 December.

Anquetil, Louis Pierre French historian, born Paris, 21 February 1723, died there, 6 September 1808. He was older brother to Abraham Anquetil Duperron, the French orientalist. He became an Augustinian canon at Sainte-Geneviève in 1741, where he was professor of philosophy and literature. He was made director of the seminary at Reims, where he wrote *Histoire civile et politique de Reims*, (3 vols, 1756–7), perhaps his best work. He held ecclesiastical positions at La Roe, Senlis, Chateau-Renard and La Villette. During the Reign of Terror, he was imprisoned in St Lazare. He was elected a member of the group dealing with moral and political sciences at the national institute, and was employed in the office of the ministry of foreign affairs. He is said to have been asked by Napoleon to write his *Histoire de France* (14 vols, 1805), considered a mediocre compilation at second or third hand, with the assistance of Mezeray, and Paul François Velly. The work nevertheless passed through several editions, and his name is remembered by it.

Ansbald Saint, abbot, died 12 July 886. We know nothing of his origins and little of his early life. He was elected abbot of the monastery at Prüm, in 860, to succeed Eigil, and under his leadership the abbey gained great renown for its flourishing religious observance. He was a close friend of **Lupus** of Ferrières, whose correspondence reveals Ansbald's concern to collate the monastery's manuscripts of classical authors, especially those of the letters of Cicero. Ansbald worked actively to increase the goods and privileges of his monastery, as indicated by the numerous diplomas, donations, exchanges, concessions of rights and immunities accorded to him; in 861, King **Lothair II** allowed him to coin money and to establish a market. In 882, the monastery was burnt by the Normans, but Ansbald was able rapidly to restore it with the help of **Charles III** the Fat. He died with a reputation of great sanctity, and several monastic martyrologies accord him the title of saint. Feast day 12 July.

Ansbert of Rouen Saint, archbishop of Rouen, born Chaussy, mid-seventh century, died Hautmont, 9 February 693. He is little known, his reputation having been eclipsed by his predecessors, SS **Ouen**, Wandrille and Lambert. Son of a distinguished and noble person, Siwin, he received an excellent education and shone in belles-lettres. He dedicated a poem to his saintly predecessor, and promoted his cult. He was brilliant at court and became chancellor but, touched by grace, he abandoned the worldly life and fled to the Benedictine abbey of Fontenelle, founded by St Wandrille. He received holy orders from St Ouen, became abbot, founded three hospitals, or hospices, for the poor, established wise rules, practised all the virtues, worked at establishing harmony. On the death of St Ouen, he was elected archbishop of Rouen in 683, and consecrated by St Lambert. His zeal was not well received, however, and his austere life caused offence. He was banished by Pepin of Heristal to a monastery at Hautmont, but was later authorized to return to Rouen; too late, however, and he died in the 'odour of sanctity', thanking God for his restitution. His body was returned to Rouen and he was buried in the abbey church. His remains were transferred to Chartres in 875; then to Boulogne and finally to Ghent in 944, but were profaned and dispersed by the Calvinists in 1578. He is mentioned in the Roman martyrology. Feast day 9 February.

Ansegis Saint, Frankish monk and abbot, Carolingian adviser, born Lyonnais, c.770, died Fontenelle, 20 July 833. He became a monk at Fontenelle in Normandy, and met **Charlemagne**, who entrusted him with various political missions. Named abbot of Saint-Germer-de-Flay, he restored the abbey, both spiritually and materially. The emperor called him to the imperial court at Aachen, and sent him to the Spanish March; **Louis I**, the Pious, made him abbot of Luxueil in 817, and of Fontenelle in 823, where he restored discipline, observance of the Benedictine Rule, and a dedication to learning, as evidenced in Fontenelle's famous library and scriptorium. He undertook a collection of Carolingian laws from 789 to 826, divided into four capitularies, which became the great authority on ecclesiastical law (books 1–2), and civil law (books 3–4), in the Frankish Empire. Feast day 20 July.

Anselm of Canterbury Saint, archbishop, born Aosta, Val d'Aosta, c.1033, died Canterbury (probably), 21 April 1109. He entered the monastic school of Bec in 1059, where he succeeded **Lanfranc** as prior in 1063, and **Herluin** as abbot in 1078. Lanfranc became archbishop of Canterbury in 1070, and Anselm succeeded him in 1089, though a dispute with King William II (Rufus) over lay investiture delayed his assumption until 1093. Conflict arose again in 1097 over church independence, and while Anselm was in Rome seeking support, the king seized the properties of his see. In 1100 William was killed and Henry I recalled Anselm, but demanded that he should again receive, from him in person, investiture in his office of archbishop, and that he should consecrate all bishops and abbots nominated by himself. Anselm again went to Rome for support and Henry then surrendered the right of lay investiture, establishing supremacy of the Papacy over the English church. Anselm is generally considered the outstanding theologian between St **Augustine** and St **Thomas Aquinas**. He asserted the harmony between faith and reason, contending that faith preceded reason, but could be demonstrated by reason, and did not rely solely on the authority of Scripture and tradition; central to this approach was 'Credo ut intelligam', and 'fides quaerens intellectum'. He was the first to successfully incorporate dialectics into theology. In his greatest work, *Cur Deus Homo*, Anselm undertakes to make plain, even to infidels, the rational necessity of the Christian mystery of the Atonement. The theory rests on three positions: that satisfaction is necessary on account of God's honour and justice; that such satisfaction can only be given by the peculiar personality of the God-man; that such satisfaction is really given by the voluntary death of this infinitely valuable person. This theory has had immense influence on the form of church doctrine and, in contrast with the subjective theory of **Abelard** and others, asserts the necessity of an objective act of atonement for man's sin. Anselm's speculations did not receive in the Middle Ages the respect and attention they deserved, perhaps due to their unsystematic character; they are not elaborate treatises like the great works of **Albert**, Aquinas and **Eriugena**. He differed from most of his predecessors in preferring to defend the faith by intellectual reasoning, instead of employing scriptural and patristic authorities. Canonized in 1163, **Clement XI** declared him a Doctor of the Church in 1720.

Anselm of Havelberg Archbishop, died at Milan, 12 August 1158. Little is known of his life until his consecration as bishop of Havelberg in 1129. An envoy of **Lothair III** to Constantinople in 1136, he took part in ecumenical dialogues on issues dividing the Greek and Latin Churches, and defended the Western Church against charges of doctrinal novelty, claiming that the growth and development of the faith, both in understanding and in institutional expression, are the means of the Holy Spirit in his continuing reformation of the Church. In 1152, Anselm, at the request of **Frederick I Barbarossa**, helped to arrange a treaty with **Eugenius III**, who rewarded him with the archiepiscopal see of Ravenna, in 1155. He died suddenly while serving the emperor at the siege of Milan.

Anselm of Laon Frankish theologian, born Laon, date unknown, died Laon, 1117. One of the most respected teachers of the late eleventh century, he directed the illustrious school of Laon with his brother Raoul, and counted among his pupils both William of Champeaux and **Abelard**; the latter ridiculed him by comparing him to the fig tree in the Gospel that, while covered in leaves, remained fruitless – an unjust charge on a man considered 'teacher of teachers'. His *Sentences* form an important work, and one of the earliest attempts by

scholasticism to systematize theological thought; they were collected according to a plan inspired by John Scotus **Eriugena**: creation, the fall of the angels and of men (original sin); the necessity of redemption; redemption and the sacraments. The *Glossa ordinaria*, once attributed to **Walafrid Strabo**, is now believed to have been compiled by glossators under his direction.

Anselm of Liège Chronicler, born near Cologne, late tenth century, died after 3 March 1056. He studied at Liège with Poppo of Stavelot, became a canon there, then deacon of St Lambert's Cathedral. Highly esteemed by Bishops Wazo of Liège, and Theoduin, for his integrity, holiness and knowledge, he chronicled the activities of the bishops of Tongres, Utrecht and Liège in his two-volume *Gesta Episcoporum*, the principal source for the history of the Diocese of Liège to 1048. In a second version, he substituted the newly discovered chronicle of **Heriger** of Lobbes for the first volume, considering it to be more accurate. Anselm used carefully the materials at hand as well as his own knowledge, and showed himself to be both well read and critical.

Anselm of Lucca Saint, bishop, born Mantua *c.*1035, died there, 18 March 1086. His uncle, Pope **Alexander II**, also Bishop Anselm of Lucca, nominated our Anselm to the see in 1073. He resigned the bishopric and retired to a monastery, but resumed it in 1075, at the insistence of **Gregory VII**, whom he firmly supported in his movement to reform the Church. He lived an austere life and sought to impose strict discipline on an unwilling chapter; he opposed the antipope, **Clement III**, and Emperor **Henry IV**, whose partisans expelled him from Lucca in 1080, and became Gregory's standing legate in Lombardy. He made a collection of canons, *c.*1083, and wrote a polemical treatise in support of Gregory against Clement, *Contra Guibertium et Sequaces eius* (1085). Feast day 18 March.

Anselm of Nonantola Saint, Lombard duke and abbot, date and place of birth unknown, died 3 March 803. Duke of Friuli, he founded the Benedictine abbey of Fanano in 750, and of Nonantola, *c.*752, which included a hospital and a hospice for pilgrims. King **Desiderius** considered him *persona* *non grata*, and banished him to Monte Cassino for several years, but **Charlemagne** restored him to his flourishing monastery. Feast day 3 March.

Ansfrid (Anfrid, Anfroi)   Saint, duke of Brabant, bishop, date and place of birth unknown, died Heiligen, 3 May 1010. Educated at the imperial school, Cologne, he loyally supported Emperor **Otto III**, and strove to suppress brigandage. In 992 he became a monk, founded a convent at Thorn, which his wife and daughter entered, and, persuaded by the emperor, he agreed to be bishop of Utrecht, where he served until he lost his sight in 1006, at which point he retired to Heiligen, a monastery he had founded. He died there, but his relics were removed and now repose in St Peter's Church, Utrecht. Feast day 3 May.

Ansgar (Anskar, Anschar, Scharies)   Saint, 'Apostle of the North', born Picardie, near Corbie, *c*.801, died Bremen, 3 February 865. He became a Benedictine monk at Corbie, taught and preached at Corvey, and thence to Denmark, where King Harold had recently converted to Christianity. He founded a school at Schleswig but, expelled by the local heathen, he returned to Corvey in 829, without having achieved any missionary success. In response to a request by a Swedish embassy, he set out with another monk, and after great hardship, reached Bjorko, where King Bjorn received them well, and there built the first Christian church; among his converts was Heriger, governor and councillor to the king. **Louis I**, the Pious, named him abbot of Corvey, and **Gregory IV**, bishop of Hamburg and papal legate to Scandinavia; **Nicholas I** named him as well bishop of Bremen in 848. In 854, again in Denmark, he converted Haavik, king of Jutland, and then King Olaf of Sweden. He did much to alleviate the horrors of the slave trade. His wish to become a martyr was denied him and he died peacefully, having been a powerful preacher, a modest, self-effacing priest and ascetic, a benefactor of the poor and the sick. He left no legacy, however, and the Scandinavian countries relapsed into paganism after his death. In Germany he is also known as St Scharies. Feast day 3 February.

Anson, Peter   Writer and artist, born Portsmouth, the son of an admiral, 22 August 1889, died Caldey Island, July 1975. For health reasons he did not enter formal education but was taught privately until at nineteen he became a student of the Architectural Association. He was attracted to the High Anglican tradition of the Church of England, and in 1910 entered the Anglican Benedictines in their abbey on Caldey Island, off the coast of Wales. He, like most of the community, became Roman Catholic in 1913. He did not take final vows, however, because of his health. In 1921 he founded the Apostleship of the Sea, and was its secretary until 1924. He spent much time in travelling, including to Assisi, as a consequence of which visit he became a Franciscan tertiary. His first book was *A Guide to Franciscan Italy* (1927), and he produced books at the rate of almost one a year from then on. In 1938 he moved to Scotland, where he lived for two decades. In 1969 he settled back at Caldey, now a Cistercian abbey, where he became an oblate. He was made a Knight of St Gregory for his services to seamen.

Anstrudis   Saint, abbess of Laon, born *c*.645, died before 709. Born in the reign of Dagobert, her parents were probably SS Blandinus and Salaberga. She entered while very young the monastery of Nôtre-Dame de Laon, founded by her mother, and became abbess at the age of twenty. One of her brothers, Baldwin, deacon of Laon, *c*.679, was treacherously murdered by Ebroim, mayor of the palace, and she nearly suffered the same fate, having been accused of acting against his interests, but her virtue and innocence were proved. Numerous miracles are attributed to her, and her relics have been venerated at St Jean de Laon since the French Revolution. Feast day 17 October.

Ansuerus   Saint, German abbot and martyr, born Mechlenburg, *c*.1040, died Ratzeburg, 15 July 1066. He became a Benedictine, and an early and zealous missionary among the pagan Slavic tribes still living around Ratzeburg. He and about 30 companions were stoned to death by pagan Wends, or Obotrites, at Ratzeburg, during which ordeal he besought his executioners to kill him last so that his companions would not apostasize, and so that he could comfort them in their sufferings. Bishop Evermond credited him with restoring sight to a blind man, and had his remains translated from the crypt in the modest church of Sankt Georg, to the cathedral of Ratzeburg. The relics perished during the Reformation, and he is remembered only in monastic martyrologies. Feast day 15 July.

Antelami, Benedetto Italian sculptor, born *c.*1150, died *c.*1230. He came from the region around Lake Como, and is known as the greatest Romanesque sculptor in northern Italy, though his only documented works are the signed architrave of the north portal of the baptistry at Parma (1196–1270), and a *Deposition from the Cross* (1278) in Parma Cathedral. The octogonal Parma baptistry is his greatest creation, for which he seems to have been both architect and sculptor. The complexity of the work suggests numerous assistants, but the unity of design – a novel iconographic ensemble of three portals, with a 'Last Judgement' tympanum, a legend of Barlaam and Josaphat, a relief surrounding the baptistry, and decoration carried into the interior, including the altar frontal – shows Antelami's close supervision of the most complex work in Italy up to that time. Attributed to him as architect are the cathedral of Borgo San Donnino (1179); and San Andrea, Vercelli (1219–27), with carved central tympanum by Antelami.

Anterus Saint, Pope 235–6. He succeeded Pontian and was of Greek extraction. He briefly reigned (43 days) during the persecution of Emperor Maximus Thrax, and though he has been represented as a martyr, this is improbable, since his name does not appear in early official lists of martyrs, and the fourth-century Liberian catalogue says that he 'fell asleep', a term used of Popes who died naturally. The first to be buried in the new papal crypt in the catacomb of **Callistus**, his feast does not appear in ancient calendars, nor in Roman books of the liturgy before the ninth century. Feast day 3 January.

Anthelm of Chignin Saint, French Carthusian reformer and bishop, born Chignin (Savoie), 1107, died Belley, 26 June 1178. A Carthusian at Portes in 1136, he rebuilt the recently damaged La Grande-Chartreuse, and became its seventh prior in 1139, after the resignation of Hugh, and the first minister-general of the Order in 1142. He supported **Alexander III** against antipope Victor IV, who rewarded him with the see of Belley in

1163, and was consecrated by Alexander himself. Alexander named him legate to England in the hope of reconciling Henry II with **Thomas Becket**, but Anthelm could not go. In 1175, **Frederick I Barbarossa** conferred on him and his successors the title of Prince of the Holy Roman Empire. His cult has been observed by the Carthusians since 1607. Feast day 26 June.

Anthelmi, Joseph French cleric and church historian, born Fréjus, 27 July 1648, died there, 21 June 1697. A theology student of François de la Chaise at Lyons, he devoted his life to the history of the Church. Within a few years he had published *De initiis ecclesiae Forojuliensis* (1680), and became involved in polemics with Pasquier **Quesnel** over the authorship of several religious works. In 1693, he published a study of St **Martin of Tours**. In 1697, exhausted by work and ill with tuberculosis, he retired to Fréjus from his post as vicar-general of the Diocese of Pamiers. He authored many works, manuscripts and notes, some of which were published as late as 1872.

Anthemius of Constantia Bishop of Constantia (ancient Salamis) during the fifth century. He is renowned for having claimed – as reported by Alexander, a monk in the sixth century – to have discovered the body of St Barnabas in 488 and, on that basis, alleged the apostolicity, and petitioned the emperor **Zeno** to confirm the independence from Antioch of the church in Cyprus. Alexander describes the event as miraculous, the result of a dream, and states, moreover, that a copy of the Gospel of St Matthew was found on Barnabas' chest. The emperor granted Anthemius' request, upholding the decision of the Council of Ephesus of 431 against a challenge of Peter the Fuller, patriarch of Antioch. Anthemius built a basilica, and established the feast of St Barnabas on 11 June.

Anthemius of Poitiers (also **Anthemus, Attenius, Aptemius**) Saint. He is named as thirteenth in the episcopal list, which suggests his being bishop of Poitiers around the year 400, but the authority for the list at this time is to be treated with great caution, according to Louis **Duchesne**. Nothing is known of his life, but his cult has been observed in the Dioceses of Saintes and Poitiers since the seventeenth century. There is no authentic document supporting the claim that he died at Jonzac, while preaching, in 400. Feast day 3 December.

Anthimus A priest, martyred at Rome under Diocletian, c.302 (third century).

Anthimus Saint, bishop of Nicomedia (Izmit, Turkey), beheaded in the Diocletian persecution of 303. He is credited with a text *De sancta ecclesia* which defines, against the heretics, the characteristics of the true Church: unity, catholicity, apostolicity; however, it may be a later addition. **Justinian I** built a church in his honour, and the legend of SS Domna and Indes credits him with a letter to persecuted communities exhorting them to fortitude and perseverance during the persecution. He declined an offer of pagan priesthood and relief from torture before he was beheaded. Feast day 27 April; in Greek calendar, 3 September.

Anthimus Saint, a hymnographer. With Auxentius he belonged to the imperial guard and to a group of lay ascetics called the 'Spondaioi', who kept vigils in the church of St Irene in Constantinople. As a priest, after 457, and leader of the Chalcedonian party, he wrote strophes, hymns and psalmody for choirs of men and women. Feast day 7 June.

Anthimus I Patriarch of Constantinople 535–6, died after 548. Bishop of Trebizond in 533, Empress Theodora had him transferred from there in 535, but Pope **Agapetus I** had him deposed from both sees, and deprived of his sacerdotal functions, because of his Monophysite leanings and epistolary relations with Severus of Antioch and Theodosius of Alexandria.

Anthimus II (of Constantinople) Patriarch June–October 1623, died Mount Athos, 1628. French policy supported him in his opposition to Cyril **Lucaris**.

Anthimus III (of Constantinople) Patriarch 1822–4, born Naxos, c.1760, died Smyrna, 1842; exiled in 1824.

Anthimus IV (of Constantinople) Patriarch 1840–1, and 1848–52, born Constantinople, c.1788, died Isle of Princes, 1878. Metropolitan of Iconium, 1825, of Larissa, 1835, and of Nicomedia, 1837. Elected patriarch February 1840, deposed in 1841; re-elected 1848, deposed again 11 November 1852; died a nonagenarian.

Anthimus V (of Constantinople) Patriarch 1841–2, born Neochorion, Turkey, died Constantinople, June 1842. Metropolitan of Agathopolis, 1815, Anchialos, 1821, Cyzicus, 1831; elected patriarch, May 1841.

Anthimus VI (of Constantinople) Patriarch 1845–8, 1853–5, 1871–3, born Isle of Koutali, c.1790; died Candili, 1878. A monk on Mount Athos, elected and deposed three times. A decisive opponent of Bulgarian Orthodoxy, he retired to Candili in 1873, and died there almost a nonagenarian.

Anthimus VII Tsatsos (of Constantinople) Patriarch 1895–6, born Janina, c.1835, died Halki, December 1913. A renowned preacher and theologian, named bishop of Paramythia, 1869, metropolitan of Ainos, 1878, of Korytsa, Leros and Kalymnos; served 22 months as patriarch and retired to Halki. He rejected the ecumenical efforts of Pope **Leo XIII**'s encyclical *Praeclara gratulationes*, 1894, in a letter published in September 1895.

Anthimus of Tyana Fourth-century bishop, who quarrelled with his friend St **Basil** (c.372) over episcopal jurisdiction in Cappadocia and Armenia, but supported Basil's anti-African offensive.

Anthony I, Kassimatas (of Constantinople) Patriarch January 821–c.January 837. Successively hegumen (abbot) of the monastery of Metropolitou in Petrion, c.815, and bishop of Sylaion. An iconoclast because of personal ambition, an active supporter of the policies of Emperor **Leo V** (813–21), by his opposition to Patriarch **Nicephorus I** and his role in the Iconoclastic Synod of 815, under Theodotus Melissemus. When he became patriarch, he excommunicated Job, patriarch of Antioch, because he had crowned the usurping emperor Thomas, who was supported by the Arab emir Mamun.

Anthony II, Kauleas (of Constantinople) Saint, patriarch August 893–12 February 901. A monk at the age of twelve, then hegumen of the monastery of the Mother of God (later Kalliou Kauleas), he initiated the canonization of St Blasius of Amorion, c.894, and, in 899, received opponents of Photius into communion with the Church, in the presence of papal legates. He strengthened the authority of the Byzantine patriarchate over the Church in Dalmatia.

Anthony III, the Studite (of Constantinople) Patriarch 974–9, died Mount Athos, 983. He became Syncellus to Patriarch Basil I, and his successor, after his deposition by Emperor John I Tzirnisces. Anthony favoured the antipope **Boniface VII** over **Benedict VII**, and was removed from office in 979, for his support of Bardas Sclerus against Basil II. Well known for his austere life, he initiated the first collection of lives of the saints of the Oriental Church, and left his monks a 'Monitum' on confession and the monastic account of conscience; he opposed the simonaical activity connected with taxes for Hagia Sophia.

Anthony IV (of Constantinople) Patriarch 1389–90, and 1391–7, died at Constantinople, May 1397. Deposed in 1390, he regained favour, and took up office eight months later. He tried to regulate the conflict between the various Byzantine-rite churches, and maintained the ecclesiastical sovereignty of Constantinople over Alexandria, despite efforts to the contrary by the Sultan of Egypt. Anthony informed Jagellon, grand duke of Lithuania and king of Poland, that he would consider union of the churches if he joined Sigismund, king of Hungary, in a Crusade against the Turks and, to this end, encouraged **Manuel II** to journey to the West in 1399. Three of Anthony's seals survive.

Anthony Bonfadini Blessed, Italian Franciscan missionary, born Ferrara, c.1422, died Cotignola, 1 December 1482. Of a noble family, he became a Franciscan at the Friary of the Holy Spirit, Ferrara, in 1439, and a missionary in the Holy Land; a renowned preacher there when he returned to Italy, at Cotignola, he died at a pilgrim's hospice. Known for his kindness and peacemaking spirit, a miracle was attributed to him during his lifetime.

The discovery of his incorrupt body a year after his death, and other reports of miracles at his tomb in Cotignola, occasioned his cult, which **Leo XIII** eventually confirmed in 1901. In 1495 his body was transferred into the church of the Observant Friary, founded by Blessed **Angelo Carletti di Chivasso**, and he protected Cotignola from calamities in 1630, 1685 and 1696. Feast day 1 December.

Anthony Neyrot Blessed, Italian Dominican martyr, born Rivoli, died Tunis, 10 April 1460. He went to Sicily to preach, contrary to the advice of St **Antoninus**, Dominican archbishop of Florence, but tired of the island and took ship to Naples in August 1458; the ship was captured by pirates, who imprisoned him in Tunis. While waiting to be ransomed, he succumbed to temptation, publicly denied Christ, became a Muslim and married, in 1459. Some months later he repented and reconciled to the Church. On Palm Sunday 1460, he publicly abjured Islam, renounced his apostasy and preached the Gospel of Christ before the Sultan, who had him executed. His body was sent first to Genoa, thence to Rivoli in 1469. **Clement XIII** beatified him in 1767. Feast day 10 April.

Anthony of Egypt (the Great) Saint, hermit and father of anchoritic monasticism, born Kome, Upper Egypt, c.251, died Pispir, 356. The son of a prosperous Coptic family, he gave away all his possessions c.269, and withdrew from society to lead an ascetical life near his home. In 285, he retired into complete isolation in an abandoned fort near Pispir, where he suffered his famous 'temptations', and began to attract followers. In 305, he emerged to give the disciples a rule, the first of anchoritic life. He retired into solitude again five years later, but re-emerged during the Arian conflict to support St **Athanasius**, who is credited with the *Vita Antonii*, the evidence for his life that has influenced the whole Christian world. In it, Anthony is depicted as the perfect man who follows moderate ascetic practices, supports Church hierarchy and performs miracles with divine assistance. Thus was initiated a tradition of monastic support for the Alexandrian patriarchate that grew into a movement for Coptic national self-determination, which reached its climax in the schism between the Coptic Church and the supporters of the Council of Chalcedon (451). Anthony died in his 'Inner Mountain', his refuge (still called Der Mar Antonios), near the Red Sea at the age of 105. Feast day 17 January.

Anthony of Padua Saint, Franciscan theologian, preacher, Doctor of the Church, born Lisbon, 15 August 1195, died Arcella, near Padua, 13 June 1231. The son of noble parents, and given the name Ferdinand at baptism, he joined the Canons Regular of St Augustine at fifteen, and for eight years practised piety and studied Scripture at Coimbra. Deeply moved by the relics of some Franciscan missionaries killed in Morocco and brought to Coimbra in 1220, a desire seized him to become a Franciscan, to preach the Gospel in Africa and to suffer a martyr's death. Accepted by the Order, he changed his name to Anthony, and went to Morocco within the year. Serious illness, however, obliged him to return, but his ship was blown off course and carried him to Sicily; he proceeded to Assisi where St **Francis** had convoked a general chapter in 1221. His reputation for preaching and learning having been established in the Romagna province, and against the heretics in France, Francis approved his appointment as lector in theology to the Order, the first to hold the post, and he taught at Montpelier, Bologna, Padua and Toulouse. He led the rigorous party in the Franciscan Order against the mitigations introduced by the general, Elias. Feast day 13 June.

Anthony of Stroncone Blessed, Italian Franciscan lay brother, born Stroncone, Umbria, 1381, died Assisi, 7 February 1461. He joined the Observant Friars Minor at the age of twelve and, like St **Francis**, refused the dignity of priesthood and remained a lay brother. He served as assistant novice master at Fiesole, 1411–20, under the saintly Thomas Bellacci, whom he helped to repress and convert the Fraticelli in Tuscany and Corsica (1420–35). He spent the last 25 years of his life at the Carceri hermitage above Assisi, and was revered for his humility, mortification, prophesies and contemplative prayer. Many important favours are reported to have been granted at his tomb between 1461 and 1475. Beatified by **Innocent XI** in 1687, twenty armed citizens forcibly translated his well-preserved body to his birthplace. Feast day 8 February.

Anthony of the Holy Ghost Portuguese theologian, canonist, bishop, born Monte Morovelho, June 1618, died Loandra, Angola, 27 January 1674. He entered the Discalced Carmelites at Lisbon in 1636, becoming lector in theology, provincial definitor and definitor for Spain. Nominated bishop of Angola by Peter II, he took possession of his see in 1673, but died the following month. Renowned as a preacher, he composed five volumes of spiritual and canonico-moral works, amongst which, *Directorium mysticum* (1677), a treatise on the spiritual life tracing the 'Three Ways' in the Fathers, St **Thomas Aquinas** and St **Teresa of Avila**.

Anthony Pavonius Blessed, Italian Dominican inquisitor and martyr, born Savigliano, *c.*1326, died Bricherasio, 9 April 1374. He entered the Dominicans at Savigliano in 1341, became a master in theology in 1365, and was appointed inquisitor-general for Liguria and upper Lombardy, where his opponents were chiefly the Waldensians, whose numbers he much reduced through his preaching and official duties. Some of them hated him so much for his persistence and success that they brutally murdered him as he left the church after preaching. In 1375, **Gregory XI** eulogized him as a martyr, and **Pius IX** approved his beatification in 1856. Feast day 9 April.

Antoine, Charles French Jesuit economist, born Fumary, 16 December 1847, died Le Dorat, 24 April 1921. He studied engineering at the Ecole des Mines, and chemistry at the Collège de France, before entering the Society of Jesus in 1869. He then taught theology in Jesuit seminaries, and published *Cours d'économie sociale* in 1896, in which he emphasized the relation between theology and the science of economics. The work had great success as a text book, and a sixth edition was brought out in 1921. Antoine became widely known, lectured at the 'Semaines Sociales' (1905–13), wrote the *Chronique sociale* for *Etudes* (1897–1906), and published numerous articles on economics. He left the Society in 1913.

Antoine, Paul Gabriel French Jesuit theologian, born Luneville, Lorraine, 10 January 1678, died Pont-à-Mousson, 22 January 1743. He entered the Society in 1693 and taught humanities, philosophy and theology, becoming professor, then rector, at

Pont-à-Mousson. In 1723 he published *Theologia universa speculativa et dogmatica*, which immediately established his reputation as one of the best theologians of his time; the work went through nine editions during his lifetime, and ten editions after his death. His *Theologia moralis universalis* of 1726 was immensely popular and brought him even more acclaim, and was published in several countries, in 60 editions. St **Alphonsus Liguori** considered Antoine's doctrine overly severe; **Benedict XIV** prescribed a Roman edition for use by students at the College of Propaganda, in 1746, and French and Italian bishops also recommended it.

Antolinez, Agustin Spanish theologian, born Valladolid, 6 December 1554, died there, 19 June 1626. An Augustinian, professor of theology at Valladolid and at Salamanca, he became bishop-elect of Ciudad Rodrigo in 1623, and archbishop of Santiago de Compostella in 1624. In addition to spiritual works on, e.g., St John of Saliagun and St **Clare of Montefalco**, Antolinez is noted for his commentary on the *Spiritual Canticle* of St **John of the Cross**, *Amores de Dios y el Alma*, which suggests that he worked from the mystical Doctor's own interpolated revision of the text, i.e. a transcription made by John of the Cross himself, perhaps bequeathed to Antolinez by his confrère, Luis de Leon. The commentary has emerged from obscurity in recent times, because of the question it raises regarding the authenticity of the text of the *Canticle*, as edited by the Carmelites. Antolinez, and later the Carmelites, did not wish the *Amores* to be published, nor have the Augustinians wished to make a claim on behalf of Antolinez, and this may help to explain their reasons.

Antonelli, Giacomo Italian cardinal and diplomat, born Sonnino, 2 April 1806, died Rome, 6 November 1876. Created a cardinal in 1847, and chosen by **Pius IX** to preside over the council entrusted with drafting a constitution, he became premier of the first ministry; when his cabinet fell, Antonelli created for himself the governorship of the sacred palaces so that he could retain constant access to, and influence over, the Pope. When violence arose in the Papal States in 1848, he arranged the flight of Pius to Gaeta, and became secretary of state of the government in exile. Upon their return to Rome in 1850, he influenced Pius in favour of a reactionary and ultramontane policy, and virtually became temporal ruler of Rome down to 1870, being nicknamed the 'Red Pope'. He obtained French aid against Garibaldi's invasion of papal territory in 1867; when the Italians did enter in 1870, he was active in the struggle beween the Papacy and the Italian Risorgimento. More a statesman than a prelate (he was never ordained a priest), his contemporaries regarded him as 'unscrupulous, grasping and a sinister personality'. When he died the Vatican finances were in disorder, with a deficit of some 45 million lire. His personal fortune, accumulated during office, was considerable, and he left nearly all of it to his family; to the Church little, and to his patron, Pius, a trifling souvenir.

Antonello da Messina Italian painter, born Messina, 1430, died Venice, February 1479. He trained at Naples, under Colantonio, and when he saw, there, a painting in oil by **Jan van Eyck**, belonging to Alphonso y Aragon, he determined to learn the new method. He went to the Netherlands and returned with his secret about 1465, then removed to Venice in 1472, where he painted for the Council of Ten, and died there. His style shows a unity – not always successful – of Italian simplicity and Flemish love of detail, a synthesis of Flemish realism, Tuscan formal composition and abstracted forms related to **Piero della Francesca** and Francesco da **Laurana**. There are extant some twenty authentic productions, consisting of renderings of 'Ecce Homo', Madonnas, saints and half-length portraits, many painted on wood. The finest of all is said to be the marvellous *Picture of a Man*, in the Berlin museum. The National Gallery, London, has three of his works, including *St Jerome in his Study*. Antonello is important in Italian painting not only for the introduction of the Flemish invention, but also for the transmission of Flemish tendencies.

Antonia of Florence Blessed, Italian Poor Clare, died at Aquila, 29 February 1472. A Florentine widow, she entered the Franciscan Third Order Regular in 1429, became prioress at Foligno, and at Aquila for thirteen years where, on the advice of St **John Capistran**, she founded a monastery under the first rule of the Poor Clares. An example of patience under the trials of a long, painful illness and of family difficulties caused by a spendthrift son, and other relatives. Her body, still whole and flexible, is kept in the Monastery of St Clare of the Eucharist in Aquila. Feast day 28 February.

Antonil, Andre João (João Antonio Andreoni) Italian Jesuit in Brazil, born Lucca, Tuscany, 8 February 1649, died Bahia, 13 March 1716. He entered the Society in 1667, and went to Brazil as secretary to visitor-general Antonio Vieira in 1681; professor of rhetoric, director of students, rector of the Collegio de Bahia and provincial. In 1711 he wrote *Cultura e opulenza do Brasil*, in Portuguese under a pseudonym, which did not have the approval of the Society; it was known that he was the author. The book gives a valuable account of the economic and social aspects of Brazil as it appeared in the early eighteenth century.

Antoninus (Antonio Pierozzi, also, de Forciglioni) Saint, Italian Dominican archbishop, born Florence, 1 March 1389, died there, 2 May 1459. He entered the Order at 15, and was soon entrusted, in spite of his youth, with the government of houses at Cortona, Rome, Naples and Florence, which he laboured zealously to reform. Consecrated archbishop of Florence by **Eugenius IV** in 1446, it is said on the advice of **Fra Angelico** he became a counsellor of popes and statesmen, and won the esteem and love of his people by his energy and resource in combating the effects of plague and earthquake in 1448 and 1453. Of his various theological works, the best known are *Summa theologica* (1477), and the *Summa confessionalis* (1472); also a general history of the world, *Chronicon* (1440–59), illustrating from the past how men should live in this world, and drawing on the Scriptures, lives of the saints and the Fathers and Doctors of the Church, decrees of Popes and councils. He also wrote on economic questions, and adapted Catholic traditions to modern conditions, maintaining that money invested in business was true capital, and that it is not therefore necessarily wrong to receive interest on it. Feast day 10 May.

Antonio de Butrio Italian professor and canonist, born Butrio, near Bologna, 1338, died Bologna, 4 October 1408. A layman, he studied civil and canon law at Bologna, Florence, Ferrara and Perugia. He went to Marseilles in 1407 to negotiate, on behalf of **Gregory XII**, the end of the schism with antipope **Benedict XIII**. After the treaty in April that year, he returned to Bologna where he died. He wrote several works designed to remedy evils in the Church, and to bring about Christian unity, which were noted for their practicality and wide diffusion.

Antonius Andreas Spanish Franciscan and scholastic, born Tauste, Saragossa, *c.*1280, died *c.*1320. He studied at Paris in the University of Lerida, under **Duns Scotus**. He became a dedicated proponent of his master's doctrine, and promulgated the 'Subtle Doctor's' teaching in numerous writings, not only commentaries, e.g. on the *Sentences*, in 1572. His works were widely read and frequently printed in the fifteenth and sixteenth centuries, and he stongly influenced the development of Scotism with writings such as *Tractatus formalitatum ad mentem Scoti* (1475); *Quaestiones super Libros 12 metaphysicae* (1482), and the *Compendiosum principum in Libros sententiarum* (1495), formerly attributed to St **Bonaventure**.

Antony (Khrapovitsky) Metropolitan of Kiev, Russian Orthodox theologian and émigré leader, born Novgorod, 17 March 1863, died Belgrade, Yugoslavia, 10 August 1936. He was successively rector of three of Russia's theological academies. In 1917 he received the largest number of votes to be the new patriarch, though the final decision was made by lot and **Tikhon** was elected. After the revolution he became leader of the Russian Orthodox Church Abroad, in Yugoslavia. He strongly opposed the declaration of loyalty to the soviet régime of Metropolitan **Sergius**. His theological works include the controversial *Moral Aspects of the Dogma of the Redemption* (1919). There is a voluminous biography in Russian by his friend Archbishop Nikon (Rklitsky)

Anunciación, Domingo de la Spanish missionary, born Fuente-Ojeguna, Estremadura, 1510, and baptized Juan de Paz, died Mexico City, 1591. He went to Mexico with his brother in 1528, and joined the Dominicans. He did missionary work to the Indians at Tepetloaxtac and learned the Indian dialects, which resulted in a *Doctrina Cristina* for use in catechetical work. He took the history of his province, begun by Andres de Moguer, down to 1580, and his in turn was completed by **Dávila y Padilla**. During a number of epidemics among the Indians, particularly in 1545 and 1547, Domingo worked among the sick and dying, which may help to explain the 100,000 Indian baptisms attributed to him. He accompanied expeditions to Florida and Alabama, during which the hardships he endured undermined his health, and he eventually returned to Mexico where he spent his last years in missionary work.

Aparicio, Sebastian de Blessed, Spanish-born pioneer colonist, born Gudina, Galicia, 20 January 1502, died Puebla, Mexico, 25 February 1600. He went to Mexico in 1533 where, by way of service to the Indians at Puebla de los Angeles, he worked as a farmer, a road builder and a trainer of young bulls, all of which trades he taught. He married twice and when the second wife died, he became a Franciscan at the age of 72, in Mexico City. Assigned the task of begging for the daily bread of the community, for 20 years he provided the convent of Puebla with all the material goods required; also noted for his humility and charity, he gave much help to all sorts of poor and needy people. He worked so many miracles in his lifetime that the bishop, Diego Romano, began the process for his beatification, but even though the miracles continued after his death, the process continued for two centuries, among the main causes for delay being his two marriages; **Pius VI** beatified him in 1789. Feast day 25 February.

Aper of Toul Saint, French bishop, born Trancault, Troyes, fifth century, died *c*.507. The seventh bishop of Toul, a late *vita* states that he served seven years, during which time he is said to have miraculously liberated three prisoners of the common law at Chalon-sur-Saône. Aper built a basilica at the gates of Toul, where he is buried, and which bore his name early in the seventh century, later becoming better known as the abbey of St Aper. His cult is popular in the ancient see of Toul and in neighbouring dioceses. Feast day 15 September.

Aphraates (a Greek form of the Persian name Aphrahat, or Pharhadh) The earliest of the Syriac Fathers, called 'The Persian Sage', he flourished in the early fourth century. An ascetic, he lived through the persecution of the Sasanid king Shapur II (310–79). What is known about him comes from his 23 treatises, or 'Demonstrations' (not homilies), the first ten of which, on faith, love, fasting, prayer, the resurrection, humility, were completed in 337; the next twelve, almost all directed against the Jews and their religious practices, in 344, and the final one in 345. The first 22 are arranged as an acrostic, each beginning with a different letter of the alphabet, and give 'a full and ordered exposition of the Christian faith', with a strong emphasis on ascetical practices. His grasp of Scripture is remarkable, but the absence of contemporary Western influence, such as the Nicene theology, would seem to indicate the isolation of the Persian Church, because of both persecution and differences of language, and the Bible may well have been his only written source.

Apollinaris, Claudius Saint, bishop of Hierapolis, early Christian apologist, fl. second century. He received his see during the reign of Marcus Aurelius (161–80), and is known as an outstanding champion of orthodoxy in the early days of Montanism. His writings include a 'Defence of the Faith', presented to Marcus Aurelius in 172, five treatises 'Against the Pagans', two 'On the Truth', and two 'Against the Jews'. His refutations of the early Montanists were highly esteemed by Serapion of Antioch, but he could not have been the author of the anti-Montanist tract cited by **Eusebius**. Apart from a few fragments, all his writings are lost. Feast day 8 January.

Apollinaris of Laodicea, the Younger Bishop, theologian and heretic, born Laodicea, Syria, *c*.300, died *c*.390. A vigorous advocate of orthodoxy against the Arians, a firm supporter of the Council of Nicea (325), and a friend of St **Athanasius** (whom he had received on the latter's return from exile in 346). He became bishop of Laodicea in 361, and noted as a theologian at Antioch, where St **Jerome** was an auditor. Most of Apollinaris' writings have disappeared, but from other sources we know that he shared with St Athanasius the conviction that only the unchangeable Divine Logos could be the saviour of man, whose mind, or soul, is inherently changeable and fallible. This led him to deny explicitly – as Athanasius did not – that Christ had a soul, being persuaded that his divine personality supplied the assumed human nature with that function; so his manhood was not complete, and he could not be a perfect example for us, nor could he redeem the whole of human nature, only its physical elements. This teaching was condemned by synods at Rome in 374–80, and by the Council of Constantinople in 381, whence his teaching was forbidden. Apollinaris left the Church in 375 and no more is heard of him.

Apollinaris of Monte Cassino Saint, Benedictine abbot, born, date unknown, died 27 November 828. Entrusted to the abbey as a young child, and eventually ordained priest, he succeeded Abbot Gisulfus in 817. During his reign the abbey reached a high point of development, both materially and spiritually; famous for his sanctity, he is said to have crossed the River Liri dryshod. His relics, placed under an altar in the chapel dedicated to him and decorated with paintings by Luca Giordano, survived the destruction wreaked on the abbey by the Allied forces in 1944. Feast day 27 November.

Apollinaris of Valence Saint, bishop, born Vienne, c.453, died Valence, c.520. The son of St Hosychius (Isicius), and brother of St **Avitus**. When he became bishop in c.490, he laboured to renew discipline in his diocese, vacant for some years, and to restore the Burgundians to the Catholic faith, who had fallen into Arianism. Exiled by King Sigismund, following the Synod of Epaon in 517, he returned the following year. Biographies have relied on his correspondence with Avitus, and records of the councils. Feast day 5 October.

Apollinarius *see* **Apollinaris of Laodicea**

Apollonia of Alexandria Saint, virgin and martyr (third century). A victim of the anti-Christian disturbances in Alexandria c.255 toward the end of the reign of Emperor Philip the Arabian, her martyrdom is described in a letter of **Dionysius**, bishop of Alexandria, to Fabius, bishop of Antioch, according to which, a mob seized 'the marvellous aged virgin Apollonia', broke her teeth and threatened to burn her alive, whereupon she leapt into a fire and was consumed. The morality of such acts has given some trouble to moralists, and St **Augustine** suggested that it would not have been suicidal in any objectionable sense of the word, if it were performed under the direct inspiration of the Holy Spirit. Although usually pictured as a young maiden, she was in fact an elderly deaconess at the time of her death, and is honoured as the patron saint of dentists. Feast day 9 February.

Aquarius, Mattia dei Gibboni Italian theologian, born Aquaro, date unknown, died Naples, 1591. He joined the Dominicans at Naples and became professor of theology at the universities of Milan, Turin, Rome and Naples (1569–75). A staunch Thomist, much influenced by **Capreolus**, he published *Ad notationes super IV libros sententiarum Joannis Capreoli*, and *Controversiae inter Divum Thomam et caeteros theologos et philosophos* (1589); and *Formalitates iuxta doctrinam Divi Thomae* (1605), edited by A. de Marcho, OP.

Aquilinas Saint, martyr, born Würzburg, c.970, died Milan, c.1015. He studied at Cologne, but left there when his fellow canons chose him as successor to the bishop; he went to Paris and left there, for the same reason. He crossed the Alps to Pavia and from there to the church of San Lorenzo in Milan. Because of his zeal in opposing the spread of Manichaeism, he made enemies of the heretics, who martyred him; his body rests in San Lorenzo in a special chapel bearing his name, and decorated with scenes from his life. He has had a continuous cult and is revered by the churches of Cologne, Würzburg and Milan, and by the canons of the Lateran. Feast day 29 January.

Aquinas, Philippus (Juda Mordechai) French Hebrew scholar, born Carpentras, c.1575, died Paris, 1650. While a rabbi at Avignon he showed great sympathy for Christianity; forced to resign his position in 1610, he became a Roman Catholic at Aquino, from which he took his Christian surname. Named professor of Hebrew at the Collège de France by Louis XIII, he had influence at court; his grandson, Antoine d'Aquin, became chief physician to **Louis XIV**. Philippus worked on the Paris Polyglot and developed the Hebrew lexicographical work of Nathan ben Jehivel and J. Buxtorf, with his own publications: *Radices breves* *linguae Sanctae* and *Dictionarium Hebraeo-Chaldaeo talmudico-rabbiniarum* (1620 and 1629).

Aquinas, Thomas   *see* **Thomas Aquinas**

Arator   Christian poet, born Milan(?), before 500, died Rome, *c.*550. Orphaned very young, he received his education from Bishop Lawrence of Milan, and the poet Eunodius. He studied classical literature and rhetoric, pursued a legal career at the court of Theodoric the Great in Ravenna for a time, and was ordained sub-deacon by Pope **Vigilius**, *c.*540. In 554 he wrote his epic poem *De Actibus Apostolorum*, comprising 2326 hexameters, modelled on the *Carmen Paschale* of Sedulius, and Vigilius allowed him to introduce it at a public reading in the church of St Peter in Chains. The poem was popular during the Middle Ages, but its inferior verse, uninspired rhetoric and flights of extravagant allegory have not been much acclaimed in later times.

Araujo, Antonio de   Portuguese Jesuit missionary, born São Miguel, Azores, 1566, died Espiritu Santo, Brazil, 1632. He entered the Society in 1582 at Bahia and, after ordination, went to do missionary work among the Tupi Indians. Zealous and gifted, Antonio mastered the Tupi language with a fluency that equalled his Portuguese. He wrote a catechetical work in Tupi, and several historical treatises containing valuable geographical and ethnographical information of the period.

Araujo, Francisco de   Spanish Dominican bishop, born Verin, 1580, died Madrid, 19 March 1664. He entered the Order of Friars Preachers at Salamanca, had a high reputation for piety and learning, and commented on most of St **Thomas Aquinas**' *Summa Theologiae*. Consecrated bishop of Segovia in 1648, he retired from his see in 1656 to a Dominican house in Madrid.

Arbez, Edward Philip   French biblical scholar, born Paris, 16 May 1881, died Washington, DC, 27 December 1967. He studied at Argentière, Alix and Issy, and went to Washington in 1901 as a candidate for the Society of St Sulpice on the 'American Mission'. He studied oriental languages at the Catholic University of America, and was ordained a Sulpician in 1904. He taught apolo-

getics, Old and New Testament and Hebrew at Menlo Park, California; and sacred Scripture and Semitic languages at the Catholic University, from 1905 until his retirement in 1951. He contributed to the *Catholic Encyclopedia* and co-founded, with R. F. Butin, the Catholic Biblical Association of America, and played a leading part in bringing out the New American Bible. He laid the groundwork, as a trustee of the American Schools of Oriental Research, for more active Catholic participation in its scholarly undertakings. He acted as adviser to the Near Eastern Affairs section of the Department of State, and the Federal Bureau of Investigation, from 1951 to 1961.

Arbogast of Strasburg   Saint, bishop, born Aquitaine, died near Strasburg, mid-sixth century. He lived as a hermit in a forest in Alsace, and, according to one tradition, became bishop of Strasburg, *c.*673, through the influence of King Dagobert II of Austrasia, who seems to have been his patron. Known for his humility, he wanted to be buried in a cemetery with criminals. He is venerated as the patron of the Diocese of Strasburg, where, however, the ancient episcopal catalogues and inscriptions on the sixth-century cathedral assign his episcopate to *c.*550. Feast day 21 July.

Arbol y Díez, Antonio   Spanish Franciscan spiritual writer, born Torellas, 1651, died Saragossa, 31 January 1726. He excelled as a teacher of philosophy and theology, as well as being a celebrated preacher. His life an intense quest for holiness, his writings are renowned in the fields of theology, homiletics, asceticism and mysticism. The list of his published works includes 33 items, some of which had as many as ten editions, e.g. *Desenganos misticos, Novenarios espirituales, La familia regulada*, all published at Saragossa. SS **Bonaventure**, **Teresa of Avila** and **John of the Cross** all influenced his mystical theology.

Arcadelt, Jakob (also **Arkadett, Archadet, Harcadelt**)   Flemish composer, born Liège?, *c.*1504; died Paris?, *c.*1567. In 1539 he left a position at Florence to teach the choristers of St Peter's, where he formed the Sistine Choir. A prolific composer of church madrigals, five books of his published at Venice, greatly stimulated the beginnings of the Venetian school of composition. He returned to

Fance in 1555, entered the service of Cardinal Charles of Lorraine, Duc de Guise, and devoted his talent to the composition of *chansons* which, with his madrigals, constitute his greatest importance as a composer. In them he succeeded in infusing the simple Italian forms with the artistic polyphony of his homeland.

Archangel of Pembroke British Capuchin, born William Barlow at Slebech, *c.*1568, died Paris, 24 August 1632. Son of a prominent Catholic family, he fled to France where he could practise his religion freely, joined the Capuchins in 1587, and became a noted reformer of convent life, notably at Port-Royal, and spiritual adviser to Angélique **Arnauld**. In 1607, Maffeo Barberini, nuncio in Paris, and later **Urban VIII**, included Archangel's name as a prospective bishop in England. In 1614 he led a group of missionary Capuchins to Brazil, and contributed to an effort to convert Hugo **Grotius**, in 1624.

Archangela Girlani Blessed, Italian Carmelite, born Eleanora, at Trino, 1460, died Mantua, 15 January 1494. Her desire to lead a strict religious life was at first thwarted by her father, who finally allowed her to enter a Benedictine convent of relaxed observance, but she later joined the Carmelites at Parma in 1477, where she became prioress. Shortly afterwards, the influential Gonzaga family requested that she found a new convent at Mantua. Renowned for her austerity, charity and spirit of prayer, she had a reputation for mystical experiences. Her body was found to be incorrupt three years after her death, and her cult confirmed in 1864. Feast day 13 February.

Archangelo of Calatafimi Blessed, Sicilian hermit, Franciscan Observant, born Archangelo Placenza, at Calatafimi, 1380, died Alcamo, 26 July 1460. His reputation for sanctity, and the miracles attributed to him, attracted so many that he could no longer continue his solitary life at Calatafimi, so he fled to Alcamo, where he organized a hospice for the poor. When **Martin V** required all hermits in Sicily to accept religious life under a Rule, he became a Franciscan of the Observance at Palermo; he returned to Alcamo to make his hospice a Franciscan foundation, and later became provincial of the Sicilian Observants. His cult was approved in 1836. Feast day 30 July.

Arcimboldi, Giovanniangelo Italian archbishop, born Milan, 1485, died there, 16 April 1555. His father served the Sforza dukes, and his uncles were archbishops of Milan. In 1514, he purchased (for 1100 gulden) the right to preach in Scandinavia the indulgence for the building of St Peter's, and became legate there, as well as from the Rhone to the Rhine. Christian II received him well in Denmark, in 1516, but his association in Sweden with rebels against Denmark two years later, ruined his mission, and Arcimboldi fled to Lubeck, where further abuses came to the attention of **Leo X**, who recalled him. However, the damage was done, and Christian invited Lutheran theologians to the Danish court, thus setting the stage for the conversion of Scandinavia to Lutheranism. This episode did not hurt his career, however; Sforza made him ambassador to the Popes from 1522, and **Clement VII** named him bishop of Novara in 1526, and archbishop of Milan in 1550, where he introduced reforms.

Arcoverde de Albuquerque Cavalcanti, Joaquim Brazilian cardinal, born Pernambuco, 17 January 1850, died Rio de Janeiro, 18 April 1930. Made bishop of Goias in 1890, then bishop of São Paulo, 1892, archbishop of Rio, 1897, he became first cardinal of Brazil and Latin America in 1905. His entire career centred on a revitalization of the Church in Brazil, which at the time failed to influence national life, though Catholics were in an absolute majority. He took an active part in the Latin American Plenary Council in Rome in 1899 and, after 1901, met annually with his suffragan bishops, the better to put the decisions of the Council into practice. These meetings were necessary antecedents, and facilitated preparation, for the important Brazilian Plenary Council held in Rio in June 1939.

Arden, Edward Victim of Elizabethan persecution, born Warwickshire, 1542, died Smithfield, 30 December 1583. His family were landowners from the time of **Edward the Confessor**, and devout Catholics. He kept a priest, Hugh Hall, disguised as a gardener, at Park Hall, his residence as High Sheriff of Warwickshire; under Hall's influence

Arden and his son-in-law, John Somerville, conspired and intrigued against Queen **Elizabeth**. Somerville's recklessness led to his arrest, and he implicated Hall and the Arden family, under torture. The three men were tried, convicted and sentenced to death, encouraged by the Earl of Leicester, who had suffered aspersions on his character by Arden. Somerville hanged himself in his cell; Mrs Arden and Hall aided the prosecution and were pardoned, but they hanged Arden for treason, protesting his innocence, and affirming his Catholicism as his only crime.

Aredius (also **Aridius, Arigius, Yrieix**) Saint, abbot, born Limoges, early sixth century, died Attane, 25 August 591. Son of an important family, he grew up in the court of Theudebert I. Attracted by his sanctity and eloquence, Bishop **Nicetius** made him a member of his clergy; he then used his patrimony to build churches, in particular the abbey of Attane, later named St Yrieix, of which he became first abbot, and followed the teachings of **Basil** and John **Cassian**. His friend **Fortunatus** celebrates Aredius in his poems, and St **Gregory of Tours** reports that many miracles were performed through his intercession. Feast day 25 August.

Aremberg, Charles d' Belgian historical and ascetical writer, born Brussels, 1593, died there, 5 June 1669. Scion of a noble family dating from the thirteenth century, he entered the Capuchin Order at Scheut in 1616, became definitor-general in Rome and provincial in his native Flanders. One of the chief protagonists for his Order, he defended in his writings the claim of the Capuchins to be authentic Friars Minor, against the opposing claims of Observant and Conventual Franciscans. Among his works are the well known *Flores Seraphici*, a sequence of vignettes of early Capuchin life, and *Epilogus totius Ordinis Seraphici*, an iconographical table of Franciscan saints in various branches, for which he produced two collections of engravings to accompany them. Also an ardent patriot, Aremberg earned a place in the history of Belgium's long quest for independence.

Arethas of Caesarea Archbishop, Byzantine theological writer and scholar, born Patras, *c.*850, died *c.*944. Archbishop of Caesarea and an outstanding figure in the intellectual and literary flowering of ninth- and tenth-century Byzantium. Arethas wrote a Greek commentary on the Apocalypse which, though based on that of Andrew, his predecessor, contains additions from other sources. He had several MSS copied at his own expense, amongst them the Codex Clarkianus of Plato (brought to England from the monastery of St John in Patmos), and the Dorvillian MS of Euclid (now at Oxford). He is also known for his polemical, apologetical and rhetorical writings, and the Arethas Codex (Paris gk 451) testifies to his scholarship. As archbishop he opposed Emperor **Leo XI**'s fourth marriage, for which **Nicholas I**, patriarch of Constantinople, wished to grant a dispensation. Being something of an opportunist, Arethas acquiesced in the dispensation granted by the next patriarch, **Euthymius I**. His pastoral interests were not forgotten, and he wrote letters and sermons for the consecration of bishops and churches.

Aretino, Pietro Italian literary figure, born Arezzo, 20 April 1492, died Venice, 1556. The son of a poor cobbler, he went to Rome, where he achieved notoriety for his slanderous pasquinades, and where his talents, wit and impudence commended him to the papal court of **Leo X** and **Clement VII**. Aretino left Rome in 1524, however, after writing a set of obscene sonnets to accompany an equally immoral series of drawings by the great painter Giulio Romano. Giovanni de Medici received him in Milan, and introduced him to **Francis I** of France, whose good graces and support he gained. When Giovanni died in 1526, Aretino found refuge in Venice, where he became rich writing comedies, sonnets, licentious dialogues and a few devotional and religious works. He led a profligate life and received large sums from nobles and princes, apparently from their fear of his satire. He became very proud and styled himself 'the divine', and 'the scourge of princes'; **Titian** painted his portrait (Pitti Palace, Florence). His comedies, five in number, are considered to be his best works, and his letters are also commended for their style. The dialogues and the licentious sonnets have been translated into French, under the title *Academie des Dames*.

Arevalo, Rodrigo Sanchez de Spanish bishop and scholar, born Santa Maria de Nieva, 1404, died Rome, 4 October 1470. Arevalo went as Castilian delegate to the Council of Basel, 1434–9, under Alfonso de Cartegena, and withdrew in protest when the Council attempted to depose **Eugenius IV**. Indeed, during his diplomatic career, as well as in his writings, he promoted supreme spiritual and temporal papal primacy, and urged ecclesiastical reforms. These anti-conciliarist ideas were expressed in his *De remediis schismatis*, in which he promoted adherence to Eugenius IV in the courts of France, Germany and Italy. **Calixtus III** made him bishop of Orviedo in 1457, **Paul II** bishop of three other sees and, from 1460, papal castellan of Castel San Angelo. His proposals for church reform are contained in *Defensorium eccsiae et status ecclesiastici*; his Latin correspondence with Italian humanists ranks him among the foremost of Spanish humanists. His writings are mostly unedited.

Argenti, Eustratios Greek Orthodox lay theologian, born 1687 in Chios, died 1757. Educated at Constantinople and Padua he was very familiar with contemporary Western theology and attempted to defend Orthodoxy from aggressive prosyletism by his writings. His conservative views on heretical baptism, the use of unleavened bread in the Eucharist and on purgatory were influential. He followed St Cyprian of Carthage in denying any validity to sacraments outside the Church.

Argentre, Charles du Plessis d' French theologian, born near Vitre, 16 May 1673, died Tulle, 27 November 1740. He studied at the Sorbonne, became vicar-general of Treguiers in 1707 and bishop of Tulle in 1725, where he distinguished himself by his holiness and erudition. By his *Apologie de l'amour*, 1698, written against F. Fénelon in the controversy over Quietism, he helped to develop a doctrine of grace in which the extremes of both the Molinist and Banezian schools might be avoided. His most important contribution is *Collectio judiciorum de novis erroribus*, a three-volume compilation of documents relative to theological controversies from the twelfth century.

Argimir Saint, Spanish martyr, born Cabra; died Cordoba, 28 June 856. He held the office of 'censor' in the administration of justice, in the Muslim government of Cordoba, from which he retired to a monastery. Certain Muslims accused

him of scurrilous derision of the prophet, Allah, and of having professed the divinity of Christ. Argimir admitted the charges before the cadi, who sentenced him to death. Christians buried his relics in the basilica of St Acisclus in Cordoba, and he is included in the Roman martyrology of 1586. Feast day 7 July.

Argyropoulos, John Byzantine scholar in Italy, born Constantinople, 1415, died Rome, 26 June 1487. A Greek humanist, one of the earliest, and one of the most famous, scholars to promote a revival of learning in the West. He went as a member of the Greek delegation to the Council of Florence (1438–9), remained in Italy, studying and teaching at Padua, where he became rector of the university. He returned to Constantinople in 1441, but after its capture by the Turks in 1453, he returned to Italy, where Cosimo de **Medici** appointed him professor of Greek. In 1471, on the outbreak of the plague, he removed to Rome, where he taught Greek literature until his death. Among his students had been Constantine **Lascaris** in Constantinople, Angelus Politianus and Johann **Reuchlin** in Italy. He is important for his influence as a teacher and for his many translations of the works of Aristotle, including the *Physics*, *Metaphysics* and *Nicomachean Ethics*, helping to diffuse his philosophy when it seemed that Aristotelianism might be overshadowed by the Quatrocentro's concentration on Plato.

Argyros, Isaac Greek monk, astronomer, born Thrace(?), c.1305, died c.1375. A student of Nikephoros Gregoras, and the leading proponent of Ptolemaic astronomy in the 1360s and 1370s. He wrote a *Construction of New Tables* and a *Construction of New Tables of Conjunction and Opposition* (of the sun and moon), for both of which the epoch is 1 September 1367. In them he recomputes for the Roman calendar and the longitude of Constantinople, the mean motions of the sun, moon, planets and syzygies that Ptolemy had tabulated in the Almagest according to the Egyptian calendar, and the longitude of Alexandria. Argyros was also a theologian and polemicist. He ranged himself with Gregoras, supporting **Barlaam of Calabria** in his principal treatise against Palamism, written probably after 1360. He wrote three anti-

Palamite treatises, including an attack on Theodore **Dexios**' concept of the light on Mount Tabor.

Argyrus, Marianus Byzantine 'Dux Italiae', Calabria, Sicily and Paphlagonia. Born the son of the Lombard Melo of Bari, *c.*1005, died Bari, *c.*1068. Held hostage in Constantinople following his father's rebellion in 1009, he returned to Italy in 1029, where he fought against Byzantine domination, and in 1042 became leader of the Norman faction. Reconciled to Byzantium, Argyrus went to Constantinople, returned to Bari in 1051 as governor of Byzantine Italy, and sought an alliance with **Leo IX**, to halt the Normans. In 1053 Argyrus and Leo were separately defeated and the Pope taken prisoner. From captivity Leo sent Cardinal **Humbert of Silva Candida** to the patriarch of Constantinople, Michael Ceroularius, who claimed that Argyrus had forged offensive papal letters, and had Argyrus' son and son-in-law arrested, leading to the Eastern schism of 1054. Argyrus strove to renew the papal/Bzyzantine alliance, but in vain, and was relieved of office in 1058.

Arias, Francis Spanish Jesuit theologian, born Seville, 1533, died there, 15 May 1605. Professor of moral philosophy at Cordoba, and rector at the colleges of Triguero and Cadiz. He is known more for his rigorous discipline and observance than for his teaching. His personal life of the spirit is known through his writings, especially *Exhortacion al aprovechamiento espiritual*, a work in which he unfolds his inner growth and development. **Francis de Sales** mentions his ascetic life in his own work, *Introduction to a Devout Life.*

Aribo of Mainz Italian archbishop, born *c.*990, died Como, 6 April 1031. Son of the noble Aribo family, he became archbishop of Mainz in 1021, and chancellor of Italy in 1025 through Conrad II, whose imperial election he had brought about. Although a brilliant man, an organizer and a writer, his domineering character and intolerance of the rights of others involved him in numerous disputes, and complicated the problems of Church and State that confronted him. He revived a controversy regarding metropolitan jurisdiction with Bishop Godehard; his harsh attitude toward the marriage of Otto and Irmgard Hannerstein became so offensive that **Benedict VIII** withdrew his fac-

ulties. He refused to permit the coronation of Empress **Gisela** in Mainz, because he doubted the validity of Conrad's marriage. He attended a Lateran Council in 1027, and died while returning from a later trip to Rome.

Arintero, Juan González Spanish natural scientist and spiritual writer, born Lugueros, 24 June 1860, died Salamanca, 20 February 1928. He joined the Dominicans at Corias in 1875, studied at Salamanca and taught natural sciences, and their relation to philosophy and theology, at Valladolid, inaugurating in 1900 the Academia de Santo Tomas. He returned to Salamanca in 1903 to teach apologetics, and remained there. More interested in ascetical and mystical theology, he abandoned the study of natural sciences and apologetics, after 1908. His major work is *Desenvolvimiento y vitalidad de la Iglesia*; in 1920 he founded *La vida sobrenatural*, a Spanish review of spirituality published by the Dominicans.

Ariosto, Lodovico Italian poet of the Renaissance, born Reggio Emilia, 8 September 1474, died Ferrara, 16 July 1533. Author of the first significant Italian dramas, and a leading force in the development of European drama. His early work attracted the attention of Cardinal Ippolito d'**Este**, who took him under his patronage, but the poet himself tells us that the cardinal was ungrateful, and deplores the time he spent under his yoke. His great work, *Orlando Furioso* (1516), a vast epic dedicated to the cardinal, who despised the poetry, is a retelling of the Roland story, and has been acclaimed as the greatest work of the Italian Renaissance; it earned him the name 'Divino Lodovico'. The poem synthesizes and symbolizes the ideals of the period, beginning with the cult of beauty and recognition of the importance of life on earth. Honoured and respected by the first men of his age, most of the princes of Italy showed him great partiality, but limited their patronage to kind words. He does not seem ever to have received any substantial mark of their love for his literature; he lived and died poor.

Arishima Takeo Japanese novelist, playwright, essayist, born Tokyo, 4 February 1878; died Karuizawa, 9 June 1923. Educated at Sapporo University, he came under the influence of the Christian leader Inazo Nitobe, through whom he met the founder of the non-church group Kanzo Uchimura. In 1900, Arishima, until then a Buddhist, accepted Christianity, expressing the quality of his new faith in a comment in his diary that nature is the 'living garment of God'. He began to doubt his Christian faith while doing his military service, and later, while studying in the USA in 1903–8, the empty formality of some American churches, and Walt Whitman's views on religion in his poems deepened his dislike of institutional Christianity. He formally left the Church in 1911. Although called a heretic, Arishima considered himself a Christian; he had a love for Christ and read the Bible faithfully. His plays, based on biblical stories such as *Daikozui no Mae* (Before the Great Flood, 1916), *Samson to Derira* (Samson and Delilah, 1915), and *Seisan* (The Last Supper), are unique in Japanese literature.

Aristides Athenian philosopher and Christian apologist, born and died in the second century. Until 1878 our knowledge of him was confined to the statement of **Eusebius**, that he was an Athenian philosopher, who presented an apology 'concerning the faith' to Emperor Hadrian. In that year, however, the Mechitharists of S. Lazzaro, Venice, published a fragment of the document in Armenian, and in 1889 J. R. Harris found the whole of it in a Syriac version at St Catherine's Monastery on Mount Sinai. While his edition was going to press, it occurred to J. A. **Robinson** that all the while the work had been available in Greek, though in a slightly abbreviated form, as a speech in a religious novel written about the sixteenth century and entitled 'The life of Barlaam and Josaphat'. Aristides sought to defend the existence and eternity of God, to point out the inadequacies of the pre-Christian concepts of the Godhead, to show that Christians had a fuller understanding of his nature than either the barbarians, the Greeks or the Jews, and that they alone have come into possession of the full truth, and live according to its precepts.

Arius Alexandrian priest and heresiarch, born Libya, *c.*250, died Constantinople, 336. Achillas, bishop of Alexandria, put him in charge of Baucalis, one of the great city churches, in 312. As a pastor, he seems to have met with success and gained a large following by his learning and ascet-

ical life. However, under the next bishop, St **Alexander**, Arius came forward as a champion of subordinationist teaching about the person of Christ, set forth in his most important work, the 'Thalia', in which the principal object was firmly to establish the unity and simplicity of the eternal God: however far the Son may surpass other created beings, he remains himself a created being, to whom the Father before all time gave an existence formed out of 'not being'. In his eyes it was blasphemy for Alexander to proclaim in public that 'as God is eternal, so is his Son, – when the Father, then the Son, – the Son is present in God without birth, ever-begotten, an unbegotten-begotten'. **Eusebius of Nicomedia** and **Eusebius of Caesarea** defended Arius, but Alexander excommunicated him. When Emperor Constantine arrived in the East in 324, he attempted to settle a 'trifling and foolish verbal difference, the meaning of which would be grasped only by the few', but in vain. The Council of Nicaea in 325, influenced by St **Athanasius**, decided, against Arius, that the Son was 'of the same substance' (homoousios) with the Father. Arius, and the bishops who refused to subscribe the creed, were excommunicated, and banished; recalled from exile in *c.*335, he returned to Alexandria, but the people raised a riot against the heretic. In 336 the emperor summoned him to Constantinople, and Bishop Alexander reluctantly assented to receive him once more into the Church, but Arius died suddenly while walking in the streets of Constantinople, the day before he was to have been formally reconciled. Although defeated at the Council, the Arians continued to trouble the Church until the Council of Constantinople in 381 recognized the Nicene doctrine as the only orthodox one.

Arlegui, José Spanish Franciscan chronicler, born Laguardia, Navarre, 1685, died, place unknown, 1750. He joined the Franciscans in 1701 and was sent to Zacatecas, Mexico, as professor, provincial in 1725, and chronicler of the province. A zealous mission worker, he promoted education and built (literally at times, cutting wood for church floors) convents and churches. He wrote treatises on theology, but his most important work is the history of Zacateca province, *Cronica de la santa provincia de nuestro P. San Francisco de Zacatecas* (1851), which incorporates some unique information on

Indian life and Franciscan catechetical efforts, closing in 1733, with the statement that the Order then had ten provinces in New Spain, 3200 religious, 397 convents, 122 missionary centres among the pagans, four apostolic colleges and 187 professorships of theology, rhetoric and the various native languages.

Armagnac, Georges d' French cardinal, diplomat, humanist, born c.1500, died Avignon, 5 June 1585. Made bishop of Rodez and governor of Armagnac in 1530, ambassador of **Francis I** to Venice, 1536–8, and to Rome, 1540–5, cardinal in 1544, archbishop of Tours, 1545–51, archbishop of Toulouse and lieutenant-general of Languedoc in 1552. Tolerant by nature, a defender of civil and religious orthodoxy, he worked against the Huguenot disturbances and civil war in the south of France. He is also remembered as a noted patron and enthusiast of letters.

Armand de Belvezer (de Beauvoir) French Dominican theologian. Born near Milau, Aveyron, second half of thirteenth century, place and date of death unknown. An early Thomist, he taught theology at Montpelier in 1326, and wrote a commentary on St **Thomas Aquinas** *De ente et essentia*, which showed him to be closer to St Thomas than to the *via moderna*. As master of the sacred palace at Avignon in 1328–34, he opposed **John XXII**'s teaching on the beatific vision, and thereby lost his favour. Most of his works are unedited.

Armellini, Mariano Italian Benedictine historian, born Ancona, 10 December 1662, died Foligno, 4 May 1737. He joined the Benedictines at Rome in 1682, studied at Monte Cassino and taught philosophy at various Cassinese monasteries, 1687–95. He had great success as a preacher, and is noted for his pastoral zeal and eloquence throughout Italy. Successively abbot at Siena, Assisi and St Felician, near Foligno, he wrote extensively on the Cassinese congregation, including the well-known *Biblioteca Benedictino-Cassinesis*, a biographical bibliography of Cassinese writers, amended other of their works, and prepared lists of the lives, writings and members of his congregation.

Armentia, Nicolas Spanish Franciscan missionary, explorer and bishop, born Basque country, 1845,

died La Paz, Bolivia, November 1909. He joined the Franciscans as a boy, went to La Ricoleta in La Paz, and was there ordained. He worked in the missions of Couendo, Ixiamas and Tumupara for thirteen years from 1870, and made many expeditions through the jungles bordering the Beni River in search of Aborigines to bring to the missions. Armentia explored the Beni River itself in 1884–5, going down the Madre de Dios, and toured the hinterland of both rivers extensively; he established relations with the Araona and Toromona tribes, and travelled to the Purus River and the Amazon. He wrote several books about his explorations, revealing his sound knowledge of zoology and botany in valuable information of the flora and fauna of the area. He wrote a grammar and lexicon of the Chipibo language. Consecrated bishop of La Paz in 1902, he proved himself a dedicated prelate in continuing his missionary apostolate.

Arminius, Jacobus (Jakob Hermandszoon) Dutch Reformed theologian, born Oudewater, 10 October 1560, died Leiden, 19 October 1609. Ordained a pastor at Amsterdam in 1588, he trained in Calvinist orthodoxy, absorbed humanist learning in the philosophy of Peter **Ramus** and, especially at Leiden, liberalizing attitudes toward religious and political freedom. His study of St Paul's Epistle to the Romans led him to doubt the harsh Calvinist doctrine of unconditional predestination, and when in 1589 he debated against D.V. Coornheert's denial of Calvin's teching, Arminius came instead to reject it himself, and was inspired to promote the milder form of a conditional predestination. His subsequent life was one of controversy, especially with F. Somarus, a colleague, when appointed to the faculty of Leiden in 1603. Charged with Socinianism and Pelagianism, he gradually clarified his own criticisms of strict Calvinism and his defence of human freedom under grace, and achieved renown as a theologian of moderation. Essentially an amiable man, he hated the zeal for an impossible orthodoxy that 'constrained the church to institute a search after crimes which have not betrayed an existence, yea, and to drag into open contentions those who are meditating no evil'.

Arnaldus Amalrici (Arnaud-Amaury) French archbishop of Narbonne. Born Narbonne, *c.*1160, died Cistercian abbey of Fontroide, 26 September 1225. A Cistercian monk, later abbot of Poblet in Catalonia and Grandselve in Languedoc, he became abbot-general in 1221. The Cistercians were traditionally involved in controversy with the Albigensians and, in 1203, **Innocent III** appointed the Fontfroide monks, Raoul and Peter of Castelman, as papal legates for Languedoc, threatened by heresy. In 1207, Arnaldus joined them, and when **Raymond VI** of Toulouse, leader of the opposing clergy, murdered Peter in 1208, Arnaldus led a crusade against the Albigenses. He captured Beziers, and perpetrated a bloody massacre, during which Arnaldus is said to have cried: 'Kill them all, God knows his children.' Innocent reprimanded Arnaldus, and he gave up any further attempts to confront Raymond, but instead tried personal negotiation, which failed, and Innocent excommunicated him. He died at Fontfroide, and his body was taken to Cîteaux for burial.

Arnauld, Antoine   Born Paris, 6 August 1560, died there, 29 December 1619. He furthered the family's reputation at the Paris bar, and in this capacity delivered a famous philippic against the Jesuits in 1594, 'Plaidoyer pour l'Université contre les Jesuites', accusing them of gross disloyalty to the newly converted Henri IV. The speech, afterwards known as the original sin of the Arnaulds, started a quarrel, continued by his own children, noted for their implacable hatred of the Jesuits, and who delighted in controversy. Antoine had twenty children by his wife, Catherine Marion, and is remembered chiefly as the father of almost all the first leaders of the French Jansenist party.

Arnauld, Antoine (The Great)   Born Paris, 5 February 1612, died Brussels, 2 August 1694. Twentieth and youngest child of the original Antoine, and by far the most distinguished of the family, he studied theology at the Sorbonne, was ordained in 1641, and came under the influence of **Saint-Cyran**, who inspired him to write *De la frequente Communion*, which did more than anything else to make the aims and ideals of Jansenism intelligible to the general public; indeed, he went beyond the teaching of predestination and grace to elaborate the practical conclusions of sacraments, particularly penance, for which he demanded perfect

contrition. The book raised a violent storm, and the Jesuits protested so vigorously, following the appearance in 1655 of his *Lettres a un duc et pair*, on Jesuit methods in the confessional, that the Sorbonne expelled him. He sought the support of the Dominicans and of **Pascal**, who defended him in his *Lettres provinciales*. When the Jansenist controversy began again in 1679, Antoine exiled himself to The Netherlands where he wrote against the Calvinists, against **Malebranche**, on Gallicanism, on philosophy, science and mathematics. However, a purely controversial writer is seldom attractive to posterity, and, but for his connection with Pascal, Antoine's name might now be forgotten.

Arnauld, Henri   Born Paris, October 1597, died Angers, 8 June 1692. He became bishop of Angers in 1649 and represented Jansenism on the episcopal bench for 43 years.

Arnauld, Jacqueline Marie Angélique   Abbess and reformer of Port-Royal, born Paris, 8 September 1591, died Port-Royal, 6 August 1661. Second daughter of Antoine, who had her named coadjutrix, with right of succession, of Port-Royal at the age of eight, and she succeeded Jeanne Boulehart as abbess at the age of eleven. At first she fell in with the relaxed discipline of the convent, until converted at sixteen, and then began a series of ruthless reforms in the direction of its original Rule; about 1623, she made the acquaintance of du Vergier, and thenceforward began to move in a Jansenist direction. In 1625 she moved the entire convent to the influential Faubourg Saint-Jacques in Paris, and in her forties met **Saint-Cyran**, under whose ascendancy as spiritual director the community became Jansenist in principle and in practice. As abbess in 1642–55, Angélique ensured the permanence of Saint-Cyran's work, and the *Fronde*, which brought more than 200 religious refugees to Port-Royal, helped her to disseminate Jansenist ideas still more widely.

Arnauld, Jeanne Catherine Agnès   Abbess of Port-Royal, born Paris, 31 December 1593, died Port-Royal, 19 February 1672. Third daughter of Antoine and younger sister of Angélique, she became abbess of Saint-Cyr at the age of six, and joined her sister at Port-Royal in 1608, where she collaborated in the reforms. Abbess of Tard at

Dijon, and of Port-Royal, 1636–42, and again 1658–61, she refused to sign the 'formulaire' of 1661. Agnes lived in her sister's shadow, but her deep spirituality greatly impressed contemporaries; her 'Le Chapelet secret du St Sacrement', championed by Saint-Cyran, was described as 'the negative theology of the mystics'.

Arnauld d'Andilly, Robert Born Paris, 1589, died there, 17 September 1674. Antoine's eldest son, his five daughters all took the veil at Port-Royal, a convent of Cistercian nuns in the neighbourhood of Versailles.

Arndt, Ernst Moritz German poet and patriot, born Schoritz, Isle of Rugen, 26 December 1769, died Bonn, 29 January 1860. Son of a prosperous farmer, he studied theology and history at Greifswald, and went to Jena in 1793, where he fell under the influence of Fichte. He qualified for the ministry as a 'candidate of theology', but philosophical doubts led him to renounce his intention to become a pastor. Lecturing in history at Greifswald in 1800, his *Von Geist der Zeit* (1806), directed against Napoleon, obliged him to flee to Sweden. Much of his thought was formulated as a reaction to anti-Christian feeling in France after the Revolution. His hopes of a union between Protestants and Catholics in a German National Church were founded on political considerations that lacked a theological basis; they were disappointed through the growing influence of Ultramontanism, and he became a sturdy representative of German Protestantism.

Arndt, Johann German Lutheran theologian, born at Ballenstedt, Anhalt, 27 December 1555, died Celle, 11 May 1621. He studied theology at Helmstedt, and was a devoted follower of **Melanchthon**. In 1583, he became pastor at Badeborn, but his Lutheran tendencies aroused the hostility of the Reformed Church authorities, who deposed him in 1590 for refusing to remove the pictures from his church. Arndt's fame rests on his writings, mainly of a mystical and devotional kind, inspired by St **Bernard**, Johann **Tauler** and **Thomas à Kempis**. His principal work, *Wahres Christentum* (1606–9), has served as the foundation of many books of devotion in most European languages, both Roman Catholic and Protestant. In it, he

dwells upon the mystical union between the believer and Christ, and endeavours, by drawing attention to Christ's life 'in' his people, to correct the purely forensic side of Reformation theology, which paid almost exclusive attention to Christ's death 'for' his people. Like **Luther**, Arndt liked the little anonymous book, *Deutsche Theologie*, of which he published an edition, and called attention to its merits in a special preface.

Arnobius the Elder Early Christian writer, date and place of birth unknown, died *c.*327. He flourished in the time of Diocletian, 284–305, and St **Jerome** refers to him as a rhetorician at Sicca in Proconsular Africa, one of his pupils being **Lactantius**. A pagan, he vigorously fought Christianity before being converted, it is said, by a dream, and he wrote his *Adversus Gentes* (or *Nationes*) (*c.*303) as a pledge to the bishop of Sicca of his sincerity. This account seems doubtful, however, for Arnobius speaks contemptuously of dreams, and his work shows no traces of having been written in a short time. The treatise is full of curious learning and defends the consonance of the Christian religion with the best pagan philosophy; he appears to have written as a recent convert, for he does not indicate an extensive knowledge of Scripture. He knows nothing of the OT, and only the life of Christ in the NT, while he does not quote directly from the Gospels; much influenced by Lucretius, he had also read Plato. The treatise is a poor source for Christian teaching, but is useful for information about contemporary pagan religions.

Arnobius the Younger Early Christian writer, date and place of birth unknown, died Rome, after 455. Probably an African, he lived as a monk at Rome from *c.*432. He wrote a mystical and allegorical commentary on the Psalms, first published by **Erasmus** in 1522, and by him attributed to the elder **Arnobius**. An edition of 1580, by De la Barre, is accompanied by a commentary on the Gospels, and both these writings reveal Arnobius to have been a semi-Pelagian, who approached orthodoxy with a recognition of the evils that befell mankind as a result of original sin.

Arnold, Eberhard Founder of the Bruderhof, born Hufenbei, Königsberg, 26 July 1883, died Darmstadt, 22 November 1935. Studied church history and theology at Erlangen, was active in the Christian Socialist and Student Christian movements, and began to seek ways to live out a Gospel-based Christian life more radically. Through his lectures and writing he began to attract others who wanted to do likewise and soon a group of families came together to form the original Bruderhof Community at Sannerz Farm. In 1930 they affiliated with a similar, if stricter, group in North America, the Hutterites. With the rise of the Nazis in Germany there was an attempt to suppress the Bruderhof and eventually the Community left the country. Eberhard, who had been ill, remained but died a few years later. Bruderhof Communities continue in England, the USA, Germany and Paraguay.

Arnold, Gottfried   German Protestant theologian and devotional writer, born Annaberg, 5 September 1666, died Perlebey, 30 May 1714. He studied theology at Wittenberg, came to know the Pietist Philipp **Spener**, and experienced a conversion to radical spiritualism. In 1693, he went to Quedlinburg, where he wrote *Die erster Liebe* (1696), an enthusiastic account of the life of the first Christians, founded on his patristic studies and especially the work of Wilhelm Cane. His chief writing, controversial and richly documented, *Unparteiische Kirchen- und Ketzer-Historie* (1699), though not as impartial as it claimed to be, maintained that the Church had fallen away from its early ideals, and that the heretics, especially the mystics, are the true Christians. In 1702, he accepted a pastorate, and his later works, mostly devotional and less eccentric, were popular, amongst which is *Historia et Descriptio Theologiae Mysticae* (1702). He is well known as an author of hymns, as translator of Miguel de **Molinos** and Mme Jeanne **Guyon**, and editor of the works of **Angelus Silesius**.

Arnold, Matthew   Poet and critic, son of Thomas **Arnold**, born Laleham, Middlesex, 24 December 1822, died Liverpool, 15 April 1888. He was educated at Rugby, Winchester and Oxford. He was appointed an inspector of schools, 1851–83, and later professor of poetry at Oxford, 1857–67. He championed the cause of 'sweetness and light' a phrase borrowed from **Swift**. His output includes work on religious themes: *St Paul and Protestant-*

ism, God and The Bible and *Last Essays on Church and Religion*. Religion he believed to be important as a moral force rather than a statement about ultimate truths.

Arnold, Thomas   Schoolmaster and headmaster of Rugby, born East Cowes, Isle of Wight, 13 June 1795, died Rugby, 12 June 1842. He was educated at Winchester and Oxford, was ordained and became a doctor of divinity. Schooling for boys in England then was at a low ebb, and sometimes left to run on primitive lines. He wrote on being appointed headmaster of Rugby School: 'My object will be, if possible, to form Christian men, for Christian boys I can scarcely hope to make.' When appointed, he expressed his aims in a letter: 'What we must look for here is, first, religious and moral principles; secondly gentlemanly conduct; and thirdly, intellectual ability.' His reform of public schools on earnest Christian lines had a profound and long-lasting effect on the educational system in Britain.

Arnold of Bonneval   French abbot, writer, date and place of birth unknown, died Marmoutier after 1156. Few facts are known of his life, other than his having been a monk of Marmoutier in 1138, and abbot of Bonneval, Diocese of Chartres, *c.*1144; also, a friend and biographer of St **Bernard of Clairvaux**, having written Book 2 of the *Vita Bernardii*, begun by **William of St-Thierry**. His other writings include discourses on the gifts of the Holy Spirit, on the seven last words of Our Lord, a sermon in praise of Our Lady, a commentary on Psalm 132 and a variety of meditations and spiritual treatises.

Arnold of Brescia   Italian church reformer, born Brescia, *c.*1100, died Rome, June 1155. An ardent adversary of the temporal power of the Popes and a man of extreme austerity, he denounced clerical licentiousness and simony, and became a leader against the political power of the bishop. Forced to return to France, *c.*1139, he became a supporter of Peter **Abelard**; at the Council of Sens in 1140, St **Bernard of Clairvaux** secured his condemnation, along with that of Abelard, on the grounds that he taught the same errors. Briefly reconciled with the Church, he then supported the Roman senate in its rejection of the temporal dominion of the Popes, and was excommunicated by **Eugenius III** in 1148. However, the senate lost control of Rome in 1152, and **Adrian IV** (Nicholas Breakspear), successor to Eugene, placed Rome under an interdict, had **Frederick I Barbarossa** seize Arnold, who condemned him to death, hanged him and threw his ashes into the Tiber. Above all an ascetic, Arnold denied to the Church the right of holding property: 'Clerks who have estates, bishops who hold fiefs, monks who possess property, cannot be saved.' He developed this belief into an assault, readily adopted by political rebels, on the Roman clergy, and in particular on the curia, which he stigmatized as a 'house of merchandise and a den of thieves'.

Arnold of Hiltensweiler Blessed, Swiss monastic founder, flourished early twelfth century, died 1127. A layman, he founded a convent at Langnan, near Berne. He appears to have been a member of the First Crusade, 1099 to 1100, and is usually represented with a banner on which there is a cross inscribed. Married, but childless, in 1122 he formally bequeathed all his property to the house of All Saints at Schaffhausen on the Rhine; he is buried at the oratory he founded at Hiltensweiler. Feast day 1 May.

Arnold of Lübeck German abbot and chronicler, he died between 1211 and 1214. First abbot of the Benedictine monastery of St John at Lübeck, he championed the Papacy in its conflict with the Hohenstaufen. He compiled the *Chronica Slavorum*, begun by Hemhold, for the years 1172–1209, an important source of information, despite errors and interpolations, about many events of the era in which **Henry the Lion**, **Henry VI**, Philip of Swabia and **Otto IV**, were active.

Arnold of Villanova Spanish physician, theologian and church reformer, born Valencia, *c*.1240, died near Genoa, September 1311. He studied theology and medicine under the Dominicans at Montpelier, *c*.1260, with Arabic physicians at Valencia, as well as Hebrew and rabbinic literature in Barcelona, under the Dominican Raymond Martini. Considered the leading alchemist and physician of his day, he frequently ministered to Popes **Boniface VIII**, **Benedict XI**, **Clement V**; and Kings Peter III, **James II** of Aragon and Frederick III of Sicily. Several of his medical works are important in placing medicine and pharmacy on a scientific basis. He wrote extensively on theology, in Latin and Catalan, but the Inquisition in Spain and Paris declared him heretical, and he thus never became well known. However, he is famous for 70 scientific works reflecting his contact with the Arabic scientific tradition, which include translations of Arabic works, commentaries on classical texts, treatises on hygiene and tracts on alchemy and other occult sciences.

Arnoldi, Bartholomaeus German Catholic apologist, born Usingen, near Frankfurt, 1465, died Würzburg, 9 September 1532. He studied at Erfurt and, as professor of philosophy, he taught the nominalist view (*via moderna*) of **William of Ockham** and **Biel**, which **Luther**, his student in 1501–5, later reflected in his theology. Luther persuaded Arnoldi to join the Augustinians for whom he taught theology, from 1514, and preached until expelled by Lutherans in 1525. Always firmly Catholic, though he attacked abuses, he rejected Luther's 95 theses, and broke with him in 1520. Thereafter he preached, and promoted reforms, for the bishop of Würzburg, Konrad von Thungen, took charge of several monasteries and preached against Luther. He examined, in a group of twenty theologians, the Lutheran Confession at Augsburg in 1530.

Arnolfo di Cambio Italian Gothic sculptor and architect, born Colle di Val d'Elsa, *c*.1245, died Florence, *c*.1302. The most renowned pupil of Nicolo Pisano, he is first mentioned as his assistant in the sculpture of the pulpit for Siena Cathedral, 1265–8; he also seems to have worked on the tomb of St **Dominic** in Bologna. He began to work independently in about 1268, and his tomb of Cardinal Guglielmo de Braye, Orvieto, 1282, with arched canopy and two angels drawing back the curtains on either side of the recumbent effigy, set the type of wall tomb for more than a century. He removed to Florence in 1296, where he directed original work on the dome of the cathedral in 1300, and where Santa Croce and, traditionally, the Palazzo Vecchio have been attributed to him. He played an important role in the development of Italian art, and led Vasari to call him the first 'modern' architect.

Arnoux, Jean French preacher and confessor of **Louis XIII**, born Riom, 19 January 1576, died Toulouse, 19 May 1636. He joined the Society of Jesus in 1592, and had great success as a gifted controversialist and preacher wherever Calvinism was prominent. His preaching in Paris attracted the attention of Louis XIII, whose confessor he became, from 1617. Two qualities characterized Arnoux's action at the court: the vigour with which he fought Protestant doctrines, while united in charity to the persons themselves; the firmness, which Voltaire qualified as heroic, in the efforts he deployed to reconcile Louis with his mother, Marie de Medici. The private advice he gave to Louis being insufficient, Arnoux, preaching to the assembled court, dared put Louis on guard against the violent advice of his entourage, which could lead to a scandal of Christianity. This brought about his dismissal in 1621, and he retired to Toulouse, where he was provincial of the Society in 1635, a year before his death.

Arnulf of Gap Saint, French bishop, born Vendôme; died Gap, 19 September 1070/9. A Benedictine monk at Sainte-Trinité, Vendôme, he went to Rome in 1061 to secure for Sainte-Trinité papal confirmation of the Roman church of St Priscia, and, for its abbot, the dignity of cardinal-priest. **Alexander II** detained Arnulf and consecrated him bishop of Gap in 1063, where he became a zealous supporter of the Gregorian reform movement of the late eleventh century. Feast day 19 September.

Arnulf of Lisieux French bishop, born Rouen, died monastery of Saint-Victor, Paris, 31 October 1184. He went to Rome, where he studied canon law, and in 1130 wrote a polemical work attacking the antipope Anacletus II. Made bishop of Lisieux in 1141, he actively engaged in controversies within the Church, and between the Church and Henry II of England, who was being offensive to **Thomas Becket**. Arnulf defended Thomas, but his efforts were seen as self-serving rather than altruistic. At the Synod of Tours in 1163, he defended the Apostolic See against the antipope, Victor IV, and **Frederick I Barbarossa**. After the Becket affair, he retired to the monastery of Saint-Victor in Paris, remaining there until his death.

Arnulf of Metz (also **Arnoul**) Saint, Frankish bishop, born near Nancy, c.582, died Remiremont, 18 July c.641. Of a noble family, he rose rapidly in the court of Theodebert II, king of Austrasia (595–612), and took an active part in securing the accession of Clothar II, in 613. Consecrated bishop of Metz, c.614, he helped Clothar's son, Dagobert, to govern his kingdom in the Ardennes. He took part in the Council of Clichy in 626–7, and of Reims in 627; after fifteen years of service to Church and State, he resigned his see and joined his friend St Romanic in a deserted place near Remiremont in the Vosges, where he spent his last years in meditation and prayer. He had been married before becoming a bishop, and had two sons, of whom **Ansegis** married (St) Begga, daughter of Pepin of Landeu, and became the father of Pepin of Heristal; Arnulf is thus the progenitor of the Carolingian dynasty. Arnulf's relics were brought back to Metz by his successor Goeric. Feast day either 18 July or 16 August.

Arnulf of Milan Historian of the archbishops of Milan, born, date and place unknown, died, Milan(?), 1077. The great-grandson of the brother of an earlier archbishop of Milan, Arnulf I (died 974), but what else we know of him is derived from his own writings. Probably a cleric, he remained faithful to the Church, and to Pope **Gregory VII** during the struggles for supremacy, and resisted the appointment of Otto as archbishop of Milan. Following the submission of **Henry IV** at Canossa during the investiture struggle, Arnulf himself yielded to Otto and took part in a delegation sent by the Milanese to promise loyalty to him. He is renowned for *Gesta archiepiscoporum Mediolanensium*, a chronicle of events, out of his own experience and that of reliable witnesses, from King Hugo of Italy (925), to the election of Rudolf of Rheinfelden (died 1080). It is a valuable source of information for the period it covers.

Arnulf of Soissons Saint, Belgian monastic reformer, bishop, born Brabant, c.1040, died Oudenbourg, 15 August 1087. He had a brief military career, and then became a monk at St Medard (Soissons), where his rigorous asceticism so impressed his fellow monks that they elected him abbot to replace Raymond, a worldly man and guilty of simony. In 1080, he became bishop of

Soissons, again to replace a man of ill-repute, Ursio, but his efforts to reform the diocesan clergy there were thoroughly repulsed and he had to leave the diocese. He founded a Benedictine monastery at Oudenbourg in Flanders, where he died; there has been a public cult since 1121. Feast day 15 August.

Arregui, Antonio María   Spanish Jesuit moralist, born Pamplona, Navarre, 17 January 1863, died Barcelona, 10 October 1942. He taught theology for thirteen years at Oña, and published *Summarium theologiae moralis* in 1918, a handbook of moral theology favoured by students for its clarity and concision. A tertian master at Manresa for twenty years, he gained fame as a director in Jesuit spirituality. In 1934, he brought out a second major work on the constitution and rules of the Society of Jesus, *Annotationes ad epitomen Instituti Societatis Jesu.*

Arregui, Domingo Lazaro de   Mexican writer. He flourished in the seventeenth century, but his date and place of birth and death are unknown. A native of the Indian village of Tepic, in 1607 he served as a sponsor for some Indians being baptized by the Jesuits in the province of New Galicia, which he knew well from several expeditions. In 1621 a description of the territory was required to support the division of the bishopric of Guadalajara, and Arregui produced the *Descripcion de la Nueva Galicia* that same year, based on personal observation and on archives of the Audiencia at Guadalajara. It has little historical perspective and no critical spirit, but he produced none the less a valuable historical document.

Arriaga, Pablo José de   Spanish missionary and author, born Vergara, 1564, died in a shipwreck near Cuba, 6 September 1622. He joined the Society of Jesus at Ocana in 1579, and went to Peru in 1585, where he spent his life as professor, or rector, of Jesuit colleges in Lima. He had a strong sense of apostleship to the Indians in rural and urban areas, particularly for the education and well-being of children, for whom he supervised the building of a school. He wrote and translated many spiritual works, including *La retorica Cristiana*, and his most important, *Extirpacion de la idolatria del Peru* (1621), which contained much information on the history and ethnology of the Quechua area, and especially of the Inca religion.

Arriaga, Rodrigo de   Spanish theologian and philosopher, born Logroño, 17 January 1592, died Prague, 7 June 1667. He entered the Society of Jesus in 1606, and taught at Valladolid and Salamanca. In 1625 he went to the university at Prague as professor of theology, becoming chancellor and finally prefect of studies. He published *Cursus philosophicus* in 1632, based on St **Thomas Aquinas**, but which showed the influence of **Suárez** in his consideration of the role of metaphysics as a distinct category.

Arricivita, Juan Domingo   Mexican missionary and historian, born Toluca, 1720, died Queretaro, 16 April 1794. He entered the Franciscans in 1735 and, though a reliable friar and a good priest, spent most of his years in posts of secondary importance in New Mexico and south-west USA. Procurator of the missions of his college in the decade from 1757, he helped make arrangements for the Franciscans to replace the expelled Jesuits in their former missions in Sonora and Lower Arizona. Named official historian of Queretaro College in 1787, to continue the work of Isidro **Espinosa**, whose chronicle of the mission College of the Holy Cross he completed in 1791. It constitutes a valuable, often first-hand, report of Franciscan missionary efforts.

Arrieta, Francisco Sales de   Peruvian archbishop of Lima, born Lima, 29 January 1768, died there, 4 May 1843. He joined the Discalced Franciscans, became director of their house of exercises in 1813, inspector of convents of the Lima province, and rector of the Third Order. In 1841 he reluctantly became archbishop of Lima, having sought, in a letter to **Gregory XVI**, to be excused from the nomination by President Gaurana. He worked to reform the clergy and monastic life in Peru, and to improve religious education, to which end he reorganized the seminary of San Toribio, and to improve the instruction of children. The most serious challenge to his work was Peruvian liberalism, particularly the actions of Manuel Lorenzo Vidaurre, whose writings demanded that the Church democratize its organizational structures; he asserted the right of the State to supervise the

Church in all temporal matters. Arrieta condemned Vidaurre's writings, but anticlerical liberals for many more years continued to oppose the Church.

Arrillaga, Basilio Mexican defender of the Church, born Mexico City, 1 June 1791, died there 28 July 1867. He joined the Society of Jesus in 1816, in which he held various offices, including provincial, and became rector of the University of Mexico, 1844–9. He lived during a troubled period of Church–State relations, and the Jesuits themselves lived a precarious existence in Mexico, for the Society was dissolved on occasion, and persecuted frequently. A dynamic and competent protagonist in the political-religious debates, Arrillaga spoke and wrote vigorously in defence of the Church against liberal Catholicism, and the antireligious action of those in charge of the government. Named an alternative deputy to the Cortes in 1821, president of the congress in the Federal District in the 1830s; Santa Anara included him in a national legislative junta in 1842, and he became an honorary Councillor of State for Maximilian.

Arrowsmith, Edmund Saint, English priest and martyr, born Haydock, near St Helens, 1585, died Lancaster, 28 August 1628. Both his parents had been imprisoned for their faith; after ordination at the English College, Douai, in 1612, he returned the following year to labour in his native Lancashire. Fearless in his apostolate, his forthright speech put him at risk; having been arrested and examined, however, the bishop of Chester released him. He joined the Society of Jesus at the London novitiate of Clerkenwell, and, betrayed on his return to Lancashire, appeared before Sir Henry Yelverton, who condemned him to death. On the way to execution in Lancaster Castle, St John Southworth, also a prisoner, gave him absolution. He refused until the end to renounce his faith: 'Tempt me no more. I will not do it, in no case, on no condition.' Canonized in 1970, his hand is preserved in the church of St Oswald at Ashton-in-Makerfield, Wigan, and has been the source of miraculous cures. Feast day 28 August.

Arrupe, Pedro Jesuit superior-general, born Bilboa, 14 November 1907, died Rome, 5 February 1991. He first studied medicine, but abandoned that to enter the Society of Jesus in January 1927. He studied theology in Belgium and Holland before being ordained in 1936. After a number of years' further study in the United States, he was sent to Japan, and was in charge of the Jesuit noviceship in Hiroshima when the atomic bomb was dropped. This experience convinced him that Christians had to promote structural changes if oppression and violence were to be overcome. Elected superior-general of the Jesuits on 22 May 1965, at a General Congregation in 1975 he proposed a modern mission, defined as 'faith that does justice'. He was accused of leading the Jesuits astray and, after suffering a stroke in 1981, the Vatican tried to take direct control of the Society by nominating a vicar-general more in sympathy, it was thought, with its own position.

Ars, Curé of see **Vianney, Jean-Baptiste Marie**

Arseniev, Nicholas Orthodox lay theologian, born Stockholm, Sweden, 1888, died New York, 18 December 1977. After the revolution he left Russia and became lecturer in Russian Culture and Religion in Königsberg, Germany, and in 1948, lecturer in NT at St Vladimir's Seminary, New York. He was a prolific writer, his most celebrated works being *Russian Piety* (1975) and *Revolution of Eternal Life* (1982).

Arsenius (Arseny Matsievich) Metropolitan of Rostov, Russian Orthodox bishop and confessor, born 1697, died Tallin (Reval Fortress) 1772. When Empress **Catherine II** began to secularize the monasteries of Russia he was one of the few to protest and he accused her personally in 1763. He was deprived of his diocese and reduced to being a monk. He continued his protest and was declared a political offender; not only being imprisoned but also being physically prevented from speaking by being gagged.

Arsenius Autorianos (Arsenios Autoreianos) Patriarch of Constantinople, 1254–60, born Constantinople, c.1200, died Prokonnesos, 20 September 1273. A monk, known as Gennadios, at the monastery on Oxeia (Princes' Islands), he became patriarch of Nicaea in 1254. Even though, after Theodore II's death, Arsenius served as protector of John IV Laskaris, he allowed himself to be used to crown the usurper Michael VIII Palaeologus in 1258. By 1260 Arsenius, aware of Michael's ambition to rule alone, refused at first to serve as patriarch, but Michael accepted in 1261, and performed a second coronation of Michael in Hagia Sophia. However, when Michael had John IV, the legitimate heir to the throne, blinded, Arsenius excommunicated him, and antagonism between the emperor and patriarch reached its limit in 1265, when a synod deposed Arsenius and exiled him to the island of Prokonnesos, where he died. His deposition led to the rise of the Arsenites and, in 1284, as a concession to them, **Andronicus II** permitted the translation of his remains to Hagia Sophia. His cult continued into the fifteenth century.

Artaud de Montor, Jean Alexis François French diplomat and biographer, born Paris, 21 July 1772, died Paris, 12 November 1849. During his diplomatic career he served as attaché at the embassy in Sweden, and took part in negotiations preceding the concordat of 1801. He then went as attaché to the embassy in Rome, where he published works on medieval painting: *Considerations sur l'état de la peinture en Italie dans les quatre siècles qui ont précédé celui de Raphael* (1808); and the catacombs: *Voyages dans les catacombes de Rome* (1810); as well as a translation of the Divine Comedy (1811). He then concentrated upon historical biography, an eight-volume history of the Popes: *Histoire des Souverains Pontifs romains* (1847); lives of **Pius VII**, **Leo XII**, **Pius VIII** (his best work), **Dante Alighieri** and an historical estimate of **Machiavelli**.

Artusi, Giovanni Maria Italian music theorist and composer, born Bologna, c.1540, died there, 18 August, 1613. A canon of the Congregation of the Saviour, a conservative student of **Zarlino**, he devoted himself to a reactionary defence of the strict contrapuntal style of the *prima prattica*, taking exception also to the *secunda prattica* of **Monteverdi** in *L'artusi, overo delle imperfettioni della musica moderna* (1600); he wrote against **Gesualdo**, Vincentino, Rose and Gabriella in that they had strayed from classical Renaissance traditions. He remained until the end a defender of the traditional style of composition, though he came to like some of Monteverdi's music.

Arundel, John English bishop, born Cornwall, died Chichester, 18 October 1477. A fellow of Exeter College, Oxford, 1420–31, ordained in 1432, chaplain and physician to Henry VI in 1453. He held prependaries at numerous cathedrals, became archdeacon of Richmond in 1457, and bishop of Chichester by papal provision in 1459, and the cathedral contains his tomb. His register is no longer extant, and there are no means now of assessing his eighteen years of episcopal administration.

Arundel, Thomas English archbishop, born Arundel, 1353, died Canterbury, 19 February 1414. The son of Richard Fitzalan, Earl of Arundel, and named bishop of Ely in 1374 by the Pope, in opposition to **Edward III** and the cathedral chapter. Translated to Canterbury in 1396, Thomas and his brother Richard, Earl of Arundel, opposed **Richard II** during his turbulent reign; the king requested **Boniface IX** to deprive Thomas of his see of Canterbury, but he regained it in 1399, under Henry IV, and retained it until his death. He strongly opposed the Lollards, held a provincial council against them at Oxford in 1428, and aided the persecution carried out against them; his *Constitutions*, issued in 1409, were intended to ensure orthodoxy in the English Church.

Arundell, Thomas Baron Arundell of Wardour, soldier and statesman, born 1560, died Wardour, 7 November 1639. Of Norman descent, Queen **Elizabeth** commended him in 1579 to serve Emperor Rudolph II of Austria, and he distinguished himself by fighting against the Ottomans in Hungary; at the siege of Gran, 1595, he became Count of the Holy Roman Empire. When he returned to England, **James I** made him Baron Arundell in 1605, and he commanded the English regiment that served Archduke Albert in Flanders against the Dutch. Active in parliament, he sat on several committees, taking the oath of allegiance in 1560. Being a Catholic, **Charles I**, at his accession in 1625, forbade Thomas to bear arms.

Ascellino (Asselino, Anselmo) Lombard Dominican, papal envoy to the Tartars. Dates and places of birth and death unknown. In 1245 **Innocent IV** sent him to exhort the Tartars to cease their depredations and become Christians. He reached mid-Persia and in 1247 and established contact with a Tartar general, Batschu, who refused him access to the Great Khan because he would not conform to Oriental protocol, thus endangering the lives of the envoys, and leading to great discomfort, hunger and insults. He returned to Europe, accompanied by two Tartar envoys to the Pope, and letters from the Khan and Batschu, that arrogantly demanded papal submission to the Tartars. There was no favourable response to any of the Pope's proposals.

Ascham, Roger English scholar and humanist, born Kirby Wiske, Yorkshire, c.1515, died London, 30 December 1568. He studied at St John's College, Cambridge, became a reader in Greek and public orator there. He wrote *Toxophilus* in 1545, a treatise on archery, which gained him some fame as a prose stylist. Briefly tutor to Princess **Elizabeth** in 1545, he became, despite his outspoken Protestant views, Latin secretary to Queen **Mary Tudor** in 1553, and later to Queen Elizabeth. His best known work, the *Schoolmaster*, presents his ideas on the psychology of learning, and the importance of educating the whole man by persuasion rather than by force. Though derivative of the ideas of **Elyot** and Quintillian, the work was well received, and it influenced later English writers on education, such as John **Locke**.

Ashbury, Francis First Methodist bishop of the USA, born Handsworth, England, 21 August 1745, died Spotsylvania, Virginia, 31 March 1816. Of a poor family, he left school at twelve to serve as an apprentice to a blacksmith. He converted at fourteen and became a lay preacher, replacing an itinerant Methodist shortly afterwards, and devoted himself entirely to preaching, under John **Wesley**. He answered Wesley's call and went to America in 1771, preached in Philadelphia, New Jersey and southern New York, forming new congregations, and enforcing Methodist discipline. True to Wesley's principle of itinerancy, he never again had a home, and continued these missionary journeys throughout the eastern states of the Union; in 1772, Wesley appointed him general assistant in America. During the Revolutionary war, Ashbury remained in America, became general superintendent at Lovely Lane Chapel, Baltimore, and the Methodist Episcopal Church in America came into being; he later used the title bishop, though this was repugnant to Wesley. He travelled widely, kept a 'journal', now invaluable to historians, and wrote hundreds of letters; his insistence on itinerancy made the remarkable growth of Methodism possible: there were about 1200 Methodists when he went to America; 214,000 at his death.

Asín Palacioss, Miguel Spanish archbishop, born Saragossa, 5 July 1871, died San Sebastian, 12 August 1944. He obtained a doctorate in theology at the Conciliar Seminary of Saragossa, and then studied Islamic philosophy and mysticism. He wrote *The Christianization of Islam*, and *Muslim Eschatology in the Divine Comedy* (1919), in which he showed that a good part of the ultra-terrestrial voyage owed less to **Dante**'s fecund imagination than to the Islamic legend of Muhammad's ascent to heaven. In the first work he demonstrated the Christian origins of the theology of Algazel (Al-Ghazali), and the practical mysticism of the school of Abenmassara and Abentofail. He held the chair of Arabic studies at Madrid, became director of the Royal Spanish Academy, and the leading scholar of Spanish–Arabic studies.

Aske, Robert Yorkshire leader of the Pilgrimage of Grace, 1536–7, born, place and date unknown, died York, 28 June 1537. Of an old Yorkshire family, he became an attorney and fellow of Gray's Inn. In 1536, rebellion broke out in Yorkshire against the restrictive enactments of Parliament, and Aske put himself at the head of a 'Pilgrimage' of 30,000, wearing the badge of the 'Five Wounds'. Religious and social elements were inextricably combined in the revolt; Aske issued a proclamation opposing Thomas **Cromwell**, and 'other evil counsellors' of **Henry VIII**, and demanded a repeal of the Statute of Uses, and an end to the suppression of monasteries. He apparently obtained from Henry a promise that the abuses would be redressed, but a fresh outbreak in West Yorkshire the same year provided a pretext for Henry to break his pledge and, in May, Aske was summoned to London and imprisoned in the Tower. He insisted that the Act of Supremacy 'could not stand with God's law', that belief in the Pope's authority was fundamental to orthodoxy, and that Thomas **Cramner** and other bishops were heretics. Charged and condemned for high treason and taken back to the North, he was hanged in chains at York.

Asola, Giovanni Matteo Italian composer of the late Renaissance, born Verona, c.1540; died Venice, 1 October 1609. A pupil of **Ruffo** in Venice, where his publications first appeared, he composed, in a conservative style, two sets of Masses in 1570; he became maestro at Treviso, 1577, and the next year at Vicenza. He returned to Venice in 1588 as a chaplain at the church of San Severo, where he remained until his death. His main works were some 40 Masses for three to eight voices, psalms for vespers and *falso bordone* settings (1575–92), three passions, a requiem Mass and a set of introits and alleluia verses (1565). He published *Psalmodia Vespertina*, containing works of various Venetian composers, in honour of **Palestrina** in 1592.

Asperger, Sigismundo (Aperger) Austrian missionary, born Innsbruck, 20 October 1687, died Paraguay, 23 November 1772. A Jesuit missionary among the Guarani Indians from 1719 until his death, and the only member of the Society not to leave the country in the expulsion of 1767, because of his physical disability. Though not a medical doctor by profession, he attained some renown for his knowledge of medicinal herbs, e.g. a cure-all from the oil of the Aguaraybi tree. He published a book, *Medicinal Prescriptions, the chief ingredients of which are the medicinal herbs of Paraguay*, now in the British Museum, which lists 88 diseases and their respective herbal remedies. Several of his studies, on dragon's blood, on Paraguayan maté, nutmeg and wild vicereine, were published in Buenos Aires in 1802. He died at the Guarani Reduction of Apostles.

Aspilcueta, Martin (Doctor Navarrus) Spanish canonist and moral theologian, born Barasoain, Navarre, 13 May 1493, died Rome, 21 June 1586. A cousin of St **Francis Xavier**, he studied at Toulouse, Salamanca and Coimbra. Consultor to the Sacred Penitentiary under three Popes: **Pius V**, **Gregory XIII** and **Sixtus V**, he published *Manuale sine Enchiridion confessariorum et paenitentium* (1588), long considered a classic. He would probably have been made a cardinal had it not been blocked by Philip II of Spain, who was deeply offended at Martin's insistence that, because of Spanish prejudice, the prosecution of the Dominican archbishop of Toledo, Bartolome de Carranza, be transferred to Rome. His numerous writings are collected in *Doctoris Navarri . . . opera* (1609).

Assemani, Joseph Aloysius Born Tripoli, Lebanon, 1710, died Rome, 9 February 1782. A brother of Joseph Simon, one of the pioneers in modern oriental studies, and professor of Syriac, later of liturgy, at the Sapienza in Rome. Besides aiding his brother in his literary labours, he edited *Codex Liturgicus Ecclesiae Universae*, a valuable collection for the study of Eastern liturgies; *Commentarius Criticus de Ecclesiis*, and *Commentaria de Catholicis Patriarchiis Chaldaeorum et Nestorianorum* (1775).

Assemani, Joseph Simon Born Tripoli, Lebanon, 27 July 1687, died Rome, 3 January 1768. He entered the Maronite college at Rome in 1703 and, following his ordination, transferred to the Vatican Library. In 1717, **Clement XI** sent him to Egypt and Syria to search for valuable MSS, and he returned with about 150 choice ones; sent again in 1735, he brought back an even more valuable collection. Named titular archbishop of Tyre, he attended the first National Maronite Council, where he used his influence to bring his countrymen into closer connection with Rome. His two great works are: *Biblioteca Orientalis* (1719–28), a collection of Syriac documents on the history of the churches of Syria, Chaldaea and Egypt, which introduced Syriac literature to the West, and parts of which have not been superseded; the edited works of St **Ephraem** Syrus, *Opera Ephraemi* (1732–46), with Latin and Greek translations, still the only complete edition. Other works include: the unfinished *Kalendaria Ecclesiae Universae* (1755), on all the saints of the world; *Italicae Historiae Scriptores* (1751); *Bibliotheca Juris Orientalis Canonici et Civilis* (1762).

Assemani, Simon Born Tripoli, Lebanon, 20 February 1752, died Padua, 7 April 1820. A grandnephew of Joseph Simon, he studied at Rome, went to Syria as a missionary and, in 1785, became professor of oriental languages at Padua, both seminary and university. He is best known for his masterly detection of the literary imposture of Vella, which claimed to be a history of the Saracens in Syria. He published important works on Arabic subjects, e.g. *Essay on the Origin, Cult, Literature and Customs of the Arabs before Muhammad* (1787), and the *Catalogue of the Marriana Library* (1787–92), containing MS extracts and essays on Arabic literature, coins, and other subjects.

Assemani, Stephen Erodius Born Tripoli, Lebanon, 1707, died Rome, 24 November 1782. Nephew of Simon and Aloysius, and the former's chief assistant in the Vatican Library, titular archbishop of Aparnea in Syria, he held several rich prebends in Italy. At the suggestion of **Benedict XIV**, he edited certain valuable MSS in *Bibliothecae Mediceae-Laurentianae et Palatinae Codium MSS Orientalium Catalogus* (1742); *Acta Sanctorum Martyrum Orientalium et Occidentalium* (1748); and *Bibliothecae Apostolicae Vaticanae Codicum MSS Catalogus*. A fire destroyed the manuscript collections prepared for the continuation of the work.

Asser, John (Asker) Bishop, biographer and chronicler, born in Menevia, Wales, died in England, 909. Studied at St David's monastery in Wales, where he was ordained. He went to the court of king **Alfred** for six months each year, spending the other six in Wales. Asser is credited both by Alfred and by **William of Malmesbury** with helping the king in his writing, notably of the *Pastoral Care* and the translation of Boethius' *De consolatione philosophiae*. He was given charge of monasteries and made bishop of Sherborne. He wrote *De rebus gestis Aelfredi*, a major source of information about his own life as well as Alfred's.

Assmayer, Ignaz Austrian composer and organist, born 11 February 1790, died Vienna, 31 August 1862. A student of Michael **Haydn**, he became organist at St Peter's in Salzburg at eighteen. He moved to Vienna in 1815 and studied with Joseph von **Eybler**, who influenced his grasp of symphonic form. His sacred works include two oratorios, two requiems and over 50 secular pieces.

Asterius of Amasea Saint, bishop, born Cappadocia, *c.*350, died Amasia, *c.*410. Little is known of his life except that he abandoned the law to enter the clergy, and became a bishop around 385. His fame rests chiefly on his *Homilies*, much esteemed in the Eastern Church, most of which have been lost, but 21 are given in full by Migne, and there are fragments of others in Photius. The eleventh homily, on the martyrdom of St **Euphemia**, contains a description of a painting of the saint, which text was used at the Second Council of Nicaea (787), against the Iconoclast. A man of great culture, Asterius' works are a valuable contribution to our knowledge of the history of preaching. Feast day 30 October.

Asterius of Cappadocia Sophist and theologian, born Cappadocia, died *c.*341. He converted to Christianity about 300 and became a disciple of **Lucian**, founder of the school of Antioch. During the persecution under Maximian (304), he relapsed into paganism and thus, though received again into the Church by Lucian and supported by the Eusebian party, could not be ordained. He is best known as an early and able defender of the semi-Arian position, and **Athanasius** styled him 'advocate' of the Arians. His chief work, the *Syntagmation*, known through excerpts quoted by Athanasius and **Marcellus of Ancyra**, is Arian in its treatment of the Son, and according to Marcellus, draws heavily on **Eusebius of Nicomedia** and other Arian-minded bishops to support his position. He wrote other treatises, including commentaries on the Gospels, the Psalms and Romans. He attended many synods and we last hear of him at the Synod of Antioch in 341.

Astrain, Antonio Spanish Jesuit historian, born Undiano, Navarre, 17 November 1857; died Loyola, 4 January 1928. He entered the Society in 1871, became editor of the *Mensajero del Sagrado Corazon* from 1890, and joined the staff of *Monumenta historia Societatis Iesu*; in 1895 he began to write a history of the Spanish Jesuits from the beginning to 1767, *Historia de la Compania de Jesus en la Asistencia de España*, of which seven volumes appeared before he died. The first volume is largely a life of **Ignatius of Loyola**, and the last four an account of the work of Spanish Jesuits in the Americas, the Pacific Islands and the Philippines.

Astrolabe (Astrolabius), Peter *see* **Peter Astralabe**

Astros, Paul Thérèse David d' French cardinal, archbishop, born Tourves, Var, 15 October 1772, died Toulouse, 29 September 1851. A canon at Nôtre Dame Cathedral, he began in 1806 to draw up the imperial catechism. When the see of Paris fell vacant in 1808, d'Astros became vicar capitular, in which position he opposed the pretensions of Bonaparte, and stood firm against the efforts of Cardinal Maury, the emperor's appointee, to take possession of the see without the approval of **Pius VII**, and was imprisoned for his pains, 1811–14. He became bishop of Bayonne in 1820, archbishop of Toulouse, 1830, and cardinal, 1850. He energetically promoted the condemnation of Lamennais, composing a censure of 56 propositions from the latter's writings, and also opposed Prosper Gueranger's attack on diversities in traditional Gallican usages in the liturgy of France.

Astruc, Jean French physician and biblical critic, born Sauve, Languedoc, 19 March 1684, died Paris, 5 May 1766. Son of a Protestant pastor, he converted to Catholicism at an early age, graduated in medicine at Montpelier in 1703, became successively superintendent of the mineral waters of Languedoc in 1721, first physician to the king of Poland in 1729, and regius professor of medicine at Paris in 1731. Of his numerous works, that on which his fame principally rests is *De Morbis Veneris libri sex* (1736). In addition, he published anonymously *Conjectures sur les mémoires originaux dont il paraît que Moyse s'est servi pour composer le livre de la Genèse* (1753), in which he pointed out that two main sources can be traced in the Book of Genesis, the Elohistic, and the Yahvistic; and, also, two dissertations on the immateriality and immortality of the soul (1755). His acute observation on the varying use of 'Elohim' and 'Yahweh' for the divine name, laid the foundation for the documentary theory developed in the nineteenth century.

Athala of Bobbio Saint, abbot, born Burgundy, *c*.570; died 10 March 627. The events of his life are recounted in the writings of his contemporary, **Jonas of Bobbio**. He spent some years in the monastery of Lerins, and in the stricter observance of Luxeuil. Nominated to replace **Columbanus**, exiled by Brunhilde in 610, he instead followed him into northern Italy, where they established the monastery of Bobbio, and there he succeeded Columbanus as abbot, *c*.615. He combated Arianism

among the Lombards and supported the Papacy in the controversy of the 'Three Chapters'. Feast day 10 March.

Athanasius Saint, bishop of Alexandria, born Alexandria, *c*.295, died there, 2 May 373. One of the most illustrious defenders of the Christian faith, a Father and Doctor of the Church, defender of the Nicene faith, friend of St **Anthony of Egypt**. He attended the Council of Nicaea (325) as deacon and secretary to Bishop **Alexander**, and succeeded him in 328. **Constantine I** banished Athanasius to Trier because of the intrigues against him of **Eusebius of Nicomedia**, the Arians, and partisans of the Miletian schism, but he returned after a successful appeal to **Julius I**. His enemies forced Athanasius from his see four more times between 335 and 366.

His writings are (a) dogmatic: *Discourses against the Arians*, being the most important; (b) historical-polemical: three apologies, of which *Apology against the Arians*, is valuable; (c) ascetical: the principal work is his *Life of Anthony*, which profoundly influenced subsequent Greek and Latin hagiography; (d) his correspondence is of prime importance for the history of Arianism and the development of Christian doctrine in the fourth century, amongst which are of note: the *Festal Letters*, annual messages to the bishops of Egypt; the *Synodal Letters* explain the Nicene faith and warn against Arian errors; four *Letters to Serapion of Thmuis*, a unified dogmatic treatise setting forth the correct doctrine of the Holy Spirit. His most famous work, *De Incarnatione*, is the second of two closely linked treatises (the other, *Contra Gentiles*), and the 'locus classicus' for the teaching of the ancient Church on the subject of salvation. In it God himself, the Word (logos), has entered into humanity and restored fallen man to the image of God in which he had been created (Genesis 1:27); by his death and resurrection he met and overcame death, the consequence of sin, thus leading mankind back to God.

Athanasius' writings are occasional pieces, born of controversy and intended for controversial ends, the abstract exposition of theological ideas being everywhere subordinated to the polemical purpose. Inspired with an enthusiastic devotion to Christ, his main distinction was his zealous advocacy of the essential divinity of Jesus; with justice has he been called 'The Father of Orthodoxy'. Feast day 2 May.

Athanasius I (of Constantinople) Patriarch, 1289–93, 1304–10, born Adrianople, 1230, died Xerolophus, 28 October 1310. He changed his name from Alexius when he entered the monastery of Thessalonica, whence he emigrated to Mount Athos, thence to the Holy Land and the founding of a monastery at Thrace. Named patriarch by Emperor **Andronicus II**, he set about stabilizing ecclesiastical discipline, and initiated regulations restricting the travel of monks and bishops, despite his own travels, opposition to which resulted in his resignation and retirement to a monastery at Xerolophus. He returned, however, in 1304, expelled the Franciscans from Constantinople in 1307, and resigned a second time in 1310, dying a short time later, at the same monastery. Most of his writings are unedited; 126 letters dealing with ecclesiastical discipline are known, as well as two catechetical instructions and an anthem in praise of the Mother of God.

Athanasius of Brest Orthodox saint, abbot and martyr, born Minsk province, 1596, died (martyred) 5 September 1648. He was born in the same year as the Union of Brest which united the Orthodox dioceses of Poland and Lithuania with Rome. He spent his whole life fighting what he regarded as a false union. This aroused much opposition even from his wealthier co-religionists. At the time of the Cossack invasions of Poland he was arrested and although no sedition could be proved against him he was tortured with hot coals and shot. His relics were later found and enshrined. Feast days 5 September and 20 July.

Athanasius of Naples Saint, Italian bishop, born 832, died Veroli, 15 July 872. Of a powerful Neapolitan family, his father being Sergius, duke of Naples, elected bishop of Naples aged eighteen. Details of his life were recorded in a vita by **John the Deacon** of Naples, who shows him to have been an exemplary cleric, renowned for personal austerity and compassion for others, especially the poor, orphans and Saracen prisoners. He rebuilt churches, reunited communities of priests and monks and championed their interests before the emperor, by whom he was much esteemed for his holiness and practical conduct of affairs. After the death of his father and brother, his nephew, young Duke Sergius, persecuted Athanasius, imprisoned him and dislodged him from his see. He sought refuge for five years from 867 with his brother Stephen, bishop of Sorento, and finally approached the emperor for a lifting of the ban and a return to his see. He died near Monte Cassino, and his remains were translated to the cathedral church in Naples in the thirteenth century. Feast day 15 July.

Athenagoras Christian apologist of the second century, died 190. A native of Athens, according to an emendator of the Paris Codex 451 of the eleventh century, he converted to Christianity, and thereafter used his learning in philosophy and rhetoric in defence of Christian truth. The inscription on the earliest MS of his principal work, the *Apology*, describes it as the 'Embassy of Athenagoras, the Athenian, a philosopher and a Christian concerning the Christians, to the emperors Marcus Aurelius Antoninus and Lucius Aurelius Commodus', etc. This statement has given rise to much discussion, but from it and internal evidence the date of the *Apology* may be fixed at about 177; it refutes accusations brought against Christians of atheism, cannibalism and incest, and attacks pagan polytheism and mythology. He is also reputedly the author of a discourse on the resurrection of the body, which answers objections to the doctrine, and attempts to prove its truth from considerations of God's purpose in the creation of man, his justice and the nature of man himself. Athenagoras' theology is strongly tinged with Platonism; he elaborated a philosophical defence of the Christian doctrine of the Trinity, and upheld the indissolubility of marriage, even in death.

Athenagoras (of Constantinople) (Spyrou) Patriarch, born Ioannina, 25 March 1886, died Istanbul, 7 July 1972. Became Greek archbishop of North America in 1930, where he did much to organize the Church. In 1948 he was elected ecumenical patriarch when he attempted, without lasting success, to reconcile the Turkish authorities to the presence of the patriarchate. After the anti-Greek pogrom of 1955 he saw his flock reduced to one-tenth of its previous strength through emigration. He worked tirelessly in ecumenical causes especially to improve relations with

Rome. He became a personal friend of Pope **Paul VI** and together they simultaneously 'lifted' the anathemas of 1054 in a ceremony on 7 December 1964.

Atienza, Juan de Spanish Jesuit educator and canonist, born Tordehumos, 1544, died Lima, 1 November 1592. He joined the Society in Spain, and went to Peru in 1581, where he founded the Collegio de San Martin in Lima, and became rector of the major seminary of San Pablo; he served as provincial from 1585, and as a valued collaborator of the archbishop of Lima, Toribio de Mogrovejo. As provincial he addressed himself to internal discipline, the organization of missions already established and the expansion of new areas, concentrating on creating and directing significant works, guided by his knowledge and experience of the situation in South America.

Atkinson, Maria Church of God missionary, born Sonora, Mexico, 1879, died 1963. She moved to Arizona in 1905 with her first husband, and after his death she married an American. In 1924 she experienced baptism in the Holy Spirit following a recovery from cancer, and in 1931 she joined the Church of God. Based in missions in Obregon and Hermosillo, she became known as 'La Madre de Mexico' in north-west Mexico.

Atkinson, Matthew (Paul of St Francis) English Franciscan missionary, born Yorkshire, 1656, died Hurst Castle, Hampshire, 15 October 1729. He had served for twelve years on the English mission when betrayed for £100 and, in 1698, condemned to life imprisonment for being a Catholic priest, a criminal offence. After complaints against liberties allowed him by his keeper, he voluntarily confined himself to his cell in Hurst Castle, to avoid causing difficulty to his goaler, for the last twenty years of his life.

Atticus of Constantinople Saint, born Sebaste, Armenia, died Constantinople, 10 October 425. Patriarch of Constantinople, 406–25, he testified against St **John Chrysostom** at the Synod of the Oak in 403, and later persecuted his followers. However, as patriarch, he realized that this quarrel with Rome weakened the prestige of his see and, to the vexation of St **Cyril of Alexandria**, who had

to do likewise, he restored Chrysostom's name to the diptychs in 421. Theodosius II approved a law requiring the consent of the patriarch of Constantinople for episcopal consecration in the Hellespont, Bithynia and Asia Minor; the Councils of Ephesus (431) and Chalcedon (451) recognized his defence of orthodox teaching against the Pelagians and the Novatians. He pained St **Augustine** with his references to the latter's Manichaean attitude to sex, attributed to him by the Pelagians, and he wrote to protest, c.420. He is listed with the saints in the Eastern Church. Feast day 11 October.

Attilanus Saint, patron and first bishop of Zamora, born, date and place unknown, died Zamora, 916. A disciple of St **Froilan** and his colleague in the organization of monastic life in northern Spain. He became bishop of Zamora in 900, and when the see was restored c.1109, after destruction by the Moors, c.986, his cult and a Cistercian *vita* became popular. It is claimed that in 1260 a shepherd discovered his relics in Zamora, part of them later being stolen and taken to Toledo. He is included in the Roman martyrology of 1583. Feast day 5 October.

Atto of Milan Italian cardinal and canonist, born, place and date unknown, died 1085. A Milanese cleric of noble birth, who though elected successor to Archbishop Wido in 1072, with the approval of **Gregory VII**, never took possession of the see of Milan due to local disturbances, and King **Henry IV**'s opposition. He fled to Rome, and was named cardinal-priest of the title of St Mark, but little is known of his Roman career. His fame rests on his *Breviarum*, a summary of disciplinary canons of some importance in Gregory's early reform measures.

Atto of Vercelli Bishop and canonist, born c.885, died 31 December 961. Of a distinguished Lombard family, and remarkable for his erudition in an unlearned age. His writings include a long commentary on the Pauline Epistles (dependent on **Augustine**, **Jerome**, **Claudius of Turin**, *et al.*), considering the question of why the Roman Epistles come first, and a collection of ecclesiastical canons dealing with such subjects as the refutation of charges against the clergy, the filling of clerical posts and the unjust seizure of church property by the laity after the death of the bishop. Some of his letters and sermons have also survived. Atto himself stands as an index to his age and as a person of notable endowments and achievements.

Attwater, Donald English lay scholar and writer, born Forest Gate, 24 December 1892, died Storrington, 3 February 1977. Of Puritan stock in Kent, he studied law and became a Catholic in 1911, giving himself to scholarly work from 1920, and becoming an authority on ancient churches of the East. Among his principal works are *Christian Churches of the East* (2 vols, 1948 and 1961); *A Catholic Dictionary* (1961); *St John Chrysostom* (1959); *Cell of Good Living* (1968), a biography of Eric **Gill**, who had influenced so deeply the renaissance of English letters of which Attwater was a part; *Dictionary of Saints* (reissued by Penguin in 1965), a continuing best-seller. He translated the early works of Nicholas **Berdiaev** from the French, as well as Yves **Congar**'s *Laity*, and collaborated with Herbert **Thurston** in the revision, scholarly updating and supplement of **Butler**'s *Lives of the Saints*, completed in 1956, seventeen years after the death of Thurston; it provided English-speaking Catholics with the most complete collection of lives of the saints available in their own language. Attwater was one of the earliest advocates of liturgy in the vernacular, and an enthusiastic ecumenist years before the term came into use.

Attwood, Thomas Musician, born London, 23 November 1765, died London, 24 March 1838. He was a chorister in the Chapel Royal, studied in Italy, and in Vienna. He was the only English pupil of **Mozart**. In England he became organist of St Paul's Cathedral and composer to the Chapel Royal. He wrote hymns, church music and anthems for the coronations of George IV and William IV.

Atwater, William English bishop, born *c*.1440, died Lincoln, 4 February 1521. At Magdalen College, Oxford, he earned a doctorate in theology and probably tutored **Wolsey**, who seems to have helped him accumulate benefices and offices for the rest of his life. Several times vice-chancellor of Oxford, in 1504 he became canon of Windsor and registrar of the Order of the Garter; chancellor of Lincoln Cathedral (1506–12), archdeacon of Lewes

(1509–12), and archdeacon of Huntingdon in 1514, when he succeeded Wolsey as bishop of Lincoln; he is buried in the cathedral there.

Aubarède, Jean Michel d'Astorg d' French ecclesiastic, born Tarbes, 1639, died Bayeux, 1692. A priest in the Diocese of Tarbes, he moved to Parmiers as canon, where he staunchly supported Bishop **Caulet**, and succeeded him in 1680. He, as Caulet before him, opposed the policy of **Louis XIV**, who annulled his election, imposed as bishop his own choice of a man earlier excommunicated by Caulet, and enforced it through the armed strength of his intendant, Nicholas Foucault. Appeals were made to **Innocent XI** and the archbishop of Toulouse for restitution of the see, but in vain, and Aubarede was imprisoned in the Bastille until the eve of his death.

Aubert, Suzanne Founder of the Daughters of Our Lady of Compassion, born St-Symphorien, Lyons, France, 19 June 1835, died Wellington, New Zealand, 1 October 1926. Determined to be a nursing nun, she trained in Paris, nursed during the Crimean War, and joined Bishop Pompallier in New Zealand in 1860. She worked with Maori girls in Auckland and in 1871 moved to Napier where she nursed, developed herbal remedies, catechized, and edited a *Maori Prayer Book* (1879). From 1883 she developed a remote congregation at Jerusalem on the Wanganui River where she broke in a farm, ran a dispensary, gathered babies and children, published *A Manual of Maori Conversation* (1885) and founded the Daughters of Our Lady of Compassion (1892). Moving to Wellington in 1899 she set up the Home of Compassion and went to Rome (1913–20) to gain papal recognition for her Order and its mission.

Aubert of Avranches Saint, Frankish bishop, born, place and date unknown, died Avranches, 725. Tradition has it that Aubert, bishop of Avranches, was told in a dream to build a church on the site of what became Mont St Michel, dedicated to St Michael the Archangel, which he undertook to do, and the church was duly erected and dedicated in 709, and entrusted to a chapter of canons. Aubert's body was translated to the abbey in 1009; his remains were dispersed during the Revolution, but the head is preserved at St Gervais in Avranches. Feast day 10 September.

Aubigné, Jean Henri Merle d'   Swiss historian of the Reformation, born Geneva, 8 August 1794, died there, 21 October 1872. The son of French Huguenot refugees (the name Aubigné being added to the family name of Merle), he studied at Berlin under W. M. L. de Wette. Pastor of the French Protestant church in Hamburg, 1819, pastor and court preacher in Brussels, 1823, and president of the consistory of French and German Protestants. In 1831 he returned to Geneva as professor of church history in the theological faculty, where he wrote his popular, but unreliable, *Histoire de la Réformation du XVI siècle* (1835–53), and *Histoire de la Réformation en Europe au temps de Calvin* (1863–78), a more finished work. He travelled frequently to Britain, and was honoured by Oxford University and by the city of Edinburgh.

Aubigné, Théodore Agrippa d'   French Huguenot writer and soldier, born Saint-Maury, 8 February 1552, died Geneva, 9 May 1630. While still young he swore to avenge the Huguenot cause when he saw the Protestant victims of the aborted 'conspiracy of Amboise', 1650. He fought with Henry of Navarre (**Henry IV**) in the French Wars of Religion, 1565, became implicated in plots against the strongly pro-Catholic regency of Marie de Medici after 1610, and sought refuge in Geneva, where he died. Aubigné expressed his revulsion at the suffering of France and the selfish indifference of her aristocratic rulers in his religious epic poem, *Les Tragiques* (1616), where attacks against the Catholics alternate with eloquent appeals to divine justice in favour of persecuted Protestants. Other major works include *Confession du très catholique sieur de Sancy* (1660), against the Protestants who, emulating Henry IV, abjured; *Les Aventures du baron de Faeneste* (1617), ridiculing the court of Marie de Medici; *Histoire universelle depuis 1550 jusqu'en 1601* (1616–26), a coolly humanist look at Protestant exploits which earned him exile in Geneva; and *Printemps du sieur d'Aubigné*, a collection of his youthful love poetry to the Catholic Diane Salviati, whom he could not marry. D'Aubigné remained true to the Huguenot cause, a fearless advocate of Huguenot interests.

Aubry, Pierre   French musicologist, born Paris, 14 February 1874, died Dieppe, 31 August 1910. He received the diploma of 'Archiviste-paleograph' from the Ecole de Chartes, Paris, in 1898, and undertook research into medieval music. He authored numerous works of lasting value, among which significant contributions of thirteenth-century musical sources and studies of the rhythm of late medieval music, e.g. *Trouvières et Troubadours* (1910). Aubry also lectured at the Institut Catholique, Schola Cantorum and Ecole des hautes études sociales. His erudite researches are at the origin of the renaissance of medieval music.

Aubusson, Pierre d'   French cardinal, born Monteil-au-Vicomte, 1423, died Rhodes, 3 July 1503. His family ruled the town of Aubusson, he joined the Order of St John of Jerusalem, and became Grand Master in 1476. Under his leadership the knights defeated an attempt by the Turks, under Mohammed II, to conquer Rhodes in 1480, which made him widely known in Europe. His memory, however, has been somewhat stained by what followed. Mohammed died in 1481 and his sons Bayezid and Jem disputed his successsion, with the latter defeated, and he fled to Rhodes under a safe conduct from Aubusson. Jem was sent to France and, despite the safe conduct, d'Aubusson accepted an annuity of 45,000 ducats from the sultan, to guard Jem in such a way as to prevent him from appealing to the Christian powers to aid him against his brother. He was kept a close prisoner for six years until handed over to **Innocent VIII** in 1489. Aubusson's reward was a cardinal's hat, and the power to confer all benefices connected with the Order without reference to the Papacy; the Order received the wealth of the suppressed Orders of the Holy Sepulchre and of St Lazarus. His reputation further suffered by his success in extirpating Judaism in Rhodes by expelling all adult Jews and forcibly baptizing their children.

Auctor of Metz   Saint, flourished *c*.451, and was a contemporary of Attila the Hun, who ravaged the region at that time. There is an extant life of Auctor written by Paul the Deacon, and Bishop Drogo of Metz transferred his relics to Maursmunster. Auctor of Trier is an unhistorical personage whose *vita* perhaps derives from that of Auctor of Metz. Feast day 10 August.

Auden, Wystan Hugh Poet, born York, 21 February 1907, died Vienna, 29 September 1973. A leading twentieth-century poet, he was educated at Oxford. He was a schoolmaster for some five years from 1930 onwards, during which period he began to publish his verse. He became the leader of a group of left-wing poets: in 1937 he spent some months driving an ambulance for the Republican forces in Spain. During World War II he became interested in Protestant Christianity, as is shown by *The Double Man*, written while he was in the USA. He moved to the United States at the outbreak of the Second World War but returned to Europe after the war was over and in 1956 became professor of poetry at Oxford. His hymn to St Cecilia was set to music by Benjamin **Britten**.

Auger, Edmond French Jesuit preacher, born Alleman, 1530, died Como, 19 January 1591. **Ignatius of Loyola** himself received Auger into the Society in 1550, and formed him in the religious life. He taught Latin at the Roman College, at Perugia and at Padua. A great preacher, vigorous and cheerful, hailed as the 'Chrysostom of France', he attracted even the Calvinists, whose heresy was spreading in southern France. Captured by Huguenots in Valence in 1562, and sentenced to death by burning, he so won over the onlookers by his preaching on the pyre, that they demanded his release. In 1564 he became the first Jesuit provincial of Aquitaine, and the close adviser and confessor of Henry III, but this aroused the hostility of the Catholic League, and he had to leave France after Henry's assassination in 1589. His important writings are his *Summary of Catholic Doctrine* (1563), and a second, smaller catechism published in 1568; both works were reprinted and translated, even into Greek, many times.

Augustin, Antonio Humanist, scholar, bishop and reformer, born at Saragossa, 26 February 1517, died at Tarragona, 31 May 1586. One of the most illustrious prelates of Spain because of his zeal and learning. His father was vice-chancellor of the kingdom of Aragon and ambassador of **Charles V** to **Louis XII** of France, and to Pope **Julius II**. His elder brother was bishop of Huesca, Jaca and Barbastro. He studied at Alcala, Salamanca and Bologna, where he took a doctorate in law in 1541, and at Padua. At the age of 25 he was the equal of the most renowned jurists of the time and he was appointed auditor of the Roman Rota in 1544 at the request of the Emperor Charles V. He was sent to England in 1555 as nuncio to Queen **Mary Tudor** and Philip II, and councillor to Cardinal Pole. He was appointed bishop of Alife in the kingdom of Naples in 1556, and of Lerida in 1561. He distinguished himself at the Council of Trent (1562–3) as an independent thinker, expressing his opinion without consideration of friends or of princes, while conducting himself with all modesty. In recognition of his efforts to carry out its reforms, he was created archbishop of Tarragona by **Gregory XIII** in 1576. One of his first tasks was to rid the diocese of corruption and crime. He convoked two diocesan synods and three provincial councils, before an early death. He was buried in the cathedral of Tarragona, being too poor to pay the expense of his own funeral rites. Augustin was a person of stature. He was concerned with the history of Roman law and his *De emendatione Gratiani dialogorum libri duo* laid the foundation for the history of the sources of canon law. His writings also include works on theology, classical philosophy and heraldry.

Augustine (Aurelius Augustinus) Saint, African bishop of Hippo Regius, born Thagaste (Souk-Ahras, Algeria), 13 November 354, died Hippo, 28 August 430. One of the four great fathers of the Latin Church, and the single most influential theologian in the history of the Church in the West. His life and personality are well known to us first and foremost in his numerous writings. His first years, up to his conversion in 387 are recounted at length in the *Confessions*, with the added charm of personal disclosure; the *Retractatones* (426–7), at the end of his life, constitutes the most exacting examination of conscience by a writer, in which he seeks to improve what was erroneous, and to make clear what was doubtful in his literary activity. His other writings, especially his sermons and letters (more than 200 have survived), are filled with traits of his character and biographical details. Finally, one of his disciples, Possidius of Calama, wrote, shortly after his death, an account of his life that is rich in information and of great historical value. Professor of rhetoric (Carthage, Rome, Milan), Augustine adhered to Manichaeism (373–83), but converted to Christianity after discovering Neoplatonic philosophy, and responding to the influence of his mother (St **Monica**), and of St **Ambrose** of Milan (386). Returning to Africa in 388, he lived a monastic life, ordained priest at Hippo in 391, and acclaimed bishop there in 395. A dedicated and effective pastor, he engaged fully in the affairs of his diocese (preaching, apologetic refutation, justice, assistance to the poor). Abroad he became one of the principal personalities of the Christian West, affirming his doctrine in the face of heresies: against the Donatists he proclaimed the universal vocation of the Church; against the Pelagians he affirmed, at the same time, the inability of man to merit his salvation and the powerful effect of grace; against the Manichaeans, finally, he argued that belief in absolute evil alongside absolute good constitutes an error. The good and the evil are bound, at the level of action, in the manner of obscurity and light. However, the evil is subordinate to the good, which alone proceeds from the divine power; evil is thus efficient only by the good that it harbours. Against their pessimism, he affirms the goodness of Creation, the work of God. Among Augustine's other principal works are: the *Soliloquies* (386–7), written when he was at Cassisiacum at the time of his conversion, on the significance of evil in the world; *De magistro* (389), in which, as in other treatises, is apparent the influence of the Neoplatonic method of thought, which for him, as for so many others, had become the bridge to Christianity; *De doctrina christiana* (396–426) and *Enchiridion* (421), two compendiums of Catholic doctrine, the first, a sort of biblical hermeneutic, which became the programme of the monastic schools, the second, a brief and concise presentation of Catholic doctrine, which he wrote at the request of a Roman layman named Laurentius; *De Trinitate* (399–422), a systematic treatise, which unlike most of his dogmatic writings, was not provoked by any special controversial emergency, and has played in the history of the dogmas of the West a role of the first rank; *The City of God* (413–24), his greatest work, the occasion for which was the sack of Rome in 410, by Alaric, as a reply to the pagans who attributed the catastrophe to the anger of the old gods against Christianity. But Augustine saw things otherwise; to him the ruin of cvilization was less important than the conflict between the two 'cities': that of the devil and that of God, which are opposed in this world and will continue to be so until the end of time. The doctrine of St Augustine is complex: it ascribes to faith the overarching role, without abandoning reason (believing, and understanding what one believes); it is a meditation on God, grasped in an interior act, rather as the Cartesian *cogito*. Always he remains faithful to a first principle: it is God who operates in man the will and the doing; and even though man is free, it is the grace of God alone which merits him the reward of heaven. If at times reason cannot penetrate the mystery, the only attitude permitted is one of humble confidence. The Pelagian controversy was the most important and the one most closely associated with his distinctive greatness as a theologian, and earned him the title 'Doctor of Grace'. He had himself been brought out of darkness into 'marvellous light' only by entering into the depths of his own soul, and finding, after many struggles, that there was no power but divine grace, as revealed in the life and death of the Son of God, which could bring rest to human weariness, or pardon and peace for human guilt. The influence of St Augustine has dominated Western theology over the centuries, and continues to occupy an important place in the history of philosophy in general, notably in epistemology, or the theory of knowledge. Feast day 28 August.

Augustine Kazotoic Blessed, Dominican bishop, born Trogir, Dalmatia, *c.*1260, died Lucera, Apulia, 3 August 1323. He entered the Order of Preachers in his youth, and studied at the University of Paris in 1286. On returning to Dalmatia he founded several convents, and undertook missions in Italy, Bosnia and Hungary. **Benedict XI** consecrated him bishop of Zagreb in 1303; he restored discipline in the diocese and fostered learning, particularly in biblical studies. Miladin, governor of Dalmatia, whose tyranny he opposed, persecuted him until **John XXII** transferred him to the see of Lucera in Apulia, where he died in a convent he had founded. Venerated for charity to the poor, he had the gift of healing. Feast day 8 August.

Augustine Novellus Blessed, Italian jurist and Augustinian religious, born Tarano, Sabina, date unknown, died near Siena, 19 May 1309. He studied law at Bologna, became chancellor to King Manfred of Sicily, and entered the Augustinian

Order, where his reputation as a jurist preceded him. Confessor to **Nicholas IV**, he went to Siena as papal legate under **Boniface VIII**. He helped to revise the constitutions of the Order and became prior-general in 1298. He resigned in 1300 and retired to Siena. **Clement XIII** confirmed his cult in 1759. Feast day 19 May.

Augustine of Ancona (Triumphus) Augustinian philosopher, born Ancona, *c.*1241, died Naples, 2 April 1328. After Giles of Rome, founder of the Augustinian school, Augustine is the most prolific theologian of his Order, though most of his writings remain unpublished. In his celebrated *Summa de ecclesiastica potestate*, on the nature and scope of papal authority, Augustine not only defends the theocratic doctrine of Giles and **James of Viterbo**, but takes it to the extreme conclusion that all authority, civil and ecclesiastical, derives solely from the Roman pontiff, who alone possesses absolute and direct power in both religious and civil domains. He wrote a famous treatise on Aristotle's *Metaphysics*, and undertook the earliest concordance of the writings of St **Augustine**, the *Mille loquium Sancti Augustini veritatis*, completed by his pupil **Bartholomew of Urbino**.

Augustine of Canterbury Saint, apostle of England and first archbishop of Canterbury, born, date and place unknown, died Canterbury 26 May 604. **Gregory I** the Great consecrated him bishop, and sent him from Rome with 30 monks, in 596, to evangelize the Anglo-Saxons. He landed at Ebbsfleet in 597, where the king, **Ethelbert of Kent**, married to a Christian, Bertha, allowed the monks to preach, giving them a ruined church in Canterbury. His preaching converted many, including the king, and he established his cathedral seat, with a monastic chapter, at Canterbury – contrary to Gregory's wish that it be at London, with another at York – and consecrated bishops for London and Rochester. His attempts at co-operation with Christian Britons and Celtic bishops in the West Country, however, failed, because of their hatred of Anglo-Saxons and their attachment to their own traditions and customs, such as their own date, not the Roman, for the observance of Easter. Augustine's mission bore fruit long after his death in the conversion of the rest of England, and in

the missionary work of Anglo-Saxons on the continent. Feast day 26 May.

Augustinis, Aemilio de Italian theologian, educator, born Naples, 28 December 1829, died Rome, 17 January 1899. He entered the Society of Jesus at Conocchia in 1855, and went to Woodstock, Maryland, in 1869, as professor of sacred Scripture and librarian. A founder and editor of *Woodstock Letters*, a news publication for Jesuits, recognized by **Leo XIII** for his contribution to theology, he succeeded his former Woodstock colleague, Cardinal Camillo **Mazzella**, as professor of dogma at the Gregorian University, Rome, and rector of the institution from 1891 to 1895.

Aunarius of Auxerre (Aunacharius) Bishop of Auxerre, born Orléans, date unknown, died Auxerre, 25 September 601. He spent his youth at the royal court of Burgundy, became a priest, and a bishop in 561, participating in councils at Paris, 573, and Macon 583 and 585. He is famous for the 45 canons issuing from a diocesan synod in *c.*588, some of which discuss marriage and superstitions, which shed interesting light on the mode of living, when pagan abuse of Christian practices still persisted. He arranged for a transcription of the martyrology attributed to St **Jerome** (592), from which all extant copies are derived. He provided vitae of his two distinguished predecessors, St Amator and St **Germanus of Auxerre**, and organized liturgical prayer in the diocese. His relics, transferred to the crypt of the abbatial church of St Germain, were seized by the Calvinists in 1567, but retrieved, and are recognized as authentic.

Aunemund of Lyons Saint, bishop, born, date and place unknown, died Macon, 28 September 658. Reared at the court of Dagobert I and Clovis II, he became bishop of Lyons. St **Bede** recounts (*Eccl. Hist.* 5.19) that in 653, St **Benedict Biscop** and Wilfrid were hospitably received at Lyons by Aunemund, who is called Dalfinus in Bede's narrative, during their journey to Rome; very impressed by Wilfrid, he offered him 'the government of a large part of France' (*ibid.*), and his niece as wife. Wilfrid declined, however, and continued to Rome, but returned to Lyons, and stayed three years, received the tonsure from Aunemund, and was present when Queen Bathildis sent soldiers and 'commanded that the bishop be put to death' (*ibid.*). However, most scholars say that Aunemund was murdered by Ebroin, mayor of the palace of Neustria. Aunemund's cult began in the ninth century. Feast day 28 September.

Auraeus Saint, fifth-century bishop of Mainz. **Rabanus Maurus**, and the oldest sources, place his martyrdom, and that of his sister St Justina, in the time of Attila (*c.*451). More recent research suggests martyrdom by the Vandals in 406, when they destroyed Mainz. His name is united with that of a certain Justinus, a deacon, as the patron saint of Heiligenstadt, but it is unlikely that Justina and Justinus are not the same person. Feast day 16 June.

Aurea of Cordoba Saint, Spanish martyr, born Cordoba, *c.*810, died Cordoba, 19 July 856. An Arab of noble descent, her father had been a Muslim and after the martyrdom of her brothers, Adolphe and John, in 825, she went to live in the monastery of Cuteclara with her mother, for 30 years. When her relatives from Seville denounced her to the Cadi, also a relative, she abandoned Christianity, but immediately returned to the faith. Denounced a second time, she remained constant and suffered death by decree of the Emir. Her body was thrown into the Guadalquivir and never recovered. She is included in the Roman martyrology of 1583. Feast day 19 July.

Aurelian of Arles Saint, French archbishop, born, date and place unknown, died Lyons, 16 June 551. Elected bishop of Arles to succeed Auxanius, and named papal-vicar for Gaul by Pope **Vigilius** in 546. He founded a monastery and a convent for women, the rule for the men being a modified form of that of St **Benedict**, and that for the nuns of St Mary of Arles modelled on the monks. He exchanged letters with Vigilius regarding the 'Three Chapters', a matter that caused concern in the West, since by agreeing with Emperor **Justinian** I that three bishops should be condemned by papal approval, the authority of the Council of Chalcedon might be weakened. Vigilius was not disposed to agree with the emperor and replied to him in non-commital terms in 558. Aurelian is interred in the basilica of the Holy

Apostles (Saint-Nizier), where his epitaph was discovered in 1308.

Aurelian of Réomé Benedictine musical theorist, flourished in the ninth century. He is important for his treatise *Musica disciplina* (*c.*830), in which he discusses the nature of Gregorian chant, in particular the modes, the earliest treatment of the melodic formulae of chant using the terminology 'protus, deuterus, tritus, and tetrardus', in authentic and plagal forms. The treatise is a juxtaposition of ancient theory and contemporary practice, and valuable for the evidence it gives for chant performance during the Carolingian era.

Aurelius and Sabigotona Saints, Spanish martyrs, born Cordoba, *c.*820, died Cordoba, 27 July 852. Of a noble Muslim father and a Christian mother, Aurelius was brought up by a Christian aunt; he married Sabigotona, also a Christian, and they lived secretly as such, but, inspired by the courage of the Christians they saw suffering under Moorish persecution, they let their faith be known publicly. With another couple, Felix and Liliose, and a monk named George from Jerusalem, they were beheaded, on orders from the Cadi. Feast day 27 July.

Aurelius of Armenia Saint, bishop in Armenia, date and place of birth unknown, died Milan, 475. Nothing is known of his early life, but a ninth-century *vita*, now lost, stated that he brought from Cappadocia to Milan the relics of St Dionysius, bishop in 335, who had died in exile. In 830 Bishop Noting of Vercelli removed his body to Hirsau, where he erected a church of which Aurelius is patron. The extant life of Aurelius is an eleventh-century revision by Abbot William of Ebersberg. Feast day 9 November.

Aurelius of Carthage Saint, bishop of Carthage from 391, died *c.*429. A close friend of St **Augustine**, and praised by him for the many practical measures he took to advance the cause of Christianity in his city. As leader of the African bishops, he presided over a long series of ecclesiastical councils, mostly at Carthage, the most important being in 411, which condemned Donatism, and in 418, which condemned Pelagius and Celestius. Some of the letters addressed to him by St Augustine, who held him in high regard, survive. Feast day 20 July.

Aurispa, Giovanni Italian humanist, born Sicily, c.1369, died Ferrara, 1459. One of the learned Italians of the fifteenth century who did so much to promote the revival of the study of Greek. From his several trips to Greece he collected some 250 MSS, which he copied, translated and distributed. He became secretary to Popes **Eugenius IV** and **Nicholas V**. Considering his long life and reputation, Aurispa produced little, and he is remembered for the extensive collection of MSS and his persistent efforts to revive and promote the study of ancient literature.

Ausonius, Decimus Magnus Roman poet and rhetorician, born Burdigala (Bordeaux), c.310, died there c.394. About 365 he became tutor to Emperor Gratian, who raised him to the consulship in 379. To judge by a few of his poems he appears to have been a (not very enthusiastic) convert to Christianity in his mature years; he tried to dissuade his former pupil Paulinus of Nola from giving his wealth to the poor and becoming a monk. His most important extant works are: *Gratianum Actio*, an address of thanks to Gratian for his elevation to the consulship; *Periochae*, summaries of the books of the Iliad and Odyssey, and *Epigrammata*, including several free translations from the Greek Anthology. Perhaps his most successful poem is *Mosella*, in which he praises the regions of the Moselle flowing by Trier, then capital of the West. Ausonius was rather a man of letters than a poet, and his wide reading provided him with material for a great variety of subjects.

Austin, John English Catholic author, born Walpole, Norfolk, 1613, died London, 1669. He left Cambridge when he became a Catholic in c.1640, and studied at Lincoln's Inn. He visited the English College at Rome in 1640 and 1646, and belonged to a Catholic literary group in London from 1650. He defended Catholicism against bigotry, joined those who advocated allegiance to the Cromwellian government and hoped for a degree of toleration and sympathy from the Independents; he used Thomas Hobbes' *Leviathan* (1651) in support of their arguments. His *Gospel Devotions with Psalms, Hymns and Prayers* was very popular, and the contents even found their way into non-Catholic collections, such as John **Wesley**'s *Collection of Psalms and Hymns* (1737).

Austreberta Saint, Merovingian abbess, born Therousanne c.635, died Pavilly Abbey, 10 February 704. Her father was apparently a member of the royal family, her mother of German royal blood, and later honoured as a saint at the abbey of Sainte Austreberta at Montreuil-sur-Mer. Betrothed while still a young girl, she instead took the veil in 655, and entered the abbey of Port-le-Grand, Ponthieu, where she became prioress for fourteen years, and abbess of the newly founded Pavilly in c.670; her rule combined **Benedict** and **Columbanus**. Her relics were venerated for protection against drought and fire, but were destroyed in the French Revolution. Feast day 10 February.

Austregisilus Saint, Frankish abbot and bishop, born Bourges, 29 Novenber 551, died there 20 May 624. Of noble parents, he lived at the court of King Guntram from about the age of 24, until he left the court, and became a priest, then abbot of St Nicetius and bishop of Bourges in 612. He attended a synod at Paris in 614, and his name appears eighth in the list of 79 bishops who signed the decrees. He is reported to have granted a hermitage at Bourges to **Amandus**, the apostle of Belgium. Feast day 20 May.

Auxilius of Naples Frankish priest and polemicist. Date and place of birth and death unknown, flourished around 890. Ordained at Rome by Pope **Formosus**, an act declared invalid according to decrees of the 'cadaveric synod' (897), and reaffirmed by **Sergius III** in 904, on the ground of general invalidity of actions by Formosus. When Sergius demanded reordination, Auxilius defended the legality of Formosus' position, on the ground that the conferring of Holy Orders ought not to be contingent upon the integrity of its ministers, and opposed re-ordination. Indeed, he believed that a council should be called to vindicate Formosus and judge Sergius. His writings in this regard include *De ordinationibus a Formoso papa factis* (PL 129:1059–74); *Infensor et defensor* (PL 120:1073–1102) and *In defensionem sacrae ordinationis papae Formosi* (Dummler, 59–95).

Avellino, Andrew Saint, preacher and reformer, born Castronuovo, Naples, 1521, died Naples, 10 November 1608. Of noble birth, he became a priest in 1545, studied canon and civil law, but abandoned that in 1548 after making the spiritual exercises under the Jesuit **Lainez**, and devoted himself to the care of souls. He joined the Theatines in 1556, after recovering from a beating by enemies of his reform of a convent in Baiano, and became superior of the community in Naples. Charles **Borromeo** asked him to found a house in Milan in 1570, and he acted as spiritual director of several institutions in Milan and Piacenza (1570–82). He left some 3000 letters of spiritual direction, some of which were published after his canonization. Feast day 10 November.

Avendano, Diego de Spanish Jesuit missionary, born Segovia, 29 September 1596, died Lima, 30 August 1688. He joined the Society in Lima, 1610, after studies at Seville, taught at Cuzco and Chaquisaca, became rector of the major seminary of Lima, and provincial in 1663. In his great work *Thesaurus indicus* he applied his knowledge of canon, civil and moral law to the solution of legal problems peculiar to the Indian environment. Not original in his approach, he did not try to be, but he was most useful for the correct administration of justice.

Aventinus (Johannes Thurmayr) German humanist and historian, born Abensberg, Bavaria, 4 July 1477, died Regensburg, 9 January 1534. He served the dukes of Bavaria, collected original documents and produced *Annales ducum Boiariae* (1522), and *Bayerische Chronik* (1533). Influenced by the humanist Konrad Celtis to write German history, he became a virulent anti-clerical and nationalist humanist (as he made clear in his works), even though a friend of Philip **Melanchthon** and **Lefèvre d'Etaples**, but he never left the Church.

Aversa, Raphael Italian Theatine theologian, born Sanseverino, 1588, died Rome, 10 June 1657. He served five times as superior-general of his congregation, and was noted for his work in scholastic theology, especially for *Theologiae scholastica universa ad mentem Santae Thomae*. He refused the episcopacy offered him by **Innocent X**, and again by **Alexander VII**.

Avila, Francisco de Peruvian Quechua scholar, born Cuzco, Peru, 1573, died Lima, 17 September 1647. A foundling, he took the name of Beatriz de Avila, who cared for him, became a priest in Cuzco, and trained in the law at Lima. He is known for his crusade against Indian idolatry and superstition, deploying his knowledge of the language and customs of the Quechua. Accused of exceeding his authority, he spent some time in prison, but was absolved and became the first Visitador de Idoltrias, under Archbishop Lobo de Guerrero. He wrote extensively and contributed to the development of Quechua literature from being merely a language of evangelism.

Avila, José Cecilio Venezuelan professor, born Pedernales, Guigue, 22 November 1786, died Caracas, 24 October 1833. A brilliant student at the Royal Pontifical University, Caracas, he was ordained in 1811, and became professor of canon law at 27. Named rector of the University of Caracas in 1825, it was largely due to his efforts that the university was saved from closure in a financial crisis, in which Avila appealed to Simón **Bolívar** for help. He induced José Vargas to come as professor of anatomy, which attracted new students, and the first centenary, celebrated in 1825, saw Avila as rector of a university of radically revived fortunes. A strong exponent of Catholic doctrine in the face of heterodox influences, he enjoyed great prestige as a preacher. His biographer said of him that he had 'an authority in the moral and ecclesiastical field which no one surpassed in his day in his country'.

Avitus Saint, French abbot, born Auvergne, midfifth century, died Chateaudun, 17 June, c.530. He left the abbey of Menat to live as a hermit at the abbey of Micy in the Loire. When Abbot Maximus died in 520, the monks sought out Avitus and made him their abbot. **Gregory of Tours** relates that Avitus pleaded unsuccessfully with King Clodinus to spare the lives of Sigismund of Burgundy and his family, who had been captured in war. He is buried in the church of Saint-Georges at Orléans. Though his oldest biography dates from the ninth century, some scholars now consider that the *vita* may confuse Avitus with another Avitus at Menat. Feast day 17 June.

Avitus of Vienne Saint, bishop, born at Auvergne, c.450, died Vienne, c.519. Alcinus Ecdidius Avitus succeeded his father, St Hesychius, as bishop of Vienne, from c.490. Being of a Roman senatorial family, he became leader of the Gallo-Roman episcopate, and exercised enduring influence on the ecclesiastical life of Burgundy. A strong advocate of closer union of Gaul with Rome, and an ardent defender of the primacy of Rome. Praised by his contemporaries for his charity and literary achievement, **Clovis**, then still a pagan, was greatly impressed by his reputation for learning. He converted the Arian Burgundian prince Sigismund to the Catholic faith. Of his many works some 90 letters, as well as homilies and poems, survive. Feast day 5 February.

Avril, Philippe French Jesuit missionary, born Angoulême, 21 July 1654, died 1698. Assigned by his superiors in the Society in 1684 to find an overland route to China, free of Portuguese interference, he reached Moscow via Syria, Armenia and the Volga, but was expelled from Russia and had to return. His account of the six-year journey, *Voyages* (1692), was translated into many languages, including English, but a promised history of Muscovy did not appear. He died in a shipwreck on a second attempt to find a route to China.

Avvakum Petrovich Russian archpriest and author, born Grigorov, Novgorod (Gorki), 1620, died Pustozersk, 24 April 1682. The son of a village priest, well educated, he had a fine literary style. He resisted the ecclesiastical reform of Patriarch **Nikon**, opposed the correction of church books by Greek scholars, and the modification of church rituals, such as the three-fingered sign of the cross. He and his followers' protests led to schism and the formation of the Old Believers. Despite exile to Siberia in 1653, then to Mezen in 1662, and being confined to an underground prison, Avvakum remained steadfast in his convictions, blurting out accusations against the reforms even as he was being burnt at the stake in Pustozersk Square. He is one of the most colourful figures in Russian church history, because of his courageous, fanatical and OT cast of mind.

Axel, *see* Absalon of Lund

Ayala, Manuel José de Spanish Jesuit, born Panama, 26 March 1728, died Madrid, 8 March 1805. Educated in Panama, he held important posts in the ecclesiastical court and royal 'audiencia'. He went to Spain in 1753 to complete his education, and rose to be first officer in the Secretariat of State, and councillor of the Indies. A driving, ambitious man, he made many recommendations for the utilization and modification of legislation dealing with the Indies, which, though not adopted by his contemporaries, were none the less responsible for his appointment to a committee formed in the eighteenth century to reform the 'Recopilacion de Indias' of 1680.

Aymard Blessed, third abbot of Cluny, date of birth unknown, died Cluny, 5 October 965. He succeeded **Odo** in 942, whose work in the Cluniac Reform he continued. In 948 Pope **Agapetus** confirmed the direct dependence of Cluny and its dependencies on the Apostolic See. Aymard resigned his office in 948 because of blindness, having provided for the election of **Majolus** as fourth abbot. In 1063 **Peter Damian** collected the oral testimony of Aymard's patience, simplicity and humility. Feast day 5 October.

Aymer de la Chevalerie, Henriette French co-foundress of the Picpus Sisters, born Château de la Chevalerie, Poitou, 23 November 1767, died Paris, 23 November 1834. Of a royal family, she and her mother were imprisoned during the Revolution for giving asylum to two priests. Upon her release she joined an association of pious laywomen in Poitiers, and was prevailed upon by her spiritual director, Abbé Couchin, to co-found the Sisters of the Sacred Heart and Perpetual Adoration, in 1797. Henriette acted as superior, and the congregation received papal recognition in 1817. The community moved to Paris in 1804, taking up residence in Rue Picpus, and expanded its apostolate to include the religious education of children along with perpetual adoration of the Blessed Sacrament.

Aymer de Lusignan Bishop of Winchester, date and place of birth unknown, died Paris 4 December 1260. The younger son of Dabella, widow of King John, and Hugh X, count of La Marche; half-brother to Henry III of England, who secured for him the see of Winchester in 1250, where he apparently spent the revenues extravagantly. He opposed, with other bishops, Henry's taxation of clerical revenues and, in 1253, he, ironically, pressed the king to allow free episcopal elections. He and his brother were obliged by the barons to flee England when he opposed the political reforms outlined in the Provisions of Oxford, 1258, which expulsion was justified to the Pope by the barons, who maintained that the Lusignan brothers had harmed the Crown by their irresponsibility, and their return would never be tolerated by the populace.

Azariah, Vendanayagam Samuel First Indian Anglican bishop, born Vellalanvilai, Tirunelveli, South India, 17 August 1874, died Dornakal, 1 January 1945. A gifted evangelist, he served as a YMCA secretary from 1895 to 1905, and founded the Indian Missionary Society in 1903. At the Edinburgh Missionary Conference in 1910 he challenged Western missionaries for their lack of friendship. In 1912 he became bishop of Dornakal. Some 200,000 joined the Church under his ministry. He worked for a united Indian Church from 1919, and was chair of the National Christian Council of India. He attended meetings of Faith and Order (Lausanne, 1927), Life and Work (Oxford, 1937) and the International Missionary Council (Tambaram, 1938). The Church of South India, formed in 1947, was a fruit of his leadership.

Azeglio, Massimo Taparelli d' Italian statesman and author, born Turin, 24 October 1798, died Turin, 15 January 1866. Descended from an ancient and noble family in the Piedmont, he produced two historical novels, pointing out the evils of foreign domination in Italy, and seeking to reawaken national feeling. He studied the political situation in the Romagna, and in 1846 wrote his famous pamphlet *Degli ultimi casi di Romagna*, in which he espoused the cause of a united Italy under the House of Savoy, in consequence of which he was expelled from Turin and Tuscany. He returned to Rome, enthused over the supposed liberalism of the new pope, **Pius IX**, and an Italian confederation under his auspices, opposed the radical wing of the Liberal party, and founded the

moderate, progressive Concordia party that upheld social and political morality, and the triumph of legality. He served as envoy to Rome, Paris and London in 1859; Cavour appointed him governor of Milan in 1860.

Azevedo, Ignacio de Blessed, Portuguese Jesuit missionary, born Oporto, 1527, martyred off the Canary Islands, 15 July 1570. He joined the Society in 1548, and became rector of the college at Braga before Francis Borgia, the general, appointed him visitor to the Jesuit missions in Brazil. Finding the missions flourishing, but short of manpower, he returned to Europe to recruit volunteers, and inspired 69 Spanish and Portuguese to come with him to Brazil. They sailed in two groups in 1570, but a Huguenot corsair, commanded by Jacques Sourie, captured them at sea, brutally slaughtered Ignacio and 39 companions on the *Santiago*, and threw their bodies into the ocean. They were beatified by **Pius IX** in 1854. Feast day 15 July.

Azevedo, Luiz de Portuguese Jesuit missionary, born Canazzedo, Montenegro, 1573, died Dambea, Ethiopia, 22 February 1634. He entered the Society in 1588, went to India in 1592 as master of novices at Goa and rector of the college at Thana. In 1605 he went as missionary to Ethiopia and made many converts among the Agaus, from the Church of Ethiopia. Later, however, when his fellow missionaries were forced to leave the country, many of his converts returned to their former allegiance; he was too infirm to leave Ethiopia and died there. He translated into Ethiopic the NT, a catechism, and instructions on the Apostle's Creed, and compiled an Ethiopic grammar.

Azor, Juan Spanish Jesuit moral theologian, born Lorca, 1535; died Rome, 19 February 1603. He taught extensively in Spain and Rome, and served on the committee that drafted *Ratio Studiorum*, the programme of studies for Jesuit institutions, which led him to write *Institutiones morales* (1600–11), a new type of moral treatise in which the basic division followed that of the commandments, not the virtues. It is considered the forerunner of modern manuals of moral theology, and **Bossuet** considered it unique in its class.

B

Baader, Franz Xaver von German Catholic social philosopher and theologian, born Munich, 27 March 1765, died Munich, 23 May 1841. He studied at Ingolstadt, Vienna and Freiburg. While residing in England and Scotland, 1792–6, he became acquainted with the works of Jakob **Böhme**, whose mystical speculation, and that of Meister **Eckhart**, were in harmony with his own thoughts on problems affecting society. He returned to Hamburg in 1796 and met Friedrich **Schelling**, by whom he was influenced, and whom, in turn, he influenced. Baader was opposed to any ethical system that does not see man's end as the realization in himself of the divine life, and to any atheistic, or secularist, concept of the State; he vigorously affirmed the need for religion and morality in society. Although he alienated Schelling with his views, Baader exerted much influence through the development of a corporative social structure based upon principles of authority, hierarchy, subordination and status. His corporativist ideas became the stuff of European social thought, and he may be considered the founder of German Catholic social teaching, a pioneer among those who strove to interest the Church and its clergy in modern social problems.

Babington, Thomas Member of Parliament, banker, philanthropist and abolitionist, born 18 December 1758, died 21 November 1837. Educated at Rugby and St John's, Cambridge, he also studied law at Lincoln's Inn. Sheriff for Leicester 1780–1, he served as MP for the same city 1800–18. Marrying a sister of Zachary Macaulay, he identified himself fully with the interests of the Clapham Sect, assisting William **Wilberforce** in the prep-aration of his case against the slave trade, and joining him in Commons lobbies on this issue, but not to the detriment of his own concern to alleviate the condition of the poor at home. He became a director of the Sierra Leone Company in 1805 and campaigned for the opening up of India to missionaries. His considerable wealth was deployed through a large range of philanthropic societies.

Babits, Mihaly Hungarian poet and man of letters, born Szekszard, 23 October 1883, died Budapest, 5 August 1941. He studied at the Cistercian Gymnasium, Pecs, and the University of Budapest, where he taught Latin and Hungarian from 1905. He published an important work, *Recitative* (1916), a collection of highly intellectual, largely impersonal poems; a translation of **Dante**'s *Divina Commedia* (1940); three autobiographical novels revealing the conflicting aspirations of an intellectual in his search for God and the meaning of life; a history of European literature (1935), in which, as a Catholic humanist, he emphasizes the Christian foundations of European culture.

Bach, Johann Christian German composer, born Leipzig, 5 September 1735, died London, 1 January 1782. The eleventh son of Johann Sebastian **Bach**, he studied with his brother Emanuel in Berlin after his father's death, and with Padre Martini in Bologna. While organist at Milan Cathedral, 1760–2, he wrote two Masses, a 'Requiem', a 'Te Deum', and other works. Having gained a reputation as a composer of opera, in 1762 he was invited to the King's Theatre in London, where his dramatic works were received with great cordiality. Appointed music master to Queen Charlotte, he became the most popular musician in England. He had converted to Catholicism while in Italy, resented by his brothers in a family that had always been Lutheran, and adhered to his new faith in Protestant England for the rest of his life. His copious works in the late baroque idiom influenced the boy Mozart, who visited Christian in London; though elegant and pleasing, his works were ephemeral in character and have been mostly forgotten.

Bach, Johann Sebastian Lutheran composer, born Eisenach, Thuringia, 21 March 1685, died Leipzig, 28 July 1750. He was orphaned by the age of ten, and was looked after by his elder brother Johann Christoph, who was the organist at Ohrdurf and taught him to play both the organ and the clavier. He trained in the choir schools of Ohrdurf and Lüneburg. He was given an appointment at court in Weimar in 1703, but the following year moved to Arnstadt as organist. He went to Mühlhausen in 1707, and returned to the ducal court at Weimar the following year. He stayed there for nine years but fell out with the duke and moved into the service of Prince Leopold of Anhalt-Cöthen, at Cöthen. In 1723 he returned finally to Leipzig. His *St Matthew Passion* and *St John Passion* are considered by many the greatest works of their kind. His *B Minor Mass* was written for the Roman Catholic Church, but not intended for liturgical performance. His music is much inspired by Lutheran chorales and his harmonizations of over 300 of these chorales continue to be used. Not all of his vast output of music, most of it for the Church, survives. He married twice. By his cousin Maria Bach, whom he married in 1707, he had seven children of whom, by her death in 1720, three had already died. Two years later he married Anna Magdalena Wilken, herself an accomplished musician, by whom he had thirteen children. By the time of his death he was almost completely blind, but continued to compose, his last, unfinished, work being *The Art of Fugue.*

Bach, Joseph German theologian, born Aislingen, Bavaria, 4 March 1833, died Munich, 22 September 1901. Ordained in 1856, he taught pedagogy and philosophy at Munich and, after the suppression of the philosophical faculty in 1888, apologetics and the history of dogma. His major work,

Die Dogmengeschichte des Mittelalters (1873–5), is still very useful; other works include *Meister Eckhart* (1864).

Bacha, Constantine Lebanese historian of the Melchite Church, born Batroun, 3 February 1870, died Holy Saviour Monastery, Saida, 12 October 1948. After studies at Holy Saviour Seminary, he joined the Salvatorians in 1893. He did much research in foreign libraries, especially Rome and Paris, and his greatest work, *History of the Catholic Melchite Community and the Salvatorian Order* (1945), is acclaimed as the authoritative source in its field. This and other manuscripts gathered by him, as well as those he translated or composed, are preserved in the archives of the library of the Holy Saviour Monastery.

Bachem, Julius German lawyer and politician, born Mülheim, 2 July 1845, died Cologne, 22 January 1918. He managed a publishing house and a printing press in 1869, taken over by his uncle Joseph, which produced the *Kölnische Volkszeitung*. With the historian Hermann Cardamus, he made the newspaper the most important voice of Catholicism in Germany. He wrote many political tracts in which he argued for a more equitable respect of citizens' rights, especially for northern German Catholics during the Kulturkampf. Elected, as a member of the (Catholic) Centre party, to the Prussian Parliament (Landtag) in 1876, he regarded the Centre party as political rather than denominational, and attempted to win non-Catholics to its ranks. As a founding member of the Görres-Gesellschaft, and through publication of the *Staatslexikon*, he contributed to the advancement and improvement of Catholic journalism.

Bachiarius Spanish monk and theologian, born probably Galicia, Spain, *c.*350, died, date and place unknown. He admired Priscillian, condemned for heresy by the councils of Saragossa in 380, and had to leave Spain the same year. He went to Rome and wrote two books, *Libellus fidei*, a defence of his orthodoxy, and *De reparatione lapsi*, an appeal to 'brothers' for clemency toward a sin of the flesh by a monk, in which he gave an excellent presentation of the Spanish penitential system at that time. He commented on the Incarnation, the Trinity and the perpetual virginity of Mary in clear and orthodox texts.

Backer, Augustine de Belgian Jesuit bibliographer, born Antwerp, 18 July 1809, died Liège, 1 December 1873. Ordained in the Society at Louvain in 1843, he remained there and continued the bibliography of writings by Jesuits, published by Pedro de **Ribadaneira** in 1608 and 1613, by Philippe de Alegambe, and by Nathaniel Southwell in 1676. With the collaboration of his brother Alois, he published the colossal *Bibliothèque des écrivains de la Compagnie de Jésus*, 7 vols, 1853–61. A second edition, containing the names of 11,000 Jesuit writers, was broader in scope, and cited important information of a personal and professional nature. Backer died before the edition could be published, but Alois brought it out three years later.

Backus, Isaac Eighteenth-century North American Baptist pastor, theologian and writer on religious liberty, born Norwich, Connecticut, 9 January 1724, died Middleborough, MA, 20 November 1806. He has been characterized as adopting the new evangelical Calvinist theology of Jonathan **Edwards** and the evangelistic methods of George **Whitefield**, both within a Baptist and voluntarist form of churchmanship, rejecting the established Congregationalism in which he was brought up. He was later imprisoned for refusing both to pay church taxes and to give service as a delegate to the Massachusetts Convention. His writings on Church–State relations were much influenced by John Locke. Baptized as a believer in 1751, he served as pastor of a congregation he had gathered at Middlesborough from 1756 until his death.

Bacon, David William American bishop, born Brooklyn, New York, 15 September 1813, died New York City, 5 November 1874. He studied at the Sulpician College, Montreal, and following ordination in 1838, and service in parishes in New York and New Jersey, was assigned to Brooklyn to organize a new parish; he became bishop of Portland, Maine, in 1855. He met the needs of a diocese, which included Maine and New Hampshire, with help from Jesuits and priests from Quebec, who ministered to Franco-Americans in northern Maine; educational and charitable needs were met by the Sisters of Mercy. He built the cathedral of the Immaculate Conception, and his diocese included 52 priests, and some 80,000, mainly Irish- and Franco-Americans, at his death.

Bacon, Francis English philosopher and statesman (Baron Verulam, Viscount St Albans), born London, 22 January 1561, died London, 9 April 1626. He studied at Cambridge, entered Parliament in 1584, and became lord chancellor in 1618. His main philosophical work lay in science, where he concluded that the methods employed in its teaching, as well as the results attained, were alike erroneous; a new method must be devised, and this was to be empiricism: the acquisition of sure and useful knowledge by the method of induction. Because of his stress on induction, Bacon has been hailed as the 'prophet' of 'experimental discovery'. He divided knowledge (philosophy) into 'divine' philosophy, to establish the existence of God as presupposed by the existence and character of the natural world, for which we must depend on revelation for knowledge of God's nature, action and purposes; and 'human' philosophy, the study of man and society, to be carried out in the same inductible way as the study of non-human nature; and maintained that every event has a cause. In this strict separation of the study of nature from the study of the divine, he directly opposed the Thomist doctrine of seeking knowledge of the supernatural through the natural. Most of the works relating to his major enterprise, *Instauratio Magna*, i.e. restoration to mankind of dominion over the universe that was lost with the Fall of Man, were published from 1620 onwards. The Royal Society owed much to Bacon's ideas and principles. The French Enlightenment recognized him as the originator of scientific advance, and Scottish philosophers praised him in the nineteenth century. He has not appealed so well to philosophers of the twentieth century, sceptical that the inductible method yields certain knowledge, and regarding induction only as a species of probability. Bacon's greatness, however, lies in 'the grandeur of his prophetic vision of science in the service of mankind and the transmission, through his writings, of his zest for, and delight in, the whole realm of learning'.

Bacon, Roger English Franciscan philosopher,

born near Ilchester, Somerset, *c.*1214, died Oxford, 11 June 1294. He studied at Oxford, and from about 1234 at the University of Paris, where he became doctor of theology, and seems to have received the complimentary title of *doctor mirabilis*. In 1250 he was again at Oxford, where his fame spread; about 1257, **Bonaventure**, general of the Franciscans, doubtful of his orthodoxy, forbade Bacon to lecture at Oxford, and placed him under supervision for ten years in Paris. However, in 1266, **Clement IV**, who had been papal legate in England, ordered him to dispatch to Rome 'without delay' an account in writing of his doctrines, which he did, in three large treatises: *Opus majus*, *Opus minus* and *Opus tertium*, outlining, in forceful terms, the causes which had hindered the progress of philosophy in the Church, and weakened Western Christendom in its struggle against Islam; he also stressed the importance of language in understanding the Bible and the value of mathematics, optics, the natural sciences and moral philosophy. We do not know Clement's opinion of the treatises, but in 1268 Bacon was allowed to return to England. In 1271, he published the first part of an encyclopaedic work *Compendium Studii Philosophiae*, in which he makes a vehement attack upon the ignorance and vices of the clergy and monks, and generally upon the insufficiency of existing studies. In 1278 his books were condemned by Jerome de Ascoli, general of the Franciscans, and he himself imprisoned for fourteen years. Roger Bacon occupies a unique place in the history of the thirteenth century. His *œuvre* constitutes a revision of the Scholastic movement at its apogee, and a programme which announces the humanist renaissance; he proposed to the Church a doctrinal direction and a new method. Taking up the concepts of St **Augustine** on civilization, Bacon pursues one goal: to restore to the Bible primacy in the intellectual life of the Church, to found on the Church the entire Christian civilization, and thereby reserve to the Holy See the moral and political direction of the world. The Bible, not the *Sentences* of **Peter Lombard**, nor the summas of the Scholastics, must be the basis of all teaching. To interpret it without error, all branches of learning must be employed: philology, the study of Greek and Semitic languages; the sacred texts must be edited and read in their original voice; the Latin versions and especially the Vulgate should be

revised according to this method. He was important above all for his rejection of blind obedience to received authority, maintaining that the Church's teaching would prevail only if it could command the support of a scientific approach, of textual criticism and of a positive theology of modern times. In an age particularly rich in great men, Roger Bacon is now considered worthy to be placed beside **Albert the Great**, Bonaventure and **Thomas Aquinas**.

Badet, Arnold French Dominican and mystical theologian, born Limoux, *c.*1475, died Toulouse, 1536. He spent most of his career in Languedoc, around Toulouse, where he forged a reputation as preacher and teacher, and of which region he became Inquisitor in 1531. This appointment, and his asssociation with Jean Caturce and other French humanists, led to his denunciation by fellow Dominicans to the Parlement of Toulouse for heresy, but he successfully refuted the charges, and remained Inquisitor. Among his writings is the notable *Destructorium haeresium* (1532).

Badia, Tommaso Italian theologian and cardinal, born Modena, 1483; died Rome, 6 September 1547. He became Master of the Sacred Palace in 1523, following many years of teaching theology at Ferrara, Venice and Boulogne, and known for his knowledge and zeal. Undaunted in his desire to preserve the integrity of the faith, he was strict in condemning error, but lenient with regard to individuals. From 1536 he belonged to the reform group of Cardinal **Contarini** and, as master of the Sacred Palace, intervened decisively for confirmation of the Society of Jesus in 1529. Created cardinal in 1542, he helped prepare the Council of Trent and, though not in attendance, he intervened from Rome even in the discussion on justification. His writings have not been published.

Badin, Stephen Theodore French missionary, born Orléans, 17 July 1768, died Cincinnati, Ohio, 19 April 1853. He went to the USA in 1792, and became the first priest ordained there, at St Mary's seminary, Baltimore, the following year. He served as vicar-general to the scattered Catholics of Kentucky, Ohio, Indiana, Illinois, Michigan and Tennessee, usually alone, and with never more than six priests to help him. He joined the Cincinnati diocese in 1826 and worked with the Pottawatomie Indian mission in Indiana, founded the first orphan asylum near South Bend, and bought the land for the university at Notre Dame. His writings include religious tracts, Latin poems and books on Catholic doctrine. His missionary labours spanned 60 years in frontier territory, and justifiably earned him the title 'Apostle of Kentucky'. In 1906, his remains were translated to Notre Dame, where they are conserved in the 'Log Chapel', an exact replica of an ancient oratory where he had often gathered his Indian followers.

Bagshaw, Christopher English controversialist, born Lichfield, c.1552, died Paris, c.1625. He studied at Oxford, went to Paris in 1582, converted to Catholicism, and studied at the English College, Rome, but was expelled as 'unwilling to take the oath'. He acquired a doctorate at Padua and returned to England in 1587 'to make converts'; captured on landing, he was imprisoned in the Tower for six years, then Wisbech Castle, where he came into conflict with the Jesuits, against whom his writings show unrelenting animosity. Freed in 1601, he returned as rector of the Ave Maria college in Paris; a controversial figure, difficult to friends and irreconcilable to the Jesuits.

Bagster, Samuel (father) Baptist Bible publisher, born London, 26 December 1772, died Windsor, 28 March 1851. He began his career in the Strand, London, as a general bookseller, but saw an opportunity to produce Bibles in languages other than English (English Bibles being a limited monopoly), beginning with a Hebrew Bible, and continuing with an edition of the Septuagint. In 1816 he brought out 'the English version of the Polyglot bible' which, having notes, evaded the rules of the monopoly. His fame was as publisher of polyglot Bibles, and of other Bible aids which he was successful in popularizing, work taken over by his sons Samuel **Bagster** and Jonathan. It was Jonathan who took over his father's firm. Bagster moved his firm in 1816 to Paternoster Row, and in 1841 published *The English Hexapla* containing six English versions of the NT.

Bagster, Samuel (son) Baptist publisher, son of the above, born London, 19 October 1800, died London, 1 July 1835. He was apprenticed to his father in 1815, and set up independently as a printer in London in 1824, printing many of his father's publications, and himself contributing *The Treasury of Scripture Knowledge* in 1834: his other two publications were both on bees.

Baillie, John Scottish theologian, born Gairloch Wester Ross, 26 March 1886; died Edinburgh, 29 September 1960. He studied philosophy at Edinburgh and theology at New College, a seminary of the United Free Church. He taught for some years in Canada and the USA from 1934, and then became professor of divinity at Edinburgh and principal of New College; students came to him from all over the world. Moderator of the Church of Scotland in 1943, and elected joint president of the World Council of Churches from 1954. In his many publications, including *The Idea of Revelation in Recent Thought* (1956) and *The Sense of the Presence of God* (Gifford Lectures, 1961–2), he showed literary grace, loyalty to a Christian faith much indebted to Calvinism, and a middle way between philosophical and theological extremes. He welcomed Barthianism, but reserved his position in *Invitation to Pilgrimage* (1942) and *A Diary of Private Prayer* (1936).

His brother, **Donald Macpherson Baillie**, *born 1887, died 1954, was equally distinguished as preacher, theologian and ecumenical statesman. He taught systematic theology at St Mary's college, St Andrews, from 1934 until his death, and published God Was in Christ (1948), for which he won international acclaim with his imaginative use of the Pauline 'paradox of grace' to illuminate Christology. Like his brother, Donald acknowledged his debt to the Calvinist faith and his Highland upbringing. He had a high regard for the Student Christian Movement and the Iona Community.*

Bailly, Vincent de Paul French Assumptionist and journalist, born Berteaucourt-les-Thennes, 2 December 1832, died Paris, 2 December 1912. He benefited from a strong Christian heritage at home – his grandfather had preserved the MSS of St **Vincent de Paul** during the Revolution, and his uncle and future mother had transported the body of the saint to Paris for interment – and this no doubt influenced his vocation. Ordained an Assumptionist at Rome in 1863, Vincent, like his father, who had been one of the founders of the

Conférences St Vincent de Paul, also was a versatile and dynamic worker, a founder of many societies, an organizer of pilgrimages, the first for lay people to La Salette, Lourdes and Paray-le-Monial. In 1876 he directed *Le Pélerin*, the journal devoted to promoting the pilgrimages; in 1883 he founded the Catholic daily paper *La Croix*, and a score of other publications connected with them. When the Assumptionists were suppressed in France in 1899, he went to Rome and, having founded houses in Belgium and England, returned to Paris in 1906, as assistant general of the congregation until his death.

Bainbridge, Christopher English cardinal and servant of **Henry VIII**, born Hilton, near Appleby, Westmorland, *c*.1463; died Rome, 13/14 July 1514. Educated at Oxford, Ferrara and Bologna, appointed bishop of Durham, 1507, archbishop of York, 1508. Henry sent him as his ambassador to the Roman curia in 1509, and he was papal legate in Italy in 1511; **Julius II** made him a cardinal. Bainbridge, like Henry, was anti-French, and an intense rivalry developed between him and Silvestre Gigli, bishop of Worcester, resident ambassador at Rome, who was pro-French, and who informed Julius in 1511 of Henry's adherence to the Holy League against France. Bainbridge was poisoned by one of his chaplains, who accused Gigli of having put him up to the murder for motives of rivalry. Bainbridge proved himself a courageous defender of English interests at the curia, and is buried in what has become the English College.

Baines, Edward Journalist and advocate of the Nonconformist Conscience, born Walton-le-Dale, 5 February 1774, died London, 3 August 1848. Having been educated at Hawkshead and Preston Grammar Schools, he was apprenticed to a local stationer. From 1795 he worked in Leeds. In 1801 he became the proprietor of the *Leeds Mercury*, a newspaper which he used to advocate Liberal and Nonconformist principles, particularly the separation of Church and State, educational voluntarism and temperance. A staunch Congregationalist, he created a family dynasty which had a considerable influence on the life of Leeds throughout the Victorian period. Served as MP for Leeds, 1834–41. His published works include *Topography of Yorkshire and Lancashire*.

Baines, Sir Edward Member of Parliament and publisher, born Leeds, 28 May 1800, died Burley, Hampshire, 2 March 1890. The son of the older Edward **Baines**, who had migrated from Unitarianism to Congregationalism, the younger Edward was a Sunday School teacher from the age of fifteen (when he also began assisting his father on the *Leeds Mercury*) but retired from the superintendency on his election as MP for Leeds in 1859, he represented the city until 1874. He made the family newspaper one of the 'authoritative organs' of the Liberal Party, and his *History of the Cotton Industry of Great Britain* (1835) remains a standard text. An advocate of free trade and self-improvement, he opposed the Corn Laws and supported Catholic Emancipation. A strong supporter of Sunday Schools, he became convinced that voluntary endeavour could never meet the nation's needs and in 1867 reluctantly but publicly changed sides, still insisting on proper controls of any extension of State activity.

Baines, Henry Wolfe Anglican bishop of Singapore and Wellington, born England, 7 February 1905, died Wellington, New Zealand, 29 November 1972. Educated at Repton, Oxford (Balliol), and at Cuddleston, he was a Student Christian Movement Travelling Secretary (1927–9), ordained deacon in 1930 and priest in 1931. He was chaplain at St John's Cathedral in Hong Kong (1934–8), vicar of St Nicholas Radford, Coventry (1938–41) and then rector of Rugby. He married Elizabeth Bartlett in 1944 and in 1949 was consecrated bishop of Singapore. During the Malayan Emergency, Baines was noted for his ecumenical commitment and encouragement of local clergy. In 1960 he became bishop of Wellington, New Zealand. He visited South Vietnam in 1971 and opposed rugby tours to South Africa under apartheid. Of imposing stature and gracious manner, he had a good voice and was known as a person of prayer as well as a listener.

Baines, Peter Augustine English Benedictine bishop. Born Kirkby, Lancashire, 25 January 1787; died Prior Park, Bath, 6 July 1843. Educated at the monastery of Lampspring, Germany, and by the Benedictines at Ampleforth, where he held many important offices, he took charge of their mission at Bath in 1817, and succeeded Bishop Collingridge as vicar apostolic of the Western District in 1829. Baines wanted to establish a seminary, but this was opposed by the Benedictines at Downside, and the matter was only finally resolved when Baines and four others left the Order and put the plan into effect at Prior Park, a mansion which he purchased. Baines had hoped for a Catholic university for lay students as well as clerics, but Prior Park never achieved that goal.

Baini, Giuseppe   Italian priest, musical critic and composer, born Rome, 2 October 1775, died Rome, 21 May 1844. Instructed in composition by his uncle Lorenzo Baini, he had a fine bass voice and was appointed musical director to the choir of the pontifical chapel in 1814. His compositions were noted specimens of the severe ecclesiastical style; one, a ten-part 'Miserere', composed for Holy Week in 1821 by order of **Pius VII**, has a permanent place in the Sistine Chapel services for Passion week. Baini held a higher place, however, as a musical critic and historian than as a composer; his life of **Palestrina** (1828) ranks as one of the best works in its class, and gave impetus to renewed scholarship and performances of Palestrina's works.

Bainvel, Jean Vincent   French Jesuit theologian, born Plougonmelen, 4 August 1858, died Paris, 29 January 1937. He taught fundamental theology at the Institut Catholique de Paris for 25 years from 1900, becoming in 1924 the first dean of the faculty of theology. Challenged by the modernist crisis, he defended the traditional; he was, however, attentive to the difficulties that arose and trained his collaborators to face up to their resolution. Other than his courses in Latin, he published two classic works: *La foi et l'acte de foi* (1908), and *Nature et surnaturel* (1920). Still popular today, because of the happy alliance of theology and spirituality, are two works published in 1919: *La dévotion au Sacré-Cœur de Jésus*, and *Le Saint Cœur de Marie*. He preached numerous retreats to priests and religious, and his spiritual direction bore much fruit.

Baius   see Bay, Michel de

Baker, David Augustine   Benedictine monk and chaplain, born Abergavenny, Wales, 9 December 1575, died London, 9 August 1641. After becoming a Benedictine he spent some time doing pastoral work in England before he moved to the Continent. He began working with some English nuns in Cambrai in 1624 and then moved on to the English monastery in Douai in 1633. It was during his stay on the Continent that he wrote most of his literature. In 1638 he returned to England to continue his work. He wrote mostly on matters of spirituality and his work was finally condensed after his death into a single volume called *Sancta Sophia* (1657), the English translation being *Holy Wisdom*.

Baker, Elizabeth V.   Pentecostal healer and educator, born *c*.1849, died 1915. Following a religious experience at a temperance lecture in Ohio, she several years later embraced faith healing after being cured of a throat condition. With her sisters, in 1895 she opened the Elim Faith Home in Rochester, New York, which was followed by the Elim Publishing House, Elim Tabernacle, and in 1906 the Rochester Bible Training School. In 1907, following news of the Welsh and Azusa Street Revivals, the Baker sisters began their own revival. The Baker sisters produced a magazine, *Trust* (from 1902), and a book, *Chronicles of a Faith Life* (2nd edition *c*.1926).

Baker, Francis Asbury   Paulist missionary, born Baltimore, USA, 30 March 1820, died New York City, 4 April 1865. In 1846 he was ordained as a Methodist minister and served at both St Paul's and St Luke's in Baltimore. He came under the influence of the Oxford Movement and resigned his pulpit. In 1853 he converted to Catholicism and joined the Redemptorist community. In 1856 he was ordained and joined four other American Redemptorist converts (George **Deshon**, Isaac **Hecker**, Augustine **Hewit** and Clarence Walworth) in missionary work on home soil. In 1858 he was released from his Redemptorist vows and joined with Deshon, Hecker and Hewit to form the Society of Missionary Priests of St Paul the Apostle (the Paulists).

Baker, H. A.   Pentecostal missionary in Asia, born 1881, died Taiwan, 1971. Baker attended Hiram College and began his pastorate for the Christian Church in Buffalo in 1909. In the same year he married Josephine Witherstay and in 1912 the couple became missionaries in Tibet. Five years later they became independent Pentecostal missionaries in China. After the revolution the Bakers worked with the Navajo, before moving to Taiwan. His books include *God in Ka Do Land* (1937), *Visions Beyond the Veil* (*c.*1938), and *Tribulation to Glory* (*c.*1951), as well as his autobiography, *Plains of Glory and Gloom* (n.d.), and a series of booklets on his ministry, *The Adullum News*.

Baker, Sir Henry Hymn editor, born Vauxhall, Lambeth, Surrey, on 27 May 1820, died Monkland, 12 February 1877. He was educated at Cambridge, took holy orders and succeeded to his father's baronetcy. He was the chairman of the editorial committee of *Hymns Ancient and Modern*, editing the texts of existing hymns, and contributing his own hymns and translations. His popular hymns include 'The King of Love My Shepherd Is' and 'O Praise Ye the Lord'.

Baker, Moses Ex-slave leader of Native Baptists in Jamaica, born British North America, 1758, died Jamaica, 1826. He escaped from America via New York to arrive in 1783 in Jamaica, where under the influence of George Liele he, with his wife, was baptized as a believer. He sought the help of Drs Rippon and Ryland of England for the slaves of Jamaica, leading to the sending out of John Rowe in 1814, the first British Baptist missionary to Jamaica. Later, though supported by Baptists and Moravians, he came under suspicion from missionaries in the mainstream societies, though he was in fact an orthodox evangelical believer. The Native Baptist movement, however, suffered from a paucity of educated leadership

Baker, Nelson Henry Roman Catholic priest, born Buffalo, USA, 16 February 1841, died Lackawanna, USA, 29 July 1936. Ordained in 1876, serving firstly as an assistant pastor in Lackawanna and then as a curate in Corning. He returned to Lackawanna in 1882 to take over the institution that later became Our Lady of Victory Homes of Charity. He was recognized by the Church by firstly becoming the vicar-general of the Buffalo diocese and then being made a domestic prelate (1902 and 1905 respectively). Later he was raised to the rank of protonotary apostolic. Our Lady of Victory included an orphanage, an industrial school, a maternity hospital and a home for infants, and aided many under Baker's leadership.

Bakhita, Josephine Blessed, Catholic nun, born southern Sudan, *c.*1869, died Schio, Italy, 8 February 1947. Kidnapped and enslaved as a child, she was eventually sold in 1883 to an Italian family, who took her home to care for their daughter. In Italy, with the support of the Church, she was declared free, was baptized on 9 January 1890 and joined the Daughters of Charity. She was considered holy during her life. The people of her town prayed for her protection during World War II and Schio was spared bomb damage, as she had promised. She was beatified on 17 May 1992. Feast day 17 May.

Bakócz, Tamás Prince primate of Hungary and cardinal, born Erdoed, Szatmar, 1442, died 15 June 1521. Educated in Hungary, Poland and Italy (where he received his doctor's degree) and fond of the arts. In 1470 he became a friend and confidant to King Matthias of Hungary. He became cardinal in 1500 and ten years later was the titular Patriarch of Constantinople. He was very influential and involved in Hungary's affairs of State and also participated in the general Roman synod's committee for the reform of the Church in 1512. After failing to be elected Pope the next year he was appointed the legate *a latere* for Hungary and after a violent but failed peasant revolt (instigated by the gentry) retired in 1516.

Balassa, Bálint Roman Catholic soldier-poet, born Kékkó, Hungary, 1551, died Esztergom, 26 May 1594. A somewhat controversial and excitable character, he would fluctuate between behaving as a saint and being involved in court cases for various felonies and incest. In 1584 he married Christine Dobó, who happened to be his cousin, but the marriage had only lasted for two years when his conversion to Catholicism nullified the arrangement. In 1594, while involved in fighting at Esztergom, he translated Edmund **Campion**'s defence of the Catholic faith, *Decem Rationes*. It was during this battle that he was fatally wounded. He wrote many poems: religious, martial and about love. He also invented new verse forms.

Balbi, Girolamo Bishop and humanist, born Venice, 1450, died 1535. Studied belles-lettres and jurisprudence at various schools in Italy. Took a lecturing post in the humanities at the University of Paris (1489). He became involved with the local humanists (Publio Fausto **Andrelini** and William Tardiff especially) and ended up exchanging angry diatribes with them. Leaving France suddenly he went to Germany for a short time and then moved to England. His argumentative nature resulted in him moving from a new post in Vienna to Prague. It was after he left Prague that he was ordained and climbed the ecclesiological hierarchy moving from Hungary to Austria and back to Italy. He wrote much but his best was on the culture of Renaissance Europe.

Balbin, Bohuslav Jesuit historian, born Königgrätz (Hradec Králové), 4 December 1621, died Prague, 29 November 1688. He became a Jesuit in 1636 and taught at Prague and elsewhere until 1662, when he gave his full attention to the study of Bohemian history. He was banished from Prague by the Habsburgs and became physically paralysed in 1683. His vast number of works include *Dispuattio apologetica pro lingua slavonica, praecipue bohemica* in defence of the Bohemian language threatened by the Habsburgs, *Miscellanea historica regni Bohemiae* on the history of Bohemia, and *Epitome rerum bohemicarum seu historia Boleslaviensis*, published in 1775, 1679–88 and 1677 respectively.

Balbo, Cesare Roman Catholic historian and statesman, born Turin, Italy, 21 November 1789, died Turin, 3 June 1853. As the son of an ambassador to France, he was influenced by the French Revolution. From 1807 to 1814 he took on various positions for the Napoleonic regime in Italy and from 1824 to 1848 he dedicated himself to Italian history. Generally a supporter of the Papacy despite his ideas. In his work *Le speranze d'Italia* (1844) he put himself firmly in the camp that wanted independence for Italy, but his refusal to accept the suggestion that the Pope could govern the country as well as the Church resulted in the book being frowned upon by Catholics.

Balboa, Miguel Cabello de Roman Catholic priest, born Málaga, Spain, 1530, died 1608. He spent much of his life travelling, but found time to write and minister to his parish at the same time. After an early career as a soldier he was ordained in 1571, and in 1572 took part in exploratory expeditions to Chocó and Quijos. In 1576 he began to write his *Miscelánea antártica* and then began travelling again the next year. During the rest of his life he finished the *Miscelánea* and visited many places including Lima, Lambayeque, Túcume, Ica, Trujillo and the jungle in upper Peru. He was also present at the Third Council of Lima.

Balde, Jakob Jesuit poet, born Ensisheim, Alsace, 4 January 1604, died Neuburg, 9 August 1668. Having studied the classics, rhetoric, law and philosophy, he entered the Society of Jesus in 1624, after which he began a teaching career in Munich, Innsbruck and (after his ordination in 1633) Ingolstadt. He was so successful that he was summoned to teach the children of Duke Albert of Bavaria, who also made Balde his historian and court preacher. In 1650 he moved to Landshut and then Amburg, but in 1654 his failing health caused him to settle in Neuburg as court preacher to Count Philip Wilhelm. Many of his poems were translated by **Herder** including *Carmina lyrica* and *Silvae*.

Baldi, Donato Italian Franciscan and biblical topographer, born Montevettolini, Pistoia, 28 March 1888, died Jerusalem, 15 February 1965. Educated at Fribourg and at the Ecole Biblique in Jerusalem. He taught biblical geography and topography at the Studium Biblicum Franciscanum from 1927 until his death, apart from the 1940s, which he spent in military service. He was a consultor of the preparatory commission for Vatican II and was made a Knight of SS Maurice and Lazarus and a Knight of the Italian Republic. A prolific writer, he published many books and articles on aspects of the Bible, church history and the Holy Land.

Baldinucci, Antonio Blessed, Jesuit preacher, born Florence, Italy, 19 June 1665, died Pofio, 7 November 1717. He joined the Society of Jesus in 1681 and was ordained in 1695. He desperately wished to become a missionary to India, but his superiors refused him because of his frail health. In 1697 he was sent to Abruzzi and Romagna as a missionary. He spent the rest of his life preaching in a very passionate and dramatic way, often carrying heavy chains or a wooden cross. He would travel to town after town (often barefoot) to preach and would beat himself publicly to convert his hearers. He had tremendous success. His death came after collapsing while ministering to the sick in his parish. In 1893 **Leo XIII** beatified him. Feast day 7 November.

Baldus de Ubaldis Lawyer and canonist, born Perugia, Italy, 1320, died Pavia, 28 April 1400. He studied law at the University of Perugia (under **Bartolo of Sassoferrato**) and graduated about 1344. He moved to Siena and then to Bologna, returning to Perugia in 1351 to take a post at the university. He worked on many doctrines of the Catholic Church and was greatly influential as it faced the Great Schism of the West and the exile of the Roman curia. In 1390 he moved to Pavia to take up another teaching assignment and died ten years later. Apart from his contribution to the canon law of the Catholic Church, he also wrote a commentary on feudal law (*Usus feudorum*).

Baldwin I of Jerusalem King of Jerusalem 1100–18, born Boulogne, 1058, died El Avish, 2 April 1118. His brother **Godfrey of Bouillon** founded the first Crusader principality in Edessa. Baldwin was crowned king of Jerusalem after his brother's death, with the support of his vassals. Despite inheriting a kingdom with terrible economic and military problems he built forts at Toron (Galilee) and Montréal (Shaubak) and extended the kingdom to Ailah on the Gulf of Aqaba. He also occupied the ports of Arsuf, Acre, Beirut, Caesarea and (with the aid of a Norwegian force) Sidon, and resisted Egyptian attacks. He enlisted the support of and rewarded the Genoese, who were influential in helping him secure the above territories.

Baldwin II of Jerusalem King of Jerusalem 1118–31, died Jerusalem, 21 August 1131. The cousin of **Baldwin I** and an experienced Crusader. He was captured in April 1123 and not released until August 1124, but the Venetian fleet he had requested earlier took Tyre in July 1124. He militarized the Knights of Malta and established the Knights Templars. He added more structure to the feudal reign of Jerusalem and was the last of the

original Crusaders. A church council was held at Nablus in 1120 and it was under Baldwin II that the kingdom of Jerusalem was recognized as superior to all the other Crusader provinces and attained a sovereignty that was never to be repeated. In 1128 Baldwin II secured his successor by marrying his daughter to Fulk V of Anjou.

Baldwin III of Jerusalem King of Jerusalem 1143–63, died Beirut, 10 February 1163. The son of Fulk V and Melisend, he was only thirteen when Fulk died; so he and his mother were both crowned. The most troublesome time for his reign was in his early years, when Edessa fell in 1144, the Second Crusade failed and his opponent Nur ed-din rose to prominence. In 1151 Baldwin was made the sole monarch of Jerusalem and in 1153 he successfully captured Ascalon, the last port still held by the Muslims. This was followed by military success against Egypt, but Nur ed-din captured Damascus. Baldwin sought an alliance with Byzantium, and even married the Emperor's daughter, but Emperor Manuel I Comnenus chose to negotiate with Nur ed-din instead. However, the historian William of Tyre saw Baldwin III as the perfect king.

Baldwin IV of Jerusalem King of Jerusalem 1174–85, died Jerusalem, 16 March 1185. Nephew of **Baldwin III** and son of King Amalric I. Like his uncle, he was also thirteen years old when his father died. He was tutored by William of Tyre, the historian who thought so highly of Baldwin III, and showed himself to be a man of great and sharp intelligence. Unfortunately, he contracted leprosy, and his ill-health meant that there were times when he was unable to rule, leading to strife and problems within the court at Jerusalem. Despite his ailment he carried on with his duties as king and showed great strength of character. In 1183 he had his nephew Baldwin V crowned in preparation for his death.

Baldwin of Brandenburg Canonist, born Brandenburg, 1230, died 1275. Baldwin of Brandenburg is a figure about whom little is known. He studied theology in Paris and wrote a brief chronicle of the Franciscan Order. He taught in one of the Franciscan seminaries in Germany, and it was during this time that he wrote a *Summa titulorum* on canon law (between 1265 and 1270), concerned mainly with the practical considerations and questions of such canon law. However, **Hostiensis** had a similar work out already and Baldwin's volume had very little success, despite several sources praising its comprehensiveness and worth in its own right.

Baldwin of Canterbury Cistercian archbishop of Canterbury, born in the Diocese of Exeter, England, date unknown, died Acre, 19 or 20 November 1190. After 1150 he tutored Gratian, nephew of Pope **Innocent II**, in Italy and soon after 1161 was appointed archdeacon of Totnes in England. He supported **Thomas Becket** in his conflict with King Henry II and withdrew to the Cistercian abbey of Ford when the situation was at its worst. In 1180 he became bishop of Worcester and then in 1184 archbishop of Canterbury. He spent time visiting the Welsh Church from 1187 to 1188 and preached the Third Crusade there. His writings include *De commendatione fidei* and *De sacramento altaris*. While he was archbishop of Canterbury he enjoyed the support of King Henry II.

Ball, Frances Mary Teresa Nun and foundress of the Irish branch of the Ladies of Loreto (Institute of the Blessed Virgin Mary), born Dublin, Ireland, 6 January 1794, died Dublin, 19 May 1861. Her wealthy silk weaver father sent her to the Institute of the Blessed Virgin Mary in England for her education. In 1822, with the support of Bishop Daniel Murray of Dublin, she founded Loreto House in Dublin. After the Emancipation of Catholics in 1829 she opened boarding, day and free schools, and in 1841 sent her Sisters to India, where they founded the first Loreto foreign mission. By 1861 there were convents in England, Ireland, Spain, Canada, India, Mauritius and Gibraltar, and by 1900 there were convents in Africa and Australia.

Ball, Henry Cleophas Assemblies of God missionary, born Brooklyn, Iowa, 1896, died 1989. Beginning as a Methodist working with Mexicans in Texas, he experienced a baptism in the Holy Spirit which led him to be ordained in the Assemblies of God in 1915. As superintendent of the Latin American Conference he organized conventions of Hispanic converts and set up indigenous churches. From 1916 he produced the influential magazine *Apostolic Light*, and later a Spanish hymn-book, *Hymns of Glory* (2nd edition 1921). In 1926 he set up the Latin American Bible Institute, for which he provided much of the syllabus. From 1953 he devoted his efforts to producing Spanish literature.

Ball, John Excommunicated priest and leader of the English Peasants' Revolt, died St Albans, 15 July 1381. His excommunication by Archbishop Simon Islip of Canterbury sometime between 1362 and 1366 was confirmed by later archbishops in 1366 and 1376. Arrested in 1381 for continuing to preach and circulating radical literature, he was in prison in Maidstone when the Peasants' Revolt began. He was freed by the revolutionaries and proceeded with them, inciting them to murder nobles and lawyers. As the revolt began to collapse, after **Richard II**'s intervention, he fled and was captured at Coventry. He was tried for treason and executed. He believed in complete social equality and seemed to share some of John **Wycliffe**'s views. He even tried (unsuccessfully) to blame Wycliffe for the revolt.

Ballerini, Antonio Jesuit moral theologian, born Medicina, Italy, 10 October 1805, died Rome, 27 November 1881. In 1826 he entered the Society of Jesus and became professor first of church history and then of moral theology (1844 and 1855 respectively) at the Gregorian University in Rome. He wrote on both church history and moral theology. Amongst his works on moral theology we find *De morali systemate s. Alphonsi M. de Ligorio*, annotations to *Compendium theologiae moralis* and *Opus theologicum morale in Busembaum medullam*, which was completed after his death by D. Palmieri. Ballerini was a firm believer in probabilism, and interpreted some Alphonsian doctrines in a manner that resulted in conflict with some Redemptorists.

Ballerini, Girolamo Roman Catholic scholar and theologian, born Verona, Italy, 29 January 1702, died there, 23 February 1781. Brother of Pietro **Ballerini**, with whom he worked very closely. Son of a surgeon and educated in Verona. He was ordained in 1725 and opposed (with his brother) the Jansenists and the Febronians. Pietro and Girolamo worked on editing patristic works, history and other theologians. This included *S. Zenonis*,

Episcopi Veronensis, sermones; S. Antonini, Archiepiscopi Florentini, Summa Theologica; and *Ratherii, Episcopi Veronensis, opera.* They also organized a new edition of the works of **Leo** the Great, ordered by **Benedict XIV**, and this is still the standard edition.

Ballerini, Pietro Roman Catholic scholar and theologian, born Verona, Italy, 7 September 1698, died there, 28 March 1769. Brother of Girolamo **Ballerini**, with whom he worked very closely. Son of a surgeon and educated in Verona. Ordained in 1722, he then became the head of a classical school in Verona. He wrote a book on usury, parts of which were condemned by **Benedict XIV** in *Vix pervenit.* Apart from the works which he edited with his brother (see above) he also wrote a history of probabilism, *Saggio della storia del probabilismo* (1736); *De vi et ratione primatus Romanorum Pontificum* (1766); and *De potestate ecclesiastica Summorum Pontificum et Conciliorum Generalium* (1765).

Balmaceda, Francisco Roman Catholic ascetic, born Ibscache, Chile, 2 October 1772, died Santiago, 2 November 1842. Studied at Convictorio Carolino and was ordained by Bishop Marán. He was heir to a great fortune but took up the life of an ascetic. He owned a hacienda and used to teach the tenants prayers and literacy, while also feeding many families from the crops grown there. After his mother's death he gave away all his wealth and property except 1,000 pesos a year and his house. He would wear heavy clothing in very hot weather and live on boiled vegetables. On 2 November 1842 he collapsed when he was on his way to say Mass for some nuns and died. Understandably, the poor of his area considered him a saint.

Balmes, Jaime Luciano Roman Catholic priest and philosopher, born Vich, Catalonia, Spain, 28 August 1810, died Vich, 9 July 1848. After studying at Vich and Cervera he was ordained in 1834 and qualified for a degree in theology the next year. He was involved in philosophy, sociology and politics and wrote books on all of these subjects. In 1840 he wrote *Consideraciones politicas sobre la situación de España* against General Espartero. While in Barcelona he founded and directed *La Civilización* (1841–3) and *La Sociedad* (1843–4) and he also wrote *El Criterio, Filosofía fundamental* and *Filosofía elemental.* The latter two of these works were aimed at students, and his purpose was to guide the youth away from the mistakes made by modern philosophy.

Balsamon, Theodore Patriarch and canonist, born Constantinople, 1105, died Constantinople, 1195. He was a deacon in the church of Hagia Sophia and was also the head legal advisor to the patriarch. Sometime between 1185 and 1191 he was elected patriarch of Antioch but did not leave Constantinople. He was mostly involved in solving problems raised by contradiction in church laws and situations where there was a clash of interest between the laws of Church and the laws of State. His main work on these topics was a commentary on the Photian *Nomocanon*, a work of fourteen titles. As well as this he expounded on the collection of Byzantine law. In the year of his death he was involved in answering questions directed to the permanent synod of Constantinople. His use of otherwise unknown documents makes him of interest to the historian.

Balthasar, Hans Urs von Roman Catholic theologian and writer, born Lucerne, Switzerland, 12 August 1905, died Basel, 26 June 1988. He studied German literature and philosophy at Vienna, Berlin and Zurich before becoming a Jesuit in 1929, and then continued his studies in philosophy in Munich and in theology at Lyons: he was ordained in July 1936 and served for a time as an assistant editor of the German Jesuit periodical *Stimmen der Zeit.* During that time he wrote the three-volume *Apokalypse der deutschen Seele*, a study of the German spiritual tradition as represented by some of its leading exponents. A deep interest in the spiritual dimension of the faith remained a constant theme. Between 1940 and 1948 he was the university chaplain at Basel, where he met, and wrote a study (in 1951) on, Karl **Barth**. He also met Adrienne von **Speyr**, converting her to Catholicism and founding a secular institute with her in 1945. He left the Jesuits in 1950 – though he retained personal friendships, particularly with Henri de **Lubac**, who had taught him in Lyons and about whom he wrote a book; he set up his own publishing house and a secular institution. In 1988 he was nominated a cardinal but died two days before receiving the red hat. In 1970 he established the international journal *Communio*, which continues to reflect his theological perspective. He wrote much on history and theology, but his most important works were theological: *Das Herz der Welt* (*Heart of the World*) (1945), *Das betrachtendes Gebet* (1955) on prayer, and the trilogy *Herrlichkeit: Eine theologische Ästhetik* (1961–9 (incomplete)), *Theodramatik* (1973–83); and *Theologik* (1985).

Balthasar of St Catherine of Siena Discalced Carmelite and mystic, born Bologna, Italy, 24 August 1597, died Bologna, 23 August 1673. He took orders at the novitiate of La Scala in Rome in 1614 after becoming interested in the Teresian reform, and was later professed in 1615. He then became professor at the Seminary for the Missions at St Paul of the Quirinale and took over much of the administration for his Order. He wrote several works. Noteworthy are the letter to Christians in the Lombardy province; his Italian translation of *Subida del Alma a Dios* and his commentary on St **Teresa**'s *Mansions*. He attempted (with some success) to balance St Teresa's teaching with that of St **John of the Cross**, who was little known in Italy at that time.

Balticus, Martinus Humanist and educator, born Munich, Germany, 1532, died Ulm, 1600. He started off at Bruck, where he learnt Greek and Latin, and then spent six years studying under Johann Mathesius and then a little time being taught by Philipp **Melancthon** in Wittenberg. He returned to Munich in 1553 to become the director of the Latin Poetenschule, but left in 1559 because of his Lutheran sympathies. He moved directly to Ulm where he began a post as director of the Latin school. This lasted until 1592. He wrote Latin elegies (*Poematum libri tres*, 1556), plays (*Adelphopolae*, 1556, *Daniel*, 1558 and *Christogonia*, 1589) and a paraphrase of the Gospels and Sunday Epistles (*Evangeliorum et epistolarum . . . sensus genuinus*, 1593).

Baltimore, Charles Calvert *see* **Calvert, Charles**

Baltimore, Cecilius (Cecil) *see* **Calvert, Cecilius**

Baltimore, George Cecil *see* **Calvert, George**

Baluffi, Gaetano First internuncio to South America and cardinal, born Ancona, Italy, 1788, died Imola, 11 November 1866. In 1835 New Granada was recognized as an independent country and Bishop Baluffi of Bagnorea was sent there by **Gregory XVI**. Two years later he was acting as the representative of the Catholic Church to several South American countries that had previously lacked such communication with Rome. In 1841 he became bishop of Camerino; **Pius IX** made him bishop of Imola and a cardinal. He was influenced by the Catholic Society, who were at odds with Archbishop **Mosquera** of Bogotá and the official policy of Rome. He wrote *La América un tiempo española, considerada por su aspecto religioso, desde su descubrimiento hasta 1843*, a book of history and apologetics that has been described by the *New Catholic Encyclopedia* as 'a bibliographical curiosity'.

Baluze, Etienne Roman Catholic scholar, born Tulle, France, 24 November 1630, died Paris, 28 July 1718. Though he became a cleric when age 15, he was never ordained. Instead he chose to devote himself to study. In 1652 and 1654 poor health demanded that he retired to Tulle until 1656. He then went to Paris to act as secretary to Archbishop Pierre de **Marca** of Paris, and when he died worked for the archbishop of Auch for a little while. In 1667 he became librarian for J. B. Colbert and collected many rare manuscripts for him, some of which he transcribed. An eye illness forced him to stop work in 1671 and in 1689 **Louis XIV** made him professor of canon law at the Collège de France before exiling him from Paris in 1710. He was allowed to return three years later without a position or pension. He died leaving a library of 10,000 printed works, which were auctioned off.

Balzac, Honoré de Novelist, born Tours, France, 20 May 1799, died Paris, 18 August 1850. After moving to Paris with his parents (1814) he studied law. In 1819 he retired to an attic he had hired in an attempt to become a writer. Later his efforts at publishing, printing and typefounding left him in debt and forced him back to writing. He produced a few works, *Les Chouans* (1829), *La physiologie du mariage* (1830) and *La peau de chagrin* (1831), which provided a dedicated fanbase, including the Polish Countess Éveline Hanska, with whom he corresponded. In 1834 he published *Le Père Goriot* and the following year he decided to link all of his novels by having characters reappear in each. Thus *La comédie humaine* (1842) was born. In 1850 he died of heart trouble, having just married.

Balzac, Jean Louis Guez de   Roman Catholic writer and critic, born Angoulême, France, 1595, died Angoulême, 18 February 1654. After an education in Paris and Leyden and a discipleship under the poet François de Malherbe, Balzac began to write his famous letters while in Rome on behalf of the archbishop of Toulouse. These were printed in 1624, and there followed *Le Prince* (1631) and *Aristippe* (1658). He also wrote *Socrate chrétien* (1652), which apparently influenced **Pascal**'s *Provincial Letters*. When he returned from Rome to France he was unable to find a position at court; so he retired to his estate near his birthplace. He wrote right up until his death, and these works continued to earn him the admiration of the French intellectuals.

Bandas, Rudolf G.   US priest, theologian and pioneer of the catechetical movement. Born in Silver Lake, Minnesota, 18 April 1896, died St Paul, Minnesota, 26 July 1969. Studied for the priesthood at St Paul and was ordained in 1921. Did further studies at Louvain before returning to teach dogmatic theology and catechetics at St Paul Seminary, where he was also rector for a time. He was one the first teachers of catechetics in the USA and wrote one of the earliest books, *Catechetical Methods* (1929). He wrote articles and lectured at national and international catechetical gatherings. In his 30-year term he made major contributions, as the first director in the Archdiocese of St Paul, to the newly established Confraternity of Christian Doctrine.

Bañez, Domingo   Dominican theologian, born Medina del Campo, Old Castile, 29 February 1528, died Medina del Campo, 22 October 1604. He studied at Salamanca University and in 1547 became a Dominican. He was an exponent of Thomism and gave lectures on St **Thomas Aquinas**'s *Summa Theologiae*. Bañez taught at Avila, Alcalá, Salamanca and Valladolid. He was elected prior of Toro, but went to Salamanca as professor. In Spain he was known as 'The brightest light of the country'. He was spiritual director and confessor to **Teresa of Avila**. He became involved in a controversy concerning Christ's freedom on the cross, which gave rise to a heated debate between Jesuits and Dominicans on the nature of grace (the De auxiliis controversy). The matter was referred to Rome. He was a prolific and vigorous writer.

Bannister, Henry Marriott   Anglican hymnologist and scholar, born Oxford, England, 18 March 1854, died Oxford, 16 February 1919. After studying at Oxford he was ordained as an Anglican deacon in 1877 and as a priest in 1878. After serving as a minister in England and Australia he devoted his time to studying medieval music, working in Oxford and Rome. During the First World War he served as sub-librarian of the Bodleian Library while studying for a D.Litt. degree. He wrote many articles and was co-editor of volumes 40 to 55 of *Analecta Hymnica Medii Aevi*, as well as editing *Monumenti vaticani di paleografia musicale latina* (1913) and *Missale Gothicum* (1917–19).

Bannon, John B.   Roman Catholic military chaplain and Confederate commissioner, born Roosky, Ireland, 28 December 1829, died Dublin, Ireland, 14 July 1913. He was ordained in 1853 and moved to St Louis in America, where he began a ministry at the cathedral and the Immaculate Conception church. In 1858 he became the pastor of St John's parish, where he built a new church in two years. In 1862 he received permission from his bishop to become a chaplain to the Confederate forces in the American Civil War. In 1863 he was granted commission as a chaplain; later that year he was released from the army and made the Confederate commissioner to Ireland. In 1864, during his visit to Rome with Bishop Patrick **Lynch** of Charleston, attempts to have the Papacy recognize the Confederacy failed. On 9 January 1865 Bannon became a Jesuit.

Bapst, John   Jesuit priest and missionary, born La Roche, Fribourg, Switzerland, 17 December 1815, died Mount Hope, Maryland, USA, 2 November 1887. He studied in Fribourg, joined the Jesuits in 1835 and was ordained in 1846. Two years later he was sent to North America to minister to the Indians at Old Town, Maine, a community seemingly much in need of moral reform, having been without a priest for some twenty years. He founded temperance societies in Maine and won many converts. He also encountered a lot of hostility in those areas where Roman Catholicism was not popular, especially in Eastport and later in Ellsworth. His efforts to establish a school in Ellsworth resulted in his being attacked, tarred and feathered, and driven out of the town. He worked at Bangor, where he built the first church, and in 1860 went to Boston as rector of the college. He was superior in the Jesuit houses in Canada, New York, and later in Providence, Rhode Island.

Baptist of Mantua   Blessed, Carmelite and poet, born Mantua, 17 April 1447, died there 22 March 1516. His father was Peter Spagnoli, a Spanish nobleman at the court of Mantua. He studied at Pavia and, having fallen out with his father, went to Venice and Ferrara, where he joined the Carmelites. Taught philosophy and divinity at Bologna before becoming reconciled with his father, when he became tutor to the duke of Mantua's children. Baptist became a distinguished, prolific Renaissance poet, much of his work inspired by the duke's family, but he was criticized for drawing too much on pagan mythology. In 1513 he was made general of the Carmelite Order. He was beatified in 1890. Feast day 23 March.

Bar, Catherine de   Nun and foundress of the Benedictine Nuns of the Blessed Sacrament, born Saint-Dié-Vosges, France, 31 December 1614, died Paris, 6 April 1698. After joining the convent of the Annunciation in 1632, she was professed just one year later. In 1639 she found herself with the Benedictines of Rambervilles after the Thirty Years War caused her to flee the convent. She transferred from the Annonciades to the Benedictines, but again war caused her to move to Montmartre. It was here that she founded the Benedictine Nuns of the Blessed Sacrament, after assuming the name Mother Mechtilde of the Blessed Sacrament. Apart from writing on spiritual matters she also wrote to figures such as St John **Eudes** and Jean-Jacques **Olier**.

Bar-Cursus (Joannes Tellensis)   Monophysite bishop and protagonist, born Kallinikos, 483, died Antioch, 538. He was originally involved in court

life, but he left to become a monk. After entering the monastic life he was ordained as bishop of Tella in northern Mesopotamia in 519, a time when Monophysites and Chalcedonians were facing each other in complex debates over Christology. When these dogmatic discussions moved to Constantinople in 533 Bar-Cursus was involved. Because of his convictions he died violently in prison. He edited a collection of canons that discussed the sacraments, and these writings are important for liturgical history, especially for the Sacrament of the Holy Eucharist.

Bar-Hebraeus (Abû al-Faraj)   Jacobite bishop and polymath, born Melitene, 1226, died Managa, Azerbaijan, 30 July 1286. Of Jewish descent, he studied medicine (his father was a physician) at Antioch and Tripoli. In 1246 he was consecrated as a bishop, and became primate of the East eighteen years later in 1264. He lived in the monastery of Mar Mattai near Mosul. He wrote two works on life and discipline in the Church (*Nomocanon* and *Ethicon*), *The Book of the Dove* on the monastic life and many others of an encyclopaedic nature, including *The Cream of Science* (on Aristotle), *The Candelabra of the Sanctuary* (a compendium of theology) and a commentary on the whole Bible entitled *The Storehouse of Mysteries*. These works were mostly written in Syriac.

Baradai, Jacob   Monophysite bishop and the founder of the Jacobite Church, born Syria, died Romanos monastery, Kaison, Egypt, 30 July 578. After becoming a monk and being ordained a priest he was sent *c.*527 to the Byzantine Court in Constantinople. He remained there until 543 when he was ordained as bishop of Edessa by Theodosius of Alexandria. He was then sent to the eastern front of the Empire as a missionary to the Arabs. There he found and consecrated a large number of Monophysites, beginning a hierarchy that was to remain established, even after his death. This Church is still known as the Jacobite (or Syrian Monophysite) Church. Baradai wrote nothing of any real value to the scholar.

Baraga, Frederic   Missionary and bishop, born Mala Vas castle, Slovenia, 29 June 1797, died Marquette, Michigan, 19 January 1868. After being educated in Ljubljana and Vienna he broke off his engagement and renounced his inheritance to enter the seminary in Ljubljana. He was ordained in 1823 and sent to Šmartno and then Metlika, in 1828, where he wrote many devotional works. He then realized his ambition to become a missionary to the American Indians in Cincinnati, Ottawa in 1831, Grand River in 1833, La Pointe in 1835 and L'Anse in 1845, all with amazing success. In 1853 he was consecrated bishop of Amazonia and in 1857 his vicariate was made a diocese. In 1866 he transferred to Marquette, where he died amongst the Indians he had gone to serve. He wrote too much to be recorded here, but his works on grammar and linguistics are still an aid to the study of the Indian language. Steps have been taken towards his beatification.

Baranzauskas, Antanas Roman Catholic poet, born near Anykščiai, Lithuania, 17 January 1835, died Seinai, 26 November 1902. Despite their humble income, his parents saw him through a good education and then into the seminary of Varniai in 1856. He then spent time at the Theological Academy at St Petersburg and was ordained in 1862. He spent the time between 1863 and 1864 studying in Munich, Innsbruck, Rome and Louvain, and then became a professor at the Theological Academy. He then taught at the seminary of Kaunas, 1867–84, and in 1884 was consecrated as the auxiliary bishop of the Kaunas diocese. Finally, in 1897, he became bishop of Seinai. He wrote a collection of songs that became popular, but his greatest work was *Anykščiai šilelis* (*The Forest of Anykščiai*), a 342-line poem written during his 1858–9 summer holiday.

Barat, Madeleine Sophie Saint, nun and foundress of the Sacred Heart Society, born Joigny, France, 12 December 1779, died Paris, 25 May 1865. In 1800 her teacher/brother (who was a priest) took her to Paris so that she could study. There she was persuaded to join a small group hoping to found a new religious order. She followed this group to Amiens and in 1802 became their superior-general and head of their school for girls. In 1804, in Grenoble, she founded the second house of the Sacred Heart Society. She spent the rest of her life attempting (with reasonable success) to extend her institute and to keep the constitution of the society safe from the attitudes of the post-revolutionary society that her pupils came from. Even the chaplain of the Amiens house was involved in attempting to reshape the constitution, but she resisted him and such change for her whole life. Feast day 25 May.

Barbara Saint. There is no historical evidence that she existed, but veneration became common from the seventh century, and she is first named in the *Martyrologium Romanum parvum*, *c.*700, the oldest Latin martyrology. Tradition places her in the third century, the beautiful daughter of a pagan, Dioscorus. Her father kept her in a tower to discourage suitors. Before he went on a journey, her father had a bath house built for her. She had three windows inserted in it to symbolize the Trinity, and on his return told her father she was a Christian. He took her before the prefect of the province, Martinianus. She was tortured and condemned to be beheaded at the hand of her father. On his way home following the execution he was struck dead by lightning. Various accounts are set in Egypt, Rome, Tuscany and elsewhere. The place of martyrdom is attributed to Heliopolis in Egypt or Nicomedia. Because of the circumstances of her father's death, Barbara was regarded as the patron saint of those beset by thunder or fire, and later of soldiers in the artillery and of miners. She is also regarded as the advocate for ensuring believers are able to receive the sacraments of Penance and Holy Communion at death. Feast day, originally 4 December, suppressed in 1969.

Barbarigo, Giovanni Francesco Cardinal, born Venice, Italy, 29 April 1658, died Padua, 26 January 1730. He was the nephew of St Gregory **Barbarigo** and cousin of Marc' Antonio **Barbarigo**. He rejected his position as ambassador of Venice at the court of **Louis XIV** so that he could become a priest. He was made bishop of both Verona, in 1697, and Brescia, in 1714, before being ordained as a cardinal in 1721. In 1723 he was also honoured with the title of bishop of Padua. It was at Padua that he was recognized as a man of true piety, for his promotion of education, reform of ecclesiastical order and visitations to hospitals. He himself paid for the works of St **Zeno**, in 1710, and St Gaudentius, in 1720, to be published, and was buried next to his uncle.

Barbarigo, Gregory Saint, Roman Catholic bishop and cardinal, born Venice, Italy, 16 September 1625, died Padua, 18 June 1697. In 1648 he was part of the Venetian embassy that went to Münster for the Treaty of Westphalia. In 1655 he was ordained after having taken a degree in law, and the next year he was helping to organize the Roman Trastevere quarter, which had been struck by the plague. In 1657 he became bishop of Bergamo and advocated the reforms of the Council of Trent in his own parish. In 1660 he was made cardinal, and then bishop of Padua in 1667. He gave much support to Christians who were under Muslim rule. He wrote *Regulae studiorum* (1690) and played an important role as a candidate at three papal conclaves, especially in 1691. He was beatified in 1761, and canonized in 1960. Feast day 18 June.

Barbarigo, Marc' Antonio Cardinal, born Venice, Italy, 6 March 1640, died Montefiascone, 26 May 1706. A promising and talented politician, he rejected that career for the priesthood and was ordained in 1671. Gregory **Barbarigo** called him to come to Padua and he became a canon in the cathedral and obtained a degree from the university. In 1676 he attended the conclave that elected **Innocent XI** and two years later was appointed to the see of Corfu. A controversy over protocol between Barbarigo and Francesco Morosini (admiral of the Venetian fleet) caused him to flee to Rome; having been cleared, he was made a cardinal in 1686 and appointed bishop of Montefiascone and Corneta in 1687 by Innocent XI. He founded the Scuole e Maestre Pie for underprivileged girls and performed an excellent pastoral role.

Barbastro, Francisco Antonio Franciscan prelate for north-west Mexico, born Aragón, Spain, 1734, died Sonora, Mexico, 22 June 1800. Barbastro became a friar of the Convento de Jesús in Zaragoza in 1754 and spent time at the Colegio of San Roque de Calamocha in 1764, and the Missionary College of Santa Cruz de Querétaro in 1770. He was made president of the missions to Sonora and had great success in preaching to the natives in their own languages, especially the Opatas. In 1783 he founded the first Sonoran school at Aconchi. He acted as vice-custos of San Carlos until the custody was dissolved in 1789 after he had convinced Charles IV that the custody harmed the missionary efforts. He worked on a history of Sonora as his *Apologia* for the Franciscans involved in the mission to the pagan world.

Barbatia, Andreas de (Andreas Siculus) Canon lawyer, born Messina, Sicily, 1400, died Bologna, 21 July 1479. Having studied medicine and then law at Bologna in 1425, he both taught and took his doctorate in canon law in 1438. He taught at Florence between 1438 and 1442, and then returned to Bologna to teach until he retired in 1478. His works include *Lecturae seu Repetitiones*; *Tractatus de Praestantia Cardinalium*; *Tractus de Cardinalibus a latere legatis* and *Tractatus de praetensionibus*. He was renowned for his legal skill and expertise, and his knowledge of both canon and civil law caused him to give advice to leaders of both State and Church. He also attracted many excellent students, including Rodrigo Borgia, who was to become Pope **Alexander VI**.

Barbatus Saint and bishop, patron of Benevento, born Cerreto Sannita, Italy, early seventh century, died Benevento, Italy, 19 February 682. St Barbatus is a comparatvie unknown until his succession to Hildebrand as bishop of Benevento in 663. He attended the sixth general council, Constantinople III, but died not long after he returned from it. His body is buried under the main altar in Benevento cathedral, and he is venerated for his work in eliminating remaining pagan superstitions amongst his people and for predicting both the invasion of Emperor **Constans II**'s army in 663 and the later lifting of the siege. There exists a ninth-century work on the life of Barbatus. Feast day 19 February.

Barbelin, Felix Joseph Jesuit pastor and educator, born Lorraine, France, 30 May 1808, died Philadelphia, USA, 8 June 1869. He moved to America after having completed his education in France and joined the Jesuits in Maryland in 1831, where he was ordained in 1835. He then taught at Georgetown University. He also served as an assistant at St Joseph's in Philadelphia before becoming a pastor there in 1844. In 1841 he inaugurated the first parish sodality and established a St Vincent de Paul Society conference and a free school for girls.

He also worked amongst Negroes, founding a school for Negro children and gathering the first Negro congregation. His humanitarian desires led also to the founding of St Joseph's Hospital and establishing St Joseph's College.

Barber, Daniel Roman Catholic convert and writer, born Simsbury, North America, 2 October 1756, died St Inigoes, 24 March 1834. A member of a very prominent New England family, he was originally a soldier in the Continental army. He left the Congregational Church to become an Episcopal minister, was ordained and began his ministry at a Claremont church. However, after 24 years, in 1818, he became a Roman Catholic. Daniel Barber wrote *Catholic Worships and Piety Explained* (1821) and *The History of My Own Times* (1827). His son Virgil Horace **Barber** and daughter-in-law Jerusha **Barber** both followed the Catholic faith and entered religious orders.

Barber, Jerusha Visitandine nun, born Newtown, USA, 20 July 1789, died Mobile, 2 January 1860. Born Jerusha Booth, she was the wife of Virgil Horace **Barber** and the daughter-in-law of Daniel **Barber**. After becoming a Catholic, both Jerusha and her husband took vows of celibacy. She entered the Visitandines and took her vows at Georgetown in 1820, changing her name to Sister Mary Austin/Augustine. She remained with the community of the Visitandines and served them and the public in Georgetown, Kaskaskia, St Louis and Mobile, where she eventually died. She and Virgil raised five children (Mary, Abigail, Susan, Samuel and Josephine), who also became valued members of various communities, including the Ursulines, the Visitandines (Josephine) and the Jesuits (Samuel).

Barber, Virgil Horace Jesuit priest and missionary, born Simsbury, USA, 9 May 1782, died Georgetown, 27 March 1847. After his education at Dartmouth College he followed in his father's footsteps and became the Episcopal pastor at St John's Episcopal Church in Waterbury in 1807–14. In 1814 he resigned his position and became principal of an Episcopal academy in Fairfield. Two years later he and his entire family were converted to Catholicism. While his wife entered the Visitandines, he entered the Society of Jesus in Boston and

was ordained in 1822. He was assigned to Claremont in 1823–4, and there he opened the first Catholic church in the area. He then took up some missionary work in Maine, and returned to work in the Georgetown area until his death.

Barberi, Dominic Saint, Passionist priest and lecturer, born near Viterbo, Italy, 22 June 1792, died Reading, England, 27 August 1849. Despite his lack of training he was accepted into the Passionist order in 1814 and made his profession the next year. In 1818 he was ordained at Rome and between 1821 and 1831 he took a post as lecturer of philosophy and theology to Passionist clerics. He spent some time as the superior of the new monastery at Lucca in Italy in 1831–3 and became provincial for southern Italy in 1833. He moved to England in 1841 and opened the first British Passionist monastery in Aston, Staffordshire, a year later. His holy life brought many to conversion, despite the fact that he was mocked and persecuted by Catholics and Protestants alike because he was an odd-looking man. He was beatified on 27 October 1963. Feast day 27 August.

Barbosa, Agostino Roman Catholic bishop and canonist, born Guimarens, Portugal, 1589, died Rome, 19 November 1649. He studied canon law in Portugal and then Rome; in 1632 he went to Madrid, where he had been offered a position as an ecclesiastical judge, and sixteen years later Philip IV saw fit to nominate him bishop of Ungento. He wrote much, but the work regarded as most important is his *Historia iuris ecclesiastici universi libri tres*. He also wrote a fairly comprehensive commentary on the Council of Trent that was later placed on the Index. He wrote a compendium of law and a juridical lexicon also. All of his works were published at Lyons, and he was noted for his incredible memory and familiarity with authors and sources.

Barbosa, Januário da Cunha Roman Catholic priest, journalist and politician, born Rio de Janeiro, Brazil, 10 July 1780, died Rio de Janeiro, 22 February 1846. Orphaned at the age of ten, Barbosa came into the custody of his uncle, who provided a good education for him and sent him to the São José seminary to become a priest. He was ordained in 1803 and, after having spent two years in Europe, worked in a Brazilian parish. In 1814 he became professor of rational and moral philosophy in the seminary and one of the leaders of the Brazilian independence party. With Joaquim Gonçalves Ledo he founded the *Revérbero Constitucional Fluminense*. He opposed the Andrada brothers, who controlled the government, and had to spend a year in exile. On returning he turned further to liberal politics and journalism, writing many satirical and scathing articles, and co-founded the monthly journal *Revista do Instituto histórico e geográfico brasileiro*. Because of their political influence, he also joined the Masons.

Barbosa, Rui Statesman, jurist and writer, born Salvador, Brazil, 5 November 1849, died Petrópolis, 1 March 1923. After gaining a law degree from São Paulo he became a journalist until 1878, when he was elected a deputy of the Liberal party. Despite his famous work on bills on humanitarian issues, he took up law again after the Conservative victory in 1885. He did become, however, vice-president and minister of finance of the Republic's provisional government. He established basic laws, such as the separation of Church and State and civil marriage. From then until his death he was a representative of Bahia in the Senate and was twice a candidate for president. He was also delegate to the Second Hague Peace Conference in 1907 and special ambassador in Buenos Aires. He was criticized by the Church because of his Masonic and secular attitude, but by his death his defence of many church interests and his successful address at the Jesuit College in 1903 won him many clerical friends.

Barclay, John Roman Catholic Latin satirical novelist and poet, born Pont-à-Mousson, Lorraine, 28 January 1582, died Rome, 15 August 1621. Educated by the Jesuits, at the age of nineteen he published the first of his Latin works. In 1603 he moved with his father, William Barclay, to London and dedicated his *Euphormionis Lusinini Satyricon* to King **James I**. Barclay published the second part of this in Paris in 1607, as well as a collection of poems under the title *Sylvae*. He also wrote an account of the Gunpowder Plot. In 1609 he arranged the publication of his father's *De potestate Papae*, denying the pope's temporal powers, which brought him into controversy with **Bellarmine** and

the Jesuits, against whom his *Euphormio* (1603) was directed. In the fourth part of his *Satyricon*, Barclay described the characteristics of European countries, especially approving of Scotland. In London in 1615 he published a collection of poems. In 1616 Barclay moved to Rome, where he completed his Latin novel *Argenis* (Paris, 1621), which inspired many later works from other writers and was translated into most of the major languages of Europe and Scandinavia.

Barclay, John Founder of the Bereans or Barclay-ites, born Muthill, Scotland, 1734, died Edinburgh, 29 July 1798. He was educated at St Andrews University and then in 1759 moved to Auchterarder, where he soon became the assistant to James Jobson. A disagreement with Jobson led him to move to Fettercairn in 1763, where he assisted A. Dow. He was censured as a heretic for promulgating immediate divine revelation in his 1766 work *Rejoice Evermore, or Christ All in All*, and despite the support of his parishioners he was not appointed to succeed Dow when he died in 1772. He moved on to Edinburgh, where he acquired a small following, and then moved to Newcastle so that he could be ordained (which he was in 1773). He started the Berean assembly in Edinburgh, marked for their zealous study of Scripture. He established communities in London and Bristol and then returned to Scotland. His chief work was *The Psalms, paraphrased according to the NT Interpretation* (1766).

Barclay, Robert Quaker apologist, born Gordonstoun, Scotland, 23 December 1648, died Ury, 3 October 1690. He was educated at the (Roman Catholic) Scots' Theological College, and joined the Quakers in 1667, a year after his father had done so. In 1673 he published his *Catechism and Confession of Faith*, and three years later he wrote his *Apology for the True Christian Religion*, which offered the Quakers as the 'True Christian Religion'. It advocated the doctrine of 'Inner Light' over and against external sources (including Scripture) and made a fierce attack on Calvinism. In his travels in The Netherlands and Germany he found favour with the Princess Palatine, Elizabeth, and the future King **James II**. He also helped William **Penn** found Pennsylvania with a Quaker constitution and became (non-resident) governor of East

New Jersey. He was often imprisoned for his convictions.

Barclay, William Scottish Catholic lawyer and political theorist, born Aberdeenshire, c.1547, died Angers, 3 July 1608. He studied at Aberdeen University. He was a member of Queen Mary's court, but c.1571 moved to Paris and Bourges to study law. He became professor of law at the University of Pont-à-Mousson and a councillor to the duke of Lorraine. In 1581 he married and had a son, John **Barclay**, who was educated partly by the Jesuits. William, however, fell out with the Jesuits, which appears to have lost him the favour of the duke, and in 1603 he decided to return to England. This move was prompted by the accession of King James, who he believed would be favourable to him after the publication of his *De Regno et Regali Potestate* (Paris, 1600) which defended the divine right of kings. James was indeed sympathetic, but before bestowing preferment on him, required him to renounce Catholicism, which he refused to do. The following year, therefore, he returned to Paris, and in 1605 he became professor of law at Angers and distinguished champion of his own views regarding the divine right of kings. James, it is said, offered him high preferment, but only on condition that he should renounce the Catholic faith, whereupon Barclay decided at the beginning of 1604 to return to Paris. The chair of civil law at Angers had been vacant since 1599, and such was the fame of Barclay in France that as soon as his return to Paris was known a deputation was sent, requesting his acceptance of the chair. In addition to this, notwithstanding the strenuous opposition of two professors, he was appointed dean of the faculty of law, the appointment being confirmed by a special decree of the university on 1 February 1605. His *De Potestate Papæ*, attacking what Barclay believed to be exaggerated papal claims, was published by his son after his death: it evoked a response from Robert **Bellarmine**.

Barco Centenera, Martín del Roman Catholic politician and poet, born Logrosán, Spain, 1535, died Portugal, 1605. In 1572 he went to La Planta to be archdeacon of the cathedral of the Assumption. during this time his duties as a priest were secondary to his role in politics. After having put down a rebellion against Juan de Garay he went to Peru for nine years, and then in 1582 he became secretary of the Lima Council. Not long afterwards he was vicar of Charcas and commissary of the Inquisition in Cochabamba, and it was the Inquisition who arrested and punished him for his directionless lifestyle. He returned to govern the Buenos Aires diocese in 1590, and then left for Europe. In 1602 he published *Argentina*, the first part of his poem. The second part was never published. He also wrote a volume called *El desengaño del mundo*.

Bardas Caesar, statesman and brother of Empress Theodora, born Paphlagonia (probably), died (assassinated) Crete, 21 April 865. He was probably educated in Constantinople, and became a director in state policy in Emperor Theophilus' last years. He also advised Empress Theodora during her regency for **Michael III** (his nephew) until displaced by the prime minister Theoctistus. He and Michael had Theoctistus murdered in 856 and Theodora (and her daughters) entered a monastery. Bardas became Caesar in 862 and helped defeat the Arabs in 863, as well as reorganizing the University of Constantinople and arguing for the revival of profane studies. Michael III's new favourite, **Basil**, falsely accused Bardas of treason and he was assassinated in front of the Emperor.

Bardenhewer, Otto Roman Catholic patristic scholar, born Münchengladbach, Germany, 16 March 1851, died Munich, 23 March 1935. He was ordained in 1875 after finishing his doctorate in classical philology at Bonn (1873). He then earned a doctorate in theology from Würzburg (1877), and taught OT at Munich. He then moved to Münster to teach OT exegesis in 1884, and two years later left to teach NT at Munich. Amongst his many writings is the five-volume reference work *Geschichte der altkirchlichen Literatur* (1913–32). From 1911 to his death he was the joint editor of the *Bibliothek der Kirchenväter* (for patristic translations) and he founded the *Biblische Studien* series (1896–1928).

Bardesanes (Bar-Daisan) Christian astrologer and philosopher, born Edessa, Mesopotamia, 154, died Edessa, 222. Born of pagan parents and educated by a pagan priest in Syria, Bardesanes was converted to Christianity when he was 25 years old. He was also ordained as either a deacon or a priest.

He wrote works in Syriac that were translated into Greek, metrical hymns (for which he has been called the father of Syriac poetry) and some lost works on astrology and on India and Armenia. The church historian **Eusebius** credits him with works against **Marcion** and Valentinus. However, Bardesanes' mix of astrology, philosophy and Christianity has left him labelled as a Gnostic, and thus a heretic. His personal doctrine was given by a disciple called Philip in the Syriac *Book of the Laws of the Countries.*

Bardo of Oppershofen Saint, archbishop, born Oppershofen, Germany, 980, died Dornloh, 10 June 1051. In his youth he was sent to the monastery of Fulda where after some time he became a monk and the director of the monastic school. He was made abbot of Werden in 1029 and in 1031 he became the leader of the monastery of Hersfield. The same year he was consecrated as archbishop of Mainz and worked hard on the construction of the cathedral, which was completed and then consecrated in 1036 in the presence of Emperor Conrad II. In 1049 Pope **Leo IX** presided over a synod that was held at Mainz. He was renowned for his preaching, leading to him being regarded as another **John Chrysostom**. He was buried in the cathedral at Mainz. Feast day 15 June.

Bardy, Gustave Roman Catholic patristic scholar, born Belfort, France, 25 November 1881, died Dijon, 31 October 1955. He was educated at the Seminary of St Sulpice and then ordained in 1906. He attended the Institut Catholique in Paris until 1909 and then lectured in theology at the University of Besançon. In 1914, with the outbreak of World War I, Bardy did military service, was wounded and decorated for valour. In 1919 he taught theology at Lille and then transferred in 1927 to Dijon, where he edited the diocesan paper *Vie Diocésaine de Dijon* for the rest of his life. He wrote and worked on more than 30 books and received doctorates in letters and in theology. His biography is called *Didyme l'Aveugle* and appeared in 1910.

Baring, Maurice Novelist, poet and literary critic, born London, 27 April 1874, died Beauly, Scotland, 14 December 1945. He was educated at Eton and Cambridge, after which he joined the British diplomatic service, 1898–1903, and spent a year in the Foreign Office. From 1904 to 1907 he was in Russia acting as a correspondent on the Russo-Japanese War for *The Morning Post.* In 1909 Baring was received into the Roman Catholic Church at the London Oratory and he befriended men such as **Chesterton** and **Belloc**. During World War I he fought in the Royal Flying Corps, and this connection led to him becoming an honorary wing commander in 1925. His faith was reflected in his novels *Passing By* (1921), *C* (1924), *Cat's Cradle* (1925) and *Daphne Adeane* (1926). His last published work was the poem *Have You Anything to Declare?* (1936).

Baring-Gould, Sabine Anglican clergyman and writer, born Exeter, England, 28 January 1834, died Lew Trenchard, Devon, 2 January 1924. He graduated from Clare College, Cambridge, and was ordained in 1865. In 1871 he became rector of East Mersea in Essex and then of Lew Trenchard in Devon from 1881 to 1924. He wrote something for almost every type of genre, from novels to hymns. The best known of his 30 novels is *Broom Squire* (1896), and of his hymns, 'Onward Christian Soldiers'. He wrote the biography *Richard Hawker of Morwenstow* (1875) as well as the hagiographies *Lives of the Saints* (15 vols, 1872–7) and *Lives of British Saints* (1907).

Barlaam and Joasaph This is in fact the title of a novel generally assumed to be written by St **John Damascene**. It is the adaptation of a Buddhist legend and tells of a monk named Barlaam who converted the Indian prince Joasaph. Joasaph becomes king and converts his entire kingdom before dying as a hermit. The text contains much discussion about the truth and meaning of Christianity. Since 1583 Barlaam and Joasaph have been venerated in the Roman martyrology, and their cult was very popular in the Middle Ages. P. Peeters argues that the text was in fact written by Euthymius, abbot of Iviron, Mount Athos, but F. Dölger's case for St John Damascene has reopened the debate.

Barlaam of Calabria Monk, theologian and bishop, born Seminara, Calabria, 1290, died Gerace, Calabria, 1350. He was educated in the Byzantine monasteries of southern Italy and taught at the Holy Saviour monastery and the Imperial University at Constantinople in 1326–7. He was involved in a public debate with Nicephorus Gregoras and then moved to Thessalonica, where he taught. In 1334 he was chosen to debate the issue of papal primacy with two envoys of Pope **John XXII**, leading him to a polemical exchange with the hesychastic monks of Mount Athos. In 1339 he was sent by the imperial court to Pope **Benedict XII** to discuss a Turkish crusade, and when he returned to Constantinople in 1341 he faced condemnation for his earlier anti-hesychastic comments. After a public retraction and a full conversion to Catholicism he was made bishop of Gerace by Pope **Clement VI** in 1342. After another failure to reunite Constantinople and the Church, he remained in his parish until his death.

Barlach, Ernst Sculptor, dramatist and artist, born Wedel, Germany, 2 February 1870, died Rostock, 24 October 1938. Barlach studied in Hamburg and Dresden. It was during his trips to Paris in 1895–6 that he was exposed to the work of artists such as Steinlen, **Millet**, Meunier and **Van Gogh**. Furthermore, a visit to Russia in 1906 led him to turn his back on his Jugendstil (Art Nouveau) influences. He made many important war memorials for Magdeburg, Hamburg and Gustrow. The one at Gustrow was destroyed by the Nazis, and they also removed 381 of his pieces from public buildings. His rich and varied experiences reveal themselves in his work, as does his humanitarian side, which express mysticism, religion and compassion for the pains of humanity.

Barlow, Ambrose (Edward) Blessed, Benedictine monk and martyr, born Barlow Hall, England, 1585, died (executed) Lancaster, 10 September 1641. Despite his Catholic background he, with many others, conformed to the Protestant Church during his youth. When he was 22 he joined the English seminary at Douai. In 1613 he was imprisoned during a visit to England and was released after a few months. He then entered the English Benedictine monks at St Gregory's, Douai, and changed his name to Ambrose. Professed in 1614 and ordained in 1617, he returned to England. He spent 24 years working amongst the poor in the districts of Manchester and Liverpool. A stroke in 1641 left him partially paralysed, and on Easter day

in the year he was arrested while preaching to his congregation in Lancashire. He refused to abandon his faith, and on 8 September was condemned to death. **Pius XI** beatified him in 1929. Feast day 10 September.

Barlow, William Augustinian monk and bishop, born (allegedly) in Essex, died Chichester, 13 August 1568. He was at one time a canon of St Osyth's and then became prior of several houses of Augustinian canons; about 1524 he became the prior of Bromehill, Norfolk. When **Wolsey**'s policy of suppression hit Bromehill, Barlow produced several polemical pamphlets that were rejected as heresy in 1529. He recanted of his harsh words and in 1535 strongly believed in reform. In 1536 he became bishop of St Asaph and not long afterwards was transferred to St David's. Arguments with his chapter resulted in his being labelled, for the second time, a heretic. In 1548 he was moved to the bishopric of Bath and Wells, but resigned when **Mary Tudor** became queen later that year. He suffered a short imprisonment and then fled to Germany, returning on Mary's death to become bishop of Chichester in 1559.

Barlow, William Rudesind Benedictine writer, born Barlow Hall, Lancashire, 1584, died Douai, 19 September 1656. Brother of Ambrose **Barlow**. In 1602 William entered the Douai College, and in 1605 he left to become a Benedictine. He was professed in Spain a year later and ordained in 1608. He took doctorates in divinity at both Salamanca and Douai and served twice as prior of St Gregory's at Douai, in 1614–20 and 1625–9. He also spent time as president-general of the English Benedictine Congregation in 1621 and as professor of theology at the College of St Vedast in Douai. In 1641 he resigned from his place as titular prior of Coventry and the place was given to his brother five days before Ambrose was condemned for his faith.

Barnard of Vienne Saint, French Benedictine, founder of the monastery at Ambronay, archbishop. Born near Lyons, c.778, died Valence, 22 January 842. He was married and a soldier but gave up both for the spiritual life, becoming a monk in 803 and archbishop of Vienne in 810. He became embroiled in the politics of the time and was forced to flee to Italy because he had sided with **Lothair** against the latter's victorious father **Louis I** the Pious. He was allowed to return to France and founded the abbey of Saints-Severin-Exupère-et-Félicien, where he spent his last years. Feast day 22 January.

Barnardo, Thomas John Irish doctor and philanthropist, born Dublin, 4 July 1845, died Surbiton, near London, 19 September 1905. He began his career in a wine merchant's, but gave it up when he became convinced of the evils of intemperance. He converted to Christianity in 1862 in the middle of a Protestant revivalist crusade in Dublin, and decided to leave for London to study medicine and become a medical missionary in China. Confronted with the destitute children on the London streets, he alerted missionary enthusiasts to the needs on their own doorstep, captured the interest of Lord **Shaftesbury**, and opened the first Ragged School in a donkey stable to teach children to read and write, to make clothes and find jobs, in 1866. He then founded the East End Mission for Destitute Children, in Stepney, 1867, the East End Juvenile Mission, with classes for children and adults, 1868, and the Stepney Boys' Home, 1870, followed by others for both boys and girls, of all faiths and none, many outside London. When he died 8,000 children were in his care and he has been described as the 'father of nobody's children'.

Barnett, Samuel Anglican clergyman active in the nineteenth-century settlement movement, born Bristol, 8 February 1844, died Hove, 17 June 1913. With Octavia Hill he was influential in the Charity Organization Society, founded in 1869. Four years later he became incumbent of St Jude's Whitechapel, described by his bishop as 'the worst parish in the diocese', and made its care his life's work. Because of this he became involved in working-class education, poor relief, the campaign for improved working-class housing, and the pension movement. He is best known for his endeavours in the university settlement movement and was himself the first warden of Toynbee Hall, in 1884–96.

Baron, Vincent Dominican theologian, born Martres, Haut-Garonne, France, 17 May 1604, died Paris, 21 January 1674. Studied under the Jesuits, then joined the Dominicans in Toulouse in 1621. Professed in 1634, he taught philosophy and theology to the Dominican students and also at the University of Toulouse. He became a well-known and respected preacher throughout southern France and entered into open debate with the Calvinists in that area. The essence of these debates was published in *L'hérésie convaincue* (Paris, 1668). From 1630 to 1659 he was prior in Toulouse, Rodez, Castres, Albi, Avignon and Paris. In his last fourteen years he devoted himself to theological writing. At the instigation of Pope **Alexander VII** he wrote and published a course in moral theology, in three volumes, based on the work of **Thomas Aquinas** in which he defended the Probabiliorist approach, steering a steady path between approaches which were either too lax or too rigorous (Paris, 1665–7).

Baronius, Caesar Venerable, cardinal and church historian, born Sora, Campagna, 31 October 1538, died Rome, 30 June 1607. He began his education at Veroli and then studied philosophy, theology and law at Naples until the 1557 French invasion forced him to move to Rome. He gained a doctorate in law in 1561 and joined Philip **Neri**'s (not yet established) Congregation of the Oratory. When the pro-Lutheran history of the Church *Centuriae Magdeburgenses* was published, the twenty-year-old Baronius was chosen to respond. His twelve-volume *Annales ecclesiastici* (1598–1607) was the eventual result. He was ordained in 1564 and in 1593 he replaced Philip Neri as provost of the established (in 1575, though reluctantly on Neri's part) Oratory. In 1596 Baronius was promoted to cardinal, a post he had at first not wanted, and in 1597 he served as Vatican librarian.

Barontius Saint, monk, birth date and place unknown, died Pistoia, Italy, c.695. Coming from a somewhat wealthy family, Barontius decided to abandon a life of pleasure and distributed his wealth to the poor, though he secretly withheld some of it. With his son, he joined the abbey of Lonray (Berry, France), where he became a monk. A series of visions on hell and purgatory that he had during an illness caused him to give away the remainder of his wealth, make a pilgrimage to

Peter's tomb in Rome, and become a hermit near Pistoia, where he presumably died. His feast day is 25 March.

Barot, Madeleine French Protestant ecumenical leader, born Chateauroux, France, 4 July 1909, died Paris, 28 December 1995. Studies at the University of Paris led her into the Student Christian Movement. After the Nazi occupation of France, in May 1940 she became first general secretary of CIMADE (Comité intermouvement auprès des évacués), which quickly came to undertake pastoral support of all internees, especially Jews. Thereby she became associated with the Resistance movement, helping many to escape abroad. After the war she was involved in the massive task of reconstruction. From 1953 to 1966 she directed the World Council of Churches' department on the Co-operation of Men and Women in Church and Society. Later working for the WCC in development education, she played a part in the founding of SOPEPAX, the WCC–Vatican joint committee on Society, Development and Peace.

Barratt, Thomas Ball Norwegian Pentecostal preacher, born Albaston, Cornwall, 1862, died 1940. In 1889 Barratt was ordained in the Methodist Episcopal Church of Norway, the country to which his father had emigrated in 1867. He founded the Oslo City Mission in 1902, and following a fund-raising visit to the USA in 1906 he became a supporter of Pentecostalism. The following year he became a freelance revivalist, leaving the Methodists in 1916 to found the Filadelfia Church. He helped establish indigenous Pentecostal churches in the Third World and Europe, and his periodical *Korsets Seier* appeared in several languages.

Barré, Nicolas French priest, educator and founder of the Schools of Charity and of the Sisters of the Holy Infant Jesus. Born in Amiens, 21 October 1621, died Paris, 31 May 1686. He entered the Order of the Minims in 1639 and became professor of theology at Paris, a position he held for twenty years. As well as teaching theology he devoted much of his time to preaching and spiritual direction, as well as to promoting free education for all. He later established Schools of Charity of the Holy Infant Jesus, in Rouen in 1662, and later in Paris.

His work was continued by one of his protegés, St John de **La Salle**. His writings on spirituality include *Lettres spirituelles* (Rouen, 1697; Toulouse, 1876) and *Maximes spirituelles* (Paris, 1694).

Barrientos, Pedro Nolasco South American Franciscan theologian and educationist, born Paraguay, 1734, died Buenos Aires, Argentina, 15 October 1810. Entered the Franciscans in 1749 and was a noted preacher, teacher and confessor before he became professor of sacred theology and rector at the University of Córdoba in 1768. Over the next eleven years he reorganized and reformed the constitution and the curriculum of the university and increased its status considerably. He was for a time counsellor to the Viceroy Don Pedro Melo of Portugal before being sent to Buenos Aires.

Barrière, Jean de la Born St Ceré, Diocese of Cahors, 29 April 1544, died Rome, 25 April 1600. He was known for reforming the Order of Cîteaux or Feuillants. He studied at Toulouse and Bordeaux. In 1573 he was ordained priest. Monks at Les Feuillants refused to accept his reforms and some attempted to poison their abbot. Some monks left for Cistercian houses. The Feuillant rule was austere: food was simple, the monks ate on the floor kneeling, they went barefoot, and slept only for four hours and on the ground. In 1581 Pope **Gregory XIII** confirmed the Feuillants as a separate congregation, and they opened houses in Rome and Paris. In 1588 he founded a Feuillantine order for women. During the Peasants' War, Barrière was condemned as a traitor and reduced to being a layman.

Barron, Edward Irish missionary bishop, born Ballyneale, Co. Wexford, 28 June 1801, died of yellow fever, Savannah, Georgia, 12 September 1854. Studied law at Trinity College, Dublin, and in 1825 entered the seminary. He was ordained in Rome in 1829 and returned to Ireland to teach at St John's College, Waterford. He spent some time as rector of St Mary's Seminary in Philadelphia, and later became pastor of St Mary's and vicar-general. He volunteered for the mission to Liberia and while he was on his way there was named prefect apostolic of Upper Guinea, his jurisdiction later being extended to cover Sierra Leone and those parts of the west coast of Africa not within other ecclesiastical jurisdiction. His missionary endeavours were frustrated when two different groups of priests died of disease, and in 1845 Barron resigned and returned to the USA, where he worked in the Indian missions for a while. Although suffering from tuberculosis, he went to minister to the sick when the yellow fever epidemic struck Georgia.

Barrow, Henry   Separatist leader and martyr, born Shipdam, Norfolk, *c.*1550, hanged Tyburn, 6 April 1593, was converted from the life of a courtier to Puritanism *c.*1580. He was arrested when visiting John **Greenwood** in prison in 1586 and confined for the rest of his life. His works were published abroad but led to his conviction and execution for publishing seditious books: *A True Description of the Visible Congregation of the Saints* (1589) and *A Brief Discovery of the False Church* (1590 or 1591). It is very unlikely that he was the author of the Marprelate tracts, though they are commonly attributed to him.

Barrow, Isaac   Mathematician and theologian, born London, October 1630, died London, 4 May 1677. His early days of education were spent at Charterhouse and Felstead before finishing his education with a degree from Trinity College, Cambridge in 1648. In 1649 he accepted a fellowship and in 1655 published his edition of Euclid's *Elements.* That year he left England to journey in eastern Europe, returning in 1659. In 1660 he was ordained and was appointed to the chair of Greek at Cambridge. From 1662 to 1664 he was professor of geometry at Gresham College and in 1664 he became the first Lucasian professor at Cambridge. His most important mathematical work was the *Lectiones Geometricae,* which appeared in 1670, the same year that he handed his teaching role to his pupil Isaac **Newton**. He spent the rest of his life in the study of divinity.

Barruel, Augustin de   Jesuit polemical writer, born Villeneuve de Berg, 2 October 1741, died Paris, 5 October 1820. In 1756 he joined the Jesuits and was exiled with them in 1762. He returned to France, still with his Order, in 1774. It was at this point that his career as a polemicist really began, with a criticism of the *philosophes* in his *Helviennes ou Lettres provinciales philosophiques* in 1781. From 1788 until 1792 he used his role as editor of the *Journal ecclésiastique* to attack the French Revolution. Between 1790 and 1791 he wrote tracts criticizing the Civil Constitution of the Clergy and in 1787 wrote a thesis highlighting the role of the Freemasons and such secret societies in the Revolution. When the Directory fell he wrote to defend the new order and returned to the restored Society of Jesus in 1815. The remainder of his life was spent writing against **Kant**.

Barry, Mother Gerald (Catherine)   Nun and administrator, born Inagh, Ennis, County Clare, Ireland, 11 March 1881, died Adrian, Michigan, 20 November 1961. As a young woman she emigrated from Ireland to America and was involved in business until 1913, when she joined the Dominican Sisters of Adrian. She made her vows in 1914 and then served the convent in several ways, including as teacher and principal in 1914–21, novice mistress in 1921–33 and prioress-general in 1933–61. While she was superior, the community membership more than doubled and two colleges and four schools were built. The Holy See requested that she act as the first executive chairman of the Sister's Committee for the National Congress of Religious in the USA in 1952, and she presided over the Chicago meeting of superiors in 1956. She received honorary degrees from the Universities of Santo Domingo, Notre Dame and Loyola.

Barry, John   Roman Catholic bishop, born County Wexford, Ireland, died Paris, 21 November 1859. He was ordained in Charleston in 1825 and then served as assistant at the cathedral and secretary to the bishop until 1828. He was then made pastor of St Mary's Church; a year later he moved to Columbia to take charge of St Peter's Church, and another year later he moved to Holy Trinity Church in Augusta. During the Seminole War in 1836 Barry was assigned to the Irish Volunteers of Charleston as chaplain. He served as vicar-general under Bishop John **England** and his successor Ignatius Reynolds, and was named vicar-general of Savannah in 1850. Upon Bishop Gartland's death Barry was made administrator of the diocese in 1854, and in 1857 he was consecrated bishop of Savannah. He attended the Fourth and Eighth Provincial Councils of Baltimore.

Barrymore, Georgianna Emma Drew Roman Catholic actress and matriarch of a family of famous actors and actresses, born Philadelphia, Pennsylvania, 1856, died Santa Barbara, California, 2 July 1893. Barrymore began her acting career in 1872 in the Arch Street Theater in Philadelphia, which was run by her mother. In 1876 she married her fellow-actor Maurice Barrymore, and continued to act, appearing with the most famous actors of her day. In 1884, under the influence of Helena **Modjeska**, she converted to Catholicism and was baptized along with her three children: Lionel, Ethel and John. In late 1892, she contracted tuberculosis and moved, in hopes of slowing the disease, to California, where she died half a year later.

Barth, Karl Theologian of the Swiss Reformed Church, born Basel, Switzerland, 10 May 1886, died Basel, 10 December 1968. He studied theology in Berne, Berlin, Tübingen and Marburg. He established his theological reputation with his *Commentary on the Letter to the Romans* (1919) and served as professor at Göttingen, 1921–5, in a new professorship established by the Reformed community there with money from the American Presbyterian Church. He subsequently held professorships in Münster, 1925–30, and Bonn, 1930–5. When he refused to take an unconditional oath to Hitler, he was dismissed and became professor at Basel until 1962. Although his father, also a pastor in the Swiss Reformed Church, was a theological conservative, Barth in his early university studies was much influenced by liberal theologians and church historians, particularly Adolf von **Harnack**. His experience as a pastor, however, and his reading of existentialists, moved him towards an increasing suspicion of philosophy. The finiteness of human beings and the unquestionable authority and otherness of God were his major theological themes, worked out in his *Church Dogmatics* (1932–67: 4 volumes, incomplete).

Bartholomaeus Anglicus English Franciscan theologian, born 1195, date of death unknown. He flourished in the thirteenth century. Was professor of theology at Paris and joined the Franciscans *c.*1225. He was sent to Magdeburg in Germany *c.*1231. Here he produced *De proprietatibus rerum*, a nineteen-volume encyclopedia, covering theology, philosophy, medicine, astronomy, chronology, zoology, botany, geography and mineralogy. It was the first important medieval encyclopedia. Many manuscripts were made of it and it was produced in many editions and translations.

Bartholomew of Braga Venerable, Dominican archbishop and theologian, born Lisbon, 3 May 1514, died Viana, 16 July 1590. In 1528, having completed his schooling, he became a Dominican friar and taught philosophy and theology for twenty years. In 1558 he accepted appointment to the archiepiscopal see of Braga, despite his doubts. In the Council of Trent sessions from 1562 to 1563 Bartholomew was very influential in the discussions about reform. During his time as archbishop of Braga he began a seminary in his palace, visited and preached in his 1300 parishes, instituted chairs of moral theology in Braga and Viana do Castelo and created a catechism. Amongst his works are *Stimulus pastorum* (1565) and *Compendium spiritualis doctrinae* (1582). He resigned in 1582.

Bartholomew of Brescia Canonist, born in the second half of the twelfth century, died Bologna 1258. Having first studied Roman law and canon law in Bologna he taught there from about 1234 onwards. He wrote much, but nothing of his own, merely revisions of other authors' works. While still a student he revised Benencasa Aretinus' *Casus Decretorum*, which was published in 1505. His greatest work was a revision of **John Teutonicus**' writings on canon law, which Bartholomew entitled *Glossa ordinaria Decreti*. It was published between 1240 and 1245 and was regarded as a very useful and comprehensive work. It was appended to most manuscripts of the *Decretum*, and continued to be added even to the printed edition of the *Decretum*.

Bartholomew of Exeter Bishop and canonist, born Normandy, 1110, died 15 December 1184. Bartholomew moved to England after having excelled in the University of Paris. He spent some time serving Archbishop **Theobald** at Canterbury before becoming archdeacon of Exeter in 1155. By 1159 he was influential enough to support Pope **Alexander III** at the London Synod. In 1161 he became bishop of Exeter, shortly after Theobald's death. He took the side of **Thomas Becket** in the debate with King Henry II, but was in favour of peace. He did indeed play an important role in bringing peace after Becket's murder in 1170. He often served as Alexander III's papal judge-delegate with **Roger of Worcester**. He wrote a *Penitentiale*, the *De libero arbitrio* and the *Dialogus contra Judaeos*.

Bartholomew of Lucca Dominican bishop, historian and theologian, born Lucca, Italy, 1236, died Torcello, 1327. He became a Dominican in Lucca and studied under **Thomas Aquinas** from 1261 to 1268. During the 1280s and 1290s Bartholomew was the prior of various houses in Tuscany. He spent the years 1309 to 1319 at the papal court in Avignon researching and writing, and was appointed bishop of Torcello in 1318. He was imprisoned, after an argument, by the patriarch of Grado. In 1323 Pope **John XXII** himself ordered his release. He died in Torcello (near Venice) four years later. His works include the *Historia ecclesiastica*, which deals with the history of the Church from the birth of Christ to 1314, books 22 and 23 (of 24) being very important sources for information on the life of St Thomas Aquinas.

Bartholomew of Marmoutier Saint, Benedictine priest and abbot, died Marmoutier, near Tours, 24 February 1084. He was abbot of the monastery at Marmoutier from 1063 and resisted Geoffrey the Bearded's attempts to claim dominion over it. The Benedictine monks under Bartholomew's rule were so well disciplined and trained that they were highly desired by many to reform old monasteries and found new ones. Even **William** the Conqueror asked for (and received) Bartholomew's monks when he founded Battle Abbey at Hastings to give thanks for his victory. Officially Bartholomew has never had a cult in his name but he has been included in many medieval Benedictine martyrologies.

Bartholomew of Rome Roman Catholic reformer and preacher, born Rome, died Mantua 1430. He was involved in attempting to bring religious reform to Venice and in reforming the monastery of Santa Maria di Fregionaia near Lucca. As a result of this work the Congregation of Canons Regular of St John Lateran was born, and Bartholomew was made prior in 1403 and from 1407 to 1408. It seems that this was the only office he held

and that the rest of his time was devoted to his preaching, which was good enough for him to be remembered for it. Some historians have attributed to him the foundation of the Congregation of St George in Alga near Venice, but this was in fact the work of Pope **Clement IX** in 1668.

Bartholomew of San Concordio (of Pisa) Dominican theologian, born San Concordio, near Pisa, 1262, died Pisa, 11 June 1347. He lectured at Lucca, Florence and Pisa and was considered a talented preacher and writer, being termed 'One of the most erudite men of his time'. During the fourteenth and fifteenth centuries his *Summa de casibus conscientiae* was used considerably. He also wrote a series of Lenten sermons, a compendium of moral theology, *Ammaestramenti degli antichi*, some treatises on virtues and vices and amongst others a collection of comments made by authors of literature and theology which he titled *De documentis antiquorum*.

Bartholomew of Simeri Saint, Basilian abbot, born Simeri, Calabria, Italy, mid-eleventh century, died Rossano, 19 August 1130. In his youth Bartholomew joined the hermit Cyril in his ascetic lifestyle. Before the end of the eleventh century he had founded the monastery of Santa Maria Odigitria in the mountains near Rossano. After 1104 he was ordained and in 1105 travelled to Rome to confirm from the Pope immunity for his monastery. During this time he appears to have paid a visit to Constantinople, where he collected gifts of icons, sacred vessels and liturgical books from the emperor and the high official of the Empire, Basil Kalimeris. Upon his return to Italy, Bartholomew organized another monastery, San Salvatore de Messina. Feast day 19 August.

Bartholomew of Trent Dominican hagiographer, born Trent, died Trent, 1251. He was a well travelled man, visiting France and Germany as well as travelling extensively in Italy. He was often present at the imperial and papal courts, and Pope **Innocent IV** sent him on at least one mission of peace to **Frederick II**. A *Summa theologica adversus sui temporis haereses* has been ascribed to his authorship, but his main work was the *Liber epilogorum* (1245–51), which was a collection of biographies of the saints and included some of his own reflections and comments. His success with this work opened the way for a new genre that added a devotional aspect and sermon illustrations to what was once purely liturgical material.

Bartholomew of Urbino Augustinian bishop and compiler, died 1350. He was a student at both the University of Bologna and the University of Paris. After 1321 he began to teach at the University of Bologna, where he began his relationship with the canonist Andreae **Joannes**, who also taught there. Bartholomew's prime work was the *Milleloquium veritatis s. Augustini* (1555), which was a compilation of about 15,000 quotations from the writings of St **Augustine**. These citations were arranged in an orderly fashion under about 1,000 subject titles. Through this he displays an incredible knowledge of the works of Augustine. He also compiled the *Milleloquium Sancti Ambrosii* (1556), and for the last three years of his life served as bishop of Urbino.

Bartholomew of Vicenza Blessed, Dominican preacher and bishop, born Vicuza, 8 September 1200, died Vicenza, Italy, 1270. In 1223 Bartholomew was responsible for the founding of the Militia of Jesus Christ for knights. In 1252 he was ordained as bishop of Limassol, Cyprus, after having been the regent of the theological faculty at the papal curia. In 1255 he was transferred to Vicenza and served as the papal envoy to England and France. At this time **Louis IX** sent him a thorn from the alleged Crown of Thorns. His main works were *An Exposition of the Canticle of Canticles* and *The Search for Divine Love*. Bartholomew seems to have been, before his episcopal career began, very active as a preacher and opponent of heretics. His cult received approval in 1793. Feast day 23 October.

Bartleman, Frank Pentecostal evangelist and commentator, born Carversville, Pennsylvania, 1871, died California, 23 August 1936. Bartleman ministered in a number of denominations, and travelled widely in America and Europe. In 1904 he moved to Los Angeles, and from 1906 he attended W. J. **Seymour**'s prayer meetings and the Azuza Street Mission. In six books, 550 articles and 100 tracts he argued for Church–State separation, for pacifism and against capitalism and communism, among other subjects. In *How Pentecost Came to Los Angeles* (1925) he chronicled the Azuza Street revival. Other works include *My Story: 'The Latter Rain'* (1909), *From Plow to Pulpit* (1924), and *Around the World by Faith* (1925).

Bartmann, Bernhard Roman Catholic theologian, born Madfeld, Germany, 26 May 1860, died Paderborn, 1 August 1938. Having spent a few years teaching, Bartmann began his study of theology at Münster in 1884. From there he went on to Würzburg, Eichstätt and Paderborn. In 1888 he was ordained and gained his doctorate in theology eight years later. In 1898 he became professor of dogma at the Paderborn faculty of theology. His main work was his *Lehrbuch der Dogmatik* (1905), which attained the status of being the most widely used German text of his time. It worked at presenting the teaching of St **Thomas Aquinas** from a biblical, patristic and historical aspect.

Bartók, Béla Unitarian musician, born Nagyszentmiklós (now in Romania), 25 March 1881, died New York, 26 September 1945. After he had finished his studies at the Royal Hungarian Academy of Music in Budapest he remained there as the principal piano teacher whilst trying to become a recognized international concert pianist. In 1905 he began to compile and study Hungarian peasant music. In 1919 he and his family became members of the First Unitarian Church in Budapest, despite having declared himself to be an atheist in 1907. He worked on the Hungarian Unitarian hymnbook, and in 1940 he emigrated to the USA, where he worked on researching folk music and performed as a concert pianist. All of his works have been published in Budapest but not yet translated.

Bartoli, Daniello Jesuit historian and author, born Ferrara, 12 February 1608, died Rome, 13 January 1685. In 1623 he joined the Jesuits as a novice at Novellera. He studied theology and philosophy at the University of Parma, and in 1636 he was ordained at Bologna. He remained in Italy while a Jesuit, despite his burning desire and frequent requests to be sent to the mission field. He earned himself a reputation as a powerful speaker and talented writer, and he was called to Rome by Vincenzo **Carafa** to write a history of the Jesuits in Italian. Apart from working on this he spent the years 1671 to 1673 as the rector of the Roman College. The finished work consisted of an introduction (*Della vita dell'istituto di S. Ignazio*) and five volumes of history (*Dell'istoria della compagnia di Gesù*) appearing in 1650 and 1653–73 respectively.

Bartolo di Fredi Renaissance painter, born Siena, 1335, died Siena, 1410. He painted religious art extensively, and his repeated experiences of the plague and Dominican preaching lent his work a serious mien. This is demonstrated by his OT cycle (finished in 1367) in the Collegiata, San Gimignano, which contains many scenes from the book of Job. His works include *Deposition* (1382), *Coronation of the Virgin* (1388) and *Adoration of the Magi* (between 1375 and 1380). His art expresses itself through ignoring realism and spatial depth without becoming absurd. He was employed to paint by many groups, but worked extensively for the Dominicans.

Bartolo of Sassoferrato Jurist, born Sassoferrato, 1313, died Perugia, 1357. He was educated at the Universities of Perugia and Bologna, first studying law under Cinus at Perugia and then under James of Belvisio at Bologna. In 1334 he also received his doctorate in law from Bologna. After much private study he took the post of professor of law at Pisa in 1339, and later moved to Perugia. His best-known work is his commentary on the Code of **Justinian**, and he is also renowned for his use of scholasticism to apply methods of Roman law to contemporary situations. His method was not forgotten upon his death and a group of jurists kept it alive. This group was termed 'Bartolists' in honour of Bartolo.

Bartolomeo, Fra Influential painter, born Baccio della Porta, Soffignano, 28 March 1475, died Florence, 6 October 1517. At a young age he joined a fellow apprentice, Mariotto Albertinelli, and entered into a partnership. When **Savonarola** was besieged in 1498 Bartolommeo, a supporter of the friar, pledged to become a monk if he was spared. In 1500 he entered the Dominicans and was assigned to the convent in Florence. He had ceased painting but was asked by the prior to work on *The Vision of St Bernard* (1504–7). It was about this time that he met and influenced the painter

Raphael. In 1508 he travelled to Venice and joined up with Albertinelli again, but the prior dissolved the partnership in 1512. Bartolomeo spent some time in Rome painting but left for Florence before his work was completed. Having contracted malaria, he spent the last years of his life painting in Florence, Lucca and elsewhere.

Bartolucci, Giulio Hebraist, born Celano, Abruzzi, 1 April 1613, died Rome, 20 October 1687. He became a Cistercian monk of the Italian congregation of the Feuillants (reformed Bernardines) in Rome and then studied theology at Mondovi and Turin. Whilst travelling through Italy he would spend much time in libraries poring over Jewish literature, and as a result he taught Hebrew at Rome and was named *Scriptor Hebraicus* of the Vatican Library. His other posts included consultor to the Congregation of the Index, superior of Cistercian houses in Brisighella and Rome, presiding at their general chapter, and titular abbot of San Sebastiano ad Catacumbas. His primary work was his four-volume account of Jewish authors and literature, *Bibliotheca magna rabbinica de scriptoribus et scriptis hebraicis*.

Barton, Elizabeth 'Prophetess' known as 'The Nun of Kent', born 1506, died London, 20 April 1534. The nineteen-year-old Barton was a servant to Thomas Cobb, steward of Archbishop William **Warham** of Canterbury, when she started slipping into trances and uttering prophecies. Her condition was attributed to divine activity by Edward **Bocking**. She became a nun in the St Sepulchre Priory (near Canterbury), and despite the scepticism of Thomas **More** and King **Henry VIII** achieved great renown. She was an outspoken opponent of the king's divorce and was consulted by Henry's enemies, such as John **Fisher**, but never by Queen **Catherine** herself. In 1533 Thomas **Cranmer**, new archbishop of Canterbury, obtained a confession of deceit from Elizabeth and she was publicly executed at Tyburn, proclaiming her own guilt.

Barzyński, Vincent Roman Catholic missionary, born Sulislawice, Poland, 20 September 1838, died Chicago, 2 May 1899. Ordained in 1861 after studying at the diocesan seminary in Lublin, Poland. After the unsuccessful anti-Russian Polish uprising of 1863 (in which he took part) he fled to Austria and France. In 1866, while in Paris, he joined the Congregation of the Resurrection and was sent to work amongst Polish Catholics in Texas, America. In 1874 he became the pastor of St Stanislaus Kostka in Chicago. In 1890 he founded a publishing house that produced a daily newspaper for Polish Catholics, *Dziennik Chicagoski*, and in 1891 St Stanislaus Kostka High School for boys. He also served as superior for the Chicago Resurrectionists and became the first provincial of the congregation's American province, 1898–9.

Basalenque, Diego   Augustinian historian and linguist, born Salamanca, Spain, 25 July 1577, died Charo, Mexico, 11 December 1651. His parents emigrated to Mexico when Diego was still young, and he joined the Augustinians when he was fifteen. He was professed in Mexico City in 1594 and after his ordination taught Augustinian students in Michoacán. He received a master of theology degree and served as prior in the monasteries of San Luis Potosí, Valladolid, and in 1623 Michoacán. He wrote two studies on native tongues, only one being published, and a history of the Augustinian order entitled *Historia de la provincia de San Nicolás de Tolentino de Michoacán del orden de N.P.S. Agustín*, which he finished in 1644 and published in 1673.

Bascio, Matteo Serafini da   Vicar-general of the Friars Minor Capuchin, born Bascio, near Pesaro, 1495, died Venice, 6 August 1552. In 1511 he joined the Friars Minor Observant of the Province of Ancona and was ordained nine years later. In 1525 he embarked on a secret journey to Rome where he sought **Clement VII**'s permission to observe the Rule of St **Francis** strictly. He became an itinerant preacher, despite the efforts of his Order to stop him. He unwittingly began a trend which resulted in the foundation of the Friars Minor Capuchin, receiving canonical approbation in 1528. He became their first vicar-general in 1529, but was unhappy, resigned soon afterwards and returned to his wandering. From 1536 onwards he appears to have shifted his allegiance from the Capuchins to the Observants, and in 1546 he served with the papal troops sent to fight the Schmalkaldic League.

Basedow, Johann Bernhard   Educational reformer, born Hamburg, Germany, 12 September 1723, died Magdeburg, 24 July 1790. During an unhappy childhood he was sent to the Hamburg Johanneum classical school and in 1744 studied philosophy and theology at the University of Leipzig. He then worked as tutor to the son of the Danish privy councillor at Borghorst. He applied the methods of naturalism he had encountered in **Rousseau**'s *Emile* while at Leipzig. His success endeared him to influential people, and Prince Leopold supported and encouraged him. In 1774 he opened his Philanthropinum school in Dessau, the first German non-sectarian school. Of his many books only his *Elementarwerk* and *Das Methodenbuch* were considered noteworthy.

Basham, Don Wilson   Bible teacher and author, born Wichita Falls, Texas, 1926, died 1989. Basham joined the Christian Church at college, and experienced baptism in the Holy Spirit in 1952. In 1955 he was ordained into the Disciples of Christ, but he resigned in 1967 to become a freelance writer and minister. His teaching emphasized the 'deliverance ministry', and he wrote on the subject in *Deliver Us from Evil* (*c.*1972). In Fort Lauderdale, Florida, he co-founded Christian Growth Ministries (CGM) with Bob Mumford, Derek Prince and Charles Simpson. He edited the CGM *New Wine Magazine* until 1986, when he began his own newsletter, *Don Basham's Insights*.

Bashīr II al-Shihābi   Maronite Christian, reformer and last Lebanese feudal lord. Born into the Shihābi family (which had entered Lebanon around 1170), died Constantinople, 1850. Succeeded as emir in 1788 and set about centralizing power, building bridges and roads, and improving the justice system. He encouraged Christian missionary work; American missionaries were in Beirut from 1823 and established the first mission school in 1834. When, with Turkish and British encouragement, the people of Lebanon revolted against Bashīr, he was taken by British ship to Malta, and later went to Constantinople, where he spent his final days.

Basil I   Byzantine emperor 867–86, born near Adrianople 812, died 886. Once he had settled in Constantinople he became a groom at the imperial court. He charmed Emperor **Michael III**, married the emperor's mistress Eudocia Ingerina, killed the Caesar **Bardas** and was crowned co-emperor in 866. After the murder of Michael, Basil founded the Macedonian dynasty, which lasted until 1056. He supported the expansion of Christianity through the Slav tribes and in 872 began his war against the Paulicians in Asia Minor. The eastern boundaries of the Empire were expanded under his command and he was responsible for beginning a revision of **Justinian**'s Code of Laws, which was completed by **Leo VI**. He also deposed Patriarch **Photius** and restored him after Patriarch **Ignatius**' death.

Basil II Byzantine emperor 976–1025, born Constantinople, 958, died 15 December 1025. He only fully claimed the throne after usurping his eunuch uncle Basil in 985. Between 976 and 979 he faced and fought off a revolt led by Bardas Sclerus, and between 987 and 989 he overcame (aided by Prince Vladimir of Kiev) another, this time led by Bardas Phocas. For his help Basil granted Vladimir his sister's hand in marriage, leading to the conversion of Russia. By 1018, after twenty years of combat, the Empire's deadliest enemy, Bulgaria, had been totally annexed. The Church there, however, was left independent of Constantinople. He also made peace in Syria with the Fatimids while fighting his campaign in the Balkans (995–9).

Basil the Great Saint, bishop and theologian, born Pontus, 330, died Caesarea, 379. Brother of **Gregory of Nyssa**. He was educated in Pontus and Athens before becoming a teacher of rhetoric in 356. In 357 he was baptized and became a hermit on his family land. It was during his time as a hermit that he began to write against the various heresies that were challenging orthodoxy. His works include *De Spiritu Sancto*, in which he defends the deity of the Holy Spirit, and *Adversus Eunomium*, in which he foreshadows the Council of Constantinople of 381 in understanding the Trinity as one substance (*ousia*), three persons (*hypostasis*). In 364 he was encouraged to leave his hermitage by **Eusebius of Caesarea**, who made him a presbyter, and he became bishop of Caesarea in 370. He also developed the Rule of St Basil, which is today still the structure for Eastern monasticism. Feast day 2 January.

Basil of Ancyra Bishop and theologian, originally a doctor, died in exile, 364. In 336 Bishop **Marcellus of Ancyra** was deposed and exiled for Sabellianism and Basil replaced him. At the 358 Synod of Ancyra Basil became the leader of the moderate Arian party. However, it was the extreme Arian party that gained the favour of Emperor **Constantius II**. Like many orthodox bishops, Basil and his followers went to Constantinople in 359 to agree to the terms of extreme Arianism. **Acacius of Caesarea** became the leader of Basil's followers, and in 360 Basil and his friends were deposed and exiled. He died in exile after having recanted his consent to the extreme Arian position. *On the True Purity of Chastity* has been attributed to him, its anatomical detail supporting the theory that Basil was once a physician. **Athanasius** wrote that Basil, apart from his rejection of *homoousion*, was nearly orthodox and 'must not be treated as [an enemy]'.

Basil (Krivocheine) of Brussels Russian Orthodox bishop and patristic scholar, born St Petersburg, 30 June 1900, died Leningrad, 22 September 1985. He left Russia after the Revolution and in 1925 became a monk of Mount Athos, where he stayed for 22 years. Afterwards he devoted his life to patristic studies. His most important work was *St Symeon the New Theologian* (English edition 1986). In 1959 he became archbishop in Brussels for the Russian Orthodox Church. He died on his first return to the city of his birth.

Basil of Soissons Capuchin theologian, date of birth unknown, died Paris, 3 March 1698. In 1635 He joined the Capuchins, and committed himself to the defence of the Roman Catholic faith. In his four-volume work *Fondement inébranlable* (1680–2) he challenges his opponents using the only common ground they had, Scripture. He defended the creed of Roman Catholicism, the sacraments, the Decalogue and prayer. He wrote *Défense invincible* (Paris, 1676) which dealt primarily with the Eucharist, and in his *La véritable décision* (Paris, 1685) he argues that the Catholic Church is the only true point of reference for matters of theology.

Basiliscus Byzantine Emperor (475–6), died Cappadocia, 477. Basiliscus was the brother of Emperor **Leo I**'s wife Verina. He showed little talent or ability, yet managed to rise to the position of consul and led the expedition against the Vandals that was destroyed in 468. After Leo died **Zeno** was crowned in 474, and Verina successfully plotted against him. He was deposed in 475 and Basiliscus crowned. Basiliscus' pro-Monophysite, anti-Chalcedon position resulted in him persecuting the orthodox clergy. The protests of the orthodox, especially the stylite Daniel and Patriarch Acacius of Constantinople, drove the people to rebellion and Verina betrayed her brother, ultimately engineering his downfall. Zeno was restored and Basiliscus (and his family) were starved to death in a cistern somewhere in Cappadocia.

Bassianus of Ephesus   Bishop, died *c*.452. Bishop Memnon of Ephesus appears to have been jealous of Bassianus' popularity as a priest and had him made bishop of Evaza in 431. Bassianus refused to occupy his see and Basil, who succeeded Memnon, appointed another bishop for Evaza and allowed Bassianus to return to Ephesus in 434. In 444 Bassanius was chosen to succeed Basil as bishop of Ephesus. In 448, however, Bassianus was deposed and replaced by Stephen. Bassianus, understandably, objected to this and took his case to the Council of Chalcedon. The Council, unable to reach a clear decision, deposed both men and appointed a new bishop for Ephesus. Bassianus vanishes from history at this stage, but both he and Stephen were awarded 200 gold solidi a year from the see of Ephesus.

Bassville, Nicolas Jean Hugou de   Diplomat and writer, born Somme, France, 7 February 1753, died (assassinated) Rome, 14 January 1793. From 1789 he supported the French Revolution and contributed to the unsuccessful *Mercure national et Révolutions de l'Europe*. In 1790 he wrote his four-volume commentary on the work of the National Assembly, *Mémoires historiques . . . de la Révolution*. In 1792 he was sent to Rome as the French ambassador to attend to the rights of French citizens. His extreme Republicanism worked against him, however, and on 13 January 1793 he suffered at the hands of an uprising on the Corso. He was stabbed in the abdomen, and died the next day after having received the last rites. Bassville's assassination became another stumbling-block to Franco-Roman peace.

Bataillon, Pierre Marie   Marist missionary, born Saint-Cyr-les-Vignes, France, 6 January 1810, died Wallis Island, 10 April 1877. After being ordained as a Marist priest he was sent, with Bishop Jean Pompallier, as a missionary to Oceania. They arrived at Wallis Island in 1837. Bataillon faced the trials and danger of his work with a courage and love that soon won the favour of the fierce Polynesian chiefs. In 1842 the entire island was converted (about 2,700 people). In the same year he also became the first vicar-general of Central Oceania. A year later he was made bishop and began successful missionary work in Fiji, Tonga and Somoa. In 1874 he opened a seminary on Wallis Island to train native clergy.

Bathilde   Saint, wife of Clovis II, king of France. Born, possibly in England, date and place unknown, died near Paris, January 680. She was a slave in the palace of Neustria. Clovis was so impressed by her beauty and goodness that he freed her and in 649 married her. She became known for her humility, prayerfulness and generosity. Clovis II died in 656. His son Clothaire III, aged five, became king and Bathilde became regent. She abolished Christian slavery and repressed the custom among clergy of buying and selling promotion in the Church. She founded religious institutions, such as hospitals and monasteries, including the abbeys of Corbie and of Chelles. When her children were grown up she withdrew to Chelles. Feast day 26 January.

Báthory family: An aristocratic Hungarian family descended from the ancient Magyar clan of Gut-Keled, which included:

>   **Báthory, Andras**   Bishop of Nagyvárad in 1333, built the cathedral there and was advisor to King Charles Robert of Hungary.

>   **Báthory, Andras**   Cardinal bishop of Ermland. Born in 1566, he died in battle on 3 November 1599 before being able to take up the position of prince of Transylvania.

>   **Báthory, Istvan**   Born in 1533 and died suddenly in 1586. He was a soldier and diplomat who was elected prince of Transylvania in 1571 and king of Poland in 1575. He enjoyed numer-

ous victories over Ivan the Terrible and the Muscovites, and over the Turks and Tartars and strengthened Poland's position in northern Europe. He supported the Roman Catholic Reform movement over the Protestants and introduced the Gregorian calendar into Poland.

Báthory, László Blessed, died c.1484, translated the Bible into Hungarian and was a member of the Order of Hermits of St Paul.

Batiffol, Pierre Roman Catholic theologian, born Toulouse, France, 27 January 1861, died Paris, 13 January 1929. After his studies at the Seminary of St Sulpice in Paris, 1878–82, he was ordained in 1884. While undertaking a post as curate in Paris he also attended the Institut Catholique and the Ecole des Hautes Etudes. From 1889 until 1898 he was chaplain in Paris at the Ecole de Ste Barbe and then he moved to Toulouse to become the rector of the Institut Catholique. Amongst his works on church history he wrote *L'Eucharistie: la Présence réelle et la Transubstantiation*, which was put on the Index in 1907, resulting in Batiffol resigning from his post as rector and returning as chaplain to the Ecole de Ste Barbe. In 1913 he revised his book on the Eucharist.

Batista, Cicero Romão Priest and object of popular devotion, born Ceará, Brazil, 1844, died Rome, 1934. After his ordination in 1870 Batista became a pastor in the impoverished region of Juazeiro in Ceará. A severe drought from 1877 to 1879 brought many people to hear his passionate sermons on repentance and the benefits of asceticism. In 1889 Batista's church experienced 'miracles' in which the Hosts turned into blood, increasing his reputation amongst the growing peasant congregation. The bishop of the diocese condemned the miracles in 1891 and Batista was banned from preaching and saying Mass. He travelled to Rome in 1898 to present his case to Pope **Leo XIII**, who permitted him only to say Mass in a private oratory. The situation was abused by the State governors and there were violent clashes between the authorities and the public, who believed themselves protected supernaturally by their *padrinho*.

Batthyány, Jozsef Hungarian prince-primate, archbishop of Esztergom and cardinal, born Vienna, 30 January 1727, died Pozsony (Bratislava), 23 October 1799. He was a first-rate orator and statesman who advised the Empress Maria Theresa and successfully mediated in the dispute between **Pius VI** and the Emperor Joseph II concerning the emperor's reforms.

Baudissin, Wolf Wilhelm Protestant OT scholar, born Sophienhof, near Kiel, Germany, 26 September 1847, died Berlin 6 February 1926. He gained his Ph.D. in theology and Semitics from Leipzig in 1870, and then taught OT at Leipzig, 1876–80, Strasburg, 1880–1, Marburg, 1881–1900 and Berlin, 1900–26. He endlessly attempted to prove that the religion of the OT had much in common with general Semitic religion. His main work in this area was his *Kyrios als Gottesname im Judentum und seine Stelle in der Religionsgeschichte*, and he also wrote other noteworthy books purely on the OT. These include *Die Geschichte des alttestamentlichen Priestertums* (1889) and *Einleitung in die Bücher des Alten Testaments* (1901).

Baudouin, François Lawyer and humanist, born Arras, France, 1 January 1520, died Paris, 1574. He met many of the leading French humanists while studying law and classical languages at Louvain. Early in his life he had sympathies with the cause of the Reformers and spent three years in Geneva as one of **Calvin**'s secretaries. He taught law at Bourges, 1549–55, Strasburg, 1556, Heidelberg, 1556–62 and Angers, 1562 onwards. About 1560 he returned to his Catholic faith and spent his time trying to reconcile Catholics and Calvinists in France. He was present at the 1561 Colloquium of Poissy but not allowed to take part. His noble attempts to bring peace between Catholics and Protestants were ignored and he was (unfairly) criticized by both parties for his apparently half-hearted stance between the two religions.

Baudouin, Louis Marie Venerable, Roman Catholic priest, born Vendée, France, 2 August 1765, died Vendée, 12 February 1835. He was ordained in 1789 after having been educated by the Vincentians at the seminary of Luçon. He then assisted his brother (who was pastor in Luçon) until after the French Revolution, when the brothers refused to take the oath of the Civil Constitution of the Clergy. They moved to Spain in 1792, and Louis' brother died in 1796. Louis returned to France, defying the persecution of the clergy by resuming a hidden apostolate. In 1802 he became a parish priest in Chavagnes and founded the Sons of Mary Immaculate of Luçon (the Priests of Chavagnes). With Gabrielle Charlotte Ranfray de la Rochette he founded, for women, the Ursulines of Jesus. In 1812 he became rector of the seminary of La Rochelle and vicar-general of Luçon in 1822. He was declared Venerable in 1871.

Baudrillart, Henri Marie Alfred Cardinal, scholar and diplomat, born Paris, 6 January 1859, died Paris, 19 May 1942. In 1890, after his training in history, he earned his doctor of letters degree. He taught at Laval, Caen, Paris and in 1883 the Institut Catholique. In 1890 he joined the Oratory and was ordained three years later. He returned to the Institut Catholique as a professor after having gained his doctorate in theology. In 1907 he became rector of the Institut Catholique and in 1921 was made titular bishop of Himeria. This was followed in 1928 by the titular bishopric of Melitene and in 1935 by the title of cardinal priest. As a scholar he contributed to the *Dictionnaire d'histoire et de géographie ecclésiastiques* and as a diplomat he played an important role in the 1921 reconciliation between France and the Pope. In 1918 he became a member of the Académie Française, in 1920 a chevalier of the Légion d'Honneur, and a commander in 1935.

Baudry of Bourgueil Bishop and poet, born Meung-sur-Loire, France, 1046, died January 1130. He received his education at the cathedral school of Angers and then entered the Benedictine Order. In 1089 he was made abbot of Bourgueil-en-Vallée and in 1107 he was made archbishop of Dol in Brittany. His poetry shows that he often tried to imitate Ovid, or at least was influenced by him. Sometime between 1100 and 1110 he wrote an account of the First Crusade that used the *Gesta Francorum* as its source. His poetry also shows a love of the natural world. As well as writing unusually 'unbishop-like' poetry he was occasionally absent from his bishopric, preferring the scenery and lifestyle of Normandy.

Bauer, Bruno Biblical critic and scholar, born Eisenberg, Germany, 6 September 1809, died Rixdorf, 15 April 1882. Very influential on some of the atheists that the Enlightenment era was producing, Bauer began his career as a Hegelian, having studied philosophy and theology at Berlin. In 1839 he became an instructor at the University of Bonn, but was dismissed in 1842 after the publication of his *Kritik der evangelischen Geschichte des Johannes* and *Kritik der evangelischen Geschichte der Synoptiker*. Both texts renounce his Hegelian past and suggest that the Gospels are nothing more than than creations from the minds of the Evangelists. His *Christus und die Cäsaren* (1877) places the first Gospel in the time of Hadrian (118–38) and the birth of Christianity during the time of Marcus Aurelius (160–80).

Bauer, Georg *see* **Agricola**

Bauer, Walter NT Greek lexicographer and church historian, born Königsberg, Prussia, 8 August 1877, died Göttingen, Germany, 17 November 1960. He did graduate studies at Marburg, Berlin and Strasburg and then taught NT exegesis at Marburg in 1902–13, Breslau in 1913–16 and Göttingen in 1916–45. As a historian he promulgated the thesis that the first Egyptian Christians were Gnostics and that it was in fact orthodoxy that was the intruder there. His main achievement was his work on Erwin Preuschen's *Griechisch-Deutsches Handwörterbuch zu den Schriften des Neuen-Testaments und der übrigen urchristlichen Literatur*, which he revised and updated until it was almost a completely new work.

Bäuerle, Hermann Roman Catholic priest and scholar, born Ebersberg, Germany, 24 October 1869, died Ulm, 21 May 1936. He studied ancient and modern philology at the University of Tübingen while also training for the priesthood, and was ordained in 1895. He was sent, as a pastor, to Ochsenhausen. He attended the Kirchenmusikschule at Regensburg from 1898 to 1899, served as court chaplain to the Prince of Thurn and Taxis and then moved back to Regensburg to lecture on harmony and counterpoint. He taught there from 1901 to 1908. During that period, in 1906, he also studied for his doctorate degree at Leipzig. After another pastoral placement he founded his Ulm music school in 1921. Bäuerle also composed music for Masses, vespers and other liturgical pieces.

Bäumer, Suitbert Roman Catholic liturgist, born Leuchtenburg, Rhineland, 28 March 1845, died Freiburg im Breisgau, 12 August 1894. In 1865 he joined the Beuron monastery and was ordained four years later. He studied at the Universities of Bonn and Tübingen. He spent the years from 1875 to 1890 (during the Kulturkampf) in Belgium and England, serving as liturgical consultant to the publisher Desclée in Tournai for its versions of the Missal, the monastic Breviary, the Vulgate and so on. His many writings were on church liturgy, monasticism and patristics. His most noteworthy work was published the year after his death, *Geschichte des Breviers*, and was influential enough to appear in a French edition ten years later.

Baumgartner, Alexander Roman Catholic scholar and literary critic, born Sankt Gallen, Switzerland, 27 June 1841, died Luxemburg, 5 October 1910. He joined the Society of Jesus in 1860 and in 1875 (after being ordained) began working on the editorial staff of the *Stimmen Maria-Laach* (later to become *Stimmen der Zeit*). The expulsion of the Jesuits from Germany led to the publication moving from place to place during Baumgartner's term. His first writings of note all appeared in *Stimmen*, including *Lessings religiöser Entwicklungsgang* (1877), *Longfellow* (1877) and the first part of his critique of Goethe that was to eventually become the three-volume *Goethe, sein Leben und seine Werke* (1885–6).

Baumgartner, Walter Theologian, born Winterthur, Switzerland, 24 November 1887, died Basel, 1969. A student of the great OT scholar Hermann **Gunkel**, he wrote his dissertation on the Lamentations of Jeremiah (Marburg, 1916). He taught at the University of Basel and was an authority on the OT and the Semitic languages. Among his many publications in these fields were a *Commentary on the Book of Daniel* (1926), *Das Buch Daniel und seine Botschaft von den letzten Dingen* (1944), and a *Dictionary of the Aramaic Part of the Old Testament in German and English* (1953). He was named an honorary member of the British Society for Old Testament Studies (1947).

Baumstark, Anton Liturgical and Oriental scholar, born Constance, 4 August 1872, died Bonn, 31 May 1948. Baumstark spent his time in scholarly pursuits, giving him some knowledge of many disciplines such as history, literature and theology. He taught various disciplines (including Oriental studies, Islam, Arabic and Semitic languages) at Heidelberg in 1898, Bonn in 1921–30, Nijmegen in 1923, Utrecht in 1926 and Münster in 1930–5. In 1901 he and Anton de Waal began the *Oriens Christianus* and in 1922 published the *Geschichte der syrischen Literatur*. With Odo **Casel** he started the *Jahrbuch für Liturgiewissenschaft* and attempted to trace the development and evolution of Christian liturgy through history. Baumstark became a supporter of the Nazi party in the last years of his life.

Baunard, Louis Pierre Roman Catholic writer, born Bellegard (Loiret), 24 August 1828, died Gruson, near Lille, 9 November 1919. He entered the seminary at Orléans and was ordained in 1852. He then taught at the minor seminary from 1852 to 1860. In 1860 he received his doctorate in letters from Sorbonne and a year later a doctorate in theology from Rome. In 1877 he became a professor at the Institut Catholique, Lille, and in 1888 became a rector there. He retired from the academic life in 1902 and moved to Gruson. The works he is most remembered for are his work of church history, *Un siècle de l'Eglise de France, 1800–1900*, and for his biographies of noteworthy religious people. These included, amongst others, St John the Apostle (1869), St **Ambrose** (1871) and St Madeleine Sophie **Barat** (1876).

Bauny, Etienne French Jesuit and moral theologian, born Mouzon, Ardennes, 1 June 1575, died St Pol de Léon, 12 December 1649. Joined the Society of Jesus in 1593 and taught humanities, rhetoric and later moral theology. As a moral theologian he was the focus of the attack by the Jansenists **Arnauld** and **Pascal** against the moral laxity of the Jesuits. Among his writings are *Sommes des péchés qui se commettent en tous états* (1640), *Pratique du droit canonique au gouvernement de l'Église* (1633), *De sacramentis ac personis sacris . . . Theologiae moralis* (1640–2), *Tractatus de censuris ecclesiasticus* (1642) and *Libri tres quibus,* *quae in contractuum ac quasi contractuum materia videntur ardua ac difficilia, enucleantur* (1645).

Baur, Ferdinand Christian   Protestant theologian and founder of the newer Tübingen school, born near Cannstatt, Germany, 21 June 1792, died Tübingen, 2 December 1860. He spent 34 years as professor at Tübingen, where he devoted himself to historical-critical research on the NT, church history, and the history of dogma. He viewed the history of primitive Christianity as a dialectical development in which two originally opposed traditions, the Jewish and the pagan or Gentile, eventually underwent a synthesis in the second and third centuries. His works include *Symbolik und Mythologie: Die christliche Gnosis* (1835), *Christianity and the Christian Churches of the First Three Centuries* (1853), and *Paul, the Apostle of Jesus Christ* (1866).

Bautain, Louis-Eugène-Marie   Catholic priest, philosopher and theologian, born Paris, France, 17 February 1796, died Paris, 15 October 1867. He was vicar-general of the Archdiocese of Paris and professor of moral theology at the Sorbonne. He held that the divine Word as revealed to humanity is the only source of all scientific knowledge, and thus philosophy must fashion its principles from Holy Scripture. The task of reason is to render evident (by the dialectical method) what has been acknowledged by faith. He wrote *La morale de l'Evangile comparée à la morale des philosophes* (1827), *La philosophie du Christianisme* (1835), and *Le chrétien de nos jours* (2 vols, 1861–2).

Bauza, Francisco   Uruguayan Roman Catholic politician, historian and orator, born Montevideo, 7 October 1851, died Montevideo, 4 December 1899. Worked as a journalist and edited the *Los Debates* newspaper. Served as a diplomat and entered the House of Representatives. He was Uruguayan representative in Brazil, a govenment minister and a senator. He introduced local and national reforms. He was one of the leaders of the Catholic cause and opposed the liberal actions of the Ateneo of Montevideo. His writings include the three-volume *Historia de la dominación española en el Uruguay*, *Estudios constitucionales* and *Estudios literarios*.

Bavinck, Johan Herman   Dutch missiologist, born Rotterdam, 22 November 1895, died 1964. After graduating from the Free University of Amsterdam and gaining a doctorate from Erlangen in 1919, he ministered to Dutch congregations in Medan and Bandung, Indonesia in 1919–26. He was then a pastor in Heemstede, Holland, 1926–9 before returning to Indonesia as a missionary in Solo and Jogjakarta, where he developed a deep understanding of Javanese spirituality. In 1939 he became the first professor of missions at Kampen Theological College and taught at the Free University of Amsterdam until 1964. He wrote on Javanese mysticism and religious psychology and lectured in America and South Africa. His missiological handbook was translated into English as *An Introduction to the Science of Missions* in 1960. His irenical influence was spread through his students, and by many others impressed by his transparent spirituality and good humour.

Bavoo also called **Allowin**   Patron saint of Ghent and of the Diocese of Haarlem, Holland, died about 653. Born into a noble family in Hesbaye, Brabant, he married but was then widowed. He converted to a life of Christian poverty after hearing a sermon preached by Armand and entered the monastery at Ghent. He travelled with Armand to France and Flanders, but then lived the life of a hermit near to the monastery. Feast day 1 October.

Baxter, Richard   English Presbyterian theologian and writer, born Rowton, Shropshire, 12 November 1615, died London, 8 December 1691. He was educated first by local clergy, then at Wroxeter, and then privately in Ludlow Castle, by its chaplain. He left Ludlow for London in 1633, but stayed only a short time before returning home to Easton-Constantine near Shrewsbury. Here he came under the influence of evangelical .preachers, one of whom invited him to take charge of a new school in Dudley. For this purpose he sought, and obtained ordination, and as well as running the school he preached. He moved to Bridgenorth, and then, at the request of the congregation in Kidderminster, to that town in 1641. His sympathies, when the Civil War broke out, were with Parliament, and he had to flee Kidderminster for Coventry, and then served as a chaplain to a regiment. Although he was a man of presbyterian views, he came into conflict with other more radical ministers. At this point he was not, for instance, opposed to the episcopacy. After the war he returned to Kidderminster, where his ministry produced a remarkable reformation in the town. He was also something of a political leader, opposing the execution of **Charles I**. He had begun to write, and his best-known book, *Saint's Everlasting Rest*, appeared when he was at Kidderminster. In 1660, at the Restoration of the monarchy, he moved to London, where he became a chaplain to **Charles II**, but withdrew from the Church of England two years later and moved to Acton. He began preaching in meeting houses, which was, after the Act of Uniformity of 1662, an offence against the law. He was several times imprisoned, but continued to preach until his death. He produced well over a hundred books. He married in 1662, his wife dying in 1681: the *Breviate of the life of Margaret, daughter of Francis Charlton* has been described as 'perhaps the most perfect of his minor writings'.

Bay, Michel de   Priest, theologian, born Mélin l'Évêque (Hennegau, Belgium) 1513, died Louvain, 16 September 1589. Studied humanities, philosophy and theology at Louvain and was ordained in 1541. He continued to study and teach theology at Louvain and in 1551 was made regius professor of sacred Scripture. In 1560 aspects of his teaching, inaugurating new methods and doctrines, were condemned by the Sorbonne. He was accused of neglecting the scholastic doctrines of original sin and justification by focusing too much on scriptural teaching. Later Jansenist teachings were built upon the foundations laid by Baius. There was some reluctance on the part of both **Pius IV** and **Pius V** to condemn him outright, and there has been much scholarly discussion about the punctuation and precise meaning of the papal bull *Ex omnibus afflictionibus*, which eventually did. Baius submitted, but not without protest. He was made chancellor of the university in 1575 but in 1580 the condemnation of his teaching was confirmed by **Gregory XIII**. Again he submitted and with the whole faculty produced a clear statement, *Doctrinae eius (quam certorum articulorum damnatio postulare visa est) brevis et quoad fieri potest ordinata et cohaerens explicatio* (1586), of the doctrine taught in the condemnation. Baius was party to the ongoing controversy between the Jesuits and Louvain in his latter years, but he died in communion with Rome.

Bayly, Albert   English hymn writer, born Bexhill, Surrey, 6 September 1901, died Chichester, Sussex, 26 July 1984. He was educated at Hastings Grammar School, became a shipwright in Portsmouth, and trained for the Congregational ministry at Mansfield College, Oxford. Several of his hymns celebrate the glory of God as reflected in the universe and many were included in the Methodist hymn-book *Hymns and Psalms*.

Bayly, Lewis   Welsh Anglican bishop, born Carmarthen and died Bangor, 26 October 1631. Studied probably at Exeter College, Oxford, and was vicar in Evesham and then in London. He was chaplain to Henry, Prince of Wales and treasurer of St Paul's. In 1616 he became bishop of Bangor in Wales. His Puritan leanings brought him into some disfavour with the court and in his diocese. He is the author of the *Practice of Piety* (3rd edition 1613) which by 1735 was in its 59th edition. It became a particular favourite among Puritans and was translated into the main European and some native American languages.

Bazin, John Stephen   Roman Catholic bishop, born near Lyons, France, 15 October 1796, died Vincennes, Indiana, 23 April 1848. Originally a seminary professor, he volunteered for the American missions in 1833 and worked for 27 years near Mobile, Alabama. From 1836 to 1847 he was vicar-general of the diocese and rector of the cathedral. An educator, he brought French Jesuits to Spring Hill College and Christian Brothers to his Boys' Orphan Asylum. In 1847 he was named bishop of Vincennes, where he succeeded in restoring good relations between the hierarchy and the clergy.

Bea, Augustin   Jesuit priest and cardinal 'of Unity', born near Donaueschingen, Germany, 28 May 1881, died Rome, 16 November 1968. He modernized the Papal Biblical Commission by bringing the historical-critical method as well as the disciplines of philology and archaeology to bear in the study of Scripture. With the Pope's approval he participated in the International Congress for Old Testament Research in Göttingen in 1935. Pope **John XXIII** named him a cardinal and appointed him president of the newly formed Secretariat for the Promotion of Christian Unity. He travelled all over Europe and the USA in the cause of ecumenism and was responsible for the Second Vatican Council's Decree on Ecumenism.

Beasley-Murray, George Raymond Baptist minister and NT scholar, born London, England, 3 October 1916, died Hove, England, 23 February 2000. Following a conversion experience, Beasley-Murray abandoned a promising musical career in order to become a Baptist minister. After some years in pastoral ministry he became a lecturer, and went on to hold a variety of academic appointments at Baptist seminaries in the UK, Europe and the USA. Through his numerous publications on NT literature and theology he became widely respected as a NT scholar, and during his term as chairman of the Baptist Union of Great Britain he was largely responsible for maintaining unity in the denomination when a serious doctrinal controversy threatened to cause a schism.

Beaton, James Primate and archbishop, born Balfour *c.*1473, died St Andrews, 1539. Studied at St Andrews, was made abbot of Dunfermline in 1504 and the following year was appointed by King James IV to the staff of the high treasurer. In 1508 he was made bishop of Galloway, then archbishop of Glasgow, and in 1522 was appointed to the see of St Andrews. He was one of the regents of James V following the death of James IV at Flodden, and supported the duke of Albany in his efforts to continue the alliance of Scotland with France, rather than with England – although he hoped to preserve peace with the latter. He began the persecution of Protestants, and Patrick **Hamilton** was executed during Beaton's administration.

Beaton, James Roman Catholic archbishop, born Auchmuty, 1517, died Paris, 24 April 1603. Studied in Paris and in 1522 became what was to be the last pre-Reformation Roman Catholic archbishop of Glasgow. Although admitting the need for reforms in the Catholic Church, and taking steps to put these in place, he was strongly opposed to the teachings of the Reformers. In early 1560, anticipating the new reformed religious settlement, Beaton fled to France and took with him many of the diocesan records and treasures. From his exile

he maintained correspondence with **Mary** Queen of Scots and James VI (see **James I**) and with leading churchmen and diplomats. In his will he left money for a Scots College in Paris, for the education of poor Scottish seminarians.

Beatrice d'Este Blessed, Italian Benedictine nun, born *c.*1191, died Gemolo, Italy, 10 May 1226. She entered the convent of St Margaret at Solarola. The community later moved to the empty monastery of St John the Baptist near Gemolo, where they adopted the Benedictine rule. Feast day 10 May.

Beatrice d'Este Blessed, Italian Benedictine nun and niece of the above, born Ferrara 1230, died there 18 January 1262. She had been promised in marriage by her parents but she herself wanted to follow the religious life. Following the death of her betrothed she joined the convent at St Lazarus and her family later had a new convent built for the community at Ferrara. Feast day 18 January.

Beatrice of Nazareth Cistercian nun, spiritual writer, born Tirlemont *c.*1200, died Notre-Dame-de-Nazareth, near Lierre (Brabant), 29 August 1268. She was educated with the Beguine community in Léau and later sent to the Cistercian abbey her father had recently founded at Bloemendael. She became a member of the community about 1217 and was made prioress of the third house that had been opened, at Notre-Dame-de-Nazareth. She wrote at length about her mystical experiences and about the spiritual life, and after her death these were published in the form of a biography. Some of her writings on the stages of the soul's ascent to union with God prefigure the writings of **Teresa of Avila** and others give an important insight into Beguine spirituality at this time.

Beatrice of Tuscany Lay ecclesiastical reformer, born Lorraine, *c.*1015, died Pisa, 28 April 1076. She exercised some political powers and in 1055 was imprisoned by the Emperor **Henry III** and sent to Germany. She was released after his death, and yielded much of her power, but with her daughter **Matilda** ruled the Canossan dominions. She collaborated with Pope **Gregory VII** in his ecclesiastical reforms, and supported the Papacy in the investiture struggle.

Beatus of Liebana Spanish monk and writer, born Liebana near Santander, died 19 February 798. He wrote against the adoptionist heresy being propounded by **Elipandus of Toledo** and Felix of Urgel, *Ad Elipandum epistulae duae* (784), and produced a twelve-volume commentary on the Apocalypse. He was tutor and advisor to Queen Adosinda of León and was responsible for the *Commentary* (776, 784, 786), important for the illuminations and illustrations in the 30 extant manuscripts from the ninth to the thirteenth centuries, which demonstrate the development of and influences on Spanish art during this period. These illustrations in turn were a major influence on the Romanesque artists of Vezelay, Saint-Benoît-sur-Loire and especially Moissac. The hymn for the feast of St James, *O Dei verbum, Patris ore proditum*, was probably written by Beatus.

Beatus of Lungern Hermit and saint, died *c.*112. He lived in a cave on what became Mount St Beatenberg, Switzerland. According to a tenth-century legend, he was of Gallic origin, and was baptized in England by St Barnabas, ordained at Rome by St Peter, and commissioned to be the apostle to the Swiss. His cave, where he was said to have fought and slain a dragon, became a place of pilgrimage. Patron of central Switzerland, he is invoked against various illnesses. His historical archetype may in fact have been a sixth-century Irish or English saint. Feast day 9 May.

Beauchamp, Richard English bishop, died Windsor, 18 October 1481. Studied possibly at Exeter College, Oxford, and practised as a canon lawyer, worked in the chancery and was royal chaplain. In 1448 he was appointed bishop of Hereford and in 1450 bishop of Salisbury. He was an efficient diocesan administrator, was emissary in the Lancaster–York struggle and later to France. Unusually, while bishop of Salisbury he was also dean of Windsor and was instrumental in the Perpendicular architectural developments made there.

Beaudenom, Leopold French Roman Catholic priest, spiritual writer and director, born Tulle, 23

November 1840, died Puteaux, 21 December 1916. Studied at the seminaries of Serrières and Tulle, was ordained in 1863 and became chaplain to the Ursulines and other religious communities in Beaulieu. In 1896, partly because of ill-health, he retired to Puteaux to write. He drew his inspiration in his spiritual direction and in his writings from **Ignatius of Loyola** and from **Francis de Sales**. His works include *Préparations et actions de grâces pour la sainte Communion* (1894), *Formation à l'humilité* (1897), *Pratique de l'examen particulier* (1898), the two-volume *Pratique progressive de la confession et de la direction* (1900), *Méthodes et formules pour bien entendre la messe* (1905), *Formation morale et religieuse de la jeune fille*, also in two volumes (1906–11), and his four-volume *Méditations affectives et pratique sur l'Évangile* (1912–18).

Beauduin, Lambert Belgian Benedictine and liturgist, born Rosoux-les-Waremme, Belgium, 5 August 1873, died Chevetogne, 11 January 1960. Studied at Liège, was ordained in 1897 and, after nine years as a member of the Aumôniers du Travail, joined the Benedictines at Mont-César. Under the direction of Columba **Marmion** he began to study and teach liturgy. In 1909 he helped begin the Liturgy Weeks and started the publication *La vie liturgique*, the name of which was early changed to *Les questions liturgiques*. He is the author of the manifesto of the liturgical movement *La piété de l'Église* (1914). In 1921 he became professor of theology at S. Anselmo, Rome, and began to take an interest in Eastern liturgy. In 1925 he founded the monastery de l'Union in Amay (Liège) and the review *Irénikon* and was a participant in the Malines Conversations on reunion between the Anglican Church and Rome. His views proved too progressive and in 1931 he was condemned by a Roman tribunal. He returned from his banishment in 1950, was applauded for his work by the patriarch of Venice, the future **John XXIII**, and lived to hear the latter's call for an ecumenical council for reunion. He is celebrated as the founding influence of the Centre Pastorale Liturgique in Paris and of the Christian renewal movement in France.

Beaufort, Henry Cardinal, ecclesiastical politician and bishop, born Beaufort-en-Vallée, France, c.1375, died Winchester, England, 11 April 1447. He became bishop of Lincoln in 1398 and of Winchester in 1405. He was made cardinal in 1417 and led crusades for **Martin V**, against the Hussites of Bohemia in 1420 and 1427. His mission in Bohemia failed because he put his troops at the disposal of the English army in France, and while his influence in Rome was terminated, his fortunes in English politics increased. He had spent three terms as chancellor and became one of the chief advisers to **Henry VI** supporting, on financial not religious grounds, peace rather than aggression.

Beaufort, Margaret ('The Lady Margaret') Mother of Henry VII, founder of educational and religious institutions, born 1443, died 1509. She was the wife of Edmund Tudor (half-brother of **Henry VI**), the father of her son. After the death of Edmund she married Henry Stafford and, after his death, Lord Stanley, who later became Earl of Derby. In 1504, however, she separated from her husband, and took vows as a religious, though she continued to reside at her manor house rather than join a convent. She played an active part in ensuring her son became king. She was friendly with John **Fisher**, who became her spiritual director, and lived a life of prayer and piety. She also gave active expression to her faith by establishing readerships (later professorships) and other educational and religious foundations at both Oxford and Cambridge, the most significant of them being St John's College, Cambridge. She was a patron of the first English printers, and herself translated devotional books from French.

Beaume, Renard de Catholic bishop, peacemaker and reformer, born Tours, France, 12 August 1527, died Paris, 17 September 1606. Successively councillor to the Parlement of Paris, and a councillor of state, bishop of Mende in 1568 and archbishop of Bourges in 1581, he was advisor to King **Henry IV**, who named him archbishop of Sens in 1594 and made him head of a commission appointed to reform the University of Paris. Although not authorized to do so, he granted conditional absolution to the king while Henry was under censure from Rome, and Rome refused to recognize his claim to Sens. He did not occupy the see until 1606. His publications include a translation of the Psalms and his funeral sermons on **Mary** Queen of Scots and **Catherine** de' Medici.

Beaumont, Geoffrey Anglican minister and musician, born Coggeshall, Essex, 1903, died Cape Town, South Africa, 24 August 1970. He was the co-founder of the Twentieth Century Church Light Music group of the 1950s and 1960s, anticipating the use of popular and pop music in the liturgy. He wrote a popular, controversial *Twentieth-Century Folk Mass*.

Beaver, Robert Pierce North American historian and documentalist of mission, born Hamilton, Ohio, 26 May 1906, died Tucson, Arizona, 20 November 1987. He studied at Oberlin College and Cornell University (Ph.D. 1933) and was in parish ministry before going to China as an Evangelical and Reformed Church missionary in 1938. He taught at Central China Union Theological Seminary in Hunan, was interned by the Japanese in Hong Kong and repatriated in 1943. He taught at Lancaster Theological Seminary, then in 1948 became director of the Mission Research Library (MRL) at Union Theological Seminary, New York. In 1955 he was appointed professor of missions at the University of Chicago Divinity School. Personally, a modest man, his writings on comity, women in mission, and *American Missions in Bicentennial Perspective* (1976) laid the foundations for a new generation of missionary scholarship. His *Occasional Bulletin from the MRL* continues as the *International Bulletin of Missionary Research*.

Becanus, Martin Jesuit priest and theologian, born North Brabant, Belgium, 6 January 1563, died Vienna, 24 January 1624. He taught theology at Würzburg, Mainz and Vienna. As confessor to **Ferdinand II** he advised him to tolerate the Augsburg Confession in Austria. After Robert **Bellarmine** he is the best-known theologian of the Counter-Reformation because of his polemical works against the Calvinists, Lutherans and Anglicans. They include *Aphorismi doctrinae Calvinistarum* (1608), a four-volume *Summa theologiae scholasticae* (1612), and *Controversia Anglicana de potestate —Regis et pontificis* (1613).

Beche, John Blessed, English Benedictine abbot and martyr, died (by execution) Colchester, 1

December 1539. Studied at Oxford and was in charge of the abbey of St Werburgh in Chester from 1515 to 1530, when he became abbot of St John's, Colchester. In 1534 he took **Henry VIII**'s Oath of Supremacy but spoke out, following the executions in 1535 of three Carthusians, of John **Fisher** and of Thomas **More**, and incurred the wrath of the king. When, three years later, Beche denied Henry's right to confiscate his abbey, he was arrested, sent to the Tower, charged with treason and released, rearrested and, despite his apparent willingness to deny Catholicism, sent for trial. He affirmed his Catholic faith, was found guilty and executed. Feast day 1 December.

Becker, Christopher Edmund   Roman Catholic missionary, ethnographer and pioneer of missionary medicine in Catholic Germany, born near Frankfurt-am-Main, 22 October 1875, died Würzburg, 30 March 1937. Ordained a priest in the Order of the Divine Saviour, he became apostolic prefect of Assam, India. On his return to Germany he founded and directed the Missionsärztliche Institute in Würzburg and became professor of missiology at the University of Würzburg. Among his works are *Indisches Kastenwesen und christliche Mission* (1921), *Ärztl. Fürsorge in Missionsländern* (1921), and *Missionsärztliche Kulturarbeit: Grundsätzliches und Geschichtliches* (1928).

Becket, Thomas   *see* **Thomas Becket**

Bede   Venerable, saint, monk and doctor of the Church, born near Sunderland, England, *c*.673, died in the monastery of Jarrow, *c*.735. He entered the monastery at Wearmouth as a boy, and was educated there by **Benedict Biscop**, but later moved to Jarrow, where he was ordained *c*.703. He wrote Scripture commentaries which display a thorough knowledge of the Fathers of the Church, both Latin and to some extent Greek: he may well also have known some Hebrew. He wrote homilies, letters, a study of chronology, and a history of his own monastery. It is, however, mainly on his *Ecclesiastical History of the English People*, completed some four years before his death, that his fame rests. Although he probably never travelled beyond the borders of the Kingdom of Northumbria, he took great care to establish facts, and wrote vividly about the figures of the early Church

in England, as well as about the political events which went to shape it. In his own day he was admired for his learning, and his writings were widely known in the Middle Ages. Feast day 25 May.

Bedingfield, Frances   Religious and educator, born Norfolk, England, 1616, died Munich, 1704. One of eleven sisters who entered the religious life, she became superior of the English Institute of Mary at Munich and, at the request of Catherine of Braganza, wife of King **Charles II**, she established a house in London. Known as Mrs Long, she also directed a school at York, where she often experienced government interference, including imprisonment. Eventually she turned the superiorship of the community over to her niece Dorothy Paston Bedingfield, and returned to Munich.

Bedini, Gaetano   Italian cardinal and diplomat, born Sinigaglia, 15 May 1806, died Viterbo, 6 September 1864. He was ordained in 1828 and went as nuncio to Vienna in 1838 and Brazil in 1846, was sub-secretary of state at the Vatican in 1848 and prolegate to Bologna in 1849 and undertook other papal diplomatic service in Italy. From 1853 to early 1854 Bedini was in the USA; having experienced the anti-Catholic feelings that existed and been the target of hostile action, he advised Rome against trying to establish an apostolic nunciature there at that time. In 1856 he became secretary of the Congregation of Propaganda Fidei and in 1861 became bishop of Viterbo-Toscanella and was later made cardinal.

Bedjan, Paul   Iranian Vincentian priest and orientalist, born Khusrawi, Iran, 27 November 1838, died Cologne-Nippes, Germany, 9 June 1920. He studied at the school of the Vincentians in Khusrawi, changed from the Chaldean to the Latin rite and in 1856 joined the Vincentians in Paris. He studied there, was ordained in 1861 and returned as a missionary to the north-west of Persia, where he worked until 1880. On his return to Europe he turned his attention to writing, translating and publishing books of Roman Catholic devotion in Neo-Syriac. He also prepared editions of ancient Syriac texts; among these are the seven-volume *Acts of the Martyrs and Saints of the East* (1890–7), the five-volume *Sermons of Jacob of Sarûg*

(1905–10) and the *Book of Heraclides of Damascus* (1910).

Bedon, Pedro Ecuadorian Dominican, painter and social worker, born in Quito about 1555 and died there on 27 February 1621. Studied philosophy at Quito and theology in Lima. In Lima he also learned from the Jesuit Bernardo **Bitti** how to paint. From 1587 he taught philosophy and theology at the Dominican school in Quito and in his own time worked with the poor through the Confraternity of the Rosary which, largely through his encouragement, had Spanish, Indian and Negro members. He founded a school of painting for the native Ecuadorians, and they copied illuminated manuscripts. He went to teach in Bogotá, where he held the chair in theology, but returned to Quito in 1596 and, along with his teaching and social service, founded three convents. He was made provincial and took up the cause of the native Indians.

Bedos de Celles, François Benedictine and organ-builder, born near Béziers, France, 24 January 1709, died St Denis, 25 November 1779. As secretary of the Benedictine Monastery of St Croix he built for the monastery church a 38-register organ, which later was moved to the cathedral of St André. He was a corresponding member of the Parisian Academy of Sciences. At their request he wrote the groundbreaking, richly illustrated work *The Art of Organ Building* in four volumes.

Bedyll, Thomas English civil servant, died September 1537. Studied at Oxford, became secretary to William **Warham**, archbishop of Canterbury, and in 1532 was made clerk of the Privy Council. He was responsible for trying to gain the support of Oxford University for **Henry VIII**'s proposed divorce from **Catherine of Aragon**. Later he was charged with getting religious leaders to sign the king's Oath of Supremacy and in overseeing the confiscated monastery lands, as well as serving on the committee judging the validity of papal bulls.

Beecher, Henry Ward US Congregational preacher and journalist, born Litchfield, Connecticut, one of thirteen children of Lyman **Beecher**, 24 June 1813, died in Brooklyn, New York, 8 March 1887. Studied at Amherst College, Massachusetts, and Lane Theological Seminary, Cincinnati, Ohio; worked as a pastor in Cincinnati and Indianapolis. In 1847 he was called to the Plymouth Congregational Church in Brooklyn and remained there until his death. He was opposed to slavery and in favour of women's suffrage and agreed with the theory of evolution. He had previously been editor of the *Independent* and in 1870 took the same position on the *Christian Union*. He was the author of *The Life of Jesus the Christ* (1871) and *Evolution and Religion* (1885).

Beecher, Lyman Congregational preacher, head of a prominent New England family, born in New Haven, Connecticut, on 12 October 1775, died Brooklyn, New York, 10 January 1863. Studied at Yale and became a disciple of Thomas **Dwight.** He served as pastor at the Presbyterian church of Easthampton, New York, from 1799, at the Congregational church in Litchfield from 1810 and at the Hanover Street church in Boston from 1826. In 1832 he helped form an American Anti-Slavery Society, which helped bring churches into the movement, and he was the first president of the Lane Theological Seminary in Cincinnati. He was the father of thirteen children: his seven surviving sons, including Henry Ward **Beecher**, entered the ministry and two of his daughters, one being Harriet Beecher Stowe, became noted authors.

Beelen, Jan Theodoor Biblical commentator, born Amsterdam, 12 January 1807, died Louvain, 31 March 1884. As professor of Scripture and oriental languages at the University of Louvain for 40 years he was responsible for the revival of oriental studies in Belgium. A prolific author of biblical studies, his commentary on Romans, a translation of the Psalms, and a study of **Clement** of Rome were his most important works.

Beethoven, Ludwig van Composer, born Bonn, Germany, 16 December 1770, the son of a singer in the chapel of the Archbishop-Elector of Cologne, died Vienna, 16 March 1827. Beethoven played the organ, viola and piano. In 1787 he was sent to Vienna by the then archbishop-elector, and there he studied briefly under **Mozart**, but returned to Bonn after only two months because of his mother's death. He also studied under **Haydn**, and it was Haydn who persuaded him to return to Vienna in 1792. He remained in Vienna giving concerts and recitals, but suffered from increasing deafness. He composed two great Masses; the *Missa Solemnis* was written for the consecration of his patron and former pupil, the Archduke Rudolph as archbishop of Olmütz. It was completed three years too late for the ceremony. The celebrated theme from his *Ninth Symphony* has become used as the anthem of the European Union and has also been adapted as a hymn tune.

Bégin, Louis Nazaire Cardinal, born La Point-Lévis, Canada, 10 January 1840, died Quebec, 18 July 1925. He taught theology and history at Laval and was principal of the normal school there before being named bishop of Chicoutimi. He was appointed coadjutor bishop of Quebec before becoming archbishop there. An advocate of improved social legislation, he founded Catholic Social Action and wrote a book on the Papacy and a history of the United States.

Bek, Anthony Bishop of Durham, born *c.*1240, died Eltham, 3 March 1311. Educated at Oxford, he accompanied Prince Edward (later King Edward I), to whom he became a leading adviser, on a Crusade. As prince-bishop of Durham he occupied an important position of power and played a significant role in the decision about the succession to the Scottish throne in 1291–2 and in the negotiations for the alliance against France. In 1306 the Pope accorded him the title patriarch of Jerusalem.

Bekynton, Thomas English bishop, diplomat and humanist, born in Beckington, near Frome, Somerset, and died in Wells on 14 January 1465. Studied at Winchester and at New College, Oxford, where he became a fellow and later sub-warden. A doctor of civil law, he went into the service of Humphrey, duke of Gloucester. About 1438 he became secretary to **Henry VI** and was one of the diplomats with Henry **Beaufort** at Calais in 1439; he supported Henry's educational foundations, Eton College and King's College, Cambridge. While still keeper of the Privy Seal, in 1443 he was made bishop of Bath and Wells. He made generous benefactions to the cathedral at Wells and to the city in general. He was a friend and correspondent of leading English and Continental humanists and

moved the style of diplomatic Latin towards that of the Italian humanists.

Belasyse, John (Baron Belasyse) Catholic parliamentarian and administrator, born Newburgh Priory, Yorkshire, 1614(?), died London, 10 September 1689. He served the English Parliament until the Civil War, in which he fought on the royalist side, becoming general of the royal forces in the north and governor of York. Having acted as an agent for **Charles II** during the Commonwealth, he later held various offices which he resigned when the Test Act removed those who wanted to remain Catholics. Impeached as a traitor during the Titus **Oates** plot, he was restored to honour by **James II**.

Belcourt, George Anthony Missionary, born Quebec, 22 April 1803, died New Brunswick, 1874. After sixteen years ministering among the Chippewa Indians he had to resign because of the hostility generated by his support of those of mixed race against officials of the Hudson Bay Company. Moving to North Dakota, he encouraged the nomadic Native Americans to adopt a more stable life-style, and built the first sawmill and grist mill in that area. His writings include *Principes de la langue des Sauvages appelés Saulteux* (1839) and an important historical eyewitness account of the annual Chippewa buffalo hunt in North Dakota.

Belford, John Louis Priest and educator, born Brooklyn, New York, 1861, died Brooklyn, 12 December 1951. Having served as superintendent of schools for the Diocese of Brooklyn, he founded St Dominic's parish in Oyster Bay, Long Island, then served as pastor in Williamsburg, where he established Epiphany parish. An outstanding preacher, he spoke out against Tammany Hall corruption, Prohibition, and the Ku Klux Klan. His prayer book for children sold 3 million copies. He was on the executive committee of the Catholic Book Club.

Bell, Eudorus First general chairman of the General Council of the Assemblies of God, born Lake Butler, Florida, 1866, died June 1923. For seventeen years Bell was a Baptist pastor, but in 1908 he embraced Pentecostalism, becoming a Pentecostal pastor in Arkansas. In 1913 his paper *Word and Witness* publicized a gathering in Hot Springs which led to the formation of the Assemblies of God, of which he became chairman. He was re-baptized during the Oneness controversy, but later returned to Trinitarianism. From 1917 to 1919 he edited the *Pentecostal Evangel*, and a selection of his columns was published as *Questions and Answers* (1923).

Bell, George Allen Kennedy   Bishop of Chichester, ecumenical statesman, born Norwich, England, 4 February 1883, died Canterbury, 3 October 1958. Educated at Christ Church, Oxford, and Wells Theological College, in 1914 he became chaplain to Archbishop **Davidson**. He was a secretary of the 1920 Lambeth conference and edited four volumes of *Documents on Christian Unity*. In 1929 he became bishop of Chichester. Involved with the emerging Life and Work movement, he supported the Confessing Church in Germany, and worked for refugees from the Hitler regime. During the war he met Dietrich **Bonhoeffer** in Stockholm and took news of German opposition to Hitler to the British government. His opposition to the area bombing of German cities was believed to have cost him the position of archbishop of Canterbury. He supported the Church of South India and was first moderator of the WCC Central Committee (1948–54).

Bell, Harold Idris   British papyrologist, born 2 October 1879, died 22 January 1967. Studied at Oriel College, Oxford, and in Berlin and Halle, and in 1903 joined F. G. Kenyon at the Department of Manuscripts at the British Museum, London. He edited the Aphrodito papyrii, which were published as volumes 4 and 5 of the *Catalogue of Greek Papyri* and added significantly to the knowledge of late antiquity. It made Bell one of the fathers, with Jean Maspero, of Byzantine papyrology. He was an active member of the Greco-Roman branch of the Egypt Exploration Society, the Hellenic and Roman Societies and the International Association of Papyrologists. With his help several significant collections of papyri were built up in Europe and America and he added new Greek words from papyri to the lexical work of Liddell and Scott. He was knighted in 1946 and was honoured by numerous learned societies and

universities. His other publications include *Jews and Christians in Egypt* (1924) on the Meletian schism, and *The Abinnaeus Archive* (1962), a study of fourth-century economic history.

Bellarmine, Robert   Saint, Jesuit cardinal, born Montepulciano, 4 October 1542, died Rome, 17 September 1621. He came from a distinguished family (his mother was a sister of Pope **Marcellus II**) and was well educated in the arts and humanities. He entered the Society of Jesus in 1560, taught classics and then was sent in 1569 to Louvain, where the following year he became the university's first Jesuit professor, lecturing on the *Summa* of **Thomas Aquinas**. While there he also produced a Hebrew grammar. In 1576 he was appointed to the Roman College of the Jesuits to teach 'controversial theology', i.e. to discuss the view of the Reformers; his *Disputationes de controversiis Christianae Fidei adversus huius temporis hereticos* were published between 1586 and 1593. His views on the indirect papal power in secular affairs nearly resulted in the first volume of this being put on the Index in 1590. In 1592 he became rector of the Roman College, and two years later provincial in Naples. In 1597 he was made papal theologian by **Clement VIII**, and a cardinal two years later. From 1602 he was archbishop of Capua, but resigned his see on becoming prefect of the Vatican Library in 1605, and from then on served in the papal curia. Apart from his disputes with Protestant theologians, he was also involved in the controversy over grace – one of the major disputants, Leonard **Lessius**, had been a student of his – and in the **Galileo** affair, in which he was somewhat sympathetic to Galileo. Also a person of great generosity towards the poor and personal austerity, he spent the last years of his life writing spiritual works. The process for his canonization began soon after his death, but was not concluded, for political reasons, until 1930. The following year he was declared a Doctor of the Church. Feast day 17 September.

Bellesheim, Alfons   German priest, church historian, born near Aachen, 16 December 1839, died Aachen, 5 February 1912. Studied at Cologne and at Tübingen under Carl von **Hefele**, then went on to study canon law and church history in Rome. He held senior posts in the Diocese of Cologne and in 1902 was made provost in the cathedral chapter at Aachen. He is noted as the first Roman Catholic of modern times to undertake a serious study of the ecclesiastical history of the British Isles. His two-volume *Geschichte der katholischen Kirche in Schottland* appeared in 1883, and a three-volume equivalent on Ireland in 1890 and 1891. He wrote biographies of Cardinals **Mezzofanti, Allen** and **Manning** and was a regular contributor of articles on theology and church history to academic journals and periodicals.

Bellesini, Stefano Blessed, Italian Augustinian, born Trent, 25 November 1774, died of typhoid, Genazzano, 2 February 1840. Joined the Augustinians in 1790 and studied in Bologna but was forced during the French Revolution to return to Trent. He was ordained in 1797 and when the religious orders were suppressed lived as a secular priest. He established a number of free schools and was appointed inspector of schools in Trent by the Austrian government. When the Augustinians were re-established Bellesini became master of novices in Rome, in Città della Piave and then in Genazzano, where in 1830 he was appointed pastor in the basilica of Our Mother of Good Counsel. He contracted typhoid while working with the sick during the epidemic there. Feast day 2 February.

Bellings, Richard Catholic historian, born near Dublin, 1600, died there 1677. He became secretary of the supreme council of the Irish Confederation and was active with the royalist forces in Ireland. When Cromwell confiscated his property he went to France, and returned when **Charles II** was restored to the throne. He wrote a supplement to Philip Sidney's *Arcadia*, a defence of Irish Catholics, and a history of the war in Ireland (1641–8).

Bellini, Gentile Venetian painter, son of Jacopo and brother of Giovanni **Bellini**, born Venice, 1429, died Venice, 23 February 1507. In 1479 he went to Constantinople and painted the portrait of Sultan Mohammed II. His series of huge paintings depicting miracles and set within great Venetian processions can be seen in the Accademia, Venice, and the Brera, Milan.

Bellini, Giovanni Venetian painter, son of Jacopo and brother of Gentile **Bellini**, born Venice,

c.1430, died Venice, 20 November 1516. His *Transfiguration*, which can be seen in the Correr, Venice, shows the influence of Paduan art, but he developed a distinctive style which can be seen in his huge paintings such as the *Coronation of the Virgin* and *St Francis*, which is in the Frick Gallery, New York. A series of Madonnas can be seen in Venice and Bergamo, and his altarpieces of the Madonna and saints are in the Accademia, the Frari church and San Zaccaria.

Bellini, Jacopo Venetian painter, born Venice, early fifteenth century, died Venice, c.1470. Father of Gentile and Giovanni **Bellini**. Probably trained in Florence. His Madonnas can be seen in the Accademia, Venice, and in the Uffizi, Florence. Two large volumes of his drawings are in the British Museum, London, and in the Louvre, Paris.

Bellintani, Mattia da Salò Italian Capuchin, preacher and spiritual writer, born Gazzane, 28 June 1534, died Brescia, 20 July 1611. He joined the Capuchins in Bergamo in 1552 and following his ordination in 1560 taught philosophy and theology and was minister-provincial. In 1575 he visited Bohemia, France and Switzerland as commissary-general of the Order. He was an acclaimed preacher, promoted the Forty Hours devotions and established the Confraternity of the Blessed Sacrament. His writings include *Corone spirituali* (1570), *Prattica dell'orazione mentale* (1573), *Trattato della Santa Oratione delle 40 Hore* (1583), a history of the Capuchins and collections of sermons.

Bellinzaga, Isabella Cristina (Lomazzi) Italian spiritual writer, born Milan, 1551, died Milan, 26 January 1624. Between 1584 and 1594, with the Jesuit Achille **Gagliardi** as her spiritual director, she wrote *Breve compendio intorno alla perfezione cristiana*. She was suspected of Quietism and the book was put on the Index from 1703 to 1900. Before this time, however, it appeared in several editions and translations and was influential in the thinking of subsequent spiritual writers including **Bérulle, Surin**, de Camillus and **Molinos.**

Belloc, Joseph Hilaire Pierre English Roman Catholic writer and controversialist, born St Cloud, near Versailles, 27 July 1870, died Guildford, Surrey, 16 July 1953. He was educated at the Oratory

School, Birmingham, under John Henry **Newman** and then at Balliol College, Oxford. He opted for service in the French army, but settled in England and took British citizenship in 1902. From 1906 to 1910 he was Liberal Member of Parliament for Salford, but did not stand in the 1910 election because he disapproved of his party's alliance with the Socialists. His writings include a continuation of John **Lingard's** *History of England* and the influential *The Servile State*, both of which were written because he was short of money with which to support wife and family, a condition which lasted through much of his life. *Europe and the Faith* (1912) expounded what he saw as the true values of Western culture as enshrined in medieval Catholicism. His travel books include *The Path To Rome* (1902), an account of a walking tour to Rome. He was made a Knight of St Gregory, though he rejected other honours, including the offer of an honorary fellowship from Balliol and the Companion of Honour. He was a close friend of, and frequent collaborator with, G. K. **Chesterton**, who sometimes provided the illustrations for his books.

Belloy, Jean Baptiste de   Cardinal, born Morangles, France, 9 October 1709, died Paris, 10 June 1808. As bishop of Glandèves he brought about peace in the Church and, on becoming bishop of Marseilles, saved that diocese from schism. He was the first bishop to resign at the Pope's request at the time of the Concordat and was then named archbishop of Paris by Napoleon. Though already an old man he was noted for his vigorous rule and was named cardinal in 1805.

Belmont, François Vachon de   Sulpician priest, born Grenoble, 2 April 1645, died Montreal, 22 May 1732. After twenty years of missionary work in Canada he was appointed fifth superior at Montreal. He erected a seminary and preached the funeral sermons for Marguerite **Bourgeoys** and bishop François de Montmorency **Laval** of Quebec. He wrote a history of Canada.

Belsunce de Castelmoron, Henri François Xavier de   Bishop, born Périgord, France, 9 December 1671, died Marseilles, 4 June 1755. As bishop of Marseilles he presided over the clergy who remained to serve the people during the plague of 1720–1 while the nobility fled. He actively combated the Jansenists and was honoured by Pope **Clement XII** and by Alexander Pope in his *Essay on Man*. He wrote a history of the Diocese of Marseilles and translated excerpts from the writings of St **Augustine** and Robert **Bellarmine**.

Beltran, Luis   Argentinian Franciscan and soldier, born Mendoza, Argentina, 8 September 1784, died Buenos Aires, 8 December 1827. He volunteered for the Chilean army and served as a chaplain in the war of independence against Spain, and had to flee with it to Argentina. As a friar his interests had lain in science, and he showed himself remarkably skilled in artillery. He served in the Argentinian army in several campaigns, rising eventually to the rank of lieutenant-colonel. He retired the year before his death. He was buried as a Franciscan.

Bembo, Pietro   Cardinal, born Venice, 20 May 1470, died Rome, 18 January 1547. A courtier of the Medicis, he enthusiastically promoted culture, became historiographer of the Venetian republic, and was appointed librarian of St Mark's. After being named cardinal by Pope **Paul III** he studied Scripture and became bishop, first of Gubbio, then of Bergamo. A highly respected man of letters, he authored a history of Venice from 1487 to 1513, a dialogue on Platonic love, a treatise on Italian, and several volumes of poems; he also edited writings of Petrarch and **Dante**.

Benard, Laurent   Benedictine, born Nevers, 1573, died Paris, 21 April 1620. He entered the Cluniac priory of St Stephen in Nevers and then, after taking his degree at the Sorbonne, became prior of the Cluniac College in Paris. He was co-founder of the Congregation of St Vannes in Lorraine and then, in order to further the reforms begun there, he founded the Congregation of St Maur.

Benavides, Alonzo de   Franciscan bishop, born San Miguel, the Azores, 1580, died on his way to Goa, 1636. As a missionary he served at several missions in Mexico and was custos of missions in New Mexico. He was appointed archbishop of Goa in Portuguese India and wrote two valuable ethnological treatises on the Indians of New Mexico.

Benedict Saint, monastic founder, born Norcia, Italy, 480, died Monte Cassino, *c.*550. He studied in Rome, was influenced by the developments in Byzantine monasticism, and his journey in faith began when he became a hermit, living in the caves, probably near Subiaco. He was gradually joined by others, many like himself from influential families. They built basic monastic accommodation, but Benedict conceived the need for a grander and more organized structure, and about 529 the community moved to Monte Cassino, where they set about the new construction. It is here too that the Rule of St Benedict, which was soon to become the guiding norm for Western monasticism, is thought to have been drawn up. There is strong claim to this being the site of Benedict's death and burial, and the resting-place of his relics, though much controversy surrounds this question. Benedict was in touch with many of the monastic and ecclesiastical leaders of his day and the community developed to the extent that another foundation, St Stephen's, was established in the Diocese of Terracina. Most of what we know of his life comes from the *Dialogues* of **Gregory the Great**, written in 593 and 594 and told to Gregory by the confrères and disciples of Benedict.

Monte Cassino was destroyed by the Lombards in 577 and a cult of the saint begins to appear after this time. Feast day: in the West 11 July, which is thought to be the date his relics were taken to Saint-Benoit-sur-Loire; 21 March is also kept within the Order, as the *transitus* or date of death, and in the East it is celebrated on 14 March.

Benedict I Pope, date of birth unknown, died 30 July 579. He was a Roman and the son of Boniface, and was called Bonosus by the Greeks. The ravages of the Lombards rendered it very difficult to communicate with the Emperor at Constantinople, who claimed the privilege of confirming the election of the Popes. Hence there was a vacancy of nearly eleven months between the death of **John III** and the arrival of the imperial confirmation of Benedict's election on 2 June 575. Almost the only act recorded of him is that he granted an estate, the Massa Veneris, in the territory of Minturnae, to Abbot Stephen of St Mark's 'near the walls of Spoleto'; and from the few words the *Liber Pontificalis* has about Benedict, it appears that he died in the midst of his efforts to cope with difficulties following the Lombard incursion.

Benedict II Pope, saint, born Rome, died 8 March 685. He became a Scripture scholar and an expert in sacred chants. He was elected to succeed **Leo II** in 683, but his consecration was delayed almost a year until 26 June 684, awaiting the emperor's confirmation. During his term, he amended the process to speed approval of papal elections by having the exarch of Ravenna confirm the election, rather than the emperor, thus eliminating long delays. Benedict was greatly respected by Emperor Constantine the Bearded, who sent him locks of his sons' hair, making them the Pope's spiritual sons. Benedict brought Macarius, the ex-patriarch of Antioch back to orthodoxy, from his Monothelitism, and restored several Roman churches. He upheld the cause of St **Wilfrid of York**, who sought the return of his see from which he had been deposed by **Theodore**. Feast day 8 May.

Benedict III Pope, date of birth unknown, died 17 April 858. The election of the learned and ascetic Roman, Benedict, the son of Peter, was a troubled one. On the death of **Leo IV** (17 July 855) Benedict was chosen to succeed him, and envoys were dispatched to secure the ratification of the decree of election by the Emperors **Lothair I** and **Louis II**. But the legates betrayed their trust in favour of the ambitious and excommunicated Cardinal **Anastasius the Librarian**. Most of the clergy and people, however, remained true to Benedict, and the legates had to yield. Benedict was accordingly consecrated on 29 September or 6 October 855. Because of dissensions and attacks from without, the kingdom of the Franks was in disorder. Benedict wrote to the Frankish bishops, attributing much of the misery in the Empire to their silence.

Benedict IV Pope, date of birth unknown, died summer of 903. Popes Benedict IV to IX inclusive belong to the darkest period of papal history; the reigns of several of them were very short. Benedict IV was a Roman, the son of Mammalus, and became Pope in the first half of 900. His high birth, his generosity, his zeal for the public good are loudly commended by the contemporary historian Frodoard, who gives him the title of 'Great'. The principal historic act of his reign was his crowning Louis the Blind as Emperor Louis III. He supported the decision of Pope **Formosus**, who had ordained him priest, upheld the cause of Stephen, bishop of Naples, and excommunicated the assassin of Fulk, archbishop of Reims.

Benedict V Pope, date of birth unknown, died Hamburg, 4 July 965. He was elected Pope in May 964 in critical circumstances. The powerful Emperor **Otto I**, had forcibly deposed the unworthy **John XII**, and had replaced him by a nominee of his own who took the title of **Leo VIII**. But at the first opportunity the Romans expelled Leo, and on the death on 14 May 964 of the lawful Pope, John XII, elected the cardinal-deacon Benedict. Otto was furious, marched on Rome, seized Benedict and put an end to his pontificate on 23 June 964. After reinstating Leo, Otto left Rome and carried Benedict with him to Germany. He was placed under the care of **Adaldag**, archbishop of Hamburg-Bremen, who treated him with great consideration; and he was even then acknowledged as Pope by some of the German clergy.

Benedict VI Pope, date of birth unknown, died August 974. A Roman, son of Hildebrand, he was elected as the successor of **John XIII**, who died 6 September 972; but the necessity of waiting for the ratification of the Emperor **Otto** delayed his consecration till 19 January 973. Nothing is known of his deeds, except that he confirmed the privileges of some churches and monasteries. The most striking event of his pontificate is its tragic close. He was seized and thrown into the castle of Sant' Angelo by a faction of the nobility headed by Crescentius I and the antipope, a deacon named Franco who called himself **Boniface VII**. There, after a confinement of less than two months, he was strangled on the orders of Boniface to prevent his release by Sicco, an imperial envoy sent to Rome by **Otto II**.

Benedict VII Pope, date of birth unknown, died *c.* October 983. Acting under the influence of Sicco (see **Benedict VI**), the Roman clergy and people elected to succeed Benedict VI another Benedict, bishop of Sutri, a Roman, son of David in October 974. **Boniface VII** opposed his authority, and, though the antipope himself was forced to flee, his party followed fiercely in his footsteps and com-

pelled Benedict to call upon **Otto II** for help. Firmly established on his throne by the emperor, he showed himself desirous of checking the tide of simony that was rising in the Church, of advancing the cause of monasticism especially in Germany, and of the conversion of the Slavs. He allowed St **Majolus of Cluny** to place his monastery under the special protection of the Holy See, which helped ensure the reform movement of the eleventh century.

Benedict VIII Pope, Theophylact, son of Count Gregory of Tusculum, born *c.*980, elected to the Papacy 17 May 1012 while still a layman, died 9 April 1024. He was a statesman of stature and obtained the support of **Henry II**, whom he crowned emperor in Rome in 1014. In 1016 the alliance of Pope, Genoa and Pisa successfully liberated Sardinia from the Spanish Saracens. He faced the most pressing problem of the age, which was reform in the Church. Benedict followed the leadership of Henry II. The Roman synod of 1014 had issued decrees concerning irregular ordinations. The Synod of Pavia in August 1020 opened with the Pope's address. It decreed degradation for non-celibate clerics in higher orders and the reduction of their offspring to the status of slavery. The emperor approved these decrees and enacted them as the law of the Empire.

Benedict IX Pope, elected 21 October 1032, died, probably, early January 1056. Born Theophylact, the son of Alberic III of Tusculum, he was made Pope by his father when still a layman, and only some twenty years old. His life had been dissolute, and did not change after his election. Though he struggled fairly successfully to free the Papacy from imperial control, he was forced out of Rome in September 1044 by the populace, who were wearied by his behaviour, and perhaps more by the domination of the Tusculani. In March the following year, however, he regained power, but was prevailed upon to abdicate two months later by the offer of a very large amount of money. He retired to the family estates near Frascati. He returned, however, seemingly by popular demand though more likely by bribery, in November 1047, and was ousted again on the orders of the emperor the following July. In December he was excommunicated by a Roman synod for simony.

Benedict X Antipope, elected 5 April 1058, resigned January 1059, died 1073 or later. Born in Rome, John Mincius at his election was cardinal bishop of Velletri and a reformer. He was elected by a small group of Roman clergy wanting to control the Papacy. He claimed at his trial, orchestrated by Hildebrand despite the fact that he had willingly resigned in 1059, that the office had been forced upon him. He was put under house arrest, and lived long enough to see Hildebrand become Pope as **Gregory VII**.

Benedict XI Blessed, Pope, born Niccolò Boccasino at Treviso, Italy, 1240, elected 22 October 1303, died Perugia, 7 July 1304. He entered the Dominican Order at the age of fourteen. In 1296 he was elected master general of the Order. As at this time hostility to **Boniface VIII** was becoming more pronounced, he issued an ordinance forbidding his Dominican brethren to favour the opponents of the reigning Pope. When Boniface died, he was unanimously elected Pope, taking the name of Benedict XI. The principal event of his pontificate was the restoration of peace with the French court. After a pontificate of eight months, Benedict died suddenly. He was beatified in 1773. He is the author of a volume of sermons and commentaries on a part of the Gospel of St Matthew, the Psalms, the Book of Job, and the Apocalypse. Feast day 7 July.

Benedict XII Third of the Avignon Popes, born Jacques Fournier at Saverdun in the province of Toulouse, *c.*1280, elected 20 December 1334, died Avignon, 24 April 1342. He studied at the University of Paris, where he received the doctorate in theology. He was abbot of Fontfroide, later bishop of his native Diocese of Palmiers, then Mirepoix, and was made cardinal by Pope **John XXII** in 1327. On the latter's death, during the conclave of 1334, he amazed the cardinals by receiving the necessary two-thirds vote. On 8 January 1335 he was enthroned as Benedict XII. Resolved to re-establish the Papacy at Rome, Benedict signalized his accession by providing for the restoration of St Peter's basilica and the Lateran. In the end he remained at Avignon, where he was responsible for the massive papal castle that still exists.

Benedict XIII Antipope, born Pedro Martinez de Luna in Aragon, *c.*1328, died Valencia, 23 May 1423. He taught canon law at Montpellier. In 1375 he was made cardinal deacon and he had the support of Castile and Aragon in favour of the Antipope **Clement VII**, whose successor he became at Avignon on 28 September 1394 until 26 July 1417, when he was deposed by the Council of Constance. He was noted for his knowledge of church law and personal integrity. His confessor was St **Vincent Ferrer**. He was adamant about his legitimate claim to the Papacy. Already in 1415 he retreated to Peniscola, where in almost complete isolation he maintained his papal claim until his death.

Benedict XIII Pope, born Peter Francesco Orsini, Palastrina, 2 February 1649, elected Pope, despite his many protestations, 29 May 1724, died 23 February 1730. At the age of sixteen he entered the Dominican novitiate against the will of his parents. On 22 February 1672, he was elevated to the cardinalate. In honour of **Benedict XI**, a saintly member of the Dominican Order, on his election he took the name of Benedict XIV, which he shortly changed to Benedict XIII as Pedro de Luna, who had previously borne the name (see above) was a schismatic. In order to encourage the foundation of diocesan seminaries, he organized a special commission (Congregatio Seminariorum). At a provincial Roman Lateran synod held in 1725, he required an unqualified acceptance of the Bull *Unigenitus* and through his efforts Cardinal de **Noailles**, archbishop of Paris, was led to accept it in 1728.

Benedict XIV Pope, born Prospero Lambertini at Bologna, 31 March 1675, elected to the Papacy 17 August 1740, died 3 May 1758. In 1694, though only nineteen, he received the degrees of doctor of theology and doctor utriusque juris (canon and civil law). On the death of **Innocent XII** he was made consistorial advocate by **Clement XI**, and shortly afterwards consultor of the Holy Office, in 1718 secretary of the Congregation of the Council. He was made bishop of Ancona in 1727 and cardinal, 30 April 1728. Between 1708 and 1727 he was promotor of the faith, and in charge of canonizations, writing the classic study of the process. When **Clement XII** died on 6 February 1740 his fame was at its highest. Through intrigues of various kinds the conclave which commenced on 17 February lasted for six months. To break the deadlock, he addressed the conclave: 'If you wish to elect a saint, choose **Gotti**; a statesman, Aldobrandini; an honest man, elect me.' He was chosen and took the name of Benedict XIV in honour of his friend and patron **Benedict XIII**. As Pope, Benedict improved relations between the Holy See and the states of Europe, both Catholic and Protestant. He engaged in reform of the Church, especially of the clergy, and continued his own scholarly interests, which won him friends and admirers even among those otherwise hostile to Catholicism.

Benedict XV Pope, born Giacomo della Chiesa at Genoa, 21 November 1854, elected to the Papacy 3 September 1914, died 22 January 1922. He studied law at Genoa and theology at the Gregorian University in Rome. He became a doctor of sacred theology in 1879. Giacomo entered the papal diplomatic service and soon caught the eye of **Rampolla**, secretary of state to **Leo XIII**. **Pius X** made him a cardinal in 1914; the same year he became Pope Benedict XV and immediately faced World War I. He urged Woodrow Wilson to use his great influence for a just peace, but expressed disappointment at the results of the Paris Peace Conference from which, at Italy's demand, the Holy See was excluded. Benedict worked successfully to improve the Holy See's diplomatic relations – in general he supported the League of Nations – and began the process which led, under his successor, to the settlement of the conflict between Italy and the Papacy. His first encyclical put an end to the persecution of Modernists. In 1917 Benedict promulgated the new Code of Canon Law, and his encyclical *Maximum Illud* of 1919 urged missionary bishops to promote an indigenous clergy. He had a particular interest in the churches of the East, founding the Congregation for the Oriental Church and the Pontifical Oriental Institute.

Benedict Biscop (also known as **Benet Biscop** and **Biscop Baducing**) Saint, abbot, Benedictine, born in Northumbria, England, *c*.628, died Wearmouth, England, 12 January *c*.690. In 674, at the mouth of the river Wear (Wearmouth), he built a church and monastery dedicated to St Peter. He is acknowledged as the founder of the joint monasteries of SS Peter and Paul at Wearmouth and Jarrow. He was the first to introduce glass into England. He organized the scriptorium in which was written the manuscript his successor St **Ceolfrid** took with him in 716 as a present to Pope St **Gregory II**: the Codex Amiatinus. **Bede**, whose work was made possible by Benedict's library, says that the civilization and learning of the eighth century rested in the monastery founded by Benedict. Feast day 12 January.

Benedict of Aniane Saint, Benedictine, born in Languedoc, France, 750, died Aachen, Germany, 11 February 821. In 774, he became a Benedictine monk at Saint-Seine near Dijon, France. When Bishop Felix of Urgel proposed that Christ was only the adoptive son of the eternal Father (Adoptionism), Benedict opposed this heresy and attended the Council (Synod) of Frankfurt in 794. He also refuted this heresy in four treatises, which were published in the miscellanies of Balusius. He and Emperor **Louis I** co-operated to their mutual benefit. The emperor made Benedict director of all the monasteries in the Empire. He compiled the *Codex regularum*, a collection of all monastic regulations, and *Concordia regularum*. Feast day 12 February.

Benedict of Benevento Saint, missionary and martyr, born Benevento, Italy, died with his four brothers and fellow missionaries John, Matthew, Isaac and Christian, near Miedzyrzec, Poland, 11 November 1005. He and his brothers followed St **Adalbert of Prague** in the mission among the Slavs, and were massacred at their hermitage by robbers who were acting on a rumour that Duke Boleslav I, who built the hermitage, had given them a great treasure. The five were buried at their hermitage, and it soon became a pilgrimage centre. Their cult was popular in the Polish church from an early date and was confirmed in 1508 by Pope **Julius II**. Feast day 11 November.

Benedict II of Cluse Venerable, abbot, Benedictine reformer, born Toulouse, *c*.1030, died Cluse, 31 May 1091. When very young he was confided by his father to the abbey of Saint-Hilaire, Carcassonne, France. He later entered the monastery of San Michele della Chiusa (Cluse), and became abbot in 1066 and was consecrated by Pope **Alex-**

ander II. Benedict then began a reform of the abbey, insisting on asceticism, humility and manual labour. When **Gregory VII** became Pope, Benedict's bishop, Cunibert of Turin, devastated the property at Cluse and put the abbey under interdict. Benedict was forced to flee. For the remainder of his life he struggled with William, Cunibert's successor.

Benedict of Peterborough English abbot, and chronicler of **Thomas Becket**, died Peterborough Abbey, England, 1193. It is thought that he was a Benedictine at Christ Church, Canterbury, England, and that his accounts of Thomas Becket are from first-hand experience. In 1174 he was made chancellor to **Richard of Canterbury**, Becket's successor, and the following year was made prior of Christ Church. In 1175 he was elected prior of Peterborough Abbey and during his fifteen years there returned the abbey to solvency and developed some of the buildings. He served in the court of **Richard I**, and wrote a *passio* of the martyrdom of Becket, parts of which are preserved in the *Quadrilogus*, and an account of Becket's miracles, which survived as a separate work.

Benedict the Levite or **Benedict the Deacon** is the name given to himself by the author of a forged collection of capitularies which appeared in the ninth century. The collection belongs to the group of pseudo-Isidorian forgeries that includes the pseudo-Isidorian recension of the Spanish collection of canons, the so-called *capitula Angilramni* (see **Angelram**), and the collection of false decretals of the Pseudo-Isidore (see **Isidore of Seville**). The name Benedict is, without doubt, an assumed one; the statements that he had been a deacon in the church of Mainz and that the collection had been made from the archiepiscopal archives of Mainz at the command of the late Archbishop Autgar (825–47) seem untrue. Nothing is known concerning the real author.

Benedict the Moor (also known as **Benedict the Black**) Saint, Franciscan lay brother, born near Messina, Italy, 1526, died Palermo, Italy, 4 April 1589; beatified in 1743, canonized in 1807. He was the son of freed slaves brought to Sicily from Africa. He was about 21 when he was publicly insulted on account of his race. The leader of a group of Franciscan hermits observed his dignified demeanour on that occasion and Benedict was invited to join the group at Montepellegrino. In 1578, Benedict was appointed superior though he was an illiterate lay brother. With understandable reluctance he accepted the office. After serving as superior, he became novice master but asked to be relieved of this post and returned to his former position as cook. Benedict is the patron of African-Americans in the USA. The surname 'the Moor' is a misnomer originating from the Italian *il moro*, 'the black'. Feast day 4 April.

Benedict the Pole (Benedict de Ponte) Franciscan missionary and interpreter, died 1247. In March 1245 Pope **Innocent IV** sent **John da Pian del Carpine** to the Great Khan of the Mongols. Benedict was his companion and interpreter. He and John reached the camp of Batu Khan in February 1246 and the camp of Kuyuk on 26 July. They saw Kuyuk proclaimed Great Khan on 24 August 1246 and departed in November. They reached Batu Khan on 9 May 1247 and then returned to Lyons via Cologne. In Cologne, Benedict gave an account of their journey to a local prelate and to a scholastic who wrote it down.

Benelli, Giovanni Italian cardinal and archbishop, papal diplomat and Vatican reformer, born Paggiole de Vernio, near Pistoia, 12 May 1921, died Florence, 26 October 1982. Studied in Pistoia, at the Gregorian University in Rome and at the Ecclesiastical Academy. He was ordained in 1943 and in 1947 became secretary to Montini, the future Pope **Paul VI**. He served in the papal diplomatic service in Dublin, Paris, Rio de Janeiro and Madrid. In 1965 he was observer to UNESCO in Paris and was in West Africa, but in 1967 the Pope called him back to the Vatican secretariat of state, responsible for implementing reforms of the curia: one of the reforms made the secretary of state co-ordinator of the work of all the curial departments. He entered into his task with great thoroughness and ensured there would be no further nepotism or abuses within the curia. His management style was direct and, in his efforts to maintain a balance between the newly formed and the traditional departments, was sometimes suspected by both. Benelli was made archbishop of Florence and cardinal in 1977. Some thought his previous influence had been too great, and he proved to have the upper hand in the conclave of 1978 when his candidate, the future Pope **John Paul I**, won the election. He was himself a contender in the conclave some months later, following the sudden death of the new Pope, and almost gained sufficient votes to be elected. But his opponents would not give in and Benelli went back to Florence, with ambitions to make it the spiritual and cultural capital of the new Europe.

Benezet Patron saint of bridges, born near St Jean-de-Maurienne, Savoy, 1165, died Avignon, 14 April 1184. While a shepherd in the south of France he received a divine commission to build a bridge over the Rhône river at Avignon. The bridge was never completed, however. He is supposed to have founded the lay Brotherhood of Bridgebuilders (Fratres Pontifices), who were particularly active in the south of France building bridges, bridge chapels, streets and pilgrim hostels. Canonized in 1233, he is patron saint of Avignon, bridge builders and shepherds. Feast day 14 April.

Benigni, Umberto Italian priest, church historian and journalist, anti-Modernist, born in Perugia, 30 March 1862, died Rome, 26 February 1934. Ordained in 1884, became secretary to the archbishop of Perugia, professor of ecclesiastical history in the seminary in Perugia and later at the Apollinaris in Rome, where he lectured in Italian and not Latin. From 1911 he taught at the Academy of Noble Ecclesiastics in Rome. He worked at the Vatican secretariat of state, was opposed to Modernism and became a leading figure in the Integralist movement and a supporter of Action Française. Much of his journalistic activity was devoted to rooting out and denouncing those suspected of Modernist tendencies, and he was a contributor to the *Catholic Encyclopedia*.

Benignus of Dijon Patron saint of Dijon, early martyr, thought to have died under Marcus Aurelius, possibly a native of Asia Minor, a disciple of **Polycarp** and a missionary to Burgundy. The basilica and abbey in Dijon are built over his tomb. Feast day 1 November.

Benjamin (Kazansky) of Petrograd Russian Orthodox saint, bishop and martyr, born Olonets,

Russia, 1874, died (shot) Petrograd, 13 August 1922. He was elected in 1917 as metropolitan of Petrograd (St Petersburg). In 1922, when the Communists started to confiscate church valuables on the false pretext of helping the famine victims of the Volga region, he agreed to give up all except the Eucharistic vessels. The offer was rejected by the government and the metropolitan was arrested and, after a dramatic show trial, was shot, with many other clergy, as a counter-revolutionary. His body was never recovered. Feast day 13 August.

Bennet, John Methodist lay preacher and Congregational minister, born near Chinley, Derbyshire, 1714, died Warburton, Cheshire, 1759. Having attended Findern Academy, Derby, he worked as a legal clerk and a packman. Following an evangelical conversion in 1742 he travelled with Benjamin **Ingham** and the Moravians. In 1743 he joined the Methodists, becoming an itinerant preacher, creating a circuit of religious groups in the northern counties. He was influential in establishing the Methodist Quarterly Meeting and Annual Conference. Largely because of his marriage in 1749 to Grace Murray (who was apparently already engaged to **John Wesley**), Bennet left Methodism in 1752 and became the founder of Congregationalism at Bolton. Gaining ordination in 1754, he supervised a church at Warburton.

Benoît, Michel Scientist, born Autun or Dijon, 8 October 1715, died Peking, 23 October 1774. After studying astronomy he went as a missionary to China, where he put his scientific skills at the service of the emperor. He designed fountains and buildings for the royal gardens, engraved maps, and taught the emperor how to use the telescope. He published his memoirs and translated the *Imitation of Christ* into Chinese.

Benoît, Pierre French Dominican, biblical scholar, archaeologist and editor, born Nancy, 3 August 1906, died Jerusalem, 23 August 1987. Joined the Dominicans in 1924, studied theology at the Dominican College in Kain, Belgium, and then went to teach at the Ecole Biblique et Archéologique Française in Jerusalem. He taught NT studies and the topography of Jerusalem. From 1965 to 1972 he was director of the Ecole, and from 1953 to 1968 was editor of its scholarly journal *Revue Biblique*. He received honours from the French government, from the Universities of Durham and Munich, was a member of the Pontifical Biblical Commission, given honorary life membership of learned biblical associations and was a founder member and first Roman Catholic president of the Society for New Testament Studies. He was a major figure in both the idea and the execution of the idea of the Jerusalem Bible, the first modern Roman Catholic Bible to be translated from the original languages. It was laid out as a work of literature, and had detailed, scholarly but accessible notes that provided a very full, critical commentary. He became very interested in and knowledgeable about archaeology and established the 'Chronique archéologique' in the *Revue Biblique* to report on new excavations. His own expertise was in the archaeology of Jerusalem. He was a theological advisor to the Second Vatican Council, contributing to the documents on revelation, the Church, religious freedom and non-Christian religions. He was editor of the Greek and Latin documents of the Dead Sea Scrolls and after the death of Roland de **Vaux** became general editor of the unpublished fragments.

Benson, Joseph Methodist minister, twice president of the Methodist Conference, born Melmerby, Cumberland, 25 January 1749, died London, 16 February 1821. In 1765 he became a teacher and underwent an evangelical conversion. Met **John Wesley** at Bristol in 1766 and was appointed classical tutor at Kingswood School. In 1769 he entered St Edmund Hall, Oxford, in the hope of entering the ministry but his association with the Methodists prevented his ordination. After a brief period at the Countess of Huntingdon's college at Trevecka (see Selina **Hastings**), Benson was dismissed for his Arminianism, but was accepted as an itinerant preacher. President of the Methodist Conference in 1798 and 1810, and secretary in 1805 and 1809. From 1803 till the time of his death served as editor of the *Methodist Magazine*. His numerous publications include a *Commentary on the Holy Bible* (1810).

Benson, Robert Hugh Roman Catholic convert and apologist, born at Wellington College (where his father was headmaster, who in 1882 became archbishop of Canterbury), 18 November 1871, died Salford, 19 October 1914. He studied at Eton and at Trinity College, Cambridge. He was ordained in the Church of England in 1895 and worked among the poor in Hackney Wick, then entered the Community of the Resurrection at Mirfield in Yorkshire. He became a Roman Catholic in September 1903. He was ordained a priest in Rome in 1904 and returned to England to support himself by writing a large number of books with a Catholic theme, several of them historical novels, of which perhaps the best known is *Come Rack, Come Rope* (1912). He was also much in demand both in England and in the United States as a preacher.

Bentley, Richard Church of England priest, classical scholar and Christian apologist, born Oulton, Yorkshire, 27 January 1662, died Cambridge, 7 July 1742. Studied at Cambridge and was tutor in the household of E. Stillingfleet, dean of St Paul's, and spent many hours studying in the library there and at the Bodleian, Oxford. He was ordained priest in 1690 and became chaplain to Stillingfleet, and in 1694 became Keeper of the Royal Libraries. In 1700 he was made master of Trinity College, Cambridge, and remained there until his death. He showed the extent of his scholarly abilities in his *Dissertation on the Epistles of Phalaris* (1697) written to refute W. Temple's claim that the *Epistles* were an authentic work. This work establishes him as the founder of higher literary and historical criticism. His other works include *The Folly of Atheism* (1692), a refutation of free-thinking which he published under a pseudonym; and *Proposals for the Edition of the Greek Testament* (1720), which anticipates later methods of biblical textual criticism.

Benziger, August Painter, born Einsiedeln, Switzerland, 2 January 1867, died New York City, 13 April 1955. Educated in England, Vienna and Paris, he became known for his portrait painting, especially his idealized style of portraiture. He painted many of the prominent people of his time, including Popes **Leo XIII**, **Benedict XV** and **Pius XI**, as well as Cardinal James **Gibbons**, Presidents William McKinley and Theodore Roosevelt, and J. P. Morgan.

Benziger, Joseph Charles Catholic publisher, born

Einsiedeln, Switzerland, 1762, died Einsiedeln, 1841. Originally the proprietor of a religious goods store in Einsiedeln, he went on to found the Benziger publishing firm and become a bookseller. In America his sons founded the firm of Benziger Brothers, which became a major publisher of Catholic books, and on which the Holy See conferred the title 'Printers to the Holy Apostolic See'.

Benzo of Alba Imperial partisan (especially of Otto III) during the investiture controversy, believed to be of southern Italian origin, died 1089/90. In addition to his intervention in mysterious negotiations in aid of an alliance between the Western and the Byzantine Empires to expel the Normans from southern Italy, he was significant as a supporter of Cadalus, who became Antipope Honorius II in opposition to Pope **Alexander II**. Because of his bitter opposition to **Gregory VII** the populace expelled him from his episcopal see.

Beran, Josef Czechoslovakian archbishop and primate, born Plzen, 29 December 1888, died Rome, 17 May 1969. Studied in Plzen and in Rome and following his ordination in 1911 returned home and served in Chyš, Prosek, Prague and Michle. He became a spiritual director, was director of the Teachers Institute of St Anne and from 1928 until 1932 taught at the University of Prague. He became rector of the seminary, held office in the archdiocesan curia and in 1936 was made a papal prelate. In 1942 he was deported by the German Gestapo to the concentration camp in Teresin and later to Dachau. In 1946 he returned to the seminary and was made archbishop of Prague. He was put under house arrest in 1949 following the Communist takeover of Czechoslovakia and, refusing to resign as archbishop, was removed and kept hidden for the following twelve years. Under the president's amnesty he was released in 1963 and was sent to villages near Tabor. In 1965 he was made cardinal and went to Rome, where he was forced to remain. He was present at Vatican Council II, where he spoke for the independence of the Church and made forceful interventions in support of the *Declaration on Religious Freedom*. He visited the USA in 1966, was warmly welcomed by both clergy and laity and was honoured by several academic institutions.

Berard of Carbio and companions Franciscan protomartyrs, sent as missionaries by **Francis** himself in 1219 and put to death in Morocco on 16 January 1220, on the orders of Sultan Aboidile (Abou Yacoub) because they persistently refused to stop preaching the Christian message. Their remains were brought back to the church of the Canons Regular of St Augustine, and were instrumental in determining the Franciscan vocation of **Anthony of Padua**. Feast day 16 January.

Berardi, Carlo Sebastiano Canonist, born Oneglia, Italy, 26 August 1719, died Turin, 1786. A member of the faculty of law at Turin, he produced the standard edition of **Gratian**'s *Decretum* (1752–7) and wrote other works on canon law which, however, are not all fully competent.

Bérault-Bercastel, Antoine Henri de Priest and historian, born Briey, Lorraine, 22 November 1720, died Noyon, 1794. He served as parish priest at Omerville and Noyon and wrote a scholarly 24-volume *History of the Church*, which originally went up to 1721 and was extended to 1844 by Hevrion. The German historian Pius Bonifatius Gams (1816–92) later produced an abbreviated edition.

Berdiaev (Berdyaev), Nikolai Aleksandrovich Religious philosopher, born Kiev, 6 March 1874, died Clamart, France, 24 March 1948. He was born into a well-to-do family, and attended the University of Kiev, where he was attracted to Marxism. This led to his arrest and exile in 1898. Six years later, with Sergei **Bulgakov** he started *Novy Put*, a journal of social and religious issues. He taught philosophy for a time in Moscow, but was again exiled, moving to Paris in 1924 where he set up a Religious Philosophical Society, and edited *Put* ('The Way'), devoted to philosophy and religion. Himself a rather left-wing Orthodox, he tried to bring together the different denominations in dialogue. His philosophy was a form of rather mystical existentialism.

Berengarius of Tours Archdeacon and initiator of Eucharistic heresy, born Tours, France, c.1000, died Saint-Cosmas island, near Tours, 1088. He studied under **Fulbert of Chartres** and in 1031 became a teacher at the school of St Martin in

Tours. In 1041 he was appointed archdeacon of Angers. His Eucharistic teaching is based on that of **Ratramnus**. Berengarius tried to explain the Eucharistic mystery as a rationalist and dialectician, which he thought superior, rather than as a believer, which he seemed to look down on. He denies the Real Presence and sees the bread and wine as mere symbols, and sees the change that happens at the consecration as being in the value and meaning the believer endows them with, not in the elements in themselves. Berengarius' teaching was condemned at a council in Rome in 1050, and later that year at Vercelli, in Paris in 1051, again in Rome in 1059 and later in 1079. At this stage Berengarius signed a formula which contained the words *substantialiter converti*, the first time these words appear in a church document. He retired to the hermitage of St Cosmas and appears to have died in communion with the Church. The major treatises which refute and correct the teachings of Berengarius are by **Lanfranc, Guitmond of Aversa** and Alger of Liège. As a result of his teaching, Eucharistic doctrine was clarified and developed.

Berger, Samuel   French Reformed theologian, born near Montbéliard, Alsace, 2 May 1843, died Sèvres, near Paris, 13 February 1900. He helped to found the Protestant theological faculty at Paris and also founded and directed its library. As professor of church history and church archaeology he researched the history of Bible translation. The Universities of Cambridge, Leipzig and Dublin recognized his scholarship with honorary doctorates. Among his works are *La Bible au seizième siècle* (1879), *La Bible française au Moyen-Age* (1880), and *Histoire de la Vulgate pendant les premiers siècles du Moyen-Age* (1893).

Bergier, Nicolas-Sylvestre   Catholic theologian and apologist, born Darney, France, 31 December 1718, died Paris, 9 April 1790. After serving as pastor at Flau(n)gebouche and professor at Besançon he was appointed canon at Paris by Archbishop Christophe de Beaumont. He collaborated with Denis Diderot on the *Encyclopédie*. Noted as one of the most significant apologists of the eighteenth century, he wrote countless polemical works defending Christianity against French deism and materialism. They include the twelve-volume

Traité historique et dogmatique de la vraie religion (1780), *Le déisme réfuté par lui-même* (1765), *La certitude des preuves du christianisme* (2 vols, 1767), and *Encyclopédie méthodique: Théologie* (3 vols, 1788–90).

Berington, Charles   Catholic bishop, born Stock, Essex, England, 1748, died Wolverhampton, 8 June 1798. Educated at Douai and the Sorbonne, he became coadjutor to Bishop Thomas Talbot, whom he was designated to succeed as vicar apostolic of the Midland district. He had, however, joined a liberal Catholic group known as the Cisalpine Club and signed the so-called 'blue books', which had been condemned by the Pope. Complicated negotiations with Rome followed which were to have ended with Berington's signing an acceptable retraction, but he died suddenly before these could be completed.

Berkeley, George   Philosopher and bishop, born near Kilkenny, Ireland, 12 March 1685, died Oxford, 14 January 1753. He was educated in Kilkenny and at Trinity College, Dublin, where he became a fellow in 1707 and taught 1709–13. He then travelled and wrote his main philosophical works. He returned to Trinity for the years 1721–4, when he became dean of Derry, then in 1734 bishop of Cloyne. While dean, he undertook to establish a seminary in Bermuda, and visited America from 1728 to 1734, settling in Newport, Rhode Island. His project failed. He left Ireland for Oxford in 1752. His philosophy was chiefly intended to refute scepticism, and defend religion, and was mainly the work of his early years. In his latter days he became famous for recommending, and defending in print, the benefits to the health of tar water. *An Essay towards a New Theory of Vision* was published in Dublin in 1709, and the *Principles of Human Knowledge* appeared there the following year. His *Alciphron* was written in Newport, and published in London on his return.

Berkeley, Lennox   British composer, born Boar's Hill, Oxford, 12 May 1903, died London, 26 December 1989. A Roman Catholic, his compositions include works for Westminster Cathedral. From 1944 to 1968 he was professor of composition at the Royal Academy of Music and was president of the Composers' Guild of Great Britain. His religious compositions include a *Missa Brevis* and a *Stabat Mater*. He was knighted in 1974.

Berlage, Anton Catholic theologian, born Münster, Germany, 21 December 1805, died Münster, 6 December 1881. After studying at Münster, Bonn and Tübingen, he became private tutor at the Academy of Münster, then professor of moral theology and professor of dogmatic theology. He was named papal chamberlain. He is the author of *Apologetik der Kirche* (1834) and *Die katholische Dogmatik* (7 vols, 1839–63).

Berlière, Ursmer Benedictine, born Gosselies, Belgium, 3 September 1861, died Maredsous, Belgium, 27 August 1932. He became professor and librarian at the Abbey Gymnasium at Maredsous and for over 40 years was editor-in-chief of the *Revue Bénédictine*. He founded and directed the Belgian Historical Institute in Rome and then became director of the Royal Library in Brussels and consultor for the historical division of the Sacred Congregation of Rites. He wrote wide-ranging works about Benedictine history, including *Mélanges d'histoire bénédictine* (1897), *L'ordre monastique des origines au XIIe siècle* (1912), and *L'ascèse bénédictine des origines à la fin du XIIe siècle* (1927).

Bernadot, Marie Vincent French Dominican, author and publisher, born Escatalens, 14 June 1883, died Labastide Leveque, 25 June 1941. Studied at the seminary in Montauban, was ordained in 1906 and joined the Dominicans in 1912. After studies in Rome he returned to the priory of Saint-Maximin in France and wrote on the spiritual life. In 1919 he founded the journal *La vie spirituelle*, whose circulation reached over 3000 in the first year. He then set up *La vie intellectuelle*, with a political, social, artistic and religious focus, and some of the best Roman Catholic minds of the day contributed to this. In 1928 he founded the publishing house Les Editions du Cerf, which later moved to Paris. His new weekly journal *Sept*, founded in 1934, soon had a circulation of of over 50,000, and Bernadot caused some controversy both by his socialist sympathies and by his suggestion that the Spanish Civil War was not a 'holy crusade'. *Sept* continued under the title *Temps présent* and under the editorship of **Maritain** and **Mauriac**, among others. He is also responsible for starting the journal *La vie chrétienne avec Notre Dame*, which became *Fêtes et saisons* and eventually *La vie catholique*.

Bernanos, Georges French novelist and playwright, born Paris, 20 February 1888, died Neuilly, 5 July 1948. He was educated in minor seminaries and at the Sorbonne. He began his career as a journalist, then volunteered for the army during the First World War, and after it worked in insurance. He published his first book in 1922, his second, *Sous le soleil de Satan* (1925), brought him fame, though he always found it difficult to provide for his wife (a collateral descendant of **Joan of Arc**) and their six children. His best-known work, *Le journal d'un curé de campagne* (*The Diary of a Country Priest*, 1938) won him the Grand Prix of the Académie Française. This was a typical work, in that its protagonist was a much less than perfect priest. Priests figure in much of his fiction, but he also wrote essays on moral and political issues, often concerned with Christianity and human rights.

Bernard Gui Dominican, bishop and historical author, born Royère (Limousin), 1261/2, died Château de Laroux, Hérault, 31 December 1331. A theology teacher, he served as bishop of Lodève (Languedoc). He was a prolific writer whose works include a hagiography of **Thomas Aquinas**, an important collection of saints' lives entitled *Speculum sanctorale*, *Flores chronicorum* (a compilation of histories of the Papacy), and a popular illustrated work, *Arbor genealogiae regum Francorum*. Having been named Inquisitor of Toulouse, he also wrote *Practica officii inquisitoris*, for which, perhaps, he is most remembered.

Bernard Lombardi Dominican prior in Avignon, died 1333. He came from Provence and entered the Order in Perpignan, receiving his master of theology degree in Paris. He was named prior of Avignon and then became provincial superior of Provence. He published *Quaestiones de Quolibet* (a commentary on the *Sentences* of **Peter Lombard**) and *Collationes de sanctis et de tempore*.

Bernard of Aosta (Menton, Mont Joux) Archdeacon, patron of mountain climbers, born probably in Italy, died Novara, 15 June 1081. He was archdeacon of Aosta for about 40 years and was respected for his preaching and loved for his goodness. He is known to all as the restorer and patron of the hospices for travellers in the Alps, under the care of the community that eventually became the Canons Regular of St Augustine.

Bernard of Besse Early French Franciscan chronicler, flourished c.1283. He was a member of the Franciscans of Cahors and was secretary to the minister-general, **Bonaventure**. He was probably living in Limoges in 1250. He wrote extensively about early friars as well as ascetical works accessible to young people. The first chapter of his *De Laudibus b. Francisci* is the oldest Franciscan hagiographic catalogue.

Bernard of Clairvaux Saint, born near Dijon, 1090, died Clairvaux, 20 August 1153. The well-educated son of a noble family, with 31 companions he entered the (Cistercian) abbey of Cîteaux in 1111, thereby saving it from probable extinction. Three years later he became abbot of Clairvaux, a new foundation, and was ordained in 1115. By the time of Bernard's death there were over 700 monks in the monastery, and the Cistercians had made some 500 new foundations. He was so convinced of the superiority of the Cistercian way of life that he was critical of other forms, particularly that of Cluny, and a lively correspondence on the matter developed between Bernard and Cluny's abbot, **Peter the Venerable**. He was much involved in church politics, backing **Innocent II** against the Antipope, and giving vigorous support (and advice) to **Eugenius III**, who had been one of his disciples. He gave equally vigorous support through his preaching to the disastrous Second Crusade. He engaged in theological debate with Peter **Abelard** and **Gilbert de la Porrée**. Much of his writing is on prayer and spiritual subjects, and he fostered devotion to the person of Christ, and to the Virgin Mary. His *Liber de diligendo Dei* ('On how to love God') is a classic, and so are his sermons on the Song of Songs. He was canonized in 1174, and declared a Doctor of the Church in 1830. Feast day 20 August.

Bernard of Compostela I (the elder) Spanish canon lawyer, died c.1220. He studied and taught canon law in Bologna and wrote a glossary to the *Decretum Gratiani* and *Quaestiones decretales*. He compiled the decretals of **Innocent III** and also was probably active in the papal curia.

Bernard of Compostela II (the younger) Spanish bishop and canon lawyer, born Vergantinas, Galicia, died Rome, 1267. As papal chaplain to Popes **Innocent IV**, **Alexander IV** and **Urban IV**, he was involved in the jurisprudence of the Roman curia. Among his works are a glossary to the decretals of Innocent IV and a fragmentary but quite detailed *Lectura* to the *Liber Extra*.

Bernard of Constance Polemicist, died Corvey, 15 March 1088. Principal of the cathedral schools in Constance and then Hildesheim, he was a firm supporter of Pope **Gregory VII**. He wrote a polemical work on the Rome Lenten Synod of 1076, directed against King Henry IV, which was formerly attributed to Bishop **Altmann of Passau** and entitled *De damnatione eorum qui papam totamque romanam synodum deauctorizare temptaverunt, et de sacramentis damnatorum*.

Bernard of Foncaude Abbot, born c.1192. He was abbot of the Praemonstratensian abbey of Fontcaude in the Diocese of Narbonne, France, and known as an opponent of the Waldensian heresy. He wrote *Tractatus contra Vallenses et Arianos* (1188).

Bernard of Kraiburg Bishop of Chiemsee and humanist, born Kraiburg, between 1410 and 1420, died Herrenchiemsee, 17 October 1477. After studying canon law in Vienna he served the archiepiscopal curia in Salzburg and became chancellor. He is one of the three participants in the dialogue *De Possest* about the essence of God written by his friend **Nicholas of Cusa**. He became bishop of Chiemsee as well as vicar-general and suffragan bishop of Salzburg. Of his works the best known is a complaint about general corruption entitled *Deploratio miseriarum sui saeculi*. He owned an extensive library, of which some 100 manuscript volumes are now in the libraries at Munich, Salzburg and Vienna.

Bernard of Montmirat Abbot and canon lawyer,

born Montmirat, southern France, 1225, died Monte Cassino, 1296. A student of Petrus de Sampsone, he taught canon law at Béziers and Toulouse. In 1286 Pope **Honorius IV** named him bishop and assigned him to various missions, including legate to England and Sweden. He composed a *Lectura* to the *Liber Extra* and a commentary on the *Novellae* of **Innocent IV**.

Bernard of Saisset Bishop, born 1232, died Parmiers, 1311. Originally abbot of the Canons Regular of St Antonin, he clashed with the Count of Foix. He was supported by Pope **Boniface VIII**, who appointed him, without the approval of the French king, the first bishop of the Diocese of Parmiers. Bernard was for a time imprisoned, but later pardoned.

Bernard of Tiron Monastic reformer, hermit, wandering preacher, prior of Saint-Savin-sur-Gartempe, founder and abbot of the reformed Benedictine monastery of Tiron, his own foundation. Born Abbeville, *c*.1046, died Fontaine-Gehard, 14 or 25 April 1117. His foundation at Tiron eventually became the mother house of a small monastic order with houses in France, Wales and Scotland. By the thirteenth century, its Scottish daughter houses had managed to secure their independence from Tiron and its Continental houses became all but indistinguishable from other Benedictine monasteries. Feast day 14 April.

Bernard of Trille Dominican theologian, born Nîmes, southern France, *c*.1240, died Avignon, 4 August 1292. He lectured in theology in various centres of Dominican studies in the south of France and became master of theology in Paris, where he composed a series of *Quaestiones disputatae*, three *Quodlibets*, and commentaries on Scripture. He strongly favoured the theology of **Thomas Aquinas** and thus became a founder of the early Thomistic school, opposing **Henry of Ghent** in the defence of certain aspects of Aquinas' teaching.

Bernardin, Joseph Cardinal, archbishop of Chicago, born Columbia, South Carolina, of Italian parents, 2 April 1926, died Chicago, 14 November 1996. He studied in Baltimore and in Washington, being ordained in 1952 and consecrated assistant bishop of Atlanta in 1966, he was general secretary and then president of the National Conference of Catholic Bishops. Archbishop of Cincinnati in 1972 and later of Chicago in 1982, he became a cardinal in 1983. He was very active on the pro-life committee of the US bishops, insisting that the issue should not be limited to the question of abortion, but to that of capital punishment, a view not wholly welcome among pro-life activists. He took a lead in establishing procedures to investigate allegations of sexual abuse against priests. Accused of abuse in 1993 by an ex-seminarian, he insisted the allegation be thoroughly examined. The young man later withdrew the charge and apologized. Bernardin spent what he knew were his last months – he died of cancer – encouraging American Catholics to find common ground and unite.

Bernardine of Siena Saint, Franciscan preacher, born near Siena, 8 September 1380, died Aquila, 20 May 1444. An orphan early in his life, he was brought up by relatives in Siena, attended school, studied humanities and philosophy and later canon law at the university. He finished in 1400 and worked with plague victims in the hospital and himself became ill. In 1402 he joined the Franciscans and was ordained in 1404. He preached, studied and wrote and in 1414 became vicar-provincial of the Observants of Tuscany. From 1417 to 1429 he met invitations to preach throughout central and northern Italy, sometimes to crowds of about 30,000 people. He was a gifted speaker, intelligent, holy, sensitive to individuals and to political situations, full of human warmth and joy. He continued his preaching in his later years until his death, but combined this with writing and with administrative office. He was one of the leading proponents of devotion to the Holy Name, and the creator of the often used YHS (or IHS) trigram, set in the middle of a radiant sun. His writings, some of which he wrote himself and others of which were written down by others, consist mainly of his sermons, but he also wrote more systematic theological works. His collected writings first appeared as the four-volume *S. Bernardini Sen. Ord. Min. Opera quae extant omnia* in 1591 and there is a recent multi-volume edition by the Franciscan Fathers of Quaracchi. Feast day 20 May.

Bernières-Louvigny, Jean de French mystic, born Caen, France, 1602, died Caen, 3 May 1659. He lived with friends in his hermitage near Caen and devoted himself to prayer, meditation and charitable deeds. Among his works are *Le chrétien intérieur* (1659) and *Les œuvres spirituelles* (1670). In 1727 a selection of his works was published as *Das verborgene Leben mit Christo in Gott*, edited and translated by the Reformed Pietist and mystic Gerhard Tersteegen.

Bernini, Giovanni Lorenzo Italian baroque sculptor and architect, born Naples, 1598, died Rome, 28 November 1680. The family moved to Rome when he was still young and he stayed there for the rest of his life, apart from a brief period in Paris in 1665 at the court of **Louis XIV**. He learned his basic skills from his father Pietro, and while still a young man he was made architect to St Peter's and superintendant of public works, a position he held for most of his life. He renovated existing churches, piazzas, fountains and tombs and designed and built new ones. He played a prominent part in the planning of civic functions such as carnivals and firework displays, and produced very many paintings as well as poems and comedies. Much of the magnificence of present-day Rome, notably the colonnade of St Peter's, is the work of Bernini, and his ability to put sculpture at the service of architecture worked to the enhancement of both.

Berno Blessed, first abbot of Cluny, born Burgundy, c.850, died 13 January 927. He joined the Benedictines at St Martin of Autun, was at the abbey of Baume-les-Messieres, and about 890 founded Gigny, becoming its superior. In 909 he was given the territory of Cluny by the Duke of Aquitaine, and he built a new abbey there which he dedicated to SS Peter and Paul. Under the Cluniac reforms it was placed under the immediate authority of the Holy See. The houses of Deols and Sauvigny were also put in Berno's charge. Feast day 13 January.

Berno of Reichenau German Benedictine monk, orator and musician, born Prüm, near Trier, died Reichenau, 7 June 1048. He was educated at Sankt Gallen, was a monk at Prüm and became abbot of Reichenau in 1008. He was a supporter of the Cluniac reforms, but tempered these, and both renewed fervour in the abbey and attracted new recruits. He went with **Henry II** to Rome for the latter's coronation in 1014 and supported his son Conrad the Younger for emperor after Henry's death. When his rival won the throne Berno supported him and later the new Emperor **Henry III**. He was at the Synod of Constance in 1043. He wrote liturgical and musical works, letters and sermons, many of which are extant.

Bernold of Constance (Bernold of St Blaise) Chronicler, born c.1050, died Schaffhausen, 16 September 1100. Educated at the cathedral school in Constance, was at the Lenten synod in Rome in 1079 and was ordained in 1084. He opposed **Henry IV** in the investiture struggle and was at the battle of Pleichfeld in 1086. His writings show him to have been against the married clergy and in favour of the superior authority of papal decrees against other sources of canon law. In his *Chronicle* he includes extracts from earlier chronicles and traces historical events from 1075 to 3 August 1100. He also wrote a treatise on the Eucharist and on the liturgy.

Bertha of Blangy Saint, French Benedictine abbess, born Arras, second half of the seventh century, died c.725. She seems to have been married with children, as she founded the monastery of Blangy about 686 and went to live there with two of her daughters. Feast day 4 July.

Bertha of Val d'Or Saint, French founder and abbess, died Avenay c.690. She lived a celibate life with Gombert, the founder of the convent of St Peter in Reims. He was murdered and Bertha founded a convent at Avenay, previously Val d'Or, and was its first abbess. It is thought that she herself was murdered by her husband's relatives. Feast day 1 May.

Bertharius Saint, Italian Benedictine abbot and martyr, born in Lombardy, early ninth century, died at the hands of the Saracens, Teano, Campania, 22 October 884. Joined the Benedictines at Monte Cassino and became abbot there in 848. He entertained the Emperor **Louis II** in 866 and gained many privileges for the monastery and he secured its exemption from episcopal jurisdiction from Pope **John VIII**. He encouraged the development of sacred studies, and many of those who studied in the monastery became bishops. His extant writings include a homily on **Scholastica**, the sister of **Benedict**, who was buried at Monte Cassino, and a poem on the life, death and miracles of Benedict himself. Feast day 22 October.

Berthier, Guillaume François Jesuit and biblical commentator, born Issoudun, France, 7 April 1704, died Bourges, 15 December 1782. He taught philosophy in Rennes and Rouen and theology in Paris and was teacher of the future Kings Louis XVI and Louis XVIII. When the Jesuits were expelled from France in 1764–74, he lived in Offenburg, and then, after the prohibition was lifted, he returned to Bourges and devoted himself to ascetic and biblical studies. Among his works are translations of and commentaries on the Psalms (1785) and Isaiah (1788) and five volumes of spiritual reflections.

Berthier, Jean Baptiste Founder of the Congregation of the Missionaries of the Holy Family, born Châtonnay, France, 24 February 1840, died Grave, Holland, 16 October 1908. Originally a member of the Congregation of the Missionaries of La Salette, he founded the Missionaries of the Holy Family in Grave in 1895 to train men with late vocations to the priesthood. The Congregation later branched out into missionary work. Berthier wrote 36 theological works, including *Le prêtre dans le ministère* (1883), *Le sacerdote* (1894), and *Compendium Theologiae* (1887). The process for his canonization began in 1953.

Berthold of Chiemsee Bishop and author of theological works, born Salzburg, 1465, died Saalfelden (Pinzgau), 16 July 1543. He became prince-bishop of Chiemsee and ordinary of Salzburg, later resigning to retire to the Cistercian monastery of Raitenhaslach in Upper Bavaria. Moving to Saalfelden, he founded a hospice and church. He is probably the author of a pamphlet titled *Onus ecclesiae*, which called urgently for church reform, and is known also for his *Tewtsche Theologey* (1528), the first systematic work of Catholic dogmatic theology in German.

Berthold of Garsten Saint, Benedictine abbot and reformer, died 27 July 1142. Became a monk at Sankt Blasien and later its sub-prior; appointed prior at Götweig in 1107 and later made abbot of Garsten, which flourished as a centre for reform during his reign as abbot, 1111–47. Feast day 27 July.

Berthold of Regensburg Franciscan preacher, born Regensburg, Germany, c.1210, died Regensburg, 14 December 1272. After studying at (probably) the Magdeburg Studium, he became lector, c.1230–4 and then preacher in 1240 at the Franciscan house at Regensburg. His preaching took him across his native Bavaria, as well as elsewhere in Germany, and to Switzerland, Czechoslovakia, Hungary, and as far as Paris; in 1263 Pope **Urban IV** directed him to preach against heresy. His sermons, marked by their simplicity, were almost certainly preached in the vernacular; however, the only sermons to survive are in Latin.

Berthold of Reichenau Chronicler, born c.1030, died 11 March 1088. He wrote a life of his teacher **Herman of Reichenau** as well as a chronicle that in parts goes up to 1066 and in parts up to 1079–80, and along with the biography of Herman comprises the final part of a world chronicle. For the years 1056–75 it takes the form of annals that are, in parts, identical with the world chronicle of **Bernold of Constance**, while the later entries plead passionately for **Gregory VII** and Rudolf of Swabia in their conflict with **Henry IV** and are among the best sources of information about this period. There are two extant versions: the shorter, simpler, and pro-imperial chronicle which stops in 1066 is probably Berthold's work (as is the *Vita Herimanni*, which precedes both versions of the continuation), whilst the longer, pro-Gregorian account, extending to 1080, is almost certainly the work of another.

Bertholet, Alfred Protestant theologian and Scripture scholar, born Basel, 9 November 1868, died Münsterlingen, Bodensee, 24 August 1951. The son of a schoolmaster, he studied in Basel, Strasburg and Berlin, becoming in 1892 pastor of a German–Dutch community in Livorno. He started to teach at Basel, becoming professor of OT in 1905, moving to Tübingen in 1913 and to Göttingen the following year. In 1928 he moved to Berlin. He became increasingly interested in comparative religion, and it was in that capacity that he was elected to the Prussian Academy of Science in 1938, the first theologian to be so honoured. He retired in 1936, and spent the war years in Bavaria, the border to his homeland being closed. He wrote a number of OT commentaries, and his interest in comparative religion is demonstrated in his co-editorship of the second edition of *Religion in Geschichte und Gegenwart*.

Berti, Giovanni Lorenzo   Catholic church historian and Augustinian, born Seuravezza, Tuscany, 27 June 1696, died Florence, 26 May 1766. He joined the Augustinian Order early in life and served as professor of theology in Siena, Florence, Padua, Rome and Pisa. He is the author of a ten-volume *Theologia historico-dogmatico-scholastica*. His four-volume *Historia ecclesiastica* provides a valuable account of the Church during the first five centuries of Christianity.

Bertilla of Chelles   Saint and abbess, born near Soissons, died Chelles, *c*.705. When young she joined the monastery of Jouarre, near Meaux, but went at the head of a small group to form the community of Chelles, a monastery refounded by **Bathilde**, the English wife of King Clovis II. Bathilde herself joined the community, as did Hereswitha, the widow of a king of the East Angles. Bertilla is said to have ruled the community for 46 years. Feast day 5 November.

Bertinus   Benedictine abbot, born Orval, near Coutances, France, *c*.615, died Sithiu, France, 5 September 709. Following his training at Luxeuil, he was called to Morinia (modern Pas-de-Calais) where he succeeded Momelin as abbot of SS Peter and Paul on the island of Sithiu. As abbot, Bertinus oversaw both the abbey and the church of Sainte-Marie on the hill. He built a small monastery at Wormhout, on property he received from a Flemish noble, for four men whom he received as monks: Quadanoc, Ingenoc, Madoc and St Winnoc. At his request, Rigobert built the church of Saint-Martin on Sithiu. Feast day 5 September.

Bertonio, Ludovico   Jesuit missionary and linguist, born near Ancona, 1552, died Peru, 3 August 1625. He joined the Society of Jesus in 1575 and from 1581 worked in Bolivia and Peru, mainly with the Aymará Indians. He wrote several works on their language. These included a grammar, a phrase book and a translation into the Aymará language of a book on the *Life and Miracles of Our Lord Jesus Christ*. Most of his books were published in Peru, on printing presses established by the Jesuits there. Some of his publications have been published again in facsimile editions.

Bertrand, Louis   Saint, Dominican preacher and missionary, born Valencia, Spain, 1 January 1526, died Valencia, 9 October 1581. Bertrand became a Dominican in 1544 and was ordained three years later. He became master of novices in Valencia in 1553 and cared for the sick during the plague of 1557, during which time he became famous for his preaching. He went to South America as a missionary in 1562, where he laboured for seven very fruitful years before returning to Spain as prior of San Onofre. After serving a term as master general, he finished his career as prior at Valencia. Said to be gifted with extraordinary graces, he was canonized in 1671 by Pope **Clement X** and named patron of the New Kingdom of Granada (Colombia) in 1690. Feast day 9 October.

Bertrand, Pierre   Cardinal and theologian, born Annonay in Vivarais, 1280, died priory of Montaud, near Avignon, 1348 or 1349. His first, very successful, career was as a lawyer. After ordination as a priest, he rapidly became a bishop, then, in 1331, a cardinal. At the 'Conférence de Vincennes' in 1329, he defended the primacy of the Church's spiritual power against attempts by the French king, Philip VI, to reduce its traditional privileges.

Bertrand of Aquileia   Blessed, Patriarch of Aquileia, born probably Montcuq, France, *c*.1260, died near Spilimbergo, Italy, 6 June 1350. After training in both canon and civil law at the University of Toulouse and holding a professorship there, Bertrand became a papal chaplain in 1318. In 1334, he was made patriarch of Aquileia, which he then set about reconquering and restoring. His success alarmed the leaders of Florence, who allied with the Pope and Venice to regain what Bertrand had conquered. In response, Bertrand called a synod at Aquileia in 1339 to affirm the protections of church officials from secular rulers. This failed, however, and Bertrand's travelling party was attacked by forces of the count of Goritz after the Synod of Padua in 1350, leaving Bertrand mortally wounded. After many miracles were credited to his intercession, his cult was approved in 1599. Feast day 6 June.

Bertrand of Comminges Saint, bishop, born Isle-Jourdain, France, c.1050, died probably Comminges, France, 16 October 1123. Nobly born, Bertrand studied in the abbey of La Chaise-Dieu before being made canon and archdeacon of Toulouse. He was elected bishop of Comminges in 1073. He was an energetic and committed leader, visiting every corner of his diocese during his 50-year tenure. In his diocese, 2 May is commemorated as the 'Great Pardon of Comminges', remembering a time when Bertrand delivered from Moorish exile a dishonest noble who once opposed him. Feast day 16 October.

Bertrand of Garriga Blessed, Dominican friar, born southern France, c.1172, died Toulouse, France, after 1230. Bertrand was a friend and follower of St **Dominic**, joining the Dominican Order in 1215. He frequently accompanied his mentor on his many travels, or else was placed in charge of the fledgling organization in Dominic's absence. In 1217, he went to Paris, returning to Toulouse as prior of St Romanus in 1218, a post he held until his death. He was made provincial of Provence in 1221 and had a reputation for prayer and piety. His cult was approved by Pope **Leo XIII** in 1881. Feast day 6 June.

Bertrand of Le Mans Bishop and saint, born c.550, died Le Mans, 30 June 623. Little or nothing is known about his early life. He was educated in the cathedral school at Paris, became an archdeacon and, in 573, bishop of Le Mans. It was a difficult time, and he was more than once driven from his see, but occupied it permanently from 605, thanks to the support of King Clotaire II. He founded an abbey to serve as a hospice for pilgrims, but is best remembered for encouraging the planting of vineyards. Feast day 30 June.

Bertulf of Bobbio Monk and saint, date of birth unknown, died 639 or 640. From a noble pagan family in Austrasia, he converted to Christianity,

becoming a monk in 620. He later transferred to the monastery of Bobbio, Italy, where he was elected abbot in 627. He preached against Arianism, which had spread to Italy. He also fought against attempts at episcopal control, persuading Pope **Honorius I** to grant his monastery exemption from the jurisdiction of the bishop of Tortona. **Jonas**, one of his monks, wrote an account of miracles attributed to the prayers of his abbot. Feast day 19 August.

Bertulf of Renty Saint, born in Germany but travelled to Flanders where he became a Christian, died in the monastery of Renty, Flanders, c.705. He became steward to Count Wamba and his wife, and with them made a pilgrimage to Rome. At the death of the count and his wife, Bertulf entered the monastery of Renty, which he had himself founded, and died there. Feast day 5 February.

Bérulle, Pierre de Cardinal, founder of the French Congregation of the Oratory, born in Champagne, France, 4 February 1575, died Paris (while saying Mass), 2 October 1629. He was educated by the Jesuits in Paris and ordained in 1599. After ordination he was chaplain to King **Henry IV**. He was instrumental in attracting nuns of the Carmelite reform to Paris and, in 1611, he established the Oratory in France, similar to, but not identical with, the Italian model created by St Philip **Neri**. Well-known for his piety and devotion to the teachings of Jesus, he wrote several works promoting Catholic doctrine and faith. He remained involved in public life and became a cardinal in 1627.

Beryllus Bishop of Bostra, died 245. The leading Arabian intellectual of his time, he was charged c.240 with propagating the heresy that Christ had no distinct divinity of his own, but derived his divinity from God the Father who indwelt him. He was challenged by **Origen**, who convinced him of the orthodox position. He is said to have written a number of letters about this exchange, but none survives.

Beschi, Costanzo Giuseppe Jesuit missionary and Tamil-language poet, born Castiglione, Venetian Republic, 1680, died Manapar, India, c.1746. Joining the Society of Jesus in 1698, he was sent to the

Madura mission in southern India in 1710. He is considered the founder of Tamil philology, having compiled several grammars, lexicons and dictionaries. He wrote doctrinal works in Tamil, but is best remembered for several long poems. He wrote *Têmbâvani* (*The Unfading Garland*, in honour of St Joseph) and *Paramartaguru Kadey* (*The Adventures of the Guru Paramarta*, a satire on non-Christian local gurus), both of which became classics.

Besold, Christof   Lawyer, teacher and high-profile convert to Catholicism, born Tübingen, Württemberg, 1577, died Ingolstadt, Bavaria, 15 September 1638. Professor of law at Tübingen, 1610–37, then of Roman law at Ingolstadt University, he learnt nine languages and studied Scripture and the early Christian writers. A Protestant, he publicly converted to Catholicism at Heilbronn in 1635. He caused controversy when he published three volumes from the Stuttgart archives, as the documents were viewed as implying that religious property confiscated in Württemberg should be restored to the Catholic Church. His writings give insights into the causes of the Thirty Years War.

Bessarion   Basilian monk, bishop and cardinal, born Trebizond, 2 January 1403, died Ravenna, 18 November 1472. The young bishop of Nicaea was a member of the Orthodox delegation to the ecumenical Council of Ferrara–Florence in 1438–9, called in response to the Turkish threat to Constantinople. He converted to Catholicism, was made a cardinal in 1439 by **Eugenius IV**, but was overlooked in successive conclaves. His scholarship, particularly his defence of Plato (*In calumniatorem Platonis libri IV*, printed at Rome, 1469), demonstrated the influence of his master Gemistos Plethon, and he actively supported Greek scholars in Italy and Italian students of Greek literature and philosophy. In 1468 he donated his library to the Republic of Venice.

Bessarion of Egypt   Hermit and saint, died 425. A native of Egypt, he became a hermit under St **Anthony** and then St **Macarius**, and established a pilgrim shelter in Jerusalem and a monastery at Sinai. He was famed for his severe asceticism, and, as with his mentors, many miracles were attributed to him. Feast day 17 June.

Bessarion of Romania   Orthodox saint and martyr, born Bosnia, 1714, died *c.*1760. He was a monk and wandering preacher in Transylvania at a time when the Empress Maria Theresa was attempting to unite the Orthodox under Rome. Like a number of other Serbian and Romanian priests and monks of the time, he was arrested and imprisoned at Kufstein in the Tyrol. The exact date of his death there is unknown. His name was entered into the Romanian Church calendar in 1950 and he was solemnly canonized with other martyrs in June 1992. Feast day 21 October.

Synaxarion I.

Bessel, Gottfried von   Christened **Johann Franz**, monk and historian, born Büchen, Grand Duchy of Baden, 5 September 1672, died Göttweig Abbey, Austria, 22 January 1749. After ordination on 21 March 1696 in the Benedictine community of Göttweig, and study in Rome, he became vicar-general in Mainz. He undertook several diplomatic missions, including negotiations between the Pope and the emperor. Appointed abbot of Göttweig in 1641, he developed the monastery as a centre of learning. His one important work is a German diplomatic history, *Chronicon Gottwicense, tomus prodomus* (Tegernsee, 1732), gathering in one volume much documentary evidence from archives and other sources.

Betancur, Pedro de San José   Venerable, Third Order Franciscan, born Tenerife, 1626, died Guatemala City, 25 April 1667. His family were poor, and his first occupation was as a shepherd. He left for Guatemala in 1650, finally arriving on 18 February 1651. He was so poor that he was forced to join the daily bread queue at the Franciscan friary. Here he befriended the missionary Fray Fernando Espino, who found him work in a local textile factory. In 1653 he entered the local Jesuit college, hoping to become a priest, but his lack of intellectual ability forced him to give this up. In 1655 he joined the Third Order of St Francis. He founded a hospital for the poor, an oratory, a school, and a hostel for the homeless. He dedicated his life to alleviating the suffering of the poor. He had small chapels erected in the poorer districts of Guatemala City. Each 18 August he would gather the children to sing the Seven Joys of the Franciscan Rosary in honour of the Virgin Mary. This custom is still practised in Guatemala today. Known as the 'St Francis of the Americas', he died in the hospital which he founded.

Betanzos, Domingo Dominican brother, missionary in the Americas, born León, Spain, date unknown, died Valladolid, September 1549, the year he returned from Mexico. A Benedictine and hermit for five years, he joined the Dominicans and went to Santo Domingo (then Hispaniola) in 1514. He founded provinces in Guatemala and Mexico, successfully opposing attempts by Tomás de Berlanga to retain Mexico within his own Dominican province. In 1516, he signed a letter from the Dominicans violently denouncing Spanish excesses against aboriginal people. In 1541, and again in 1543, he urged moderation in Indian policy in an individual *parecer* (opinion), but in a markedly more temperate manner.

Betanzos, Pedro de Franciscan brother, missionary in the Americas, born Betanzos, Galicia, date unknown, died Chomez, Nicaragua, 1570. One of the first Franciscans in Guatemala, he established the Church in Nicaragua. He was said to speak fourteen Indian languages. He was one of the authors of the earliest book in a Guatemalan language, published by the Franciscans in Mexico in 1553 (no copy known). He opposed the Dominicans who used the aboriginal word for 'god' in their teaching: he urged that it could not portray the Christian God, as it represented a general world spirit, not a personal deity.

Bethge, Eberhard Lutheran theologian and biographer, born Warchau, Germany, 28 August 1909, died Rengsdorf, Germany, 18 March 2000. The son of a pastor, Bethge studied theology in various universities in Germany and Austria, and was briefly a member of the Hitler Youth, but became disillusioned and joined the Confessing Church, entering its seminary and there encountering Dietrich **Bonhoeffer**, then the seminary's director. The two became close friends (Bethge married Bonhoeffer's niece), and the exchange of letters between them forms an important part of Bonhoeffer's theological writing. Bethge was himself arrested in 1944, but was freed by the advancing Russian army. He then held various positions in the Lutheran Church, including, between 1953 and 1961, that of pastor to the German community in London. He returned to Germany to head a pastoral college in Rengsdorf. There he wrote his major biography of Bonhoeffer, published in 1967, and he went on to produce a number of other books on various aspects of Bonhoeffer's theology.

Betti, Ugo Italian dramatist, born Camerino, 4 February 1892, died Rome, 9 June 1953. Betti began writing poetry while a prisoner during the First World War. Following his release he trained as a lawyer, became a magistrate, and also wrote the first of his 25 plays. Recurrent themes in all of these are the problems of sin and evil; written from a clearly Christian perspective, the various allegorical motifs and metaphors Betti employs portray concepts such as atonement, sacrifice and redemption, thereby pointing to the Christian faith as the resolution of those problems.

Bewerunge, Henry Roman Catholic musicologist, born Lethmathe, Germany, 7 December 1862, died Maynooth, Ireland, 2 December 1923. Bewerunge studied music at Würzburg University, after which he studied for the priesthood. His ordination in 1885 was followed by further musical studies and a year spent as cantor at Cologne Cathedral. In 1888 he was appointed professor of church music at St Patrick's College, Maynooth, and in 1914 he moved to University College, Dublin, where, apart from a brief absence during the First World War, he spent the rest of his career. Bewerunge was a noted authority on Gregorian chant, and the author of numerous monographs and articles on Roman Catholic church music, the most significant being *Die vatikanische Choralausgabe* published in 1906–7.

Beyerlink, Laurent Lawrence Belgian theologian and ecclesiastical writer, born Antwerp, April 1578, died Antwerp, 22 June 1627. Ordained in 1602, he taught at the seminary of Antwerp, served as superior there and held other church appointments in the diocese. He both preached and wrote extensively. His works include a volume on the lives of popes and other famous people, and an encyclopedia which eventually reached eight volumes (published in Venice, 1707). The entries ranged from serious theological essays to frivolous trivia. His role was largely editorial, assembling in publishable form information in the main researched by others.

Beza, Theodore   French Calvinist pastor and theologian, born Vézelay, France, 24 June 1516, died Geneva, Switzerland, 7 October 1605. Converted to Protestantism in 1548, he went to Geneva and formally regularized an earlier clandestine marriage, becoming professor of Greek in Lausanne in 1549. Moving back to Geneva, he became first rector of Jean **Calvin**'s enormously influential newly inaugurated Academy, June 1559, later becoming the leader of the Swiss Calvinists on Calvin's death in 1564. Never separated from his fellow Huguenots, he defended godly resistance to oppressive authority. A prolific theological and historical writer and textual critic, his *Confession de la foi chrétienne* (1560) was an important popular exposition of Calvinist beliefs, whilst his *Vita Calvini* (1564) was more a panegyric than an accurate biography. Arguably his Calvinism was more brittle than that of Calvin himself: it is to him, for example, that the concept of double predestination has been attributed: this is spelt out in his *Tabula Praedestinationis*.

Bhengu, Nicholas   African evangelist, born Zululand 1909, died 1986. Bhengu was the son of a Lutheran evangelist, but although he attended Bible training college he took up work as a court interpreter before becoming an evangelist himself. He became affiliated with the South African Assemblies of God, and used preaching tours in America and Europe to raise funds. By 1959 he had become very influential and had helped create over 50 churches. He believed in an 'apostle' system of church leadership, and in 1974 he became a fellow of Selly Oak. In 1949 he wrote *Revival Fire in South Africa*.

Bianchi, Francesco Saverio Maria   Barnabite saint and mystic, born Arpino, Italy, 2 December 1743, died Naples, 31 January 1815. He wished to become a priest but, because of parental opposition, studied law at Naples instead. In 1762 he joined the Barnabites there, and was eventually ordained priest. Almost all of his ministry was exercised at Naples. Became superior in the College of Portanova in 1773, and professor of theology at Naples in 1778. Widely regarded as a wise and learned man, his care and concern for the poor gradually took precedence over his academic labours, particularly after a mysterious ecstasy on the feast of Pentecost, 1800. Became famous for performing miracles, which reputedly included stopping the flow of lava from Vesuvius in 1804 and 1805. From 1804 he suffered from a terrible disease which affected his legs, making walking impossible. He was a wise spiritual counsellor. Feast day 13 January.

Bianchini, Francesco   Deacon and historian, born Verona, Italy, 13 December 1662, died Rome, 2 March 1729. Protégé of Cardinal Peter Ottoboni, later Pope **Alexander VIII**, then of his nephew, another Cardinal Peter Ottoboni. A distinguished scholar, member of learned societies, he was secretary of the commission for the reform of the calendar, and historiographer of the 1725 Lateran synod. His publications on the Church's calendar include *A Solution of the Paschal Problem* (Rome, 1703). He edited (1718–28) three volumes of an edition of the *Liber Pontificalis* (his nephew Giuseppe Bianchini edited the fourth volume). He became a deacon in 1699.

Biber, Heinrich Johann Franz von   Church composer, born Wartenberg, Bohemia, 12 August 1644, died Salzburg, Austria, 3 May 1704. Biber spent much of his life in the service of the archbishop of Salzburg, for whom he composed many Masses, requiems, litanies and vespers, including the *Missa Sti Henrici* (1701) and the *Fifteen Mysteries of the Life of Mary* (1674). He often composed in the popular *concertato* style. Biber is known for introducing innovations in violin-playing by employing a variety of techniques including double stops, wide skips and tuning the strings of the violin to other than usual pitches for special effect (*scordatura*).

Bichier des Ages, Jeanne Elisabeth   Saint, cofoundress of the Daughters of the Holy Cross of St Andrew, born Le Blanc, near Poitiers, France, 5 July 1773, died Paris, 26 August 1838. After the death of her father in 1792, she conducted a successful lawsuit against the Revolutionary government to save the family's property from confiscation. Jeanne settled with her mother at Béthines-Poitou, and followed a pattern of prayer and good works. She was the central figure amongst resistance to the Constitutional clergy. In 1805, along with five companions, she founded a community at La Guimetière. The community was approved by the bishop of Poitiers in 1816. As superior, Jeanne guided the community through rapid growth, and by 1830 there were over 30 houses. Ill health forced her to retire to Paris for the rest of her life. Feast day 26 August.

Bickell, Gustav   Oriental scholar, born Kassel, Germany, 7 July 1838, died Vienna, Austria, 15 January 1906. Bickell was a noted authority on Semitic languages, on which he published numerous works. During his career he held academic posts at several universities in Germany and Austria, and made a particular study of the relationship of Syriac and Hebrew poetry. Bickell came from a Protestant family but converted to Roman Catholicism in 1865 and was ordained priest in 1867.

Bickell, Johann Wilhelm   Canon lawyer, born Marburg, Germany, 2 November 1799, died Kassel, Germany, 23 January 1848. After studying law at Marburg, he taught canon law there from 1820. In 1832, he began to practise law, and in 1846, became a legal consultant of the Ministry of Justice. He was primarily interested in the sources of canon law. His written works include *Ueber die Enstehung der beiden extravaganten Sammlungen des Corpus iuris canonici* (Marburg, 1825), *De paleis quae in Gratiani decreto occurunt disquisitio* (Marburg, 1827) and *Geschichte des Kirchenrechts* (vol. 1, Giessen, 1843; vol. 2, 1849, posthumously from Bickell's notes).

Bickersteth, Edward   Anglican clergyman and secretary of the Church Missionary Society, born Kirby Lonsdale, Westmorland, 19 March 1786, died, Watton, Hertfordshire, 28 February 1850. Following practice as a solicitor in Norwich, under the influence of the evangelical movement he moved into deeper religious commitment. In 1815 he was invited by Josiah Pratt, secretary of the Church Missionary Society, to become his assistant, a task which became the deputation secretary of the society, which made Bickersteth *de facto* an itinerant ambassador for Anglican evangelicalism. He was also asked to conduct an investigation into

the society's affairs in West Africa, which he undertook early the following year. It was natural that in 1824 he should succeed Pratt as secretary. He resigned his secretaryship in 1830 to become rector of Watton in Hertfordshire at a time when uncertainty overtook central evangelical counsels. He was the principal Anglican promoter of the Evangelical Alliance. Both through his ever-active pen and by his ubiquitous presence he commended a thoughtful and balanced evangelicalism in the tradition of Charles **Simeon**.

Biddle, John   English Unitarian and polemicist, born Wotton, Gloucestershire, 1615 (baptized on 14 January that year), died in prison in London, 22 September 1662. He studied at Magdalen Hall, Oxford, from where he graduated in 1638, then became master of the Free School in Gloucester. He wrote a tract entitled *Twelve Arguments against the Deity of the Holy Ghost* for which he was imprisoned. He later published two tracts against the doctrine of the Trinity, despite a penalty of death, approved in 1648, on all those who denied the doctrine. He was saved by friends among the Independent Parliamentarians. Biddle's unorthodox views caused him to be imprisoned on numerous occasions, as well as spending a period of time banished by Cromwell to the Scilly Isles. He died in prison of disease contracted in the dirty conditions.

Biel, Gabriel   Theologian, born Speyer, Germany, 1425(?), died Tübingen, Germany, 1495. He was vicar of Mainz cathedral, superior of the Brethren of the Common Life at Butzbach and provost of the church at Urach before founding the University of Tübingen with Count Eberhard. From 1484 he was the university's first professor of theology. A nominalist of the Ockham school, he wrote on the canon of the Mass and papal authority as well as a commentary on the *Sentences* of **Peter Lombard** and many sermons. As a political economist he also discussed the work of merchants, taxation, peasant land, the devaluing of currency and a just price.

Bielski, Marcin   Polish chronicler, born on his noble family's estate of Biała, Sieradz province, Poland, 1495, died Biała, 1575. He studied at Cracow University and fought against the Tartars and the Wallachians. He wrote extensively, largely on historical subjects, the first to do so in Polish. His most ambitious work is *Kronika Świata* (*Universal Chronicle*), a universal history from the earliest times, including a history of Poland from 550 onwards. He wrote a history of warfare, which contains useful information about the Polish army. He composed satirical poems on the contemporary political situation, published after his death.

Biener, Friedrich August Church lawyer, born Leipzig, Germany, 5 February 1787, died Dresden, 2 May 1861. His legal career included a professorship in law at the University of Berlin from 1810 and an appointment as councillor of justice in 1832. His primary interest lay in the history of law. His published works include *Historia authenticarum* (Leipzig, 1807), *Geschichte der Novellen Justinians* (Berlin, 1824–49), *De collectionibus canonum Ecclesiae graecae* (Berlin, 1827) and *Beiträge zur Geschichte der Inquisitions-Prozesses und der Geschworenengerichte* (Leipzig, 1827).

Biffi, Eugenio Roman Catholic missionary and bishop, born Milan, Italy, 22 December 1829, died Barranquilla, Colombia, 8 November 1896. Following his ordination in 1853 Biffi entered the seminary of Foreign Missions in Milan. He was sent to Colombia in 1856, but persecution forced him to withdraw. He spent several years in missionary work in Central America before returning to Colombia as bishop of Cartagena in 1882. He established numerous schools and welfare agencies in the diocese, and was held in great affection by his people.

Bihl, Michael Franciscan historian, born Filsdorf (now in France but at that time in Germany), 10 May 1875, died Metz, 24 April 1950. After joining the Franciscans in 1896, Bihl was ordained in 1902 and spent almost the rest of his life at the Franciscan Collegio di S. Bonaventura, Quaracchi. During his long tenure as head of its historical section he became a recognized authority on Franciscan history, and for over 30 years edited the *Archivum Franciscanum Historicum*.

Bihlmeyer, Karl Roman Catholic church historian and patristic scholar, born Aulendorf, Germany, 7 July 1874, died Tübingen, Germany, 27 March 1942. Apart from a brief period of pastoral work following his ordination in 1897, Bihlmeyer spent his entire career as professor of church history at Tübingen University. He wrote or edited numerous books and articles of church history, and although the early Church was his main interest he was also well known for his research into medieval German mysticism.

Bijns, Anna Roman Catholic poet and apologist, born Antwerp (Belgium), 1493, died Antwerp, 1575. Little is known of Bijns' life except that she was a teacher and never married. Her poetry first appeared in 1528, with new works of *Refereinen* (a form akin to French ballads of the time) appearing in 1548 and 1567. Her poems are chiefly religious, her themes chiefly reflecting a deep (if sometimes moralizing) love of Christ, Mary and the Church and her opposition to the doctrines of Martin **Luther.** She also praised the beauty of nature, though she rejected the naturalism of the nascent Renaissance. She is often styled one of the last writers of the Middle Ages.

Bilhild Saint and abbess, *fl.* early eighth century. Although she is listed in a ninth-century Fulda calendar, the details of her life are only known from legends written in the twelfth century, which describe her as a noblewoman from Veitshöchheim near Würzburg who, at the age of seventeen, married Duke Hetan I of Thuringia. After his death, she fled to her uncle Bishop Rigibert of Mainz, became a nun and founded the monastery of Altmünster, near Mainz. Feast day 27 November.

Bilio, Luigi Cardinal and Barnabite, born Alessandria, Italy, 25 March 1826, of poor parents, died Rome, 1 January 1884. At an early age he joined the Barnabites at Genoa, and after teaching philosophy at various Barnabite colleges, left for Rome in 1857 to teach theology. After holding a number of ecclesiastical offices, including consultor of the Holy Office and of the Congregation of the Index, he was made a cardinal in 1866. Bilio was greatly admired as a moderating force in Rome, a role particularly evident when he was one of the presidents at the First Vatican Council. He remained considerate toward the views of the minority group in discussions concerning papal infallibility.

Among other ecclesiastical offices, Bilio served as bishop of the suburbicarian Diocese of Sabina and is believed to have declined election to the Papacy at the conclave of 1878.

Billerbeck, Paul Lutheran theologian, born Bad Schönfliess, Germany, 4 April 1853, died Frankfurt an den Oder, Germany, 23 December 1932. Unusually, Billerbeck pursued his scholarly research in parallel with his ministry as a Lutheran pastor, rather than as an academic. He is renowned for his four-volume *Kommentar zum NT aus Talmud und Midrasch* (1922–8), which broke new ground by showing that the study of Jewish and Rabbinical literature greatly enhances the understanding of the NT.

Billiart, Marie Rose Julie Foundress of the Sisters of Notre Dame de Namur, born Cuvilly, France, 12 July 1751, died Namur, Belgium, 8 April 1816. A French peasant woman, severely paralysed for much of her life, she founded her congregation in 1804 with her great friend Françoise Blin de Bourdon (an aristocrat), to teach the 'poorest of the poor', anywhere in the world. She was among the first to insist on a superior-general from among her own Sisters. At the end of the twentieth century there are over 3000 Sisters throughout the world belonging to her congregation.

Billick, Eberhard Theologian, Carmelite priest, opponent of the Reformation, born Cologne, 1499 or 1500, died Cologne, 12 January 1557, before consecration as auxiliary bishop of Cologne. He entered the Carmelites in 1513, first became a prior in 1531, was provincial of lower Germany from 1542, reforming and expanding the Order. He exposed the bishop of Cologne, Hermann von Wied, as a supporter of the Reformation, revelations eventually leading to the bishop's excommunication. He denounced the Reformation in letters and other writings, angering **Luther** and **Melanchthon**. He participated in the disputations of Worms (1540), Ratisbon (1541 and 1546) and Augsburg (1547).

Billot, Louis Theologian, born Sierck, France, 12 January 1846, died Golloro, Italy, 18 December 1931. Billot was ordained in 1869 and entered the Society of Jesus. After serving preaching ministries

in Paris and Laval, he taught theology at the Catholic University of Angers, the Jesuit scholasticate on the Island of Jersey and the Gregorian University in Rome. Billot was an opponent of Modernism and Liberalism and contributed to the encyclical *Pascendi*, which condemned Modernism. In 1911, he was made a cardinal by **Pius X**. Supportive of the condemned Action Française, he resigned from the office of cardinal under pressure from **Pius XI** in 1927 and advised others to conform to the orders of the Pope. His works include *De Verbo Incarnato* (1892), *De Ecclesiae sacramentis* (1894–5) and *Disquisitio de natura et ratione peccati personalis* (1894).

Billuart, Charles-René Dominican preacher and theologian, born Revin, Ardennes, 28 January 1685, died Revin, 20 January 1757. Ordained in 1708, he taught philosophy and theology, served several terms as prior at Douai and Revin, and was twice provincial. He preached courses in Liège and Maastricht, gaining fame as an incisive speaker. His major work is a monumental commentary in nineteen volumes on the *Summa* of St **Thomas Aquinas**, *Summa S. Thomae hodiernis Academiarum moribus accomodata* (Liège, 1746–51). He followed this with a compendium on the same subject (Liège, 1754). Both were published in numerous editions.

Billy, Jacques de Benedictine monk and scholar, born Guise, France, 1535, died Paris, France, 25 December 1581. Educated in the humanities in Paris and in law at Orléans and Poitiers, Billy followed these studies with Greek and Hebrew in Lyons and Avignon. Though he served as abbot of Saint-Michel-en-l'Herm in Vendée and Notre Dame des Châtelliers in Ile de Ré, he is better known for his translations of Greek Fathers (such as **Gregory of Nazianzus**, **John Damascene** and **John Chrysostom**) into Latin and French. His most noted original work was his Greek dictionary *Locutiones graecae*.

Binchois, Gilles Composer, born Mons (Belgium), *c.*1400, died Soignies (Belgium), 20 September 1460. From about 1430, Binchois was a chaplain in the Burgundian court. His compositions were polyphonic, using the best of the techniques known in his day. His sacred music –

Masses, Magnificats and hymns – was highly esteemed and used the full range of human voices, but it was his *chansons* (a type of song) that were most influential on those composers who followed him, particularly Josquin **Desprez** and Jan van **Ockeghem**, who wrote a *Déploration* when Binchois died.

Binet, Etienne Jesuit priest, born Dijon, 1569, died Paris, 4 July 1639. He joined the Jesuit Order at Novellera in Italy, and later returned to France, where he played an increasingly important role in Jesuit affairs. He held the post of rector of the Jesuit college at Rouen and Paris, and was successively provincial of the provinces of Paris, Champagne, and Lyons. An important figure in the renewal of religious life in seventeenth-century France, he was noted as a preacher and spiritual writer of repute, producing more than 40 books. He was a close friend of both St **Francis de Sales** and St Jane Frances de **Chantal**. He was one of the great religious figures of his day.

Bingham, Joseph Church historian, born Wakefield, September, 1668, died Havant, near Portsmouth, 17 August 1723. He was educated at Wakefield and Oxford, becoming a fellow of University College in 1689. He resigned in 1695 after being accused of preaching tritheistic doctrine. In 1695 he became rector of Headbourne near Winchester and in 1712 also took the benefice of Havant. In the controversy over lay baptism he advocated the practice. In 1706 he wrote *The French Church's Apology for the Church of England*, claiming that the Huguenots were closer to the Church of England than to English Dissenters. Between 1708 and 1722 he published his best-known work, *Origines Ecclesiasticae: or the Antiquities of the Christian Church*, a systematic explanation of the hierarchy, structure, rites, calendar and discipline of the early Church which was translated into Latin in Halle, Germany, and abridged for a Catholic audience in 1788. He died in straitened circumstances, having lost his savings in the South Sea Bubble.

Binius, Severin Priest and editor of the texts of church councils, born Randerath, near Aachen, Germany, 1573, died Cologne, 14 February 1641. He spent most of his life at Cologne, where he was rector of the university from 1627 to 1629. He became vicar-general of the Diocese of Cologne in 1631, a post he held until his death ten years later. He published the histories of **Socrates**, **Theodoret**, **Sozomen** and **Evagrius Scholasticus.** His main work, however, was his edition of the *Concilia generalia et provincialia*, published at Cologne in 1606.

Binney,   Thomas Congregational minister, preacher and writer, born Newcastle-upon-Tyne, 30 April 1798, died London, 24 March 1874. For 40 years minister at the King's Weigh House Church in London, he has been called 'the representative and architect of nineteenth-century dissent'. Chairman of the Congregational Union in 1848, he opposed the establishment of the Church of England the more forcefully as ritualism grew within it, campaigned for secular education, and was active in the Sunday School, Domestic Mission and Ragged School movements. Concerned for improvements in worship, he exercised a powerful ministry among young people.

Biondo, Flavio Humanist, historian, and curial secretary, born Forlì, Italy, late 1392, died Rome, 4 June 1463. Biondo (or Blondus as he signed himself) was the scriptor of apostolic letters for four Popes from 1433 until his death. He married in 1423, fathered ten children, and lived and died without seeking riches. He was content with his service to the papal court and his historical work, chiefly on contemporary history (*Historiarum ab inclinatione Romanorum imperii decades*, 1483) and Roman antiquity (*Italia illustrata*, 1453, *Romae triumphantis libri X*, 1460, and *Roma Instaurata*, 1471). He was important for the development of an idea of a 'Middle Age', ushered in by the barbarian conquest of Rome, and for the stirring of interest in antiquarian studies.

Birinus Saint, bishop of Dorchester, England, died Dorchester 649 or 650, though his relics were later moved to Winchester. Birinus was possibly of German ancestry, though a priest in Rome. He came to England with the encouragement of Pope **Honorius I**, and was consecrated bishop for this purpose in Genoa. He arrived in England in 634, intending, it seems, to travel to the furthest parts of the island, but settled in Dorchester, where he converted the king of the West Saxons. Feast day 5 December.

Birkenmajer, Alexander Roman Catholic medieval historian, born Czernichow, Poland, 8 July 1890, died Warsaw, Poland, 30 September 1967. He worked with the manuscript collection at the Jagiellonian University library, Cracow, where he studied medieval science and philosophy until, in 1929, he gained the chair of history of science. After World War II, when he was imprisoned in a concentration camp, he returned to the Jagiellonian Library and worked to reorganize other war-damaged libraries. In 1952 he was elected to the Committee of History of Science and Technology of the Polish Academy of Sciences. He published numerous works on manuscripts and medieval learning.

Birks, Thomas Rawson Anglican clergyman and leading nineteenth-century evangelical scholar, born Staveley, Derbyshire, 28 September 1810, died Cambridge, 19 July 1883. From a Nonconformist background, he graduated at Trinity College, Cambridge, became an Anglican, and married the daughter of Edward **Bickersteth** when serving as his curate. From 1850 to 1871 he served as honorary secretary of the Evangelical Alliance, and succeeded F. D. **Maurice** in the chair of moral philosophy at Cambridge in 1872, a position held until his death. He has been identified as the leader of scholarly evangelicalism in the second half of the nineteenth century. In 1853 he rejected dogmatic inerrancy but when questions were raised about his apparent denial of the concept of everlasting retribution, he resigned from the secretaryship and executive council of the Evangelical Alliance, though not from membership.

Bishop, Edmund Roman Catholic historian and liturgiologist, born Totnes, England, 17 May 1846, died Barnstaple, England, 19 February 1917. After a short time as personal secretary to Thomas **Carlyle**, Bishop worked as a civil servant and pursued his research interests in his spare time. Following his conversion to Roman Catholicism in 1867, his intention was to become a monk at Downside Abbey; this ambition was thwarted, but he retained strong links with Downside for the rest of his life. Bishop's many writings on the history

of liturgy made a lasting contribution in this field; most of his significant works were collected and published posthumously in 1918 as *Liturgica Historica*.

Bishop, William Founder of the Glenmary Home Missioners, born Washington, DC, 19 December 1885, died Glendale, Ohio, 11 June 1953. Following studies at Harvard University and St Mary's Seminary, Baltimore, Bishop was ordained in 1915. As a pastor in Clarksville, Maryland, he became aware of rural concerns and was instrumental in founding the Archdiocesan League of the Little Flower (with Michael J. **Curley**) to assist needy rural pastors and the Archdiocesan Rural Life Conference of Baltimore in 1925. In the 1930s, he compiled statistics that led to the 'No-Priest Land' map, which illustrated US counties with no resident priests. In 1937, he was invited by Archbishop John T. **McNicholas** of Cincinnati to found the first Catholic home missions society. In 1949, he began a seminary in Glendale, Ohio. He also organized the Glenmary Lay Brothers Society and the Glenmary Home Mission Sisters.

Bismarck, Otto von German statesman, born Schönhausen, 1 April 1815, died Friedrichsruh, 30 July 1898. Having studied law at the Universities of Göttingen and Berlin, Bismarck entered politics in 1847. He held a succession of offices including diplomatic representative of Prussia at the federal diet at Frankfurt and ambassador to Russia and France. King William I appointed him Prussian prime minister and foreign minister in 1862. His most notable political accomplishment was the unification of the German Empire. In 1871, he was appointed the first imperial chancellor as well as prince. He held this office until Emperor William II dismissed him in 1890 over domestic issues. Following the publication of the *Syllabus of Errors* in 1864 and the declaration of papal infallibility by Vatican I, Bismarck launched the Kulturkampf as the means to promulgate the idea of the liberal state. He met with significant Roman Catholic opposition, which contributed to his eventual downfall.

Bitti, Bernardo Jesuit painter, born Camerino, Italy, 1548, died Lima, Peru, 1610. Bitti became a Jesuit brother in 1568. In 1575, he was sent to

Lima, Peru, to respond to a need for churchmen who were skilled in trades and crafts. He later worked in Cuzco, La Paz, Potosí and Chuquisaca. Much of his work was executed in Juli, a town on Lake Titicaca where a Jesuit mission to the Aymará Indians had been established. He characteristically painted in the Italian Mannerist style, a technique to which South American painters remained faithful even after it disappeared from European usage. His surviving works include a retable in the church of San Miguel, Sucre, and numerous paintings in Lima.

Black, William Methodist missionary, born Huddersfield, England, 1760, died Halifax, Nova Scotia, 6 September 1834. In 1775 he emigrated with his parents to Nova Scotia in Canada. At the age of nineteen he became a Methodist convert, and by the age of twenty he was already a lay preacher. He travelled throughout Nova Scotia, and was later placed in charge of the Nova Scotia mission. In 1789 he was ordained deacon and then elder, and became superintendent of the Methodist societies in British North America. Around this time he travelled to the Windward Isles and Bermuda. He successfully appealed to England for more lay preachers. In 1827 his wife and two children all died. He remarried a year later. He is thought of as the father of Methodism in Nova Scotia.

Blackman, John Carthusian writer, born in the Diocese of Bath and Wells, England, 1407–8, died probably Somerset, England, January 1485(?). Blackman began his career at Oxford, where he became a fellow of Merton College in 1439 and subwarden in 1443. He also served in Eton College and in King's Hall, Cambridge. In 1457, he entered the Carthusian London Charterhouse (though probably not as a monk) and later moved to Witham Charterhouse in Somerset. He is mostly associated with King **Henry VI**, about whom he composed a noted essay around 1480. He copied many manuscripts of academic and devotional worth, leaving these at his death to the Witham Charterhouse.

Blackwell, George First archpriest of England, born Middlesex, England, c.1545, died London, 25 January 1612. He studied initially at Trinity College, Oxford, where he was elected to a fellowship in 1566. This he relinquished because of his Roman sympathies and in 1574 entered the English College at Douai. Ordained in 1575, he worked for over twenty years in England. In 1598 Pope **Clement VII** appointed him archpriest over the seminary priests in England. Difficulties soon arose when a small number of priests objected to the new office, and to Blackwell's style of leadership, in particular his pro-Jesuit policies, even though he was not a Jesuit himself. After two appeals to Rome, the result of which confirmed him in office, his powers were greatly restricted by a brief of 5 October 1602, which also severed Jesuit connections. Following the Gunpowder Plot of 1605 an Oath of Allegiance was imposed in England, which was bitterly opposed by Rome. Blackwell, however, advocated that Catholics should take the oath, and did so himself. He was deposed in 1608, being replaced by George Birket, and died in Clink prison.

Blaise (Blasius) Bishop of Sebaste and martyr, died c.316. According to a late and unreliable legend, he was martyred under Licinius, after being caught hiding in a cave. He is said to have performed numerous miracles, especially among the sick, such as saving the life of a child who was almost choked by a fish-bone: he is invoked against throat diseases. He is also invoked for the cure of diseases in cattle, and is the patron saint of woolcombers. One of the fourteen 'auxiliary saints' or 'Fourteen Holy Helpers', his cult was traditionally strong in Germany, particularly in the sixteenth century. Feast day 3 February (formerly 15 February) in the West; 11 February in the East.

Blake, Eugene Carson North American Presbyterian minister and ecumenical leader, born St Louis, Missouri, 7 November 1906, died Stamford, Connecticut, 13 July 1985. Blake held numerous offices in the USA, including that of Stated Clerk of the United Presbyterians in the USA and President of the National Council of Churches of Christ in the USA (1954–7) having started his career with missionary service in India. An ardent advocate of the civil rights movement, he was jailed in 1963 for leading an anti-segregationist demonstration. Beyond the USA he represented his church on a number of international bodies, including the governing bodies of the World Council of Churches of which he became the second general secretary in 1966, serving until 1972.

Blake, William Writer and artist, born London, 28 November 1756, the son of an Irishman, died London, 12 August 1827. He was apprenticed as an engraver from 1771 to 1778, and studied at the Royal Academy of Art. He produced watercolours and engravings, first commercially and then increasingly to illustrate his own writings. His mystical writing includes *The Marriage of Heaven and Hell* and *The Gates of Paradise* (both 1793). His work *Songs of Innocence and Experience* was published in 1789 and his *Illustrations to the Book of Job* was published only a year before his death. He wrote the words for 'Jerusalem': set to music by **Parry** and arranged for orchestra by **Elgar**, it has almost become an alternative English national anthem. He believed himself, throughout his life, to be supported by visitations from the spiritual world, and he was certainly supported in many vicissitudes by faithful friends and a devoted wife.

Blakely, Paul Lendrum Jesuit journalist, born Covington, USA, 29 February 1880, died New York, 26 February 1943. Blakely became a Jesuit novice in 1897 and was ordained in 1912. He joined the staff of *America*, the Jesuit weekly review, for which he eventually became chief editorial writer. In his long career he contributed some 4000 articles to this journal, dealing with diverse subjects such as education, history, and constitutional and social issues. Blakely disliked unfettered capitalism and was a consistent champion of workers' rights.

Blanc, Anthony Archbishop of New Orleans, born Sury, France, on 11 October 1792, died New Orleans, 20 June 1860. He was ordained at Lyons on 22 February 1816 by Bishop Louis W. **Dubourg** of Louisiana, whom he accompanied back to America, where he became a missionary in Indiana. He remained there until the beginning of 1820. The following 40 years were spent ministering in Louisiana, first as a parish priest, then as vicar-general, administrator of the Diocese of New Orleans, and finally, from 1850, its first archbishop. During his episcopacy the diocese trebled in population, and Blanc established parishes for people of different ethnic origins.

Blanche of Castile Queen of France, born Palencia, Spain, 1188, died Maubuisson, France, 26 November 1252. The daughter of Alfonso VIII of Castile, Blanche married the future **Louis VIII** in 1200. She served as regent for her son **Louis IX** during his minority in 1226–34, and when he went on his own Crusade in 1248–52. She was an able ruler, controlling her unruly barons and founding the University of Toulouse, and a supporter of the Pope, helping to suppress the Albigensians and founding the Cistercian cloister of Maubuisson. Among her other children were the Blessed **Isabelle of France** and **Charles of Anjou** (ruler of Sicily, 1266–82).

Blanchet, Francis Norbert Archbishop, born St Pierre, Quebec, Canada, 3 September 1795, died Portland, Oregon, 18 June 1883. After being educated at the local parish school, and at seminary in Quebec, he was ordained on 18 July 1819. For a brief time he was stationed at the cathedral in Quebec City, before being sent to minister to the Acadians and the Micmac Indians in New Brunswick. In 1827 he became pastor of the parish of St Joseph de Soulanges in Montreal. He was later appointed vicar-general for the Oregon country, and set up missions at Cowlitz and among the French Canadians in Willamette Valley. Along with Pierre Jean **De Smet**, SJ, and Modeste Demers, he drew up a plan for the ecclesiastical organization of the Oregon country. This was approved and a vicariate apostolic was erected in Oregon. Blanchet was created titular bishop of Philadelphia (later changed to Adrasus). He travelled to Europe and had several audiences with Pope **Gregory XVI**. He successfully argued for the creation of an ecclesiastical province from his vicariate, with an archbishop and suffragan bishops. He became archbishop of Oregon City (now Portland), with both his brother and Demers as suffragans. He took a number of missionaries back with him from Rome, but missionary activity among the Indians became almost impossible following the Whitman massacre in 1847, which led to bigotry along with problems with those who believed clergy to have been somehow responsible. He convened the first Provincial Council of Oregon in February 1848, travelled widely in South America, gaining financial support for his diocese, and attended the First and Second Plenary Councils of Baltimore. In 1869 he attended the First Vatican Council, at which he strongly supported the declaration of papal infallibility. In 1862 he established his residence at Portland, retiring in 1880.

Blandina Virgin martyr, died Lyons, 177. A young slave-girl arrested together with her mistress, she was martyred alongside Pothinus, the bishop of Lyons, and a number of others. She is said to have died tied to a stake as to a cross, a Christ-like victim, sending her companions on ahead of her to God, and making a great impression on pagan onlookers. Feast day 2 June in the West, 25/26 July in the East.

Blandrata, Giorgio Unitarian physician and lay church leader, born Saluzzo, Italy, 1515, died Gyulafehérvár, Transylvania (now in Romania), 1588 or 1590. Blandrata studied medicine in Pavia and served as court physician abroad. In 1556 he fled to Geneva after becoming an anti-Trinitarian. After opposing **Calvin** in Geneva over Trinitarian doctrine, he moved to Poland, where he became influential in the Minor Church. In 1563, he became court physician in Transylvania, where he supported the Unitarian Church in Transylvania and won over King John Sigismund to the anti-Trinitarian cause. He is later said to have lost interested in the Unitarian Church and befriended many Jesuits at court, though he was still a Unitarian when he died.

Blanqui, Andres Jesuit architect, born Campioni, near Milan, Italy, 25 November 1677, died Córdoba, Argentina, 1740. In 1716 he entered the Society of Jesus and travelled to Rio de la Plata in Argentina. He completed his novitiate at Córdoba in Argentina. Along with another young Jesuit architect, Juan B. Primoli, he dedicated his life to the construction of public and private buildings such as cathedrals, churches, convents and schools.

Blarer, Ambrosius Protestant reformer, born Constance, Germany, 4 April 1492, died Winterthur, Switzerland, 6 December 1564. Ambrosius Blarer was a Benedictine monk at Alpirsbach in the Black Forest when he came into contact with Philip **Melanchthon** while studying at Tübingen. He maintained correspondence with him after his return and was eventually convinced by his brother

Thomas **Blarer** and the spirit of Protestantism to join the Lutheran cause. He left his abbey in 1522 and returned to his home in Constance, where he became a zealous preacher and advocate for the Reformation. He continued his preaching and ministry in Württemberg and later in Switzerland.

Blarer, Diethelm Benedictine monastic reformer, born place unknown, 1503, died St Gall, Switzerland, 18 December 1564. Diethelm Blarer became a Benedictine in 1523 and then abbot of St Gall in 1530, soon after which he was forced into exile to Mehrerau. He became the abbot in Mehrerau in 1532 and from this position persuaded the civil leaders in St Gall to restore the abbey there. He worked very hard for the restoration of sound spiritual life among the monks of Mehrerau and St Gall and was influential in the restoration of many of the cloisters and abbeys for women in Switzerland.

Blarer, Gerwig Benedictine reformer, born Constance, Germany, 25 May 1495, died Weingarten, Germany, 30 August 1567. After becoming a monk at the abbey of Weingarten in 1513, Gerwig Blarer studied canon law in Freiburg, Vienna and Ferrara. He was made abbot of Weingarten in 1520 and abbot of Ochsenhausen, Germany, in 1547 under pressure from the Holy Roman Emperor **Charles V.** He was a vigorous defender of traditional Catholicism, against the Protestants and sometimes even against the Jesuits as well, laying the foundation for the preservation of Roman Catholicism throughout Swabia in southern Germany.

Blarer, Jakob Christoph Roman Catholic bishop and reformer, born Rosenberg, Switzerland, 11 May 1542, died Prunktrut, Switzerland, 18 April 1603. Jakob Blarer was made bishop of Basel in 1575, and upon assuming his see found it to be in spiritual as well as financial disarray. Through able management and staunch support of the Council of Trent, he resisted the spread of Protestantism in north-western Switzerland and effected a renewal of his diocese. He also founded a Jesuit college in Prunktrut, his residential see. He is often cited as one of the leading Roman Catholic Counter-Reformers in Switzerland.

Blarer, Ludwig Benedictine reformer, born Constance, 1483, died 26 February 1544. Ludwig Blarer became a Benedictine at St Gall, Switzerland, sometime serving as cellarer. He was made administrator of Einsiedeln, Germany, in 1528 and abbot there in 1533. Pope **Clement VII**, because of the growing religious unrest, also granted him the normally episcopal powers of administering confirmation and establishing churches. He is now considered to be an important transition figure, supporting reform but choosing to effect that reform from within the communion of the Roman Catholic Church.

Blarer, Thomas Politician and Protestant reformer, born Constance, Germany, after 1492, died Gyrsburg, Switzerland, 19 March 1567. Thomas Blarer studied law at Freiburg before coming to Wittenberg to study theology. There he came under the influence of Martin **Luther**, later convincing his brother Ambrosius **Blarer** to leave St Gall and join the Protestant cause. He returned to Constance, where he supported the Protestant cause in the political arena, serving as mayor of the city for ten years in 1537–47, before being compelled to leave the city. He also took part in the discussions among the reforms aimed at reaching an agreement on the Lord's Supper.

Blastares, Matthew Byzantine monk and canon lawyer, died 1340. Almost nothing is known of Blastares' life except that he was a monk on Mount Athos, Greece, and then in Thessalonika, Greece, at the Isaia monastery there. He is known almost solely for his encyclopaedic compendium of civil and canon law called the *Syntagma*, which also includes a lexicon of Latin legal terms and commentaries on some of the laws. The work was often translated and influenced the later legal codes of the Byzantine Empire and surrounding nations. Blastares also wrote treatises against the Latin (Roman) Church and the Jews.

Blasucci, Domenico Venerable, Redemptorist clerical student, born Ruvo del Monte, Lucania, Italy, 5 March 1732, died at Caposele, Avellino, 2 November 1752. He was the younger brother of Peter Paul Blasucci, the third superior-general of the Redemptorists. At the age of eighteen he was himself received into the Congregation. Noted as a man of great piety, purity and devotion, he was

famed as the **Aloysius Gonzaga** of the Alphonsian Congregation. A man of great austerity, he modeled himself on the Redemptorist novice master and superior Paul Cafaro.

Blenkinsop, Catherine Educator, born Dublin, 18 April 1816, died Emmitsburg, USA, 18 March 1887. She joined the Sisters of Charity of Emmitsburg in 1831, taking the name of Euphemia. She worked in schools in New York and Baltimore, before becoming assistant at the mother house at Emmitsburg in 1855. She directed the work of the Sisters of Charity in the Southern states during the American Civil War, and became mother superior of the Order in the United States in 1866.

Blenkinsop, Peter J. Jesuit educator, born Dublin, 19 April 1818, died Philadelphia, 5 November 1896. The family emigrated to America in 1826 and Peter, like his younger brother, William **Blenkinsop**, attended St Mary's College, Baltimore in 1830–3. In 1834 he became a Jesuit and taught at Georgetown College, Washington, DC. Ordained in 1846, he became teacher and treasurer at the College of the Holy Cross, Worcester, Massachusetts, becoming the foundation's fifth president in 1854. Made a number of missionary journeys throughout New England. He ministered for a time at St Joseph's Church in Philadelphia, before returning to the College of the Holy Cross in 1873. He cared for the mission at Leicester, Massachusetts until 1880, when he returned to Georgetown. From 1882 until his death, he was based at the church of the Gesu, Philadelphia.

Blenkinsop, William A. Roman Catholic missionary, born Dublin 1919, died Boston, USA, 8 January 1892. He was the brother of Catherine and Peter **Blenkinsop**. Studied at St Mary's College, Baltimore, where he also taught for a time. He was ordained in 1843. After ordination he was greatly involved in missionary work in western Massachusetts, and fostered a spirit of ecumenism between Catholics and Protestants during a period of great mistrust. In 1864 he became pastor of SS Peter and Paul in south Boston.

Bliss, Kathleen English Anglican ecumenical leader, born London, 25 July 1908, died Midhurst, 13 September 1989. A close friend and collaborator of J. H. **Oldham** for over twenty years and editor of *The Christian Newsletter* from 1945 to 1994, she was a main speaker at the first assembly of the World Council of Churches at Amsterdam in 1948 and was the author of the famous phrase articulating the desire of the churches: 'We intend to stay together.' As general secretary of the Church of England's Board of Education, 1957–66, she was much involved in the governing bodies of both the British Council of Churches and the WCC and played a key role in integrating the World Council of Christian Education into the WCC. Latterly a lecturer at the University of Sussex, she had a fertile pen on women's, ecumenical and religious issues.

Blondel, Maurice French philosopher, born Dijon, 2 November 1861, died Aix-en-Provence, 3 June 1949. Educated in Dijon and at the Sorbonne, he taught at the Collège Stanislas, Paris, at Lille and at Aix-en-Provence. He retired in 1927, having almost lost his sight. His published works include *La pensée*, *L'Etre et les êtres* (a reworking of his controversial Ph.D. thesis *L'action*), *Le procès de l'Intelligence*, *Le problème de la mystique*, *Le problème de la philosophie catholique*, *Patrie et humanité* and two volumes of a trilogy entitled *La philosophie et l'esprit chrétien*. He influenced modern philosophy with his ideas on action and his exploration of relations between philosophy and religion and between science and belief.

Blosius, Francis Benedictine spiritual writer, born Donstienne, 1506, died Liessies, 7 January 1566. He was employed for a time as a page at the court of the Emperor **Charles V.** At the age of 14 he entered the Benedictine abbey of Liessies. Regarded as a monk of outstanding ability and discipline, he became coadjutor abbot in 1527 (aged just 21) and abbot in 1530. The standards of the abbey had been fairly relaxed, which was characteristic of the time. As abbot, Blosius was faced with a number of scandals. He was zealous in attempting to reform the abbey and impose greater discipline. His spiritual writings display a sympathy with the mysticism of **Dionysius** and affective prayer.

Bloy, Léon Henri Marc French Roman Catholic writer, born Périgueux, 11 July 1846, died Bourg-la-Reine, 3 November 1917. Raised in a Masonic family, he replaced the anticlericalism of his youth by a fervent Catholicism following a mystical religious experience of which little is known. His faith is reflected in his various writings, such as his two novels *Le désespéré* (1887) and *La femme pauvre* (1890), which are characterized by a romantic, mystical and passionate style which puzzled many of his contemporaries. Bloy has since been recognized as genuinely original, and a significant figure in the circle of French Catholic writers of the early twentieth century whose other members include **Péguy** and **Claudel**.

Blume, Clemens Jesuit hymnologist, born Billerbeck, Germany, 29 January 1862, died Königstein, Germany, 8 April 1932. Blume became a Jesuit at sixteen, and following ordination he became a collaborator in the hymn publishing project known as the *Analecta Hymnica*, on which he worked for many years. His wide-ranging textual research into the history and development of the Latin hymn was an important early contribution to hymnology. His ultimate concern was to ensure that such study should result in the enrichment of contemporary worship, rather than being pursued for its own sake.

Blumhart, Johann Christoph Protestant evangelist, born Stuttgart, Germany, 16 July 1805, died Bad Boll, Göppingen, Germany, 25 February 1880. Educated at Tübingen, he taught at Basel from 1830 until he became a pastor at Möttlingen, Württemberg in 1838. Here he developed his gifts in evangelism and healing. Between 1852 and 1880 he established a centre for healing and pastoral counselling at Bad Boll, which influenced the British and American healing movements and later Pentecostalism. Informed by Swabian Pietism, his eschatological thought anticipated the theology of Karl **Barth** and others. His collected works were published posthumously in three volumes (1886–8). His son Christoph Friedrich Blumhart became director of Bad Boll on his death.

Bobadilla, Nicolás Alfonso de Companion of St **Ignatius of Loyola**, born Bobadilla, Spain, *c.*1509, died Loreto, Italy, 23 September 1590. Bobadilla studied rhetoric, logic, philosophy and theology at Valladolid and Alcalá in Spain before going to Paris to finish his studies in 1533. There he fell in with Ignatius, travelled with him to Rome, and was ordained there in 1537. He spent most of his career as a travelling missionary and preacher, first in Italy, but later in Germany, 1541–8, Valtellina, Italy in 1558–9 and Dalmatia (modern Croatia and Bosnia-Herzegovina) in 1559–61. He was a very controversial figure, and was barred from several Jesuit deliberations by the Pope and expelled from Germany by **Charles V**. He left an autobiography, which contains useful information about the early Society of Jesus, as well as reform plans for the Church, a tract on the importance of daily Communion, and various treatises on theology and exegesis.

Bobola, Andrew Saint and martyr, born Sandomir, Poland, 1591, died Pinsk, 16 May 1657. After becoming a Jesuit in 1609 he worked as a parish priest in Vilna (Vilnius), Lithuania, and was superior at Bobrinsk. Despite strong anti-Catholic opposition he was a successful preacher. In 1652, with the support of Prince Radziwill, he founded a Jesuit centre at Pinsk and invited other Jesuits to leave their places of hiding and join him. In 1657 the Cossacks attacked Pinsk, capturing Bobola. He was killed slowly and cruelly. He was canonized in 1938. Feast day 31 May.

Boccaccio, Giovanni Author, born Paris, 1313, died Certaldo, Italy, 21 December 1375. He was educated at Florence and Naples before deserting his studies to join the literary group at the court of Anjou. In 1340 he returned to Florence and worked as a diplomat from 1348. From *c.*1338 he began writing legends, allegories and satire which influenced the work of **Chaucer** and others. His best-loved work is *Decameron*, published in 1353. He also wrote a significant life of *Dante* in 1364 and from 1356 to 1364 *De genealogis deorum gentilium*, an important dictionary of classical mythology. Towards the end of his life he became reflective and religiously devout.

Boccherini, (Ridolfo) Luigi Composer, born Lucca, Italy, 19 February 1743, died Madrid, 25 May 1805. He was taught the violoncello by his father, and was an accomplished professional by the age of thirteen. In 1757 he travelled to Rome, where he was introduced to the **Palestrina** style. His recitals and published works gained widespread admir-

ation. In 1768 he was named composer to the Infante Don Luis of Spain. Later patrons included Friedrich Wilhelm II of Prussia and Lucien Bonaparte, French ambassador to Madrid. A gentle Christian, he wrote a number of religious works. Latterly he has been regarded as the peer of pre-**Mozart** classicists. In 1927 his body was returned to Lucca, the place of his birth.

Bocken, Placidus Canonist, born Munich, Bavaria, Germany, 13 July 1690, died Salzburg, Austria, 9 February 1752. He entered the Benedictine Order and was ordained in 1713. Eight years later he became professor of canon law at Salzburg. He worked there for twenty years, becoming vice-chancellor of the university in 1729, and being counsellor to four of the city's bishops and to the abbot of Fulda. In 1741 he resigned from the university and two years later became superior of Maria Plain. Between 1735 and 1739 he published a significant book on canon law and several smaller works on the Decretals.

Bocking, Edward Benedictine monk, born East Anglia, England, died Tyburn, England, 20 April 1534. He studied at Oxford, becoming a doctor of divinity there in 1518. In 1526 in Canterbury he entered the Benedictine Order. When Elizabeth **Barton** began having visions and became known as 'the Holy Maid of Kent' he went to investigate and may have influenced the political nature of her statements. In 1534, at a time of political and religious change, he and six others were arrested and accused of treason against King **Henry VIII**, for which they were convicted and hanged.

Bodey, John Roman Catholic martyr, born Wells, Somerset, England, 1549, died Andover, England, 2 November 1583. He studied at Winchester and Oxford before he converted to the Roman Catholic faith. He then went to Douai to study law, returning to England to get married. He was arrested in 1580 and remained in prison for three years. Along with John Slade he was found guilty of refusing to accept the supremacy in matters spiritual of Queen **Elizabeth** and was hanged. He was beatified in 1929. Feast day 2 November.

Bodin, Jean French Catholic politician and political philosopher, 'the Aristotle of the sixteenth century', born Angers, 1529/30, died of plague, Laon, 1596. To minimize the conflicts of religious faction, Bodin sought to strengthen the authority of the monarch, who would receive recognition from the heads of families in return for protection offered. The first to differentiate between the State and government, Bodin still believed that the stars made their impact on the history of States. However he was also committed to the importance of environment, including climate, in determining human behaviour. This led him to adopt historical and comparative approaches to political philosophy, which he explained in his *Method for the Easy Understanding of History* (1566). Author of a model explaining the contemporary price revolution, he also wrote on the family, identifying practices such as infanticide as devil-originated. Deeply religious, he was the author of *The Demonology of Sorcerers* and a keen advocate of witch-trials. He criticized **Machiavelli** for his secular appraisal of the State, and became an early advocate of religious toleration, believing the truth of religions to be beyond the competency of the magistracy. His writings demonstrate a fascinating mixture of the liberal and the conservative.

Boece, Hector Scottish chronicler, born Dundee, *c.*1465, died probably Aberdeen, Scotland, 1536. Boece was made the founding principal of the University of Aberdeen by its founder Bishop William **Elphinstone**. His chief work was an uncritical work of the history of Scotland entitled *Scotorum historiae* (1527). It was very popular, serving as the source for Holinshed's *Historie of Scotland* and so, secondarily, giving **Shakespeare** the plot for *Macbeth*, but was based on poor earlier chronicles and at least one deliberate forgery. The untrustworthiness of this history was eventually proven by Thomas **Innes**, but not until almost 200 years after its first appearance.

Boehm(e) *see also* **Böhm(e)**

Boehm, Martin Co-founder of the Church of the United Brethren in Christ, born Conestoga, Pennsylvania, 30 November 1725, died Conestoga, 23 March 1812. He was the son of a German-born blacksmith, a Mennonite elder. In 1756 Martin became a Mennonite preacher and later came under the influence of disciples of George **White-**field. An association with Philip William **Otterbein** of the Reformed Church led to the establishment of the Church of the United Brethren in Christ. Theologically he was very close to early Methodists, amongst whom he had many associates. Boehm was active as a preacher among German settlers in Pennsylvania, Virginia and Maryland. In 1800 he became bishop of the Church of the United Brethren.

Boehmer, Justus Henning Lutheran lawyer and hymn-writer, born Hanover, Germany, 29 January 1674, died Halle, 29 August 1749. Having studied philosophy and jurisprudence at Jena, he became a lawyer in Hanover. He became professor of law at Halle in 1701, and was subsequently promoted to various offices in the Prussian government, becoming finally chancellor of the duchy of Magdeburg. He was appointed director of the University of Halle by William I of Prussia in 1731. He is particularly noted for his interest in Roman law studies and for the influence he had upon the development of the canon law of the Reformed Church. He wrote a number of hymns, but mainly in his younger days.

Boehner, Philotheus Heinrich Franciscan scholar, born Lichtenau, Germany, 17 February 1901, died St Bonaventure, USA, 22 May 1955. Boehner became a Franciscan in 1920 and was ordained in 1927. He held a number of academic posts, pursuing research and publishing books on both medieval philosophy and botany. He went to Canada in 1939 to join the Pontifical Institute of Medieval Studies, where he undertook research on **William of Ockham.** On the outbreak of World War II Boehner entered the USA and became an American citizen, becoming the first director of the Franciscan Research Center at St Bonaventure University, and initiating the publication of a number of academic journals, including the new series of *Franciscan Studies*.

Boethius, Anicius Manlius Severinus Philosopher, martyr and saint, born Rome, *c.*480, died Pavia, 524. A member of the Anician family, he was brought up by Q. Aurelius **Symmachus** and married his daughter Rusticiana. He translated into Latin many of the works of Greek philosophers, including Plato, Aristotle and Pythagoras and wrote treaties on logic, mathematics, geometry and music. His best-known theological treatise is *De Trinitate*. His philosophical work *De consolatione philosophiae* was especially influential in medieval thought. Often considered the last Roman philosopher and first Scholastic theologian, he was also involved in the politics of the day, being appointed consul in 510 and later master of offices. He was executed for defending an ex-consul against charges of treason. Canonized in 1883. Feast day 23 October.

Boethius of Sweden (or **Boethius de Dacia**)   Born probably Denmark, early 1200s, place and date of death unknown. Boethius was a secular cleric who taught philosophy at Paris and was part of the condemned Averroist movement there in the late 1200s. He later became a Dominican in Dacia (modern Romania and Bulgaria). He was a rigorous defender of philosophy's independence from religion, but he tried to reconcile his philosophical ideas (such as the eternity of the world, and the denial of creation and the resurrection) with Christian faith. He wrote commentaries on Aristotle and three original works: *De summo bono*, *De sompniis* and *De aeternitate mundi*.

Bogarín, Juan Sinforiano   Roman Catholic archbishop, born Mbuyapey, Paraguay, 21 August 1863, died Asunción, Paraguay, 25 February 1949. Bogarín studied with the Lazarist Fathers, was ordained in 1887 and served as curate and diocesan secretary at the cathedral of Asunción. Only seven years later he was made bishop of Paraguay by **Leo XIII**. In this office he ministered for over 50 years, for the first 35 years of which he was the country's only bishop. During his episcopacy he managed to visit the whole of the vast diocese several times, travelling on horseback, and strengthening the organization and infrastructure of the Roman Catholic Church in Paraguay. He was eventually elevated to the status of archbishop and in 1940 became the first president of Paraguay's new council of state.

Bogomił of Gniezno (also known as **Theophilus of Gnesen**)   Saint, archbishop of Gniezno, died either Dubrow, Poland, 1092, or Uniejow, Poland, 1182. There is surprisingly little accurate information about him, and the extant sources disagree: he probably resigned as archbishop of Gniezno in 1080 (or possibly 1172), after serving only five years, and lived as a hermit until his death twelve years later. Venerated as a saint during the Middle Ages; his cult was approved in 1925. Feast day 6 or 10 June.

Bogue, David   Congregationalist minister and pioneer missionary educator, born Coldingham, Berwickshire, 1 March 1750, died Brighton, 25 October 1825. He studied in Edinburgh (1762–71) and was licensed to preach in the Church of Scotland. Rejecting patronage, he taught in London and in 1777 became an Independent minister at Gosport near Portsmouth, where he began to take in students for the ministry. His appeal in 1794 'To the Evangelical Dissenters who practise Infant Baptism' helped found the London Missionary Society, in 1795. He advocated proper training for missionaries and was active in the British and Foreign Bible Society and the Religious Tract Society. His *History of Dissenters* was first published in 1809. He had a special interest in India. By his death some 115 missionary students had passed through his academy, 50 going to India. Yale University awarded him a DD in 1815.

Bohic, Henri   Canon lawyer, born Saint-Mathieu, Brittany, France, 1310, died 1351. Few details are known of Bohic's career. He studied canon law in Paris and Roman law in Orléans before becoming a counsellor to John IV of Brittany near the start of the Hundred Years War with England. He taught canon law at Paris around 1335 and wrote *Distinctiones* (published posthumously in 1498), a commentary on the Decretals of Pope **Gregory IX**. Bohic opposed a purely technical conception of canon law, and his work is important in the study of the conflicting streams in canon law in the fourteenth century.

Böhler, Peter   Moravian bishop and missionary, born Frankfurt am Main, Germany, 31 December 1712, died of a stroke London, 27 April 1775. Educated at the Frankfurt Gymnasium and Jena University. Converted under Spangenberg, he worked as a preacher at Leipzig and Jena. In 1737 he was ordained into the Moravian ministry and sent on a missionary journey to Savannah. In April 1738, en route to America, founded the Fetter

Lane Society in London and was instrumental in bringing about **John Wesley**'s 'heart warming experience' of 24 May. Following a period of preaching in Yorkshire he went to Pennsylvania in 1742. On 10 January 1748 he was appointed a Moravian bishop. In 1753 he went to America for the third time, returning to England in 1764.

Böhm, Dominikus   Church architect, born Jettingen, Germany, 23 October 1880, died Cologne, Germany, 6 August 1955. Böhm was among a number of architects who revolutionized church architecture in the first half of the twentieth century, consciously rejecting the styles of earlier periods in favour of a modernist approach. In the 1920s and early 1930s he designed notable churches in Mainz, Leverkusen, Hindenburg and Cologne which are regarded as landmarks of Christian architecture. Böhm was forced to abandon modernism by the rise of the Third Reich, which regarded it as decadent, and although he was able to be more experimental after 1945, his post-war church designs never quite achieved the same impact as his earlier ones.

Böhm, Hans   Lay religious preacher, born near Helmstadt, Germany, c.1450, died Würzburg, Germany, 19 July 1476. Called 'Hansel the drummer', Böhm was a shepherd who entertained people with his drum and pipes before claiming to having a vision of Mary. On 24 March 1476, he burned his drum in front of the church in Niklashausen, claimed that Mary told him she was to be especially venerated in that place, and began preaching a combination of penance and revolutionary communist-like social reform. He attracted thousands from southern Germany. When he called on them to take up arms, he was arrested by Bishop Rudolf of Würzburg and burned as a heretic. His influence lived on, however, and the Niklashausen church had to be destroyed a year later to prevent the continuation of his movement.

Böhm, John Phillip   Founder of the German Reformed Church in the United States, born Hochstadt, Germany, 1683 (baptized 25 November that year), died Hellertown, Pennsylvania, 29 April 1749. He was the son of a Protestant minister and worked for a time as a schoolmaster at Worms

before moving to North America in 1720. There he became a lay leader of a settler congregation, and was later ordained into the Dutch Reformed Church in New York, 1729. He ministered in Pennsylvania. Böhm opposed attempts to unite the Reformed congregations with the Moravians. In 1747, along with Michael Schlatter, he formed the Synod of the Reformed Church in Pennsylvania.

Böhme, Jakob   Lutheran theosophical writer and mystic, known as *philosophus Teutonicus*, born Alt-Seidenburg, Germany, 1555, died Görlitz, 17 November 1624. The son of a farmer, he became a shepherd and then a shoemaker. He underwent a series of mystical experiences, maintaining that his writings (the first of which was published in 1612) were the result of what he had learned through these experiences. Arousing suspicion, he was ordered to cease writing by the municipal authorities of Görlitz. He continued to publish, but opposition, notably from the Lutheran pastor Gregorius Richter, led him to leave for Dresden in 1624, though he returned soon afterwards. His writings are obscure. Scholars are divided as to whether they display pantheistic or dualistic thought. God the Father is the 'Urgrund', the indefinable matter of the universe, known in the Son, and expressed in the Spirit. The Godhead has two wills, one good and one evil. These two wills lead God to create. Humanity can avoid hell by uniting to Christ in faith.

Bohr, Niels   Roman Catholic physicist, born Copenhagen, Denmark, 7 October 1885, died Copenhagen, 18 November 1962. He became professor of theoretical physics in Copenhagen University from 1916 until his retirement in 1956. In 1921 he founded, and directed, the Institute of Theoretical Physics in Copenhagen. In 1922 he won the Nobel Prize for physics. Having fled Nazi Europe, he assisted in the atomic energy project at Los Alamos, USA. After World War II he worked on the peaceful uses of atomic energy. He wrote *Compound Theory of Nuclear Reactors* (1936), *Mechanism of Nuclear Fission* (1939) and papers which laid the basis for quantum mechanics.

Boileau-Despréaux, Nicolas   Poet, born Paris, 1 November 1636, died Paris, 13 March 1711. Having been educated at Beauvais, he respected the wishes of his family by continuing his studies in law. However, from the age of 21 he used his private income to support himself whilst writing poetry. He followed the style of Juvenal and Horace both in poetry and in the criticism of literature. He is known for his *Epistles* of 1660, *Le Lutrin* published in 1674 and *L'art poétique.* From his earliest works he introduced a new poetic method to French literature and remains a significant figure in classical poetry, influencing, among others, Alexander Pope.

Boisgelin de Cuce, Jean de Dieu Raymond de Cardinal archbishop, born Rennes, France, 27 February 1732, died Angervilliers, 22 August 1804. He entered the Church at an early age, and by 33 he had already risen to the position of bishop of Lavour, his speedy promotion largely due to the fact that he belonged to an influential Brittany family. At the age of 38 he became archbishop of Aix. He showed himself to be a good leader, both as pastor and administrator. He became a leading figure in the Roman Catholic Church during and after the French Revolution, defending the Church and refusing to take the oath supporting the Civil Constitution (he had been elected to the Assembly after the Revolution). His stance led to a ten-year exile in England, returning after Napoleon's rise to power. In 1802 he became archbishop of Tours and was made a cardinal by Pope **Pius VII**.

Bolanos, Luis de Franciscan founder of the first reductions in Paraguay, born Marchena, Spain, *c.*1550, died Buenos Aires, 11 October 1629. After becoming a Franciscan, was ordained deacon, and then left for South America with the Juan Ortiz de Zarate expedition in 1572. He learnt a great deal about the language and culture of the natives, and quickly began to visit the Indians of Guayra and Villa Rica and to found pueblos or reductions. He was ordained priest in 1585, while guardian of the Franciscan friary of Asunción. He continued his missionary activity and foundations until his retirement to the Franciscan house in Buenos Aires.

Bolívar, Simón Liberator of Latin America, born Caracas, 24 July 1783, died Santa Marta, Venezuela, 17 December 1830. Born of a rich *criollo* American-born land-owning family; his tutor educated him in principles derived from **Rousseau** and the European Enlightenment, before completing his education in Europe, where he experienced Napoleon's self-coronation. The following year in Rome he called on God to witness that he would not rest until his native land had been liberated from Spain. Thus, as romantic man of action and subsequently a cult figure, he became the leader of the Caracas rebels of 1810 but was all too soon disappointed at the disjunction between his ideals of justice and liberty – he embraced the freeing of slaves and upheld the ideal of religious toleration – and local responses, which he sought to galvanize into effective action following the declaration of independence in 1811. Although he had ideals of co-operative action between the different South American states which he hoped might embrace unity of purpose as set out at the Congress of Panama in 1826, he had in the end to confess that these territories were 'ungovernable' and so his high ideals for the new world ended in disillusion before his premature death. The priority of authority rather than the fruits of freedom was the legacy left to the emerging republics, with the ideal of the old Catholic monarchy of Spain, reconciling cultural diversity and political unity, left in ruins.

Bolland, Jean Jesuit hagiographer, born Julemont, Diocese of Liège, 13 August 1596, died Antwerp, 12 September 1665. He joined the Jesuits in Malines in 1612, and for a time taught humanities in colleges of the Society located in what is now Belgium. In 1630 his provincial asked him to undertake the gathering together of material on the saints begun by Heribert **Rosweyde**, who had died the previous year. Bolland collected a group of fellow Jesuits at Antwerp dedicated to a critical study of the lives of the saints. This group became known as the Bollandists after their founder. The first two volumes of the *Acta Sanctorum*, containing information for the saints commemorated in January, appeared in 1643, the next three, with the saints for February, in 1658. The work continued until the suppression of the Society of Jesus in 1773, and began again in 1837. The Bollandists are now located in a Jesuit college in Brussels.

Bollig, Johann Jesuit theologian, born Kelz, Germany, 8 August 1821, died Rome, Italy, 9 March 1895. Ordained in 1853, Bollig became professor of oriental languages at the Roman College and Pontifical University in 1855. From 1862 until 1864 he lectured on dogmatics in the Lebanon, and on returning to Rome was made a consultor to the Congregation of Propaganda. During Vatican I he was a papal theologian, and in 1877 was made prefect of the Vatican Library.

Bologna, Giovanni Sculptor, born Douai, 1529, died Florence, 13 August 1608. He trained under Jacques Dubroeucq before going to Rome, but on his return journey from Rome to Flanders he stopped at Florence. This became his home for the rest of his life. Bologna developed a form of sculpture that can be viewed from all angles. Among his famous works are the Neptune Fountain in Bologna, *Florence Triumphant over Pisa*, *Samson and a Philistine*, and *The Rape of the Sabines*. Bologna's work is noted for its realism.

Bolsec, Jerome Hermes Controversialist and physician, born Paris, died Lyons, *c.*1585. Originally a Carmelite friar in Paris, he adopted Protestantism *c.*1545 and worked in the Chablais as a physician. During visits to Geneva he engaged John **Calvin** in debates over predestination which led to his arrest in October 1551. He was banished from Geneva, a light sentence secured for him by other Swiss Protestants who disagreed with Calvin's view on predestination. Bolsec continued to attack Calvin's theology whilst travelling through France and Switzerland. His views were finally condemned at the Synod of Lyons in 1563. Before his death he returned to the Roman Catholic Church, settled in France and wrote hostile biographies of Calvin (1577) and Theodore **Beza** (1582).

Bolshakoff (Bolshakov), Serge Nikolaevich Russian Orthodox lay theologian and historian, born St Petersburg, 9 August 1901, died Hauterive, Switzerland, 24 September 1990. He emigrated from Russia in 1918 and studied in Estonia, Belgium and Oxford. He wrote extensively on ecumenical and historical themes as well as comparative spirituality. His most important works are *Russian Nonconformity* (1950) and *Foreign Missions of the Russian Orthodox Church* (1943). He had close relations with a number of Orthodox monastic elders.

Bolzano, Bernhard Mathematician, born Prague, 5 October 1781, died Prague, 8 December 1848. He was ordained and began lecturing in Prague from 1805. He was dismissed from his teaching post in 1820, accused of introducing rationalism into his teaching. He concentrated on private study and took a particular interest in mathematics. He became well known for his theories of differentiation, of parallel lines and of functions of one real variable as well as the binomial theorem and his work on infinity. His best-known treatises are *Science of Religion* (4 vols, 1834) and *Science of Knowledge* (4 vols).

Bomberg, Daniel Publisher and printer, born Antwerp, Belgium, 1470–80, died Venice, Italy, 1549. Bomberg established a printing press in Venice, Italy, in 1515 and began a long and distinguished career in publishing books. Though a number of important books on law, grammar and liturgy came from his presses, he is chiefly known for his publication of Hebrew and Aramaic works, printing over 200 of them in his life. He printed his first Hebrew Bible in 1516–17 (edited by Felix Pratensis) and his second (edited by Jacob ben Chayyim) in 1524–5. With the permission of Pope **Leo X**, he also printed the first complete Babylonian Talmud (1522–3).

Bombolognus of Bologna Dominican theologian, flourished 1265–70. A contemporary of **Thomas Aquinas** though not a follower of him, Bombolognus taught theology at San Domenico in Bologna, which then consisted of lectures on the *Sentences* of **Peter Lombard**. His commentary on that book is the first by a Dominican in Italy and shows a reliance on Italian traditions, rather than those of Paris, normally in evidence in such commentaries. He is also noted for supporting a doctrine of the sanctification of Mary before her birth in place of the Immaculate Conception.

Bona Saint, patroness of travel hostesses, born Pisa, Italy, *c.*1156, died Pisa, 29 May 1207. A pious child, St Bona joined the Canons Regular of St Augustine as a young woman, serving St Martin's Church in Pisa. She had a vision that instructed her to make a trip to the Holy Land, which she did, where she met a hermit who told her what other places to go and when to return home.

Returning to Pisa, she was attacked by Saracens and molested by highwaymen. For the rest of her life, she lived in seclusion except for pilgrimages to Santiago de Compostela and Peter's tomb in Rome. She was named patroness of Italian travel hostesses by **John XXIII** in 1962. Feast day 29 May.

Bona, Giovanni Cardinal, born Mondovi, Piedmont, Italy, 1609, died Rome, 28 October 1674. Of French ancestry, he joined the Cistercian Order at Pignerola and worked for 15 years in Turin before becoming prior at Asti and then abbot at Mondovi. From 1651 the entire Cistercian Order came under his direction. He is known for his works on ascetics, the most popular being *Manuductio*. He also studied patristic commentaries on the Mass and wrote comprehensive studies of Psalter use and the liturgy of the Mass. He was made a cardinal in 1669.

Bonal, Raymond Founder of the Congregation of the Priests of St Mary, born Villefranche, France, 15 August 1600, died Agde, France, 9 August 1653. He was educated at Cahors and Toulouse, studying both theology and canon law. He was ordained and in 1632 established a community of priests which was to follow the exemplary life and work of St **Francis de Sales**. His Congregation was popular and in 1665 gained papal recognition. Bonal also founded a seminary and a college at Toulouse. After his death the Congregation declined and eventually merged with the Lazarists a century later.

Bonald, Louis Gabriel Ambroise de Statesman and theorist, born at Le Monna, France, 2 October 1754, died Paris, 21 November 1840. He was educated by the Oratorians of Juilly and came under the influence of the philosophy of **Malebranche**. He lived abroad during the French Revolution, returning under Napoleon. He was very influential during the period of the Restoration monarchy, and was elected to the Académie Française in 1816. Bonald opposed liberalism and was the leading voice and theorist of the ultraroyalists. Following the Revolution of 1830, he resigned his peerage and retired to La Monna. His writings on social and political theories embody and epitomize traditionalism. In a sense they represent a challenge

to Enlightenment rationalism by establishing a theory by which society can be well ordered. The theory depends upon a hierarchical structure, which included a union of an absolute political power with an absolute religious power. Since God must have revealed all truth to the first man, it followed that tradition rather than reason was the only means by which one could attain truth. Bonald's views were not explicitly condemned by the Roman Catholic Church, but the 'fideism' which they implied was condemned by implication in 1855.

Bonaparte, Charles Joseph Roman Catholic lawyer and politician, born Baltimore, USA, 9 June 1851, died Baltimore, 28 June 1921. Great-nephew of Napoleon. Under Theodore Roosevelt's presidency, he served as legal adviser to the Board of Indian Commissioners (where he opposed corruption and increased federal funding for mission schools) and then, in the cabinet, as secretary of the navy (where he supported Roosevelt's expansionist policies) and later as attorney general. In this position he was influential in the reform of the civil service. He favoured the separation of Church and State, often acting as intermediary between the two. He left public office with Roosevelt in 1909 to work in his law practice and crusade for Negro rights.

Bonaparte, Lucien Ornithologist and political activist, born Paris, 4 May 1803, died Paris, 29 July 1857. The nephew of Napoleon, he studied in Italy and moved to Philadelphia, USA, in 1822. There he worked on Wilson's *Ornithology*, including more than 100 birds he had discovered, and wrote articles for scientific journals. He returned to Italy in 1828 and on the death of his father in 1840 was crowned prince of Canino and Musignano. He joined the anti-papal political party and became vice-president of the republican assembly. He fled Italy for France in 1848 and in 1854 took direction of the Jardin des Plantes. He published several important works between 1827 and 1858, the most popular being *Geographical and Comparative List of Birds in Europe and North America* (1838).

Bonar, Horatius Free Church minister and hymn-writer, born Edinburgh, 19 December 1808, died Edinburgh, 31 July 1889. He was educated in

Edinburgh, and became minister at Leith and Kelso. He returned to Edinburgh as minister of the Chalmers' Memorial Church in 1866. In 1843, the year he married, he left the Church of Scotland and helped to found the Free Church of Scotland, being elected moderator of the Free Church of Scotland's General Assembly in May 1883. He wrote psalm paraphrases and about 600 hymns, of which his most popular is 'Fill Thou My Life, O Lord My God'.

Bonaventure Franciscan saint, cardinal and Doctor of the Church, born Viterbo, Italy, 1221, died Lyons, 15 July 1274. He both studied and taught in Paris. His book *The Poverty of Christ* arose from attacks on mendicant friars by other professors at Paris. Between 1257 and 1274 he was minister general of the Friars Minor, aiming for a middle way in the tensions between radicals and moderates. In 1264 he established one of the earliest Marian confraternities, the Society of Gonfalone. In 1273 he became cardinal bishop of Albano. He prepared the programme for the second Ecumenical Council of Lyons, which brought union with the Greeks. His works include a commentary on the *Sentences* of Peter Lombard, *Perfection of Life*, *Soliloquy* and many biblical commentaries, sermons, a life of St **Francis** and a commentary on the Franciscan rule. He was canonized in 1482 and made Doctor of the Church in 1588. Feast day 14 July.

Bondolfi, Pietro Founder of the Bethlehem Fathers, born Rome, Italy, 10 April 1872, died Immensee, Switzerland, 27 June 1943. Following service as an archivist of the Diocese of Chur and priest to the parish of St Moritz, Bondolfi became director of the Bethlehem school in Immensee in 1907. The school had been founded to prepare priests for mission and service in poor dioceses. In 1921, Bondolfi was named the first superior general of the Bethlehem Fathers. From this office, he encouraged missionary interest in Switzerland, sending his first missionaries to China in 1924. He wrote *Der Geist des Kindes von Bethlehem* in 1938.

Bonet, Juan Pablo Priest, writer, and statesman, born Jaca, Spain, c.1560, died Barcelona (?), c.1620. He served as a diplomat for the king of Spain but he also wrote on the education of deaf-mutes,

inspired by his deaf-mute brother. He was the first to use lip-reading, and established the Municipal Institute for deaf-mutes in Barcelona.

Bonet, Nicholas Theologian, born Tours, France, c.1280, died perhaps Malta, before 27 October 1343. Bonet joined the Franciscan Order and taught at Paris, where he became a disciple of John **Duns Scotus**. Philip VI of France appointed him as his private chaplain. He also served Pope **Benedict XII** as legate to the Great Khan of the Tartars, and **Clement VI** made him bishop of Malta, though he lived but a short time in that office. His most influential writings are *Theologia naturalis* (1505) and *Formalitates in via Scoti* (1489).

Bonfrère, Jacques Jesuit biblical scholar, born Dinant, Belgium, 12 April 1573, died Tournai, 9 March 1642. He joined the Society of Jesus in December 1592 and taught at Scots College, Douai, of which he eventually became rector, for many years. Wrote a number of biblical commentaries in which he displays erudition and an extensive knowledge of Hebrew and biblical geography.

Bonhoeffer, Dietrich Lutheran pastor, theologian and martyr, born Breslau, Germany, 4 February 1906, died Flossenburg, Germany, 9 April 1945. Raised as a member of the upper class in Berlin, Bonhoeffer studied theology in Berlin under Adolf von **Harnack** and at Union Theological Seminary in New York, USA, under Reinhold **Niebuhr**. He was also influenced by the early writings of Karl **Barth**. Upon his return to Berlin, Bonhoeffer worked against the 'Nazification' of the German churches, and soon took a pastorate in London, returning only when the Confessing Church (whose members resisted Hitler) founded its own seminaries. After a month-long stay at Union Theological Seminary in 1939, he chose to return to, and remain in, Germany despite the growing crisis. Involved in a plot to kill Hitler, Bonhoeffer was imprisoned in 1943 and hanged two years later after the plot failed. His writings include *The Cost of Discipleship* (1937), *Life Together*, and his posthumously published *Letters and Papers from Prison*.

Boniface (Wynfrith) Archbishop, saint, missionary

to Germany, born Crediton, Devon, England, 680, martyred Dokkum, Frisia, eve of Pentecost (5 June) 754. Went to Frisia in 716 to work under **Willibrord.** Given papal authority for his mission in 719; worked in Bavaria and Thuringia. He gained more converts when he countered traditional belief by cutting down the oak of Thor near Fritzlar. From 741 he was given authority to reform the Frankish church, which he did by holding a number of councils. He founded an abbey at Fulda *c.*743 and became archbishop of Mainz *c.*747. His influence extended papal authority. In 752 he resigned his see to return to evangelistic work in Frisia. Feast day 5 June.

Boniface I Pope and saint, born Rome, died Rome, 4 September 422. Having been the papal representative in Constantinople, he was elected to the Papacy on 28 December 418 in a disputed election, when he was already quite old and frail. Boniface was ordered out of Rome by the Emperor Honorius, because the prefect of the city supported the other candidate for the Papacy, but his rival succeeded in infuriating the imperial government and Boniface was recognized on 3 April 419. He was indefatigable in promoting the authority of the Papacy, and supported **Augustine** and the other North African bishops in the controversy with the Pelagians. Feast day 4 September.

Boniface II Pope, born Rome, though of German ancestry, died Rome, 17 October 532. He was elected to the Papacy on 22 September 530, though by a minority of the clergy: the majority, angered that the previous Pope, **Felix IV**, had effectively nominated Boniface as his successor on his deathbed, elected **Dioscorus**. But Dioscorus died very shortly afterwards, and Boniface was acknowledged by all as the rightful Pope. He tried to re-establish unity by lavish gift-giving, but again alienated the clergy by attempting, unsuccessfully, to secure the election of a pro-German to the Papacy to succeed him, but in this he failed.

Boniface III Pope of Greek ancestry but born in Rome, elected 19 February 607, died Rome, 12 November the same year. Boniface had been created a deacon by **Gregory I**, who had sent him as papal ambassador to Constantinople in 603. He established, and retained, very good links with the emperor in Constantinople, who at Boniface's behest formally recognized the church of Rome as the head of all churches. Boniface, whose own election may have been held up because of rivalries in Rome (Pope **Sabinian** had died over a year earlier), issued instructions that there was to be no discussion of the papal succession during a Pope's lifetime, or for three days after his death.

Boniface IV Pope and saint, elected 15 September 608, died 8 May 615. The son of a doctor from Valeria, Italy, he became a deacon under Pope **Gregory I** and in 591 is mentioned as papal treasurer. In his pontificate he tried in many ways to emulate Pope Gregory. Like Gregory, he turned his home into a monastery. He also held a synod in Rome to regulate monastic life. This synod was attended by the bishop of London, to whom he gave letters for the English, for the king of Kent, and the archbishop of Canterbury. He received a letter of criticism from **Columbanus** over his predecessor's behaviour in a doctrinal dispute, and received permission to turn the Pantheon into a church dedicated to the Virgin Mary. Feast day 25 May.

Boniface V Pope, elected 23 December 619, died 25 October 625. Nothing is known of his early life except that he was a Neapolitan by birth. He continued his predecessor **Boniface IV**'s interest in the conversion of England, but he was more concerned with the prerogatives of the diocesan clergy and less with the monastic communities. He was described as 'compassionate and kindly', and he distributed all his considerable personal fortune to the poor.

Boniface VI Pope, elected April 896, in which month he also died. He was born in Rome, the son of a bishop, and had twice been degraded from clerical status for immorality: the choice of Boniface was forced upon the Church by a rioting mob. He died of gout only a fortnight after his election.

Boniface VII Antipope, born Rome, and named Franco, elected June/July 974, deposed, returned summer 980, fled again March 981, returned for a third time August 984, died Rome, 20 July 985. Boniface was a cardinal deacon at his election, which was effectively a coup against Pope **Benedict**

VI, who was the choice of the Emperor **Otto I**. Benedict was imprisoned and Boniface consecrated. When the imperial representative in Italy hurried to Rome to overturn the appointment, Boniface had him murdered. This act turned the people of the city against him, and he had to flee Rome, taking the papal treasury with him. He returned to Rome in the summer of 980 in circumstances that are unclear, though he had to abandon the city again when the Emperor **Otto II** came to Rome at Benedict's request. After the death of Otto he returned again in the pontificate of the unpopular **John XIV**, who was deposed and subsequently murdered. When Boniface died unexpectedly – there were stories that he, too, had been murdered – his body was dragged through the streets and mutilated.

Boniface VIII Pope, born Anagni, Italy, c.1235, elected 24 December 1294, died Rome, 11 October 1303. Born Benedict Gaetani of a noble and influential Italian family, Boniface VIII spent his early career serving the curia in minor capacities after studying civil and canon law in Bologna. He was created cardinal in 1281, played a role in the 1290 Council of Paris, helped to persuade Pope **Celestine V** to abdicate the papal throne and was subsequently elected to fill the position. His nearly nine-year reign was spent in conflict with both secular rulers (particularly Philip the Fair of France) and the powerful **Colonna** family, and in frankly promoting his own Gaetani family. Though he made a significant contribution to canon law, he was dogged by accusations of usurping the papal office and misusing it throughout his reign. That reign ended in 1303 when Philip's minister **Nogaret** seized the city of Anagni, from which Boniface was going to excommunicate the king. Though he was not physically attacked, the encounter shattered Boniface's health, and he died several weeks later.

Boniface IX Pope, born Pietro Tomacelli, Naples, c.1350, elected 2 November 1389, died Rome, 1 October 1404. An able ruler who succeeded **Urban VI** as Pope of the Roman obedience and made notable progress in reversing the political and economic damage caused by his predecessor. The Jubilee of 1390 helped swell papal coffers, as did financial sharp practice. Renewed control of the Papal States was not, however, matched by a resolution of the papal schism, which was fought out with his Clementine opponents in the parallel contest for the Neapolitan throne. Otherwise noted as a nepotist and as the Pope who canonized **Bridget of Sweden**.

Boniface of Savoy Blessed, Carthusian monk and archbishop of Canterbury, born c.1207, died Savoy, 14 July 1270. He was the son of Thomas I, count of Savoy, and returned to Savoy in his old age. He joined the Carthusian Order whilst still a boy and in 1234 was elected bishop of Belley in Burgundy. In 1241 he was elected to succeed St **Edmund of Abingdon** at Canterbury, but because of a delay in confirmation of this office, he did not arrive until 1244. He attended the Council of Lyons in 1245 and only returned to Canterbury in 1249, when he was enthroned. During his tenure he carried through a number of financial reforms. He also made two visitations of his province – once before going to the council and once afterwards – which met with a degree of hostility among his clergy. Feast day 14 July.

Bonitus of Clermont Saint and bishop, died Lyons, 706. He had been chancellor to Sigebert III, king of Austrasia, and was recommended for the see of Clermont in the Auvergne by his brother, who died in that post in 689. Bonitus was duly consecrated, but he came to doubt the legality of the procedure, resigned the see and retired to the abbey of Manglieu. He died returning from a pilgrimage to Rome. Feast day 15 January.

Bonizo of Sutri Bishop, born Cremona, Italy, c.1045, died there 14 July 1090. He was ordained bishop of Sutri in 1074, having been a subdeacon in Piacenza. During his episcopacy he was papal legate to Cremona, attended ecclesiastical councils and published works which include treatises on church history, sacraments, theology, canon law and schism. He was imprisoned in 1082 by the Antipope Clement III (**Guilbert of Ravenna**), having been captured by Emperor **Henry IV**. After a year he escaped and went to Tuscany. He was translated to the see of Piacenza but was refused entry to the diocese and was killed by anti-papal militia.

Bonnechose, Henri Marie Gaston de Cardinal, archbishop of Rouen, born Paris, 30 May 1800, died Rouen, 28 October 1883. Ordained in 1833, he became a member of the Society of St Louis. In 1844 he became superior of the community at St-Louis des Français in Rome. Consecrated bishop of Carcassonne in 1847, he was subsequently bishop of Evreux, 1854, and archbishop of Rouen, 1858, becoming a cardinal in 1863. Within the French Senate, a member of which he had became in 1863, he was a strong defender of the Church. He also took an active part in the First Vatican Council. Bonnechose was one of the founders of the Institut Catholique de Paris.

Bonnefoy, Jean-François Theologian, born Lausonne, France, 12 June 1897, died Grottaferrata, Italy, 9 May 1958. Bonnefoy was received into the Franciscan Order in 1915 and ordained in 1924. He pursued doctoral studies at the Institut Catholique in Toulouse and taught in Toulouse and Rome. He concentrated his scholarly interests on developing the theology of John **Duns Scotus** (particularly the necessity of the incarnation – regardless of Adam's sin – and the sinlessness of Mary) and the spirituality of St **Bonaventure**. His written works include *Christ and the Cosmos*, 'L'Immaculée dans le plan divin' (*Ephemerides Mariologicae*, 8, 1958) and *Le Saint-Esprit et ses dons selon s. Bonaventure* (Paris, 1929).

Bonner, Edmund Bishop of London, born *c*.1500, died in Marshalsea prison, London, 5 September, 1569. He studied canon and civil law at Oxford and engaged in diplomatic work for **Henry VIII** from 1527, visiting, among others, Pope **Clement VII**, King **Francis I** of France, and Emperor **Charles V**. In 1538 he became bishop of Hereford and the following year bishop of London. He enforced the Act of Six Articles but during **Edward VI**'s reign became unhappy with the developments of Protestantism. He was deprived of his see in 1549 for disobeying the instructions of the Privy Council. Restored by Queen **Mary** in 1553 he worked for the return of England to Catholicism. On **Elizabeth I**'s succession to the throne he refused to swear the oath of the Act of Supremacy and was once again deprived of his see and imprisoned.

Bonnet, Joseph Organist, born Bordeaux, France, 17 March 1884, died Sainte-Luce-sur-Mer, Quebec, 2 August 1944. A Benedictine Oblate, Bonnet became organist at Saint-Eustache in Paris in 1905, and in 1906 was awarded the first organ prize at the conservatory. In 1906, he embarked upon a world tour that lasted until his death in 1944, presenting little-known organ works from the seventeenth, eighteenth and nineteenth centuries. These works were later collected into the six-volume *Historical Organ Recitals*. Minutes after his performance of César **Franck**'s three *Chorales* at the Eiffel Tower radio, Hitler began his invasion of Paris. He spent the last years of his career heading the organ departments at the Eastman School of Music (Rochester, New York) and the Conservatoire Nationale of the Province of Quebec. He also published several collections of organ works for concert and study.

Bonnetty, Augustin French Roman Catholic philosopher, born Entrevaux, France, 9 April 1798, died Paris, 26 March 1879. For a time he was intended for the priesthood, and spent four years at seminary before deciding against ordination. Bonnetty left for Paris, where he became part of a wide circle of Catholic intellectuals. In 1830 he founded a review entitled *Annales de philosophie chrétienne*, which he edited for the rest of his life. Philosophically he was a fervent defender of fideism and traditionalism. Bonnetty argued that the only valid problem, from a philosophical point of view, was the nature of man's religious belief, and that all human knowledge has its origin in a direct revelation of God to Adam and Eve. Furthermore, man is incapable of discovering truth without revelation. His theories regarding truth and revelation led him to condemn Scholasticism and this resulted in conflict with Rome, which insisted that he subscribe to a number of propositions which effectively exonerated scholasticism. Bonnetty, a faithful Catholic, agreed without hesitation.

Bonomelli, Geremia Bishop and writer, born Brescia, Italy, 12 September 1831, died Brescia, 3 August 1914. After ordination in 1855, he taught in Brescia and served as pastor in Lovere. Consecrated bishop of Cremona in 1871, he worked especially in the pastoral field and to reconcile science and religion. He founded the Opera Bonomelli to assist Italian emigrants. He owned to writing an anonymous article (*La realta della Roma e cose*) when it was placed on the Index. He published many articles and books on religious and socio-economic problems, and many of his letters and sermons were printed.

Bononius Saint, abbot, born Bologna, Italy, mid 900s, died Lucedio, Italy, 30 August 1026. A Benedictine monk of St Stephen's in Bologna, he became a disciple of St **Romuald**, who sent him to preach in Syria and Egypt, and he wished to become a hermit on Mount Sinai. In 990, however, his bishop recalled him in order to make him the abbot of Lucedio. As abbot, his major concern was monastic reform. Pope **John XIX** canonized him. Feast day 30 August.

Bonosus Pope *see* **Benedict I**.

Bonsirven, Joseph Scholar, born Lavaur, France, 25 January 1880, died Toulouse, 12 February 1958. Following his ordination in 1903, Bonsirven successively taught biblical studies at the major seminary in Albi, France and the Pontifical Biblical Commission. His doctoral thesis on rabbinic theology was rejected in 1910 and he was barred from teaching. He was imprisoned during World War I and during this time **Benedict XV** appointed him to teach biblical studies and theology to imprisoned seminarians. He became a Jesuit in 1919 and spent the rest of his life teaching in Belgium, France and the Pontifical Biblical Institute in Rome. His publications include commentaries on the NT, the Apocalypse volumes in the *Verbum Salutis* series (Paris, 1951), *Le judaïsme palestinien au temps de Jésus-Christ* (1934–5) and *Exégèse rabbinique et exégèse paulinienne* (1939).

Bonvin, Ludwig Jesuit composer, born Siders, Switzerland, 17 February 1850, died Buffalo, New York, 18 February 1939. Bonvin became a Jesuit in 1874 in Holland. Following his ordination in 1885 in Liverpool, England, he studied music theory, early church music and composition. He settled at Canisius College in Buffalo and conducted the college's chorus and orchestra from 1887 to 1907. His scholarly interests were concerned with the notation of early music. Bonvin's compositions included liturgical Masses, litanies, vespers services, hymns and instrumental works.

Bonzel, Maria Theresia Founder of the Poor Sisters of St Francis Seraph of Perpetual Adoration, born Olpe, Germany, 17 September 1830, died Olpe, 5 February 1905. Baptized Aline, she studied with the Ursulines at Cologne and became a Franciscan tertiary in 1851, at which time she took the name Theresia. She founded the Poor Sisters to care for and teach needy children as well as to attend to the needy sick. During her lifetime, the Poor Sisters increased to over 700 members and spread to the USA, in 1875, and Austria.

Boonen, Jacques Archbishop of Malines, born Antwerp, 11 October 1573, died Brussels, 30 June 1655. He first studied law at Louvain, qualifying in 1596, but later entered upon an ecclesiastical career, and was ordained in 1611. After holding a number of ecclesiastical offices he eventually became archbishop of Malines (Belgium). A controversial figure, Boonen was a rigorist who strongly advocated the application of the decrees of the Council of Trent. He was a friend and admirer of Cornelius **Jansen**, his suffragan, and petitioned Rome in an attempt to reverse the papal condemnation of Jansenism.

Booth, Catherine Born Catherine Mumford, Ashford, Derbyshire, England, 17 January 1829, died of cancer, Clacton, England, 4 October 1890. The daughter of a Wesleyan preacher, she joined the Wesleyan church of Brixton, London, as an adult but was expelled for her religious enthusiasm. In 1855 she married William **Booth**, who had also been expelled, and they had eight children. Together they established an itinerant ministry of Gospel preaching before returning to London and establishing the Christian Revival Association (later known as the Salvation Army) in Whitechapel in 1864. Catherine ran the women's work, inspiring the evangelism of the 'Hallelujah lasses', as well as continuing her preaching ministry. The global popularity of her work and that of the Salvation Army was evident at her funeral at Olympia, which was attended by 36,000 people.

Booth, Joseph Missionary to southern Africa, born Derby, England, 26 February 1851, died

Weston-super-Mare, England, 4 November 1932. Emigrated to Australia before going to Africa in 1892, when he established the Zambezi Industrial Mission in Malawi. He also worked in South Africa, Lesotho, Britain and the USA and was a Baptist, Seventh Day Baptist and Seventh-Day Adventist. He had a radical approach to missionary work championing pro-African causes, as laid out in his book *Africa for the Africans* (1897), and influencing many African nationalists, including John **Chilembwe**. As a result he was mistrusted by colonial settlers and mainline missionaries. In 1915 he was unjustly blamed for Chilembwe's uprising and deported from Lesotho to Britain.

Booth, Lawrence Archbishop of York, chancellor of England, born Lancashire, England, died Southwell, England, 19 May 1480. The half-brother of William **Booth**, Lawrence began his career as master of Pembroke Hall, Cambridge, in 1450. He was Queen Margaret's chancellor and highly favoured at the English court, which led to his receiving several ecclesiastical posts, including dean of St Paul's, London, in 1456. He was made bishop of Durham in 1457, which gave him grounds of favour with the new king when the Yorkist Edward IV came to power. He was chancellor of England for one year, 1473–4 and in 1476 was made archbishop of York, though his political involvements meant that he likely spent very little time there.

Booth, William Archbishop of York, born Lancashire, England, died York, England, 12 September 1464. Though he did not have a university education, William Booth practised law at Gray's Inn, London, before assuming a series of minor church offices. In 1445, the wife of **Henry VI**, Queen Margaret, made him her chancellor, and through that he became bishop of Coventry and Lichfield. A papal bull installed him as archbishop of York in 1452, and he helped his brother Lawrence **Booth** become the queen's new chancellor. Though he held no other important office until his death, he remained active in politics, freed by a dispensation of **Calixtus III** from actually fulfilling his pastoral duties in York. Still, after his death he was remembered in York as a benefactor of the lower clergy.

Booth, William Founder of the Salvation Army,

born Nottingham, England, 10 April 1829, died London, 20 October 1912. As a Methodist, he was converted in 1844. He became a revivalist preacher in 1846, which took him to London in 1849. Six years later he married Catherine Mumford, who worked closely with him. He left the Methodists in 1861 and founded the Christian Mission. Its aim was to work with the poor, through preaching the Gospel and offering practical support. The Army spread throughout the world from 1880 onwards and Booth spent much time travelling and speaking at meetings. In 1890 *In Darkest England and the Way Out* was published, in which he suggested ways of improving the social conditions of the poor.

Borda, Andrés de Franciscan theologian, born Mexico City, date unknown, died Mexico City, 1723. In 1697 he became the first Franciscan to receive a doctorate from the University of Mexico, and held the chair of theology, in the tradition of John **Duns Scotus**, at the university from 1688 until his retirement in 1711. After his retirement he became theological consultant to the Inquisition in Mexico City. He wrote widely, and was greatly admired as a theologian in his day.

Bordoni, Francesco Franciscan theologian and historian, born Parma, Italy, 25 April 1595, died Parma, 7 August 1671. At the age of just fifteen he became a Franciscan (Third Order Regular). He studied and then taught theology at the Studium Parmense. He became master of novices and then prior and provincial in the province of Bologna. He later became minister general of the Order. He was a prolific writer on theology, history and canon law.

Borgess, Casper Henry Roman Catholic bishop, born Kloppenburg, Hanover, Germany, 1 August 1824, died Kalamazoo, Michigan, USA, 3 May 1890. Having settled in the United States, he studied at Cincinnati and Philadelphia and was ordained in 1848. He worked at Columbus until he was appointed to a parish church in Cincinnati in 1859. In 1870 he became titular bishop of Calydon and coadjutor of Detroit. Later the same year he was made bishop of Detroit. During his episcopacy the Roman Catholic population of his diocese became mainly English- rather than

French-speaking. On resigning in 1888 he was made titular bishop of Phacusa.

Borgia, Cesare Cardinal, born Rome, September 1475, died Viana, Navarre, Spain, 12 March 1507. A member of the infamous Borgia (Borja) family and son of Cardinal Rodrigo de Borgia (Pope **Alexander VI**), Cesare was legitimized by both Pope **Sixtus IV** in 1480 and Ferdinand II of Aragon in 1481, allowing him to receive certain church benefits. He served a number of church offices, eventually climbing to archbishop of Valencia in 1492, at the tender age of seventeen. He was made cardinal by his father in 1493, made a deacon in 1494, but declined ordination to the priesthood in 1498 on account of his unrestrained lifestyle. He tried to create a small feudal state for himself in Romagna during the War of Naples, but Alexander's death led to his imprisonment by his successor Pope **Julius II**; he eventually escaped to France and died fighting for the king of France in Viana.

Borgia, Francis Saint, Jesuit, great-grandson, on his father's side, of Pope **Alexander VI** and, on his mother's, of King Ferdinand of Aragon, born near Valencia, 28 October 1510, died Rome, 30 September 1572. Married Eleanor de Castro in 1528 and enjoyed a privileged position at the court of the Emperor **Charles V**, becoming viceroy of Catalonia in 1539. On his father's death he succeeded him as duke of Gandia and retired with his wife and eight children to the family estates there. Eleanor died suddenly in 1546 and soon after Francis asked to join the Society of Jesus. On the advice of **Ignatius of Loyola** he waited a further three years until his children were settled, and meanwhile studied theology at the university he had founded at Gandia. Francis was ordained in 1551, became commissary general of the Jesuits in Spain in 1554 and father general of the Order in 1565. Under his influence the Society was greatly strengthened and enjoyed both reform and expansion in Europe, the Far East and the Americas. Francis was widely recognized as a good and holy man, as well as an efficient administrator, and up to his death remained sensitive to the welfare of his family and the needs of the poor and sick. Feast day 10 October.

Borgia, Jofré Prince of Squillace, born Rome, 1481, died Squillace, Italy, January(?) 1517. A son of Cardinal Rodrigo de Borgia, who later became Pope **Alexander VI**, Jofré was legitimized by his father, though the latter doubted that he was, indeed, the boy's father. He married Sancha, a noblewoman of Aragon, in 1494, and was given the principality of Squillace in extreme southern Italy by Alfonse II of Naples. After the death of his first wife, he married again, led a short and uneventful life, and died leaving his son Francesco to inherit his lands and title.

Borgia, Juan Duke of Gandia, ecclesial military leader, born Rome, 1476, died Rome, 14 or 15 July 1497. A son of Cardinal Rodrigo de Borgia (Borja) (later Pope **Alexander VI**), Juan became duke of Gandia at the age of twelve upon the death of his brother Pere-Luís **Borgia** in 1488. In 1493, he married María Enríquez, cousin to the king of Aragon and formerly betrothed to Juan's brother. He lived in Valencia for a time to consolidate his ducal holdings but returned to Rome when he was named a commander of church military forces, who were battling **Charles VIII** of France. His losses against the king forced him back to Rome, where he was assassinated (possibly at the instigation of his brother Cesare **Borgia**) and his body thrown in the Tiber.

Borgia, Lucrezia Duchess of Ferrara, born Subiaco, Italy, April 1480, died Ferrara, Italy, 24 June 1419. Probably the most infamous daughter of the Borgia family and a child of Cardinal Rodrigo de Borgia (Pope **Alexander VI**), Lucrezia lived with relatives in Rome until betrothed by her father the Pope to the count of Cotignola, Giovanni Sforza, in order to build an alliance with Milan. She was granted a divorce when the Sforzas allied themselves with King **Charles VIII** of France. She later married the duke of Bisceglie and had a son by him before the duke was assassinated on orders of Lucrezia's brother Cesare **Borgia**. She then married the future duke of Ferrara in 1500. Despite her affairs and other scandals in her household, she was supposed to be deeply religious in her later years and gave her husband seven children.

Borgia, Pere-Luís Duke of Gandia, born Rome,

c.1468, died Rome, August 1488. He was the son of Cardinal Rodrigo de Borgia, later Pope **Alexander VI**. When he was about fifteen, his father gave him a sum of money and a barony and sent him to Spain, where he was arrested a year later in a dispute between the cardinal and King Ferdinand II of Aragon. The king was eventually forced to recognize Pere-Lluís's nobility and sold him the dukedom and title of Gandia in late 1484. Though engaged to a cousin of the king in 1486, he died before the marriage could take place, leaving his brother Juan **Borgia** as his heir.

Boris I of Bulgaria First Christian ruler of Bulgaria, born 827, died in a monastery, 7 May 907. In the face of military pressure, Boris' decision to accept baptism from the Byzantine church in 864 introduced Christianity amongst the Slavs and Bulgars of Bulgaria. The refusal of the Byzantine church to grant autonomy to his church compelled him to turn to Rome for missionaries and bishops in 866. The Bulgarian church returned to the Byzantine fold in 870, but in 880, Rome and Constantinople reached an agreement that placed the Bulgarians under Roman jurisdiction. Political factors and distance prevented Rome from significant oversight and the Church remained largely influenced by Constantinople. In 885, Boris accepted refugee clergy of the Slavonic rite who fled from Moravia after the death of **Methodius**. Their work was particularly successful amongst the Bulgarian Slavs. Upon his retirement, Boris appointed his son Vladimir to the throne. Vladimir's relapse into paganism caused him to resume power for a brief period while he established his son Symeon as the favoured successor.

Boris and Gleb Saints, princes of Kiev, died 1015. They were the sons of **Vladimir** I of Kiev and his wife Anne of Constantinople who, on the death of their father, shared with other brothers their father's dominions, as was the custom. Their half-brother, Svyatopolk, who wished to reunite the country, made war on his two brothers. Boris refused to fight against his brother, and was murdered beside the River Alta, calling on the passion of Christ. Gleb was subsequently assassinated on a boat travelling down the Dnieper to Kiev. When in 1020 Svyatopolk was himself overthrown by another brother, Yaroslav of Novgorod, the two murdered brothers were reburied in the church of St Basil at Vyshgorod, where their tomb became a centre of pilgrimage, and of miracles. They were regarded as martyrs in the Russian church, and in 1724 Pope **Benedict XII** approved their cult for the western church. Their feast day is 24 July.

Borromeo, Charles Saint, cardinal, born Rocca di'Arona, Italy, 2 October 1538, died Milan, Italy, 3 November 1584. Of aristocratic parentage, he had his first benefice aged twelve. From 1552 he studied canon and civil law at Pavia. In 1560 he was made cardinal and archbishop of Milan by his uncle **Pius IV**. A leader in the Catholic Reformation, he was very influential in the third and last group of sessions of the Council of Trent. He reformed the see of Milan by insisting on higher morals and discipline, introducing a more effective structure and establishing seminaries for the training of clergy. He also founded an Order of Oblates, reorganized a Confraternity of Christian Doctrine for educating children and showed concern for the poor and sick. His reforms were not always popular but they were adopted elsewhere in Europe. He was canonized in 1610. Feast day 4 November.

Borromeo, Federigo Cardinal, born Milan, Italy, 18 August 1564, died Milan, 22 September 1631. He was educated at Bologna, at Paris and from 1580 at Rome. In 1587 he was made a cardinal and became archbishop of Milan in 1595. He was renowned as an excellent preacher and attentive in the formation of his priests. During the famine and plague of 1627 to 1628 he organized the feeding of over 2000 people daily. This concern for the poor cost the lives of 95 priests when they also contracted the plague. He established the Ambrosian Library in 1609 and permitted it to be opened to the public. His own writings are extensive.

Borromini, Francesco Architect, born Francesco Castelli at Bissone, Lake Lugano, on 25 September 1599 (the name Borromini was adopted later), died Rome of a self-inflicted wound, 2 August 1667. He went to Rome in 1616 and worked under the notable architects Maderno and Bernini. Given to fits of restlessness and melancholy, he was a brilliant, though controversial architect. Particularly notable are his designs for S. Carlo alle Quattro Fontane; S. Agnese a Piazza Navona; S. Philip Neri;

the Collegio di Propaganda Fide; and his renovations to St John Lateran.

Bortniansky, Dmitri Stepanovich Musician, born Glukhov, Ukraine, 29 November 1751, died St Petersburg, 10 October 1825. He studied in St Petersburg and Italy. He was given charge of what became the Imperial Chapel Choir, bringing it to a high state of excellence. He wrote much church choral music, unaccompanied in the tradition of the Greek church.

Boscardin, Maria Bertilla Saint, Roman Catholic nurse, born Brendola, Italy, 6 October 1888, died Treviso, Italy, 20 October 1922. Baptized Anna Francesca, she became a part of the Dorothean community at Vicenza in 1905. As a novice to the Dorotheans, she worked as a kitchen maid in a hospital in Treviso. She made her religious profession in 1907, taking the name Maria Bertilla. She continued to nurse in the Treviso hospital with children stricken with diphtheria as her special charge. She was known for her display of courage and faith to wounded soldiers during the latter part of World War I. Feast day 20 October.

Bosch, David Jacobus South African missiologist, born near Kuruman, South Africa, 1929, died in a car accident, 15 April 1992. He studied at the Universities of Pretoria and Basel (Th.D., 1957) and served as a Dutch Reformed missionary in the Transkei. He founded the Southern African Missiological Society (SAMS) in 1968 and was first editor of its journal *Missionalia*. He became professor of missiology at the University of South Africa (UNISA) in 1971. He was known for his gracious pastoral and spiritual sensitivities, enjoyed the trust of diverse groups of Christians, and in his magisterial *Transforming Mission* (1991) produced the summative work of classic twentieth-century missiology.

Bosco, John Saint, religious founder, born into a peasant family in Becchi, Turin, 16 August 1815, died Turin, 31 January 1888. From a very early age he had a sense of his vocation to help other poor boys. He entered the seminary in Chieri in 1831 and studied there and in Turin. While in Turin he used to gather and teach the young homeless boys, and his vocation to continue this work was con-firmed by Joseph **Cafasso**. After his ordination, and with his mother as housekeeper, he gave shelter to some of the boys who came for instruction; this developed, with workshops being added so that the boys could learn trades. He built a church and larger accommodation and in 1856 he had 500 boys coming for recreation and instruction, 150 residents, and four workshops, one of which had a printing press. His methods were to encourage study and prayer, and to use a caring, unintrusive discipline with the boys. In 1859, after much thought, prayer and preparation, he founded the Pious Society of St Francis de Sales to continue and develop this work. In 1872 a similar organization of Sisters to work with girls and young women, the Daughters of Our Lady Help of Christians, was founded. Both developed quickly and their work continues throughout the world. Feast day 31 January.

Boscovich, Ruggiero Giuseppe Jesuit priest, astronomer, mathematician, philosopher, born Ragusa (Dubrovnik), 18 May 1711, died Milan, 13 February 1787. He studied at the Jesuit college in Ragusa before entering the Jesuit novitiate at Rome in 1725. A brilliant scholar, he eventually became professor of mathematics at the Collegium Romanum. Wrote various scientific, mathematical and astronomical treatises, and was ordained in 1744. In 1745 he published *De viribus vivis*, his first philosophical work, in which he put forward a new theory on the nature of matter. In subsequent years he became famous throughout Europe, in 1760 being made a Fellow of the Royal Society of London. After the suppression of the Jesuits in 1773, Boscovich went to Paris and became director of optics for the Marine. He remained for some nine years, after which time he returned to Italy because of ill-health.

Boso Cardinal and papal chamberlain, birth place and date unknown, died Rome, 1178. Cardinal Boso was either an Englishman (as noted in a necrology of Bologna) or of Lombardian origin and began his curial career as a papal scriptor. In 1154–5 he was appointed papal chamberlain by Pope **Adrian IV**, which made him an overseer of the Lateran treasury and all the papal finances. He was created cardinal in 1156, served the Pope for a time in Portugal and held the Castel Sant' Angelo in Rome for Pope **Alexander III** against the Anti-pope Victor IV in the contested papal election of 1159. His writings include the *Liber Censuum* and biographies of the two Popes he served.

Bossi, Marco Enrico   Church musician, born Salò, Italy, 25 April 1861, died at sea 20 February 1925. Following music studies in Bologna and Milan, Bossi held a number of positions including organist of Como cathedral, professor of organ and harmony at Naples Conservatory, and director of the music school of Santa Cecilia Academy, Rome. He reformed Italian organ technique, performance, design and pedagogy through the publication of his *Metodo di studio per l'organo moderno* (1889). He also composed Masses, motets, sonatas, organ concerti, orchestral suites, *Fantasia sinfonica* for organ and orchestra, choral works and oratorios.

Bossuet, Jacques Bénigne   Catholic bishop, born Dijon, France, 27 September 1627, died Paris, 12 April 1704. Educated at Dijon, Metz, Paris and under **Vincent de Paul**, he was ordained priest in 1652. He became a well-known preacher and apologist against the Protestants, combining clarity of thought with passionate belief. He was consecrated bishop of Condom in 1669 and was tutor to the Dauphin between 1670 and 1681. During this time he wrote *Exposition de la doctrine catholique sur les matières de controverse* (1671), *Traité de la connaissance de Dieu et de soi-même* (1677) and *Discours sur l'histoire universelle* (1681). He was translated to the see of Meaux and became increasingly involved in French ecclesiastical issues, approving in 1685 of the revocation of the Edict of Nantes. He wrote against Protestants in *Histoire des variations des Eglises protestantes* (2 vols, 1688) and against Mde **Guyon** in *Relation sur le quiétisme* (1698).

Boste, John   Saint, martyr of Durham, born Dufton, Westmorland, England, *c.*1543, died Dryburn, near Durham, England, 24 July 1594. Trained at Oxford, Boste became a Roman Catholic in 1576 despite having taken the Oath of Supremacy. In 1580, he travelled to the English College at Rheims, France, to train for the priesthood, and returned to England in 1581. He travelled secretly around the country, mostly in the north, in the livery of Lord Montacute, illegally promoting the Roman Catholic faith. He was betrayed and arrested in September 1593. After serving time in the Tower of London and refusing to reveal other Roman Catholics, he was sent to Durham for trial. He was accused of high treason, waived his right to a trial to spare a jury the guilt of his blood, and died forgiving his executioners and inspiring his colleagues. He was canonized as one of the **Forty Martyrs of England and Wales**. Feast day 24 July.

Bostius, Arnold (Arnold van Vaernewijck)   Carmelite theologian, born Ghent (Belgium), 1445, died Ghent, 4 April 1499. Bostius was the spiritual director of the Carmelite nuns in Ghent. A committed humanist, he promoted classical studies and kept contact with other humanists, including **Erasmus**. He also promoted the Immaculate Conception and wrote works on Mary's patronage of the Carmelites (*De patronatu et patrochinio Virginis Mariae*) and historical works about his Order (*De illustribus viris, Speculum historiale* and *Breviloquium tripartitum*).

Boswell, James   Man of letters, born Edinburgh, 29 October 1740, died London, 19 May 1795. He was the eldest son of the Presbyterian Lord Auchinleck. He was received into the Catholic Church as a young man but kept his conversion secret, for fear of the penalties that would be imposed at that time. Although he studied and qualified as a lawyer, he was far more interested in literature. His *Account of Corsica* (1768) and *Essays in favour of the Brave Corsicans* (1769) were published following his own visit to the island in 1766. In 1785 he published his *Tour to the Hebrides*, which followed a tour through Scotland during which he was Samuel **Johnson**'s guide. His most famous writing was his *Life of Samuel Johnson*, published in 1791. He was a man of great humour, but of questionable morals.

Bosworth, Fred Francis   Pentecostal evangelist and healer, born 1877, died 1958. Originally associated with Alexander Dowie's church, Bosworth became a Pentecostal in 1906, and in 1910 he founded a church in Dallas. From 1914 to 1918 he was a member of the executive presbytery of the Assemblies of God, but he resigned over their insistence on speaking in tongues as the only evidence of Spirit baptism. With his brother he held dramatic healing meetings in various parts of America and Canada, and he organized radio evangelism in Chicago. His final years were concerned with African evangelism. In 1924 he wrote *Christ the Healer* (revised 1948).

Botticelli, Sandro   Italian painter, born Florence, 1445, died Florence, May 1510. Born Alessandro di Mariano Filipepi, the man who came to be called Botticelli was the son of a tanner. After his initial studies under Lippi and Verrocchio, he worked independently on frescos in Mercanzia, Pisa and Rome, including the Sistine Chapel. He eventually returned to Florence and enjoyed the patronage of powerful and important people, until old age diminished his popularity and success. Initially Botticelli painted both religious works (*Adoration of the Magi* and numerous Madonnas) and secular (*The Birth of Venus*), but the influence of **Savonarola**'s preaching made him renounce pagan themes. He is recognized as one of the most important painters of the fifteenth century.

Botulf (Botolph)   Saint and abbot, born in England or possibly Ireland, died possibly Boston, Lincolnshire, *c.*680. The earliest life comes from four centuries after his death, from which it seems he travelled for a time with his brother Adulf in Germany, before returning to England to found a monastery in 654 which is generally identified as having been at Boston, though all trace of it was destroyed at the Danish invasions. Feast day 17 June.

Boturini Benaducci, Lorenzo   Historian, probably born Sondrio, Italy, 18 April 1698, died Madrid, 1749. After a period of study he travelled to Mexico City in 1736, there becoming interested in the shrine of Our Lady of Guadalupe at Tepeyac, and in particular the tradition of the apparition of the Virgin Mary there in December 1531. Boturini collected many Mexican documents relating to Indian history, as well as antiquities. He also raised money in order to place a crown on the statue of the Virgin at Guadalupe. In 1742 he was accused of promoting devotion to Our Lady of Guadalupe without royal authorization. His documents and antiquities were seized, and, in February 1743, he was imprisoned. Sent to Spain, he was put ashore at Gibraltar by English pirates, who had plundered his ship. He eventually arrived in Madrid penniless, but was later given an annual pension and named the official chronicler and historian of the New World. In 1749 he completed the first volume of his *Historia general de la América septentrional*, though this was never published.

Botvid   Saint and lay evangelist, born Sweden, date unknown, died Sweden, *c.*1120. Botvid was a pious layman concerned with promoting Christianity in Sweden, who was killed by a slave he had freed. Little else is known of his life. His relics were honoured from soon after his death, several offices were composed for him, and he is portrayed in iconography with an axe and a fish. Feast day 28 July.

Bouchard, James (Indian name **Watomika**)   Jesuit missionary, born Muskagola, Kansas, *c.*1823, died California, 27 December 1889. His mother was of French descent, but had been captured by Indians of the Delaware tribe, and adopted by them with the name Monotwan, 'White Fawn'. She married an Indian called Kistalwa, and their son was named Watomika, meaning 'Swift Foot'. Following the death of his father in a skirmish with the Sioux, Watomika was taken by a Presbyterian missionary to Ohio, where he studied for the ministry. He later converted to Roman Catholicism, became a Jesuit, and was ordained in 1855. He was the first American Indian to be ordained in the United States. After many years in the Midwest, he went to California, where he was greatly in demand as a preacher, retreat leader and lecturer. He also worked as a missionary in the mining camps and towns of California.

Boudon, Henri Marie   French spiritual writer, born La Fère, 14 January 1624, died Evreux, 3 August 1702. He was educated at Rouen and Paris, was named archdeacon of the Diocese of Evreux in 1655, and was ordained soon after. He sought to cleanse his diocese of ecclesiastical abuses and restore discipline, which aroused a great deal of opposition. In 1664 Bishop Henri de Maupas went to Rome for the canonization of St **Francis de Sales**. Boudon was given sole charge of the diocese. Because of opposition to his reforms, he became the subject of a number of false accusations. This led to his suspension from office, pending investigation. He bore the situation with great patience, and was affirmed to be innocent of the charges in 1674, and was reinstated. He wrote widely on spiritual matters, and his works, which enjoyed great popularity, were translated into many languages. The process for his canonization was begun in 1885.

Bouelles, Charles de (Carolus Bovillus) Roman Catholic theologian and philosopher, born Saucourt, France, *c.*1470, died Noyon, France, *c.*1553. De Bouelles was a disciple of Jacques **Lefèvre d'Étaples** and for most of his adult life professor of theology at Noyon. He wrote and lectured on a broad variety of topics, but is best known for his theological–philosophical synthesis of **Pico della Mirandola** and **Nicholas of Cusa**, as can be found in his *De sapiente*. He was also influenced by Nicholas in the matter of prayer, in which he stressed the soul's internal disposition and the importance of praise, as seen in his *De indifferentia orationis* (1529).

Bouillon, Emmanuel Théodore de la Tour d'Auvergne Cardinal and diplomat, born Turenne, France, 24 August 1643, died Rome, 2 March 1715. He was educated at the College of Navarre and the Sorbonne, in Paris. He was created a cardinal in 1669, at the personal request of **Louis XIV**, and later became his chief almoner. He lost favour with the king, largely due to his attempts to increase his family's fortune, and was exiled to Cluny. He later regained the king's support and was appointed the royal representative in Rome, only to find himself out of favour once more. He refused to obey the king's summons back to France, and remained in Rome as dean of the cardinals and directed the conclave that elected Pope **Clement XI**. He finally submitted to the king and retired from public life, first at Cluny, and then in Holland, though he eventually returned to Rome.

Boulainvilliers, Henri de Historian and philosopher, born Saint-Saire, France, 11 October 1658, died Paris, 23 January 1722. He originally embarked upon a military career as a royal musketeer, but left military service after the death of his father in order to take care of the family affairs. He became interested in history and philosophy, and wrote extensively. His writings display a dis-

satisfaction with the absolute monarchy of **Louis XIV**, tracing, as he does, the decline of the French state from the rule of individual nobles to the absolute rule of the monarch, in which the nobles are little more than servants of the king. Boulainvilliers also studied comparative religions, though from the standpoint of a Christian who regarded other religions as being derived from the one true religion of Christ, or being of purely human origin.

Bouquillon, Thomas Joseph Theologian, born Warneton, Belgium, 16 May 1842, died Brussels, 5 November 1902. Educated at the major seminary in Bruges, Bouquillon entered the Capranica in Rome and was ordained in 1865. He received his doctorate from the Gregorian University in Rome in 1867 and returned to the seminary in Bruges to teach moral theology. In 1889, he was invited by Bishop John **Keane**, the first rector of the Catholic University in America, to teach as part of the original faculty. Bouquillon's scholarly interests focused on the theologians of sixteenth- and seventeenth-century Spain and the Netherlands. He played a significant role in the foundation of the University's library by choosing the initial 30,000 volumes of the theology collection. In 1891, he published a pamphlet that embroiled him in the controversy named after him, a dispute concerning the religious instruction of Catholic students and the building of parochial schools. Bouquillon published over 50 articles and *Theologia moralis fundamentalis* (1903), *De virtutibus theologicis* (1890) and *De virtute religionis* (1880).

Bourassa, Henri Roman Catholic politician and journalist, born Montreal, Canada, 1 September 1868, died Outremont, Canada, 31 August 1952. He worked as a journalist in Ontario and Montreal before becoming founder and editor-in-chief of Montreal's nationalist newspaper *Le Devoir* in 1910. In 1896 he was elected as an Independent Liberal to the House of Commons, where he served, with breaks and representing different counties, until 1935. He was a moving spirit in the Ligue Nationaliste and a leader of the Canadian nationalists. His most important books are *Que devons nous à l'Angleterre* (1915) and *Hier, aujourd'hui, demain* (1916).

Bourbon, Jeane-Baptiste de Counter-Reformation abbess of Fontevrault, born 22 February 1608, died Fontevrault, 16 January 1670. The illegitimate daughter of **Henry IV** and Charlotte des Essarts, she was abbess of the royal monastery of Fontevrault for 43 years. Despite much opposition from the community, she continued and completed the reform of Fontevrault begun under Marie de **Bretagne**, and arranged for the publication of new editions of the two twelfth-century *vitae* of **Robert of Arbrissal** in the *Acta Sanctorum*, as well as a number of other hagiographical works related to her Order's founder.

Bourchier, Thomas Cardinal, archbishop of Canterbury, born, place unknown, *c.*1410, died Kent, England, 30 March 1486. Of high birth, Bourchier began his career by graduating from Oxford and serving a term as the university's chancellor, 1434–7. He was ordained and served several minor posts before being involved in a dispute for the see of Worcester in 1433, finally being named to the post in 1435. After serving there and at Ely, he was made archbishop of Canterbury in 1454. He supported the Yorkist cause in the party struggles of the 1450s and loyally crowned and served King Edward IV, who had him made cardinal in 1467. He spent most of his career in politics, crowning three kings and leaving the ecclesiastical administration of his diocese to suffragans and officials.

Bourdaloue, Louis French Jesuit preacher, born Bourges, 20 August 1632, died Paris, 13 May 1704. In 1648 he became a Jesuit and for many years taught humanities and morals at various Jesuit colleges. In 1666 he began preaching, gaining a great reputation for a series of sermons delivered before **Louis XIV** and his court from 1670 onwards. His published sermons are somewhat dry, though it was noted in his day that he had great oratorical power. The sermons are mainly concerned with moral theology and its application. He was called the 'king of orators and the orator of kings'.

Bourdeille, Elias de Franciscan cardinal, archbishop, born Perigord, France, 1413, died near Tours, France, 5 July 1484. The son of a noble family, Elias joined the Franciscan Order in Périgueux, France, in 1423. He took advanced studies at Toulouse and preached at Mirepoix before being named bishop of Périgueux in 1437, in which capacity he attended the Council of Florence. In 1468, he became the confessor of Louis XI and was consequently made archbishop of Tours. Despite his close relationship to the king, he adamantly defended papal rights against those of secular rulers and influenced Louis to repeal the Pragmatic Sanction. Nine months before his death, he was created cardinal by Pope **Sixtus IV.** He wrote a justification of the beatification of **Joan of Arc** and a work against Gallicanism.

Bourgeois, Louis Huguenot musician, born Paris *c.*1510. He went to Geneva with **Calvin** and became master of the choristers there. He was musical editor of the first French psalter and compiled several others. He lived later in Lyons and Paris, where he was living in 1561, but the date of his death is unknown.

Bourgeoys, Marguerite Saint, foundress, born Troyes, France, 17 April 1620, the daughter of wealthy parents, died Montreal, Canada, 12 January 1700. After several unsuccessful attempts to become a nun, she travelled to Canada in 1653. In 1658 she opened the first school in Montreal, and later a school for Indians, a mission, a boarding school, and a school for training the poor. She was joined by other girls from France and Canada, including two Indian girls. These formed themselves into a religious community which was distinct from the cloister in that the sisters were itinerant, and would travel where they felt they were most needed. The Congregation de Notre Dame, which gained ecclesiastical approval in 1698, refused endowments and gifts of money, supporting themselves instead by sewing and manual work, and living with austerity. After a fire in 1683, in which most of their buildings were destroyed, the community was left destitute. They once again began to build a new school, and a chapel of pilgrimage dedicated to Our Lady, Notre Dame de Bon Secours. Marguerite, along with the other sisters, assisted in the manual labour needed in this building project. She was canonized in 1982. Feast day 12 January.

Bourget, Ignace Bishop of Montreal, born Saint-Joseph-de-Lévis, Canada, 30 October 1799, died

Montreal, 8 June 1885. Bourget was educated in Quebec and at Montreal. In 1836, when the Diocese of Montreal was created, he became vicar general, and by 1840 was the second bishop of the diocese. As bishop he spent some time in Europe, from 1841, trying to encourage priests and religious orders to come to Montreal, where there was a great need. In addition he himself founded religious orders in the diocese. Bourget was a man of action, but also possessed a deep spirituality. Doctrinally he was very much an ultramontanist, supporting the doctrine of papal infallibility.

Bourgoing, François Oratorian superior general, born of a noble family in Paris, 18 March 1585, died there, 18 March 1662. He became curé of Clichy, a position he held until 1611, when he resigned in favour of **Vincent de Paul**. He then joined the Oratory founded by Pierre de **Bérulle.** Bourgoing taught extensively at a number of seminaries, before going to Flanders at the request of the archbishop of Malines in 1626. Here he founded Oratorian houses at Louvain, Maubeuge and Mons. In 1630 he returned to France, and in 1641 became the third superior general of Bérulle's foundation. An authoritarian superior, he nonetheless was a wise and competent administrator and one of the leading figures in the seventeenth-century religious revival in France. He was a prolific writer on spiritual matters.

Bourne, Gilbert Roman Catholic bishop, born, place and date unknown, died Silverton, England, 10 September 1569. After an early career at Oxford, Bourne served in several ecclesiastical posts under King **Edward VI**. Although he complied with the Protestant Edward, when the Roman Catholic **Mary** Tudor came to the throne he returned to Roman Catholicism. Queen Mary made him a royal preacher, and his eloquence in defending Catholicism and his patron Bishop **Bonner** won him the bishopric of Bath and Wells in 1554. Though he zealously promoted a return to Roman Catholic worship and doctrine, he seems to have been a kind man, and no one was executed in his diocese for their religious views. He was removed by Queen **Elizabeth** in 1558, refused to take the Oath of Supremacy, was imprisoned in the Tower of London, and eventually died under house arrest.

Bouscaren, Timothy Jesuit priest, educator, born Cincinnati, USA, 17 August 1884, died Cincinnati, 10 February 1971. Ordained in 1929, he taught at Detroit University, Loyola College, Chicago, Mundelein Seminary, the Gregorian University in Rome and West Baden College. He later served as procurator general of the Jesuits and as consultor to the Congregations of the Faith, of the Council and of Religious. After being professor emeritus of canon law at West Baden, he taught at Bellarmine Theology School, Illinois. He wrote *Ethics of Ectopic Operations* (1933), *Canon Law Digest* (1933–69), *Canon Law Digest for Religious* (1963–9) and *Canon Law: A Text and Commentary* (1946).

Bousset, Wilhelm German biblical scholar, born Lübeck, 3 September 1865, died Giessen, 8 March 1920. Bousset taught biblical studies in Göttingen in 1896–1916 and Giessen in 1916–20. He cofounded the school of comparative religion in Göttingen and applied its principles to NT studies. His scholarly work concentrated on the influence of Hellenism upon early Christianity. He maintained, contrary to A. von **Harnack**, that the history of dogma was not one of the Hellenization of Christianity but that the early Church had been deeply influenced by Hellenism from the beginning. The significant turning point in the Church's history came not with the end of the NT but in the transition from the belief in an immediate return of the Son of Man to the Gentile proclamation of the Lord already present with his people. Bousset's thought influenced **Bultmann** and his school. His notable writings include a commentary on Revelation (1896), *Die Religion des Judentums im neutestamentliche Zeitalter* (1902) and *Kyrios Christos* (1913).

Boutrais, Cyprien Marie Carthusian author, born Paris, 10 June 1837, died Vedana, Italy, 18 August 1900. Boutrais was ordained in 1863 and became a Carthusian at the Grande-Chartreuse. He managed the Carthusian printing operation at Montreuil-sur-Mer in 1885–8 and served as prior at La Valsainte (Switzerland), Glandier (France) and Vedana (Italy). His published works include the life of Blessed Ayrald (1880), *La Grande Chartreuse par un chartreux* (1881) and several works addressing the role of the Carthusians in the development of devotion to the Sacred Heart of Jesus.

Boutroux, Etienne Emile Marie Roman Catholic philosopher of science, born Montrouge, France, 28 July 1845, died Paris, 22 November 1921. As conference master of the Ecole Normale, he influenced a generation of French philosophers and philosophers of science. In his acclaimed doctoral dissertation, he attacked the determinism of the academic rationalists and suggested that the human quest for an absolute could be found in morality and religion. His major works are *Science and Religion in Contemporary Philosophy* (1909), *Historical Studies in Philosophy* (1912), *William James* (1912), *Natural Law in Science and Philosophy* (1914) and *Contingency of the Laws of Nature* (1916).

Bouts, Dirk (Thierry) Painter, born Haarlem, Netherlands, *c.*1415, died Louvain, Belgium, 1475. Bouts came from Holland to Flanders around 1448 to marry the daughter of a wealthy family in Louvain, where he was made official city painter in 1468. In his art, he was influenced by Jan van Eyck and Roger van der Weyden but developed a psychological intensity and a balance of figure and landscape that was all his own. He also introduced a new type of focal point perspective. His most noted words are the *St Erasmus Altarpiece* and *Altarpiece of the Blessed Sacrament*, both painted for the church of St Peter in Louvain.

Bouvet, Joachim Missionary, born Le Mans, France, 18 July 1656, died Beijing, China, 28 June 1732. As a Jesuit astronomer and geographer he was sent with five others by King **Louis XIV** to China to gather scientific information. He arrived at the court of Emperor Kang-hsi (Kangxi) in 1688 and helped him by writing mathematical works in Tatar which were translated into Chinese later on. The emperor sent Bouvet back to France with gifts for Louis XIV. Returning to China again in 1699, accompanied by ten missionaries, Bouvet became an interpreter for the emperor's son, and between 1708 and 1715 co-ordinated a survey of the Empire. He wrote a life of the emperor, who permitted him to evangelize. He was both a successful missionary and a scientist.

Bouvier, Jean Baptiste Roman Catholic bishop, born Saint-Charles-la-Forêt, France, 16 January 1783, died Rome, 28 December 1854. He was ordained in 1808 and lectured in theology and philosophy in various institutions. Between 1819 and 1834 he was vicar general of Le Mans and superior of the seminary there. He was ordained bishop of Le Mans in 1834. In 1853 his best-known work, *Institutiones theologicae*, was published and was used extensively as a textbook in seminaries. A friend of Pope **Pius IX**, he supported the dogma of the Immaculate Conception, which was proclaimed in 1854, and opposed the Jansenists.

Bova Benedictine abbess, seventh century. The place and date of Bova's birth are unknown (though according to **Flodoard of Rheims**, her father was Sigebert, king of Austrasia, and her sister St Baudry of Montraucon), died Rheims, 24 April 673. Bova was the first abbess of Saint-Pierre, Reims, to which she introduced the Benedictine rule. Feast day, shared with her niece and probable successor Doda, 24 April.

Bowet, Henry Archbishop of York, born, place unknown, *c.*1350, died Yorkshire, England, 20 October 1423. A doctor of both civil and canon law, Bowet accompanied Bishop Henry **Despenser** on his crusade to Flanders in 1382. He then spent a time as an official of the Roman curia in 1385–90. In 1396, John of Gaunt had him made constable of Bordeaux, and he joined Bolingbroke (later Henry IV of England) when the latter was forced into exile. His wealth and property were confiscated by **Richard II**, but when Henry IV came to power all was restored and he was made bishop of Bath and Wells. Despite his evident lack of management skills, he was made archbishop of York in 1407, after which time he became less involved in matters of state.

Bowman, Thea (born **Bertha**) African-American Catholic Franciscan, born Mississippi, 1937, died Canton, Mississippi, 30 March 1990. The only black member of the religious Order she had joined aged sixteen, she became committed to developing a black way of being Catholic. Instead of black Catholics being expected to conform to a white culture, she wanted them, for example, to use song and dance in church as the black Protestants did. After completing a doctorate in English, she worked as a teacher, preacher and evangelist in Mississippi and Louisiana. She addressed meetings all over the country, encouraging Catholics to support a spirituality that affirmed the complex identity of African-Americans.

Boyce, William Composer and organist, born London, 1710, died Kensington, London, 7 February 1779. He was a chorister at St Paul's cathedral, and organist of the Chapel Royal as well as at a number of other churches around London. He composed church music and edited a collection of cathedral music. His collection of his own compositions, *Lyra Britannica*, extended to six volumes.

Boyle, Robert Scientist and apologist, born Lismore, Ireland, 25 January 1627, died London, 7 January 1692, 'The father of chemistry and the son of the Earl of Cork', Boyle played a leading role in the founding of the Royal Society in 1662. He advanced the cause of science by experimental work in chemistry, physics and anatomy, exploring in particular the circulation of the blood in the human body, and, by use of air pumps, establishing the proportional relationship between the elasticity and pressure of air, which led to the establishment of the law named after him. Having himself studied ancient languages, he became a generous promoter of the printing of Bibles in Welsh, Irish and some Indian languages, the NT in Turkish and the Gospels and Acts in Malay. He used his directorship of the East India Company to promote Christianity in Company territories, and also sought to promote the spread of the gospel in New England. He declined ordination, the provostship of Eton and a peerage. Seeking to harmonize new discoveries in science with Christian faith, he endowed the Boyle Lectures for the defence of Christianity against unbelievers.

Bracken, Thomas Roman Catholic convert, poet, politician and journalist, born Clones, Ireland, 21 December 1843, died Dunedin, New Zealand, 16 February 1898. Orphaned at the age of nine, he emigrated to Australia and thence to Dunedin. In 1875 he established and edited Dunedin's *Sunday Advertiser*, where his poem 'God Defend New Zealand' (later adopted as the country's national

anthem) first appeared. From 1885 he edited Dunedin's *Evening Herald*. He served twice as a Member of Parliament and in 1896 converted to Catholicism. His publications include *Behind the Tomb* (1871), *Musings in Maoriland* (1892), *Paddy Murphy's Annual* (1886) and *Tom Bracken's Annual* (1896).

Bracton, Henry de Priest and canon lawyer, born Devon, England, *c.*1210, died Exeter(?) before September 1268. Coming from a wealthy family and possibly educated in law at Oxford, Bracton served various posts in the Diocese of Exeter and entered the service of Henry III in 1239. In 1244, he became a judge, in which capacity he also served for a time on the king's counsel 1255–6. Bracton's chief fame comes from his legal writings *De legibus et consuetudinibus Angliae* and a *Note Book*.

Bradford, John Protestant martyr, born Manchester, England, *c.*1510, died London, 1 July 1555. He studied law at the Inner Temple but *c.*1547 went to Cambridge to study theology, having been thus convinced by the preaching of Hugh **Latimer**. After receiving his MA in 1549 he became a fellow of Pembroke Hall and taught John Whitgift. He was ordained deacon in 1550 and became chaplain to Nicholas **Ridley**, bishop of London. He was a good preacher and champion of the Protestant faith for which he was imprisoned in the Tower of London soon after **Mary** succeeded the throne in 1553. There he wrote *The Hurt of Hearing Mass* (published *c.*1561) and defended predestination against other prisoners who supported the doctrine of free will. He remained loyal to Protestantism during his trial and was burnt as a heretic at Smithfield.

Bradford, William Governor of Plymouth, USA, born Austerfield, Yorkshire, England, 1590, died Plymouth, MA, 19 May 1657. He joined the Scrooby congregation of Separatists in 1606 before moving to Amsterdam and then Leiden in The Netherlands, where he worked as a weaver. He sailed to America aboard the *Mayflower* in 1620 and was elected governor of Plymouth the following year after the death of John Carver. Respected by the electorate, he remained governor until 1656 and assisted the founding of the New England Confederacy. He worked with the Indian population and was present at the 1647 Synod at Cambridge. His book *Of Plymouth Plantation* remains an informative source on the colony.

Bradley, Denis Mary Roman Catholic bishop, born Castle Island, Kerry, Ireland, 25 February 1846, died Manchester, New Hampshire, USA, 13 December 1903. He settled in Manchester from the age of eight and was educated at Holy Cross College. In 1871 he was ordained at Troy, New York. He worked first in Portland, Maine, where he was made diocesan chancellor, and then ministered in Manchester. He was consecrated bishop of the new see of Manchester in 1884 and held its first synod in 1886. He did much to establish an efficient organizational system in the diocese and offered good pastoral care to the scattered congregations of Roman Catholics.

Brady, Matthew Francis Roman Catholic bishop, born Waterbury, Connecticut, USA, 15 January 1893, died Burlington, Vermont, 20 September 1959. He studied at St Thomas Seminary, Bloomfield, CT, Louvain and New York and was ordained in 1916. After serving in the First World War as a chaplain he returned to St Thomas to teach from 1922 to 1932. He was consecrated bishop of Burlington in 1938 and became bishop of Manchester, Vermont, in 1944. He presided over several committees until his death: the Education Department of the National Catholic Welfare Conference in 1950–6, the US Bishops' Committee for Confraternity of Christian Doctrine in 1956–9 and the National Catholic Education Association in 1957–8.

Brady, Nicholas Frederic Roman Catholic convert, financier and philanthropist, born Albany, NY, 25 October 1878, died Philadelphia, PA, 27 March 1930. He entered his father's utility business on graduation from Yale and doubled the family fortune. He was a skilled financier, merged several public utility companies and directed over 100 concerns during the course of his career. His pioneering work in labour relations extended security benefits for employees. He converted to Catholicism in 1905 and in 1929 was awarded the Ordine Supremo del Christo in recognition of his charitable works and contribution to the study of the moral problems of capitalism.

Brady, William Maziere Historian, born Dublin, Ireland, 8 January 1825, died Rome, 19 March 1894. He was educated at Trinity College, Dublin, and on being ordained served in Anglican parishes in Maynooth, Kilkeedy, Dublin, Farrahy, Confert and Kibery, and was chaplain to the viceroy. He edited records of parishes and wrote on the history of the Church in Ireland during the reign of **Elizabeth I** and on the contemporary Anglican Church in Ireland. After a visit to Rome in 1873 he converted to Roman Catholicism. He continued his research from the Vatican, publishing *Episcopal Succession in England, Scotland and Ireland, 1400–1875* and *Annals of the Catholic Hierarchy in England and Scotland, 1585–1876*. He wrote for the London Catholic journal *The Tablet* and corresponded with Prime Minister **Gladstone** on political issues.

Brahe, Tycho Astronomer, born Knudstrup, Denmark, 14 December 1546, died Prague, 24 October 1601. He studied at the Universities of Copenhagen and Leipzig. As an astronomer he recognized the need for accuracy and precision in all observations, and built instruments to enable this. In 1576 he was granted an island by the king of Denmark, on which he built two observatories. He believed the Aristotelian system to be incorrect, but also rejected the Copernican doctrine because he found it to be incompatible with Scripture. Instead he argued for a system where the planets circled the sun while the sun in its motion circled a stationary earth. In 1597 Tycho left Denmark for Prague, following a disagreement with the king.

Brahms, Johannes Composer, born Hamburg, Germany, 7 May 1833, died Vienna, Austria, 3 March 1897. A musical child, he trained as a concert pianist. In 1862 he went to Vienna and the following year became conductor of the Choral Academy. Considered the best symphony and chamber music composer of the Romantic era, he was not a church musician but was well versed in the Lutheran church music tradition and edited much of it. He composed sacred motets after **Schütz** and **Bach**. His best work, *A German Requiem*, was first performed in 1868 and is one of the greatest choral works of the nineteenth century; it uses words from the German Bible and has no relation to the Roman Mass.

Brainerd, David　Missionary to the Delaware Indians, born Haddam, Connecticut, 20 April 1718, died Northampton, Massachusetts, 2 October 1747. Under the influence of the emerging Great Awakening, Brainerd became an early example of missionary zeal. However, he was expelled from Yale without a degree for questioning the religious standing of one of his instructors. His place in missions history owes more to Jonathan **Edwards'** publication of his journal, which became an evangelical classic, than to visible success of his missionary endeavours during his short life.

Bramante, Donato　Architect, born near Urbino, Italy, 1444, died Rome, Italy, 11 April 1514. Though he began his career as a painter, Bramante is best known as an architect and engineer of domes. True to the spirit of the Renaissance, he studied Roman ruins to learn ancient construction techniques and then began designing domes, beginning in Milan in 1480–90, where he worked on the east end of S. Maria presso S. Satiro. In 1499, he went to Rome, where his Tempietto of S. Pietro in Montorio of 1502 is considered the first and best example of High Renaissance architecture. He also had grand plans for St Peter's, but his death prevented their completion.

Brambach, Wilhelm　Roman Catholic scholar and historian, born Bonn, Germany, 17 December 1841, died Karlsruhe, Germany, 26 February 1932. In his early life he worked on classical philology and musicology, later becoming professor of classical philology at Freiburg and district librarian at Karlsruhe. Here he uncovered early liturgical books showing the role of the abbey of Reichenau in the development of Gregorian chant. His works include *Das Tonsystem und die Tonarten des christlichen Abendlandes im Mittelalter* (1881), *Die Musikliteratur des Mittelalters bis zur Blüte der Reichenauer Sängerschule* (1883) and *Gregorianisch: Bibliographische Lösung der Streitfrage Über den Ursprung des gregorianisches Gesang* (1895).

Brammart, Johannes　Carmelite theologian, born Aachen, Germany, c.1340, died Cologne, Germany, 8 September 1407. After becoming a Carmelite, Brammart began his theological studies in Paris, but finished them in Bologna, probably because of his ideas about the Great Western Schism. He served as the provincial of the German Carmelites from 1384 to 1404 and helped to found the University of Cologne. His only work, *Lectura super I Sententiarum*, which was never published, shows him holding to voluntarism and an ambiguous mix of nominalism and realism.

Brancati, Lorenzo　Franciscan cardinal, born Lauria, Italy, 10 April 1612, died Rome 30 November 1693. In 1630 he became a Minor Conventual and lectured in philosophy and theology at the Roman University. He was appointed consultor to the Congregation of the Holy Office and later became librarian to the Vatican Library. In 1681 he was made a cardinal but retained a humble obedience to the vows of his Order. He published a commentary on Books 3 and 4 of **Duns Scotus'** *Sentences*, wrote on missiology and on prayer.

Brandsma, Titus　Carmelite priest and martyr, philosopher, historian of mysticism, born Friesland, Holland, 23 February 1881, died Dachau, Germany, 26 July 1942. He entered the Carmelites in 1898 and in 1905 was ordained. He edited a newspaper in Oss, where he founded a Catholic library and several schools. He was professor and rector of the Catholic University of Nijmegen, where he specialized in medieval mysticism and was spiritual director of the Union of Dutch Catholic Journalists. Under Nazi occupation, he persuaded newspaper editors to reject Nazi propaganda. He was imprisoned by the Nazis and killed in Dachau.

Brangwyn, Sir Frank　Roman Catholic painter and book illustrator, born Bruges, Belgium, 13 May 1867, died Ditchling, England, 11 June 1956. After exhibiting in the Royal Academy, he travelled to Asia Minor and Africa, financing himself by his drawings. He was elected an associate, and later made a fellow, of the Academy and was knighted in 1941. He was the first living artist to have a retrospective show at the Academy. His interior decorations include those in Swansea's Civic Centre (*The War Memorial Compositions*), in the Skinners' Hall, London, in the Houses of Parliament, Ottawa, and in Radio City, New York.

Branham, William　Pentecostal healing evangelist, born Barkesville, Kentucky, 6 April 1909, died

Amarillo, Texas, 1965. Branham claimed to have been guided throughout life by an angel that he met in a cave in 1946. In 1933 he led a revival in Jeffersonville, Indiana, and his dramatic tent meetings led to the post-1945 healing revival. Branham was popular in Trinitarian Pentecostal churches, despite his insistence on 'Jesus only' baptisms. He also taught prosperity; that he was the angel of Revelation 13:17; and that the world would end in 1977 following the World Council of Churches being taken over by Catholics. His book *Footprints on the Sands of Time* appeared in 1975.

Branly, Edouard   Roman Catholic physicist and inventor, born Amiens, France, 23 October 1844, died Paris, France, 24 March 1940. He conducted research into electricity and invented the coherer, a device essential to wireless telegraphy. He also researched the effect of ultra-violet light on charged bodies and the electrical conductivity of gases. He became Commander of the Order of St Gregory the Great, was nominated Chevalier of the Legion of Honour, received the grand prix at the Paris Exposition and the Prix Osiris. His papers were chiefly published in *Comptes rendus*. He wrote *Cours Elémentaire de physique* and *Traité Elémentaire de Physique*.

Brann, Henry Athanasius   Roman Catholic scholar, born Parkstown, West Meath, Ireland, 15 August 1837, died New York City, USA, 28 December 1921. He settled in the USA in 1849 and was educated in Wilmington, Delaware, New York and St Sulpice, Paris. He was ordained in Rome in 1862 and taught theology at Seton Hall College, New Jersey. Between 1862 and 1864 he worked in several parishes. He became a Paulist in 1867. He was principal of Wheeting College, Virginia and parish priest in New York until his death. In 1910 he was made a monsignor. A prolific writer on a range of subjects including aspects of Catholic doctrine and a biography of Archbishop **Hughes** (1892), his most famous book is *Age of Unreason*, published in 1880. He also wrote *History of the American College, Rome* (1912).

Brant, Sebastian   Poet, born Strasburg, Alsace, *c.*1458, died Strasburg, 10 May 1521. Educated at Basel he taught there from 1484, receiving his doctorate in 1489. In 1485 he married Elizabeth

Burg. He worked with the Basel printers, editing, proof-reading and advertising their publications. When Maximilian became emperor in 1486 he wrote a poem of praise. His famous satire *Das Narrenschiff* (*Ship of Fools*) was published in 1494 and was widely appreciated, going through six editions before Brant died. In 1498 he wrote *Varia Carmina*. He was syndic of Strasburg from 1501 and later became city clerk and chancellor whilst retaining his involvement in literary circles.

Brask, Hans   Roman Catholic bishop, born Sweden, 1464, died Danzig (now Gdansk, Poland), 30 July 1538 or 1539. After studies in Rostock and Griefswald, Brask was first provost, in 1510, then bishop, in 1513, in Linköping. As bishop, he energetically promoted Scholasticism and wrote several works now lost. He supported the Swedish national cause against Denmark, but vehemently opposed the introduction of Lutheran doctrines there. He continued to battle with **Luther**'s supporters in Sweden, who included the king, from 1522 until 1527. At that time, the Diet of Västerås deprived all bishops of their power and property, made the Church subject to the Swedish Crown and made Lutheranism the state religion. Brask went into exile in Danzig.

Brasseur de Bourbourg, Charles Etienne   Missionary and archaeologist, born Bourbourg, France, 8 September 1814, died Nice, France, January 1874. Aged 31, he went to Quebec, Canada, where he taught church history. In 1846 he was appointed vicar general to the Diocese of Boston. After a visit to Rome he went to Mexico City and became chaplain of the French legation. Between 1854 and 1865 he travelled throughout Central America, working in Guatemala as church administrator and in Mexico with a French scientific team. During this time he studied Indian languages and ethnology and published several important works on Latin American history.

Brauer, Theodor   Roman Catholic economist, educator and writer, born Cleve, Germany, 18 January 1880, died St Paul, USA, 19 March 1942. He held a variety of trades union and academic appointments before becoming director of the Institute for Social Research and professor of labour economics and social legislation at Cologne

University, and director of the Labour School of the Christian Trades Unions in Königswinter. He was dismissed from his directorships and jailed by the Nazis. He later emigrated to the USA. His many publications include *The Catholic Social Movement in Germany* (1932) and *Thomist Principles in a Catholic School* (1943).

Braulio Saint and bishop, born possibly in Seville, died Saragossa, 651. He was a disciple of St **Isidore**, and was elected bishop of Saragossa in 631. He attended the Fourth, Fifth and Sixth Councils of Toledo, and was zealous in imposing discipline upon the clergy. He was renowned for his personal asceticism. He wrote a life of, and a poem to, St Emilian, and some letters of his are extant. He is also said to have completed some works of St Isidore. Feast day 26 March.

Braun, Joseph Jesuit priest, archaeologist and liturgist, born Wipperfurth, Germany, 31 January 1857, died Pullach, Germany, 8 July 1947. He was ordained in 1881 and entered the Society of Jesus in 1890. He taught archaeology and art history in Valkenburg, Frankfurt and Pullach. His many publications on archaeology, iconography and liturgy include *Des christliche Altar in seiner geschichtlichen Entwicklung* (1924), *Die liturgische Gewandung im Occident und Orient nach Ursprung und Entwicklung: Verwendung und Symbolik* (1907), *Sakramente und Sakramentalien* (1922) and *Liturgisches Handlexikon* (1924).

Braun, Placidus Benedictine historian, born Bavaria, 16 February 1756, died Augsburg, 23 October 1829. He became a monk of the abbey of SS Ulrich and Afra in Augsburg, and was ordained priest in 1779. As the librarian and archivist of the abbey, he published catalogues and descriptions of the books and manuscripts that they possessed. After the French Revolution, during which time the abbey was suppressed, Braun became involved in historical study in the Diocese of Augsburg.

Brauns, Heinrich Roman Catholic priest, government minister, born Cologne, Germany, 3 January 1868, died Lindenburg, Germany, 19 October 1939. He was ordained in 1890 and worked as a curate and then on the staff of the Volksverein, where he later became departmental head and course director. He subsequently became a delegate to the Weimar National Assembly, a member of the Reichstag and minister of labour, during which time he promoted social welfare policies, enacted the Labour Tribunal Law and established unemployment insurance. His writings include *Christliche Gewerkschaften oder Fach-Abteilungen in Katholische Arbeite-vereinen* (1904), *Das Betriebs-trategesetz* (1920) and *Lohnpolitik* (1921).

Bray, Thomas Philanthropist and pioneer Anglican mission strategist, baptized Chirbury, Shropshire, 3 May 1658, died London, 15 February 1730. Ordained priest in 1681, he became rector of Sheldon, Warwick, in 1690. In 1696 he published his *Lectures upon the Church Catechism*. He was instrumental in founding the Society for the Propagation of Christian Knowledge (SPCK) in March 1699 to provide Christian libraries in the American colonies. It also supported parochial libraries in Britain and from 1710 contributed to the Danish–Halle Mission in Tranquebar, India. After visiting Maryland in 1700, Bray obtained a royal charter for the Society for the Propagation of the Gospel in June 1701. He was appointed to St Botolph Without, Aldgate, London, in 1706 and in 1723 created the Associates of Dr Bray for the evangelization of African–American slaves.

Brehier, Louis Byzantine scholar, born Brest, France, 5 August 1868, died Rheims, France, 13 October 1951. He led a reclusive life, teaching in schools and then as professor of ancient and medieval history at the University of Clermont-Ferrand. A prolific writer on art history and the history of Greek–Latin relations during the Middle Ages, his publications include *Le schisme oriental du XI siècle* (1900), *L'Eglise et l'Orient au Moyen Age*, *L'art chrétien* (1918), *L'art byzantin* (1924), *La sculpture et les arts mineurs byzantins* (1936), *Le style roman* (1946), *Le monde byzantin* (1947–50).

Bremond, Henri Priest and sometime Jesuit, spiritual writer, born Aix-en-Provence, France, 31 July 1865, died Arthez d'Asson, France, 17 August 1933. He entered the Society of Jesus in 1882 and was ordained ten years later: he spent this decade in Britain, and remained interested in things English, writing lives of Thomas **More** and John Henry **Newman**. As a professor and editor of the Jesuit monthly *Etudes*, he conducted research and wrote on religious thought and the importance of the mystical tradition. He left the Jesuits in 1904, but remained a priest, taking charge of the funeral of George **Tyrrell** when the local bishop had refused him a Catholic burial. For this he was for some months suspended from the exercise of his priesthood. He was elected a member of the French Academy in 1923. His works include *Poésie et prière* (1925), *Dans les tempêtes* (1926), *Introduction à la philosophie de la prière* (1929), *Divertissements devant l'Arche* (1930) and *La poésie pure* (1933), though he is chiefly remembered for his eleven-volume – and still incomplete – *Histoire littéraire du sentiment religieux en France* (1916–33).

Brendan of Birr   Sixth-century Irish abbot. Little is known of Brendan's life except that he was associated with **Brendan of Clonfert**. He appears only as a figure in accounts of other saints but was referred to as 'the chief of the prophets of Ireland'. His primary monastery was located at Birr, County Offaly. Feast day 29 November.

Brendan of Clonfert   Saint and abbot, born, perhaps near Tralee, Ireland, *c.*486, died Clonfert, Ireland, *c.*578. Little is known about his life, though his father's name is given as Findlugh, and it is claimed he was for some years as a child in the charge of St **Ita**. He became a monk, and possibly the founder *c.*559 of the monastery at Clonfert, to which he gave a rule of life. There is a well-known story of his setting off with some 60 monks in coracles to find the 'Islands of the Blessed': these are usually discounted as legends, but he may well have travelled to Scotland. Feast day 16 May.

Brennan, Christopher John   Roman Catholic poet, born Sydney, Australia, 1 November 1870, died Sydney, 5 October 1932. Having matriculated at Sydney University, he won a scholarship to study in Berlin but returned without getting a degree, to work as a librarian and to teach in Sydney University, where he became professor of German and comparative literature. He was a good linguist, widely read in the literature of Greece, Rome, France, Germany and Italy, and influenced by the English Victorian poets. Some consider him Aus-

tralia's finest poet. His poems are published in the collection *Poems 1913*.

Brennan, Francis   Cardinal, dean of the Roman Rota, born Shenandoah, USA, 7 May 1895, died Philadelphia, USA, 2 July 1968. He was ordained in 1920 and later became professor of moral theology at St Charles Borromeo seminary. He was the first American to be assigned to the Roman Rota. In 1967 he was consecrated bishop and designated cardinal, and served as assistant on the Cardinals' Commission for the Prefecture of Economic Affairs of the Holy See. While in Rome he also served as prefect of the Congregation for the Discipline of the Sacraments, as president of the Vatican Court of Appeal, and on several Congregations.

Brent, Charles Henry   First Protestant Episcopal Church bishop of the Philippines, ecumenical leader, and opponent of the opium trade, born Newcastle, Ontario, Canada, 9 April 1862, died Lausanne, Switzerland, 27 March 1929. He studied at Trinity College, Toronto, was ordained priest in 1887 and served in Boston until 1901, when he was appointed bishop in the Philippines by the Episcopal Church in the USA. The Edinburgh Missionary Conference of 1910, which he attended, represented a call to Christian unity, for which he became a tireless worker. He became bishop of Western New York in 1917 and was president at the first Faith and Order conference in 1927. Known for his disciplined spirituality and informed social conscience, his published writings are largely devotional. From 1926 to 1928 he was in charge of Episcopal churches in Europe.

Brentano, Clemens Maria   Poet, born Thal-Ehrenbreitstein, Germany, 8 September 1778, died Aschaffenburg, Switzerland, 28 July 1842. He was educated at Jena and Heidelberg and married twice. He wrote *Das Knaben Wunderhorn* (3 vols) between 1805 and 1808 in collaboration with Achim von Arnim: this was a collection of folksongs which gave him prominence in the Romantic movement. He left his second wife, travelled through Europe and finally settled in Berlin in 1818. Here he returned to the Roman Catholic faith into which he had been baptized. In 1833 he went to Munich to work with Joseph **Görres** and his circle of Catholic scholars. He wrote *Romances of the Rosary* and recorded the stigmata of Anna Katharina **Emmerich**. His collected works were published posthumously between 1851 and 1855.

Brentano, Franz Sometime Roman Catholic priest, philosopher and psychologist, born Marienberg, 16 June 1838, died Zurich, Switzerland, 17 March 1917. Nephew of Clemens **Brentano**. He entered the Dominicans in his youth but left while a novice. He was ordained in 1864 and lectured at Würzburg University, where he became professor of philosophy until he resigned over the doctrine of infallibility and abandoned the priesthood. He was professor at Vienna University and then a lecturer until blindness forced him to retire. A precursor of the phenomenologist philosophers, his major works were *Psychologie des Aristoteles* (1867), *Psychologie von empirischen Standpunkt* (1874) and *Vom Ursprung sittlicher Erkenntnis* (1889).

Brenz, Johann Lutheran reformer, born Weil der Stadt, Germany, 1499, died Stuttgart, Germany, 11 September 1570. Brenz met **Luther** in Heidelberg in 1518 and became convinced by his ideas. He was evangelical minister at Schwäbisch-Hall for 24 years, writing a catechism and supporting Luther in the Sacramental Controversy with **Zwingli** and his followers. After 1534, he worked under the newly restored Duke Ulrich in Württemberg, establishing schools and orphanages, reforming Tübingen University, and even composing a 'Swabian Confession' for consideration at the Council of Trent, though it was completely rejected.

Bresee, Phineas Franklin Nazarene general superintendent, born Delaware County, New York, 31 December 1838, died Los Angeles, 13 November 1915. A Methodist pastor and presiding elder in Iowa and California, his passion to serve the urban poor and promote the Wesleyan–holiness revival led to an independent congregation in inner city Los Angeles in 1895. A regional denomination grew from this which merged with similar ones in the east and south in 1907–8, creating the Church of the Nazarene. Bresee was the first general superintendent elected by the united body. He edited *The Nazarene Messenger*, a weekly, and was founding president of Pasadena College (now Point Loma Nazarene University).

Bretagne, Marie de Reforming abbess, born 1424, died at the Fontevrault priory of Madeleine d'Orléans, 19 October 1477. She was the daughter of Richard, Comte d'Etampes, and Marguerite d'Orléans, and was the first of a series of Bourbon abbesses of the royal monastery of Fontevrault, 1457–77. Her extensive reforms – so opposed by some members of the community that she had for a time to take refuge in the priory of Madeleine d'Orléans – included the creation of a definitive rule for the community based on the Rules of SS **Benedict** and **Augustine**, supplemented by the original statutes of the Order, approved by Pope **Sixtus IV** in 1475.

Breton, Valentin Marie Franciscan priest and spiritual writer, born Besançon, France, 18 November 1877, died Paris, France, 6 July 1957. Having entered the Franciscan Order, he emigrated to Canada to escape the persecution of religious congregations and was ordained in Quebec in 1907. He later returned to France, where he served at the Franciscan church in Paris. His life was dedicated to preaching, writing and spiritual direction. His works include *The Community of Saints* (1934), *Franciscan Spirituality* (1957) and *Life Poverty* (1963).

Breuil, Henry Edouard Prosper Roman Catholic priest, prehistorian and pioneer of palaeolithic studies, born Mortain, France, 28 February 1877, died L'Isle-Adam, France, 14 August 1961. Ordained in 1900, he worked in prehistoric scholarship, laying the foundations of western European prehistory. He traced pictures from the walls of Spanish and French caves and produced volumes of illustrations. He held professorial appointments in Fribourg University, the Sorbonne, the Institut de France and the Collège de France. He received many academic honours and travelled widely, notably to study Bushman art in South Africa. He wrote 27 books, mainly illustrated, and 878 articles.

Brevicoxa (Jean Courtecuisse) Theologian, born Haleine, France, mid-1300s, died Geneva, Switzerland, 4 May 1423. Courtecuisse spent his academic career at Paris, beginning his studies there in 1367, teaching after 1389, and serving as dean of the Faculty of Theology from 1416 to 1421, when he was made bishop of Paris. Because of opposition from England, he was transferred to the episcopal see at Geneva a year later. His speaking ability and learning earned him the title *doctor sublimis*, and he played an important role in ending the Great Western Schism. A conciliar theologian, his *Tractatus de fide et ecclesia* teaches that the Pope must be subordinate to church councils.

Březina, Otokar Roman Catholic poet and essayist, born Počátky, Czech Republic, 13 September 1868, died Jaroměřice, Czech Republic, 26 March 1929. He worked as a schoolteacher in a number of small towns in Moravia, where he wrote poetry and prose. He was a literary perfectionist and consequently repolished his work for years before having it published. Deeply influenced by Christian tradition, his works view the physical universe through the discoveries of modern science. He published two main collections, *Tajemné dálky* (1895) and *Svitáni na Západě* (1896).

Brian Boru King of Ireland, born County Clare, Ireland, 941, died Clontarf, Ireland, 23 April 1014. Born in a little-known town, Brian, through his exceptional abilities as both soldier and statesman, was made king of Munster in 978 and high king of Ireland in 1002. He helped his claim to rule all of Ireland by supporting the claim of Armagh to to ecclesiastical power over the same territory. He promoted learning and the arts and fought to free his realm from the influence and forces of the Norse (and those Irish who allied with them), whom he died fighting at the battle of Clontarf on Good Friday 1014.

Briand, Jean Olivier Roman Catholic bishop, born Plérin, Brittany, France, 1715, died Quebec, Canada, 25 June 1794. Ordained in 1739, he worked under Bishop Pontbriand in Canada, becoming diocesan administrator after Pontbriand's death. He negotiated for leniency from the British after the 1759 siege of Quebec. In 1766 he was ordained bishop of Quebec. He continued to work for the rights of Roman Catholics, seeing through the Habeas Corpus Act and the Quebec Act, which granted religious freedom to Catholics, and a

rewriting of the Test Act in compliance with papal approval. His passionate sermons ensured that Canada remained loyal to Britain when the Americans attacked.

Briant, Alexander Martyr, born Somerset, England, 1556, died Tyburn, England, 1 December 1581. He was educated at Oxford and converted to the Roman Catholic faith. He went to Douai to study for ordination. In 1579 he was sent back to England. Two years later he was captured in London and taken to the Tower, where he was tortured to compel him to reveal the hiding place of Father Persons. Whilst imprisoned he became a Jesuit. He was hanged, drawn and quartered along with Edmund **Campion** and Ralph Sherwin. In 1886 he was beatified. Feast day 1 December.

Brice Saint and bishop, died 444. He studied in Marmoutier under St **Martin of Tours**. He was ordained but was an ambitious priest, envious of his tutor. In 397, after Martin's death, he was consecrated bishop of Tours and ministered with little care for those in his see. In 430 he was evicted from his diocese and spent seven years in exile in Rome, during which time his character was reformed. When he returned to Tours *c*.437 his ministry had been so transformed that he was proclaimed a saint on his death. Feast day 13 November.

Briceno, Alonso Franciscan philosopher and theologian, born Santiago, Chile, 1587, died Trujillo, Venezuela, 15 November 1668. In 1605 he entered the Franciscans, and quickly gained a reputation as a teacher. Greatly interested in **Duns Scotus**, he published works on him which reveal his clarity of mind and brilliance as a scholar. After holding a number of important ecclesiastical offices in Chile, Briceno was appointed bishop of Nicaragua in 1646. In 1649 he was transferred to Caracas.

Briçonnet, Guillaume Cardinal, born Tours, France, 1445, died Narbonne, France, 14 December 1514. Of noble birth, he served the French Crown in financial administration. After the death of his wife he was ordained and made bishop of St Malo. He continued his involvement in politics, accompanying the French army into Italy to support Ludovico Sforza's claim to Naples. He received his cardinalate in 1495 as a reward for taking French forces out of Italy and restoring relations between King **Charles VIII** and Pope **Alexander VI**. He also gathered the sees of Toulon and Rheims in 1497 and Nîmes in 1507. He crowned **Louis XII** in 1498, supported his policy of limiting papal power, and was responsible for the anti-papal council at Pisa for which he was excommunicated. Louis rewarded him with St Germain-des-Prés Abbey and the governorship of Languedoc. His cardinalate was restored by **Leo X** and he was made archbishop of Narbonne.

Briçonnet, Guillaume   Bishop, born Tours, France, 1472, died Montereau, France, 24 January 1534. Son of Cardinal Guillaume **Briçonnet**, he rose rapidly to become bishop of Lodève, chaplain to the queen and abbot of St Germain-des-Prés. He served the French King **Louis XII** as ambassador in Rome to Pope **Leo X**. Taking his ecclesiastical duties seriously, he improved the monastery at St Germain, encouraged discipline and study for his clergy, and dealt severely with abuses and immorality. He held several synods at Meaux to organize and enforce his reforms. A patron of letters, he also enlarged the monastery's library.

Briçonnet, Robert   Bishop, born France, died Moulins, France, 26 June 1497. He was the son of Jean Briçonnet, Lord of Varennes, and brother to Cardinal Guillaume **Briçonnet**. After ordination he became canon at Orléans and then abbot of Vaast at Arras through Guillaume's influence. In 1493 he was consecrated archbishop of Rheims. He was appointed chancellor and given responsibility over the royal finances by King **Charles VIII**.

Bridel, Bedřich   Czech Jesuit poet, born Vysoké Mýto, 1619, died Kutná Hora, Bohemia, 15 October 1680. Bridel's poetry remained largely unknown until rediscovered by Professor Vašica of Charles University in the 1920s. Several volumes have been published and are recognized as a significant component of Czech literary history. His work is characterized by vivid imagery and the use of grammatical structure and sounds to emphasize the dramatic. Bridel's influence can be seen in the work of **Macha** as well as several modern Czech authors. His works include *Co Bůh? co člověk?*

(1658), *Jesličky* ('The Manager'; a collection of hymns and prayers) and several legends, including the life of St Ivan.

Bridge, Sir Frederick   Musician, born Oldbury, Worcestershire, 5 December 1844, died London, 18 March 1924. He was an organist at various churches, being appointed to Manchester cathedral in 1869, and then assistant organist at Westminster Abbey in 1875 and permanent organist in 1882, taking charge of the music at many national events. When the Royal College of Music opened in 1883 he was appointed a professor, and in 1890 he was elected professor of music at Gresham College. He composed much church music and carols, and assisted in the editing of the *Westminster Abbey Hymnbook* and the *Wesleyan Hymnbook*.

Bridges, Robert   Poet and hymnologist, born Walmer, Kent, 23 October 1844, died Boars Hill, Oxford, 21 April 1930. He was educated at Eton and Oxford, studied medicine at St Bartholomew's Hospital, London, and practised as a doctor. He lived at Yattendon, Berkshire, and compiled *The Yattendon Hymnal*. He was made Poet Laureate. One of his well-known hymn translations and paraphrases is of a Neander hymn as 'All My Hope on God Is Founded', sung to the tunes 'Meine Hoffnung' and more popularly 'Michael', by Herbert **Howells**. But for Bridges' publishing the poems of the Jesuit Gerard Manley **Hopkins** long after his death, Hopkins might have been a poet virtually unknown to us.

Bridget   *see* **Brigid**

Bridget of Sweden   Saint, patron of Sweden and religious founder, born Upland, Sweden, June 1302/3, died Rome, Italy, 23 July 1373. A daughter of the governor of Upland, Bridget was the mother of eight children, including St **Catherine of Sweden**. Upon the death of her husband in 1344, she retired to a Cistercian monastery, where she experienced visions leading her to establish a contemplative order at Vadstena in 1346. In 1349, she moved to Rome to secure confirmation of her Order. She is known for her charitable works, urging church reform, and pleading for the restoration of the Papacy to Rome from Avignon. Her Order was confirmed by the Pope in 1370, and she was canonized in 1391. Her writings and the records of her visions have been the topic of much theological discussion and critique. Feast day 23 July.

Bridgett, Thomas Edward Roman Catholic convert and priest, author, born Derby, England, 20 January 1829, died London, England, 17 February 1899. He left Cambridge University without graduating to avoid taking the oath recognizing royal supremacy over the Church of England, and became a Roman Catholic. After studying in Holland, he was ordained in 1856 and worked thereafter in England and Ireland as a missioner. His works include *Our Lady's Dowry* (1875), *The History of the Holy Eucharist in Great Britain* (1881), *The Life of the Blessed John Fisher* (1888), *Blunders and Forgeries* (1890) and *The Life of the Blessed Thomas More* (1891).

Bridgewater, John Roman Catholic theologian, born Yorkshire, England, 1532(?), died probably Trèves, France, 1596(?). After studies at Oxford and Cambridge, Bridgewater served a series of minor ecclesiastical posts, mostly in south-west England, before being elected rector of Lincoln College in Oxford in 1563. In 1574, he resigned all his ecclesiastical posts and benefices to go abroad, and probably never returned to England. He may have been a Jesuit, and he wrote two polemical works of theology while in France, both of which were directed against Protestant attacks and doctrines.

Brieuc or **Briocus** Saint and abbot, born possibly Cardiganshire, Wales, died Saint-Brieuc, Brittany, sometime in the fifth or perhaps sixth century. He is said to have been miraculously converted from paganism, educated in France but, after his return to England, summoned back to France by a dream. He founded a monastery near Tréguier on the Brittany coast, and a second one at Saint-Brieuc. He is said to have lived almost 100 years. Feast day 1 May.

Briggs, Charles Augustus Presbyterian biblical scholar, born New York, USA, 15 January 1841, died New York, 8 June 1913. He served as a pastor in New Jersey before becoming professor of Hebrew at Union Theological Seminary and edit-ing the *Presbyterian Review*. His inaugural address as professor of biblical theology at Union led to his trial for heresy and suspension from the ministry in 1893. In 1899 he was ordained priest of the Protestant Episcopal Church and later became professor of symbolics and irenics at Union. He worked for the reunion of Catholics and Protestants. His principal work was *Commentary on the Book of Psalms* (1906).

Bright, John Member of Parliament, Quaker statesman and reformer, born Rochdale, Lancashire, 16 November 1811, died One Ash, 27 March 1889; buried in the Quaker burial ground in Rochdale. He achieved fame alongside Richard Cobden as leader of the Anti-Corn-Law movement and later as a campaigner for parliamentary reform. Opposing all monopolies and protectionism, including the Anglican Establishment, he entered public life in opposition to church rates. In all his much-respected public life Bright was motivated by his Bible-based Quaker faith. An MP from 1843, he became member for Manchester in 1847 and for Birmingham ten years later, representing the city for more than 30 years, becoming president of the Board of Trade in 1868. He opposed the hysteria over Papal Aggression, spoke against Jewish disabilities, and was a consistent spokesman on behalf of peace issues.

Brightman, Edward Sheffield Methodist minister, philosopher, born Holbrook, USA, 20 September 1884, died Newton, USA, 25 February 1953. He studied at the Universities of Boston, Berlin and Marburg, and taught at several American universities before joining Boston University from 1919 to 1953. He was an inspirational teacher and the leading American exponent of the philosophy of personalism. His books include *Introduction to Philosophy* (1925), *The Problem of God* (1930), *The Finding of God* (1931), *Moral Laws* (1933), *A Philosophy of Religion* (1940) and *Person and Reality: An Introduction to Metaphysics* (1958), and he wrote many articles.

Brigid Saint, abbess, born Offaly, Ireland, c.460, died Kildare, c.528. After making her religious profession, Brigid founded a church on the Liffey plain called Cill Dara (Kildare) or 'the church of the oak'. Nearby lived a hermit named Conleth who ruled a community of men as bishop and abbott. Conleth's monks shared a church with Brigid's nuns, thus forming the only double monastery to have developed in Ireland. In addition to ruling her community, Brigid was remembered for her acts of charity. She was known as the 'Mary of Gael' and devotion to her spread with the work of the Irish missionaries and pilgrims to the Continent. Brigid is recognized as one of the three patron saints of Ireland. Her life story is told in a seventh-century work. Feast day 1 February.

Brihtwald   *see* **Brithwald**

Brinkley, Stephen   Printer, Roman Catholic, born England, died Rouen, *c.*1590. During the persecution of Roman Catholics in England under Queen **Elizabeth I** Brinkley aided clergy and Catholics who were at risk of arrest. He was part of George Gilbert's group which raised money for the cause, and with seven others he ran the printing press which had been established by Robert Persons. They published many tracts by Edmund **Campion** and others. Brinkley was captured in 1581 and tortured in the Tower of London. Although his assistant William Catter was executed, Brinkley was released in 1583. He went first to Rome and then to Rouen, where he took over the printing of Catholic books from George Flinton in 1585.

Brisacier, Jacques Charles de   Director of the seminary of the Paris Foreign Missionary Society, born Blois, France, 18 October 1642, died Paris, 23 March 1736. After a time as commendatory abbot of Saint-Pierre de Neuvillers and chaplain to Queen Marie Thérèse, he entered the seminary of the Paris Foreign Missionary Society around 1670. From 1681 to 1736 he was superior of the society. During his tenure some 49 missionaries were sent to the Far East. Many new buildings were erected, including the church of the society and the seminary buildings. A man of deep spirituality and piety, he was greatly admired by his contemporaries.

Brisson, Louis Alexandre   Roman Catholic priest and founder of religious Orders, born Nancy, France, 23 June 1817, died Nancy, 2 February 1908. He was ordained in 1840. While serving as chaplain in Troyes, his superior encouraged him to found the Oblate Sisters of St Francis de Sales and the Oblates of St Francis de Sales. He worked for the spread of faith in mission territories.

Bristow, Richard   Roman Catholic theologian, born Worcester, England, 1538, died Harrow, 21 October 1581. Educated at Christ Church College, Oxford, Bristow was honoured as a student by being chosen with Edmund **Campion** to debate before Queen **Elizabeth** during her visit to the university in 1566. During a debate with Lawrence Humphrey, his Roman Catholicism became evident, and he thought it politic to leave the country. He went first to Louvain, then in 1573 became the first student of the English College of Douai to be ordained. At Douai he served as prefect of studies, pro-rector and teacher of biblical studies. With William **Allen**, he revised and corrected Gregory **Martin**'s translation of the NT in 1581. Amongst his published works are *A briefe treatise ... conteyning sundry worthy motiues unto the Catholic faith* (1574), *Demaundes to bee proposed of Catholickes to the heretickes* (1576) and *A reply to William Fulke in Defence of M. D. Allen's Scrole of Articles and Book of Purgatorie* (1580).

Brithwald   Archbishop of Canterbury, born *c.*650, died Canterbury, 19 January 731. Sometime about 670 the palace of the kings of Kent at Reculver was converted into a monastery, of which Brithwald was made abbot. He was elected eighth archbishop of Canterbury on 1 July 692, two years after the death of his predecessor, **Theodore**, and was consecrated in Lyons a year later. It was a difficult period in the history of the English church, particularly because of conflicts with **Wilfrid**, but he handled the situation well.

Brithwald of Wilton   Saint, abbot and bishop, birth place and date unknown, died probably Glastonbury, England, 22 April 1045. Brithwald was a monk at the abbey of Glastonbury before being made abbot of the same and bishop of Wiltshire (Ramsbury) in 995. Even though his episcopate lasted 50 years, there is no record of his life or activity. He was remembered as a benefactor of Glastonbury, where his tomb lies, and for a vision in which he foresaw the succession of **Edward the Confessor** to the English throne. Feast day 22 January.

Britten, Benjamin   The most highly esteemed British composer of his time, born Lowestoft, 22 November 1913, died Aldeburgh, 4 December 1976. He studied under Frank Bridge and at the Royal College of Music. Britten was known for his originality, imagination and gift for setting words. His *Mass for Westminster Cathedral* was a totally new concept. Opinions vary about his *War Requiem*, which combined the text of the Roman Catholic Mass with that of the poetry of the war-poet Wilfrid Owen. His many choral works also include a *Hymn to St Cecilia*, *A Ceremony of Carols*, *Rejoice in the Lamb* and *Cantata Misericordium*.

Broadway, Lucy   Born Melrose, Roxburghshire, Scotland, 9 August 1858, died Canterbury, 22 August 1929. She industriously collected folk songs and folk carols, some of which were later published in hymn-books.

Broederlam, Melchior   Painter, flourished in Flanders (Belgium) 1381–1409. The first record of Broederlam is as court painter to the count of Flanders and then to the duke of Burgundy, Philip the Bold, whom he also served as a personal assistant. His main work seems to have been with the decorative arts, painting furniture, banners, tournament harnesses and such. His only confirmed surviving work is a pair of wings that decorate the altarpiece from Chartreuse de Champol (Dijon, France), which are very skilfully done and evince an important step in the history of such arts in Flanders.

Broglie, Albert de   Roman Catholic statesman, publicist and historian, born Paris, France, 13 June 1821, died Paris, 19 January 1901. He edited *Le Correspondant* in the 1850s and was a frequent contributor to this and other periodicals defending Catholic interests and moderate liberalism. While on the National Assembly and later the Senate, he served as ambassador to London, as president of the Council of Ministers, as foreign minister, as minister of the interior and as premier. His most noteworthy publication, *L'Eglise et l'empire romain au IV siècle*, gained him a seat in the French Academy in 1862.

Brogue, Maurice Jean de   Roman Catholic bishop, born Paris, 5 September 1766, died Paris, 20 June 1821. He was educated at St Sulpice, Paris, and, after fleeing France during the Reign of Terror, was made canon at Posen. In 1803 he went back to France and became almoner to Napoleon. In 1805 he was consecrated bishop of Acqui, Italy, and in 1807 of Ghent, Belgium. He became disenchanted with the emperor and was imprisoned for four months in 1811 for voting against Napoleon's demand that the Pope accept his church appointments. In Ghent he fought to regain the rights of Catholics which had been rescinded in 1815 by William of Nassau, but was deported.

Brollo, Basilio   Franciscan vicar apostolic to China, born Gemona, Italy, 25 March 1648, died San-yuan, China, 16 July 1704. He became a friar in 1666, and was ordained priest in 1674. He arrived in China in 1684, and took the name Yeh Tsun-hsiao. Between the years 1685 and 1700 he acted as pro-vicar to Bishop Bernardino **Della Chiesa**. In spite of illness he visited many of the missions, taking up residence at Nan-ching (Nanjing) in 1692. He was named vicar apostolic of Shan-hsi, arriving there in May 1701. In 1703 he moved to San-yuan to set up his headquarters there, but fell ill and died there.

Bromyard, John of   Dominican preacher, born probably Herefordshire, England, date unknown, died probably Hereford, England, 1352(?). A student of Oxford, Bromyard served the Diocese of Hereford as a preacher and confessor from 1326 to 1352. He is best known for his *Summa praedicantium*, a handbook for preachers with moral teaching and illustrative material arranged in alphabetical order. The book was very popular in the late Middle Ages, going through several printings and circulating throughout Europe.

Brondel, John Baptist   Roman Catholic bishop, born Bruges, Belgium, 23 February 1842, died Helena, USA, 3 November 1904. Two years after his ordination at Mechlin in 1864, he emigrated to America, where he worked as a pastor in Washington territory. He was consecrated bishop of Vancouver Island in 1879. He was named administrator of the vicariate apostolic of Montana, and when the Diocese of Helena was created in 1884, became its first bishop. Here he promoted the building of schools, hospitals and churches, and founded a mission among the Cheyenne Indians.

Bronisława Blessed, Premonstratensian nun, born Kamien, Silesia, Poland, 1203, died near Cracow, Poland, 29 August 1259. Of a noble birth and related to both St **Hyacinth** and Blessed **Ceslaus of Silesia**, Bronisława entered the Premonstratensian convent near Cracow at the age of sixteen. She was reportedly a model of mortification, virtue and the contemplative life. She had a vision in which she saw St **Hyacinth** being carried to heaven by Mary, after which she devoted almost all her time to contemplative prayer. The city of Cracow considers her their patron, and Pope **Gregory XVI** confirmed her cult in 1839. Feast day 1 September.

Brontë, Charlotte Novelist, born Thornton, Yorkshire, 21 April 1816, died during pregnancy, 31 March 1855. She lived most of her life in Haworth, Yorkshire, except when working as a teacher, which took her as far as Brussels, or visiting literary circles in London once her fame was established. The publication of *Jane Eyre* in 1847 brought her success and was followed by *Shirley* (1849) and *Villette* (1852). Her main characters are independent women who struggle with the role society expects of them, as typified by Jane Eyre's decision not to marry St John Rivers and accompany him to the mission field.

Brontë, Emily Jane Novelist, born Thornton, Yorkshire, 30 July 1818, the fourth of five sisters who included the novelists Charlotte Brontë and Anne, died Haworth, Yorkshire, 19 December 1848. With her sisters she was mainly educated at home in her father's parsonage at Haworth. The writing of imaginative prose and poetry in childhood was preparation for her only published novel *Wuthering Heights* (1847). With its desire for freedom and a spiritual union with nature, *Wuthering Heights* pulsates with intensity and passion and is recognized as one of the great English novels.

Bronzino, Angelo Roman Catholic painter and poet, born Monticelli, Italy, 1503, died Florence, Italy, 1572. Bronzino studied under Raffaelino del Garbo and Jacopo da Pontormo and aided them in their decorative work for the Medici family. On his own, he painted a number of religious and allegorical works, which are usually categorized as Mannerist but some of which show the subtle influence of **Michelangelo.** His work is known for its clarity, attention to the human figure, and for cold, pallid colours.

Brooks, James Bishop, born Hampshire, England, May 1512, died in prison in Gloucester, 20 March 1560. He was educated at Oxford and became master of Balliol College from 1547. He was renowned as an accomplished preacher. In 1554 during the reign of the Roman Catholic Queen **Mary** he was consecrated bishop of Gloucester. He was the papal sub-delegate on the royal commission trial of the Reformers Thomas **Cranmer**, Hugh **Latimer** and Nicholas **Ridley**, refusing on legal grounds to degrade the latter two. He was imprisoned when **Elizabeth I** succeeded to the throne in 1558, and died there two years later.

Brooks, Phillips American episcopal minister, preacher and bishop, born Boston, Massachusetts, 13 December 1835, died Boston, 23 January 1893. A graduate of Harvard, he was ordained into the Protestant Episcopal Church in 1859. From 1862 to 1869 he served as rector of Holy Trinity, Philadelphia, and as rector of Holy Trinity, Boston, from 1869 to 1891, when he became bishop of Massachusetts. Author of the Christmas carol 'O Little Town of Bethlehem', he moved his congregations on from the last remaining vestiges of an inherited Calvinism and commended the liberal theology of F. D. **Maurice** and F. W. Robertson in England to an American public through his warm personality and oratorical skills. His influential *Lectures on Preaching* were delivered at Yale in 1877. He championed a positive and optimistic American search for self-fulfilment. Emphasizing goodness rather than sin, he advised 'Believe in yourself and reverence your own human nature; it is the only salvation from brutal vice and every false belief', an absolute contradiction of all that Calvinism stood for.

Brosig, Moritz Roman Catholic composer and teacher, born Fuchswinkel, Silesia, 15 October 1815, died Breslau, Silesia (now in Poland), 24 January 1887. He became music director of Breslau Cathedral in 1853 and was later appointed to the faculty of Breslau University. He was prominent in a group of musicians who reacted against the restrictive Caecilian principles concerning church music, and attempted a reconciliation of concerted music and Caecilian principles. His theoretical works include *Modulations Theorie* (1866), *Handbuch der Harmonie Lehr und Modulation* (1874), *Über die alten Kompositionen und ihre Wiedereinführung* (1880). His musical works include seven Masses and twenty volumes of organ pieces.

Brou, Alexandre Jesuit spiritual writer and historian, born Chartres, France, 26 April 1862, died Laval, France, 12 March 1947. He entered the Society of Jesus in 1880 and studied mainly in England. He taught literature at Canterbury, the island of Jersey and Laval, and wrote extensively on Jesuit spirituality. His publications include *S. François Xavier* (1914), *St François Xavier: conditions et méthodes de son apostolat* (1925), *Les Jésuites de la légende* (1906), *Les Exercices Spirituels de St Ignace, histoire et psychologie* (1922), *La spiritualité de St Ignace* (1914) and *St Ignace, maître d'oraison* (1925).

Broun, Matthew Heywood Campbell Journalist and author, born Brooklyn, New York, 7 December 1888, died New York City, 19 December 1939. Educated at Harvard, he worked on the *Morning Telegraph* from 1910 and the *Tribune* from 1912. He was a war correspondent in France during the First World War. He became a columnist for the New York *World* in 1921 and for the *Telegram* in 1928. He was unsuccessful in his attempt to join Congress as a Socialist in 1930. In 1933 he established the American Newspaper Guild. He wrote many books including *Things at Night* (1922), *Sitting on the World* (1924), *Gandle Follow His Nose* (1926), *Christians Only* (1931) and the autobiographical *The Boy Grows Older* (1922). He also edited the *Connecticut Nutmeg*, lectured and painted. In the year of his death he became a Roman Catholic.

Brouns, Thomas English bishop, jurist and administrator, born *c.*1381, died Hoxne, Suffolk, 6 December 1445. Educated at Oxford, his ecclesiastical life began as sub-dean at Lincoln Cathedral in 1414. He also became canon at Lincoln, prebendary at Welton Westhall and archdeacon of Stow,

1419. He moved to Canterbury, 1425–9, serving as auditor of causes and chancellor. He started diplomatic work for Henry V and **Henry VI** from 1420 until 1434. He was made bishop of Rochester in 1435 and Norwich in 1436. His tenure at Norwich was mixed, the citizens attacking the palace and priory, yet he interceded on the city's behalf with **Henry VI** and left provision in his will for the education of six boys at Oxford.

Brouwer, Christoph Dutch historian, born Arnhem, 10 November 1559, died Trier, Germany, 2 June 1617. He entered the Society of Jesus on 12 March 1580, was ordained and made rector of the college at Fulda and then at Trier. His historical work centred on the Archdiocese of Trier and resulted in 26 volumes. He was objective and detailed, and did not edit the works of unflattering revelations. This aroused hostility, and publication was prevented by the curial advisors of the archbishop. The Jesuits eventually printed the works in France. They include *Antiquitates et Annales Trevirenses et Episcoporum Trevirensis Ecclesiae Suffraganorum* (1670), *Venantii Honorii Clementiarii opera* (1603), *Hrabanus Maurus poemata* (1617), *Sidera illustrium et sanctorum vivorum* (1616) and *Antiquitatum Fuldensium libri 4* (1612).

Browe, Peter Austrian theologian and historian, born Salzburg, 22 December 1876, died Baden-Baden, 18 May 1949. He entered the Jesuits in 1895 and specialized in research in medieval moral and pastoral theology, which he taught at Maastricht, Valkenburg, Frankfurt and Immersee. He was also interested in medieval religious folklore. He wrote extensively on the historical development of Eucharistic devotion: *De Frequenti Communione in Ecclesia Occidentali* (1923), *De Ordaliis* (1932–3), *Die Verehrung der Eucharistie im Mittelalter* (1933), *Die Häufige Kommunion im Mittelalter* (1938), *Die eucharistischen Wunder des Mittelalters* (1938) and *Die Pflichtkommunion in Mittelalter* (1940).

Brown, Leo Cyril Jesuit economist, mediator, academic, born Stanberry, USA, 28 April 1900, died St Louis, USA, 3 May 1978. Having entered the Society of Jesus, he taught at St Louis University where, after ordination in 1934, he became director of the Institute of Social Science, president of the Catholic Economic Institute, director of the Institute of Social Order, regent of the School of Law, and professor of economics. He gained national renown as arbiter in labour disputes, serving as president of the National Academy of Arbiters and chairman of the Atomic Energy Labour Management Panel. His national and international arbitration work led to his being awarded the first special mediator award by the Federal Mediation and Conciliation Service. His many books include *Impact of New Labor Law on Union–Management Relations* (1948), *The Shifting Distribution of the Rights to Manage* (1950) and *Tripartite Wage Determination in Puerto Rico* (1966).

Brown, Raymond E.   Sulpician priest and biblical scholar, born New York City, 22 May 1928, died St Patrick's Seminary, Menlo Park, California, 8 August 1998. Brown began his priestly career by entering St Mary's Seminary, Baltimore, and went on to study at Catholic University, Washington, DC. He was ordained priest for the diocese of St Augustine, Florida, in 1955. He studied for a doctorate in theology at St Mary's, where he also taught, and for one in Semitic languages at Johns Hopkins University. From 1971 to 1990 he taught at Union Theological Seminary, New York. He published a great many books and articles, but is best known for *The Gospel According to John* (2 vols, 1966, revised edition 1970), *The Epistles of St John* (1982), *The Birth of the Messiah* (1977, revised edition 1993), *The Death of the Messiah* (1994) and *An Introduction to the New Testament* (1997). He also was one of the editors of the highly successful *Jerome* (later *New Jerome*) *Bible Commentary* (1968, 1990).

Brown, William Adams   Presbyterian theologian, born New York, 29 December 1865, died New York, 15 December 1943. He studied at Yale, Union Theological Seminary, New York, and in Berlin, and was ordained in 1893. He was interested in the ecumenical movement and in Christian social work. He was Roosevelt Professor of systematic theology from 1898 to 1930 at the Union Theological Seminary, New York. His main writings are *The Essence of Christianity* (1902), *Christian Theology in Outline* (1906), *Modern Theology and Preaching of the Gospel* (1914), *The*

Church in America (1922), *Imperialistic Religion and the Religion of Democracy* (1923).

Browne, Michael   Dominican cardinal, born Grangemockler, Ireland, 6 May 1887, died Rome, Italy, 31 March 1971. He was ordained in 1910. While professor of philosophy at Rome's Angelicum University, he served as rector magnificus at the Pontifical University of St Thomas and master of the Sacred Apostolic Palace. He was elected master general of the Dominicans in 1955 and made cardinal in 1962. During Vatican II, he served as vice-president of the Doctrinal Commission and of the commission for the revision of the schemas on the Sources of Divine Revelation. He participated in the commission for the revision of the Code of Canon Law.

Browne, Robert   Puritan, born Tolethorpe, Rutland, England, *c.*1550, died Northampton, 1633. While studying at Corpus Christi College, Cambridge, he felt the call to establish independent congregations at Norwich and elsewhere along Presbyterian lines. For this he went to prison. His relative William Cecil, Lord Burleigh, freed him and he went to Holland with his supporters. After an unsuccessful period in Scotland, he returned to the Church of England. His changed views are contained in *A Reproof of Certain Schismatic Persons* (1588). In 1591 he became rector of Achurch, which post he held until his death in Northampton gaol, on a charge of assaulting a policeman.

Browning, Robert   English poet, born Camberwell, London, 7 May 1812, died Venice, 12 December 1889. The son of a banker and largely self-taught (though he spent one year at the newly opened London University in 1828), Browning, after an initial interest in atheism, came to be a fully committed Christian. His poetry expresses his own philosophical and theological difficulties and does not offer solutions to others. His works encounter both his Low Church Protestant background and his growing understanding and acceptance of Catholicism. His extreme individualism rules out the place of a church and the meaning of the sacraments, yet the doctrines of atonement and original sin are apparently accepted. His works are numerous and include *Pauline* (1833), *Paracelsus* (1835), *Sordello* (1840), *Christmas Eve* (1850), *Men* *and Women* (1855) and *Easter Day* (1880). He married Elizabeth Barratt, also a poet.

Brownson, Josephine van Dyke American teacher and author, born Detroit, 26 January 1880, died Grosse Pointe, Michigan, 10 November 1942. Educated by the Religious of the Sacred Heart, she herself started working life as a teacher. In 1930 she resigned and concentrated on the Catholic Instruction League which she had started to benefit children in public schools. Her method of religious teaching, which became standard for catechists, is laid out in *Stopping the Leak* (1926), *Catholic Bible Stories* (1919) and *Living Forever* (1928). She was given the Laetare medal of the University of Notre Dame, and the papal decoration Pro Ecclesia et Pontifice.

Brownson, Orestes Augustus American preacher, journalist, editor and philosopher, born Stockbridge, Vermont, 16 September 1803, died Detroit, Michigan, 17 April 1876. He grew up on a farm with little formal education but a great appetite for reading, which in practice was limited for the most part to religious books. He first joined the Presbyterians in 1822, but four years later was ordained a Universalist minister. His liberal views led him away from this church into being a freelance preacher. It was at this period that he wrote *New View of Christianity, Society and the Church* and *The Labouring Classes*. He was always interested in social issues. and helped to found the Workingmen's Party, but was not convinced of the value of political action. He then became a Unitarian minister and set up his own church in a working-class area of Boston. He worked on several journals, including the *Boston Quarterly Review*, which he founded in 1838 and refounded in 1844 as *Brownson's Quarterly Review*, the same year that he, much to everyone's surprise because he had attacked Roman Catholicism, became a Catholic. His editorship led to his being perhaps the most influential Catholic layman in nineteenth-century America. He developed an interest in Continental Catholicism, and in social and political views being expressed particularly in France. They found expression in *Lacordaire and Catholic Progress* (1862) and *Civil and Religious Freedom* (1864). These books expressed views of the kind condemned by the Syllabus of Errors of 1864, which

he accepted, and spent the rest of his life repenting his past liberalism.

Bruce, Frank M. American Catholic publisher, born Milwaukee, Wisconsin, 1886, and died there 1953. He joined his father William George **Bruce** and brother William C. in the family firm in 1906 and with his brother made it a major American Catholic publishing house. He was a founder and first president of Serra International and president of the National Association of Publishers and Church Goods Dealers.

Bruce, Frederick Fyvie Biblical scholar, born Elgin, Scotland, 12 October 1910, his father an evangelist for the Christian Brethren, died Buxton, England, 11 September 1990. Bruce was a brilliant classicist who became gradually drawn to biblical studies as a result of his personal evangelical faith. He lectured in biblical studies at Sheffield University from 1947 until 1959, when he was appointed Rylands Professor of biblical criticism and exegesis at Manchester University, a post he held until his retirement in 1978. Bruce was equally at home in both the OT and NT, and his many publications gained him a worldwide reputation for meticulous scholarship. Less radical in his conclusions than the liberal scholars who at that time formed the majority of academic theologians, Bruce did much to restore the intellectual respectability of a more confident attitude towards biblical literature.

Bruce, William George American publisher, born in Milwaukee, Wisconsin, 17 March 1856, died Milwaukee, 13 August 1949. He received little education and started working life as a cigar maker. He later worked on newspapers and founded the *American School Board Journal* (1891) and *Industrial Arts and Vocational Education* (1914). His business, which became known as The Bruce Publishing Co. was taken over by his two sons William C. and Frank M. **Bruce**. Bruce himself spent the rest of his life in civic work. He was given the Vercelli and Laetare medals and named a Knight of St Gregory as an outstanding Catholic layman.

Bruchési, Louis Joseph Paul Napoléon Canadian archbishop, born Montreal, Quebec, 29 October 1855, died Montreal, 20 September 1939. Following education in Montreal, France and Italy, he gained a doctorate in theology. He was ordained on 21 December 1878 at St John Lateran alongside a fellow student who was to become **Benedict XV.** He was a well known theologian and orator, and taught dogma at the Grand Seminary of Quebec. After a period as secretary to the archbishop, he succeeded to the post in 1897.

Brück, Heinrich   German ecclesiastical historian, born Bingen, 25 October 1831, died Mainz, 5 November 1903. He studied for the priesthood in Mainz and was ordained there in 1855, taught church history at Mainz, becoming professor in 1862. He became bishop of Mainz in 1899. He is known for his methodical work in the study of the eighteenth and nineteenth centuries, which he was one of the first Catholic historians to undertake. His work can appear defensive, as it was written during the Kulturkampf. His main works are *Die rationalistischen Bestrebungen in katholischen Deutschland* (1865), *Geschichte der katholischen Kirche in Deutschland im 19. Jh.* (5 vols, 1887–1905), *Die Kulturkampf Bewegung im Deutschland 1807–1900* (2 vols, 1901–5) and *Lehrbuch der Kirchengeschichte* (1874).

Bruckner, Anton   Austrian composer and organist, born Ansfelden, 4 September 1824, died Vienna, 11 October 1896. He was inspired by Wagner. He went to the choir school at St Florian, was organist of Linz cathedral and moved to Vienna. He was a deeply devout Roman Catholic. His greatest contributions to music are his nine magnificent large-scale symphonies often having mystical and religious qualities, three Masses and a Te Deum. He also wrote small-scale sacred pieces but surprisingly little music for organ.

Brueghel, Pieter (the Elder)   Flemish painter, born probably Antwerp, c.1525–30, died Brussels, 9 September 1569. Pieter is the most famous of a family of Flemish painters. He was thought to have been of peasant stock but is now more usually believed to have been an educated townsman. His work is satirical and treats of religious and political subjects. His style is said to be influenced by the Dutch painters Bosch and Patinir. Many paintings can be interpreted as being a comment on the pretensions of the rich and famous and the hypoc-

risy and indifference shown to Christ by his contemporaries. His best-known works are *Tower of Babel* (1563), *Christ Carrying the Cross* (1564), the five 'calendar' landscapes (1565), *The Census Taking at Bethlehem* (1566), and *The Adoration of the Magi in the Snow* (1567).

Brumel, Antoine   Renaissance composer of sacred music, born in Flanders or France, c.1460, died c.1525. He was employed as a musician at Chartres in 1483 and Notre-Dame in Paris in 1498 and eventually became maestro for Duke Alfonse I of Ferrara. His main compositions are *Missa Et Ecce Terrae Motus*, *Missa de Beata Virgine*, *Mater Patris* and *Laudate Dominum*. The latter is one of the earliest Psalm texts in a motet setting.

Bruneau, Joseph   French Sulpician educator, born Sainte-Gaumier, 18 April 1866, died Evian-les-Bains, ?26 August 1933. After a Catholic education in various seminaries and the Institut Catholique, he was ordained on 15 July 1889. Five years later he was sent to the USA, where he taught in seminaries, specializing in philosophy, dogmatic theology and Scripture. He was director of the choir at Baltimore and actively supported the Maryknoll Missionaries. His main writings are *Harmony of the Gospels* (1898), *Our Priesthood* (1911) and *Our Priestly Life* (1928); he also translated a number of English and American devotional works into French.

Brunelleschi, Filippo   Italian architect, born Florence, 1377, died Florence, 15 April 1446. His early working life was as a sculptor and silversmith. His training in mathematics led to his discovery of the laws of linear perspective which was so influential for the development of renaissance art. These laws are seen to perfection in the cupola of S. Maria del Fiore (1421–36), which he built without any scaffolding. His interest was in the use of space and the pictorial properties of the surfaces of walls, leading viewers to feel themselves in control of the space in which they are immersed. Other important buildings are the Loggia of the Foundling Hospital, the Old Sacristy, and the Pozzi Chapel.

Bruni, Leonardo Aretino   Italian humanist and historian, born Arezzo, c.1369, died Florence, 9 March 1444. He was secretary to **Innocent VII** but found the ecclesiastical arguments around the Western Schism unacceptable and returned to Florence as the secretary of the Signoria. The last years of his life were spent in historical writings in which he broke with previous tradition and highlighted the struggle for liberty over the forces of tyranny. His well-known and well-received work was *The Twelve Books of Florentine History or the History of Florence*. He also translated St **Basil**, Plutarch, Aristotle, Plato and Xenophon into Latin.

Brüning, Heinrich   Roman Catholic statesman and academic, born Münster, Germany, 26 November 1885, died Norwich, VT, 30 March 1970. As secretary general of the German Trades Union Confederation he worked to create an interconfessional progressive conservative party. From 1929 he was leader of the Reichstag Centre Party, whilst remaining critical of the Weimar parliamentary system. He became chancellor of Germany in 1930 but was forced to resign by the Nazis and left the country. He subsequently held appointments as professor of government at Harvard University and professor of political science at Cologne University.

Brunini, John B.   American lawyer, born Vicksburg, Mississippi, 25 December 1868, died Vicksburg, 8 November 1954. He studied law at the University of Virginia and set up the firm of Brunini and Hirsch. He was successful in establishing the right of a nun to inherit property in the Bolto case for the Sisters of Mercy, which led to a repeal of the law prohibiting bequests to religious institutions. He was politically active, active in professional and Catholic organizations and was the first person from Mississippi to be named a knight of St George.

Brunner, Francis de Sales   Swiss missionary, born Mümliswel, 10 January 1795, died Schellenberg, Liechtenstein, 29 December 1859. He was ordained 6 March 1819 after joining the Benedictines at Mariastein. In 1829 he left and joined the Trappists in Alsace. In the revolution of 1830 it was necessary to return to Switzerland, where he worked as a missionary under the papal nuncio; he then became estranged from the Trappists. He joined the Society of the Precious Blood in 1838, set it up in Switzerland and with his mother founded there the Precious Blood Sisters. He and his companions

went to the USA in 1843. He recruited in Europe for the American foundation and is buried at Schellenberg, where he had established a convent.

Brunner, Heinrich Emil   Swiss Reformed Church theologian, born Winterthur, Switzerland, 23 December 1889, died Zurich, 6 April 1966. He studied theology in Zurich and then Berlin, where Adolf **Harnack** was his most significant mentor. After graduating in 1913 he taught for a time in a secondary school in England, which laid the foundation for his later involvement with the ecumenical movement. He was ordained in the Reformed tradition, was minister of the church at Obstalden 1916–24 while continuing his theological studies, and was appointed professor of systematic and practical theology in Zurich in 1924. He taught there until 1953, and then in Tokyo until 1956. He first supported Karl **Barth** in opposing theological liberalism but then incurred Barth's wrath when he suggested that some knowledge of God may be gained from creation, and the two of them became firm theological opponents. Author of nearly 400 books and articles, the most widely known being *The Mediator* (1927) and *The Divine Imperative* (1932). He delivered the Gifford Lectures in 1947–9.

Brunner, Sebastian   Austrian priest, born Vienna, 10 December 1814, died Vienna, 26 November 1853. He was ordained in 1838 and was active in his parish, becoming friendly with Anton **Günther** and Metternich with whom he collaborated. He became certain of the need for Catholic renewal in Austria and contributed to this by his writings. He was editor of the *Wiener Kirchenzeitung*, campaigning against Protestantism and Josephinism. His writing against Austrian liberals was often strongly anti-Semitic. The principal ones are *Woher? Wohin?* (1855), *Die theologische Dienerschaft am Hofe Josef II* (1868), *Die Mysterien der Aufklärung in Österreich* (1869).

Bruno   Saint, founder of the Carthusian Order, born *c*.1032, died La Torre, Calabria, 6 October 1101. He studied at Rheims, Tours and, *c*.1048, theology at Cologne, probably being ordained *c*.1055. His working life started as canon of St Cunibert's, Cologne; he then taught at the cathedral school of Rheims, where the future

Urban II was one of his pupils. He rose through the ranks of the cathedral clergy, but, scandalized by the life of Bishop Manasses, he decided to enter religious life. Initially this was as a hermit under the guidance of St Robert of Molesme, who founded Cîteaux, then under the protection of Bishop St Hugh of Grenoble. Bruno founded a community in the mountains near Grenoble. This was to become the Grande Chartreuse. The (Carthusian) monks lived a quasi-eremitical life, but in a monastery, a rule of life more in common with the early Egyptian monks than with the Benedictines. In 1090 Urban summoned him to Rome, where he lived in a hermitage he established in the baths of Diocletian. When Urban fled south, Bruno went too, and and was offered the bishopric of Reggio, which he refused. Instead he founded a hermitage in La Torre, where he died. Feast day 6 October.

Bruno, Giordano   Italian philosopher, born Nola, near Naples, 1548, died by burning at the stake in Campo dei Fiori, Rome, 17 February 1600. He joined the Dominicans at Naples in 1562 but was accused of unorthodoxy, and fled in 1576. He spent the next seventeen years on the move, first at Toulouse, at Paris, in England (from 1583 to 1585, when he published some of his more important cosmological works), in Paris again and at various cities in Germany. He was captured in Venice in 1592, examined by the Inquisition and sent to Rome. He was an anti-Aristotelian, and a supporter of Copernicus' theories, but the chief charge against him at the time was of pantheism.

Bruno de Jésus-Marie   French Carmelite writer on religious psychology, born Jacques Froissart at Bourbourg, 25 June 1892, died Paris, 16 October 1962. He entered the Discalced Carmelites in 1917. In poor health he left but re-entered in 1920 at Avon-Fontaine. He was ordained in 1924. He became lifelong editor of Études Carmélitaines in 1930, which he developed as a forum for religious psychology. He organized the first Congress of Religious Psychology. He was awarded the Académie Septentrional in 1948 and the Rose d'Or in 1957. His main works are St Jean de la Croix (1929), La vie d'amour de St Jean de la Croix (1944), Madame d'Acarie, épouse et mystique (1937), and Le livre d'amour (1961).

Bruno of Cologne   Saint, archbishop, born c.925, and died Rheims, 11 October 965. He was of royal birth, son of Emperor Henry I, the Fowler. and became abbot of monasteries at Lorsch near Worms and Corvei on the Weser. He was ordained in 950 and travelled with his brother Henry II to Italy the following year. His appointment to the archbishopric of Cologne in 953 enabled him to further the ecclesiastical and temporal policy of his brother Emperor Otto I, which led to a greater degree of peace in his domains. His life was written by the monk Ruotger. Feast day 11 October.

Bruno of Magdeburg   German chronicler, died after 1084. Little is known of his life and his historical writings are thought unreliable. He was probably a cleric with Archbishop Werner of Magdeburg. He wrote Liber de bello Saxonico, which covers the eight years 1073–81, dedicating it in 1082 to Bishop Werner of Merseburg. His writings favour the Saxons against Henry IV. Though his writings lack impartiality, he did however include unaltered letters and papers of the Magdeburg and Merseburg archbishoprics, and his writings give a good impression of contemporary life.

Bruno of Querfurt   Saint, bishop, monk and martyr, born Saxony, c.970, died Prussia, 14 February 1009. During the early part of his life he became a canon at Magdeburg cathedral and was attached to the court of Emperor Otto III. He travelled widely with Otto and dedicated his life to missionary work among the Slavs and Baltic peoples, emulating St Adalbert of Prague, his educator in childhood. He entered monastic life inder St Romuald, founder of the Camaldolese at Pereum, near Ravenna; his name in religion was Boniface. In 1008 he went to Poland with colleagues and attempted to bring peace between the Poles and Germans. He was martyred with eighteen companions after crossing from Poland into Prussia. His main works are a life of Adalbert of Prague and an account of the martyrdom of the Five Polish Brothers. Feast days 15 October, 19 June.

Bruno of Segni   Saint, Italian bishop and abbot, born Asti of a noble family, c.1040 or 1050, died Segni, 18 July 1123. He studied at Bologna and Siena, where he became a canon. He was a friend of Pope Gregory VII, who made him bishop of

Segni in 1079, and a counsellor to **Urban II** and **Paschal II.** He accompanied Urban to the Council of Clermont in 1095; on his return he was thrown into prison by the count of Segni. He became a monk at Monte Cassino and was elected abbot in November 1107, while retaining his bishopric. He publicly condemned the Concordat of Sutri of 1111 between Paschal II and **Henry V** of Germany, which brought him into conflict with the Pope, who forced his return to his bishopric. He was eminent in the field of exegesis and theology, and **Gueranger** thought him one of the great liturgists of his time. Feast day 18 July.

Bruno of Würzburg Saint, Austrian bishop and imperial counsellor, born c.1005, died Persenberg near Linz, 27 May 1045. He was of royal blood, a member of the royal chapel and imperial chancellor of Italy in 1027–34. He was elected bishop of Würzburg in 1034, where he rebuilt the cathedral and contributed to improving education. During his tenure, the cathedral school expanded. He died suddenly on the way to Hungary and is buried at Würzburg. He was not formally canonized but appears in a martyrology of 1616. Feast day 17 May.

Bruté de Rémur, Simon William Gabriel American bishop, born Rennes, Brittany, 20 March 1779, died Vincennes, Indiana, 26 June 1839, He was educated locally and trained as a printer. During the French Revolution he visited imprisoned priests and nobles, taking messages and the Sacrament. He first studied medicine in Paris and then entered the Society of Saint-Sulpice, being ordained in 1808. He went to America in 1810, taught in Baltimore and Emmitsburg and acted as pastor. In 1834 he was made bishop of Vincennes. His work in this post, a frontier mission field, required him to return to Europe to seek funds and clergy, and to set up a seminary to serve the needs of his large see. His memoranda, diaries and letters are of historical significance.

Bruyère, Jeanne Henriette Cécile French abbess, born Paris, 12 October 1845, died Ryde, Isle of Wight, 18 March 1909. As a child she was educated by **Gueranger**, abbot of Solesmes, who appointed her superior of the first group of postulants of his new convent of Benedictine nuns at Solesmes. Two

years later she was made abbess, which she remained for 38 years. During this time two new foundations were made, but anticlerical laws forced her removal to the Isle of Wight in 1901. She wrote a much-used and well-known book on prayer, *La vie spirituelle et l'oraison d'après la Sainte Ecriture et la tradition.*

Bryennios, Joseph Byzantine preacher and theologian, born c.1350, died c.1438. There is little known of his life. He spent twenty years in Crete, then occupied by the Venetian Republic, as an Orthodox missionary. In 1402 he became a monk at the Studion monastery outside Constantinople and was sent by the Patriarch Matthew I to Cyprus in 1406 to negotiate links between the church there and Constantinople. From 1416 to 1427 he was a monk of the Charsianeites monastery. At the time he was a well-known preacher, and renowned for his erudition. He was a vigorous defender of Orthodox theology against Rome. He also praised Muslim tolerance. His writings were rediscovered in 1768 by Eugenius **Bulgaris.**

Bryennios, Philotheus Orthodox metropolitan and patristic scholar, born Constantinople, 26 March 1833, died Heybeli Ada, near Istanbul, 1918. He was educated in Leipzig, Berlin and Munich. He taught church history at Chalki and was director of the Ecclesiastical academy at Constantinople. He became metropolitan of Serres in Macedonia in 1875 and subsequently of Nicodemia. In 1877 he found in the Hospice of the Holy Sepulchre, Constantinople, and later published, a Greek parchment codex containing the text of the hitherto unknown *Didache*, the *Epistle of Barnabas* and the *Letter of Clement of Rome to the Corinthians.* He represented the Orthodox Church at an assembly of Old Catholics at Bonn (1875).

Bubwith, Nicholas English bishop and ambassador, born Menthorpe, near Bubwith, Yorkshire, died Wookey, Somerset, 27 October 1424. During his life he had tenure of many ecclesiastical positions, starting as a chancery clerk, through canonries and prebendaries at Exeter, Wells, York, Salisbury, Chichester, Lincoln and St Paul's. Eventually he was made bishop of London in 1406, Salisbury in 1407, and Bath and Wells in 1407. He acted as ambassador to the Council of Constance and as an envoy to Scotland. During his life he endowed poor churches, a cathedral library and almshouses.

Bucceroni, Gennaro Italian Jesuit theologian, born Naples, 22 April 1841, died Rome, 18 February 1918. He joined the Jesuits on 7 September 1856. Following political turmoil in Italy, he went to Belgium, where he studied philosophy and theology. He returned to Rome and taught moral theology at the Gregorian University from 1884 until his death. He was involved in the preparation of the Code of Canon Law.

Bucelin (Buzlin), Gabriel Swiss Benedictine church historian, born at Diessenhofen, Switzerland, 27 December 1599, died Weingarten, Germany, 9 June 1681. From 1621 he studied at Weingarten abbey, becoming a monk in 1617 and being ordained on 23 April 1624. He served as novice master in Feldkirch in 1625 and then for five years at Weingarten. He started writing here but from 1632 made a number of journeys from the abbey, which was threatened by war, eventually moving to Switzerland because of the threat, and then to Admont. He was able to resume writing here and served as prior of St John's Priory in 1651–81, after which he returned to Weingarten in poor health. His main works are *Historia universalis nucleus* (Augsburg, 1658) and *Germania topochromo-stemmato graphica sacra et profana* (4 vols, Augsburg, 1655–78).

Bucer (Butzer), Martin, German Reformer, born Schlettstadt, Alsace, 1491, died Cambridge, 28 February 1551. He joined the Dominicans in 1506, studied Hebrew and Greek at Heidelberg, was ordained, and came into contact with Martin **Luther** in 1518. In 1521 he asked for papal dispensation from his vows, which was granted. He obtained an incumbency at Landstuhl, and married a former nun, one of the first of the Reformers to marry. He began to preach Lutheranism in 1523 and was excommunicated, taking refuge in Strasburg, where his father now lived. His views, especially on the Eucharist, became more radical than those of Luther's, and closer to **Zwingli**'s. He attempted to mediate between Zwingli and Luther and after the death of the former became leader of the Reformed Churches in Switzerland and southern Germany, taking part in conferences between Protestants and Catholics, the most significant of which was that at Regensburg in 1541, attended by **Contarini** and **Pflug** for the Catholics, and by **Melanchthon** and Bucer for the Protestants. On his return to Strasburg he discovered that his wife and several children, as well as his closest associate, had died in the plague. Strasburg, however, began slowly to turn against Bucer's views, and in 1549 he came to England – he had been consulted by **Henry VIII** and by **Cramner** – and was made Regius Professor of divinity at Cambridge. He was made welcome by **Edward VI** and others – the king increased his stipend – but he died soon afterwards. He was buried at Great St Mary's Church, Cambridge, but in the reign of **Mary Tudor** his body was exhumed and publicly burnt.

Buchanan, Claudius East India Company chaplain, missionary strategist and publicist, born Cambuslang, Scotland, 12 March 1766, died Broxbourne, Hertfordshire, 9 February 1815. After study at Glasgow University he moved to London. Following a spiritual crisis in 1790 John **Newton** encouraged him to go to Queen's College, Cambridge. Ordained Anglican priest in 1796, at Charles **Simeon**'s suggestion he was appointed an East India Company chaplain and served at Barrackpore in 1797–9, and Calcutta in 1799–1808. To publicize the cause of the India mission he donated some £2600 for prize essays in 1803 and 1805. His *Memoir of the Expediency of an Ecclesiastical Establishment for British India* (1805), *Star in the East* (1809), and *Christian Researches in Asia* (1810) were major contributions to the successful campaign for the inclusion of missionary clauses in the East India Charter of 1813 and the appointment of the first bishop for India in 1814.

Buchanan, George Scottish humanist and Protestant writer, born Killearn, Stirlingshire, 1 February 1507, died Edinburgh, 28 September 1582. Educated in Paris and Portugal, he taught humanities in France, Scotland and Portugal. On his return to Scotland in 1560/1 as a Calvinist he acted as 'instructor' to Mary Queen of Scots and James VI (later **James I** of England). Academic appointments followed, and his writings *Rerum Scoticarum historia* (1582) and *De jure regni apud Scotos*

(1579) are said to have contributed to the revolution of 1567 and the deposing of Mary Queen of Scots. He is best known for his publication of the Casket Letters in the *Detectio Mariae Reginae Scotorum*. He was well known as a political theorist but considerable controversy has surrounded the accuracy of his historical writings and his antagonism to Mary Queen of Scots.

Buchez, Philippe Joseph Benjamin French Christian Socialist, born Matagne-la-Petite, 31 March 1796, died Rodez, 12 August 1865. He qualified in medicine in 1824 but went on to develop revolutionary ideas based on Christian Socialism. With Armand Bazard he founded Le Charbonnerie Française, which hoped to depose the Bourbons and institute a constitutional assembly. He converted to Catholicism in 1829, but did not practise, thereby hoping to reach a wider audience with his ideas of Social Christianity. He saw the ideals of the French Revolution as a direct development of the truths of Christianity, in particular the selfless service of one's fellow human beings. His main works are the journals *L'Européen* (1831–2, 1835–8), *Revue Nationale* (1847–8) and *L'Atelier* (1840–50) and *L'Histoire parlementaire de la Révolution française* (1833–8), *L'essai d'un traité complet de philosophie au point de vue du catholicisme et du progrès* (1838–40).

Buchman, Frank Nathan Daniel Founder of the Oxford Group ('Moral Rearmament'), born Pennsburg, Pennsylvania, 4 June 1878, died Freudenstadt, Germany, 7 August 1961. Of a Lutheran family, he entered the Lutheran ministry as a pastor in a poor quarter of Philadelphia, where he also founded a boys' home. He then worked as a student chaplain. He attended in 1908 an address on the atonement at the Keswick Convention, England, and had a conversion experience. Thereafter he took up evangelistic work and travelled widely. His technique of evangelization was to hold 'house parties' of men, and one such, in 1921 in Oxford, gave its name to the movement renamed by Buchman in 1938 as Moral Rearmament. His approach was to emphasize national and social morale in place of individual salvation. He established the headquarters of MRA first at Caux, near Montreux, and later at Lucerne.

Buchner, Alois German theologian, born Murnau, Bavaria, 20 April 1783, died 29 August 1869. He became a Benedictine novice but his monastery was suppressed. He continued his studies at Landhut and was ordained in 1806. Thereafter he taught dogma at Dillingen in 1818, Würzburg in 1824 and Munich in 1827. He then became rector of the theological faculty at Passau, 1840–57. His main works are *Summa Theologiae Dogmaticae* (4 vols, Sulzbach, 1838–9) and *Enzyklopädie und Methodologie der theologischen Wissenschaft* (Sulzbach, 1837).

Bückers, Hermann Joseph Roman Catholic Scripture scholar. Born 23 February 1900 at Uedem, Niederrhein, died 6 May 1964 at Henef, near Cologne. He joined the Redemptorists in 1921 and was ordained in 1926. His studies in the seminary and in Scripture at the Pontifical Biblical Institute led to a doctorate in sacred Scripture in 1937. His thesis on the immortality of the soul in the Book of Wisdom caused controversy, as he sought to show that the rational thought of the OT author and the influence of Hellenism on Jewish Wisdom literature were the basis for the doctrine of immortality. He taught OT exegesis at Hennef and officiated as rector there, as well as provincial of the Cologne Redemptorists. His main works are a new translation of the OT into German, and much biblical commentary and criticism.

Buckler, Reginald English Dominican spiritual writer, born London, 14 February 1840, died Grenada, West Indies, 18 March 1927. He followed his three elder brothers, two of them subsequently Dominicans, into the Catholic Church at the age of fifteen. In 1856 he entered the Order of Preachers at Woodchester, where Reginald replaced his birth name Henry. He was ordained in 1863 and spent the next 63 years in several Dominican houses, serving as novice master twice. At the age of 71 he volunteered for the mission in Grenada. His most important book, *The Perfection of Man by Charity* (1889), became a spiritual classic and was published twice under this name and also as *Spiritual Perfection Through Charity* (1912). His other main works were *A Spiritual Retreat* (1907, 1924), *Spiritual Instruction on Religious Life* (1909), *Spiritual Considerations* (1912) and *An Introduction to the Spiritual Life* (1957).

Budde, Karl Ferdinand Reinhardt OT scholar, born Bensberg, near Cologne, 13 April 1850, died Marburg, 29 January 1933. His work concentrated on OT criticism and he contributed substantially to this field within the framework set up by J. **Wellhausen**. His academic posts included professorships at Strasburg in 1889–1900 and Marburg in 1900–21. His writings include many commentaries and the well-respected *Religion of Israel* (1899).

Budé, Guillaume French scholar of Greek studies, born Paris, 26 January 1467, died there 20 August 1540. He was thought to be the best Greek scholar of his day, even above **Erasmus**. His important work *Commentarius Linguae Graecae* (1529) was a significant contribution to the study of Greek literature at the time. He was well known also for establishing the Collège de France for the study of Greek, Latin and Hebrew, an event which marked a revival of classical studies in France. It was believed that he had leanings towards Lutheranism, but if so did not act upon them. He was the royal librarian, and established the collection at Fontainebleau which became the seed of the Bibliothèque Nationale. His main works are *Annotationes in XXIV Pandectarum libros* (1508), *De asse et partibus eius libri V* (1515), *De contemptu rerum fortuitarum libri III* (1521–6), *De Philologia libri II* (1530), *De transitu Hellenismi ad Christianismi libri III* (1534), and the *Epistolae*, which include letters written to Thomas **More**, Erasmus, **Sadoleto**, **Bembo**, **Rabelais** and **Vives**.

Budenz, Louis F. Roman Catholic journalist, writer and lecturer, born Indianapolis, USA, 17 July 1891, died Newport, USA, 27 April 1972. Involved in the labour movement as a writer (editing *The Carpenter* and *Labour Age*) and organizer, he turned increasingly to Communism. In 1920 he became publicity director for the American Communist Party, editing its newspaper *The Daily Worker* and serving on its national committee. He left the party in 1945, rejoined the Church and taught at Notre Dame and Fordham Universities. His extensive anti-Communist writings include *This is My Story* (1947), *Men Without Faces* (1950) and *The Techniques of Communism* (1954).

Bufalo, Gaspare del Saint, Italian founder of the Society of the Precious Blood (CPPS). Born Rome, 6 January 1786, died Rome, 28 December 1837. He was educated at the Roman College and ordained in 1808. He gained a reputation for visiting the sick, caring for the homeless and teaching the catechism, and he helped his spiritual director Canon Francesco Albertini establish a pious union of the Precious Blood in the church of San Nicola in Carcere. He was later exiled for four years (and for some of the time imprisoned) for refusing to swear allegiance to Napoleon I. After his return to Rome in 1814 with papal support he established the Society of the Precious Blood, on 15 August 1815, and opened its first house in Umbria. He also helped Blessed Maria de **Mattias** to found the Precious Blood Sisters. He was beatified 18 December 1904, canonized 12 January 1954. Feast day 21 October.

Buffier, Claude French philosopher, born Warsaw, 25 May 1661, died Paris, 17 May 1737. Born of French parents who returned to Normandy when he was young, he joined the Jesuits in 1679 and then taught literature in Paris and philosophy and theology in Rouen. He argued against the Jansenist recommendations of his archbishop and was exiled. On his return he worked on the *Journal de Trévoux* and wrote on religion, philosophy and pedagogy. He is known for being an original thinker and demonstrated the influence on his thinking of **Descartes**, **Locke** and **Malebranche** in his *Traité des premières verités*.

Bugenhagen, Johann Lutheran theologian, born Wolin in Pomerania (hence his nickname Pomeranus), 24 June 1485, died Wittenberg, 20 April 1558. He was educated locally, then at the University of Greifswald, and opened a school at Treptow an der Rega, which flourished. In 1509 he became a priest, and took charge of the parish in Treptow. He was attracted to Lutheranism through reading **Luther**, and went to Wittenberg in 1521, where he entered the university, gave well-received lectures and became parish priest in 1525. In 1535 he became a member of the university's faculty of theology. Although his home remained in Wittenberg for the rest of his life, he travelled widely in Germany helping to organize the Reformed churches, and was invited to Denmark in 1537 for the same purpose. While there – he stayed until 1539 – he also helped to reorganize the university in Copenhagen. He wrote a number of biblical commentaries as well as other theological works, and assisted **Melanchthon** in revising Luther's translation of the Bible into German. He became a close friend of Luther, officiating at his marriage and at his funeral. He had always also been an admirer of **Erasmus**, and after 1548 he was alienated from some of his friends by his readiness to reach a compromise over reform.

Buglio, Ludovico Italian missionary and author, born Mineo, Sicily, 26 January 1606, died Peking (Beijing), China, 7 October 1682. By the time he was sixteen he had joined the Jesuits, and was sent to China fifteen years later. In 1642 in Szechwan he was joined by Gabriel de Megalhaens, but their missionary work was interrupted when they were imprisoned first by the bandit Chang Hsien-chung and then by the emperor for alleged collaboration with the bandit. They were able to continue with missionary work from 1659 and he translated **Thomas Aquinas**' *Summa Theologiae* into Chinese (30 vols, Peking, 1654–79).

Bugnini, Annibale Roman Catholic bishop and liturgical reformer, born Civitella del Lago, Italy, 1912, died Rome, 3 July 1982. Ordained in 1936, he was later appointed secretary of the preparatory commission for draft schemata on liturgical matters for Vatican II, and subsequently secretary of the commission formed to implement the council's liturgical reforms. Having served as secretary of the Sacred Congregation for Divine Worship, he became a titular archbishop of Diocletiana. He was appointed as pro-nuncio in Tehran, where he was involved in negotiations for the release of American hostages and in the defence of Roman Catholic and Protestant clergy during the Khomeini regime.

Bulgakov, Sergei Nikolaevich Russian Orthodox priest and theologian, born Livny, Russia, 16 June 1871, died Paris, 12 July 1944. He was the son of a priest, but as a student was a Marxist revolutionary. He returned to belief before the Revolution, and in exile he headed the St Sergius Theological Institute in Paris from 1925 to 1944. His theological works on 'sophiology' were condemned by many Russian bishops but he continued to write.

His chief works are *The Orthodox Church* (1935) and *La Sagesse de Dieu* (1938). He is the most important theologian of the so-called 'Paris school' of the Russian emigration.

Bulgaris, Eugenius Greek Orthodox theologian, born Corfu, 10 August 1716, died 29 May or 10 June 1806. He entered the monastery of Vatopedi on Mount Athos in 1749, after studying at Padua and lecturing in Janina. He taught at Vatopedi and Constantinople. His teaching methods were at odds with the tradition, and he lost his job and went to Leipzig. He was taken up by **Catherine II**, made librarian and ordained in 1775. He became archbishop of Khersan. He later retired to the monastery of St Alexander Nevski. He wrote widely on theology, philosophy, history, physics and mathematics. His main work is a dogmatic theology written in the Scholastic manner (Venice, 1872).

Bull, George Evangelical clergyman and social reformer, born Stanway, Essex, 12 July 1797, died Almeley, Herefordshire, 20 August 1865. Joined the navy at the age of ten, leaving it six years later. In 1818 he was appointed as a schoolteacher at the Christian Institution in Sierra Leone. Because of ill-health he returned to England in 1820. Ordained deacon in 1823 and priest in the following year. From 1826 to 1840 he was curate of Bierley near Bradford. An active supporter of the Ten Hours Movement, temperance and education, and an opponent of the 1834 Poor Law. In 1840 he went to Birmingham before retiring to Herefordshire in 1864.

Bullinger, Johann Heinrich Swiss Reformer, born, the son of a priest, Bremgarten near Zurich, 18 July 1504, died Bremgarten, 17 September 1575. He was taught by the Brethren of the Common Life at Emmerich, and then attended the University of Cologne. Returning to Switzerland in 1523, he taught at the Cistercian monastery near Cappel until 1529, but in 1528 a sermon by **Zwingli** led him to adopt the principles of the Reformation. In 1529 he became pastor at Bremgarten in succession to his father, and married a former nun. Two years later he succeeded Zwingli as chief pastor of Zurich, a post he held until his death. He was involved in the debates among the Reformers, especially over the Eucharist, and was responsible for both Helvetic Confessions, the later one, of 1566, more Calvinist in tone than the one twenty years earlier, reflecting Bullinger's own development. Many of the Protestant refugees from England in the reign of **Mary Tudor** came to Zurich, which in part accounts for his influence on the English church under **Elizabeth**. He wrote a great many theological works, including a life of Zwingli.

Bullough, Sebastian Dominican priest, biblical philologist, linguist, born Cambridge, England, 17 May 1910, died Stone, England, 31 July 1967. He became a Dominican in 1931 and was ordained in 1937. He studied in Rome until World War II and then taught at Blackfriars School, later becoming prior of the novitiate house in Woodchester, lecturer in theology at Oxford University, and preacher and lecturer in Hebrew at Cambridge University. He contributed to many periodicals on scriptural subjects and wrote *Five Minor Prophets* (1953) and contributed to the *New Catholic Commentary on the Holy Scriptures*.

Bultmann, Rudolph Karl German NT scholar and theologian, born Wiefelstede, Germany, 20 August 1884 and died Marburg, 30 July 1976. The son of a Lutheran pastor, he was educated in the classics at his local school in Oldenburg, and then in theology in Tübingen, Berlin and Marburg. He taught for a year in the school in Oldenburg before returning as a tutor to Marburg in 1907. He taught in the university there from 1912 to 1916, when he went to Breslau, as an assistant professor, then in 1920 as professor to the University at Giessen, returning to Marburg in 1921 as professor and remaining there for the rest of his life. His radical methodological scepticism, most clearly expounded in *Die Geschichte der synoptischen Tradition* ('The history of the synoptic tradition'), written while he was at Breslau and published in 1921, used form criticism to determine what of the Gospel narrative reflects the material which may be said to belong to Jesus' own teaching. In 1926 he published *Jesus*, in which he demonstrated the accretions of myth with which the early Christians had encrusted the figure of Christ, 'demythologizing' the Christian message so that only the fact of the crucified Christ is necessary for Christian

faith. The controversy surrounding the concept of demythologizing was examined in Bultmann's five-volume *Kerygma und Mythos*. He also wrote a number of commentaries on the NT, in particular on the Gospel of John.

Bunderius, Jan Dominican theologian, born Ghent, 1481, died Ghent, 8 June 1557. He joined the Dominicans in 1507, studying at Louvain and then teaching theology at Ghent. He served both as prior at Ghent and as provincial vicar in 1550. He became inquisitor for the Diocese of Tournai in 1542 and is known for his rigorous writings against Reformers. His main work was *Compendium dissidic quorumdam haereticorum atque theologorum* (Paris, 1540).

Bunsen, Christian Carl Josias von (Chevalier Bunsen) German diplomat and amateur theologian, born Korbach, Prussia, 25 August 1791, died Bonn, 28 November 1860. He studied theology in Marburg and Göttingen before going on a tour of Europe. In 1817 he married an Englishwoman, Frances Waddington, and he attributes to her influence his abiding interest in theology. The year after his marriage he entered the diplomatic service. His diplomatic skills were used in sensitive matters of the relations between Germany and Rome when he was minister at the Prussian legation in Rome, and also as ambassador to London in 1841–54. He had a high profile as a representative of European Protestantism in England and attempted the setting up of a joint Lutheran and Anglican bishopric in Jerusalem. His many writings include *Hippolytus and His Age* (4 vols, 1852), *Christianity and Mankind* (7 vols, 1855), *Gott in der Geschichte* (3 vols, 1857–8) and *Vollständiges Bibelwerke für die Gemeinde* (9 vols, 1858–70).

Bunting, Jabez Methodist minister and connexional statesman, born Manchester, 13 May 1779, died London, 16 June 1858. Though his background was radical, revivalist and dissenting, he became the architect of a high Wesleyan doctrine of the ministry and of connexional authority. He entered the Methodist itinerancy in 1799 and served in numerous circuits both in the North of England and in London until placed at the denominational headquarters from 1833, where he 'filled the chief posts of influence and authority', converting, it has been said, a society into a church. The problem for Methodism was that John **Wesley**'s authority was largely personal and at his death the connexion had failed to evolve an institutional model adequate to the needs of an expanding Methodism. This Bunting provided, with his own emphasis on keeping distance between the religious work of Methodism and the many radical movements that sprang up in England after the Napoleonic Wars. The price was several reform secessions in the 1820s, 1830s and 1840s, which severely limited Wesleyan Methodism's numerical expansion. Bunting served as president of conference successively in 1820, 1828, 1836 and 1844.

Bunyan, John Nonconformist minister, preacher and author, born Elstow, Bedfordshire, 1628 (baptized 30 November), died London, 31 August 1688. He was drafted into the parliamentary army in 1644 and possibly served until 1646, when he returned to his native village and, in 1648, married. His wife brought to the house a number of religious books which he began to read, leading to his conversion. He practised his father's trade of a tinker, frequently working in Bedford, and it was there that he joined in 1653 a religious community founded by John Gifford, moving to Bedford two years later. He was ordained deacon in the church, and began to preach, at first privately but later in public. At the Restoration he defied the prohibition against holding illicit services and was imprisoned from 1660 to 1672, being released after **Charles II**'s Declaration of Indulgence, though he was imprisoned again, briefly, in 1675. On his release in 1672 he took up the ministry of the church in Bedford he had first joined, and spent the rest of his life ministering there, or preaching around England. He wrote *Grace Abounding*, a spiritual autobiography, in 1666 while in prison, *The Holy City* the year before, *A Confession of My Faith* in 1672, *The Life and Death of Mr Badman* in 1680 and *The Holy War* in 1682. *Pilgrim's Progress*, which has always been his most-read book, was written in 1672, during his second imprisonment. He championed hymn singing. *Pilgrim's Progress* was set to music by **Vaughan Williams**. Percy Dearmer adapted a song from *Pilgrim's Progress* as a hymn 'Who Would True Valour See'. Vaughan Williams set this to the folk tune 'Monks Gate' in

The English Hymnal, since when it has been very popular.

Buonaccorsi, Filippo (Callimaco Esperiente) Italian humanist and philosopher, born San Gimignano, near Siena, 2 May 1437, died Cracow, Poland, 1 November 1496. He founded the Roman Academy with Pomponio Leto and was exiled with other members of the Academy for their part in the plot against Pope **Paul II** in 1468. His writings suggest that he denied the immortality of the soul, questioned the separation of soul and body, supported the sovereignty of the State and argued for the independence of morality from religion. He left historical writings, letters, poems and his main work, *Consilium Callimachi*.

Buonaiuti, Ernesto Italian writer, born Rome, 25 June 1881, died Rome, 20 April 1946. He was ordained in 1903 and then taught philosophy and ecclesiastical history in Rome. Believed that church doctrine had to come to terms with historical scholarship, and with scientific advance, the outlook associated with the Modernists. He wrote *Il programme dei modernisti* (1907), translated into English by George **Tyrrell**, as a response to the Holy See's condemnation of Modernism. His *Rivista di scienza della religioni* (1916) was condemned by the Holy Office, *Ricerche religiose* was placed on the Index in 1925 – indeed, all his works were condemned no less than three times over the years – and he was excommunicated in 1925. In 1931 he was dismissed also from his academic post for refusing to take an oath in support of Fascism. He was visited when dying by an emissary from the Pope authorizing reconciliation without retraction, but he died excommunicated.

Buonpensiere, Enrico Italian Dominican theologian, born Trelizzi, near Bari, 26 October 1853, died 18 February 1929. He joined the Dominicans in 1869 and studied at the College of St Thomas, Rome. He received his doctorate, lectured in many subjects and became rector in 1897. From 1909 to 1925 he taught dogma at the Lateran University. He wrote commentaries on most of the dogmatic tracts of St **Thomas Aquinas** and was recognized as an expert in the field.

Burchard of Worms Bishop, born Wesse, 965,

died Worms, 20 August 1025. He was a very influential bishop of his time. He was from a noble family of Hesse, studied at St Florian in Coblenz and at the monastery at Lobbes in Flanders. He entered the service of Willigis of Mainz, and **Otto III** promoted him to the bishopric of Worms in 1000. He was one of the leaders of the reform movement in Germany, concerned in particular for the formation of the clergy of his diocese, and for education in general. With the assistance of Oldbert of Gembloux, a monk of Lobbes, he produced an important collection of canon law, the *Decretum Collectarium*, which was commonly known by his name, the 'Brocardus'.

Burchard of Würzburg Saint, bishop, born in Wessex, England, died Germany, 2 February 753 or 754. He became a Benedictine monk and *c.*732 followed St **Boniface** to Germany as a disciple and collaborator. He was made the first bishop of Würzburg in 741 or 742. He travelled to Rome, attended synods in Germany and Franconia and was entrusted with ambassadorial duties by Pepin III. Buried in the cathedral at Würzburg, his relics were translated to the monastery of St Andrew which he had founded. Feast day 14 October.

Burckhardt, Jakob Swiss historian, born Basel, 25 May 1818, died Basel, 8 August 1887. He was the son of a Calvinist pastor, and studied theology, history and philology at the University of Basel, where he was professor of history from 1845 until his death. His views of a society dominated by an élite are said to have influenced his historical writings and give a distorted view, for instance, of fourth-century civilization. His writings have been severely criticized since the 1920s, but in recent years his reputation as a philosophical historian is being revised.

Bureau, Paul French sociologist and moralist. Born Elboeuf (Seine-Maritime), 5 October 1865, died Paris, 7 May 1923. He studied law at Rouen and the Institut Catholique of Paris, becoming professor of international law at the latter in 1902. His work as a sociologist prepared the way for Henri Bergson, added *Weltanschauung* to the social factors developed by Tourville, thus avoiding sociological determinism, and emphasized the role of the individual in social development. He opposed

Durckheim and refused to give collective consciousness a reality over and above individual life. His main works are *La crise morale des temps nouveaux* (1907), *L'indiscipline des mœurs* (1920) and *Introduction à la méthode sociologique* (1923).

Burgoa, Francisco de Mexican Dominican chronicler, born Antequera (Oaxaca), *c.*1600, died Zaachile or Teozapotlán, 1681. He was descended from the conquistadores of Oaxaca. He was professed in 1620 in the province of San Hipólito and was ordained in 1625. He worked in many parishes and learnt the local Zapoteca and Mixteca languages, which gave him access to indigenous traditions and legends. He travelled widely in Europe, visiting convents, libraries and museums in order to improve the culture of his country. His order conferred on him many offices, including vicar general and provincial. His main works are historical and geographical, recording the arrival of Dominicans in Mexico, and histories of monasteries.

Burgon, John William Anglican priest and theologian, born Smyrna, Turkey, 21 August 1813, died Chichester, England, 4 August 1888. Worked for his father's merchant company until it collapsed in 1841, and was subsequently educated at Worcester College, Oxford. Fellow of Oriel College, Oxford, 1846, vicar of the University Church, 1863, dean of Chichester, 1876. He was an old-fashioned High-Churchman who became involved in many of the controversies of his day, generally adopting an extreme position, and usually on the losing side. Denounced the disestablishment of the Irish church in 1869, the appointment of A. P. **Stanley** as a select preacher in 1872, the new BCP Lectionary in 1879, the education of women at Oxford in 1884. A textual critic and staunch upholder of the *textus receptus* of the NT, he published *The Last Twelve Verses of the Gospel according to St Mark Vindicated* in 1871, and *The Revision Revised* in 1883.

Buridan, John *see* **John Buridan**

Burigny, Jean Lévesque de Scholar, born Rheims, 1692, died Paris, 8 October 1785. He developed a scholarly interest in ancient and modern history, theology and philosophy. He wrote on the authority of the Pope (4 vols, 1720), pagan theology (1724), biographies of Plotinus, **Grotius**, **Erasmus** and **Bossuet**, and histories of Sicily and Byzantine revolutions. In 1756 he received membership of the Académie des Inscriptions et Belles-Lettres.

Burke, Thomas Nicholas Dominican friar, born Galway, 8 September 1830, died Tallaght, 2 July 1883. He received his training in Perugia and Rome in the 1840s and was ordained in 1853, returning to Ireland in 1855 to found a novitiate and house for his Order in Tallaght. In 1864 he succeeded Dr **Manning** as preacher of the Lantern sermons in English at the church of Santa Maria del Popolo. He was present at Vatican I as theological adviser to Bishop Leahy of Dromore. In the early 1870s he was visitor to the American Province of St Joseph. His reputation as a speaker went before him and he was booked to give some 400 lectures, besides sermons. He spoke, amongst other subjects, against the English occupation of Ireland. During a course of lectures in New York in 1872 he attacked J. A. **Froude**'s position on the relations between England and Ireland and published them as *English Misrule in Ireland* (1873) and *Ireland's Case Stated in Reply to Mr Froude* (1873).

Burkitt, Francis Crawford NT, patristic and Semitic scholar, born London, 3 September 1864, died Cambridge, 11 May 1935. He entered Trinity College, Cambridge, to read mathematics, but after Part I of the Tripos changed to theology. After his degree he stayed on to teach, being appointed to his first university post in 1903. He subsequently held the Norrisian chair of divinity at Cambridge from 1905 until 1935. He was noted for his contributions to the study of the Syriac versions of the NT and wrote dozens of articles for the *Journal of Theological Studies*. He also published on early church history: *Christian Beginnings: Three Lectures* (1924); *Church and Gnosis: The Morse Lectures 1931* (1932), as well as articles on Franciscan subjects including *The Study of the Sources of the Life of St Francis* (1926).

Burne-Jones, Sir Edward Artist, born Birmingham, 28 August 1833, died London, 17 June 1898. He was educated at Oxford, where he befriended William **Morris**. He then came under **Rossetti**'s influence. His work, exhibited in the Grosvenor Gallery, London, brought him to public attention, and he became known for his romantic, dreamlike, melancholy, historical subjects. His religious works include *Days of Creation*. He designed stained glass windows which were executed by William Morris. He was parodied in Gilbert and Sullivan's aesthetic opera *Patience* as the aesthetic character Bunthorne. Burne-Jones' work appears in several churches.

Burnett, Peter Hardeman Lawyer, first American governor of California, born Nashville, Tennessee, 15 November 1807, died San Francisco, 16 May 1895. He was a member of the Church of the Disciples or Campbellites (a secession from the Baptists) but was converted to Roman Catholicism through the writings of Bishop Purcell of Cincinnatti and was received into the Church of Rome in June 1846. He became the first American governor of California in 1850. He wrote on early constitutional and political development and published a powerful apology for Roman Catholicism, *The Path Which led a Protestant Lawyer to the Catholic Church* (1860).

Burns, James Founder of Burns & Oates publishers, born into a Presbyterian minister's family in Montrose, Forfarshire, Scotland, 1808, died of cancer, London, 11 April 1871. Educated at a Presbyterian college in Glasgow, but in 1832 moved to London and took up work at a publisher's. Very soon set up his own firm, published many of the High Anglican publications of the period and eventually, along with many of those he published, converted to Roman Catholicism in 1847. The firm was soon publishing most of the major British Roman Catholic writers: John Henry **Newman**, who had been responsible for Burns' conversion, wrote his novel *Loss and Gain* (1848) to support the company, which had lost business because of the owner's change of religion. His widow joined the Ursuline community in Pittsburgh, Pennsylvania, and their five children all went into religious life.

Burns, James Aloysius US priest and educationist, born Michigan City, Indiana, 13 February 1867, died Notre Dame, Indiana, 9 September 1940. Originally went to Notre Dame to study printing but joined the Congregation of the Holy Cross there in 1888. Studied in Watertown, Wisconsin, and at Notre Dame and was ordained in 1893. Was superior of Holy Cross Seminary in Washington, DC, from 1900 and gained his doctorate from Catholic University in 1906. He became president of Notre Dame in 1919; under his direction it underwent a major reorganization which resulted in increased enrolment and income. He was a founder member and first vice-president of the US National Catholic Educational Association and held senior posts in his religious Order. Among his publications are *Principles, Origin and Establishment of the Catholic School System* (1908), *Growth and Development of the Catholic School System* (1912) and *Catholic Education – A Study of Conditions* (1917).

Burns, William Chalmers Evangelist and pioneer Presbyterian Church of England missionary in China, born Kilsyth, Scotland, 1 April 1815, died Yingkou, China, 4 April 1868. He studied law in Edinburgh and theology in Glasgow and was involved in revivals in Dundee and Kilsyth, where he developed his gifts as an evangelist. After time in Ireland and Canada, in 1847 he was ordained and appointed to China as the first missionary of the Presbyterian Church of England. His itinerant ministry laid the foundation for their work in Guangzhou, Xiamen, Shanghai, Shantou and Fujian. Known as 'the man of the Book', he translated Bunyan's *Pilgrim's Progress* and the metrical Psalms and wrote a number of hymns in Chinese.

Burrows, Eric Norman Bromley English Jesuit orientalist, born Ramsgate, Kent, 26 March 1882, died in a car crash, Oxfordshire, 23 June 1938. Studied at Oxford, joined the Roman Catholic Church after his graduation in 1904 and the following year joined the Jesuits. Studied oriental languages in Beirut, and Akkadian and Sumerian in Rome. Between 1924 and 1930 he took part in the archaeological expeditions to Kish and to Ur, and in 1935 published his *Ur Excavations, Texts, II: Archaic Texts*, a study of the oldest documents found at Ur and a major contribution to oriental studies. *The Oracles of Jacob and Balaam* and *The Gospels of the Infancy and Other Biblical Essays* were published after his death.

Burrus, Petrus Belgian theologian and neo-Latin poet, born Bruges, 4 June 1430, died Amiens, France, 25 April 1507. Lived for many years in Paris and possibly studied canon law at the university there. He worked as a private tutor and in 1495 became a canon in Amiens. His work in both prose and poetry was published in two volumes in 1503 and 1508.

Burtsell, Richard Lalor US priest, canonist and civic leader, born New York City, April 1840, died Kingston, New York, 5 February 1912. Studied for the priesthood at the Sulpician Seminary in Montreal, Canada, and at the Propaganda College in Rome, graduating with doctorates in theology and philosophy. He was ordained in 1862 and worked in New York parishes; he founded Epiphany parish in 1867 and St Benedict the Moor parish in 1883. For five years from 1887 he worked as canonical adviser to Edward **McGlynn**, and in 1890 became parish priest of St Mary's parish in Kingston, where he spent the rest of his life. He played an active role in civic life in Kingston as a member of the Board of Trade, founder and president of the city hospital and trustee of the city library. He wrote for scholarly journals and was a contributor to the *Catholic Encyclopedia*. He was made papal chamberlain in 1905 and domestic prelate in 1911.

Bus, Cesar de French founder of two religious congregations, born Cavaillon, Comtat Venaissin (now in France), 3 February 1544, died Avignon, 15 April 1607. Spent his youth as a soldier (fighting the Huguenots), as an artist and poet, and then had a life of pleasure in Paris for some years before returning to Cavaillon and his studies. He was ordained priest in 1582 and became known for his work in preaching, teaching and charity. In 1592 he set up the Secular Priests of Christian Doctrine, known as the Doctrinaires, a congregation devoted, as the name suggests, to preaching and teaching Christian doctrine. He later established a similar congregation for women, the Filles de la Doctrine Chrétienne. His *Instructions familières* in five volumes were published in Paris in 1666.

Busenbaum, Hermann German Jesuit and moral theologian, born Notteln, Westphalia in 1600, died Münster, 31 January 1668. He entered the Society of Jesus in 1619 and after ordination taught classics and moral philosophy and theology to Jesuit students. He was rector at Hildesheim and Münster and became confessor and adviser to C. B. von Galen, the prince-bishop of Münster. His major work, *Medulla theologiae moralis facili ac perspicua methodo resolvens casus conscientiae ex variis probatisque auctoribus concinata*, soon became the standard work of moral theology used in seminaries for the next two hundred years.

Bushnell, Horace US Congregational minister and pioneer of liberal theology, born at Bantam, near Litchfield, Connecticut, 14 April 1802, died Hartfield, Connecticut, 17 February 1876. He studied law at Yale and became a tutor there in 1829, but joined the theology department in 1831. In 1833 he was appointed pastor to the north Congregational church in Hartford, Connecticut, and remained in active ministry there until 1859. In his work he stressed the symbolic nature of language and the immanence of God in creation. His writings include *Christian Nurture* (1847), *God in Christ* (1849), *Christ in Theology* (1851), *Nature and the Supernatural* (1858), *The Vicarious Sacrifice* (1866) and *Forgiveness and Law* (1874).

Busnois, Antoine Composer and poet, born France, died Bruges, 6 November 1492. He was chaplain at the court of Burgundy from 1467 and was later in Bruges. Composed Masses, Magnificats, motets and chansons. His works, many of which were adapted by later composers, include *Fortuna desperata*, *Missa L'Homme armé*, *Victima paschali* and *Antoni usque limina*: the last-named, unusual for its time, includes a part for Anthony's symbol, a bell. Busnois also composed the words for many of his pieces.

Buss, Franz Joseph Ritter von German Catholic lawyer and statesman, born Zell, Baden, 23 March 1803, died Freiburg im Breisgau, 31 January 1878. Studied philosophy, law and medicine at Freiburg, became city attorney and lectured at the university, where he became embroiled in matters of religion and politics. Attempted to found a centre for the comparative study of European legislation and jurisprudence, but this never came to fruition, although some of the material collected was published between 1835 and 1846. Served for four terms as a member of the Lower House in Baden

and from 1874 to 1877 in the Reichstag, and did much here, in other political positions and in his writings, to strengthen the position of Catholics. Publications include *Methodology of Canon Law* (1842), *Influence of Christianity on Law and State* (1844) and a *Defence of the Jesuits* (1853). He was awarded both the Order of the Iron Crown and the Order of Gregory the Great.

Bustamante, Carlos Maria Mexican historian and politician, born Oaxaca, Mexico, 4 November 1774, died Mexico, 29 September 1848. Studied law, engaged in the struggle to gain independence from Spain, for which activity he was imprisoned several times, and, in the several senior government posts he held, fought to keep Mexico a republic. He argued for the rights of the Catholic Church, including the return of the Jesuits to Mexico. He edited and published the work of several early Mexican historians including the late sixteenth-century Fray Bernardino de Sahagún's *Historia general de las cosas de Nueva España*. His other writings include *Cuadro histórico de la revolución mexicana* (1843–6), *Historia del Emperador D. Augustín Iturbide* (1846) and *El Nuevo Bernal Díaz o sea historia de los anglo-americanos en México* (1847). His autobiography was published in 1833.

Butin, Romanus French Marist priest, orientalist, born Saint-Romain d'Urfé, 3 December 1871, died Washington, DC, 8 December 1937. Studied in France and then at Dodon in Maryland, USA, and was ordained as a Marist priest in 1897. Gained a doctorate in Semitic languages from the Catholic University of America and taught there from 1912 until he died. As well as three books, he wrote numerous articles and book reviews and was instrumental in setting up the Catholic Biblical Association of America.

Butler, Alban Roman Catholic priest, historian, author of the *Lives of the Saints*, born Appletree, Northants, England, 10 October 1710, died St Omer, France, 15 May 1773. Studied and, after his ordination in 1735, taught at Douai, where he began work for his *Lives*. Travelled through Europe, where he continued to collect material, and worked as a mission priest in the English Midlands before becoming chaplain to the duke of

Norfolk. Went as tutor to the duke's nephew to Paris, where he eventually completed the *Lives*. The work, containing some 1600 biographies, was published in London between 1756 and 1759. In 1766 Butler was appointed president of the English College at St Omer, where he led a more active life than he had perhaps expected, as adviser and vicar general in the service of the bishops of the surrounding dioceses. His other writings include *Life of Mary of the Holy Cross* (1767); some time after his death Charles **Butler**, his nephew, edited and published his *Travels* (1791), *Meditations* (1791) and *The Life of Sir Tobie Matthews* (1795).

Butler, Charles Roman Catholic lawyer, writer, leading member of the Committee for Catholic Emancipation, born London, 14 August 1750, died there 2 June 1832. Nephew to Alban **Butler**. Educated at Douai, then returned to England to study law. His ambition to join the Bar was frustrated because he was a Catholic, so from 1775 he practised, and enjoyed much acclaim, as a conveyancer. He fought for the repeal of the Penal Laws as secretary to the Catholic Committee, and its publications *The Blue Books* were largely his work. In 1791 the laws were partially repealed and Butler was called to the Bar. He continued to work for Catholic Emancipation, which was achieved three years before his death. Married with three children, he was also a prolific writer and published works on law (including canon law), church music, Roman Catholic history and politics and biographies of leading religious figures including Alban Butler, **Fénelon**, **Bossuet**, **Thomas à Kempis**, **Erasmus** and **Grotius**.

Butler, Edward Cuthbert Benedictine abbot and scholar, born Dublin, 6 May 1858, and died Clapham, London, 1 April 1934. Educated at Downside, he joined the Benedictines in 1876. He was the first head of the Downside house of studies at Cambridge from 1896 and in 1906 became second abbot of Downside. He resigned in 1922 and moved to Ealing Priory, where he remained until his death. His writings include a study and text of the *Lausiac History of Palladius* (1898 and 1904); a Latin edition of the *Rule* of St **Benedict** (1912); and studies on various aspects of the Benedictine Order, the *Benedictine Monachism* (1919). He also wrote *Western Mysticism* (1922), a biography of

Bishop **Ullathorne** (1926) and a history of the First Vatican Council (1930).

Butler, Joseph Moral philosopher (opponent of Thomas Hobbes) and bishop of Durham, born Wantage, England, 18 May 1692, youngest of the eight children of a Presbyterian draper, died Bath, 16 June 1752. Educated at the dissenting college at Tewkesbury but turned to the Church of England, went to Oriel College, Oxford, in 1714 and in 1718 was ordained priest. He spent the next eight years at the Rolls Chapel, and his famous *Fifteen Sermons* delivered here were published in 1726. He held pastoral posts in the north-east of England and continued his writing. His *Analogy of Religion*, written to demonstrate, against the Deists, that Christianity was not unreasonable, was published in 1736. He was clerk of the closet to Queen Caroline and then appointed to the see of Bristol in 1739 and to Durham in 1750: he had earlier refused the archbishopric of Canterbury. As bishop of Bristol he met John **Wesley**, told him he disapproved of his methods, and asked him to leave his diocese, which Wesley refused to do.

Butler, Josephine Elizabeth English social reformer, born Glendale, Northumberland, England, 13 April 1828, died Wooler, Northumberland, 30 December 1906. She experienced a religious call to work for the moral well-being and elevation of women, and early on campaigned for women's higher education. In 1866 she settled with her husband in Liverpool and began to work tirelessly to help women out of violence, poverty and prostitution. In 1869 she set up the Ladies' National Association for the Repeal of the Contagious Diseases Acts, and in 1875 the International Federation for the Abolition of the State Regulation of Vice. She published her *Personal Reminiscences of a Great Crusade* in 1896. Her other writings include pamphlets, memoirs of family members, several works on abolition, including *The Hour Before the Dawn* (1876), and a *Life of St Catherine of Siena* (1898).

Butler, Marie Joseph Educationist, religious superior, born Kilkenny, Ireland, 22 July 1860, died Tarrytown, New York, 23 April 1940. Her early education was with the Sisters of Mercy and she entered the Congregation of the Sacred Heart in Béziers, France, in 1876. She was sent first to Portugal but in 1903 headed the Congregation's second foundation in the USA, on Long Island. She oversaw a huge programme of development and by the time of her death there was a novitiate for the Order in Ireland and another in New York, three Marymount colleges and about a dozen schools in the USA, and another two dozen education institutions world-wide.

Butler, Mary Joseph Benedictine abbess, born Callan, Co. Kilkenny, December 1641, died Ypres, Flanders, 22 December 1723. Educated by the English Benedictine sisters in Ghent, she joined the Order when she was fourteen and was professed at sixteen. Was sent to the Irish Benedictine abbey of Our Lady of Grace in Ypres in 1683 and was elected abbess in 1686. In 1688, at the invitation and with the financial support of **James II**, she went to Dublin, where she established a house and school. After the Battle of the Boyne in 1690 the convent was sacked and the nuns returned to Ypres. Despite great poverty and hardship, Dame Mary succeeded in keeping the abbey open.

Buxton, Thomas Fowell Christian politician, brewer, philanthropist and missionary strategist, born Castle Hedingham, Essex, England, 6 April 1786, died Overstrand, Norfolk, 19 February 1844. From a Quaker family, he was educated at Trinity College, Dublin. In London from 1807, he became a partner in Truman's brewery, and attended Wheler Street Chapel under the ministry of the Church Missionary Society secretary Josiah Pratt. He supported prison reform and became MP for Weymouth in 1818. From 1821 he was prominent in the abolition of slavery campaign, taking over the leadership from **Wilberforce**. His *African Slave Trade and Its Remedy* (1839) advocated a 'native agency' and his 1841 Niger River expedition pioneered a new phase of West African Christian mission despite its tragic loss of life. He was created baronet in 1840.

Buxtorf, Johannes (the Elder) Christian Hebraist and grammarian, born Kamen, Westphalia, 25 December 1564, died Basel, 13 September 1629. He was a student of Johannes Piscator at Herborn and was appointed professor of Hebrew at Basel in 1591. He produced an edition of the Rabbinic

Bible (1618–20), *Epitome radicum hebraicarum et Chaldaicarum* (1607), *De abbreviaturis Hebraicis* (1613) and *Praeceptiones grammaticae de lingua Hebraea* (1605), all advancing the understanding of Hebrew grammar and literature. His *Synagoga Judaica* and its German version *Juden Schul* (1603) are anti-Jewish in tone; the latter running to many editions, fuelling the spread of institutionalized Christian anti-Semitism.

Buxtorf, Johannes (the Younger) Christian Hebraist, born Basel, 13 August 1599, died Basel, 16 August 1664, son of the above. He continued his father's lexicographic work and succeeded him as professor of Hebrew at Basel in 1629. He inherited his father's passion for acquiring rare Hebrew MSS and editions and corresponded widely with influential Jews of his day on Hebrew bibliography. He produced valuable work of his own including *De lingua Hebraicae origine et antiquitate* (1644); and translations into Latin of both Maimonides' *Guide to the Perplexed* (1629) and *Cuzari*, a philosophical work of Jehudah Halevi (1660).

Buyl, Bernal Spanish monk, first vicar apostolic of the New World, born near Tarragona, 1445, place and date of death unknown. Joined the Benedictines in Montserrat and was ordained in 1481. Became acquainted with King Ferdinand and in 1488 acted as ambassador to France for the king. Soon after, he left the Benedictines and joined **Francis of Paola**'s Order of Minims in France; in 1492, with the authority of Ferdinand, Buyl established the Order in Spain. The following year the king sent him, with the second expedition of **Columbus**, as vicar apostolic to the Indies, but after a quarrel with Columbus over the latter's treatment of the Indians Buyl returned to Spain. He spent some time in Rome as ambassador for both the king and his Order.

Buys, Johannes de Jesuit theologian and writer, younger brother of Petrus de **Buys**, born Nijmegen, Netherlands, 14 April 1547, died Mainz, 30 May 1611. Joined the Society of Jesus in 1563, studied in Rome and taught theology at Mainz. His early writings are mainly polemical works attacking Protestantism, but in his later work he concentrated more on ascetics and piety. He published new editions of earlier church writers, and among his own writings are *Enchiridion piarum meditationum* (1606) and *Viridarium christianarum virtutum* (1610).

Buys, Petrus de Jesuit, theologian and older brother of Johannes de **Buys**, born Nijmegen, Netherlands, 1540, died Vienna, 12 April 1587. Entered the Society of Jesus in Cologne in 1561 and in 1567 was appointed novice master. He began editing the *Catechism* of Peter **Canisius**, which was seen as a weapon against the Reformers and first published in four volumes between 1569 and 1570. In 1571 he went to Vienna and taught Scripture and Hebrew, at the University and the Jesuit College respectively, and was later rector of the College of Nobles there. In 1584 he was part of a team brought together in Rome to plan a programme of study for the whole Jesuit Order.

Byrd, William Elizabethan composer, born Lincoln, *c.*1543, died Stondon Massey, Essex, 4 July 1623. He was organist of Lincoln cathedral and a gentleman of the Chapel Royal. His music, of striking beauty, reflects the religious controversies of its time. He wrote first for the Anglican and later for the Roman Catholic Church. His later activities are shrouded in secrecy because of religious persecution of Catholics, but he managed to remain in Queen **Elizabeth**'s favour. He composed English church music, three Masses, Latin church music and gradualia. Byrd's sublime three Masses are said never to have been performed after his death until they were revived 400 years later by Sir Richard **Terry** at Westminster Cathedral.

Byrne, Andrew First Roman Catholic bishop of Little Rock, Arkansas, born Navan, County Meath, 5 December 1802, died Helena, Arkansas, 10 June 1862. He emigrated to America at the behest of Bishop **England** to be a volunteer helper in the mission of the Diocese of Charleston. He was ordained 11 November 1827 and became bishop of Little Rock in 1844. He encouraged missionary and educational activity and, at his death, left the diocese well established, with churches, schools and academies actively supported by Irish missions.

Byrne, Edmund Archbishop of Dublin, born about 1656 in County Carlow, died in about 1723.

Educated at the Irish College in Seville, Spain, and ordained there in 1679. He remained to do doctoral studies then returned to Ireland as parish priest at St Nicholas, near Dublin, in 1698. In 1707 he was appointed archbishop and took up residence in Dublin, the first archbishop to do so since 1692. Despite the many difficulties of exercising his office under penal conditions, he managed to hold a diocesan synod in 1712. He was a supporter of the use of the Gaelic language, and promoted the document *Unigenitus*, the constitution of **Clement XI** against the Jansenists.

Byrne, Patrick James Maryknoll priest, missionary, first apostolic delegate to Korea, born Washington, DC, 26 October 1888, and died of pneumonia, while on a forced march, Ha Chang Ri, Korea, 25 November 1950. Educated at St Charles College, Catonsville, Maryland, and then at St Mary's Seminary in Baltimore, but soon after his ordination as a diocesan priest he entered the Catholic Foreign Mission Society at Maryknoll. In 1923 he founded a mission in north Korea and became prefect apostolic of Pyongyang four years later, a post he held until 1929, when he became vicar general of the CFMS. Opened a mission in Japan in 1935 and remained in Japan throughout World War II. In 1947 he returned to Korea as the first apostolic delegate there. He was arrested under the Communist regime in 1950 and imprisoned in Pengyang; on his release towards the end of October, he went with 700 other prisoners on the 100-mile 'death march' to the Manchurian border and died en route.

Byrne, William Irish missionary and educator, born County Wicklow, Ireland, 1780, died of cholera Bardstown, Kentucky, 5 June 1833. Forced to become the family breadwinner early in life, he had little education. Went to the USA in 1805 and studied at Mount St Mary's College, Emmitsburg, St Mary's Seminary, Baltimore and then at St Thomas' Seminary in Bardstown, Kentucky. In 1819 he was one of the first to be ordained priest there by the recently consecrated Bishop David. He worked in Kentucky as a missionary and in 1821 opened St Mary's College in Bardstown. By the time of Byrne's death some 1200 boys had been educated there, many of those in turn contributing to the education of others in some of the remoter parts of Kentucky.

Byrne, William Roman Catholic priest, educationist, born Kilmessan, County Meath, Ireland, 8 September 1833, died Boston, Massachussetts, 9 January 1912. Went to the USA in 1853 and was educated at St Mary's College in Wilmington, Delaware, and at St Mary's College, Emmitsburg, Maryland. In 1864 he was ordained priest for the Diocese of Boston and became diocesan chancellor in 1864. He founded the Boston Temperance Missions and began to work for penal reform. In 1874 he was made rector of St Mary's Church, Charlestown, Massachusetts, and in 1881 became president of Mount St Mary's College, helping turn round the financial fortunes of the college and saving it from closure. The library there is named after him. He remained a governor of Mount St Mary's but returned to parish ministry in 1884 as rector of St Joseph's in Boston. His major publication is his *History of the Catholic Church in the New England States*, published in 1899.

C

Caballero, Antonio Founder of modern Franciscan missions in China; born Baltanás, Spain, 1602, died Kuang-chou, China, 13 May 1669. Joined the Franciscans in 1618 and was ordained in 1626. He went to China in 1633 and worked in Fu-chien and Chiang-nan, but was forced to leave. He was appointed prefect apostolic of China in 1643 and returned there in 1649. He was banished to Kuang-chou in 1665, with the Jesuits and Dominicans. He wrote many essays and books, including *T'ien Ju Yin* ('Catholicism and Confucianism Compared'), 1664.

Caballero y Góngora, Antonio Spanish archbishop of Bogotá and viceroy of New Granada; born Priego, Córdoba, 1723, died Córdoba, March 1796. Studied in Granada, was ordained and became canon of Córdoba, and in 1775 bishop of Mérida, Yukatan, Mexico. In 1778 he was sent to Bogotá, where he became involved in the insurrection of the Comuneros in 1781. He took over the office of viceroy when the previous incumbent died and in 1784 moved his residence to Cartagena, which was threatened by the British. He ordered an expedition to explore the flora of New Granada and when in 1785 there was an earthquake he used his personal funds to help repair some of the damage. He left South America in 1789 to take up his new office as bishop of Córdoba.

Cabanilles, Juan Bautista José Spanish priest, composer and organist, born in Algemesi, Valencia on 4 September 1644, died Valencia, 29 April 1712. He became organist of the cathedral in Valencia in 1665 and was ordained in 1668.

Cabasilas, Nicholas Saint, Byzantine mystic, born 1320, died 1390. His major work is *Concerning Life in Christ*, and in it he outlines how spiritual union with Christ can be achieved through the sacraments of Baptism, Confirmation and the Eucharist. He was sympathetic towards **Gregory Palamas** in the Hesychast controversy, and in a short pamphlet defends Palamism against Nicephorus Gregorias. Feast day 20 June.

Cabasilas, Nilus Byzantine theologian, metropolitan of Thessalonica, born Thessalonica about 1298, died about 1363. Uncle and teacher of Nicolas **Cabasilas**. Although at first apparently neutral he eventually sided with **Gregory Palamas** in the Hesychast controversy and tried to win over Nicephorus Gregorias but eventually wrote an *Antigramma* against him. Although at one time sympathetic to the theology and method of **Thomas Aquinas** and others he eventually found it at least expedient to refute these writers of the Latin church.

Cabassut, Jean French Oratorian priest and theologian, born Aix, France, 1604, died Aix, 1685. Taught canon law at Avignon and was also well read in church history and moral theology. His writings include *Notitia Conciliorum* (1668), *Notitia ecclesiastica historiarium, conciliorum . . .* (1680) and *Juris canonici theoria et praxis* (1660).

Cabrera, Miguel Mexican painter, born Antequera (Oaxaca), 1695, died Mexico City in 1768. His teacher was Xuarez and he was influenced also by **Murillo**, and was given the nickname 'the Mexican Murillo'. He and his students were never short of commissions from both religious and secular organizations and from individuals. Examples can be seen in the Pinacoteca de San Diego in Mexico City, in St Ignatius Church in Polanco and in the Museo de Historia at Chaputelpec.

Cabrera, Pablo Argentinian priest and scholar, born San Juan, Cuyo, on 12 September 1857, died Córdoba, 29 January 1936. He was largely self-taught but developed scholarly knowledge and understanding of history, ethnography, archaeology and music. He grew up in Córdoba and knew all the archives in the city thoroughly. He developed a more accurate understanding of the civil and ecclesiastical history, and of the archaeology, of Argentina. He also corrected many ethnographic errors. He published over 450 books and articles, including *Ensayos de etnografía argentina* (1910), *Tesoros del pasado argentino* (1911), *Universitarios de Córdoba* (1916), *Córdoba de la Nueva Andalucía* (1917), *Los aborígenes del país de Córdoba* (1930), *Los Comenchingones* (1931), *Etnologia argentina* (1931) and *Espigando en el preterito cordobes* (1932).

Cabrini, Francis Xavier *see* **Francis Xavier Cabrini**

Cabrol, Fernand Benedictine liturgical scholar, born Marseilles, 11 December 1855 and died Farnborough, 4 June 1937. He was a member of the community at Solesmes, France, where he was professed in 1877. He was sent to England in 1896 as prior of the new house at Farnborough, Hampshire, where in 1903 he was elected abbot. His publications include *Le Livre de la prière antique* (1900) and *L'Angleterre chrétienne avant les Normands* (1909). He co-edited, with H. **Leclercq**, the *Monumenta ecclesiae liturgica* (1900–13) and the *Dictionnaire d'archéologie chrétienne et de liturgie* (1903–53). He also produced a widely used edition of the Roman Missal.

Cacciaguerra, Bonsignore Italian priest and spiritual writer, born Siena, 1494, died Rome, 30 June 1566. After a vision he gave up his life as a merchant in Palermo and made pilgrimages in Italy and to Santiago de Compostela in Spain. In 1545 he went to Rome to study for the priesthood and in 1547 was ordained. He was a friend of St Philip **Neri**. He became chaplain at San Girolamo della Carità and began his mission to encourage the frequent reception of Communion among the faithful. His writings include *Trattato della communione* (1557), *Trattato della tribolazione* (1559) and his two-volume *Lettere spirituali* (1564–75).

Cacucabilla (Cacucila, Cucacilla) *see* **Kakubilla**

Cadbury, Henry Joel American Quaker NT scholar, born Philadelphia, 1 December 1883 and died Bryn Mawr, PA, 7 October 1974. Educated at Haverford College and at Harvard. Went on from teaching at Haverford to Andover, Bryn Mawr and then to Harvard, where he taught from 1934 to 1954. A Lukan scholar, he was a form critic and led the way in redaction criticism. His scriptural publications include *The Making of Luke–Acts* (1927), *The Peril of Modernising Jesus* (1937), and *Jesus, What Manner of Man* (1947). With Kirsopp **Lake** and F. J. Foakes-Jackson he played a major part in the production of the five-volume *Beginnings of Christianity*. He played an active role in the work of the Quakers and wrote on George **Fox** and the history of Quakerism.

Caedmon Earliest English Christian poet, died *c*.680. Caedmon was a tone-deaf labourer at Whitby monastery who received the gifts of song and composition. Encouraged by the abbess, **Hilda**, he began to compose religious verse based on biblical and doctrinal themes. **Bede** writes that Caedmon was inspired to turn the Scriptures into Anglo-Saxon verse. Many works are ascribed to him with little authority but his poetry had a popular appeal as it set biblical stories and the Lord's life, death, resurrection and ascension to metre, all prefaced by a Hymn to the Creator. Bede gives a translation in Latin and observes that 'by his songs the minds of the many were often turned to despise the world and to seek the heavenly life'.

Caedwalla King of Wessex, born about 659, died Rome towards the end of April 689. He was only king for a couple of years but during that time he had brought a lot of the surrounding kingdoms under his dominion and Wessex became very powerful. He was a friend of St **Wilfrid**. He was the first Anglo-Saxon king to make a pilgrimage to Rome, where he was baptized by Pope **Sergius I**

and where, several days later, he died. He was buried in St Peter's on 20 April.

Caesaria Saint, first abbess of a convent in Arles established in about 512 by her brother, **Caesarius of Arles**, who also wrote the Rule. Born Chalon-sur-Saône about 465, died Arles 530. The nuns worked with the poor and sick, in girls' education and in dressmaking for themselves and for others outside the convent. They also transcribed books and engaged in daily study, and were enjoined to bathe regularly (though not in Lent) for the sake of their health. Her community also enjoyed the privilege of being exempt from episcopal authority, with the power to make all decisions concerning the community held within the community itself. Feast day 12 January.

Caesaria Saint, second abbess of the convent at Arles and possibly a relative of the first abbess; died about 559. She commissioned **Cyprian of Toulon** to write the biography of **Caesarius of Arles**, the founder of the convent. She also had the sermons of Caesarius, as well as the works of **Augustine**, transcribed and sent to various parts of Gaul.

Caesarius of Arles Saint, monk of Lérins and archbishop of Arles, France. Born Chalon-sur-Saône, Burgundy, about 470, died Arles, 27 August 543. Became bishop in about 503, did much to reform laws affecting both Church and State and helped establish Arles as the primatial see in Gaul. At the Council of Orange in 529 he played a leading role in ensuring that Semi-Pelagianism was condemned. He was an acclaimed preacher and wrote two monastic Rules, one each for monks and nuns. The latter was written for the convent which he started and which was headed by his sister, **Caesaria**. Both Rules were later taken on by other Orders. His biography was written by **Cyprian of Toulon**. Feast day 27 August.

Caesarius of Heisterbach Cistercian writer, born Cologne about 1180, died Heisterbach near Cologne, 1240. His early education was at the school of St Andrew in Cologne, where he studied the Church Fathers and the Latin classical writers. He entered the Cistercians in 1199 at Heisterbach, near Königswinter on the Rhine, and soon became

novice master and, in 1228, prior. He was a prolific writer and his twelve-volume *Dialogue of Visions and Miracles* was one of the most popular books of the period. He also wrote a life of **Engelbert of Cologne** and one of **Elizabeth of Hungary**, and his *Dialogus Miraculorum* (c.1219–23) and other writings on miracles give valuable insights into the popular beliefs and events of the period.

Caesarius of Nazianzus Physician and saint, born probably Arianzum, Cappadocia (Nenisi, Turkey), c.330, died Bithynia, 369. Younger brother of **Gregory of Nazianzus**, he studied at Alexandria and held various offices at the imperial court in Constantinople, including that of court physician. He survived the Constantinople earthquake of 368, and resolved to adopt a spiritual life. He was baptized, but died, in debt, not long afterwards. Gregory wrote a funeral panegyric for him, which is the source of most of our information. There also exists a set of four dialogues with Gregory attributed to Caesarius, but they are clearly inauthentic, deriving from a much later period. Feast day 25 February in the West; 9 March in the East.

Caesarius of Speyer One of the earliest companions of St **Francis of Assisi**, acclaimed preacher and first minister provincial of the Friars Minor in Germany. Born in the later twelfth century in Speyer, died 1239. Enjoyed early success in winning converts from the Albigensians, but in 1212 had to flee to Paris. Studied under Conrad of Speyer, before going to the Holy Land where, in 1217, he joined the Franciscans. In 1221 he returned to Italy with Francis and later that year was sent to establish the Order in Germany. He retired from the post of minister provincial in 1223 and it is believed that, in co-operation with Francis, he is the author of the Rule written that same year.

Cafasso, Joseph Saint, Italian priest, moral theologian and spiritual director, born in Castelnuovo d'Asti, Piedmont, 15 January 1811, died Turin, 23 June 1860. Studied at Chieri, was ordained in 1833 and did further studies in Turin, at the Institute of St Francis, where the emphasis was on combating the Jansenist tendencies prevalent in northern Italy. He became lecturer in moral theology at the Institute and in 1848 was made rector. One of his students was John **Bosco**. Besides his work in the seminary he did a lot of work with the laity: he gave lectures, preached, gave spiritual direction and was confessor. His writings include *Meditazione e instruzione al clero* (1892). Feast day 23 June.

Caffarelli Borghese, Scipione Cardinal. Born Rome, 1576, died 2 October 1633, he was the son of Francesco Caffarelli and Ortensia Borghese and a nephew of Camillo Borghese, who became Pope **Paul V**. Due to his uncle's influence Scipione was made cardinal of San Grisogono in 1606. He also held a number of other prominent positions in the Catholic Church, including legate to Avignon, 1607; archpriest of the Lateran prefect of the Congregation of the Council and abbot of San Gregorio on the Coelian, 1608; librarian of the Roman Church, 1609; head of the Grand Peniteniary and archbishop of Bologna, 1610; and *Camerlengo* of the Roman Church and prefect of briefs, 1612. His influence declined following the death of Pope Paul V. He is most notable for the building of the Villa Borghese at Rome, and for starting the collection of art treasures that were housed there.

Cagliero, Juan Salesian missionary, cardinal and bishop of Frascati, born Castelnuovo, 11 January 1838, died Rome, 28 February 1926. He was taught by John **Bosco** and joined the Salesians in 1854. He was ordained in 1862 and taught and composed music. In 1857 he led the first Salesian mission to Latin America and founded houses in Argentina and Uruguay. On his return to Italy two years later he was made spiritual director to the Society. In 1885 he went to Patagonia and served as vicar apostolic there until 1904. In 1908 he was sent by the Pope to San Jose de Costa Rica, as apostolic delegate to Central America. He was made cardinal in 1915 and in 1921 became bishop of Frascati.

Cahensly, Peter Paul Founder of the St Raphael Society for the Protection of Emigrants, born Limburg an der Lahn, Germany, 28 October 1838, died 25 December 1923. He was an active member of the St Vincent de Paul welfare society. While preparing to go into the family business he became aware of the conditions suffered by emigrants from European countries to the Americas and resolved to do something to alleviate some of their problems. He gathered data about all aspects of the emigrants' journey, spoke at religious gatherings, established missions, chaplains and welfare programmes at ports, and lobbied the churches, governments and business. In 1871 the St Raphael Society was set up, initially to help German Catholic emigrants, but later it encompassed Italians, French, Belgian and other Europeans. Cahensly battled on behalf of the Society and those it served, first as secretary and then as president. He also held secular political roles in local and regional government and from 1885 to 1915 was a member of the Prussian House of Delegates and from 1898 until 1903 a Centre Party member of the Reichstag. An American branch of the Society was established in 1883 but it sparked off a huge controversy. Those who were in favour of what became known as 'Americanism', close identification between Catholics and the USA, were upset and angered by Cahensly's call for the preservation of national languages and cultures through national chaplains, churches, Masses and language lessons. The situation was eventually resolved and Cahensly was both vindicated and honoured.

Caird, Edward Scottish philosopher, master of Balliol College, Oxford. A younger brother of John **Caird**, he was born Greenock, 22 March 1835, died Oxford, 1 November 1908. Educated at Glasgow, St Andrews and then Oxford, where he was given a fellowship, at Merton, in 1864. In 1886 he became professor of moral philosophy at Glasgow, a post he held for 27 years. In 1893 he was elected master of Balliol. He was an advocate of women's higher education and supported education for the working class in helping establish Toynbee Hall in London's East End and Ruskin College in Oxford. His writings include works on Kant, Hegel and Comte, *The Evolution of Religion* (1893) and *The Evolution of Theology in the Greek Philosophy* (1904), based on two series of Gifford Lectures.

Caird, John Scottish philosopher and theologian, principal of Glasgow University. Older brother of Edward **Caird**, he was born Greenock, 15 December 1820, died Greenock, 30 July 1898. Educated at Glasgow, he was ordained into the Church of Scotland and held several pastoral posts before becoming professor of theology at Glasgow in 1862 and in 1873 its principal. His publications include collections of sermons and *Introduction to the Philosophy of Religion* (1880). In *The Fundamental Ideas of Christianity*, based on his Gifford Lectures and published posthumously in 1899, his main concern was to show that Christian ideas are in accordance with reason, not contrary to it.

Cairns, David Smith Scottish theologian, born Stitchel, Roxburghshire, Scotland, 8 November 1862, died Edinburgh, 27 July 1946. He left Edinburgh University after a crisis of faith, and attended the United Presbyterian Theological Hall from 1888. In 1895 he became minister in Ayton, Berwickshire, and in 1907 professor of dogmatics and apologetics at the United Free Church College, Aberdeen. He was later principal. He chaired the 1910 World Missionary Conference commission which produced *The Missionary Message in Relation to Non-Christian Religions*. He lectured in America, China and Japan. His writings include *The Faith that Rebels* (1928) and *The Riddle of the World* (1937). He supported the incipient Iona Community, and was known for his personal diffidence, sensitivity, humour and love of poetry, especially Browning.

Caius, John Founder and first master of Gonville and Caius College, Cambridge, born at Norwich, 6 October 1510, died London, 29 July 1573. He studied in Norwich and at Gonville Hall, Cambridge, where he obtained a good knowledge of Greek. In 1539 he left for Italy and on 13 May 1541 he was created MD of the University of Padua. He stayed for a time on the Continent, visiting libraries in Italy and France, and encountering a number of major figures among the Reformers. He returned to England and lectured at Cambridge on anatomy for twenty years. He was appointed physician to **Edward VI**, and retained the post of royal physician until 1568, when his Catholicism could no longer be overlooked. Nine times president of the College of Physicians. A loyal Roman Catholic whose Mass vestments were burned by loyal Protestants, in the wake of the St Bartholomew's Day Massacre, while he sent them to the stocks. Author of a significant book on *Sweating Sickness* (1552), and with his considerable wealth he endowed Gonville Hall, coming to be regarded as its second founder.

Cajetan (Gaetano) Saint, founder of the Theatines, born Vicenza, October 1480, died Naples, 7 August 1547. He was educated at Padua University and graduated as a doctor of law. He served the papal court and founded a pious confraternity in Rome, the Oratory of Divine Love, gathering about him many of the devout of the city. He was ordained priest in Rome, 1516. He returned home to Vicenza two years later but returned to Rome in 1523, where he determined to establish a congregation of priests who would reform the standards of religious life. One of his co-founders of this congregation was Caraffa, then bishop of Theate, but later to become Pope **Paul IV**: it was from the title of his see that the organization took its name, 'the Theatines'. The members were bound by vow, living in common and engaged in preaching and pastoral work, mainly among the poor and sick. A number of houses were founded in Italy, including one at Naples, where he died. Cajetan also founded pawnshops to help, not to exploit, their users. He was canonized in 1671. Feast day 7 August.

Cajetan, Constantino Benedictine and scholar, born in Syracuse, Sicily, 1560 died Rome, 17 September 1650. Joined the Benedictines in 1586 and was called to Rome to work in the archives. He was made custodian of the Vatican Library, a post he held under four Popes, and until his death. He wrote biographies of numerous saints, on the primacy of the See of Rome, and tried to argue that many works, including the Spiritual Exercises of St **Ignatius of Loyola**, derived from the works of Benedictines.

Cajetan, Tommaso de Vio Dominican cardinal and theologian, born of Italian nobility in Gaeta, 20 February 1469, died Rome, 9 August 1534. He entered the Dominican Order against his parents' wishes in 1484. He studied at several universities in Italy, became professor of philosophy at Padua then of theology at, successively, Brescia and Pavia. He was appointed general of the Order in 1508, a cardinal in 1517, bishop of Gaeta in 1519, and legate to Hungary in 1523. He tried to get Martin **Luther** to recant and opposed the projected divorce of **Henry VIII**. His main goal was to defend orthodox philosophy and theology intellectually, including the monarchical supremacy of the

Pope. His main writing – he produced well over 100 titles – was a commentary on the *Summa Theologiae* that was a defence of **Thomas Aquinas** against **Duns Scotus** and the Protestant reformers, but even so, his original thinking and his freer biblical interpretations sometimes caused anxiety among his more conservative colleagues.

Calancha, Antonio de la   Augustinian monk, born in what is now Sucre, Bolivia, 1584, died 1 March 1654. Studied in Lima, Peru, and joined the Augustinians there. He became rector of the college of San Ildefonso and was later prior in Lima. His main work, *Coronica moralizade de la orden de N.S.P.S Agustin en el Peru*, published in two volumes (1638 and 1653), is an important source of information on the indigenous peoples of Peru and Bolivia.

Calas, Jean   French Calvinist, born near Castres, Tarn, 19 March 1698, died, by execution, Toulouse, 10 March 1762. At the time of his death he was a prosperous merchant and had been living in Toulouse for about 40 years. In 1760 one of his sons, Louis, had become a Catholic and another, Marc-Antoine, had also expressed an interest in converting. The family appears to have been opposed and when, in October 1761, Marc-Antoine was found hanged in his father's warehouse, Jean Calas was suspected of murder. He was arrested and in March of the following year was condemned, and put to death the next day. Voltaire took up the case to prove Calas' innocence, and through letters and pamphlets the case became world famous. Several plays and books were written about the affair. In March 1765 a tribunal in Paris declared Calas innocent.

Caldara, Antonio   Composer, born Venice, about 1670, died Vienna, 28 December 1736. He was a pupil of Legrenzi, travelled in Spain and Italy and in 1716 went to live in Vienna, where he remained for the rest of his life. He was assistant chapelmaster to J. J. **Fux**. Known mainly for his vocal writing, he composed Masses and cantatas and his work is regarded as a good example of Austrian baroque. It includes a sixteen-part *Crucifixus* and *Missa in contrapunto canonico*.

Calderón de la Barca, Pedro   Spanish dramatist and priest, born Madrid (?), 17 January 1600, died Madrid, 25 May 1681. He was educated by the Jesuits in Madrid, and studied law and philosophy at Salamanca and Alcalá in 1613–19. He served in the army and fought in The Netherlands and in Italy, and against the rebels in the 1640 rebellion in Catalonia. He managed the theatre of Bueno Retiro in Madrid, but in 1651 he entered the priesthood and retired to Toledo, being recalled to the court after ten years. He exercised his dramatic skills and became chaplain of honour to Philip IV. Continued to write for church, court and theatre until his death. Catholic and Castilian at heart, he reflected the Spanish way of life, writing 72 outdoor plays for the Corpus Christi festival; 118 of his regular dramas are extant, the most well-known being *El divino Orfeo*.

Calderwood, David   Controversial Scottish ecclesiastic and historian, born probably Dalkeith, Midlothian, Scotland, 1575, died 1650. Educated at Edinburgh University, and in 1604 became minister of Crailing in Roxburghshire. One of the main opponents of **James** VI's efforts to reintroduce episcopacy to Scotland, he was deprived of his right to attend church courts and effectively publicly silenced. The king later engaged in argument with him, with the result that Calderwood was first imprisoned and then exiled. He went to Holland and lived there until the death of the king in 1625. He became pastor of Pencaitland, Lothian, in 1641 and was one of three writers responsible for drawing up the service book of the Church of Scotland, the *Directory for Public Worship*. He wrote numerous polemical pamphlets but his major publication is his *History of the Kirk of Scotland*, still important for the light it throws on the Church in Scotland in the sixteenth and seventeenth centuries.

Caldwell, Mary Gwendoline   Founding financier of what was eventually Catholic University of America, born in Louisville, Kentucky, 1863, died on the liner *Kronprinzessin Cecile*, anchored outside New York, 10 October 1909. Her parents died while she was still quite young and she inherited a very large sum of money. In 1884, through her friend Bishop John Lancaster Spalding, she offered $300,000 to help found a national Catholic school of theology and philosophy. In 1899 she was awarded the Laetare medal by the University of Notre Dame.

Calecas, Manuel Byzantine theologian, rhetorician and opponent of Hesychasm, later a Dominican. Born Constantinople, died Lesbos, 1410. Little is known of Manuel's life but he may have been related to John Calecas, patriarch of Constantinople, 1334–47. His attempt to found a school was unsuccessful, possibly because his approach was judged to be too gentle. About 1390 he was introduced to Aristotelian philosophy by Demetrius Cydones, and he taught himself Latin to study the works of **Thomas Aquinas**. Forced to leave Constantinople because of his opposition to Hesychasm, he travelled through Italy and the Orient and, late in life, entered the Dominican Order at Lesbos. Amongst his many written works were a Greek translation of **Boethius**' *De Trinitate*, **Anselm of Canterbury**'s *Cur Deus Homo*, and a Christmas Mass of the Ambrosian Rite, and a Mass of the Holy Spirit from the Roman Missal.

Calénus, Henri (van Caelen) First follower of Jansen, born Beringen, Belgium, 1583 died Brussels, 1 February 1653. Studied at Louvain and became a friend of Cornelius **Jansen**, later bishop of Ypres. Following his ordination he worked from 1609 to 1624 in the parish of Asse, near Brussels, and for the last half of this time looked after the deanery of Alost. In 1624 he was sent to the parish of St Catherine in Brussels and worked with Jansen to introduce the Oratorians into the Low Countries. He was canon and from 1642 archdeacon in Malines and became vicar-general to Archbishop **Boonen**. He worked on Jansen's *Augustinus* after Jansen's death and at his request, and it was published in 1640. When it was condemned by Rome he put up a strong defence of the work but eventually submitted. Nevertheless, he was never able to take up the See of Ruremonde offered him by the king of Spain.

Calepino, Ambrogio Augustinian monk and lexicographer, born in Calepio, Bergamo, *c.*1435, died *c.*1511. He entered the Augustinians in 1458, and became a specialist in the Italian language. Compiled a Latin–Italian dictionary which appeared in 1502. There were many editions, and it eventually, long after its compiler's death, turned into a polyglot dictionary covering eleven languages. 'Calepinus' became a synonym for dictionary.

Calès, Jean French Jesuit, OT exegete, born Larzac in the Dordogne, 6 August 1865, died Vals-près-Le-Puy, Haute-Loire, 1 August 1947. All of his scholarly life was spent at the Jesuit College of Vals, where he collaborated with the NT scholar Ferdinand Prat. He wrote a book on the life and work of Prat, as well as the two-volume *Livre des Psaumes traduit et commenté* (1936) and numerous articles for learned journals.

Calixtus I Pope 217–22 and saint, died 222. Originally, it seems, a Roman slave, he was then (according to **Hippolytus**) involved in some kind of fraudulent banking activities and was sent to the mines in Sardinia. Released at the request of Marcia, consort of Commodus, he was ordained by **Victor I**, and subsequently became chief minister and successor to Pope **Zephyrinus.** He was attacked (unfairly) by Hippolytus for being a patripassian (i.e. believing that God the Father suffered in the sufferings of Christ), and for too lightly readmitting to communion those found guilty of sexual misdemeanours. He was in charge of the catacombs on the Appian Way which came to be named after him. He himself was probably martyred. His tomb in Trastevere, excavated in 1960, is still venerated. Feast day 14 October.

Calixtus II Pope, born *c.*1050 as Guido, son of William, count of Burgundy, died Rome, 14 December 1124. He became the archbishop of Vienne in 1088 and showed himself a prelate in the reforming tradition of **Gregory VII**. He was chosen as Pope on 2 February 1119 by a small group of cardinal electors who were at the abbey of Cluny when Pope **Gelasius II** died there. Calixtus was crowned at Vienne exactly a week after his election. His election was not at first recognized in Germany, but when agreement to do so was finally reached, at the beginning of 1122, the Pope used this opportunity to settle the struggle between the emperor and the Papacy over control of the Church. The Concordat of Worms of September 1122 carefully distinguished the spiritual authority of bishops from their temporal responsibilities, and while granting the emperor a say in the latter, denied him any rights over the former. Calixtus also held the reforming First Lateran Council in 1123.

Calixtus III Pope 1455–8, born Alfonso de Borja (Italianized as Borgia), Játiva, Valencia, 31 December 1378, died Rome, 6 August 1458. A client of the Spanish Antipope **Benedict XIII** and of the kings of Aragon, Borja became bishop of Valencia and a cardinal in 1444. During his brief pontificate the Christian powers rejected his calls to reconquer Constantinople, which had fallen to the Turks in 1453, though they scored a major victory against the Ottomans at Belgrade in 1456. Calixtus was a notable nepotist, his nephew Rodrigo Borgia, the future **Alexander VI**, being most conspicuous among the many Spaniards who benefited from the Pope's patronage. Calixtus showed no interest in humanistic scholarship.

Calixtus, Georg Lutheran theologian born in Medelby, Schleswig, 14 December 1586, died Helmstedt, 19 March 1656. He was educated at Helmstedt and influenced by the theology of **Melanchthon**. He travelled extensively in Roman Catholic and Calvinist countries in 1609–13, and became professor of theology at Helmstedt in 1614–56 and the leading protagonist in the syncretistic controversy which preoccupied the Lutheran Church through the early part of the seventeenth century. He attempted to create a theological system to bring about reconciliation between Catholics, Lutherans and Calvinists, based on the Scriptures, the Apostles' Creed and the doctrines of the first five centuries, but he was charged with heresy and accused of apostasy at the Conference of Thorn of 1645. His views were later championed, but no more successfully, by Leibniz.

Callahan, Patrick Henry US Roman Catholic layman, industrial reformer, born in Cleveland, Ohio, 15 October 1865, died Louisville, Kentucky, 4 February 1940. Started his career in baseball (as a member of the Chicago White Sox) but later went into business and eventually became president of the Louisville Varnish Company. He devised a plan whereby the workers would take a share in company profits and wrote and lectured to spread this idea. He was an active member and chair of committees of the Knights of St Columba on religious prejudice, on war activities and on peace.

He was also publicly vocal as a spokesman for Catholic committees on industrial problems, Prohibition, the New Deal, and against child labour and racial prejudice. In 1922 he was made a Knight of St Gregory.

Callan, Charles Jerome Dominican theologian, born in Lockport, NY, 5 December 1877, died Milford, Connecticut, 26 February 1962. Studied at Canisius College, Buffalo, and joined the Dominicans in Springfield, Kentucky. He was ordained in 1905 and went to do further studies in Fribourg, Switzerland. In 1909 he became professor of philosophy and biblical exegesis at the Dominican House of Studies in Washington, DC. In 1915 he went to teach at the Maryknoll Seminary in New York State and in 1940 he was appointed consultor of the Pontifical Biblical Commission. He was a prolific writer, producing some sixteen works in biblical studies, theology and liturgy in collaboration with John A. **McHugh**, two with Thomas Reilly and seven others on his own. He was co-editor with McHugh of the *Homiletic and Pastoral Review*.

Callewaert, Camille Belgian Roman Catholic priest, historian of liturgy, born Zwevegem, Belgium, 1 January 1866, died Bruges, 6 August 1943. Studied in Courtrai, Roulers, and then went to Louvain to study canon law, historical criticism and church history. He was ordained in 1889 and in 1893 became assistant at the cathedral in Bruges. In 1894 he became professor of church history at the major seminary, in 1903 was given the chair in liturgy, and from 1907 to 1934 was rector. From 1910 to 1921 he was also professor of liturgy in the University of Louvain, and in 1929 was made a domestic prelate. He was active in promoting interest in the liturgy beyond the seminary, began liturgical study groups and organized the Dutch liturgical week. His published work includes the three-volume *Liturgicae Institutiones* (1919–37).

Calliergis, Zacharias Greek editor and publisher, born in Rethymnon, Crete, 1473, died in or after 1524. He came to the West during the Renaissance period and copied, edited, printed and published numerous Greek texts. He worked in Venice and in Rome, where he set up the first Greek presses. He printed and published the then most comprehensive Greek dictionary, *Etymologicum magnum*, as well as influential editions of the works of Aristotle. From 1515 he appears in Rome and is last referred to in 1524.

Callistus I etc. Popes *see* **Calixtus**

Callistus I Patriarch of Constantinople, monk, Byzantine preacher and hagiographer, died Serres, 1363. He was a disciple of **Gregory Sinaites** and a fellow monk of **Gregory Palamas** and lived in the monastery of Iviron on Mount Athos. He was one of the signatories of the Hagiorite *Tome* of 1341, the manifesto for the Hesychasts, the proponents of a form of inner mystical prayer condemned by its opponents as superstition. In 1350 he became patriarch of Constantinople and the following year held a synod which canonized Hesychastic practices. In 1353 he was deposed briefly but regained his position the following year. He oversaw widespread pastoral reorganization and reform as well as the spread of Hesychasm. He wrote many homilies and the biographies of several monks, including Gregory Sinaites.

Callistus II Patriarch of Constantinople (Xanthopulus), Byzantine spiritual writer who lived in the monastery of Xanthopulus. He was patriarch in 1397 and was co-author, with Ignatius, also of Xanthopulus, of the tract *Century*. This contained 100 sections on Hesychastic (a form of mystical prayer) ascetical practices which was later part of the *Philokalia* of **Nicodemus the Hagiorite**. It seems to have avoided incurring the condemnation of the opponents of Hesychasm, because it made the efficaciousness of ascetical practices dependent on the action of God's grace.

Callistus Angelicudes (Melenikeotes, Meliteniotes, Telecudes) Follower of **Gregory Palamas**, mystical writer, active in the fourteenth century. He is probably the founder of a monastery and wrote several tracts on Hesychastic (a form of mystical prayer) spiritual practices and doctrine.

Callus, Daniel Angelo Philip Maltese Dominican medieval scholar, born in Malta on 20 January 1888 and died there on 26 May 1965. Joined the Dominicans in Malta and studied there, in Fiesole, in Florence and in Rome. From 1914 to 1921 he taught at the Theological College of Malta. Later in 1921 he went to England, to the Dominican House of Studies at Hawkesyard, Staffordshire, where he taught until 1923. He was regent of studies in Viterbo and in Malta, and in 1932 returned to England and settled at Blackfriars, Oxford. He was at the centre of the study of medieval thought and learning at the university) and from 1942 to 1954 was regent of studies at Blackfriars. He studied and lectured internationally and wrote extensively. *Oxford Studies Presented to Daniel Callus* (Oxford Historical Society, New Series 16, 1964) contains a bibliography of his work.

Cally, Pierre French philosopher and theologian, born Mesnil-Hubert near Séez, died Caen, 31 December 1709. In 1660 he was made professor of philosophy and eloquence at the University of Caen and remained in Caen for the rest of his life. In 1675 he became president of the Collège des Arts and in 1684 took charge of the parish of St Martin. He tried to win over the Protestants, but his book on the Eucharist was condemned by his bishop. He also published an edition of Boethius' *De consolatione philosophiae*, with major annotations (1695), and *Discours en forme d'homélies sur les mystères* (1703), a study of the Jesus of the Gospels. His major work however was a defence of **Descartes**, *Universae philosophiae institutiones* (1695).

Calmet, Augustin (Antoin) French Benedictine, biblical exegete and historian, born Ménil-la-Horgne (Meuse), France, 26 February 1672, died Senones, France, 25 October 1757. Studied at Breuil and at Pont-à-Mousson and joined the Benedictines in St Mansuy in Toul, being professed in 1689. Studied philosophy in Toul and theology in Münster and was ordained in 1696. He taught at Moyen-Moutier and at Paris and held various posts in his Order, becoming abbot of Senones in 1728. In his work he balanced the spiritualizing and mystical interpretations of Scripture of **Bossuet** with more literal interpretations. His works include the 26-volume *Commentaire littéral sur tous les livres de l'Ancient et du Nouveau Testament* (1707–16), *Dictionnaire historique . . . de la Bible* (1719) and the three-volume *Histoire ecclésiastique et civile de la Lorraine* (1728).

Calov, Abraham (Calovius) Lutheran theologian, born Mohrungen, Germany, 16 April 1612, died Wittenberg, Germany, 25 February 1686. Calov taught theology at several German universities before being appointed to the University of Wittenberg in 1650. He sought to defend orthodox Lutheranism against theological compromise, and to this end was a prolific writer and controversialist, engaging in polemics against Roman Catholics, Lutheran revisionists and other Protestants. His most important work is a twelve-volume systematic theology, *Systema Locorum Theologicorum*, which is regarded as one of the significant works of seventeenth-century Lutheranism.

Calvert, Cecilius (Cecil) Second Lord Baltimore, founder of Maryland, USA; born England, 1606, died London, 30 November 1675. Granted the charter of Maryland on his father George **Calvert**'s death, he sent his brothers to administer the colony, remaining in England to handle sectarian conflicts arising from the charter. Though a Roman Catholic, Calvert granted religious tolerance to all faiths, and sheltered Puritans from persecution. He poured personal funds into the new colony, and granted it a large degree of self-government. He clashed with the Jesuits on many occasions. Despite his active involvement, ongoing conflicts over the charter denied him the opportunity to visit the colony.

Calvert, Charles Third baron of Baltimore, proprietary governor of Maryland; born in London, England, 1629, died Surrey, England, 20 February 1715. The grandson of George **Calvert**, he administered the Maryland charter (1661–84), becoming its proprietor on his father's death in 1675. He negotiated boundary disputes with Pennsylvania's William **Penn**, as well as sectarian issues in England concerning the charter. After the Protestant revolution of 1688, he was stripped of his proprietary standing in 1691, and was charged with treason against Ireland for his Catholicism. The charges were later revoked, but the charter was never returned.

Calvert, George Colonist, statesman, born Kiplin, North Yorkshire, England c.1580, died London, 15 April 1632. Knighted in 1617 after a successful political career, he went on to become secretary of state, 1619–25. He surrendered his office upon becoming a Roman Catholic, but remained in royal favour and was made first baron of Baltimore in the Irish peerage. After establishing colonies in Newfoundland and Avalon, Calvert travelled to America and requested a charter for the region that is now Maryland. He returned to England, but died before the charter was granted. His son, Cecilius **Calvert** (Baltimore), received it in his stead.

Calvet, Jean French Roman Catholic priest, critic and literary historian, born in Castelnau-Montratier in the Lot, 17 January 1874, died Sèvres, near Paris, 26 January 1965. Studied at Montfauçon, Cahors and Toulouse and was ordained in 1896 and did further studies at Toulouse and at the Institut Catholique in Paris. He taught in Toulouse from 1904 to 1907, and in Paris at the College Stanislaus from 1907 to 1921, when he was made professor of literature at the Catholic Institute. He became dean there in 1934. He wrote widely on literature, and his writings more particularly related to religion include *La Litterature religieuse de François de Sales à Fenelon* (1938), *Bossuet* (1941), *St Vincent de Paul* (1948) and *Moliere, est-il chretienne?* (1950). He also contributed to the *Catholic Encyclopaedia*.

Calvin, Jean (Cauvin) Protestant reformer, born Noyon, France, 10 July 1509, died Geneva, Switzerland, 27 May 1564. Calvin was originally a classicist with no apparent interest in religion. This changed c.1533, when he experienced a religious conversion which also led him to embrace Protestantism. In 1536 he published the first edition of *Institutes of the Christian Religion*, his famous compendium of Protestant theology. The following year Guillaume **Farel** persuaded Calvin to assist him in consolidating Protestantism in Geneva. In 1538 they presented a reform programme to the city council which aimed to turn the city into a model Christian community, but this provoked a bitter controversy which forced them to leave. For a while Calvin lived in Strasburg, but in 1541 the councillors of Geneva invited him to return. Initially reluctant, Calvin eventually agreed, securing the acceptance of his presbyterian system according to which all citizens of Geneva came under the moral authority and discipline of the Church. In 1559

Calvin published the final edition of the *Institutes*, and founded the Geneva Academy for the training of ministers. This attracted students from many Protestant areas, through whom Calvin's 'Reformed' churchmanship spread to other parts of Northern Europe. Calvin's influence in both religious and secular fields has been profound, and he is generally recognized as a seminal figure in the development of Western culture.

Calvo, Carlos Argentinian diplomat, writer, born Montevideo, 26 February 1822, died Paris, 3 May 1906. Studied in Argentina and travelled abroad, returning home in 1852 after the fall of Rosas. He joined the diplomatic service and held senior posts in Montevideo. He was representative in England for Paraguay, and as special emissary to the Vatican from Argentina helped restore diplomatic relations between the two. He served in most European countries and was one of the founders of the Institut de Droit International in 1887. He was a member of the Academy of Moral and Political Science of Paris and received top French and German honours. The famous Calvo Clause, inserted in certain agreements between states, and the Calvo Doctrine, prohibiting the use of force and pressure a state might exert on another to obtain payments of claims in certain circumstances, both take their name from him. Among his writings, *Derecho internacional teória y practica de Europa y America* (1868) has been translated into many languages, including Chinese, and has had great influence on the development of international law. His other works include *Manuel de droit international public et privé* (1881) and *Le Dictionnaire de droit international public et privé* (1885).

Camaiani, Pietro Italian bishop and papal nuncio, born, Arezzo, 1 June 1519, died Ascoli, Piceno, 27 March 1579. He went into the service of Duke Cosimo of Florence in 1539 and was his agent at the Council of Trent. He joined the papal curia in 1551, was nuncio to **Charles V** and at Naples and was able to mediate in problems between the Habsburgs and the Papacy. In 1566 he was made bishop of Ascoli and implemented the Tridentine reforms in both letter and spirit. He was special nuncio at the court of Philip II.

Câmara, Hélder Pessoa 'Brother of the poor' and Roman Catholic archbishop of Olinda and Recife, Brazil, born Fortaleza, Ceará, Brazil, 1909, died Olinda, 27 August 1999. Ordained priest in 1931, he became archbishop in 1964 until his retirement in 1985. He was secretary of the National Conference of Brazilian Bishops for twelve years from 1952 and helped the formation of the Latin American Conference of Bishops. He put world development on the Church's agenda at Vatican II, brought clergy and laity into the administration of his diocese and reformed the education of priests. He was restricted by the military government between 1968 and 1977, but defended human rights, acted out a 'preferential option for the poor' and travelled as a prophetic voice for Third World peoples. His simplicity, charity, clarity of vision and saintliness won international respect. His writings have been widely translated.

Camerarius, Joachim (Kammermeister) Lutheran reformer and scholar, born Bamberg, Germany, 12 April 1500, died Leipzig, Germany, 17 April 1574. Camerarius was an outstanding Greek scholar, and studied at several German universities, including Wittenberg, where he became a Lutheran. Subsequently he pursued a successful academic career, notably at the Universities of Tübingen and Leipzig. He participated in the Imperial Diets at Speyer in 1526 and 1529, and at Augsburg in 1530, where he helped draft the Augsburg Confession. He wrote a biography of his lifelong friend **Melanchthon**, and collected a number of important documents written by prominent Reformers. A theologically moderate Lutheran, Camerarius also took part in several discussions with Catholics exploring the possibility of reunion.

Cameron, John Scottish theologian, Huguenot, born Glasgow, 1579, died Montauban, France 1625. Studied at Glasgow and in 1600 went to France and became professor at the Protestant University of Sedan. He did further studies in Paris, Geneva and Heidelberg and held the chairs of divinity at Saumur, 1618–20 and Glasgow, 1622–3. He was not at home with the more extreme Presbyterians in the Scottish Church and returned to live and teach at Montauban. His earlier work displays his concern to bridge the divide between **Arminius** and orthodox Calvinism on the question of whether Christ died for all or only for the elect and on this question wrote a series of tracts starting with *De triplici Dei cum homine foedere* (1608).

Cameron, John Canadian Roman Catholic bishop and educator, born South River, Antigonish County, Nova Scotia, 16 February 1826, died Antigonish, 6 April 1910. Studied at the College of Propaganda in Rome and was ordained priest in 1853. Was made professor and director of a school in Arichat, Nova Scotia, and in 1855 took charge of St Ninian's parish, Antigonish. He taught at the newly opened St Francis Xavier College (later University) and was made rector, a post he held for some 50 years. In 1887 he became bishop in Antigonish and opened schools and parishes as well as developing and strengthening the position of St Francis Xavier College as a centre of Catholic learning in the region.

Cameron, Richard Scottish Covenanter, born Falkland, Scotland, *c.*1648, died (in a skirmish with troops), Ayrdsmoss, Scotland, June 1680. Cameron came from an Episcopalian background, but became a Presbyterian following a conversion experience and joined the Covenanters, an outlawed movement which opposed the imposition of episcopacy in Scotland. He was an eloquent and powerful preacher in the Covenanter cause, and was one of the principal authors of the Sanquhar Declaration, which defied the authority of **Charles II** and accused him of tyranny. As a prominent outlaw Cameron was constantly sought by the authorities and was forced to live as a fugitive. He was eventually discovered by English troops, but was killed in the ensuing skirmish.

Camillus of Lellis Saint, patron of the sick and of nurses, Italian founder of the Ministers of the Sick, born Bacchianico, Naples, 1550, died Rome, 14 July 1614. He was a soldier and a gambler in his youth but from about 1575 began to live a reformed life. He made several attempts to join a religious order without success, partly because of infirmities which lasted throughout his life. He took an interest in the plight of the sick, and his experience as a nurse in the hospital of St Giacomo in Rome made him determined to improve their care. He was ordained priest in 1584 and set about founding a congregation which, in addition to the vows of poverty, chastity and obedience, would take a fourth vow to care for the sick and especially those with the plague. The congregation spread quickly and Camillus became its first superior-general. He introduced several reforms including isolation of those with infectious and contagious diseases and the importance of fresh air, cleanliness and diet. He also stressed the need for spiritual as well as physical care for the dying, and his brothers were the first such to accompany soldiers into battle. Feast day 14 July.

Campana, Emilio Italian Roman Catholic priest and theologian, born Signora (Val Colla, Ticinio), 1874, died Lugano, 8 June 1939. Studied at Pollegio, Lugano and the Propaganda College in Rome and specialized in Marian studies. He was ordained in 1897 and went to teach dogmatic theology at Lugano, where he spent the rest of his life. He was made theologian to the bishop of Lugano in 1914, and from 1927 until 1932 was rector. Among his writings are the highly acclaimed *Maria nel dogma cattolico* (1923) and the two-volume *Maria nel culto cattolico* (1933). He also made a study of Mary in art.

Campanella, Tommaso Italian Dominican philosopher, born Stilo, Calabria, 5 September 1568, died Paris, 21 May 1639. Joined the Dominicans and undertook the usual studies but rejected Aristotelian teachings and defended and promoted those of Telesio. He was arrested in 1599, imprisoned in Naples, tortured and tried for heresy and in 1602 was sentenced to life imprisonment. He was released in 1626, spent some time at the priory of Santa Maria sopra Minerva, was brought before Pope **Urban VIII** and on his advice fled to France in 1634 where he lived out his days at the priory of St Jacques. In his philosophy he attempted a synthesis of traditional Scholastic teachings and the naturalistic doctrines prevalent at that time, and his work tended towards the Platonizing tendencies of Augustinianism and anticipated **Descartes** in asserting self-consciousness as the basis of knowledge.

Campbell, Alexander Founder of the Disciples of Christ, born Ballymena, Ireland, 12 September 1788, died Bethany, USA, 4 March 1866. Campbell entered the Presbyterian ministry in America in 1812. He subsequently became convinced that the essence of Christianity consisted in baptism and belief in the divinity of Christ, holding that the churches should unite on this basis alone, rather than on detailed doctrinal confessions. He joined the Baptists, but his insistence that the act of baptism had redemptive efficacy caused him to split from them. Campbell's revivalist preaching met with considerable success, and in 1832 he and his followers united with Barton W. Stone's Christian Connection as the Disciples of Christ. This became one of the largest denominations in America, though it was weakened by splits in later years.

Campbell, James Marshall   Roman Catholic priest, Greek scholar and educationist, born in Warsaw, NY, 30 September 1895, died Washington DC, 25 March 1977. Studied at Hamilton College, Clinton, NY, Princeton and the Catholic University of America, where he gained his doctorate in Greek in 1922, and then studied theology at the Sulpician Seminary. He was ordained in 1926, taught at Catholic University and in 1934 became dean of the College of Arts and Sciences there, a post he held until 1966. During his tenure he did much to raise standards of learning and teaching in the College and, as an inspector, beyond it. He published *The Influence of the Second Sophistic on the Style of the Sermons of St Basil the Great*; *Greek Fathers* (1930) and, with R. J. Deferrari, *A Concordance of Prudentius* (1932), but his life's work, *Greek Attitudes toward Chastity from Homer to Plato*, was unfinished.

Campbell, John McLeod   Presbyterian minister and theologian, born Kilninver, Argyle, 1800, died Roseneath, 27 February 1872. After education at Glasgow and Edinburgh Universities he became rector of Row, in Dumbartonshire, in 1825. His views on assurance and his preaching of universal atonement both caused controversy and led to his dismissal from the Presbyterian ministry in 1831, as a result of which he became an independent minister. Campbell expounded his views in his classic work *The Nature of the Atonement*, published in 1856, arguing that the basis for atonement lay in the spiritual context of Christ's sufferings, rather than any penal or quasi-legal quality which could be attached to them.

Campbell, Royston Dunnachie Ignatius   Poet and satirical writer, born Durban, Natal, South Africa, 2 October 1901, died in a road accident in Setubal, Portugal 23 April 1957. He was born into a Presbyterian family but married a Catholic, Mary Garman, in 1922 and in 1935 converted to Roman Catholicism. In 1937 he was war correspondent with Franco's forces for the Catholic weekly the *Tablet* and from 1942 to 1944 served in the British Army in East Africa. After the war he worked for the BBC and was joint editor of a Catholic review, *Catacomb*, and when this folded in 1952 he went to live in Portugal. Like many Catholics at this time he had Fascist sympathies and was anti-Communist. His writings include three volumes of *Collected Poems* (1949–60) and his translation *Poems of St John of the Cross* (1951). He also wrote plays, satires, a study of *Lorca* (1952) and one of *Portugal* (1957).

Campbell, Thomas Joseph   US Jesuit writer and educator, born New York City, 29 April 1848, died Monroe, NY, 14 December 1925. Joined the Jesuits in Canada and in 1870 went to teach classics at St John's College (later Fordham University), New York. Studied philosophy and science at Woodstock, Maryland, and in 1876 went to teach rhetoric at his old college of St Francis Xavier. Studied French literature, church history and theology at Louvain in Belgium and was ordained in 1881. After his return to the USA he became president of St John's College and in 1888 became Jesuit provincial, instigating many educational and spiritual initiatives for lay people. He also made plans for a US Jesuit periodical, which eventually appeared as *America* and for which he served as editor from 1910 to 1914. He held several pastoral posts and lectured in American history at Fordham. His writings include the three-volume *The Pioneer Priests of North America* (1908–19), the two-volume *The Pioneer Laymen of North America* (1915) and *The Jesuits, 1534–1921* (1921).

Campeggi, Camillo   Italian Dominican theologian, born Pavia *c.*1500, died Sutri, 1569. He was Dominican inquisitor at Pavia, Ferrara and Mantua and was the Pope's theologian at the Council of Trent (1561–3). In 1568 he became bishop of Nepi and Sutri. He published mainly editions of texts including *De potestate papae et concilii generalis* (1563) and works by Torquemada and Ugolini.

Campeggio, Lorenzo Cardinal, canon lawyer, reformer; born Bologna, 1472 or 1474, died Rome, 25 July 1539. A civil lawyer, entered the priesthood after being widowed. Influential in Germany and England during the Reformation, he shared legate's duties in England with **Wolsey**. He heard the divorce trial between **Henry VIII** and **Catherine of Aragon** in 1529, but avoided entering a judgement, at papal request. Though a proponent of aggressive church reforms himself, he was opposed to co-operation with Protestant reformers, and negotiated a deal with the German Emperor that resulted in the Council of Trent.

Campion, Edmund Saint, Jesuit priest and martyr, born London, England, 1540, died (executed) London, 1 December 1581. An Anglican deacon, Campion was received into the Roman Catholic Church at Douai after doubts concerning Protestantism led him to study at the English College. In 1573 he joined the Society of Jesus, was ordained priest, and in 1580 taught in Prague and participated in the first Jesuit mission to England. On arrival he publicized his mission in a pamphlet popularly known as 'Campion's Brag'. He subsequently disseminated further pamphlets intended to encourage dispirited English Catholics, and challenging Protestants to debate. Campion was eventually arrested in 1581 and tried for high treason, resulting in his execution at Tyburn. He was canonized in 1970. Feast day 25 October.

Canal, José de la Spanish Augustinian, church historian, born Uceda, near Santander, 11 January 1768, died Madrid, 17 April 1845. Studied in Burgos and joined the Augustinians there in 1785. Taught philosophy at Salamanca and at Burgos, then became librarian at Salamanca from 1789 to 1800. He spent four years in Toledo before going to teach at San Isidro in Madrid. He was suspected of liberalizing tendencies but was later appointed to work on the monumental and comprehensive *Espagna Sagrada*, which had already reached its 42nd volume. He and his fellow worker, Antolin Merino, travelled around Spain researching archives to continue the work, and in 1819 they published volumes 43 and 44. Between 1826 and 1832 volumes 45 and 46 which Canal worked on alone, were published. His other writings include enlarged editions of earlier historial works, a *Manuel del Santo Sacraficio de la Misa* and several translations from French. He was an active member of and held several senior offices in the Royal Academy of History, and belonged to other learned historical societies.

Cañas y Calvo, Blas Chilean priest, founder of children's homes, born Santiago, 3 February 1827, died Santiago, 23 March 1886. He studied at the seminary in Santiago and was ordained in 1849. He was professor of theology at Santiago, preached in the city and acted as chaplain to a convent. In 1856 he founded La Casa de María, to provide housing and education for poor girls, and founded a community of sisters to run it. Homes were subsequently opened in Valparaiso and in Mendoza, Argentina. In 1872 a similar house, Patrocinio de San José, was opened for boys and was later given into the care of the Salesians.

Candido, Vincenzo Italian Dominican, moral theologian, born Syracuse, Sicily, 1572, died Rome, 7 November 1654. He joined the Dominicans in Rome and in 1609 was made provincial of the province of Sicily and in 1633 of the province of Rome. He was prior of the Minerva three times and between 1642 and 1649 was vicar-general of the Order. Between 1617 and 1642 he held the post of penitentiary on several occasions at St Mary Major and in 1645 he was made master of the Sacred Palace. He is the author of *Illustriorum disquisitionum moralium* (1637–43) and in this and in his response to Jansenism his approach is laxist.

Candidus A companion and scholar of **Alcuin**, accompanied the latter to Gaul in 792 and was a tutor in the palace school of **Charlemagne**, succeeding Alcuin as master in 796. Alcuin's commentary on Ecclesiastes is dedicated to him.

Candidus Bruun of Fulda Benedictine, studied in the court of **Charlemagne**, and in 822 became head of the monastery in Fulda. His philosophical writings include *Dicta de imagine mundi* and *Dicta Candidi*.

Canfield, Benedict *see* **Fitch, William Benedict**

Canisius, Henricus Canon lawyer and Roman Catholic historian; born Nymwegen, Geldern, 1548, died Ingolstadt, 2 September 1610. The nephew of St Peter **Canisius**, he studied at Louvain, and was professor of canon law at Ingolstadt. He produced many significant works, including *Summa Juris Canonici, Praelectiones Academicae Comment. in lib. III decretalium, De Sponsalibus et Matrimonio*, and a historical collection re-edited by Basnage and published as *Thesaurus Monumentorum ecclesiasticorum et historicorum*.

Canisius, Peter Saint, Jesuit theologian, born Nijmegen, Netherlands, 8 May 1521, died Fribourg, Switzerland, 21 December 1597. Canisius studied theology at Cologne and Mainz, after which he became a Jesuit and founded a house of the Order in Cologne. He was a staunch defender of Roman Catholic beliefs in opposition to Protestantism, and was the author of the *Summa Doctrinae Christianae* (or *Catechismus Major*), which was published in 1555 and has subsequently appeared in over 130 editions. In 1556 he was appointed provincial of Upper Germany, and founded several Jesuit colleges. Protestantism's ultimate failure to establish itself in Southern German territories was largely due to the vigour with which Canisius revived and consolidated Roman Catholicism in those areas. He was canonized in 1925 and simultaneously made a Doctor of the Church. Feast day 21 December.

Cannon, James US Methodist bishop and social reformer, born Salisbury, Maryland, 13 November 1864, died Chicago, Illinois, 6 September 1944. Studied at Randolph-Macon College in Ashland, Virginia, and at Princeton, and in 1888 entered the ministry. He spent six years in pastoral posts, was a college president for 24 years and a bishop for twenty. During these times he edited religious periodicals, founded a summer assembly and campaigned through several organizations against alcohol. He also worked to improve the social conditions of the poor and worked in ecumenism. His ecumenical activity did not prevent him, however, from campaigning and successfully lobbying the Southern Democrats against A. E. Smith, not just because Smith was in favour of repealing the Prohibition legislation but also because he was a Roman Catholic.

Cano, Alonso (Alexis) Carthusian, sculptor, painter and architect, born Granada, Spain, 19 March 1601, died Spain 3 or 5 October 1667. After studying in Seville, he went to Madrid, where he was given the post of court architect and painter. He moved on to Valencia, where he joined the Carthusians, was professed, then returned to Granada. Many of his artistic works survive; among them paintings and sculptures found in Lebrija, Granada and Malaga. His architectural work includes Granada Cathedral.

Cano, Melchior Spanish Dominican and theologian, born Tarancón (Cuenca), 6 January 1509, died Toledo 30 September 1560. He entered the Order in 1523, in Salamanca, and, from 1527, studied under **Francisco de Vitoria**, whose successor, as Professor of Theology, he became in 1546, after teaching in Valladolid and Alcalá. In 1551 he was the representative at the Council of Trent of the Emperor **Charles V**, who then created him bishop of the Canary Isles, a post he promptly resigned to return first to Valladolid and then to Salamanca, where he became prior and, in 1557, provincial. The appointment was opposed by **Bartolomé de Carranza**, who taught him at Valladolid and was then archbishop of Toledo. Pope **Paul IV** annulled the election as provincial, but his successor **Pius IV**, reinstated him, and Cano returned to Salamanca from Rome, where he had been pleading his case. He died the same year. His major work is *De locis theologicis*, which he began to publish in 1543 and completed in the year of his death. In it he discusses systematically the sources of theology, including philosophy and history, and it is the first significant work to do so. He was a man of great energy and strong views, and an opponent of the Jesuits.

Canossa, Maddalena Gabriella Blessed, religious foundress, born Verona, Italy, 2 March 1774, died Verona, 10 April 1835. She was educated privately by her uncle and from 1799 devoted herself to the care of poor girls. In 1800 she gave housing to some of these girls and three years later opened a school for them. She was joined by others and in 1808 founded the Daughters of Charity of Canossa (Canossian Sisters), whose apostolate was to education and nursing. Feast day 10 April.

Canova, Antonio Sculptor, born Possagno, Treviso, Italy, 1 November 1757, died Venice, 13 October 1822. Considered one of the greatest sculptors in modern times, Canova was an innovative Neoclassicist, and in 1815 negotiated the return of many art treasures seized from the Papal States by Napoleon. His works include *Theseus and the Minotaur*, now in Venice; monuments to Popes **Clement XIII** and **XIV**, both in Rome; a bust of Napoleon, now in Washington; depictions of Popes **Pius VI** and **VII**; a statute of George Washington for the State House in Raleigh, North Carolina; and the bronze *Pietà*, now in Possagno.

Cantù, Cesare Poet, Roman Catholic historian; born Brivio, Italy, 8 December 1807, died Milan, 11 March 1895. After discontinuing his seminary studies, Cantu taught literature, and eventually wrote the *Ragionamenti sulla Storia Lombarda nel secolo XVII* (1832), which contained liberal political views and for which he was imprisoned for over a year. His 1838 work *Margherita Pusterla* documents his imprisonment. In later years he spent time in political exile, and was also a member of the Italian parliament, 1859–61. Other significant historical works include *Storia universale, Storia dei cent' anni 1750–1850*, and *Storia degli Italiani*.

Cantwell, John Joseph Roman Catholic archbishop of Los Angeles, born Limerick, 1 December 1874, died 30 October 1947, was educated at the Jesuit College in Limerick and studied at St Patrick's Seminary, Thurles, Ireland. He was made priest in 1899 and emigrated to California, where he became bishop of Monterey and Los Angeles, 1914–22. He was bishop of Los Angeles and San Diego, 1922–36, and was foremost in the Legion of Decency for the Improvement of Motion Pictures. He was made archbishop of Los Angeles in 1936.

Canute King of England born about 995, the son of King Sweyn of Denmark, died Shaftesbury, England, 12 November 1035. In 1015 he made his second and this time successful attempt to invade England. He defeated Edmund, son of Ethelred, and took all the lands north of the Thames, and following Edmund's death was proclaimed king of all England. On the death of his brother Harold he

became king of Denmark and ten years later defeated Olaf II Haroldsson and took Norway as well. He was now second in power to the Holy Roman Emperor. He made generous benefactions to the Christian Church and in 1026 went on pilgrimage to Rome.

Canute IV King of Denmark, saint and martyr, born c.1043, died Odense, 10 July 1086. Canute was the third son of Sweyn II (Estridsen) and father of Charles the Good. Elected king in c.1080, he defended the interests of the Church in his reign, defeated and converted to Christianity the pagans of Courlund and Livonia and had a reputation for stern justice. He led expeditions to England in 1075 and supported the Saxons against William the Conqueror in 1085, only to be foiled by his brother Olaf's treachery. He was assassinated in Denmark by rebels and canonized by Pope **Paschal II** in 1100. Feast day 19 January.

Canute Lavard Danish saint, patron of the Danish guilds, nobleman, born about 1096, died by assassination at Haraldsted, near Ringsted, Denmark, 7 January 1131. He was educated at court and about 1115 became prince of the Wends in eastern Holstein and tried to convert them to Christianity. He was killed by supporters of Magnus, son of King Kniels, and to whose succession to the throne he posed a threat. Civil war ensued, and following reports of miracles at Canute's tomb a chapel was built on the spot where he had been killed. He was canonized in 1169. Feast day 7 January or 25 June.

Capaccini, Francesco Italian cardinal and papal diplomat, born Rome, 14 August 1784, died Rome, 15 June 1845. He was ordained in 1807 and taught astronomy at the University of Naples. In 1815 he joined the papal diplomatic service, where he took on increasingly senior roles. In 1826, with the future Pope **Gregory XVI**, he was appointed to negotiate the concordat with the Low Countries. He went there two years later and in 1830 went on to London to the conference on the independence of Belgium. He went on diplomatic missions to Berlin, Vienna, Naples and Portugal. In 1844 he was made cardinal.

Capecelatro, Alfonso Archbishop of Capua, cardinal, Roman Catholic historian; born Marseilles,

5 February 1824, died Capua, 14 November 1912. Of Italian descent, he joined the Oratory of St Philip **Neri**, at Naples, was ordained priest in 1847 and appointed archbishop in 1880. He was made a cardinal in 1885. His written work includes biographies of SS **Peter Damian**, **Catherine of Siena**, Philip Neri, and **Alphonsus Liguori**, as well as a *Life of Jesus Christ*, intended in part as a rebuttal of **Renan**'s *Life of Christ*.

Capelle, Bernard Benedictine abbot, born Namur, 18 February 1884, died Louvain, 12 October 1961. He was ordained priest in 1906 and professed as a Benedictine in 1919 at the abbey of Maredsous. In 1928 he became coadjutor abbot of Mont-Cesar, Louvain, and abbot in 1942. From 1936 he taught history of liturgy at Louvain. His writings include *Le Texte du psautier latin en Afrique* (1913), *Pour une meilleure intelligence de la Messe* (1946) and *An Early Euchologium: The Der-Balizeh Papyrus Enlarged and Re-edited* (1949, with C. H. Roberts). He was also a regular contributor to Benedictine and other learned journals.

Capéran, Louis French priest, theologian and writer, born Saint-Gaudens, 15 April 1884, died Toulouse, 9 January 1962. He was canon of the cathedral in Toulouse. He was a prolific writer and wrote about contemporary thought and the evangelizing roles of the Roman Catholic laity. His works include *Foi laïque et foi chrétienne: La Question du surnaturel* (1938), *L'Anticléricalisme et l'affaire Dreyfus 1897–99* (1948), *Histoire contemporaine de la laïcité française* (1957), *France nouvelle et Action Catholique* (1942), *La Méthode du prêtre: Leçons et lectures sur les preuves de la religion*, *Manuel à l'usage des écoles, des catéchismes et des mouvements de jeunesse*. He also made popular translations of the Gospels.

Capgrave, John Augustinian, theologian, historian; born Lynn, Norfolk, England, 21 April 1393, died Lynn, 12 August 1464 or, less likely, 1484. Ordained in 1417 or 1418, he possibly studied at both Cambridge and Oxford. He joined the Augustinians and was made provincial of the Order in England. He is incorrectly credited with John of Tynemouth's *Nova Legenda*, which he arranged and edited. His numerous works include sermons, biblical commentaries, a work on the creeds, and *A Chronicle of England from the Creation to 1417*. Many unpublished manuscripts survive.

Capillas, Francis de Blessed, Spanish Dominican missionary and martyr, born Baquerin de Campos, Spain, 18 August 1607, died by beheading at Fukien, China, 15 January 1648. He joined the Dominicans and went to Manila in 1631. He was ordained and from 1633 to 1641 worked in Cagayan and Babuyanes. He was sent to China, via Formosa, in 1642 and returned with Francisco Diaz to Fukien during the Tartar invasions. In 1647 Christianity was outlawed and almost immediately Francis was arrested and tortured, and later beheaded. Feast day 15 January.

Capitanio, Bartolomea Saint, religious co-founder, born Lovere, Lombardy, 13 January 1807, died Lovere, 26 July 1833. She joined the Poor Clares in Lovere when she was eleven but returned home in 1824 and opened a school in her house. Two years later she started a hospital in Lovere and acted as counsellor to many young people as well as writing devotional works, prayers and guides to the spiritual life. In 1832 she and Vincenza **Gerosa** dedicated themselves to God and founded the Sisters of Charity of Lovere. Feast day 26 July.

Capito, Wolfgang (Köpfel) Swiss scholar and Reformer, born Alsace, 1478, died Strasburg, 4 November 1541. Studied at Ingelstadt, Heidelberg and Freiburg, and after his ordination in 1515 he moved to Basel and met **Erasmus.** He became increasingly persuaded by the arguments of **Luther** and, with Martin **Bucer**, became the chief proponent of these views when he settled in Strasburg in 1523. He and Bucer drew up the Tetropolitan Confession in 1530 and collaborated with Haller in consolidating the Reformation in Berne. He signed the Wittenberg Concord of 1536, though he seemed to share **Zwingli**'s views on the Eucharist. He wrote a Hebrew grammar as well as commentaries on several OT books.

Cappa y Manescau, Ricardo Spanish Jesuit and historian, born Madrid, 25 October 1839, died Madrid, 8 November 1897. He began his career as a seaman and in 1866 joined the Jesuits in Cadiz. Studied in Spain and France and in 1872 was sent to Quito as professor of cosmography and astronomy. He later went to Lima and during the War of the Pacific in 1878 was volunteer chaplain in the Peruvian Army. He went to teach at the Immaculata School, but the outcry following the publication of his *Historia compendiada del Peru* forced him to flee to Bolivia and thence to Spain, where he re-edited and expanded the work he had begun. It eventually appeared in twenty volumes (1889–97) and as well as tracing secular events includes a discussion of the influence of Christianity on the culture of South America.

Capponi, Gino   Count, Roman Catholic historian, statesman and writer; born Florence, Italy, 13 September 1792, died 3 February 1876. Capponi was deeply involved in academic affairs, assisting with many projects, including the periodicals *Antologia*, *Giornale Agrario Toscano*, the *Guida dell'Educatore*, and the *Archivio Storico Italiano*, and also involved himself in the Amerigo Vespucci controversy. He involved himself in politics, and in 1848 he became head of a ministry, then later, a senator. His written work includes *Storia della Repubblica di Firenze*, a history of Florence; and *Scritti editi ed inediti*, a collection of his lesser works, published after his death.

Capranica, Domenico   Cardinal, canon lawyer, statesman and theologian; born Capranica, Palestrina, Italy, 1400, died Rome, Italy, 14 July 1458. A secretary to Pope **Martin V**, he was given a cardinalate in 1423 or 1426, which after some controversy was recognized in 1432. He was responsible for twelve embassies for the Holy See, and founded the Collegio Capranica. He mediated successfully between the Holy See, the princes of Germany, and King Alfonso of Naples. He was considered a likely successor to the Papacy, but died before this could happen.

Caprara, Giovanni Battista   Cardinal, born Bologna, 29 May 1733, died Paris 27 July 1810. After being ordained priest, Caprara served as a vice-legate and nuncio, and was made cardinal. He was ill-equipped to protect the Church's interests against Emperor Joseph II and others; it is probably for this reason that Napoleon Bonaparte chose him as his court's papal legate in 1801, a post he held until **Pius VII**'s imprisonment in 1809.

Caprara, who had been made archbishop of Milan in 1802, remained at the French court until his death.

Capreolus, John   Dominican theologian, born Rodez, France, *c.*1380, died Rodez, 6 April 1444. Capreolus became a lecturer at the University of Paris in 1407, where he lectured on the *Sentences* of **Peter Lombard**. He was subsequently made regent of studies at Toulouse before returning to Rodez in 1426, where he remained for the rest of his life. His four books known collectively as the *Defensiones* were an important apologia for traditional Thomist philosophy, which by Capreolus' time had been in a long decline, and played a key role in reviving its authority.

Carabantes, José de   Capuchin theologian, born Aragon, Spain, 27 June 1628, died Galicia (?), 11 April 1694. Carabantes devoted himself to evangelising Native Americans in Spanish America. In 1678, he wrote *Lexicon, seu vocabularium verborum, adverbiorum, etc.* and *Ars addicendi atque docendi idiomata* to assist others working missions in the region. An account of his life was written shortly after his death by Diego Gonzales de Quiraga; it was published in Madrid in 1705.

Caracciolo, Francis (Ascanio)   Saint, co-founder of the Clerks Regular Minor, born into a distinguished religious family at Villa Santa Maria, Abruzzi, Italy, 13 October 1563, died Agnone, Italy, 4 June 1608. He was ordained in Naples in 1587 and later joined Fabricius Caracciolo Marsicovetere and John Augustine Adorno and helped draw up the Rule for the Clerks Regular Minor. Their intention was to engage in charitable works, and to be engaged in perpetual adoration of the Blessed Sacrament, and in addition to poverty, chastity and obedience they took a fourth vow, not to aspire to any ecclesiastical office. Adorno became the first superior and Francis Caracciolo followed him in 1591 and remained in office until 1598. During this time the Order spread to Rome, and Francis himself established houses in Madrid, Valladolid and Alcala in Spain. He retired to a life of contemplation in 1607 but the following year went to negotiate the transfer of a house from the Oratorians in Agnone and died there after a brief illness.

Caracciolo, Landolf Franciscan bishop and theologian in the tradition of **Duns Scotus**, born in Naples, 1287, died Amalfi, 1351. He probably studied at Naples and then at Paris. He became minister provincial in Naples in 1324, in 1327 was made bishop of Castellammare and in 1331 was transferred to Amalfi. After 1343 he went on several diplomatic missions for Queen Joanna I of Anjou. His writings include 35 manuscripts of *Commentary on the Sentences*, a *Commentaria moralia in quatuor Evangelia*, *Postilla super Evangelia dominicalia* as well as sermons, tracts and commentaries on biblical themes and on the Immaculate Conception.

Caracciolo, Roberto Franciscan bishop, born Lecce, Kingdom of Naples, 1425, died Lecce, 6 May 1495. A Neapolitan noble, he was described as a 'second Paul' for his great preaching ability. As papal nuncio in Milan he preached a crusade against the Turks. He was made preacher apostolic by Pope **Paul II**, preacher of the realm by Ferdinand I of Naples, and became royal confessor to his son Alphonse. In 1475 he became bishop of Aquila and was transferred to Aquino in 1477. With this title he became bishop of Lecce in 1485. His sermons were widely read – early works appear in his *Opera varia* (Venice, 1479), and more complete collections appeared later.

Carafa, Alfonso Cardinal and librarian, born Naples, 1540, died Naples, 26 August 1565. Of the noble Neapolitan dynasty and nephew to Pope **Paul IV** (Gian Pietro Carafa), he became cardinal in 1557 and was named *bibliothecarius* of the Vatican Library. After other members of the Carafa dynasty were exiled in 1559, he was the only member of the family to remain in the favour of Pope **Pius IV**.

Carafa, Antonio Cardinal and scholar, born Naples, 25 March 1538, died Rome, 13 January 1591. Nephew to Pope **Paul IV** (Gian Pietro Carafa), his canonry was temporarily deprived when members of the noble Carafa family were exiled in 1559. He was restored by **Pius V**, and made cardinal in 1568. He was prefect of the Congregation of the Council, and was a member of the congregations that corrected the Missal, the Breviary and the Vulgate. A Greek scholar, he prepared

an edition of the Septuagint which was published in Rome in 1586. He left manuscript notes on the pontificate of Paul IV.

Carafa, Carlo (I) Cardinal, born Naples, 1517, died (by strangulation in the Castel Sant' Angelo) Rome, 4 March 1561. Of the noble Neapolitan dynasty, he was a nephew of Pope **Paul IV**. Although uneducated, he was a close adviser to his uncle and arranged his anti-Spanish policy, which led to war against Philip II. He was made cardinal in 1555. In 1559 his uncle exiled him from Rome when his debauched lifestyle and political intrigue became known. Carlo worked to install Cardinal de' Medici as **Pius IV**, but after further investigation Carlo was condemned for high treason. In 1567 he was posthumously rehabilitated by **Pius V**.

Carafa, Carlo (II) Venerable, priest, born Mariglianella (Naples), 1561, died Mariglianell, 8 September 1633. Of the noble Neapolitan dynasty that had produced Pope **Paul IV**, he was ordained in 1599 after time spent with the Jesuits and the Spanish military. He gave all his possessions to the poor and helped to organize missions for the people in 1601. He opened a house for his *Pii Operarii* in Naples in 1606, a congregation which has survived to the present. Miracles were attributed to him following his death.

Carafa, Carlo (III) Bishop, born Naples 1584, died Averso, 7 April 1644. Of the noble Neapolitan dynasty that had produced Pope **Paul IV**, he became bishop of Aversa (Naples) in 1616. As nuncio to the imperial court from 1621 he helped **Ferdinand II** select candidates for sees, reform colleges and arrange restitution of church buildings seized by Protestants. He was also knowledgeable about the religious problems of Germany and Bohemia. In 1641 he published the *Commentaria de Germania sacra restaurata*.

Carafa, Carlo (IV) Papal nuncio and cardinal, born Naples, 1611, died Rome, 19 October 1680. He succeeded to his uncle **Carlo III**'s see of Aversa (Naples) and in 1653 became nuncio to Switzerland. The following year he was transferred to Venice, and from 1658 to 1664 he was at the court of Emperor Leopold. In 1664 he became cardinal, his see passing to his brother Paolo.

Carafa, Oliviero   Cardinal, born Naples, 1430, died Rome, 20 January 1511. Of the noble Neapolitan family, he was uncle to Pope **Paul IV.** A jurist, he became archbishop of Naples in 1458 and cardinal in 1467 as reward for making peace between **Sixtus IV** and King Ferdinand of Naples. In 1503 he became cardinal-bishop of Ostia and dean of the Sacred College of Cardinals. The crypt chapel in Naples Cathedral, the chapel of St Thomas Aquinas in the church of Santa Maria sopra Minerva at Rome, and the cloister of Santa Maria della Pace are due to his patronage. His palace in Rome was a retreat for artists and writers.

Carafa, Pierluigi   Nuncio and cardinal, born Naples, 31 July 1581, died (during a conclave) Rome, 15 July 1655. Of the noble Neapolitan family, in 1624 he became vice legate to the governor of Fermo and bishop of Tricarico (Potenza). As nuncio to Cologne he set up colleges in Lower Germany and a university at Münster. He also effected reforms and introduced the Capuchins and Jesuits into the Palatinate and the Dioceses of Trier, Fulda and Constance. He rebuilt his diocesan cathedral, but resigned his see to become legate to Bologna and prefect of the Congregation of the Council in 1645.

Carafa, Rosa di Traetto   Venerable, Franciscan tertiary, born Naples, 6 April 1832, died Naples, 2 May 1890. Of the noble Neapolitan family and descended from the dukes of Traetto, she joined the Order of the Servants of the Sacred Heart. She suffered continual painful illness but enjoyed gifts of prayer which encouraged many vocations to the Order. The cause for her beatification began in 1907.

Carafa, Vincenzo   General of the Jesuits, born Andria, 9 May 1585, died Rome, 8 June 1649. Of the noble Neapolitan family, he entered the Jesuit novitiate in 1604. After ordination he taught philosophy and made the Congregation of the Nobles at Naples into a charitable centre. In 1624 he dedicated himself to those with plague, and in 1648–9 he organized food for thousands during an outbreak in Rome before he himself succumbed.

He became seventh Jesuit general in 1646 while he was provincial of Naples. As Luigi Sidereo, he wrote *Fascetto di Mirra* (1635) and *Camino del Cielo* (1641), both ascetic works. His confraternity Bona Mors still exists.

Caraman, Philip   Jesuit historian and writer, born Elstree, Middlesex, 11 August 1911, died Dulverton, Devonshire, 6 May 1998. He was educated at the Jesuit colleges of Stonyhurst and Campion Hall, Oxford. His chief works concern Jesuit hagiography – for example lives of SS Edmund **Campion**, Robert **Southwell** and Henry **Garnett** and of the secular priest Cuthbert **Mayne**. His translation of John **Gerard**'s *Autobiography of an Elizabethan* (1951) was notable. His final book, *Tibet: the Jesuit Century*, enshrines his exact scholarship in both archives and on the ground. He was editor of the Jesuit journal *The Month* from 1948 until in 1959 when he became vice-postulator for the cause of the **Forty Martyrs**. While working on Jesuit archives in Rome he placed later scholars much in his debt by his re-cataloguing and by unearthing much new material on the Jesuit missions in Paraguay. Caraman ended his days as parish priest of Dulverton in Devonshire.

Caramuel, Juan Lobkowitz   Cistercian bishop, theologian and mathematician, born Madrid, Spain, 23 May 1606, died Vigevano, Italy, 8 September 1682. He wrote many books on mathematics, religion, politics and science. A laxist in his moral theology, he used mathematics in moral theology. Several of his more speculative works were put on the Index, although he satisfied the Pope in 1655. He was titular abbot and vicar for Cistercian abbeys in England, Ireland and Scotland, and later abbot in the Diocese of Mayence, where he became a suffragan bishop. Emperor **Ferdinand II** gave him the abbeys of Montserrat and Vienna, and he became vicar general to the archbishop of Prague. His works include *Theologia fundamentalis*.

Caravaggio, Michelangelo Merisi da   Painter, born Caravaggio, 28 September 1573, died (of malaria) Port 'Ercole, 18 July 1610. Creator of 'realism' as opposed to 'mannerism' in Italian painting, he adopted a plain style. After apprenticeship in Milan, he worked in Rome, and after being charged with manslaughter there, he painted in Naples, Malta, Syracuse and Messina. From 1598 to 1600 he worked on the stories of St Matthew in the Contravelli chapel of S. Luigi dei Francesi, and in 1600–1 on altarpieces in the Cerasi chapel of St Paul in S. Maria del Popolo. His realism led to his *Death of a Virgin* (1606) being refused by the brothers of S. Maria della Scala.

Carayon, Auguste Jesuit and bibliographer, born Saumur (Maine-et-Loire), France, 31 March 1813, died Poitiers (Vienne), 15 May 1874. He joined the Jesuits in 1841 following ordination and worked as a librarian and procurator, despite poor eyesight. He re-edited books on asceticism and ecclesiastical history, and in *Bibliographie historique de la Compagnie de Jésus* (1864) edited a list of 4,370 works on the Society of Jesus. Between 1863 and 1886 he collected *Documents inédits concernant la Compagnie de Jésus* in 23 volumes.

Cardano, Geronimo (Girolamo) Mathematician and physician, born Pavia, Italy, 24 September 1501, died Rome, 20 September 1576. After studying medicine at Padua he became a country doctor at Sacco. In 1534 he attained a chair in mathematics and medicine in Milan, and later in Pavia and Bologna. In 1545 he produced his *Ars Magna* on algebraic theory. He ended his life pensioned by Pope **Gregory XIII** after a short period of imprisonment due to a false accusation of heresy. Other works are *De Subtilitate Libri XXI* (1550) and *De Rerum Varietate Libri XVII* (1557). His *Omnia Opera* appeared in 1663.

Cárdenas, Bernardino de Franciscan missionary, writer and bishop, born La Paz, 1579, died near Santa Cruz de la Sierra (now in Bolivia), 20 October 1668. A speaker of native languages, he was made visitor and official delegate to all the indigenous population of the area in 1629 after several years of missionary work. Later, he condemned the sale of coca and alcohol to natives. In 1640 he became bishop of Paraguay. From 1644 he quarrelled with the Jesuit Reductions, being driven out in 1651. In 1662 he was transferred to Santa Cruz de la Sierra. In 1634 he wrote *Memorial y relación verdadera . . . de cosas del Reyno del Peró.*

Cárdenas, Juan de Jesuit theologian, born Seville,

1613, died Seville, 6 June 1684. He was a Jesuit from age fourteen, and wrote a number of ascetical works. Most well-known was his *Crisis theologica bipartita* (1670) on moral theology, which argued for moderate probabilism and opposed rigorism; 65 propositions in the work were condemned by Pope **Innocent XI** in 1679, to which Cárdenas responded with *Crisis theologica in qua plures selectae difficultates ex morali theologia ad lydium veritatis lapidem revocantur ex regula morum posita a SS D N Innocentis XI PM . . .,* published three years after his death.

Cardiel, José Jesuit missionary and geographer, born La Guardia, Spain, 18 March 1704, died Faenza, Italy, 6 December 1781. He entered the Jesuits aged sixteen, was ordained and in 1729 went to Buenos Aires. He joined the Guaraní Reductions and worked with various indigenous tribes. In 1768 he was deported to Italy, where he worked on studies and maps of Paraguay. His writings include *Carta-relación* (1747), *Declaración de la verdad* (1758) and *Breve relación* (1771). In 1936 his maps were reproduced in *Cartografía jesuítica del Río de la Plata.*

Cardijn, Joseph-Leon Belgian cardinal, founder of Young Christian Workers (YCW), born into a working-class family in 1882, died 1967. Studied for the priesthood and was ordained in 1906. He was one of the pioneers of the movement for the ministry of the laity in the Roman Catholic Church. After his ordination he went on to do studies in the social sciences at Louvain and became a secondary schoolteacher. In 1915 he was working in a parish and also overseeing Catholic social work in Brussels and began to work with young factory workers, many of whom were completely alienated from the Church and from Christianity. He was aware that while there were organizations to help students who went into further education, there was none for those who went straight to work. His method of 'SEE (what is actually happening in one's own and in others' lives), JUDGE (this in terms of the Gospel values), and ACT (to improve the situation in accordance with these values)' was found to be very helpful by the young workers and indeed by others keen to witness to their faith in the world. Cardijn was in great demand throughout the world and spent much of the remainder of his life helping the movement develop. His book *Laïcs en première ligne* (1963) contributed to the shape of the *Document on the Laity* of the Second Vatican Council, where Cardijn was a *peritus* (i.e. a theological adviser). He was made a cardinal in 1965.

Cardoso, Manoel Carmelite composer, born Fronteira, Portugal, 1566, died Lisbon, Portugal, 24 November 1650. He became a Calced Carmelite in 1588, following musical studies in Evora, and in 1589 joined the Convento do Carmo at Lisbon. In 1631 he conducted the royal choir in Madrid, and he instructed the future King João IV of Portugal in music. He produced a book of Magnificats in 1613, which was followed by three books of Masses and in 1648 a book of Holy Week music.

Carey, Mathew Author, economist and publisher, born Dublin, Ireland, 28 January 1760, died Philadelphia, 16 September 1839. A writer, his protests about the treatment of Irish Catholics led him to Newgate Prison, after which he sailed for the USA. In 1785 he began the *Pennsylvania Herald*, and in 1792 set up as a bookseller and publisher. He also organized the Hibernian Society for the relief of Irish immigrants, and in 1802 became director of the Bank of Pennsylvania. His works include *Olive Branch* (1814), *Essays on Banking* (1816) and *An Appeal to the Wealthy of the Land* (1836).

Carey, Thomas F. Dominican psychologist and theatre producer, born Chicago, Illinois, USA, 19 June 1904, died New York City, New York, USA, 8 May 1972. Carey joined the Dominican Order in 1926 and was educated in psychology at the Catholic University of America, where he also served as an assistant professor. Convinced of the benefits of using drama to forward the Christian message, he founded an institute for performing arts in Washington, DC. While serving as assistant national director of the Holy Name Society in 1940–52, he founded the Blackfriar's Guild Theater, an off-Broadway theatre in New York. He helped produce some 43 original plays, some of which went on to Broadway and television. He continued producing until the Blackfriar's Guild was forced to close some six weeks before his death.

Carey, William Baptist missionary, born Paulers Pury, Northamptonshire, England, 17 August 1761, died Serampore, India, 9 June 1834. As an apprentice shoemaker he converted from Anglicanism, receiving believers' baptism in 1783, and was ordained, successively ministering to congregations at Moulton in Northamptonshire and Leicester. In 1792 his enthusiasm for foreign missions was instrumental in the formation of the Baptist Missionary Society, and he volunteered as its first missionary. His party arrived in Bengal in 1794, and in 1800 he moved to Serampore, where he established a school and printing press. Appointed professor of Sanskrit, Bengali and Marathi at the newly established Fort William College, Calcutta, in 1801, Carey published translations of the Bible in Bengali and also grammars and dictionaries in Sanskrit, Marathi, Punjabi and Telegu. He also translated part of the *Ramayana*, and helped to establish a number of schools and colleges. He was also a noted botanist and a fellow of the Linnaean Society, the London Horticultural Society and the Geological Society and received a doctorate from Brown University, Rhode Island. In 1792, with Andrew Fuller, he wrote *An Enquiry into the Obligations of Christians to use means for the Conversion of the Heathens . . .*

Carileffus Saint, bishop and hermit, born Aquitaine, died *c*.540. A monk of either the abbey of Ménat or that of Micy, after ordination he became a solitary by the river Anille in the Diocese of Le Mans. The abbey of Anille (later Saint-Calais) was built in commemoration of him. He was buried in Saint-Calais, and after a period in Blois, his bones were returned there in 1663. Feast day 1 July.

Carissimi, Giacomo Composer, born Marino, 18 April 1605, died Rome, 12 January 1674. After being based at Tivoli and Venice, he became *maestro di cappella* of San Apollinare in Rome in 1629. He introduced the secular *stile moderno* into sacred music, and his development of the non-liturgical Latin oratorio resulted in that form becoming artistically significant. He taught other significant musicians, and his work was much used by **Handel**.

Carleton, William Novelist, born Prillisk, Ireland, 1794, died Dublin, 30 January 1869. His career began with the sketch 'The Lough Derg Pilgrim', published in the *Christian Examiner* with anti-Catholic polemic added by Caesar Otway. He was later associated with Thomas Davis of the Young Ireland movement, although he never joined. Carleton recorded the lives and conversations of ordinary people, and Yeats saw him as Ireland's greatest novelist. His works include *Traits and Stories of the Irish Peasantry* (beginning 1830), *The Emigrants of Ahadarra* (1839), *Fardorougha the Miser* (1839), *Valentine McClutchy* (1845), *The Black Prophet* (1847), and lesser works such as *Jane Sinclair* and *Father Butler*.

Carlo, William Roman Catholic historian and philosopher, born New York City, New York, USA, 1921, died Ottawa, Canada, August 1971. After education at St Joseph's College, Westchester, New York and the Pontifical Institute of Medieval Studies in Toronto, Carlo held several professorships at different colleges and universities, including lecturer in anatomy and psychiatry at the Albert Einstein College of Medicine and professor of philosophy at St John's University, Boston College and the University of Ottawa, where he was a member of the University Senate. His main works are *Philosophy, Science and Knowledge* (1967) and *The Ultimate Reducibility of Essence to Existence in Existential Metaphysics* (1966).

Carlstadt (Andreas Bodenstein) First Reformer to celebrate the Eucharist in the vernacular. Born Carlstadt, Germany, c.1480, died Basel, Switzerland, 24 December 1541. Studied at Erfurt, Cologne and Wittenberg, and from 1502 taught at Wittenberg, where, in 1512, he presided at Luther's doctoral graduation. He defended Scholasticism against **Luther**'s criticisms but later changed his views and took an extreme position on the need for grace. He was excommunicated in 1520, and in 1522 he married. He found himself in conflict with Luther, who he saw as not going far enough in his demands for reform. In 1523 he resigned from Wittenberg and went to Orlamünde as a preacher. In 1529 he fled to Switzerland and, after abandoning his opposition to infant baptism, he was appointed preacher and professor of Hebrew at Basle.

Carlyle, Aelred Abbot, founder of the first Anglican Benedictine monastery, born Sheffield, England, 7 February 1874, died Corston, near Bath, 14 October 1955. After several unsuccessful attempts, he established a monastery on Caldey Island, South Wales, in 1906. He worked to reconcile Benedictine and Roman Catholic practices with Anglicanism, but failed to obtain official ecclesiastical sanction. After refusing to meet the demands of Charles **Gore**, bishop of Oxford, Carlyle and a majority of his community converted to Roman Catholicism in 1913. He resigned as abbot in 1921, and he went to British Columbia. In 1936, Carlyle became a diocesan priest of the Archdiocese of Vancouver. He returned to England in 1951 and renewed his monastic vows at Prinknash Abbey, Gloucestershire, where his old community had moved in 1928.

Carlyle, Thomas Historian and critic, born Ecclefechan, Scotland, 4 December 1795, died London, 5 February 1881. He brought Transcendentalism into Britain through a translation of Goethe's *Wilhelm Meister* (1824) and a biography of Schiller (1825), after the Calvinist faith he had lost at university was replaced in an experience described in *Sartor Resartus* (1833–4). He was critical of the utilitarian values of England and prophesied decline without heroic leadership. Works include 'Signs of the Times' (1829), 'Characteristics' (1831), *French Revolution* (1837), *Chartism* (1839), *Critical and Miscellaneous Essays* (1839), *Heroes and Hero-Worship* (1841), *Past and Present* (1843), *Cromwell* (1845), *Latter-Day Pamphlets* (1850), *Frederick the Great* (1852–65), 'Shooting Niagara' (1867) and *Reminiscences* (1881).

Carman, Harry James Educator and social historian, born Greenfield, New York, 22 January 1884, died New York, 26 December 1964. A Roman Catholic, he was a school and college teacher who joined the history department of Columbia University and became dean in 1943. He helped manage a fund for black students and educational programmes for unions. As a historian, he wrote works such as *Lincoln and the Patronage* (1943), *Jesse Buel, Agricultural Reformer* (1947) and *Guide to Principal Sources for American Civilisation* (1960–2).

Carmichael, Amy Missionary to India, born Millisle, Belfast, Ireland, 16 December 1867, died

Dohnavur, Tirunelveli, India, 18 January 1951. Educated privately, of intense personality and earnest Christian commitment, she was strongly influenced by the Keswick movement. As their first commissioned missionary, she set off for Japan in 1893, relocated to Sri Lanka, returned to Britain and wrote the first of many books, *From Sunrise Land* (1895). In 1895 she headed for Bangalore, mastered vernacular Tamil, and took charge of a band of women evangelists whose stories she told in *Things As They Are* (1903). This passionate corrective of other views was followed by *Overweights of Joy* (1906) and *Lotus Buds* (1909). Her children's rescue mission, the Dohnavur Fellowship, was registered in 1927 but dated from 1901. Bedridden after a fall in 1931, 'Amma's' last years were filled with visitors and writing. She never returned to Britain.

Carmody, Martin Henry Knights of Columbus executive, attorney, lecturer and writer, born Grand Rapids, Michigan, 23 January 1872, died Grand Rapids, 9 December 1950. He became Deputy Supreme Knight in 1909 and Supreme Knight in 1927. In this capacity he organized aid to the victims of natural disasters and scholarships to Catholic schools. He became Knight of the Grand Order of the Cross in 1929 and Secret Chamberlain to the Pope two years later. He also received honours from the French and Mexican governments. Many of his works appeared in *Columbia* magazine.

Carnesecchi, Pietro Secretary to **Clement VII**, born Florence, 24 December 1508, died (executed as a heretic) Rome, 1 October 1567. From 1536 he was associated with Bernardino **Ochino** and Peter Martyr **Vermigli**, and in 1541 joined the group of Reginald **Pole** in Viterbo. He was first tried for heresy in 1546, four years after Ochino and Vermigli apostatized, but was acquitted. In 1552 in Venice he showed support for Lutheranism, and was condemned by **Paul IV**. After Paul's death the condemnation was annulled, but under **Pius V** he was subjected to a year-long trial, after which he was beheaded and burnt.

Carney, Andrew Merchant and philanthropist, born Ballanagh, Ireland, 12 May 1794, died Boston, Massachusetts, 3 April 1864. A successful businessman, he founded the Carney Hospital in South Boston in 1863 and assisted in the foundation of Boston College, which opened the following year. He also supported Theobald **Mathew**'s temperance work, St Vincent's Orphan Asylum, the Church of the Immaculate Conception in Boston, the House of the Guardian Angel in Boston, and unemployed textile workers in Lawrence, Massachusetts. He also performed business services for Bishop John Fitzpatrick.

Carnoy, Jean Baptiste Priest and cytologist, born Hainaut, Belgium, 22 January 1836, died Schuls, Switzerland, 6 September 1899. Following ordination at Tournai, he studied biology at Bonn, Leipzig, Berlin, Vienna and Rome before returning to church duties in Belgium in 1868. In 1876 he joined Louvain University and established what was perhaps the earliest school of cytology in the world, using his own funds. In 1884 he founded the periodical *La Cellule*. His publications include *Manuel de microscopie* (1879) and *Traité biologie cellulaire* (1884), the only volume of a projected series.

Caro, Miguel Antonio Politician, jurist and writer, born Bogotá, 1843, died Bogotá, 1909. A Jesuit-educated militant politician, he defended the rights of the Church and became the main author of Colombia's constitution. As vice-president he ruled from 1892 to 1896 during the absence of the president, heading the moderate Nationalist Party. His works include a Latin grammar (with Rufino José Cuervo), translations of Virgil, mystical poetry, philological works such as *Tratado del Participio* and *Del uso en sus relaciones con el lenguaje*, and philosophical works such as *Estudio sobre el utilitarismo*, against utilitarianism.

Caro Rodríguez, José María Cardinal, born San Antonio de Petrel, 1866, died Santiago de Chile, 1958. He taught in Santiago's seminary until 1911, when he became apostolic vicar of Tarapacá, and subsequently titular bishop of Milas. Residing in Iquique, he started a news sheet, *La Luz*, and held public ceremonies to counter anti-religious feeling. He was transferred to La Serena in 1925, from where he made many visits into the interior. In 1939 he became archbishop of Santiago, founding a seminary, opening the shrine of Maipú and concerning himself with social problems. In 1945 he became cardinal. He wrote 33 books and pamphlets, including *Misterio*, a polemic on Freemasonry.

Carocci, Horacio Jesuit missionary and linguist, born Florence, 1579, died Tepotzotlán, Mexico, 14 July 1662. He was ordained in 1608, three years after arriving in Mexico, and was sent to a school in Tepotzotlán for speakers of Mazahua, Nahuatl and Otomí. In 1625, he was granted money to pay the natives to help prepare an Otomí grammar and dictionary. In 1645 he produced these for the Nahuatl language. In 1649 he became rector of the main seminary, and in 1653 of the school and novitiate in Tepotzotlán.

Caron, Redmond Franciscan theologian, born near Athlone, Westmeath, Ireland, *c.*1605, died Dublin, May 1666. He taught theology and philosophy in St Anthony's College and became canonical visitor of the Irish Franciscan province, although his acts here were annulled. Between 1651 and 1665 he served in Ghent, Antwerp, Paris, Flanders and Britain, before settling in Dublin. In 1661 he supported the Remonstrance, a statement of grievances and allegiance to **Charles II**. His works include *Loyalty Asserted* and *Remonstrantia Hibernorum contra Louvanienses*, both defending the Remonstrance, as well as a book of apologetics and a missiology for regular clergy (both 1653) and a general work on missiology (1659).

Carossa, Hans Catholic novelist and poet, born Tölz, Bavaria, 15 December 1878, died Rittsteig bei Passau, 8 December 1956. He was a physician until the late 1930s, although his first prose work, *Doktor Bürgers Ende*, appeared in 1913. His first book dealt with a doctor's suicide, and was followed by the poem *Die Flucht, Gedicht aus Dr Bürgers Nachlass* (1916). Other works include *Rumänisches Tagebuch* (1924), about his work as an army doctor, *Der Artz Gion* (1931), about war, and two works about the Nazi period – *Aufzeichnungen aus Italien* (1948) and *Ungleiche Welten* (1951). From 1922 to 1956 he also wrote volumes of autobiography.

Carothers, Warren Fay Pentecostal pastor and ecumenist, born Lee Country, Texas, 1872, died 1953. Corothers entered the Methodist ministry in 1896, but in 1905 he joined Charles Parnham's Apostolic Faith movement, becoming field director the next year. In 1912 he split with Parnham and in 1914 joined the Assemblies of God. An advocate of unity, he helped draft the 1921 AG resolution on 'World-wide Co-operation', but in 1923 he set up independently in Houston. He wrote *The Baptism with the Holy Spirit* (1906–7) and *Church Government* (1909), and published a journal promoting unity, *The Herald of the Church*. Carothers also had a legal career.

Carpaccio, Vittore Painter, born Venice, *c.*1455, died there early in 1526. His real name was Scarpazza. In the Venetian school he formed the link between painters such as Jacobello del Fiore and the classic masters such as **Giorgione** and **Titian**. Carpaccio was taught by Bastiani, and he was also influenced by **Mantegna** and Pietro **Lombardo.** In 1501 he was commissioned to paint the, extant, *Lion of St Mark* for the Doge's palace. He spent most of his life painting for schools or religious confraternities of artisans or foreigners, for which he produced his celebrated *Life of St Ursula*. His paintings can be seen in galleries throughout Europe, and many of those which depict the lives of the saints can be found in Venetian churches, notably San Giorgio de Schiavoni. His work is bound up with the golden age of the republic of Venice, and he is often regarded as the most quintessentially Venetian of all painters.

Carpani, Melchiore Barnabite missionary, born Lodi, Italy, 1726, died Lodi, 8 July 1797. He entered the Barnabites aged eighteen, and in 1764 he left Italy for missionary work in Ava and Pegù, Burma. He was the first to examine Burmese script, and attempted to develop a Burmese typeface. However, he was recalled to Rome in 1774 following an assassination attempt, and from 1775 to 1785 he was superior of the College of San Giovanni at Lodi. He wrote *Alphabetum Burmanum* (1776) and *Memorie sopra la vita di Hyder Ali Khan* (1782), an important biography of an Indian general.

Carpentras (Elzéar Gênet) Composer and priest, born Carpentras (Vaucluse), France, 1475(?), died Avignon, 14 June 1548. He became *maestro di cappella* Under **Leo X** in 1518, following periods in the papal choir and the court of **Louis XII**. In 1521 he moved to Avignon, returning to Rome only for the period 1524 to 1526. He introduced oval 'Briard' noteheads, and used *falso bordone* and Hebrew melismas. His works include five four-part Masses, a book of hymns with biographical details, Magnificats, three-voiced cantica and the *Liber Lamentationum Hieremiae prophetae Carpentras* (1532).

Carpzov, Benedikt Lutheran jurist, born Wittenberg, 27 May 1595, died Leipzig, 30 August 1666. Of a prominent Saxon family, he was brother of the theologian Johann Benedikt **Carpzov (I)**. He joined the bench at Leipzig in 1620, becoming a law professor in 1645. In 1653 he became privy councillor at Dresden, and he was judge again in Leipzig from 1661. He is seen as the father of German penal law, and he systemized Lutheran church law and episcopal polity in his *Jurisprudentia ecclesiastica* (1649).

Carpzov, Johann Benedikt I Lutheran pastor and theologian, born Rochlitz, 22 June 1607, died Leipzig, 22 October 1657. Of a prominent Saxon family, he was brother of the jurist Benedikt **Carpzov**. He became professor of theology at Leipzig in 1645 and mediated in the syncretistic controversy. In 1665 he wrote *Isagoge in libros ecclesiarum luth. symbolicos*. His son Johann Benedikt **Carpzov (II)** followed the same career, and his son Samuel Benedikt **Carpzov** became a court preacher.

Carpzov, Johann Benedikt II Lutheran pastor and theologian, born Leipzig, 24 April 1639, died Leipzig, 23 March 1699. Of a prominent Saxon family, he shared the name and the profession of his father, and was brother of court preacher Samuel Benedikt **Carpzov**. In 1665 he became professor of ethics, in 1684 of theology, and in 1679 he became pastor of St Thomas's Church. He opposed Pietism, and in *De jure decidendi controversias theologicas* (1696) wrote against August Hermann **Francke**, Philipp Jakob **Spener** and Christian Thomasius.

Carpzov, Johann Gottlob Lutheran theologian and Hebrew Bible scholar, born Dresden, 26 September 1679, died Lübeck, 7 April 1767. Of a prominent Saxon family, he was the son of court preacher

Samuel Benedikt **Carpzov**. In 1713 he became professor of Hebrew at Leipzig, and in 1730 superintendent at Lübeck. He opposed Moravians and Pietists, and in *Introductio ad libros canonicos bibliorum VT* (1714–21) he rejected biblical criticism and defended verbal inspiration.

Carpzov, Samuel Benedikt Lutheran preacher, born Leipzig, 17 January 1647, died Dresden, 31 August 1707. Of a prominent Saxon family, he was the son of the theologian and pastor Johann Benedikt **Carpzov (I)**, and had a brother with the same name and profession as his father (see above). In 1674 he became court preacher in Dresden, in 1680 superintendent and in 1693 senior court preacher. Unlike his son, Johann Gottlob, he wavered in his opinion of Pietism.

Carr, Henry Superior general of the Basilian Fathers, born Oshawa, Canada, 8 January 1880, died Vancouver, 28 November 1963. He joined the novitiate in 1900 and was ordained in 1905. His career was in the organization of higher education. He made St Michael's College the Catholic college of Toronto University, and served as superior for ten years from 1915. In 1929 he founded the Pontifical Institute for Mediaeval Studies in Toronto, serving as president until 1936. He then established a Catholic college for Saskatchewan University, becoming principal from 1942 to 1948. He later organized St Mark's College at British Columbia.

Carr, Thomas Matthew Augustinian, born Dublin, 1755, died Philadelphia, 29 September 1820. He established the Augustinians in the USA, arriving in Philadelphia in 1796. In August that year he was made vicar-general, acting as superior of the American Augustinian missions and prior of the Philadelphia community. He was given responsibility for Pennsylvania east of the Susquehanna in 1799. A parish was established in Philadelphia in 1801, and the Brothers of the Order of the Hermits of St Augustine was incorporated in 1804. In 1811 he established a secondary school for classics and religious studies. He wrote *The Spiritual Mirror* (1812).

Carracci, Agostino Engraver and painter, born Bologna, 15 August 1557, died Parma, 23 February

1602. He was the brother of Annibale **Carracci** and the cousin of Ludovico **Carracci**. He was apprenticed to a goldsmith and was primarily an engraver, as well as being the main articulator of the three's ideas. In 1597 he joined his brother at the Farnese Palace in Rome, and from 1599 until his death he worked on the Palazzo Giardino in Parma.

Carracci, Annibale Painter, born Bologna, 3 November 1560, died Rome, 15 July 1609. With his brother Agostino **Carracci** and cousin Ludovico **Carracci**, Annibale helped to replace mannerism in painting with the study of life models and past examples. The three opened a studio and academy in 1582, and worked together on frescoes at the Palazzi Fava, 1583–84, and Magnani-Salem, 1588–91. Annibale produced altar screens in Bologna, and in 1595 began work on the Farnese Palace in Rome. Here he produced allegorical works and scenes from Ovid with simulated architectural mouldings. Later he produced works with tragic elements and naturalistic landscapes, and invented the modern caricature.

Carracci, Ludovico Painter, born Bologna, 1555 (baptised 21 April), died there, 13 November 1619. He was the cousin of Annibale and Agostino **Carracci**. From around 1570 to 1580 he studied under Prospero Fontana, and then Passignano and probably Camillo Procaccini. He also travelled to various towns in Italy to examine local traditions. His works use patterns of light and dark and were often dramatic, such as his *Holy Family with St Francis* (1591).

Carranza, Bartolomé de Dominican archbishop and theologian, born Miranda de Arga (Navarra), Spain, c.1503, died Rome, 2 May 1576. He became master of theology in Rome in 1539, and for two periods between 1545 and 1552 he was imperial theologian at the Council of Trent. He worked for Catholic restoration in England and Flanders, and in 1557 he became archbishop of Toledo. As a Reformer, however, in 1559 he was accused by the Inquisition of Lutheranism and imprisoned. In 1566 he was brought to Rome, where **Pius V** died before he could acquit him. **Gregory XIII** made him retract sixteen theological propositions weeks before he died.

Carrel, Alexis Biologist and surgeon, born Ste. Foy-lès-Lyons, France, 28 June 1873, died Paris, 5 November 1944. In 1912 he won a Nobel Prize for his work on suturing blood vessels and transplants, and he also researched tissue survival and growth outside the body. In 1914 he established a military hospital in Compiègne and with H. D. Dakin developed an antiseptic that did not harm cells. He also examined Lourdes and identified himself as a Catholic just before he died. His works are *Man the Unknown* (1936), *Culture of Organs* (with C. A. Lindbergh, 1939), *Prayer* (translated 1947), *Voyage to Lourdes* (translated 1950), and *Reflections on Life* (translated 1952).

Carreño, Alberto Maria Historian, economist, sociologist and philologist. Born Tacabuya, Mexico, 7 August 1875, died Mexico City, Mexico, 5 September 1962. During a long career Carreño gained a reputation for erudite scholarship in a wide range of disciplines. From 1927 to 1929 he was a professor at Fordham University in America, and was also private secretary to the archbishop of Mexico City. His literary output reflected the breadth of his interests, but of particular significance are his works on the history of Mexico, and of Mexican–American relations.

Carrière Joseph Priest of Saint-Sulpice, moral theologian, born La Panouze-de-Cernon, near Rodez, France, 19 February 1795, died Lyons, 23 April 1864. Entered the seminary of Saint-Sulpice in 1812 and was ordained in 1819. Taught postgraduate courses in moral theology at the seminary. In 1829 he went to the USA as official visitor to the Sulpician houses and accepted the invitation to attend the First Provincial Council of Baltimore. A well-respected figure, he was appointed thirteenth superior of the Society of Saint-Sulpice. He published books on moral theology, including marriage and annulment. He had tried to argue that the French state had the power to annul marriages, but under pressure from Rome conceded that this power lay with Rome alone. He was one of the first writers to discuss theology in relation to the Code Napoléon.

Carroll, Charles Of Carollton. American statesman, born 19 September 1730, Annapolis, Maryland into a wealthy and powerful Catholic family of Irish origin, died near Baltimore, 14 November 1832. A revolutionary leader and signatory of the Declaration of Independence, and cousin of John **Carroll**, he was educated by the Jesuits in Maryland, in St Omer, Bruges and Paris, finishing his legal studies in London. In the 1770s he was much involved in the pamphlet war on behalf of the colonies. He became the first senator from Maryland to the US Senate, 1789–92. His stand for the Revolutionary cause was an inspiration to American Catholics. After 1800 he devoted himself to the development of the Carroll estates in Maryland, Pennsylvania and New York. Like his cousin John he was a firm believer in the separation of Church and State. When he died he was deemed the wealthiest citizen in the USA.

Carroll, Daniel Roman Catholic politician and American patriot, born Upper Marlborough, America, 22 July 1730, died Rock Creek, USA, 7 May 1796. Carroll's business interests, and wealth gained through inheritance and marriage, made him one of the new aristocrats of eighteenth-century America. He entered politics in 1777 and was sympathetic to the philosophical and religious principles of the American independence movement. He served in a number of public offices until 1795. His brother John **Carroll** was the first Roman Catholic archbishop of Boston.

Carroll, Howard Joseph Roman Catholic bishop, born Pittsburgh, USA, 5 August 1902, died Washington DC, USA, 21 March 1960. Carroll was ordained in 1927 following studies at universities in America and Europe. He served in parochial ministry from 1928 to 1938, during which time he also lectured in philosophy. Subsequently he went on to hold positions of responsibility in a number of both Catholic and national organizations, and in 1955 became the first bishop of Altoona-Johnstown in Pennsylvania, instigating a building programme that included the new diocese's cathedral. Carroll's varied contributions to American Catholicism won widespread recognition, and he was the recipient of numerous honours and accolades.

Carroll, John First Catholic bishop in the United States, born Upper Marlborough, Maryland, 8 January 1735, died Baltimore, 3 December 1815. He was educated by the Jesuits in Maryland and in St

Omer. In 1753 he joined the Society of Jesus and for the next two decades he was a student and teacher in the Jesuit houses in the Austrian Netherlands. When the Society was suppressed in 1773 he returned to America in 1774 to support the cause of independence. He went with his cousin Charles **Carroll** and Benjamin Franklin on a vain mission to get the French-Canadians to join the American side. On the recommendation of Franklin, Rome appointed Carroll the superior of the American Mission. His first report to Rome estimated the American Catholic population as 25,000, or 1% of the total population. **Pius VI** appointed Carroll bishop of Baltimore in 1788 and Carroll was ordained bishop 15 August 1790 at Lulworth Chapel in England. At his request **Pius VII** erected four new American dioceses in Boston, New York, Philadelphia and Bardstown, Kentucky, and Baltimore was raised to the rank of an archdiocese. Throughout his episcopate he established schools, seminaries and colleges but was also plagued by 'the wandering clerical fraternity' as he called the disruptive Irish priests who often joined forces with lay trustees to challenge episcopal authority. He held firm views on the separation of Church and State, on the spiritual role of the Papacy rather than on any administrative role, but he never advocated an 'independent' American Catholic Church and yet was always committed to the American experiment in religious liberty and freedom of conscience. His piety had nothing in common with the devotional romanticism of the nineteenth century.

Carroll, John Patrick Roman Catholic bishop, born Dubuque, USA, 22 February 1864, died Fribourg, Switzerland, 4 November 1925. Ordained in 1889, Carroll held academic posts at St Joseph's College, Dubuque, until becoming bishop of Helena, Montana, in 1902. He founded a new cathedral and a diocesan college, which was later named after him. Carroll became well-known in America as a powerful orator, and delivered addresses at a number of major public occasions. He died in Switzerland while en route to Rome.

Carroll, Walter Sharp Papal diplomat, born Pittsburgh, USA, 18 June 1908, died Washington DC, USA, 24 February 1950. Following an academic career and a brief time as a curate in Pittsburgh, Sharp was appointed attaché in the Vatican secretariat of state and US military vicar delegate. During World War II he represented the Holy See in a number of locations, principally to further the welfare of prisoners of war, work for which he was later honoured by the Vatican. After the war he was the Vatican's representative in the International Refugee Organisation in Geneva.

Carter, William Printer of Catholic books in Queen Elizabeth's reign, hanged, drawn and quartered at Tyburn, London, 11 January 1583. He was an apprentice to John Cawood, Queen **Mary Tudor**'s printer and printer to **Elizabeth I**. Carter became secretary to Nicholas Harpsfield, the theologian and historian and biographer of Thomas **More** and **Cranmer**. Carter secretly printed Catholic books, tracts and pamphlets against Elizabeth I and her regime in the years 1579–82. He was part of a Catholic printing industry to cope with the works of **Campion** and Parsons. He was imprisoned in the Tower in July 1582 and executed for treason at Tyburn.

Cartwright, Thomas Leading English Puritan, born Hertfordshire, 1535, died Warwick, 27 December 1603. Educated at Cambridge, first at Clare Hall and then at St John's College. He was among those who had to leave Cambridge while **Mary** was queen, but returned after her death, and in 1562 he was made a fellow of Trinity. He spent four years in Ireland from 1565, and returned to Cambridge but was deprived of his fellowship in 1570, because of his strong Puritan views, and went to Geneva. He returned in 1572 but, following the publication of works critical of the religious establishment, a warrant for his arrest was issued and he again left the country. He eventually returned in 1585 and became chaplain in Warwick, under the patronage of the Earl of Leicester. He was arrested and imprisoned in 1590 but, by the influence of the king and of Burghley, was freed two years later. He spent some time on Guernsey before retiring to Warwickshire.

Carvajal, Bernardino López de Cardinal bishop, born Plasencia, Spain, 1456, died Rome, 16 December 1523. Carvajal held various bishoprics in Spain before being made a cardinal in 1493. He was sent as legate to Germany in 1496. In a clash with Pope **Julius II** over foreign policy, Carvajal was among a cabal of dissident cardinals which convened a council at Pisa and summoned Julius to appear before it. Carvajal was excommunicated, along with his companions, but was absolved and restored when he later pledged his loyalty to Julius' successor, **Leo X**.

Carvajal, Gaspar de Dominican missionary, born Estremadura, Spain, c.1500, died Lima, Peru, 1584. Entered the Dominicans and went to Peru as a missionary. He was part of the unsuccessful exploratory expedition of Gonzalo Pizarro which returned to Quito in 1542 with only eighty of the four hundred people who had set out. He was posted to the mission at Tacuman and later became provincial of the Order.

Carvajal, Juan de Cardinal, papal diplomat, born Truxillo, Estremadura, Spain, c.1400, died Rome, 6 December 1469. Studied both canon and civil law and became auditor of the Rota in Rome, and City Governor. He spent most of his life as official legate of the Holy See throughout Europe. Between 1441 and 1448, he was mainly in Germany, during which time, 1446, he was made cardinal by **Eugenius IV**. From 1455 to 1461 he was in Hungary helping prevent the progress of the Ottoman Empire and the Islamic religion. On his return to Rome he was consecrated cardinal-bishop of Porto and Santa Rufina.

Carvajal, Luisa de Born Jaraizejo, Spain 2 January 1568, died London, England, 2 January 1614. She had a vocation to minister to Catholics in England. She was brought up in Pamplona, where she was known for her saintliness. She remained unmarried, but did not become a nun. Instead she founded a group of ladies devoted to prayer. In London she continued this work, visiting recusant Catholics, often in prison. She tended to the Benedictine John Roberts before his martyrdom. Twice she too was imprisoned, but the Spanish ambassador in London secured her release.

Carve, Thomas Historian and traveller, born Mobernan, Co. Tipperary, 1590. His name is often written 'Carue', 'Carew', or in Irish 'O'Corrain'. The date of his death is conjectural in the 1670s.

After being fostered with the Butlers of Ormond he went to Oxford and was ordained priest and became chaplain to Walter Butler for four years. In the 1630s he travelled much in the Germanies and wrote up a curious but valuable *Itinerary* published in Mainz in April 1639 and dedicated to the Marquis of Ormonde. In 1640 he was made chaplain general of English, Scots and Irish forces fighting under Walter Devereux on the Continent. But he resided in Vienna as notary apostolic and brought out the second and third parts of his *Itinerary*, a valued source for the Thirty Years' War and the Civil War in England, as well as containing a description of Ireland and a curious account of London's buildings. His full writings were translated and reprinted in London in 1859.

Casa, Giovanni della Archbishop and poet, born near Florence, 28 June 1503, died Montepulciano, 14 November 1556. After his ordination he worked in the papal civil service in Rome, and became archbisop of Benevento in 1544, though he was made papal representative in Venice, and never resided in his see. His post terminated in 1549 and he retired to the country, but was recalled to Rome a year before his death to be secretary of state – though to his disappointment he was never made a cardinal. He is best remembered for his lyric verse, some of which reflects on the vanity of ambition, and a manual of etiquette, *Il Galateo* (1551–4).

Casale, Giacinto da Capuchin preacher and papal diplomat, born Casale dai conti Natta, Italy, 21 January 1575, died Casale dai conti Natta, 18 January 1627. An important personage in the Catholic Reformation, Casale was by birth the count of Alfiano. He joined the Capuchins in Venice, in 1601, and soon began preaching through the country. He also preached in Prague, in 1606, and helped to reconcile Emperor Rudolph II with his brother. This success led to many diplomatic missions all over Europe, including helping Pope **Gregory XV** to ensure a majority of Catholic electors for the Empire, for which success he was offered – but declined – the cardinal's hat. He also wrote ten volumes of sermons and several works on ascetic practice.

Casani, Pietro Venerable, Piarist, born Lucca,

Italy, 8 September 1570, died Rome, 17 October 1647. He was a companion of **Joseph Calasanctius**, the founder of Piarist schools, for which he wrote a Latin grammar. He became secretary-general and rector of St Panteleon, Rome, and was the author of works on theology and exorcism. In Germany, he was effective in preaching and in raising money for charity. Ladislas IV invited him to Poland to inspect proposed sites for Piarist schools. The process of his beatification, introduced in 1922, was held up by the loss of the relevant documents.

Casas Martínez, Felipe de Jesús Saint, proto-martyr of Japan. Born Mexico City, 1 May 1572, died Nagasaki, Japan, 5 February 1597. Of Spanish parentage, at seventeen he joined the Franciscans in Puebla, left to become a merchant and went to Manila. Here he rediscovered his vocation, took the habit and was ordained in 1593. On 18 October 1596 the ship in which he was travelling back to Mexico was wrecked on the coast of Japan. He was taken into the Franciscan convent of Miyaco, Kyoto, but shortly afterwards the Japanese authorities ordered the execution of the missionaries, with whom he requested to be included, and they were all crucified. He was beatified 14 September 1627 and canonized 8 June 1862. Feast day 6 February (martyrs of Japan).

Casaubon, Isaac Classical scholar, born Geneva, Switzerland, 18 February 1559, died London, England, 1 July 1614. He was appointed professor of Greek at the Academy of Geneva, where he had been educated, in 1581. As a Protestant, he was not allowed to accept a chair at the University of Paris, but was made royal librarian. **Scaliger** called him 'the most learned man in Europe'. He was one of the genuine fraternity of scholars who transcended the religious division. A man of broad sympathy and exactness of judgement, greatly influenced by patristic studies, opposed to extremes both of Catholicism and of Calvinism, he found his true home in the Church of England. His most important works were editions of Suetonius, Athenaeus and Theophrastus.

Casava, Girolamo Cardinal, born Naples, 13 July 1620, died Rome, 3 March 1700. He studied and practised law in Naples. Cardinal Pamphily advised him to become a priest. When Pamphily became Pope **Innocent X**, Casava became his private chamberlain and was promoted to become governor of various Italian towns. At Camerino he became a friend of Bishop Altieri, who, when he became Pope **Alexander VII**, sent Casava on a mission to Malta. Casava was governor of the conclave which elected **Clement IX** pope. He was ordained cardinal and **Innocent XII** made him Vatican librarian. In Rome, Casava had to consider various controversial legal matters brought before the Holy See, including Quietism, the Gallican question, and the Chinese rites controversy between the Jesuits and the Dominicans. He founded and endowed the large Casanatense Library in Rome.

Casavant, Joseph Canadian organ-builder, born 1807, died St Hyacinthe, Canada, 9 March 1874. He made sixteen organs, among them those installed in the Catholic cathedrals of Ottawa and Kingston, Canada. He insisted on the highest quality in his instruments, a tradition carried on by his sons, and Casavant organs are to be found all over North America and in many parts of the world.

Casciolini, Claudio Composer of church music, born Rome, 9 November 1697, died there, 18 January 1760. He was choirmaster at San Lorenzo in Damaso in Rome, but none of his compositions was published in his lifetime. There are some MSS in the university library of Westphalia, Germany, and of his works in modern editions, the *Angelus Domini Descendit*, an Easter motet for two choirs of four voices, demonstrates his brilliance in the Roman baroque tradition.

Casel, Odo Liturgist and prominent figure in the twentieth-century liturgical movement, born Koblenz-Lützel, 27 September 1886, died 28 March 1948. Became a Benedictine monk of Maria Laach in 1902. From 1922 to his death he was spiritual adviser at Holy Cross Abbey, Herstelle. His thoughts, especially on the Eucharist, are contained in several papers including *Jahrbuch für Liturgiewissenschaft*.

Casgrain, Henri Raymond French-Canadian historian, born Rivière-Ouelle, Province of Quebec, 16 December 1831, died Quebec City, 11 February 1904. Educated at the college of Sainte Anne de la Pocatière, he was ordained in 1856 and in 1860 appointed to the cathedral parish of Quebec, becoming chaplain of the convent of the Good Shepherd there in 1861, but retired with eye trouble in 1870. Intensely patriotic, he wrote about the religious and social development of his country in narratives and historical essays about its life and customs and was a leader of the group of intellectuals known as the Ecole de Québec. His most important work was *Montcalm et Lévis* (1891).

Cashwell, Gaston Pentecostal preacher, born Sampson County, North Carolina, 1862, died 1916. Cashwell began as a Methodist minister, but in 1903 he joined A. B. **Crumpler**'s Pentecostal Holiness Church. In 1906 he travelled to Azusa Street, where he experienced speaking in tongues and the end of his racial prejudice. On return to Carolina, he spread Pentecostalism in the Holiness churches. Leaders of the Church of God and of the future Assemblies of God had their first Pentecostal experiences at Cashwell's meetings. In 1909, the 'apostle of the South' became an independent pastor. From 1907 he published a paper, *Bridegroom's Messenger*.

Casimir Patron saint of Poland and Lithuania, born Cracow, 1458, died of phthisis at Grodno, 4 March 1484. A member of the Polish royal family who, to the disappointment of his relatives, led a life of prayer, philanthropy and penance. He was canonized in 1522. Feast day 4 March.

Casoni, Filippo Cardinal and papal secretary of state, born Sarzana, Italy, 6 May 1733, died Rome, 9 October 1811. After studying at the Sapienza he was sent as papal vice-legate to Avignon, a State of the Church, in 1789, where there was revolutionary unrest which he tried to settle by distributing free grain, establishing new municipalities and reducing his own and the Pope's authority. **Pius VI** saw this as weakness, and in 1790 Casoni was sent to Nice as vice-legate until 1794 and thence to Madrid as nuncio. Here he found Spanish nationalism arrogating the plenitude of faculties to bishops, episcopal consecration to the Crown, and whatever concerned Roman tribunals to the Spanish Rota. All these changes Casoni persuaded the king to abrogate. He was created cardinal 28 February 1801.

Caspar, Erich Protestant medievalist and historian of the Papacy, born 14 November 1879, died Berlin, 22 January 1935. He studied at Heidelberg, Bonn and Berlin, where his doctoral thesis indicated the direction of his life's work, which was to be the study of papal history and of the Papal States. A methodical, skilled and scholarly investigator, his most penetrating works were his essays on **Gregory I** and St **Bernard of Clairvaux** in *Meister der Politik*, and his magisterial *Geschichte des Papstumms* (7 vols, 1930–3), which remains basic to the understanding of both the Papacy and European development.

Caspicara (nickname 'Scarface') of **Manuel Chili** Ecuadorian sculptor and painter of Amerindian descent. His dates of birth and death are unknown, though his authenticated works date from 1790 to 1810. His thorough knowledge of anatomy, eye for detail and love of colour animate his works, examples of which are in Quito and in the monastery of San Francisco. He was the last Amerindian representative of Ecuadorian art.

Cassander, George Roman Catholic theologian, born Pitthem, Belgium, 24 August 1513, died Cologne, 3 February 1566. Studied at Louvain and later taught at Bruges and Ghent. His most famous work, *De Officio . . . Religionis Dissidio* (1561), was an attempt to reconcile the differences between Roman Catholics and Protestants. It was presented to the Colloquy of Poissy in 1561 but caused offence to both sides. In his *Consultatio* (1577) he tried to put a Catholic interpretation on Protestant teaching.

Cassant, Marie Joseph Trappist-Cistercian, born Casseneuil-sur-Lot, France, 6 March 1879, died abbey of Notre Dame du Désert, 17 June 1903. He wanted to be a priest, but was not thought to be physically or intellectually strong enough for the priesthood. In 1894 he became a choir religious in the Trappist-Cistercian abbey of Notre Dame du Désert, where he was professed on 24 May 1900. With the help of his spiritual father André Malet, later the abbot, who recognized his spiritual perception, he was ordained priest 12 October 1902.

His cause for beatification was introduced at Rome, 19 February 1956.

Cassian, John Monk and theologian who introduced Eastern monasticism to the West, born Dobrudscha, Scythia, 360, died Marseilles, 435. Educated in a monastery at Bethlehem before spending about fifteen years as a hermit in the Egyptian desert. Studied in Constantinople with St **John Chrysostom**, who ordained him as deacon. In about 415 he settled in Marseilles, France, and founded the monasteries of SS Peter and Victor for men, and St Saviour for women. His books include *The Institutes*, which lays down the rules of the monastic life, and *The Conferences*, which describes his discussions with certain monastic leaders. He also wrote *De Incarnatione Domini*, a work in seven books, containing the teachings of **Nestorius**. The East treats him as a saint, but he is not recognized as such by the West.

Cassian of Nantes Blessed Capuchin missionary and martyr, born Nantes, France, 15 January 1607, died Condar, Ethiopia, 7 August 1638. He entered the Capuchin novitiate in 1623 and in 1633 was sent to their mission in Cairo, where he joined Father Agathangelus. The behaviour of local Catholics obstructed their labours, and intending to work for the reunion of Copts with Rome, they entered Ethiopia in 1637, disguised as Coptic monks. They were discovered and sent to Condar for trial. Given the choice of conversion to the Coptic faith or hanging, they chose death. **Pius X** beatified them on 23 October 1904. Feast day 7 August.

Cassiano da Macerata Capuchin priest, missionary and scholar, born Macerata, Italy, 1708, died Macerata, 4 February 1791. He received the habit in 1728 and in 1738 was sent to Tibet, arriving at the mission at Lhasa in 1741, and from there went to Nepal, where mission work was impeded by persecution as well as by local Christians. Recalled to Rome in 1756, he wrote his recollections of missionary work, and a Tibetan grammar which was published by the Holy See in 1773.

Cassiodorus Roman monk and writer, born at Squillace, Italy, 485, died 580, at his monastery of Vivarium in Calabria. Trained as a lawyer, he held various positions in the civil service, including praetorian prefect. Served as counsellor to Theodoric, king of the Ostrogoths. Became a monk in 540. Founded a monastery at Vivarium. He encouraged religious scholarship and copying of manuscripts, thereby contributing greatly to the preservation of culture during the Dark Ages. His works include the *Institutiones* and his *De Anima*.

Castagno, Andrea del Renaissance painter, born Castagno, Italy, 1419, died Florence of the plague, August 1457. Spent most of his life in Florence painting frescoes for the Church and the Medici family. His most important works include *The Last Supper* and other images of the death of Christ painted for the convent of Sant' Apollonia between 1445 and 1450.

Castaneda, Carlos Eduardo Educator and historian, born Camargo, Mexico, 11 November 1896, died Austin, Texas, 5 April 1958. After studies at the University of Texas he taught at the Catholic University of America, Washington DC, then at the University of Texas as professor of history from 1946 until his death. His principal works are *The Mexican Side of the Texan Revolution* (1928) and *Our Catholic Heritage in Texas 1519–1950* (7 vols, 1936–58). In addition to his ecclesiastical distinctions he was president of the American Catholic Historical Association 1939–40, and during World War II regional director of the Fair Employment Practices Committee in the south-west.

Castaneda, Francisco de Paula Franciscan journalist and defender of the Church in Argentina, born Buenos Aires, 1776, died Parana, 12 May 1832. Ordained in 1800, after teaching at the University of Córdoba he returned to Buenos Aires. In 1815 during the religious persecution being carried out by the government as clergy reform, he published six newspapers simultaneously, attacking those who were trying to appropriate convents and conventual property, for which he was exiled six times. Believing in the power of literacy and art to counter demagoguery, he established schools wherever he could.

Castellanos, Juan de Historian, born Alanis, Spain, 1522, died Tunja, Colombia, 27 November

1607. After studies in Alanis and Seville he went to South America in 1539, where he worked as a soldier and then a miner before being ordained in 1544. Eventually he was given the benefice of Tunja, where he lived until his death, writing *Elegias de varones illustres de Indias*, which dealt successively with the conquest of Mexico; the conquest and history of Venezuela and of various provinces including Cartagena; Sir Francis Drake; and the history of Granada. He is one of the most authoritative early historians of South America.

Castelli, Benedetto Astronomer and hydrologist, born Brescia, Italy, 1578, died Rome, 9 April 1643. He became a monk at Monte Cassino in 1595, and from 1604 he closely cooperated with **Galileo** in techniques for making better telescopic observations. Together with Filippo Saleriati they observed the Medici planets and sun spots in 1611. Castelli became reader in mathematics and physics at the University of Pisa in 1613 and then began to specialize in hydraulics, writing a standard work on the measurement of running water. Summoned to Rome by **Urban VIII** he founded a school and continued to study hydraulics, astronomy, mechanics and physiology.

Castellino da Castelli Priest and religious educator, born Menaggio, Italy, c.1476, died Milan, 21 September 1566. At 60, without much diocesan support in the absence of the archbishop, Charles **Borromeo**, he founded the first school in Milan to teach Christian doctrine to children, and by 1566 there were 30 schools with more being established all over northern Italy. When Borromeo returned, recognizing the importance of the schools to the Counter-Reformation, he rapidly promoted them, with the result that Castellino's pioneering work was less recognized.

Castellio, Sebastian (Chateillon) Humanist and biblical scholar, born St Martin-du-Fresne, Burgundy, France, 1515, died Basel, Switzerland, 29 December 1563. He studied in Lyons, became a Protestant and met **Calvin**, who made him rector of the college in Geneva in 1541, but his liberal views on exegesis prevented his being ordained. Moving to Basel in 1545, he became professor of Greek in 1553, where he had continuing differences with Calvin and **Beza** over exegesis, theological questions about the Trinity and predestination, and the persecution of religious opponents. He published the most important and influential manifesto of the sixteenth century in favour of toleration. Deeply learned in Latin, Greek and Hebrew, he translated the whole Bible into both Latin and popular vernacular French.

Castellvi, Marcellino de Capuchin linguist and anthropologist, born Castellvi de la Marca, Catalonia, Spain, 11 September 1908, died Bogotá, Colombia, 25 June 1951. One of five brothers who became Capuchins, he entered in 1924, studied at the Gregorian University in Rome, was ordained and was assigned to the apostolic mission at Sibundoy in south Colombia in 1931, where he remained. While working as a priest, he founded the Linguistic and Ethnological Research Centre of Colombian Amazonia, assembled a prestigious library and museum of anthropological sciences and published the journal *Amazonia Colombiana* as well as works on linguistic investigation, Amerindian ethnology and the methodology of folk studies.

Castiglione, Baldassare Diplomat and writer, born Casatico, Italy, 6 December 1478, died Toledo, 2 February 1529. Educated in Milan he spent most of his life as a diplomat in the courts of Spain and Italy. In 1528 he wrote his most well known work *Il Cortegiano* (*The Courtier*), a Renaissance treatise which provides a unique picture of sixteenth-century social, political and religious life. In 1524 he was appointed apostolic protonotary, and three years later he became papal nuncio to the court of **Charles V** in Spain.

Castiglione, Giuseppe Painter and Jesuit missionary, born Milan, 19 July 1688, died Peking (Beijing), 16 July 1766. After an art training he entered the Jesuit novitiate in 1707, completed it in Portugal and was sent to Peking in 1715. Here he was known as Lang Shih-ning and became a favourite artist and architect at the imperial court, where he was active under three emperors, the last of whom, Ch'ien Lung, was a notorious persecutor of Christians, but out of regard for Castiglione allowed him to intercede for them. Castiglione was the only European painter to be included in the Chinese *History of Painting* of 1800.

Castillo, Andraca y Tamayo, Francisco del Poet, born Lima, Peru, 2 April 1716, died Lima, December 1770. In 1734 he entered the Order of Our Lady of Mercy as a lay brother. Near blindness made reading impossible, but he had an amazingly retentive memory. He was a prolific composer of romances and satires, but for philosophical and moral depth his best work is on religious themes, such as that on the passion and death of Christ from the four Gospels, and his translation of the *Te Deum* based on the *Epistolas Familiares* of Antonio de **Guevara**.

Castillo y Guevara, Francisca Josefa del Nun and writer, born Tunja, Colombia, 1671, died there 1742. She entered the Poor Clares at eighteen and was three times abbess, becoming known for her visions and ecstasies. On the order of her confessor she wrote her *Autobiografía* (Philadelphia, 1817), and *Sentimientos espirituales* (Bogotá, 1843 and 1942). She deeply loved God, and her books show sound knowledge of the Bible and of doctrine. She was one of the best Colombian writers of the eighteenth century.

Castner, Gaspar Jesuit missionary, born Munich, 7 October 1665, died Peking (Beijing), 9 November 1709. He entered the Society of Jesus in 1681 and became professor of philosophy at Regensburg in 1695. By 1697 he was in Macao, where he saw to the erection of a memorial church on the island of Sanchwan, where St **Francis Xavier** had died. He represented the bishops of Nanking and Macao at Rome in discussions concerning Chinese translation and rites. A notable cartographer, on his return to China the emperor made him president of the Bureau of Mathematics and tutor to the prince.

Castorena y Ursua, Juan Ignacio de Bishop of Yucatan and first Mexican journalist, born Zacatecas, 31 July 1668, died Mérida, 13 July 1733. He studied under the Jesuits in Mexico City, was awarded a doctorate in theology at Avila, Spain, then became resident theologian at the nuncio's office in Madrid. He returned to Mexico City as a canon of the cathedral, censor of the Inquisition and rector of the university. In 1721 he established a school for girls and was made bishop of Yucatan in 1729. He founded the influential monthly *Gas-*

eta de Mexico in 1720, which supplied religious, commercial, maritime and social news and book reviews.

Castro, Agustín Pablo   Jesuit scientist and humanist, born Córdoba, Mexico, 24 January 1728, died Bologna, 23 November 1790. He was ordained in Mexico City in 1752 and had various posts teaching philosophy between 1756 and 1763 but became ill while at Tepotzotlán, though he managed to write his *Cursus Philosophicus*. He enhanced the reputation of the University of Merida, Yucatan, by his teaching of moral theology, canon law, jurisprudence and civil law. On the expulsion of the Jesuits in 1767 he and his companions went to Bologna, where he produced literary works characterized perhaps by curiosity rather than depth.

Castro, Ignacio de   Historian and educator, born Tacna, Peru, 31 July 1731, died Cuzco, 1792. He was a foundling, looked after by Domingo de Castro, a priest. He gained a doctorate in theology from the Jesuit University of San Ignacio, and became rector of the college of San Bernardo in 1778, where he remained for the rest of his life. He was secretary to the creole bishop Juan Manuel de Moscoso y Peralta in 1780, during the rebellion of the Tupac Amara, and wrote the first history of Cuzco, posthumously published in 1795, as well as devotional treatises.

Castro, Mateo de   First Brahmin bishop of the Latin rite, born Divar, near Goa, India, *c.*1594, died Rome, 1668 or 1669. Converted by Theatines, his studies under Franciscans in Goa were completed in Rome through the College of Propaganda. He was ordained and sent to evangelize the Brahmins of India, but clashed with the bishop of Goa, whose appointment was under Portuguese royal patronage. The Holy See solved this problem by establishing apostolic vicariates, and Castro was the first to be appointed, to Idalkan, a native state bordering Goa. Here he established a seminary for, and as a titular bishop ordained, Brahmin clergy, to more opposition from the Portuguese. He was apparently no diplomat, which set back the efforts of the Papacy to foster a native episcopacy, and returned to Rome.

Caswall, Edward   Priest and writer, born Yateley,

Hampshire, 15 July 1814, died Edgbaston, Birmingham, 2 January 1878. He was ordained in the Anglican Church, but like other figures in the Oxford Movement, followed John Henry **Newman** into the Roman Catholic Church and joined Newman's Oratorian Order in Birmingham. He contributed hymns to *Lyra Catholica*, and his hymns continue to be used in the Roman Catholic Church and outside, including *Hark! a Herald Voice is Calling, Earth Has Many a Noble City* and *Glory Be To Jesus*.

Cataldino, José   Jesuit missionary, born Fabriano, Italy, April 1571, died Reduction of San Ignacio Mini, Paraguay, 10 June 1653. Ordained before becoming a Jesuit in 1602, he reached Lima 1604 and was appointed to the mission of Tucaman and Paraguay, arriving in Asunción in 1605. He and a fellow Italian, Father Mascetta, began gruelling evangelical work in Guaira in 1609. He founded the Reductions of San Ignacio Mini and Loreto before becoming superior of all Paraguayan missions and founding the Reductions of San Pablo, San José and Encarnación. Eleven years later he was put in charge of the Amerindians of Villarica, and spent his final years working for the conversion of the native people of Uruguay.

Cataldo, Joseph Mary   Jesuit missionary, born Terracina, Italy, 17 March 1837, died Pendleton, Oregon, 9 April 1928. Ordained in Liège in 1862, he was sent to Santa Clara College, California, to study and teach, after which he worked among the Nez Percé, Coeur d'Alène and Spokane native Americans until 1877, when he was appointed superior of the Jesuit Rocky Mountain Mission, from where he sent out missionaries to tribes in Montana, Wyoming, Washington and Oregon as well as to the Alaskan Eskimos. Replaced as superior in 1893, he was freed to work again with the tribes and with settlers in the Pacific northwest. He had a particular affection for the Nez Percé, for whom he wrote a life of Christ and a prayer book in their language, one of the eight Native American languages which he learnt.

Cataldus of Rachau   Saint, bishop and patron of Taranto, born Ireland, early seventh century, died Taranto, Italy, *c.*671. His life story comes from legends of the twelfth century. He is said to have become a monk at Lismore, and later, when bishop of Rachau, and when returning from a pilgrimage to the Holy Land, to have been wrecked off Taranto. Here he became bishop, reformer and builder of churches. He is venerated for his miracles in Italy and in Sens and Auxerre in France. Feast day 10 May.

Catherine II Empress, born Stettin, Prussia, 2 May 1729, died St Petersburg, 17 November 1796. Her marriage to the future Peter III of Russia was unhappy. Shortly after Peter's accession in 1762 he was murdered and she became empress. She converted from Lutheranism to Orthodoxy, but her principles were those of the Enlightenment, and her policy to increase the power of the nobility, to closely control the serfs, and to expand abroad. She saw the need for the education of the upper classes and founded specialist academies. For this reason she did not allow **Clement XIV**'s Brief of Suppression of the Jesuits of 1773 to be carried out in Russia.

Catherine de' Medici Queen consort of Henry II of France, born Florence, 13 April 1519, died Blois, 5 January 1589. Daughter of the Florentine ruler Lorenzo de' Medici. In 1533 she married the duc d'Orléans, who became king of France in 1547 as Henry II. In 1560, after the death of her husband and son, she ruled as regent for her second son Charles IX, until 1563 when he was crowned king. Her domestic policy consisted of maintaining a balance between the Huguenots and the Catholics. In 1572, fearing the influence of the Huguenots, she brought about the St Bartholomew's Day Massacre, resulting in the deaths of 50,000 Huguenots.

Catherine de' Ricci Saint, Dominican contemplative of the Counter-Reformation, born Florence, 23 April 1522, died Prato, 2 February 1590. She was professed at fourteen in the Dominican convent of San Vicenzio, Prato, of which she was prioress from 1560 to 1590. From Holy Week 1542 and thereafter for twelve years she relived Christ's passion from Thursday noon to Friday at 4 p.m. People of all classes, including many religious leaders drawn by her ecstatic experience and (Savonarolan) spirituality, came to her for advice and help. She was beatified in 1732 and canonized in 1746. Feast day 13 February.

Catherine of Alexandria Saint, martyr. Legends coming from a number of tenth-century sources say that as a result of protesting to the emperor Maxentius about the persecution of Christians she was tortured on the wheel and decapitated in 305. Her cult became popular especially in Italy. Feast day 25 November, suppressed in 1969.

Catherine of Aragon The first wife of King **Henry VIII**, born Alcalá de Henares, Spain, 16 December 1485, died Kimbolton, Huntingdon, 7 January 1536. The daughter of Ferdinand V and Isabella I of Aragon and Castile. She married Arthur, son of King Henry VII, in 1501, but Arthur died six months later. She married Henry VIII in June 1509, bearing him six children, but only Mary surviving. Henry, in 1533, had the marriage annulled, having secretly married Anne Boleyn four months earlier. In 1534 Pope **Clement VII** declared the first marriage to Catherine to be valid. Henry then passed a series of Acts which created the Anglican Church. The Succession Act of 1534 officially decreed Catherine's marriage as void.

Catherine of Bologna Also known as Catherine de Vigri, patron saint of artists, born Bologna, 8 September 1413, died Bologna, 9 March 1463. Educated at the royal court at Ferrara, Italy. Became a nun in 1432. In 1456 she founded a convent of Poor Clares at Bologna, later becoming its abbess. Throughout her time at the convent she experienced visions and revelations. She also revealed a talent for calligraphy. Her main work is *The Spiritual Armour* (1438). Canonized in 1712. Feast day 9 March.

Catherine of Genoa Saint and mystic, born Genoa, 1447, died Genoa, 15 September 1510. Due to a religious crisis in 1473 Catherine Fieschi, and her husband, spent the rest of their lives caring for the sick and needy. From 1490 to 1496 she was matron of a hospital caring for victims of the plague. Her works include the *Trattato del Purgatorio* and the *Dialogo*. Canonized in 1737. Feast day 15 September.

Catherine of Racconigi Blessed, born Racconigi, Piedmont, Italy, 24(?) June 1486, died Caramagna, Piedmont, 4 September 1547. A weaver, she gave her wages to the poor, vowed virginity and received the habit of a Dominican tertiary from her Dominican confessor in 1513. She received the stigmata, prophesied and at Caramagna offered herself as a victim for sinners and the maintenance of peace. **Pius VII** authorized her Mass and Office on 9 April 1808 and she is commemorated in the Order of Preachers. Feast day 4 September.

Catherine of Siena Caterina Benincasa, saint and mystic, born Siena, 1347, died of exhaustion at Rome, 29 April 1380. Experienced visions from the age of seven and the pain, but not the manifestation, of the stigmata. In 1360 became a tertiary of the Dominican Order at Siena and soon gathered around her a group of followers or 'Caterinati'. In 1376 she visited Pope **Gregory XI** at Avignon as a mediator between the Papacy and Florence. In 1378 she went to Rome to aid Pope **Urban VI** in the reform of the Church. Her works include the *Dialogo*, which contains descriptions of her ecstatic experiences, and her dictated *Letters*. Canonized in 1461. Declared patron saint of Italy in 1939. Feast day is 29 April.

Catherine of Sweden Katarina Ulfsdotter, saint, born 1331, died Vadstena, 24 March 1381. The daughter of St **Bridget** of Sweden. In 1373 succeeded her mother as superior of the Brigettines. Spent most of her life gaining recognition for her mother and the Bridgettines. A supporter of Pope **Urban VI** against the Antipope. Recognized as a saint but never formally canonized. Feast day 24 March.

Catherine Tomas Saint, Canoness Regular of St Augustine, born Valdemuzza, Majorca, May 1531, died Palma, Majorca, 5 April 1574. An orphan, at sixteen she entered the convent of St Mary Magdalene in Palma at her confessor's insistence as she had no dowry. She was aware of her spiritual gifts but tried to hide them as they involved her in controversy; she was said to have the gift of prophecy, converse with angels, to suffer attacks from devils, and to have foretold the day of her death. She was beatified in 1792 and canonized in 1930. Feast day 5 April.

Cathrein, Viktor Jesuit moral philosopher, born Brig, Switzerland, 8 May 1845, died Aachen, Germany, 10 September 1931. A Jesuit by 1863, he was a leading neo-Thomist professor in the German province. He attacked positivism and the idea that morality can be separated from religion. His criticism of socialism in *Der Sozialismus* was influential on Catholic thought.

Catrik, John Bishop and royal envoy, born Catterick, Yorkshire, died Florence, 28 December 1419. Having graduated in canon and civil law at Oxford in 1406, he held benefices in Lincolnshire before becoming bishop of St David's, 1414, Coventry, 1415, and Exeter, 1419, though as the king's proctor at Rome in 1414, a diplomat from the English court to France and Burgundy, and as head of the English delegation to the Council of Constance in 1414–17, and with **Martin IV** at the curia thereafter, he must have been largely an absentee in his dioceses.

Catrou, François Jesuit historian and writer, born Paris, 28 December 1659, died, Paris, 18 October 1737. Admitted to the novitiate in 1668, he found his niche from 1701 to 1713 as the first editor of the journal *Mémoires de Trévoux pour servir à l'histoire des sciences et des beaux arts*, a powerful influence against Protestants, Jansenists and Encyclopaedists. He published histories of the Mogul empire, of the Anabaptists, of Protestant fanaticism, and *Histoire Romaine* (21 vols, Paris 1725–37).

Cattaneo, Lazzaro Jesuit missionary, born Sarzana near Genoa, 1560, died Hangchow, 16 January 1640. He entered the Society of Jesus at Rome in 1581; was in Goa in 1588 as superior of the Malabar coast mission. By 1593 he was in Macao, from where he went to Chaoking to study Chinese with Matteo **Ricci**, and accompanied him to Peking in 1598. An influential Chinese convert, Sin Kwang-Ki, invited him to Shanghai as its first missionary. From 1611 he worked in Kiangsu province, retired to Hangchow in 1622 and spent his remaining years in writing and the study of linguistics.

Cauchie, Alfred Henri Joseph Belgian historian, born Haulchin in Hainault, 26 October 1860, died Rome, 22 February 1922. He was professor of church history at the University of Louvain, where he established, with **Ladeuze**, the *Revue d'histoire* *ecclésiastique* (1900), and was one of the founders of the Institut Historique Belge in Rome, which he directed, 1919–22. His particular studies were on the investiture struggle, Jansenism and the religious history of Belgium, which were published in learned journals.

Caulet, François Etienne Bishop, opponent of royal patronage, born Toulouse, 19 May 1610, died Pamiers, 7 August 1680. A Jesuit, he became director of the seminary of St Sulpice in Paris in 1642, and in 1644 bishop of the largely Protestant Diocese of Pamiers. Possibly in sympathy with the moral rigorism of Jansenism, he was one of the five French bishops who refused to sign the papal formulary condemning it. From 1665 he opposed **Louis XIV**'s efforts to extend his rights to the revenues of vacant bishoprics until then exempt: deprived of temporalities, Caulet continued his resistance until death.

Caunton, Richard Papal chaplain and royal envoy, born Pembrokeshire, Wales, died June or July 1465. Between 1437 and 1446 he pursued the king's business in various countries of Europe, was the proctor at Rome for the king and for a number of English bishops, and served as clerk of the Apostolic Camera and papal chaplain. He was granted an Oxford doctorate in canon and civil law in 1450 and appointed a papal chaplain in 1453. He had held livings in south Wales when he was appointed to the archdeaconries of Salisbury from 1446 and St David's from 1459 until his death.

Caussade, Jean Pierre de French Jesuit and mystic, born Quercy, 7 February 1675, died Toulouse, 8 December 1751. In 1693 he became a Jesuit at Toulouse. Travelled widely as a preacher. Defended mysticism against the advocates of Quietism. He was condemned in 1687. His writings include his *Letters of Spiritual Direction* and a *Treatise on the Abandonment to God's Will.*

Caussin, Nicholas Jesuit confessor of **Louis XIII**, born Troyes, France, 27 May 1583, died Paris, 2 July 1651. He became a Jesuit in 1607, a preacher in 1620, and in 1637 he became Louis XIII's confessor. In helping Louis to be reconciled with his estranged wife Anne of Austria, he opposed

Cardinal **Richelieu**, for which he was later exiled to Quimper. After the deaths of Richelieu in 1642 and Louis in 1643 he returned to Paris. His chief work was *Cour saint* (5 vols, Paris, 1624).

Cavalieri, Francesco Bonaventura Italian mathematician, born Milan, 1598, died Bologna, 3 December 1647. Became a Jesuit at an early age. Appointed professor of mathematics at Bologna in 1629. Famous for the contribution he made to geometry, particularly for his principle of indivisibles.

Cavallera, Ferdinand Jesuit scholar, born Le Puy, France, 26 November 1875, died Toulouse, 10 March 1954. He entered the Society of Jesus in 1892 and was ordained in 1906. After his doctoral thesis on the Schism of Antioch he became professor of theology at the Institut Catholique of Toulouse, where he extended the syllabus to include courses on social thought in the Church, 1926, and patrology, his particular interest, 1932. He was a founder and director of the *Bulletin de littérature ecclésiastique*, the *Revue d'ascétique et de mystique* and the *Dictionnaire de spiritualité ascétique et mystique*. Among other works, his *St Jérome* (1920) was highly praised.

Cavalli (Pier), Francesco Influential Italian opera composer, born Crema, Italy, 14 February 1602, died Venice, 14 January 1676. In 1617 he became a member of the choir at St Mark's, Venice, where he stayed the rest of his life, holding various posts. His most famous operas include *La Didone* (1641) and *L'Egisto* (1643).

Cavallini, Pietro One of the founders of Italian painting, born Rome, 1250, died 1334. His most famous works include the frescoes at Santa Maria Donna Regina, Naples, the walls of the nave of San Francesco of Assisi and the *Last Judgement* fresco at Santa Cecilia, Trastevere.

Cavanaugh, John Joseph US Roman Catholic priest and educationist, born Owosso, Michigan, 23 January 1899, died Notre Dame, Indiana, 28 December 1979. Started his career as a businessman, joined the Congregation of the Holy Cross and was ordained in 1931. Studied in the USA and at the Gregorian University in Rome. In 1933 he returned to Notre Dame and became prefect of religion. In 1938 he was made assistant provincial of the US province of the Congregation, in 1940 became vice-president of the University of Notre Dame and in 1946 was appointed president. He held this post for six years and during that time secured its financial future, restructured and reformed its teaching and research programmes and ensured its place in the mainstream of US academic life. In 1952 he became director of the Notre Dame Foundation, was chaplain to St Mary's College, Notre Dame, and held positions in public service and spoke up for civil rights. He was a friend of the Kennedy family and served them notably around the time of J. F. **Kennedy**'s assassination.

Cavazzoni, Girolamo Organist and polyphonist, born Urbino, Italy, c.1520, son of Marco Antonio **Cavazzoni**, died Venice, 1577. He is remembered for his extensive volume of keyboard music *Intervolatura cioè recercari canzoni Himni Magnificati* (Venice, 1542) and three organ Masses of 1543, which display considerable originality.

Cavazzoni, Marco Antonio Composer and organist, born Urbino, Italy, c.1490, died Venice(?), c.1570. He served **Leo X**, and was organist at Choggia Cathedral, 1536–7, and singer at St Mark's, Venice, under Willaert, 1545–59. His *Recerchari, Motetti, Canzoni* (Venice, 1523) is the second earliest printed organ music and shows a development away from current vocal style.

Cave, William Anglican divine and patristic scholar, born Pickwell, Derbyshire, 1637, died Windsor, 4 July 1713. Ordained 1662, he served mainly in London parishes and in 1684 became a canon of Windsor and chaplain to **Charles II**. His principal works, *Apostolici* (1677), *Ecclesiastici* (1682) and *Scriptorum Ecclesiasicorum Historia Litteraria* (1688 and 1698), were erudite and lucid. He was censured by Continental Protestants and Catholics for his attempt in a tract of 1685 to identify Anglicanism with the primitive Church, and all his work was put on the Index in 1693.

Cavell, Edith Louisa Born Swardeston, Norfolk, 4 December 1865, executed Brussels, 12 October 1915. The daughter of a Norfolk vicar, she became a governess in Belgium, 1890, but five years later took up nursing after caring for her father during an illness. She returned to Belgium in 1907, where she became the first matron of the hospital in Brussels which was taken over by the Red Cross during the First World War. After the Battle of Mons, 23 August 1914, she became involved in helping Allied soldiers to escape, and on 5 August 1915 was arrested by the German secret police. She pleaded guilty, was tried and was executed, despite pleas by Spanish and American officials in Brussels to spare her life.

Cavo, Andrès Mexican historian, born Guadaljara, 21 January 1739, died Rome between 1794 and 1800. He entered the Society of Jesus in 1759 and was a catechist in the north-west mission until the expulsion of Jesuits in 1767, a situation unbearable to him, so he became secularized. He wrote the *Historia Civil y Politica de Mejico* covering the years 1521 to 1766, lost for many years but discovered in the library of the bishop of Tenagra and published in 1836.

Caxton, William First English printer, born Tenterden, Kent, probably in 1422, died London, 1491. He was apprenticed to a London merchant and worked for a time in Bruges, Belgium, negotiating commercial treaties with the dukes of Burgundy. While there he learned the new art of printing, possibly in Cologne, and in 1476, when he set up his press at Westminster, he had already published an English book while in Bruges. Using six distinct fonts of type, he published nearly 80 separate books between 1477 and his death, including **Chaucer** and **Malory**'s *Morte d'Arthur*, many translations from the French and some portions of the biblical text in English in his translation of *The Golden Legend*, but the Constitutions of Oxford prevented him from printing and distributing the English Bible as a whole.

Cayet, Pierre Victor Theologian, born Montrichard, France, 1525, died Paris, 10 March or 22 July 1610. He became a Calvinist, studied in Geneva and was appointed minister of Montreuil-Bonnin near Poitiers. After 1593 he followed Henry of Navarre to Paris. Accusations of sorcery caused him to lose favour with the Calvinists, and he returned to Catholicism in 1595. He conducted a paper war against Calvinism in 1596–9, and was ordained priest in 1600. A work of 1605 in which he denied the authority of the Pope over bishops was put on the Index. He would not retract, and like Henry his religious loyalty was in doubt.

Cecilia (Probably legendary) saint and martyr of the second or third century, and patroness of music. Many poetical, prose and musical works were written in her honour. Among authors were **Dryden** and **Auden**. Among composers were **Purcell** and **Britten**. Feast day 22 November.

Cecilia of the Nativity (Cecilia Morillas) Discalced (i.e. sandal-wearing) Carmelite, spiritual writer and poet, born Valladolid, Spain, 1570, died Valladolid, 7 April 1646. Professed in 1590 and sent to the new convent at Calahorra, she was twice elected prioress, and influenced the Discalced Carmelite Friars to go there. Her writing on the spiritual pilgrimage was not published until the twentieth century.

Cecilia Romana Blessed, Dominican nun, born Rome, c.1200, died Bologna, c.1290. She moved with her community from the monastery of Sta Maria in Tempulo, Rome, in 1221 to the reformed monastery of St Sisto, founded that year by St **Dominic**, and they renewed their vows. He sent three of them to the newly formed monastery of St Agnes at Bologna, where in 1237 Cecilia became prioress. Her eyewitness recollections of St Dominic were preserved in writing by another nun in 1280. Feast day 9 June.

Cedda, or **Cedd** Bishop and saint, the brother of Saint **Chad**, the date of his birth is unknown, died of the plague at Lastingham, Yorkshire, 26 October 664. Raised at Lindisfarne, where he was instructed by St **Aidan**. Sent by Bishop **Finan** in 653 to convert the Mercians. Also went as a missionary to preach to the East Saxons. Made bishop of the East Saxons in 654. Founded the abbey of Lastingham, and monasteries at Bradwell-on-Sea and Tilbury. Feast day 7 January.

Ceillier, Rémi Ecclesiastical historian, born Bar-le-Duc, France, 14 May 1688, died Flavigny, 26 May 1761. He entered the Benedictine monastery of Moyen-Moutier, 1704, was ordained in 1710

and thereafter taught theology, becoming prior of St Jacques de Neufchateau, 1718, and of Flavigny-sur-Moselle, 1733. With help he wrote the *Histoire générale des auteurs sacrés ecclésiastiques* (23 vols, 1729–63) a full if diffuse record down to mid-thirteenth century.

Celestine I Pope and saint, born in the Roman Campagna, date unknown, elected to the Papacy 10 September 422, died Rome, 27 July 432. He was active in reconstructing Rome's churches after the devastation of 410, and he also suppressed as far as he could Novatianism in the city. He was active in asserting the authority of the Papacy and sent St **Germanus of Auxerre** to Britain in 429 to convert the followers of **Pelagius** and reputedly sent **Palladius** as the first bishop in Ireland. He became involved in the Nestorian controversy, condemning **Nestorius** after a synod of Rome in 430 and giving his support to the decisions of the Council of Ephesus (431), where Nestorius was excommunicated. Feast day 27 July.

Celestine II (Teobaldo Buccapecus) Elected Pope and assumed the name Celestine II, 15 or 16 December 1124 but resigned, or more probably died, a few days later. Because he was not consecrated he is not recognized officially as a Pope.

Celestine II (Guido di Città di Castello) Born in Città di Castello, Umbria, elected 26 September 1143, died 8 March 1144. Guido had studied under Peter **Abelard**, whom he much admired, and himself a considerable scholar, he had served as a papal legate under **Innocent II**, who had recommended him (among others) on his deathbed. Celestine, however, reversed some of Innocent's policies, most notably removing the interdict which had been placed on **Louis VII** of France.

Celestine III Pope, born Giacinto Bobo about 1106, elected March or April 1191, died 8 January 1198. He had been a student under **Abelard**, whom he supported, and was appointed cardinal in 1144 by **Celestine II**, who had been a fellow student. He served the papal court for 47 years as cardinal deacon and was 85 when chosen as Pope. A learned and pious man, yet indecisive, his pontificate was dominated by the burgeoning power of **Henry VI** (whom Celestine crowned in 1191) and the Holy Roman Empire. Celestine wished to abdicate at Christmas 1190, but under a condition (naming his successor) which the cardinals would not accept.

Celestine IV   Pope, born Goffredo Castiglioni at Milan, about 1187, elected 25 October 1241, died 10 November 1241. He served the Church in Milan before being appointed cardinal priest of St Mark's in 1227 and cardinal-bishop of Sabina in 1239. On 25 October 1241 he succeeded **Gregory IX** as Pope, after a much disputed election. The ten cardinal electors (two were held prisoner by the Emperor) were so deeply divided that it seemed unlikely they could reach agreement. They were therefore locked in a Roman palace for sixty days, making Celestine IV the first Pope to be elected in a conclave. He died less than a month after his election, which suggests that the choice was decided by the cardinals' determination to escape their confinement.

Celestine V   Pope and saint, born Pietro da Morrone in Isernia, Italy, about 1215, elected Pope 5 July 1294, resigned 13 December the same year, died 19 May 1296. He became a Benedictine monk c.1232, later living a solitary life in the Abruzzi mountains and founding a religious order, originally called the Hermits of St Damian, but changing to the Celestines on his election as Pope. However, being eighty years of age, and politically and administratively naïve, he resigned in December of the same year (an act known as 'the great refusal'). His successor, **Boniface VIII**, who had pressured him into the resignation, held him prisoner in the castle of Monte Fumone until his death. He was canonized in 1313 under pressure from the king of France, a vigorous opponent of Boniface. Feast day 19 May.

Cellini, Benvenuto   Sculptor and goldsmith, born Florence, 3 November, 1500, died Florence 13 February 1571. In 1516, due to his riotous living, he was exiled to Siena. While living in Rome he briefly became **Michelangelo**'s pupil. He received patronage from Pope **Clement VII** and Pope **Paul III**. In 1540 he resided at the court of **Francis I** of France but was forced to leave in 1545. On returning to Florence he worked for Cosimo de' **Medici**. His most important works include *The Nymph of*

Fontainebleau and the statue of *Perseus and Medusa*. His autobiography provides insights into the ecclesiastical and social life of Italy in the sixteenth century.

Cennick, John   Methodist preacher and Moravian missionary, born Reading, 12 December 1718, died London, 4 July 1755. Converted in 1737. On meeting with George **Whitefield** in London in May 1739 he was appointed as master at the Kingswood school. At Bristol, on 14 June 1739, he preached in public and became the first Methodist lay preacher. He carried out aggressive evangelism in various localities but particularly in Wiltshire. Disagreeing with, **John Wesley** on Christian perfection and adopting Calvinistic views, he was expelled from Methodism in 1741. In December 1745 he became a Moravian. From 1746 to 1751 he was influential in establishing Moravianism in Ireland. Ordained as a Moravian deacon in 1749. He wrote numerous hymns, including 'Children of the Heavenly King' and 'Lo, He comes with clouds descending'.

Ceolfrid of Wearmouth   Saint, Anglo-Saxon monk, born northern England, c.642, died Langres, France, 25 September 716. He entered the monastery at Gilling at eighteen, moved to the monastery of Ripon in 664 and was ordained under the Roman rite. **Benedict Biscop** asked him to help build the abbey of St Peter at Wearmouth in 672, and in 678 he accompanied Benedict to Rome for ideas and supplies, and returned with John the arch-chanter, who taught the monks to sing the Roman liturgy. Benedict asked Ceolfrid to establish a second abbey, at Jarrow, which was dedicated in 685. With their splendid libraries, the two foundations were foremost in England for their transcriptions of the Gospels. Ceolfrid died at Langres on his way to Rome with a copy, the *Codex Amiatinus* (the oldest extant MS of the Vulgate) in 716. Bede said that Ceolfrid brought him up. Feast day 25 September.

Cepeda, Francisco   Dominican missionary and official of the Inquisition, born Spain, 1532, died Guatemala, 1602. He entered the Dominican convent of San Domingo de Murcia in Andalusia and before 1560 was sent to Guatemala, where he became prior of the convent at Zacapula and served as a commissary of the Inquisition. He was elected provincial in 1593 and is remembered for his simplified grammar of various indigenous local languages.

Cepeda Álvarez, Felix Alejandro Claretian scholar, born La Serena, Chile, 19 November 1854, died Madrid, 29 January 1930. A graduate in law, ordained 1876, he entered the Claretian mission in Santiago in 1889 and was sent to Spain, where in 1895, having become provincial, his administrative and organizational ability was recognized, and he went to Mexico to direct the province in 1895. He founded missions there and in the USA and also wrote some theology and history.

Cerbonius Saint, bishop of Populonia. Nothing is known of his birth, he died Isle of Elba, *c*.580. When the Vandals drove the bishops out of Africa, he went with St Regulus (died 542) to Tuscany and was made bishop of Populonia. When Totila, king of the Ostrogoths (died 552), exposed him to a bear in punishment for sheltering Roman soldiers, it failed to attack him and he was freed, but the Lombards exiled him to Elba, where he lived the thirty years until his death. Feast day 10 October.

Cerfaux, Lucien Belgian NT scholar, born Presles, Belgium, 14 June 1883, died Lourdes, France, 11 August 1968. Studied in Tournai, at the Belgian College, and the Gregorian University in Rome and spent a year at the Pontifical Biblical Institute there. From 1911 to 1930 he was professor of sacred Scripture in the seminary in Tournai and latterly taught also at the Catholic University in Louvain, where he had the chair in NT studies from 1930 until 1954. He was a member of the Roman Catholic Biblical Commission and was a *peritus* at Vatican Council II. He was a member of the editorial board of several learned journals, founded *Studia Hellenistica* and was co-editor of *Ephemerides theologicae Lovanienses*. In 1949 he helped found the Colloquium Biblicum Lovaniense and was its first president. His early interests were in the environment of the NT and in Gnosticism. His later concerns with exegesis are seen in his publications *The Church in the Theology of St Paul* (1942), *Christ in the Theology of St Paul* (1951)

and *The Christian in the Theology of St Paul* (1962). He also wrote on the synoptic Gospels.

Cerioli, Constanza Blessed, foundress, born Soncino, Italy, 28 January 1816, died Comonte di Seriate, 24 December 1865. In 1835 she married a wealthy widower, had three children, who died, and was widowed in 1854. Thereafter she devoted her money and energy into the care of orphan girls through her foundation in 1857 of the Sisters of the Holy Family at Bergamo, and was helped by Giovanni Caponi, of the Brothers of the Holy Family, to look after orphan boys. She was beatified in 1950. Feast day 24 December.

Cerone, Domenico Pietro Music teacher, born Bergamo, Italy, 1566, died Naples, 1625. He was in Spain by 1592 as priest and cantor in chapels of Philip II and Philip III, and in Italy in 1608 serving at the Spanish Chapel in Naples. He published a book on musical theory and practice, which is a valuable exposition of sixteenth-century counterpoint.

Cerqueira, Luis de Bishop of Japan, born Vila de Alverto, Portugal, 1551, died Nagasaki, 16 February 1614. He entered the Jesuit novitiate in 1566 and, after service in Rome, Coimbra and Evora, where he was awarded a doctorate in 1593, he was sent as coadjutor to the bishop of Japan. Via Goa and Macao, he arrived in Nagasaki in 1598, became bishop and remained there till his death.

Certon, Pierre Musician and choirmaster, born ?Melun, France, *c*.1510, died Paris, 22 February 1572. He worked in Paris at Notre Dame in 1529 and at the Sainte Chapelle from 1532, where he was master of the choirboys and perpetual chaplain until his death, writing much polyphonic music as well as popular songs.

Cervantes Saavedra, Miguel de Spanish writer, born Alcalá de Henares, 29 September 1547, died Madrid, 23 April 1616. In 1559 he went to Rome, where he entered the service of Cardinal Guido Acquaviva. He joined the Spanish army, fighting the Turks at the naval battle of Lepanto, losing the use of his left hand. In 1575 he was captured by Barbary pirates and taken to Algeria as a slave. Returning to Spain in 1580 he began to write, publishing numerous plays and his pastoral novel *La Galatea* (1585). Gaining employment with the government, he was imprisoned for alleged corruption. While in prison he wrote the first part of *Don Quixote* (1605), the second part appearing ten years later.

Cesalpino, Andrea Botanist and physician, born Arezzo, Italy, 6 June 1519, died Rome, 23 February 1603. He studied anatomy at Pisa and Padua and medical botany at Pisa, where he became professor of pharmacology in 1549, and founded the botanic garden there in 1553. The most original and philosophical botanist since Theophrastus, whose work he revived, he was the author of *De Plantis* (1583), which **Linnaeus** acknowledged. He propounded a theory of the circulation of the blood and in his later years was **Clement VIII**'s physician.

Cesarini, Alessandro Cardinal, died 13 February 1542. A member of an important gonfalonier ('standard-bearer', i.e. magistrate) family, he was made cardinal in 1517 and served under **Paul III** as legate to the Emperor **Charles V** and to France. He was involved in the preparations for the Council of Trent.

Cesarini, Giuliano Cardinal and papal ambassador, date of birth unknown but possibly 1398, died 1444. A member of the Roman nobility, he was educated at Perugia and Padua. Became a papal diplomat, influential in the mission against the Hussites in 1419 and representing the Pope in France in 1425 and England in 1426. Appointed cardinal in 1426. In 1442 he preached in Hungary for a crusade against the Turks. He was killed while fleeing from the defeat of the Christian army at Varna on 10 November 1444.

Ceslaus of Silesia Blessed, Dominican priest, born Kamien, Poland, c.1184, died Wroclaw, 15 July 1242. With his relative St **Hyacinth** (St Iaccho in Poland) he joined the Dominicans in Rome c.1218. Ceslaus founded the first Dominican house in Prague and in Wroclaw. St **Hedwig**'s spiritual director, he was believed to have saved Wroclaw from a Tartar siege by his prayers. His cult was confirmed by **Clement XI** in 1713. Feast day 17 July, 20 July in Wroclaw.

Ceuppens, Francis Biblical scholar, born Tirlemont, Belgium, 14 September 1888, died Brussels, 28 February 1957. He entered the Dominican Order in 1907, was ordained in 1912 and taught Scripture in Louvain, 1914–21, and in Ghent, 1921–7. Thereafter he was professor of Scripture at the Pontifical Institutum Angelicum in Rome. His most important work was five volumes of biblical theology, Scripture-based Catholic doctrine, largely for students.

Chabham, Thomas de English pastoral theologian, born 1170, died 1240. Educated in Paris about 1190, he became vicar of Sturminster Marshal in 1206 and was sub-dean of Salisbury until at least 1239. He wrote for priests in a new style: on 'how to preach effectively' and, more influentially, on 'how to be a good confessor', which was widely copied, and printed at Cologne and Louvain in 1485.

Chabot, Jean Baptiste Orientalist, born Vouvray, France, 16 February 1860, died Paris, 7 January 1948. Ordained in 1885, he gained a doctorate from Louvain in 1892. He then pursued Syriac studies at the Collège de France and in 1903 was one of the founders of the *Corpus scriptorum christianorum orientalium*, a collection of texts and translations of the works of Syriac, Coptic, Arab and Armenian Fathers. He edited Phoenician and Aramaean inscriptions for the Académie des Inscriptions et Belles Lettres.

Chad Anglo-Saxon monk, bishop and saint, died 2 March 672. A disciple of **Aidan** at Lindisfarne. Succeeded his brother **Cedda** as abbot of Lastingham. In the absence of **Wilfrid**, he was appointed bishop of York by King Oswy in 665. **Theodore** of Tarsus, on becoming archbishop, challenged Chad's consecration, and in 669 Chad retired to Lastingham, later becoming bishop of Lichfield. Feast day 2 March.

Chaine, Joseph Biblical scholar, born Lyons, France, 24 December 1888, died Lyons, 24 March 1948. Ordained in 1913, he studied in Jerusalem, 1919–20, and from 1927 he was professor of Scripture at the Institut Catholique of Lyons. He published critical editions of the *Letter of James* (1927), *Introduction to the Prophets* (1932), the *Catholic*

Epistles (1939), and the *Book of Genesis* (1948), and was involved for many years with the *Catholic Encyclopaedia*.

Challoner, Richard English Roman Catholic bishop and writer, born Lewes, Sussex, 29 September 1691, died London, 12 January 1781. Educated at Douai, France. Taught philosophy and divinity at Douai from 1713 until 1730. Served as a missionary priest in London from 1730, becoming a bishop in 1741. In 1758 he became vicar apostolic of the London district. His many publications include *Garden of the Soul* (1740), a popular prayer book, and a revised edition of the *Douai Bible* (1749–52).

Chalmers, James London Missionary Society (LMS) missionary to the Cook Islands and Papua New Guinea, born Ardrishaig, Argyllshire, 4 August 1841, killed Goaribari Island, Papua, 8 April 1901. He responded to a call to mission in 1854 in the United Presbyterian Church, worked as a city missionary in Glasgow, studied under Henry Robert Reynolds at Cheshunt College (1862–4) and did missionary training with the LMS at Farquhar House. He was ordained to the Congregational ministry in 1865 and sailed for the Cook Islands, reaching Rarotonga in 1867. For ten years he trained Pacific Island missionary teachers and developed local leadership. He joined the London Missionary Society's New Guinea Mission in 1877, made links with village leaders and staffed stations along the southern coast with Pacific Island and Papuan teachers. He opposed colonization and indentured labour, published vocabularies and ethnographic material and laid an important base for later Melanesian anthropology.

Chalmers, Thomas Presbyterian theologian, preacher and leader of the Free Church of Scotland, born Anstruther, Fife, 17 March 1780, died Edinburgh, 30 May 1847. He was educated at St Andrews, licensed to preach in 1799. In 1803, he became minister of Kilmany, Fife. In 1809 he was struck down with consumption and underwent a deep religious crisis. Re-emerging as an evangelical philanthropist, he served as pastor of the Tron Church, Glasgow, 1814–19, and St John's, 1819–23. Professor of moral philosophy at St Andrews from 1823 to 1828, he helped inspire the

first generation of Church of Scotland missionaries to India. He then became professor of theology at Edinburgh until 1843. Served as moderator of the Church of Scotland, 1831–2, and raised funds for over 200 new churches. In 1843 he led 470 clergymen from the Church of Scotland to form the Free Church of Scotland. First principal of the Free Church College in Edinburgh. His publications include the *Institutes of Theology* (1843–7).

Chalmers, William Theologian, born Aberdeen, died Paris, 1678. He trained for the priesthood at the Scots College, Rome, and became first a Jesuit and then an Oratorian. He is known for his rejection of the teaching that grace is efficacious only with the co-operation of the will, and for his defence of physical influence which determines the will, in *Antiquitatis de novitate victoria* (Fastembourg, 1634) and *Dissertatio theologica de electione angelorum et hominum ad gloriam* (Rennes, 1641).

Chaminade, Guillaume Joseph Founder of the Marianists and the Marianist Sisters, born Périgueux, France, 8 April 1761, died Bordeaux, 22 January 1850. After studies in Périgueux, Bordeaux and Paris he was ordained in 1784, and gained a doctorate in 1785. As a non-juring priest he was forced into exile in Spain, 1797–1800, then returned to France, where, to fight religious indifference through education and social service, he founded the Marianist Sisters in 1816, and in 1817 the Marianists. The congregations spread rapidly in Europe, America and Asia.

Champagnat, Marcellin Joseph Benoit Blessed, founder of the Marist School-Brothers, born Le Rosey, Loire, France, 20 May 1789, died Notre Dame de L'Hermitage, Loire, 6 June 1840. He was one of the seminarians ordained in 1816 who had the idea of founding a teaching and missionary organization which fostered devotion to Mary, and his part was to organize the teaching brothers on its foundation in 1817. His experience enabled him to write the *Guide des Ecoles* for them in 1853. Feast day 6 June.

Chandler, Joseph Ripley Journalist, born Kingston, Massachusetts, 1826, died Philadelphia, Pennsylvania, 10 July 1880. He was part-owner of the *Gazette of the United States*, 1826–47, editor of

Graham's American Monthly Magazine of Literature, 1848, and his *Grammar of the English Language* (revised 1848) was widely used in the public schools. He became a Catholic in 1849. Three times elected to Congress, he was appointed the US minister to the Two Sicilies in 1858. A prison inspector, 1861–80, he pressed for penal reform. He pleaded for religious tolerance in *The Beverley Family or the Home Influence of Religion* (1875).

Chandler, Theophilus Parsons Architect, born Boston, Massachusetts, 1845, died Delaware County, Pennsylvania, 1928. He studied architecture at Harvard and Paris and set up practice in Philadelphia, 1870, where he helped to organize the Pennsylvania School of Architecture and was its first director. He is best known for the variety of his church designs.

Chanel, Peter French priest and the first martyr of the South Seas, born at Cuet in the Diocese of Belley, France, in 1803, died 28 April 1841. After being ordained for the diocese and serving for four years in the parishes of Ambérieux as a curate and then as parish priest at Crozet, he became one of the earliest members of the Missionary Society of Mary (the Marists). In 1836 he went as a missionary to the New Hebrides. He was murdered by natives on the island of Futuma, after the ruler's son had become a Christian. Canonized in 1954. Feast day 28 April.

Chang, Agneta Korean Catholic nun and martyr, died Korea, 1950. From a Catholic family, she and a cousin were among the first Koreans to join the American-based Maryknoll Sisters in 1921. After her novitiate in New York, she returned to Korea, where she helped develop the first Korean Catholic women's congregation. As this was in the North, they were disbanded when the communists took over in 1949. Disabled following an old back injury, and unable to comply with an order to report for compulsory civil defence work, she was taken away by soldiers. Her congregation later learnt that she had been shot.

Channing, William Ellery Unitarian minister, writer and philanthropist, born Newport, Rhode Island, 7 April 1780, died of typhoid fever, Bennington, Vermont, 2 October 1842. Graduated from Harvard University in 1798. Spent two years as a private tutor in Richmond, Virginia. Licensed to preach in 1803 and appointed minister of the Federal Street Congregational Church, Boston, remaining there until his death. By preaching and writing, he put forward pacifist, prohibitionist and, after a visit to the West Indies in 1830, abolitionist views. Following a trip to Europe in 1822 he began writing literary essays. By 1819 he had become the acknowledged head of the Unitarians in New England. Due mainly to his efforts the American Unitarian Association was formed in 1825. His writings include *Unitarian Christianity* (1819).

Chantal, Jane Frances Fremiot de Saint, foundress of the Order of the Visitation. Born Dijon, France, 28 January 1572, died Moulin, 13 December 1641. She married Christophe, Baron de Chantal, in 1592 and they had four children. After her husband's death in 1601, Jane resolved not to remarry and took a vow of chastity. She became the spiritual daughter and friend of **Francis de Sales** and in 1610, with his help, founded the first house of the Visitation Order at Annecy. She was well liked and her Order, for young girls and for widows who were not called to the austerities of the existing Orders, grew rapidly. By the time of her death there were 86 Visitation houses. Feast day 12 December.

Chao Tzu Ch'en Chinese theologian, born Deqing, Zhejian, China, 14 February 1888, died Beijing, 21 November 1979. He had a solid classical Chinese education, attended Soochow University and graduated about 1911. He went to the United States in 1914, obtaining his MA and BD degrees at Vanderbilt. He taught at Soochow from 1917, then at Yenching University, Beijing, from 1926, where he became dean of the School of Religion, 1928–56. His *Christian Philosophy* (1925) and *Life of Jesus* (1935) related Christian faith to China's social needs. Following imprisonment by the Japanese in 1942, he wrote a *Life of Paul* (1947) and *My Prison Experience* (1948). He was active in the Chinese National Christian Council and the YMCA, attended International Missionary Council meetings in 1928, 1938 and 1947, and was president of the World Council of Churches from 1948 to 1951.

He identified with the Three-Self movement, but suffered during the Cultural Revolution.

Chapeauville, Jean   Theologian and historian, born Liège, 5 January 1551, died Liège, 11 May 1617. He tried to enforce the Tridentine reforms and established a seminary in Liège. He made a collection of original documents relating to the history of Liège, and wrote a three-volume history of its bishops (Liège, 1612–16).

Chapelle, Placide Louis   Diplomat and archbishop, born Runes, France, 28 August 1842, died New Orleans, Louisiana, 9 August 1905. He emigrated to the USA at seventeen, studied at St Mary's Seminary, Baltimore and was ordained in 1865. After working in Baltimore and Washington DC, he was appointed coadjutor to the archbishop of Santa Fé, New Mexico, in 1891, and archbishop in 1894. He wiped out the huge debts of the archdiocese by levying an extra assessment on the parishes, which alienated many priests, as did his frequent (but unsought) absences from 1898 as apostolic delegate to Puerto Rico and chargé d'affaires of the Philippines. On one of his upstate visitations he heard that yellow fever had broken out in New Orleans, whither he returned and himself died of it.

Chapman, John   Biblical and patristic scholar, born at Ashfield, Suffolk, 25 April 1865, died in London, 7 November 1933. Educated at Oxford University. Ordained deacon in the Anglican Church in 1889. On entering the Roman Catholic Church in 1890 he joined the Benedictine Order, being ordained priest in 1895. For one year in 1913 he served as superior to the religious community on Caldey Island. In 1922 he became prior of Downside and abbot seven years later. His works include *John the Presbyter and the Fourth Gospel* (1905) and *Studies on the Early Papacy* (1928).

Chappotin de Neuville, Hélène de   Foundress of the Franciscan Missionaries of Mary, born Nantes, France, 21 May 1839, died San Remo, Italy, 15 November 1904. She entered the Society of Mary Reparatrix in 1864 and from 1865 to 1876 worked in the Madura Missions of India, of which she was provincial superior at 29. She founded the Institute

of Missionaries of Mary in 1877. In 1882 it was affiliated with the Franciscans and she was received into its Third Order. Her *Méditations liturgiques et franciscaines* was posthumously published (5 vols, Paris, 1896–8).

Chappuis, Maria Salesia   Venerable visitation nun, born Souhières, France (now Switzerland), 16 June 1793, died Troyes, 7 October 1875. She entered the Visitation Order in 1814, was superior and novice mistress at Troyes in 1826–37 and at Paris 1838–44, and collaborated with Louis Bresson in founding the Oblate Sisters of St **Francis de Sales**, 1866, and the Oblates of St Francis de Sales, c.1871. Her cause for beatification was introduced in 1897.

Chapt de Rastignac, Armand   Blessed, theologian, born Périgot, France, 2 October 1729, died Paris, 3–5 September 1792. As vicar-general of the Diocese of Arles, he attempted at the Estates-General meetings in 1789 to prevent church properties being taken over, published *Question sur la propriété des biens ecclésiastiques* (Paris, 1789) and signed protests against the anti-clerical laws of the Constituent Assembly. He was arrested, imprisoned and killed in the massacres of September 1792. He was beatified in 1926. Feast day 2 September.

Charbonneau, Joseph   Archbishop, born Lefaivre, Ontario, Canada, 31 July 1892, died Victoria, British Columbia, 19 November 1959. Ordained at Grand Seminary, Montreal, 1916, he studied at the Catholic University of America and the Canadian College at Rome. He was vicar-general of the Ottawa diocese, first bishop of Hearst, Ontario, 1939, and archbishop of Montreal, 1940. His particular concerns were immigration, education and welfare; he opposed the provincial government's labour legislation for its lack of social justice and supported the workers in their strike at Asbestos in 1949. He resigned and retired to the convent of the Sisters of St Anne in Victoria, British Columbia, for health reasons in 1950.

Charbonnel, Armand François Marie de   Missionary and educator, born Monistrol-sur-Loire, 1 December 1802, died Crest, Drome, 29 March 1891. He joined the Society of Priests of St Sulpice in Paris and was ordained in 1825. Sent to

Canada, he worked in Montreal, 1840–7, and became bishop of Toronto in 1850, where he founded St Michael's College. He divided the diocese in 1856, making Hamilton and London new dioceses, then resigned and joined the Capuchins at Rieti, Italy, in 1860. For his last ten years he preached in France for the Society for the Propagation of the Faith.

Chardon, Louis French mystic, born Clermont, 1595, died Paris, 17 August 1651. Entered the Dominican Order in 1618, spending most of his life at a convent at Paris. His main work is *La Croix de Jésus* (1647), in which he describes his doctrine of the mystical life and his emphasis on spiritual desolation.

Chardon, Matthias Charles Theologian, born Yvois, Carignan, France, 22 September 1695, died abbey of St Arnoul, Metz, 20 October 1771. He was novice master at the Benedictine abbey of St Vannes, Verdun, where he taught philosophy and theology until its general chapter deposed him in 1730 for having refused to sign the Constitution *Unigenitus* of **Clement XI** of 1713, which condemned recent developments in Catholic faith and practice. His *Histoire des Sacrements* (6 vols, Paris, 1745) is a valuable account of their celebration and administration.

Charlemagne King of the Franks and emperor of the Romans, born Aix-la-Chapelle, 2 April 742, died 28 January 814. On the death of his father Pepin, he ruled jointly with his brother Carloman the realm of the Franks. In 771, on the death of his brother, he took possession of all the inheritance and commenced extending Frankish rule, bringing large parts of Western and Central Europe, not only under his own control, but under the authority of the Roman church. In 773 he began a campaign to conquer and Christianize the Saxons and Frisians North of France, and the Lombards of northern Italy. He also fought in Spain, and in 796 conquered the Avars in modern-day Hungary. On Christmas Day 800 Pope **Leo III** crowned him Roman Emperor. In the management of the Empire he gathered scholars from all over Europe, built churches and monasteries and strengthened the Church.

Charles I King of Great Britain and Ireland, second son of James VI of Scotland, born Dunfermline, 19 November 1600, beheaded London, 30 January 1649. Came to England in 1604 and succeeded to the throne in 1625. Being out of sympathy with the English Parliament, which was Calvinistic and anti-Roman, he forbade the preaching of Calvinist dogmas and pledged himself to tolerance of English Catholics. His efforts to impose a new prayer book in Scotland were one of the several causes of the civil war between the supporters of Charles and those of Parliament, which the Royalists effectively lost. Charles was tried, and condemned to death. In 1627 he was presented with a Greek MS of the Bible dating from the fifth century and older than any biblical MS previously available in the West. It became known as *Codex Alexandrinus* and led to much greater accuracy in Bible translation.

Charles II (the Bald) German emperor, born Frankfurt am Main, 13 June 823, died Avrieux, 6 October 877. He fought for the Pope against the Saracens in Italy, for which he was made emperor by **John VIII** in 875. Grandson of **Charlemagne**, he was the first ruler of France proper. He confirmed the Carolingian donations to the Roman church and was known for welcoming scholars to his court.

Charles II King of England, Scotland and Ireland, born London, 29 May 1630, died there 6 February 1685. Fought in the early stages of the Civil War, before fleeing to The Hague. He invaded England from Scotland in 1651 but was defeated by Cromwell at Worcester. After spending nine years in exile he landed at Dover on 25 May 1660 and was crowned king on 23 April 1661. Edward Hyde, first earl of Clarendon, appointed chief minister, restored the supremacy of the Church of England. With the passing of the Act of Uniformity 1662 2000 ministers were ejected from their livings, thus strengthening Nonconformity rather than suppressing it. Other statutes such as the Corporation Act (1661), the Conventicles Act (1664), the Five Mile Act (1665), and the Test Act (1673) led to widespread persecution of these dissenting ministers and their congregations. His reign also saw the 'Popish plots' of Titus **Oates**, leading to renewed persecution of Roman Catholics. On his death-bed he declared his allegiance to the Roman Catholic Church.

Charles III (the Fat) Frankish king and German emperor, born Bavaria(?), 839, died Neidingen on the Danube, 13 January 888. He became heir to the whole domain of Charlemagne in 884, but the political will was for separation and in 887 he was deposed, his régime collapsed and the Carolingian Empire dissolved with the final separation of German-speaking from French-speaking peoples.

Charles IV Holy Roman Emperor, born Prague 14 May 1316, died Prague, 29 November 1378. In 1346 crowned king of Germany and Bohemia. Due to the fact that Pope **Clement VI** secured Charles' election as monarch, and due to the alliance that he made with the Papacy, Charles was known as 'the priests' king'. In 1355 he was crowned emperor by Cardinal Peter of Ostia. He gained ecclesiastical independence for Bohemia, establishing the archbishopric of Prague in 1344.

Charles V Emperor and Spanish king, born Ghent, Flanders, 24 February 1500, died at the monastery of Yuste in Spain, 21 September 1558. Became king of Spain in 1516 and Holy Roman Emperor in 1519. A devout Catholic, throughout his reign he believed it was his divinely appointed duty to defend Christendom from its enemies, such as the Turks, and the Church from Lutheranism. The Diet of Worms in 1521, attended by Charles, condemned Luther's works. However, the Protestant princes gained autonomy by the Peace of Augsburg, 1555. Due to increasing pressure to reconcile the desire of the Papacy to destroy the Protestant Reformation and his need for Protestant allies, he abdicated in 1556.

Charles VII King of France, born Paris, 22 February 1403, died Mehun-sur-Yèvre, 22 July 1461. Crowned king of France, 1422. During his reign the Hundred Years' War with England was brought to an end. Under Charles' mediation the Gallican church approved the decrees of the Council of Basel and affirmed its liberties, particularly in granting benefices. **Calixtus III** was unsuccessful in persuading Charles to join a crusade against the Turks.

Charles VIII King of France, born Amboise, 30 June 1470, died Amboise (due to an accident), 8 April 1498. Crowned king of France in 1483. Almost his entire policy was to extend the power of the House of Anjou. In 1495 Pope **Alexander VI** formed an alliance with Milan, Venice and Austria against Charles, forcing him to return to France.

Charles Martel Ruler of the Frankish kingdom of Austrasia (north France and southern Germany), called 'Martel' or 'the hammer' due to his defeat of the Moors, born about 688, died Quierzy, 741. Son of Pepin of Herstal and grandfather of **Charlemagne**. On the death of his father in 714 Charles, an illegitimate son, was imprisoned by the father's widow. He escaped and was proclaimed mayor of the palace. Following a war between Austrasia and Neustria Charles became king of all the Franks. He did much to protect Christendom against the encroaching power of Islam by defeating the Moors at Poitiers in 732 and driving them out of the Rhône Valley in 739.

Charles of Anjou Founder of the Angevin dynasty, born March 1227, died Foggia, 7 January 1285. Crowned king of Naples and Sicily by Pope **Clement IV** in 1266. He carried out successful military campaigns in Tunisia, Albania, Corfu and Italy. From 1277 onwards the Pope, attempting to maintain political stability, allowed Charles freedom in the Papal States. However, the last few years of his life witnessed the weakening of his hegemony.

Charles of Blois Blessed, Franciscan tertiary, born c.1319, died Auray, France, 29 September 1364. Greatly respected as a saint and wonder-worker, he fought the English de Montforts for his family territory claimed by them, from 1341, and was their captive 1347–56. The Franciscans propagated his cult, which **Urban V** condemned. Investigations of it were held up by the Great Schism and it was not authorized until 1904. Feast days Blois, 12 June, Vannes, 14 October.

Charles of Sezze Saint, Franciscan lay brother and ascetical writer, born Sezze, Italy, 19 October 1613, died Rome, 6 January 1670. He joined the Reformed Franciscan province in Rome, 1635 and after ten years of intense self-abnegation he experienced ecstatic union. He wrote at length on the spiritual life, and his autobiography has been compared with that of St **Teresa of Avila**. He was beatified in 1882 and canonized in 1959. Feast day 7 January.

Charles of the Assumption (Charles Bryas) Theologian, born Saint-Ghislain, Belgium, 1625, died Douai, France, 23 February 1686. He joined the Discalced Carmelites at Douai in 1653, and was ordained in 1659. Here he taught theology, eventually became prior and later served two terms as provincial superior of the Carmelites in Belgium and France. His great study was the relationship between predestination and grace, on which he published, without the permission of his superiors, *Pentalogus diaphoricus* in 1678, a work probably ahead of its time, in which, for example, he said that a penitent who confesses the same mortal sins each week ought to be absolved by his confessor. The book was put on the Index in 1684.

Charles of Villers Blessed, abbot, born Cologne, died Hocht near Maastricht, Netherlands, *c*.1215. He entered the Cistercian abbey of Himmerod in 1184 or 1185, was prior at Heisterbach 1191 and abbot of Villers 1197–1209, when he resigned and returned to Himmerod but was later summoned to organize a foundation at Hocht. Feast day 29 January.

Charlevoix, Pierre François Xavier de Jesuit explorer, born St Quentin, France, 24 October 1682, died La Flèche 1 February 1761. He entered the Society of Jesus in 1698 and was sent to teach at the Jesuit College at Quebec, *c*.1705–9, then at the Collège Louis le Grand, Paris, 1709–20, when the French regent commissioned him to find a new route to western Canada, but after long journeys he was unsuccessful in this. From 1733 to 1755 he edited *Mémoires de Trévoux*, a Jesuit monthly journal. Among his historical works the most valuable is his *Histoire de la Nouvelle France* (Paris, 1744); he was the only traveller of the time to describe the interior of North America, in this the first general history of Canada, which had a valuable appendix recounting native Indian life and customs.

Charnetsky, Nicholas Redemptorist priest and bishop of the Greek-Catholic Church in the Ukraine, died L'viv, Ukraine, 2 April 1959. Charnetsky studied theology in Rome, and was ordained to the priesthood in 1909. The following year he became professor in the seminary in Stanislav, but in 1919 he entered the Redemptorist Order. He was consecrated a bishop in 1931, and was made exarch in 1939, his appointment being confirmed by the Pope in 1941. He had charge of areas in both the Ukraine and Poland, though the Greek-Catholic Church of which he had oversight had been officially suppressed in some of these areas. He was arrested by the Soviet government, along with other Greek-Catholic bishops, in April 1945, and although sentenced to five years' hard labour he was not released until 1956, by which time he had become very ill.

Charonton, Enguerrand Painter, born Laon, France, 1410, died Provence(?), *c*.1466. He is said to have created a new style of Provençal painting influenced by both Flemish and Italian sources, and his authenticated works represent an intense and systematic study of Mary unusual in his time.

Charpentier, Marc Antoine Composer, born Paris, *c*.1634, died Paris, 24 February 1704. Having studied in Italy he became the leader of Italianate musical taste in France and held various musical posts before that at the Sainte Chapelle in 1698. Among some powerful works was an opera, *Médée* (Paris, 1693), and over twenty oratorios, of which *La Reniement de St Pierre* is the best known.

Charron, Pierre French theologian and philosopher, born Paris, 1541, died Paris, 16 November 1603. Studied law at the Sorbonne, Orléans and Bourges, but entered the Church. Served as preacher to the queen of Navarre and as canon of Bordeaux from 1576. In 1594 he became vicargeneral at Cahors and later canon of Condom. His works include *Discours chrétiens* (1589), containing a criticism of the Protestant League, and *Les trois Vérités* (1594), and *De la Sagesse* (1601) which present his scepticism and a vindication of Catholicism.

Chatard, Francis Silas Fifth bishop of Vincennes (now Indianapolis), born Baltimore, 13 December

1834, died Indianapolis, 7 September 1918. He graduated in medicine from the University of Maryland in 1856, but in 1857 entered the Urban College of Propaganda Fide at Rome and by 1863 was vice-rector of the American College, Rome and rector in 1871. Having returned to the USA to solicit help for the college in 1877, he was appointed bishop of Vincennes by **Leo XIII** in 1878. A vigorous leader, he reorganized schools, founded hospitals, raised the status of priests, built the cathedral of SS Peter and Paul and wrote for *Catholic World*.

Chateaubriand, François Auguste René, Vicomte de French writer, statesman and Christian apologist, born St Malo, Brittany, 4 September 1768, died Paris, 4 July 1848. Raised in a noble family, was educated at Dol, Rennes and Dinan. Served as a soldier in the French army. In 1791 he explored the east coast of North America. Returning to France he was wounded in 1792 and fled to England. Gaining favour with Napoleon, he obtained a diplomatic post in 1800, but later resigned. Under the Bourbons he was appointed ambassador to Great Britain in 1822 and minister of Foreign Affairs in 1823. By virtue of his writings, particularly his novels, he is regarded as being a forerunner of Romanticism. In his *The Genius of Christianity* (1802) he emphasized the uniqueness of Christianity with regard to other world faiths, while in *Essay on the Revolutions* (1797) he describes his early religious criticisms and doubts.

Chatel, Ferdinand Toussaint Priest, founder of the Eglise Catholique Française, born Gannat, France, 9 January 1795, died Paris, 13 February 1857. Ordained in 1818 and an army chaplain 1821–30, he was reprimanded for expressing unorthodox opinions in periodicals. He then founded the Eglise Catholique Française, propounding some ideas derived from the Enlightenment, abolishing auricular confession and using a vernacular liturgy. His sect's political radicalism caused the police to close the Paris chapel in 1842, and he was imprisoned for a time, but by 1843 he was back in Paris urging women's emancipation, divorce and socialism. The movement failed and he died poor and alone.

Chaucer, Geoffrey Poet, born London, c.1340, died London, 25 October 1400. He came from a learned and courtly background, and became comptroller to the Petty Customs of the Port of London. He was allowed a deputy, which gave him time to complete his epic *Canterbury Tales*. Later he was appointed clerk of the king's works. He is buried in Poets' Corner, Westminster Abbey, where a monument is erected to him. He is regarded as one of the greatest of English poets. *The Canterbury Tales* is based on the idea of a party of twenty-nine pilgrims setting out for Canterbury and includes many religious figures and much insight into human character.

Chaumont, Henri Ascetic and spiritual director, born Paris, 11 December 1838, died Paris, 15 May 1896. Educated in the seminary of St Sulpice and ordained in 1864, he made the teaching and spirit of St **Francis de Sales** his own, and his *Directions spirituelles de St François de Sales* (Paris, 1870–9), a best-seller, put him in demand as a preacher and spiritual director. He founded societies for lay women in 1872, priests in 1876 and laymen shortly after. They meet in local autonomous groups and follow his careful method of planned meditations, readings and religious exercises to help them live a holy life in their particular situation.

Chaundler, Thomas Humanist, born Wells, Somerset, c.1417, died 2 November 1490. Educated at Winchester and New College, Oxford, he was ordained in 1444, awarded a doctorate in theology in 1445, became warden of New College in 1454 and chancellor of the university in 1457–61 and 1472–9, when he entered royal service and was made dean of Hereford. He helped introduce Renaissance studies into England.

Chautard, Jean Baptiste Reformed Cistercian abbot, ascetic and writer, born Briançon, France, 12 March 1858, died Sept-Fons near Moulins, 29 September 1935. He entered the Trappist monastery at Aiguebelle near Valence at nineteen, in 1897 became abbot of Chambarand near Grenoble, and in 1899 became abbot of Sept-Fons, where he remained, basing his teaching on the rule of St **Benedict** and the writings of St **Bernard of Clairvaux**. In 1903 when the Trappists were threatened with dissolution by the French government, Chautard defended them before the Senate and the threat was removed.

Chavara, Kuriakos Elias Founder and first superior-general of the Syro-Malabar Carmelites, born Kainakari, Kerala, India, 1805, died Coonemmavu, Kerala, 3 January 1871. Ordained in 1829, he founded a Carmelite congregation in 1855 and became vicar-general of Virapoly in 1861. A great exponent of the power of print, he designed his own press in 1844 and published ten books in five years. In 1887 he published *Deepika*, now the oldest daily paper in Malayalam, and in 1902 *Flower of Carmel*, the most widely circulated Catholic magazine in Kerala.

Chávez de la Rosa, Pedro José Bishop and reformer, born Cadiz, Spain, 27 June 1740, died Cadiz, 26 October 1821. He was sent to Peru and consecrated in Lima as bishop of Arequipa, 1788. This was a neglected diocese, and he carried out a thorough reform of its buildings, discipline and the curriculum of the seminary, thus preparing a generation of men outstanding in public life in the early years of the republic. Not surprisingly he was opposed, and he resigned in 1805 to return to Spain. He bequeathed his library to the seminary of Arequipa and the rest of his possessions to the orphanage he founded there.

Chavoin, Jeanne Marie Foundress, born in Coutouvre, Beaujolais, France, 1786, died 1858. Collaborated with Jean-Claude **Colin** in starting the Marist Sisters, the female branch of the Society of Mary or Marists. Her work helped pave the way for the active, non-cloistered apostolate for women religious.

Checa y Barba, José Ignacio de Archbishop of Quito, born Quito, Ecuador, 4 August 1829, died Quito, 30 March 1877. Ordained in 1855, bishop of Ibarra, 1866, archbishop of Quito in 1868, his aim was to raise the spiritual and intellectual standard of his clergy. He stood aloof from contemporary politics, until a Franciscan took advantage in his preaching of the currently proclaimed freedom of thought and was prevented by the police from continuing. Checa y Barba protested against the subjection of sermons to censorship, warned his people against 'heretical publications' and refused to accede to government requests. He died on Good Friday after drinking from the chalice at the close of the liturgy, and an autopsy

revealed he had been poisoned by strychnine, but no one was prosecuted.

Cheffontaines, Christophe de Theologian, born near Saint-Pol de Lyons, Brittany, 1512, died Rome, 26 May 1595. He joined the Franciscan Observants in 1532 and studied in Paris, from when he applied his energy to opposing the Huguenots. After a period as provincial in Brittany, he was elected minister general of his Order in 1571 and for eight years toured its houses stiffening adherence to its original principles. His principal work was *Deffence de la foi de nos ancetres* (Paris, 1570). Some of his works were censured and three of them put on the Index.

Chelidonia Saint, anchoress, died Subiaco, Italy, 13 October 1152. Anything known about her comes from the history of the monastery of Subiaco written by Guglielmo Capisacchi, who was professed there in 1525 and completed the work in 1573. He claimed to have used an anonymous life of the saint, who had been abbess of a nearby convent before becoming a recluse distinguished for prophecies and miracles, and whose remains were buried under the altar of Subiaco in 1578. Feast day 13 October.

Chemnitz, Martin Lutheran theologian, born Treuenbrietzen, Germany, 9 November 1522, died Brunswick, Germany, 8 April 1586. Chemnitz was a lecturer at the University of Wittenberg, where his original interests were in mathematics and astrology. Forced to leave Wittenberg by the Smalcaldic Wars, he spent some years at Königsberg, where he began to study theology. He later returned to Wittenberg, becoming a close friend of **Melanchthon**. In 1554 he moved to Brunswick, where he was active in church leadership, remaining there until his death. Chemnitz was largely responsible for consolidating and stabilizing Lutheran theology in the unsettled period following Luther's death; he drafted much of the Formula of Concord, and wrote important works on Christology and the Eucharist, and an influential Lutheran critique of the Council of Trent.

Ch'eng Ching-Yi (Cheng Jingyi) Chinese church leader, born Beijing, 1881, died 1939. He attended theological school in Tianjin and followed his father into London Missionary Society ministry. He travelled to Britain and assisted in Bible translation from 1903 before returning to pastor a church in Beijing. He sought independence from mission control and in 1910 informed the Edinburgh Missionary Conference that Western denominations did not interest Chinese Christians. He became secretary of the China Continuation Committee, 1913–22, which prepared the way for the National Christian Conference of 1922. He was appointed secretary of the National Christian Council in 1924 and, despite his failing health, in 1934 became secretary of the Church of Christ in China. He was a vice-president of the International Missionary Council in 1928–38 and attended their Jerusalem and Tambaram meetings.

Chenu, Marie Dominique Dominican theologian, medievalist, born Soisy-sur-Seine, France, 7 January 1895, died Paris, 11 February 1990. Having entered the Dominican Order in 1913, he taught at Le Saulchoir, where he later became regent of studies and wrote *Une Ecole de Theologie – Le Saulchoir* (1937), which was placed on the Index. During the German occupation, he worked to renew urban Catholicism and in France's priest-worker movement, papal disapproval of which led to his being relieved of his teaching duties. He was theological adviser to the African bishops at Vatican II. His writings on Aquinas are collected in *La Parole de Dieu – La Foi Dans L'Intelligence* (1964).

Cherubini, Luigi Composer, born Florence, 14 September 1760, died Paris, 15 March 1842. He composed a Mass at thirteen, and later studied at Milan and Bologna, 1778–80, when he wrote twenty motets in the style of **Palestrina**. Between 1780 and 1806 he wrote eight operas, living in Paris from 1788 and becoming professor of counterpoint at the Conservatoire in 1795. Napoleon did not care for his music, and he went to Vienna in 1805, where he met **Beethoven** and **Haydn**. He was ill and depressed on his return to France after the outbreak of war with Austria, but while recuperating at the château of the prince de Chimay he was asked by the local music society to write a Mass for them. This set his creative spirit going again and he subsequently wrote some powerful church music, of which the most memorable

examples are his Requiems in C minor and D minor.

Cherubino of Avigliana Blessed, born Avigliana, 1451, died Avigliana, 17 September 1479. An Augustinian from Piedmont whose family name was Tosta, he was noted for his piety, obedience and ardent devotion to the Crucifixion. Reports of his life make particular mention of his angelic purity. According to a local tradition in Avigliana, after his death the sound of celestial bells announced his soul's arrival in heaven, and for some time afterwards his body gave off the fragrance of lilies. His cult was confirmed by **Pius IX** in 1865. Feast day 20 February.

Cheshire, Leonard Group Captain and Roman Catholic philanthropist, born Chester, 7 September 1917, died Le Court, Hampshire, 31 July 1992. Educated at Stowe School and studied law at Merton College, Oxford. He became a Group Captain in the RAF during the Second World War, serving with Bomber Command, and completed a hundred bombing missions, often at low altitude on heavily defended German targets: he commanded the 'Dambusters' squadron. He was awarded the Victoria Cross, Britain's highest decoration for bravery, in 1944, as well as many other distinctions. His experience as British observer at the dropping of the atomic bomb on Nagasaki, 1945, however, together with a conversion to Roman Catholicism, led him to devote the rest of his life to the relief of suffering. Founder of Cheshire Foundation Homes for the Sick in 1952 (there were 270 of them in England and elsewhere at the time of his death), and co-founder of the Ryder–Cheshire Mission for the Relief of Suffering. He married Sue, Baroness **Ryder** of Warsaw, in 1956. He was awarded the Order of Merit in 1981.

Chesterton, Gilbert Keith Prolific and versatile essayist, novelist and poet, born London, 29 May 1874, died Beaconsfield, Bucks, 14 June 1936. He was educated at St Paul's School and then attended Slade School of Art, though he never practised professionally as an artist beyond illustrating the novels of his friend Hilaire **Belloc**. Chesterton began his career as a journalist. He is best known for his series of Father Brown detective stories, beginning with *The Innocence of Father Brown*

(1911). Chesterton was received into the Roman Catholic Church in 1922 by his friend Father O'Connor, the original of Father Brown, though his attraction to the faith had long been signalled. He also wrote lives of leading religious characters including *St Francis of Assisi* and *St Thomas Aquinas* (1933), as well as of literary ones such as *Browning* (1903) and *Dickens* (1906). In 1925 he launched *G.K.'s Weekly*, a successor to *New Witness*, established in 1912 by his brother Cecil and Belloc. His style was characterized by a strong sense of humour and a rather too frequent use of paradox.

Chevalier, Jules Religious founder, born Richelieu, France, 15 March 1824, died Issoudun, 21 October 1907. Originally a shoemaker's apprentice, he was eventually ordained in 1851, and appointed curate of Issoudun, where he remained until his death. In 1854 he founded the Sacred Heart Missionaries and was their superior general until 1901. His principal works are *Notre Dame du Sacré Coeur de Jésus* (1895) and *Le Sacré Coeur de Jésus* (1900).

Chevalier, Ulysse French priest and historian, born Rambouillet, 24 February 1841, died Romans, Dauphiné, 1923. Famous for the publication of his six-volume edition of the *Bibliothèque Liturgique* (1893–7) and the *Répertoire* (1877–1903) containing a list of all persons named in books, and all places of historical significance, referred to in the medieval period.

Cheverus, Jean Louis Lefebvre de Bishop, born Mayenne, France, 28 January 1768, died Bordeaux, 19 July 1836. He was educated at the Collège Louis le Grand, Paris, and ordained in 1790. Having refused to take the oath required by the Civil Constitution of the Clergy, he fled to England in 1792 and taught French and mathematics at a Protestant school in Wallingford, until 1794, when he founded a church for émigrés in Tottenham. In 1796 he went to Boston, Massachusetts, and worked among the Native Americans in Maine, for which he received a pension from the State of Massachusetts. During an epidemic of yellow fever he was tireless in serving the sick. He was appointed the first bishop of Boston in 1810, and for the next thirteen years travelled widely in the diocese, fostering friendly relationships between the Catholics and Protestants. Indeed, when in 1824 Louis XVIII summoned him back to France, 226 Protestants petitioned for him to stay. Appointed bishop of Montauban, then a peer of France, 1827–30, he set up a retirement scheme for the Bordeaux clergy in 1829, and an association for the care of 167 children left fatherless by a fishing disaster in 1836.

Chezard de Matel, Jeanne Marie Religious foundress, born Matel, France, 6 November 1596, died Paris, 11 September, 1670. She set up the Institute of the Sisters of the Incarnate Word and the Blessed Sacrament, which was authorized in 1633, but not formally established until 1639 at Matel, and finally approved in 1644. As her writings were full of erudite theological terms, though she was practically illiterate, Cardinal **Richelieu** was suspicious and ordered her to write her autobiography, which completely authenticated her integrity.

Chichele, Henry Archbishop, born *c.*1362, died 12 April 1443. A product of Winchester and of New College, Oxford, he was bishop of St David's from 1408, and took part in the 1409 Council of Pisa, which resulted in three papal claimants rather than the previous two. Translated to Canterbury in 1414, his period in office coincided with **Martin V**'s reassertion of papal authority after the Council of Constance. For upholding England's anti-papal Statutes of Provisors and Praemunire, Chichele was deprived of his legatine powers, while the archbishop of York and bishop of Winchester were made cardinals and therefore ranked above him. He founded All Souls College, Oxford (1438).

Chidwick, John Patrick Chaplain and educator, born New York City, 23 October 1862, died there 13 January 1935. Ordained at Troy, New York, in 1887, he was serving as chaplain aboard the US battleship *Maine* when it was blown up in Havana harbour, Cuba, in 1898, and his heroism became known nationwide. In the Archdiocese of New York he was a police chaplain, pastor and founder of a high school, president of the college of New Rochelle and from 1909 to 1922 rector of St Joseph's Seminary at Dunwoodie. Appointed a papal chamberlain, he served as pastor of St Agnes' parish in New York City until his death.

Chiericati, Francesco Bishop, born Vicenza, after 1482, died Bologna, 5 December 1539. After legal studies at Padua, Bologna and Siena, Chiericati served Cardinals Matthäus Schiner and Adriano Castellesi. He found favour with **Leo X**, who appointed him nuncio to England, 1515–17, Spain, 1519 and Portugal, 1521. In Spain he met the future **Adrian VI**, during whose brief pontificate Chiericati was made bishop of Teramo in the Abruzzi, 1522 and was nuncio to the Diet of Nuremberg (also 1522), where he presented papal pleas for united action against the Turk and enforcement of the anti-Lutheran Edict of Worms. For **Clement VII** he undertook embassies to Prussia and Muscovy.

Chigi, Agostino Banker, entrepreneur and patron of art, born Siena, 1465, died Rome, 10 April 1520. Deftly negotiating changes of regime at the Vatican, Chigi was banker to **Alexander VI**, **Julius II** and **Leo X**, becoming the richest banker of his generation. Much of his wealth was derived from the lease, granted by Alexander in 1500, to exploit the alum mines at Tolfa in the Papal States, alum being a rare commodity used in cloth production. The Roman villa now known as the Farnesina, designed by Peruzzi and decorated by many leading artists including **Raphael**, is an enduring monument to Chigi's worldly success.

Chigi, Angela Blessed, a member of the influential Chigi family, she belonged to a congregation of hermits of St Augustine, living a holy life in Siena, where she died in 1400. She was never officially beatified.

Chigi, Flavio Cardinal, born Sienna, 11 May 1631, died Rome, 3 September 1693. When Fabio Chigi became Pope **Alexander VII** in 1655, he made three of his nephews cardinals, among whom was Flavio, who was appointed his legate and librarian. The family library, which he enlarged, was his particular concern. It is now in the Vatican Library and contains about 3000 manuscripts and many volumes of archival materials.

Chigi, Giovanni da Lecceto Blessed, born Maciareto near Siena, Maciareto, 1300, died 28 October 1363. He became a lay brother with the Augustinians of Lecceto and led an exemplary life in Vallas-

pra, Siena and Pavia, and later once again in Siena. Feast day 28 October.

Chigi, Giuliana Blessed, possibly connected with the famous Chigi family. After being widowed four times, she spent her remaining years as a tertiary of St Augustine and died in Siena in 1400.

Chigi, Sigismondo Cardinal and legate to the Order of Malta, born 1649, died 1678. He was another nephew to be appointed cardinal by his uncle **Alexander VII**.

Chigi-Albani, Agostino Lived in the second half of the seventeenth century and was another of **Alexander VII**'s nephews. He acquired for himself and his family the title of Marshal of the Church and Guardian of the Conclave.

Chilembwe, John Nationalist and leader of an Independent Church, born *c.*1871 near Chiradzulu, Malawi, died January 1915. Influenced by Joseph **Booth** in the 1890s. He was baptized in July 1893 and studied in the USA from 1897, where he was ordained by the National Baptist Convention. In 1900 he formed the Providence Industrial Mission. He became increasingly concerned about the mistreatment of Africans on colonial estates until the policy of conscription for World War I pushed him to stage a military uprising in January 1915. It was unsuccessful, but his subsequent death gave him martyr status in the struggle against colonial rule.

Chillenden, Thomas Prior of Christ Church, Canterbury, England, died 15 August 1411. He became a Benedictine at Christ Church in 1364, studied canon law at the Roman curia from 1378 to 1379, and was awarded an Oxford doctorate in canon law in 1383. An outstanding administrator, after the decline in population after the Black Death he leased church lands on favourable terms, with the returns of which he was able to undertake a rebuilding programme at Canterbury Cathedral. He declined an election to the See of Rochester in 1400, and in 1409 was the representative of the province of Canterbury to the Council of Pisa.

Chimalpain, Domingo Native Mexican historian, born Amecameca, Mexico, 1579, died Mexico City,

1660. A layman, he lived most of his life in the service of the church of San Antonio Abad in Mexico City. Among his existing works are two in the Nahuatl language, *Ocho relaciones historicas* (Copenhagen, 1949–52) and *Memorial breve de la fundacion de la ciudad de Culhuacan* (Stuttgart, 1958).

Chiniquy, Charles Pascal Temperance advocate, excommunicated priest, born Kamouraska, Canada, 30 July 1809, died Montreal, 16 January 1899. Ordained in 1833, he became an ardent advocate of temperance. Having served in various parishes before founding a temperance society in 1840, he was excommunicated in 1856 as a schismatic and eventually received into the Presbyterian Church as an official preacher and moved to Montreal in 1875. He published *Cinquante ans dans l'Eglise de Rome* (1885) and *Quarante ans dans l'Eglise du Christ* (covering 1859 to 1899 and published posthumously).

Chisholm, Caroline Philanthropist and social worker, born Woolton, Northampton, England, 3 May 1808, died London, 27 March 1877. She married Captain Archibald Chisholm in 1830, an officer in the East India Company's service. In 1832 she opened schools for soldiers' daughters at Madras; in 1841 a home for female immigrants in Sidney, Australia. In 1842 she published her report *A Brief Account of the Sydney Immigrants' Home*, the first publication by an Australian woman. Came to London in 1846 and wrote on emigration. Returned to Australia in 1854 but came back to England twelve years later.

Chlodulf of Metz Bishop and saint, died 696 or *c.*663. Son of **Arnulf of Metz** and brother-in-law of St Begga, he became bishop of Metz in either 652 or 656. A ninth- or tenth-century catalogue accords him a 40-year episcopate, but it is not clear if his death should be placed as late as 696, since his successor's signature is on a charter of 667. His bones are in the former Benedictine church of Lay-Saint-Christophe, near Nancy, and in St Arnulf's, Metz. Feast day 8 June.

Chmielowski, Adam (Brother Albert) Polish saint and well-known artist, especially for his painting of the *Ecce Homo*, born Cracow, 20 August 1845,

died Cracow, 25 December 1916. He was a student of engineering in both Poland and Belgium, then of art in Paris and Munich. As a politically active student he took part in the 1863 uprising against Russia, in which he lost a leg. He decided to adopt a form of religious life, and founded the Congregation of the Brothers of the Third Order of St Francis Servants of the Poor (the Albertines), and a similar Congregation of Albertine nuns. He devoted his life to work with the sick, the poor, orphans (he had himself been orphaned at an early age) and the homeless. Karol Wojtyla wrote a play around his life, *Our God's Brother*. As Pope John Paul II, Wojtyla canonized him on 12 November 1989. Feast day 25 December.

Choiseul du Plessis Praslin, Gilbert de Bishop, born Paris, 1613, died Paris, 31 December 1689. Having been awarded a doctorate from the Sorbonne in 1640, he became bishop of Comminges in 1644 and of Tournai from 1671. He founded schools and seminaries and raised money to feed the poor during a famine. He is chiefly remembered for championing the Jansenists and for his spirited advocacy of greater autonomy for the French Church. His *Mémoires touchant la religion* (3 vols, Paris, 1681–5) explain his defence of 'Gallican liberties'.

Choiseul, Etienne François de French statesman, born Lorraine, 28 June 1719, died Paris, 8 May 1785. At the request of Madame de Pompadour, Louis XV made him ambassador to Rome in 1754–7, during which time he arranged the alliance between the Bourbon rulers of France and Austria against Prussia. He improved the French army and navy and reopened trade with India. On behalf of the Bourbons, while claiming to uphold religion, he set about the suppression of the Jesuits which was accomplished in 1773 by **Clement XIV**. Choiseul was eventually alienated from Louis XV by madame du Barry.

Chong Yak-Jong, Augustine Early Korean Catholic theologian and martyr, born near Seoul, 1760, beheaded 1801. He came from a noble family, studied widely, and encountered Christianity through I Sung-Hun (1756–1801), who had investigated the new ideas associated with the Catholics in Beijing and baptized Chong in 1786. In 1791

Chong survived persecution. He compiled a Korean catechism which was still in use in 1932 and republished in 1986 (H. Diaz, *A Korean Theology, Chu-Gyo Yo-Ji: Essentials of the Lord's Teaching*). However, he was tried in 1797 and again a year later. Chong stated before his execution that becoming a Christian was something 'I would never regret, even if I have to die a thousand times'.

Choron, Alexandre Etienne Musician and innovator, born Caen, France, 21 October 1772, died Paris, 29 June 1834. He published the scores of Italian and German classics from 1804, reorganized training schools for church choirs, and directed church festivals 1811–15. From 1815 to 1817 he was director of the Paris Opéra, but was forced to resign for bringing in too many unknown composers, after which he etablished the Institution Royale for religious and classical music but had to close it when the government subsidy ceased with the revolution of 1830. With F. J. Fayolle he produced in 1810–11 the notable *Dictionnaire historique des musiciens*.

Christaller, Johannes Gottlieb Basel Mission linguist and translator in Ghana, born Winnenden, Germany, 19 November 1827, died Stuttgart, 16 December 1895. After training at the Mission House in Basel, he was sent to Ghana, where he arrived in January 1853. He taught at the Basel Mission Seminary at Akropong-Akuapem and worked on Scripture translation and literature production. He returned to Europe in 1868 with the text of the Bible in Twi which was published in 1871. Based in Schondorf, he published a scientific grammar of the Twi language in 1875. His monumental *Dictionary of the Asante and Fante Language* – called Tshi (Twi) (1881, 1933) established the language in literature and worship and provided a basis for understanding Akan religious, social and moral ideas. From 1883 he edited *The Christian Messenger*, Ghana's oldest Christian periodical.

Christian of Prussia Cistercian missionary and first bishop of Prussia, died Poland, 4 December 1245. He was created a missionary bishop by Innocent III in 1215. A metropolitan with the right to establish dioceses and consecrate bishops, his aim was to convert the Prussians without destroying their independence. This brought him into conflict with the Teutonic knights, whose intention was colonization. They managed to get the Cistercian mission handed over to the Dominicans, and Christian had to withdraw to Poland.

Christian of Stablo Monk and scholar, born Burgundy or Aquitaine, first half of the ninth century, died Stablo, Lower Lorraine (now Stavelot, Belgium), after 880. A man of independent mind, he was one of the few accomplished Greek scholars of the time. He taught that history, not allegory, is the clue to understanding Scripture, and his *Commentary on St Matthew's Gospel* broke new ground in explaining the original meaning and grammatical implications of the text.

Christiana of Lucca Blessed, born Santa Croce sull' Arno, Italy, 1240, died there, 4 January 1310. After a pilgrimage to Monte Gargano and Assisi she founded an Augustinian convent at Santa Croce in 1279. Acclaimed for her holy life, she was known for her devotion to the Eucharist and to the Blessed Virgin Mary. Her cult was officially recognized in 1776. Feast day 18 February.

Christina of Hamm Blessed mystic. She was born in Westphalia, Germany, and died in 1490. Little is known of her life. She is mentioned in *Fasciculus temporum* (1482), where it is stated that she bore the signs of the stigmata on her hands, feet and side. This was said to have occurred shortly after her baptism in 1464 as a young girl. Her name at the time was Stine. A popular cult grew up around her. Feast day 22 June.

Christina of Markyate Recluse. Born in Huntingdon, England, to a noble family and died in *c.*1155. She secretly took a private vow of virginity on a visit to St Albans as a child, which was challenged at the age of sixteen by the advances of Ralph Flambard, bishop of Durham. Thereafter followed a difficult time for Christina in maintaining her vow in opposition to the wishes of her parents. She was locked up, but when she discovered she was supported by Ralph d'Escures, the archbishop of Canterbury, she arranged to escape with the help of a local hermit. She fled to Flamstead, where she hid for two years with the hermit Alwen and then moved to Markyate, where a cell was built for her. She afterwards had to put herself under the protection of Thurstan, the archbishop of York, but she returned to Markyate in 1123. She had come to know the abbot of St Albans, where her brother was a monk, and he persuaded her to make her profession as a nun, after which she was left in comparative peace. She became a spiritual adviser to the abbot. In 1145 the abbot established a convent of nuns at Markyate, with her as prioress, and ten years later she sent a gift of embroidery to the English Pope, **Adrian IV**.

Christina of Spoleto Blessed, Swiss Augustinian. She was born at Porlezza, Lugano, c.1435 and died at Spoleto, Italy, 13 February 1456. She was born Augustina Camozzi, the daughter of a respected doctor. She married and was widowed young. This part of her life was lived in a worldly way, but she converted and entered the Third Order Regular of St Augustine at Verona, where she was given the name Christina. She led an ascetic and penitential life of such severity that she easily became the subject of veneration and had to move frequently to avoid this. Her remains are held at S. Gregorio Maggiore, Spoleto. Feast day 13 February.

Christina of Stommeln Blessed, German Beguine. She was born at Stommeln, Cologne, 1242, died Stommeln, 6 November 1312. Her origins were from a well-off peasant family, and she became a Beguine at Cologne. She aroused opposition in her community because of her austere and pious life, and she returned to Stommeln, where in 1267 she acquired the Dominican Peter of Dacia as her spiritual director. Her spiritual experiences were recorded by him and later her parish priest, but were of a nature to attract doubt and hostility. Despite this she remained steadfast in faith. Her relics kept today at Jülich are still venerated. Feast day 6 November.

Christina of Sweden Queen. Born Stockholm, 8 December, 1626, died Rome, 19 April 1689. She succeeded to the throne at the age of five, but under a regency until 1644. Her father had instructed that she be given the same education as a boy might receive, and her court was visited by many learned men from across Europe, including **Grotius** and **Descartes**. The early years of her reign were concerned with the ending of the Thirty Years War. She abdicated in 1654 and was received into the Roman Catholic Church at Innsbrück. She then moved to Rome, where she once again attracted scholars, though her own unconventional behaviour rather shocked the Romans. Though there is no reason to question the reality of her faith, she was not uncritical (especially of the Inquisition) and she certainly seemed to embrace ideas which were not compatible with it. She was constantly short of money and twice attempted to regain the throne of Sweden. She left a collection of works on theology, church history, philosophy, civil law and medicine, now housed in the Vatican Library.

Christine of Pisan French author. Born Venice 1364, died France, c.1430. She accompanied her astrologer and physician father to the court of Charles V of France. She was well educated, and after the death of her father and her husband, and in need of money, she started writing prose and poetry for publication. Some of the longer pieces were written against the contemporary attitudes towards women. She also wrote historical and philosophical works, including *Dittié a Jeanne d'Arc*, in honour of **Joan of Arc**, the only one written after she had entered the Dominican convent at Poissy where her daughter was a nun.

Christopher Saint, dates unknown. According to the Western tradition he lived in Asia Minor in the third century, he was a giant of a man, earning his living by carrying people across a river. On one occasion he carried a child who, on becoming almost too heavy to bear, revealed himself to be Jesus Christ, and the saint to be carrying the entire world upon his shoulders. He was later martyred for his faith during the Decian persecution. He is the patron saint of travellers. Feast day, now abolished, 25 July.

Christopher Maccassoli Blessed, Franciscan, born Milan, between 1415 and 1420, died Vigevano, Italy, 1485. He joined the Observants, the stricter branch of the Franciscans, in 1435, was ordained and assigned to preaching. He reformed and enlarged the priory at Vigevano. In 1890 **Leo XIII** authorized a Mass in his honour in the Diocese of Vigevano and among the Franciscans. Feast day 11 March.

Christopher of Romandiola Blessed, (also called Christopher of Cahors), companion of St **Francis of Assisi**, born Romandiola, Italy, c.1172, died Cahors, France, 31 October 1272. When he was parish priest of Romandiola, he joined Francis, and was one of the first Franciscans sent to work in Aquitaine. Not a preacher, he led a life of prayer and service to the sick and outcast. His cult was confirmed by **Pius X** in 1905. Feast day 31 October.

Chrodegang of Metz Bishop and saint, born at Liège in Brabant, 712, died Metz, 6 March 766. A relative of King Pepin, he became a chief minister to **Charles Martel** and to his successor, Pepin III. In 742 he was appointed bishop of Metz, but continued to hold political office. In 748 he founded the abbey of Gorze, near Metz. A leading ecclesiastical reformer, he drew up a communal rule, c.755 which promoted a common life while allowing clerics to retain property and maintain links with diocesan officials. He also introduced Roman chant and liturgy at Metz. Feast day 6 March.

Chrysanthus and Daria Martyrs and saints, died c.300. Their stories derive from sixth- or seventh-century Roman legends, which are confused. Evidently born of an Egyptian patrician father, Chrysanthus was baptized at Rome in the reign of Numerian. Resisting his father's attempts to arrange a marriage for him, he married Daria, a former Greek priestess of Minerva, whom he converted and persuaded to live with him in chastity. Denounced as a Christian, he so impressed under torture that the tribune Claudius, his wife, two sons and a company of soldiers were converted (whereupon they were summarily executed). Chrysanthus and Daria are said to have been buried alive; in some versions, Daria was first sent to a brothel, where she was said to have been protected by a lion. Their relics were taken to Prüm then to Münsterreifel in the ninth century. Feast day 25 October.

Chrysanthus (Khrisanf) Shchetkovsky Russian Orthodox bishop and missionary, born 1871, died Yelizavetgrad 1906. He graduated from the Kazan Theological Academy, which specialized in missiology and linguistics. After five years working among the Buddhist Kalmyks, he was appointed to head the Orthodox mission in Korea in 1900. He consecrated a church in Seoul and started the translations of liturgical books in Korean. He had extremely good relations with local Buddhist monks and is the real founder of the Orthodox Church in Korea.

Chrysoberges, Andrew Byzantine Dominican scholar, birth not known, died Famagusta, Cyprus, 1451. He had opposed the Hesychast idea, prevalent in the Eastern Church, that the union of the mind with the heart could be accomplished by carefully controlled breathing during prayer. He became a papal diplomat, and **Martin V** sent him to the Council of Constance, 1414–17, convoked to end the Great Schism; **Eugenius IV** sent him both to the Council of Basel, 1431–49, to deal with the idea that a general council is superior to the Pope, in which he failed, and to the Council of Florence, 1438–45, whose object was reunion with the Greek Church. He spoke in favour of the *filioque* clause, which the Greeks said was an unlawful addition to the Creed, but they eventually agreed, and union was promulgated in 1439. He became apostolic legate to Cyprus in 1447.

Chrysogonus Martyr and saint, died 304. Little is known of his life, but according to Roman legend he was arrested during Diocletian's persecution, and his martyrdom probably took place at Aquileia. From the sixth century, he is associated with St Anastasia of Rome as a spiritual mentor and correspondent. In the eighth century, the Frankish king Pippin the Short considered him his personal protector. His name is mentioned in the canon of the Roman Mass. He is venerated particularly in northern Italy. Feast day 24 November in the West, 22 December in the East.

Chrysoloras, Manuel Classical scholar, born Constantinople, 1350, died Constance, 15 September 1415. In 1394 the beleaguered Byzantine emperor **Manuel II** sent Chrysoloras to the West to seek support against the advancing Ottomans. Coluccio Salutati, chancellor of the Florentine republic, caused him to be invited to Florence as professor of Greek, a post he held between 1397 and 1400, after which he returned to the East. Chrysoloras inspired a generation of Florentine patricians and scholars, including Leonardo **Bruni**, with enthusiasm for ancient Greek literature and culture. He returned to the West in 1408, travelling widely before his death during the general council at Constance.

Chrytraeus, David (Kochhafe) Protestant theologian and historian, born Ingelfingen, Württemberg, 26 February 1531, died Rostock, 25 June 1600. He was the son of a Lutheran pastor, and educated at Tübingen, Heidelberg and Wittenberg, where he was taught by **Melanchthon**. He became a professor at Rostock in 1548 and taught theology there from 1561. A gifted organizer, he drew up statutes for the reform of the University of Rostock and other universities. He was a church historian, and a respected theologian. His *De Studio Theologiae* (1562) was found particularly helpful by students.

Ciasca, Agostino Cardinal and orientalist, born Polignano a Mare, Italy, 7 May 1835, died Rome, 6 February 1902. He entered the Order of St Augustine in 1856 and was ordained in 1858. He had a deep knowledge of several Near-Eastern languages, particularly Arabic and Coptic, in 1866 became professor of Hebrew in the College of Propaganda, and at Vatican Council I interpreted for speakers in these languages. In 1888 he discovered and published a valuable Arabic version of **Tatian**'s *Diatessaron*. He helped to organize some missions to the Congo and in 1899 was made a cardinal.

Cibot, Pierre Martial Jesuit missionary and scientist, born Limoges, France, 14 August 1727, died Beijing, 8 August 1780. He entered the Society of Jesus in 1743 and was sent to Beijing in 1748, where he remained. A devoted missionary and eager student of Chinese science, he made many contributions to *Mémoires concernant l'histoire, les sciences, les arts, les moeurs, les usages etc. des Chinois* (16 vols, Paris, 1776–89).

Cicognani, Amleto Giovanni Apostolic delegate, cardinal, Vatican secretary of state, born Brisighella, Italy, 24 February 1883, died Rome, Italy, 17 December 1973. Ordained in 1905, he was official of several Congregations in Rome before becoming apostolic delegate to the USA. He was named a cardinal and Vatican secretary of state by Pope **John XXIII**. He served as dean of the college of cardinals, was a member of several Vatican commissions, and was a leading figure at Vatican II, where he served as president of the Commission for the Oriental Churches. His writings include *Sanctity in America* (1939) and *Canon Law* (1925).

Ciconia, Johannes Walloon musician, born Liège, Belgium, *c.*1335–40, died Padua, Italy, December 1411. His friendship with **Clement V**'s niece and his musical talents brought financial security with work at Avignon, after which Cardinal **Albornoz** in 1358 granted him a canonry at Cesena and **Urban V** granted him one at St John the Evangelist, Liège, about 1372. He returned to Padua in 1401 as canon and precentor at St John's. His five-part *Nova Musica*, which remains unpublished, blends the French tradition in which he was trained with the Italian style, and demonstrates the musical innovations of the fourteenth century.

Cienfuegos, Alvaro Jesuit theologian, born Anguerina, Spain, 27 February 1657, died Rome, 19 August 1739. He entered the Society of Jesus in 1676, taught philosophy at Compostela, 1688–91, then theology at Salamanca. The Emperor Charles VI had him named cardinal, after which he was the Emperor's legate in Rome until his death. His principal works were *Aenigma Theologicum*, on the Trinity (2 vols, Vienna, 1717), and *Vita Abscondita*, on the Eucharist (Rome, 1728), through which, he held, the communicant becomes an instrumental 'engine' of the Word. This notion did not recommend itself to contemporary theologians.

Cienfuegos, José Ignacio Reforming bishop, and leader of the 'Catholic Enlightenment' in Chile, born 1762, died Talca, 1845. He was ordained in 1785, was in Talca until 1813, and was made bishop of Concepción in 1830. As a member of the government's education commission, he brought about the union of the Tridentine Seminary with the newly-founded lay National Institute for Human, Philosophical and Scientific Studies, so that enlightened and liberal ideas should be disseminated among the secular clergy. He was in favour of clerical reform, including the selection of parish priests by the people, for which he was accused of trying to usurp episcopal jurisdiction. He retired to Talca in 1837.

Cieplak, Jan Bishop, born Dabrowa Gorniczna, Poland, 17 August 1857, died Jersey City, USA, 17 February 1926. After studies at St Petersburg from 1878 he was ordained in 1881 and became a professor at the Catholic Academy there. He was consecrated bishop of Evaria and auxiliary bishop of Mogilev in 1908. After the Russian Revolution he was accused of conspiring with the papal nuncio in Warsaw, arrested as a counter-revolutionary and sentenced to death in 1923. The pressure of the Papacy and the US and British governments brought about his release and deportation in 1924. He had been named archbishop of Vilna but died when on a tour of the USA. His cause of beatification was introduced in 1960.

Cingria, Alexandre Pioneer of the modern renewal of sacred art, born Geneva, 22 March 1879, died Lausanne, 8 November 1945. He was a painter, mosaicist and costume designer, but his greatest works were in stained glass, which reflected his joyous faith. His early work is to be seen in Carouge, a village near Geneva, and his last, *Orpheus charming the beasts* is in the University of Geneva. In 1920 he founded the Society of St Luke for progressive painters and sculptors whose work was not always well-received by other Catholics.

Cisneros, García de Spanish Benedictine abbot, monastical reformer and ascetic, born Cisneros, Castile, 1455 or 1456, died Montserrat, 27 November 1510. Cousin of Cardinal **Ximénez**, he entered the Benedictine monastery at Valladolid in 1475, and was a leader in centralizing and reforming monastic observance in the newly united Spain of **Ferdinand** and **Isabella**. His *Exercises of the Spiritual Life* (1500) made him an important bridge between mediaeval monastic piety and the spiritual analysis of **Ignatius of Loyola** and the later Spanish mystics.

Civezza, Marcellino da Franciscan missiologist and historian, born Civezza, Italy, 29 May 1822, died Leghorn 1906. He entered the Franciscan Order in 1831 and was ordained in 1845. His gift for researching and writing history was recognized

by the Order and he was requested to write *Storia universale delle missione Francescane*, a magnificent and scholarly achievement (9 vols, 1857–95).

Clara, Jeronimo Emiliano Defender of the Church in Argentina, born Villa del Rosario, province of Córdoba, 29 December 1827, died Córdoba, 29 December 1892. As archdeacon of the Cathedral of Córdoba, he founded the Daughters of Mary Immaculate, but came to prominence in 1883 as the implacable opponent of the laws being promulgated in Buenos Aires to destroy the influence of the Church by secularizing education and promoting civil marriage. A number of professors at the University of Córdoba who supported his protest were sacked, and he himself was imprisoned for a time but was released in 1884.

Clare Saint, foundress of the Poor Clares. Born Assisi, 1194, died Assisi, 11 August 1253. She was born into a well-to-do family but gave up her possessions and joined St **Francis of Assisi**, being clothed by him in the Franciscan habit in the church of the Portiuncula on March 1212. As other women attracted to the Franciscan way of life joined her, including her sister **Agnes of Assisi**, a community was founded at San Damiano of which Clare was abbess – her mother and another sister also joined. The Rule she drew up was approved by the Pope just two days before her death. Her remains are in the S. Chiara in Assisi. She was canonized in 1255. Feast day 11 (formerly 12) August.

Clare Gambacorta Blessed, Italian Dominican reformer. Born Pisa, 1362, died Pisa, 17 April 1419. Born into a ruling family, she was married for political convenience at the age of twelve and widowed three years later. The following year she joined the Poor Clares but met opposition from her family. Eventually her family conceded and she joined the Dominicans, founding her own community and in 1382 the convent of S. Domenico. The way the convent was run attracted vocations of quality and she exerted reforming influence on the Dominicans. She was remembered for pardoning the murderers of her father and brothers, for the fragrance which accompanied her in life and death and for the fact of the incorruptibility of her tongue, when her body was exhumed after 13 years. Feast day 17 April.

Clare of Montefalco Saint, Italian Augustinian. Born in Montefalco, Umbria, c.1275, died Montefalco, 17 August 1308. Initially Clare followed the Franciscan Rule but in 1290 joined her sister Joan at the Augustinian convent at Montefalco. She succeeded her sister as abbess and encouraged the community away from quietism and towards penitential works. She was known for ecstasies, and for the gifts of miracles and the discernment of spirits. Her body is preserved intact, and it is claimed that her heart displays instruments of the Passion. Feast day 17 August.

Clare of Rimini Blessed, Italian Franciscan tertiary, mystic. Born Rimini, 1262 or 1282, died Rimini, 10 February 1320 or 1346. She was born into a well-to-do family, married young and lived a worldly life until her conversion at the age of 34. She joined the Third Order and lived a life of penance, prayer and service of the poor after the death of her husband. She lived with companions near the Poor Clare convent but was not enclosed. Her feast day is not in the Franciscan calendar. Feast day 10 February.

Clarenbaud of Arras Scholastic of Chartres, France, born c.1110, died c.1180. (As he possessed some relics of St **Thomas Becket**, who was killed in 1170, he must have lived until after that date.) He studied at Paris and from c.1152 to 1156 was provost of Arras. He is known for his theological writing; when monks told him they could not understand the commentary of **Gilbert de la Porrée** (c.1080–1154, one of the Chartres school) on the smaller works of **Boethius**, he wrote one himself, in which he criticized both Gilbert's obscurities and **Abelard**'s application of dialectical principles to the doctrine of the Trinity. He was influenced in his account of creation by **Thierry of Chartres**, a contemporary exponent of Platonic theories applied to Christian belief. He thought that ignorance of creation led to heresies; in his view creation can be seen as a transition from non-being to being in interwoven steps which occur in the order predetermined by God.

Claret de la Touche, Louise Visitandine and mys-

tic, born Saint-Germain-en-Laye, France, 15 March 1868, died Vische, 14 May 1915. She entered the Order of the Visitation at Romans in 1890 and in 1902 recorded a revelation of Christ's saying 'Margaret Mary showed my heart to the world; you will show it to the priests'. By 1913 there was such opposition to this message that she was no longer allowed to continue in the community. As a result she founded another, at Vische, which followed the Rule of the Visitation but was distinguished by its austerity and its use of the full office. Now called Bethany of the Sacred Heart, it sponsors L'Alliance Sacerdotale for the encouragement of priests to study and imitate the mercy of the Sacred Heart.

Claret, Anthony Mary Saint and founder of the Missionary Sons of the Immaculate Heart of Mary or Claretians, born Sallent, Spain, 23 December 1807, died in the Cistercian monastery of Narbonne, 24 October 1870. He was ordained priest at Vich in 1835. Ill-health caused him to leave a Jesuit novitiate in Rome. He returned to pastoral work in Sallent, conducting missions and retreats in Catalonia. At Vich he founded the Missionary Sons dedicated to preaching missions. He was appointed archbishop of Santiago, Cuba in 1850 and made many enemies in his attempts at reform. He resigned his see in 1858 and became director of the Escorial and confessor to Queen Isabella II. He attended Vatican Council I in 1869/70. He retired to Prades in France but had to flee to a Cistercian monastery when the Spanish ambassador demanded his arrest. An important figure in the revival of Catholicism in Spain, he was canonized in 1950. Feast day 24 October.

Claritus Blessed Italian monastic founder. Born Florence, c.1300, died convent of Chiarito, Florence, 25 May 1348. Though he delighted in the divine services of Florence Cathedral, Claritus married rather than take Orders; he engaged in public affairs and in charitable works, assisting young women to enter the religious life. To this end he founded a convent under the Rule of St Augustine, known as Chiarito (Regina Coeli). His wife, Nicolosia, and daughter joined the community, the former becoming its first abbess; Claritus ministered to their needs until his death. His tomb is in the convent, and his body in the church of the Dominican Sisters, Al Sodo. Feast day 6 May.

Clarke, Mary Frances Mother, Irish-born foundress. Born Dublin, 2 March 1803; died Dubuque, Iowa, 4 December 1887. Mary Clarke and three friends went to Philadelphia as missionary teachers in 1833. With the help of the Reverend Terence Donaghoe, she founded the Sisters of Charity of the Blessed Virgin Mary. In 1843, Bishop Mathias Lorcas and Pierre **de Smet**, SJ, asked her to serve in Dubuque; in 1896 she applied for pontifical status for her community, which **Leo XIII** approved in 1885. Clarke governed her community for 54 years, leaving behind schools that pioneered the nineteenth-century movement for women's colleges.

Clarke, Maura Maryknoll missionary sister, born Bronx, New York, 13 January 1931, died by shooting near San Salvador, El Salvador, 2 December 1980. She graduated from Maryknoll College and after teaching in a mixed race school in the Bronx, she was assigned to the Maryknoll mission in Nicaragua. After the 1972 earthquake, she worked in OPEN 3, a resettlement camp. In 1980 she went to El Salvador, where she worked with refugees, searched for the missing, buried the dead and generally supported the victims of oppression and injustice. In a notorious event, which horrified world opinion, Sister Maura was with other missionaries, Ita **Ford**, Dorothy **Kazel**, and Jean Donovan, near San Salvador when the women were stopped by soldiers, tortured, raped, shot and buried in shallow graves. The soldiers responsible were eventually found and brought to justice.

Clarke, Samuel Metaphysicist and theologian, born Norwich, England, 11 October 1675, died London, 17 May 1729. Educated at Cambridge University. Appointed chaplain to the bishop of Norwich in 1698. In 1706 he became rector of St Benet's, London, and then at St James's, Westminster, three years later. His Boyle Lectures of 1704 and 1705 on rational theology were published in 1716 entitled *A Discourse concerning the Being and Attributes of God etc.* Other publications include *Three Practical Essays on Baptism, Confirmation, Repentance* (1699), a Latin translation of Newton's *Opticks* (1706) and his *Scripture Doctrine of the*

Trinity (1712). Invited to succeed Newton as master of the Mint in 1727 but declined.

Clarke, William Newton Baptist theologian, born Cazenovia, New York, 2 December 1841, died Deland, Florida, 14 January 1912. He graduated from Madison University and Colgate Theological Seminary, and became pastor of Newton Center, Massachusetts, and Olivet Baptist Church, Montreal, Canada. He became professor of the NT at Baptist Theological School, Toronto, then professor of Christian theology at Colgate Seminary. In his *Outlines of Christian Theology* he took an historical and experiential approach. He interpreted the Bible via his personal experience.

Clarus Abbot and saint, born near Vienne, early seventh century, died Vienne, 1 January 660. A monk of St Ferreol Abbey, he also served as spiritual director of St Blandina Convent, where his mother and sister were nuns, before becoming abbot of the monastery of St Marcellus at Vienne, *c.*625. Numerous miracles are attributed to him; his cult was officially confirmed by **Pius X** in 1903. He is the patron saint of tailors. Feast day 1 January.

Claudel, Paul Louis Charles Marie French Catholic diplomat and writer, born Villeneuve-sur-Fère, France, 6 August 1868, died Paris, 23 February 1955. Having experienced a deep religious crisis in 1886 he became a Roman Catholic. He entered the French diplomatic corps in 1892, and rising rapidly within the service, was appointed ambassador at Tokyo in 1922, then to Washington in 1927 and Brussels in 1933: he retired in 1935. Famous for his poetry and plays, much of which emphasized religious themes such as salvation and spiritual conflict. His published works include the collection of poems entitled *Cinq Grandes odes* (1910) and his play *Le Soulier de Satin* (1929), in which he developed the idea of the sacrificial life. He was elected to the French Academy in 1946. He was the brother of Camile Claudel, the sculptress.

Claudianus Mamertus Philosopher and writer, born perhaps Vienne, *c.*425, died *c.*474. Younger brother of St **Mamertus** of Vienne, he grew up in Lyons, and received a solid education in literature and rhetoric. He was a life-long friend of Sidonius

Apollinaris, who prized his intellectual gifts. His chief work was a three-book treatise, *On the State of the Soul* (*c.*470), written against **Faustus of Riez**. Drawing heavily on Platonist authors and on **Augustine**, he argued that the soul was immaterial. The work was popular in the Middle Ages. He also left a well-known letter in which he complained of the cultural condition of early-fifth-century Gaul.

Claudius and companions Martyrs and saints, died Aegeae, Cilicia, *c.*285. The history behind the legends is very difficult to access, but the three brothers Claudius, Asterius and Neon, and two women, Domnina and Theonilla, together with Domnina's child, were martyred for their Christian confession. Feast days 23 August (West); 23 October and 27 January (East).

Claudius of Condat Bishop, abbot and saint, born perhaps Franche-Comté, early seventh century, died Condat, 6 June 693. The accounts of his life are legendary, but he was apparently already elderly when he was appointed to Condat. He was then called to be bishop of Besançon; he later resigned this see and retired to monastic life at Condat. The abbey there was dedicated to his memory, and its church became a pilgrimage site. His relics were discovered in 1213, but were lost during the French Revolution. Feast day 6 June.

Claudius of Turin Bishop, date of birth unknown although it is believed that he was Spanish, died in about 827. Master of the Royal Schools of Aquitaine. Appointed bishop of Turin in 817. Disregarding papal authority he criticized many traditional teachings of the Roman Church including the use of relics, pilgrimages and the intercession of the saints. Famous also for his biblical commentaries.

Claver, Peter Jesuit missionary and saint, to use his own words, was 'the slave of the Negroes for ever', born Verdú, Spain, 1580, died Cartagena, Colombia, 9 September 1654. Entered the Society of Jesus in 1602. Went to Colombia in 1610 as a missionary. In 1616 he was ordained priest. Spent the rest of his life caring for the slaves arriving from West Africa. During the last four years of his life he suffered from paralysis and was neglected

by his servant. Canonized in 1888. Feast day 9 September.

Clavigero, Francisco Javier Jesuit authority on Mexican history, born Vera Cruz, Mexico, 9 September 1731, died Bologna, Italy, 2 April 1787. In Mexico, Clavigero found and investigated documents on Mexican history. When the Jesuits were expelled from Mexico in 1767 Clavigero went to Bologna, where he founded a literary society and continued his research into the native people of Mexico. He produced *Historia Antica de Messico* in 1780, which listed sources, was well researched and catalogued Indian writers. In his writings he favoured the native Indians rather than the Spaniards, and he exaggerated the aboriginal culture of the Mexican sedentary tribes. His *Storia della California* was published posthumously.

Clavius, Christopher (the Latinized form of his name **Christoph Clau**) Jesuit mathematician and astronomer, born Bamberg, Bavaria, 1538, died Rome, 12 February 1612. He entered the Society of Jesus in 1555, and studied in Coimbra. He was summoned to Rome and spent the rest of his life teaching. His friends included **Galileo Galilei**. He was much concerned with the calendar reform that was carried out under **Gregory XIII** (hence the 'Gregorian calendar') and it remains Clavius' greatest achievement.

Claymond, John English humanist, born Frampton, Lincolnshire, *c.*1468, died 19 November 1537. He went up to Magdalen College, Oxford, and was elected a fellow. Bishop Richard **Foxe** of Winchester invited Claymond to become master of St Cross Hospital in his diocese and later arranged for him to be president first of Magdalen College then of Corpus Christi College, which Foxe had founded. Foxe shared his wish to revive classical learning. Claymond wrote to **Erasmus** and knew Thomas **More**; he left his library to Corpus Christi College.

Clemens, Alphonse Henry Roman Catholic social scientist, born St Louis, Missouri, 19 August 1905, died Washington DC, 19 September 1977. He studied at St Louis University, then at Fontbonne College, St Louis, where he introduced an undergraduate course in family life. He worked in St Louis in World War II in the Office of Price

Administration and the National Labor Relations Board. In 1946 he joined the Catholic University in Washington as associate professor in sociology, and he opened a marriage and family counselling centre. He wrote *Marriage and the Family, Design for Successful Marriage* and *The Cana Movement in the US.* Also he brought the Cana Conference idea to Washington.

Clemens, Carl Lutheran theologian and writer, born Sommerfeld, near Leipzig, 30 March 1865, died Bonn, 8 July 1940. He taught at Halle and was professor of religions at Bonn from 1910. He applied the principles and methods of comparative religion to the NT, and he studied Christianity in the context of its civilization. He also researched ancient religions. In the 1920s and 1930s he produced, or collaborated in, many books on religious history, such as *Die Religionen der Erde* (Munich 1927) and *Fontes Historiae Religionuin* (7 vols, Bonn, 1920–36).

Clemens, Wenzeslaus Saxon duke and archbishop. Born Hubertusberg Castle, 28 September 1739, died Marktoberdorf, Swabia, 27 July 1812. The youngest son of Friedrich August II, king of Poland, Clemens, thanks to his noble rank, advanced rapidly in the Church, and became archbishop of Trier. He inaugurated reforms in monastic and devotional life inspired by Enlightenment objectives, and participated in the Congress of Ems of 1786, which drew up a list of articles mostly directed against the Roman curia. In 1794 he fled to Augsburg ahead of the armies of the French Revolution.

Clemens non Papa, Jacobus Jacob Clement, priest and composer, born Middelburg, *c.*1510/15, died Dixmuide, 1555/6. The peculiar nickname of this prolific Franco-Flemish composer can be dated to the time he entered into a business relationship with the Antwerp composer and music publisher Tielman Susato and was probably a joke rather than the result of any confusion with the late Pope **Clement VII** (died 1534). In 1544–5 Clemens was succentor at Bruges Cathedral and was later employed by the Marian Brotherhood in 's Hertogenbosch; he also enjoyed the patronage of Emperor **Charles V.** His output included Mass settings, motets and chansons.

Clement I (Clement of Rome) Saint, bishop, Church Father, fl. *c.*96. Early sources name Clement as the second or third bishop of Rome, although the exact connotation of that title at this early date is unclear. Numerous early Christian writings were once attributed to him, although now only the epistle known as 1 Clement is regarded as genuine. This is valuable for the light it sheds on the nature of early Christian ministry and church organization, and the early history of the Church in Rome. Little else is known of the author, and later accounts of his life are too obviously embellished with legends to be reliable. Feast day 23 November (Western calendar), 24 or 25 November (Orthodox calendar).

Clement II Reformer and Pope, elected 24 December 1046, died, probably of lead poisoning, near Pesaro, 9 October 1047. Originally called Suidger, he came from a well-to-do Saxon family, had been canon of Halberstadt, a member of the royal chapel of King **Henry III** of Germany, and was bishop of Bamberg, from 1040. He was made Pope at the instigation of King Henry, whom he crowned as emperor immediately after his election. The choice of a German was welcomed as breaking the hold of Roman families over the Papacy. During his short pontificate he tried to enhance the authority of the Papacy following the immorality and vice of his predecessor **Benedict IX.** His reforms included the calling of the Synod of Rome, which condemned simony. Despite being Pope, he never resigned the See of Bamberg.

Clement III Antipope, *see* **Guibert of Ravenna**

Clement III Pope, born Paolo Scolari in Rome, elected to the Papacy 19 December 1187, died Rome late March 1191. He came from a wealthy family and had been archpriest of Sta Maria Maggiore before becoming cardinal-bishop of Palestrina. He managed to settle the dispute between the commune of Rome and the bishop of Rome, allowing the Papacy's return to the city. Although in general a peacemaker, he promoted the Third Crusade for the recapture of Jerusalem from Saladin. He was responsible for the removal of the Scottish Church from the jurisdiction of the See of York.

Clement IV Pope, born Guy Foulques near Nîmes in France, c.1195, the son of a judge, elected 5 February 1265, died, Viterbo 29 November 1268. Originally a capable and successful jurist, he became a priest following the death of his wife, then bishop of Le Puy in 1257. In 1259 he became archbishop of Narbonne, and cardinal-bishop of Sabina two years later. He was sent by **Urban IV** to England to express papal support for the king against the barons, and was elected while he was still travelling back to the papal court, then in Perugia. He financed the invasion of Sicily, invested **Charles of Anjou** as its king in 1266, and gave his backing to Charles' project to recapture Constantinople, which had been captured by the Byzantine Emperor Michael VIII, despite Michael's offering the hope of church union if Clement should try to dissuade Charles. He supported the work of the mathematician and philosopher Roger **Bacon**. His bull *Licet ecclesiarum* made the claim that the appointment to all benefices belonged to the Papacy by right, an important stage in the centralizing of church government.

Clement V Pope, born Bertand de Got, c.1260 in Gascony, France, elected Pope at Perugio 5 June 1305, died Roquemaure, 20 April 1314. After studying canon law in Orléans and Bologna he was appointed bishop of Comminges in 1295 and archbishop of Bordeaux four years later. Because of political disturbances in Rome, Clement moved the papal residence to Avignon in 1309, bringing him under the influence of Philip IV and commencing the 'Babylonian captivity' of the Papacy which lasted till 1377. At Philip's request Clement suppressed the Knights Templar: in 1311 he convened the Council of Vienne, by order of which this was achieved. Clement encouraged scholarship, founding the University of Perugia in 1307 and creating the chairs of Asian languages at Oxford and Paris. He promulgated the *Constitutiones Clementinae* in 1311, thus contributing to the development of canon law.

Clement VI Pope, born Pierre Roger in Corrvèze, France, c.1291, died Avignon, 6 December 1352. A French Benedictine abbot, appointed cardinal in 1338 and elected Pope on 7 May 1342. He centralized church finances, bringing them directly under the control of the Papacy. He was criticized for the luxuriance of his court and his practice of nepotism. However, he displayed uncommon charity and philanthropy during the period of the Black Death (1348–50). He was a protector of the Jews, welcoming them to Avignon.

Clement VII Antipope 1378–94, born Robert of Geneva, 1342, died Avignon, 16 September 1394. The son of Count Amadeus III of Geneva, he was successively bishop of Thérouanne and bishop of Cambrai before being made a cardinal. In 1378 he was among those who voted for **Urban VI** but rapidly regretted the promotion of so unstable a character. Dissident cardinals declared Urban's election void and elected Robert in his stead. Taking up residence in the papal enclave of Avignon, he replicated the administrative machinery of the Roman curia and enjoyed the support of France, Burgundy, Naples, Savoy and Scotland, while England and the Empire remained loyal to Urban.

Clement VII Pope, born Giulio de' Medici, Florence, 26 May 1478, illegitimate son of Giuliano de' Medici and nephew of Lorenzo de' Medici (il Magnifico); elected to the Papacy 19 November 1523, died Rome, 25 July 1534. As cardinal and archbishop of Florence from 1513, he ruled his native city on behalf of his cousin **Leo X**. During his own pontificate, Italy was convulsed by war, Clement being a mere pawn in French and imperialist hands. In 1527 imperialist troops besieged the Pope in Castel Sant' Angelo and sacked the city of Rome. In such circumstances, Clement was not well placed to respond either to the Lutheran threat in Germany or to the schism in England. He did, however, refuse **Henry VIII** his divorce from Catherine of Aragon, thus precipitating the break between England and Rome, partly at least under the influence of **Charles V**, who was Catherine's nephew. He crowned Charles as Emperor in 1530 – the last such coronation by a pope – but then tried to repair relations with France by arranging, and presiding at, the marriage of his grand niece to a son of the King of France.

Clement VIII Reforming Pope, born Ippolito Aldobrandini in Fano, Italy, 24 February 1536, elected Pope 30 January 1592, died Rome, 5 March 1605. Having been trained at Padua, Perugia and

Bologna, he became a cardinal in 1585. As Pope he was influential in the conversion of **Henry IV** of France to the Roman church, in the weakening of Spanish dominance of the Papacy and in establishing the Treaty of Vervins in 1598, thus establishing peace between France and Spain. He appointed **Francis de Sales** as bishop of Geneva in an attempt to bring the Swiss back into Catholicism. His many reforms included the publication of a revised edition of the Latin Vulgate, the Breviary and the Missal, and the extension of the Vatican Library.

Clement IX Pope, born Giulio Rospigliosi in Pistoia, 27 January 1600, elected Pope 20 June 1667, died Rome, 9 December 1669. He studied at the Jesuits' Roman College, then theology and law at Pisa, before entering the service of the Papacy. He rose through the ranks to become nuncio in Madrid, and then cardinal and secretary of state under **Alexander VII**, having been governor of Rome under Alexander's predecessor **Innocent X.** His pontificate was characterized by the rise of Gallicanism and a policy of appeasement towards the Jansenists. The failure of Venice's attempt to recover Crete from the Turks, despite all Clement's efforts to support Venice, hastened his death.

Clement X Pope, born Emilio Altieri in Rome, 12 July 1590, elected Pope 29 April 1670, died Rome, 22 July 1676. He had studied under the Jesuits in Rome, and taken a degree in law. He worked as a lawyer for a time before his ordination in 1624, and then served in the papal diplomatic service. He was appointed cardinal in 1669 by **Clement IX**, only a few months before the latter's death. He was troubled by the advance of Turkish forces, and gave financial support to John Sobieski, the future king of Poland, to oppose them. He was firm against the growing influence of Gallicanism.

Clement XI Pope, born Giovanni Francesco Albani in Urbino, 23 July 1649, elected Pope 23 November 1700, died Rome, 19 March 1721. After studies in the classics in Rome, he entered the papal civil service, working mainly in the Papal States, before being made secretary of briefs in 1687 and a cardinal in 1690. As Pope he was known for his scholarship, acquiring several important additions to the Vatican Library, including manuscripts from the East. He made the feast of the Immaculate Conception a holy day of obligation in 1708 and issued two bulls, *Vineam Domini Sabaoth* (1705) and *Unigenitus* (1713), against Jansenism. He was unsuccessful in intervening in the events leading up to the War of the Spanish Succession of 1701–14.

Clement XII Pope, born Lorenzo Corsini into an influential Florentine family, 7 April 1652, elected Pope 12 June 1730, died Rome, 6 February 1740. A lawyer by training then a curial official and papal treasurer, he became a cardinal in 1706. As Pope, despite constant ill-health (possibly due to diabetes), he tried to re-establish the authority of the Papacy, especially against the encroaching power of France. He condemned Freemasonry and encouraged missionary activities. He became totally blind in 1732.

Clement XIII Pope, born Carlo della Torre Rezzonico in Venice, 7 March 1693, elected to the Papacy 6 July 1758, died Rome, 2 February 1769. Educated by the Jesuits at Bologna and became a doctor of law at Padua. He became a cardinal in 1737 and a reforming bishop of Padua six years later. Following the expulsion of the Jesuits from Portugal, France, Spain, Naples and Parma, as Pope he resisted pressure from all over Europe to suppress the Order, and indeed published a bull indicating his support for the Jesuits, and supported also their propagation of devotion to the Sacred Heart.

Clement XIV The Franciscan Pope who suppressed the Jesuits, born Giovanni Vincenzo Antonio Ganganelli in Sant' Arcangelo, near Rimini, Italy, 31 October 1705, elected Pope 19 May 1769, died Rome, 22 September 1774. Educated by the Jesuits and Piarists, he became a Franciscan in 1723. He taught theology and philosophy at convents in Oscoli, Milan and Bologna, dedicating one of his several books to them in 1743. He was made a cardinal in 1759 by **Clement XIII**, and though hitherto friendly towards the Society of Jesus, began to distance himself from it. After his election he was clear that the only way to re-establish good relations with the European powers was to suppress the Jesuits, which he did in 1773 with the bull *Dominus ac Redemptor*. Though he enriched

Rome, he spent the last years of his pontificate in deep depression, and with a morbid fear of assassination.

Clement, Caesar English Roman Catholic priest, born Louvain, 1561, died Brussels, 28 August 1626. He entered the English College in Rome in September 1579, and was ordained in Rome in September 1586. He never went to England, though he visited Italy and Spain. He became dean of St Gudule's, Brussels, in 1617 after being a canon for ten years. He served as vicar general of the king of Spain's army in Flanders. He was related to John **Clement**, probably being his illegitimate son.

Clement, John Doctor and scholar, born Yorkshire, c.1500, died Mechlin, 1 July 1572. He was educated at St Paul's School and at Oxford. Clement became a tutor to St Thomas **More**'s children and married Margaret Gibbs, who lived and studied with More's family. He was reader in rhetoric and then professor of Greek at Corpus Christi College, Oxford. He became a member of the College of Physicians and later its president. **Henry VIII** chose Clement to treat **Wolsey** when he was dangerously ill in 1529. In the reign of Edward VI, Clement was exempt from the general pardon, he returned to England in **Mary**'s reign working as a doctor in Essex, but left when **Elizabeth I** became queen. Clement translated epistles and homilies from Greek to Latin. He may have been the natural father of Caesar **Clement**.

Clement of Alexandria Church Father, born c.150, died c.215. Clement is known only through his writings, few details of his life having come down to us. It is known that he taught in Alexandria, probably towards the end of the second century, and it is possible that he died as a martyr, though this cannot be established with any certainty. In his writings Clement attempted to refute the charge of pagan philosophers that Christianity was a religion fit only for the ignorant. He argued that in fact it was the fulfilment of all that Greek philosophy aspired to, demonstrating this by frequent use of the terminology and concepts of Platonism in his expositions of Christian theology.

Clement of Ireland Saint. Born Ireland, mid-eighth century, died on the Continent, after 828.

He succeeded **Alcuin** as head of **Charlemagne**'s palace school, and though Theodulf of Orléans, Alcuin and Einhard all opposed his methods of instruction, Clement retained his position until c.826; among his students were Modestus of Fulda and the future emperor Lothair I. Clement is the author of Ars Grammatica, in three parts: De philosophia, De mentis and De barbarismo, a valuable text for its extensive quotations from earlier authors. Feast day 20 March.

Clement the Bulgarian (Clement of Ochridia) Saint. Born Macedonia, date unknown, died Ochridia, Yugoslavia, 27 July 916. A pupil of SS **Cyril** and **Methodius**, Clement accompanied the latter to Moravia; the German bishops expelled him after Methodius' death, and he found refuge in western Bulgaria and became bishop of Velitsa, c.893. He founded the monastery of St Panteleimon, where he is buried, and three churches. He is the father of Slavonic literature, and his works include liturgical texts translated from the Greek, homilies and lives of the saints, e.g. the Life and Encomium of St Cyril Feast days 17 and 27 July.

Clenock, Maurice Welsh priest, date of birth uncertain, died at sea, 1580. He studied law at Oxford, and during **Mary**'s reign he entered the service of Cardinal **Pole**, then rose to successively more prestigious posts in England and Wales. In 1558 he was due to be appointed bishop of Bangor, but when **Elizabeth I** became queen, he travelled to Rome and resided in the English Hospital, becoming its warden. Pope **Gregory XIII** ordered the hospital to become a college for the conversion of England and made Clenock its rector; Cardinal **Allen** judged Clenock unsuitable. When Clenock was accused of favouring the minority Welsh students at the expense of the English students, the Pope appointed a new rector and Clenock returned to being warden. In 1580 he retired to Rouen. He died when his ship to Spain was lost at sea.

Clérambault, Louis Nicolas Born Paris, 19 December 1676, died Paris, 26 October 1749. French composer and organist. He studied the organ with André Raison, to whom he later dedicated his Livre d'Orgue. Clerambault was organist at various Paris churches and of the Maison Royale de St Cyr, near Versailles. He was widely esteemed as a composer of French cantatas and as organist. His instrumental music includes pieces for harpsichord. His choral music includes a *Te Deum, Magnificat* and motets, including some for the church of St Cyr.

Clerk, John English bishop, date of birth unknown, died London, 3 January 1541. He was educated at Cambridge and Bologna, was ordained and held posts in southern England, culminating in his being appointed dean of Windsor and judge in the court of the Star Chamber. Clerk served in diplomatic missions on behalf of **Wolsey** and King **Henry VIII**, liaising with Rome. He was appointed master of the rolls, then succeeded Wolsey as bishop of Bath and Wells. In 1540 Clerk visited the duke of Cleves, to explain King Henry's divorce from Anne of Cleves. At Dunkirk, he was taken ill, poisoning being suspected; he died and was buried at St Botolph's, Aldgate, London.

Clermont-Tonnerre, Anne-Antoine Jules de French cardinal. Born Paris, 1 January 1749, died Toulouse, 21 February 1830. Ordained in 1774, Clermont-Tonnerre became bishop of Châlons-sur-Marne in 1781, and a deputy to the Estates General in 1789; he refused the oath of loyalty to the Civil Constitution of the Clergy in 1791, and went into exile in Belgium and Germany. After the Concordat of 1801, he returned to France and resigned his see; appointed to Toulouse in 1820 and a cardinal in 1822, he worked zealously to restore discipline and fought for the restoration of all the Church's rights.

Clichtove, Josse Humanist theologian, born Nieuwpoort, Flanders, 1472/3, died 22 September 1543. A disciple of Jacques **Lefèvre d'Etaples**, whose scholarly lapses he defended against the attacks of Nöel Béda, although Clichtove's own editions of the Christian Fathers also contained errors which **Erasmus** eagerly corrected. A conscientious priest who avoided pluralism, he was interested in pastoral theology and clerical reform, all of which was confirmed by association with the evangelical Briçonnet family. Clichtove taught the young Guillaume **Briçonnet**, future bishop of Meaux. In the 1520s he drew closer to the conservative Béda and was the first influential author in France to oppose **Luther**.

Clifford, John Baptist leader, born Sawley, Derbyshire, 16 October 1836, died London, 20 November 1923. He began work in a lace factory at the age of ten, but was unusually studious and in 1850 underwent a conversion experience. He went on to study at the Midland Baptist College, Leicester, and in 1858 became minister first of Praed Street Baptist Church and, when his congregation expanded, of the Baptist Church at Westbourne Park, London, one of the most notable places of worship in the city. He continued his academic career, graduating in three different faculties of London University. He was an ardent preacher and denominational leader who believed that Christianity related to the whole of life and he was a great liberalizing force in theology, resisting Baptist pressures (notably from C. H. **Spurgeon**) to reject modern biblical criticism and adopt a creed, 1887. He opposed state aid for denominational schools and led the 'passive resistance' to the Education Act of 1902. He was from 1905 to 1911 the first president of the Baptist World Alliance, and thereafter almost to the end of his life its vice-president. He was made a Companion of Honour in 1921.

Clifford, Richard English bishop. Born, place and date unknown, died London, 20 August 1421. Known as a 'king's clerk' from 1380, Clifford enjoyed royal favour under **Richard II**, and went to prison on that account in 1388. The new king, Henry IV, agreed in 1400 to his consecration as bishop and sent him to Worcester, then to London, after which he resigned the privy seal and took little part in secular affairs. He presided at the heresy trials of Sir John **Oldcastle** and John Clayton, and favoured the election of **Martin V** at the Council of Constance. He is buried in St Paul's, London.

Climent, José Spanish bishop, born Castellon de la Plana, Valencia, Spain, 1706, died there, 25 November 1781. He studied at Valencia, where he later taught theology. He worked as a parish priest and in 1766 was made bishop of Barcelona. He founded hospitals, established schools and produced publications inexpensively to spread knowledge. He translated several religious works into Spanish. In Barcelona he stopped a revolt against the imposition of military conscription. He declined, on grounds of conscience, promotion to the far wealthier see of Malaga.

Clitherow, Margaret English saint and martyr, known as the 'Martyr of York', born 1556, died 29 October 1586. She was converted to Catholicism in 1571. Arrested in 1586 for hiding priests and executed, being crushed to death. In 1970 she, and thirty-nine other martyrs, were canonized by Pope **Paul VI.** Feast day 29 October.

Clorivière, Joseph Pierre Picot de French-born soldier, priest. Born Brittany, 4 November 1768, died Washington, DC, 29 September 1826. Clorivière graduated from the Royal Military School in Paris, but resigned his commission in 1791 and associated himself with the counter-revolutionists, being active in the plot to assassinate Napoleon Bonaparte in 1800. He escaped to Savannah, Georgia, became a priest in 1812 and ministered to refugees from Santo Domingo in Charleston, South Carolina; obliged to surrender his appointment, he retired to the Visitation Convent in Georgetown, Washington, in 1818.

Clotilde Frankish queen and saint, born Lyons or Vienne, c.474, died Tours, 3 June 545. A Burgundian princess, she married **Clovis**, king of the Franks, c.492/3, and was instrumental in his conversion to Christianity. After his death in 511, she witnessed bitter internecine strife in her own household. She retired to the abbey of St Martin at Tours, where she devoted herself to a life of piety and good works which became much celebrated in legend. She was buried beside her husband in Paris, in the basilica of the Holy Apostles. Her body was cremated in 1793 to avoid profanation; her ashes were kept in Paris. Feast day 3 June.

Cloud (Clodoald, Clou) Hermit and saint, born 524, died Nogent, near Paris, c.560. Grandson of King **Clovis** of the Franks, he lost his own father, King Clodomir of Orléans, in a family feud, and saw his two brothers murdered by an uncle. Protected by his grandmother, St **Clotilde**, he was sent to Provence. He became a hermit and disciple of St Severinus, revoked his claim to the Frankish throne, and later built a hermitage at Nogent; by 811 it was known as St Cloud. Feast day 7 September.

Clovis King of the Franks, born Tournai, c.465, died Paris, 511. Clovis became king of the Franks in 481 and soon began an aggressive campaign of territorial expansion, conquering much of Roman Gaul. Around the turn of the fifth/sixth centuries he married the Christian princess **Clotilde.** Under her influence he was converted to Christianity and baptized, at Rheims, 25 December 496 or 497 along with many of his subjects. He continued to expand the Frankish kingdom, and in 507 won a crucial battle over Alaric, the Arian king of the Visigoths. In these campaigns Clovis was strengthened by the support of the Church, which his conversion had secured, thus beginning the process through which the Franks came to be regarded as the natural temporal guardians of the Catholic faith in the West.

Coady, Moses Michael Educationist, born East Margaree, Nova Scotia, Canada, 3 January 1882, died Antigonish, Nova Scotia, 8 July 1959. He studied at St Francis Xavier University, Antigonish, in Washington DC, and in Rome. In Canada he taught at St Francis Xavier High School and University. He became the first director of St Francis Xavier University's extension department. The federal government appointed Coady and his department to tutor fishermen, and promote economic co-operation and credit unions. These initiatives were successful in improving the fishermen's lives. Coady's book *Masters of Their Own Destiny* (1939) is an account of this economic co-operation. Pope **Pius XII** created him a domestic prelate.

Coakley, Thomas Francis Roman Catholic priest, educationist and writer, born Pittsburgh, Pennsylvania, 20 February 1880, died Pittsburgh, 5 March 1951. He was educated in Pittsburgh, and worked as a clerk and for various companies. After ordination in Rome he was assigned to Pittsburgh's St Paul's Cathedral. In the First World War he served as a chaplain in France and Germany. He returned to become a parish priest in Pittsburgh. He founded schools and was the first director of the De Paul Institute for deaf and speech-defective children.

Cobo, Bernabé Jesuit, natural scientist and historian, born Lopera, Jaén, Spain, 26 November 1580, died Lima, 9 October 1647. He sailed for the

West Indies, and reached Santo Domingo and then Lima. There he studied at the Jesuit College and in 1601 joined the Jesuit Order. In 1615 he was posted to the mission of Juli, and worked in Peru until *c.*1630, when he was sent to Mexico. He travelled through Bolivia, Peru, Central America and Mexico. His great *Historia del Nuevo Mundo*, part of which is lost, or was never completed, is an exhaustive study of the Indies; also of the Indians, and the Spaniards at Lima.

Cochlaeus, Joannes German Catholic controversialist, born Wendelstein, 1479, died Breslau, 10 January 1552. Born Johann Dobneck, of peasant origins, he was educated by an uncle, taught in Nuremberg, and studied law in Bologna and theology in Ferrara, gaining a doctorate in Ferrara in 1517. He moved to Rome, where he was ordained priest, and returned to Germany in 1519. Though at first sympathetic to Martin **Luther**, he became advisor to the papal legate at the Diet of Worms, and his attitude to the Reformer became increasingly hostile. He took part in all the major German debates, but was not invited to the Council of Trent, which he took as a slight. He took Luther as his chief adversary, examining his writings to demonstrate inconsistency and incoherence. His many polemical writings coloured Catholic views of the Reformation. From 1528 to 1539 he was chaplain to the Duke of Saxony, and canon of the cathedral at Meissen, but when Saxony converted to Protestantism he moved to Breslau, where he remained for the rest of his life.

Cochran, William Bourke Irish-born US Congressman. Born Sligo, 28 February 1854, died Washington, 1 March 1923. Cochran emigrated to New York in 1871, became a member of Congress first in 1866, and several times thereafter, as a Democrat, until 1922. He defended the interests of organized labour, participated as a moderate in the Irish movement in America, opposed Prohibition and resisted restrictions on immigration and naturalization. An adviser to three archbishops, a member of the Third Order of St Francis, founder of the New York Perpetual Adoration Society, Cochran became a Knight Commander of the Order of St Gregory the Great.

Coclico, Adrianus Petit Protestant Flemish Renaissance composer. Born Flanders, *c.*1500, died Copenhagen, 1562. Little has come down about his early life, and his first known activity is as a Protestant in Wittenberg in 1545. He led an unsettled life, wandering from town to town teaching, studying and composing, with no permanent position. Around 1552 he published in Nuremberg a collection of motets, the *Musica Reservata*, and his theoretical treatise *Compendium musices*. Noted as a theorist, Coclico stressed the relation of music and poetry, giving pride of place to poet-composers, who best understood the emotional meaning of words, as well as the demands of music.

Codde, Pieter (Coddaeus) Dutch archbishop and Oratorian. Born Amsterdam, 27 November 1648, died Utrecht, 18 December 1710. From an aristocratic family, Codde went to Paris, joined the Congregation of the Oratory and became archbishop of Sebaste in 1689. The Jesuits accused him of Jansenism and he had to vacate his see in 1702; he wrote three statements in his own defence: *Declaratio*, *Responsiones* and *De morte Christi pro omnibus*, but the Inquisition condemned and deposed him in 1704. He refused to sign the anti-Jansenist decree of **Alexander VII**; the Schism of Utrecht in 1723 resulted from this unsettled question.

Codrington, Thomas Catholic chaplain to King **James II**, born probably at Sutton Mandeville, Wiltshire, died St Germain, February 1693 or 1694. He was educated at Douai and ordained there in 1676, then summoned to Rome to act as Cardinal **Howard**'s secretary and chaplain. He returned to England in 1684 and two years later became one of the king's chaplains. In Rome, Codrington had joined the Institute of Secular Priests Living in Community, and attempted to introduce the scheme to England, but Bishop **Giffard** suppressed the Institute in England. He returned to the Continent with James II, and died at the court in exile, probably of smallpox.

Cody, John Patrick Cardinal, born St Louis, Missouri, 24 December 1907, died Chicago, Illinois, 25 April 1982. He studied in Rome and was ordained there, becoming a member of the staff of Giovanni Montini, later Pope **Paul VI**. In the USA, Cody served as secretary to Archbishop John J.

Glennon of St Louis, then diocesan chancellor. In 1954 he was consecrated bishop of St Joseph Missouri and in 1956 moved to the Diocese of Kansas City–St Joseph as coadjutor to Archbishop O'Hara. Cody became first coadjutor bishop, in 1961, and then archbishop of New Orleans in 1964 and, taking a firm stand on racial justice, de-segregated the schools, amid difficulties. In 1965 he became sixth archbishop of Chicago and was created a cardinal, assisting with the implementation of the Second Vatican Council decrees. He reorganized his diocese. He was ultimately involved in a grand jury investigation for allegedly improperly diverting funds, accusations which brought on the heart attack which occasioned his death.

Coeffeteau, Nicolas French Dominican and bishop, born Château-du-Loir, Main, France, 1574, died Paris, 21 April 1623. He studied at Sens, became a Dominican and taught philosophy in Paris. He held various posts including that of vicar-general of the French congregation. He was appointed preacher to King **Henry IV.** In 1617 he became titular bishop of Dardainia and administrator of Metz diocese. He prevented the spread of Calvinism and restored the practice of the Roman Catholic faith. Though appointed to the Diocese of Marseilles, a coadjutor took responsibility, and Coeffeteau stayed in Paris up to his death. He wrote about the Eucharist and was a skilful writer and a moderate voice in a period when religious controversies could be violent.

Coello, Claudio Spanish painter, born Madrid, c.1642, died Madrid, 20 April 1693. He studied under Francisco Rizi. With Josef Donoso, he collaborated in the decoration of ecclesiastical buildings and palaces in Madrid. Coello decorated the ceiling of the vestry in Toledo Cathedral and painted frescoes in the Augustinian church at Saragossa. He was painter to King Charles II of Spain and to Toledo Cathedral. Coello's masterpiece is the altarpiece for the sacristy in El Escorial, which contains about 50 portraits. He is regarded as the last important master of the seventeenth-century Madrid School.

Cogley, John Roman Catholic journalist, born Chicago, 16 March 1916, died Santa Barbara, California, 28 March 1976. He attended Loyola Uni-

versity, Chicago, and joined the Catholic Worker movement. From 1942 to 1945 he served in the United States Air Force. He founded *Today* magazine, became executive editor of *Commonweal*, and contributed to many other publications. He headed a study on the (McCarthyite) blacklisting of the those in the entertainment industry and served as Church–State adviser in the John F. **Kennedy** presidential campaign. He joined the *New York Times* and published a book, *Catholic America*. After *Humanae Vitae*, he joined the Episcopal Church and was ordained deacon.

Cogulludo, Diego López de Spanish Franciscan, dates of birth and death uncertain. He came from Alcalá de Henares in Spain and became a Franciscan in San Diego in 1629. He lived in Yucatan, where he became lector in theology, father guardian and father provincial. In his book *Historia de Yucatan*, published in Madrid in 1688, he used information from Bishop Diego de **Landa**, but the book also resulted from his own field research.

Cohen, Hermann German musician and writer, born into a Jewish family in Hamburg, Germany, 10 November 1820, died Spandau, 20 January 1871. In Paris he studied music under **Liszt**, and in 1847 had a religious experience which led to his conversion to Christianity. He founded monasteries in France and London and toured Germany and France as a preacher. In the Franco-Prussian War he went to Switzerland. He wrote religious books including *Catholicisme en Angleterre*. His musical compositions include a setting of the Mass.

Coke, Thomas Methodist bishop and missionary, born Brecon, Wales, 1741, died at sea en route to India, 3 May 1814. Educated at Jesus College, Oxford, he became an Anglican curate in South Petherton until 1777, when he was dismissed for Methodist tendencies. He became the most important of John **Wesley**'s recruits from the Anglican clergy. He was appointed superintendent of the London circuit in 1780 and chair of the Irish Conference in 1782. In 1784 he was ordained by Wesley for the superintendency of Methodism in the newly independent United States and assumed the title of bishop. Coke visited North America nine times. He was appointed chair of the first Methodist missionary committee in 1790, and its president in 1804. He married late in life and devoted his own and his wife's fortune to the cause. His last voyage was to establish Methodist mission work in India and South Africa.

Cola di Rienzo *see* **Rienzi, Cola di**

Colbert A distinguished family of seventeenth- and eighteenth-century France, the most celebrated member being Jean-Baptiste (1619–83), comptroller general of finances under **Louis XIV**.

Colbert, Charles-Joachim Nephew of Jean-Baptiste. Born Paris, 11 June 1667, died Paris, 8 April 1738. Having been vicar general of his cousin, the archbishop of Rouen, he became bishop of Montpelier in 1696 and a leading figure in the Jansenist controversies. He opposed the bull *Unigenitus*, and maintained his resistance in pastoral letters and instructions, encouraging hostility to the Jesuits whom he held responsible for all the ills of the Church. Well-intentioned toward his flock, he produced the *Catéchisme de Montpellier*, often re-edited, but finally placed on the Index in 1721 because it contained formulae of a Jansenist flavour.

Colbert, Jacques-Nicolas Son of Jean-Baptiste. Born Paris, 1654, died 10 December 1707. His literary merits, and even more the status of his father, got him elected to the Académie Française, where Jean Racine received him in 1678. In 1691 he became archbishop of Rouen, and showed himself enlightened and charitable toward the Protestants, mitigating to the extent possible the harsh effects of the revocation of the Edict of Nantes.

Colbert, Michel Born Paris, 1633, died there, 29 March 1702. He entered the Order of Prémontré (the Norbertines), and became abbot general in a manner sufficiently irregular as to require several years before being approved by the Holy See, until his death. During an industrious and fertile career he left many writings, e.g. *Lettre d'un abbé à ses religieux sur la nécessité de bien vivre et de faire son salut*; and *Lettre d'un abbé à ses religieux sur le culte qu'il faut rendre à Dieu*.

Cole, Henry Dean of St Paul's, born Godshill, Isle of Wight, *c.*1500, died in Fleet Prison, London, February 1579 or 1580. He was educated at Winchester and Oxford and became a fellow and later warden of New College, Oxford. At the Reformation he conformed to the Church of England, but soon afterwards returned to the Catholic faith, and resigned his posts and benefices. In Queen **Mary**'s reign, he became a canon of Westminster, then dean of St Paul's and a vicar-general for Cardinal **Pole**. He was assigned to debate with **Cranmer**, **Ridley** and **Latimer**, and to preach before Cranmer just before his execution. Cole was sent to suppress heresy in Ireland, but it seems his commission to do so was stolen, and he had to return to England. After **Elizabeth I** succeeded as queen, he was fined, deprived of his preferments and imprisoned. He was in the Fleet Prison for nearly twenty years before his death there.

Coleman, Walter (or Colman) English Franciscan poet. Born Cannock, Staffordshire, date unknown, died London, 1645. Educated in France, Coleman became a Franciscan of the Strict Observance in 1625, returned to England as a missionary and went to prison in 1627; released, re-arrested and condemned to death at the Old Bailey in 1641, Charles I commuted the sentence, but Coleman died in Newgate Prison after a lengthy illness. He published *La Dance Machabre, or Death's Duell*, a poem of 262 stanzas dedicated in French to Queen Henrietta Maria.

Colenso, John Anglican bishop and schismatic, born St Austell, England, 24 January 1814, died Pietermaritzburg, South Africa, 20 June 1883. Colenso was appointed bishop of Natal in 1853, and soon provoked controversy by his toleration of polygamous marriages contracted by indigenous Christians prior to their conversion. Further upset was caused in 1861 by his commentary on St Paul's Epistle to the Romans, in which he rejected the doctrine of eternal punishment, and in 1862 by a monograph on the Book of Joshua which cast doubt on its historical reliability. In 1863 Colenso was deposed from his bishopric, but successfully appealed. Excommunication followed, but his considerable local popularity enabled him to continue ministering schismatically until his death. The schism in the diocese was not finally healed until 1911.

Coleridge, Henry James Jesuit writer, born Devon, 20 September 1822, died Roehampton, Surrey, 13 April 1893. Educated at Eton and Oxford, he was elected a fellow of Oriel College and was ordained an Anglican priest. Coleridge helped to start *The Guardian* newspaper. He became a disciple of John Henry **Newman** and in 1852 he joined the Roman Catholic Church and went to Rome to study. In 1856 he was ordained, returned to England and joined the Jesuit Order. In London he became editor of *The Month*, and later also of the *Messenger*. He wrote studies of the lives and letters both of St **Francis Xavier** and of St **Teresa of Avila.** He succeeded in completing *The Public Life of Our Lord* shortly before his death.

Coleridge, Samuel Taylor Poet and philosopher, born 21 October 1772 at Ottery St Mary, Devon, where his father was the vicar and master of the local grammar school, died London, 25 July 1834. He was educated at Christ's Hospital and then at Jesus College, Cambridge, but abandoned his original intention of seeking ordination and joined the Dragoons. His military career was short-lived, and he returned briefly to Cambridge, married, and considered becoming a Unitarian minister. He had already begun to publish verse, and he came into contact with **Wordsworth** and other poets. With the Wordsworths he travelled to Germany, where he was impressed by German philosophy. He continued to travel, though his addiction to opium, partly overcome by 1816, had a deleterious effect on his skills as a poet. From *c.*1810 he thought of himself as a Christian, though his version was hardly orthodox, believing as he did that the chief test of Christianity was its beneficent effects in civil life, and expressing a distrust of all rational argument for religious truth. He did, however, believe that there should be no conflict between science and religion, a view not common at the time.

Colet, John Dean of St Paul's, London, born in possibly December 1466, died probably at Sheen, 16 September 1519. He studied at Oxford, possibly at Magdalen College, and then *c.*1493 went to France and Italy. It was this tour which aroused his interest in the reform of the Church, and in particular of the clergy. He was in England in 1496, and was ordained on 25 March 1497. That autumn he delivered a series of lectures on the NT at Oxford which displayed the influence of the Italian Neoplatonists, particularly **Ficino** and Pico della Mirandola, and a dislike of the Scholastic method of theologizing. He lectured again the following year, when **Erasmus** was among his hearers: the two became friends. He repeated his series of lectures annually until, in 1504, he was appointed dean of St Paul's, London, bringing him into regular contact with his friend Thomas **More.** He continued to live simply, even though the following year he inherited his father's fortune. He founded a lecture series at St Paul's and, in 1509, St Paul's School, where 153 boys of any nationality were to be instructed in Christianity, and in Latin and Greek. When in 1511 he was chosen to preach against Lollardy, he took the opportunity to criticize failings in the Church, and was charged with heresy, though the archbishop of Canterbury dismissed the accusations. He then went on to criticize the wars engaged in by **Henry VIII**, saying that he thought the new king would have brought in an era of peace. He was summoned to see Henry at Greenwich, but the two parted amicably. He completed the statutes for his new school in 1518, putting it under the control of the Mercers' Company rather than leaving it in clerical control. He was by this time quite ill, and talked of retiring to the Carthusian monastery at Sheen. He did not do so, but died in his lodgings at Sheen.

Colette Franciscan saint, born Calcye, Picardy, 13 January 1381, died Ghent, 6 March 1447. In 1398, after the deaths of her parents, she became a Franciscan tertiary and lived as a hermit near the abbey church at Corbie, where her father had been a carpenter. On the foundation of her holiness and austerity was built a conviction, inspired by visions, that her mission was to recall communities of Franciscan nuns, Poor Clares, to the purity of their original Rule. In addition to reforming existing houses, she founded seventeen new ones of so-called Colettines, mostly in Flanders, France and Savoy. She was canonized in 1807. Feast day 6 March.

Colgan, John Franciscan hagiographer of Irish saints, born Carndonagh in Co. Donegal, *c.*1592, died Louvain, 1658. He was ordained priest in Louvain in 1618, where he entered the Franciscans and became professor of theology. Though he planned to write a complete biographical dictionary of all the Irish saints he only managed to cover those whose festivals occur in January, February and March. But he also published extremely detailed lives of SS **Patrick**, **Brigid** and **Columba** and a life of John Scotus **Eriugena**. His *Acta Sanctorum ... Hiberniae* was published in Louvain in 1645.

Coligny, Gaspard II de   Huguenot leader, born Châtillon-sur-Loing, 16 February 1519, died Paris, 24 August 1572. At age 22 Coligny went to court, served in the Italian campaign, was appointed colonel general of the infantry, made admiral of France and fought in the Spanish campaign. Only from 1560 did Coligny support the Reformation. He demanded religious tolerance for the Huguenots, hoping the reformed religion would create an orderly, just nation. On the death of the Prince of Condé, Coligny became the Huguenot leader. His army in southern France progressed to the upper Seine, resulting in the Peace of Saint-Germain. He found favour with Charles IX but the Huguenots were wrongly blamed for an assassination attempt and Coligny was killed in the notorious St Bartholomew's Day Massacre.

Colin, Frederick Louis   Sulpician priest, born Bourges, France, 1835, died Montreal, Canada, 27 November 1902. After studying science he joined the seminary of Saint-Sulpice in Paris and was ordained. In 1862 he moved to Canada, and took up various posts before becoming from 1881 superior of the priests of Saint-Sulpice in Canada. In Montreal he promoted higher education. In 1885 he founded the Canadian College in Rome, and in Canada he established Laval University. He helped to institute th chair of French literature, at his own expense, disseminating in Canada interest in French language and literature.

Colin, Jean-Claude   Venerable, founder, born in Les Barberies, near St Bonnet-le-Troncy, France, 7 August 1790, died Notre Dame de la Neyliere, 28 February 1875. Studied at the seminary of St Irenaeus in Lyons, was ordained priest in 1816 and served as assistant priest in Cerdon until 1825. Despite opposition from the local bishop, who wanted to see the establishment of a diocesan congregation, Colin gained approval from **Gregory XVI** in 1836 for the Society of Mary or Marists to be set up as an Order, with simple vows, to extend beyond diocesan jurisdiction. Colin became the first superior general in the same year and held this office until his resignation in 1854, by which time he had established communities in many parts of the world. He spent the remainder of his life completing and revising the Constitutions of the Society, which gained final approval in 1873.

Coll y Prat, Narciso   Spanish archbishop. Born Cornellá de Ter, Gerona, 1754; died Madrid, 28 December 1822. Coll y Prat became archbishop of Caracas in 1810, just before the new regime declared independence from Spain. During the years of warfare that ensued, though a loyal appointee of the king of Spain, Coll respected and obeyed the republican authorities. He tried to be a good pastor, preventing cruelty, interceding on behalf of those on either side who were in need or persecuted, and maintaining religious services; all this to the satisfaction of Simón **Bolívar**, who kept him in office. However, the king recalled him to Spain in 1816 to answer charges of disloyalty, and Coll justified his actions in two extensive memorials.

Collier, Peter Fenelon   Irish-born publisher. Born Myshall, 12 December 1849, died New York City, 24 April 1909. Collier's family settled in Dayton, Ohio, in 1866, and Peter set himself up in the business of Catholic and Irish national, as well as general reference, book publishing. He began a magazine, *Collier's Weekly*, which first brought the works of standard authors, encyclopaedias and reference works to the attention of the average family. The magazine continued under his son, Robert, and had a circulation of 4 million at its demise in 1959.

Collins, Joseph Burns   Sulpician priest and catechetical leader, born Waseca, Minnesota, 7 September 1893, died Washington DC, 23 January 1975. He studied in Minnesota and Rome. In the USA he taught at various colleges, joined the Society of Saint-Sulpice, and finally taught at the Catholic University of America. He became interested in catechizing children and adults, and directed the National Center for the Confraternity of Christian Doctrine. He published many books and articles. Pope **Paul VI** awarded him the Pro Ecclesia et Pontifice medal.

Collius, Francesco (Collio) Milanese theologian. Born Milan, date unknown, died Milan, 1640. Collius entered the Oblates of St Charles and served as grand penitentiary for the Diocese of Milan. Three works are ascribed to him: *Conclusiones in sacra theologia numero MCLXV una cum variorum doctorum opinionibus*; *De sanguine Christi libri quinque in quibus de illius natura, effusionibus ac miraculis copiose disseritur*, and the *De animabus paganorum*, which questions the probability of well-known biblical and pagan personages of antiquity having attained salvation.

Colloredo, Hieronymus Viennese archbishop. Born Vienna, 31 May 1732, died Vienna, 20 May 1812. The second son of Prince Rudolph Joseph, Colloredo became prince-bishop of Salzburg in 1772, where he improved education and promoted literary and artistic efforts. His place in church history, however, is due to his enlightened ideas aimed at a simple Christianity, purified of all incidentals and externals, which failed because opposed by the conservative classes, but mostly due to being implemented without having sufficiently prepared a sympathetic reception among the people.

Colman of Cloyne Bishop and saint, born Munster, Ireland, 530, died 606. He became a poet and royal bard at Cashel. At the age of 50, he was baptized by St **Brendan of Clonfert** and given the name Colman; he was ordained and worked in Limerick and Cork, where he became the first bishop and patron of Cloyne. He is said to have taught St **Columba**. He built the first church at Cloyne, and another at Kilmaclenine. Feast day 26 November.

Colman of Kilmacduagh Born Kiltartan, County Clare, seventh century. Apparently made an unwilling bishop, Colman lived as a hermit in the Burren district, and founded a great monastery at Kilmacduagh. Feast day 29 October.

Colman of Lindisfarne Bishop and saint, died 8 August 676. A native of Ireland, he became a monk at Iona before going to Northumberland, where he became bishop of Lindisfarne in 661. As bishop he supported King Oswy's defence of the Celtic tradition against Romanizing trends. At the Synod of Whitby in 664, he pleaded unsuccessfully for the retention of the Celtic date of Easter, and other traditions, including the Celtic tonsure. He left Lindisfarne for Iona then Ireland, and spent the rest of his life at the monastery of Innisboffin, Co. Mayo. Feast day 18 February.

Colman of Lynally (also known as **Colman Macusailni**) Abbot and bishop, born Glenelly, Tyrone, c.555, died Lynally, 26 September 611. The nephew of St **Columba**, who greatly influenced him. Around 590 he built a monastery at Offaly called Lann Elo (Lynally); he also founded and became first abbot of Muckamore, then bishop of Connor. He was probably the author of a work entitled *Alphabet of Devotion*.

Colmar, Joseph Ludwig Roman Catholic bishop, born Strasburg, 22 June 1760, died Mainz, 15 December 1818. After ordination he worked at Strasburg, and continued to work secretly as a priest during the French Revolution. After Napoleon had appointed him bishop of Mainz he opened a seminary, and restored parishes, schools and Catholic life, all in a parlous state after the Revolution. To improve knowledge of the faith he inaugurated a system of catechetical instruction in his diocese. During the epidemics of 1813 and 1814, he tended the sick and dying. He edited a collection of old German hymns, compiled prayer books, and seven volumes of his sermons were published.

Coloman Saint, Irish pilgrim. Born in Ireland, tenth century; died Stockerau, near Vienna, 17 July 1012. While travelling to the Holy Land he had the misfortune to be taken for a spy, tortured and hanged from a tree. Miracles were reported at the place of his execution, and his cult spread through south Germany, Austria and Hungary. He is invoked by young women looking for a good husband, by farmers, and for protection against pestilence. He is a patron saint of Austria. Feast day 13 October.

Colombini, John *see* **John Colombini**

Colonna, Ascanio Duke of Marsi and head of Colonna family, born 1490s, died Naples before 24 March 1557. The son of Fabrizio **Colonna** and of Agnese, daughter of Federigo da Montefeltro, duke of Urbino, Ascanio inherited his ducal title in 1520. In 1521 he was appointed grand constable of Naples, as his father had been, and in 1522 was unsuccessful in his claim to the disputed duchy of Urbino. From 1524 he served **Charles V**, taking an active part in military campaigns against the French and was the Emperor's governor at Velletri. He was no less active in support of Cardinal Pompeo **Colonna**'s anti-papal rebellion.

Colonna, Fabrizio Duke of Marsi, born between 1450 and 1460, died Aversa, 20 March 1520. The son of Odoardo Colonna, he succeeded to his father's ducal title in 1465. Though destined to be a cleric, in 1481 he joined the Neapolitan troops sent to counter the Turkish invaders at Otranto, and a distinguished military career ensued, combining service with Ferdinand of Aragon in the Italian Wars with open hostility towards the Colonna family's traditional Orsini rivals. **Innocent VIII** favoured the Colonnas, as **Sixtus IV** and **Alexander VI** did not; not surprisingly, Fabrizio supported Giuliano della Rovere against Rodrigo Borgia (Alexander VI) in the 1492 papal election.

Colonna, Giovanni Cardinal, born between 1450 and 1460, died Rome, 26 September 1508. Fifteenth-century Rome witnessed intense rivalry between the noble Orsini and Colonna families, reflected on a smaller scale in the Sacred College of cardinals. **Sixtus IV** favoured the Orsinis. When the War of Ferrara opened in 1482, the Colonnas sided with Naples against the Pope. On 2 June Cardinals Giovanni Colonna and Giovanni Battista Savelli were arrested and held in Castel Sant' Angelo until November 1483. Colonna had been a cardinal and bishop of Rieti since 1480. At the French invasion of Italy in 1494 he sided with **Charles VIII** against **Alexander VI.**

Colonna, Pompeo Cardinal, born Rome, 12 May 1479, died near Naples, 28 June 1532. He played an active, pro-Spanish part in the Italian Wars and entered the Church for dynastic reasons. On the death of his uncle Cardinal Giovanni **Colonna** he became bishop of Rieti in 1508, but was temporarily deprived of the see after a rebellion against **Julius II** in 1511. **Leo X** made him bishop of Terni in 1520. For **Clement VII** he was cardinal vice-chancellor and legate to the imperial court in 1524, but a brief military attack on Rome again resulted in the temporary loss of his benefices in 1526–7. From 1530 he was bishop of Monreale.

Colonna, Prospero Cardinal, died Rome, 24 March 1463. He benefited from the nepotism of his uncle **Martin V**, who created him a cardinal in 1426. After Martin's death in 1431 relations between the Colonna family and the Venetian **Eugenius IV** deteriorated so rapidly that the Pope excommunicated them within weeks of his election. They were excommunicated again in 1433 after allying with the condottiere Niccolò Fortebraccio against Eugenius. In the conclave of 1447 Prospero was the preferred candidate of the king of Naples. Aside from political machinations he was interested in Roman antiquity and, together with Cardinals Alain de Coëtivy and **Bessarion**, prepared the canonization of **Catherine of Siena.**

Colonna, Prospero Soldier, born Lavinio, near Rome, c.1460, died Milan, 31 December 1523. The son of Antonio, prince of Salerno, his military career spanned three decades of the Italian Wars. **Alexander VI**'s hostility towards the Colonna family accounts for Prospero joining **Charles VIII** of France when the latter entered Rome in 1494. From 1495 he was Aragonese captain-general and fought loyally for Ferdinand of Aragon and the Neapolitan kings. When the action moved to northern Italy, so did he, fighting for the Sforza of Milan against the French invaders, who briefly took him prisoner at Merignano in 1515. He became supreme commander of the imperial–papal army in 1521.

Colonna, Vittoria Poet, born Marino, 1490, died Rome, 25 February 1547. The daughter of Fabrizio **Colonna** and Agnese da Montefeltro, herself the daughter of the cultivated Federigo da Montefeltro of Urbino, Vittoria is remembered for the sonnets she wrote under the title of 'Rime', for her membership of the spirituali, religious reformers who were sympathetic to Lutheranism but who, in many cases, remained within the Church, and for her friendship in later years with fellow poet

Michelangelo. Many of her sonnets were written to express her grief after the death of her husband, the marquis of Pescara. Cardinal Reginald **Pole** was her spiritual adviser.

Colum, Padraic   Poet and playwright, born Longford, Ireland, 1881, where his father was the master of the workhouse, but brought up on his grandfather's farm in Co. Cavan; died Enfield, Connecticut, 11 January 1972, though he is buried in Dublin. He founded the *Irish Review* with Thomas McDonagh and James Stephens in 1912. His first collection of poems, *Wild Earth*, came out in 1907, his collected *Poems* appeared in 1953. His work has a strong Christian background. His best known lyrics are 'Cradle Song' and 'She moved through the Fair' and 'The Burial of St Brendan'. Most of his professional life was spent lecturing in comparative literature at Columbia University, New York.

Columba (sometimes **Colum** or **Columcille)**   Saint, born Gartan, Donegal, Ireland, 7 December 521, died Iona, Scotland, 8 June 597. He studied in schools at Moville and Clonard, became a priest and founded churches in Ireland. He set out on missionary work, and in 563 settled on the island of Iona, off the west coast of Scotland, where he arrived on the eve of Pentecost and founded a monastery. It may be that political reasons drove him to leave Ireland. It seems there was a dispute between Columba's clan and King Diarmid, the king-overlord, which ended in a battle (Cuil Dremne) in which, it was claimed, 3,000 were killed. He was censured by the Church for his involvement, and may have decided to leave the country as a result: the twelve who set off with him were all relatives. Eventually, it is sometimes alleged, he converted the whole of northern Scotland: certainly monks from Iona evangelized the Picts, the Scots and the Northern English. Columba continued, however, to maintain contact with Ireland, and may even have been partly responsible for yet another battle. He died in the abbey church, just after naming a relative as his successor. His name is attached to a traditional Irish hymn tune, which was first published in the Irish Church Hymnal (1874) and often sung to the words *The King of Love My Shepherd Is*. Feast day 9 June.

Columba and Pomposa   Spanish virgin martyrs. Born Córdoba, *c*.830 and *c*.840, died Córdoba, 17 and 19 September 853. The sisters built the monastery of Tabanos. The Muslim authorities martyred Columba, who had witnessed to Christ and renounced belief in the prophet Muhammad; Pomposa repeated Columba's profession of faith before the *cadi*, and likewise suffered death. Christians recovered their bodies from the Guadalquivir river, and buried them in a basilica outside Córdoba. Both are included in the Roman martyrology Feast days 17 and 19 September.

Columba of Rieti   Blessed, Italian Dominican tertiary. Born Angelella Guadagnoli, Rieti, 2 February 1467, died Perugia, 20 May 1501. Having vowed virginity, Columba lived as a recluse, but left her seclusion aged nineteen, and travelled to Perugia, where she founded the convent of St Catherine in 1490. Civic rulers and members of the hierarchy sought her advice, and she had remarkable influence as a peacemaker. Feast day 20 May.

Columbanus   Saint, monk and missionary, born Leinster, Ireland, *c*.543, died Bobbio, Italy, 23 November 615. In *c*.590 Columbanus left the monastic community in Ireland of which he was a member, and with a small group of followers commenced an itinerant preaching ministry. Sailing to Gaul he revitalized the moribund church there, though his adherence to the traditions of the Celtic church proved unpopular with local bishops. He was eventually forced to leave Gaul and moved on to evangelize the heathen Alemanni people before finally settling in Bobbio, which later developed into an important monastic centre. Feast day 21 November (23 in Ireland).

Columbus, Christopher   Explorer, probably born Genoa, *c*.1451, died Valladolid, 20 May 1506. His protracted campaign to secure patronage for a proposal to sail westwards across the Atlantic to reach Cathay (China) finally yielded support from **Isabella of Castile** and Ferdinand of Aragon. There followed four transatlantic voyages, in 1492–3, 1493–6, 1498–1500, 1502–4, in the course of which he explored Hispaniola, Cuba, Jamaica and other Caribbean islands, departing from conventional practice by conquering territory in the name of the Crown of Castile instead of merely founding trading stations. Columbus increasingly thought of himself as the 'bearer of Christ' to the New World.

Comboni, Daniel Roman Catholic missionary bishop to Sudan, born Limone, Italy, 15 March 1831, died Khartoum, Sudan, 10 October 1881. Studied at the Missionary Institute of Don Mazza, Verona, and was ordained in 1854. He joined the Holy Cross team in their work with the Dinka in 1857, where the slave trade and the high mortality of missionaries slowed progress. His ill-health forced him to return to Italy, where he worked to ransom African slaves and educate them. For three years he was vice-rector of the African colleges in Verona. From 1864 he devised a Plan for the Regeneration of Africa which suggested the training of Africans in Africa for the spread of the Gospel. The papal approval of his plan led to the establishment of the Verona (Comboni) Fathers and the Cairo Institute in 1867 and the Verona Sisters in 1872. He returned to Sudan in 1873 to work among the Nuba, founding a school and an ex-slave village.

Comenius, Johannes Amos (Jan Komensky) Moravian educational philosopher, born Niwnitz, or Coma, in the modern Czech Republic, 28 March 1592, died Amsterdam, Netherlands, 15 November 1670. Comenius' early career was spent as a pastor in the Unitas Fratrum (Moravian Brethren); subsequently he travelled extensively to undertake research into educational methods, resulting in his *Didactica Magna* of 1657. He later established a school in Hungary based on his ideals. His last years were spent in The Netherlands. His most significant work, *De rerum humanarum emendatione Consultatio*, was lost for many years and was not published in full until 1966. Comenius regarded the purpose of education as the development of Christian character, which would eventually open the way for a reunified Christendom. His educational philosophy was far in advance of its time, and his principles are still highly regarded by educationalists today.

Comgall Abbot and saint, born Dalriada, *c.*520, died Bangor, 10 May 602. He is said to have undertaken military service, then studied at Clonard and Clonmacnoise. He spent some time on an island in Lough Erne, where he was ordained and

began zealously to promote monasticism. He founded the abbey of Bangor in the late 550s, imposing a strict Rule. **Columbanus** was his most prominent student. He made missionary journeys to Iona and elsewhere in Scotland, and his name became known also on the Continent, probably as a result of the activities of Columbanus' disciples. Feast day 11 May.

Comitoli, Paolo Spanish Jesuit theologian. Born Perugia, 1544 died Perugia, 18 February 1626. Comitoli took part in a commission charged with producing a new edition of the Septuagint in 1587. A staunch defender of papal authority in the controversy of **Paul V** against the Venetian doge and senate, he wrote *Trattato apologetico* on the subject, but Cardinal **Bellarmine** had to intervene to clarify his position. As a moral theologian, Comitoli opposed probabilism, and wrote *Catena in Job*, *Responsa moralia*, and *Doctrina contractuum*.

Commendone, Giovanni Francesco Italian cardinal. Born Venice, 17 March 1524, died Padua, 25 December 1584. Commendone went to Rome in 1550 and entered the service of **Julius III**, who sent him to London in 1553 on a secret mission to Queen **Mary Tudor**, to evaluate the religious and political situation, and the possibility of a Catholic restoration. Later he went to Germany in 1561, to invite the followers of **Luther** to participate in the conciliar sessions at the Council of Trent; the invitation was met with a firm refusal. Entrusted with other delicate and important missions by **Paul IV**, **Pius IV** and **Pius V**, Commendone's untiring zeal, diplomatic skill and deeply religious sense of responsibility contributed greatly to the revival of Catholicism in Central Europe.

Commer, Ernst German philosopher, theologian and priest, born Berlin, 18 February 1847, died Graz, Austria, 24 April 1928. He became a doctor of civil and canon law, was ordained priest, and studied in Germany and Rome. He taught in Regensburg, Liverpool, Münster, Breslau and Vienna. He founded the *Jahrbuch für Philosophie und Speculativ Theologie*, and Pope **Pius X** commended Commer for his work on the Catholic reformer Hermann Schell.

Compère, Loyset Composer, born Hainault,

c.1445, died St Quentin, 16 August 1518. One of the wave of Franco-Flemish composers who dominated musical life in western Europe during the fifteenth century, Compère was possibly a pupil of **Ockeghem**. Although he seems to have been prolific, little of his work survives. There is documentary evidence of his presence at the Sforza court in Milan in the 1470s, but he received French nationality in 1494 and accompanied **Charles VIII** on the invasion of Italy in 1494–5.

Con, George (Conn, Connaeus) Scottish papal agent. Born Aberdeen, date unknown, died Rome, 10 January 1640. Educated at the Scots College in Paris and Rome, and at Bologna, Con entered the service of Cardinal Monalto, and later of Cardinal Barberini, **Urban VIII**'s secretary of state, who sent him to England in 1636 as papal representative to Queen Henrietta Maria. He made some converts at court, and was a friend of **Charles I**, a fellow Scot, with whom he discussed ways of improving the situation of English Catholics. He published in Latin some tracts on Scottish affairs and a life of Mary, Queen of Scots.

Conaty, Thomas James Educationalist and bishop, born Killmallough, Cavan, Ireland, 1 August 1847, died Coronado, California, 18 September 1915. In 1850 his family emigrated to Taunton, Massachusetts. He studied to be a priest at Montreal, Canada, and Worcester, Massachusetts. He became a parish priest in Worcester, was active in the Irish Nationalist movement and in abstinence societies. He was appointed second rector of the Catholic University of America (and a titular bishop), where he coordinated the newly established schools. In 1903 he was appointed sixth bishop of Monterey–Los Angeles. In his time there were great increases in the Catholic population of California, and in the number of priests, churches and educational institutions. He was active in efforts to preserve the old mission stations in the state.

Conceicáo, Apolinário da Portuguese Franciscan writer. Born Lisbon, 23 July 1692, died, probably Brazil, c.1759. Conceicáo became a lay brother in Rio de Janeiro, and undertook to collect biographies of Franciscan lay brothers of saintly reputation, a task on which he spent much of his life in Lisbon and elsewhere in Europe. He published, in four volumes, biographies of 2350 brothers under the title *Pequenos na terra, grandes na céu*; he also published a more valuable historical work, *Primazia seráfica*, dealing with the Franciscan missions in Brazil.

Concina, Daniello Dominican, born Clauzetto or San Daniele, Friuli, Italy, 1687, died Venice, 21 February 1756. He studied at the Jesuit College at Görz, Austria, but joined the Dominican Order. In 1717 he was appointed to the monastery of Forli. He became well known in Italy as a preacher, but he was also a controversialist, his first book, *Commentarius Historico-Apologeticus*, refuting the opinion that St **Dominic** had borrowed his ideas from St **Francis of Assisi**, while his book *Storia del Probabilismo e Rigorismo* criticized the Jesuits. Pope **Benedict XIV**, however, praised it. Concina's *Theologia Christiana Dogmatico-Moralis* had to be eprinted in later editions with a partial retraction, dictated by the Pope.

Condren, Charles de French spiritual director. Born Soissons, 15 December 1588, died Paris, 7 January 1641. Condren joined the Congregation of the Oratory, established in France by Cardinal de **Bérulle**, and became his successor in 1629. The most effective interpreter of de Bérulle, he enlarged his concepts; the central doctrine became the total dependence of man on God the Creator and devotion to the Word Incarnate, the supreme priest and perfect victim, who offered the one sacrifice worthy of the Creator. Among his many admirers were St **Vincent de Paul** and St Jane Frances de **Chantal**. After his death, his followers published *Discours et lettres*; *L'Idée du sacerdoce et du sacrifice de Jésus-Christ*; *Considérations sur les mystères de Jésus-Christ*.

Conforti, Guido Maria Italian bishop, religious founder. Born Ravadese, Parma, 30 March 1865, died Parma, 5 November 1931. Conforti helped to set up the Pontifical Missionary Union of the Clergy, but because of poor health could not himself engage in missionary activity; he founded instead in 1898, the Xaverian Missionary Fathers. In 1902, **Pius X** asked him to become bishop of Parma, where he worked with great dedication, holding diocesan synods, making pastoral visitations of his 300 parishes, organizing congresses, and thus demonstrating care for the diocese, as well as zeal for souls in the wider world.

Congar, Yves Marie-Joseph Dominican priest and theologian, born Sedan, France, 13 April 1904, died Paris, 22 June 1995. He joined the noviceship of the Dominican Order in Amiens in 1925, was professed in December 1926, went to study theology at Le Saulchoir, then located in Belgium, and was ordained priest on 25 July 1930. In 1932 he went back to Paris for further studies, particularly of the problem of unbelief, and came to know the leading Thomists of the period such as **Gilson** and Jacques **Maritain** and, through Maritain, Emmanuel **Mounier**. He returned to Le Saulchoir to teach fundamental theology, especially ecclesiology, and in 1937 he launched with the Paris firm of Éditions du Cerf the series 'Unam Sanctam'. The first volume was his own *Chrétiens désunis: principes d'un 'oecuménisme' catholique* (ET *Divided Christendom: A Catholic Study of the Problems of Reunion* (1939)), which set new standards for the relationship of the Roman Catholic Church with other Christian bodies. In the same year he visited England, where his host was the future archbishop of Canterbury, Michael **Ramsey**, then principal of Lincoln Theological College. At the outbreak of the war he was mobilized to serve as a military chaplain, but was captured and from 1940 to 1945 was imprisoned in Germany. On his release he was associated with the weekly *Témoignage Chrétien*, founded by Christians who had been involved in the French resistance against German occupation. *Vraie et fausse réforme dans l'église* appeared in 1950 and *Jalons pour une théologie du laïcat* in 1953, arguing in the latter book that ecclesiastical structures ought to be reformed to allow lay people to play a more active role in the life of the Church. Troubles with his superiors continued, and he was forbidden in 1947 to publish an article about the relationship of the Roman Catholic Church to other Christian churches then preparing to establish the World Council of Churches. Another article, on the priest-worker movement in France, caused the master general of the Dominicans to send him into exile, first – and at his own request – to the École Biblique in Jerusalem, and then for a year from November 1954 to December 1955 to the Dominican house in Cambridge, England. The accession to the papal throne of **John XXIII** in 1958 radically altered Congar's standing in the Church. He was invited to be a member of the preparatory commission for the Second Vatican Council, and helped to draft many of the conciliar documents, including the council's opening 'Message to the World'. His most important work after the council was the three-volume *Je crois en l'Esprit Saint* (1979–80, ET *I Believe in the Holy Spirit* (1983)). On 26 November 1994 Pope **John Paul II** named him a cardinal, but, because he was too ill to go to Rome, Cardinal Johannes Willebrands enrobed him in the insignia of a cardinal in the chapel of Les Invalides on 8 December.

Connaughton, Luke Roman Catholic author, born Bolton, Lancashire, 2 June 1917, died Oulton, Stone, Staffordshire, 2 September 1979. He began training for the priesthood, but eventually became a journalist. He was literary editor of the hymnbook *Sing a New Song to the Lord*. He sometimes used pseudonyms such as Peter Icarus. Some of his hymns are popular in the Catholic Church, for example *Reap Me the Earth*, set to music by three different composers, and reprinted in many hymnals.

Connell, Francis J. Redemptorist priest and theologian, born Boston, Massachusetts, 29 January 1881, died Washington DC, 12 May 1967. He studied in Boston, became a Redemptorist and was ordained in New York. He studied at the Angelicum in Rome and then taught moral theology at the Catholic University in Washington DC. He was subsequently rector of Holy Redeemer College, Washington, and professor in the sacred sciences at St John's University, Brooklyn, New York. He was a versatile scholar, writer, administrator and preacher. As well as writing books on moral theology he was associate editor of the *American Ecclesiastical Review*. His work included radio and TV appearances and he was active in theological and Marian societies. Among the awards he received was that of Pro Ecclesia et Pontifice from Pope **Pius XII**. In the Second Vatican Council he served as a member of the briefing panel for English-speaking reporters.

Connelly, Cornelia US religious foundress, born in Philadelphia, Pennsylvania, 15 January 1809, died St Leonard's, Sussex, England, 18 April 1879.

She married an Episcopalian rector, Pierce Connelly. In 1835, as a joint decision, she became a Roman Catholic, Pierce resigned from his ministry and the following year he was received into the Catholic Church in Rome. In 1840 Pierce took steps to fulfil his sense of call to the Catholic priesthood and, accepting this, Cornelia and their children went to live in the Sacred Heart Convent in Rome. In 1845, following Cornelia's solemn vow of chastity, Pierce was ordained. Cornelia went to England and in 1846 founded the Society of the Holy Child Jesus, with an apostolate to teaching. Schools were opened in England, France and in the USA and, after her death, in other parts of the British Isles, Europe and Africa. Pierce's vocation was short-lived: he left the priesthood and expected Cornelia to leave her work and come back to live as his wife, which she discerned, even at the expense of having her children taken away from her, was not what she should do. She continued to work for the approval of the Rules of the Society, but this was not accomplished until after her death.

Connery, John Richard Jesuit moral theologian, born Chicago, Illinois, 15 July 1913, died 22 December 1987. After entering the Society of Jesus he studied at West Baden College, Indiana, and the Pontifical Gregorian University, Rome. He taught moral theology at West Baden College, served as provincial of the Chicago province, then returned to teaching at Loyola University, Chicago, where he became Cardinal Cody professor of theology. He also taught at Georgetown University and was a consultant on medical ethics to the hospital there. He wrote for *Theological Studies* and other periodicals. He took a stand on medical and sexual problems, as in his survey *Abortion: The Development of the Roman Catholic Perspective*, 1977.

Connolly, Francis Xavier Educationist and writer, born New York City, 24 June 1909, died New York City, 17 November 1965. He studied in New York, and became full professor then chairman of the English department at Fordham College. During the Second World War, he served as a lieutenant in the US Navy. Though he had wide-ranging interests, he specialized in Victorian literature. He wrote *The Art of Rhetoric* and *A Rhetoric Casebook*.

He helped to found the Catholic Poetry Society of America, and with John B. **Brunini** edited four volumes of poetry. His interest in Gerard Manley **Hopkins** resulted in a novel, *Give Beauty Back*.

Connolly, Hugh Benedictine authority on Syriac and early Christian liturgy, born Werajel, Austria, 12 July 1871, died Bristol, England, 16 March 1948. He studied at the English Benedictine abbeys of Belmont and Downside, where he was ordained priest. He studied at Cambridge, became superior of St Benet's House and lectured on Syriac in the university as well as serving on the board of *Oriental Studies* at Cambridge. He edited *The Downside Review* and was a prolific and versatile writer.

Connolly, John Dominican bishop, born Slane, Ireland, c.1750, died New York, 6 February 1825. He was educated at Drogheda, and studied at Liège and Louvain. In Rome he was attached to the Irish Dominican House, San Clemente, where he became prior. In 1814 he was appointed second bishop of New York, and installed in 1815. Here he encountered a vast, populous diocese, with only four priests and three churches. He introduced the Sisters of Charity, built many churches and founded an orphanage.

Connolly, Thomas Louis Capuchin archbishop of Halifax, Nova Scotia, born County Cork, Ireland, 1815, died Halifax, Nova Scotia, 27 July 1876. Connolly studied in Rome, where he joined the Capuchins, and was ordained in Lyons, France. After some years' work in Ireland he went in 1842 to Nova Scotia as secretary to Bishop Walsh, bishop of Halifax, later first archbishop, at a time when there were bitter relations between Catholics and Protestants. In 1852, Connolly was appointed bishop of St John and in 1859 was translated to Halifax as second archbishop. He was diplomatic, tactful, interested in public affairs, so the bitterness between the two communities declined. At the First Vatican Council he took a prominent part, initially opposing the dogma of infallibility, but accepting it once it had been promulgated. After his death, he was described as 'a true Canadian'. He had opposed Fenianism.

Conon Pope, elected 21 October 686, died Rome,

21 September 687. Son of an army officer, he was educated in Sicily and ordained priest at Rome. He was elected Pope as a compromise figure, in lieu of candidates favoured by the clergy and the military respectively. Already old and in poor health, he proved a somewhat gullible leader: his mistakes included the appointment of Constantine of Syracuse to administer the Holy See's patrimony in Sicily. He was the recipient of a letter dated 17 February 687 from Justinian II stating that the decrees of the Third Council of Constantinople had been endorsed by the Byzantine clergy. He is buried in St Peter's Basilica.

Conrad Bosinlother Blessed, Benedictine abbot and reformer, born near Trier, Germany, died at Oberwang, near Mondsee, 15 January 1145. When Abbot Conrad of Siegburg became bishop of Regensburg in 1126, he chose Conrad Bosinlother – a monk of Siegburg – to reform the small episcopal abbey of Mondsee. He was perhaps too successful in his reforms, for when he placed his abbey directly under the Holy See (with his bishop's permission) in order to secure his reforms, he was clubbed to death by some of the abbey's tithe-payers. Feast day 15 January.

Conrad of Bavaria Blessed, Italian Cistercian monk. Born *c.*1105, place unknown, died Modugno, 17 March 1154. The son of Henry the Black, Conrad spent some years at Clairvaux under St **Bernard**'s tutelage before going to the Holy Land to live as a hermit. Towards the end of his life he set out for Clairvaux hoping to die with Bernard, but the saint predeceased him, and Conrad ended his days as an anchorite in Modugno. Feast day 14 February.

Conrad of Constance Saint. Born Germany, date unknown, died Constance, 26 November 975. Educated at the cathedral school of Constance, Conrad became bishop there and though he abstained from any political activity, Emperor **Otto I** held him in great esteem. His name is associated with churches in Einsiedeln, Rheingau and St Trudpert, and the chapel of St Maurice in Constance. Feast day 26 November.

Conrad of Gelnhausen German theologian. Born Gelnhausen, *c.*1320, died Heidelberg, 13 April

1390. Conrad studied and taught at Paris and became procurator of the German nation at Bologna. He is significant for two tracts, *Epistola brevis* and *Epistola concordiae*, in which he pronounced himself in favour of a general council, after the fashion of the Apostles, to bring the Western Schism to an end. His writings had little immediate effect, but they did influence later proponents of the conciliar theory.

Conrad of Mazovia Polish prince. Born in Poland, *c.*1190; died there, 31 August 1247. A son of Casimir II, Conrad inherited Mazovia and Kujawy, and cooperated with the Prussian bishops in founding the Knights of Dobrin, to safeguard the Christians of Prussia against the Teutonic Knights, and to Christianize the pagans. This step proved ineffective and Conrad, together with the bishops, invited the Teutonic Knights to accept the land of Chelmno as their base of operations; however, by exploiting the concessions made to them they acquired control over Prussia and made it into a Germanic state. Conrad is severely condemned in Polish history for his lack of political foresight in not anticipating the consequences of his actions.

Conrad of Megenburg German medieval scholar. Born Megenburg, *c.*1309, died Regensburg, 14 April 1374. Educated at Erfurt and Paris, Conrad became pastor of St Ulrich's Cathedral in Regensburg. Among his more famous works is *Buch der Natur*, a translation from the Latin *Liber de natura rerum* by the Dominican Thomas of Cantimpré, being the first work of natural history to appear in German, and the source of all subsequent writings on that subject in German until the sixteenth century.

Conrad of Offida Blessed, Franciscan, founder of the Celestines, born Offida, near Ancona, Italy, *c.*1241, died Bastia, Umbria, 12 December 1306. At Ascoli he entered the Order of Friars Minor, was ordained and became an impressive preacher. He modelled himself on St **Francis of Assisi** and lived in poverty, always walking barefoot. When Brother **Leo of Assisi**, St Francis' companion, was dying he bequeathed his writings to Conrad. Pope **Celestine V** gave Conrad permission to separate from the main body of Franciscans and to found the Celestine congregation. Pope **Boniface VIII** suppressed the Celestines and Conrad returned to the main Order. Conrad was giving missions at Bastia when he died. Later his remains were reburied in Perugia Cathedral. In 1817 he was declared blessed. Feast day 19 December.

Conrad of Ottobeuren Blessed, Benedictine abbot, died 27 July 1227. Elected abbot of Ottobeuren in 1191; was twice forced to rebuild his monastery during his 34-year reign. Feast day 27 July.

Conrad of Parzham Saint, Bavarian Capuchin lay brother. Born Parzham, 22 December 1818, died Altötting, 21 April 1894. Born into a farming family, Conrad pronounced his solemn vows in 1852 and served, 'through devotion to the Mother of God and the Blessed Sacament', the friary at Altötting as doorkeeper for 41 years, attending to a constant stream of pilgrims, and to the poor, with charity, meekness and patience. Canonized 40 years after his death, his relics are enshrined in the church of St Anne close by the monastery. Feast day 21 April.

Conrad of Querfurt German bishop. Born, date and place unknown, died Würzburg, 3 December 1202. Conrad became bishop of Hildesheim and Würzburg in 1194 and, as chancellor of Philip of Swabia, led the so-called German Crusade of 1197, which raised the Teutonic Order of St Mary's Hospital at Jerusalem to the rank of Teutonic Knights in 1198. **Innocent III** excommunicated him and deprived him of his see, but he regained Würzburg in 1201 after seeking papal pardon in Rome. Conrad then shifted his allegiance from Philip to the Guelph Emperor **Otto IV**. He was assassinated by one of his own household.

Consalvi, Ercole Italian cardinal and statesman, born Rome, 8 June 1757, died Anzio, Papal States, 24 January 1824. He entered the papal government and became an auditor in the curia. When the French occupied Rome, he became secretary of the Venetian conclave, which elected **Pius VII** as Pope, under Austrian protection. Pius VII created Consalvi cardinal and secretary of state. In Paris, Consalvi negotiated the concordat between France and the Papacy. Napoleon, however, forced Consalvi's resignation and imprisoned the Pope. At the Congress of Vienna, Consalvi managed to obtain the restitution of the Papal States. He reached agreements with secular powers to preserve the political independence of the Papacy.

Considine, John J. Priest and authority on missions, born New Bedford, Massachusetts, 9 October 1897, died Maryknoll, New York, 1982. He entered the Missionary Society at Maryknoll, studied for the priesthood, and in Rome served as procurator-general for the society. He researched world-wide missionary activity. On behalf of the Vatican he served on assignments in Ethiopia, Asia, the East Indies and Africa. He wrote of his travels in his book *Across a World*. In Washington DC he helped to organize the mission secretariat meetings. Cardinal **Cushing** set up a Latin American Department which Considine headed. At Maryknoll he founded a missionary journal, *Channel*.

Consobrino, João (Sobrinho) Portuguese Carmelite theologian. Born Lisbon, early fifteenth century, died Lisbon, 11 January 1486. A professor of theology and canon law at Lisbon, Consobrino is noteworthy for his work *De institia commutativa, arte campsona ac alearum ludo*, an important contribution to the doctrinal formulation of economic problems.

Constabilis Saint, Benedictine abbot, born Tresino, Italy, *c.*1090, died La Cava, 17 February 1124. Entered the abbey of La Cava at the age of seven, was made coadjutor to Abbot Peter in 1118 and was elected the fourth abbot of La Cava in March 1122, but died after serving for only two years. Venerated as the founder and patron of the town of Castel Abbate. Feast day 17 February.

Constans I Roman emperor, born *c.*323, died (killed in a military rebellion) in the Pyrenean fortress of Helena, January 350. Constans became emperor of the western Roman Empire on 9 September 337, following the death of his father, **Constantine I**. He supported the Nicene bishops of the Western Church, who upheld the full deity of Christ in opposition to the predominantly Arian bishops in the East. They were supported by the eastern emperor, Constans' brother **Constantius II**. Constans' strong support for the anti-Arian party had a restraining effect on Constantius' pro-Arian stance, but when Constans was killed in 350

Constantius became sole emperor, and he then proceeded to force the Catholic Church to accept Arian theology as its official doctrine.

Constans II Pogonatus   Byzantine emperor, born Constantinople, 7 November 630, died Syracuse (murdered in his bath), 15 September 668. The son of Constantine III, he became emperor in 641 at the height of the monothelite controversy and at a time when his empire was under pressure on its borders. He suffered a severe defeat at the hands of the Arabs in 655, and conducted campaigns against the Slavs in Macedonia from 656. He sought to resolve the monothelite controversy by issuing in 647/8 the Typos Decree, which prohibited further discussion of the number of wills or energies in Christ. This led to a rift with Rome, and the deposition of Pope **Martin I**, who refused to accept the edict. In *c.*662 he left for Italy, went to Rome and eventually settled in Syracuse, where he was killed.

Constantine   Pope, elected 25 March 708, died Rome, 9 April 715, a Syrian by birth. The *Liber Pontificalis* describes his visit to the East in 710–11, where he was warmly received by Justinian II at Nicomedia. When Justinian was assassinated in December 711, Constantine refused to recognize his successor, Philippicus (though he was soon deposed and replaced by an orthodox candidate, Anastasius II). Constantine authorized the English monastery of Bermondsey and Woking to choose its own abbot in 713, and he received the professions of the Mercian king Coinred and the East Saxon prince Offa at Rome in 709.

Constantine I (the Great)   Roman emperor, born Naissos (Nis, Serbia) *c.*273, died Nicomedia (now Izmit, Turkey), 22 May 337. While in Britain in 306 Constantine was declared emperor of the western Roman Empire in succession to his father, Constantius Chlorus. In Rome his position was usurped by Maxentius, and not until 312 was Constantine able to challenge him. Prior to their crucial battle Constantine apparently had a vision of the Cross, which convinced him that he should fight under its sign. He proceeded to win a decisive victory at the Battle of the Milvian Bridge, which he duly attributed to the Christian God, and in the Edict of Milan of 313 jointly decreed with the

eastern emperor Licinius that within the Roman Empire Christianity would no longer be an outlawed religion. In 324 Constantine became emperor over both East and West, and established a new imperial capital at Byzantium, subsequently renamed Constantinople. During his reign he enacted legislation which positively discriminated in favour of the Church, and reflected Christian ethical principles. Taking a keen interest in ecclesiastical affairs, he convened the first ecumenical council of bishops, at Nicaea in 325, and his numerous endowments stimulated the building of churches throughout the empire. There has been much argument over the exact nature of Constantine's commitment to Christianity, but the evidence suggests that it was genuine, though his understanding of it could be confused or even syncretistic. In keeping with a common practice of the time, he deferred his baptism until near death. In some parts of the Orthodox Church he is regarded as a saint. Feast day 21 May.

Constantine III Leichudes   Patriarch of Constantinople, scholar and statesman, born *c.*1000, possibly in Constantinople, died there, 10 August 1063. Leichudes was one of the intellectual leaders of the city in the mid-eleventh century, and became first minister under **Constantine IX**, falling from favour around 1055, at the end of Constantine's reign. However, Michael VI sent him on an embassy to Isaac Comnenus, who, when he had displaced Michael, chose Leichudes as patriarch of Constantinople in 1059, to succeed Michael Cerularius. He reciprocated the favour by giving Isaac ecclesiastical tonsure during his illness and abdication. Most of the information about Leichudes, as a distinguished scholar, wise administrator and admirable churchman, has been provided by his friend Michael **Psellus** in his *Chronographia* and *Funeral Oration*.

Constantine IV Pogonatus   Byzantine emperor, born *c.*652, died Constantinople, possibly 10 July 685. He became emperor in 668. He oversaw the defence of Constantinople during the Arab siege and blockade, 674–8. At the Third Council of Constantinople in 680 he pressed for a restoration and reinforcement of Chalcedonian Christology, abandoning the policy of his Heraclid dynasty; the council affirmed that Christ possessed two wills, not one (i.e. the dyothelite position). Constantine suffered a series of setbacks at the hands of the Bulgars, but in general strengthened and stabilized his empire.

Constantine V Byzantine emperor and iconoclast theologian, born Constantinople, 718, died Strongylon, Bulgaria, 14 September 775. He became emperor in 741. He checked Arab and Bulgar invasions of Byzantium; his reign however saw the final loss of central Italy, when Ravenna fell to the Lombards in 751. In 754 he presided over an Eastern council at Hiereia near Constantinople, which claimed to be the seventh ecumenical council, and denounced the veneration of icons. A vigorous programme of destruction of images, persecution of monasteries and sporadic martyrdoms followed. The Second Council of Nicaea in 787 reversed the assembly's enactments.

Constantine VII Byzantine emperor, called Porphyrogenetos ('born in the purple chamber'), born Constantinople, 17 or 18 May 905, died 9 November 959. He was son of **Leo VI**, and succeeded his uncle Alexander in 913, ruling jointly with his father-in-law, **Romanus I Lecapenus**, but gradually lost power to him. However, Constantine banished the sons of his father-in-law and ruled alone after 945. Constantine was known for his generosity in alleviating taxes on the poor. He was, however, more interested in study than statesmanship; he patronized the arts and literature; and wrote a biography of **Basil I**. His book *De Ceremoniis Aulae Byzantinae* described the elaborate Byzantine ceremonial.

Constantine IX Monomachos ('Fighter in single combat'), born *c.*980, died Constantinople, 11 January 1055. He was Byzantine emperor from 1042 when he became the third husband of the Empress Zoe and co-ruler of the Byzantine Empire with her. However, during his reign, he neglected the defence of the empire, reduced the army, spent extravagantly on luxuries, lavishly endowed two monasteries and debased the coinage. Southern Italy was lost to the Normans: an attempt to ally the Byzantine Empire with the Papacy against the Normans was unsuccessful. He gathered intellectuals about him, and established a law school in Constantinople.

Constantine XI Palaeologus Byzantine emperor. Born Constantinople, 1404, died there, 29 May 1453. Son of **Manuel II Palaeologus**, he received the Greek Peloponnesus as his share of the empire; he tried unsuccessfully to settle the Unionistic controversy in the Church, although he duly accepted the promulgation of the decree of the Council of Florence in 1452. The last emperor of Byzantium, he commanded the defence of Constantinople in the siege by Muhammad II, and died valiantly during the final assault.

Constantine of Barbanson Capuchin theologian from the Low Countries. Born Barbanson, near Beaumont in the Hainaut, *c.*1581, died Bonn, 25 November 1631. He joined the Capuchins in Brussels, and went to their province in the Rhineland, where he distinguished himself as a master of the spiritual life, especially in regard to the pre-quietistic mysticism of the times. His most important writings are *Les Secrets sentiers de l'amour divin*, and *Anatomie de l'âme et des opérations divines en icelle.*

Constantine the African Perhaps a merchant, then physician, and Benedictine monk, born Carthage, between *c.*1010 and 1015, died Monte Cassino, 1087. He spent much of his adult life travelling in the Near East; it is unknown if he was born a Christian or if he later converted from Islam. When he returned to Carthage his use of Arab medicine led to his being accused of practising magic, he was expelled from the city, and took up a position with **Robert Guiscard**, Duke of Salerno. His connexion to the medical school at Salerno is uncertain; he may have been a professor there prior to becoming a monk at Monte Cassino during the reign of Abbot Desiderius (later Pope **Victor III**), *c.*1078. He is best known for his translations of Graeco-Arabic medical texts, but it is uncertain how many of the texts that bear his name he actually composed.

Constantius II Roman emperor, born 7 August 317, died Mopsoukrene, Cilicia, 3 November 361. One of the sons of **Constantine I**, Constantius became emperor of the eastern Roman Empire in 337 on the death of his father, and became sole emperor in 350 when his brother **Constans**, the western emperor, was murdered in a rebellion.

Though generally benevolent towards the Church, he favoured the theology of the Arians, who denied the full deity of Christ. This was reflected in the ecclesiastical policies he pursued, and in 359 he imposed a creed on the Church which, for a brief period, made the official Catholic faith explicitly Arian.

Constantius of Fabriano   Blessed, Italian Dominican. Born Fabriano, 1410, died Ascoli, 24 February 1481. A man of exceptional holiness, Constantius became prior of the Dominican Congregation of the Strict Observance, professor of theology at Bologna and Florence, and prior of the convents at Fabriano and Perugia, and at Ascoli in 1470, where he died. **Pius VII** approved his cult in 1814. Feast day 25 February).

Contarini, Gasparo   Cardinal, theologian and diplomatist, born Venice, Italy, 16 October 1483, died Bologna, Italy, 24 August 1542. Contarini came from a prominent Venetian family, and became a diplomatist following a brilliant student career. He also gained a reputation as a theologian, publishing several works which were so highly regarded that despite being a layman he was created a cardinal in 1535. Contarini was deeply involved in the ultimately abortive attempts to heal the breach with Lutheranism, notably at the Conference of Regensburg (Ratisbon) of 1541. His religious experience made him not unsympathetic to some aspects of Lutheran theology, and his treatise on justification, written in the hope of promoting reconciliation, was regarded by some Roman Catholics to be conciliatory to the point of compromise.

Contarini, Giovanni   Patriarch of Constantinople, born into the Contarini family in Venice c.1370 and died in the abbey of San Giorgio Maggiore, Venice, 1451. Studied at Oxford and Paris, and on his return to Venice, though still a sub-deacon, was made patriarch of Constantinople in 1409. He went as papal nuncio for **Gregory XII** to Germany in 1414 and was at the Council of Constance in 1415, where he was commissioned to negotiate Gregory's abdication. **Martin V** transferred Contarini to Alexandria in 1422 (because there were two patriarchs of Constantinople, both appointed during the Western Schism) but by 1424 he was

back in Constantinople. From 1418 to 1427 he was also administrator of the Diocese of Cittanova nell'Estuario, near Asola in Italy. Information about his life is found mainly in his correspondence with his brothers.

Contenson, Guillaume Vincent de   Dominican, born Altivillare, Diocese of Condon, France, 1641, died Creil-sur-Oise, 26 December 1674. At age seventeen he joined the Dominican Order and taught philosophy at Albi and theology at Toulouse. He was considered a brilliant preacher and attempted to get away from dry Scholasticism. In his theology he used impressive images borrowed from Scripture. His main work is *Theologia Mentis et Cordis*, published posthumously in 1681.

Conti, Sigismondo de'   Historian, born Foligno, 1432, died Rome, 23 February 1512. A career in papal service, culminating in the office of papal secretary for **Sixtus IV**, **Innocent VIII**, **Alexander VI** and **Julius II**, enabled him to compile the *Historia sui temporis* (History of his own time), dedicated to Julius II and covering the period 1475–1510. This effectively continued the history of the Papacy where Platina (Bartolomeo de' Sacchi) had left off. Conti had been educated at the Roman Studium, travelled with Giuliano della Rovere (the future Julius II) in France and Burgundy (1480–1) and was in contact with many important literary figures.

Conway, John D.   Priest and writer, born Pleasantville, Iowa, 16 May 1905, died Davenport, Iowa, 5 February 1967. He studied in Knoxville and Davenport, Iowa, then at Louvain, where he was ordained priest. In Rome he attended the Gregorian University and in the USA was chancellor of the Davenport diocese. In the Second World War he became an army chaplain. From 1946 onwards he served skilfully in the diocesan marriage tribunal, then became pastor of St Thomas More parish, and the University Student Centre at the University of Iowa. He served as president of the Canon Law Society of America. Pope **Paul VI** appointed him papal chamberlain, and Pope **John XXIII** a domestic prelate. Conway was a prolific author. His *Question Box* in Davenport's *Catholic Messenger* was syndicated by over fifty diocesan newspapers.

Conway, William Cardinal archbishop of Armagh and Primate of All Ireland. Born in Dover St, now the Falls Road area of Belfast, 1913, died Armagh, 17 April 1977. Educated by the Christian Brothers, at Queen's University, Belfast, and at Maynooth, he was ordained in 1937 and a DD followed in 1938. He studied canon law at Rome's Gregorian University, 1938–41. He held chairs of moral theology and of canon law at Maynooth until 1958 and was editor of the *Irish Theological Quarterly*. In 1950 he published *Problems of Canon Law*. He became auxiliary to Cardinal D'Alton in 1958 and was then appointed as archbishop of Armagh and Primate of All Ireland on 9 September 1963, being created cardinal by **Paul VI** in 1965. He was very active at Vatican II and was one of the chairmen of the synod of bishops in 1967. Trocaire, an agency to develop aid to the Third World from Irish Catholics, was mainly his initiative. Conway was a member of the pontifical commission for the revision of canon law carrying out the first major revision since 1918.

Cook, J. A. Bethune English Presbyterian missionary to Singapore, born South Shields, England, 1854, died 13 July 1926. Inspired by Livingstone and educated at Westminster College, Cambridge, in 1881 he was appointed by the English Presbyterian Church to work amongst Singapore Chinese. He arrived in Singapore in 1882 after language study in South China, and guided the emerging Chinese Presbyterian churches growing through migration and conversion. He established new congregations and expanded the dialect groups involved. Committed to 'three-self' principles he established a Presbyterian synod in 1901. He convened meetings of Protestant missionaries in Singapore, was a leader in moral and temperance movements and anti-opium campaigns, and wrote for the Christian and secular press. His *Sunny Singapore* was published in 1907. He retired in 1924.

Cook, Thomas Baptist founder of the Thomas Cook travel agency, born Melbourne, Derbyshire, 22 November 1808, died Stonegate, 18 July 1892. Apprenticed as a wood-turner he afterwards entered a Loughborough printing and publishing firm which produced books for the General Baptist Association. He joined the local Association of Baptists and travelled throughout Rutland as a missionary. As secretary to the South Midland Temperance Association in Market Harborough, his success in arranging the first publicly advertised railway excursion in England, from Leicester to Loughborough and back in 1841 for a temperance meeting, led him to organize more excursions at home and abroad. As business developed he published handbooks for tourists and subsequently issued vouchers for hotel expenses and, from c.1846, a monthly magazine, *Excursionist*. In 1872 he undertook a journey around the world to prepare the way for tourists, leaving his son in charge of the firm.

Cooke, Terence Seventh archbishop of New York, born New York City, 1 March 1921, died New York City, 6 October 1983. He was ordained priest in St Patrick's Cathedral. He studied for a degree in social work in Chicago and Washington DC. He was assigned to the Youth Division of Catholic Charities, taught at Fordham University and became Cardinal **Spellman**'s secretary. Cooke became auxiliary bishop of New York in 1965 and subsequently succeeded Spellman as archbishop. The day on which he was installed was that on which Martin Luther **King** was assassinated. That evening, in Harlem, Cooke pleaded for racial peace. In 1969 Cooke was made a cardinal. He was regarded as a fine, hard-working administrator, with excellent communication skills. He appointed black and Hispanic auxiliary bishops, and visited American servicemen abroad.

Cooper, John Montgomery Priest and anthropologist, born Rockville, Maryland, 28 October 1881, died Washington DC, 22 May 1949. He studied in the North American College in Rome and after ordination was assigned to Washington DC's St Matthew's Cathedral. In 1920 he became a full-time member of the Catholic University, with a dual interest in religion and anthropology. His specialism was cultural anthropology, on which he published widely, doing fieldwork among North American Indians. In 1934 he was appointed head of a new anthropology department. He was secretary of the American Anthropological Association. He collaborated in the *Handbook of South American Indians* (1949).

Copernicus, Nicolaus Astronomer, born Torun, Poland, 19 February 1473, died Frauenberg, Poland, 24 May 1543. The formulator of the heliocentric theory of the universe, Copernicus had been brought up by his uncle, Lucas Watzelrode, bishop of Warmia. Through this family connection he later become a canon of the cathedral of Frauenberg, and here carried out his astronomical researches. The heliocentric theory was expressed in *De Revolutionibus Orbium Coelestium*, published in 1543 (Copernicus received it from the printer just hours before his death). The apparent contradiction of Scripture which the theory entailed caused fierce controversy during the seventeenth century, especially as a result of **Galileo**'s support. The work was placed on the Index of Prohibited Books in 1616, but subsequent research by later astronomers put the truth of heliocentrism beyond doubt. *De Revolutionibus* was removed from the Index in 1758.

Corbinian of Freising Saint, born Chatres, near Melun, France, 670, died Obermais, 8 September 725. Baptized Waldegiso, his mother changed his name to Corbinian. He lived as a solitary at Chatres, and organized his own community of disciples. On a visit to Rome (possibly by then as a bishop), he was commissioned by **Gregory II** to evangelize Germany. He settled at Freising, Upper Bavaria, but had to flee to Meran after denouncing the prospective marriage of his patron, Duke Grimoald, to his brother's widow. On the death of Grimoald, he returned to Bavaria and founded a monastery at Obermais, where he spent the rest of his days. His emblem of the bear derives from the legend that he compelled a bear who had killed his pack-horse to take over the horse's job. Feast day 8 September.

Corbishley, Thomas Jesuit writer and ecumenist, born Preston, England, 30 May 1903, died London, 11 March 1976. He joined the Society of Jesus at fifteen, and had a distinguished academic career before being appointed master of Campion Hall, the Jesuit house at Oxford University, in 1945 in succession to Martin **D'Arcy**. He then became superior of the main London community of Jesuits at Farm Street until 1966, and remained there for the rest of his life. He was very active in ecumenical circles, and was also active in promoting the idea of European integration among British Christians (there is an annual 'Corbishley Lecture' on that theme mounted by a society of which he was a member). He was a regular broadcaster and a writer in both the national and the religious press. His published books include studies of Ronald **Knox** (1964) and **Teilhard de Chardin** (1971), as well as a translation of the *Spiritual Exercises* of **Ignatius of Loyola** (1963).

Corcoran, James Andrew US Roman Catholic priest, theologian, editor and linguist, born Charlestown, South Carolina, 30 March 1820, died Philadelphia, 16 July 1889. Studied at the College of Propaganda, Rome, and was ordained priest in 1842. He taught in the seminary in Charlestown, did parish work and, with Patrick Lynch, edited the *United States Catholic Miscellany*, the first US Catholic literary periodical. He supported the South in the Civil War and later did parish and diocesan work and was chosen as the US theologian to go to the First Vatican Council, where he was in favour of the teaching on papal infallibility. He was appointed to the chair of theology at the new seminary at Overbrook near Philadelphia and remained there for the rest of his life. In 1876 he became chief editor of the newly founded *American Catholic Quarterly Review*. In 1883 he became secretary to the Third Plenary Council of Baltimore, and in 1884 he was made a domestic prelate.

Cordell, Charles English Roman Catholic priest, born Holborn, Middlesex, 5 October 1720, died Newcastle upon Tyne, 26 January 1791. He was educated at Douai and ordained in December 1744. In 1748 he returned to England and served in Arundel Castle, Sussex, until 1755, when he went on to Leeds, then the Isle of Man and finally Newcastle upon Tyne. He was a scholarly man and declined the presidency of the English College at St Omer. He supported the Jacobite cause. He translated many books, including *The Divine Office for the Use of the Laity, Bergier's Deism Self-refuted, Caraccioli's Life of Pope Clement XIV, The Letters of Pope Clement XIV* and two versions of the Catechism.

Córdoba, Antonio de Spanish Franciscan theologian. Born Spain, 1485, died Guadalajara, 1578. Córdoba participated in the Council of Trent at the request of **Philip II**; he wrote several treatises on moral theology, the major ones being *Quaestionarium theologicum* and *Summa casuum*.

Córdoba, Pedro de   Spanish Dominican missionary. Born Córdoba, 1482, died Santo Domingo, 1521. Córdoba, believing himself to have a missionary calling, went to Santo Domingo in 1510, where he established the first convent of the Holy Cross province of the Dominican Order; he also founded missions on Española, Cuba, and at Cumaná on the mainland. His writings remain mostly unedited, but his *Doctrina cristiana para instrucción de los indios, por manera de historia* (1544), published in Mexico, has been influential.

Córdova, Matías de   Mexican Dominican educator, born Tapachula, Chiapas, 20 April 1768, died Chiapas, 1828. Having studied at the seminary of Ciudad Real de San Cristóbal de Las Casas, Córdova went to Guatemala, where he joined the Dominicans and became a humanistic scholar; he wrote poems, epigrams and various other works. He published a treatise on Indian problems, their aptitudes, and peaceful ways of converting them; also *Método facil de enseñar a leer y escribir*, which intended to popularize primary education. He is the author of a moral fable-poem, *La Tentativa del León y el Exito de su Empresa*.

Córdova y Salinas, Diego de   Peruvian Franciscan historian, born Lima, 1591, died there, 1654. He was commissioned in 1620 to prepare a history of the Franciscan province of Peru, and began by visiting elderly friars and taking depositions of their reminiscences. His great work *Crónica franciscana de las provincias del Perú* is a monumental history of the work and plans of the Franciscan provinces in almost all Spanish South America, during the first century after Pizarro's conquest.

Corelli, Arcangelo   Italian composer and violinist, born Fusignano, 17 February 1653, died Rome, 8 January 1713. He went to Rome, where he was a violinist at the French Church and played in the orchestra of the Teatro Capranica, and remained there except for brief visits to Modena and Paris. Corelli had a powerful patron in Cardinal Benedetto Pamphili, and Queen **Christina of Sweden** was an admirer. **Handel** as a young man met Corelli in Rome. Corelli taught Geminiani and Locatelli, and founded modern violin technique. He was an influential composer, but not a prolific one. He created the concerto grosso form and wrote trio sonatas and concerti grossi. A famous work is his *Christmas Concerto*.

Corker, James Maurus   English Benedictine, born Yorkshire, 1636, died Paddington, London, 22 December 1715. In 1656 he took his vows at the abbey of Lamspringe, near Hildesheim, Germany, and in 1665 returned to England as a missionary priest, where Titus **Oates** implicated him in the 'Popish plot'. Corker was imprisoned in Newgate, acquitted from involvement in the plot, but then arrested for being a priest. He was sentenced to death, but reprieved to remain in Newgate. It is alleged that he converted a thousand Protestants while there. A fellow prisoner was Oliver **Plunket**, archbishop of Armagh. When **James II** became king in 1685, Father Corker was retained at court as an ambassador to the prince-bishop of Bavaria. However, during the Glorious Revolution Corker had to flee to the Continent. He became abbot of Cismar, near Lubeck, but in 1696 he returned to England as a missioner. He wrote pamphlets proving the innocence of those blamed in the Popish plot.

Cormier, Hyacinth Marie   Dominican priest and writer, born Orléans, France, 8 December 1832, died Rome, Italy, 17 December 1916. Cormier joined the Dominican Order after being a priest of the Diocese of Orléans. He was provincial of the Toulouse province, and served as prior in various houses. He became 'socius' or assistant to the master general, Fr Fruhwirth, and then became procurator general. He restored Dominican provinces and established new ones, continuing the work of Henri **Lacordaire**. In 1909 he established in Rome what is now the Pontifical University of St Thomas. His writings such as *Instructions de Novices* and *Quinze Entretiens sur la Liturgie Dominicaine* consolidated his work. He was a confidant of Pope **Pius X**, and in 1945 his cause for beatification was introduced.

Cornaro, Elena Lucrezia Piscopia   Born Venice, 5 June 1646, died Padua, 26 July 1684. A Venetian patrician who devoted her life to a combination of piety and scholarship. At the age of nineteen she became a secular Benedictine oblate, taking the name of Scolastica. Her academic reputation was confirmed when, in 1678, she became the first woman to be awarded a university degree, a Paduan doctorate in philosophy. Her studies were principally theological, but the bishop of Padua opposed the granting a doctorate in that discipline on the grounds that a woman could not preach or administer the sacraments.

Corneille, Pierre French poet and playwright, born Rouen, 6 June 1606, died Paris, 1 October 1684. He studied with the Jesuits in Rouen, and then law at Caen, being admitted to the bar in 1624. Four years later he was appointed to a post in the Admiralty. The following year, 1629, however, his first play was produced in Paris. For a time he was under the patronage of Cardinal **Richelieu**, but fell from favour and returned to Rouen the year before his most famous play, *Le Cid* was produced (1636), which is said to mark a major turning-point in the history of French theatre. From then on he wrote with great regularity, but not always with success, and when *Pertharite* proved a failure in 1653 he gave up working as a dramatist, and undertook a translation of **Thomas a Kempis'** *Imitation of Christ*. He was a devout Catholic, serving as churchwarden in his parish in Rouen, and selling his house to provide a dowry for his daughter when she became a nun. In 1659 he began again to write plays, but never quite achieved the success of his earlier years.

Cornelius Pope and saint, elected March 251, died June 253, a Roman by birth. After the martyrdom of **Fabian** under Decius in 250, the See of Rome was vacant for fourteen months, prior to his election. Cornelius faced strong opposition from the supporters of **Novatian**, who had directed the Church in the meantime. The Novatianists objected to his fairly lenient policy towards those who had lapsed during the persecution; however, the majority of bishops supported him. Several of his letters survive, including two to **Cyprian**. Exiled under Gallus' persecution, he is said to have been martyred at Centumcellae (Civitavecchia); he was buried in Rome. Feast day 16 September.

Cornelius of Zierikzee Dutch Franciscan Observant in Scotland. Born Island of Schouwen, Zeeland, 1405, died Antwerp, *c.*1470. He led seven friars to establish in 1447 Franciscan life in Scotland in response to **James I**'s request to the province of Cologne for learned and pious religious. Zierikzee was highly popular and gained for the Order noble and educated members, who had studied at Paris and Cologne. He accepted five buildings offered to him in Edinburgh by James II and administered friaries there, at St Andrews and at Perth. He returned to Cologne in 1462 and died a saintly death in the monastery at Antwerp. His remains were burned by the Calvinists in 1566.

Cornely, Rudolph German Jesuit scriptural scholar, born Breyell, Germany, 19 April 1830, died Trier, Germany, 3 March 1908. As a Jesuit he studied oriental languages in the Lebanon, Egyptology in Paris, and taught these at Maria Laach, and was later professor at the Gregorian University in Rome. He founded the magazine *Die Katholischen Missionen*. He planned the *Cursus Scripturae Sacrae*, collaborating with others, and wrote the introduction. Then he wrote commentaries on St Paul's epistles and on the book of Wisdom.

Cornwallis, Thomas English colonial official. Born England, *c.*1603, died England, *c.*1676. Of the Catholic gentry, Cornwallis joined a small group chosen by Lord Baltimore (Cecilius **Calvert**) to preside over homesteads in Maryland in 1634. He played an important role in assuring the success of the colony that became the foundation of English Catholic life in the New World, and had a long career in the council and in the assembly. He was instrumental in having passed, over the opposition of Lord Baltimore, the Ordinance of 1639 and its Toleration Act; he also defended the Jesuit missionaries in their litigation with Baltimore over land tenure. As a captain in the militia, he led the Marylanders against incursions by the Virginians, Puritans and Indians.

Coronel, Juan Franciscan missionary, born Torija, Spain, 1569, died Mérida, Mexico, 1651. He studied at the University of Alcalá de Henares and joined the Franciscans in Seville. In 1590, he was sent to Yucatan, Mexico. He mastered the Maya language and was able to teach it: **Cogulludo**, the historian, was one of his pupils. Coronel published at least two books in Maya, of which one was a catechism. He lived austerely and always travelled barefoot.

Corrado, Giovanni Baptista Italian Dominican theologian, born Perugia, 1536, died Perguia, 1606. Corrado taught canon law and moral theology in the Order's *studia* for many years, and wrote manuals on casuistry and canonical questions.

Correggio Italian Renaissance master painter, born Correggio, a small city near Modena, of comfortably-off parents, the Allegri, and named Antonio, about 1494, died Modena, 5 March 1534. Though he developed a subtle personal style in oil and fresco, he was also influenced by both **Leonardo da Vinci** and **Raphael**. His specifically religious themes such as *The Vision of St John* (1520) in the dome of S. Giovanni Evangelista in Parma and the dynamic freedom in his remarkable *Assumption of the Virgin* (1530) in the cathedral of the same city anticipate the baroque designs of a century later. These paintings on ceilings and cupolas of churches and convents directly aided the devotions of worshippers. *The Holy Night*, a Nativity (*c.*1530) in the Dresden Gallery, his *Ecce Homo* in the National Gallery, London, and *The Mystic Marriage of St Catherine* in the Louvre are among the more famous of his paintings outside Italy. About forty major works can be confidently assigned to him.

Corrigan, Michael Augustine Archbishop of New York, born Newark, New Jersey, 13 August 1839, died New York City, 5 May 1902. In Maryland he studied at Emmitsburg, and in Rome was one of the first students of the North American College. He returned to the USA to work in Newark diocese and helped to establish Seton Hall College and Seminary, New Jersey. He served as vicar-general and was appointed bishop in Newark. He cared especially for the needs of the Italian population, and promoted schools, hospitals and orphanages. Corrigan became coadjutor archbishop of New York and prevented the Italian government taking over the North American College in Rome. In 1886 he became archbishop of New York. Corrigan made the diocese administratively efficient and helped to complete St Patrick's Cathedral.

Corrigan, Patrick US Roman Catholic priest, born Longford, Ireland, 1 January 1835, died Hoboken, New Jersey, 9 January 1894. He arrived in the USA aged thirteen, and studied at Wilmington, Delaware, and at seminaries in Dublin, Ireland, and Baltimore, Maryland. As a priest he served in the Diocese of Newark, New Jersey, finally at Hoboken. He advocated that priests in the USA be given a say in the appointment of US bishops and that the Church there be in harmony with the spirit of the US Constitution. Corrigan clashed with Bishop Winand M. Wigger, was given an ecclesiastical trial and was forced to resign. He helped to sponsor a bill to make New Jersey Roman Catholic schools part of the state system, but the bill failed, and as a result, a school he had built had to close.

Corrigan, William Raymond Jesuit and historian, born Omaha, Nebraska, 28 January 1889, died St Louis, Missouri, 19 January 1943. He entered the Society of Jesus after studying at Creighton University, Omaha, and at St Louis University, and was then sent to the Jesuit mission in Belize, British Honduras, where he developed an interest in mission history. He studied theology in Barcelona, and was ordained there, going on to further studies in The Netherlands, in France, and at Bonn and Munich Universities. He completed a doctorate in Munich on Rome's relations with the church in North America. He was head of the department of history at St Louis University from 1932 until his death and wrote *The Church and the Nineteenth Century*.

Corsini, Neri Cardinal, born Florence, 11 May 1685, died Rome, 6 December 1770. The Corsinis were a powerful trading family of Florence from the thirteenth century almost to the present day, raised to the nobility by Pope **Urban VIII** in 1629. They produced four cardinals, of whom this Neri was the third. He represented Cosimo III de' Medici at The Hague, London, and Paris, until Cosimo's death in 1723. Neri then went to Rome with his uncle, Cardinal Lorenzo, later Pope **Clement XII**. In 1730 Neri was made cardinal. A year earlier he had bought the Riario Palace. After restoring it, he developed the library started by his great uncle, also Cardinal Neri, and added to by Clement XII. This collection was opened to the public in 1754. He played a major role in the conclave of 1740 which elected **Benedict XIV**, unsuccessfully gathering votes for a rival candidate. He nonetheless played an important part in the pontificate of Benedict, being created archpriest of St John Lateran. Corsini had pro-Jansenist sympathies.

Corsini, Pietro Cardinal, born probably in Florence, died Avignon, France, 6 August 1405. Pietro was the first of the Corsini cardinals (see above) and was a cousin of the Carmelite St **Andrew Corsini**. After legal studies he moved to the papal court at Avignon and became bishop of Volterra in 1362, of Florence a year later, and of Porto in 1374. He was made ambassador to **Charles IV** in 1364, and cardinal in 1370. The next year he was made prince of the Empire. Pietro was the author of a tract on Pope **Urban VI** and the Western Schism.

Cortese, Gregorio Benedictine theologian and cardinal, born Gian Andrea Cortese at Modena, 1483, died Rome, 21 September 1548. The Paduan educated Cortese enjoyed the favour of Giovanni de' Medici (**Leo X**) early in his career, but became disillusioned with life in Rome and joined the Benedictine Order, thereafter acquiring a reputation as a theologian and monastic reformer. In 1536 he was recalled to Rome to contribute to the wider movement for ecclesiastical reform. **Paul III** made him a cardinal and bishop of Urbino in 1542. His erudition was expressed in philosophical, theological, historical and other scholarly works, most of which remain unedited.

Cortona, Pietro Berrettini da Painter and architect, born Cortona, Italy, 1 November 1596, died Rome, 16 May 1669. A pivotal figure of Roman high baroque. Although impressive as a painter, his architectural works are among the finest of the period. The Palazzo Barberini in Rome features his massive ceiling fresco *Allegory of Divine Providence and Barberini Power*, completed between 1633 and 1639. This is a major example of illusionism. He also worked on the Pitti Palace for the grand duke of Tuscany, including *Allegories of Virtues and Planets*, which covers seven ceilings. Among his architectural works are the church of the Academy of St Luke, and the lower church of Sta Martina,

with its curved façade. This element is further developed in the two-storey church of Santa Maria della Pace. His work was valued by Cardinal **Mazarin**, and in 1664 he was invited to submit designs for the Louvre; the competition was won by **Bernini**. Under a pseudonym, he was a co-author of *Trattato della pittura*, expounding the ideals of the Counter-Reformation.

Cosgrove, Henry Roman Catholic bishop, born Williamsport, Pennsylvania, USA, 19 December 1833, died Davenport, Iowa, 22 December 1906. He was taught by pioneer priests, among whom was his special adviser, Joseph **Crétin**, who became the first bishop of St Paul, Minnesota. He studied philosophy and theology, and after completing his studies at the St Louis diocesan seminary, was ordained in 1857. He served in Davenport as priest, pastor, rector of the cathedral and vicar-general to the bishop. In 1884, he succeeded the bishop, who had died the previous year, thus becoming the first American-born bishop west of the Mississippi river. He was an outstanding preacher, and worked on behalf of Catholic schools and orphanages, and of Catholic immigrants. He is buried under the main vestibule of Davenport's cathedral of the Sacred Heart, which he built.

Coskery, Henry Archdiocesan administrator, born Frederick County, Maryland, USA, 19 July 1808, died Baltimore, Maryland, 27 February 1872. Ordained for the Baltimore archdiocese in 1834, he served at several Maryland missions, and in 1837 was sent to Ellicott's Mills. After building St Paul's Church there, he went to Baltimore Cathedral in 1839. In 1843, he became rector and vicar-general, posts he held until his death. He administered the archdiocese after the deaths of three archbishops, preferring to stay in Baltimore rather than take the bishopric of Portland, Maine, to which he was appointed in 1854. He was instrumental in bringing the Brothers of the Christian Schools to Baltimore.

Cosmas and Damian Martyrs and patron saints of physicians, perhaps died *c.*302. Their lives are very obscure; legend suggests they practised medicine without charge at Rome, and became known as the 'silverless ones'. Both are said to have been martyred under Diocletian. Their cult was already strong in the fifth century. A church was constructed in their honour by **Felix IV** in the 520s; other Roman churches have also commemorated them. They are mentioned in the canon of the Roman Mass. Feast day 26 (previously 27) September in the West; 1 July (also 1 November) in the East.

Cosmas Indicopleustes (Cosmas 'the Indian navigator') Geographer, died *c.*550. A merchant of Alexandria, he may have become a monk. He is famous for his *Christian Topography* (*c.*547), which argues against Ptolemaic astronomy by setting out various fantastic astronomical theories intended to harmonize with the Bible. The work is valuable for its geographical information, especially on Sri Lanka, and for its witness to the spread of the Christian Church at this period. In exegesis, Cosmas followed **Theodore of Mopsuestia**; in doctrine, he was probably a Nestorian.

Cosmas of Aitolia Greek Orthodox saint and martyr, born in the province of Aitolia, 1714, died (martyred) near Berat, Albania, 24 August 1779. He became a monk on Athos and in 1760 started to preach throughout Greece and Albania. He established schools in more than 200 villages and preached against ignorance and social injustice. He was accused of treason to the Turkish authorities and hanged. His continuous veneration made him the principal one of the numerous Greek 'new martyrs' of the period of Turkish rule. Canonized in Constantinople 1961. Feast day 24 August.

Cosmas of Prague Bohemian historian, born *c.*1045 in Prague, Bohemia, died there, 21 October 1125. Cosmas was born of a knightly family and was taught in Prague and Liège. He was ordained 11 June 1099 in Gran, Hungary, and became a member and ultimately the dean of the chapter of St Vitus' Cathedral in Prague. At the same time, he was married and had a son (his wife was named Bozetecha, and his son Henry or Zdic, who later became bishop of Olmutz). Cosmas was the first writer of Bohemian history; his *Chronica Bohemorum* consists of three volumes.

Cosmas the Melodian Greek liturgical hymn writer, born Jerusalem, *c.*706, died *c.*760. Also called Hagiopolites. Adopted by the father of **John**

Damascene, he and John studied with an Italian monk. Around 732, he entered the laura (or Lavra) of St Sabas, near Jerusalem. In 743 he became bishop of Maïuma, near Gaza. His poetry is well-known, and especially valued are the fourteen canons (chants) for Easter, Christmas and the Exaltation of the Holy Cross, which form parts of the Byzantine liturgy. In the East, he is revered as a saint. Feast day October 14 in the Eastern Church.

Costa ben Luca Christian philosopher, born Baalbek, Syria, *c.*864, died Armenia, *c.*923. Also known as Qusta-ibn-Luqa; Constabulus, Constabulinus. He translated Aristotle into Arabic. He is held to have written four chapters on the difference between spirit and soul. *De differentia animae et spiritus* was to be extracts from Plato, Aristotle, Theophrastus and Galen. Costa ben Luca agrees with Galen that the spirit is present in the body, almost as a liquid or gas. But where Galen discusses the functions in human beings in terms of the spirits of the liver, heart and brain, Costa ben Luca leaves out the liver and imposes his own definitions of spirit and soul. The work was translated from Arabic into Latin in the twelfth century; in the thirteenth century it was a required text in the Paris arts curriculum.

Costigan, John Canadian politician, born St Nicholas, Quebec, 1 February 1835, died Ottawa, 29 September 1916. Registrar of deeds and a judge of the Inferior Court of Common Pleas, in 1861 he became a member of the Canadian House of Commons. He lost the seat in 1866, won again the following year, and served until 1905. He held ministerial posts in several Conservative governments, and from 1896 supported the Liberals. In 1907, he became a senator. A spokesperson for Canadian Irish Catholics, he authored the Costigan Resolutions, which favoured Irish home rule; these passed the House of Commons in 1882.

Coton, Pierre Jesuit spiritual writer, born Néronde (Loire), France, 7 March 1564, died Paris, 19 March 1626. After entering the Society of Jesus in 1583, he studied philosophy and theology at Milan, Rome and Lyons. In France, he became famous for his work in defending the Church against the Huguenots. His influence led to the reestablishment of the Jesuits in France in 1603. He later became confessor to **Henry IV**; his influence was resented by Calvinist factions. After Henry's assassination, his position became untenable and in 1617 he left the court. In 1622 he became provincial of Aquitaine, and two years later provincial of Paris. As part of an important circle of writers and thinkers, he was instrumental in the rebirth of spirituality. Among his best known works are the two-volume *Institution catholique* (1610), *Lettre déclaratoire de la doctrine des Pères Jésuites* (1610) and *Méditations sur la vie de Notre Sauveur Jésus Christ* (1614).

Cottam, Thomas Blessed, Jesuit martyr, born 1549, died London, May 1582. He completed his degree at Oxford in 1568. While teaching in London he converted to Catholicism under the influence of Thomas Pound. In 1577 he went to Douai, later attracting other English converts there. He was ordained in 1580, but poor health stopped his being accepted by the Society of Jesus. After spending time in Rome, Lyons and again in Douai, he returned to England. He was arrested at Dover on the basis of information from an English priest-catcher named Sledd. He escaped, but rather than endanger the man who had helped him, Cottam gave himself up. After imprisonment and torture, he was tried and condemned in 1581. He was received into the Society of Jesus before his execution at Tyburn. In 1886, he was beatified. Feast day 4 May.

Cottolengo, Giuseppe Benedetto Saint, born Bra, Kingdom of Sardinia (now Italy), 3 May 1786, died Chieri, 30 April 1842. He was ordained in 1811 and served as a canon in Turin from 1818 to 1827. He became aware of the great need for medical and social services. He founded the hospital known as Piccola Casa della Divina Providenza (the Little House of Divine Providence). This became a massive complex, serving the mentally ill, the aged, those with physical disabilities, penitent women and orphans. It also trained the religious in nursing skills. He founded fourteen religious congregations, including the Brothers and Sisters of St Vincent de Paul (Cottolenghine), the Daughters of Compassion, and the Hermits of the Holy Rosary. This network of caring institutions continued to grow and still thrives. In 1917 Cot-

tolengo was beatified, and in 1934 he was canonized. Feast day 29 April.

Cotton, Emma L. Pentecostal evangelist and healer, born Louisiana, 1877, died Compton CA, 27 December 1952. Cotton emerged from the Azusa Street revival, where she experienced a healing from nasal cancer. In 1916 she held healing services in San Jose, and in the 1930s she founded several independent churches. She co-pastored one with her husband Henry, who was accredited by the Church of God in Christ. In April 1939 she produced one issue of a projected paper, *Message of the 'Apostolic Faith'*.

Cotton, John Puritan clergyman, born Derby, England, 4 December 1585, died Boston, Massachusetts, 23 December 1652. After receiving his MA, he went on to the strongly Puritan Emmanuel College, Cambridge. He was ordained in 1614. He served as a vicar in Boston, Lincolnshire, from 1612 to 1633, becoming more Puritan and less Anglican. After being prosecuted for his nonconformity, he fled to the Massachusetts Bay Colony. He became the highly popular teacher of the First Church of Boston. He held that government should have the ultimate power to ensure conformity; many of his beliefs became law. He wrote a catechism, *Milk for Babes, Drawn out of the Breasts of Both Testaments* (1646), new prayers, and a defence against the clergyman Roger **Williams**. His works on Congregationalism include *The Way of the Churches of Christ in New England* (1645) and *The Way of Congregational Churches Cleared* (1648).

Couderc, Marie Victoire Thérèse Blessed, foundress of the Religious of the Cenacle, born Sablieres (Ardeche), France, 1 February 1805, died Lyons, 26 September 1885. In 1826, taking the name Thérèse, she joined a teaching congregation at Aps. A hostel she started for female pilgrims to the tomb of St John Francis **Regis** soon evolved into the Congregation of the Cenacle, with Thérèse appointed superior in 1828. Here women made retreats following the Spiritual Exercises of St **Ignatius of Loyola**. The Jesuits, who oversaw the institution, strongly shaped the nature of the growing congregation. In 1837 she made her perpetual vows and renounced her own authority. The congregation then went through a period of chaos and mismanagement. Thérèse herself was slighted and humiliated, but bore all this stoically. From 1855 until her death, she again served in positions of responsibility. In 1951 she was beatified. Feast day 26 September.

Coudrin, Pierre Marie Joseph Founder of the Congregation of the Sacred Hearts of Jesus and Mary (Picpus Fathers) and Picpus Sisters, born Soussay-les-Bois (Vienne), France, 1 March 1768, died Paris, 27 March 1837. Because of the anti-clerical climate of revolutionary France, he was ordained secretly in 1792. He would not subscribe to the Civil Constitution of the Clergy, and had to carry out his religious duties covertly through fear of arrest. He and Henriette **Aymer de la Chevalerie** founded a society of missionaries for men in 1792, and five years later another society for women. He set up a number of colleges and was vicar-general of Rouen, Mende, Séez and Troyes. His beatification is under consideration.

Coughlin, Charles Edward Roman Catholic priest and broadcaster, born Hamilton, Ontario, 25 October 1891, died Bloomfield Hills, Michigan, 27 October 1979. Choosing the priesthood over a career in politics, he was ordained in Detroit in 1923. In 1930, while pastor of the Shrine of the Little Flower, he started broadcasting. His radio programmes proved popular, but his early support of Roosevelt soon turned to rabid criticism. His magazine *Social Justice* attacked not only communism but also the financial establishment and the Jews. He became linked with the anti-Semitic, pro-Nazi Christian Front organization; *Social Justice* was distributed at one of their rallies in 1939. In 1942 the magazine was found guilty of violating the Espionage Act. Church authorities then forbade Coughlin to broadcast. In 1966, still at the Shrine of the Little Flower, he retired. Among his books are *Christ or the Red Serpent* (1930) and *The New Deal in Money* (1933).

Coughlin, Mary Samuel Mother, religious superior, educator, born Faribault, Minnesota, 7 April 1868, died Sinsinawa, Wisconsin, 17 October 1959. Sister of the Congregation of the Most Holy Rosary from 1886. She taught until 1901 when she was elected bursar general. She was elected mother

general in 1910. Under her, the congregation thrived and expanded within the USA and abroad. She was involved in research both for the Institutum Divi Thomae, in Cincinnati, and for the Vatican Library in Rome. She helped to draft *Guiding Growth in Christian Social Living*, for the Commission on American Citizenship of the Catholic University of America, Washington, DC. Among the many schools she started were five for black pupils; she also welcomed black women into the congregation. Loyola University, in Chicago, awarded her an honorary degree of doctor of law. From 1935 to 1937, she was the first president of the American Dominican Mothers General Conference.

Coulton, George Gordon Protestant historian, born King's Lynn, England, 15 October 1858, died Cambridge, 4 March 1947. Educated in England and France, he became an Anglican deacon in 1883. He found parish work unsuitable and turned to teaching. After almost thirty years in preparatory schools, he was appointed a lecturer at St John's College, Cambridge, in 1910, and was a fellow from 1919 until his retirement in 1934. From 1940 to 1944 he was a guest lecturer at the University of Toronto. He was an authority on medieval history, with a special interest in social conditions. His work led him to criticize the medieval Church and the monasteries. Notably, he was involved in controversy with the Catholic writer Hilaire **Belloc**. Among his books are *Chaucer and His England* (1908), *Five Centuries of Religion* (1923–50) and *Inquisition and Liberty* (1938).

Couperin, François Born Paris, 8 December 1668, died Paris, 11 September 1733. He came from a large musical family and to distinguish him from the others he is often known as 'Couperin le Grand'. Like his father Charles, he was organist of St Gervais, Paris. He became organist to **Louis XIV** in 1693, and in 1717 composer of chamber music to the king, as well as teacher of the harpsichord to the royal children. He was particularly well known as a harpsichordist, and influenced J. S. **Bach**, but he also wrote church music and organ music including versets for organ designed to accompany the Mass.

Couppé, Louis Missioner in Oceania, born Romorantin, France, 26 August 1850, died Douglas Park, Australia, 20 July 1926. He was ordained in 1874 and six years later joined the Sacred Heart Missionaries. In 1884 he went to Melanesia, establishing the office of mission procurator for his congregation at Sydney, Australia, in 1886. He devoted his life to exploring and studying Oceania and expanding missionary work throughout the vast area. He established schools and ensured that his missions had means for survival by supporting plantations and woodworking shops. He left a robust Catholic community, including over three dozen nuns from the indigenous population. In 1926, he became titular archbishop of Hierapolis.

Courtenay, Peter Bishop, born 1432, died Winchester, 23 September 1492. The Courtenays were a powerful Devonshire family. Peter Courtenay came from the Powderham branch and was related to Richard **Courtenay**, bishop of Norwich (d. 1415). He studied at Oxford and Padua before receiving benefices in rapid succession and being made bishop of Exeter in 1478, where he undertook a number of building projects. Although he initially accepted Richard of Gloucester's usurpation in 1483, he supported the duke of Buckingham's rebellion and joined Henry Tudor in his Breton exile. A flurry of appointments and translation to the See of Winchester in 1487 followed the Tudor victory in 1485.

Courtenay, Richard Bishop, born c.1381, died Harfleur, France, 15 September 1415. He was nephew of archbishop William **Courtenay** and related by marriage to Henry IV. He studied law at Oxford and became its chancellor in 1406. In 1411 his resignation was forced in a dispute with Henry IV over archbishop Thomas **Arundel**, a strong opponent of the Lollards. Courtenay had tried to block Arundel's coming to Oxford, still home to Lollard sympathizers, but the king took Arundel's side. Courtenay, however, was quickly restored. In 1413 he was consecrated bishop of Norwich. He later joined the royal council and became treasurer of the royal household. In 1414 he led a peace mission to France, but its failure only exacerbated a hostile situation. He died in the siege of Harfleur. He is buried in Westminster.

Courtenay, William Archbishop of Canterbury, born near Exeter, Devon, England, 1341 or 1342, died Maidstone, Kent, 31 July 1396. He was the great-grandson of Edward I and uncle of Bishop Richard **Courtenay**. He studied law at Oxford and became chancellor of the university 1367. He was consecrated bishop of Hereford in 1370 and of London in 1375. In 1381 he became archbishop of Canterbury. In the spring of 1382 he called a council – the Blackfriars, or 'Earthquake', Council, in London – that condemned 24 of John **Wycliffe**'s ideas. This led to a convocation in November that saw the crushing of the proponents of Wycliffe's ideas at Oxford. He used the support of **Richard II** against Wycliffe, and this put Courtenay in direct opposition to Wycliffe's protector, John of Gaunt. Courtenay defended the Papacy, but also defended the clergy against both papal and royal control. He was buried in Canterbury Cathedral.

Coussa, Acacius Cardinal, born Aleppo, Syria, 31 August 1897, died Rome, 29 June 1962. A member of the Order of Basilians, he was ordained in 1920. Serving in the Roman curia, he was involved in the Oriental Church. He was adviser to the Congregation for the Oriental Church and on the commission for the revision of the Oriental Code. In 1961 he was consecrated titular bishop of Gerapoli in Syria, and he became prosecretary for the Congregation for the Oriental Church. He became a cardinal in 1962. Among his works are *Epitome praelectionum de iure ecclesiastico orientali* (1921) and *E praelectionibus in librum secundum Codicis iuris canonici – De Personis: de clericis in specie* (1953).

Coussemaker, Edmond Henri de Musicologist, born Bailleul, France, 19 April 1805, died Lille, 10 January 1876. By profession a lawyer and a judge, he composed music and is held to be among the most eminent of French musicologists. His research was in medieval music, and he uncovered new material on Gregorian chant, notation and musical theory, the troubadours, folk music and liturgical drama. He found the Mass of Tournai. In addition to significant legal studies, he published widely on music, including *Drames liturgiques du moyen-âge* (1860), *Scriptorum de musica medii aevi nova series* (1874) and *Histoire de L'harmonie au moyen-âge* (1852, 1865). He held both the French Legion of Honour and the Order of Leopold of Belgium.

Coustant, Pierre French patristic scholar, born Compiègne, France, 30 April 1654, died abbey of St-Germain-des-Prés, near Paris, 18 October 1721. After a Jesuit education, he entered the Benedictine monastery of the Maurist Congregation of Saint-Remi at Rheims in 1671. Ten years later, in Paris, he assisted with an edition of St **Augustine**. His edition of the works of St **Hilary** was published in 1693. His last great work was the editing of the papal letters, from **Clement I** to **Innocent III**. The year 1721 saw the publication of the first volume of *Epistolae Romanorus Pontificum*, covering the years AD 97 to 440. He wrote *Vindiciae Manuscriptorum Codicum* (1706) and *Vindiciae Veterum Codicum* (1715), both in defence of the Maurist editions of the Fathers in response to the Jesuit B. Germon, who had impugned their sources.

Couturier, Paul Irénée Abbé, French ecumenist, born Lyons, 29 July 1881, died there, 24 March 1953. Ordained in 1906, he studied science, and became a member of the staff of the Institut des Chartreux at Lyons. Work with Russian refugees and exposure to the work of Cardinal D. J. **Mercier** led to his involvement with the ecumenical movement. In 1933 he inaugurated a Triduum – three days of prayer for church unity. Two years later this became an octave – eight days of prayer for the unity of all Christians, from 18 to 25 January. (The idea of an octave starting on the first Sunday of January had been initiated in the mid-1800s by the Evangelical Alliance.) The Anglican P. J. Wattson was also instrumental in this. In 1939 this octave became the 'Week of Universal Prayer'. Couturier organized conferences and many tracts were published by the Dombes group, which he formed. In 1952 he was made honorary archimandrite by the patriarch of Antioch.

Couturier, Pierre Marie Alain Pioneer of modern liturgical arts movement, born Montbrison, France, 15 November 1897, died 9 February 1954. In 1919, he studied painting in Paris. There he joined the newly founded Ateliers d'Art Sacré, concentrating on his chosen speciality of stained glass. He was ordained as a Dominican in 1930. He worked on frescoes and stained-glass windows in Dominican houses in Oslo, Paris and Rome. Some works showed the influence of El **Greco**. He was in North America when war broke out and stayed there until 1946, when he returned to his post as co-director of the review *Ars Sacra*. He was also involved in the design and building of several churches. He wrote many articles, and his books include *Art et Catholicisme* (1941) and *Chroniques* (1946), both published in Montreal.

Coux, Charles de Precursor of social Catholicism, born Paris, France, 1787, died Guerande, 16 January 1864. In 1830 he became an editor of *L'Avenir*. He wrote on socio-economics and the exploitation of workers by the industrial system. He himself believed that workers' and masters' associations would be a fairer way to control prices and wages than government regulation. *L'Avenir* was suspended in 1831 and he turned to organizing conferences and publishing his lectures. He gradually became less forceful and after the revolution of 1848 began to withdraw totally from public affairs. He was a major influence on the scholar Antoine **Ozanam**, founder of the Society of St Vincent de Paul.

Covarrubias y Leyva, Diego de Jesuit and jurist, born Toledo, Spain, 25 July 1512, died Madrid, 1577. In 1534 he received a doctorate in canon law from the University of Salamanca, where he became a professor. He also served as a judge, and was named to several bishoprics. His works and opinions became models of legal thought for almost two centuries. He lectured and wrote extensively on the Indies and the question of Spanish colonial practices, largely as an apologist for the Spanish conquest and slavery of the indigenous peoples.

Coverdale, Miles Biblical translator, bishop and Protestant reformer, born York, England, 1487 or 1488, died London, 20 January 1569. In 1514 he became an Augustinian friar. He immersed himself in biblical studies, under the influence of his prior Robert Barnes, who was tried for heresy in 1526. By the late 1520s he was preaching against the Mass, confession, and praying before statues; his views forced him into exile. In 1529, in Hamburg, he helped William **Tyndale** translate the Pentateuch. He then translated the Bible, while based in

Antwerp. In 1539, Coverdale's translation was printed in Paris; under Thomas **Cromwell**'s patronage 2,500 copies were issued in England as the 'Great Bible'. A revised edition, in 1540, carried an introduction by **Cranmer**. After **Henry VIII**'s death, he returned to England and was made bishop of Exeter. With Mary's accession, he went back to the Continent. There, together with John **Knox**, and under the influence of **Calvin**, he oversaw the production of the Geneva, or 'Breeches', Bible. In 1559 he returned to England. He continued to preach and was a leader of the Puritans.

Cowper, William   Poet of the evangelical revival, born Berkhamsted, Hertfordshire, where his father was rector, 15 November 1731, died Dereham, Norfolk, 25 April 1800. He was educated at Westminster School, trained as a lawyer, being called to the bar in 1754, had a nervous breakdown, and retreated to the country. He returned to the law, acting for some years as a commissioner for bankruptcy, but suffered from recurring mental illness – he became convinced he was eternally damned – and retreated again to the country, residing at Huntingdon, near Cambridge, then at Olney. There he came under the influence of John **Newton**, curate of Olney, with whom he became friends. They collaborated in *Olney Hymns* (1779). His hymns, such as *God Moves in a Mysterious Way*, set to the tune *London New*, remain popular. Three years later *Poems* was published, a collection mainly of moral satires. A number of other works appeared subsequently, including the comic ballad *John Gilpin*.

Cram, Ralph Adams   Architect, born Hampton Falls, New Hampshire, 16 December 1863, died Boston, Massachusetts, 22 September 1942. The son of a Unitarian minister, he trained as an architect. In 1888, he became an Anglo-Catholic. He wanted his work to embody spiritual values and was influenced by **Ruskin**'s rejection of the Classical. He embraced the Gothic style as the only form that 'could enhance the reality of the liturgy'. He designed a number of churches and cathedrals, including New York City's cathedral of St John the Divine; and it was he who set Gothic as the style for US college and university buildings. Cram did also work in Classical, Byzantine and American Colonial styles. From 1914 to 1921 he was profes-

sor of architecture at the Massachusetts Institute of Technology. Among his books are *Church Building* (1901), *The Gothic Quest* (1907), *The Catholic Church and Art* (1931).

Crampon, Joseph Theodore   Biblical scholar, born Franvillers, at Corbie (Somme), France, 4 February 1826, died Paris, 16 August 1894. Prior to his ordination he studied Latin, theology and Hebrew. He was ordained in 1850 and for five years was a professor at the minor seminary of St Riquier. He then served as chaplain for the bishop of Amiens and the Holy Family Sisters. He translated the Bible from the original languages. Only the first volume was published in his lifetime; publication of the remaining five volumes was completed in 1904. A one-volume edition with notes was also published that year.

Cranach, Lucas ('The Elder')   Painter, born Cranach, Upper Franconia (now Kronach, Germany), 1472, died Weimar, Saxe-Weimar, 16 October 1553. Born Lucas Müller, he changed his name while in Vienna. He was a strong influence in the Danube School and his work at this time was innovative and emotionally charged. It includes a *Crucifixion* (c.1500), *St Jerome in Penitence* (1502), *St Francis Receiving the Stigmata* (c.1502), and *Rest on the Flight into Egypt* (1504). From 1505, most of his career was spent as court painter at Wittenberg to the Elector Friedrich the Wise of Saxony. Although still fine, his later work lacks power. It is worth noting that he had commissions from both Protestant and Roman Catholic churches. **Luther** was a personal friend and it is through Cranach's portraits that the faces of Luther, his wife and associates are known today. Indeed, he has been called the 'chief pictorial propagandist of the Protestant cause in Germany'.

Cranmer, Thomas   Archbishop, born Aslockton, Nottinghamshire, 2 July 1489, died Oxford, 21 March 1556. A Cambridge theologian who assimilated the ideas of the Continental Reformers and found favour with **Henry VIII** by providing intellectual support for the divorce campaign. On William **Warham**'s death in 1532, Henry rewarded the apparently pliant Cranmer with the archbishopric of Canterbury. In that capacity he annulled not only the Aragon marriage, but also those of

Anne Boleyn and Anne of Cleves. His theological views found expression in the 1549 and 1552 versions of the Book of Common Prayer. At Mary's accession he was found guilty of treason, but his life was spared. After a period in prison, he was again sentenced, was degraded, and signed recantations which he renounced immediately before his execution.

Crashaw, Richard Poet, born London, c.1613, died Loreto, Italy, 1 August 1649. His father was a Puritan clergyman and poet, and Crashaw was baptized by James **Ussher**. He was educated at Charterhouse and Cambridge, where he became a fellow of Peterhouse. While there his piety developed, especially under the influence of Nicholas Ferrar, although he was also much inspired by **Teresa of Avila**, who had fairly recently been canonized. After the sacking of Cambridge by the Parliamentary army he refused to sign the Covenant and was deprived of his fellowship. He went to France, where he became a Roman Catholic and was introduced to Queen Henrietta Maria, who in turn gave him introductions to people of influence in Rome. He first served Cardinal Palotta, and later became a canon of the church of Loretto, Italy. His religious poetry is often regarded as ecstatic and transcendental, but too complicated for modern taste. His chief work is *Steps to the Temple*, published in 1646 just before he left England. A volume of Latin poems had been published in 1634.

Crasset, Jean Jesuit spiritual writer, born Dieppe, France, 13 January 1618, died Paris, 4 January 1692. He entered the Society of Jesus in 1638. He taught and went on to become a renowned preacher. His campaign against Jansenism saw him placed under an interdict for five months when he accused a number of clergy of holding Jansenist views. Prayer and contemplation were prime among his interests. He wrote books for those on retreat that adapted the Jesuit method of prayer for the layperson. He worked with lay groups, including children, the poor and workers. He also wrote religious poetry. Among his works are *Méthode d'oraison avec une nouvelle forme de méditations* (1672); *Vie de Madame Helyot* (1683), containing his own ideas on contemplation; *La Véritable devotion envers la sainte Vierge* (1679); and two books of guidance on retreat, *Le Chrestien en solitude* (1674) and *Le Manne du désert* (1674).

Crathorn, John Dominican scholar and lecturer, fl. Oxford c.1340, died 1360. He lectured on the Bible and the *Sentences* of **Peter Lombard**, the standard theology textbook of its time. His comments prompted the appendage of the *Sex articuli* to **Robert Holcot**'s commentary on the *Sentences*. He tried to reconcile the teachings of **Thomas Aquinas** with empiricism and nominalism. His, however, was an earlier, fundamental nominalism, not that of **William of Ockham**, who argued that theological truth could not be arrived at by means of reason. Crathorn's *Quaestio de universalibus* questioned the arguments not only of Ockham and **Duns Scotus**, but also of Aquinas himself.

Crawley Boevey, Mateo Born Tingo, Peru, 18 November 1875, died Valparaiso, Chile, 4 May 1960. Having been educated by priests of the Congregation of the Sacred Hearts of Jesus and Mary, the Picpus Fathers, he entered their novitiate in 1891 and was ordained seven years later. In 1903 he founded the Catholic University of Valparaiso. He became popularly known as Father Mateo. In 1907 he began the crusade of the Enthronement of the Sacred Heart. **Pius X** instructed him to make the sanctification of the family through dedication to the Sacred Heart his main work. He preached in many countries and held numerous retreats for the clergy. In Italy, at the request of the Papacy, he spoke on Catholic Action. He founded the Tarcisians in 1917. Ten years later he started a movement of night adoration by the laity. His published conferences are included in *Jesus, King of Love* (1933) and *Holy Hour* (1943).

Creagh, Richard Archbishop, born Limerick, Ireland, c.1515, died London, 14 October 1585. He was educated with the aid of a grant from the Emperor **Charles V** at Louvain. He returned to Limerick in 1555, where his zeal and learning attracted David Wolfe, the papal nuncio, who sent him to Rome in 1560 with commendation that he be raised to the See of Armagh. **Pius IV** consecrated him on 17 March 1564, at the same time strengthening the primacy of Armagh. Shipwrecked on his return, Creagh was arrested while offering Mass and sent to the Tower of London in January 1565 but made a dramatic escape into Belgium and thence to Spain. In August 1566 he returned while Shane O'Neill in Ulster, his patron, was at the height of his independence. Creagh was yet again captured in Connaught and sent to Dublin to be tried for treason. Though acquitted by jury he was kept prisoner until he escaped yet again. His freedom was short-lived for he was recaptured in Kildare in 1567 and once more sent to the Tower, where he remained for the next eighteen years. It is alleged that he was poisoned there. Among his writings the more significant are: *De lingua Hibernica*; *Vitae sanctorum Hiberniae*; and a work of apologetics, *De Controversiis de fidei*

Creighton, Edward Businessman and philanthropist, born near Banesville, Belmont County, Ohio, 31 August 1820, died Omaha, Nebraska, 5 November 1874. He surveyed and supervised construction of the telegraph line from Omaha to Salt Lake City. His initial fortune came about when Western Union bought the Pacific Telegraph company in which he had an interest. Prudent investment increased this substantially. During his lifetime he donated much to Catholic charities, and his wife's will carried the request that $200,000 be used to found Creighton College (now University) in Omaha. His work was carried on by his brother John **Creighton**.

Creighton, John Businessman and philanthropist, born Licking County, Ohio, 15 October 1831, died Omaha, Nebraska, 7 February 1907. Brother of Edward **Creighton**, he also had his astute business sense and dedication to Catholic charities. His generosity established the first two US monasteries of the Poor Clares and St Joseph–Creighton Hospital. But most of his philanthropic efforts went toward the development of the university begun with Edward's money – $1 million during his lifetime and a further $1,250,000 in his will. In 1895 he became a Knight of St Gregory and a papal count; in 1904 he was made a 'founder' in the Society of Jesus.

Creighton, Mandell Historian and Anglican bishop, born Carlisle, England, 5 July 1843, died London, 14 January 1901. He was an academic and a clergyman. He was a lecturer and fellow at Merton College, Oxford, where he obtained his degree in 1867. Three years later he was ordained a deacon. After some years as a vicar, he was appointed bishop of Peterborough in 1891 and of London in 1897. He was a gifted administrator, a fine speaker, and took an interest in educational reform. From 1884 to 1890, he held the first Dixie professorship of ecclesiastical history at Cambridge; from 1886 to 1891 he was the first editor of the *English Historical Review*; and from 1894 to 1901 he was the first president of the Church Historical Society. His great work was the highly regarded *History of the Papacy from the Great Schism to the Sack of Rome*, published 1882–94.

Crétin, Joseph Bishop, born Montluel, Ain, France, 10 December 1799, died St Paul, Minnesota, 2 February 1857. He was ordained in 1823, and served as curate, then pastor, until 1838. That year he was invited to go to a new diocese in Dubuque, Iowa. From 1839 to 1850 he was its vicar general. In 1850 he became the bishop of the new diocese of St Paul, a post he held for six years. Crétin was responsible for attracting hundreds of Catholic immigrants. He also invited Benedictine priests; the abbey of St John is now the world's largest Benedictine community.

Crétineau-Joly, Jacques Augustin Marie Journalist and historian, born Fonte-Pay-le-Comte (Vendée), France, 23 September 1803, died Vincennes (Seine), 1 January 1875. After studying for a short time at a seminary and teaching philosophy for an even shorter time, he went to Italy and was secretary to the French ambassador to the Holy See. He was against the French Revolution and became involved with royalist publications. He wrote poetry and many works on French history. His greatest work was the six–volume history of the Jesuits, *Histoire religieuse, politique et littéraire de la Compagnie de Jésus*, published 1844–46. This work is notable in that it had the full cooperation of the superior general of the Jesuits, who granted him access to their archives.

Crichton-Stuart, John Patrick Marquis, scholar and philanthropist, born Island of Bute, Scotland, 12 September 1847, died Commock, Ayrshire, 9 October 1900. He inherited his title in 1848. He converted to Catholicism in 1868 after studying history at Christ Church, Oxford. He became a benefactor of both St Andrews and Glasgow Universities. He owned land in Wales, and supported the development of Welsh vineyards. He also contributed to the port of Cardiff, whose mayor he was from 1890 to 1891. One of his special interests was the history of Scotland, and he was a firm believer in Scottish home rule. He wrote on a range of subjects, but was noted for his liturgical works. In 1879 he published his translation of the Roman Breviary.

Criminali, Antonio Jesuit protomartyr, born Sissa, near Parma, 7 Feburary 1520, died Punnaikayel, India, May 1549. Little is known of his life prior to **Ignatius of Loyola**'s receiving him into the Society of Jesus in April 1542, after which he was sent from Italy to Portugal and ordained priest at Coimbra, 6 January 1544. He sailed to India and reached Goa in 1545, three years after the arrival there of St **Francis Xavier**. There followed a period of intense missionary work in the Jesuit missions along the coast of southern India. Criminali was killed when Portuguese soldiers provoked the local Indians to attack a missionary residence.

Crimmins, John Daniel Philanthropist, born New York City, 8 May 1844, died New York City, 9 November 1917. After studying at St Francis Xavier College, New York City, he joined his father's company as a building contractor. Eventually he took over the business. As the city developed, so did the company and his personal fortune. He became valued as a labour arbiter and was involved in Democratic Party politics. He was commissioner of parks, a presidential elector, and was a delegate to the state constitutional convention. His philanthropic activities supported schools and hospitals and built a Dominican monastery. He was a trustee of St Patrick's Cathedral, to which he donated generously. Irish-American history was a strong interest and he was a member of the Friendly Sons of St Patrick. In 1905 he published *Irish American Historical Miscellany*.

Crisogóno de Jésus Sacramentado Discalced Carmelite writer and lecturer, born Villamorisca, Leon, Spain, died Usúrbil, Gaipuzcoa, 5 March 1945. Born Lawrence Garrachón. He studied in the minor seminary of the Discalced Carmelites at Medina del Campo and was professed in the monastery of Segovia in 1920. He was ordained in 1927, having completed studies in theology and philosophy. He then became professor of philosophy at Avila. He continued his studies in France, where he remained during the Spanish Civil War. He died while conducting a retreat. Although relatively young, he left a substantial body of work, including *San Juan de la Cruz: Su Obra Cientifica y Su Obra Literaria* (1929) and *Compendio de Asetica y Mistica* (1933).

Crispin and Crispinian Martyrs and saints, died *c*.285. Traditionally said to have come from a noble Roman family, they fled to Soissons, where they set up as shoemakers, and took only such money as was offered to them for their work. They are regarded as the patron saints of shoemakers, cobblers and other leather-workers. Another legend suggests (probably wrongly) that they were martyred in Rome, from where their bones were taken to Soissons and elsewhere. Yet another tradition associates them with Faversham in Kent. Feast day 25 October.

Crispin of Viterbo Blessed, Capuchin lay brother, born Viterbo, Italy, 13 November 1668, died Rome, 19 May 1750. Born Pietro Fioretti, he was educated by the Jesuits and worked as a shoemaker until 1693 when he joined the Capuchins, taking the name Brother Crispin. He worked in the kitchen, the garden and the infirmary. He was devoted to Mary Immaculate. He was known for his unfailingly happy disposition and work on behalf of the poor. He was also believed to be capable of miracles, and people on all levels went to him for help. He was beatified in 1806, and the canonization process began in 1923, and is still under way. Feast day 21 May.

Crispina Martyr and saint, died 304. A native of Thagara in Africa, she was a wealthy matron who was arrested during Diocletian's persecution and tried at Thebeste. On refusing to sacrifice to the gods, she was beheaded, probably with other martyrs. She is often mentioned by St Augustine, who preached a panegyric in her honour. Feast day 5 December.

Crispolti, Filippo Journalist and senator, born

Rieti, Italy, 25 May 1857, died Rome, 2 March 1942. He wrote and edited a number of Catholic publications and was an early member of the Italian Catholic movement. In 1919 he became deputy of the Italian Popular Party, a Catholic organization, and three years later was elected a senator. He was a member of the Noble Pontifical Guard and devoted much of his energy to creating links between the Catholic aristocracy and the more middle-class members of the Italian unification movement, the Risorgimento. He remained firmly opposed to the Popularists in the Catholic movement. He wrote poetry and novels, lives of the saints and memoirs. These works include *Il laicato cattolico italiano* (1890), *Questioni vitali* (1908), *Ricordi personali: Pio IX, Leone XIII, Pio X, Benedetto XV* (1932), and *Corone e porpore* (1936).

Croce, Giovanni dalla   Priest and composer, born Chioggia, near Venice, Italy, *c.*1557, died Venice, 15 May 1609. Known as Il Chiozzotto, from his birthplace, he was a leading composer of his day. He became maestro di cappella at St Mark's in Venice, in 1603. Although he wrote much secular music designed for popular entertainment, he is best known for his sacred music. His work is a prime example of the Venetian style as it was shaped during the Renaissance. From 1585 to 1622, his madrigals and canzonets were published in seven books. His sacred music was published from 1591 to 1622.

Croke, Thomas William   Archbishop, born Ballyclough, County Cork, Ireland, January 1823 or 1824, died Thurles, County Tipperary, 22 July 1902. He studied in Paris and Rome, and became a priest in 1847. He taught theology in Paris and may have fought at the barricades in 1848, an early manifestation of his later involvement in radical politics. At the First Vatican Council he was theologian to Bishop Keane of Cloyne. In 1870 he became bishop of Auckland, New Zealand. Upon returning to Ireland in 1875, he became bishop of Cashel and Emly. He was a strong supporter of Irish culture and of home rule. His opinions led to difficulties with the British government, but the support of Dublin's Archbishop Walsh and Westminster's Cardinal **Manning** saved him. Eventually he distanced himself from Parnell's Irish Parliamentary Party and ceased all political involvement.

Cromwell, Oliver   'Lord Protector' of England, born Huntingdon, 25 April 1599, died London, 3 September 1658. he was educated in Huntingdon and then at Sydney Sussex College, Cambridge. He went to London to study law, but returned to Huntingdon to manage his father's estates. He was elected to Parliament for the town in 1628, and in 1640 for Cambridge, after which he was active in the Puritan interest during the 'Long Parliament'. When the Civil War broke out between Royalists and Parliamentarians he raised and trained the 'New Model Army', which he used with devastating effect against the forces loyal to King Charles I and, after the king's defeat and execution, against insurrection in Scotland and Ireland. He dismissed the Long Parliament in the Spring of 1653, and was appointed 'Lord Protector' the following December. He now attempted to impose Puritan practices both on the country as a whole and on the Church of England. He refused the title of King, but was succeeded – briefly – by his son. His body, buried in Westminster Abbey, was disinterred at the restoration of the monarchy in 1660, and buried at Tyburn, London's chief place of execution.

Cromwell, Thomas   Minister of the English Crown, Earl of Essex, 1540, born London, *c.*1485, died London, 28 July 1540. A man of humble origins, Cromwell returned from obscure continental adventures to enjoy the favour of Cardinal **Wolsey**. An MP from 1523, he entered royal service after Wolsey's fall in 1529, supporting Protestant doctrines and royal supremacy over the Church. From 1535 he was the king's principal adviser in ecclesiastical affairs, styled Vicar General and Vice-Gerent in Spirituals. He had been employed by Wolsey in the suppression of small monasteries for financial gain, a pattern writ large between 1536 and 1540 when he supervised the dissolution of all England's monastic houses. He engineered **Henry**'s ill-fated marriage with Anne of Cleves, contributing to his own fall from power. Two months after his ennoblement he was executed for treason.

Crotch, William   Musician, born Norwich, 5 July 1775, died Taunton, Somerset, 29 December 1847. He was an infant musical prodigy, and aged thirteen he was admitted to Christ Church, Oxford, as a theological student. At fourteen his oratorio *The Captivity of Israel* was performed. He became organist of Christ Church, Oxford, professor of music at 22, and principal of London's newly formed Royal Academy of Music. He wrote church music, including hymn tunes, anthems and chants.

Crotus Rhubianus, Johannes Scholar, born Johann Jäger, Dornheim, Thuringia, 1480, died *c.*1545. Of peasant origins, Jäger was educated at the Universities of Erfurt and Cologne, obtaining a doctorate from Bologna in 1517, and adopted the name Crotus Rhubianus in 1509. Between 1510 and 1517 he was headmaster of the abbey school at Fulda. A close associate of the leading German humanists Ulrich von **Hutten** and Johann **Reuchlin**, he was the principal author of *Epistolae obscurum vivorum* (Letters of obscure men, 1515–17), the satire aimed at Reuchlin's Scholastic adversaries. Although he knew **Luther** personally from 1501, he refused to break with the Church and wrote an anti-Lutheran *Apologia* (1531).

Crowley, Patrick Edward Railroad executive, born Cattaraugus, New York, 25 August 1864, died Mount Vernon, New York, 1 October 1953. Over 54 years, he worked his way up from messenger on the Erie Railroad to retire as president of the New York Central. During World War I he served as Federal manager of the government-controlled railroad system. In recognition of his abilities and work for Catholic charities he received honorary degrees from two Catholic universities and became a Knight of Malta.

Crowther, Samuel Adjai (Ajayi) First African Anglican bishop, born Osogun, Yorubaland (Western Nigeria), *c.*1807, died, Lagos, 31 December 1891. Captured as a slave about 1820, and liberated by the Royal Navy in Sierra Leone, he became a Christian, attended the Church Missionary Society (CMS) Fourah Bay Institution and assisted in the study of African languages. He joined the ill-fated Niger expedition of 1841 and went to England for study and ordination. The CMS saw in Crowther the future embodiment of their ideals of a native pastorate and in 1857 he was sent up the Niger with an entirely African staff. In 1864 he was made bishop. Noted for sensitivity in his engagement with Islamic leaders, in the 1880s his authority was undermined by a brash new generation of English missionaries. His *Yoruba Vocabulary* was the first such work by an African native speaker. His other publications included *Journal of an Expedition up the Niger* (1841).

Cruce, Emeric French writer, born *c.*1590, died 1648. He may have been a monk. In 1623 he published a work that argued against the necessity of war and called for a permanent court of arbitration where rulers or their appointees would discuss international disputes, and make decisions based on moral principles. This court would include countries beyond Europe, including those of Africa and Asia. He also advocated free trade and social welfare. The title of this innovative work was *Le Nouveau Cynée ou Discours d'estat représentant les occasions et moyens d'establir une paix générale et la liberté de commerce par tout le monde.*

Cruden, Alexander Presbyterian biblical scholar and publisher, born Aberdeen, 13 May 1699, died Islington, London, 1 November 1770. Prevented by ill-health from entering the Presbyterian ministry, he became a teacher in 1720, and moved to London in 1722, settling there permanently in 1732, opening a book shop in the Royal Exchange. A man of extreme religious views (and occasionally considered sufficiently insane to be incarcerated) he assumed the title of 'Alexander the Corrector' and went through the county reproving Sabbath breaking and profanity. In 1737 he began work on his *Complete Concordance to the Old and New Testaments*, containing over 225,000 biblical references. It was completed in a year, being first published in 1737 with a dedication to Queen Caroline, who died within a month of its publication, thus frustrating Cruden's attempts to win an influential patron. He died at prayer, and was discovered still on his knees.

Cruger, Johann Musician, born Gross-Breesen, near Guben, Prussia, 9 April 1598, died Berlin, 23 February 1662. After leaving the University in the middle of his theology studies, he became the cantor of St Nicholas' Church in Berlin. He also taught at the gymnasium of the Grey Friars until 1662. He worked toward developing congregational singing and was an esteemed musician and tune composer. The Thirty Years' War affected his mental and physical energy and his musical output, but he recovered and went on to compose again. His works include 71 chorales and a number of hymn collections, of which his *Praxis pietatis melica* was valued above all others in its time.

Crumpler, Ambrose Blackman Holiness evangelist, born near Clinton, North Carolina, 1863, died there 1952. A Methodist preacher, Crumpler joined the Holiness Movement in 1890. He set up the North Carolina Holiness Association in 1897 and later, after his departure from Methodism, the Pentecostal Holiness Church. In 1908, when this new denomination came under the influence of Gaston **Cashwell**, Crumpler returned to the Methodists. He claimed never to have sinned following his 1890 experience, and he published a periodical, the *Holiness Advocate*. He also practised law.

Cruz, Gaspar da First Dominican missionary to China, died Setuval, Portugal, 1570. After work in India and Cambodia, he became the first Dominican missionary in China. Although forced to leave, he later wrote his own recollections of China, utilizing the work of Galeotto Pereira, who had been a prisoner there. He died of the plague before he could be named bishop of Malacca.

Cruz, Juan de la Spanish theologian and preacher, died *c*.1567. He was a Dominican known for his great learning, piety and sense of discipline. In 1538 he was sent to Portugal to restore a sense of order. He was a professor and several times served as a prior. Among his works are the three-volume *La Historia de la Iglesia* (1541), *Diálogo sobre la necessidad, obligación y provecho de la oración* (1555), and *Crónica de la Orden de Predicadores* (1567).

Cucchi, Marco Antonio Sixteenth-century Italian canon lawyer. This Paduan professor made his name as the author of *Institutiones iuris canonici* (Pavia, 1565; Venice, 1565) in four books, a work noted for its clarity and for being the first attempt to present the subject in a systematic fashion.

Cuero y Caicedo, José de Bishop and political leader, born Cali, Ecuador, 1734, died Lima, Peru, 5 October 1815. He was well-born and rose quickly in the Church, eventually becoming bishop of

Quito. He was also a member of the Patriotic Society of Friends of the Country and became involved in its struggle for freedom from Spain. He held posts in the revolutionary juntas, that of president of the second one. He sought to involve the clergy in the revolution, even those who supported the king. He fled Quito and was transferred to Lima.

Cuevas, Mariano Jesuit historian, born Mexico City, Mexico, 18 February 1879, died Mexico City, 31 March 1949. He was ordained in 1909 and spent most of his life engaged in historical research and publication. The work was carried out in archives around the world. Unique and best known of his many works, the five-volume *Historia de la iglesia en Mexico* (1921–8) has run to five editions.

Cullen, Paul Cardinal, born Prospect, County Kildare, Ireland, 29 April 1803, died Dublin, 24 October 1878. Ordained in Rome in 1829, he became rector of the Irish College there. He was instrumental in the establishment of a Catholic university in Ireland. In 1850 he was made archbishop of Armagh, and in 1852 of Dublin. He was involved in the national movement of the early 1850s, but soon found himself at odds with the more extreme nationalists. In 1853, he forbade clergy in his archdiocese to participate in politics. In 1866 he was made the first Irish cardinal. During the First Vatican Council he helped frame the doctrine of papal infallibility.

Cullmann, Oscar Lutheran theologian, was born at Strasburg, 25 February 1902, died Chamonix, France, 16 January 1999. He began his academic career as director of the Protestant seminary in Strasburg in 1926, and transferred to the Protestant faculty of theology at the University of Strasburg in 1930, where for eight years he was professor of NT exegesis and of church history. In 1938 he moved to the University of Basel until his retirement in 1972, but he also taught in Paris and in the Waldensian faculty in Rome. He had a close interest in ecumenism, and was an observer at the Second Vatican Council. He produced over 30 books, on the NT and on Johannine studies in particular, and an ecumenically influential work on St Peter. His last book was *Prayer in the New Testament*, published in 1995.

Cummings, Jeremiah Williams Born Washington DC, 15 April 1814, died New York City, 4 January 1866. Ordained in Rome in 1847, he returned to New York as curate of the old St Patrick's Cathedral. The following year he became the first pastor of St Stephen's parish. It soon developed a reputation for the high quality of its services and music. Cummings wrote books and articles. One article in *Brownson's Review* criticized Catholic education and the training of priests. This brought him into conflict with Archbishop Hughes, who responded in print. Cummings contributed to *Appleton's Encyclopedia* and wrote *Italian Legends* (1859), *Songs for Catholic Schools* (1862), and *Spiritual Progress* (1865).

Cummins, George David Evangelical clergyman, bishop, born near Smyrna, Delaware, 11 December 1822, died Lutherville, Maryland, 26 June 1876. Having run a circuit of the Methodist Episcopal Church, he studied to be a minister of the Protestant Episcopal Church and was ordained in 1847. He was assigned to a number of important parishes and proved himself a fine preacher. In 1866 he became assistant bishop of Kentucky. He soon got involved in a controversy within the church concerning ritual. In 1873, after much pressure and soul-searching, he broke away and organized the Reformed Episcopal Church, becoming its first bishop.

Cumont, Franz (-Valéry-Marie) Archaeologist and philologist, born Aalst, Belgium, 3 January 1868, died Brussels, 25 August 1947. Having been a professor at Ghent 1896–1910, and curator at the Brussels Royal Museum 1899–1913, he turned to private research. Discoveries in Syria and Turkey showed connections between the Mithraic cult and Zoroastrian Mazdaism. He also saw Iranian religious influences on Jewish and Graeco-Roman culture. His work on Roman paganism, among other fields, had a great impact on the Protestant theory of the history of religions. His works include *After Life in Roman Paganism* (1922) and *Les Religions orientales dans le paganisme romain* (1929).

Cunialati, Fulgenzio Theologian, born Venice, Italy, 22 February 1685, died Venice, 9 October 1759. His pseudonym was Mariano (degli) Amatori. He joined the Dominicans in 1700 and taught philosophy and theology at Conegliano. In the dispute on probabiliorism, which culminated in a long argument between the Jesuits and the Dominicans, he, as a Dominican, predictably argued in favour of probabiliorism. His great work, presenting moral solutions drawing on the principles of **Thomas Aquinas**, is *Universae theologiae moralis accurata complexio*, published in 1752.

Cunibert of Cologne Bishop and saint, died *c*.663. Brought up at the court of Clotaire II, he was ordained and became archdeacon of the church at Trier. He was appointed bishop of Cologne around 625. An important royal counsellor, he was appointed one of the two guardians of Dagobert I's son, Sigebert, as king of Austrasia. He attended several synods, and promoted the evangelization of the Frisians. Feast day 12 November.

Curci, Carlo Maria Jesuit writer, born Naples, Italy, 2 September 1810, died Careggi (Florence), 19 June 1891. He wanted to preach and teach Hebrew and Scripture, but got caught up in one controversy after another. He rose to the defence of the Jesuits and the Church and the temporal power of the Papacy. His journal *Civiltà Cattolica* became a powerful voice. Following the conflict between Church and State, he began to publicize his opinion that the 'civil hegemony of the Holy See was not a matter of dogma' and that the Pope should give up any territorial claims. In 1877 he was dismissed from the Jesuits and three of his books were placed on the Index. Just before he died he consented to undergo a condemnation of his opinions and was re-admitted to the Society.

Curley, James Astronomer, born Athleague, County Roscommon, Ireland, 26 October 1796, died Georgetown, Washington DC, 24 July 1889. He entered the Jesuits in 1827 and taught mathematics and astronomy at Georgetown. He designed and oversaw the construction of the Georgetown Astronomical Observatory, finished in 1844. Soon after, he accurately calculated the meridian of Washington DC, but this was disputed by government figures and only proven after 1858.

Curley, Michael Joseph Archbishop, born Athlone, County Westmeath, Ireland, 12 October 1879, died Baltimore, Maryland, 16 May 1947. He was ordained in Rome in 1904 and was sent to the USA. In 1914 he became bishop of St Augustine, Florida. The Catholic population and number of churches dramatically increased. Twice he came into conflict with the law, first when the state legislature stated its intention to inspect all convents. In the second clash a law was passed forbidding white women to teach black children. Curley fought and challenged the state to arrest the nuns. The law was declared unconstitutional. In 1921, in Baltimore, he became the country's youngest archbishop. He made Catholic education a priority. He was a strong proponent of lay retreats and Catholic lay organizations. In 1939 he was also made the first archbishop of Washington DC.

Curran, John Joseph Labour arbitrator, born Hawley, Pennsylvania, 20 June 1859, died Wilkes-Barre, Pennsylvania, 7 November 1936. He was ordained in 1887 and worked at several parishes. In the late 1890s his life was changed when he witnessed the plight of the coal miners. He encouraged miners to join the United Mine Workers of America, in an effort to strengthen the union. He went on to become a valued arbitrator in disputes, most notably in the anthracite strike of 1902, when he acted in negotiations with President Roosevelt and the union's leader. His skills led to a successful conclusion.

Currier, Charles Warren Bishop, born St Thomas, West Indies, 22 March 1857, died Baltimore, Maryland, USA, 23 September 1918. He was ordained as a Redemptorist in 1880, in Amsterdam. He went to the USA, but recurring illness led to his being dispensed from his vows as a Redemptorist in 1891. For the next two decades he worked with the Archdiocese of Baltimore, as a pastor, then with the Bureau of Catholic Indian Missions. In 1913 he was made bishop of Matanzas, Cuba. Ill-health forced him to resign in 1915 and he returned to Baltimore. He was appointed to the titular see of Etalonia. He was a respected authority on Spanish-American affairs, and represented the US government at international conferences. His most important work was the *History of Religious Orders* (1894). He also wrote *The Rose of Alhambra*

(1897), *Mission Memories* (1898), and *Lands of the Southern Cross* (1911).

Curtis, Alfred Allen Bishop, born Rehoboth, Delaware, 4 July 1831, died Baltimore, Maryland, 11 July 1908. He was ordained as an Episcopal minister in 1859. In 1872, in England, **Newman** received him into the Catholic Church. He returned to Baltimore and studied at St Mary's Seminary. He was ordained in 1874. His work on the cathedral staff there was impressive, and in 1886 he was made bishop of Wilmington. He was very active and his diocese thrived. It took its toll on his health and he resigned in 1896, and was made titular bishop of Echinus. In 1897 he retired to Baltimore, where he acted as vicar-general for Cardinal **Gibbons**.

Cusack, Thomas Francis Bishop, born New York City, USA, 22 February 1862, died Albany, New York, 12 July 1918. He was ordained in 1885. In 1904 he was made titular bishop of Themiscyra and auxiliary for the Archdiocese of New York. In 1915 he became bishop in Albany. Conversion and missions for Catholics were the focus of his work. He set up offices of Catholic charities and the Society for the Propagation of the Faith. His reputation continued to be high, as shown by a biography published sixteen years after his death entitled *A Short Sketch of the Life of Bishop Cusack: America's Uncanonized Saint.*

Cushing, Richard Cardinal, born Boston, Massachusetts, 24 August 1895, died Boston, 2 November 1970. He was ordained in 1921 and spent his whole career in Boston. After an unpromising pastoral start he worked for the Society for the Propagation of the Faith for twenty years, eventually becoming its director. In 1939 he became auxiliary bishop, and in 1944 archbishop, the youngest in the Church. His tenure was marked by the modernization of his archdiocese and by his commitment to ecumenism, although the latter did not extend to his approval of the underground church movement where Catholics and Protestants worshipped jointly. He was prepared to speak out for what he felt was right. Such a case occurred in 1949 when he was forced to excommunicate a Jesuit who denied that salvation could be found outside the Catholic Church. Although Cushing never came down on the side of contraception, only counselling patience, he made positive comments about Dr John Rock's work in the field. He came to public attention in 1961 at the J. F. **Kennedy** inauguration; just under four years later he officiated at the president's funeral Mass in Washington DC.

Cuspinian, Johannes (Johannes Spiessheimer) Humanist and diplomat, born Schweinfurt, Germany, December 1473, died Vienna, Austria, 19 April 1529. He studied humanist subjects and also medicine, in which he received his doctorate in 1499. He was leader of the humanist circle in Vienna and had his portrait painted by Lucas **Cranach** the Elder. He was also a member of the entourage of the Emperor Maximilian I. As such, he was instrumental in arrangements for meetings between rulers and the marriages of royal children. His great achievement was to find and publish ancient manuscripts. He was distressed by the military actions of the Turks and was instrumental in saving manuscripts from threatened or conquered cities. Among his greatest works, published posthumously, are a history of Roman, Greek and Turkish emperors (1540) and a history of Roman consuls to **Justinian I** (1553).

Cuthbert of Canterbury Archbishop, died 25 October 758. Of noble parentage, he served as abbot of Lyminge, Kent, bishop of Hereford before being appointed archbishop of Canterbury in 740. He was a friend of St **Boniface**, and received letters from him urging him to promote various moral ideals and to discourage women from making solo pilgrimages to Rome. In 747 he called a provincial synod at Clovesho, which passed 30 canons on the duties of the clergy and confirmed various feasts. He established the feast of Boniface as a martyr in 754. He was the first archbishop of Canterbury to be buried in his own cathedral church rather than in St Augustine's Abbey.

Cuthbert of Lindisfarne Bishop and saint, born *c*.636, possibly near Melrose in Scotland, died Farne Island, 20 March 687. A monk at Melrose, he accompanied his abbot, Eata, to Ripon, where they established a monastery. Refusing to conform to Roman practices, the two were expelled and returned north, though they opted to obey the Roman position at the Synod of Whitby in 664. Cuthbert became prior of Melrose in 664, then prior of Lindisfarne. After a time on Farne Island, he was elected bishop of Hexham in 684, and was consecrated bishop of Lindisfarne at Easter 685. His tenure was short but active. He retired again to Farne, where he died. Buried on Lindisfarne, his body was moved several times, before being interred in Durham in 995. A large cult grew up around him. His shrine was destroyed in 1539–40. His tomb was opened in Durham Cathedral in 1827. Feast day 20 March.

Cuthbert of Wearmouth Abbot and student of **Bede**, died *c*.770. He entered the abbey of Jarrow in 718 and was taught by Bede. He became abbot of Wearmouth–Jarrow sometime after 747. He is remembered especially for his letter to his fellow disciple Cuthwine, describing Bede's deathbed scene. He corresponded also with St **Boniface** and with Bishop Lull of Metz, to whom he sent copies of Bede's works.

Cuthburga Anglo-Saxon queen, abbess and saint, died Wimbourne, *c*.725. Daughter of Coenred and sister to King Ine, she was wife of King Aldfrith of Northumberland (died 705). She became a nun at Barking and subsequently founded the nunnery of Wimborne, perhaps with other helpers. Feast day 31 August.

Cyneburg (Kyneburg) Abbess and saint, died Castor, Northants, *c*.680. Daughter of Penda, the pagan king of Mercia, she was wife of Alcfrith, son of Oswy of Northumbria. Possibly on his death in *c*.664, she became abbess of the convent at Castor, Northamptonshire. Along with her sister St Cyneswide and another relative, St Tibia, she was venerated at Peterborough Abbey, to which her relics were taken in the tenth century. Feast day 6 March.

Cynewulf Anglo-Saxon poet, thought to have written around the early ninth century. This name is spelled in runic symbols in the epilogues of four religious poems. *Elene* and *Juliana* are legends of saints. *Elene* is the most highly regarded and tells of St **Helena** finding the true cross. Also attributed to him is the second part of *Christ*; Cynewulf's contribution is the Ascension and is based on a homily by **Gregory I**. *The Fates of the Apostles* is only a fragment and it recounts legends of the apostles after they dispersed. There are other unsigned poems that have been attributed to Cynewulf, but this is debatable. *The Dream of the Rood* had also been attributed to him, but this is no longer thought to be the case. There is no evidence of his identity, though some say he may have been a clergyman because of Latin references within the work. The original dialect appears to have been from northern England.

Cyprian Bishop, martyr and saint, born probably Carthage, *c.*200, died Carthage, 14 September 258. Elected bishop of Carthage in 248, he fled during the Decian persecution, but governed his church by letter from exile. On his return in 251, he dealt strictly with those who had lapsed. He took a high view of the Church as the sole place of salvation, and argued, against Pope **Stephen I**, for the rebaptism of schismatics. Banished under Valerian, he tried to hide, but was eventually caught and put to death. His writings include *On the Unity of the Catholic Church*; a series of ascetical and pastoral treatises; and a highly important collection of practical letters, which constitute a major historical resource. Feast day 16 September in the Roman Missal; 26 September in the Book of Common Prayer, altered to 13 September in the Alternative Service Book and elsewhere.

Cyprian of Toulon Bishop and saint, died by 549. Consecrated bishop of Toulon before 517, he participated in various synods and was a vigorous opponent of so-called 'Semi-Pelagianism' at the Council of Orange in 529. He was himself criticized for holding theopaschite views, a charge on which he defended himself in a still-extant epistle to Maximus of Geneva. He is the main author of a part of a life of his friend **Caesarius of Arles**. Feast day 3 October.

Cyril Saint, born Thessalonica (Saloniki), Greece, 826 or 827, died Rome, Italy, 14 February 869. He is the younger brother of St **Methodius**; together they are 'the apostles of the Slavs'. He was a scholar, linguist and theologian. He was born Constantine, and took the name Cyril when he became a monk. When young he had a reputation as a philosopher. In 860 he was part of a mission to the Khazars. In 862 he went to Moravia, where he taught in the vernacular. In preparation, he devised the Glagolitic alphabet. Copies of the Scriptures were produced in this script. In 867 he returned to Rome, where he saw the new Slavonic liturgy celebrated. He died only 50 days after becoming a monk. He was buried in San Clemente in Rome. Together with Methodius, he was canonized by the Eastern Church soon after his death; Rome followed only in 1880. Feast day 11 May in the Eastern Church; 7 July in the Roman calendar.

Cyril Orthodox patriarch of Bulgaria, born Sofia 1901, died there 7 March 1971. He was consecrated bishop in 1936 and during the German occupation defended the Jews of Sofia. He was elected patriarch, with Communist approval, in 1953, being the first to hold that title since the fourteenth century. He was perhaps the most scholarly of the Orthodox leaders promoted under Communist rule and did much to improve theological education. He wrote on Bulgarian church history, and nine volumes of his sermons have been published.

Cyril Lucaris Patriarch of Constantinople, born Candia, Crete, 13 November 1572, died (strangled) Constantinople, 27 June 1638. He studied theology in Italy but became strongly anti-papal after witnessing the union council of Brest in 1596 (see **Athanasius of Brest**). He was three times appointed patriarch with the help of Protestant ambassadors and in 1629 published his famous *Confession of Faith* which was unequivocally Calvinist in theology. The resulting protests eventually led to his murder by the Turks. His writings were condemned by four separate Orthodox councils.

Cyril of Alexandria Patriarch, theologian and saint, born Alexandria, 375, died Alexandria, 27 June 444. He succeeded his uncle Theophilus as patriarch of Alexandria in 412, despite strong opposition. He prosecuted a vigorous campaign against various pagan, Novatianist and Jewish opponents, and may have been complicit in the murder of Hypatia, a distinguished Neoplatonist philosopher. He is chiefly famous for his fierce opposition to **Nestorius** on the person of Christ, 430–1. A theologian of considerable acumen, his emphasis on Christ's divinity fostered what would become the monophysite view that Christ had only one nature. A gifted writer, he left many letters, homilies and commentaries, and a number of anti-heretical dogmatic tracts. Feast day 9 June in the East; 27 June (formerly 9 February) in the West.

Cyril of Constantinople Prior of Mount Carmel, died c.1234. Very little is known about Cyril aside from his position as prior. He is said to have been a prophet although this is disputed (one prophecy is variously attributed to him as well as to **Cyril of Jerusalem**, and an angelic oracle concerning the procession of the Holy Spirit is supposed to have been given to him while he was saying Mass, and which was applied by Telesphorus of Cosenza to the Western Schism).

Cyril of Jerusalem Bishop and saint, born perhaps Jerusalem, c.315, died there, 18 March 386. Little is known of his early years. Bishop of Jerusalem from c.348, he found himself exiled several times for offending his Arian superior in Caesarea, **Acacius**. His orthodoxy was investigated by **Gregory of Nyssa** in 379, but proved satisfactory. He is famous for a series of *Catechetical Lectures* which were published in his name (though some scholars attribute them to his successor, **John**). They offer a valuable insight into the liturgy of the Palestinian Church, and place a strong emphasis on the Eucharistic real presence and on the efficacy of baptism for the remission of sins. Feast day 18 March.

Cyril of Scythopolis Monk and hagiographer, born Scythopolis (now Beisan in Israel) c.525 of parents who kept a hospice for travelling monks, died after 557 in the great laura of St Sabas. In 543 he became a monk and went to Jerusalem. After a time as an anchorite on the banks of the Jordan, in 544 he attached himself to the monastery of St Euthymius, but in 555 was expelled with a group of monks because of a controversy over the teachings of **Origen**. They joined the 'new laura' in Bethlehem, but two years later he entered the neighbouring community of Sabas. He produced a detailed and popular series of the lives of seven Palestinian abbots, most prominently St **Sabas.**

Cyril of Turov Monk, bishop, died 1182. As a monk, hermit and then bishop of Turov (near Kiev), Cyril was an important figure in early Rus-sian Christianity. He was a biblical scholar known for his allegorical interpretations, his sermons and his devotional writings. Feast day 28 April.

Cyrion Catholicos of Mzcheta, E. Georgia, c.598 – after 609, died there c.610. On his accession, he was in communion with the monophysite Church of Armenia, but in 600 he returned to the Catholic faith. This led to a dispute between the Iberian church and the monophysite Armenian Church from 602, which was further complicated by rivalry in a southern Iberian diocese. In 608/9 he and his church were excommunicated by Abraham, the Armenian catholicos, an event which proved a major root of long-term discord between the two nations.

Cyrus of Panopolis Imperial official, bishop and poet, born Panopolis, Egypt, died, perhaps at Cotyaeum, c.457. He came to the attention of the Empress Eudoxia through his poetry, and was eventually promoted, c.435, to being Prefect of the city of Constantinople and, in 441, to the post of Consul. An extremely efficient administrator, he completed the walls of the city, built a church and oversaw much urban development. Accused of being ambitious for the crown, he was forced into exile as bishop of Cotyaeum in Phrygia. He was, however, also driven from that post, and died as a private landowner.

Czerski, Johann Apostate priest, born Warlubien, East Prussia, 12 May 1815, died Schneidemühl, Germany, 22 December 1893. He was ordained in 1842. In 1844, having been suspended for concubinage, he founded the Christian Apostolic Catholic Community. This group rejected major areas of the Church's teaching, including papal primacy, fasting, celibacy and indulgences and the remission of sins. Czerski offered Communion as two species and the liturgy was in the vernacular. In 1845 he was degraded from the priesthood and formally excommunicated. He went on to co-found the German Catholic movement with Johann **Ronge**. His ideas became more radical, and he eventually rejected Christianity and ended his days as an itinerant preacher for the Religious Society of Free Congregations.

Dablon, Claude Jesuit missionary and pioneer, born Dieppe, France, c.1618, died Quebec, Canada, 3 May 1697. He went to Canada and in 1655 began working among the Iroquois in the area that is now Syracuse, New York. He went on to become Jesuit superior general in New France. He set out to find the 'Northern Sea', in 1661. Together with another Jesuit, Claude **Allouez**, he created the 'Map of the Jesuits', which recorded all the posts the two priests visited on Lake Superior. In 1678 he published a description of Father Jacques **Marquette**'s Mississippi River exploration of 1673.

Dabrowski, Joseph Educator, born Zontance, Russian-held Poland, 27 January 1842, died Detroit, Michigan, USA, 15 February 1903. In 1863 he fought with Polish forces against those of the czar. For the next three years he was a refugee in Europe and the USA. He then went to Rome, where he was ordained in 1869. That same year he immigrated to Wisconsin. His career was devoted to supporting Polish Catholicism and developing Polish education. He established schools, brought in the Felician Sisters to teach and had textbooks printed in Polish. He oversaw the growth of the Felicians and also ensured that there were a number of priests who spoke Polish and English.

Dahlmann, Joseph Jesuit orientalist, born Coblenz, Germany, 14 October 1861, died Tokyo, Japan, 23 June 1930. He studied languages and archaeology, receiving his doctorate in 1902. Then he was sent to China, Japan and India, with a view to the return of the Jesuit missions to Japan. In 1908, he became the first German Jesuit sent to Japan after the founding of the Catholic College, Tokyo, where he served as professor of Indology and German literature from 1913 to 1930. For much of this time he was also a professor at the Imperial Japanese University.

Dahmen, Peter Jesuit missionary, born Renland, near Trier, Germany, 9 March 1880, died Gladbach-Rheydt, 5 December 1935. He entered the Society of Jesus at the age of eighteen and was soon sent to India to be based at the mission in Madura. When he returned to Europe, he spent the remainder of his life writing. Most of these works dealt with aspects of the missions. Indeed, his last, unfinished, work was to be an authoritative biography of the Jesuit missionary Roberto de **Nobili**. In 1924 he had already published *Un Jésuite brahme, Robert de Nobili*.

Dahood, Mitchell J. Biblical scholar, born Anaconda, Montana, USA, 2 February 1922, died Rome, 8 March 1982. He entered the Society of Jesus in 1941 and from 1948 to 1951 he studied Semitic languages at Johns Hopkins. In 1956 he joined the Faculty of Near Eastern Studies of the Pontifical Biblical Institute in Rome as professor of Ugaritic. He also taught Phoenician and the language of ancient Ebla. From 1956 to 1974, he served as director of the antiquities collection. He published extensively and the focus of his work was the reinterpretation of the biblical text in the light of the North-west Semitic languages. He was the author of the three-volume translation and commentary on the Book of Psalms in the Anchor Bible series. He was known for his rigorous scholarship and generous spirit.

Daig Saint and bishop, died 587. Daig mac Cairill is said to have been a pupil of **Finnian of Clonard**. Early legends say he had been a scribe or a metalworker. He was probably not consecrated as a bishop; nor, contrary to legend, was his patron Kieran of Clonmacnois. He is the patron of Iniskeen, on the borders of Louth and Monaghan. Feast day 18 August.

Daillé, Jean Protestant scholar and preacher, born Chatelleraut, France, 6 January 1594, died Charenton, 15 April 1670. He was a protégé of the Protestant leader Phillipe **Du Plessis-Mornay** and later tutor to his grandchildren. After his ordination, he soon gained fame for his views and was moderator of the last national synod of the Reformed Church in 1659. He held that the Church Fathers were no longer relevant. For this he was attacked by both Protestants and Catholics. He also tried to prove that all Christian doctrine is clearly stated in, or can be deduced from, Scripture. A Calvinist, he agreed with Moïse **Amyraut**, who believed in a less extreme predestination by means of a doctrine of conditional grace. Among his works are *Traité de l'employ des saints Pères* (1632) and *Apologie des Églises Réformées* (1633).

Dain, Marie Alphonse Palaeographer and Byzantinist, born Chavignon, France, 3 April 1896, died Paris, 10 July 1964. He was a Christian humanist. After an education thoroughly grounded in the classics, he spent his life as an academic promoting the cause of Greek and Latin. He was dean of the Free Faculty of Letters in Paris and director of the catalogue of Greek manuscripts at the Bibliothèque Nationale. He served as president both of the Société des Etudes Latines and of the Association des Etudes Grecques; and vice president of the Association International des Etudes Byzantines. A fierce patriot, he became a much decorated war hero. Among his works are *Les Manuscrits d'Onasandros*, *Inscriptions grecques de musée du Louvre*, *La Tradition du texte d'Héron de Byzance*, *La Tactique de Nicéphore Ouranos*, *Histoire du texte d'Élien le Tacticien*, *Le 'Corpus perditum'*, *La Collection florentine des tacticiens grecs*, and *Sophocles*.

Dake, Finis Jennings Pentecostal author and pastor, born 1902, died 1987. *Dake's Annotated Bible* (1961–3) is now a favourite Pentecostal Bible.

Dake studied at the Central Bible Institute in the 1920s, following ordination into the Assemblies of God. As a pastor in Zion City, Illinois, he helped to establish Shilo Bible Institute in John **Dowie**'s house. Dake left the AG in 1937 following a jail term for taking a sixteen-year-old girl across state borders. After time with the Church of God, he became an independent evangelist. His many works include *Revelation Expounded* (2nd edn 1950), and *God's Plan for Man* (1949).

Dalberg, Adolf von Prince-abbot of Fulda, born 29 May 1678, died Hammelburg on the Saale, Lower Franconia, 3 November 1737. To renew Fulda as a centre for learning, he established a university. It had faculties of law and medicine and philosophy and theology, the latter formed by combining the Jesuit and Benedictine schools. When the Jesuits were suppressed, control passed to the Benedictines, but following secularization of the monastery in 1802 they too gave up control in 1805.

Dalberg, Johann Friedrich Hugo Nepomuk Eckenbrecht von Clergyman and musician, born Herrnsheim, Germany, 19 May 1752, died Aschaffenburg, 26 July 1812. He completed his religious studies and was canon in three major cathedrals. His interests were wide-ranging, but he eventually focused on musical theory and aesthetics. He composed in a style much like that of **Mozart**, wrote a number of vocal works, and performed as pianist. His writing was influenced by **Rousseau** and the German critic and poet Johann **Herder**.

Dalberg, Johann von Humanist and bishop of Worms, born Oppenheim, Germany, 14 August 1455, died Heidelberg, 27 July 1503. He became chancellor of the University of Heidelberg in 1481 and was appointed to his bishopric the following year. As a diplomat of some ability he carried out a number of missions for the Elector of the Palatinate and Emperor Frederick III. He also had a lifelong interest in classical literature. Because of him both Worms and Heidelberg attracted a variety of humanist scholars. He assembled an invaluable collection of rare books and manuscripts.

Dalberg, Karl Theodor von Archbishop, born Herrnsheim, Germany, 8 February 1744, died

Regensburg, 10 February 1817. He was ordained in 1788 and was consecrated bishop later that year. He went on to be named bishop of Constance in 1800 and archbishop of Mainz and Worms in 1802. That year he also became bishop of Regensburg, which in 1805 became a metropolitan see. That made him elector and archchancellor of the Empire and primate of Germany. In 1806 he became president of the newly declared Confederation of the Rhine; later Napoleon made him grand duke of Frankfurt. A humanist by nature, he had been strongly influenced by Febronianism, a form of German Gallicanism that sought to diminish the power of the Pope, particularly in temporal matters. He tried to mould a national church based on Febronian principles, but the Pope made concordats with individual German rulers, so Dalberg's attempt came to nothing. His period of secular power likewise came to an end with the fall of Napoleon.

Dalberg, Wolfgang von   Elector and archbishop of Mainz, born 1537, died Aschaffenburg, 5 April 1601. He seems to have owed his appointment in 1582, in the heated atmosphere of post-Reformation Germany, to his ability to compromise. He did begin by being so agreeable toward the Protestants as to seem lacking in any will at all. He worked so hard at maintaining a moderate stance that he refused to put into effect the reforms of **Gregory XIII**'s *In coena Domini*. After the Council of Trent and with the growing radicalism of the Reformation, however, he responded to the papal legate's pressure and embarked upon a programme of reform.

Dale, Robert William   Congregational minister, theologian and activist, born Newington Butts, south London, 1 December 1829, died Birmingham, 15 March 1895. After study at Spring Hill College, which he subsequently did much to move to Oxford, he became assistant to Angell James, minister of Carr's Lane Chapel, Birmingham, becoming co-pastor in 1854 and sole pastor from 1859 until his death. A leading force in the urban renewal of Birmingham and its educational provisions in particular, Dale co-operated closely with Joseph Chamberlain and George Dawson, so that 'Dale of Birmingham' became a name to conjure with amongst Nonconformists. Education was too

great a concern to leave entirely to voluntary agencies; only a national system would prove capable of meeting the interests of the nation's young, but one which was not allowed to become a vehicle for the aggrandisement of the established church. He wrote extensively on historical and theological topics, including works on the atonement, the enhancement of deeper understandings of Congregational polity and liturgical practice, and the adoption of conditional immortality. He served as chairman of the Congregational Union in 1869, but withdrew from it in 1888 owing to differences articulated at the autumn assembly by pro-home-rulers, which Dale believed to be secularizing the Union. In 1891 he was first moderator of the International Congregational Council.

Dalgairns, John Dobree   Theologian, born Guernsey, Channel Islands, 21 October 1818, died Burgess Hill, Sussex, UK, 6 April 1876. A follower of **Newman**, he converted to Catholicism in 1845 and was ordained the following year. In 1849 he joined the London Oratory and became its superior in 1863. He became a famous preacher and was a member of the Metaphysical Society. He was a gifted historian and student of philosophy. He was also widely read in the works of the German scientists, allowing him to debate on an equal footing with Thomas Huxley. A chronic striving toward perfection took a terrible toll that resulted in paralysis, mental illness and death. He wrote lives of the English saints for Newman's series. Among his other works are *The Devotion to the Sacred Heart of Jesus* (1853) and *The Holy Communion, its Philosophy, Theology and Practice* (1861).

D'alton, Edward Alfred   Historian, born Lavallyroe, Ballyhaunis, County Mayo, Ireland, 5? November 1859, died Ballinrobe, County Mayo, 25 January 1941. He was ordained in 1887. Although not completing his degree, he sought chairs of history in Cork and Dublin. After several pastoral assignments, he became dean and vicar-general of the Archdiocese of Tuam in 1930. He wrote many works on Irish history. But their initial historical objectivity gave way to partisanship and lack of judgement. He unquestioningly sided with the Young Ireland movement against Cardinal Cullen. His *History of Ireland* was published from

1903 to 1910 and covered the years to 1908; a third edition, published between 1920 and 1925, covered the years up to 1925.

Daly, Malachy Bowes, Sir Politician and philanthropist, born Quebec City, Canada, 6 February 1836, died Halifax, Nova Scotia, 26 April 1920. He became a lawyer and was elected to the Canadian House of Commons in 1878, serving as deputy speaker from 1882 to 1886. In 1890 he began a period of 20 years as lieutenant governor of Nova Scotia. Throughout his life he was an active philanthropist, and was president of the St Vincent de Paul Society of Halifax.

Damasus Hungarian writer and teacher of Roman Catholic canon law, died c.1205. Not much is known of the life of Damasus, except that he taught and worked in Bologna. It has been asserted incorrectly in the past that he was Bohemian or Italian. Some of his known works are: *Brocarda* (Brocardia); *Quaestiones*; *Summa titulorum*; *Apparatus to the constitutions of the fourth Lateran council* (1215); *Glosses on the Decretum of Gratian*; *Apparatus to the first two Compilationes Antiquae, including some of Tantred's glosses*; *Glosses on the tree of consanguity*.

Damasus I Pope and saint, born Rome, c.304, elected 1 October 366, died Rome, 11 December 384. Of Spanish descent. He became a deacon and was ordained priest under Pope **Liberius**, whose successor he became. He was elected by a majority of the Roman clergy, despite violent opposition from a rival, Ursinus, and his supporters. He was a staunch opponent of heresy, especially Arianism; he also did much to consolidate the strength of the Church of Rome, promoting local martyr cults and building churches. In his old age, he commissioned **Jerome** to commence a revision of the Latin Bible, a project which laid the foundations of the Vulgate version. Feast day 4 (formerly 11) December.

Damasus II Pope. Born in Bavaria, and named Poppo, consecrated 17 July 1048, died Palestrina, 9 August the same year. He was bishop of Brixen, in the Tyrol, a see he kept even during his short pontificate. He was part of the entourage of the Emperor **Henry III** during his visit to Italy in 1046, and stayed on to play a part in the Roman synod of 5 January 1047. This may have encouraged Henry to think of him as Pope on the death of **Clement II**, though Poppo appears to have been unenthusiastic. Because of support for the Antipope **Benedict IX**, he was for several months prevented from entering Rome. His choice of name indicates a desire to return to the imagined purity of the early Church, but his ability to impose a programme of reform was never tested.

Damian *see* **Cosmas and Damian**

Damian Bishop and saint, died Pavia, c.4 April 715. Son of a noble family, he became a priest and was present at the Synod of Milan in 680, where he opposed the monothelite theology that in the incarnate Christ there was only one will. He composed a letter in the name of the Synod's bishop, Mansuetus, to the emperor, which was read at the third Council of Constantinople in the same year. Elected bishop of Pavia c.685, he sought to mediate between the Byzantine emperor and the Lombards. He had a reputation for his learning and his sanctity. He visited Constantinople not long before his death. Feast day 12 April.

Damiano de Fulchieri Blessed, died Reggio, 1484. There is no known detailed contemporary record of the life of this Dominican. However, nineteen years after his death at Reggio, there appeared the first manifestations of his cult and the citizens declared him to be one of their patrons. The Dominican Order obtained official confirmation of the cult in 1848. Feast day 26 October.

Damien of Molokai (Joseph de Veuster) Missionary to the Hawaiian leper colony on Molokai, born Tremelo, Belgium, 3 January 1840, died Molokai, 15 April 1889. He joined the Congregation of the Sacred Hearts of Jesus and Mary (Picpus Fathers) in 1859 taking the name of Damien. Arriving in Honolulu in March 1864 he was ordained priest 21 May that year. In 1873 he volunteered to serve the asylum on Molokai Island. Out of a chaos of neglect he brought order, hope and support for the community, and built houses, churches, an orphanage and a hospital. By 1885 he himself had contracted leprosy but continued his ministry with the help of others from his congregation and the Franciscan Sisters of Syracuse. His remains were removed to Louvain in 1936 and he was beatified in 1994.

Dandoy, George Teacher and journalist, born Hemptinne, Belgium, 5 February 1882, died Calcutta, India, 11 June 1962. He was ordained as a Jesuit in 1914, after several years of missionary work in India. In 1922 he started a monthly publication, *Light of the East*. It never reached a circulation over 3,000, but its influence was profound, and the clergy in India began to view the religions and cultures of the East with respect rather than ignorance or arrogance. This insightful magazine ceased publication in 1946. From then until 1962 Dandoy lectured in apologetics at St Xavier's College in Calcutta.

Dandrieu, Jean François Late baroque musician, born Paris, c.1682, died Paris, 17 January 1738. He was a composer and organist. In 1705 he took over the organ at St-Merry; in 1721 he succeeded to the organ of the Chapel Royal. He also took on St-Barthélemy in 1733, where his sister succeeded him on his death. He wrote numerous works, among which are three volumes of harpsichord music, and after his death an album of organ music was published. In 1718 he published *Principes de l'accompagnement du clavecin*.

Daniel, Gabriel Jesuit historian, born Rouen, France, 8 February 1649, died Paris, 23 June 1728. He entered the Society of Jesus in 1667. He taught theology and then became librarian at the Society's house in Paris. He wrote essays attacking Cartesian philosophy (1690), and **Pascal** and the Jansenists (1694). In 1713 he published his greatest work, the three-volume *Histoire de France depuis l'établissement de la monarchie française*. **Louis XIV** made him the country's official historiographer and awarded him a pension. In 1721 he published the two-volume *Histoire de la milice française*. Throughout his career he wrote frequently for the Jesuit *Journal de Trévoux*.

Daniel of Belvedere Friar Minor, martyr and saint, born Calabria, died 10 October 1227. Inspired by the missionary martyrdom of St **Berard** in 1219, five Friars Minor left Tuscany as missionaries to Morocco. Daniel, who became their superior, joined them in Spain. Immediately upon their arrival in the Moroccan city of Ceuta they loudly began to preach Christianity and to denounce Islam. Soon they were captured and brought before the sultan, who ordered them to be held in prison for a week. After that, since they continued their refusals to deny Christianity, they were condemned and beheaded. Their feast day is October 13.

Daniel Palomnik Russian abbot and pilgrim, born (probably) Chernigov, Little Russia, c. mid-eleventh century, died (possibly) Tartu, Estonia, 9 September 1122. What little is known about him comes from internal evidence in his account of his pilgrimage to the Holy Land, the *Pilgrimage of the Abbot Daniel*; he is probably the same Abbot Daniel who was made bishop of Yurev (modern Tartu, Estonia) in 1115. He accompanied King **Baldwin I of Jerusalem** on an expedition against Damascus in either 1106 or 1108, as well as visiting most of the important biblical sites. His account of this pilgrimage also shows the co-operation and mutual respect between Greek and Latin clergy in the Holy Land after the First Crusade.

Daniélou, Jean Jesuit theologian and cardinal, born Neuilly-sur-Seine, France, 14 May 1905, died Paris, 20 May 1974. He became a Jesuit in 1929, and rose to cardinal 40 years later. In 1943 he became a professor at the Institut Catholique in Paris. His life's work was centred on Christianity and culture, and he focused on early Christianity, especially Jewish Christianity, and the Church Fathers, notably **Origen** and **John Chrysostom**. He was a key figure in Ressourcement, the theological renewal movement of the mid-twentieth century. He was an expert at the Second Vatican Council, where he was a consultant in the drafting of *Gaudium et Spes*, the document that redefined the relationship between the Church and the world. He took part in several ecumenical dialogues. Among his works are *Histoire des Doctrines Chrétiennes avant Nicée* (1958–78; ET 1964–7), *Sacramentum Futuri* (1950; ET 1960), and *Prayer: The Mission of the Church*.

Daniel-Rops, Henri Writer and ecclesiastical historian, born Epinal (Vosges), France, 19 January 1901, died Chambary (Savoie), 27 July 1965. He taught history under his family name Petiot. 'Daniel-Rops' was his pseudonym. World War I left him questing and angry. In 1932 he joined the New Order, an intellectual movement that demanded large-scale changes in society. He found his own vehicle for change in his dormant Catholicism, and it permeated his writing. In 1934 his most famous novel was published: *Mort où est ta victoire* (published in English 1946). Essays and a novel followed that stressed the importance of Christianity for the safety of the world. In 1941 he began a series of twelve books on biblical and church history. The first, translated into English in 1949 as *Israel and the Ancient World*, was a sensation. (Under its French title *Le Peuple de la Bible*, it had been seized by the Gestapo when it appeared in 1943.) He continued to write, lecture and edit until his death.

Dannenmeyer, Matthias   Catholic historian born Öpfingen, Württemberg, 13 February 1744, died Vienna, Austria, 8 July 1805. Freiburg made him professor of polemics and church history in 1772. Fourteen years later Emperor Joseph II brought him to the University of Vienna. In 1788 he completed his textbook of church history, *Institutiones historiae ecclesiasticae Novi Testamenti*. It was the standard work in theology schools for ten years. The Church condemned it because of its implicit Josephinism, the reforming principles of Joseph II that were based on Febronianism. Dannenmeyer lost his Vienna post in 1802, but a year later was made curator of the university's library.

Dante Alighieri   Poet, born Florence, Italy, May 1265, died Ravenna, 13 or 14 September 1321. By his mid-teen years, Dante had begun to establish himself as a poet. Early influences included Cavalcanti and Guinizelli. Brought to a spiritual crisis by the untimely death of his childhood beloved, Beatrice, he attended lectures in philosophy and theology, beginning in late 1293. He became active in the political life of Florence, siding with those who challenged the temporal authority of the Church. He was banished from Florence by **Boniface VIII** in 1302 and spent the rest of his life in exile. He remained actively supportive of the sovereign authority of the Emperor, contributing treatises such as the *Monarchia* (1309) to the debate. His works include the *Vita Nuova* (1296), the *Convivio* (1305) and *The Divina Commedia*.

Darboy, Georges   Archbishop of Paris, born Fayl-Billot in Haute-Marne, France, 16 January 1813, died Paris, 24 May 1871. He was ordained in 1836, rising to become archbishop of Paris in 1863. He was a good bishop, but Gallican in spirit. At the First Vatican Council he worked against the definition of papal infallibility, and even tried to have **Napoleon III** stop the discussion. He left Rome the night before the final vote, but once it had passed he acted in accordance with the definition. He refused to leave Paris during the siege of 1870–1, and was arrested. He was executed, probably on the orders of Ferra, who controlled the revolutionary police. As he was shot in the courtyard of La Roquette prison, Darboy blessed his executioners.

Darby, John Nelson   Founder of the 'Exclusive' or Darbyite branch of the Plymouth Brethren. Born London, 18 November 1800, died Bournemouth, 29 April 1882. He was educated at Westminster School and Trinity College, Dublin, and was called to the Irish bar in about 1825. He was ordained an Anglican minister but, uneasy about denominationalism and State–Church associations, left in 1827 to join A. N. **Groves**' newly formed 'Brethren', a group attempting to return to a more scripturally based form of Christianity. The name 'Plymouth Brethren' was given to the group because its centre of activity was for a time in Plymouth, England. Disputes over eschatology and the control of assemblies broke out, and in 1845 Darby formed a breakaway group. He moved to Bristol and there was yet another split, the first of several that were to occur in his lifetime. He travelled widely, settling for some time in Germany and later in France. He visited Canada several times in the 1860s, the USA in the early 1870s, and in 1875 went to New Zealand and then to the West Indies. Darby accepted the main tenets of orthodox Protestantism. He also introduced a new form of thinking called 'dispensationalism', a system of dividing history into the periods (dispensations) of God's dealings with humanity, which is still very influential among Christian fundamentalist churches. Similarly prevalent are forms of his eschatological thinking, usually called pre-millennialism. His early writings include *Nature and Unity of the Church of Christ* (1828), and his later *The Sufferings of Christ* (1858) and *The Righteous-*

ness of God (1859), both of which caused controversy inside and beyond the Brethren. He translated the OT into German and the NT into French, and wrote devotional works and also hymns. His collected writings, edited by W. Kelly, were published in 32 volumes between 1867 and 1883.

D'Arcy, Martin Cyril Jesuit theological philosopher, born Bath, 15 June 1888, died London, 20 November 1976. He was ordained in Rome in 1921. He was master of Campion Hall, Oxford, 1933–45, and provincial of the English Jesuits 1945–50. While at Oxford, he created a significant art collection. D'Arcy followed the example of **Thomas Aquinas** as a model for rational thought. He wrote on moral philosophy, but for an audience wider than theological scholars. In 1956, in *The Mind and Heart of Love*, he defines love as it exists in Christianity. That is, agape, a selfless love, that of God for man. D'Arcy suggests it is to be found in friendship or in the love between two people. His other works include *St Thomas Aquinas* (1930) and *The Nature of Belief* (1931).

Daria *see* **Chrysanthus and Daria.**

Darwin, Charles Robert Naturalist, born Shrewsbury, Shropshire, England, 12 February 1809, died Downe, Kent, 9 April 1882. Although his formal attempts at study were medicine and theology, he abandoned both for his passion: nature. In 1859 his milestone work was published – *On the Origin of Species by Means of Natural Selection, or the Preservation of Favoured Races in the Struggle for Life*. The book seemed to pit science and religion against each other. His later book *The Descent of Man and Selection in Relation to Sex* appeared in 1871, and linked humans to the apes and proposed the theory of sexual selection. Darwin's own religious inclination became increasingly agnostic.

Daudet, Léon Writer and political activist, born Paris, 16 November 1867, died St-Remy-de-Provence, 2 July 1942. Following medical studies at the University of Paris in 1885–91, Daudet embarked upon a prolific political and literary career. With Charles **Maurras**, he founded Action Française in 1908, and spearheaded activity against Jews, Dreyfus, Freemasonry and Members of Parliament.

Pope **Pius XI** condemned Action Française in 1927, but Daudet did not personally submit to this action until 1939. His writings include over one hundred books and many articles, several of which were listed on the Index (*Le Voyage de Shakespeare*, 1927 and *Les Bacchantes*, 1932). Topics covered were medicine, psychology, politics and literary criticism. Daudet's literary style contributed to his popularity as a French pamphleteer.

David I King of Scotland, born *c.*24 May 1080, died Carlisle, 24 May 1153. The sixth son of Malcolm III and **Margaret of Scotland**, he became king in 1124. He continued his mother's policy of establishing Anglo-Norman religious communities in his kingdom. A just and saintly ruler – and something of a collector of monasteries – he founded at least twelve of the major Scottish monastic houses and reorganized six Scottish dioceses.

David, Armand French Lazarist missionary and naturalist, born Espelette (Basses Pyrenées), France, 7 September 1826, died Paris, 10 November 1900. He was ordained in 1862. He was sent to China and spent many years exploring and recording the flora and fauna of that country. In 1865, in northern China, he observed a unique deer, *Elaphurus davidianus*, or, more commonly, Père David's deer. The only specimens now exist in zoos and game parks; there are none in China. In 1872, Père David was admitted to the Academy of Science. His publications include *Voyage en Mongolia* (1875), *Second voyage d'exploration de l'ouest de la Chine* (1876), *Journal de mon troisième voyage d'exploration dans l'Empire chinois* (1875) and *Plantae Davidianae* (1884–6), which catalogued his plant collections. He also contributed numerous learned articles.

David, Franz Born Kolozsvár (Cluj), Romania, *c.*1510, died Deva, 15 November 1579. He became the superintendent of the Hungarian Evangelical (Lutheran) Church in 1557, of the Calvinist Reformed Church in 1564, and of the anti-trinitarian Reformed Church in 1566. As court preacher, he argued for toleration. When the Unitarian Church split in the early 1570s, he led the more extreme faction. He was against praying to Christ and in favour of incorporating Jewish practices.

He was put into prison, and died the same year. He came to be seen and esteemed as the source of Hungarian Unitarianism.

David, John Baptist Mary Missionary and bishop, born Couëron, France, 4 June 1761, died Nazareth, Kentucky, USA, 12 July 1841. He was ordained as a Sulpician in 1785. He fled France in 1791 and sailed to the USA, where he was assigned to Maryland. He then taught philosophy at Georgetown College, in Washington, DC. He was spiritual director of the Sisters of Charity, then went to Kentucky. He was made titular bishop of Mauricastro and coadjutor of Bardstown, Kentucky. Although a candidate for several significant sees, he preferred to serve as confessor and adviser to the bishop of Bardstown, with whom he had come from France. He was an unassuming man who carried out a number of assignments well and with dignity.

David of Augsburg Franciscan mystic, born early thirteenth century, probably at Augsburg, died there, 19 November 1272. A Franciscan at the monastery at Ratisbon (Regensburg), David served as master of novices, for whom he wrote the *Formula Novitiorum* – a highly regarded work at times mistakenly attributed to **Bernard of Clairvaux** or **Bonaventure**. David also wrote treatises in German notable for their fine language and their common-sense yet eloquent spirituality. After 1250 David, together with **Berthold of Regensburg**, made missionary/preaching tours. David also participated in the inquisition against the Waldensians.

David of Dinant Pantheistic philosopher, thought to have died after 1215. Born either at Dinant (Belgium) or Dinan (Brittany), David was a teacher, probably in Paris. His work *Quaternuli* (Little notebooks) was condemned in 1210 at a provincial council and again at the council of 1215, and ordered to be burned 'before Christmas'. None of David's writings survive; he is described by both **Thomas Aquinas** and **Albert the Great**, according to whom he taught that God and intellect and matter are one substance. Details of David's death are unknown; presumably he escaped punishment for his pantheistic teachings by fleeing from France.

David of Himmerod Saint, Cistercian mystic, born Florence, *c.*1100, died Himmerod Eifel, Germany, 11 December 1179. David, after his studies in Paris, entered the monastery of Clairvaux in 1131, but in 1134 went to the abbey of Himmerod in obedience to St **Bernard**. He was renowned for his mysticism and miracles, and was venerated from the time of his death, becoming the patron saint of mothers. His biography was written by Peter of Trier, *c.*1204, emphasizing his inner holiness rather than miracles. Feast day 11 December.

David of Vastmanland (of Munktorp) Monk, missionary, believed bishop, saint, died Munktorp, *c.*1080. David was an English monk who went to Sweden as a missionary. Bishop Sigfrid of Vaxio sent him to Vastmanland, where he founded a monastery at Munktorp. He is thought to have been the first bishop of Vasteras, and to have been a successful missionary, a holy man and a performer of miracles. Feast day 15 July.

David of Wales Bishop, saint (patron saint of Wales). Birth unknown, died 601. According to the tenth-century *Annales Cambriae* he was bishop of Mynyw or Menevia, now St David's. David took part in the Synod of Brefi *c.*560. Much of the written information concerning him is legend. Feast day 1 March.

Davidson, Randall Thomas Anglican archbishop, born Edinburgh, 7 April 1848, died London, 25 May 1930. Following legal and historical studies at Trinity College, Oxford, Davidson was ordained and served in a succession of ecclesiastical positions including resident chaplain to the archbishop of Canterbury, Archibald Tait, dean of Windsor, bishop of Rochester, bishop of Winchester and archbishop of Canterbury, 1903–28. Significant interests and activities included efforts to prevent the negotiation of papal recognition of Anglican Orders, negligible support of the Malines Conversations between Anglicans and Roman Catholics and the revision of the Anglican Prayer Book, ultimately rejected by Parliament in 1927 and 1928.

Davies, (Henry) Walford Musician, born Oswestry, Shropshire, 6 September 1869, died Axbridge, Somerset, 11 March 1941. He was educated at

Windsor and the Royal School of Music, and held various posts as an organist. He became professor of music at University College, Aberystwyth, and later Master of the King's Musick. He helped to edit and compile many hymn-books and his hymn tune for *God Be in My Head* is popular in churches, including Unitarian churches. His best known piece of music is his march written for the RAF.

Davies, William   Venerable, Welsh Roman Catholic priest and martyr, born probably Crois in Yris, Denbighshire, North Wales, died Beaumaris Wales, 27 July 1593. Studied at Rheims, was ordained priest in 1585 and returned to minister in Wales. In 1591 he was arrested at Holyhead and imprisoned in Beaumaris Castle. He was, it seems, able to celebrate Mass and receive visitors who wanted to consult or convert him. He was a popular figure and was moved from prison to prison in an attempt to stem the flow of his popularity and in renewed attempts to get him to convert. He was eventually returned to Beaumaris, where, despite opposition by the populace, he was hanged, drawn and quartered. Feast day 27 July.

Dávila y Padilla, Agustín   Archbishop of Santo Domingo and chronicler, born Mexico City, 1562, died Santo Domingo, 1604. Graduated from the University of Mexico in 1578 and entered the Dominican Order the following year. He held various positions, teaching philosophy, theology and Latin in Mexico and Europe before being appointed chronicler of the Indies in 1589. Noted as an orator, he was preacher to Philip III, who presented him with the archbishopric of Santo Domingo in 1599. He arrived in his see in 1601 and became involved in a controversy concerning the distribution of Lutheran Bibles, in which he tried to protect the indigenous peoples while allowing for the confiscation of the Bibles. He wrote *Historia de la fundación y Discurso de la Provincia de Santiago de México de la Orden de Predicadores*, (Madrid, 1596 and Brussels, 1625).

Davis, Henry   Jesuit moral theologian, born Liverpool, England, 1 December 1866, died Heythrop College, Oxfordshire, 4 January 1952. Educated in St Francis Xavier's College and entered the Jesuit novitiate in 1883. Graduated in classics from Lon-

don University and in 1903 became prefect at Stonyhurst College in Lancashire. From 1911 to 1951 he was professor of moral theology first at St Beuno's College and later at Heythrop, and continued to be involved in Jesuit formation. His major work is *Moral and Pastoral Theology* (London, 1935) in four volumes. He revised **Suárez**'s *De Legibus* in 1944, and his last important work was an edition of St **Gregory** I's *Pastoral Care.*

Dawson, Christopher   Historian, born Hay Castle, Wales, 12 October 1889, died Budleigh Salterton, Devon, 25 May 1970. He was educated at Winchester and Trinity College, Oxford, and shortly afterwards became a Roman Catholic. He was a scholar of independent means – he did not hold a major teaching position until 1930 when he gained a lectureship at the University of Exeter – which gave him leisure to write. His *The Age of the Gods* (1928) argued that religion was at the root of every culture – and much of his other writing can be understood as an examination of how Christianity (by which he really meant Roman Catholicism) was at the root of European civilization. He was a natural choice, therefore, to assist Cardinal **Hinsley**'s Sword of the Spirit during the war years, aided by Barbara **Ward**, and also with Ward to edit the *Dublin Review*. After the war he gave the Gifford Lectures in Edinburgh University, and he was invited to be the first incumbent of the Chauncey Stillman chair of Roman Catholic studies at Harvard, where he lectured from 1958 to 1962. His other works include *Progress and Religion* (1929), *The Making of Europe* (1932), *Religion and the Modern State* (1935) and *Religion and Culture* (1952).

Day, Dorothy   Pacifist, social activist, founder of *The Catholic Worker*. Born in Bath Beach, Brooklyn, NY, 8 November 1897, died Maryhouse, a Catholic settlement house for homeless women in New York City's Lower East Side, 27 November 1980. She did not take up a university place she had won, but worked as a journalist for the *Socialist Call* in New York and lived a bohemian-like existence. The birth of her daughter in March 1926 was a major turning-point in her life. In December 1928, she was baptized into the Catholic Church. In 1933 she met Peter **Maurin** and through his teaching came to see how her faith related to the social order. She opened a house of hospitality for the poor and started *The Catholic Worker*, and the remainder of her life was given over to working towards peace and social justice.

Day, George Bishop of Chichester, England, during the reign of **Henry VIII**, born probably at Newport, Shropshire, 1501, died London, 2 August 1556. After being educated at Cambridge, gaining a DD in 1527, he became chaplain to Bishop **Fisher** of Rochester, master of St John's, and in 1537 vice chancellor of Cambridge. In 1540 Day helped in revising the *Bishops' Book*, which emerged as the *King's Book* in 1543. In the latter year he became bishop of Chichester. In **Edward VI**'s reign he preached against the destruction of altars, was summoned before the council, imprisoned, and deprived of his bishopric. He was released in **Mary**'s reign and restored to his see.

Day, Victor Diocesan administrator, born Desselghem, Belgium, 29 March 1866, died Helena, Montana, 7 November 1946. Educated in Belgium at the college of Saint-Amand, Courtrai, Roulers and Bruges. Ordained in 1891, and spent two years in Bruges before leaving for the Diocese of Helena, where he was to spend the remaining 45 years of his life, serving under five bishops. Four times he acted as administrator of the diocese during periods when the See of Helena was vacant. He also helped to plan and build the cathedral of St Helena. He was made a domestic prelate by **Pius X**. Among Day's published works were his translations of Gottfried **Kurth**'s *The Church at the Turning Points of History* (1918) and *What Are the Middle Ages?* (1921). He also compiled *An Explanation of the Catechism* (1924) and translated Part 2 of Jacques Bénigne **Bossuet**'s *Discourse on Universal History* (1928). He was an occasional contributor to journals and periodicals, and a life member of the American Catholic Historical Association and a member of the Medieval Academy of America.

De Andrea, Miguel Argentinian bishop and sociologist, born Navarro, Buenos Aires, 1877, died Buenos Aires, 1960. He was ordained in Rome in 1899 and held various posts in his native city, including that of rector of the Catholic University. From 1912 until his death he was parish priest of San Miguel. He was consecrated titular bishop of Temnos in 1919, and served as founder and adviser of the Argentine Popular Union and of the House of Working Women. In 1923, following the death of Archbishop Espinosa, the president of Argentina urged the Holy See to appoint De Andrea as his successor, but the Holy See refused to do so. De Andrea was a man of action, who worked ceaselessly to implement the directives of the Roman Catholic social encyclicals. In 1919 he organized a campaign to build low-cost housing developments for workers.

De Bruyne, Donatien Benedictine, Bible textual critic, born Neuve-Église, West Flanders, Belgium, 7 October 1871, died Bruges, Belgium 5 August 1935. After his ordination for the Diocese of Bruges in 1895, he did graduate studies in theology at Louvain in 1895–9, and from 1901 to 1903 taught sacred Scripture in the Grand Seminary at Bruges. He entered the abbey of Maredsous, Belgium, and made his religious profession in 1905. In 1907 he was appointed to the Pontifical Vulgate Commission and the abbey of St Jerome, Rome. From 1921 to 1925, he served as sub-prior of Maredsous and editor of the *Revue Bénédictine*, of which he was co-editor from 1929 until his death. He returned from Rome to Maredsous in 1933, when he began cataloguing the manuscripts of the Grand Seminary at Bruges. De Bruyne's contributions to textual criticism of the Latin versions of the Bible include an extensive investigation and cataloguing of biblical, patristic and liturgical manuscripts; an exhaustive study of the beginnings of the Latin Vulgate in Spain; an edition of the *Vetus Latina* versions of 1 and 2 Maccabees; and a study of the *Vetus Latina* versions of the Canticle of Canticles, Ecclesiasticus, Wisdom, Psalms, Tobias, Esther and Judith.

De Concilio, Januarius Vincent Theologian, author, born Naples, Italy, 6 July 1836, died Jersey City, New Jersey, 22 March 1898. Studied in Naples and Genoa and was ordained for the Diocese of Newark, New Jersey, in 1860. In 1865 he became the first pastor of St Michael's in Jersey City, where he built the church, rectory and school, and constructed an orphanage and academy. In 1892 he was given the degree of doctor of divinity by Georgetown University, Washington, DC. De

Concilio was involved in the causes for Italian emigrants and wrote pamphlets deploring the neglect of Italians in America, as well as frequent articles for the *Freeman's Journal*. Among De Concilio's works were *Catholicity and Pantheism* (1873), *The Knowledge of Mary* (1878), *The Elements of Intellectual Philosophy* (1878), *The Doctrine of St Thomas on the Right of Property and Its Use* (1887), *The Harmony Between Science and Revelation* (1889) and *Child of Mary* (1891). He also wrote two plays, *The Irish Heroine* and *Woman's Rights*.

De Courcy, Henry   Historian, foreign correspondent, born Brest, France, 11 September 1820, died Lawrence, Massachusetts, 14 May 1861. He came to New York in 1845 as the business agent of the Paris glass company of Saint-Gobain. Here he also acted until 1856 as correspondent for the Paris publication *L'Univers* of Louis **Veuillot**. His writings on Catholic affairs in North America influenced French opinion. In America he was best known for his work, translated by John Gilmary Shea in 1856, on *The Catholic Church in the United States: a Sketch of its Ecclesiastical History*. Orestes **Brownson**, a convert and a Yankee, attacked the book. Because much of the writing was polemical, De Courcy, for business reasons, adopted the name C. de Laroche-Heron, and wrote *Les Servantes de Dieu en Canada* (1855); as De Courcy he published *Lettres inédites de J.-M. et F. de La Mennais adressées à Mgr. Bruté, de Rennes, ancien évêque de Vincennes* (1862).

De Hueck Doherty, Catherine   Pioneer of social doctrine of the Roman Catholic Church, born Nijni-Novgorod (present Gorki), Russia, 15 August 1896, died Combermere, Ontario, Canada, 14 December 1985. As a nurse she was decorated for bravery in World War I. After the Russian Revolution, she went to England, where she was received into the Catholic Church. In 1921 she emigrated to Toronto and in the slum area opened Friendship House, which served meals, handed out clothes and ran classes in the social teachings of the Church. After some local opposition she moved to the USA and in 1938 opened Friendship House in Harlem, NY, but problems also arose here, and in 1947 she moved to Ontario, where she established Madonna House. Her writings in

spirituality include *Poustinia*, *Sobornost* and *The People of the Towel and the Water*.

De Koninck, Charles   Philosopher and theologian, born Thourout, Belgium, 29 July 1906; died Rome, 13 February 1965. De Koninck went to Detroit with his parents as a child but returned to Belgium in 1917 to attend the college at Ostend. He entered the Dominican Order but was dispensed from his vows for reasons of health and married Zoe Decruydt in 1933: they had twelve children. He pursued graduate studies at Louvain, receiving his Ph.D. in 1934; subsequently he received the STD from Laval, where he was professor of natural philosophy from 1934 until his death. The American Catholic Philosophical Association awarded him the Cardinal Spellman–Aquinas medal in 1964 for his sometimes controversial efforts to apply Thomistic teaching to the modern world. He was theological assistant to Cardinal Maurice **Roy** at Vatican Council II, the only layman in such a position. He was concerned with the morality of the contraceptive pill and developed a complex but clear argument in favour of its use. De Koninck's principal works are *De la primauté bien commun* (Quebec, 1943), *Ego Sapientia, La sagesse qui est Marie* (Quebec, 1943), *La Piété du Fils, études sur l'Assomption* (Quebec, 1954), *The Hollow Universe* (London, 1960), *Le Scandale de la Médiation* (Paris, 1962).

De la Croix, Charles   Belgian missionary, born Hoorbeke-St-Corneille, Belgium, 28 October 1792, died Ghent, 20 August 1869. Studied at Ghent and took part in the attempt to stop the appointment of a bishop by Napoleon I. He was imprisoned but after the fall of the empire resumed his studies and was ordained priest by the bishop of Louisiana, **Dubourg**, and went with him to the USA. In 1818 he was sent, as a missionary and to look after the building of a seminary, to Barrens, Perry County, Missouri. He went later to St Louis, where he prepared the ground, both physically and spiritually, for the arrival in 1823 of Belgian Jesuit missionaries. He worked in Belgium and in Louisiana before returning to become canon of Ghent Cathedral, where he remained until his death.

De la Ramée   *see* **Ramus, Peter**

De La Taille, Maurice   Jesuit theologian, born Semblançy (Indre-et-Loire), France, 30 November 1872; died Paris, 23 October 1933. After secondary schooling in England under the exiled French Jesuits, he entered the Society of Jesus there in 1890. He studied philosophy at Jersey and theology at Lyons and was ordained at Tours in 1901. From 1905 he taught theology at Angers, and from 1919, at the Gregorian University, Rome. Served as a military chaplain during World War I. His writings include *Mysterium fidei de augustissimo Corporis et Sanguinis Christi sacrificio et sacramento*, and *Elucidationes in tres libros distinctae* (1921 and 1924), *Esquisse du mystére de la foi suivie de quelques éclaircissements* (Paris, 1925), which was translated in 1930 to form, along with further papers written in the intervening years, *The Mystery of Faith and Human Opinion Contrasted and Defined* (London, 1930).

De Lisle, Ambrose Lisle March Phillipps   Philanthropist, writer, born Garendon Park, Leicestershire, England, 17 March 1809, died there 5 March 1878. His friendship with a French priest led to his secret conversion to Catholicism at the age of sixteen. In 1833 he married into the old Catholic family of the Cliffords of Chudleigh. He established the Cistercians in Leicestershire, introduced the Rosminians into the country and initiated a revival in plainchant. Together with George Spencer (who owed his conversion to De Lisle), he founded the Association of Universal Prayer for the Conversion of England and later established the Association for Promoting the Unity of Christendom.

De Luca, Giuseppe   Writer and publisher, born Sasso da Castelda, in the Diocese of Potenza, southern Italy, 13 September 1898, died Rome, 19 March 1962. De Luca entered the seminary at Ferentino in 1909, but two years later went to the Roman Seminary, where he was a contemporary, and friend, of the future cardinals Alfredo **Ottaviani** and Domenico Tardini. He was ordained on 30 October 1921 and became a priest of the Diocese of Rome, where he continued his studies in classics and palaeography. From 1923 to 1948 he was chaplain to an old people's home run by the Little Sisters of the Poor, and for part of that time served as archivist to one of the Vatican departments. He built up an immense library of some 100,000 volumes, and wrote a great deal, though much of it under pseudonyms. In 1943 he established a publishing house, Edizioni di Storia e Letteratura, which specialized in learned monographs in many different languages. His own best known work was the *Archivio Italiano per la storia della pietà*, the first volume of which (there were three) appeared in 1951. A correspondence with the future **John XXIII** began when Roncalli was appointed nuncio in Paris, and the friendship endured until De Luca's death. On 18 February 1962 Pope John received him in private audience and announced his intention of appointing De Luca prefect of the Vatican Library, with the task of bringing together the various curial archives for the benefit of researchers. On 12 March, however, De Luca was taken into hospital: the Pope visited him two days before his death.

De Meester, Marie Louise   Foundress of the Missionary Sisters of St Augustine, born Roulers, Belgium, 8 April 1857, died Heverlee, Belgium, 10 October 1928. She established a novitiate in Belgium in 1908; in 1910 she began missions in the Philippines and the Virgin Islands; and in 1919 set up the congregation's first American house in New York City. This foundation later served as a procuratorial centre for the Caribbean missions. After returning to Belgium in October 1919, she accepted further missions in the Congo and China and directed the construction of a new motherhouse in Heverlee, near the University of Leuven, Belgium.

De Neve, John   Rector, born Evergem, Belgium, 5 July 1821, died Lierre, Belgium, 11 April 1898. He was educated at St Nicholas's College and at the major seminary in Ghent, Belgium. After his ordination in 1847 he was assistant pastor at Renaix and Waerschoot, Belgium, until he left for Detroit, Michigan in October 1856. He became the first resident pastor at Niles, Michigan, where he remained until 1859 when Bishop Peter Paul **Lefèvre** appointed him rector of the American College of Louvain, Belgium. The college flourished under his administration, which, apart from a period of about eight years when he suffered a mental illness, lasted until his retirement in 1891.

De Smet, Pierre Jean Jesuit, founder of Indian missions, born Termonde, Belgium, 30 January 1801, died St Louis, Missouri, 23 May 1873. He went to the USA in 1821, entered the Society of Jesus and was ordained in 1827, being then sent to the mission in Iowa, where he remained until 1839. He visited the Rocky Mountains area and in 1841, with five companions, founded St Mary's Mission near Missoula, Montana, and in 1844 a mission on the Willamette river near St Paul, Oregon. He was recalled to St Louis, and made provincial treasurer and secretary. During the 1850s and 1860s he visited the Great Plains and the Rocky Mountains as an agent of the federal government. In 1864 he alone could enter the camp of Sitting Bull; his last journey West, in 1870, was to establish a mission among the Sioux. His principal published works include *Letters and Sketches* (Philadelphia, 1843), *Oregon Missions and Travels* (New York, 1847), *Western Missions and Missionaries* (New York, 1863), and *New Indian Sketches* (New York, 1865).

De Valera, Eamon Revolutionary, Christian statesman and President of the Irish Republic, born 14 October 1882 in New York of a Spanish father and an Irish mother, from Knockmore in Co. Limerick, who brought him up there after being widowed when Eamon was two years old, died, Dublin, 29 August 1975. He was educated in Cork, at Blackrock College, and at University College Dublin. He taught mathematics and lectured for the Royal University at Loreto, Holy Cross and University Colleges. In 1908 he joined the Gaelic League, Sinn Féin and the Gaelic Athletic Association, all of which with the Irish literary revival heightened national consciousness. During the Easter Rising of 1916 he commanded the 3rd Brigade Irish Volunteers at Boland's Mill and was the last to surrender. His death sentence was commuted to life imprisonment, but he was released in 1917 and shortly afterwards was elected Sinn Féin Member of Parliament for East Clare, a seat he held until 1959. In 1918 he was again imprisoned in Lincoln Gaol but escaped in February 1919 and went to the USA to float the Dáil Eireann External Loan and to secure recognition for an All Ireland Irish Republic. After the Anglo-Irish Treaty De Valera led the anti-treaty republican movement as IRA director of operations in the civil war, pledging unalterable opposition to the partition of

Ireland. He was president of the Free State, 1932–7; taoiseach (prime minister) 1937–48, 1951–4, 1957–9 and president of the Republic of Ireland 1959–73. De Valera was the architect of the new Irish Constitution in December 1937 and for the neutrality of the Free State during the Second World War – or the Emergency as it was known in Ireland. His two major political aims – the restoration of the Irish language and the ending of partition to achieve a 32-county Gaelic republic – appear no nearer fruition than when he first put them forward. His spiritual ideals for Ireland, as the home of a people living the godly life in adequate self-sufficiency in a rural economy, and as a nursery of Christian missionaries, may be left to historians to evaluate. Pope **John XXIII** bestowed on him the Order of Christ.

De Wette, Wilhelm Rationalist Protestant theologian and exegete; born near Weimar, Germany, 12 January 1780, died Basel, 16 June 1849. He received his education at Jena and Weimar, where J. G. von **Herder** and **Griesbach** influenced his future thinking. He taught theology and Scripture at Heidelberg, Berlin and Basel. De Wette's writings include: *Lehrbuch der Einleitung in die Bucher des Alten und Neuen Testaments* (1817); *Lehrbuch der hebr.-jüdied Archaologie* (1814); and *Kurzgefasstes exegetisches Handbuch zum Neuen Testament* (1836–48), which established De Wette's reputation and influence as a scholar.

De Wulf, Maurice Historian of medieval philosophy; born Poperinge, Belgium, 6 April 1867, died Poperinge, 23 December 1947. As a student at the University of Louvain, De Wulf followed the courses given by the future cardinal **Mercier** on the philosophy of St **Thomas Aquinas**, during the years from 1885 to 1891, and was named professor at the Institut Supérieur de Philosophie at Louvain (1893–1939). In 1900, De Wulf published the *Histoire de la philosophie médiévale*, which promoted the Scholastic revival. In 1910 he published a *Histoire de la philosophie en Belgique*. Following his wartime conferences in the USA and Canada, De Wulf held a chair of the history of medieval philosophy at Harvard, which he occupied from 1920 to 1927.

Deane, Henry Archbishop of Canterbury, chancellor of Ireland, died Lambeth Palace 15 February 1503. A canon regular of St Augustine, he was prior of Llanthony, near Gloucester, from 1467 to 1501. He was chancellor of Ireland in 1494, became bishop of Salisbury in 1500 and archbishop of Canterbury in 1501. From 1500 to 1502, he was Keeper of the Great Seal, and he was chief commissioner in the negotiations for the marriage of Princess Margaret and James IV of Scotland, from 1501 to 1502.

Dease, Mary Teresa Missionary nun, member of the Institute of the Blessed Virgin Mary, born Dublin, Ireland, 7 May 1820, died Toronto, Canada, 1 July 1889. In 1847, immediately after her profession, at Rathfarnham, Dublin, she went as a pioneer missionary to Toronto. In 1851 she became superior and accepted responsibility for the first convent of her institute in America. She was superior general until her death, at which time Loreto schools flourished in many cities of Ontario and in Illinois.

Dechamps, Victor Auguste Cardinal, theologian, born in Melle near Ghent, Belgium 6 December 1810, died Mechlin, Belgium, 29 September 1883. He entered the seminary at Tournai in 1832, attended Louvain University and was ordained in 1835, and soon after joined the Redemptorists at Saint-Trondied. In 1836 he became professor of dogma and Scripture at the Redemptorist scholasticate in Wittem until 1840. His main writings include *Entretiens sur la Démonstration de la Foi* (1856); *Lettres Theologiques* (1861); and *La Question Religieuse* (1861). In his religious community he was several times rector, and became provincial superior from 1851 to 1854. He became bishop of Namur in 1865 and two years later bishop of Malines. At Vatican Council I (1869–70), with Cardinal **Manning**, he led the 'Infallibilists', and his apologetic views on revelation and the credibility of the Church were used in the constitution *De Fide*. He was made a cardinal in 1875.

Dechevrens, Antoine Jesuit scholar of Gregorian chant, born near Geneva, Switzerland, 3 November 1840, died Geneva, 17 January 1912. Dechevrens entered the Society of Jesus in 1861 and during his studies was choirmaster in Paris. Later he was appointed professor of philosophy and theology at the Catholic University in Angers. From 1874 onward he pursued the scholarly work on chant begun by Lambillote. He is the author of *Du rhythme dans hymnographie latine* (1895), *Etudes de science musicale* (1898), *Les Vraies mélodies grégoriennes* (1902), *Composition musicale et composition littéraire* (1910), and the posthumous *Les Ornaments dans le chant grégorien* (1913), together with studies on Chinese and Arabian music.

Decius, Philippus (Philippe de Dexio) Professor of canon and civil law, born Milan, Italy, 1454 died Siena, 1536. He taught law in Paris and later in Siena. In 1502 he was auditor of the Roman Rota. While teaching at Siena in 1505, he instigated a meeting of cardinals opposing Pope **Julius II** in favour of King **Louis XII**. He was excommunicated and fled to France, where he taught at Valence. He returned to Italy to reside in Pisa. Important works include the *Commentaria in Decretales*; the *Repetitiones* (Pisa, 1490); and *Consilia* (Lyons, 1565). His writings on the authority of a general council and the Council of Pisa appear in *Goldast's Monarchia S. Romani Imperii* (1614–21).

Deferrari, Roy J. Classics scholar and educator, born at Stoneham, Massachusetts, 1 June 1890, died Washington, DC, 24 August 1969. He received his Ph.D. from Princeton in 1915, and was a faculty member there from 1915 to 1918. After serving in the Army Air Service in World War I, he began his half-century of work at the Catholic University of America. Was professor of Greek and Latin, and chairman of the Committee on Affiliation, which helped thousands of schools. He was awarded thirteen honorary degrees and was created a Knight of St Sylvester. With colleagues and students at CUA he produced a number of indexes and concordances on: **Thomas Aquinas'** *Summa Theologicae* (1956), Luke (1940), Ovid (1939), **Prudentius** (1932), and Statius (1943). He also edited CUA publications, produced Latin textbooks and did many translations.

Deharbe, Joseph Jesuit catechist and theologian, born Strasburg, 1 April, 1800, died Maria-Laach, 8 November 1871. He entered the Society of Jesus in 1817 and, after teaching for eleven years at the Jesuit College in Brieg, Switzerland, became a missionary and catechist. He and Peter Roh, SJ, established the Academy of St Charles Borromeo at Lucerne in 1845. Two years later, when persecution broke out in Switzerland, he barely escaped to Germany alive. The rest of his life was spent chiefly in giving confessions in Germany and in revising his *Katholischer Katechismus oder Lehrbegriff* (Zurich, 1847; Ratisbon, 1848), which won immediate acclaim and in 1853 was introduced officially throughout the whole Kingdom of Bavaria. Within the next fifteen years, it was widely used in Europe and became the catechism most frequently employed in the USA until past the turn of the century, and in some places into the 1930s.

Dehon, Leon Gustave French Roman Catholic priest and founder of the Congregation of the Priests of the Sacred Heart, born La Capelle-en-Thierache, France, 14 March 1843, died Brussels, Belgium, 12 August 1925. He was educated at the Sorbonne, Paris, and was ordained in Rome. He attended the First Vatican Council, returned to France as an assistant priest and founded his Oblates of the Sacred Heart. He took the name Jean du Coeur de Jésus and became his congregation's superior for life. Dehon moved the headquarters to Brussels. Pope **Benedict XV** gave the congregation formal approbation, and now it has houses in many countries.

Deicolus of Lure Saint. Born Leinster, died 18 January *c.*625. Deicolus is one of the famous Irish *peregrini minores*. He accompanied **Columbanus** to Luxeuil in France, and journeyed with him, until ill-health forced him to stop, when Columbanus was expelled in 610. Deicolus built a hermitage in the vale of Orignon, and was eventually joined by others. This became the abbey of Lure. Feast day 18 January.

Deimel, Anton Jesuit orientalist and scholar of Sumerian, born in Olpe, Westphalia, 5 December 1865, died Rome, 7 August 1954. He entered the Society of Jesus in Blijenbeek, Netherlands, in 1888 and pursued his initial cuneiform studies under the guidance of J. N. Strassmaier, from 1904 to 1907. From the founding of the Pontifical Biblical Institute in 1909, he occupied the chair of Assyriology, becoming emeritus in 1941. Deimel wrote numerous books, monographs and articles dealing with Near Eastern and biblical subjects. He did

pioneering work in the publishing and interpretation of Sumerian texts from the early third millennium, especially from Fara: *Die Inschriften von Fara*, 3 vols (Leipzig, 1922–4). He founded the scholarly publication series *Orientalia* (1920) and *Analecta Orientalia* (1931). His chief contribution remains his mammoth *Sumerisches Lexikon*, in four volumes (Rome, 1925–50), the first standard lexicon of significant scope for the Sumerian language.

Dekkers, Eligius (Jan) Benedictine scholar, born Antwerp, 20 June 1915, died Steenbrugge, 15 December 1998. He entered the Benedictine Order on 9 October 1933 in the abbey of Steenbrugge (near Bruges), where he later became abbot and honorary abbot. He was involved in the Flemish movement, published on liturgical history, edited some important texts of **Tertullian** and **Augustine**'s *Enarrationes in Psalmos*, but his main achievement is the founding of the Corpus Christianorum series, which is today, with its *Series Latina*, *Series Graeca*, *Series Apocryphorum* and *Continuatio Medievalis*, probably the most wide-ranging collection of definitive editions of texts.

Del Prado, Norbert Dominican theologian, born Lorio, Asturias, Spain, 4 June 1852, died Fribourg, Switzerland, 13 July 1918. Professed as a Dominican at Ocaña, Spain. He was sent to Manila in 1873, was ordained in 1875, and became professor of humanities and moral theology in 1887. From 1891 until his death he taught moral theology at the University of Fribourg. His principal publications were: *De gratia et libero arbitrio* (3 vols, 1907) and *De veritate fundamentali philosophiae christianae* (1911), which deals with the real distinction between essence and existence.

Del Rio, Martin Antoine Jesuit humanist, jurist and scholar, born Antwerp, Belgium, 17 May 1551, died Louvain, Belgium, 19 October 1608. Studied classics and philosophy at Paris, and law at Douai, Louvain and Salamanca, where he received a doctorate in 1574. He became fluent in nine languages and wrote many books on the classics. Don Juan of Austria, governor of the Spanish Netherlands, took him into his service, aged 28, as vice chancellor and general procurator of the Senate of Brabant. He wrote a legal commentary, *Ex miscellaneorum scriptoribus digestorum, codices et* *institutionum iuris civilis interpretatio* (1580). After the death of his patron in 1578, Del Rio entered the Jesuit novitiate at Valladolid. During the next twenty years he studied at Douai, Liège, Louvain and Graz and wrote commentaries on Scripture, Mariology and polemics. His *Disquisitionum magicarum libri* (1599) had a baneful effect in promoting witch trials.

Delanoue, Jeanne Saint, foundress of the Sisters of St Anne of Providence, born Saumur, France, 18 June 1666, died Saumur, 17 August 1736. Following an early life dedicated to making money she repented and experienced an ecstasy in which her vocation to help the poor was made known. She began this at once, living in incredible austerity. Her home became known as 'the house of providence' and was formally made into a religious house in 1704. She established 'houses of providence' in Brézé and Puy-Notre-Dame, feeding and housing thousands of homeless in a famine winter, by what seemed miraculous means. She was canonized in 1982. Feast day 16 August.

Delany, Selden Peabody Episcopal, then Roman Catholic, pastor and writer, born Fond du Lac, Wisconsin, 24 June 1874, died Highland Mills, NY, 5 July 1935. In 1896 he graduated from Harvard University, where he was converted from Presbyterianism to High Church Episcopalianism. Three years later, after study at Western Theological Seminary, Chicago, he was ordained to the Episcopal ministry. He held various positions until, in 1915, he became curate at the church of St Mary the Virgin, New York City, where he edited the *American Church Monthly*; he was promoted to rector in 1930, but that year he resigned his rectorship and received conditional Roman Catholic baptism at Our Lady of Lourdes Church, New York City. Following study at the Beda College, Rome, he was ordained on 17 March 1934. On his return to New York, he became chaplain at Thevenet Hall, Highland Mills, NY, where he remained until his death. He described the process of his conversion in *Why Rome?* (1930), where he stated that the primacy of the Papacy was the chief obstacle to his conversion. Delany was also the author of *Rome from Within* (1935) and *Married Saints* (1935).

Delehaye, Hippolyte Jesuit scholar and hagiographer, born Antwerp, Belgium, 19 August 1859, died Brussels, 1 April 1941. Studied at Louvain and Innsbruck, became a Jesuit in 1876, joined the Bollandists in 1891, and took charge of the group in 1912. Delehaye was a highly competent, and much respected, historian who applied critical method to the lives of the saints. His publications include *Les Legendes Hagiographiques, Les Origines du Culte des Martyrs, Les Passions des Martyrs et Les Oeuvres Litteraires*. He also assisted in the preparation of catalogues of the hagiographical manuscripts in the Paris Bibliothèque Nationale and in the Vatican.

Delfino *see* **Dolfin.**

Delgado, José Matías Bishop and political leader, born San Salvador, El Salvador, 24 February 1767, died San Salvador 12 November 1832. He was appointed pastor of San Salvador in August 1797, and headed the region's first revolutionary uprising of 5 November 1811. When Mexico tried to annex all of the Central American provinces, only El Salvador protested. When Central America reasserted its independence, Delgado was overwhelmingly elected president of its First National Constituent Assembly. The Diocese of El Salvador was created by political edict in 1824 with Delgado as bishop and became the subject of much controversy between the government and Rome, who instructed Delgado to renounce his office under pain of being branded a schismatic.

D'Elia, Pasquale Jesuit missionary, born Pietra Catella, Campo Basso, 2 April 1890, died Rome, 18 May 1963. Pasquale became a Jesuit in 1904. Following his theological studies at Woodstock College, Maryland, and ordination in 1920, he went to Shanghai, where he taught in Jesuit institutions from 1921 to 1934. He also edited an edition of the Chinese classics and included a European vernacular commentary. From 1934 to 1963, he taught mission studies at the Gregorian University in Rome. His scholarly interests included political conditions and early Jesuit missionary activity in China. His work *History of the Catholic Church in China* (Studia Missionalia, Rome, 1950, 1–68) is recognized as an important contribution to early Jesuit history in China.

Delitzsch, Franz Julius Lutheran exegete, Hebraist and scholar of rabbinical literature: born Leipzig, 23 February 1813, died Leipzig, 4 March 1890. Despite his early poverty, he pursued the study of theology, Hebrew and rabbinical literature. His teaching career began in Rostock in 1846–50, and from there he went to Erlangen, 1850–67, and finally to Leipzig, 1867–90. The great esteem in which Delitzsch was held is evident from the title of 'the venerable' bestowed even during his lifetime. His interest in rabbinical studies and Judaism eventually produced a translation of the NT from the Greek into Hebrew (1877; 12th edition 1901). His commentaries on the Prophets: Isaiah (1872), the Minor Prophets (1880), Ezekiel (1884), Jeremiah (1890), and the Psalms (1880) and Proverbs (1880) established him as the representative of the conservative wing of Protestant exegesis. However, toward the end of his prolific writing career he abandoned some of the conservative tone evident in his previous works and made notable concessions to rationalistic criticism. Besides his commentaries and his masterpiece, *Die Bücher des Neuen Bundes aus dem Griechischen ins Hebräische übersetzt*, by which he intended to promote the conversion of the Jews, Delitzsch wrote a book on Messianism, *Messianische Weissagungen in geschichtlicher Folge* (1890). He was the father of the eminent Assyriologist Friedrich **Delitzsch**.

Delitzsch, Friedrich Orientalist, early Assyriologist, born Erlangen, 3 September 1850; died Langenschwalbach, 19 December 1922. Son of Franz **Delitzsch**, he took his doctorate at Leipzig in 1873, specializing in Sanskrit. He studied Assyriology under E. Schrader in Jena from 1873 to 1874 and taught Assyriology in Leipzig, Breslau and Berlin until 1920. Delitzsch introduced many orientalists to the field of Assyriology. His books for students laid the groundwork for a systematic approach and he wrote numerous scientific treatises on other Semitic languages, Sumerian and oriental geography. His famous lecture on *Babel und Bibel* (1902) launched an attack on the original and inspired character of the OT books, culminating in *Die Lese-und Schreibfehler im Alten Testament* (1920) and especially *Die grosse Täuschung* (1920), in which he claimed that the early history of Israel was a fraud perpetrated on the Jewish people by post-Exilic schools.

Della Chiesa, Bernardino Bishop and vicar apostolic, born Venice, 8 May 1644, died Lin-ch'ing, China, 21 December 1721. He was sent by the Holy See to China to enforce the subjection of all missionaries to the vicars and to terminate the Portuguese and Spanish patronage. He sailed in October 1680 with Basilio **Brollo** and three others, spent two years in Siam, and entered China by Kuang-chou on 27 August 1684. Upon Bishop François Paullu's death on 29 October, he succeeded him as vicar apostolic of Fu-chien vicariate and general administrator of all China missions. Rumours of the division of China into three dioceses under Portuguese patronage made his position uncertain. Finally, in 1700, armed with the bull naming him bishop of the new diocese of Pei-ching, he took possession of his see, made a pastoral visit, and settled at Lin-ch'ing, Shan-tung. In line with the imperial decree of 17 December 1706, he requested and was granted the imperial certificate to remain in China for life, and asked his missionaries to do likewise. His greatest merit was to have established the hierarchical church and to have fostered peace and harmony among missionaries in China under trying circumstances.

Della Robbia, Luca Sculptor, probably born Florence, July 1399/1400, died Florence, 20 February 1482. As a conventional sculptor Luca is best known for his cantoria (singing gallery) for the cathedral in Florence (Florence, Museo dell'Opera del Duomo, 1431–8), soon matched by that of **Donatello**, but the family workshop he headed is famous for the distinctive coloured, glazed terracotta work which it pioneered. Employing a formula which they kept secret, Luca produced the roundels of the Apostles (c.1444) for the Pazzi Chapel, S. Croce, Florence, but those of babies on the façade of the Ospedale degli Innocenti (foundling hospital), were probably by his nephew Andrea (1435–1525).

Della Somaglia, Giulio Maria Cardinal, papal secretary of state, born Piacenza, Italy, 28 July 1744; died Rome, 30 March 1830. Secretary of the Congregation of Indulgences and Relics, 1774, and of the Congregation of Rites, 1784. After being created cardinal in 1795, he suffered imprisonment during the French occupation of Rome. He attended the conclave at Venice in 1800, after which he was sent as legate by **Pius VII** to discuss with the governor of Rome the Pope's arrival in the Eternal City. Della Somaglia was one of thirteen cardinals, out of 27 invited, who refused to attend the wedding of Napoleon I and Archduchess Marie Louise of Austria, because of the manner of the annulment of the Emperor's previous marriage. As a result he and the other cardinals were deprived of their benefices and exiled, Della Somaglia being sent to Mazières and then to Charleville. Upon Napoleon's downfall, Della Somaglia governed Rome in March–June 1815, until the return of Pius VII. He became bishop of Frascati in 1814, secretary of the Holy Office in 1814, and bishop of Ostia and Velletri in 1820. **Leo XII** named him secretary of state, 1823–8, but handled most negotiations himself. Despite the widespread urge for self-determination of peoples, the Pope and his secretary of state strove to maintain royalty in its traditional role and made every effort to restrain republican forces throughout Italy and elsewhere.

Delp, Alfred German Jesuit and martyr, born Mannheim, Germany, 15 September 1907, hanged Plotzensee Prison, 2 February 1945. A Jesuit since 1926, he was ordained in 1937 and served for a time as editor of the Jesuit journal *Stimmen der Zeit*, 1939–41, after which he was put in charge of a parish in Munich. During World War II he belonged to a clandestine anti-Nazi group aiming to create a new Christian society after the war. In the summer of 1944, he was arrested and accused of treason when the group was discovered. In prison, awaiting his execution, he wrote a series of outstanding meditations on the meaning of Advent and Christmas, reflecting on the paradoxical encounter between God, who is love and life, and the world, which is filled with war and death.

Delphina of Signe Blessed, Franciscan tertiary, born Provence, France, 1283 or 1284, died Apt, France, 26 November 1358 or 1360. In 1299 Delphina, daughter of Count William of Glandèves, was married to **Elzéar of Sabran**, with whom she lived in continence. In 1317 Elzéar was summoned to the court of King Robert of Naples, where Delphina formed a life-long friendship with Queen Sanchia. After the death of her husband in 1325, she returned to Provence and lived as a recluse in

absolute poverty, devoting herself to works of mercy. She was buried beside him in Apt. In 1694 **Innocent XII** confirmed her cult, which had been introduced under **Urban V**. Feast day 26 September; in her Order, 9 December.

Deluil-Martiny, Marie de Jésus (Marie Caroline Philoméne) Foundress of the Daughters of the Heart of Jesus, born Marseilles, France, 28 May 1841, died Marseilles, 27 February 1884. Under the guidance of Jean Calage, SJ, she founded in 1873 in Belgium a contemplative congregation of women to make reparation to the Sacred Hearts of Jesus and Mary and to pray for priests, and took the name Marie de Jésus. The institute's constitutions were definitively approved by the Holy See in 1902. She adopted devotion to Mary as 'virgin and priest'. In 1916 the Holy Office published a decree forbidding representations of Mary in priestly vestments; and in 1927 it prohibited the spread of this devotion among the faithful, but permitted the Daughters to practise the devotion within the confines of the congregation. The congregation spread in France, Belgium, Austria, Italy, Switzerland and The Netherlands. Marie was shot to death by an anarchist employed at the mother house. Her cause for beatification was introduced in 1921.

Demetrian of Khytri Monk, bishop, saint, died c.912. Demetrian was born at Sika, Cyprus, the son of a priest. Upon the death of his wife he became a monk at St Anthony's Monastery, later being elected abbot and serving for 40 years. Against his will he was made bishop of Khytri (Cerca) and ruled for 25 years. Once, when Saracens raided Cyprus during his episcopate, he succeeded in persuading them to set their Christian captives free, rather than selling them into slavery. Feast day 6 November.

Demetrius Chomatianus Archbishop and Greek canonist. He occupied the See of Ochrida from 1217 to 1234 and is noted for his letter to (St) **Sava** (Sabas), archbishop of Serbia, which dealt with the jurisdictions of the churches of Ochrida and Ipek in 1220, and the coronation of the despot Theodore Ducas in 1223; and his correspondence with the patriarch of Nicaea, German II, in relation to the consecration of the bishop of Serbia, which Demetrius did not consider canonical. These exchanges of letters are important for the history of Byzantine canon law of the epoch.

Demetrius of Alexandria Bishop. Birth unknown, died Alexandria, 232. Demetrius was ordained bishop of Alexandria in 189, and governed for 43 years. Coptic sources mention his peasant origin. He appointed **Origen** head of the catechetical school in Alexandria, but subsequently condemned him for his (alleged) self-castration after Origen was ordained by extraneous bishops. His act of deposing Origen from the priesthood is usually held to be one of jealousy, although there is evidence that doctrinal matters also contributed.

Demetrius of Rostov Russian Orthodox saint, bishop and writer, born near Kiev, 1651, died Rostov, 28 October 1709. He was appointed metropolitan of Rostov in 1702, one of a number of Kievans promoted to church positions by Tsar Peter I, who approved of their rather 'Westernized' theology. He is chiefly famous for his enormous *Lives of the Saints*, in twelve volumes, which has been very influential in Russia and was the first collection to give a proper place to local saints. He was canonized in 1757 at a time when such events were extremely rare. Feast day 28 October.

Demetrius of Sirmium (or Thessalonika(?)) Soldier, martyr, saint, died 304. Patron saint of Belgrade. Demetrius has many churches in the Balkans dedicated to him. Suffered in the early fourth century under Maximian. Demitrius became especially popular in the East, where he was called the 'Great Martyr'. Feast day 26 October (East); 8 October (West).

Demochares (Antoine de Mouchy) Theologian and canonist, born Ressons, Picardy, 1494, died Paris, 8 May 1574. After having been appointed rector of the University of Paris in 1539, he received a doctorate in theology from the Sorbonne a year later. He then served as professor at the Sorbonne and as canon penitentiary of Noyen with the title of 'inquisitor fidei'. After attending the Council of Trent in 1562 and the Synod of Rheims in 1564, he was sent to investigate the orthodoxy of the university and colleges of Paris. In 1547 he edited the first critical edition of the *Decretum* of **Gratian**.

Dempsey, Bernard William Jesuit economist, born Milwaukee, Wisconsin, 21 January 1903, died there, 23 July 1960. He attended Marquette University, Milwaukee, from 1920 to 1922, entered the Society of Jesus in September 1922, and was ordained 24 June 1936. He received a Ph.D. in economics from Harvard in 1940, and taught economics for the next twelve years at St Louis University. In 1952, Dempsey went to New Delhi, India, as professor of economics at Nirmala College. In 1953 he returned to St Louis, and in 1954 joined the Department of Economics of Marquette University. He wrote about 300 articles on economics. His major interests were the economic implications of the papal encyclicals. Founder and early president of the Catholic Economic Association, he assisted Hiram C. Nicholas in founding the Council of Profit Sharing Industries.

Dempsey, Mary Joseph Franciscan hospital superintendent, born Salamanca, NY, 14 May 1856, died Rochester, Minnesota, 29 March 1939. At Rochester she entered the Third Order Regular of St Francis of the Congregation of Our Lady of Lourdes in 1878. She was teaching in Ohio in 1889 when St Mary's Hospital was opened in Rochester by Mother Alfred. Sister Mary Joseph was assigned to the new hospital, and was soon made head nurse. In 1892 she was appointed superintendent, a post she held until her death. Under her direction, the institution grew into a modern 600-bed hospital. In 1906 she founded St Mary's School of Nursing. In 1915 she participated in the organization of the Catholic Hospital Association of the USA and Canada, serving as its first vice president. Although her activities were chiefly confined to St Mary's, her reputation in medicine was international.

Dempsey, Timothy Roman Catholic priest and founder of charitable institutions, born Cadamstown, Offaly, Ireland, 21 October 1867, died St Louis, Missouri, 6 April 1936. He studied for the priesthood at Mullingar and Carlowe, and on 14 June 1891 he was ordained for the USA. After seven years as a curate in Missouri he was appointed pastor of St Patrick's, St Louis, in 1898, and in 1923 was made a domestic prelate. Early in his career he became active in the rehabilitation of paroled convicts and then in other areas of social work. His personality and sympathy for the unfortunate made him a popular counsellor and aided his success as a peacemaker in industrial disputes and gang wars. He is buried in the 'Exiles' Rest' cemetery, which he had established.

Dempster, Thomas Scottish scholar, born Cliftbog, possibly 23 August c.1579, died Bologna, Italy, 16 September 1625. He studied at Cambridge, Louvain, Rome, Douai and Paris. He held various teaching posts – in humanities at Toulouse, oratory at Nîmes, civil law at Pisa and humanities at Bologna. **Urban VIII** knighted him. Dempster composed Latin poetry. He wrote *Historia Ecclesiastica Gentis Scotorum*, published in Bologna in 1627.

Dengel, Anna Medical missionary, foundress, physician, born Steeg, Austria, 16 March 1892; died Rome, Italy, 17 April 1980. In 1919 she graduated from medical school. After a nine-month residency in Claycross, England, she left for St Catherine's Hospital in Rawalpindi, India. For four years she served as the only doctor to 10,000 sick and dying women and children. She became convinced that numbers of professionally trained women were needed to effect real healing among the people. At the same time she felt called to a religious vocation. An Austrian priest persuaded her to establish a new congregation to respond fully to medical mission needs. In 1924 Dengel travelled to the USA to make her cause known and Michael J. **Curley**, archbishop of Baltimore, gave permission to begin the new foundation. Four women gathered in Washington, DC, on 30 September 1925, to begin the Medical Mission Sisters. The congregation was granted full canonical status on 11 February 1936 when Pope **Pius XI** lifted the ban on sisters being doctors. Superior general of the Medical Mission Sisters from 1925 to 1967, Dengel spearheaded their growth to over 700 members serving in 50 health facilities in 33 countries.

Denifle, Heinrich Seuse Dominican historian of the Middle Ages, born Imst (Tirol), 16 January 1844, died Munich, 10 June 1905. While a student at Brixen, Denifle (baptismal name, Josef Anton) decided to enter the Dominican Order in Graz. From 1870 to 1880 he devoted himself exclusively to his Order's work as a teacher and preacher in Graz. When Pope **Leo XIII** commissioned a new edition of the works of **Thomas Aquinas**, Cardinal **Zigliara**, the chairman of the commission, brought Denifle to Rome as his collaborator in 1880. In 1883 Leo appointed him one of the three assistant papal archivists. This position determined Denifle's subsequent research as a historian. In an effort to make Vatican sources accessible, he cultivated ties with the directors of the various historical institutes in Rome. Upon conclusion of his work on the history of the University of Paris, Denifle returned to Rome in 1899, devoting all his time to visiting Austrian and German archives and libraries to collect material for his work on **Luther**. He died in Munich on his way to Cambridge. Denifle's merit as a historian lies chiefly in his investigation of the history of late medieval thought. His writings include pioneer works on the history of the universities in the Middle Ages. His study on Luther, which presents the Reformer as the product of a decadent age, became his best-known publication and the object of the most violent criticism. Denifle discovered a copy of the hitherto unknown Luther commentary on the Epistle to the Romans, dating from 1515–16.

Denis Patron saint of France, date and place of birth unknown, died Paris, c.250. According to **Gregory of Tours**, in the sixth century, he was one of seven bishops sent to convert Gaul, and was subsequently martyred. Denis was once considered to have been the author of the Pseudo-Dionysian writings. Feast day 9 October.

Denis *see also* **Dionysius**

Denis, Maurice French painter, engraver and writer on art, born Granville, Manche, France, 25 November 1870, died Paris, 13 November 1943. Like his fellow student Pierre Bonnard, he was influenced by Gauguin. They and others joined the Symbolist movement, and later founded the school of Nabism, from a Hebrew word meaning inspiration or prophecy. They revived decorative mural painting. Denis had a highly religious nature. He visited Italy and was inspired by **Giotto** and **Piero della Francesca**. Denis' murals are in many French churches, at Le Vesinat; and the ceiling of the Théâtre Champs Elysées, Paris, and he helped revive religious painting in France. With Georges **Desvallières**, he founded the Studios of Sacred Art.

Denis the Carthusian Theologian and mystical writer, called the Ecstatic Doctor, born Ryckel, Belgium, 1402 or 1403, died Roermond, Holland, 12 March 1471. After leaving the university at Cologne as a master of arts in 1424, in that or the following year he became a Carthusian at Roermond. From 1432 until 1434 he held the office of procurator. **Nicholas of Cusa** insisted upon having him as assistant during his reform visitations in the Rhineland in 1451 and 1452. He was put in charge of a Carthusian foundation at Bois-le-Duc in 1465, but in 1469 resigned because of failing health and returned to Roermond. Denis was a prolific writer, his works filling 42 volumes in quarto, with two index volumes, in the Montreuil–Tournai–Parkminster edition (1896–1935). There are fourteen volumes of commentaries on Scripture, and commentaries on Pseudo-Dionysius, **Peter Lombard**, **Boethius**, and **John Climacus**, and he wrote a compendium of the *Summa Theologiae* of St **Thomas Aquinas**. Among his minor works are 21 treatises aimed at the reformation of the Church and of Christian society. There are also some letters written to princes on this topic, and others about a crusade against the Turks. In consequence of several revelations he had a premonition of the calamities threatening the Christian world if a reformation did not take place in time. Although an eclectic, Denis was no mere compiler. He sifted critically and organized his diverse sources with a powerful analytic and synthetic mind. The many editions of his commentaries and spiritual treatises in the sixteenth century testify to their popularity. SS **Ignatius of Loyola**, **Francis de Sales** and **Alphonsus Liguori** read and quoted him often. Denis was much concerned to lead souls to contemplation. His most important work on the subject is his *De contemplatione*. He thought contemplation in the highest sense to be a negative knowledge of God, by which the soul, inflamed by love, aided by the gift of wisdom and a special illumination, arrives at ecstatic union with God. This negative knowledge of God supposes a positive one, which attributes in an infinite degree to the Creator every perfection found in creation. The positive knowledge of God, through the operation of the gift of wisdom and special illumination,

sometimes becomes 'savoury' (wisdom is 'sapientia', derived from 'sapere', 'to savour') and produces an experience of contact of loving knowledge with God. This experience in itself deserves to be called true mystical contemplation. But the contemplative may progress further, that is, to an awareness that the perfections of creatures, however purified his concept of them may be, fall infinitely short of God's excellence. Therefore, drawn on by illuminating graces, the contemplative turns away from the contemplation of God in the mirror of creation and tries the 'negative way'. He now sees God as not good, not wise, and so on, because these attributes, the concept of which is derived from creatures, are incapable of expressing what God really is. Denis sometimes referred to God as 'superbonissimus, supersapientissimus', i.e. more than supremely good or more than supremely wise. Realizing this, the contemplative prefers to remain in silent adoration before the Inconceivable One, 'smiting with a sharp dart of longing love upon that thick cloud of unknowing' (see the *Cloud of Unknowing*, ch. 6). When the soul's love is sufficiently purified and intensified, it may, by a special grace and for a short time, 'enter and penetrate an inner keep, outside of which knowledge must remain'. No one can understand such things unless he has experienced them. The influence of the Pseudo-Dionysius on the mystical doctrine of Denis is highly significant, as it was also on the older Carthusian authors, **Hugh of Balma** and **Guigo de Ponte**. Denis, however, did not limit himself to a treatment of the sublime. His *Opuscula* deal also with such topics as the devout recitation of the Psalms, meditation, the combating of inconstancy of heart, mortification, the reformation of the inner man, progress, the custody of the heart.

Denomy, Alexander Joseph Canadian medievalist, born Chatham, Ontario, Canada, 21 June, 1904, died North Scituate, Massachusetts, 19 July 1957. Educated at Assumption College, Windsor, Ontario, Canada, he entered the Congregation of Priests of St Basil at Toronto, and was ordained on 30 June 1928. After advanced studies at the University of Toronto (MA, 1928), and Harvard University (Ph.D., 1934), he was appointed in 1935 professor of the history of comparative literature at the Pontifical Institute of Mediaeval Studies,

Toronto, and taught there until his death. He twice received a Guggenheim fellowship for research in European libraries, and was fellow of the Royal Society of Canada and corresponding fellow of the Medieval Academy of America. Among his publications are *The Old French Lives of St Agnes* (1938). He was editor of volumes 6 to 18 of *Medieval Studies* (1945–56).

Dens, Pierre   Theologian, born near Antwerp, 12 September 1690, died Malines, 15 February 1775. He studied at the Malines Oratory and at Louvain, was ordained in 1715 and was sent to teach theology to the monks of Affligem Abbey. In 1773 he took his licentiate in theology and began to teach at the Malines seminary, where he was president from 1735 until his death. He served also as a pastor from 1729 until he was appointed a canon and cathedral lecturer in theology in 1737. He became archpriest of the Malines canons in 1754. He devoted his Sundays to explaining the catechism to working people, and supported a school for poor girls. The fourteen-volume work that made his name well-known, *Theologia ad usum seminariorum et sacrae theologiae alumnorum*, was published after his death. He shaped the material into clear and precise questions and answers, following generally the order of the *Summa Theologiae* of St **Thomas Aquinas**, but passing quickly over speculative matters and lingering on those he deemed practical.

Denzinger, Heinrich Joseph   Theologian, born Liège, Belgium, 10 October 1819, died Würzburg, Germany, 19 June 1883. Ordained in 1844, he began teaching theology at Würzburg in 1848. He contributed to the renewal of sacred science in the nineteenth century by his many theological works of a positive-historical orientation. Chief among them were: *Vier Bücher von der religiösen Erkenntnis* (Würzburg, 1856–7) and *Ritus Orientalum, Coptorum, Syrorum et Armenorum* (Würzburg, 1863–4). His best-known work, used by all theologians, is the *Enchiridion Symbolorum et Definitionum*. First published at Würzburg in 1854, it has appeared in at least 35 editions.

Deochar (Theoker, Dietker, Gottlieb)   Saint, Benedictine abbot, died Herrieden, c.832. Deochar, a monk at Fulda, then a follower of **Alcuin** at Charlemagne's court, became the first abbot of the monastery at Haserode (Herrieden) in Franconia which Charlemagne built, c.795. David was 'missus—Regis' in Regensburg, was the first of the signatories to the synod of Mainz, and died at a very old age. Feast day 7 June.

Deodatus of Nevers   Saint, bishop, date and place of birth unknown, died St Dié, 18 June 679. Deodatus is the founder of the monastery of Jointures. He obtained land for the monastery from King Childeric, also obtaining exemption from the jurisdiction of the bishop of Toul. Both the monastery and the town that grew around it (St Dié) bear his name. His 'life' written in 1048 contains some extra legendary material. Feast day 19 June.

Descamps, Albert-Louis   Biblical scholar, theologian, bishop; born Escanaffles, Belgium, 27 June 1916, died Ottignies, Belgium, 15 October 1980. He entered the diocesan minor seminary, 1933–4, and studied philosophy at the Catholic University of Louvain, 1934–7; the study of theology at Tournai was interrupted by military service when he served as a stretcher-bearer. He was ordained a priest on 5 October 1940, and returned to Louvain to pursue graduate studies in theology and obtained the STD in 1945. He then moved on to teach in the Pontifical Biblical Institute in Rome, 1946–7, and at Tournai, obtained the Louvain degree of Sacrae Theologiae Magister in 1950, and in 1956 became professor of NT studies at Louvain. His academic career was interrupted by his nomination as auxiliary bishop of Tournai in 1960 and rector of the Catholic University of Louvain in 1962, where he had the difficult task of presiding over a rapidly growing university and the division of the university into two autonomous institutions, the French Université Catholique de Louvain and the Flemish Universiteit Katholieke te Leuven during the political upheavals of the time. In 1968, Descamps accepted the title of honorary rector and resumed his academic career at Louvain-la-neuve. He was appointed secretary of the reorganized Pontifical Biblical Commission by **Paul VI** in 1974 and continued to hold that position until his death in a car accident.

Descartes, René   Philosopher, mathematician and scientist who could lay claim to be the founder of modern philosophy, born La Haye, in Touraine, 31 March 1596, died Stockholm, 11 February 1650. He was educated from the age of eight by the Jesuits at the College Royal in La Flèche in Anjou: it was said by his critics, especially Thomas Hobbes, that he wrote his defence of transubstantiation 'which he knew to be against his reason' in deference to his Jesuit teachers, and he suppressed his *Le Traité du Monde*, which maintained the two then 'heretical' doctrines: the rotation of the earth and the infinity of the universe. Of his devotion to the Church there is no doubt; he remained sincere and loyal to the end of his days. He spent brief periods in the Universities of Paris and Poitiers. He became a soldier of fortune in the Dutch and Bavarian armies, travelling widely in Europe between 1620 and 1628. He was present at the siege of La Rochelle. From 1629 to 1649 he lived in Holland; in 1649 he went as tutor to Queen **Christina of Sweden**, a patroness of scholars, but the Scandinavian winters proved too much for him. He was the first philosopher since Aristotle not to accept the current systems and foundations laid by his predecessors in his attempt to complete a philosophic edifice de novo. His teachings were accepted by the Académie des Sciences on its foundation in 1666 and his followers were legion; the Jesuits were at first favourable to his philosophy, but their later opposition led to the suppression of Cartesianism in 1663. In character he was vain and never showed a trace of doubt regarding the strength of his own position; he sneered at **Galileo**'s work and complained that **Pascal** 'has too much vacuum in his head'. Mathematics was his greatest strength; and in physics his greatest contribution was in the field of optics: in both he prepared the way for the discoveries of **Newton** and **Leibniz**. In his famous *Discours de la Méthode pour bien conduire sa raison et chercher la vérité dans les sciences* (1637) his proofs of the existence of God are derived from SS **Augustine** and **Anselm of Canterbury**. His greatest achievement must be the creation of a philosophic method, based on his dictum 'Cogito, ergo sum' ('I think, therefore I am'), and elaborated in his monumental *Principia Philosophiae* (1644), which gave a systematic and comprehensive account of the universe. His (unfinished) *Regulae ad directionem Ingenii* ('Rules for the direction of the Understanding') was not published until 1701.

Deshayes, Gabriel   Religious founder, born Beignon (Morbihan), France, 6 December 1767, died Saint-Laurent-sur-Sèvre (Vendée), France, 28 December 1841. He was a deacon when the French Revolution forced him to flee to Jersey in the Channel Islands, where he was ordained in 1792. He returned then to France and exercised his ministry. In 1805 he became pastor in Auray (Morbihan) and began reestablishing parish missions, recalling religious orders, providing welfare agencies, and opening schools. In conjunction with Michelle Guillaume he founded the Sisters of Christian Instruction of Saint-Gildas-des-Bois in 1807. In the rectory he organized in 1816 a community of teaching brothers that merged with another group to form the Brothers of Christian Instruction of Ploërmel. His role in the foundation of the Brothers of Christian Instruction of St Gabriel began in 1821. In 1839 Deshayes founded the Brothers of St Francis of Assisi to conduct agricultural schools. This group fused in 1899 with the Salesians. After joining the Montfort Fathers in 1820, Deshayes served in 1821–41 as superior general of this institute and of the Daughters of Wisdom, both being foundations of St Louis **Grignion de Montfort**. Deshayes also organized special institutions for the care of the deaf and mute.

Deshon, George   Missionary, author, born New London, Connecticut, 30 January 1823, died New York, NY, 30 December 1903. Deshon was raised as an Episcopalian. In 1839 he entered the US Military Academy at West Point (Ulysses S. Grant was his room-mate). Graduating second in his class, Deshon remained at the Academy to teach mathematics and ethics. Under the influence of General Rosecrans, he became a Catholic in 1850. He resigned his captaincy to enter the Redemptorists and was ordained on 28 October 1855. With three other Redemptorist converts he gave missions throughout the Eastern seaboard of the USA. In 1858, **Pius IX** released him and his missionary companions to form the Paulist Fathers. The new order put his practical business sense to good use. In 1873, at the request of the bishops of the USA, Deshon interceded with President Grant on behalf of the Catholic Indians. He was elected third superior general of the Paulist Fathers and continued in that office until his death. In addition to writing for the *Catholic World*, he published *Parochial Sermons* (New York, 1901), and the *Guide for Catholic Young Women* (New York, 1860), which ran to 25 editions and had a larger sale than any other Catholic book of its day.

Desideratus of Bourges   Saint, bishop. Birth unknown, died Bourges, 8 May 550. A councillor of King Chlotar and keeper of his seal. At the request of the king he gave up the monastic life, eventually becoming bishop of Bourges in 543. He was present at the Synod of Orléans held under King Childebert I in 549. He is held to be the founder of the church of St Symphorien at Bourges. Feast day 8 May.

Desiderius of Cahors   Saint, bishop. Born Obrège *c.*590, died Cahors, 15 November *c.*655. Desiderius was born into a Gallo-Roman family in the service of the kings of the Franks. He had a brilliant ecclesiastical and civil career, being treasurer of King Clotaire II of Cahors. Desiderius became bishop of Cahors after the murder of his elder brother (Rusticus). He built much in the city, and created many rural parishes in his diocese. Writings include sixteen letters by him, and twenty addressed to him. Feast day 15 November.

Desiderius of Langres   Saint, bishop, martyr. Birth unknown, died Langres, 407 or 411. Desiderius suffered martyrdom with many of his people at the hands of the Vandals in either 407 or 411, although his death during an earlier invasion cannot be ruled out. Desiderius is the patron saint of St Dizier. Feast day 23 May.

Desiderius of the Lombards   King, duke. Birth unknown, death unknown. Dates of rule, 756–74. Desiderius was king of the Lombards, whose land was bisected by a strip of land under papal authority. Initially Desiderius recognized papal authority, but he was persuaded by his nobility to invade the region to secure a unified Lombard kingdom in 773–4. The kingdom fell to the Franks, and Desiderius spent the rest of his life in a Frankish monastery.

Desiderius of Vienne   Saint, bishop. Birth unknown, died by assassination at Vienne, *c.*606. Desiderius was born of Christian parents and educated in grammar and religious studies. He refused

a number of bishoprics before accepting the position of bishop of Vienne in 595. Desiderius was deposed on a morals charge at the instigation of Queen Brunhilde. After four years he was restored, but because he continued to reprove the queen and her son Theodoric II he was arrested and assassinated. Feast day 23 May.

Desiderius Rhodonensis   Saint, bishop, martyr. Birth unknown, died 17 September 690. Desiderius was martyred whilst returning from a pilgrimage to Rome, by order of King Childeris II. Desiderius was buried at the place of his murder in an oratory. This chapel was later known as Saint-Dezier-l'Evêque. Feast day 18 September.

Desmaisières, María Miguela of the Blessed Sacrament   Saint, foundress of the Handmaids of the Blessed Sacrament and of Charity, Sisters, Adorers; born Madrid, 1 January 1809, died Valencia, 28 August 1865. María de la Soledad Miguela Desmaisières Lopez de Dicastillo, Viscountess of Jorbalén, early displayed zeal for the ascetical life and for charitable works. During a cholera epidemic in Madrid she attended the plague-stricken, 1834, and set up home assistance boards to aid them. In 1845 she established a home for 'fallen' or endangered young women. To perpetuate this work she founded her religious congregation in 1859, and acted as superior general until her death. Papal approval came in 1866. Men who had preyed on these women caused the foundress to be slandered, but by 1865 the institute numbered seven houses. The Order has since grown in Europe, Latin America and Japan. María died after contracting cholera while attending her own religious during an epidemic. She was beatified 7 June 1925, and canonized 4 March 1934, by Pope **Pius XI**. Feast day 25 August.

Despenser, Henry   English bishop, born *c.*1343, died Norwich, 23 August 1406. After studying civil law, he was made bishop of Norwich in 1370 by papal provision, even though he was only 27, because of the prominence of his family. He suppressed the Peasants' Rebellion of June 1381 in East Anglia, delivering Peterborough and its monks from the rebels and hanging three captive rebels at Wymondham on his own authority. In 1382 Pope **Urban VI** commissioned him to raise and conduct an English Crusade against the French supporters of the Avignon Antipope **Clement VII** in Flanders. The indulgences, with absolution from punishment and guilt, which were conceded to him for the Crusade by the Pope, stimulated the project. Parliament supported the Crusade, but it ended in disaster, and on his return Despenser was impeached by the Commons for the misconduct of the war, found guilty by the Lords, and condemned to lose the temporalities of the see in 1383. However, these were restored in 1385. A steadfast supporter of **Richard II**, he only reluctantly accepted Henry IV in 1399. He is buried in Norwich Cathedral.

Desurmont, Achille Redemptorist ascetical writer, born Tourcoing, France, 23 December 1828, died Thury-en-Valois, 23 July 1898. Professed as a Redemptorist in 1851 and ordained in 1853, he became successively prefect of seminarians, professor of theology and provincial of the French province of his congregation from 1865 to 1887, and again in 1898. In spite of his administrative and pastoral activities, he made a considerable contribution to spiritual literature. The contents of his *Rapports de Notre Règle avec la fin de Notre Institut* (1854) are evident from the title. His principles of pastoral practice are found in his posthumous work, *La Charité sacerdotale* (Paris, 1899). He founded the periodical *La Sainte Famille*, and published his *Oeuvres Complètes* (12 vols, Paris, 1906–13). He was steeped in the ascetical spirit of St **Alphonsus Liguori**, and his works represent an expression and adaptation of that spirit to contemporary needs.

Desvallières, Georges French painter of pronounced Catholic fervour who worked for a modern renewal of religious art; born Paris, 14 March 1861, died Paris, 4 October 1950. From his mother's side (Legouvé), Desvallières inherited a tradition of culture and artistic taste. He was first apprenticed to Delaunay, who sent him to the studio of Gustave Moreau. During his earlier years he was indecisive about religion. He travelled widely in Europe in 1882–1902 and painted mostly mythological subjects with elegant nudes or studies of the theatrical milieux of Montmartre and London, and by exception an occasional religious subject. In 1903 he was active in founding the Salon d'automne. During this period he was influenced by **Huysmans** and Léon **Bloy**, who had become his friend. His two celebrated works, now at the Musée d'Art Moderne, Paris, *The Sacred Heart* (1905) and *Christ at the Column* (1910), contain the theme of redemptive suffering that was to dominate his work after World War I. During the war he served as a commandant with his two sons, Richard and Daniel; the latter was killed in 1915. Desvallières vowed to paint only religious works if he should survive the war. In 1919, with M. **Denis**, he founded the Ateliers d'art sacré, hoping to inspire a rebirth of church ornamentation in the spirit of medieval artisans. In his paintings he often sacrificed quality in his attempt to achieve spiritual significance through a shocking expressionism. Among his many church decorations are works at: Chapelle de la Cité du Souvenir, Paris (1931); St John the Baptist Church, Pawtucket, Rhode Island (1931); and the Church of the Holy Spirit, Paris (1934–6, Stations of the Cross).

Deusdedit I Saint, Pope. Born Rome, elected 19 October 615, died 8 November 618. He had previously served as a priest in Rome for 40 years. Deusdedit was Pope during turbulent times, as the Lombards sought freedom, but he remained loyal to the Emperor **Heraclius**. During his reign he had to contend with earthquakes and plague. Deusdedit was known for his care towards diocesan clergy as opposed to the monks. Feast day 8 November.

Deusdedit of Monte Cassino Saint, abbot and martyr, died 834. Elected abbot of Monte Cassino in 828, Deusdedit was captured by Prince Sicard of Benevento, who wanted to appropriate the abbey's property, and died in captivity. Feast day 9 October.

Devanandan, Paul David Indian Christian theologian, born Madras, 9 July 1901, died, Dehra Dun, India, 10 August 1962. He studied at Nizam College, Hyderabad, and Madras University before going to the United States in 1924, where he gained his BD at the Pacific School of Religion in Berkeley, California, and his doctorate from Yale in 1931 (*The Concept of Maya*, 1950). That year he returned to India as professor of philosophy and the history of religions at the United Theological

College, Bangalore. In 1949 he became general secretary of the YMCA at New Delhi. He was ordained a presbyter of the Church of South India in 1954 and in 1956 became director of what became the Christian Institute for the Study of Religion and Society (CISRS). He edited the journal *Religion and Society* with M. M. Thomas, laying an important groundwork for Hindu–Christian dialogue.

Devas, Charles Stanton Roman Catholic political economist, born Windsor, England, 26 August 1848, died 6 November 1906. Educated at Eton and Balliol College, Oxford, having been received into the Church before entering the university, he immediately took a prominent part in Catholic activities, especially in the campaign that enabled Catholics to enter universities. He was among the pioneers of the Catholic social movement in England. Devas' writings influenced several generations of Catholic social students, and his *Political Economy* (1892) became a standard textbook in Catholic colleges. He was professor of political economy at the short-lived Catholic University College of London and examined in that subject at the Royal University of Ireland for nine years. He linked social science with ethics in opposition to the current view that ethics were irrelevant. Other important works include *Key to World Progress* (1906); *Studies in Family Life* (1886).

Devine, Arthur Passionist theologian and devotional writer, born Sligo, Ireland, 1 December 1849, died St Paul's Retreat, Mount Argus, Dublin, 20 April 1919. He entered the Passionist Order in 1865, was ordained in 1872 and was lector of theology for almost 30 years at St Joseph's, Highgate Hill, London. From 1884 to 1887 he was consultor to the provincial of his Order. During the last twelve years of his life he taught theology, Scripture and canon law at Mount Argus. While in England he followed the developments of the Oxford Movement with great interest, and through his preaching and direction led many Anglicans into the Catholic Church. He was also interested in the revival of the Irish language and preached in it frequently. Chief works are *Auxilium Praedicatorum: a Short Gloss upon the Gospels* (3 vols, Dublin, 1884); *The Sacraments Explained* (1918); *The Creed Explained* (1923).

Dexios, Theodore Fourteenth-century Byzantine monk and anti-Palamite theologian, died Thessalonika(?), *c*.1360. A monk from Nicephorus Gregoras, he joined **Gregory Akindynos** in his propaganda against Palamism in Thessalonika and repudiated the use of the dialectical method in theology. He wrote a four-part work against John VI Cantacuzenus and the Tome of the Synod of 1351. He expressed an agnostic attitude in regard to the essence of the Light of Mount Tabor, and he claimed that as the divine essence was incomprehensible, theologians who attempted to discuss it were temerarious. This opinion brought him into conflict with his anti-Palamite friend Isaac **Argyros** (died 1375), and he wrote three short apologies to justify his position. While he favoured the mystical elements put forward in the theories of **Gregory Palamas**, he maintained it was both foolish and impossible to give any explanation beyond that which was furnished by the Gospels.

Dezelić, Velimir Croatian poet and novelist, born Zagreb, Croatia, 21 Febuary, 1864, died Zagreb, 7 February 1941. He was the first Croatian author to react against Liberal Modernism and religious indifference. The son of author Djuro Dezelic (died 1907), he studied medicine in Vienna and physical sciences in Zagreb, winning a doctorate in philosophy. He was librarian after 1894 and director in 1910–20 of the library of the University of Zagreb, and then, until retirement, employed in the state archives, and he was active in literature, library science, archive work, historiography and biography, and in various literary, social, national and religious organizations. He was active in the Croatian Catholic Movement from its beginning in 1900, taking part in various congresses. The undisputed ideologist and representative of Croatian Catholic literature, he headed various Catholic cultural and literary associations and for fifteen years edited the literary review *Prosvjeta* ('Culture').

Dhorme, Edouard Paul Biblical scholar, orientalist, born Fleurbe, Pas de Calais, France, 15 January 1881, died Paris, 19 January 1966. In December 1899 Dhorme went to Jerusalem, where at the *Ecole biblique et archeologique française* he became a professed member of the Dominican Order in 1900 and was ordained a priest in May 1904. He remained there as professor, and from 1923 to 1931 as director. In that year he left the Order and the Church, married and returned to France. There he became professor at the *Ecole des hautes études Sorbonne* from 1933 and at the *College de France* from 1945. He was co-director of the *Revue de l'histoire des religions* from 1935 and of the *Revue d'Assyriologie* from 1944. He never completely broke contact with his former colleagues in Jerusalem; some months before he died he received the sacraments of the Church, and he was buried from the parish church at Becon-les-Bruyeres. Dhorme's scholarly accomplishments included a number of important studies in biblical exegesis and related historical and linguistic subjects. When the Ugaritic texts were discovered at Ras Shamra, he was allowed access to those materials and assisted in their decipherment. His many publications include: *Choix de textes religieux assyro-babyloniens* (1907), *Les Religions de Babylonie et d'Assyrie* (1945, 1949) and portions of the collection entitled *Peuples et Civilizations* (Paris, 1950). During his years of retirement he published a two-volume translation of the OT, the *Bible 'de La Pleiade'* (Paris, 1956, 1959). Dhorme's work shows a rigorous attention to linguistic and historical details balanced by equal attention to a comprehensive overview of the material at all points. His popular writings display zeal to share the scholar's discoveries with a larger public.

Di Rosa, Maria Crocifissa Saint, foundress of the Handmaids of Charity, born Brescia, Italy, 6 November 1813, died Brescia, 15 December 1855. After her mother's death in 1824, Paolina Francesca Maria (her name at baptism) was entrusted for her education to the Visitandines in 1824–30. Then she took charge of her father's household and developed a talent for organization and supervision. During a devastating cholera epidemic in 1836, Paolina and her companion Bagriella Bornati won wide admiration by caring for the sick. Her religious congregation, founded in 1840, was popularly called at first the Hospitable Adorers. Maria Crocifissa went to Rome in 1850 and obtained approval of her institute's Rule. Basic to her spirituality was the imitation of Christ's sorrowful life; this led her to infused contemplation and inspired her with the idea of aiding the sick and the poor, the sorrowful members of Christ's Church. The

chapel in the mother house at Brescia is her burial place. She was beatified 26 May 1940, and canonized 12 June 1954. Feast day 15 December.

Diadochus of Photike Bishop, ascetic and theologian. Born *c*.400, died 474. bishop of Epirus Vetus (Photike). An anti-monophysite, his major work was the *Discourse on the Ascension of Our Lord Jesus Christ*, which proclaims the glorification in a single divine hypostasis of Christ's human nature. He was also one of the Chalcedonian signatories of a letter of support for Emperor **Leo I**. Other works include the ascetic *Vision of St Diadochus, Bishop of Photice in Epirus*, which is mystical in character. Diadochius also wrote *The Hundred Gnostic Chapters*, which speak of the experiential knowledge of the Spirit.

Diana, Antonino Theatine moral theologian who strongly influenced the development of casuistry in the seventeenth and eighteenth centuries, born Palermo, Sicily, *c*.1585, died Rome, 20 July 1663. Before taking his vows in the Theatine Order in 1630, he had become famous as a counsellor in moral matters. **Urban VIII**, **Innocent X** and **Alexander VII** esteemed him highly and named him examiner of bishops. In 1629 Diana published at Palermo *Resolutiones morales*. The work's immediate success compelled him to make repeated additions to it; when completed (1659), the twelve-volume collection contained 6,000 cases or moral problems. During the following century it was republished frequently, in either original or abridged versions. When rigorism set in at the end of the eighteenth century, Diana's reputation waned quickly, but his name still epitomizes an epoch in modern casuistry.

Díaz, Manuel Jesuit missionary to China and astronomer, born Castello Branco, Portugal, 1574, died Hangchow, China, 1 or 2 March 1659. He is called 'junior' to distinguish him from Manuel Díaz, SJ (1559–1639), who was a Portuguese missionary in Eastern India. Díaz junior entered the Society of Jesus in 1592 and sailed for the Indies in 1601. He arrived in China in 1610, taught theology for six years at Macao, worked in the missionary fields of Fukien and Chekiang in South China and, as the first vice-provincial of China for eighteen years, travelled extensively throughout the orient. He published several works in Chinese on ascetical theology and on astronomy; they include *Tai i luen* (dissertation on the incarnation), and *Cheng king tche kiai* (on the Gospels).

Díaz y Barreto, Pascual Jesuit Mexican archbishop, born Zapopan, Jalisco, 22 June 1875, died Mexico City, 19 May 1936. He studied at the Tridentine Seminary of Guadalajara and was ordained 17 September, 1899. He entered the Society of Jesus in 1903 and was sent to the Colegio Maximo in Oña, Spain, to perfect his philosophical studies and then to Enghien, Belgium, where he received his doctorate. On his return to Mexico, he held various positions. He was consecrated bishop of Tabasco in 1923, but lived only a short time in his see. During the rebellion there he saved the life of Tomás Garrido Canabal, but when Garrido Canabal recovered the governorship, he expelled the bishop. Díaz y Barreto went to Mexico City, where he served as secretary for the Episcopal Committee organized to unify measures taken to protect the Church from persecution. He was exiled in January 1927. In 1929 he accompanied Archbishop Ruíz y Flores to Mexico. In June the Holy See appointed Díaz y Barreto archbishop of Mexico. Persecution increased: the state restricted severely the number of churches and the number of clergy in his diocese. He himself had to perform all sorts of activities. These weakened his health. His funeral was marked by a moving demonstration of grief on the part of the Catholic population.

Díaz y Clusellas, Josefa Argentine artist, born Santa Fé, 13 April 1852, died Villa de Rosario, Córdoba, 24 September 1917. Studied under the painter Hector Facino, whom she soon surpassed in ability. She used her free hours to decorate church and chapel altars. When she was nineteen, her works were well known in the province, and in 1874 the legislature of Santa Fé honoured her with a gold medal for her talent. She collaborated with the government in honouring heroes and government figures such as Justo José de Urquiza. In May 1894, she took her vows at the convent of the Sisters of the Adoration. She continued working but now was interested only in religious subjects. She was the first artist of Santa Fé whose works had real value.

Dibelius, Martin Biblical scholar, born Dresden, Germany, 14 September 1883, died Heidelberg, 11 November 1947. Dibelius spent his life as a teacher of biblical studies at Berlin, 1910–1915, and Heidelberg, 1915–47. With K. L. Schmidt, R. **Bultmann**, M. Albertz and G. Bertram, he founded the Formgeschichte (form criticism) school. By making use of categories such as paradigm, Novelle (short story), exhortation, legend and myth, Dibelius and his colleagues attempted to determine the context or Sitz im Leben (life situation) of such forms, and then used this information as a significant tool in biblical interpretation. Other scholarly interests lay in the area of NT ethics. Dibelius' works include *Die Formgeschichte des Evangelium* (1919); *Botschaft und Geschichte* (1952–3), as well as many biblical commentaries.

Dicconson, Edward Roman Catholic professor of theology, vicar apostolic of the (English) Northern district, 1740–52, born Wrightington Hall, Lancashire, 1670; died Finch Mill, Wrightington, 24 April 1752. Educated at Douay College, he was ordained there in 1700, and the following year became procurator, and later vice president. He was largely instrumental in getting Douay cleared of charges of Jansenism. After twenty years as professor and official at Douay he was sent to the English mission in 1720 and, though his name was frequently put forward for a bishopric, it was not until he was past 70 that he was appointed to the Northern district. In 1736 the vicar apostolic sent him to Rome to urge the Franciscan observance of the decree of **Innocent XII** concerning the relations between the regular orders and the bishops, and also to remove the Jesuits from their charge over the English College in Rome. In the latter he was successful. On 19 March 1740 he was consecrated at Ghent as titular bishop of Malla for the Northern district, and as such was instrumental (with Bishops John Stonor and Francis Petre) in obtaining from **Benedict XIV** *Apostolicum Ministerium* laying down the rules for the government of the English mission. He was afflicted with a stammer that prevented him from preaching. In his last years he wrote a detailed account of his agency in Rome in four volumes.

Dickinson, Emily Elizabeth America's greatest woman poet and letter-writer, born 10 December

1830 in Amherst in Massachusetts, where her father was a lawyer and later Congressman, died there, 15 May 1886. Apart from a visit to Washington she spent her life as a virtual recluse, spending her days tending to her father until his death in 1874. Only two of her poems were published in her lifetime, but after her death her sister Lavinia discovered a cache of over 1000 poems and had them published in three series (1890, 1891, 1896). Further collections followed, *The Single Hound* (1914); *Further Poems* (1929) and *Bolts of Melody* (1945). Thomas H. Johnson prepared a three-volume variorum edition of all her poetry – *The Poems of Emily Dickinson*, containing 1175. Her massive literary correspondence was published in 1958, *The Letters of Emily Dickinson*. Her writings evoke a deep New England Puritanism and yet she achieved much dramatic tension from her religious doubts, finding it difficult to accept orthodox religious faith and yet craving the stability that such faith can bring. Nature, love, religion and mortality are the dominant themes of her work.

Didacus of Alcalá Saint, Franciscan lay brother and ascetic, born St Nicolás del Puerto, Spain, 1400, died Alcalá, Spain, 12 November 1463. He was at first a mendicant hermit, but he later entered the monastery of Arizafa in Córdoba and was an exemplar of virtue, especially of humility and simplicity. He was sent to the Canaries in 1441–9 and became guardian of the Franciscan mission and converted many. In 1450 while in Rome for the canonization of **Bernardine of Siena**, he served the sick in the convent of Aracoeli. In 1456 he was sent from Salicetum in Castile to a new monastery in Alcalá, where he was revered for penances, miracles and a divinely infused knowledge of theology. After death his severely mortified body did not suffer rigor mortis or corruption. Miraculous cures were reported immediately. In 1562 his body was taken to the bedside of Carlos, son of Philip II, to effect his cure. His canonization, requested by Philip in 1564, was obtained in 1588. Feast day 12 November.

Didacus of Azevedo Blessed, bishop of Osma; died Osma, 30 December 1207. As prior, Didacus (Diego de Acebes) collaborated with Bishop Martin Bazan in transforming the cathedral chapter of Osma into a chapter of canons regular; St **Dominic**

was elected his subprior. Didacus was chosen bishop of Osma in 1201. In 1203, and again in 1205, with Dominic as companion, he went to Denmark to negotiate the marriage of Ferdinand, son of Alphonsus VIII. In 1206, after **Innocent III** had refused him permission to resign his bishopric to preach to the Cumans, he reorganized the preaching against the Albigenses on the pattern of Christ and the Apostles, a plan that was later fully realized in the Order of Preachers. He established a community of women at Prouille, which later became the Order's first monastery. Feast day 6 Febuary.

Didymus the Blind Theologian. Born Alexandria, *c.*313, died Alexandria 398. Didymus was a director of the catechetical school in Alexandria, a staunch supporter of Nicene trinitarianism. He was greatly influenced by **Origen**, showing a development of Origen's scriptural exegesis. He was ultimately condemned as an Origenist in Constantinople in 553. Major works: *On the Holy Spirit*; *Against the Manichees*; only fragments survive of the rest of his vast literary output. There have been some recent discoveries of commentaries (Job, Zechariah, Genesis, Psalms), but authenticity is uncertain.

Dieckmann, Hermann Jesuit theologian, born Osnabrück, Germany, 2 July 1880, died Valkenburg, Holland, 15 October 1928. He joined the Society of Jesus in 1897 and began to teach fundamental theology at Valkenburg in 1915. The most mature product of his theological works in his complete treatise *Theologia Fundamentalis* in 2 vols: *De ecclesia* (Freiburg, 1925); *De revelatione Christiana* (Freiburg, 1930). While the work has merit in its use of the findings of studies in comparative religion, it is somewhat dated because of its polemic aimed at liberal Protestants, especially at Adolf von **Harnack**.

Diego of Cadiz Blessed, Spanish Capuchin preacher, born Cadiz, Spain, 30 March 1743, died Ronda (Malaga, Spain), 24 March 1801. José Francisco Lopez Camoño took the name Diego after joining the Capuchins in 1759. After ordination in 1766 he dedicated his religious life largely to preaching missions in Spain, Portugal and the Levant, but he won his greatest renown in Andalusia. He delivered more than 20,000 sermons, sometimes as many as fifteen a day, to audiences that often numbered 15,000 to 20,000. His most common themes were the Holy Trinity and the Blessed Virgin under the title of Shepherdess of Souls and of Peace. Diego was in great demand as a confessor and impressed people as much by his asceticism as by his eloquence. Diego led the resistance to the influence of French Enlightenment in the Spanish court, but he met opposition there. When the armies of the French Revolution invaded Spain, Diego crusaded for national independence. A valuable source for knowledge of his life and spirituality is contained in his published correspondence. Diego was beatified 23 April 1894. Feast day 24 March.

Diego of Estella Franciscan ascetical-mystical theologian (known also as Diego de San Cristóbal), born Estella, Navarre, 1524, died Salamanca, 1 August 1578. After studying at Toulouse, he joined the Friars Minor in Salamanca. In 1552 he went to Portugal but by 1561 he was again in Spain. He preached, at the request of St **Teresa of Ávila**, for the opening of her convent in Salamanca. His best-known works are the ascetical *Libro de la vanidad del mundo* (Toledo, 1562) and the mystical *Meditaciones devotisimas del amor de Dios* (Salamanca, 1576). Both these works are strongly Augustinian and have appeared in many editions and languages up to the present. His commentary on St Luke was censured by the Inquisition.

Diekamp, Franz Theologian, born Geldern, Rhineland, 8 November 1864, died Münster, 10 October 1943. After his ordination in 1887 he spent some time in parish work. In 1889 he taught at the Münster theological seminary, and in 1898 was a lecturer at the University of Münster. In 1904 he was named professor, and until 1933 taught patrology, history of dogma, church history and dogmatic theology. Diekamp advanced the science of patrology and history of dogma by his editions of and commentaries on the Fathers. His works are distinguished by an extraordinary accuracy, thoroughness and clarity. In 1902 he founded the *Theologische Revue*, and in 1923 he became editor of the *Münsterische Beiträge zur Theologie*. Of his numerous writings the following are especially important: *Die Gotteslehre des hl. Gregor v. Nyssa* (Münster, 1896), *Die origenistischen Strei-* *tigkeiten im 6. Jahrhundert u. das 5. allg. Konzil* (Münster, 1899), *Doctrina Patrum de incarnatione Verbi* (Münster, 1907), *Über den Ursprung des Trinitätsbekenntnisses* (Münster, 1911). His best-known work, representing the most important German effort in a Thomistic direction, is *Katholische Dogmatik nach den Grundsätzen des hl. Thomas* 3 vols, (Münster, 1912–14).

Diepenbrock, Melchior von German cardinal, theologian, born Bocholt, Westphalia, 6 January 1798, died Johannesburg Castle, 20 January 1853. He studied at the French Academy in Bonn, which he left for disciplinary reasons. During the campaign against France in 1814–15, he served as a lieutenant in a Prussian regiment. Influenced by Johann Michael Sailer, he reformed his life, studied political science at the University of Landshut and prepared for the priesthood at Mainz, Münster and Regensburg. He was ordained in 1823. In 1845 Diepenbrock became prince-bishop of Breslau (Wroclaw), where he resisted the encroachments on the rights of the Church. He succeeded also in his opposition to Deutschkatholizismus, a religious movement with pronounced rationalistic tendencies. In 1850 he was created cardinal. His interest in mysticism led him to write **Henry Suso**'s *Leben und Schriften* (1829). *Geistlicher Blumenstrauss aus spanischen und deutschen Dichtergarten* (1829) contains translations of Spanish and German mystics.

Dieringer, Franz Xavier Theologian, born Rangeningen, Germany, 22 August 1811, died Veringendorf, 8 September 1876. He studied at Tübingen and was ordained at Freiburg im Breisgau in 1835. After teaching in seminaries he was called to the chair of dogma and homiletics at the University of Bonn, where Hermesianism had all but destroyed the reputation of the theological faculty. Dieringer founded and edited a journal, *Katholische Zeitschrift für Wissenschaft und Kunst* (Cologne, 1844–9; since 1849 called *Katholische Vierteljahrschrift*), to provide a forum for orthodoxy; and for many years his writing and teaching did much to restore balance to theological thought in Germany. He also wrote against A. Gentler. He was a founder and for many years president of the Verein vom hl. Karl Borromäus. In 1853 he was named a canon of Cologne, though permitted to retain his chair at Bonn. Three times he was proposed for the episcopacy, but he was vetoed. Though he had taught papal infallibility, he at first opposed its definition as inopportune and later as wrong in itself. After it was defined, he accepted it but resigned his professorship and his dignities to become a parish priest.

Dietrich of Nieheim (Niem) Chancery official in the Roman curia, publicist of the Western Schism, born Brakel, Westphalia, *c.* 1340, died Maastricht, Netherlands, March 1418. Supported by **William of Ockham**, **Marsilius of Padua** and Alexander of Roes, he gave the first comprehensive presentation of conciliarism in his *Dialogus de schismate* (1410), in which he called for the reunion and reform of the Church. His *Avisamenta* (1414) contains the programme for the Council of Constance. As a representative of the historically conservative approach to the Empire, he stressed the right of the German emperors to call a general council of the Church. He was an intimate of several Roman Popes; in 1395 **Boniface IX** tried in vain to bestow upon him the bishopric of Verden (Germany). The Anima, the German hospital in Rome, claims him as its founder.

Dietz, Peter Ernest Labour priest, journalist and member of the Society of the Divine Word, born New York, NY, 10 July 1878, died Milwaukee, Wisconsin, 11 October 1947. In 1900, after his early education at Holy Redeemer School, New York City, Peter entered the novitiate of the Society of the Divine Word in Moedling, Germany. Three years later he returned to the USA and was ordained a diocesan priest on 17 December 1904. Dietz early displayed interest in social questions, and he held many positions, both pastoral and journalistic, that allowed him to further Catholic social teaching. Dietz defended trade-unionism. His Militia of Christ for Social Service, an organization of Catholic trade-unionists, effectively combated the influence of socialism. He pioneered in setting up an industrial council plan among the building trades in Cincinnati during the 1920s. Dietz's public career ended abruptly in 1923 when Catholic members of the Chamber of Commerce protested to Archbishop **McNicholas** that his influence on labour had interfered with their business. Dietz, forced to close his academy at Ault Park, withdrew from the Archdiocese of Cincinnati

and spent the next 24 years building St Monica's, Milwaukee, into a large and important parish.

Díez Laurel, Bartolomé Blessed, Franciscan martyr, born Puerto de Santa Maria, Spain; died Nagasaki, Japan, 17 August 1627. His real name was Díaz Laruel. He was a sailor, and while living in Acapulco, Mexico, he requested permission to enter the Franciscan Order. He took the habit of a lay brother on 13 May 1615 in Valladolid (Morelia), Mexico, but he did not persevere. He again took the habit on 17 October 1616 in the same convent, where this time he was professed on 18 October 1617, as a lay brother. At the end of 1618 he was in the convent of San Francisco del Monte in Manila. There he learned and practised medicine in a hospital. In 1623 he went to work as a missionary in Japan, where he disguised himself as a physician. At Pentecost in 1627 he was imprisoned in Nagasaki, and in August of the same year he was martyred. Feast day 18 August.

Digby, Everard Born Stoke Dry, Rutland, 16 May 1578, executed London, 30 January 1606. He attended Queen **Elizabeth I** at court, but was converted by John **Gerard** in 1599, and his wife and mother followed him in Catholicism. He was knighted in 1603 at Belvoir Castle by **James I**, but was implicated in the Gunpowder Plot and was deserted by his companions when besieged in Holbeach House in Gloucestershire, 8 November 1605. He was captured, tried in Westminster Hall and executed.

Digby, George Second earl of Bristol. Born Madrid, October 1612, while his father was ambassador there, died Chelsea (his house there had once been Thomas **More**'s), 20 March 1677. He was educated at Magdalen College, Oxford. Before his conversion he first attacked Catholicism in correspondence with his relative Sir Kenelm **Digby**. He fought for **Charles I** at Edgehill but gave up his command after quarrels both with moderate politicians and with Prince Rupert. He fled to France and became a lieutenant-general in the French army in 1648, but being caught out in an intrigue against Cardinal **Mazarin** he was forced to flee France for England where he was appointed secretary of state to **Charles II** in 1657. His political enemies had him subsequently deprived of the seals of office on account of his Catholicism. Digby wrote comedies and translations from French. In 1663 he intrigued unsuccessfully against Clarendon.

Digby, Kenelm Christian author, diplomat, Roman Catholic recusant and naval commander, born Gayhurst, Buckinghamshire, 11 July 1603, died London, 11 June 1665. He entered Gloucester Hall, now Worcester College, Oxford, in 1618, but left two years later without taking a degree. He was already deeply in love with Venetia Stanley, but his mother, who disapproved of the match, persuaded him to go abroad. He visited Paris, and Angers, but fled to Florence to escape the importunities of Queen Marie de Médicis. In 1623 he joined Prince Charles, the future **Charles I** in Madrid, and he accompanied him back to England, where he married Venetia in 1625. In 1628 as commander he defeated a French and Venetian fleet in Scaneroon (Alexandretta). On his return to England he professed Protestantism but soon returned to Catholicism *c.*1630, then published *Conference with a Lady about choice of a Religion* (1638). He was removed from the House of Commons in 1641 because he appealed to English Catholics to support Charles I against the Scots. He fought a duel in defence of Charles I in Paris. In 1644 he became chancellor to Queen Henrietta Maria; pleaded Charles I's cause with Pope **Innocent X** but quarrelled with him and left Rome in 1645. He returned to England but was banished again in 1649. He tried to get toleration for English Catholics from Oliver **Cromwell** without success. John Evelyn visited him in Paris in 1651, and there Digby also became friendly with René **Descartes**. At the Restoration he was allowed to return to England, where he retained his office of chancellor to Queen Henrietta Maria but was, in fact, forbidden the court. When the Royal Society was founded he became a member of its council. After his wife's death Sir Kenelm retired to Gresham College. He published a criticism of Thomas **Browne**'s *Religio Medici* (1643): *Of the Immortality of Man's Soul* (1644). He also wrote *Of Bodies* and is supposed to have discovered the necessity of oxygen to the life of plants and claimed to have discovered a 'sympathetic powder' for the cure of wounds, to be applied to the weapon which caused the wound!

Digby, Kenelm Henry Roman Catholic convert and writer, born Clonfert, Ireland, where his father was dean, 1800, died London, 22 March 1880. He was educated at Trinity College, Cambridge, where he graduated in 1819. His particular interest was the medieval period, and his studies of Scholasticism occasioned his conversion to Catholicism. He published his first book, *The Broad-Stone of Honour*, in 1822 and the eleven-volume *Mores Catholici*, a compilation of material on the religious, social and artistic life of medieval Europe, between 1831 and 1841.

Dintilhac, Jorge (Louis Eugene) Peruvian educator, member of the Picpus Fathers, born Provins, France, 13 November 1878, died Lima, Peru, 13 April 1947. He entered the Congregation of the Sacred Hearts of Jesus and Mary (Picpus Fathers) in October 1895 and pursued ecclesiastical studies in France, Spain, Chile and Peru, where he received a doctorate in theology from the University of San Marcos. As a university student in Lima, Dintilhac became interested in the education of boys. The school conducted by the Picpus Fathers in Lima, called La Recoleta, had opened in March 1893 with 22 students. Through the students, Dintilhac became aware of the confusion at the University of San Marcos, which most of the graduates of the Recoleta attended. In 1916 Dintilhac was authorized to apply to the Ministry of Education for permission to begin the Catholic University of Peru, and permission was granted on 24 March 1917. Classes began 15 April, 1917, with ten students and with Dintilhac as rector. Later it was designated a pontifical university by the Holy See. During the 30-year rectorship of Dintilhac, the university developed five faculties.

Dinus Mugellanus (Rossoni) Roman law jurist of the postglossator period, born near Florence, 1253, died Bologna, *c.*1300. He studied jurisprudence at Bologna, receiving his doctorate *c.*1278. He taught at the University of Pistoia for five years. In 1284 he returned to Bologna to teach civil law. He spent some time in Rome (*c.*1297), where he contributed to the compilation of the *Liber Sextus* of Pope **Boniface VIII**. It is believed that Dinus compiled the 88 rules of law that are appended to this collection. He is the author of several works, the most important being *Ordo iudicarius* (*c.*1298–9), a commentary on the rules of law in which he developed a new method of interpretation. He is especially noted for his influence in the field of the rules of law.

Diodore of Tarsus Priest, bishop and monk. Birth unknown, died Tarsus, c.393. Diodore sided with Melitius in the Antiochene schism. Exiled to Armenia in 372 by Emperor Valens, he was recalled and ordained bishop of Tarsus in 378. Diodore was head of a school of scriptural exegesis at Antioch (Literalist). He wrote many commentaries and a theoretical work entitled *On the difference between theory and allegory*. Diodore was instrumental in formulating a literal method of exegesis that ran counter to the allegorical exegesis of Alexandria. Diodore played a prominent part in the Council of Constantinople in 381. Many of his writings disappeared as a result of the Nestorian controversy.

Dionigi da Piacenza Capuchin missionary, born Flaminio Carli in Piacenza, Italy, 1637, died Venice, Italy, 21 April 1695. In 1652 he entered the Bologna province of the Capuchin Order. He laboured in the Congo from 1667 to 1671, after which he went to Brazil. After returning to Italy, he was sent in 1678 to the missions of Asia Minor, Persia and Russian Georgia. In Georgia he served as pro-prefect of the mission. He spent his last years in Venice. Dionigi's two books narrating his experiences caused a sensation among his European contemporaries. The English rendering is by J. Pinkerton in *A General Collection of the Best and Most Interesting Voyages and Travels* (vol. 16, London, 1888).

Dionysius Pope, 22 July 260 to 26 December 268. Birth unknown though of Greek descent, died Rome, c.267. Dionysius is considered one of the most important Popes of the third century. He reorganized the community at Rome, and called a synod which condemned both the Sabellian and Marcionite tendency of breaking up the Trinity into three hypostases. Dionysius also helped the Cappadocian communities which had been devastated by foreign invasions.

Dionysius Exiguus Monk, born Dobrudscha, c.470, died Rome, 550. A Native of Scythia Minor,

Dionysius was one of the main mediators of Greek ecclesiastical culture to the West. He was a renowned translator (fluent in Latin and Greek), canonist and computist. He is considered as one of the founders of medieval culture. His collection of Greek and Latin canons places him as a founder of canon law. Dionysius was instrumental in the acceptance by the West of the Alexandrian nineteen-year Easter cycle. He also replaced the Era of Diocletian chronology with the Christian Era, in which he placed the date of Jesus' birth on 25 December 753 AUC.

Dionysius of Alexandria Bishop. Birth unknown, died Alexandrai, 265/6. Little is known of Dionysius before he was made bishop of Alexandria in 248, although it is suggested he was of a wealthy background. During the Decian persecution in 249 Dionysius left Alexandria to hide in Mareotis, and later the Libyan desert, for which he was subsequently rebuked. In 251 Dionysius supported **Cornelius** against **Novatian** in the contest for the bishopric at Rome. Dionysius intervened in the trinitarian controversy in Libya Pentapolis, siding against the incumbent bishop of Ptolemais. Dionysius vindicated his actions in his work *Refutation and apologia*, fragments of which are cited by **Athanasius**.

Dionysius of Corinth Bishop, birth unknown, died Corinth, 180. The only chronological certainty concerning Dionysius is a letter written to Bishop Soter of Rome (166–75), in which he defends his actions concerning a judgement given to the bishops of Pontus. The letter to Soter reveals that Dionysius was consulted by the bishops of Pontus as to whether they should receive into the Church 'all those who were converted from every kind of sin'. Dionysius judged that they should admit them into the Church. The letters are summarized by **Eusebius of Caesarea**.

Dionysius of Paris, Dionysius the Carthusian *see* **Denis**

Dionysius of the Nativity (Pierre Berthelot) Blessed, missionary and protomartyr of the Discalced Carmelite Reform, born Honfleur, France, 12 December 1600, died Sumatra, 27 November 1638. He was a professional navigator and cartographer, captured by Dutch pirates and imprisoned at Java on his first expedition to the Indies. After his release he settled in Malacca and worked for the Portuguese, assuming command of a ship. His voyages brought him into contact with the recently founded Discalced Carmelite monastery at Goa, and in 1634 he entered the Order. After his ordination in 1638, his superiors assigned him as the chaplain of an expedition to Sumatra and appointed a lay brother, Blessed Redemptus of the Cross, as his companion. When the expedition arrived at Sumatra, both men were captured by the natives and martyred when they refused to apostatize to Islam. **Leo XIII** beatified them in 1900. Some of Dionysius' cartographic work is in the British Museum. Feast day 29 November.

Dioscorus Deacon, born Alexandria, died 14 October 530. Dioscorus was a deacon at Rome, sent on a mission to Theodoric by Pope Symmachus in 507, and sent by Hormisdas on a mission to Constantinople in 519. He was proposed, but rejected, as bishop of Alexandria. He was elected Pope on 17 October 530, in opposition to **Boniface II**, who had been elected by a minority. Boniface anathematized him, but his memory was restored by **Agapetus**.

Dioscorus of Alexandria Archdeacon, patriarch, saint. Birth unknown, died 4 September 454 at Gangra. Dioscorus accompanied **Cyril of Alexandria** to the Council of Ephesus in 431, succeeding Cyril in 444. He supported **Eutyches** against **Flavian**, provoking violence. Dioscorus was anathematized at the fourth ecumenical council, at Chalcedon in 451, and was exiled to Asia Minor. He is venerated as a saint by the non-Chalcedonian churches.

Dishypatos, David Fourteenth-century Byzantine Hesychast and theological polemicist, died Constantinople, c.1353. He was a monk and apparently worked in close contact with **Gregory Palamas.** He wrote (c.1347) a short but important account of the controversy between Palamas and **Barlaam of Calabria** for Empress Anne of Savoy. He is credited with the diatribe (logos) against Barlaam and Gregorius Akindynos addressed to **Nicholas Cabasilas**; and a polemic poem in 468 verses against Akindynos. These works have remained

unedited. To Dishypatos is attributed also a canon of the Mass dedicated to St George, the martyr, but he is no longer credited with a section of the patristic florigelium.

Dix, Gregory Monk and liturgical scholar, born George Eglington Alston (Gregory was his religious name) at Woolwich, 4 October 1901, died Nashdom Abbey, 11 May 1952. He was the son of an Anglican priest, and inherited his father's interests. He attended Westminster School, then read Modern History at Merton College, Oxford, where he also displayed a talent for rowing. In 1923 he was appointed a lecturer at Keble College. He was ordained in 1925, and joined the Anglican Benedictines, being sent to West Africa. He had to return in 1929 because of ill-health, and went to live at Nashdom, where he became a novice in 1936, and took solemn vows four years later. He was elected prior in 1948. His major works were a study of **Hippolytus'** The Apostolic Tradition (1937) and The Shape of the Liturgy (1945). In 1949 he received the degree of Doctor of Divinity from Oxford.

Dix, William Hymn-writer, born Bristol, 14 June 1837, died Cheddar, Axbridge, Somerset, 9 September 1898. He studied at Bristol Grammar School. He translated hymns from Greek and Abyssinian, and wrote many original hymns, which appeared in Hymns, Ancient and Modern (1861), such as With Gladness Men of Old.

Długosz, Jan Priest, educator, Polish historian (also known as Johannes Longinus), born Brzeznica, Poland, 1415, died Cracow, Poland, 19 May 1480. After higher studies at the University of Cracow, he was ordained in 1440. He was appointed secretary to the bishop of Cracow, and he later became a canon of the cathedral. He was one of the Polish delegates to the Council of Basel. As a special envoy of Polish church authorities to Pope **Eugenius IV**, with whom he reconciled the University of Cracow, he returned with the cardinal's hat for the bishop. Shortly before his death Długosz was named archbishop of Lvov but was not consecrated. Among his works is especially the outstanding Annales seu chronicae inclyti regni Poloniae, libri XII, a twelve-volume history of Poland written in classical Latin between 1455 and

1480. Długosz also emphasized the importance and advantages of the traditional role of the Catholic Church in Poland. Through his many charities he founded a home for university students and built monasteries and churches.

Doane, George Hobart Diocesan administrator, born Boston, Massachusetts, 5 September 1830, died Newark, New Jersey, 20 January 1905. Although he graduated in 1852 from Jefferson Medical College, Philadelphia, Pennsylvania, he decided to enter the ministry and was ordained a deacon in the Protestant Episcopal Church, New Jersey, of which his father was bishop. In 1855 he became a Catholic; and after study at the seminary of St Sulpice, Paris, and the Collegio Pio, Rome, he was ordained for the Diocese of Newark on 13 September 1857. He became pastor of the Newark Cathedral, secretary to the bishop and chancellor of the diocese. He served briefly as chaplain in the First New Jersey Brigade during the Civil War. Afterwards he was instrumental in collecting funds to save the North American College in Rome. Doane was named protonotary apostolic in 1889. He was appointed theologian for Bishop John Salpointe at the Third Plenary Council of Baltimore. After attending the council, he was named to the diocesan posts of consultor, dean and member of the cathedral committee.

Dobrizhoffer, Martin Jesuit missionary and author, born Friedberg, Bohemia, 7 September 1718, died Vienna, 17 July 1791. He entered the Austrian province of the Jesuits, 19 October, 1736. He was already ordained when he arrived in Buenos Aires as a member of the expedition of Father Orosz on 1 January 1749. For eighteen years he worked among the Abipon Indians in Gran Chaco and among the northern tribes of the Guarani. After the expulsion of the Jesuits in 1768, he returned to Austria and lived in Vienna until his death. From 1773 he was preacher at the court and Empress **Maria Theresa** frequently invited him to tell his experiences as a missionary. His excellent, objective work on this subject, the *Historia de Abiponibus* (3 vols, 1783–4) puts Dobrizhoffer among the pioneers of ethnology.

Dodd, Charles Harold Congregationalist minister and biblical scholar, born Wrexham, 7 April 1884,

died 22 September 1973 at Goring-on-Thames. He studied classics at Magdalen College, Oxford, then theology at Mansfield College to prepare for the Congregational ministry. He was ordained in 1912, serving in Warwick between 1912 and 1915, but was then invited back to Mansfield to be lecturer and later professor of NT Greek. In 1930 he became professor of biblical criticism and exegesis at Manchester, and in 1935 Norris-Hulse professor of divinity, Cambridge, the first non-Anglican to be appointed. He retired from the post in 1949. He published over twenty books, mostly on the NT, including *The Parables of the Kingdom* (1935), *Epistle to the Romans* (1935), and *The Interpretation of the Fourth Gospel* (1953). His last work, published in 1970, was *The Founder of Christianity*. He was vice-chairman of the NT panel for the *New English Bible*, published in 1970, and its general director from 1949. He was made a fellow of the British Academy in 1946, and a Companion of Honour in 1961.

Dodd, John Born 20 November 1916, died 11 January 1987. RAF corporal, Japanese prisoner-of-war, who found rehabilitation difficult until becoming a prison visitor and discovering that his experience in Changi gave him an empathy with the inmates. He was the founder of the Langley House Trust, set up by Christian Teamwork to cope with recidivist problems by providing a half-way house for offenders. He opened his own home to offer newly-released convicts a temporary respite between prison and the outside world, from which developed more permanent and supportive communities.

Doddridge, Philip English Presbyterian minister and theologian, born London, 26 June 1702, died Lisbon, 26 October 1751. He studied theology in Leicestershire and, being unwilling to subscribe to the Toleration Act, became a Nonconformist minister in Kibworth, 1723, and in Market Harborough, from 1725 to 1729, where he opened an academy, moving it to Northampton when he took charge of a congregation there: he was ordained a presbyter in Northampton on 19 March 1730. He founded there a charity school in 1737, and participated in the institution of a county infirmary in 1743. He opposed rigidity, proclaimed tolerance and committed himself to uniting Nonconformity.

Author of a number of works, of which *Free Thoughts on the Most Probable Means of Reviving the Dissenting Interest* (1730), and a collection of sermons, *On the Rise and Progress of Religion in the Soul* (1745), are perhaps the most significant. His *Family Expositor* of 1739, the final volume appearing posthumously in 1756, a commentary on the NT, was very popular in the eighteenth century. He also composed many hymns, including 'O God of Bethel' and 'Ye servants of the Lord'.

Dodo of Asch   Blessed, premonstratensian hermit; died Asch, Friesland, 30 March 1231. After several years of a marriage reluctantly contracted, he became a Premonstratensian canon of Mariengaard, and his wife entered a convent. Permitted to live as a hermit in a cell at Bakkeveen, Dodo practised extraordinary austerities for many years. About five years before his death he moved to a sanctuary at Asch. His reputation for sanctity and wonder-working attracted the sick of every kind and many were cured. Stigmata were found on his body when he died, but they may have been caused by the fall that killed him. His feast has been celebrated by the Premonstratensians in Spain at least since 1636. Feast day 30 March.

Dolcino, Fra   Heretical leader of the Apostolici, born Diocese of Novara, Italy, died Vercelli, 1 June 1307. The son of a priest or hermit, he was raised by a priest from Vercelli who obtained a good education for him. Dolcino ran away in 1291 and joined the sect of the Apostolici or Pseudo-Apostles founded by Segalelli. Upon the latter's execution on 18 July 1300, Dolcino succeeded him as leader. His eloquence, agreeable manners and skilful interpretation of Scripture won him nearly 4000 disciples. The sect's plundering led Pope **Clement V** to assist the people of Novara to organize a Crusade, and on 23 March 1307, Dolcino was captured by the Crusaders. He was executed by the civil authority, and his body was cut into pieces and burned. The Pseudo-Apostles practised absolute poverty and obeyed God alone, allowing the Roman Church no authority, because of the wickedness of its prelates. Two of Dolcino's letters (August 1300 and December 1303) outlined his doctrines. He awaited the return of the Church to evangelical poverty and to virtue under the leadership of his disciples. He predicted that after the inevitable extermination of contemporary Popes and cardinals, God would then choose the sovereign pontiff.

Dolfin, Pietro   Camaldolese monk, born Venice, 24/25 November 1444, died Venice, 15 January 1525. This Paduan-educated patrician entered the Camaldolese house of S. Michele di Murano, Venice, in 1462. He was elected abbot in 1479, and general of the Order in 1480, moving to its headquarters at Camaldoli in Tuscany and initiating various reform programmes. The Venetian Senate proposed him for a number of vacant bishoprics as well as for the cardinalate, but these bids were unsuccessful. His fellow Venetians Vincenzo Querini and Tommaso Giustiniani entered the Camaldolese Order in 1510, four years before Dolfin renounced the generalship and returned to Venice.

Dolfin, Zaccaria   Cardinal, born Venice, 29 May 1529, died Rome, 19 December 1583. As bishop of Lesina in Dalmatia from 1553 he was appointed nuncio to Emperor **Ferdinand I** at Vienna in July 1560, with a mission to obtain his assent for the reopening of the Council of Trent. The emperor's strong resistance caused Dolfin to be criticized for not presenting the papal position with sufficient force, but he eventually prevailed. He was then sent throughout middle and upper Germany to inform lay and ecclesiastical princes about the reconvening of the council, and was made a cardinal in 1565.

Dölger, Franz Josef   German Roman Catholic church historian, born Sulzbach am Main, 18 October 1879, died Schweinfurt, 17 October 1940. He studied at the University of Würzburg in 1899–1904, when he was awarded his doctorate in theology: he had been ordained there in 1902. He then travelled to Rome, Sicily and North Africa, a journey which aroused his interest in the adaptation of Christianity to the culture in which it found itself. This was to remain his abiding concern, which gave rise to the foundation of the journal *Antike und Christentum* in 1929, in which he published more than 150 articles. He was also cofounder of the *Reallexikon für Antike und Christentum*. He taught first at Würzburg (1906–8), then in Rome. From 1912 he was professor at the University of Münster, moving in 1926 to Breslau and in 1929 to Bonn. He was also interested in the history of the liturgy – his first book, in 1906, was an historico-theological work on the sacrament of confirmation. In 1955 the university of Bonn founded the Franz Josef Dölger Institute.

Döllinger, Johann Joseph Ignaz von Roman Catholic priest and church historian, born Bamberg, 28 February 1799 and died Munich, 10 January 1890. He was ordained in 1822 and taught at Aschaffenburg and at Munich. In his early career he was in favour of a German church with no state connections, ruled only from Rome. Later he became critical of the temporal power of the Pope and defended the liberalism that the First Vatican Council tried to suppress. He was critical of the council and especially of the doctrine of papal infallibility. He was excommunicated in 1871 because he refused to submit to the decisions of the council, moved closer to the Old Catholic Church in Germany, but worked for reunion with Rome. In 1873 he became president of the Bavarian Academy of Sciences. His writings include his three-volume *Reformation* (1845–8), *Luther* (1851), *Hippolytus und Kallistus* (1853), *Heidenthum und Judenthum* (1857), *Christentum und Kirche* (1860), *Die Papstfabeln des Mittelalters* (1863), *Geschichte der Moralstreitigkeiten in der römisch-katholischen Kirche seit dem 16. Jahrhundert* (1889, with F. H. **Reusch**) and *Briefe und Erklärungen über die vatikanischen Dekrete* (1890).

Dominic Saint, founder of the Order of Preachers, or Dominican friars, and the Dominican Sisterhoods, born at Calaruega into the Castilian family of Guzmán, *c.*1170, died Bologna, 6 August 1221. Little is known about his early life: he was educated at the University of Palencia and began his priestly life as a canon of the cathedral at Osma, becoming prior of the chapter there *c.*1201. In that year he went with his bishop to Denmark on a diplomatic mission, and passing through the Languedoc encountered Albigensianism. On their way home, both Dominic and his bishop visited Rome to ask permission to evangelize in Russia, but **Innocent III** encouraged them to combat heresy nearer home. A visit to Cîteaux, whose monks were charged with combating Albigensianism, persuaded him that they were adopting the wrong approach. Dominic became convinced that

there was a need in the Church for a body of trained preachers to safeguard and spread divine truth. He also established a convent at Prouille of nuns who were mostly converts from heresy, and devised for them a Rule of life of enclosure, prayer and penance. Pope Innocent III gave his blessing to the new order and the bishop of Toulouse employed his preachers throughout his diocese. The Order was officially licensed by Pope **Honorius III** in 1216, and its members were to live on alms. In organization Dominic imprinted an indelibly democratic character on the Order of regular consultations and of elections to offices. He spent the rest of his years establishing houses throughout Italy, France and Spain. Feast day 4 August.

Dominic Gundisalvi (Gundissalinus, Dundisalvi) Philosopher, translator, archdeacon of Segovia, died *c.*1170. Dominic probably studied in France; later he lived and worked in Toledo, Spain. He translated many Arabic philosophical works into Latin, working together with the Jewish Avendauth (Ibn Daub). Dominic's translations include Avicenna's *De Anima* and *Metaphysica*, Algazel's *Summa theoricae philosophiae*, Avicebron's *Fons vitae*. Dominic is not considered to be an original thinker but was a precise and fluent translator.

Dominic Loricatus Saint, Benedictine hermit and follower of **Peter Damian**, died near San Severino, 14 October 1060. After his parents made a gift which he considered to be simoniacal to the bishop who ordained him, Dominic became a hermit and lived a life of heroic penance: he gained the name 'Loricatus', the armoured one, after his ascetical practice of wearing a metal breastplate over his bare skin. Sometime around 1040, he joined Peter Damian at Fonte Avellana, who described his penitential practices in a letter to Pope **Alexander II**. Feast day 14 October.

Dominic of Silos Saint and abbot, born *c.*1000, died Silos, 20 December 1076. Dominic was born at Canas, Navarre, Spain, into a peasant family. He was a shepherd as a youth, later becoming first a Benedictine monk and later prior at San Millan de Cogolla Monastery. When Garcia III of Navarre claimed some of the monastery's land, he refused to surrender it, instead becoming abbot at San Sebastian Monastery at Silos. His reforms at San

Sebastian transformed it into a great spiritual centre famous for its scriptorium and art. Dominic is also known for rescuing Christian slaves from the Moors and is credited with miracles of healing. Saint **Dominic**, founder of the Order of Preachers, was named after Dominic of Silos because, it was claimed, his mother had a vision of the earlier St Dominic, who promised she would bear a son. Feast day 20 December.

Dominic of Sora   Saint, abbot, born *c*.951, died *c*.1031. Dominic was born at Foligno, Etruria, Italy. As a Benedictine monk, he is known for his work in building many monasteries across Italy. St Dominic died at Sora, one of his foundations. He was invoked as a protection against thunderstorms. Feast day 22 January.

Dominic of the Causeway   Saint, hermit and builder, died *c*.1109. Dominic was a Basque born at Villoria, Spain. He wanted to become a Benedictine but was refused several times, and so lived as a hermit. For a while he followed St **Gregory of Ostia**, but after his death returned to the life of a hermit. As he lived on the road to Compostela, he tried to help the many pilgrims by building a highway, a bridge and a hospice. Feast day 12 May.

Dominici, Giovanni   Blessed, Dominican and cardinal, born Giovanni Banchini, Florence, 1355/6, died Buda, 10 June 1419. Banchini entered the Dominican Order at S. Maria Novella in his native city in 1374. He became a preacher of note who was devoted to reform of his Order and critical of both the papal schism and that between the Eastern and Western churches. In 1408 he was made archbishop of Ragusa and a cardinal. **Martin V** sent him on a legation to Hungary and Hussite Bohemia, but he died before the mission could be completed. His cult was confirmed in 1832. Feast day 10 June.

Domitian of Ancyra   Bishop. Birth unknown, died Ancyra, 550. Together with Theodore Askidas, Domitian headed the Origenists of Palestine at the beginning of the sixth century. Domitian owed his position as bishop of Ancyra to influence by **Leontius of Byzantium**. With Theodore, Domitian was influential in the condemnation of the 'Three Chapters' (an edict served by **Justinian I** in opposition to Nestorianism) in 548.

Domitian of Maastricht   Saint, bishop. Born France, date unknown, died Huy(?), 560. Domitian was bishop of Tongeren but was transferred to Maastricht. He was present at the Councils of Clermont (535) and Orléans (549). Dominitian was an evangelist who converted the valley of the Mense, founding both churches and hospitals. He is the patron saint of Huy, in Belgium. According to legend he killed a dragon. Feast day 7 May.

Domnolus of Le Mans   Saint, abbot, bishop. Birth unknown, died Le Mans, 1 December 581. Domnolus was abbot of St Laurent in Paris. He declined the bishopric of Avignon, but in 539 he was appointed bishop of Le Mans. He attended the Synod of Tours in 567. Domnolus was responsible for the building of several churches and a hospice for pilgrims on the Sarthe river. Reputedly a man who worked many miracles. Feast day 16 May.

Domnus of Antioch   Bishop, birth unknown, died 271/2. Son of Bishop Demetrian, Domnus was elected bishop of Antioch in 268 after Paul of Samosata's excommunication. However, Paul with Zenobia's support kept possession of the see until 271/2, when Emperor Aurelian decided the dispute in favour of the orthodox party.

Domnus of Antioch   Bishop, birth unknown, died Jerusalem, 449. Domnus was a nephew of **John of Antioch**, his predecessor as bishop of Antioch. Domnus denounced **Eutyches** as monophysite in tendency, provoking a violent response. He was attacked by the Syrian monk Barsumas, who was a supporter of **Cyril of Alexandria**. Subsequently Domnus exonerated Eutyches. Domnus was deposed and replaced by Maximus, and he returned to the convent of St Euthymies, near Jerusalem, where he had lived before accepting the See of Antioch.

Donatello (Donato di Niccolò di Betto Bardi)   Sculptor, born Florence, 1386 or 1387, died Florence, 13 December 1466. Following his apprenticeship with Lorenzo **Ghiberti**, Donatello became the leading sculptor of his day, spearheading an artistic revival along with the architect Filippo **Brunelle-**

schi and the painter **Masaccio**. His extensive Florentine output included the figures of SS Mark, George and Louis of Toulouse for the Orsanmichele niches, the harrowing polychrome wood figure of St Mary Magdalene (Florence, Museo dell'Opera del Duomo, *c*.1456–60), and the bronze David (Florence, Bargello, 1440s/50s) for Cosimo de' **Medici**. Between 1443 and 1457 he was based in Padua and created the equestrian statue of the condottiere Gattamelata (1447–53).

Donatus of Besançon   Saint, bishop, monk. Born *c*.590 Upper Burgundy, died Besançon(?), before 660. Donatus took to the monastic life at an early age at Luxeuil, under the guidance of St **Columbanus**. Whilst bishop of Besançon in 624, Donatus founded a men's monastery, to which he gave a Rule combining those of St Columbanus and St **Benedict**. He also founded a women's monastery, giving it a Rule based on those of St Columbanus, St Benedict and St **Caesarius of Arles**. Feast day 7 August.

Donatus of Carthage   Bishop, born *c*.270 at Casae Nigrae, died in exile, 355. Donatus may have been bishop at the time of the Great Persecution (303–5). He opposed any collaboration with 'pagan' authorities. Opposed election of Caecilian as bishop in succession to Mensurius, eventually leading the main opposition. Arbitration by Pope **Miltiades** (311–14) cleared Caecilian and pronounced against Donatus. North African Christians supported Donatus. Emperor **Constantine I** subsequently also found against Donatus, but from 317 to 347 the majority of African Christians accepted him as bishop. Asked Emperor **Constans I** to recognize him as bishop in 346, but rejection and ensuing riots saw him arrested and exiled.

Donne, John   Dean of St Paul's and leading metaphysical poet, born London in the early part of 1572, died London, 31 March 1631. He was educated at Oxford and then Cambridge and in 1592 became a member of Lincoln's Inn. He served in two expeditions led by the Earl of Essex. He was brought up a Roman Catholic, related on his mother's side to Thomas **More**, but by 1598, when he became secretary to the Keeper of the Great Seal, he must have already joined the Church of England. He wrote two satires against Rome, and

more specifically against the Jesuits (his mother had been sister to an English Jesuit), *Ignatius His Conclave* and *Pseudo-Martyr*. He lost his post as secretary, and was briefly imprisoned, after a secret marriage to his employer's niece, and for a time was in considerable poverty. He was supported by Thomas Morton, later bishop of Durham, who encouraged him to become a clergyman, as did the king. He eventually took orders in the Anglican Church and was soon after made dean of St Paul's, where he became renowned as a preacher. In the early part of his life he wrote largely secular poetry; his *Holy sonnets* and much of his other religious verse, though certainly not all, belong to the period of his ministry, as does the *Hymne to God the Father*. He had an obsession with death, wrote a treatise on suicide and some poems on funerals, and is depicted, for his monument in St Paul's, standing upright in a shroud.

Donus   Pope, born Rome, birth date unknown, though he was an old man when elected to the Papacy on 2 November 676, died Rome, 11 April 678. Donus was the recipient of a vague but conciliatory letter from Theodore, patriarch of Constantinople, seeking an end to the monothelite controversy. Emperor **Constantine IV** Pogonatus also sent a conciliatory letter, but Donus died before he received it. Donus rebuilt and decorated several churches, including putting a marble pavement in the atrium of St Peter's, and disbanded a Nestorian monastery.

Dooley, Thomas Anthony   American Catholic doctor, born 17 January 1927 St Louis, Missouri, died New York City, 18 January 1961. He served in the US Medical Corps during World War II, and then studied medicine at St Louis University. He was commissioned in the naval Medical Corps in 1953, and helped to evacuate Vietnamese from North Vietnam. His experiences led him to resign from the navy and devoted himself to founding medical centres in South-East Asia. He helped to found Medical International Corporation (Medico) to run these centres. He lectured widely in the United States, and wrote two books on his experiences.

Doria, Andrea   Admiral and statesman, born Oneglia, Liguria, 30 November 1466, died Genoa, 25 November 1560. A member of one of the most illustrious families of republican Genoa, Doria devoted much of his long life to mercenary warfare. From 1515 he was in French employment, remaining so after the Spanish capture of Genoa in 1522. Although the French recaptured it in 1527, Doria's contract expired in 1528 and he transferred his services to the Emperor **Charles V**, who later created him prince of Melfi. In later life he was not only first citizen of Spanish-protected Genoa, but the most famous admiral of the age.

Dorotheus of Antioch   Priest. Birth unknown, died Antioch, c.305. Dorotheus was a mid-third-century priest of Antioch. He taught **Eusebius of Caesarea**, who informs us that Dorotheus was put in charge of the Tyre purple works. Dorotheus learned Hebrew to aid his understanding of Scripture, and he was well-versed in Greek culture.

Dorotheus of Gaza   Abbot. Birth unknown, died Gaza, c.550. In c.525 Dorotheus was given a collection of letters direction by the recluses Baranuphius and John in Abbot Seridos' monastery. When Dorotheus was in charge of his own monastery he left his disciples a similar collection of letters. Dorotheus made a synthesis of Palestinian monastic literature, taken from the *Apophthegmata*, the Cappadocians, **John Chrysostom**, Mark the Hermit and Isaiah of Scete.

Dorothy   Martyr, saint, birth unknown, died Alexandria, c.305. Dorothy (also Dorothea) lived in Alexandria and suffered martyrdom in the Diocletian persecution. Mentioned by both **Eusebius of Caesarea** and **Rufinus**. According to legend as Dorothy was being taken to martyrdom she was mocked by a lawyer named Theophilus, who asked her to send him fruits from the garden to which she was going. At the time of her execution an angel appeared to her with a basket of fruit, which she sent to Theophilus, who subsequently became a Christian. Feast day 6 February.

Dosithea of the Kiev Caves   Russian Orthodox saint and recluse, born near Riazan, 1721, died Kiev, 25 September 1776. She entered the St Sergius monastery disguised as a boy. As her parents were searching for her she moved to Kiev, living under the name Dositheus the Hermit, at the great Kiev Caves monastery. Thousands visited her for advice, including the Empress Elizabeth and the future St **Seraphim of Sarov**. She is therefore regarded as a precursor of the Hesychast and monastic revival in Russia. Only after her death did the monks find that she was a woman. Canonized in Ukraine as a local saint in 1994. Feast day 25 September.

Dositheus   Patriarch of Jerusalem, born Peleponnese, 31 May 1641, died Constantinople, 7 February 1707. Appointed patriarch in 1669, he held a local council (the 'Synod of Bethlehem') to combat Protestant influence in the Orthodox East. The council's 'Confession' (written by Dositheus) was accepted throughout the Orthodox world. He also founded a printing press at Jassy in Moldavia to disseminate Orthodox literature in the Turkish empire – the first such press in the East.

Dostoevsky, Feodor Mikhailovich   Russian novelist, writer and thinker, born Moscow, 11 November 1821, died St Petersburg, 28 January 1881. In Moscow he graduated as a military engineer but turned to writing. His political interests led him to be arrested and he was exiled to Siberia. In his writing he expressed his hatred of bourgeois society and his sympathy with the working classes. His writing is characterized by power and deep insight. He attempted to justify the ways of God to man. Dostoevsky's famous works include: *Crime and Punishment*, *The Gambler*, *The Idiot*, *The Possessed* and *The Brothers Karamazov*.

Dow, Lorenzo   Transatlantic revivalist, born Coventry, Connecticut, 16 October 1777, died Georgetown, DC, 2 February 1834. Admitted on trial by the Methodists in 1798, he was never fully authorized by conference, doubtless because of his restless and visionary spirituality. Nonetheless, he spent many years travelling as a Methodist revivalist, serving as a most effective preacher amongst the American frontiers people, travelling it has been calculated some 250,000 miles in his ministry in North America, the West Indies and Europe, where he linked up with some of the more exotic Methodist sects of the early nineteenth century, and became the promoter of the camp meeting. A decided opponent of slavery, he was a convinced republican.

Dowdall, George Counter-reformation friar and archbishop of Armagh, born Drogheda, Ireland, 1487, died London, 15 August 1558, three months before the accession of **Elizabeth I**. The Dowdall family benefited from the dissolution of the monasteries under **Henry VIII**, but George went on to become prior of the Crutched or Crossed Friars at Ardee. Though Anglo-Irish, he was sponsored by the O'Neill for the See of Armagh and he accompanied O'Neill to the English court in 1542 acting as an intermediary with the Crown. The following year he was appointed to Armagh. Dowdall as archbishop had a firm statesmanlike grasp of the political realities of his time, was an outstanding ecclesiastic and sincere pastor, staunch in orthodoxy. Under **Edward VI** he opted for exile in 1551 rather than abandon the Mass for the Second Book of Common Prayer, claiming he 'would never be bishop where the Mass was abolished'. With the government's enforcement of the Edwardian reforms Dowdall's recalcitrance embarrassed the government because hitherto he was unwaveringly loyal to the Crown and had played a key role in controlling O'Neill. However, under **Mary Tudor** he was restored to Armagh and to a life interest in the Ardee monastic properties in 1554.

Dowdall, James Irish layman and martyr, born Wexford or Drogheda, died by hanging in Exeter, England, 20 September 1600. He was a merchant in Drogheda who traded with England and France. On his way back from France in 1598 his ship ran aground in Devonshire, England, and he was arrested, imprisoned and tortured but would not recant his papal allegiance, so he was sentenced to be hanged, drawn and quartered.

Dowie, John Alexander Faith healer and founder of Zion City, Illinois, and the Catholic Christian Church, born Edinburgh, 25 May 1847, died Chicago, 9 March 1907. Dowie was a Congregational minister and then an independent evangelist in Australia, before emigrating to America in 1888. Based in Chicago, he taught that prayer should replace medicine in healing. His denomination was founded in 1895, and Zion City, with 6000 inhabitants, at the turn of the twentieth century. He announced himself to be Elijah the Restorer, but due to financial mismanagement of Zion City he

was discredited. He produced a periodical, *Leaves of Healing*.

Dowland, John Roman Catholic composer and lutenist, born probably in London, though it is possible he was Irish, in 1563, died possibly in London, buried 20 February 1626. He graduated as a bachelor in music from Oxford, and left England, possibly because of his Catholicism, to enter the service of the duke of Brunswick in 1594. He subsequently travelled widely on the Continent and, it has been suggested, spied on his fellow Catholics in Rome, which enabled him to return to England, where he was in 1596. He became court lutenist in Denmark the following year, and stayed in Copenhagen until 1605. He arranged some of the tunes in Thomas Este's *Whole Book of Psalms*, but is largely remembered for the simple melody of his songs, which are still frequently sung.

Doxopatres, Neilos (Nilus the Archimandrite) Byzantine theologian and historian, died Sicily(?). c.1150. At one time notary to the patriarch of Constantinople, then head of the law school, Neilos was invited to Sicily by Roger II (1130–54). At Roger's request, Neilos wrote the history and a geographical-statistical survey of the five patriarchates, demonstrating an anti-Roman, pro-Eastern viewpoint. He is assumed to be the same person as Johannes Doxopatres, who wrote a large theology, two volumes of which are extant and address creation, anthropology, paradise, original sin, the incarnation and Christology.

Doyle, James Warren Irish Augustinian and bishop, born near New Ross, Co. Wexford, 1786, died Carlow, 16 June 1834. Studied at the Augustinian College at New Ross and joined the Order in the early 1800s. He was sent to Portugal, where he continued his studies, helped the Portuguese during the French invasion and acted as interpreter at court. He returned to Ireland, was ordained and taught logic at New Ross and later at Carlow College. In 1819 he was made bishop of Kildare and Leighlin and fought vigorously for Catholic Emancipation, joining the Catholic Association, as well as working to improve education and welfare in his own diocese.

Doyle, William Joseph Gabriel Jesuit military chaplain, notable ascetic. Born in Dalkey, Co. Dublin, 3 March 1873, died during the 3rd Battle of Ypres, 16 August 1917 in World War I. Doyle was educated at Ratcliffe College, Leicestershire. He was also a student and member of staff of many Jesuit colleges, notably Clongowes, Belvedere, Stonyhurst and Enghien in Belgium. He was ordained priest in 1907. Fr Willie Doyle became celebrated as a giver of retreats and was remarkable for the intensity of his spirituality, and yet his asceticism attracted controversy and criticism. He became a military chaplain to the 16th Irish Division of the British Army in 1916; his courage was legendary in administering the sacraments to soldiers in the line of battle and won him the Military Cross for gallantry.

Dracontius, Blossius Aemilius Poet, born c.450–60, died Carthage, c.505. Dracontius was of a senatorial family, who were moved to Carthage, Africa. He was taught by Felicianus in the classics, dedicating himself to law until 484. Dracontius was imprisoned on Gunthamund's orders due to the contents of a *carmen ignotum* written in praise of either **Zeno** or Theodoric. Dracontius' poems include *Satisfacto* (written to Gunthamund to solicit his pardon and grace) and *Laudes Dei*. His later work includes *Epithalamium Ioannis et Vitulai*, his last work in captivity, and *Epithalamium in fratribus dictum*, written after he regained his liberty.

Drew, Samuel Methodist lay preacher, 'the metaphysical shoemaker', born St Austell, Cornwall, 6 March 1765, died Helston, Cornwall, 29 March 1833. Child of a Methodist small farmer, he was apprenticed to shoemaking, from which he absconded. His conversion under the ministry of Adam Clarke in 1785 became a conversion not only to faith but also to education. A class leader and local preacher, he thus became perhaps the most outstanding example of an evangelical autodidact. His writings, in which he engaged in debate with Tom Paine, were philosophical, historical and theological, and showed an indebtedness to John **Locke**. His scholarship was recognized by the award of an Aberdeen MA in 1824.

Drexel, Jeremias German Jesuit spiritual writer and preacher, born Augsburg, 15 August 1581, died Munich, 19 April 1638. Although a Lutheran by birth, he converted to Catholicism and was educated by the Jesuits, which Order he joined in 1598. He studied philosophy and theology in Ingolstadt, and was ordained at Eichstätt in 1610. He taught at Munich, Augsburg and Dillingen before becoming, in 1615, court preacher at Munich to Maximilian I. He began to write in 1620, and by his death was the best-known spiritual writer of the day.

Drexel, Katherine American religious foundress, born Philadelphia, 26 November 1858, died Cornwells Heights, Pennsylvania, 3 March 1955. She was born into an extremely wealthy banking family, and inherited a massive fortune which she wished to give to a missionary congregation for the evangelizing of the black and native American population of the United States. She asked the advice of Pope **Leo XIII**, who suggested that she herself become a missionary. She therefore entered the novitiate of the Sisters of Mercy at Pittsburgh in 1889, but two years later founded, in her family's summer house at Toresdale, Pennsylvania, the Blessed Sacrament Sisters for Indians and Coloured People. Her 49 foundations in the USA included Xavier University in St Louis in 1915.

Driver, Godfrey Rolles Scholar of Semitic languages, born Oxford, 20 August 1892, died Oxford, 22 April 1975, the son of Samuel Rolles **Driver**. After studies at New College, Oxford, he served in the army, 1915–19, being awarded the Military Cross. He was appointed fellow of Magdalen College, Oxford, in 1919, and became professor of Semitic philology. His publications include a grammar of colloquial Arabic, editions of Babylonian laws, Aramaic documents and Ugaritic mythological texts, *Problems of the Hebrew Verbal System* (1936) and *Semitic Writings* (1948). From 1933 to 1940 he was editor of the *Journal of Theological Studies*. He was chairman of the OT panel for the *New English Bible*, which appeared in 1970, and joint director of the project with C. H. **Dodd** from 1965. He was knighted in 1968.

Driver, Samuel Rolles Regius professor of Hebrew and canon of Christ Church, Oxford, born Southampton, 2 October 1846, died Oxford, 26 February

1914. Although originally from a Quaker family, after studies, and a fellowship, at New College, he was offered the canonry of Christ Church and professorship of Hebrew when still only a deacon in the Church of England. He spent all his life in Oxford. He was a member of the OT panel for the *Revised Version of the Bible* (1885). His literary contribution to the world of OT scholarship, and particularly his commentaries on Genesis, did much to make German OT scholarship better known and more acceptable to the English-speaking world. Other writings include *A Treatise on the Use of the Tenses in Hebrew* (1874), *Introduction to the Literature of the OT* (1891), and several OT commentaries.

Droste-Hülshoff, Annette Elisabeth von Leading German poet and baroness, born Schloss Hülschoff, near Münster, Westphalia, 10 January 1797, died Meersburg, Baden, 25 May 1848. She came from a Roman Catholic aristocratic Westphalian family, was educated by tutors, and was introduced to poetry by Levin Schuking, a young novelist, and her ward, seventeen years younger, for whom she developed unrequited love. She had a deeply religious nature. She wrote a cycle of religious poems, *Das Geistliche Jahr*, The Spiritual Year. Nature and religion inspired her. Also she wrote a novella, *Die Judenbuche*, about a Westphalian villager. In her lifetime she went unrecognized, but is now regarded as one of the greatest nature poets, and the greatest female poet of Germany.

Drouin, Hyacinthe René (Drouven) Dominican theologian, born Toulon, *c*.1680, died Ivrée, 30 September 1740. He entered the Order in 1696 and was professed in 1697. In his early life he studied and taught in Paris, receiving a masters degree in 1713. He was appointed professor of theology at the University of Caen in 1719. His primary work was *De re sacramentaria contra perduelles hereticos*, in two volumes (1765).

Drumgoole, John Christopher Irish Roman Catholic social worker, born 15 August 1816, Granard, Co. Longford, died New York, 28 March 1888. On arriving in New York aged eight he began his schooling at St Patrick's Cathedral School, but was unable to continue because he had to support his widowed mother. He was not able to enter the

seminary of Our Lady of Angels until the age of 49: ordination followed four years later. He is internationally known for his work with homeless children, founding homes and schools and being influential in bringing into being a New York law providing for homeless children to be placed in homes of their own religion.

Druthmar Saint, monk and abbot, died Corvey, 15 February 1046. He entered a community at Lorsch and was made abbot at Corvey, Westphalia, in 1014. His reputation for learning and observance of the monastic discipline enabled him to bring the monks to a greater degree of observance. His body and that of Unsdorf of Corvey (d. 983) were exhumed in 1100, after which a cult developed. A statue of the seventeenth century at Corvey gives him the title Blessed. Feast day 13 August.

Druzbicki, Gaspar Jesuit writer and preacher, born Druzbice, Poland, 6 January 1590, died Posen, 2 April 1662. He entered the Society of Jesus in 1609; thereafter followed several years of teaching, especially of logic, and he was novice master and rector of colleges at Kalisz, Ostrog and Posen. He was twice provincial. He wrote extensively in both Latin and Polish. His ascetical writings are mostly on the religious life and include a series of meditations.

Dryden, John Poet, dramatist and critic, born 9 August 1631, Aldwinkle All Saints, Northamptonshire, died London, 1 May 1700. He was a celebrated author, publishing his first volume of poetry, *Heroic Stanzas*, in 1659 to commemorate the death of Oliver **Cromwell**. *Religio Laici*, written in 1682, was a defence of Anglicanism, but, having been fairly uninterested in religion until his fifties, he converted to Roman Catholicism in 1686 following the accession of **James II**. *The Hind and the Panther* was in praise of his new faith, in which he remained for the rest of his life, losing as a result the title of poet laureate.

Du Bellay, Jean Cardinal, diplomat and religious reformer, born Gratigny, 1492, died Rome, 16 February 1560. He was born into a powerful family and after being licensed in law at the University of Orléans, he was given the abbacy of a monastery in Picardy, then had a string of appointments to bishoprics in Bayonne in 1524, Paris in 1532, and to the archbishopric of Bordeaux in 1545. He resigned as bishop of Paris in 1551 and retired to Rome – he had been made a cardinal in 1535. He took part in diplomatic missions for **Frances I** to England, Rome and Germany, promoting peace, church reform and conciliation. He wrote three books of poems, and his unpublished letters are held in the Bibliothèque Nationale.

Dublanchy, Edmond   Marist theologian. Born Bruville, 21 January 1858, died Differt, Luxemburg, 26 January 1938. He studied theology and became a deacon before entering the novitiate of the Society of Mary, Dundalk, Ireland. He was professed and ordained on 1 and 2 October 1881 respectively. Dublanchy worked as a teacher in several countries for the Society but is best known for his written work. His interests were in the controversy around salvation outside the Church, Thomism, and in support of papal temporal power. Main works: *De Axiomate Extra Ecclesiam Nulla Salus* (1895), and *La Voix de Pierre* (1926).

Dubois (François Clément), Théodore   Composer and organist. Born Rosnay (Marne), 24 August 1837, died Paris, 11 June 1924. He studied at the Paris Conservatoire and was a colleague of César **Franck** at Ste Clothilde. He succeeded Saint-Saëns as organist at the Madeleine. He composed widely but is best known for his religious music. His main compositions are *Seven Last Words of Christ* (1867), and a *Mass in B Minor* (1914). He also wrote a standard work on counterpoint and fugue.

Dubois, Guillaume   French cardinal. Born Brive-la-Gaillande, 6 September 1656, died Paris, 10 August 1723. His early life was spent as a tutor and then, also as a tutor, in the service of the brother of the king. This influence helped him rise in status, and in 1715 he became a member of the Council of State. He took part in several diplomatic missions, including securing an Anglo-French alliance against Spain, and became foreign minister in 1718. He was ordained in 1720, became archbishop three months later, cardinal a year later, and prime minister in 1722.

Dubois, John   American bishop, born Paris, 24 August 1764, died New York City, 20 December 1842. His schooling was in company with **Robespierre** and Desmoulins, but he entered a seminary and was ordained in 1787. His pastoral work was interrupted by the French Revolution and he escaped to Norfolk, Virginia. He became an American citizen, did missionary work and built the first Catholic church in Frederick, Maryland. He spent some years establishing and developing a seminary at Emmitsburg, affiliating both it, and himself, to the Society of St Sulpice – though the link did not survive. He was appointed bishop of New York in 1826. His appointment was not popular with the Irish who formed in New York the majority of the Catholic community, but his work in the see was successful and initial hostility was replaced by affection.

Dubois, Louis Ernest   French cardinal, archbishop. Born St-Calais, 1 September 1856, died Paris, 23 September 1929. He was ordained in 1879 and served in the capacity of curate, pastor, vicar general and almoner in Le Mans. He served as bishop of Verdun in 1901–9, rising to archbishop of Bourges in 1909, through his support for the Holy See's directives on the separation of Church and State. He became cardinal of Rouen and then Paris, during which time he travelled widely on official business. He worked for conciliation with cultural associations and began radio broadcasts of sermons. His main written works are *Vie de St Joseph* (1927), and *Paroles Catholiques* (1928).

Dubois, Pierre   Probably born near Coutances, *c.*1250, died northern France, *c.*1321. His early life in Paris included a period at law school and lectures by **Thomas Aquinas**. He is known for his attack on papal power and his advocacy of secular leadership of the Church – the view of the French monarchy at the time – which he believed would promote peace in Europe and the expansion of Christianity. He also advocated the setting up of schools of oriental languages.

Du Bos, Charles   French author and critic. Born Paris, 27 October 1882, died La Celle St Cloud, 5 August 1939. He had a Catholic education as a boy, but lost his faith while at Oxford, 1900–1, studying philosophy. He worked in publishing, and as a writer. He produced a collection of critical essays in seven volumes, on the works of Byron, Mauriac and Gide among others, called *Approximations* (1922–37). He was also published posthumously in 1945 in *Qu'est-ce que la littérature?* which includes an 'Hommage' by a number of well known writers. In 1927 he returned to Catholicism, and in his last years of life taught in Catholic universities in the United States.

Dubourg, Louis William Valentine French bishop. Born Cap Française, Santo Domingo, 14 February 1766, died Besançon, 12 December 1833. He went to France as a small child, was ordained probably in 1788 but escaped to Baltimore, Maryland during the French Revolution. There he entered the Society of St Sulpice. He served in teaching posts, becoming president of Georgetown College, and founding St Mary's College in 1803. He was appointed bishop of Louisiana during the Civil War. During his tenure a Catholic cathedral was constructed here, schools founded and a seminary opened. A rift was caused over the official appointments, and Dubourg resigned in 1826. He was nominated for the Diocese of Montauban and became archbishop of Besançon in 1833. In 1830 he published a concordance to the four Gospels

Dubricius Saint, also known as **St Dyfrig or Devereux**, monk and bishop. It is claimed that he was born near Madely in Herefordshire and died Bardsey Island(?), c.550. He was one of the earliest and most important saints of South Wales. There is little verifiable information about his life but he became the subject of many medieval legends and was mentioned in *The Book of Llandaff* and *The Life of Benedict*. **Geoffrey of Monmouth** cites him as archbishop of Caerleon and claims that he crowned King Arthur. He is also said to have been bishop of Llandaff and to have had his headquarters at Henllan near Ross on Wye and at Moccas. He is credited with having set up many monastic establishments, and a number of churches in Wales are dedicated to him. He is said to have died as a hermit on Bardsey Island. Feast day 14 November.

Du Cange, Charles Dufresne French historian and philologist, born Amiens, 18 December 1610, died Paris, 23 October 1688. He was educated by the Jesuits at Amiens, then studied law at the University of Orléans, but through a convenient marriage became treasurer of that region, a lucrative post that allowed him much time for research. He moved back to Paris in 1668. The range of his knowledge was immense, but he is best known for his philological work on Late Latin and Byzantine Greek. The three-volume dictionary he published on Late Latin in 1678, *Glossarium ad scriptores mediae et infimae latinitatis*, continues to be in use as the most complete reference work on the subject.

Ducas, Demetrius Byzantine scholar, born in Heraklion and died c.1527 in Crete. In the first decade of the sixteenth century he was working in Venice for Aldus **Manutius**. As a pioneer of Hellenic studies in Spain he published at his own expense the first two Greek books printed in the Iberian peninsula. He was principal editor of Cardinal **Ximénez'** Polyglot Bible, was chief editor of the Greek NT edition of the Septuagint and edited a number of other Greek works. Contemporary reference to him disappears in 1527 after the sack of Rome, where he also taught.

Duccio di Buoninsegna Artist, born Siena, c.1255–60, died there, c.1318–19. There is little documentary information on Duccio and few works attributed to him with certainty. He is credited with being the first great master of the Sienese school of painting and every subsequent Sienese master depended in some way on his work. His major works are the Rucellai Madonna and the Maestà altarpiece held in the Uffizi and Siena Cathedral Museum respectively. His art form while within the Italo-Byzantine style added new ingredients of elegance, sentiment and sense of colour harmony and refined craftsmanship.

Duchesne, André French historian, born Touraine, May 1584, died Paris, 30 May 1640. He was both a royal and ecclesiastical historiographer, writing a history of the House of Burgundy and of the Popes down to **Paul V**.

Duchesne, Louis Priest, historian and academic, born Saint-Servan-sur-Mer, 13 September 1843, died Rome, 21 April 1922. His interest in Christian archaeology was sparked by his years as a student in Rome. After ordination in 1867 he spent four years teaching, then went on to higher studies. His 1877 dissertation was on the *Liber Pontificalis* and laid the groundwork for his important two-volume edition of the *Liber* (1886–92). He was appointed professor of church history. His radical treatment of the early Papacy, and of early Christianity in general, led to his being denounced by the Congregation of the Index, but he was defended by his rector. However, he resigned the professorship in 1885, and moved to the Ecole supérieur des Lettres until, in 1895, he was appointed to the Ecole archéologique française at Rome. He became a member of the French Academy in 1910. His critical approach gave rise to opposition within the Roman Catholic Church and his three-volume history of the early Church (1906–10) was put on the Index in 1912.

Duchesne, Rose Philippe Saint, nun and missionary. Born Grenoble, 29 August 1769 into a merchant family, died St Charles, Missouri, 18 October 1852. Educated in early life by the Visitation nuns, she was prevented from joining the community by her father and therefore devoted herself to good works. She bought the convent buildings in 1802 and after failing to revive the religious life there she joined the Society of the Sacred Heart at the invitation of its foundress. Professed in 1804, she eventually realized her calling to be a missionary in America. Here she and other sisters established schools first at St Charles, and in New Orleans, St Louis and elsewhere. In old age she attempted to set up a school for Native Americans at Sugar Creek (Kansas). Age, health and language difficulties frustrated this attempt, and she died ten years later in conditions of extreme personal poverty. She was canonized in 1988. Feast day 17 November.

Duesberg, Hilaire Benedictine biblical scholar, born Verviers, Belgium, 29 August 1888, died Strasburg, France, 11 March 1969. He joined the Benedictine Order in 1907 and was ordained in 1914. He worked in Ireland and Jerusalem, returning to Belgium to publish many books and articles on biblical subjects and give numerous retreats and conferences. During and after World War II, he was professor at Fribourg University. He was elected to the Royal Belgium Academy of French Language and Literature and edited *Bible et la Vie*

Chrétienne. His main works include *Les Scribes Inspirés* (1965), *Ecclesiasticus* (1966) and *Adam, Père des Hommes Modernes* (1968).

Dufay, Guillaume Composer, born possibly in Flanders, *c.*1400, died Cambrai, 27 November 1474. He was a choirboy at Cambrai and returned there as a canon after living for a time in Italy. He was well known and celebrated in his time, and more than 200 of his works survive, including eight Masses. He instigated the use of the *cantus firmus* Mass and was very influential with Renaissance composers.

Duff, Alexander Pioneer Church of Scotland missionary to India, born Moulin, Perthshire, 25 April 1806, died Sidmouth, Devon, 12 February 1878. Influenced by Thomas **Chalmers** at St Andrews University and a key figure in the group of students who set their hearts and minds on overseas mission, Duff was appointed headmaster by the Church of Scotland. In Calcutta from 1830, Duff articulated a philosophy of mission based on English higher education as intrinsically evangelistic. As practised by a gifted teacher this was successful for a time. While back in Scotland from 1834 he wrote *India and India Missions* (1839) and *Missions the Chief End of the Christian Church* (1839). In India again from 1840 to 1851, and 1855 to 1863, he returned to be convenor of the Free Church foreign mission committee and in 1867 was appointed to the first ever chair of missions.

Duff, Edward Aloysius American Catholic priest, born Philadelphia, 31 May 1881, died Philadelphia, 11 February 1943. He studied at several colleges and seminaries before being ordained on 21 June 1911. He served as assistant at Charleston Cathedral and chaplain to the Navy in various capacities throughout his life. He travelled in these roles to London, Paris and Venice and accompanied the body of the Unknown Soldier to the United States. He became Chief of Navy Chaplains in 1936 and retired in 1938.

Duffy, Charles Gavan Journalist and politician, born Monaghan, Ireland, 12 April 1816, died Nice, France, 9 February 1903. He began his career as a journalist in his home town, then moved to Dublin and in 1839 was appointed editor of the Ulster

Catholic paper *The Vindicator*, a post he held for three years, returning to Dublin in 1842, where he founded *The Nation* as a paper of the movement for home rule. In the famine he espoused more radical views, but in 1852 was elected to Parliament for New Ross, Co. Wexford. Disillusioned with politics, he left for Australia in 1854, where he was persuaded to stand for the state parliament of Victoria, rising to the rank of prime minister. He left Victoria in 1880, and devoted the remainder of his life to writing, including *Young Ireland* (1884) and *My Life in Two Hemispheres* (1903).

Duffy, Francis Patrick Canadian Catholic military chaplain, born Cobourg, Ontario, 2 May 1871, died New York, 26 June 1932. He was educated at Catholic colleges and seminaries in both Canada and New York and was ordained in Cobourg on 6 September 1896. He taught philosophy and edited the *New York Review*. He later became World War I's best-known chaplain, and his statue in Times Square is the first ever erected on public land in New York State. He was highly decorated, receiving the Distinguished Service Cross, Distinguished Service Medal and Legion of Honour.

Dugdale, William Historian, born near Coleshill, Warwickshire, 12 September 1605, died Blythe Hall, also near Coleshill, 10 February 1686. His antiquarian interests took him into heraldry, eventually becoming Garter King of Arms. He was a royalist, and went into exile in 1648. Before the Civil War he had met Roger Dodsworth, who was collecting material on the foundation of monasteries in the North. During his exile he collected material on monastic foundations, and the first volume of his main work, the *Monasticon Anglicanum*, appeared in 1655, a year after Dodsworth's death. The third and final volume came out in 1673. His other works include *Antiquities of Warwickshire* (1656), *History of St Paul's Cathedral* (1658) and the three-volume *The Baronage of England* (1675–6).

Duggan, Alfred Leo British novelist and biographer, born Buenos Aires, 1903, died Ross-on-Wye, Herefordshire, 14 April 1964. Of Irish and American parentage, he came to England in 1905 to be educated at Eton and Balliol College. At the age of twenty he advocated atheism, but soon returned to

the Church and remained a devout Catholic for the rest of his life. His first novel, *Conscience of the King*, was written at the age of 49, to be followed by fourteen other works plus the educational books *Arches and Spires* (1962) and *Growing Up In 13th. Century England* (1962).

Duglioli, Helena Blessed, born Bologna, 1472, died Bologna, 23 September 1520. She married Benedetto dall'Oglio in 1489. After his death thirty years later she devoted herself to a life of prayer and mortification. She died aged 48 and is buried at S. Giovanni di Monte. After her death she was venerated for the holiness of her life and was beatified in 1828. Feast day 23 September.

Duhamel, Jean-Baptiste French Roman Catholic priest, scientist, philosopher and theologian, born Vire, Normandy, 11 June 1624, died Paris, 6 August 1706. Studied in Caen and Paris, was an Oratorian for ten years but left and took charge of the parish of Neuilly-sur-Marne before becoming chancellor of the church at Bayeux. He was the first secretary of the Académie des Sciences in 1666, a post he held until 1697. He wrote widely in science and philosophy, but among his religious writings, approached with scientific rigour, are his seven-volume *Theologia speculatrix et practica* (1690), *Institutiones biblicae* (1698) and *Biblia sacra Vulgata editionis* (1705).

Duhem, Pierre Maurice Marie French philosopher and physicist, born Paris, 10 June 1861, died Cabrespine, 14 September 1916. His work in thermodynamics was in advance of his time, and he is known for his contribution to the history of science, for reviving interest in medieval science and for his work in the philosophy of science. In particular his written works present the view that scientific theories and models are not direct descriptions or explanations of the world but can be used as predictive and psychological devices. Among his major works is the ten-volume *Système du monde*, the first volume of which appeared in 1913. He was a devout Roman Catholic and his *Physique du croyant* (1905) was an attempt to reconcile his science with his faith.

Du Houx, Jeanne A mystic, born Pinczon France, 2 September 1616, died Colombier, 26 September

1677. She had an early call to the religious life but was subjected to an arranged marriage. Her husband, however, joined her in charitable works, and after his early death she entered the Visitation Convent at Colombier. She divided her time here between activity in the world and the contemplative life. A vision of St Jane Frances de **Chantal** taught her abandonment while communications with souls in purgatory characterized her spirituality. Her simplicity is said to identify her spirituality as Salesian while her emphasis on 'putting on the Spirit of Jesus Christ' identifies her with the school of **Bérulle**.

Duhr, Bernard   German Jesuit and historian, born Cologne, 2 August 1852, died Munich, 21 September 1930. He entered the Order in 1872 and was ordained in 1887. He is one of the greatest authorities on Jesuit history, specializing in the period 1550 to 1800. His best-known works are *Die Studienordnung der Gesellschaft Jesu* (1906) and the still indispensable *Geschichte der Jesuiten in den Ländern deutscher Zunge* (1907–28).

Dujčev, Ivan   Bulgarian Orthodox medievalist, born Bulgaria, 1907, died Sofia, 1986. Having conducted extensive research into the history of Bulgaria, he became convinced of the importance of Western religious influences, especially during the seventeenth and nineteenth centuries. He was ostracized by the intellectual community during the early stages of communist rule, but was eventually reinstated and made a member of the Academy of Science of Bulgaria in 1981. He bequeathed his document collection to the University of St Clement of Ohrid in Sofia, where it is now the Ivan Dujčev Centre for Slavo-Byzantine Studies.

Dumont, Henri   Belgian composer of church music, born Villers l'Evèque, 1610, died Paris, 8 May 1684. He changed the Walloon family name de Thier to the French form Du Mont in 1635. He was a chorister and then organist at the church of Notre Dame in Maastricht and then organist at Paris in 1640. Queen Marie Thérèse appointed him chamber harpsichordist in 1660, and in 1663 he was named as a maître de chapelle in the Chapelle Royale. He composed numerous pieces, including five plainchant Masses, motets and keyboard works.

Dumoulin, Jean (Joannes Molinaeus)   Belgian canonist and theologian, born Ghent, 1525, died Louvain, 29 September 1575 by starvation. He was appointed to the chair of canon law in 1557 at Louvain. In 1573 he went to Rome to seek suppression of the government's subjection of certain abbeys to new bishoprics. This attempt failed and his orthodoxy was questioned. He went into seclusion, where he starved to death. He published the *Decretum* of **Ivo of Chartres** (1562).

Dunin, Martin von   Polish archbishop, born Wal near Rawa, 11 November 1774, died Poznán, 26 December 1842. He was ordained in 1797 after studying in Rome. He served as canon and then archbishop of the Sees of Gnièzo and Poznán. He attempted to bring about peace between the Prussian government and its Polish subjects but ran into difficulties over the issue of mixed marriages, insisting that children of such marriages be educated as Catholics. This stance led to legal restrictions on his movements and then to house arrest. Under King Friederich Wilhelm IV Dunin was able to return to his see and was known for his pious and benevolent ministry.

Dunn, Joseph   American Celtic scholar, born New Haven, Connecticut, 26 August 1874, died there, 9 April 1951. On graduation from Yale University he taught Latin at the Catholic University of America and was then fellow in Gaelic at Harvard. Celtic studies at Freiburg im Breisgau and Rennes followed, and he was appointed to a chair of Celtic at the Catholic University of America in 1904. He translated *Le Vie de St Patrice: Mystère Breton* (1909), *Taín Bó Cuailnge* (1914) and a *Life of St Alexis* (1920). He also produced a grammar of the Portuguese language.

Dunne, Finley Peter   American humorist and journalist, born Chicago, 10 July 1867, died New York, 24 April 1936. He was a journalist and editor of the *Chicago Journal* (1897–1900). He developed a satirical way of working and created a famous philosopher-bartender 'Mr Dooley', who commented on and became famous for his American-Irish satire on contemporary events and people. He wrote *Mr Dooley in Peace and War* (1898) and many other books.

Dunne, M. Frederic American Cistercian abbot, born Ironton, Ohio, 25 April 1874, died Knoxville, Tennessee, 4 August 1948. He became the first American Cistercian (Trappist) abbot, although his first attempt to enter the Trappist abbey of Gethsemane at the age of twenty was discouraged by the then abbot, a Frenchman who advised him to study instead for the diocesan priesthood. He did, however, enter Gethsemane and was ordained in 1901. He progressed through the ranks and became abbot in 1935, eventually presiding over a community of more than 200 monks.

Dunne, Peter Masten American Jesuit historian, born San José, California, 16 April 1889, died San Francisco, 15 January 1957. He entered the Society of Jesus in 1906 and was ordained in England in 1921. His life was spent in writing, initially for the Jesuit magazine *America*, and teaching at Santa Clara College and Los Gatos. His first book, *Mother Mary of St Bernard*, was published in 1929, and he subsequently wrote works on Hispanic America and the Jesuit missions, many articles and book reviews. He was elected president of the Pacific Coast branch of the American Historical Association in 1955.

Duns Scotus, Johannes Franciscan, priest, philosopher, theologian and teacher, born 1265, probably at Moxton, near Roxburgh, died Cologne, 8 November 1308. He was taught by an uncle at the friary at Dumfries, and entered the Order. He went to Oxford c.1290 and was ordained in 1291. From 1293 to 1296 he was a student in Paris, but then returned to Oxford to lecture on the *Sentences* of **Peter Lombard**, 1297–1301. He studied, and then taught, at Paris again until 1307, when he was sent to teach at Cologne, where he died. He wrote commentaries on Aristotle, and many other works in his short lifetime, but his most important work is the commentary on the *Sentences*, based on his notes from his Oxford lectures. His thought incorporated elements from **Augustine** within the Aristotelianism influential at the time. In particular he advocated that love and will were of first importance in distinction from the primacy of knowledge and reason of St **Thomas Aquinas**. He is also known as the first theologian of note to defend the Immaculate Conception and the inevitability of the Incarnation irrespective of the Fall. The Scotist system was particularly influential in medieval times and was accepted by the Franciscans as a basis for doctrine. In the Middle Ages he was known by the nickname of 'Doctor subtilis' – 'the subtle teacher', and is listed in the Franciscan calendar of saints.

Dunstable, John (Dunstaple) Musician and mathematician, born 1370, Dunstable, Bedfordshire, died London, 24 December 1453 and is buried at St Stephen's, Walbrook. Nothing is known of the early part of his life. He became famous Europe-wide for being one of the earliest musicians to lay the foundations of the great schools of music of the fifteenth century. He was chief musician in England and is first mentioned in the *Proportionale* of John Tractus (1445–1511). There were many claims to his influence, such as inventing counterpoint, which were challenged by continental writers but it seems that this notwithstanding, an English school of music advanced for its time existed even prior to Dunstable. Examples of his music are held in the British Museum and Lambeth Libraries.

Dunstan Saint, archbishop of Canterbury, abbot, minister and ascetic, born 909 near Glastonbury, died Canterbury, 19 May 988. He came from a noble family, and was educated at Glastonbury Abbey, then in the household of his uncle, who was archbishop of Canterbury. From there he went to the court of King Athelstan, was professed at Glastonbury and made abbot in c.940. Under his guidance, the full observance of the Rule of St **Benedict** was reinstated. Between 945 and 955 he was minister and treasurer to King Eadred. He had to go into exile after he had criticized the conduct of King Edwig, which gave him the opportunity to see for himself the style of reformed monasticism on the Continent. He was recalled from exile by King Edgar in 959 and with him began the reform of Church and State. In 970, at a meeting at Winchester, there was promulgated the *Regularis Concordia*, establishing the norms by which monastic life should be observed. It reflected many of the practices Dunstan had encountered on the Continent. A number of monasteries were reformed under Dunstan's influence. He was made archbishop of Canterbury in 960, and showed the same determination to reform the lives of the secular clergy. He was also known as a musician, illuminator and metalworker. Feast day 19 May.

Du Pac de Bellegarde, Gabriel   French Jansenist historian, born at Bellegarde (Aude), 17 October 1717, died Utrecht, 13 December 1789. He joined the Jansenist party as a young lawyer and was then appointed canon in Lyons. His views however led to the loss of this post and he moved to a seminary in Holland. He defended the schismatic Church of Utrecht but also attempted reconciliation with Rome. He was a professional historian whose work contributed extensively to the archives of the Ancienne Hérésie. His main works are *Mémoires Historiques sur l'affaire de la Bulle Unigenitus dans les Pays-Bas* (1755), *Histoire abrégée de L'Eglise métropolitainé d'Utrecht* (1765) plus biographies of Van **Espen** and Antoine **Arnauld**.

Dupanloup, Félix Antoine Philibert   Priest, educator and bishop, born St Felixin the Savoie, 3 January 1802, died Lacombe, 11 October 1878. He was an illegitimate child, brought up by his mother in Paris. He was ordained in 1825 and worked in the parishes of Madeleine and St Roch. He was noted for his new educational methods, particularly for the development of the 'Catechism of St Sulpice'. He was made bishop of Orléans in 1849. The rest of his life was spent in influencing educational policy, and he also obtained the right for the Church to run voluntary schools. He was one of only two who voted against the dogma on papal infallibility in 1870, though eventually he accepted the view of the majority. He published widely in the form of letters and panegyrics, his main works being *La Haute Education Intellectuelle* (1850) and *La Femme Studieuse* (1869).

Duperron, Jacques Davy   Cardinal and statesman, born a Calvinist in Berne, Switzerland, 25 November 1556, died Paris, 5 September 1618. His father was a Calvinist minister, but Duperron was received into the Roman Catholic Church by Jesuits in 1577 or 1578, having been converted, it was claimed, by reading the *Summa Theologiae* of **Thomas Aquinas**. He was closely associated with both Henry III and **Henry IV**. The latter made him bishop of Evreux in 1591 and himself converted to Catholicism under Duperron's guidance in 1593. Duperron's later life was spent in the midst of religious controversy and public dispute. He became cardinal in 1604, and French ambassador to the Papacy. He was made archbishop of Sens in 1606. In this role he mediated the reconciliation of the Pope and Venice. His main works are *Réplique à la réponse du sérénissime roy de la Grande Bretagne* (1620) and *Traité de l'eucharistie* (1622).

Dupin, Louis Ellies   Theologian, born Paris, 17 June 1657, died Paris, 6 June 1719. His writing on early church history aroused hostility because of his unconventional views. However, his *Nouvelle Bibliothèque des Auteurs Ecclésiastiques* in 60 volumes (1686–1719), was not placed on the Index until 1757. He had Gallican sympathies and connections with Port-Royal but is not considered a Jansenist. He is also known for his attempt in later life to bring about reconciliation between Anglican and Roman Catholic Churches through his friendship with Archbishop W. Wake.

Du Plessis, David Johannes   Pentecostal ecumenist, born Twenty-four Rivers, near Cape Town, 7 February 1905, died Pasadena, 1987. Born to Pentecostal parents, Du Plessis was ordained into the Apostolic Faith Mission (AFM) in 1930. In 1936 he became general secretary. In 1947 he attended the first Pentecostal World Conference in Zurich, resigning as general secretary and organizing future world conferences. In 1952 he made contact with the World Council of Churches, and following Vatican II he acted as co-chairperson in Roman Catholic/Pentecostal dialogue sessions. He was the first non-Catholic to receive the Benemerenti award, and he gained the name of 'Mr Pentecost'. In the 1930s he edited the AFM *Comforter/Trooster* magazine, and a collection of his writings appeared in 1961 as *The Spirit Bade Me Go*. Two books were produced from interviews with him: *A Man Called Mr. Pentecost* (1977) and *Simple and Profound* (1986).

Du Plessis-Mornay, Philippe   Huguenot and statesman, born Normandy, 1549, died at his castle in La Fôrete-sur-Sèvre, Poitou, 1623. His family became Protestant after the death of his father in 1559. He studied in Paris, fought in the second War of Religion, where he survived the St Bartholomew's Day Massacre in 1572, and went to England. He fought for the Huguenots and acted as diplomatic agent for William of Orange and Henry of Navarre. He returned to France and worked for the union of the Protestant churches. In 1589 he became governor of Saumur and built a Protestant church and academy there. He helped bring about the Edict of Nantes in 1598. He published several works including: *Traité de L'Eglise* (1578), *De la Vérité de la religion chrétienne* (1581), *De l'Institution, usage et doctrine du saint sacrement de l'eucharistie en l'Eglise ancienne* (1598), and *Mysterium Iniquitatis seu Historia Papatus* (1611).

Duprat, Guillaume French bishop, Catholic Reformer, born Issoire, 1507, died Beauregard, 22 October 1560. The son of the archbishop of Sens and St Benoît-sur-Loire, he succeeded to the bishopric of Clermont at the age of 23 following the death of his uncle, the previous incumbent. He took part in the Council of Trent in 1545, contributing to discussion on Holy Scripture, tradition and the sacraments. He founded the first Jesuit seminary in France and was involved in the training of preachers by establishing colleges at Billom and Mauriac.

Durán, Diego Spanish Dominican chronicler, born Seville, 1537, died Mexico, 1588. He went to New Spain as a child and entered the monastery of St Dominic, Mexico City, in 1556. He began his Chronicle in 1574 and finished it in 1581. The manuscript discovered in the National Library in Madrid in the nineteenth century includes treatises on the Mexican calendar, Mexican religious ideas and practices and a history of Mexico. He had sympathy for the culture and wished it to be retained but Christianized and hoped that his Chronicle would help missionaries to understand Indian religions.

Durand, Alfred Jesuit exegete and semiticist, born Chantemerle (Drome), 12 March 1858, died Lyons-Fourrière, 31 July 1928. He was ordained in the Society of Jesus in 1890 and studied in England, France and Lebanon. After studying Semitic languages, Egyptology and Assyriology, he became professor of sacred Scripture at Hastings, England. His main works are *L'Evangile selon S. Matthieu* (1927), *L'Evangile selon S. Jean* (1927), *L'Enforce*

de Jesus-Christ (1927). The latter part of his life was engaged in conducting retreats for priests.

Durand de Maillane, Pierre-Toussaint Canonist, born S. Renigius, Provence, 1 November 1729, died Aix, 15 August 1814. He took a prominent role in the French Revolution. He was influential in tempering the measures put in place against religion and in formulating policies concerning religion. He wrote on the history of the revolution, on the history of canonical institutes and a 'Plan de Code civil et uniform pour toute la République française'.

Durandus, William French canonist, liturgist, bishop, born about 1235, Puimisson, Beziers, Provence, died Rome, 1 November 1296. Studied law at Bologna and later taught at Modena. He was given titular canonries at Beauvais and Chartres by **Clement IV**, and was auditor to **Gregory X** at the Second Council of Lyons in 1274, for which he drew up the decrees. He became papal governor in Romagna and established the town of Urbania. In 1286 he became bishop of Mende, Narbonne, but his nephew, also William, administered the diocese until 1291. He returned to Italy in 1295, but would not accept **Boniface VIII**'s offer of the archbishopric of Ravenna. His most famous work is his eight-volume *Rationale divinorum officiorum* (1286), giving the laws, customs, symbolism and ceremonies of the Roman rite. He also wrote *Speculum Legatorum, Speculum Judiciale, Brevarium, sive Repertorium juris canonici, Brevarium glossarum et textuum juris canonici* and *Commentarius in canones Concilii Lugdunensis II.*

Durandus of Aurillac French Dominican theologian, born 1280, Auvergne, dates given for his death are variously 1330, 1332 or 1335. He joined the Order at Clermont. There is disputed evidence that he is the 'Durandellus', author of *Evidentiae contra Durandum* (c.1330). He took part in theological debate in the presence of Philip VI and opposed in writing the Pope's view against the proposition 'whether the souls of the blessed possess the beatific vision before the day of the last judgement'. It is claimed he was the author of *Scripta in 4 Libros sententiarium*, which has not yet been found.

Durandus of Saint-Pourçain   Dominican, bishop and Scholastic philosopher, born Saint-Pourçain in the Auvergne, 1275, died Meaux, 10 September 1334. He entered the Order at Clermont, and was sent to Paris to study theology. His commentary on the *Sentences* of **Peter Lombard**, probably written 1307–8, is critical of the teaching of **Thomas Aquinas**. He revised the work several times, but propositions from his writings were condemned by the master general of the Dominicans in 1313. By this time, however, Durandus had been summoned to the papal court at Avignon, and he became successively bishop of Limoux, of Le Puy and of Meaux. He also wrote on the origins of political authority, and on the beatific vision – a work to which **John XXII** took exception. He was an early teacher of nominalism (the theory of knowledge which holds that universal concepts have no independent reality but are simply names to identify things with similar characteristics). He also taught a strong contrast between faith and reason, and that in the Eucharist the existence of bread and wine was not in opposition to the presence of Christ.

Durandus of Troarn   Abbot, born Normandy, 1010, died Troarn, 11 February 1088. He became abbot of Troarn in 1059. He is best known for his writings on the Eucharist. He stressed the spiritual nature of the change of the elements in the Eucharist into the identical Body and Blood of Christ and was one of the first writers to speak of Christ's presence in the Eucharist as 'substantial'.

Durante, Francesco   Italian composer, born Fratto Maggiore, 31 March 1684, died Naples, 13 August 1755. He was head of the conservatoire in Naples from 1742 to 1745. He is known for his wide variety of compositions in church and chamber music.

Duranti, William (the Younger)   French bishop, born Puymission, died Cyprus, July 1330. He was the nephew of William Duranti (**Durandus**) the Elder. He also was appointed bishop of Mende in 1305. He was given the task by **Clement V** of reporting on conditions in Italy, and of investigation into a canonization cause and into the Templars. He also wrote a piece criticizing abuses in the Church, including centralization of power

in the papal court. There followed the attempt to investigate Duranti himself, but his position at the French court protected him. In 1329 he was given with others the task of organizing a Crusade.

Durbin, Elisha John   American Catholic missionary, born near Boonesboro, Kentucky, 1 February 1800, died Shelbyville, Kentucky, 22 March 1887. He entered St Thomas Seminary in 1816 and was ordained 21 September 1822. During his 60 years of missionary work he rode in excess of 500,000 miles on horseback and became known as the 'Patriarch Priest of Kentucky' and 'Apostle of Western Kentucky'. During this time he was in charge of western and southwestern Kentucky (10,000 sq. miles). His ministry was extensive, including the people living along the railroad, and Catholics in Indiana and Illinois, and, as chaplain, the Franciscan sisters at Shelbyville.

Dürer, Albrecht   Roman Catholic painter and engraver, born Nuremberg, Germany, 21 May 1471, died Nuremberg, 6 April 1528. He worked as a goldsmith, in copperplating and wood engraving. His religious paintings at Munich and Florence are well known. He travelled to Italy, where he was influenced by Giovanni **Bellini**, and to The Netherlands, where he met, among many others, **Erasmus,** of whom he later produced a portrait. His work was a link between Italian art and the Gothic north, his woodcuts in particular influencing Italian painters. They were used as biblical illustrations in many languages. He remained in the Catholic faith but was sympathetic to the reforms of Martin **Luther**.

Durkin, Martin Patrick   American Catholic labour leader and government official, born Chicago, 18 March 1894, died Washington DC, 13 November 1955. He trained in plumbing, heating and engineering and in later life worked extensively for the Plumbers Union, of which he became president in 1943. He was a delegate to the Independent Labour Organisation in Geneva in 1948 and elected vice-president of the Catholic Conference on Industrial Problems in 1950.

Durocher, Marie Rose   Blessed, Roman Catholic, foundress of a religious congregation, born St Antoine, Canada, 6 October 1811, died Longueuil,

Canada, 6 October 1849. She worked in Beloeil parish, where she established the first Canadian parish sodality with help from the Oblates of Mary Immaculate. In 1843, at the request of the bishop of Montreal, she co-founded the Congregation of the Sisters of the Holy Name of Jesus and Mary at Longueuil – which was canonically established in 1844. She worked to promote the religious and general education of poor young women and set up schools for 400 students. She was beatified on 23 May 1982. Feast day 6 October.

Dürr, Lorenz German Catholic biblical scholar, born Oberschwarzach, Bavaria, 7 April 1886, died Regensburg, 26 February 1939. He was ordained in 1910. After studying oriental languages he taught OT studies at Bonn in 1921, and was professor at Brauberg in 1925, Freising in 1933, and Regensburg in 1937. He specialized in the relationship between the OT and the literatures of the ancient Near East. His many writings encompassed both scientific publications and those for a more popular but educated laity.

Duruflé, Maurice French organist and composer, born Louviers, Eure, 11 January 1902, died Paris, 16 June 1986. He was a pupil of Dukas. His music includes organ pieces, motets based on Gregorian themes and a Requiem. This and other music wonderfully incorporates plainsong, yet achieves an original, seraphic, mystical spirit.

Durych, Jaroslav Czech poet and novelist. Born Turnov, Bohemia, 2 December 1886, died Prague, 1962. In early life he studied medicine and served in the medical corps in the army. He started writing in his late twenties, publishing poetry and a novel. A second novel, *Sedmikráska* (1925), followed, plus editing work. He developed an interest in literary theory and began the study of the baroque style which appeared in several of his novels. His main work is a study of beauty and evil, *Bloudení* ('Wandering', 1929).

Dutt, Toru Anglo-Indian poet, born Calcutta, 4 March 1856, died 30 August 1877. She was the daughter of a Christian family who moved to Europe in 1869. After education in France and England she returned to India and with her sister Aru began translation of French works. Her interests were in French Romanticism, as is evident in the works she published herself and those of her sister. She studied Sanskrit, spoke English and French, and her mother tongue was Bengali, and she wrote in all these languages. She used classical Indian themes in her works without prejudice to her Christianity. Her main works are, *Sita, Our Casuarina Tree, Ancient Ballads and Legends of Hindustan* and many others.

Dutton, Joseph Brother, soldier, lay missionary, born Stowe, Vermont, April 1843, died Honolulu, 26 March 1931. Dutton found the breakup of his marriage difficult, which gave impetus for change in his life. He became a Roman Catholic in 1883 and spent two years as an oblate at the monastery of Our Lady of Gethsemane, Kentucky. He offered his services to the leper settlement in Hawaii and worked there until his death in 1930. He worked closely with Fr Joseph Daunier, nursing lepers and attempting to improve conditions for them.

Duval, George Logan Merchant philanthropist, born Brooklyn, 14 July 1855, died New York, 16 March 1931. He started working life in business, working in California and Chile. He donated large amounts to Catholic charities and was honoured both in Chile and with the Laetare Medal, in 1919, from the University of Notre Dame, Indiana. On his death he willed $2 million to Catholic charities.

Duval, Jean (Bernard of St Theresa) French Carmelite bishop and councillor, born Clamecy, 22 April 1597, died Paris, 4 October 1669. He entered the novitiate of the Discalced Carmelites in Paris and became well known as a preacher and superior. In 1638 he became first bishop of Baghdad and apostolic vicar for Persia. At the age of 45 he returned to Paris and established a seminary for Eastern missions. His skills led to his recognition by **Louis XIV** as a councillor, in which capacity he served for the rest of his life. He is known for his expertise in oriental languages and compiled both Turkish and Persian dictionaries.

Duvergier de Hauranne, Jean Abbé de Saint-Cyran, spiritual director and writer, born Bayonne, France, 1581, died Paris, France, 11 October 1643. He studied in Louvain, where he became friendly with **Jansen**. He was ordained in 1618 and created

Abbé de Saint-Cyran in 1620, a commendatory title which allowed him to continue living in Paris. He was associated with the beginnings of the French Oratory. He defended **Bérulle** and Richard Smith against the Jesuits. His opposition to Cardinal **Richelieu** resulted in his imprisonment, during which time he continued his work of spiritual direction. He later worked with the Visitation Nuns and with Port-Royal. His publications include *Theologie Familière* (1639), *Le Coeur Nouveau* (1642) and posthumously published letters of direction.

Duvernay, Ludger Canadian journalist, born Montreal, 1799, died Montreal, 28 November 1852. He began working life as a journalist and co-founded *La Minerve*, the paper of the Patriot Party. He is known for establishing the feast of St John the Baptist as a public holiday for French Canadians. His defence of his compatriots led to imprisonment and accusations of treachery and he exiled himself to Burlington, Vermont. Following the amnesty of 1842 he returned to Canada and restarted the party paper. He is commemorated in a monument at Côtes-des-Neiges Cemetery.

Duverneck, Frank American painter, etcher and sculptor, born Covington, Kentucky, 9 October 1848, died Cincinnati, Ohio, 3 January 1919. His decorative work in churches in the USA drew on the 'Munich Style'. He went to Munich, where he started an art school. He and his students, 'The Duverneck Boys', then went to Italy, where he did his most important etching work. In 1888 Duverneck returned to Cincinnati, taught, and painted religious murals for St Mary's Cathedral, Covington.

Dvořák, Antonín Czech composer, born Nelahozeves, 8 September 1841, died Prague, 1 May 1904. The son of a butcher, he showed early musical talent and studied at the organ school in Prague. He started working life playing the viola in an orchestra and in 1874 became church organist at St Adalbert's. During this time his compositions began to be noticed, particularly by **Brahms**, who recognized his ability. He is known for his *Slavonic Dances*, *Stabat Mater*, *Rusalka* and *Armida*, and the *Ninth Symphony*, 'From the New World'. This last was written while he was director of the New York Conservatory.

Dvořák, Max Austrian art historian, born 14 June 1874, died Grusbach bei Znaim, 8 February 1921. He was professor at Vienna University and then director of the Institute of Art History and curator of the Central Committee for the Preservation of Historical and Artistic Monuments. He used the history of ideas method in the context of art history. His approach provided new insights into early Christian art, such as the concept of metaphysical space and the body as image of the soul. He suggested that the purpose of Christian art is spiritual experience not sensual pleasure.

Dwenger, Joseph Gerhard American bishop, born Maria Stein, Ohio, 7 September 1837, died Fort Wayne, 22 January 1893. He was born of Prussian immigrant parents and attended Holy Trinity school in Cincinnati. On the death of both parents he was cared for by the Society of the Precious Blood. He was ordained in 1859 and supervised the seminary programme until 1864. He then became the youngest bishop (of Fort Wayne) in the USA. His particular interest was in developing orphanages. In late life he was subject to accusations associating him with the **Cahensly** controversy which were unfounded.

Dwight, Thomas Roman Catholic convert, surgeon, born Boston, USA, 13 October 1843, died Nahant, USA, 8 September 1911. He converted to Catholicism in 1856. In 1883 he became Parkman professor of anatomy at Harvard University, and in 1893 president of the Association of American Anatomists. In later life he focused on research into anatomical variations, which led him to attempt to reconcile theories of evolution and Catholic teaching. He served as president of the Catholic Union of Boston and of the Society of St Vincent de Paul. His publications include *Variations of the Bones of the Head and Foot* (1907) and *Thoughts of a Catholic Anatomist* (1911).

Dwight, Timothy American Congregational minister, theologian and educator. He was born Northampton, Massachusetts, 14 May 1752, died New Haven, Connecticut, 11 January 1817. He was the grandson of the well known theologian Jonathan **Edwards**. A precocious child, he was found at the age of six preaching from the Bible to a group of Native Americans. His early interests were literary and he belonged to a small literary group called the Connecticut Wits. He became military chaplain in 1777. He was a pastor at Greenfield, Connecticut in 1783 and in 1795 president of Yale. He became a noted theologian and evangelist at Yale. He helped establish 'evangelical orthodoxy', stressing the practical aspects of personal religion and rejecting the metaphysics of determinism.

Dyer, Samuel London Missionary Society missionary to Malaya and inventor of Chinese metallic type, born Greenwich, England, 20 January 1804, died Macao, 24 October 1843. After studying mathematics and law at Cambridge, in 1824 he joined the LMS and married Maria Tarn before leaving for Malaya in 1827. Their daughter Maria later married James Hudson **Taylor**, founder of the China Inland Mission. In Penang, Dyer studied Hokkien and began statistically analysing Chinese characters before developing steel punches and copper matrices. His linguistic abilities, strategic planning and attention to detail resulted in high quality fonts of importance in the history of Christian printing in China. The Dyers moved to Melaka in 1835 and returned to England in 1839. He was in Singapore in 1842 and Hong Kong in 1843. As well as articles in the *Calcutta Christian Observer*, *Chinese Repository* and *Periodical Miscel-*

lany, his publications included *Vocabulary of the Hokkien Dialect* (Singapore, 1838).

Dyfrig *see* **Dubricius**

Dykes, John Anglican hymn-writer and composer, born Kingston-upon-Hull, 10 March 1823, died Ticehurst, Sussex, 22 January 1876. He was educated at Cambridge, was ordained, and became a minor canon and precentor of Durham Cathedral. He was involved in a dispute over ritual with his Low Church bishop and moved to St Leonard's, Sussex. He composed anthems, church music and over 300 hymns, of which a high proportion survive in use. His melodies are deeply embedded in the consciousness of English-speaking Christians and non-Christians, as set to the words of *Eternal Father*, *Praise to the Holiest*, *The King of Love* and *Lead Kindly Light*.

Dympna (Dimpna) Saint, seventh-century martyr. There is very little historical information. The legend is said to be largely folklore. She was said to be of royal birth and escaped an incestuous infatuation by her father by fleeing to her confessor St Gerebernus at Antwerp. Her father traced them to Gheel and found them living as solitaries. They were both killed immediately. The bodies were translated in the thirteenth century. This event was accompanied by many cures of epileptics and the mentally ill, whose patron saint she became. Gheel has become well known for its progressive work with mentally ill people. Feast day 15 May.

E

Eadmer Historian and theologian, born Canterbury, 1060, died Canterbury, 1128. He was brought up in the monastery of Christ Church at Canterbury and as an adult became a member of the household of St **Anselm of Canterbury**, to whom he was devoted, and accompanied him in exile. He is best known for his *Life of St Anselm* and for lives of several early English saints. He also wrote an important source book for the historical period 1066 to 1122, and his theological treatise *De conceptione sanctae Mariae* is an important early source for the doctrine of the Immaculate Conception. He was offered the bishopric of St Andrews in 1120 but was never consecrated.

Ealdred of York (Aldred) Archbishop, died York, 11 September 1069. He was a powerful presence both politically and in the Church. His lifetime encompassed within it the reigns of both Harold II and **William I** and Matilda; the latter he certainly crowned and probably the former also. He was a monk at Winchester, becoming abbot at Tavistock *c.*1027, bishop of Worcester in 1046, and then archbishop of York in 1060. He travelled on state business and was involved in the wars of the time. He reformed and strengthened the dioceses in which he served. After his submission to William the Conqueror, he served faithfully but was an opponent of oppression of the Anglo-Saxon population.

Ebbe (Aebbe, Ebba) Saint, abbess, born Northumbria, died Coldingham, 683. She was the daughter of Ethelfirth, king of Northumbria. On his death **Edwin** conquered Northumbria and Ebbe fled to Scotland. She took profession at Coldingham and later became abbess. She had a reputation for wisdom and holiness. In late life she was warned by the priest Adaman that her community needed reform under threat of dire punishment. Reforms were instituted for a short time but lapsed. After her death the monastery burnt down, but Ebbe's reputation remained and revived in the twelfth century after her relics were discovered. They are now held at Durham and Coldingham. Her name is remembered at St Abb's Head. Feast day 25 August.

Ebbe the Younger Saint, abbess, martyr, died 870. She is said to have been martyred at Coldingham by Vikings. She and her community are said to have preserved their virtue by cutting open their noses and lips with a razor, engendering disgust in the raiders, who shortly after burnt down the monastery and the community. A thirteenth-century shrine is spoken of, and a feast of dedication of the altar of St Ebbe on 22 June is referred to in a Coldingham manuscript. It is not known whether it refers to this or an earlier Ebbe.

Ebbo Saint, abbot and hermit, born Tonnerre, towards the end of the seventh century, died Arce near Sens, *c.*750. His early life as a district administrator was distasteful to him and he professed at St Pierre le Vif near Sens, where he later became the abbot. He is credited with having saved the city of Sens from the Saracens' siege by the power of prayer. His later years were spent in solitude and meditation. He was buried at St Pierre. Feast day 27 August.

Ebbo of Rheims (Ebo) French archbishop, born

c.775, died Hildesheim, Germany, 20 March 851. His parents were in the employ of the royal household and Ebbo was educated with Prince Louis, the future **Louis I** the Pious. On Louis's succession to the throne he appointed Ebbo as librarian and later as archbishop of Rheims. This relationship was fraught, and Ebbo supported Louis's son **Lothair (I)** against his father. The attempted dethronement failed and Ebbo was imprisoned and deposed from his see. After a brief respite on the death of Louis he was exiled to Hildesheim, where he died. His main written work is *Evangeliarum*, and there are several other, minor works.

Ebendorfer, Thomas Austrian historiographer, theologian, diplomat, born Haselbach, 10 August 1388, died Vienna, 12 January 1464. Of peasant background, he gained a doctorate in theology in 1428. He served as a canon at St Stephen's in Vienna and spent much of his life in diplomatic and state activities, retiring to academic work when his relationship with Emperor Frederick III cooled. He wrote *Chronicle of the Emperors* and the *Austrian Chronicle*.

Eberhard of Einsiedeln Blessed, abbot, birth not known, died 14 August 958. He was of noble birth and became provost of Strasburg Cathedral early in his life. He developed a reputation for piety and gave up this office in 934 in order to establish the hermitage of Einsiedeln with Berno of Metz. The community here thrived and Eberhard gave family money to establish a monastery of which he was the first abbot. The monastery prospered and had a reputation for generosity which came to the fore during the great famine of 942. Pilrimages took place to his tomb until his relics were lost around 1789 during the French Revolution. Feast day 14 August.

Eberhard of Rohrdorf Blessed, abbot and statesman, born c.1160, died 10 June 1245. He was of noble birth, entering a Cistercian monastery at the abbey of Salem, becoming abbot in 1191. A reputation for humility was gained alongside his competence, and he was highly regarded by his contemporaries. His abbacy was one of the most famous and existed between the death of **Frederick I Barbarossa** and the end of the Hohenstaufen regime. He was appointed by **Innocent III** to investigate some difficult questions of ecclesiastical politics, including negotiating a peace between Philip of Swabia and Pope Innocent III. He resigned office in 1240 owing to advanced age and was written into the Cistercian martyrology following his death. Feast day 14 April.

Eberhard of Tüntenhausen Saint, shepherd, born Freising, died Bavaria, c.1370. He is a folk saint, not canonized, and was buried under the altar at Tüntenhausen in Bavaria. He is the patron saint of shepherds and domestic animals, and is invoked in cases of cattle sickness and for good weather. His cult is first mentioned in a letter in 1428, and according to testimony given at a hearing in 1729–34, it is said that the earth taken from his grave and used as medicine for sick animals never diminished. Iron and wooden figures of animals were left at his grave. Feast day 12 September (also 28 or 29 September).

Eberlin, Johannes Evangelical preacher and writer, born Kleinkötz, c.1470, died Leutershausen, before 13 October 1533. He entered the Franciscan monastery at Heilsbronn but was expelled in 1520. He had in this time encountered the teaching of **Luther**, and in 1521 published his *Die 15 Bundgnossen*. In this he postulates a utopian state called Wolfaria which involved both socio-political and religious reform. He travelled as an evangelist and married. He wrote several volumes of reform tracts and treatises. In later life his writings became more moderate following the inability of the Reformers in Germany to maintain their early moral standards. He also produced a German translation of Tacitus' *Germania*.

Eccleston, Samuel American archbishop, born Kent County, Maryland, 27 June 1801, died Washington, DC, 22 April 1851. He was educated as a Catholic following the second marriage of his Episcopalian mother to a Catholic. He entered a seminary in 1819 in opposition to some of his relatives. After ordination and entry to the Society of St Sulpice he was sent to study at Issy in France. On returning to Baltimore he succeeded to the archbishopric in 1834. Baltimore thrived during his tenure, St Charles College opened, schools were opened by the Christian Brothers and Visitation nuns, and the number of priests nearly doubled.

Echard, Jacques Dominican bibliographer, born Rouen, 22 September 1644, died Paris, 15 March 1724. He entered the Dominican Order in Paris in 1659, where he remained until his death, but for an unexplained exile of several months to Gonesse. He was prior of the convent of the Annunciation in Paris and an appellant against the bull *Unigenitus* in 1717. He was appointed to complete the Dominican bibliography from notes left by J. Quétif. This work, *Scriptores ordinis praedicatorum* (2 vols.), was published 1719–21 and is known for its thoroughness and accuracy.

Echter von Mespelbrunn, Julius German prince-bishop, born Mespelbrunn, 18 March 1545, died Würzburg, 13 September 1617. He was born into the nobility and became first a member of chapter, then dean and then was elected prince-bishop of Würzburg in 1573. After eighteen months' preparation he was ordained and then consecrated in 1575. He was helped by Jesuits in the Counter-Reformation and is said to have reclaimed 100,000 Protestants. He was known as ascetic and pious and in early life had leanings towards humanism. As others of his time did, he persecuted witches.

Eck, Johann German theologian, born Egg (Eck) an der Günz in Swabia, 15 November 1486, died Ingolstadt, 10 February 1543: also known as Johann Maier 'of Eck'. He was a man of wide, humanistic, learning and studied at the Universities of Heidelberg, Tübingen, Cologne and Freiburg, in which last he began to tutor. He lectured on the *Sentences* of **Peter Lombard** in 1506, and graduated as doctor in 1510. In that year he was invited to become professor of theology at Ingolstadt. Despite being on good terms earlier in life with Martin **Luther** he became his sharpest opponent. He was prominent in arousing Catholic opposition to Protestantism and played a substantial part in securing Luther's excommunication in 1520. He helped to prepare the Council of Trent, and took part in many debates with the Reformers, such as those at Augsburg in 1530 and Regensburg in 1541. His writings include a defence of charging interest on loans, and of indulgences, and commentaries on Aristotle and Petrus Hispanus. He is also known for producing a Bible in German dialect for Catholic use.

Eckbert of Schönau Abbot and theologian, born in the Rhineland before 1132, died Schönau, 25 March 1184. Of noble birth, in early life he had strong church connections, but following a visit to Rome entered a Benedictine monastery at the abbey of Schönau. His writings reflect a later devotion to the Sacred Heart. He is also known for his anti-Cathar writings. His main works are *Sermones contra Catharos*, *Stimulus Amoris* and *Soliloquim seu Meditationes*.

Eckhart, Anselm von German missionary born Bingen, 4 August 1721, died Polotsk, Russia, 29 June 1809. He entered the Society of Jesus in 1740 and in 1753 was sent on missionary work to Brazil. He was at first successful but later imprisoned for eighteen years in Lisbon by the Portuguese. He was released after the death of Joseph I of Portugal and returned to Bingen. He then went to Russia and applied for admission to the Polish Jesuits, who had escaped the consequences of the papal bull which had suppressed the Society of Jesus elsewhere. He remained there for the rest of his life.

Eckhart, Johann Georg von German historian, born Duingen, 7 September 1664, died Würzburg, 1 February 1730. He became assistant to Leibniz and then professor at Helmstedt in 1706. He served the royal family as councillor, historian and librarian. He fled Cologne in 1723 for unknown reasons and converted to Catholicism in 1724. His works include *Corpus Historicum Medii Aevi* (1723), *Animadversiones Historicae et Criticae* (1727) and *Commentarii de Rebus Franciae Orientalis et Episcopatus Wirceburgenses* (1729).

Eckhart, Meister Dominican monk, preacher and mystic, born Hochheim in Thuringia, *c.*1260, died Cologne, 1327. He entered the Dominican convent at Erfurt at a young age and progressed in the Order, studied in Paris and Cologne (under **Albert the Great**) and then once again in Paris, where he taught. He left Paris finally in 1313 to live first in Strasburg, to 1323, and then in Cologne. He held various offices in his Order, including prior of Erfurt, and in 1304–11 was provincial of Saxony. He was a well known and popular preacher at both Strasburg and Cologne. His attempts to express the inexpressible engendered ambiguities with doctrinal orthodoxy, and despite much popular support he was tried before the court of the archbishop of Cologne in 1326. He appealed to the Pope but died during the investigation. Two years later **John XXII** condemned 28 propositions drawn from his writings as heretical or dangerous, but he himself escaped censure – the Pope insisting that Eckhart had recanted before his death.

Eckhel, Joseph Hilarius von Jesuit historian, numismatist, born Enzesfeld, 13 January 1737, died Vienna, 16 May 1798. He was educated by and ordained in the Society of Jesus, for whom he taught at Loeben, Steyr and Vienna. Illness forced him to retire from teaching, and he turned to archaeology and numismatics. He became director of the numismatic section at the Imperial Museum in Vienna and professor of antiquities and auxiliary historical sciences at the University of Vienna. His main work, *Doctrina Nummorum Veterum*, is a seminal study of numismatics.

Eddy, Mary Baker Founder of Christian Science, born Mary Baker, Bow, New Hampshire, 16 July 1821, died Chestnut Hill, Massachusetts, 3 December 1910. Her early education was spasmodic, though in later life she claimed to have read a great deal, and even to have studied Greek and Hebrew. At the age of seventeen she became a member of the local Congregational church. Her first husband died after some six months of marriage: she gave birth to a son, George, but retreated for a time into inertia, living with her sister or with her father. In 1853 she married an itinerant dentist, but they separated in 1866 and divorced seven years later. It was about the time of the separation that she began to develop a method of spiritual healing, based originally upon the methods of Phineas Parkhurst Quimby, whom she had herself consulted in 1862. She set up in 'practice' with a young man called Richard Kennedy, a partnership which lasted only two years, but proved profitable. She now began to work out a theory for what she was doing, published as *Science and Health* in 1875, the basic principle being that the distinction between mind and matter was unreal, and that all disease can be cured through the mind. The eternal mind is revealed in Christ – hence Christian Science. A group was growing around her and, in 1877, she married one of them, Asa Eddy (she was hitherto, from her first mar-

riage, Mary Glover). Her husband was expelled a year later from the nascent church for alleged immorality, and much time was subsequently spent in litigation with him. In 1883 she established, and began to edit, *The Christian Science Journal*. The *Christian Science Monitor* was begun two years before her death.

Edes, Ella B. American Catholic journalist, born New England, 7 December 1832, died near Pescina, Italy 27 February 1916. She was baptized in 1852 and moved to Rome in 1866, where she was secretary to a cardinal. She then became Rome correspondent of various newspapers, including the *Tablet* (London), *New York Herald* and many other Catholic and secular newpapers. Her interests were in Roman ecclesiastical events, about which she recorded and corresponded. These writings are preserved in the archives of the Archdioceses of Baltimore, New York and St Paul, the Diocese of Rochester and the American Catholic Historical Society of Philadelphia. Following ill-health, she returned to northern Italy, where she died.

Edgeworth de Firmont, Henry Essex Irish Priest, born Edgeworthtown, Co. Longford, 1745 died, Mitau in Latvia, 22 May 1807. He was the son of a Protestant rector who converted to Catholicism and lived in Toulouse. Edgeworth was educated by Jesuits and later ordained. He was confessor to both the sister and the brother of Louis XVI. He attended them to the scaffold and in 1796 escaped to England. His last post was as chaplain to Louis XVIII.

Edigna Blessed, patron against theft, died Puch near Fürstenfeldbruck in Bavaria, 26 February 1109. She is said to have taken a vow of virginity. Her father, a French king, instructed her to marry, but she escaped to Bavaria. Legend says that she lived in a hollow tree. This was the site of a miraculous flow of holy oil, after her death. The flow ceased when merchants tried to sell it for gain. She is buried at Puch and still honoured there. Feast day 26 February.

Edmund of Abingdon Saint, archbishop, born Abingdon, Berkshire, 20 November 1180 died in self-imposed exile at Pontigny, 16 November 1240.

He studied at Oxford and then at Paris, taught the new logic at Oxford *c.*1194–1200, then returned to Paris for theological studies. He was treasurer at Salisbury Cathedral by 1222, and was appointed to Canterbury in 1233. He failed in his efforts to prevent royal interference in the management of ecclesiastical affairs, and was on his way to visit the papal curia when he died. He was canonized by **Innocent IV** in 1247. Feast day 16 November.

Edmund the Martyr   Saint, king and martyr, born 840, died Hellesdon, Norfolk, 20 November 869. Although the son of a king of 'Saxony', he was adopted by the East Angles as their king and succeeded to the throne in 865. His rule ended with the invasion of the Danes when as a Christian he refused to share his kingdom with the Dane Ingwar. He was shot with arrows and beheaded. A cult grew up quickly and his eventual burial place in the tenth century at Bury St Edmunds became a place of pilgrimage. Feast day 20 November.

Edward   Saint, king and martyr, born 963, died by stabbing at Corfe in Dorset, 18 March 978. He succeeded to the English throne in 975 on the death of his father Edgar the Peaceful against the wishes of his stepmother Queen Elfrida. He was murdered three years later, allegedly on the instructions of Queen Elfrida. He was first buried at Wareham and then translated to Shaftesbury. Miracles were reported at his tomb, and he was officially announced a martyr in 1001. Feast day 18 March.

Edward III   English king, born Windsor Castle, 13 November 1312, died Sheen in Surrey, 21 June 1377. He was the son of Edward II and Isabella and succeeded to the throne in 1327. He was not in power however until Isabella and her lover Roger Mortimer fell from favour. His reign was relatively stable and marked by wars, successful to him, with Scotland and France. These wars imposed heavy taxation upon the country. He is associated with the passing of the anti-papal Statutes of Provisors (1357), attempting to prevent foreign clerics being 'provided' by the Papacy with English benefices, and Praemunire (1353), limiting the right of appeal to Rome

Edward VI   King of England, born Hampton Court, 12 October 1537, died Greenwich, 6 July 1553, son of **Henry VIII**, whom he succeeded in 1547. He studied Greek, Latin, French and amateur astronomy at Cambridge. As king, he reacted against trends at the close of his father's reign and encouraged a programme of religious reform. Many who had fled to the Continent returned. He made John **Knox**, **Ridley**, **Latimer** and Hooper court preachers, affirmed his devotion to the Bible at his coronation, ordered a copy in English to be installed in every parish church, and instructed that the Epistle and Gospel in the Communion Service be read in English. Editions of **Tyndale**, **Coverdale** and the Great Bible poured from the press. In 1553 he gave the palace of Bridewell to the Corporation of London as a 'workhouse', and in the same year converted the old Grey Friars' Monastery into Christ's Hospital.

Edward the Confessor   Saint, king, born Islip, 1003, died London, 5 January 1066. He was educated at Ely and in Normandy, succeeding to the throne on the death of his half-brother. He had a reputation for piety and his reign was peaceful though interspersed with internal struggles between his Saxon supporters and the Norman advisers Edward had brought with him. On his death this disunity and disputed succession resulted in hostilities. He is known for the building of the abbey of St Peter at Westminster. He was a popular saint in the Middle Ages and at one time considered to be England's patron saint. He was canonized in 1161. Feast day 13 October.

Edward the Elder   English king, born *c.*870, died *c.*924. He was the son of **Alfred the Great** and succeeded to the throne of Wessex in 899. He is credited with returning to English rule the whole of the Danelaw south of the Humber. He also succeeded to control of Mercia after the death of his sister Aethelfraed and in this capacity subdued the Welsh Britons of Strathclyde, the Norsemen of Northumbria and the Scots.

Edwards, Jonathan   American Congregationalist theologian and philosopher, born East Windsor, Connecticut, 5 October 1703, and died New Jersey, 22 March 1758, Princeton, New Jersey. The son and grandson of Congregationalist pastors, he studied at Yale, and was ordained in 1727 to his grandfather's Congregational church in North-ampton, Massachusetts. His preaching at North-ampton sparked a religious revival, to him a sign of God's grace already active, rather than a means to obtain grace. His views are analysed in his *Faithful Narrative of the Surprising Works of God* (1737). His evolution into a strict Calvinist alien-ated his congregation, and he was dismissed from his post in 1750. He then went to Stockbridge as successor to David **Brainerd**. In 1757 he agreed to become president of Princeton University. He wrote a life of Brainerd, on free will, and on virtue, but his greatest work is *A Treatise concerning Religious Affections* (1746).

Edwin Saint, Northumbrian king, born North-umbria, 585, died at the Battle of Heathfield, 6 October 633. He was banished early in life from his kingdom by the king of Bernicia, who con-quered his realm, but he regained it in 617 and later became the most powerful monarch in Eng-land. He married **Ethelburga**, the Christian daugh-ter of the Kentish King Eadbald in 627 and was converted to Christianity by her chaplain **Paulinus**. Paulinus was made bishop of York, where Edwin began the building of a church. This was inter-rupted by further invasion of his kingdom by Mercian and Welsh kings, by whom he was defeated. Feast day 12 October.

Eeden, Frederick Willem van Dutch poet and social reformer, born Haarlem, 3 April 1860, died Bussum, 16 June 1932. He was a doctor and an early psychotherapist known for using hypnotism. He established two co-operative living exper-iments, Walden in Bussum and Van Eeden Colony in the USA. They closed in 1907 and 1949 respec-tively. His poetry encompasses his ideas and expe-riences ranging from theosophy and occultism to mainstream Christianity. His concerns became eschatological in character.

Egan, Maurice Francis American literary critic, academic and diplomat, born Philadelphia, 24 May 1852, died Brooklyn, 15 January 1924. His parent-age was Irish-American and he was educated at La Salle College. He first worked as a journalist and editor and then became professor at the University of Notre Dame and the Catholic University of America. As a diplomat he helped in the purchase

of the Virgin Islands and was sent as a minister to Denmark. His main works are the *Sexton Maginnis Stories*, the *Ghost of Hamlet* (1892), *Studies in Literature* (1899), *Ten Years Near the German Frontier* (1919) and *Recollections of a Happy Life* (1924).

Egan, Michael Franciscan bishop, born Limerick, Ireland, 1761, died Philadelphia, 22 July 1814. He became a Franciscan in Belgium in 1779 and was ordained in Bohemia. He was guardian of several friaries, St Isidore's College, Rome, and Ennis, Roscrea and Castelyons friaries in Ireland. He went to the USA, where he was unsuccessful in establish-ing a province of the Franciscan Order but became bishop of Philadelphia in 1808 at the request of John **Carroll**.

Egaña, Mariano Chilean politician and jurist, born Santiago, 1 February 1793, died Santiago, 24 June 1846. He was part of the independence move-ment from an early age. As secretary to the national government he was imprisoned when Spanish power was restored in 1814. After the defeat of the Spanish he was minister of govern-ment and foreign affairs and travelled on a diplo-matic mission to England. On his return to Chile in 1829 he was an influential political figure and was instrumental in establishing the constitution in 1833. He had shown admiration for the consti-tutional monarchy of England. He wrote *Elementos de derecho público constitucional*.

Egbert Saint, monk and hermit born Northum-bria, 639, died Iona, 24 April 729. His early life was spent as a monk at Lindisfarne. He travelled to Ireland to seek learning and to further his spiritual life. At this time he vowed never to return to Northumbria and was also instrumental in sending St **Willibrord** and others to evangelize Germany. Following a vision, the last thirteen years of his life were highly devotional and he lived as a hermit on Iona. Whilst there he introduced the Roman method of calculating Easter, which had been resisted by the monks. He died on Easter Sunday, on the first occasion of the new obser-vance. Feast day 24 April.

Egbert Archbishop, died York, 19 November 766, born into the Northumbrian royal household, received a monastic education, was sent to Rome and ordained there, and was then made bishop of York in 732. **Bede** urged him to apply for the pallium, granted in 735, thus constituting York an archdiocese. **Alcuin** was a pupil at the cathedral school in his time. He corresponded with **Boniface**, and wrote a work on liturgy, and one on the rights of the clergy.

Egbert of Liège Poet and rhetorician, born c.972 of a noble German family, and probably educated at the cathedral school in Liège where he worked as a teacher of grammar, rhetoric and dialectic. He produced the *Fecunda Ratis*, a manual of wisdom in extracts derived from the Bible, patristic sources and contemporary folklore. It has literary relevance for its demonstration of medieval appreciation of satire.

Edigio Maria of St Joseph Blessed Italian Franciscan lay brother, born near Taranto, Italy, 16 November 1729, died Naples, 7 February 1812. He entered the monastery at Taranto in 1754 after working as a ropemaker to support the family. A spiritual experience of note led him to a devout life of simplicity and serenity. He was drawn to the activities of the Sodality of Our Lady of the Rosary, and to devotion to Mary and Joseph and he was held in high esteem by the sick and poor of Naples. Feast day 7 February.

Egino Blessed, German Benedictine abbot, birth date unknown, died Augsburg, 15 July 1120. He was banished from his monastery in 1098 owing to political opposition and fled to Switzerland. From here he was sent on a mission to Pope **Paschal II**. He was able to return to Augsburg in 1106 and in 1109 became abbot. He was a noted reformer and preacher but came into conflict with his bishop, the simoniacal Hermann. He fled again in 1118 and died at the Camaldolese monastery of San Michele at Pisa and is buried there. Feast day 15 July.

Ehrhard, Albert Byzantinist, church historian, patrologist, born Herbitzheim, Alsace, 14 March 1862, died Bonn, 23 September 1940. He was ordained in 1885, gained a doctorate in theology in 1888 and became professor of church history at the Grand Seminaire, Strasburg in 1889. Academic posts followed at Würzburg, Vienna, Freiburg im Breisgau and Bonn. His main interests were editing sources of theology, hagiography and homiletic literature of the Greek church. He wrote, among others, *Forschungen zur Hagiographie der Griechischen Kirche* (1897), *Die Altchristliche Literatur und Ihre Erforschung seit 1880* (1894), *Überlieferung und Bestand der Hagiographischen und Homiletischen Literatur der Griechischen Kirche* (1936–52).

Ehrle, Franz Jesuit cardinal and medievalist, born Ising in Württemberg, 17 October 1845, died Rome, 31 March 1934. Educated by Jesuits, he entered the Society of Jesus in 1861. He left Germany in 1873 because of the Kulturkampf, and lived for four years in Ditton Hall, Lancashire, where he was ordained in 1876, being sent to Rome in 1880 after a period of travel around Europe. He specialized in the study of medieval manuscripts, was prefect of the Vatican Library, 1895–1914, and with H. S. **Denifle** was the founder of the scientific study of Scholasticism. Important works are *Historia Bibliothecae Romanorum Pontificum*, a history of the Vatican Library (1890), *Der Sentenzenkommentar Peters von Candia* (1924) and *I più antichi statuti della facoltà teologica del l'Università di Bologna* (1932).

Eichenberg, Fritz Quaker artist, born Cologne, Germany, 24 October 1901, died USA, 30 November 1990. After his art studies he became a wood engraver but, being Jewish, left Germany in 1933. After his wife's death in 1938, he became a Quaker. He created many wood engravings illustrating **Dostoevsky**, Tolstoy and the **Brontë** sisters. In 1949, Dorothy **Day**, editor of the *Catholic Worker*, asked him to contribute his art to her newspaper, judging correctly that images could reach audiences who did not read the articles. He produced many powerful works, including a Black Crucifixion and representations of Christ as one among contemporary homeless and hungry Americans.

Einhard Author, born c.770, died Seligenstadt, 14 March 840. Little is known of Einhard's life. He was born into a noble family and was of Frankish birth, entered the service of the Emperor and is known for his famous biography of his employer **Charlemagne**.

Eisengrein, Martin Theologian and preacher, born Stuttgart, 28 December 1535, died Ingolstadt, 4 May 1578. He came from a Protestant family but converted to Roman Catholicism at university in 1558. He was ordained in 1560 and later was influential in the Catholic Restoration in Bavaria. He was sent on diplomatic missions by Duke Albert V, took part in religious discussions and debates, held academic posts and was preacher at the court of Maximilian II.

Eisengrein, Wilhelm Church historian, born Speyer, 1534, died Rome, 1584. He was a nephew of Martin **Eisengrein**. He became noted for his refutation of **Flacius Illyricus** in the *Centuries* of Magdeburg: he published only two volumes of a proposed 16-volume work at Ingolstadt (1566) and then *Harmonia Ecclesiae Historica Adversus Centurias Magdeburg* (1576) in Speyer.

Eisenhofer, Ludwig Liturgist, Munich, born 1 April 1871, died Eichstätt, 29 March 1941. He was ordained in 1895 and worked as a teacher of patrology, liturgy and church history at Eichstätt. His main interest was in historical method and he wrote a respected guide to the problems of liturgical history and literature which is still a reliable and wide-ranging source of information. His main works are *Handbuch der Katholischen Liturgie* (1932–7) in 2 vols., and a revision of Thalhofer's book of the same title (1883–93).

Ekkehard of Sankt Gallen (I) Teacher and poet, born Thurgau, *c.*910, died Sankt Gallen, 14 January 973. He came from a noble family and became dean of the monastery. He was offered the abbacy but declined. On a pilgrimage to Rome he developed a friendship with Pope **John XIII**. He composed religious poetry and hymns, and a Latin epic based on a German folk saga, *Waltharius*, is attributed to him, but his authorship is said to be doubtful.

Ekkehard of Sankt Gallen (II) (Palatinus) Died Mainz, 23 April 990. He was the nephew and pupil of **Ekkehard**. His life was spent both in the monastery and at the court of Emperor **Otto I**. He also served as provost of the cathedral of Mainz. He taught at the school of Sankt Gallen and was also an author.

Ekkehard of Sankt Gallen (III) Teacher, chronicler, born *c.*980, died 21 October 1060. He served as director of the cathedral school in Mainz and was known for his excellence in ecclesiastical music. In 1031 he returned to the monastery and worked on a chronicle of Sankt Gallen, which had been started by Ratpert. He was able to bring the chronicle up to date and it remains an important historical source, although it is said to contain inaccuracies. His main other work, *Liber Benedictionum*, is taken from metrical writings on the walls of Mainz Cathedral.

Elbel, Benjamin Franciscan moral theologian, born Friedburg, Bavaria, *c.*1690, died Soeflingen near Elm, 4 June 1756. He joined the Order of Friars Minor Recollect and became minister provincial of Strasburg. He taught theology in seminaries and other institutions, his chief interest being in moral theology. His main works are *Theologiae moralis decalogalis et sacramentalis per modum conferentiarum casibus practicis illustrata* (1731) and a history of his Order: *Ortus et progressus ordinis minorum S. Francisci ultra quinque saecula* (1732).

Elder, George Educator, born Hardin's Creek, Kentucky, 11 August 1794, died Bardstown, Kentucky, 28 September 1838. He entered the seminary of St Mary's, Baltimore, in 1816, was ordained in 1819 and founded a school for boys of Bardstown, begun in the basement of St Joseph's Seminary. After a time as a parish priest, Elder returned as president of St Joseph's. A fire broke out there in 1838 and Elder strained his heart while fighting it, hastening his death.

Elder, William Henry Archbishop, born Baltimore, 22 March 1819, died Cincinnati, 31 October 1904. He entered the seminary of Mt St Mary's College, Emmitsburg, and became a deacon in 1842. He was ordained priest in Rome in 1846 and on returning home became professor of dogmatic theology at Emmitsburg. He continued to teach here until made bishop of Natchez, Mississippi. His tenure was marked by the Civil War and the depredations of yellow fever. He was promoted in 1880 to the Archbishopric of Cincinnati, where he presided over an archdiocese in deep difficulties with its finances. His tenure was noted for its wisdom and evenhandedness.

Eldrad (Heldrade, Hildradus) Saint, abbot, born near Aix, Provence, died Novalese, Turin, 13 March between 840 and 845. He was born into a noble family and entered the Benedictine monastery of SS Peter and Andrew at Novalese after a lengthy pilgrimage in Spain and Italy. He was elected abbot c.826. The abbey was already known as a cultural centre and for its library. During his abbacy it developed as a hospice for pilgrims crossing the Alps. It is also recorded that as abbot he was given the monastery of Appagni by **Lothair I** in 825. Feast day 13 March.

Eleutherius (Eleutherus) Pope, of Greek ancestry, died Rome, c.189–92. He was bishop of Rome in the reigns of Marcus Aurelius and Commodus. **Eusebius of Caesarea** gives his accession as AD 177. His tenure of the bishopric probably coincided with the heresy of Montanus, and of Basilides, **Valentine**, Cerdo and **Marcian**, although exact dates are difficult to place. Letters from **Irenaeus** to Eleutherius deal with these matters, and Irenaeus also visited him in Rome.

Eleutherius of Tournai Saint, bishop, born Tournai, c.456, died there, c.531. Information about Eleutherius comes from the *Vita S. Medardi* (c.600), where he was said to have spent his early life at court. He was of Gallo-Roman birth and became both count and bishop of Tournai. He is said to have developed a thriving Christian community there. His first *Vita* was written about 900, thus factual information about him is unreliable. Events credited to him such as the diocesan synod of 520 and certain writings are not definitely credited. Feast day 20 February.

Elfleda Saint, abbess, born Northumbria, 653, died Whitby, 8 February 714. She was consecrated in infancy to the religious life by her father King Oswin of Northumbria and her mother Enfleda in thanksgiving for the successful outcome of a battle. She spent her early life with **Hilda**, who was then abbess of Hartlepool. Later at Whitby Abbey both she and her mother became abbesses, during which time the *Life of Gregory the Great* was written there. She was a friend of **Cuthbert of Lindisfarne** and **Wilfrid**. As a skilled mediator she effected the reconciliation of Wilfrid, bishop of York, and the church in Northumbria at the Synod of the river Nidd (705). Her relics were discovered and translated at Whitby, c.1125. Feast day 8 February.

Elgar, Edward Roman Catholic composer of the early twentieth century, also conductor, born Broadheath, Worcestershire, 2 June 1857, died Worcester, 23 February 1934. He was largely self-taught. He succeeded his father as organist of St George's Roman Catholic Church, Worcester. He married in 1899 and settled in Malvern: after his wife's death in 1920 he composed little. His works include two organ sonatas, and several oratorios, such as *The Apostles* and *The Kingdom*. His Christian masterpiece is *The Dream of Gerontius* (1900), a consummate setting, in which he matched the romantic, mystical genius of Cardinal **Newman**'s masterful poem. This, with the *Enigma Variations* (1899), established his reputation. The well-known 'Pomp and Circumstance' marches were written between 1901 and 1907: the first contains the tune now called 'Land of Hope and Glory'. He was knighted in 1904, in 1924 became Master of the King's Musick and was created a baronet in 1931.

Elguero, Francisco Mexican lawyer and writer, born Morelia, Michoacán, 14 March 1856, died there 17 December 1932. He was a great defender of Catholicism, linking the defence of it with that of Spanish civilization, in particular stressing the need to preserve the purity of the Castilian language. In a time of anti-Catholic laws and institutions he finally went into exile to Cuba, following the revolution of Carranza. Here and on his return he wrote extensively as a journalist, poet and religious commentator. His main works are *La Immaculada* (1905), *Senilias poéticas* (1920), *Commentarios a pensiamentos religiosos* (1924) and *Museo Intelectual* (1930).

Elias bar Shinaya Nestorian metropolitan, author and historian, born Nisibis (Nusaybin) on the Turkish/Syrian border, 11 February 975, died there after 1049. He entered the monastery of Michael at Mosul, and then Shem'ôn, was ordained in 994, became bishop of Beit-Nûhadra in 1002 and metropolitan in 1008. He wrote, in both Syriac and Arabic, works on canon and civil law, a Syriac grammar and dictionary, hymns and homilies. His most well known and important work is *Chronography* – a history of the Church from 25 to 1018, which includes sources, now lost, from which he worked. Other works are the *Book on the Proof of the Truth of the Faith*, *Book of the Translator*, *Book on the Removal of Suffering* – this last on how to acquire interior peace.

Elias Ekdikos Greek theologian and author, born in the twelfth century, he is often confused with Elias the metropolitan of Crete. His writings include scholia on early Church Fathers and writings showing Byzantine doctrine of the movement of human beings towards perfection. The former include works on the homilies of **Gregory of Nazianzus**, **John Climacus** and Elias of Charan. His most famous work of Byzantine doctrine, *Didactic Anthologion*, uses a device of three steps towards perfection, the Exodus as the cleansing of the body, Crossing the Red Sea as the cleansing of the soul and Crossing the Desert as the final purification.

Elias of Cortona Franciscan minister general, born near Assisi, died Cortona, 22 April 1253. He joined the Order in its first years and became a friend of St **Francis**. He was with St Francis on his deathbed and was charged with building the basilica at Assisi in his memory. He became minister general in 1233 and the Order flourished. He was, however, unable to use power wisely and antagonized many. In 1239 he was excommunicated, though he repented on his deathbed.

Elias of Jerusalem Saint, Arabic patriarch and theologian, born Aila, 20 July 430, died 518. He lived as an anchorite in early life, but on the uprising of the monophysite persecution fled to Palestine and lived at the laura in Sahel. He became patriarch of Jerusalem in 494. His life was marked by the controversies and allegiances surrounding monophysitism. His position was complex: he adhered to the Council of Chalcedon and entered into communion with Constantinopolitan patriarchs but suffered from a misrepresentation of his position by Emperor **Anastasius I**, to whom he had made a profession of faith. He was exiled to Aila in 516 when he refused to sign a monophysite formula. Feast day 4 July.

Elias of Reggio (Spelaiotes) Saint, born Reggio di Calabria, *c*.865, died Meluccà in Calabria, 11 September 960. His name Spelaiotes means cave-dweller, and this is where he ended his life, as a hermit in a cave near Meluccà. He entered monastic life at the age of nineteen, and lived as a hermit near Rome. He then lived with a companion Arsenios at Armo. They both then spent some eight years at a hermitage at Patras, but Elias returned to the monastery of Saline in Calabria. He returned to eremitic life, where he stayed till his death. A group of disciples joined him at the hermitage. Feast day 11 September.

Elias of Thessalonika Saint, monk, born Enna, Sicily, 823, died Thessalonika, Greece, 17 August 903. Baptized as John, he was sold into slavery in 838 following the Saracen invasion of Sicily, but was redeemed a few years later. As an act of thanksgiving he undertook a pilgrimage to the Holy Land, changing his name to Elias in honour of the patriarch of Jerusalem. When eventually he returned to Sicily he established a monastery before setting out on a second pilgrimage, and was later received by the Pope. Subsequently Elias was summoned to appear at the court of the Eastern Emperor at Byzantium, but died at Thessalonika en route. Feast day 17 August.

Eligius of Noyon (Tournai) Saint, bishop, born Limousin, *c*.588, died Limoges, 30 November 660. Eligius was from an old Gallo-Roman family, apprenticed as a goldsmith, under the king's treasurer, in the mint of Limoges. While still a layman he founded the monastery of Solignac, and another for women at Paris. Eligius entered the clergy in 639 and was appointed bishop of Noyon in 641. At Noyon he founded a monastery and discovered the relics of St Quentin and St Paitus. He re-evangelized areas of his diocese that had reverted to paganism under the influence of Barbarian invasions. Feast day 1 December.

Eliot, Charles William Leading Unitiarian, American educator, born Boston, Massachusetts, 20 March 1834, died Northeast Harbor, Maine, 22 August 1926. After studies at Harvard he was appointed assistant professor of mathematics and chemistry there. In Europe he studied chemistry and the education system. Returning to the USA, he was appointed professor of chemistry at the Massachusetts Institute of Technology. For forty years, from 1867 to 1907, he was Harvard's president and raised the college from provincial status to an internationally recognized institution. Eliot influenced secondary education, raising standards. He urged the inclusion of foreign languages and mathematics in schools. He edited *Harvard Classics*, a 50-volume set of world literature. He was a great spokesman for the Unitarian Church, and wrote *The Religion of the Future*. Also his writings include *The Happy Life*, *The Durable Satisfactions of Life* and *Twentieth Century Christianity*. He was twice invited to be US ambassador to the UK.

Eliot, Thomas Stearns Poet and writer, born St Louis, Missouri, 26 September 1888, died London, 4 January 1965. He was born into a Unitarian family and educated at Smith Academy, Harvard, the Sorbonne and Oxford. He was a student of philosophy during this period, and it was this which brought him to Oxford, but in 1911 he showed his poetry to Ezra Pound, who persuaded him to stay in Britain. He became a teacher for eighteen months, a bank official for nine years, and finally a director of the publishing company Faber and Faber. He became a British subject in 1927, and a member of the Church of England in the Anglo-Catholic tradition. Much of his poetry has a religious theme. His play *Murder in the Cathedral* (1935) was written for Canterbury Cathedral and was filmed. He became professor of poetry at Harvard. His books include *The Idea of a Christian Society* (1939). He was awarded the Nobel Prize for Literature in 1948.

Elipandus of Toledo Archbishop and heretic, born Spain, 25 July 717, died there, c.807. Appointed archbishop of Toledo in 783, Elipandus held a form of adoptionism, which basically teaches that the man Jesus was indwelt by the second person of the Trinity, so that there are thus two personalities in the Incarnation, one human and one divine. The detail of Elipandus' teaching is uncertain, since no reliable record of it has survived, but it was condemned as heretical by the Council of Frankfurt in 794.

Elizabeth I Queen of England, 1558–1603, born Greenwich, 7 September 1533, died Richmond, 24 March 1603. By the age of ten the daughter of **Henry VIII** and Anne Boleyn had been declared legitimate and restored to the line of succession. This early initiation into the world of religious politics served her well during the reign of her sister **Mary**, when the princess outwardly conformed to Catholicism. After her own accession she sought to strike a balance between the religious extremes of the previous reigns, being styled supreme governor rather than supreme head of the Church, and appointing Protestant bishops while making slight amendments to the 1552 Book of Common Prayer. Puritans such as Archbishop Grindal criticized this cautious policy. The evolution of Elizabeth as a Protestant heroine may be traced through English military aid sent to the Dutch rebels, the consequent war with Spain, her excommunication by Pius V in 1570, the persecution of English Catholics in the 1580s, the execution of Mary Stuart, Queen of Scots in 1587, and the English defeat of the Spanish Armada in 1588.

Elizabeth Feodorovna Grand duchess, Orthodox saint, nun and martyr, born Darmstadt, Germany, 1 November 1864, died (martyred) Alapaevsk, Russia, 18 July 1918. Daughter of the grand duke of Hesse and sister of the future Empress Alexandra, she married Grand Duke Sergius of Russia and became Orthodox in 1891. After her husband's assassination in 1905 she founded a convent in Moscow to care for the poor and sick. She was arrested during the Revolution and with one faithful nun was sent to Alapaevsk, near Ekaterinburg. There she was killed by being thrown alive down a mine shaft. Her body was eventually taken to Jerusalem to a convent she had helped to found. Feast day 5 July.

Elizabeth of Hungary Saint, and Hungarian princess, born Bratislava, 1207, died of exhaustion, Marburg, 17 November 1231. Following the death of her husband while on crusade in 1227, she and her three children were exiled from court. She lived as a Franciscan tertiary at Marburg. She sold her jewellery and clothes, and used the proceeds to build a hospital. Carrying out various works of charity she had a concern for the poor, particularly lepers, the sores of whom she often washed. Believed to have performed miracles, she was canonized by Pope **Gregory IX** in 1235. Feast day 17 November.

Elizabeth of Portugal   Saint, a queen famous for her piety and acts of charity, born Saragassa(?), 17 November 1271, the daughter of Peter III of Aragon, died Estremoz, Portugal, 4 July 1336. At the age of twelve she married the king of Portugal, who allowed her to continue with the many pious devotions she was accustomed to observe. She established a hospital and an orphanage. She acted as a peacemaker, successfully resolving disputes between rival royal factions. During her later years she retired to a house she had built beside a convent of Poor Clares she had founded near Coimbra. Feast day 4 July.

Elizabeth of Ranfaing   Venerable, French foundress, born Remiremont, 30 October 1592, died Nancy, 14 January 1649. Elizabeth had been coerced into marriage with an aged nobleman, who maltreated her, and, a widow at 24, she opened a refuge in Nancy, with her three daughters, for fallen women. Her congregation, become Our Lady of Refuge, was approved by the Holy See in 1634, and attracted other houses of refuge, under the patronage of St Ignatius, and the Rule of St Augustine as a guide. Members were classified according to the moral status of their lives, and the rule specified that penitents proper should always constitute at least two-thirds of the community, so as to ensure the apostolic nature of the congregation.

Elizabeth of Schönau   Saint, Benedictine, born c.1129, died Schönau, 18 June 1165. She was professed at Schönau in 1147 and became superior in 1157. She was the subject of ecstasies and visions of many kinds but feared that she may have been deceived. She was instructed by Abbot Hildelin to report them to her brother Egbert, priest at Bonn. He put them in writing and they were published in three books of visions. She and her brother were certain of the authenticity of her visions, but doubt was cast on them by Eusebius Amort, who claimed they were imaginary or illusions of the devil as they sometimes conflicted with history or other revelations. Feast day 18 June.

Elizabeth of the Trinity   Blessed, Carmelite nun, born Elizabeth Catez, near Bourges, France, 18 July 1880, died of Addison's disease, Dijon, 9 November 1906. Emphasizing holiness of life, in her writings she taught the possibility of the individual believer attaining the image of God by reliving the mysteries of the Incarnate Word. She has been beatified. Feast day 8 November.

Elizalde, Miguel de   Jesuit theologian, born Echalar, Spain, 1616, died San Sebastian, Spain, 18 November 1678. He became a Jesuit in 1635, and taught theology and philosophy at several seminaries before becoming rector of the Jesuit College in Naples. His theology of revelation was unusual for its time in giving a prominent place to human reason, and although it was little recognized in his own day it became highly regarded during the nineteenth century.

Ellacuría, Ignacio, and companions   Six Jesuit priests, killed El Salvador, 16 November 1989. As had other priests in the country before them, notably Oscar **Romero** and Rutilio **Grande**, the Jesuits who ran the University of Central America denounced repression and injustice in the country as a major factor in the ongoing civil war. Ellacuría, a theologian, developed intellectual arguments linking their faith with their solidarity with the poor. They also tried to promote negotiations between government and opposition. They were shot at night on the orders of the military commanders, who told the soldiers they were the intellectual authors of the uprising. The housekeeper and her daughter were also killed.

Ellard, Gerald   Jesuit liturgical scholar, born Commonwealth, USA, 8 October 1894, died Boston, USA, 1 April 1963. Ellard became a Jesuit in 1912 and was ordained in 1926. Most of his career was spent as professor of liturgy and church history at St Mary's College, Kansas. A keen student of the history of liturgy, he became respected internationally for his scholarship in this field. He was the author of several significant books on liturgy and Christian worship, and was a keen advocate of the liturgical renewal movement.

Ellenbog, Nikolaus   Benedictine humanist scholar, born Biberach, Germany, 18 March 1481, died Ottobeuren, Germany, 6 June 1543. He joined the

Benedictines at Ottobeuren Abbey in 1504 following studies in medicine and philosophy at several universities. He was ordained in 1507 and proceeded to serve the abbey in a variety of offices. He also maintained a life of study, corresponding with several of the most prominent scholars of the day, notably **Erasmus** and **Reuchlin**. Ellenbog was the author of several minor treatises, and through his influence Ottobeuren became a notable centre of humanist scholarship.

Ellis, Jane E. Historian of the Russian Orthodox Church, born Liverpool, 3 August 1951, died Oxford, 30 June 1998. She was a member of the evangelical wing of the Church of England, and her interest in Russia was sparked by a campaign in the late 1960s to smuggle Bibles into the country. She studied Russian at Birmingham University and graduated in 1973, immediately joining Keston College, then located in Kent. She was on the editorial board of Keston's journal *Religion in Communist Lands* from the outset, and was its editor from 1981 to 1986. Her major study *The Russian Orthodox Church: A Contemporary History* (1986) was translated into Russian as well as Italian, and ten years later she published *The Russian Orthodox Church: Triumphalism and Defensiveness.*

Ellis, John Tracy Roman Catholic priest and church historian, born 30 July 1905, died Washington, DC, 16 October 1992. Between 1938 and 1963, and 1978 and 1989, he taught at the Catholic University of America. From 1941 to 1963 he was managing editor of *The Catholic Historical Review.* His most famous major work (he published a dozen books and some 400 articles) is a two-volume biography of *Cardinal Gibbons* (1952), but he is also particularly remembered for a lecture given in 1955, 'American Catholics and the Intellectual Life', and subsequently published, in which he criticized the scholarly achievements of the American Catholic Church.

Ellis, Philip Michael English Benedictine bishop, first vicar apostolic of the Western District, England, born 1652, died Segni, 16 November 1726. From a Protestant family, he converted to Roman Catholicism in his youth and went to study in Douai, where he was ordained. He returned to England in 1685 and was a royal chaplain before

being made vicar apostolic of the newly created Western District in 1688. He was imprisoned the same year but was soon released and went to Paris and then to Rome, where his understanding of the situation in England was put to good use. In 1704 he was made bishop of Segni, where he rebuilt the monastery of Santa Chiara and opened it as a seminary for the diocese.

Ellul, Jacques Social critic and theologian, born Bordeaux, 6 January 1912, died Bordeaux, 19 May 1994. He was brought up in a non-Christian family, but publicly stated he was a Christian in 1932, joining the French Protestant Church. His early studies were in law, and he completed a doctorate in Roman law at the University of Bordeaux in 1936. By this time he was a political radical, though he never joined either the Socialist or the Communist Party. He was, however, a student of Marx and an active opponent of Fascism. He was attracted to the personalist philosophy espoused by Emmanuel **Mounier**, though he parted company with Mounier in 1938. His political beliefs led to his dismissal from his post in the faculty of law at Strasburg by the Vichy government, and he fled to the countryside with his family, where he acted as a Protestant pastor, though he never received any formal theological training. At the liberation of Bordeaux he became the city's deputy mayor, but became disillusioned with the ability of politicians to institute reforms in society, and left office in 1947. He was involved with the World Council of Churches from its beginning, but broke with it because of its political position in 1966. He served on the National Synod of the French Reformed Church, and, with his wife Yvette, was very active in their parish of Pessac, where for a long time he was pastor. At the University of Bordeaux he was both professor of the history and sociology of institutions (his major work is a five-volume *Histoire des Institutions*) and professor in the Institute of Political Studies. He retired from the University of Bordeaux, to which he had been appointed secretly in 1943, in 1980. His first book, *The Theological Foundation of Law*, was published in 1946, though the book which made him well-known outside his immediate circle was *The Technological Society*, published in English in 1964, though the French edition had appeared a dozen years earlier. He was not, however, solely concerned with 'technology' in the sense of machines, and preferred to use the word 'technique', by which he meant a totality of methods used to achieve efficiency, and it is this 'technique' which now shapes society. In his theological writing he was very influenced by the writings of Karl **Barth**, with a strong emphasis on the Fall and the belief that revelation alone can be the source of a Christian's knowledge of God. He was particularly concerned with the role of ethics in a totalitarian state, advocating anarchy as the appropriate political stance for a Christian.

Elmo Saint, bishop of Formiae, in Campania, Italy, martyred c.303. According to legend he was tortured during the Diocletian persecutions and died of his wounds. Another legend states that he died by having his intestines wound out of his body on a windlass. Feast day 2 June.

Elmo (Peter González) Dominican preacher and missionary amongst the Spanish fisher-folk, born 1190, died Easter Sunday 1246. He was later adopted as the patron saint of sailors. Feast day 14 April.

Elmsley, John Roman Catholic civic leader and businessman, born York (now Toronto), Canada, 19 May 1801, died Toronto, 8 May 1863. Formerly an officer in the Royal Navy, and from a staunch Protestant background, Elmsley converted to Roman Catholicism following marriage to a Catholic. He became a Sunday School teacher, then a churchwarden. From various business interests he accumulated considerable wealth, with which he paid off the debts incurred in the building of St Michael's Cathedral, Toronto. Through the allocation of building plots to a number of Roman Catholic religious orders, Elmsley also encouraged the establishment of schools and centres for charitable work in the same city.

Elphinstone, William Scottish bishop and statesman, born Glasgow, 1431, died Edinburgh, 25 October 1514. After studying at Glasgow University he was ordained a priest and became reader in canon law at the University of Paris. In 1474 he was appointed rector of Glasgow University, in 1481 bishop of Ross, and bishop of Aberdeen two years later. He was sent by James III and James IV on diplomatic missions to England and France. He was lord chancellor briefly in 1488 and Keeper of the Privy Seal in 1492. He was the founder of Aberdeen University.

Elwell, Clarence Roman Catholic bishop and educator, born Cleveland, Ohio, USA, 4 February 1904, died Columbus, Ohio, USA, 16 February 1973. After attending parish schools in Cleveland, Elwell studied for the priesthood and was ordained in Innsbruck, Austria, in 1929. He served four years as an assistant pastor before entering education administration, which would be his life's work. He directed schools, served as school superintendent and was eventually ordained a bishop in 1962, and made vicar for Catholic education in the Diocese of Cleveland, where he improved the quality of education and helped to develop textbooks. In 1968 he was moved to Columbus, where he worked until his death.

Elyot, Thomas Diplomat, author and MP, born Wiltshire, c.1490, died Cambridgeshire, 20 March 1546. The favour of Cardinal **Wolsey** brought Elyot appointments in local government, but his reputation at court was assured by the publication of the *Boke called the Governour* (1531), a treatise on the education of a statesman, after which he was appointed ambassador to the imperial court. His other works, in which the influence of **Erasmus** and Pico has been traced, include a Latin-English dictionary. As a friend of Thomas **More** his loyalty to the Reformed doctrine was doubted, a doubt which Elyot maintained was unjustified.

Elzéar of Sabran Count of Ariano, saint, born in the castle of Saint-Jean, Provence, 1285, died Paris, 27 September 1325. He studied in an abbey of St Victor at Marseilles, and though he married in 1299 (Blessed) **Delphina** of the House of Glandèves, they both took vows of chastity. At the death of his father he returned home to claim his inheritance, and though he was met with hostility by his vassals, he won them over. In 1312 he led an army to aid the Pope against the Emperor **Henry VII**, and in 1324 he was sent as the king of Naples' ambassador to Paris, which is where he died. He was a Franciscan tertiary, and was buried in the Franciscan habit. He had a reputation for generosity and kindliness, and **Urban V**, Elzéar's own godchild, formally recognized his sanctity, though the proclamation of it took place under **Gregory XI**.

Embury, Philip The pioneer of American Methodism, born Ballingrane, Ireland, 29 September 1728, died due to an accident mowing, Salem, New York, August 1773. Following an evangelical conversion experience in 1752 he joined the Methodist society and became a local preacher six years later. In 1760 he emigrated to America, living as a schoolteacher. Due to the influence of Barbara Heck he resumed his preaching, firstly in his own house, later establishing a chapel on the site of the present John Street Church in New York. In 1769 he moved to Camden, New York, where he formed a society which later became the Troy Conference.

Emebert of Cambrai Saint, bishop, birth unknown, death uncertain but before 645. Identification of Emebert is problematic. Emebert is held to have been bishop of Cambrai-Arras after 627, and before 645, and could possibly have been chorbishop of Brabant. No other certain life details are available. Feast day 15 January.

Emeric of Hungary Blessed, prince, died 1031. Son of St Stephen, first king of Hungary, Emeric/Imre had been his father's choice for successor, but died in a hunting accident. Feast day 4 November.

Emerson, Ralph Waldo Unitarian philosopher, poet and essayist, born Boston, Massachusetts, 1803, died Concord, 27 April 1882. After studying theology at the Harvard divinity school he was ordained into the Unitarian ministry and became the pastor of the Second Church in Boston. In 1831 he became a lecturer and writer, and travelled to Europe in 1832, meeting with **Carlyle**, Wordsworth and **Coleridge**. He founded the Transcendentalists, a group of New England Idealists. His pantheistic Unitarianism and ethical Idealism were expressed in his book *Nature* (1836) and in his other works, the divinity school *Address* (1838), *Essays*, first series (1841) and the *Essays* (1844). He also wrote *Poems* (1846, 1847–8).

Emery, Jacques-André French priest, born Gex, 26 August 1732, died Paris, 28 April 1811. He studied at St Sulpice in Paris, and was ordained priest. He taught in seminaries, was vigorously anti-Gallican, and became superior-general of the seminary, and Society, of St Sulpice. To some extent foreseeing the Revolution, he attempted to reform the clergy and prepare them for it. In Paris, the archbishop having been exiled, Emery acted as administrator of the diocese. He regarded taking the 'oath of Liberty and Equality' as acceptable, regarding this as a civil and political matter only, but opposed the Civil Constitution of the Clergy. During the Revolution, he was imprisoned and narrowly escaped execution. On the closure of French seminaries, some Sulpicians were sent to America, where the first seminary was established at Baltimore. In the presence of Napoleon, Emery defended papal rights.

Emiliani, Jerome Saint, and founder of the Clerks Regular of Somascha – named after the town where they founded their first house – born Venice, 1481, died Somascha, 8 February 1537 while ministering to victims of disease. As a soldier in the Venetian army he was in command of a fortress at Castelnuovo, near Treviso, which was captured, and he was imprisoned. During the imprisonment he underwent a conversion and determined to devote his life and energies to plague and famine victims and especially to orphans (he was named the patron saint of abandoned children and orphans in 1928). He founded homes, hospitals and orphanages throughout northern Italy and a house for repentant prostitutes. It is claimed that he was the first to teach catechism to children by using the question-and-answer method. His congregation was approved by the Papacy in 1540, but he was not canonized until 1767, by Pope **Clement XIII**. Feast day 8 February.

Emmanuel Bishop, born possibly at Cremona, Italy, *c*.1225, died Adwert, Netherlands, 1 October 1298. Details of Emmanuel's early life are unclear, but he is known to have been professor of canon law at the University of Paris during the second half of the thirteenth century. Subsequently he became bishop of Cremona, a post which for political reasons he was forced to resign in 1295. He spent the last three years of his life at the Cistercian abbey at Adwert, where he was much venerated after his death.

Emmerham (Emmeram) Saint, martyr, preacher, possibly a bishop, born Acquitaine, died Helfendorf, *c.*660. Emmerham's original name was Hainhramm. He was patron of the monastery at Sankt Emmeram, where his remains were translated in 737 when he was being honoured as a martyr. No other facts are known about his life. In art he is shown in bishop's robes, either pierced by a lance, or bound to a ladder and mutilated. Feast day 22 September.

Emmerich, Anna Katharina Roman Catholic mystic and stigmatic, born 8 September 1774, near Coesfeld, Germany, died Dülmen, 9 February 1824. Her parents were poor peasants and she worked for a farmer, and then as a seamstress and finally as a domestic servant for a number of years before in 1802 entering an Augustinian house at Agnetenberg, Westphalia, staying there till it closed in 1812. About that time she became seriously ill and began to show the stigmata of the Passion on her body. Her visions were taken down by Clemens **Brentano** and published posthumously, *The Dolorous Passion of Our Lord Jesus Christ* appearing first, in 1833. Lives of Christ, and of the Virgin Mary, were later constructed from Brentano's notes.

Emmons, Nathaniel Congregational minister, born East Haddam, Connecticut, 20 April 1745, died 23 September 1840, Franklin, Massachusetts. He graduated at Yale in 1767 and in 1773 became the minister of the Congregational chapel at Franklin, a pastorate lasting 54 years, until he resigned in 1827. He trained numerous students for the ministry in his own house. He was editor of the *Massachusetts Missionary Magazine* and co-founder and president of the Massachusetts Missionary Society. He was a moderate Calvinist and an abolitionist.

Emrys ap Iwan (Robert Ambrose Jones) Methodist scholar and critic, born Abergele, Wales, 24 March 1851, died Rhewl, Wales, 6 January 1906. Following studies in Europe and a period working as a teacher, Jones became a Methodist minister in 1833. His desire to spread the Gospel in Welsh led him to study the Welsh language and its literature, on which he became a noted authority. A strong advocate of the promotion of Welsh culture, which he regarded as an integral part of Wales's Christian heritage, he opposed the planting of English-speaking churches in Welsh-speaking areas.

Emser, Hieronymus German priest, theologian, editor and essayist, and for long Martin **Luther**'s bitterest opponent, born Ulm, Germany, 16/26 March 1478, died Dresden, Germany, 8 November 1527. Emser studied at the Universities of Tübingen and Basel. At Erfurt, he lectured on classics, and became the duke of Saxony's secretary. He wrote tracts against Luther and also entered into a controversy with the Swiss theologian **Zwingli**. He wrote a defence of the *Canon of the Mass* and published a German translation of the NT from the Vulgate, a rival edition to Luther's New Testament of 1522. Luther burned Emser's writings with the papal bull of excommunication.

Emygdius of Ancona Saint, bishop, martyr, birth unknown, died Ancona, 5 August 303/4. According to legend, Emygdius was a barbarian from Trier who converted to Christianity there. At an early age he went to Rome and undertook vigorous missionary activity under the guidance of Pope **Marcellus I**. He was beheaded at Ancona under the Diocletian persecution of 303/4, with SS Eupolus, Germanus and Valentinius. In his cult he is considered an effective protector against earthquakes. Feast day 5 August.

Encina, Juan del Poet, dramatist and composer, born Juan de Fermoselle, Salamanca, 12 July 1468, died León, 1529/30. Encina occupies a pivotal position in the history of both music and drama in Spain. The patronage of the Catalan Pope **Alexander VI** and of Spanish nobles enabled him to travel and transmit the Italian tradition of secular theatre to his native land. He was the principal contributor to the *Cancionero musical de palacio* (Palace songbook, 1495), an anthology of plays and poems, thereby becoming the first Spanish dramatist whose plays were printed. His pastoral poetry frequently developed popular songs for more refined ears.

Engel, Hans Ludwig Roman Catholic canon lawyer, born Castle Wagrein, Austria, *c.*1630, died Grillenberg, 22 April 1674. He studied at the Benedictine monastery of Melk, then law at the

University of Salzburg. He became successively a doctor of civil and canon law, was ordained priest, and became professor of canon law at the university. In 1669 he became vice-chancellor of the university. He wrote many works on law, notably *Collegium Universi Juris Canonici* (Salzburg, 1671–4).

Engelbert Abbot of Admont, born Völkersdorf, Styria, c.1250, died 12 May 1331. He studied at Admont, Prague and Padua. He was abbot of Admont for almost thirty years, but resigned to devote himself to prayer and study. He was a learned and versatile writer on moral and dogmatic theology, philosophy, history, political science, Scripture, natural sciences and even music. He believed civil and papal authority should be separate, and foresaw the fall of the Holy Roman Empire.

Engelbert of Cologne Bishop and saint, born Berg, 1185, assassinated near Schwelm, 7 November 1225. Due mainly to family connections he quickly ascended the ecclesiastical hierarchy, becoming archbishop of Cologne in 1217. He spent most of his life as a statesman, being guardian of King Henry VII, son of the Emperor **Frederick II**, and was murdered by political opponents. The immediate cause of his death, however, which he himself had expected and had prepared for, was his defence of a convent of nuns against the oppression of their supposed protector. He was therefore honoured as a martyr. Feast day 7 November.

Engelhardt, Zephyrind (Charles Anthony) Franciscan missionary and historian, born Bilshausen, Germany, 13 November 1851, died Santa Barbara, USA, 27 April 1934. Emigrating to America with his parents at a young age, Engelhardt joined the Franciscans in 1873 and was ordained in 1878. He became a missionary and worked among the Menominee and Ottawa Indians, in whose languages he wrote several Christian books. He also wrote a large number of histories and journal articles chronicling the activities of the Franciscans and Catholic missions in America, which are regarded as standard works in these fields.

England, John Roman Catholic bishop and theologian, born Cork, Ireland, 23 September 1786, died Charleston, South Carolina, 11 April 1842. Following his ordination in 1808 he lectured at Cork Cathedral, becoming president of the diocesan college of St Mary four years later. In 1820 he was appointed as bishop of Charleston. In this episcopal office he established schools and religious communities, such as the Sisters of Our Lady of Mercy. In 1833 he was sent as the papal legate to Haiti. As a writer he founded the *United States Catholic Miscellany*, and his theology is contained in his collected works, published in 1849.

Ennodius, Magnus Felix Bishop and rhetorician, born probably at Arles, Southern Gaul, 474, died Pavia, Italy, 17 July 521. He was educated, was ordained and then taught in Pavia. He acted as secretary to his uncle Laurentius, bishop of Milan, at the Synod of Palmaris in 501, and as a supporter of **Symmachus** as Pope, wrote a reply to the objections raised by the supporters of the defeated archpriest Laurentius, *Libellus adversus eos qui contra synodum scribere praesumpserunt*. Shortly after 513 he returned to Pavia as its bishop. He wrote poems, epigrams, inscriptions, biographies, letters, treatises on both pagan and Christian rhetoric, and his autobiography.

Eoban Saint, bishop, birth unknown, died Dokkum, 5 June 754. Eoban was an Anglo-Saxon missionary and bishop in The Netherlands. Originally a messenger for St **Boniface** he later became his amanuensis. He was sent to England by Boniface and elevated to chorbishop. He accompanied Boniface on his last mission amongst the Frisians, and was martyred with him at Dokkum. Feast day 5 June.

Eon of Stella (also known as **Eudo of Brittany, Eudes de l'Etoile, Eys, Eon, Eons, Euno, Evus)** Heretic, probably born Loudéac, Brittany, died in captivity, Rheims, c.1148. The best account of his life is found in **William of Newburgh**. Around 1145, Eon began preaching in the forests of Brittany; he soon organized his many followers into a new church, whose bishops and archbishops he named Wisdom, Knowledge, and Judgement, as well as after the Apostles. Eon was convinced that the phrase at the end of prayers, 'Through Him (*per eundem*) our Lord' referred to him, and declared himself to be the son of God. He carried a forked staff with him: when the fork pointed upwards, two-thirds of the world belonged to God and one-third to him; the proportions were reversed when it pointed downwards. When he explained this to the council summoned by Archbishop Samson of Rheims, they laughed and mocked him – and ordered him to be imprisoned, where he quickly died.

Eparchius Monk, priest, born Perigord, France, c.504, died Angoulême, France, 1 July 581. Eparchius entered the monastic life despite parental opposition, while he was still young. He served there under Abbot Martin, gaining a reputation for virtue and the gift of miracles. He left the monastery to live in solitude at Angoulême, but the bishop of the area obliged him to receive ordination to priesthood. Eparchius accepted disciples, but required them to live completely dependent upon providence, and to be devoted to prayer.

Ephrem the Syrian Saint, poet, theologian, born Nisibis, c.306, died Edessa, c.373. Ephrem is the most important Syrian Church Father, and greatest poet of the patristic period. Born of Christian parents Ephrem grew up under the tutelage of Bishop Jacob, with whom he founded the theological school of Nisibis. Ephrem was a 'son of the covenant' (rather than a 'monk') living in abstinence and virginity within the Christian community. Many legends arose concerning his life through monastic circles. Ephrem's works are many and include hymns and poems. Feast day 28 January/1 February, Syrian Church; 28 January, Byzantine rite; 9 July, Coptic rite; 9 June, Latin Church.

Epimarchus (Epimachus) Saint, died c.250. Linked to Gordian. Epimarchus suffered martyrdom in Alexandria, but his body was taken to Rome. Gordian, martyred later in Rome, was buried in the tomb of Epimarchus. Thereafter they were venerated together. Feast day 10 May.

Epiphanius of Constantia Monk, bishop, saint and Church Father. Born near Eleutheropolis, Palestine c.315, died at sea in May 402. A native Syrian, Epiphanius studied classics in Egypt, and also knew Coptic and Hebrew. He founded a monastery at Eleutheropolis and remained there for 30 years before his ordination. In 367 he was selected for the See of Constantia. A strong supporter of Athanasian doctrine, he opposed the Arians and Origenists. Epiphanius broke allegiance with Melitius over *homoousios*. Epiphanius opposed philosophy. His *Ancoratus* (374) deals with the Trinity and opposes Apollinarianism. His *Panarion* (374, 376) is a tract against heretics. He also produced *De mensuris et ponderibus*, and *De duodecim gemmis*. Feast day 12 May.

Epiphanius of Constantinople Patriarch, place and date of birth unknown, died Constantinople, 5 June 535. Epiphanius was consecrated patriarch of Constantinople in 520. He ratified the union with Rome and frequently corresponded with Pope **Hormisdas**. Epiphanius tried to bring Thessalonika under his own jurisdiction, supporting the revolt in 531 of two bishops who opposed the election of Stephen of Larissa.

Epiphanius of Pavia Saint, bishop, born 438, died Pavia, 496. Epiphanius became bishop of Pavia in 466 after a rapid ecclesiastical career. He worked towards peace during a time of strife, and intervened in disputes between various Germanic kings. He contributed to the rebuilding of Pavia, and obtained its exemption from tribute. Feast day 21 January.

Epping, Joseph Jesuit astronomer and Assyriologist, born Neuenkirchen, near Rheine, Westphalia, 1 December 1835, died Exaeten, Holland, 22 August 1894. He studied at Münster and specialized in mathematics. He joined the Society of Jesus at Münster and later became professor of mathematics and astronomy at Maria-Laach. When the president of Ecuador asked for Jesuits to settle at Quito, Epping was one of those who went, becoming professor of mathematics there. He wrote a geometry textbook in Spanish at this time. Owing to political upheavals, Epping had to return to Europe, and settled in Holland, living at Blijenbeck and Exaeten. He undertook a mathematical investigation of and wrote on the Babylonian astronomical tables.

Eppinger, Elizabeth (Mother Marie Alphonse)

Religious, foundress of the Daughters of the Divine Redeemer, born Niederbronn, France, 9 September 1814, died Niederbronn, 31 July 1867. From a poor family, as a child Eppinger had only a limited education, partly due to chronic ill-health. In 1846 she began to experience ecstatic visions and revelations, which various religious examiners came to accept as genuine. She also experienced a remarkable physical healing, and in 1848 took religious vows. In 1849 she founded the Daughters of the Divine Redeemer, devoted to the care of the sick and poor. Under her religious name of Mother Marie Alphonse she administered the Order with great competence, and by the time of her death it had 372 sisters in 72 houses.

Epstein, Sir Jacob Sculptor, born New York City, 10 November 1880, died London, 21 August 1959. He studied at the École des Beaux-Arts in Paris and moved to London: in Paris he designed an angel for Oscar Wilde's tomb. His work, which often proved controversial, includes a large number of Christian themes, though he was in origin a Russian-Polish Jew: *Genesis, Ecce Homo, Jacob and the Angel*, and the monumental sculpture *St Michael and the Devil* for Coventry Cathedral.

Eptadius Saint, born Autun, France, c.490, died Montelon, France, 550. Eptadius was married at twenty, and shortly after was struck by a fever. He received a vision of three holy women, which rekindled his faith. He recovered from his fever, and led a life of austerity and penance. Bishop Flavian tried to ordain him, but Eptadius fled. He was appointed a bishop by King **Clovis** I, but refused the dignity. As a compromise he accepted priesthood, withdrawing to a monastic community in Cervon. He was noted for his charity. Feast day 24 August.

Equiano, Olaudah (Gustavus Vassa) Calvinist and anti-slavery campaigner, Igboland (Nigeria), born c.1745, baptized 1759, died Middlesex, England, 31 March 1797. An Igbo who was captured by slave traders about the age of ten. Worked in Barbados, Virginia and England. He had an experience of salvation in 1774. His request, in 1779, to be ordained and sent to Africa as a missionary was turned down by the bishop of London. Instead he became a leader of Africans in London and worked with Granville Sharp on abolitionist campaigns, becoming an effective lobbyist. He wrote his autobiography, *The Interesting Narrative of the Life of Olaudah Equiano, or Gustavus Vassa* (1789), to further the cause. It was an enormous success, and brought him both fame and modest wealth. Three years later he married Susannah Cullen of Soham near Cambridge. They had two daughters.

Erasmus, Desiderius Humanist scholar, born Rotterdam, 28 October 1466, died Basel, 12 July 1536. Educated at Gouda and with the Brethren of the Common Life at Deventer, before becoming an Augustinian canon at Steyn in 1487 and being ordained priest in 1492: he became an arch-critic of monasticism and his monastic obligations were nullified in 1517. From 1495 he studied in Paris, encountering the Scholastic theology of which he became so notable a critic. In 1499 his pupil and patron William Blount, Lord Mountjoy, invited him to England for the first of three visits. John **Colet** encouraged his rejection of Scholastic theology, and urged him to apply his scholarship to Scripture rather than the pagan ancients. Between 1506 and 1509 he travelled in Italy, receiving his doctorate in theology at Turin in 1506 and working closely with the Venetian printer Aldus **Manutius**, who published the revised edition of his *Adagia* (1508). During his final English sojourn he celebrated his friendship with Thomas **More** by writing the *Moriae encomium* (*Praise of Folly*, 1511) and taught Greek and divinity at Cambridge at the invitation of John **Fisher**. Thereafter he proceeded to Basel to prepare his Greek edition of the NT with Latin translation. His life continued to be that of an itinerant scholar, translating and editing many of the Greek Fathers, but his movements were increasingly determined by the unfolding Reformation. His long-standing criticisms of Scholastic theology and clerical corruption heralded the Reformation; combined with his refusal to break with Rome, he succeeded in becoming reviled by both sides and his works long remained on the Index.

Erastus Or, more correctly, Thomas Lieber or Liebler (he used the Latin form in his writings), Zwinglian theologian and doctor, born Baden, Switzerland, 7 September 1524, died Basel, 31 December 1583. Though of poor parents, he succeeded in studying at the Universities of Basel, Bologna and Padua, and by 1558 was professor of medicine at the University of Heidelberg. He became much engaged in theological controversy, and was for a time accused of Unitarianism and in 1570 excommunicated by the presbyterate of Heidelberg. He was soon afterwards reinstated, but resigned his chair, and returned to Basel. In the course of these controversies he wrote his *Seventy-Five Theses*, not published until after his death, in which he argued that, with a godly ruler, there is no need for any other authority in the Church. It was from this belief, which constituted only a small part of his theology, that the term 'Erastianism' was derived.

Erben, Karel Jaromír Poet and folklorist, born Miletin, in the modern Czech Republic, 7 November 1811, died Prague, 21 November 1870. Trained as a historian and by profession an archivist, Erben underook extensive research into traditional Czech poetry and folklore, recording many works which hitherto had existed only orally. He also wrote a number of original poems and songs in traditional styles. One aspect of Czech folklore which came to prominence as a result of Erben's research was its strong Christian tradition.

Erchempert Monk, historian and poet, late ninth century. Little is known of Erchempert's life apart from the fact that he was a monk at the monastery of Monte Cassino. He was the author of a history of the Lombards of southern Italy during the eighth and ninth centuries, which is the main contemporary source of information on the history of this region for that period. Erchempert is known also to have written poetry, although only small fragments of this have survived.

Erconwald of London Bishop, monk, saint, born Lindsey, *c.*630, of royal blood, died Barking Abbey, 30 April 693. Erconwald was attracted to the monastic life, and founded a community at Cherts, and an abbey at Barking under the direction of his sister. In 675 he was appointed bishop of London. He enlarged his cathedral and diocese. He worked for the reconciliation of **Wilfrid** of York and **Theodore** of Canterbury. After eleven years as bishop he retired to Barking. He was buried at St Paul's Cathedral. Feast day 14 Novemer or 30 April.

Erhard Saint, bishop, missionary, born Narbonne, France, died Regensburg, Germany, dates unknown. Details of Erhard's life are unclear, the main information coming from a mid-eleventh-century monk. Erhard is reputed to have been a zealous missionary and the founder of seven monasteries. He was also a regional missionary bishop with a great reputation for sanctity. Feast day 8 January.

Eric of Sweden King and saint, died at Uppsala, 18 May 1161. On becoming king of Sweden in 1150 he aimed at converting the Finns to Christianity. However, he was killed when Uppsala was attacked by a Danish prince. Due mainly to the efforts of Eric's son Cnut to present his father as a martyr, Eric became the national saint of the Swedes. Feast day 18 May.

Eriugena, John Scotus Irish scholar and one of the first representatives of Scholasticism, born about 810, died about 877. According to tradition he was born in Ireland of Scottish parents. In about 847 he was appointed supervisor of the court school of Charles I, king of France. He translated into Latin the works of Dionysius the Pseudo-Areopagite. He was involved in the controversies surrounding predestination, emphasizing the place of free will in salvation, and the Eucharist, denying the real presence. The Councils of Valence (855), Langres (859) and Vercelli (1050) condemned his treatise *De Divina Praedestinatione* (851), and the Council of Sens condemned his *De Divisione Naturae* (870) in 1225.

Erkembodo Saint, bishop, abbot, birth unknown, died Thérouanne, 12 April 734. He was accepted into the abbey of SS. Peter and Paul at Thérouanne before 709, and became fourth abbot of the monastery in 717. Erkembodo developed the abbey's liturgical practices and intensified its life of prayer. He also bought neighbouring lands to increase the property of the monastery. In 720 he became bishop of Thérouanne, and became the object of a popular cult. Feast day 12 April.

Erlembald Saint, Milanese reformer, died Milan,

Italy, 28 June 1075. After the death of his brother **Landulf**, Erlembald, a knight and a member of the influential Cotta family, led the military forces supporting the ecclesiastical reform of Milan. The opposition to the reform, led by Archbishop Guido Velate (d. 1071), had the support of Emperor **Henry IV** and was ascendant until the election of Pope **Gregory VII** in 1073; Erlembald was killed in a street battle against the anti-reformers in 1075 and was canonized by Pope **Urban II** twenty years later. Feast day 27 June.

Ermelinde Saint, place and date of birth unknown, died 29 October, at the end of the sixth century. Ermelinde belonged to a rich family in Brabant, which had connections with the Carolingian family of Pepin I. According to legend Ermelinde left home to avoid an arranged marriage, taking up a life of asceticism in a hermitage, first at Beauvechan, later at Meldaert, Belgium. It was alleged that she founded a monastery at Meldaert. Feast day 29 October.

Ermenburga Saint, Anglo-Saxon queen. Birth unknown, died Thanet, *c.*695. Also known as Domna Ebba, or Domneva. Married when young to Mereweld, son of Penda, by whom she had three daughters and one son. She was given estates on Thanet as compensation for the death of her brothers in battle. Ermenburga retired there on the death of her husband, and founded the abbey of Thanet. She was succeeded as abbess by her daughter. Feast day 19 November.

Ermengarde of Bretagne Pious noblewoman, of the late eleventh and early twelfth centuries. The sister of Fulk V of Anjou, she wanted to join **Robert of Arbrissal**'s new monastic community at Fontevrault, but was persuaded by Robert that she should instead stay in the world. In a letter written *c.*1109, he provides her with a Rule suitable for 'a mother and a princess', and instructs her to embrace voluntary poverty, be merciful to the poor, and show moderation in all things.

Ermenrich of Passau Benedictine bishop, born Passau, Germany, *c.*814, died there 26 December 874. He is possibly the monk also known as Ermenrich of Ellwagen, the author of a number of minor works which contain useful historical data.

They are also regarded as good evidence of the standard of learning that could be acquired in the monastic schools. He also undertook a missionary journey to Bulgaria.

Ermin Saint, abbot. Born Herly, France, late seventh century, died Lobbes, Belgium. Ermin was born of a noble family and became chaplain and confessor to Madelgar, bishop of Laon. He entered the monastery of Lobbes, after befriending Abbot Ursmar. On Ursmar's resignation Ermin became abbot in 711/12. Together with Ursmar he is patron saint of Lobbes. Feast day 25 April.

Erminfrid Saint, monk. Date and place of birth unknown, died seventh century. Of noble stock, Erminfrid spent part of his youth at the court of Chlothair II. In 625 he retired (with his brother) to the area of Cusance for a life of piety. In 627 Erminfrid entered the Celtic monastic life at Luxeuil. He inherited the empty nunnery at Isalia in Cusance, and restored it, to re-establish monastic life there for men, under the guidance of **Eustace of Luxeuil**. Feast day 25 September.

Erminold of Prüfening Abbot, died 6 January 1121. Sources about Erminold's childhood are unreliable, but they say that he was brought to the monastery of Hirschhau at a young age. He was elected abbot of Lorsch, but resigned when his election was disputed. Later he became prior in 1114 and abbot in 1117 of Prüfening Monastery. Because of the strictness of his Rule, some of his monks attacked him, resulting in his death.

Ernest of Pardubice Archbishop, born Hostinec, modern Czech Republic, 1297, died Roudnice, modern Czech Republic, 30 June 1364. Ernest was ordained following studies in Prague, Bologna and Padua. In 1338 he was made dean of St Vitus' Cathedral chapter in Prague, and became bishop of that city in 1343, a position which was elevated to an archbishopric the following year. His administrative skills helped to reform the local clergy, something helped by the moral influence of the *devotio moderna*. He initiated the building of the present St Vitus' Cathedral in 1344, and founded Charles University in 1348, of which he became rector. A trusted counsellor to the Emperor **Charles IV**, Ernest was spoken of as a papal candidate in 1362, but his desire for retirement ruled him out.

Ernest of Zwiefalten   Abbot, saint and martyr, died Mecca, 1148. Not much is known of Ernest's early life; he was abbot of Zwiefalten in Swabia for five years. Because of disruptive factions at the monastery, he abdicated and set off on pilgrimage to the Holy Land together with Bishop **Otto of Freising**, who accompanied Conrad III to the Crusades. Ernest, according to legend, was tortured and killed in Mecca by Saracens. Ernest is regarded as a saint at Zwiefalten but has not been officially recognized. Feast day 7 November.

Errázuriz y Valdivieso, Crescento   Roman Catholic archbishop and historian, born Santiago, Chile, 28 November 1839, died Santiago, 5 June 1931. A member of the Chilean aristocracy, following ordination Errázuriz developed an interest in the history of the Chilean church, on which he became an authority, and edited a Catholic newspaper. In 1919 he became Archbishop of Santiago and became embroiled in the Chilean Church–State controversy of the time. Errázuriz denounced proposals to separate Church and State, fearing that it would open the door to persecution. His opposition was unsuccessful, and the separation occurred in 1925. Largely because he saw it as a bulwark against communism, Errázuriz then became sympathetic to the nascent Chilean Fascist movement, though he died before its true nature had become apparent.

Erthal, Franz Ludwig von   Prince-bishop, born Lohr on the Main, 16 September 1730, died Würzburg, 16 February 1795. He studied theology at Mainz, Würzburg and Rome, and jurisprudence at Vienna. In 1762 he became president of the secular government of Würzburg. He took part as Imperial Commissioner in the Diet of Ratisbon and became prince-bishop of Würzburg and of Bamberg. He defended papal rights against Febronianism, was concerned for the welfare of his people, founded a hospital and used his private means for charities. He improved education and the economic conditions of rural life and civil administration.

Erthal, Friedrich Karl Joseph von   Last elector and archbishop of Mainz, born Mainz, 3 January 1719, died Aschaffenburg, 25 July 1802. Friedrich was educated at Rheims, became canon of the cathedral at Mainz, and rector of the university. From 1760 to 1774 he was plenipotentiary of the Electorate of Mainz at the imperial court of Vienna. He became elector and archbishop of Mainz and later prince-bishop of Worms. He became a supporter of free-thinking and Febronianism. Erthal suppressed a Carthusian monastery and two nunneries at Mainz and used their revenues to meet the expenses of the university. With the archbishops of Cologne, Trier and Salzburg, he convened the Congress of Ems, where anti-papal articles were drawn up, attempting to reduce the Pope to *primus inter pares*.

Esbjörn, Lars Paul   Lutheran minister, born Hälsingland, Sweden, 16 October 1808, died Ostervala, Sweden, 2 July 1870. After graduating from Uppsala University, Esbjörn became a Lutheran pastor and teacher. During his ministry he came under the influence of Pietism, which awakened in him a concern for the spiritual condition of migrant Swedes in America. In 1849 Esbjörn moved there, subsequently establishing a number of Swedish congregations and a seminary. He eventually returned to Sweden in 1863 to resume local pastoral ministry, in which he continued to work until his death.

Esch, Nicholaus van   Mystical theologian, born Oisterwijk, near Hertogenbosch, Holland, 1507, died 19 July 1578. He studied philosophy, theology and canon law at Louvain. After being ordained he settled in Cologne as private tutor to a number of young men. There he became friendly with members of the Carthusian Order. His health did not allow him to join the Order, but he lived in the monastery and followed its Rule. He was appointed pastor at Diest, and founded several seminaries according to the rules laid down by the Council of Trent. Esch wrote mystical theological works. After his death he was commonly spoken of as 'the saintly father Eschius'.

Eschmann, Ignatius T.   Dominican philosopher and theologian, born Dusseldorf, Germany, 13 November 1898, died Toronto, Ontario, Canada, 11 April 1968. After serving as a machine gunner for the Germans in World War I, Eschmann joined the Order of Preachers in 1920. He studied and taught theology at the Angelicum in Rome, Italy, until 1936. After getting in trouble with both the German hierarchy and civil authorities for his support of Pope **Pius XI**'s encyclical *Mit brennender Sorge*, Eschmann moved to Canada, where he became a Canadian citizen, worked on a critical edition of **Thomas Aquinas**, and taught at the University at Saint Michael's College and the Pontifical Institute of Medieval Studies in Toronto.

Escobar, Andrés de   Benedictine bishop and theologian, born Lisbon, Portugal, *c.*1366, died (?)Florence, Italy, *c.*1440. Most of Escobar's career was spent in the papal curia. He was the author of a variety of treatises which were widely read in the sixteenth and seventeenth centuries, and which dealt with aspects of churchmanship and ritual, spiritual authority, and the reform of the clergy, which was one of his special concerns.

Escobar, Marina de   Mystic, born Valladolid, Spain, 8 February 1554, died Valladolid, 9 June 1633. As an adult she devoted herself to the promoting of piety in others, with the Venerable Luis de Ponte as her spiritual guide. She founded a branch of the Order of the Holy Saviour or Brigittines. From the age of 50, she was bedridden. By divine command, as she believed, she wrote revelations which De Ponte had published after her death, in six books. They concern the means by which God has led her, revelations about the mysteries of redemption, God and the Blessed Trinity, guardian angels and the Blessed Virgin Mary, and souls in purgatory.

Escriva de Balaguery Albas, José María   Blessed, founder of Opus Dei, born Barbastro, Spain, 9 January 1902, died Rome, 26 June 1975. Educated by the Piarists in Barbastro, then in the State Instituto in Logroño before entering the seminary there in 1918. He subsequently studied in Saragossa and Madrid. It was in Madrid in 1928 that he decided to found Opus Dei, though it was some time before it took its final form. During the Spanish Civil War he had to flee Spain, but then returned to Burgos, in the hands of the Nationalists, to begin his work again. He moved the headquarters of Opus Dei to Rome in 1947, and

remained there until his death, apart from many journeys to visit members of the organization. He was beatified by **John Paul II** in 1992. Feast day 26 June.

Esglis, Louis-Philippe Mariauchau d'   Eighth bishop of Quebec, born Quebec, Canada, 23 April 1710, died 4 June 1788. He studied at Quebec Seminary, was ordained priest and appointed pastor of St Pierre-d'Orléans. After 35 years of ministry, he was appointed coadjutor bishop of Quebec in 1772, the first native Canadian to be appointed a bishop. When Bishop **Briand** resigned as bishop of Quebec, d'Esglis succeeded him. In turn, Bishop d'Esglis nominated a coadjutor in Jean-François **Hubert**, but the British government withheld its approval until 1786. Bishop d'Esglis tried unsuccessfully to obtain priests from France.

Eskil   Bishop and martyr, born possibly in England, died at Strängnäs, Sweden, *c.*1080. According to tradition he accompanied Sigfrid on an evangelistic mission to Sweden, the Swedes having relapsed into paganism after the first missionary journeys of St **Ansgar** in the ninth century. He was consecrated bishop at Strängnäs, and it was there he was stoned to death at a pagan gathering. Feast day 12 June.

Eskil of Lund   Archbishop, born in Germany to a noble family, *c.*1100, died at Clairvaux, France, 6/7 September 1180. He was educated at the cathedral school of Hildesheim and became provost of the cathedral of Lund, Sweden, in 1131, appointed to the post by his uncle, who was the first archbishop of that city. In 1137 he succeeded his uncle, and was very diligent in the administration of his diocese. He completed a new cathedral, reformed the standards of clerical life and encouraged monks to settle in his diocese, especially Cistercians. He was particularly impressed by **Bernard of Clairvaux** and wished to join the Cistercians, but Bernard insisted he was more needed in Lund as its bishop. In 1153, hearing of Bernard's death, Eskil made a pilgrimage to his tomb, and on his return journey was imprisoned. Until 1168 he was unable to settle back in his diocese for political reasons, and he spent most of his time in the abbey at Clairvaux. In 1177 he resigned the archbishopric and returned to Clairvaux to spend the final years of his life as a monk.

Espada y Landa, Juan José Díaz de   Roman Catholic bishop, born Arróyave, Spain, 1756, died Havana, Cuba, 13 August 1832. Between 1802 and his death, Espada exercised a zealous reforming ministry in the Diocese of Havana which was to have a transforming effect on Cuban society. He founded schools and hospitals, gave assistance to impoverished areas through church initiatives and encouraged numerous charitable causes. Although his single-mindedness made some enemies, for the most part his reforming vision earned widespread affection and respect.

Espen, Zeger Bernard van   Priest, canon lawyer, born Louvain, 9 July 1646, died Amersfoort, Netherlands, 2 October 1728. He studied at Louvain, was ordained priest, and became a doctor of civil and canon law. He taught law at the University of Louvain, but resigned in order to devote himself to study. His work *Jus Canonicum Universum* became famous, though controversial: he defended the Gallican theories and exaggerated the authority of civil power. Similarly he exalted the power of the bishops at the expense of the religious orders. Because of his anti-papal stance, he was approached by Jansenists to pronounce on the legitimacy of the Jansenist bishop of Utrecht. He declared him legitimate, even though the Holy See had withheld its permission. The bishop of Mechlin subsequently suspended Espen, who fled to Maastricht, then Amersfoort, where he found protection in the Jansenist community. His works were put on the Index.

Espence, Claude Togniel de   French theologian, born Châlons-sur-Marne, 1511, died Paris, 5 October 1571. He entered the College of Navarre and was later made rector of the University of Paris. The Sorbonne queried some propositions in his Lenten sermons and he was asked to explain or retract them. He took part in theological consultations associated with the Council of Trent, at Mélun, Bologna and Orléans. At the Council of Poissy he argued in favour of the infallibility of the Church. An anonymous treatise on the veneration of images was censored by the Sorbonne, and he was believed to be its author, and was asked to subscribe to the sixteenth article of the faculty, directed against Protestants. He wrote theological works, treatises, discourses, sermons, conferences and poems.

Espinar, Alonso de   Franciscan missionary, place and date of birth unknown, died at sea, 1513. One of the first Christian missionaries in the New World, Espinar established a friary in Santo Domingo, which became the headquarters of the province of the Holy Cross, of which Espinar was made provincial. He subsequently founded a hospital, and oversaw missions by friars to the Caribbean and South America. He had a comparatively enlightened attitude towards the Indians, and encouraged basic Spanish education for their leaders. Espinar died at sea while returning from Spain, from where he had been escorting a group of friars who were on their way to join his mission.

Espinareda, Pedro de   Franciscan missionary, date and place of birth unknown, died Zacatecas, Mexico, 1576. Nothing is known of Espinareda prior to his missionary journey to the New World from Spain in 1553. He and a small band of friars worked initially among nomadic Indians, and subsequently he made exploratory journeys into other unevangelized regions of Mexico. The missionary community Espinareda headed grew in size, and eventually became established as the Custody of Zacatecas.

Espinosa, Isidro Félix de   Franciscan missionary and historian, born Querétaro, Mexico, November 1679, died Querétaro, February 1755. Ordained in 1703, Espinosa initially worked as a missionary in north-east Mexico, where he was able to secure the reopening of a number old Franciscan missions. He then founded six new missions in the north of the country. In 1721 Espinosa was elected guardian of the college of Querétaro. This saw the end of his own missionary activities, but it enabled him to write a number of important works chronicling the history of Franciscan missions in Mexico.

Esquiú, Mamerto   Franciscan bishop and theologian, born San José, Argentina, 1826, died Córdoba, Argentina, 1883. As bishop of Córdoba, Esquiú became well known in Argentina during the nineteenth century because of his involvement and interventions in public affairs, which did much to bring stability to the country. Through numerous writings he also made significant contributions to Catholic theology in such areas as moral theology, Christology and metaphysics. Esquiú was widely revered and respected for his piety and Christian charity, and among Argentinians is considered a saint.

Este, Alessandra d'   Cardinal, born Ferrara, Italy, 1568, died Rome, 13 March 1624, of an illness contracted during the papal election of the previous year. A man of considerable linguistic ability and general culture, he was created cardinal by **Clement VIII** in 1599. Although rather morally lax as a young man (he fathered a daughter, who afterwards became a nun), he developed a strong devotional life in later years, though he never ceased to promote the interests of his family. Among the Este dynasty of churchmen, as bishop of Reggio from 1621, Alessandro earned a reputation for pastoral sensitivity. A learned man, he was also a generous patron of the arts: in 1621 he persuaded **Gregory XV** to endow the Villa d'Este at Tivoli, which he had occupied – and embellished – from 1605 to the Este family in perpetuity.

Este, Alfonso d'   Franciscan, died 1644. A member of a long-established Lombard family. Following the death of his wife, Isabella of Savoy, he was ordained as a Capuchin in 1630. His work for the apostolate took him to the Tyrol and Vienna.

Este, Ippolito d'   Cardinal, born Ferrara, 20 November 1479, died Ferrara, 2 September 1520. The son of Ercole I d'Este, duke of Ferrara, Ippolito was appointed archbishop of Esztergom at the age of seven, thanks to the intervention of his maternal aunt Beatrice d'Aragona, queen of Hungary, but he later exchanged it for the more lucrative See of Eger. Other benefices held by this notable pluralist included the archbishopric of Milan and the bishoprics of Ferrara, Modena, Narbonne and Capua. He was also a military commander, collector of antique sculpture and patron of Ariosto, who wrote *Orlando furioso* while in the cardinal's service.

Este, Ippolito, d'   Italian cardinal and papal legate to France, born Ferrara, 25 August 1509, the son

of Lucrezia **Borgia**, daughter of Pope **Alexander VI**, and Alfonso d'Este, died Rome, 1 December 1572. He was made archbishop of Milan at the age of ten and became known as the supporter of French interests in Rome in his period of office as legate of the Holy See to France. He was a great patron of the arts and built the celebrated Villa d'Este in Tivoli near Rome, wherein he assembled a great collection of paintings and sculptures.

Este, Leonello d'   Marquis of Ferrara (1441–50), born Ferrara, 21 September 1407, died Ferrara, 1 October 1450. Leonello, whose name reflected courtly enthusiasm for Arthurian legends, was one of the many illegitimate children acknowledged by Niccolò III d'Este. Educated in letters by the humanist Guarino da Verona and in arms by the condottiere Braccio da Montone, he balanced the creation of a highly cultured court with the astute political sense required of the ruler of a second-rate state wedged between expansionist Venice, Milan and Florence. In 1438 the ecumenical council called to seek unity between the Orthodox and Latin churches met briefly in Ferrara before being forced to transfer to Florence.

Este, Louis d'   Cardinal, born Ferrara, Italy, 25 August 1509, died Tivoli, Italy, 2 December 1586. One of the numerous Este cardinals, Louis entered the Church on the insistence of his family and became a cardinal in 1561. He twice sought to renounce holy orders in order to marry, but on both occasions papal permission was refused. He completed the building of the sumptuous Villa D'Este at Tivoli, typical of a propensity for profligate spending which left him permanently in debt.

Este, Rinaldo d'   Cardinal, born Modena, Italy, 1618, died Rome, Italy, 1672. Formerly a distinguished soldier, he later joined the Church and became bishop of Reggio, and subsequently of Montpelier.

Este, Rinaldo d'   Cardinal, born 1655, died 1737. Made a cardinal in 1681, he subsequently renounced holy orders in order to marry and thus maintain the line of succession of his family.

Esther John   Christian missionary, one of ten Christian martyrs commemorated in 1999 by the erection of a statue in Westminster Abbey, London. Born Qamar Zia, 14 October 1929 in India, found murdered in her home in Chichawatni, near Sahiwal, in the Punjab, 2 February 1960. She went to a government school when she was young and then to a Christian school when she was seventeen. After partition her family moved to Pakistan, and in her late twenties she left home for Karachi, where she became a Christian. She worked in an orphanage, and during this time changed her name. In 1955 she went to Sahiwal, where she worked and lived in a mission hospital before entering the United Bible Training Centre in Gujranwala. She graduated in 1959 and joined a group of US Presbyterian missionaries based in Chichawatni, from where she evangelized, taught literacy skills and worked alongside the local women. Her brutal murder the following year remains a mystery.

Estienne, Robert Printer-publisher, born Paris, 1503, died Geneva, 7 September 1559. Son of the printer Henri Estienne (d. 1520), Robert's independent career coincided with **Francis I's** enthusiasm for both Evangelisme and the classical revival. His output reflected a similar range of interests, with classical authors including Terence, Plautus and Virgil, an edition of the Bible (1527) and the *Thesaurus linguae latinae* (1528). In 1539 he was appointed 'Printer to the King in Hebrew and Latin', and the same in Greek in 1544. Estienne moved to Geneva in 1550, where he printed Protestant texts, including Calvin's *Institution de la religion chrétienne*.

Estius, Gulielmus Roman Catholic scholar, born Gorcum, Netherlands, 1542, died Douai, France, 20 September 1613. During a long academic career, of which 30 years were spent at the University of Douai, Estius established a reputation for biblical, historical and theological learning which made him one of the most widely read Catholic scholars of the period. He was particularly renowned for a commentary on the NT Epistles, which for generations was regarded as the standard exposition of these writings.

Estouteville, Guillaume, d' Cardinal, born Normandy, *c.*1412, died Rome, 22 January 1483. Already bishop of Angers when made a cardinal by

Eugenius IV in 1439, d'Estouteville was transferred to the archbishopric of Rouen in 1453, before becoming cardinal-bishop of Porto in 1457 and of Ostia in 1461. The wealth and luxurious lifestyle of this pluralist prelate caught the attention of contemporary chroniclers, and his death occasioned a major redistribution of benefices. He was a major player in the politics of the papal court and responsible for the building or repair of a number of churches and palaces in Rome, Ostia and Frascati.

Estrada, José Manuel Roman Catholic educationalist and politician, born Buenos Aires, Argentina, 13 July 1842, died Asunción, Paraguay, 17 September 1897. Estrada first became well-known in Argentina as a political journalist. He was subsequently invited to teach at the Colegio Nacional of Buenos Aires, and pursued an academic career for the next twenty years, though continuing to be a prominent commentator and speaker on public affairs. In 1882 he was elected to the Argentine congress as a national deputy, and following the 1890 revolution was made minister plenipotentiary in Paraguay, where he died. Estrada's devout Catholicism deeply influenced his politics, and he resisted any attempts to separate Church and State, which he thought would lessen the Church's influence in society and render it liable to persecution.

Ethelbert of East Anglia King, saint, martyr. Date and place of birth unknown, martyred by the orders of Offa II of Mercia, in 794. Ethelbert is described as a pious youth disposed to celibacy, but persuaded to marry Elfthryth, Offa's daughter. Ethelbert became patron saint of Hereford. Feast day 20 May.

Ethelbert of Kent King, saint, born 550, died Canterbury, 24 February 616. Ethelbert was head of the confederation of Anglo-Saxon kingdoms south of the Humber, and was the first Christian king of England. He was married to Bertha, a Christian princess, wife of a Frankish king who ruled in Paris. He welcomed **Augustine of Canterbury** as missionary and allowed him freedom of action and a place to stay at Canterbury. Ethelbert was baptized *c.*601 and built several churches. There is also a code of law attributed to him. He is thought to have reigned for 56 years. Feast day 24 February.

Ethelbert of York   Archbishop, date and place of birth unknown, died York, 8 November 780. Ethelbert was related to Archbishop **Egbert**, who appointed him as director of the school of York. He was a teacher of rhetoric and grammar. Ethelbert succeeded Egbert as archbishop in 767. He undertook restoration of the cathedral at York, including 30 altars in the renovations. Ethelbert retired in 778, having consecrated the cathedral, and was buried there.

Ethelburga   Saint, abbess, birth unknown, died 644. Ethelburga (also known as Tata) was the daughter of King Albert and Bertha. Ethelburga married the pagan King **Edwin** of Northumbria, and travelled to meet him accompanied by her chaplain **Paulinus**, who became the first bishop of York. Together with Paulinus Ethelburga spread Christianity to the north. After she gave birth to a daughter Edwin converted to Christianity. On his death (in battle) Ethelburga returned to Lymynge and founded an abbey. Feast day 12 October.

Ethelburga   Saint, abbess, died 676. Ethelburga was the sister of Bishop **Erconwald of London**, and the first abbess of the double monastery at Barking. Feast day 11 October.

Ethelburga   Saint, abbess, birth unknown, died 695. Ethelburga was the sister of **Etheldreda** of Northumbria, and was the abbess of Faremontiers when she died. Feast day 7 July.

Etheldreda of Northumbria   Queen, abbess, saint, born Exning, Suffolk, c.630, died from the plague, Ely, 23 June 679. Etheldreda was the daughter of Anna, King of East Anglia. She was married to Tonbert, a prince of the Gyrvii. Tonbert endowed to her what is now known as Ely. Etheldreda lived in virginity with him, entering a convent after his death. She was married again, for diplomatic reasons, to Egfrid, once more living in virginity. She returned to the convent after twelve years, eventually becoming abbess at Ely. Etheldreda foretold her own death. Feast day 23 June.

Ethelhard of Canterbury   Archbishop, died Can-

terbury, 12 May 805. Consecrated as archbishop of Canterbury in 793. Due to the opposition of the Kentish nobility to a Mercian archbishop he was forced to flee in 796. On regaining his position, with the support of Pope **Leo III**, he strengthened the authority of the See of Canterbury.

Ethelnoth of Canterbury   Archbishop, died Canterbury, 29 October 1038. Ethelnot served as a monk of Glastonbury and dean of Christ Church, Canterbury, before **Wulfstan** of Worcester, the archbishop of York, consecrated him as archbishop of Canterbury in 1020. **Benedict VIII** gave him the pallium during a visit to Rome in 1022. He served King **Canute** as chief adviser. The king bestowed upon Ethelnoth the earliest known writ of judicial and financial authority given to an English prelate. He arranged for the removal of the martyr **Alphege of Canterbury**'s relics from London to Canterbury in 1023. Details of Ethelnot's life are recorded in the *Anglo-Saxon Chronicle*, as well as in the writings of **Florence of Worcester**, Simeon of Durham, **William of Malmesbury** and **Gervase of Canterbury**.

Ethelwold of Winchester   Saint, bishop and reformer, born Winchester, 908, died Beddington, Surrey, 1 August 984. Trained at Glastonbury under St **Dunstan**. About 954 he was given the task of re-establishing Abingdon Abbey. In 963 consecrated bishop of Winchester. With St **Oswald of York** he helped to reform English monasticism, expelling the secular clerks from Winchester, Chertsey and other establishments. He founded several monasteries including Peterborough and Ely. He translated the Rule of St **Benedict** and the *Regularis concordia* into English. Feast day 1 August.

Ett, Kaspar   Composer and musicologist, born Eresing, Germany, 5 January 1788, died Munich, Germany, 16 May 1847. Following musical studies, Ett became music director of the court church of St Michael in Munich, in 1816, where he spent his entire career. An enthusiast for the polyphonic style of the late Renaissance, he revived many neglected works of that period, notably those of **Lasso**. Ett also wrote a considerable number of original compositions, in which the influence of polyphony is much in evidence.

Eubel, Konrad Franciscan historian, born Sinning, Germany, 19 January 1842, died Würzburg, Germany, 5 February 1923. Ordained in 1868, Eubel spent twenty years in Rome as penitentiary of St Peter's. During his time there he compiled a massive listing of all the Popes, cardinals and bishops of Christendom, arranged in alphabetical order according to the Latin names of the dioceses.

Eucherius of Orléans Saint, bishop, born late seventh century, died 738. Eucherius was born into an influential Merovingian family and was destined for the monastic life from an early age. He was professed at the Benedictine abbey of Jumièges c.709. Seven years later he was elected bishop of Orléans, against his will. He was arrested due to family allegiances in 732, by **Charles Martel**, and sent into exile in Cologne. Eucherius was subsequently allowed to return to the abbey of Saint-Trond. Feast day 20 February.

Eudes, John Saint and missionary, born Ri, Normandy, 1601, died Caen, 19 August 1680. Having been educated by the Jesuits he became a priest in 1625 and served in the Oratory at Paris. For several years he worked as a missionary in various regions of France. In 1641 he founded the Order of Our Lady of Charity, a charity formed to care for fallen women. In 1643 he established at Caen the Congregation of Jesus and Mary (the Eudists). He is best known for promoting the devotion to the Sacred Hearts of Jesus and Mary. His written works include *Le Coeur admirable de la Mère de Dieu* (1670) and *La Vie et le royaume de Jésus* (1637). He was beatified in 1909 and canonized in 1925. Feast day 19 August.

Eugendus of Condat Saint, abbot, born c.450, died Condat, 1 January 510 or 517. Eugendus was entrusted to SS Romanus and Lipicinus as a child, who had earlier founded the monastery of Condat (today Saint-Claude). Eugendus stayed there until his death, esteemed for humility and learning. He was renowned for his knowledge of Greek, which was unusual for his day. Eugendus rebuilt the monastery, patterning its life on the Eastern monasticism of **Basil the Great** and John **Cassian**. Feast day 1 January.

Eugene *see* **Eugenius**

Eugenia Saint, abbess, birth unknown, died 735. Eugenia succeeded her aunt (St **Odilia**) as abbess of Hohenburg, Alsace in 722, leading the community until her death in 735. Her father was Duke Adalbert of Alsace. She had two sisters, Attala and Gunlid. Eugenia was revered for her holy life and wise government. Feast day 25 December.

Eugenicus, Mark Archbishop, born Constantinople, 1391, died June 1444. Took the name of Mark when he became a monk at the age of 26. His early career ran in parallel with that of the future Cardinal **Bessarion**, in that he was a disciple of the Platonic philosopher Gemistos Plethon, was promoted to the archbishopric of Ephesus when Bessarion received Nicaea, and was one of the orthodox representatives at the Council of Ferrara–Florence (1438–9). At that point their careers diverged for, while Bessarion supported the union agreed at Florence in 1439, Mark of Ephesus opposed it vehemently.

Eugenius I Saint, Pope, born Rome, elected to the Papacy 10 August 654, died Rome, 2 June 657. Eugenius was brought up in the Church's ministry from childhood. As an elderly presbyter he was elected Pope after the deposition of **Martin I**, by Emperor **Constans II.** The main theological issue of his reign concerned the nature of the will of Christ. Eugenius had the reputation of a conciliatory Pope, dispatching envoys to Patriarch Peter in 654–6 at Constantinople. In 655 they agreed a new communion, affirming two natures in Christ, each having one will, yet also affirming that when Christ was a person he possessed only one will. The Roman people rejected the theological compromise and schism once again broke out. Feast day 2 June.

Eugenius II Pope, place and date of birth unknown, elected to the Papacy 5 June 824, died Rome, 27 August 827. Eugenius was the cardinal-priest of St Sabina, enthroned as Pope by Co-emperor **Lothair I.** Eugenius restored order in the papal domains guaranteeing fidelity to the emperor on the part of papal subjects. During his pontificate iconoclasm arose anew. Eugenius gave papal permission for theologians to examine the question of icons in 825.

Eugenius III Blessed, Pope and reformer, born Pisa as Bernardo Pignatelli, elected to the Papacy 15 February 1145, died Tivoli, 8 July 1153. Possibly prior of a house in Pisa, he met and was much influenced by **Bernard of Clairvaux**, and subsequently became a Cistercian monk at Clairvaux and then abbot of SS Vincent and Anastasius. In 1145 he became the first Cistercian to be elected as Pope. Between 1146 and 1148 he was forced into exile due to his refusal to accept certain political reforms in Rome. He promoted the Second Crusade and authorized Bernard of Clairvaux to preach it. He reformed clerical morality and monastic observance. In 1872 his cult was approved by **Pius IX**. Feast day 8 July.

Eugenius IV Pope, born Gabriele Condulmer, Venice, c.1383, elected 3 March 1431, died Rome, 23 February 1447. The early career of this Venetian patrician was moulded by the patronage of his uncle **Gregory XII**. As Pope he continued the work of **Martin V** in reestablishing papal authority in Rome and the Papal States, but Roman hostility drove him into exile in Florence in 1433–43, where the curia offered employment to leading humanists. He was a tenacious anti-conciliarist, the Council of Basel in its schismatic phase going so far as to 'depose' him. The Ottoman threat to Constantinople prompted Eugenius to call an ecumenical council at Ferrara and Florence, but reconciliation between Greeks and Latins proved to be short-lived.

Eugenius of Toledo Saint, monk, archbishop, born Toledo, unknown date, died Toledo, 13 November 657. Eugenius was from a royal Visigothic family of Spain, who became a cleric in the cathedral of Toledo, and a monk at Saragossa. Eugene studied theology and literature. He was appointed an archdeacon by his uncle (Bishop **Braulio**). In 645 he became archbishop of Toledo, being appointed by King Chindswinth. He was a small man in frail health, but well known for his spiritual and intellectual activity. Eugenius was active in the councils of Toledo from 646 to 656. Writings include a volume of prose and a treatise *De Trinitate* (both lost) and a collection of short poems. Feast day 13 November.

Eugenius Vulgaris Grammarian, place and date of birth unknown but was contemporary with Pope **Sergius III** (904–11). Vulgaris lived in southern Italy and was known for his knowledge of classical and Byzantine culture. He supported the controversial election of **Formosus** to the papal office (891–6) but later submitted to Sergius III. His works include *Insimulator et actor*, *De cause formosiana libellus* and letters and poems.

Eulogius (Evlogii Georgievskii) Metropolitan, Russian Orthodox émigré leader, born near Tula, 1868, died Paris, 1946. He rose to prominence before the revolution, becoming bishop in 1903 and an elected member of the Duma in 1907. From 1921 until his death he headed the main Russian diocese for western Europe, centred in Paris. There he gathered a number of intellectuals to teach at the St Sergius Theological Institute. He broke both with the Church in Russia (Metropolitan **Sergius**) and with the Russian Church Abroad (Metropolitan Antony II) and placed his diocese under Constantinople. He wrote a fascinating autobiography, *The Path of My Life* (1947) – unfortunately never translated.

Eulogius of Alexandria Saint, theologian, monk, patriarch, born Antioch, died Alexandria, 607. Eulogius was a monk who became a priest and abbot of the Deipara Monastery at Antioch. In 580 he became Patriarch of Alexandria. He was a Chalcedonian who followed the doctrine of St **Basil the Great** via **John the Grammarian**. He denied ignorance in Christ, a doctrine which became part of the ordinary magisterium of the Church through Pope **Gregory I**. Eulogius corresponded with the Pope between 595 and 600, concerning the Patriarch of Constantinople. Eulogius also wrote against Novatianism and Severian monophysites. Feast day 13 September; 13 February (Greek).

Eulogius of Córdoba Saint and martyr, born Toledo, died Córdoba, 859. During a period of persecution carried out by occupying African Muslims Eulogius was imprisoned. During his incarceration he wrote letters of encouragement to Saints Flora and Mary, also in prison. He wrote the *Memorandum of the Saints*, an account of the sufferings of the Church during that period of persecution. Appointed as archbishop of Toledo in

859, he was arrested again before he could be consecrated. Refusing to deny his faith he was beheaded. Feast day 11 March.

Eunomius of Constantinople. Bishop, theologian, born Cappadocia, *c.*335, died Dakora, Cappadocia, *c.*394. Eunomius was the chief exponent of Anomoeanism. He joined Aetius in Alexandria as disciple and secretary, following him to Antioch. Aetius ordained him deacon. Eunomius became bishop of Cyzicus in 360 or 366, but was forced to resign due to his theological views. After the death of Aetius in 366 Eunomius assumed leadership of the radical wing of Arianism. He was often exiled, eventually dying at the family estate in Dakora, Cappadocia. Little remains of his literary output.

Euphemia of Chalcedon Saint, martyr, birth unknown, suffered martyrdom at Chalcedon, 16 September 303. A large cult grew concerning Euphemia, and she was the object of **Asterius of Amasea's** panegyric *c.*400. The Council of Chalcedon in 451 was held in her basilica, and gave her cult a decisive impetus. Euphemia's cult is fundamental within Orthodoxy. Feast day 1 September.

Euphrasia Saint, ascetic, born Constantinople, 380, died Egypt, about *c.*410. Euphrasia was the daughter of Antigonus, a senator of Constantinople, who died shortly after her birth. She was related to Emperor **Theodosius I** (379–95), who arranged a betrothal to the son of a wealthy senator when she was five years old. Two years later she left Constantinople when her mother moved to Egypt, settling near a convent of nuns. At the age of seven she insisted on joining the nuns, declining her betrothal at the age of twelve. She transferred her fortune to Emperor Arcadius (395–408) to be used for charity. She died aged 30. Feast day 13 March.

Eusebia of Hamay Saint, abbess, birth unknown, died 16 March 680/689. Eusebia was elected abbess of Hamay at the age of twelve (some records say aged 23). This enabled the abbey to gain the patronage of a powerful family. When the abbess of Hamay, St **Adalbald**, was murdered, Eusebia's mother Rictrude transferred the community to Marciennes. Eusebia eventually returned the community to Hamay, where she ruled until her death. Feast day 16 March.

Eusebia of Saint-Cyr Saint, abbess, died Marseilles, France, 838. Little is known factually of Eusebia's life. She may have lived as early as the fifth or sixth century, though her traditional death date is recognized as 838. She was a Benedictine nun who served as abbess of Saint-Cyr in Marseilles. According to her epitaph, she was martyred at the hands of the Saracens with 39 other nuns. Her tomb is located in the church of Saint-Victor in Marseilles. Feast day 20 September (in Marseilles, 12 October).

Eusebius Saint, Pope. Of Greek ancestry, elected 18 April 310, died Rome, 21 October the same year. Eusebius succeeded **Marcellus I** and immediately became embroiled with Heraclius in the controversy regarding the *lapsi*, who claimed the right to be received back into ecclesiastical communion without submitting to penance. Emperor Maxentius exiled both Eusebius and Heraclius to Sicily. Feast day 17 August.

Eusebius of Caesarea (in Palestine) Bishop, historian, theologian, born Caesarea(?), *c.*265, died there(?), *c.*340. Eusebius was educated in Caesarea by Pamphilius, a disciple of **Origen**. During the persecution by Diocletian Eusebius escaped by fleeing to Tyre and then to Egypt. He was arrested and imprisoned, but returned to Palestine due to the Edict of Tolerance in 311. Became bishop of Caesarea in 313, and was immediately involved in the Arian controversy, in which he sided with **Arius**, but not sharing the more extreme views of the movement. He took part in the Council of Nicaea in 325. Eusebius' literary work was considerable and took in various fields: historiography, exegesis, philology, theology.

Eusebius of Emesa Bishop, theologian, born, Edessa, *c.*300, died Antioch, before 359. Eusebius was of Syrian origin, but Greek education. He was a pupil of **Eusebius of Caesarea** and completed his education at Antioch and Alexandria. Eusebius was offered the See of Alexandria, but declined. He was elected bishop of Emesa soon afterwards, but was accused of astrology and had to leave his position. He was reinstated through the intervention of George of Laodicea. Eusebius' work includes commentaries, and homilies, which often appeal to peace and concord. His trinitarian theology stresses the Son's subsistence to the Father and had a great influence upon homoousian theology.

Eusebius of Nicomedia Bishop, born Syria, died Constantinople, c.342. In his early life Eusebius was a disciple of **Lucian of Antioch**, and subsequently became the leader of the Arian party in the first half of the fourth century. He was bishop of Berytus (Beirut), but became bishop of Nicomedia. He used his influence on **Arius'** behalf. Eusebius was exiled due to his support of Arius even though he had signed the Creed of Nicaea in 325. Eusebius returned from exile in 328/9. He baptized **Constantine I** in 337. He was translated from Nicomedia to Constantinople in 339.

Eusebius of Samosata Saint, bishop, birth unknown, died Samosata, due to being hit on the head by a brick thrown by a female supporter of **Arius**, 22 June 380. Eusebius was bishop of Samosata in 360, and supported the election of Melitius to the See of Antioch. He was an opponent of Arianism. Eusebius became closely involved with **Basil the Great** and **Gregory of Nazianzus**. In 374 he was exiled to Thrace due to his orthodox stance, but was recalled by Emperor Gratian. Feast day 22 June, East; 21 June, West.

Eusebius of Vercelli Saint, bishop, born Sardinia, unknown date, died Vercelli, 1 August 371. Eusebius was a strong supporter of orthodoxy in the Arian conflict. He was bishop of Vercelli from 340. After the synod of Milan in 355 he was exiled to the East, returning in 362, in the reign of Julian. Eusebius lived with his clergy at Vercelli under monastic rule. Three written works survive. He also made a Latin translation of **Eusebius of Caesarea**'s *Commentary on the Psalms*. Feast day 2 August.

Eustace, Maurice Irish martyr, born Castlemartin, County Kildare, Ireland, died Dublin, November 1581. He was educated at the Jesuit College in Bruges, Flanders, and wanted to join the Jesuit Order, but his father was opposed. Maurice returned to Ireland, where he was appointed a cavalry officer. He secretly he took holy orders, however, and his servant – or, according to some, his younger brother who wished to inherit the family estate – reported him to his father, who had Maurice arrested and imprisoned in Dublin. He was tried for high treason, found guilty and hanged.

Eustace of Luxeuil Saint, abbot. Born Burgundy, c.560, died Luxeuil, France, 2 April 629. Eustace became a monk at Luxeuil towards the end of the sixth century and was eventually placed in charge of the monastic school there. He followed his abbot, **Columbanus**, into exile c.610, but was sent back to take up the leadership of the monastery c.612. Eustace was in conflict with Agrestius over the latter's support for the Three Chapters. Agrestius was condemned at the Synod of Macon, 626–7, on Eustace's instigation. Feast day 29 March.

Eustachio, Bartolomeo Italian physician and anatomist, born San Severino, Ancona, Italy, 1520, died Rome, August 1574. He knew Latin, Greek and Arabic and studied medicine and anatomy. He became physician to Cardinal **Borromeo**, then to Cardinal Guilio della Rovere, whom he accompanied to Rome. Eustachio became professor of anatomy at the Sapienza, reorganized as the Roman University by Popes. He was the greatest anatomist in Italy of his time. He became physician to Cardinal Peretti, afterwards Pope **Sixtus V**. Eustachio's true merit was not recognized until long after his death when his *Tabulae Anatomicae* were published in 1714. He gave his name to the stirrup bone in the ear and the canal connecting the ear and the mouth, hence Eustachian tube, though he was not the first to discover it.

Eustathius of Antioch Saint, bishop, born Syria, died Thrace, 336. A native of Side, Eustathius was bishop of Beroea before being translated to Antioch, where he took the see from 324 to 327. Eustathius attended the Council of Nicaea in 325, being given a position of honour. When he returned to his diocese after the council he banished many of his clergy, accusing them of Arianism. He was uncompromising in his support of the Nicene position. This brought conflict with **Eusebius of Caesarea**. Eustathius was subsequently accused of Sabellianism, and deposed at a council at Antioch. He was banished to Thrace by **Constantine I.** His work survives in fragments. Feast day 16 July.

Eustathius of Sebaste Bishop, born Caesarea in Cappadocia, *c.*300, died Sebaste, after 377. In his younger days Eustathius was a disciple of **Arius** at Alexandria, and throughout his life he vacillated in his attitude to the Nicene cause. He took the role of bishop of Sebaste, *c.*357. His main interests were not theological but monastic. Eustathius had a great influence upon **Basil the Great**, and it is possible that he authored the 'shorter rules' of Basil. Subsequently the relationship foundered, due to issues of the position of the Spirit in trinitarian theology. Eustathius became a leading spirit in Asia Minor in the Macedonian heresy.

Eustochia Calafato Blessed, Poor Clare abbess, born Messina, Sicily, 25 March 1434, died Messina, 20 January 1468. Renowned for her beauty, Smargada Calafato came from a noble family and joined the Poor Clares in *c.*1446, taking the name Eustochia. In 1458 she was given papal permission to found a community of more rigorous discipline, under the Rule of the Franciscan Observants, which was eventually established at Monte Vergine, and of which she became abbess. During her relatively short life she gained a reputation for piety and devotion which led to her beatification in 1782. Feast day 20 January.

Eustochium, Julia Saint, born *c.*370, Rome, died *c.*419, probably Bethlehem. The daughter of St **Paula**, the two were in contact with St **Jerome**, and were ultimately forced to leave Rome when a letter concerning virginity written by Jerome to Julia in 385 (Ep. 22) caused controversy. They travelled through Syria and Egypt before building four monasteries in Bethlehem, for which Julia assumed responsibility in 404 after her mother's death. Feast day 28 September.

Eustochium of Padua Blessed, Benedictine, born 1444, Padua, Italy, died there, 13 February 1469. St Eustochium was born to a nun in Padua, and baptized Lucrezia Bellini. After joining the Benedictines at the age of seventeen, she appears to have suffered from some kind of mental disorder,

and was treated for demonic possession by way of imprisonment, exorcism and at times food deprivation for four years. Upon her death soon after her profession, her body was reportedly found with the name of Jesus burned on her breast. Feast day 13 February.

Euthymius I Patriarch, born Seleucia, Isauria, *c.*834, died Constantinople, 5 August 917. As a youth, Euthymius joined a community of monks on Mount Olympus, Bithynia. He later served as abbot of St Theodora in Constantinople and confessor to Emperor **Leo VI** the Wise (886–912), whom he convinced to protect officers in **Photius'** party. He reigned as patriarch of Constantinople from 907 to 912. He was embroiled in the political and marital intrigues of the emperor, eventually suffering banishment. The Greek church recognized him as a saint in 991. His Vita extols his virtues as a preacher, but very few of his sermons survived. He has been associated with a history of the first seven ecumenical councils and the synod of Photius' rehabilitation, but these may have been written by another monk Euthymius (1410–16).

Euthymius the Great Saint, priest and monk, born 377, Melitene, Armenia, died 20 January 473, near Jericho. He was ordained in Melitene and supervised monasteries there until 405, after which he lived as a monk near Jerusalem, and then near Jericho from 411. Despite his attempts at solitary life, he attracted many converts, and was ultimately consecrated a bishop by Patriarch Juvenal of Jerusalem to minister to them. One of few supporters of the Council of Chalcedon at the time, 451, he influenced some to abandon their allegiance to **Eutyches.** Feast day 20 January.

Euthymius Zigabenus Byzantine theologian and exegete, died Monastery of the Holy Virgin, Constantinople, *c.*1120. Because of confusion with another monk, Zigabenus of Peribleptos, little is known of his life, except that, at the command of the Emperor **Alexus Comnenus**, he wrote *Panoplia Dogmatike*, against all heresies, a work highly praised by **Anna Comnena**. The first chapter refutes the old heresies in an array of patristic texts; the new heresies are treated independently in the following 21 chapters, and include those from the time of the Jews to Zigabenus' own contemporaries: Armenianus, Paulicianus, Messalianus, Musulmans and Bogomils, the latter being the more interesting since knowledge of them was first written down by Euthymius Zigabenus, monk of Peribleptos (above). He wrote commentaries on the Psalms, the Four Gospels and the epistles of St Paul, in which he uses mainly patristic sources, especially St **John Chrysostom.** His works are the more remarkable for the account they take of the literal sense of the Bible, unusual among the later Greek exegetes.

Eutyches Archimandrite and theologian, born Constantinople, c.378, died 454. Proposed a Christology in which Christ had a single nature, a blend of human and divine. For this view he was deposed as head of his monastery by the patriarch of Constantinople. He appeared at the Synod of Constantinople in 448 and was condemned. His appeal resulted in the 'Robber Council' of Ephesus in 449, which reversed the 448 ruling. He was condemned once again by the Council of Chalcedon in 451. His most significant surviving work is *Confessions of Faith.* Some letters also survive.

Eutychian Saint, Pope, born in Tuscany, reigning from 4 January 275 until his death, probably in Rome, 7 December 283. Limited details of his life survive, perhaps because of the Diocletian persecution, which followed shortly after his death. He himself, however, ruled the Church at Rome at a relatively trouble-free period, and seems to have brought stability and organization to the Church, evidenced in the expansion of official Christian cemeteries at the time. Feast day 7 December.

Eutychius of Alexandria Melchite patriarch, born Cairo, 876, died 11 May 940. He left practising medicine to join a monastery, becoming patriarch of Alexandria in 933. He was a prolific writer, with many works surviving in part. Among them are works of theology, medicine and history. One, pertaining to the ongoing division between the Melchites and Monophysites, is titled *Discussion Between a Christian and an Infidel.* His most important surviving work is *Nazm al-Gawahir,* a chronicle of world history from the biblical period until 938.

Eutychius of Constantinople Patriarch and saint, born Phrygia, c.512, died Constantinople, 22 April 582. First a monk then an archimandrite, he found favour with Emperor **Justinian I,** who ensured his succession to the patriarchate. He later fell foul of Justinian and was deposed, only to be recalled some twelve years later by Justin II, in 577. He briefly denied the doctrine of resurrection of the body but recanted after discussion with St **Gregory** the Great, the future Pope, then papal representative in Constantinople. Surviving writings include a letter to Pope **Vigilius** and a portion of a *Discourse on Easter.* Feast day 6 April.

Evagrius Ponticus (Evagrius of Pontus) Deacon, monk and theologian, born Pontus, Greece 346, died Egypt, 399. Studied under **Basil** the Great until 379, then under **Gregory of Nazianzus.** He was also influenced by **Origen** and **Gregory of Nyssa** and participated in the Council of Constantinople in 381. He lived in various monastic communities in Egypt from 382 until his death. His works, including the *Praktikos,* the *Gnostikos* and the *Kefalaia gnostika,* were influential to both Christian spirituality and Islamic Sufism. He was condemned several times from the sixth century for his use of Origen's work.

Evagrius Scholasticus Church historian, born Colele, Syria, c.536, died Antioch, c.600. A lawyer, he lived in Antioch and wrote a six-book history spanning the years from 428 to 594. Although tending towards an unquestioning acceptance of legend, he also made excellent use of sources, making his work a worthy early source.

Evans, Christmas Baptist minister and evangelist, known as 'the Welsh Bunyan', born at Esgair-Waun, Cardiganshire, Wales, 25 December 1766, died Swansea, 19 July 1838. On the death of his father in 1775 he was raised by a relative who treated him cruelly. He worked as a farm labourer receiving some tuition from David Davis, a Presbyterian preacher. Converted in 1783 he was baptized five years later in the river Duar. Ordained in 1789 he became an itinerant preacher travelling throughout Caernarvonshire. One-eyed, and dramatic in style, he gained a reputation as a fiery evangelical preacher. While serving as a minister on Anglesey he adopted Sandemanian views. Regaining orthodox belief, he acted as minister to a chapel at Caerphilly in 1826–8; Cardiff in 1828 and Caernarvon in 1832.

Evans, Philip Blessed, martyr, born Monmouth, England, 1645, died Cardiff, 22 July 1679. Evans became a Jesuit in 1665, and after his ordination in Liège in 1675, he worked in South Wales. In 1678, he became a target as part of Titus **Oates'** plot to persecute Catholics. Late that year, a price was placed upon his head by John Arnold of Abergavenny, a justice of the peace and hunter of priests. Following his arrest on 2 December, Evans refused to take the oath of allegiance and subsequently was imprisoned for three weeks of solitary confinement. In May of 1679, he was brought to trial and convicted of being a priest. He was executed in July. Feast day 22 July.

Evaristus Saint, Pope, birthdate unknown, died *c.*109, probably 26 October, probably Rome. The *Liber Pontificalis* states he was of Greek ancestry, as well as giving certain unreliable data about his pontificate; but no reliable information survives. He succeeded **Clement I** *c.*100 during the reign of Trajan. His usual designation as martyr is unproven. Feast day 26 October.

Evdokimov, Paul Nikolaevich Russian Orthodox lay theologian, born St Petersburg, 2 August 1900, died Meudon, France, 16 September 1970. He settled in Paris in 1923 and in 1951 became professor of moral theology at the St Sergius Orthodox Institute. He also lectured at several Catholic and ecumenical institutes. He wrote on many theological subjects, including iconography, marriage and sexual ethics, and largely in French. *L'Orthodoxie* (1959) is usually considered his greatest work, though his theology has been criticized for being expressed with too much poetic vagueness.

Eve of Liège Blessed, nun, recluse, died *c.*1265. Eve lived in solitude and contemplation at Liège, Flanders. Together with Juliana of Cornillon, she laboured to establish the feast of Corpus Christi, which was sanctioned by Pope **Urban IV** in 1264. Feast day 26 May.

Everard of Béthane Author, died *c.*1213. Author of the *Graecismus*, Everard was formerly confused with **Everard the German**.

Everard of Ypres Teacher, cleric, writer, born Ypres, Belgium, died Clairvaux, *c.*1199. Everard studied under **Gilbert de la Porrée**, then became a cleric in 1162–5 under Hyacinth, the future **Celestine III**. For most of his life he taught at the University of Paris, writing a compendium of canon law, a letter to **Urban III** addressing alleged errors regarding the Trinity, and his main work, *Dialogue between Ratius and Everard*. In the latter work Everard uses a fictional Greek character, Ratius, to propound the views of Everard's former teacher, Gilbert.

Everard the German (Eberhard, Evrardus) Poet, schoolmaster, died *c.*1230. Everard studied at Paris and Orléans, and taught at Bremen and Cologne. His principal achievement was the didactic poem *Laborintus*, written after 1212 but before 1280. The poem has more than 1200 verses which encompass descriptions of classical works, praise of the classics, philosophy, mathematics, natural science and the evaluation of some 30 poets and their works. The poem is important historically, culturally and linguistically. Everard has sometimes been confused with **Everard of Béthane**, who wrote the *Graecismus*.

Evergislus (Ebergesilus, Ebregislus) Saint, monk, fifth-century bishop of Cologne. He is said to have died a martyr, killed by pagan thieves, in Tongres, Belgium. His martyrdom seems improbable and his whole life, presuming it to be not entirely legendary, may have been somewhat later. Feast day 24 October.

Evodius of Antioch Saint, bishop, first century. Multiple sources indicate him as the first bishop of Antioch after St Peter. He appears in various later martyrologies, but there is no surviving primary source evidence to indicate that he was martyred. He was succeeded by St **Ignatius of Antioch**. Feast days 29 April and 7 September (Eastern rites) and 6 May (Roman rite).

Evroul (Evroult, Ebrulf) Saint, abbot, born possibly Bayeux, Normandy, 626, died 12 December, 706. A married nobleman, he joined a monastery and later became a hermit. His wife became a nun. Feast day 29 December.

Evroul of Saint-Fuschien-au-Bois Saint, abbot, born Beauvais, France, sixth century, died Oroër, France, 25 July c.600. Venerated in the areas where he had been active, his remains were transferred to Beauvais in 838. Little is known for certain about his life. There are different stories about how he came to be made abbot at Saint-Fuschien-au-Bois. One version credits the bishop of Beauvais, another says the monks petitioned to have him, and yet another that the king's influence was the determining factor. Some scholars believe that he actually lived a hundred years later. Feast day 25 July; 27 July in Beauvais.

Ewald, Georg Heinrich August German Protestant Hebrew scholar, born Göttingen, 16 November 1803, died Göttingen, 4 May 1875. He developed the scientific study of the Semitic languages and is considered the founder of the historical comparative approach. A professor of oriental languages and exegesis at Göttingen and Tübingen Universities, he developed a complicated theory to explain how the Pentateuch was composed, not supported by other scholars. A prolific writer, his best-known work is *Geschichte des Volkes Israel* (History of the People of Israel), which he worked on for many years. The third edition, published 1864–8, ran to seven volumes.

Ewald the Black Saint, martyr, priest, born Northumbria, died Old Saxony, c.695. After meeting St **Willibrord**, he and fellow Northumbrian priest Ewald the Fair set out on missionary activities c.690. While the guest of a Saxon overlord, his subjects murdered the two priests, fearing they would convert him and jeopardize their own religion. Feast day 3 October.

Ewald the Fair *see* **Ewald the Black**

Ewart, Frank J. Pentecostal preacher and author, born Australia, 1876, died Belvedere, California, 1947. Ewart emigrated to Canada in 1903, where he was dismissed from his Baptist ministry in 1908 following a Pentecostal experience. In 1911 he became assistant to William Durham in Los Angeles, and later became his successor. He was also ordained in the United Pentecostal Church. Ewart spread the non-trinitarian Oneness doctrine through Pentecostalism via his journal *Meat in Due Season*. His books include *The Name and the Book* (1936), *Jesus, the Man and the Mystery* (1941), *The NT Characters X-Rayed* (1945) and *The Phenomenon of Pentecost* (1947).

Ewing, Charles Lawyer, general, born 6 March 1835, Ohio, USA, died 20 June 1883, Washington, DC. The son of Thomas **Ewing**, he served with the Union Army during and after the American Civil War, for which he was cited for bravery. He resumed practising law in 1867 in Washington, DC, where he dealt with Catholic Indian affairs at the appointment of the archbishop of Baltimore. The first commissioner of the Bureau of Catholic Indian Missions, he received a papal knighthood in 1877.

Ewing, Thomas Lawyer, statesman, born 28 December 1789, West Liberty, Virginia, USA (now Liberty, West Virginia), died 26 October 1871, Lancaster, Ohio, USA. A prominent lawyer, Ewing represented Ohio in the US Senate and was an early advocate for the abolition of slavery. He was a prominent advisory figure to Presidents Harrison, Taylor, Lincoln and Johnson. He supported and advised the government during the American Civil War and helped avert a possible conflict with England during Lincoln's administration. He was received into the Roman Catholic Church shortly before his death in 1871. His children with wife Maria Boyle included prominent Catholic lawyer Charles **Ewing**.

Ewostatewos (Eustatius) Ethiopian monk, born c.1273, died 1352, Armenia. He influenced the establishment of the Debra Maryam Monastery in Tigre, and began the significant Ethiopian movement which observed the Sabbath as well as Sunday. He failed to obtain the Patriarch of Alexandria's approval for this and so spent the last fourteen years of his life in exile. His followers were persecuted and excluded from the priesthood, but later the movement was accepted by the Ethiopian church. His reforms also included a religious revival which led to the evangelization of newly conquered areas, the introduction of Christian marriage and the development of a rich hagiographic literature.

Exuperius of Toulouse Saint, bishop, born in the

fourth century, died after 410. Praised by St Jerome for his generosity to his subjects and to the monks of Palestine, Egypt and Libya. He wrote to Pope Innocent I for clarification regarding canonical Scriptures, and a reply, *Consulenti tibi*, dated February 405, contains the canon of Scriptures as it is accepted today. It includes the deutero-canonical books recognized by the Roman Catholic Church. St Jerome mentions him as living in 411, the latest primary source reference. Feast day 28 September.

Eybler, Joseph von Catholic composer, born Schwechat, Austria, 8 February 1765, died Vienna, 24 July 1846. He composed a wide range of religious and secular music in the high classical tradition, including 32 Masses, seven Te Deums, oratorios, operas, symphonies and chamber music. His Requiem in C-minor (1802) is considered his best work. Having nursed Mozart before his death in 1791, he was asked by Mozart's widow to complete her husband's Requiem, but refused the commission. By 1794, he was choirmaster at the Carmelite church and the Schottenkirche. He succeeded Salieri as chief court chapel master on 16 June 1824.

Eyck, Jan van Flemish painter, born Maaseik, *c*.1390, buried at Bruges, 9 July 1441. His brother Hubert (died 1426) began the best-known of Eyck's paintings, the *Adoration of the Lamb* altarpiece in the cathedral at Ghent. It is a deeply religious painting, the greatest achievement of fifteenth-century Flemish art. It reveals both a Gothic delight in detail of costumes and jewellery, but also a new realism and an innovative use of light. Jan was first employed by Count John of Holland, and worked at The Hague from 1422 to 1425. He then entered the service of Philip, Duke of Burgundy, both as a painter and as a confidential agent. In the latter capacity he went to Portugal to negotiate Philip's marriage. As a painter, he worked mainly in Bruges and Lille, under the patronage of the Burgundian court and Italian merchants. He continued to paint portraits and, especially, religious works, including a number of Madonnas, but his best-known canvas is *The Arnolfini Wedding* of 1434 ('Jan van Eyck was here' appears in an inscription over the mirror hanging in the background of the picture).

Eyck, Hubert van Painter and illuminator, born Maeseyck, *c*.1366, died Ghent, 18 September 1426. He founded a school of painting in Bruges with younger brother *Jan van Eyck*, inspiring painting schools across Northern Europe. He is referred to as a master painter in a document dated 1413, but no other biographical information survives. The brothers painted the three-piece altarpiece *The Adoration of the Lamb*, portions of which are found at St Bavo's at Ghent and museums in Brussels and Berlin. This work is often attributed solely to Jan, but the inscription on the work indicates that Jan completed the work after his brother's death.

Eymard, Pierre Julien Saint, priest, born La Mure d'Isère, France, 4 February 1811, died there, 1 August 1868. He founded the Society of the Blessed Sacrament for men and the Servants of the Blessed Sacrament for women. Dedicated to Eucharistic devotion, he wrote, among other works, *La Sainte Communion* and *L'Eucharistie et la Perfection Chrétienne*. He was also responsible for the founding of the Archconfraternity of the Blessed Sacrament and the Priests' Eucharistic League. Feast day 2 August.

Eyre, Thomas Roman Catholic priest, born Glossop, Derbyshire, 1748, died Ushaw, near Durham, 8 May 1810. He trained for the priesthood at the English seminary at Douai, and left for the mission in England in 1775, working mainly in the northeast of the country. In 1794 he founded St Cuthbert's College for a number of displaced ordination candidates, at the bidding of Bishop Gibson. In 1808 the students were moved to a new estate named Ushaw, and he became the first president of the college. The college remains one of England's major seminaries for candidates for Roman Catholic priesthood.

Eyston, Charles Roman Catholic antiquary, scholar, born East Hendred, England, 1667 into a well-established recusant family, died there, 5 November 1721. He was known for his piety and charity, and reportedly preserved the Blessed Sacrament in his home in the post-Reformation period. His writings include *A Little Monument to the Once Famous Abbey and Borough of Glastonbury* and an unpublished manuscript, *A Poor Little Monument to All the Old Pious Dissolved Founda-*

tions of England: or a Short History of Abbeys, all sorts of Monasteries, Colleges, Chapels, Chantries, etc.

Eyzaguirre, José Alejo Chilean Catholic priest, born Santiago, Chile, 13 July 1783, died there, 4 August 1850. As a result of his life-long opposition to government intervention in matters of ecclesiastical authority, he never became a bishop. The government prevented his first appointment as auxiliary bishop of Santiago and, in 1845, he resigned as archbishop-elect of that diocese in protest at government interference. He was a delegate to, and later the president of, the constitutional congress for two years from 1823. He was a councillor of state from 1844 until his death, at which time he was also dean of the cathedral.

Eyzaguirre, José Ignacio Víctor de Chilean Catholic priest, lawyer and politician, born Santiago, Chile, 25 February 1817, died in the Mediterranean on board ship, 16 November 1875. He combined academic positions at the University of Chile with political life as a deputy until 1852, when he left for Europe because political developments were compromising his position as a priest. In 1858, he founded the South American College in Rome, after travelling for two years around Latin America to raise support for it. He published a *History of Chile* (1850) and accounts of his travel experiences from a Catholic perspective. He published *Historia eclesiástica, política y literaria de Chíle* (1850); *El Catolicismo en presencia de sus disidentes* (Paris, 1855); *Los intereses católicos en América* (1859).

F

Faber, Frederick William   Priest and hymn-writer, born Calverly, Yorkshire, 28 June 1814, died London, 26 September 1863. He was educated at Harrow and Oxford, where he became a fellow of Magdalen College in 1837; he was ordained in the Church of England two years later. His family faith had been Calvinistic but, under the influence of John Henry **Newman**, he became Roman Catholic: on 16 November 1845, he was received into the Roman Church at Northampton, several of his friends being received at the same time. They formed a community in Birmingham under the title of Brothers of the Will of God, ('the Wilfridians'). He was ordained priest on 3 April 1847, and given charge of the parish of Cotton in Staffordshire. The Wilfridians entered the Oratory of St Philip Neri, and established a house in London of which Faber immediately became superior in 1849. Faber wrote poetry, theological treatises and hymns for the Catholic Church.

Faber, Johann Augustanus   Swiss Dominican theologian, born Fribourg, 1475, died c.1531. He probably joined the Dominicans in Augsburg, Germany, and it was there he spent most of his life. In 1511 he became vicar general of the Order in Upper Germany and was prior in Augsburg for twenty years. He was court preacher and royal counsellor to the Emperor Maximilian I and to **Charles V**. He was a friend of **Erasmus** and although he sympathized with the Reformers in their desire to revive classical learning, he broke off with them over the extent of their doctrinal and ecclesiastical reforms.

Faber, Johannes   German theologian and bishop, born Leutkirch, Württemberg, 1478, died Vienna, 21 May 1541. Studied theology and canon law at Tübingen and Freiburg, then became minister at Lindau, Lutkirch, vicar general of Constance in 1518, and chaplain to King Ferdinand I of Austria in 1524. In 1530 he was made bishop of Vienna. He was a lifelong friend of **Erasmus**, was himself not uncritical of certain aspects of Church practice, but his early friendships with other Reformers, including **Melanchthon** and **Zwingli**, came to an end when he realized the extent of their proposed reforms. From his *Malleus Haereticorum, sex libris ad Hadrianum VI summum Pontificem* of 1524, he has been given the description 'hammer of heretics'. He wrote his *Opus adversas nova quaedam dogmata Martini Lutheri* in 1552. He debated with the Reformers and took pains to persuade them of their errors and to stem the spread of their ideas. He was a great preacher and his other works consist of homilies and treatises against the Reformers and in defence of Roman orthodoxy.

Faber, Peter   Saint, Jesuit, born Villaret, Savoy, 13 April 1506, died Rome, 1 August 1546. In 1525 he went to Paris to study and shared lodgings with **Francis Xavier**. He also met **Ignatius of Loyola** and became one of his earliest associates. He was ordained in 1534 and took vows with the incipient Society of Jesus in the same year. In 1537 he led the small group to Venice to meet up again with Ignatius and from there he travelled to Rome. He was sent as the Pope's representative to the Colloquy of Worms in 1540 and Regensburg the following year. He was shocked both by the problems wrought by the Reformers and by the decadent Church against which they were protesting. He set about reforming the clergy rather than arguing with the Reformers. At the end of the year he was called back to Spain by Ignatius but within six months was back in Germany, where he laboured in Speyer, Mainz and Cologne for another nineteen months. In 1544 he went back to Spain, where he taught and preached in all the main cities, but his health was weakening and after journeying to Rome in 1546, to meet up again with Ignatius, he developed a fever and died. Feast day 8 August.

Fabian Saint, Pope, martyr, pontiff from 10 January 236 until his martyrdom in Rome on 20 January 250. Born in Rome, he appears to have been influential politically, negotiating a previously unknown level of peace and social tolerance for the Church. A respected leader, Fabian's life was brought to an end when Emperor Decius renewed persecution against the Church upon his accession. He was buried originally at San Callistus, but his remains were discovered in 1915 at the church of San Sebastiano. Feast day 20 January.

Fabiola Saint, widow, died Rome, 399. Born of the wealthy patrician family Fabia or Fabii, she divorced her husband, reportedly for his immoral living, then married again. After her husband's death, she repented publicly for breaching the Church canons concerning divorce and spent the rest of her life in the service of the poor and the sick. She went to Bethlehem in 395, where she lived with SS **Paula** and **Julia Eustochium**. She was in contact with St **Jerome** and some letters between them survive. She eventually returned to Rome, where she continued to serve until her death. Fabiola, with St **Pammachius**, is known to have founded a hospital for the poor in Rome, as well as a hospice at Porto. Feast day 27 December.

Fabri, Filippo Franciscan philosopher and theologian, born Spinata di Brisighella, Italy, 1564, died Padua, 28 August 1630. He was a professor at the University of Padua and a respected commentator on **Duns Scotus**. His writings include *Philosophia naturalis Scoti in theoremata distributa*, *Commentaria in quatuor libros sententiarum Duns Scoti*, a treatise *De Sacramento Ordinis, poenis et censuris ecclesiasticis* and *Commentaries on the Metaphysics of Aristotle*.

Fabricius, Johannes Albert Lutheran scholar, born Leipzig, 11 November 1668, died Hamburg, 30 April 1736. He had originally begun studying medicine, but abandoned it for theology. He was employed in Hamburg first as a librarian, then as a teacher of rhetoric and ethics. His primary endeavour was bibliography, and his collections of ancient texts remain an excellent source for historical study. His most significant writings were *Bibliotheca Graeca*, *Bibliotheca Latina*, *Bibliotheca Latina Mediae et Infimae Aetatis*, *Codex Apocryphus Novi Testamenti* and *Codex Pseudepigraphus Veteris Testamenti*.

Facundus of Hermiane Bishop, birth details uncertain, died North Africa, after *c.*571. A supporter of the Three Chapters, he became embroiled in the Monophysite dispute, and was excommunicated for a period after the Second Council of Constantinople (553). His apologetical writings are valuable source materials for the controversy, and include *Pro Defensione Trium Capitulorum*, *Contra Mocianum Scholasticum* and *Epistola fidei catholicae in defensione trium capitulorum*.

Fagnani, Prospero Roman Catholic canon lawyer, born Sant'Angebo in Vado, 1588, died Rome, 1678. A doctor in both canon and civil law, he was the secretary of the Congregation of the Council for fifteen years. At the request of Pope **Alexander VII** he wrote a detailed commentary on the Decretals of **Gregory IX**, *Jus canonicum seu commentaria absolutissima in quinque libros Decretalium* (published in Rome in 1661). This work was praised by **Benedict XIV** and it is still referred to in the interpretation of canon law today.

Falconieri A noble Florentine family, which has included:

Falconieri, Alessandro Cardinal and papal civil servant, born Rome, 8 February 1657, died Rome, 26 January 1734. **Clement XI** appointed him governor of Rome after he had restored law and order in the surrounding countryside. He continued in that post under **Innocent XIII** and **Benedict XIII** and was created a cardinal by Benedict in 1724.

Falconieri, Alexius Saint, monk, founder of the

Servite Order, born Florence, 1200, died Mt Senario near Florence, 17 February 1310. Alexius was born into a well-off merchant family. He joined the Laudesi, a fellowship which venerated the Virgin, and met there six other monks who, together with Alexius, had a vision of Mary. Soon afterwards, the seven founded the Servite Order, which grew to a membership of 10,000 after only a few years. Alexius begged funds for the new Order on the streets of Florence. On his deathbed, he had a vision of the infant Jesus.

Falconieri, Julia Saint, foundress of the Sisters of the Third Order of Servites, born Florence, 1270, died there, 19 June 1341. Julia was born into a respected Florentine merchant family. Her uncle was St Alexius **Falconieri**. Devout from youth, Julia founded the Third Order, remaining the superior until her death. The Order cared for the sick and did works of mercy. On her deathbed, desiring to receive Communion but being unable to because of vomiting, Julia asked for the host to be placed on her chest. The host disappeared, Julia died, and a cross such as had been on the host was said to have appeared on her chest. Feast day 19 June.

Falconieri, Lelio Lawyer and cardinal, great-uncle of Alessandro **Falconieri**, born Florence, 1585, died Viterbo, 14 December 1648. He practised law in Rome before working for Popes **Paul V**, **Gregory XV** and **Urban VIII** as a governor, councillor and diplomatic representative. The government in Brussels did not receive him when he arrived as nuncio in 1635, believing he favoured the French. He became a cardinal in 1643 and went to Bologna as the papal legate. He was a good administrator, helping the poor and contributing to a measure of reconciliation between opposing political factions.

Falkner, Thomas Jesuit priest, born Manchester, England, 6 October 1707, died Shropshire, 30 January 1784. A surgeon by profession, he became ill in Buenos Aires and was cared for by a Jesuit superior there about 1731. In 1732 he converted to Roman Catholicism and joined the Jesuits. He served as a missionary in Patagonia for 30 years until the Jesuits' expulsion from South America in 1768. He returned to England and served as a

chaplain until his death. His writings include an account of his time in Patagonia and an unpublished work concerning the properties of American botanical products.

Fallon, Michael Francis Canadian Catholic bishop, born Kingston, Ontario, 17 May 1867, died London, Ontario, 22 February 1931. After studying in Rome, he joined the Oblates of Mary Immaculate in Holland and was ordained on 29 July 1894. He taught at Ottawa University, where he was vice-rector, then worked as a parish priest. He was the elected American provincial of his Order from 1904 to 1909, when he became bishop of London, Ontario. The son of an Irish immigrant, he was well known as a strong advocate of Home Rule in Ireland. He edited *Shorter Poems by Catholics* (London, 1930).

Fallon, Valère Belgian Jesuit and economist, born Namur, 24 May 1875, died Louvain, 21 January 1955. After ordination in 1907, he studied political and social sciences, then taught at the Jesuit college, Louvain, and at the Institut Supérieur Zénobe Gramme, Liège. He was one of the founders of the Ligue des Familles Nombreuses in 1921, and of the International Population Union in 1928. He pioneered demographic studies in Belgium, publishing a number of works, notably on the Belgian system of family allowances. He was chaplain to the Belgian armed forces from 1914 to 1918 and again from 1939 to 1940.

Famian (Famianus) Saint, monk, priest, born Cologne *c.*1090, died Galese, Italy, 8 August 1150. Famian went on pilgrimages to the Holy Land, to Rome and to Compostella, afterwards becoming a hermit, and then, when a monastery was built nearby at Osera, a monk in the Order of Cîteaux. He once more went off to the Holy Land, and on his return died at Galese, where a church bears his name. Feast day 8 August.

Fan Noli Albanian Orthodox bishop, writer and political leader, born Thrace, Turkey, 6 January 1882, died Boston, USA, 13 March 1965. He helped to obtain independence of Albania in 1912 and served as prime minister until the coup of King Zogu. He was already bishop when he was forced to leave his country, eventually settling in

America where he headed the Albanian parishes and spent the remainder of his life translating liturgical books and Western classics into Albanian. He also encouraged the use of English in church. He was a talented musician and biographer of Beethoven.

Fara (Fare, Burgundofara) Saint, abbess, born Burgundy 595, died Meaux, 657. A noblewoman in the court of King Theodebert, she defied demands by her father, Count Agneric, that she marry. St **Eustace** intervened and eventually the two made peace. She was professed in Meaux in 614, and a few years later persuaded her father to build her an abbey, later known as Faremoutier-en-Brie, which she ruled as abbess for 37 years. The sister of SS **Faro** and Cagnoald, she was responsible for the formation of SS Gibitrudis, Sethrida, Hildelid and others. She has been associated with several miracles. Feast day 3 April.

Farel, Guillaume Protestant reformer of Switzerland, born Gap, France, 1489, died Neuchâtel, Switzerland, 13 September 1565. Taught in moderate Meaux, France, for a time before being expelled as a radical. He was highly influential in the acceptance of the Reformation in Geneva and was a close supporter of Jean **Calvin**. A prolific writer, his most important work was the theology manual *Sommaire: C'est une brieve declaration d'aucuns lieux fort necessaires a un chacun chrestien pour mettre sa confiance en Dieu et a ayder son prochain.*

Farges, Albert French Catholic priest and theologian, born Beaulieu, France, 1848, died Beaulieu, 9 June 1926. Ordained priest with the Sulpician Order in 1872, he was teacher and director in several seminaries and professor of philosophy at the Institut Catholique in Paris. He contributed to a revival of interest in the philosophy of **Thomas Aquinas**. His essays on the theories of Aristotle and Aquinas were published in nine volumes as *Études Philosophiques pour vulgariser les théories d'Aristote et de S. Thomas et leur accord avec les sciences* (Paris, 1885–1907). He lectured and wrote on ascetical and mystical theology, with reference to Aquinas and **Teresa of Ávila**.

Farlati, Daniele Jesuit and Church historian, born San Daniele del Friuli, Italy, 22 February 1690, died Padua, 25 April 1773. He joined the Society of Jesus in 1707, becoming a priest in 1722. He spent the remainder of his life working on a history of the Church in Illyria, a region in the Balkans along the Adriatic coast. After his first collaborator, the Jesuit Filippo Riceputi, died in 1642, he worked with Giacomo Coleti, another Jesuit. The first volume of *Illyricum sacrum* appeared in Venice in 1751. Farlati completed five volumes and, after his death, Coleti published the final three volumes.

Farley, John Murphy Cardinal, born 'John Farrelly' at Armagh, Ireland, 20 April 1842, died New York, USA, 17 September 1918. Ordained priest in New York in 1870, he was appointed secretary to Cardinal **McCloskey** two years later, changing his name to 'Farley' at the same time. He was ordained auxiliary bishop of New York in 1895, then archbishop in 1902. He improved the archdiocese's parochial and seminary education facilities, and was interested in the Catholic University, women's education, and immigrants. He was made a cardinal in 1911. His major writings are a biography of Cardinal McCloskey and a history of St Patrick's Cathedral.

Farmer, Ferdinand Jesuit missionary, born Weisenstein, Württemberg, Germany, 13 October 1720, died Philadelphia, Pennsylvania, 17 August 1786. Ordained as a Jesuit priest around 1750. Farmer (originally 'Steinmeyer') was first sent to China, then transferred to Pennsylvania to serve German immigrants there, arriving in 1752. From 1758, he based himself in Philadelphia and travelled extensively as a missionary in the region to minister to existing congregations and to found new ones, including the first Catholic congregation in New York City. He was an early member of the American Philosophical Society, corresponding with scholars in Europe. He was a trustee of Pennsylvania University.

Farnese, Alessandro Cardinal, born 7 October 1520, died Rome, February 1589. A grandson of Pope **Paul III**, the teenager was given the rank of cardinal-deacon of the Title of Sant' Angelo in 1534. Other offices followed, including vice-chancellor of the Holy Roman Church and bishop of Monreale, Sicily, and afterwards further bishoprics, and in 1580 he became cardinal-bishop of Ostia and Velletri. He served as Paul III's legate in the severing of ties with England, founded a Jesuit college in Sicily in 1552, advocated for Tridentine reform, and was known for his interest in the poor.

Farnese, Odoardo Created cardinal in 1591, died 1626. He was papal legate in Parma and a member of the first Congregation for the Propagation of the Faith, when he was described as one of the outstanding cardinals. He was regent for his nephew, Duke Odoardo, during the latter's minority.

Farnese, Ranuccio Grandson of **Paul III**, born Vetulano, 11 August 1530, died Parma, 28 October 1565, created cardinal by him in 1545. He was known for his academic interests and was also a papal legate.

Faro of Meaux Saint, monk, bishop, probably born in Burgundy, died *c.*675, probably in Meaux. The son of a nobleman and brother to SS **Fara** and Cagnoald, Faro was a chancellor in the court of King Dagobert I. He left his position to become a monk, and by 637 was the bishop of Meaux. **Bede** mentions him as assisting St **Hadrian** of Canterbury, but otherwise little is known of his episcopate. Feast day 3 April.

Farquhar, John Nicol Scottish missionary to India, born Aberdeen, 6 April 1861, died Manchester, 17 July 1929. After apprenticeship to a draper and study at Aberdeen and Oxford he went to India in 1891 as a lay educational missionary for the LMS. He taught at Bhowanipur, Calcutta, for eleven years. While on the staff of the YMCA in India, in 1902–23, he wrote *Gita and the Gospel* (1903), *The Crown of Hinduism* (1913) and *Modern Religious Movements in India* (1915). Still regarded for his scholarship and his popularization of a missionary theology of religion based on a fulfilment model (Matthew 5:17), he was an excellent linguist with a detailed, empathetic understanding of Hinduism. He returned to Britain for health reasons in 1923 and was professor of comparative religion at the University of Manchester until his death.

Farrar, Frederic William Clergyman and writer, born in the fort at Bombay, India, where his father was a Church Missionary Society chaplain, 7 August 1831, died Canterbury, 22 March 1903. He was educated at King's College, London University, where he was much influenced by F. D. **Maurice**, and at Trinity College, Cambridge, where he afterwards became a fellow. He taught at Marlborough College, and then at Harrow. He returned to Marlborough as head in 1871, but in 1876 he became a canon of Westminster and rector of St Margaret's parish. An honorary chaplain to Queen Victoria, he later became archdeacon of Westminster and a chaplain to the House of Commons. In 1893 he became dean of Canterbury. He wrote many theological works, including the enormously popular *Life of Christ*, *Life and Works of St Paul* and *Eternal Hope*, but his earliest publications were novels, and he is also remembered for his children's stories, including *Eric, or, Little by Little*.

Farrell, Walter American Dominican theologian and writer, born Chicago, Illinois, 21 July 1902, died River Forest, Illinois, 23 November 1951. He joined the Order on 14 September 1920 and was ordained on 9 June 1927. He obtained the degree of master in sacred theology in Rome in 1940, the highest honour in his Order. He wrote *A Companion to the Summa*, published in four volumes (1938 to 1942), and contributed to the *Thomist*, a quarterly review he had helped to start in 1939. He preached, led retreats and lectured on theology. He was a US navy chaplain during World War II.

Farrer, Austin Marsden English philosopher and Christian apologist, born into a Baptist family in Hampstead, London, on 1 October 1904, died Oxford, 29 December 1968. Studied at St Paul's School and at Balliol College, Oxford, joined the Church of England and following his ordination as priest in 1929 he worked at All Saints', Dewsbury. He returned to Oxford in 1931 as chaplain and tutor at St Edmund Hall; in 1936 he became fellow and chaplain of Trinity and in 1960 warden of Keble College. One of his concerns was to discern a natural philosophy most suited to Christian belief. His publications include *Finite and Infinite* (1943), *The Freedom of the Will* (1958), *The Glass of Vision* (his 1948 Bampton Lectures), a collection of sermons, *The Crown of the Year* (1952) and *Saving Belief* (1964).

Farrow, John Catholic film director and writer, born Sydney, Australia, 10 February 1906, died Beverly Hills, California, 28 January 1963. His first successful film in Hollywood was *My Bill*, directed in 1937. Discharged from active service on medical grounds, he received the New York Film Critics' award for best direction in 1943 for his film *Wake Island*. Among his other films are *Two Years before the Mast*, *Back from Eternity*, *Botany Bay*, *Submarine Command* and *Sea Chase*. He wrote several books, notably *Damien the Leper* (1937), *Pageant of the Popes* (1942) and *The Story of Thomas More* (1954). He was awarded a papal knighthood, and an honorary rank of Companion of the British Empire. He was married to the actress Maureen O'Sullivan.

Farrow, Lucy Pentecostal pastor and missionary, born Norfolk, Virginia, nineteenth century, died twentieth century. Farrow was born a slave, but later became a Holiness pastor in Houston. In 1905 she became a governess for Charles **Parham**'s family, and after experiencing speaking in tongues she persuaded Parham to enrol William **Seymour** as a student. When Seymour began his ministry in Los Angeles, he sent for her. Farrow preached in Norfolk, Houston and New Orleans, and she spent several months from December 1906 preaching to the freed slaves in Liberia. Her last years were spent in a cottage behind the Azusa street mission.

Fastred de Cavamiez Blessed, Cistercian abbot, born Hainaut, died Paris, 1164. Fastred was received into the Cistercians at Clairvaux by St **Bernard**, and in 1148 became the first abbot of the abbey of Campron in Hainaut, then the successful abbot of Clairvaux in 1157, and finally of Cîteaux in 1162. Feast day 21 April.

Faulhaber, Andreas Catholic priest and martyr, born Glatz, Silesia (now Klodzko, Poland), 21 May 1713, died Glatz, 30 December 1757. The Prussian authorities executed him for refusing to reveal the details of a confession. A Prussian soldier, a deserter during the Seven Years' War, told his interrogators that he had confessed his action to Faulhaber who, by implication, had condoned it. Although the man retracted his statement, the priest was imprisoned and executed. His body hung from the gallows for 30 months, but did not decay. Austrian troops took it down on 26 July 1760 and buried it in the church in Glatz.

Faulhaber, Michael von Cardinal, born Klosterheidenfeld, Germany, 6 March 1869, died Munich, 12 June 1952. Ordained in 1892, von Faulhaber was an accomplished theologian, particularly in the areas of the OT and patristics. He was consecrated bishop of Speyer in 1910 and was named archbishop of Munich in 1917, being created cardinal in 1921. He wrote on contemporary issues and was outspoken against the Nazi regime, and against capitalism. He published a number of works, especially on scriptural themes, including a study of women in the Bible.

Fauré, Gabriel Urbain French composer known for the refinement of his music, and organist, born Pamiers, Ariège, 12 May 1845, died Paris, 4 November 1924. In Paris he was a pupil of Saint-Saëns. He became organist of the Madeleine and director of the Paris Conservatoire. His Church music is known for its seraphic calm. His *Requiem* of 1887 was not performed in England until much later, and became a popular piece outside the Christian context in the 1990s.

Faure, Giovanni Battista Jesuit theologian, born Rome, 25 October 1702, died Viterbo, 5 April 1779. He wrote numerous works of theology and Church history, several of them critical of contemporary attitudes. In one, published anonymously, he attacked the mainly Dominican inquisitors for condemning books arbitrarily. The Inquisition responded by placing the work on the Church's Index of Prohibited Books. His theological criticism of Jansenism was attacked for being too lenient with individual Jansenists. When Pope **Clement XIV** suppressed the Jesuits in 1773, he was held in the prison of Sant'Angelo for two years for fear he would encourage resistance to the Pope through his polemical writings.

Faust, Mathias Constantine Franciscan, born Oberbimbach, Germany, 30 March 1878, died New York, USA, 27 July 1956. At nineteen, he joined the Franciscans in New Jersey; he was ordained priest in 1906. He held jurisdiction over much of the Americas during World War II as a delegate of the Franciscan minister general. He was responsible for the establishment of St Bonaventure University's Franciscan Institute and the Academy of American Franciscan History. After the war he continued to hold positions of responsibility, most notably that of the Order of Friars Minor's procurator general, in which he was responsible for the Order's relationship with the Holy See.

Faustus of Riez Saint, abbot and bishop, born England, c.410, died c.490. Already bishop of Lérins, he became bishop of Riez, in Provence, c.460, but left his see under duress for some years after opposing Euric, the Visigoth king. A proponent of early Semi-Pelagian theology, most particularly in his work *De gratia Dei*, the Second Council of Orange condemned him in 529; however, he is revered in Southern France. Feast day 28 September.

Favier, Alphonse French Catholic missionary and bishop in China, born Marsonnay-la-Côte, near Dijon, France, 22 September 1837, died Peking (Beijing), China, 3 April 1905. Joining the Vincentian Order in 1858, he was sent to China in 1862. He became auxiliary bishop of Peking in 1897 and vicar apostolic of North Chihli (now Hopeh) in northern China in 1899. Under his leadership, 3500 Christians besieged in Peking's Northern Church held fast for two months during the Boxer Rebellion in 1900. Afterwards, he was an important mediator between China and the Europeans. He wrote a book on Peking, *Pékin, Histoire et Description* (Lille, 1900).

Fawcett, John Baptist minister, educationalist and hymn-writer, born near Bradford, Yorkshire, 6 January 1740, died Hebden Bridge, Yorkshire, 25 July 1817. Converted as a teenager by the preaching of George **Whitefield**. Originally a Methodist, he joined the Baptists in 1759, and was ordained a minister in 1764, serving as pastor of the Wainsgate and Hebden Bridge church. Influential in the founding of Horton Academy, Bradford, later to become Rawdon College. He wrote several hymns including 'Blest be the Tie that Binds'. His published works include *The Constitution and Order of a Gospel Church* (1797) and a *Commentary on the Bible* (1811).

Fay, Cyril Sigourney Webster Priest and diplomat, born Philadelphia, Pennsylvania, 16 June 1875, died (of influenza) New York City, 10 January 1919. Ordained an Episcopalian priest in 1903, he taught in a seminary and joined a group of clergymen called the 'Companions of the Holy Saviour'. When the Episcopal Church opened its pulpits to clergy of other denominations, he and others in the 'American Oxford Movement' became Catholics. He was ordained as a Catholic priest in Baltimore on 21 June 1921. During World War I, when in Italy for the Red Cross, he took part in negotiations intended to enable the Vatican to participate in the post-war peace conference.

Febei, Francesco Antonio (Foebus) Catholic writer on canon law, born Orvieto, 17 March 1652, died Rome, 2 May 1705. After entering the Society of Jesus on 12 November 1667, he was a teacher of canon law, philosophy and theology at the Roman College. He wrote two works that were popular for many years. The first, *Institutionum iuris canonici libri IV*, published in Rome in 1698, was a lucid and comprehensive summary of canon law for those embarking on the subject. The second, *De regulis iuris*, was published in Venice in 1735, thirty years after his death.

Febronius *see* **Hontheim**.

Federer, Charles Antoine Antiquarian and Methodist layman, born in Switzerland, 18 October 1837, died Bradford, Yorkshire, 5 November 1908. Educated at St Gall and Lausanne. Arriving in England in 1857, he worked as a teacher at Bakewell, Gildersome and Wetherby before settling in Bradford. In about 1864 he renounced his Roman Catholicism and became a Methodist, joining the White Abbey Wesleyan Chapel. Founder of the Bradford Historical and Antiquarian Society and editor of the *Bradford Antiquary* and the *Yorkshire Magazine*. His published works include *Materials for French Translation*. His extensive collection of literature (much of which relates to Nonconformity in Yorkshire) now forms an important archival deposit at the Central Library, Bradford.

Federer, Heinrich Swiss Catholic German-language novelist and priest, born Berne, 7 October 1866, died Zurich, 29 April 1928. Ordained in 1893, he gave up working in a parish in 1899 as a result of ill health – he suffered from severe asthma – but also in order to concentrate on writing. He published numerous works in which realistic descriptions were combined with a moral and religious inspiration. He wrote three novels containing very poetical descriptions of Catholic life in Switzerland, two autobiographical novels about his youth as well as several books about the people and landscape of Italy.

Fedotov, George　Russian Orthodox historian and educator, born Saratov, 1 October 1886, died New York, 1 September 1951. Probably the greatest Church historian of the Russian emigration, he lived in Paris before World War II and in America thereafter, where he was active in Church affairs. His most important work was *The Russian Religious Mind* – he completed the first volume (1946) on the Kiev period, but unfortunately only part of the second (1966).

Feehan, Patrick Augustine　Catholic archbishop, born County Tipperary, Ireland, 29 August 1829, died Chicago, Illinois, 12 July 1902. Emigrating with his family in 1850, he was ordained in Missouri on 1 November 1852. First a seminary teacher, then a parish priest, he became known during the American Civil War for his work with war victims. As bishop of Nashville, Tennessee, from 1865, he rebuilt churches destroyed during the war, recruited priests from Ireland and attended the first Vatican Council in Rome. In 1880, he became the first archbishop of Chicago, where he helped to organize the second Catholic congress in 1893 and undertook a major building and expansion programme.

Feeney, Leonard　Jesuit priest, writer, born Lynn, Massachusetts, 15 February 1897, died Still River, Massachusetts, 30 January 1978. Ordained in 1928, he taught at Boston College, edited the Jesuit journal *America* and ministered at Harvard before forming a religious community with Catherine Goddard Clarke in 1949. He adhered strictly to the position that salvation was impossible outside the Church, was consequently expelled from the Jesuits in 1949 and excommunicated in 1953. In 1972, his excommunication was lifted, and he and most of his community returned to the Church. His writings include *Fish On Friday*, *Boundaries* and *You'd Better Come Quietly*.

Feijó, Diogo Antônio　Catholic priest and regent of Brazil, born São Paulo, Brazil, August 1784, died São Paulo, 10 November 1843. Ordained on 25 February 1809, he worked as a priest until 1821, when he went to Lisbon as a deputy to the Cortes. As Brazilian minister of justice in 1831–2, and later as regent in 1835–7, he is credited with saving the country from revolution during some turbulent years. He remained a senator until his death. As a liberal political reformer, he held views that were not always in accord with the Catholic Church and supported the idea of married priests.

Felbiger, Johann Ignaz von　Augustinian canon regular and schools reformer, born Gross-Glogau, 6 November 1724, died Pressburg, 17 May 1788. A canon regular from 1746, he worked on reforming educational methods in Catholic schools in Silesia and Prussia. From 1774, he worked for Empress Maria Theresa of Austria, from 1778 to 1782 as chief director of the Austrian educational system. He established teacher-training colleges, replaced tutorials by classroom teaching and introduced a system of teaching through questions and answers instead of expecting pupils to learn by rote. He wrote a catechism and several books on teaching methods.

Feldmann, Franz　German Catholic priest and biblical scholar, born Hüsten, Westphalia, 17 May 1866, died Bonn, 9 February 1944. Ordained in 1891, from 1900 he taught OT exegesis at Paderborn and then, from 1903, at Bonn University. He had an excellent grasp of Semitic languages and biblical theology. As far as he could, given the attitudes in his Church, he drew on the research of contemporary Protestant scholars. For instance, he accepted the possibility that more than one person had composed the book of Isaiah. He published many books, notably in 1926 the so-called *Bonner Bibel*, a series of commentaries he had edited.

Felici, Pericle　Cardinal, canon lawyer, secretary general of the Second Vatican Council, founder of the review *Communicationes*, born Segni, Italy, 1 August 1911, died Foggia, 22 March 1982.

Ordained in 1933 he went on to do doctoral studies and was awarded his doctorate in 1938. He was rector of the Pontifical Institute of Jurisprudence, spiritual director at the Pontifical Roman Seminary and from 1943 taught moral theology at the Lateran University. He was made titular archbishop of Samosata in 1960. As secretary general to the Council he played a key role during Vatican II: preparing preliminary papers, co-ordinating meetings and summarizing discussions. In June 1967 he was made cardinal and became president of the Pontifical Commission for the revision of the Code of Canon Law. He served on a number of sacred congregations and commissions and published academic articles on moral theology and canon law.

Felicissimus and Agapitus   Saints, deacons, martyrs, died in the catacombs of Praetextatus, 6 August 258. Attendants to Pope **Sixtus II**, they died with him at the hands of Roman soldiers by order of the Emperor **Valerian**. Sixtus was beheaded, and the deacons were probably executed in the same way, along with an estimated five others. The martyrs were buried together at the cemetery of Callistus. **Gregory IV** gave their bones to Abbot Gozbald of Niederaltaich for his church at Isarhofen. Their martyrdom is detailed in the Roman Martyrology and in a letter by St **Cyprian**. Feast day 6 August.

Felicity (Felicitas)   *see* **Perpetua and Felicity**

Felix I   Saint, Pope from 3 January 269 until his death on 30 December 274. Few details survive, but he is thought to have been a Roman by birth. He is known to have ordered the deposition of the renegade bishop **Paul of Samatosa**, but little else is known of his activities. Feast day 30 May.

Felix III (II)   Saint, Pope from 13 March 483 until his death on 1 March 492. He excommunicated Patriarch Acacius of Constantinople and was responsible for the first schism of the Eastern and Western Churches, and also excommunicated many Catholics who had been forcibly rebaptized by Arian Vandals. Feast day 1 March.

Felix IV (III)   Saint, Pope from 12 July 526 until his death on 22 September 530. A 58-day gap between Felix and his predecessor, **John I**, suggests a struggle for the Papacy; Felix was consecrated on the orders of Theodoric, the Ostrogoth king of Italy. He wrote 25 propositions concerning grace, which were adopted at the Council of Orange (529), and posthumously affirmed by **Boniface II**, thus ending the Pelagian controversy.

Felix V   *see* **Amadeus VIII of Savoy**.

Felix of Cantalice   Saint, Capuchin priest, born Cantalice, Abruzzi, on an unknown date, died Rome, 18 May 1587. A shepherd and labourer, Felix was devoted to austerity and prayer, and was received into the Capuchins in 1543. He became a questor in Rome for the Order, and preached and challenged powerful and poor alike, often with St Philip **Neri**. He had a special interest in the spiritual formation of children but was also consulted by learned adults on this issue, despite his lack of education. He is buried in the church of the Immaculate Conception in Rome. Feast day 18 May.

Felix of Nicosia   Blessed, Capuchin lay brother, born Nicosia, Sicily, 5 November 1715, died Nicosia, 30 May 1787. A cobbler's apprentice, Felix made several attempts to join a religious order, before becoming a Capuchin lay brother in 1743. He wandered as a beggar for the monastery – a common practice among poor and uneducated monks – and was known for his ministry of preaching, converting and tending to the sick. He was beatified in 1888.

Felix of Nola   Saint, confessor, priest, died 260, probably in Nola. Felix, in the company of Paulinus, was tortured but not killed for professing his faith. His apostolate afterwards, based at his church in Nola, was characterized by reports of miracles. Feast day 14 January.

Felix of Valois   Saint, monastic founder of the Order of the Holy Trinity for the Redemption of Captives, born 1127, died Cerfroid, 4 November 1212. Perhaps of royal Valois blood, perhaps simply from the Valois province, Felix at an early age left all to live in contemplation in a wood (now Cerfroid Monastery). Joined by **John of Matha**, who suggested to him the founding of an Order,

Felix journeyed to Rome where he and John presented the idea to Pope **Innocent III**. The two were kindly received and confirmed to the task of beginning their Order, which grew in 40 years to 600 monasteries around Europe. Feast day 20 November.

Fell, Margaret Early Quaker leader and wife of George **Fox**, born Dalton-in-Furness, Lancs, 1614, died at Swarthmore Hall, Ulverston, 23 April 1702. Born Margaret Askew, she married Judge Thomas Fell of Swarthmore, and bore him nine children. In 1652 a Quaker meeting was held in her house, led by Fox, and she and most of her family were converted, though not Fell himself, who was absent. He, however, seems to have made no complaint about the continuing use of Swarthmore for meetings of the Quakers. She went to London in 1660 to petition **Charles II** on behalf of Fox, who had been arrested in her house, and to attempt to obtain toleration. She was herself arrested in 1663 for allowing meetings at Swarthmore, and was not finally released until mid-1668, by which time the hall had been made over to her son. She, however, continued to reside there when not accompanying Fox, whom she married in Bristol in 1669 (Fell had died in 1658), on his journeys around England. She was arrested again in 1670, possibly through the machinations of her son who wanted possession of Swarthmore, but was freed the following year. After Fox's death she played less of a role in the Society of Friends, though in 1697 she went to London to thank William III for his toleration of Quakers.

Felton, John Blessed, martyr, died London, England, 8 August 1570. His wife Mary was servant and childhood friend to Queen **Elizabeth I**, and the Catholic family was allowed access to the clergy without recrimination as a consequence. In this way, Felton obtained copies of **Pius V**'s papal bull excommunicating Elizabeth. He published them in England. When confronted, he admitted his involvement, and was tortured. He sent a ring to Elizabeth by way of reconciliation but maintained belief in papal supremacy. He was executed at St Paul's Cathedral, his corpse was desecrated as that of a rebel. He was beatified in 1886.

Feneberg, Johann Michael Roman Catholic priest,

born Oberdorf, Allgau, Bavaria, 9 February 1751, died Vöhringen, near Ulm, 12 October 1812. Ordained in 1775, he taught at several gymnasiums, but was removed in 1793 on suspicion of sympathy towards Illuminism. He went on to parish work and was an active pastor, despite losing a leg after a horse-riding accident. When he gave shelter to his kinsman, priest and mystic Martin Boos, he fell under suspicion of heresy, but after repudiating key errors of which he was accused, he was allowed to return to his post. Boos himself, who embraced Reformed doctrine, was condemned.

Fénelon, François de Salignac de la Mothe Philosopher, theologian, Roman Catholic archbishop, born at the Château Fénelon, near Cahors, France, 6 August 1651, died Cambrai, 7 January 1715. He studied first at Cahors and then at Paris, being ordained in 1675. He worked for a time in a parish served by the priests of St Sulpice, whose seminary he had attended. There he gained a reputation for eloquence in preaching. He became much in demand as a spiritual guide, especially by the more eminent members of Parisian society (including Mme **Guyon**) and was named archbishop of Cambrai by **Louis XIV** in 1695. However, the first volume of his *Telémaque* (1697) was thought to be a criticism of the king, and he lost royal favour, being obliged to spend the rest of his life in his diocese rather than at court as hitherto. Spiritually, he was influenced by Quietism but was careful to remain orthodox; parts of his *L'Explication des maximes des saints sur la vie interieure* (1697) were nonetheless condemned by the Holy See in 1699. He accepted the condemnation, ensuring that it was published in his own diocese. He continued his spiritual direction, and gained a reputation as an opponent of Jansenism. His many writings include political and philosophical, as well as spiritual and theological, works.

Fenlon, John F. American Catholic priest and teacher, born Chicago, Illinois, 23 June 1873, died Holland, Michigan, 31 July 1943. Ordained in Chicago on 19 June 1896, he joined the Sulpician Order two years later and studied theology and oriental languages in Rome. On his return, he taught in various institutions at the same time as holding several positions in his Order. His final posts from December 1925 were as president of St Mary's Seminary and University and provincial superior of the Sulpicians in the USA. He helped to set up the National Catholic Welfare Conference and contributed to many Catholic publications.

Fenwick, Benedict Joseph   Jesuit, bishop, born Maryland, USA, 3 September 1782, died Boston, 11 August 1846. Ordained in 1808, he served as a pastor and educator. After serving in positions of leadership within the Jesuit Order, he was consecrated bishop of Boston in 1825. His episcopate saw a fivefold explosion of the Catholic population in his diocese, which then included New England. Accordingly, much of his episcopate was dedicated to providing more churches, clergy, relief organizations, defence against sectarian violence, and Catholic education. He founded a Catholic newspaper, known first as the *Catholic Sentinel*, then *The Pilot*, which is still published today.

Fenwick, Edward Dominic   Dominican, bishop, born Maryland, 19 August 1768, died Ohio, 26 September 1832. Fenwick was ordained in 1793, taught in Belgium and England, and was granted permission to establish the Dominican Order in the USA in 1804. He started communities in Kentucky, then Ohio, and in 1821 was appointed first bishop of Cincinnati. Starting with six priests, Fenwick built the diocese up over a decade to include a college and seminary, 22 churches, 24 priests, and the presence of the Sisters of Charity and the Dominican Sisters.

Fényi, Gyula   Jesuit priest and astronomer, born Sopron, Hungary, 8 January 1845, died Kalocsa(?), Hungary, 25 May 1927. Fényi entered the Society of Jesus in 1864 and encountered astronomy as a formal science when he was sent to teach at the Jesuit college in Kalocsa, where the archbishop of that town, Cardinal Lajos Haynald, had established an observatory in 1878. He became director of the Haynald observatory in 1885, and remained in that post until 1913, though he continued to make observations for another four years. During these years he only once left the observatory in order to make a brief visit to Granada for the total eclipse of the sun in 1905. His studies of solar prominences are still used by astronomers as the basis of

their divisions of the various types. One of the craters on the moon was named after him in 1971.

Feo, Francesco   Composer, born Naples, 1691, died there, 28 January 1761(?) At a time when composers in southern Italy were writing simpler, 'democratic', works, in contrast to the more complex 'aristocratic' music in the north, he was considered a leader of the Neapolitan baroque school, notably for his liturgical works. These include Masses, motets, a Requiem and *Magnificat*. He contributed to the development of the 'cantata Mass', in which the solo sections are like arias. He began as a composer of opera. His first opera, *L'Amore Tiranico Ossia Zenobia* (1713), is a good example of the Neapolitan style, with the orchestra providing only a simple accompaniment.

Feodorov, Leonid   Russian Catholic exarch, born St Petersburg, Russia, 4 November 1879, died Vyatka (or Kirov), 7 March 1935. He first studied to be an Orthodox priest but, in 1902, went to Italy and became a Catholic priest, ordained in Constantinople in 1911. He insisted that Russian converts to Catholicism should keep to a Russian rite, free of Latin influences. Returning to St Petersburg in 1914, he was deported to Tobolsk. In 1917, both the Orthodox leaders and the Pope named him exarch (leader) of Russian rite Catholics. In 1923, he was tried and sent to prison. Released and rearrested in 1926, he spent the rest of his life as a prisoner.

Ferdinand   Blessed, prince, born Portugal 29 September 1402, died Fez, Morocco, 5 June 1443. Though not a cleric, he was offered appointment as a cardinal, which he refused. In 1437 he led a force against the Moors which took control of strategic Ceuta, eventually offering himself hostage in exchange for the safe passage of his men. As a prisoner of Salà ben Salà, he was subjected to torture, solitary confinement and slavery until his death, despite rescue efforts. His secretary, João Alvarez, once freed, wrote his biography, and returned his body to his birthplace.

Ferdinand I   Holy Roman Emperor, born Alcalá de Henares, 10 March 1503, died Vienna, 25 July 1564. Brother of Emperor **Charles V**, he was a ruler in his own right in Germany, Bohemia and

Hungary, and became Emperor in 1558 after Charles' abdication. Though he remained a loyal Catholic, he was conscious of the need to bring peace to his dominions by reaching a compromise on religious conflicts. He therefore negotiated between warring Catholic and Protestant factions and was responsible for the conciliatory Peace of Augsburg in 1555.

Ferdinand II Holy Roman Emperor, born Graz, 9 July 1578, died Vienna, 15 February 1637. The grandson of **Ferdinand I**, he was very devout and much influenced by the Jesuits: he took a vow to sacrifice land and life before his religious principles. He fought successfully to suppress Protestantism in his territories, particularly Bohemia.

Ferdinand III (of Castile) King and saint, born near Salamanca c.1201, died Seville, 30 May 1252. He was the son of Alfonso IX of León and was brought up there. In 1217 he was crowned king of Castile, succeeding his cousin Henry. On Alfonso's death in 1230 Ferdinand was accepted as king of León, so both kingdoms were reunited. Ferdinand conquered Andalucia, securing it from the Moors, and he accepted the submission of the king of Murcia. Ferdinand captured Seville. The remaining Muslim kingdoms of Niebla and Granada came under Castile's sway. He re-established the University of Salamanca. At his death he was popularly acclaimed a saint. He was buried in Seville Cathedral dressed not as a king but as a Franciscan. He is the patron saint of prisoners, the poor and local rulers. In 1671 he was canonized for his services to the Crusades. His emblem is a greyhound. Feast day 30 May.

Ferdinand V (of Castile) Spanish king, born Aragon, Spain, 1452; died Madrigalejo, 23 January 1516. Entitled to Aragon by birth, he married **Isabella of Castile** in 1469, and ruled there first as her consort, then on behalf of their daughter, who was mentally ill. He was extremely religious and, together with Isabella, introduced the Inquisition in 1478, and expelled from their possessions Muslims and Jews who refused to convert to Christianity. He gained control by conquest of Sicily, Naples, and of Navarre, becoming king of all Spain by 1512.

Fernández de Piedrahita, Lucas Catholic bishop and historian, born Bogotá, Colombia, 1624, died Panama, 1688. A canon of the cathedral in Bogotá, he was elected capitular vicar in 1654 to look after the archdiocese in between archbishops. Accused of wrongdoing, he was sent to Spain for investigation, where he was finally cleared. He returned to America as a bishop. During his protracted stay in Spain, he wrote *Historia General de las conquistas del Nuevo Reino de Granada*. The first part, twelve volumes published in 1688, takes the history up until 1553. The second part was lost after his death.

Fernández Truyols, Andrés Jesuit Scripture scholar, born Manacor, Majorca, 15 December 1870, died Barcelona, 3 November 1961. Ordained in 1894, from 1909 he worked in Rome at the Pontifical Biblical Institute, becoming vice-rector, 1914–18, then rector, 1918–24. He helped to found an offshoot of the Institute in Jerusalem and worked there from 1929 to 1947, when he returned to Europe. He wrote extensively, his 11 books and 120 articles including biblical commentaries, a life of Christ and studies on Palestinian topography. He founded two periodicals: *Biblica* (1920–) and *Verbum Domini* (1921–). He proposed the theory of the *sensus plenior* in biblical hermeneutics.

Férotin, Marius Benedictine writer on the history of the liturgy, born Châteauneuf-du-Rhône, France, 18 November 1855, died Farnborough, England, 15 September 1914. Having become a monk at the monastery of Solesmes in France in 1876, he then lived at Silos, Spain, 1881–92, and at Farnborough, 1885–1914. He was a specialist on the Mozarabic liturgical rite as well as on the history of Spain. He wrote numerous studies in Spanish, French and Latin and collaborated on the *Dictionnaire de la Bible* and other publications. He made several important discoveries, notably identifying the author of the *Peregrinatio Aethriae* as the Spanish nun Aetheria (Egeria).

Ferrandus (of Carthage) Deacon, died before April 548, probably in Carthage. Little is known of Ferrandus, besides his position in the Church in Carthage, but his work *Breviatio canonum* is of historical interest, collating the rulings of the early Councils.

Ferrari, Bartolomeo   Venerable, co-founder of the Catholic Order of the Barnabites, born Milan, 1499, died there, 25 November 1544. He founded this Order with a friend, Anthony **Zaccaria**, with a mission to defend the Catholic faith against heresy and to work for moral reform. Helped by his brother, who worked at the papal court, he was able to obtain approval for his project from Pope **Clement VII** in 1533, with the bull *Vota per quae vos*. Ordained around 1532, he became general of his Order in 1542. He was declared venerable by Pope **Urban VIII** in 1634.

Ferraris, Lucio   Franciscan canonist, born Solero, Italy, died 1763. A prolific writer, Ferraris produced an impressive collation of religious knowledge, *Prompta Bibliotheca canonica, juridica, moralis, theologica, necnon ascetica, polemica, rubricistica, historica* (1746), and spent much of his life amending and adding to this work.

Ferrata, Domenico   Cardinal and papal diplomat, born Gradoli (Viterbo), 4 March 1847, died Rome, 10 October 1914. After first teaching canon law in Rome, he entered the papal diplomatic service in 1879. He held numerous posts during his career. He mediated between the cantons and dioceses in Switzerland, 1883–8. He was nuncio in Brussels in 1885 and Paris in 1891. He was made a cardinal in 1896. From 1899, he was prefect of four congregations one after the other and then, in 1913, secretary of the Holy Office (1913). He had recently been appointed secretary of state by Pope **Benedict XV** when he died.

Ferreira de Melo, José Bento Leite   Roman Catholic priest and politician, born Campanha, Brazil, 6 January 1785, died (assassinated) Pouso Alegre, Brazil, 8 February 1844. Ferreira entered the priesthood after originally intending to follow a career in the army. In 1821 he was elected to the provincial government, and subsequently became a national deputy. Politically radical, his vocal support for liberal principles made him one of the most prominent Brazilian politicians of his time. Inevitably his views aroused opposition, which ultimately led to his assassination at the hands of political enemies.

Ferreri, Zaccaria   Bishop, born Vicenza, Italy, *c.*1479, died Rome, before September 1524. He first joined the Benedictines and then the Carthusians but left the Order to become a supporter of the inchoate attempt to revive the conciliar movement, and was forced to take refuge in France when this was outmanoeuvred by **Julius II**'s calling of the Lateran Council of 1512. Following the accession of **Leo X**, Ferreri returned and was absolved. In 1519 he became bishop of Guardalfiera, and was also made a nuncio to Russia and Poland. Although never a supporter of Lutheranism, Ferreri was concerned by abuses in the Church and consistently argued for the necessity of reform.

Ferretti, Gabriele   Blessed, Franciscan, born Ancona, Italy, 1385, into the family of the counts of Ferretti, died in the convent of S. Francesco ad Alto, 9 November 1456. He became a member of the Friars Minor Observant in Ancona against the wishes of his family. He became guardian of the convent of S. Maria ad Alto in 1425, and was elected provincial *c.*1434. The minister general sent him to preach in Bosnia in 1438, but his brethren solicited **Eugenius IV** to release him from this post as they had need of his talents. He was in 1449 named guardian of S. Francesco ad Alto. Feast day 12 November.

Ferretti, Gabriele   Cardinal, born Ancona, Italy, 31 January 1795, died Rome, 13 September 1860. From a noble family, and related to **Pius IX**, Ferretti held a series of high ecclesiastical offices in the first half of the nineteenth century. He was created cardinal in 1839, and appointed secretary of state in 1847, but resigned after only a few months in office over a question of foreign policy. He eventually became cardinal-bishop of Sabina. Ferretti was a moderate liberal, but he tended to implement half-measures which satisfied nobody. Despite this he was generally respected by his contemporaries for his sincerity and piety.

Ferretti, Paolo Maria   Benedictine musicologist, born Subiaco, Italy, 3 December 1866, died Bologna, Italy, 23 May 1938. Ferretti became a Benedictine in 1884 and studied theology in Rome, subsequently becoming abbot of San Giovanni Evangelista in Parma. In 1913 he joined the faculty of the Scuola Superiore di Musica Sacra, and was appointed its president by **Pius XI** in 1922. Ferretti devoted his life to the study of Gregorian chant, on which he became an internationally recognized authority through his many publications.

Ferrini, Contardo Blessed, Italian Catholic university professor and writer, born Milan, Italy, 4 April 1859, died Suna (Novara), 17 October 1902. In 1881, he became a Franciscan tertiary and took a vow of celibacy. Having studied ancient classics and ancient law, he became professor of Roman law at Messina University in 1887, moving on to Modena and Pavia. He published a number of legal studies, notably on private and penal law in ancient Rome, as well as biographical reconstructions of the lives and work of several lawyers of that time. He was beatified on 13 April 1947. Feast day 17 October.

Fesch, Joseph Cardinal, born Ajaccio, Corsica, 3 January 1763, died Rome, 13 May 1839. As a young priest he arrived in France, serving under his kinsman, Napoleon Bonaparte in the Italian army. Ordained archbishop of Lyons in 1802, and made cardinal in 1803; he was instrumental in having Napoleon crowned, and later worked to minimize his nephew's political estrangement from the Church, with limited success. Fesch was instrumental in recalling the Jesuits and the Brothers of Christian Doctrine. His loyalty to the pontiff eventually caused him to lose favour with Napoleon, and he ended his days in Rome.

Fessler, Joseph Bishop and secretary of Vatican Council I, born Lochau, near Bregenz, in the Vorarlburg, 2 December 1813, died St Pölten, 25 April 1872. Studied at Feldkirch, Innsbruck and Brixen and was ordained priest in 1837. He was professor of ecclesiastical history and canon law at the theological school in Brixen from 1841 to 1852 and professor of canon law at the University of Vienna from 1856 to 1861. He became assistant bishop of Brixen in 1862 and bishop of St Pölten, near Vienna, in 1864. In 1867 he was named assistant at the papal throne and two years later was appointed to oversee preparations for the forthcoming Vatican Council, and to be secretary to it. He had written an earlier book on provincial councils and diocesan synods (1849) and now published his *Das letzte und das nächste allgemein*

Konzil (1869). After the Council he became embroiled in the discussions on papal infallibility and wrote *Die wahre und die falsche Unfehlbarkeit der Päpste* (1871) in response to an attack by Dr Schulte of Prague University. It presents a moderate view and was approved of at least by **Pius IX**. Fessler's other writings include the two-volume *Institutiones Patrologiae quas ad frequentiorem SS Patrum lectionem promovendam concinnavit J. Fessler* (1850–1).

Festa, Costanza Composer, born Rome, c.1490, died there, 10 April 1545. He is especially remembered as the composer of the first Italian madrigals. His works of sacred music include Masses, motets, hymns, *Magnificats* and a *Te Deum* still sung at the Vatican in the twentieth century. He is believed to have been composer to the French King **Louis XII** early in his career, because he is mentioned by **Rabelais** in his *Quart Livre* and four of his works are included in the French Codex Medici. He influenced the style of **Palestrina** and composed music in most of the forms current during the Renaissance.

Fetis, François Joseph Composer, historian, born Mons (Belgium), 25 March 1784, died Brussels, 26 March 1871. He studied at the Paris Conservatoire, and then stayed on there as librarian until 1833, when he was appointed director of the newly established Brussels Conservatoire. A distinguished musician and writer, his most significant written work was *A General History of Music*.

Févin, Antoine de French Renaissance composer and singer, born Arras(?), France, c.1470, died Blois, 1511 or 1512. Attached to the chapel of **Louis XII**, his many elegant compositions include 10 Masses, about 30 motets as well as 17 chansons, which the king thought the best of their kind. His graceful melodies and contrasting voice parts have been compared to the music of **Josquin des Prez**, his better-known contemporary. Josquin actually used two of Févin's motets as bases for some of his own compositions. Variously called 'gentil Févin' and 'felix Jodoci [Josquin] aemulator', he was appreciated by **Rabelais** and is an important precursor of later French court music.

Fey, Clara Foundress of the Sisters of the Poor

Child Jesus, born Aachen, Germany, 11 April 1815, died Simpelveld, The Netherlands, 8 May 1894. Fey founded her religious order in 1844, consolidating a work first begun in 1837 when she and several others had opened a school for poor children. Despite poor health she continued to work as superior general of the Order until her death. During the Kulturkampf of **Bismarck** the community was forced to leave Germany, and was re-established in The Netherlands.

Ficino, Marsilio Philosopher and priest, born Figline, near Florence, 19 October 1433, died Careggi, near Florence, 1 October 1499. The banker Cosimo de' **Medici** commissioned Ficino to translate all the texts then attributed to Plato, though the idea of a formal Platonic academy at Cosimo's villa at Careggi is inaccurate. Ficino's Platonic philosophy is best expounded in the *Theologia Platonica de immortalitate animae* (Platonic theology concerning the immortality of the soul, 1469–74), **Lefèvre** and **Colet** being among those influenced by it. A work on astrology and white magic, *De triplici vita* (On the threefold life, 1489), was condemned by the Church.

Figliucci, Felix Dominican humanist theologian, born Siena, 4 May 1518, died there, 28 April 1584. Figliucci studied philosophy at Padua, served on the staff of Cardinal del Monte (later Pope **Julius III**) and attended the Council of Trent. Writing mainly in Italian, during his lifetime his reputation as a scholar was considerable, and he wrote (or translated) a large number of books.

Figueiredo, Jackson de Roman Catholic writer and lay activist, born Aracajú, Brazil, 9 October 1891, died Rio de Janeiro, Brazil, 4 November 1928. In his student days Figueiredo rebelled against the Catholicism in which he had been brought up and was a leader in an anarchistic and anticlericalist movement. He subsequently became reconciled to the Church, and thereafter sought to encourage Christian ideals through his writings, principally through the journal *A Ordem*, which he founded in 1921.

Filaret (Vasily Mikhailovich Drozdov) Russian Orthodox metropolitan, born Kolomna, near Moscow, 26 December 1782, died Moscow, 19 November 1867. Ordained to the priesthood in 1809, he was appointed rector of St Petersburg Theological Academy in 1812 and member of the Holy Synod in 1819. In 1821 he became archbishop of Moscow, and in 1826 he was made metropolitan of Moscow. In 1842, the Holy Synod banned Filaret from participation in its activities because of disputes over his project of a translation of the Bible into Russian. A wealth of his work has been published; his most significant writing is his *Longer Catechism* (1823).

Filelfo, Francesco Scholar, born Toltentino, 25 July 1398, died Florence, 31 July 1481. A brilliant scholar in rhetoric, eloquence, languages and moral philosophy, Filelfo taught philosophy in Padua and Venice, before travelling to Constantinople, where he married. After a series of diplomatic posts, he taught in Florence, but was forced to leave there in 1434 after conflicts with Cosimo d' **Medici**. In Milan, he was honoured by Filippo Maria Visconti. In 1474 he went to Rome to teach, but left after conflicts with Pope **Sixtus IV**, eventually returning to Florence, dying soon after his return. A collection of his prose was published as *Convivia Mediolanensia*.

Filippini, Lucy Saint, born Tuscany, Italy, 13 January 1672, died Montefiascone, Italy, 25 March 1732. An orphaned, highly gifted child, Lucy was found as a young girl by Cardinal **Barbarigo**, explaining the faith to crowds in the marketplace in Corneto. He took her to be raised and instructed by the Poor Clares in Montefiascone. As an adult, she founded places of Christian education for girls and women across Italy, including one in Rome at the request of Pope **Clement XI**. She is buried at the cathedral in Montefiascone. Feast day 25 March.

Filippucci, Alessandro Francesco Saverio Jesuit missionary, born Macerata, Italy, 5 January 1632, died Macao, China, 15 August 1692. Filippucci became a Jesuit in 1651 and sailed as a missionary to China in 1660. He worked in Macao until 1671, and then in Kwantung Province, where his residence was destroyed in an uprising. From 1680 to 1683 he was provincial for Japan, and from 1684 to 1688 superior in Canton, subsequently becoming visitor to the Chinese and Japanese missions.

Filippucci defended the Jesuits in the Chinese rites controversy, and collected many letters of **Francis Xavier**, which were later included in standard editions of his works.

Fillastre, Guillaume Cardinal, born La Suze, Maine, *c.*1348, died Rome, 6 November 1428. When the French Crown and the Sorbonne sought to resolve the papal schism by rejecting **Benedict XIII** at the 1406 Synod of Paris, the canon lawyer Fillastre defended the Antipope, claiming that princes did not have the right to judge Church affairs and that General Councils have no authority over Popes. **John XXIII** made him a cardinal in 1411, but was rejected by Fillastre when the latter became a conciliarist. **Martin V** sent him on diplomatic missions to France and made him archpriest of S. Giovanni in Laterano.

Fillastre, Guillaume Benedictine and bishop, born *c.*1400, died Ghent, 21 August 1473. Nephew of the elder **Fillastre**, he had been prior or abbot of various houses before obtaining his doctorate from Louvain in 1436. He was successively bishop of Verdun, 1437–49, Toul, 1449–60 and Tournai, 1460–73. When the citizens of Toul refused to recognize his temporal authority he placed them under an interdict, but **Nicholas V** considered this too severe. A close adviser of Philip the Good and Charles the Bold, dukes of Burgundy, he was chancellor of the Order of the Golden Fleece from 1462 and delivered Philip's funeral oration in 1467.

Fillion, Louis Claude Roman Catholic biblical scholar, born Saint-Bonnet-de-Joux, France, 25 June 1843, died Issy, France, 12 October 1927. Following ordination in 1867, Fillion became a Sulpician and held academic appointments in Rheims and Lyons before being appointed professor at the Institut Catholique in Paris. In 1903 he was appointed a consultor of the Pontifical Biblical Commission. He wrote numerous articles and books on various biblical themes, a number of which were written with non-academics in mind.

Finan of Lindisfarne Saint, abbot, bishop, died 9 February 661. The Irish monk succeeded St **Aidan** to the See of Lindisfarne in 651 and, according to St **Bede**, engaged in missionary activity in Northumbria. His baptism of Paeda, a prince of Mercia,

and Sigbert or Sigebert, ruler of the East Saxons, led to a strong Christian presence in those kingdoms. He favoured Celtic customs and the Irish method of calculating Easter over traditions emerging from Rome. Feast day 9 February.

Fink, Louis Mary (Michael) Benedictine bishop, born Triftersberg, Germany, 12 July 1834, died Kansas City, USA, 17 March 1904. Fink left his native Germany *c.*1850 to settle in America. He became a Benedictine in 1854 and was ordained in 1857. He served as priest in a number of parishes before becoming prior of St Benedict's Priory in Atchison, Kansas, in 1868. Subsequently Fink was made bishop of Kansas when the diocese was established in 1877. In what was then an unruly frontier town, Fink helped bring stability by establishing Christian mission centres, and by encouraging Catholic settlements in the area. He was acutely aware of the problems of the working classes, many of whom were Catholic immigrants, and supported trade unions and improvements in working conditions.

Finn, Francis James Jesuit priest, novelist, born St Louis, USA, October 1859, died Ohio, 2 November 1928. He joined the Jesuits in 1877 and, after teaching at boys' schools in Kansas and Ohio, he was ordained in 1893. He continued to teach in Cincinnati. He founded a free school and served as a pastor in later years. He wrote many stories for Catholic boys. Among his popular titles were *Percy Wynn*, *Tom Playfair*, *His Luckiest Year*, and *Sunshine and Freckles*.

Finney, Charles Grandison Evangelist, born Connecticut, USA, 29 August 1792, died 16 August 1875. Finney left a legal career and was ordained by New York's Presbytery of Oneida in 1824. While travelling as a revivalist preacher, he joined Oberlin College, Ohio, as professor of theology, and converted to Congregationalism in 1837. In 1851 he became the college president, still travelling to preach at revival meetings. He is credited with transforming revivalism in the USA. Among his writings are *Lectures on Revivals of Religion* and *Lectures on Systematic Theology*.

Finnian of Clonard Saint, monk, born *c.*470, possibly at Idrone, County Carlow, Ireland, died Clonard, c.549–52, probably on 12 December. A great biblical scholar, Finnian founded a number of monasteries in Ireland, including Clonard, in County Meath, which was known for its strength of biblical training. He is often referred to as a bishop but this seems unlikely. Among his students were SS **Columba**, Ciaran of Clommacnois and **Brendan of Clonfert**. It seems likely that he wrote *The Penitential of Finnian*, although **Finnian of Moville** has also been suggested as its author. Feast day 12 December.

Finnian of Moville Saint, abbot, born Ireland c.495, died 579. After studying with SS Colman of Dromore and Mochaw of Noendrum, he founded a monastery at Bromin, in Louth, and another at Moville, in County Down, where his students included St **Columba**. He may have written *The Penitential of Finnian*, although **Finnian of Clonard** seems the more likely author. Feast day 10 September.

Finotti, Joseph Mary Jesuit priest, author, born Ferrara, Italy, 21 September 1817, died Central City, Colorado, 10 January 1879. After joining the Jesuits in 1833, he went to Maryland, USA, in 1845 and was ordained in Georgetown, District of Columbia, in 1847. He ministered in Maryland and Virginia until 1852, then went to Massachusetts. He edited the Catholic journal *The Pilot* and served as a pastor there until 1876, when he went to Nebraska, then Colorado. Among his writings are *Life of Blessed Paul of the Cross*, *Month of Mary*, and, best known, the incomplete *Bibliographica Catholica Americana*.

Fintan of Clonenagh Saint, abbot, born Leinster, c.524, died 17 February, probably in 603, though 594 has also been suggested. Taught by St Columba of Terryglass, he founded a monastery in Clonenagh, where students of his austere discipline included St **Comgall** of Bangor. When soldiers came to his monastery bearing the heads of their enemies, he is reported to have had them buried in the monks' cemetery in order that the monks might pray for them. Feast day 17 February.

Fintan of Rheinau Saint, hermit, born Leinster, died 879. After being abducted as a slave by Viking raiders, the young Fintan escaped by swimming

from the Orkneys to Scotland, where he was sheltered by a bishop. After making a pilgrimage to Rome, he went to the Benedictine abbey in Sabina, then travelled to an island on the Rhine, near Schlaffhausen. There he joined a group of Irish hermits and remained there until his death. A missal, believed to have belonged to him, is preserved at St Gall Library. Feast day 15 November.

Fintan of Taghmon (Munnu, Mundus) Saint, abbot, died Taghmon, or Teach Munnu, County Wexford in 635. A monk for eighteen years, he travelled to join the Iona Community, but was told St **Columba** had left word before his death instructing him to found an abbey of his own instead. He did so in Taghmon. At the Synod of Magh Lene in 630, he sought to retain Celtic liturgical rituals, but the decision to adopt the Roman liturgy prevailed. Feast day 21 October.

Finzgar, Franc Saleski Roman Catholic priest and writer, born Doslovice (Slovenia), 9 February 1871, died Ljubljana (Slovenia), 2 June 1962. Ordained in 1894, Finzgar served as a parish priest until his retirement in 1936. He began writing poetry as a young man, and continued his literary activities in parallel with his parochial ministry. He went on to write several novels and plays which have established him as one of the leading Slovene writers of the early twentieth century. In his writings Finzgar frequently drew on his own experiences, notably his portrayal of the exploitation of factory workers, which he had encountered while a priest in an industrial parish.

Firmian, Leopold Anton Eleutherius Roman Catholic archbishop, born Munich, Germany, 27 May 1679, died Salzburg, Austria, 22 October 1744. He held a variety of ecclesiastical appointments before being appointed archbishop of Salzburg in 1727. He enabled the Jesuits to establish a number of retreat and mission houses in his diocese, and in 1731 issued an edict which ejected Protestants from it, causing over 20,000 to leave.

Firmian, Leopold Ernst Cardinal, born Trent, Italy, 22 September 1708, died Passau, Germany, 13 March 1783. Nephew of Leopold Anton **Firmian**, he became bishop of Passau in 1763, and was made a cardinal in 1772. He supported missions for the laity and was concerned to improve the education of the clergy.

Firmian, Leopold Max Roman Catholic archbishop, born Trent, Italy, 11 October 1766, died Vienna, Austria, 29 November 1831. He became archbishop of Vienna in 1822, prior to which he held appointments elsewhere in Austria and Germany.

Firmicus Maternus, Julius Rhetorician and writer, died *c.*351. Probably of Sicilian origin and aristocratic blood, he was converted to Christianity as an adult. Prior to his conversion, he produced the *Mathesis*, a learned eight-book moralizing treatise on astrology. His most significant text as a Christian is his *On the Error of the Profane Religions*, produced at Rome around 347, appealing to **Constantius II** and **Constans I** to destroy pagan idols with violent zeal. A sole medieval codex of the work was discovered at Minden in the sixteenth century.

Firmilian Bishop and saint, died Tarsus, 268, bishop of Caesarea from *c.*230. He was educated at the feet of **Origen** in both Cappadocia and Palestine. He supported St **Cyprian** against Pope **Stephen I** in his contention that those who had lapsed had to be rebaptized on their return to the Church; a letter by him on this theme survives in Cyprian's correspondence. In 264 he was in charge of the first of the Synods of Antioch held to investigate the views of **Paul of Samosata**; he died *en route* to the second. Feast day 28 October in the East.

Firmin of Amiens Bishop of Amiens, martyr and saint, died *c.*303. Very little is known of his life, except that he was possibly a native of Pamplona, who was converted and became a missionary bishop, traditionally the first bishop of Amiens; he was martyred there during the Great Persecution. A later bishop, Firmin the Confessor (with whom he is often confused), built the church of St Acheul over his tomb. His relics were translated to Pamplona in 1186. Feast day 25 September.

Fischer, Johann Kaspar Ferdinand Composer and musician, born Germany, *c.*1650, died Rastatt, Germany, 27 March 1746(?). Apart from the fact

that he is known to have been music director for the margrave of Baden in the late seventeenth century, no details of Fischer's life are known. His musical compositions, consisting of both sacred and secular works, are written in the late baroque style of Lully, and helped to popularize this style in Germany.

Fischer von Erlach, Johann Bernhard Austrian architect, born Graz, 20 July 1656, died Vienna, 5 April 1723. Von Erlach trained in the baroque tradition in Italy and became one of the great masters. His highly ornamented structures feature high transepts and oval-shaped cupolas, and include Salzburg's Collegiate Church and Vienna's St Charles Borromeo. In later years his strong Italian style was moderated by French neoclassicism, as shown in the Hofbibliothek in Vienna, considered one of his finest works.

Fisher, Geoffrey Francis Anglican archbishop, born Higham-on-the-Hill, near Leicester, England, 5 May 1887, died Sherborne, 17 September 1972. He became bishop of Chester in 1932 and was translated to London in 1939, where he concerned himself with the Churches' Main War Damage Committee. He became archbishop of Canterbury in 1945 and was committed to ecumenism. He met with the patriarchs of Constantinople and Jerusalem and with Pope **John XXIII**, as well as giving autonomy to the Church communities in Africa and Asia. A high point of his period in office was the coronation of Queen Elizabeth II. He worked towards the revision of the Anglican canon law, and retired in 1961.

Fisher, John Saint, bishop, theologian and martyr, born Beverley, Yorkshire, 1469, died London, 22 June 1535. He was educated at Cambridge, ordained priest in 1491 and gained the patronage of Lady Margaret **Beaufort**, whose confessor he became in 1497, encouraging her patronage of the University of Cambridge, where she founded a chair of divinity in 1503 and Christ's College in 1505. St John's, its sister college, was supervised by Fisher in 1511 and Fisher persuaded **Erasmus** to lecture in Greek there 1511–14. He became president of Queens' College as well as chancellor of the University and, in 1504, bishop of Rochester. Although he strongly opposed the teachings of

Martin **Luther** he was a dedicated and scholarly humanist and not opposed to moderate reforms in the Church. He became confessor to Queen **Catherine of Aragon** in 1529 and opposed **Henry VIII**'s attempts to divorce her as well as his title of Supreme Head of the Church in England and the Supremacy Act of 1534. He was condemned for not reporting the subversive prophecies of Elizabeth **Barton** and for his refusal to take the Oath required by the Act of Succession and was imprisoned in the Tower with Thomas **More**. In 1535, to the additional fury of Henry VIII, Pope **Paul III** created Fisher cardinal. He was put on trial, condemned for treason and beheaded on Tower Hill. Fisher's theological work on the real presence in the Eucharist later influenced the Fathers at the Council of Trent. His complete Latin *Opera* were first published in 1597 at Würzburg. Some of his works against Luther, *Assertionis Lutheranae confutatio* (1523), and a body of vernacular sermons, especially one on the Penitential Psalms (1508), were published in England. **Pius XI** canonized Fisher and More in 1935. Feast day 9 July.

Fishta, Gjergj Franciscan priest, poet and statesman, born Fishta, Albania, 23 October 1871, died Shkoder, Albania, 30 December 1940. From a family of farmers, Fishta was educated by Franciscans, joining them himself in 1887. Ordained in 1894, he taught in a seminary and then briefly worked as a parish priest before returning to teaching. Fishta was a keen student of Albanian culture, and in 1912 he founded a cultural magazine which he edited until his death. His own poetry is of considerable merit, and often reflects the traditional lyric style of Albanian folksong. Fishta also took an active role in Albanian politics; in 1921 he became vice-president of the Albanian parliament, representing Albania at many international conferences during the 1920s, and was internationally honoured by numerous awards.

Fitch, William Benedict Capuchin friar, also known as 'Benedict Canfield' or 'William Fitch of Little Canfield' in Essex, was born there in 1563 and died in the Capuchin house in Paris, 21 November 1611. He was a student of law in the Middle Temple but went to Douai to become a priest and then joined the Capuchins in Paris in 1586. He was sent to the English mission in 1589 but was imprisoned for his faith for three years. Fitch wrote general devotional works and became master of novices in Rouen. He was admired as a preacher, both in English and French.

Fitton, James Roman Catholic priest, missionary, born Boston, Massachusetts, 10 April 1805, died Boston, 15 September 1901. Ordained in 1827, he travelled throughout New England on missionary activities, served as a pastor, and built a church in Rhode Island, and in 1840 founded an education facility for young Catholic men in Worcester, Massachusetts. He continued his pastoral and missionary activities, building four more churches before his death. He deeded the college to Bishop Benedict **Fenwick** of Boston in 1842, who gave its responsibility to the Jesuits. It would eventually become Holy Cross College.

Fitzalan, Henry Twelfth earl of Arundel and godson of King **Henry VIII**, after whom he was named and whom he accompanied to France in 1532, born *c.*1511, died London, 24 February 1579. He was governor of Calais, 1540–3, made Knight of the Garter in 1544 and Lord Chamberlain of England, an office he retained under **Edward VI** though alternately disloyal to Warwick and to Somerset. He supported **Mary Tudor** in secret but openly raised the City of London against Northumberland, who attempted to subvert the succession of the Catholic Mary to the throne in favour of Lady Jane Grey and her male heirs. On Mary's succession Arundel became lord steward of the household and a member of the Privy Council, offices which he retained at the accession of **Elizabeth I**. She made him chancellor of Oxford University in 1559. He resigned his lord stewardship in 1564 and was rapidly out of favour at court and rarely attended the Council. Arundel led a Catholic party which aimed at deposing Elizabeth, marrying Mary Stuart (Queen of Scots) to the duke of Norfolk and ousting the Cecil faction, which had developed an aggressive policy towards Spain. By 1572, however, the duke of Norfolk was in the Tower on multiple charges of treason and Arundel put under house arrest. He was restored briefly to the Council by Leicester's influence. With the discovery of the Ridolfi Plot, in which he was implicated, Arundel was imprisoned.

Fitzalan-Howard, Bernard Marmaduke Sixteenth duke of Norfolk, earl marshal and hereditary marshal of England born Arundel Castle, Sussex, 30 May 1908, died Arundel, 31 January 1975. He was educated at the Oratory School, Birmingham, but failed responsions for his place at Christ Church, Oxford. He succeeded to the title in 1917. He joined the Sussex Regiment in 1928, and saw active service in France. His official duties as the premier duke and hereditary marshal entailed masterminding state occasions: the funeral of King George V in 1936, the coronation of George VI originally intended for Edward VIII, the coronation of Elizabeth II in 1953, the funeral of Winston Churchill, and the investiture of the Prince of Wales at Caernarfon in 1969. In parallel with these duties he was the official spokesman for the Catholic laity of England. In 1970 he participated in the canonization of the **Forty Martyrs of England and Wales** including his ancestor St Philip **Howard**.

Fitzalan-Howard, Henry Fifteenth duke of Norfolk, eldest son of Henry Granville **Fitzalan-Howard**, born London, 27 December 1847, died there 11 November 1917. He succeeded his father at the age of thirteen. He was educated at the Oratory School, Birmingham, and since Oxbridge was then not open to Catholics Henry was sent abroad to travel. At Constantinople he resided with his uncle Lord Lyons, who had a formative influence on him. As a member of the House of Lords he was indefatigable on educational matters. Throughout his life he maintained close relations with the Vatican. He presided over the coronations of Edward VII in 1902 and George V in 1911. A great builder of churches he was passionately devoted to the Gothic style and flamboyant stained glass. The chapel at Arundel Castle is one of his notable monuments.

Fitzalan-Howard, Henry Granville Fourteenth duke of Norfolk, born 7 November 1815 in London, educated privately and at Trinity College, Cambridge, died Arundel Castle, 25 November 1860 at the age of 45. He represented Arundel in Parliament from 1837 to 1850 and Limerick from 1850 to 1852. He opposed the Ecclesiastical Titles Bill in 1850 and became the friend and confidant of Count **Montalembert**, who became his biographer. The duke published much on the condition of British Catholics in 1847 as well as Lives of Philip **Howard**, earl of Arundel, and of Anne Dacres, his wife. At his death in 1860 Cardinal **Wiseman** published a panegyric on the duke emphasizing his extensive alms and charities in the liberal way he administered his vast patrimony. Montalembert called him 'the most pious layman of our times'.

Fitzgerald, Edward Roman Catholic bishop, born Limerick, Ireland, 28 October 1833, died Arkansas, USA, 21 February 1907. Brought to the USA in 1849, he was ordained priest in 1857, and began pastoral work. Ordained bishop of Little Rock, Arkansas, in 1866, he voted against papal infallibility at the First Vatican Council and participated in the Third Plenary Council in Baltimore. He supported Catholic school education, the growth of religious orders, immigration, and the first African-American church in his diocese, until, suffering from poor health, he resigned in 1906.

Fitzgerald, John Roman Catholic businessman, statesman, born c.1739, died Virginia, USA, 2 December 1799. After settling in Alexandria, Virginia, Fitzgerald served in the American Civil War as a soldier and secretary to George Washington. After being wounded, he turned his attention to politics and was mayor of Alexandria, 1792–4. He assisted in raising funds towards the building of Alexandria's first Roman Catholic church, St Mary's, and continued to serve in various official capacities in Alexandria until his death.

Fitzgibbon, Mary Irene Roman Catholic social worker, born London, England, 11 May 1823, died New York City, 14 August 1896. After emigrating to the USA with her family at the age of nine, Catherine Fitzgibbon entered the Sisters of Charity in 1850 and took the name 'Mary Irene'. After teaching for a few years she was made responsible for the care of the abandoned children often left at the convent. This was to be her ministry for the rest of her life; she founded the New York Foundling Asylum (later Hospital) in 1869, of which she was the superior, and the organization she developed over the next 27 years was eventually caring for some 100,000 children. It had expanded to include a maternity hospital, a children's convalescent home, a TB clinic, and a day nursery for working mothers.

Fitzpatrick, Edward Augustus Roman Catholic writer and educationalist, born New York City, 29 August 1884, died Milwaukee, 13 September 1960. Fitzpatrick taught in high schools in New York before becoming an education administrator in Wisconsin. Subsequently he held senior appointments at a number of universities and colleges in that state. He wrote for or edited a number of educational journals, and his philosophy of education was deeply influenced by his own Christian faith.

Fitzpatrick, John Clement Roman Catholic archivist, historian, born Washington, DC, 10 August 1876, died Washington, 10 February 1940. Much of his archival work took place at the Library of Congress, where he worked as an assistant chief and then acting chief of the manuscripts division. He edited a nine-volume collection of the works of George Washington, was president of the American Catholic Historical Society, and was involved in the reintroduction of the military award, the Purple Heart. His *Notes on the Care, Cataloguing, Calendaring, and Arranging of Manuscripts* remained the main authoritative manual for archivists for over twenty years.

Fitzpatrick, Thomas Bernard Roman Catholic businessman and philanthropist, born Grafton, USA, 17 December 1844, died Boston, 15 January 1919. From starting at a junior level, Fitzpatrick rose to become president of Brown, Durrell and Company, then one of the largest business corporations in the eastern USA. An Irish-Catholic, his financial backing helped establish many Catholic hospitals, schools and orphanages. Fitzpatrick's philanthropy was recognized in 1905 when Notre Dame University awarded him its Laetare Medal.

Fitzsimon, Henry Jesuit missionary and theologian, born Dublin, 31 May 1566, died Kilkenny, Ireland, 29 November 1643. At first an ardent Protestant while at Hart Hall, Oxford, but converted to Catholicism by Thomas Darbyshire and admitted to the Society of Jesus in 1592, he later held the chair of philosophy at the English College, Douai. In the 1590s he became an energetic missionary in Dublin openly conducting services. Adam Loftus, Protestant archbishop of Dublin, regarded Fitzsimon with particular disfavour and had him arrested, examined and imprisoned, 1599–1604. Fitzsimon appears to have admitted the illegality of Queen **Elizabeth I**'s excommunication but at the same time 'making lewd and frivolous distinctions'. Even in prison he continued his preaching and disputing with James **Ussher** and other Protestant divines. After release under **James I** he spent some time in Spain, Flanders and Rome and became a chaplain to the army in Bohemia in 1620 – he wrote a history of that campaign. He returned to Ireland in 1630. In Rome he had written *Words of Comfort to Persecuted Catholics* (1607) and other minor and devotional works.

Flacius Illyricus, Matthias Lutheran theologian, born Albona, on the south-east of Istria (hence the Latinized form of his name 'Illyricus' – his surname was 'Vlacich', Latinized in 'Flacius'), 3 March 1520, died Frankfurt am Main, 11 March 1575. The nephew of a Franciscan executed for Reformation sympathies, he studied alongside radical Lutheran reformers at Wittenberg (and became professor of Hebrew there, 1544–9) and while there came into contact with Martin **Luther**, coming to think of himself in later years as the true upholder of Lutheran doctrine. His strongly held beliefs, and his argumentative nature, meant he did not stay long in any academic post. He came into conflict with **Melanchthon** and others over conciliation with Roman Catholics. His writings include *Catalogus Testium Veritatis* and *Clavis Scripturae Sacrae*, though he is best known for his history of the Church, the *Magdeburg Centuries* (1559–74).

Flanagan, Edward Joseph Roman Catholic priest, born Ireland, 13 July 1886, died Berlin, 15 May 1948. After emigrating to the USA, he was ordained in 1912. He ministered in parishes in Nebraska, and founded a homeless men's refuge in 1913. In 1917 he established a tiny nondenominational orphanage in Omaha. Eventually this would become a large, self-governing village, known as Boys' Town. Boys' Towns were established in many countries and continue to serve boys all over the world today.

Flavia Domitilla Imperial Roman matron, regarded since the fourth century as a martyr and saint, died *c.*100. Daughter of the Emperor Vespasian, she was married to Domitian's cousin, Titus Flavius Clemens. Domitian banished her to the island of Pandateria when he executed Clemens in 95. According to the Roman historian Cassius Dio, she (like her husband) was accused of 'atheism', which may or may not imply Christian belief. **Eusebius of Caesarea** says she suffered as a Christian; similar claims for her husband were not made until the early ninth century. The cemetery of Domitilla on the Via Ardeatina outside Rome was used as a Christian burial-ground. Feast day 12 May.

Flavian of Constantinople Patriarch and saint, died Hypaepa, Lydia, 449. Patriarch of Constantinople 446–9, in 448 he excommunicated the archimandrite **Eutyches** for heresy concerning the person of Christ. In August 449, under imperial pressure, the decision was reversed, and Flavian and other bishops were deposed at a council in Ephesus. The Roman legates to the meeting, who had brought a Tome from Pope **Leo I** in support of Flavian, were physically attacked – Leo described the gathering as a 'Robber Synod' (*Latrocinium*). Flavian died not long after the council, probably from similar maltreatment. His remains were brought to Constantinople by the Empress Pulcheria, and he was vindicated and declared a martyr at the Council of Chalcedon in 451. Three of his letters are preserved among the works of Leo. Feast days 16/17/18 February and 12 November in the East, 18 February in the West.

Fleming, Patrick Franciscan priest, born County Louth, Ireland, 17 April 1599, died Benesabe, Bohemia, 7 November 1631. Christopher Fleming joined the Franciscans in 1617, taking the name 'Patrick', and was ordained in Rome. In 1630 he became founding superior of a Franciscan seminary in Prague, but fled the city when the elector of Saxony threatened Catholics there. Outside the city he and his deacon were confronted and murdered by a band of Lutherans. Two of his works of Irish Catholic history were published after his death as *Collectanea Sacra*. The case for his canonization was opened in 1903.

Fleming, Thomas Franciscan, archbishop, born 1593, died 1655. After being ordained a priest, he taught at the Franciscan College of Louvain. In 1623, he was appointed archbishop of Dublin. He sided with the Confederates during the Confederate War, and opposed Old Irish interests. He and other prelates helped bring about a brief reconciliation with Ormond in 1649. He was subject to such severe persecution by the **Cromwell** government that after his death, a successor could not be appointed until 1669.

Flemming (Flemying), Robert Dean of Lincoln Cathedral, co-founder with his uncle Bishop Richard Flemming of Lincoln College, Oxford, and early Renaissance scholar, born probably at Lincoln, died there 1483. He was chosen dean of Lincoln in 1451, but the chapter being in dispute with the bishop of Lincoln, Robert went to Italy in pursuit of learning among the celebrated scholars and universities, particularly in Padua, Florence and Rome. He formed a firm friendship with the librarian of the Vatican, **Platina**, famous for his *Lives of the Popes*. Pope **Sixtus IV** favoured Flemming as a diplomat in the then complicated affairs of the Holy See. He returned to England in 1465 and donated his collection of translations, writings and manuscripts to Lincoln College. He then became prebend of Leighton Manor in Lincoln Cathedral.

Flesch, Rosa Franciscan religious, born Schönstatt, Germany, 24 February 1826, died Waldbreitbach, Germany, 25 March 1906. In her youth Margarete Flesch claimed to have experienced visions. In 1851 she and some companions began charitable works and ten years later began to build a convent. She took religious vows in 1863, with the name 'Rosa', and then established a hospital at Waldbreitbach. Known as the Sisters of Our Lady of the Angels, her congregation was given episcopal approval in 1869. During the Franco-Prussian War she cared for the wounded, even on the battlefield, as a result of which she herself was wounded. Within a few years the community had twenty-one houses, but Flesch was removed as superior general in 1878, and for the rest of her life was forced to serve in a menial capacity.

Fletcher, John William Evangelical Anglican and

Methodist theologian, born Nyon, Switzerland, 11 September 1729, died Madeley, 14 August 1785. His original name was 'de la Fléchière'. Educated in Geneva, he came to England in about 1750 and worked as a private tutor. Having met the Methodists, he had an evangelical conversion in 1754. In 1757 he was ordained as deacon and priest, becoming the vicar of Madeley in Shropshire. In 1768 he was appointed as superintendent of Lady Huntingdon's College at Trevecka near Brecon, resigning three years later. He became an intimate friend of John **Wesley** and was designated as his successor. He was a leading advocate of the doctrine of Christian Perfection. His writings include his *Checks to Antinomianism* (1771).

Flete, William Augustinian friar, mystic, died *c*.1383, perhaps in Lecceto, Italy, perhaps in England. The Cambridge-educated monk left England for a stricter discipline in Italy, and settled in Lecceto, near Siena, with others of his Order. He became a great friend of St **Catherine of Siena**. He was invited to Rome by Pope **Urban VI** to assist during the papal schisms, but declined. He wrote several unpublished manuscripts, including a eulogy to St Catherine, which survives in the public library in Siena, and a treatise on temptation, a copy of which survives in the university library at Cambridge.

Fleury, André-Hercule de Cardinal, born Lodève, 26 June 1653, died Paris, 29 January 1743. A student of Cardinal de Bonzi, he was ordained bishop of Fréjus in 1698. He resigned his see in 1715 to tutor Louis XV. After the young king came of age, he gave control of the government to Fleury, which he retained until his death. He was appointed cardinal in 1726 and was a key figure against the Jansenists in France.

Fleury, Claude Priest and Church historian, born in Paris, 6 December 1640, died there, 14 July 1723. Educated by the Jesuits, he first studied and practised law. Ordained in 1669, he taught in the royal household, and was appointed commendatory abbot at Loc-Dieu in Aveyron. A friend of both **Bossuet** and **Fénelon**, he played a conciliatory role in the Quietism controversy, and was confessor to Louis XV. A prolific writer, his most significant work was *Histoire ecclésiastique*, a

twenty-volume history of the Church to the year 1414.

Fliche, Augustin French Church historian, born Montpellier, 19 November 1884, died there, 20 November 1951. Studied in Paris and was professor of medieval history at Montpellier from 1919 until 1946. He was a member of the Académie des Inscriptions et Belles-lettres from 1941 until his death. His dissertation was on the reign of Philip I of France and was published in 1912. He made a study of **Gregory VII** and the Gregorian reform and his *Polémique religieuse à l'époque de Grégoire VII* was published in 1914, followed by *Les Prégrégoriens* (1916), *St Grégoire VII* (1920) and the three-volume *La Réforme grégorienne* (1924–7). His largest project, however, which he edited in co-operation with Victor **Martin**, was the *Histoire de l'Église depuis les origines jusqu'à nos jours*. The first of the fifteen volumes he edited appeared in 1934. He also wrote for learned journals and lectured throughout Europe.

Flick, Lawrence Francis Doctor of medicine, born Pennsylvania, USA, 10 August 1856, died Philadelphia, USA, 7 July 1938. Shortly after receiving his medical degree in 1879, Flick was diagnosed with tuberculosis, and in his bid to cure himself pioneered research of and treatment for the disease. He founded institutions for the care of sufferers, including the poor and African Americans. A Catholic and an avid historian, he also founded the American Catholic Historical Society and the American Catholic Historical Association. He wrote several medical texts on tuberculosis, as well as *The Study of History from a Christian Point of View*.

Flodoard of Rheims Historian, born Épernay, France, 894, died Rheims, 28 March 966. He was loyal to the politically embattled Archbishop Arthold, who took him in his entourage to Rome, where he was ordained in 936 by Pope **Leo VII**. He was rewarded by being made archivist in the cathedral at Rheims, and later with election to the bishopric of Tournay, though he was never able to take up the post. In 963 he retired to the monastery of St Basil. His most significant historical works are *Historia Remensis ecclesiae*, an account of the history of the Church of Rheims, and

Annales, a historical narrative of the period 919–66.

Florence of Worcester English chronicler and monk of Worcester, where he died, 7 July 1118. He was the author of *Chronicon ex chronicis*, which begins with the Creation and ends in 1117 but which from *c.*1106 becomes of value as an independent authority, accurate, honest and fair but without the literary flair of a **William of Malmesbury**. The basis of his work was a chronicle of Marianus Scotus, an Irish hermit of Fulda and later of Main, but he supplements Marianus from now lost chronicles, from the writings of **Asser** and a free translation from the Anglo-Saxon Chronicle.

Florensky, Paul (Pavel Aleksandrovich) Russian Orthodox priest, scientist, theologian and martyr, born Azerbaijan, 9 January 1882, died (probably shot) 15 December 1943. He became a priest, while continuing with philosophical and scientific research. He refused to leave Russia after the Revolution and the Communists permitted him to lecture and even to help in the 'electrification of the Soviet Union'. In 1933 he was imprisoned and finally died or was shot at Solovki Island. He was called the 'Russian Leonardo' and his literary output was enormous. His most important theological works are *The Pillar and Ground of Truth* (1914) and *Iconostasis* (1922).

Florent, François Roman Catholic canon lawyer, born Arnay-le-Duc, France, *c.*1590, died Orléans, France, 29 October 1650. Florent studied at Toulouse and became professor of law at Orléans in 1630. His contemporary reputation as an authority on canon law was considerable, and led to his appointment as professor of canon law at Paris in 1644, becoming dean of the law school there in 1649. He wrote a number of books dealing with various aspects of canon law.

Florentina Virgin and saint, fl. around Seville *c.*600. The sister of **Fulgentius of Ecija** and of **Leander** and **Isidore of Seville**, she seems to have been given a convent by Leander, who wrote for her community a work celebrating consecrated virginity and setting out a Rule of 31 chapters for virgins. Isidore dedicated his work *On the Catholic*

Faith Against the Jews to her. Her relics were discovered along with those of Fulgentius near Guadalupe *c.*1320, and shared between the Escorial and the Murcia in 1593. The cult of Florentina, patroness of Plasencia, dates from the fifteenth century. Feast day: 20 June.

Florentius Radewijns Monk, born near Utrecht, 1350, died Deventer, 24 March 1400. An early member of the Brethren of the Common Life, he succeeded **Groote** as head of the community at Deventer, The Netherlands. He was also responsible for the establishment of a monastery at Windesheim in 1387. His is reported as the first communal house of the Brethren.

Florez, Enrique Augustinian priest, theologian, archaeologist, Church historian, born Valladolid, Spain, 14 February 1701, died Madrid, 20 August 1773. Florez joined the Order of St Augustine at fourteen and spent his life in scholarship. He wrote more than half of the mammoth 51-volume history of the Spanish Church *La España Sagrada, ó teatro geográfico-histórico de la Iglesia de España*, completed after his death by his fellow priests. Among his other works was the five-volume *Cursus Theologiae*, and *España carpetana; medallas de las colonias, municipios, y pueblos antiguos de España*, a general history of Spain during Roman occupation.

Florinus Saint, fl. in Switzerland, seventh century. Florinus is the patron saint of the Diocese of Chur in Switzerland. He is the subject of a number of miracle stories which are obviously legendary, and hardly any reliable details of his life have survived.

Florovsky, George Vasilievich Russian Orthodox priest and theologian, born Odessa, 28 August 1893, died Princeton, New Jersey, 11 August 1979. On leaving Russia he taught himself theology while living in Czechoslovakia. From 1926 to 1948 he was professor of patristic and systematic theology at St Sergius Institute in Paris. Thereafter he lived in America, where he helped to establish St Vladimir's Theological Seminary. He championed the Greek patristic revival in Orthodox theology and his works have been extremely influential. The most important is *Ways of Russian Theology*, a lengthy historical survey of the effects of various

Western influences on Russian Orthodoxy and the importance of a 'return to the Fathers'.

Florus of Lyons Deacon, theologian, died Lyons, c.860. Few details survive of his life, but a letter signed by Florus to the bishop of Narbonne, c.827, makes clear that he is at this time a deacon of the Church at Lyons, and is apparently a highly regarded theologian. Throughout his life his writings portray him as a man interested in and consulted about issues important in the local Church. His works include *De iniusta vexatione ecclesiae Lugdunensis*, *De expositione Missae* and a criticism of John Scotus **Eriugena**, *Liber adversus Johannem Scotum*.

Flotte, Pierre Statesman, born France, c.1260, died (killed in battle) Courtrai, France, 11 July 1302. As the chief adviser on foreign affairs for Philip IV of France, Flotte was deeply involved in the struggles between him and **Boniface VIII**. Flotte proved an effective advocate for Philip's position, but avoided attacking Boniface personally. He was killed at the Battle of Courtrai, which was occasioned by the dispute.

Flower, Joseph Roswell Leader in the Assemblies of God, born Belleville, Canada, 1888, died 1970. Flower became a Pentecostal in 1907. In 1911 he and his wife Alice Reynolds helped to establish a Bible school in Indiana and an organization for communication between Pentecostal Churches. In 1913 Flower became a pastor, and in 1914 he became secretary-treasurer of the Assemblies of God, the first of several administrative positions. Flower championed Trinitarianism in the Assemblies of God. From 1913 he and Reynolds published the *Christian Evangel*, later known as the *Weekly Evangel* and now as the *Pentecostal Evangel*.

Floyd, John Jesuit priest, missionary, author, born Cambridgeshire, 1572, died St Omer, 16 September 1649. In 1606, as a missionary priest in England, Floyd was imprisoned for visiting a Catholic captive; upon his freedom the following year, he was banished. Despite this he spent much of his life evading capture in England and, under many pseudonyms, engaged in many polemical discussions of the day. Among his writings are *The Overthrow of the Protestant Pulpit Babels*, *Hypocrisis*

Marci Antonii de Dominis detecta sui censura in ejus libros de Republica Ecclesiastica and *An Answer to Francis White's Reply to Mr Fischer's Answer to the Nine Articles Offered by King James to Father John Fischer*.

Focher, Juan Franciscan lawyer, born probably in France, date unknown, died Mexico City, 1572. Focher went to Mexico (then known as New Spain) in 1540, where he proved an effective Church organizer and administrator. He wrote a number of treatises concerning the organization and method of evangelism, which became the de facto manuals for the Franciscan missionaries in that region, and which had a lasting influence on the later development of Mexican civil law.

Fogazzaro, Antonio Novelist, born Vicenza, Italy, 25 March 1842, died there, 7 March 1911. He studied law at Turin, and abandoned Catholicism for a time, but on recovering his faith he became an influential Catholic layman. His many writings attempted to reconcile Catholicism both to the new theories of **Darwin**, and to the newly emerging Italy. His 1898 work *Ascensioni umane* attempted to align traditional Catholic teaching and evolution. His 1905 novel *Il Santo* was condemned by Rome.

Foggia, Francesco Composer, born Rome, 1603, died Rome, 8 January 1688. Foggia held a variety of court and ecclesiastical appointments during his musical career. His compositions, of which a large number survive, consist entirely of sacred music. Stylistically they represent something of a transition between the Roman and baroque traditions.

Foik, Paul Joseph Roman Catholic priest, writer and librarian, born Stratford, Canada, 14 August 1879, died Austin, Texas, 1 March 1941. Ordained in 1911, Foik was librarian and archivist at Notre Dame University for twelve years before moving to St Edward's University in Austin. During his time there he held a variety of academic positions, among them librarian, professor of foreign languages, and dean of the College of Arts and Letters. Foik was also noted as a historian of American Catholic history, and edited or contributed to a number of major reference works and historical journals.

Folcwin Saint, bishop, born late 700s, died Ekelsbecke, France, 14 December 855. Folcwin became bishop of Thérouanne, Pas-de-Calais, France, around 816. He belonged to an illegitimate branch of the Carolingian dynasty, which was no doubt one factor in his appointment. He attended the Synod of Paris in 846 as well as other synods, and he helped secure the relics of St **Omer of Thérouanne** for the abbey of Saint-Bertin. His biography was written about a hundred years after his death by **Folcwin of Lobbes**. Feast day 14 December.

Folcwin of Lobbes Abbot, chronicler, born *c.*935, died Lobbes, 990. The grand-nephew of St **Folcwin** of Thérouanne, Folcwin became a monk in 948 at Saint-Bertin, succeeding to the bishopric of Lobbes in 965. He wrote a history of abbots of Lobbes, and a history of the miracles of Ursmar and **Ermin**. All emphasized documentary evidence and distrusted mere oral tradition.

Foley, James Thomas Roman Catholic journalist, born Asphodel, Canada, 26 April 1863, died London, Canada, 5 March 1932. A graduate of the University of Ottawa, Foley was ordained in 1892 and served in a number of parishes before being invited to become editor of the influential *Catholic Record* in 1912, a post he held until his death. In his editorials Foley wrote on a wide range of subjects, which proved significant in moulding Canadian Catholic opinion on current affairs and social matters as well as on more obviously religious questions.

Foliot, Gilbert Ecclesiastical politician and bishop, born Normandy, died spring 1187. He became a monk at Cluny and Abbeville and soon advanced to being prior of Cluny, abbot of Gloucester and bishop of Hereford, in 1148, and to the bishopric of London, 1163. He strongly opposed the election of **Thomas Becket** to the primacy and in 1162 refused obedience to him as metropolitan. During Becket's absence in France Foliot administered the Archdiocese of Canterbury. For his support of King Henry II against Becket on the question of criminous clerks Foliot was excommunicated in 1167. He appealed to the Pope, who gave licence to **Bartholomew of Exeter** to absolve him from the censure at Rouen in 1170. But again defying Becket he took part in the coronation of the young Henry, and was once more excommuicated and not absolved until 1172 when he was cleared of all part in Becket's murder. As Bishop of London, Foliot exercised much influence over King Henry II and his family until his death.

Follet, René Jesuit orientalist, born Hodeng-au-Bosc, France, 18 May 1902, died Rome, 29 January 1956. Ordained in 1934, Follet became a student of Assyriology, and in the course of studies in Ankara became stranded there by the outbreak of World War II. He joined the Pontifical Biblical Institute in 1946, where he lectured in Semitic studies for the rest of his life. Much esteemed as a teacher, Follet's written output was comparatively small; a major work on Babylonian history he had been engaged on was still unfinished at his death.

Fonck, Leopold Jesuit biblical scholar, born Wissen, Germany, 14 January 1865, died Vienna, Austria, 19 October 1930. Fonck was ordained in 1889 following studies in Germany and Rome, and became a Jesuit in 1892. He continued theological studies at various European universities, and for seven years taught at the University of Innsbruck before joining the Gregorian University in 1908. The following year **Pius X** founded the Pontifical Biblical Institute, and appointed Fonck to be its first rector. He served in this capacity until 1919, and oversaw much of the important formative work which established the Institute's ethos and infrastructure. Subsequently Fonck became the editor of *Biblica*, the Institute's journal, but in his last years he devoted himself to pastoral ministry in Prague and Vienna.

Fonseca, José Ribeiro da Roman Catholic bishop, born Evora, 3 December 1690, died Porto, 16 June 1752. After joining the Franciscans in Ara Coeli, Rome, in 1712, he became minister general of the Order and devoted himself to restoring discipline with reported diplomacy and skill. Between 1731 and 1741, the *Annales Ordinis Minorum* of **Wadding** were published under his direction in seventeen volumes. After declining episcopal ordination several times, he accepted John V of Portugal's nomination to the See of Oporto.

Fonseca, Peter da Jesuit priest, theologian, born

Cortizada, Portugal, 1528, died Lisbon, 4 November 1599. Considered a brilliant philosopher at Evora, where he lectured, he wrote *Institutionum Dialecticarum Libri Octo, Commentariorum in Libros Metaphysicorum Aristotelis Stagiritae* and *Isagoge Philosophica*, all considered central texts in Europe for over a century. He served as superior in Lisbon, assisted **Gregory XIII** and resolved the problem of grace and free will in his writings, a solution later developed by his student, Luis de **Molina**.

Fontana, Carlo   Papal architect, born near Como, Italy, 22 April 1638, died Rome, 16 February 1714. He came to Rome *c.*1656 as a student of **Bernini**. Fontana's work is in the tradition of late baroque, moving towards neoclassicism in his later years. He was responsible for the tombs of Queen **Christina of Sweden**, Pope **Clement XI** and Pope **Innocent XII** in St Peter's, the Grimani and Bolognetti palaces, and the fountain in the piazza of St Peter's, all in Rome; Loyola College, in Spain; and the restoration of the Library of Minerva.

Fonte, Pedro José   Roman Catholic archbishop, born Linares, Spain, 13 May 1777, died 11 June 1839. Archbishop Lizana of Mexico invited Fonte to become his vicar general in 1802, the same year Fonte had been ordained. Fonte succeeded Lizana in 1816, the see having been vacant since his death in 1811. From 1820 onwards the Mexican independence movement became increasingly powerful, and when the country gained its independence in 1821 Fonte returned to Spain. When Spain finally recognized Mexico's independence in 1837, he was ordered by the Pope either to return to his see or to resign, and he chose the latter.

Forbes, Alexander Penrose   Anglican bishop, theologian and hagiographer, born Edinburgh, 6 June 1817, died Dundee, 8 October 1875. He was educated at Haileybury and Glasgow University and sailed to India to work in the civil service. But his health broke down, and he returned to England, graduating from Brasenose, Oxford, in 1844 and being ordained priest of St Saviour's, Leeds, in that year. During his time at Oxford he had come under the influence of the Tractarian movement. In 1848 he was consecrated bishop of Brechin. He laboured much to further Tractarian principles

and was censured for promulgating the doctrine of the Real Presence in 1860. In 1864 he edited the *Arbuthnot Missal* and in 1872 published edited Lives in *Kalendars of Scottish Saints.*

Forbes, John   Capuchin priest, born Scotland, 1570, died Termonde, 2 August 1606. The son of a Protestant father and a Catholic mother, he converted to his mother's religion in 1587. To dissuade him, his father arranged a marriage to a Protestant noblewoman, but John fled. He eventually reached the Capuchin Order in Tournai in 1593. Despite continuing attempts by his father and friends to stop him, he was eventually ordained and became a chaplain at Dendermond. He wrote in defence of Catholicism to his kinsman King **James** VI of Scotland (I of England) and died in an epidemic after becoming missionary apostolic of Scotland.

Forbin-Janson, Charles de   Roman Catholic bishop, and founder of missionary associations, born Paris, France, 3 November 1785, died Aggalades, near Marseilles, 11 July 1844. Ordained in 1811, he participated in efforts to re-Christianize post-revolutionary France, helping to found the Missionaires de France with Abbé Jean Bauzan. As bishop of Nancy from 1824, he was notable for his opposition to Gallicanism. Leaving France after the 1830 revolution, he made a successful preaching tour of US cities in 1839–41, subsequently working in Canada and among indigenous American peoples. He helped Pauline-Marie **Jaricot** to start the Society for the Propagation of the Faith and in 1843 he founded the Association of the Holy Childhood.

Forcellini, Egidio   Lexicographer, born near Treviso, Italy, 26 August 1688, died Padua, 4 April 1768. He came from a poor background and had little early education, but entered the seminary at Padua in 1704. He became assistant to the lexicographer Facciolati, and worked on revising the Latin dictionary of **Ambrogio Calepino**. With Facciolati he conceived the idea of a completely new Latin lexicon and under his mentor's direction set to work reading the whole Latin corpus. In 1724 this work was interrupted when he became professor of rhetoric and director of the seminary at Ceneda, but he took it up again on his return to Padua in

1731. It was not until 1771, three years after Forcellini's death, that the four-volume *Totius Latinitatis Lexicon*, upon which all modern Latin lexicons are based, was published.

Ford, Ford Madox   Novelist, poet and editor, born 'Ford Hermann Hueffer' at Merton, Surrey, England, 17 December 1873, died Deauville, France, 26 February 1939. Grandson of the artist Ford Madox Brown, he published his first novel in 1892, and the same year was received into the Roman Catholic Church. He served with the Royal Welch Fusiliers during World War I, and moved to France in 1922, living there and in the United States until his death. As founder of the *Literary Review* in 1908 (and later the *Transatlantic Review* in 1924), he was notable for his encouragement of new authors, including D. H. Lawrence and Ezra Pound. As a novelist, Ford's best-known works are *The Good Soldier* (1915), and the wartime tetralogy *Parade's End*, featuring *Some Do Not* (1924), *No More Parades* (1925), *A Man Could Stand Up* (1926) and *Last Post* (1928), which deal in particular with differences in sexual and religious attitudes among the upper middle classes.

Ford, Francis Xavier   Roman Catholic bishop and missionary, born Brooklyn, New York, 11 January 1892, died (in prison) Canton, China, 21 February 1952. Ordained in 1917, he travelled to China the following year, founding the Maryknoll Seminary for Chinese students in Yeoungkong/Yang-chiang in 1921, and a convent in 1922. In 1925, he headed a new mission in Kwangtung/Mei-hsien, and was made a bishop in 1935. He remained during World War II, helping Chinese refugees fleeing the Japanese invasion. Under the Communist government, Ford was subjected to persistent harassment, and was arrested on charges of anti-Communism and espionage in December 1950. He suffered public beatings during his transfer to Canton prison, where his death in February 1952 was not revealed outside China for a further six months.

Ford, Ita   Maryknoll missionary sister, born 1940, died (by shooting) El Salvador, 2 December 1980. She had worked in Chile, Nicaragua and El Salvador for many years in the midst of war, poverty and injustice. She was returning to El Salvador from a meeting in Nicaragua when the van carrying her and three fellow missionaries Maura **Clarke**, Jean Donovan and Dorothy **Kazel**, was stopped by soldiers of the El Salvadorean army. The women were tortured and two of them raped before they were all shot and buried in shallow graves. The incident caused international outrage and pressure was brought so that all the soldiers responsible were eventually brought to justice.

Ford, Jeremiah Denis Mathias   Philologist and scholar of Romance languages and literature, born Cambridge, Massachusetts, 2 July 1873, died there, 14 November 1958. He taught at Harvard University throughout his career, and was chairman of the Department of Romance Languages and Literature between 1911 and 1943. In addition, he researched and taught widely in Europe, particularly in France and Spain. His major works focused on Old Spanish language and literature, also editing textbooks and original texts of Spanish, Italian and Portuguese authors. Among many other positions, he was editor of *Speculum*, president of the Dante Society, 1922–40, and the American Catholic Historical Association, 1935.

Ford, Patrick   Journalist, social and economic reformer, born Galway, Ireland, 12 April 1835, died, Brooklyn, New York, 23 September 1913. Arriving in the USA as an orphan in 1842, he had become editor and publisher of the Boston *Sunday Times* by 1859. In 1870 he founded the weekly *Irish World and American Industrial Liberator and Gaelic American*, through which he championed Irish independence, economic reform in the USA, and a variety of other progressive social and economic causes. Notably, his prominence in the USA's large Irish community enabled him to generate support for many Irish independence issues: for example, raising financial support for the 1880–1 Land League agitations through a network of 2500 American branches.

Foreiro, Francisco   Dominican theologian and Scripture scholar, born *c.*1510, died Lisbon, in his native Portugal, 10 January 1581. Became theological adviser to King John III of Portugal, and later to King Sebastian. He went as Sebastian's representative to the Council of Trent, where he distinguished himself as both scholar and preacher. He was the first secretary of the Index of Prohibited

Books, helped to develop the Roman Catechism and to reform the Breviary and Missal. He became provincial of the Order in Portugal in 1568. His writings include a Hebrew lexicon, commentaries on the Prophets and on Job, and reflections on the Gospels.

Formosus Pope, born *c.*816, probably in Rome, died there, 4 April 896. Elected Pope on 6 October 891, he appears to have been a very holy man and his early missionary activities were a great success. However, both before and during his pontificate he was enmeshed in controversies over political and papal succession. After his death his body was exhumed, on the orders of his successor, **Stephen VI**, and 'tried' for the canonical offence of changing sees. The corpse was found guilty and Formosus' pontificate, including the ordinations he had carried out, declared invalid. The papal garments were then ripped, three fingers of the right hand severed and the corpse thrown into the strangers' graveyard and thence into the Tiber, from where it was recovered by a monk. Stephen died in August 897 and his second successor, **Theodore II**, called a synod which reversed all the decisions of the 'Synod of the Cadaver' and had the body of Formosus re-interred in St Peter's, with full honour.

Fornari-Strata, Maria Victoria Blessed, foundress of the contemplative order of the Annunciation, the 'Celestial Annunciades' or 'Blue Nuns', born Genoa, Italy, 1562, died Genoa, 15 December 1617. After the death of her husband she took a vow of chastity and lived a holy life, bringing up her six children – five of whom joined religious orders. When they were all settled she set about establishing her new contemplative order. Maria Victoria and ten companions took solemn vows in 1605. Communities were established early on in Burgundy, France and Germany. The Order, which makes altar linens and vestments, is regarded by some as being rather rigid. Feast day 12 September.

Forsyth, Peter Taylor Congregational minister and theologian, born Aberdeen, 12 May 1848, died Hampstead, 11 November 1921. From 1901 he was principal of Hackney College, Hampstead, after a number of years in local Church ministry. His theology is notable for the centrality given to the need for atonement through the cross, where Christ is both reconciler and reconciled (as in his 1910 book, *The Work of Christ*). His other main writings include *The Cruciality of the Cross* (1909), *The Person and Place of Jesus Christ* (1909), *The Christian Ethic of War* (1916), *The Justification of God* (1916) and *The Soul of Prayer* (1916).

Fortescue, Adrian Blessed, Knight of St John, martyr, born Punsborne, Hertfordshire, *c.*1476, died by execution in London, 10 July 1539. A country gentleman, he was present at the Field of the Cloth of Gold in 1520. Second cousin to Anne Boleyn, he was arrested and released in 1534, and arrested and imprisoned in the Tower in 1539. He was not accused of any specific act of treason, but of 'sedition and refusing allegiance', and was beheaded in July 1539. He was beatified by **Leo XIII** in 1895.

Fortescue, Adrian Roman Catholic priest, orientalist, liturgist, artist, musician and controversialist, born Perth, 14 January 1874, died London, 11 February 1923. Educated at the Scots College, Rome, and Innsbruck, he was ordained on 27 March 1898, and proceeded to a doctorate in divinity in Innsbruck, in 1905. From 1907 he was founding rector of the parish of St Hugh's, Letchworth, where he pioneered the ideals later espoused by the liturgical movement. He supported his parish by his literary work, principally *The Greek Fathers and the Orthodox Eastern Church* (1908), *The Mass* (1912), *The Ceremonies of the Roman Rite Described* (1917) and *The Early Papacy* (1920).

Fortunato of Brescia Morphologist, philosopher, theologian and member of the Franciscan 'Friars Minor' (of the Lombardy Reform), born Brescia, 1 December 1701, died Madrid, 11 May 1754. He became secretary general of his Order, and in his academic work brought together many of the teachings of Scholastic philosophy with findings in the natural sciences. He pioneered studies in anatomical observation using the microscope, followed much later by Bichat and Cuvier, and was one of the first to distinguish between organs and tissues.

Fortunatus, Venantius Honorius Clementianus

Latin poet and bishop, born Treviso, near Venice, c.530, died c.610. He travelled widely in Europe, and was for a time spiritual director to the former Queen **Radegunda** and her abbess **Agnes of Poitiers** at Holy Cross Monastery, Poitiers, where he served as steward and then chaplain. He was encouraged to publish his poetry (which wove classical forms with a more medieval mysticism and symbolism) by his friend St **Gregory of Tours**. His *Vexilla Regis* and *Pange Lingua Gloriosi* came to form part of the Office of Holy Week in the Western Church. He became bishop of Poitiers in c.599.

Forty Martyrs of England and Wales Between 1535 and 1680 some 357 English and Welsh Roman Catholics were put to death for their beliefs. Of these, 199 have been beatified and the forty most popular of these were canonized, as representative of the whole group, on 27 October 1970. The group includes twenty religious and thirteen secular priests, four laymen and three laywomen.

Fosdick, Harry Emerson American Baptist minister and divine, born Bufalo, New York, 24 May 1878, died Bronxville, New York, 5 October 1969. Ordained in 1903, he worked as a pastor and also taught homiletics at Union Theological Seminary, New York. An evangelical liberal of modernist persuasion, he resigned from the pastorate of a Presbyterian church after pressure from conservatives to adhere to traditional Presbyterian doctrine, before becoming pastor of the Baptist Riverside Church, New York, 1926–46. His approach to preaching was highly influential, and he wrote thirty books, including: *The Meaning of Prayer* (1915), *The Modern Use of the Bible* (1924), *Successful Christian Living* (1937), *Living Under Tension* (1941) and *A Faith for Tough Times* (1952). *On Becoming a Real Person* (1943), which sought to apply insights from the psychological study of personality to religion, became a best-seller.

Fouard, Henri Constant Roman Catholic biblical scholar and priest, born Elbeuf, near Rouen, 6 August 1837, died Elbeuf, 3 December 1903. After theological studies at St Sulpice, he was ordained in 1861, taking his doctorate in 1876 for a dissertation on the Passion of Christ. He taught at Rouen until 1883 and became canon of Rouen Cathedral in 1884. In both his role as a consultor to Pope **Leo XIII**'s Pontifical Biblical Commission of 1903 and in his major works (collected as *Les Origines de l'Église*), he sought to defend a traditional Catholic interpretation of Scripture against 'higher criticism' while advocating the use of newer techniques and theories where useful.

Foucauld, Charles Eugène de Explorer, Roman Catholic priest and hermit, born Strasburg, 15 September 1858, died (assassinated, probably by Senoussi tribesmen) Tamanrasset, Algeria, 1 December 1916. After an early military career, he undertook a two-year expedition in the Sahara, detailed in *Reconnaissance au Maroc* (1888). Stirred by the religiosity of the desert tribespeople he had met, he returned to the Catholic faith in 1886, and spent some years as a Trappist in France and Syria, 1890–7. After his ordination in 1901, he returned to the desert to live as a hermit, studying local languages and gaining respect from both the tribes and French soldiers for his charitable works. He wrote Rules for communities of 'Little Brothers' and 'Little Sisters', which since his death have inspired a number of fraternities, emphasizing both contemplation and life and work in the wider community.

Fourier, Peter *see* **Peter Fourier**

Fournet, André Hubert Saint, Roman Catholic priest and co-founder of the Daughters of the Holy Cross of St Andrew, born Maillé, near Poitiers, France, 6 December 1752, died La Puye, near Poitiers, 13 May 1834. Ordained in 1776, he was among those who, after the Revolution, refused to take the oath required under the Civil Constitution of the Clergy. For a number of years he continued to say Mass in his former parish – often in secret. During the time of Napoleon, he took on greater responsibility for the churches in the Maillé area. In 1797, he met St Jeanne Elisabeth **Bichier des Ages**, encouraging her to form a religious community dedicated to the care and education of the poor and sick (the Daughters of the Holy Cross of St Andrew), for which Fournet wrote the Rule. He was beatified in 1926 and canonized in 1933. Feast day 13 May.

Fournier, Paul Roman Catholic historian and

scholar of canon law, born Calais, 26 November 1853, died Paris, 14 May 1935. Between 1880 and 1914, he served as professor of Roman law and of the history of canon law at the University of Grenoble, and became professor of law and of the history of canon law at the University of Paris in 1921, a position he held until his death. His main work concerned the history of canonical collections, and is summarized in *Histoire des collections canoniques en Occident depuis les fausses décrétales jusqu'au décret de Gratien* (1931–2), written in collaboration with the historian Gabriel Le Bras.

Fournier, St John Mother, Roman Catholic nun and foundress of the Sisters of St Joseph of Philadelphia, born Arbois, France, 13 November 1814, died Philadelphia, USA, 15 October 1875. After teaching with the Sisters of St Joseph of Lyons in St Louis until 1847, she was sent to Philadelphia to staff an orphanage, and throughout the rest of her life established two orphanages and 38 parochial and private schools in the city. In 1858, she set up a permanent mother house in Philadelphia, and the Rule of this community received papal approbation in 1896.

Fox, George Founder of the Society of Friends, born Drayton-in-the-Clay (now Fenny Drayton), Leicestershire, England, July 1624, died London, 13 January 1691. Initially an apprentice shoemaker, he left family and friends to begin nearly four years of travelling in search of enlightenment. In 1646 he ceased attending church, increasingly trusting what he called the Inner (or Inward) Light of the Living Christ. He began his preaching ministry in 1647, travelling widely and quickly gaining followers. His main teaching was that truth was revealed directly by God to the soul of the individual. He was imprisoned on a number of occasions for blasphemy and for disrupting church services. A skilled organizer as well as a charismatic preacher, he was able to develop a stable structure for the growing movement of Friends, based from 1652 at Swarthmore Hall, near Ulverston. He also undertook missionary journeys to Ireland in 1669, the West Indies and America in 1671–3, Germany in 1677 and The Netherlands in 1677 and 1684. In later life he campaigned for greater toleration, and against a variety of social evils. His well-known *Journal* first became public in 1694.

Foxe, John Historian of the English Protestant Church, 'martyrologist' and Anglican priest, born Boston, Lincolnshire, 1516, died London, April 1587. A Protestant, he was fellow of Magdalen College, Oxford, 1539–45, and later tutor to a number of noble families, before fleeing to continental Europe upon the accession to the throne of the Roman Catholic Queen **Mary Tudor** in 1553. Here he became acquainted with other Protestant refugees, and began to write (in Latin) on the history of Christian persecutions. This work he revised and expanded several times. It was published in English in 1563 as *Acts and Monuments* popularly known as 'Foxe's Book of Martyrs'. Its sympathetic account of the struggles of Protestant martyrs (particularly in the reign of Queen Mary) became hugely popular, and the book continues to provide valuable evidence on the oral culture of early Protestantism. Foxe was ordained in 1560 and devoted much of the rest of his life to writing, and preparing new versions of the 'Book of Martyrs'.

Foxe, Richard Bishop of Winchester, and founder of Corpus Christi College, Oxford, born Ropesley, Grantham, 1448(?), died 1528. Probably educated in Oxford, Cambridge and Paris, he was appointed bishop of Winchester by Henry VII, 15 October 1487. He was translated to the bishopric of Bath and Wells in 1492, was made bishop of Durham in 1494 and became bishop of Winchester in 1501. Throughout this period he undertook extensive diplomatic work for the king, and continued to remain influential into the reign of **Henry VIII**. In later years, his role was eclipsed by that of Thomas **Wolsey**, and Foxe devoted more time to Church matters. Influenced by the New Learning of the northern European Renaissance, he founded Corpus Christi College, Oxford, in 1515–16.

Foy (Faith, Foi) Saint, born Agen, France, 290, died, by burning, 303. Her shrine at Conques, on the pilgrimage route to Santiago, notable for its bejewelled gold reliquary, was popular in the Middle Ages and continues to flourish today. St Foy is included in the Sarum calendar and has several churches in England named after her, probably because some of her relics were taken to Glastonbury. Feast day 6 October.

Franca Saint, fl. eleventh century. She began her religious life as a solitary in Fermo, Italy, before taking vows and entering the convent, it is thought, of San Angelo in Pontano. Towards the end of her life she resumed the eremitical life in Fermo. Feast day 1 October.

Franca, Leonel Jesuit priest, founder and first rector of the Pontifical Catholic University of Rio de Janeiro, spiritual leader and writer, born São Gabriel, Rio Grande do Sul, Brazil, 6 January 1893, died Rio de Janeiro, 3 September 1948. He taught first at the Colégio Anchieta, Rio de Janeiro, and then, from 1928 until his death, at the Colégio S. Ignacio, Rio de Janeiro, also writing and lecturing extensively on philosophy, apologetics, sociology and education. From 1939, he organized the first Catholic faculties of the University of Rio de Janeiro, and became its first rector in 1940. As well as being a talented confessor and spiritual director, he also gained prominence as an adviser to many government figures. He wrote fourteen books, including *Nocoes da história da filosofia*, which ran to numerous editions.

Franca Vitalta Cistercian saint, born Piacenza, Italy, 1175, died 25 April 1218. She joined the Bendictine convent of St Syrus when she was seven and was professed there when she was fourteen. Not long after this she was made abbess, but appears to have been rather severe, and was deposed. She later became abbess of the Cistercian convent at Pittoli. Feast day 26 April.

Frances d'Amboise Saint, born Thouars, 28 September 1427, died Nantes, 4 November 1485. She was raised at the court in Brittany and was married, unhappily at first, to Duke Peter of Brittany. Eventually her husband joined her in charitable work among the poor and newly established religious communities. She was a friend of Blessed John Soreth, general of the Carmelites, and became a Carmelite herself after her husband's death, at the convent she had helped establish in Nantes. Feast day 4 November.

Frances of Rome Saint, born into a rich noble family in Rome, 1384, died there, 9 March 1440. Although at first reluctant to marry, she remained devoted to her husband, Lorenzo Ponziano, until his death. From early in her marriage and along with her sister-in-law she strove to live a simple, prayerful life, accompanied by work with and for the poor and sick of Rome. The two younger of her three children died in childhood. She survived the plundering of the family homes in Rome and Campagna, and the exile of her husband and son. The family was reunited in 1414 and much of their property restored. Frances nursed Lorenzo until his death in 1417, when she retired to live with the religious community of the Oblates of Mary which she had founded at Tor de'Specchi. Feast day 9 March.

Frances Xavier Cabrini Saint, foundress of the Missionary Sisters of the Sacred Heart, first US citizen to be canonized, born near Lodi, Italy, 15 July 1850, died Chicago, USA, 22 December 1917. The youngest of thirteen children, she had hoped to become a missionary to China but her parents sent her to be educated as a teacher. She taught for several years following her parents' deaths, took religious vows and established one of the earliest congregations of missionary sisters. Her intention to go to China was thwarted when **Leo XIII** encouraged her to go to the USA. For the rest of her life she travelled throughout Europe and the Americas establishing congregations, schools, hospitals, orphanages and clinics. Feast day 13 November.

Franceschi, Gustavo Juan Roman Catholic priest, philosopher and sociologist, born Corsica, 1871, died Montevideo, Argentina, 11 June 1957. He was ordained in 1902, and, among many appointments, was chaplain to the chapel of El Carmen, secretary of the Argentine Social League, advised Catholic students' and teachers' organizations and directed the review *Justicia Social*. He wrote and preached extensively on the social doctrines of the Catholic Church, and was professor of sociology and Catholic social thought at the Catholic University of Buenos Aires between 1917 and 1941. From 1933, he directed *Criterio*, a review for which he wrote regular articles on a wide spectrum of subjects, many of which later appeared in book form.

Francesco Bartholi Franciscan writer and preacher, born towards the end of thirteenth and died towards the end of the fourteenth century. He studied in Perugia and Cologne, but spent most of his life in his home town of Assisi. He taught theology there, at Santa Maria degli Angeli, for five years from 1320. In 1332 he was guardian of San Damiano and in 1334 was at the Sacro Convent. At this time he wrote his *Tractatus de indulgentia S. Maria de Portiuncula*, which gives significant information about and insight into the early days of the Franciscan Order. The manuscripts of his volume of sermons and concordance on the Passion are preserved in Assisi.

Francesco Maria of Camporosso Saint, Italian Capuchin lay brother, born Camporosso (Imperia), 27 December 1804, died Genoa, 17 September 1866. He joined the Capuchin Order in 1821, pronouncing his solemn vows four years later. He was alms gatherer for the friary in Genoa for 40 years, gaining a wide recognition for the spiritual advice and catechetical instruction he gave while on his begging rounds. He died of cholera, having caught the disease from those whom he was nursing, during the epidemic of 1866. He was beatified in 1929 and canonized in 1962. Feast day 20 September.

Franchi, Alessandro Cardinal, secretary of state to the Vatican, born Rome, 25 June 1819, died there, 31 July 1878. During a long diplomatic career, he held appointments in Spain (where he helped negotiate an important agreement in 1859) and Tuscany, becoming papal nuncio to Spain in 1868 and a cardinal in 1873. He was influential in securing the election of Cardinal Vincenzo Gioacchino Pecci as Pope **Leo XIII**, who appointed him as his secretary of state in 1878. In the few months before his death, he began negotiations with the German government which would subsequently lead to a resolution of the Kulturkampf.

Franci de' Cavalieri, Pio Italian scholar and hagiographer, born Veroli, Italy, 31 August 1869, died Rome, 6 August 1960. After studying classical philology, he began work as a scriptor (researcher) in the Vatican Library in 1896, becoming honorary conservator in the Library's Sacred Museum, 1921–48. His main field of work was hagiography, and he wrote widely on this subject, including nine volumes of *Note agiografiche* for the Studi e Testi series. He also jointly edited and compiled bibli-ographies of Greek and Latin manuscripts, and prepared several editions of ancient works, including the *Menologion of Basil* (1907).

Francia, José Gaspar de Dictator of Paraguay, called 'El Supremo', born Ascunción, Paraguay, 6 January 1766, died Ascunción, 20 September 1840. He was a scholar of philosophy and theology, who also practised law and spoke several languages. From 1789 until his resignation he was professor of theology at the Seminario San Carlos. Having been elected *alcalde* (mayor) in 1808, he became deputy to the Spanish Cortes in 1809. After the declaration of Paraguayan independence in 1811, he served in the first ruling triumvirate. He became consul of the republic in 1813, named 'temporary dictator' the following year and 'perpetual dictator' in 1816.

Francis I King of France, born Cognac, 12 September 1494, died Rambouillet, 31 March 1547. He succeeded his cousin **Louis XII** to the throne in 1515. His reign reflected the increasing importance of the monarchies and the development of nation-states in Europe, as well as the decline of papal and civil imperialism. His second war against the Emperor **Charles V**, in which Francis forged an alliance with the Italian princes, including **Clement VII**, brought about the sack of Rome in 1527. While he favoured the Protestant princes in Germany, and encouraged intellectual debate along humanistic and Protestant lines, he later discouraged the promotion of Protestant ideas among the common people.

Francis de Sales Saint, Roman Catholic bishop, joint founder of the Visitandines, born Thorens, France, 21 August 1567, died Lyons, 28 December 1622. Born into an aristocratic family, Francis gave up a promising career in public service in favour of the priesthood. He was ordained in 1593 and appointed provost of Geneva. Here he strove to reconvert the Calvinists of the Chablais region, and his preaching drew back thousands into the Catholic fold. Appointed bishop of Geneva in 1602, he became the spiritual director for Jane Frances de **Chantal**, with whom he formed the Visitandine Order in 1610. His spiritual instructions were published as the *Introduction to the Devout Life* (1608) and *Treatise on the Love of God* (1616), and both became deeply influential. He was canonized in 1665. Feast Day 24 January.

Francis Mary of the Cross see Jordan, Johann Baptist.

Francis of Assisi Saint, founder of the Franciscans, born 'Giovanni de Bernadone' at Assisi, Italy, c.1181, died Assisi, 3 October 1226. Francis came from a prosperous family and as a youth led a carefree and reckless life. He repented following a serious illness, dedicating himself to a life of prayer and service to the poor and the sick. Subsequently he renounced his wealth, embraced poverty and began itinerant preaching. He soon attracted a number of disciples, for whom he drew up a Rule characterized by simplicity of life. This was given papal approval in 1212, thereby establishing the Franciscan Order. Known as 'Friars Minor', Francis's followers travelled extensively in their preaching journeys, Francis himself visiting Spain, Eastern Europe and Egypt. In 1221 he founded an order of tertiaries, who sought to live out Franciscan ideals while still remaining in the world. Francis's ideals, simple piety and lifestyle all combine to make him probably the supreme model of Christian sanctity. The alleged manifestation in his body of the stigmata (i.e. the wounds of Christ), in 1224, is often regarded as symbolic of this. He was canonized in 1228. Feast day 4 October.

Francis of Geronimo (di Girolama) Saint, Jesuit, born near Taranto, Italy, 17 December 1642, died Naples, 11 May 1716. He went to study at the Gesu Vecchio in Naples and, four years after his ordination there, entered the Society of Jesus in 1670. Despite his desire to go as a missionary to the East, he obeyed his superiors and spent the next 40 years in apostolic work in and around Naples. He enlisted the support of ordinary workers in his ministry, in what became known as the 'Oratorio della Missione'. He went to the people: in the streets and squares, in the prisons and hospitals, and even in the ships. He was an imaginative and dramatic speaker who drew vast crowds to his short sermons, to his longer missions and to the confessional. Feast day 11 May.

Francis of Marchia Franciscan theologian, born Appignano d'Ascoli, Italy, c.1290, died after 1344.

He studied in Paris and enjoyed the Scholastic titles of Doctor succinctus and Doctor praefulgidus. He became lector in Avignon, where he came out in support of **Michael of Cesena** in the Franciscan poverty controversy. He was expelled from the Franciscans in 1329 but accepted back into the Church again in 1344. His writings greatly influenced some of the leading Oxford Franciscans. His Quaestiones super sententias follows the teaching of **Duns Scotus**.

Francis of Meyronnes French Franciscan theologian, known by the title Doctor illuminatus, born Meyronnes, Provence, c.1285, died Piacenza, Italy, after 1328. He was a student at the University of Paris, where he was much influenced by the work of **Duns Scotus**. In 1323 he went to Avignon. **John XXII** sent him to Gascogne to attempt to broker peace between **Edward III** of England and Charles IV of France. He became embroiled in the Franciscan controversy over poverty and in 1324 was made minister provincial of Provence. He was a leading Mariologist and propounded Mary's Immaculate Conception, divine maternity and Assumption. His writings include philosophical, theological and political works as well as many sermons.

Francis of Osuna Spanish Franciscan priest and writer, born Osuna, Spain, c.1497, died 1542. Studied at Salamanca and was much given to prayer and contemplation. In 1527 he published his Abecedario espiritual, which was to have a profound influence on **Teresa of Ávila**. He spent the next five years in Seville and was then sent to attend Franciscan chapters at Toulouse in 1532 and Paris in 1533. He spent some time in Flanders and was elected Franciscan commissary general to the Indies, but never took up this post.

Francis of Paola Saint, founder of the Order of Minims, born Paola, Italy, 27 March 1416, died Tours, France, 2 April 1507. As a youth his parents placed him in a friary, awakening in him a vocation to the ascetic life. Aged twenty he retired to a cave by the sea, where others joined him and a religious brotherhood developed. Officially established in 1474 as the Order of Minims, it was characterized by charitable works and an austere lifestyle. Francis became renowned for his sanctity, and numerous miracles were attributed to him. He spent the last 25 years of his life in France, having been summoned by the dying Louis XI for spiritual consolation, subsequently becoming the spiritual director of Louis's son, **Charles VIII**. He was also involved in important diplomatic missions. Feast day 2 April.

Francis Solanus Franciscan saint, born Cortilla, Spain, 10 March 1549, died Lima, Peru, 14 July 1610. He joined the Order of Friars Minor in Montilla in 1569 and, after a period as master of novices, was sent to Peru in 1589. He spent the next twenty years there, engaged in missionary work. He learned many of the local languages and dialects and won the affection of many throughout Peru. Feast day 24 July.

Francis Xavier Saint, pioneer Jesuit missionary to Asia, born Castle Xavier, Navarre, Spain, 7 April 1506, died Shangchuan Dao Island, China, 3 December 1552. He studied at the University of Paris (MA, 1530) along with **Ignatius of Loyola**. A founding member of the Society of Jesus, he was ordained priest in 1537. He was assigned to missions in the East and arrived in Goa in May 1541. He worked with children and the poor and baptized thousands from October 1542 to December 1544. He then visited Sri Lanka, 1544–5, Melaka (Malacca) and the Moluccas. In Japan in August 1549 he worked with state and religious leaders. In 1552 he returned to Goa and then Melaka preparing to go to China, but died in sight of his goal. Many of his letters survive, and also his catechisms. He was canonized in 1622 and proclaimed Patron of Missions, 14 December 1927.

Franciscan Martyrs of China Died 1900. It is estimated that over 100,000 Christians were put to death in the Boxer Rising which took place under the Dowager Empress Tz'u-hsi. In 1946, 29 of these, mostly Franciscan priests, brothers, sisters and tertiaries, were beatified to represent the wider group. They were: Theodore Balat, Andrew Bauer, Mary Adolphine Dierk, Elias Facchini, Bishop Antoninus Fantosanti, Bishop Francis Fogolla, Mathias Fun-Te, Joseph Mary Gambaro, Caesidius Giacomantonio, Bishop Gregory Grassi, Mary Emiliana Grivot, Mary of Peace Guiliani, James Ien-Kutun, Mary Amandina Jeuris, Mary of Ste

Nathalie Kerguin, Mary of St Justus Moreau, Mary Clare Nanette, Thomas Sen, Peter Tchang-Pau-Nien, John Tciang, another John Tciang, Philip Tciang, Francis Tciang-Iun, James Tciao-Tcieum-Sin, Simon Tcing, Patrick Tun, Peter U-Ngan-Pau, John Van, Peter Van-al-man.

Franciscus de Accoltis Lawyer, born Arezzo, c.1417, died Pisa, 1485. He was a teacher of law and canon law in several universities. His written work concentrated on canon law and includes *Conciliate* (1531).

Franck, César Auguste French composer, organist and teacher, born Liège (Belgium), 10 December 1822, died Paris, 8 November 1890. Although a musically gifted child, his development as a major composer came comparatively late. After a short-lived virtuoso career, he was for many years a church organist and taught organ, keyboard and composition. He became organ professor at the Paris Conservatoire in 1872 and taught several of the younger generation of French composers, including d'**Indy**. Influenced by the Viennese tradition, **Liszt** and Wagner, Franck nevertheless developed his own style which was both contrapuntal and lyrical. A key figure in the development of modern harmony, he was instrumental in shifting the focus of French music from the operatic to the symphonic form. His symphonic, chamber and keyboard works are generally regarded as his most significant, and include the *Six pièces* for organ, Violin Sonata, String Quartet, Piano Quintet, *Variations symphoniques* and the D Minor Symphony.

Franck, Sebastian Humanist and Reformer, born Dnauwörth, Germany, 20 January 1499, died Basel 1542 or 1543. He studied at Ingolstadt, was ordained to the priesthood, then became a Lutheran in the 1520s. His ideas became increasingly radical, and he was forced to leave several German cities, settling for his last few years in Basel. His religious and theological ideas can be found in his three-volume *Chronica* (1531) and in his German edition of Althamen's treatise against the Anabaptists, *Dilliage* (1528).

Francke, August Hermann Pietist and educationalist, born Lübeck, Germany, 22 March 1663, died Halle, 8 June 1727. He was attracted to Pietistic forms of religion and held teaching positions at Leipzig, from 1685, and at the University of Halle, from 1691. He opened a poor school in his house, an orphanage, a dispensary and publishing house, institutes later to be referred to as 'Franckesche Stiftungen'. He engaged in debate with both orthodox and Enlightenment opponents and, supported by the Prussian King Frederick William I, was instrumental in having the philosopher Christian Wolff removed from Halle in 1723. He was much influenced by his mentor, P. J. **Spener**, but his teaching had the more legalistic bent that was to mark later German Pietism.

Franco, Hernando Polyphonic composer, born near Alcántara, Spain, c.1532, died Mexico City, 28 November 1585. Was a choirboy at the cathedral in Segovia from the age of ten. The professor of canon law at the University of Mexico, Matheo Arévalo Sedeño, encouraged Franco to take the position of chapelmaster at Guatemala Cathedral. After some problems there he went, in 1575, to Mexico City Cathedral. His works include sixteen highly praised *Magnificats* (inspired by the works of Cristóbal de **Morales**), Psalm settings, the *Salve* and various responses. Two pieces written in Aztec text in the Valdés Codex of 1599 are by a local composer who took Franco's name.

Franco Lippi Blessed, Carmelite lay brother, born near Siena, Italy, 1211, died Siena, 11 April 1291. He led a life of crime until he became blind at about the age of 50. He repented and went on pilgrimage to Santiago de Compostella and regained his sight. He journeyed to Rome and the returned to Siena, where he lived as a hermit. He continued this life after he became a Carmelite lay brother, living in a small cell near to the chapel of Our Lady. In about 1340 his body was exhumed and some of his relics removed to Cremona. He first appears in Carmelite liturgy in 1672.

Franco of Cologne Musical theorist, fl. between 1250 and 1280. Notable for his system of musical notation which clearly sets out metre and rhythm, and enabled the development of polyphony. His major work is the *Ars cantus mensurabilis*, of about 1260. Several aspects of his method were used into the sixteenth century. A three-part motet by Franco is referred to by Jacob of Liège, who describes Franco as *Teutonicus*. He was a papal chamberlain and preceptor of the Hospital of St John of Jerusalem in Cologne.

Frangipani Roman noble family, several members of which exercised considerable influence on Popes and Emperors during the eleventh, twelfth and thirteenth centuries, their allegiance shifting according to circumstances. The family owned considerable land and property in Rome, including the *Turris cartularia* which held part of the papal archives for some time, and throughout what is now Italy. **Cencio** helped to obtain the election of **Alexander II** in 1061 by supporting Hildebrand, and in 1084 helped **Robert Guiscard** in his efforts to free **Gregory VII**. **Giovanni**, Cencio's son, gave refuge to **Urban II** in 1093. **Leone** was appointed in 1108 by **Paschal II** as governor of Benevento. **Cencio II** supported **Henry V** against Pope **Gelasius II**, and imprisoned the Pope in 1118. Frangipani support shifted back to the Papacy and the high point of the family's power came in 1124 when their candidate, **Honorius II**, was elected Pope. This support continued throughout the remainder of the century. In the thirteenth century, however, they helped **Frederick II** in his struggles against Pope **Gregory IX** and against **Innocent IV**. This allegiance did not last, and by the end of Frederick's reign the family was once again supporting the Papacy. The family's influence in Rome began to decline after this time, but the influence of the Neapolitan branch of the family lasted until the seventeenth century. The Frangipani of Fruili branch of the family still exists.

Influential women members of the Roman branch of the family include **Aldruda**, Countess of Bertinoro, who helped lead the troops in the liberation of Ancona in 1174, **Jacoba**, who was a friend and supporter of **Francis of Assisi**, and **Giovanna**, mother of Pope **Benedict XIII**. Other major family members include: **Guglielmo**, archbishop of Patras, who died about 1337; **Muzio**, who led the papal auxiliaries to France in 1569; **Silvester**, Dominican provincial and writer, who died in 1667, and **Benedict XIII** (Pietro Francesco Orsini), Pope and Dominican, who died in 1730.

Notable members of the Neapolitan branch include: **Giovanni**, count of Astura, who captured Conradin of Swabia in 1268; **Fabio Mirto**, bishop, governor of the Marches and of Perugia, nuncio to

Paris, participant at Council of Trent, died in 1587; **Ottavio Mirto**, bishop then archbishop, nuncio, governor of Bologna, died 1612; and **Ottavio Fraja**, Benedictine, librarian at Monte Cassino, palaeographer, who died in 1843.

Frankenberg, Johann Heinrich Roman Catholic archbishop, and primate of the Netherlands, born Grosglogau, Silesia, 18 September 1726, died Breda, Holland, 11 June 1804. From a Silesian noble family, he was ordained in 1750 and rose quickly through the hierarchy of the Church. He was made archbishop of Malines by Empress Maria Theresa, and cardinal by Pope **Pius VI**, in 1778. While the early years of his archiepiscopate were largely free from tension, Church and emperor increasingly clashed over questions of mixed marriages and religious toleration. This came to a head in 1786–9, when Frankenberg refused to send pupils to a seminary founded by the emperor. Episcopal seminaries were briefly re-established in 1789, but on the outbreak of civil war in that year, Frankenberg was forced to leave the country. He returned with the restoration of Austrian rule, but was forced to flee again in 1797, having opposed further measures which were antagonistic to the Church.

Franko, Ivan Ukrainian writer, born Nahuievychi, West Ukraine, 15 August 1856, died Lvov, Halychyna, 1916. He was a passionate advocate of Ukrainian independence and wrote novels, poetry and drama on the economic hardship and political repression of the Ukrainian people. The son of a village blacksmith, he studied philosophy at the Universities of Lvov and Vienna. Unable to gain a professorship at home, and declining to leave Ukraine to take up other academic positions, he worked for a time on a Polish socialist periodical, writing widely within the Marxist–socialist tradition (although he later became disillusioned with this). His Catholic religious faith remained throughout his life, and remained influential in his writing. Two of his major works which deal with religious themes are *Pans'ki Zharty* ('Landowner's Humour', 1887) and *Moišeš* ('Moses', 1905).

Fransen, Pieter Frans Belgian Jesuit, theologian and writer, born Doornik (Tournai), Belgium, 10 December 1913, died Heverlee, Louvain, 2 December 1983. He joined the Jesuits in 1930, studied philosophy and theology at Louvain and taught dogmatic theology there from 1947 to 1967. He also taught at Innsbruck and in 1966 was named dean of theology at Haverlee. He helped form the Centre for Ecclesiastical Studies, a seminary consortium of several religious orders. In 1969 he became chairman of the newly created English language programme at Louvain and had overall responsibility for the teaching of sacramental and mystical theology, ecclesiology and the hermeneutics of conciliar texts. He was one of the major exponents of renewed understandings of the Church and of the new theological thinking leading up to and following the Second Vatican Council. He lectured worldwide, was on the editorial board of *Louvain Studies, Bijdragen, Collationes* and *Tijdschrift voor Theologie*, and contributed to learned journals and Christian periodicals. Among his writings are *Divine Grace and Man* (1962), the three-volume *Intelligent Theology* (1969), *New Life of Grace* (1971) and he edited and contributed to *Authority in the Church* (1983).

Franzelin, Johannes Baptist Jesuit priest, cardinal and theologian, born Aldein, Tyrol, 15 April 1816, died Rome, 11 December 1886. He entered the Society of Jesus in 1834, becoming prefect of studies and confessor at the German College in Rome in 1853, and professor of dogmatic theology at the Roman College in 1857. He was papal theologian at the First Vatican Council (1869–70), drafting the constitution on the nature of the Church *Dei Filius*, which was accepted after extensive revision. He wrote extensively, publishing both a widely used theology course and more detailed dogmatic works, including *De Divina Traditione et Scriptura* (1870). He also participated in debates with Orthodox and Protestant theologians on the nature of the Holy Spirit. He was made a cardinal in 1876.

Fraser, Alexander Campbell Idealist philosopher and minister of the Free Church of Scotland, born Ardchattan, Argyllshire, where his father was minister, 3 September 1819, died Edinburgh, 2 December 1914. Held the post of professor of philosophy at Edinburgh from 1856 to 1891. He specialized in the study of George **Berkeley**, whose philosophy greatly influenced Fraser's own views – though he never sought to impose these on his students. His works include a volume on *Berkeley* for the Blackwood's Philosophical Classics (1881), *The Philosophy of Theism*, prepared as the Gifford Lectures for 1885–6, and *Biographia Philosophica* (1904), which sets out the development of his philosophical position.

Frassen, Claude Franciscan theologian and philosopher, born near Péronne, France, 1620, died Paris, 26 February 1711. He entered the Franciscan Order in 1637 and the following year went to Paris first as a student and later as professor of philosophy and theology, specializing in the work of **Duns Scotus**. In 1662 Frassen was elected definitor general of the Franciscans and in that capacity took part in the general chapters at Toledo and Rome. He was well regarded by civil and religious authorities alike. His *Scotus Academicus*, which has appeared in several editions since the first (Paris 1672–7), is regarded as one of the most authoritative and accessible treatments of the works of Scotus.

Frassinetti, Giuseppe Roman Catholic pastor, writer and founder of the Sons of Mary Immaculate, born Genoa, 15 December 1804, died there, 2 January 1868. Brother of Bl. Paola **Frassinetti**. He was ordained in 1827, and was pastor of St Sabina, Genoa, from 1839 onwards, where he earned a reputation as 'the Italian Curé d'Ars'. In addition to his energetic pastoral ministry, he also wrote extensively. His works, which were widely read for many years, included *Compendia della teologia dogmatica* (1839), *Gesù Cristo regola del sacerdote* (1852), *Il conforto dell'anima divota* (1852), *Manuale practico del parocho novello* (1863) and *Compendia della teologia morale* (1865–6). In 1939 his cause for beatification was introduced in Rome.

Frassinetti, Paola Blessed, Roman Catholic foundress of the Dorothean religious congregation, born Genoa, 3 March 1809, died Rome, 11 June 1882. Sister of Giuseppe **Frassinetti**. Owing to ill-health, she was prevented from fulfilling her early wish of joining a religious community, and so in 1834 she founded her own institute for the education of girls from all levels of society. The Dorotheans were granted papal approval in 1863. New houses were founded across Italy and in Portugal and Brazil, with Paola Frassinetti serving as superior general until she died. She was beatified on 8 June 1930.

Frayssinous, Denis Roman Catholic bishop and apologist, born Curières, Aveyron, France, 9 May 1765, died St Géniez, Aveyron, 12 December 1841. A member of the Society of St Sulpice (a society for committed clergy devoted to study and spiritual development) from 1788 to 1806, he taught at the Society's seminary for six years and, after the French Revolution, secretly undertook pastoral work. As a notable apologist for Catholicism, he preached widely and organized conferences (at one time banned by Napoleon). The conferences were later published as *Defense du christianisme* (3 vols, 1825). A royalist and moderate Gallican, he was court preacher and royal almoner to Louis XVIII, became titular bishop in 1822 and minister of ecclesiastical affairs, 1824–8. After the July Revolution in 1830, he left public life.

Frederick I Barbarossa German king and Holy Roman Emperor, born 4 March 1122 or 1123, died by drowning in the River Saleph, Cilicia, 10 June 1190. Following the death of his uncle, Conrad III, Frederick was elected king of the Germans and crowned in March of 1152. He had hoped to re-establish Carolingian and Ottoman ideals of empire by strengthening royal power but failed in this mission in part because of the opposition by princes such as **Henry the Lion** as well as his interests in Italy. He was crowned Emperor in 1155. His relationship with the Papacy was fraught with power struggles culminating in the defeat of the imperial army by the Lombards at Legnano in 1176.

Frederick II Of Germany, Holy Roman Emperor and king of Sicily, born near Ancona, 26 December 1194, died Apulia, 13 December 1250. His father, the Hohenstaufen Emperor **Henry VI**, and his mother, Constance of Sicily, both died when he was very young. His guardian, Pope **Innocent III**, helped Frederick wrest power from the Guelph emperor **Otto IV**, and he was eventually crowned Emperor in 1220. To achieve his aim of consolidating and centralizing imperial power in Italy he introduced measures to reduce the power of the Papacy, earning him several excommunications.

He went on a Crusade to the Holy Land in 1228 and crowned himself king of Jerusalem, continuing his struggles with the Papacy on his return.

Frederick III of Saxony Elector, born Torgau, 14 January 1463, died Lochau, 5 December 1525. Known as 'the Wise', Frederick succeeded to the position of elector in 1486 and worked to strengthen the power of the prince by reforming the administration of his territory. He founded the University of Wittenberg and is best known for his support, protection and guidance of the Protestant reformer Martin **Luther**, whom he invited to teach at Wittenberg. Such interventions on Luther's behalf as blocking his extradition to Rome, negotiating for his appearance before Cardinal **Cajetan** in 1518, and arranging for his sojourn in the Wartburg Castle after the Diet of Worms in 1521 were significant to the overall establishment of the Reformation.

Frederick of Mainz Archbishop, date and place of birth unknown, died Mainz, 25 October 954. Appointed archbishop of Mainz in 937, and presided over the Synod of Augsburg (952). A friend of the Emperor **Otto I**, he nevertheless took part in two rebellions, in 938 and 953, in defence of the Church's rights and against Otto's ecclesiastical policies. Frederick was highly regarded as a preacher and reformer, and he founded St Peter's in Mainz as a collegiate church.

Fredoli, Berenger Cardinal, born Vérune, France, *c.*1250, died Avignon, 11 June 1323. He was professor of canon law at Bologna and held various senior ecclesiastical positions, including that of chaplain to Pope **Celestine V**. He became bishop of Béziers in 1294. **Boniface VIII** appointed him to assist in the compilation of the text of the Decretals known later as the *Liber Sextus*. He became cardinal in 1305 and cardinal-bishop of Frascati in 1309. His works, mainly on canon law, include *Oculus*, a commentary on the *Summa* of the cardinal of Ostia, *Inventarium juris canonici* and *Inventarium speculi judicialis*.

Free, John English Renaissance scholar, humanist, probably born London *c.*1430, died Rome *c.*1465. He was educated at Bristol and Balliol, Oxford, and became clerk to the Diocese of Bath and Wells.

In 1456 he was sent by the bishop of Ely, William Gray, to study in Ferrara under Guarini da Verona. He polished his Latin, learned Greek and associated with several leading humanists. He studied at Padua, where he became a doctor of medicine sometime after 1461. He enjoyed the patronage of the earl of Worcester, and later, after he had moved to Rome, of Pope **Paul II**. His works include translations of *Laus Calvitii* and *De insomniis* both by Synesius of Cyrene.

Freeman, Hobart Pastor and faith healer, born Ewing, Kentucky, 1920, died 1984. As a Baptist, Freeman taught at Grace Theological Seminary from 1961 to 1963; that year, however, he left over doctrinal matters and started his own Church in Winona Lake, Indiana. Freeman claimed to have been healed of polio, and he taught that medicine was demonic. Freeman achieved media notoriety in 1978: two of his congregation were sentenced to prison for allowing their child to die rather than be treated, and Freeman was indicted over another death. Freeman wrote *Introduction to Old Testament Prophets*, published by Moody, in 1969.

Frelinghuysen, Theodore Jacobus Dutch Reformed pastor, contributor to the development of Pietism and to the revival in America known as the Great Awakening, born Westphalia, Germany, 6 November 1692, died after May 1747. He studied for the ministry in both Holland and Germany and was ordained as a Reformed pastor in Holland in 1717. Two years later he went to minister to the Dutch congregations in New Jersey, where his efforts to impose stricter spiritual discipline, on pain of excommunication, involved him in controversy. He promoted the increased use of English in services and from 1737 worked towards greater autonomy for the American Dutch Reformed Churches.

French, Thomas Valpy Anglican bishop, born Burton-on-Trent, 1 January 1825, died Muscat, 14 May 1891. He studied at University College, Oxford, of which he became a fellow in 1848. The following year he was ordained priest, and in 1850 was sent by the Church Missionary Society to be principal of St John's College, Agra. Periods in India alternated with incumbencies in England. He founded the divinity school at Lahore, and became the first bishop of Lahore in 1877, a post he resigned a decade later. In 1891, shortly before his death, he became a missionary in Muscat.

Freppel, Charles Emile Roman Catholic theologian, apologist and writer, born Obernai, Bas-Rhin, France, 1 June 1827, died Angers, 22 December 1891. He was professor of homiletics (later also of patristics) at the Sorbonne from 1855, bishop of Angers from 1869, and closely involved in the First Vatican Council (1869–70), where he strongly supported the doctrine of papal infallibility. An opponent of laicism, he regularly defended the Church as a deputy to the French Chamber from 1880. He was particularly critical of state efforts to intervene in social problems, believing these were to be solved through individual action and moral renewal. He wrote over 40 books, including *Examen critique de la Vie de Jésus par E. Renan* (1863) and *La Révolution française* (1889).

Frere, Rudolph Walter Howard Anglican bishop, liturgist and musicologist, born Cambridge, England, 23 November 1863, died Mirfield, Yorkshire, 2 April 1938. He was a High Churchman with extensive knowledge of medieval liturgy, particularly in the 'English' (as opposed to 'Roman') tradition. Ordained in 1887, he was a curate in Stepney, East London, before joining the new Community of the Resurrection, Mirfield, in 1892 (he served as superior twice between 1902 and 1922). He was bishop of Truro from 1923 to 1935, and took part in the Malines Conversations between the Anglican and Roman Catholic Churches, 1921–7. Among his publications were *The Use of Sarum* (2 vols, 1898, 1901), *The Principles of Religious Ceremonial* (1906) and editions of the *Winchester Troper*, *Sarum Gradual* and *Hymns, Ancient and Modern* (1909 edn).

Frescobaldi, Girolamo Baroque composer and keyboard virtuoso, born Ferrara, Italy, mid-September 1583, died Rome, 1 March 1643. He held a number of positions as a church organist in Italy and in 1607 spent a year in Flanders in 1607, then a leading centre of keyboard playing. In 1608 he became organist of St Peter's, Rome, and was engaged there for most of the rest of his life, apart from a six-year period at the court of Ferdinando II de' Medici in Florence. During his lifetime he gained considerable fame across Europe for his virtuoso keyboard playing. He composed for both voice and keyboard, although his reputation mainly rests on the latter works (including canzonas, toccatas, ricercares and in particular the capriccios of 1624). His music, much of which is highly contrapuntal in style and requires high technical ability, reflects the shift from Renaissance to baroque styles of composition which took place in his lifetime.

Frey, Johann Baptist Roman Catholic biblical scholar, born Ingersheim, Alsace, 26 April 1878, died Rome, 19 May 1939. His area of expertise was in the study of Judaism in the time between the Testaments, writing his doctorate on *Le Théologie juive au Temps de Jésus Christ comparée avec la Théologie de le Nouveau Testament*. He studied in Chevilly, Rome and Paris, and became a consultor to the Pontifical Biblical Commission in 1910 and secretary in 1925, a period during which conservative scholarship held sway. He wrote widely on the Jewish faith in early Christian times, and vol. 1 of his collection of Hebrew inscriptions was published as *Corpus inscriptionum Judaicarum* in 1936 (vol. 2, posthumously, 1952).

Freytag, Walter Missiologist, teacher and ecumenist, born Nieudietendorf, Thuringia, Germany, 1899, died Heidelburg, 24 October 1959. Of Moravian background, he studied theology and philosophy at Tübingen, Marburg and Halle. Unable to become a missionary in China, in 1928 he became director of Deutsche Evangelische Missionshilfe. He taught missiology at Hamburg and Kiel until removed by the Nazis. A notable speaker and teacher, and known for being a good listener, he left few major writings. He travelled widely in India, New Guinea, China and America and attended all the meetings of the International Missionary Council from Jerusalem in 1928 to Ghana in 1957–8. He strove to bring Church and mission closer together, and to avoid polarization between ecumenical and evangelical groups. Sensitive to the changing realities of mission, he was a passionate supporter of the integration of the International Missionary Council with the World Council of Churches in 1961.

Fridelli, Xaver Ehrenbert Austrian Jesuit, missionary and cartographer, born Linz, Austria, 11 March 1673, died Peking, 4 June 1743. He joined the Jesuits in 1688 and in 1705 was sent to China, where he made a major contribution to the cartographical survey of the empire. He was for many years rector of one of the four Jesuit churches in Peking.

Frideswide   Saint, born between 650 and 680, died traditionally Oxford, 19 October 735, but the oldest source suggests 727. Little is known of her life, but traditionally she was a consecrated virgin, the first abbess of a convent founded in Oxford by her father, a local Anglo-Saxon ruler. After refusing an offer of marriage from the 'king of Leicester', she was by a miracle transported from Oxford and into hiding, and her suitor was struck blind (or dead – the accounts vary here) for persisting in his attempts to marry her. Her monastery was recorded as having been sacked by Danish armies in the early eleventh century, but refounded by Augustinians in 1122. From the twelfth century until the dissolution of the remaining monasteries in 1538 her shrine was a place of pilgrimage. Feast day 19 October.

Friedberg, Emil Albert   Protestant scholar of canon law, born Konitz, Prussia, 22 February 1837, died Leipzig, 7 September 1910. After studying in Heidelberg and Berlin, he taught law in Berlin, Halle, Friedburg and Leipzig, the last from 1868 to 1910. As a leading figure in Church law and an exponent of the view that the Church should be subordinate to the State, his ideas were influential in the development of Church–State policy in Prussia during the Kulturkampf. He made an edition of *Corpus Iuris Canonici* (1878–81, 1922–8) and *Quinque compilationis antiquae* (1882), and co-edited the *Zeitschrift für Kirchenrecht* (named the *Deutsche Zeitschrift für Kirchenrecht* after 1891).

Friedel, Francis   Marianist priest, author and educator, born Cleveland, Ohio, 8 August 1897, died Dayton, Ohio, 12 February 1959. He studied in Dayton, Fribourg, Switzerland (where he was ordained in 1927), and Washington, DC. He was awarded a Ph.D. by the University of Pittsburgh in 1950. He wrote widely, and his major works include *The Mariology of Cardinal Newman* (1928) and *Social Patterns in the Society of Mary* (1951).

He was president of the American Catholic Sociological Society and of Trinity College, Sioux City, Iowa, 1943–9. Between 1949 and 1953 he was dean of the College of Arts and Sciences at the University of Dayton, and also took a close interest in community welfare.

Friedrich, Johann   Roman Catholic (later Old Catholic) Church historian, born Poxdorf, Upper Franconia, 5 June 1836, died Munich, 19 August 1917. He taught theology at Munich from 1862, and was involved in the First Vatican Council as secretary to Archbishop (later Cardinal) Hohenlohe of Ephesus. He was a strong opponent of the doctrine of papal infallibility (on the grounds of historical indefensibility), and was excommunicated in 1871 after refusing to accept the conciliar decrees. He was a member of the Old Catholic Church in Germany but left after it repealed a policy of celibacy for its priests. From 1872, he was professor of theology at Munich, and his many writings on Church history include: *Die Kirchengeschichte Deutschlands* (2 vols, 1967–9) and *Geschichte des vatikanischen Konzils* (3 vols, 1877–87).

Frigidian of Lucca   Bishop and saint, died Lucca, c.588(?). Apparently of Irish origin, he settled as a hermit in Italy, where he acquired a reputation for his sanctity and was chosen bishop of Lucca. After his death, his cult spread beyond Tuscany into other regions of Italy and Corsica; his relics, miraculously discovered in the eighth century, are in a church dedicated to his memory in Lucca. Most of our information about him comes from a Life of which the earliest manuscripts are from the eleventh century; many scholars doubt much of its account, and in one case date Frigidian as early as the third century. Feast day 18 March, 20 March in Ireland.

Frins, Victor   Jesuit theologian and author, born Aachen, Germany, 17 April 1840, died Bonn, 13 April 1912. He joined the Society of Jesus, and after his studies taught at Regensburg, Ditton Hall near Liverpool and St Bueno's at St Asaph, Wales. He was particularly influenced by Juan de **Lugo**, the seventeenth-century Spanish theologian. A specialist in moral theology and Scholastic theology, his works include *Doctrina S. Thomae Aquinatis de cooperatione Dei* (1893), *De actibus humanis onto-*

logicae et psychologice consideratis (1897), *De actibus humanis moraliter consideratis* (1904) and *De formanda conscientia* (1911).

Frith, John Protestant martyr, born Westerham, England, *c.*1503, died (burnt as a heretic) London, 4 July 1533. Frith was appointed a junior canon at Cardinal College, Oxford (later Christ Church), by Thomas **Wolsey**, its founder, in 1525. Subsequently he came under the influence of Lutheranism, for which he was imprisoned in1528. He escaped to Germany, where he assisted William **Tyndale** in his translation of the Bible. Frith returned to England in 1532, but a privately circulated dissertation he had written on the nature of the sacraments (in which he denied the doctrines of purgatory and transubstantiation) fell into the hands of Chancellor Thomas **More**, who had him arrested on a charge of heresy. Frith refused to recant and was burned at the stake at Smithfield.

Fritz, Samuel Jesuit missionary and Amazon explorer, born Trautenau, Bohemia, 9 April 1654, died Jéveros, Ecuador, 20 March 1725(8?). He joined the Jesuits in 1673 and was sent as a missionary to Quito in 1684. He worked among the Indian people of the Upper Marañon for the next 42 years. He was gifted in art and crafts and enjoyed considerable linguistic abilities and diplomatic skills. He mapped the area between Perua and Quito, thus helping settle some of the territorial disputes between the Spaniards and the Portuguese, and he charted the course of the Amazon River. He was the first to demonstrate that the Tunguragua was the real source of the Marañon.

Froben, Johann Scholar and printer, born Hammelburg, Germany, *c.*1460, died Basel, Switzerland, 26 October 1527. Froben established a printing press in 1491 in Basel, where he had studied, and commenced publishing the scholarly works which soon gained the press a widespread reputation for accuracy and high editorial quality. Froben's most famous publication was the 1516 edition of the Greek NT edited by his friend **Erasmus**, who subsequently prepared several editions of the Fathers for Froben's press. The business eventually suffered because Froben was reluctant to publish the writings of the Reformers.

Froberger, Johann Jakob German composer organist and keyboard player, born Stuttgart, Germany, baptized 19 May 1616, died Héricourt, near Montbéliard, France, 7 May 1667. In 1637 he became a court organist at Vienna, but then became a pupil of **Frescobaldi** in Italy. Froberger visited Belgium, Germany, Holland, France and England. He wrote a vast number of works for harpsichord and organ. Only two religious vocal works are extant, an *Alleluia* and *Apparuerant Apostolis.*

Fröbes, Joseph Jesuit philosopher, psychologist and author, born Betzdorf (now in Germany), 26 August 1866, died Cologne, 24 March 1947. He was the leading Catholic expert on experimental psychology in Germany, and wrote a number of influential books, including *Lehrbuch der experimentellen Psychologie* (2 vols, 3rd edn, 1923–9), *Psychologia speculativa in usum scholarum* (2 vols, 1927) and *Compendium psychologiae experimentalis* (rev. edn, 1948). He entered the Jesuit Order aged sixteen, spent some years teaching mathematics and sciences, and after ordination in 1900 taught philosophy. He then studied and trained in psychology, before becoming professor of philosophy and founder of a psychological laboratory at a Jesuit college in Holland, where he taught for over twenty years.

Frohschammer, Jakob Roman Catholic priest and Idealist philosopher, born Illkhofen (now in Germany), 6 January 1821, died Bad Kreuth, Germany, 14 April 1893. He was for many years professor of philosophy at the University of Munich, and sought to understand faith in the context of natural reason, insisting that the philosophy should be independent of Church control. When in 1862 he declined to withdraw three of his books, he was suspended. He argued that reality finds its fundamental base in imagination ('phantasie'). The created world is the tangible manifestation of the transcendent imagination of God, which is the active force in the creation and development of the universe. His books include *Über den Ursprung der menschlichen Seelen* (1854), *Einleitung in die Philosophie* (1858) and *Die Phantasie als Grundprinzip des Weltprozesses* (1877).

Froilan Saint, Spanish Benedictine, born Luga in

the Galicia region of Spain, 832, died 905. With his companion, **Attilanus**, and with the authorization of Alfonso III of Oviedo, he led the restoration of monastic observance at Moruruela in Old Castile and later throughout Western Spain. He became abbot and later bishop of Léon. He was included in the Roman Martyrology in 1724. Feast day 3 October.

Froude, James Anthony English historian and biographer, born Dartington, England, 23 April 1818, died Salcombe Harbour, 20 October 1894. Brother of Richard Hurrell **Froude**. He became a fellow of Exeter College, Oxford, in 1843, was ordained deacon in 1844, became rector of St Andrews University in 1868 and Regius professor of modern history at Oxford in 1892. His extensive writings on the history of England and its colonies, while highly partisan and sometimes factually inaccurate, nevertheless made a notable contribution to scholarship. His major works include the *History of England from the Fall of Wolsey to the Defeat of the Spanish Armada* (12 vols, 1856–70), *Life of Thomas Carlyle* (4 vols, 1882–4) and *The English in Ireland in the Eighteenth Century* (1872–4).

Froude, Richard Hurrell Tractarian (leading figure in the early stages of the Oxford Movement), born Dartington, England, 25 March 1803, died Dartington, 28 February 1836. He became fellow and tutor of Oriel College, Oxford, in 1826 and 1827 respectively, and was ordained in 1829. While at Oxford, he became acquainted with High Church views through his friendships with John Henry **Newman** and John **Keble**, whom he helped to introduce. Despite being plagued by illness, Froude frequently worked together with Newman and Keble, and made three contributions to *Tracts for the Times*. Extracts from his private papers (published posthumously as *Remains*, part 1, 1838; part 2, 1839) caused considerable controversy for their apparent criticism of the Reformation and approval of clerical celibacy and devotion to the Virgin Mary.

Froumund of Tegernsee Monk, educator, poet, born possibly near Regensburg, Germany, *c*.960, died probably at the abbey of Tegernsee, 20 October 1008(?). Originally a Benedictine at Tegernsee, Froumund studied in Cologne, residing and working at the abbey of Pantaleon. Back at Tegernsee, along with the monk Wigo, 990–5, and bishop Liutold of Augsburg, he took part in the reform of the Feuchtwangen Abbey. Froumund was ordained *c*.1005 and spent the rest of his life at his abbey teaching and writing verse. His correspondence reflects Bavarian life and monasticism of his day.

Fructuosus Saint, bishop and martyr, died 21 January 259. He was bishop of Tarragona and was arrested with two of his deacons during the Valerian persecutions. Under interrogation he refused to recognize the Roman gods or sacrifice to the image of the emperor, and with his deacons was burnt in the amphitheatre. Feast day 21 January.

Fructuosus of Braga Saint, Spanish monk, archbishop, died Braga, *c*.665. He lived alone in a desert area of Galicia and was eventually joined by numerous pupils, and so was established the monastery of Complutum, the first of many monasteries founded by Fructuosus. In 654 he was made bishop of Dumium, and in 656 archbishop of Braga. His remains were moved to Compostella. He is usually shown with a stag, which he allegedly saved from hunters. Feast day 16 April.

Frumentius Saint, bishop, 'Apostle to the Abyssinians', born Tyre(?), *c*.300, died *c*.380. As a young man Frumentius was captured by Abyssinians while on a trading journey. At Axum he was shown favour by their king, who made him his secretary. Following the king's death his queen persuaded Frumentius to help govern the country until the crown prince was of age. As a Christian, Frumentius used his position as a platform for evangelism, with considerable success. When he was eventually released he reported his work to **Athanasius**, who appointed him bishop of Axum *c*.340. Frumentius took the title 'Abuna' (Our Father), still used by primates of the Abyssinian Church. Feast days Orthodox calendar, 30 November, Coptic calendar, 18 December, Western calendar, 27 October.

Frutolf of Michelsberg Monk, historian, musicologist, died 17 January 1103, abbey of Michelsberg, Bamberg, Germany. Frutolf, a Benedictine teacher in the Michelsberg monastic school, wrote a history of the world to 1101 called the *Chronicon*.

This was a remarkable and readable work, drawn from numerous sources, but overshadowed by a plagiarized version by Ekkehard of Aura, died 1125. Frutolf also produced several musicological works, i.e. *Breviarim de musica*, *Tonarius* and perhaps the *Rithmimachia*.

Fry, Elizabeth Quaker philanthropist and prison reformer, born Norwich, England, 21 May 1780, died Ramsgate, 12 October 1845. An approved Quaker minister from 1811, she became concerned with prison conditions in 1813, and began to give Bible readings to female prisoners in Newgate gaol. There in 1817 she founded the Association for the Improvement of the Female Prisoners in Newgate, offering education, paid employment and religious instruction. She campaigned widely in both Britain and Europe on prison reform, particularly for the rights of female prisoners (e.g. for the right to female warders), and undertook further philanthropic work. Her works include *Observations on the Visiting, Superintendance and Government of Female Prisoners* (1827), and extracts from her letters and papers were published in a *Memoir* edited posthumously by her daughters.

Fry, Franklin Clark Lutheran minister, Church president, born Bethlehem, Pennsylvania, 30 August 1900, died New Rochelle, New York, 6 June 1968. Ordained in 1925, he gained a doctorate and served as pastor of a church in Ohio until 1944. From then until 1962, he was president of the United Lutheran Church in America. As a skilled organizer, he was an important figure in the creation of the Lutheran Church in America, and was appointed its first president in 1962. He was an important figure in the US ecumenical movement and also served as chairman of the central committee of the World Council of Churches.

Fuente, Michael de la Spanish Carmelite and spiritual writer, born Valdelaguna, near Madrid, 2 March 1573, died Toledo, 27 November 1625. After his profession as a Carmelite in 1594 he studied philosophy and theology at the University of Salamanca and became novice master in Toledo, where he spent the rest of his life. He wrote a Rule for the Carmelite Third Order, important for the group's development. He is reported to have experienced states of ecstasy and levitation and to have

had the gift of prophecy. His body was found incorrupt several years after his death. He is the author of the important ascetical and mystical work *Libro de las tres vidas del hombre corporal, racional y espiritual* (Toledo, 1623).

Fugger, Jakob Banker, born Augsburg, Germany, 6 March 1459, died Augsburg, 30 December 1525. Fugger entered his family's textile business in 1478, and within a few years his business acumen had secured him an immense fortune. He cultivated business contacts with the Habsburgs and the Holy See, becoming the principal moneylender to these and other powerful families of the time. In 1513 Fugger lent Albert of Brandenburg the funds necessary to enable him to accumulate a number of German benefices. Albert secretly arranged to repay Fugger with half the proceeds of the sale of a new indulgence. The scandalous manner in which this was peddled angered Martin **Luther**, provoking him to compose his '95 theses' of 1517, and thereby triggering the Reformation.

Fulbert of Chartres Bishop, scholar, born probably near Rome, *c.*960, died at Chartres, 10 April 1028. He was educated at Rheims and one of his teachers was Gerbert, the future Pope **Sylvester II**. He was chancellor of the church of Chartres and treasurer of St Hilary's in Poitiers. In 990 Fulbert opened a school at Chartres which eventually drew scholars from all over Europe. In 1007 he was made bishop of Chartres but continued to teach. The cathedral burned down in 1020 and Fulbert began an even more splendid building in its place, financed by several European monarchs. Though not a monk himself he was friendly with many monks of his time and did a lot to reform the clergy. He left many writings including letters, treatises, hymns and sermons.

Fulcher of Chartres Priest and chronicler of the First Crusade, born *c.*1059, died Palestine(?), *c.*1127. Present at the Council of Clermont (1095), Fulcher gives a valuable eyewitness account of the council where Pope **Urban II** preached the First Crusade, which Fulcher joined first as chaplain to Count Stephen of Blois and then, from 1097, **Baldwin I**, later the count of Edessa and king of Jerusalem. After Baldwin became king of Jerusalem in 1100, Fulcher served as a royal chaplain and canon of the Holy Sepulchre; he may also have been prior of Mount Olivet. In 1101, he began writing the *Historia Hierosolymitana*, an unusually reliable account of the First Crusade and the Latin Kingdom of Jerusalem.

Fulcoius of Beauvais Archdeacon, writer, born Beauvais, died Meaux, *c.*1200. Fulcoius wrote three volumes of poetry (*Uter*, epitaphs and letters, *Neuter*, Lives of SS **Agil**, Blandinus, **Faro** and **Maurus**, and *Uterque*, about Christ and the Church). He also wrote letters to political and ecclesiastical leaders which illustrate the conditions of the time and the obstacles to the reform of Pope **Gregory VII**. Fulcoius' writings are enhanced by his use of the classical poets and the Fathers.

Fulcran of Lodeve Saint, bishop, died Lodeve, 1006. According to the Life written in the fourteenth century by one of his successors (Bernard Guidonis), Fulcran came from a respected family and dedicated himself to the Church as a youth. He was conscrated bishop of Lodeve, France, on 4 February 949, strove to uphold morality in his diocese, especially among the clergy, and rebuilt many churches and convents. Revered as a saint after his death, his preserved body was burned by Huguenots in 1572. Feast day 13 February.

Fulgentius, Fabius Planciades Writer, fl. late fifth century. Nothing is known of his life, except that he may have come from Carthage. Attributed to him are the *Mythologiae*, a series of allegorical interpretations of pagan myths; an allegorical interpretation of Virgil's *Aeneid*; and the *Expositio sermonum antiquorum*, a far-fetched explanation of 62 obsolete Latin words illustrated from a wide range of authors, with many false citations. Another text, attributed to a Fabius Claudius Gordianus Fulgentius, *On the Ages of the World and of Man*, is similar in style to Fulgentius' works. All of these treatises were widely read in the Middle Ages, when they were mistakenly attributed to **Fulgentius of Ruspe**.

Fulgentius of Ecija Bishop and saint, born probably Seville, *c.*540–60, died probably Ecija, *c.*619. One of four saintly siblings of a distinguished Hispano-Roman family (see **Florentina, Isidore of Seville, Leander**), he became bishop of Ecija and attended the Councils (or Synods) of Toledo (610) and Seville (619). Around 1320 his relics were discovered near Guadalupe, which led to claims that he was bishop of Cartagena; in 1593 they were shared between the Escorial and the See of Cartagena, where he had become patron saint. His cult is immemorial in Spain. Some Spanish breviaries falsely attribute to him writings by **Fulgentius of Ruspe** and Fabius Planciades **Fulgentius**. Feast day 14 January.

Fulgentius of Ruspe Saint, bishop, born North Africa, *c.*460, died Ruspe, near Tunis, 1 January 533. He was a former Roman civil servant who became a monk, and was appointed bishop of Ruspe in North Africa early in the sixth century. Fulgentius was a staunch Nicene, which brought him into conflict with the Arian King Thrasamund; as a result Fulgentius twice suffered banishment. His admiration for the theology of **Augustine** of Hippo is evident in his writings. Feast day 1 January.

Fulk of Neuilly Blessed, priest and preacher of the Fourth Crusade, died Neuilly-sur-Marne, 2 March 1201. Nothing is known of his early life. From 1191, he served as a priest in the church of Neuilly-sur-Marne near Paris. A brilliant preacher, acording to Villehardouin, Fulk inspired Count Thibault III of Champagne to ask Pope **Innocent III** to organize the Fourth Crusade, and later Fulk preached the Crusade across France, though he died before the Crusade began. Feast day 2 March (unofficial cult).

Fuller, Andrew Baptist theologian and preacher, born Wicken, Cambridgeshire, 6 February 1754, died Kettering, Northamptonshire, 7 May 1815. Agricultural labourer who, at the age of sixteen, was converted and became a member of Soham Baptist Church, eventually becoming its pastor in 1775. Rejecting hyper-Calvinism he adopted a moderate form of Calvinism as expressed in his book *The Gospel Worthy of all Acceptation* (1785). From 1782 until his death he ministered to a church at Kettering. He was appointed the first secretary of the Baptist Missionary Society in 1792. His other writings include *The Gospel its own Witness* (1799) and *The Calvinistic and Socinian*

Systems Examined and Compared as to their Moral Tendency (1793).

Fumo, Bartolommeo Italian Benedictine, theologian, born Villon, near Piacenza, died 1545. He is best known for his *Summa casuum conscientae, aurea armilla dicta*. It contained a digest of all similar works from the thirteenth century on and refutes what Fumo sees as the errors of probabilism. His other works are *Philothea, opus immortalis animi dignitatem continens, Expositio compendiosa in epistolas Pauli et canonicas* and *Poemata quaedam*.

Funder, Friedrich Austrian Roman Catholic journalist, born Graz, Steiermark, Austria, 1 November 1872, died Vienna, 19 May 1959. His early journalistic career was with the left-wing Catholic *Reichspost*, becoming editor in 1902. He was a close ally of Archduke Franz Ferdinand (until the latter's assassination in 1914) and had supported his political reforms. In the inter-war years he worked closely with the chancellor of the republic, Ignatz Seipel. As a strong opponent of National Socialism, he was arrested after the German annexation of Austria and placed in the concentration camp at Dachau (and later at Flossenburg). In 1945 he began the Catholic weekly *Die Furche*, in which he sought reconciliation between rival political parties. In the 1950s he served as president of a number of international Catholic press organizations.

Funes, Dean Gregorio Roman Catholic priest and leading figure in the Argentine independence movement, born Córdoba, Spain, 25 May 1749, died Buenos Aires, Argentina, 10 January 1829. Trained in civil and canon law, he was dean of Córdoba Cathedral from 1804 and rector of the Colegio de Monserrat and the University of Córdoba, 1808–13. He participated in the revolution for Argentine independence in 1810, and as a member of the first provisional government helped to draft several decrees and constitutions. In his politics he was a liberal, a democrat and a federalist. He advocated a measure of state religious tolerance, while favouring a close partnership between the state and the Roman Catholic Church.

Funk, Franz Xaver von Church historian and expert on patristics, Roman Catholic priest, born Abtsgmünd (Germany), 12 October 1821, died Tübingen, 24 February 1907. He gained his doctorate in 1863 and was ordained the following year. He began his teaching career at the University of Tübingen in 1866, becoming professor in 1875. An exponent of the 'scientific' approach to history, his main works include *Lehrbuch der Kirchengeschichte* (1886, many times revised) and a collection of articles and reviews, *Kirchengeschichteliche Abhandlungen und Untersuchungen* (3 vols, 1897–1907). He made an edition of the post-Apostolic Fathers, *Opera Patrum Apostolicorum* (2 vols, 1878–81), and editions of the *Doctrina XII Apostolorum* (1887) and *Didascalia et Constitutiones Apostolorum* (2 vols, 1905).

Furlong, Thomas Irish Roman Catholic bishop and founder of three religious institutes, born County Wexford, Ireland, c.1803, died Wexford, 12 November 1875. After ordination, he taught at St Patrick's College, Maynooth, becoming in turn professor of humanities in 1829, rhetoric in 1834 and theology in 1845. As bishop of Ferns from 1857, he encouraged a more personal spirituality and greater observance of Sundays and holy days. In 1866 he began the Missionaries of the Blessed Sacrament, an institute dedicated to preaching at missions and retreats. He also founded the nursing and teaching order the Sisters of St John of God, in 1871, and the Institute of Perpetual Adoration, which gained papal approval in 1875.

Fursey Saint, Irish abbot or bishop, and missionary, born near Lough Corrib, Ireland, died Mezerolles, France, c.650. He became a monk and founded a monastery in the Diocese of Tuam, before travelling to England in c.630. He was welcomed by King Sigebert of East Anglia, who gave him lands to found a monastery at Burgh Castle, near Yarmouth. After the defeat of Sigebert in battle, Fursey travelled to Gaul, where he founded a monastery at Lagny-sur-Marne. His remains were first translated to a shrine in 654, and he was widely venerated in the Middle Ages, partly as a result of an account of his visions of heaven and hell, written by **Bede**. Feast day 16 January.

Fürstenberg, Franz Egon von German Catholic bishop and politician, born Bavaria, 10 April 1625, died Cologne, 1 April 1682. A son of the Bavarian commander-in-chief, Egon von Fürstenberg-Heiligenberg. Together with his brother Wilhelm (see below) he went to the Jesuit school in Cologne, and entered the service of Prince Maximilian Heinrich of Bavaria. Later, under the influence of Cardinal **Mazarin**, both became active in promoting French interests and helped create the Rheinischer Bund between France and the major German cities and states. **Louis XIV** gave Franz the bishopric of Strasburg. Both brothers suffered the loss of their property and income at the hands of the Emperor Leopold I, but these were restored under the Treaty of Nijmegen in 1679.

Fürstenberg, Franz Friedrich Wilhelm von   German Catholic priest, politician and educational reformer, born Herdringen, Westphalia, 7 August 1729, died Münster, 16 September 1810. He studied at Cologne, Saltzburg and at the Sapienza in Rome and was ordained in 1757. He became vicar general of the Diocese of Münster in 1770, a post which involved numerous secular duties. In this capacity Fürstenberg brought about reforms in religious and civil administration, education, economics, agriculture and the military. In 1773 he set up a college of medicine. In education he emphasized the sciences over the classics, included the study of German on the timetable, and established a college especially to train teachers for this new, more practical, curriculum.

Fürstenberg, Wilhelm Egon von   German cardinal and politician, born in Bavaria, 2 December 1629, died Paris, 10 April 1704. Brother of Franz Egon (see above), with whom he shared political interests and activities. On the death of his brother, Wilhelm was appointed to take over the See of Strasburg and in 1686 **Innocent XI** appointed him cardinal. When the Bavarian Prince Maximilian Heinrich died Wilhelm, against the wishes of the Pope, had himself elected to the powerful See of Cologne and headed the government. The election was declared null and void and after further wranglings Wilhelm was banished to his abbey of St-Germain-des-Prés, where he eventually died.

Fux, Johann Joseph   Austrian composer and music theorist, born Hirtenfeld, near Graz, Styria, Austria, 1660, died Vienna, 13 February 1741. After studies at Jesuit universities in Graz and Ingoldstadt he settled in Vienna, where he became successively court composer, choirmaster at St Stephen's Cathedral; then at the imperial court vice-kapellmeister and kapellmeister. He was primarily a composer of Church music, but also composed an opera for the 1723 coronation festival, and his book *Gradus ad Parnassum* became a respected rule book for composers. He admired **Palestrina** and some of Fux's music is in Palestrina's style. He wrote over 600 works – oratorios, about 80 Masses, three Requiems, motets and about 50 church sonatas.

G

Gabriel of St Mary Magdalen Discalced Carmelite and writer on mysticism, born 'Adrian Devos' at Bevere-Audenaerse (Belgium), 24 January 1893, died Rome, 15 March 1953. He made his vows in 1911 and studied in Courtrai (Belgium) and Dublin. During the First World War he was wounded twice and decorated in the course of service with the Belgian sanitation corps. After his ordination in 1920, he taught philosophy and theology, 1920–6, before serving successively as professor, vice-rector and prefect of studies at the International College of the Discalced Carmelites in Rome. In 1941 he founded the journal *Vita Carmelita* (from 1947 the *Rivista di vita spirituale*).

Gabriel Sionita Maronite Bible translator, born Edden, Lebanon, 1577, died Paris, 1648. Went to Rome at the age of seven, where he learned Latin, Syriac and some Hebrew as well as studying theology. Along with another Maronite, John Hesronita, Gabriel accompanied Savary de Breves to Paris to work on the Parisian Polyglot of the Bible. He was appointed professor of Semitic languages at the Sorbonne, received his doctorate in 1620 and was ordained to the priesthood in 1622. His contribution to the Polyglot included revising and translating into Latin nearly all the Arabic and Syriac texts. His other publications include a Latin translation of the Arabic Psalter (with John Hesronita and Victor Sciala) (1614); the first part of an Arabic grammar (1616); a *Geographia Nubiensis* (1619); and treatises on Syrian philosophy, and Islam and Christianity.

Gabrieli, Andrea Composer, born Venice, *c.*1510, died there, 30 August 1585. Long recognized as one of the great masters of Renaissance music, Gabrieli began his musical career as a chorister. He travelled north of the Alps before becoming an organist at San Geremia in Venice, and finally in 1566 at St Mark's, remaining there for the rest of his life. His virtuosity as an organist was famous in Venetian society, while his many compositions, including Masses, *Magnificats* and settings of the Psalms, and a rich corpus of secular music, all show him to have been equally talented as a composer. A pioneer of homophony, his music epitomizes the grandeur and colour of Renaissance Venice. Among his many pupils was his similarly talented nephew Giovanni **Gabrieli**.

Gabrieli, Giovanni Composer of the Venetian school and organist, born Venice, *c.*1553–6, died Venice, 12 August 1612. The nephew of the composer Andrea **Gabrieli**, he worked at the court of Duke Albrecht V in Munich, before becoming organist at St Mark's, Venice (from 1585 until his death). Many of his works were written for the worship and ceremonial of St Mark's, and reflect the large musical resources at his disposal there. His compositions include over 80 *symphoniae sacrae*, 40 organ works, and 30 madrigals. His canzonas and sonatas are notable for their creative use of instrumentation. He also edited many of his uncle's works for publication, and was influential as teacher to several northern European composers, including Heinrich **Schütz**.

Gaforio, Franchino Italian composer, born Lodi, 14 January 1451, died Milan, 25 June 1522. Following positions at Mantua, Genoa and Naples, most of Gaforio's career was spent as *maestro di capella* at Milan Cathedral. His output includes most genres of sacred music, and three volumes of musical theory. A traditionalist, he opposed musical innovations favoured by a younger generation of composers.

Gagarin, Ivan Sergeevich   Writer and (from 1843) Jesuit priest, born Moscow, Russia, 1 August 1814, died Paris, 19 July 1882. He was born into a high-ranking family and joined the Russian diplomatic corps. While living in Paris (where he was secretary to the Russian embassy from 1838) he met many influential figures within French Catholicism, and converted from Orthodoxy to Catholicism. He joined the Society of Jesus, with whom he taught philosophy and ecclesiastical history, 1849–55. Later in life he wrote widely, and his works include *La Russie sera-t-elle catholique?* (1856), *Les Starovàres, L'église russe et le Pape* (1857) and *L'Église russe et l'Immaculée Conception* (1868). He also worked for the union of the Roman Catholic and Russian Orthodox Churches.

Gage, Thomas   Traveller and writer, born Haling, Surrey, *c.*1595, died Jamaica, 1656. His father sent him to Spain to study with the Jesuits, and he afterwards joined the Dominican Order, being sent by them to the Philippines and then to Central America. Gage lived for a period among the Indians of Nicaragua and Panama. He returned to Europe in 1637 and after a visit to Loreto renounced his Catholicism in a recantation sermon at St Paul's in 1641, then joined the Parliamentarians in the Civil War. He was rector of Acrise and in 1651 of Deal. He joined the naval commander Robert Venables, becoming his chaplain during his conquest of the Spanish West Indies. Gage's most notable among his several writings is *The English-American: his Travail by sea and land* (1648). This contained rules for learning Central American languages and became influential, being translated into most European languages in the late seventeenth century.

Gagliano, Marco da   Priest and composer, born Gagliano, Italy, *c.*1575, died Florence, 24 February 1642. Succeeding his teacher Bati as *maestro di capella* of San Lorenzo in Florence, and remaining there for his entire career, Gagliano was an early representative of the new baroque style of composition which became fashionable in the courts of Europe during the seventeenth century. In addition to his secular works, some of which were written for the Gonzaga and Medici families, Gagliano also produced a considerable amount of sacred music, though in some cases only the texts have survived.

Gagliardi, Achille   Jesuit ascetic and spiritual director, born Padua, Italy, 1537, died Modena, 6 July 1607. Studied at Padua and entered the Society of Jesus in 1559. He taught philosophy in Rome and theology at Padua and Milan and then became director of several Jesuit houses in Northern Italy. He was well respected by, among others, Charles **Borromeo**, then archbishop of Milan, and it was at his insistence that he published in 1584 his *Catechismo della fede cattolica*. His other works on mysticism and asceticism, published after his death, include *Breve compendio intorno alla perfezione christiana* (1611) and *Commentarii in Exercizia spiritualia S.P. Ignatii de Loyola* (1882).

Gaguin, Robert   Humanist scholar and ecclesiastical diplomat, born Callone-sur-Lys, France, *c.*1433, died Paris, 22 May 1501. A professor at the Sorbonne, where he was dean of the faculty of canon law, Gaguin numbered **Erasmus** and **Reuchlin** among his pupils. His letters form a valuable historical source regarding the introduction of humanist ideals in Paris. Later in his life Gaguin became involved in ecclesiastical diplomacy, and in the course of various missions visited Italy, England (where he was known to Thomas **More**), and Germany. These missions also brought him into contact with other prominent humanist scholars of the time. Gaguin wrote a number of theological works, and also made several French translations of Latin verse and prose.

Gailhac, Pierre Jean Antoine   Roman Catholic priest and founder of the Religious of the Sacred Heart of Mary, born Béziers, France, 14 November 1802, died Béziers, 25 January 1890. Ordained in 1826, he taught theology in his Montpellier seminary for eight years (at which he was the only professor to refuse the government's order to sign the 1682 Declaration of the French Clergy). He also worked as a hospital chaplain in Béziers, 1830–49, and opened an orphanage and a women's refuge. In 1849 he founded the Religious of the Sacred Heart of Mary to look after both orphans and the education of girls. In 1860 he was acquitted of poisoning two nuns (a crime to which the real culprit later confessed). The cause for his beatification was introduced in 1953.

Gairdner, James Historian and archivist, born Edinburgh, Scotland, 22 March 1828, died Pinner, England, 4 November 1912. From 1846 until his retirement in 1893, he worked at the Public Record Office, London, becoming assistant keeper of records in 1859. An expert on the English Reformation, he produced editions of the *Calendar of Letters and Papers of the Reign of Henry VIII* (1862–1905) and *The Paston Letters* (1872–5). His own works are notable for their efforts to redress what Gairdner saw as an unwarranted bias against the Catholic case in histories of the English Reformation. These include *The English Church in the Sixteenth Century* (first published 1902) and *Lollardy and the Reformation in England* (4 vols, 1908–13). A Presbyterian in early life, he later shifted his allegiance to Anglo-Catholicism.

Gairdner, William Henry Temple Anglican missionary and Islamic scholar, born Ardrossan, Scotland, 1873, died Cairo, Egypt, 22 May 1928. Following ordination in the Church of England, in 1898 Gairdner went as a missionary to Egypt, where he made a detailed study of Arabic and Islamic culture. In order to make the worship of the Arabic Anglican Church feel less alien to converts from Islam, he strove to make the Church reflect its surrounding culture as much as possible. He became a leading Arabic and Islamic scholar, and produced one of the first grammars of colloquial Arabic in 1917. In addition to his numerous scholarly publications, Gairdner also wrote many hymns and devotional works, in both Arabic and English.

Gaius Pope and saint, elected 17 December 283, died Rome, 22 April 296. The *Liber Pontificalis* describes him as a Dalmatian, and a relative of the Emperor Diocletian, but this is doubtful. He is said to have insisted on a strict observance of the clerical orders, and assigned deacons to the seven ecclesiastical districts of Rome. He was perhaps imprisoned along with the future popes **Sixtus II**

and **Dionysius** in 257; other accounts associate him with later persecution. The details are decidedly confused. Buried in the cemetery of Callixtus, his body was transferred to the church of St Caius in 1631 by Pope **Urban VIII**. Feast day 22 April.

Galano, Clemente Roman Catholic missionary and theologian, born Sorrento, Italy, c.1610, died Leopolis, Poland (now Lvov, Ukraine), 14 May 1666. From 1626 until his death Galano was involved in the mission to reunite the Armenian Church with Rome. Early negotiations were encouraging, but when a less sympathetic Armenian patriarch was appointed following the death of his more conciliatory predecessor, Galano was forced to break off contact and return to Rome. Subsequently he went to Poland to work among Polish Armenians, and although he did not live to see the final success of this mission, the final healing of the schism was achieved shortly after his death, largely as a result of his skill and diplomacy.

Galantini, Hippolytus Roman Catholic layman, founder of the Institute of Christian Doctrine, born Florence, Italy, 12 October 1565, died Florence, 20 March 1619. A silk weaver by trade, Galantini dedicated himself to God's service as a youth, although the poor health from which he suffered throughout his life prevented him from joining a religious order. Galantini's vision was to establish a confraternity dedicated to providing an education for poor children. This he did in 1581, but setbacks and frustrations meant that it was not until 1602 that its work could begin as the Institute of Christian Doctrine. Galantini's works of charity, coupled with his pious and ascetic nature, resulted in his beatification in 1825. He has also been adopted by the Franciscans, who now regard him as one of their tertiaries.

Galberry, Thomas Roman Catholic bishop, and first provincial of the Augustinian Order in the USA, born Naas, County Kildare, Ireland, 28 May 1833, died New York City, 10 October 1878. Arriving in the USA with his family in 1851, he joined the Augustinians the following year and was ordained in 1856. Between 1858 and 1872 he worked as pastor successively in Philadelphia, New York State and Massachusetts, and was president of Villanova College, Philadelphia, 1872–5. He became superior of the Augustinian Order of the USA in 1866, and was made first principal of the province of St Thomas, Villanova, in 1874. He became bishop of Hartford, Connecticut, in 1876.

Galdinus Saint, cardinal and archbishop, born Milan, Italy, *c*.1100, died Milan, 18 April 1176. Born of a noble Milanese family, Galdinus served as chancellor in Milan and cardinal-priest in Rome before being made archbishop of Milan and papal legate for Lombardy in 1166. As such, he worked to repair the damage done by the Victorine schism and the Cathari as well as rebuild his city after it was destroyed by **Frederick I Barbarossa**. He died while preaching and was soon canonized by **Alexander III**. Feast day 18 April.

Galen, Clemens August Graf von Cardinal and bishop, born Dinklage, Oldenburg, Germany, 16 March 1878, died Münster, 22 March 1946. Of noble birth, he joined the Jesuits and was ordained in 1904. After parish ministry in Berlin and, from 1929, Münster, he became bishop of Münster in 1933. His 1932 book *Die Pest des Laizismus und ihre Erscheinungsformen* attacked the irreligiosity of post-World War I Germany. He was a consistent opponent of the Nazi regime (with little thought for his own safety), and was severely critical of its policies on race, the indoctrination of youth and the enforced euthanasia of 'unwanted' social groups. He also opposed the Nazi confiscation of religious property. It appears he remained largely free from harassment because Hitler feared von Galen's arrest would turn Westphalia against the Nazi dictatorship. Von Galen was made cardinal shortly before his death in 1946.

Galgani, Gemma Saint, Italian mystic and stigmatic, born Borgo Nuovo di Camigliano, near Lucca, 12 March 1878, died Lucca, 11 April 1903. Born of poor but devout parents, her initial wish to become a Passionist nun was thwarted by serious illness. On several occasions between 1899 and 1901 she displayed the stigmata and other marks of Christ's Passion, and experienced several ecstasies and visions of Christ, the Virgin Mary and her guardian angel. Also known for her patience, obedience and poverty in the face of her physical afflictions, she was beatified in 1933 and canonized in 1940. The publication of her correspondence with her spiritual director (1941) was important in spreading the popularity of her cult. Feast day 11 April.

Galileo Galilei Physicist and astronomer, born Pisa, 15 February 1564, died Florence, 8 January 1642. Galileo is renowned for his discoveries in physics and astronomy, and for his conflict with the Roman Catholic Church concerning the Copernican (heliocentric) theory of the universe. Although usually portrayed as a clash between science and religion, the dispute arose not over the theory itself, but rather Galileo's insistence that it entailed reinterpreting Scripture – an idea anathema to the Church. For this reason, in 1616 he was forbidden to propagate the theory publicly, an injunction he disobeyed in 1632 with the publication of his *Dialogue*. Consequently, he was summoned to Rome and forced to recant. The Church has since recognized that Galileo's condemnation was unjust.

Galitzin, Elizabeth Nun and religious administrator, born St Petersburg, Russia, 22 February 1797, died St Michael's, Louisiana, 8 December 1843. She entered the Society of the Sacred Heart, taking her final vows in Paris in 1832. As secretary general to the foundress of the Order, she participated in its sixth general council in 1839, was elected assistant general, and in 1840 travelled to America to introduce extensive reforms to the Order. She also founded several convents, but the strong-handed way in which she imposed the reforms drew resentment from some quarters. She later regretted this and returned to America in order to restore the original organization after Pope **Gregory XVI** confirmed the Society's original rules. On her visit, she contracted yellow fever while nursing the sick during an epidemic.

Gall Saint, monk and missionary, born Ireland, *c*.550, died Swabia (modern Switzerland), *c*.640. Gall became a monk at Bangor in Ireland, later travelling to Gaul among a group of missionaries led by **Columbanus**. Subsequently their journey took them to Swabia, where Gall stayed for the rest of his life as a hermit and evangelistic preacher. After his death the reputed site of one of his hermitages grew into an important monastic centre (with a famous library), which was named 'St

Gallen' (or 'St Gall') after him. Feast day 16 October.

Gall of Clermont Bishop and saint, born Clermont, 486, died Clermont, 551. Of an eminent family (**Gregory of Tours** was his nephew) he became a monk at Cournon, a deacon at Clermont, then a cantor at the chapel of Theodoric. He served as bishop of Clermont from 526 until his death. He participated in various synods, convening one at Clermont in 535, and was noted for his charitable acts and for his humility. Feast day 1 July.

Gallagher, Hugh Patrick Roman Catholic priest, missionary and editor, born Donegal, Ireland, 12 May 1815, died San Francisco, USA, 10 March 1882. He left Ireland for the USA in 1832, studied for the priesthood and was ordained in 1840. For some years he worked as pastor in Pennsylvania, taught theology, campaigned on temperance issues and spoke out on behalf of Irish immigrants (including writing editorials for the *Pittsburgh Catholic*). In 1852 he moved to the new Archdiocese of San Francisco, where he founded several institutions, including the *Catholic Standard* in 1853, and St Joseph's in 1861, including a church, free school and convent. He also undertook missionary work in the gold and silver mining areas of the West Coast, establishing the first Catholic church in Nevada.

Gallagher, Simon Felix Roman Catholic priest and missionary, born Ireland, 1796, died Natchez, Mississippi, 13 December 1825. Arriving in the USA in 1793, he was sent to minister at a church in Charleston, South Carolina, where he was a popular preacher, organized the Hibernian Society and taught at the college. A controversial figure, he had a stormy relationship with his church trustees and in 1800 was briefly suspended for intemperance. From 1812 to 1818 he was engaged in a long-running struggle for control with his French assistant priest **Clorivière**, leading to Gallagher's suspension by the archbishop. Although reinstated in 1820, he left the diocese soon afterwards, working in several other American states until his death.

Gallandi, Andrea Roman Catholic patristic scholar, born Venice, Italy, 7 December 1709, died Venice, 2 January 1779. An Oratorian priest, Gallandi compiled an important edition of patristic writings, *Bibliotheca graeco-latina veterum Patrum antiquorumque scriptorum ecclesiasticorum*, the fourteen volumes of which were published between 1765 and 1781. He also published a significant collection of writings on the history of canon law, *De vetustis canonum collectionibus dissertationum sylloge*, in 1778.

Gallifet, Joseph François de Jesuit priest, notable for his work in spreading devotion to the Sacred Heart, born Aix, France, 2 May 1663, died Lyons, 1 September 1749. He was rector at Vesoul, Lyons and Grenoble and later provincial of the Lyons province. As assistant for France he spent the years from 1723 until 1732 in Rome, returning to be rector of Lyons until his death. His major work *De cultu Sacrosancti Cordis Dei ac Domini Nostri Jesu Christi*, published in 1726, met with much criticism at first, but by the time of his death Gallifet saw the establishment of over 700 confraternities of the Sacred Heart.

Gallitzin, Amalia Leader of the Münster Circle in the German Catholic revival, born Berlin, 28 August 1748, died Münster, 27 April 1806. Mother of Demetrius Augustine **Gallitzin**. The daughter of a Prussian count, she married the Russian Prince Dimitri Gallitzin in 1768, separating from him in 1775. In 1779 she moved to Münster and, as a devotee of the French Enlightenment, focused her energies on studying. With Franz Friedrich von **Fürstenberg** she formed the Münster Circle, a group containing a number of leading Catholic intellectuals, and devoted to the discussion of philosophy, pedagogy and Christian perfection. Around 1786, she returned to the Catholic faith into which she had been baptized, and became an active member of the Westphalian Catholic community.

Gallitzin, Demetrius Augustine Roman Catholic priest and missionary, born The Hague, Holland, 22 December 1770, died Loretto, Pennsylvania, 6 May 1840. Son of Amalia **Gallitzin**. He converted to Catholicism in 1787 and, in 1792, travelled to America at his mother's suggestion. He was ordained in 1795, the first priest to have been wholly trained in the USA. He served mainly in the new western frontier states and by 1799 had established a church in Cambria County, Pennsylvania, in a place later called Loretto. Here, he attempted to build a model Catholic frontier settlement, buying land which he sold cheaply to Catholic settlers (although relations with them were initially strained). The area still has a strong Catholic population. He later became vicar general of Western Pennsylvania.

Gallo, Andrés María Colombian nationalist and Roman Catholic priest, born Tuta, Boyaca Colombia, 2 February 1791, died Bogotá, 14 April 1863. He fought on the republican side in the war for independence, and narrowly escaped the death penalty after the royalist return to power in 1816. He served on the council of justice and federal congress and was ordained in 1818. He served in parish ministry for many years, at one point helping to supply **Bolívar**'s army and serving as a military chaplain. He was several times a senator and representative, eventually becoming vice-president of the senate. He refused a bishopric on three occasions, but became vicar general of the Archdiocese of Bogotá in 1859, defending the Church against the dictator General Tomás de Mosquera.

Gallo, Maria Francesca of the Five Wounds Saint, Franciscan religious and mystic, born Naples, Italy, 25 March 1715, died Naples, 8 October 1791. Baptized 'Anna Maria Rosa Nicoletta', she was deeply pious from childhood and became a Franciscan tertiary in 1731, devoting herself to works of charity. She is said to have had the gift of prophecy, and among numerous mystical experiences is reputed to have manifested the stigmata. During her lifetime she suffered much misunderstanding, as well as poor health and intense spiritual conflicts. She was canonized in 1867. Feast day 6 October.

Galtier, Paul Theologian and Jesuit priest, born Jouanesq, Aveyron, France, 9 February 1872, died Rome, 20 January 1961. He joined the Society of Jesus in 1892, was ordained in 1904, and taught at Enghien, Belgium, 1907–38, and the Gregorian University, Rome, 1939–57. He wrote several major works on the indwelling of God, including *De SS. Trinitate in se et in nobis* (1953) and *L'Habitation en nous des trois personnes* (1953). He

also wrote on Christology, proposing Christ the Redeemer as the end of creation, e.g. in *De incarnatione et redemptione* (1947) and *Les deux Adam* (1947). He was also a leading expert on the history of Christian penance, writing *De paenitentia tractatus dogmatico-historicus* (1957) and *Aux Origines du sacrement de pénitence* (1951).

Galvin, Edward J. Roman Catholic bishop and founder of the Columban Fathers, born Cookstown, County Cork, Ireland, 23 November 1882, died Navan, Ireland, 23 February 1956. Ordained in 1909, he served as a curate in Brooklyn, New York, before offering himself for missionary work in China, in 1912. He initially worked in Shanghai, later returning to Ireland to enlist more volunteers, and founded St Columban's Missionary Society, in 1916. In 1920, he returned to China for missionary work in Hanyang (Hubei province), eventually becoming bishop of Hanyang in 1946. He remained there throughout difficult conditions in World War II, but after Communist rule was established in the area, he spent three years under house arrest, eventually being expelled from China in 1952.

Galvin, William Leland Roman Catholic lawyer and leading civic figure, born Baltimore, Maryland, 27 December 1886, died Baltimore, 12 April 1960. He worked as a lawyer in the firm of Galvin and McCourt, becoming legal adviser to the Roman Catholic Archdiocese of Baltimore in 1924. He also served as treasurer of the Catholic University of America, 1938–60, and on the Maryland State Department of Public Welfare, and State Planning Commission, both 1939. Among his many other interests, he was governor/board member of several Baltimore hospitals and schools, and held a number of business directorships. He was honoured by the Roman Catholic Church as a Knight Commander of St Gregory, 1939, and a Knight of the Holy Sepulchre, 1953.

Gambacorta, Peter (Peter the Hermit) Blessed, hermit and religious founder, born Pisa, Italy, 16 February 1355, died Venice, 17 June 1435. Although a member of Pisa's ruling family, Gambacorta opted for a life of seclusion and went to live in the wilderness near Urbino. He was joined there by other hermits, as a result of which he formed the Poor Hermits of St Jerome, which was given papal recognition in 1421. Other foundations of the Order were established in Venice, Pesaro and Treviso. Gambacorta's asceticism was severe, and on one occasion brought him before the Inquisition. He was beatified in 1693, but his Order ceased to exist in 1933 when it was suppressed because it had become too small.

Gams, Pius Bonifatius Church historian and Benedictine, born Mittelbuch, Württemberg, Germany, 23 January 1816, died Munich, 11 May 1892. After studies at Tübingen, he was ordained in 1839, and served as professor of history and theology at Hildesheim between 1847 and 1855. In 1855, he joined the Benedictine monastery of St Boniface in Munich. His major works are *Kirchengeschichte von Spanien* (5 vols, 1862–79), a vast but unselective history of the Church in Spain before 1492, and *Series Episcoporum* (1873, supplemented 1879 and 1886), a see-by-see catalogue of all bishops in communion with Rome, throughout the history of the Church.

Gandavo, Pero de Magalhaes Roman Catholic historian, born Braga, Portugal, *c.*1550, date and place of death unknown. Gandavo was a school headmaster, and made a trip to Brazil in order to record the hitherto unresearched history of that country. The fruit of this research was a book published in 1576, in which he describes the discovery and settlement of Brazil by the Portuguese, its native inhabitants and their way of life (and results of Christian proselytizing), geography and natural history. The breadth of Gandavo's study of Brazil earned him the epithet 'Little Herodotus'.

Gandolf of Binasco Blessed, Franciscan hermit, born Binasco, Italy, late 1100s, died Polizzi Generosa, Sicily, *c.*1260. Gandolf was a model Franciscan, joining the Order while **Francis of Assisi** was still living. He abstained from fine foods, dressed only in coarse clothes and spent long nights in prayer. His quest for holiness and solitutde took him to a hermitage near Polizzi Gererosa in Sicily, where he acquired a great reputation for holiness and eloquence among the townspeople. He was especially noted for his devotion to Mary and to the Passion. He was beatified by Pope **Gregory XV** in 1621. Feast day 17 September.

Gangolf Saint, martyr of uncertain identity, died possibly 670. This figure has been variously identified as (a) an attorney associated with the abbey of Beza in France, (b) a friend of St **Ceolfrid** and of **Bede**, or (c) a noble Burgundian warrior. He was apparently murdered at the behest of an unfaithful wife, as a result of which he has been traditionally revered as a martyr to marital fidelity. Feast day 11 or 12 May.

Gänsbacher, Johann Roman Catholic composer of Church music, born Sterzing, southern Tyrol, 28 May 1778, died Vienna, 13 July 1844. From a musical family, he initially studied law and philosophy, before studying music with Albrechtsberger and Abbé Vogler from 1801 (and again with Vogler in 1810 after a period as a musician and teacher). He served in the 1813 uprising against Napoleon, became choral director of a Jesuit church in Innsbruck, and from 1824 was kapellmeister of Vienna Cathedral. His 216 surviving works, mainly written in the Viennese classical style, include 35 Masses, eight Requiems, many hymns and cantatas, and a number of instrumental works. He was a long-standing friend of both Meyerbeer and Weber.

Gansfort, Wessel (Wessel of Gansfort) Humanist theologian, born Groningen, Holland, *c.*1420, died Groningen, 4 October 1489. A major figure of the late medieval Devotio Moderna, he was educated by the Brethren of the Common Life and subsequently studied at a number of European universities. He taught in Paris for sixteen years, then visited Italy, where he came into contact with Renaissance humanism. He returned to teach in his native Groningen *c.*1474. Gansfort's influence was considerable: the notable humanists **Reuchlin** and Rulolphus **Agricola** were among his pupils, and his writings were known to **Luther**; Gansfort in fact anticipated a number of Luther's ideas, hence he is often described as a 'Reformer before the Reformation'.

Ganss, Henry George Roman Catholic priest, author and musician, born Darmstadt, Germany, 22 February 1855, died Lancaster, Pennsylvania, 25 December 1912. He was ordained in 1878, serving in Pennsylvania as parish priest in Milton, Carlisle and Lancaster. He was also chaplain to the US government Indian School (at Carlisle) and later became financial agent of Catholic Indian missions. He contributed (mainly historical) articles to a number of periodicals, and was an expert on Martin **Luther**. He was also a performer (on piano and organ), conductor and composer. His works include five Masses (influenced by the style of early nineteenth-century Vienna) and the hymn 'Long Live the Pope'.

Gante, Pedro de   Franciscan missionary to Mexico, born Ayghem-de-Saint-Pierre, Flanders, 1486, died Mexico City, April 1572. He was educated by the Brethren of the Common Life, but joined the Franciscans as a lay brother. He was in the first group of missionary Franciscan friars to arrive in Mexico in 1523. After learning the Nahuatl language he launched a massive campaign to convert the Indians with the help of his Indian students. Gante is credited with founding numerous churches, schools and hospitals in Mexico City.

Garabito, Juan de Santiago y León   Roman Catholic bishop, born Palma, Spain, 13 July 1641, died Guadalajara, Mexico, 11 July 1694. From a noble family, Garabito studied at Salamanca and held a series of ecclesiastical offices before being made bishop of Guadalajara in 1677. Although this provided him with a rich living, he allocated a large proportion of this income for the care of the needy, and lived very simply himself. He was devoted to the needs of his flock and became renowned for his sanctity. In order to foster communication he insisted that all priests in his diocese had to learn the local language.

Garakonthie, Daniel   Iroquois chief and Roman Catholic convert, born c.1600, died Onadaga, America, 1676. Garakonthie was a member of a peace delegation which met with the French at Montreal in 1654, and remained with them as a goodwill hostage. He came to admire the French, and befriended Simon le Moyne, a French Jesuit, through whom Garakonthie came to embrace Christianity, taking at his baptism the name 'Daniel'. In order to understand the Bible he soon learned to read and write, and earnestly desired to spread the Christian Gospel among his people.

Garampi, Giuseppe   Cardinal, historian and diplomat, born Rimini, Italy, 29 October 1725, died Rome, 4 May 1792. Well educated, and with a keen interest in ecclesiastical history, Garampi was made prefect of the Papal State Archives in 1751. On a number of occasions he was chosen for important papal diplomatic missions in various parts of Europe. During the course of these travels Garampi was also able to pursue his historical interests, and amassed a large library of manuscripts and books. He was made a cardinal in 1785.

Garcés, Francisco Tomás Hermenegildo   Franciscan missionary and martyr, born Moratadel Conde, Spain, 12 April 1738, died by the Colorado River in America, 19 July 1781. Ordained in 1763, Garcés volunteered for missionary work and after training was sent to minister to Native Americans in California and Arizona, where he arrived in 1768. He made four extended missionary journeys, during the course of which he travelled great distances through hostile territory. He was martyred by Yuma Indians while attempting to pacify a rebellion.

Garcés, Julián   Roman Catholic bishop, born Munébrega, Spain, 1447, died Puebla, Mexico, 1542. A member of the aristocracy, Garcés had a reputation as a learned and able preacher, as a result of which he became confessor to Bishop Rodríguez de Fonseca at the court of **Charles V**. Through Fonseca's recommendation, Garcés was subsequently appointed to become a bishop of the new see of Tlaxcala in Mexico, in 1526. On arriving in Mexico the following year he commenced an especially fruitful ministry among the Mexican Indians, claiming at one time that he was making 300 converts a week. He supported the rights and equality of the Indians, and his representations on their behalf to **Paul III** may have been responsible for the papal bull of 1537 which confirmed their right to be accorded the full dignity of human beings.

García Diego y Moreno, Francisco   First Roman Catholic bishop of the Californias, born Lagos, Jalisco, Mexico, 17 September 1785, died Santa Barbara, California, 30 April 1846. He joined the Franciscan Order, and was ordained in 1808. He then served at the Franciscan College, Zacatecas, Mexico, also undertaking missionary preaching and writing a handbook for mission priests. In 1833, he was sent (as prefect) with a group of other friars to lead mission work in the Californias, part of a strategy to use Mexican instead of Spanish missionaries. He became bishop of the Californias in 1840, and began a seminary at Santa Ines in 1844, although the progress of the diocese was impeded by difficult conditions.

García Moreno, Gabriel President of Ecuador, born Guayaquil, Ecuador, 24 December 1821, died (assassinated) Quito, 6 August 1875. Active in opposition to the ruling governments while a law student, he was elected a city councillor for Quito and then interim governor of Guayaquil in 1847. During a visit to Europe, he was influenced by the Catholic revival, and defended the arrival of the Jesuits in Ecuador in the early 1850s, in the face of opposition from Ecuador's Liberal president. Exiled in 1853, he spent some years in Paris, where he experienced a renewal of his Catholic faith. Later, in 1859, he was a leading figure in an armed insurrection against the government. While by no means wholly successful, he was elected president, 1860–5, and made a concordat with the Catholic Church in 1862. After a conservative revolution in 1869, he accepted a further term of office, continuing his work of improving Ecuador's educational and transport infrastructures. Fears that he would seek to tighten his grip on power led to his assassination.

García Villada, Zacarías Historian and Jesuit priest, born Gatón de Campos, Valladolid, Spain, 16 March 1879, died (shot by Republican militia) Vicélvaro, near Madrid, 1 October 1936. A Jesuit from 1894, he wrote and lectured widely on Spanish history. His major work, *Historia eclesiástica de España* (3 vols in 5), was completed in 1936, despite the loss of many of his historical sources when the Jesuit Instituto Católico in Madrid was set on fire in 1931. His *El destino de España en la historia universal* (1936) argued that the greatest eras of Spanish history had come during times of notable devotion to Roman Catholicism. He also published editions of manuscripts and chronicles, textbooks and more popular works.

García Xerez, Nicolás Dominican priest and bishop, born Murcia, Spain, 1746, died Guatemala,

31 July 1825. He studied at the Dominican monastery of Murcia before travelling to the Indies for missionary work. He became bishop of Nicaragua in 1807, taking up the post three years later. Although those who favoured Nicaraguan independence were seeking to remove all Spaniards from office, García Xerez remained. He gave cautious support to the break with Spain and influenced the 1821 proclamation of Nicaraguan independence, although some distrusted his moderate views. That same year, a dispute broke out over whether Nicaragua should be annexed to Mexico, and in the ensuing conflict García Xerez was exiled, in 1814, to Guatemala, where he died.

Gardeil, Ambroise Theologian and Dominican priest, born Nancy, France, 29 March 1859, died Paris, 2 October 1931. He joined the Dominicans in France in 1878 and from 1884 taught theology on the Gold Coast for many years, eventually becoming Dominican provincial regent of studies. An expert in theological methodology, he was arguably the leading Dominican theologian of his time. Among the most important of his works were *La Crédibilité et l'apologétique* (1908), *Le donné révélé et la théologie* (1910) and *La Structure de l'âme et l'expérience mystique* (1926). He was also co-founder of the *Revue Thomiste*, and contributed many articles to it. After 1911, he left his teaching post to concentrate on writing and preaching.

Gardiner, Harold Charles Editor, journalist, author and Jesuit priest, born Washington, DC, 6 February 1904, died Denver, Colorado, 3 September 1969. He joined the Jesuits in 1922 (ordained 1945) and spent a number of years studying philosophy, theology and literature. He was literary editor of the Catholic periodical *America*, 1940–62, and afterwards staff editor on literary subjects for the *New Catholic Encyclopedia*. He also chaired the editorial board of the Catholic Book Club, 1948–62. He also lectured and wrote widely, particularly on the relationship between morality, literature and censorship. His works include *The Great Books* (ed.; 4 vols, 1947–53), *Fifty Years of the American Novel* (ed.; 1951), *Catholic Viewpoint on Censorship* (1958) and *In All Conscience* (1959).

Gardiner, Stephen Bishop and Lord Chancellor

of England, born Bury St Edmunds, England, c.1490, died London, 12 November 1555. After an early career as master of Trinity Hall, Cambridge, Gardiner was appointed secretary to Thomas **Wolsey**, and was involved in diplomatic missions attempting to secure the annulment of **Henry VIII**'s marriage to **Catherine of Aragon**. In 1529 Gardiner became one of the king's secretaries, and became bishop of Winchester in 1531. Theologically conservative, Gardiner sought to maintain Catholic doctrine in the Church of England, but the advance of Protestantism during **Edward VI**'s reign made his position difficult and he was twice imprisoned. On her accession in 1553 **Mary Tudor** appointed him Lord Chancellor, but his influence in this office was minimal, partly because of chronic ill health.

Garembert (Walembert) Venerable, Premonstratensian abbot, born Wulpen (Belgium), c.1084, died Bony, France, 31 December 1141. Garembert founded a religious community in Bony in 1118, which evolved into a double (both men and women) Augustinian monastery, of which he was the abbot. In 1134, he affiliated his community with the new Premonstratensians in order to promote a more austere life. Two years later he moved the monastery to Mont-Saint-Martin, and in 1137 he retired as abbot in order to return to Bony and govern the nuns, who had remained there.

Garesché, Edward Francis Mission aid organizer, author and Jesuit priest, born St Louis, Missouri, 27 December 1876, died Framingham, Massachusetts, 2 October 1960. After a brief legal career, he joined the Jesuits in 1900 (ordained 1912). He worked on the periodical *America*, then served with the Sodality of Our Lady, 1913–22, founding its periodical *The Queen's Work*. He then became involved in medical/hospital work. He was director of the Catholic Medical Mission, 1929–60, and founded several organizations for the care of the sick, including the International Catholic Guild of Nurses, in 1928, the Daughters of Mary Health of the Sick, in 1935 and the Sons of Mary Health of the Sick, in 1952. He wrote over 40 books, and numerous articles and leaflets.

Garesché, Julius Peter Union soldier in the American Civil War, born near Havana, Cuba, 26 April 1821, died (in battle), Murfreesboro, Tennessee, 31 December 1862. He became a Catholic while studying at Georgetown College, Washington, DC, 1833–7. While there, he helped set up the first branch of the St Vincent de Paul Society in the city, and wrote for two local periodicals. Graduating from the US Military Academy in 1841, he served in the war against Mexico, eventually becoming a lieutenant colonel and chief of staff to General William S. Rosencrans. In 1851, he received the Order of Knight of St Sylvester from Pope **Pius IX**. He was killed in the Battle of Stones River.

Garet, Jean Augustinian theologian, born Louvain (Belgium), early sixteenth century, died (Belgium), 21 January 1571. Subprior of the monastery of St Martin in Louvain, during the theological upheavals of the Reformation, Garet was a staunch upholder of traditional Catholic doctrines. He wrote numerous works in defence of these, notably a treatise on the Eucharist published in 1561, in which he sought to demonstrate that the Church Fathers affirmed a doctrine of the Real Presence. Garet was offered the bishopric of Ypres, but refused it on the grounds of poor health.

Garicoïts, Michael Saint, Roman Catholic priest and founder of the Bétharram Fathers, born Ibarre, Basses-Pyrénées, France, 15 April 1797, died Bétharram, 14 May 1863. Born of a poor peasant family, he was ordained in 1823. After a period of parish work, in 1826 he became professor at the seminary of Bétharram. While he was serving as its superior, 1831–3, the seminary was moved to Bayonne, but Garicoïts stayed to found, in 1832, the Bétharram Fathers, a congregation devoted to mission and teaching work. He also founded numerous schools and colleges. A leading figure in efforts to re-Christianize the Basses-Pyrénées and re-establish a Church presence in that region, he was beatified in 1923 and canonized in 1947. Feast day 14 May.

Garin, André Oblate Father and missionary, born Côte-Saint-André, Isère, France, 7 May 1822, died Lowell, Massachusetts, 16 February 1895. Having joined the Oblates of St Mary Immaculate in France in 1842, he was ordained in Canada in 1845. After this, he spent twelve apparently difficult but diligent years as a missionary to the indigenous peoples of Saguenay, Hudson Bay and Labrador. In 1866, he was invited to Massachusetts with other Oblates to found a parish for Franco-Americans, establishing the first chapel in Lowell in 1868. He ministered there for the remainder of his life, founding a further three churches.

Garnerius of Rochefort Monk, bishop and writer, born probably near Rochefort, *c.*1140, died Clairvaux (Luxemburg), after 1225. Related to the nobility of Rochefort-sur-Brévon, France, Garnerius (Garnier) became a Cistercian monk and later served as prior, 1175, and abbot, 1187, of Clairvaux. By 1193 he was also bishop of Langres. He supported the Third Crusade and was the person to whom **Richard I** of England wrote, asking for reinforcements. In 1199 conflicts with Pope **Innocent III** forced his resignation and retirement to Clairvaux. His works include *Contra Amaurianos*, as well as a few sermons, which show him to be a good representative of late twelfth-century monastic theology.

Garnett, Henry Jesuit superior and martyr, born Heanor, Derbyshire, 1555, died London, 3 May 1606. He was educated at Winchester and then went to study law in London. For two years he was corrector of the press to Tottel, the government law printer, during which time he resolved to become a Roman Catholic. He journeyed to Spain and then to Italy and became a Jesuit novice in 1575. He was appointed professor of Hebrew at the Roman College, and for a time taught mathematics there in place of Christopher **Clavius**. Clavius strongly opposed his desire to return to England, but this was granted, and he landed in July 1586 accompanied by Robert **Southwell**. He succeeded William Weston as superior of the Jesuits on the English mission and became a peacemaker in the 'stirs' among the Catholic prisoners at Wisbech Castle. Garnett was accused of complicity in the Gunpowder Plot and arrested, after three days' search, at Hindlip Hall. Garnett was imprisoned in the Tower and brought before the Privy Council at least 23 times but condemned on his admission of conversations with one of the plotters, Catesby. Garnett published a translation with appendices of *Summa Canisii* (1590) as well as *Treatise on Schism*.

Garnett, Thomas Saint, English Jesuit martyr, born London, 1575, died London, 23 June 1608. Nephew of Henry **Garnett**. He studied at St-Omer and at the English College, Valladolid. He came to England with the Benedictine Mark Barkworth and was admitted to the Society of Jesus in 1604. He was seized at the port on his way to the Jesuit novitiate in Flanders and sent to the Tower of London. In 1606 he was among the 46 priests banished from the country. Later he was betrayed to the civil authorities by the apostate priest Rouse and was executed at Tyburn. He was canonized in 1970 as one of the **Forty Martyrs of England and Wales**.

Garr, Alfred Goodrich Pentecostal missionary and pastor, born Danville, Kentucky, 1874, died 1944. As a pastor in Los Angeles, Garr became the first white pastor to experience glossolalia at the Azusa Street Mission. He resigned from his Church and became a missionary, supported by the mission. With his family, he pastored in India, Hong Kong and Japan, overcoming his initial disappointment at not being able to speak the local languages miraculously. In 1930 he settled in Charlotte, North Carolina. In 1940 he opened a short-lived Garr School of Theology.

Garraghan, Gilbert Joseph Historian and Jesuit priest, born Chicago, Illinois, 14 August 1871, died Chicago, 6 June 1942. He joined the Society of Jesus in 1890 and was ordained in 1904. He taught at various universities and colleges, and was twice assistant to the Jesuit provincials of Missouri, 1911–21 and 1927–8, before becoming professor of history at St Louis University, 1925–32, and research professor at Loyola University, Chicago, from 1932. An expert on the early history of the Roman Catholic Church (particularly the Jesuits) in midwestern America, his works include *Catholic Beginnings in Kansas City* (1919), *Catholic Church in Chicago* (1921), *Chapters in Frontier History* (1934) and *Jesuits in the Middle United States* (3 vols, 1938).

Garrigou-Lagrange, Réginald Dominican theologian and philosopher, born Auch, France, 21 February 1877, died Rome, 15 February 1964. A Dominican from 1897, he taught philosophy and theology in Le Saulchoir, Belgium, 1905–9, and then fundamental, dogmatic and spiritual theology at what is now the Pontifical University of St Thomas Aquinas, Rome, 1909–60. He was a leading proponent and developer of a classical interpretation of the theology of St **Thomas Aquinas**, writing *La Synthèse thomiste* (1946), a major commentary on *Summa Theologiae* (7 vols, 1938–51) and a defence of Thomistic proofs of the existence of God, *Dieu, son existence et sa nature* (1915). He was also a leading writer on apologetics, and his *De revelatione ab ecclesia proposita* (1918, revised edn 1932) was widely read.

Garstang, John Archaeologist, born Blackburn, England, 5 May 1876, died Beirut, Lebanon, 12 September 1956. He was a leading expert on the archaeology of the Middle East, and particularly of the Hittites (as in his 1910 work *The Land of the Hittites*). He was honorary professor of Egyptian archaeology at the University of Liverpool from 1902 and later professor of methods and practice of archaeology. He directed several major excavations, for example, in northern Syria in 1907, Turkey in 1908 and 1911, Ethiopia, 1909–14, and Jericho, 1930–6. He was director of the British School of Archaeology in Jerusalem, 1920–6, and founded the British Institute of Archaeology in Ankara in 1947, becoming its president.

Garvan, Francis Patrick Roman Catholic lawyer, public official and president of the Chemical Foundation, born East Hartford, Connecticut, 13 June 1875, died New York City, 7 November 1937. Initially working as a lawyer and an assistant district attorney, he was director of the bureau of investigation of the Alien Property Custodian, becoming Custodian in 1919. He was also Assistant Attorney General of the US, helping to reorganize the FBI. He was first president of the Chemical Foundation, in 1919, an organization formed to support the development of the chemical industry, securing several important German chemical patents for the US. He posthumously received the Mendel Medal from Villanova University, 1938, for the most significant contribution to science in the USA by a Roman Catholic.

Garvin, John E. Author and Marianist brother, born San Antonio, Texas, 24 February 1865, died Washington, DC, 7 October 1918. He joined the Society of Mary, graduated from the University of Dayton, Ohio, in 1886, and then studied mathematics and physics at Stanislaus College, Paris. His main contribution was as a teacher and speaker to conferences of American religious and the American Catholic Educational Association. His writings include *The Centenary of the Society of Mary in America* (1917), a translation (from French to English) of Henri Rousseau's *Life of Guillaume Joseph Chaminade* (founder of the Marianists), and contributions to *Apostle of Mary*.

Gasbert de Laval Archbishop, date and place of birth unknown, died Narbonne, 3 January 1347. During his ecclesiastical career Gasbert held a series of appointments, among them bishop of Marseilles, archbishop of Arles and archbishop of Narbonne. He founded the chapel of All Saints at Arles Cathedral, and transferred the relics of a number of saints to a new reliquary. He also endowed scholarships for the education of young priests at the college of Toulouse.

Gascoigne, Thomas Theologian, born Hunslet, England, 5(?) January 1403, died Oxford, 13 March 1458. He was educated at Oxford, and despite several opportunities to assume high ecclesiastical office, stayed there for the rest of his life to devote himself to scholarship. He was a prominent figure in university life, several times holding the office of chancellor or vice-chancellor. Gascoigne upheld the established order of Church and State in the face of the attacks of the Lollards, though he shared their concerns with the manifest clerical abuses of the time. His *Dictionarium theologicum* is a valuable contemporary source on the Church of the period.

Gasparri, Pietro Cardinal, secretary of state to two Popes, codifier of canon law, born Ussita, Macerata, Italy, 5 May 1852, died Rome, 18 November 1934. After eighteen years as professor of canon law at the Institut Catholique, Paris, in 1901 he became secretary to the Congregation for Extraordinary Ecclesiastical Affairs. Between 1904 and 1916, he oversaw the codification of canon law, a task originally expected to take 25 years. He was made cardinal in 1907, and became secretary of state to Pope **Benedict XV** in 1914, giving him particular support throughout World War I. Continuing as secretary of state under Pope **Pius XI**, Gasparri was important in formulating the Lateran Pacts (establishing the Vatican as a sovereign city state, and giving Catholicism a privileged position in civil life), which were signed with Mussolini in 1929.

Gasperi, Alcide de Italian Roman Catholic politician, premier of Italy, born Pieve Tesino, Trentino, Austria-Hungary, 3 April 1881, died Selia, Italy, 19 August 1954. An advocate of the social teaching of Pope **Leo XIII** from his student days, he edited *Il Trentino* (the Catholic journal of the Popular Party) before being elected to the Austrian Reichsrat in 1911. After World War I (during which he had run relief camps for Italians ejected from Trentino by Austria) he was elected to the Italian parliament, 1921. He was a consistent opponent of Fascism, and was arrested and imprisoned in 1927, although ill-health forced his release a year later. He then worked in the Vatican Library, 1929–43, but in 1942 restarted the Popular Party as the Christian Democrats. From 1945 to 1953 he served as Italian premier, implementing industrial and agrarian reform and advocating European unity, alignment with the West and the maintenance of the Lateran Pacts with the Vatican.

Gasquet, Francis Neil Aidan Cardinal, Benedictine and historian, born London, England, 5 October 1846, died Rome, 4 April 1929. He was prior of Downside Abbey, 1878–85, but after resigning on health grounds, he undertook historical research on monasticism and the English Reformation. His books include *Henry VIII and the English Monasteries* (2 vols, 1888–9) and *Religio religiosi, the Object and Scope of the Religious Life* (1918). He participated in the Commission on Anglican Orders, 1896, and was abbot-president of the English Benedictine Congregation, 1900–14. He became first president of the International Committee for the Revision of the Vulgate, from 1907, and was made cardinal in 1914. During World War I he secured a British government envoy to the Vatican. He was later prefect of the Vatican archives, 1917, and Vatican Librarian, 1919.

Gassendi, Pierre Scientist and philosopher, born near Digne, Provence, 22 January 1592, died Paris, 24 October 1655. He studied rhetoric at Digne and philosophy and later theology at Aix. He was appointed canon and later provost, in 1625, of the cathedral at Digne. Although he became professor of mathematics at the Collège Royal de France in 1645, his interests were more in astronomy, and in 1647 he published his *Institutio astronomica*. In philosophy he is notable for his attempts to revive the Epicurean system and for his opposition to Aristotelianism. Hobbes was one of his many correspondents, and **Descartes** was one of those with whom he found himself in controversy. He was a respected amateur astronomer and corresponded with, among others, **Galileo** and **Kepler**. His six-volume *Opera omnia* was published in Lyons in 1658 and in Florence in 1727.

Gasser, Vinzenz Ferrer Prince-bishop, born Inzing, Tyrol, 30 October 1809, died Brixen, 6 April 1879. Ordained in 1833, he taught at the seminary in Brixen from 1836 to 1855 and was elected to the Frankfurt national assembly in 1848. As prince-bishop of Brixen from 1856, he was a staunch defender of Catholicism as the uniquely legitimate faith in Tyrol. He played a leading role in the First Vatican Council (1869–70), notably for drafting the decree on papal infallibility (approved, with minor amendments, in 1870). Earlier in the Council he had participated in the revision of the schema on the Catholic faith against atheism, materialism and pantheism, and successfully argued that the primacy of the Pope did not limit the ordinary authority of bishops.

Gastoldi, Giovanni Composer, born Caravaggio, Italy, c.1550, died Milan, 4 January 1609. Many details of Gastoldi's life are unknown or uncertain, but he is known to have worked in Milan, and probably in Mantua also. Most of his surviving works are secular pieces, largely dance pieces, songs and madrigals. A small quantity of sacred music has also survived, though little known, and includes Masses, motets and settings for various Offices.

Gaston, William Joseph Federalist politician and judge, born New Bern, North Carolina, 19 September 1778, died Raleigh, North Carolina, 23 January 1844. A leading figure in the public life of North Carolina, he sat in either the state Senate or state House of Representatives for a total of 30 years.

He formulated several state statutes, and was elected to the state supreme court in 1833, although (as a Roman Catholic) this violated a state constitution that only Protestants were permitted to hold public office. He was instrumental in widening this to admit all Christians. He also championed the causes of several oppressed minorities, making several important judgments in favour of slaves and ex-slaves. As a member of Congress, in 1813 and 1815, he was leader of the anti-war Federalists, and a noted speaker.

Gastoué, Amédée French Roman Catholic musicologist and composer, born Paris, 19 March 1873, died Clamart, Seine, 1 June 1943. He was professor of chant at the Schola Cantorum, later also lecturing at the Institut Catholique, Paris, and serving on the Pontifical Commission on Chant. He compiled several catalogues on musical subjects, wrote several teaching aids for use in Church music and published *Les Origines du chant romain* (1907), which summarizes his research. As a composer, his writing reflected his passion for early music, and was closely related to the liturgy. His works include Masses, motets, instrumental works, a *Stabat Mater*, a *Tantum Ergo* and many editions of early music works.

Gatterer, Michael Jesuit pastoral theologian, born Oberrasen, South Tyrol, 21 September 1862, died Innsbruck, 6 June 1944. Ordained in 1885 and a Jesuit after 1888, he taught at Innsbruck from 1892, becoming professor of moral theology, homiletics and catechetics. He taught that love for God should characterize each stage of any theological enquiry, while basing such an enquiry in the teaching of the Roman Catholic Church. He also advocated that in the religious instruction of children, the child's own beliefs, doubts and concerns should be the starting-point for catechesis. His works include *Katechetik* (1909), *Die Erstkommunion der Kinder* (1911), *Elementarkatechesen* (1923) and (with A. Gruber) *Das Religionsbuch der Kirche* (4 vols, 1928–30).

Gattinara, Mercurino Arborio di Statesman and cardinal, born Vercelli, Italy, 10 June 1465, died Innsbruck, Austria, 5 June 1530. Gattinara studied law at Turin University, became a successful advocate, and was then appointed professor of law at the University of Dôle. He subsequently became a member of the court of Margaret of Austria, where he first came into contact with the future **Charles V**. In 1513 Gattinara was made president of the Council of The Netherlands, but later fell into disfavour and retired to a monastery. On becoming emperor, Charles recalled Gattinara and appointed him to be his grand chancellor. He retained this office until his death, and proved to be an influential and astute adviser. He was created a cardinal and bishop of Ostia by **Clement VII** in 1529.

Gaucherius Saint, Augustinian abbot, born Meulan-sur-Seine, France, c.1060, died near Limoges, France, 9 April 1140. After obtaining a good liberal education, Gaucherius moved to a hermitage near Limoges to live a contemplative life when he was eighteen. As other groups of contemplatives soon gathered around him, he founded a Augustinian priory there, which was called Saint-Jean of Aureil. He later also founded an Augustinian convent for women. His disciples included St Stephen of Muret and St Faucherius, and he was canonized by Pope **Celestine III** in 1194. Feast day 9 April.

Gaudentius of Gniezno Saint, first metropolitan of Gniezno, born c.960–70, died, probably Gniezno, Poland, c.1006–10. Gaudentius became a Benedictine in Rome in 988 and was ordained there. Around 996, he went on a missionary journey to Prussia with his brother St **Adalbert of Prague**, who was martyred there. He returned to Rome in 999 to help with the canonization of his brother. While there, he was consecrated as a bishop and in March of 1000 was made archbishop in Gniezno. Little is known for sure of his activity as bishop, but in 1036 his relics were brought to Prague (Czech Republic). He has long been venerated as a saint, but his canonization has never been officially ratified. Feast day 25 August.

Gauderich of Velletri Bishop, died c.896. As bishop of Velletri, Gauderich was one of the principal counsellors of Pope **John VIII**. Gauderich had been exiled in 867, but was soon recalled and in 868 ordained the Slav disciples of **Cyril** who had arrived in Rome. He took a prominent role in the Photian controversy, but was later instrumental in securing **Photius'** rehabilitation. Gauderich also commissioned an account of the miracles of St

Clement from John Hymmonides, but he was unable to finish this before his death and Gauderich completed it himself. This work contains important source material relating to the lives of SS **Cyril** and **Methodius**.

Gaudí y Cornet, Antonio Architect, born Reus, Catalonia, 25 June 1852, died Barcelona, 10 June 1926. A graduate of the Escuela Superior de Arquitectura, Barcelona, much of his most famous work is inspired by the forms and shapes of the natural world, combined with medieval symbolism and academic revivalism. This is best seen in his work on the Sagrada Familia Church, Barcelona, e.g., the Nativity façade of the east transept (1891), which blends plant and mineral shapes with cubistic towers. He completed designs for the Sagrada Familia nave shortly before his death. His other notable works include Güell Park (1900–14), the helical roof of the Sagrada Familia parochial school (1909) and the Colonia Güell Chapel (1898–1914), in which the stress mechanics coming to bear on the building are reflected in its physical shape.

Gaulle, Charles de Leader of the French Resistance, and president of the Fifth French Republic, born Lille, 22 November 1890, died there 9 November 1970. After service in the French army in World War I, he was an instructor in military theory at the École Supérieur de la Guerre from 1922, controversially advocating the creation of an elite professional army. After the fall of France in 1940, he went to England to organize the Free French resistance, becoming a national hero. Initially head of the post-war provisional government, he resigned soon afterwards, frustrated with peacetime politicians and methods. Civil unrest in 1958 prompted those seeking strong government to call for de Gaulle's return. Back in power, he founded the Fifth Republic and served twice as President. During this time, he granted independence for Algeria, clashed with America over French involvement in Indo-China, and championed Europe as a third force to rival the USA and the USSR. He resigned in 1969 after failing to achieve the margin of success he sought in his referendum on the constitution, called in response to the widespread unrest of 1968.

Gaume, Jean Joseph Writer and Roman Catholic priest, born Fuans, Doubs, France, 5 June 1802, died Paris, 19 November 1879. He was briefly professor of dogmatic theology at Nevers, 1827–8, and was later vicar-general of Nevers, 1843–52, before being removed by the bishop in a dispute over the value of the classics in teaching children. Gaume controversially argued that the central place of the classics in education was the primary factor in the de-Christianization of France (see *Le Ver rongeur des sociétés modernes, ou la paganisme dans l'éducation* (1851)). The dispute became the subject of **Pius IX**'s encyclical *Inter multiplices* (1854), which reasserted the value of pagan classics but recommended they be studied alongside early Christian writings. Gaume wrote 45 other works, on a variety of subjects.

Gauntlett, Henry Musician, born Wellington, Shropshire, 9 July 1805, died London, 21 February 1876. He was an organist, praised by **Mendelssohn**, and played the organ in the first performance of *Elijah*. He helped to edit many hymn-books and was said to have composed about 10,000 hymn tunes. His tune 'Irby', to Mrs **Alexander**'s words 'Once in Royal David's City', has usually been the introductory hymn in the annual King's College, Cambridge, Service of Nine Lessons and Carols, since it was devised in 1913.

Gauzelin of Toul Saint, bishop, date and place of birth unknown, died Toul, 7 September 962. A member of a noble Frankish family, Gauzelin became bishop of Toul, France, in 922. He overcame the turbulent political climate of the times to introduce a number of ecclesiastical reforms during his episcopate, and founded or encouraged the development of a number of religious houses. Feast day 7 September.

Gay, Charles Louis Roman Catholic priest and spiritual writer, born Paris, France, 1 October 1815, died Paris, 19 January 1892. Ordained in 1845, he gained a significant reputation as a preacher and spiritual director in the ascetic, Christ-centred spiritual tradition of the Oratorian Fathers. His spiritual direction was rooted in the principle that clear instruction in the Christian faith should precede the giving of advice. He became vicar-general, then bishop, of Poitiers, and participated in the First Vatican Council

(1869–70). His works include *De la vie et des vertus chrétiennes* (2 vols, 1874) and *Elévations sur la vie de notre Seigneur Jésus Christ* (2 vols, 1879).

Gebhard II of Constance Saint, bishop, born probably Bregenz (Austria), 949, died Constance, Germany, 27 August 995. The son of the count of Bregenz, Gebhard was educated in Constance under Bishop **Conrad of Constance** and was made his second successor by Emperor **Otto II**. As bishop, his major concern was monastic reform. To this end he founded an abbey, which was consecrated with the relics of Pope **Gregory I** and named after him but eventually came to be called Petershausen, because of its resemblance to St Peter's in Rome. Despite Gebhard's best efforts, the abbey never became the major centre he had hoped for. He is buried under the abbey church, and his cult is officially followed only in the former Diocese of Constance.

Gebhard III of Constance Bishop, born Zähringen, Germany, c.1050, died Constance, Germany, 12 November 1110. Though born of a noble family, Gebhard began his religious career as a simple monk. He was made bishop of Constance by Otto of Ostia and papal legate when the latter became Pope **Urban II**. As legate, he supported the cause of Rome during the turbulent time of Emperor **Henry IV**. He was driven out of Constance in 1103 and rallied support behind the emperor's rebellious son **Henry V**. In 1107, he was reprimanded by Pope **Paschal II** for his support of Henry V, removed as papal legate, and spent his last years to caring for his diocese.

Gebhard of Salzburg Blessed, archbishop, birth date and place unknown, died Salzburg (Austria), 15 June 1088. Gebhard was chaplain to Emperors **Henry III** and **Henry IV** and ambassador to Greece before being made archbishop of Salzburg in 1060. As such, he expanded his archdiocese, promoted monasticism, and successfully supported Pope **Gregory VII** over **Guibert of Ravenna**. He also wrote a description of the investiture controversy that occurred during his tenure. Henry IV drove him from his see, allowing him to return only two years before his death. The process for his canonization began in 1629.

Gebizo Saint, monk, birth place and date unknown, died near Venafro, Italy, 21 October 1078 or 1087. The first records of Gebizo find him making a pilgrimage in 1060 from Cologne, Germany, to Monte Cassino, Italy, where he became a Benedictine. He was known for his austere eating practices and his love of prayer and silence. Even near his death, as he was suffering greatly from an painful abscess on his chest, he continued to ask God for additional sufferings. Though called a saint by all his earliest chroniclers, there is no tradition of his veneration. Feast day 21 October.

Geddes, Alexander Catholic biblical scholar, born Ruthven, Scotland, 14 September 1737, died London, England, 26 February 1802. He was ordained in 1764 after studying in Paris, but left parish work in 1779 to undertake biblical and literary studies in London under the patronage of Lord Petrie. His rationalistic views included questioning whether all Scripture was inspired and Moses' authorship of the Pentateuch. His works include *Critical Remarks on the Hebrew Scriptures* (1800) and *A Modern Apology for the Roman Catholics of Great Britain* (1800). He began, but did not complete, a new translation of the Bible, which did not find acceptance within the Catholic community.

Gee, Donald Pentecostal author and pastor, born London, 1891, died London, 1966. Gee, a sign painter, became a Pentecostal in 1913 and a pastor in 1920. From 1945 to 1948 he was chairman of the British Assemblies of God. He travelled widely, and he helped to organize international conferences. From 1951 to 1964 he was principal of the Assemblies of God Bible School at Kenley, Surrey. As well as hundreds of articles, Gee wrote over 30 books, including *Concerning Spiritual Gifts* (1928), *Upon All Flesh* (1935), *After Pentecost* (1935) and *The Pentecostal Movement: A Short History and an Interpretation for British Readers* (1941).

Geiler von Kayserberg, Johannes Catholic theologian and preacher, born Schaffhausen, Switzerland, 16 March 1445, died Strasburg, Germany, 10 March 1510. He studied at Freiburg and Basel Universities, was elected rector at Freiburg University in 1477 and appointed cathedral preacher in Strasburg in 1478. He was a scholar and a member of a group of early German humanists, but not a radical. His sermons, concerned mainly to criticize moral decadence, corrupt legal practices and monastic laxity, provide important information on the social mores of his day. His published sermons are mostly transcripts. Strasburg became Protestant soon after his death.

Geissel, Johannes von Cardinal, born Gimmeldingen, Germany, 5 February 1796, died Cologne, Germany, 8 September 1864. He was ordained in 1818, became bishop of Speyer in 1836, archbishop of Cologne in 1845, and cardinal in 1850. He was involved in the promotion of clerical education, improved Church–State relations under King Frederick William, promoted the continued construction of Cologne Cathedral, was responsible for the Cologne provincial council, and directed the first conference of the German episcopate at Würzburg, a conference which was important in Church renewal.

Gelasius I Pope and saint, born Rome, died there 21 November 496. Succeeding **Felix III** on 1 March 492, he strongly affirmed his position against the Caesaro-papist tendencies of the Emperors. Within the Church Gelasius affirmed the *primatus iurisdictionis* of the bishop of Rome and his supreme authority, even over against decisions of episcopal synods. Further, he argued for the divine origin of the sacerdotal and the political power, claiming their mutual autonomy as well as the greater value of the bishops' sacred authority. In Rome he dealt with Manichaeism and Pelagianism while also suppressing the last outbursts of paganism. Feast day 21 November.

Gelasius II Pope, elected 24 January 1118, died Cluny, 29 January 1119. Born 'John of Gaeta', he had studied at, then entered, the monastery of Monte Cassino. He was made a cardinal-deacon in 1088, and the following year became chancellor of the Roman Church, a post he held for 30 years. After his election to the Papacy he was imprisoned by one of the Roman factions, and then, because of the advance of the Emperor, had to flee the city for his home city of Gaeta, where he was consecrated. The Emperor set up an Antipope, and though Gelasius was able to return to the Rome after the Emperor left, he judged it unsafe, and left

for France, where he held a synod at Vienne. He fell ill while there, and went to the monastery at Cluny to die.

Gelasius of Caesarea Bishop, born *c*.335, died Caesarea *c*.395. In 367 he became bishop of Caesarea in Palestine. Being a convinced Nicene, he was expelled under the Arian-minded Emperor Valens. He returned for good in 379 with the accession of **Theodosius I**. Not much of his writings has survived. Following a suggestion of his uncle **Cyril of Jerusalem**, he wrote an *Ecclesiastical History*, a continuation of **Eusebius of Caesarea**'s. In defence of Nicene orthodoxy he wrote *Against the Anomoeans*. Like his uncle, he also compiled an interpretation of the Creed for catechumens.

Gélin, Albert Catholic OT exegete, born Amplepuis, France, 3 October 1902, died Lyons, 7 February 1960. He was ordained in 1926, appointed professor of sacred Scripture at the major seminary of Lyons in 1931. He was on the theological faculty of Lyons University from 1937, and from 1947 acted as superior of the Maison Saint-Jean at the University. His main works are *Les Idées maîtresses de l'Ancien Testament* (1959), *Jérémie* (1952), *Problèmes d'Ancien Testament* (1952), *Les Pauvres de Yahvé* (1956) and *L'Âme d'Israël dans le livre* (1958).

Gemelli, Agostino Catholic psychologist and philosopher, born Milan, Italy, 18 January 1878, died Milan, 15 July 1959. He studied medicine, physiology, biology and philosophy at various European universities. Following a period outside the Church, he entered the Franciscan Order and was ordained in 1908. His dominant interest became psychology, including its practical aspects, on which he advised his government during both world wars. He was founder and rector of the Catholic University of the Sacred Heart in Milan, professor of psychology and director of a psychological research centre, and president of the Papal Academy of Sciences. He published numerous works in psychology, theology and philosophy.

Generbrard, Gilbert Benedictine, exegete and Hebraist, born Riom, France, 12 December 1537, died Saumur, France, 14 March 1597. He entered the Benedictines as a youth, was consecrated bishop in 1592 and appointed archbishop of Aix-en-Provence. He opposed the succession of the Protestant Henry of Navarre to the French throne as **Henry IV**, but rendered submission to him when he became Catholic. He was accused by the *parlement* of Provence of *lèse majesté* and exiled from the area after the public burning of his *De sacrarum electionum jure* (1593). He published numerous works on OT exegesis, rabbinical literature, patristics, theology and liturgy.

Genesius of Arles Martyr and saint, died *c.*303 or *c.*250. He was a catechumen and during his military service, while he was stationed in Arles, fulfilled the function of chancellor. During a persecution (Diocletian's or possibly Decius') he deserted and took flight. According to his *Passio* he did so because he had refused to register the edict of persecution. He tried to escape his persecutors by swimming to the other side of the Rhône but was taken and beheaded. His cult was soon held in high esteem. Feast day 25 August, dedication of his basilica in Arles 16 December.

Genesius of Clermont Saint and bishop, died Clermont, 662. He became bishop of Clermont in the Auvergne by popular demand and, despite journeying to Rome to seek permission to lead a solitary life, continued to hold the position. He built a hospice, a monastery and St Symphorian's Church (where he is buried and which was later renamed St Genesius'). Feast day 3 June.

Genesius of Lyons Saint and bishop, died Lyons, 11 November 678. He became bishop of Lyons in 658 and served as chaplain to Queen **Bathilde**. Feast days 1, 3, 4 and 5 November.

Genesius the Comedian Saint and martyr, patron of actors, died Rome, 303. His enacted 'baptism', performed as part of an anti-Christian satire before the Emperor Diocletian, led him to publicly confess the faith, whereupon the emperor had him tortured and beheaded. Feast day 25 August.

Geneviève Saint, patroness of Paris, born Nanterre, France, 422, died Paris, *c.*500. At the age of seven she was inspired by a sermon to consecrate her life to God. She took the veil at fifteen and, when her parents died, moved to Paris. When Childeric the Frank besieged Paris, she made sorties to get provisions for the city. When Attila the Hun threatened to invade, she persuaded the Parisians to pray instead of abandoning the city; Attila changed his route and was defeated at Orléans. She is reputed to have saved Paris after her death, notably from an epidemic in 1129. Feast day 3 January.

Genicot, Edouard Jesuit moral theologian, born Antwerp, Belgium, 18 June 1856, died Louvain, Belgium, 21 February 1900. He entered the Society of Jesus in 1872 and became professor of moral theology at Louvain University in 1889. His *Theologiae moralis institutiones* (1896) became the standard moral text in many seminaries. His other main work is *Casus conscientiae* (1901).

Gennadius I of Constantinople Patriarch, about whose life little is known. He was patriarch of Constantinople between August/September 458, died 25 August 471. For his entire life he was committed to the anti-Monophysite struggle and the upholding of the decisions of the Council of Chalcedon (451). As patriarch he held a synod against simoniacs and enjoyed fame as a miracle-worker. He wrote some exegetical and dogmatic treatises as well as disciplinary texts and homilies, most of which are lost. In what remains one detects a literalist reading of the Scriptures, showing familiarity with the rules of Antiochene exegesis.

Gennadius II of Constantinople Patriarch, Orthodox theologian and scholar, born Constantinople, 1405, died Mt Menoikeion, 1472. He translated **Thomas Aquinas** into Greek, opened a philosophy school and became preacher-in-ordinary at court. In 1450 he became a monk and changed his name from 'Scholarius' to 'Gennadius'. To obtain military assistance for Constantinople, he sought to unite the Greek and Latin Churches, but eventually came to oppose their union. He was captured when Constantinople fell, but was chosen to serve as its patriarch by Sultan Muhammad II. He sought several times to escape the position and finally abdicated. His literary output was vast.

Gennadius of Astorga Saint and bishop, patron of Astorga, died Bierzo, Spain, 936. He restored the monastery of San Pedro de Montes in 895 and became bishop of Astorga in 899. He fostered Benedictine monasticism and built an oratory for hermits in 920 and three hermitages. He resigned his see to become a solitary. Feast day 25 May.

Gennadius of Marseilles Theological writer, died Marseilles, 505. He was a presbyter of the Church of Marseilles and compiled heresiological treatises against, among others **Nestorius**, **Pelagius** and **Eutyches**. The only authentic work, however, that survives is his *De viris illustribus* (*On Famous Men*), a continuation of **Jerome**'s work of the same name. Gennadius' catalogue of fifth-century Christian writers was composed in three stages and concluded between 476 and 480. Gennadius followed Jerome's basic model while putting in his own accents, e.g. in the greater attention given to monastic culture and a greater ecclesiological interest.

Gennings, Edmund Saint, Catholic martyr, born Lichfield, England, 1567, died London, 10 December 1591. He was born a Protestant but was inspired to become a Catholic while serving as a page to Richard Sherwood, and in 1584 went to Paris to study for the priesthood. Ordained in 1590, he returned to England and tried unsuccessfully to convert his brother, the only family member then alive, to Catholicism. He was arrested while saying Mass in a private house in London. He and the house's owner were accused of treason and executed. He was cannonized in 1970 as one of the **Forty Martyrs of England and Wales**. Feast day 10 December.

Gennings, John Franciscan provincial, born Lichfield, England, 1570, died Douai, 12 November 1660. He was born a Protestant but was inspired by his elder brother Edmund **Gennings**'s martyrdom to become a Catholic. He was ordained in 1607 in Douai and returned to England. In 1614 he joined the Franciscan Order. The defunct English Franciscan province was revived in 1629, following his work at the provincial college in Douai, and he was himself appointed provincial in 1629, being re-elected in 1634 and 1640.

Gentile da Fabriano Italian painter of the Umbrian school, born Fabriano, 1370, died Rome,

1427. His style, with its minute naturalistic detail, owes much to Lombard and Venetian art, and was influential in northern Italy. Much of his work, which included several frescoes, is lost. His surviving panel paintings include *The Adoration of the Magi* (in the Uffizi, Florence) and *The Quaratesi Altar* (divided between London, Florence, Washington and the Vatican).

Geoffrey Hardeby English Augustinian theologian, born Hardby, Leics, died 21 May 1385, is said to have been buried in London. He entered the Augustinian Order at Leicester while studying at Oxford, and was appointed master regent at the Oxford Monastery in 1357. He defended the Augustinians against the charges brought against them concerning poverty and property by Richard Fitzralph and the Canons Regular. He was the Order's delegate to Padua and was twice elected prior provincial for England.

Geoffrey of Bayeux Blessed, second abbot of Savigny, died 1138. After the death of **Vitalis of Savigny**, the founder and first abbot of Savigny, in 1122, Geoffrey, a former Cluniac monk, was elected as his successor. In many ways the creator of the Congregation of Savigny, Geoffrey created the organizational framework for Savigniac expansion, and by the time of his death in 1138, the Congregation, which later merged with the Cistercians, had grown to include some 29 monasteries.

Geoffrey of Clairvaux Cistercian abbot and author, born Auxerre, France, 1120, died Hautecombe Abbey, France, 1188. He studied under Peter **Abelard** and was inspired to join the Cistercian order by **Bernard of Clairvaux** himself, to whom he acted as secretary during the Council of Rheims' discussions on the Gregorian reform. He became abbot of Clairvaux (1161) of Fossanova (1170) and of Hautecombe (1176). His main work is a collection of the letters of Bernard of Clairvaux and the completion of his biography, which gives accounts of Bernard's work with the Albigensians and during the Second Crusade.

Geoffrey of Dunstable Benedictine abbot, born Maine, France, died St Albans, England, 1146. He headed a school in Dunstable, after studying in Paris. He joined the community at St Albans to compensate for the loss by fire of their scripts which he had borrowed for a miracle play which he was staging. In time he became prior and later abbot of the community, and was responsible for an extensive building programme at St Albans and for saving the abbey from demolition during King Stephen's civil wars.

Geoffrey of Monmouth Bishop and historian, born Monmouth, Wales, 1100, died Llandaff, 1155. He taught at Oxford and, in 1152, became bishop of St Asaph but is unlikely to have ever visited his see, because of the Welsh rebellion. His major work *Historia Regum Britanniae*, which covers the history of Britain from the fall of Troy to the Anglo-Saxon conquests and includes Arthurian and Celtic material, is now regarded as pseudo-history.

Geoffrey of Vendôme Cardinal and Benedictine abbot, born Angers, France, 1070, died Angers, 26 March 1132. He was elected abbot of Sainte Trinité at Vendôme in 1093 while only a deacon. He supported Pope **Urban II** against **Guibert of Ravenna**, and was consecrated cardinal-priest of St Prisca on the Aventine in 1094. In a series of polemics, he argued that simony and lay investiture were heretical. He served as papal legate to the Councils of Clermont, Saintes and Rheims, and supported the Gregorian reform. His letters are a valuable source of information on twelfth-century Church politics.

Geoffrey of Vinsauf Poet and teacher of rhetoric, born Vinsauf, France, died Vinsauf, 1220. Little is known about him other than that he was English and travelled to Rome. His hexameter poem on the art of poetry, *Poetria nova*, provided a template for metrical poetry and influenced poetic theory until the Renaissance. His other works include *Documentum de Modo et Arte dictandi et versificandi* and *Summa de coloribus rhetoricis*.

Geoffrey of York Chancellor of England and archbishop, born in England, 1152, died Grandmont, France, 8 December 1212. He was the illegitimate son of Henry II and reared with Eleanor of Aquitaine's children. Elected bishop of Lincoln in 1173, he delayed ordination and consecration to defend Henry against a rebellion. In 1182, still unconsecrated, he resigned the bishopric and a year later became Chancellor. He was named archbishop of York as a reward for faithfulness to Henry and consecrated at Tours in 1191. Following an argumentative episcopacy, he withstood King John's demand for clerical taxes and was forced to flee England. He died in exile.

George Saint and martyr, patron of England, soldiers, knights, archers and armourers, died Lydda, Palestine, 303. He was probably a soldier martyred in the persecutions of Diocletian and Maximian. The legend of St George and the dragon appears in Irish mythology and the martyrology of **Bede**. He appeared in a vision at the siege of Antioch during the First Crusade. **Richard I**'s army fought under George's patronage and **Edward III** founded the Order of the Garter under it. In the later Middle Ages, he became patron of Venice, Genoa, Portugal and Catalonia. His popularity declined with the introduction of guns. Feast day 23 April.

George Cedrenus Byzantine chronicler, probably a monk, died 1110. He wrote *Synopsis istorion*, chronicling the history of the world from the Creation to 1057 when Isaac Comnenus ascended to the throne, which is largely derived from **Theophanes the Confessor**, Pseudo-Symeon, **George Hamartolus** and others, and partly copied verbatim from John Skylitzes.

George Hamartolus Byzantine chronicler and monk, died 875. Nothing is known of his life except that he was a monk. His *Chronicle*, which runs from the Creation to 842, is valuable not in itself but because it is copied from a variety of sources which have since been lost.

George of Saxony Catholic opponent of Lutheranism, born Dresden, Germany, 27 August 1471, died Dresden, 17 April 1539. He inherited the Duchy of Saxony, the Margravate of Meissen and the cities of Leipzig and Dresden, which passed to his Lutheran brother on his death. He supported Church reform, but opposed **Luther** when he split with Rome. He advocated a universal council to define doctrine and institute overdue reforms, and vainly sought Rome's authority to introduce monastic reforms in his territories, from which he had banned anti-Catholics. He supported the League of Dessau and its successor bodies which opposed Protestantism.

George of Trebizond Humanist, born Crete, Greece, 4 April 1395, died Rome 1486. A Byzantine by birth, George settled in Italy and became a key agent for the dissemination of Greek learning in the West. He taught, translated and copied Greek works in Venice, Mantua, Florence and Rome. Important translations included the works of Aristotle, Plato and Ptolemy and the writings of Greek fathers such as **Eusebius of Caesarea**, Cyril of Alexandria, St **Basil** and **John Chrysostom**. He served as interpreter for the papal curia during the Council of Florence from 1438 to 1439.

George Syncellus Byzantine chronicler, died 815. The only source of knowledge about him is his chronicle, which records that he came from Palestine, received the title *syncellus*, became secretary to Patriarch **Tarasius**, and retired to a monastery to compose his *Chronicle*. This runs from the Creation to the start of the reign of Diocletian in 284, and is second only to **Eusebius** in giving an understanding of early Christian chronology.

Gerald de Barri *see* **Giraldus Cambrensis**

Gerald of Aurillac Saint and nobleman, born Aurillac, France, 855, died Aurillac, 13 October 909. Despite inheriting the family titles, he chose to enter the religious life. He established the abbey of Aurillac following several pilgrimages to Rome. He was renowned for his justice, devotions and gift of healing. Feast day 13 October.

Gerald of Braga Benedictine saint and bishop, died Bornes, Spain, 5 December 1108. Having entered the Benedictine Order, he was invited by the primate of Spain, a fellow Benedictine, to join him in re-establishing Christianity in Spain following the defeat of the Moors. He was consecrated bishop of Braga in 1096, and his see was restored to metropolitan status in 1100. Feast day 5 December.

Gerald of Mayo Saint and abbot, born Winchester(?), England, died Mayo, Ireland, 732. He was among the English and Irish monks who left Lindisfarne with St **Colman** when the Synod of Whitby disallowed the Celtic date of Easter in Northumbria. The group founded a monastery off the Mayo coast and later a house on the mainland for the English monks. He succeeded St Colman as abbot of the latter. Feast day 13 March.

Geraldini, Alejandro Catholic bishop and humanist, born Italy, died Santo Domingo, 8 March 1524. He was titular bishop of Vultutara from 1494 and, having served the Crown of Castile in various capacities and been nominated by **Charles V** as bishop of Santo Domingo, was consecrated in 1516 and sent there, where he constructed the first cathedral in the Americas. He described his arrival in Santo Domingo in *Itinerarium ad regiones sub aequinoctiali plaga* and honours his cathedral in a Latin ode.

Gerard, John Jesuit missionary, born Etwall Hall, Derbyshire, England, 4 October 1564, died Rome, 27 June 1637. His *Autobiography of a Hunted Priest* records his return, after joining the Society of Jesus in Rome, to England, where he worked to re-establish Catholicism. He was arrested and imprisoned without trial in the Tower of London, but made a remarkable escape to continue his missionary work. He crossed to Calais when his arrest was ordered after the Gunpowder Plot. Thereafter he served as English penitentiary at St Peter's, Rome, novice instructor in Louvain, rector of the Jesuit house in Liège, and rector of the English Jesuits at Ghent.

Gerard, Richard Recusant, born Staffordshire, England, 1635, died London, 22 March 1680. He was converted to Catholicism and became friendly with the Jesuits, for whom he administered some property. Arrested as a conspirator when he came to London to testify in favour of a group of Catholic peers, he was impeached following Titus **Oates**' revelation of the Popish Plot. He died in prison awaiting trial.

Gerard of Abbeville Theologian, born Abbeville, France, *c.*1220, died Paris, 8 November 1272. Appointed master (teacher) of the University of Paris, papal subdeacon, regent master in theology and archdeacon of Ponthieu, he came to be recognized as leader of the movement to expel the mendicant orders from the universities. He opposed the mendicants and their privileges in his writings and sermons and was in turn attacked by them, particularly by the Franciscans. His *Contra adversarium perfectionis Christianae* elicited responses from **Thomas Aquinas** and **Bonaventure**, and his *Liber apologeticus* was attacked in a Franciscan pamphlet. Writings opposing him came to be known as *contra Geraldinos*.

Gerard of Brogne Saint, abbot and monastic reformer, born Stave (Belgium), 880, died Brogne Abbey (Belgium), 3 October 959. He rebuilt an oratory in Brogne to house the relics of St Eugene, replaced its clerics with monks, and became its abbot in 923. He was commissioned to restore regular observation of the Benedictine Rule at the abbey of Saint-Ghislain in Hainaut, and reformed the monasteries of Saint-Bavo, Saint-Pierre (where he became abbot), Saint-Bertin and Saint-Amand in Ghent, and the monastery of Saint-Remi in Rheims. His work paved the way for the Gregorian reform. Feast day 3 October.

Gerard of Brussels Geometer, died 1250. Nothing is known of his life save that he wrote *Liber de motu* (*c.*1250) and that he is the likely author of *Algorithmus demonstratus*, which concerned lines, areas and solids in rotation and contributed to the development of kinematics.

Gerard of Cambrai Bishop and theologian, born in Saxony, died Cambrai, France, 14 March 1051. He was bishop of Arras and Cambrai, accompanied Emperor **Henry II** on various expeditions, and continued the monastic reforms instituted by **Gerard of Brogne**. He was responsible for bringing some Italian Cathar-type heretics before a synod in Arras in 1025, an account of which he gives in *Gesta Episcoporum Camaracensium*.

Gerard of Clairvaux Blessed, born near Dijon, died Clairvaux, 13 June 1138. He entered the Cistercian Order, despite initial reluctance, after being impressed by the fulfilment of his brother **Bernard**'s prophecy that he would be wounded, captured and freed following a battle. He accompanied Bernard to the foundation of Clairvaux and became its cellarer until his death, which is lamented by Bernard in his *Sermones in Cantica.* Feast day 30 January.

Gerard of Cremona Translator, born Cremona, Italy, 1114, died Toledo, 1187. Having studied in Italy, he was attracted by the New Learning in Toledo, a city which had recently been recaptured by the Christians from the Muslims. In Spain, he studied Arabic and became a prolific translator from Arabic into Latin of works that had hitherto been the preserve of the Muslim world and that would transform Scholasticism. Many branches of learning were renewed following his translations of Aristotle (in particular *Posterior Analytics*, *De naturali auditu* and *Liber caeli et mundi*), and of Avicenna, Alkindi, Alfarabi, Euclid, Ptolemy and others.

Gerard of Csanad Saint, martyr, bishop and abbot, born Sagrado, Italy, 980, died Buda, Hungary, 24 September 1046. He studied in Bologna and became abbot of the Benedictine abbey of San Giorgio. Following some time as a hermit in Bel, he tutored the son of King **Stephen** I of Hungary, who appointed him bishop of Csanad, where he worked to Christianize the south-east Hungarian tribes by means of founding mission parishes with monks of various nationalities trained in Csanad. He was martyred in Buda by the deceased King Stephen's opponents. His only extant writings are *Deliberatio Gerardi Moresanae Episcopi supra Hymnum Trium Puerorum*. Feast day 24 September.

Gerard of Sauve-Majeure Saint and Benedictine abbot, born Corbie, France, 1025, died near Bordeaux, 5 April 1095. He was a child oblate of Corbie Abbey, where he later served as a cellarer. He accompanied the abbot on pilgrimage to Rome, where he was ordained, and cured through the intercession of St **Adalard**. He was unsuccessful in re-establishing regular observance when abbot of Saint-Vincent, but consequently constructed a new abbey on land given to him at Sauve-Majeure, and later built a priory at Semoy and an abbey at Broqueroie, all of which prospered. Feast day 5 April (21 June in Poitou).

Gerard of Toul Saint and bishop, born Cologne, Germany, 935, died Toul, France, 23 April 994. He served as a canon in Cologne before being designated bishop of Toul. Here he completed the foundation of the Saint-Mansuy Abbey, erected a convent for women in honour of St Gengoult, founded the Maison-Dieu, and rebuilt the cathedral. Feast day 23 April.

Gerard of Villamagna Blessed, Franciscan hermit, born Villamagna, Italy, 1174, died Villamagna, 13 May 1245. He went on Crusade while serving as page to a Florentine knight, was captured by the Saracens and, on being released, travelled as a pilgrim to Jerusalem. On returning to Italy, he joined the Third Order of St Francis and lived as a hermit. Feast day 23 May (13 May in Florence).

Gerard of York Archbishop of York, died Southwell, England, 21 May 1108. He was rewarded with the bishopric of Hereford following a secret mission to Rome. He became archbishop of York despite **Anselm**'s opposition, was embroiled in the Canterbury–York quarrels over primacy and forced to profess canonical obedience to Canterbury. He supported Henry I in his rivalry with Anselm, this leading to his misrepresenting the Pope's views to Henry, an offence for which he was briefly excommunicated. He was eventually reconciled with Anselm, but the conflict left him with many enemies. Some of his letters are printed in Anselm's correspondence.

Gerasimus Saint and anchorite, born Lycia, died Palestine, 5 March 475. He founded a monastery near the Jordan River following a pilgrimage to the Holy Land c.451. During Lent he took no nourishment apart from the Eucharist. Tradition has it that he removed a thorn from the paw of a lion who thereafter became the monastery's pet. Feast day 5 March.

Gerberon, Gabriel Benedictine, Jansenist theologian and historian, born Saint-Chalais, France, 12 August 1628, died Paris, 29 March 1711. He joined the Benedictine Order and taught in several monasteries. While preparing an edition of the works of St **Anselm** for publication, he became interested in the Scholastics and thence in Jansenism. He subsequently moved to the Low Countries. Having aroused the hostility of the bishops, he was arrested in Brussels, extradited to France and imprisoned. He published many theological and historical works including *Histoire générale du jansénisme* (1700) and *Lettres de Monsieur Cornelius Jansenius* (1702).

Gerbert von Hornau, Martin Benedictine abbot and liturgical scholar, born Horb am Neckar, Germany, 12 August 1720, died Sankt Blasien, 13 May 1791. He joined the Benedictine Order at the abbey of St Blaise, where he was ordained and in 1764 elected abbot. While serving as abbey librarian, he conducted extensive research into medieval music theory and history. He restored plainchant in his community. His many important works on liturgy and music include *Scriptores ecclesiastici de musica sacra potissimum, Cantu et musica sacra a prima ecclesiae aetate usque ad praesens tempus* and *Iter Alemannicum*.

Gerbet, Olympe Philippe French philosopher, theologian and bishop, born Poligny, 5 February 1798, died Perpignan, 8 August 1864. He was ordained priest in 1822. A liberal in his youth (he admired Félicité de **Lamennais**), he became increasingly conservative with age. After ten years in Rome, he became professor of sacred eloquence at the Sorbonne, vicar-general of Amiens and bishop of Perpignan. His works include *Des doctrines philosophiques sur la certitude dans leurs rapports avec les fondements de la théologie, Introduction à la philosophie de l'histoire, Rapports du rationalisme avec le communisme* and *Esquisse de Rome chrétienne*.

Gerbillon, Jean François Jesuit superior general of the French mission to China, born Verdun, France, 11 June 1654, died Peking (Beijing), China, 22 March 1707. He entered the Society of Jesus in 1670 and was among the first group of French Jesuits to be sent to China by **Louis XIV**. There he instructed the emperor on geometry and philosophy, served as interpreter at the signing of the first Russo-Chinese peace treaty, accompanied the emperor on several expeditions into Tartary, and supervised the building of the French church in Peking.

Gerhard, Johann Lutheran theologian, born Quedlinburg, Germany, 17 October 1582, died Jena, 17 August 1637. Having studied philosophy, medicine and theology at Wittenberg, Marburg and Jena, he was appointed superintendent of the churches of Heldburg in 1606 and professor of theology at Jena University in 1616. He worked with the movement which unsuccessfully attempted to develop a supreme tribunal for the Lutheran Church. His theological publications include *Loci theologici* and *Confessio Catholica*, and he wrote many devotional and exegetical works.

Gerhardinger, Karolina Foundress of the School Sisters of Notre Dame, born Stadtamhof, Bavaria, 20 June 1796, died Munich, 9 May 1879. At eighteen she told her school headteacher she wanted to be a nun, but he persuaded her to found a community of itinerant teaching sisters, along the lines attempted unsuccessfully in the seventeenth century by St **Peter Fourier**, using Pestalozzi's teaching methods. She was not allowed to take her vows until her community had demonstrated its self-sufficiency. A decree introducing her cause for beatification was proclaimed in 1952.

Gerhoh of Reichersberg Gregorian reformer, statesman and theologian, born Polling, Bavaria, 1093, died Reichersberg, 27 June 1169. He was involved throughout his life in conflicts between the Church and the Holy Roman Empire. After the failure of his reform proposal at the Lateran Council he withdrew to monastic life, and sought the introduction of the Rule of St Augustine for his monastery. He was ordained thereafter at Regensburg. Appointed provost of the Augustinian monastery of Reichersberg in 1132, he had to flee because he refused to support the imperial papal candidate. His many works on clerical reform and Church–State relations include *Exposito in Psalmos*.

Gerlach Saint and anchorite, born Houthem, The Netherlands, 1100, died Houthem, 1177. On the accidental death of his wife, he abandoned his estates and knightly life and went on pilgrimage to Rome, where Pope **Eugenius III** agreed to his spending seven years in the Holy Land caring for the poor and the sick. When he returned to Rome, Pope **Adrian IV** agreed to his continuing this work in his native town. Here he lived in a huge hollow tree, which was felled with episcopal approval after critics said they suspected him of hiding gold in it. Feast day 5 January.

Germaine of Pibrac Saint, born Pibrac, France, 1579, died Pibrac, 1 June 1601. She was forced by her unloving stepmother to live with the sheep from the age of eight, and was continually neglected by the family thereafter. Working as a shepherdess in her small community, she acquired a reputation for patience and kindness. Tradition has it that sheep gathered around her staff were kept safe from wolves while she attended Mass. When her grave was opened to take another body in 1644, her body was found to be intact. Feast day 15 June.

Germanus I Patriarch of Constantinople and saint, born *c*.650, died Platanion, *c*.742. His father was executed in 669 and Germanus himself was castrated at this occasion. He became bishop of Cyzicus *c*.705 and was patriarch of Constantinople between 11 August 715 and 17 January 730. He first supported the Emperor **Leo III** but the latter's policy of iconoclasm caused many conflicts, leading to Germanus' forced resignation. Many of his works (e.g. letters, homilies on the Virgin) were destroyed. Germanus was excommunicated in 754 but rehabilitated by the Second Council of Nicaea (787). Feast day 12 May.

Germanus II Patriarch of Constantinople, born Anaplous, *c*.1175, died Nicaea, June 1240. He was a deacon at Hagia Sophia at the fall of Constantinople to the Latins in 1204, and fled. He was elected patriarch in exile in 1223 and worked to prevent schisms in the Byzantine Church following the fall of Constantinople. To that end he wrote to Pope **Gregory IX** to seek Church union, but came to appreciate the impossibility of this after receiving envoys from Rome at Nicaea, and wrote a number of theological works against the Latins. Though he had strong views of his own authority as ecumenical patriarch, he recognized the title of 'Patriarch of the Bulgarians', but would not agree to the Bulgarian Church becoming autocephalous. He sought reunion with the Armenians, without success.

Germanus of Auxerre Saint and bishop, born Auxerre, France, 378, died Ravenna, Italy, 31 July 448. Having studied in Rome and entered the imperial civil service, he was dispatched to Gaul as military governor. Elected bishop of Auxerre, he distributed his fortune by endowing churches and monasteries, worked to found coenobite monasticism, visited Britain to combat Pelagianism, led British forces in a bloodless battle against Picts and Saxons, promoted clerical education, and sought the alleviation of taxes in his diocese. He died in Ravenna working to prevent reprisals for a revolt in Brittany. Feast day 31 July according to the Roman Martyrology but 3 August in Wales.

Germanus of Münster-Granfelden Saint and abbot, born Trier, Germany, 610, died Münster-Granfelden, 21 February 675. After his father's death he was brought up by the bishop of Trier and later became a disciple of St **Arnulf of Metz**. He moved to the monastery of Luxeuil, where the abbot, St Walbert, recommended him as abbot for a new monastery at Münster-Granfelden. Here he opposed peasant oppression and was consequently murdered by its perpetrator, Boniface, the brother and successor of Duke Gondo, who had sought his appointment as abbot. Feast day 21 February.

Germanus of Paris Saint and bishop, born Autun, France, c.496, died Paris, 28 May 576. He was ordained in 530 and appointed administrator and later abbot of St Symphorin. He was elected bishop of Paris, where he continued to live an austere life, presided over the Third and Fourth Councils of Paris, attended the Second Council of Tours, miraculously restored King Childebert's health, founded an abbey (later known as Saint-Germain-des-Prés), and worked to bring peace to the Merovingian kingdom. Feast day 28 May.

Germerius Saint, abbot and statesman, born Vardes, France, 610, died Saint-Germer-de-Flay, 660. As a nobleman, he served at the court of Dagobert I and Clovis II. He founded the monastery of Isle (now Saint-Pierre-aux-Bois), left his wife and secular career to enter the monastery of Pentale (now Saint-Samson-sur-Risle), where he became abbot but which he left after a quarrel to become a hermit for five years. He later founded the abbey of Flay (now Saint-Germer-de-Flay), where he was made abbot. Feast day 16 May.

Gero of Cologne Saint and archbishop, died 28 June 976. He was sent to Constantinople to request the hand of Romanus II's daughter Anna in mar-

riage to Emperor **Otto I**'s son, but received instead that of Theophano, niece of the Eastern Emperor John I Tzimisces. He also returned with the relics of St **Pantaleon**. He founded a Benedictine monastery in Thankmarsfeld (which later transfered to Nienburg) and the abbey of Gladbach. He is associated with the Gero Codex of the Gospels given to Cologne Cathedral.

Gerold Saint and hermit, born 920, died Sankt-Gerold, near Mitternach, Germany, 10 April 978. At the age of 38, he gave his lands to the Benedictine abbey of Einsiedeln, where his two sons were monks, and built himself a hermitage on a site presented to him by a friend. On his death his sons lived in his cell guarding his tomb, on which spot the abbots of Einsiedeln later built a church: rebuilt after being destroyed in the Reformation, this now houses his relics. He is depicted in pictures with two haloed sons or freeing a bear trapped by hounds. Feast day 19 April.

Gerosa, Vincenza Saint, co-foundress of the Sisters of Charity of Lovere, born Lovere, Lombardy, 29 October 1784, died Lovere, 28 June 1847. Her family were wealthy but quarrelsome, which led to her mother's dying in poverty and Gerosa having to be carefully advised on retaining her patrimonial rights. On inheriting the family fortune, she converted one of her houses into a hospital. She later became co-foundress of a religious institute with Bartolomea **Capitanio**, after whose death she ran it herself. When it gained ecclesiastical approval, she was elected superior. Feast day 28 June.

Gerson, Jean le Charlier de Chancellor of the University of Paris, reformer and mystic, born Gerson, France, 14 December 1363, died Lyons, 12 July 1429. The eldest of twelve children of devout parents, he entered the Collège de Navarre in Paris when fourteen years old, and formed a close friendship with its rector, Pierre d'Ailly. After d'Ailly was appointed bishop of Puy in 1395 he replaced him as chancellor of the University of Paris until his death. For political reasons, however (he had made an enemy of the duke of Burgundy), he was unable to return to Paris after the Council of Constance of 1419. He moved instead to Lyons and worked to bring peace to the Church during a turbulent period, taking a stand on all the major issues of his day, in particular the dispute between the Avignon Papacy, to which on the whole he remained loyal, and the Papacy in Rome. His many publications include *De unitate Ecclesiae*, *De vita spirituali animae*, *Mémoire sur la réforme de la faculté de théologie* and *De theologia mystica*.

Gertrude of Nivelles Saint and abbess, born Landen, 626, died Nivelles, 17 March 659. She is venerated in Holland and Belgium and known as a patroness of travellers. St **Iduberga**, her mother, founded a convent at Nivelles on the death of Gertrude's father. Gertrude succeeded her as its abbess. She lived such a life of asceticism that *c.*656 she stepped down from the abbacy and gave her last three years completely to devotional prayer. Feast day 17 March.

Gertrude the Great Saint, German mystic, born Eisleben, 6 January 1256, died Helfta, Thuringia, 17 November 1302. From the age of five she lived at the convent of Helfta. Following a conversion experience at the age of 25, she led a contemplative life. She is known as one of the first to practise devotion to the Sacred Heart. Her main written works are the *Exercitia spiritualia* and the *Legatus Divinae Pietatis*. The former is a series of meditations, the latter includes an account of her mystical experiences, which centred on the person of Christ and had an effect upon the development of the spirituality of the Cistercian Order, to which Gertrude's monastery was loosely affiliated. Feast day 16 November.

Gerulf Saint and martyr, born Meerendra (Belgium), 732, died Ghent (Belgium), 750. Legend has it that, while riding home from his confirmation at the monastery of Saint-Bavo at Ghent, his godfather was possessed by the devil and threatened to kill him despite Gerulf's warning that he would go to hell if he did. His mother realized what had happened when his horse returned riderless, and had him buried at a church in Meerendra. After several miracles it was moved to the monastery at Dronghem. Feast day 21 September.

Gervaise, François Armand Catholic abbot and historian, born Paris, 1660, died at the monastery of Le Reclus, Diocese of Troyes, 1751. Educated by the Jesuits, he joined the Discalced Carmelites and then the reformed Cistercians at La Trappe, where he became abbot in 1696. Forced to resign following quarrels, he drifted from monastery to monastery. He published a large number of biographies and critical studies including *Histoire de l'Abbé de Rence et de sa réforme*. Objections regarding *Histoire générale de la réforme de l'Ordre de Cîteaux* (1746) resulted in a royal *lettre de cachet* confining him to the monastery of Le Reclus.

Gervase and Protase Martyrs and saints. Milanese martyrs unknown until **Ambrose** discovered their bodies in 386. On 19 June he had them transferred to a recently built basilica, where they were put under the altar. This was important in two respects: the placing of relics under the altar became part of the dedication ceremony of churches and, secondly, the finding (*inventio*) of the relics by Ambrose caused many other similar findings and translations in north Italy. About Gervase and Protase themselves we know nothing, since their *Passio* has no historical value. Feast day 19 June.

Gervase of Canterbury English monastic chronicler, born *c.*1141, died Canterbury, *c.*1210. He was professed as a monk of Christ Church, Canterbury, in the presence of **Thomas Becket**, and spent most of his life there working as monastic historian. His major work *Chronica* is continued in *Gesta Regum*, which gives valuable information on King John. His other works include *Actus Pontificum Cantauriensis Ecclesiae* (a history of the archbishops of Canterbury from **Augustine** to **Hubert Walter**), a *Mappa mundi* (a topographical work, not an atlas) and an account of the burning of Canterbury Cathedral in 1174.

Gervase of Melcheley English grammarian and poet, died *c.*1241. The information about his life is uncertain, except that he wrote poetry from about 1200. He may have visited Rome in 1214 while serving as secretary to the archbishop of Canterbury, and may perhaps have studied at the Universities of Paris and Oxford. His principal work is *De arte versificatoria et modo dictandi*. He also wrote verses and an epitaph for William Marshal, regent of England.

Gervase of Rheims Archbishop, born Coemont,

France, 2 February 1008, died Rheims 4 July 1067. He succeeded his uncle as bishop of Le Mans in 1036, but was impeded in the exercise of his episcopal office by Geoffrey of Anjou, who had him imprisoned, releasing him seven years later only on threat of excommunication by Pope **Leo IX** and in return for the gift of Château-du-Loir. In 1055 he was promoted to archbishop of Rheims. He also served as Chancellor. He crowned Philip I.

Gervase of Tilbury English medieval cleric and author, born Tilbury, c.1140, died in England c.1234. Though apparently born in Tilbury, he spent some of his youth in Rome and then, having taught law at Bologna University, returned to the English court, where he wrote *Liber facetiarum*. He served Henry II's son-in-law (King William II of Sicily) and grandson (Emperor **Otto IV**). He accompanied Otto, who made him regent of the Kingdom of Arles, to Rome for his imperial coronation and wrote for him *Otia Imperialia*, a book of knowledge interesting for its insights into the Pope–Emperor relationship and the knowledge available to the medieval mind. He returned to England after Otto IV's defeat at Bouvines.

Gervin of Oudenburg Saint and abbot, born in Flanders, died Forest of Cosfort, Flanders, 17 April 1117. He became a Benedictine monk and priest at Bergues-Saint-Winoc following a journey to Rome and two pilgrimages to Jerusalem. He left the monastery to be a hermit but, while near Oudenburg in 1095, was elected abbot of the monastery there. He resigned in 1105 to live in the forest near the abbey. Feast day 17 April.

Gery of Cambrai Saint, bishop and patron of Cambrai, born Carignan, France, died Cambrai, 11 August 625. Mageric, bishop of Trier, conferred the tonsure on him and promised to ordain him when he had learned the Psalter by heart. He was chosen by the people of Cambrai to replace Mageric as bishop, and consecrated by the archbishop of Rheims in 584. As bishop, he opposed paganism, built a church to St **Medard**, attended a Council in Paris in 614, and went on pilgrimage to Tours. Feast day 11 August.

Gesenius, Heinrich Friedrich Wilhelm Lutheran orientalist and exegete, born Nordhausen,

Germany, 3 February 1786, died Halle, Germany, 23 October 1842. He studied at the Universities of Helmstadt and Göttingen and in 1811 was appointed professor of theology at Halle University, where he taught linguistics and made an important contribution to Hebrew studies. His many scholarly writings include *Der Prophet Jesaia* (1820–1), *Hebräisch und chaldäisches Handwörterbuch* (1810–12), *Thesaurus philologico-criticus linguae Hebraeae et Chaldaeae Veteris Testamenti* (1829–58) and *Hebräische Grammatik* (1813).

Gesualdo, Carlo Prince of Venosa, composer, born Naples, Italy, c.1560, died Naples, 8 September 1613. He travelled widely in Italy, where he met the chief literary and musical figures of his day. He is particularly renowned for his settings of some of Tasso's poems to music as madrigals. He published much of his religious music in two books of *Sacrae Cantiones* (1603) and a volume of compositions for Holy Week, though these were overshadowed by his madrigals. There is substantial support for the never-proved allegation that he arranged the murder of his wife and her lover.

Geulincx, Arnold Calvinist philosopher, born Antwerp, 31 January 1624, died Leiden, Holland, November 1669. He was professor and, from 1654, dean at the University of Louvain, but his Jansenist and later Calvinist sympathies – he attacked both Scholasticism and monasticism – led him to resign in 1658 and move to Leiden, where he converted to Calvinism. He developed Cartesian thinking along different lines from **Descartes**, seeing the *cogito* not as confirmation of the existence of a thinking substance but as consciousness of total dependence on a God who determines what humans can and cannot perceive, thereby rendering pointless any act of will. His theories, known as Occasionalism, influenced the work of **Malebranche** and Spinoza.

Gevaert, François Auguste Roman Catholic, musicologist, born Huysse (Belgium), 31 July 1828, died Brussels, 24 December 1908. He taught at the Ghent Conservatory when only fifteen, thereafter studying opera composition at the Jesuit College in Melle before being appointed director of the Paris Opéra. He later became director of the Brussels Conservatory. He is remembered chiefly for his studies in Greek music and Gregorian chant, between which he attempted to establish a connection. His main works are *Histoire et théorie de la musique de l'Antiquité*, *Les Problèmes musicaux d'Aristote*, *Les Origines du chant liturgique de l'Église latine* and *La Mélopée antique dans le chant de l'Église latine*.

Gezzelinus Blessed, hermit, died in the city of Luxemburg, 6 August 1138. He lived as a hermit in the forests around Grünenwald near Luxemburg for some fourteen years without any clothes or shelter, foraging for his food. The Cistercians claim that he was a member of their Order because a monk, Achard of Clairvaux, gave him the habit of **Bernard of Clairvaux**. He was buried in the Benedictine abbey church of Maria-Münster in Luxemburg. Feast day 6 August.

Gfrörer, August Friedrich Church historian, born Calw, Württemberg, Germany, 5 March 1803, died Karlsbad, 6 July 1861. In obedience to his family he studied theology at Tübingen, and after ordination served as a Lutheran pastor in Württemberg. He became unsympathetic to Lutheranism, resigned his post and, from 1830, was appointed to a post in the library in Stuttgart. There he continued his historical studies, and published a five-volume work on the history of early Christianity and a study of the history of the Thirty Years' War which demonstrated a growing sympathy to Catholicism. In 1846 he was appointed to the Catholic University of Freiburg-im-Breisgau, and in 1853 became a Catholic. His Catholic sympathies were rooted in his research on the Catholic Middle Ages and the work of Archbishop Hermann von Vicari during the religious conflict in Baden. He supported the reunion of the Christian confessions as a means of reviving the political unity of Germany.

Ghebre, Michael Blessed, martyr and theologian, born Mertoule-Miriam, Ethiopia, 1790, died Cerecia-Ghebaba, Ethiopia, 28 August 1855. As a Monophysite monk he was renowned for his holiness and theology. Following a visit to Rome, he recast his theology to take account of Catholic Christology, but was suspected of Arianism by his metropolitan. He subsequently became a Roman Catholic, establishing a seminary at Gaula and

translating the catechism and Catholic theological works into Ethiopian languages. He was later ordained and became a member of the Vincentian Congregation. In 1855 he was imprisoned at the instigation of the metropolitan and died in chains. Feast day 1 September.

Ghellinck, Joseph de Belgian Jesuit and theologian, born Ghent, 30 October 1872, died 4 January 1950. On 23 September 1889 he entered the novitiate and in October 1906 he became professor in Louvain. He founded the series Spicilegium Sacrum Lovaniense. As head of the library of the Jesuit College he became engaged in reconstituting the University Library, burnt down in 1914. As researcher he distinguished himself by some 150 publications and 1000 reviews in the fields of medieval theology and canon law, history of doctrine, patrology, Christian Latin and library history. In 1949 he became doctor *honoris causa* of the faculty of theology.

Ghéon, Henri (Henri Vangeon) Roman Catholic poet and dramatist, born Bray-sur-Marne, France, 15 March 1875, died Paris, 13 June 1944. He co-founded *La Nouvelle Revue française*, and wrote poetry and social dramas. On Christmas Day 1915 he was impressed by a marine officer to return to the Church. Thereafter he concentrated on writing biographies of the saints and religious dramas, including *Secrets of the Saints*, *Three Plays*, *St Anne and the Gouty Rector*. Considering true theatre to exist only where there is a common bond uniting the writer and actors, he founded Les Compagnons de Notre-Dame, where the link was faith.

Ghiberti, Lorenzo Italian sculptor, born Florence, 1378, died Florence, 1 December 1455. Trained as a goldsmith, he won the competition to design the north doors of the baptistery in Florence, the 28 panels of which depict NT scenes. His work was completed in 1424 and so admired that he was commissioned to design the east doors, with OT scenes, as well. His work is considered to mark the transition from Gothic to Renaissance in Italian art. His *Commentarii* includes the earliest autobiography by an artist.

Ghirlandaio, Domenico Italian fresco painter, born Florence, 1449, died Florence, 11 January

1494. Trained as a goldsmith, he became a skilled fresco painter and chronicler of Florentine life. He taught the fresco technique to **Michelangelo**. He was commissioned to do two frescoes for the Sistine Chapel, and painted many religious subjects, among them *The Annunciation*, *The Life of St Finn*, *The Last Supper* and *The Adoration of the Shepherds*.

Gianelli, Anthony Saint, founder and bishop, born Cereta, Italy, 12 April 1789, died Piacenza, Italy, 7 June 1846. He was ordained in 1812 following an education in Genoa, and taught rhetoric until 1823. He was appointed archpriest at Chiavari in 1826 and consecrated bishop of Bobbio in 1838. He acquired a great reputation as a preacher, a retreat conductor, a writer of tracts and discourses, and a correspondent. He founded the Daughters of Our Lady of the Garden and the Oblates of St Alfonsus for Clerical Formation. Feast day 7 June.

Gibalin, Joseph de Jesuit priest and teacher of canon law, born Mende, France, 22 February 1592, died Lyons, France, 14 December 1671. He taught canon law at a Jesuit college, specializing in the changes brought about by the Council of Trent. He wrote *Disquisitiones canonicae de clausura regulari*, *De irregulantibus et impedimentis canonicis sacrorum ordinum*, *Disquistiones canonicae et theologicae de sacra jurisdictione in ferendis poenis et censuris ecclesiasticis*, *De usuris commerciis Gallico et Romano*, *De simonia* and *Sententia canonica et hierapolitica*.

Gibault, Pierre Roman Catholic missionary, born Montreal, Canada, 7 April 1735, died New Madrid, USA, 15 August 1802. He was ordained following theological training in Quebec and moved to Illinois territory where, from 1777, he served as the sole priest following the expulsion of the Jesuits. He approved the revolutionist cause, despite being threatened with suspension by his bishop, and his support was a deciding factor in General George Roger Clark's campaign. In 1782 he left for the Mississippi area, and later moved on to New Madrid, where he became pastor.

Gibbes, Nicholas Sydney (Archimandrite Nicholas) Orthodox monk and priest, born Rotherham,

Yorkshire, 1876, died London, 24 March 1963. He was selected to teach English to the Tsarevich Alexis and the daughters of Emperor **Nicholas II** of Russia. After the Revolution he insisted on joining them in Tobolsk but was not permitted to go to Ekaterinburg, and so escaped death. Among Russian exiles in Harbin, Manchuria, he became Orthodox in 1934 and subsequently a monk and priest. He returned to England in 1936 and thereafter ministered to Orthodox communities in London and Oxford. Regrettably he left no autobiography. He strongly rejected the claims of Anna Anderson to be the Grand Duchess Anastasia.

Gibbon, Edward English historian, born Putney, 27 April 1737, died London, 16 January 1794. He entered Magdalen College at fifteen and two years later went over to Catholicism. He was sent to Lausanne where, influenced by Calvinism, he abandoned Catholicism. He made several long journeys, e.g. to Italy, and it was on Rome's Capitol Hill that he conceived the idea and plan of his chief work, *The Decline and Fall of the Roman Empire* (1776–88). The main cause for the fall he attributed to Christianity; only **Athanasius** was in his eyes worthy of praise. This work and his other writings reveal Gibbon as the enlightened intellectual: a well-educated man of the world, with a sense of humour and a disdain for Christianity.

Gibbons, James Cardinal, born Baltimore, USA, 23 July 1834, died Baltimore, 24 March 1921. In 1868 he was consecrated to work as a bishop in North Carolina and, in 1872, also became bishop of Richmond. Appointed bishop of Baltimore in 1877, he presided over the Council which gave birth to the Catholic University of America, of which he was chancellor. He became a cardinal in 1886 and did much to interpret the free spirit of America to the Holy See and the Church to America. His works include *The Faith of Our Fathers*, *Our Christian Heritage*, *The Ambassador of Christ* and *A Retrospective of Fifty Years*.

Gibbons, Orlando Composer and organist, born Oxford, 25 December 1583, died Canterbury, 5 June 1625. In 1596 he became a member of the choir of King's College, Cambridge, where his brother was in charge. He took a degree at Cambridge in 1606, by which time he had already been organist of the Chapel Royal for two years. He was appointed organist at Westminster Abbey in 1623. He composed much Church music. His 'Song I' and 'Song 34' are popular as hymn tunes.

Gibbs, Armstrong Composer, born Great Baddow, near Chelmsford, Essex, 10 August 1889, died Chelmsford, 12 May 1960. He was educated at Winchester, Cambridge and the Royal College of Music. He is known chiefly as a song composer and wrote three hymns for Charterhouse School.

Gibbs, James Roman Catholic architect, born Aberdeen, Scotland, 23 September 1682, died London, England, 5 August 1754. He studied architecture in Rome during his grand tour, and established a practice in London under Tory patronage. He was appointed as surveyor to the commissioners for building 50 new churches in London and, although he lost the appointment on the accession of the Whigs, his private practice flourished. He designed St Mary-le-Strand and St Martin-in-the-Fields in London and the Radcliffe Camera, now part of the Bodleian Library, at Oxford. His publication *A Book of Architecture* is a source of country house designs.

Giberti, Gian Matteo Italian bishop, born Palermo, 20 September 1495, died Verona, 30 December 1543. He served on the secretariat of Cardinal Guilio de' Medici (later **Clement VII**) and was associated with the Oratory of Divine Love, which promoted the austere life and Church reform. He was appointed bishop of Verona in 1524 but did not go there until released from being taken hostage during the sack of Rome. As a bishop, he insisted on clerics living religiously, supported intellectual activity and promoted Church reform. He was papal legate to the conference of Catholic and Protestant theologians at Worms in 1540.

Gibieuf, Guillaume Oratorian theologian and philosopher, born Bourges, France, 1580, died Paris, 6 June 1650. He became superior at the Oratory in Paris on the death of its founder Cardinal **Bérulle**. He was visitor of the Carmelite nuns and superior of Saint-Magloire, but turned down the See of Nantes. His teaching and practice were on Bérullian lines and he opposed Jansenism,

despite similarities between his work and **Jansen**'s *Augustinus*. He published *Vie et grandeurs de la Très Sainte Vierge Marie* and *De Libertate Dei et creaturae*.

Gibson, Hugh Simons Roman Catholic diplomat and humanitarian, born Los Angeles, USA, 16 August 1883, died Geneva, Switzerland, 12 December 1954. He worked in the US foreign service in Honduras, London and Havana and assisted President Hoover's relief work in Europe after the First World War. Subsequently he served as US minister to Poland and to Switzerland, and then as US ambassador to Belgium, Brazil and Belgium. He converted to Catholicism just before the Second World War when he was active in relief work. His many books include *Rio*, *Belgium*, *Problems of Lasting Peace* and *Basis of Lasting Peace*.

Gibson, John Campbell Scottish missionary to South China, born Glasgow, 10 January 1849, died Glasgow, 25 November 1919. After education in Glasgow and training for ministry in the Free Church of Scotland in 1874 he went to Swatow (Shantou) in South China as a Presbyterian Church of England missionary. He advocated the use of Romanized script translations and contributed to the Easy Wen-li translation of the NT. He supported the union and independence of Chinese Churches and his Duff Lectures were published as *Mission Problems and Mission Methods in South China* (1901). He was joint chairman of the 1907 Shanghai Mission Conference and chaired the Edinburgh 1910 Commission on the Church in the Mission Field. He was moderator of the Presbyterian Church of England in 1910 and of the first General Assembly of the Presbyterian Church in China in 1919.

Giffard, Bonaventure Catholic bishop, born Wolverhampton, England, 1642, died Hammersmith, London, 12 March 1734. He was educated at Douay College and was the first student to attend St Gregory's, Paris. He returned to England to work in the slums of London and the Midlands. In 1688 he was consecrated bishop, made first vicar apostolic of the Midlands district, and appointed by King **James II** as president of Magdalen College, Oxford. He was captured while trying to escape to the Continent and served two years in prison. Made vicar apostolic of the London district in 1703, and leader of the persecuted Catholics, he was arrested five times.

Gifford, William Benedictine and archbishop, born Gloucestershire, England, 1554, died Rheims, France, 11 April 1629. He studied at the English Colleges in Rheims and Rome. He was ordained in 1582 and was dean of Lille from 1595 and later a university professor in Rheims, summoned there by Cardinal William **Allen**, in whose household he lived. After Allen's death he was for some time in the household of St Charles **Borromeo**. He was accused of fomenting opposition to the Jesuits in the English College in Rome; he was himself sympathetic to the possibility of an accord between English Catholics and the Crown. He joined the Benedictines in 1608, became prior of Dieulouard, founded the English monasteries of St Malo and St Edmund's, Paris, helped to establish the English Benedictine Congregation, and was the first president and reformer of Fontevrault. Having served as assistant bishop (with the rank of archbishop) in Rheims, in 1622 he succeeded to the archbishopric itself, thereby becoming the senior nobleman in France. Though he received this preferment through his friendship with the Guise family, he served his diocese well until his death, being renowned as a preacher.

Gigli, Giovanni Bishop and papal official, born Lucca, Italy, 1434, died Rome, 25 August 1498. After being sent to England by Pope **Sixtus IV** as a collector of papal dues, he made a career serving the English Church, as papal subdeacon, and then as protonotary apostolic. In 1490 he became resident English proctor at Rome. He held canonries in Wells, St Paul's, London, Lichfield, Lincoln and Salisbury, and was archdeacon of London and Gloucester. He was consecrated in Rome as bishop of Worcester, but died before being able to visit his see. He is buried in the English College in Rome.

Gigot, François Ernest Roman Catholic scriptural scholar, born Lhuant (Indre), France, 21 August 1859, died New York, USA, 14 June 1920. He was ordained following studies in Vienna, Limoges and Paris and joined the Society of St Sulpice. He emigrated to America, where he served as professor of dogmatic theology, philosophy and Scripture in several seminaries. In 1906 he resigned from the Sulpicians and joined the diocesan clergy of New York. He was author of several books, including *General Introduction to the Study of the Holy Scriptures* and *Special Introduction to the Study of the Old Testament*.

Gihr, Nikolaus Roman Catholic writer, born Aulfingen, Germany, 12 December 1839, died St-Peter-im-Schwarzwald, Germany, 25 June 1924. Ordained in Rome, he worked at the seminary of St Peter in Freiburg as spiritual director, then as tutor and finally as rector. His work is valuable because of its extensive coverage of the history of the Mass and includes *Das heilige Messopfer, dogmatisch, liturgisch und aszetisch erklärt*.

Gilbert Blessed, Cistercian abbot, born England, died Toulouse, France, perhaps 17 October 1167, or possibly 1168. He was abbot of Ourscamp, near Compiègne, from 1143, and was elected abbot of Cîteaux, with responsibility for all Cistercian houses, in 1163. In that capacity he won from Pope **Alexander III** exemption for his Order from all episcopal jurisdiction, but he failed to settle, as he attempted to do, the conflict between Alexander and the Emperor **Frederick I Barbarossa**. When **Thomas Becket** took refuge from Henry II in the Cistercian abbey of Pontigny, Gilbert pressed him to find some other sanctuary, fearful of reprisals against the Cistercians by the English king. He is sometimes called 'the Great' or 'the Theologian', probably through a confusion with other Gilberts; no treatises can be assigned to him with certainty. He was, however, included by the Cistercians among the 'blesseds' of their Order. Feast day on 17 October.

Gilbert, Robert Bishop of London and academic, died London, 22 June 1448. In 1398 he was elected fellow of Merton College, Oxford, where he spent most of his life, serving on the committee which drew up the heresies that graduands had to promise to abjure, and being appointed warden of Merton in 1417. He was granted a canonry in Lincoln in 1407 and made dean of York in 1426. He was a member of the English delegation at the Council of Constance, dean of the Chapel Royal and prebendary of Osbaldwick in York. He was consecrated bishop of London in 1436.

Gilbert Crispin Benedictine abbot and writer, died probably 1117. He was a monk at Bec and later abbot of Westminster, summoned there by **Lanfranc**: he is reported to have ruled the abbey for 32 years. Influenced by, and friendly with, St **Anselm**, his writings give a flavour of Anselm's intellectual milieu and of the problems he sought to resolve, particularly in connection with the Jewish controversy. His numerous writings include *Disputatio Iudaei et Christiani* (dedicated to Anselm), and a Life of **Herluin**, abbot of Bec, which is an important source for the history of that monastery.

Gilbert de la Porrée Theologian and philosopher, born c.1080, died Poitiers, 4 September 1154. He was taught by both Bernard of Chartres and **Anselm of Laon**. He was chancellor of Chartres Cathedral and lectured in Paris before being consecrated bishop of Poitiers. His supposed views on the Trinity, expressed in a commentary on **Boethius**, led to his being accused of four errors at a consistory convened after the Council of Paris in 1148; but he agreed with the profession of faith drawn up by St **Bernard** as a reply to the errors, and was acquitted. His numerous works, many still in manuscript and several wrongly attributed, include writings on the Psalms and on the Pauline Epistles, and on the writings of Boethius.

Gilbert of Holland (Hoyland) Cistercian abbot, born possibly near Holland, Lincolnshire, died at the abbey of Rivours, near Troyes, France, 1172. He was abbot of Swineshead, near Holland, by c.1150, and was still there c.1167, but was possibly exiled because of his support for **Thomas Becket**, in which case he would have left England c.1170. He wrote in the style of St **Bernard of Clairvaux** a commentary on the Song of Songs.

Gilbert of Neuffontaines Premonstratensian (Norbertine) saint and abbot, born Auvergne, France, 1110, died abbey of Neuffontaines, France, 6 June 1152. After the Second Crusade, he gave half his possessions to the poor and half to rebuild a convent at Aubeterre and a monastery at Neuffontaines. He joined the Premonstratensian Order on

completion of the monastery and became its first abbot. Many cures are attributed to him, and his intercession is believed to benefit children. Feast day 6 June.

Gilbert of Saint-Amand Benedictine chronicler and poet, died Saint-Amand, France, 7 December 1095. He was dean of the church of Saint-André and entered the Benedictine Order at Saint-Amand-les-Eaux. When the monastery was damaged by fire, he arranged the fund-raising for its restoration by taking the relics of St **Amandus** through neighbouring regions and seeking the saint's intercessions for the protection of the communities in return for funds. His *Carmen de incendio monasterii Sancti Amandi* recounts the tour and the resultant miracles. He may also have written a poem on the fire.

Gilbert of Sempringham Monastic reformer and founder of the Order of Sempringham, the only medieval English monastic order, born Sempringham, Lincolnshire, between c.1083 and 1089, died Sempringham, 4 February 1189. The son of a Norman knight, Jocelin, and an Englishwoman, he was educated first in Lincolnshire and then (probably) in Paris; he returned to Lincolnshire and established a school, almost certainly at Sempringham. Before 1123 he became a clerk in the household of the bishop of Lincoln, and was ordained by Alexander the Magnificent in 1123. By 1131 he had returned to Sempringham, where he established a small religious community of seven women, which by 1147 had grown so large that he went to Cîteaux in an attempt to incorporate his monasteries into the Cistercian Congregation. Reluctant to take on the administration of a small and isolated monastic order, the Cistercians declined his request; Pope **Eugenius III** gave his approval to the Order – made up of both double monasteries and communities for men – in 1148, and, by the time of Gilbert's death, the Order had grown to nine double monasteries and four houses of canons. He was canonized by Pope **Innocent III** in 1202. Feast day 4 February.

Gilbertus Anglicus Canon lawyer, born in England, died 1225. Virtually nothing is known of his life other than that he may have entered the Dominican Order in Bologna. His chief work is a collection of letters from the pontificate of **Alexander III** which comprises five books and is used in various other collections.

Gilby, Thomas   Dominican theologian and editor, born Birmingham, England, 18 December 1902, died Cambridge, England, 29 November 1975. Gilby entered the Dominicans after studies at Cambridge, was ordained in 1926, studied further at the University of Louvain and then was sent to teach at Hawkesyard Priory in Staffordshire. From 1939 to 1948 he served as a naval chaplain, and then spent the rest of his life in Cambridge. He published a large number of books, particularly on the philosophy and theology of **Thomas Aquinas** (he had an especial interest in medieval political thought), but his most enduring memorial is the 60-volume Latin–English edition of the *Summa Theologiae*, published 1965–76.

Gildas (the Wise)   Saint, historian, born probably Dumbarton, Scotland, *c.*516, died Houat, Brittany, 570. He was educated in Wales by **Illtyd** and knew St **Samson** and Peter of León. He became a monk and went to Ireland and ministered and preached both there and in northern Britain. He made a pilgrimage to Rome and on the way back retired to live a solitary life on the island of Houat. He established a monastery at Rhuys in Brittany and has been honoured in that region ever since. His major work is *De excidio et conquestu Britanniae*, which outlines the history of Britain from the time of the Roman invasion down to his own period. He also berates several of the British kings and rebukes the clergy. Feast day 29 January.

Giles   Saint, abbot and hermit, patron of cripples, beggars and blacksmiths, possibly born Athens, Greece, died Saint-Gilles, *c.*720. According to some sources he came from Greece to Marseilles, where he lived as a hermit near the mouth of the Rhône and influenced Flavius Wamba, king of the Goths, to build the monastery for him which became the abbey of Saint-Gilles; but it is possible that this story was concocted by the monks of Saint-Gilles to free themselves from the authority of the bishop of Nîmes. According to legend he later became confessor to a King Charles of France, though it is unclear who this might be. His tomb became a place of pilgrimage. Feast day 1 September.

Giles of Assisi   Blessed, Franciscan, companion of St **Francis**, born 1190, died Perugia, Italy, 22 April 1262. He joined Francis as his third companion in 1208 and accompanied him to Rome, where the approval of Pope **Innocent III** was obtained for the new Order and he received the tonsure. He lived in a series of remote hermitages, becoming famous for his mystical raptures, and finally in Monteripido, where he was visited by **Gregory IX** and St **Bonaventure**. His *Dicta* denounce relaxation and intellectual pride. He was the only one of Francis's companions to be beatified. Feast day 23 April.

Giles of Corbeil   Canon of Notre Dame, physician, born Corbeil, 1165, died Paris, 1224. Having studied medicine at Salerno University and taught it in Montpellier and Paris, he became physician to King Philip Augustus of France. His medical writings, which include *De pulsibus*, influenced medical thought and practice for several centuries. He also wrote *Hierapigra ad purgandos prelatos*, criticizing the clergy.

Giles of Foscarari   Canon lawyer, born Bologna, Italy, died Bologna, 1289. He came from a prominent Bolognese family and was personally held in high regard. He was the first layman to teach canon law at Bologna University and spent a short time in the service of Charles I of Naples (**Charles of Anjou**. It was decreed at his death that those assisting at the funeral of any canon lawyer could be vested in scarlet, an honour previously reserved for knights and professors of civil law. His works include *De ordine iudiciario* and *Lectura in Decretales*.

Giles of Lessines   Dominican philosopher and scientist, born Lessines (Belgium), 1235, died 1304. He entered the Dominican Order, probably at Valenciennes, and studied under **Albert the Great**, probably at Cologne, and is likely to have attended **Thomas Aquinas**' lectures in Paris. His various treatises include *De essentia motu et significatione cometarum*, *De concordia temporum*, *Tractatus de crepusculis*, *De unitate formae* and *De usuris*.

Giles of Rome   Archbishop, theologian and general of the Augustinian Hermits, born Rome, 1243, possibly a member of the **Colonna** family, died

Avignon, France, 22 December 1316. He joined the Hermits of St Augustine at the age of fourteen and was sent to study in Paris, where he had **Thomas Aquinas** as a teacher. On returning to Italy in 1280, he became provincial and then in 1292 general of the Order. In 1295 he was appointed archbishop of Bourges by **Boniface VIII**. He wrote prolifically on the issues of his day – his works include *De regimine principum*, *De renuntiatione Papae* and *De Summi Pontificatus potestate* – and was involved in numerous disputations. Of these writings the first mentioned is the best known: it was written for his pupil, the future Philip the Fair of France; the second was inspired by the resignation of Boniface's predecessor in the Papacy, **Celestine V**; and the third may have been the basis for Pope Boniface's bull *Unam Sanctam*.

Giles of Santarem Blessed, Dominican preacher, born Vaozela, Portugal, 1184, died Santarem, Spain, 14 May 1265. He was endowed with five ecclesiastical benefices when young and squandered their proceeds studying medicine in Paris and going on to practise necromancy. His religious conversion prompted him to return to Spain, where he entered the Dominican Order at Palencia. As a travelling preacher and teacher, he became acquainted with many prominent people. He was twice elected provincial of the Spanish province. Feast day 14 May.

Giles of Viterbo Cardinal, scholar and reformer, born Viterbo, 1469, died Rome, 11 November 1532. He joined the Augustinians at Viterbo, and became a renowned preacher. When appointed vicar general of the Augustinians he worked to reform the Order, encouraging higher study and a return to the full common life. He served Emperor Maximilian I as papal agent, was nominated cardinal in 1517, was papal legate to Spain in 1518, and was a serious candidate for the papacy in 1521. He wrote poetry, edited philosophical works, wrote a survey of Christian history and compiled a theological commentary. Most of his writings remain unpublished.

Gilij, Filippo Salvatore Jesuit missionary and ethnographer, born Legona, Italy, 26 July 1712, died Rome, 1789. After entering the Society of Jesus he travelled to Colombia, where he was later ordained

and worked as a missionary in the Orinoco area. When the Jesuits were expelled in 1767, he returned to Rome. He is renowned for his *Saggio di storia americana*, a much-translated source of information on the history, religions and language of Colombia.

Gill, Eric Sculptor, engraver, writer and typographer, born Brighton, Sussex, 22 February 1882, the son of a clergyman belonging to the Countess of Huntingdon's Connexion, died Uxbridge, Middlesex, 17 November 1940. He studied at Chichester School of Art. He moved to London to train as an architect in 1899, but abandoned this to devote himself to lettering, whether in signs, title pages of books, engravings, etc.: he originated ten printing types, including Perpetua (1925) and Gill Sansserif (1927). In 1907 he moved to Ditchling in Sussex, where he established a small printing-press. In 1913 he joined the Roman Catholic Church, being given a commission to engrave the Stations of the Cross for Westminster Cathedral the same year, and later became a Dominican tertiary. He founded a quasi-monastic community at Ditchling which included married people and was sometimes popularly known as the married monk. In 1924 he left Ditchling for Capel-y-ffin, where he devoted himself for four years to sculpture. The remainder of his life he spent at Piggots, a house near High Wycombe. Among his major works in addition to the Stations of the Cross are *Prospero and Ariel* at Broadcasting House, London, *Christ Driving the Moneylenders out of the Temple* at Leeds University, many war memorials, *Mother and Child* and the *Creation of Adam* at Geneva. His major written work is *Christianity and Art*.

Gille, Albert Catholic journalist, born Amsterdam, Holland, 30 September 1878, died Watford, England, 26 October 1950. After becoming a Jesuit, he was sent to the Calcutta mission, ordained in Bengal, and appointed professor of rhetoric at the Papal Seminary in Kandy. He became editor of the *Catholic Herald of India* and was such an ardent campaigner that, on attending the Mission Congress in Rome, he was barred from returning to India amid much adverse press comment. He left the Jesuits in 1934. He published *Catholic Plea for Reunion*, *To Xavier's Tomb*, *Christianity at Home* and *Professional Prayers*.

Gillespie, Angela Superior of the Congregation of Sisters of the Holy Cross, born Brownville, USA, 21 February 1824, died Notre Dame, USA, 4 March 1887. While studying in Washington, she organized a parochial school, won acceptance of religious instruction for Catholics in state schools, and opened a Sunday school for Negroes. On entering the Community of the Holy Cross Sisters in Michigan, she was transferred to Notre Dame, Indiana, where she introduced many advanced courses and published the *Metropolitan Reader* series. During the Civil War she established eight hospitals and staffed two hospital ships. She was appointed provincial superior in 1869 and later founded a teacher-training institute.

Gillet, Martin Stanislaus Dominican master-general and philosopher, born Louppy-sur-Loyson, France, 14 December 1875, died Rome, 4 September 1951. He was professed at the priory of Amiens and studied at Louvain and Fribourg University. He became professor of moral philosophy at the Institut Catholique in Paris, provincial of the Dominican province of France and, in 1927, master-general of the Order. In 1946 he was named titular archbishop of Nicaea. His many writings include *Le Fondement intellectuel de la morale d'après Aristote*, *L'Éducation du caractère*, *L'Éducation du coeur*, *L'Éducation de la conscience* and *La Conscience chrétienne et justice sociale*.

Gillis, James Martin Roman Catholic editor and author, born Boston, USA, 12 November 1876, died New York, 14 March 1957. Having joined the Paulist Fathers, he was ordained in 1901, studied at the Catholic University of America, taught in Washington, and did missionary work. In 1922 he became editor of *Catholic World* and was renowned for his outspoken conservative opinions. From 1928 he published the newspaper column 'Sursum Corda : What's Right with the World'. He was a radio speaker on *Catholic Hour*. His prolific authorship includes *False Prophets*, *Christianity and Civilization*, *The Paulists* and *This Mysterious Human Nature*.

Gillmann, Franz Roman Catholic priest and canon lawyer, born Landstuhl, Germany, 22 September 1865, died there 23 October 1941. He was ordained in Speyer, appointed professor of canon law at Würzburg University, and made a papal domestic prelate. He is renowned for his research into the history of the canon law of the twelfth and thirteenth centuries, both in the East and in the West.

Gillow y Zavalza, Eulogio Gregorio Roman Catholic archbishop, born Puebla, Mexico, 11 March 1841, died Ejutla, Mexico, 18 May 1922. He was ordained in Mexico in 1865, having studied in England, Belgium and Rome, where he gained a doctorate in canon law. In 1887 he was consecrated bishop of Antequera, which was elevated to an archbishopric three years later. He helped to develop the Mexican railway system and did much to improve his archdiocese, but the Mexican revolution forced him into exile in 1910. He was considered for a cardinalate but not appointed, because of political opposition.

Gilmour, Richard Roman Catholic bishop and educationist, born Glasgow, Scotland, 28 September 1824, died St Augustine, USA, 13 April 1891. His parents emigrated to America, where his conversion at a temperance rally when he was thirteen led to his baptism and eventual ordination. He was consecrated bishop of Cleveland in 1872, where he improved Catholic schools, introduced the *Gilmour Readers* and *Gilmour Bible History*, introduced several religious orders, built several churches and hospitals, encouraged native vocations and improved Catholic awareness and esteem. He was an advocate of the establishment of a Catholic university.

Gilson, Etienne Henri Roman Catholic philosopher and historian of philosophy, born Paris, 13 June 1884, died Cravant, near Auxerre, 19 September 1978. He studied at the Sorbonne, and then became a schoolmaster before being appointed in 1913 to the University of Lille, where he first began his studies of medieval philosophy. He was taken a prisoner of war during World War I and continued his studies in prison camps. On release he became a full professor at the University of Strasburg, before being summoned in 1926 to a specially-created chair in medieval philosophy at the Sorbonne. Six years later he was elected to the Collège de France, and withdrew from the Sorbonne. He lectured at the Collège throughout the war years and until his retirement in 1971. He lectured widely in both Britain and North America. Many of his publications have been translated, and he exercised enormous influence on the study of Scholastic theology and, more particularly, philosophy. Though in the first period of his life he was concerned especially with the history of medieval thought, from the 1930s onwards his interests moved more to metaphysics.

Ginoulhiac, Jacques Marie Achille   Roman Catholic bishop and theologian, born Montpellier, France, 3 December 1806, died Montpellier, 17 November 1875. Following ordination, he was appointed professor of philosophy and natural science and later professor of theology at Montpellier. In 1839 he became vicar general of Aix, in 1852 bishop of Grenoble and in 1870 archbishop of Lyons. He worked to prevent misunderstanding between the Church and modern society. At Vatican Council I, he advocated the freedom of theological investigation and opposed papal infallibility. He wrote *Histoire du dogme catholique pendent les trois premiers siècles, Sermon sur la Montagne* and *Les origines du christianisme.*

Gioberti, Vincenzo   Roman Catholic philosopher and statesman, born Turin, Italy, 5 April 1801, died Paris, 26 October 1852. He was ordained to the priesthood in 1825. He came under the influence of Giuseppe Mazzini, which led to his arrest for suspected political intrigue. Following exile in Paris and Belgium, he returned to Turin, where he became president of the Chamber of Deputies and, later, president of the Council of Ministers of King Victor Emmanuel II. He returned to Paris in voluntary exile in 1851 and died there. His philosophy, which may be seen as theistic or pantheistic, is summarized in the formula 'being creates the existent and the existent returns to being'. His works, which were placed on the Index, include *Il rinnovamento civile d'Italia, Protologia* and *Riforma cattolica.*

Giocondo, Giovanni   Architect, engineer, archaeologist and humanist, born Verona, Italy, 1433, died Rome, 1515. Little is known of his life other than that he was appointed by Pope **Leo X**, along with **Raphael** and Antonio da Sangallo, as architect of St Peter's. He probably constructed the Palazzo di Poggio Reale in Naples and the fortifications at Padua and Treviso, and diverted the Brenta River to protect Venice. He published *The Letters of Pliny the Younger, Breviarium Historiae Romanae of Aurelius Victor* and *The Commentaries of Julius Caesar,* and illustrated Francesco di **Giorgio**'s works on architecture.

Giorgio, Francesco di   Painter, sculptor and architect, born Siena, Italy, 25 September 1439, died Siena, 1501. He was employed as a military engineer by the duke of Urbino, at whose court he executed a series of bronze reliefs. Several of his masterpieces are in Siena Cathedral. From 1495, serving as an official of the Sienese government, he visited and advised the cities of Milan, Florence, Rome, Naples and Lucca. He was the chief architect of Santa Maria della Grazie in Cortona, and wrote *Trattato di architettura.*

Giorgione da Castelfranco   Painter, born Castelfranco, Italy, 1477, died Venice, October 1510. He lived in Venice and died of the plague while working with **Titian** on frescoes for the Fondaco dei Tedeschi. Opinions vary as to the number of paintings that can be accurately ascribed to him, because many of his works were completed by others and he had many imitators. His paintings include *The Tempest* (Accademia, Venice), *The Ordeal of Moses* and *The Judgement of Solomon* (Uffizi, Florence), *The Three Philosophers* (Kunsthistorisches Museum, Vienna), and *Fête Champêtre* (Louvre, Paris).

Giotto di Bondone   Painter, born Vespignano, Italy, 1266, died Florence, 8 January 1336. He studied under Cimabue and revolutionized Florentine painting by using three-dimensional sculpture figures for models. His earliest authenticated frescoes are those in the Arena Chapel. He was commissioned to execute the great mosaic of the Navicella in St Peter's, Rome, and probably worked at the frescoes in the church of San Francesco, Assisi. He decorated four of the chapels in Santa Croce in Florence and the great hall of Castelnuova in Naples. In 1334 he was recalled to Florence to supervise the construction of the campanile of the cathedral.

Giovanna Maria of the Cross   Venerable, poetess

and foundress of two convents of Poor Clares, born Roverto, Italy, 8 September 1603, died Roverto, 26 March 1673. In 1650 she founded the convent of Poor Clares of St Charles in Roverto and became its abbess. In 1672 she founded the convent of Poor Clares of St Anne in Borgo Valsugana and was influential in founding a Carmelite convent nearby. She worked to establish peace during the Thirty Years' War. She wrote *Evangelici spirituali sentimenti*, an unpublished autobiography and much poetry, becoming known as 'first poetess of the Trentino'.

Giraldus Cambrensis (Gerald de Barri) Archdeacon and historian, born Manorbier Castle, Wales, *c*.1147, died 1223. A descendant of a Welsh royal family, he became archdeacon of Brecon. When Henry II in 1176 opposed his succeeding his uncle as bishop of St Davids, he went to study in Paris. Although he accompanied Henry's son to Ireland and supported the Third Crusade, Henry died without offering him any preferment. When he was in 1199 again elected to succeed as bishop of St Davids, the archbishop of Canterbury refused his approval and years of litigation following an appeal to the Pope got him nowhere: Giraldus believed, probably correctly, that the English would not permit a Welshman to become bishop of St Davids. His most valuable work is *Expugnatio Hibernica*.

Girard, Jean Baptiste Swiss Roman Catholic priest and educationalist, born Fribourg, 1765, died 1850. Trained for the priesthood at Lucerne, from 1805 to 1823 he taught at a school at Fribourg and then for the next eleven years at Lucerne. From 1834 he wrote books on education such as *The Mother Tongue* (1847) and *Cours éducatif* (1844–6), which had a profound influence on educational thinking.

Gisela Blessed, queen of Hungary, born *c*.973, died *c*.1060. Following the death of her husband **Stephen I**, she involved herself in affairs of state. Many virtues are ascribed to her, but it is postulated that these were to contrast her with her husband's successor, Peter I. She probably died in exile or in a convent; her reported death and tombstone at Passau are not considered reliable. She is not normally honoured as a saint, although she is still under consideration by the Holy See. Feast day 7 May.

Gislebertus French sculptor, flourished early twelfth century, born Autun, France. He worked on the abbeys at Cluny and Vézelay. At the cathedral of St Lazarus he executed work, including the west tympanum. His most greatly admired works are the *Last Judgement* on the west doorway at Autun, and an *Eve*. At Autun he also created 60 capitals.

Gislenus Saint, abbot, hermit in Hainaut, France, born *c*.650, died Ursidong, 9 October 681. He founded and governed the monastery of SS Peter and Paul. Legend has it that a bear he saved from a hunt showed him the site of the future monastery. Supposedly he was born in Attica and became a monk, and bishop of Athens. He is said to have resigned his see, travelled to Rome and then Hainaut, met St **Amandus**, and settled on the River Haire. Feast day 9 October.

Giusti, Giuseppe Italian poetical satirist, born Monsummano, 1809, died Florence, 1850. After two short periods as a law student at Pisa, following the revolution of 1848 he sat in the Tuscan legislative assemblies and the constituent assembly. His poetry, mainly consisting of political satire against the Habsburg rule in Italy, first appeared in *La ghigliottina a vapore* (1833), *Poesie italiane* (1844) and *Versi* (1845). His most famous work is *Sant' Ambrogio* (1847).

Giustiniani, Agostino Bishop, born 'Pantaleone Giustiniani' at Genoa, *c*.1470, died at sea, 1536. Against the wishes of his distinguished family, he became a Dominican in 1484, was forced to leave, but returned in 1488, taking the name 'Agostino'. His kinsman Cardinal Bandinello Sauli secured for him the Corsican bishopric of Nebbio in 1514, the income from which supported his linguistic studies. His principal work was the polyglot *Psalterium octuplex* (1516), presenting in parallel columns Massoretic Hebrew, Septuagint, Aramaic Targum and Arabic texts with modern Latin versions of the first three; in the eighth column was material from rabbinical sources. Plans for a complete Polyglot Bible were thwarted by Sauli's fall.

Guistiniani, Lorenzo   *see* **Lawrence Justinian**

Gladstone, William Ewart   Anglican statesman and author, born Liverpool, 29 December 1809, died Hawarden, 19 May 1898. After studying at Eton and Christ Church, Oxford, where he gained a double First, he entered Lincoln's Inn in 1833 to study law, though he was never called to the Bar and was already a Member of Parliament (from December 1832). He joined the Liberal Party and was four times prime minister. He was throughout his life closely associated with the Church of England, and was openly devout. In politics he favoured the gradual emancipation of slaves, accepted the repeal of the Corn Laws, supported Disraeli's first Reform Bill (1859), and introduced and passed the Irish Church Disestablishment Bill of 1869. He opposed the first Opium War with China (1840), the Ecclesiastical Titles Bill (1851; a reaction against the re-establishment in England of a Roman Catholic hierarchy), the Bill for establishing the divorce court (1857), and the Bill for removing theological tests for university degrees (1865). He founded St Deiniol's Library at Hawarden in 1895. His publications include *The State in its Relations with the Church* (1838), *Church Principles Considered in Their Results* (1840), an edition of Joseph **Butler**'s *Analogy*, and *Sermons and Studies Subsidiary to Works of Bishop Butler* (1896).

Glareanus, Henricus   Humanist scholar, born 'Heinrich Loriti' at Mollis, near Glarus, Switzerland, June 1488, died Freiburg, 27/28 March 1563. After studies at the University of Cologne, the layman Glareanus abandoned Scholastic theology. He was crowned poet laureate by Emperor Maximilian I in 1512, thereafter being master of residential schools in Basel in 1514–17, Paris in 1517–22, and Freiburg, 1529–63, where he was also professor of poetry. He edited many classical Latin authors and wrote on geography and mathematics; his most original work was in musical theory: *Isagoge in musicen* (Basel, 1516) and *Dodecachordon* (Basel, 1547). Though sympathetic to his friend **Zwingli**, he was closer to **Erasmus** and remained within the Roman Church.

Glennon, John Joseph   US cardinal, born Hardwood, County Meath, Ireland, 14 June 1864, died Dublin, 9 March 1946. Educated at St Mary's College, Mullingar, and All Hallows College, Dublin. At the age of 22 he was ordained priest and emigrated to the USA. He served in various parishes, and became bishop of Kansas City, Missouri. As archbishop of St Louis for 43 years, he organized 47 parishes, built schools and a seminary, and constructed a large cathedral. In 1946 Pope **Pius XII** made him a cardinal, but he died in Dublin on his journey back from his ordination in Rome.

Glodesindis   Saint, abbess, born Metz, France, 570, died there 600. Glodesindis' father tried to give her in marriage against her wishes. Glodesindis fled to the cathedral of Metz. She was taken to Trier by her aunt, and instructed in the monastic life. On her return to Metz she founded a monastery of about 100 nuns.

Glycas, Michael   Byzantine author known as 'Grammaticus', born probably in Corfu, *c.*1118, died *c.*1200. Little is known of his life. He was blinded by Manuel I in 1159 for a political offence. Famous for his *Biblos Chronike* (World Chronicle), which traces the history of the world from the Creation to the death of **Alexius I** in 1118.

Goar, Jacques   French liturgiologist, born Paris, 1601, died there, 23 September 1653. Entered the Dominican Order in 1619. Lecturer at the convent at Toul. In 1631 became prior of the convent of St Sebastian in Chios, Greece; in 1637 appointed prior of San Sisto, Rome. Settled in Paris, writing extensively on the Greek liturgy, research which was later published in his *Rituale Graecorum* (1647).

Goar of Trier   Saint, priest, hermit, date of birth unknown, died 570. Goar is held to have come from Aquitaine, in the days of Childebert I, king of the Franks. He built a chapel and hermitage near Oberweld. Goar was renowned for his hospitality. There are conflicting accounts of his life which have given rise to different opinions as to his dates: as well as the sixth century, he could be placed in the eighth century.

Godfrey, William   Cardinal, born Liverpool, 25 September 1889, died 22 January 1963. He was educated at Ushaw College, County Durham, and in Rome and was consecrated archbishop in 1938.

He had an unusual career in being apostolic delegate to Great Britain, linking Rome with the British Roman Catholic hierarchy from 1938 to 1953. He held various international offices and was rector of the English College in Rome. He was created archbishop of Liverpool in 1953, translated to Westminster as the seventh archbishop in 1956 and created a cardinal in 1958.

Godfrey of Amiens Bishop, ecclesiastical reformer and saint, died Soissons, 8 November 1115. Little is known about his early life. Appointed bishop of Amiens in 1104. Attempted to reform the Church by enforcing clerical celibacy, removing simony and organizing religious communes. Facing stern opposition he withdrew to the monastery of the Grande Chartreuse. Feast day 8 November.

Godfrey of Bouillon One of the leaders of the First Crusade, born Baisy (Belgium), c.1061, died Jerusalem, 18 July 1100. In 1082 he was created duke of Lower Lorraine by Emperor **Henry IV**. Godfrey and his brothers **Baldwin** and Eustace led the First Crusade, arriving at Constantinople in December 1096. In 1099, after capturing Nicaea and Antioch in the previous year, he captured Jerusalem. Having rejected the title of 'King of Jerusalem', he was given the title 'Advocate of the Holy Sepulchre'. In August 1099 he defeated the Egyptians at Ascalon. Because of his piety and bravery, he became the subject of several legends and sagas.

Godfrey of Fontaines French philosopher and theologian, born Fontaines-les-Hozémont, Lower Lorraine, before 1250, died Paris, after 1305. He was prominent in the medieval controversy over faith. In Paris he studied under St **Thomas Aquinas**. He taught at the University of Paris, latterly as regent or dean of the faculty. Godfrey was a proponent of Aristotelianism, in contrast to the Christian interpretations of Aristotle by Thomas Aquinas and **Duns Scotus**. He wrote quodlibets and scholia (annotations) on St Thomas Aquinas' *Summa Theologiae*.

Godfrey of Saint-Victor French Augustinian, theologian and poet, born c.1125, died Paris, c.1194. He studied at Paris and entered the abbey of Saint-Victor. However, because of an unsympathetic

superior, he left the abbey and retired to a rural priory. Here he wrote *Microcosmos*, on man's natural and spiritual nature. In verse he wrote *Fons philosophiae*, on knowledge. His writings summarized an early medieval Christian humanism. He eventually returned to Saint-Victor.

Godo Saint, abbot, date of birth unknown, died Oyes, 26 May 690. Godo was the nephew of St Wandville, the founder of a monastery at Fontenelle. Godo was a member of the monastery until 661, when he left to found his own community at Oyes.

Goes, Hugo van der Painter, born Ghent, c.1440, died Rode Klooster, near Brussels, 1482. Nothing is known of his life prior to his admission to the Ghent painters' guild in 1467, after which he received commissions for more or less ephemeral works. From 1475 he was a lay brother of a priory near Brussels, where he suffered a temporary mental breakdown in 1481. None of his works are signed, but his masterpiece is undoubtedly the *Portinari Altarpiece* (Uffizi, Florence, 1473–8), commissioned for the Florentine hospital of S. Maria Nuova by Tommaso Portinari, agent of the Medici bank in Bruges.

Gogarten, Friedrich Protestant theologian, born Dortmund, 13 January 1887, died Göttingen, 16 October 1967. In 1917 he became pastor at Styelzendorf, Thuringia, and in 1925 at Dorndorf. Appointed professor of systematic theology at Breslau in 1931 and at Göttingen in 1935. A dialectical theologian, he was influenced by Martin Buber's 'I–Thou' philosophy. His writings include *Religion und Volkstum* (1915), and *Entmythologisierung und Kirche* (1953), in which he defended various aspects of **Bultmann**'s demythologizing.

Gogol, Nikolai Vasilevich Russian writer and dramatist, born Sorochinsk, 31 March 1809, died 4 March 1852. While living at St Petersburg in 1829, he published his poem *Hans Kuechelgarten*. Working as a civil servant, he wrote his *Ukrainian Tales* (1831–2), including 'The Terrible Vengeance', which deals with the conflict of good and evil. In 1831 he worked as a teacher and for one year, in 1834, lectured at the University of St Petersburg. In 1842 he published the first part of

Dead Souls, in which he criticized the corruption of the ruling classes. His other works include *Taras Bulba* (1833) and *The Government Inspector* (1836). Disillusioned by criticisms of his work, he entered a monastery, burnt his manuscripts, and died of starvation.

Góis, Damião de Portuguese humanist, born Alenquer, 2 February 1502, died Alenquer, 30 January 1574. Travelled widely in Europe in the service of King John III of Portugal. A pupil and friend of **Erasmus**, he studied at Padua University. While living at Louvain, he was taken prisoner by the French. Following his return to Portugal in 1545 he became chief keeper of the royal archives. His writings causing offence, he was arrested in 1571 and imprisoned at the monastery of Batalha.

Goldsmith, Oliver Playwright, novelist and poet, born in Pallasmore, Ireland, 10 November 1728, died of a fever, London, 4 April 1774. Educated at Trinity College, Dublin. On being rejected for the Church he decided to go to America, then to study law at London, but lost his money gambling. He studied medicine at Edinburgh in 1752, but staying only two years, he went to Leiden, where again he lost money playing cards. Following a 'Grand tour', during which he lived as a busker, he worked as a physician then as an usher at Milner's Academy at Peckham. From about 1758 he began to write, his most famous works including *The Vicar of Wakefield* (1766) and *She Stoops to Conquer* (1773).

Goldwell, James Bishop, born Great Chart, Kent, died 15 February 1499. Goldwell's career was paralleled by those of a number of fifteenth-century English bishops, being the king's proctor in Rome, from 1471, and receiving a bishopric because of his proximity to the Pope: **Sixtus IV** appointed him to Norwich in 1472. In the 1460s Edward IV sent the Oxford-educated Goldwell on a series of political missions abroad, while he accumulated minor benefices at home, but his later years were occupied with building projects at Norwich and elsewhere. He was the great-great-uncle of Thomas **Goldwell**, Bishop of St Asaph.

Goldwell, Thomas Bishop of St Asaph in North Wales, born possibly in Kent, England, *c*.1505, died Rome, 3 April 1585. He studied at Oxford, and

possibly received the living of Cheriton, near Folkestone, in 1531. He was strongly opposed to **Henry VIII**'s religious policy, and attached himself to Reginald **Pole**, to whom he was later to administer the last rites. He moved to Rome, to a post at the English 'hospital' (now the English College) but in 1547 joined the Theatine Order in Naples. He was allowed to return with Pole to England, and in 1555 was appointed to the bishopric of St Asaph, where he re-introduced the pilgrimage to St **Winefride**'s well at Holywell, and attempted to restore the traditional faith. After the accession of **Elizabeth I** he abandoned St Asaph and returned to Rome, then in 1561 to Naples, where he became superior of the Theatine house. He was the only English bishop at the Council of Trent. He was for a time an assistant to Charles **Borromeo**, the reforming archbishop of Milan. He spent most of the rest of his life in Rome, although in 1580 he set out to accompany Edmund **Campion** and Robert **Persons** to England. He was taken ill at Rheims, and summoned back to Rome by the Pope.

Gomarus, Franciscus Dutch Calvinistic theologian, born Bruges, 30 January 1563, died Groningen, 11 January 1641. Studied at Strasburg, Neustadt, Oxford, Cambridge and Heidelberg. Pastored a congregation at Frankfurt from 1587 to 1593. In 1594 appointed professor of theology at Leiden. In 1611 he became preacher at the Reformed church at Middelburg. Appointed professor at Saumur in 1614 and at Groningen four years later. He was an opponent of Arminianism, attending the Synod of Dort (1618). He took part in the revision of the Dutch OT.

Gombert, Nicolas Composer, born *c*.1495, died *c*.1560. A Fleming believed to have been pupil of **Josquin des Prez**, Gombert was prolific in the production of both sacred and secular works, writing approximately 160 motets, ten Mass settings and 70 songs. Between 1526 and 1540 he was in the service of Emperor **Charles V**, whose early years had been spent in The Netherlands at the court of his aunt Margaret of Austria, a notable patroness of musicians.

Gonet, Jean Baptiste Dominican theologian, born Béziers, France, *c*.1616, died Béziers, 24 January

1681. Educated at Languedoc, Gonet became a Dominican c.1633. He then took his doctorate in theology at Bordeaux, where he remained as a professor of theology until his retirement in 1677. A noted champion of Thomism, Gonet's most famous work is his *Clypeus theologiae thomisticae contra novos ejus impugnatores* (definitive edition 1681). He worked to disprove charges of Calvinism in Thomistic theology and to answer questions raised by Jansenism. He is also known as one of a few theologians who did not find heresy in **Pascal**'s *Lettres provinciales*, for which opinion he was suspended from teaching for three years, 1660–3.

Góngora y Argote, Luis de Spanish poet and dramatist, born Córdoba, 11 July 1561, died there, 23 May 1627. Educated at the University of Salamanca. Ordained as a priest, eventually becoming chaplain to Philip III. His works include *Fábula de Polifemo y Galatea* (1613) and *Soledades* (1613). His style of writing came to be known as 'Gongorism'.

Gonsalvus Hispanus Franciscan theologian and general, born Galicia, Spain, date unknown, died Paris, France, 13 April 1313. Gonsalvus was educated at Paris, taking his bachelor's of theology there in 1288 and his master's in 1303. He served as part of a Spanish delegation to Pope **Nicholas IV** in 1289 and as provincial of the Franciscan provinces of Santiago de Compostela, 1290–c.1297, and Castile, 1303–4, before being elected the fifteenth general of the Order in 1304. Though he left a few works of philosophy and theology, his importance stems from his preserving the integrity of his Order during the great debates over Franciscan poverty, which reached a new height during his tenure as general.

Gonzaga, Aloysius *see* Aloysius Gonzaga.

Gonzaga, Ercole Cardinal, bishop of Mantua, born Mantua, Italy, 23 November 1505, died Trent, Italy, 2 March 1563. A member of the ruling Gonzaga family of Mantua, Ercole was appointed bishop of Mantua in 1521 (or 1525), following his cousin Sigismondo. As bishop, he studied at the University of Bologna, was created cardinal in 1527 and served as legate to Emperor **Charles V** when the latter came to Italy in 1530. Encouraged by his friends Gasparo **Contarini** and Cardinal Gian Matteo **Giberti**, he began reforming his diocese by careful visitation of his churches. From 1540 to 1556 he served as the chief regent of Mantua for his two nephews, and the city prospered under his leadership. He was serving as president of the Council of Trent when he died in 1563.

Gonzaga, Scipione Cardinal, born Mantua, Italy, 11 November 1542, died San Martino, Italy, 11 January 1593. A scion of the ruling Gonzaga family of Mantua, Scipione Gonzaga was educated by his relative Cardinal Ercole **Gonzaga** and studied in Bologna and Padua, where he later founded the Academy of the Ethereals. He served Pope **Pius IV** in Rome as personal chamberlain before becoming bishop of Mende, France. He was created cardinal in 1587, soon after being named by Pope **Sixtus V** as patriarch of Jerusalem. He was known as a patron of literature (including the noted author Torquato **Tasso**) and himself wrote three volumes of *Commentarii*, which are noted for their highly polished Latin.

González, Roque Blessed, Jesuit missionary and martyr, born Asunción, Paraguay, 1576, died Rio Grande do Sul, Brazil, 15 November 1628. After his ordination in 1599, González felt his work to be the evangelization of the indigenous South Americans. After serving as priest and vicar general of his own diocese, he entered the Society of Jesus in 1609. In 1615, he left his diocese to found the settlement of the Reduction of Itapúa among the natives of Rio Grande do Sul in Brazil. He founded several other settlements before being killed by the natives he served in the Reduction of Todos los Santos. He was beatified in 1934, the first martyr of South America to be so recognized. Feast day 17 November.

González Dávila, Gil Roman Catholic historian, born Ávila, Spain, c.1570, died Ávila, 25 April 1658. After studying in Rome in the service of Cardinal Pedro de Deza, González returned to Spain in 1592 to serve in the cathedral of Salamanca. Upon being appointed archivist there in 1607, he began his life's work of chronicling the ecclesiastical history of Spain, the so-called *Teatro eclesiástico*, upon which he worked for his entire life and which was not published in its entirety until after his death. In 1617 he was made chief chronicler of Castile and in 1643 chief chronicler of the Spanish possessions in the New World. During his life, he also published specific ecclesiastical histories of Salamanca and Madrid and a biography of Don Alonso Tostado de Madrigal.

González de Santalla, Tirso Jesuit theologian and general, born Arganza, Spain, 18 January 1624, died Rome, 27 October 1705. González became a Jesuit in 1643, taught theology and philosophy at the University of Salamanca and travelled as a preacher before being elected the thirteenth general of the Society of Jesus in 1687. He was involved in the disputes over probabilism that dominated Jesuit moral theology at the turn of the eighteenth century. His major work on the subject, *Fundamentum theologiae moralis* (1694), was endorsed by Pope **Innocent XI** and supported a position called 'probabiliorism', but it was deemed too strict by many of González' Jesuit colleagues.

González Flores, Anacleto Roman Catholic journalist and organizer of Catholic lay action, born Tepatitlán, Mexico, 13 July 1888, died Guadalajara, early April 1926. Coming from a large and poor family, González studied theology in San Juan de los Lagos before moving to Guadalajara to study law. In the face of the anti-Catholic position of the government, he worked actively with Catholic worker groups, youth groups and study groups to defend the rights of Catholics in Mexico. When President Plutarco Calles began to move against the Roman Catholic Church in 1926, González called upon Roman Catholics to resist, non-violently at first but later in open rebellion. He was arrested for his role in the Cristeros rebellion on 1 April 1926, then later beaten and shot.

González Holguín, Diego Jesuit linguist, born Cáceres, Spain, 1552, died Mendoza, Argentina, 1617 or 1618. After becoming a Jesuit in 1568, González came to the New World in May 1581. He began in Lima, Peru, then moved to Cuzco in 1584 and Quito, Ecuador, in 1586. Although occasionally involved in missionary work, his chief contributions were academic, becoming proficient in the Quechua language and publishing a grammar and dictionary of that language. He was also known for his moderate views in dealing with the

affairs of the native South Americans, especially the issue of forced labour (*encomiendas*), which he allowed but argued against its abuse.

González Suárez, Federico Bishop, historian and statesman, born Quito, Ecuador, 12 April 1844, died Quito, Ecuador, 1 December 1917. Coming from a very poor family, González served in the Ecuadorian army and spent ten years as a Jesuit before leaving the Society to be ordained a secular priest by the bishop of Cuenca. In Cuenca, he developed an interest in history. He was elected to Congress, moved to Quito and became a well-known and well respected public figure. He was named bishop of Ibarra in 1894, a see he governed tightly but well. He wrote books on aboriginal history, a four-volume history of Ecuador and a book of biographical studies.

González y Díaz Tuñón, Ceferino Dominican cardinal and philosopher, born San Nicolás de Villoria, Spain, 28 January 1831, died Madrid, Spain, 29 November 1894. González began his ecclesiastical career by entering the Philippine province of the Dominicans in 1844, travelling there in 1849, where he was ordained. After teaching at the University of Santo Tomás, 1859–66, he returned to Spain. He was made bishop of Córdoba in 1875, and archbishop of Seville in 1883 and of Toledo in 1886. He was created cardinal in 1884. He propounded a view of Thomism as an open, rather than closed, system, and wrote a number of works on the interplay of Thomism and science. His last publication, *La Biblia y la ciencia*, influenced the ideas of both **La Grange** and Pope **Leo XIII**.

Goodier, Alban Jesuit archbishop and writer, born Lancashire, England, 14 April 1869, died Teignmouth, England, 13 March 1939. Goodier became a Jesuit in 1887, was ordained in 1903 and by 1915 served as superior in London. That year he was called to Bombay to resolve a dispute at the Jesuit University there and was made archbishop of the city four years later. The touchy political situation there induced him to resign his see in 1926, becoming titular archbishop of Hierapolis and auxiliary for Cardinal Bourne in London. His influential writings reveal him as a scholarly man of great piety. Among his works are *The Passion and Death of Our Lord Jesus Christ* (1933) and

Introduction to the Study of Ascetical and Mystical Theology (1939).

Goodman, Godfrey Anglican bishop of Gloucester, born Ruthin, Denbighshire, England, 10 March 1583, died Westminster, 19 January 1656. Educated at Westminster and Cambridge, Goodman began his clerical career in Essex, serving as a rector of a country parish from 1606 to 1620, after which he rose quickly through the ecclesiastical ranks to become bishop of Gloucester in 1625. His sermons showed his orientation towards Roman Catholic belief about the Eucharist, and he was eventually removed from his see for seeming to be too Catholic by Archbishop William **Laud**. He was imprisoned for joining other English clergy in protest against the Puritan Parliament and died without property or title. In his will he finally owned his spiritual allegiance to the Church of Rome. His most noted works are *The Fall of Man* (1616) and the history *The Court of King James the First*.

Goodspeed, Edgar Johnson American Bible translator and papyrologist, born Quincy, Ilinois, 23 October 1871, died Los Angeles, 13 January 1962. Educated at Denison University, Yale University, and the Universities of Chicago and Berlin. From 1898 to 1937 he lectured at Chicago University and from 1938 to 1951 at the University of California. His books include *The New Testament: An American Translation* (1923), *An Introduction to the New Testament* (1937) and *A Life of Jesus* (1950). He was one of the scholars who worked on the Revised Standard Version of the NT in 1930.

Goossens, Pierre Lambert Roman Catholic archbishop, born Perck (Belgium), 17 July 1827, died Mechelen (Malines), Belgium, 2 January 1906. Ordained in 1850, Goossens served as professor and pastor in Mechelen from 1851 until 1856, when he was made secretary to the archbishop. He was made vicar general of the archdiocese in 1878, bishop of Namur in 1883 and archbishop of Mechelen in 1884. He served the Church in Belgium at a difficult time, working to balance the external forces of secularism and the internal conflicts between liberal and ultramontane Roman Catholics. He supported Belgium's working class through social works but also ensured the continuing importance of the middle class through the establishing of humanities education. However, his authoritarian personality slowed the advance of the neo-Thomism promoted by Cardinal Désiré **Mercier**.

Goossens, Werner Roman Catholic theologian, born Sint-Niklaas-Waas, Belgium, 12 April 1899, died Sint-Niklaas-Waas, 19 November 1949. Educated at the Roman Catholic seminary in Ghent and the Catholic University of Louvain, Goossens obtained a master's degree in theology and was long-time professor of dogmatic theology at the seminary in Ghent. He argued for adherence to critical facts during the movements for the proclamation of new Marian dogmas and made important contributions to theology in *Les Origines de l'eucharistie, sacrement et sacrifice* (1931) and *L'Église, corps mystique du Christ d'après St Paul* (1949).

Göpfert, Franz Adam Roman Catholic priest and moral theologian, born Würzburg, Germany, 31 January 1849, died Würzburg, 18 April 1913. Ordained in 1871, Göpfert served as professor of moral theology at the University of Würzburg from 1879 until his death. He was the first person to attempt a German edition of the typical Latin moral theological textbook: *Moraltheologie* (3 vols, 1897–8). He also wrote ecclesiological works, including *Die Katholicität der Kirche* (1876) and *Der Eid* (1883).

Gorazd (Pavlik) of Prague Orthodox saint, bishop, missionary and martyr, born Moravia, 1879, died 4 September 1942. He was one of a group of Czech Catholic priests who broke from Rome in 1919. Most drifted towards liberal Protestantism but one group, led by Gorazd, became Orthodox and he was consecrated bishop for them in 1921 by the Serbian patriarch. He worked tirelessly to establish his new local Church and to translate liturgical books into Czech. During the German occupation, the assassins of Heydrich hid under the Orthodox cathedral in Prague and the bishop accepted full responsibility. He was tortured and shot by the Nazis, who then executed many of his clergy. Recognized as a local saint by the Serbian Church in 1961, and canonized in Prague in 1987. Feast day 22 August.

Gordon, Andrew Benedictine monk and physicist, born Cofforach, Angus, Scotland, 15 June 1712, died Erfurt, Germany, 22 August 1751. After travelling around Europe for a while, Gordon became a Benedictine in Scotland, was ordained, studied law in Salzburg and finally became professor of natural philosophy in Erfurt. He is best known for his spectacular experiments with static electricity. Among his works are *De concordandis mensuris* (1742), *Phaenomena electricitatis exposita* (1744), *Varia ad philosophiae mutationem spectantia* (1749) and *Philosophiae experimentalis elementa* (2 vols, 1751–2).

Gore, Charles Church of England bishop, born Wimbledon, 22 January 1853, died London, 17 January 1932. He studied at Harrow and Balliol College, Oxford, and in 1875 was awarded a fellowship at Trinity College. He was ordained in 1878, was vice-principal of Cuddesdon College, 1880–3, and then served for a time as the first principal and librarian at Pusey House, Oxford, 1884–93. He helped to found the Community of the Resurrection at Mirfield, serving as its first superior, 1898–1901. He was a canon of Westminster from 1894 to 1902, and then bishop of Worcester, 1902–5, though his consecration had to be delayed because of challenges to the orthodoxy of his belief. In 1905 he went as bishop to Birmingham, and in 1911 to Oxford as bishop, a post from which he resigned in 1919. He moved to London to teach at King's College, serving as its dean 1924–8. He supported revision of the Book of Common Prayer in 1928. He worked closely with other Churches, though he was a critic of Roman Catholic claims, even during the Malines Conversations organized by Cardinal **Mercier**, in which he took an active part. His many publications include *Lux Mundi* (1889), *The Body of Christ* (1901) and *The Reconstruction of Belief* (1926).

Goretti, Maria Teresa Martyr and saint, born Corinaldo, Italy, 16 October 1890, died there, 6 July 1902. A peasant girl, responsible for the care of her family following the death of her father. On 5 July 1902 she was mortally wounded by Alessandro Serenelli, a young man who stabbed her with a stiletto while attempting to rape her. She died the next day after forgiving him. Canonized in the presence of her killer in 1950. Feast day 6 July.

Gorgonia Saint, born Nazianzus (Cappadocia; today part of Turkey), *c*.329, died Iconium (Konya) *c*.370. She was the eldest daughter of the bishop of Nazianzus, Gregory the Elder, and the sister of **Gregory of Nazianzus**, who composed a funeral oration on her. Born in a Christian family, she married young, was baptized just before marriage and had her husband and children also baptized. During her fairly short life she exhibited truly Christian virtues. Feast day 9 December.

Gorham, Joseph Roman Catholic educator, born Drexel Hill, Pennsylvania, 19 March 1907, died Washington, DC, 7 July 1966. After secondary education in Catholic parochial schools and study in Philadelphia, Gorham earned his theology degree in Rome, where he was ordained in 1933. He returned to the United States and soon became a Catholic school administrator in Philadelphia. In 1945, he joined the Catholic University of America, where he actively promoted education of Catholic nuns, was widely regarded for his excellence in teaching school administration, and edited the *Catholic Educational Review*. Pope **Pius XII** named him a domestic prelate in 1952.

Goríbar, Nicolás Javier Roman Catholic painter, born probably around Quito, *c*.1670, date and place of death unknown. Goríbar began his artistic career as an apprentice to Miguel de Santiago. There is a record of the baptism of his first child in 1688, but little is actually known of his life. He was associated somehow with the Jesuits of Quito, his series of sixteen prophets adorning their cathedral there and his name being found in the dedication of an academic thesis on the Jesuit province of Quito in 1717. He also executed a series of the kings of Judah and a number of other scenes and portraits from the OT. Like his mentor, he seems to have illustrated the faith of the people of his city.

Görres, Johann Joseph von German Catholic writer, born Coblenz, 25 January 1776, died Munich, 29 January 1848. In 1797 he published a republican periodical *Das rote Blatt*. Appointed teacher of natural science at Coblenz in 1800 and later at Heidelberg, 1806–7. Edited the *Zeitung für Einsiedler*. In 1814 he founded the newspaper *Rheinischer Merkur*. Forced to flee, he lived in Switzerland, where he formally returned to the Roman Catholic Church in 1824. In 1827 he became professor of history at Munich. His works include *Deutschland und die Revolution* (1819) and *Christliche Mystik* (1836–42). He was influential in the spread of Catholic ideas in Germany.

Gorriti, Juan Ignacio de Roman Catholic priest and politician, born Jujuy, Argentina, 1766, died Sucre, Bolivia, 1842. Gorriti studied at and received his doctorate from the University of Córdoba and served in several parishes before becoming archdean of the cathedral in Salta and chaplain in Belgrano's army. He wrote effectively in the cause of Argentine independence in 1811, supported a government for the new country similar to that of the United States, and was later elected as a deputy. He changed his mind on federalism, joined the Unitarian political party and became governor of Salta in 1829. He soon fled to Bolivia, however, to escape reprisal by the Federalists and became rector of the Colegio Junín. In exile he wrote his noted *Réflexiones* (1836), which contain his thoughts on sociology, education and politics.

Gosling, Samuel Roman Catholic priest and liturgist, born Stone, Staffordshire, England, 18 April 1883, died Alton, Stoke-on-Trent, 8 October 1950. Gosling served as an army chaplain during World War I, during which time he became convinced of the need to use vernacular languages for Roman Catholic liturgy. As the idea was so revolutionary at that time, he waited until 1942 to publish his suggestion. This led to his founding the English Liturgy Society in 1943 and the periodical *The English Liturgist*, and directly influenced the founding of the American Vernacular Society. Gosling maintained his cause against sometimes bitter opposition. Thirteen years after his death, his view was officially vindicated by the Constitution on the Sacred Liturgy (1963) of the Second Vatican Council.

Gossec, François-Joseph South Netherlands composer who worked in France, born Verginies, Hainaut, 17 January 1734, died Passy, near Paris, 16 February 1829. He is best known for his works

inspired by and celebrating the French Revolution, and a *Te Deum* which in its demand for 1200 singers and 300 instruments anticipates Berlioz – it was performed on the anniversary of the fall of the Bastille. Gossec was a choirboy at Antwerp Cathedral, director of the Concert Spirituel and later became conductor at the Opèra. His large catalogue of music includes pieces for wind band such as his *Marche Religieuse*, oratorios, and Church music including motets, as well as extensive secular music.

Goswin Saint, Benedictine abbot and scholar, born Douai, died Anchin, near Douai, 9 October 1165 or 10 October 1166. After studying in Paris, where he was a fierce opponent of Peter **Abelard**, Goswin taught as a canon of Douai and *c*.1112 entered the nearby monastery of Anchin. A monastic reformer, he was responsible for the reform of three monasteries, and as prior of St Médard of Soissons gave shelter to his old adversary Abelard after his condemnation by the Council of Soissons in 1121. In 1131, he became abbot of Anchin, where he encouraged the production of illuminated manuscripts. Feast days 7 and 9 October.

Gotti, Vincenzo Lodovico Dominican theologian and cardinal, born Bologna, Italy, 5 September 1664, died Rome, 18 September 1742. After entering the Order of Preachers at the age of sixteen, Gotti studied in Forlì and Salamanca and taught philosophy and theology at Mantua, Bologna and Faenza. From 1715 to 1717 he served as inquisitor general in Milan, during which time he wrote *La vera chiesa di Cristo* (1719) against a Calvinist Swiss pastor. In 1728 he was made titular patriarch of Jerusalem and created cardinal, in which capacity he served as a member of ten different Sacred Congregations. As a cardinal, he continued to write, mainly on the authority of the Pope and the reformation of the clergy.

Gottschalk Saint, king and martyr, born northern Germany, date unknown, died Lenzen on the Elbe, 7 June 1066. Gottschalk was a prince being educated at the monastery in Lüneburg when he left around 1030 in order to avenge the murder of King Uto, his father, by the Saxons. His rebellion was quashed, and he found himself in exile in Denmark, where he served King **Canute**, and then came to England with Sweyn and married his daughter. He returned to native land to rule in 1043 and worked to Christianize his realm with the aid of **Adalbert of Bremen**. He was killed in an anti-Christian uprising against Adalbert. Feast day 7 June.

Gottschalk of Limburg (of Aachen) Benedictine prior, chaplain, poet, born c.1010–20, died 24 November 1098. Gottschalk resided in Limburg (on the River Hardt), where he studied the forgotten works of **Irenaeus** and Abundius. He was also prior of the Aachen church of the Virgin, then chaplain of **Henry IV**, to whom he dedicated his sequence hymns. He served finally in Klingenmuenster. Though Gottschalk wrote a short theological dissertation, he is known primarily for a set of 22 or 23 poetical sequences for use in Masses for the feasts of saints and angels, which remained popular in German liturgical books until the sixteenth century. His work uses much biblical imagery and tends to be somewhat dogmatic, though not without some poetic feeling or a mystical touch.

Gottschalk of Orbais German theologian and poet, born possibly Mainz, 803, died Hautvillers, 30 October 868. As a child he was entered as an oblate in the abbey at Fulda but later left the monastic life. Ordained priest at Rheims in 835, he studied **Augustine** and developed a doctrine of double predestination. Preached and taught extensively in Italy and the Balkans. Censured for heresy at the Synods of Mainz in 848 and of Quiercy in 849, he was deposed as a priest and imprisoned at the abbey of Hautvillers, where he died.

Goudimel, Claude French composer, born Besançon, 1514, died Lyons, 28 August 1572. Taught at Rome and Lyons. Famous for his settings of the metrical Psalms and his Latin Church music. He was killed in the anti-Huguenot riots of 1572.

Goudin, Antoine Dominican philosopher and theologian, born Limoges, France, c.1639, died Paris, 25 October 1695. After entering the Dominican Order in 1657, Goudin was recognized for his scholastic ability while still a student in Limoges. He was sent to Avignon, France, to reorganize the programme of theological studies there and was

later, 1669, elected prior of Brives, France. He earned his doctorate in Paris and taught there at Saint-Germain and Saint-Jacques, where he was later also prior. Involved in the Molinist/Thomist debates of the late 1600s, Goudin's most noted work is a compendium of Scholastic philosophy entitled *Philosophia juxta inconcussa tutissimaque divi Thomae dogmata* (1671).

Gounod, Charles François French composer and conductor, born Paris, 17 June 1818, died St-Cloud, 17 October 1893. He studied at the Paris Conservatoire, and then in Rome. Returning to Paris he became for a time the organist in the chapel of the Missions Etrangères. He studied for the priesthood but decided not to be ordained. He spent the Franco-Prussian war of 1870 in England. His opera *Faust* is his masterpiece and his *Messe de Ste Cecile* his greatest Mass, inspired by a mix of imitation sixteenth-century polyphony, military music and lush operatic scenes. His choral works became popular in Britain as a result of their publication by Novello & Co., the inexpensive printing of vocal editions and rise in popularity of choral societies. His genius lies in filling his music, including his Church music, with trenchant tunes and succulent harmony. His music, once extremely popular, was by the twentieth century regarded as sentimental, and his Church music too sanctimonious. He wrote oratorios, Masses, Requiems and other Church music.

Gousset, Thomas Marie Joseph Cardinal and theologian, born Montigny-les-Cherlieu, France, 1 May 1792, died Rheims, 22 December 1866. Ordained in 1817, Gousset achieved note as a moral theologian with his *Le Code civil commenté dans ses rapports avec la théologie morale*, published in 1827. He became vicar general of Besançon in 1832, and bishop of Périgueux three years later. In 1840 he was made archbishop of Rheims, and continued to publish, most notably his *Théologie morale* (2 vols, 1844). Created cardinal in 1850, Gousset was an early leader of the ultramontanist cause in France and worked to oppose Gallicanism.

Gower, John Poet, born Kent, 1325/30, died London, August–October 1408. Apart from his friendship with **Chaucer**, little is known of the life of this man of means. His poems illustrate social conditions in England at the time of the Peasants' Revolt and demonstrate the rise of native English over French literary culture. *Speculum meditantis* or *Mirour de l'Omme* is an allegorical treatise on virtues and vices, written in French. The Latin *Vox Clamantis* was written *c*.1382. In the English *Confessio Amantis* (*c*.1390) a lover, in old age, meets the goddess of love and confesses the sins he has committed against love; each of the seven books is dedicated to a mortal sin.

Goyau, Georges Roman Catholic Church historian, born Orléans, France, 31 May 1869, died Bernay, France, 25 October 1939. Educated in Paris and Rome, Goyau served in the Red Cross during World War I before becoming professor of mission history at the Institut Catholique, Paris, in 1927. During his academic career, Goyau served the Roman Congregation of Rites as a historical counsellor and wrote more than 100 works, including his most noted ecclesiastical history of Germany (*Allemagne religieuse*, 1898–1913), a religious history of France and about 170 articles for the *Catholic Encyclopedia*. In 1922 he was made a member of the French Academy and praised by Pope **Pius XII** upon his death.

Goyeneche y Barreda, José Sebastián de Roman Catholic archbishop, born Arequipa, Peru, 20 January 1784, died Lima, Peru, 19 February 1872. After studies in theology and law at Lima and San Marcos, Goyeneche practised civil law for a couple of years before being ordained in 1807. In 1817, he was appointed bishop of Arequipa. During the emancipation of Peru, he was one of the few bishops to remain at his post and guide the Church in Peru through that politically turbulent time. In 1832, Pope **Gregory XVI** made him apostolic delegate to Peru and in 1859 he was made archbishop of Lima, where he worked to reform religious orders and restore the seminary there.

Gozzoli, Benozzo (Benozzo de Lese) Goldsmith and painter, born Florence, *c*.1420–2, died Pistoia, 4 October 1497. After training as a goldsmith and assisting his master Lorenzo **Ghiberti** on the Florentine Baptistery doors, Gozzoli broke that contract in order to assist the painter Fra **Angelico** in Rome and Orvieto. Gozzoli's fame now rests on the brightly coloured *Journey of the Magi* fresco

cycle (1459–61), created for Piero de' Medici in the chapel of the Palazzo Medici, Florence. The impression of a one-work master is reinforced by the fact that his OT fresco cycle (1467–*c*.1484) in the Campo Santo, Pisa, was seriously damaged in 1944.

Grabmann, Martin Roman Catholic historian and theologian, born Winterzhofen, 5 January 1875, died Eichstätt, 9 January 1949. He was ordained priest in 1898 and after doctoral studies in Rome was appointed professor of theology and philosophy at Eichstätt in 1906. He later lectured at the Universities of Vienna in 1913 and Munich, 1918–39. He returned to Eichstätt in 1943. He made a significant contribution to manuscript research and in describing the development of Scholasticism. His works include *Die Geschichte der scholastischen Methode* (1909–11) and *Thomas Aquinas* (1928). The Grabmann Institute at the University of Munich for philosophical and theological research, founded by Michael Schmaus, his successor at Munich, was named after him.

Grace, William Russell Roman Catholic politician and philanthropist, born Queenstown, Ireland, 10 May 1832, died New York, USA, 21 March 1904. The son of an Irish businessman, Grace travelled with his father to Peru in 1850 to work in shipbuilding. After ill health forced him to leave Peru, he went to New York and set up William R. Grace and Company, a mercantile empire dealing mostly in South American goods. His Grace steamship line established the first regular service to Peru's west coast, and Grace's company helped to refinance Peru's national debt (under the Grace–Donoughmore contract, 1890). He was also the first Roman Catholic mayor of New York City, 1880–8, and founder of the Grace Institute in 1897, an organization to train women in vocational skills.

Graf, Georg Roman Catholic priest and orientalist, born Münsingen, Germany, 15 March 1875, died Dillingen, Germany, 18 September 1955. Graf was a pastor by vocation but by avocation he was ardently interested in Christian Arabic literature. This interest was manifest in his wide travels to libraries of unpublished Christian Arabic literture (such as in Jerusalem, Cairo and the Vatican) and his works on history (*Geschichte der christlichen arabischen Literatur*, 5 vols, 1944–53) and lexicography (*Verzeichnis arabischer kirchlicher Termini*, 1954). In 1930, because of his work, he was made honorary professor in Munich and in 1946 made a domestic prelate.

Graffin, René Roman Catholic priest, editor and publisher, born Pontvallain, France, 22 March 1858, died Sainte-Radegonde-en-Touraine, 3 January 1941. After theology studies in Rome and language studies in Innsbruck, Graffin moved to Paris, where in 1886 he founded the oriental languages programme at the Institut Catholique de Paris. He edited and directed several series of oriental texts and studies, including the *Revue de l'Orient chrétien* (30 vols, 1896–1938, 1946), *Patrologia syriaca* (3 vols, 1894–1926), and *Patrologia orientalis* (25 vols, 1907–42), for which he prepared many of his own typefaces. He was made domestic prelate in 1906 and consultor to the Congregation for the Oriental Church in 1917.

Grande, Rutilio Jesuit martyr, born El Paisnal, El Salvador, 1928, killed near there, 12 March 1977. At first a pious but conventional priest after his ordination in 1959, he was changed by Vatican Council II. From 1965 he worked for nine years at the seminary of San Salvador, encouraging the students to live with the peasants instead of among the elites. Seen as a dangerous radical, he had to resign but, as parish priest of Aguilares, he established base communities and continued to denounce oppression. He was murdered after preaching an outspoken sermon denouncing the attitudes of the wealthy.

Granderath, Theodor Jesuit Church historian, born Giesenkirchen, Germany, 19 June 1839, died Valkenburg, The Netherlands, 19 March 1902. Ganderath became a Jesuit in 1860 and taught canon law, 1874–6, and theology, 1876–87, to Jesuits at Ditton Hall, England. He also lectured at the Gregorian University in Rome, 1897–8. He is best remembered for his editing of the documents of the First Vatican Council (*Acta et decreta Concilii Vaticani*, 1890), which he took over from Gerard Schneemann, and his posthumously published history of that Council, *Geschichte des Vatikanischen Konzils* (1903–6), still considered a valuable, if somewhat one-sided, historical resource.

Grandidier, Philippe André French Roman Catholic priest, archivist and historian, born Strasburg, 29 November 1752, died Strasburg, 11 October 1787. A protégé of Cardinal Louis de Rohan, Grandidier was an exceptional student, finishing his education by the age of thirteen. While waiting to be ordained, he organized the archives of Strasburg and by the age of 24 had published two volumes (of a projected eight) of a historical work proving the spuriousness of numerous legends and supposed papal bulls (*Histoire de l'Évêché et des Évêques de Strasburg*, 1777). Though he abandoned that work under pressure from his clerical colleagues, he continued to study and write history, including the unfinished *Histoire ecclésiastique, militaire, civile et littéraire de la province d'Alsace* (1787).

Grandin, Vital Oblate missionary and bishop, born St-Pierre-la-Cour, France, 8 February 1829, died St Albert, Canada, 3 June 1902. In 1851, Grandin joined the Oblates of Mary Immaculate, was ordained in 1854 and sent as a missionary to Canada, where he began work in Île-à-la-Crosse, Saskatchewan. In 1857, he became auxiliary bishop of St Boniface (but did not learn of this until 1859). In 1871, he moved from Île-à-la-Crosse to St Albert upon becoming bishop there. He interceded during the Métis revolt, 1855, and as bishop strongly defended the rights of both Indians and Catholics. His cause for canonization was introduced in 1937.

Grandmaison, Léonce de Jesuit theologian, born Le Mans, France, 31 December 1868, died Paris, 15 June 1927. Grandmaison became a Jesuit at the age of eighteen, and studied on the island of Jersey and in Le Mans. In 1899 he was made professor of apologetics at Fourvière and later in Hastings, England. From 1908 he was the editor of *Études* and was the founding editor of *Recherches de science religieuse* in 1910. Most of Grandmaison's career was spent defending the Church against relativist and Modernist attacks. His most important work is his *Jésus Christ: sa personne, son message, ses épreuves*, published posthumously.

Grant, Thomas Roman Catholic bishop, born Ligny-les-Aires, France, 25 November 1816, died Rome, 1 July 1870. Born in France of Irish parents, Grant studied in Durham, England, and Rome, where he was ordained in 1841. From 1844 to 1851, he was rector of the English College in Rome. In Rome he also served as the secretary to Cardinal Charles **Acton** and was involved in the negotiations that restored the English hierarchy in 1850. A year later, he was made the first bishop of Southwark and worked hard to organize and expand his see. He died attending the First Vatican Council, where he was generally reputed to be the ablest of all the English bishops.

Granvelle, Antoine Perrenot de Statesman and cardinal, born Ornans, Franche-Comté, 20 August 1517, died Madrid, 21 September 1586. Educated at Padua and Louvain. Granvelle's fortunes were determined by his service to **Charles V** and **Philip II**. For Charles, he negotiated with German Lutheran princes and represented the Emperor at the Council of Trent. When Philip left the Low Countries for Spain, Granvelle remained as his principal agent, but headed the Spanish government at the time of the annexation of Portugal, 1580–1. He held the bishoprics of Arras, from 1538, Malines, 1560–82, and Besançon, from 1584, and was made a cardinal in 1561.

Grassell, Lorenz Roman Catholic priest and bishop-elect, born Ruemannsfelden, Germany, 18 August 1758, died Philadelphia, Pennsylvania, October 1793. Prevented from completing his Jesuit novitiate by the suppression of the Order in Germany, Grassell was ordained a secular priest *c.*1780 and sent to Philadelphia in 1787. In Philadelphia, he worked among German immigrants and other settlers at St Mary's Church. His outstanding pastoral work and support of Archbishop John **Carroll** led to his nomination as Carroll's coadjutor bishop. However, before the appointment could be made official, Grassell died ministering to the sick during a yellow fever epidemic in his city.

Grassi, Anthony Blessed, provost of Fermo Oratory, born Fermo, Italy, 13 November 1592, died Fermo, 13 December 1671. Grassi joined the local Oratory, founded by St Philip **Neri**, when he was eighteen and remained a member until his death. In 1625, three years after Philip Neri was canonized, Grassi made a pilgrimage to honour him and devoted his life to imitating him. He was elected provost of the Oratory in 1635 and was re-elected to the post twelve times, despite his continued protestations, holding the office until his death. He was personally known for his mortified life, for hearing confessions (up to five hours a day), and for guiding the Oratory into being an example of the Rule of St Philip Neri. Feast day 13 December.

Grassi, Antonio Roman Catholic bishop and papal diplomat, date and place of birth unknown, died probably Tivoli, Italy, 1491. Nothing is known of the origin of this Italian churchman before his appointment as an auditor of the Rota (a papal chaplain and consultant) by Pope **Pius II** in 1462. He was Pope **Sixtus IV's** nuncio to the Holy Roman Empire and Emperor Frederick III for one year, 1478–9, and finished his career as bishop of Tivoli, where he was appointed in 1485 by Pope **Innocent VIII**.

Grassi, Gregorio Blessed, Franciscan bishop and martyr, born Alessandria, Italy, 13 December 1833, died Taiyüanfu, Shansi, China, 9 July 1900. Grassi joined the Order of Friars Minor in 1848, was ordained in 1856 and left for mission work in China in 1861. During his missionary work, he was made titular bishop of Ortosia and vicar apostolic for the Shansi province of North China. Along with a fellow bishop, seven nuns, five seminarians, and the household servants, he was martyred in his episcopal residence during the Boxer Rebellion in 1900. He was beatified in 1946 by Pope **Pius XII**. Feast day 4 July.

Gratian Lawyer and founder of the science of canon law, born near Orvieto, 1090, died Bologna, *c.*1160. Little is known of his life. Having become a Camaldolese monk he taught at the monastery of SS Felix and Nabor at Bologna. Famous for his *Concordia discordantium canonum* ('Concordance of discordant canons') or *Decreta* (1140), a compilation of canon law and commentary which remained the authoritative textbook of canon law within the Roman Catholic Church until 1917. It is believed that he was created cardinal by Pope **Alexander III**.

Gratian, Jerome Carmelite reformer and theologian, born Valladolid, Spain, 1545, died Brussels (Belgium), 21 September 1614. The son of **Philip II**'s secretary, Gratian attended the University of Alcalá, was ordained in 1570 and joined the Carmelites in 1572 because he was impressed with the reform initiated by St **Teresa of Ávila**. He won Teresa's confidence and was elected the first provincial of the Discalced Carmelites in 1581. However, upon Teresa's death and the finishing of his term, he fell out with his successor, was charged with rebellion and expelled from the Order. His appeals to Rome failed. In 1593 he was captured by Turkish pirates. Freed to return to Rome in 1596, he was allowed to live among the Calced Carmelites. In 1600 he returned to Spain, in 1607 accompanied Philip II to Brussels, and remained there until his death. Although a controversial figure, his importance for the early years of the Teresian reform is unquestionable.

Gratius, Ortwin Theologian and humanist, born Holtwick, Germany, 1480, died Cologne, 22 May 1542. Gratius (van Graes) graduated from Cologne in 1506, taught there, and served as an editor for the Quentell publishing house. His *Orationes quodlibeticae* (1508) enhanced his humanist reputation, but his later work (specifically opposing the humanists Hermann von dem Busche and Johann **Reuchlin** and translating the anti-Semitic Johann Pfefferkorn) made him powerful enemies who eventually ruined his reputation. His *Fasciculus rerum expetendarum ac fugiendarum* (1535), a collection of early reformist writings (from, for example, Lorenzo Valla and John **Wycliffe**), was later placed on the Index of Prohibited Books.

Gratry, Auguste Joseph Alphonse Roman Catholic priest, philosopher and theologian, born Lille, France, 30 March 1805, died Montreux (Switzerland), 7 February 1872. Gratry cared little for religion until the age of seventeen, when he became convinced of the futility of worldly ambitions. In 1826/27 he returned fully to the Roman Catholic Church, studied in Strasburg and was ordained in 1834. In 1840, he went to Paris to be the director of the Collège Stanislas. He later served in the École Normale and the Oratory before becoming professor of moral theology at the Sorbonne in 1867. His works, which include *De la connaissance*

de Dieu (1855) and *La sophistique contemporaine* (1861), contributed to the revival of Christian philosophy, though they give a greater role to 'heart knowledge' of God than to the intellect.

Gratz, Peter Roman Catholic biblical scholar, born Mittelberg, Allgäu, Germany, 17 August 1769, died Darmstadt, Germany, 1 November 1849. After education in Ausberg and Dillingen, Gratz was ordained in 1792, and served the parish of Unterhalheim, where he became interested in NT studies. His first exegetical work, *Neuer Versuch, die Entstellung der drei ersten Evangelien zu erklären* (1812), which advanced the idea of a Hebrew original behind the Synoptic Gospels, earned him a position at the University of Ellwangen. In 1819, he helped found the *Theologische Quartalschrift* in Tübingen and accepted a position at the University of Bonn, where he would remain until 1826. He finished his career serving on the city council and school board of Trier, Germany. His works include a *Novum Testamentum graeco-latinum* (2 vols, 1820–1) and the posthumously published *Kritischer Commentar über das Evangelium des Matthäus* (2 vols, 1921–3).

Grebel, Conrad Swiss Anabaptist theologian who carried out the first adult baptism of modern times, born Zurich, Switzerland, 1498, died of plague Maienfeld, July/August 1526. Originally a humanist, following a religious crisis in 1522 he became a follower of **Zwingli**. However, reaching the conclusion that infant baptism was unscriptural, he disagreed with Zwingli and formed a group of Anabaptists in Zurich in 1525. Having been reproved by the Council of Zurich in 1526, he was imprisoned but later escaped.

Grechaninov, Aleksandr Tikhonovich Russian composer famous for his religious compositions, born Moscow, 25 October 1864, died New York, 3 January 1956. Educated at the Moscow Conservatory from 1881 to 1890 before working at St Petersburg. He composed numerous operas, string quartets, symphonies and Church music which brought him an imperial pension. However, in the aftermath of the Revolution of 1917 his religious music was seen as being controversial and he consequently moved to Paris in 1925. In 1940 he went to live in New York.

Greco, El Painter of the Spanish School, born 'Domenico Theotocopuli', Candia, Crete, 1541, died Toledo, Spain, 7 April 1614. In Venice, El Greco ('The Greek') was a pupil of **Titian** and was influenced by other Venetian masters. After periods in Venice and Rome he left, probably c.1577, for Toledo, where he was influenced by Spanish mysticism and executed work for churches, painting *The Stripping of Christ* for the cathedral. His paintings include *Christ's Agony in the Garden*, *The Holy Trinity* and *The Martyrdom of St Maurice*.

Gredt, Joseph August Benedictine philosopher, born Luxemburg, 30 July 1863, died Rome, 29 January 1940. After philosophical studies in Luxemburg, Gredt was ordained in 1886. He travelled to Rome for further study and in 1891 became a Benedictine. He served as professor of philosophy at San Anselmo in Rome from 1896 until his death. A proponent of the neo-Thomistic revival inaugurated by **Leo XIII**, Gredt's work focuses on metaphysics and is true to the Scholastic method. His major work is his *Elementa philosophiae aristotelico-thomisticae* (2 vols, 1899–1901), a manual of philosophy. He also defended a 'natural' philosophical realism, arguing for the reliability of the senses against the so-called 'critical realist' view, in *De cognitione sensuum externorum* (1924).

Greene, (Henry) Graham English Catholic journalist and writer, born Berkhamsted, Hertfordshire, 2 October 1904, died Vevey, Switzerland, 3 April 1991. His father was headmaster of Berkhamsted School, which Greene attended, but from which he ran away. He went on to study at Balliol College, Oxford, where, in 1926, he converted to Roman Catholicism. From 1926 to 1930 he worked for *The Times*, and then, until 1940, *The Spectator*. He published a book of verse, *Babbling April*, in 1925, and his first novel, *The Man Within*, four years later. But it was with *Stamboul Train* (1932; filmed two years later) that his reputation began to grow. These early 'thrillers' were fairly successful, as was his screenplay for *The Third Man* (1949), but his more powerful novels such as *Brighton Rock* (1938; filmed 1948), *The Power and the Glory* (1940; filmed 1962), *The Heart of the Matter* (1948) and *The End of the Affair* (1951) reflect some of the moral issues of Catholicism. During the Second

World War Greene worked for the British Foreign Office, and after the war he continued to travel widely, many of his experiences being reflected in the settings of his novels. Greene spent the latter part of his life in the South of France.

Greenwood, John Separatist leader and martyr, born c.1560, hanged Tyburn, London, 6 April 1593. Greenwood was chaplain to Robert, Lord Rich, a prominent Puritan, before moving to London, where he became identified with the Separatists. He was arrested at a conventicle meeting in 1586 and spent most of the rest of his life in prison. In 1592 he was briefly released and appointed teacher to Francis **Johnson**'s Separatist congregation in London. He was the author of *A Plaine Refutation of Mr Giffards Short Treatise*, which dramatically converted Francis Johnson from Presbyterianism to the Separatist cause.

Grégoire, Henri Historian, born Huy, Belgium, 21 March 1881, died Rosières, Belgium, 28 September 1964. A scholar of all things Greek, Grégoire received his doctorate in Liège, Belgium, and furthered his studies in Germany and France before serving on the international commission charged with investigating the administration of the Belgian Congo, 1904–5. After this, he spent a year in Palestine and three years in Greece and went on numerous archaeological expeditions before returning to Brussels to teach. He was a founding editor of *Byzantion* in 1924 along with Paul Graindor, and published works on almost every aspect of Greek and Byzantine language and history, his most noted being *Les Persécutions dans l'Empire romain* (1964).

Grégoire, Henri Baptiste Bishop in the French Constitutional Church, born Vého, France, 4 December 1750, died Paris, 28 May 1831. Grégoire was ordained in the Roman Catholic Church in 1775 and ministered in Marimont and Embermenil before being elected a clerical representative to the French Estates-General in 1789. He argued and voted for the Civil Constitution of the Clergy and upon its adoption was made Constitutional bishop of Blois. Throughout the ensuing French Revolution and the coming of the Empire under Napoleon (whom he opposed), Grégoire worked to secure a place for the Church in France. He resigned his see in 1802 but continued his political career. A confirmed Jansenist and the de facto leader of the Constitutional Church, Grégoire published many works, including a history of royal confessors in France and a history of religious sects.

Gregorčič, Simon Roman Catholic priest and poet, born Vrsno (Slovenia), 15 October 1844, died Gorizzia (Slovenia), 24 November 1906. Considered one of the best Slovene authors, Gregorčič was ordained in 1867 after theological studies in Gorizzia. He served as parish priest in Kobarid and Rihenberk before heart disease forced him into a sort of early retirement, first in Gradišče and then in Gorizza. Nicknamed the 'nightingale of Gorizzia', Gregorčič had a difficult life. Though he wrote mostly about his native land and the simple people who inhabited it, his work contains the evidence of much suffering and struggle. His poetry first appeared in 1882, with subsequent volumes following in 1888, 1902 and 1906.

Gregorovius, Ferdinand Historian, born Neidenburg, East Prussia, 19 January 1821, died Munich, 1 May 1891. Studied Lutheran theology at Königsberg and was a self-taught historian whose life's work was a history of Rome in the Middle Ages (*Geschichte der Stadt Rom im Mittelalter*, 1859–71), which evolved into a history of the Papacy. In spite of his extensive archival research, Gregorovius felt alienated from the German academic establishment, though **Döllinger** remained a friend. When the history of Rome was placed on the Index, Gregorovius, an ardent supporter of Italian unification, hoped that the civic authorities or even **Bismarck** were the real targets. In his history of the Papacy Ludwig von **Pastor** set out to counter the influence of Gregorovius.

Gregory I ('the Great') Pope and saint, born Rome, of a patrician family, c.540, consecrated Pope 3 September 590, died Rome, 12 March 604. He had a legal education and in 572/3 he became *praefectus urbis*, a position which allowed him to develop his organizational skills. In 575, however, after the death of his father, he abandoned his secular career and founded a monastery in the family palace on the Caelian Hill. In 578 he was ordained deacon and was sent the following year as papal nuntius to Constantinople. He returned to Rome and his monastery in 585, and in 590 he became Pope. He tried, but failed, to avoid the appointment by writing to the emperor. He came into office as the city was under a plague, and did a great deal to relieve suffering and provide food. To do this efficiently he reorganized the Curia and the revenues from the land the Church owned, as well as trying to establish peace in the peninsula. He established good relations with Visigothic Spain, and sent **Augustine**, a monk, to evangelize the English: throughout his pontificate he encouraged the growth of monasticism. He was a vigorous upholder of the prerogatives of the bishop of Rome, which meant that his relationship with Constantinople was tense. In 591 he wrote *Pastoral Care*, a reflection on the role of the bishop, which was formative for medieval bishops. His many other theological writings, his homilies and letters and his reform of the liturgy assured him a prominent place in the history of theology and Christian worship. Feast day 3 September

Gregory II Pope, saint, born Rome, 669, elected Pope 19 May 715, died Rome, 11 February 731. From a wealthy family, he had acted as treasurer in the Lateran while he was a subdeacon, and as deacon had been part of a diplomatic mission to Constantinople in 710–11. He possessed considerable political skills, and in 729 persuaded an alliance of Lombards and Byzantines not to lay siege to Rome. He repaired the city walls and restored churches, as well as the abbey of Monte Cassino, which the Lombards had devastated. He gave active support to **Boniface** in the evangelization of Germany. He rejected Emperor Leo III's demand that he approve of his iconoclastic campaign, and rejected iconoclasm as heretical, adding that theology was the business of priests and not of princes. Feast day 29 January.

Gregory II Patriarch of Constantinople 1283–9, born Cyprus, 1241, died Constantinople, 1290. Baptized George, he studied in Cyprus and travelled extensively throughout the Greek East before becoming a cleric in Constantinople. Initially he strongly supported the movement for reunion with Rome, then in 1283 changed sides. In opposition to John Beccos, he published a *Tome on Faith*, which proposed a controversial account of the procession of the Holy Spirit; despite defending himself in a *homologia* and in a letter to the Emperor **Andronicus II**, he was forced to resign. He died in a monastery the following year. Among his other writings were encomia, treatises on rhetoric and mythology, a life of the monk St **Lazarus the Confessor** of Mount Galesius, an autobiography and a collection of letters.

Gregory II Vkajaser   Saint, head of the Armenian Church (*katholikos*) and translator, born Cappadocia, 1025, died 1105. Gregory 'Martyr-Lover', the son of Gregory Magistros, was elected catholicos in 1065. He travelled to Rome to discuss union with the Latin Church with Pope **Gregory VII** in 1074 and maintained a correspondence with him after that. During his travels in Palestine and Egypt, he collected many stories of Armenian martyrs, eventually publishing them as a set of Acts. He also translated, with his disciples, **Proclus'** commentary on Revelation and his biography of **John Chrysostom** into Armenian. Feast day 3 August.

Gregory III   Pope, saint, of Syrian origin, died Rome, 28 November 741. He was chosen by acclaim and consecrated 18 March 731. One of his first acts was to hold a synod in Rome to condemn iconoclasm, which annoyed the emperor, but Gregory also aided the emperor in the struggle against the king of the Lombards in Italy, which restored relations with Constantinople. Gregory strengthened the walls of the city and twice sent embassies to **Charles Martel** to ask for help from the Franks. Though none came, it established a pattern for the future. Gregory gave his backing to **Boniface**'s evangelization of Germany, and improved links between Rome and England. Feast day 10 December.

Gregory III   Patriarch of Constantinople 1443–51, born Constantinople, 1400, died Rome, 1459. He became a monk, superior of the monastery of the Pantocrator, and confessor to the Emperor **John VIII Palaeologus**. Initially, at the Council of Ferrara–Florence in 1439–41, he opposed reunion with Rome; he then opted to sign the formula of union, and campaigned vigorously for its acceptance against strong clerical and monastic opposition. In 1450 he retired to the Peloponnese, then

in 1452 went to Rome, where he presided over the Greek territories under Venetian control until his death. He composed the emperor's letter to the patriarch of Alexandria on reunion, two apologies on the same subject, a commentary on the Creed, and various theological tracts.

Gregory III Pahlav   Head of the Armenian Church (*katholikos*) and writer, born c.1093, died Rumkaten, 1166. Gregory was elected catholicos in 1113. Aside from combating the schism of David of Aghtamar, he maintained close contact with the Latin Church. He continued his predecessors' contact with Rome, maintaining consistant correspondence with Popes **Honorius II**, **Innocent II** and **Eugenius III** (from whom he received the pallium, a symbol of orthodoxy and authority) and attended the Latin Councils of Antioch (1139) and Jerusalem (1142), after which he accepted the doctrine of Chalcedon. He left a large body of letters, liturgical writings and hymns.

Gregory IV   Pope, born Rome, consecrated 29 March 828, died Rome, 25 January 844. A cardinal-priest at his election, he was a firm supporter of papal authority, put to the test when the French clergy objected to his support for **Lothair I** rather than Lothair's father **Louis I**. He accompanied Lothair to France, but had to return to Rome when Louis triumphed. His attempts to mediate in subsequent dynastic struggles were unsuccessful. He consecrated **Ansgar** as bishop of Hamburg, giving him responsibility for missions to Scandinavia. He did much rebuilding in Rome, and erected a fortress as Ostia to try to contain the threat from the Saracens in the south of Italy.

Gregory IV Tegha (Gregory Tłay)   Head of the Armenian Church (*katholikos*) and writer, born 1133, died 1193. Gregory became catholicos in 1173, following his uncle. Unlike **Gregory III Pahlav**, he initially pursued union with the Byzantine Church rather than with Rome. However, in the Synod of Hromkla in 1179, the confession of faith that he signed was much more amenable to Pope **Lucius III** in Rome than to the Greeks, and in response to it the Pope sent Gregory the pallium, a symbol of orthodoxy and authority. His writings include an 'Elegy on Jerusalem' bemoaning the Muslim siege of the city in 1187, and a collection of letters describing his troubles with priests who wanted to keep the Armenian Church independent.

Gregory V Pope, born 'Bruno', son of Duke Otto of Carinthia, in 972, elected 3 May 996, died Rome, 18 February 999. He was a member of the imperial chapel, and accompanied the Emperor **Otto III** in his invasion of Italy. At Ravenna, Bruno was presented to the Roman delegation who had come to meet Otto as the new Pope (the first ever German). Although he was at first accepted, opposition in Rome drove him out for a time and he returned only with Otto's aid, his authority being established by the brutal suppression of his opponents. Though dependent for his survival on Otto, Gregory was able to display a degree of freedom, but he died suddenly, still only 25 years old.

Gregory V (Angelopoulos) Patriarch of Constantinople, saint and martyr, born Arcadia, Peloponnesus, 1745, died (martyred) Constantinople, 10 April 1821. He was elected ecumenical patriarch in 1797, was twice deposed by the Turkish authorities and twice reinstated, becoming patriarch finally in 1819. He concerned himself always with his flock: the entire Orthodox population of the Turkish Empire. The declaration of independence by the southern Greeks on 25 March 1821 enraged the sultan, and many massacres of Christians followed. On Easter morning the patriarch was hanged on his own gate, having refused the ritual offer of freedom in return for conversion to Islam. His body was taken to Odessa and eventually to Athens. He was canonized in 1921. Feast day 10 April.

Gregory VI Pope, born 'John de Gratiano' at Rome, elected 1 May 1045, deposed 20 December 1046, died, possibly at Cologne, November 1047. He was a highly principled and respected senior member of the Roman clergy, and provided the funds to persuade **Benedict IX** to abdicate. He was then himself elected. But this transaction seemed rather too obviously simoniacal, even if well-intentioned. At the Synod of Sutri (1046), the Emperor **Henry III** declared him deposed. One of those who followed him into exile was his chaplain Hildebrand, the future **Gregory VII**.

Gregory VII Pope, saint, born 'Hildebrand' in Tuscany, c.1020, elected 22 April 1073, died Salerno, 25 May 1085. Hildebrand appears to have been a monk, possibly in Rome, and certainly spent some time at Cluny. He was chaplain to **Gregory VI** and accompanied him into exile; having identified himself clearly with the reform party, he returned to Rome in 1049 with the newly appointed **Leo IX**. He became a deacon, papal treasurer, and prior of the monastery of St Paul Outside the Walls, and an important figure in papal politics in the reigns of successive Popes. He was elected by popular acclaim. He was determined to make the Roman see the effective law-making and law-enforcing authority in Western Christendom, and began by a series of synods aimed to improve the moral status of the clergy, particularly opposing simony and clerical marriage, imposing an oath of obedience on bishops and threatening to remove them if they did not impose the papal demands upon their clergy. He also wanted them to make regular visits to Rome to report on their success in carrying out papal policies. He was also deeply opposed to the system of lay investiture, according to which monarchs conferred benefices on the senior clergy, thus effectively controlling them. This was incompatible with Gregory's policies. At the Synod of Worms, summoned by the German king **Henry IV** early in 1076, the bishops attending declared Gregory deposed: Gregory responded by declaring Henry suspended from his royal power (rather as recalcitrant bishops were suspended from the exercise of their office). At Canossa in 1077 Henry asked pardon, which was granted. However, when a rival was chosen as king of Germany, Rudolf of Swabia, Gregory backed him, after the failure of his efforts to mediate between the two. This proved a costly mistake. In 1080 Henry had an Antipope elected. In 1084 Gregory had to take refuge in Castel Sant'Angelo, and **Robert Guiscard**'s efforts to free him, though successful, so alienated the people of Rome that the Pope had to flee with Robert to Salerno. Feast day 25 May.

Gregory VIII Pope, born 'Albert de Mora' at Benevento, c.1110, elected 21 October 1187, died Rome, 17 December 1187. He was a Canon Regular of St Augustine, made a cardinal by **Adrian IV** and promoted to be chancellor of the Roman

Church in 1178. An influential member of the Curia, he was elected Pope at Ferrara, and was intent on promoting peace in Europe, to prepare the way for a new Crusade, when he died suddenly.

Gregory IX Pope, born 'Hugolino' at Anagni, c.1160, elected 19 March 1227, died Rome, 22 August 1241. A son of the count of Segni and a nephew of **Innocent III**, he studied law at Paris and Bologna, was made a cardinal in 1198 by his uncle, and bishop of Ostia in 1206. He was a great supporter of the Dominicans and Franciscans, and a personal friend of St **Francis** himself. His pontificate opened with a clash with the Emperor **Frederick II**, who wished to renege on his undertaking to launch a Crusade. Gregory effectively forced him to go, and then undertook a campaign against him in Italy, while the Emperor was still in the Holy Land. Frederick returned, captured the Papal States and would only release them in 1230 once all ecclesiastical censures had been removed. Five years later Frederick accused the Pope – wrongly – of having fomented opposition to him in Lombardy. An imperial invasion of Sardinia, a vassal of the Papacy, led to Gregory's excommunicating Frederick again in 1239, and freeing the Emperor's subjects from their obedience to him. The Emperor invaded Italy and was advancing on Rome when Gregory died. Gregory was extremely active against heresy, creating an Inquisition directly under his control, despite the complaints of local bishops, and using the Dominicans in particular in the role of inquisitors. He was a great supporter of the religious orders in general.

Gregory X Pope, blessed, born 'Teobaldo Visconti' at Piacenza, 1210, elected 1 September 1271, died Arezzo, 10 January 1276. Elected at Viterbo after a vacancy of three years, Gregory had studied in Paris, had been a canon of Lyons and archdeacon of Liège before becoming a chaplain to the future King Edward I of England, and accompanying him to the Holy Land, where he was when he learnt of his election to the Papacy though he was not yet a priest. He returned to Rome, was ordained and consecrated. His pontificate was dominated by his desire for a new Crusade, for which he needed, and worked very successfully for, peace in Europe, and for a reunion of the Churches of East and West. The crusade was launched at the Second Council of Lyons (1274), which was attended by representatives of the Byzantine Emperor Michael VIII Palaeologus. The Council promulgated the constitution *Ubi periculum*, which was intended so to regulate conclaves that future papal elections would not drag out as long as the one which elected Gregory himself.

Gregory XI Pope, born 'Pierre Roger de Beaufort' near Limoges, 1329, elected 30 December 1370, died Rome, 27 March 1378. He had been made a cardinal at the age of nineteen by his uncle **Clement VI** and then sent to study law at Perugia. He was a pious man, and convinced that his major task after his election was to return the Papacy from Avignon to Rome. To do so he needed to re-establish control over the Papal States; his efforts to assert this led to conflict with Florence, and a general revolt in the Papal States themselves. A peace with Florence was negotiated, and the revolt suppressed. The harshness exercised by one of his commanders at Cesena led to such hostility towards Gregory that, although he managed to return to Rome in September 1377, he had for a time to retire for safety to Anagni.

Gregory XII Pope, born 'Angelo Correr', Venice, c.1325, died Recanati, 18 October 1417. Venetian patrician who had been bishop of Castello and patriarch of Constantinople prior to his election in 1406 by cardinals of the Roman obedience. Although he swore to abdicate if elected and undertook half-hearted negotiations with the Avignon Antipope **Benedict XIII**, both were overtaken by events when in 1409 conciliarists at Pisa deposed them, electing first **Alexander V** and then **John XXIII** in their place. Gregory finally bowed to pressure from the Council of Constance in 1415 and was made bishop of Porto and legate to the March of Ancona for what little remained of his life.

Gregory XIII Pope, born 'Ugo Buoncompagni' at Bologna, 1 January 1502, elected 14 May 1572, died Rome, 10 April 1585. He went to Rome in 1539 after law studies at Bologna (during which time he fathered a son), and was ordained. He was an efficient lawyer and administrator and rose through the ranks of the papal civil service, attending the Council of Trent (1561–3) as an expert in canon law. He became a cardinal in 1565, then papal legate in Spain. It was his success there, and the good relations he had established with **Philip II**, that led to his election as Pope. He was a major figure in propagating the reforms of Trent in the Church, especially in improving the standards of the clergy. He opened colleges across Europe, frequently handing them over to the Society of Jesus, whose Roman College he reconstructed and endowed (it was eventually renamed the Gregorian University in his honour); he founded colleges in Rome for a number of different nationalities, including the English. His commitment to Catholicism took a more militant turn when he helped to promote the Catholic League against the Huguenots, backed a (failed) invasion of Ireland, and furthered plots against **Elizabeth I** as well as encouraging Philip II in The Netherlands, seeing it as a jumping-off point for an invasion of England. The advance of Lutheranism in Germany was halted in his pontificate, and was reversed in Poland, though he had no success in Sweden and talks with Russia collapsed. He was an important patron of missionary activity in the New World and in South-East Asia, especially of that undertaken by the Jesuits, whose headquarters at the Gesù in Rome he completed. He also built the Quirinal Palace. His name has been given to the (Gregorian) calendar reforms introduced during his pontificate in Catholic lands.

Gregory XIV   Pope, born 'Niccolò Sfrondati' at Somma, near Milan, 11 February 1535, elected 5 December 1590, died Rome, 16 October 1591. A friend in his youth of Charles **Borromeo**, he studied at Perugia, Padua and Pavia, graduating finally in law. In 1560 he became bishop of Cremona, taking part in the third session of the Council of Trent. He became a cardinal in 1583. As Pope he proved weak. He was also ill, and depended heavily upon his inefficient and self-seeking nephew Paolo Sfrondati, who became his cardinal secretary of state in 1590. Paolo gave his support to Spanish interests against the French, even sending a subsidy to Paris to win that city's allegiance to the Guise family against Henry of Navarre (**Henry IV**). Moderate Catholics rallied to Henry, however, hastening his conversion and frustrating papal policy. Otherwise, in the internal affairs of the Church,

Gregory was active in furthering the reforms, such as episcopal residence, introduced by Trent.

Gregory XV   Pope, born 'Alessandro Ludovisi' at Bologna, 9 January 1554, elected 9 February 1621, died Rome, 8 July 1623. He was educated first at Rome by the Jesuits, then at the University of Bologna, where he graduated in law in 1575, whereupon he decided to seek ordination. He began a legal career in the papal curia under **Gregory XIII**, showed himself to be a particularly able negotiator, and was regularly used in diplomatic and important legal positions. In 1612 he became archbishop of Bologna, and a cardinal four years later. As archbishop he was active in improving the training of the clergy. After his election he made significant changes to the procedure for conclaves, forbidding any cardinal to vote for himself, and requiring a two-thirds majority for an election. He also established the Congregation for the Propagation of the Faith (Congregatio de Propaganda Fide), appointing to it some of the most capable prelates available to him, to oversee the missionary work of the Church. In Europe he aided the expansion of Catholicism by supporting financially and in other ways Maximilian of Bavaria against his Protestant rival.

Gregory XVI   Pope, born 'Bartolomeo Alberto' at Belluno, 18 September 1765, elected 2 February 1831, died Rome, 1 June 1846. He joined a Camaldolese monastery near Venice, taking the name 'Mauro'. After ordination in 1787 he taught, then, in 1795, came to Rome, where he stayed for the rest of his life, except when driven out, 1807–14, by the Napoleonic occupation. He rose through the ranks of his Order, turned down a bishopric, but accepted a cardinal's hat in 1825, though this was kept secret for a year. He had a strong interest in theology and in 1799 he published *The Triumph of the Holy See*, upholding the independence of the Church from all political interference and defending, long before it became an official teaching, the doctrine of papal infallibility. He was faced on his election with a revolt in the Papal States, which was crushed with the help of Austrian troops. He demonstrated the same intransigence in his defence of Catholicism. He rejected the overtures of Félicité de **Lamennais** and condemned his ideas in his encyclical *Mirari vos* (1832), rejecting freedom of conscience and of belief, and the freedom of the press, as pernicious notions. Such was his belief in obedience to lawfully constituted authority that he denounced the Polish revolt against the Tsar in 1831, and in 1844 wrote to the Irish clergy telling them to stay out of politics. On the other hand he also denounced slavery in his brief *In supremo* (1839) and encouraged the development of an indigenous clergy in mission territories. He was, indeed, much devoted to the Church's missionary activity, which revived during his pontificate.

Gregory Akindynos Byzantine priest, monk, and theologian, born Prilep, Bulgaria, *c.*1300, died place unknown, *c.*1349. Educated in Thessalonica, Greece, under **Gregory Palamas**, Gregorius was also a friend of **Barlaam of Calabria**. He was thus caught between the two when they clashed over Hesychasm around 1335. After failed attempts to mediate between them, Gregorius sided with Palamas in 1338. He was later convinced that Barlaam was right and, under the direction of John XII Calecas, patriarch of Constantinople, wrote against Palamas (*c.*1344). When Palamas' views were finally vindicated, Gregorius was posthumously declared a heretic, his views being considered so dangerous that both the Emperor John IV Cantacuzenus and the Patriarch **Philotheus Coccinus** worked personally to combat them.

Gregory Dekapolites Byzantine monk and saint, born Eirenopolis, Isaurian Decapolis, *c.*780, died Constantinople, 20 November 842. After completing his early education, he spent fourteen years in a monastery in Isauria whose archimandrite was his maternal uncle, Symeon. He then wandered extensively in Asia Minor, Greece and Sicily, settling for periods in Syracuse and Thessalonica, from where he visited Mount Olympus and Constantinople. He survived the second wave of persecution in the Iconoclastic controversy unscathed. A Life, written in the 840s, has been attributed to Ignatius the Deacon, but the ascription is disputed. Feast day 20 November.

Gregory Magistros Armenian prince and writer, born Ani, *c.*990, son of Prince Vasak Pahlawuni, lord of Bjni, died Taron, 1058. He was educated at Ani, particularly in Greek literature. He played an active political role from the 1030s, prosecuting various military campaigns. In 1045 at Constantinople he was forced to accede to the annexation of Ani by Byzantium, in return for other territories. Given the honorary title *magistros* in 1048, he was appointed *dux* of the Byzantine province of Mesopotamia. He built numerous churches and greatly enriched the cultural life of Armenia, teaching philosophy and science himself. Among other works, he wrote a 1000-line verse epitome of the Bible, and translated into Armenian Euclid's *Elements* and a number of Plato's dialogues; more than 80 of his letters survive, written to intellectuals, churchmen and political leaders.

Gregory Narek Armenian mystical poet, theologian and saint, born *c.*951, son of Xosrov, bishop of Anjevac'i, died Narek, *c.*1001. Educated by his uncle, a philosopher, he lived in Narek Monastery, and refers to himself as a priest. He seems to have acquitted himself of heresy charges by performing various miracles. He appears to have spent his later life as a cave-dwelling anchorite on the shores of Lake Van. He composed 95 mystical meditations on the book of Lamentations (copies of his text were prized as talismans), a number of hymns and panegyrics, a commentary on the Song of Songs, and a letter on heresy. Feast day 27 February.

Gregory of Agrigentum Bishop and saint, born near Agrigento, Sicily, 559, died Agriento, probably 604 (though some estimates suggest later, even 638). He studied in Byzantine monasteries in Palestine and was ordained deacon in Jerusalem. After visits to Antioch, North Africa and Constantinople, he went to Rome and was appointed bishop of Girgenti (Agrigento). A plot was laid to besmirch his reputation by the discovery of a prostitute at his home, but he was cleared of the charge. He wrote a major Greek commentary on Ecclesiastes, in ten books. Feast day 23 November.

Gregory of Antioch Patriarch of Antioch, 570–93, preacher and writer. A monk at the Byzantine monastery in Jerusalem and Sinai and at the laura of Pharan, he was elected patriarch of Antioch by Justinian II after the deposition of **Anastasius I**. Well respected by both civil and ecclesiastical leaders, on one occasion he quelled a rebellion of the Byzantine army at Litarba; his speech is recorded by **Evagrius.** He left many sermons and writings, of which one discourse on the Resurrection and two on the baptism of Christ survive. He is renowned for having won back into unity the Monophysites in his patriarchate.

Gregory of Bergamo   Bishop and theologian, born Bergamo, Italy, late 1000s, died 9 June 1146, probably martyred. Gregory was a Vallumbrosan monk who became bishop of Bergamo in 1133. He was a friend of **Bernard of Clairvaux** and an active ecclesiastical reformer. As a theologian, he is best known for his teachings about the Eucharist, found in *Tractatus de veritate corporis et sanguinis Christi* (1130–40). He believed in the real presence of Christ in the elements, which he also took as symbolizing the Church as the Mystical Body of Christ.

Gregory of Catina   Archivist and chronicler, born Catina, Italy, *c*.1060, died abbey of Farfa (near Rome), *c*.1132. Around 1092, Gregory was placed in charge of the archives of the Benedictine abbey of Farfa where he was a member, and spent the rest of his life in research on the documents and records contained therein. He transcribed many of the documents into the *Regestum Farfense* and the *Liber largitorius*, which contain both histories of Farfa, Italy and the Church and contemporary information about geography, topology and agriculture. His *Chronicon Farfense* contains notes and observations on papal pronouncements and medieval law.

Gregory of Cerchiara   Saint, abbot, born Cassano all'Ionio, Calabria, Italy, *c*.930, died abbey of Burtscheid, Germany, 1002. Gregory began his career as a Basilian monk and abbot at Cerchiara. He fled to Rome after the Saracen invasion and there, with the help of Empress Theophano, founded San Salvatore around 990. The Empress then sent him to Germany, where he founded and became abbot of a monastery (SS Apollinaris and Nicholas) that became the centre for much dispersion of Byzantine culture and Christianity in Germany. His cult is only found among the Basilians at Burtscheid. Feast day 4 November.

Gregory of Einsiedeln   Blessed, abbot, born probably in England, early 900s, died Einsiedeln,

Germany, 996. Of noble English descent, Gregory was married early but left his virgin wife, with her consent, to become a monk in Rome. He came to Einsiedeln in 949 and became abbot in 964. He knew the English monastic reforms of **Dunstan** of Canterbury and regulated Einseideln according to the English *Regularis concordia*. He was favoured by the German Emperors **Otto I** (to whom he was related by marriage), **Otto II** and **Otto III**, who all enriched the abbey and helped establish its reputation. That reputation led **Gebhard II of Constance** to request monks from Gregory when he founded Petershausen. Miracles were said to occur at Gregory's tomb after his death. Feast day 8 November.

Gregory of Elvira   Bishop and saint, date of birth unknown, died Elvira (near Granada) in old age after 392, possibly even after 403. He became bishop of Elvira (Spain) *c*.359. A fervent anti-Arian, he did not subscribe to the formula of Rimini (359). He also fought against Priscillianism. Among his works we find a defence of the *homoousios* (*De fide*) preserved in two recensions, and several exegetical writings among which is the earliest Western typological exegesis of the Song of Songs. His exegesis is allegorical throughout and shows familiarity with Jewish explanations of the OT. Feast day 24 April.

Gregory of Nazianzus   Bishop, theologian and saint, born *c*.330 of a Christian family (his father was bishop of Nazianzus), died Arianzos, 390. He was a close friend of **Basil** of Caesarea and **Gregory of Nyssa** (together known as the 'Three Cappadocians') and received a brilliant literary education in Caesarea, Alexandria and Athens. He was baptized in 358 and turned to the monastic life. Around Christmas 361 his father ordained him a priest. Because of his own ecclesiastical policy, Basil wanted him to become bishop of Sasima, a very small place in the middle of nowhere. Gregory refused this appointment and remained in Nazianzus. Later he went to Constantinople, where he became the leader of the small orthodox Neo-Nicene community in a largely Arian city. There he also preached his five *Theological Orations*, which gained him the designation 'the theologian'. He presided over the Council of Constantinople in 381. Soon after, he went back to Nazianzus and in

383 retreated to his estate, where he died. Gregory was a fierce defender of the Nicene orthodoxy and of the divinity and consubstantiality of the Spirit. He strongly influenced later theological developments. Feast day 2 January.

Gregory of Nyssa Saint, bishop and theologian, born Caesarea, in Cappadocia, between 335 and 340, died Nyssa, in Armenia, after 394, one of the greatest speculative theologians of the early Church and instrumental in the development of what was to become the 'orthodox' doctrine of the Trinity. Born of a wealthy Cappadocian family, brother of **Macrina the Younger** and **Basil** of Caesarea, he was probably married to Theosebeia and became bishop of Nyssa in 372, on Basil's instigation. As a consequence of ecclesiastical politics he was in 374(?) accused of maladministration and removed from his see. In 378 he was able to return and after Basil's death took over his leadership of the Neo-Nicene party. At the Council of Constantinople (381) he played a prominent role and delivered the funeral oration for the local bishop Meletius. Another testimony to his rise was his being asked to deliver the funerary orations for the emperor's wife and daughter. Among his writings, the most influential is undoubtedly his *Life of Moses*, an allegorical reading of Exodus describing the journey of the soul towards God. There are many exegetical commentaries (on Ecclesiastes, the Song of Songs and the Beatitudes), a biography of Macrina and an encomium on Basil and many theological treatises, such as *Contra Eunomium*. Feast day 9 March.

Gregory of Ostia Saint, bishop and papal legate, birth date and place unknown, died Logroño, Navarre, Spain, 9 May 1044. Gregory was a Benedictine monk in Rome and abbot of the monastery of SS Cosmas and Damian from 998 to 1004. Known for his piety and learning and favoured by Pope **Benedict IX**, he was elected bishop of Ostia 1033/4 and made librarian or chancellor in the Roman Church as well. He was sent by the Pope as his legate to Navarre in 1039, where he reportedly freed the kingdom from locusts by making the sign of the cross. In 1754, his veneration was officially approved for Navarre. Feast day 9 May.

Gregory of Rimini Philosopher and theologian, born Rimini, late thirteenth century, died Vienna, November 1358. A member of the Hermits of St Augustine, he studied in Italy and Paris and taught in Bologna, Padua and Perugia. In 1341 he returned to Paris, and in 1345 became director of the Sorbonne. Becoming general of his Order in 1357, he began a programme of reforms, but died the following year. He espoused a thoroughgoing Augustinian theology, and taught that unbaptized infants are damned (his opponents dubbed him *tortor infantium*, the torturer of infants); philosophically, he extended the nominalist thinking of **William of Ockham**. He wrote on Augustinian principles, and produced a number of exegetical and moral treatises. His ideas probably influenced the theology of Martin **Luther**.

Gregory of Tours Bishop, historian, and saint, born Clermont-Ferrand, probably November 538, died Tours, 17 November 594. Of an eminent Gallo-Roman family, he became bishop of Tours in 573. An opponent of King Chilperic, he won royal favour for his support for King Guntram's campaign against the aristocracy. Around 576 he began his monumental *History of the Franks*, a well-informed, if somewhat disorganized and ambitious, work which became an indispensable resource for early French history. He also produced a series of eight works on miracles, which reflect a decidedly credulous attitude, and other writings on the Fathers, the Psalms, and the Church offices. Feast day 17 November.

Gregory of Utrecht Associate of St **Boniface** and saint, born Trier, 707, died Utrecht, 25 August 776. From a leading Merovingian family, he was so impressed by an exposition of St Boniface at the convent of Pfalzel, where his grandmother was abbess, that he became a devoted disciple of the saint, who in 754 appointed him abbot of St Martin's, Utrecht. It became a great missionary and scholarly centre. On the martyrdom of St **Eoban** in 755, he assumed the administration of the See of Utrecht, though he was never formally consecrated bishop in the ensuing twenty-year period. Feast day 25 August.

Gregory Palamas Greek Orthodox saint and mystic, born Constantinople of a noble family with connections to the imperial court, 1296 or 1297, died Thessalonica, 14 November 1359. After studies at the university in Constantinople he entered a monastery on Mount Athos at the age of 22. In 1325, however, he and several companions fled to Thessalonica to escape Turkish raids. He was ordained priest there, but established a hermitage near Beroea and lived there largely in silence until 1331, when he returned to Athos, but continued to live his eremitical life. He was attacked by the monk **Barlaam** from Calabria for his 'hesychastic' (= silence or rest) spirituality. His defence of Hesychasm was expressed in nine books, written between 1338 and 1341. In 1345 he became archbishop of Thessalonica, and in 1354/5 was held for ransom by the Turks. He was canonized in 1368. Feast day both 14 November and the second Sunday of the Great Lent, the latter commemorating his victory over Barlaam.

Gregory Sinaites Hesychast monk, writer and saint, born near Clazomenae, late thirteenth century, died Paroria, Thrace, probably 27 November 1346. Captured by the Turks in his youth, on his release he fled to Cyprus, where he became a monk. He spent some time on Mount Sinai, before moving to Mount Athos via Jerusalem and Crete. In Crete, he studied with Arsenios and learned the pioneering meditative Jesus prayer ('Lord Jesus Christ, Son of God, have mercy on me', repeated over and over again), which he introduced to Athos. Turkish raids led him to flee to Paroria, where c.1325 he established a monastery on Mount Katakekryomene, which attracted Greek and Slav devotees and earned aid from the Bulgarian tsar, Ivan Alexander. His main writing was the *Most Beautiful Chapters*, a series of 137 short essays on the contemplative life; he also wrote on Hesychastic prayer and on the Transfiguration. One of his disciples, the future Patriarch **Callistus I**, composed his biography. Feast day 27 November (8 August among the Slavs).

Gregory Thaumaturgus Bishop and saint, was born of a pagan family in Neocaesarea (Pontus; today part of Turkey), c.213, died there, c.270–5. After his conversion to Christianity at the age of fourteen he studied rhetoric and law. In Caesarea in Palestine he met **Origen** and studied philosophy and exegesis for five years with him, while also receiving a training in spirituality. When leaving

Caesarea, Gregory delivered a long farewell speech thanking his master. Back home he became bishop of Neocaesarea, where he performed many miracles. We also have a (probably genuine) Trinitarian creed from his hand, showing Origenian influence. Feast day 17 November.

Gregory the Illuminator Saint, born c.260, died c.328, at his See of Ashtishat. Probably an Armenian by birth, he converted to Christianity in Caesarea in Cappadocia. On his return to Armenia, King Tiridates II tried to force him by torture to revert to paganism. Gregory refused and was thrown in a pit where he stayed for fifteen years. He was released to cure the king, who had gone mad as a consequence of a love affair. Gregory healed the king, who then converted to Christianity. Gregory became the first bishop and the apostle of the Armenians. Feast day 30 September.

Gregory the Wonder-Worker *see* **Gregory Thaumaturgus**

Gressmann, Hugo Old Testament scholar, born Mölln, Germany, 21 March 1877, died Chicago, 6 April 1927. He studied at Göttingen University and was a lecturer at Kiel University, where the wrote *The Source of Israelite-Jewish Eschatology*. He was an advocate of the religious-historical approach. He visited the German Evangelical Institute for the Study of Antiquity in Jerusalem, then became professor at Berlin. His other writings include *Old Oriental Texts and Pictures*, *Moses and His Time* and *The Beginning of Israel*. *The Messiah* was published posthumously in 1929.

Grétry, André Ernest Modeste Composer, born Liège (Belgium), 8 February 1741, died Montmorency, near Paris, 24 September 1813. Grétry wrote: 'Woe to the artist enslaved by rules who does not dare yield to the flight of his genius.' He composed a Mass which entitled him to study in Rome, 1761–5. He wrote some 50 operas, and many romances (songs); he also composed some small-scale choral pieces such as motets.

Grey, William Bishop, died Ely, 4 August 1478. Noble birth assisted Grey's accumulation of minor benefices, which, in turn, funded his studies at Balliol College, Oxford (he was chancellor of the university in the early 1440s), Cologne, Florence, Padua and Ferrara. In Italy he was taught by Guarino da Verona, acquired knowledge of Greek and possibly Hebrew, patronized the humanist Niccolò Perotti, and was an avid collector of manuscripts, which were duly bequeathed to Balliol. In 1449 he was appointed king's proctor at the Roman curia, which led to his elevation to the bishopric of Ely in 1454.

Griesbach, Johann Jakob Lutheran biblical scholar, born Butzbach, Germany, 4 January 1745, died Jena, 12 March 1812. He studied at Tübingen, Halle and Leipzig and became professor at Jena in 1775, devoting himself to a critical revision of the NT text. He set out fifteen canons of textual criticism, classified manuscripts into Alexandrian, Western and Byzantine, drew up a list of readings which he thought superior to those he inherited and published a Greek edition of the NT in 1774–7, and another in 1796–1806, thus laying the foundations for all subsequent work. He also coined the term 'synoptic' for the first three Gospels and published *Commentarius criticus* (1811). The 'Griesbach hypothesis', named after him, reflects his belief that Mark's was the final Gospel to be written, and that it draws on Matthew's and Luke's.

Griffin, Bernard William Cardinal, born Birmingham, 21 February 1899, died Polzeath, Cornwall, 20 August 1960. He studied at Cotton College and Oscott College, then from 1922 to 1927 at the English College, Rome, being ordained in Rome in 1924. He worked as a parish priest, showing particular concern for the orphanage in his parish. He was appointed assistant bishop in Birmingham in 1938, and archbishop of Westminster in 1943. He was always interested in social issues, but was faced in the aftermath of the Second World War with the development in Britain of a new structure for education, and of the Welfare State. With neither of these was he entirely happy. He was made a cardinal in 1947.

Griffith, Patrick Raymond Dominican missionary bishop, born Limerick, 15 October 1798, died Cape Town, 18 June 1862. After entering the Dominicans, he studied in Lisbon and Rome, and was ordained in 1821. After some years back in Ireland, in 1837 he was appointed first vicar apostolic of the Cape of Good Hope; after consecration in Dublin, he arrived in Africa in 1838. He established several mission stations in the Cape Peninsula and in the Eastern Cape, and over the years 1841–51 constructed St Mary's Cathedral in Cape Town. He resigned in 1862, after presiding over a massive expansion of the Catholic presence in the Cape Colony.

Griffiths, Bede Monk and sannyasi, born England, 17 December 1906, died in his ashram at Shantivanam, India, 13 May 1994. Educated at Oxford, he attempted first to establish a small community in two cottages in the Cotswolds. This experiment ended in a spiritual and psychological crisis and in 1932 he became a Catholic, joining Prinknash Priory, a Benedictine monastery, soon afterwards. He developed an interest in Eastern ways of prayer and in 1955 went to India, where he worked to develop links between the spirituality of Europe and India while remaining committed to Christianity. He learnt Indian spiritual disciplines and the Hindu classic texts and wrote many books on his vision of Christ hidden in the world's religions. He helped to found a monastic ashram in Kerala, where the monks lived and dressed as sannyasi, Hindu holy men, and in 1968 to establish Saccidananda Ashram, where the liturgies were both Christian and Hindu.

Griffiths, Thomas Roman Catholic bishop, born London, 2 June 1791, died London, 12 August 1847. He became a Catholic in boyhood, and was educated at St Edmund's College; he was ordained in 1814, and was president of his college 1818–33. After being appointed coadjutor of the London district and titular bishop of Olena, in 1836 he succeeded to the vicariate. He opened numerous missions for Irish immigrants to London, and spearheaded a large amount of charitable work.

Grignion de Montfort, Louis-Marie Saint, religious founder, born Montfort-sur-Meu, France, 31 January 1673, died St-Laurent-sur-Sèvre, 28 April 1716. He was ordained a priest in Paris, and worked at Nantes, then Poitiers. Here he founded a religious congregation, the Daughters of Wisdom. Then he founded the Montfort Fathers, for missionary and retreat work, and to spread devotion to the Blessed Virgin Mary. Pope **Clement XI** named him missionary for France, and Grignion preached in parishes in western France. His work *True Devotion to the Blessed Virgin* was discovered only posthumously, in 1842. He was beatified in 1888 and canonized in 1947. Feast day 28 April.

Grillmeier, Alois   German theologian and Jesuit cardinal, born Pechbrunn, 1 January 1910, died Unterhaching, near Munich, 13 September 1998. He studied at the episcopal school in Regensburg before joining the Society of Jesus in April 1929. He was ordained priest in 1937 (together with Alfred **Delp**). The war prevented his studying in Rome and he took his doctorate in Freiburg in 1942. After two years of military service he began teaching theology, moving to Sankt Georgen, the Jesuit theological faculty in Frankfurt, in 1950. The following year he edited a large collection of essays by various writers to commemorate the 1500th anniversary of the Council of Chalcedon. His own essay in the first of the volumes was expanded, and appeared in English as *Christ in Christian Tradition* in 1965. His study of this theme was planned to appear in three volumes, but it also expanded until it became his life's work, even after he retired in 1978. He had attended the Second Vatican Council as the theologian of the bishop of Limburg, and helped to draft the conciliar documents on the Church and on revelation. He was created a cardinal in November 1994.

Grimani, Domenico   Cardinal bishop and humanist, born Venice, 22 February 1461 and died Rome, 27 August 1523. Studied at Padua and was an associate of the leading humanists of his day. In 1493 he was made cardinal and in 1497 became patriarch of Aquileia. In 1511 he was made bishop of Porto and during the League of Cambrai defended the rights of Venice. He developed a large collection of art and books and left his library to the monastery of San Antonio de Castello in Venice.

Grimbald   Scholar and saint, born Thérouanne, Flanders, perhaps *c.*825, died Winchester, 8 July 901. He became a monk of the abbey of Saint-Bertin, rising to become its prior. He was invited to England by King **Alfred** *c.*887. According to legend, he declined the offer of the archbishopric of Canterbury on the death of Ethelred. He was appointed prior of the planned New Minster at Winchester, but died before its completion. None of his writings survives, but he exercised an important role in bringing manuscripts to England and in promoting scholarly activity. He was commemorated by the community of the New Minster. The fourteenth-century *Breviary of Hyde Abbey* is influenced by a lost medieval Life. Feast day 8 July.

Grimshaw, William   Evangelical clergyman and perpetual curate of Haworth, born at Brindle, Lancashire, 14 September 1708, died Haworth, 7 April 1763. Educated at Blackburn Grammar School and Christ's College, Cambridge. Following his ordination in 1731 he briefly served as curate at Littleborough near Rochdale, then Todmorden. From 1742 to his death he was curate of Haworth. Although experiencing an evangelical conversion at Todmorden he was greatly influenced by William Darney in 1744. He became **Wesley**'s chief assistant in establishing Methodism in the north of England, creating and regulating the 'Great Haworth Round'. On 18 October 1748, he conducted the first Methodist Circuit Quarterly Meeting, an idea put forward by John **Bennet**.

Grisar, Hartmann   German Jesuit and Church historian, born Coblenz, 22 September 1845, died Innsbruck, Austria, 25 February 1932. Studied in Coblenz, Münster and Innsbruck. He was ordained and joined the Jesuits in 1868 and did further studies in Rome. In 1871 he was made professor of Church history at Innsbruck, where he remained until 1889. He was a proponent of the historiographical principles of Leopold von **Ranke**. In 1877 he helped found *Zeitschrift für katholische Theologie*. In 1899 he went to live in Rome and began historical and archaeological research on the city. He returned to Innsbruck because of ill-health and began a study of **Luther**: his approach is psychological and although less hostile than others before him is still negative in tone. His writings include a collection of studies of early Rome, *Analecta Romana* (1899), *Geschichte Roms und der Päpste* (1901), *Luther* (3 vols, 1911–12), *Lutherstudien* (6 vols, 1920–3), *Der deutsche Luther im Weltkrieg und in der Gegenwart* (1924) and *Martin Luthers Leben und sein Werk* (1926). His later works include *San Gregorio Magno* (1904), *Das Missale im Licht der römischen Stadgeschichte* (1925) and *Marienblüten: Systematische Marienlehre aus dem grossen Marienwerk des Petrus Canisius* (1930).

Grocyn, William English priest and scholar, born Colerne, Wiltshire, *c.*1446, died Maidstone, Kent, October 1519. He studied at Winchester and New College, Oxford, taught at Oxford, then travelled to Italy, 1489–91, where he met many scholars, including Aldus **Manutius**. In Oxford he was reputed to be the first to lecture in Greek. He then became rector of St Lawrence Jewry in London, the church at which Thomas **More** worshipped. He was one of a group of English humanists, and was a friend of **Linacre**, More, **Colet** and **Erasmus**. He finally became warden of All Hallows College, Maidstone, though still retaining, until 1517, St Lawrence Jewry. A monument to him was erected in the church at Newton Longueville, at which he also held a benefice.

Groote, Gerardus Magnus Founder of the Brethren of the Common Life, born Deventer, The Netherlands, October 1340, died of the plague Deventer, 20 August 1384. Of an upper-class family, he had a distinguished academic career in Paris and taught in Cologne and elsewhere. In 1374, he adopted a life of Christian asceticism, and after a period in the monastery at Munnikhuizen became a missionary lay-preacher at Utrecht. His licence was revoked in 1383 for his outspoken attacks on clerical abuses; his appeal against the sentence was unanswered when he died. With a few friends, he formed the Brethren of the Common Life (having previously launched a similar movement for women), whose vocation was to devotion and simplicity of life. He wrote a number of works on spirituality and morality. His Life was written by **Thomas à Kempis**.

Grotius, Hugo Jurist and theologian, born Delft, 10 October 1583, died Rostock, 28 August 1645. Of a prominent family, he was a child prodigy, studying at Leiden aged twelve and practising law at sixteen. At eighteen he was appointed historian of the States General, and later held other offices, including advocate fiscal. He evoked the wrath of the Calvinists for his Arminian views, and was sentenced to life imprisonment, but escaped by being smuggled in a box of books to Paris. There he published *On the Law of War and Peace* (1625), whose grounding of justice in natural law rather than in theology has earned him the title of the father of international law. He returned to Holland, was again banished, and served latterly as ambassador of Sweden in Paris. He wrote some pioneering annotations on OT exegesis; his main religious work was *On the Truth of the Christian Religion* (begun 1622), a practical guide for Christians which upheld a strong natural theology and Christ-centred ethic.

Groves, Anthony Norris Plymouth Brethren founder and missionary, born Newton, Hampshire, England, 1 February 1795, died Bristol, 20 May 1853. Groves studied chemistry, learnt dentistry, and opened a surgery in Plymouth in 1814. After his conversion and marriage to his cousin Mary Thompson, he moved to Exeter. He applied to the Church Missionary Society as a missionary and took examinations at Trinity College, Dublin, before deciding ordination was unbiblical. After discussions with others who helped found the Brethren movement he received believers' baptism in 1829 and sailed for St Petersburg en route to Baghdad. Mary and their daughter died in 1831. In 1833 he relocated to India and published *On the Liberty of Ministry in the Church of Christ* (1834). In the 1840s he precipitated a break with the 'exclusive' wing of the Brethren movement. His broad sympathies, advocacy of the 'faith principle' and simple lifestyle had a lasting impact.

Grueber, Johannes German Jesuit, missionary to China, explorer, born Linz, 28 October 1623, died en route from Rome to China, 1665. He became a Jesuit in 1641 and was sent to China in 1656, where he was professor of mathematics at the court in Peking (Beijing). He was sent to Rome in 1661; unable to travel by sea because of a Dutch blockade, he travelled (with Albert de Dorville, who died at Agra on the journey) overland across China and Tibet to India and thence overland to Europe. The journey took 214 days. The route had never been conceived before and caused a sensation, as well as providing new knowledge about Tibet and the Himalayas. Grueber attempted an overland route back to China via Russia, but died en route.

Grueber's journals were published as *China illustrata* by Athanasius **Kircher** in 1667.

Grundtvig, Nikolai Frederik Severin Danish Lutheran reformer, born Udby, 8 September 1783, died Copenhagen, 2 September 1872. An authority on Anglo-Saxon and Norse literature, after certain religious experiences he turned his attention to reforming the Lutheran Church in Denmark. He was critical of the way in which the Church was dominated by the State and of the rationalism of its theology and in 1824 founded a movement (Grundtvigianism) to try to rectify this. It helped bring about a better understanding of ecclesiology and the place of the sacraments in the Church. From 1839 until he died he held the post of preacher at the Vartov Hospital in Copenhagen. He also helped found the Folk High Schools in Denmark.

Grünewald, Matthias Painter (known during his lifetime as 'Mathis Gothart Nithart') born Würzburg, *c.*1460(?), died Halle, August 1528. Almost nothing is known of his life, except that he lived in the Upper Rhine area. He is famous for his altarpiece for Isenheim near Colmar, one panel of which pictures John the Baptist pointing, with very long index finger, to the crucified Jesus, and bears the inscription 'He must increase: I must decrease' (John 3:30). He also painted numerous other crucifixion scenes, a celebrated depiction of the *Meeting of St Erasmus and St Maurice*, and a possible self-portrait. His work influenced twentieth-century Expressionism.

Guadagni, Bernardo Gaetano Cardinal bishop, born Florence, 14 September 1674, died Rome, 15 January 1759. He obtained his doctorate in civil and canon law in Pisa in 1694 and was a canon in the cathedral at Florence when he entered the Discalced Carmelite Order in 1700. After serving as a provincial of the Tuscan province, he was named bishop of Arezzo in 1724. When **Clement XII** was elected Pope, Guadagni, his nephew, was summoned to Rome, created a cardinal in 1731, and nominated to the Curia. During three pontificates he was a secretary to the Consistory, counsellor to many other congregations, and vicar of Rome from 1732 to 1759. He was nominated to be bishop of Frascati in 1750 and of Porto and S.

Rufina in 1756. He was a man remarkable for virtue, devoted to the reform of morals and the care of the poor; his cause for beatification was introduced in 1761 and 1763. He was the first cardinal of the Discalced Carmelites.

Guajázar Valencia, Rafael Roman Catholic bishop and evangelist, born Cotija, Mexico, 27 April 1878, died Mexico City, 6 June 1938. Guajázar Valencia had a strong evangelistic vocation and began his first preaching journey in 1901, only eight days after ordination. His preaching missions were ended by the Mexican revolution, but he continued to evangelize by travelling in disguise with the revolutionary armies, preaching as often as possible and at considerable risk. He was finally forced to flee the country, but returned in 1920 as bishop of Veracruz. Persecution of the Church was then severe, but when it finally ended the Church emerged stronger than it had been at the beginning, largely thanks to Guajázar Valencia's determined resistance and considerable bravery.

Gual, Pedro Franciscan missionary, apologist, founder and restorer of influential religious institutions in Peru, born Canet del Mar, Barcelona, Spain, 1813, died Lima, 1890. He received his primary education in Italy, arrived at the Peruvian Missionary College of Ocopa in 1845, and in 1852 founded the famous missionary college of the Descalzos in Lima. He became a general commissary of the Order in charge of the missionary colleges and visitor of Franciscan provinces. Gual was from the very beginning the driving force behind the religious restoration initiated by Andrés Herrero in the South American Pacific republics. He set up or consolidated the string of Colegios de Propaganda Fide that arose in Peru, Bolivia, Chile, Ecuador and Colombia. He was an inexhaustible supporter and organizer, by his example and writings, of the missions popular among the faithful. He attacked the enemies of the Church, Jansenist, liberal, Masonic and atheist, with his powerful lectures and publications, which he aimed especially against **Renan**, Jacolliot and De Santis. These publications were widely circulated among the learned Peruvians. He successfully refuted also Vigil and other Peruvian writers who spread heretical and demoralizing doctrines in his *Equilibrio entre las dos potestades* (1832), *La moralizadora del* *mundo* (1862), *La vida de Jesús* (1869), *La India cristiana* (1880) and many other works.

Guala of Bergamo Blessed, Dominican bishop, born Bergamo, Lombardy, *c.*1180, died Astino, 3 September 1244. When **Dominic** preached at Bergamo in 1217 Guala (Walter) Roni (Romanoni) received from him the habit of the Order of Preachers. In 1221 he became prior of the Dominican convent at Brescia. At this time he had the vision of the glory of St Dominic, whose death, unknown to Guala, had just occurred. He established the convent at Bergamo (1222), was associated with the founding of the nuns' convent of St Agnes at Bologna (1225) and soon after became prior of St Nicolas there. Both **Honorius III** and **Gregory IX** recognized his prudence and diplomatic skill by sending him to handle difficult missions. In 1229–30 he was elected as bishop of Brescia, where he continued his diplomatic activities. Exiled from his see in 1239, Guala spent his last years in penitential retirement with the Benedictines at Astino. **Pius IX** beatified him in 1868. Feast day 3 September.

Guanella, Luigi Blessed, religious founder, born Fraciscio di Campodocino (Sondrio), Italy, 19 December 1843, died Como, Italy, 24 October 1915. Guanella came from a poor family, entered the diocesan seminary in 1854 and was ordained in 1866. During his pastoral works in the village of Savogno he had so great a concern for the spiritual and temporal needs of his parishioners that they built a monument in his honour shortly after his death. While pastor in Pianello Lario, he opened a hospice for orphaned and abandoned children in 1878. He started similar institutions in several Italian cities. To perpetuate his work, Guanella founded the Daughters of St Mary of Providence and also a religious congregation for men, the Servants of Charity, originally, known as the Sons of the Sacred Heart, 1904. Both institutions have spread to other countries, especially to Switzerland. Visits to these regions stimulated Guanella to aid Italian immigrants. Through his friendship with Davide Albertario and Giuseppe Toniolo he also became a pioneer leader in the social question. Guanella promoted the apostolate of the press and wrote about 50 popular devotional, historical and pedagogical works. Feast day 24 October.

Guardini, Romano Philosopher of religion and pioneer of the liturgical movement, born Verona, 17 February 1885, died Munich, 1 October 1968. While at the University of Tübingen he developed his love of liturgy from attending the Benedictine services at the abbey of Beuron. Ordained priest in May 1910, he continued his studies at Freiburg and began a long teaching career in the philosophy of religion at Bonn, Berlin, Tübingen and finally at Munich, from 1948 to 1963. He became a leader in the renewal of Catholicism in the inter-war years. As a professor of philosophy his main aim was to show the relevancy of the Christian faith to modern realities. To enliven liturgical spirituality, he wrote *The Spirit of the Liturgy* (1918) but he is especially remembered for his life of Christ, *The Lord* (1937). His thought and work anticipated much of the teaching of Vatican II.

Guarinus of Palestrina Saint, cardinal bishop, born Bologna, Italy, *c.*1080, died Palestrina, Italy, 6 February 1159. Around 1104, Guarinus, who was already a priest, joined the Augustinian Order in Mortara, Italy. Twenty-five years later, upon the death of the bishop of Pavia, he was elected bishop by popular acclaim, no doubt because of his reputation for virtue, love for the poor and exemplary monastic life. He refused the honour and was imprisoned. He escaped, only to be forced by Pope **Lucius II** to accept a cardinal's hat and the See of Palestrina near Rome. Pope **Alexander III** canonized him immediately after his death. Feast day 6 February.

Guarinus (Guérin) of Sion Saint, Benedictine and Cistercian abbot, bishop of Sion (Switzerland), born Pont-à-Mousson, Lorraine, *c.*1065, died Aulps, Savoy, 27 August 1150. Guarinus entered the monastery of Molesme around 1085; in 1094, he and several others left that monastery in order to lead a more retired life at Aulps, of which he became the second abbot in 1110. After a visit from **Bernard of Clairvaux**, Guarinus arranged for Aulps to become part of the Order of Cîteaux in 1136; two years later, he became bishop of Sion. He died while visting Aulps and was buried there. Feast day 30 August in the Diocese of Sion, 14 January in the Cistercian Order.

Guarnerius *see* **Irnerius**

Guasto, Andrea del Founder and superior of the Congregation of Centorbi, born Castrogiovanni, Sicily, 16 August 1534, died Regalbuto, 7 September 1627. He became a part of a group of about 200 hermits who lived in the mountains around Argira under the direction of Philip Dulcettus. Guasto gained a reputation of sanctity. He suggested the hermits changed from the Third Order of St Francis to the First Order of St Augustine. On 2 February 1579, **Gregory XIII** approved the change, but only after the president of Sicily lent his support did Andrea and twelve confrères receive the Augustinian habit, on 22 May 1585, from Melchior Testai of Regalbuto, their first moderator. In 1591 the remaining hermits were united and led a common life, living by the work of their hands. This Congregatio Heremitarum Siciliae, from 1602 renamed the Congregatio Centrum Urbium, after Centorbi, the first monastery, grew to nineteen houses until suppressed in 1873.

Gubernatis, Domenico de Franciscan historian, born Sospitello, Diocese of Turin, date unknown, died Turin, 1690. Little is known about his life. His fame as a historian rests on his authorship of the monumental work whose six-line title is usually shortened to *Orbis Seraphicus*. He was selected to undertake this work about 1670 by the minister general of the Franciscans. As conceived by Gubernatis, it was to be a universal history of the Franciscan Order in 30 volumes. Only seven ever appeared, but the work remains a singular specimen of seventeenth-century historiography and probably the most precious history of the Order, with the single exception of **Wadding**'s *Annales*. The first four volumes, published by Gubernatis himself at Rome and Lyons between 1682 and 1685, concern the internal history of the Order. He also published a volume on missionary history (Rome, 1689). Gubernatis' plan was continued by Cavalli da Cueno, who produced a volume on the history of the provinces (Turin, 1741), and by Marcellino da **Civezza** and Theophil Domenichelli, authors of a second volume of missionary history.

Gudula Saint and virgin, patroness of Brussels, born mid-seventh century, died Ham, *c*.712. Apparently born into a noble family of Brabant, she was educated at the abbey of Nivelles and devoted her life to prayer and works of charity,

living at Ham near Alast. After her death, her remains were moved to Brussels, being placed in the church of St Michael in 1047, where her cult developed soon afterwards. She is typically depicted with a lantern, according to the legend that when a demon blew out her taper it was miraculously rekindled. Feast day 8 January.

Gudwal (Gurval, Goal) Missionary and saint, died *c*.640. Very little is known of his life. Probably Welsh or a Briton (perhaps from Cornwall), he was an early missionary to Brittany. He established the monastery of Plec near Locoal and several others elsewhere, and perhaps became a regional bishop. The chapel of St Stephen at Guer was probably his hermitage. His relics were moved to Picardy, then to Ghent. He now tends to be identified with Gurval, the successor of St **Malo** at Aleth. Feast day 6 June.

Guéranger, Prosper-Louis-Pascal Priest who restored Benedictine monasticism to France, born Sablé-sur-Sarthe, 4 April 1805, died Solesmes, 30 January 1875. He opposed Gallicanism: he aimed for local liturgies to be abolished and for Catholicism in France to come more under the control of Rome (the ultramontane viewpoint). In France, Benedictine Orders had died out in the Revolution. He acquired the ancient abbey site of Solesmes, rebuilt the abbey and became abbot. He revived liturgical life and wrote *Institutions liturgiques*, which restored the Roman liturgy. After his death the abbey of Solesmes pioneered the restoration of plainsong, which became the official music of the Roman Catholic Church, confirmed by Pope **Pius X** in his *Motu Proprio* of 1903.

Guercino Italian painter Giovanni Francesco Barbieri, an originator of the baroque pictorial style, born Cento, near Bologna, February 1591, died Bologna, 22 December 1666. Guercino ('Squint-eye) was educated by local masters, and his early work was influenced by Ludovico **Carracci**, whose *Madonna with St Francis and Donors* was in Cento. In 1616 Guercino visited Bologna, and five years later followed the newly elected Bolognese Pope, **Gregory XV**, to Rome. There, particularly in his illusionistic *Aurora* fresco for the ceiling of Casino Ludovisi, he introduced his dynamic, colourful and form-dissolving style, which was fundamental to later developments of Roman high baroque decorative painting. Unfortunately, influenced by Domenichino and G. B. Agucchi, he began to change from his flowing, decorative *sfumato* to a dry linear clarity, which was less appealing visually though perhaps more 'correct' theoretically. Although he returned to Cento in 1623, his work consistently tended to this unexcited classicism, until he moved to Bologna after Guido **Reni**'s death in 1642. At that time no trace of his original style remained. In his youth Guercino painted a number of frescoes, but after *c*.1630 he limited himself mainly to oils. He also drew superbly in pen and in chalk, both atmospheric figure studies and landscapes.

Guerin, Theodore Mother of the Sisters of Providence of St Mary-of-the-Woods, born Brittany, France, 2 October 1798, died St Mary-of-the-Woods, Indiana, USA, 14 May 1856. Her parents, Laurent and Isabelle Guerin, christened her 'Anne Thérèse'. After early education at a private school, she undertook the care of her invalid mother until 1823, when she entered the recently founded Congregation of the Sisters of Providence. After taking her vows on 8 September 1825, she was appointed superior of the school in the industrial town of Renhes, where she remained for eight years. When transferred to Soulaines, she was noted for the excellence of her methods in teaching mathematics. In 1840, answering an appeal from Bishop Celestine de la Hailandriere of Vincennes, Sister Theodore and five companions left to establish a motherhouse in Indiana. Upon arriving, Mother Theodore opened an academy for girls, chartered in 1846, the first in Indiana. She also established the motherhouse and Institute of St Mary's and ten schools during her sixteen years of labour. A process for her canonization began in 1956.

Guerra, Elena Blessed, foundress of the Oblate Sisters of the Holy Spirit, born Lucca, Italy, 23 June 1835, died Lucca, 11 April 1914. Elena was born of a well-to-do pious family, and was educated by a tutor. She was active in works of charity from an early age and eventually organized a number of young girls into an association following a common life and called the Pious Union of Spiritual Friendship. From these disciples she chose the first members of her congregation, founded in 1872 in honour of St **Zita**, to spread devotion to the Holy Spirit. The institution received the approval of the Holy See in 1911 as the Oblate Sisters of the Holy Spirit, but it is more commonly known as the Sisters of St Zita. In her efforts to promote devotion to the Holy Spirit, Elena wrote frequently to Pope **Leo XIII**, whose encyclical *Divinum Illud Munus* (1897) rewarded her efforts. She wrote some short devotional works, and was the teacher of St Gemma **Galgani**.

Guerrero, Francisco Spanish composer, born Seville, 4 October 1528, died Seville, 8 November 1599. At the age of seventeen he became choirmaster at St Jaén's Cathedral, Andalucia. At Seville Cathedral he was successively a singer, assistant choirmaster and choirmaster. He visited Rome, Venice and Jerusalem: because his music was published in Seville, Venice, Paris and Rome, a facility not available to all his contemporaries, he achieved fame. His Church music is considered typically Spanish. In Latin he composed Masses, Requiems, motets and settings of the *St Matthew* and *St John Passions*. Sometimes he adapted secular songs to sacred texts; he also wrote religious songs in Spanish.

Guerric of Igny Blessed, Cistercian abbot and theologian, born Tournai, *c*.1070–80, died Igny, France, 19 August 1157. Before becoming a Cistercian monk at Clairvaux *c*.1125, he was a cathedral canon and *magister scholarum* at Tournai. Elected abbot of Igny in 1138, he is best known for his sermons. Feast day 19 August.

Guevara, Antonio de Spanish Franciscan and writer, born Trecerio, Spain, *c*.1480, died Mondonedo, 3 April 1545. He joined the Franciscans and was appointed court preacher, royal chronicler, and bishop of Guadix, and then of Mondonedo. His book translated as *The Golden Boke of Marcus Aurelius* was influential in the sixteenth century as a model for rulers. Other works include *Scorn of Court Life and the Praise of Village Life* and *The Caesars*. In *The Perfect Prince*, Guevara invented the legend of the Danube peasant who shames the Roman Senate with his appeal against the unfairness of conquest.

Guevara y Lira, Silvestre Fifth archbishop of

Caracas, Venezuela, born Chamarizapa, Anzoátegui, 31 December 1814, died Caracas, 20 February 1882. Having been vicar-general of the Diocese of Guayana and senator in the National Congress, he was consecrated archbishop of Caracas on 6 February 1853. The first seventeen years of his episcopate were characterized by fruitful activity which commanded respect and admiration. He completely restored the cathedral, in ruins since the earthquake of 1812; reorganized studies and the discipline of the seminary and thus raised the prestige of the clergy. He succeeded in getting the Venezuelan government to accept a concordat with the Holy See. However, the concordat was never ratified by the government. For the next twelve years, during the regime of Guzmán Blanco, Guevara was the focus of the most serious political-religious conflicts in the history of Venezuela. He was expelled from the country for not being submissive to the autocratic rule of the president. In 1877, with the end of Guzmán's regime, the new president authorized the return of Guevara, who spent the last five years of his life surrounded by affection and widespread veneration of the faithful.

Guibert, Joseph de Jesuit theologian, born L'Isle-sur-Tarn, France, 14 September 1877, died Rome, 23 March 1942. Guibert became a Jesuit in 1895 and was ordained in 1906. Following studies at the Sorbonne, he taught theology at seminaries in France and Belgium, and during World War I served as an army chaplain. In 1919 he founded the journal *Revue d'ascétique et de mystique*, with the intention of furthering the study of spirituality in an intellectually disciplined fashion. In 1922 Guibert moved to the Gregorian University, Rome, to teach ascetical and mystical theology, remaining there until his death. He wrote an important treatise on mystical theology, and a study of the history and spirituality of the Jesuits.

Guibert of Gembloux French Benedictine abbot, born Gembloux, *c*.1125, died, probably in the monastery of Florennes, 22 February 1213. He entered the abbey of Gembloux after studying there, but from 1177 to 1180 was at Bingen to assist the abbess **Hildegarde**. He visited the shrine of St **Martin** at Tours, and much of his writing concerns St Martin. In 1188 or 1189 he became abbot of Florennes, and in 1193 of Gembloux. In both houses he restored monastic discipline. He resigned the abbacy early in the thirteenth century, and retired as a simple monk to Florennes.

Guibert of Nogent Benedictine abbot and historian, born Clermont-en-Beauvais, 10 April 1053, died Nogent, 1124. Of noble birth, he was a child oblate at the Benedictine abbey of Flavigny; he became abbot of Nogent-sous-Coucy in 1104. He is best known for two works: his autobiography, *De vita sua*, which is an important source for medieval daily life, and the *Gesta Dei per Francos*, an account of the First Crusade.

Guibert of Ravenna Antipope Clement III, born Parma, *c*.1025, died Città Castellana, September 1100. A nobleman, he was a member of the imperial court by 1055 and was elected imperial chancellor for Italy in 1058. Despite helping to develop the papal election decree of 1059, he played an important role in the election of the Antipope Honorius II in 1061. In 1072, Emperor **Henry IV** named Guibert archbishop of Ravenna, and with the support of Hildebrand (later Pope **Gregory VII**), he was consecrated as such by Pope **Alexander II**. Guibert broke with Hildebrand shortly after the latter became Pope in 1073, and became the leader of those opposed to the Gregorian reform; he was excommunicated in 1078. In June 1080, anti-Gregorians declared that Gregory had been wrongly elected, and on 25 June Guibert was declared to be Pope Clement III. Despite this, Guibert was not Henry's puppet: he was a capable administrator, a staunch opponent of simony and a defender of papal rights.

Guibert of Tournai Franciscan spiritual, teacher, preacher, born Tournai, France, *c*.1210, died Tournai, 7(?) October 1284. He was born Guibert Aspis de Muriel Porte, of noble lineage; his only brother, Henry, also a teacher, died before him. After being brought up by Bishop Gautierer of Marvy (d. 1251), he studied at Paris, where he eventually obtained a master's degree in theology. Attracted to contemplation, he became a Franciscan (*c*.1235), but his superiors assigned him to teaching. He may have been a participant in the first crusade of **Louis IX**, 1248–54, for it is known through the *De viris illustribus* attributed to **Henry of Ghent** that Guibert wrote a history of this crusade, *Hodoeporicon*. Furthermore, several sermons addressed *Ad crucesignatos* are extant. He was the author of a commentary on the *Sentences*, but this has disappeared. He collected excerpts from the Fathers and Seneca in *Pharetra* (edited 1866). Guibert's writings are effusive and wander from the main topic. A mystic, he often followed **Bonaventure** but was sometimes an original thinker.

Guicciardini, Francesco Historian and politician, born Florence, 6 March 1483, died Sancta Margherita a Montici, near Florence, 22 May 1540. He was involved in much political, papal and military activity in Italy. He was a friend of **Machiavelli**. His political aphorisms were described as 'corruption codified and elevated to a rule of life'. He was appointed successively Florentine ambassador to Aragon, papal governor of Modena and Reggio, and governor of Romagna under Pope **Clement VII**. Guicciardini was instrumental in the creation of the League of Cognac. He became papal lieutenant general, worked for the restoration of the Medicis and became governor of Bologna. His *Storia d'Italia* was the most important contemporary history of Italy in the sixteenth century.

Guidi, Ignazio Scholar of oriental Christian texts, born Rome, 31 July 1844, died Rome, 18 April 1935. He acquired a vast knowledge of oriental languages from clergy in Rome, and from 1876 to 1919 taught Hebrew and comparative Semitics at the University of Rome – adding to them, from 1885, Ethiopic languages and history. Although he never visited Ethopia he published a dictionary of Amharic, and many translations, and a survey, of its literature. His works gave rise to the *Corpus Scriptorum Ecclesiasticorum Orientalium*, and to the *Patrologia Orientalis*.

Guido III of Spoleto German emperor, 21 February 891–December 894. Of Frankish ancestry, he was duke of Spoleto and Camerino. He expanded his domain, encroaching on papal territory and conspiring with Byzantium against the Emperor **Charles III** the Fat. After competing unsuccessfully for the Frankish crown in 887, he was elected king of Italy after defeating Berengar, margrave of Friuli, at the Trebbia in 889. Pope **Stephen V** had no option but to give him the imperial crown. In 894

Guido resisted a combined assault from Berengar and Arnulf. He had his son **Lambert** recognized as his successor in 892.

Guido da Siena Pioneering Tuscan painter, born *c*.1220, fl. 1260s, place and date of death unknown. Influenced by Byzantine art and by the North Italian school of the Berlinghieris, his masterpiece is the altarpiece for S. Domenico in Siena, the *Madonna and Child Enthroned*, now in the Palazzo Pubblico. The work is signed and dated 1221, but was probably painted *c*.1280, the inscription being added in the early fourteenth century to commemorate 1221 as the date of St **Dominic**'s death. His other paintings include the reliquary shutters and the polyptych *Madonna and Child and Four Saints*, both in the Pinacoteca of Siena; further works hang in various galleries in Europe and the USA.

Guido de Baysio Canonist, born Reggio d'Emilia, died Avignon, 1313. He was a student in Bologna under the canonist Johannes de Anguissola and the professor of civil law Guido de Suzaria. In 1295 he received from **Boniface VIII** a canonry and precentorship in Chartres. A year later he was made archdeacon of Bologna. There he taught canon law and was installed as a professor. His main work was the *Apparatus ad Decretum*, called *Rosarium*. It is a canon law classic and remains indispensable for Guido's knowledge of older canonical writings. His aim was to append material from the decretists and earlier decretals not used in the *glossa ordinaria* on the *Decretum* of **Gratian**. His *Tractatus* was written at the time of the Council of Vienne. It defends Pope Boniface and deals with the question of the Templars.

Guido De Brès Protestant martyr and author of the Belgic Confession, born Mons, near Brussels, 1522, executed Valenciennes, 31 May 1567. A refugee in London in 1548 because of his support for the Reformation, including selling Bibles and preaching, from 1552 he developed an itinerant ministry based in Lille. He was forced to move to Frankfurt in 1556. A meeting with **Calvin** led him to Geneva, where he was ordained in 1558 before returning again to the Low Countries, to Tournai. There he married Cathérine Ramon. Caught in the Low Countries' revolt against Spain, from 1561 he was once more on the run. He was eventually captured, imprisoned and hanged. His 'Belgic Confession' (*Confession de foi des Églises Réformées*, Rouen, 1561) was translated and adopted by a number of synods, becoming after 1619 one of the major standards of the Dutch Reformed Church.

Guido Marramaldi Blessed, Dominican preacher and inquisitor, born Naples, Italy, mid-fourteenth century, died Naples, *c*.1391. He was born to a noble Neapolitan family. Guido entered the Dominican Order and studied philosophy and theology there. He gained a reputation as a public orator. His preaching inspired the inhabitants of Raguza to erect a Dominican convent. He later became an inquisitor. He was buried in the chapel of the Rosary in San Domenico. His burial place quite soon became the centre of a cult and he received the name of 'Blessed Guido', but his cult has never received official approbation.

Guido of Anderlecht Confessor and saint (known in Flemish as St Wye), died Anderlecht, 12 September 1012. Apparently the son of Brabant parents, he became a sexton in the church of Our Lady in Laeken near Brussels. After a period as a merchant, he sought to atone by undertaking a seven-year pilgrimage to Rome and Jerusalem. Thereafter he spent the brief remainder of his life in Anderlecht. Miracles attested near his tomb awakened veneration of him. Our only information comes from a dubiously reliable twelfth-century Life. Feast day 12 September.

Guido of Arezzo Pioneering musician, born near Paris, *c*.992, died perhaps Avellan, *c*.1050. He became a monk at St Maur des Fossés. He moved to a monastery at Pomposa, then went to Arezzo *c*.1034. There he perfected his system of musical notation (attracting the attention of Pope **John XIX**): he added two lines to the then-used red (F) and yellow (C) lines, and made use of the spaces in between, thus establishing rhythm as well as melodic interval. He wrote several musical treatises, and his innovations shaped the course of Western music for centuries.

Guido of Cortona Blessed, Franciscan priest, born Cortona, *c*.1187, died Cortona, 12 June 1247. As a wealthy young man, he showed such impressive hospitality to St **Francis of Assisi** that he was invited to join the new Franciscan Order. He founded the hermitage of Le Celle near Cortona, and lived as an ascetical priest. He was renowned for a number of miracles. His cult was approved in 1583. Feast day 16 June.

Guido of Pomposa Abbot and saint, born Casamari, near Ravenna, *c*.1010, died Borgo San Domnino, near Parma, 31 March 1046. After living for a period as a hermit, he went to the abbey of Pomposa, where he soon became abbot, and turned it into one of the chief monasteries of northern Italy. **Peter Damian** was invited to lecture there *c*.1039–41. Invited to accompany **Henry III** to the Synod of Sutri in 1046, he took sick and died *en route*. Temporarily buried at Parma, in 1047 his remains were taken to Speyer in Germany. Feast day 4 May (translation), 31 March in Speyer.

Guido the Lombard Blessed, born probably Milan, late eleventh century, died *c*.1150. Two conflicting accounts exist of his life. He is associated with the establishment of the Humiliati, a guild of men and women who worked in the wool trade in Lombard cities and dedicated themselves to the evangelical life. Some legends picture him receiving the Order's Rule from **Bernard of Clairvaux**. The male branch of the Order was suppressed in 1571; a few female communities persist in Italy. Guido is revered by them and by the Church of Milan. Feast day 6 December.

Guigo I Carthusian leader and writer, born 1084, died Grande Chartreuse, 27 July 1136. Guigo became a Carthusian in at the abbey of La Grande-Chartreuse in 1106 and was elected prior three years later. He is best known for his *Consuetudines Cartusiae* (1121–7), a codification of Carthusian rules and customs from the earliest days which eventually became the Rule for the Order. He was respected and admired by **Bernard of Clairvaux** and **Peter the Venerable**. Aside from the *Consuetudines*, Guigo wrote a Life of St **Hugh of Grenoble** and a book of *Meditationes*, often called one of the greatest spiritual masterpieces of the twelfth century.

Guigo II Carthusian writer, died Grande Chartreuse, 1188. Guigo became prior of the abbey of La Grande-Chartreuse and general of the Carthusian Order in 1173, resigning from the latter office in 1180. He is best known for his *Scala Paradisi* (or *Scala Claustralium*, translated into Middle English as *A Ladder of Four Rungs*), which describes the way of spiritual perfection in four stages – reading, meditating, praying and contemplating – a formula later taken over by **John of the Cross**. Like his namesake, he also wrote a book of *Meditationes*.

Guigo de Ponte   Carthusian mystical writer, died 29 October 1297. He was prior of the charterhouse of Mont-Dieu from 1290. While he was a monk he wrote a still unedited treatise *De contemplatione*. He distinguished three main types of contemplation: natural, which arises from finding the Creator mirrored in His creation; scholastic, which is an acquired wisdom, an experimental knowledge that results from finding God in Scriptures; and divinely infused, which is truly mystical. Real mystical contemplation meant for him an 'overshadowing of the darkness in the chamber of heart'. It is evident that he relied on Pseudo-Dionysius.

Guilday, Peter   Educator, Church historian, born Chester, Pennsylvania, 25 March 1884, died Washington, DC, 31 July 1947. He was the second of twelve children of Irish parents. He had his schooling in Philadelphia, received a scholarship and studied theology in Louvain, Belgium, for two years. Guilday was ordained in 1909 and then did his graduate work in history at Louvain. In 1914 he received an invitation from the rector of the Catholic University of America, where he taught till his death. He was the editor of the *Catholic Historical Review* and in 1919 founded the American Catholic Historical Association. He worked out a programme for master's and doctor's degrees at the University. Through these means and his writings, he made his mark on the revival of American Catholic history. He wrote *An Introduction to Church History*, *A History of the Councils of Baltimore* and a study of *The English Catholic Refugees on the Continent, 1558–1795*, intended to be in two volumes, although only the first was completed (1914).

Guiney, Louise Imogen   Roman Catholic poet, editor, essayist, born Roxbury, Massachusetts, 7 January 1861, died Chipping Campden, England, 2 November 1920. She received her education in Elmhurst, Providence, at the convent of the Sacred Heart. Her father's death – he died of wounds received in the Battle of the Wilderness – left a deep imprint on her: the 'knight' symbol pervades much of her writings. Her first published poems were 'Songs at the Start' (1884) followed by *Goose Quill Papers* and *The White Sail*. She published *A Roadside Harp* in 1901, which she thought to be the best of her works. She was appointed as a postmistress in Auburndale, Massachusetts, but soon had to resign due to public resistance. She moved to England in 1901 and started undertaking research on forgotten and neglected authors. Her estimate of Henry **Vaughan** initiated a new revival of interest in him. With Geoffrey Bliss, SJ, she compiled *A Catholic Anthology from St Thomas More to Pope*.

Guiraud, Jean   French historian and journalist, born Quilan (Aude), 24 June 1866, died near Paris, 11 December 1953. (He should not be confused with his brother, the historian Paul Giraud, 1850–1907.) Guiraud, a very talented student, went to the École Normale Supérieure in 1885. In Rome he was a member of the École Française and specialized in medieval religious history. In 1898 he was offered a professorship of medieval history. He did decisive work on the Albigensian heresy. He strongly opposed the separation of State and Church in France in 1905. Twelve years later he quit his university career and acted as the director of *La Croix*, a prominent Catholic newspaper in Paris. In his later years he started to write a history of the medieval Inquisition which he never completed, though he produced two valuable volumes, *Histoire de l'Inquisition au Moyen-Âge*.

Guise, Charles de Lorraine de   Cardinal, born Joinville, 17 February 1524, died Avignon, 26 December 1574. A member of the illustrious House of Lorraine, he became archbishop of Rheims in 1538 and first cardinal of Guise (later of Lorraine) in 1547. He attempted to bring the Inquisition to France, and prosecuted a strong policy of intolerance towards doctrinal dissenters. He defended Catholic views against Theodore **Beza** at the Colloquy of Poissy (1561), and defended Gallicanism at the Council of Trent (1562–3), calling for Church reforms and denouncing Pope

Pius IV. He attempted (unsuccessfully) to have Trent's decrees proclaimed throughout France. He had varying relations with French kings, having crowned Henry II, Francis II and Charles IX. A patron of such literary figures as **Rabelais** and **Ronsard**, he was a generous benefactor of the University of Rheims. His literary legacy consisted largely of letters and sermons.

Guitmond of Aversa Theologian, born Normandy (France), early 1000s, died Aversa, Italy, *c.*1090–95. Guitmond became a Benedictine at La Croix-Saint-Leufroy, then moved to the abbey of Bec to study under **Lanfranc**, and was finally appointed bishop of Aversa by Pope **Urban II** in 1088. Guitmond is best known for his theological opinions on the Eucharist, found in his work *De corporis et sanguinis Domini veritate*, which was an argument against **Berengarius**' denial of the Real Presence. Guitmond was an early proponent of a doctrine much like transubstantiation and was the first to talk about the 'accidents' of the bread and wine.

Guizar Valencia, Rafael *see* **Guajázar**.

Guizot, François-Pierre-Guillaume Huguenot historian and politician, born Nîmes, France, 4 October 1787, died Val-Richer, 12 October 1874. He was brought up in Geneva and became professor of history at the Sorbonne, Paris. He favoured constitutional monarchy, and was successively appointed a deputy, minister of the interior, then education minister. His Guizot Law of 1833 established that secular primary education should be available to all. Later he became ambassador to England, foreign minister and then premier of France, but he was forced to resign in the 1848 revolution. He wrote books on the history of France.

Gumbert of Ansbach Abbot, bishop and saint, born Ansbach, died there perhaps *c.*790. Details of his life are obscure: later legend describes him as a great lord who renounced the world and bestowed his wealth on the Church. Before 748, on family lands at Ansbach, he founded St Mary's Abbey; in 786, on the guarantees of immunity and free election of abbots, he handed it over to **Charlemagne**, who *c.*800 gave it to Bernwelf of Würz-

burg. Known as St Gumbert Abbey by the early tenth century, it moved to St Stefan in Würzburg. The community was suppressed in 1563. The cult of Gumbert is still active in Vilchband. Feast day 15 July (11 March until the tenth century).

Gummar Hermit and saint, born Embleheim, died Nivesdonck, *c.*775. From a distinguished Brabant household, he became a courtier of **Pepin III**. On the king's recommendation, he married Guinimaria; the marriage was not a success, and after eight years he obtained a separation from her. Thereafter he lived as a recluse, and along with St Rumold founded the abbey of Lierre in Flanders, whose patron saint he became. He was one of the most celebrated miracle-workers of the Low Countries. Feast day 11 October.

Gundecar Blessed, bishop, born probably near Eichstätt, Germany, 10 August 1019, died Eichstätt, 2 August 1075. Educated at the Eichstätt cathedral school, Gundecar was a canon there and then chaplain to Empress Agnes *c.*1045 before Emperor **Henry IV** named him bishop of Eichstätt in 1057. He was completely devoted to his diocese, building a cathedral, dedicating more than 100 churches and preparing the so-called *Gundecarianum*, a ritual and liturgical manual used in the education of his priests. His cult spread in consequence of reported miracles at his grave and translation of his relics in 1309. Feast day 2 August.

Gundlach, Gustav German Jesuit and social theorist born Geisenheim (Rheingau), 3 April 1892, died Mönchengladbach, 23 June 1963. He joined the Jesuits in 1912, was ordained in 1923, undertook graduate studies at Berlin and became professor at the seminary of Sankt-Georgen in Frankfurt am Main. In the 1930s, with the rise of the National Socialists, he went to teach at the Gregorian University, Rome. He became director of the Catholic Social Sciences Centre at Mönchengladbach just before his death. His economic and social ideas were those of the solidarism school of Heinrich Pesch, based on natural-law theory and on neo-Scholastic thinking. Gundlach has been a major influence on Catholic social thought and is credited with having introduced the term 'subsidiarity' into social and political parlance. He contributed widely to learned journals and a two-volume collection of his work, *Die Ordnung der menschlichen Gesellschaft* appeared after his death (1964–5).

Gundulić, Ivan (Giovanni Gondola) Croatian poet and dramatist, born Dubrovnik, Republic of Venice, 8 January 1589, died there, 8 December 1638. His epic poem *Osman*, written in 1626, was a great Renaissance achievement. It describes Sultan Osman II's defeat by the Poles in Bessarabia.

Gunkel, Hermann Protestant theologian and OT scholar, born Springe, near Hanover, 23 May 1862, died Halle, 11 March 1932. He held teaching appointments at Göttingen, Halle and Berlin, becoming professor of OT theology at Halle in 1920. A prominent member of the history of religions school, he sought to trace the origins of Hebrew ideas in Babylonian and Egyptian myths; he also pioneered the application of structural form criticism to Genesis, the NT and the Psalms, arguing that oral traditions lay behind the scriptural poetry. He left a number of influential monographs and commentaries on these themes.

Guntbert of Saint-Bertin Monk, born Cormont, *c.*810, died after 868. He was the son of a rich landowner, who during a memorable trip to Rome dedicated his son to St Peter. In accordance with his father's will Guntbert entered the monastic school of Saint-Bertin as a resident student. Together with his father, he donated gifts to the monastery of Sithiu and the collegiate church of Sainte-Maire. Though the two separated after 820, they remained on good terms. Guntbert as a diligent student copied and illuminated antiphonaries for Saint-Marie and the abbeys of Bergues-Saint-Winnoc and Saint-Bertin; he is known for founding a famous scriptorium at Saint-Bertin. After being named provost, he was ordained in 844. His relations with the abbey deteriorated, however, and in 868, old and ill, he left for Rome to petition the Pope for justice. There is no further record of his life.

Günther, Anton Roman Catholic priest and philosopher, born Lindenau, near Leitmeritz, Bohemia, 17 November 1783, died Vienna, 24 February 1863. At Prague he studied philosophy and jurisprudence, then became tutor to the household of Prince Bretzenheim at Brunn, near Vienna. He studied theology at Vienna, then at Raab, Hungary, where he was ordained priest. He lived privately in Vienna and attracted a theological following, contributing to the Viennese *Literary Chronicle* and writing books in which he expounded his individual system of philosophy and speculative theology. His speculative system initiated a far-reaching movement and he had many followers. He received honorary degrees from the Universities of Munich and Prague. However, in Rome, the Congregation of the Index began investigating his writings in 1852. In 1857 they were placed on the Index. This was a bitter blow and he wrote nothing thereafter. After the First Vatican Council most Güntherians joined the Old Catholic movements.

Günther of Niederaltaich Saint, monk, born probably 955, died Hartmanice, Bohemia, 9 October 1045. Of a noble Thuringian family, Günther led a rather pagan youth until the spiritual direction of Godard of Hildesheim helped him reform his life. He became a Benedictine in Rome and later moved to Niederaltaich, Germany. He turned down the offer to become an abbot in order to found a hermitage in the Bavarian forest. His hermitage helped open the trade route between Bohemia and Passau and was the goal of many pilgrims. He was the spiritual adviser to emperors, founder of monasteries and political mediator. He is also the patron of the abbey of Brevnov (Czech Republic), where his tomb was located until its destruction in 1420.

Günther of Pairis Cistercian writer, died at the abbey of Pairis, Alsace, *c.*1220. He was a minor literary figure of the late twelfth and early thirteenth centuries. It is likely that he came from the Basel region. Before entering the monastery he lived at the court of **Frederick I Barbarossa**, where he taught Conrad, the emperor's eldest son. His earliest work, the *Solimarius*, written *c.*1180 and dedicated to Conrad, is a verse narrative of the First Crusade. It is often said to be in large part a poetical version of the *Historia Hierosolymitana* of **Robert of Rheims**. He produced another piece of work on the Fourth Crusade, which purports to give an eyewitness account of the expedition, as recounted by a certain Abbot Martin. The authenticity of this was called into question by many until two scholars, G. Paris and A. Pannenberg, working independently of each other, recently established the claim that his works are authentic.

Gunthildis   It is possible that three saints bore the same name: (a) an Anglo-Saxon nun from Wimborne, England, a follower of **Lioba** who became an abbess in Thuringia; (b) an abbess whom Gundecar II, bishop of Eichstätt, lists in his Pontifical; he transferred her remains from Suffersheim to his cathedral, where she was honoured among the twelve founders of Eichstätt; (c) a maidservant, venerated at the abbey of Plankstetten in the Diocese of Eichstätt, though buried at Suffersheim.

Gurian, Waldemar   Political scientist, historian and publicist, born St Petersburg, Russia, 13 February 1902, died South Bend, Indiana, 26 May 1954. When his parents moved to Germany he converted from Judaism to Catholicism. Waldemar attended schools in The Netherlands and Germany and received his doctorate from Cologne. He was the editor of *Kölnische Volkszeitung*. He outlined his objectives in a memorable lecture 'The Catholic priest', and criticized the cultural and political nihilism of Nazism. In 1937 the University of Notre Dame appointed him to be the head of the political science department, where two years later he founded the *Review of Politics*. He was recognized in the United States as an excellent interpreter of Soviet affairs. He wrote numerous articles as well as his well-known work *Bolshevism: Theory and Practice*.

Gury, Jean Pierre   Jesuit moral theologian, born Mailleroncourt, Haute-Saône, 23 January 1801, died Mercoeur, Haute-Loire, 18 April 1866. In 1824 he entered the novitiate of the Society at Montrouge and four years later was sent to Rome to pursue further theological studies. When he returned he worked as a minister (bursar) and in 1834 was also invited to be the professor of moral theology at the scholasticate at Vals. He was appointed to teach at the Roman College, now the Gregorian University, but was forced to return to Vals when the revolution came in 1848. He published his first major work, *Compendium theologiae moralis*, in 1850. Gury's aim was to apply moral principles to contemporary issues. His reasoning was of a very high standard and he was brilliant in

carefully detailing the issues with which he dealt. Gury's other work on moral theology, *Causus conscientiae in praecipuas quaestiones theologiae moralis*, became such a great success that it bore a considerable influence on the topic well into the twentieth century.

Guthlac   Hermit and saint, born England, c.674, died Crowland, Lincs, 11 April 714. Related to the royal house of Mercia, he became a monk at Repton, then c.699 moved to an island in the Fens near the site of the subsequent Crowland Abbey, which was founded in his honour by King Ethelbald in 716. He lived a life of extreme asceticism. His life is depicted on the late twelfth-century Guthlac Roll, now in the British Library. His cult was particularly strong in the English Midlands in the Middle Ages. Feast day 11 (in some calendars 12) April.

Guthrie, Donald   NT scholar, born Ipswich, England, 21 February 1916, died Northwood, England, 8 September 1992. Guthrie's academic potential was spotted while he was still a student at the London Bible College, and he was invited to join its faculty before he had even graduated. He spent his entire career at the college as a NT lecturer (overcoming acute shyness and a bad stammer), and through his writings gained a worldwide reputation as a biblical scholar. As an Evangelical, Guthrie's theological position was unfashionable in academic circles, but his courteous and irenic approach, allied to sound and persuasive scholarship, won him widespread respect. Along with F. F. **Bruce**, Guthrie played a large part in rehabilitating the academic credibility of Evangelical scholarship in the latter half of the twentieth century.

Gutiérrez de Padilla, Juan   Composer, born probably Andalusia, c.1593, died Puebla, Mexico, April 1664. After appointments in the collegiate church of Jérez de la Frontera and Cádiz Cathedral, 1616, he was appointed to Puebla Cathedral in 1629 (consecrated in 1649), where he remained for the rest of his career, except for a brief suspension in 1634. An elegant baroque composer, his extant works include four double-choir Masses, a *St Matthew Passion*, a collection of motets and many Spanish *villancicos*.

Gutiérrez, Rodríguez Bartolomeo Blessed, Augustinian missionary and martyr, born Mexico City, c.1580, burnt alive, Nagasaki, Japan, 3 September 1632. He became an Augustinian friar in 1596, was ordained, and went to the Philippines in 1606 before going to Japan in 1612 and becoming prior of Ukusi. Temporarily exiled, 1614–18, he was seized in 1629, imprisoned for three years and tortured before being put to death along with six others. He was beatified in 1867. Feast day 28 September.

Guy *see also* **Guido**.

Guy de Montpellier Founder of the Order of the Holy Spirit, born Montpellier, died Rome, March 1208. Very little is known of his life. He founded a hospital and an Order of the Hospitallers of the Holy Spirit in Montpellier c.1180, a lay community recognized by **Innocent III** in 1198. Invited to Rome, he was placed in charge of the hospital of Sancta Maria in Saxia. His Order spread to several countries, assuming both lay and clerical members and taking on increasingly military associations, but its main purpose continued to be the care of the sick.

Guy of Bazoches French chronicler, born c.1146, died 1203. His family took its name from a holding in the neighbourhood of Soissons. Towards the end of the twelfth century he composed a biased chronicle of an expedition to the Holy Land. In the nineteenth century there were discovered other, hitherto unknown, works: *Liber historiarum*, *Libellus de mundi*, *Liber apologeticus* and so on. All these works had an overall title: *Liber Apologie Contra Maledicos vel Comographia* [sic], *id est excerpta vel Abbreviationes Diversarum Hystoriarum*, which was divided into eleven books. The first three of these deal with apologetics, the fourth is a study of the regions of the world, while the remaining seven form a history of the world from the Creation to the death of **Richard I** of England in 1199.

Guyon, Jeanne-Marie French Roman Catholic mystic, born Montargis, France, 13 April 1648, died Blois, 9 June 1717. She advocated extreme Quietism, in conflict with the Roman Catholic Church. Her influence, however, had an enormous impact on **Fénelon**, leading to a rupture with his close friend **Bossuet**. She wrote the *Short and Very Easy Method of Prayer*. She was arrested, but after the intervention of Madame de **Maintenon**, second wife of **Louis XIV**, was released. Quietism was condemned and she was again arrested, imprisoned in the castle of Vincennes, then in the Bastille, and was condemned by Pope **Innocent XII**. Finally she retired to Blois.

Guzmán y Lecaros, Joseph Javier Franciscan priest and the first historian of Chilean independence, born Santiago, 1759, died Santiago, 1840. He was a distinguished member of the Franciscan convent in that city. In 1782 he was appointed to be a teacher of sacred theology. He was influenced by Enlightenment ideas, and this inspired him to join the patriotic cause and fight against Spanish domination of Chile. His preaching was persuasive and influential during the time of the struggle for independence. He had a highly successful career both in the Church and as a writer. In 1833 the government appointed him to edit the first history of Chile. The merit of this was not so much in the historical research which went into it, but in the challenge posed by a pioneering task.

Gwyn, Richard Saint, Welsh schoolmaster and Roman Catholic martyr, born Llanidloes, Montgomeryshire, died Wrexham, 17 October 1584. He was educated at St John's College, Cambridge, and became a schoolmaster at Overton, Flintshire (Clwyd). He married, and had six children, three of whom survived infancy. He was eight times arraigned for recusancy, several times fined, tortured or placed in the stocks. The eighth time he was condemned to death. He was canonized by Pope **Paul VI** in 1970 as one of the **Forty Martyrs of England and Wales**.

H

Haas, Francis Joseph Roman Catholic bishop, educator and writer, born Racine, Wisconsin, 18 March 1899, died Grand Rapids, Michigan, 29 August 1953. Educated at St Francis Seminary, Milwaukee, he was ordained in 1913 and taught literature there, before completing a doctorate at the Catholic University of America. He taught sociology at Marquette University and edited the journal *Salesianum*. He was involved in numerous public bodies, including the League of Nations Association and the American Association for Social Security. Director of the National Catholic School of Social Service 1931–5, he taught at the Catholic University. He played a significant role in numerous labour relations and governmental agencies, and from 1935 to 1953 was on the conciliation board of the US Department of Labor. He became monsignor in 1937, and was consecrated bishop of Grand Rapids, Michigan, in 1943. His publications include *Shop Collective Bargaining* (1922) and *Man and Society* (1930).

Haberl, Franz Xaver German priest and music authority, born Oberellenbach, Bavaria, 12 April 1840, died Regensburg 5 September 1910. Ordained a priest at Passau, he went to study in Rome, and returned to Regensburg, where he founded a school of Church music. Best known for his edition of **Palestrina**'s music, **Pius IX** made him an honorary canon of Palestrina Cathedral. His works included many Church music collections, an edition of **Frescobaldi**'s organ works and a catalogue of the Sistine Choir manuscripts.

Habert, Isaac Bishop, controversialist and theologian, born Paris, *c.*1600, died Pont-de-Salars, near Rodez, 15 September 1688. During his early career he published books of poetry. He received his doctorate in theology from Sorbonne in 1626, was named a canon at Notre Dame Cathedral and was also a preacher of the royal court. He was very much an opponent of the new theological trend of Jansenism, which he compared with **Calvin**'s doctrine. He conducted a fierce polemic with Martin de Bacos, who promoted the idea that Peter and Paul shared authority over the Roman Church. Hence he issued his work *De Cathedra seu Primatu Singulari S. Petri*. He was appointed to Vabres as a bishop in 1645.

Hadalinus Saint, born Aquitaine, died Celles, *c.*690. Along with his teacher, St Remaclus, he spent a time as a recluse in the wilderness of Cougnon, and later lived in Remaclus' abbey at Stavenot. He founded the monastery of Celles, near Dinant-sur-Meuse, whose eleventh-century Romanesque church survives. In 1338 the monastery moved to Visé, where Hadalinus was patron; it was suppressed in 1797. He is invoked against children's ailments. Feast days 3 February and 11 October.

Hadeloga Saint, died Kitzingen, Upper Bavaria, *c.*750. According to a twelfth-century Life, she was the daughter of **Charles Martel**. To escape an arranged marriage, she fled and established a double monastery at Kitzingen, Franconia, allegedly under inspiration from St **Boniface**, *c.*745. She was subsequently reconciled with her father, who bestowed generous endowments on the monastery. She was esteemed for her care for the poor. The monastery was secularized in 1544. Feast days 2 February and 20 March.

Hadewych (Hadewig, Hedwig) Blessed, born c.1150, died 14 April c.1200. She was the daughter of **Hildegunde**. Together they founded the convent of Meer in 1165. This was a Premonstratensian convent near Brüderich in Prussia. She became prioress after her mother in 1183. She, her mother and her brother, the prior of the monastery at Kappenberg, are all counted among the blessed.

Hadoindus Bishop and saint, died 20 August c.653. Evidently of a noble family, he became bishop of Le Mans in c.623. He established the abbey at Evron, aided in the founding of the monastery of St Lonegisilus and attended the Councils of Clichy, c.627, and Rheims, 627–30. He inherited wealth from a rich patron named Alan, and bequeathed it to the church of Le Mans in 643. Buried in the church of Saint-Victor; his cult was already evident by the ninth century, when his relics were exhumed and placed in the cathedral church of Le Mans. Feast day 20 January (in Le Mans diocese, 20 August).

Hadrian Popes *see* **Adrian**

Hadrian of Canterbury Saint, archbishop of Canterbury, born Africa, c.630, died Canterbury, 9 January 709. He twice declined Pope **Vitalian**'s offer of the archbishopric of Canterbury while serving as abbot of a monastery near Naples; on the third asking, he proposed the Greek monk **Theodore** of Tarsus, and was asked to go with him to England as a guide and counsellor, along with **Benedict Biscop**. Arriving c.670, Hadrian became head of the abbey of SS Peter and Paul (later St Augustine's), where he presided over a regime of remarkable scholarly industry. Along with Theodore, he did much to organize the pastoral affairs of the English Church as a stable provincial body. He is buried in the church of his monastery at Canterbury. Feast day 9 January.

Haffelin, Kasimir von German cardinal, diplomat, born Minfeld (Rhine Palatinate), 3 January 1737, died Rome, 27 August 1827. Soon after his ordination he obtained the position of court chaplain to Karl Theodor, prince-elector of the Palatinate,

with whom he moved to Munich in 1778. Five years later he became the vice-president of the Spiritual Council in Munich. In 1787 his career achieved its climax when he became a titular bishop, and in 1790 he received the title of baron with the accompanying prefix 'von'. He was the ambassador of Bavaria to the Holy See and to Naples. His religious-political view, embracing Gallicanism and Febronianism, changed after the fall of Montgelas in 1817 to a much more orthodox one. He played an important part in arranging the Bavarian concordat. He was made cardinal in 1818.

Hagerty, James Leo Educator, born San Francisco, California, 31 January 1899, died San Francisco, 11 September 1957. He received his basic education in his home city and graduated from St Mary's College, Oakland, California, in 1919. After graduation he was invited to teach there, where he stayed for 38 years. He became the chairman of the department of philosophy and the dean of the School of Arts and Letters. He was a great proponent of the 'World Classic Programme', which he made a basis for the liberal arts curriculum. He played an active role in cultural and religious life and was the editor as well as the co-founder of *Moraga Quarterly* and served as associate editor of *New Scholasticism*. He established the Western Branch of the American Catholic Philosophical Association and was the chairman of it. In 1936 he supported the establishment of the Catholic Action Programme in San Francisco.

Haid, Leo Michael Benedictine abbot and bishop, born near Latrobe, Pennsylvania, 15 July 1849, died Belmont, North Carolina, 24 July 1924. He was admitted in 1868 to the novitiate at St Vincent Abbey, Latrobe, and the following year he made his profession. After being ordained in 1872 he worked at St Vincent College, Latrobe, as a professor, secretary and chaplain. In 1885 he was elected to be first abbot of the monastery in Garibaldi, North Carolina, which had been founded as a priory in 1876. The next year he opened a seminary and started to set up a school, which was named St Mary's College. He exercised a great influence on the townsfolk and succeeded in persuading them to change the name of the town from Garibaldi to Belmont. Thus the abbey was renamed too. In 1887 Haid was appointed vicar apostolic of North Carolina as titular bishop of Messene.

Haidt, John Valentine *see* **Haydt**

Haimo *see also* **Haymo**

Haimo of Auxerre Monk and exegete, died Auxerre(?), *c*.855. Having apparently studied with Murethach, an Irish grammarian, he became a monk of St Germain of Auxerre, and went on to teach **Heiric of Auxerre**. At some point he seems to have served as abbot of Sasceium. He wrote a large body of biblical commentaries, homilies, glosses and other didactic texts, which were widely used in the Middle Ages and which form an important historical source. Some of his works were published under the name of Bishop **Haymo of Halberstadt** (died 853).

Haimo of Landecop Blessed, Cistercian monk, born Landecop, Brittany (France), date unknown, died abbey of Savigny, France, 30 April 1173. Haimo was a member of the abbey of Savigny for all his spiritual career. During his life, he was known for his great piety and his spiritual visions. His life resisted the politics of his area, both serving Henry II of England as friend and confessor and giving spiritual advice to **Louis VII** of France. His renown also brought his monastery many gifts. Many miracles were attributed to his intercession after his death, and the annals of Savigny record many of his visions.

Hainmar of Auxerre Bishop, martyr and saint. Little is known of his life, but he served as bishop of Auxerre *c*.717–31, apparently without ever being formally consecrated. Perhaps more active as a military commander than as a churchman, he led two of **Charles Martel**'s expeditions against Aquitaine. He subsequently quarrelled with the king and was imprisoned in Bastogne (Luxemburg); he escaped, but was captured near Toul and executed. Feast day 28 October.

Hales, Stephen English clergyman, botanist and physiologist, born Bekesbourne, Kent, 17 September 1677, died Teddington, near London, 4 January 1761. At Cambridge he studied divinity, science, botany and chemistry, was ordained and held a parish post at Teddington. Among other things he was the first to measure blood pressure and heart capacity. In London his ventilator inventions were applied to St George's Hospital and to two prisons. John **Wesley** wrote of him: 'How well did science and religion agree in this man of sound understanding.' Hales was a founder member of the Society of Arts.

Halifax, Charles Lindley Wood Second Viscount Halifax, High Church Anglican, president of the English Church Union, born London, 7 June 1839, died Hickleton, 19 January 1934. Studied at Eton and at Christ Church, Oxford. He helped establish the Society of St John the Evangelist (Cowley Fathers) in 1865 and considered joining. From 1868 until 1919, and from 1927 until his death, he was president of the English Church Union and was involved in most of the controversies in the Anglican Church at that period. A chance meeting with the Abbé **Portal** on Madeira in 1890 led to a particular interest in the reunion of the Roman Catholic and Anglican Communions, leading to discussions which came to an end with the publication of the bull *Apostolicae Curae*, condemning Anglican Orders as invalid. In the 1920s he reopened the question with Cardinal **Mercier** of Malines, giving rise to the Malines Conversations, the report of which, after they, too, had failed, he published in 1928.

Halinard of Lyons Abbot, archbishop and reformer, born Burgundy, France, died Rome, 29 July 1052. Halinard came from a noble house, was educated at Langres and entered the Benedictine Order at St Bénigne, becoming abbot there in 1031. In 1046 he was consecrated archbishop of Lyons. He was an ardent promoter of the Cluniac monastic reform and assisted Pope **Leo IX** with both ecclesial synods (in Rome and Rheims) and political diplomacy (in Germany, France and Italy). He was even proposed as Pope once himself. He was a man of education and piety, but there is no tradition of his cult.

Hall, Ronald Owen Anglican bishop of Hong Kong, born Newcastle, England, 22 July 1895, died Oxford, 22 April 1975. He survived World War I, was awarded the Military Cross, studied at Brasenose College, Oxford, and Cuddesdon and became active in the Student Christian Movement. He was ordained priest in 1921 and attended the World Student Christian Federation conference in Peking (Beijing) in 1922, where he formed close friendships with Chinese Christian leaders. He married that year and was in parish ministry in Newcastle, 1926–32, before being appointed bishop of Hong Kong, 1932–66. He initiated social welfare projects and was sympathetic to the Chinese revolution. His *Art of the Missionary* (1940) became a classic. He spent the war in China and was the first bishop to ordain a woman, Li Tim-oi, to the Anglican priesthood. In post-war Hong Kong he energetically built schools and churches. He retired in 1966.

Hallahan, Margaret Mary Foundress of the English congregation of St Catherine of Siena of the Third Order of St Dominic, born London, 23 January 1803, died Stone, Staffordshire, 11 May 1868. She came from a very poor Irish family and had only two years of elementary education at an orphanage at Somers Town in London. She then began 30 years of service as a maid and nurse. She lived in Bruges, Belgium, and became a Dominican tertiary in 1837. In 1842 she returned to England, and in 1844 founded a small community of Third Order Dominicans in Coventry. Bishop **Ullathorne**, then vicar apostolic but afterwards bishop of Birmingham, gave encouragement. Other foundations were made but in 1853 the whole community there was transferred to St Dominic's at Stone, which became the motherhouse of the congregation. Mother Hallahan's devoted Christian life and indefatigable energy as well as excellent administrative skills led her to set up five convents, several schools and orphanages, four churches and a hospital for incurables. Her cause for beatification was introduced in 1936.

Haller, Johannes Roman Catholic historian, born Keinis, Estonia, 16 October 1865, died Tübingen, 24 December 1947. Educated in Dorpat, Berlin and Heidelberg, he held teaching posts in Rome, Marburg and Giessen, before becoming a professor at Tübingen in 1913, where he taught until his death. He wrote a five-volume *Concilium Basiliense*, but he is famed above all for his massive three-volume history of the Papacy, *Das Papsttum,*

Idee und Wirklichkeit (1934–45; second edition in five volumes, 1950–3). He also published a considerable amount on German history, in particular exploring the influence of papal decretals on medieval Germany.

Haller, Karl Ludwig von Roman Catholic jurist, born Berne, 1 August 1768, died Solothurn, 20 May 1854. From an old patrician family, he entered Swiss government service aged fifteen and travelled as a legate. From 1801 to 1806 he was secretary of the council of war in Vienna; recalled to Berne, he became professor of political law, a member of the great council and a privy councillor. In 1821 he was dismissed, following his profession of Catholic faith. After a spell in Paris, he went to Solothurn, and was elected to the great council. He wrote extensively, being most famous for his six–volume work on political theory, *Restauration der Staatswissenschaften* (1816–25), in defence of a natural-law theory of leadership by a propertied class.

Haller, Leonhard Roman Catholic theologian and bishop, born Denkendorf, Germany, early sixteenth century, died Eichstätt, 23 March 1570. He became involved in pastoral ministry in Munich in 1533. Some time after, he moved to Eichstätt, where he achieved recognition as a preacher and served in several posts. He was appointed auxiliary bishop to Moritz von **Hutten**, bishop of Eichstätt, in 1540. He also served as a vicar general of the diocese under Bishop Martin von Schaumberg. For a short period he was the representative of the bishop at the Council of Trent at a time when the Council was considering the possibility of acceding to the demands of **Luther** to the extent of allowing reception of Communion under both species.

Haller, Michael Roman Catholic priest, composer and teacher, born Neusaat (Upper Palatine), Germany, 13 January 1840, died Regensburg, 14 January 1915. He studied at the Benedictine monastery at Metten, after which he attended the seminary at Regensburg, where he was ordained in 1864. He worked at Regensburg Cathedral and was engaged in the revival of Renaissance polyphony. He was the music director of the 'Old Chapel' in Regensburg and a composition teacher at the music school. He took a lead in the German

Caecilian Society and gained a reputation as an interpreter of Renaissance vocal works. His works include fourteen Masses, as well as many other sacred settings, and chamber music. He restored the missing parts of some of **Palestrina**'s works and edited 27 motets of **Marenzio**.

Hallerstein, Augustin von Jesuit missionary to China and scientist, born Ljubljana (Slovenia), 27 August 1703, died Peking (Beijing), 29 October 1774. He studied theology in Austria, after which he embarked for China from Lisbon in 1736. His reputation as a mathematician had already preceded him to the Chinese court. The young Emperor Chi'en Lung became so interested in him that he was appointed to the Bureau of Astronomy and Mathematics in 1739. Seven years later he secured the position of president, the last Jesuit to hold this post. For more than 30 years he was engaged in the astronomical observations and computations particularly esteemed by the Chinese because they were essential for their yearly cycle of holidays and feasts. Because of his scientific work he gained toleration for the promotion of Christianity. Hallerstein was elected to be a foreign associate of the Royal Society of London.

Hallinan, Paul Roman Catholic archbishop, born Painesville, Ohio, 8 April 1911, died Atlanta, Georgia, 27 March 1968. Educated at the University of Notre Dame and St Mary's Seminary, Cleveland, he was ordained in 1937. He served as a military chaplain in World War II, then as a chaplain at Western Reserve University, Cleveland (where he also completed a doctorate in philosophy), before being appointed bishop of Charleston, South Carolina, in 1958. In 1962 he was consecrated first archbishop of Atlanta. He was a well-respected leader, ecumenist and popular expositor of Catholic teaching.

Hallum, Robert Bishop, born Warrington, Lancashire, sometime during 1361–70, died Gottlieben Castle, near Constance, 4 September 1417. An Oxford graduate, he received his doctorate in canon law in 1403, then becoming chancellor of the university. He was made bishop of Salisbury by **Gregory XII** in 1407. He attended the Council of Pisa in 1409. When the Antipope **John XXIII** wanted to create him cardinal, he declined because

of Henry IV's objections. Hallum was the chief representative of the English nation at the Council of Constance, where he worked closely with Emperor Sigismund to guard the unity of the Church. He played a key role by achieving, through his personal influence, the suspension of **John XXIII**. He was also a member of the committee which investigated charges brought against the Antipope **Benedict XIII**. His burial place is Constance Cathedral.

Hallvard Vebjörnsson Saint, patron saint of Oslo, place and date of birth unknown, died near Drammen, Norway, 1043. The only information about Hallvard's life comes from legends. According to them, he was a relative of **Olaf II** and died while defending a lady who had been wrongly accused of stealing. His cult is mainly confined to Norway, Iceland and parts of Sweden, and he is usually pictured in Swedish and Norwegian iconography with a millstone. Feast day 15 May.

Hamann, Johann Georg German Protestant thinker, born Königsberg, Prussia, 27 August 1730, died Munich, 21 June 1788. He was largely self-educated, and worked at Riga and Courland. Though a friend of **Kant**, Hamann was impatient with rationalistic abstractions and Kant's systematic idealism. Viewing truth as a necessary unity of reason, faith and experience, he attempted to reconcile philosophy and Christianity. In the twentieth century, his writings were edited in six volumes. He was known as the 'Magus of the North', and was a prophet of the *Sturm und Drang* movement.

Hamer, Fannie Lou Black American civil rights activist, born Mississippi, 1917, died 14 March 1977. An enslaved share cropper, in 1962 she heard a call for blacks to register as voters. She did so, she and her family were evicted, and from then on she worked for the civil rights movement. Arrested in 1963, she suffered permanently as a result of her mistreatment in prison. In 1964, she became nationally known when she attended the Democratic Party National Convention to challenge – unsuccessfully – the legitimacy of the all-white official Mississippi delegation. Her actions were rooted in her conviction that 'Christ was a revolutionary person'.

Hamilton, Patrick Scottish Protestant martyr, born 1504, died St Andrews, 29 February 1528. The son of Sir Patrick Hamilton of Kincavel, Linlithgow, as a boy he was made titular abbot of Ferne in 1517; he studied at Paris and St Andrews. Influenced by Martin **Luther**'s writings in the mid-1520s, he visited Wittenberg and Marburg, where he wrote a set of *Loci Communes* (*Patrick's Places*), and made contacts with Luther and **Melanchthon**. He returned to Scotland in 1527, where he managed to convert Alexander Alesius, who had been elected to confute his views. Charged with heresy by Archbishop **Beaton** in early 1528, he was burnt at the stake.

Handel, George Frideric Composer, born Halle, Germany, 23 April 1685, died London, 14 April 1759. His father was court surgeon at Halle, and intended his son to study law, even banning all musical instruments in his house. He relented, however, under pressure from the duke, who noticed George's interest in music, and allowed him to study under the local organist. In 1696 he went to Berlin, to the court of the Elector of Brandenburg, where he was much fêted, and on his return to Halle entered the university, possibly in deference to his (by now late) father's wishes. In 1703, however, he went to Hamburg until 1706, then visited Italy, where he was well received. In 1710 he came to London. That same year he was appointed to the court of the elector of Hanover as kapellmeister, but fell out with him because of his frequent absences. When the elector became George I of England friends achieved a reconciliation by arranging for a specially composed piece by Handel, the *Water Music*, to be played as the king's barge went down the Thames. Handel took on British nationality so successfully that his music, often Christian or British patriotic in associations or spirit, is regarded as typically British. In later years he turned to writing oratorios. His oratorio *Messiah*, with its Hallelujah Chorus, has remained popular. His setting of *Zadok the Priest* is performed at coronations.

Haneberg, Daniel Bonifatius Orientalist, biblical scholar, Benedictine abbot and bishop, born Lenzfried, near Kempten, Bavaria, 16 June 1816, died Speyer, Rhine Palatine, 31 May 1876. He attended the University of Munich, where he was profoundly influenced by J. J. I. von **Döllinger**. He was ordained in 1839. While at university he specialized in Semitic languages. From 1842 he taught OT and oriental studies at the university, but in 1850 he entered St Boniface Abbey at Munich. Four years later he was elected its abbot. He first opposed the papal claim for infallibility then accepted it. He declined three offers to be bishop of Trier, Cologne and Eichstätt, finally agreeing to be consecrated bishop of Speyer. He is most well known for his theory, which Vatican Council I condemned, that it is the subsequent approbation of the Church which constitutes the inspired nature of the books of the Bible. He later repudiated this belief. His most significant works are *Die religiösen Altertümer der Bibel* and *Geschichte der biblischen Offenarung*.

Hanna, Edward Joseph Roman Catholic archbishop, born Rochester, New York, 21 July 1860, died Rome, 10 July 1944. Educated in Rome, Munich and Cambridge, he was ordained in Rome in 1885. After holding teaching positions in Rome, 1886–7, and in seminaries in Rochester, 1887–1912, he was appointed titular bishop of Titiopolis and auxiliary of San Francisco in 1912, and became archbishop of San Francisco in 1915. From 1919 to 1935 he was chairman of the National Catholic Welfare Conference Committee; in the 1930s he also worked in arbitration and in the promotion of Christian–Jewish relations. He resigned his see in 1935 and became titular archbishop of Gortyna.

Hannibaldus de Hannibaldis Dominician theologian and cardinal, born Rome, died Orvieto, 1272. He joined the Dominican Order at Santa Sabina, Rome, then studied theology under St **Thomas Aquinas** in Paris. He was the successor of Aquinas in the chair for foreign Dominicans. He wrote a commentary on the *Sentences*, formerly attributed to Aquinas. This work is one of the best and earliest examples of Thomism. When he returned to his native land, Italy, he was named cardinal-priest by Pope **Urban IV** in 1262. Three years later he was legate of **Clement IV** in supporting the claims of **Charles of Anjou**. Soon after the death of Urban IV, Aquinas dedicated the last three books of the *Catena aurea* (1265–8) to his former disciple.

Hanno   *see* **Anno of Cologne**

Hansiz, Markus   Austrian Jesuit historian, born Völkermart in Carinthia, 25 April 1683, died Vienna, 5 September 1766. At the age of fifteen he entered the Society of Jesus and was ordained in 1708. He then taught in Vienna and at Graz. He began his historical work in 1717 on the *Germania sacra*. Though he spent a lifetime on the work, it has never been completed. He did, however, undertake detailed research and confronted difficult controversies about the evaluation of evidence relating to local traditions, the historicity of many of which he challenged. Much of his material remained unpublished. He produced three volumes, of which the first deals with the history of Lorch and Passau, the second with Salzburg, and the third tries to survey the early history of Regensburg.

Hanthaler, Chrysostomus (Johannes Adam)   Cistercian historian, born Mehrnbach bei Ried, Austria, 14 January 1690, died Lilienfeld, 2 September 1754. He entered the Cistercian community of Lilienfeld in 1726 and thereafter studied in Vienna. There he became interested in genealogy, history and numismatics. Having finished his studies he returned home and became librarian at his abbey. He dedicated his life entirely to collecting and publishing historical documents. By his death his diligent work had produced 24 volumes in folio, just a few of which were published during his lifetime. Apart from this interest, his major work was the *Fasti Campililienses*, a thoroughly documented history of Austria from the beginnings to 1500. His patriotism and professional pride persuaded him to forge several alleged chronicles of early Austrian history.

Hanxleden, Johann Ernst   Jesuit missionary in India, born Osterkappeln, near Osnabrück, 1681, died Palur, India, 21 March 1732. He joined the Society of Jesus in 1699 and volunteered for the East India Mission. He left from Augsburg with two priests, neither of whom survived the voyage. Hanxleden was a brilliant linguist who knew Sanskrit, East Syrian and Malayalam. He was among the first Europeans, together with de **Nobili** and Heinrich **Roth**, to study Sanskrit, and he was one of the first to write a Sanskrit grammar. He also compiled two lexicons, one Sanskrit–Portuguese and another Malayalam–Portuguese. In addition he was an inspired poet and songwriter, composing many religious poems and songs in Malayalam. Most of his works which survived are in the Vatican Library and in the library of the University of Coimbra.

Hardey, Mary Aloysia   Mother, religious superior, born Piscataway, Maryland, 8 December 1809, died Paris, France, 17 June 1886. The descendant of a Maryland colonial Catholic family, she received her education at the convent of the Sacred Heart, Grand Coteau, Louisiana, and entered the novitiate there in 1825. She was professed in 1833 and only three years later she became the superior of the convent at St Michael's, Louisiana. She founded the first house of the missionary society of her Order in New York City. This convent on Houston Street later became Manhattanville College. She was superior there for 25 years and in 1844 she became the vicar of all houses of the society of the Eastern states and of Canada. In 1871 she was sent to Paris to represent the houses within the British Empire and in North America.

Hardouin, Jean   French Jesuit and scholar, born Quimper, Brittany, 22 December 1646, died Paris, 3 September 1729. The son of a bookseller, he joined the Society of Jesus in 1660. From 1683 to 1713 he taught, and was librarian, at the Jesuit Collège Louis-le-Grand at Paris. He was thought to have an unrivalled knowledge of Christian antiquity, and was invited by the assembly of the French clergy in 1685 to produce a collection of the decrees of the Church Councils, the *Conciliorum Collectio Regia Maxima: Acta Conciliorum* (12 vols, 1714–15), the distribution of which the French government held up for a decade because it seemed to contradict the Gallican 'liberties'. He also wrote for the Jesuit *Journal de Trévoux* on a great variety of topics, including numismatics. He was a vigorous polemicist, with some peculiar views – he argued, for instance, that **Arnauld**, **Descartes**, **Jansen** and others were atheists.

Hardt, Hermann von der   Lutheran Church historian, born Melle, Westphalia, 15 November 1660, died Helmstedt, 2 February 1746. He was a teacher at Jena and Leipzig, where the famous

German Pietist A. H. **Francke** founded with him a *Collegium philobiblicum*. In 1688 he became librarian and secretary to Duke Rudolf August von Braunschweig, through whose influence he obtained a professorship at Helmstedt, where he was responsible for teaching oriental languages and biblical studies. When he changed his religious convictions from Pietism to rationalism, his teaching posts were gradually withdrawn. He wrote on the Council of Constance and on **Luther** as well as on exegesis.

Harduwijn, Justus de Flemish poet and Catholic priest, born Ghent, 11 April 1582, died Oudegem, 21 June 1636. His interest in poetry was fostered by his father. He was educated at the Jesuit College of Ghent and took his law degree under Justus **Lipsius** in 1605. He was appointed to the vicarages of Oudegem and Mespelarein in 1607. The Pléiade strongly influenced his early poems and he mainly dealt with love themes. The ecclesiastical authorities denounced his early attempt as 'Venuswhining'. From 1614 he devoted his talents to furthering the Counter-Reformation. His themes touched upon devotion and repentance in *Goddelicke lof-sanghen* and ascetic contemplation is the theme in his *Goddelycke Wenschen* (1629), which was a free translation of *Pia desideria*. He translated and published the Counter-Reformation pamphlet of **Jansen**.

Harent, Etienne Jesuit theologian, born Gex, France, 25 December 1845, died Dole, 5 February 1927. He joined the Society of Jesus in 1864. He taught systematic theology at Meld in 1883, at Lyons in 1899, and, because of French anticlerical legislation, at Canterbury in 1901 and at Ore Place, Hastings, in 1906. He wrote several, highly successful theological treatises: *De vera religione*, *De fide*, *De ecclesia*, *De gratia* and *De ordine*, which were frequently republished. He is especially known for writing important monographs on hope, faith, belief and salvation of unbelievers for the *Dictionnaire de Théologie Catholique*. He also showed great interest in religious psychology and history, but is best remembered as a Scholastic theologian.

Häring, Bernhard German moral theologian, born Böttingen, 10 November 1911, died Gars am Inn, 3 July 1998. The eleventh child of twelve born to a peasant family, he attended the Redemptorist school at Gars am Inn, and in 1933 joined the noviceship of the Order, also at Gars. Though his first intention was to be a pastor or a missionary in Brazil, he developed an interest in moral theology, which his Order fostered. He was ordained in 1939, and during the war served as a medical orderly, including on the Russian front. After the war he studied at Tübingen, taking as his doctoral topic 'The holy and the good'. He returned to Gars to teach moral theology, but moved to the Order's faculty, the Alphonsianum, in Rome in 1949. He retired back to Gars in 1988. His two major works were *Das Gesetz Christi* (*The Law of Christ*; one volume in 1954, but three by 1961) and *Frei in Christus* (*Free and Faithful in Christ*; three volumes, 1974), but in all he wrote some 80 books and many articles. **John XXIII** wrote to him to thank him for *Das Gesetz Christi*, and Häring was much involved in the Second Vatican Council, but was an outspoken critic of **Paul VI**'s encyclical *Humanae vitae*, and of some of the writings of Pope John Paul II. His criticisms brought him into difficulties with the Congregation for the Doctrine of the Faith, a conflict which coincided with the onset of cancer. After his retirement he continued to uphold a non-legalistic moral theology, and was a prophetic voice in the Catholic Church, to which he always remained loyal.

Harlay, Achille Jurist, born 7 March 1536, died 21 October 1619. He succeeded his father as president of the Paris court, and was one of the most distinguished lawyers of his age. He was adviser to **Henry IV** and strongly supported the Gallican opposition to papal hegemony. He was also very much opposed to the Jesuits and after the assassination of Henry he publicly accused them of instigating the crime. He persuaded the royal court to condemn the books of Juan de Mariana and of Cardinal Robert **Bellarmine**. He had to resign from his office because of ill health. He wrote only one book, entitled *Coutume d'Orléans*, which was published in 1585.

Harlay, Achille Baron de Sancy, littérateur, bishop, born Paris, 1581, died Paris, 20 November 1646. At a young age he was given three abbeys and became a bishop of Lavour. He was an ambassador to the Turkish court, but resigned because of hostility towards him. He was loyal to **Richelieu** and Louis XIII and in appreciation of his loyalty the bishopric of Saint-Malo was bestowed on him. As Richelieu had intended, from that position he persecuted several bishops of Brittany. He had an excellent collection of ancient Hebrew Bibles, now exhibited at the Bibliothèque Nationale in Paris. He mastered oriental and modern languages and wrote poetry and political tracts. He was also the editor of Richelieu's *Mémoires.*

Harlay, François de Theologian, archbishop of Rouen, born Paris, 1586, died Château de Gallion, 22 March 1653. He was a very talented student of philosophy who at a very early age received the wealthy abbey of St-Victor. He was sympathetic to papal claims, an attitude which angered the Gallican bishops, especially his superiors. He became the archbishop of Rouen in 1616. His zealous reforms in social as well as religious areas caused fierce conflict with the Jesuits, which he resolved by establishing a theological school in the archiepiscopal palace. When, however, he was not created a cardinal he altered his stance, and directed his anger against the Pope in a pamphlet, *Ecclesiasticae historiae liber primus.*

Harlay-Chanvallon, François de Archbishop, nephew of François de **Harlay,** born 14 August 1625, died Conflans, 6 August 1696. After a remarkable academic career he moved into an ecclesiastical career as a prelate and courtier. He received the rich abbey of Jumièges from his uncle, then succeeded to the archbishopric in 1651. He was appointed to be the archbishop of Paris in 1671 and became a close adviser to **Louis XIV** on Church-related issues. He was as ambitious as his uncle and hoped to succeed **Mazarin** as Louis' first minister. In return for his service the king transformed the Archdiocese of Paris into a peerage, with the rank of duke. Chanvallon consecrated the secret marriage of Louis and Madame de **Maintenon.** He also participated in discussions over the rights of Huguenots, discussions which led to the revocation of the Edict of Nantes in 1685. He was as harsh and relentless an enemy of Jansenism as he was of Protestantism. He was shrewd and cunning, much criticized for his private life, as well as for his political and ecclesiastical conduct.

Harless, Gottlieb Christoph Adolph von Lutheran theologian, born Nuremberg, Germany, 21 November 1806, died Munich, 7 September 1879. Harless studied theology at Erlangen and Halle, where at first his theological outlook was influenced by the prevailing rationalism. Subsequently his views changed to a more classically Lutheran position, which he held for the rest of his life. During his career Harless held a number of both academic and ecclesiastical posts, and became Germany's most prominent representative of Lutheran orthodoxy during the mid-nineteenth century.

Harlez, Charles Joseph de Orientalist, born Liège, Belgium, 21 August 1832, died Louvain, 7 July 1889. Shortly after receiving his doctorate he felt a strong call to be a priest. He had a long teaching career, starting in 1858. From 1871 he was a professor at the University of Louvain, where his main research interest was in the religions of Asia, on which topic he wrote many articles and books. He was the first to produce a French translation of *Avest.* He was a recognized expert on the Chinese, and in particular on ancient Chinese religion. He was the editor of *Revue Catholique,* which under his editorship changed its name to *Le Museon.* Among his more important works are *Les origines du Zoroastrisme, Le Vedisme* and *Brahmanisme et Christianisme.*

Harmel, Léon Born La Neuville-lez-Wasigny, Ardennes, 17 January 1829, died Nice, 25 November 1915. He was the owner of a textile factory with a vision of forming a family of workers, thereby transforming his whole enterprise into a Christian corporation. His work was recognized by the early leaders of Catholic social action and blessed by **Pius IX:** he himself was strongly ultramontane and in 1887 he organized a pilgrimage of workers to Rome. **Leo XIII** and **Pius X** both supported his work. To make the social work of the Church better known Harmel set up Secretariats du Peuple, gave popular lectures and promoted Christian circles for social studies all over France. He was reluctant to join the Christian Democrat Party and had some reservations about his own role, believing that social work should be the task of priests. Léon Harmel was himself a Franciscan tertiary, with the result that French Catholic social action tended to have a Franciscan spirituality.

Harnack, Adolf von Lutheran Church historian and theologian, born 7 May 1851, Dorpat (Germany), died 10 June 1930, Heidelberg. After studies in Dorpat and Leipzig he became a professor in Leipzig, Giessen, Marburg and Berlin. In his research and teaching in the NT and the early Church he wanted to confront Christian faith with the historical-critical method. This resulted in many conflicts with the Lutheran Church. Of more than 1600 publications two in particular ought to be mentioned, *Lehrbuch der Dogmengeschichte* and *Mission und Ausbreitung des Christentums*. Harnack was in his time undoubtedly the leading figure of German Protestantism.

Harold, Francis Franciscan historian, born Limerick, Ireland, early seventeenth century, died Rome, 1685. His family was extensively involved in the Franciscans. His relatives included Luke **Wadding**, an uncle; Bonaventure Baron, a cousin; and Anthony, Thomas and Francis (junior) Harold, nephews. He was educated in Rome at St Isidore's College and was sent to Prague in 1642, then to Vienna and finally to Graz, whence he moved back to Rome in 1665 to be successor to Luke Wadding as chronicler of the Order. Though compared with his uncle he was a less talented historian, he collected a great deal of material – but published little of it.

Harold, William Vincent Dominican missionary, born Dublin, c.1785, died Dublin, 29 January 1856. He entered the Dominicans in Portugal, where he was ordained. After a spell back in Ireland, he emigrated to the United States. An eloquent and popular preacher, he was appointed co-pastor of St Mary's Cathedral, Philadelphia, and became vicar general. He became embroiled in a dispute with his bishop over the activities of his uncle, who had also come to the city; he was deposed and returned to Ireland in 1813. Reappointed in Philadelphia in 1821, he ended up in further trouble. Refusing a transfer to Cincinnati, he appealed (unsuccessfully) to the US government that he was being moved against his will. He was deprived of his clerical faculties and returned to Ireland. Reinstated there, he became provincial of his Order, 1840–4.

Harris, Howell The 'Welsh Boanerges', one of the founders of Calvinistic Methodism in Wales, born Talgarth, South Wales, 14 January 1714, died Trevecka, Breconshire, 21 July 1773. Worked as a schoolteacher at Llangorse and Llangasty. He underwent an evangelical conversion on Whit Sunday 1735. After a brief time at Oxford University he applied for ordination but was refused, owing to his alleged 'enthusiasm'. From 1736 he preached throughout Breconshire and Radnorshire. In 1737 he first met Daniel **Rowland** and began to itinerate with him. They parted company in 1751 because of doctrinal differences. In 1752 he founded the religious community at Trevecka.

Harris, William Educator and philosopher, born North Killingly, Connecticut, 10 September 1835, died Providence, Rhode Island, 5 November 1909. He entered Yale in 1854, where he espoused philosophical idealism. He left college and went to the Midwest as a teacher, becoming superintendent of St Louis, 1868–80. His St Louis system became a national high-school model, promoting scientific and manual subjects and encouraging the establishment of school libraries. With Susan E. Blow, he introduced the kindergarten system in 1873. He served as US Commissioner of Education 1889–1906. A prolific writer, he was the founder editor of the *Journal of Speculative Philosophy*; his major work was *Psychologic Foundations of Education* (1898), whose ideas were however soon outdated by the influence of John Dewey.

Harris, William Wadé Prophet and evangelist, born Half-Graway, Cape Palamas, Liberia, c.1860, died April 1929. He became a Methodist lay preacher and in 1888 married Rose Farr and joined the staff of the US Episcopal Mission. Tension with the bishop and collaboration in a failed pro-British plot led to dismissal and jail, 1909–10. An experience of the Angel Gabriel fired a vision of obedience to the Great Commission as a black Elijah. In the Ivory Coast Harris preached a radical rejection of fetishes and local spiritual powers and sent tens of thousands of converts crowding into Catholic and Protestant missions for instruction by bewildered missionaries. In the 1920s many of his converts were gathered into the Methodist Church despite differences over polygamy. The Église Harris was founded in 1931.

Harsányi, Lajos Hungarian poet and novelist, born Nagyimánd, 1883, died 1960. He received his education from the Benedictines, hence the importance of the liturgy to his literary work. He entered the seminary at Györ and was ordained in 1907. Harsányi's poetry is a literary reflection of his understanding of Catholic Church history; in it the whole world and every living being is seen as sanctified by the mysteries of faith.

Hart, Charles Aloysius Roman Catholic educator and philosopher, born Ottawa, Illinois, 6 September 1893, died Washington, DC, 29 January 1959. Educated in Illinois, at St Paul's Seminary, Minnesota, and the Catholic University of America (gaining his doctorate in philosophy in 1930), he was ordained in 1919. From 1921 he was on the faculty of the Catholic University, and from 1933 also taught philosophy at Notre Dame College, Baltimore. He founded the Catholic Evidence Guild of Washington, and was national secretary of the American Catholic Philosophical Association, 1930–59. He was made a domestic prelate by **Pius XII** in 1957. He wrote *The Thomistic Concept of Mental Faculty* (1930), *Metaphysics for the Many* (1957), and *Thomistic Physics* (1959), as well as many papers of a neo-Scholastic bent.

Hartmann, Anastasius Capuchin bishop, missionary to India, born Altwis, Lucern Canton, Switzerland, 20 February 1803, died Patna, Bihar, India, 24 April 1866. He entered the Capuchins at Baden, Germany, in 1821 and was ordained four years later. Hartmann taught theology and philosophy for a while before leaving for India as a missionary. He was appointed first vicar apostolic of Patna. He recruited missionaries to Patna and engaged in an extensive school-building programme. He was transferred to Bombay, but then returned to Rome as an adviser on India for the Vatican's Congregation of Propaganda. He promoted the establishment of Capuchins in the USA and from 1858 to 1860 was the director of the missions of his Order. He returned to Patna in 1860 as vicar apostolic. Hartmann wrote a Hindustani Catechism (1853) and two books on psychology. The cause for his beatification was introduced in 1906.

Hartmann of Brixen Blessed, abbot and bishop, born Polling, Germany, c.1090, died Brixen, Italy, 23 December 1164. Hartmann became an Augustinian at Saint Nicholas in Passau, Germany, and in 1122 was moved to Salzburg to take charge of the new Augustinian chapter there. From there he was called to lead communities in Herren Chiemsee in 1128 and Klosterneuburg in 1133. He was made bishop of Brixen in 1140/41 and soon founded an Augustinian priory near there, in Neustift. His saintly life allowed him to rise above politics, earning him the respect of both Pope **Alexander III** and **Frederick I Barbarossa**. His veneration has been allowed in Brixen since 1784. Feast day 23 December.

Hartwich of Salzburg Blessed, archbishop, born c.955, died Salzburg (Austria), 5 December 1023. Hartwich was the last scion of the noble Aribo-Sponheim family and served as archbishop of Salzburg from 991 until his death. His noted charity earned him grants and privileges from Holy Roman Emperors **Otto II** and **Henry II**. He is most known for his rennovation of the Salzburg cathedral school and the many monasteries around the city. His veneration dates back to the 1200. Feast day 14 June.

Harty, Jeremiah James Roman Catholic archbishop, born St Louis, Missouri, 5 November 1853, died Los Angeles, 29 October 1927. He studied in St Louis and at St Vincent's College, and was ordained in 1878. After parish posts in his native city, he was appointed archbishop of Manila in the Philippines. He arrived in 1904; the first provincial council of the Islands was convoked in 1907. He transferred to Omaha, Nebraska, in 1916.

Hartzheim, Joseph Jesuit priest, professor, author, born Cologne, 11 January 1694, died Cologne, 14 January 1772. He received his education from the fathers of the Society of Jesus, which he entered in 1712. He was a professor from 1724 to 1736 at Cologne, then resigned to be the regent of the Gymnasium of Ticoronaum in Cologne. His main writings are concerned with the natural sciences and with history. He was active in the modernization of educational methods and textbooks. He was one of the editors of a collection of Church Councils, the *Concilia Germaniae*.

Harvey, Nedellic Dominican theologian and philosopher, referred to as 'Doctor rarus', born Brittany, *c.*1250–60, died Narbonne, 7 August 1323. He entered the Order in 1276. The next record of him comes in 1301, when he is mentioned in a list of those who were present at the provincial chapter of Rouen. In the conflict between **Boniface VIII** and Philip the Fair he opposed the Pope and was loyal to the French king. In 1308 he was elected master general of the Dominicans. He worked extensively on the canonization of **Thomas Aquinas**. His literary output was enormous. He wrote *Quaestiones super sententias, Quaestiones disputatae* on theology and *Quaestiones de praedicamentis, De recognitione primi principi*. He was very familiar with Aquinas' writings, yet he occasionally adopted positions incompatible with Thomistic metaphysics. His own philosophy is more eclectic than Thomistic. However, a great merit is awarded to him for the canonization of Aquinas.

Hase, Karl August von German ecclesiastical historian, born 1800, died 1890. Taught at Tübingen and Leipzig and from 1830 to 1883 was professor at Jena. His writings include a *Life of Christ* (1829) and *Kirchengeschichte* (1834).

Hassard, John Rose Greene Journalist, critic, biographer, born New York, 4 September 1836, died there, 18 April 1888. His parents were Episcopalian, but he became Catholic in 1851. He served as a secretary to Archbishop John **Hughes** till the prelate's death, then wrote a biography in 1866 based on the archbishop's private letters. He was approached to compile articles for the *New American Encyclopedia* and became editor of the *New York Tribune*. He was also the first editor of the *Catholic World*. He became New York correspondent for the *London Daily News* and wrote many essays and reviews for the *Catholic World* and *American Catholic Quarterly Review*. He produced books of which the most significant is *History of the United States* (1878). It was widely used in Catholic schools as a textbook. His interest was wide enough even to write on Wagner, *Wagner at Bayreuth* (1877).

Hasse, Johann Adolph German Roman Catholic composer, born Bergedorf, near Hamburg, baptized 25 March 1699, died Venice, 16 December 1783. He studied in Italy with Porpora and Alessandro **Scarlatti**. He served the elector of Saxony and settled in Italy, where he was known as 'Il Sassone', the Saxon. He wrote over 60 operas in Italian and also composed Church music. His catalogue in this field alone is vast, comprising oratorios, Masses, Requiem Masses, Mass sections, offertories, Psalm settings, antiphons, hymns and motets.

Hassler, Hans Leo von German composer and organist, born Nuremberg, 26 October 1564, died Frankfurt am Main, 8 June 1612. He studied in Venice with Andrea **Gabrieli**. Returning to Germany, he worked at Augsburg, Nuremberg and Dresden. He wrote both Protestant and Catholic Church music. His tune 'Mein Gemüt ist mir Vervirret' was adapted by J. S. **Bach** as 'O Haupt voll Blut und Wundun' in the *St Matthew Passion*. Hassler's Church works include Masses, Psalm settings and a litany.

Hastings, James Editor of the *Expository Times* and *Encyclopaedia of Religion and Ethics*, born Huntly, Scotland, 26 March 1852, died Aberdeen, 15 October 1922. Educated at Aberdeen University and Free Church College, he was in Free Church and then United Free Church pastoral ministry in Kinneff, 1884–98, Dundee, 1898–1901, and St Cyrus, 1901–11, while managing to edit a prodigious succession of encyclopaedias as well as the *Expository Times*, which he founded in 1889. His work of supporting faith by publicizing the best scholarship of his day continued from his retirement to Aberdeen in 1911 until his death. His *Encyclopaedia of Religion and Ethics* (Edinburgh, 1908–26) has remained in print.

Hastings, Selina Countess of Huntingdon, early Methodist leader and founder of the Countess of Huntingdon's Connexion, born 24 August 1707, died London, 17 June 1791. The daughter of Washington Shirley, Earl Ferrers, she married the earl of Huntingdon in 1728, joined the Methodists in 1739 and, following her husband's death in 1746, gave herself to social and religious work, introducing the upper classes to Methodism, mainly by appointing Anglican priests as her private chaplains, one of whom was George **Whitefield**. Following Whitefield's death in 1748 she became trustee of his foundations in the USA, assumed the leadership of his followers, established a college to train ministers (the forerunner of Cheshunt) and registered her chapels as dissenting places of worship under the Toleration Act.

Hatto of Reichenau Bishop and abbot, born 763, died Reichenau, 17 March 836. The founder of Reichenau's monastic school, he served as a counsellor to **Charlemagne**, who appointed him bishop of Basel in 802, abbot of Reichenau in 806 and ambassador to Constantinople in 811. He resigned his offices in 816, and lived simply as a monk until his death. The author of a significant collection of diocesan statutes for Basel, he also wrote an account of a vision of the next world experienced by his disciple, Wettin, which was versified by **Walafrid Strabo**. The cathedral in Reichenau-Mittelzell is his.

Hatzfeld, Johannes Church musician, folksong specialist, born Benolpe, Germany, 14 April 1882, died Paderborn, 5 July 1953. He was endowed with exceptional musical and spiritual talents. He studied under A. Sandberger and T. Kroyer. He worked for eight years as a priest and immersed himself in religious education. He became a crucial and energetic figure in the revival of German folksong. He promoted his interest in folksong through public lectures, writings and compositions. He produced a valuable collection of folkmusic as the director of Volksvereins-Verlag in Munich. He was the cofounder of the International Society for New Catholic Church Music in 1929. He received, as a recognition of his lifetime work, a doctorate from the University of Munich.

Hauck, Albert Lutheran Church historian, born Wassertrüdingen, Germany, 9 December 1845, died Leipzig, 7 April 1918. Following ordination Hauck spent several years in pastoral ministry before taking up an appointment as professor of Church history at Erlangen in 1878. In 1889 he moved to a similar position at Leipzig, where he also served as dean and rector. Of the many works which he wrote or edited during his career, the most significant is his five-volume history of the

Church in Germany, which is still highly regarded by scholars.

Hauge, Hans Nielsen Norwegian Lutheran lay preacher and revivalist, born Thune, Norway, 3 April 1771, died Bredtcedt, Norway, 29 March 1824. He came from a poor family. He underwent a religious conversion in 1796, as a consequence of which he started travelling all across Norway preaching about the need for conversion. He soon became very well known, and organized others to preach the Gospel. He was loyal to the established Church and opposed to any breakaway from the mainline tradition, yet he was charged with violating the law of assembly. He was put in gaol several times and when he came out of prison in 1811 after seven years, he was a broken man. Hauge wrote more than 30 books. His follower Elling Nielsen carried his ideas across the Atlantic to the United States in 1838 and founded the Norwegian Evangelical Lutheran Church.

Haughery, Mary (Gaffney) Philanthropist, born County Cavan, Ireland, *c.*1813, died New Orleans, Louisiana, 9 February 1882. She was nine years old when she lost her parents, and was brought up by a Welsh woman. She had an unfortunate marriage as she lost her husband and infant daughter soon after they moved to New Orleans. She was successful in business, starting a dairy and then a bakery shop, which she developed into the one of biggest enterprises of the South. She was virtually illiterate, yet she had a remarkable business career and amassed more than $500,000, of which most went to charity. She supported St Vincent's Infant Asylum by substantial donations. Her religious tolerance led her to make bequests not only to Catholic but also to Protestant institutions and to Jewish orphan asylums.

Haupt, Paul Protestant Assyriologist and biblical scholar, born Görlitz, Silesia, 25 November 1858, died Baltimore, Maryland, 15 December 1926. After studies in Leipzig and Berlin, he taught at Göttingen before moving to the United States in 1885 to become professor of Semitics at Johns Hopkins University, where he founded the Oriental Seminary. He did pioneering (though now dated) work in Sumerology and Assyriology; his most famous project was his *Polychrome* or *Rain-*

bow Bibles, which used colours to highlight various literary sources: the sixteen volumes of *The Sacred Books of the Old Testament* (1896–1904) and a modern English version with commentary, *The Sacred Books of the Old and New Testament* (6 vols, 1899–1904).

Hauréau, Jean Barthélémy French scholar and librarian, born Paris, 8 May 1812, died there, 29 April 1896. After working in politics, journalism and romantic literature, he realized his real vocation was as a librarian, which career he began at Le Mans in 1838. A year later he was offered a job at the Bibliothèque Nationale in Paris. His main interest was the Middle Ages. He wrote a number of distinguished works: *Notes sur les Montagnards* was followed by a four-volume *Histoire littéraire du Maine*, and by *Histoire de Sablé* and *Histoire de la philosophie scolastique*. This last work was commended by the French Academy in 1850, which so encouraged him that he expanded it into three volumes (1872–80). He served as one of the directors of the *Histoire littéraire de la France*. He also compiled an important manuscript catalogue of the *incipits* of Latin manuscripts in the Bibliothèque Nationale.

Hauteserre, Antoine Dadin de (Alteserra) Canon lawyer and historian, born Cahors, France, 1601, died Toulouse, 1682. Among his best-known publications is a four-volume work on canon law, published in 1651, *Dissertationum iuris canonici libri quatuor*. Three years later he produced the fifth and sixth volumes. The first two volumes deal with administrators established by bishops for their dioceses; the following two treat of taxes; and the final two discuss the clergy and legislation relating to them. He wrote a commentary on the decretals of **Innocent III**. Other important works include *Notes sur les Vies des Papes* and *Traité des ascétiques*.

Haüy, René Just Roman Catholic priest, mineralogist, originator of the science of crystallography, born Saint-Just, France, 28 February 1743, died Paris, 3 June 1822. A son of poor weavers, he was, however, a precocious child and attracted the attention of the local Premonstratensian prior. He was sent to school, and his parents were then persuaded to send him to Paris, where he studied at the Collège de Navarre. His main interests there lay in physics and electricity. He was appointed to Notre Dame as a metropolitan canon and was elected to be a member of the Académie des Sciences in 1783. After the Revolution he was appointed minister of mines and was a professor of mineralogy at the Museum of Natural History. The restoration period brought him hardship, for he lost his pension and had to live in Spartan simplicity. His most important publication is *Traité de cristallographie* .

Havergal, Frances Ridley Hymn-writer, born Astley, Worcestershire, 14 December 1836, died of peritonitis, 3 June 1879. Her father, William Henry Havergal, was also a well-known hymn-writer. Educated at schools at Worcester and Düsseldorf. She began writing poems at the age of seven. From 1861 she published hymns and poems for *Good Words* and other magazines. In 1866 she returned to Astley for a brief period before moving to Leamington. She edited her father's work, *Havergal's Psalmody*, for the press. Her hymns include 'Take my Life', 'Who is on the Lord's Side' and 'Like a River Glorious'.

Havey, Francis Patrick Author, educator, born County Meath, Ireland, 4 March 1864, died Baltimore, Maryland, 13 March 1945. He was educated in New Haven, Connecticut, then studied philosophy at St Bonaventure College, Allegany, New York. He pursued his theological studies at St John Seminary, Brighton, Massachusetts. He spent his novitiate in France. After returning to the United States he was approached to be a professor of Church history at St Joseph's Seminary, Dunwoodie, NY (1898–1904), and later (1915–17), church history and ascetical theology at St Mary's Seminary, Baltimore. In between he served as Rector of the house of philosophy at his alma mater in Brighton, Massachusetts; and professor of Church history and ascetical theology. He taught moral theology at Sulpician Seminary in Washington, DC, until 1925. His main works include *Meditations on Passion and Eastertide*, *The Way of the Cross in the Seminary*, *Vesting for the Altar* and *Retreat Companion for Priests*.

Hawkins, Denis John Bernard English Catholic philosopher, born Thornton Heath, London, 17

July 1906, died Godalming, Surrey, 16 January 1964. He was educated at Whitgift School, Croydon and at the Gregorian University, Rome, where he received two doctorates, one in philosophy the other in theology. Hawkins was ordained in 1930, the year before he returned home to various curacies. He was appointed parish priest of Esher in 1940 and Godalming a decade later. In 1956 he was made an honorary canon of the diocese. Though he never held an academic post, he devoted his life to the study of philosophy, reinterpreting **Thomas Aquinas** in the light of the philosophical systems of **Locke** and Hume. This he did in a number of short works: *Causality and Implication* (1937), *Criticism of Experience* and *Being and Becoming* (both 1945), and *The Essentials of Theism* (1949). His most popular book, however, was probably his *Sketch of Medieval Philosophy* (1946).

Hawks, Edward Roman Catholic priest, teacher and writer, born Abergavenny, South Wales, 17 February 1878, died Philadelphia, Pennsylvania, 22 January 1955. At the age of 21 he emigrated to Canada, where he spent some years as a lay missionary to the miners in northern Canada. Hawks attended the Episcopalian seminary at Nashotah, and joined the Companions of the Holy Saviour. When the Episcopal Church changed its canon law in 1907 to allow non-Episcopalians to preach before its congregations, the Companions regarded this 'open pulpit' amendment as a rejection of the historic priesthood and episcopacy. As a consequence Hawks resigned his position as an instructor at Nashotah. He entered the Catholic Church in 1908 and became a priest in 1911. During World War I he was a chaplain in the Canadian army. He moved to Philadelphia in 1919 and founded a parish dedicated to St **Joan of Arc**, remaining its priest until his death.

Hawthorne, Rose Foundress of the Servants of Relief for Incurable Cancer, born USA, 20 May 1851, died New York, 9 July 1926. Married in 1871, she and her husband became Catholics in 1891 but separated two years later (he was an alcoholic). Discovering that cancer patients in New York were expelled from hospital, she began to look after them in her own flat. After her husband's death, she became a Dominican nun in

1900 and in 1906 started her own congregation, taking the name 'Mother Alphonsa'. Her Order continues to follow her rule that no money should be accepted from the patients, their families or the state.

Hay, George Roman Catholic bishop, born Edinburgh, 24 August 1729, died Aquhorties, Aberdeenshire, 15 October 1811. Born an Episcopalian, he studied medicine at Edinburgh; converted to Roman Catholicism in 1749, he studied at the Scots College, Rome, and was ordained in 1758. He served as assistant to Bishop Grant in Banffshire, and was consecrated as coadjutor bishop in Lowland Scotland in 1769 and vicar apostolic in 1778. He lobbied extensively for the abolition of Scottish laws discriminating against Catholics, and oversaw the publication of the first English Catholic Bible in Scotland (1796–7).

Hayden, James Edward (Jerome) Benedictine monk, priest and psychiatrist, born Pittsburgh, Pennsylvania, 2 December 1902, died Brighton, Massachusetts, 18 July 1977. Educated in medicine and theology at the Universities of Pittsburgh and Louvain, in 1939 he became a monk of St Anselm's Benedictine Monastery, Washington, DC, and took the name 'Jerome'; he was ordained priest in 1947. After further studies in psychiatry and theology in the United States and Canada, he taught at the Catholic University of America and served as president of a school for retarded girls in Washington. In 1957 he was invited to found a Catholic Institute for Psychiatry in Boston, where he spent the rest of his career promoting research into mental health.

Haydn, Franz Joseph Composer, born Rohrau, Lower Austria, 31 March 1732, died Gumpendorf, near Vienna, 31 May 1809. He was a choirboy at St Stephen's Cathedral in Vienna and a devout Roman Catholic. In 1761 he entered the employ of the Esterhazy family, and remained with them for most of the time until 1790. After that time he travelled, including to England, where he was made a doctor of music by the University of Oxford in 1791. He settled in Vienna, and for a short time **Beethoven** was among his pupils, though the relationship was not a satisfactory one. Though known mainly for his instrumental music, he wrote several religious works, including Masses, oratorios and *The Seven Words of the Saviour on the Cross*. His oratorio *The Creation*, with its highly imaginative depiction of Chaos, is regarded by many as his greatest Christian work.

Haydn, Michael Composer, born Rohrau, Lower Austria, 14 September 1737, died Salzburg, 10 August 1806. He was the younger brother of Franz Joseph **Haydn** and has been overshadowed by him in reputation. He was a choirboy at St Stephen's Cathedral, Vienna, and settled in Salzburg as musical director to the archbishop, refusing a post with the Esterhazy family offered him by his brother. He wrote Church music often inscribed 'O.a.m.D.Gl.', 'Operatum ad maiorem Dei gloriam': 'Done for the glory of God.'

Haydt, Johann Valentin (John Valentine Haidt) Significant colonial religious painter and Moravian preacher, born Danzig, Germany, 4 October 1700, died Bethlehem, Pennsylvania, 18 January 1780. His father was a goldsmith in Berlin and after his schooling he travelled extensively in Europe to study the work of the great painters. While in London he joined the Moravian Church, and encountered Count **Zinzendorf**, who encouraged him to paint religious topics for churches all over Britain and Germany. Unfortunately many of these were destroyed in World War II. The Moravian Church sent him to Bethlehem, Pennsylvania, in 1754, where he continued painting portraits of Moravian dignitaries and other religious subjects. More than 70 of his paintings are known to survive, most of which can be seen in Wachovia Museum, Winstons-Salem, North Canolina.

Hayes, Carlton Joseph Huntley Roman Catholic historian, diplomat, born near Afton, New York, 16 May 1882, died Afton, 3 September 1964. He attended Columbia University, New York City, and went on to become a lecturer in modern European history there. After serving in the US army during World War I he became a full professor in 1919 and Seth Low Professor in 1935. He was a well-known specialist in Atlantic history, publishing *British Social Forces* and *Political and Social History of Modern Europe* (1916). His broad field of interest can be seen since he also researched modern nationalism and published *Essays on National-*

ism (1926) and *The Historical Evolution of Modern Nationalism* (1931). His career became controversial when he was sent as ambassador to Spain and was said by his critics to have been biased in favour of Franco. He resigned in 1945. He received several honorary degrees from many universities, such as Columbia, Detroit and Fordham, and the American Catholic Historical Association elected him as president. Hayes was the founder of the National Conference of Christians and Jews and was the co-chairman from 1928 to 1946.

Hayes, Patrick Joseph Cardinal and founder of Catholic charities, born New York City, 20 November 1867, died Monticello, New York, 4 September 1938. He studied in Washington, DC. In New York, he worked successively as chancellor of the archdiocese, then auxiliary bishop, and became the first Roman Catholic bishop of the armed forces, in charge of chaplains in the army and navy. After World War I, he became the fifth archbishop of New York and was created a cardinal in 1924.

Haymarus Monachus (Haymar) Monk, Latin patriarch of Jerusalem, poet, died 1202. A Florentine monk, probably of Corbizzi, who held a number of significant posts, including that of archbishop of Caesarea, 1181–92, before being appointed patriarch of Jerusalem in 1192, though he resided at Acre, Jerusalem itself being occupied by Muslims. He wrote a poem on the battle for Acre, *De expugnatione civitatis Acconensis*.

Haymo *see also* **Haimo**

Haymo of Faversham English Franciscan, born Faversham, Kent, died Anagni, Italy, 1244. At the University of Paris he achieved fame as a preacher and joined the Order of Friars Minor. He attended the general chapter of the Order at Assisi. After this, Haymo probably came to England, and lectured at Oxford in the Franciscan School. The Holy See sent him to Constantinople to negotiate for the reunion of the Latin and Greek Churches. He was active lecturing in Tours, Bologna and Padua, and Pope **Gregory IX** employed him to revise the Roman Breviary. Haymo became general of the English Franciscan province, then minister general of the Order. He preferred the Franciscans to live by their own labour and grow crops rather than beg. In an epitaph he was celebrated as 'the highest glory of the English'. He left a treatise on the ceremonies of the Mass.

Haymo of Halberstadt Monk, bishop and theologian born late eighth century, died Halberstadt, 28 March 853. We know very little of his life except that he was a monk at Fulda, studied at Tours under **Rabanus Maurus** and attended the lectures of **Alcuin**; he taught at Fulda between 815 and 820, and became bishop of Halberstadt in 840. Trimethius calls Haymo 'a most learned man, a penetrating interpreter of Scriptures'. Some works previously attributed to him, however, are the writings of Haymo of Hirschau and it is difficult to decide which of them wrote the remainder. He wrote on dogmatics, and produced spiritual works as well as history, such as his *De vanitate liborum, Sive de amore coelestis patriae libri tres*. His *Historiae sacrae epitome* is a history of early Christianity up to the death of Emperor **Theodosius I**. His name appears in the Benedictine Martyrology for 27 March.

Haynald, Ludwig Cardinal, born Szécsény, Hungary, 3 November 1816, died Kalocsa, 4 July 1891. Educated in Budapest and Vienna, he was ordained in 1839 and acquired his doctorate in theology in 1841. From 1842 to 1846 he taught in the seminary at Gran. After a period as secretary to Archbishop Kopçcsy, and some further travel and study, in 1848 he was appointed chancellor, but was dismissed for refusing to publish the Hungarian parliament's declaration of independence. He became coadjutor to the bishop of Transylvania in 1851, and succeeded him in 1852. He resigned in 1861, and became titular archbishop of Carthage. In 1867 he was appointed archbishop of Kalocsa-Bács. He attended the First Vatican Council in 1870, where he opposed, but ultimately accepted, papal infallibility. He was created a cardinal in 1879.

Haze, Maria Theresia Foundress of the Daughters of the Holy Cross of Liège, born Liège (Belgium), 27 February 1782, died Liège, 7 January 1876. As a child, she went through difficult times, her parents' property being confiscated and the family persecuted during the French Revolution. With Canon

Jean Habets (d. 1876) she founded her religious order in 1833. The sisters' work covered wide areas of social, as well as spiritual, activities – teaching in schools, nursing the sick, taking care of needy women, especially of women in jail. Her congregation spread to England, Germany and India during her lifetime. Her cause for beatification was introduced in 1910.

Healy, George Peter Alexander Roman Catholic portrait painter, born Boston, Massachusetts, 15 July 1813, died Chicago, Illinois, 24 June 1894. Born of an Irish family and receiving no formal training he started painting with the encouragement of the popular artist Thomas Sully. From 1830 he painted portraits and had made enough money by 1834 to travel to Paris. There he studied in Antoine Jean, Baron Gros' studio and copied in the Louvre. He soon established his own studio and became well known. From 1855 to 1867 he lived in Chicago, and again from 1892 till his death. He painted many famous contemporaries: **Pius IX**, for example, **Bismarck, Liszt, Guizot**, Gambetta and **Emerson**, and no fewer than eleven US Presidents. The French king Louis Philippe was his patron. His paintings have historical value, but are not otherwise highly regarded.

Healy, James Augustine Roman Catholic bishop, born Macon, Georgia, 6 April 1830, died Portland, Maine, 5 August 1900. The son of an Irish plantation owner and a black slave, he was educated at Holy Cross, Montreal, and Paris, and ordained in 1854. He was appointed secretary to the bishop of Boston, chancellor in 1855, vicar general in 1857, and pastor of St James', Boston, from 1866. In 1875 he became second bishop of Portland, Maine, which he served until his death. He worked to promote outreach activities, not least to French-Canadians, and to extend the Church's work in schools and orphanages.

Healy, John Irish Roman Catholic archbishop, historian and author, born Ballinafad, County Sligo, 14 November 1841, died Tuam, County Galway, 16 March 1918. He attended school at Summerhill College in Athlone and went on to St Patrick's College, Maynooth, in 1860. He was ordained in 1867. He pursued a teaching and pastoral career and was the editor of the *Ecclesias-*

tical Record. He became bishop of Clonfort in 1896, built a cathedral and founded a residential seminary. He was a conservative in politics and was much opposed to land agitation, which occasioned some unpopularity for him. His major works include *Ireland's Ancient Schools and Scholars* (1890) and *The Life and Writings of St Patrick* (1905). He greatly helped the development of Catholic higher education in Ireland, and the National University owes him much.

Healy, Patrick Joseph Roman Catholic Church historian, born Waterford, Ireland, 26 July 1871, died Washington, DC, 18 May 1937. Ordained in New York in 1897, he studied at the Catholic University (doctor of philosophy, 1903, published 1905), and pursued further work in Bonn and Heidelberg. After a brief spell as a parish priest in New York, he joined the faculty of the Catholic University, and from 1910 served as Patrick Quinn Professor of Church History and several times as dean of the faculty of theology. He edited the *Catholic University Bulletin* 1911–14, and wrote much on early Church history and Church–State relations. A notable ecumenist, he worked for many years on a history of US Christianity from Protestant sources, though no evidence of the work was found among his papers on his death.

Heath, Nicholas Archbishop of York, born London, *c.*1501, died London, December 1578. He was educated at Oxford, and Christ's College, Cambridge, where he became a fellow. After ordination, he was appointed archdeacon of Stafford, and bishop of Rochester, and then of Worcester. He refused to accept the form of the ordination rite proposed by **Cranmer**, and was briefly imprisoned and deprived of his see. On Queen **Mary**'s accession, he was restored, then elected archbishop of York, and he consecrated Cardinal **Pole** as archbishop of Canterbury. He became Lord Chancellor, proclaimed **Elizabeth I** queen, but resigned warning Elizabeth against religious changes and then refused to crown her. He was imprisoned in the Tower of London, where he died.

Heber, Reginald Bishop, hymn-writer, born Malpas, Cheshire, 21 April 1783, died Trichinopoly, India, 3 April 1826. He was educated at Oxford and won the Newdigate Prize for his poem *Pal-*

estine, later set to music by **Crotch**. He was ordained, became vicar of Hodnet, Shropshire, and later bishop of Calcutta. He wrote *Hymns Written and Adapted to the Weekly Church Service of the Year*, many of which remain popular. Tennyson regarded his hymn 'Holy, Holy, Holy! Lord God Almighty' as the finest hymn ever written.

Hebert, Marcel Roman Catholic priest, philosopher and proponent of a theory of religious symbolism which denied personality in God, born Bar-le-Duc, France, 22 April 1851, died Paris, 12 February 1916. He was educated at Saint-Sulpice and wrote on modern philosophical issues and on such philosophers as **Kant**, Voltaire, Schopenhauer and **Renan**. His two most significant works are *Souvenirs d'Assise* (1899) and the article 'La Dernière idole' (1902). He questioned the Thomistic proof for the existence of God along broadly Kantian lines. God seemed to him a category of the 'Ideal', immanent and unknowable. Because of his views he was obliged to abandon his priesthood and was given a teaching post at the new socialist university recently established in Brussels. He was never reconciled to the Church.

Hecker, Isaac Thomas Founder of the Catholic Paulist Fathers, born New York City, USA, 18 December 1819, died New York City, 22 December 1888. The son of German immigrants, he was a Methodist, Mormon, Transcendentalist and Unitarian before becoming a Roman Catholic in 1844 and being ordained a Redemptorist in England in 1849. Against Catholic values of the time, he believed that democracy and Catholicism were compatible and wanted to both Americanize Catholicism and convert America. Permitted by the Pope in 1856 to found the Congregation of St Paul the Apostle, his aim was to persuade Protestants that the Catholic Church was not an enemy of liberty. To this end he urged the use of the press, and in 1865 started the monthly *The Catholic World*, which he edited until his death.

Hedda Bishop and saint, died 9 July 705. A monk and abbot, probably of Whitby, in 676 he was made bishop of the divided Wessex diocese, first at Dorchester, then at Winchester. He served as an adviser to King **Ine** on the drawing up of the king's legal code. He was a chief benefactor of Malmesbury. Many miracles were attested at his tomb. Feast day 7 July.

Hedley, John Cuthbert Benedictine bishop and writer, born Morpeth, Northumberland, England, 15 April 1837, died Cardiff, Wales, 11 November 1915. He entered the Benedictines at Belmont Abbey in 1854 and was ordained in 1862. He was consecrated bishop auxiliary in 1873 and upon the death of Dr Joseph Brown, OSB, in 1881 he succeeded him as diocesan bishop of Newport and Menevia. He wrote on theology, philosophy, asceticism and history. His most widely known books are *Lex Leviatrum* (1906), *The Holy Eucharist* (1906) and *Retreat* (1894). He was a prominent spokesman of the English bishops and played a decisive role in seeking permission from the Pope for Catholic students to attend Oxford and Cambridge. His diocese was divided in 1895, and he was thenceforth bishop of Newport only.

Hedwig *see* **Hadewych**

Hedwig Saint, born Andechs, *c*.1174, died Trebnitz, 12 or 15 October 1243. She was of noble birth, monastery educated and said to have married Henry I of Silesia at the age of twelve. The marriage brought relations with Silesia closer and Hedwig was prominent in affairs of state. She had a reputation for fortitude and piety, enabling the foundation of new monasteries and support of existing ones. She encouraged her husband to found the first house of religious women in Silesia. Piety, gentleness and austerity gave her the reputation of a saint while still alive. She is the patron saint of Silesia. Feast day 16 October.

Heenan, John Carmel Cardinal, born Ilford, Essex, 6 January 1905, died London, 7 November 1975. He was educated at Ushaw College, County Durham, and at the English College, Rome. He was ordained in 1930, served in parishes in the East End of London, and in 1947 became superior of the Catholic Missionary Society. In 1936 he travelled to Russia in the guise of a lecturer in psychology, and during the war he became well-known as a broadcaster. He was appointed bishop of Leeds in 1951, then archbishop of Liverpool in 1957 and translated to Westminster as the seventh archbishop in 1963. He was created a

cardinal in 1965. He wrote several books, including a biography of Cardinal **Hinsley**, and his own (partial) autobiography, *Not the Whole Truth* and *A Crown of Thorns*.

Heeney, Cornelius Roman Catholic merchant and philanthropist, born Ireland, 1754, died Brooklyn, New York, 3 May 1848. He arrived at New York in 1784 and founded a fur business with John Jacob Astor. Being unmarried, he devoted his fortune to charity and religion. He was a driving force in organizing the setting up of St Peter's Church in 1785 and was its first trustee and treasurer. He also helped to acquire the site for St Patrick's Cathedral. He was one of the first Catholics to hold a public office in New York. In 1835 he retired from his business and moved to his estate in Columbia Heights, Brooklyn. A year later he donated land adjacent to his property for a parish church, a school and an orphanage. His generous donations to religious as well as to social causes amounted to more than $2,000,000.

Heerinckx, James Franciscan ascetical and mystical theologian, born Melkwezer, Belgium, 31 December 1877, died Rome, 24 March 1937. He joined the Franciscan province of St Joseph in 1894 and was ordained on 2 March 1901. He taught theology and acted as a rector of St Seraphic College in Lokeren until 1921, when he was appointed to Rome as penitentiary of the Lateran Basilica. From 1924 he became a professor of mystical and ascetical theology at the Pontifical Athenaeum Antonianum. He wrote for the *Dictionnaire de spiritualité* and various periodicals. His publications, mostly in Latin, include among the most important, *Introductio in theologiam spiritualem asceticam et mysticam* (Turin, 1931). He devoted considerable time to studying the spirituality of SS **Anthony of Padua** and **Charles of Sezze**.

Hefele, Karl Joseph von German theologian and historian, born Unterkochan, Württemberg, 15 March 1809, died Rottenburg, 5 June 1893. He attended the University of Tübingen and after ordination was appointed by the Catholic faculty of theology of Tübingen to the department of Church history. He was then elected bishop of Rottenburg. He was an accurate scholar and a fine teacher. He wrote many articles and introduced Christian archaeology into the academic curriculum. His nine-volume history of the Councils of the Church (the two last volumes were contributed by **Hergenröther**) was an outstanding contribution to scholarship. He was honoured by universities and by the government. As bishop of Rottenburg he attended the First Vatican Council; initially opposed to the declaration of papal infallibility, he later submitted, promulgating the decrees of the Council in his diocese.

Hegemonius Author, fl. mid-fourth century. Nothing is known about his life, but he is regarded as the author of the *Acta Archelai*, a vital source on Manichaeism, consisting of a purported dialogue between Archelaus, a fictional bishop of Kashkar, Mesopotamia, and Mani. Contrived as a stylized polemic against Manichaean beliefs, the work was composed in Greek, but the full text is known only in Latin; some Greek fragments are preserved in **Epiphanius**. **Jerome** mistakenly attributed the work to the character of Archelaus himself and believed it was originally written in Syriac. According to **Photius**, it was first ascribed to Hegemonius by one Heraclian of Chalcedon.

Hegesippus A Greek-speaking Jewish Christian, possibly from Palestine. In the years 160 to 180 he was in Rome, where he finished his composition of five books of *Hypomnemata* (memories). This work, used and quoted by **Eusebius of Caesarea**, intended to narrate, without error, the tradition of the apostolic preaching. It is a fierce polemic against Gnosticism.

Hegius, Alexander Humanist scholar and teacher, born probably Heeck, Westphalia, 1433, died Deventer, 7 December 1498. He was a pupil of Rudolphus **Agricola** and became a priest. In 1469 he was appointed rector of a school in Wesel, and in 1474 became head of Deventer. A prominent teacher in an important centre, he taught, among others, **Erasmus**, Murmellin and Mutianus.

Hehn, Johannes Roman Catholic OT and oriental scholar, born Burghausen, Germany, 1 January 1873, died Würzburg, 9 May 1932. He received his doctorate from the University of Würzburg and also studied under Friedrich **Delitzsch** at Berlin University. He received his professorship at Würzburg in 1903, and lectured there on the OT and oriental languages until his death. He was eager to point out the relationship between the OT and the ancient Middle East, drawing attention to ties between the culture of Israel and those of the other Middle Eastern peoples. His biblical works include *Sünde und erlösung nach biblischer und babylonischer anschauung* (Leipzig, 1903), *Der Israelitische Sabbath* (3rd edn, Münster, 1909) and *Die biblische und babylonische Gottesidee* (Leipzig, 1913).

Heiler, Friedrich Lutheran historian and ecumenist, born Munich, Germany, 30 January 1892, died Munich, 28 April 1967. Though he came from a Roman Catholic family, Heiler, who studied the phenomenon of religions, assumed a posture of 'evangelical catholicity' by joining a Lutheran communion in 1918 but not separating himself from the Roman Catholic Church, at least in his own mind. From 1920 until his retirement in 1960 (with a break of ten years during the Second World War), Heiler was professor of the history of religions in the Lutheran faculty of the University of Marburg. He wrote many works on ecumenism, religious authority and other religions, which he treated with great empathy. Upon his retirement, he returned to Munich, where he taught as an emeritus until his death.

Heim, Karl Lutheran theologian, born Frauenzimmern, Württemberg, 20 January 1874, died Tübingen, 30 August 1958. He studied at Tübingen and worked initially as a pastor and schoolmaster before becoming an academic theologian, first in Halle, 1907–14, then Münster, 1914–20, then Tübingen, from 1920. From a Pietist background, he emphasized the gulf between faith and reason, and the transcendence of faith over scientific knowledge. He espoused a personalist-existentialist philosophy. He wrote a number of works, of which the most famous is *Glauben und Denken* (1931–4; translated as *God Transcendent*, 1935); other English translations of his texts include *Jesus the World's Perfecter* (1959) and *The World: Its Creation and Consummation* (1962). He published his autobiography in 1957.

Heimbucher, Maximilian Joseph Roman Catholic theologian and historian, born Miesbach, Bavaria,

10 June 1856, died Miesbach, 24 August 1946. He taught dogmatics and apologetics at the University of Munich between 1887 and 1891 and at the theological seminary in Bamberg from 1891 to 1924. His best-known publication is *Die Orden und Kongregationen der Katholischen Kirche*. He was a very meticulous researcher, and the data he compiled for this volume are still regarded as one of the very best resources on the history, statistics and bibliography of the religious orders and congregations of the Catholic Church.

Heimerad Wandering priest, hermit and saint, born Messkirch, Baden, of serf parents, died Mount Hasungen, near Cassel, 28 June 1019. He was ordained, served for a time in Baden, then as a chaplain to the lady of his parents' estate. After a pilgrimage to Rome and Jerusalem, he wandered around Germany, settling for a while at Hersfeld Abbey, then in an abandoned church given to him in Westphalia. An eccentric, he made himself very unpopular in a number of places, being publicly flogged at Paderborn; elsewhere he was revered as a saint. Ultimately he settled in a forest near Cassel, where he built a hermitage. A popular cult grew up around his tomb, where many miracles were attested; it has never been officially approved. Feast day 28 June.

Heimo of Michelsberg Chronicler, date and place of birth unknown, died abbey of Michelsberg, Bamberg, Germany, 3 July 1138. Heimo became an Augustinian canon in 1108 and spent most of his life on his work *De decursu temporum ab origine mundi*, which purports to chronicle the history of the world from the Creation, as well as co-ordinate dates of the Popes with other Roman leaders and discuss the history of man's slavery to sin and liberation through Christ. Heimo also worked out the dates of Easter up through 1595. His work does not contain much of real historical value for historians today, but does represent the type of work being done at Michelsberg in the early 1100s.

Heinisch, Paul Roman Catholic priest and biblical scholar, born Leoschütz, Silesia, Germany (today's Glubzyce in Poland), 25 March 1878, died Salzburg, Austria, 11 March 1956. He was ordained in 1902 and pursued further studies at Breslau University, where he obtained his doctorate in theology. He taught there for three years from 1908 and then became a professor of OT studies at Strasburg and afterwards at the Catholic University of Nijmegen. He was a very prolific author, publishing a book in every other year in his 40-year career. His most significant work is *Das Buch der Weisheit* (Exegetisches Handbuch zum Alten Testament; Münster, 1912). He also wrote several other commentaries on books of the OT, in the Bonner Bibel series – on Ezekiel, Genesis, Exodus, Numbers and Leviticus.

Heinrich, Johann Baptist Roman Catholic priest and neo-Thomistic theologian, born Mainz, 15 April 1816, died there, 9 February 1891. He first studied law and received his doctorate in canon law as well as in civil law. Beginning his career as a lecturer in law, he later shifted his interest to theology and in 1844 entered the seminary at Mainz. Seven years later he became a professor of dogmatic theology there. He was the editor of *Der Katholik*, a well-known journal of pastoral theology. He worked for the Piusverein, promoting religious freedom throughout Germany. He wrote on dogmatic theology, criticizing the teaching of **Döllinger** and also the liberal views of D. F. **Strauss** and J. E. **Renan**.

Heiric of Auxerre Teacher and hagiographer, born Herz, 841, died Auxerre, 876. He entered the monastery of St Germanus at Auxerre as an oblate in childhood, and studied at Ferrières, 859–60, and Soissons, 862–5, where he came into contact with John Scotus **Eriugena**. He returned to Auxerre, where he taught for the rest of his life. One of the most learned classical scholars of the early Middle Ages, he wrote a notable metrical life of St **Germanus of Auxerre**, a survey of Germanus' miracles, and a medley of classical and theological quotations.

Heirich, Leo Franciscan pastor, born Östrich, Germany, 15 August 1867, assassinated Denver, Colorado, 23 February 1908. He was christened 'Joseph' and brought up in the Diocese of Cologne, Germany, but emigrated to the United States, where in 1886 he joined the Friars Minor at Paterson, New Jersey. He was ordained in 1901 at Newark, New Jersey, and for sixteen years worked as a pastor in churches entrusted to the Franciscan

Province of the Most Holy Name of Jesus. He was then appointed to the parish of St Elizabeth in Denver. Shortly after arriving in Denver, however, an anarchist shot him out of hatred of the clergy and of Christianity.

Heiss, Michael   Roman Catholic archbishop and writer, born Pfahldorf, Bavaria, 12 April 1818, died La Crosee, Wisconsin, 26 March 1890. He attended the Latin School at Eichstätt and was ordained in 1840. For a short time he was a missionary in Kentucky and in 1866 at the Second Plenary Council of Baltimore he recommended the establishment of two new dioceses, to one of which he was appointed. He became the titular archbishop of Hadrianople and coadjutor of Milwaukee. He was an ardent supporter of local, especially parochial, schools and a great proponent of the use of the German language, which greatly aggravated the already difficult situation about national churches in the USA. He was also a great supporter of papal infallibility.

Helen of Skovde (Sköfde)   Saint, martyr, born in the twelfth century. Information about her life comes from the twelfth-century St Brynolph, bishop of Skana in Sweden. Of noble birth, she remained a widow following the death of her husband and spent the rest of her life in charitable and pious works. She built the church at Skovde. She was falsely accused by her daughter's relatives of instigating the murder of her son-in-law by his own servants. She went on pilgrimage to the Holy Land but was killed by the same relatives on her return in about 1160. She is buried at Skovde and many cures of the sick and disabled were reported at her intercession. She was long venerated, and the subject of many pilgrimages. Feast day 31 July.

Helen of Udine   Blessed, Augustinian tertiary, born Udine, c.1396, died there, 23 April 1458. In deep grief after the death of her husband, Antonio dei Cavalcanti, she entered the Augustinian Third Order at the age of 40. She lived a life of penance, prayer and good works. Miracles are credited to her in life and after death. Feast day 23 April.

Helena   Empress and saint, born Drepanum (Bithynia), c.255, died c.330. Of humble origins she became the concubine of Constantinus Chlo-

rus, who later rejected her. Their son, **Constantine I**, recalled her to court in 306 and made her *augusta*. She performed works of charity and erected many church buildings. She made a pilgrimage to Jerusalem and on Golgotha believed she had found the True Cross, a fragment of which she placed in Rome in the S. Croce. Her cult, often associated with that of her son, quickly developed in East and West. Feast day 18 August.

Helentrudis   Saint, hermitess, died Neuenheerse, Westphalia, Germany, c.950. Also known as 'Helmtrud' or 'Hiltrud', Helentrudis is named by Bishop Imad of Paderborn in his Martyrology of 1052. According to the *Passio of St Ursula* (c.975), she reportedly had a vision of St Cordula, one of the virgins supposedly killed by the Huns in Cologne, in which Cordula described her martyrdom. The *Regnante Domino*, another source of legends about St Ursula, describes pilgrimages to Helentrudis' grave and miracles that occurred there. Feast days 31 May and 22 October.

Helgesen, Poul   Danish humanist and Carmelite monk, born Varberg, Danish Sweden, c.1485, died 1535. He became professor of theology at Copenhagen, and was provincial superior of the Carmelites in Scandinavia. He championed Roman Catholicism against Lutheran reforms in Denmark, though he did criticize the Roman Catholic Church for its worldliness and the sale of indulgences. He produced several works and translated **Erasmus**.

Helinand of Froidmont   Cistercian writer, chronicler and poet, born Pronleroy, France, c.1160, died at the monastery of Froidmont, c.1229. He was born into a noble family and entered the monastery of Froidmont in 1194, shortly afterwards becoming prior there. His many works include 28 sermons, which reveal his knowledge of theology, and his considerable familiarity with the Scriptures and the classics. His *Les vers de la mort* written in Old French was extremely popular and is one of the earliest examples of the 'Danse Macabre' literature. A *Chronicon* in 49 books covers a period from 634 to 1204. His *Epistola* contains an exposé of the singular theory that novices are not free to leave their Orders. Venerated as a Saint by the Cistercians. Feast day 3 February.

Helmond Chronicler and priest, born in the Harz region of Saxony, Germany, *c.*1120, died Bosau, Holstein, Germany, after 1177. Of peasant origin, Helmond became a Benedictine at Neumünster and a priest in Oldenburg, 1156, and served the parish of Bosau from around 1163 until his death. He is best known for his *Chronica Slavorum* (vol. 1, 1168; vol. 2, 1172), an important historical source for information about Saxon history, especially for the years 1072–1172, and for the activities of leaders like Duke **Henry the Lion**, Margrave Albert I ('the Bear') of Brandenburg, and Adolf II of Schauenburg.

Héloïse Abbess, born *c.*1098 and died at the abbey of the Paraclete, Nogent-sur-Seine, 15 May 1164. She was the seventeen-year-old niece of Fulbert, canon of Notre Dame, who hired Peter **Abelard** as her tutor. They fell in love, fled to Brittany and there Héloïse gave birth to their son **Peter Astralabe**. On their return to Paris, Héloïse entered the convent of Argenteuil, eventually becoming prioress. In 1128 this convent closed, and the community transferred to the Paraclete, a monastery built by Abelard at Nogent-sur-Seine: Héloïse became its first abbess. She and Abelard were both buried at the Paraclete, but the bodies were later taken to Paris and buried in 1817 at the Père Lachaise cemetery, in the same grave.

Helwys, Thomas English Baptist divine, born in possibly Askham, Nottinghamshire, 1550, died probably in London, 1616. He seems to have studied at Gray's Inn and emigrated to Holland to avoid persecution. There he became convinced of the importance of believers' baptism and received it from John **Smyth**, as a result of which they were both excommunicated. On returning to London he founded the first General Baptist congregation in England, at Pinners' Hall, London, in 1612, and published his *Mystery of Iniquity*, the first sustained plea by an English divine for universal religious toleration and a denial of the right of the state to legislate on matters concerning a person's relationship with God.

Helyot, Hippolyte Franciscan historian, born Paris, January 1660, died Paris, 5 January 1716. Known as 'Le Père Hippolyte'. He entered the Franciscan friary in Paris, and twice visited Rome.

He wrote informatively on Roman Catholic religious congregations in *Histoire des Ordres monastiques, religieux et militaires*, which was completed by Père Maximilien Bullot.

Hemma Blessed, Carolingian queen, born *c.*808, died Regensburg, 31 January 876. She married Louis the German and had seven children. She became patroness and abbess of the Benedictine convent at Obermünster. Her tombstone is at Sankt Emmeram and she is reputed to be buried there, although the convent at Obermünster lays claim to her body. Feast day 31 January.

Hemmingsen, Niels Protestant theologian, born Errindler, Lolland, 8 (or 22) May/4 June 1513, died Roskilde, Copenhagen, 23 May 1600. Educated at Wittenberg under Philipp **Melanchthon**, he became a professor at the University of Copenhagen, where he obtained a doctorate of theology in 1557. A prolific (if not very original) writer, he produced some key works of early post-Reformation Danish theology, including *Enchiridion theologicum* (1557), *De lege naturae* (1562) and *Syntagma institutionum* (1574). Accused of having Calvinist tendencies over his views on the Eucharistic Real Presence, he was dismissed from his post in 1579, and spent the rest of his life as a canon at Roskilde.

Hémy, Henri Friedrich Musician, born Newcastle upon Tyne, England, 12 November 1818, died Hartlepool, 10 June 1888. He held various teaching and organist posts in north-east England. He compiled collections of Roman Catholic music: *Easy Hymns for Catholic Schools* and *The Crown of Jesus Music*. He is most famous for having adapted the music of a folk tune, 'Bonnie Dundee', as the hymn 'Hail Queen of Heaven' to words by John **Lingard**. It has become one of the most popular traditional Catholic hymns in Britain, and the tune appears in hymnals of other denominations.

Henana Syriac theologian, born Adiabene, died Nisibis, *c.*610. Educated in the school of Nisibis under Abraham, he became its director in 572, despite strong opposition. He sought to abandon Nestorian theology for Chalcedonian orthodoxy, and endorsed the principle of a communication of idioms between the two natures of Christ. He was accused of Origenism and fatalism, and provoked controversy for failing to share the Persian Church's traditional veneration for the exegesis of **Theodore of Mopsuestia**. He wrote numerous scriptural commentaries, and other tracts on the Creed, on Golden Friday (the Friday after Pentecost), and on the so-called fast of the Ninevites; only fragments of his work survive.

Hennepin, Louis Missionary and explorer, born Ath, Hainaut (Belgium), 12 May 1626, died Rome, March 1701. He joined a French Order of Friars Minor and voyaged with La Salle to Canada, where he began ministering to the Iroquois Indians. They reached the site of Peoria, Illinois, where they established a fort. Hennepin explored the upper Mississippi River and was captured by Sioux Indians. He was taken to falls which he named the Falls of St Anthony, now the site of Minneapolis, Minnesota. However, the same year, Hennepin was rescued, returned to France and wrote accounts of his travels, *Descriptions de la Louisiane*. Later he published *Nouvelle découverte d'un tres grand pays situé dans L'Amérique*.

Henricus Aristippus Scientist and translator, died Palermo, Sicily, *c*.1163. Of Norman background, he was a clerk who became master of the palace school in Sicily, and tutored the future **William I**. Archdeacon of Catania in 1156, and ambassador to Constantinople in 1158, he was for a time the chief official at William's court, before he fell out of favour; he died in prison. In 1156 he produced the first Latin translation of Plato's *Meno* and *Phaedo* (hence his sobriquet of Aristippus, after Socrates' disciple). He also translated Book 4 of Aristotle's *Meteorologica*, and a number of other classical and Christian Greek texts, into stylish Latin, and wrote notes on books and libraries in Sicily. His interest in the natural sciences led him to conduct hazardous researches on Mount Etna.

Henry First African Roman Catholic bishop, born Kongo, *c*.1496, died Kongo, *c*.1530. In 1508 he was part of a group of youths sent by his father, King **Afonso I**, to Lisbon, where he trained as a priest. In 1514 he was Afonso's envoy in Rome to swear fealty to the Pope and in 1521 the Pope agreed to the request of the king of Portugal that he be consecrated bishop. Officially he was an auxiliary of the Diocese of Funchal because the Portuguese feared an independent diocese in Kongo. His ministry to his large diocese was hampered by his ill health and a lack of priests. He represents the often-thwarted aspirations of his father to make Kongo a Christian country.

Henry II German king, Holy Roman Emperor and saint, born Hildesheim(?), 6 May 972, died Grona, near Göttingen, 15 July 1024. Son of Henry, duke of Bavaria, he succeeded his cousin **Otto III** as king in 1002. He devoted his energies to consolidating German power, spending much of his early reign in campaigns in the East and in Lombardy. In 1007 he established and generously endowed the See of Bamberg. He was crowned Emperor at Rome by **Benedict VIII**, 14 February 1014. He intervened controversially, though with Rome's support, in ecclesiastical affairs, and supported the nascent monastic reform movement. His piety became legendary; he was canonized in 1146 (as was his wife, **Kunigunde**, in 1200). Feast day 13 (formerly 15) July.

Henry III German king and Holy Roman Emperor, born Osterbeck, 28 October 1017, died Bodfeld, 5 October 1056. Son of Emperor Conrad II and Gisela, he became duke of Bavaria and Swabia in 1027, joint king in 1028, and succeeded his father as Emperor in 1039. In 1043 he invaded Hungary, and settled the Austrian–Hungarian border as the Leitha and March Rivers, a frontier which endured until 1919. From 1044 to 1050 he was at war with Godfrey, duke of Upper Lorraine, and latterly with the barons of the Low Countries. A devout Christian ruler, Henry urged Church reforms; at the Synod of Sutri in 1046, the power-struggle between **Benedict IX**, **Sylvester III** and **Gregory VI** was condemned; **Clement II** was elected in their stead, and he crowned Henry Emperor in Rome in 1046.

Henry IV German king and Holy Roman Emperor, born Goslar, 11 November 1050, died Liège (in battle against his son, **Henry V**) 1106, and buried at Speyer. Son of **Henry III**, he succeeded in 1056 and became of age in 1065. After conquering the Saxons in 1075, he became embroiled in a conflict with Pope **Gregory VII** over the Pope's prohibitions of simony and clerical marriage; he was excommunicated after declaring Gregory deposed. When the Saxons rebelled again, he was reconciled with the Pope at Canossa in 1077. In 1080 he was excommunicated again, but at the Council of Brixen in 1084 he endorsed an Antipope who was enthroned as **Clement III**; Clement crowned him as Emperor. Relations with Rome remained bad, and Henry's last years were marked by disorder, including serious revolts within his own household. His death saved Germany from civil war.

Henry IV (of France) King of France who ended the religious wars and began the Bourbon dynasty, born Pau, 14 December 1553, died Paris, 14 May 1610. Although baptized a Catholic, he was raised as a Protestant and joined the Huguenot forces at La Rochelle in 1568. The St Bartholomew's Day Massacre marred his marriage in 1572 to Margaret of Valois. On 25 July 1593 at St-Denis he gave up Protestantism; but on 13 April 1598 he issued the edict of toleration at Nantes, which gave the Huguenots civil liberty and freedom of worship. He later married Marie de Médicis and their son was the future Louis XIII.

Henry V German king and Holy Roman Emperor, born 8 January 1081, died Utrecht, 23 May 1125. Co-ruler with his father from 1098, in 1105 he forced his father to abdicate, and was crowned Emperor by the Pope in 1106. Initially he continued his father's controversial practice of lay investiture, but in 1107 **Paschal II** outlawed it. He conducted military campaigns against the Bohemians, Hungarians and Poles, and in 1110 invaded Italy. He extorted concessions from Paschal, imprisoning him for a time. He was excommunicated by both Paschal and his successor, **Gelasius II**. In 1122 he signed the Concordat of Worms with **Calixtus II**, which surrendered his claims to investiture, and guaranteed free clerical elections and the restoration of Church property; he was received back into the Church. He campaigned against the rebel **Lothair** of Saxony, and planned a campaign against **Louis VI** of France, in alliance with Henry I of England, whose daughter Matilda he had married in 1114.

Henry VI Holy Roman Emperor from 14 April 1191 to 28 September 1197, born Nijmegen, The Netherlands, 1165, died Messina, Sicily, 1197. He was the second son of **Frederick I Barbarossa** and Beatrice of Burgundy, crowned king of Germany in 1169, of Italy in 1189, of Sicily in 1194 and Emperor in 1191. The three major objectives of his brief reign were to gain the assent of the German princes to the principle of hereditary succession of the Hohenstaufen line; to achieve a permanent territorial settlement with the Papacy; and to liberate the Kingdom of Jerusalem. He failed in all three.

Henry VI (of England) King of England from September 1422 to 1471, founder of Eton College and King's College, Cambridge, born Windsor, 6 December 1421, died London, 21 May 1471. After the death of Charles VI, he became king of France as well in terms of the Treaty of Troyes of 1420. In 1453 he lost his mind and Richard of York was appointed protector. When he recovered in 1455, civil war, the War of the Roses, broke out between the king and the Yorkists. He was imprisoned in the Tower of London, restored briefly, and executed by Edward IV.

Henry VII Holy Roman Emperor from 1308 to 1313, born 1274, died 1313. He was duke of Luxemburg from 1288 and succeeded Albrecht I as Emperor in 1308. In 1310 he acquired the crown of Bohemia for his son John and journeyed to Italy in the same year to combat the Guelphs and Ghibelines. In Milan in 1312 he was crowned king of Italy and later at St John Lateran in Rome he was crowned Emperor by the papal legate of Pope **Clement V**. He died near Siena while making preparations for a Crusade to Naples. He is buried in Pisa. **Dante** praises him in his *Paradiso* as the liberator of Italy.

Henry VIII (of England) King of England from 1509 to 1547, born Greenwich, 28 June 1491, died Windsor, 28 January 1547. For his book against **Luther** in 1521, *Defence of the Seven Sacraments*, Rome gave him the title 'Defender of the Faith'. Henry, a nominal Catholic, wanted to control the Church in England. His so-called 'divorce' was in fact an addition to his conflict with Church authorities. In 1532 the Convocation of the English Clergy yielded to him their legislative independence, Lord Chancellor Thomas **More** resigned, a little later Archbishop **Warham** died and the way was set for Thomas **Cranmer**. With this the die was cast.

Henry, Matthew   Presbyterian minister and Bible commentator, born near Whitchurch, Shropshire, 18 October 1662, died 22 June 1714. Educated at the academy of Thomas Doolittle of Islington. Although commencing the study of law at Gray's Inn, London, in 1685, he was ordained as a Presbyterian minister in 1687 and supervised a dissenting chapel at Chester, located on Crook Lane. In 1712 he took charge of the dissenting church at Hackney, London. In November 1704 he commenced his famous commentary on the Old and New Testaments, reaching the book of Acts by the time of his death, the remainder completed by various dissenting ministers using Henry's notes.

Henry Murdac   Cistercian monk and archbishop of York, died Sherborne, 14 October 1153. He embraced the monastic life under St **Bernard** at Clairvaux, and established a monastery at Vauclair, Laon, but left after a dispute with a neighbouring abbot. He then became abbot of Fountains Abbey in Yorkshire. His term of office was brief, but saw Fountains' status considerably increase. He intervened controversially in a dispute at York, and ended up seeing Fountains sacked. In 1147, with Bernard's backing, he was appointed to succeed his enemy, William Fitzherbert, at York, and was consecrated on 7 December; rejected by the clergy, he was enthroned only in January 1153. A dispute broke out with Durham; he died in flight. An intransigent and pugnacious figure, he nevertheless did a vast amount for the furtherance of the Cistercian cause in England.

Henry of Blois   Cluniac monk and bishop of Winchester, born c.1095, died 8 August 1171. He was the most influential individual in the English Church between **Anselm of Canterbury** and **Thomas Becket**. He was fourth son of Stephen, count of Blois; grandson of **William** the Conqueror; and brother of King Stephen of England. He was appointed bishop of Winchester in 1129. On King Henry II's accession in 1154 he left England for Cluny, where he reorganized the abbey's finances. After his return in 1158 he strove

to keep peace between Henry II and the new archbishop Thomas Becket.

Henry of Bolzano   Blessed, ascetic, born Bolzano, Italy, c.1250, died Treviso, 10 June 1315. After the death of his wife and his son, he began to live in extreme poverty, devoting himself to humble trades, prayer and penance. Famed for his holiness at the time of his death, large crowds attended his funeral, and his tomb in the cathedral of Treviso became a goal for pilgrimages. Paduan Peter of Baone, later bishop of Treviso, wrote a biography of Henry in 1381. **Benedict XIV** confirmed the cult for the Diocese of Treviso and **Pius VII** extended it to Trent.

Henry of Bonn   Blessed, Rhineland nobleman, born c.1100, died Lisbon 1147. Henry set out from Cologne on 27 April 1147 for the Second Crusade. He was among the first who responded to the plea of Alfonse I of Portugal to help free Lisbon from the Saracens. Henry fell during the siege of Lisbon. After his burial at St Vincent's Church, miracles were reported at his grave and this led to his veneration as a martyr.

Henry of Clairvaux   Blessed, Cistercian abbot, cardinal, born Burgundian castle of Marcy, died 1 January 1198. He became a Cistercian in 1155 and abbot of Clairvaux in 1176. He served the Popes by a mission to Archbishop Henry of Rheims in 1162 and by reconciling King Henry II of England with the Church of Canterbury in 1178. He had been active in reconciling the Albigensians and in 1181, as cardinal archbishop of Albano, assumed leadership of that mission. Before his death he persuaded **Frederick I Barbarossa** to join the Crusade, arranged for treaties between France and England, and enrolled Philip Augustus and Henry II in what was the Third Crusade.

Henry of Diessenhofen   Chronicler, born c.1302, died 22 December 1376. Henry studied law at Bologna, was a canon at Beromünster and later Constance, where he became administrator of the cathedral chapter from 1371 to 1372. He spent a great part of his time at the papal court at Avignon and there began to write his *Historia ecclesiae* to cover the years 1316 to 1361, as a continuation of the work of **Bartholomew of Lucca**. Henry added a twenty-fifth book to Bartholomew's 24 and seems also to have made additions to Bartholomew's history. The *Historia ecclesiae* is a highly valuable collection of source material.

Henry of Friemar Theologian and preacher, *Magister Parisiensis*, born *c.*1245, died Erfurt, Germany, 18 October 1340. He is known as the author of numerous ascetical-mystical treatises, among which are *Tractatus de quattuor instinctibus*, *Tractatus de decem praeceptis* and *Explanatio Passionis Dominicae*. A great wealth of ascetical and mystical material is also found in his sermons. He was the first Augustinian to write an account of the origin and development of his Order, after its establishment in its modern form in 1256: *Tractatus de origine et progressu Ordinis Fratrum Heremitarum Sancti Augustini*.

Henry of Ghent Scholastic philosopher and theologian, known as *Doctor solemnis* and *Summus Doctorum*, born Ghent, *c.*1217, died Tournai, 29 June 1293. He actively supported the condemnation of Latin Averroism in 1277, joined other masters at the University of Paris in opposing their chancellor Philip of Thory in 1284 and was a violent opponent of the mendicant orders between 1282 and 1290. He attended the Council of Lyons in 1274 and took an active part in the Synods of Sens, Montpellier, Cologne and Compiègne. His contemporaries sometimes referred to him as *Doctor reverendus* and also *Doctor digressivus*.

Henry of Gorkum Theologian, born Gorkum, The Netherlands, *c.*1386, died Cologne, 1431. He was a Thomistic theologian who obtained the *magister artium* from the University of Paris in 1418. From 1419 until his death, he taught in Cologne. He was founder and rector of the Gymnasium Montanum, canon of the basilica of St Ursula and pro-chancellor of the University of Cologne. He was active on the side of Thomism in the famous debate between the followers of **Albert the Great** and **Thomas Aquinas**. Major works were *Quaestiones in partes St Thomae*, *De praedestinatione* and *De justo bello*.

Henry of Harclay English theologian and ecclesiastic, born *c.*1270, died Avignon, 25 June 1317. Master of arts at Oxford by 1296, he was ordained for the Diocese of Carlisle in 1297 and before 1310 was master in theology. From 11 December 1312 until his death, he was chancellor of the University of Oxford and directly involved in the University's dispute with the Dominicans about graduation in theology. For this reason he went to the Roman curia in Avignon, where he died. In the debate between Thomists and Scotists, he favoured **Duns Scotus**. His most important work was *Quaestiones ordinariae*.

Henry of Heisterbach Blessed, Cistercian abbot, born *c.*1180, died *c.*1244. Born of a noble family and educated in Paris, Henry became a canon of the church of St Cassius in Bonn. About 1200 he entered the Cistercian abbey of Heisterbach, where he was elected abbot in 1208. His reign marked a high point in the history of Heisterbach and he was effective in founding the daughter-house at Marienstatt. He encouraged the important literary activity of **Caesarius of Heisterbach**, and served the Church and secular governments as a counsellor, ambassador and preacher of a Crusade.

Henry of Herford Historian, theologian, philosopher, born Hervorden, Westphalia, early fourteenth century, died Minden, 13 October 1370. He entered the Dominican Order at St Paul's, Minden, and was definitor for the province of Saxony in 1340. His chief work is the *Liber de Rebus memorabilioribus*, ending at the year 1355. Unedited works include a treatise on the Immaculate Conception and a *Catena aurea* on theological and philosophical subjects. In 1377 his remains were transferred to a place of honour by order of Emperor **Charles IV**.

Henry of Herp (Harphus van Erp) Flemish mystical writer, born probably at Erp, The Netherlands, *c.*1405, died Mechelin, 22 February 1477. He joined the Brethren of the Common Life and was rector of the house at Delft and later founder and rector at St Paul's in Gouda. He was one of the most influential representatives of the Devotio Moderna. He established the monastery in the Zoniën forest near Brussels. A great number of his works were collected and published by the Cologne Carthusian Bruno Loer under the title *Theologia mystica*. Henry is strongly dependent on van **Ruysbroeck**. Roman censors issued a corrected version of his writings in 1586.

Henry of Huntingdon English churchman and chronicler, born near London, c.1085, died Huntingdon, 1155. Trained by a certain Albinus of Angers, he was ordained priest before 1110 and made archdeacon of Huntingdon the following year. At the request of Alexander, bishop of Lincoln, he began the composition of *Historia Anglorum*, which took **Bede**'s work as its foundation. He later added three books, written in epistolary form: *De summitatibus*, addressed to important people, including King Henry I, *De miraculis* and *De contemptu mundi*.

Henry of Kalkar Carthusian writer and reformer, born Kalkar, near Cleves, 1328, died Cologne, 20 December 1408. He studied at Cologne and Paris, where he completed his master's degree in 1357. He was made prior of the charterhouse of Arnhem in 1368 and had a great influence on Gerard **Groote**. For twenty years he was visitator of the Rhine province and promoted reform that enabled his Order to survive the Western Schism. He had an important influence on the Devotio Moderna and for a while was proposed as the author of the *Imitation of Christ*. His published works are *Exercitatorium monachale*, which appeared at Cologne under the name of **Denis the Carthusian**, and a chronicle *Ortus et decursus Ordinis Cartusiensis*.

Henry of Lausanne Heretic, died Toulouse, c.1145. He was originally a Benedictine monk but was dismissed for improper behaviour. He later became a penitential preacher and denounced, with a lot of popular support, the worldliness and immorality of the clergy. He was anti-sacerdotal and anti-sacramental, rejecting baptism of children and the Eucharist. He was expelled from the Diocese of Lavardin by Bishop **Hildebert**. After the death of **Peter de Bruys** he became the leader of his sect. He retracted his errors at the Council of Pisa but then returned to his earlier position. He was condemned by the bishop of Toulouse, where he died. He cleared the way for the Waldensians and the Albigensians.

Henry of Livonia Chronicler of the Baltic Church, born near Magdeburg, Germany, last quarter of the twelfth century, died after 1259. He is also known as 'Henry de Lettis' and was probably a Saxon. He went to Livonia c.1205 to join the household of Albert I of Riga. Ordained in 1208, he settled among the Letts, who were being converted to Christianity and conquered by Saxon knights and missionaries. Around 1225 he began his *Chronicle*, in which he traced the conquest of the Baltic by the Saxons. This was later presented to the papal legate Bishop William of Modena, for whom Henry was an interpreter.

Henry of Mechelen Scholastic philosopher, born Mechelen, 24 March 1246, died Liège, 1311. He translated treatises of Abraham ben Ezra (1092–1167) from Hebrew into Latin or French. At the request of his friend **William of Moerbeke** he wrote an astrological work, *Magistralis compositio astrolabii*. His most famous work, containing 537 chapters, was *Speculum divinorum et quorundam naturalium*, which was written for the instruction of the young Guido of Henegouwen, bishop of Liège. *Speculum* is particularly important for the history of medieval Platonism and a valuable record of philosophical controversies at Paris in the late thirteenth century.

Henry of Merseburg Franciscan canonist, born Merseburg, beginning of the thirteenth century, died Magdeburg, c.1276. He taught ecclesiastical law at the Franciscan house of studies in Magdeburg and in Erfurt. As early as 1242 he wrote a short *Summa titulorum* of the Decretals of **Gregory IX**. A number of unknown Franciscans wrote later supplements to Henry's work, known as *Apparatus*, *Quaestiones practicae* and *Casus in summam Henrici*. In the fourteenth century another Franciscan put all of the writings into one work.

Henry of Newark Archbishop of York, probably born in Newark, died York, 15 August 1299. He began his career c.1270 as a clerk to King Edward I. His entire life was one of service to King and State. In 1277 he was in Rome on a mission for Edward. In 1281 he was arbitrating a dispute with subjects of the count of Holland. In 1283 he was fixing dues and collecting subsidies in the Diocese of Durham for the Welsh wars. In 1290 he was installed as dean of York. On 1 May 1296 he was elected archbishop of York and was ordained by the bishop of Durham on 15 June 1298.

Henry of Oyta Secular priest, Scholastic philosopher and theologian, born Oyta, The Netherlands, c.1330, died Vienna, 20 May 1397. He studied at Prague and then Erfurt, then returned to Prague. In 1371 at the papal court at Avignon he was denounced for his teachings, but was absolved after a trial which lasted two years. In 1378 he went to Paris, where he obtained the degree of doctor of theology. When the theological faculty was instituted at the University of Vienna, Henry obtained a chair there and later became dean. Along with Henry of Langenstein he is considered a founder of that university.

Henry of Saint Ignatius Carmelite theologian, born Ath (Belgium), c.1630, died near Liège, 1 April 1719. He entered the Carmelites in 1646 and was ordained in 1652. He taught theology for many years and held administrative positions in three Carmelite provinces. He was an indefatigable controversialist and was a strong opponent of Molinism and of the Jesuits. He advocated a rigid morality that had tinges of Jansenism. His best-known work, *Ethica amoris*, was condemned by the bishop of Liège, the Holy Office and the *parlement* of Paris. His works were put on the Index. Other major works were *Theologia vetus fundament. Ad mentem Joannis de Bacchone* (1667) and *Molinismus profligatus* (1715).

Henry of Settimello Priest and poet, also known as 'Henry of Florence' and 'Henry the Poor', born near Florence, mid-twelfth century, died c.1194. He came from a poor family and studied at the University of Bologna. His claim to recognition is based on a narrative poem, *De diversitate fortunae et philosophiae consolatione*, which was widely read in the Middle Ages. The poem, written c.1194, is arranged in four books and is concerned with the ills of this life that can only be overcome through education. He was in fact a minor figure in the literary life of the late twelfth century, and he made use of classical authors and contemporary writers.

Henry of Uppsala Saint, bishop and martyr, died Köylio, Finland, c.1156. He is a somewhat enigmatic figure. An Englishman who was probably already in Rome when Cardinal Nicholas Breakspear, the later Pope **Adrian IV**, was sent in 1151 as papal legate to Scandinavia. Henry went with him and was ordained bishop of Uppsala by the legate in 1152. The new bishop impressed St **Eric**, the king of Sweden. The bishop accompanied King Eric on a campaign against pagan marauders in Finland and converted many Finns to Christianity. A convert named Lalli refused to do the penance required of him for murder and killed the bishop. From an early date Henry has been venerated as the patron saint of Finland. By 1296 the cathedral at Abo (Turku) was already dedicated to him. In 1300 his remains were translated there.

Henry of Vitskól Blessed, Cistercian abbot, birth date and place unknown, died presumably Vitskól, Denmark, 11 February late 1100s. Henry joined the Cistercians at Clairvaux, where he was noticed by the then abbot, **Bernard of Clairvaux**. In 1143, he was sent to the abbey of Alvastra, Sweden, and became the founding abbot of the abbey at Varnhem seven years later. Forced by external conflict to leave Sweden, he became first abbot of Danish King Waldemar I's new monastery at Vitskól in 1158. In 1166, he worked to found a new monastery at either Oem or Clara-Insula. Feast day 11 February in the Cistercian calender, but he has no official cult.

Henry of Zwiefalten Blessed, Benedictine monk, born c.1200, died Ochsenhausen, Germany, 4 November 1262. Henry was a respected knight in his youth before becoming prior of the Ochsenhausen Priory in 1238. Though few details are known of his life, as prior he seems to have been most concerned with the expansion of the priory library. However, he also helped obtain endowments that helped to decorate the priory church. During his life, he was renowned for great sanctity and also for healing powers. His cult seems to have been late in getting established, which may be why he is normally referred to as 'Blessed' rather than 'Saint'.

Henry Suso Blessed, Dominican spiritual writer, born probably Constance, 21 March 1295, died Ulm, 25 January 1366. He initially entered the Dominican house at Constance, but at eighteen went through a conversion experience; he went to study at Cologne, where he was deeply influenced by Meister **Eckhart**. Around 1326 he published *The Little Book of Truth*, a speculative exposition of Eckhart's teaching. Deprived of his position in

1330, he adopted an itinerant preaching ministry in Switzerland and the Upper Rhine. He served as prior of Constance 1344–6, but his community, the Friends of God, was then exiled and dispersed. He moved to Ulm in 1348, where he spent the rest of his life. He left two collections of letters, and *The Little Book of Eternal Wisdom* or *Clock of Wisdom*, produced in German and Latin, a meditative study much read in the fourteenth and fifteenth centuries. A cult grew up shortly after his death, approved in 1831. Feast day 23 January (formerly 2 March, then 15 February).

Henry the Lion Duke of Saxony, born 1129, died Brunswick, 6 August 1195. Son of Henry the Proud, duke of Saxony and Bavaria, he was born in Ravensburg and succeeded his father as duke of Saxony in 1139. In 1154 **Frederick I Barbarossa** gave him responsibility for Bavaria, which he regained for his family as personal property in 1156. He founded Munich and the Dioceses of Lübeck, Ratzeburg and Schwerin. After Frederick Barbarossa's death in 1190, King **Henry VI** of Germany took the field against him but made peace at Fulda in July 1190.

Henry the Navigator Portuguese prince who initiated the great age of exploration, born Oporto, 4 March 1394, died Cape St Vincent, 13 November 1460. As a result of his patronage the islands of Porto Santo and Madeira and the Azores were colonized, and the Cape Verde Islands discovered. He recruited mathematicians, chart makers, and skilled shipmasters and ended up collecting charts, sailing directions and geographical information. Thanks to him the caravel type of sailing vessel was developed and proved highly useful in explorations. Henry had limited success but his labours produced great results after his death.

Henschenius, Godfrey Jesuit, hagiographer, born Venray (Limburg), 21 June 1601, died Antwerp, 11 September 1681. Studied at the Jesuit College of Bois-le-Duc and joined the Jesuits in 1619. He taught Greek poetry and rhetoric and was ordained in 1634. He was sent to Antwerp in 1635 and remained there until his death. He collaborated with **Bolland** in his work but his main occupation was on the *Acta sanctorum*, seventeen volumes of

which he worked on. He was also first librarian of the Museum Bollandianum in Antwerp.

Heraclius Byzantine emperor, born *c.*575, died February 641. Son of the exarch of Ravenna, he became emperor in 610, having overthrown the regime of the tyrannical Phokas. At that time the empire faced many challenges: Slavs and Avars invading the Balkans, the Persians pressing on the eastern frontier and many internal revolts. After the emperor's initial successes against the Avars and the Persians, the Arabs invaded and overran large parts of the empire. In religious matters Heraclius advocated the middle way of monenergism which satisfied neither Chalcedonians nor Monophysites. In Heraclius' time Latin lost the status of an official language, the empire becoming completely Greek.

Herbert, Edward (Lord Herbert of Cherbury) Philosopher, historian and diplomat, born Eyton-on-Severn, near Wroxeter, 3 March 1583, into an English aristocratic family, died London, 29 August 1648. He was an older brother of the poet George **Herbert** and a close friend of **Donne**, Ben Jonson and Carew. He was educated at University College, Oxford, where he taught himself French, Italian and Spanish, as well as music. In 1600 he moved to London and was presented at court. He was a skilled horseman, and also a skilled fencer: during his continental travels from 1608 to 1611 he became involved in duels while visiting Italian cities. He was appointed ambassador to France in 1619 and while there he published his chief philosophical work, *De veritate*, an attack on empiricism which was much admired by **Descartes** and which influenced the later-seventeenth-century philosopher John **Locke**. Though he is sometimes called the father of English Deism his real affinity lay with the Cambridge Platonists. He had serious disagreements with King **James I** about the French marriage of **Charles** to Henrietta Maria. He stayed a royalist during the Civil War, even accompanying Charles on his Scottish expedition, 1639–40, and was imprisoned in the Tower for royalist speeches in the Lords in 1642 but released on submitting to Parliament. His *Life of Henry VIII* was published in 1649. He wrote his autobiography up to 1624, which was printed by Horace Walpole in 1764, but it scarcely mentions his serious pursuits. He was also the author of several theological works which argued for the existence of God and the importance of duty.

Herbert, George Anglican priest and poet, born Montgomery, Wales, 3 April 1593, died Bemerton, near Salisbury, 1 March 1633. He came from a noble family, the brother of Edward **Herbert**, and was educated at Westminster School and Cambridge, where he became a fellow and public orator. He was briefly MP for Montgomery, 1624–5, but in 1630, under the influence of **Laud**, he was ordained and chose to live quietly as a parson in the country. At Bemerton in Wiltshire he looked after his parish with great pastoral care. His religious poetry is magnificent and some poems, such as 'Come my Way my Truth my Life', have been set to music as hymns. His collection *The Temple, or Sacred Poems* was published posthumously in 1633, as was his *A Priest to the Temple* (1652), pastoral guidance for country parsons.

Herbigny, Michel d' Jesuit bishop and orientalist, born Lille, 8 May 1880, died Aix-en-Provence, 24 December 1957. He joined the Society of Jesus in 1897 and after ordination in 1910 taught Scripture and theology in Belgium until 1921, when he moved to the Gregorian University in Rome. He was put in charge of the Pontifical Oriental Institute, and was instrumental in the foundation of the Russian College in 1929. He was a specialist in Russian affairs, and worked to alleviate the famine there in the early 1920s. He was consecrated bishop in 1926 to work secretly in Russia to prevent the total suppression of the Roman Catholic Church there. For reasons never revealed he was suddenly relieved of these responsibilities, and made an assistant to the papal throne in 1934. He was sent to the Jesuit noviceship, where he spent the remainder of his life.

Herculano de Carvalho e Araújo, Alexandre Portuguese historian, novelist and poet, born Lisbon, 28 March 1810, died Santarem, Portugal, 13 September 1877. He was a liberal opponent of the tyrannical Dom Miguel and was exiled to Paris and London. But he returned to Portugal with the small army which ousted Dom Miguel. Herculano became editor of *O Panorama*, an imitation of the English *Penny Magazine*. Elected to the Cortes he campaigned for democratic reform of education. He became librarian of the Royal Library of Ajuda, and wrote historical novels, and his important *Historia de Portugal*. He founded two newspapers, in which he attacked centralist politics and the power of the clergy. He enjoyed national prestige as a liberal and historian. He advocated civil marriage, and criticized in 1871 the new dogmas of papal infallibility and of the Immaculate Conception.

Herder, Benjamin German Catholic publisher, son of the founder of the Herder publishing company, born 31 July 1818, died 10 November 1888. Educated in publishing by his father and in Paris, he travelled through Europe as a young man and his experiences determined him to help free and revive the Catholic Church in Germany. He became a major publisher of Catholic scholarly works in biblical studies, theology, hagiography, Church history and catechetics. He published the *Bible for Students*, which was translated into 60 languages. His major publication was the *Kirchenlexikon*, which was years in the making and published between 1847 and 1860. He also began to publish a 31-volume Theologische Bibliotek (1882–1930) and published a five-volume *Konversations-Lexikon* (1853–7).

Herder, Hermann German Catholic publisher, son of Benjamin **Herder**, born 1864, died 1937. He broadened the scope of the firm's publishing to include philosophy, political science, law, archaeology, religion and politics, and eventually went into publishing more widely in science and the arts. He published papal encyclicals and began Ludwig von **Pastor**'s sixteen-volume *History of the Popes* (1886–1933). He built a new publishing plant in Freiburg and extended the firm to Vienna, Rome, Barcelona, Tokyo and St Louis, USA. The firm continued to develop and expand under Hermann's son-in-law, Theophil Herder-Dorneich, who took over in 1937, resisted Nazi pressures to conform, and oversaw the reconstruction necessary after World War II and the firm's global expansion. In 1957 Herder and Herder was established in New York.

Herder, Johann Gottfried von German philosopher and theologian, born Kohrungen, East Prussia, 25 August 1744, died Weimar, 18 December 1803. He was influenced by **Kant**'s teachings and studied theology at Königsberg University. He was appointed court preacher at Bückeburg. On Goethe's recommendation he became superintendent of the Weimar church district. Herder helped to found German Romanticism. He was a leading figure in the 'Sturm und Drang' (storm and stress) literary movement. He published many works, including popular poetry, and *Outline of a Philosophy of the History of Man*. Herder helped to develop a philosophy of mind, art and history. Also he published collections of German folksongs.

Hereford, Nicholas Lollard, died *c.*1420. He was ordained priest in 1370. As a fellow of Queen's College, Oxford, he came under the influence of the ideas of John **Wycliffe** and made them his own in his writing and preaching. He was excommunicated and went to Rome to appeal against this but was imprisoned there. He escaped and on arrival back in England continued his preaching, was again arrested and imprisoned, but seems to have recanted. In 1394 he became a canon of Hereford and in 1397 treasurer. He joined the Carmelites and was professed in 1417.

Hergenröther, Josef German cardinal and Church historian, born Würzburg, 15 September 1824, died the abbey of Mehrerau, on Lake Constance, 3 October 1890. He was educated in his home town, then at Rome, where in 1848 he was ordained priest. He did doctoral studies at the University of Munich, where he briefly taught theology before returning to Würzburg as professor of canon law and ecclesiastical history. During the 1860s he took issue with **Döllinger** over the role of the Papacy, and was appointed a consultor to the commission preparing the First Vatican Council. In 1864 he had refused a bishopric, but in 1879 was made a cardinal and put in charge of the Secret Archives of the Vatican, then being opened up to scholars by **Leo XIII**. He early established his credentials as a historian. He proved in 1852 the attribution to **Hippolytus** of the recently discovered *Philosophoumena*, and produced a major, three-volume work on the Patriarch **Photius**, which appeared in 1867–9. He was a defender of the infallibility of the Papacy, and attacked Döllinger in his *Anti-*

Janus, Döllinger having produced an attack on the Council under the pseudonym 'Janus'.

Heribert of Cologne Saint, archbishop, born presumably Worms, Germany, *c.*970, died Cologne, 16 March 1021. Heribert was the son of the count of Worms, where he was educated and where he began his ecclesiastical career as a canon. After serving his friend **Otto III** as chancellor of first Italian, 994, then German, 998, affairs, he became archbishop of Cologne in 999. His bull of canonization from Pope **Gregory VII** is most probably a forgery, but he was known for his great piety and care for the poor. Feast day 16 March.

Heriger of Lobbes Writer, born Louvain (Belgium), middle 900s, died Lobbes (Belgium), 31 October 1007. Heriger entered the abbey of Lobbes early in life and became abbot there in 990. He was the teacher of Wazo of Liège and friend of **Notker of Liège**, but he is most known for his literary endeavours. His chief works are a history of Liège from the 300s to the 600s, entitled *Gesta episcorum Tungrenstium, Trajectensium et Leodiensium*; *Epistola ad quemdam Hugonem monachum*, a work of chronology; and several Lives of saints, most notably *S. Landoaldi et sociorum translatio*. He also wrote on mathematics and compiled patristic texts for use in the Eucharistic controversies.

Herincx, William Franciscan theologian, bishop, born Helmon, North Brabant, 1621, died 17 August 1678. He studied at Louvain, joined the Franciscans and in 1653 became lecturer in theology at Louvain. At the request of his superiors he drew up a course of study for use in Franciscan schools and this, the *Summa theologica scholastica et moralis*, was published in 1660. The work is predominantly Scotist but draws on the teaching of **Bonaventure** and **Thomas Aquinas**. Its probabilist approach brought criticism from the more rigorist wings of the Church. Herincx held senior office in his Order and in 1677 was made bishop of Ypres, a post he held for less than a year.

Herluin of Bec Blessed, founder and first abbot of Bec, born Brionne, Normandy, *c.*995, died Bec, Normandy, 26 August 1078. A knight in the service of the count of Brionne until the age of 38, he became a hermit and founded a monastic community for his followers on his land near Bonneville. In 1035 Bishop Heribert of Lisieux ordained him and named him first abbot of Bec; his zeal attracted two Italians, **Lanfranc** and **Anselm**, both of whom served long terms as prior of Bec and as archbishop of Canterbury. Lanfranc introduced the usages of Bec to England and consecrated the abbey church at Bec in 1077, just a few months before Herluin's death. Feast day 26 August.

Herluka of Bernried Blessed, nun, born Swabia, Germany, mid-tenth century, died convent of Bernried, Augsburg, Germany, 1127. Not much is certain about Herluka's life. She began her cloistered life at Epfach, where she carried on an extensive correspondence with a nun named 'Deimoth', which apparently evinced great familiarity with the events of her day. She was expelled from Epfach for her pro-papal activies and retired to the convent at Bernried, where she died. Her correspondence has been lost, but from what is known she appears to have been well educated and at least moderately influential in her day. Feast day 18 April.

Herman Joseph Saint, Premonstratensian mystic and writer, born Cologne, Germany, 1150, died convent of Hoven, Cologne, 7 April 1241(?). Having had spiritual visions from an early age, Herman joined the Premonstratensians when he was twelve and was sent from Steinfeld Abbey to Frisia to finish his schooling, after which he returned. At Steinfeld, he served as chaplain of the local Cistercian nuns and was noted as a clockmaker. His exemplary life led him to be called 'Joseph'. Some of what he wrote is now lost, but his surviving hymns and prayers (including possibly the *Summi Regis cor aveto*, the earliest hymn about the Sacred Heart) reveal an affectionate piety that foreshadows the Devotio Moderna. His cult was approved in 1958. Feast day 7 April or 24 May.

Herman of Alaska Orthodox saint, monk and missionary, born Serpukhov, Russia, *c.*1760, died Spruce Island, Alaska, 15 November 1836. He was sent to Alaska, with twelve other monks, from the famous monastery of Valaam, to evangelize the Aleuts. By 1823 he was the sole survivor. His ascetic life, gentleness with Indians and settlers alike and love of children made him a highly successful missionary, though he was never ordained priest. His last years were spent in seclusion but his memory was always treasured by the local population. He was canonized 9 August 1970. Regarded as the Orthodox patron saint of North America. Feast day 12 December.

Herman of Reichenau *see* **Hermannus Contractus**

Herman of Salza Grand master of the Teutonic Knights, born Thuringia, Germany, last third of the 1100s, died Salerno, Italy, 20 March 1239. Herman became the grand master of the Teutonic Knights in Syria in 1209 and soon began what was to be a lifelong vocation, keeping peace between the Pope and the Holy Roman Emperor. He was friends with **Frederick II** and persuaded the Pope to crown him Emperor. He and his knights served variously in Hungary under King Andrew II, 1211–25, and in Prussia, 1226, where the knights were given control of a large area of yet-to-be-converted Prussians. After reconciling the Emperor and the Pope again in 1230, he went with the former to Jerusalem in 1230 for the Sixth Crusade. In 1237 he saw the Livonian Knights incorporated into his Order.

Herman of Scheda Abbot and writer, born Cologne, Germany, *c.*1107, died abbey of Scheda, Paderborn, Germany, 1170 (or perhaps 1198). Also known as 'Herman the Jew', he was converted to Christianity out of Judaism while in Mainz on business around 1128. He joined the Premonstratensians at the abbey of Kappenberg, was ordained in 1134 and was named abbot of Scheda (a dependent of Kappenberg) in 1143. He is best known for his autobiography *Opusculum de vita sua* (Patrologia Latina 170), which was written to exhort other Jews to convert to Christianity and in which Herman shows himself to be amazed by the graces he had received. He is also thought to be the author of the *Vita Godefredi*, a biography of an early Premonstratensian in Germany.

Herman of Schildesche Augustinian theologian and administrator, born Schildesche, Germany(?), 8 September *c.*1290, died Würzburg, 8 July 1357. Herman, also known as 'Herman of Westphalia', became an Augustinian at Herford, and studied theology, probably at least some of the time at Paris. He taught in Germany before moving to Paris to teach in 1330, where he also received the bachelor's and master's degrees in theology. He also served as an Augustinian provincial before moving to Würzburg in 1340, where he lectured in theology and was the first vicar general of his Order. Herman wrote many works on various aspects of theology, of which two – the *Speculum manuale sacerdotum* on pastoral theology and the *Introductorium iuris* – saw wide circulation in his own day.

Herman the German Blesed, Dominican missionary, flourished early 1200s. Virtually nothing is known about the life of Herman, except that he was brought into the Dominican Order by St **Dominic** himself, that he co-founded a Dominican house at Friesach in 1219 (the first such house in Germany), and that he later served in Silesia (Poland). He is often grouped together with **Ceslaus of Silesia** and St **Hyacinth**, who were also among Dominic's first followers.

Hermannus Contractus Monk and scholar, born Saulgau, Württemberg-Hohenzollern, Germany, 18 July 1013, died abbey of Reichenau, Germany, 24 September 1054. Also known as 'Herman the Lame' or 'Herman of Reichenau', this son of the count of Altshausen overcame great physical impairment to become a scholar in many areas of thought. He spent his entire life in the abbey of Reichenau on Lake Constance, placed there by his father at the age of seven and taking monastic vows in 1043. He wrote many works, including the *Chronicon*, a list of important events from Christ's birth, and the *De sancta cruce* and *Rex regum Dei agne*, which were part of many sung Latin Masses. A local cult surrounding him was confirmed in 1863, but he is not normally regarded as a saint.

Hermenegild Saint, beheaded Tarragona, Kingdom of the Visigoths, in Spain, 13 April 585. He was son of Leovigold, king of the Visigoths in Spain, and was brought up in the Arian faith. Hermenegild married Ingund, a devout orthodox Catholic, and was converted to Catholicism, partly through her influence and partly through that of the bishop of Seville. Hermenegild rebelled against his father but was defeated. He knew of his forth-

coming death and was fully prepared for it when his father's soldiers appeared. Feast day 13 April.

Hermericus *see* **Adso of Montier-en-Der**

Hermes, Georg German Roman Catholic theologian and philosopher, born Dreierwalde, Münster, 22 April 1775, died Bonn, 26 May 1831. He was educated at the University of Münster, was ordained, and became professor at Münster and then at Bonn. He gave his name to the philosophical doctrine of Hermesianism, explaining Christianity through rationalism. His views spread through Germany. Pope **Gregory XVI** condemned his writings in 1835 and they were placed on the Index of Prohibited Books. The First Vatican Council reaffirmed this in 1869–70.

Herrad of Landsberg Abbess and compiler, born chateau of Landsberg, Alsace (France), c.1130, died Hohenberg, Germany, 25 July 1195. Virtually nothing is known about Herrad before she became abbess of Mont Sainte-Odile in Hohenberg in 1167. The abbey prospered under her leadership, and its level of learning is exemplified in the work Herrad compiled, called *Hortus deliciarum*. The *Hortus deliciarum* was a compendium of thought from the twelfth century, consisting of various spiritual texts but known especially for its more than 300 miniatures.

Herrgott, Marquard German Benedictine, historian, born Freiburg, 9 October 1694, died Krozingen, near Freiburg, 9 October 1762. Studied at Freiburg and Strasburg and was a tutor in Paris for two years. He joined the Benedictines at St Blasien in the Black Forest and was sent to Rome to study theology. He was ordained in 1718 and returned to St Blasien and worked and studied at St Gall, Vienna and St-Germain-des-Prés. In 1728 he went as diplomatic representative for the Estates of Breisgau at the imperial court of Vienna. In 1737 he was made imperial councillor and historiographer but came into conflict with the court in 1749 and went to take up office in his Order. His writings include *Vetus disciplina monastica* (1726), a history of St Blasien Monastery and of the Diocese of Constance, and *Genealogia diplomatica Augustae Gentis Hapsburgicae* (1737), which he continued and finished as *Monumenta Augustae Domus Austriacae*.

Herrick, Robert Clergyman and poet, born London and baptized there on 24 August 1591, buried Dean Prior, Devon, 15 October 1674. Educated at Westminster School, he was originally apprenticed to a goldsmith, his father's trade, but at the age of 22 went to Cambridge. He took holy orders in 1623 and was later appointed to the parish of Dean Prior, where, except for the period from 1647 to 1660, when he was deprived of his living because of his royalist sympathies, he remained until his death. Though he is best known for his graceful secular poetry, he also wrote religious poems under the title of *Noble Numbers*.

Hersende of Montsoreau First prioress of Fontevrault, died Fontevrault before 1112. The twice-widowed sister of Hubert of Champagne, she was a nun at Fontevrault and was chosen by **Robert of Arbrissel** to be that community's first prioress, where she was responsible for governing the men and women of the double monastery.

Hertling, Georg von German Roman Catholic statesman and philosopher, born Darmstadt, 31 August 1843, died Ruhpolding, Germany, 4 January 1919. He was a devout scholar, and became professor at Bonn and then Munich. He founded the Görres-Gesellschaft to promote Roman Catholic studies. He became parliamentary leader of the Catholic Centre Party. Under King Ludwig III of Bavaria, he became prime minister and foreign minister. In 1917 he became imperial chancellor, though power was in the hands of the military, and in 1918 he resigned.

Hesychius of Jerusalem Saint, monk, Church historian and theologian, active in the fifth century. In 412 he seems to have been a presbyter in Jerusalem. His *Church History*, now lost, was cited at the Council of Constantinople in 553 and reveals him as a supporter of **Cyril of Alexandria** in his stand against Nestorianism, and opposed to the Christology of **Theodore of Mopsuestia**. He played an active role in support of the Alexandrians leading up to the Council of Chalcedon. His writings, which survive only in part, included com-

mentaries on most of the Bible, and sermons. Feast day in the Greek Church 28 March.

Hettinger, Franz Roman Catholic priest and theologian, born Aschaffenburg, Germany, 13 January 1819, died Würzburg, 26 January 1890. Educated in Rome, Hettinger's entire academic career was spent at the University of Würzburg, which, along with his colleagues and friends Josef **Hergenröther** and Heinrich Joseph **Denzinger**, he helped to bring to international prominence. He taught preaching and apologetics and succeeded Denzinger as professor of dogma. His many works include *Apologie des Christenthums* (1863), *Aus Kirche und Welt* (1885) and *Timotheus, Brief an einen jungen Theologen* (1891). He was also quite a scholar of the works of **Dante**. Pope **Leo XIII** named him a domestic prelate in 1879.

Hetzenauer, Michael Capuchin biblical scholar, born Zeel, Austria, 30 November 1860, died Rome, 8 August 1928. Hetzenauer became a Capuchin when he was eighteen and was ordained in 1885, when he began teaching at the Capuchin seminary in Innsbruck, Austria. Known for his piety as well as his scholarship, he was appointed in 1904 to the pontifical seminary of St Apollinaris (now Lateran), where he worked to combat the influences of Modernism. In 1914, he was made a consultor to the Pontifical Bible Commission. His works include commentaries on Genesis and the genealogies of Jesus and critical editions of the Greek NT and the Latin Vulgate.

Heuser, Jerman Joseph Roman Catholic priest and scholar, born Potsdam, Germany, 28 October 1852, died Overbrook, Pennsylvania, 22 August 1933. Heuser arrived in America from Germany in 1870 to study at St Charles Seminary in Overbrook, where he also taught in the preparatory department. Ordained in 1876, he was made a professor, teaching languages and Scripture at St Charles until his retirement in 1927. Heuser's influence stems largely from his founding and editing of the *American Ecclesiastical Review*, which promoted literary as well as scholarly endeavours, and from his serving as general censor of Catholic publications in the United States from 1907 to 1927.

Hewit, Augustine Francis Associate founder of the Paulist Order, born Fairfield, Connecticut, 27 November 1820, died New York, 3 July 1897. Hewit originally studied to be a Congregationalist minister before joining first the Episcopal Church in 1843 under the influence of the Oxford theologians and then the Roman Catholic Church in 1846. Ordained in 1847, he professed as a Redemptorist in 1950, only to be released from his vows eight years later to help Isaac **Hecker** found the Paulists. He helped to write the constitutions of the new society and oversaw it when Hecker took ill. He was elected superior general in 1889, and as such helped to found St Paul's College in the Catholic University of America and the Paulist Press (originally Columbus Press) in 1891.

Heywood, Oliver The pioneer of Presbyterianism in the West Riding of Yorkshire, born Little Lever, Bolton, Lancashire, March 1630, died Northowram, Yorkshire, 4 May 1702. Having undergone a religious experience at an early age by the teaching of 'an ancient godly widow woman', he 'went up to Cambridge, and was placed in Trinity College'. Following his ordination at Bury, Lancashire, in 1652, he served as curate at Coley, near Halifax. As a result of his refusal to give his assent to the Act of Uniformity of 1662, he was deprived of his living and, constantly in fear of fines and imprisonment, he undertook regular preaching tours throughout Yorkshire and Lancashire. During such evangelistic excursions he established numerous Presbyterian Churches, the main ones being those at Bingley and Northowram.

Hickey, Antony Irish Franciscan professor of theology and philosophy, born Dunmoylan, County Limerick, c.1586, died St Isidore's College, Rome, 26 June 1641. He studied at Louvain, where he became a professor, and was then posted to Cologne. In 1619 he was sent to Rome to assist Luke **Wadding**. He supported the advance of Hugh **O'Reilly**, friend to the Observant Friars, to the See of Armagh against his English rivals in Rome and was the promoter of the Franciscan Order's causes at Rome in 1639. His most notable publications are a complete edition with commentary of the works of **Duns Scotus** (1639) and, under the pseudonym 'Dermitius Thadaei', *Nitela*

Franciscanae religionis, an apologia for the Franciscans.

Hickey, Joseph Loysius Augustinian prior general, born Chicago, Illinois, 30 May 1883, died 1955. After studies at Villanova College (now University), Hickey joined the Augustinians in 1903 and was immediately sent to Rome, where he was ordained and received his doctorate. From 1910 he served many functions at the main American Augustinian community in Villanova, until 1925, when he was elected assistant general of the Order at the chapter in Rome. In 1947, he became the first American prior general of the Augustinians, in which capacity he served until 1953, helping to rebuild the Order after World War II (especially in Italy), and serving numerous assignments for the Holy See and the Congregation of the Sacraments in Rome.

Hicks, Elias Quaker preacher, born Westbury, New York, 19 March 1748, died Jericho, New York, 27 February 1830. The son of a Quaker farmer, Hicks began a lifelong campaign against slavery when in 1776 he was asked by the Westbury Meeting to urge Quakers to free their slaves. Beginning in 1781, he travelled America with this message, his travels described in his *Journal* (1832). Doctrinally, Hicks downplayed the role of Scripture and sacrament and denied the deity of Christ. His teaching garnered many followers and occasioned a split among the Quakers at their Yearly Meetings in 1827–8.

Hidalgo y Costilla, Miguel Mexican Catholic priest, revolutionary and the father of Mexican independence, born Corraleyo, near Guanajuato, Mexico, 8 May 1753, died Chichuachua, 31 July 1811. Most of his life he was a diligent parish priest in Dolores, promoting agriculture and industry. However, in 1810 he rang the Dolores church bells, initiating a revolutionary movement. Mexican Indians and Mestizos followed his banner of the Virgin of Guadalupe, protectress of Mexican Indians. They captured Guanajuato and other cities. With an army of 80,000, he marched on Mexico City but his supporters failed him and he was defeated at Aculo. He was finally defeated at Calderón in 1811, attempted escape, was caught, dismissed from the priesthood and shot. Through his initiative, his name became a revolutionary symbol.

Hidulf Saint, monastic founder, born probably Regensburg, Germany, date unknown, died abbey of Moyenmoutier or Bonmoutier, France, 11 July 707. Hidulf was first a monk in Trier, Germany, at Saint-Maximin's. He later served as a sort of auxiliary bishop for the Diocese of Trier before retiring to a hermitage in the Vosges Mountains. Other hermits gathered to him, and together they founded the abbey of Moyenmoutier. Feast day 11 July.

Hidulf of Lobbes Saint, monastic benefactor and monk, date and place of birth unknown, died Lobbes (Belgium), 23 June 707. Hildulf was a Frankish nobleman and a good friend of Pepin of Heristal. In the later part of the seventh century, he aided St **Landelin** and St Ursmar in their work of founding an abbey in Lobbes. After the death of his wife, St Aya, Hildulf joined the abbey and lived as a monk until his death.

Higden, Ralph or Ranulf *see* **Ralph Higden**

Hilarion of Gaza Monk and saint, born 291, died Cyprus, 371. His Life by **Jerome** is our only source about this Palestinian monk. A student in Alexandria he was converted and frequented the desert cell of St **Anthony of Egypt**, whose ascetic way of life he was soon to imitate. Disciples joined him from 329 onwards. Near the end of his life he travelled widely, seeking solitude in Egypt and elsewhere, finally dying in Cyprus. Feast day 21 October.

Hilarius of Mende Bishop and saint, died *c.*540. A tenth- or eleventh-century Life describes him as a hermit who lived on the banks of the Tarn and attracted a group of followers, for whom he built a monastery; this is probably unreliable. He was made bishop of Mende before 535. Nothing is known of his episcopate, except that on one occasion he offered shelter to St **Leobin** of Chartres, and that he attended the Synod of Auvergne in 535. Feast day 25 October.

Hilarius of Sexten Capuchin moral theologian, born Sexten (Sesto), Italy, 15 December 1839, died

Merano, Italy, 20 October 1899. Born Christian Catterer, Hilarius became a Capuchin in 1858. After his ordination in 1862, he did pastoral work until 1872, when he began teaching moral theology in Merano at the Capuchin convent there. He also served as the Capuchin provincial for Tirol, 1889–92. He wrote a compendium of theology and a tract on the sacraments for the use of his students. He also contributed many articles on moral theological questions to the *Linzer Quartalschrift*.

Hilary Pope, born Sardinia, elected 19 November 461, died Rome, 29 February 468. Archdeacon to **Leo I**, he was one of the papal delegates at the notorious 'Robber Synod' at Ephesus in 449. As Pope, he strengthened Rome's hold over the Church in Gaul and Spain, and held a number of councils in Rome to settle Western disputes. He rebuilt numerous churches in Rome, and constructed the chapel of St John the Evangelist in the baptistery of St John Lateran to commemorate his escape at Ephesus. He rebuked the Emperor Anthemius for tolerating the spread of the Macedonian heresy at Rome; he also sent an encyclical to the East endorsing the confessional statements of Nicaea (325), Ephesus (431), Chalcedon (451), and Leo's *Tome to Flavian* (449).

Hilary of Arles Bishop and saint, born *c.*401, died Arles, 5 May 449. A relative of St **Honoratus**, he became a monk at Lérins, then succeeded Honoratus as metropolitan bishop of Arles, *c.*430. He presided over notable gatherings such as the First Council of Orange (441) and the Council of Vaisson (442). In 444, having deposed a local bishop, Chelidonius of Besançon, exceeding thereby his metropolitan authority, he was deprived of his powers by Pope **Leo I**, who obtained from the Emperor Valentinian the right to direct Roman control over the Church in Gaul. He wrote a Life of Honoratus which survives; he also produced letters and poetry. Feast day 5 May.

Hilary of Chichester Bishop, died Chichester(?), 1169. He was elected bishop of Chichester in 1146, consecrated 1147, and though elected archbishop of York the election did not get papal approval. In 1148 Hilary was responsible for a reconciliation between King Stephen and Archbishop **Theobald**. He lived and practised at the Roman curia for some years and became familiar with all the then developments in canon law. As bishop he was keen to assert his rights of visitation and abbots' duty to attend his synods but he failed to enforce this episcopal jurisdiction over the abbot of Battle Abbey. In the acrimonious debates over criminous clerks between King Henry II and **Thomas Becket**, Hilary opposed Thomas: at the Council of Northampton in 1163 Hilary with five other bishops urged Becket to resign his position as archbishop and they formed a powerful embassy to Pope **Alexander III** at Sens, where King Henry II's disputed and celebrated Constitutions of Clarendon were condemned. Hilary urged Becket to make his peace with the king and then went on personally to absolve all those excommunicated by Becket. He died in 1169 before the murder of Becket in his own cathedral of Canterbury.

Hilary of Orléans Poet, pupil of Peter **Abelard**, early twelfth century, dates and places of birth and death unknown. On the basis of an assertion by Mabillon, he was long thought to have been an Englishman, but this is generally now thought not to be the case. A pupil of Abelard at the Paraclete *c.*1125, one of his poems is a lament that Abelard has forced his pupils to take lodgings in a nearby town so that his hermitage is undisturbed. His work is a collection of lyrics, miracle plays and poems that mix piety (a poetic *Vita* of the anchoress Eve of Wilton) and secular pleasures (including several poems addressed to beautiful young boys).

Hilary of Poitiers Bishop and saint, born Poitiers, start of fourth century, died Poitiers, 367. Bishop of Poitiers (France) from *c.*350, he was an anti-Arian. Exiled to Phrygia by the Synod of Béziers (356), he became acquainted with Eastern theology, especially with the work of **Origen**. In the Trinitarian conflicts he mediated between the Homoousians and the Homoiousians. In 361 he returned to Gaul. His moderate theological position is reflected in his works, such as *De Trinitate*. His exegesis is allegorical, as shown in his commentaries on the Gospel of Matthew and on the Psalms. Feast day 14 January.

Hilda of Whitby Saint and abbess, born Northumbria, 614, died Whitby, 17 November 680.

Hilda (Hild) was the great-niece of King **Edwin** of Northumbria and became a Christian at the age of thirteen, baptized by **Paulinus** at York in 627. St **Aidan** appointed her abbess of a convent at Hartlepool in 649, the earliest nunnery in Northumbria; and in Whitby she founded the first double monastery (for men and women) in 657, an innovation from Gaul, and, though richly endowed by the Northumbrian dynasty, she ruled it with great wisdom. Many of the Anglo-Saxon nobility of Northumbria entrusted their daughters to Hilda's care. Whitby became a nursery for English bishops and it was there that **Caedmon** was encouraged to write vernacular poetry. **Bede** also tells us that it was from Whitby that we have the earliest surviving Anglo-Saxon hagiographical writing, in a Life of Pope **Gregory I** *c.*700. When the Synod of Whitby met in 664 to settle the Paschal controversy between the Roman and Celtic traditions, she argued in favour of keeping Celtic religious customs, including their dating of Easter. But when the decision to follow Roman customs was made under the leadership of St **Wilfrid**, Hilda concurred while **Colman** left with a splinter party of both English and Irish monks. Feast day 17 November.

Hildebert of Lavardin Archbishop and author, born Lavardin, France, *c.*1056, died Tours, 18 December 1133. Educated at the cathedral school at Le Mans, he became an archdeacon there in 1091, and was elected bishop of Le Mans in 1096 and archbishop of Tours in 1125. His ecclesiastical career was difficult: shortly after his election to the See of Le Mans, he quarrelled with King William II, who ordered him to England in 1099, where he was all but a prisoner until the next year; as archbishop of Tours he had numerous difficulties with King **Louis VI**. Besides being a skilful preacher, he was an able administrator and bishop: he expelled the popular but heretical preacher **Henry of Lausanne** from his diocese, attended the First Lateran Council in 1123, and presided over the provincial Synod of Nantes in 1127. He is, however, best known for his literary work and mastery of Latin style.

Hildebrand, Dietrich von Roman Catholic philosopher and moral theologian, born Italy, 1889, died New Rochelle, New York, 30 January 1977. After studying philosophy under Husserl in Göttingen, Hildebrand became a Catholic in 1914. He taught at Munich from 1924 to 1933, when he was forced to flee to Florence. After sojourns in Austria, France and Spain, he settled at Fordham University in New York in 1942, where he remained until 1960. Hildebrand's chief aim in his writing and teaching was to defend what he saw as traditional Catholicism against secularism and liberalism. To this end, he wrote, among others, books on moral theology (*Christian Ethics*, 1952, and *True Morality and its Counterfeits*, 1955), on the Church (*Trojan Horse in the City of God*, 1967) and in defence of *Humanae vitae* (*In Defence of Purity*, 1970).

Hildegard of Bingen (Hildegaard) Saint, abbess, authoress, musician and German mystic, born Böckelheim, 1098, died Bingen, 17 September 1179. She was brought up by the Blessed **Jutta** and had religious experiences from an early age. These caused her embarrassment and confusion so that she was reluctant to talk about them. In later life however she was persuaded to write them down and obtained the approval of both the archbishop and the Pope. She was skilled in healing and in musical composition. She had a wide influence in her time and has recently again become well known for the breadth of her learning and teaching. Her main work recording her visions is the *Scivias* but she wrote many other works and letters. Miracles were reported during her life and after her death. Feast day 17 September.

Hildegard of Kempten Blessed, wife of **Charlemagne**, born 758, place of birth unknown, died Thionville (France), 30 April 783. Hildegard was born into a family allied with the dukes of Swabia. The second wife of Charlemagne, she was the mother of **Louis I** the Pious. She contributed greatly to the rebuilding of the abbeys of Kempten and St Arnulf of Metz. Though she was buried in the latter abbey, the sisters of Kempten obtained her relics in 872, and she has been venerated as blessed since the late 900s. Feast day 30 April.

Hildegunde of Meer Blessed, place and date of birth unknown, died Germany, 6 February 1183. Of noble birth, after her husband's death she joined the Premonstratensians and founded the convent of Meer in 1165 and became the first

prioress. Her son was involved in the sack of Rome with **Frederick I Barbarossa** and to expiate his sin she built a monument. Her daughter **Hadewych** succeeded her as prioress and both are recognized as among the blessed. Feast day 6 February.

Hildegunde of Schönau Cistercian, place and date of birth unknown, died Schönau Abbey, 20 April 1188. Her merchant father dressed her as a man and named her 'Joseph'. He took her on a pilgrimage to Rome and died during the journey. She then entered the Cistercian abbey of Schönau but died during the novitiate and was discovered to be a woman only after her death. The story was well known and she became venerated by Cistercians. There are other such stories however from the earliest days of monasticism. The earliest record of 'Joseph''s life is from Berthold, who shared the novitiate with her.

Hildelide (Hildelithe) Saint, Anglo-Saxon Benedictine abbess, born France, c.650, died Barking, c.717. Of royal birth she entered a monastery in France (Chelles or Faremoutiers). She was invited to Barking Abbey by **Erconwald**, bishop of London, to train his sister St **Ethelburga**. Hildelide became second abbess there until her death. **Bede**, **Boniface** and **Aldhelm** admired her and *De laudibus virginitatis* by Aldhelm was dedicated to her. Feast days 24 March, 3 February.

Hildigrim Saint, bishop and missionary, date and place of birth unknown, died Halberstadt, Germany, 19 June 827. St **Ludger**'s brother, Hildigrim was his brother's pupil and companion, travelling with him to Rome in 784 and then Monte Cassino. After serving for a time as abbot of Werden, Germany, he became bishop of Châlons-sur-Marne in 802. He went from there to be bishop of Osterwiek and spent the last eight years of his life in active missionary work as the bishop of Halberstadt.

Hilduin of Saint-Denis Royal chancellor and translator, born c.775, place of birth unknown, died Prüm, Germany, 22 November c.855–9. The cousin of **Louis I** the Pious of France, Hilduin was the student of **Alcuin** and teacher of **Hincmar** of Rheims and **Walafrid Strabo**. In 815 he was made abbot of Saint-Denis-en-France and during 819–22 was archchaplain to his cousin. He participated in the Council of Paris (825) but his involvement in a rebellion against Louis I resulted in his exile in 831. He was recalled through Hincmar's influence and devoted the rest of his life to reforming the abbey of Saint-Denis. His Life of St **Denis** aided the mistaken identification of him with Dionysius the Pseudo-Areopagite, whose works Hilduin also translated in 831–4. He finished his life as the archchancellor of **Lothair I** and archbishop designate of Cologne.

Hilton, Walter Devotional writer and mystic, date and place of birth unknown, died Thurgarton, Nottinghamshire, 24 March 1396. He quite possibly studied canon law at Cambridge. He became a hermit but was later a professed Augustinian at Thurgarton. His best-known work is the *Scala perfectionis*, Part One of which shows how the soul must obliterate the image of sin, replacing it with the image of Christ, and Part Two compares the active ascetic life of faith with the contemplative life of feeling and describes the beginnings of contemplation. His writing is influenced by **Augustine**, **Gregory** the Great and Richard **Rolle** and by the author of the *Cloud of Unknowing* – it is unlikely that he was the author of this last. The *Scale of Perfection* was first printed by Wynkyn de Worde in 1494.

Hincmar Archbishop of Rheims, born of noble parents *c*.806, died Epernay, 21 December 882. He was educated by Abbot **Hilduin** at the abbey of Saint-Denis, and accompanied Hilduin to the court of **Louis I** the Pious in 822. He later returned to the abbey, but in 840 was called into the service of **Charles II** the Bald. In 845 **Sergius II** raised him to the See of Rheims. Hincmar restored the archbishopric to all those rights and lands previously appropriated into lay hands and he became a keen reformer of the clergy, though his conduct towards them led to conflict with the Papacy. He had a wide knowledge of Roman civil and canon law and of theology. Hincmar was one of the first to attack the predestinarian heresy of **Gottschalk of Orbais**, in his *De Praedestinatione Dei et libero arbitrio*, which he followed up by a work on the Trinity, *De una et non trina deitate*. As a reformer of both the clergy and laity he condemned King **Lothair II**'s repudiation of his wife, Queen Theut-

berga. At the Council of Soissons in 863 he supported Pope **Nicholas I** in the condemnation of the Pseudo-Isidorian Decretals and in 869 he exercised his primatial rights in consecrating Charles the Bald at Metz. By insisting on his episcopal privileges he came into conflict both with the Frankish kings and occasionally with the Papacy; he stated his position in a forthright tract, *De jure metropolitanorum*, and at the same time wrote a Life of St **Remigius**, the founder of his see, to prove the primacy of Rheims over the other bishoprics and persisted in the right of St Remigius' successors to crown the kings of France. His opinions on the duties of kings are enshrined in his *Instructio ad Ludovicum regem* and in his *De Regis persona et regio ministerio*, which he dedicated to Charles the Bald. On the Norman invasion of 882 Hincmar fled to Epernay and died there.

Hincmar of Laon Bishop, born France, *c*.820–40, died, place unknown, 879. A young orphan, Hincmar became a ward of his uncle and namesake, Archbishop **Hincmar** of Rheims, who secured his appointment as bishop of Laon in 858. Hincmar soon began working to expand his power, challenging the authority of the king in his diocese. In 869, **Charles II** the Bald had him seized and in retaliation Hincmar placed an interdict on his diocese. This was revoked by his uncle and led to a conflict between the two, eventually leading to Hincmar of Laon's banishment and blinding by the Synod of Douzy (871). The banishment was lifted in 879 by Pope **John VIII**, but Hincmar died soon after.

Hindemith, Paul German composer, viola player and theorist, born Hanau, near Frankfurt am Main, 16 November 1895, died Frankfurt am Main, 28 December 1963. He studied at Munich, played in cafés, led the Frankfurt Opera orchestra, joined a string quartet and taught in Berlin. In the 1920s his music was often associated with bizarre expressionist subjects. Also he wrote in a neo-baroque or neoclassical style, as in his *Kammermusik Op. 24 No 1*, and encompassed jazz. He pioneered *Gebrauchsmusik*, utility music for amateurs. His best-known works are *Mathis der Maler*, *Nobilissima visione* and *The Four Temperaments*, and he also wrote organ sonatas, a Mass and *Ite, angeli veloces*, a cantata. The Nazis banned his opera *Mathis der Maler*, considering his music 'bolshevistic'.

Hinderer, Roman Jesuit missionary and cartographer, born Reiningen, Alsace, France, 21 September 1669, died Wutsin, China, 26 August 1744. A Jesuit in Mainz, Germany, since 1686, Hinderer was sent to China in 1707 to assist the Jesuits in their efforts to map parts of China for Emperor K'ang-hsi. The emperor allowed him to travel and preach Christianity through his empire, and he met with great success, which he attributed to his devotion to the Sacred Heart. He served as a papal representative to the missions in China, Japan and Tonkin and also wrote books on the Mass and the rosary for his Chinese converts.

Hingston, Sir William Hales Roman Catholic surgeon, born Hinchinbrook, Quebec, Canada, 29 June 1829, died Montreal, Quebec, 19 February 1907. After medical studies at McGill University in Montreal and the University of Edinburgh, Hingston returned to Canada to have a long and distinguished surgical career. In 1875 he was elected mayor of Montreal, was knighted in 1895 and earned the high Roman Catholic honours of Knight Commander of the Order of St Gregory and the medal *Pro Ecclesia et Pontifice*. He made a number of surgical and medical advances in his career, organized Canada's first board of health, and supported the vaccination against smallpox.

Hinschius, Paul Lutheran canonist and professor of law, born Berlin, Germany, 25 December 1835, died Berlin, 13 December 1898. Hinschius studied civil and canon law at Heidelberg and Berlin and from 1872 to 1898 exerted a profound influence on thinking about law, both civil and ecclesiastical, in Germany. This influence was in large measure due to his edition of the Pseudo-Isidorian Decretals and his large work on canon law in Germany, *Das Kirchenrecht der Katholiken und Protestanten in Deutschland: System des katholischen Kirchenrechts mit besonderer Rücksicht auf Deutschland* (6 vols, 1869–97). Though his work influenced Protestants and Roman Catholics alike, many suspect his involvement in the anti-Catholic legislation of Prussia during the Kulturkampf of the late nineteenth century.

Hinsley, Arthur Cardinal archbishop of Westminster, born Carlton, near Selby, Yorkshire, 25 August 1865, died Buntingford, Hertfordshire, 17 March 1943. He studied at the local Catholic school, then at Ushaw College, near Durham, and the English College, Rome, and gained a DD from the Gregorian University. He was ordained priest in 1893 and returned to Ushaw to teach, then went to Keighley as parish priest. Hinsley founded St Bede's Grammar School in Bradford and was its headmaster, but he also taught at the seminary at Wonersh before becoming rector of the English College, Rome, 1917–30. He was parish priest at Sutton Park, 1904–11, and Sydenham, 1911–17. He became a domestic papal prelate in 1917 and in 1926 titular bishop of Sebastopolis and the following year visitor apostolic to Africa. From 1930 to 1934 he was delegate apostolic and titular archbishop of Sardis, and the following year appointed archbishop of Westminster. He was raised to the cardinalate in 1937. In the early years of the Second World War he launched the 'Sword of the Spirit' movement to rejuvenate the Christian cause against Nazism.

Hippolytus of Rome Bishop and saint, born *c.*170, died Sardinia, 235, the last ecclesiastical author in the West writing in Greek. About his career we know only that he was an Antipope at the time of **Calixtus I** (217–22) and that he suffered exile in Sardinia. A prolific writer, most of his works (commentaries, especially on the books of the OT, heresiological, apologetical and chronographical tractates) survive only in fragments, the authenticity of which it is often difficult to ascertain. Feast day 3 August in the Roman calendar, 30 January in Orthodox Churches.

Hirscher, Johann Roman Catholic theologian, born Altergarten, Württemberg, 20 January 1788, died Freiburg, 4 September 1865. After education at the University of Freiburg, Hirscher was ordained in 1810. In 1817, he was a professor of moral and pastoral theology at Tübingen and from 1837 until his retirement in 1863 he taught at Freiburg. A co-founder of the *Theologische Quartalschrift*, Hirscher propounded, in his *De genuina missae notione* (1821), Masses in the vernacular, full Communion (under both kinds) for the laity and the abolition of private Masses. He also wrote a devotional moral theology and many works on catechesis. His works were often placed on the Index of Prohibited Books and considered very controversial, but history has shown him to be simply a man much ahead of his time. Many of his ideas were officially adopted by the Roman Catholic Church at the Second Vatican Council, 100 years after his death.

Hittorf, Melchior   Roman Catholic liturgist, born Cologne, Germany, c.1525, died Cologne, 1584. Hittorf's fame rests entirely on his collection and publication of the works of medieval liturgists and parts of the ancient Roman Ordinal in his *De Divinis Catholicae Ecclesiae Officiis ac Ministeriis* (1568). The work, still valuable for its completeness, was designed to support Catholic liturgy against the growing tide of the Reformation in Germany.

Hitze, Franz   Roman Catholic priest and politician, born Hanemicke, Germany, 16 March 1851, died Bad Nauheim, 20 July 1921. Educated in Paderborn and Würzburg, Hitze was ordained in 1878. In 1880 he was made executive secretary for a Catholic industrial association named Arbeiterwohl. His political career began in 1884, when he was elected to the Prussian house of representatives, 1884–93, 1898–1912, and to the Constitutive National Assembly, 1884–1921. In 1893 he also became a professor at Munich. In all he did, Hitze concerned himself with the relationship of workers to government and the ideas of social welfare, especially with workers' rights. His influence was felt all over Germany and was responsible for the founding of many Catholic social action groups.

Hłond, Augustyn   Cardinal and primate of Poland, born Brzeczkowice, Poland, 5 June 1881, died Warsaw, 22 October 1948. Hłond became a Salesian in Turin, Italy, in 1897, studied in Rome and was ordained in Cracow in 1905. After World War I, he was made the first bishop of Kadowice in 1925 and a year later archbishop of Gniezno-Poznan and primate of Poland. He escaped to Rome when the Germans invaded Poland but was eventually taken captive in France in 1944; he was freed by American troops a year later. He worked to help Catholicism in Poland recover after the Nazi occupation and also worked to secure free-

doms for the Church under the new Communist regime. He is buried in St John's in Warsaw.

Hobart, John Henry   Bishop, writer and educator, born Philadelphia, 14 September 1775, died Auburn, New York, 12 September 1830. In New York he founded the Protestant Episcopal Theological Seminary. Later he became a professor and was well-known as a preacher, emphasizing 'evangelical truth and apostolic order'. Having done extensive writing, he founded the Protestant Episcopal Tract Society and Protestant Episcopal Press. He became assistant bishop of New York. His writings include *Essays on the Subject of Episcopy* and *An Apology for Apostolic Order and its Advocates*. Hobart helped the culture of the Church of England to expand into the USA.

Hoberg, Gottfried   Roman Catholic priest and biblical scholar, born Heringhausen, Germany, 19 November 1857, died Freiburg, Germany, 19 January 1924. Ordained in 1881 after studies in Paderborn and Münster, Hoberg obtained his doctorate in theology and philosophy at Bonn. From 1887 to 1890, he taught OT at Paderborn before moving to Freiburg to teach, first NT, 1890–4, then OT, 1894–1919, until his retirement. He was made a member of the Pontifical Biblical Commission in 1903, supported conservative Catholic views against Modernism, and contributed to the investigation of various exegetical problems of the Pentateuch. His publications include commentaries on the Psalms and the Pentateuch, a catechism and an introduction to the Bible.

Hocedez, Edgar   Jesuit theologian, born Ghent, Belgium, 1 July 1877, died Fayt-le-Manage, Belgium, 5 September 1948. Hocedez became a Jesuit in 1895, and his superior initially had him working on articles for the *Analecta Bollandiana*, but his talents for theology persuaded them to let him teach the subject. He taught in the Orient for a time before going to the Catholic University of Louvain, Belgium, in 1912. From 1919, he taught theology at Louvain until 1928, when he moved to Rome to direct the doctoral theological programme at the Gregorian. He fled Rome during World War II and eventually returned to his native Belgium. He served as editor of the *Nouvelle Revue Théologique*, 1920–6, and published many books, but his masterwork is generally agreed to be his *Histoire de la théologie au XIXᵉ siècle* (3 vols, 1949–52).

Hochwalt, Fredrick G. Roman Catholic priest and educator, born Dayton, Ohio, 25 February 1909, died at sea on the liner *Coronia*, 5 September 1966. After studying in Dayton and Cincinnati, Hochwalt was ordained in 1935 in the Archdiocese of Cincinnati. He served as a pastor and school-teacher there for two years before pursuing advanced degrees at the Catholic University of America. In 1944, he succeeded George **Johnson** as director of the Department of Education for the National Catholic Welfare Conference, a post he held until January 1966. A strong advocate of Catholic education and a well-known national leader in education, Hochwalt served on numerous international commissions, received twelve honorary doctorates, and published many articles on various aspects of education.

Hodge, Charles US Presbyterian theologian, born Philadelphia, 27 December 1797, died Princeton, New Jersey, 19 June 1878. He studied theology at Princeton and later returned to become professor of biblical literature, then of theology. He travelled in Europe, meeting prominent theologians, and studied in Paris, Halle and Berlin. He represented the Calvinist conservative view of the Bible and stressed its verbal infallibility. Hodge was elected moderator of the General Assembly (Old School) of the Presbyterian Church. His books include *Systematic Theology*, *The Constitutional History of the Presbyterian Church in the USA* and *What Is Darwinism?*

Hodges, Melvin Lyle Assemblies of God missionary and author, born Lynden, Washington, 1909, died 1988. Hodges began his missionary career in El Salvador in 1936 following a ministry in Colorado. He soon became general superintendent of the Pentecostal churches in Nicaragua and in 1954 field director of missions to Latin America. In 1953 he produced *The Indigenous Church*, the first Pentecostal book on missiology. In 1980 he became Noel Perkin Professor of Missions at the Assemblies of God Theological Assembly. His other works include *Spiritual Gifts* (1964), *A Guide to*

Church Planting (1973) and *The Indigenous Church and the Missionary* (1978).

Hoehn, Matthew Benedictine librarian and prior, born Newark, New Jersey, 4 February 1898, died Newark, 12 May 1959. After studying at St Anselm's College, Manchester, New Hampshire, Hoehn became a Benedictine at St Mary's Abbey, Newark, where he was ordained in 1925. He taught chemistry at St Anselm's and St Benedict's Preparatory, Newark, where he also served as a librarian. He was appointed prior of St Mary's in 1946, and in 1948 he published his *Catholic Authors: Contemporary Biographical Sketches, 1930–47*, with a supplement published in 1952. The library at St Benedict's Preparatory in Newark is named the Matthew Hoehn Memorial Library in his honour.

Hoensbroech, Paul von Lutheran polemicist, born near Geldern, Germany, 29 June 1852, died Berlin-Lichterfelde, Germany, 29 August 1923. Count Hoensbroech was of a Catholic noble family. Educated by the Jesuits, he joined the Order in 1878 after trying, unsuccessfully, to practise law in Geldern. He was ordained in 1886 and studied in Berlin, where he came under the influence of Adolf von **Harnack** and Heinrich von Treitschke. He left the Jesuits in 1892, publicly became a Protestant and married in 1895 and wrote extensively against his former religious order. His books include the autobiographical *Fourteen Years a Jesuit* (1909–11), and two other books which strongly attacked the Jesuits as deceptive, fraudulent and irreligious (*Das Papsttum in seiner sozialkulturellen Wirksamkeit*, 2 vols, 1900–2, and *Der Jesuitenorden*, 2 vols, 1926–27). His work served as a model for the anti-Catholic literature of the Nazis.

Hofbauer, Clement Saint, Redemptorist priest, born Tasswitz, Moravia, 26 December 1751, died Vienna, 15 March 1820. Clement (originally 'John') entered Vienna University and was later ordained. He lived in Warsaw, and set up Redemptorist houses in Switzerland and Germany. Napoleon ordered the closure of the Redemptorist community in Warsaw, so Hofbauer moved to Vienna, continuing his work in establishing Redemptorist houses in Europe. He was canonized in 1909 and named patron saint of Vienna. Feast day 15 March.

Hoffman, Johann Christian Konrad von German Lutheran theologian, born Nuremberg, 21 December 1810, died Erlangen, 20 December 1877. Studied in Berlin and in Erlangen, where in 1838 he became lecturer in theology. He spent three years as professor of theology at Rostock before returning to Erlangen, where he remained until death. His writings include a work on the theology of prophecy in the Old and New Testaments, published in two volumes between 1841 and 1844, and the three-volume *Der Schriftbeweis*, published between 1852 and 1856, in which he refutes the theory of a vicarious Atonement. In addition to later works which defend this position he also wrote an (unfinished) eight-part NT commentary, *Die hl. Schriften des Neuen Testaments*, published between 1862 and 1878.

Hoffman, Melchior Anabaptist preacher, born Schwäbisch Hall, Germany, before 1500(?), died Strasburg, Germany, 1543. Hoffman was a tradesman and lay preacher who, with a recommendation from Martin **Luther**, preached around northern Europe, especially the Baltic countries. However, his theology was always suspect and caused uproar everywhere he went. He joined the Anabaptists in Strasburg in 1529, was rebaptized, and continued preaching. He claimed to be one of the two witnesses from Revelation (11:3) and promised the 1000-year reign of the saints. His Christology influenced that of **Menno Simons**. In 1533, he returned to Strasburg, where he was put in prison until his death.

Hofinger, Johannes Jesuit catechist, born Tyrol, Austria, 21 March 1905, died New Orleans, Louisiana, 14 February 1984. After studies in Salzburg and Rome, Hofinger became a Jesuit in 1925. After completing his doctorate in catechesis in 1937, he went to China to teach at the seminary in Kinghsien. From 1949 to 1958, he taught at the seminary in Manila. His later years were spent promoting international conferences in liturgy and catechesis and lecturing around the world on his 'kerygmatic approach' to religious education. He wrote numerous books, including *The Good News and its Proclamation* (1968) and *Pastoral Life in the Power of the Spirit* (1982), and founded the journal *East Asian Pastoral Review*.

Hofmann, Georg Jesuit Church historian, born Friesen, Germany, 1 November 1885, died Rome, 9 August 1956. After studies in Rome, Hofmann was ordained in 1912 and joined the Society of Jesus in 1918. He then studied Church history in Munich and from 1922 until his death was professor of oriental ecclesiastical history at the Pontifical Oriental Institute, Rome. Although he wrote some monographs and prepared critical editions of documents relating to Rome and the Eastern patriarchies, he is mostly known for initiating and editing the critical edition of the documents of the Council of Florence, the *Concilium Florentinum, documenta et scriptores*.

Hogan, John Baptist Sulpician rector, born near Ennis, County Clare, Ireland, 24 June 1829, died Paris, France, 29 September 1901. Hogan studied for the priesthood in Bordeaux through the aid of a priest-uncle in Périgueux. In 1849 he went to Paris to study at the seminary of Saint-Sulpice, joined the Sulpicians in 1851, was ordained the following year and began teaching dogma at the seminary. In 1863 he turned his attention to moral theology and liturgy and in 1884 was sent to the USA and became the first president of St John's Seminary, Brighton, Massachusetts. From 1889 to 1894 he was president of the Divinity College at the Catholic University of America but returned to St John's to serve another term as president from 1894 to 1901. He became ill, resigned and returned to France, where he died suddenly. His writings include articles in scholarly journals and two books, *Clerical Studies*, a collection of his articles which appeared between 1891 and 1895 in *Ecclesiastical Review*, and *Daily Thoughts*, a series of meditations for clergy.

Hogan, John Joseph Roman Catholic bishop, born County Limerick, Ireland, 10 May 1829, died Kansas City, Missouri, 21 February 1913. Studied in Ireland and in 1848 he went to the United States to study for the priesthood. He was ordained for the Diocese of St Louis, Missouri, in 1852 and worked in parishes there. In 1857 he volunteered to pioneer new territories in northern Missouri, living a life largely in the saddle and serving along the new railroad. In 1865 he refused to take the oath that clergy were supposed to take under the Missouri state constitution. The case went to the

US Supreme Court and the oath was declared to be unconstitutional. In 1868 Hogan was appointed the first bishop of the new Diocese of St Joseph, Missouri, and was also made bishop of Kansas City when that diocese was created in 1880. He oversaw both until 1893, after which time he governed Kansas City alone. Both dioceses flourished under his episcopate, new religious communities came to work there, numbers of parishioners increased dramatically and new churches, including the cathedral of the Immaculate Conception in Kansas City, were built. His writings include *On the Mission in Missouri* (1892) and *Nautical Distances and How to Compute Them* (1903).

Hogan, William Anti-Catholic campaigner, born Ireland, 1788, died Nashua, New Hampshire, USA, 3 January 1848. Originally a Roman Catholic priest of Limerick in Ireland, Hogan went to the United States, seemingly with the intention of becoming a Protestant minister. In 1820, he moved to Philadelphia and persuaded the lay trustees of St Mary's Cathedral to reject the leadership of Bishop Conwell. A public dispute ensued and Hogan proposed the founding of an American Catholic Church with a congregational organization and order. He was forced to resign his position at St Mary's, in retaliation for which the trustees closed the cathedral. From then on Hogan worked as an anti-Catholic lecturer and pamphleteer, publishing *Popery as It Was and Is* and *Nunneries and Auricular Confession*. He was appointed US consul in Nuevitas, Cuba, in 1843.

Hoger of Bremen-Hamburg Saint, archbishop, date and place of birth unknown, died 20 December 916(?). Hoger was a monk at the abbey of Corvey when he became the assistant to **Adalgar**, archbishop of Bremen. He followed Adalgar as archbishop, holding the diocese together in the face of the onslaught of both Slavs and Magyars. Nothing is known of the rest of his career but his long-standing reputation for holiness. He was buried at St Michael's Church in Bremen, but his remains were moved to the main cathedral around 1036.

Hogg, Alfred George Presbyterian missionary, philosopher and theologian, born Ramleh, Alexandria, Egypt, 23 July 1875, died Elie, Fife, 31 December 1954. Son of American United Presbyterian missionaries, he was educated in Edinburgh (receiving his MA in 1897) and in Halle, 1902. He was appointed to Madras Christian College in 1903 as a lay missionary and remained for 35 years, becoming principal in 1928. He married Mary Paterson in 1907 and was ordained by the Edinburgh United Free Presbytery in 1915. His publications include *Karma and Redemption* (1910), *Christ's Message of the Kingdom* (1911) and *Redemption from this World* (1922). Known as an acute thinker who refused easy answers, he provided an alternative voice to **Kraemer**'s at the 1938 meeting of the International Missionary Council. He then returned to Scotland, assisted in parishes during the war, and retired to Fife.

Hohenbaum van der Meer, Moritz Benedictine historian, born Spörl, Serbia, 25 June 1718, died abbey of Rheinau, near Schaffhausen, Switzerland, 18 December 1795. In 1730, Hohenbaum entered the abbey of Rheinau as a student. He became a Benedictine in 1734 and was ordained in 1741. Three years later, he began teaching at the abbey and became prior in 1758, a post he held until 1794. While prior, Hohenbaum was also the archivist for the abbey, and during his life he wrote a number of monographs on various aspects of the history of the abbey, the Benedictines and the area in Switzerland where he lived. His method was very close to that of the Maurists, though he had no personal contact with that group.

Holaind, René Jesuit educator, born Moulins, France, 27 July 1836, died Woodstock, Maryland, USA, 20 April 1906. Holaind entered the Society of Jesus in 1851 in Avignon, where he later taught before moving to the United States in 1861. He studied at Boston College and in Alabama and taught at a number of Jesuit secondary schools before becoming, in 1895, professor of ethics at Woodstock College. He later taught at Georgetown. During the debates in the 1890s over the role of public and parochial schools, he defended a strong position on behalf of the parochial schools in his *The Parent First* (1891). His other works include *Ownership and Natural Right* (1887) and *Natural Law and Legal Practice* (1889).

Holden, Henry Roman Catholic theologian, born

Chaigley, Lancashire, 1596, died Paris, March 1662. Holden studied theology in Douai from 1618 to 1623 under an assumed name before taking his doctoral degree at the Sorbonne in Paris and being made vicar general of the archbishop of Paris. After a failed term as superior of St Gregory's Seminary in Paris, he was made superior of the famous 'Blue Nun' community in Paris in 1659. He wrote on the debates about the timeliness of having bishops present again in England, even travelling to Rome to debate the question, and on other theological questions of the day.

Holes, Andrew Priest and diplomat, born Bromston, Cheshire, c.1400, died Salisbury, 1 April 1470. After attending Oxford as student and fellow, Holes held ecclesiastical posts in Anglesey and York before going to Rome, where he was a papal chamberlain and proctor for the king, 1437–44. While in Italy, he earned a doctorate in canon law in 1439 and purchased many books, which influenced the humanist movement in England when Holes returned there in 1444. Back in England, he acquired more religious benefices, and even served as Keeper of the Privy Seal from 1450 to 1452. His personal influence, though not specifically his thought, did much to advance the cause of humanism in Britain.

Holguín, Melchior Pérez Roman Catholic painter, born Cochabamba, Bolivia, c.1660, died Potosí, Bolivia, after 1724. Holguín spent his life and career in Potosí, where he became one of the most interesting and important painters in South America. Little is known of the details of his life, but his work influenced art in Bolivia for more than 100 years. His style was a combination of Spanish and Flemish influences, his subjects were almost always religious, and his figures were real individuals rather than the prototypes that were more typical of South American painting. His most noted works are *St Peter of Alcántara* and *Rest on the Flight into Egypt.*

Holl, Karl German Evangelical Church historian, born Tübingen, 15 May 1866, died Berlin, 23 May 1926. He was professor in Tübingen, 1900–6, and, from 1906, in Berlin. The focal point of his research was Greek patristics, characterized by a strong philological approach (see his edition of

Epiphanius, but also his study on **Amphilochius**). He reached a wider audience with his study on **Luther**, prepared during World War I, the source-critical approach of which strongly influenced Luther research while also stimulating the so-called 'Luther renaissance'.

Hollaz, David Lutheran theologian, born Wulkow, Poland, 1648(?), died Jakobshagen (Dobrzany), Poland, 17 April 1713. After education in Erfurt and Wittenberg, Hollaz (or 'Hollatius') served in Putzerlin, Stargard and Colberg before becoming pastor of the Lutheran church in Jakobshagen in 1692, where he served until his death. He is best known for his *Examen theologicum acroamaticum* (1717), probably the last textbook of the period of Lutheran orthodoxy. Though not highly original, the work is clear and well organized and is imbued with a devotional spirit, though it does deal quite sharply with the growing Pietistic influence in Lutheran Churches at that time.

Hollis, Christopher Author and politician, born Axbridge, Somerset, 29 March 1902, died Mells, Somerset, 5 May 1977. He was educated at Eton and Balliol, Oxford, where he became president of the Union in 1923. He converted to Catholicism in 1924 and was appointed history master at Stonyhurst, the Jesuit College, in 1925, where he taught until 1935. That year he became visiting professor at Notre Dame University, Indiana, where he engaged in economic research, until the outbreak of the war. Between 1939 and 1945 he served as an intelligence officer in the RAF. After the war he was elected Conservative Member of Parliament for the Devizes division of Wiltshire, 1945–55. He was also the parliamentary reporter for *Punch*. After retiring to Somerset in 1955 he became the author of some 30 works on varied subjects, from a biography of St **Ignatius of Loyola** and the foundation of the Jesuits to works on Soviet Communism, monetary reform and foreign policy. Perhaps his biographies are best known, especially those on **Erasmus**, Thomas **More**, **Dryden** and Dr **Johnson**. He published two autobiographical works, *Along the Road to Frome* (1958) and *The Seven Ages* (1974), as well as a work of recollections, *Oxford in the Twenties: Recollections of Five Friends* (1976).

Hollweck, Josef German Roman Catholic canon lawyer, born Pfaffenhofen, 16 January 1854, died Eichstätt, 10 March 1926. Ordained in 1879, Hollweck spent his entire career as professor of canon law at the lyceum in Eichstätt, though he lectured on many other topics as well. In 1906, he was also made dean of the Eichstätt cathedral chapter. Hollweck was very active in the codification of canon law and wrote many books on it, including *Das kirchliche Bücherverbot* (1897) and *Lehrbuch des katholischen Kirchenrechts* (1900).

Hollý, Ján Slovakian Roman Catholic priest and poet, born Borsky Sväty Mikulás, 24 March 1785, died Madunice, Slovakia, 14 April 1849. After theological study in Trnava, Hollý was ordained in 1808 and served parishes in Pobedim, Hlohovec and lastly Madunice, where most of his work was composed. His work is mainly about Slavic culture and identity. Among other works, he wrote three long epics about real and mythical Slavic history, a collection of very patriotic elegies and odes and a collection called *Selanky* (Idylls). His work influenced many younger writers, and his collections of classical translations also enriched the culture of his native Slovakia.

Holst, Gustav Composer and music educator, born Cheltenham, 21 September 1874, died Ealing, Middlesex, 25 May 1934. He became an Anglican church organist, studied at the Royal College of Music, helping to maintain himself by playing the trombone in brass and dance bands, moving on, after finishing his studies, to orchestras. He then held various teaching posts, principally at St Paul's School for Girls in London, but gave them up in 1907 to concentrate on composing. He is known for his interest in world religions, especially Eastern. *The Planets* is his outstanding work, but he also wrote choral works such as *The Hymn of Jesus*, choral *Hymns from the Rig Veda* and hymn tunes. The tune to the hymn 'I Vow to Thee My Country' has been adapted from *The Planets*.

Holt, John Priest, schoolmaster and grammarian, born Sussex, died before 14 June 1504. He was ordained in 1495 and a year later called by Archbishop John **Morton** to oversee his school at Lambeth Palace. There he composed what became the first significant Latin grammar to be published in England, his *Lac puerorum* or *Mylke for Children*. He was noted by Anthony à Wood to be 'the most eminent grammarian of his time'. In 1500, he was made schoolmaster of the Chichester Prebendal School and two years later was appointed schoolmaster to Prince Henry (later to become **Henry VIII**). His will was proved on 14 June 1504.

Holtzmann, Heinrich Julius Lutheran biblical scholar, born Karlsruhe, Germany, 17 June 1832, died Baden-Baden, 4 October 1910. An important, prolific and influential scholar, Holtzmann taught at Heidelberg, 1858–74, and Strasburg, 1874–1904. His works include *Kanon und Tradition* (1859), *Lehrbuch der historisch-kritischen Einleitung in das NT* (1885), commentaries on the Gospels and Pastoral Epistles, a NT theology and several volumes of the commentary series Hand-Commentar zum NT, which he himself founded and edited.

Holtzmann, Walther German Roman Catholic historian, born Eberbach-Neckar, 31 December 1891, died Bonn, 25 November 1963. After work in Rome, Holtzmann began lecturing in Berlin in 1926, after which he was professor of medieval history in Halle, 1931–6, and Bonn, 1936–55. He also directed the German Historical Institute in Rome from 1953 to 1961. Most of his scholarly work resulted in critical editions of historical sources and monographs related thereto. He also wrote significant historical works on the medieval Papacy as part of the *Regesta Pontificum Romanorum: Italia pontificia*, begun by Holtzmann's mentor Paul **Kehr**.

Holweck, Frederick Roman Catholic priest and author, born Baden, Germany, 29 December 1856, died St Louis, Missouri, 15 February 1927. Holweck went to the United States at the age of twenty in order to attend a seminary, and was ordained in 1880. He spent most of his career working in parishes in St Louis. He published a book on saints (*Biographical Dictionary of the Saints*, 1924) and on liturgical festivals (*Calendarium liturgicum festorum Dei et Dei Matris*, 1925) and was an editor for several periodicals (including the *St Louis Catholic Historical Review*). Made a domestic prelate in 1923, Holweck was named vicar general of the Diocese of St Louis a year before his death.

Holywood, Christopher Irish Jesuit superior, born Dublin, 1562, died there, 4 September 1626. Born of Irish nobility, Holywood became a Jesuit in Verdun, France, in 1584. After studies in Pont-à-Mousson and teaching at Dole and Padua, Italy, Holywood was appointed superior of the Jesuit mission to Ireland. However, he was arrested in Dover in 1598, and spent several years in prison before being released to France in 1603 and eventually making it to Ireland the next year. Despite poor health and eyesight, he was a competent administrator for the Order, increasing the number of Jesuits in Ireland from 7 to 44 and combating the 'Protestantizing influences' of the British government.

Holzhauser, Bartholomew Roman Catholic priest and clerical reformer, born Langna, Germany, 24 August 1613, died Bingen, Germany, 20 May 1658. Ordained at Ingolstadt, Germany, in 1639, Holzhauser was struck by the moral laxity at the university there. He envisioned a congregation for secular clergy that would encourage their sanctification, which they could then live out as an example in their parish and seminary work. This he eventually founded at Tittmoning, Germany, as the Institutum Clericorum Saecularium in Communi Viventium, often called the 'Bartholomites'. The initial request for papal approval was denied, but it was eventually granted in 1680. The constitution for the congregation was used for the next 200 years as a model in many seminaries.

Honoratus of Amiens Saint, bishop of Amiens, born probably in Port-le-Grand, France, died c.600, Amiens. The biography of Honoratus (late eleventh century at the earliest) is unreliable; but it says that he lived at the time of Pope **Pelagius II** (579–90). After his death, veneration of Honoratus spread and in 1060 cures were attributed to him when his relics were elevated. Various churches are dedicated to him; the Faubourg and Rue Saint-Honoré in Paris are named after him. He is the patron of bakers. Feast day 16 May.

Honoratus of Arles Saint, abbot, born probably in the region of Northern Gaul, to an illustrious family, died c.430. He is known as an exemplary ascetic, and information pertaining to him comes from the commemorative sermon given on the anniversary of his death by his relative and successor **Hilary**. Honoratus travelled widely in his early life, particularly to the East. He travelled with his brother, but upon his death Honoratus returned to the West. Honoratus was the founder and first abbot of the monastery of Lérins. He became bishop of Arles in 427, succeeding the brief episcopate of Euladius. Nothing remains of his writings. Feast day 16 January.

Honorius I Pope, born in the Campagna, elected 27 October 625, died Rome, 12 October 638. One of the most controversial of Roman pontiffs because he seems to have embraced a heresy. In response to a letter from Patriarch Sergius of Constantinople, who was seeking to end the debate over the nature of Christ, Honorius wrote that there could be only one will in Christ, a doctrine known as 'monothelitism'. This was welcomed in the East, and adopted by the Emperor **Heraclius**, but was rejected after Honorius' death as heretical. He showed himself an active, peacemaking bishop in Italy, and encouraged the mission to the English. He took effective control, secular as well as spiritual, of the city of Rome, repaired the aqueducts, built churches, and administered efficiently the papal estates. He was very much in the mould of Pope **Gregory I**, even to the support he gave to monks: it is not clear that he was one himself, though he turned his family home into a monastery, and brought the monastery of Bobbio directly under the control of the Papacy, the first case (it was June 628) of what became a common practice, to have members of religious houses independent of their local bishops.

Honorius II Pope, born 'Lamberto Scannabecchi' at Imola, elected 21 December 1124, died Rome, 13 February 1130. Scannabecchi was a canon regular who had risen to prominence under **Paschal II**, who made him a cardinal in 1117, and had taken part in the negotiations for the Synod of Worms of 1122, which effectively settled the investiture contest, or so he thought. Honorius and his supporters wished now to concentrate on reform within the Church, a task for which they believed the canons regular were particularly suited: Honorius sanctioned the establishment of the Premonstratensian canons, or Norbertines, as well as the Knights Templar. In France he brought to an end disputes between **Louis VI** and the French bishops, and managed to persuade the English king to allow papal legates once again to enter the country.

Honorius III Pope, born 'Cencio Savelli' at Rome, elected 18 July 1216, died 18 March 1227. A member of the Roman aristocracy, he had been a canon of Santa Maria Maggiore before becoming a cardinal in 1193. He was an efficient administrator and was credited with improving the finances of the Roman Church. He was also tutor to the future Emperor **Frederick II**, whom he crowned in St Peter's in 1220, exacting a promise that he would go on a Crusade. Frederick himself, however, was more concerned to consolidate his power in Italy, though he agreed to go on the Crusade by the summer of 1227 or be excommunicated. Within the rest of Europe, Honorius negotiated peace between rival monarchies to prepare for the Crusade. He gave approval to both the Franciscan and the Dominican Orders, both newly founded, and gave the Dominicans the responsibility of combating the Albigensian heresy, effectively creating the Inquisition in the process.

Honorius IV Pope, born 'Giacomo Savelli' at Rome, 1210, elected in Perugia, 2 April 1285, died Rome, 3 April 1287. A grand-nephew of **Honorius III**, he had been created cardinal in 1261. He was a popular choice at Rome and although elected at Perugia was crowned in Rome and lived there. He was concerned to try to return Sicily to the House of Anjou – **Charles of Anjou** had been closely linked with the Savelli family – but Charles' heir renounced the title. He also had little success in establishing better relations with **Rudolf** of Habsburg, whom he was expecting to crown as Emperor, an event which never happened. In internal Church matters he encouraged the newly founded Dominicans and Franciscans, giving them responsibility for the Inquisition, and he encouraged the study of oriental languages at Paris, in the hope that this might lead to a reunion of the two halves of Christendom.

Honorius Magister Archdeacon and canon lawyer, born probably England, middle 1100s, died Richmond, England, c.1210–13. Honorius was an English decretalist (a canon lawyer who commented on **Gratian**'s *Decretum*) who worked until 1190 in Paris, where he wrote his only work, *Summa decretalium questionum*, a didactic study of the *Decretum*. He later taught at Oxford until 1195, when he began working for Bishop **Geoffrey** Plantagenet of York. He was appointed archdeacon of Richmond in 1198 but did not actually assume the office until after a long struggle with the English Crown and a papal pronouncement in 1202. He also served as a proctor for King John in Rome in 1205, but was imprisoned by the king a few years later for debts owed to the Crown. Details of his death are not known.

Honorius of Autun Writer, born c.1080 or 1090, died c.1156. Traditionally associated with Autun, he has been identified with a priest of Autun named 'Honorius', who later became a monk at Regensburg and concealed his identity with the pseudonym 'Augustodunensis', after the site of a supposed victory of **Charlemagne**. His most celebrated work, the *Elucidarium* (Clarification), exists in numerous manuscript translations in French, Provençal, Italian, Old Norse, Gaelic and English, as well as in many early printed editions. Often labelled derivative, his work is important as a witness to what his contemporaries considered respectable learning.

Honorius of Canterbury Saint, missionary, fifth archbishop of Canterbury, died 30 September 653. Honorius was sent by Pope **Gregory I** to Kent, probably with the second group of Roman monks in 601, and became archbishop c.627. Honorius' reign of consolidation was successful, including the sending of Felix of Dunwich to evangelize the East Angles, and the appointment in 644 of the first English bishop, the Kentish Ithmar of Rochester, who in 655 consecrated Frithona, the first English archbishop of Canterbury. Feast day 30 September.

Hontheim, Johann Nikolaus von Historian and theologian, born Trier, 27 January 1701, died Montequentin (Luxemburg), 2 September 1790. He travelled through Europe to Rome, where he was ordained, and worked at Trier, where he was appointed auxiliary bishop and vicar general. Hontheim, using the pen name 'Justinus Febronius' wrote *De statu ecclesiae et legitima potestate Romani Pontificis* ('Concerning the State of the Church and the Legitimate Power of the Roman Pope')

(1763). This book was placed on the Index of Prohibited Books. It is from his pen name that we get 'Febronianism', the German equivalent of Gallicanism, opposing the ultramontane view that all Church matters should rightly fall under the Pope's authority. Hontheim also wrote three histories of Trier.

Hooke, Samuel Henry Biblical scholar and oriental linguist, born Cirencester, 21 January 1874, died Buckland, 17 January 1968. Studied at Jesus College, Oxford, taking degrees in theology and oriental languages. Originally a member of the Plymouth Brethren, he joined the Church of England while at Oxford. From 1913 to 1925 he was professor of oriental languages and literature, Victoria College, Toronto, and then professor of OT studies, King's College, London, until 1942. For 23 years he was editor of the *Palestine Exploration Quarterly*. He was director of *The Bible in Basic English* (1949), made from original texts and published by Cambridge University Press. He was best known for his work on *Myth and Ritual* (1933) and numerous other books on the OT.

Hooker, Richard Anglican theologian, born Heavitree, near Exeter, c.1554, died Bishopsbourne, near Canterbury, 2 November 1600. He was fellow of Corpus Christi College, Oxford, and in 1559 became assistant professor of Hebrew. He married and in 1584 was appointed rector of Drayton Beauchamp and the following year Master of the Temple. In 1591 he was made rector of Boscombe in Wiltshire and in 1595 rector of Bishopsbourne. His major work is his treatise *Of the Laws of Ecclesiastical Polity* (Books 1–4, 1593 and Book 5, 1597; Books 6–8 not appearing until after his death, 1648, 1662), in which he bases his views of ecclesiastical and civil authority on a theory of natural law. It is a defence of Anglicanism against both Rome and the Puritans, and was much admired even by his adversaries, including Cardinal William **Allen**. The Church, argued Hooker, evolved organically, and so the Church of England, though Reformed, was in direct continuity with the medieval Church in England. The Church, he wrote, was a political society with authority to make its own laws – he developed a social contract theory which influenced later political theorists in England. The strength of the book lay not only in its arguments, but in the elegant prose in which it was composed. Some claim Hooker as possibly the greatest theologian the Church of England has ever had, and he is in some parts of the Anglican communion venerated as a saint. Feast day 3 November.

Hooker, Thomas Nonconformist minister, born Markfield, Leicestershire, 7 July 1586, died Hartford, Connecticut, 7 July 1647. He preached fervent evangelical sermons in Essex and Surrey. In the religious climate of the time, he was called to appear before the Court of High Commission and was dismissed for nonconformity. He sailed to Massachusetts and became pastor at New Towne, now Cambridge, of a group of Puritans who came to be called 'Mr Hooker's Company'. Hooker later founded a new community at Hartford, Connecticut. He objected to suffrage being restricted to Church members, and he became known as the 'father of American democracy'. He wrote *A Survey of the Summe of Church Discipline*, *The Souls Implantation* and *The Application of Redemption*.

Hoonacker, Albin van OT theologian, born Bruges, Belgium, 19 November 1885, died Bruges, 1 November 1933. Most of Hoonacker's academic career was spent as professor of OT exegesis at the University of Louvain, where he had also been a student. He wrote a number of significant works on the historical criticism of the OT, and Jewish religion in the OT period.

Hoover, Willis Pentecostal missionary, born Freeport, Illinois, 20 July 1856, died Chile, 1936. Hoover was originally a Methodist who became a missionary in Chile as the result of an inner call. He established a congregation in Iquique in 1891, later becoming superintendent of that district. In 1902 he became pastor in Valparaiso. In 1910 he resigned his ministry and membership of the Methodist Episcopal Church following his Pentecostal experience. He set up the Iglesia Methodista Nacional and, following a split, in 1932 he founded the Iglesia Evangelica Pentecostal de Chile. These are now the two largest Protestant groups in Chile.

Hopkins, Gerard Manley Jesuit priest and poet, born Stratford, Essex, 11 June 1844, died Dublin, 8 June 1889. He was brought up in the Anglican

Church and educated at Highgate School and Oxford University. He was received into the Roman Catholic Church by John Henry **Newman** in 1866 and joined the Jesuits two years later. He taught at Stonyhurst College, and was then appointed professor of Greek at University College, Dublin. He believed he ought to abandon writing poetry on becoming a Jesuit, but in 1876 the death of a group of German nuns, refugees from the Kulturkampf, led to his writing *The Wreck of The Deutschland*. Hopkins is now known for the richness, density, complexity and 'sprung rhythm' of his poems, many of which are on religious themes, or are inspired by the countryside around the college in North Wales where he studied theology. He tried to express the inner essence of objects, hence his term 'inscape'. He was almost unknown as a poet in his lifetime. His poetry was brought to public attention by Robert **Bridges** in 1918. His poems have inspired composers such as Lennox **Berkeley**, Edmund **Rubbra** and Egon **Wellesz**.

Hopper, Christopher Wesleyan Methodist preacher, regarded as the first Methodist preacher to visit Scotland, born Low Coalburne, County Durham, 25 December 1722, died Bolton, Lancashire, 5 March 1802. Worked as a merchant's apprentice and a wagon driver transporting coal. Challenged by the preaching of John and Charles **Wesley**, who visited the Newcastle area in 1742–3, he experienced an evangelical conversion on hearing a sermon given by Jonathan Reeves. On joining the Methodists he worked as a teacher and an itinerant evangelist. He was influential in establishing Wesleyan Methodism in the Yorkshire Dales, Cumbria and Lancashire, as well as visiting other areas of Britain.

Hormisdas Saint, bishop of Rome, elected 20 July 514, died, Rome, 6 August 523. Possibly of Persian ancestry by his name, but born in Frosinone, Italy, Hormisdas was of a wealthy family and had been married: his son became Pope **Silverius I**. As bishop of Rome, Hormisdas was deeply concerned in the separation of the Eastern and Western Churches following the Henoticon of Emperor **Zeno** and the demand of Emperor **Anastasius I** that the Council of Chalcedon (451) be repudiated. Hormisdas fought this monophysitism by means of a formula of faith which, after the emperor's

sudden death in a storm, all Eastern bishops signed (Holy Thursday, 28 March 519). Feast day 6 August.

Hort, Fenton John Anthony NT scholar, born Dublin, Ireland, 23 April 1828, died Cambridge, England, 30 November 1892. He was educated at Trinity College, Cambridge, which he entered in 1846 and where he later became a fellow and professor. He was ordained in 1856, and served for fifteen years in the parish of St Ippolyts cum Great Wymondley, near Hitchin. In 1872 he returned to live in Cambridge, as a fellow of Emmanuel College and six years later was elected Hulsean Professor of Divinity. He was an associate of Brooke Foss **Westcott** and with him worked on an edition of the NT, the prototype of the NT in the English Revised Version of the Bible. Hort's *Introduction to the New Testament RV* is widely admired.

Horton, Douglas Congregationalist Christian ecumenist and administrator, born Brooklyn, New York, 27 July 1891, died Berlin, New Hampshire, 21 August 1968. Educated at Princeton, Edinburgh, Oxford and Tübingen, Horton was among the first to introduce Karl **Barth** to the English-speaking world with his translation of Barth's *Word of God and Word of Man* in 1928. After serving as a minister in several churches, he became, in 1938, chief executive officer of the Congregational Christian Churches, leading that Church into the merger that formed the United Churches of Christ. He also participated in the foundation of the National Council of Churches in the USA and the World Council of Churches (chairing the Faith and Order Commission from 1957 to 1963) and served as dean of Harvard Divinity School, 1955–9.

Hosius (Ossius) Bishop, born 256, died Córdoba, 358. Bishop of Córdoba (Spain) from *c*.300, he became a confessor during the Diocletian persecution. At the request of **Constantine I**, he assumed an intermediary role in the Arian controversy. Thus he played an important role in the Councils of Antioch (325), Nicaea (325) and Serdica (343). After 350, when the West had come under the Arian-minded **Constantius II**, he refused to yield to Arian pressure: only after torture did the centenarian subscribe in 357 to **Athanasius'** condemnation. In this context he wrote a letter to Constantius, arguing for a separation between Church and State.

Hosius, Stanislaus Cardinal, born Crakow, Poland, 5 May 1504, died Capranica, Papal States, Italy, 5 August 1579. He was made bishop of Chelmno, Poland, then of East Prussia. He campaigned in the Counter-Reformation. At the Synod of Piotrków, he proclaimed the Roman Catholic faith, later expressed in his *Confessio Catholicae Fidei Christiana*. As a cardinal he presided at the Council of Trent.

Hoss, Crescentia Blessed, Franciscan mystic, born Kaufbeuren, Germany, 20 October 1682, died Kaufbeuren, 5 April 1744. Crescentia demonstrated a sense of piety from childhood. She entered the Kaufbeuren Franciscan convent, where she eventually became mistress of novices and superior. Her reputation for sanctity and devotion was enhanced by her claims to a number of visions and other mystical experiences. She was beatified by **Leo XIII** in 1900.

Hostiensis Cardinal and canon lawyer, born Susa (Segusio), Turin, Italy, *c*.1200, died Lyons, France, 25 October or 6 November 1271. Hostiensis (Henry of Segusio, Enrico Bartolomei) studied both civil and canon law in Bologna, taught at Paris in 1239 and served in various ecclesiastical posts: bishop of Sisteron, 1243, archbishop of Embrun, 1250, papal legate and finally cardinal, 1262. He is chiefly known for his influential works on canon law, including the *Summa 'Copiosa'*, a synthesis of Roman and canon law, and *Lectura in quinque libros decretalium*, a commentary on decretals.

Houbigant, Charles François Oratorian biblical scholar, born Paris, 1686, died there, 31 October 1783. He entered the Oratory in 1704 and went on to teach classics at Juilly, rhetoric at Marseilles and philosophy at Soissons. He returned to Paris and became head of the Conference of Church Antiquities and Discipline at the seminary of St Magloire. He became deaf, so devoted himself to study, learning oriental languages. His first work was a vocabulary of Hebrew roots. He published his *Prolegomena in Scripturam Sacram*, a Latin

translation of the Psalms, and an edition of the Hebrew Psalter. *Biblia Hebraica cum notis criticis* was his great work, to which he devoted twenty years. Also he translated English books into French. Works found at his death include a Life of Cardinal de **Bérulle**, a treatise on the coming of Elias and a Hebrew grammar.

Houck, George Francis Roman Catholic diocesan chancellor, born Tiffin, USA, 9 July 1847, died Lakewood, USA, 26 March 1916. A son of German immigrants, Houck was ordained in 1875. After two years in parochial ministry he was appointed first chancellor of the Diocese of Cleveland and secretary to the bishop, serving in this position until 1909. Houck's administrative skills exercised over his long period of service made important contributions to the development of the diocese. In 1909 he retired to become a convent chaplain.

Houghton, John Saint, Carthusian martyr, born Essex, *c*.1487, died Tyburn, London, 4 May 1535. After taking a degree in law from Christ's College, Cambridge in 1506, he studied privately for the priesthood and served as a secular priest for several years until entering the London Charterhouse around 1515. Served as prior of Beauvale, Nottinghamshire, 1530–1; unanimously elected prior of the London Charterhouse in 1531. Imprisoned in the Tower for refusing to swear to the Act of Succession, 1534; he was martyred at Tyburn, 4 May 1535. Feast day 4 May.

Houselander, Frances Caryll A convert to Catholicism at the age of six and outstanding English spiritual writer, born Bath, 29 September 1901, died London, 12 October 1954. Although she lacked formal theological training, her writings evince remarkable psychological and theological insights. Her childhood is memorably recorded in *A Rocking Horse Catholic*. She devoted her life to helping others, especially abused children; the main focus of her life was to see and act out the presence of Christ in every person. One of her first major works, *This War is the Passion* (1941), stressed the building of the Kingdom of God here and now in all of human life. Her other works, in plain unsentimental prose, such as *The Reed of God*, *The Risen Christ*, *The Flowering Tree*, *Stations of the Cross* and *The Comforting of Christ*, had and have a wide readership. Her letters were collected and published by Maisie **Ward** as *The Letters of Caryll Houselander* (1973).

Houtin, Albert Historical theologian, born La Flèche, France, 4 October 1867, died Paris, 28 July 1926. Following ordination in the Roman Catholic Church in 1891, Houtin taught in a seminary before moving to Paris in 1901. During the first decade of the twentieth century he gradually moved away from Christianity, and by 1912 had abandoned it; eventually he came to regard all religions as fraudulent belief systems arising from a fundamental insincerity in human nature. From 1913 he worked at the Musée Pédagogique, becoming its director in 1919. Houtin wrote a number of works on the history of doctrine, notably on the history of Modernism in French Catholicism.

Howard, Francis William Roman Catholic bishop and educator, born Columbus, Ohio, 21 June 1867, died Covington, Kentucky, 18 January 1944. Ordained in 1891, Howard served four years in parish work before studying at Columbia University, New York, and at Rome. He ministered to the Holy Rosary parish in Columbus from 1905 to 1923, when he was named bishop of Covington. As bishop, he established so-called 'Bishop's Schools', elite boys' academies, in his diocese and also continued his work of promoting Catholic education through the National Catholic Education Association as secretary general, 1904–28, president, 1929–35, and chairman of its advisory board, 1936–44.

Howard, Philip Saint, born 28 June 1557, died 19 October 1595. He was the son of Thomas **Howard**, fourth duke of Norfolk who was executed in 1572. As a consequence of his father's fall from favour, Philip did not succeed to the title of Duke of Norfolk, and was known as the Earl of Surrey until in 1580 he succeeded his grandfather as earl of Arundel. After a rather dissolute youth he turned to religion when his chances of preferment at **Elizabeth** I's court had diminished. Under the inspiration of his wife, Anne Dacre, for whom he had been betrothed at the age of twelve, and of Edmund **Campion**, he converted to Catholicism, being received into the Church in September 1584 by the Jesuit William Weston. He was arrested as

he tried to leave England the following year, and was imprisoned in the Tower of London. He was found guilty of treason but the death sentence was not carried out. It has been alleged that he was poisoned: as he lay dying he asked to see his wife and children, and this was refused unless he conformed, which he would not do. In 1970 he was canonized as one of the **Forty Martyrs of England and Wales**. His body is in Arundel, at the cathedral, dedicated to him and to Our Lady. Feast day 19 October.

Howard, Philip Thomas Dominican and cardinal, born London, 21 September 1629, died Rome, 17 June 1694. He was a member of the illustrious family of the dukes of Norfolk. He joined the Dominican Order at the age of sixteen, and was professed in 1646. He was chosen to deliver a Latin address to the general chapter in Rome, which he did on the need for the conversion of England, to which cause he became devoted. After being ordained in 1652 he founded a priory in Flanders at Bornhem, where he was the first prior. In the reign of **Charles II**, Father Howard was made grand almoner to Queen Catherine of Braganza, living at St James's Palace, and with influence at court. An outbreak of anti-Catholic hostility forced him to retreat to Bornhem. Pope **Clement X** made him a cardinal in 1675; he took up residence in Rome and rebuilt the English College there. He co-operated with **James II** in having four vicars apostolic in England, an arrangement which lasted until 1840, when the number was doubled. In Rome he assisted in conclaves for the election of Popes **Innocent XI**, **Alexander VIII** and **Innocent XII**.

Howard, Thomas Earl of Surrey, 1514–24, third duke of Norfolk, 1524–54, born 1473, died Kenninghall, Norfolk, 25 August 1554. A 'natural councillor' of the Tudor monarchs, he found success as a soldier, against the Scots and in suppressing the Pilgrimage of Grace in 1537 and Wyatt's rebellion in 1554, but lacked diplomatic skill. Although he engineered the fall of abler men, Cardinal **Wolsey** and Thomas **Cromwell**, his ambitions were frustrated by the disgrace of his nieces, the Queens Anne Boleyn and Catherine Howard, and by the rise of Edward Seymour, earl of Hertford. From 1533 until **Mary**'s accession in 1553 he languished in the Tower of London.

Howard, Thomas Fourth duke of Norfolk, born Kenninghall, Norfolk, 10 March 1538, died London, 2 June 1572. English nobleman involved with the Catholic and Protestant affairs of Mary, Queen of Scots, and **Elizabeth I** of England respectively. He was the son of Henry Howard, earl of Surrey, who was put to death in 1547. He was restored to his father's title in 1553, succeeded his grandfather as duke of Norfolk in 1554 and became Earl Marshal. He commanded English forces that invaded Scotland. After Mary's flight to England, Scots noblemen and others attempted, unsuccessfully, to persuade him to marry Mary so that she might be restored to Scotland. Several Roman Catholic nobles in the North attempted a revolt and in 1569 Queen Elizabeth had Norfolk arrested. He was released but drawn into a plot for a Spanish invasion of England, was imprisoned in the Tower of London and executed.

Howard, Timothy Edward Roman Catholic politician and lawyer, born Ann Arbor, USA, 27 January 1837, died South Bend, USA, 9 July 1916. Howard's early career was spent teaching at the University of Notre Dame, which he left in 1879 in order to devote himself to politics. He subsequently held numerous public offices in the state of Indiana, and also wrote many books, among them a history of Notre Dame University. Towards the end of his career he returned there as professor of law.

Howells, Herbert Composer, born Lydney, Gloucestershire, 17 October 1892, died Putney, London, 23 February 1983. He studied at the Royal College of Music, succeeding **Holst** as a professor at the College, and later became King Edward Professor of Music at London University. He received many awards, including the Companion of Honour. He wrote much music on Christian themes, including *Requiem*, *Sine Nomine* and *Hymnus Paradisi*. His tune 'Michael', set to the words 'All My Hope on God is Founded', is popular.

Hronský, Jozef Cíger Novelist, born Zvolen (Slovakia), 23 February 1896, died Lujan, Argentina, 13 July 1960. Hronský was a teacher by profession, but soon turned to writing, eventually producing a large number of novels and short stories. Now regarded as classics of Slovak literature, they portray the turbulence of Slovakia's early national development in the aftermath of the First World War, and the social and ideological issues involved in this. Hronský also became director of the Slovak Institute, which under his leadership acted as an important stimulus for the study of Slovak folklore and culture. Following the Communist occupation of Slovakia, Hronský came under suspicion through both his patriotism and his Christian faith, and he was arrested. He succeeded in escaping, and finally settled into exile in Argentina, where he continued to write until just before his death.

Hrotsvitha *see* **Roswitha of Gandersheim**

Hroznata Blessed, Premonstratensian crusader and monastic founder, born Tepl, Bohemia (Czech Republic), *c.*1170, died Alt-Kinsburg (near Eger, Hungary), 14 July 1217. Hroznata was a member of the court of Henry Bretislav, prince-bishop of Prague, until the death of his wife and young son brought about a religious transformation in his life. He founded a Premonstratensian monastery at Tepl and joined the Crusade of Emperor **Henry VI**. When the Crusade failed, he returned to Bohemia, founded a convent on his family estate in Choteschau, and joined the abbey at Tepl as a monk and governor of the abbey's temporal affairs. He was killed by local nobles jealous of the abbey's revenues. His cult was confirmed in 1897. Feast day 14 July.

Hubert, Jean François Roman Catholic bishop of Quebec, born Quebec, Canada, 23 February 1739, died Quebec, 17 October 1797. The son of a tradesman, Hubert was the first ordinand of the re-established Roman Catholic hierarchy in Quebec in 1766. After serving as professor at and superior of the seminary in Quebec and working in missions in Illinois and Michigan, Hubert was made assistant bishop of Quebec in 1786 and bishop there in 1788. As bishop he encouraged Catholic education, harboured refugee priests from the French Revolution, and worked against the founding of a non-denominational university in the province, which he saw as a threat to the province's Catholicity.

Hubert Walter Archbishop of Canterbury and Chancellor of England, born Dereham(?), late middle 1100s, died between Canterbury and Boxley, 13 July 1205. Raised by his uncle, the renowned lawyer Ranulf de Glanville, Hubert began his ecclesiastical career as dean of York in 1186. He was made bishop of Salisbury in 1189, and in 1190 accompanied King **Richard I** on the Third Crusade, serving as both pastor to the crusaders and diplomat for the king. He was elected archbishop of Canterbury in 1193 and served as administrator of England for King Richard from 1194 to 1198. In 1199, King John made him Chancellor of England. Hubert had a reputation as a very worldly cleric, but his work in his churches seems also to show evidence of true piety.

Hubmaier, Balthasar Early German Reformer and leader of the Anabaptists, born Friedberg, near Augsburg, Bavaria, 1485, died, by burning, Vienna, 10 March 1528. He studied at the Universities of Fribourg and Ingolstadt, and became a doctor of theology. At Regensburg he became cathedral preacher, and then a pastor at Waldshut. He read **Luther** and became a supporter of **Zwingli**. In Switzerland he became leader of the Anabaptists, a prominent Protestant Reformation group which favoured adult baptism. However, he was persecuted by the Zwinglians and forced to flee. He continued his Anabaptist preaching in Augsburg, then in Nikolsburg, Moravia. He had been implicated in a peasants' revolt in Waldshut against Austrian rule and was arrested in Nikolsburg, handed over to the Austrian authorities and executed.

Huby, Joseph Jesuit biblical scholar, born Châtelaudren, France, 12 December 1878, died Laniscat, France, 7 August 1948. Ordained in 1910, Huby spent his entire career as an academic, holding positions in England and France, and for the last ten years of his life was on the staff of the academic journal *Études*. He wrote numerous books and articles, among them a number of important NT commentaries, several of which appeared in the Verbum Salutis series which Huby himself founded. In 1940 he was appointed a consultor to the Pontifical Biblical Commission.

Huc, Évariste Régis Vincentian missionary, born Caylus, France, 1 June 1813, died Paris, 26 March 1860. His Order sent him to Macau, and he lived in South China, Peking and Hei-Shui. With two others he set out from Dolon Nur (now To-Luh) and reached Lhasa, Tibet. They spent some time in a Lama monastery and learned the language. However, the Chinese imperial commissioners expelled them. Huc returned to Europe and left the Vincentians. He wrote of his travels in *Souvenirs d'un Voyage dans La Tartarie, le Thibet et la Chine*, which was translated into English.

Hucbald of Saint-Amand French musical theorist, composer, scholar and priest, born at or near Tournai, *c.*840, died Saint-Amand, 20 June 930. He was a pupil of his uncle, the scholar Milo of Saint-Amand. He is the first known person to have written a theory of Western music which is extant, *De harmonica institutione*, describing notes and music. As an abbot, he aimed to instruct the monastic choir how to sing chants. He also composed music for saints' feast days. Several other theoretical works, once attributed to him, are now thought to be written by others.

Huddleston, John Benedictine, royal chaplain, born Farington Hall, Lancashire, 15 April 1608, died 1698, buried in London, 13 September 1698. When aged twenty, he was sent to St Omer's College, then went to the English College at Rome and was ordained priest. In 1651 when residing at Moseley, Staffordshire, as chaplain to the Whitgrove family, King **Charles II**, after his defeat at Worcester, took refuge there. **Cromwell**'s troops searched the house but Charles and Huddleston escaped discovery, being shut away in the priest's hole. At some time after this, but before 1660, he entered the Benedictine Order. In 1660, at the Restoration, Huddleston was invited to live at Somerset House, London, under the protection of the Queen Dowager Henrietta Maria; he was then appointed chaplain to Queen Catherine. In 1678, amid all the anti-Catholic feeling aroused by the Popish Plot, the House of Lords ordered that Huddleston should be able to live freely like the king's Protestant subjects. Allegedly, when Charles II lay dying, Huddleston received him into the Catholic Church. On the accession of **James II**, Huddleston continued to live at Somerset House.

Huddleston, Trevor English Anglican missionary bishop, born 15 June 1913, died Mirfield, April 1998. After studying at Wells Theological College and Christ Church, Oxford, he was ordained in 1937 and entered the Community of the Resurrection at Mirfield. In 1943 he went to Johannesburg, where he became provincial of his Order in 1949, returning to the Community in England in 1955. He was appointed bishop of Masasi, Tanzania, 1960–8, suffragan bishop of Stepney, 1968–78, bishop of Mauritius and archbishop of the Indian Ocean, 1978–83. He was a firm believer in universal brotherhood and the need to apply it universally, particularly in the light of his experiences in South Africa with its racial policies, exposed in his best-known book, *Naught for Your Comfort* (1956). He was able to return to South Africa in 1991.

Hudson, Daniel Eldred Roman Catholic journalist, born Nahant, USA, 18 December 1849, died Notre Dame, USA, 12 January 1934. Hudson was a member of the Congregation of the Holy Cross and spent his entire career as editor of the Congregation's weekly journal *Ave Maria*, taking up this appointment in 1875, the year of his ordination. He remained as editor until his retirement in 1928, and under his editorship the journal became influential in fostering devotion to the Virgin Mary, and helped mould Catholic opinion on various religious issues of the day.

Hueber, Fortunatus Franciscan historian and theologian, born at Neustadt on the Danube, c.1659, died Munich, 12 February 1706. He became successively a general lector in theology, cathedral preacher, provincial in Bavaria, then definitor-general and chronologist of the Order in Germany. He made formal visitations of Franciscan provinces in Bohemia and Hungary. The elector of Cologne appointed Hueber his theologian. Hueber left twenty literary works, the best known being *Menologium Franciscorum*, on the lives of the beatified and saints of the Franciscan Order.

Huerta, Juan Ambrosio Roman Catholic bishop, born Lima, Peru, 7 December 1823, died Lima, 9 June 1897. Following his ordination in 1847 Huerta was made responsible for restoring the Lima Seminary, and stayed there in various positions for seventeen years. In 1865 he was made bishop of Puno, and did much to establish the infrastructure of the Church in what was then a new diocese. The complications of the political situation, and poor health, forced his retirement in 1874, but he was persuaded to re-emerge in 1880 to become bishop of Arequipa, a position he held until 1893. Huerta was one of the most able teachers and preachers in the Peruvian Church during the nineteenth century, upholding traditional doctrine in the face of theological compromise and endeavouring to protect the rights of the Church in the face of political opposition.

Huet, Pierre-Daniel French scholar and critic of **Descartes**, born Caen, France, 8 February 1630, died Paris, 26 January 1721. Orphaned when very young, he studied with the Jesuits and quickly established a reputation for remarkable learning. When he was twenty he was invited to the court of Queen **Christina of Sweden**, where he found in the Royal Library fragments of a commentary on St Matthew by **Origen**, which text he edited. He was chosen assistant tutor (under **Bossuet**) to the Dauphin and in 1685 he was made bishop of Soissons (he had been ordained priest in 1676), though he exchanged this for Avranches. He became bishop there formally only in 1692, and showed himself a diligent pastor. However, he resigned the see in 1699, receiving instead the abbacy of Fontenay and moving to Paris, where he lived with the Jesuits. At his death he left them his important library of 9000 volumes. He refuted Descartes' dictum 'Cogito ergo sum' (I think therefore I am), believing, as a fideist, that truth arises from faith rather than reason. He wrote *Demonstratio evangelica* and *Traité de la faiblesse de l'esprit humain*. His interests also included chemistry, anatomy and painting and, aged 86, he published *Histoire du commerce et de la navigation des anciens*.

Hug, Johann Leonard Roman Catholic priest and biblical scholar, born Constance, 1 June 1765, died Freiburg, 11 March 1846. In 1791, two years after his ordination, he became professor of OT at the University of Freiburg, and the following year professor of NT: it was for his NT studies that he became best known.

Hügel, Friedrich von *see* **von Hügel, Friedrich**

Hugh Etherian Theologian, born Pisa, *c.*1115, died Velletri, 1182. Also referred to variously as 'Hugo Eterianus', '(A)Etherianus' or 'Heterianus', Hugh studied theology in France and Italy as a layman. He travelled with his brother, **Leo Tuscus**, to Constantinople after 1150 to work as Emperor Manuel I's adviser on affairs related to the theology of the Latin Church and questions of reunification with it. With his brother, he wrote, at the emperor's request, a work on the Filioque controversy, showing how the doctrine had Greek as well as Latin roots, which they also sent to Rome. He also wrote a work on souls after death and a translation of important texts from the Greek Fathers. Pope **Lucius III** made him a deacon and a cardinal in 1182, a few months before his death.

Hugh of Amiens Archbishop of Rouen, born Amiens, *c.*1080, died Rouen, 11 November 1164. Educated at the cathedral school of Laon, he became a Cluniac monk and was appointed prior of Lewes and in 1123 first abbot of Reading. (Reading, King Henry I's burial place, had close links to Cluny but was never a formal member of the Cluniac Order.) With King Henry's support, he introduced the feast of the Immaculate Conception at Reading, although he himself apparently did not teach it. He was made archbishop of Rouen in 1130, and was a much-sought-after arbitrator of ecclesiastical and secular disputes.

Hugh of Balma Carthusian mystic. The only information we have about Hugh's life is that he was a monk and later prior of the charterhouse of Meyriat and that he wrote *De theologia mystica* (also called *Viae Sion lugent*) between 1246 and 1297. The book, one of the first systematic attempts to describe the mystical or inner life according to the 'three ways' (purgative, illuminative and unitive), has sometimes been attributed to **Bonaventure**. Similar in many ways to the *Cloud of Unknowing* and the Hesychasm of the Eastern Church, it is highly influenced by the writings of Pseudo-Dionysius and in turn has had an influence on many mystic writers down through the centuries.

Hugh of Bologna Priest and writer, flourished early 1100s. Also known as 'Hugues' or 'Ugo', Hugh is best known for his work on the composi-

tion of official letters and acts (the so-called *ars dictaminis*) entitled *Rationes dictandi prosaice*, which is mostly a collection of official letters to serve as models from Cicero, through **Gregory** the Great, up to his own time. He was also probably a teacher of rhetoric and writing in schools and chanceries.

Hugh of Bonnevaux Saint, Cistercian monk and abbot of Bonnevaux, born Châteauneuf d'Isère, France, *c.*1120, died Bonnevaux, 1 April 1194. A nephew of St **Hugh of Grenoble**, he entered the Cistercian monastery of Miroir about 1138. Elected abbot of Léoncel in 1162 and of Bonnevaux in 1166, he founded three daughter-houses. His efforts led to **Frederick I Barbarossa**'s recognition of **Alexander III** in 1177. Feast day 1 April.

Hugh of Cluny Saint, sixth abbot of Cluny, born Burgundy, 1024, died Cluny, 29 April 1109. Son of Count Dalmace of Semur, he was educated by Bishop Hugh of Auxerre and entered Cluny in 1038. Made prior in 1048 and elected abbot the following year; his 60-year reign marked the high point of the Cluniac reform and the papal confirmation of Cluny's temporal and spiritual privileges. He took part in many Church Councils, was appointed by the Papacy to diplomatic missions to Hungary and Germany, and was at Canossa for Emperor **Henry IV**'s reconciliation with Pope **Gregory VII**. Canonized 1 January 1120. Feast day 29 April.

Hugh of Die Gregorian reformer, archbishop and papal legate, also known as 'Hugh of the Romans', born *c.*1040, died Susa, Italy, October 1106. After serving as a precentor of Lyons Cathedral, he was consecrated bishop of Die in 1074 and archbishop of Lyons in *c.*1082–3. Papal legate in France, 1075–87, primate of the French Church, 1082–3. An early patron and supporter of the Cistercians, he fought – successfully – to institute reform in France, but was excommunicated at the Council of Benevento (1087) for criticizing Pope **Victor III**. **Urban II** restored him as papal legate, and he accompanied Urban on the preaching tour of France in 1095–6 that led to the First Crusade, and he went on crusade to the Holy Land in 1100.

Hugh of Digne Franciscan administrator and

writer, born Digne, c.1218, died Hyère(?), c.1254–7. Regarded as a forerunner of the Franciscan Spirituals, Hugh came from Provence in the south of France and was the brother of St Douceline. He served most of his career in southern France, inspiring the formation of the Order of Friars of the Sack and his sister's Order of Beguines, which he served as spiritual director. A follower of the doctrines of **Joachim of Fiore**, Hugh is best remembered for his two works on poverty, *De finibus paupertatis* and *Tractatus de paupertate inter zelatorem paupertatis et inimicum domesticum*, which promote a strict but not rigid view of poverty, and for his exposition of the Franciscan Rule (c.1242).

Hugh of Flavigny Benedictine abbot and chronicler, born near Verdun, France, 1065, died after 1115. Related to Emperor **Otto III**, he entered the abbey of Saint-Vanne in Verdun at a young age; when the monks were expelled by Thierry, bishop of Verdun, they took refuge at Saint-Benigne in Dijon, where Hugh was befriended by Abbot Jarento. Elected abbot of Flavigny-sur-Ozerain (which had been without an abbey for seven years) in 1096 and installed on 22 November 1097, he was dismissed by Bishop Norgaud of Autun in September 1099. He put his case to two different synods, but when Norgaud was deposed for simony, he was not reinstated as abbot.

Hugh of Fleury Benedictine priest, historian and biographer, died Fleury-sur-Loire, after 1118. Also known as 'Hugh of Sainte-Marie', and should not be confused with Hugh of Fleury of Canterbury, who died in 1124. The author of an ecclesiastical history dedicated to Countess Adela of Blois, he also wrote a chronicle of the kings of France, as well as a *Tractatus* addressed to Henry I of England, outlining his stand during the investiture crisis, and several other works.

Hugh of Fossess Blessed, first Premonstratensian (Norbertine) abbot general, born Fosses, near Namur, c.1093, died Prémontré, 10 February 1164. An episcopal chaplain before joining **Norbert of Xanten** and the Premonstratensians, he succeeded St Norbert as abbot in 1128. He guided the Order through its early rapid expansion, and wrote its first constitutions as well as the first *Vita Norberti*.

His cult was approved in 1927. Feast day 10 February.

Hugh of Fouilloy Augustinian canon, prior and theologian, born Fouilloy, near Corbie, between 1100 and 1110, died Saint-Laurent-au-Bois, 7 September c.1172–3. Probably educated at the Benedictine abbey of Corbie, he joined the nearby Augustinian priory of Saint-Laurent-au-Bois, which later became a dependency of Corbie. He became prior in 1153. Many of his works were wrongfully attributed to his contemporary **Hugh of Saint-Victor**.

Hugh of Grenoble Saint, bishop and reformer, born Châteauneuf d'Isère, France, 1052, died Grenoble, 1 April 1132. His father, a soldier, became a Carthusian; before his ordination, Hugh was a cathedral canon at Valence and he entered the service of the papal legate, **Hugh of Die**. In 1080, at the age of 27 and still not yet ordained, he was elected bishop of Grenoble (he was ordained immediately after his election, and was consecrated by Pope **Gregory VII** in Rome). On his election, his see was in urgent need of reform; in the course of his 52-year episcopate, he was successful in reforming Grenoble, although he thought himself a failure. A friend of **Bruno** the Carthusian, his Life was written by **Guigo I**, prior of La Grande-Chartreuse. He was canonized by Pope **Innocent II** in 1134. Feast day 1 April.

Hugh of Honau Theologian, born Alsace, France, died Alsace, flourished late 1100s. A canon regular and scholar in the court of **Frederick I Barbarossa**, Hugh served as the Emperor's legate to Emperor Manuel I in Constantinople, travelling there in 1171 and again in 1179. There he befriended **Hugh Etherian** and from him obtained some important translations of Greek texts concerning the distinction between nature and person in God, which he later incorporated into his work *A Book concerning the Difference between Nature and Person* (1180). His other major work, an earlier one, is entitled *A Book concerning Homoousion and Homoiousion*.

Hugh of Lincoln Saint, Carthusian bishop (and the first Carthusian to be canonized), born Avalon, France, 1140, died London, 16 November 1200. Educated by Augustinian canons, he left the

Augustinian house of Villard-Benoît to join La Grande-Chartreuse, of which he later became procurator. In 1179, he was made prior of Witham by Henry II, who had founded that charterhouse after the murder of **Thomas Becket**. He became bishop of Lincoln in 1186, rebuilt the cathedral, and served as royal ambassador and papal judge-delegate; three kings and three bishops carried his coffin at his funeral. He was canonized in 1220. Feast day 17 November.

Hugh of Lincoln Also known as 'Little St Hugh', died Lincoln, aged nine, 27 August 1255. His body was found in a well: a Lincoln Jew named 'Koppin' confessed under torture that Hugh was scourged, crowned with thorns and crucified; Koppin and eighteen of his supposed accomplices were executed – allegations of ritual murder by Jews being widely believed in the Middle Ages. Feast day 27 August.

Hugh of Newcastle Franciscan philosopher and disciple of **Duns Scotus**, dates of birth and death uncertain, but he flourished in the early decades of the fourteenth century as he is found in attendance at the chapter in Perugia in 1322. He wrote much on Antichrist and is buried in Paris.

Hugh of Pisa *see* **Huguccio**

Hugh of Remiremont Cardinal, early advocate and later opponent of the Gregorian reform, also known as 'Hugo Candidus', born Lorraine, *c.*1020, died after 1098. He left Remiremont for Rome in 1049 and was created cardinal-priest of S. Clemente by Pope **Leo IX**. In 1061, he opposed the reform party and supported the Antipope **Honorius II**, but returned to the reforming camp by 1063, when he was absolved by Pope **Alexander II** and made his legate to Spain. He was again made legate to Spain under Pope **Gregory VII**, whose election he supported, and played an active role in the Gregorian reform. In 1075, however, he left the Gregorian camp, and played an important role in **Henry IV**'s Synod of Worms in January 1076; he was excommunicated later that year and deposed in 1078. He signed the decree deposing Gregory VII at Brixen in 1080; supported the Antipope Clement III, **Guibert of Ravenna**, for whom he served as legate to Germany (and as

such, he was again excommunicated, by the Synod of Quedlinberg in 1085); and was one of the schismatic cardinals who signed the proclamation against Pope **Urban II** in August 1098.

Hugh of Saint-Cher Dominican administrator and biblical scholar, born Saint-Cher, France, *c.*1200, died Orvieto, Italy, 19 March 1263. After studies at Paris, Hugh entered the Dominican Order at St Jacques in Paris in 1225. In 1226, while continuing his studies in theology, he was elected provincial of France, a post he held until 1230 and again from 1236 to 1244. He also served as vicar general, 1240–41. In 1244 he became the first Dominican cardinal and served the Curia at the Council of Lyons (1245), and as legate to Germany, 1251–3, where he was the first to sanction the feast of Corpus Christi (in Liège). Hugh's best-known works are resources on the Bible, including a Latin Concordance (1240) and a set of exegetical notes called the *Postillae*.

Hugh of Saint-Victor Philosopher and mystical theologian, born Saxony, late eleventh century, died Paris, 11 February 1141. Very little is known about his early life, and the extant sources are not in agreement. From *c.*1120 until his death he was master at the school of Saint-Victor; many works attributed to him are in fact the work of others, and as a result there has been some degree of misrepresentation of his teaching.

Hugh of Trimberg Poet and teacher, born Oberwerrn, Germany, *c.*1235, died Bamberg, Germany, *c.*1314. Teacher and eventually rector of the collegiate school of St Gandolf in Bamberg, Trimberg was the author of a number of didactic poems, of which the most influential and best known is *Der Renner* (The Runner), dating from the turn of the thirteenth and fourteenth centuries. Written in German and with nearly 25,000 verses, it attacks the sinfulness of the world and mocks the foibles of human nature. It was in wide circulation for some 500 years.

Hughes, Angela Roman Catholic sister and social administrator, born Annaloghan, Ireland, *c.*1806, died New York City, 5 September 1866. The sister of Archbishop John J. **Hughes**, Ellen emigrated to America with her parents in 1818 and entered the

Sisters of Charity in 1825, taking the name 'Mary Angela'. She was involved in the care of needy children, and subsequently helped establish missions, schools, convents and hospitals in the New York area. She became assistant to the mother general of the New York sisterhood in 1849, becoming mother general herself in 1855. From 1861 until her death she was superior of St Vincent's Hospital in New York, which she herself had founded in 1849.

Hughes, Hugh Price Methodist minister, preacher and chief founder of the 'Nonconformist Conscience', born at Carmarthen, Wales, 8 February 1847, died London, 17 November 1902. Attended Richmond College, 1865–9. Served as minister at churches in Dover, Brighton, Tottenham, Dulwich and Oxford. From 1881 he was the leader in London of the Methodist 'Forward Movement'. In 1885 he commenced and edited the *Methodist Times*, using it as an instrument of social reform and political agitation. He began the West London mission in 1886, giving a series of popular services in St James's Hall, Piccadilly. One of the founders of the Free Church Congress and, in 1896, the first president of the National Free Church Council, in 1898 he was appointed president of the Wesleyan Methodist Conference. He was influential in establishing a chain of 'Central Halls' in various localities as centres of evangelism and social welfare.

Hughes, John Joseph American prelate, born Annaloghan, County Tyrone, Ireland, 24 June 1797, died New York, 3 January 1864. From Ireland he emigrated to the USA, was ordained and later, in 1838, created coadjutor bishop of New York. He succeeded to the vacant see as fourth bishop in 1842. He founded St John's College, Fordham, now Fordham University. He led the campaign for parochial schools, and was created the first archbishop of New York in 1850. His achievements were many and varied: founding the *Catholic Herald* newspaper, defending Catholic schools against the Know-Nothing movement, and fighting the radical Irish press. During the Civil War he helped end the critical draft riots in the city, and visited Europe as President Lincoln's personal agent, successfully counteracting pro-Southern feeling in France, Rome and Ireland. In Rome, he founded the North American College. In

1858 he laid the cornerstone of St Patrick's Cathedral, New York City.

Hughes, Philip Roman Catholic priest and Church historian, born Manchester, England, 11 May 1895, died South Bend, Indiana, 6 October 1967. After studying at St Bede's College, Manchester, and the Catholic University of Louvain, Belgium, Hughes spent some time in Rome, where he was ordained in 1920. He served for a time in parish work, 1924–31, before becoming archivist of Westminster Diocese, until forced to resign in 1943 because of poor health. In 1954 he became professor of Church history at the University of Notre Dame, Indiana, teaching there until ill health forced his retirement in 1963. His fame chiefly rests on his *History of the Church* (3 vols, 1933–47) and his important *History of the Reformation in England* (3 vols, 1951–4). In 1957, he was made a domestic prelate by Pope **Pius XII**.

Hughes, Thomas Jesuit historian, born Liverpool, England, 24 January 1849, died Rome, 14 June 1939. Hughes became a Jesuit in 1866 and worked initially as a missionary among Native Americans in Missouri before completing his training for the priesthood. Following ordination in 1878 he taught at the University of St Louis, and in 1894 was among those nominated to contribute volumes to the comprehensive history of the Society of Jesus then being planned. Hughes moved to Rome to work on this project and eventually contributed four volumes to the series. These cover the history of the Jesuits in North America, and achieved authoritative status as soon as they were published.

Hugo, Charles Hyacinth Norbertine bishop, abbot, historian, born St-Mihiel, Department of Meuse, France, 20 September 1667, died 2 August 1739. Hugo entered the Norbertine Order at Pont-à-Mousson and became a priest, receiving 'Louis' as his religious name. He studied at the abbey of Jovillier and then at Bourges University. He taught theology at Etival in Lorraine, and he was named prior of St Joseph's, Nancy, in 1700. In 1710 he was chosen coadjutor abbot of Etival, and in 1722 was elected abbot. He was created a bishop in 1728. He published a great many works, the more important ones being on the history of the Norbertines (the Premonstratensians) and on the history of Lorraine. The general chapter of his Order encouraged his work, naming him historiographer of the Order and urging all abbots to provide him with material. Two volumes of the *Annales* had been published, and a third was in the hands of the censors, when he died.

Hugolino of Gualdo Cattaneo Blessed, Augustinian prior, born Bevagna, Italy, date unknown, died Gualdo Cattaneo, Italy, 1 January 1260. Little is known of Hugolino's life except that he received a Benedictine community in Gualdo into the Augustinian Order, becoming its prior two years before his death. A local cult evolved which encouraged charitable penitential works, and the Augustinians have venerated him as a saint since 1482. Against this history, however, there is evidence that the Hugolino of Gualdo Cattaneo was the same man as the fourteenth-century monk Hugolino Michaelis of Bavagna, who founded a monastery in the area around 1340, which eventually became Augustinian in 1437. Evidence for neither history is conclusive.

Hugon, Edouard Dominican theologian, born Lafarre, France, 25 August 1867, died Rome, 7 February 1929. Hugon joined the Dominicans in 1885 and was ordained in 1892. His entire career was spent teaching philosophy and theology in a number of seminaries, and he eventually became one of the first professors at the Pontifical Institute Angelicum on its foundation in 1910. He was the author of numerous theological treatises and articles, dealing with a variety of subjects, such as Thomism, metaphysics, spirituality and Christology.

Huguccio (Hugh of Pisa) Canon lawyer, born Pisa, Italy, early to mid 1100s, died Ferrara, Italy, 30 April 1210. Huguccio studied and taught canon law at Bologna, there becoming the mentor of Lotharius of Segni (later Pope **Innocent III**). On 1 May 1190 he was appointed bishop of Ferrara, where he lived and worked until his death. A master of grammar as well as law, he wrote several well-known lexicographical studies (such as the *Liber derivationum* and the *Summa artis grammaticae*), but his influence is most profoundly felt through his commentary on the *Decretum* of **Gratian**, *Summa super decreta*. Making use of most

of the greatest ecclesiastical minds of his day, Huguccio's *Summa*, with its analysis and its exposition, influenced the course of canon law at the point when it was being definitively codified, thus affecting the juridical practice of the Church for hundreds of years.

Hull, Ernest Reginald Jesuit author and editor, born Manchester, England, 9 September 1863, died Roehampton, England, 19 July 1952. A convert from the Church of England, Hull became a Jesuit in 1888. After working on literary pursuits, he was sent to Bombay (Mumbai), India, in 1902, to edit the *Catholic Examiner*, the diocesan paper, which he ran until 1924, bringing the paper into great repute and pioneering the Catholic press for all of India. From 1924 to 1932, he served as the archivist for the archbishop of Bombay. Upon returning to England he continued his writing career. His literary output was prodigious, covering all areas of Christian life. His most important work, *Man's Greatest Concern: The Management of Life* (1918), was translated into Chinese and several Indian languages.

Hulst, Maurice d' (Le Sage d'Hauteroche) Priest, writer and orator, born Paris, 10 October 1841, died Paris, 6 November 1896. Hulst studied at St-Sulpice in Paris and at Rome, where he was awarded a doctorate of divinity. On his return to Paris he was engaged in mission work, and in the Franco-Prussian War he became an army chaplain. Hulst helped to found and organize the free Catholic University in Paris, and in 1880 became its rector, which post he held for fifteen years. In 1892 he was elected deputy for Finistère, and loyally responded to **Leo XIII**'s 'ralliement', or call to French Catholics to support the republican government, although his own sympathies were royalist. His chief efforts, however, were devoted to encouraging the clergy to study the sacred sciences and he helped to organize the International Scientific Congresses of Catholics. From 1891 until the year of his death he preached the Lenten conferences at the cathedral of Notre Dame, and his sermons from there and elsewhere – he was much admired as a preacher – were subsequently published. His publications also include two biographies and articles on social and educational issues in particular. The latter were published in four volumes.

Humbeline Blessed, Benedictine prioress, born Dijon(?), c.1091, died priory of Jully, before 1136. The sister of **Bernard of Clairvaux**, Humbeline was married to a wealthy nobleman. After her brother refused to see her on account of her worldly finery, she felt convicted of her worldly life. On her brother's urging, she began living a life of prayer and fasting. After two years, she entered the priory of Jully with her husband's consent, later becoming prioress there. Feast day 12 February.

Humbert of Maroilles Saint, abbot, born in Méziéres-sur-Oise, died Maroilles, 25 March c.680. Humbert, according to tradition, was a monk and priest at Laon. When, upon his parents' deaths, Humbert inherited the family estate, he retired and made two pilgrimages to Rome. In 675 he gave his land to the monastery of Maroilles by a document which is still in existence, becoming also the first abbot of that monastery. Some legends claim that he became a bishop. Feast day 25 March.

Humbert of Romans Dominican master general, born Romans, near Vienne (France), c.1194, died Valence (France), 14 July 1277 (or 15 January 1274). Humbert became a Dominican in 1224 after receiving his master's of arts in Paris. Two years later he was appointed professor of theology. In 1236 he was elected to the priorship of Lyons and in 1240 became the provincial of the Roman province. After also serving as provincial of France, he was elected master general of the Order in 1254, a post he held for nine years. As master general, he helped the Order solidify its academic and administrative practice and complete a reform of its liturgy. In 1264, he retired to Valence in order to write works on the Order and on asceticism. These works are still influential within his Order.

Humbert of Silva Candida Cardinal, papal legate and canonist, born Lorraine, c.1000, died Rome, 5 May 1061. One of the great churchmen of the eleventh century, he entered Moyenmoutier as a novice in 1015, where he studied law, theology and Greek. Appointed first archbishop of Sicily and later cardinal-bishop of Silva Candida by Pope **Leo IX**, he was a strong proponent of reform, albeit theologically extremist: he rejected the validity of heretical and simoniacal sacraments. In 1054 he was sent to Constantinople, and here his intransigence proved to be disastrous: his mission ended in failure and the excommunication of the Greek patriarch, Michael Cerularius.

Hume, (George) Basil English Benedictine monk, cardinal, born Newcastle upon Tyne, 2 March 1923, died London, 17 June 1999. He was educated at Ampleforth College, Oxford and Fribourg. He was ordained priest in 1950, taught at Ampleforth and was elected abbot in 1963. It came as a surprise to many people when in 1976, from such a background, he was made archbishop of Westminster and cardinal. He was known for his prayerfulness, for his ability to listen to different sides of arguments and for his courage to take a stand on issues of importance. As cardinal he won the affection and respect not only of Roman Catholics, but of leaders and members of other Christian denominations and of other faiths, and of politicians at home and abroad. Just before he died he was awarded the Order of Merit by Queen Elizabeth II. His writings include *Searching for God* (1977), *In Praise of Benedict* (1981), *To Be a Pilgrim* (1984), *Towards a Civilisation of Love* (1988), *Light in the Lord* (1991), *Remaking Europe* (1994), *Basil in Blunderland* (1997) and *The Mystery of the Cross* (1998). He gave many interviews and was involved in numerous broadcasts and wrote and presented the film *Return of the Saints*, made in 1984.

Hume, Nelson Roman Catholic educator, born New York City, 12 January 1881, died New Milford, Connecticut, 14 June 1948. After studying at St Francis Xavier College in New York and teaching in the metropolitan area, Hume founded his own school, which he directed for six years. In 1915, after completing a doctorate at Georgetown University, Hume founded the Canterbury School in New Milford, a school run by lay people under the auspices of the bishop, John Nilan. He was treasurer and headmaster of the school until his death, and in 1938 was made Knight of the Order of St Gregory the Great by Pope **Pius XI**.

Humiliana de Circulis Blessed, Franciscan tertiary, born Florence, December 1219, died Florence, 19

May 1246. After five difficult years of marriage, Humiliana became a widow with two young girls. Because of the children, she could not fully join an Order as a nun and so became a member of the Third Order of the Franciscans, or a tertiary, devoting her life to prayer, penance, church attendance and helping the poor. She was known for her meekness and courage, and miracles were ascribed to her even during her lifetime. **Innocent XII** confirmed her cult in 1694. Feast day 19 May in Florence, 15 June in the Franciscan Order.

Hummel, Johann Nepomuk Austrian composer, pianist and child prodigy, born Pressburg, 14 November 1778, died Weimar, 17 October 1837. As a youth he studied under **Mozart**, and lodged with him. Later his teachers included Clementi, Albrechtsberger, Salieri and Joseph **Haydn**. Hummel performed as a pianist in Germany, Holland and Great Britain. In Austria he was kapellmeister, succeeding Haydn, to Prince Esterhazy, and later worked at Stuttgart and Weimar, where he knew Goethe. Hummel worked in the Viennese classical tradition, as his Mass settings reveal. His catalogue includes a *Te Deum* and other sacred pieces, including many Masses. Many of Hummel's sacred compositions dating from 1804–11 were written for the Esterhazys' chapel, and are usually scored for solo voices, choir and orchestra.

Hummelauer, Franz von Jesuit scholar, born Vienna, Austria, 14 August 1842, died 's-Heerenberg, The Netherlands, 12 April 1914. Hummelauer became a Jesuit in 1860 and studied for the priesthood in Germany and in England, where he continued to study for some years following his ordination. In 1884 he co-founded the Cursus Scripturae Sacrae commentary series with R. **Cornely** and J. **Knabenbauer**, and contributed several OT commentaries to this series. In 1903 he became a consultor to the Pontifical Biblical Commission, but a treatise on Catholic exegetical methodology which he published in 1904 caused such controversy that he withdrew completely from academic life. He worked in pastoral ministry in Germany for three years before retiring to the novitiate of 's-Heerenberg.

Hunegundis (Hunegonde) Saint, foundress of the monastery of Homblieres, born Lemblais, Picardy, died Homblieres, *c.*690. Hunegundis was forced to marry by her parents, but at the same time vowed virginity and promised God to become a nun. She and her husband travelled to Rome, where the Pope granted her request for the veil. Back in France, she founded the monastery of Homblieres (near Saint-Quentin). Feast day 25 August.

Hunfried Saint, Benedictine bishop, died Thérouanne, France, 8 March 870. Hunfried became a monk as a young man and as abbot of Prüm was elected bishop of Thérouanne in 856. Thérouanne was sacked by the Normans in 861, but after initial discouragement Hunfried saw it rebuilt. Subsequently he became abbot of Saint-Bertin, and attended a number of important Church Councils held in France. Feast day 8 March.

Hunt, Duane Garrison Roman Catholic bishop, born Reynolds, USA, 19 September 1884, died Salt Lake City, USA, 31 March 1960. From a Methodist family, Hunt embraced Roman Catholicism in 1913 while a postgraduate student at the University of Chicago. He subsequently studied for the priesthood and was ordained in 1920. Hunt served a number of parishes in the Diocese of Salt Lake City, and became its bishop in 1937. He was a gifted preacher and became well known as a Catholic apologist through a weekly radio programme he presented, which was influential both in overcoming anti-Catholic prejudice and in encouraging the faithful.

Hunt, Walter (Venantius) Theologian in the Carmelite Order, died Carmelite Friary in Oxford, 28 November 1478. It is likely he was a professor of theology at the University of Oxford. He represented the English bishops as theologian at the Council of Ferrara and was the personal theologian of Pope **Eugenius IV** when he moved that council to Florence, 1438–9. He was the leading exponent of the Western Latin view on the reunion of the Western Church with the Eastern Churches. He wrote some 30 lost Latin treatises, among them an *Apologia* for the monastic life in general and that of the friars in particular, and a diatribe against preaching by women.

Huntingdon, Countess of   *see* **Hastings, Selina**

Hunton, George K. Roman Catholic civil rights advocate, born Claremont, New Hampshire, 24 March 1888, died New York City, 11 November 1967. After graduating in law from Fordham University, New York, Hunton began working for indigent defendants in the inner city of New York. After serving in World War I, he began a successful private law practice. In 1931, he began working to raise funds for the Cardinal Gibbons Institute, a Catholic school for African Americans. In 1934, with John **La Farge**, SJ, he helped found the Catholic Interracial Council of New York. He was an advocate for civil rights along with Jewish and Protestant colleagues.

Huonder, Anton Jesuit missiologist, born Chur, Switzerland, 25 December 1858, died Bonn, Germany, 23 August 1926. Ordained in 1889, Huonder became well known within the Jesuits for his spirituality, and his abilities as a preacher and retreat director. He also took a keen interest in mission, and through his influential writings promoted the concept of indigenous clergy as an alternative to what he regarded as the unhealthy Eurocentrism then characterizing much missionary effort.

Hurley, Michael Augustinian religious, born Ireland, c.1780, died Philadelphia, USA, 15 May 1837. Hurley emigrated to the USA with his family as a child, and c.1797 became the first American candidate for the Augustinians. He studied for the priesthood in Italy and was ordained in 1803, after which he returned to America, holding a variety of clerical posts before becoming Augustinian superior in the USA in 1826. He encouraged charitable work among orphans and the poor, and in 1832 was commended by the civic authorities of Philadelphia for his ministry during a cholera epidemic.

Hurtado, Caspar Spanish Jesuit theologian and orator, born Mondejar, New Castile, 1575, died Alcalá, 5 August 1647. Studied at Alcalá and became a professor there, but in 1607 he resigned and joined the Jesuits. Lectured in theology at Murcia, Madrid and Alcalá, where he remained until his death. He wrote mainly on sacramental theology, including his *De Eucharistia, sacrificio missae et ordine* (1620), *De matrimonio et censuris* (1627) and *Disputationes de sacramentis et censuris* (1633), and he wrote *De Incarnatione Verbi* (1628), *De beatitudine, de actibus humanis, bonitate et malitia, habitibus, virtutibus et peccatis* (1632) and *De Deo* (1642).

Hurter, Hugo von Theologian, born Schaffhausen, Switzerland, 11 January 1832, died Innsbruck, 10 December 1914. A convert to Catholicism, he was a student at the Germanicum in Rome from 1849 to 1856, being ordained in 1855. After leaving the Germanicum he joined the Society of Jesus and in 1858 was appointed to the theology faculty of Innsbruck University. His works include surveys of theology and selections from the writings of the Fathers of the Church. His chief work, however, was his *Nomenclator literarius theologiae catholicae*, published first in three, then in five, volumes, which lists all known writers on theology and associated disciplines from the Fathers of the Church to the year 1910, providing brief biographies of each, listing their works, and describing their characteristic teachings.

Huss (Hus), John Bohemian religious reformer, martyr, born Husinec (Czech Republic), c.1369, burned at the stake at the Council of Constance, 6 July 1415. He studied at Prague University, where he went on to lecture in theology, 1398, and where he became dean, 1401. He was a popular preacher in the Bethlehem Chapel in Prague, and he was much influenced by the ideas of John **Wycliffe**. In 1408 he defied a papal directive to stop preaching, and this led to his excommunication in 1411. His main work, *De Ecclesia* (1413), led to a summons to appear before the Council of Constance. When he refused to recant he was executed. His angry followers started the Hussite Wars, which lasted until the middle of the century. Feast day 6 July.

Husslein, Joseph Caspar Jesuit social theorist, born Milwaukee, USA, 10 June 1873, died St Louis, USA, 19 October 1952. Husslein became a Jesuit following graduation and was ordained in 1905. He taught English at St Ignatius' College in Cleveland, where he was attracted to socialism and became a regular contributor to the journal *America*, becoming an associate editor in 1911. He later helped found the School of Social Work at Fordham University, New York, and the School of

Social Service at St Louis University. Husslein was also active in a number of Catholic social initiatives, and wrote or edited over 200 books on various social issues.

Hutchinson, Anne Religious enthusiast and American pioneer, baptized Alford, Lincolnshire, 20 July 1591, died Pelham Bay, Long Island, August or September 1643. The daughter of a Lincolnshire clergyman, Francis Marbury, she married William Hutchinson in 1612, and emigrated to Boston, Massachusetts, where her eldest son had gone, in 1634. There she developed her religious ideas in meetings of women held in her house. Following a trial for sedition and heresy she was banished from the state and went with a few friends to Rhode Island, where in 1638 she acquired some land from the Indians and set up a new democracy. After her husband's death in 1642 she moved to a new settlement, where she and all fifteen members of her family were murdered by Indians.

Hutin, Madeleine (Little Sister Magdeleine of Jesus) Foundress of the Little Sisters of Jesus, born France, 1898, died Rome, 6 November 1989. She was the daughter of an army doctor stationed in Tunisia, with a great love of Africa. Inspired by the life of Charles de **Foucauld**, she went to Algeria in 1936 where, with the support of the Little Brothers, she established a congregation for women along the same lines. The Little Sisters live in small fraternities, always among the poor, entering into the lives of their often non-Christian neighbours and combining manual work with contemplative prayer. Madeleine travelled to many countries to encourage fraternities, notably to Russia and Eastern Europe, and the Order is now established worldwide.

Hutten, Christoph Franz von Bishop, born Mainburg, Germany, 19 January 1673, died Würzburg, 25 March 1729. Von Hutten was known as a patron of the arts and of learning. He rose from dean of Würzburg Cathedral to bishop in a brief ecclesiastical career.

Hutten, Franz Christoph von Cardinal, bishop, born Wisenfeld, Germany, 6 March 1706, died Bruchsal, Germany, 20 April 1770. An aristocratic cardinal and bishop, Hutten was also a patron of the arts whose court was famous for its splendour. He also promoted both lay and clerical education, and endowed numerous churches.

Hutten, Moritz von Bishop, born Arnstein, Germany, 26 November 1503, died Eichstätt, Germany, 6 December 1552. After study at Ingolstadt, Hutten held a variety of clerical appointments, eventually becoming bishop of Eichstätt in 1539. Untainted by the clerical abuses common at that time, he worked hard to reform the clergy in his diocese. He attended the Council of Trent in 1543 and presided at the Regensburg Colloquy of 1546.

Hutten, Ulrich von Humanist scholar, born Steckelberg, near Fulda, 21 April 1488, died island of Ufenau, Lake Zurich, August 1523. A descendant of the Franconian knights, Ulrich von Hutten embodied a German nationalism which was already evident among late-fifteenth-century writers, reacting against the imperialism of papal Rome, and consequently became a fervent supporter of **Luther**. His intellectual formation came from the monastery at Fulda and a number of German universities, finding expression in poems, treatises and contributions to the *Epistolae obscurorum virorum* (Letters of obscure men, 1515–17), defending **Reuchlin** against his Scholastic critics. His last days were spent under the protection of **Zwingli**.

Hutter, Jakob Itinerant hat-maker and founder of the Hutterites, born probably Moos, South Tyrol, date unknown, died, burned at the stake, Innsbruck, 25 February 1536. He was an Anabaptist and founded a group in Moravia devoted to pacificism and the common ownership of property. Because they refused to accept infant baptism and reintroduced the practice of believers' baptism, the sect was much persecuted, having to keep moving from Moravia to Transylvania, to the Ukraine and eventually to North America, where small colonies still exist in South Dakota and more recently in Canada. Moravian Anabaptists, like so many of the sixteenth-century sects, regarded any true religious reform as necessarily involving social betterment. Hutter himself left Auspitz, Moravia, for the Tyrol because of persecution, and was arrested in Clausen in 1535.

Huvelin, Henri   Roman Catholic spiritual director, born Laon, France, 7 October 1838, died Paris, 10 July 1910. By refusing the offer of a professorship at the Institut Catholique following his ordination in 1867, Huvelin turned his back on an academic career in favour of pastoral ministry. He ministered as priest of Saint-Sulpice in Paris for 35 years, where his wisdom as a counsellor and spiritual director gained him a wide reputation. Although Huvelin himself never published anything, many of his spiritual directions and counsels were recorded and published by those who had benefited from them, notably Friedrich **von Hügel**.

Huygens, Constantijn   Dutch Calvinist statesman, poet and playwright, born The Hague, 4 September 1596, died there, 28 March 1687. He studied at Leiden, London and Oxford. As a diplomat he frequently visited England, where he befriended **Donne** and **Bacon** and was knighted by **James I**, and Venice. Huygens translated some of Donne's poetry, which he introduced to Holland. As a poet, he was complex and intellectual. His collected poems, written between 1658 and 1672, were published as *Korenbloeinen* (Cornflowers). He was the father of Christiaan Huygens, the Dutch mathematician, physicist, astronomer and playwright.

Huysmans, Joris-Karl   French novelist, born Paris, 5 February 1848, died Paris, 12 May 1907. He worked in the French Ministry of the Interior. His novels trace a journey from Baudelaire and **Zola** to devout Catholicism. His early work, influenced by naturalistic novelists, includes *Marthe, histoire d'une fille* and *Sac au dos*. Later he wrote violent and individual novels. They are partly autobiographical, as in *En route*, *La Cathédrale* and *L'Oblat*, set at Ligugé Abbey, near Poitiers.

Huyssens, Peter   Jesuit architect, born Bruges (Belgium), June 1577, died Bruges, June 1637. Huyssens became a lay brother in the Jesuits in 1597, and following architectural studies designed the earliest baroque church in the Low Countries, the Jesuit church in Maastricht (1606). This was followed by the church of St Charles Borromeo in Antwerp, on which he collaborated with **Rubens**. The opulence and expense of Huyssens' later designs attracted opposition from within the Jesuits (it was felt that they were incompatible with the Order's principles of simplicity and poverty), but he went on to complete a royal chapel for Duchess Isabella in 1628, and his masterpiece, St Peter's in Ghent, in 1633, held by many to be the finest example of baroque architecture in Belgium.

Hyacinth (Iaccho)   Saint, Polish Dominican missionary, born Duchy of Oppeln, 1185, died Cracow, 15 August 1257. He is said to have been of noble birth and met St **Dominic** on a visit to Rome in 1220. He was professed at Santa Sabria and became superior of a small group of brothers. He carried out missionary work in Denmark, Sweden and Norway and as far as the Black Sea. There is doubt about some of the facts of his life. Feast day 17 August.

Hydatius   Historian, bishop, perhaps of Chaves (Portugal), born Lemica, *c*.395, died, perhaps in Galicia, after 468. Hydatius chronicled and annotated lists of consuls from 509 BC to AD 468, and continued the chronicle of **Jerome** for 379–468. He wrote against the Sueves, Manichaeism and Priscillianism; his writings are somewhat uneven but valuable as eyewitness accounts of barbarian invasions of Spain. Hydatius was also a priest, 416, bishop, 427, and legate to Aetius, 431.

Hyginus   Saint, bishop of Rome. **Eusebius** records that Hyginus reigned from 138 (the year of the death of **Telesphorus**) to 142, when he died; however, the *Liber Pontificalis* claims that he was a philosopher of Athens who reigned four years and is buried in the Vatican near St Peter (modern excavations do not uphold this), while the Liberian catalogue says that his reign was twelve years long. The Roman Martyrology lists him as a martyr, but this is unsupported by other sources. **Irenaeus** writes that during the reign of Hyginus, the Gnostic forerunners of **Marcion**, Valentinus and Cerdo, arrived in Rome. Feast day 11 January.

Hynd, David   Nazarene medical missionary, born Perth, Scotland, 25 October 1895, died Manzini, Swaziland, 14 February 1991. He and his wife, Nema, were both ordained ministers and medical professionals who went to Africa in 1925. He supervised construction of Raleigh Fitkin Memorial Hospital in Manzini, Swaziland, and was its chief administrator and head of surgery until 1962. He founded the Red Cross of Swaziland in 1931. RFM Hospital became the anchor of a wider medical programme that included a leprosy clinic, over a dozen other clinics and dispensaries throughout Swaziland, a training programme for nurses, and an orphanage.

Hypatius of Ephesus Bishop, dates of birth and death unknown. Metropolitan of Ephesus between 531 and 537/8, he supported on various occasions **Justinian I** in his anti-Monophysite policy. So, at the Council of Constantinople in 536, he was the orthodox spokesman when Severus of Antioch and other Monophysites were condemned. Hypatius composed an episcopal decree on Christian burial, preserved incised in stone, and commentaries on the Psalms, on the Minor Prophets and on Luke, as well as *Quaestiones miscellaneae* (answers to questions of a suffragan bishop).

Hyvernat, Henri Roman Catholic oriental scholar, born Loire, France, 30 June 1858, died Washington, DC, 29 May 1941. Hyvernat became chaplain at the French church in Rome following his ordination in 1882, and while there studied for a doctorate at the Pontifical University. On completion he was appointed professor of Assyriology and Egyptology at the Roman Seminary, and in 1889 became a founding member of faculty at the Catholic University in Washington, DC, remaining there until his death. During his long academic career Hyvernat published numerous books and articles, and his detailed research on the manuscripts of early Coptic Christianity made a permanent contribution to the study of this subject.

I

Ibarra y González, Ramón Roman Catholic archbishop and educationalist, born Olinalá, Mexico, 22 October 1853, died Mexico City, 1 February 1917. After study and ordination in Rome, where his scholarship won a papal medal, Ibarra returned to his native Mexico in 1883, becoming bishop of Chilapa in 1889, and of Puebla in 1902. This became an archdiocese in 1903. He founded numerous schools, a seminary and a university, and encouraged the establishment of hospitals and other charitable institutions for the poor, including the native population. The religious persecution which was inflicted on the Mexican Church during the early twentieth century brought about the collapse of most of these initiatives, and at the time of his death Ibarra was in hiding.

Ibn al-'Assāl Canon lawyer, flourished 1235–43. Little is known about the life of Ibn al-'Assāl except that he was chief of protocol to Cyril III, Coptic patriarch from 1235 to 1243. For a synod in 1239, he compiled a compendium of law (both ecclesiastical and civil) of the Monophysite Coptic Church, which is called the *Nomocanon* of Ibn al-'Assāl. Manuscripts of the work still survive, and two Arabic editions were published in 1908 and 1927 in Cairo.

Icazbalceta, Joaquín García Roman Catholic historiographer, born Mexico City, 21 August 1825, died 26 November 1894. Taught by private tutors and lacking a formal university education, Icazbalceta began literary and historical studies as a young man. His most lasting contribution to scholarship consists of his meticulous and exhaustive research into the documentary sources of Mexican history,

and although a devout Catholic his conclusions were never influenced by his faith, and remained balanced and impartial. Icazbalceta's erudition and learning earned him a wide reputation, and during his lifetime he was the recipient of numerous honours and awards.

Ida of Boulogne Blessed, noblewoman, born Bouillon (Belgium), *c.*1040, died 13 April 1113. Ida was the daughter of Duke Godfrey II (of Lower Lorraine) and niece of Pope **Stephen IX**. She married the count of Boulogne, Eustace, around 1057 and was the mother of King **Baldwin I of Jerusalem**. Her life was noted for the practice of virtue and for her generosity, particularly to Saint-Bertin, Affligem, and the convent at Nivelles. She was also a correspondent of **Anselm of Canterbury**. Feast day in the Diocese of Arras and Bayeux 13 April.

Ida of Herzfeld Great-granddaughter of the Emperor **Charlemagne** and an unofficial saint, date and place of birth unknown, died Herzfeld, Westphalia, 4 September 825. She was brought up at the court of Charlemagne and eventually married to one Egbert (not of Kentish fame) but was widowed early and spent the rest of her life in doing good works, moving from her estate at Hofstadt to Herzfeld in Westphalia where her son Warin became a monk. She built a convent there and continued her exemplary life, helping the poor until her death.

Ida of Leeuw Blessed, Cistercian nun, born Leeuw (Belgium), died convent of La Ramée, Brabant (Belgium), *c.*1260. Ida entered the convent of La

Ramée at some time after 1216. There she was known for her love of learning and for certain mystical graces given her. During the sixteenth and seventeenth centuries her cult spread throughout Flanders. Feast day 30 October.

Ida of Louvain Blessed, Cistercian nun, born Louvain (Belgium), early 1200s, died abbey of Roosendael, near Mechelen (Belgium), c.1300. A nun at the abbey of Roosendael, Ida was said by her biographer to have been gifted with great mystical graces and by the stigmata. Though the historicity of much of her biography is doubtful, her feast was granted to the Benedictines as well as the Cistercians by Pope **Clement XI** in 1719. Feast day 13 April.

Ida of Nivelles Blessed, Cistercian nun, born Nivelles (Belgium), c.1190, died convent of La Ramée, Brabant (Belgium), 11 December 1231. Ida originally joined Kerkhem Abbey, near Louvain (Belgium), when she was sixteen and then moved with her community to La Ramée in 1215. She was reputed to have been given mystical graces and was devoted to the Passion of Christ and the Blessed Sacrament. She is also said to have offered her sufferings for harassed priests and religious. After long such sufferings due to illness, she died aged 32. Feast day 12 December at La Ramée.

Iduberga (Ida, Itta) Saint, abbey foundress, born c.592, died Nivelles (Belgium), 8 May 652. Iduberga was born the daughter of a count of Aquitaine and was married to the mayor of the palace, Pepin of Landen. (Two of her daughters, Begga and **Gertrude**, were later, after their mother, also declared to be saints.) After the death of her husband, she founded the abbey of Nivelles, freely giving herself and all her property to the endeavour. The first nuns for the new abbey came from Ireland; Iduberga was the first abbess, succeeded by her daughter Gertrude. Feast day 8 May.

Ignatius (Brianchaninov) Russian Orthodox saint, spiritual writer and elder, born Vologda province, 5 February 1807, died Babaevsky monastery, 30 April 1867. He gave up a successful military career to become a monk, against the wishes of Emperor Nicholas I. In 1857 he was consecrated bishop but after four years he retired owing to ill health and became a recluse at a remote monastery. There he wrote a large number of spiritual works for both monks and laypeople. His theology was rather anti-Western for the time – certainly more so than his near contemporary, St **Theophan the Recluse**. His classics *The Arena* and *On the Prayer on Jesus* are available in English. Canonized in Russia in 1988. Feast day 30 April.

Ignatius of Antioch Bishop and saint, born Antioch(?), died Rome, c.107. We only know something about the end of his life. As bishop of Antioch he was arrested and taken to Rome. During this journey he visited several Christian communities in Asia Minor; he met **Polycarp** at Smyrna and exchanged letters. In sum seven of these letters have been preserved. They contain vestiges of an early theology of martyrdom and of a triple *ordo* (bishop, priest and deacon) in which the bishop has the central role. Today the authenticity of these letters is a much debated issue, even to the point of denying Ignatius' existence. Feast day 17 October.

Ignatius of Laconi Saint, Capuchin religious, born Laconi, Sardinia, 10 December 1701, died Cagliari, Italy, 11 May 1781. Francis Ignatius Vincent Peis came from a poor peasant family; he never learned to read or write. Even as a child he was known for his piety, which eventually led him to join the Capuchins in Cagliari in 1721 as a lay brother. Over the course of the next 60 years he served the Order through the seeking of alms and works of charity, and miracles were also attributed him. He was canonized in 1951. Feast day 12 May.

Ignatius of Loyola Saint, founder of the Society of Jesus, born into a noble family, castle of Loyola, Spain, 1491, died Rome, 31 July 1556. Ignatius (Iñigo) spent his youth in the service of the treasurer to the royal house of Castile, and then in the service of the duke of Nájera. He was technically a cleric, though not a priest, and served mainly on diplomatic missions. He was, however, caught up in the battle for Pamplona and had his leg broken by a French canonball on 20 May 1521. During his convalescence he was converted, chiefly by reading the Life of Christ by **Ludolph of Saxony**, and spent a year as a hermit near Montserrat, composing what became his *Spiritual Exercises*. He went on pilgrimage to Jerusalem, then spent more than a decade studying, finally at Paris, where he gathered a group of six like-minded individuals, including **Francis Xavier** and **Lainez**, who took vows together in a chapel on Montmartre on 15 August 1534. Two years later they gathered again at Venice, hoping to travel to Jerusalem, but as this proved impossible they put themselves at the disposition of the Pope. They were ordained in 1537. The bull to create a religious order was approved by Pope **Paul III** in September 1540, and Ignatius was elected the first superior general of the Society the following year. He spent the rest of his life running the Order from its headquarters in what is now the Gesù in Rome. Feast day 31 July.

Ildefonsus of Toledo   Saint, archbishop, born early seventh century, died Toledo, 23 January 667. He entered as a very young man the monastery of Agali, of which he became abbot. With his inheritance he founded a convent for women religious. He participated in the Eighth and Ninth Councils of Toledo, the city of which he was archbishop between 657 and 667. His *De viris illustribus* is a colourless continuation of earlier homonymous works. His *De perpetua virginitate Sanctae Mariae* made him the founder of the Spanish cult of Mary. Feast day 23 January.

Ilga   Blessed, hermitess, died *c.*1115. Ilga (Hilga, Helga) gave her name to a spring in Schwarzenberg in the forest of Bregenz (Austria), near the site of her hermitage. The spring is said to cure diseases of the eye. Traditionally, she is the sister of Blessed **Merbot** and Blessed Diedo. Nothing else is known about her. Feast day (unofficial cult) 8 June.

Illtyd (Illtud)   Saint, monk, founder of a monastic school at what is now Llantwit Major, Vale of Glamorgan, born *c.*450, died *c.*525. Illtyd was a Welshman who, by one account, went to Britain, joined King Arthur's court, and was later converted by St Cladoc in Glamorgan. He was helped by the chieftain Merchion to build a church and monastery, which became a centre for scholarship. Legend has it that the school was originally on an island which Illtyd miraculously rejoined to the mainland. This legend may stem from Illtyd's teaching of practical skills as well as religion, such

as improved ploughing practices and how to reclaim land from the sea. Feast day 7 February.

Illyricus, Thomas   Franciscan theologian, born Vrana (Zadar, Croatia), *c.*1485, died Mentone, France, 1528. Illyricus became a Franciscan in Italy and during the course of his life preached in many parts of Europe. He was made inquisitor general in Savoy by **Clement VII**. Illyricus' extant writings consist of sermons and polemics against Protestantism, but show also that he regarded Ecumenical Councils as superior in authority to the Pope.

Imelda   Blessed, born Bologna, *c.*1321, died 12 May 1333. Of noble birth she entered the Dominican cloister at Valdipietra. At that time Holy Communion was given from the age of twelve. Imelda being only eleven stayed in her place while the nuns received Communion. It is reported that the host appeared above her head. The priest then gave her First Communion, at which point she died in the rapture of thanksgiving. Beatified in 1826, in 1910 she became patroness of first communicants. Feast day 13 May.

Imma (Emma, Imina, Immina)   Saint, Benedictine abbess, died *c.*570. The Life of Imma (twelfth century) says that she was the daughter of the duke of Thuringia, Hetan II, who erected a church in Würzburg on the Burgberg (Marienburg). Imma began a monastery there, then moved to another location at Karlsburg am Main (Karlstadt). Feast day 25 November or 10 December.

Indrechtach   Saint, martyr, date and place of birth unknown, died 854. Celtic chronicles record that Indrechtach was an abbot of Iona martyred by Saxons while travelling to Rome. **William of Malmesbury** also records the story of a certain Indract, who was murdered near Glastonbury while returning from Rome, but opinion is divided over whether or not the two are identical. Feast day 5 February.

Indy, Vincent d'   French Roman Catholic composer, born Paris, 27 March 1851, died Paris, 2 December 1931. Studied in Paris, served in the Franco-Prussian War, then became a pupil of César **Franck**, who persuaded him to turn from law to music. With Bordes and Guilmant, d'Indy founded the Schola Cantorum, a music academy. On its curriculum was the study of sixteenth- and seventeenth-century music, **Palestrina**, J. S. **Bach** and plainsong. He wrote biographies of **Beethoven**, Wagner and Franck. D'Indy was a prolific composer. His best-known work is his *Symphonie sur un chant montagnard français*. He wrote nine sacred vocal works, including canticles and motets, often with organ or harmonium accompaniment. Also he wrote solo pieces for the organ and harmonium and a stage work, *La Légende de Saint Christophe*.

Ine Saint, king of the West Saxons, died Rome, 726. He established new laws and encouraged religious development by founding monasteries, notably Glastonbury, and giving money to those already in existence. He abdicated and went with his wife, Ethelburga, on pilgrimage and to live out their days in Rome. While there they founded a home for English pilgrims, which it has been claimed was the origin of the English College. It is thought that Ine and Ethelburga are buried in the church of San Spirito in Sassia.

Infessura, Stefano Chronicler, born Rome, 1435, died Rome, *c*.1500. His family belonged to the minor nobility of Rome and his profession was that of law, rising through public office in the town of Orte to become a lecturer in civil law at the University of Rome, but his reputation rests on his history of Rome, *Diario della città di Roma*, from the death of **Boniface VIII**, 1303, to April 1494. In this work, one of the most important for fifteenth-century Roman history, Infessura demonstrates devotion to republican ideals and support for the Colonna family.

Inés de la Cruz *see* **Juana Inés de la Cruz**

Inge, William Ralph Christian Platonist, and dean of St Paul's Cathedral, whose views earned him the nickname 'The Gloomy Dean', born Crayke, Yorkshire, 6 June 1860, died Wallingford, Berkshire, 26 February 1954. He went to Eton and King's College, Cambridge, and he returned to both as assistant master and fellow respectively. He became a fellow of Hertford College, Oxford, and was ordained in the Anglican Church. He was appointed professor of divinity at Cambridge. His work includes *Christian Mysticism*, *Personal Idealism and Mysticism* and *Faith and its Psychology*. To his surprise, in 1911 he was appointed dean of St Paul's Cathedral, London. He lectured on the philosopher Plotinus at St Andrews University, bringing Plotinus' ideas to public attention. Inge's widest popularity, however, stemmed from his pessimistic columns in *The Evening Standard*. Other publications include *Outspoken Essays*, *God and the Astronomers* and *Christian Ethics and Modern Problems*.

Ingegneri, Marc'Antonio Italian composer, born Verona, *c*.1547, died Cremona, 1 July 1592. He was a choirboy at Verona Cathedral and at Cremona he became *maestro di cappella*. His catalogue of music for choir includes Masses, sacred songs, responses, lamentations and small-scale sacred pieces. Ingegneri was a friend of Bishop Niccolò Sfrondati, later Pope **Gregory XIV**, to whom Ingegneri dedicated music. He produced nine volumes each of sacred music and madrigals. Until 1898 his *Responses* were attributed to his student, **Monteverdi**, but **Haberl** discovered these were by Ingegneri.

Ingenuin (Genuinus, Geminus) Bishop, died *c*.605. According to **Paul the Deacon**'s 'History of the Langobards', Ingenuin defended the schismatic position in the Three Chapters controversy at the Pseudosynod of Maran (590). He subscribed to the schismatic letter (591) to Emperor Maurice; later Ingenuin changed his position to an orthodox one.

Ingham, Benjamin Revivalist preacher and founder of the Inghamite Church, born Ossett, Yorkshire, 11 June 1712, died Abberford, 2 December 1772. Educated at Batley Grammar School and Queen's College, Oxford, where he joined the 'Holy Club', the first group of Methodists. Ordained in 1735 he went with John and Charles **Wesley** to Georgia, returning to England in 1737. Prohibited from preaching in the Diocese of York in 1739 he began 'field preaching' throughout northern England, establishing a 'connexion' of religious societies, many of which he handed over to the Moravians in 1742. In 1741 he married Lady Margaret Hastings. Ingham was later influenced by Sandemanianism, teaching which led to the break-up of the Inghamite societies, only 13 out of 80 remaining loyal to him. He published a hymn-book in 1748 and *A Discourse on the Faith and Hope of the Gospel* (1763).

Inglis, Charles First Anglican bishop of Nova Scotia, born Glencolumbkille, Donegal, Ireland, 1734, died near Halifax, Nova Scotia, 24 February 1816. As a young man he worked in a church school in Pennysylvania. He returned to England, was ordained priest and on returning to America he tried to convert the Mohawk Indians in Delaware. He moved to New York but, as he supported the British in the War of Independence, his church was burned down. He went to Nova Scotia, was made a bishop and founded a church academy which later became the University of King's College, Halifax.

Ingrid Elovsdotter Dominican religious, born Skänninge, Sweden, date unknown, died Skänninge, 1282. After being widowed, Ingrid Elovsdotter founded the first cloister for Dominican nuns in Sweden in 1281. She was said to have worked miracles, and a canonization process was initiated in 1405. This was never completed, and her cult and relics both vanished during the Reformation.

Innes, Thomas Roman Catholic priest, historian and antiquary, born Drumgask, Aberdeenshire, 1662, died Paris, 28 January 1744. He studied at the college of which his brother Lewis was principal, Scots College, Paris, and the College of Navarre in Paris. He became prefect of studies and, in 1727, vice-principal at the Scots College, after some years working on the mission in Scotland. He wrote much on the history of Scotland, including *Critical Essay on the Ancient Inhabitants of the Northern Parts of Britain* (1729) and *Civil and Ecclesiastical History of Scotland*, which was edited for the Spalding Club by George Grubb in 1853.

Innitzer, Theodor Austrian cardinal, born Weipert, Bohemia, 25 December 1875, died Vienna, 9 October 1955. He became a priest, taught at Vienna and became rector of the university. Austrian chancellor Johann Schober made Innitzer minister of social welfare. In 1932 he became archbishop of Vienna and in 1943 a cardinal. After Germany occupied Austria in 1938, he denounced Nazism and sheltered Jews. After the war he

attempted to restore the Austrian Church and separated himself from politics.

Innocent Saint, bishop, died *c*.380. According to his legends he was imprisoned during the persecution of Diocletian and later fled to Rome, where he was made a deacon and later bishop, possibly the first, of Tortona, Italy. Feast day 17 April.

Innocent I Saint, Pope from 21 December 401 to 12 March 417, born Rome, died there. A man of great ability and firm resolution in asserting the powers of the papal office, Innocent succeeded his father, **Anastasius I**; he insisted on a uniform discipline in the Western Church based on Roman ways and custom. He endorsed the decision on the Pelagian controversy taken at Carthage in 416, and so informed the fathers of the Numidian synod, **Augustine** being one of their number. He tried to defend his friend St **John Chrysostom** against Theophilus of Alexandria, but could not save him from exile. He is commemorated as a confessor of the faith. Feast day 28 July.

Innocent II Pope from 14 February 1130, born 'Gregorio Paparesci dei Guidoni' at Rome, died Rome, 24 September 1143. After the death of **Honorius II**, the chancellor, **Aimeric of Santa Maria Nuova**, with a minority of cardinals clandestinely elected Paparesci that same night, and enthroned him at daybreak in the Lateran. The majority of cardinals refused to accept the coup, and elected Petrus Leonis **Pierleoni** as Anacletus II. Both elections were irregular and an eight-year schism resulted, but through the efforts of **Bernard of Clairvaux**, Innocent was ultimately declared the rightful Pope. His reign is significant in that he steered the Church once for all in the direction of the wide-ranging reforms called for by **Nicholas II** in 1059.

Innocent III Pope from 8 January 1198, born 'Giovanni Lotario, conti di Segni' at Anagni, 1160/1, died Perugia, 16 July 1216. Unanimously elected, while still a deacon, on the day of **Celestine III**'s death, Lotario saw himself as the vicar of Christ (*Vicarius Christi*). He used every opportunity to strengthen his political power in the cities and kingdoms which formed the patrimony of St Peter. His great triumph was victory over King John of

England, who refused to accept Innocent's nomination of Stephen **Langton** to the See of Canterbury; he imposed an interdict on the kingdom and threatened John with a Crusade. In 1213 the king consented and agreed to hold England and Ireland as fiefs of the Holy See, subject to an annual tribute; for years the Pope virtually ruled England through his legates. Perhaps his greatest achievement was Lateran Council IV, which in 1215 promulgated a series of pastoral constitutions that affected the Church for the next three centuries.

Innocent IV   Pope from 25 June 1243, born 'Sinibaldo Fieschi' at Genoa, *c.*1200, died Naples, 7 December 1254. Fieschi was elected in the middle of a crisis with Emperor **Frederick II** at the end of an eighteenth-month vacancy since the death of **Celestine IV**. He declared Frederick deposed, and did all in his power to undermine his authority in Germany and Italy. He pushed to an extreme **Innocent III**'s claims to pontifical authority, notably in *Eger cui lenia*, which served to cloak an unlimited personal ambition, and unblushing nepotism. He continued the activity of the Inquisition and, in *Ad extirpanda*, authorized the use of torture. Innocent lowered the prestige of the Papacy, because he used his spiritual powers to raise money, buy friends and injure foes, but is remembered as a canon lawyer of some eminence, and a notable patron of learning.

Innocent V   Blessed, Pope from 21 January 1276, born 'Pierre de Tarantaise' at Champagny, Savoy, *c.*1224, died Rome, 22 June 1276. A Dominican, he held a chair in theology at Paris, and collaborated with **Albert the Great** and **Thomas Aquinas** in preparing a new rule of studies for his Order; a friend of the great Franciscan **Bonaventure**, he preached his funeral sermon. He succeeded **Gregory X**, and confirmed **Charles of Anjou** in his office of imperial vicar of Tuscany. He resumed Gregory's negotiations with Byzantine Emperor Michael VIII Palaeologus to implement Church union, and demanded that Greek clergy take personal oaths accepting the Filioque, and the primacy of the Pope; but he died as the envoys bearing these stiff demands were boarding the ship at Ancona. Feast day 22 June.

Innocent VI   Pope from 18 December 1352, born 'Etienne Aubert' at Mons, Limousin, 1282, died Avignon, 12 September 1362. He succeeded **Clement VI** as the fifth Avignon Pope. Shaky in health and indecisive, but intent on reform, he did not flinch from resorting to prison and the stake to ensure obedience in religious orders. He used the military skill of Cardinal **Albornoz** to defeat usurpers who had seized the States of the Church; the cost of this enterprise caused the failure of a Greek proposal for reunion of the Churches, because Innocent could not raise an army to fight the Turks. He had frequently expressed a desire to return to Rome, but death thwarted his plans.

Innocent VII   Pope from 1404, born 'Cosimo de' Migliorati' at Sulmona, Abruzzi, *c.*1336, died Rome, 6 November 1406. An experienced churchman who was collector of papal taxes in England for ten years, archbishop of Ravenna and Bologna, and legate to Tuscany and Lombardy, but made little impact as Pope, requiring Neapolitan support to suppress the revolt in Rome which followed his election. By 1404 Western Europe had been divided between the 'obediences' of the Roman and Avignonese Popes for 26 years. Resolution of the schism was perceived to lie with the French backers of the Avignon Antipope **Benedict XIII**, but civil war convulsed the kingdom.

Innocent VIII   Pope from 1484, born 'Giovanni Battista Cibo' at Genoa, 1432, died Rome, 25 July 1492. One of the less distinctive Popes of the fifteenth century, his election was engineered by Cardinal Giuliano della Rovere, nephew of the previous Pope, **Sixtus IV**, and subsequently Pope himself as **Julius II**. Della Rovere remained the most powerful political operator in Rome throughout Innocent's pontificate. Relations between the the Papacy and other states featured war with King Ferrante of Naples and the marriage of Innocent's son, Franceschetto, with **Lorenzo de' Medici**'s daughter Maddalena. With regard to cultural patronage, Innocent was among the less notable of the Renaissance Popes.

Innocent IX   Pope from 29 October 1591, born 'Giovanni Antonio Fachinetti' at Bologna, 20 July 1519, died Rome, 30 December 1591. As bishop of Nicastro, Fachinetti participated in the Council of Trent, and became papal nuncio at Venice in 1566, where he negotiated the grand alliance that defeated the Turks at Lepanto in 1571. He succeeded **Gregory XIV**, strove to improve the organization of the Curia, followed a pro-Spanish policy in France, repressed banditry around Rome and regulated the course of the Tiber. A scholarly man, he commented on Aristotle's *Politics*, and wrote on other subjects.

Innocent X Pope from 15 September 1644, born 'Giovanni Battista Pamfili' at Rome, 7 March 1572, died Rome, 1 January 1655. Elected on the death of **Urban VIII**, despite opposition from France because of his pro-Spanish views, Innocent broke the power of the Barberini, nephews of his predecessor and defended by Cardinal Jules **Mazarin**. His most doctrinal decision had to do with the Jansenist controversy in France, when he condemned, in the bull *Cum occasione*, five propositions taken from the *Augustinus* of Cornelius **Jansen**, though he failed to stifle the dispute. Throughout his pontificate Innocent was dominated by his sister-in-law, Olimpia Maidalchini, of insatiable ambition and rapacity, whose influence was baneful and much resented.

Innocent XI Blessed, Pope from 21 September 1676, born 'Benedetto Odescalchi' at Como, 19 May 1611, died Rome, 12 August 1689. Greatly loved for his piety and generosity while bishop of Novara. **Louis XIV** of France opposed his election to succeed **Clement X**, and he had to struggle continuously against the absolutism of Louis in Church affairs. For a similar reason, he disapproved of the measures taken by **James II** of England to restore Roman Catholicism, and especially of the Declaration of Indulgence, which allowed full liberty of worship. A process of canonization, begun by **Clement XI** in 1714, was long delayed because Innocent had shown favour to the Jansenists, but in 1956 in the altered atmosphere of the twentieth century **Pius XII** announced his beatification. Feast day 13 August.

Innocent XII Pope from 12 July 1691, born 'Antonio Pignatelli' near Spinazzola, 13 March 1615, died Rome, 27 September 1700. Antonio became a cardinal under **Innocent XI**, and succeeded **Alexander VIII** as a compromise, after a conclave of five months. Devoted to the poor, he took firm

actions to suppress nepotism and to reform religious life. He sought reconciliation with France, and brought about the withdrawal by **Louis XIV** of the Declaration of the French Clergy, which obliged bishops to subscribe to the Four Gallican Articles denying the Pope any authority in temporal affairs. He put an end to the haggling over the five Jansenist propositions, and declared in 1696 that nothing was further from his intention than to modify the teaching of his predecessor in regard to this heresy.

Innocent XIII Pope from 8 May 1721, born 'Michelangelo de' Conti' at Poli, near Palestrina, 13 May 1655, died Rome, 7 March 1724. He succeeded **Clement XI** following Emperor Charles VI's veto of the early favourite, Cardinal Paolucci, and adopted the name of **Innocent III**, from whose family he was descended. He endorsed Clement's *Unigenitus* against the Jansenists, and insisted on their submission to his constitution. Innocent had a deep aversion to the Jesuits and took a firm stand in the controversy over Chinese rites, insisting on the Society's obedience. In international affairs he was concerned for economic and cultural development, but constant illness overshadowed his short reign.

Innocent of Alaska (John Veniaminov) Russian Orthodox saint, missionary and bishop, born Anginskoe, Russia, 26 August 1797, died Moscow, 31 March 1879. His missionary work started in the Aleutian Islands of Alaska, which was then Russian. He devised alphabets for several local languages and translated St Matthew's Gospel. He was appointed bishop in 1840 and established a seminary, founding an enduring local Church in Alaska. In 1868 he was recalled and appointed metropolitan of Moscow. He was perhaps the greatest of all Orthodox missionaries. His primary catechism, *An Indication of the Way into the Kingdom of Heaven*, was written in the Fox Aleutian dialect and from that later translated into Russian and English. He was canonized in 1977. Feast days 31 March and 6 October.

Innocent of Irkutsk (Kulchitsky) Russian Orthodox saint, missionary and bishop, born Chernigov, 1680, died Irkutsk, 27 November 1731. He was consecrated bishop in 1721 for Peking, but was refused entry by the Chinese emperor. He was then sent to the new Irkutsk Diocese in central Siberia where he renewed the missionary work and trained translators. His labours and the climate eventually proved fatal. He was canonized in 1804 and his relics were recently recovered and re-enshrined, 1990. Often called 'the Apostle of Siberia'. Feast day 26 November.

Innocent of Le Mans Saint, French bishop, died *c*.542. Probably became bishop of Le Mans in 524 and was at the Synods of Orléans in 533 and 541. He did much in his diocese to restore the cathedral, churches and convents.

Innocent of Maronia (Marona) Bishop, died *c*.550. Innocent was a Byzantine bishop in Maronia, east of Thessalonika on the coast of Thrace, and is remembered only through his writings. He participated in a colloquy between orthodox and Monophysite bishops in Constantinople in 532, writing a description of the event. He also wrote a defence of the Theopaschite formula ('one of the Trinity has suffered in the flesh'). Innocent maintained that Jesus Christ was not two Sons, Son of God and Son of Man, but only One, who suffered in his assumed human nature.

Innocenzo of Berzo (Giovanni Scalvinoni) Capuchin priest, born Niardo, Italy, 18 March 1844, died Bergamo, Italy, 3 March 1890. Giovanni Scalvinoni was educated in Brescia and ordained in 1867, following which he became assistant to the priest of Berzo. He then moved back to Brescia to become rector of the seminary, where he gained a reputation for sanctity. He took the name 'Innocenzo' on joining the Capuchins in 1874, becoming assistant master of novices and a preacher and confessor.

Intorcetta, Prospero Jesuit missionary, born Piazza, Sicily, 28 August 1625, died Hangchow, China, 3 October 1696. Arriving in China in 1657, the early period of Intorcetta's work was made difficult by persecution, and for a while he was imprisoned. He returned to Rome in 1672 to defend the Jesuits in the Chinese rites controversy, and on his return to the Far East in 1674 he became visitor to the missions in China and Japan. Intorcetta was one of the first Westerners to pro-

duce a study of Confucius. He also wrote a study of Chinese politics and ethics, and made a Chinese translation of the *Spiritual Exercises* of **Ignatius of Loyola**.

Ireland, John Dean of Westminster, born Ashburton, Devon, 8 September 1761, died Westminster, 2 September 1842. Studied at Oriel College, Oxford, and was appointed vicar of Croydon in 1793 and in 1816 became dean of Westminster. He funded scholarships and other posts at Oxford, including the John Ireland Chair of Exegesis of Holy Scripture. Since 1947 this has been in NT only.

Ireland, John Roman Catholic archbishop of St Paul, Minnesota, born Burnchurch, County Kilkenny, baptized 11 September 1838, died St Paul, Minnesota, 25 September 1918. His family moved to the USA in 1848, and eventually settled in St Paul. Ireland was sent by the bishop of St Paul to a minor seminary in France, and then to a major seminary at Montbel, near Toulon. He was ordained in St Paul in 1861, served in a parish, briefly, then as a military chaplain during the Civil War. He was put in charge of the cathedral of St Paul in 1867, and was made assistant bishop in 1875. In 1884 he took over the diocese, which four years later became an archdiocese. He was a fervent American patriot, and was concerned that Catholic immigrants were not being integrated adequately into American life: his efforts to aid this process led in part to the charge of 'Americanism'. However, his clear views on the relationship between Church and State (and his command of French) made him **Leo XIII**'s choice in 1892 to commend to French Catholics a more sympathetic relationship with their government. He held up, before a Parisian audience, the ideal he saw at work in the United States. When the controversy arose about the Knights of Labor, it was Ireland, with Cardinal **Gibbons**, who ensured that the organization was not condemned – Ireland went personally to Rome to plead the case. He was active on social issues, and was especially a campaigner for total abstinence from alcohol. When the US government gave to the French a statue of Lafayette, it was Ireland they chose to take it to France: in return he was awarded the Legion of Honour. He was one of the moving forces behind the establishment of the

Catholic University in Washington, but was equally concerned about the parochial schools, and the standard of clergy education, in his own diocese. His essays were published in 1896 as *The Church and Modern Society*.

Ireland, John Composer, born Bowden, Cheshire, 13 August 1879, died Washington, Sussex, 12 June 1962. He was educated at the Royal College of Music and worked as an organist for the Anglican Church, but devoted himself to composition. He wrote a variety of works, including *These Things Shall Be* for orchestra and chorus. His compositions include hymn tunes. His hymn 'Love Unknown' and the Christmas song 'Holy Boy' are popular.

Ireland, Seraphine Roman Catholic religious superior and educator, born Kilkenny, Ireland, July 1842, died St Paul, Minnesota, 20 June 1930. Ellen Ireland was ten when her parents emigrated to the United States and sixteen when she joined the Sisters of St Joseph as 'Sister Seraphine'. Working in education, she was named provincial superior of her Order in 1882. From then until her retirement in 1921, Mother Seraphine worked to supply the Order's educational and medical institutions with qualified teachers and nurses and to secure accreditation and funding for the schools. Her Order more than quadrupled in membership under her leadership and she expanded it territorially as well.

Irenaeus of Lyons Bishop and saint, born Smyrna(?), c.140(?), died Lyons, c.202(?). Probably a native of Asia Minor, he may have lived in Rome for some time. In 177 he was presbyter of the Greek-speaking community of Lyons (France). During a persecution he was sent to Rome with the 'Letter of the Martyrs of Lyons and Vienne'. After his return he became bishop of Lyons and intervened to exhort Pope **Victor I** (189–98) to have patience with the bishops of Asia in their disagreement about the date of Easter. His main work is the *Adversus omnes haereses*, a refutation of diverse Gnostic currents. His martyrdom is unhistorical. Feast day 28 June.

Irene Byzantine empress and Greek Orthodox saint, born Athens, c.752, died Lesbos, 9 August

803. She married the future Byzantine emperor Leo IV in 769. On the death of her husband, she became co-emperor and guardian of their son Constantine VI. She was a devoted Iconodule, and her husband is said to have refused to sleep with her after discovering two icons in her room. During her regency she weakened the empire by removing competent generals who were Iconoclasts. She instigated the Council of Nicaea of 787, which restored icons. She was briefly deposed, 790–2, and in 797 she dethroned and blinded her son, allowing her to reign alone as empress for five years, the first woman to achieve this in Byzantium. In 802, however, she herself was deposed and exiled to the islands of Prinkipo, and then Lesbos. The Eastern Church regards her as a saint. Feast day 9 August.

Irene of Portugal Saint, died 653. She is mentioned in the tenth-century Antiphony of León as 'Virgo in Scallabi Castro'. References appear in later *Vitae* where she is described as a beautiful nun of noble birth in Thomar. She rejected the advances of her spiritual director, who gave her a potion to make her appear pregnant. A jealous former suitor had her killed. Her body is said to have floated down river and to have become miraculously entombed in a pool at Scallabis on the Tagus in 653. The town changed its name to 'Santarem' ('Santa Irene', 'Ira', 'Eriä'). Feast day 20 October.

Irmengard (Ermengard) Blessed, German abbess, born Munich, c.832, died Chiemsee, 16 July 866. Of royal birth, her father Louis the German made her abbess of the Benedictine convent at Buchau and then of the royal abbey at Chiemsee. She was said to have led a life of penance and virtue, devoting her life to the women in her care. She is buried in the monastery church at Chiemsee. Feast day 17 July.

Irmgardis of Cologne Saint, countess of Aspel, died on pilgrimage to Rome, c.1085. Irmgardis was an heiress who spent her fortune founding cloisters, churches and charitable institutions. Much legendary material is told of her life, and she might have resided at Süchteln (where a chapel was erected to her honour) before moving to Cologne to spend the rest of her life in doing works of charity. Her personality is somewhat in dispute; she is often confused (perhaps correctly) with Irmentrud of Aspel.

Irmhart, Öser Theologian, date and place of birth unknown, died Augsburg, Germany, c.1360. Öser originally studied law before ministering to churches in Austria, and became a canon of Augsburg Cathedral in 1358. Among the corpus of his about 30 extant works is a translation of a treatise on the Messiahship of Jesus written by a Jewish rabbi, Rabbi Samuel, who had converted from Judaism to Christianity in the eleventh century.

Irmina Saint, Benedictine abbess, died Trier(?), 24 December 710. The Life written in the 1100s is considered unreliable, but portrays Irmina as the daughter of Dagobert I. She was engaged to be married but her fiancé died before the wedding, so Irmina became a nun. She is thought to have founded the monastery of Ohren (Trier), where she was abbess. Irmina was generous to English and Irish monks, giving land to **Willibrord** and his monks for their monastery (Echternach). Feast day 30 December.

Irnerius (Guarnerius) Jurist, born Bologna, Italy, c.1050, died Bologna, c.1130. By the age of twenty, Irnerius was teaching didactics and rhetoric at Bologna. Encouraged by Countess **Matilda of Tuscany**, he devoted himself to the study of law and in 1084 founded a school of jurisprudence at Bologna that was to influence juridical studies throughout Europe. He was the first to use marginal glosses to expound on Roman law, a practice that became customary after him. His surviving works include the first medieval system of Roman jurisprudence, entitled *Summa codicis*, and *Quaestiones de juris subtilitatibus*.

Irving, Edward Presbyterian pastor and a founder of the Catholic Apostolic Church, born Annan, Dumfries, 4 August 1792, died Glasgow, 7 December 1834. Irving ministered in London from 1822 following ordination in Scotland. Influenced by **Coleridge** and **Carlyle**, he urged his congregation to seek charismata. In 1833 he was expelled from the Presbyterians, after which he set up what later became the Catholic Apostolic Church, although he only held a minor position in it. He wrote *For*

the Oracles of God, Four Orations. For Judgement to Come, and Argument in Nine Parts (1823), *Babylon and Infidelity Foredoomed by God* (1826) and *The Orthodox and Catholic Doctrine of Christ's Human Nature* (1830).

Irwin, Benjamin Hardin Holiness preacher, born near Mercer, Missouri, 1854, died after 1905. Hardin was a Baptist preacher, and in 1891 he had a Holiness sanctification experience and joined the Wesleyan Methodist Church. In 1895 he experienced a 'baptism of fire' which he interpreted as the 'third blessing'. He organized the Fire-Baptized Holiness Association in 1895, stressing OT dietary laws and baptisms of dynamite, lyddite and oxidite. In 1900 he left the Association to Joseph **King** after confessing to 'gross sin'. He may have adopted Pentecostalism in 1906, but his later career is unknown. In 1898 he began the *Live Coals of Fire* periodical.

Isaac, Heinrich Composer, born c.1450, died Florence, 26 March 1517. Isaac's origins are obscure and he has been described as German and Flemish. He was in Florence by 1474, where he acted as tutor to the children of **Lorenzo de' Medici** between 1485 and 1493. At various times he found employment at the imperial court in Innsbruck and with the Este of Ferrara, a dynasty particularly notable for their patronage of musicians in the late fifteenth and early sixteenth centuries. Isaac's most important work was a series of motets entitled the *Choralis Constantinus*.

Isaac of Langres (the Good) Saint, bishop, born early ninth century, place unknown, died Langres, France, 880. Following the destruction by Normans of the monastery of Saint-Bénigne, Isaac was made responsible for its reconstruction. He is known to have taken part in the Councils of Soissons and Troyes, and from 859 until his death he was bishop of Langres. Feast day 18 July.

Isaac of Monte Luco Monk, died c.550. Isaac was a Syrian who, to escape the Monophysite persecution, went to Italy, where he embraced the life of a hermit on Monte Luco. After seeing a vision of the Virgin, he established a laura-like community of trained disciples. He was known for his gifts of prophecy and miracles. Feast day 11 April.

Isaac of Stella   Cistercian abbot and theologian, born England, c.1100, died Étoile (Stella), near Chauvigny, c.1169. Much of what we know about Isaac comes from sermons and other written work: he probably began his career in the curia of **Theobald of Canterbury** and studied theology in Paris, and was almost certainly a priest before entering Cîteaux in 1145. In 1147, he was made abbot of Stella, and he later established a community of monks on the island of Ré, about two miles from La Rochelle.

Isaac the Great   Saint, head of the Armenian Church (*katholikos*), born 345, died Ashtishar, 7 September 439. Isaac was the son of St **Nerses** and a descendant of St **Gregory the Illuminator**. He studied at Constantinople, where he married. After the death of his wife at a young age, he became a monk. He became the tenth catholicos, in c.389. Isaac gained from Constantinople the recognition of the metropolitical rights of the Armenian Church, and terminated the dependence of the Church upon Caesarea. Isaac was active in national Armenian literature. With St **Mesrop** he also translated much of the Bible into Armenian. In 425 he was deposed by the Persians but allowed to regain his see owing to popular support. Feast days: St Sahak in the American Church, 9 September and 25 November.

Isabella of Castile   Queen of Castile, 1474–1504, born Madrigal, 22 April 1451, died Medina del Campo, 26 November 1504. The daughter of Juan II of Castile, she succeeded her half-brother Enrique IV, but her claim was initially contested in a period of civil war. Her lightning marriage in 1469 to the future Ferdinand II of Aragon (**Ferdinand V** of Castile) anticipated the union of their kingdoms. By their judicious use of patronage and propaganda, the monarchs imposed order and royal authority throughout their domains. The Castilian capture of Granada in 1492 concluded the centuries-old Christian *reconquista* and was rapidly matched by a policy of forced conversion of Jews.

Isabelle of France   Blessed, born France, March 1225, died Longchamp, Paris, 23 February 1270. The daughter of the French king **Louis VIII**, Isabelle refused all her suitors, including a politically expedient marriage to the son of the Holy Roman Emperor, in order to devote her life to charity and hospital work. This work was often done through the Franciscan Order, which she highly favoured, though she refused to join. She also founded a convent of Poor Clares at Longchamp, and even drafted its Rule. Her cult was granted by **Leo X** in 1521. Feast day 8 June.

Isaias Boner   Blessed, Augustinian friar, born Cracow, Poland, c.1400, died Cracow, 8 February 1471. Isaias studied at the University of Padua, where he subsequently became a lecturer in theology. He was visitor of the province of Poland in 1438, and in 1452 vicar general of Bavaria. He also taught at the University of Cracow in the 1460s. During his lifetime he was much venerated for his sanctity and Christian character, and although never officially beatified his name bears the prefix 'blessed' among Augustinians.

Isfried   Saint, Premonstratensian bishop, date and place of birth unknown, died c.1204, probably 15 June. Isfried was a canon and provost before becoming bishop of the new Diocese of Ratzeburg, Germany, in 1180. He devoted himself to the Christianization and Germanization of the heathen tribes east of the Elbe and was called the 'soul' of the Premonstratensians in North Germany. He also served as confessor to **Henry the Lion**. He is said to have practised great self-denial, and miracles were ascribed to him while he was yet alive. His cult was approved by Pope **Benedict XIII** for the Premonstratensians around 1725.

Isho-dad of Merv   Nestorian bishop and theologian, born Merv (in modern Iran), in the ninth century. Few details of Isho-dad's life have survived beyond the record of his birthplace and the fact that he was bishop of Hedatta on the Tigris. His writings, mainly biblical commentaries, are valuable for their extensive quotations of earlier theologians, notably **Theodore of Mopsuestia** and others in the Monophysite tradition. As such they occupy an important place in the history of biblical interpretation.

Isidore of Kiev   Metropolitan and cardinal, born Peloponnese, c.1385/95, died Rome, 17 April 1464. Byzantine envoy to the Council of Basel, charged with obtaining union between the Eastern and Western Churches, but he returned to Constantinople without concluding a deal. He was appointed metropolitan of Kiev in 1436, a city then under Lithuanian control. With **Bessarion**, he belonged to the Orthodox contingent at the Council of Ferrara–Florence (1438–9), which agreed an act of union in 1439. **Eugenius IV** made them both cardinals in 1439, before sending Isidore as legate to Russia to apply the union, but he met with hostility in Moscow and returned to Italy. Made patriarch of Constantinople in 1459.

Isidore of Pelusium   Saint, Egyptian presbyter and monk, born Alexandria, c.360, died c.435. A presbyter in Pelusium, he was forced to leave the city and lived from 405 in a monastery. His more than 2000 letters reveal a well-educated man, full of divine wisdom. He was also a trained exegete, rejecting excessive use of allegory. Theologically he was orthodox (anti-Arian), attacking both heretics and pagans. He was not afraid to rebuke high officials, even Emperor Theodosius II and the Patriarch **Cyril of Alexandria**. Feast day 4 February.

Isidore of Seville   Bishop and saint, born Cartagena, c.560, died Seville, 4 April 636. The youngest child of a Spanish Romanized family devoted to the Church: his sister **Florentina** entered a convent and his two brothers, **Leander** and **Fulgentius of Ecija**, both became bishops. In 600/1 he succeeded Leander as bishop of Seville. In this function he presided over the Second Synod of Seville (619) and the Fourth Synod of Toledo (633). He was a prolific writer. His most important work is the *Etymologiae*, an encyclopaedia of classical and Christian culture in twenty books. Feast day 4 April.

Isidore the Farmer   Saint, patron of farmers and of Madrid, born Madrid, Spain, 1070, died Madrid, 15 May 1130. Isidore was reputedly married to St Maria de la Cabeza, thus constituting one of the rare husband/wife sainthoods, but his wife is a latecomer to the story. He was employed by Juan de Vergas for most of his life. He was said to have led an unusually devout life and was associated with miracles even when he was alive. His growing reputation for holiness was crowned

with his canonization in 1622 by Pope **Gregory XV**. Feast day 15 May.

Ita of Killeedy   Saint, nun, born c.475 in the present county of Waterford, Ireland, died 15 January 570. Ita resided at Cluain Credhail (County Limerick), which has since been known as Killeedy (i.e. 'The church of St Ita'). She was known for her austerities, miracles and prophecies, and inspired other Irish saints, such as **Brendan of Clonfert**, Pulcherius (Mochoemog) and Cummian Fada. Feast day 15 January.

Ivanios, Mar (Givergis Thomas Panikervirtis)   Syrian-Jacobite archbishop, born Mavelikkara, India, 18 September 1882, died Trivandrum, India, 15 July 1953. He was ordained as a priest in the Syro-Jacobite Church of the Malkankar Rite in 1909, following study at Madras Christian College. He helped to gain autonomy for the Syro-Jacobean Church in India, and in 1925 he took the name 'Mar Ivanios' on his appointment as bishop, subsequently becoming metropolitan in 1928. During this period he had also been involved in the Malines Conversations, which eventually led to the reunion of the Syro-Jacobean Church with Rome in 1930. Thereafter Ivanios worked hard and travelled widely in the cause of ecumenism. He also established many schools and churches, and wrote several articles on the liturgy and language of the Syriac churches.

Ivo   Saint, patron of St Ives in Huntingdonshire, England, and the village of Saint Ive (pron. 'eve') in Cornwall. Ivo may not have been a real person; when bones with a bishop's insignia were found c.1001 at Slepe near Ramsey Abbey, the name and legend were linked with them. Feast day 3 February.

Ivo of Chartres   Saint, bishop and author, born Chartres, France, c.1040, died 23 December 1115. After studying at Paris and Bec, he was a parish priest in Picardy and provost of the Canons Regular at Saint-Quentin in Beauvais before becoming bishop of Chartres in 1090. A prolific writer, he contributed to the establishment of the seven sacraments, and is perhaps best known for his moderate stance in the investiture crisis: for Ivo, there was no objection to the king investing a properly chosen candidate after a canonical election, as everyone would understand that the king was only conferring temporal power. Feast day 23 May.

Ivo of Helory Saint, patron of lawyers, born the manor of Kermartin, Brittany, 17 October 1253, died Trédrez, France, 19 May 1303. He studied philosophy, canon law and theology in Paris and civil law in Orléans. He became a diocesan judge in the Rennes district and later in his own diocese of Tréguier, where he became known as the poor man's advocate. He was not ordained until 1284. He was a parish priest at Trédrez and at Lovannec, where he built a hospital in which he ministered to the ill and poor himself. was sought out as a mediator and advocate and noted for the austerity and piety of his life. He was canonized by Pope **Clement VI** in 1347. Feast day 19 May.

J

Jacob of Serugh (Sarug) Syrian bishop and saint, born Hawra (district of Serugh), *c*.451, died 29 November 529. He visited the famous school of Edessa but broke with it because of its Nestorian tendency. He became a priest and then a *periodeuta* (a supervisor of clergy). In 519 he became bishop of Batnai. His large, exclusively Syriac, literary heritage reveals a (moderate) Monophysitism. Noteworthy are his *memre* (rhythmical homilies). He was a pastorally oriented bishop who did not engage in the Christological controversies of his time, though certainly not unaware of them. Feast day 29 November for the Syrians, 5 April for the Maronites.

Jacobazzi, Domenico (Iacovazzi) Canon lawyer and cardinal, born Rome, 1444, died 2 July 1527. His rise through the ranks of the Roman curia from the 1480s onwards was capped by appointments to the bishopric of Lucera in southern Italy in 1511 and the sacred college of cardinals in 1517. Author of *De computatione dotis in legitimam*, his major work, *De concilio*, was published postumously (Rome, 1538, Paris, 1672, and Venice, 1584).

Jacobis, Giustino de Saint, Italian Vincentian (Lazarist) missionary bishop to Ethiopia, born San Fele, Italy, 1800, died Alghedien, Eritrea, 31 July 1860. He was ordained in 1824, became prefect apostolic of a new mission to Ethiopia in 1839 and in 1847 was made vicar apostolic. He had great sympathy for the Ethiopian Church and used its liturgy. In turn, internal dissent in the country encouraged more openness towards Roman Catholicism. In 1844 he built a seminary at Gwela and a school for Ghe'ez and Catholic theology. His mission was particularly successful among the mountain tribes. His good relations with Ethiopian authorities declined after the appointment in 1855 of Abuna (Metropolitan) Salama, who saw de Jacobis as a rival. He was arrested but his work continued through the many priests he had ordained – some of them married – and the Roman Catholic Church continued to grow. He was canonized in 1939.

Jacobus de Voragine Blessed, Dominican archbishop and writer, born Varazze, near Genoa, *c*.1230, died Genoa, 13 July 1298. He entered the Dominicans at the age of fourteen and achieved fame as a popular preacher in Lombardy. He was elected provincial of Lombardy in 1267, and was elected archbishop of Genoa in 1286, but he refused the office. He was chosen once more in 1292, and this time was obliged to undertake the office at a very disturbed time, socially and politically, in the city. His enduring fame, however, rests upon *The Golden Legend*, a compilation of the lives of popular saints, some of them legendary, and some feast days. Later dismissed as unhistorical, the work was not intended as a factual record but a means to encourage devotion among ordinary Christians by describing the deeds of earlier Christians. Feast day 13 July.

Jacopone da Todi Italian poet and Franciscan, born Todi, *c*.1228–30, died Collazone, 25 December 1306. Probably first a lawyer, he entered the Franciscan Order in 1278, adhering to the branch of the Spirituals. He fiercely fought for the ideal of poverty as well as for Church reform, even subscribing to a document in which the removal of Pope **Boniface VIII** was demanded. He was excommunicated and in 1298 imprisoned. Five years later **Benedict XI** released him. Besides numerous prose works in Latin, Jacopone also wrote 92 superb *laudi spirituali* which are often of an almost ethereal beauty.

Jacques de Molay Last grand master of the Templars, born Molay, Haute-Saône, France, between 1243 and 1254, died Paris, 19 March 1314. Other than that he became a Templar at Beaune *c.*1265, little is known about him before he was promoted grand master of the Order of the Temple in 1298. In 1307, he rejected a plan to merge the Templars and the Hospitallers, and was granted papal permission to study the Order's moral condition; it is unknown if this study – probably a plan by Pope **Clement V** to prevent the French king, Philip IV ('the Fair'), taking over the Order's assets – ever took place. Jacques de Molay was arrested in October 1307, and pleaded guilty to charges of heresy. He soon retracted his plea; the Templars were condemned at a national council in Tours in May 1308, and some five years later, a committee of French cardinals sentenced him to life imprisonment. He again retracted, and Philip IV ordered him to be burned at the stake as a relapsed heretic. There is no evidence to suggest that he was guilty of any of the charges brought against him.

Jacques de Vitry Cardinal and preacher of the Crusade, born Rheims, *c.*1170, died Rome, 1240. He studied in Paris, and as a regular canon he developed an interest in the Beguines, a religious movement for women: he wrote the Life of the Beguine leader **Mary of Oignies** (d. 1213), and secured papal recognition of the movement in 1216. He preached against the Albigensian Cathars in 1213. Appointed bishop of Acre in 1216; his letters are a valuable source for the study of the Fifth Crusade. In 1228, he was appointed cardinal-bishop of Tusculum.

Jaeger, Lorenz Cardinal and ecumenist, born Halle, Germany, 23 September 1892, died Paderborn, Germany, 2 April 1975. After serving as a soldier in World War I, Jaeger studied for the priesthood, was ordained in 1922 and worked in pastoral ministry until 1941, when he was named bishop of Paderborn. He was an active participant in the preparations for the Second Vatican Council and in the Council itself, and was created a cardinal in 1965 by Pope **Paul VI**. A keen supporter of the post-conciliar position on ecumenism, Cardinal Jaeger was influential in the setting up of the Secretariat for Promoting Christian Unity and personally founded the Johann Adam Möhler Institute for ecumenical studies in his own diocese. His works include *The Ecumenical Council, the Church and Christendom* (1961) and *A Stand on Ecumenism: The Council's Decree* (1965), a commentary on the decree on ecumenism of the Second Vatican Council.

Jaffray, Robert Alexander Christian and Missionary Alliance missionary in Asia, born Toronto, Canada, 16 December 1873, died Celebes, Dutch East Indies, 29 July 1945. Converted under the ministry of the Alliance's founder, A. B. **Simpson**, Jaffray trained at the New York Missionary Training Institute and was sent to Wuzhou, South China. He helped found the Alliance Bible School (now the Alliance Seminary in Hong Kong) and his Chinese-language *Bible Magazine* circulated around the world. In 1916 Jaffray opened a station in Tourane (now Da Nang) Vietnam and the Evangelical Church of Vietnam remains the largest Protestant Church body in Vietnam. In 1928 he sent Chinese missionaries to Borneo and in 1931 he and his family settled in Makassar (now Ujung Pandang) in the Celebes. He was arrested by the Japanese in 1942 and died in captivity.

Jägerstätter, Franz Martyr, born St Radegund, Austria, 1907, beheaded Berlin, 9 August 1943. A peasant in a small village, and a married father of three daughters, he opposed the Nazis and had always declared he would not serve in Hitler's army. When his call-up papers came, he presented himself and declared this to the authorities. Everyone, including his local priest and bishop, tried to persuade him to change his mind. But he maintained his conviction that, as a Christian, he had to oppose Nazism and that to serve in Hitler's army would be to condone it. An American scholar discovered this 'solitary witness' in the 1960s.

Jagiello (Władysław) Saint, grand duke of Lithuania, 1377–81, 1382–1401, supreme duke of

Lithuania, 1401–34, and king of Poland, 1385–1434, born 1351, died Gródek, 31 May 1434. From his father he succeeded to the grand duchy of Lithuania, a land whose rulers were still pagan. His marriage to Jadwiga of Poland, daughter of Louis the Great, king of Poland and Hungary, created the united kingdom of Poland-Lithuania. It also occasioned his own baptism at Cracow. His policies undermined the Teutonic Knights, who began their steady retreat into Germanic lands. Władysław ruled alone after the death of Jadwiga in 1399. He was canonized in 1997.

James I King of Aragon, born Montpellier, France, 2 February 1208, the son of King Pedro II, died Valencia, 2 February 1276. Known as 'the Conqueror', he succeeded his father as king of Aragon in 1213, aged five. In 1229 he began his conquest of the Balearic Islands, gaining full control in 1235. He then began a campaign which led to the capture of the Moorish city and kingdom of Valencia. He instituted a new legal code in 1247 and later resolved the conflicting territorial claims of France and Aragon through the Treaty of Corbeil in 1258. For the remainder of his life he attempted to remove the Moors from the Spanish peninsula. Towards the end of his life he divided his kingdom between his two sons, an act which would later lead to conflict.

James I King of England and VI of Scotland, born Edinburgh, 19 June 1566, the only son of Lord Darnley and Mary, Queen of Scots, died London, 5 May 1625. Became king of Scotland on the abdication of his mother in 1567. Entered alliance with England in 1596 through the Treaty of Berwick. Married **Anne of Denmark** in 1589. Succeeded to the English throne on the death of **Elizabeth I** in 1603. Upheld the connection between the divine right of kings and the apostolic succession and consequently quarrelled with Parliament, in which there was a strong Puritan influence. Authorized a new translation of the Bible in 1611. Concluded peace with Spain in 1604. His leniency towards Roman Catholics led to the Gunpowder Plot in 1605. Generally unpopular in England, whose subjects were already suspicious of the monarchy, and regarded him as a foreigner.

James II King of Aragon, born 1267, died Barce-

lona, November 1327. He became king of Aragon in 1291, and was also king of Sicily from 1286. Known as 'James the Just', he continued the expansionist policies of his predecessors – invading Castile, 1291–1301, briefly seizing Gibraltar, 1309, and conquering Sardinia, 1323–4. He also held Muslim Tunis, Bugia and Tlemecen as tributaries; and was able to secure a protectorate over Christians in the Holy Land. In 1317 he replaced the Knights Templar with his own Knights of Montesa. Under the Anagni Treaty of 1295 he had surrendered Sicily to Anjou–Papacy disposition – but connived at its retention by his brother, Frederick III. He was appointed captain general of the Church by **Boniface VIII**. James was also a patron of the arts, and founded the University of Lérida in 1300.

James II King of England, born London, 14 October 1633, the third son of **Charles I**, died St-Germain, 6 September 1701. As duke of York he fought in the Civil War and was captured after the surrender of Oxford. Having escaped to the Continent, he served with the French army. At the Restoration he became Lord High Admiral. He was received into the Roman Catholic Church around 1670. Attempts to pass an Exclusion Bill keeping him from the succession failed, and he ascended the throne in 1685. Initially conciliatory towards the Established Church, his Roman Catholic allegiance soon led to conflict, particularly after the attempted rebellion by the duke of Monmouth when James began taking repressive measures against churchmen who opposed him. His pro-Catholic position led to an invasion by the Protestant William of Orange and James fled to France in 1688. After an attempt to recover Ireland was defeated at the Boyne in 1690, James returned to France, where he died eleven years later.

James VI King of Scots *see* **James I**, King of England

James, Montague Rhodes Biblical scholar, antiquary and palaeographer, born Goodnestone, Kent, 1 August 1862, died Eton, 12 June 1936. He studied at Eton and King's College, Cambridge. He became assistant director of the Fitzwilliam Museum in 1886, and was director from 1893 to 1908. He became a fellow of King's College, Cambridge, in 1887 and lecturer in divinity. He was dean in 1889–1900, tutor 1900–2, provost 1905–18, vice-chancellor of Cambridge University 1913–15, provost of Eton 1918–36. He catalogued the Western manuscripts at Cambridge, Lambeth Palace, Eton, John Rylands, Westminster Abbey and Aberdeen University libraries. He studied apocryphal literature and wrote extensively on medieval arts and literature.

James de Blanconibus Blessed, Dominican monk, also known as 'James Bianconi of Mevania', born Bevagna (Mevania), Umbria, 7 April 1220, died 22 August 1301. He joined the Dominican Order at Spoleto at the age of sixteen, and studied theology and philosophy at Perugia, where he was also ordained. James was a noted preacher and attacked Nicolaitanism (the defence of a married clergy) so successfully that it was eliminated from Umbria. He founded the Dominican priory of St George in Bevagna, and also directed the establishment of a convent of Benedictine nuns. A visionary – he was gifted with a vision while praying in front of a crucifix, and fearing the loss of his soul, in which he was comforted by being bathed in the blood from the side of Christ. On 15 August 1301 he received a further vision in which he was instructed to prepare himself for death. He died a week later. His intact remains are at Bevagna.

James (Iakov) Netsetov of Alaska Saint, Alaskan Orthodox priest and missionary, born island of Unalaska, 1802, died Sitka, 26 July 1864. He was a disciple of St **Innocent of Alaska** and one of the first local priests. He worked among several native groups, translating the NT and liturgical books and devising writing systems for the different languages. He kept a valuable journal during his missionary years. Canonized in America in 1994. Feast day 16 October.

James of Certaldo Blessed, Camaldolese monk and priest, born Certaldo, date unknown, the son of a knight of Volterra, died 13 April 1292. He became a monk at the abbey of San Giusto at Volterra in 1230. After refusing the office of abbot twice, he finally accepted, only to resign the office shortly after to continue his work as parish priest of the monastery church. Here he served as a noted pastor for 40 years.

James of the Marches Saint, Franciscan, born Monteprandone, Italy, 1391, died Naples, 28 November 1476. From a poor family he was nevertheless able to take a doctorate in civil law at the University of Perugia. In 1416 he entered the Franciscans at Assisi, and after his ordination in 1420 taught and preached throughout Italy. He travelled throughout Europe and was commissary of the Friars Minor in Bosnia. He was a member of the Observant branch of the Order, and was active with his confrère **John Capistran** in efforts towards reform and unity. Feast day 28 November.

James of Viterbo Blessed, Augustinian, bishop of Benevento and then Naples, born 1255, died 1308. His *De regimine christiano* was one of the earliest discussions of ecclesiology. Feast day 13 February.

James of Voragine *see* **Jacobus de Voragine**

Janáček, Leoš Czech composer, born Hukvaldy, Moravia, 3 July 1854, died Ostrava, Moravia, 12 August 1928. He was a choirboy at the Augustinian monastery at Brno and studied at the Prague organ school. He founded his own organ school in Brno. He was fascinated by the rhythms and intonation of folksong and speech, and is best known for his operas. Notable among his religious compositions is his *Glagolitic Mass*.

Jane Françoise de Chantal *see* **Chantal, Jane Frances Fremiot de**

Janequin, Clément Composer, born Châtellerault, near Poitiers, *c.*1485, died Paris, a poor man, 1558. He spent his early life in the Bordeaux region, where he studied for the priesthood. In 1530 he moved to Angers, where he served as *maître de chapelle* from 1537. He built up a considerable reputation as a *chanson* composer and had a number of his works published. In 1549 he settled in Paris. When in his seventies, he decided to become a student at the University of Paris.

Jansen, Cornelius (the Elder) Biblical scholar, born Hulst, Flanders, 1510, died Ghent, 11 April 1576. Studied theology and Eastern languages at Louvain and went on to teach Scripture at the Premonstratensian abbey of Tongerloo until 1542. For the next ten years he ran a parish. After he gained his doctorate, in 1562, he became professor of theology at the University of Louvain and represented the University at the last sessions of the Council of Trent. He became bishop of the new see of Ghent, and devoted himself to stemming the development of Protestantism and to enacting the decrees of Trent. Jansen's writings include the *Concordia evangelica* (1549), a later *Commentarius in Concordiam et totam historiam evangelicam* (1572), commentaries on Proverbs, Psalms and Ecclesiasticus and, published after his death, *Annotationes in Librum Sapientiae* (1577).

Jansen, Cornelius Otto Flemish theologian, born Acquoi, 28 October 1585, died of the plague, Ypres, 6 May 1638. He studied at the Universities of Utrecht, Leuven (Louvain) and Paris. In Paris he met Jean Duvergier de Hauranne (the future Abbé de **Saint-Cyran**), with whom he spent the years 1612–17 in study, at Bayonne and Champré. It was during this time that he conceived a plan of action against the theologians of the Counter-Reformation, and which led to his work the *Augustinus*. This would, in turn, lead to the formation after his death of the movement known as 'Jansenism'. In 1617 he became the director of a newly founded college at Leuven. In 1628 he started work on the *Augustinus*, a work which advanced radical theories of grace and justification, and which was published posthumously. It was later condemned as heretical. In 1636 he was consecrated bishop of Ypres.

Janssen, Johannes German Roman Catholic historian, born Xanten, Prussia, 10 April 1829, died Frankfurt am Main, Germany, 24 December 1891. Studied at Münster, Louvain and Bonn and settled in Frankfurt. His *History of the German People from the Close of the Middle Ages* (1876–94) suggested that the high point in German cultural achievement was prior to the Lutheran reformation, an interpretation naturally rather more agreeable to Roman Catholics than to Protestants.

Januarius Saint and (probably) bishop of Beneventum (Italy): according to the earliest liturgical tradition and his earliest *Passio*, this martyr was decapitated, together with his six companions, near Pozzuoli on 19 September 305. In 432 his relics came to Naples, where they, despite some temporary translations, are still kept today. Januarius also is the city's patron saint. Since the fourteenth century a blood miracle is regularly witnessed: the saint's blood, which is preserved in two *ampullae*, becomes fluid again. Feast day 19 September.

Jaricot, Pauline-Marie Foundress, born Lyons, France, 22 July 1799, died Lyons, 9 January 1862. As a teenager she took a personal vow of virginity and began a prayer circle for servant girls, the Réparatrices du Sacré-Coeur de Jésus-Christ. She began to gather in from the members of this group, and from others, regular donations for the propagation of the Catholic faith, on a sort of 'pyramid collecting' basis. In 1822 this organization became the Society for the Propagation of the Faith. In 1826 she founded the Association of the Living Rosary, which ensured the rosary was said regularly among its members. She also promoted learning and social welfare and reform projects.

Jarret, Bede English Dominican, preacher, historian and spiritual writer, born Greenwich, 22 August 1881, died London, 17 March 1934. Studied at the Jesuit school, Stonyhurst, and joined the Dominicans in 1898, changing his name from 'Cyril' to 'Bede'. Studied at Woodchester and Hawkesyard and in 1904 went to Oxford, the first Dominican in modern times to do so. Following further studies in Louvain he did parish work in London and in 1914 was made prior. From 1916 to 1932 he was provincial in England. He opened a house of studies in Oxford and a house in Edinburgh, and extended the work of the English province to South Africa. His publications include *Medieval Socialism* (1913), *St Antonino and Medieval Economics* (1914), *Meditations for Layfolk* (1915), *Living Temples* (1919), *Religious Life* (1920), *The English Dominicans* (1921), *St Dominic* (1924), *Social Theories of the Middle Ages* (1926), *A History of Europe* (1929), *The Space of Life Between* (1930) and *No Abiding City* (1934).

Javouhey, Anne-Marie Blessed, religious, born Jallanges, France, 10 October 1779, died Paris, 15 July 1851. During the French Revolution she helped her family to house many nonjuring priests, one of whom encouraged her religious vocation. In 1800 she spent a short time in the novitiate at the convent of the Sisters of Charity of St Joan Antida at Besançon, and then later, in 1803, with the Trappistines in Switzerland. In 1806, with her three sisters, she founded a school and association of St Joseph in Chalon-sur-Saône, and in 1807 founded the Sisters of St Joseph of Cluny to conduct schools and orphanages and to aid the sick and elderly. In 1817 she travelled to Senegal in an attempt to encourage boys into the priesthood. Having little success, she later set up hospitals in Gambia and Sierra Leone. In 1828 she established a colony of enfranchised slaves. She spent much of her time visiting the many foundations which had grown up. At her death, there were 118 houses with 700 sisters in France alone, with 300 sisters in Africa, and sisters in India, Tahiti and South America.

Jean (in medieval names) *see* **John**

Jeanne Marie de Maille Blessed, Franciscan tertiary, mystic and recluse, born Roche-Saint-Quentin, near Tours, France, 1332, of noble birth, died Tours, 28 March 1414. At the age of sixteen she was married to Robert de Sille, but remained a virgin. When he died in 1362, she was dispossessed by his family and she returned to Tours. Here she spent her days living in a simple house near to the church of St Martin in prayer and good works. Later she became a recluse, living near Clery. In 1377 she entered the Third Order of St Francis at Tours. She prayed unceasingly for an end to the Western Schism and also sought to reform the morals of the court of Charles VI and Isabelle.

Jedin, Hubert German Roman Catholic priest and Church historian, born Grossbriesen (Germany), 17 June 1900, died Bonn, 16 July 1980. After studies in Breslau, Munich and Freiburg and several long periods of research in Rome, Jedin was professor of medieval and modern Church history in Bonn between 1946 and 1965. His research focused on the Reformation and on the history of Councils, his most important work being a four-volume *History of the Council of Trent*. Between 1962 and 1965 he was a *peritus* (a specialist adviser) during the Second Vatican Council. During the later years of his life, 1962–79, he edited a *Handbuch der Kirchengeschichte* in ten volumes that became a standard work – translated at first as *A Handbook of Church History* and afterwards simply as *History of the Church*.

Jeffreys, George Founder of the Elim Foursquare Gospel Alliance, born Nantyffylon, Wales, 28 February 1889, died Clapham, 26 January 1962. Jeffreys became a Pentecostal in 1911, and left his work in the Co-operative Stores to train as a missionary in Preston. With his brother Stephen **Jeffreys**, he preached in Wales and London, and he attended the Sunderland Convention in 1913. He established his first Church in Belfast in 1916, and made highly successful preaching tours across Britain, with trips to Europe and North America. In 1939 he resigned from the Elim Church following disagreements about Church government, and in 1940 set up the Bible-Pattern Church Fellowship in Nottingham.

Jeffreys, Stephen Pentecostal evangelist, born 1876, died 7 November 1943. A coal miner in Maestig, Wales, he and his brother George **Jeffreys** were converted to Pentecostalism during the Welsh revival. He worked closely with the Assemblies of God of Britain and Ireland, preaching widely in Britain and making tours to Canada, the USA, New Zealand, Australia and South Africa. His hugely popular preaching was accompanied with supernatural experiences, including a widely reported vision of the Man of Sorrows on a wall of the Island Place Mission, Llanelly, in 1914.

Jerome (Hieronymus, Sophronius Eusebis) Saint, exegete and theologian, born Stridon (Dalmatia), *c.*345, died Bethlehem, 419/20. His was one of the greatest intellects and most versatile minds of antiquity. During his restless life he travelled the entire Roman Empire, took up in various places a monastic lifestyle and became secretary of Pope **Damasus I**. Most of all, however, he was an erudite scholar who mastered the legacies of the Latin, Greek and biblical literature and realized the importance of reading the Bible in the original language. His most lasting contribution has been the Latin translation of almost the entire Bible (the Vulgate). There is also his *De viris illustribus*, biographies of monks, Latin translations of Greek works, homilies, letters and much more. Feast day 30 September.

Jerome of Prague   Reformer, born Prague, *c.*1370, died Constance, 30 May 1416. Little is known of his early life. He studied in his home town and came under the influence of John **Huss** and of Wycliffite philosophy. He left Prague for Oxford in 1398, where he studied the writings of John **Wycliffe**, taking the ideas with him to Paris, Prague, 1402, Jerusalem, 1403, Paris again, 1404, Heidelberg and Cologne, 1406. Back in Prague in 1407, he became involved in religious controversy, and tried to spread Wycliffite philosophy to neighbouring countries. Suspected of heresy he fled to Moravia but later returned to Prague. In 1415 he followed Huss to Constance but escaped when he realized the danger. Following the death of Huss on 6 July, he was brought back in chains and the Council successfully appealed for him to repudiate his beliefs to prevent a further execution. He later withdrew his abjuration and was condemned to the stake in 1416.

Jerrold, Douglas Francis   English publisher and writer, born Scarborough, Yorkshire, 1893, died London, 21 July 1964. He studied at Westminster School and New College, Oxford. His time at Oxford was cut short owing to the Great War, and in 1914 he enlisted. Having served with distinction at Gallipoli and in France, he was later wounded and transferred to the Ministry of Food, and then to the Treasury. In 1923 he joined the publishing firm of Ernest Benn, transferring to Eyre and Spottiswoode in 1928, where he remained for the rest of his working life. It was through his initiative that the company acquired Burns, Oates and Washbourne, who were publishers to the Holy See. Jerrold was briefly the company chairman. He founded a Conservative monthly and the *English Review*. Right-wing in his politics, he was staunchly anti-pacifist between the wars, and wrote a wide range of material – political, historical, propaganda and novels. During the Spanish Civil War he wrote for the nationalists, and was awarded the Cross of Isabella the Catholic.

Jewel, John   Bishop, born Buden, Devonshire, 24 May 1522, died Monkton Farleigh, 23 September 1571. He was educated at Merton and Corpus Christi Colleges, Oxford. He was elected a fellow of Corpus Christi in 1542. He became one of the leading intellectuals of the Reforming party in England, though he signed anti-Protestant articles during the reign of **Mary**. In 1555 he fled to Frankfurt, where he opposed the more advanced Calvinist views of John **Knox**. He travelled to Strasburg, where he met **Peter Martyr Vermigli**, with whom he journeyed to Zurich. He returned to England upon the accession of **Elizabeth I** and was consecrated bishop of Salisbury in 1560. From this point Jewel became a strong defender of the Anglican settlement, most notably in his *Ecclesiae Anglicanae*, published in 1562. He administered his diocese with great energy and was responsible for building the cathedral library.

Jieron (Jeron, Hieron)   Saint, priest, missionary and martyr. There are differing traditions concerning his birth, which place him in Egmond, Holland, England and Scotland. Little is known of him save that he was a missionary to the Frisians. He was captured and brought before a tribal assembly and was questioned, before being tortured and killed. It is said that he bore witness to his faith with great bravery. His head is at Noordwijk, which was the scene of his martyrdom around 856. Other relics are at St Adalbert's monastery in Egmond.

Joachim de Fiore (Flore)   Cistercian abbot and mystic, born Crelino, Calabria, *c.*1135, died abbey of St Martin, Canale, near Cosenza, 30 March 1202. His Life was written by his secretary, Luke, who became archbishop of Cosenza. He was well educated (his father was a lawyer) and travelled to Constantinople and to the Holy Land, had spent some time as a hermit and then as a visitor at the Cistercian monastery of Sambucina before entering the Benedictines at the monastery of Corazzo, of which he became abbot in 1178, and changed the rule of life to that of the Cistercians. He left Corazzo, however, and spent the year 1183 at the monastery of Casamari, where he began to work on his major treatises, *Concordie Novi ac Veteris Testamenti*, *Expositio in Apocalypsim* and the *Psalterium decem chordarum*. He was encouraged in his work by Popes **Lucius III** and – later – **Clement III**. He returned to Corazzo, but left again in 1189, settling as a hermit in the mountains of Pietralta where, on Mt Nero, he founded the monastery of St John of Fiore, which soon became the motherhouse of a new religious order, approved by **Celestine III** in 1196 (and which lasted, following the Cistercian Rule, until 1505). It was Joachim's belief, expressed particularly in the *Concordie*, that history was divided into three ages: that of the Father (until the end of the Old Testament), that of the Son (which was just, in his view, coming to an end), to be followed by the age of the Spirit. His teachings had a considerable impact on certain sections of the Franciscans, and on many others in the Middle Ages and beyond. Joachim was condemned by the (local) Council of Arles in 1263.

Joan   Pope. There is little to substantiate the story of a female Pope, and most scholars now treat it as legend. The story emerged in the thirteenth century. It is said that either *c.*1100 or *c.*855 a woman wearing male dress and living as a noted scholar became Pope. She held the throne for two years and then gave birth to a child during a procession to the Lateran and died straightaway. This story was widely believed in the Middle Ages.

Joan of Arc   Saint, visionary and martyr, born Domrémy, Lorraine, 6 January 1412, died Rouen, 30 May 1431, by being burned at the stake. As a child she experienced visions and heard voices which called her to a mission to save France. In 1429 she made her way to the French court, and, following the examination of her claims by theologians, **Charles VII** allowed her to lead an expedition to Orléans. Dressed in white armour and carrying a banner with the symbol of the Trinity and the words 'Jesus Maria', she was successful in relieving the city. Six months later she was taken prisoner, sold to the English, tried before the bishop of Beauvais and accused of witchcraft and heresy. She partially recanted, but on 23 May 1431 she once again put on male dress, was condemned as a relapsed heretic and burnt. She was rehabilitated by the Church in 1456, but not declared a saint until 1920. Feast day 30 May.

Joan of Aza   Blessed, the mother of St **Dominic**, born in the Castle of Aza, Old Castile, *c.*1140, died Calaruega between 1190 and 1203. Having borne two sons she prayed at the shrine of St **Dominic of Silos** for a third child. Her prayer having been answered, she resolved to name the child 'Dominic' in gratitude.

Joan of France   Saint, foundress of the Franciscan Annunciades, born Nogent-le-Roi, 23 April 1464, died Bourges, 4 February 1505. The sister of **Charles VII** of France. Joan was despised by her father, probably owing to the fact that she was deformed from birth. Aged just two months she was betrothed to the duke of Orléans and was later sent to his chateau to be trained in court etiquette. At the age of twelve her marriage was solemnized, though she was badly treated by the duke, who later (as King **Louis XII**) had the marriage annulled. Joan was now free to fulfil her lifelong ambition of founding a religious community. The Franciscan Annunciades were a community dedicated to acts of charity. The community Rule was approved in 1501 and a second house was founded at Bourges the following year. Joan adopted the name 'Sister Gabriella Marie' and made her profession, though she never lived in the community itself. Feast day 4 February.

Joan of Orvieto   Blessed, Dominican tertiary and mystic, born Carnaiola, near Orvieto, 1264, died Orvieto, 23 July 1306. Having refused a proposed marriage, she entered the Third Order of St Dominic, where her director was **James de Blanconibus**. She received frequent visions as well as the stigmata. In spite of her own protestations she was venerated by the local townsfolk as a saint during her own lifetime. She was tireless in her care of the poor and sick. It was said that the best way to be assured of her prayers was to do her an injury.

Joan of Portugal   Blessed, religious, born Lisbon, 6 February 1452, died of a fever, Aveiro, 12 May 1490. She was the eldest child and heiress to Alfonso V of Portugal. Ignoring family pressure to marry, and determined to remain chaste, she resolved to enter a convent. In 1475 she assumed the Dominican habit at the convent of Jesus at Aveiro, though she was never professed nor did she give up control of her property.

Joan of Santa Lucia   Blessed, religious, born Bagno, Italy, 4 September (year unknown), died Bagno, 16 or 17 January *c.*1105. She joined the Camaldolese convent of St Lucia at Bagno. Little else is known of her life. In 1287 her remains were transferred to the parish church at Bagno. Some time later the cessation of the plague in the town was ascribed to her intercession. She became the town's patroness in 1506.

Joan of Signa   Blessed, virgin and recluse, born Signa, near Florence, *c.*1245, died 9 November 1307. At the age of 23 she became a recluse at a cell in Signa, leading a life of austerity and prayer for over 40 years. She had the reputation of being a miracle-worker. Joan is claimed by the Franciscans, the Carmelites, the Vallumbrosan monks and the Augustinians as a tertiary, though there is no direct evidence to support the claims. In 1348 the cessation of an epidemic at Signa was attributed to her intercession.

Joanna Angelica de Jesus   Brazilian nun, born Salvador, Balua, 11 December 1761, died Salvador, 20 February 1822. Of Baluan Portuguese ancestry, she entered the Conceptionist Franciscan convent of Lapa, Salvador, in 1782, and became one of the Reformed Nuns of Our Lady of the Conception in 1783, clerk in 1797, vicar in 1812, abbess in 1817 and again in 1821. When fighting broke out in the city between the Portuguese and Brazilians in 1822, she resisted the entry of Portuguese troops into the convent and was killed by them.

Joannes   *see also* **John**

Joannes Andreae   Canon lawyer, born probably at Bologna, *c.*1270, died there 7 July 1348. Becoming doctor of canon law at the University of Bologna at some time between 1296 and 1300, he was a professor of this subject until dying of the plague. He undertook several diplomatic missions both for Bologna and for the papal legate. In his writings he collected important statements of preceding canon lawyers and expressed his own ideas from them, his greatest work being the Novella Commentaria series (*c.*1338–46). He was the first historian of canon law.

Joasaph   *see* **Barlaam and Joasaph**

Joasaph (Bolotov)   Russian Orthodox saint, bishop and missionary, born near Tver, 22 January 1761, died (drowned) off the Alaskan coast, 1799. He became a monk and later abbot at the Valaam Monastery and was appointed to head the famous mission to Russian America (Alaska). After a suc-

cessful beginning he was appointed first bishop of Kodiak for Alaska. He was consecrated bishop in Siberia but shipwrecked before he could enter his diocese. Revered still as the first Orthodox bishop of America. Feast day 22 January.

Joasaph of Belgorod   Russian Orthodox saint and bishop, born Poltave province, 8 September 1705, died 10 December 1754. He was appointed bishop of Belgorod through the direct intervention of Empress Elizabeth and became a zealous pastor, constantly travelling around his vast and poor diocese. Miracles were attributed to him in his lifetime and even more so after his death, when his tomb became a shrine for pilgrims. He was not canonized until 1911, one of the last such ceremonies before the Revolution. Feast day 10 December.

Job of Pochaev   Orthodox saint and abbot, born Poland, 1551, died Pochaev, 28 October 1651. Early in his life he became a monk and lived in various monasteries until in his old age he became abbot of the famous shrine of Pochaev, in what is now western Ukraine. He opposed the Polish efforts to unite the Orthodox Church to Rome to the end of his life, especially by the printed word. His body was found incorrupt and the tomb was visited by pilgrims from both Churches from then on. Feast day 28 August.

Jocelin of Brakelond   English monk, Church historian, died *c.*1216. Entered the abbey of Bury St Edmunds, his home town, in 1173 and in 1182 became chaplain and companion to Abbot Sampson. He later became guestmaster and almoner. He wrote a history of the abbey which was later used by **Carlyle** in his *Past and Present.*

Jocelin of Glasgow   Bishop, died Melrose, 17 March 1199. Little is known of his life. He was abbot of Melrose in 1170 and bishop of Glasgow 1175–99. In 1176 he attended the Council of Northampton. In 1181 he was sent by William the Lion, king of Scotland, to Rome in an attempt to obtain removal of an interdict. At Glasgow Cathedral he was responsible for building the crypt, the choir, the Lady Chapel and the central tower.

Jocelin of Wells (Josceline) Bishop, born Wells, died 19 November 1242. He became bishop of Bath and Glastonbury, 1206–18, and of Bath (and Wells) alone, 1206–42. At Wells he built the nave, choir and west front, as well as the earliest part of the palace. He is mentioned in the preamble to the Magna Carta (1215), and witnessed its confirmation in 1236. In 1224 he took part with Stephen **Langton**, archbishop of Canterbury, against Falkes de Breaute. He is buried in Wells Cathedral.

Jocham, Magnus Theologian, born Rieder-bei-Immerstadt, Germany, 23 March 1808, died Freising, 4 March 1893. After doing pastoral work from 1841 to 1878, he became professor of moral theology at the Freising Lyceum. He wrote *Moraltheologie, oder die Lehre von Christi, Leben nach den Grundsetzen der Katholische Kirche* (1852–4), in which, against contemporary rationalism and moralism, he urged a moral theology fulfilled by the sacramental system.

Jogues, Isaac Saint, Jesuit and North American martyr, born Orléans, January 1607, died Ossernenou, Canada (now Auriesville, New York), 18 October 1646. Arriving in Canada in 1636, he lived with other Jesuits among the Huron Indians, the only tribe to tolerate them. In 1642, Mohawks captured and tortured them, then kept him as a slave. He escaped and returned to France in 1644, showing his mutilated hand as proof of his story. The Jesuits wanted him to stay in France and become a public speaker, considering that his dramatic story would serve to encourage vocations. But he chose to return to Canada, where he was eventually killed by Mohawks. Feast day 19 October.

Johannes *see* John

Johannitius (Hunainbu Ishāq) Arabic scholar, born al-Hirah, Euphrates, 808, died Baghdad, probably 1 December 873. Of a Nestorian Christian Arabic family, he studied Arabic and medicine. His writings were mostly translations of medical works into Syrian and Arabic and were scholarly, although intrigues in the caliph's court brought him imprisonment and excommunication. Despite his firm Christian faith, he and his helpers prepared the way for the growth of medieval Muslim civilization in science and scholarship.

John I Saint, Pope, born in Tuscany, consecrated 13 August 523, died Ravenna, 18 May 526. Senior deacon on his election, and already old, he was pro-Eastern in sentiment, and introduced the Alexandrian method of dating Easter to the West. He went to Constantinople on instructions of Theodoric, king of Italy, to dissuade the emperor from persecuting Arians on the Italian peninsula. John was treated with great respect by the emperor, but he refused to grant Theodoric's demand that Arians who had been forced to convert to Catholicism should be free to revert to Arianism. Theodoric was furious, but John died suddenly in Ravenna before the king could wreak vengeance. Feast day 18 May.

John II Pope, consecrated 2 January 533, died Rome, 8 May 535. He was a priest of San Clemente, and named 'Mercury': he changed it on his election (the first Pope known to have done so) because it was the name of a pagan god. He managed to maintain good relations both with the king of Italy and with the Emperor **Justinian I** in Constantinople. In the continuing controversy over the nature of Christ, John appears to have contradicted Pope **Hormisdas** when he accepted a dogmatic formulation favoured by Justinian that Hormisdas had rejected.

John III Pope, consecrated 17 July 561, died Rome, 13 July 574. The son of a Roman senator and originally called 'Catelinus'. Little is known about his pontificate, though much happened in Italy, in particular the drive southwards of the Lombards. John went to Naples to persuade the emperor's representative in Italy, Narses, to return to Rome. This he did, but John's action was ill received by the people of Rome, and he went to live on the Appian Way, just outside the city.

John III Scholasticus Patriarch of Constantinople, born Antioch, *c*.503, became patriach January 563, died 31 August 577. John was born of a clerical family at Antioch. He was a lawyer by profession, ordained priest by Domninus, who made him apocrisiary at Constantinople. **Justinian I** called John to replace the deposed patriarch **Eutychius**

in 565 (this fulfilled a prophecy given by Simon Stylites the Younger). John treated Eutychius and the Monophysites harshly. After John's death Eutychius returned to his see, and exacted revenge. John is linked to several works, the *Synagogē of 50 Titles*, the *Collectio of 87 Chapters*.

John III Ducas Vatatzes   Eastern Orthodox saint, Byzantine emperor, born Didymoteicho, 1193, died Nymphaion, 3 November 1254. He was the son-in-law of Theodore I, whom he succeeded in 1222. Twice John III defeated his rivals and conquered Asia Minor. He allied himself with the Bulgarian Tsar Arsen and besieged Constantinople. On Arsen's death, John annexed territory in Bulgaria. He was involved in negotiations with the Holy Roman Empire – he married, after his first wife died, the daughter of the Emperor **Frederick II** – and the Papacy, in an attempt to win back Constantinople, which was still occupied by the Latins (he was ruling from Nicaea). He improved agriculture, stockbreeding, built hospitals and poorhouses, and was revered as St John the Merciful.

John III Sobieski   King of Poland and conqueror of the Turks in Hungary, born Olesko, Ukraine, 17 August 1624, died Wilanow, near Warsaw, 17 June 1696. Fought in the Polish–Swedish war 1655–60 and against the Cossacks and Tartars in 1667. In 1668 he was appointed commander in chief of the Polish army. Having defeated the Turks at Khotin in 1673 he was elected king of Poland. In March 1683 he signed a treaty with Leopold I, Holy Roman Emperor, against the Turks, defeating them at the Battle of Kahlenberg in the same year.

John IV   Pope, born in Dalmatia (his father was legal adviser to the emperor's representative in Ravenna), he was archdeacon of Rome, consecrated 24 December 640, died Rome, 12 October 642. He held a synod in Rome to condemn monothelitism: a decision which the Emperor Heraclius accepted but the patriarch of Constantinople rejected. Dalmatia was being overrun by Slavs and Avars, and John sent money to ransom captives. He wrote to the Irish, criticizing them for holding Easter on the same date as the Jewish Passover.

John IV   Saint, patriarch of Constantinople, died 2 September 595. First a deacon at Hagia Sophia, later patriarch, 582–95, under Emperors Tiberius II and Maurice, John was popular at court as well as renowned for his asceticism – hence his nickname 'John the Faster'. He is known primarily for his assumption of the title 'ecumenical patriarch', the apparent arrogance of which proved controversial to Pope **Gregory I** and other primates. At his death, John left only a cloak, a blanket and a prayer stool. Feast day 12 September.

John IV Otznetzi   *see* **John of Otzun**

John V   Pope, a Syrian deacon who had taken a leading part in the Third Council of Constantinople, unanimously elected 23 July 685, died Rome, 2 August 686. Politically astute, and a learned man, he was ill for most of his pontificate.

John V Palaeologus   Byzantine emperor from 1341 to 1391, born Didymoteicho, 18 June 1332, died Constantinople, 16 February 1391. John succeeded his father in 1341, but a civil war broke out and the conflict was only resolved when John married Cantacuzenus' (the usurper's) daughter in 1347. He and Cantacuzenus were crowned co-emperors at Constantinople. In 1354 he succeeded in forcing his father-in-law to abdicate. The Ottoman Turks were advancing towards Constantinople, and in an attempt to get Western assistance, John accepted papal supremacy in 1369. This had no practical effect, and John decided to become an Ottoman vassal. Revolts within his own family forced him to break up the empire into principalities, himself controlling the capital.

John VI   Pope, a Greek by birth, elected 30 October 701, died Rome, 11 January 705. Little is known of his pontificate, except that he saved the life of the imperial representative in Italy, and that during these years the Lombard king came to within a short distance of the city, and John had to spend much money getting him to withdraw, and ransoming his prisoners. **Wilfrid** of York came to Rome during John's pontificate, and his appeal was upheld.

John VI of Constantinople   Patriarch, died 715. John was deacon and librarian of the patriarchate of Constantinople. He was appointed patriarch in 712 by the Emperor Philippicus. After Philippicus' fall it was John who crowned the new emperor, Anastasius II. John sent the Pope his *Epistula ad Constantinum papam*, a synodal letter in which he justified his acceptance of the patriarchate as given by Philippicus, and maintained that he had given an oath of orthodoxy in the presence of the Roman apocrisiaries.

John VII Pope, a Greek, the son of a Byzantine imperial official, elected 1 March 705, died 18 October 707. Although thought to be too subservient to the emperor in Constantinople, he also managed to achieve good relations with the Lombards. Highly gifted, and artistic, he had churches rebuilt and redecorated – though rather in the Byzantine style.

John VII of Constantinople Patriarch of Constantinople, born Constantinople, towards the end of the eighth century, died in prison, before 863. He was a leading Iconoclastic theologian during the second phase of Iconoclasm. Of Armenian origin, he was ordained *c.*806. His first attack on the veneration of icons came in 813 when he was asked by the Iconoclast Byzantine emperor **Leo V** to compile a handbook of biblical and patristic texts against the veneration of images. This work, which is no longer extant, was used at the Iconoclast Council of 815. For a time he took charge of the education of the future emperor, Theophilus, and on his accession became syncellus. He became patriarch in January 837. The death of Theophilus in January 842 marked the end of Iconoclasm. John was deposed and excommunicated.

John VIII Pope, born Rome, elected 14 December 872, died – he was poisoned then clubbed to death – 16 December 882. He was elected at a very troubled time, when there was great need to defend Rome against Saracen invaders. John built walls and established the first papal fleet. He tried, but failed, to establish an alliance in southern Italy against the Saracens, and supported **Charles II** the Bald as emperor in the vain hope that he would help to defend Italy. When Carloman demanded the imperial crown after Charles' death, John would not grant it, and was imprisoned in Rome by some of Carloman's supporters – whom John had earlier excommunicated. When he was freed, John went to Provence to find an alternative to Carloman, eventually deciding on **Charles** the Fat, whom he crowned in 881. John also tried to win the support of Constantinople, the price of which proved to be the recognition of **Photius** as patriarch. The council which met in Hagia Sophia in November 879 (regarded in the East as the Eighth General Council) was manipulated by Photius: John simply agreed to its decisions, adding the rider that he agreed so long as his legates had kept within his instructions, thus achieving the required unity between the Churches. He was the first Pope to have been assassinated.

John VIII (of Constantinople) Patriarch, born Trebizond, 1005, died Constantinople, 2 August 1075. Born into a humble family, he taught in the law school in Constantinople from 1045, becoming its head, and was prominent in the revival of letters and the reorganization of law. In 1054 he retired to a monastery at Bithynian Olympas and became its abbot in 1063. He was however summoned back to the capital to become patriarch of Constantinople on 1 January 1064. As such he dealt vigorously with administrative problems, and tried to obtain reunion with the Armenians. He wrote a number of legal works.

John VIII Palaeologus Byzantine emperor, 1425–48, born 1392, died Constantinople, 31 October 1448. Succeeded his father **Manuel II Palaeologus**, whose example he followed in looking to Latin Christendom for support as the Ottoman threat loomed over ailing Byzantium. John went further by favouring union between the Latin and Greek Churches as a means of saving the remnant of his empire, and accordingly headed the Orthodox delegation which accepted **Eugenius IV**'s invitation to the Ecumenical Council of Ferrara-Florence (1438–9). His failure to defend the union against its Orthodox critics contributed to its rapid collapse. John was succeeded by his brother **Constantine XI**, the last Byzantine emperor.

John IX Pope, born Tivoli, elected January 898, died January 900. He immediately convened a synod and annulled the sanctions placed on the (dead) **Formosus** and his supporters. It was also agreed that the election of a Pope should be by bishops and clergy of the city alone, and imperial representatives were to attend the consecration. At a subsequent synod at Ravenna these decisions were confirmed, and the right to appeal to the emperor was confirmed.

John X Pope, born Tossignano in the Romagna, ordained at Bologna, and then deacon and afterwards archbishop of Ravenna, elected March or April 914, deposed May 928, died 929. John was well known in Rome, to which he was a frequent emissary from Ravenna, and a capable and vigorous leader. It was for these qualities that he was chosen: Rome needed a strong leader against the Saracens, which he proved to be, constructing an alliance and defeating them decisively, with the help of Constantinople, in 915. John took part in the battle. He was equally at home in ecclesiastical affairs, and re-established good relations with the patriarch of Constantinople. In Rome itself he was something of a reforming Pope, but his attempt to keep independent from the powerful senatorial families led to his being deposed, imprisoned in Castel Sant'Angelo and probably suffocated.

John X (of Constantinople) Patriarch, born Constantinople, died Didymoteicho, Bulgaria, June 1206. He became patriarch of Constantinople on 5 August 1198, and fled to Bulgaria when the city was sacked during the Fourth Crusade. He exchanged letters with Pope **Innocent III**, but opposed any attempt at reunion between the Eastern and Western Churches by denying the primacy of the Papacy, arguing that the primacy sprang not from Peter but from Rome's position as capital of the Roman Empire. He assisted the Byzantine–Bulgarian alliance of 1204, but refused to join the government-in-exile after the fall of Constantinople to the Latins. He resigned as patriarch in 1206, just one or two months before his death.

John XI Pope, born Rome, possibly the illegitimate son of Pope **Sergius III**, elected February or March 931 through the influence of his mother, **Marozia**, died Rome, December 935 or January 936. He strengthened the position of the Cluniacs, but was thrown into prison by his half-brother **Alberic II of Spoleto**, after Alberic had risen against the third marriage of Marozia, imprisoning

her, driving her new husband out of the city, and confining John to the Lateran.

John XI (of Constantinople) (Beccus) Patriarch, born Nicaea *c.*1235, died in the fortress of St George, Bithunia, March 1297. From 1254 to 1266 he was sacristan of the patriarchate of Constantinople, and served on several diplomatic missions. He was imprisoned in 1273 for opposing the Emperor Michael VIII Palaeologus' short-lived submission to Pope **Gregory X**, made for political reasons. In captivity he studied theology, which led him to recognize papal supremacy. His action brought about the abdication of the patriarch of Constantinople in 1275, and John succeeded him on 26 May that year. Clerical and imperial opposition to his belief compelled him to abdicate in 1279. He was reinstated that same year, but was deposed in December 1282 and was eventually exiled to St George, where he died in poverty.

John XII Pope, born Rome, *c.*937, elected 16 December 955, died in the Campagna, 14 May 964. Named 'Octavian', and the illegitimate son of **Alberic II of Spoleto**, the virtual ruler of Rome, he was made Pope in compliance with his late father's instructions, and despite his complete lack of interest in religion. He was, however, interested in the reform movements in monasticism. Papal territories in northern Italy were being attacked by Berengar I, king of Italy, so John sought the assistance of **Otto I**, the German king, offering him the imperial crown. Otto came to Rome, was crowned, guaranteed the papal domains, and told John to improve his dissolute way of life. After Otto had gone John started to intrigue with Berengar's son. Otto came back, John fled and was deposed. He was able to reinstate himself a few months later in Otto's absence, but fled again on his return. He died, it was said, of a stroke while in bed with a married woman.

John XIII Pope, born Rome, the son of John Episcopus, elected 1 October 965, died 6 September 972. He had been librarian under **John XII**, then bishop of Narnia in Umbria. He was the Emperor **Otto** I's choice for the Papacy, and as such was resented by the people of Rome. John was first imprisoned, then exiled, but reinstated by Otto, who then supported him. John in return raised Magdeburg to an archbishopric, something Otto wanted. John performed the wedding of a Greek princess to Otto's son (**Otto II**), in a vain attempt to reunite the two parts of the empire.

John XIII Patriarch of Constantinople, born c.1250, died Constantinople c.1319. After a career in imperial administration, he was made patriarch of Constantinople, although a layman and married, by the Emperor **Andronicus II Palaeologus** in the hope of ending factional disputes in the Church. His wife entered a convent, and he was consecrated in 1315, but he resigned through illness in May 1319 and retired to the monastery of Kyniotissa in Constantinople. He was well known in his time as a writer and a teacher.

John XIV Pope, born Pavia, elected December 983, died Rome, 20 August 984. Peter Capenova was an official of **Otto II**'s court, then bishop of Pavia from 966: he changed his name on his election, imposed on the Roman people by Otto. Otto, however, died almost immediately after, and without his protection John was vulnerable. He was imprisoned in Castel Sant'Angelo and died there, possibly of starvation.

John XIV Patriarch of Constantinople, born Apros, Thrace, c.1283, died Constantinople, 29 December 1347. The Emperor John VI Cantacuzenus made him patriarch in 1334 although he was a married priest and the father of a family. Being involved in disputes in the Church, particularly over **Gregory Palamas**, whom he at first supported and then, in 1344, excommunicated, he was deposed on 2 February 1347, imprisoned and exiled to Didymoleichon; but he returned to Constantinople, where he died. A collection of his disciplinary, dogmatic and canonical decisions form an important source for the history of the period.

John XV Pope, born Rome, elected mid-August 985, died March 996. John, the son of a priest, was a cardinal-priest on his election by senior members of the papal curia and of the city. He had little political influence but involved himself in the organization of the Church in Europe at large and in 993 became the first Pope formally to canonize a saint – Ulrich, bishop of Augsburg. An avaricious

man, he so alienated his clergy that he had to flee Rome, taking refuge in Sutri. He appealed to the German king **Otto III** for help, and Otto advanced on Rome, forcing the people who had driven out John to invite him back so as to avoid the wrath of Otto. John had however died before Otto reached Rome.

John XVI Antipope, born 'John Philagathos', a Greek from Calabria, appointed February 997, deposed May 998, died 26 August 1001. John held various appointments under **Otto II**, then was tutor to **Otto III** and archbishop of Piacenza. When it was decided that Otto should have a Byzantine princess as his wife, John went to Constantinople as ambassador. While **Gregory V** was in exile in Pavia, John went to Rome and was elected Pope by the faction opposed to Gregory. Otto, however, gave his support to Gregory, and marched on Rome. Though John fled, he was captured, mutilated, degraded from his priestly rank, paraded around the city sitting backwards on a donkey, then shut up in a monastery for the rest of his life.

John XVII Pope, born 'John Sicco' at Rome, elected 16 May 1003, died Rome, 1003. Little or nothing is known of him, except that he must have been the nominee of one of the powerful Roman families.

John XVIII Pope, born 'John Fasanus', elected 25 December 1003, died June or July 1009. He was cardinal-priest of St Peter's at his election, which he probably owed to one of the powerful families of Rome. It seems likely, however, that he wanted to break free of their control by inviting the German king **Henry II** to the city. He also seems to have re-established friendly relations with Constantinople. He was active in Church affairs in both Germany and France, and canonized five Polish martyrs. It is possible that he retired to a monastery before his death.

John XIX Pope, born 'Romanus', a brother of **Benedict VIII**, and a member of the family of the counts of Tusculanum, still a layman when elected to the Papacy on 19 April 1024, died 20 October 1032. He had been active in the politics of the city of Rome before his election, which he appears to have achieved by bribery. By judicious use of his resources he seems to have consolidated his position in Rome, despite the scandal of being elevated from the rank of layman to bishop in one day. Outside Rome his authority was less obvious. Relations with Constantinople seem to have deteriorated, and although he crowned Conrad II as Emperor (in the presence, among others, of England's King **Canute**), Conrad frequently overruled his decisions when they affected his dominions. (Canute, for his part, obtained the waiver of all fees for granting the pallium in return for the annual 'Peter's Pence'.)

John XX Pope: through a miscalculation, there was never a John XX.

John XXI Pope, born 'Pedro Julião' at Lisbon, c.1215, the son of a doctor, elected 8 September 1276, died Viterbo, 20 May 1277. Pedro, known in scholarly circles as 'Peter of Spain', had studied in Paris and taught medicine at Siena. He became dean of Lisbon and archdeacon of Braga, but became personal physician to Pope **Gregory X**, who created him a cardinal. As Pope, he made it clear that he was going to continue his scholarly pursuits, which had included a widely used textbook on logic, *Summulae logicales*, a treatise on the soul, and another on the eye, and a manual of popular medicine, *The Poor Man's Treasury*. He retired to his study in the palace at Viterbo, and for the most part left it to others to run the Church. He was, however, concerned to broker peace in Europe so that the monarchs might be ready for a Crusade, and attempted an agreement with the Tartars to make common cause against the Muslims. The Byzantine emperor Michael VIII Palaeologus, afraid that a further attempt might be made by the Latins to retake Constantinople, made his submission to Rome, along with the Patriarch **John XI** Beccus, but this had no lasting effect on relations between the two Churches. Pope John died when the roof of his new study fell upon him.

John XXII Pope, born 'Jacques Duèse' at Cahors, c.1244, elected 7 August 1316, died Avignon, 4 December 1334. He had studied law at Montpellier, became bishop of Fréjus in 1300, chancellor successively to Charles II of France and Robert of Naples, bishop of Avignon, 1310, and a cardinal in

1312. Although old at his election, over two years after the death of his predecessor **Clement V**, he was an experienced administrator, and his reform of the papal finances greatly improved its income. He also increased papal control over the appointment of bishops. In 1317 he published the *Extravagantes*, a collection of canon law which became standard. He clashed with the Franciscans, under their minister general **Michael of Cesena**, over the radical claim that they should own nothing at all because Christ and the apostles owned nothing. This declaration he declared to be heretical. The majority of the Franciscans submitted, but Michael of Cesena and **William of Ockham** did not, taking refuge with the Pope's adversary **Louis** of Bavaria. In his bull *Quia vir reprobus* the Pope declared that the right to own property predated the Fall, and therefore was not a consequence of sin. The conflict with Louis was over the succession to the Empire, contested by Louis and Frederick the Fair of Austria. Louis, who was also backed by **Marsilius of Padua**, supported those hostile to John in Italy, and was excommunicated. Louis then marched on Rome, and had himself crowned, installing an Antipope. This attempt to browbeat John did not, however, last long, and the Antipope submitted to John. John himself, however, ran into theological difficulties over the beatific vision, arguing in a series of sermons that the dead would not enjoy the beatific vision until after the Last Judgement – a view he to some extent retracted on his own deathbed. John established bishoprics in the Near East and in India, and started the university at Cahors.

John XXIII Antipope (though this is questionable), born 'Baldassare Cossa' at Naples, elected 17 May 1410, resigned 29 May 1415, died Florence, 22 November 1419. Born into a noble family, Baldassare was a sailor before studying law at Bologna and becoming archdeacon of Bologna and papal treasurer. In 1402 he became a cardinal and was sent as legate to the Romagna and Bologna. His profligacy was legendary, at least before his election during the Great Schism by the cardinals of the Pisan faction (or 'obedience'). He had wide support, both politically and militarily, and conformed to the decisions of the Council of Pisa at least to the extent of calling a reform council to meet in Rome, where, given military support, he had been able to establish himself. This council condemned the writings of John **Wycliffe** and excommunicated John **Huss**. His support began to melt away, however. He had to flee from Rome to Florence, and seek the aid of the Emperor Sigismund. Sigismund wanted a council to decide between the three claimants, and John had to agree to call one at Constance. There all three claimants were called upon to abdicate. John agreed to do so, but then fled the city. He was brought back and, after accusations of gross misconduct and of simony, he resigned. He was imprisoned in Germany, but released in 1419, when he made his way to Florence, submitted to **Martin V**, and shortly afterwards died.

John XXIII Pope, Angelo Giuseppe Roncalli, born into a peasant family at Sotto il Monte near Bergamo, 25 November 1881, elected 28 October 1958, died 3 June 1963. He attended the village school, the seminary in Bergamo, and the S. Apollinare Institute in Rome, where he gained a doctorate in theology in 1904. He became secretary to the reforming bishop Radini-Tadeschi of Bergamo, and served in the army in the First World War. His researches in the Ambrosian Library in Milan for his work on Charles **Borromeo** brought him into contact with the future **Pius XI**, then the librarian of the Ambrosianum, who sent him, with the title of archbishop, on diplomatic missions to Bulgaria in 1924 and Turkey and Greece in 1934. He was sent as papal nuncio to France in 1944. He became cardinal in 1953, and the same year was made patriarch of Venice. When elected Pope, his pontificate was expected to be a stop-gap, but in calling the Second Vatican Council to meet in 1961 he decisively influenced the nature of Roman Catholicism. His major concern throughout his pontificate, and the direction he set for the Council, was pastoral rather than dogmatic. He became personally very popular, and was able to open channels of communication between the Roman Catholic Church and the Soviet bloc, making way for his successor **Paul VI**'s 'Ostpolitik'. He promoted dialogue between Catholicism and other Christian denominations, and with the Jews.

John and Paul Saints and martyrs, died *c.*361. John and Paul were martyred in Rome during the reign of Julian the Apostate, 361–3; their legend, which is not historically reliable, claims that they were eunuchs of Constantina, daughter of **Constantine I** (the Great); that they were converted, then beheaded secretly by the emperor's command and buried in their house on the Caelian Hill. This house was built into a Christian basilica in the second half of the fourth century by the senator Byzantius and his son **Pammachius**, and is still one of the most important memorials of early Christianity in Rome. Feast day 26 June.

John Baconthorpe Carmelite theologian, born Baconsthorpe, Norfolk, *c.*1290, died London, *c.*1346. A grand-nephew of Roger **Bacon**, brought up in a Carmelite monastery, possibly that of Blakeney, near Walsingham in Norfolk, he studied at Oxford, graduated at Paris and *c.*1321 returned to preach at Oxford, like **Wycliffe** later, that priestly power was subordinate to the kingly. He seems also, and rather oddly, to have been an opponent of the privileges of the mendicant orders in the universities. He was the English provincial of the Carmelites from 1329 to 1333, when he appears to have been dismissed, perhaps for granting the Papacy too much authority in the annulment of marriages. He was summoned to Rome in 1333, and he taught there, while continuing to play an important role in the governance of the Carmelites. He seems to have opposed Pope **John XXII** over the issue of the beatific vision. He was back in England by 1346. His writings are said to number some 120 works, and include commentaries on the Bible and on Aristotle's works. He was particularly expert in the philosophy of Averroes. He was given the title of 'the Resolute Doctor'.

John Baptiste de la Salle *see* La Salle, John Baptiste de

John Baptist of the Conception Blessed, Trinitarian reformer, writer and mystic, born Almadovar del Campo, Spain, 10 July 1561, died Córdoba, Spain, 14 February 1613. He studied philosophy at Almadovar and theology at Baeza and Toledo. In 1580 he entered the Trinitarian Order and was admired for his virtue, mortification and prayerfulness. He was professed in 1581 and was made official preacher at La Guardia and Seville. In 1594 he was made superior at Valdepenas. He was a prolific writer on theology and mysticism. At Valdepenas he reformed (though he said *restored*) the Order by adding the use of sandals and other austerities to the Rule. He established nineteen houses of the Discalced Friars. Today these Discalced Trinitarians form the surviving branch of the Trinitarian Friars as founded by **John of Matha** and **Felix of Valois** in 1198.

John Bassandus Blessed, religious, reformer and diplomat, born Besançon, France, 1360, died Collemaggio, 26 August 1445. In 1378 he entered the Augustinian monastery in Besançon and in 1390 the Celestines in Paris. He was later sent to found a monastery in Amiens, where he became the director of St-Collette. Between the years 1411 and 1441 he was prior in Paris, and provincial of France five times. During this period he travelled extensively. He was sent by **Charles VII** of France on a diplomatic mission to try to persuade the Antipope **Felix V** to resign his claim to the Papacy. This mission was unsuccessful. In 1443 he was called upon by Pope **Eugenius IV** to reform the monastery at Collemaggio.

John Beleth Liturgical scholar, born probably in England, died France(?), *c*.1182. He was perhaps the rector of a theological school in Paris, where he was known for his sermons, but is most important for his *Rationale divinorum officiorum*, which is almost the sole means of knowing about the twelfth-century liturgy.

John Benincasa Blessed, Servite hermit, born Florence, Italy, 1376, died Monticelli, 9 May 1426. At a very young age he entered the Servite house at Montepulciano, and became a hermit on Mount Montagnata, near Siena, at the age of 25. He was a rigorous ascetic, and was often sought out by the locals for spiritual advice. It is said that his death was announced by the spontaneous ringing of the local church bells.

John Berchmans Saint, born Diest (Belgium), the son of a shoemaker, 13 March 1599, died Rome, 13 August 1621. Amid the religious controversy in The Netherlands, he was educated in Diest by Premonstratensians, then at the seminary in Malines as a servant to one of the cathedral canons, and finally, in 1615, at the newly opened Jesuit college in Malines. Influenced by news of Jesuit martyrs, he became a novice at Malines, during which time his mother died and his father was ordained and became a canon of Malines. In 1618 he went (on foot) to study philosophy in Rome. Feast day 26 November.

John Bosco Saint, priest, founder of the Salesian Order, born near Turin, 1815, died Turin, 31 January 1888. Experienced religious visions from about the age of nine, and dedicated his life to the care, education and training of vulnerable boys and young men. Entered the seminary in 1831 and went on to further theological studies in Turin. Beginning with combined Sunday schools and re-creation activities for boys, he went on to set up evening classes and eventually, with his mother as housekeeper, took some homeless boys into their home. Later he set up hostels where, in addition to receiving food, shelter, education and spiritual guidance, they could learn a trade. A positive and encouraging, rather than punitive, approach was taken in matters of discipline. In 1859 Don Bosco established the Pious Society of St Francis de Sales to continue and develop all the aspects of his work, which in 1872 was extended to girls and young women. By the time of his death there were about 750 Salesians in over 60 houses in Europe and in North and South America. Feast day 31 January.

John Buridan Philosopher, born possibly Bethune, *c*.1300, died St-André-des-Arcs, near Arras, *c*.1370. After visiting the papal curia at Avignon, he taught for the rest of his life at the University of Paris, becoming its rector in 1328. In 1342 Pope **Clement VI** made him a canon of Arras Church, and in 1348 the bishop of Paris made him chaplain of St-André-des-Arcs Church; and in 1358 he established peace between Picardy and England, probably dying soon afterwards. His commentaries displayed his philosophy, especially important for his theories about the motion of the spheres and falling bodies. In that respect he was a precursor of **Leonardo da Vinci**, **Copernicus** and **Galileo**, though most famous for 'Buridan's Ass', the argument that an ass, placed equidistant from two equally attractive bales of hay, would die of starvation because unable to choose.

John Calderini Canon lawyer, born Bologna, *c*.1299, died there, 1365. The son of a leading family of the city, he studied canon law under **Johannes Andreae** at the University of Bologna. He became a doctor of canon law *c.*1325 and taught the subject from 1330 to 1359. He undertook many diplomatic missions for Bologna, going in 1360 to ask Pope **Innocent VI** to accept the governance of the city, and in 1362 to Avignon to congratulate Pope **Urban V** on his election. His works include the selection of his *Concilia* published at Rome in 1472.

John Camillus Bonus of Milan   Saint, bishop, died 660. John Bonus was bishop of Milan; he was also called 'John the Good', owing to his good works. He participated in the Lateran Council of 649, and was a vigorous opponent of the Monothelites. Feast day 10 January.

John Canonicus   Spanish Scotist, probably a Catalan named 'Juan Marbres', a canon of Tortosa Cathedral and master of arts of Toulouse, died 1250. He wrote *Quaestiones super Physicorum Aristoteles*, a defence of the ideas of **Duns Scotus**, which was very influential during the later Middle Ages.

John Cantius   Saint, Polish priest and theologian, born Kenty, near Oswiecim, Poland, 1390, died Cracow, 24 December 1473. Studied philosophy and theology at the Academy of Cracow, was ordained priest and became professor of theology at Cracow. He worked in a parish for a time but returned to Cracow as professor of sacred Scripture and remained in this post until his death. Feast day 23 December.

John Capistran   Saint, Franciscan, born Capistrano, Italy, 1386, died Villach, 23 October 1456. He studied in Perugia and became governor there in 1412. He married but the marriage was never consummated and when John decided some time later to join the Franciscans, which he did in 1416, the marriage was annulled. He went with **Bernardine of Siena** on his preaching tours and undertook some preaching himself. He was ordained in 1420 and became a preacher renowned throughout Italy. He also helped in the Franciscan reforms and was sent several times as ambassador for the Holy See to France and Austria. He travelled through Europe preaching against the Hussites. In 1454 he

was at the Diet of Frankfurt and accompanied Hunyady throughout the campaign against the Turks. He wrote mainly against the heresies of his day.

John Chrysostom   Saint, and bishop of Constantinople, probably the greatest preacher of the early Church, born Syrian Antioch, between 344 and 354, died in exile in the small town of Comana (Pontus, today in Turkey), 14 September 407. After an outstanding education he turned his back on a worldly career and had himself baptized. He became a lector and studied exegesis with Theodore of Tarsus. Then he retired to the mountains near Antioch to live a severely ascetic life. However, his health suffered too much and after six years he returned to the city, in 378. In 381 he became a deacon, in 386 a presbyter. In 398 he was more or less coerced to become bishop of Constantinople. Chrysostom did not succeed in establishing good relations with the imperial court. Because of his attempts to reform the clergy of Constantinople and the enmity of Theophilus of Alexandria, he was twice exiled. He died during the second term of exile. Among his writings, his homilies particularly stand out. Most of them are exegetical or theological, while always betraying a genuine concern for the less privileged. Feast day 13 September in the Roman calendar, 13 November in the Orthodox one.

John Chrysostom of Saint-Lô   Franciscan spiritual director and writer, born Saint-Frémond, near Bayeux, France, 1594, died Paris, 26 March 1646. He entered the Third Order Regular of St Francis at sixteen, by 1634 he was provincial of the province of France and in 1640 provincial of the province of Saint-Yves. He was the confessor of Marie de Médicis and Anne of Austria. He had great influence as a spiritual director, and his surviving works include *Exercises de piété et de perfection* (Caen, 1654).

John Climacus (Scholasticus)   Monk, abbot, born before 579, died *c.*649. John was a monk at Sinai, first in a community, then as a solitary. At the age of 60 he was elected abbot of the monastery of Sinai. His major work is the *Ladder of Divine Ascent*. He was asked to write this work by John, the superior of the monastery of Raithu. In 30 steps or chapters John Climacus explains the devices dangerous to monks, and the virtues that distinguish them. However, the editions of the work are many, and as yet there is no single critical edition available.

John Colombini Blessed, founder of the Congregation of Jesuati, born Siena, Italy, c.1300, died en route to Aquapendente, 31 July 1367. He was a rich and influential businessman who gradually left behind materialism and sought the spiritual life and service to the poor and sick. With the eventual acquiescence of his wife he began a life of apostolic poverty. He attracted many young men to join him, and the families of the richer and more influential among them caused him to be banished from Siena. He and a group of followers traversed Tuscany preaching and serving the poor and on their return to Siena were welcomed and honoured. They were eventually approved by **Urban V**, a week before Colombini died. Their main apostolate was the care of the sick, especially those with the plague, and the burial of the dead. They also led a life of prayer and mortification. Abuses crept into the Congregation and it was suppressed in 1668. Feast day 31 July.

John da Pian del Carpine (John of Plano Carpine) Franciscan explorer, born probably Piano della Maggiane (formerly Pian di Carpini), near Perugia, c.1180, died probably in Italy, 1 August 1252. An early companion of St **Francis**, he was a Franciscan warden in Saxony in 1222 and provincial of Germany in 1228. In April 1245 he was sent on a mission by Pope **Innocent IV** to the Mongols, where he attended the Great Khan's enthronement. On his return he was made archbishop of Bar (Antivari). His *Istoria Mongalorum quos non Tartoros* was the first detailed European report on the Mongols and one of the best sources for information about them in the thirteenth century.

John Damascene Saint, theologian, born into an influential family in Damascus, c.650, died Mar Saba monastery, near Jerusalem, before 754. After a career at the caliph's court, he retired c.725, when Christians were excluded from government offices, to the monastery of St Sabas, near Jerusalem. Later he received priestly ordination. In the Iconoclast controversy he defended the veneration of images. His most important work is the *Source of Knowledge*, a kind of systematic theological compendium (including a catalogue of heresies). He also wrote moral, ascetic and homiletic works. Feast day 4 December.

John de *see also* **John of**

John de Britto Blessed, Jesuit missionary, born Lisbon, Portugal, 1 March 1647, died, by beheading, Oreiour, India, 11 February 1693. He was brought up at court and joined the Jesuits in 1662. He was sent to Madura in Southern India and was in Goa in 1673. He did the 30-day 'Spiritual Exercises' in Ambalacarte, near Crangamore, joined a noble caste and learned the languages of India before proceeding to Madras and Vellore. He was imprisoned in 1684 and then expelled but returned to India in 1691. Two years later he was executed following his attempts to get the newly converted Teriadevan to dismiss all but one of his wives.

John de Deo Canon lawyer, born Silves, Portugal, c.1199, died Lisbon, 15 March 1267. A professor at the University of Bologna, he wrote many treatises on decretists and decretalists which, though not particularly original, are useful for the indication he gives of his sources. He was appointed a judge several times by Popes **Innocent IV** and **Alexander IV**. Returning to Portugal, he was archdeacon of Santarem in Lisbon in 1260 and was a judge and arbiter in lawsuits there.

John de Fantutiis Canon lawyer, born Bologna, died there, 26 May 1391. He taught canon law at Bologna and acted in a legal capacity for the city. His works include an incomplete commentary on *Decretum Gratiani* and *Lectura super Clementem*.

John de Feckenham Benedictine abbot, born Feckenham, Worcestershire, c.1512, died Wisbech Castle, Cambridgeshire, c.October 1584. He was sent from the Benedictine abbey of Evesham to Gloucester Hall, Oxford, where he graduated as a bachelor of divinity in 1539. After the dissolution of the monasteries, he was from 1540 successively chaplain to Bishops Bell and **Bonner**. Upon Queen **Mary**'s accession he was made dean of St Paul's Cathedral, London, in 1554 and mitred abbot of the refounded Westminster Abbey. Queen **Elizabeth I** deposed him and sent him to the Tower of London 'for railing against the changes that had been made' in 1560, and in 1577 he was committed to the charge of Richard Cox, bishop of Ely.

John de Grey (Gray) Bishop, born Norfolk, died St Jean d'Audely, near Poitiers, 18 October 1214. Bishop of Norwich from 1200 to 1214, he was elected through King John's influence to the See of Canterbury in 1205, but Pope **Innocent III** annulled this in Stephen **Langton**'s favour. Having lent money to John, he was placed by **Matthew Paris** among the king's evil counsellors, and he was excluded from the general absolution of 1213. As justiciar of Ireland from 1210 he remodelled the coinage on the English pattern. While bishop-elect of Durham, he died when returning from Rome.

John de Grocheo Musician, lived in Paris at the end of the thirteenth century, died *c*.1310. His treatise *Musica* (*c*.1300) has full information about contemporary music, and since reference is also made to his own sermons, he was probably a priest.

John de Lignano Canon lawyer, born Milan *c*.1320, died 16 February 1383. He studied at Bologna and by 1350 was a doctor. After defending the Church in the disputes between the Papacy and Bologna from about 1350, he secured peace in 1377 and became the Pope's first vicar general at Bologna, which rewarded him with an honorary citizenship. During the Western Schism he supported **Urban VI**'s election. His most important works were *De bello* and *De pace* about the problems of war and peace.

John de Muris Musician, born France, *c*.1300, died *c*.1351. A philosopher and mathematician also, he was prominent in calendar reform under **Clement VI** at Avignon. His *Ars novae musicae* (1319) influenced the development of liturgical music in the later Middle Ages.

John de Offord (Ufford) Bishop, died of the plague at Tottenham, 20 May 1349. He was probably educated at Cambridge University, of which he became a doctor of civil law in 1334. He was Dean of the Arches in 1328, archdeacon of Ely in 1335, Keeper of the Privy Seal in 1342, dean of Lincoln in 1344 and Lord Chancellor of England from 1345 to 1349. From 1328 he was much employed by King **Edward III** in negotiations with European courts and with the Papacy. He was made archbishop-elect of Canterbury in 1348, but died before he could be consecrated.

John de Ponteys Bishop and diplomat, born Diocese of York, died Wolvesey, 4 December 1304. His family probably came from Pontoise, France. Pastor of Welwick, Yorkshire, in 1264 and rector of Tavistock, Devon, in 1275, he became a papal chaplain and legal adviser to Archbishop John **Peckham** at the papal curia in 1281. He became bishop of Winchester in 1282, he was Edward I of England's envoy to Paris and Gascony in 1283–5 and served the king of France at the Curia in 1297–1301. Though often abroad, the register of his visitations shows that he did not neglect his diocese.

John de Ridevall Franciscan philosopher, died *c*.1345. Also known as 'John of Musca'. A doctor of theology in about 1331, he was lector of the Franciscans' Oxford house from 1331 to 1332. A number of theological and philosophical works are attributed to him, including commentaries on Ovid's *Metamorphoses* and **Augustine**'s *De Civitate Dei*. Like **John of Wales** (d. 1???), he presented classical mythology as a moralizing subject-matter for the use of preachers.

John de Rupella *see* **John of La Rochelle**

John de Sacobosco Mathematician and astronomer, died Paris, *c*.1250. ('Sacrobosco' is probably derived from Holywood or Halifax in England.) He probably taught at the University of Paris. His main works were *Agorismus* (arithmetic), the *Sphere*, and *De anni ratione* (ecclesiastical computation), which preserve existing knowledge of the subjects rather than display original scientific method. It is his short *Tractatus de sphaera*, a study of the globe and other astronomical matters, which brought him fame. The book was extremely popular despite its many errors, and appeared in many editions.

John de Saint-Pol (St Paul)   Archbishop of Dublin, born Owston, Yorkshire, *c.*1295, died Dublin, 9 September 1362. He was a clerk in Chancery before 1318, joint guardian of the Great Seal and Master of the Rolls in 1334, and prebendary of Chichester in 1336. In 1340 **Edward III** imprisoned him for corruption, but he was released in 1343 and restored to the Chancery. Appointed archbishop of Dublin in 1349, he became also Chancellor of Ireland in 1350–6 and a privy councillor in 1358. He enlarged Holy Trinity Cathedral (now called Christ Church), Dublin.

John de Seccheville (Sicheville, Sicenvilla, Sackville)   Philosopher and diplomat, died *c.*1290. Called also 'John de Driton'. He was educated possibly at Oxford and at Paris University, which sent him on a delegation to Rome. In 1258 during the Barons' War he returned to England to be secretary to the duke of Gloucester and in 1259 mediated between Henry III of England and **Louis IX** of France in their peace negotiations. He wrote in Paris in about 1263 his chief work, *De Principiis naturae*, favouring the Averroistic outlook.

John Discalceatus   Blessed, born Saint-Voregay, Brittany, *c.*1280, died Quimper, 15 December 1349. Becoming a Franciscan friar in 1316, he went barefoot for over thirteen years and was devoted to charitable deeds, even giving away his clothes. He died of a plague. Many miracles led him to be popularly held a saint and commemorated in the Franciscan Order, but this never attained ecclesiastical approval. Feast day 15 December.

John Faventius   Canon lawyer, born Faenza, Italy, died there, 1187. He was a student and professor at Bologna until *c.*1174 when he returned to Faenza. His main work was a *Summa* on the *Decretum* of **Gratian**, which extended the knowledge of the teaching of the early decretists.

John Garsias   Canon lawyer, born Spain, died Bologna, 1290. He was a canon of the cathedral of St James of (Santiago de) Compostella and taught at Bologna from *c.*1277. In 1280 his students persuaded him to begin his commentary on **Gratian**. He was the first professor to be paid by public authorities. Most of his writings remain unpublished.

John Gilbert   Dominican friar, bishop and diplomat, died London, 28 July 1397. He was bishop of Bangor, 1372–5, Hereford, 1375–89, and St Davids, 1389–97, and treasurer of England, 1386 to May 1389 and August 1389 to 1391. In 1385 he went on an embassy to King Charles VI of France to negotiate a peace, but was only partly successful; and in 1384 he founded the Cathedral Grammar School at Hereford. Thomas **Walsingham** described him as more eloquent than trustworthy, but he had the general reputation of being efficient and conscientious.

John Grandison (Grandisson)   Bishop, born Ashperton, Herefordshire, *c.*1292, died Chudleigh, Devon, 16 July 1369. He was a prebendary of York in 1309 and of Lincoln in 1317, archdeacon of Nottingham in 1310 and chaplain to Pope **John XXII** and papal legate in 1327. Appointed bishop of Exeter by provision and consecrated at Avignon in 1327, he completed the nave of his cathedral and erected the episcopal throne.

John Gualbert   Saint, abbot and founder of the Vallumbrosans, born Florence, Italy, *c.*995, died Passignano, Italy, 12 July 1073. Soon after the murderer of one of his kinsmen asked for his forgiveness on Good Friday, John became a Benedictine monk at S. Miniato in Florence. He went to Camaldoli in search of a more ascetic way of life at some time before St **Romuald of Ravenna**'s death in 1027, but around 1030 he left Camaldoli to lead an eremitic life at Vallombrosa. The monastery he founded at Vallombrosa in 1038 incorporated *conversi* to perform manual labour. Feast day 12 July.

John Italus   Philosopher, born Southern Italy, *c.*1025, died after 1082. He was an influential teacher at the University of Constantinople from 1055, and his writings included commentaries on Plato and on Aristotle's logic, but his popularity was resented by the Byzantine clergy. Being twice condemned by a synod at Constantinople in 1082, he was banished to a monastery, and his works were publicly burned.

John Joseph of the Cross   Saint, Franciscan, born on the Island of Ischia, Southern Italy, 15 August 1654, died Santa Lucia del Monte, Naples, 5 March

1734. He joined the Franciscans of the Alcantarine Reform in Naples in 1670 and lived a life of great austerity. In 1674 he founded a monastery in Piedmont di Alife, himself assisting in its construction. He was ordained in 1677 and became novice master in Naples, then the superior of the monastery in Piedmont, and in 1702 was made vicar provincial of the Alcantarine Reform in Italy. Even during his own lifetime he had a great reputation for miracle-working.

John Klenkok Canon lawyer, born Buken, Hanover, died Avignon, 17 June 1374. He was a doctor *utrisque iuris* probably of the university at Bologna before joining the Augustinians at Herford, becoming their provincial of Saxony in 1363 and 1367–8 and a professor at Prague in 1370. In his treatise *Decadecon* he criticized the civil law of Eastern Germany and was condemned by the Inquisition amid a popular outcry.

John Kochurov Russian Orthodox saint, priest and martyr, born Riazan, 13 June 1871, died (martyred) Tsarskoye Selo, December 1917. He served the Orthodox immigrants in Chicago, where he built a cathedral and did much to help the Uniates (Greek Catholics) to return to Orthodoxy. He was loved and accepted by many different ethnic groups. In 1907 he returned to Russia and was appointed to a church in Tsarskoye Selo near St Petersburg. Here he became the first clergyman to suffer in the Revolution. According to most accounts he was dragged over the railway tracks by Bolshevik sailors until he died. The recently restored church of St Sofia in Tsarskoye Selo contains his icon and was paid for by the Orthodox of Chicago. Feast day 8 December.

John Kynyngham (Cunningham) Theologian, born Suffolk, died York, 12 May 1399. Joining the Carmelites at Ipswich, he studied at Oxford and was provincial of his Order from 1393 until his death, being among John of Gaunt's Carmelite confessors. He vigorously opposed **Wycliffe** and was a member of the synod at Blackfriars in 1382 which condemned Wycliffe's writings.

John Lapus Castilioneus Canon lawyer, born Florence, Italy, died 27 June 1381. He studied under **John Calderini** and **John de Lignano** at Bologna,

becoming a doctor in 1355. He was professor of law at Florence from 1378, when he headed the Guelph party governing the city and went on missions to **Gregory XI** and **Urban VI**. Being accused of wishing Florence to be under papal temporal power, he fled for his life from the city, but Charles of Durazzo made him professor of law at Padua and, on becoming king, appointed him his personal representative to the Pope. Among his writings, the *Tractatus hospitalitatis* was the first study of the privileges and juridic significance of works of charity.

John Lathbury (Lathbery) Franciscan theologian, born possibly at Lathbury, Buckinghamshire, died Reading, 1362. Ordained in 1329, he was by 1343 a Franciscan at Oxford, where he was after 1350 a doctor of divinity and apparently regent master. Famous as a theologian throughout the later Middle Ages, his best-known work, *Commentary on Lamentations*, was one of the earliest books issued by the University Press, being printed at Oxford in 1482.

John le Blund (Blunt) Divine, born 1180, died 1248. Educated at Oxford and Paris, he returned to Oxford as a teacher *c.*1229, where he collaborated with **Edmund of Abingdon** in the introduction of Aristotelian philosophy. He was a canon of Chichester and chancellor of York. He was nominated archbishop of Canterbury by Peter des Roches, bishop of Winchester, and elected in 1232, but when the Pope refused his assent, the election was annulled.

John le Moine Cardinal, canon lawyer, born Crécy-en-Ponthieu, 1250, died Avignon, 1315. He studied theology and philosophy at Paris, becoming a doctor both in canon and in civil law. He was dean of the church of Bayeux from 1288 to 1292, was made a cardinal by Pope **Celestine V** and cardinal and vice-chancellor of the Roman Church by Pope **Boniface VIII**. Best known for his *Apparatus* of 1301 on the *Liber Sextus* of Boniface VIII (1298), which went into many editions, he developed an important basis for the constitution and rights of the college of cardinals.

John Le Romeyn (Romanus) (the Younger) Divine, son of John Le Romeyn the Elder, born *c.*1230, died Bishop Burton, near Beverley, Yorkshire, 11 March 1296. Educated at Oxford, he became prebendary of Lincoln in 1258, chancellor of Lincoln in 1275, professor of theology at Paris in 1276, prebendary of York in 1279 and archbishop of York in 1285. He was engaged in a dispute with Anthony **Bek** concerning the relations of the See of Durham to that of York. He rebuilt the nave of York Minster, built the chapter houses at York and Southwell and extended the choir of Ripon Cathedral.

John Lobedau Blessed, Franciscan, born Torun, Pomerania, c.1231, died Chelmo, Poland, 9 October 1264. He became a Franciscan at Torun and was then sent to Chelmo. Pious, learned and devout, on account of miracles reputedly performed through his intercession he became the patron of sailors and fishermen. His cult was approved in Poland on 31 October 1638. Feast day 9 October.

John Lutterell Philosopher, theologian and mathematician, died Avignon, 17 July 1335. In 1317 he became a doctor of divinity and chancellor of the University of Oxford. He represented the University in its dispute with the Dominicans, who claimed that they need not have an arts degree before proceeding to a doctorate of divinity, but he resigned as chancellor in 1322 after a conflict with the scholars and masters of the University. He then lived at Avignon until 1329. He was a prebendary of Salisbury in 1319 and of York in 1334. He returned to Avignon in 1334, but died there the following year. He wrote a number of works, including one against the nominalism of **William of Ockham**, and two on the beatific vision.

John Malalas Byzantine chronicler, died c.577. The name 'Malalas' is Syriac in origin and is equivalent to 'the Rhetor'. Nothing is known of John's life. His work, which exists in Greek, includes a 'Chronology' or 'Universal History', in seventeen books, in a Monophysite vein. An eighteenth book is more orthodox. The surviving text goes up to 563, and influenced similar compositions, both Eastern and Western.

John Morosini Blesssed, founder of S. Giorgio,

Venice. Born Venice, and died there 1012. A kinsman of **Peter Orseolo**, the Venetian doge and hermit who resigned to enter the religious life, he accompanied **Romuald of Ravenna** to Cuxa in 978, and led a coenobitic life there. Unlike his companions Romuald of Ravenna, Peter Orseolo, and John Grandenigo, he did not become a hermit, and eventually returned to Venice, where he founded the monastery of S. Giorgio. Feast day 5 February.

John of *see also* **John de**

John of Acton Canon lawyer, died November 1349. He became a doctor of canon law at Oxford about 1311 and at Cambridge about 1330. He was a canon of Lincoln in 1329, rector of Willingham by Stow, Lincolnshire, in 1330, an official of the court of York in 1335 and prebendary of Welton Rivall in about 1343. He is chiefly known for his commentaries on the ecclesiastical constitutions of Otho and Ottobone.

John of Antioch Bishop, died 441. Details of his early life are unknown. He became bishop of Antioch in 429, and was a friend of **Nestorius**, to whom he gave active support during the latter's dispute with **Cyril of Alexandria**. John is regarded as the leader of the moderate Easterners in the Nestorian controversy. He was late in arriving at the Council of Ephesus (431) and proceedings against Nestorius began in his absence. Upon his arrival John held a counter-council which condemned Cyril and vindicated Nestorius. Cyril and John were eventually reconciled in 433 on the basis of a compromise theological formula, which caused anxiety in the patriarchate of Antioch and lost John many supporters.

John of Appleby Church lawyer, probably born Appleby, Cumbria, date unknown, died between 24 September and 1 October 1389. He studied civil law and received a doctorate, probably from Oxford, at some time before 1359. He worked as a lawyer until 1361, when the convent of Durham retained him as an adviser. This was a position that he held until his death. Between 1365 and 1389 he was dean of St Paul's, London, and was present at the condemnation of the doctrines of John **Wycliffe** at the Blackfriar's Synod in 1382. In

1372 he was used on diplomatic missions by King **Edward III**. In his will he remembered the church of Appleby and the poor of the parish.

John of Ávila Blessed, Spanish mystic, born near Toledo, 1500, died 1569. He studied law, 1514–15, before devoting himself to a life of austerity and prayer. He later studied philosophy under Domingo de **Soto** at Alcalá. Upon the death of his parents he sold all of his property, was ordained priest in 1525 and was prepared for missionary work in Mexico. He was dissuaded from this path by the archbishop of Seville, who encouraged him to revive the faith in Andalusia. John became one of the most effective preachers of his age, although he was summoned before the Inquisition for preaching of the dangers of wealth. He was subsequently acquitted. After a nine-year ministry in Andalusia, John returned to Seville. He later visited many other Spanish towns, despite being in great physical pain for the last seventeen years of his life. He was a friend of St **Teresa of Ávila**, and was responsible for the conversion of St **Francis Borgia** and St **John of God**. He was beatified in 1894.

John of Bastone Blessed, Sylvestrine monk, born early thirteenth century, died Fabriano, Italy, 24 March 1290. He taught grammar at Fabriano. He later became a priest, and was resident as a Sylvestrine Benedictine in the monastery of Monte Fano for 60 years.

John of Beverley Saint, bishop of York, born Harpham, Humberside, died 7 May 721. He studied at Canterbury under St **Hadrian**. Became a monk at **Hilda**'s monastery in Whitby. Succeeded Eata as bishop of Hexham in 687, where he was renowned as a man of piety who cared for the poor and the handicapped. Ordained **Bede** both deacon and priest. Succeeded Bosa as bishop of York in 705. Founded the monastery of Beverley and retired there in 717. In 1307 his relics were translated – Henry V ascribed his victory at Agincourt, on the feast day of the translation, to John's intercession. Feast days 7 May (death), 25 October (translation).

John of Biclaro Abbot and historian, born into the Catholic Visigothic nobility at Scallibis, Lusitania (Portugal), c.540, died Gerona(?), c.622. He studied for sixteen years in Constantinople then returned to Spain, where his faith led to his exile to Arian Barcelona. Upon the death of Leo Vigild in 586, he founded the monastery of Biclaro (location unknown). As its abbot, he wrote its Rule, which is not now extant, but his chronicle (567–90) describes from personal experience Spanish, Visigothic, Byzantine, Lombard and North African history during that period.

John of Bridlington Saint, prior of St Augustine's, Bridlington, born Thwing, near Bridlington, died 1379. He studied at Oxford. Became canon at St Augustine's and eventually prior, 1362. He was greatly loved, and regarded as a man of deep piety alongside a great ability as an administrator, exercising the duties of his office with considerable success. He was canonized by **Boniface IX** in 1401. There is a fifteenth-century stained glass window of him in Morley, Derbyshire. Feast day 21 October.

John of Caramola Blessed, Cistercian monk and ascetic, born Toulouse, date unknown, died Sagittario, 26 August 1339. He was for many years a hermit on Mount Caramola in Italy, living a life of great austerity. He was reputedly given the gift of prophecy. Owing to illness, he gave up the life of a hermit and became a lay brother at the Cistercian monastery of Santa Maria of Sagittario at Chiaramonte. He continued to live an austere life, feeding upon a little bread and water. It is said that his bed was so small that it was impossible to lie down in a normal position. After his death many miracles were attributed to his intercession.

John of Châtillon Saint, abbot and bishop, born Châtillon, Brittany, c.1098, died 1 February 1163. He is also known as 'John de Craticula' (of the grate), owing to the iron grating around his tomb. He became bishop of Aleth and transferred the see to the Isle of Aaron, which he renamed 'Saint-Malo'. He was also abbot of the Saint-Croix monastery of the Canons Regular of St Augustine at Guingamp. While bishop, he was involved in lengthy litigation when he tried to replace monks from Marmoutier with the canons regular in his cathedral.

John of Cornwall Theologian, born probably at St

Germans (he is sometimes referred to as 'de Sancto Germano'), Cornwall, *c*.1125, died *c*.1199. He went to France to study under **Peter Lombard** and **Robert of Melun** in Paris, returning to England *c*.1163. He appears then to have taught theology and canon law at Oxford. He became archdeacon of Worcester, and it seems was twice put forward as archbishop of St Davids. The only work which can be ascribed to him with certainty is the *Eulogium ad Alexandrum III*, a work which has led some to think he knew Pope **Alexander III** personally, which in turn may have meant he studied in Italy. The *Eulogium* is an attack on the Christological doctrine of Peter **Abelard**.

John of Damascus   *see* **John Damascene**

John of Dukla   Blessed, patron of Poland and Lithuania, born Dukla, Poland, 1414, died Lvov, 1484. He became a Franciscan conventual, and was guardian at Krosno and Lvov, and then custos. A model of charity and virtue, he became blind in later years, though he continued to minister, preach and hear confessions. His tomb is in the church of the Bernardines at Lvov, where many miracles have been reported.

John of Dumbleton   Philosopher, born presumably in Dumbleton, Gloucestershire, died *c*.1349. A fellow of Merton College, Oxford, in 1338–9 and of Queen's College, Oxford, from 1340 to *c*.1348, he is supposed to have died of a plague. In September 1332 he was presented to a living near Henley, but resigned it two years later, and is thought to have remained at Oxford for the rest of his life. His chief work was the *Summa logicae et philosophiae naturalis*, which prepared the way for later mathematical surveys.

John of Egypt   Saint, hermit, born Lycopolis, Egypt, *c*.300, died 394. A carpenter by profession, he joined a monastery at an early age and later became a hermit in a cave on Mount Lykos. Here he remained for the rest of his life, living a life of great austerity. He was widely sought out for spiritual advice, communicating only through a small window. Reputed to have the gift of prophecy, he was known as 'the Seer'. According to tradition he foretold the victories of the Emperor

Theodosius I over Maximus and Eugenius, as well as the death of Theodosius in 395.

John of Ephesus   Monophysite bishop and ecclesiastical historian, born near Amida, *c*.507, and consequently also known as 'John of Amida' as well as 'John of Asia', died 586. Initially a monk, he was forced to live a nomadic life following the anti-Monophysite decrees of Justin I. Arriving in Constantinople he gained the support of the Empress **Theodora I**, and through her that of **Justinian I**. At some time around 542 he became titular bishop of Ephesus. John was a successful missionary in Lydia and Caria in Asia Minor, and was said to have baptized some 70,000 souls. As a result of his Monophysite views he was imprisoned under Justin II. Following his release he led a nomadic life until his death. John of Ephesus is the most important early Church historian in the Syriac language.

John of Epirus   Orthodox saint and martyr, born Albania, *c*.1789, died (martyred) Ithaca, 23 September 1814. Unusually for a martyr of the Turkish period he was born a Muslim and not baptized until adulthood. After baptism he married and led an obscure life but was discovered by the authorities. He was executed, but his body was secretly buried in a nearby monastery. Feast day 23 September.

John of Falkenberg   Dominican writer, born Falkenberg, Pomerania, Prussia, died Italy or Falkenberg, 1435. He became a Dominican and studied at Kammin. He taught philosophy and theology. John supported **Gregory XII**, the legal Pope, refusing to accept the jurisdiction of his Dominican superior, Bernard de Datis. John wrote that the king of Poland and his party were idolaters and that it was acceptable to oppose them, even to kill the king, following the extreme view of Jean Petit. John claimed that only the Pope was infallible in matters of faith. He was imprisoned, ultimately in Rome.

John of Fécamp   Benedictine abbot, reformer and theologian, born Ravenna(?), 990, died Fécamp, Normandy, 22 February 1078. A nephew of the reforming abbot **William of Volpiano**, he entered his uncle's monastery, Fruttuaria, and followed him to Dijon. In 1017, he was elected prior of the abbey of Fécamp and in 1028 he was elected abbot. Part of the eremitical movement of monastic reform in the tradition of **Romuald of Ravenna**, he was also a mystical theologian – although many of his works have long been attributed to others – and designed a spiritual programme for the monks of Fécamp.

John of Freiburg (Rumsik) Writer, born perhaps Haslach, Germany, date unknown, died Freiburg, 10 March 1314. He was a lecturer at Freiburg im Breisgau, and his most important work was the *Summa confessorum* (1280–98). He made pastoral theology a science by relating its material to speculative moral principles, especially those of St **Thomas Aquinas**.

John of Garland Writer, born England, *c.*1195, died Paris(?), *c.*1272. At Oxford University he became interested in wide studies about which he later wrote. He went to Paris *c.*1217, settled in the Clos de Garlande (hence his name) and for the rest of his life taught Latin language and literature at the university there, except in 1229–32, when he was the first professor of Latin at the new University of Toulouse. He wrote on contemporary history, medieval hymnology and language, and compiled dictionaries. His works, written mainly for his students, are important for the study of medieval Latin.

John of God Saint, founder of the Brothers Hospitallers, born Portugal, 1495, of Christian parentage, died Granada, Spain, 8 March 1550. After a pious upbringing he later renounced the practice of religion and became a soldier. At about the age of 40 he rediscovered his faith. He hoped for martyrdom in Morocco, but when this was denied him he journeyed to Spain, coming under the influence of **John of Ávila** in 1538. He became somewhat excessive in his piety, devotion and penitence, but later directed his energies towards helping the poor and sick, founding the 'Brothers Hospitallers'. He was canonized in 1690. In 1886 he was declared patron of hospitals and sick people by Pope **Leo XIII**. Feast day 8 March.

John of Gorze Blessed, abbot, born Vandiers, France, late ninth century, died Gorze Abbey, 974.

Also known as 'Jean de Vandiers'. He was the son of an affluent landowner, and studied at Metz and later at the abbey of Saint-Mihiel. After the death of his father he took care of the estate, but continued his studies at Toul. Upon returning from a pilgrimage to Rome, he came under the influence of Einold, the archdeacon of Toul. In 933 he followed Einold to the abbey of Gorze, where, with their companions, they re-established monastic discipline. In 953 he travelled to Córdoba as envoy to **Otto I**. Following the death of Einold, John succeeded him as abbot of Gorze, where he played a major role in the monastic reform movement of which Gorze was the centre.

John of Hauteville Poet, born Auville, France, flourished late 1100s. John perhaps studied at Oxford or Paris and might even have been a Benedictine monk at the abbey of St Albans in England. His most famous work is the long satiric epic *Architrenius* (*c.*1184), dedicated to Walter of Coutances when he was made archbishop of Rouen. The work of some 4300 lines tells the story of a young man's search for true Nature and pokes fun at such things as academics and presumptuous clergy. The work was one of the few medieval ones to be respected by Renaissance humanists.

John of Hoveden Poet, born London, died Howden, Yorkshire(?), after 1275. Several thirteenth-century men were called 'John of Hoveden' (now Howden, Yorkshire); this may be the so-called 'astrologer', who was born in London and reputedly educated at Oxford. By 1268 he was certainly clerk of Queen Eleanor of Provence (Henry III's queen), was probably prebendary of Howden Collegiate Church and known as canon and prebendary of the King's Free Chapel, Bridgnorth, Shropshire. His greatest mystical poem is *Philomena* on Christ's birth, passion and resurrection. He held a high position among English poets and was the precursor of the great fourteenth-century mystics.

John of Jandun Writer, born Jandun, Ardennes, France, *c.*1275, died Montalto, 15 September 1328. He studied and taught at Paris University and in 1316 became a canon at Senlis. Describing himself as 'a mimic of Aristotle and Averroes', he wrote commentaries on Aristotle emphasizing truths demonstrated by reason rather than those revealed by faith. His connection with **Marsilius of Padua**'s anti-papal *Defensor pacis* forced him to leave Paris in 1324 and gain **Louis** of Bavaria's protection. The work was condemned by Pope **John XXII** in 1327. Louis appointed him bishop of Ferrara in 1328, but it is doubtful whether he was consecrated.

John of Jerusalem Bishop, born late fourth century, died 417. He succeeded **Cyril** as bishop of Jerusalem in 387. Along with **Jerome** and **Rufinus of Aquileia**, he was an enthusiastic supporter of **Origen**. The friendship between John and Jerome later turned to open hostility when the latter joined with **Epiphanius of Constantia** in attacking John. As a consequence John refused access to the Bethlehem monks to the sacred places in Jerusalem and also refused to baptize their converts or bury their dead. In 396 Jerome retaliated by publishing *To Pamachius, against John of Jerusalem*, a violent attack on the bishop. An attempted reconciliation ultimately failed. John was later criticized for welcoming **Pelagius** to Jerusalem. Responding to a complaint at a diocesan synod that Pelagius taught a doctrine opposed by **Augustine**, John replied, 'I am Augustine here.'

John of Jesus Mary Carmelite educator and writer, born 'Juande San Pedro y Ustarro' at Calahorra, Logrono, Spain, 27 January 1564, died Montecompatri, 29 May 1615. He joined the Discalced Carmelites at Pastrani, 1593, and was a professor at the Colegio Complutense and at a friary of Genoa where he was ordained priest in 1590. Present at the general council of the Carmelite Order of 1593, which decreed the separation of Reform from the old Order of Carmel, he was concerned with the novitiate at St Ann's of Geneva in 1493–8 and at La Scala, Rome, in 1599–1611. Active in founding the Italian congregation, he became its general in 1611 and retired in 1614 to the friary of St Sylvester, Montecompatri. He produced 65 mystical writings.

John (Sergeyev) of Kronstadt Russian Orthodox saint, priest and healer, born near Archangel, Russia, 19 October 1829, died Kronstadt, 20 December 1908. A married priest who served a poor parish at the naval base near St Petersburg. He undertook extensive charitable and educational projects and transformed his church liturgically, with daily liturgies, frequent Communion and public confession (because of the numbers involved). Popular as a healer throughout Russia, he travelled widely and attended the dying Emperor Alexander III. His published works were many but the most famous was *My Life in Christ*, a spiritual diary which was translated into English and presented to Queen Victoria. He prophesied the Revolution in the clearest terms. He was canonized by the Russian Church Abroad in 1964 and inside Russia after the fall of Communism in 1990. Feast day 20 December.

John of La Rochelle (de Rupella) Franciscan philosopher and theologian, born La Rochelle, France, c.1195, died Paris(?), 8 February 1245. He became a Franciscan friar and master of theology in 1238. He partly wrote a *Summa theologicae disciplinae*, much of which was later incorporated into the so-called *Summa* of **Alexander of Hales**, by whom he was much influenced. He wrote also a *Summa de anima*, the first Scholastic text on psychology.

John of La Verna Blessed, Franciscan priest, born Fermo, near Ancona, Italy, date unknown, died La Verna, 9 August 1322. At the age of ten he joined the Augustinian canons, and three years later the Franciscans. After residing in hermitages in both Ancona and Fermo, he eventually settled in a hermit's cell at La Verna, at some time around 1290. He is reputed to have had the gift of prophecy along with mystical experiences. These included visions of the Blessed Virgin Mary, the Sacred Heart, St **Francis** and St **Lawrence**. In the later years of his life he preached widely throughout Tuscany.

John of Langton Bishop, born, it is thought, at Church Langton, Leicestershire, died Chichester, 19 July 1337. Little is known of his early life, but it is probable that he studied at Oxford. He had an early career in the royal chancery and later became Keeper of the Rolls. Between 1292 and 1302 he was Chancellor of England under King Edward I, a function he was later to repeat between 1307 and 1310, under Edward II. In 1305 he became bishop of Chichester. A moderate, he helped to negotiate the Treaty of Leake in 1318. After the overthrow of Edward II he retired from politics.

John (Pommers) of Latvia Orthodox saint, martyr and archbishop, born near Riga, 1876, died (martyred) 12 October 1934. Born of a Latvian family recently converted to Orthodoxy, he was consecrated bishop in Russia, but on Latvia becoming independent, he was elected archbishop of Riga. He worked tirelessly to reconcile the Russian and Latvian members of his flock and did much to publicize the persecution of the Church in the Soviet Union. In 1934 agents of the Soviet secret police, the NKVD, managed to enter the country, destroy his papers, torture him and burn him alive below the cathedral at Riga. Feast day 29 September.

John of Lichtenberg (Piccardi, Teutonicus) Dominican friar, died *c.*1320. Having lectured at the Dominican priory in Cologne, he studied in Paris from 1307 to 1312, except when he was provincial of the German province in 1308–10. He accompanied **Henry VII**, Holy Roman Emperor, to Italy in 1311–12. Pope **Clement V** named him bishop of Regensburg in 1313, but the cathedral chapter had already made another appointment. In his writings he was an important early Thomist commentator.

John of Lodi Saint, Benedictine monk, born Lodi, Italy, *c.*1025–30, died Gubbio, 7 September 1105. After an education in the liberal arts, he joined a group of hermits at Fonte Avellana sometime around 1065. He became the travelling companion of St **Peter Damian**, whose Life he wrote following the latter's death. In 1080 he became prior to the hermitage at Fonte Avellana. In 1104 he became bishop of Gubbio. Feast day 7 September.

John of Matera Saint, Benedictine monk, also known as 'John of Pulsano', born Matera, in the Kingdom of Naples, 1070, died Pulsano, 20 June 1139. He spent many years moving from one monastic house to another in a bid to find one which was conducive to his severe mortifications. For many years he lived as a hermit, and founded a small monastery at Ginosa, which was later dispersed by the Normans. While preaching at Bari he narrowly escaped being burned as a heretic.

Around 1130 he founded a community at Pulsano which adopted a strict Benedictine rule. He ruled over the monastery until his death.

John of Matha Saint, founder of the Trinitarian Order, about whom very little is known save that he was born in Provence, founded his Order for the redemption of captives, and died at Rome on 17 December 1213. Later biographies, which give abundant details about his life, are based on fabricated records of the fifteenth and sixteenth centuries. Feast day 8 February.

John of Mecklenberg Bishop and martyr. He was one of many missionaries who preached the faith in Iceland during the eleventh century. At some time after 1055 he was made the first bishop of Mecklenberg and was sent to witness among the Slavic tribes, including the Wends in Saxony. In 1066, during an uprising, he was captured. Refusing to deny his faith he was tortured, having both his hands and his feet amputated. Decapitated, his head was impaled on a spike and offered to the tribal god Redigast. He has erroneously been called the first American martyr because the territory Veindland (land of the Wends) is wrongly associated with Vinland, the reputed Norse settlement in North America.

John of Mirecourt French Cistercian monk, philosopher and theologian, flourished fourteenth century, died *c.*1350. He was from the Vosges Mountains in Lorraine and was called the 'White Monk' from his habit. In Paris in 1345 he obtained his bachelor's degree in theology. He wrote a commentary on the *Sentences* or theological theses of **Peter Lombard**. The university faculty censured 63 propositions for being unorthodox, but after John's 'Apology', these were reduced to 41. He believed that we cannot deduce the existence of God, because our senses are fallible.

John of Monte Corvino Franciscan, archbishop, founder of the mission to China, born Monte Corvino, Southern Italy, 1246, died Peking, 1328. He set off for China in 1289 with the Dominican Nicholas of Pistoia and a merchant, Peter of Luca-longo. They went to Persia and thence by sea to India, where they stayed for just over a year, in the course of which Nicholas died. John reached China in 1294 and pursued his missionary activities unhindered. In 1299 he built a church in Peking, followed six years later by a second, which also included workshops and housing for 200 people. He learned and used the language and translated the NT and Psalms. In 1304 he was joined by Arnold of Cologne and in 1307 another seven Franciscans were sent to join him, though only three arrived, and John was consecrated archbishop of Peking. He continued his missionary activities and was acclaimed by all as a saint.

John of Monte Marano Saint, bishop and monk. He lived in the late eleventh century and is reputed to have been a Benedictine monk. He became bishop of Monte Marano in Italy in 1074. A champion of the poor, he is also reputed to have performed many miracles. There is a tradition which claims that he was a disciple of **William of Vercelli**, the founder of the abbey of Monte Vergine, although this has no historical foundation. Feast day 17 August.

John of Montfort Saint, Knight Templar, died Nicosia, Cyprus, 1177/8. A nobleman and crusader, he was wounded in a battle at Jerusalem against the Saracens and taken to Cyprus, where he died. His body was interred at the abbey church of Beaulieu in Nicosia, where he was venerated until the Turkish conquest of 1571. Feast day 24 May.

John of Montmirail Blessed, Cistercian monk, born twelfth century, died 29 September 1217. He was a loyal knight in the service of King Philip II Augustus of France. He turned his back on a worldly life and founded a hostel near his castle, where he personally cared for the sick. In later life he left his wife and children and became a Cistercian monk at the abbey of Longpont in the Diocese of Soissons. He displayed extraordinary devotion to the virtues of obedience and humility.

John of Musca *see* **John de Ridevall**

John of Naples Dominican Thomist theologian, born Naples, date unknown, died there, 1340. He taught as a master at Paris University until 1317 when the general council of Pamplona made him lector in the Dominican college at Naples, and he spent the last years of his life at the priory of San Domenico Maggiore. He was often consulted in current controversies, including those about Franciscan poverty; and he worked hard to promote the beatification and canonization of St **Thomas Aquinas**.

John of Nepomuk Saint, born Bohemia, *c.*1340, martyred in Prague, 20 March 1393. As vicar general of the Archdiocese of Prague, he incensed Wenceslas IV by resisting the monarch's attempts to suppress an abbey in order to create a see for one of his favourites. There is also a tradition that he angered the king by refusing to betray the queen by breaking the seal of the confessional. As a consequence, and on the king's orders, he was drowned in the River Vltava. His recovered body became the centre of veneration. He was canonized in 1729. Feast day 16 May.

John of Otzun (Hovhannes IV Otznetzi) Head of the Armenian Church (*katholikos*), born Otzun, 650, died Diorin, 729. He became the *catholicos* in 718 and held a synod to reform the Armenian Church and another at Manzikert in 726 to consider the Syrian (Jacobite) Church, and the patriarch of Constantinople, **Germanus I**, wrote to him urging the Armenian Monophysites to unite with the Byzantine Church. His theological and canonical books led him to be called 'the Philosopher'.

John of Oxford Bishop, died Norwich(?), 2 June 1200. Employed by King Henry II of England on a number of important foreign missions, he was sent to request Pope **Alexander III** to sanction the Constitutions of Clarendon, which attempted to define the legal relations between Church and State. In 1166 he was excommunicated by **Thomas Becket** for recognizing the Antipope Paschal III, but received absolution from Alexander. In 1170 he escorted Becket back to England and by his firmness prevented the archbishop's enemies from attacking him when he landed. John was consecrated bishop of Norwich in 1175, and in 1179, along with two other bishops, was appointed 'archi-justiciarius' on the reconstruction of the judicial system.

John of Paris (John Quidort) Dominican theologian, born 1250, died Bordeaux, 22 September

1306. He studied at the University of Paris. John wrote extensively, his most notable works being a defence of **Thomas Aquinas** against Franciscan attack, and his tractate on 'Regal and Papal Power' (1302–3), a work which was moderate in nature and which shunned contemporary theory by refusing to make either spiritual or temporal authority subservient to the other.

John of Parma Blessed, Franciscan minister general, born Parma, 1209, died Camerino, 19 March 1289. He taught logic at Parma for many years, during which time he became a Franciscan, around the year 1233. Studied in Paris. A popular preacher and teacher he was elected minister general of his Order in 1247. He travelled widely throughout Europe. Endeavoured to restore the Order to its original standards of asceticism and discipline. He worked tirelessly in an attempt to reunite the East and West, though without success. His austerity of life made him many enemies and he was accused of heresy in Rome. He resigned his office in 1257, retired into the hermitage of Greccio and lived a solitary life for over 30 years. He was sent on a mission to Greece in a further attempt at reunification, but died on his way. Feast day 22 May.

John of Plano Carpine *see* **John da Pian del Carpine**

John of Ragusa (John Stojković) Dominican theologian, bishop, born Ragusa, *c.*1395, died Lausanne, October or November 1443. He joined the Dominicans, studied in Paris and in 1420 became master of theology there. In 1422 he was one of the representatives of the University at the Council of Pavia and in 1431 papal theologian at the Council of Basel. He was legate of the Council of Constantinople between 1435 and 1437 to try to bring about reunion, and managed to get the Eastern emperor and the patriarch to send a delegation to Basel to try to bring this about. In 1438 he was sent on behalf of the Council to the Emperor Albert II and when he returned joined the dissidents. He was made bishop of Ardsijsch and two years later the Antipope **Felix V** made him cardinal-priest of Sisto. His writings include a treatise on the Church, a sermon on Communion under both kinds which formed part of the debate he had had with the Hussites, a treatise on reunion

with them, and a similar work on reunion with the Greeks.

John of Ravenna Archbishop, born *c.*812, died *c.*864. Archbishop of Ravenna from 850, he supported the Emperor **Louis II** and opposed Popes **Leo IV** and **Nicholas I**, oppressing the clergy and laity and even murdering a papal legate with the support of his brother Gregory, duke of Emilia. Nicholas I excommunicated him in 861, but he was forced to make peace with a synod at Rome and swear fidelity to the Pope, only in 863 to support the two archbishops of Cologne and Trier in their dispute with the Papacy concerning King **Lothair II**'s divorce, for which he was deposed.

John of Reading Franciscan theologian, born England, *c.*1285, died Avignon, 1346. He was an early follower of **Duns Scotus**, whom he knew personally. He lectured on the *Sentences* of **Peter Lombard** at Oxford, and became the forty-fifth regent master of theology around the year 1320. He opposed the theories of **William of Ockham**. From around 1322 he was teaching at Avignon, where he was consulted by **John XXII** on theological matters.

John of Réomé Saint, monk, born Courtangy, *c.*450, died Menetreux, 28 January 544(?). He became one of the pioneers of the monastic life in Burgundy. He became a monk at Lérins, and later, at the instigation of his bishop, founded a monastery at Réomé (now Menetreux) called Saint-Jean-de-Réomé or Moutier-Saint-Jean-en-Auxois. Here he introduced the Rule of **Macarius of Alexandria**. He had a reputation for sanctity, and many miracles were attributed to him.

John of Riga *see* **John (Pommers) of Latvia**

John of Ripa Franciscan theologian, died 1370. He joined the Franciscan friary of Ripatransone in the March of Ascoli near Pinceno. He was a disciple of **Duns Scotus**, with whom he often disagreed in his original approach, and he probably lectured on the *Sentences* of **Peter Lombard** at the University of Paris in about 1357 and was a professor there until about 1368. He sought to explain the character of the beatitude communicated by God to his creatures.

John of Rodington Franciscan Scholastic, born Rodington (Rodendon, Rodin) on the River Roden, *c.*1290, died Bedford, 1348. A member of the Franciscan friary at Stamford, after becoming doctor of divinity at Oxford he was lector of the Order there in about 1325–8 and after about 1340 became its provincial minister in England. Perhaps dying of the Black Death, he left several manuscripts.

John of Saint-Samson Carmelite mystic, family name 'Jean du Moulin', born Sens, France, 29 December 1571, died Rennes, 14 September 1636. Blind since childhood, he became in Paris in 1597 familiar with the mystics of The Netherlands and Rhineland. In *c.*1606 he became a Carmelite lay brother and then entered the reform of Touraine as 'John of Saint-Samson'. He was very influential as a spiritual adviser, and his mystical writings were published at Rennes in 1658–9.

John of Saint Thomas Spanish philosopher and theologian, born 'Juan Poinsat' at Lisbon, Portugal, 9 July 1589, died, possibly of poisoning, Fraga, near Barcelona, Spain, June 1644. In Madrid he became a Dominican. He taught theology at Madrid, in Piacenza, Italy, and at the University of Alcala, Spain. King Philip IV in Madrid made him his adviser and confessor. During a military campaign, John wrote *De donis Spiritus Sancti*. He became one of the Spanish inquisitors. He wrote a *Course in Theology* and *Course in Philosophy*, his *Cursus philosophicus* becoming a basis for Roman Catholic teaching on the psychology of knowledge.

John of Salerno Blessed, Dominican friar, born Salerno, *c.*1190, died Florence, 9 August (or 10 September) 1242. He received the habit from St **Dominic** himself, who sent him to introduce the Order into Florence. In Florence he founded the priory of Santa Maria Novella and, later, the monastery of Dominican nuns at Ripoli. He was commissioned by **Gregory IX** to preach against the heretical Patarines, a Manichaean sect. Feast day 29 August.

John of Salisbury Bishop and philosopher, born Salisbury, *c.*1115, died Chartres, 25 October 1180. He studied in Paris under Peter **Abelard** and Alberic of Rheims during the years 1136–8. He later studied at Chartres, before returning to Paris in 1140. He was presented to **Theobald** (archbishop of Canterbury) by St **Bernard** in 1148 and became his secretary, *c.*1150 to 1161, during which time he was sent on a number of important missions. He then became secretary to **Thomas Becket**, who succeeded Theobald. He supported Becket in his quarrel with Henry II, and was present at Canterbury on 29 December 1170, when Becket was murdered. In 1176 he became bishop of Chartres, where he remained until the end of his life. An accomplished Latinist and philosopher, he was one of the leaders of the literary renaissance of the twelfth century.

John (Maximovich) of San Francisco Russian Orthodox saint, bishop and missionary, born Kharkov, 4 June 1896, died Seattle, 2 July 1966. He emigrated to Yugoslavia after the Revolution and became monk and priest. Consecrated bishop of Shanghai in 1934 he remained there until after the war, when he managed to arrange the evacuation of most of his flock to America. As bishop in Paris he received various Dutch and French groups into the Orthodox Church. In 1963 he was appointed archbishop of San Francisco. An extraordinary ascetic and man of prayer, miracles were attributed to him in his lifetime and continue at his shrine today. Canonized by the Russian Church Abroad on 2 July 1994. Feast day 19 June.

John of Scythopolis Bishop of Scythopolis, Byzantine theologian, flourished sixth century. He wrote tracts against Monophysite heresies and affirmed that Christ was both God and man, the doctrine affirmed by the Council of Chalcedon of 451.

John of Seville (Hispalensis) Writer and translator, born Spain, probably Seville, died again probably Seville, Spain, *c.*1157. A Christian of the Mozarabic tradition, John of Seville was a scholar of astrology and astronomy as well as languages. He wrote about ten works in Latin (the best are two on the sciences of the stars – *De judiciis astrologicis* and *De astrolabio* – and one on mathematics – *Liber algorismi de practica arithmatica*) but is probably better known for his translations from Arabic of some works of al-Fargani, al Battani, Maslama of Madrid and al-Zarkali. He is thought by some to be the same person as **John of Spain**, but their original works are different enough to indicate that they were indeed two different people.

John of Spain (Hispanus) Archbishop and philosopher, birth date and place unknown, died Toledo, Spain, 1166. John was a convert from Judaism. In 1149 he was elected bishop of Segovia and at some time later archbishop of Toledo. His importance stems, not from his original philosophical contribution, but from his adept synthesis and dissemination of Arabic philosophy (Avicennian Aristotelianism), which had a profound effect on European philosophy from the time of its introduction. His chief works, all written with his disciple **Dominic Gundisalvi**, are *Tractus de anima, Liber de causis* and *Liber de causis primis et secundis*. He is sometimes confused with **John of Seville**.

John of Sterngassen Dominican theologian and mystic, died *c*.1328. Said to be a close disciple of **Thomas Aquinas**, he was a contemporary of Meister **Eckhart** and brother of Gerard and author of the popular *Pratum animarum*. As a master of theology, he taught in the Dominican priories of Strasburg and at Cologne, where he lived from 1310. His principal work, a commentary on the *Sentences* of **Peter Lombard**, show him to be an avowed Thomist. He often wrote of Aquinas as 'Doctor Noster' and mainly followed his Aristotelianism.

John of the Cross Saint, Carmelite mystic and poet, joint founder of the Discalced Carmelites, born 'Juan de Yepes y Álvarez' at Fontiveros, Spain, 24 June 1542, died Ubeda, Spain, 14 December 1591. He became a Carmelite friar in 1563, but the laxity of the Order caused disillusionment. He sought admission to the Carthusians, but **Teresa of Ávila** persuaded him to remain in the Carmelites and seek reform from within, and with her he formed the Order of Discalced (i.e. without shoes, but meaning in effect Reformed) Carmelites. Meeting opposition he was imprisoned in 1577, but escaped, subsequently holding various positions in the Discalced Carmelites. Further opposition saw him banished to Andalusia in 1591, where he died. His poems and other writings are among the great masterpieces of Spanish literature, notably *The Spiritual Canticle, The Dark Night of*

the Soul, The Ascent of Mount Carmel and *The Living Flame of Love*. He was canonized in 1726. Feast day 14 December.

John of Thoresby Archbishop and Chancellor, born probably North Thoresby, East Lincolnshire, died Bishopsthorpe, Yorkshire, 6 November 1373. In the royal service from 1330, he became notary in Chancery in 1336, Master of the Rolls in 1341 and Keeper of the Privy Seal in 1345–7. He was a commissioner to treat with France in 1345 and attended **Edward III** at Calais. He was made bishop of St Davids in 1347 and of Worcester in 1349. Chancellor of England in 1349–56, he was guardian of the kingdom during Edward's absence in France in 1355. As archbishop of York from 1351, he secured an agreement that the archbishop of York was the 'Primate of England' and the archbishop of Canterbury the 'Primate of All England'.

John (Maximovich Vasilkovsky) of Tobolsk Russian Orthodox saint, missionary and bishop, born Chernigov province, 1651, died Tobolsk, 10 June 1715. Archbishop of Chernigov, 1697–1711, then metropolitan of Tobolsk and all Siberia, where he became a very active missionary in his vast diocese. He wrote a number of theological and spiritual works in Latin, as was the custom at that time. Canonized 1916. Feast day 10 June.

John of Valence Saint, bishop, born Diocese of Lyons, date unknown, where he was later ordained priest and became a canon of Lyons Cathedral, died 21 March 1145. He wished to enter the monastic life at Cîteaux, but went instead on pilgrimage to Santiago de Compostella. Encouraged by a dream, he eventually entered Cîteaux in 1114. In 1118 he was sent to found the monastery of Bonnevaux. He later established four daughter-houses. In 1141 he became bishop of Valence. He was noted for his care of widows and orphans, and for his commitment to social justice. Feast day 26 April.

John of Vercelli Blessed, Dominican master general, born 1200(?), died Montpellier, 30 November 1283. He taught civil and canon law at Paris, and later at Vercelli. Around 1230 he was received into the Dominican Order and by 1245 had become prior of Vercelli. In 1255 he was appointed vicar general for Hungary, and, in 1256, prior of San Nicolo at Bologna. Between the years 1257 and 1264 he was provincial of Lombardy, and from 1264 to 1283, sixth master general of the Order. In this post he personally visited nearly every house of the Order, with the exception of those in Spain. He presided at twenty general chapters, and sent many encyclical letters. He urged perfect obedience to the constitution of the Order. He was responsible for the building of the Arca, into which the body of St **Dominic** was translated. In 1278 he declined the patriarchate of Jerusalem. Feast day 1 December.

John of Viktring Cistercian abbot, born c.1285, died Viktring, Carinthia, c.1345. Elected abbot of the Cistercian abbey of Viktring in about 1312, he became Albrecht II's chaplain in Vienna in 1341 and the Patriarch **Bertrand of Aquileia**'s chaplain in 1342. His *Liber certarum historiarum* began as a chronicle of the world and ended as a history of the House of Austria. He ably supported the Habsburg cause and was attached to the monastic ideals of his Order.

John of Waldby Augustinian preacher and writer, died c.1373. By 1354 he had a doctorate at Oxford, when he probably became provincial of the Augustinians in England. Five of his fourteen works survive. These were all sermons changed into devotional reading texts. Thus his name and ideas were widely circulated through the *Mirour of Life* of William of Nassington. He was an important English mystical writer, depending largely upon St **Bernard** and **Augustine**.

John of Wales Canon lawyer, died c.1220, but nothing known of him except that he was a Welshman. In about 1210–15, he wrote an *apparatus* to the *Compilatio tertia antiqua* and put together and glossed the *Complicatio secunda antiqua*, a collection of decretal letters before the great compilation commissioned by Pope **Gregory IX** in 1234.

John of Wales Franciscan theologian, died Paris, April 1285. A lector in the Franciscan friary at Oxford in about 1257–8 and regent master at Paris in 1281–3, he was one of five masters in theology chosen to examine **Peter John Olivi** and employed

by Archbishop John **Peckham** to negotiate between the English and Welsh. His writings, marked by practical wisdom and piety, include biographical and moral works.

John of Wales Franciscan theologian, died c.1380. He was a lector at the Franciscan friary in Oxford from about 1349, taking part in a riot against the chancellor of the University; later he was for many years a lecturer at the friary in London. He was appointed a papal chaplain in April 1372 and envoy of the king of England to the Roman curia in September 1377. His London hospice was robbed of horses, books, money and plate in 1378, but these were returned by order of the king.

John Parenti Italian Franciscan friar, born probably Curta Castellani, died 1235. He joined the Franciscan Order soon after its foundation in 1209, became the provincial minister of Spain in 1219 and from 1227 to 1232 was minister general. He developed the Friars Minor into an educated and effective Order. Among his achievements were securing the canonization of St **Francis of Assisi** by Pope **Gregory IX** in 1228 and the translation of the saint's relics to Assisi in 1230. He resigned his post in 1232.

John Parvus Theologian, born Caux, France, c.1360, died Hesdin, France, 15 July 1411. He taught at the University of Paris, where he was known for his lectures on the Western Schism (c.1403) and especially on tyrannicide. In 1407 King Charles VI's brother, Louis, duke of Orléans, was murdered by his brother, John the Fearless, duke of Burgundy, who summoned Parvus to defend him. In 1408 Parvus delivered his *Justificatio ducis Burgundiae* before the king, who pardoned John the Fearless. Parvus went to the duke of Burgundy's estate at Hesdin and wrote answers to attacks on his *Justificatio*. The bishop of Paris condemned this work in 1414, but the condemnation was eventually withdrawn at the duke's insistence.

John Paul I Pope, born 'Albino Luciani' at Canale d'Agordo, near Belluno, into a working-class, socialist, family, 17 October 1912, elected 26 August 1978, died 28 September 1978. He studied in the local seminary, and at Rome's Gregorian

University. He was ordained on 7 July 1935, served in his local parish, then in the seminary in Belluno. He became vicar general to the bishop of Belluno and in 1958 bishop of Vittorio Veneto. A very popular and successful bishop, he became patriarch of Venice in 1969, and a cardinal in 1973. His election to the Papacy was intended to mark a turning away from the Vatican's curial establishment, and, in holding a press conference and choosing to be invested with his office rather than enthroned as pontiff, this seemed likely, but he died only a month after the conclave. He published, while at Venice, *Illustrissimi*, letters on topics of the day addressed to characters from history and fiction.

John Peckham   *see* **Peckham, John**

John Pelingotto   Blessed, born Urbino, Italy, 1240, died there, 1 June 1304. Belonging to a leading local family, he joined the Third Order of St Francis in 1255 and devoted himself to prayer and the service of God. In 1300 he made a pilgrimage to Rome for the celebration of Pope **Boniface VIII**'s jubilee year, where he was described as 'the holy man from Urbino'. After his death he was buried in the chapel of St Francis in his native city. His cult was approved by Pope **Benedict XV** on 12 November 1918. Feast day 1 June.

John Philoponus   Scholar, lived in Alexandria from *c*.490 to *c*.575. Of, presumably, Alexandrian and Christian origin, he developed into a universal scholar whose works encompassed knowledge of astronomy, mathematics, grammar and medicine. In philosophy he was very well at home in the works of Aristotle, on which he wrote many commentaries. In the theological field he was a Monophysite. His Aristotelian realism, however, led him to acknowledge in the Trinitarian sphere the existence of three separate hypostases, resulting in the accusation of tritheism. Philoponus ('lover of labour') was an industrious writer on all these subjects. Many of these writings were lost.

John Scotus Erigena   *see* **Eriugena, John Scotus**

John Stratford   *see* **Stratford, John**

John Teutonicus   Glossator, died Halberstadt,

Germany, 25 April 1246. He was provost of the collegiate chapter of St Maria, and, after studying civil and canon law at Bologna, was an important glossator, or commentator, teaching there until *c*.1220. His chief work was the *Glossa ordinaria* on the *Decretum* of **Gratian** (*c*.1218), which is still a basic source for research into the history of canon law.

John the Almsgiver   Saint, patriarch of Alexandria, born in Cyprus of a good family, date unknown, died Amathus, Cyprus, 11 November 619 or 620. After completing his education he took on secular work, and married. At some time after, he was widowed and without children living, and renounced all his goods and consecrated himself to the Church. As patriarch of Alexandria, he was a staunch defender of Chalcedonian orthodoxy against Monophysitism. Although a builder of churches and teacher of clergy, John's main reputation is of charity. He sought to eradicate misery by daily distributions to the poor, and created nurseries, orphanages and hospitals. He worked throughout Egypt, Syria and Jerusalem. Feast day 23 January.

John the Deacon of Naples   Hagiographer, born Naples, *c*.880. Educated by the priest **Auxilius**, he was deacon of St Gennaro in Naples by 906 when he assisted in the translation of the relics of St Sosius from Miseno to Naples. While still young he compiled a chronicle of the bishops of Naples from 762 to 872. He is best remembered for his lives of the saints **Severinus**, **Januarius**, Sosius, Procopius and the Forty Martyrs of Sebaste.

John the Deacon of Rome (Hymonides)   Writer, born *c*.824, died *c*.881. He was probably a monk of Monte Cassino, who was first at the court of **Charles II** the Bald, king of the Western Franks, and after 875 probably papal secretary to Pope **John VIII**, at whose request he wrote the *Vita Gregorii Magni*, which, as he used the registers of Pope **Gregory I**, is an important source for historians.

John the Deacon of Rome   Writer, died *c*.1170. When a canon of the Lateran, he was asked by Pope **Alexander III** and Prior John of the Lateran to produce the third edition of *Descriptio Lateran-*

ensis ecclesiae, which he called *Liber de sanctis sanctorum ecclesiae*, and which attempted to prove the precedence of the Lateran canons over those of the Vatican and includes much legendary material.

John the Deacon of Venice   Chronicler, died *c.*1009. He is noted for his *Chronicon Venetum*, probably the oldest history of Venice. Covering its beginning to 1008, it is a particularly valuable source for the reign of the Doge Peter II Orseolo (991–1009), whose friend and chaplain he was, and whom he admired as a successful ruler of this great age for the city. He acted as the doge's envoy to the Emperor **Otto III**, for whom he arranged a secret visit to Venice in 1001.

John the Silent   Monk, bishop, born at Nicopolis, Armenia, 8 January 454, died 13 May 558. Of a wealthy family, John distributed his inheritance after his parents' deaths, retaining enough to build a church and monastery where he and ten friends lived in austerity. Against his wishes he was made bishop of Colonia (Taxara) in 481. During his episcopate he fought the oppression of the Church by Pasinius, his brother-in-law. Later he returned to monastic life – first (anonymously) under St **Sabas** at the laura near Jerusalem, and afterwards as a solitary and perpetually silent hermit in the desert. Feast day 13 May.

John Vianney   *see* **Vianney, Jean-Baptiste Marie**

John Vincentius   Saint, bishop and hermit, died probably 12 December 1012. A bishop in the area of Ravenna, he fled the city, it is said, because of his great popularity and became a hermit on Monte Pirchiriano, Piedmont, where he assembled around him a group of hermits called Santa-Maria della Celle. There he built a chapel which by 1000 became the abbey of San Michele di Chiuse, and in 1006 he assisted in the foundation of San Salutore in Turin. Feast day 21 December.

John Walwayn   Historian, died July 1326. In the Falkirk campaign of 1298 he accompanied Sir Robert de Tony (or Thorny), the Swan Knight, as a confidential clerk employed by Humphrey de Bohun, earl of Hereford. He had other official posts, but his importance in English history depends upon his possible authorship of *Vita*

Edwardia Secundi, a Latin life of King Edward II of England.

John Welles (Wells)   Benedictine monk of Ramsey, died Perugia, 1388. He was a doctor of divinity at Oxford *c.*1377 and for thirteen years principal of Gloucester College, founded in the late thirteenth century for the education of Benedictine monks (now Worcester College). He was a determined opponent of **Wycliffe**, condemning his doctrines at Oxford and at the Earthquake Synod in London during 1382. He was an envoy from the English Benedictines to Pope **Urban VI** in 1387.

John Zonaras   *see* **Zonaras, John**

Johnson, Francis   Separatist pastor, born Richmond, Yorkshire, March 1562, died Amsterdam, January 1618. He was imprisoned and ejected from his fellowship at Oxford for Prebyterianism in 1589 and went to serve as preacher to merchants at Middelburg. There he was converted to the Separatist cause by the work of **Barrow** and **Greenwood** and returned to London but by 1598 was pastor of the Amsterdam Separatists. In 1610 Johnson reverted to Presbyterianism and was ejected by Henry **Ainsworth** from the Amsterdam Church. He co-wrote the Separatist confession of faith *Confessio fidei* (1598) and wrote works defending Separatism and, later, Presbyterianism: *A Short Treatise concerning Tell the Church* (1611).

Johnson, George   Professor and administrator, born Toledo, Ohio, 22 February 1889, died Washington, DC, 4 June 1944. Educated at St John's University, Toledo, St Bernard's Seminary, Rochester, New York, and the North American College, Rome, where he was ordained in 1914. He gained a doctorate in education at the Catholic University of America, Washington, DC, and was diocesan superintendent of schools at Toledo in 1919–21 and professor of education at the Catholic University in 1921–44. By serving on Roman Catholic educational organizations and presidential committees, he exercised a national educational influence. Pope **Pius XII** made him a domestic prelate in 1942.

Johnson, James ('Holy Johnson')   Anglican bishop in Nigeria, born Sierra Leone, *c.*1836, died Bonny,

Nigeria, 18 May 1917. Educated at Fourah Bay Institution, he joined the Church Missionary Society (CMS) in 1858 and was ordained in 1863. He ministered for eleven years in Freetown, where he encouraged the native pastorate ideal and promoted the concept of an independent Anglican Church in Africa. In 1874 he was transferred to Nigeria, where he worked in Lagos and as superintendent of the CMS Yoruba Mission (1877–9). His ability, zeal and championing of 'ethiopianism' were mistrusted by a generation of white missionaries who wanted increased control over the developing African Church. Nevertheless, he was finally appointed assistant bishop of Western Equatorial Africa in 1900 with oversight of the Niger Delta and Benin.

Johnson, Lionel Pigot   Poet and critic, born Broadstairs, 15 March 1867, died London, 29 September 1902. He was a scholar of Winchester College. Between 1884 and 1886 he edited *The Wykehamist*. He studied at New College, Oxford, where he graduated with a first in 1890. He then pursued a literary career in London. In 1891 he became a Roman Catholic. In 1895, he published his first volume of poetry, which displays a 'catholic puritanism'. Published *Ireland and Other Poems*, which displays a great love of Ireland, in 1897, *The Art of Thomas Hardy* in 1894 and *Post Liminium: Essays and Critical Papers* (posthumously in 1911).

Johnson, Samuel   Writer, critic and lexicographer, born Lichfield, Staffordshire, 18 September 1709, died London, 13 December 1784. After an unsettled early life Johnson moved to London in 1737. He began writing for *The Gentleman's Magazine*, for which he reported parliamentary debates. In the following years his literary reputation grew, and the publication of his famous *Dictionary* in 1755 established him as one of the outstanding men of letters of his day. He was renowned for his sparkling wit and conversation, immortalized in the biography by James **Boswell**. Johnson was a devout Anglican, and his occasional sermons, prayers and meditations reveal a deep and genuine piety.

Joinville, Jehan de   Feudal lord and historian, born probably at Joinville, Champagne, *c*.1225, died 14 December 1317. As lord of Joinville he was the seneschal of the counts of Champagne and a supporter of **Louis IX** and his successors. He wrote towards the end of his life an Old French biography of Louis, with whom he had crusaded in 1248–54: he had been one of the chief witnesses for the canonization of the king. While on the crusade he wrote a manual of the Christian faith, his *Credo*.

Jolenta of Hungary   Blessed, Poor Clare nun, born Hungary, *c*.1235, the daughter of King Bela IV of Hungary, died Gniezno, 1298 or 1299. Her mother was the daughter of the emperor of Constantinople. She was also the grand-niece of St **Hedwig**; niece of St **Elizabeth of Hungary**; and sister of **Margaret of Hungary**. At the age of five she was put in the care of her sister **Kunigunde**, queen of Poland. She later married Duke Boleslas VI the Pious of Kalisz. With him she founded the Poor Clare convent at Gniezno. In 1279 the duke died and Jolenta, along with her youngest daughter, joined Kunigunde (also widowed) in the Poor Clare convent at Stary Sacz. Jolenta later moved to Gniezno, where she became abbess.

Jolivet, Régis   Roman Catholic priest and philosopher, born Lyons, 8 November 1891, died there, 4 August 1966. Jolivet studied at the Lyons seminary, and was ordained in 1914: he fought and was wounded in World War I. After advanced studies in philosophy in Lyons and Grenoble, he taught for a number of years before being appointed master of lectures at the Catholic University of Lyons in 1926. In 1929 he was awarded his doctor's degree and made full professor and in 1933 founded the University's school of philosophy. He was a chaplain to the First North African Division in World War II. Jolivet wrote many works on a whole range of philosophical issues, was a member of many academic societies, and was made a knight of the Legion of Honour by the French government in 1961.

Jommelli, Niccolò   Italian composer, born Aversa, near Naples, 10 September 1714, died Naples, 25 August 1774. He studied in Aversa and Naples and is best known for his operas and Church music. He wedded together elements from German, French and Italian music, and in his operas had a great feeling for drama. He was nicknamed 'the

Italian Gluck' for his operatic work. He worked at St Peter's, Rome, as *maestro coadjuture* of the papal choir. He worked in Bologna and in Venice, where he composed the oratorios *Isaac Figura del Redentore* and *La Betulia Liberata*. He went to Stuttgart, where he produced operas and had performed a *Miserere* and a *Te Deum*, and then travelled to Portugal. His religious music includes cantatas, oratorios, Passions, Masses, Requiems and small-scale sacred pieces.

Jon Ogmundsson Saint, bishop, born Breidabolsstadur, Iceland, 1052, died 23 April 1121. He travelled extensively, perhaps even as far as Rome. He brought back with him from his travels Saemund the Learned, who founded the famous Icelandic school at Oddi. Ogmundsson was a priest in Breidabolsstadur when it was decided to divide Iceland into two dioceses. He became the first bishop of Holar. During this time he was responsible for renaming the days of the week in Iceland, to rid them of their pagan association.

Jonah ben Jishaq, Jehudah Learned Jewish convert to Christianity, born Safed, Galilee, 28 October 1588, died Rome, 26 May 1668. He had been a rabbi but converted to Roman Catholicism and took the name of John the Baptist in Poland. The king of Poland sent him to purchase precious stones at Constantinople, where the Venetian ambassador saved him from execution for espionage. He went to Italy and taught Hebrew and Aramaic at Pisa and Rome and translated the Gospels into Hebrew.

Jonah (Pokrovsky) of Manchuria Russian Orthodox saint and bishop, born Kaluga, 1888, died Manchuria, China, 1925. He escaped with the White armies to China after the Revolution and was consecrated bishop for the exiles. During the three years he was bishop he cared for his flock and shared their poverty. He contracted blood-poisoning, owing to the lack of medical supplies. Miracles were attributed to him after his death and it was through the efforts of his surviving flock, and their descendants in America, that he was canonized by the Russian Church Abroad, on 13 September 1996. Feast day 7 October.

Jonas, Justus German Reformer, born 'Jodocus

Koch' at Nordhausen, 5 June 1493, died Eisfeld, 9 October 1555. He studied at the Universities of Erfurt and Wittenberg. He became professor of law at Erfurt and canon of the church of St Severus in 1518, becoming rector of the university one year later. He is attributed with the introduction of Greek and Hebrew into the curriculum. He was a great admirer of both **Erasmus** and **Luther**, and followed the latter to the Diet of Worms in 1521. He was appointed professor of law at Wittenberg by the elector of Saxony, and played a prominent role in the Protestant Reformation. In 1546 he preached at Luther's funeral, and later translated the writings of both Luther and **Melanchthon**. In 1553 he was appointed superintendent at Eisfeld, where he died.

Jonas of Bobbio Hagiographer, born Susa, Piedmont, *c*.600, died *c*.666. From 618 he was at the abbey of Bobbio, except for being a missionary with St **Amandus** in northern France in 639–42 and abbot of St-Amand-les-Eaux in 652–3. He is known chiefly through his Lives of such figures as Bishop Vedas of Arras, Abbot **John of Réomé** and St **Columbanus**.

Jonas of Orléans Frankish bishop and theologian, born Aquitaine, *c*.779, died Orléans, 843. He was bishop of Orléans from 818. His *De cultu imaginum* expressed his concern with the question of the veneration of images. He sought to moderate between Iconoclasm and image worship, holding that the purpose of images was for the adornment of churches, commemoration and instruction, but not to uphold a superstitious cult amounting to adoration.

Jonatus Benedictine abbot, died *c*.691. Jonatus was a follower of **Amandus**, also named the 'Apostle of the Belgians'. Amandus called Jonatus from the abbey of Elnon to become abbot at Marchiennes (the double monastery), near Douai.

Jones, David English Roman Catholic painter and poet, born Brockley, Kent, 1 November 1895 (and baptized 'Walter', a name he jettisoned), died Harrow, 28 October 1974. He studied art in London before serving in France as an infantryman during the First World War: he admired soldiers and wished to re-enlist, but instead returned to the study of art. He became a Roman Catholic in 1921, and went to work with Eric **Gill**, being engaged for a time to one of Gill's daughters. His long poem on World War I, *In Parenthesis*, published in 1937, the following year won the Hawthornden prize. His other major poetical work, about the history of Britain, was *The Anathemata*, published in 1952 to acclaim. He was also distinguished for his painting and engraving. Shortly before his death he was made a Companion of Honour. Having lived in many places in England and Wales, after 1947 he settled in Harrow.

Jones, Griffith Founder of the Welsh circulating schools, born into a Nonconforming family in Carmarthenshire, 1683, died Llanddowror, 8 April 1761. He became an Anglican, was ordained in 1708 and was made rector of Llanddowror in 1716. He promoted social and religious reforms and in 1730, backed by the Society for Promoting Christian Knowledge, inaugurated a very successful system of peripatetic teachers of Welsh-language Bible study. He produced several Welsh-language publications, including an annual report of the circulating schools, *Welsh Piety*.

Jones, John (Buckley) Saint, Franciscan priest and martyr, born Clynog Fawr, Wales, 1559, died Southwark, London, 12 July 1598. In around 1590 he joined the Franciscan Order at Pontoise in France, was professed in 1591, and returned to England in 1592. In 1597 he was arrested and imprisoned on the charge that as a priest ordained abroad he had returned to minister in England. He was found guilty by his own admission and was executed. He was canonized by Pope **Paul VI** in 1970 as one of the **Forty Martyrs of England and Wales**.

Jones, Rufus Matthew American Quaker, born South China, Maine, 25 January 1863, died Haverford, Pennsylvania, 1948. He was educated at Haverford College and in Europe. From 1889 to 1893 he was principal of Oak Grove Seminary, and from 1904 to 1934 professor of philosophy at Haverford College. He wrote extensively, his most notable works being *A Dynamic Faith* (1901), *Social Law in the Spiritual World* (1904), *Studies in Mystical Religion* (1909), *Spiritual Reformers in the Sixteenth and Seventeenth Centuries* (1914), *The

Later Periods of Quakerism (1921), *The Faith and Practice of the Quakers* (1927), *New Studies in Mystical Religion* (1927), *George Fox* (1930), *The Testimony of the Soul* (1936).

Jones, William Ambrose Roman Catholic missionary bishop, born Cambridge, New York, 21 July 1865, died Philadelphia, Pennsylvania, 17 February 1921. Ordained in 1890, he was engaged in pastoral work in New England until 1899 when, following the Spanish–American War, he was sent to Cuba, where he achieved the formation of three parishes and the Pontifical University of St Thomas of Villanova (confiscated by Castro in 1961). He was consecrated bishop of San Juan, Puerto Rico, in 1907.

Jong, Johannes de Cardinal, ecclesiastical historian, born Nej, Ameland Island, The Netherlands, 10 September 1885, died Amersfoort, The Netherlands, 8 September 1955. After ordination in 1908, he studied in Rome until becoming professor of ecclesiastical history in the major seminary at Rijsenburg in 1914 and rector there in 1931. He was appointed (after becoming coadjutor in 1935) archbishop of Utrecht in 1936. During the German occupation of The Netherlands he was widely recognized as a resistance leader. He opposed the dissolution of the Catholic Workers' Association in 1941 and the persecution of Jews. He was made a cardinal in 1946 and retired in 1951.

Jordan, Edward Benedict Professor, born Dunmore, Pennsylvania, 17 December 1884, died Washington, DC, 19 July 1951. In 1909 he gained a doctorate at the Propaganda College, Rome, and was ordained in 1909. He then taught at Mount St Mary's College, Scranton, Pennsylvania, until 1921 when he became a professor at the Catholic University of America, Washington, DC. He was named a domestic prelate by Pope **Pius XI** in 1936 and became the national director of the International Federation of Catholic Alumni in 1943. He wrote on the philosophy of education and the theology of evolution.

Jordan, Johann Baptist (Francis Mary of the Cross) Religious founder, born Gurtweil, Baden, Germany, 16 June 1848, died Tafers, Switzerland, 8 September 1918. He was ordained priest in 1878, the year the Kulturkampf began in Germany, and went to Rome to study oriental languages. After a visit to the Holy Land in 1880 he conceived the idea of an organization embracing all levels in society, clerical and lay, men and women, in a common apostolate to promote and defend Catholicism. In the event he founded the Salvatorians – though they did not acquire that name until 1894 – a congregation of priests and brothers, being its superior general until 1915. To aid the Salvatorians, in 1883 he established the Franciscan Sisters of the Sorrowful Mother and in 1888 the Sisters of the Divine Saviour.

Jordan Forzate Blessed, monk, born Padua, c.1158, died Venice, 1248. He studied law before becoming a Camaldolese monk. He later became prior of San Benedetto Novello in Padua, the rebuilding of which he instigated. In 1231 he was appointed examiner in the canonization process of **Anthony of Padua**. He also played a decisive role in the quarrel between **Frederick II** and the Popes as *doctor decretalium* of the city council of Padua. In 1237 he was imprisoned by Ezzelino III of Romagna, but was freed by Frederick in 1239, and took refuge in Aquileia. He finally settled in the monastery of Della Celestia in Venice, where he died. His body was moved to the cathedral of Padua in 1810. Feast day 7 August.

Jordan of Giano Franciscan chronicler, born Giano, Italy, c.1195, died Magdeburg, Germany, after 1262. He entered the Order c.1218 and was ordained in 1223. He held several Franciscan posts in Central Europe, finally becoming provincial vicar of Saxony in 1242. Commissioned by the provincial chapter, he wrote a chronicle of the Order in Germany from 1207 to 1262, which was continued until the end of the fifteenth century and is an important source for its early history.

Jordan of Osnabrück Writer, died 15 April c.1284. Little is known of his life beyond a mention as *scholasticus*, *canonicus* and *magister* in Osnabrück's archives, presumably because of his studies. He wrote a short treatise praising the Holy Roman Empire, *De prerogativa Romani Imperii*, in c.1256–73.

Jordan of Quedlinburg Augustinian scholar and author, born Quedlinburg, Saxony, c.1300, died Vienna, c.1380. He lectured in Augustinian monasteries in Erfurt and Magdeburg and was provincial of Saxony in 1341–51. He reorganized the Augustinians into a mendicant order. His chief influence was spiritual, as shown in his writings. He may have been attracted, like other Augustinians, to Vienna by the foundation of its university in 1365.

Jordan of Saxony Blessed, Dominican, second master general of the Order of Preachers, born Diocese of Mainz, died in a shipwreck while returning from the Holy Land, 13 February 1237. He later lectured in Paris. Here he received the habit on Ash Wednesday 1220. By 1221 he had already become provincial of the Lombardy province, which at that time was the most important province in the Order. Shortly after, he succeeded St **Dominic** as master general. He visited many houses of the Order, enlarging and strengthening them. A preacher of some note, he encouraged many vocations to the religious life (it is said he encouraged more than 1000 vocations to the Dominican Order). A great writer on spiritual matters, his letters of spiritual direction are still read to this day. He also wrote the first Life of St Dominic.

Jordanis Historian, place and date of birth unknown, died 560. Biographical details of Jordanis' life are uncertain. He was *notarius quamvis agramatus* to the noble Gunthiges Baza, or the royal family of the Amalings. Later, he settled in Italy and was part of **Cassiodorus**' community of Vivarium. He joined Catholicism from the Arian sect. He is mentioned as a bishop in 551. His historical work *De summa temporum vel origine actibusque gentis Romanorum* is a compendium of universal history from Adam to Justinian. His second work, *De origine actibusque Getarum*, is a summary of Cassiodorus' lost *History of the Goths*.

Jordanus de Nemore Mathematician, died 1250, may have been identical with **Jordan of Saxony**, the second general master of the Dominican Order (1222–37). An inventive student of statistics, he wrote various mathematical books, which were widely copied and cited, and he exercised a considerable influence on the development of medieval mathematics.

Jorg, Josef Edmund   Journalist and politician, born Immerstadt, Germany, 23 December 1819, died Burg Trausnitz, near Landshut, 18 November 1901. He supported the Roman Catholic, conservative cause against the liberal, nationalist outlook of the Progressive Party, which was influential in the newly united Germany. From 1849 he was leader of the Patriotic Party in the Bavarian provincial diet, a member of the parliament of the German Customs Union (Zollverein) and a delegate of the Centre Party in the German parliament, when he unsuccessfully opposed the alliance of Bavaria with Prussia. Though politically conservative, he pioneered social reforms in Germany.

Jørgensen, Jens Johannes   Poet and biographer, born Svendborg, Denmark, 6 November 1866, died Svendborg, 29 May 1956. Studied zoology at Copenhagen. His early writing embraced naturalism and symbolism, and later he became interested in mysticism and religion. After his conversion to Roman Catholicism in 1896 he lived mostly in Assisi, Italy. Outside Denmark his hagiographies of *St Francis of Assisi* and *St Catherine of Siena* are well known. Inside Denmark he is known primarily as a poet, for his 'Blossoms and Fruits', 'Funen' and other poems. Also he wrote about travelling, as in *Pilgrimsbogen*.

Joris, David   Religious reformer and agitator, born Ghent or Bruges, Flanders, *c.*1501/2, died Basel, Switzerland, 25 August 1556. By trade he was a painter of stained glass and settled in Delft, in The Netherlands. Initially, as an exponent of Lutheranism, he attacked the Roman Catholic Church. In 1528 at The Hague he was sentenced to three years' imprisonment for his religious beliefs. Also he was involved in controversies involving the Anabaptists, who supported adult baptism. Joris declared himself to be the third David, after King David and Christ the son of David, and was viewed as a messiah who would redeem the world. With his disciples, he settled at Basel and became a highly regarded citizen. He took the name 'Jan van Bruges' and wrote extensively, including his *Wonder Book*. After his death he was tried as a heretic; his body was exhumed and burned at the stake.

Jornet e Ibars, Teresa   Blessed, religious, also known as 'Teresa of Jesus', born Aytona, Spain, 9 January 1843, died Valencia, 26 August 1897. Her parents were pious peasants. She joined the Poor Clares, but was forced to return home owing to ill health. She later founded her own religious community to provide care for the elderly. Later, along with ten companions, she took the habit at Barbastro, but soon transferred the motherhouse to Valencia, where it remains to this day. She continued to be superior general until her death. By this time the institute had 103 houses. Feast day 26 August.

Josaphat   *see* **Joasaph**

Josaphat Kuncevyc   Saint, bishop and martyr, born Volodymyr, Volyns'kyj, the Ukraine, 1580, died Vitebsk, 12 November 1623. He entered the monastery of the Holy Trinity in Vilnius in 1604. He was a man of deep spirituality, prayer and asceticism. In 1617 he became bishop of Polock (Polotsk) and was noted for his tireless preaching. He supported the Union of Brest, which had been concluded in 1596. He was killed by some opponents of the union of the Ukrainian-Belorussian Church with Rome. Josaphat was the first Eastern saint to be formally canonized by the Roman Catholic Church.

Joscio   Blessed, monk. Virtually nothing is known of his life, save that he was a monk at Saint-Bertin in France, where he died on 30 November 1163. According to legend five roses are said to have sprouted from his head after death, each bearing a letter of the name 'Maria'. His grave was under the small choir altar at Saint-Bertin, and the miracle of the roses was depicted in the ambulatory of the choir. Feast day 30 November.

Joseph I of Constantinople   Patriarch of Constantinople, born Asia Minor, *c.*1200, died Nicaea(?), 23 March 1283. A priest at the imperial court of Nicaea, he became a monk at the monastery of Mount Galesios between Smyrna and Ephesus. He was excommunicated by the Patriarch **Arsenius Autorianos** for interfering with his jurisdiction. After the deposition of Arsenius, and the brief patriarchate of Germanus III, Joseph was himself enthroned in 1267. He opposed attempts at reunification with the Roman Church following the Council of Lyons (1274), and vowed never to recognize Rome until it gave up its error or until a panorthodox council ruled on the matter. He was urged to reconsider by the Emperor Michael VIII Palaeologus, but remained intransigent. Joseph retired from the patriarchate over this issue, but was reinstated by Emperor **Andronicus II** in 1282. On his death, Joseph was hailed as a confessor by the emperor.

Joseph II Holy Roman Emperor, born Vienna, 13 March 1741, died there, 20 February 1790. He ruled Austria and its dominions from 1765, at first alongside his mother, Maria Theresa (to 1780), who made all the important decisions. Both he and his mother were concerned to reform the administrative and educational structures of their country, and he introduced both religious equality and the emancipation of the Jews. He clashed with the Papacy, reforming the Church along lines which separated it from Rome. He also dissolved many religious houses, as well as establishing new parishes. The thinking which lay behind his policy (known as 'Josephinism') may have been aimed less against the Church than at the renewal of parochial life, and of education, which depended heavily on the clergy. Pope **Pius VI** visited Joseph in Vienna, and Joseph in turn visited Rome, but these negotiations achieved little. He was not successful in his foreign policy, and succeeded only in alienating his subjects in Hungary and the Austrian Netherlands.

Joseph Calasanctius Saint, in religion 'a Matre Dei', founder of the Piarists, born Peralta de la Sol, Aragon, 1556, died Rome, 25 August 1648. He studied at several Spanish universities before being ordained priest in 1583. He went to Rome in 1592, where he was patronized by the Colonna family. He became greatly involved in working with the poor and homeless and in their education. He was influential in the founding of the first free school in Rome in 1597. He founded the Piarist Order further to facilitate the work of educating the poor. He was canonized in 1767. Feast day 27 August.

Joseph Cottolengo *see* Cottolengo, Giuseppe Benedetto

Joseph of Cupertino Saint, Franciscan priest, born in poverty at Cupertino, Italy, 17 June 1603, died Osimo, 18 September 1663. He had a very unhappy childhood and was resented by his mother, who was widowed shortly after his birth. He was refused admission by the Conventual Friars Minor and was then dismissed by the Capuchins as a result of his awkwardness. He finally became a stable boy at the Franciscan convent of La Grotella, near Cupertino, where he was admitted as a novice in 1625. Though very backward in his studies he was ordained priest in 1628. His life from then on was one of extreme austerity, accompanied by a series of miracles and ecstasies which included levitation. Because of the disturbance caused by this he was not allowed to take part in community duties for some 35 years, and was even denounced to the Inquisition. In 1639 he was removed from the curiosity of the people to Assisi and then to the convent of the Capuchins in 1653. Finally, in 1657, he was removed to the Conventual house at Osimo, where he remained in strict seclusion for the rest of his life. He was canonized in 1767. Feast day 18 September.

Joseph of Exeter (Josephus Iscanus) Latin poet, born Exeter, about whom very little else is known, fl. 1190. He studied at Gueldres, and accompanied Archbishop **Baldwin of Canterbury** to the Holy Land in 1188. His most notable poem, *De Bello Trojano*, which had been known under the names of Dares Phygius and Cornelius Nepos, was first published as his own in Frankfurt as late as 1620, and was later edited by Jusserans in 1877.

Joseph of Leonessa Saint, Capuchin monk, born Leonessa, Italy, 8 January 1556, died Amatrice, Italy, 4 February 1612. The son of a nobleman, he was orphaned at fifteen and was brought up and educated by his uncle, Battista, who was a professor at Viterbo. In January 1573 he joined the Capuchin Order, and was later ordained to the priesthood. A noted preacher, he arrived in Contantinople in 1587, where he ministered to galley slaves and preached in the city. This led to great hostility, and his imprisonment. On his release he attempted to enter the royal palace, but was caught and was condemned to death by the sultan. Having been left hanging by hooks through his hand and foot for three days, he was released. He returned to Italy, where he became widely known for his preaching and his care for the poor and sick.

Joseph of Methone Scholar and bishop, born 'John Phisradensis', probably in Candia, Crete, c.1429, died Methone, 9 August 1500. Being opposed in his support for the Byzantine union with Rome, he sought Venetian and papal help. Cardinal **Bessarion** made him 'head of the Oriental Churches' and 'Vice-Proto papas' c.1466–81. When appointed bishop of Methone, he was about to revisit Crete in 1500 but hearing of a Turkish threat to Methone, he went there, cross in hand, to meet the attacking Turks and was killed.

Joseph of the Holy Spirit (Joseph Barroso) Carmelite theologian and writer, born Braga, Portugal, 26 December 1609, died Madrid, 27 January 1674. Commonly known as 'the Portuguese' to distinguish him from a similarly named 'the Andalusian', he entered the Discalced Carmelites in 1632 and after ordination assisted in the establishment of several foundations. He declined the offer of a bishopric made to him by the king of Portugal because of his fame as a theologian and preacher. His writings are important because he used many works and manuscripts not now extant.

Josquin des Prez (des Prés, Despres) French musician, born Condé-sur-L'Escaut, Hainaut, now in northern France, c.1440, died Condé-sur-L'Escaut, 27 August 1521. He was highly regarded as a composer. He travelled to Italy and became a member of the papal choir. He composed many items of Church music, most of which lay forgotten until rediscovered by Dr Charles Burney in the eighteenth century.

Jouffroy, Jean Benedictine cardinal, abbot and diplomat, born Luxeuil, France, c.1412, died Rully, Burgundy, 24 November 1473. He taught canon law at the University of Pavia, 1435–8, and defended the Papacy at the Council of Ferrara. He then became the diplomatic adviser of Duke Philip the Good of Burgundy, who made him bishop of Arras in 1453. Pope **Pius II** sent him as legate to rescind the Pragmatic Sanction of Bourges in 1461. He then became a cardinal in 1461, bishop of Albi in 1462 and abbot of Saint-Denis in 1464.

Jouon, Paul Jesuit grammarian of Semitic languages, born Nantes, France, 26 February 1871, died Nantes, 8 February 1940. Becoming a Jesuit at Canterbury, England, in 1890, he was ordained at Lyons, France, in 1901. After studying at Innsbruck and Paris in 1907–8, he taught Hebrew at St Joseph's University, Beirut, and then at the Pontifical Biblical Institute until 1920, when his health failed, and he engaged in scholarly research, publishing mainly lexicographic studies and works of textual criticism.

Journet, Charles Cardinal and theologian, born Vernier, Switzerland, 26 January 1891, died Fribourg, Switzerland, 15 April 1975. Journet was educated at the major seminary in Fribourg, ordained there in 1917, became professor of dogmatic theology there in 1924 and stayed there until his retirement in 1970. In 1965, he was created cardinal by Pope **Paul VI**. A specialist in Thomistic theology and in ecclesiology, Journet worked on the pre-conciliar theological commission of the Second Vatican Council, where his work and understanding were influential. The founding editor of the journal *Nova et vetera*, Journet wrote many and varied works, including *The Church of the Word Incarnate* (1955), and *The Dark Knowledge of God* (1948).

Jouvancy, Joseph de Jesuit historian, born Paris, 14 September 1643, died Rome, 29 May 1719. Entering the Society of Jesus in 1659, he taught classics in several French colleges until he was summoned in 1699 to Rome to complete a history of the Jesuits, which occupied the rest of his life. In 1715 the *parlement* of Paris banned this work as contrary to the power of the French Crown, and in 1722 it was put on the Index for discussing the Chinese rites controversy. Among his other works, the most important was *Christianus litterarum magistris de ratione discendi et docendi* (1691), which Jesuit professors adopted as a standard classical textbook.

Jovius, Paulus Bishop, Italian historian, born Como, Milan, 19 April 1483, died Florence, 10 December 1552. In Rome, Jovius came under the patronage of **Leo X** and of Cardinal Guilio de' Medici, later Pope **Clement VII**. Jovius became bishop of Nocera. He wrote a history of Florence in Latin. In his retirement, he settled at Lake Como and his art collection became renowned.

Joyeuse, Henri, duc de Comte de Bourchage, Capuchin friar, a son of Guillaume de Joyeuse, a Roman Catholic and royalist, born Courzia, Languedoc, September or October 1562, died Rivoli, 28 September 1608. As governor of Anjou in 1585 he captured Angers from the duke of Condé, for which he was appointed governor of Touraine, Maine and Perche. He became a Capuchin Friar Minor in 1588 as 'Ange de Joyeuse', but was persuaded to lead the Catholic League of Languedoc in the Wars of Religion. Pope **Clement VIII** exclaustrated him from the Order, and **Henry IV** made him lieutenant-governor of Languedoc and marshal of France. He re-entered the Capuchins in 1599 and was twice a provincial of the Order.

Juan de los Angeles Franciscan theologian and preacher, born probably near Oropesa, Ávila, 1536, died Madrid, 1609. He joined the Franciscan Friars Minor c.1562 and was transferred to the province of San José, Madrid, and spent the rest of his life travelling to preach, confess and write. He directed the Infanta Sor Margarita de la Cruz and her mother the Empress Maria. After being guardian of San Antonio in Guadal-Aja in 1595 and San Bernadino in Madrid in 1598, he was elected provincial governor of San José until 1603. He wrote numerous religious works.

Juan de Yepes y Álvarez *see* John of the Cross

Juan Diego Blessed, Mexican witness to Our Lady of Guadalupe, died 1548(?). A Christian Indian from the village of Cuauhtitlan, he saw a vision of Mary on three occasions, the first on 9 December 1531. She appeared on a hill at Tepeyac, near what is now Mexico City, as a young Indian girl speaking Nahuatl, his own language. She told him to instruct the bishop to build her a shrine on the hill. The Spanish bishop refused to believe that the Virgin could appear as an Indian or choose an Indian as her messenger until her image was mysteriously imprinted on Juan's cape. The Virgin of Guadalupe, as she is known, remains a potent symbol to all Mexicans. Feast day 9 December.

Juana Inés de la Cruz Poetess and dramatist, fam-ily name 'Inés de Asbaje y Ranirez de Castillana', born San Miguel Nepantla, near Mexico City, 12 November 1648, died Mexico City, 17 April 1695. After being lady-in-waiting to the viceroy's wife, 1665–7, she became a nun and from 1669 spent her life in the convent of St Jerome in Mexico City. She was prominent as a poetess in her own lifetime, but in later life gave up her literary activities to care for the plague-stricken – she died as a consequence of nursing the sick.

Juanes, Juan de Painter, real name 'Vicente Juan Masip', born Fuente la Higuera, Valencia, Spain, c.1500, died Bocairente, 21 December 1579. His paintings, almost all of religious subjects, introduced the Italian Renaissance to the Valencian school, such as *The Last Supper*, oil on a panel, in the Prado at Madrid, probably part of the reredos above an altar.

Juárez, Gaspar Jesuit canon lawyer and naturalist, born Santiago del Estero, Argentina, 1731, died Rome, 1799. He became a Jesuit in 1748 and taught canon law at Córdoba University until, when expelled in 1767, he went to the Papal States, where he studied biology and established in Rome a garden of American plants. He publicized throughout Europe the work of Maria Antonia San José de la Paz, who promoted a wider understanding of the 'Spiritual Exercises' of St **Ignatius of Loyola**.

Juárez, José Painter, born c.1615, died c.1660. The son of Luis **Juárez**, he was probably superior to his father, his paintings showing a knowledge of perspective and composition, harmonious colouring and precise, certain design. Some of his best works are in the Museo de San Diego, Mexico City.

Juárez, Luis Painter, born probably Mexico City, c.1575, died c.1635. He enjoyed contemporary approval as an artist. His works include the great retable of the Jesus Maria Monastery, Mexico (1631), and the important series for the La Merced and El Carmen Monasteries (1631–3). Many of his paintings are in the Museo de San Diego, Mexico City, including the oil on canvas *San Ildelfonso*.

Jud, Leo Swiss Reformer, born Germar, Alsace,

1482, died Zurich, 19 June 1542. At Basel University he studied medicine, but turned to theology and became a pastor in Alsace and then Zurich. In 1523, Jud devised a new vernacular baptismal service and in 1536 a new catechism. He supported **Zwingli** and believed that Church and State should be independent of one another. He was active as a translator, and translated the Bible into German.

Judde, Claude Jesuit spiritual director, born Rouen, 19 December 1661, died Paris, 11 March 1735. He became a Jesuit in 1677 in Paris, where he studied. After his ordination he taught at the Collège de Claremont. He was an instructor of priests at Rouen from 1709 to 1713, rector of the Paris novitiate from 1721 to 1722 and finally rector of the Collège St Thomas until his death. He wrote nothing apart from his notes for retreats and conferences. A collection of these was published by the Abbé Lenoir Duparc, *Oeuvres spirituelles de P. Judde*. He was an important representative of the continuing mystical tradition in Jesuit spirituality.

Judge, Thomas Augustine Founder of missionary congregations, born Boston, Massachusetts, 23 August 1868, died Washington, DC, 23 November 1933. Of Irish immigrant parents, he entered the Congregation of the Mission (Vincentian Fathers) at Philadelphia, Pennsylvania, where he was ordained in 1899. To assist the clergy faced by Latin immigrants defecting from the Church, he founded a lay apostolate in Brooklyn, New York, in 1909. Later known as the Missionary Cenacle Apostolate, this was extended to many New England parishes; and from them evolved, under his direction, as the Missionary Servants of the Most Holy Trinity

Judicael of Quimper Saint, king of Brittany, died *c.*647–58. A source of many legends, Judicael was the last independent king of Brittany. According to Fredegar, King Dagobert I insisted that the Bretons obey his rule; King Judicael responded and a peaceful solution was reached with the help of Bishop **Ouen** of Rouen and **Eligius of Noyon**. Apparently Judicael became a Benedictine monk later in life at the abbey of Saint-Jean-Baptiste (later called Saint-Meen-Gael). Feast day 17 December; in the Diocese of Quimper, 16 December.

Judith of Niederaltaich Saint, anchoress, died *c.*799. According to legend, Judith was the aunt or cousin of a certain Salome (perhaps Edburga, daughter of King **Offa** of Mercia), an Anglo-Saxon princess who had become an anchoress at Altaich (Niederaltaich), Bavaria, in a cell attached to a monastery. Judith came to find Salome and built a cell for herself as well, embracing the anchorite life and many difficulties. Judith outlived Salome, and when she died was buried with her. Feast day (with Salome) 29 June.

Judson, Adoniram Pioneer Baptist missionary, born Malden, USA, 9 August 1788, died at sea, 12 April 1850. Originally a Congregationalist minister, Judson was a founder of the American Board of Commissioners for Foreign Missions, America's first missionary society, in 1810. In 1812 he and his wife sailed for Burma, thus becoming America's first missionaries. During the voyage they became convinced of their need for adult baptism, which took place in India, and in 1814 they were recognized as Baptist missionaries. Once in Burma Judson learnt Burmese and exercised an especially fruitful ministry among the Karen tribe. He also worked on a translation of the Bible and a Burmese–English dictionary. He remarried twice, his first and second wives (and two children) having succumbed to disease.

Jugan, Jeanne Blessed, foundress of the Little Sisters of the Poor, born Petites-Croix, Brittany, 25 October 1792, died Pern, France, 29 August 1879. She spent twenty years working in a hospital at St Servan, and then in domestic service – in the latter occupation she used to accompany her employer visiting the sick and needy, and teaching catechism. In 1837 she established a small house with a friend in St Servan, joined the following year by a young woman who had been entrusted to her charge. They began by chance to look after the sick and elderly and in May 1842 the small group established themselves as a religious community, with Jeanne as superior. She was re-elected the following year, but Auguste Le Pailleur, the priest moderator of the group, dismissed her as superior: she was not even invited to the first general chapter of her Order in 1847. Though the Order she had founded went from strength to strength she gained no recognition of her work in her lifetime, apart from an award of 3000 francs from the French Academy in 1845 in recognition of her charitable work. For a time she was allowed both to beg, and to assist in the foundation of new houses, but in 1852 she was sent to remain inactive for the rest of her life in the community's motherhouse. When she died, there were 2400 Little Sisters of the Poor, caring for 20,000 aged poor in 177 houses. She was beatified by Pope John Paul II in 1982.

Jugie, Martin Assumptionist theologian, born Aubazine, France, 3 May 1878, died Lorgues, France, 29 November 1954. After joining the Assumptionists in 1895 he took the name 'Martin' and was ordained in 1901. He was professor of oriental theology from 1902 to 1914 at a seminary near Istanbul, then taught in various other colleges until 1952, and was consultor for the Oriental Church from 1935 to 1954. He wrote widely in oriental theology and was a leading exponent of the ecumenical movement.

Julian of Cuenca Saint, bishop and patron saint of Cuenca, born Burgos, Castile, 1127, died Cuenca, 28 January 1208(?). He taught theology at Palencia before becoming archdeacon of Toledo in 1182. In 1196 he became the second bishop of Cuenca, a city which had been captured from the Moors in 1177. As bishop he was responsible for drawing up the constitutions of the cathedral chapter. He was renowned as a pastor who cared for the poor and the sick. A number of miracles were attributed to him, including one in which he provided grain for the city. After his death his shrine became a place of pilgrimage where cures were reputedly effected.

Julian of Eclanum Bishop and theologian, born into an aristocratic family in Southern Italy, c.385, died Sicily, before 455. He received an excellent philological and philosophical education. He married Titia in 403 and was ordained first deacon, 407/8, and then bishop of Eclanum, 417/18. His refusal to subscribe to the anti-Pelagian *Epistola tractoria* of Pope **Zosimus** led to his removal. All his efforts to get an Ecumenical Council convoked failed, as well as his attempts to be reinstated. He died as a teacher in Sicily. Julian is probably most famous for the extensive theological polemic he had with **Augustine** in the latter's old age on issues such as original sin and predestination.

Julian of Halicarnassus (Helicarnassus) Monophysite bishop and heretical faction leader, died after 527. Julian was expelled from his see by **Justinian I** in 518 and took refuge in Alexandria. His theological position has been named 'aphthartodocetism', and teaches that Christ's body was incorruptible; that his suffering and death were real, but possible only because he willed passivity on his normally incorruptible body. Julian's opponents called those holding this doctrine 'Phantasiastae' (those teaching that Christ had only a phantom or apparent body).

Julian of Le Mans Saint, traditionally first bishop of Le Mans, France, died c.400(?). Unreliable sources claim that Julian was a Roman nobleman and evangelist in the Le Mans area, where many churches are dedicated to him. His cult was probably popularized by Henry II, born at Le Mans and baptized in the church of St Julian. Julian's legend claims that he performed miracles, calling him one of Christ's 72 disciples and Simon the Leper. He is occasionally confused with the perhaps mythical Julian the Hospitaller. Feast day 27 January.

Julian of Norwich English anchoress and mystic, born Norwich, c.1342, died there, c.1413. There is little definite evidence of her life. She is said to have lived as an anchoress against the walls of St Julian's Church, Norwich. Her main work is *The Sixteen Revelations of Divine Love*, which records and explains her visions and 'shewings'. It was written after twenty years' meditation on her experiences. The crux of the work is the activity of Divine Love, and the evil which comes from human will but is also the source of clearly revealing Divine Reality.

Julian of Saba Saint, monk, born Heliopolis, Syria, c.300, died Orshoene, c.377/80. Julian lived first in a cave in the desert of Orshoene, between Antioch and the Euphrates, with a group of disciples. He built a church in Sinai on the rock where God was said to have appeared to Moses. He refuted Arian claims of allegiance between 364 and 378. Feast day 18 October in the East, 17 January in Rome.

Julian of Speyer Franciscan musician and poet, born Speyer, c.1200, died Paris, c.1250. Also known as 'Julianus Teutonicus', Julian was a chapelmaster at the French court after his education at Paris but resigned to become a Franciscan around 1225. He set to music the poetic offices of **Francis of Assisi** and **Anthony of Padua** (though his authorship of the music for the latter is sometimes doubted). These offices became a model for many to follow and influenced the popularity of sequences, or poetic structures for parts of the Mass.

Julian of Toledo Saint, bishop, born Toledo, 642, died there, 6 March 690. Julian was of Jewish descent, educated in the Toledian episcopal school under Bishop **Eugenius**. He became bishop of Toledo in January 680. He played a part in the deposition of King Wamba and the election of Ervigius. Julian called the Twelfth–Fifteenth Councils of Toledo and presided over them all, and had his diocese accepted as the primary see in Spain. He engaged in conflict with Rome, confirmed the acts of the Sixth Ecumenical Council and was censured by Pope **Benedict II**. Major works include the controversial *Apologeticum*, a treatise 'on last things', and three books of anti-Jewish polemic. Feast day 8 March.

Juliana of Liège Blessed, abbess and visionary, born Retinnes, near Liège, 1192, died Fosses, near Namur, 5 April 1258. An orphan, she joined the Augustinian convent of Mont Cornillon, where in 1222 she became prioress. As the result of a vision she dedicated herself to establishing the feast of Corpus Christi, persuading her local bishop to allow its celebration: he fixed the day as the first Thursday following the octave of Trinity Sunday. The feast was extended to northern Europe in her own lifetime and, six years after her death, to the whole Church (by **Urban IV**, who had been archdeacon of Liège). Juliana herself, however, was exiled from Mont Cornillon and spent her final years first at a monastery in Namur and then as a recluse at Fosses.

Julicher, Adolf Lutheran NT scholar, born Falkenberg, Germany, 26 January 1857, died Marburg, 2 August 1938. After a parish ministry at Rummelsberg from 1882, he became professor of theology at Marburg, 1889–1923, where his special studies concerned Old Latin versions and NT exegesis. His principal work was *Die Gleichnisreden Jesu* (2 vols, 1886–9), in which he said that the parables must be taken as real similes and not as allegories, a view which anticipated the theory of form criticism. His careful critical introduction to the NT, *Die Einleitung in das Neue Testament* (1894), was widely acclaimed and re-edited several times.

Julius I Saint, Pope from 6 February 337, died 12 April 352. He was dragged into the Arian controversy when **Athanasius** and **Marcellus**, both condemned and in exile in Rome, sought his support. Julius took their part and managed to have the emperors convene a synod in Serdica (Sofia). After the departure of the Easterners, Julius' decision in favour of Athanasius and Marcellus was approved by the Westerners, who in this way accepted the right of bishops condemned by a provincial council to appeal to the Roman see. The episode shows a glimpse of the very gradual unfolding of the theory of papal primacy. Feast day 12 April.

Julius II Pope, born 'Giuliano della Rovere' at Albissola, near Savona, 5 December 1443, elected to the Papacy 1 November 1503, died Rome, 21 February 1513. He came from an impoverished noble family, but his uncle Francesco della Rovere became **Sixtus IV** in 1471 and as a result Giuliano was created cardinal, and given many benefices and bishoprics. After helping to secure the election of **Innocent VIII**, largely through bribery, he began to take a leading role in the affairs of the Papacy, but was forced to flee to **Charles VIII** of France in 1492 when Rodrigo Borgia was elected as **Alexander VI**, returning to Rome only after Alexander's death in 1503. After the brief pontificate of **Pius III** he was himself elected Pope in the same year. He increased the temporal power of the Papacy, removed Cesare **Borgia** from Italy, brought Perugia and Bologna to submission, and joined the league against Venice. When Venice had been defeated he turned against France, hitherto his principal ally. **Louis XII** responded by calling a council at Pisa to depose the Pope (1511). When the council, which moved to Milan, declared Julius suspended in 1512, he called a council at the

Lateran and won the Emperor Maximilian I over to his side. He was a patron of Renaissance art – through his generosity the painting of the Sistine Chapel was commissioned, along with the statue of Moses by **Michelangelo** in San Pietro in Vincoli, and **Raphael**'s frescoes in the Vatican. He laid the cornerstone of the basilica of St Peter's, the sale of indulgences for which brought about Martin **Luther**'s 95 theses.

Julius III Pope, born 'Giovanni Maria Giammaria Ciocchi del Monte' at Rome, 10 September 1487, elected to the Papacy 8 February 1550, died Rome, 23 March 1555. He studied jurisprudence at Perugia and Siena, and in 1511 he was made archbishop of Siponto, and held administrative posts in both Rome and the Papal States. Following the sack of Rome in 1527 he was taken hostage by the imperial forces. He opened the Council of Trent in 1545 as papal legate and was its first president. After a somewhat stormy conclave he was elected Pope in 1550. He was a great supporter of the Jesuit Order and, at first, of Church reform, but towards the end of his life lost interest in reform. In 1553, following the death of **Edward VI** of England, he was responsible for sending Cardinal Reginald **Pole** to England as legate. He was a patron of Renaissance art, and protector of **Michelangelo**.

Julius Africanus, Sextus Writer, born *c*.160, died Nicopolis, Palestine, *c*.240. Julius was an official under Septimius Severus, and was charged to organize a library in the Pantheon at Rome. He was in Heraclas' school at Alexandria and a contemporary of **Origen**. His work survives in fragments; his *Chronicles*, from the creation of the world until 221, places biblical dates with facts concerning Greek and Roman history. The work is based in Millenarian ideals. His *Kestoi* (stitches) was a miscellaneous work dealing mainly with secular matters.

Jungmann, Bernard Catholic theologian, born Münster, Germany, 1 March 1833, died Louvain, Belgium, 12 January 1895. Ordained in 1857, he taught philosophy to seminarians at Roulers from 1861, and dogma at Bruges from 1865 to 1871, when he moved to the University of Louvain to teach Church history, until 1880. In each of these institutions he produced important textbooks:

Demonstratio Christiana (Roulers, 1864), *Institutiones theologiae dogmaticae specialis* (Brussels, 1868), *Institutiones theologiae dogmaticae generalis* (Regensburg, 1874), *Dissertationes selectae in historiam ecclesiasticam* (7 vols, Regensburg, 1880–7).

Jungmann, Josef Andreas Jesuit theologian and liturgical scholar, born Sand, South Tyrol (in pre-First World War Austria), 16 November 1889, died Innsbruck, Austria, 6 January 1975. Ordained in 1913, Jungmann joined the Society of Jesus in 1917. From 1925 until 1963 (excluding the time when Hitler closed the faculty) he taught at the University of Innsbruck, in pastoral theology, catechetics and liturgy. An expert particularly on the meaning and history of the Latin liturgy, Jungmann was appointed to the Preparatory Commission for the Second Vatican Council and was highly esteemed as the *peritus* of the Commission for Liturgy. He wrote many books on liturgy, including *The Liturgy of the Word* (1966) and *The Mass: an Historical, Theological and Pastoral Survey* (1976).

Jungmann, Joseph Jesuit priest and theologian, born Münster, Westphalia, 12 November 1830, died Innsbruck, Austria, 26 November 1885. He studied in the local gymnasium before going to the German College, Rome, in 1850. He was ordained priest in 1855, a year after completing his doctorate. In 1857 he joined the German province of the Society of Jesus, and after his noviceship was appointed to the theology faculty of the Jesuits in Innsbruck, where he was professor of homiletics and catechetics, with a special interest in liturgy. His chief writings, however, all touched on aesthetics, and his approach to this subject denoted Jungmann as an early exponent of neo-Scholasticism.

Junilius Africanus Exegete, Byzantine imperial official, died before 550. Junilius, an African, served Emperor **Justinian I** from 541 to 549 as 'Quaestor Sacri Palatii'. At the same time, he possessed a good knowledge of Scripture and theology. Junilius translated into Latin a Greek introduction to scriptural exegesis by the Persian Paul, at the urging of his friend Primasius, bishop of Hadrumentum. This work, *Instituta regularia divinae legis*, was very influential in the early Middle Ages.

Junker, Hubert   Roman Catholic biblical scholar, born Merlscheid, Germany, 8 August 1891, died Trier, Germany, 26 April 1971. Junker was ordained in 1915, worked in parish work in Trier and Ahrweiler and earned his doctorate from the University of Bonn in 1922. He taught at Bonn, 1927–31, and Passau, 1931–8, before returning to the seminary in Trier in 1938. In 1950, he was a founding member of the Theological Academy of Trier, became rector there two years later and stayed there until his retirement in 1962. A prominent advocate of form criticism, Junker's book on the subject was suppressed by Rome until the 1943 papal encyclical *Divino afflante Spiritu* vindicated his position. He also wrote important commentaries on Genesis, Deuteronomy and the Minor Prophets.

Jurieu, Pierre   Calvinist theologian and polemicist, born Mer, the Orléanais, France, 24 December 1637, died Rotterdam, 11 January 1713. He was educated at Saumur, then at Sedan, by his grandfather Pierre Dumoulin, and he completed his studies in Holland and in England, where he received Anglican ordination. On returning to France, however, he was re-ordained and took up his father's parish at Mer. He became professor of Hebrew at Sedan, but when **Louis XIV** closed the college he became minister of the Walloon church in Rotterdam. Among his more influential books are *Lettres pastorales adresses aux fidèles de France*, in three volumes, 1686/7, published in Rotterdam but banned from France, and therefore becoming popular there with French Protestants. His *Histoire du Calvinisme et du Papisme* forecast the downfall of Antichrist (the Papacy) in 1689. It was his *La Politique du clergé de France* which led to his fleeing France for Holland. His defence of Protestantism also involved him in bitter attacks against Bishop **Bossuet** and against the Jansenists in his *Histoire et critique des dogmes et des cultes* (1704), which was translated into English in 1715.

Justel, Christopher   Calvinist canonist, born Paris, 5 May 1580, died Paris, June 1649. He acted as secretary first to **Henry IV** and later to the duc de Bouillon but his principal interest was in Eastern and African canon law. His celebrated works were on universal canon law (1610), African, Greek and Latin canon law, with notes (1615), **Photius'** collection of canon law (1615) and that of **Dionysius Exiguus** (1628).

Justin Martyr   Saint, Christian apologist, born Samaria, *c*.100, died Rome, by beheading, *c*.165. He was trained in philosophy, particularly Stoicism and Platonism, and became a Christian in about 130. He continued to teach, but now his teaching was in the defence and explanation of Christianity to Jews and pagans alike, first in Ephesus where he engaged in his famous 'Dialogue with Trypho the Jew' and later in Rome, where he opened a school. His *Apologies* (*c*.155 and 161) meet accusations against Christianity and endeavour to explain its beliefs and practices to pagan minds.

Justinian I   Roman emperor, born Tauresium, Illyricum, *c*.482, died Constantinople, 14 November 565. In 521 he was proclaimed consul and in 527 *augustus*, then emperor. He made great contributions to the military, the law, the Church and to architecture.

Justinianus   Bishop of Valencia, died there, mid-500s. Justinianus served during the reign of King Theudes (531–46). He subscribed the acts of the Council of Valencia (546) and wrote in opposition to Arianism and Donatism. Some believe that **Ildefonsus'** *Liber de cognitione baptismi* is actually an adaptation of the book by Justinianus. A short biography of Justinianus was written by **Isidore** in his *De viris illustribus*.

Justus of Canterbury   Saint, missionary to England, fourth archbishop of Canterbury, born Rome(?), died Canterbury, 10 November *c*.627. Most of what is known of Justus comes from **Bede**, who tells us that Justus was one of the second wave of missionaries sent to England by **Gregory I** (the Great) in 601. He was made bishop of Rochester by **Augustine of Canterbury** in 604. Following a pagan backlash he fled to Gaul but returned and in 624 was made archbishop of Canterbury.

Jutta   Blessed, German recluse, born *c*.1090, died Disibodenberg, *c*.1136. She became a recluse near Mons St Disibodi and was joined in 1106 by St **Hildegard**, who was then aged eight. A group of noblewomen gathered around them, to whom Jutta acted as prioress. On her death she was succeeded by Hildegard. Feast day 22 May.

Jutta of Fuchsstadt   Blessed, German Cistercian abbess, died 1250. A group of pious women living in an independent community at Essleben, wishing to live by a Rule, founded a Cistercian convent at Heiligenthal. Jutta was its first abbess, 1234–50. Pilgrimages were made to her tomb before the high altar. Her relic, an arm to which a golden cup was attached, was said to cure the sick, and was held at the Julius Hospital in Würzburg but is now lost. Commemoration 29 November.

Jutta of Sangerhausen   Saint, German anchoress, born Sangerhausen, died Kulmsee, Prussia, 12 May 1260. Although wanting to enter religious life, she married to please her parents. After her husband's death she settled as an anchoress in Prussia, nursing the sick and lepers. Her spiritual directors were **John Lobedau** and Bishop Heideinreich. Her devotion was to the Sacred Heart of Jesus. Feast day 5 May.

K

Kaas, Ludwig Roman Catholic priest and politician, born Trier, Germany, 23 May 1881, died Rome, 15 April 1952. Having studied in Rome, he was ordained in 1909, studied law at Bonn and became professor of canon law at Trier in 1918. His interest in German politics led to his election to the National Assembly in 1919, to the Reichstag from 1920 and as a delegate to the League of Nations in 1926. As chairman of the (Catholic) Centre Party from 1928, his fear of socialism led him to press for a coalition with German nationalists, and to be one of those responsible for the Act which enabled Hitler as Chancellor to become dictator. After the dissolution of his party in 1933 he went to Rome. Friend and adviser of **Pius XII** and secretary of the Congregation of St Peter's Basilica, he directed the archaeological investigations concerning the burial place of St Peter underneath it.

Kačič-Miošić, Andrija Franciscan Croatian poet, born Brist, Makarska, June 1704, died Zaostrog, Makarska, 14 December 1760. Having become a Franciscan in 1720 he studied philosophy and theology at Buda, 1721–7, and was ordained in 1728. He taught philosophy at Zaostrog, 1730–5, then was *lector generalis* at Sibenik until 1743. He worked on the construction of the monastery on the island of Brac, c.1745–50, went to Venice for a year and on his return tried to help flood victims in Zaostrog, where he contracted pneumonia and died. His first book, on **Duns Scotus**, was an introduction to philosophy mainly for his students (1752), but his *Pleasant Conversation of the Slavic People* (1756) was a well-researched prose and verse epic recounting tales of heroism and faith in which democracy and toleration were advocated, and aroused a new sense of nationhood.

Kagawa Toyohiko Protestant social reformer, born into a wealthy family in Kobe, Japan, 10 July 1888, died Tokyo, 10 April 1960. His early education was in a Buddhist monastery, but he converted to Christianity in his teens and was rejected by his family. He subsequently studied at the Presbyterian College, Tokyo, and Princeton Theological Seminary, USA. Worked in the slums on his return in 1917 as an evangelist and social reformer. A leader in the Japanese labour movement, founding the Federation of Labour, 1918, the Farmers' Union, 1921, and the National Anti-War League, 1928. In 1940 he was imprisoned as a pacifist. A leader in the post-war women's suffrage movement and in the process of democratization. Wrote numerous books, including the autobiographical *Across the Death Line* (1920).

Kahle, Paul Ernst Lutheran pastor and OT scholar, born Hohenstein, East Prussia, 21 January 1875, died Düsseldorf, 24 September 1964. He studied theology and oriental languages in Marburg and Halle and from 1899 undertook an examination of Hebrew, Samaritan, Syriac and Arabic manuscripts in Berlin, London, Oxford and Cambridge. From 1903 to 1908 he worked in Cairo as head of the German School there, and as a pastor. In Cambridge he studied some of the manuscripts found in the Cairo Geniza and questioned the possibility of reconstructing the original text, on the ground that no recension was the result of a single act but rather the end result of much editing and revision. He attributed agreements between the Septuagint and the Samaritan Pentateuch to the fact that they came from the same 'common' tradition. After appointments in Jerusalem, Halle and Giessen, he went as professor to Bonn, and began to work with Rudolf **Kittel** on the *Biblia Hebraica*. In 1938 he emigrated to England with his family, and remained a British citizen even after returning to work in Bonn and Münster after the war.

Kakubilla (Cacucabilla, Cacucila, Cucacilla)   Saint, a mythical saint popular in the fifteenth century. It is said that her name, which is reminiscent of 'Columcille', goes back to St **Columba**, who was invoked against demons and thunderstorms. In Germany the saint was invoked against rats and mice, and in the abbey church of Adelberg in Württemberg there is a portrait of a saint with two mice bearing the title 'Cutubilla'.

Kalley, Robert   Protestant medical missionary, born Glasgow, 8 September 1809, died Edinburgh, 17 January 1888. Brought up a Presbyterian, after graduating MD at Glasgow in 1838 he went independently to Madeira, where his medical, educational and evangelical ministry provoked Portuguese opposition and he was expelled in 1848. After work in Ireland, Malta and Lebanon he went to Brazil in 1855, where in Rio de Janeiro he established a Congregational Church, the oldest Protestant Church in the country, and was prominent in the pressure for religious liberty. He retired to Scotland in 1876.

Kamel, George Joseph   Jesuit missionary and botanist, born Brunn, Moravia, 21 April 1661, died Manila, 2 May 1706. He became a Jesuit in 1682, working as an infirmarian and botanist, and in 1688 established a herb garden and pharmacy at the Jesuit College in Manila, from where he sent botanical specimens to Europe and reported the medicinal properties of *Strychnos ignatii* (St Ignatius' bean). The first and third parts of his treatise on Philippino plants were published by John Ray in his *Historia generalis plantarum* (3 vols, 1686–1704), and his drawings are in the Jesuit archives at Louvain and in the British Museum.

Kane, William Humbert   US Dominican theologian and philosopher, born Chicago, 12 July 1901, died

Oak Park, Illinois, 10 June 1970. Made his first profession in 1921 and was ordained in 1927. Besides studying philosophy and theology, and in preparation for going as a missionary to China, which never came about, he studied medicine in Washington. He was then sent to Rome to do a doctorate in philosophy and thereafter taught philosophy at, and was later president of, the Dominican house of studies (which became a pontifical faculty of philosophy in 1944) in River Forest, Illinois. Between 1948 and 1951 he taught in Rome before returning to River Forest to establish the Albertus Magnus Lyceum for the study of philosophy and science.

Kant, Immanuel   German philosopher, born into a Lutheran family in Königsberg, East Prussia, 22 April 1724, died Königsberg, 12 February 1804. Studied mathematics, physics and philosophy in Königsberg, then worked as a private tutor. In 1755 he returned to Königsberg and spent fifteen years as unsalaried professor at the university. In 1770 he was appointed professor of philosophy and he remained in this post until 1797. His earlier writings, largely based on the teaching of Christian Wolff, were on mathematics and physics and about the principles and possibility of metaphysical knowledge. It is his later works of 'Critical Philosophy', however, that have exercised most influence on Christian thought. These include and are translated as *Critique of Pure Reason* (1781), *Foundation for the Metaphysics of Morals* (1785), *Critique of Practical Reason* (1788), *Critique of Judgement* (1790) and *Religion Within the Limits of Reason Alone* (1793). Kant denied the possibility of a simple a priori rational knowledge of reality. He argued that all knowledge needed an empirical element, and this idea threatened customary thinking in metaphysics which claimed it was possible to have knowledge of that which transcended nature, traditionally God, freedom and immortality. In Kant's scheme the three main proofs for the existence of God, the Ontological, Cosmological and Teleological Arguments, were not possible. Kant turned to ethics and especially to conscience to supply this knowledge, arguing that in our understanding and experience of duty we know freedom and knowing freedom leads us to a knowledge of immortality and of the Divine Being. For Kant religion is little more than morality, and there is little or no place for the mystical, for the historical or for a personal redeemer. However, his moral imperatives – the concept of universality and the injunction to treat all people as an end and not as a means only – and the autonomy of ethics, underlie liberal democracy and enable a global morality which does not depend on adherence to the Christian faith.

Karlstadt, Andreas Rudolf Bodenstein von (Carlstadt) Radical Protestant reformer, born Karlstadt, Germany, c.1480, died Basel, Switzerland, 24 December 1541. Karlstadt taught at the University of Wittenberg. He went through a spiritual crisis in 1515, but found consolation in the doctrines of his colleague Martin **Luther**, and became one of his early disciples. Karlstadt's celebration of Communion on Christmas Day 1521 was the first to reflect Protestant eucharistic theology. The next day he announced his engagement, thereby renouncing clerical celibacy. While Luther was in hiding following the Diet of Worms, Karlstadt introduced radical Church reforms in Wittenberg. His radicalism eventually proved too much for Luther, and Karlstadt was forced to leave. He finally settled in Switzerland, and was a professor at Basel from 1534 until his death.

Karnkowski, Stanisław Archbishop of Gniezno and primate of Poland, 1581–1603, born 10 May 1520, died Łowicz, Poland, 8 June 1603. Having become bishop of Włocławek in 1567 he began to implement the Tridentine reforms, which brought many of his people back into Catholicism. He made, in 1579, a collection of synodal laws relating to his province and supported Jacob Wujek in translating the Bible into Polish.

Kasper, Katharina Foundress of the Poor Handmaids of Christ, born Dernbach, near Montabaur, Germany, 26 May 1820, died Dernbach, 2 February 1898. In 1848 in Dernbach she founded her congregation to care for the sick, which was approved by the diocese in 1851. Largely because of the Church–State antipathy in Prussia, her movement was established in the USA in 1868 and in England in 1875. Her cause for beatification was introduced in 1946.

Kasprowicz, Jan Poet and translator into Polish

of European classics, born Szymborze, German Poland, 12 December 1860, died Zakopane, Poland, 1 August 1926. He studied at the Universities of Leipzig, Breslau and Lvov and became a journalist and a professor of comparative literature at Lvov University. In his early poems he is concerned with social justice and depicts the suffering of the poor. His cycle of poems *To a Dying World* is concerned with the sufferings of humanity, and his *Book of the Poor* reveals his religious faith. He translated from English, German, French and Italian.

Katerkamp, Johann Theodor Hermann Theologian and Church historian, born Ochtrup, Westphalia, 17 January 1764, died Münster, Westphalia, 9 June 1834. Ordained in 1787, he was private tutor to the family of Droste-Vischering in Münster, where he remained until 1806. He became provisional professor of Church history in 1809 and ordinary professor of Church history, canon law and patrology in 1819 at the University of Münster, where he produced the first major modern Catholic history of the Church, *Kirchengeschichte* (Intro. and 5 vols, Münster, 1819–34).

Katschthaler, Johannes Cardinal, born Hippach-Zillertal, Tyrol, 29 May 1832, died Salzburg, 27 February 1914. Ordained in 1856, he became professor of dogmatic theology at Salzburg in 1864, and of apologetics and the history of dogma at Innsbruck in 1865. In 1877–88 he wrote his important work *Theologica dogmatica specialis*, then in 1891 he was appointed auxiliary bishop and in 1900 prince-archbishop of Salzburg. Having become a cardinal in 1903, he led the opposition to the 'Away from Rome' movement which found Catholicism in Austria too political. In his leisure moments he pursued the history of Church music.

Katterbach, Bruno Franciscan palaeographer and archivist, born Düsseldorf, Germany, 16 September 1883, died Rome, 29 December 1931. He entered the Franciscan Order in 1901, studied at Fulda and was ordained in 1909. After studies at the Antonianum in Rome, he was appointed archivist and professor of palaeography and diplomatics in the Vatican Archives School, 1913–16, 1920–31. His most valuable work was the *Inventorium Registro-*

rum Supplicationum ab anno 1342 ad 1899 (Rome, 1932).

Katzer, Frederick Francis Xavier   Third Roman Catholic archbishop of Milwaukee, Wisconsin Diocese, born Ebensee, Austria, 7 February 1844, died Fond du Lac, Wisconsin, 20 July 1903. Ordained in Milwaukee, 1866, he was appointed bishop of Green Bay, Wisconsin, in 1875. In 1890 he led the objections to compulsory education and the use of English. Many Catholics were unhappy with his appointment as archbishop in 1891, finding him too German, and later with his outright opposition to 'Americanism', the Catholic movement which wanted the Church to adapt to contemporary cultural ideals by emphasizing, e.g., humanitarianism and democracy and depreciating, e.g., humility and subjection to authority, and to minimize differences with other Christians.

Kaulen, Franz Philipp   Catholic theologian and exegete, born Düsseldorf, Germany, 20 March 1827, died Bonn, 11 July 1907. He was ordained in 1850, gained a doctorate in theology in 1862, became professor of OT exegesis at the University of Bonn, 1880, and a member of the Pontifical Biblical Commission in 1903. He discussed the authenticity of the Vulgate in *Geschichte der Vulgata* (Mainz, 1868), surveyed contemporary Catholic study of the Bible in *Einleitung in die Heilige Schrift des Alten und Neuen Testaments* (5th edn, Freiburg, 1911–13) and completed **Hergenröther**'s work on the second edition of Wetzer and Welte's *Kirchenlexicon* (12 vols, Freiburg, 1882–1903).

Kautzsch, Emil Friedrich   Protestant OT philologist and teacher, born Plauen, Vogtland, Germany, 4 September 1841, died Halle, Germany, 7 May 1910. After study at Leipzig, he taught there, 1869–72, and at Basel, 1872–80, Tübingen, 1880–8, and Halle, 1880–1910. He was independent-minded and moderately liberal in his attitude towards OT criticism, and his acclaimed revisions of **Gesenius**' *Hebrew Grammar* (1878–1909), his *Aramaic Grammar* (1884) and German translations of the OT and of the Apocrypha exhibit his penetrating scholarship.

Kavanagh, Edward   Catholic Congressman, diplomat and governor, born Newcastle, Maine, 27 April 1795, died Damariscotta Falls, Maine, 22 January 1844. He abandoned his intention of becoming a priest to rescue the family shipbuilding business, after which he studied law and drafted the Catholic memorial to the Maine Constitutional Convention of 1819. He was elected to both houses of the Maine legislature and then to Congress, 1831–5. He negotiated the first treaty between Portugal and the USA, and became the first Catholic governor of New England.

Kazel, Dorothy   US Ursuline missionary, born Cleveland, Ohio, 30 June 1938, died by shooting, San Pedro Nonualco, El Salvador, 2 December 1980. She entered the Ursuline Order in 1960 and took her final vows in 1968. She studied for several years and in 1974 went to Costa Rica and thence to El Salvador as a missionary of the Cleveland Diocese. As the political situation in El Salvador worsened she worked alongside the refugees and the bereaved, and following the killing of Oscar **Romero** in 1980 she wrote to Jimmy Carter to protest at the way US money was being used to terrorize and kill innocent people. Driving back from the airport some months later with her co-worker Jean Donovan and two Maryknoll sisters, Ita **Ford** and Maura **Clarke**, they were set upon, abducted, tortured, raped and then shot and dumped by the roadside by five national guardsmen. It was four years, and then only following massive international outrage at the murders, before the murderers were arrested, tried, found guilty and imprisoned for their crime.

Keane, Augustus Henry   Catholic journalist, born Cork, Ireland, 1 June 1833, died London, 3 February 1912. After studies at the Propaganda Fidei College in Rome, and at the University of Dublin, he found his niche in journalism. In 1862 he became editor and in 1864 proprietor of the only Catholic newspaper published in Scotland, the *Glasgow Free Press*. He used it to campaign with increasing force on behalf of Catholic Irish immigrants against the alleged partiality of the Scots vicars apostolic. In 1868 the newspaper was condemned by the Congregation for the Propagation of the Faith and went out of publication, though as a result the Scottish hierarchy was reorganized in 1878. Keane went to London, pursued ethnology and related subjects, and became professor of

Hindustani at University College, for which he was awarded a government pension of £50 a year.

Keane, John Joseph   Archbishop and first rector of the Catholic University of America, born Bally-shannon, Donegal, Ireland, 12 September 1839, died Dubuque, Iowa, 22 June 1918. He was ordained in 1866 and assigned to St Patrick's, Washington, DC, where he helped to found the Catholic Total Abstinence Union of America in 1872 and the Catholic Young Men's National Union in 1875. His gifts were recognized and he was appointed bishop of Richmond, Virginia, in 1875. Here he gave lectures which eased tensions between Protestants and Catholics. His next assignment was the foundation of the Catholic University of America, but his brilliance as an organizer was offset by his reputation as a danger-ous theological liberal. **Leo XIII** removed him to Rome for a time but when the Catholic University got into financial difficulty he was sent back to raise funds for it. In 1900 he was appointed arch-bishop of Dubuque. Here he put his energy into founding schools and colleges and campaigning against alcoholism. When his health failed he retired to the Catholic rectory there until his death.

Keasberry, Benjamin Peach   Independent Prot-estant missionary, born Hyderabad, India, 1811, died Singapore, 6 September 1875. After a semi-nary education in the USA, he went to Singapore in 1837 with the London Missionary Society. When the mission closed he remained, indepen-dently to educate and evangelize Malays in local congregations and in his successful boarding school founded in 1848–9, for whom he translated and printed stories and textbooks. He appealed for funding from missionary societies in Britain and the USA, but none responded and after his death the school had to close, and the congregations became Presbyterian.

Keating, Geoffrey   Writer and Roman Catholic priest, born Burgess, near Clonmel, County Tip-perary, c.1570, died near Burgess, before 1644. Educated at a Latin school near Cahir, he was later ordained to the priesthood. From around 1603 he studied at the College of Bordeaux in France, where he became a doctor of theology. In 1610 he returned to Ireland, but was forced to flee after an outspoken sermon. Little is known of his sub-sequent life, save that he travelled throughout Ireland gathering material for a history of the country. As well as his history, he wrote extensively and is regarded as the greatest prose stylist in Irish Gaelic. He was buried in the chapel of Tubrid, near Clonmel.

Keble, John   Anglican priest and poet, born Fair-ford, Gloucestershire, 25 April 1792, died Bourne-mouth, 29 March 1866. He was educated at Oxford, where he gained a double first and was elected a fellow of Oriel. He was ordained in 1816, and on leaving Oxford in 1823 took up a variety of curacies, returning to Oxford in 1831 as profes-sor of poetry, a post he held for a decade: his volume of religious poems *The Christian Year* (1827) had become extremely popular. In 1833 he gave a sermon on 'National Apostasy' at the Oxford University Church of St Mary the Virgin, a sermon which is generally regarded as initiating the Oxford Movement, in which he was deeply involved. After John Henry **Newman** joined the Roman Catholic Church, Keble became leader of the Oxford Movement. In 1836 he accepted the living of Hursely in Hampshire, where he spent the rest of his working life as an assiduous parish priest until in 1864 his wife's health occasioned a move first to Cornwall and then to Bournemouth. He is commemorated by Keble College, Oxford.

Kedermynster (Kyderminstre), Richard   Abbot of Winchcomb, Gloucestershire, c.1487, died c.1531. He was one of the English representatives at the Lateran Council of 1512. Richard defended the retention of benefit of clergy as applied to minor orders.

Keeble, Samuel Edward   Methodist minister and social reformer, born London, 1853, died there, 5 September 1946. Ordained in 1878, with history and economics his chosen study, his life's work was to convince Methodism that the way to change society was not by the stricter avoidance of specific vices. He became editor of the left-wing *Methodist Weekly*, and in 1905 established the Wesleyan Methodist Union for Social Service. He achieved the admission of women to the Conference in 1909. His most influential works were *Industrial*

Day-Dreams (London, 1896) and *The Christian Responsibility for the Social Order* (London, 1921).

Keegan, Robert Fulton Roman Catholic priest and charity administrator, born Nashua, New Hampshire, 3 May 1888, died New York City, 4 November 1947. He was ordained in New York in 1915, then studied sociology at the Catholic University of America. In 1919 he was appointed the first director of New York's Catholic Charities, which he succeeded in developing into the largest charitable organization in the USA, with a social welfare department. The organization became a model for other charitable foundations, public as well as nonsectarian, some of which elected him their president. In 1933 he became pastor of the Blessed Sacrament Church, New York.

Keely (Kiely, Keily), Patrick Charles Church architect, born Ireland, either Kilkenny, 9 August 1816, or Thurles, 9 August 1820, died Brooklyn, New York, 11 August 1896, having emigrated to the USA in 1841. He attained success with his large, wide, neo-Gothic buildings intended primarily for preaching; and among the sixteen cathedrals he designed are Rochester, Chicago, Boston, Providence and Erie, while St Francis Xavier Church, New York, is one of the better-known of the 500 or more churches.

Kehr, Paul Fridolin Protestant historian of the Papacy, born Waltershausen, Germany, 26 December 1860, died Wässendorf, near Würzburg, 9 November 1944. He taught history at Marburg in 1893, and was made professor of medieval history at Göttingen in 1895. His outstanding research concerned the development of the Papacy until the time of **Innocent III**, about which he instigated a scrupulous scientific and critical investigation. The first volume of *Regesta Pontificum Romanorum* (Rome, 1906) was followed by others (and continuing), bringing together manuscripts from all the archives of Europe, set out on Kehr's regional and diocesan plan. With financial assistance from **Pius XI**, in 1931 he founded the Pius Institute ('Piusstiftung') for research into papal documents and medieval poetry.

Keiley, Anthony M. Catholic politician and jurist, born Paterson, New Jersey, 12 September 1833, died Paris, 27 January 1905. Brought up in Petersburg, Virginia, he was called to the bar, then served in the Confederate army. He was a member of the Virginia House of Delegates, 1864–71, mayor of Richmond, Virginia, 1871–6, city attorney, 1875–85, and chairman of the Democratic State Committee, 1881. In 1885 he was appointed US minister to Italy, but the Italian government refused to accept him, because he had criticized the nationalist seizure of Rome; and the same year Austria-Hungary refused to accept him, because of his Jewish wife. His gifts were eventually used at the International Court of First Instance in Cairo, of which he was appointed judge in 1886, and in 1894 he was US representative at the Higher Court of Appeals at Alexandria, from which he resigned in 1902; he thereafter served as president of the National Irish Catholic Benevolent Union.

Kekela, James Hunnewell Protestant missionary, born Mokuela, Hawaii, 1824, died Honolulu, 29 November 1904. He was trained for the ministry at Lahainaluna Seminary in 1847, and became the first ordained minister in Hawaii, in 1849. With finance from the United Church of Christ in Hawaii, he established a mission in the Marquesas, and in 1864 he was brought to the notice of Abraham Lincoln and the US people when he negotiated the ransom of the captain of a US whaling ship, captured in revenge for the kidnapping of the son of a Marquesas chief by Peruvian slavers. The mission remained small, but his 45 years of steadfast work was not forgotten.

Keller, James G. Maryknoll priest, founder of the Christophers, born Oakland, California, 27 June 1900, died New York City, 7 February 1977. Joined Maryknoll in 1921, studied at the Catholic University of America and was ordained in 1925. Founded the Christophers, based on the idea that every person can do something to make the world a better place, in 1945. In the same year he published *You Can Change the World*, which became a best-seller. He published a newsletter which went seven times a year, free, to 750,000 people, wrote a newspaper column, made regular radio broadcasts and began the Christopher Awards for work in the media which helps improve the world. The title of his autobiography, *To Light a Candle*, reflects the Christophers' motto, taken from a Chinese proverb, 'It is better to light one candle than to curse the darkness.'

Kelley, Francis Clement Roman Catholic bishop, founder of the Catholic Church Extension Society of the USA, born Prince Edward Island, Canada, 24 November 1870, died Oklahoma City, 1 February 1948. Educated at Laval University, Montreal, he was ordained in 1893 for the Diocese of Detroit, Michigan, and became pastor of Lapeer parish. In 1905 he founded and was president for nineteen years of the Extension Society, during which time its revenue eventually amounted to almost $1,000,000 annually. He founded and edited the *Extension Magazine*, which had more than 300,000 subscribers in his time. He took a great interest in the situation of the Church in Mexico, which he represented at the peace conference after World War I, and during the Carranza revolution he established a seminary for exiled Mexicans at Castorville, Texas. In Austria he worked for the relief of post-war famine, for which the Austrian government awarded him the Great Golden Cross of the Order of Merit. His conversations with Prime Minister Vittorio Orlando of Italy helped bring about the conditions for the Lateran Treaty of 1929, by which the Vatican City was established as a sovereign state, and he was awarded a knighthood in the Order of St Maurus and St Lazarus by the Italian government in 1930. In 1915 he was made a domestic prelate, that is, an official of the papal court, and soon afterwards a member of the college of notaries attached to it. In 1924 he became bishop of Oklahoma City and Tulsa, where he staunchly opposed the Ku Klux Klan.

Kellner, Heinrich Catholic patrologist and liturgist, born Heiligenstadt, Germany, 26 August 1837, died Bonn, 6 January 1915. From 1867 to 1874 he taught theology in a seminary in his home town, then from 1882 to 1915 patrology, liturgics and catechetics at the University of Bonn. Besides versions of **Tertullian**'s writings, he produced a classic work of liturgical research and historical method, *Heortologie* (Freiburg, 1900), a study of religious festivals throughout the liturgical year.

Kelly, Eugene Catholic banker and philanthropist, born County Tyrone, Ireland, 25 November 1808, died New York City, 19 December 1894.

Having emigrated to the USA in 1834, he established dry goods stores in Maysville and St Louis before moving to California in 1850, where in addition to the dry goods business he founded a bank. Six years later in New York he founded the Kelly and Company bank, from which he retired in 1894 to manage his $15,000,000 estate. He was president of the National Federation for Irish Home Rule and treasurer of the Irish Parliamentary Fund. A member of the original board of trustees of the Catholic University of America, he donated to it $100,000. He was appointed Chamberlain of the Cape and Sword, a papal honour given to only two US citizens before then.

Kelly, Gerald Andrew Jesuit moral theologian, born Denver, Colorado, 30 September 1902, died Kansas City, 2 August 1964. After his early education in Denver, he became a Jesuit and was awarded a master's degree in arts and a licentiate in theology at St Louis University. He was ordained in 1933 and went to the Gregorian University at Rome, where he attained a doctorate in theology in 1937. On his return to the USA he taught moral theology to Jesuits at St Mary's, Kansas, for 26 years. His special concern was medico-moral problems, and he was chairman of the committee which formulated the ethical code of the Catholic Hospitals Association. He received the Cardinal Spellman Award for theology in 1953. An independent thinker, he approached moral problems objectively, dealing with them simply and clearly in his many lectures to priests, nuns, physicians, nurses and social workers. Among other works of his, the critical accounts of current thinking in moral theology, in *Theological Studies*, published between 1946 and 1952, helped theological students, and his many articles in the *Linacre Quarterly*, helped physicians and nurses.

Kelly, Michael Vincent Roman Catholic pastoral theologian, born Adjala, Ontario, 31 July 1863, died Toronto, 24 July 1942. He was educated at St Michael's College and the University of Toronto, from where after his graduation in 1887 he entered the Congregation of Priests of St Basil at Beaconsfield, England, and returned to Toronto for ordination in 1891. His concern was to help priests to be good pastors, and his works reflect this, in *Zeal in the Classroom* (Toronto, 1922), *Some of the*

Pastor's Problems (Toronto, 1923) and in collaboration with Canon J. B. Geniesse, a study of the problems arising from mixed marriages (Rome, 1923). His *First Communicant's Catechism* was translated into Slovak and Spanish. From 1922 to 1936 he was assistant superior general of the Congregation.

Kelly, Thomas Protestant hymn-writer, born Stradbally, Queen's Counts, Ireland, 13 July 1769, died Dublin, 14 May 1855. Educated at Trinity College, Dublin, and ordained into the Church of Ireland in 1792, his evangelicalism caused the archbishop to forbid his preaching in Dublin. He eventually rejected the idea of a national Church, as well as ordination, and resigned. He was wealthy, and used his money to help those suffering distress in the famine of 1849, and to build churches where he preached. The seventh edition of his hymns (Dublin, 1853) contained 765 hymns, for which he composed most of the tunes. The best known are 'The Head that Once was Crowned with Thorns', 'We Sing the Praise of Him who Died' and 'Look, ye Saints, the Sight is Glorious'.

Kelvin of Largs, William Thomson, Baron Physicist, born Belfast, Ireland, 26 June 1824, died Netherhall, Scotland, 17 December 1907. Professor of natural philosophy at Glasgow for 53 years, he was a pioneer of the sciences of thermodynamics and geophysics. Lord Kelvin was one of the greatest physicists of his time, formulating the 'Kelvin scale' of absolute temperature, inventing numerous electrical instruments and doing important early work on the process of electric power transmission. He was a man of sincere Christian faith, finding no difficulty in reconciling this with the scientific discoveries of his time, and disagreed with fellow scientists who attempted to use these as a weapon to attack Christian beliefs.

Kemble, John Saint, Roman Catholic priest and martyr, born near Hereford of a Wiltshire family, 1599, died Hereford, 22 August 1679. He studied at the English College, Douai. He was ordained priest in 1625 and returned to England, where he set up mission centres in Herefordshire and Gwent. After the Popish Plot (1678), and at the age of 80, he was arrested and tried for being a seminary priest. Sentenced to be hanged, drawn

and quartered, he was first taken to London and offered release if he would give details of the (non-existent) plot. He was then sent back to Hereford prison. On 22 August 1679 the sentence was carried out. Kemble was canonized in 1970 by Pope **Paul VI** as one of the **Forty Martyrs of England and Wales**. Feast day 25 October.

Kemp (Kempe), John Cardinal and archbishop, born Wye, Kent, *c*.1380, died 1454. He was a fellow of Merton College, Oxford. He became prominent in the ecclesiastical courts and was made Dean of the Arches in 1415. He was successively bishop of Rochester, 1419, Chichester, 1421, London, 1421, archbishop of York, 1425, and archbishop of Canterbury, 1452. He was much employed as a diplomat by Henry V, and was a member of **Henry VI**'s council and supporter of Cardinal **Beaufort**. He became Chancellor of England in 1426. In the years following 1430 he strongly supported peace with France. A keen supporter of the Lancastrian cause he was far more a politician than a churchman and spent little time in the care of his dioceses. Nevertheless he was made a cardinal in 1439.

Kemp, Thomas English bishop, born *c*.1414, died 28 March 1489. He studied at Oxford. In 1433 he became a canon of Lincoln, largely owing to the influence of his uncle, Archbishop John **Kemp**. In 1435 he became canon of York, where his uncle was archbishop, and between 1436 and 1442 he was archdeacon. In 1442 he became archdeacon of Richmond and, in 1449, of Middlesex. In 1450 he was consecrated bishop of London by his uncle, and remained so for the rest of his life. Most notably during this period he attempted to mediate between **Henry VI** and the Yorkists before the Battle of Northampton. He was a considerable benefactor to Oxford, particularly Merton College, the Divinity School and the Library.

Kempe, Margery English mystic and authoress, born Lynn, Norfolk, *c*.1373, died Lynn, *c*.1433. Her father was John Brunham, several times mayor of Lynn. She married John Kempe of Lynn in 1393, and had fourteen children. In 1413, with his consent, she separated from her husband and went on pilgrimage, visiting English shrines (and people – she visited **Julian of Norwich**), the Holy Land and Santiago de Compostella. She returned to Lynn in

1425 to nurse her husband, and after his death went to Norway and Denmark. Her travels, her visions and her reflections were written down by two secretaries as *The Book of Margery Kempe*. She spoke against all pleasure and attracted some hostility and accusations of Lollardy. She was outspoken in her views but displayed great compassion for the sins of the world.

Ken, Thomas   Anglican bishop, writer, born Little Berkhamsted, Hertfordshire, 1637, died Longleat, Longbridge Deverill, Wiltshire, 19 March 1711. He was educated at Winchester School and Oxford. He was ordained and held various posts, including a fellowship at Winchester. In 1675 he went on a tour of the Continent: he is afterwards said to have remarked that a visit to Rome firmly decided him against Catholicism. In 1679 he was appointed chaplain to the wife of William of Orange. In 1685 he became bishop of Bath and Wells, but was deprived in 1691 for refusing to take the oath to William. He wrote several famous morning, evening and midnight hymns as well as *The Practice of Divine Love*. Since the early eighteenth century, his prayer 'Glory to Thee, my God, this Night', set to **Tallis**'s canon, has been popular.

Kenedy, John   Founder of the oldest American Catholic publishing firm, born County Kilkenny, Ireland, 13 April 1794, died New York City, 25 June 1866. He emigrated to the USA in 1815 and settled in Baltimore, where he established a bookshop. He began publishing in 1834 with the popular abridgement by Edward Damphoux of Alfonso **Rodriguez**' *Practice of Christian Perfection*. The business became profitable and he moved to New York in 1846, where he and his successors expanded it, specializing in Catholic works.

Kennedy, Eugene R.   US church architect, Knight of St Gregory, born Brooklyn, New York, 31 January 1904, died Boston, Massachusetts, 7 November 1986. Studied in the USA and then in Paris and Rome and worked for, and from 1954 was head of, the architectural firm Maginnis and Walsh. Among his church architecture are the RC cathedrals in Baltimore and Ogdensburg, New York, and the upper church of the National Shrine of the Immaculate Conception, next to the campus of the Catholic University in Washington, DC.

Kennedy, James   Pioneer Protestant missionary, born near Aberdeen, Scotland, 11 May 1815, died 1 December 1899. A graduate in medicine and theology of Edinburgh and Aberdeen Universities, he went to India with the London Missionary Society in 1839. At Calcutta he revised the Hindustani translation of the NT, and translated the book of Jeremiah into the language, for the British and Foreign Bible Society. After preaching tours he set up a mission at Kumaon, Rani Ghat. He recognized the causes of the Indian Mutiny, which he survived, and helped to rebuild after it, saying that there should be a reduction of taxes and more self-government if India were to prosper. He wrote a *Commentary on the Letter to the Romans* in Hindustani and *Life and Work in Benares and Kumaon* (1877).

Kennedy, John Fitzgerald   US President, born Brookline, Massachusetts, 29 May 1917, died (assassinated) Dallas, Texas, 22 November 1963. 'JFK' was a member of the political dynasty founded by Joseph P. Kennedy, who had been US ambassador to the UK. He was elected to Congress in 1947, to the Senate in 1952 and President in 1960, being the youngest person and the first Roman Catholic to hold this office. Included in his cabinet (as attorney-general) was his younger brother, Robert F. Kennedy. JFK instigated a number of civil rights reforms, many aimed at correcting injustices suffered by black Americans, making him unpopular with right-wing white extremists. JFK was shot as he was being driven through Dallas in an open car, his supposed assassin being one Lee Harvey Oswald. Oswald was himself killed soon afterwards, and a number of questions surrounding the assassination remain unanswered.

Kenneth (Canice, Cainnech, Canicus)   Saint, Irish abbot, born County Derry, c.521, died 599. Educated by St **Finnian** at Clonard. Became a close friend of St **Columba** of Iona. Founded monasteries across Ireland, most notably Aghaboe in Laois, Drumahose in Derry and Cluian Bronig in Offaly. He frequently visited Columba at Iona, where a cemetery and a church were dedicated to him. An effective preacher, he also spent periods of his life as a hermit, especially on deserted islands. In his solitude he copied books, including a manuscript of the four Gospels. In Scotland his principal church was Inchkenneth in Mull; other churches which bear his name include Kilchennich in Tiree, Kilchainie in South Uist and the abbey of Cambuskenneth. Some churches in Kintyre and Fife claim to have been founded by him. His journeys to Scotland included one with St Columba to King Brude at Inverness. Feast day 11 October.

Kenney, James Francis   Catholic archivist and historian, born Maryville, Ontario, 6 December 1884, died Ottawa, 4 June 1946. His special interests were medieval history and the development of the Irish language. He graduated BA at Toronto in 1907, MA at Wisconsin in 1908 and PhD at Columbia in 1910. He taught at St Michael's College, Toronto, 1910–11, and then after a year's research was employed at the Dominion of Canada Archives, where he published a catalogue of the pictures in the Archives in 1925. In 1926 he became director of historical research at the Public Archives. His *Sources for the Early History of Ireland: An Introduction and Guide* was outstandingly valuable to scholarship. The first volume, *Ecclesiastical* (New York, 1929), was to be followed by the second, *Secular*, but he died before its completion. He was president of the American Catholic Historical Association, 1932, founder of the Canadian Catholic Historical Association, 1933, and a fellow of the Royal Historical Society and of the Royal Society of Canada.

Kennicott, Benjamin   Biblical scholar, born Totnes, 4 April 1718, died Oxford, 18 August 1783. He studied at Wadham College, Oxford, from 1744. A brilliant scholar he published two dissertations while still an undergraduate. He was a fellow of Exeter College, Oxford, 1747–71, Radcliffe librarian, 1767–83, canon of Christ Church, 1770–83. His life's study, in which he was aided by his wife, was the Hebrew text of the OT. Between 1776 and 1780 he published his *Vetus Testamentum Hebraicum cum variis lectionibus*, in which he drew the important conclusion that the variants in the Hebrew MSS of the OT were so slight as to be of little importance in determining the correct text.

Kenraghty, Maurice   Catholic martyr, born Kilmallock, Ireland, died Clonmel, 30 April 1585. Chaplain to the rebel earl of Desmond, he was captured in 1583 and imprisoned in Clonmel. During Passiontide 1585, Victor White, a local citizen, bribed the jailer to release him for one night to administer the sacraments. The jailer betrayed them. Kenraghty escaped but White was arrested. To save him, Kenraghy surrendered himself instead, and was condemned to death for treason. Offered a pardon if he acknowledged the spiritual supremacy of the queen, he refused and was hanged, drawn and quartered.

Kenrick, Francis Patrick   Roman Catholic archbishop, born Dublin, 3 December 1796, died Baltimore, USA, 8 July 1863. He studied for the priesthood at the College of the Propaganda in Rome, was ordained in 1821, and went to Bardstown, Kentucky, where he taught theology, Church history and liturgy, at St Joseph's College. He became well known both for his incisive defence of Catholic doctrines and, from 1830, when he was coadjutor of the bishop of Philadelphia, for his opposition to and final defeat of the lay trustees' authority to name pastors, which he accomplished by convoking the first diocesan synod to enact legislation for the purpose. He used the synods of 1842 and 1847 to enforce uniform discipline among the thousands of new immigrants. He was opposed to involvement in political affairs, and the diocesan *Catholic Herald* which he founded became unpopular because of its conservative attitude. He wrote textbooks on moral and dogmatic theology for seminarians, 1834–40, and for the Catholic public *The Catholic Doctrine on Justification* (Philadelphia, 1841) and *The Primacy of the Apostolic See Vindicated* (Philadelphia, 1845). His opposition to the use of the King James Version of the Bible for all pupils in the public schools, instead of their being allowed to use the version of their Church, gave him the name, wrongly, of wanting to remove the Bible from the schools. This exacerbated an already difficult situation, and in 1844 rioters burnt St Michael's and St Augustine's and destroyed St Phillip's. Kenrick temporarily closed the churches and gave the keys to the local authorities, a peaceable action which brought converts into the Church. In 1851 he was made archbishop of Baltimore. Seen as the leading moral theologian of the time, he was asked by **Pius IX** in 1853 to collect the opinions of American bishops on a definition of the doctrine of the Immaculate

Conception. Of a sternly independent temperament, during the American Civil War he became unpopular with those in his diocese who favoured the South, because he taught that national loyalty was above state patriotism. He helped the poor through the profits of his books, and was an advocate of temperance.

Kenrick, Peter Richard Roman Catholic archbishop, born Dublin, Ireland, 17 August 1806, died St Louis, Missouri, 4 March 1896. After his education at St Patrick's College, Maynooth, and ordination in 1832, his brother, Francis Patrick **Kenrick**, then coadjutor of the bishop of Philadelphia, invited him to be rector of the cathedral, president of the seminary and vicar general there in 1833. He became coadjutor at St Louis in 1841, to administer the diocese while Bishop **Rosati** was in Haiti. Rosati died in 1843, and Kenrick replaced him. When St Louis was raised to an archbishopric in 1847 he became its first archbishop and during his time the Catholic population of the diocese rose from 100,000 to 200,000. In 1869–70 at the First Vatican Council he opposed the doctrine of papal infallibility because it was not going to involve the agreement of all the world's bishops, as well as for a number of practical reasons, and he published his views in *Concio*, a pamphlet which was condemned by the Congregation of the Index, though not listed on the Index. While in Rome he asked for a coadjutor and Patrick J. **Ryan** was appointed. On his return Kenrick went into virtual retirement until 1884 when Ryan became archbishop of Philadelphia and he resumed the official duties, but in 1890 the pastors of the diocese asked Cardinal **Gibbons** for another coadjutor. Bishop John Kain was appointed in 1893 and named archbishop of St Louis in 1895, when Kenrick was named titular archbishop of Marcianopolis.

Kent, Corita (Frances) Artist and social activist, born Fort Dodge, Iowa, 20 November 1918, died Boston, 18 September 1986. Joined the Sisters of the Immaculate Heart of Mary in 1936 and taught art at the Order's college. She left religious life (though she retained her religious name, 'Corita') in 1968 and moved from California to Boston, Massachusetts. Although best known for her silkscreens, her work includes the design for the 1985 US Postal Service 'Love' stamp. Much of her work was done, often on a voluntary basis, for social causes: against hunger and war and for human development and social responsibility. It can be found in galleries in the major US and European cities.

Kentigern Missionary bishop and saint, also known as 'Mungo', died Glasgow, *c.*612. According to legend, he was born in southern Scotland the grandson of a British prince, and taught by St Serf in a monastic school at Culross. He became bishop of the Britons of Strathclyde and founded the Church of Glasgow. He spent a period away from Scotland to avoid persecution, in Wales, where he established the monastery of Llanelwy (St Asaph), and in Cumbria. His reputed tomb stands in Glasgow Cathedral. We are heavily dependent on a dubious twelfth-century Life for what we know of his career. Feast day 14 January.

Keogh, James Catholic editor and theologian, born Enniscorthy, Ireland, 4 February 1834, died Pittsburgh, 10 July 1870. His family settled in Pittsburgh in 1841, where he was educated. At the College of the Propaganda, Rome, he gained a doctorate in philosophy, 1851, and in theology, 1855. Ordained in 1856 he served at Latrobe, Pennsylvania, for a year and in 1857 was appointed professor of dogmatic theology at St Michael's Seminary, Pennsylvania. Here he edited the *Pittsburgh Catholic* but after disagreements about the way both the seminary and the newspaper were managed, in 1865 he moved to St Charles' Seminary, Philadelphia, becoming the first editor of the *Philadelphia Catholic Standard* in 1866. He was under consideration to be the American representative for the preparation of the First Vatican Council but ill health overtook him and he retired in 1868.

Keogh, John Roman Catholic priest and leader of the Newman movement in the USA, born Philadelphia, 29 November 1877, died there, 14 October 1960. He was ordained in 1909, and became the first full-time chaplain of Catholic students at the University of Pennsylvania in 1913, and the first national chaplain of the Federation of College Catholic Clubs, later known as the Newman Club Federation, 1917–35. He continually pressed bishops to set up Newman studies in secular colleges and universities. He was pastor of St Gabriel's, Philadelphia, from 1938. One of the founders of the John Henry Newman Honorary Society, he was its chaplain 1945–60, as well as president of the Catholic Total Abstinence Union for many years.

Keough, Francis Patrick Roman Catholic archbishop, born New Britain, Connecticut, 30 December 1889, died Washington, DC, 8 December 1961. He studied for the priesthood at Hartford (Connecticut), Issy, France, and Rochester, New York. After ordination in 1916 for the Hartford diocese, where he gained experience in administration, he became bishop of Providence, Rhode Island, in 1934. Here his knowledge of French helped him to resolve difficulties between French- and English-speaking Catholics and his administrative gifts enabled him to rescue the diocese from debt. He was made archbishop of Baltimore in 1947. This led to other heavy responsibilities with the National Catholic Welfare Conference. He became head of its education department in 1949, legal department in 1953 and social action department in 1954. He was chairman of its administrative board, 1950–2 and 1955–9, when he put his weight behind the 1958 statement of the American Catholic hierarchy against racial discrimination. He oversaw the building of Baltimore Cathedral in 1959. His calm temperament enabled him to deal with great problems step by step, and he never lost his lifelong concern for the needs of deprived children.

Kepler, Johann German astronomer, born Weil der Stadt, 27 December 1571, died Regensburg, 15 November 1630. His family were Lutherans in a largely Catholic city. He studied in Tübingen, where he encountered the Copernican system, and was recommended to teach in the Protestant seminary in Graz. When the Counter-Reformation arrived in Graz, Kepler, a devout Protestant with Calvinist leanings, at first attempted to stay, but eventually moved to Prague with his wife and family, at the invitation of Tycho **Brahe**, whose work he had studied. Tycho and he first met in February 1600, and after Tycho's death, Kepler became imperial astronomer. His work resulted in the 'three laws of planetary motion', the first two of which drew upon Tycho's observations, but the

third was entirely Kepler's. In 1612 he became professor of mathematics in Linz, but in 1626 moved to Ulm, in the employ of Wallenstein. His first wife and one of their three children died in 1611. He remarried, and fathered six more children. He worked, and published, on optics as well as astronomy: *Somnium*, published posthumously, describes a journey to the moon, and how the earth would seem from there.

Kerby, William Joseph Catholic sociologist, born Lawler, Iowa, 20 February 1870, died Washington, DC, 27 July 1936. He studied for the priesthood at St Francis' Seminary, Milwaukee, Wisconsin, and was ordained at Dubuque in 1892. He gained a licentiate in theology at the Catholic University of America, where he became interested in the new science of sociology. He returned to teach at (what was later named) Loras College, Dubuque, but when the university was considering the inclusion of sociology in the curriculum, he was asked to go to Europe for study at Bonn and Berlin, and at Louvain, where he gained a doctorate in social and political science, 1897. He became the virtual originator of scientific social work among Catholics in the USA, helping to found the National Conference of Catholic Charities in 1910, and organizing the first systematic education of Catholic social workers, now called the National Catholic School of Social Service. He edited the *St Vincent de Paul Quarterly*, 1911–17.

Kerle, Jacobus de Composer of Church music, born Ypres, Flanders, *c.*1532, died Prague, 7 January 1591. He became organist at Orvieto Cathedral, Italy, in 1555, and then, when employed by Cardinal Truchsess von Waldburg in 1562, he composed polyphonic music for a set of prayers for the success of the Council of Trent, and its popularity influenced the Council's decision to keep polyphonic Church music. The same year Kerle published six Masses in Venice and after 1571 many motets in Nuremberg, Munich and Prague.

Kerll, Johann Kaspar von Composer and organist, born Adorf, Saxony, 9 April 1627, died Munich, 13 February 1693. Archduke Leopold Wilhelm of Austria sent him to study in Rome under **Carissimi** and **Frescobaldi**. Kerll returned to Munich as kapellmeister, where he produced operas. In

Vienna he became organist of St Stephen's Cathedral, assisted by **Pachelbel**. Kerll wrote Church music in a variety of styles, including Masses, Requiems and *Magnificats*.

Kern, Fritz Historian, born Stuttgart, 28 September 1884, died Mainz, 21 May 1950. He studied at Lausanne, Tübingen and Berlin, was a professor at Kiel, 1909–13, and at Frankfurt, 1914–22, then at Bonn he was professor of both medieval and modern history. Opposed to Nazism, he lived in Switzerland during World War II, then returned to Bonn. His interest was in the study of world history, particularly that of prehistoric cultures, by scientific methods. He founded the Institute for European History at Mainz, where he became a Catholic shortly before his death. His *Historia Mundi* was published posthumously (10 vols, Berlin, 1953–61).

Kersuzan, François Marie Roman Catholic bishop and champion of Haiti, born Grandchamp, Brittany, 25 March 1848, died Morne Lory, Haiti, July 1935. Ordained in 1871, he served in the cathedral of Port-au-Prince until 1884, and as auxiliary bishop until 1886, when he became bishop of Cap-Haitien. His frequent diocesan visitations enabled him to confront voodoo, and his establishment of secondary and primary education countered superstition. In 30 years of political upheaval he defended the accused or suspected, and during the American occupation he became not only the spokesman for the Church but the representative of the Haitian people. Illness from 1925 forced his retirement to a life of prayer in 1929 in the Collège de Notre-Dame du Secours Perpétuel, which he had founded in 1904.

Ketcham, William Henry Roman Catholic priest and missionary, born Summer, Iowa, 1 June 1868, died Washington, DC, 14 November 1921. Ordained in 1892 at Guthrie, Oklahoma, he served the settlers and Indians in the Northern Indian Territory, then as missionary to the Choctaw, where he built up a network of congregations, churches and schools. From 1901 to 1921 he was director of the Bureau of Catholic Indian Missions. He won the right of Indians to use tribal funds for the education of their children in mission schools and saw to the schools' financial security. His work

was recognized by his appointment to the US Board of Commissioners of Indian Affairs, where he was responsible for many improvements to federal schools and hospitals for Indians.

Ketevan of Georgia Queen, orthodox saint and martyr, died 13 September 1624. She lived at a time when Georgia was divided internally and threatened by both the Turkish and Persian Muslims. In 1615 the Persian shah invaded the country and Ketevan was imprisoned for ten years in Shiraz. She always refused to accept Islam and was eventually tortured to death with hooks and red-hot coals, at a public ceremony. This was witnessed and recorded in detail by visiting Augustinian friars. Feast day 13 September.

Ketteler, Wilhelm Emmanuel von German Roman Catholic bishop and social reformer, born Münster, Westphalia, 25 December 1811, died Burghausen, Bavaria, 13 July 1877. He had considered becoming part of the Prussian civil service when persecution of the Catholic Church changed his mind. He studied at Munich and at Münster and in 1846 was ordained priest: four years later he became bishop of Mainz. In 1848 he attracted public attention as a member of the Frankfurt National Assembly. He was also a member, once German unity had been achieved, of the Reichstag, though only for a year, 1870–71. His fame depended largely on his social commitment, expressed in *The Labour Question and Christianity* (1864), which argued for a more equitable distribution of wealth through the establishment of workers' associations and cooperatives. At the First Vatican Council he opposed the declaration of the dogma of papal infallibility, and left Rome before the final vote, though he said he had always believed in papal infallibility itself.

Kevan, Ernest Frederick English Baptist minister and educator, born London, 11 January 1903, died there, 28 August 1965. Kevan held Baptist pastorates in London before being invited in 1942 to become the principal and first full-time faculty member of a new evangelical and interdenominational Christian training college, subsequently named the London Bible College – though his term of office is usually dated from 1946 when the College admitted its first few students. From its initial intake, under Kevan's leadership the College steadily grew in size and established a reputation for combining traditional evangelical piety with intellectually credible scholarship. Kevan was renowned for his down-to-earth approach to theological study, and showed particular insight in discerning and bringing out the gifts of students who at first sight appeared to have little potential.

Kevenhoerster, John Bernard Roman Catholic bishop and first vicar apostolic of the Bahamas, born Alten-Essen, Prussia, 1 November 1869, died Bahamas, 9 December 1949. His family settled in the parish of St Joseph, Minneapolis. In 1887 he began his studies for the priesthood at St John's Abbey, Collegeville, Minnesota, entered the noviti-ate in 1892 and made his vows as a Benedictine in 1893. In 1907 he became pastor of St Anselm's, Bronx, where he built a school, a church and one of the first public playgrounds in New York City. In 1929 he was made vicar forane of the Bahamas, bishop in 1933 and vicar apostolic in 1941. In his service to the poor he established missions, churches, grammar schools and a teaching sisterhood.

Key, Francis Scott Episcopalian leader of the Sunday School movement, born Frederick County, Maryland, 1 August 1779, died Baltimore, Maryland, 11 January 1843. Having graduated from St John's College, Annapolis, he became an attorney. A lay reader, he was one of the founders of the interdenominational American Sunday School Union in 1824, and from 1830 established Sunday Schools along the Western frontier. He is remembered today as the author of the US national anthem, 'The Star-spangled Banner'.

Khomiakov (Ch'homyakov), Aleksei Stepanovich Russian Orthodox lay theologian and philosopher, born Moscow, 1 May 1804, died near Riazan, 25 September 1860. A prominent 'Slavophile' whose writings were regarded with suspicion in Russia, he was the most important Orthodox lay theologian of the nineteenth century and is still revered by his co-religionists of both left and right. His long essays *The Church is One* (1863), on ecclesiology, and *On the Western Confessions of Faith* (1864) have been the most influential.

Kierkegaard, Søren Aabye Lutheran philosopher and theologian, born Copenhagen, Denmark, 5 May 1813, died Copenhagen, 11 November 1855. Kierkegaard studied theology, philosophy and literature, and wrote a series of theological/philosophical works which exerted a profound influence on the development of twentieth-century theological and philosophical thinking. They include *Either–Or*, *Philosophical Fragments*, *The Concept of Dread*, *Concluding Unscientific Postscript* and *Sickness Unto Death*. Kierkegaard argued that truth does not exist objectively, but only becomes actualized as it is experienced and affirmed by the individual, hence his dictum 'truth is subjectivity'. In the same way, Kierkegaard held that God is 'wholly other', and can only genuinely be known by personal encounter through faith in Christ.

Kigosi, Blasio A founder of the East African Revival, Anglican, born Buganda, c.1909, died Kampala, 25 January 1936. In 1928 he was ordained deacon and sent to Galini, Rwanda. Along with his brother, Simeoni Nsimbambi, he was affected by the charismatic movement which took place there during the famine of 1929–30. As a result he spent the next few years as an itinerant preacher calling people to repentance and faith. In 1935 he was a leader in the Revival convention in Kabale. He was invited to speak at the synod in Kampala but died of tick fever before he could deliver his appeal to 'Awake'. Given posthumously, it had a great impact on the synod and revival spread throughout Uganda and beyond. Those influenced by the Revival became known as 'Balokole' or 'saved ones'.

Kilham, Alexander Preacher and founder of the Methodist New Connexion, born Epworth, Lincolnshire, 10 July 1762, died Nottingham, 20 December 1798. He became a Methodist local preacher in 1782, and in 1783 with Robert Carr Brackenbury, one of John **Wesley**'s itinerant preachers, he established a Methodist society in the Channel Islands. Wesley accepted him as an itinerant in 1785. After Wesley's death in 1791 he was stationed in Aberdeen, where the influence of Presbyterianism and also of revolutionary liberty intensified his opposition to the Church of England, his advocacy of the celebration of the Lord's Supper by itinerants and a Church government shared between laymen and ministers. He published these views in *The Progress of Liberty among the People called Methodists, to which is added the Outlines of a Constitution* (Alnwick, 1795), for which he was expelled in 1796. He founded the Methodist New Connexion in 1797, which held to Arminian theology and the itinerant system, but Church government was in the hands of equal numbers of laymen and itinerants.

Kilham, Hannah Quaker missionary and pioneer of African language study, born Sheffield, Yorkshire, 12 August 1774, died at sea off Liberia, 31 March 1832. Brought up in the Society of Friends, Hannah Scurr was married to Alexander **Kilham** for a few months before his death. She rejoined the Society in 1803 and established a girls' school in Sheffield where she taught until 1821, but gradually her chief interests became the anti-slavery movement and the education of Africans. She learned the Wolof and Mandinka languages from two sailors in London, and then, sponsored by the Society, opened a girls' school in the Gambia in 1823. From there she went to Sierra Leone, because many African languages were spoken there, where she opened the first bookshop, and in 1828 published *Specimens of African Languages spoken in the Colony of Sierra Leone*. In 1830 she took charge of a school for girls rescued from slavery, near Freetown, where teaching was in Yoruba and Mende.

Kilian of Aubigny (Chillen) Hermit, died 670. Kilian was Irish but lived in France; little is known of him. Legend says that upon returning from a pilgrimage to Rome, he met **Faro**, bishop of Meaux, who gave him land at Aubigny (near Arras) for a hermitage. Feast day 13 November.

Kilian of Würzburg Monk, possibly bishop, missionary, martyr, born *c*.640, died *c*.689. Born in Ireland, Kilian went to pagan Würzburg as a missionary, along with Colman, a priest, and Totnan, a deacon, arriving in 686, and saw the conversions of Duke Gozbert and many of his subjects in East Franconia and Thuringia. However, the duke had married his brother's widow, Geilana, and Kilian informed him that this was unlawful for a Christian. Geilana, while her husband was absent, murdered the three missionaries, burying them along with their vestments, books and sacred vessels.

Although their work did not continue, **Boniface** found evidence of it upon his arrival in Thuringia. Feast day 8 July.

Kilmer, Alfred Joyce US Roman Catholic poet, born New Brunswick, 6 December 1886, died near Seringes, France, 30 July 1918. He studied at Rutgers and Columbia Universities. He modelled his poetry on Coventry **Patmore** and the seventeenth-century metaphysical poets. He is most famous for his poem 'Trees' and its lines: 'I think that I shall never see / A poem lovely as a tree' and 'Poems are made by fools like me, / But only God can make a tree'. He wrote several books and edited *Dreams and Images*, a collection of modern Roman Catholic poetry. He was killed in action in World War 1 and posthumously awarded the Croix de Guerre.

Kilvert, Robert Francis Anglican clergyman and diarist, born 3 December 1840, died Bredwardine, Hereford, 23 September 1879. He was educated at Oxford. He was ordained in 1864 and served as his father's curate for two years, then held sundry other curacies until appointed to Bredwardine two years before his death. His diary, which he began in 1870 and which, thanks to his widow, has survived, though incomplete, gives a fascinating insight into the life of an English country clergyman.

Kim, Andrew Blessed, Roman Catholic priest and martyr, born in Tchoung-Echeng Province, Korea, 21 August 1821, died 16 September 1846. The son of Korean converts to Catholicism (his father was martyred in 1839), in 1836 he trained for the priesthood in China, returning to Korea in 1842. In 1844 he was ordained deacon, and in 1845 he was ordained priest in Shanghai. He was the first native Korean priest. Following his ordination he returned once more to Korea, where he had been given the task of arranging for more missionaries. He was arrested, tortured and then beheaded. On 25 July 1925 he was beatified, along with a further 78 Korean martyrs. In 1949 the Pope designated him the principal patron of the clergy in Korea. Feast day 5 July.

Kimbangu, Simon Founder of the Église de Jésus-Christ sur la terre par le Prophète Simon Kimbangu, the largest African-initiated Church, born Nkamba, Congo, *c.*1889, died in prison in Elizabethville (Lubumbashi), 1951. Educated briefly at the Baptist mission he was refused work as a catechist. Married Mwilu Marie, who led the movement after his death. His healing ministry, from March to September 1921, became a revival movement. Kimbangu preached repentance, obedience to God and monogamy, and he attacked idolatry. The colonial administration and the missionaries considered the movement to be politically dangerous and Kimbangu was arrested and spent 30 years in prison. The Church existed as an underground movement until 1957. In 1959 Joseph Diangienda, Kimbangu's youngest son, became its spiritual head.

Kimpa Vita, Beatrice Prophetess, born Kongo, *c.*1684, died Kibangu, Kongo, 2 July 1706. Possessed by St **Anthony of Padua** she preached a gospel which claimed Jesus to be Kongolese, burnt objects of superstition (including crosses) and called the people back to the ancient capital of São Salvador. Her messengers preached throughout the kingdom. Distrusted by the ruling elite and considered a heretic by the Capuchin monks, she and her consort 'Saint John' were arrested and burnt to death. Drawing on Christian piety and elements of traditional religion, she headed a mass movement at a time of political uncertainty and social change which continued after her death.

Kindekens, Peter Roman Catholic priest and founder of the American College at Louvain, born Denderwindeke, Belgium, died Detroit, Michigan, 23 March 1873. Ordained in 1842, he became the bishop of Detroit's vicar general, pastor at St Anne's Cathedral and first director of St Thomas' Seminary in 1846. While representing his bishop at Rome he pressed unsuccessfully for an American College there, so proposed one at Louvain. In 1857, with support from his bishop and money from Belgium and Germany, he opened the college and in the three years before returning to his vicariate-general at Detroit he sent nine missionaries to America.

King, Joseph Hillery First bishop of the Pentecostal Holiness Church, born Anderson County, South Carolina, 1869, died Anderson County,

1946. King became a Methodist minister in 1891, but in 1897 he joined Benjamin **Irwin**'s Fire-Baptized Holiness Association, quickly succeeding him as leader. A meeting with G. B. **Cashwell** in 1907 led to the Association's becoming Pentecostal and joining the Pentecostal Holiness Church. King became that Church's general superintendent in 1917, following a period in charge of world missions. In 1937 he became bishop. In 1909 he founded the *Apostolic Evangel* magazine, and he wrote *From Passover to Pentecost* (1911).

King, Martin Luther, Jr Baptist minister and civil rights campaigner, born Atlanta, Georgia, 15 January 1929, died (assassinated) Memphis, Tennessee, 4 April 1968. An inspirational leader and a powerful orator, King championed the cause of black civil rights in the USA. His successful challenge in the US Supreme Court to the legality of segregation laws in southern states was a watershed in this campaign. King believed in peaceful protest and non-violence, and he was awarded the Nobel Peace Prize in 1964. While greeting supporters from a hotel balcony on a visit to Memphis in 1968, he was shot dead by James Earl Ray, a white supremacist.

Kinghorn, Joseph Baptist minister and theologian, born Gateshead, County Durham, England, 17 January 1766, died Norwich, Norfolk, 1 September 1832. Trained for the ministry at Bristol, he became minister at Norwich in 1789 before his ordination in 1790, and remained there for the rest of his life. A man of broad sympathies and an accomplished scholar, he was widely read in classical, rabbinical, biblical and patristic writing, as well as in contemporary German theology. From 1799 he ran a small school for intending missionaries. He was a member of the Speculative Society for free discussion and wrote for the *Baptist Magazine*, *Eclectic Review* and *Evangelical Magazine*. When the East India Company's charter came to be revised in 1813 he successfully petitioned through the bishop of Norwich for the Baptist Serampore mission.

Kingsley, Charles Novelist and historian, born Holne, Dartmoor, Devon, 12 June 1819, died Eversley, Hampshire, 23 January 1875. He was educated at King's College, London, and Cambridge, was ordained in the Anglican Church and in 1844 became rector of Eversley and later professor of modern history at Cambridge, 1860–9. He was successively canon of Chester and a canon of Westminster, as well as being chaplain to the queen from 1873. He was influenced by the writings of **Carlyle** and became a Christian Socialist. His novel *The Saint's Tragedy* is a drama with the heroine St **Elizabeth of Hungary**. His novels *Yeast* and *Alton Locke* show his concern for the poor. He was anti-Catholic, as shown in *Westward Ho!* (1855), and was involved in controversy with John Henry **Newman**. He celebrated the 'muscular Christianity' values of being cheerful and robust.

Kino, Eusebio Francisco Jesuit missionary and explorer, born Segno, Tyrol, Italy, 10 August 1645, died Magdalena, Mexico, 15 March 1711. He was educated in Germany, joined the Jesuits, and was sent to what is now Mexico and Lower California. He was a missionary to Indians in Northern Mexico and Southern Arizona. He founded missions, and is said to have explored the sources of the Rio Grande and the Colorado and Gala Rivers. He helped the Indians diversify their agriculture and opposed slavery of Indians in Mexican silver mines. He prepared and published maps of Lower California, and wrote *Favores Celestiales*, translated as *Kino's Historical Memoir of Pimeria Alta*.

Kirby, Luke Saint, Roman Catholic priest and martyr, born Richmond, North Yorkshire, *c.*1548, died London, 30 May 1582. He received a university education in England before attending the English College, Douai. He was ordained priest in 1577, and returned to England in 1580. He was immediately arrested at Dover and was imprisoned and tortured. In November 1581 he was tried for an alleged and fictitious plot against the queen, along with Edmund **Campion**, Ralph Sherwin and Alexander **Briant**. He was sentenced to be hanged, drawn and quartered. The execution itself was delayed until 30 May 1582. He was canonized by Pope **Paul VI** in 1970 as one of the **Forty Martyrs of England and Wales**. Feast day 25 October.

Kircher, Athanasius Jesuit priest and scholar, born Geisa, Thuringia, 2 March 1601, died Rome, 27 November 1680. As a boy in the Jesuit College at Fulda he learned Greek, and he learned Hebrew

from a rabbi. He joined the Society of Jesus at Paderborn in 1618 and studied there, at Cologne and at Koblenz. The Thirty Years' War was raging, he left Germany, worked at Avignon and settled in Rome, at the Roman College, in 1634. He established a museum of science there. The invention of the magic lantern has been ascribed to him: he described it in a publication in 1646. He had an enormous range of interests, and was one of the first to study Coptic in an attempt to decipher Egyptian hieroglyphics. He wrote on China, on music and on magnetism among very many other topics.

Kiril *see* **Cyril**

Kirk, Kenneth Escott Anglican bishop of Oxford and moral theologian, born Sheffield, 21 February 1886, died Oxford, 8 June 1954. He studied at St John's College, Oxford, and was ordained into the Church of England in 1912. From 1914 to 1919 he was a chaplain to the armed forces, then a tutor, Keble College, Oxford, until 1922, when he was appointed fellow of Trinity College, until 1933. In that year he became professor of moral and pastoral theology and canon of Christ Church, until 1937, then bishop of Oxford, until his death. His publications include *The Vision of God* (1931; the Bampton Lectures for 1928), *Commentary on the Epistle to the Romans* (1937) and *The Apostolic Ministry* (1946). He was on the Anglo-Catholic wing of the Church of England, and assumed particular responsibility for the development of religious communities within the Church, and he supervised the compilation of *The Directory of Religious Life*, first published in 1943.

Kirkland, Sarah (Mrs John Harrison, Mrs William Bembridge) Primitive Methodist itinerant preacher, born Mercaston, England, *c.*1794, died Alfreton, Derbyshire, 4 March 1880. She began to preach in 1813–14, and was shortly afterwards called out as an itinerant. Powerful and effective, she was the first woman Primitive Methodist itinerant preacher. She retired from the itinerancy before 1825 but remained a preacher and class-leader until her death.

Kirlin, Joseph Catholic writer, born Philadelphia, Pennsylvania, 20 March 1868, died Philadelphia,

26 November 1926. Having graduated in arts at La Salle, Philadelphia, and theology at the Catholic University of America, he was ordained in 1892 and served at St Patrick's Church, Philadelphia. In 1907 he founded there, and served for many years, the Most Precious Blood parish. He published *The Life of the Most Rev. Patrick John Ryan* (1903) and *Catholicity in Philadelphia* (1909), which was not successful. In 1920 he was named a papal chaplain, and began writing again. He contributed to *Emmanuel*, the magazine of the Priests' Eucharistic League, and from his articles developed *One Hour with Him* (1923), *Our Tryst with Him* (1925) and *With Him in Mind* (1926). Shortly before his death he became president of the Catholic University Alumni Association and of the American Catholic Historical Association.

Kirsch, Johann Peter   Catholic historian of papal finances, born Dippach, Luxemburg, 3 November 1861, died Rome, 4 February 1941. Ordained in 1884, he was in Rome 1884–90, where his methodical research into papal finances of the thirteenth and fourteenth centuries led to a better understanding of the Reformation. He investigated early Christian places of worship, especially in relation to the liturgy. He was one of the authors of a four-volume *Church History* (Freiburg, 1930–49) and contributed 249 articles to the *Catholic Encyclopedia*.

Kissane, Edward   Catholic biblical scholar, born Lisselton, County Kerry, Ireland, 14 May 1886, died Maynooth College, Ireland, 21 February 1955. Having graduated in philosophy, theology and sacred Scripture at the Pontifical Bible Institute in Rome he became the first professor of Scripture in St Augustine's Seminary, Toronto, 1913–17, and then professor of OT exegesis and oriental languages at Maynooth, 1917–55. His outstanding work in the scientific study of the Bible is seen in *The Book of Job* (Dublin, 1939), *The Book of Isaiah* (2 vols, Dublin, 1939) and *The Book of Psalms* (2 vols, Dublin, 1953–54). He was appointed a member of the Royal Irish Academy in 1943, a domestic prelate in 1945 and awarded D.Litt. by the National University of Ireland in 1946.

Kite, Elizabeth Sarah   Catholic authoress and archivist, born Philadelphia, Pennsylvania, 4 December 1864, died Philadelphia, 5 January 1954. Having studied at universities in Germany, France and England, she taught science in San Diego, California, 1893–5, and in Nantucket, Massachusetts, 1898–1903. Brought up a Quaker, in 1906 she became a Catholic. In 1909–18 while studying mental deficiency and degeneracy at the Psychological Laboratory, Vineland, New Jersey, she became interested in the historical connections of the USA with France. She received the medal of Secours aux Blessés in 1918, and was made a chevalier of the Légion d'Honneur for her research into the role of France in the American War of Independence. She served the American Catholic History Society as archivist and was awarded life membership in 1948.

Kittel, Gerhard   Protestant NT scholar, son of Rudolf **Kittel**, born Breslau, 23 September 1888, died Tübingen, 11 July 1948. He taught at Kiel, 1913–17, Leipzig, 1917–21, Greifswald, 1921–26, Tübingen, 1926–39, Vienna, 1939–43. His research in these years was into the Jewish background of the NT and in 1931 he became the first editor of the great *Theologisches Wörterbuch*, a NT dictionary in which the semantics of every word have been traced. His book *The Jewish Question* (1939) was thought anti-Semitic, and various magazine articles on the same subject led to his imprisonment by the Allies after World War II and forced his retirement to the Benedictine abbey at Beuron.

Kittel, Rudolf   Protestant OT scholar, born Eningen, Württemberg, 28 March 1853, died Leipzig, 20 October 1929. He became professor of OT at Breslau in 1888 and at Leipzig in 1898. His work on the religion of the People of Israel (Leipzig, 1921; 2nd edn 1929) revealed his independent judgement. He further traced their spiritual development, showing Israel's relationship to the general religious history of the ancient Near East, and incorporating archaeological discoveries in a history of the People of Israel (3 vols, Gotha, 1923 and 1925; Stuttgart, 1927–9). His critical edition (with the assistance of others) of the Hebrew Scriptures, *Biblia Hebraica* (Leipzig, 1905–10), remains a classic of Bible scholarship.

Kivebulaya, Apolo (Waswa)   Ugandan missionary

and Anglican canon, born Buganda, *c.*1864, died Mboga, Congo, 30 May 1933. He is buried, as he requested, with his head pointing towards the forest and the Wambuti (pygmies), to whom he had brought the Gospel. As a young man he was a mercenary in the Ugandan civil wars. Offering himself as an evangelist to Toro in 1895 soon after his baptism, he worked there and in the Mboga area of Congo until his death. Ordained in 1903, he suffered imprisonment and chain-gang work but was sustained by a vision of Christ. In 1921, he expanded his mission to include the Wambuti and other forest peoples, often despised by others.

Kivengere, Festo Anglican bishop, born Uganda, *c.*1919, died of leukaemia, 1988. Training first as a teacher he was ordained priest in 1967. He was a great preacher and evangelist and a leader in the East African Revival. He launched the East Africa branch of the African Evangelistic Enterprise. He was bishop of Kigezi from 1972 but had to flee Uganda in 1977 after the murder of Archbishop Janani **Luwum** by Idi Amin's forces. He returned to his diocese once Amin was overthrown but remained critical of Milton Obote's human rights abuses. In 1982 he aided Rwandan refugees in Uganda despite their unpopularity, and in 1983, against ecclesiastical opposition, he ordained three women to the priesthood.

Kiwanuka, Joseph First modern African Roman Catholic bishop, born Buganda, 1892, died 22 February 1966. He was educated at Bukalasa and Katigondo seminaries and ordained in 1929. After further study in Rome he became the first African doctor of canon law and joined the White Fathers missionary society. In 1939 he was ordained as vicar apostolic and bishop of Masaka, and in January 1961 he became archbishop of Rubaga (Kampala). In 1964 at Vatican II he celebrated the canonization of the Uganda martyrs. During his episcopate he wielded great political influence and he also furthered the work of the Church by sending many priests to study abroad and establishing elected lay parish councils.

Kjeld Saint, also known as 'Ketllus' or 'Exuperius', born Vennig, near Randers, Denmark, *c.*1105, died 27 September 1150. He became canon regular at the cathedral of Our Lady in Viborg. He later became provost, lost the office as a result of excessive generosity, but was later reinstated by Pope **Eugenius III**. He preached in favour of the expedition against the Wends in 1147, and had planned to lead the Slavic missions. His cult is confined to Denmark.

Klee, Heinrich Catholic theologian, born Münstermaifeld, Rhineland, 20 April 1800, died Munich, 28 July 1840. At Mainz, he taught Church history and exegesis, 1824, philosophy, 1825, and from 1829, dogma and exegesis at Bonn and then, from 1839, once more at Mainz, as successor to **Möhler**. Open to contemporary philosophy but with an understanding of the development of dogma, he was able to counter **Hermes**' attempt to adjust Catholic theology to the theology of **Kant**. He published *Die Beichte* (Mainz, 1829), *Lehrbuch den Dogmengeschichte* (2 vols, Mainz, 1837–8) and *Katholische Dogmatik* (Mainz, 1835).

Klein, Félix Roman Catholic priest and writer, born Château-Chinon, France, 12 July 1862, died Hannecourt, France, 31 December 1953. Having been ordained in 1885, he studied then taught at the Institut Catholique in Paris. His translation of Walter Elliott's *Life of Father Hecker* (1896) was criticized for its support for 'Americanism' – the policy of democratizing and liberalizing Catholicism, and he was forced to withdraw it, though he continued to press for greater democracy in France.

Kleinschmidt, Beda Franciscan historian and liturgist, born Brakel, Germany, 12 October 1867, died Paderborn, Germany, 7 March 1932. He became a Franciscan in 1888, was ordained in 1892 and thereafter taught in his Order's houses, where his love of Christian art and religious folklore were expressed. He was one of the founders of the liturgical movement in Germany, and after 1914 of *Franziskanische Studien* and other Franciscan journals.

Kleist, James Jesuit biblical scholar and classicist, born Hindenburg, Silesia, 4 April 1873, died St Louis, Missouri, 28 April 1949. He became a Jesuit in The Netherlands in 1891, and emigrated to the USA in 1897, where he had a long teaching career in various colleges and universities. He had a great knowledge of Latin and Greek, and was the founder of the *Classical Bulletin*, but he is best known, with Joseph **Lilly**, for his English translation of the NT from the Greek text (1954).

Klesl, Melchior Cardinal and Austrian statesman, born Vienna, 19 February 1552, died Wiener-Neustadt, 18 September 1630. A convert to Catholicism, after the award of a doctorate by the University of Vienna he was ordained and appointed its chancellor. He set himself to bring Austria back to Catholicism, and therefore excluded Protestants from studying or teaching at the University. In 1598 he became bishop of Vienna, and in 1615 a cardinal. By this time he had become chancellor to the Archduke Matthias, and remained in this position when Matthias became Emperor. During Protestant unrest in Bohemia he persuaded Matthias to reject all complaints. He came to recognize that this policy exacerbated the trouble but when he tried to reverse it, some archdukes found their opportunity to bring him down, and in 1618 put him under virtual house arrest, from which he was rescued by the Pope's call to Rome in 1622.

Kleutgen, Joseph Jesuit philosopher and theologian, born Dortmund, Germany, 9 April 1811, died Kaltern, Tyrol, 13 January 1883. He became a Jesuit in 1834, and from 1837 to 1843 taught at the University of Freiburg. Severely conservative, he set himself to counteract the diluting effects on Catholic theology of contemporary thought, principally the ideas of **Kant**, Hegel and **Schelling**, by restoring traditional Scholastic method. During Vatican I he helped to formulate *De Fide Catholica*, and in 1878 Pope **Leo XIII** made him prefect of studies and professor of dogmatic theology at the Gregorian University in Rome. Of his projected eight volumes of *Institutiones theologicae* he lived to complete only the first, *De Ipso Deo* (Regensburg, 1881).

Klopstock, Friedrich Gottlieb Poet, born Quenlinburg, Germany, 2 July 1724, died Hamburg, 14 March 1803. He studied theology in the Universities of Jena and Leipzig, 1745–8, and published *Der Messias* in 1748, which was so well received that he was invited to join the group of poets at the Danish court. Here his theme, often expressed, was the celebration of God's incarnation and continuing creativity in time and in human life. In the last three decades of his life he published religious *Odes* describing the experiences inspired by the love of God, and patriotic ones describing true heroism.

Klubertanz, George P. US Jesuit and philosopher, born Columbus, Wisconsin, 29 June 1912, died 5 July 1972. Entered the Society of Jesus in 1931 and was ordained priest in 1944. Did doctoral studies in Toronto under Etienne **Gilson**. From 1949 until 1952 he taught philosophy at St Louis, Missouri, and from 1952 until 1970 he was dean of the College of Philosophy and Letters at the university. His writings include *Introduction to the Philosophy of Being* (1952, 1963), *The Philosophy of Human Nature* (1953), as well as writings on **Thomas Aquinas** and on moral philosophy. He was a good administrator and his other practical skills included electronic and mechanical engineering and cooking.

Klug, Ignaz Roman Catholic priest, psychologist and writer, born Keilberg, Germany, 31 July 1877, died Passau, 3 January 1929. Ordained in 1900, he became professor of moral theology and Christian sociology at Passau. His particular field of research was the will, its freedom and limitation. He had the gift of writing in a popular style, and his *Kriminalpedagogik* (Paderborn, 1930) and *Willensfreiheit und Persönlichkeit* (Paderborn, 1932) were well received, as were his articles on questions of belief and doubt.

Klupfel, Engelbert Augustinian theologian, born Wipfeld, near Würzburg, 18 January 1733, died Freiburg im Breisgau, 8 July 1811. He became an Augustinian in 1751, and after studying philosophy in Switzerland and Germany he taught philosophy in his Order at Oberndorf, Mainz and Constance. From 1767 to 1805 he was professor of theology at the University of Freiburg im Breisgau. A man of his time, the Enlightenment, in that he denied papal infallibility and discounted Scholasticism, he was yet never attracted to rationalism. His *Institutiones theologiae dogmaticae* (Vienna, 1789) became the standard Austrian compendium of theology.

Knabenbauer, Joseph Jesuit biblical scholar, born

Deggendorf, Germany, 3 March 1839, died Maastricht, The Netherlands, 12 November 1911. He became a Jesuit in 1857, then taught at Feldkirch, Austria, 1860–4. Having studied classics, philosophy, theology and exegesis, 1864–72, he was appointed professor of OT and NT at Ditton Hall, England, 1872–95. From there he went to The Netherlands, where he remained for the rest of his life. His knowledge of the works of the Fathers and of medieval and contemporary biblical scholars caused his commentaries on many books of both Testaments, in the Cursus Scripturae Sacrae series (collaborating with R. **Cornely** and F. von **Hummelauer**) published between 1886 and 1913, to be highly regarded.

Knight, William Bishop of Bath and Wells, born London, 1476, died Wiveliscombe, Somerset, 1547. He was educated at Westminster School and New College, Oxford, where he became a fellow in 1493. **Henry VIII** of England sent him on missions to Spain, Italy and the Low Countries during the years 1512–32. In 1515 he was appointed chaplain to Henry VIII, and then archdeacon of Chester, 1522, of Huntingdon, 1523, canon of Westminster, 1527, archdeacon of Richmond, 1529, and bishop of Bath and Wells, 1541.

Knoll, Albert Capuchin theologian, born Brunico, Italy, 12 July 1796, died Bolzano, Italy, 30 March 1863. He joined the Capuchin Order in 1818, in which he taught for 27 years, and was its definitor 1847–55. His textbook for seminarians, *Institutiones theologiae dogmaticae generalis* (Innsbruck, 1852), went through fifteen editions by 1904; his preaching manual *Predigten für die Sonntag* (Bressanone, 1867) was highly successful; and his *Institutiones theologiae theoreticae* (6 vols, Turin, 1853–9), intended for a wider public, reached twelve editions by 1892.

Knöpfler Alois Catholic Church historian, born Schomberg, Germany, 29 August 1847, died Schomberg, 14 July 1921. Having studied philosophy and theology at Tübingen, 1867–74, he was ordained in 1874. He became professor of Church history and patrology at Passau, 1880, and of Church history at Munich, 1886–1917. He established the Church history seminar at Munich, and its publications, which reached 45 volumes

(Munich, 1899–1920), made it widely respected. In 1895 he published *Lehrbuch der Kirchengeschichte*, which presented the Catholic attitude to Church history while retaining a certain objectivity.

Knowles, David Benedictine priest and monastic historian, born 'Michael Clive' Knowles at Studley, Warwickshire, 29 September 1896, died Sussex, 21 November 1974. He was educated at Downside and Christ's College, Cambridge, and became a Benedictine monk at Downside Abbey in 1914. Ordained deacon in 1921, priest in 1922. Studied at the Benedictine house of Sant' Anselmo, Rome, 1922–3. Finding that teaching clashed with a life of prayer, he considered founding a new community. This idea was rejected by Rome. Moved from Downside to Ealing Priory, 1933. Left the community in 1939. Fellow of Peterhouse, Cambridge, 1944–63; professor of medieval history, Cambridge, 1947; Regius professor of modern history, 1954–63. Fellow of the Royal Historical Society, of which he was president, 1956–60; and of the Society of Antiquaries. Major works include *The American Civil War* (1926), *The Monastic Order in England* (1940) and *The Religious Orders in England* (3 vols, 1948–59).

Knox, Edmund Arbuthnott English Evangelical Anglican bishop, born Bangalore, India, 6 December 1847, died Shortlands, Kent 16 January 1937. He studied at Corpus Chrisit College, Oxford, and was a fellow at Merton from 1869 to 1884. He worked in several parishes and was made suffragan bishop of Coventry in 1894 and then bishop of Manchester in 1903. He was one of the main figures in the Evangelical wing of the Church of England at that time and was noted for his great preaching. He held very successful missions on Blackpool sands, then a favoured holiday location in the north-west of England. He championed the cause of Church schools, and opposed both the Revised Prayer Book and liberal biblical interpretation. His writings include *Sacrifice or Sacrament?* (1914), *On What Authority?* (1922), *The Tractarian Movement, 1833–1845* (1933). Knox retired in 1921 and spent his final years in Kent at a house bought for him by his former diocese.

Knox, James Robert Cardinal, born 2 March

1914, died 1983. He was educated at St Ildephonsus College, New Norcia, Australia, and the Pontifical Urban College de Propaganda Fide, Rome. Ordained priest in 1941, he became vice rector of the Pontifical Urban College de Propaganda Fide in 1945, and remained in this post until 1948. He was attached to the secretariat of state of Pope **Pius XII**, 1948–50, was secretary of apostolic internunciature in Tokyo, 1950–3, titular archbishop of Melitene in 1953, apostolic delegate to British East and West Africa, 1953–7, apostolic internuncio in India, 1957–67, and archbishop of Melbourne, 1967–74. He was created a cardinal in 1973 and from 1974 filled a number of positions at the Vatican, including prefect of the Sacred Congregation for the Discipline of the Sacraments and of the Sacred Congregation, and member of the Sacred Congregation for Evangelization of Peoples.

Knox, John Calvinist reformer, born near Haddington, Scotland, *c.*1513, died Edinburgh, 24 November 1572. A notary by profession, Knox was led by the preaching of the Lutheran George **Wishart** in the mid-1540s to embrace Protestantism, and he became a leader of the Protestant cause in Scotland. In 1551 he was appointed chaplain to **Edward VI** of England, but when **Mary Tudor** succeeded him Knox fled to the Continent. Settling in Geneva, he was profoundly influenced by the theology and Presbyterianism of **Calvin**. Returning to Scotland in 1559, Knox began to reform the Scottish Church along Calvinist lines, but clashed repeatedly with Mary Stuart, Queen of Scots, following her accession in 1561. Her abdication in 1567 paved the way for the triumph of Knox's reforms, though these were not completed until after his death. His *History of the Reformation of Religion within the Realm of Scotland* is an important contemporary source for the period.

Knox, Ronald Arbuthnott Roman Catholic apologist, Bible translator, writer and broadcaster, born Kibworth, England, 17 February 1888, died Mells, England, 24 August 1957. A brilliant scholar and academic, son of E. A. **Knox**, he became fellow and chaplain of Trinity College, Oxford, in 1912. He moved away from the evangelical Anglicanism of his upbringing towards Catholicism, being received into the Roman Catholic Church in 1917.

Ordained priest in 1919, he taught at St Edmund's College, Ware, until 1926, when he was appointed Roman Catholic chaplain at Oxford. In 1939 he resigned to concentrate on a new translation of the Bible, the NT appearing in 1945 and the OT following in 1949, both being widely praised. Knox published many works of popular apologetics, and *Enthusiasm*, an important study of religious emotionalism. He was also a frequent and popular broadcaster.

Knudson, Albert Cornelius Methodist minister, OT scholar and theologian, born Grandmeadow, Minnesota, 23 January 1873, died (place not known) 28 August 1953. After studies at the Universities of Minnesota, Boston (Massachusetts), Jena and Berlin, and some teaching in the USA, he was appointed Boston University School of Theology's professor of Hebrew and OT exegesis, 1906, of systematic theology, 1921–43, and dean, 1926–38. His eclectic theology derived from the idea of **Kant** that consciousness perceives every event to have a cause, which became for Knudson the belief that there is a valid objective induction to be made from the religious sense. From **Schleiermacher**, he became persuaded that religion is a sense of absolute dependence; and from **Ritschl**, whose conviction that justification is achieved in the community of the Church as the subject of Christ's redemptive work, Knudson derived his teaching on the importance of practical, ethical and social Christianity. From Parker Browne came his personalism, by which he did not mean individualism, but the spiritual freedom and responsibility of human beings in community. He published *Religious Teaching in the OT* (New York, 1918), *The Doctrine of God* (New York, 1930), *The Doctrine of Redemption* (New York, 1933) and *The Validity of Religious Experience* (New York, 1937).

Knutson, Kent Sigvart President of the American Lutheran Church (ALC), theologian, born Goldfield, Iowa, 7 August 1924, died of Jacob-Creutzfeldt disease in Minneapolis, 12 March 1973. He graduated in chemical engineering from Iowa State University in 1947, went to work for an oil company but soon after entered Luther Seminary, St Paul. In 1954 he was ordained into the Evangelical Lutheran Church, later part of the ALC, and worked as a pastor in New York, before joining the faculty of Luther Seminary. He became president of Wartburg Seminary in Dubuque in 1969 and president of the ALC the following year. He was involved in national and international Lutheran organizations, in dialogue with Roman Catholics and with Anglicans, and was on the central committee of the World Council of Churches.

Kochurov, John   *see* **John Kochurov**

Kohlmann, Anthony   Jesuit defender of the integrity of the confessional, born Kaiserberg, Alsace, 13 July 1771, died Rome, 11 April 1836. After ordination in 1796 he first joined the Congregation of the Sacred Heart, but transferred to the Society of Jesus in 1800, before emigrating to the USA. From Georgetown College, Washington, he worked on missionary extensions in Maryland and Pennsylvania. He was based in New York 1808–15, and while rector of St Peter's came to public notice in 1813. Having been told by a penitent in the confessional of the theft of goods, he undertook to restore them to the owner, James Keating, who took the matter to court in an attempt to force Kohlmann to reveal the identity of the thief. The defence lawyer, a Protestant, upheld Kohlmann's refusal on the grounds of the liberty of conscience guaranteed by New York State's constitution, and the four Protestant judges confirmed his right to silence. Other states followed suit. Kohlmann returned to Georgetown College and then went to the Gregorian University in Rome in 1824, serving as consultor to the college of cardinals.

Kolbe, Frederick Charles   Roman Catholic priest and educator, born Paarl, Cape Province, 1854, died Cape Town, 12 January 1936. While on a law scholarship in London he became a Catholic. Cardinal Henry **Manning** sent him to the English College in Rome and he was ordained in 1882. Having returned to South Africa he taught in Catholic schools and pioneered Catholic teacher training, but his great desire to see a Catholic university in South Africa was unfulfilled. However, he was appointed to the board of governors of the University of Cape Town and of the Cape of Good Hope, where he was also an examiner. He founded the *South African Catholic Magazine* in 1891, and his gifts as an educator were recognized both within Catholicism and in the South African universities.

Kolbe, Maximilian Maria   Saint, Franciscan priest, born Zduńska Wola, Poland, 8 January 1894, died (executed) Auschwitz, Poland, 14 August 1941. Kolbe joined the Franciscans in 1910 and was ordained in 1919. He taught at a Polish seminary and founded a religious community which published Christian journals and newspapers. Following the German occupation of Poland, these publications assumed a patriotic, anti-German stance, leading inevitably to Kolbe's arrest and imprisonment, in the Auschwitz concentration camp. There he exercised a solicitous priestly ministry to other prisoners, which culminated in offering himself for execution in the place of a younger man with a wife and family. Kolbe was canonized by fellow-Pole John Paul II in 1982, and in the presence of the man he had saved. Feast day 14 August.

Kollár, Jan   Slovak poet and priest, born Mošovce, Slovakia, 29 July 1793, died Vienna, 24 January 1852. He was educated at the University of Jena, became a pastor in Pest to the Slovak Protestants and finally professor of Slavonic archaeology in Vienna. He encouraged literary co-operation between Slavs. Among his work is the epic poem *The Daughter of Slava*.

Köllin, Conrad   Dominican and Thomist commentator, born Ulm, Germany, *c.*1476, died Cologne, 26 August 1536. He became a Dominican in 1492, studied philosophy and theology at Ulm and matriculated at Heidelberg in 1500. Following the award of his master's degree in 1507, he was made prior of the Dominican community and dean of theology, where he earnestly opposed Lutheranism. He lectured on **Thomas Aquinas** and his *Summa Theologica*, publishing his commentary on it in 1523 (Cologne). As a result of Köllin's work, Aquinas' *Summa* replaced **Peter Lombard**'s *Sententiarum libri quattuor* (*c.*1155–8) as the standard theological textbook.

Kollwitz, Käthe   German artist, born Königsberg, East Prussia, 1867, died Berlin, 22 April 1945. Married to a doctor who practised in a working-class district of Berlin, she was committed to representing the suffering of the poor through her art. Already a socialist, she became a pacifist following her experiences in World War I, during which her son was killed. Her work was banned under the Nazis. Her husband died in 1940, her grandson was killed in action in 1942, but she continued to draw, believing that this was her personal vocation and her contribution to building a better society.

Kolping, Adolf Roman Catholic priest and pioneer of Catholic social work in Germany, born Kerpen, near Cologne, 8 December 1813, died Cologne, 4 December 1865. A shoemaker, spare-time learning enabled him at 28 to study at the Universities of Munich and Bonn, 1841–4. He was ordained in 1845 and sent to Eberfeld, where he came across an organization for young workers which gave him the key to his life's work. He moved to Cologne in 1849 and, partly as an antidote to rationalist socialism, he founded a Catholic association of young journeymen with the aim of enabling them to become trustworthy, responsible members of society. He required the men to be efficient at their work, provided them with opportunities for self-improvement, and based everything on down-to-earth Christianity. At his death there were 26,000 members in Germany and the USA.

König, Eduard Evangelical theologian, Hebraist and exegete, born Reichenbach, Saxony, 15 November 1846, died Bonn, 10 February 1936. He studied and taught philosophy and theology at Leipzig, and was professor at Rostock, 1888–1900, and Bonn, 1920–22 emeritus. He believed in the divine origin of Hebrew religion, but also the importance of tradition, though he had little time for the evolutionary theory of its history. His dictionary of Hebrew and Aramaic was well received and his *Historisch-Kritisches Lehrgebäude der hebräischen Sprache* (3 vols, 1881–97) became a classic.

Konings, Anthony Redemptorist moral theologian, born Helmond, Holland, 24 August 1821, died Ilchester, Maryland, 30 June 1884. He was professed in 1843 and ordained in 1844. He was professor of moral theology and canon law in the Redemptorist house at Wittem, and provincial of the province of Holland, 1865–8. In 1870 he moved to the USA, to the Redemptorist seminary at Ilchester, where he functioned widely as a consultant on theological and canonical questions. His *Theologia moralis S. Alfonsi* (Boston, 1874) went to six editions, and his *Commentarium in facultates apostolicas* (New York, 1884) was well received.

Kontonglu, Photios (Fotis) Greek Orthodox iconographer and writer, born Kydoniai, Asia Minor, 1896, died Athens, 13 July 1965. He studied painting in Paris but after the expulsion of the Greeks from Asia Minor in 1922 he settled in Athens and became an enthusiast for Byzantine art, declaring its superiority over Western religious art. He himself frescoed the walls of dozens of churches in Greece and America and acquired many disciples. He also encouraged the revival of Byzantine iconography by a number of articles, often rather polemical in tone, which also deal with theological matters.

Koppers, Wilhelm Roman Catholic priest (of the Society of the Divine Word) and anthropologist, born Menzelen, Germany, 8 February 1886, died Vienna, 23 January 1961. He was ordained priest in 1911 and became professor at the University of Vienna in 1928 and director of the Institute for Ethnology, posts he held until his retirement, apart from the war years, when, because of his strong anti-Nazi views, he had to flee to Switzerland. He did field research in Tierra del Fuego and in India. His books include *Primitive Man and his World Picture*.

Kornmüller, Utto Benedictine composer and music historian, born Straubing, Germany, 5 January 1824, died Metten, Germany, 13 February 1907. Ordained in 1847, he became a Benedictine in 1858 and then choir director at Metten. His historical studies influenced the reform of Church music and the correct observance of the liturgy through his *Der Katholische Kirchenchor* (1868) and his great reference work *Lexikon der kirchlichen Tonkünst* (1870).

Kostka, Stanislaus Saint and patron of Poland, born Rostkovo, Poland, 28 October 1550, died Rome, 15 August 1568. Born into the Polish nobility, he studied at the Jesuit College in Vienna.

Against family opposition, he managed to enter the Jesuit novitiate of St Andrew in Rome in 1567, where he lived for a few months in faith and spiritual fervour. He was canonized in 1736. Feast day 13 November.

Kotliarevs'kyi, Ivan Petrovich Ukrainian folklorist and satirist, born Poltava, Ukraine, 9 September 1769, died Poltava, 20 October 1838. As a young man he travelled about collecting legends and folksongs and in his spare time writing material for the comic operas performed in the local theatre. In 1798 he published *Eneida*, a satirical and humorous version of the *Aeneid*. At 27 he joined the army to fight against Napoleon, after which he became supervisor of a children's home. Towards the end of his life he was absorbed in religious mysticism.

Kotsiubyns'kyi, Mykhailo Ukrainian novelist and short-story writer, born Vinnitsa, Ukraine, 17 September 1864, died Chernigov, Ukraine, 25 April 1913. He attended Shargorod Seminary, then worked as a teacher and statistician. He was concerned to integrate Ukrainian writing into the European mainstream. His best-known novel is *Fata Morgana.* His works were translated into other languages and some were made into films.

Koudelka, Joseph Maria Roman Catholic bishop, born Chlistovo, Bavaria, 8 December 1852, died Superior, Wisconsin, 24 June 1921. The family emigrated to Manitowoo, Wisconsin, in 1865, where he studied at St Francis' Seminary and was ordained in 1875. He served in Cleveland, Ohio, until 1882, spent a year as editor of *Hlas*, a Bohemian magazine published in St Louis, then returned to Cleveland as pastor of St Michael's, where he built the parish church and school. His perceived mission was to immigrants, particularly Slavs, and he was consecrated bishop of Germanicopolis in 1908. He built up the Diocese of Milwaukee with churches, schools and hospitals and was the first auxiliary bishop of special jurisdiction appointed in the USA.

Kovalevsky, Evgrav Evgrafovich (Bishop Jean de St-Denis) Orthodox missionary in France, born St Petersburg, 26 March 1905, died Paris, 30 January 1970. He came to France in 1920 and studied theology. The remainder of his life was devoted to the establishment of a distinctively French form of Orthodoxy. He helped to revive the long extinct Gallican rite and established a number of parishes. His very idiosyncratic method and strong personality made him and his group suspect to most of the Orthodox hierarchy. He was however consecrated bishop in 1964 by St **John (Maximovich) of San Francisco**. Following the latter's death he led his flock into a rather uncanonical status, which still causes controversy.

Koyi, William Xhosa evangelist to the Ngoni, Malawi, born near Thomas River, South Africa, 1846, died of tuberculosis at Njuyu mission station, Malawi, June 1886. He was baptized by the Methodists *c.*1869 and educated at the Lovedale Institute of the Free Church of Scotland between 1871 and 1876. He volunteered for service with the Livingstonia Mission and, while he worked briefly at Cape Maclear and Bandawe, he is best known for gaining the trust of the Ngoni. His language and culture were related to those of the Ngoni and the relationships he developed paved the way for further work. Just before his death he learnt that the Ngoni chief had agreed to the establishment of the first schools in the area.

Kozeluh, Jan Antonin Composer, born Welwarn, Bohemia, 26 June (?)1747, died Vienna, 7 May 1818. An accomplished classical musician, he composed ballets for the national theatre in Prague, 1771–8, then found work in Vienna as pianist, teacher and composer. In 1792 he followed **Mozart** as composer to Leopold II and remained in this post until his death, producing a range of operas, oratorios and ballets.

Kraeling, Carl Lutheran oriental scholar, born Brooklyn, New York, 10 March 1897, died New Haven, Connecticut, 14 November 1966. Graduated from Columbia University in 1918, was ordained as a Lutheran pastor in 1920 and for the next nine years taught at the Lutheran Seminary in Philadelphia. From 1929 to 1950 he taught NT and then Near Eastern languages and literature at Yale Divinity School. From 1950 until 1960 he was director of the Oriental Institute at the University of Chicago, and stayed on to teach oriental archaeology for a further two years. During his last years he was visiting scholar to Dumbarton Oaks in Washington, DC. He was involved at a national and international level with the main orientalist organizations, lectured annually in Jerusalem and directed the Jerash excavation. He was one of those most instrumental in enabling scholars to have access to the Dead Sea Scrolls.

Kraemer, Hendrick   Dutch Reformed missiologist, lay theologian and ecumenical leader, born Amsterdam, 17 May 1888, died Driebergen, The Netherlands, 11 November 1965. Kraemer studied Javanese in Leiden before working for the Dutch Bible Society in Indonesia, 1922–37. He was professor of the history and phenomenology of religion at Leiden University, 1937–47, and first director of the Ecumenical Institute in Bossey, 1948–55. His *Christian Message in a Non-Christian World* (1938), prepared for the International Missionary Council meeting in Madras, was very influential. Kraemer was an excellent linguist with a deep understanding of Islam, of the importance of independent Churches, the role of the laity and the encounter between God and man in the midst of social and religious crises.

Kramp, Joseph   Jesuit liturgist, born Kerpen, near Cologne, 19 June 1886, died Frankfurt, 14 June 1940. He became a Jesuit in 1905, and was a chaplain in World War I. He had a strong influence over the German Catholic youth movement but his main interest was in pre-Tridentine theology and in bringing the liturgy into line with earlier practice. His most influential works in these connected spheres were *Messliturgie und Gottesreich* (3 vols, Freiburg, 1921) and *Eucharistia* (Freiburg, 1924).

Krapf, Johann Ludwig   Lutheran pioneer missionary to East Africa, born near Tübingen, Germany, 1810, died Kornthal, Germany, 26 November 1881. Studied at the Basel Missionary Training Institute before going to Ethiopia in 1837 with the Anglican Church Missionary Society. His evangelism to the Galla (Oromo) frustrated by King **Tewodros II**, he went to the East African coast in January 1844. In 1846 he established a base at Rabai with Johann Rebmann. Together they explored the interior and worked on local languages. He translated the NT into kiSwahili and St Mark's Gospel into kiKamba and published *Vocabulary of Six Languages* and

Travels and Missionary Labours in East Africa (1860). Broken in health he returned to Europe in 1855 but went back to Mombasa to aid the Methodist Mission in 1862.

Krasiński, Zygmunt   Polish count and poet, born Paris, 19 February 1812, died there, 23 February 1859. With **Mickiewicz** and Słowacki, he was one of the three Polish messianic poets but mostly lived and worked outside Poland. Krasiński studied law at Warsaw University and then studied at Geneva. His father supported Polish independence, a theme reflected in Krasiński's poetry. Two poetic dramas are his best-known works – *The Undivine Comedy*, which is the first literary expression of class war, and *Irydion*. His poem 'The Moment Before Dawn' presents Poland in the Christ-like image of sacrifice leading to resurrection.

Kraus, Franz Xaver   Catholic Church and art historian, born Trier, Germany, 18 September 1840, died San Remo, Italy, 28 December 1901. Ordained in 1864, he became professor of Christian art at Strasburg in 1872, and of Church history at Freiburg im Breisgau in 1878, positions from which he raised archaeology and art history to the status of independent disciplines. During the repression inspired by **Bismarck**, who feared Catholicism would imperil the unity of the German Empire, he tried to make a bridge between it and contemporary culture, and between State and Church, as his diaries published in Cologne by H. Schiel in 1957 reveal. His *Lehrbuch der Kirchengeschichte* went through four editions in his lifetime (Trier, 1872–96).

Krauth, Charles Porterfield   Lutheran leader and theologian, born Martinsburg, Virginia, 17 March 1823, died Philadelphia, Pennsylvania, 2 January 1883. Educated at Gettysburg college and seminary, he became pastor of churches in Maryland, Virginia and Pennsylvania before moving to Philadelphia in 1859 as editor of the magazine *The Lutheran*. On the foundation of the Lutheran Theological Seminary in Philadelphia, 1864, he was elected professor of systematic theology, and was the organizer and first president of the General Council in 1867. During 1868–83 he was professor of philosophy in the University of Pennsylvania. He defended original Lutheran doctrine and traditional practice in the magazine and in *The Conservative Reformation and its Theology* (Pennsylvania, 1872).

Krishna, Pal First Bengali Baptist evangelist, born Barigram, Bengal, 1763, died Sylhet, India, August 1822. Baptized in 1800, he was ordained in 1804. He preached twelve to fourteen times a week in the streets of Calcutta before moving his base to Sylhet. He was an effective open-air preacher and hard-working pastor, as well as a musician.

Krizanić, Juraj Dominican and the 'Father of Pan-Slavism', born Oberh, Croatia, c.1617, died near Vienna, 1683. Ordained in 1642, his aim was to convert Russia to Catholicism, and in 1647 he travelled to Warsaw, Smolensk and Moscow, back to Poland and then to Rome, where in 1652 he wrote treatises about Russia and the Orthodox Church without permission from the Office of Propaganda. Concealing his Catholic priesthood, he went again to Moscow and worked as a translator for Tsar Alexis. In 1661, in exile in Siberia, he wrote *Politika*, an (unsuccessful) appeal to the Tsar to unite all Slavs against Germany. On his release in 1676 he became a Dominican in Vilna, and died when chaplain to the Polish army during the Turkish siege of Vienna in 1683.

Kromer, Martin Catholic bishop, historian and diplomat, born Biecz, near Cracow, Poland, 1515, died Heilsberg, East Prussia, 23 March 1589. Having studied at Cracow, Bologna and Rome, he became secretary to Prince (later King) Sigismund II August, whom he served as a diplomat to Rome and Trent. He wrote a history of Poland up to 1506 (1555) but his principal work was *Polonia sive de situ, populis, moribus, magistratibus, et republica regni Poloniae* (1577). As a bishop from 1579, as a patron of the Jesuits and through his polemical tracts, sermons and catechism in Polish he strove against Lutheranism and Calvinism.

Kugler, Franz Xaver Jesuit astronomer and Assyriologist, born Königsbach, Pfalz, Germany, 27 November 1862, died Lucerne, Switzerland, 25 January 1929. He studied the physical sciences at Heidelberg and Munich, where he gained a doctorate in chemistry. In 1886 he became a Jesuit in The Netherlands and was ordained in 1893. His interest had by then turned to ancient Near-Eastern history and scholarship. From 1897 he taught mathematics at Valkenburg (The Netherlands), where he researched Babylonian chronology, astronomy and biblical history from cuneiform sources. His *Sternkunde und Sterndienst in Babel* (3 vols, 1907–35) was recognized as an important source book for future scholars.

Kuhlman, Kathryn US healing evangelist, born 1907, died 1976. An evangelist from the age of sixteen, she founded the Kuhlman Revival Tabernacle in 1933 and the Denver Revival Tabernacle in 1935. Marriage to a divorcee who had left his wife for her then damaged her credibility until they parted. From 1946 healings and being 'slain in the Spirit' became important parts of her ministry (although not glossolalia). She preached at several locations across America and had a radio and television ministry. In 1972 she received an honorary doctorate from Oral Roberts University.

Kuhn, Johannes Roman Catholic theologian, born Wäschenbeuren, Germany, 19 February 1806, died Tübingen, 8 May 1887. Having studied theology at Tübingen, he was ordained in 1831, and thereafter was professor of NT exegesis at Giessen, 1832, and Tübingen, 1837, and professor of dogma at Tübingen, 1839–82. He was appointed a permanent member of the State Tribunal in 1856 and of the Board of Peers in 1868. He believed that by countering heresy through discussion and reason, religious differences could be resolved. He is best known for his *Katholische Dogmatik* (4 vols, Tübingen, 1846–68).

Kukučín, Martin Catholic Slovak novelist, born Jansenova, Slovakia, 17 May 1860, died Zagreb, Yugoslavia, 21 May 1928. As a young man he studied medicine in Prague, but spent his adult life in Croatia and South America, where he was converted to Catholicism. His novel about village life was the first expression of realism in Slovak literature but his greatest work was *Mat Vola* ('Fatherland Calls', 5 vols, 1926–7), a dramatization of the life of Croatian immigrants in South America, whither he had gone after World War I, disappointed by the political and social condition of Slovakia. Written in popular idiom and with psychological insight, *Mat Vola* displayed a knowledge of social problems and a hope that its portrayal of the peasants' stoic heroism would reinspire the national spirit of the people.

Kundig, Martin Roman Catholic priest and civic leader, born Switzerland, 19 November 1805, died Milwaukee, Wisconsin, 6 March 1879. Ordained in 1829 for the Diocese of Cincinnati, Ohio, he was sent to Detroit, Michigan, where in 1834 during a cholera epidemic he set up relief services and established a hospital. He became the superintendent of a poorhouse in Wayne County, and from this time developed a lifelong interest in free public schooling, which in turn led to an appointment as regent at the University of Michigan, Ann Arbor. His gift for organization brought about his transfer to Wisconsin to help immigrants with land purchase. Here he founded temperance societies and the first free school in Wisconsin, in the basement of his church, St Mark's, Kenosha.

Kunigunde Saint, empress of Germany, born c.980, died convent of Kaufungen, Hesse, 3 March 1033 or 1039. The daughter of a count of Luxemburg, Kunigunde married Duke Henry IV of Bavaria around 998. When her husband became Emperor **Henry II**, she was crowned empress in 1014. She was a strong advocate and adviser to her husband but is better remembered for giving her dowry to found the Diocese of Bamberg (1007). In 1024, after her husband died, she entered the convent of Kaufungen, which she had founded in 1017. Many miracles are told of her life, and legend says (probably because their marriage was childless) that she and her husband took vows of perpetual virginity. She was canonized in 1200. Feast days in Bamberg 3 March and 9 September.

Kunigunde Blessed, patroness of Poland and Lithuania, born c.1224, died Stary Sacz, Poland, 1292. Daughter of King Bela IV of Hungary, in 1239 she married Prince, later King Boleslas V (the Chaste). It was a marriage in which sexual abstinence coexisted with lifelong harmony, and saw the establishment of hospitals, churches and convents and help for the work of the Franciscans. Widowed in 1279, she withdrew to the convent of Poor Clares which she had founded at Stary Sacz. When the Turks invaded Poland in 1287 the nuns took

refuge in Pyenin. The castle was besieged, but after her prayers for its safety the Turks withdrew. Pope **Clement XI** named her patroness of Poland and Lithuania in 1715. Feast day 24 July.

Kurth, Godefroid Catholic historian and Belgian patriot, born Arlon, Luxemburg province, Belgium, 11 May 1847, died Asshe, near Brussels, 4 January 1916. He was professor of medieval history at Liège from 1877, and after his retirement from teaching in 1906 director of the Institut Historique Belge in Rome. Here he pursued research into the Merovingian age and the etymology of Belgian place-names, and continued his advocacy of Christian democracy. In 1909 he gave the opening address at the Belgian Catholic Conference at Mechlin, on 'The Church and Education', which was said to have been a decisive moment in the liturgical movement.

Kurtz, Benjamin Lutheran newspaper editor, born Harrisburg, Pennsylvania, 28 February 1795, died Philadelphia, Pennsylvania, 29 December 1865. Licensed by the Pennsylvania Synod in 1815 he served parishes in Washington County, Maryland. An advocate of modernized and 'Americanized' Lutheranism and of revivalism, as editor of the *Lutheran Observer*, 1833–62, he was able to influence many Lutherans to become assertive evangelicals, against the wishes of the more conservative members. His was a religion of the heart, and he was one of the founders in 1858 of the Lutheran Mission Institute of Selingsgrove, Pennsylvania, which trained half-educated young men to become Lutheran pastors and revivalists in poor churches. This caused regret to many because it diluted the Lutheran reputation for an educated, intellectual ministry.

Kutschker, Johann Rudolph Cardinal and canonist, born Wiese, Silesia, 11 April 1810, died Vienna, 27 January 1881. Ordained in 1833, in 1835 he became professor of moral theology at Olmütz. From 1857 to 1876 he was an official in the Ministry of Education, and during this time he was made suffragan bishop and vicar general. In 1876 he became archbishop of Vienna, and in 1877 a cardinal. Not adversarial by nature, he was the better able to mediate in Church politics. Among his many works on the canon his most extensive is *Das Eherecht der katholische Kirche nach seiner Theorie und Praxis* (5 vols, Vienna, 1856–9).

Kuyper, Abraham Dutch theologian and statesman, born Maassluis, The Netherlands, 29 October 1837, died The Hague, 8 November 1920. He studied at the University of Leiden and worked as a pastor at Beesd in Gelderland, in Utrecht and later in Amsterdam. He entered The Netherlands' lower chamber, and broke with the national Church, forming the Free Reformed Church. In forming a reformist Christian Conservative ministry, he managed to forge a collaboration between the Calvinist and Catholic groups. From 1901 to 1903 he was prime minister. He was a fine speaker and writer, and had great influence. At Princeton University, he proposed a scientific concept of Calvinism, influencing family, Church, State and society. His writings include *The Encyclopedia of Theology* and *The Work of the Holy Spirit*.

Kvitka, Hryhorii Federovych Catholic Ukrainian writer, born Osnova, near Kharkov, 18 November 15001788 (Julian calendar), died Osnova, 8 August 1843. When he was a young man, the restoration of his eyesight lost through illness gave him a love for God which coloured all his work. He directed the Kharkov theatre, 1812–16, was district marshal of the nobility, 1817–28, and judge (later president) of the Kharkov criminal court from 1840. His most important novel, *Marusia* (1833) was the first of many attractive depictions of peasant women. He believed in natural human goodness, though also in the justice of God which punishes the sinner in this life, as in *Perekotypole* (1843), and in Nature as God's instrument. His comic operetta *Svatannia na Honcharivtsi* (1836) is still popular.

L

Labadie, Jean de French spiritual writer and Reformer, born Borg, near Bordeaux, 13 January 1610, died Altona, 13 January 1674. He entered the Society of Jesus in 1625, but left in 1639 on the grounds of ill health. He then became a diocesan priest, serving in Bordeaux, Paris and Amiens. He was growing increasingly attracted to Calvinism, and he became a member of the Reformed Church in Montauban in 1650. He was a pastor there, as well as teaching theology, from 1652 to 1657, and in 1659 became a pastor in Geneva. In 1666 he became a preacher at Middelburg, in The Netherlands, but there set up his own sect about 1670. He and his followers valued the personal inspiration of the Holy Spirit over the Bible, did not believe in infant baptism nor in the presence of Christ in the Eucharist. His sect died out in the 1730s.

Labastida y Dàvalos, Pelagio Antonio de Catholic archbishop and scholar, born Zamora, Mexico, 21 March 1816, died Coacaleco, Tlalnepantla, Mexico, 4 February 1891. Ordained in 1838, he graduated in canon law in 1839 and taught literature, philosophy and Spanish until he was appointed bishop of Pueblo in 1855. Accused of attacking the government from the pulpit, he went into exile and travelled about Europe. He was made archbishop of Mexico in 1863 but went to Rome in 1867 because of the unrest in Mexico. He was a member of the commission on ecclesiastical discipline at Vatican Council I, and returned to Mexico in 1871. Political life was dominated by liberals with whom he had little in common, though the president, Porfirio Diaz, presented him with a crozier on the fiftieth anniversary of his ordination in 1888.

Labat, Jean Baptiste Dominican missionary and writer, born Paris, 1663 or 1664, died there, 6 January 1738. After his profession in 1685 he lectured at Nancy then worked in Martinique and Guadeloupe, where eventually he was made an apostolic prefect and beat off a British expedition in 1703. This was misrepresented in France and he was recalled and confined to a cloister in Toul, but was released after the Dominican superior general intervened. He left France and travelled in Spain and Italy, returning only after the death of **Louis XIV** in 1715, when he wrote his celebrated memoirs, *Nouveau Voyage aux Isles d'Amérique* (6 vols, Paris, 1722) and *Voyages en Espagne et en Italie* (8 vols, Paris, 1722).

Labbe, Philippe Jesuit scholar, born Bourges, 10 July 1607, died Paris, 17 March 1667. He became a Jesuit in 1623; he taught for a time at the Jesuit College at Bourges but his real interest was in compiling material on many topics, including hagiography, ecclesiastical and secular history, geography and Greek prose. His most important work was a compilation of the Church Councils, *Sacrosancta Concilia ad regiam editionem exacta*, and before his death, he had produced volumes 1–8 and 12–15. The remaining volumes were completed by G. Cossart, a fellow Jesuit, but not published until 1671–3. In 1627 he was made procurator general for his superior general.

Laberthonnière, Lucien Oratorian modernist theologian, born Chazelet, France, 5 October 1860, died Paris, 6 October 1932. Ordained as an Oratorian, he taught philosophy at the college at Juilly in 1887, was appointed superior at the École Massillon in Paris in 1898 and rector at Juilly in 1900. He edited *Annales de le philosophie chrétienne*, 1905–13, a journal supporting the views expressed in Maurice **Blondel**'s *L'Action* (1893), finding the essence of life in action rather than in an intellectual system like Scholasticism, and asserting that consequences rather than origins were the test of truth. His *Annales* and six of his other works were put on the Index and he was forbidden to publish, though he continued to write.

La Bigne, Marguérin de Patrologist and theologian, born Bernières-le-Patry, Normandy, 1546, died Paris, 1589. After study at Caen and Paris, with a doctorate from the Sorbonne, he became a canon of Bayeux and dean of Le Mans. His interest in the principal early Fathers led him to make the first inclusive collection of their works, the *Bibliotheca veterum patrum et auctorum ecclesiasticorum* (1575–9), which was augmented in later editions (1618, 1644) and finally named the *Maxima bibliotheca sanctorum patrum* (27 vols, 1677).

Laborans Cardinal and canon lawyer, born Pontorma, Italy, early to mid 1100s, died probably Rome, *c*.1190. Educated at Frankfurt and Paris (where he received the rank of *magister*), Laborans became a canonicus at Capua before 1160. He was made a cardinal-deacon in 1173 and cardinal-priest seven years later. As a decretalist (a canon lawyer who commented on the *Decretum* of **Gratian**), his best-known work is the *Codex Compilationis*, an attempt to reorder and update the *Decretum*. He also wrote several theological works, including *De vera libertate* (1144–61) and *De relativa praedictione personae in divinis* (1180–90).

Labouré, Catherine Saint, mystic, born Fain-lès-Moutiers, France, 2 May 1806, died Paris, 31 December 1876. Though discouraged by her family, she entered the Daughters of Charity of St Vincent de Paul in 1830. During her novitiate in Paris she began to experience visions, of which the most enduring was that of the Blessed Virgin Mary displaying a medal of herself and saying 'Have a medal struck after this model. All who wear it will have great graces. They should wear it round the neck.' The medals were produced from 1832. Catherine went to the convent at Reuilly, Paris, in 1831 and remained there. Her mystical experiences continued for the rest of her life. Feast day 28 November.

Labré, Benedict Joseph Saint, 'the Beggar of Rome', born Amettes, France, 25 March 1748, died Rome, 16 April 1783. Rejected as unsuitable by the religious orders to whom he applied, he found his vocation in pilgrimage. In 1770 he began a pilgrimage on foot to Rome, living on alms. On the way he decided to go to all the principal places of pilgrimage in Europe, always walking, sleeping rough and taking nothing except a cloak and a few books, and sharing what he was given with other beggars. He reached Rome in 1776, spent his nights in the Colosseum and his days in different churches, particularly those which celebrated the Forty Hours devotion, which he loved and did what he could to promote. He died in Holy Week 1783 and was popularly proclaimed to be saint. He was canonized in 1881. Feast day 16 April.

Labriolle, Pierre de Historian and patrologist, born Asnières, France, 18 June 1874, died Nantes, 28 December 1940. After classical studies in Paris, from 1904 he taught at Laval University, Montreal, the Collège Stanislaus in Paris, the Lycée at Rennes and the University of Fribourg in Switzerland. Learned in patristics and expert in the Latin of the early Christian period, he published short biographies of *St Vincent of Lérins* (1906), *St Jerome* (1907) and *St Ambrose* (1908), *Histoire de la littérature chrétienne* (1910) and *La crise montaniste* (Paris, 1913). He founded the *Bulletin d'ancienne littérature et d'archéologie chrétienne* in 1911, and in 1916 entered the Académie des Inscriptions et Belles Lettres, being much respected for his scholarship, in particular for his translations of the Latin texts of the early Christian centuries.

La Chaize, François de Jesuit confessor of **Louis XIV**, born Château d'Aix, Loire, 25 August 1624, died Paris, 20 January 1709. He entered the Jesuit novitiate in 1639, was ordained in 1656 and professed in 1658. Louis XIV selected him as his confessor in 1675, a position he retained until his death. He dealt mildly with the king during his adulterous life with Madame de Montespan, which was said to have eventually resulted in his conversion. He was influential in the appointment of bishops, but incurred the displeasure of **Innocent**

XI for holding Louis back from directly attacking the Jansenists and the Huguenots.

Lachat, Eugène Catholic bishop, born Montavon, Switzerland, 14 October 1819, died Balerna, Switzerland, 1 November 1886. Ordained in 1842 he served in Italy and Alsace before returning to work in Switzerland in 1850. He was appointed bishop of Basel in 1855 at a period of social and political reform, and having supported papal infallibility at Vatican Council I he found himself opposed and isolated by the Swiss press for censuring priests who did not accept it. When five of the seven cantons in his diocese deposed and expelled him he went to Lucerne and built a seminary there. He resigned his bishopric in 1884 and was made titular archbishop of Damietta (Egypt).

Lachelier, Jules Idealist philosopher, born Fontainebleau, 27 May 1832, died there, 18 January 1918. He was a student then a teacher at the École Normale Supérieure but resigned rather than destroy his students' faith, and worked on the university's administrative staff 1875–1910. He rejected realism, the belief that externally perceived objects immediately known have real existences, and based his idealism on an absolute mechanical determinism: he thought that all things, including the will, are determined.

La Colombière, Claude de Blessed, Jesuit preacher, born St-Symphorien-d'Ozon, France, 2 February 1642, died Paray-le-Monial, 16 February 1682. He became a Jesuit at Avignon, and after ordination taught rhetoric at Lyons, 1670–3, before becoming rector of the Jesuit College at Paray in 1675. His effective preaching brought him to the notice of the duchess of York, wife of the future British king **James II**, and an appointment as a court preacher at St James's Palace in 1676. The conspiracy of Titus **Oates**, who in 1678 falsely alleged that there was a Catholic plot to assassinate **Charles II** and that La Colombière was involved, led to his imprisonment for five weeks and his enforced return to France. His London sermons were published with his other works in a critical edition (6 vols, Grenoble, 1900–1).

Lacombe, Albert Catholic missionary, born St Sulpice, Montreal, 28 February 1827, died Midna-

pore, Alberta, 12 December 1916. Ordained in 1849, he spent his life in the service of the Cree and Blackfoot Indians. He worked with Bishop Alexandre **Tache** of the Oblates of Mary Immaculate and was professed in that Order in 1856. From 1865 to 1872 he tried to involve the Indians of the West in agriculture, and in 1873 during unrest he was a government intermediary. While the Canadian Pacific Railway was being built, he looked after the workers and in 1883 prevented their being massacred by the Blackfeet. He was on the Board of Education for the Northern Territories, 1886–92, and in 1899 helped the government to make a treaty with the Indians, in whose language he wrote some important books.

Lacombe, George Catholic historian of medieval philosophy, born San Francisco, California, 1 January 1886, died Paris, 1 November 1934. Ordained in 1910, he was a chaplain in the US army in World War I, then in 1923 he entered the École des Chartes in Paris, and became a delegate of the American universities to the International Committee of Historical Sciences. His contribution to the history of medieval thought was to provide the basic contemporary material for it and he undertook to prepare the catalogue of all medieval MSS of Aristotle's works. The first of two volumes was published in 1935.

Lacordaire, Jean Baptiste Henri French Dominican preacher, born Recey-sur-Ource, Burgundy, 12 May 1802, died Sorèze, 20 November 1861. He was brought up in Dijon, where he lost his faith through reading **Rousseau**. He studied law, and practised at the Paris bar, but soon regained his faith and entered the seminary at Issy in 1824. He was ordained in 1827. He served as chaplain to nuns and to university students in Paris, but found this unsatisfactory, and for a time wished to be a missionary. However, he encountered Félicité **Lamennais**, and engaged with his crusade in France, writing for *L'Avenir*. When *L'Avenir* was suppressed by Rome, Lacordaire submitted, and returned to preaching, at which he was a great success. In 1836 he preached the Lenten conferences in Notre Dame in Paris. By this time he had decided that the only hope for the Church was the restoration of the religious orders. He took the Dominican habit in Rome in 1839, receiving the religious name 'Henri Dominique'. By the end of the following year he was back in the pulpit of Notre Dame, preaching on 'the vocation of the French nation'. He now turned his energies to refounding the Dominican Order in France: the first house was opened in Nancy in 1843, and a province was erected in 1850. Lacordaire was twice prior provincial, 1850–4 and 1858–61. He had, however, considerable problems with one of his former disciples, Alexandre Jandel, who had become master general of the Dominicans and was trying to impose on France a much stricter regime than that which Lacordaire had intended. He continued his popular sermons at Notre Dame, and was elected to the Académie Française in 1860. Beyond his sermons, journalism and correspondence, which have all been republished, he produced a number of other books, including a highly successful life of St **Dominic**.

Lacroix, Alphonse François Pioneer Protestant missionary in Bengal, born Lignières, near Neuville, Switzerland, 10 May 1799, died Calcutta, 18 July 1859. In 1820 he was appointed by The Netherlands Missionary Society to go to the Dutch trading station at Chinsurati. When this came under British rule in 1825 he joined the London Missionary Society and though persecuted worked in the fishing villages south of Calcutta. Opposed to education in English, he used the vernacular in all his missionary work. He moved to Bhowanpore in 1837 where his great height and effective vernacular preaching made him a well-known figure. He was a founder of the ecumenical Calcutta Missionary Council, a monthly meeting of all missionaries and ministers and the precursor of the Church of North India.

Lacroix, Claude Jesuit moral theologian, born Dahlem (Luxemburg), 7 April 1652, died Cologne, 1 or 2 June 1714. He became a Jesuit in 1673 and was ordained in 1684. He taught philosophy at Cologne and moral theology at Münster and Cologne. There were 25 editions of his *Theologia moralis* (8 vols, Cologne, 1707–14), but after his death parts of one of the later editions (1757) were used by the Jansenists to attack the Jesuits. Condemned by the *parlement* of Paris, it was publicly burned in Toulouse.

Lactantius (Lucius Caecilius Firmianus Lactantius) Author, born Proconsular Africa, *c*.250–60, died Gallia (Trier?), *c*.320. Under Diocletian (turn of the century) he was in Nicomedia, where he taught rhetoric and where he met the young **Constantine I**. It was probably there that he converted to Christianity. He suffered from Diocletian's persecution, echoes of which are to be found in his writings (cf. *De mortibus persecutorum*). Near the end of his life he was called to Trier by the new emperor, Constantine, to be tutor of his son Crispus. Lactantius was a stylish writer but his theological reflection is not very sophisticated.

Lacunza y Diaz, Manuel de Jesuit theologian and biblical scholar, born Santiago, Chile, 19 July 1731, died Imola, Italy, 18 July 1801. He became a Jesuit in 1747 and was ordained in 1755. He went to Italy in 1767 where he wrote *Venida del Mesias en gloria y majestad*, which was finished in 1790 (Cadiz, 1812), and translated into several languages, but banned by the Holy Office in 1824 and again in 1941, probably because of its millenarianism, a popular theme with the Protestants of the Pietist movement in the eighteenth century and with the Adventists of the twentieth century, but possibly also because of its criticism of the Roman curia and of the Fathers, and praise of Judaism.

Lacy, Edmund Bishop of Exeter, son of Stephen Lacy of Gloucester, died Chudleigh, Devon, 18 September 1455. He was elected a fellow of University College, Oxford, in 1391, and made a doctor of theology in 1414. Soon after 1431 he was appointed dean of the chapel in Henry V's household, and bishop of Exeter in 1420. He suffered from a bone disease, and probably because of that set up a cult of the Archangel (St) Raphael, whose name means 'healer' and who was therefore associated with healing, and for whose feast on 24 October he composed an Office. Miraculous cures were said to have taken place at Lacy's tomb in Exeter.

Ladeuze, Paulin Catholic exegete and patrologist, born Harvengt, Belgium, 3 July 1870, died Louvain, 10 February 1940. He specialized in a study of the eastern Fathers at Louvain, where he was ordained in 1892 and wrote his doctoral thesis on coenobitism in the fourth and fifth centuries. In 1900 he founded, with A. **Cauchie**, the *Revue d'histoire ecclésiastique*. From 1900 to 1909 he taught patrology and the Coptic and Egyptian languages, personally inspiring a generation of orientalist scholars. In 1909 he became rector of Louvain and in 1913 with the Catholic University of America set up the Corpus Scriptorum Christianorum Orientalium. After World War I he restored the damage to the university, particularly the library. Though progressive, he did not make any excessive allowances to Modernism.

Ladislaus of Gielniow   Blessed, Franciscan missionary, born Gielniow, Diocese of Gniezno, Poland, *c.*1440, died 4 May 1505. Educated at Cracow, he became a Franciscan and in 1487 the provincial of the Polish Bernardine province. He founded an Observant convent (i.e. one where the Rule of St Francis was strictly carried out) as a training centre of missionaries for Lithuania. He wrote poems on the Passion of Christ and on the Blessed Virgin Mary, in whose honour he introduced a special rosary. He was beatified in 1750, and in 1753 proclaimed patron of Poland and Lithuania. Feast days 4 May and 25 September.

Ladislaus of Hungary   Saint, king of Hungary, born Poland, 1040, died Nitra (in modern Slovakia), 29 July 1095. Elected king (against his will) by the Hungarian nobles in 1077, the early years of his reign were troubled by opposition from his cousin Solomon, a rival claimant to the throne, which took twelve years to subdue. Once this was achieved, Ladislaus, an ardent champion of Christianity, devoted himself to the evangelism of his pagan subjects. He built many churches, and enacted enlightened civil and religious laws. He was canonized in 1192. Feast day 27 June.

Laet, Carlos Maximiano Pimenta de   Brazilian Catholic journalist, born Rio de Janeiro, 3 October 1847, died there, 7 December 1927. Though he graduated as an engineer from the Escola Central in 1873, the same year he was named a professor of Portuguese, and words were henceforth his business. A firm Catholic and monarchist, when Brazil became a republic he fought the development of the current anti-religious ethos and the secularizing teachers of the day through his weekly

columns in the *Jornal do Brasil*. For this defence of Catholicism he was made a Roman count. His *A Heresia Protestante* (1907) concerned the intercession of angels and saints.

Laetus   Saint, bishop and martyr, died *c.*484. King Huneric of the Vandals, an Arian, had decreed that all Catholic churches in Africa be closed and the possessions of their clergy be turned over to Arian clergy. Laetus, bishop of Leptis Minor, was imprisoned and burned at the stake; other bishops of Byzacene (Fusculus, Germanus, Mansuetus and Praesidius) were tortured and driven into the desert, where they also lost their lives. Feast day 6 September.

La Fage, Juste Adrien Lenoir de   Catholic pioneer scholar of plainsong, born Paris, 27 March 1805, died Charenton, 8 March 1862. A chorister from the age of six, he worked with **Choron**, the enthusiast for church choirs, as a student and assistant, then after a year's study in Rome became chapelmaster at St-Étienne-du-Mont in Paris where he replaced the obsolescent bass wind instrument with an organ. He was deeply influenced by Gregorian chant, and his publications contributed to liturgical and musical scholarship. He founded and edited *Le Plain-chant* and published his views in *Cours Complet de Plain-chant* (2 vols, 1855–6).

La Farge, John   Painter and writer, born New York, 3 March 1835, died Providence, Rhode Island, 14 November 1910. He originally intended to pursue a career in law, but a visit to Europe in 1856 changed the direction of his life. He toured the galleries, met intellectuals in Paris and Pre-Raphaelite painters in England, and found a gift for painting. On his return to the USA, he painted landscapes and flowers from 1860 to 1876, and became a member of the committee set up to establish the Metropolitan Museum of Art in New York City. Thereafter he concentrated on murals and stained glass in public buildings, notably in the church of the Ascension, New York City. He developed an interest in the art of the Pacific Islands and Japan, and his *Considerations of Painting* (1895) and *An Artist's Letters from Japan* (1897) revealed a gift for lively writing.

La Farge, John   US Jesuit priest and social activist,

born Newport, Rhode Island, 1880, the son of the painter and stained-glass worker John **La Farge**, died 24 November 1963. Read classics at Harvard, then studied theology with the Jesuits at Innsbruck, and later joined the Society. He was sent as hospital and prison chaplain to Blackwell's Island, New York City, and then to the parish of Leonardtown, Maryland, and became aware of how deeply embedded in American society racism still was. In 1926 he joined the staff of the Jesuit periodical *America* and worked constantly to bring about interracial justice and equality, decades before the rise of the civil rights movement. In the 1930s he was one of the founders of the Catholic Interracial Council and in 1938, at the invitation of **Pius XI**, wrote a draft for an encyclical on the 'sin and heresy' of racism. The Pope died and his successor, **Pius XII**, did not proceed with the encyclical. La Farge believed that combating racism should be at the top of the Catholic Church's agenda and to the extent that this was not the case it strayed from its true mission.

Lafitau, Joseph François Jesuit, author and missionary, born Bordeaux, 1 January 1681, died there, 3 July 1746. He entered the Society of Jesus in 1696 and in 1711 was sent to New France (Canada) to work among the Iroquois Indians at Sault St Louis. He was recalled to France in 1717 where he remained as writer and professor. His best-known works were a treatise, *Moeurs des Sauvages Américains comparés aux moeurs des premier temps* (Paris, 1724), on the liquor traffic between French traders and the Indians, and a work on ginseng, *Mémoire concernant la précieuse plante ging-sang de Tartarie* (Paris, 1718).
.

Laflèche, Louis François Richer Canadian Roman Catholic bishop, born St Anne de la Pérade, Quebec, 4 September 1818, died Three Rivers, Quebec, 14 July 1898. He studied at Nicolet College, Quebec, was ordained in 1884 and went to the North East where he mastered the native Indian languages. In 1849 he was appointed titular bishop but by 1851 was in North Dakota successfully directing the defence of 60 mixed-race Indians against the Sioux tribe. He returned to Canada in 1856 to teach at Nicolet and was appointed its president in 1859. His sermons and pastoral letters

dwelt on the current social and politico-religious questions and he is regarded as one of the fathers of French-Canadian nationalism.

La Fontaine, Jean de French poet, born Château-Thierry, July 1621, died Paris, 13 April 1695. In 1641 he entered the seminary of the Oratoire to prepare for the priesthood but left to train in law, after which he took a government post as superintendent of rivers and forests at Château-Thierry. He had a gift for satire and poetry, which he combined in various comedies and tales, but his genius truly showed itself in his *Fables*, which sparkle with life and originality. Books 1–6 appeared in 1668, 7–11 in 1678–9 and 12 in 1693. After years of indifference he returned to Christian life in 1692.

Lagarde, Paul Anton German Protestant orientalist and political philosopher, born Berlin, 2 November 1827, died Göttingen, 22 December 1891. Lagarde held the professorial chair of oriental languages at Göttingen from 1869 until his death. His life's ambition (never completed) was to publish a critical edition of the Septuagint. His fervour for German culture and his nationalism and patriotism developed into anti-Semitic tendencies that rested on religious-ethical grounds, not on racial theoretical principles. Some of his most important works are *Der Pentateuch koptisch* (1867), *Onomastica juxta Hebraeos Hieronymi* (1874), and *Mitteilungen* (4 vols, 1884–91).

La Grange, Marie Joseph Dominican biblical scholar, born Bourg-en-Bresse, France, 7 March 1855, died St-Maximin, France, 10 March 1938. He joined the Dominican Order in 1879 and in 1890 founded the École Pratique d'Études Bibliques, in Jerusalem, followed in 1892 by the *Revue Biblique [Internationale]*. His particular field of study was the Pentateuch, but his advanced views on the literary methods and sources of its authorship led to his being forbidden to continue in this field, so he turned to the NT. His magisterial commentaries on *Marc* (1911), *Luc* (1920), *Matthieu* (1923) and *Jean* (1923) did much to revive Catholic interest in the Bible.

La Haye, Jean de Franciscan preacher and biblical scholar, born Paris, 20 March 1593, died there, 16

October 1661. He became a Franciscan in Spain, and was professed in 1613. He taught philosophy and theology before returning to France in 1620 with a reputation for good preaching, and was appointed court preacher to Louis XIII. He wrote two enormous commentaries, *Biblia Magna* (5 vols) and *Biblia Maxima* (19 vols), which exhibit his scholarship but are overloaded with detail and repetition.

Lainez, Diego (Laynez) Theologian, successor of **Ignatius of Loyola** as General of the Society of Jesus, born Almazan, Castile, 1512, died Rome, 19 January 1565. He studied in Alcalá and was one of the six companions who joined Ignatius in Paris in 1534. He became professor of Scholastic theology and was sent to Germany to combat Lutheranism. He played a decisive part at the Council of Trent as one of the Pope's theologians and in 1561 he took the leading part in the discussions between the Catholics and Huguenots at Poissy. At the same time he had the Jesuit colleges in France put on a legal footing. In his completion of the Order's Constitutions and in the reorganization of its government Lainez, who became vicar general of the Society after Ignatius' death, and general in 1558, may be considered the second founder of the Society. He wanted its members to be free of the daily recitation of the Divine Office in choir; Pope **Paul IV** thought otherwise, and also wanted the Jesuits to limit the general's office to a period of three years. They complied with Paul IV's injunctions but Lainez quietly dropped these restrictions after his death. Lainez was an astute diplomat and could see the possibilities for the Society over a wider field than envisaged by Ignatius. He gave the Society the direction it has since followed in the educational, pastoral and evangelical fields. His *Disputationes Tridentinae* were published in two volumes in 1886.

Lake, Kirsopp Biblical scholar, born Southampton, England, 7 April 1872, died Pasadena, California, 10 November 1946. He was educated at St Paul's School, London, and Lincoln College, Oxford. He was ordained as an Anglican minister in 1896 with a curacy at St Mary the Virgin, Oxford, where he wrote *The Test of the New Testament*. In 1904 he moved to Leiden University as professor of NT exegesis, where he published

his *Historical Evidence of the Resurrection of Jesus Christ*, a work which cast doubt on the physical resurrection. In 1914 he transferred to Harvard, where he was successively professor of early Christian literature, ecclesiastical history and history. His *Earlier Epistles of St Paul* (1911), which emphasized the Hellenistic influence on primitive Christianity, was attacked by the Roman Catholic Church as a denial of the divinity of Christ.

Lalande, Michel Richard de (Delande) Church music composer and organist, born Paris, 15 December 1657, died Versailles, 18 June 1726. In 1683 he was selected by King **Louis XIV** as a director of the Royal Chapel, soon afterwards a permanent director, and he was associated with the court for almost three decades. He was considered one of the greatest composers of religious music, especially the grand motets of which he composed over 70. His works became a staple of Paris concerts, known as *Le Concert Spirituel*. In addition he composed music for ballets and dramatic works, including one entitled *Symphonies for the King's Suppers*.

Lallemant, Jacques Philippe Jesuit theologian, born St-Valéry-sur-Somme, 8 September 1660, died Paris, 24 August 1748. He entered the Society of Jesus in 1677 and devoted the greater part of his life combating Jansenism. His 31 published works include *Journal historique des assemblées tenues en Sorbonne pour condamner les Mémoires de la Chine* (Paris, 1700); seven letters concerning the controversy over the Chinese rites (Paris, 1702); an abridged history of the judgements of the Church against the teachings of Jansen; *Réflexions morales avec notes sur le Noveau Testament traduit en français* (12 vols, Paris, 1713–25); and translations of the Psalms.

Lallemant, Louis Jesuit, born Châlons-sur-Marne(?), 30 October 1587, died Bourges, 5 April 1635. He was educated at the Jesuit College at Bourges, entered the novitiate at the age of eighteen and was ordained in 1621, becoming professor of philosophy and of theology there, later master of novices. He consigned nothing to writing but the essence of his spiritual philosophy was summarized and published in 1694 by P. Louis Champion, SJ, entitled *La Vie et la doctrine spirituelle du*

P. Louis Lallemant de la Compagnie de Jésus. This work highlighted Lallemant's emphasis on the importance of the gifts of the Holy Spirit, combined with union to Christ in prayer, as preparation for apostolic work, and his insight and spiritual teaching became an inspiration for both missionaries and writers on mysticism.

Lalor, Teresa Nun and foundress of religious houses, born Ballyragget, County Kildare, c.1769, died Washington, DC, 9 September 1846. With two companions and under the direction of Bishop Leonard **Neale**, SJ, in 1797 she founded what was to become the first house of Visitation Nuns, an Order with its origins in Annecy c.1610. Initially the foundation, whose members were simply known as the 'Pious Ladies,' followed a quasi-Jesuit Rule but subsequently obtained that of the Visitation Order, in which order Teresa took her vows in 1816. She established a free school for girls, and the sisterhood, expanded to Mobile in 1832 and to Baltimore in 1837. She remained as superior for twenty years, relinquishing office in 1819 to revert to the ranks of the community.

Lamartine, Alphonse Marie Louis de Prat de Statesman, historian and romantic poet, born Mâcon, France, 21 October 1790, died Paris, 1 March 1869. He was educated at Lyons and by the Pères de la Foi at Belley until 1809. He then went on a two-year Italian tour. He entered the Gardes du corps but during the Hundred Days he took refuge in Switzerland. In 1820 he published his first book, *Méditations poétiques et religieuses,* which won him instant fame as a poet. He then entered the diplomatic service as secretary to the embassy at Naples. In 1824 he was transferred to Florence, where he stayed for five years and wrote *The Last Canto of Childe Harold* and in 1829 *Harmonies poétiques et religieuses.* He received the Legion of Honour from Charles X and was elected to the Academy. His greatest prose work, *Histoire des Girondins,* published in 1847, was declamatory and republican. He declared for the Provisional Government, becoming minister for foreign affairs and from being a man of letters and lyrical poet Lamartine became an orator and one of the foremost statesmen in Europe. However, in January 1849 he failed to get elected to either the Presidency or even to the Legislative Assembly. With unremitting literary labour he set about repairing his fortunes with a host of histories on the 1848 revolutions, on the restoration, on Turkey and on Russia, biographical studies and miscellanea. He was much involved in the major literary trends of his time, especially the romantic revival of **Rousseau** in France and the revival of legitimism and the Catholicism of **Bonald** and Joseph de **Maistre**.

Lamas, José Benito Uruguayan patriot, sometime Franciscan, later a diocesan priest, born Montevideo, 14 January 1787, died there, 9 May 1857. He entered the Franciscan Order in Montevideo but was in Buenos Aires during the 1810 revolution where he became a suspect of the Spanish authorities. He celebrated his first Mass on New Year's Day 1812 in Buenos Aires and thereafter moved between that city, Córdoba and Mendoza, returning to Montevideo in 1814. He was confessor to the Chilean patriot Miguel Carrera, who was publicly executed. After leaving his Order in 1824, he returned to the newly independent Republic of Uruguay and was appointed rector of Montevideo Cathedral in 1838, a senator in 1852, and vicar apostolic in 1854. He died three years later of yellow fever working among the native poor.

Lambeck, Peter (Lambecius) Librarian, born Hamburg, 13 April 1628, died Vienna, 4 April 1680. From 1645 to 1647 he studied at Amsterdam, Leiden and Paris, where he received a doctorate of law. He moved on to Rome, where he was tutored by his uncle, Holstenius, the papal librarian, returning to Hamburg as professor of history in 1653, and becoming rector in 1664. Because of academic and marital problems he returned to Rome, where he was received into the Catholic Church. Finally he transferred to Vienna, where the Emperor Leopold appointed him librarian and historiographer and where Lambeck made a scholarly contribution in cataloguing the rich resources of the imperial library.

Lambert, Louis Aloysius Roman Catholic priest, editor and publicist, born Charleroi, Pennsylvania, 13 April 1859, died Newfoundland, New Jersey, 25 September 1910. Enlisting as an army chaplain during the Civil War, he saw action at Forts Henry and Donelson and at the Battle of Shiloh. He founded and edited the *Catholic Times,* New York,

1877–80, the *Catholic Times*, Philadelphia, 1892–4, and *Freeman's Journal*, New York, 1895–1910. Although often engaged in controversy with his former superior, Bishop Bernard **McQuaid** of Rochester, Lambert was in demand as an essayist, lecturer and literary editor, and in 1892 the University of Notre Dame, Indiana, conferred on him an honorary doctorate of law.

Lambert de La Motte, Pierre Roman Catholic priest and missionary bishop, born La Bossière, France, 28 January 1624, died Juthia, Siam (Thailand), 15 June 1679. He was ordained in 1655 and sent to Rome to take part in discussions with the various apostolic vicars. In 1658, with the titular Bishop François Pallu, he co-founded the Paris Missions Seminary, and in 1659 he was appointed titular bishop of Beirut and apostolic administrator of southern China. In 1660 he set out on foot, crossing Egypt, Persia and India, reaching Siam in 1662. He founded a seminary in Siam, later ordaining priests there and in Tonkin. He also founded the congregation of the Lovers of the Cross for women in Indo-China and Siam.

Lambert of Hersfeld Benedictine abbot and author of a universal history, born *c*.1025, died *c*.1081–5. Educated at Bamberg, he became a monk at the Benedictine monastery of Hersfeld and was ordained in 1058. He left Hersfeld in 1077 (primarily because of his enthusiasm for the Cluniac reform movement and his opposition to Emperor **Henry IV**), for the abbey of Hasungen, and after that abbey adopted the reforms of Cluny, he was elected abbot in 1081. He is best known for his *Annales*, a world history he wrote at Hersfeld, *c*.1077–9, which is particularly useful for understanding the ecclesiastical mentality of the eleventh century and has caused him to be compared to both Sallust and Tacitus: it has been noted that his *Annales* are more famous for their form than their credibility.

Lambert of Maastricht Saint and bishop, born Maastricht *c*.633–8, died Liège, *c*.698–705. Following the death of Childeric II, Ebroin, mayor of the palace, exiled Lambert from his see at Maastricht to the abbey of Stavelot, where he remained for seven years. After the assassination of Ebroin, order was re-established by Pepin of Herstal; Lam-

bert resumed his bishopric. Later, Lambert became a missionary bishop in Kempenland and Brabant. Lambert died violently in Liège, only a village at that time. It is generally believed that he was martyred for his condemnation of the adultery of Pepin with the sister of his wife, who then became the mother of **Charles Martel**. The city of Liège grew up around his relics. Feast day 17 September.

Lambert of Saint-Bertin Benedictine abbot and reformer, born *c*.1060, died Saint-Bertin, 22 June 1125. A nobleman, he entered the abbey of Saint-Bertin *c*.1070, where he taught grammar, theology, philosophy and music. He was elected abbot in 1095, and set about reforming his monastery, bringing it under the Cluniac reform. He should not be confused with **Lambert of Saint-Omer**, who may have belonged to the same monastery.

Lambert of Saint-Omer Encyclopaedist, died *c*.1125. A canon of Saint-Omer, as was his father before him, he was the author of an encyclopaedia of general knowledge, the *Liber floridus*, which he completed in 1120. Encompassing most fields of knowledge, it is a compilation of (mostly) unacknowledged extracts from ancient and medieval authorities ranging from Pliny to **Bede**. Nothing is known of his career; he has been frequently confused with **Lambert of Saint-Bertin**, who may have belonged to the same monastery.

Lambert of Spoleto German emperor, date of birth unknown, died in a hunting accident near Marengo, Italy, October 898. He was crowned co-emperor with his father by Pope **Formosus** in 892, thereby inheriting a conflict with Berengar I of Fruili. In 895 Rome was captured by Arnulf, king of the East Franks, who, in turn, was crowned emperor by Formosus. Following an agreement with Berengar and on the death of Formosus, Lambert re-entered Rome accompanied by his mother. A macabre ceremony ensued in which the new Pope, **Stephen VI**, ordered the exhumation and condemnation of his predecessor and in which Lambert's participation is debatable. In 898, shortly before his demise, Lambert's authority over Rome and the Papal States was confirmed at the Synod of Ravenna and he issued a series of reforming decrees.

Lambertenghi of Como, Geremia Blessed, Franciscan priest (called 'Master of the Cloister'), born Como, Italy, 1440, died Valverde, 25 March 1513. He joined the Order at the age of twenty and entered the convent of St Donato, near Como, where he succeeded to the offices of preacher, vicar and prior to various communities. His love of austerity and devotion to the Passion of Christ led to an intensity of penitential practices which are alleged to have included the use of an iron chain to discipline his body, and sleeping in a coffin into which nails had been driven. Miraculous powers have been attributed to him and his body is reported to be incorrupt in Forli Cathedral.

Lambin, Denis (Dionysius Lambinus) Humanist, born Montreuil-sur-mer, Picardy, France, c.1519, died Paris, 1572. He studied at Amiens, and in Paris as a student and as teacher. He left Paris in 1548 to become a lecturer at the University of Toulouse. The following year he was appointed secretary to Cardinal Touron, with whom he made extended visits to Italy and in whose employ he prepared his editions of the classics, returning to Paris as Royal Reader in Greek at the Collège de France from 1560 to 1572. His celebrated works included editions of Aristotle's *Ethics* and *Politics*, and the writings of Cicero and Lucretius. Lambin's death was hastened by grief over the violence during the massacre of St Bartholomew's Day, in which his friend Peter **Ramus** was killed.

Lambing, Andrew Arnold Roman Catholic priest, author and historian, born Manorville, Pennsylvania, 1 February 1842, died Wilkinsburg, Pennsylvania, 4 December 1918. He entered St Michael's Seminary, Glenwood, Pennsylvania, in 1863 and was ordained in 1869. His first assignment was to St Francis College, Loretto, with later appointments in Pittsburg and Wilkinsburg. He wrote extensively for magazines and religious publications such as the *American Ecclesiastical Review*, and he was also an authority on the early history of Western Pennsylvania. His *History of the Catholic Church in the Dioceses of Pittsburg and Allegheny* (1880) is described as a landmark in American historiography, as are his *American Catholic Historical Researches* (1886).

Lambruschini, Luigi Cardinal and papal secretary of state, born Sestri Levante, Italy, 16 May 1776, died Rome, 12 May 1854. He studied at St Margherite Ligure, joined the Barnabite Order, continuing his philosophical and theological studies in Rome, and was ordained in 1799. After teaching at Barnabite colleges, in 1814 he began his long career in the Curia as consultor, 1814, and secretary, 1816, contributing to concordats with Tuscany, 1815, Naples, 1818, and Russia, 1847. He was appointed bishop of Genoa in 1819, and nuncio to France in 1826 but the French government demanded his recall, accusing him of partisanship in their domestic politics. He was created cardinal in 1831 and was an unsuccessful candidate for the Papacy in 1846. An ultraconservative, he was a fervent upholder of Church doctrine and the rights of the Holy See, and described as 'an enemy of new ideas'.

Lamennais, (Hugues) Félicité Robert de Philosopher, theologian and politician, born into a mercantile family in St-Malo, 29 June 1782, died Paris, 27 February 1854. He was largely self-taught, and though at first a rationalist, under the influence of his brother Jean-Marie **Lamennais**, the founder of the Brothers of Christian Instruction, he returned to the Church and was ordained in 1816. He was convinced that belief was indispensable to action and that religion was the most powerful leaven of the community. He had a large and influential following, including **Montalembert**, **Lacordaire** and **Chateaubriand**. His *Essai sur l'indifférence en matière de religion* – the first of four volumes appeared in 1817 – deeply affected Catholic Europe in its attack on the anti-Christian thinkers; he advocated that only in a free society could Catholics hope to evangelize the new age. Total religious liberty, the disestablishment of the Church, freedom of education, of the press and decentralization of government, the full restoration of Catholic belief, with the Pope as supreme authority, were advocated by him and his followers. In *De la Religion* (1826) he denounced the Gallicanism of the French Church as disloyalty to the Papacy. With his friends he contributed to the new liberal Catholic newspaper *L'Avenir* and though it lasted only a year it had a profound effect on the thought and politics of the nineteenth century. In 1832 Lamennais went to Rome to persuade **Gregory XVI** to lead a crusade on behalf of religious and political freedom. Not only did the Pope refuse to see him, in his encyclical *Mirari vos* he condemned all that *L'Avenir* had stood for. Lamennais produced his *Paroles d'un croyant* outlining his Utopian society, which was in turn condemned by Pope Gregory in *Singulari nos*, whereupon Lamennais left the Church. Subsequently his philosophy became increasingly pantheistic, his politics increasingly democratic: his *Le Pays et le gouvernement* (1840) earned him a year's imprisonment from the French government. He was elected to both the Constituent Assembly and to the legislature in 1848, but failed to persuade others of his views, and died outside the Church, and in isolation.

Lamennais, Jean-Marie-Robert de Blessed, French Roman Catholic priest, founder, born St-Malo, 1780, the older brother of Félicité **Lamennais**, died Ploërmel, Brittany, 1860. He studied privately and under the Abbé Vielle, who had asylum in the family household during the Revolution, and was ordained in 1804. He became vicar general to several bishops, during which time he helped establish, following the Revolution, schools, colleges, seminaries and convents. He helped found the ultramontane Congregation of St Peter, and in 1817 founded the Institute of the Brothers of Christian Instruction, modelled on John Baptiste de **La Salle**'s congregation, but with an apostolate to serve the poorer country districts. By the time of Lamennais' death there were some 800 members of the congregation working in France and in the French colonies. The motherhouse was in Ploërmel, where a statue was erected in his honour. He collaborated in a number of the early publications which appear under his brother's name.

La Moricière, Louis Christophe Léon French general and commander-in-chief of the papal army, born Nantes, 5 February 1806, died Amiens, 11 September 1865. After distinguished service with the French army in Algeria during the 1830s, he became a deputy in the French parliament in 1847. A republican, he commanded the National Guard in the 1848 revolution, and when **Napoleon III** came to power in 1852 he was exiled for nine years. Eventually convinced that only the Papacy could morally renew Europe, he renounced republicanism and reverted to Catholicism. In 1860 he

accepted command of the papal Zouaves in the war for the Papal States. He was defeated and resigned, refusing papal honours. He retired to Amiens and did charitable and social work for the rest of his life.

Lamormaini, Wilhelm Jesuit administrator and teacher, born Duchy of Luxemburg, 29 December 1570, died Vienna, 22 February 1648. He received his doctorate at Prague, entered the Society of Jesus in 1590 and was ordained in 1596. From 1600 he taught philosophy and theology at Graz in Austria, becoming rector of the Jesuit College in 1614. After a short period in Rome, 1621–3, he moved to Vienna to act as spiritual counsellor and confessor to the Emperor Frederick II where he became involved in Habsburg politics. On the death of the Emperor in 1637 Lamormaini was appointed rector of the University of Vienna, and between 1643 and 1645 was provincial of the Austrian province of the Society, during which time he encouraged the growth of Jesuit institutions in the Habsburg domains.

Lamy, Bernard Oratorian, philosopher and theologian, born Le Mans, France, June 1640, died Rouen, 29 January 1715. He entered the Order in 1657, was ordained in 1667 and taught at the University of Angers from 1673 to 1675. His academic life involved him in major controversies, including attacks on the theories of Aristotle, and challenging the divine right of kings. The publication of his *Harmonia sive concordia quatuor evangelistarum* (1689) questioned the date of Christ's celebration of the Passover. Among his many treatises *Demonstration de la vérité et la sainteté de la morale chrétienne* is described as his masterpiece. He was a disciple of **Malebranche**, whose philosophy he helped to promote in France.
·

Lamy, François Soldier, Benedictine monk and philosopher, born Montyreau in the Diocese of Chartres, 1636, died St-Denis, 4 April 1711. Abandoning his military career after a duel, he entered the Order in 1659. He taught Cartesian philosophy at St-Maur, 1670, St-Quentin and Soissons, 1672–3, and theology at St-Germain-des-Prés, 1674–5. Thereafter Lamy retired to solitude at St-Denis and, because of his adherence to Cartesianism, was prohibited from teaching by King **Louis XIV**. Among Lamy's principal writings were *De la conaissance de soi-même*, in which he challenged **Malebranche**'s endorsement of Quietism, and his refutation of Spinoza in *Le nouvel athéisme renversé*. His *Traité de la conaissance et L'amour de Dieu*, published posthumously in 1712, is described as a work of rare distinction.

Lamy, John Baptist Roman Catholic archbishop, born Lempdes, Puy-de-Dôme, 11 October 1814, died Santa Fe, 13 February 1888. He studied in his home diocese of Clermont-Ferrand and was ordained in 1838. Soon recruited for the missions he began his remarkable career of apostleship in New Mexico, the territory then including Arizona and parts of Colorado. The extent of the diocese involved him in many perilous journeys through the Santa Fe trail but his tireless efforts saw rapid progress of the faith, the foundations of lay Catholic education and, with the Loreto Sisters, the first hospital and an orphanage. From ten priests in 1850, there were 37 by 1865, 45 new churches and four convent schools. In 1875 Santa Fe was raised to an archdiocese and Lamy became the first incumbent. Widely respected and loved by Catholics, Protestants and Jews alike, a memorial resolution was passed by the Territorial Congress of New Mexico in 1888, and his life's work was the basis for the classic novel by Willa Cather, *Death Comes to the Archbishop*.

Lamy, Thomas Joseph Roman Catholic priest and oriental and biblical scholar, born Ohey (Belgium), 27 January 1827, died Louvain, 30 July 1907. He studied at Floreffe and at the theological seminary at Namur, and was ordained in 1852. He received his doctorate in theology at Louvain in 1859 and continued teaching Hebrew, Syriac and sacred Scripture until 1900. His many publications included *Sancti Ephraem Syri Hymni et Sermones* (Louvain, 1882–1902) and *Introductio in Sacrum Scripturum* (2 vols, Mechlin, 1866). In 1885 he was appointed domestic prelate to Pope **Leo XIII**, and in 1903 a consultor of the Pontifical Biblical Commission by Pope **Pius X**.

Lancelotti, Giovanni Paolo Canonist and teacher, born Perugia, Italy, 1522, died Perugia, 23 September 1590. He received his doctorate in law at Perugia in 1546 where he became a professor. His classes followed the division of the *Corpus Iuris Civilis Institutiones* into persons, things and actions instead of the customary commentary on the Decretals. Invited to Rome by Pope **Paul IV** to produce a canonical volume which would correspond to *Institutes of Justinian*, Lancelotti's work was not approved by the Pope or his successor, **Pius IV**, but, when published privately in 1563, it was widely used in academic schools.

Lancicius, Nicholas (Laczycki) Venerable, Jesuit ascetical writer, born Nesvizh (Nieswiesz), Lithuania, 10 December 1574, died Kannas (Kovo), 16 March 1652. Through his studies he abandoned Calvinism in 1590 and two years later entered the Society of Jesus at Cracow, moving on to Rome, where he was ordained in 1601. In 1608 he transferred to the Academy of Wilna in Poland, where he taught Hebrew, Scripture and theology, becoming rector at Kalisz and Cracow, and provincial of the Lithuanian province from 1631 to 1635. His many books on the spirit and organization of the Society of Jesus include *De Meditationibus rerum divinarum* and *De praestantia instituti S.J.* In 1650 **Bolland** published Lancicius' collected works in two volumes (Antwerp), subsequently translated into several languages.

Landa, Diego de Franciscan missionary and bishop, born Cifuentes, Guadalajara, Spain, date unknown, died Mérida, Yucatán, Mexico, 21 April 1579. Professed as a Friar Minor at Toledo, soon after his ordination he went to Yucatán to serve the Maya Indians, where he immersed himself in their language and culture, and in 1561 was elected first minister provincial of St Joseph of Yucatán and Guatemala. Criticized for employing stern measures against native practices of idolatry, he returned to Spain to defend his actions and was finally absolved in 1569 and appointed bishop of Yucatán in 1572. During his return to Spain he wrote the treatise *Rellacion de las cosas de Yucatán*, which by 1864 had had eight editions, translations into several languages, and was a useful guide to modern students of Mayan life.

Landelin (Landelinus) Saint, hermit, abbot, born Vaux, France, died *c.*686. At eighteen he turned to a life of violence and crime together with other young men, but reformed his life when one of his friends was killed. Becoming a hermit at Lobbes, his godliness attracted disciples, whom he formed into a monastery in 654. Seeking solitude, he travelled to Aulen, to Wallens and finally to Crespin. In each place he attracted followers whom he organized into communities. He served as abbot in Crespin until his death. Feast day 15 June.

Landgraf, Artur Michael Auxiliary bishop and medievalist, born Traunstein, Bavaria, 27 February 1885, died Bamberg, 8 September 1958. He studied at Eichstätt, Innsbruck and Rome, was ordained at Bamberg in 1918 and there taught dogmatic theology. During the periods 1929–30 and 1937–9 he lectured at the Catholic University of America in Washington, DC. He was consecrated auxiliary bishop of Bamberg in 1943 and dean of Bamberg Cathedral in 1950. His research into the history of dogma and theological literature produced many critical editions of medieval texts and works on the development of theological thought. His scholarship was recognized by the award of honorary doctorates, including those of the Universities of Bologna and Innsbruck.

Landini, Francesco Musician, born Fiesole or Florence, c.1325, died Florence, 2 September 1397. The history of Italian Renaissance music is often traced back to Landini, the most famous Italian musical figure of the fourteenth century. Though renowned as a composer, organist, poet, singer and instrument maker, the more remarkable for his blindness, little is known of his life. He held offices in the Florentine churches of S. Trinità and S. Lorenzo, but his greatest impact was felt in the composition of secular songs, of which 'Ecco la primavera' is the most famous. The humanist Cristoforo Landino (1429–98) was his great-nephew.

Landívar, Rafael Jesuit humanist, born Old Guatemala City (now Santiago), 27 October 1731, died Bologna, Italy, 27 September 1793. He was educated locally and obtained an MA at the University of San Carlos. In 1745 he joined the Jesuit Order at Tepoztlan, near Mexico City, and was ordained in 1755. When the Jesuits were expelled from Latin America in 1767 he transferred to become parish priest in Bologna, where he devoted his time to writing. His epic work *Rusticatio mexicana*, acclaimed by his contemporaries in America and Europe, was published in 1781 in Modena and in 1782 in Bologna. It consists of 5000 lines in Latin hexameters, divided into fifteen books and an appendix, and gives a description of all aspects of the geography, flora, fauna, social customs and pastimes of New Spain. Landívar's remains were transferred from Bologna to Guatemala in 1950.

Lando Pope, elected July/August 913, died February/March 914. A Roman of Sabian ancestry about whom very little is known. He is thought to have been one of several early Popes created by Theophylactus, a consul and senator, in the exercise of an office, reputed to have been shared by his wife and daughter, which controlled the temporalities of the Papacy. During Lando's brief tenure nothing is recorded of good or evil and he may have been simply a tool of the contemporary Roman aristocracy.

Landoald Saint, missionary to The Netherlands, died c.688. Landoald is believed to have been a Lombard who became a priest in Rome, and was sent by Pope **Martin I** along with **Amandus** and others as missionaries to The Netherlands. Landoald was supported by Childeric II of Austrasia, and ministered in the Maastricht area, building a church in Winterhoven. Feast day 19 March.

Landry (Landericus) Saint and bishop of Paris, benefactor, died c.660. Landry as bishop of Paris was known for his concern for the poor. During one famine, he even sold church fixtures to provide food for the hungry. He was the founder of St Christopher's Hospital, which eventually became the famous Hôtel-Dieu. Feast day 10 June.

Landry Saint, abbot, bishop, died c.730. Landry, the son of Vincent Madelgarius and St Waldetrud, was the abbot at Soignies Abbey (Hainaut, Belgium) and Hautmont (Nord, France). Later he served as a missionary bishop in the area of Brussels (Melsbroek). His relics lie at the collegiate church of Soignies; he is venerated there and in Melsbroek. Feast day 17 April.

Landulf of Evreux Saint, bishop, died before 614. All that is reliably known about Landulf is that he was bishop of Evreux, and that *c.*600 he exhumed the relics of Taurinus, who had been the first bishop of Evreux (late fourth century), building a church to honour him. Feast day 13 August.

Lanfranc Archbishop, born Pavia, Italy, *c.*1005, died 1089. After an early life as an itinerant scholar, he came to northern France and entered the abbey of Bec in 1042, where he rapidly gained a reputation as an able monastic administrator, being appointed prior in 1045. In 1063 he was appointed abbot of St Stephen's, Caen, at first making an enemy of **William** of Normandy, by opposing his marriage to a cousin. This rift was subsequently healed, and Lanfranc became William's most trusted counsellor, being made archbishop of Canterbury in 1070 following the conquest of England. He continued to employ his organizational skills in this office, overhauling the administration of the English Church. Lanfranc also wrote a number of theological treatises, the most important of which is *De corpore et sanguine Domini*, which anticipates the later doctrine of transubstantiation.

Lang, Andreas Benedictine abbot, born Staffelstein, Upper Franconia, *c.*1450, died 23 October 1502. In 1483 or thereabouts he became the third abbot at the abbey of Michelsberg, Bamberg, continuing the reforms of his predecessors which aimed at restoring the disciplines of Bursfield, and also towards improving the economic and material situation of the abbey. He took a special interest in the monastery's school and library, and collected material on the history of the bishopric of Bamberg, his own abbey, and on the Benedictine saints. His written works include *Catalogus sanctorum ordinis Sancti Benedicti*, and manuscripts of his writings are preserved in the Staatsbibliothek and the Staatsarchiv at Bamberg.

Lang, John Dunmore Presbyterian minister and Australian political campaigner, born Greenock, Scotland, 25 August 1799, died Sydney, Australia, 8 August 1878. Educated at the University of Glasgow, he went as the first permanent Presbyterian minister to Australia in 1823, with a desire to establish a moral society of solid yeomen through education and religion. After a visit to the USA in 1840 he returned to campaign for a decentralized democracy and independence from Brit-

ain, and in 1843 became the representative for Port Phillip. He established a Scots church in Sydney but in both religion and politics his overbearing manner alienated support. He wrote many books and pamphlets and was the owner-editor of several newspapers, but his principal legacy was his *History of the Colony of New South Wales*, of which four editions were published (Sydney, 1834–75) and which was influential among immigrants.

Lang, Matthäus Statesman and cardinal, born Augsburg, 1468, died Salzburg, 30 March 1540. From a bourgeois background, nevertheless in 1494 he entered the service of the Emperor Maximilian I and, thereafter, became indispensable to him, firstly as secretary and later as counsellor. During this period he acquired numerous benefices and ecclesiastical offices. His diplomatic skills included negotiating the League of Cambrai in 1508, and the Settlement in Vienna in 1515 which gave the thrones of Bohemia and Hungary to the Habsburgs. He was elevated to a cardinalate in 1512 but was not ordained until 1519, becoming prince-archbishop of Salzburg, where he had to encounter and overcome rebellious nobles, citizens and peasants. Throughout he maintained an authoritarian and conservative stance in both governmental and religious affairs.

Lang, (William) Cosmo Anglican archbishop, born Fyvie Manse, Aberdeenshire, 31 October 1864, died Kew, Surrey, on his way to the railway station, 5 December 1945. His father was a minister in the Church of Scotland, and the family moved to Edinburgh and to Glasgow, where he attended the university. He later went on to Oxford, studying classics and then modern history. He entered chambers to study for the bar, but in 1888 won a fellowship at All Souls, Oxford. Shortly afterwards he decided to seek ordination in the Church of England, and studied at Cuddesdon. He was ordained priest in 1891, and after some parochial experience in Leeds, was elected fellow of Magdalen College, Oxford. In 1896 he went to a large parish in Portsea, and in 1901 became a canon of St Paul's and suffragan bishop of Stepney. He was very active in arousing concern for the poverty of the East End of London, and he became an obvious choice for preferment: he was enthroned as archbishop of York in January 1909: twenty years later, in December 1928, he was enthroned as archbishop of Canterbury. He was almost immediately struck down by illness, and to recuperate went on a number of cruises on the yacht of his friend John Pierpoint Morgan. This gave him the opportunity to become more acquainted with the Orthodox Churches, the ecumenical movement being one of his prime concerns. One of his achievements was to assist the British Museum in purchasing the Codex Sinaiticus. As archbishop of York he had sometimes sided with the Liberals in the House of Lords; as archbishop of Canterbury he showed himself more conservative. He was close to the monarchy, but was criticized for his broadcast after the abdication of Edward VIII: it was widely believed that he had helped the prime minister to bring the abdication about. He resigned in March 1942 and retired to a cottage at Kew Green, assisted by a generous gift from Pierpoint Morgan.

Langdon, John   Benedictine and bishop of Rochester, born Kent, date unknown, died Basel, Switzerland, 30 September 1434. In 1398 he entered the Benedictine Order at Christchurch, Canterbury, becoming sub-prior c.1411. He had graduated with a BD in 1400, a DD in 1411 and in that same year was appointed as one of the twelve Oxford scholars enquiring into the works of John **Wycliffe**. A champion of orthodoxy and a distinguished preacher, he persevered in the suppression of heresy. In 1421 he was appointed to the See of Rochester and consecrated by Archbishop **Chichele** in 1422. In 1430, as a royal counsellor, he was engaged in hearing petitions and employed on embassies to the court of King **Charles VII** of France. He was interred in the choir of the Carthusian monastery at Basel. His principal written work, *Anglorum chronicon*, has not survived.

Langlais, Jean   Blind French organist and composer, born La Fontenelle, Ille-et-Vilaine, France, 15 February 1907, died Paris, 8 May 1991. He studied at the Paris Conservatoire under Dupré, Dukas and **Messiaen** and held various organist posts in Paris. He composed organ music, a Passion and several Masses. His Church music became popular in Britain in the 1950s.

Langland, William   Author of *Piers Plowman*, born

perhaps at or near Cleobury Mortimer, Shropshire, c.1330, died, possibly in or near Bristol, c.1400. Very little is known about his life beyond what can be gathered from his writings, but these suggest that he may have been educated at the monastery of Great Malvern and that he was a cleric, though apparently not a priest. He appears to have spent much of his life in London. His poem, which comments on the many issues of the time, especially poverty, is presented as if revealed in a series of visions.

Langton, Stephen   Archbishop of Canterbury, cardinal, biblical scholar, born c.1150, died probably 9 July 1228. He studied at the University of Paris and was made cardinal in 1206 by **Innocent III**, who also supported his nomination to the See of Canterbury, a nomination opposed by King John. He was consecrated by the Pope at Viterbo but was prevented from occupying his see until 1213. Langton sided with the barons against the king and was a prominent supporter of the Magna Carta. The Pope excommunicated the barons but Langton would not publish the order and was suspended from his post from 1215 to 1218, during which time both John and Innocent died. On his return Langton inaugurated clerical reforms, including better education, and made improvements to the system of pastoral care. In 1220 he translated the remains of his predecessor **Thomas Becket**. The division of the books of the Bible into chapters is thought to be the work of Langton.

Lanigan, John   Roman Catholic ecclesiastical historian, born Cashel, Ireland, 1758, died near Dublin, 7 July 1828. After his ordination in Rome he moved to Pavia in Italy, where he was appointed professor of Hebrew, sacred Scripture, and ecclesiastical history, receiving a doctorate of divinity in 1794. After Napoleon's troops occupied Pavia, Lanigan returned to Ireland in 1796 but was suspected of Jansenism and met with much local opposition. A proposed appointment at the newly opened college at Maynooth did not happen. From 1799 he worked with the Royal Dublin Society, becoming their librarian in 1808. His accumulated knowledge resulted in *An Ecclesiastical History of Ireland from the First Introduction of Christianity ... to the Beginning of the Thirteenth Century* (4 vols, 1882).

Lanspergius, Johannes Justus Carthusian and spiritual writer, born Landsberg, Bavaria, 1490, died Cologne, 10 August 1539. He entered the Charterhouse of St Barbara in Cologne in 1509 and, apart from the years 1530–5, spent his adult life in that city. He was influential as a preacher, writer of devotional treatises, and as a spiritual director. Two of the earliest Jesuits, St Peter **Faber** and St Peter **Canisius**, came under his influence. Lanspergius was convinced that the remedy for the contemporary evils resulting from the Reformation was an increase in the efficacy of divine love in the souls of men and, to this end, he was an eloquent and fervent apostle of devotion to the Sacred Heart.

Lantbert of Freising Saint and bishop, place and date of birth unknown, died 19 September 955 or 957. He was appointed bishop of Freising in 937 or 938, presiding during the Hungarian invasion and domestic opposition to the Emperor **Otto I**. He was present at the Synod of Augsburg in 952 and he has been venerated locally as a saint since the eleventh century. The few details of his life have been supplemented by legends associated with his childhood, the period of the Hungarian invasions and the ravaging of his city, and to the safe deliverance of the cathedral due to Lantbert's prayers. Feast day 18 or 19 September.

Lanteri, Pio Brunone Founder of a religious order, born Cuneo, Italy, 12 May 1759, died Pinerolo, Turin, 5 August 1830. Ill health forced Lanteri to leave the Carthusians and he studied for the secular priesthood, receiving a laureate in theology at the University of Turin in 1782. He declined all preferments and devoted himself to apostolic and charitable work among students, seminarians, soldiers and workers. He was active in the Amicizia Christiana, an association founded by Nikolaus von Diessbach, SJ, which utilized the press and secret meetings similar to Freemasonry. In 1815 Lanteri was co-founder of the Congregation of the Oblates of the Virgin Mary, approved by the Holy See in 1826 and numbering 200 centres by 1963. The cause for his beatification was introduced in Rome in 1952.

Lantrua, Giovanni Blessed, Franciscan priest and martyr, born Triona, Italy, 15 March 1760, died

Changsha, China, 7 February 1816. He joined the Order in 1777 and was ordained in 1784, serving in Italy until he left for China in 1798, his long journey delaying his arrival until 1800. His apostolate in the provinces of Hunan, Hupen and Kiaugsi was conducted, despite political unrest and religious persecution, from 1802 to 1815, when he was arrested, tortured and put to death by strangulation. His remains were taken to Macao in 1819 and later to Rome, where they rest in the church of S. Maria in Aracoeli. He was beatified in 1910 and the cause for his canonization was introduced soon afterwards.

Lapide, Cornelius a (Cornelis Cornelissen van den Steen) Jesuit, teacher, born Bocholt (Belgium), 18 December 1567, died Rome, 11 or 12 March 1637. He studied theology at Douai and Louvain, entered the Society of Jesus in 1592 and was ordained three years later. He taught sacred Scripture at Louvain from 1596 to 1616 and then at the Roman College from 1616 to 1636. His extensive knowledge, combining Hebrew, Greek, Latin, theology, classical philosophy and Church history, enabled him to produce prodigious commentaries which were esteemed by his contemporaries, and he was a lively and popular lecturer. His most significant work, *Commentaria in omnes Divi Pauli Epistolas* (Antwerp, 1614), eventually reached 80 editions.

Lapini, Anna Maria Foundress of a religious order, born Florence, 27 May 1809, died there, 15 April 1860. Anna Maria Fiorelli's desire to enter religious life was thwarted owing to family pressure and in 1835 she married Giovanni Lapini, a situation which caused her much heartache and disappointment. Her husband, however, died in 1844. In 1848 she founded the Order of the Poor Daughters of the Holy Stigmata of St Francis, which followed the Rule of the Third Order of St Francis. Anna and her companions received their habits in 1850 and their Order, while steadily increasing in numbers, was finally approved by the Holy See in 1888. By 1961 there were 123 houses, mostly in Italy. Anna's life of great poverty and suffering through ill health was recognized when her cause for beatification was introduced in 1918.

La Pira, Giorgio Italian jurist and politician, born

Pozzallo, 9 January 1904, died Florence, 8 July 1977. From 1933 he was professor of Roman law at the University of Florence, and became the representative of the Christian Democratic Party in Italy's Constituent Assembly after World War II. He served in the post-war Christian Democrat government, but in 1951 became mayor of Florence. As he had in government, he worked to improve the conditions of the poor, and engaged in dialogue with the Communist Party. During the war in Vietnam he embarked on a personal peace mission. He was always on the left of his party, and was a committed Catholic with an ascetic lifestyle.

La Puente, Luis de   Venerable, Jesuit writer, born Valladolid, 11 November 1554, died there, 16 February 1624. He became a Jesuit in 1574, and was regent of studies and professor of theology in Oviedo and Valladolid, 1596–9. His principal interest and gift were in spiritual direction, and he is remembered for the insight, compassion and sound doctrine of his principal works: *Meditaciones de los Misterios de nuestra Fe* (2 vols, Valladolid, 1605), of which there were more than 260 complete or partial editions in many languages, the *Guia espiritual* (Valladolid, 1609) and *De la perfeccion del Christiano en todos sus estados* (4 vols, Valladolid, 1612–16).

Lardner, Nathaniel   Nonconformist minister, biblical and patristic scholar, born Hawkshurst, Kent, 6 June 1684, died Hawkshurst, 24 July 1768. He was educated in Kent and at a Presbyterian academy in London, and from 1694 to 1703 continued his studies at Utrecht and Leiden. His preaching career began in 1709 and, despite increasing deafness from the 1720s onwards, he continued thus until 1751. In 1745 he had received his doctorate from Marischal College, Aberdeen, and in 1746 became the London correspondent for the Scottish Society for Propagating Christian Knowledge. His best-known written work was *Credibility of Gospel History* (1727).

Larkin, John   Jesuit priest, born Newcastle upon Tyne, 2 February 1801, died New York City, 11 December 1858. He entered the seminary of St-Sulpice in Paris and was ordained in 1827. He taught philosophy at the Sulpician College in Montreal c.1830 and in 1841 entered the Society of Jesus in Louisville, Kentucky. In 1846, with fellow Jesuits, he joined the staff of St John's College, Fordham, New York, five years after the College's foundation. In 1851 he became president of the College but left in 1854 to carry out pastoral work in England. In 1857 he returned to New York as parish priest at St Francis Xavier's Church, dying the following year.

La Rochefoucauld, François de   Cardinal, born Paris, 8 December 1558, died Sainte-Geneviève, 14 February 1645. He was educated at the Jesuit College at Clermont and was appointed abbot of Tournus at the age of fifteen, proving to be an excellent administrator. After more education at Rome, he was made bishop of Clermont in 1584, where he successfully countered Protestantism. He supported the decrees of the Council of Trent, except where they impinged on the ancient rights of the French Church or the French monarchy. He refused to recognize **Henry IV** as king until he converted to Catholicism, after which the two related well and the king pressed for him to be made cardinal in 1607. He advised the court during the minority of Louis XIII, and was made Great Almoner of France in 1618 and president of the State Council in 1619. He resigned his offices in 1621 and devoted himself, as abbot of Sainte-Geneviève and vice-dean of the College of Cardinals, to the reform of religious orders.

La Rochefoucauld-Bayers, François Joseph   Blessed, bishop of Beauvais, born Angoulême, France, 28 March 1755, died Paris, 2 September 1792. As a representative of the clergy in the States General of 1789, he defended the privileges of the clergy and of the court. As a result both he and his brother, Pierre Louis, bishop of Senlis, were shortly afterwards declared 'enemies of the constitutional monarchy' and taken to the notorious prison of Carmes. They were both murdered in the general massacre of political prisoners on 2 September 1792. Feast day 2 September.

Larraga, Francisco   Dominican theologian, born near Pamplona, Navarre, date unknown, died Pamplona, 1723. He entered the Dominican Order, was ordained in his native city and taught moral theology there, and at St Paul's School in

Burgos, where he was a master of sacred theology. Among his written works were *Panegyrique de S. Catherine de Sienne* (Burgos, 1697) and a series of 55 tracts entitled *Promptrario del teologia moral* (Pamplona, 1708), with a critical edition of the latter two centuries later (Ávila, 1919).

Lárrain, Gandarillas' Joaquin Archbishop and educator, born Santiago, Chile, 13 October 1822, died San Bernardo, Chile, 26 September 1897. He was ordained to the priesthood in 1847 and was chosen to be the rector of the diocesan seminary, the foundation stone being laid in 1854 with the first students entering three years later. Lárrain became a member of the department of theology and humanities of the University of Chile, a member of Congress, an adviser on public education, vicar capitular of the Diocese of Chile, and titular archbishop of Anazarba. The first rector of the Catholic University of Chile in 1888, he was known for his culture, industry and, especially, his piety and promotion of devotion to the Virgin Mary.

Larrañaga, Damas Antonio Priest, patriot and scholar, born Montevideo, 10 December 1771, died there, 6 February 1848. He studied with the Franciscan fathers in Montevideo, continued in Buenos Aires, and was ordained in Rio de Janeiro in 1798. His particular interests were the study of medicine and natural sciences. He was also sympathetic to the revolutionary movement of 1810 and, with other patriotic religious, was expelled from Montevideo by the Spanish authorities. When Uruguay became an independent state, Larrañaga was elected a senator, and in 1824 appointed vicar apostolic. In the latter role he pursued a religious and moral apostolate with fervour, including the foundation of a home for abandoned children, and the first public library. His legislative proposals included restrictions on the use of the death penalty, and the abolition of slavery. At his death he was honoured by the government of Montevideo with a funeral befitting a general of the republic.

Larsen, Lars Peter Danish missionary to India, born Baarse, Denmark, 8 November 1862, died Denmark, 23 June 1940. The son of a blacksmith, he went to university supported by a local landowner, and in 1889 he was sent to Madras by the Danish Missionary Society. He became independent in 1899 and worked among students under the Young Men's Christian Association. In 1910 he joined the new United Theological College in Bangalore, and was shortly after made principal, 1911–24. Combining devotional piety with liberal theology, he was a widely appreciated speaker, though distrusted by confessional Lutherans. From 1924 to 1932 he was engaged with the revision of the Tamil Bible, and retired to Denmark in 1933. An outstanding linguist and scholar he wrote in Danish, English and Tamil, including *Hindu-Aandsliv og Kristendommen* (1907).

La Salle, John Baptiste de Saint, founder of the Institute of the Brothers of the Christian Schools (the De La Salle Brothers), born Rheims, 30 April 1651, into a wealthy and noble family, died St-Yon, Rouen, 7 April 1719. He entered the seminary of St-Sulpice, Paris, in 1670, and was ordained priest in 1678. Inspired by a layman, he assisted in the establishment of schools and recruited teachers for them, accommodating the teachers in his own house. In 1683 he resigned his canonry at Rheims, distributed his wealth to the poor and devoted his energies to the improvement of teachers. With twelve of his teachers he founded the Institute of the Brothers of the Christian Schools, which did not get papal approval until 1725. La Salle established teachers' colleges at Rheims in 1687, Paris in 1699 and St-Denis in 1709 and at the same time steadily increased the number of schools for boys under his control. He wrote his revolutionary *Conduite des écoles chrétiennes*, which advocated replacing individual instruction with class-room teaching, then a new idea, and giving such lessons in the vernacular. In 1698 he opened a college for the aristocratic Irish followers of **James II** who had followed him into exile in France. La Salle encountered much opposition from the secular masters, from the Jansenists, and from his own Brothers of the Institute because of reported severity in the training of his novices. His fledgling Institute weathered these storms as De La Salle Schools spread throughout France and Italy and, during and after the French Revolution, into the British Isles and eventually throughout the world. The founder retired in 1717 to St-Yon. His other main writings are *Les devoirs du chrétienne* (1703), *Recueil de differents petit traites à la usage des Frères des Écoles Chrétiennes* (1711), and several books of meditations. Many subsequently founded religious congregations were modelled on his ideas. Pope **Leo XIII** canonized him in 1900 and **Pius XII** named him patron of teachers in 1950. Feast day 15 May.

Lasance, Francis Xavier Writer of devotional books, born Cincinnati, Ohio, 24 January 1860, died Cincinnati, 11 December 1946. He was educated at Xavier College, Cincinnati, and ordained in 1883. For seven years he served as curate and pastor in several parishes in the Cincinnati diocese but had to abandon parish work in 1890 on account of ill health. From that time onwards, until his death, he wrote devotional works on the Eucharist, spiritual books for religious and children, and he compiled several missals.

Lascaris, Constantine Born Constantinople, 1434, died Messina, Sicily, 1501. A student of John **Argyropoulos**, he was taken prisoner by the Ottomans in 1453, but paid a ransom and travelled to Italy. By 1460 he was teaching Greek in Milan, where his pupils included the duke's daughter Ippolita Sforza. When she married Alfonso, duke of Calabria, Lascaris went with her to Naples. A visit to Rome in 1466 resulted in Cardinal **Bessarion** selecting him to teach at the Basilian monastery in Messina, 1467, where he was based for the remainder of his life. Lascaris' Greek grammar was the first dated Greek printed book.

Lascaris, John Leading Byzantine Scholar, born Constantinople, 1445, died Rome, 7 December 1534. An exile in Italy after the fall of his native city in 1453, he studied at Padua and his subsequent itinerant career did much to widen appreciation for Greek scholarship throughout Western Europe. For **Lorenzo de' Medici** he searched for manuscripts in the former Byzantine Empire. He was professor of philosophy at the Florentine Studium, 1492–5, but transferred his allegiance to **Charles VIII** of France and served as **Louis XII**'s ambassador in Venice, 1504–9, where he belonged to the circle of the printer Aldo **Manutius**. His later career was spent teaching in Rome, Milan and Paris.

Las Casas, Bartolomé de Spanish Dominican, bishop, campaigner, born Seville, *c.*1474, died Madrid, 1566. He trained and practised as a lawyer and in 1502 went with Ovando, governor of Antilles, to Hispañola (Haiti), where he became increasingly concerned about the plight of the native populations at the hands of the colonists. He was ordained and is reputedly the first priest to have said his first Mass in the New World. He turned his attention to the welfare of the Indians, pleading their cause in Spain and in America and berating the colonists. Many of the native populations had died because of imported diseases and ill-treatment and Las Casas was in favour of the employment of limited numbers of black slaves, many already living in other parts of the New World, to help in the work of the colonies. He was it seems solicitous of their welfare too however, and while not against slavery was against a wholesale 'slave trade'. In Venezuela he undertook an unsuccessful project to bring the Indians solely under the care and protection of the Church. In 1522 he joined the Dominicans and continued to work to overcome some of the injustices suffered by the Indians. It was largely because of his efforts that the New Laws of the Indies of 1542 came into being. In 1543 he was appointed bishop of Chiapa in Mexico. He spent only four years there, returning to Spain, where he continued his campaigns on behalf of the Indians. Among his many publications his *Destrucción des las Indias* (1552) is the most notable.

Laski, Jan Chancellor and primate of Poland, born Laski, Poland, 1456, died Kalisz, Poland, 19 May 1531. In 1505 he compiled the 'Laski Statutes', the first official edition of Polish law. In 1510 he became archbishop of Gniezno and thereby primate of Poland. An ardent foe of the Teutonic Knights, he sought to annex East Prussia to Poland. He later opposed the Peace of Cracow (1525). Towards the end of his life, he was suspected of aiding the Turks through his nephew Jerome. He was also a vigorous foe of Lutheranism. He edited a number of editions of canonical decrees and statutes.

Laski, Jan Religious reformer and nephew of Archbishop Jan **Laski**, born Laski, Poland, 1499, died Pinczow, 8 January 1560. From 1524 to 1526 he travelled throughout Western Europe and befriended **Zwingli**, **Farel** and **Erasmus**. Erasmus left him his library. He was ordained in 1521. He came more and more under the influence of Protestantism and eventually married. The *Emden Catechism* was in a great part his work. He was befriended by Thomas **Cranmer** and became head of the congregation of Protestant refugees of Austin Friars in London. He eventually returned to Southern Poland, where he became head of the Calvinists.

Lasso, Orlando di (Lassus)   Composer, born Mons, Hainaut (Belgium), 1532 according to his epitaph, died Munich, 14 June 1594. He began his musical career in his home town but later studied in Naples and in Rome, where for a year he was choirmaster at St John Lateran, 1553–4. He returned to Hainaut on the death of his parents, and travelled in France and England before settling at Antwerp. In 1556 he went as tenor to the court of Albert V, duke of Bavaria, in Munich and in 1563 became choirmaster. He spent the rest of his life there, was awarded honours by Church and State, and produced some 2000 works – among them 60 Masses, 80 settings for the *Magnificat* and about 500 motets.

Lasso de la Vega, Rafael   Roman Catholic bishop in Gran Columbia during the independence period, born Panama, 21 October 1764, died Quito, Ecuador, 6 April 1831. Ferdinand VII presented him as bishop of Mérida and he was confirmed by papal bull in 1815. He worked against the independence movement and suspended priests who supported it; however when the break from Spain was accomplished, he supported it and backed **Bolívar**. He was a senator in 1823–4 and was selected vice-president of the congress. He published a number of reports and sermons.

Lasuen, Fermind Francisco de   Franciscan missionary in North America, born Vitoria, Cantabria, Spain, 7 June 1736, died Carmel, California, 27 June 1803. He became a Franciscan in 1751 and volunteered for the Indian missions in the New World. Junipero **Serra** sent him to found the Mission San Juan Capistrano. He was later placed in charge of San Diego, until 1785 when he was chosen president of the missions of Upper California. Between 1786 and 1798 he founded nine missions, bringing the total establishment to eight-

een. From 1795 he was commissary of the Holy Office of the Inquisition.

Lateau, Louise   Stigmatic, born Bois d'Haine, Belgium, 29 January 1850, died Bois d'Haine, 25 August 1883. A child of poor parents, Louise is reported to have had good health until an accident at the age of thirteen, after which it declined steadily. In 1868 she began to have 'visions' and she was gradually stigmatized, with the wounds bleeding on Fridays, when she would fall into ecstasy. She ate little and became bedridden in 1876 and, finally, was believed to subsist solely on Holy Communion. Her condition aroused great interest in Belgium and an ecclesiastical commission attempted to investigate her condition but was unable to give an explanation. A German physician, Professor R. Virchow, considered her to be a fraud.

Lathrop, Alphonsa   Foundress of a religious order and authoress, born Lennox, Massachusetts, 20 May 1851, died Hawthorne, New York, 9 July 1926. Rose was the daughter of the author Nathaniel Hawthorne (1804–64) and in 1871 she married George Parson Lathrop, journalist, historian and poet (1851–98). In 1891, after a legal separation from her husband, Rose converted to Roman Catholicism and trained as a nurse at the Memorial Hospital, New York City. In 1899 she wrote *Memories of Hawthorne* to raise funds for her first Home for Incurables. The following year she took her vows as a Dominican tertiary, adopting the name 'Alphonsa', and founding the Order of Relief for Incurable Cancer. The motherhouse of her Order, Rosary Hill Home, Hawthorne, was founded in 1900. Two biographies, K. Burton's *Sorrow Built a Bridge*, and M. Joseph's *Out of Many Hearts*, were published in 1937 and 1961 respectively.

Latimer, Hugh   Protestant bishop and martyr, born Thurcaston, Leicestershire, *c.*1485, died (burnt as a heretic), Oxford, 16 October 1555. Latimer became a Cambridge University preacher in 1522. His sermons increasingly displayed Lutheran ideas, but despite clashes with authority he escaped censure until 1532. The appointment of Thomas **Cranmer** as archbishop of Canterbury in 1533 and the break with Rome in 1534 helped restore Latimer to favour. In 1535 he was appointed bishop of Worcester, but resigned in 1539 following the reassertion of Catholic doctrine in the 'Six Articles'. The Protestantism of **Edward VI**'s reign saw his freedom to preach restored, but **Mary Tudor**'s restoration of Catholicism in 1553 led to his final arrest. Charged with heresy, Latimer refused to recant and, with Nicholas **Ridley**, was burnt at the stake at Oxford.

Latomus, Bartholomaeus Humanist and controversialist, born Arlon (Luxemburg), *c.*1490, died Koblenz, Germany, 3 January 1570. While studying humanities at Freiburg *c.*1517, he became acquainted with **Erasmus**, and went on to teach philosophy at Trier and Cologne. In 1534 he was appointed professor of Latin eloquence at the Royal College of France but was recalled to Trier to act as counsellor to the new elector, Ludwig Van Hagen, accompanying the elector's archbishop to Speyer, Worms and Regensburg. Latomus became involved in numerous controversies concerning the Reformation and its supporters, among them Johannes **Sturm** of Strasburg, Martin **Bucer**, Petrus Dathenus and Jacob Andrea.

Latomus, Jacobus (Jacques Masson) Theologian, born Cambron (Belgium), *c.*1475, died Louvain, 29 May 1544. He studied in Paris and entered Louvain University in 1510, being appointed doctor of theology there in 1519, and rector in 1537. He became involved in numerous controversies and theological arguments, and the major part of his writings were directed against **Luther** and his adherents. These resulted in fierce disputes: one of Latomus' attacks against the Reformers was directed at William **Tyndale**. On a separate front in 1519 Latomus challenged the humanists and the Erasmian school of opinion which upheld the necessity of knowledge of Scripture as the true basis of theology. His combined writings were collected by his nephew, J. Latomus.

La Tour du Pin, Charles Humbert René (Marquis de la Charce) Catholic social reformer, born Arrancy, France, 1 April 1834, died Lausanne, Switzerland, 4 December 1924. While a military prisoner during the Franco-Prussian War of 1870–1 he came to believe that the French defeat was the result of liberalism in religion and of social injustice. Thereafter his whole concern was the way in which the State, which for him meant the monarchy, and the Church should improve the conditions of working people. His ideas were published in *L'Association Catholique* and because he participated in the 'Fribourg Union' of thinkers led by Cardinal **Mermillod**, they were incorporated into the encyclical of 1891, *Rerum novarum*, particularly with the part dealing with the State, and in that year he published his *Aphorismes de politique social*. His ideas included a rejection of republicanism, the restoration of the monarchy, the provision of a just wage and a wider distribution of property. Du Pin did not understand the spirit of the day, and when in 1892 the Pope wrote to the French cardinals 'Accept the Republic ... submit to it as representing power come from God', he knew he was isolated. The German occupation of his estate in World War I drove him out of France.

Latourette, Kenneth Scott Orientalist, missiologist and historian of mission, born Oregon City, Oregon, 8 August 1884, died (hit by an automobile) Oregon City, 26 December 1968. He was educated at McMinnville College (BS, 1904) and at Yale (BA, 1906, MA, 1907, PhD, 1909) and spent a year travelling for the Student Volunteer Movement before teaching at Yale-in-China, Chungsha, Hunan, for two years. He taught at Denison University, Granville, Ohio, from 1916, was ordained to the Baptist ministry in 1918, and became professor of missions at Yale, 1921–53. A disciplined, clear writer more than an inspiring lecturer, Latourette was devoted to his students, and steadily produced what became the backbone of modern mission historiography. His *History of the Expansion of Christianity* (7 vols, 1937–45) can appear optimistic, but it set high standards by its fairness, and by its placing of mission history in the context of Church and world history.

Latreille, Pierre-André Roman Catholic priest and zoologist, born Brives, France, 29 November 1762, died Paris, 6 February 1833. Abandoned by his parents, he was befriended by the renowned mineralogist Abbé **Haüy**. In 1778 Latreille entered the Collège Lemoine in Paris and was ordained in 1786. He spent his leisure hours in the study of entomology. When he was in Paris at the outbreak of the Revolution he was imprisoned and sentenced to deportation but, fortuitously, when he found a rare insect in his cell the prison doctor was instrumental in obtaining his release. In 1799 he was put in charge of the entomological department of the Museum of Natural History, and in 1814 was elected a Member of the French Academy. Latreille has been considered the founder of the science of entomology. His principal written work was *Histoire naturelle générale et particulière des Crustacés et Insectes* (14 vols, Paris, 1802–5).

La Trobe, Benjamin Moravian leader, born Dublin, 10 April 1728, died London, 29 November 1786. Of Huguenot descent and Baptist upbringing, he joined the Moravian Brethren in London in 1741 and became the 'ordinary', or principal preacher, at Fulneck, their centre in Yorkshire, 1750–2 and 1757–67, travelling round the country in the intervening years to visit Moravian nurseries and schools. When the Moravian Society for the Furtherance of the Gospel was reconstituted in 1768 he successfully negotiated with the British government for the establishment of a mission in Labrador. He upheld the policy of not proselytizing, and of forming societies of which the members remained within their original Churches.

Lattey, Cuthbert Charles Jesuit scholar, born London, 12 May 1877, died Heythrop, Oxfordshire, 3 September 1954. He was educated at Beaumont College, and Campion Hall, Oxford. He entered the Society's novitiate in 1894 and was ordained in 1908. The greater part of his life was spent at St Beuno's College in North Wales, and at Heythrop, where he was professor of Scripture and fundamental theology. He edited the *Westminster Version of the Sacred Scriptures*, completing the NT (1913–35) but only parts of the OT. He was a founder member of the Catholic Conference on Ecclesiastical Studies, and contributed to, and edited, publications emanating from the Cambridge Summer School of Catholic Studies. Lattey was one of the pioneers in the revival of Catholic biblical studies in England.

Laud, William Anglican archbishop, born Reading, 7 October 1573, died (executed) London, 10 January 1645. Laud was ordained in 1601 following education at Oxford. He disliked the Calvinism of the contemporary Church of England, preferring pre-Reformation liturgy and ritual. These views were shared by **Charles I**, and with his backing Laud rose in the ecclesiastical hierarchy, eventually being appointed archbishop of Canterbury in 1633. Laud proceeded to restore many pre-Reformation rituals, bringing him into bitter conflict with the Puritans, who regarded this as a preparation for the restoration of Roman Catholicism. When the Puritan party gained control of Parliament in 1641, Laud was impeached and imprisoned. In 1644 a mockery of a trial found him guilty of a specious charge of high treason, and he was beheaded on 10 January 1645.

Laudomar (Launomar) Saint, hermit, abbot, died Chartres, c.590. Laudomar's first short Life was written shortly after his death, most likely by a disciple. Laudomar studied with the priest Chirmirius, then was ordained and served as a pastor in Chartres. Later he became a hermit at La Perche, where his reputation for holiness and miracles grew. So many disciples gathered that he went to found the monastery of Curbio (c.570) and became the first abbot. After his death his relics were translated to Blois and a monastery built in his honour and named after him – Saint-Lomar, 924. Feast day 19 January.

Laudus (Lô) Saint, bishop of Coutances, died c.568. Not much is known about Laudus, except that he took part in councils at Orléans in 533, 538 and 541. He buried Paternus in 549. His name was given to Saint-Lô (Manche), and to a college and railway station at Angers. Feast day in the Sarum calendar and elsewhere 22 September.

Laugier, Marc Antoine Humanist, sometime Jesuit priest, 1727–56, and apparently a Benedictine one also, 1756–69, born Manosque, France, 22 January 1713, died Paris, 5 May 1769. A man of many callings, he was editor of the *Gazette de France*, a diplomat, historian, art critic, but principally identified as an architectural theorist. His theories were controversial but, nevertheless, influenced his contemporaries, including J. Souflett, architect of the Panthéon in Paris. A member of the Academies of Angers, Marseilles and Lyons, Laugier's first book, *Essai sur l'architecture* (Paris, 1753; London, 1755), was an eloquent testimony of neoclassicism.

Laurana, Francesco   Sculptor, born Vrana, near Zara (now Zadar, Croatia), 1425, died Marseilles, before 12 March 1502. Although from Venetian-held territory, Laurana's active life was divided between the Kingdom of Naples and the Provençal court of René of Anjou. In 1453 he contributed to the decoration of the triumphal arch façade of Castel Nuovo, Naples, for King Alfonse I, and a series of portrait busts of ladies of the Aragonese court are attributed to him. He was possibly related to Luciano Laurana (c.1420/5–79), the architect and military engineer best known for designing the cortile of the ducal palace at Urbino for Federico da Montefeltro.

Laurand, Louis   Jesuit and French classical scholar, born Gien, 9 July 1873, died Laval, 26 December 1941. He entered the Society of Jesus in 1891 and taught classics to young students of the Order for nearly 40 years. His *De M. Tulli Ciceronis studiis rhetoricis* (1907) established his reputation as a specialist on Cicero. He later published a critical edition, with French translation, of Cicero's *De amicitia*. He is best known for *Manuel des études grecques et latines*. (1930). He had a passion for solid, objective scholarship and was sharply critical of hypotheses that ignored the texts or went beyond their evidence.

Laurence   *see* **Lawrence**

Laurentius de Piv   Lawyer and teacher, born Bologna, died there, 1397. From 1365 until his death he taught the Decretals. Though not note-worthy as an author, he produced *Lectura super Decretum*, *Reportationes super Clementinis*, drawn up by his student **Zabarella** from his class notes, *Consilia*, and *Tractatus de juribus incorporalibus*.

Laurin, Franz Xaver   Roman Catholic priest and teacher, born Jesney (Bohemia), 21 April 1829, died Notre Dame am Sande, 16 October 1913. He was ordained in Prague in 1854 and received his doctorate in theology in Vienna in 1858. He taught at Prague until 1863, when he went to Vienna. There he held several posts, finally occupying the chair of decretal law until his retirement. He is more noted for his teaching than for his research. His principal works include *Décret de Gratien*

(1863), *Vaderland* (1875) and *Introductio in Corpus juris canonici* (1889).

Lauzon, Pierre de   Jesuit missionary, born Poitiers, 26 September 1687, died Quebec, 5 September 1742. He joined the Society of Jesus in 1703. He studied the Huron and Iroquois languages at L'Ancienne Lorette, near Quebec. He was later assigned to Sault St Louis, near Montreal. In 1732 he was appointed superior of the Jesuits in Canada and automatically became rector of the College of Quebec, where he remained for seven years. Upon completion of his office he returned to Sault St Louis but owing to poor health he could stay there for only two years.

Laval, François de Montmorency   First bishop of Quebec, born Montigny, France, 30 April 1623, died Quebec, 6 May 1708. Educated by Jesuits in Paris, he inherited the family title and estate after two older brothers had died in battle, but was determined to be a priest. He was ordained in 1647 and became archdeacon of Evreux, but in 1659 he was chosen as 'apostolic vicar' of New France by **Alexander VII**. The Diocese of Quebec, directly dependent on Rome, was established in 1674. He also served on the Quebec Council. He was spiritual mentor to the colony and refused the sale of alcohol to the Indians. Laval was a keen supporter of missions to the Indians and founded a seminary which in 1852 became Laval University.

La Valette, Jean Parisot de   Grand master of the Knights of St John (after 1523 known as the Knights of Malta, or Knights Hospitallers), born Toulouse, 1494, died Malta, 21 August 1568. He joined the Order as a military brother and fought the Muslims in North Africa and off Sicily. Elected grand master in 1557 he put the finances straight, then joined the viceroy of Sicily in an attack on Tripoli, which failed. He succeeded, however, in having his Order represented at the Council of Trent. He repelled a Turkish attack on Malta in 1565 and built up its defences, which included the new town of Valetta (Valletta). The Pope offered him a cardinal's hat, but he refused it.

Lavater, Johann Kaspar   Swiss Calvinist theologian, philosopher and poet, born Zurich, 15 November 1741, died there, 2 January 1801. He began studying Protestant theology in 1759. Later a writer of deep feeling and vivid imagination, he won wide fame by his religious writing: his *Schweizerlieder* (1767) and especially his four-volume *Physiognomische Fragmente zur Beförderung der Menschenkenntnis und Menschenliebe* (1775–8). He rebutted atheism and was also generally tolerant of Catholics, which led some to suspect that he was a crypto-Catholic.

Lavelle, Louis Philosopher, born St-Martin-de-Villéreal, France, 15 July 1883, died St-Martin-de-Villéreal, 1 September 1951. In 1921 he received a doctorate from the Lycée Fustel de Colanges, Strasburg, and was appointed professor of philosophy at the Sorbonne, 1932–4, and at the Collège de France, 1941–51. He was Inspector General of National Education in 1941, and elected to the Académie des Sciences Morales et Politiques in 1947. Many of his theories were drawn from the writings of St **Augustine** of Hippo, and of Nicolas **Malebranche**. His major written works included *La Conscience de soi* (1933), *La Présence totale* (1934), *La Mal de la souffrance* (1940) and *Introduction à l'ontologie* (1947).

Lavelle, Michael Joseph Vicar general, educator, born New York, 30 May 1856, died there, 17 October 1939. Shortly after his ordination in 1879, Lavelle was appointed to St Patrick's Cathedral in New York, where he spent all of his priestly life. He was appointed rector in 1887. Under his rectorship the cathedral, which had opened for public worship a month before his ordination, was gradually completed. He was a close friend of Archbishop Michael **Corrigan** and vicar general under Cardinals Patrick **Hayes** and Francis **Spellman**.

Lavigerie, Charles Martial Allemand Cardinal and historian, born near Bayonne, France, 31 October 1825, died Algiers, 26 November 1892. He was educated in Paris at St-Sulpice, ordained in 1849, and was professor of ecclesiastical history at the Sorbonne from 1854 to 1856. He resigned his professorship to become director of the Society for the Promotion of Education in the Near East. 'C'est', he wrote, 'que j'ai connu enfin ma vocation.' He was consecrated bishop of Nancy in 1863, archbishop of Algiers in 1867 and, aspiring to convert North Africa to Christianity, he founded

the Order of Missionary White Fathers in 1868. Pope **Leo XIII** elevated Lavigerie to the cardinalate in 1882, and two years later he became primate of Africa and archbishop of the restored See of Carthage (now Tunisia). His remaining years were spent in promoting anti-slavery, and his Order received final approval from Pope **Pius X** in 1908. On 12 November 1890, when receiving officers of the French navy in port in Algiers, he proposed a toast calling upon Catholics in France to support the Republic. He did this under pressure from the Vatican, which was eager to establish better relations with France: the 'Ralliement', as it was called, failed to persuade Catholics, or to mollify the French government.

Law, William English devotional writer, born King's Cliffe, Northamptonshire, 1686, died King's Cliffe, 9 April 1761. He was educated at Emmanuel College, Cambridge, being elected a fellow in 1711. Refusing to take the oath of allegiance to George I in 1714, he was deprived of his fellowship and remained a 'Nonjuror' for the rest of his life. His most famous work is the *Serious Call to a Devout and Holy Life* (1728), which had a decisive influence on many English Evangelicals, including John and Charles **Wesley**. He also wrote *The Spirit of Prayer* (1749, 1752) and *The Spirit of Love* (1752, 1754). He founded schools and did other works displaying his social concern.

Lawrence Martyr and saint, died Rome, 10 August 258. One of the deacons of Pope **Sixtus II** (257–8), he was martyred in the persecution under Valerian. According to a tradition preserved by various early writers, when ordered to surrender the treasures of the Church he presented the poor, saying, 'These are the Church's treasure'; for this he is said to have been slowly roasted to death on a gridiron. The scene is much depicted in art, but many scholars believe the story unreliable. A chapel was built over his tomb in **Constantine**'s time, at S. Cyriaca on the Via Tiburtina, which in turn became linked with the late-sixth-century San Lorenzo fuori le Mura. His sainthood is much celebrated in the Roman tradition, in the Canon of the Mass and in the Litanies. Feast day 10 August.

Lawrence, Robert Saint, Carthusian monk and

martyr, born Dorset(?), date unknown, died Tyburn, London, 4 May 1535. He gained his degree in law at Cambridge in 1508 and, after his profession at the London Charterhouse, became prior at Beauvale in 1531. In 1535, following King **Henry VIII**'s Act of Supremacy, Lawrence with two fellow priors sought to negotiate with Thomas **Cromwell**. But he proved obdurate and all three were imprisoned in the Tower, tried in Westminster Hall, and condemned to be hanged, drawn and quartered. Lawrence is one of the **Forty Martyrs of England and Wales** canonized by Pope **Paul VI** in 1970. Feast day 25 October.

Lawrence Justinian   Saint, first patriarch of Venice and spiritual writer, born Venice, 1381, died there, early January 1456. At the age of nineteen he entered the Canons of San Giorgio, was appointed superior at Vicenza in 1407, and became four times general of the congregation between 1423 and 1431. Appointed bishop of Castello in 1433, he transferred to Venice in 1451. He was noted for the simplicity of his personal life, his charity and apostolic zeal but, above all, for the depth of his spiritual writings. In fifteen written works and a collection of sermons, there was one dominant theme derived from his own early mystical experience of a vision of the Eternal Wisdom. The essence of his teaching was the theory that all spiritual development was founded in and progressed through an understanding of the Incarnate Word espoused to the Wisdom of Love. He was canonized in 1690. Feast day 5 September.

Lawrence of Brindisi   Capuchin Franciscan theologian and saint, born Brindisi, Kingdom of Naples, 22 July 1559, died Lisbon, 22 July 1619. Cesare de' Rossi was educated by his uncle at St Mark's in Venice and when sixteen joined the Capuchins at Verona, taking the name 'Lawrence'. He pursued his higher studies particularly in the biblical languages at the University of Padua. He became definitor general of his Order in 1596 and was frequently re-elected to that position. He was sent on missions to convert the Jews in Germany and to combat Lutheranism, in the course of which Lawrence and his companions founded friaries at Prague, Vienna and Gorizia. In 1602 he was elected vicar general of the Capuchins. He was sent by the Emperor to persuade Philip III of Spain to join the Catholic League and while on that diplomatic mission he founded a Capuchin house in Madrid. Lawrence was chosen as peacemaker in several royal disputes, being sent as papal nuncio to the court of Maximilian of Bavaria. In 1618 he was again called out of retirement by the rulers of Naples to intercede for them with Philip III against the duke of Osuna's tyranny. After persuading the king, who was in Lisbon, to recall Osuna, he returned to his lodging and died there. Lawrence's main writings are in the nine volumes of his sermons, but he also wrote a commentary on Genesis and several treatises against **Luther**. He was canonized by **Leo XIII** in 1881 and made a Doctor of the Church by Pope **John XXIII** in 1959. Feast day 21 July.

Lawrence of Canterbury   Saint, second archbishop of Canterbury, died 2 February 619. According to the Venerable **Bede**, Lawrence, one of thirteen monks who left Rome with **Augustine** in 595 and arrived in Britain in 597, shared in the work there and was consecrated bishop by Augustine in 604 as his successor. Discouragement with and fear of the paganism of King Eadbald tempted him to flee to Gaul. A vision of St Peter, who flogged him for his intended desertion, left visible stripes on his back. Showing this evidence to Eadbald resulted in the king's conversion and evangelization of Kent and neighbouring provinces. Feast day in England 3 February.

Lawrence of Durham   Benedictine prior and poet, born Waltham, England, c.1099, died France, 17 March 1154. He became a monk at Durham, where **Aelred** of Rievaulx was one of his pupils. Lawrence's holiness and learning led to his appointment as precentor and chaplain palatine but, following the usurpation of his patron, Bishop Geoffrey Rufus in 1141, Lawrence was exiled, as described in his *Diaglosi*. He was recalled in 1149 and was appointed prior of Durham. During a visit to Rome c.1153, Pope **Anastasius IV** granted Lawrence's request for an indulgence for pilgrims who visited the shrine of St **Cuthbert of Lindisfarne** in Durham Cathedral.

Lawrence of Ripafratta   Blessed, Dominican friar, reformer and preacher, born Ripafratta, near Pisa, 23 March 1373 or 1374, died Pistoia, 28 September

1456. He joined the Dominican Reformed Congregation in Italy and was a leading figure in the reforms inaugurated by Blessed **Raymond of Capua**. Lawrence was appointed professor of philosophy and theology at the priories of Fabriano and Pistoia, and also as prior. He was noted for his austerity and charitable works, and was counsellor to St **Antoninus** when the latter was archbishop of Florence. Lawrence's cult was approved by Pope **Pius IX** in 1851.

Lawrence of Spain Bishop, date and place of birth unknown, died 15 December 1248. He studied and wrote at the University of Bologna from 1210 to 1215, and on Roman law at Azo. He is referred to as 'Magister Laurentius' in documents in Orense Cathedral in Spain, where he was bishop from 1218 or 1219 until his death. Many of his writings and glosses are still in manuscript although the authorship of some are not attested but the greater part of *Glossa Ordinaria* is attributed to him, and possibly a gloss on the Decrees of Pope **Innocent III**'s Fourth Lateran Council of 1215.

Lawrence of Villamagna Blessed, Franciscan friar and preacher, born Villamagna, Abruzzi, Italy, 15 May 1476, died Ortona, 6 June 1535. The son of a noble family, he overcame family objections and entered the Order at the friary of Our Lady of Grace at Ortona. During the course of his studies he showed exceptional ability and, after his ordination, specialized in preaching, in which he was markedly successful. His eloquence was generally acknowledged and he preached in almost every city in Italy. Several miracles were attributed during his lifetime, and veneration of him was approved by Pope **Pius XI** in 1923.

Lawrence of the Resurrection (Nicholas Herman) Discalced Carmelite lay brother and mystic, born Herimesil, Lorraine, France, 1611, died Paris, 12 February 1691. He served in the army for eighteen years and then took the habit of the Order in Paris, working as a lay brother cook for 30 years until disabled by blindness. His reputation for holiness survived him in a few spiritual notes and edifying letters which were preserved after his death by Joseph de Beaufort, vicar general of the Diocese of Paris. The basic collection was published in 1693 under the title *Maximes spirituelles*.

Lawrence O'Toole (Lorcan ua Tuathail) Saint, archbishop of Dublin, born probably near Castledermot, County Kildare, 1128, died Eu, Normandy, 14 November 1180. He was taken as a hostage when aged ten, and released to the bishop of Glendalough two years later. He was educated there and became abbot in 1148. In 1161 he was elected the second archbishop of Dublin. He was a reformer, removing the secular canons from Christ Church, Dublin, and bringing in the Rule of the Canons Regular of Arrouaise, taking the habit himself. He took a leading part in opposing the Anglo-Norman invasion of Ireland of 1169–70. He was at the reforming Synod of Cashel of 1172, to which Pope **Alexander III** had sent letters urging acceptance of the English king Henry II as overlord. In 1175 he was at the Council of Windsor representing Rory O'Connor, high king of Ireland. In 1179 he travelled through England to Rome to attend the Third Lateran Council. In 1180 he acted as a peacemaker between the English and Irish kings but Henry II had the ports closed to prevent Lawrence's return; he was on his way following Henry II to the Continent when he took ill and died in the house of the Arrouaisan Canons at Eu, in which cathedral he is buried. He was the first Irishman formally to be canonized (in 1225). Feast day 14 November.

Layamon Author of the Middle English poem *Brut*, a priest, connected with the parish of Areley Kings, Worcestershire, flourished *c*.1200. *Brut* is a romantic chronicle based on the French *Roman de Brut* of Wace. Layamon's version is a retelling of legendary tales of the Britons up to the year 689, the verse written in rhyming couplets and with alliteration. It has been described as 'perhaps the greatest poem between the Anglo-Saxon period and the time of Chaucer'. It was the basis for future writers of Arthurian legends, and is extant in two copies in the British Museum Library.

Laycock, Geoffrey Music educationist and Catholic hymn-book music editor, born York, 27 January 1927, died Norwich, 21 May 1986. He studied at York Minster and at the Royal College of Music. He became principal lecturer in music at Keswick Hall College, Norwich. He successfully commissioned new music from leading Roman Catholic composers for the *New Catholic Hymnal* (1971) and contributed original arrangements. Hymns from this book continue to be republished throughout the English-speaking world in hymnals of many denominations. In Britain hymns from this book are used more outside the Catholic Church than inside.

Laymann, Paulus Jesuit, canonist, born Arzl, near Innsbruck, Austria, 1574, died Constance, 13 November 1635. He entered the Society of Jesus in 1594 and was ordained in 1603. On completion of his studies in law he taught at the University of Ingolstadt until 1609, at the Jesuit Institute in Munich from 1609 to 1625, and on canon law at Dillingen University from 1625 to 1632. Laymann was recognized as one of the century's great authorities on canon law and moral theology. Of his written works, the most important was *Theologia moralis in quinque libros partita* (Munich, 1625). His *Jus canonicum seu commentaria in libros decretales* was published posthumously (3 vols, Dillingen, 1666–8). The accusation that he advocated extreme measures in cases of accusations of witchcraft has been refuted.

Laynez, Diego *see* **Lainez, Diego**

Lazarus the Confessor Saint, stylite and founder, born near Magnesia, 968, died Mount Galesius, 8 November 1054. He began his religious life as a solitary and then entered the monastery of St Sabas, near Jerusalem, where he was ordained. Lazarus founded three monasteries near Ephesus, one in honour of the Saviour, the second of the Resurrection, and the third of the Mother of God at Mount Galesius. From a stylite pillar near the monastery church he directed the monastic life, drawing up a Rule for the spiritual guidance of the monks, and in relation to their temporal tasks, emphasizing the need to care for the poor.

Lea, Henry Charles US Protestant historian, born Philadelphia, 19 September 1825, died there, 26 October 1909. Indifferent health in his youth inclined him to a studious life, in particular towards research into medieval ecclesiastical history. His literary and historical reputation is based principally on his *History of the Inquisition of Spain* (4 vols, New York and London, 1906–7), followed by *Inquisition in the Spanish Dependencies* (New York, 1908). He also wrote studies of auricular confession and indulgence, and of priestly celibacy in the Western Church. These historical writings have been superseded by later researches.

Leander of Seville Bishop and saint, born Cartagena (Spain), *c.*540, died Seville, 600. After the untimely death of his father he took care of the education of his younger brother, later to be known as **Isidore of Seville**. Afterwards he embraced the religious life and did his best to spread Catholicism among the Arian Visigoths. He was exiled to Constantinople, where he met **Gregory I** the Great. After his return he was entrusted with the tutelage of Prince Reccared and with his initiation in the Catholic faith. As bishop of Seville, from 584, he convened some local synods. Leander wrote among other works a *De institutione virginum*. Feast day 27 February.

Lebbe, Frédéric Vincent Catholic missionary to China, born Ghent, Belgium, 19 August 1877, died Chongqing, China, 24 June 1940. Inspired by the martyrdom of the Vincentian Perboyre, he joined the Order in 1895 and left for China in 1901. Completing his studies in Peking (Beijing), he was ordained priest 28 October 1901. Radically committed to China and the Chinese Church in dress, language and attitude, he organized Catholic Action and helped publish Catholic newspapers. In 1916 he denounced attempts to annex land in Tientsin and was sent back to Europe, 1920–7. He laid the groundwork for the ordination of six Chinese bishops in 1926 and the 1939 revocation of the condemnation of Chinese rites. He obtained Chinese citizenship in 1928. Captured by Communists in 1940, he died soon after his release.

Lebon, Joseph-Marie Belgian Roman Catholic priest, theologian and patristic scholar, born Tamines, 18 December 1879, died Namur, 12 June 1957. He was ordained priest in 1903, completed his studies at the Louvain Faculty of Theology in 1909 (master in theology) and immediately succeeded P. **Ladeuze** as professor at the same institution. His research focused on the Monophysite movement but later he also studied earlier authors, such as **Athanasius**. He taught a wide array of subjects: NT, early and medieval Church history but also Syriac and Armenian patrology.

Le Brun, Pierre French liturgical scholar and Oratorian priest, born Brignoles, 11 June 1661, died Paris, 6 January 1729. He studied theology at Marseilles and Toulouse and taught philosophy at Toulon and theology at Grenoble. After 1690 he taught at the Oratorian seminary of Saint-Magloire, where he lectured on Church history. He had a wide variety of interests, but the main interest was liturgy as his principal work, *Explication littérale, historique et dogmatique des prières et des cérémonies de la sainte messe* (4 vols, 1716–26), demonstrates. He also supported a greater participation by the laity in the liturgy. He edited a prayer book for the laity, *Heures ou manuel pour assister à la messe* (1716).

Lebuff, Francis Peter Jesuit, author and editor, born Charlestown, South Carolina, 21 August 1885, died New York City, 27 May 1954. He was educated at Gonzaga College, Washington, DC, entered the Society of Jesus in 1901 and was ordained in 1915. From 1920 to 1922 he was regent of the School of Law at Fordham University, New York, publishing a book on jurisprudence, and dean of their School of Social Service from 1923 to 1926. Thereafter he joined the staff of the publication *America*, and became editor of *Thought*. From 1939 he devoted his time to writing articles and pamphlets on current topics and devotional subjects, and he founded the Jesuit Philosophical and Anthropological Associations, as well as becoming director of the Catholic Press Association.

Lebuinus (Lebwin) Saint, monk, patron of Deventer, Holland, born into an Anglo-Saxon family in England, died Deventer, *c.*780. He had a monastic education, was ordained priest and went to Utrecht, whence he was sent as a missionary to Overyssel. He built a chapel at Wulpe, by the River Yssel and then a larger church and residence at Deventer which was later sacked by Saxons trying to stop the spread of Christianity. Lebuinus escaped and determined to take up the matter with the Saxon Assembly. He proclaimed to the gathered Saxon leaders the Christian message and foretold their own downfall if they persisted in their idolatry. He was only spared death by the intervention of one of their own noblemen, Buto, who told of the miraculous cure of one of his servants and persuaded the gathering to practise tolerance and respect towards the Christians. Lebuinus returned to rebuild his church but it was destroyed again by Saxons soon after his death. Feast day 12 November.

Le Camus, Émile-Paul-Constant-Ange French Roman Catholic bishop, theologian, NT scholar and preacher, born Paraza, France, 24 August 1839, died Malvisade, France, 28 September 1906. Studied in Carcassonne, at St-Sulpice, Paris, and in Rome and was ordained in Carcassonne in 1862. He became a noted preacher and gave the Lenten Sermons in Avignon and was made an honorary canon. He was theologian to the bishop of Constantine (Algeria) at Vatican Council I. He acted as director of two schools and in 1887 retired to concentrate on NT studies. He travelled to the East, and was called upon to preach in Paris and Rome and in the south of France. In 1897 he became canon at Carcassonne and in 1901 bishop of La Rochelle and Saintes. His writings include *La Vie de Notre Seigneur Jésus-Christ, Voyages aux Sept Églises de L'Apocalypse, Notre voyages aux pays biblique, L'Oeuvre des Apôtres, Les Enfants de Nazareth* and *Vraie et fausse exégèse*. He also wrote on seminary formation and theological study and a *Mémoire adressé à MM. les députés membres de la Commission des Congrégations*.

Le Camus, Étienne Cardinal, born Paris, 1632, died Grenoble, 12 September 1707. The scion of a noble family, he was antipathetic to the religious life which was chosen for him. He received his doctorate at the Sorbonne in 1650 and was appointed almoner to King **Louis XIV** from 1653 to 1669, a phase of Le Camus' life marked by scandal and dissipation. He retired from the court and, under the influences of **Bossuet** and Nicholas Pavillon, bishop of Alet, he transformed his lifestyle to one of piety and austerity. In 1671 he was appointed bishop of Grenoble, where his reputation for sanctity became legendary. He was conspicuous in his respect and affection for Protestants, and he strongly opposed violence towards them. In 1686, despite royal displeasure, he received papal approval and was elevated to the rank of cardinal.

Leclerc, Jean Biblical scholar, born Geneva, 19

March 1657, died Amsterdam, 8 January 1736. He was brought up in Calvinism, but after studies at Grenoble and Saumur became an Arminian in theology. In 1684 he became professor of philosophy and Church history at the Remonstrant College at Amsterdam. He held radical views on the inspiration of Scripture and did not accept that Job, Proverbs, Ecclesiastes and the Song of Songs were inspired, nor the Mosaic authorship of the Pentateuch. His works include *Liberii de Sancto Amore Epistolae Theologicae* (1679), *Sentiments de quelques théologiens de Hollande* (1685) and *Bibliothèque universelle et historique* (26 vols, 1686–93).

Le Clerc du Tremblay, François An intimate adviser of Cardinal **Richelieu**, born Paris, 4 November 1577, died Rueil, near Paris, 18 December 1638. Better known by his religious name, 'Father Joseph of Paris'. Richelieu sent him to the Diet of Regensburg, where he is credited with having frustrated the plan of **Ferdinand II** to have his son elected to succeed him as Emperor. Richelieu had wanted to make him his successor and asked that he be named cardinal. He left a number of spiritual writings, among them *Introduction à la vie spirituelle* (1626).

Leclercq, Henri Benedictine, scholar, archeologist and historian of the early Church, born Tournai, Belgium, 4 December 1869, died London, 23 March 1945. A naturalized Frenchman, he was professed at Solesmes in 1896, transferred to Farnborough, England and was ordained in 1898. From 1914 onwards he lived in London and, apart from a chaplaincy to the Sisters of Sion, spent the major part of his time at the British Museum Library. He was a prolific writer and editor, especially on the subject of Latin Christianity. His major works, inspired by his mentor Dom Fernand **Cabrol**, were *Monumenta ecclesiae liturgica* (4 vols, Paris, 1903–12) and the *Dictionnaire d'archéologie chrétienne et de liturgie* (15 vols, 1907–53); the latter work, completed after his death, however, has been criticized because of its inaccuracies.

Le Conte, Antoine (Contius) Jurist, born Noyon, France, 1526, died Bourges, 1577. A cousin and an adherent of **Calvin** he became an authority on civil law, teaching at Bourges and Orléans. In addition he became a respected canonist on account of his edition of **Gratian**'s *Decretum* (Paris, 1556) and the companion edition of the *Corpus Iuris Canonici* (Antwerp, 1570).

Ledesma, Pedro de Dominican theologian, born Salamanca, *c.*1550, died there, 9 September 1616. He was professed in 1563 and taught theology for more than 40 years at Segovia, Ávila and Salamanca, where he held a chair in moral theology and liturgy from 1604, and that of dogmatic theology from 1608. He was noted for his virtuous life as well as his erudition, on the latter, particularly, his defence of the theology of his fellow Dominican **Bañez**. Among his written works were a two-volume commentary on the sacramental theology of St **Thomas Aquinas** and *De divinae gratiae auxiliis* (1611).

Ledóchowski, Miescyław Hałka Cardinal, count, born Gorki, near Klimontów, Poland, 29 October 1822, died Rome, 22 July 1902. He studied at Radom, Warsaw and Rome, and obtained doctorates in theology and canon law. Ordained in 1845, he served in the papal secretariat, and as apostolic delegate in Columbia and Chile. He was consecrated bishop in 1861, and archbishop of Gniezno and Poznan in 1866 but came into conflict with the Prussian government of **Bismarck** during the Kulturkampf, was arrested and detained from 1874 to 1876, being made cardinal in 1875. On his release he was exiled, but continued to issue regulations affecting his diocese from Rome to the irritation of the Prussian government. He resigned his archbishopric in 1886, after the conflict had been settled. Highly regarded by the Papacy, he served as prefect of the Congregation for the Propagation of the Faith from 1892 to 1902. In 1927 his body was returned from Rome to be buried in the cathedral at Poznan.

Ledóchowski, Władimir Jesuit, born Loosdorf, Austria, 7 October 1866, died Rome, 13 December 1942. A nephew of Cardinal Miescyław **Ledóchowski**, he studied law at Cracow, and for the secular priesthood at Tarnoro and in Rome. In 1889 he joined the Society of Jesus, was ordained in 1894 and progressed steadily from rector of the College at Cracow to become superior general of the Order in 1915. During his term of office,

1915–42, the number of missions and missionaries increased rapidly. He was responsible for the new codification of the Order's constitution and the reorganization of the superior general's curia. He gave impetus to higher studies in Jesuit institutions, notably the promotion of spirituality, inspired by the 'Spiritual Exercises' of St **Ignatius of Loyola**, and to Sodalities of the Blessed Virgin, and the Apostleship of Prayer.

Lee, Ann Anglo-American mystic, commonly known as 'Mother Ann', born Manchester, England, the daughter of a blacksmith, 29 February 1735, died Watervliet, near Albany, New York, 8 September 1784. She was illiterate, and was employed first as a factory hand and then as a cook in the Manchester Infirmary. Though not originally a church-goer, in 1758 she joined the 'Shakers', a small group which had seceded from the Quakers. After brief periods of imprisonment for preaching in the streets – suffering which confirmed her as the leader of the group – in 1774 she emigrated with her followers to America, where two years later they established the first Shaker settlement, a few miles outside Albany, New York. She was again imprisoned in 1780 for refusing to promise to obey the law, and after her release went on a prolonged, and highly successful, missionary journey.

Lee, Edward Archbishop of York, born Kent, 1482, died York, 13 September 1544. He graduated at Oxford in 1503, proceeded to Cambridge (perhaps on account of the plague) for his MA, with his BD finally confirmed in 1515. A biblical scholar himself, early in his career Lee became involved in a long and bitter dispute with **Erasmus** over the latter's *Commentary on the New Testament*, accusing the author of plagiarism. Lee was a childhood friend of Thomas **More** and a protégé of Cardinal **Wolsey**. In 1518 he was appointed chaplain to King **Henry VIII** and he served the king on diplomatic missions to Austria in 1523, Spain in 1529 and Bologna in 1530. He supported the king in his opposition to papal interference in English affairs but was thought to be uneasy over the Act of Royal Supremacy, and the divorce from Queen **Catherine**. Whatever his reservations, Lee observed the tradition of obedience with his fellow bishops,

Gardiner, Tunstall and **Bonner**, and he was an opponent of **Tyndale**.

Leen, Edward Irish devotional writer and a member of the Congregation of the Holy Ghost, born County Limerick, 17 August 1885, died Dublin, 10 November 1944. He studied in Dublin and Rome, was ordained in 1914, spent two years as a missionary in Nigeria and became dean of Blackrock College in 1922 and president in 1925. His works were of a highly devotional nature, such as *Progress through Mental Prayer* (1935), *The Holy Ghost* (1936), *Why the Cross?* (1938) – which dealt with the problem of pain – and *The Church before Pilate* (1939). He also wrote the controversial *What is Education?* in 1943.

Leeuw, Gerardus van der Protestant theologian and leading representative of the phenomenological interpretation of religion, born The Hague, 18 March 1890, died Utrecht, 18 November 1950. He was a professor at the University of Groningen, 1918–50, but served also as minister of education, art and science in the Dutch government from 1945 to 1946. Influenced by R. **Bultmann**, he was concerned primarily with the systematic description of the phenomenon of religion, in which the history of religion has a central place. His concept of the primitive was criticized by his successor at Groningen, T. P. van Barren, in his book *Wij Mensen*.

Lefèvre d'Étaples, Jacques Priest and humanist, born Étaples, Picardy, c.1460, died Nérac, March 1536. Arguably the leading French humanist of his generation, like **Erasmus** he studied in Paris and Italy, moved from the editing of classical texts to biblical and patristic ones, and found himself in the unenviable position of actively promoting ecclesiastical reform while remaining loyal to Rome. He was a close associate of Guillaume **Briçonnet**, the reforming bishop of Meaux, but the increasingly controversial nature of 'Évangelisme' caused Lefèvre to flee to Strasburg in 1525, after which sanctuary was offered by **Francis I**'s sister Marguerite, queen of Navarre.

Lefèvre, Peter Paul Roman Catholic bishop and missionary, born Roulers, Bruges (Belgium), 29 April 1804, died Detroit, Michigan, 4 March 1869.

He studied at the Lazarist seminary in Paris, was sent to Missouri to complete his theological studies and was ordained there in 1831. His early missionary activities extended to eight stations in Missouri, four in Illinois and two in Wisconsin. Consecrated as bishop in 1841, he became coadjutor and administrator of the Detroit district. In 1844 he introduced the Daughters of Charity to Michigan, he recruited priests from Belgium, and in 1857 he co-founded the American College in Louvain. From a territory comprising at the outset 25 churches and 18 priests, at the time of his death there were 160 churches and 88 priests.

Le Fort, Gertrud, baroness von   Roman Catholic poetess, born into a noble Prussian family at Minden, Germany, 11 October 1876, died Oberstdorf, 1 November 1971. While she was young her family moved a great deal, and as a consequence she did not have normal schooling. She therefore could only be admitted as an auditor into the University of Heidelberg. There, until 1913, she attended the lectures of Ernst **Troeltsch**, whom she later followed to Berlin, and whose *Glaubenslehre* she edited in 1925. She had published her first verses in 1893, and her first short stories, under the pseudonym 'Gertrud von Stark', in 1897. Her best-known work, *Hymns to the Church*, appeared in 1924. She was increasingly drawn to Roman Catholicism and became a Catholic in Rome in 1926. She continued to write verse, short stories, novels and even an historical detective story, which attracted critical approval, and in the years following World War II she was awarded a considerable number of honours and prizes.

Lefort, Louis-Théophile   Belgian Roman Catholic priest, Coptic scholar, born Orchimont, 1 August 1879, died Louvain (Leuven), 30 September 1959. He was ordained priest in 1901 and was a professor at the University of Louvain from 1906 to 1950. He edited many Coptic works, e.g. the writings of **Pachomius** and the Coptic translations of the writings of **Athanasius**. He set up a large photo-archive of Coptic manuscripts from all over the world. This archive was twice destroyed in the course of the world wars (1914 and 1940) and each time was built up again by Lefort.

Le Gaudier, Anthony   Jesuit theologian and spiritual writer, born Château-Thierry, 7 January 1572, died Paris, 14 April 1622. At seventeen he entered the Society of Jesus in Belgium. In his career he served as rector at Liège and at Paris. During his years as rector at Paris, 1618–21, he published his works on the spiritual life. Written originally in Latin, they were translated into French and other languages. They include *De sanctissimo Christi Jesus Dei et hominis amore paraeneticum in quo ejus amoris causae praxis et fructus exponuntur* (1619) and *De vera Christi Jesus Dei et hominis imitatione* (1620).

Legge, James   Congregationalist missionary to China and pioneer Sinologist, born Huntly, Scotland, 20 December 1815, died Oxford, 29 November 1897. A member of Huntly Congregational Church, Legge studied at Kings College, Aberdeen, MA in 1835, and Highbury College, London. In 1839 he married Mary Morison and the London Missionary Society appointed him to the Anglo-Chinese College at Melaka. In 1840 he took over as principal and following the Opium War of 1839–42 moved the College to Hong Kong. He ministered to English and Chinese congregations and translated the Chinese classics. He developed a deep appreciation for Confucius and believed that the early religion of China had been monotheistic. In 1876 he was appointed to the newly created chair of Chinese at Oxford University. He never retired and his translations remain in print.

Le Gobien, Charles   Jesuit historian, born St Malo, France, 20 December 1653, died Paris, 5 March 1708. He joined the Society of Jesus in 1671 and taught at the Society's schools in Tours and Alençon. He was appointed procurator for the Jesuit missions in China and in 1697 published a letter on the progress of religion in that country, followed by a history of the Chinese emperor's edict in favour of Christianity. In 1702 he began his *Lettres édifiantes*, an annual publication of selected letters from Jesuit missionaries in China and the East Indies, editing the first eight volumes himself. Some of these letters were translated in 1714 and 1720 into English and German respectively. They were widely circulated, and were in part responsible for the vogue for 'chinoiserie' in France and elsewhere.

Le Hir, Arthur Marie Sulpician priest and Scripture scholar, born Morlaix, France, 5 December 1811, died Paris, 18 January 1868. He entered the Society of St Sulpice in 1833 and taught Scripture and Hebrew until his death. He contributed several articles to the Jesuit publication *Les Études Religieuses*, but most of his works were published posthumously. Among them were *Les Psaumes* (1876) and *Les trois grands prophètes Isaie, Jérémie, Exéchiel* (1877). His student **Renan** said of him: 'He was a scholar and a saint. He was both to an eminent degree.'

Lehmann, Paul Medievalist, born Braunschweig (Brunswick), Germany, 13 July 1884, died Munich, 4 January 1964. He taught at the University of Munich from 1911 on. His contribution to medieval studies was to expand his study of the early Middle Ages to include the entire medieval millennium. In his numerous works, Lehmann single-handedly advanced the knowledge of Latin palaeography and codicology, of the history of medieval libraries, and the tradition of their holdings, and of the history of medieval Latin literature. Among his important works is *Die Parodie im Mittelalter*.

Lehmkuhl, August Jesuit, theologian and moralist, born Hagan, Westphalia, 23 September 1834, died Valenkenburg, The Netherlands, 23 June 1918. He was ordained in 1862 and taught Scripture and moral theology at Maria Laach, and then, exiled because of the Kulturkampf, at Ditton Hall in England, until 1880. Thereafter he returned to the Continent to write articles and two major works: *Theologia moralis* (2 vols, Freiburg, 1883) and *Casus conscientiae* (2 vols, Freiburg, 1902–4). Lehmkuhl applied the principles of St **Thomas Aquinas** and St **Alphonsus Liguori** to contemporary problems relating to social and economic justice. He was one of the pioneers in developing the social teaching of the Roman Catholic Church.

Lehodey, Vital Trappist Cistercian monk, ascetic, author on mysticism, born Hambye, France, 17 December 1857, died Coutances, 6 May 1948. After his ordination in 1880, Alcime Jude Lehodey spent nine years in diocesan work before entering the Trappist abbey at Bricquebec in 1890, taking the name 'Vital'. He was appointed prior in 1892 and abbot in 1895, retiring on health grounds in 1929. He wrote three major works: *Les Voies de l'orasion mentale* (Paris, 1908), the *Directoire spirituelle* (Bricquebec, 1910) and a revision of the Cistercian Order's *Directoire* of 1869 in which he stressed the importance of charity and contemplation, in contrast to the excessive pessimism in an earlier version.

Leibniz, Gottfried Wilhelm German philosopher and mathematician, born into a Lutheran family in Leipzig, 1 July 1646, died Hanover, 14 November 1716. He studied law at the University of Leipzig, 1661-6, and at Altdorf, where he entered the service of the elector-archbishop of Mainz as a political and legal adviser. In that capacity he was sent, in 1672, to Paris, where he met Antoine **Arnauld**, to whom he proposed his ideas for the reunion of the Lutheran and Roman Churches. He was working both on philosophical issues and on mathematical ones: in 1673 he demonstrated to the Royal Society of London a model of a calculating machine he had invented, and a couple of years later he laid the foundations for the calculus. But he was also a practical man, and made an important contribution to developing the economy of Hanover, where he became a councillor to the duke of Brunswick-Lüneburg in 1678. He became court adviser to, and historian of, the House of Brunswick in 1685, and in 1691 librarian at Wolfenbüttel. He helped found the Prussian Academy of Sciences in 1700. Much of his philosophy, written very largely in opposition to **Descartes** – whose teaching, he believed, was destructive of faith – was concerned with the problem of God and of the soul, and the integration of science and religion. His best-known philosophical work, *La Monadologie*, was written in 1714 (published, in German translation, in 1720). He became well known in both philosophical and scientific circles across Europe, and was awarded the rank of baron by the Emperor. He was also much admired by the Tsar Peter the Great, whom he met several times.

Leidradus of Lyons Archbishop of Lyons, born in the ancient province of Noricum, died Soissons, 28 December 817. Through his friend **Alcuin** he received an invitation to **Charlemagne**'s court, where he was Alcuin's favourite disciple. In 797 or 798 he succeeded Ado as archbishop of Lyons. He promoted the transcription of numerous MSS but was especially the restorer of churches and monasteries. He organized his clergy into a college of canons, priests and deacons. Besides a letter to Charlemagne, he wrote a theological treatise for the emperor entitled *Liber de sacramento baptismi*.

Le Jay, Claude (Jajus) Jesuit theologian, born Mieussy, near Geneva, Switzerland, 1504, died Vienna, Austria, 6 August 1552. He studied at La Roche and, following his compatriot Peter **Faber** to Paris, gained his MA in 1534. He was professed with St **Ignatius of Loyola** as one of the founder members of the Society of Jesus. He obtained his doctorate at Bologna in 1542 and was sent by Pope **Paul III** to lecture on Scripture at Ingolstadt, and thereafter at Vienna. Le Jay took an active part in the early years of the Council of Trent (1545–63) when he was one of two theologians who drafted decrees on sacred Scripture and tradition.

Lejay, Paul Classical and patristic scholar, born Dijon, France, 3 May 1861, died Paris, 13 June 1920. After his seminary studies he entered the École des Hautes Études, was ordained in 1890 and appointed professor of Latin philology at the Institut Catholique in Paris, a post he held until his death. His writings included complete and partial editions of Virgil, Horace and Lucan but Lejay was noted in particular for his brilliant articles and reviews in scholarly journals such as *Revue critique d'histoire et de littérature* and *Revue de philologie, de littérature et d'histoire anciennes*. In addition he contributed to **Mangenot**'s *Dictionnaire de la théologie catholique*.

Lejeune, Jean Oratorian and preacher, born Dole, France, 1592, died Limoges, 19 August 1672. He studied theology at the University of Dole and became a canon at Arbors. In 1611 he renounced his canonry and entered the Oratory, devoting his life thereafter to preaching missions and Advent and Lenten courses throughout France. At the age of 37 he was suddenly struck blind but, with the aid of a devoted confrère, he continued preaching. His disability appeared to strengthen his apostolate and he was nicknamed 'Le Père Aveugle'. In 1662 a collection of 362 of his sermons was published, later republished under the revised title of *Le Missionaire de L'Oratoire* (Lyons, 1825–7).

Leloutre, Jean Louis Roman Catholic priest and missionary, born Morlaix, France, 26 September 1709, died Nantes, 1772. In 1737 he was ordained at the seminary of the Paris Foreign Mission Society and destined for a parish in Annapolis, Nova Scotia, but he was detained in Cape Breton Island. Selected as missionary to the Acadian Micmac Indians ('Acadia' being the French name for Nova Scotia), in 1754 he was appointed vicar general of Quebec. He was taken prisoner by the English at the fall of Fort Beausejour and from 1758 to 1763 was held on Jersey. On his release after the Treaty of Paris he returned to France, where he took part in arrangements for the settlement of the Acadian Indians at Belle-isle-en-mer, Canada.

Le Maistre, Isaac (Le Maître de Sacy) French Jansenist, born Paris, 29 March 1613, died Pomponne, 4 January 1684. With his brother, Antoine, he was prominent in the early history of Jansenism and of the sectarians at Port-Royal, known as 'les solitaires'. He was ordained in 1649, became spiritual adviser to other 'Solitaires' but, following an edict of Pope **Alexander VII**, Le Maistre was imprisoned in the Bastille from 1666 to 1668. Thereafter he spent most of his life in exile, contributing to the spread of the Jansenist heresy in France through his interpretations of the Scriptures and the writings of the Church Fathers. Among his best-known works was *Tradition du Noveau Testament* (2 vols, Amsterdam, 1667), condemned by Pope **Clement IX** in 1669.

Le Masson, Innocent Carthusian author, born Noyon, 21 December 1627, died 8 May 1703. He entered the Carthusian Order at Mont-Renaud in 1645 and became prior there eighteen years later. In 1675 he became prior of Grande-Chartreuse and general of the Order. After fire destroyed the monastery, he designed the new buildings and reconstituted the archives and produced what was later known as the *Disciplina Ordinis Cartusiensis*. He preserved Carthusian spirituality from the dangers of Jansenism and combated Quietism, particularly among Carthusian nuns, whose houses he himself visited. He composed the *Semaine du Sacré-Coeur* for them.

Leme da Silveira Cintra, Sebastião Second Brazilian cardinal, born São Paulo, 20 January 1882, died Rio de Janeiro, 17 October 1942. He did much to promote priestly vocations and Eucharistic weeks, founded the Catholic Confederation to co-ordinate Catholic Action Associations and rebuilt the cathedral and episcopal palace. He was responsible for the huge statue of Christ the Redeemer overlooking Rio. During the revolution against Vargas, he founded the Catholic Electoral League. His last important act was the foundation of the Catholic University of Rio de Janeiro in 1941.

Lemire, Jules   Roman Catholic priest and legislator, born Hazebrouck, France, 23 April 1853, died Hazebrouck, 7 March 1928. Early in adult life he became interested in social doctrines, including those of Frédéric Le Play and Cardinal **Manning**, dedicating a book to the latter in 1893. The same year saw the beginning of his politico-social activities as Christian Democratic deputy for his native Department, maintaining a stance as a 'progressive priest', thereby incurring ecclesiastical suspicion and suspension from 1914 to 1916, until this was lifted by Pope **Benedict XV**. Lemire concentrated his energies on spreading the doctrine of *Rerum novarum*, and on Christian Democracy, intervening on numerous social questions in the Chamber of Deputies. He was the first to petition for a ministry of labour and, in his final years, was a successful mayor of his own town of Hazebrouck.

Lemke, Peter Henry   Benedictine monk and missionary, born Rhene, Mecklenburg, 27 July 1796, died Carrolltown, Pennsylvania, 29 November 1882. He studied at the Lutheran Cathedral School and at the University of Rostock, and he was licensed as a Lutheran minister in 1823. However, after reading the works of **Luther** in more detail he abandoned that faith, converted to Catholicism by 1824, and was ordained in 1826. Sent as a missionary to Pennsylvania in 1834, he founded Carrolltown in 1853, taking his Benedictine vows at La Trobe two years later. He moved on to Kansas and New Jersey, retiring finally to Carrolltown.

Lemmens, Jacques Nicolas   Belgian pianist, organist, and composer, born Zle-Parwijs, 3 January 1823, died Linterpoort, 30 January 1881. Named

professor at the Brussels Conservatoire in 1849, he attempted to merge the J. S. **Bach** and the plainchant traditions. His most famous work, *École d'orgue*, based on his teaching experience, was adopted by many conservatoires. He later founded in Malines the school for Catholic organists and choirmasters and later the Society of St Gregory. His principles for reform of Church music adumbrated those of **Pius X**'s *motu proprio* of 1903.

Lemmens, Leonhard   Franciscan historian, born near Aachen, 19 November 1864, died Rome, 10 February 1929. He entered the Franciscans in 1878 and was ordained in 1888. He was the leading Franciscan historian of the time. After serving as professor in various fields in Germany he went to Rome, where he was annalist for the Order from 1899 to 1901. From 1924 to 1929 he lectured in mission history at San Antonio. His principal areas of research were early Franciscan history, the Reformation era in Saxony, and mission history.

Lemnius, Simon   Neo-Latin poet, translator and polemicist, born Chur, Switzerland, c.1511, died Chur, 24 or 29 November 1550. He studied at Munich and Ingoldstadt, and matriculated at Wittenberg in 1534. Two books of *Epigrams* brought him into conflict with **Luther** and in 1538 he was banished from his university. In 1540 he returned to teach at Chur and, on a visit to Bologna, 1543–4, he was crowned poet in recognition of his work *Amores* (1542). Lemnius translated the *Odyssey* into Latin (Basel, 1549) but a nine-volume epic in Latin celebrating the Swiss victory over Maximilian I, written in 1499, was not published until 1874. In his own epitaph Lemnius styled himself 'preclarus carmine vates'.

Lemos, Tomás de   Dominican and theologian, born Rivadavia, Spain, c.1546, died Rome, 23 August 1629. With **Álvarez** he represented the Dominican position in controversy with the Jesuits over free will and the efficacy of grace, precipitated by the publication of **Molina**'s *Concordia liberi arbitrii cum gratiae donis*. Lemos upheld the Augustinian-Thomistic interpretation but, despite the efforts of Pope **Clement VIII**, the dispute was unresolved. At its close Lemos was offered a bishopric by the king of Spain but he declined and retired to the priory of Santa Maria Sopra Minerva in Rome. His celebrated work *Panoplia gratiae* (4 vols, Liège, 1676) was attacked by the Inquisition but vigorously defended by the Dominicans.

Lenormant, Charles Historian and Egyptologist, born Paris, 1 June 1802, died Athens, 24 November 1859. He studied at the Lycée Charlemagne and the Lycée Napoléon and, although he entered the Faculty of Law, he became intensely interested in the study of Egyptian archaeology. In 1836 he was named curator of books at the Royal Library, and was elected to the French Academy in 1839. A mission to Greece in 1841 aroused his interest in the origins of Christian civilization, which, in turn, stimulated his faith. His writings include *Questions historiques* (Paris, 1845) and *Les Associations religieuses dans la société chriétienne* (Paris, 1866), and he became editor-in-chief of the publication *Le Correspondent* from its foundation until 1855.

Lenshina, Mulenga Alice Foundress of the Lumpa Church, Zambia, born Kasomo *c.*1919, died Lusaka, 7 December 1978. In 1953 she reported to the Scottish Presbyterian mission that she had had a vision of Jesus. Her faith was encouraged and she was baptized in November 1953. She composed hymns and began preaching to large crowds, opposing sorcery, polygamy and beer drinking. Her style became so radical that she and her followers were suspended from the Church in 1955. She established Christian villages with herself as chief and preached apocalyptic messages. Prior to Zambian independence she encouraged her followers to tear up their party political cards, which resulted in violent clashes with Kenneth Kaunda's United National Independence Party. With independence, Alice was detained until 1975 and her movement banned. It continued underground in small pockets of the country.

Lenz, Peter (Desiderius) Benedictine monk, painter, architect and sculptor, born Haigerloch, Germany, 12 March 1832, died Beuron, 28 January 1928. He studied at Munich Academy from 1850 to 1858 and was professor at the Nuremberg Artistic Handicrafts School until 1862. He then moved to Italy and while there was influenced by Egyptian art. In 1862 he entered the abbey of Beuron as an artist-oblate, taking his final vows in 1892. He founded the school of Beuronese art with

the purpose of renewing sacred art in an era of naturalism. His sculptures represented classical and mythological subjects and he became renowned for his frescoes and mosaics at Beuron, Monte Cassino and other religious foundations in Belgium, Prague and Emmaus.

Leo *see* **Marinus and Leo**

Leo I ('the Great') Pope and saint, elected Pope 29 September 440, died 10 November 461. Previously he had been an influential deacon at the papal court, as his political mission to Gallia on request of the Empress Galla Placidia shows. As bishop of Rome he applied himself to establish unity within the community by reacting against, for example, both the Priscillianists and Manichaeans. This concern for the purity of faith also guided his actions on the international scene, foremost in the Nestorian controversy. Meanwhile he asserted the primacy of the Roman bishop, against the claims of the political capital, Constantinople. On the political level he tried to defend his fellow-citizens against the invasions of the Vandals and the Huns. Of his writings, 97 sermons and 143 letters were preserved. Feast day 10 November in the Roman calendar, 18 February in Greek Orthodox Churches.

Leo I Byzantine emperor (457–74), born Thrace, *c.*400, died Constantinople, 474. He became emperor while serving as a tribune, on the death of **Marcian**. He upheld the Chalcedonian theology, despite some hesitation under Monophysite pressure. He sent a famous circular letter to the Eastern bishops asking their view of the theology of Chalcedon, and, with their strong endorsement, banished **Timothy Ailouros** as bishop of Alexandria. His other laws forbade simony in episcopal elections, and restricted the behaviour of monks. Unsuccessful against the Vandals in Africa in the 460s, he turned against the Arians in 471.

Leo II Saint, Pope from 17 August 682, born Sicily, date unknown, died Rome, 3 July 683. Leo succeeded **Agatho**, and seems to have been elected in June 681, but had to wait some eighteen months before receiving the imperial mandate from **Constantine IV Pogonatus** necessary for his consecration. The only fact of historical interest with regard to Leo is that he approved of the decision at the Council of Constantinople (681) to condemn **Honorius I** as a supporter of heresy in the Monothelite controversy. During Leo's pontificate the dependence of the See of Ravenna upon that of Rome was finally settled by imperial edict. Feast day 3 July.

Leo II of Armenia   Ruled as prince from 1187 to 1198 and as King Leo II from 1198 to 1219, died Armenia, 1219. Called 'the Magnificent', he brought the provinces of Cilicia under his control and sought recognition both from the Byzantine Empire under Theodore Lascaris in Nicaea and from the West. He co-operated with the Crusaders under **Frederick I Barbarossa**, recognized the overlordship of German Emperor **Henry VI**, received papal recognition from **Celestine III**, and had himself anointed king by the head of the Armenian Church (**katholikos**) Gregory Aspirat. He encouraged efforts at reunion with Orthodox and Roman Churches.

Leo III   Saint, Pope from 27 December 795, born Rome, date unknown, died Rome, 12 June 816. Leo succeeded **Adrian I**, and his pontificate covered the last eighteen years of the reign of **Charlemagne**. Although unanimously elected, he aroused the hostility of Adrian's relatives, and after a violent physical assault in 799, he fled to Charlemagne's court at Paderborn; escorted back to Rome, he was fully rehabilitated. Shortly afterwards, on Christmas Day 800, Leo crowned Charlemagne in St Peter's, and the assembled crowd acclaimed him as Emperor of the Romans. Leo accepted the dogmatic correctness of the Filioque, but judged inopportune the emperor's request in 810 to include it in the Nicene Creed. Assisted by the emperor's rich gifts, Leo did much to adorn the churches of Rome and other cities of Italy. Feast day 12 June.

Leo IV   Saint, Pope from 10 April 847, born Rome, date unknown, died Rome, 17 July 855. Leo succeeded **Sergius II**, and his pontificate was chiefly distinguished by his efforts to repair the damage done by the Saracens, who sacked Rome in 846. He built and fortified with a 40-foot-high wall a suburb on the right bank of the Tiber still known as the 'Civitas Leonina'. In 853 he is said

to have 'hallowed' the young **Alfred** as future king of England. He sought to bring under his authority Anastasius Bibliothecarius (**Anastasius the Librarian**, later an Antipope) and **Hincmar** of Rheims, but the history of this struggle belongs rather to the reign of **Nicholas I**. Feast day 17 July.

Leo V   Byzantine emperor (known as 'Leo the Armenian'), born Armenia, died by assassination in Constantinople, 24/25 December 820. He inaugurated the Second Iconoclastic period of the Byzantine Empire, having earlier distinguished himself as a general serving in the Anatolakon district under the Emperors Nicholas I and Michael I. In 813, after a battle near Adrianople, he deserted and deposed Michael I. In 815 he deposed the Orthodox patriarch, **Nicephorus I of Constantinople**, and called a local council to reimpose the Decrees of the Iconoclastic Synod of Hieria of 754. On Christmas Eve 820 Leo condemned Michael the Armenian to death on a charge of treason but was himself assassinated during the Christmas celebrations in the basilica of Hagia Sophia.

Leo V   Pope from August to September 903, born, place and date unknown, died Rome, early 904. A parish priest at Priapi, near Ardea, south of Rome, Leo succeeded **Benedict IV**. As he was not a member of the Roman clergy, it is not known how he came to be elected; perhaps because, since the clergy and nobility could not agree on a local candidate, they settled for a stranger of whose high repute they had heard from **Auxilius** (champion of **Formosus**, Pope 891–6). After only 30 days, one of his clergy, Christopher, overthrew him, flung him into prison and installed himself in his place.

Leo VI   Byzantine emperor, born, possibly in Constantinople, 19 September 866, died Constantinople, 11 May 912. He was educated under the supervision of **Photius**, the patriarch of Constantinople, and, when he succeeded his father **Basil I** in 886, began his reign by sending Photius into exile and replacing him with his own brother, Stephen. He was regarded by succeeding generations as a wise ruler, and he did indeed reform the administrative and legal system as well as writing religious verse, compiling laws and publishing homilies. He fell foul with the patriarchate over his four marriages, especially the fourth, when he married his concubine after she had produced for him an heir. The marriage was, however, approved by Pope **Sergius III**.

Leo VI Pope from May to December 928, born Rome of the upper class, died December 928. Leo succeeded **John X**, who had been deposed by **Marozia** (daughter of Theophylact) and her party, and died in the Castel Sant'Angelo, mid-929, probably murdered. Nothing is known of Leo's reign, except that he ordered the bishops of Dalmatia to obey their archbishop, John of Spalato, to whom he had granted the pallium, and to be content with their territorial boundaries.

Leo VII Pope from 3 January 936, born Rome, date unknown, died Rome, 13 July 939. Leo succeeded **John XI** and owed his elevation to **Alberic II of Spoleto**, prince of Rome, who ruled the city with absolute control. He appears to have been seriously interested in promoting ecclesiastical and moral reform; he brought St **Odo of Cluny** to Rome, hoping that he would give impetus to a spiritual revival. Leo's surviving letters indicate his interest in Cluny and Subiaco, whose rights he confirmed. He forbade the forced conversion of Jews, but allowed archbishop Frederick of Mainz, who was his legate for Germany, to expel them from the cities, unless they accepted the Christian faith.

Leo VIII Pope from 4 December 963, born Rome, date unknown, died there, 1 March 965. Elected at the instance of **Otto I**, by the synod which deposed **John XII**, Leo, still a layman, having been put through all the intermediate orders with unseemly haste, received consecration two days later, this being unacceptable to the people. In 964 the Emperor withdrew from Rome, Leo fled and was deposed by a synod led by John, on whose sudden death, however, the populace chose **Benedict V** as Leo's successor; but Otto returned, laid siege to the city and compelled the acceptance of Leo. A few days later Leo held a synod which deposed and degraded Benedict.

Leo IX Saint, Pope from 12 February 1049, born 'Bruno', son of Count Hugh of Egisheim, in Alsace, 21 June 1002, died St Peter's, Rome, 19 April 1054. Leo succeeded **Damasus II**, and his reign marks the beginning of papal reform from its decadence of the past century and a half. He did much to foster a new ideal of the Papacy: at the Easter Synod (1049), celibacy was enforced on all clergy; shortly afterward councils promulgated decrees against simony and clerical unchastity. Leo travelled extensively, pressing home the need for renewal, assisted by Hildebrand (**Gregory VII**), **Humbert of Silva Candida** and **Peter Damian**; he condemned **Berengarius of Tours** for his Eucharistic doctrine that no material change in the elements is needed to explain the Eucharistic Presence. His later years were marred by military defeat by the Normans at Civitate in 1053, as well as a breach with Michael Cerularius and the Eastern Church. Feast day 19 April.

Leo X Pope from 11 March 1513, born 'Giovanni de' Medici' at Florence, 11 December 1475, died Rome, 1 December 1521. Leo succeeded **Julius II**, and soon disappointed the high hopes that had been placed upon him. He continued the Lateran Council called by Julius, and eventually concluded a concordat with **Francis I** of France, which firmly established royal influence over the French Church (1516). Having squandered the fortune left by Julius, Leo resorted to selling indulgences to finance a projected crusade against the Turks and the construction of St Peter's. This became the occasion of Martin **Luther**'s 95 theses at Wittenberg, and Leo excommunicated him with the bull *Exsurge Domine* (1520). He bestowed the title 'Defender of the Faith' on **Henry VIII** of England, in recognition of his book defending the seven sacraments against Luther. Leo and his curia failed to appreciate the significance of the revolution taking place in the Church, and when he died suddenly of malaria, he left Italy in political turmoil, northern Europe in growing religious disaffection, and the papal treasury deeply in debt.

Leo XI Pope from 1 April to 27 April 1605, born 'Alessandro Ottaviano de' Medici' at Florence, 2 June 1535, died Rome, 27 April 1605. A nephew of **Leo X** through his mother, Francesca Salviati, Alessandro succeeded **Clement VIII**, and adopted his uncle's name. He was entirely pro-French in his sympathies (he had been legate to France), and persuaded Clement to absolve **Henry IV** from the excommunication laid upon him. While generally welcomed, the new Pope was elderly and in frail health; he caught a chill while taking possession of the Lateran and died before the month was out.

Leo XII Pope from 28 September 1823, born 'Annibale della Genga' at Castello della Genga, near Spoleto, 22 August 1760, died Rome, 10 February 1829. Named cardinal-priest of Santa Maria Maggiore and vicar general of Rome by **Pius VII**, Leo owed his election to the votes of the *zelanti*, conservatives who wished to break with the liberal policies of Pius and with Cardinal **Consalvi**'s political and doctrinal moderation. Leo's domestic policy was one of extreme reaction: he condemned the Bible societies, instituted severe ghetto laws that led many Jews to emigrate, hunted down the liberal Carbonari, and the Freemasons; a pervasive system of espionage sapped the foundations of public confidence. His endeavours to restore contact between the Papacy and the faithful suffered from a narrow clerical outlook that failed to understand the world developing around him. His death was received by the populace with unconcealed joy.

Leo XIII Pope from 20 February 1878, born 'Vincenzo Gioacchino Pecci' at Carpineto Romano, 2 March 1810, died Rome, 20 July 1903. Leo succeeded the conservative **Pius IX**, and he sought, within the framework of traditional teaching, to bring the Church to terms with the modern age. He continued the policies of Pius against socialism, communism and nihilism (*Quod Apostolici muneris*), against Freemasonry (*Humanum genus*) and on marriage (*Arcanum illud*). He increased centralization and concentrated religious orders and congregations at Rome. His distinctive contribution was to open a dialogue between the Church and society; he directed Catholics to the philosophy of St **Thomas Aquinas** (*Aeterni Patris*), and condemned 40 propositions from the works of Antonio **Rosmini-Serbati** contradicting his doctrine. He fostered study at the Vatican of astronomy and natural sciences, called on Catholic historians to write objectively and in 1883 opened the Vatican archives to all scholars. Leo's most famous manifesto, *Rerum novarum* (1891), upheld private property, the just wage, workers' rights and trade unions; its advocacy of social justice earned him the title 'the workers' Pope'. He invited Greeks and Protestants to unite with Rome, but rejected the concept of union as a federation of Churches (*Satis cognitum*). He encouraged Anglican aspirations to union, and in 1895 appointed a commission to investigate Anglican ordinations; they were rejected as invalid (*Apostolicae Curae*, 1896). Relations remained friendly between the English court and the Vatican; he supported the British government in Ireland, but was disappointed that this did not lead to formal diplomatic relations. A man of deep conservative piety, Leo promoted the spiritual life of the Church in many encyclicals dealing with the redemptive work of Christ, the Eucharist, devotion to the Virgin Mary and the rosary; in 1900 he consecrated the whole human race to the Sacred Heart of Jesus. He encouraged the work of the missions, especially the formation of a native clergy. Under Leo, the Papacy acquired a prestige unknown since the Middle Ages.

Leo, Leonardo Baroque composer of opera and Church music, born near Brindisi, 5 August 1694, died Naples, 31 October 1744. After the death of **Scarlatti** he became first organist in the royal chapel at Naples. As choirmaster for the royal chapel from 1744, he composed Mass propers for the Sundays of Lent in a cappella style to replace the concertato music previously favoured. His well-known eight-voice *Miserere* for two choirs and basso continuo may have drawn other Neapolitan composers to the a cappella style.

Leo Diaconus Historian of one of the most brilliant and fruitful periods of Byzantine history, born Kaloe, Asia Minor, *c*.950, died after 992. He came as a young man to Constantinople and was ordained a deacon there. In 986 he took part in **Basil II**'s campaign against the Bulgarians. About 992 Leo published a history of the period 959–76 in ten books. His sources were oral reports of eyewitnesses and his own observations. His works are invaluable for the early stages of Russian history because of his data on Svyatoslav and the war with the Greeks.

Leo Luke Saint, abbot, born Corleone, Sicily, *c*.885, died Monteleone, Calabria, *c*.980. Became a monk at a young age at the abbey of St Philip in Argira; Arab raids led him and many of his fellow-monks to Calabria, *c.*940, where he became a disciple of St Christopher of Collesano. He succeeded St Christopher as abbot at the monastery he founded near Monteleone, serving for more than twenty years until his own death. Feast day 1 March.

Leo Marsicanus Monk and chronicler of Monte Cassino, also known as 'Ostiensis', born *c.*1046, died 22 May 1115. He entered Monte Cassino – aged fourteen – where he subsequently became abbey librarian. In 1101 **Paschal II** created him cardinal-bishop of Ostia. Leo has been called the most important medieval Italian historian. He is the author of *Chronica Casinensis monasterii*, which goes from St **Benedict** to 1057. Guido and a not always reliable Peter the Deacon continued it to 1139. His other works include *Historia peregrinorum* and *Vita S. Mennatis*.

Leo of Assisi Franciscan friar, disciple, secretary and confessor to St **Francis of Assisi**, born end of the twelfth century, died Assisi, 14 or 15 November 1271. The date of his entry to the Order is not known but he was one of a small group of the most trusted companions of St Francis during the latter's final years. After the death of Francis, Leo became the leader in the struggle within the Order over the maintenance of strict poverty and he came into sharp conflict with **Elias of Cortona**, who is reported to have treated Leo harshly. Leo retired to a hermitage and spent the remainder of his life writing in defence of the spiritual aspects of Francis's life and teaching. The claim that Brother Leo wrote the *Speculum perfectionis* cannot be proved, although he may have inspired its contents.

Leo of Cava Saint, Benedictine abbot, born Lucca, Tuscany, died La Cava, 12 July 1079. Alferius, founder of La Cava, designated Leo to be his successor at the moment of his death in 1050. A humble and charitable man, Leo was often in conflict with Gisulf II, prince of Salerno, who was neither. Leo selected Alferius' nephew Peter as his coadjutor and successor, whose strictness proved to be unpopular with the monks of La Cava. His Life was written by Abbot Hugh of Venossa, a former monk of La Cava; his cult was approved by Pope **Leo XIII** in 1893. Feast day 12 July.

Leo of Cava Blessed, Benedictine abbot, died 19 August 1295. Elected abbot of La Cava in 1268, he encouraged the development of the abbey's scriptorium and built the monastery's cloister and chapel of San Germano. The abbey suffered greatly during his reign owing to the Sicilian Vespers and the subsequent loss of their Sicilian holdings. Feast day 19 August.

Leo of St John Carmelite of the Touraine Reform, born Rennes, 9 July 1600, died Paris, 30 December 1671. He was a friend of **Richelieu** and later of **Mazarin**, whose policies he generally supported. He was a conciliator in the Jansenist conflict, maintained important political, religious and intellectual relations with the royal family, great statesmen, the nobility, intellectuals, St **Vincent de Paul**, **Innocent X** and many cardinals. He was a precursor of **Bossuet** and wrote *Traité de l'éloquence chrétienne* (1655). He was neither a Thomist nor among the 'devout humanists' and was a major instrument in spreading **Bérulle**'s spirituality.

Leo of Vercelli Bishop of Vercelli from *c.*998–9, poet, and trusted adviser of **Otto III**, died Vercelli, 10 April 1026. Whether he was of German or Italian origin is disputed. As bishop he regarded himself as 'bishop of the Empire'. He energetically enforced the imperial decrees reintegrating Church property and governed the counties of Vercelli and Santhia conferred upon him by Otto III. His loyalty to **Henry II** of Germany contributed largely to Henry's ultimate victory. Leo on occasion expressed his imperialist enthusiasm in Latin verses that showed considerable literary skill.

Leo Thaumaturgus Saint, bishop, miracle-worker, died *c.*785. Leo was bishop of Catania, Sicily. He was a well-respected figure, especially by Emperor Leo IV, who invited him to court in Constantinople, and by Emperor Constantine VI, who requested his intercession. The name 'Thaumaturgus' means wonder-worker. Feast day 20 or 21 February.

Leo Tuscus Byzantine courtier, born Pisa, *c.*1110, died after 1182. He and his brother **Hugh Etherian** held a high position in the court of Emperor Manuel I Comnenus (1143–80). Leo acted as official interpreter and engaged in various literary pursuits. An early translation of the Liturgy of St **John Chrysostom** from Greek to Latin is attributed to him. His main work is a counter-attack against the famous tract *Against the Franks*, written during the Cerularian controversy of *c*.1054. He titled his work *De haeresibus et praevaricationibus Graecorum*.

Leobard Saint, Benedictine recluse, died *c*.593. Leobard's parents wished him to marry, but after their death he became a recluse in Tours, under the direction of **Gregory of Tours**, where he remained for 22 years. Leobard also founded and became the first abbot of the abbey of Mormoutier. Feast day 18 January; in Tours, 13 February.

Leobard (Liuberat) Saint, abbot, died *c*.665. Leobard was a disciple of Waldebert and founded the abbey of Maursmunster *c*.660. Feast days 31 December and 25 February.

Leobin (Lubin) Monk, abbot, bishop of Chartres, born near Poitiers, died *c*.558. He worked at the monastery of Noailles and was a hermit with **Avitus**. Later, at an abbey near Lyons, Leobin was tortured by raiders who had attacked the monastery. Forced to reveal the location of the treasury, Leobin was left for dead, but eventually recovered and returned to monastic life. Ultimately, Leobin was appointed bishop of Chartres, participated in councils in Paris and Orléans, and enacted reforms.

Leodegar (Leger) Saint, bishop of Autun, born *c*.616, died 679. He was devoted to monastic reform in Germany. As abbot of St Maxentius, he introduced the Rule of St **Benedict**. In 653 he was made bishop of Autun and imposed the same Rule on all religious houses in his charge. He became involved in a dispute over claims to the throne and was eventually banished, blinded, tortured and beheaded. He was soon revered as saint and a following emerged throughout France. Feast day 2 October.

León, Luis de Augustinian friar, biblical scholar, mystic and poet, born Belmonte, Spain, 1527, died Madrigal de las Torres, 23 August 1591. He was professed at Salamanca in 1544, appointed to a theological chair there in 1561, and a chair in sacred literature in 1571. St **John of the Cross** was one of his pupils. Ecclesiastical intrigues and academic rivalries overshadowed his life. He was denounced to the Inquisition for an unauthorized translation of the Canticles, and criticism of the text of the Vulgate, and he was imprisoned from 1572 to 1576. His prose masterpiece, the mystical treatise *De los nombres de Cristo*, was published in 1583–5, and his lyrical poems, including *La vida retira* and *Noche serena*, appeared posthumously in 1631. Nine days before his death he was elected provincial of the Augustinian Order in Castile.

Leonard Saint and hermit of the sixth century, virtually unknown until the eleventh century. He is alleged to have been the son of a Frankish nobleman and was converted by St **Remigius of Rheims**, Apostle of the Franks. After his conversion he lived in a cell at Noblac, near Limoges, where he founded an abbey. Unexpectedly his cult spread rapidly in the twelfth century, possibly stemming from a legend of the returning crusader who had offered thanksgiving for his release at Leonard's shrine. Although his historical existence is unproven, in England alone 177 churches are dedicated to him, and two towns, one in Sussex and one in Dorset. He is the patron of prisoners, peasants and horses. Feast day 6 November.

Leonard of Port Maurice Saint, Franciscan friar, born Porto Maurizo, Liguria, 20 December 1676, died Rome, 26 November 1751. He was educated at the Jesuit College in Rome and professed as a Franciscan in 1697. From 1709 he was based in Florence, where he initiated a 40-year apostolate of missions, combining preaching, Lenten courses, retreats and the promotion of devotions, in particular the Way of the Cross. From 1730 he conducted similar missions in Rome, Umbria, Genoa and the Marches. He was employed (unsuccessfully) by Pope **Benedict XIV** as an emissary in a political dispute between the feuding Corsicans and their overlord in Genoa. Leonard is buried in S. Bonaventura al Palatino in Rome; he was canonized in 1867 and declared patron of popular missionaries in 1923. Feast day 26 November.

Leonardi, John Saint and founder, born near Lucca, Italy, *c*.1541, died Rome, 9 October 1609. After practising for a time as a pharmacist in

Lucca, he was ordained priest in 1572 and became a fervent reformer dedicated to combating Protestantism and promoting the Counter-Reformation. In 1574 he founded the Order of Clerks Regular of the Mother of God, which received episcopal sanction in 1583 and papal approval in 1595. He was prominent in charitable works and initiated the Confraternity of Christian Doctrine, which encouraged the training of laymen in the Church. Leonardi was supported by St Philip **Neri**, and he co-founded at Rome the Colegio Urbano, which, under the charge of the Congregation for the Propagation of the Faith, still trains priests for the foreign missions. The mother-church of the Clerks Regular is Sta Maria Campitelli in Rome, where Leonardi's relics are kept. He was canonized in 1938. Feast day 9 October.

Leonardo da Vinci   Polymath, born Vinci, Italy, 15 April 1452, died Cloux, France, 2 May 1519. The illegitimate son of a Florentine notary and a peasant woman, he studied painting in Florence until 1482, and in 1483 moved to Milan, where he produced many of his artistic masterpieces. From 1499 until his death he led a somewhat nomadic existence during which he concentrated on scientific speculations and experimentation. Leonardo's many achievements are so famous that a further description of them is unnecessary. He broke new ground by infusing his paintings with an expressiveness and sense of movement absent from the static representation typical of earlier artists. This is probably seen at its finest in the *Last Supper*, which is also a powerful illustration of the way in which Leonardo's style radically altered the portrayal of religious subjects.

Leonides of Alexandria   Saint, scholar, father of **Origen**, martyr, born *c*.155, died 202. Leonides taught his young son the Scriptures and encouraged the brilliance of the future theologian. Later, as **Eusebius** writes, he was condemned to death by Lactus, the prefect of Egypt, during the persecution of Christians under Septimius Severus. His property was confiscated and he was beheaded. Feast day 22 April.

Leonin (Leoninus)   Composer, possibly Magister Leoninus, fl. Paris, *c*.1163–1201. A composer at Notre Dame in Paris he is described as 'avant garde', the first polyphonist to compose music of great style and beauty; it was performed firstly in Notre Dame and, thereafter, elsewhere in Europe. According to the thirteenth-century theorist Anonymous IV, Leonin compiled the celebrated *Magnus liber organi*, which contained two-part settings of the solo portions of the graduals, alleluias and responsories for all the principal feasts of the Church year.

Leonius   Blessed, Benedictine abbot and reformer, died 26 October 1163. Educated by Benedictines, he became a monk at the age of 22 and embraced the ideals of the Cluniac reform. He served as prior of Hesdin until being made abbot of Lobbes in 1131. He served in that office until being elected abbot of Saint-Bertin in 1137, where he established a school. A friend of St **Bernard of Clairvaux**, he took part in the Second Crusade.

Leontius Armenius (Ghevod)   Priest, historian, died *c*.790. An Armenian, Leontius wrote a lengthy *History of the Apparitions of Muhammad*, to please Prince Sciabuh Bagratum. This history covered the period 632–774 quickly, then detailed the Arab invasion of Armenia till 790. The history is the only record of the period 662–789 in Armenia, and is particularly valuable as the author was an eyewitness.

Leontius of Byzantium   Theologian, died Constantinople 543. Little is known about his life. In all probability he was the Palestinian monk and supporter of the teachings of **Origen** who arrived in Constantinople in 531. There he engaged for many years in theological discussions with the anti-Chalcedonians, attending the synod of 536. He himself always remained a staunch defender of the Chalcedonian Christological definition and laid down his opinions in several tractates. In his theology Leontius was especially influenced by the Cappadocians and by Neoplatonic commentaries on Aristotle.

Leontius of Fréjus   Bishop of Fréjus, born probably at Nîmes, late 300s, died Fréjus, probably *c*.433–8. The establishment of the monastery of Lérins by **Honoratus** is the most important known event during the episcopate of Leontius; the relationship between the monastery and the bishop was cordial, and the independence of Lérins was assured by the Third Council of Arles, which signalled the beginning of the giving of many privileges to monasteries. In 445, Pope **Leo I** quarrelled with Honoratus, stripping him of many of his prerogatives, which were given to a successor of Leontius' of the same name. Stories of Leontius preaching to Teutonic tribes in his old age, or of his martyrdom, are unproven.

Leontius of Jerusalem   Monk and polemical theologian; though also living in the first half of the sixth century, he is to be distinguished from his namesake of Byzantium. We do not know anything at all about his life. Two tractates are preserved: *Contra Monophysitas* and *Contra Nestorianos*. He expounds in these writings a theology which is of Chalcedonian inspiration.

Leopardi, Giacomo   Count, scholar, philosopher and poet, born Recanti in the March of Ancona, Italy, 24 June 1798, died of cholera in Naples, 14 June 1837. The son of parents allegedly unsympathetic to his congenital disability, and in spite of increasing physical handicaps, frustrated hopes and emotional disappointments, he transcended all these reversals in his philosophic writings and superb lyrical compositions. By the age of sixteen he had mastered Greek, Latin and Hebrew and in 1825 undertook an edition of the works of Cicero. However, his fame is based on the exceptional quality of his lyric poetry, compared in spirit to that of Shelley. Among Leopardi's best-known poetic works are *Appresamento della morte*, *Diaria d'Amore*, *Cazzoni* and *Ginestra*.

Leopold of Austria   Saint, margrave, born Gars, c.1075, died 15 November 1136. He was educated by St **Altmann of Passau**. Initially loyal to Pope **Innocent II** in the investiture contest, he changed his allegiance to support the Emperor **Henry V**, and he married Agnes, the Emperor's widowed daughter. Of his six sons, two were distinguished: the historian **Otto of Freising** and Archbishop Conrad of Salzburg. Leopold refounded the Canons Regular at Klosterneuburg in 1108, later founding the Cistercian abbey at Heiligenkreuz, and the Benedictine monastery at Kleinmariazell. He renounced his claim to the German throne in 1125, and is buried at Klosterneuburg. Canonized

in 1485, he was declared national patron of Austria in 1663. Feast day 15 November, a national holiday in Austria.

Leopold of Gaiche   Blessed, born Gaiche, 1732, died Monteluco, 2 April 1815. He became a Franciscan in 1751, was ordained in 1757 and taught philosophy and theology. In 1768 he began 47 years of missionary activity in Umbria and the Papal States. When Napoleon seized the Papal States and suppressed religious houses, Leopold withdrew to a hut. He was imprisoned briefly for his refusal to take an oath to the new regime. After Napoleon's fall in 1814, Leopold withdrew to Monteluco and spent his last months in prayer. He wrote *Diario delle S. Missioni*.

Lépicier, Alexis   Cardinal, theologian, born Vaucouleurs, France, 28 February 1863, died Rome, 20 May 1936. At the age of 29 he was appointed by **Leo XIII** to the chair of dogmatic theology left vacant by his former professor, Francesco Satolli, who had been appointed first apostolic delegate to the United States. He held the post for 21 years. His prodigious theological work culminated in his *Institutiones theologicae dogmaticae ad textum S. Thomae concinnatae*. In December 1927 **Pius XI** made him a cardinal and the following year he became prefect of the Congregation of Religious.

Lepidi, Alberto   Dominican philosopher and theologian, born Popoli, 1838, died Rome, 1922. He taught theology in the spirit of **Thomas Aquinas** at Flavigny, 1870, Louvain, 1874, and Rome, 1855. His lectures were a curious mixture of Aristotelian Thomism and Graeco-Christian mysticism. His *Examen philosophico-theologicum de ontologismo* (Louvain, 1874) clearly asserts the teaching of St Thomas on the origin of ideas. Lepidi is remembered as a prominent contributor to the neo-Scholastic movement for his work in reorganizing the course of theological studies for the Dominicans, especially in the French province.

Lepkyi, Bodhan   Ukrainian poet and writer, born Krehulets', 9 November 1872, died Cracow, 21 July 1941. He was son of the priest-writer Marko Murawa. At the outbreak of World War II he was vacationing in the Ukraine but escaped the Russian occupation by fleeing to Cracow, where he died shortly after. His literary activity began in 1894. His earliest works appeared in the periodicals *Dilo* and *Zirka*. He often wrote about the destruction of his native land and the dangers of Communism. His most noteworthy work is his six-volume trilogy *Mazepa* (1926).

Le Plat (Jodocus) Canonist, born Malines (Belgium), 18 November 1732, died Koblenz, Germany, 6 August 1810. He studied law at Louvain, obtaining his first chair, in Roman law, in 1768, and a second, in canon law, in 1776. He achieved prominence by opposing the theory of the Pauline privilege and became a supporter of Josephinism, a concept with Austrian origins which advocated reform of Church–State relations. He was forced to flee to The Netherlands, where he was welcomed by the Jansenists, with whom he collaborated in writing *Nouvelles ecclesiastiques*. He was appointed rector of the School of Canon Law in 1806 and remained there to his death.

Le Quien, Michel Dominican theologian and historian of the Eastern Church, born Boulogne, France, 8 October 1661, died Paris, 12 March 1773. He was educated at Plessis College, Paris, entering the Order at the age of twenty, and spending most of his adult life at St-Honoré. He mastered Arabic, Hebrew and Greek, and in 1690 published *Defense du texte hébreu et de la version Vulgate*. He vigorously opposed the validity of Anglican Orders, entering into a long controversy with P. Le Courager, 1725–31. Le Quien's valuable work entitled *Oriens Christianus*, a synthesis of the history of Oriental patriarchates and bishoprics before and after the Crusades, was published posthumously (3 vols, Paris, 1740).

Lercaro, Giacomo Cardinal, participant in Vatican II, born Quinto al Mare, 28 October 1891, died Bologna, 18 October 1976. He was created cardinal-priest, 12 January 1953; and received the red hat and title of S. Maria in Traspontina, 15 January 1953. Lercaro participated in the conclave of 1958, attended Vatican Council II and was a member of the Board of Presidency, 1963–5. He participated in the conclave of 1963; was president of the 'Consilium' for liturgical reform, 1966–8; attended the first Ordinary Assembly of the World Synod of Bishops, Vatican City, 29 September to 29 October 1967. He resigned pastoral government of the Archdiocese of Bologna on 12 February 1968. He was also papal legate to 39th International Eucharistic Congress, in Bogotá, Colombia, 27 August 1968.

Lercher, Ludwig Jesuit theologian, born Hall, Australia, 30 June 1864, died Innsbruck, 5 August 1937. He became a Jesuit in 1891 and professor of theology at the University of Innsbruck in 1899. Through his lectures and writings he exercised a great influence over clergy reform. His main work was *Institutiones theologicae dogmaticae* (Innsbruck, 1924–34), which combines a solid presentation of theology with an emphasis on its ascetical relevance.

Leroquais, Victor Martial Roman Catholic priest and specialist in liturgical manuscripts, born Saint-Germain-de-Tallevende, 7 September 1875, died Paris, 1 March 1946. Ordained at Paris on 9 June 1900, he became assistant pastor at Lisieux and later pastor at Bény-sur-Mer, 1906–12. At his own expense he published a series of inventories of liturgical books found in French public libraries: *Les Bréviaires manuscripts des bibliothèques de France* (1934) and *Les Pontificaux manuscripts des bibliothèques de France* (1937). He gave courses at the École Practique des Hautes Études and a series of lectures at the École des Chartres.

Le Roy, Eduoard French Catholic philosopher and mathematician, born Paris, 18 June 1870, died Paris, 1 November 1954. Le Roy developed the evolutionary philosophy of Henri **Bergson** in the direction of a Christian 'psychistic' idealism and succeeded to Bergson's chair at the Collège de France in 1921. In holding that theoretical science is only a system of symbols and not a penetration into ultimate reality, he opposed philosophies that tended to substitute abstract concepts for an intuition of life. His phenomenology of evolution bears many resemblances to the thought of his friend Pierre **Teilhard de Chardin**.

Le Saux, Henri French Benedictine priest and pioneer of inter-religious dialogue, born St-Briac, 30 August 1910, died Indore, India, 7 December 1973. He entered the Benedictines at Kergonan in 1929, but soon developed a desire to live his monastic vocation in India. When he learned that, in 1939, another French priest, Jules **Monchanin**, had already gone to India, in 1948 he asked, and was given, permission to join him, and together they founded an ashram at Shantivanam in Tamil Nadu, Le Saux taking the name 'Swami Abhishiktananda'. In the early 1960s he built a small ashram beside the Ganges at Uttarkashi, and settled there permanently in 1968. His spirituality was much influenced by Indian holy men. His major work was *Sagesse hindoue mystique chrétienne* (1965). The English translation, *Saccidananda* (Delhi, 1974), perhaps more accurately reflected Le Saux's beliefs.

Lescot, Pierre Canon of Notre Dame, Paris, and architect, born possibly at Paris, *c.*1515, died there, 10 September 1578. His activities are unrecorded before 1544 and after 1559 but it is known that he collaborated with the sculptor Jean Goujon, who may have influenced Lescot's architectural style. His first known work was the screen at St Germain l'Auxernois, built 1541–4 but dismantled in 1745. His reputation rests on the rebuilding of the Louvre, which occupied his time from 1546 until his death. He is credited with erecting the south-west corner of the square court of the palace, considered one of the most perfect examples of French Renaissance style. Apart from his canonry he received the title of Counsellor to the Kings, **Francis I**, Henry II, Francis II and Charles IX.

Le Senne, René French philosopher, born Elbeuf-sur-Seine, 8 July 1882, died Paris, 1 October 1954. With Louis **Lavelle** he established the collection *Philosophie de l'Esprit* in 1934. He also directed the *Logos* and *Caractères* collections of the Presses Universitaires de France and presided at the International Institute of Philosophy in 1952 and 1953. Le Senne's vision of the world is harsher than that of Lavelle. He refused to give privilege to any particular value, or even charity. God alone is the perfectly determining and indeterminable value for all determined values. Even in future life, he seemed to await a sort of perpetual purgatory.

Lessius, Leonardus Flemish Jesuit and theologian, born Brecht, 1 October 1554, died Louvain, 15 January 1623. After studies in Louvain, Douai, Liège and Rome he returned in 1584 to Flanders to start teaching at the Jesuit house of studies in Louvain. Lessius was an original thinker and an admired teacher, which led to tensions within the theological faculty (for example, about the theology of grace). From 1601 he was relieved from teaching and published several important studies. *De iustitia et iure* on economico-ethical questions, addressing the needs of his time, is the most important. Near the end of his life he turned to asceticism and mysticism.

Lestonnac, Jeanne de Saint, French religious foundress, born Bordeaux, 1556, died there, 2 February 1640. From a strongly Catholic background, which included her uncle, Michel de **Montaigne**, Jeanne devoted herself to works of charity in Bordeaux and eventually, in 1607, founded the Order of Notre Dame (Company of Mary), as a counterpart to the Society of Jesus, for the education of young girls. She remained superior of the congregation until 1622, when, a victim of malicious gossip, she lost her position; but she obtained redress two years later. Jeanne devoted her remaining years to her Company, and **Pius XII** canonized her in 1949. Feast day 2 February.

Lesueur, Elisabeth French spiritual writer, born Paris, 16 October 1866, died 3 May 1914. She was educated privately in Paris and in 1889 was married to Dr Felix Lesueur, who lost his faith to atheism but, contrary to his expectations, it increased the faith of his wife, who embarked on an ascetic life, adopting as her motto 'Each soul that perfects itself, perfects the world'. She maintained habits of gentleness, silence and believing in the influence of the individual encounter. Her *Journal* was published posthumously in 1917, the same year in which her husband was reconciled to the Church, and at the age of 69 he was ordained as a Dominican priest.

Le Tellier, Charles Maurice Roman Catholic archbishop, born Turin, 1643, died Rheims, 22 February 1710. Destined from childhood for an ecclesiastical career, from his ordination onwards he developed pronounced Gallican opinions. In 1668, at the age of 25, he was nominated coadjutor to François Barberini, archbishop of Rheims, whom he succeeded in 1671. In 1679 he became a councillor of state, and in 1688 a Commander of the Order of the Holy Spirit. In his writings he opposed the Jesuits, Molonists and Jansenists, and his contemporaries described his manner as 'haughty'. He bequeathed his renowned library of 50,000 volumes to the abbey of Ste-Geneviève.

Le Tellier, Michel Jesuit, theologian and confessor to King **Louis XIV** of France, born near Vire, Normandy, 16 December 1643, died La Flèche, 2 September 1719. He entered the Society of Jesus in 1661 and for 28 years taught humanities, philosophy and biblical exegesis at Louis-le-Grand in Paris, becoming rector of the college and Jesuit provincial. In 1708 he was chosen as the king's confessor and he influenced the monarch to close the Jansenist enclave at Port-Royal. Le Tellier's writings were strongly anti-Jansenist in tone and he moved towards the condemnation of Pasquier **Quesnel**'s *Reflexions morales*. In support of his own Order he defended the Jesuit practices of allowing Confucian rites to their converts in China.

Leuren, Peter German Jesuit canonist, born Cologne, 13 May 1646, died Coblenz, 16 November 1723. Named rector of the Society's college at Coblenz. Leuren's writings on canon law include *Forum beneficiale*, a comprehensive study on the law of benefices; *Vicarius episcopalis*, a treatise on the practical problems of the vicar general; and *Forum ecclesiasticum*, a general presentation of canon law according to the teachings of ancient and modern authors.

Leutred (Leufred, Leufridus, Leufroy) Saint, monk, abbot, died 738. Born near Évreux, France, Leutred was educated locally, and at Condat and Chartres. For a time he taught boys, then became a hermit and later a monk under the Irish Sidonius of Rouen. Eventually he returned home and built the monastery of La-Saint-Croix-Saint-Ouen, later called La-Saint-Croix-Saint-Leufroy, where he served until his death. Feast day 21 June.

Levadoux, Michael French Sulpician missionary, born Auvergne, 1 April 1746, died Puy, 13 January 1815. Levadoux went to Baltimore in 1791 to assist in the foundation of the first seminary of the Society of Saint-Sulpice in America; he subse-

quently worked in Illinois among the Indians, in the French settlements at Cahokia, Kaskaskia and Prairie du Rocher, and later in Detroit as pastor of St Anne's parish. He left there in 1802 because of ill health and returned to France in 1803.

Le Vacher, Jean Roman Catholic missionary, French consul and martyr, born Ecouen, France, 15 March 1619, died Algiers, 28 July 1683. He was ordained in 1647 in the Congregation of the Missions and in the same year was sent to Tunis by St **Vincent de Paul** as missionary to the Christian slaves. From 1648 to 1653 and again from 1657 to 1666 he acted as French consul in Tunis as well as holding apostolic appointments there and in Carthage. On his return to Algiers from France in 1668 he was appointed vicar apostolic in Algiers, Tripoli, Tunis and Morocco. When a French military force invaded Algiers in 1683 he refused to renounce his faith and was cruelly martyred. The cause for his beatification was introduced in 1923.

Leven, Stephen A. American Roman Catholic bishop, born Blackwell, Oklahoma, 30 April 1905, died Oklahoma, 29 June 1983. Leven studied at a seminary in Louvain, visited London, where he participated in the preaching apostolate of the Catholic Evidence Guild, and adapted their methods to a street-preaching ministry in Oklahoma, describing it as 'the way St Paul converted the Gentiles'. Having become auxiliary bishop in San Antonio, Texas, he attended Vatican Council II, and then became bishop of San Angelo in 1969, where he remained until his resignation in 1979.

Levi, Peter Chad Tigar English Roman Catholic poet and translator, born Ruislip, Middlesex, 16 May 1931, died London, 1 February 2000. Born into a Jewish family who had converted to Roman Catholicism, he joined the Society of Jesus and was educated at Heythrop College and at Campion Hall, Oxford. Levi published several volumes of poetry, including *Collected Poems, 1955–1975*. A man of catholic interests and eclectic learning, his poems mingle imagery and themes from classical antiquity, British history and pre-history, Christianity and domestic life. Levi left the Jesuits in 1977 to marry, lectured at Christ Church, Oxford, and wrote a volume of autobiography, *The Flutes of*

Autumn (1983). He was elected professor of poetry at Oxford in 1984.

Lewis, Clive Staples   Professor of literature, Christian apologist and novelist, born Belfast, 29 November 1898, died Oxford, 22 November 1963. He was educated at Malvern and Oxford, staying on to teach at Oxford as a fellow of Magdalen College until 1954, when he became professor of medieval and Renaissance English at Cambridge. He had been an agnostic, but gradually and rather reluctantly he converted to Christianity, a process he described in *A Pilgrim's Regress* (1933). Although he wrote a number of important works of literary criticism he is better known for his religious and ethical works, particularly perhaps *The Screwtape Letters* (1942), a series of letters from a senior devil to his nephew. There is also a clear religious theme in his science fiction, and in the children's books for which he is best known, such as *The Lion, the Witch and the Wardrobe*.

Lewis, David   Saint, Welsh Jesuit martyr, born Monmouthshire, 1617, died Usk, 27 August 1679. Brought up a Protestant, Lewis became a Catholic in Paris, in 1632, studied at the English College, Rome, joined the Society of Jesus in 1644, and returned to South Wales in 1648, where he served as parish priest for 28 years. During the Titus **Oates** plot, his apostate servant, James, and his wife betrayed Lewis; tried and condemned for his priesthood and hanged, drawn and quartered, he died at Usk. He was canonized in 1970, among the **Forty Martyrs of England and Wales**. Feast day 27 August.

Lewis, Edwin   English-born Anglican theologian in America, born Newbury, 18 April 1881, died Morristown, New Jersey, 28 November 1959. Educated and ordained in Newfoundland, Lewis joined the faculty of Drew Theological Seminary, Madison, New Jersey, where he taught for 35 years. His early writings, namely, *Jesus Christ and the Human Quest*, marked him as a liberal but, influenced by Karl **Barth**, he championed a gospel of revelation, comprehended only in the light of faith, as outlined in *A Christian Manifesto*, *A Philosophy of the Christian Revelation* and *The Creator and the Adversary*. This shift in orientation developed from

intensive Bible study while undertaking his great work as editor of the *Abingdon Bible Commentary*.

Lewis, Frank J.   American Roman Catholic philanthropist, born Chicago, 9 April 1867, died there, 21 December 1960. Lewis made a fortune in building materials and chemicals, and withdrew from the business world at the age of 60 to devote his life to philanthropy. He contributed millions to Catholic charities and educational institutions in Chicago, for which largesse he received several honorary degrees, and knighthoods in the Order of St Gregory, the Order of St Sylvester and the Order of Pius IX, as well as being made a papal count of the Holy Roman Empire.

Leyser, Polycarp   German Lutheran historian, born Wunsdorff, 4 September 1690, died Helmstedt, 7 April 1728. A professor of history and poetry, Leyser published a large number of essays in these fields, and is especially remembered for his *Historia poetarum et poematum medii aevi*, containing selections, most of them for the first time, from some 700 medieval Latin poets, which text has remained a landmark in the history of medieval Latin literature.

Lezana, Juan Bautista de   Spanish Carmelite theologian, born Madrid, 23 November 1586, died Rome, 29 March 1659. Influenced by Michael de la **Fuente**, Lezana lectured on Aristotle and **Thomas Aquinas**; he became a consultor to the Congregations of the Index and of Rites, in Rome, where he lived from 1625 until his death. He wrote a history of the Carmelites, including its 'prehistory', up to 1513: *Annales sacri, prophetici et Eliani Ordinis Beatudine Virginis Mariae de Monte Carmeli . . .*, noted for its important documentation, and an account of the beliefs of the Carmelites about their past.

L'Hôpital, Michel de   French statesman and advocate of religious toleration, born Aigueperse, Auvergne, 1507, died Vignay, 13 March 1573. After studying law at Padua, 1523–9, he joined his father in Rome until 1534 when he returned to France to practise law. In 1547–8 he represented Henry II at the Council of Trent, some of whose acts he opposed because they conflicted with the established rights of the French Church vis-à-vis the

Pope. In 1554 he became superintendent of finances and in 1560 **Catherine de' Medici** appointed him Chancellor of France. In 1561 he successfully appealed to the States General for greater toleration for the Huguenots, but in 1562 the soldiers of the duc de Guise massacred a number of them and in protest L'Hôpital withdrew to Vignay. He returned to Paris in 1563 after the promulgation of an edict protecting the rights of Huguenots. The cardinal of Lorraine accused him of supporting them, and Catherine accused him of increasing religious strife, so he largely retired from public life in 1568. Shocked by the massacre of St Bartholomew's Day, 1572, thought to have been instigated by Catherine, he finally had to resign the Chancellorship in 1573.

Liberatore, Matteo   Italian Jesuit philosopher, born Salerno, 14 August 1810, died Rome, 18 October 1892. Liberatore passed from eclecticism to Thomism about 1850, and used the epistemology of St **Thomas Aquinas** to refute the theories of **Locke**, **Kant** and especially of Antonio **Rosmini-Serbati**; he made a genuine contribution to the understanding of the natural law and to the restoration of Thomism in Italy. His *Institutiones philosophicae*, which went through eleven editions, reflects his own intellectual conversion to St Thomas's thought. He helped to found the influential *Civiltà cattolica* in 1850, and edited the periodical until his death.

Liberatus of Carthage   Archdeacon, historian, died *c.*567. In 535, as spokesman for the African Churches, Liberatus was sent as legate, along with 217 bishops, to Rome and Pope **Agapetus I**, with the mission to consult him about several questions. In following years Liberatus again acted as ambassador in Church matters, especially in regard to and opposition of **Justinian**'s edict against the Three Chapters (544). To 'rest his mind' from these ecclesiastical journeys, Liberatus used his spare time to write a brief, but important, history of two heretical movements, the Monophysites and the Nestorians (*A Short Account of the Affair of the Nestorians and Eutychians*).

Liberius   Pope, died 366. His pontificate (17 May 352 to 24 September 366) was thoroughly coloured by the Arian controversy. He supported **Athana**sius against the Arian-minded Emperor **Constantius II** but could not prevent Athanasius' condemnation in Arles (353) and Milan (355). Himself exiled to Thrace, he gave in, subscribed to the Creed of Sirmium and returned to Rome, where he successfully faced the Antipope Felix II. After the death of Constantius he took up again the defence of the Nicene Creed, but to little avail. He built the Basilica Liberiana (the present S. Maria Maggiore).

Libermann, Francis Mary   French Roman Catholic priest, founder, born Saverne, Alsace, 12 April 1804, died Paris, 2 February 1852. Born into a Jewish family, his father a rabbi, Jacob studied the Talmud and Hebrew at Metz and during this time he read a copy of the Gospels in Hebrew. Three of his brothers had already become Catholics and Jacob followed suit. He was baptized in Paris in 1826 and took his Christian names. In 1827 he entered the seminary of St-Sulpice but was taken ill and went to recover and study at Issy, where, with Le Vavasseur and Tisserand, he developed the idea of forming a congregation with an apostolate to former slaves. He went to Rome and gained approval, returned and was ordained in Amiens in 1841 and a few months later the novitiate for the Congregation of the Immaculate Heart of Mary opened in La Neuville. The Congregation flourished and they were soon invited to begin their work in Mauritius, Haiti and especially in Africa. In 1848 they joined with the earlier formed Congregation of the Holy Ghost, who had a similar apostolate, and Libermann became superior general of the combined congregation. His writings include a two-volume *Lettres spirituelles, Écrits spirituels* and *Commentaire sur l'Évangile de Saint-Jean*.

Liccio, John   Blessed, Italian Dominican preacher, born Càccamo, *c.*1426, died there, 1511. Influenced by Pietro Geremia, John joined the Order as an adolescent in the monastery of Santa Zita in Palermo, founded the monastery of the Holy Spirit in Polizzi in 1469, and that of Càccamo in 1487. Throughout his life, Liccio demonstrated a spirit of profound humility and total dedication to the poor. Miracles were associated with him during his life and during the transfer of his relics, which led to his beatification by **Benedict XIV** in 1753. Feast day 14 November.

Licinius (Lesin) Saint and bishop of Anjou, born c.540, died c.616. As a cousin of King Clotaire I of Neustria, Licinius became a courtier at the age of twenty, and was made count of Anjou by King Chilperic. However, when his fiancée contracted leprosy, he decided to become a monk. Later, in 586, he was elected bishop of Anjou and spent the remainder of his life in the ministry to his diocese. Licinius is known for his compassion for the poor and is credited with miracles. Feast day 13 February.

Lidanus Saint, Benedictine abbot and monastic founder, born Antina, Sicily, c.1026, died Sezze, Italy, 1118. Lidanus probably began his monastic career at Monte Cassino, which he is said to have entered at an early age. He later founded and headed the monastery of St Cecilia at Sezze, where he is remembered for his help in draining the Pontine marshes and where his relics are still venerated. Feast day 2 July in Sezze and 27 April and 18 July elsewhere.

Liddell, Eric Church of Scotland missionary, and athlete, born Tientsin, China, 1902, died Weihsien, China, 1945. A son of Scottish missionaries, Liddell gained fame as an all-round sportsman while at Edinburgh University. He represented Scotland in both athletics and rugby, and famously won a gold medal in the 400 metres at the 1924 Olympic Games – having changed from his favoured 100 metres which required him to compete on a Sunday. He shared his parents' missionary vocation and in 1925 he returned to China to join the staff of the Anglo-Chinese Christian College. In 1942 he was placed in a Japanese internment camp, winning the respect of all through his Christian character and attentiveness to the needs of other internees. He died from a brain tumour shortly before the camp was liberated.

Lidgett, John Scott English Methodist reformer, born Lewisham, near London, 10 August 1854, died Epsom, 16 June 1953. Ordained a Wesleyan Methodist minister in 1876, Lidgett, noted as a preacher with a passion for social justice, founded the Bermondsey Settlement for the poor in 1891, and remained its warden for 58 years. He edited the *Methodist Times* for eleven years, and later the *Contemporary Review*. He advocated Methodist union and, in 1932, succeeded in bringing together the Wesleyan, the Primitive and the United Methodist Churches in Britain. His publications include *The Idea of God and Social Ideals*, *God and the World* and *Salvation*.

Liégé, Pierre-André French Dominican preacher and theologian, born Coiffy-le-Bas, 22 June 1921, died Paris, 9 February 1976. Liégé succeeded Yves **Congar** at Le Saulchoir in Paris, and taught at the Institut Catholique, where he developed the programme of pastoral theology. He attended Vatican Council II as *peritus* to French bishops, in particular to Paul-Joseph Schmitt of Metz. He published *Adultes dans le Christ*, which stressed the necessity of maturity in faith and the normative value of the adult community, which emphasis he hoped would form the basis for renewal in the Church.

Liénart, Achille French cardinal, born Lille, 7 February 1884, died there, 15 February 1973. Ordained in the Order of St-Sulpice in 1907, Liénart became bishop of Lille in 1928. Dedicated to social justice, he sided with the workers during a bitter strike in 1929, winning Vatican support for the right and duty of Catholics to form labour unions; **Pius XI** appointed him cardinal the following year. An advocate of Catholic Action, he condemned both atheistic materialism and economic liberalism. During the German occupation, he publicly opposed forced labour and assisted victims of Nazi oppression. He founded Ad Lucem, an organization to send Catholics to mission fields, and went to Cameroon in 1947 to inaugurate the enterprise in Africa. Liénart played an important role at Vatican II, where he insisted on the Council's freedom in the choice of discussions; he revised the *Schema on the Sources of Divine Revelation*, and advocated a strong statement on behalf of the Jews. His pastoral work reflected his theological views across the range of issues facing the Church in modern times.

Liendo y Goicoechea, José Antonio Costa Rican Franciscan natural scientist, born Cartago, 3 May 1735, died Guatemala City, 1814. Liendo first taught philosophy at the University of San Carlos de Guatemala, and then *philosophia recentior*, which included optics, geometry, astronomy and geography. In 1780 the government appointed him president of a commission to investigate a cure for smallpox. Elected provincial of the Franciscan province of Guatemala in 1802, he continued to promote pure and applied science, and took an effective interest in scientific projects.

Lietbert of Cambrai-Arras Saint, bishop, born Brabant (Belgium), date unknown, died probably Cambrai (France), 23 June 1076. Lietbert followed his uncle as bishop of Cambrai in 1051 and spent much time defending his flock from the machinations of the local civil authorities. He was briefly exiled from his see by those authorities but returned to lead a pilgrimage to the Holy Land around 1054. He was unable to complete the pilgrimage because of the growing Saracen threat. Feast day 23 June.

Lietzmann, Hans Lutheran NT and patristic scholar and Church historian, born Düsseldorf, 2 March 1875, died Berlin, 25 June 1942. Lietzmann succeeded Adolf von **Harnack** as professor of Church history at Berlin in 1924, having been professor at Jena since 1905. He was one of the editors of the *Handbuch zum Neuen Testament* series of commentaries, to which he himself contributed the volumes on Romans, Corinthians and Galatians. He edited the *Zeitschrift für Neutestamentliche Wissenschaft* from 1920 until his death, and his four-volume *History of the Early Church* remains a standard work. Lietzmann also made significant contributions to patristic studies, such as his important critical edition of the works of **Apollinaris**, *Apollinaris von Laodicea*, published in 1904.

Lightfoot, Joseph Barber Anglican scholar and bishop, born Liverpool, 13 April 1828, died Bournemouth, 21 December 1889. Lightfoot was an outstanding classics and divinity scholar at Cambridge, which led to his appointment as Hulsean professor of divinity in 1861 and Lady Margaret professor in 1875. He wrote three important commentaries – on Galatians, Philippians, and Colossians with Philemon – which are still highly regarded by NT scholars. He also wrote two important studies of the Apostolic Fathers Clement of Rome (**Clement I**) and **Ignatius of Antioch**, and was a member of the NT revision panel for the Revised Version of the Bible. In 1879 he was

appointed bishop of Durham; despite a relative lack of parochial experience he carried out his episcopal duties with an energy and zeal which made him very popular in his diocese, especially among poorer, working-class people, for whom he had a particular concern.

Ligutti, Luigi G. Italian-born Roman Catholic pastor and ecumenist, born Udine, 21 March 1895, died Rome, 28 December 1984. Ligutti emigrated to the USA as a young man, became a priest in Des Moines in 1917, and developed a pastoral philosophy of rural sociology expressed in a work co-written with John Rawe, SJ, *Rural Roads to Security*. Named secretary of the National Catholic Rural Life Conference in 1937, Ligutti joined forces with leaders in the liturgical movement to make Catholics aware of the importance of rural life and its problems. His programme found an echo in other Christian Churches, thus laying the foundation of an ecumenical co-operation. Appointed Vatican observer to the UN Food and Agriculture Organization in 1948, he helped draft **John XXIII**'s *Pacem in terris*. He established *Agrimissio* to assist missionaries in fostering rural values in the Third World.

Lilly, Joseph American biblical scholar, born Cape Girardeau, Missouri, 1 July 1893, died St Louis, 21 March 1952. Ordained a Vincentian in 1918, Lilly taught sacred Scripture at the Catholic University of America, and became secretary of the Catholic Biblical Association in 1942. With James **Kleist**, he published (1954) an English translation of the NT, made direct from the Greek text, known as the Kleist-Lilly version.

Lily, William (Lilly, Lilye) Grammarian and humanist, born Odiham, Hampshire, c.1468, died London, 1522. A graduate of Oxford University, Lily travelled extensively in Europe and the Middle East, where he learned Greek. Returning to England, in 1512 he became the first headmaster of St Paul's School in London. He was possibly the first person to teach Greek in London, and two Latin grammars he produced, *Grammatices rudimenta* (c.1509) and *De octo orationis partium constructione libellus* (1513), formed the basis of *An Introduction of the Eight Parts of Speech*, **Henry VIII**'s official Latin grammar of c.1540. This subsequently became known (inaccurately) as 'Lily's Grammar'. It became the standard Latin textbook for generations of scholars, and provided the exegetical and polemical tools used by both Catholic and Protestant divines in later religious controversies.

Lima e Silva, Luis Alves Duke of Caxias, Brazilian political personality, born Rio de Janeiro, 25 August 1803, died there, 7 May 1880. Lima became marshal of the army in 1866, and fought against Oribe, who tried to dominate Uruguay, and Lopez, the dictator of Paraguay. One of the great leaders of the Conservative party in Brazil, and three times president of the Council of Ministers, he received many honours. Though a member of the Masonic Order, he was an exemplary Catholic and arranged an amnesty for the bishops as the decisive factor in the solution of the religious question.

Linacre, Thomas Physician and classical scholar, born c.1460, died London, 20 October 1524. He received his early education in Greek learning at the cathedral school at Canterbury. He entered Oxford c.1480 and was elected a fellow of All Souls College in 1484. He accompanied his former schoolmaster William Celling when the latter was sent as papal envoy by **Henry VIII**, but Linacre stayed at Bologna, becoming the pupil of Angelo Poliziano or Politian and Valla both there and at Florence, where he was the companion of the sons of **Lorenzo de' Medici**; one of them later elected as Pope **Leo X**. At Padua he graduated in medicine in 1496. At Venice he became the friend of a further group of humanist scholars, especially the celebrated printer Aldus **Manutius**. About 1501 he was called to the English court to tutor Prince Arthur and also appointed King **Henry VIII**'s physician. Linacre was responsible for founding the Royal College of Physicians in 1518. He lectured at Oxford in 1510 and though not ordained priest until 1520 he held several benefices. Linacre was a progenitor of the New Learning; he could number **Erasmus** among his pupils, to whom he taught Greek. He helped **Colet** plan a regime of studies at St Paul's, though Colet could not use the elaborate Latin grammar *Rudimenta Grammatices* that Linacre had composed for the Princess Mary (it was too difficult for the young boys). Linacre founded lectureships at both Oxford and Cam-

bridge; wrote many other grammatical works; his only medical writings were translations of Galen.

Lindsay, Gordon Healer and director of the Christ for the Nations Institute, born 1906, died Dallas (during a worship service), 1 April 1973. As William **Branham**'s manager, he started the *Voice of Healing* magazine in 1948 (later *World-Wide Revival* and *Christ for the Nations*), which reported on a number of healing ministries. He organized conventions of healers and world-wide missions. His institute, for charismatic and Pentecostal theology, was opened in 1970. His 250 books and pamphlets include *The World Today in Prophecy* (1953), *God's Master Key to Success and Prosperity* (1959) and *All About the Gifts of the Spirit* (1962).

Lindworsky, Johannes German Jesuit psychologist, born Frankfurt, 21 January 1875, died Essen, 9 September 1939. During his philosophical studies in Holland, Lindworsky met Joseph **Fröbes**, who introduced him to psychology and prompted his training in the discipline at Bonn and Munich under Oswald Külpe. He successfully propounded a theory of will that integrated experimental with theoretical psychology of thought and volition. His translated works include *Experimental Psychology*, *Theoretical Psychology* and *Training of the Will*.

Line, Anne Saint, English martyr, born Dunmow, late 1560s, hanged Tyburn, London, 27 February 1601. From a Calvinist family, Anne Heigham became a Catholic and married Roger Line, also a convert. After his death in exile in Flanders in 1594, Anne managed a household established in London by John **Gerard**, SJ, as a refuge for priests. When Gerard escaped from the Tower in 1597, she came under suspicion, and moved to another location, but she and others were arrested after Mass in 1601. Tried and executed for harbouring a priest, even though the charge could not be proved, because the celebrant had escaped, Anne was canonized in 1970 as one of the **Forty Martyrs of England and Wales**. Feast day 27 February.

Lingard, John Roman Catholic priest and historian, born Winchester into a Catholic family, 5 February 1771, died Hornby, Lancashire, 17 July 1851. He was educated at the English College, Douai, which he entered in September 1782. He was a particularly brilliant student, and was retained to teach philosophy. He began theology there in 1792, but left for England as a result of the French Revolution and took up residence at Crook Hall, Durham, where he was in charge of the refugees from Douai. He was ordained in 1795 and, when Ushaw College was opened in 1808, became its vice-president. In 1811, when a new president was appointed to Ushaw, he was offered a comparable position at Maynooth, which he refused, and retired to Hornby. His eight-volume *History of England* (1819–30), of which there were five editions before his death, won for him international renown, and even a pension from Queen Victoria. Pope **Pius VII** awarded Lingard the triple degree of doctor of divinity, civil law and canon law, and there is some evidence that he was created cardinal in 1826. Lingard was also a devotional writer of much influence and his *New Version of the Four Gospels*, based on the Greek texts rather than on St **Jerome**'s Vulgate, was much used in the early Victorian era.

Linnaeus, Carolus (Carl von Linné) Swedish botanist, born Råshult, Småland, 23 May 1707, died Uppsala, 10 January 1778. He was the son of a Lutheran pastor, and throughout his life retained his piety. He studied at the Universities of Lund and Uppsala, receiving a degree in medicine from the latter. Always interested in botany, he became a lecturer in that subject at Uppsala in 1730, two years later undertaking a botanical survey of Lapland. His book *Systema naturae* appeared in 1735 and the *Genera Plantarum* two years later. His system for naming plants by organizing them according to their make-up became the standard method for establishing the taxonomy of flowers. He visited England, Holland and France to meet fellow scientists, and on his return to Sweden settled, in 1738, in Stockholm, where he practised as a doctor of medicine, becoming professor of medicine at Uppsala in 1741. The following year he became professor of botany at the same university. In that post he classified not only plants but also animals and even minerals, publishing numerous books. He was invited by its king to move to Spain in 1755, which he declined. He was ennobled in 1761.

Linus Saint, regarded as the first bishop of Rome after the Apostles Peter and Paul and conventionally given the dates *c.*68–*c.*78 for his pontificate. Nothing is really known with certainty about Linus. An early Christian by this name sends greetings, possibly from Rome, in 2 Timothy 4: 21. **Irenaeus** and **Eusebius of Caesarea** both mention him as bishop. Feast day 23 September.

Lioba (Leoba, Liobgytha) Saint and abbess, born Wessex, England, *c.*700, died near Mainz, 780. A nun and relative of **Boniface**, Lioba corresponded with the missionary bishop. When Boniface in 748 wrote to ask for nuns to help him in Germany, 30 were sent, including Lioba, whom he made abbess at Bischofsheim in Mainz. The Life written by Rudolf of Fulda 50 years after Lioba's death on the testimony of four of her companions paints a charming picture of the abbess's wisdom, zeal and holiness, and of her nuns, required to learn Latin, and industrious in the scriptorium, the kitchen, the bakery, the brewery, the garden, and in prayer. Feast day 28 September.

Lippi, Filippo Renaissance painter and one-time Carmelite friar, born Florence, *c.*1406, died Spoleto, 9 October 1469. He was orphaned when only two, and placed in a Carmelite house near Florence, and took vows as a Carmelite in 1420, though his subsequent behaviour demonstrated that he was wholly unsuited to the life of a member of a religious order. He was released from his vows by Pope **Pius II** and allowed to marry – though by that time he was already the father of Filippino Lippi (born in 1458). His artistic talents were recognized and he received many orders for his work from Cosimo de' **Medici**, among others. His principal works include *Coronation of the Blessed Virgin*, painted for the cathedral of Spoleto (1441), and *Vision of St Bernard* (1447). He is buried in Spoleto Cathedral.

Lippomano, Luigi (Aloysius Lippomanus) Italian bishop, born Venice, 1500, died Rome, 15 August 1559. One of the presidents of the Council of Trent, Lippomano became bishop of Bergamo in 1538. **Paul IV** sent him as nuncio to the Imperial Diet at Augsburg in 1555, and then to Poland, where he supported the resistance to Protestant incursions there. His writings were essentially apologetic and of a popular nature, the best-known being the hagiographic anthology *Sanctorum priscorum patrum vitae . . .*

Lipsius, Justus Flemish moral theorist, humanist and classical scholar, born Overijse, near Brussels, 18 October 1547, died Louvain, Brabant, 23/24 March 1606. Successively he was appointed to chairs at Jena, Leiden and Louvain. He became a leading editor of Latin texts, and edited Tacitus and Seneca. Lipsius regarded ancient philosophy not just as history, but as a guide to practical morality.

Lipsius, Richard Adelbert Liberal Protestant theologian, born Gera, Germany, 14 February 1830, died Jena, 19 August 1892. He studied at the University of Leipzig, and stayed on to teach there, becoming a professor in 1859. Two years later he moved to Vienna, then in 1865 to Kiel, where he was attacked by the Lutheran bishop for his liberal views. He was made professor of systematic theology at Jena in 1871 and held the post until his death. He wrote a number of works on the interpretation of early apocryphal literature. These include *Die Apokryphen, Apostelgeschichten und Apostellegenden* (4 vols, 1883–90). He also researched into early papal history and concluded that St Peter was never in Rome. He was a liberal in his theology and his systematic works include *Philosophie und Religion* (1885). He also published a commentary on Galatians, Romans and Philippians (1891).

Lisboa, Antonio Francisco (Alejadinho) Brazilian sculptor and architect, born Villa Rica, Brazil, 9 August 1738, died Mariana, 18 November 1814. His nickname 'Alejadinho' means little cripple. He was of mixed Negro/Portuguese origin. He designed and decorated churches, e.g. at Congonhas Do Campo and Oure Preto.

Lisboa, Cristovão de Portuguese Franciscan missionary, born Lisbon, c.1590, died convent of St Anthony de Curral, 19 April 1652. Sent to Brazil with eighteen friars by King John IV after 1621, Lisboa, who had quasi-episcopal authority, acted as first *custos* of the Franciscan vice-province of Maranhão-Pará, and became the foremost champion of the rights of Indians in the area, though he had little success in enforcing the *aldeiamento* laws on their behalf, especially in Pará. He returned to Portugal in 1636 in broken health.

Liszt, Franz Hungarian composer and pianist, born Raiding, Hungary, 22 October 1811, died Bayreuth, 31 July 1886. An infant prodigy as a pianist, he was sent to study in Vienna, then to play and study in other European cities, eventually settling in Paris in 1823. In 1848, after many travels, he went to Weimar to direct opera. He resigned the appointment in 1861 and returned to travelling Europe. In 1865, despite two liaisons and three children, he received minor orders in the Roman Catholic Church. His vision to 'unite the theatre and the church' was never achieved, as it was the result of his romantic, imaginative fantasy rather than a response to liturgical priorities in the Christian Church. His visionary masterpieces in the field of religious music include a *Prelude and Fugue* on the initials B A C H for organ, and a choral *Stations of the Cross*, the latter rarely performed until this century. Other works include *The Legend of St Elizabeth, Christus* and *Hungarian Coronation Mass.*

Litta, Alfonso Milanese cardinal, born Milan, 1608, died Rome, 28 August 1679. From a noble family, Litta became archbishop of Milan in 1652; a vigorous administrator, he corrected the abuses of his clergy, and defended the rights of the Church against the king of Spain.

Litta, Lorenzo Milanese cardinal, born Milan, 23 February 1756, died Monteflavio, 1 May 1820. From the same family as Cardinal Alfonso **Litta**, Lorenzo became a titular archbishop in 1793, and went to St Petersburg as papal legate in 1796. He influenced Tsar Paul to restore the Basilian Order as well as Church property confiscated by **Catherine II**. Forced to leave Russia in 1799, Lorenzo returned to Rome, where he became a cardinal and papal treasurer. Napoleon exiled him, 1809–14, when he refused to attend Bonaparte's second marriage; during this period he wrote *Lettres diverses*, refuting the Gallician Articles of 1682.

Little, Andrew George English historian, born Manchester, 10 October 1863, died Sevenoaks, Kent, 22 October 1945. Having gained extensive knowledge of Franciscan MSS, Little produced the famous *Grey Friars in Oxford* (1892), and became a fellow of the British Academy. He taught history at the University College of South Wales at Cardiff from 1892 – he was made a professor in 1898 – and palaeography at Manchester, and founded the British Society of Franciscan Studies, remaining its general editor until its demise in 1937. He retired from his post at Cardiff in 1901 because of ill health, and spent the rest of his life as an independent scholar. His *Initia operum latinorum* (1904) is an essential reference for MSS of the thirteenth, fourteenth and fifteenth centuries.

Litz, Damian German-born educator and Marist, born Eschenbach, 15 August 1822, died San Antonio, Texas, 24 February 1903. Litz entered the Society of Mary in France in 1844, and volunteered to pioneer their educational work in America. For more than 50 years he founded and organized schools in the principal cities of the USA, conducted by his congregation. In addition he wrote a weekly column for German Catholics in the *Volkszeitung* of Baltimore, which the press in other cities, Cincinnati, Philadelphia and San Antonio, carried under the title 'Unter Uns'.

Liutbirg Saint, German anchoress, date and place of birth unknown, died *c*.880. Little is known of Liutbirg's early life, but she was enclosed, *c*.824, by Bishop Thiatgrim of Halberstadt in a hermitage near the church at Wendhausen. She there instructed young girls in Church music and handicrafts, and offered her prayers and counsel to those who sought them, among whom were Bishop **Haymo of Halberstadt** and Bishop **Ansgar** of Bremen. Feast day 28 February.

Liutprand of Cremona (Liudprand) Bishop and historian, born northern Italy, *c*.920, died 972. He came from a distinguished family, was educated at the court of Pavia and became a deacon of the cathedral. He went as ambassador for Berengar II, for whom he was chancellor, to the Emperor **Constantine VII** Porphyrogenitus in 949. He learned Greek and familiarized himself with the history of the Byzantine Empire. After his return he quarrelled with Berengar and went to the court of **Otto I** of Germany and in 961 when Otto became king of Lombardy he made Liutprand bishop of Cremona. He acted on several occasions

as ambassador for Otto after he had become Emperor, and took part in 963 in the assembly in Rome which deposed Pope **John XII** and later in the election of **John XIII**. In 968 he went as ambassador to Constantinople for Otto, after his invasion of Byzantine territory in Southern Italy. Liutprand's writings include *Relatio de legatione Constantinopolitana ad Nicephorum Phocan*, an account of his mission in 968; and the *Antapodosis sive Res per Europam gestae*, dealing with events from 887 to 950, and the *Historia Ottonis*, taking the story from 960 to 964, are among the main sources for the history of Italy at this time.

Liutwin of Trier Saint, bishop, died Rheims, 29 September *c*.717–22. Liutwin, of a Frankish noble family, founded the monastery of Mettlach in 690. In 705, after the death of his uncle Basinus, he became bishop of Trier. Later, perhaps because of the generosity of **Charles Martel**, he also became bishop of Rheims and Léon. Luitwin was buried in his monastery of Mettlach; his son Milo became bishop of Trier and Rheims. Feast day 29 September.

Livarius of Metz (Livier) Saint, martyr, date and place of birth and death unknown. A twelfth-century legend has it that Livarius was martyred by the Huns at Marsal, south of Metz, in 451, but if there is any historical basis to the legend he is more likely to have been a martyr in the Hungarian incursions of the ninth or tenth centuries. His relics were removed in the tenth century to the abbey of Saint-Vincent in Metz, and thence to church of St-Polyeucte in Metz, now the church of St Livarius. Feast day 17 July.

Livingstone, David Scottish missionary and explorer, born Blantyre, 19 March 1813, died village of Ilala, Zambia, 1 May 1873. He came from a very poor, but devout, family and had to work in a cotton factory from the age of ten. He was determined to become a missionary, and in 1836 went to Glasgow to undertake both a study of theology and some courses in medicine. Two years later he joined the London Missionary Society, and in 1840 went to the Cape of Good Hope. There he worked in what later became Bechuanaland but gradually moved north into the continent, discovering Lake Ngami and the Victoria Falls. He returned to England in 1856, but two years later went back to Africa under the auspices of the government to explore the Zambezi River, encountering as he did so Portuguese slave traders, of whom he gave an account in *The Zambesi and its Tributaries* (1865). He was in England 1864–5, but returned to Africa at the request of the Royal Geographical Society to settle a dispute about the source of the Nile. He reached the Congo, which he believed to be the Nile, but was taken seriously ill. He was found at the village of Ujiji by Henry Morton Stanley, sent by the *New York Herald* to locate him. He died near Lake Bangweulu, which he had discovered, and his body was brought back to be buried in Westminster Abbey.

Lizárraga, Reginaldo de   Spanish Dominican missionary, born Medellín, Spain, 1539, died Asunción, Paraguay, November 1609. Taken by his parents to the New World, Lizárraga entered the Order in Lima. Having been named bishop of Imperial, Chile, in 1599, he could not take up his see, because of an Indian uprising, and moved to the see of Asunción, in Paraguay. The more important of his surviving works is *Descripción y población de las Indias*, referred to by Caillet-Bois as 'a little encyclopaedia of practical knowledge'.

Llorente, Juan Antonio   Spanish historian, born Rincón del Soto, Aragon, 30 March 1756, died Madrid, 5 February 1823. Ordained in 1779, and already strongly influenced by Jansenism and the Enlightenment, Llorente became a commissioner of the Inquisition. He supported Joseph Bonaparte, and when the French occupied Spain, he administered the Church property confiscated by the new regime; the subsequent French defeat forced him to go to France. He wrote many books, of which his chief work is *Histoire critique de l'Inquisition d'Espagne*.

Lloyd, John   Saint, Welsh martyr, born Brecon, 1630(?), hanged Cardiff, 22 July 1679. John Lloyd studied at Valladolid and laboured in the Welsh mission for 25 years until the outbreak of the Titus **Oates** persecution, when he was arrested on the charge of saying Mass, and imprisoned in Cardiff Castle. No other charges were made against him, but their Roman Catholic priesthood sufficed to condemn him and a fellow priest, Philip **Evans**, in

May 1679. He was canonized in 1970 as one of the **Forty Martyrs of England and Wales**. Feast day 22 July.

Lloyd-Jones, David Martyn   Calvinistic Methodist/Congregationalist minister, born Cardiff, 20 December 1899, died Ealing, England, 1 March 1981. Regarded by many as perhaps the greatest preacher of the twentieth century, Lloyd-Jones originally trained as a doctor and was assistant to Lord Horder, physician to King George V. He abandoned medicine in favour of the pulpit on becoming convinced that many ailments were spiritual in origin rather than physical. He ministered in Wales from 1927 until 1939, when he joined G. Campbell **Morgan** at Westminster Chapel in London, succeeding him as minister in 1945. Characterized by penetrating spiritual analysis, Lloyd-Jones' meticulously crafted sermons attracted large congregations to his Sunday and weeknight services. After resigning from Westminster Chapel in 1968 he travelled widely as a guest speaker, remaining active until shortly before his death.

Loaysa, Jerónimo de   Archbishop, Spanish Dominican missionary in Peru, born Trujillo, 1498, died Lima, 25 October 1575. A short first assignment in the Indies in 1530 persuaded Loaysa that the missions required much support, and when recalled to Spain, he took a strong position in their favour, denouncing the abuses of colonists. Appointed bishop of Cartagena in 1537, he then transferred to the archdiocese of Lima. Loaysa founded many parishes, built convents and, most importantly, founded the hospital de Santa Ana, where Indians were cared for and given religious instruction, and in 1550 a school for Indian children.

Lobo, Duarte   Portuguese composer and Roman Catholic priest, born Alentego, *c.*1563, died Lisbon, 24 September 1646. Lobo was cathedral chapel-master in Lisbon from *c.*1594 until his death, and in his later years rector of the Seminário de São Bartolomeu, where he taught such eminent theorists as António Fernandes and João Álvares. His fame is attested in copies, both MS and printed, of his works, found at Seville and Mexico City Cathedrals.

Lobo, Jerónimo Portuguese Jesuit missionary, born Lisbon, 1595, died Portugal, 1678. Ordained at Coimbra, Lobo went first to Goa, 1622, and then to Abyssinia, 1625; when the Catholic emperor died in 1632, the plight of the Ethiopian mission became desperate, and the Jesuits were expelled in 1634. Lobo returned to Rome and, assigned to Goa as rector and provincial, he remained there almost twenty years. One of his two works concerning Ethiopia was published in 1699, and remains in the library of the Royal Society, London.

Lochner, Stefan German painter and master of the Cologne school, born Meersburg am Bodensee, bishopric of Constance, c.1400, died Cologne, 1451. He is believed to have studied in The Netherlands. About 1430 he settled in Cologne, but revisited The Netherlands, where he met Jan van **Eyck**. His best-known work is the triptych over the altar at Cologne Cathedral. Other work includes *St Jerome in his Cell*, *Madonna with the Violet*, *Madonna in the Rose Bower* and *Presentation in the Temple*.

Locke, John English philosopher and advocate of free thinking and toleration, born Wrington, Somerset, 29 August 1632, died High Laver, Essex, 28 October 1704. He seems to have considered becoming a clergyman of the Church of England, but eventually studied medicine because he had come to distrust religion – though in his ideal commonwealth all religions would be tolerated except Roman Catholicism, and also atheism. He was profoundly influenced by the works of **Descartes** and his stress on human reason. Locke's system is a synthesis of rationalism and empiricism. He also supported religious liberty in his *Letters concerning Toleration* (1689, 1690 and 1692). He published *Two Treatises of Government* (1690), which became influential in the next century. The focus of his philosophical thought is found in *Essay concerning Human Understanding* (1690), in which he attacks the Platonist notion of 'innate ideas'. Pure reality cannot be grasped by the human mind and therefore there is no sure basis for metaphysical thinking. Towards the end of his life he moved in Deist circles, though he remained a practising member of the Church of England.

Loening, Edgar German Roman Catholic historian and canon lawyer, born 1843, died Halle, 19 February 1919. A professor at several universities, latterly at Halle until his death, Loening's major work is *Geschichte des deutschen Kirchenrechts*, a study of the rights of the Church from the era of **Constantine** and **Clovis** through the Merovingian period. The treatise received almost immediate praise and brought a new awareness of the institutions of the Church and recognition by the State.

Löffler, Klemens German Roman Catholic historian, born Steinbach, 30 January 1881, died Cologne, 18 March 1933. Director of libraries for both the university and the city of Cologne, Löffler's interest lay chiefly in the cultural history of the Church; he is known for his *Papstischgeschichte von den Anfängen bis zur Gegenwart*, written with Franz Xaver Geppelt, a study of the whole course of papal relations.

Löhe, Johann Konrad William Lutheran pastor, born Fuerth, Germany, 21 February 1808, died Neuendettelsau, 2 January 1872. He was ordained in 1831 having studied at Nuremberg, Erlangen and Berlin. He worked in a number of parishes before settling in Neuendettelsau and marrying Helene Andreae in 1837. He supported the work of missionaries in New Guinea and in Missouri and Iowa, publishing a periodical, *Kirchliche Mittheilungen aus und leber Nord-Amerika*, which explained their work. He also supported the Innere Mission, which provided evangelistic and social activities within Germany. An influential preacher and thinker he published sermons, devotional writing and works on liturgy, the nature of the Church (*Three Books about Church*) and issues of order and form of service (*Agenda*).

Lohelius, Johann (Lohel) Premonstratensian archbishop, born Ohre (Eger), 1549, died Prague, 2 November 1622. Lohelius received the Premonstratensian (Norbertine) habit in 1573, and spent much of his early career restoring the abbey of Strahov, first as prior, then as abbot from 1586. Appointed bishop of Prague in 1612, he had to flee when the Calvinists took control, but returned when the imperial forces defeated the Protestants at White Mountain in 1620.

Lohmeyer, Ernst German NT scholar, born Dorsten, Westphalia, 7 August 1890, died September 1946. Lohmeyer taught at the University of Breslau, but his strong anti-Nazi stand caused his transfer to the University of Greifswald, in Prussia, in 1945. Arrested that year for unknown reasons, he is assumed to have died somewhere behind the Iron Curtain. He is regarded as one of the leaders in the Redaktionsgeschichte school. He wrote the *Foundations of Pauline Theology* and contributed to the study of early Church history in *Christian Worship*, *Caesar Worship* and *Social Questions in Primitive Christianity*. He made valuable commentaries on Matthew and Mark for H. Meyer's *Kritisch-exegetischer Kommentar über das Neue Testament.*

Loisy, Alfred Firmin Biblical scholar, born Ambrières, France, 28 February 1857, died Paris, 6 June 1940. Loisy served as a rural Roman Catholic priest before moving to Paris in 1881 to pursue further study at the Institut Catholique, where he became a professor. His studies made him a convinced Modernist, arguing that traditional doctrines needed reinterpreting in the light of historico-critical scholarship. This led to his dismissal in 1893, and his writings were placed on the Index of Prohibited Books in 1904. Loisy became increasingly hostile to orthodox Christianity, and was excommunicated in 1908. He became a professor at the Collège de France in 1909, and over the next twenty years published a series of works on the origins and development of Christian doctrine, which in its traditional sense Loisy appears to have rejected.

Lombardo, Pietro Italian Renaissance sculptor known for his churches and tombs, born Carona, Italy, *c.*1425, died Venice, June 1515. His earliest work is in Parma, but he moved to Venice, where he spent the remainder of his life. Lombardo designed **Dante**'s tomb in Ravenna, and tombs for many nobles in Venice. He was the architect and chief sculptor of the church of Maria dei Miracoli in Venice, and master mason of the Palazzo Ducale (Doge's Palace) in Venice. Lombardo in his work was often assisted by his sons Tullio and Antonio.

Lomenie de Brienne, Etienne-Charles de French cardinal and statesman, born Paris, 9 October 1727, died Sens, 19 February 1794. He became bishop of Condom, and then archbishop of Toulouse. Queen Marie Antoinette influenced his appointment as a minister of finance in 1787, but owing to the government's difficulties in imposing taxation, France became virtually bankrupt and he resigned. He was made archbishop of Sens and later a cardinal. However, his life was overshadowed by the French Revolution and he died in prison.

Lonergan, Bernard John Francis Canadian Jesuit theologian, born Buckingham, Quebec, 17 December 1904, died Pickering, Ontario, 26 November 1984. Lonergan studied at Heythrop College, Oxfordshire, and the Gregorian University, Rome; much influenced by Edmund Husserl, his theology employed a 'transcendental method' of intellectual awareness and reflexion. In *Grace and Freedom: Operative Grace in the Thought of St Thomas Aquinas*, Lonergan traces the evolution of the theology of grace from St **Augustine**, and analyses the thought of Thomas on causality, the divine transcendence and human liberty. In *Insight: A Study of Human Understanding*, he actualizes his theory of the unified structure of understanding, how the reader can arrive at a conception of the world, coherent and open, called 'emerging probability'. The results of *Insight* led to a unity for all theology, and in *Method in Theology*, he shows how the transcendental procedure can transform the practice of theology through linked mental operations, both progressive and cumulative. The 'method' imposes on those who seek authenticity the obligation of a threefold conversion: moral, religious and intellectual. More than twenty volumes of Lonergan's collected works are being published by the Lonergan Research Institute, University of Toronto.

Longland, John Bishop, born England, 1473, died 7 May 1547. He was educated at Oxford and was a fellow of Magdalen College. Between 1508 and 1513 he was given three benefices in the West Country. In 1514 he became canon at Salisbury and then dean. Seven years later he was ordained bishop of Lincoln and worked to reform the diocese. He began preaching at the royal court *c.*1518 and became **Henry VIII**'s confessor. Believing firmly in royal supremacy, he supported the king in his divorce of **Catherine of Aragon**. He was well known as an accomplished preacher and humanist and was a friend of **Erasmus**.

Longo, Maria Laurentia Venerable, foundress of the Capuchinesses (Franciscan Sisters), born Barcelona, 1463, died Naples, 1542. She married a Catalan, Juan Llonc, who died in 1507. In her widowhood Maria Laurentia became active in the Oratory of Divine Love of St **Cajetan**, and in 1521–2 founded a hospital for incurables in Naples. In 1535 she established a convent which initially followed the Rule of St **Clare** of Assisi, later that of the Capuchin friars. Her belief was that personal sanctification was achieved by working in the service of others, and in poverty and with humility. Her Order was approved by Pope **Paul III** in 1538, and the process for her beatification was introduced in 1892.

Loofs, Friedrich German Lutheran theologian, born Hildesheim, 19 June 1858, died Halle, 13 January 1928. He was a student of **Harnack** at Leipzig and of **Ritschl** at Göttingen. After some years in Leipzig, he became professor of Church history in Halle. His general area of research was the history of dogma, resulting in his magnum opus: *Leitfaden zum Studium der Dogmen-Geschichte* (1890). His main specializations were the Trinitarian dogma in the early Church and research into **Luther**. He also took positions in contemporary debates, such as those regarding the Religionsgeschichtliche Schule and the Leben Jesu Forschung.

Loos, Cornelius Flemish Roman Catholic theologian, born Gouda, c.1546, died Brussels, 3 February 1595. Loos took Holy Orders and became a professor at Mainz, where he denounced the rebellion in the Low Countries. When a professor at Trier, he condemned the witch-burning craze, for which he was imprisoned at the instigation of the nuncio, Ottavio **Frangipani**, and wrote a book on the subject, *De vera et falsa magia*, but the Church authorities proscribed it. He died before being arraigned for his third trial.

Lopez, Gregory First Chinese bishop, born Lo Wên-tsao in Fukien province, c.1615, died 1691. He became a Christian as an adult and was baptized by the Franciscans. After studying at Manila he became a Dominican and in 1654 was the first Chinese person to be ordained priest. He had a successful ministry but refused an episcopal see in 1674. In 1679 the Pope persuaded him to become bishop of Basilopolis, Bithynia, and vicar apostolic of Nanking. However, he was not consecrated until 1685, because the Dominicans in Manila disapproved of his opinion in the rites controversy of the accommodation of Chinese culture to Christianity. He died before he could be translated to the new diocese of Nanking. There was no other Chinese bishop until 1918.

López, Ludovico Spanish Dominican theologian, date and place of birth unknown, died Spain, 27 September 1595. López taught theology in Spain and in Colombia, where the plantation owners persecuted him for his strong stand on behalf of the Indians. He went to Spain to plead their cause, and died there. An important work is his *Intructorium conscientiae*.

López Capillas, Francisco Mexican composer, born perhaps Spain, c.1612, died Mexico City, 18 January 1673. López succeeded as organist-chapelmaster in the cathedral at Mexico City in 1654, and came to be regarded as the most profound and prolific composer of Masses in Mexican history. The works preserved in the cathedral archives include *Aufer a nobis* and *Super Alleluia*, based on his own motets; a *Missa Batalla* in the tradition of Victoria's nine-voiced *Pro Victoria*; and an essay on the technique of Mass composition that is considered among the most impressive musicological documents in colonial literature.

López de Mendoza Grajales, Francisco Spanish missionary, born Jerez de la Frontera, date unknown, place and date of death unknown. López accompanied the expedition of Pedro Menéndez de Avilés to St Augustine, Florida, in 1565, and the following year became pastor of the first white settlement in what is now the USA. In a letter written to the king of Spain, López named himself 'Vicar of Florida', and spoke of being troubled by a slight illness; it is not known how long he remained in St Augustine after this, nor where he ended his life.

López y Vicuña, Vicenta María Saint, Spanish foundress, born Cascante, Navarre, 22 March 1847, died Madrid, 26 December 1890. From a middle-class family, Vicenta studied in Madrid, and became interested in the life of young working girls; she lived a common life there with a small group for five years. In 1876 she founded the Daughters of Mary Immaculate for Domestic Services, and pronounced vows two years later. The congregation received papal approval in 1888 and soon spread to elsewhere in Europe and to Latin America; the Daughters numbered some 2000 in 81 houses by 1961. Vicenta was canonized in 1975. Feast day 26 December.

Loras, Jean Mathias Pierre French-born Roman Catholic bishop in the USA, born Lyons, 30 August 1792, died Dubuque, Iowa, 19 February 1858. Loras volunteered for mission work in Mobile, Alabama, in 1828 and became first bishop of Dubuque in 1837, where he encouraged religious foundations, namely, the Cistercian abbey of New Melleray, Loras College, Mount St Bernard Seminary, the Sisters of Charity of the Blessed Virgin Mary, the cathedral and the school. He successfully mediated between the preponderantly French clergy and the increasingly numerous Irish laity, and laid the foundations for what is now one of the most flourishing American dioceses.

Lord, Daniel Aloysius American Jesuit writer and educator, born Chicago, Illinois, 23 April 1888, died St Louis, Missouri, 15 January 1955. A gifted communicator, Lord published some 30 books, 300 pamphlets, 65 booklets, 50 plays, 12 musicals, 6 pageants, a syndicated column, 'Along the Way', and 900 transcripts for radio transmission. His greatest accomplishment was the revival of the Sodality movement, which he turned from another devotional practice into a nationally recognized instrument to draw young people into the Church, and, together with his fellow-Jesuit Edward **Gar-esché**, he edited the *Queen's Work*, from 1913. He co-authored the Motion Picture Code and the Legion of Decency; he organized the National Leadership School and the Summer School of Catholic Action, which attracted hundreds of thousands over the years.

Lord, Robert Howard American educator, author and Roman Catholic priest, born Plano, Illinois, 20 July 1885, died Boston, Massachusetts, 22 May 1954. Educated at Harvard and in Europe, Lord was appointed an adviser to the American Peace Commission at the end of the Great War; a specialist in Polish and German matters on the American Delegation to the Paris Peace Conference, he became a friend of Jan Paderewski, the first Polish premier. Lord converted to the Roman Catholic Church in 1920, became a priest in Boston and pastor of St Paul's, Wellesley, in 1944. He published *The Second Partition of Poland, Some Problems of the Peace Conference* and *The Origins of the War of 1870*.

Lorenzana, Francisco Antonio de Spanish archbishop and cardinal, born León, 22 September 1722, died Rome, 17 April 1804. In 1766, Charles III appointed Lorenzana archbishop of Mexico, where he tried to eliminate superstition, improve the training of the clergy and ameliorate the social conditions of his flock. Named archbishop of Toledo in 1772, he published the works of its principal writers in *SS Patrum Toletanorum opera*. Pope **Pius VI** created him a cardinal in 1789, and Charles IV appointed him envoy to the Holy See. He supported the Pope when Bonaparte invaded Italy, and resigned his see in 1800 to assist the new pontiff, **Pius VII**, during the political trials which followed.

Lorenzo de' Medici ('The Magnificent') Statesman, ruler, patron, born Florence, 1 January 1449, died there, 9 April 1492. He became head of the family in 1469, and in charge of the bank, half of the profits of which came from dealing with the papal curia. Pope **Sixtus IV** supported the Pazzi conspiracy launched by a rival Florentine banking house in 1478: Lorenzo and his brother were attacked in the cathedral in Florence, and his brother was killed. Lorenzo worked to improve relations with the Papacy: his middle son, Giovanni, entered the Church, was made a cardinal when only thirteen, and eventually became **Leo X**. The bank was re-established in Rome, but Lorenzo preferred to see himself as less a business man than a humanist and scholar: he was a patron of the arts, and of ecclesiastical reform movements (he brought **Savonarola** to Florence), and wrote religious (and other) verse.

Lorenzo Giustiniani *see* **Lawrence Justinian**

Lorenzo Monaco, Piero di Giovani Italian monk and painter, born Siena, *c.*1370/71, died Florence, 1425. He joined the Camaldolese Order and lived in a monastery in Florence. Among his best known paintings are *Madonna and Child, Coronation of the Virgin, Life of a Hermit* and *Adoration of the Magi*. Much of his work can be seen in Florence.

Lossky, Nikolai Onufrievich Russian Orthodox philosopher, born Kreslavka, Vitebsk, 6 December 1879, died Sainte-Geneviève des Bois, Paris, 24 January 1965. Lossky studied at Berne, St Petersburg and Moscow, and taught at Bratislava, before going to St Vladimir Orthodox Russian Theological Seminary in New York. God and his Kingdom are the starting-point for Lossky's moral philosophy and aesthetics; he named his epistemology 'intuitivism', and advocated a concrete ideal realism, in contrast to the anti-intellectualism of Henri **Bergson**.

Lossky, Vladimir Nikolaevich Orthodox lay theologian, born Göttingen, Germany, 8 June 1903, died Paris, 7 February 1958. Son of the Russian philosopher Nikolai **Lossky**, he studied in Paris and was a disciple of Etienne **Gilson**. He then taught theology and was very concerned with the ecumenical challenges of the different theologies of East and West. His most influential works are *The Mystical Theology of the Eastern Church* (1957), *The Meaning of Icons* (with L. **Uspensky**, 1952) and *The Vision of God* (1983).

Lotbinière, François Louis Chartier de Canadian apostate, born Quebec, 13 December 1716, died perhaps New York State, 1784. From a distinguished founding family of French Canada, de Lotbinière, after his wife's death, became a Franciscan Recollect, but left them, spent periods in and out of several religious congregations, and extended intervals of time in a state of apostasy. He became pastor at St Laurent de l'Isle d'Orléans, 1770–2, and, again placed under interdict by his cousin, Bishop d'**Esglis**, he went to the USA in 1784.

Lothair I Frankish emperor, born 795, died abbey of Prüm, 28 September 855. He was the son of Louis I the Pious. Lothair became ruler of Bavaria, and then co-emperor. Later he received the government of Italy. Pope **Paschal I** crowned him co-emperor in Rome. After the Treaty of Verdun, he returned Italy, Burgundy, the Low Countries and some French prisoners. Lothair divided his empire among his three sons and retired to the monastery of Priiln.

Lothair II Frankish king, born *c.*835, died Piacenza, Italy, 8 August 869. His attempt to have his marriage dissolved led to a struggle with Pope **Nicholas I**. He had been forced by his father to marry Theuthberga. However, she remained childless and he wished to marry his mistress Waldrada, by whom he had children. Lothair induced the archbishops of Cologne and Trier to attempt to dissolve the marriage. Synods of Aachen dissolved the marriage, but Pope Nicholas I reversed these decisions. Pope **Adrian II**, who succeeded Nicholas, promised that the question would be considered in council but Lothair died before this could take place.

Lothair III (Lothair the Saxon) German king and Holy Roman Emperor, born early June 1075, died Breitenwang (Austria), 3/4 December 1137. As duke of Saxony he went to Italy to support the election of Pope **Innocent II**, who later crowned Lothair as Emperor. He returned to Rome to drive the Antipope **Anacletus II** from Rome.

Lotti, Antonio Italian composer of Church music and operas, born Venice or Hanover, *c.*1667, died Venice, 5 January 1740. In Venice he studied under Legrenzi. At St Mark's Cathedral he began as a chorister, became organist and finally choirmaster. He composed oratorios, a Requiem, Masses and motets. Most of his Church music is unaccompanied, such as a celebrated *Miserere*.

Lotto, Lorenzo Venetian painter of the High Renaissance, born Venice, *c.*1480, died Loreto, 1556. In his first dated work, *St Jerome* (1500), Lotto heralded the style of Venetian painting later developed by **Giorgione** and **Titian**. Pope **Julius II** invited him to Rome in 1508 and Roman classicism influenced his later work. Among his greatest paintings are his large altarpieces in Venice – *St Bartholomew, St Dominic, The Holy Spirit, St Ber-*

nardino – the great *Crucifixion* of Monte San Giusto and the *Madonna of the Rosary*.

Loughlin, James F. American educator, author and Roman Catholic priest, born Auburn, New York, 8 May 1851, died Barbados, West Indies, 17 March 1911. Ordained for the Archdiocese of Philadelphia, Loughlin served as pastor and diocesan leader. A founder of the Catholic Summer School of America, he wrote and lectured on Church history, co-edited the *American Catholic Quarterly Review* and contributed sermons to the secular *Philadelphia Ledger*. He was prominent in the formation of the National Union of Catholic Young Men's Societies, and was spiritual director of the Archdiocesan Union of Young Men.

Loughlin, John Irish-born American bishop, born County Down, 20 December 1817, died Brooklyn, New York, 29 December 1891. Loughlin went to the USA as a young man, and became bishop of Brooklyn in 1853, where he faced many problems of immigration and the accompanying demand for churches, schools and charitable agencies, compounded by a shortage of priests, religious and financial resources; however, his work there laid a strong foundation for the future development of the jurisdiction.

Louis I (the Pious) Third son of **Charlemagne**, born 778, died 840. He was appointed king of Aquitaine by Charlemagne, and joint emperor in 813. Louis' reign was marked by controversy and disturbance, largely owing to struggles with his sons. In 833 he was deposed by the Assembly of Compiègne and made to appear in penitent's garb. At Metz, in 835, he was restored and remained in power until the year of his death. Despite his weak leadership, he was devoted to learning and monastic reform in Germany.

Louis II Frankish emperor, born, c.822, died near Brescia, Italy, 12 August 875. The eldest son of **Lothair I**, Louis succeeded his father in 855 and received the imperial title from Pope **Leo IV**. His reign of twenty years was marked by bitter territorial altercations with Pope **Nicholas I** and the Byzantine emperor **Basil I**, which further diminished the patrimony of **Charlemagne** and, with the

final loss of Lotharinga, his realm became the pawn of his relatives.

Louis IV (of Bavaria) Holy Roman Emperor, born Munich, 1 April 1282, died Fürstenfeld, 1348. Son of Duke Louis of Bavaria, Louis claimed the German throne in 1314 after the death of **Henry VII**. When Pope **John XXII** refused to recognize him, Louis countered with the Sachsenhausen Appellation (1324), accusing the Pope of heresy for having condemned the doctrine of absolute poverty; John excommunicated Louis and condemned him as a usurper. In 1327, Louis invaded Italy and had himself crowned Emperor; John invalidated his coronation, but Louis declared John deposed and set up an Antipope, Nicholas V. Louis sought reconciliation with John's successor, **Benedict XII**, but Philip VI of France intervened to oppose every effort; Louis vigorously defended his crown until his death.

Louis VI (of France) King, born Paris, 1081, died there, 1 August 1137. Known as 'Louis le Gros' he succeeded his father Philip in 1108 and with him can be considered the more active of the Capetian kings of France, indeed one of the founders of that dynasty. He was an exceptional benefactor of the Church, especially in the restoration of monasteries plundered by feudal brigands. He became the patron of the new monastic foundations at Cîteaux, Prémontré and Fontevrault. He chose his chief ministers from the abler clergy, then normal royal practice in Western Europe. Étienne de Garland, archdeacon of Notre Dame, became his chancellor and seneschal of France and was therefore all-powerful with the king, until 1127, when the celebrated canonist **Ivo of Chartres** and St **Bernard** attacked his policies and Louis then demoted him; **Suger** the administrator of Saint-Denis then came to the fore at court – but his work in Church and State belonged to the next reign. Louis is sometimes credited with freeing the serfs and called 'Father of the Communes' but both claims have been shown by historians to be undeserved.

Louis VII (of France) King, born 1120, died Paris, 18 September 1180. He was crowned by Pope **Innocent II** in 1137, and the same year married Eleanor, heiress of Aquitaine. He continued the consolidation of royal power during the first half of his reign which had been begun by his father **Louis VI**. He launched a Crusade, preached and supported by St **Bernard**, at Vézelay in 1146, setting out for the Holy Land in 1147 on the overland route to Syria. The expedition was a humiliating disaster and he returned to France in 1149. For the rest of his reign he became increasingly religious and inefficient in government. His marriage to Eleanor was annulled in 1152, whereupon she married Henry Plantagenet, count of Anjou and from 1154 king (Henry II) of England. Louis was now faced with territorial aggrandizements on both sides of the Channel; but with the aid of the Papacy he staved off the Angevin threat by cleverly fomenting discord in the family of Henry II. Louis befriended **Thomas Becket** and the cause of Pope **Alexander III** but he also tried to reconcile Becket with Henry II and this paved the way for the Pope to reconcile the two kings in 1177 at Vitry. By his third wife, Adele, Louis had as heir the future Philip Augustus (b. 1165) and had him crowned at Rheims in 1179.

Louis VIII (of France) King, born Paris, the eldest son of Philip Augustus, 5 September 1187, died Montpensier, 1 November 1226. He was anointed king of France at Rheims in 1223. His brief reign was marked by the Montfort claim to the County of Toulouse and the resumption of the Albigensian Crusade in the south of France which he led himself in 1226, the year of his death. This led to the submission of Count **Raymond VII of Toulouse** to his widow **Blanche of Castile** and the eventual absorption of Languedoc into the royal desmesne. Blanche was the granddaughter of King Henry II of England and she bore Louis twelve children, the eldest and successor being St **Louis IX**. At the invitation of the rebellious barons in 1215 'to pluck them out of the hand of this tyrant' (i.e. King John), Louis led an (ultimately unsuccessful) invasion of England to claim the throne, on the correct assumption that John had murdered his nephew Arthur of Brittany. The Papacy had forbidden the enterprise, excommunicating the English rebels and the French troops.

Louis IX (of France) Saint, king, born Poissy, 25 April 1214, died of fever near Tunis during a Crusade in North Africa, 25 August 1270. He inherited the throne when only twelve, but took over the government of his country only in 1235. His way of life, even as a child, was characterized by great religious devotion, and as king, with a concern for justice and the building of churches and hospitals. He was also a very considerable politician and exercised control over his barons, repressing several rebellions. He led France into two Crusades, one from 1248 to 1254, part of which time he spent in captivity, and the other in 1270, against Tunis, although he fell sick and died almost immediately on his arrival. **Robert de Sorbon** was a friend and occasional confessor of the king, who encouraged, and financially assisted, him in the foundation of what eventually became the Sorbonne. Feast day 25 August.

Louis XII (of France) King, born Blois, 27 June 1462, died Paris, 1 January 1515. He was son of Charles, duc d'Orléans. He succeeded to the dukedom in 1465. As a boy he was forced to marry his saintly relative **Joan of France**. After becoming king of France he annulled his marriage and married Anne of Brittany. He was involved in disastrous, over-ambitious European wars, but was popular in France, being known as the 'père du peuple'. He improved justice for his poorest subjects and kept France free from civil war.

Louis XIV (of France) King, born Saint-Germain-en-Laye, 16 September 1638, died Versailles, 1 September 1715. Louis inherited the throne in 1643, but until 1661 the effective ruler of France was Cardinal **Mazarin**, who left the country strong politically, administratively and culturally. Louis had a deep concern with religious questions and favoured the Roman Catholic Church, persecuting both Jansenists and Huguenots, the latter especially through his revoking of the Edict of Nantes in 1685. He took a close interest in the controversy surrounding Quietism, and was eager for its condemnation, by the Pope preferably, but if need be at least by the archbishop of Paris. Towards the Papacy he showed himself a strong and determined Gallican. He was expansionist in policy and led France into four wars which turned other nations against her and weakened her considerably.

Louis d'Aleman Blessed, French cardinal archbishop, born Arbent-en-Bugey, c.1390, died

Salonne, near Arles, 17 September 1450. A canon lawyer, Louis took a lead at the Council of Basel (1439), and nominated **Amadeus VIII of Savoy** as Antipope Felix V, for which **Eugenius IV** excommunicated him. However, he recanted when Felix abdicated, and **Nicholas V** restored him to his previous position. He died with a reputation for sanctity; **Clement VII** proclaimed him blessed in 1527. Feast day 17 September.

Louis of Arnstein Venerable, Premonstratensian count and lay brother, born Arnstein, Germany, 1109, died Gummersheim, Germany, 25 October 1185. Louis and his wife entered the Premonstratensian Order in 1139, mutually agreeing to do so. He converted his ancestral home into a Premonstratensian abbey, gave away his material goods to the Order and to relatives, and helped to found five religious houses. Though he lacks an official beatification, he does have a feast – 25 October.

Louis of Besse French Capuchin, pioneer of the social apostolate, born 'Alphonse Eliseus Chaix' at Besse-sur-Issole, 17 October 1831, died San Remo, Italy, 8 October 1910. Inspired by the example of Blessed Bernardine of Feltre, Louis fostered the cause of the working classes through societies and popular banks, as well as the periodical *Union économique*. He wrote a biography, *Le Bienheureux Bernardine de Feltre*, and spiritual works such as, *Éclaircissement sur les oeuvres mystiques de St Jean de la Croix* and *La Science et la prière*.

Louis of Casoria Venerable, Italian Franciscan religious founder, born 'Arcangelo Palmentieri' at Casoria, Naples, 11 March 1814, died Posillipo, 30 March 1885. Louis established a society for Catholic intellectuals and the periodical *Carità*, and undertook charitable enterprises throughout Italy, including hospitals and refuges, homes for the handicapped and the elderly. He founded the Brothers of Charity at Naples in 1859, and the Grey Sisters of St Elizabeth in 1862, both congregations for the education of poor children.

Louis of Granada Spanish Dominican mystic, preacher and writer, born Granada, 1504, into the de Sarria family, died Lisbon, 31 December 1588. He entered the convent of the Holy Cross at Granada in 1524 and, showing himself an excellent student of philosophy, he was sent to the College of St Gregory in Valladolid for theology. He quickly established a reputation as a preacher and for his holiness of life, and became confessor for Queen Catherine of Portugal. He became provincial of his Order in Portugal in 1557 and remained there for the last three decades of his life. His works include *A Sinner's Guide*, first published in 1555, and *Memorial of the Christian Life*. He also produced a study of the art of preaching which achieved widespread distribution across Europe.

Louise de Marillac *see* **Marillac, Louise de**

Louise of France (Thérèse de St-Augustin) Venerable, Carmelite nun, born Versailles, 15 July 1737, died St-Denis, 23 December 1787. The daughter of King Louis XV, Louise entered the Carmelite convent at St-Denis in 1770, where she exercised considerable spiritual influence as novice mistress and prioress. She dedicated herself to penances for the conversion of her father, to the Rule and to the Church; she wrote a series of meditations on the Eucharist, and a spiritual testament. Her cause for beatification was introduced in 1873.

Louise of Savoy Blessed, widow and Poor Clare, born Savoy, 28 December 1462, died Orbe, Switzerland, 24 July 1503. The daughter of Blessed **Amadeus IX of Savoy** and Yolanda of France, granddaughter of **Charles VII** and niece of Louis XI, Louise married Hugh of Orléans; when he died in 1490, she dispersed her fortune and entered the Poor Clare monastery at Orbe. She became an exemplary religious and an inspiring abbess, noted for her hospitality to the Franciscan friars. Pope **Gregory XVI** confirmed her cult in 1839. Feast day 24 July.

Löw, Joseph Austrian Redemptorist and liturgical scholar, born Vienna, 23 July 1893, died Rome, 22 September 1962. Ordained in 1919, called to Rome in 1935 and appointed vice relator in the historical section of the Congregation of Rites, Löw helped to confirm the cult and beatification of, among others, Kateri **Tekakwitha**, the first North American Indian candidate for canonization. He published works on the history of the liturgy and on

Redemptorist history and founded the *Spicilegium Historicum CSSR*.

Lowe, Enoch Louis American Roman Catholic lawyer, governor, born Frederick, Maryland, 10 August 1820, died New York City, 23 August 1892. Educated by the Jesuits at Clongowes Wood College, Dublin, and at Stonyhurst, England, Lowe became governor of Maryland in 1851, despite his Roman Catholicism, and his young age. During the Civil War he tried, without success, to draw his native state into the Confederacy, and went into exile in Georgia. In 1866 he refused to sign the oath imposed on all 'rebel' lawyers before they could resume the practice of law in Maryland, and went to New York State.

Lowe, John English Augustinian (or Austin) friar and theologian, born *c.*1382, died Rochester, 3 September 1467. Lowe became confessor to **Henry VI** in 1432, bishop of St Asaph in 1433 and of Rochester in 1444. He vigorously combated heresy, was a bitter foe of the Lollards and contributed to the downfall of Bishop Reginald **Pecock**. A humanist, Lowe assisted in the foundation of Eton College, 1442, and King's College, Cambridge, 1444, and bequeathed his important library to Austin Friars in London.

Loyola, Ignatius *see* **Ignatius of Loyola**

Loyson, Charles French Old Catholic priest, born Orléans, 10 March 1827, died Paris, 9 February 1912. Loyson joined the Sulpicians in 1850, left them and entered the Dominicans in 1859, and then the Discalced Carmelites the same year, with the name 'Père Hyacinthe'; he became a dynamic preacher at Notre Dame de Paris. He left the Church in 1868, in protest over papal infallibility; excommunicated the following year, he married the religiously pathological Emily Mariaman, an American convert of his, and became pastor of the Old Catholic Church in Geneva; in 1879 he founded the schismatic L'Église Catholique Gallicane, but the venture failed and could not be revived, despite his efforts. Among his writings are *La Société civile dans ses rapports avec le Christianisme* and *Les Principes de la réforme catholique*.

Lozano, Pedro Spanish Jesuit historian, born Madrid, 16 June 1697, died Humahuaca (Argentina), 8 February 1752. Ordained in Argentina, Lozano spent nine years caring for the sick and dying in Santa Fe before being appointed historiographer of the province in 1730; he travelled widely through the area of La Plata (Argentina, Paraguay and Uruguay). In 1751, he prepared a reply to the Treaty of Limits, which transferred some of the Jesuit Reductions to Portugal. Among his chief works are *Historia de la Compañia de Jesús de la Provincia del Paraguay* and *Historia de la conquista del Paraguay, Rio de la Plata y Tucumán*.

Lubac, Henri de Jesuit priest, cardinal and theologian, born Cambrai, France, 20 February 1896, died Paris, 4 September 1991. He came from a middle-class family, and was educated first by nuns, and then by the Society of Jesus in Lyons. After leaving school he began to study law in Lyons, but at the end of the first year, in October 1913, he entered the Society, but was mobilized during the First World War, and was twice wounded in action. He was then sent to study in England, returning to France for a year, 1923–4, in order to teach. He completed the final two years of his theological studies in Lyons, and was ordained priest on 22 August 1927. After his final year of spiritual training as a Jesuit, he was appointed to the chair of theology and the history of religions at the Jesuit faculty of Fourvière in Lyons. He held this post until 1947, including during the Second World War, though his association with the French Resistance made life very difficult for him. He was a contemporary of, and close friends with, a number of Jesuit thinkers, including Pierre **Teilhard de Chardin**, about whom he wrote several books, Jean **Daniélou** (in collaboration with whom he began the series of texts Sources Chrétiennes), and Hans Urs von **Balthasar**. His best-known works include the often reprinted *Catholicisme: les aspects sociaux du dogme*, first published in 1938, and *Surnaturel*, which appeared in 1946. The subtitle of this latter work was 'historical studies', and it was the dedication to the history of theological ideas which especially marked de Lubac's writings. He was, in the 1940s, a leading member of the 'nouvelle théologie' school of religious thinking, several members of which were condemned for their ideas (though not by name) in Pope **Pius XII**'s 1950 encyclical *Humani generis*. He was removed from his teaching post, but continued to give retreats. A selection from his retreat conferences to priests was published in 1952 as *Méditations sur l'église*. He was rehabilitated in the Church when Pope **John XXIII** named him an adviser to the Preparatory Commission for the Second Vatican Council. He then became a *peritus*, or expert adviser, to the bishops gathered for the Council, and was especially important in the document on the Church, *Lumen Gentium*, and that on the role of the Church in the modern world, *Gaudium et Spes*. In 1969 **Paul VI** made him a member of the International Theological Commission. He was also held in very high regard by Pope John Paul II, who created him cardinal in 1983. De Lubac had wished to refuse this honour, but was not allowed to do so. He succeeded, however, in ensuring that, unlike almost all other cardinals, he was never ordained a bishop. His last years he spent in retirement in Paris.

Lubieniecki, Stanisław Polish Socinian knight, historian, born Raków, 23 August 1623, died Hamburg, 18 May 1675. Ordained in the 'Minor Church', formed by anti-Trinitarians in 1565, after being excluded from the synod of the Unitarian Reformed Church, Lubieniecki petitioned Charles X Gustav of Sweden, whose troops occupied Cracow, to protect the Minor Church. This plea went unanswered, since the Jesuits secured the suppression of the Unitarian College at Raków in 1638, and the Socinians (after Socinus, who led the Unitarians until 1604) were expelled from the realm and all traces of them disappeared from Poland. An important work, *Historia reformationis Polonicae*, is a major source of Polish religious history, from his perspective.

Lucaris, Cyril *see* **Cyril Lucaris**

Lucas, Fielding American Roman Catholic publisher, born Fredericksburg, Vermont, 13 September 1781, died Baltimore, Maryland, 12 March 1854. The leading publisher of Baltimore, and latterly the country's major Catholic book publisher, Lucas's list between 1838 and 1841 included 154 Catholic titles of a popular dogmatic, apologetic and devotional nature. He also published in widely circulated editions *The Metropolitan Catholic Almanac and Laity's Directory*, which he acquired in 1833.

Lucas, Frederick English Roman Catholic journalist, born London, 30 March 1812, died Staines, 22 October 1855. From a well-known Quaker family, Lucas converted to the Roman Catholic Church in 1839, and contributed significantly to the revival of Catholic life in England when he founded *The Tablet* (1840), as a weekly journal for the educated laity. His political sympathies were with the Whigs and he warmly espoused the Irish cause for Home Rule, being returned to Parliament for an Irish seat. He edited *The Tablet* from Dublin from 1849 for about three years, but there was little English Catholic support for the Irish cause, and his chronic financial situation worsened. The Irish bishops, obedient to Rome, discouraged the clergy from supporting the movement for the repeal of the Union, and his efforts to have Rome modify their policy were of no avail. John Wallis acquired *The Tablet* after Lucas's death and sold it subsequently, in 1868, to Herbert **Vaughan**, future cardinal archbishop of Westminster.

Lucas, Henry S. American Roman Catholic historian, born Jamestown, Michigan, 6 March 1889, died Seattle, Washington, 29 December 1961. From a Dutch background, Lucas furthered his interest in the spiritual dimension of the cultural life of the late Middle Ages, at Leiden and Ghent, and taught at the University of Washington for 38 years; he converted to the Catholic Church in 1947. Notable among his historical studies are *The Renaissance and Reformation* and *Netherlanders in America: Dutch Immigration to the US and Canada*.

Luce, Alice Eveline Pentecostal indigenous Church pioneer, born Cheltenham, Gloucestershire, 1873, died San Diego, Texas, 1955. Luce received the Pentecostal experience in 1910 while an Anglican working for the Church Missionary Society. In 1915, in Texas, she joined the General Council of the Assemblies of God, and in 1926 founded the Berean Bible Institute in San Diego to train Hispanic ministers. In 1921 she wrote 'Paul's Missionary Methods', a three-part article in *The Pentecostal Evangel* promoting indigenous Churches. She also wrote *The Messenger and His Message*

(1925), *The Little Flock in the Last Days* (1927) and *Pictures of Pentecost* (n.d).

Luce, Clare Boothe American playwright and politician, born New York City, 10 March 1903, died Washington, DC, 9 October 1987. She was privately educated, and became associate editor of *Vogue* and later of *Vanity Fair*. She was married twice, her second husband being magazine publisher Henry R. Luce. She was elected to the US House of Representatives for the Republican Party and campaigned for the election of Eisenhower in 1952, as a reward for which he made her ambassador to Italy, 1953–7, the first ever US woman in such a post. Briefly she became a member of President Reagan's Foreign Intelligence Advisory Board. She became a Catholic in 1945, and was nominated for an Oscar for the script for the film *Come to the Stable*. She also edited *Saints for Now* (1952).

Luchesius of Poggibonsi Blessed, Franciscan tertiary, born Gaggiano, Italy, *c*.1181, died Poggibonsi, Italy, 28 April 1260. Luchesius was a merchant with a reputation for greed when he underwent a religious conversion. Afterwards, upon meeting St **Francis of Assisi**, *c*.1213, he and his wife sold their possessions (excepting only a small field that he farmed) and devoted their lives to charity. They were the first to be admitted by Francis into his Third Order, in 1221. Luchesius is said to have been gifted with ecstatic prayer and the miracle of levitation. His cult was confirmed in 1694. Feast day 28 April.

Lucian of Antioch Saint and martyr, born *c*.240, possibly in Samosata, died Nicomedia, 7 January 312. It seems that he was a priest living an ascetic life. During the persecutions under Maximinus Daia he was brought before the emperor in Nicomedia, where he was questioned, leading to his suffering the martyr's death. It is probably best to abandon the idea that he was the founder of the Antiochene school of exegesis as well as the idea that he was **Arius'** predecessor. Feast day 7 January in the calendar of the Roman Church, 15 October in the Orthodox Churches.

Lucić, Ivan (Lucius, Lucio) Croatian Roman Catholic historian, born Troju, Dalmatia, 1604, died Rome, 2 August 1679. Lucić studied at Padua and Rome, and researched the Dalmatian and Vatican archives to write the first scholarly history of the Croatian people up to 1420, *De regno Dalmatiae et Croatiae*; also, historical writings on the Illyrian province of Dalmatia, *Lucii inscriptiones Dalmatiae*, and a history of Troju.

Lucie-Christine French Roman Catholic mystic, born 12 February 1844, died 17 April 1908. Lucie-Christine Bertrand married at 21, and mothered five children; a musician much appreciated in the *salons*, she left behind sixteen notebooks of around 2600 pages covering the last 38 years of her life, apparently intended for her spiritual director. She had taken the name 'Sister Marie-Aimée de Jésus' in her spiritual life. After her death, Augustin **Poulin**, SJ, condensed and published the notebooks under the title *Journal spirituel de Lucie-Christine (1870–1908)*.

Lucifer of Cagliari Bishop, died *c*.370. In the Arian controversy, Lucifer, bishop of Cagliari, stood on the Nicene side. In 353 he was sent as a messenger of Pope **Liberius** to hand over a letter to the Emperor **Constantius II**, in which the Synod of Arles was refuted and a new one proposed. At that gathering, in Milan in 355, he refused to condemn **Athanasius** and was exiled. He thus spent many years in the East – in Syria, Palestine and Egypt. In Antioch, before he returned, he ordained Paulinus, a presbyter, as bishop of the Nicene community. His highly polemical writings are important for the text of the *Vetus Latina*.

Lucius Legendary first Christian king of Britain, died 175. His life is very obscure. According to the *Liber Pontificalis*, he was a Britain who after his conversion appealed to Pope **Eleutherius** for Christian teachers to be sent to Britain; he and many of his subjects were baptized, and the apparatus of pagan cults was converted to Christian use. In later legends he is conflated with Lucius, first bishop (and martyr) of Chur, and is said to have been the son of Simon of Cyrene and a convert of St Timothy. Adolf von **Harnack** argued that the *Liber Pontificalis* passage confuses 'Britain' with 'Britis', a name for Edessa, and suggested that the king there mentioned was in fact the mid-second-century Abgar IX [VIII] of Edessa.

Lucius I Saint, Pope from 25 June 253, born Rome, died 5 March 254. Along with his predecessor, **Cornelius**, he was banished to Civitavecchia by the Emperor Gallus, but allowed to return by Gallus' successor, Valerian. He took a liberal approach towards those who lapsed in persecution, despite pressure from the Novatianists. He is the recipient of a warm letter from **Cyprian**, who salutes him as an honoured confessor. Though honoured as a martyr, he appears to have died a natural death. He was buried in the cemetery of Callistus; part of his epitaph has been recovered. Feast day 4 March.

Lucius II Pope from 12 March 1144, born 'Gherardo Caccianemici' at Bologna, date unknown, died Rome, 15 February 1145. Created cardinal-priest at Santa Croce by **Calixtus II**, Caccianemici served frequently as papal legate of **Honorius II**. No details of his election as successor to **Celestine II** are known, but during his pontificate, reactionaries under Giordano Pierleoni, brother of the late Antipope Anacletus II (Petrus Leonis **Pierleoni**), set up a senate independent of the Holy See and its rule. To restore his authority in Rome, Lucius took up arms and led an unsuccessful assault on the Capitoline, where the senate was installed, during which he suffered serious injuries, and died shortly afterwards in the monastery of San Gregorio.

Lucius III Pope from 1 September 1181, born 'Ubaldus Allucingoli' at Lucca, c.1110, died Verona, 25 November 1185. Received into the Cistercian Order by St **Bernard of Clairvaux**, named cardinal-bishop of Ostia and Velletri by **Adrian IV**, Lucius succeeded his patron **Alexander III**, and resided outside Rome, mostly at Velletri and Anagni. Elderly, honest (one of only two cardinals judged by **Thomas Becket** to be unamenable to bribery), he called a Council at Verona (1184) which condemned the neo-Manichaeans (Cathars), against whom he instituted an episcopal Inquisition.

Lucy Saint, martyred 303. Tradition claims that St Lucy was a native of Syracuse who practised her faith through the distribution of goods to the poor during the persecution of Diocletian. For doing so she was given over to the political authorities by the man to whom she was engaged. She was much venerated by the early Church, as is demonstrated by the Canon of both the Roman and the Ambrosian Mass. Feast day 13 December.

Ludger of Münster Saint, bishop, and missionary to the Saxons, born of wealthy parents near Utrecht, 744, died Münster, 26 March 809. He was impressed by the missionary work of St **Boniface** and, after studies in Utrecht, went to York to study under **Alcuin**, and there he was ordained deacon. He was ordained priest at Cologne in 777. In 775 he continued the missionary work of **Lebuinus** at Deventer. Later he evangelized the Frieslanders while living in Dokkum. In 785 he visited Rome, then entered the monastery of Monte Cassino. But in 787 **Charlemagne** called at the monastery, and sent him to evangelize the Saxons of Westphalia. He built an abbey at what came to be called Münster (after 'monasterium') and in 803 he was appointed bishop of the region. He died while continuing his evangelistic work and was buried in the Benedictine monastery in Werden. Feast day 26 March.

Ludmila Saint and martyr, patroness of Bohemia, born near Melnik, Bohemia, c.860, died Tetin Castle, near Poderrady, 15 September 921. She married Borivoj, the first Czech prince to adopt Christianity, and helped him to establish Christianity in their region. They built Bohemia's first Christian church, near Prague. She was responsible for bringing up her grandson **Wenceslas**, who became king c.921; it was an attempt to prevent her influencing Wenceslas that led to her assassination, by strangling. She was immediately hailed by Christians as a martyr. Feast day 16 September.

Ludolf of Corvey Saint, abbot, date and place of birth unknown, died abbey of Corvey, Germany, 13 August 983. Ludolf became abbot of Corvey in 965 and was known for his deep spirituality, for his promotion of the monastic school (which gained a good reputation under his leadership), and for having the gift of extrasensory perception. He was also known as a dutiful follower of Rome, where he once went on pilgrimage, and for surrounding his abbey with a high protective wall. Feast days 13 August, 21 February and 5 June.

Ludolph of Ratzeburg Saint, Premonstratensian bishop, date and place of birth unknown, died Wismar, Germany, 29 March 1250. Little is known of Ludolph before he became bishop, except that he was a member of the Premonstratensians. Upon becoming bishop of Ratzeburg, Germany, in 1236, Ludolph imposed his strict Premonstratensian Rule on his cathedral chapter. He was known for his spiritual discipline and for his conflicts with the local civil authorities. His struggles with Duke Albert of Sachsen-Lauenburg, including being imprisoned and ill-treated, eventually led to his death. He was canonized in the 1300s. Feast day 29 March.

Ludolph of Saxony (Ludolph the Carthusian) Spiritual writer, born presumably Saxony, though the exact location is unknown, c.1300, died Strasburg, 13 April 1378. He spent 30 years as a Dominican and then became a Carthusian in Strasburg in 1340. In 1343 he became prior of the Charterhouse at Coblenz, but in 1348 returned to being an ordinary monk, first at Mainz and then at Strasburg. His two main works are A *Commentary on the Psalms* and his *Vita Christi*, first printed in 1447, which is both a devotional and a theological work, and which achieved immense popularity. It is possible that Ludolph influenced the *Imitation of Christ*.

Ludovicus Bologninus Italian canon lawyer, born Bologna, 1447, died Florence, 28 July 1508. Ludovicus taught at Bologna and Florence; Pope **Innocent VIII** made him a consistorial advocate and appointed him ambassador to **Louis XII** at both Genoa and Paris. Among his works, which give the impression of being a compilation of contemporary authors, are *Interpretationes novae ad omnes textus utriusque iuris* and *Tabula consiliones abbatis Panormitani*.

Lueger, Karl Austrian Roman Catholic politician, born Vienna, 24 October 1844, died Vienna, 10 March 1910. He studied at Vienna University, and as a councillor exposed corruption. He was elected to the Austrian Reichstat, and helped to found the Christian Social Party, which he later led. As mayor of Vienna, he helped to modernize the city, developing schools and hospitals. He introduced universal suffrage in Vienna.

Lufthildis (Leuchteldis, Liuthild, Lufthold, Luchtel) Saint, virgin. Tradition has it that Lufthildis flourished in Germany in the ninth century, and that she retired to a hermitage, having been persecuted by her stepmother for her generosity to the poor. Miracles having occurred after her death, her grave became the centre of a cult for the cure of head and ear maladies, first reported by **Caesarius of Heisterbach** in 1222. Her bones were translated in 1623 and enclosed in a marble sarcophagus in 1902. Feast day 23 January.

Lugo, Francisco de Spanish Jesuit theologian, born Madrid, 1580, the elder brother of Juan de **Lugo**, died Valladolid, 17 December 1652. He joined the Society of Jesus in Salamanca in 1600 and was sent, at his own request, to Mexico, where he first taught theology. He taught subsequently in Spain, Rome and finally once more in Spain at Valladolid. While in Mexico, de Lugo wrote a commentary on the entire *Summa* of St **Thomas Aquinas**, but it was lost in an attack by Dutch pirates on the fleet in which he was returning to Spain. He subsequently wrote *De principiis moralibus actuum humanorum, Theologica scholastica* and *De septem ecclesiae sacramentis*.

Lugo, Juan de Jesuit cardinal and theologian, born Madrid, November 1583, the younger brother of Francisco de **Lugo**, died Rome, 29 August 1660. His father sent him to study law at Salamanca but instead he entered the Society of Jesus in 1603 in imitation of his brother. After teaching theology at several Spanish colleges, he went to Rome in 1621 and found fame as a theologian and then in 1643 was appointed cardinal by **Urban VIII**, to whom, at the suggestion of the Jesuit general, he had dedicated his *De justitia et jure* (1642). His main theological concern was the Mass, but he also had a considerable interest in moral questions, and his fame rests particularly on *De justitia et jure*. He also produced, among other books, six volumes of studies of moral 'cases'.

Lukáš of Prague Czech Protestant theologian, bishop, born Prague, c.1460, died Mladá, Boleslav, 11 December 1528. Reared as an Utraquist, who advocated reception of Holy Communion under both species (*sub utraque specie*), Lukáš became a leader of the Unitas Fratrum, the Czech Society of Brethren; he did much to promote the development of it into a Church, including in the membership a cross section of society, and learned clergy; he was elected bishop of the Unity in 1500. The hymn-book he edited in 1501 is considered to be the first Protestant hymnal. He had contacts with Martin **Luther** in the 1520s, and brought the Brethren into the mainstream of Protestantism.

Luke Belludi Blessed, Italian Franciscan, born near Padua, *c.*1200, died there, after 9 June 1285. From a rich family, Belludi received the habit of the Friars Minor from St **Francis** himself, became a close companion of St **Anthony of Padua**, and attended him at his death at Arcella in 1231. As provincial minister he continued building the great basilica in which are enshrined Anthony's remains and Luke's own. Pope **Pius XI** confirmed his cult in 1927. Feast day 17 February.

Luke of Armento Saint, monastic founder, born Sicily, early 900s, died Armento, Italy, 19 October 993. Luke began his monastic career at a Greek monastery in Agira. From there he moved to a hermitage in Reggio di Calabria. He left there around 959 seeking to escape the Saracen raids. He spent seven years in Noa, then moved to San Giuliano and finally to Armento around 969. Everywhere he went, he restored churches, engaged in charitable work, and founded religious communities. Feast day 13 October.

Lull (Lullus) Missionary saint, bishop, successor of **Boniface** of Fulda, a monk of Malmesbury Abbey, England, died Hersfeld, 787. A cousin of Boniface, Lull went out to help in the missionary work in Germany, eventually succeeding him at Boniface's death as bishop in Mainz. Lull's correspondence reveals an appreciation for books and a desire to build a library of books from England, as well as pastoral concerns and zeal for the observance of the canons. He founded a monastery at Bleidenstadt in Nassau, and refounded the abbey of Hersfeld in Hesse, where he retired in his old age. Feast day 16 October.

Lull, Raymond (Ramon Llull) Early missionary to Muslims, born Palma, Majorca, *c.*1235, stoned to death, Bougie, Algiers, 29 June 1315. He spent his youth in the court of Aragon, and was converted in 1257, becoming a hermit and then a Franciscan tertiary. His goal became to preach, write books to convince unbelievers, and set up colleges to train missionaries to Islam. He engaged Muslim and Jewish scholars in debate and travelled widely, including to Paris, where he taught for a time, to find support for his plans to evangelize the Islamic peoples, but had little success other than the foundation of the College of Miramar in 1276 for the study of Arabic. He attempted to build a system whereby one could fathom all religious truth by way of logical argument. In one of his works, *Ars magna* he tried to show that all possible knowledge could be deduced from first principles. This resulted in his condemnation by **Gregory XI** in 1376.

Luna Pizarro, Francisco Javier de Peruvian Roman Catholic prelate and political leader, born Arequipa, 3 December 1780, died Lima, 9 February 1855. Ordained in 1806, Luna Pizarro went to Spain, where, during the war with Napoleon, he developed liberal political views. Returning to Luria, he joined the Metropolitan Assembly, and when Peru broke with Spain, Luna Pizarro presided over the first constituent congress of the Republic; he spent his career there in support of civil liberties. In 1845 Pope **Gregory XVI** named him archbishop of Lima, where he promoted Church discipline and began restoration of the seminary.

Lunn, Arnold Sir, Christian apologist, popular theological writer, born Madras, India, 18 April 1888, died London, 2 June 1974. Son of Sir Henry Lunn (1859–1939), founder of the Lunn travel agency, he was educated at Harrow and Balliol College, Oxford, though he failed his degree. He became celebrated first as a mountaineer and skier of distinction, eventually writing many books on both sports, notably a *History of Skiing* (1927). He invented the modern sport of downhill and slalom skiing, and was responsible for their introduction to the Olympic Games. During the Second World War, Lunn was a press correspondent in the Balkans, Chile and Peru. In 1929 his *Life of John Wesley* became a minor classic. He had been brought up as a Methodist but was attracted to Roman Catholicism. With Ronald **Knox** he produced *Difficulties* in 1932, but converted to Catholicism the following year when, with C. E. M. Joad, he wrote *Is Christianity True?* The following year he wrote a popular Life of St Peter **Claver**, *A Saint in the Slave Trade* (1934). He co-wrote with G. G. **Coulton** *Is the Catholic Church Anti-social?* (1946) and published a partial autobiography, *Come What May* (1941), followed by his memoirs, *Unkilled for So Long* (1946). Lunn was knighted in 1952. His final books were characteristic apologia for the Christian faith: *And Yet So New* (1968) and *The Christian Counter-attack* (1969).

Lupold of Bebenburg German canon lawyer and bishop, born Swabia-Franconia, *c.*1297, died Bamberg, 28 October 1363. Lupold studied at Bologna and became bishop of Bamberg in 1353. He supported Emperor **Louis IV** in his struggle with the Anjou Papacy, without being himself antipapist. His most important work, *Tractatus de iuribus regni et imperii*, distinguished the roles of the secular and the spiritual in Christian society, expressing ideas that influenced the Golden Bull of 1356, which regulated the law affecting German emperors and princes until 1806.

Lupus, Servatus Abbot of Ferrières and humanist, born in the Diocese of Sens, *c.*805, died Ferrières, *c.*862. He entered Ferrières for his education, which he completed at Fulda under **Rabanus Maurus**. He made his abbey an important centre of learning and was a chief figure in the Carolingian Renaissance, but he was also deeply involved in politics and even on occasion took command in battle, supporting **Charles II** the Bald, to whom he owed his election as abbot on 22 November 840. In his principal theological work, *Liber de tribus questionibus* (850), he defends Augustinianism, arguing that human free will is affected by the Fall and defending double predestination. Lupus also compiled *Collectaneum de tribus questionibus* on these issues, which showed that he was interested in and acquainted with the early Fathers. He produced a number of saints' Lives, and there survives a collection of his letters, demonstrating an elegant literary style.

Lupus of Sens (Loup) Saint and bishop, born Orléans, *c.*573, died Brienon, near Sens, *c.*1 September 623. Educated and ordained by his maternal uncles, the bishops of Orléans and Auxerre, in 609 he was appointed bishop of Sens, with popular support. He spent a time in exile in Picardy for his support for Sigebert of Austrasia, where he is said to have made many converts. He was restored in 614, and attended the Council of Paris in that year. Buried in the monastery of Sainte-Columbe-les-Sens, which he had founded; his relics were translated to a new church in 853. Many churches in France are dedicated to him. He is invoked by epileptics. Feast day 1 September.

Luque, Crisanto Bolivian Roman Catholic prelate, born Tunja, 1 February 1889, died Bogotá, 7 May 1959. Ordained in 1916, and named bishop of Tunja in 1932, Luque promoted the mass educational enterprise known as 'Escuelas Radiófonicas de Sutatenza'. Made archbishop of Bogotá in 1950, he formed the Consejo Episcopal Latinoamericano (CELAM), which has been of great significance for the Church in Latin America, publishing the Medellín Documents in 1968 as a firm declaration of the Roman Catholic Church's intent to put itself on the side of human rights and of the poor. Luque embodied these principles in his pastoral work when he inaugurated a parochial system in the new *barrios* of Bogotá, to which poor people fled from the bandit-infested interior. He at first recognized the *coup d'état* led by General Rojas in 1953, but when it took the path of dictatorship, he sided with the students and the people who overthrew the dictator. Thanks to his promotion of Catholic principles, the Church gained prestige, respect and acceptance.

Lussy, Melchior Swiss soldier and Roman Catholic leader, born Stans, Switzerland, 1529, died Stans, 14 November 1606. He represented the Swiss Catholic cantons at the Council of Trent, and served four Popes – **Paul IV**, **Pius IV**, **Gregory XIII** and **Gregory XIV**. Lussy served in papal and Venetian armies

Lutgardis Cisterian nun and mystic, born Tongeren (Belgium), 1182, died Aywières (Belgium), 16 June 1246. At the age of twelve, Lutgardis was sent to a convent, presumably because her father had lost her dowry in a business venture. She became a nun at the age of twenty because of a vision of Christ. For the next twelve years, she had numerous mystical visions and experiences. Around 1216, she left the Benedictines for the stricter Rule of the Cistercians, living at their abbey in Aywières. Known for her spiritual wisdom as well as her visions and prophecies, Lutgardis is considered one of the leading mystics of the 1200s.

Luther, Martin Church reformer and minister, born Eisleben, 10 November 1483, died there, 18 February 1546. The son of a miner, he studied at Magdeburg and Eisenach before attending Erfurt University. In Erfurt he joined the Augustinian community. He was ordained priest in 1507 and the following year became a lecturer on Scripture at the University of Wittenberg, a post he held until his death. In his exegesis he developed the theory of justification by faith alone. He became critical of various aspects of Church teaching and practice, particularly after a visit to Rome in 1510–11, but his anger was roused by the sale of indulgences to help fund the rebuilding of St Peter's in Rome. In 1517 he posted his 95 theses, criticizing the doctrine of indulgence on the door of the castle church. (There is some doubt whether there was any physical nailing to the door.) The theses were widely distributed and naturally aroused hostility from the Church authorities. Luther was supported by **Melanchthon. Leo X** now sent Cardinal **Cajetan** to negotiate, but in 1520 Luther published his *Address to the Christian Nobles of Germany* and his *On the Babylonish Captivity of the Church*. He was excommunicated, taking refuge in Wartburg castle, where he began translating the Bible into German. The Lutheran movement spread quickly and congregations grew up all over Germany. Later he promoted reformation rather than destruction of the Church. Changes which followed included the substitution of a German service for Latin Mass, proclamation of the Gospel by preaching, congregational hymn-singing, catechizing, and married clergy – Luther himself married a former nun, Katherine von Bora, in 1525. His hymns helped to spread his beliefs, such as 'Vom Himmel Hoch', 'Christ Lag in Todesbanden', and the great rallying call of the Reformation, 'Ein' Feste Burg'.

Luthuli, Albert South African freedom fighter, African National Congress leader, Zulu chief, born Groutville, a Christian mission reserve in Natal, 1898, died in a train accident 21 July 1967. The son of a local Zulu chief he was educated at Adams College and became a teacher. He was elected chief in Groutville and began to fight for the end of apartheid. He joined the ANC and when as a result the minority white government dismissed him as chief he became ANC leader. He was repeatedly imprisoned and released, defended along with other ANC leaders by Nelson Mandela in 1955 – when charges of high treason laid against him were dismissed – and because of the ANC's promotion of political education and peaceful protest he was awarded the Nobel Peace Prize in 1960. He remained a committed Christian all his life, finding in his faith the motivation for his action, even if he did have to urge the officials of the Christian Churches to support the struggle for freedom. He refused to go along with many of the other freedom fighters who saw Christianity only as an additional weapon in the hands of the oppressors.

Luwum, Janani Anglican archbishop of Uganda, Rwanda, Burundi and Boga-Zaire, born east Acholi district, Uganda, 1922, killed Kampala, Uganda, 17 February 1977. In 1948, while a teacher, he was converted through the East Africa Revival movement. He was ordained priest in 1956 and was a teacher and then principal at Buwalasi Theological College from 1962. He was consecrated bishop of Northern Uganda in 1969 and became archbishop in 1974 during the violent reign of President Idi Amin. His criticism of Amin led to his murder by the armed forces. News of his death shocked the world and brought to public attention the brutal events taking place in Uganda. He is one of the notable twentieth-century martyrs.

Lwanga, Charles Saint, Ugandan Roman Catholic martyr, born Buddu County, *c.*1860, died Namugongo, 3 June 1886. The chieftain of the Kabaka of Buganda, Mwanga, launched a fierce persecution of Christians in 1886, following reproaches by Joseph Mukasa, a Catholic, for sexually abusing the pages of his court. Charles Lwanga was in charge of the boys kept by Mwanga, many of whom had converted to Catholicism, and fifteen of them chose death rather than abjure their faith; they were immolated on a huge funeral pyre, and the executions greatly increased the converts to Catholicism. Charles, and 21 others, were beatified in 1920 and canonized in 1964. Pope **Pius XI** declared him patron of youth and Catholic Action for sub-Saharan Africa. Feast day 3 June.

Lynch, Baptista Mother, American Roman Catholic foundress, born Cherau, South Carolina, 2 November 1823, died Columbia, South Carolina, 28 July 1887. Professed in Cincinnati; her brother Patrick **Lynch**, bishop of Charleston, invited her and others to Columbia, where she founded the Convent and Academy of the Immaculate Conception in 1858; the community flourished until devastated by the Civil War. Mother Baptista returned to Columbia only in 1887, and the community again prospered.

Lynch, Dominick Irish-born Roman Catholic merchant and philanthropist, born Galway, 1754, died the Bronx, New York, 5 June 1825. As manager of his father's commercial house in Bruges, Lynch amassed a fortune during the American Revolution, and by selling flax in Ireland. He moved to New York in 1785, where he combined China trade investments with real estate. He made many donations to Catholic causes and helped to build the first permanent Catholic church in New York City, 1786. His estate in Westchester County passed to the Christian Brothers, who converted it to the Academy of the Sacred Heart.

Lynch, John Irish scholar and patriot, born Galway, c.1599, died St-Malo, France, c.1673. Ordained in France in 1621, Lynch returned to Ireland to teach, but because he opposed the 1641 rebellion, made an enemy of its leader, Owen Roe O'Neill, as being Anglo-Irish in his sympathies; he fled to France, where he remained. An historian of repute, he published *Cambrensis eversus*, a refutation of the anti-Irish work of **Giraldus Cambrensis** in the twelfth century, and *Alithonologia*, an account of the Irish people during the reign of **Elizabeth I**.

Lynch, John Joseph Irish-born Roman Catholic missionary archbishop, born Clones, County Monaghan, 6 February 1816, died Toronto, 12 May 1888. Ordained a Vincentian in 1843, Lynch went to the USA as president of St Mary's of the Barrens, a Lazarist college in Missouri, and founded the Seminary of Our Lady of the Angels,

at Niagara Falls, in 1856. He succeeded to the See of Toronto in 1860, and became its first archbishop in 1867. He supported the definition of papal infallibility at Vatican Council I, and convened the first Provincial Council of Canada (1873).

Lynch, Patrick Nelson Irish-born Roman Catholic bishop in the USA, born County Monaghan, 10 March 1817, died Charleston, South Carolina, 26 February 1882. Ordained in Rome, Lynch became assistant at the Charleston Cathedral, and edited *The United States Catholic Miscellany*, a diocesan weekly in Charleston. Named bishop of Charleston, in 1864 the Confederate government sent him to Rome to plead its cause before **Pius IX**; President Andrew Johnson forgave him his complicity and he returned to his diocese in 1865. The Civil War destroyed much Church property and Lynch devoted the postwar years to rebuilding. He attended Vatican Council I and wrote accounts of the proceedings in the *Catholic World*.

Lyndwood, William Bishop of St Davids and ecclesiastical lawyer, born Lindwood, near Market Rasen, Lincolnshire, c.1357, died London, 21 October 1446. He was educated first at Cambridge then at Oxford, where he graduated as a doctor of laws. He held various legal positions in the English Church: in 1414 he was made 'officialis', or judge, for the Diocese of Canterbury, then under Archbishop **Chichele**, and was rewarded with a number of benefices. In 1426 he became Dean of the Arches. He also undertook public service, particularly diplomatic, and in 1433 became Keeper of the Privy Seal. In 1442 the Pope promoted him to the bishopric of St Davids; he was consecrated on 21 October that year in St Stephen's Chapel, Westminster, where his will afterwards directed that he be buried. His *Provinciale* (1433) consists of five books containing the synodical constitutions of Canterbury from Archbishops **Langton** (1222) to Chichele (1416), accompanied by a gloss in particularly elegant Latin. It is the standard collection of English ecclesiastical legislation.

Lynskey, Elizabeth Mary American Roman Catholic educator, born Minneapolis, Minnesota, 28 September 1896, died Minneapolis, 30 November 1954. A teacher of political science at Hunter

College for many years, she founded the Catholic Association for International Peace, 1942, and acted as liaison officer for the Association, to the USA Mission to the United Nations. The War Department sent her to Austria in 1948 as a consultant on social studies. A contributing editor to *The Commonweal*, she also wrote on international questions, and published *The Government of the Catholic Church*.

Lyonnet, Stanislaus French Jesuit biblical scholar, born Saint-Étienne, 23 August 1902, died Rome, 8 June 1986. Lyonnet taught classical philology at Izeure, NT at Lyons-Fourvière and, from 1943, at the Pontifical Biblical Institute, where he wrote *Les origines de la mission arménienne de la Bible et la Diatesseron*. He published several books and many articles, among the more important being *De peccato et redemptione*, his well-known 'Les Épîtres de St Paul aux Galates et aux Romains', in the *Bible de Jérusalem*, and his classic article in English, 'St Paul: Liberty and Law'. Lyonnet's openness to the views of others gave rise to criticism from more-conservative scholars, and he was suspended from teaching, 1962–4, during which time he gave lectures to the French-speaking bishops at Vatican II.

Lyte, Henry Francis Minister and hymn-writer, born Ednam, near Kelso, Roxburghshire, 1 June 1793, died Nice, 20 November 1847. He was educated at Trinity College, Dublin, and served as a curate in Ireland and England. His best-known hymns are 'Abide With Me', popular at funerals, and 'Praise, My Soul, the King of Heaven'.

M

Ma Liang, Joseph (Ma Hsiang-pai) Roman Catholic Chinese scholar and educator, born Chinkiang, Kiangsu, 1840, died Shanghai, 1939. From a family who were Catholic since the time of Matteo **Ricci**, and ordained by the Jesuits in Shanghai, Ma Liang left the Society in 1876 and entered government service; he returned to the practice of his faith in later years, though not to the exercise of his priesthood. Ma Liang had a high reputation as a Chinese and a Latin scholar; he published a translation into Mandarin, with commentary, of the NT, and a biography of St **Thérèse of Lisieux**. A collection of his writings, *Ma Hsiang-pai hsiensheng wen-chi*, has been published since his death.

Maasen, Friedrich Bernhard Canon law historian, born near Innsbruck, Austria, 1823, died Wiltern, Germany, 9 April 1900. An advocate who was prevented from taking public office by his conversion to Roman Catholicism. In 1851 he began university teaching and became professor at Innsbruck in 1857, Gratz in 1860 and Vienna in 1871. Although he first opposed the decrees on papal infallibility put forward by the First Vatican Council, he later defended the claims of the Roman Catholic Church, during the anti-Catholic movement in Germany of the 1870s. His two most renowned works on canon law are *Geschichte der Quellen und der Literatur des Canonischen Rechts im Abendlande bis zum Ausgange des Mittlelaters* (1870) and *Pseudoisidorstudien* (1885).

Mabillon, Jean Monk of the Congregation of St Maur, historian and palaeographer, born St Pierremont, Ardennes, 23 November 1632, died Paris 27 December 1707. He studied at the University of Reims, then joined the abbey of St Remi, being professed there in 1654. He transferred to the abbey at Nogent-sous-Courcy two years later, and two years after that to Corbie, where he was ordained in 1660. In 1664 he was sent to Paris, to the monastery of St Germain-des-Prés, where he remained for the rest of his life, apart from the many journeys he made mainly around France, but also, in 1883, around Germany and Switzerland, and, in 1685–6, through Italy, in search of manuscript collections. He published accounts of these journeys, describing the manuscripts he found. His particular concern was with the history and traditions both of his Benedictine Order and of the Maurist Congregation in particlar, defending it against attacks from the Abbé de **Rancé**. His major work, *De re diplomatica* (Paris, 1681), which effectively invented the science of palaeography, was, however, directed against the accusations of the Jesuit Daniel van **Papenbroeck** who had claimed that ancient charters upon which the Maurist claims depended, were forgeries. A supplement to this work, *Librorum de re diplomatica supplementum*, appeared in 1704. He also published the works of St **Bernard** and of Peter de Celle. Other major works were the nine-volume *Acta sanctorum ordinis Sancti Benedicti* (Paris, 1668–1701) and the *annales ordinis sancti Benedicti* (4 vols, Paris, 1703–7: two further volumes were completed after his death by others). He also published a number of shorter works on the liturgy, on relics and on a Christian death – this last appeared in 1702, dedicated to the Queen of England.

Macarius III (of Cyprus) (Makarios Mouskas)

archbishop of Cyprus, born near Paphos, 13 August 1913, died Nicosia, 3 August 1977. He became a novice at the age of thirteen. In 1948 he was elected bishop of Kition and in 1950 archbishop of Cyprus and leader of the Greek community. He played a prominent role in Cyprus' struggle against Britain in the 1950s, and after independence (which he had always opposed, in favour of union with Greece) became its first president. As well as his political role he improved clerical education and subsidized Orthodox mission in Kenya (where the seminary bears his name).

Macarius Chrysocephalos   Greek bishop and exegete, born c.1300, died August 1382. Macarius became a monk in 1327, bishop of Philadelphia in 1336 and, later, 1340s, metropolitan judge, *catholicos*, of the empire under **John V Palaeologus**. He wrote a life of Meletius Galesiotes, in which he advocated, as did his subject, continued separation of the Eastern Church from Rome. His major works are exegetical texts: one on Genesis, three tomes on Matthew and 24 tracts on Luke, for which he depended on Nicetas of Heraclea.

Macarius Magnes   Bishop and apologist, died 425. His life is completely obscure, though he has been identified with a bishop of Magnesia who participated in the Synod of the Oak at Chalcedon in 403. He was the author of a five-book apology against Neoplatonist objections to Christian belief, which was cited by the ninth-century Iconoclasts in support of their views. The work draws on Porphyry. The manuscript was lost, and the text was not available until the nineteenth century, when another poor quality manuscript was discovered in Athens; this too has apparently been lost. There are also fragments of a set of homilies on Genesis falsely attributed to him.

Macarius of Alexandria   Saint, acetic and writer, died c.394. Also called 'Macarius the Younger' or 'Politicus' to distinguish him from his contemporary **Macarius of Egypt.** During the persecution of Valens, 364–78, he was banished by the Arian patriarch of Alexandria, Lucius. He has been credited with some 30 regulations for monks in the Nitrian desert and a sermon on the eschatology of souls, among other writings.

Macarius of Altai (Makary Glukharev)   Russian Orthodox missionary in Siberia, born Viazma, 1792, died Bolkhov, 18 May 1847. He became a monk and priest and was appointed to the Altai mission in southern Siberia. He acquired extensive knowledge of the local languages and worked out a sophisticated missionary strategy and theology. He is one of the greatest Russian missionaries of recent centuries.

Macarius of Corinth (Notaras)   Orthodox saint, bishop and spiritual writer, born Corinth, 1731, died Chios, 17 April 1805. Both as bishop and writer he helped to sustain and revive the Greek Church under Turkish rule. He is most famous as the co-compiler (with St **Nicodemus of the Holy Mountain**) of the *Philokalia*; in fact he was probably the more important figure in the publication of this collection.

Macarius of Egypt   Saint, writer and ascetic, also called 'Macarius the Elder' or 'the Great', born c.300, died c.390. He was a native of Egypt and for most of his life lived in the wilderness of Scete, at that time the focal point of Egyptian monasticism, and was widely regarded as a holy man. Since the sixteenth century he has been recognized as the writer of some 50 homilies – though it is possible that these belong to another, unknown 'Macarius'.

Macarius of Jerusalem   Saint, bishop of Jerusalem, elected 312, died c.333. He has been regarded as the Macarius who was labelled an 'uneducated heretic' by **Arius** in his letter to **Eusebius of Nicomedia**. He attended Nicaea (325) and there is a tradition that he actively participated in the debate against the Arians. Macarius was of the opinion that Jerusalem ought to have precedence over Caesarea. **Constantine I** drafted a letter assigning construction of the church of the Holy Sepulchre to Macarius.

Macarius (Makary) of Optina   Russian Orthodox saint and elder, born Kaluga, 1788, died Optina Hermitage, 7 September 1860. He gave up a brilliant career to become a monk and was appointed confessor at Optina in 1836. Thereafter he received visitors from all over Russia. His letters of spiritual advice form five published volumes. He was influential in spreading the practice of the Jesus Prayer and helped translate patristic texts into modern Russian. His *Russian Letters of Spiritual Direction* are available in English (1944). Feast days 7 September and 11 October.

Macarius of Pelecete Saint, Byzantine monk, born Constantinople, *c.*750, died 'Aphrysia' (unknown island), 829. Macarius entered the monastery of Pelecete in Bithynia, succeeded St Hilarion as abbot, and received ordination from **Tarasius**, patriarch of Constantinople. Renowned for his holiness and miracles, Macarius opposed the Iconoclast Emperor **Leo V** the Armenian, and suffered imprisonment and torture. Freed by Michael II, he continued to refuse to accept the heretical teaching, and was exiled, as a septuagenarian, to the island where he died. Feast day 1 April.

Macarius Scottus Blessed, Benedictine abbot, born Ireland or Scotland, *c.*1100, died probably monastery of Sankt Jakob, Germany, 1153. Marcarius was a Benedictine at the abbey of Regensburg, when, in 1139, he was made abbot of the monastery of Sankt Jakob. He was known as a holy man and even made a journey to Rome to obtain relics for his community. His body was moved to the abbey church in 1615, and after this many miracles were attributed to his intercession. Feast day 23 January.

McAuley, Catherine Venerable, Irish religious foundress, born Dublin, 29 September 1778, died there, 11 November 1841. Her parents were named 'McGauley', but her mother adopted 'McAuley' after her husband's death in 1783. Catherine's mother lived until 1798, spending all her inheritance, and her three children were brought up by non-Catholic relatives. Catherine, however, made the acquaintance of a couple called Callaghan, recently returned from India, and in 1809 went to live with them. Although they, too, were Protestants (both later converted to Catholicism) they encouraged Catherine's desire to continue in her faith. Catherine inherited all their fortune – they were otherwise childless – and in 1827 with the money founded a house for herself and a few companions in Baggot Street, Dublin. It was to serve as a women's residence, an orphanage and a school. Catherine's original intention was to create a society of lay women dedicated to charitable

works, but the archbishop of Dublin recommended that, for it to survive, it ought to become a religious congregation. Catherine and two friends entered the novitiate of the Presentation Nuns in Dublin in 1830, and were professed in December the following year, whereupon they returned to their own house and admitted, early the next month, seven of their companions into the Order Catherine had decided to call the 'Sisters of Mercy'. She adapted the rule of life of the Presentation Order for her own nuns, and her Rule was approved by the Vatican in 1841. Several foundations were soon made in Ireland, the first in London in 1839, and in Pittsburgh, USA, in 1846.

MacAuley, Geneviève Garvan Brady American Roman Catholic philanthropist, born Hartford, Connecticut, 11 April 1884, died Rome, 24 November 1938. Geneviève MacAuley inherited a fortune from her husband in 1930, and made many benefactions to Catholic organizations. Chairman of the Girl Scouts of America and president of the World Council of Girl Scouts, she organized national relief and welfare to alleviate widespread distress during the winter of 1932. She was decorated by the Belgian and French governments for war service, and received the *Pro Ecclesia et Pontifice* medal from both **Pius X** and **Pius XI**.

McAvoy, Thomas American historian, born Tipton, Indiana, 12 September 1903, died Notre Dame, Indiana, 5 July 1969. Ordained a priest of the Holy Cross in 1929, McAvoy taught at Notre Dame, where he specialized in Catholic history and organized the manuscript collection into one of the richest archives for the study of American Catholic history. He contributed many articles to the *New Catholic Encyclopedia* and, of his many works, *The Americanist Heresy in Roman Catholicism, 1895–1900* won the American Catholic Historical Association's prize in 1963. He edited the quarterly *Review of Politics* for many years.

McCaffrey, John Henry American educator, born Emmitsburg, Maryland, 6 September 1806, died there 26 September 1881. Ordained in 1838, McCaffrey served as president of St Mary's College for 34 years, during which time the College provided 26 bishops and archbishops to the American Church; he refused a bishopric himself. Active as a theologian in several Councils of Baltimore, Mc-Caffrey wrote a catechism in 1865 which became the format of the famous *Baltimore Catechism*.

McCarthy, Joseph Raymond   Roman Catholic US senator, born near Appleton, Wisconsin, 14 November 1908, died Bethesda, Maryland, 2 May 1957. His tough policy of alleging Communist sympathies in US citizens resulted in the coining of the term 'McCarthyism'. He was a Wisconsin attorney, became a judge, served in the Marines in World War II and was elected to the US Senate. In the early 1950s he claimed that 205 Communists had infiltrated the State Department and began a crusade against all suspected Communists in American public life. However, the televised proceedings which he led against US army officers and civilians revealed to all viewers his brutal tactics. Opinion turned against him, and the Senate condemned him for conduct contrary to Senate traditions. As a result of his crusade, some US citizens, including employees of the Hollywood film industry, found themselves unemployable.

McClellan, William Hildrup   American OT exegete, born West Chester, Pennsylvania, 25 March 1874, died Woodstock, Maryland, 8 May 1951. Ordained an Episcopalian minister, McClellan became a Catholic and a Jesuit priest, in 1918. He taught OT at Woodstock and contributed frequently to biblical periodicals. His treatise on the Old Latin Psalter was serialized in the first 22 numbers of the *Catholic Biblical Quarterly*.

McCloskey, John   First US cardinal, born Brooklyn, New York, 10 March 1810, died New York City, 10 October 1885. He was educated in Maryland, where he was ordained, and in Rome. On his return to New York he became the first president of St John's College (later Fordham University), and later archbishop of New York – during which time he finished the construction of St Patrick's Cathedral. He was made cardinal in 1875.

McCloskey, William George   American Roman Catholic bishop, born Brooklyn, New York, 10 November 1823, died Louisville, Kentucky, 17 September 1909. Named first rector of the North American College, Rome, in 1859, McCloskey had to cope with the difficult financial circumstances

created by the American Civil War. Appointed bishop of Louisville, where he remained 41 years, he greatly expanded Catholic institutions, and showed himself a zealous shepherd, though his authoritarian disposition led to controversies with his own clergy and religious in the diocese.

McCormick, Richard   American Jesuit theologian, born Cleveland, Ohio, 3 October 1922, died Notre Dame, Indiana, 12 February 2000. Ordained in 1953, McCormick became professor of Christian ethics at Notre Dame in 1986. Among his many books are *Notes on Moral Theology* (a collection of reviews on moral theology for the Jesuit), *Theological Studies, Medicine in the Catholic Tradition, The Critical Calling: Moral Dilemmas since Vatican II* and *Corrective Vision: Explorations in Moral Theology*. He edited, with Charles Curran, eleven volumes of *Readings in Moral Theology*, and published many articles in scholarly and popular publications. In 1995 he received both the Reinhold Niebuhr Award for the promotion of justice, and the Catholic Book Club's Campion Award in recognition of his eminence as 'scholar, writer and defender of the faith'.

MacDonald, Alexander   Scottish poet and patriot, born Dalilea, Argyllshire, *c.*1700, died Sandaij, Invernesshire, *c.*1770. Employed as a young man by the Protestant Society for Promoting Christian Knowledge, MacDonald produced *A Gaelic and English Vocabulary* (1741), the first Scottish-Gaelic vocabulary to be separately printed; however, his subsequent composition of 'Galick songs stuffed with obscene language', caused his dismissal from the Society in 1745. About this time MacDonald converted to the Roman Catholic Church, and served in the Jacobite Rising of 1745; he may have written the *Journal and Memoirs of Prince Charles' Expedition into Scotland, 1745–46*, and he did become Charles' Gaelic tutor. His *Gaelic Verse* is notable for its vigorous vocabulary, its ribald verses, and the passion with which it expresses the Highlanders' attachment to the Jacobite cause.

McDonald, Allan   Scottish folklorist and poet, born Fort William, 25 October 1859, died Isle of Eriskay, Hebrides, 8 October 1905. Ordained at the Scots College, Valladolid, Spain, in 1882, McDonald returned to Scotland as parish priest of both Daliburgh on South Uist, and of Eriskay. As pastor of an impoverished Gaelic-speaking population, he used the rich oral Gaelic dialect to compose a hymnal, and his poetry reflects the local, deeply spiritual culture. He is portrayed by Neil Munro in *Children of the Tempest* and in *The Brave Days*.

McDonald, Barnabas Edward American religious and youth leader, born Ogdensburg, New York, 20 July 1865, died Santa Fe, New Mexico, 22 April 1929. A Christian Brother, McDonald founded St Philips Home for urban working boys in 1902, and Lincoln Agricultural School in 1909, pioneering the use of the 'cottage system'. He served as director of Catholic Charities in Toronto, where he introduced Catholic Scouting, and organized the Columban Squires of the Knights of Columbus. At Notre Dame University, he introduced a programme to train youth workers, subsequently copied by schools of social work in other universities; a director of more than 40 youth organizations, he received many awards.

MacDonald, John Scottish Roman Catholic nobleman, eighth laird of Glenaladale, born Glenaladale, *c.*1742, died Tracalie, Prince Edward Island, 1811. Having investigated the persecution of Catholic Jacobites in South Uist, Hebrides, MacDonald promoted emigration to the colonies, and purchased a tract of land on Prince Edward Island; more than 500 Scots from South Uist and the mainland went to his new estates. During the American Revolution, Glenaladale raised the Royal Highland Regiment; for his loyalty to the Crown, the king offered him the governorship of Prince Edward Island, but he could not accept, because the Popish Recusants Act of 1672 was still in force.

MacDonnell, Alexander Roman Catholic bishop of Kingston, Ontario, born Glengarry, Scotland, 17 July 1762, died Dumfries, Scotland, 14 January 1840. He was ordained in 1787, having studied at Paris and Valladolid. He worked in Badenoch before becoming the first resident Catholic priest in Glasgow, in 1792. Instrumental in forming the Glengarry Fencibles he became their chaplain, the first Catholic chaplain in the British army. When they disbanded in 1802 he obtained land for them in Canada and joined them in 1804. He was made

vicar general of the province in 1807, was ordained auxiliary bishop in 1820 and made bishop of the new Kingston diocese in 1826. During his episcopacy, priests and congregations increased tenfold. Loyal to the government, he was appointed a member of the legislative assembly of Upper Canada in 1831. The town of Alexandria, Ontario, is named after him.

McDonnell, Thomas John American Roman Catholic bishop, born New York City, 18 August 1894, died Huntington, West Virginia, 25 February 1961. Ordained in 1919, McDonnell became national director of the Society for the Propagation of the Faith in 1936, auxiliary bishop of New York in 1947 and bishop of Wheeling, West Virginia, in 1951. Appointed by the governor to various state commissions, he ensured that the 'Name of God' figured in the preamble to the state constitution.

McDougall, Francis Thompson Anglican bishop of Labuan and Sarawak, born Sydenham, 30 June 1817; died November 1886. He spent his childhood in Malta and Corfu, trained as a surgeon in London (MRCS 1839, FRCS 1854) and studied at Magdalen College, Oxford (BA 1844, MA 1845). He married Harriette Bunyon in 1843. At the request of Rajah James Brooke, they went to Kuching, Sarawak in 1848. McDougall became bishop of Labuan in 1855 and of Sarawak in 1856. He survived a Chinese revolt in 1857, but his enthusiasm in attacking 'pirates' in 1862 brought controversy and he was remembered more as a doctor and sailor than as a missionary. They left Sarawak in 1867 and in 1868 he became vicar of Godmanchester. His *Book of Common Prayer* in Malay was published in 1858 and his Malay catechism in 1868.

MacEachen, Evan Scottish Roman Catholic Gaelic scholar, born Arisaig, 1769, died Tombae, 9 September 1849. Ordained at the Scots College, Valladolid in 1798, MacEachen returned to Lismore as a professor, and to pastoral work in Strathglass and Aberdeenshire. He translated from the Scottish Gaelic nearly all the extant devotional literature before 1850: *The Abridgement of Christian Doctrine*; Lorenzo Scupoli's *Spiritual Combat*; **Thomas à Kempis'** *The Imitation of Christ*; the *Declaration* *of the British Catholic Bishops (1838)*; the NT; and Bishop **Challoner**'s *Meditations*.

MacEachen, Roderick A. American catechist and Roman Catholic priest, born Shawnee, Ohio, 28 December 1873, died St Leo's Abbey, Florida, 30 June 1965. Ordained in 1901, MacEachen did graduate studies in Prague, Budapest and Rome; he became a key figure in the abortive attempt to compile a universal catechism, so as to comply with the decree *De Parvo Catechismo* (1870). He returned to lecture in catechetics at the Catholic University of America, and retired to Florida. He published numerous catechisms, several of which he himself translated into European languages, and received the Floriant award in recognition of his contribution to Catholic education in Florida.

Macedo Costa, Antonio de Brazilian Roman Catholic bishop, born Maragogipe, Bahia, 7 August 1830, died Barbacena, Minas Gerais, 21 March 1891. Ordained in Paris in 1857, Macedo Costa returned to Brazil in 1859, and became bishop of Pará in 1861. He condemned interference of the State in the spiritual jurisdiction of the Brazilian Church. He fought against Freemasonry's infiltration of the religious orders, for which he was briefly imprisoned. Transferred to the primatial see of Bahia in 1890, Macedo Costa did not take possession of his archdiocese, although he assumed the presidency of the Brazilian hierarchy, and contributed much to the prestige of the Church at the time of the Republic.

MacElwane, James Bernard American Jesuit geophysicist, born Port Clinton, Ohio, 28 September 1883, died St Louis, Missouri, 15 December 1956. Ordained in 1918, MacElwane studied physics at the California Institute of Technology, Beverly, became a professor of geophysics, and published *Physics of the Seismograph*; he founded the Jesuit Seismological Association. His works include 133 technical papers and two books. During World War II, he was a member of the Research and Development Board of the Department of Defense. He served as a member of the board of the National Science Foundation in 1954, and was elected a member of the National Academy of Sciences.

McEntegart, Bryan J. American Roman Catholic archbishop and social worker, born New York City, 5 January 1893, died Brooklyn, 30 September 1968. Ordained in 1917, McEntegart served the Catholic Charities of the Archdiocese of New York in various capacities, and held positions as secretary of the Catholic Near East Welfare Association, and as director of the War Relief Services. While bishop of Ogdensburg, he founded a diocesan newspaper, built a cathedral, a preparatory seminary in Queen's County and established pension and medical plans for all diocesan employees.

McFarland, Francis Patrick American Roman Catholic bishop, born Franklin, Pennsylvania, 16 April 1819, died Hartford, Connecticut, 2 October 1874. Ordained in 1845, McFarland became bishop of Hartford in 1858, then still a missionary diocese, and succeeded in obtaining the services of several religious communities expert in education and the social services. Despite poor health and primitive travelling conditions, McFarland was assiduous in attending to the affairs of his diocese, and ensuring the best use of resources available in the pioneer territory. He attended Vatican Council I in 1869.

McGarry, William James American Jesuit exegete and educator, born Hamilton, Massachusetts, 14 March 1894, died New York City, 23 September 1941. McGarry taught sacred Scripture at Weston College, became president of Boston College in 1937 and first editor of *Theological Studies* from 1939 until his death. His chief concern was to place the Scriptures at the centre of the devotional lives of the faithful, to which end he published numerous articles and philosophical notes on the Mystical Body, as well as *Paul and the Crucified*, *Unto the End* and *He Cometh*.

McGarvey, William American priest and author, born Philadelphia, Pennsylvania, 14 August 1861, died San Diego, California, 27 February 1924. Ordained an Episcopalian minister in 1886, McGarvey became a Catholic in 1908 and, ordained in 1910, was appointed rector of the church of the Holy Infancy, Bethlehem, Pennsylvania, where he founded and directed a house for Catholic students at Lehigh University. He published *The Council of Nicaea*, *The Doctrine of the Church of England and* *of St Thomas and the Real Presence* and *The Ceremonies of Low Mass.*

McGavran, Donald Anderson Founder of the Church Growth movement, born Damoh, India, 15 December 1897, died 10 July 1990. He graduated from Butler University, Yale Divinity School and Columbia University (Ph.D.) and served as a Disciples of Christ missionary in India, 1923–54. Stimulated by the work of Wascom Pickett, he sought to discover the 'reproducible principles' contributing to Church growth. In 1961 he established the Institute of Church Growth in Eugene, Oregon, and in 1965 became founding dean of the School of World Mission and Institute of Church Growth at Fuller Theological Seminary. He had the knack of asking uncomfortable questions, was taken seriously by ecumenical and other critics, and challenged the individualism of the evangelical tradition. If he found it hard to provide answers to some more penetrating theological concerns, he remains significant for his questions, and the inspiration of his commitment that God's lost people should be found.

McGee, Thomas D'Arcy Journalist, nationalist, Young Irelander, born Carlingford, County Louth, 13 April 1825, assassinated at his house in Ottawa, 7 April 1868. McGee emigrated to Boston in 1842 and worked as a clerk on the *Boston Pilot*, which he later edited. His growing reputation and political activities brought him to the notice of the Young Ireland movement. He was soon appointed London correspondent to their papers *The Freeman's Journal* and *The Nation* and to these he contributed much patriotic poetry. He was sent to Scotland to secure help for the 1848 rising but his mission was aborted and he was sheltered by Dr Maginn, the bishop of Derry, whose Life he published in 1857. The bishop aided his escape back to America, where he founded *The American Celt* and *The New York Nation*; his editorials and articles demonstrate that he had changed his views from physical force to constitutional measures for nationalist Ireland. The Irish American republicans accused him of treachery and held him partially responsible for the failure of the 1848 rebellion. He, however, blamed the Catholic priesthood and hierarchy. He moved to Canada and settling in Montreal he founded another paper, *The New Era*,

in 1857. He became an MP, and held government office, taking a prominent part in guiding Canada towards Dominion status and federation. At this stage he threw himself unreservedly into the cause of Catholicism apart from any form of nationality. He denounced the Fenian raids into Canada and was assassinated outside his own house in Ottawa. His writings include *The Life of Art MacMurrough* (1847), *Irish Writers of the Seventeenth Century* (1847), *Irish Settlers in North America* (1852) and a popular *History of Ireland* (3 vols, 1862–9). McGee's collected poetry, for which he is best remembered, was published by Mrs John Sadleir in New York in 1869.

McGivney, Michael Joseph Roman Catholic priest and founder of the Knights of Columbus, born Waterbury, Connecticut, 12 August 1852, died Thomaston, 14 August 1890. Ordained in 1877, McGivney conceived the idea, while a curate at St Mary's Church, New Haven, of a benevolent Catholic society of laymen pledged to a life of charity, fraternalism, unity and patriotism; he named the organization the 'Knights of Columbus', incorporated in 1882, of which he served as chaplain until his death. The Knights dedicated a monument to McGivney in Waterbury in 1957.

McGloin, Frank Irish-American jurist, born Gort, Galway, 22 February 1846, died New Orleans, 1921. Taken to New Orleans as an infant, McGloin served in the Confederate army during the Civil War, became a lawyer in 1866 and served two terms as senior justice of the court of appeals of Louisiana. Named president of the Society of the Holy Spirit, he was active in the St Vincent de Paul Society and in the Federation of Catholic Societies. He published *The Light of Faith* and *The Mystery of the Holy Trinity*, and became a Knight Commander of the Order of St Gregory in 1910.

McGlynn, Edward American Roman Catholic priest and social reformer, born New York City, 27 September 1837, died Newburgh, New York, 7 January 1900. Named pastor of St Stephen's parish in New York City, McGlynn became distressed by the plight of his unemployed and poverty-stricken parishioners. He began to study political economy, and supported the single-tax doctrine of Henry George as the fundamental remedy for poverty;

this earned him the censure of Rome and excommunication in 1887. Reinstated in 1892, McGlynn continued to defend the single-tax theory, and helped to found the Anti-Poverty Society, which advocated an apostolic rather than a pedagogical ministry and support for public over parochial schools. At his funeral were prominent all the Protestant ministers, and the one Jewish rabbi in Newburgh.

McGowan, Raymond Augustine   American labour expert, born Brookfield, Missouri, 23 June 1892, died Kansas City, 13 November 1962. Named director of the Department of Social Action of the National Catholic Welfare Conference, McGowan became a leading authority on labour and industrial relations; he founded the Catholic Conference on Industrial Problems and organized conferences throughout the USA. President Franklin D. Roosevelt appointed him to a commission to study the organic law of Puerto Rico. He founded the Catholic Association for International Peace and the American Catholic Social Action Confederation. He published *Towards Social Justice* and numerous articles on the papal encyclicals.

McGrath, James   Irish-American Roman Catholic missionary, born Holy Cross, Tipperary, 26 June 1835, died Albany, New York, 12 January 1898. Ordained an Oblate of Mary Immaculate in 1859, McGrath taught at Ottawa University, and in 1866 went to Buffalo, New York, from where he conducted parochial missions throughout the northeastern USA. He proposed a separate Oblate province in America, and became its first provincial in 1883, with foundations from Massachusetts to Mexico; he made his mark as a church builder and an early advocate of parochial schools.

Macgrath, John Macrory   Irish historian, born Munster, Ireland, died *c*.1475. His main work is his *Cathreim Thoirdhealbhaigh*, which is a history of the wars of Thomond from 1194 to 1318. Among other things it details the failure of O'Brien and O'Neill to unite against the invaders, and the subsequent victory of the Anglo-Normans at the Battle of Downpatrick in 1259. It was written in Irish and has been translated into English.

MacGregor, James   Scottish folklorist, dean of Lismore, born Fortingall, Perthshire, *c*.1480, died there, 12 December 1551. MacGregor and his brother Duncan collected the 178 poems by 45 Scottish and 21 Irish poets of what is called the *Book of the Dean of Lismore*, a text of great philological value that illustrates the relations between Western Scotland and Ireland from an early date. It has the merit of being a treasure trove of lyric poetry, compiled from the oral recitation of strolling bards, written in Scots, and now in the Advocates Library, Edinburgh. MacGregor is buried in the church at Inchordin.

McGroarty, Julia   Religious foundress, founded Trinity College, Washington DC, born Inver, Donegal, 13 February 1827, died Peabody, Massachusetts, 12 November 1901. Taken to the USA as a child, Sister Julia of the Sisters of Notre Dame de Namur established a school for black children in Philadelphia, became superior of the Sisters west of the Rocky Mountains, and later of their houses in California. An able administrator, she founded some fourteen convents, prepared a course of studies in her schools and introduced a system of general examinations. Her great achievement was to establish at the Catholic University of America, which did not then admit them, the Trinity College for women.

McGuire, Martin R. P.   American patristic scholar, born Witinsville, Massachusetts, 30 December 1897, died Washington, DC, 15 March 1969. Appointed professor, in 1946, and head of the department of Greek and Latin at the Catholic University of America, McGuire gained renown for his classical scholarship and many publications. *An Introduction to Classical Scholarship* and *The Political and Cultural History of the Ancient World* are among his principal works. He was editor of the *Catholic Historical Review*, an editor of *The Fathers of the Church: A New Translation*, and directed the fifteen volumes of *The New Catholic Encyclopedia* that appeared in 1967.

McGurk, Bryan   Dean and vicar general of the Archdiocese of Armagh, born Termonmagurk, County Tyrone, *c*.1622, died Armagh gaol for the Catholic faith, 13 February 1713. He was ordained in 1660 and spent the first twelve years of his ministry in his native and neighbouring parishes.

In 1672 he was appointed 'dean and prior of the Culdees', and was one of Oliver **Plunket**'s vicars general in his campaign of reform: McGurk was given specific jurisdiction over the Diocese of Raphoe. From 1660 to 1678 the persecution of Catholic clergy had been desultory but with rumours of the Popish Plot in that year, leading clergy, including McGurk, were arrested. Throughout frequent arrests, trials and acquittals McGurk successfully outwitted the authorities, but his efforts were frequently hampered by the malice of clergy he had previously censured. In 1681/2, during Oliver Plunket's imprisonment, and later, he administered the archdiocese. Plunket from prison sent his name forward to the Holy See as a worthy pastor for a vacant see. But Rome appointed Dominic Maguire, honorary chaplain to the Spanish ambassador at the English court: when the latter fled to Paris about 1693 McGurk again took charge of the archdiocese, until his final imprisonment and death in Armagh gaol.

Mácha, Karel Hynek Czech poet, born Prague, 16 November 1810, died Litomerice, Bohemia, 5 November 1836. The son of a Prague artisan, Mácha first wrote in German, but when he began to write in Czech, he found a new vitality reflected in the dramatic imagery of baroque religious hymns, legends and chronicles. He wished to portray the vast theatre containing the splendours of the universe, at the centre of which is man, close to his Creator and yet far from him. His major work *Maj* (May) is a glorification of the month of flowers in all its dramatic beauty.

MacHale, John Irish Roman Catholic bishop, born Tubbernavine, County Mayo, 6 March 1791, died Tuam, 4 November 1881. He began his education in one of the hedge-schools but went later to Castlebar, where he learned French, Italian, German, Latin, Greek and Hebrew, and then to Maynooth, where he studied and later taught theology. He was ordained in 1814 and became professor of theology in 1820. In 1825 he was made coadjutor bishop of Killala. He wrote, preached and corresponded tirelessly in the cause of Catholic Emancipation. In 1834 and against the express wishes of the British government, **Gregory XVI** appointed him bishop of Tuam. He founded schools, run by religious orders, for boys and girls,

supported Daniel **O'Connell**'s Repeal of the Union and opposed the Charitable Bequests Bill. In the famine of 1846–7 he used every means open to him to ensure that as much food as possible was acquired and distributed to those in need. Following the death of O'Connell, MacHale maintained the pressure on the British government to legislate in favour of the Irish, continued to defy ministers and hindered diplomatic relations between Westminster and Rome. He attended Vatican Council I and voted against the document on papal infallibility, though he afterwards submitted. He preached every Sunday in Irish and translated prayers, hymns, a catechism, parts of Scripture and Homer's *Iliad* into Irish. His other publications include the 'Hierophilus letters,' written against the Irish Established Church, and *On the Evidence and Doctrines of the Catholic Church*.

McHardy, William Duff Presbyterian Scripture scholar, born Cullen, Banffshire, 26 May 1911, died Cullen, 9 April 2000. He was educated at Aberdeen, Edinburgh and Oxford Universities, gaining a Ph.D. for an edition of the Syriac (i.e. Peshitta) version of the book of Ecclesiasticus. He taught at Selly Oak, Birmingham, for three years, at Oxford from 1945 as a lecturer in Aramaic and Syriac, from 1948 at London as professor of OT studies and finally at Oxford as regius professor of Hebrew, in 1960. He had been ordained a Presbyterian minister while at Edinburgh, which meant he could not hold the canonry at Oxford traditionally associated with the regius professorship. He was one of the leading Hebrew scholars of his day and was a member of the team which produced the New English Bible in 1970, and he directed the group which produced the Revised English Bible of 1989.

Machaut, Guillaume de Priest, poet and composer, born probably in Rheims, 1300, died there, 1377. He was secretary to John, duke of Luxemburg and king of Bohemia, and later served Charles V of France. He became a canon of Rheims, where he spent much of his life. Machaut was the main French composer of the fourteenth century and the most prolific. His *Messe de Notre Dame* is the first complete setting of the Ordinary of the Mass composed by one individual. Also he composed 23 motets and secular music.

Machebeuf, Joseph Projectus French-born Roman Catholic bishop and missionary, born Riom, 11 May 1812, died Denver, Colorado, 10 July 1889. Ordained in 1836, Machebeuf went with John Baptist **Lamy** to the USA, and served at the mission in Ohio, building churches and advocating temperance. He then went to New Mexico to serve under Lamy, who sent him to Denver to care for the mining population in their booming communities. In 1887 the territory of Colorado became a diocese, and Machebeuf its first bishop, at Denver. He proved himself a great administrator, and by 1889 there were 102 churches and chapels, an orphanage, 16 parish schools, 9 academies, a protected home, a college for men, and 40,000 Catholics in his diocese.

Machen, John Gresham Orthodox Presbyterian leader, born Baltimore, USA, 28 July 1881, died Bismark, North Dakota, 1 January 1937. He was educated at Johns Hopkins and Princeton and travelled in Europe before teaching NT at Princeton, 1906–29. He was ordained by the New Brunswick Presbytery in June 1914 and took a strong reformed stand in the Fundamentalist–Modernist controversy. His *Christianity and Liberalism* (1923) remains in print. He helped lay the basis for Westminster Theological Seminary, founded in Philadelphia in 1930, and in 1935 was expelled from the Presbyterian Church in the USA for his leadership of the Independent Board of Foreign Missions. It was widely recognized that the PCUSA had over-reacted, but many left to form the Presbyterian Church of America, later the Orthodox Presbyterian Church. Machen was a careful scholar remembered also for his political libertarianism.

Machiavelli, Niccolò Politician and political theorist, born Florence, 3 May 1469, died there, 21 June 1527. He emerges first in 1494 as an official of the Florentine republic and served on numerous diplomatic missions. In 1513, after being pardoned from a charge of conspiracy against the Medici, he was forced into retirement and turned to literature. He had little time for religion, considering it mainly as a means of social control – in that regard he admired Islam more than Christianity. He was antagonistic towards the Papacy (though he wrote his most famous work, *Il principe*, in the hope of re-ingratiating himself with the Medicis, and particularly with the Medici Pope **Leo X**), because they had kept Italy divided.

McHugh, Antonia American religious superior, born Omaha, Nebraska, 17 May 1873, died St Paul, Minnesota, 11 October 1944. A Sister of St Joseph of Carondelet in St Paul, Antonia McHugh contributed much as teacher, dean and president to the development of the College of St Catherine, from 1911 to 1937. A genuine academic leader, she created one of the outstanding Catholic colleges in the USA, the first to merit a chapter of Phi Beta Kappa; she received the honour of membership in the White House Conference on Child Health, and the *Pro Ecclesia et Pontifice* medal in 1931.

McHugh, John Ambrose American Dominican theologian, born Louisville, Kentucky, 2 November 1880, died Ossining, New York, 9 April 1950. Assigned to the Order's house of studies in Washington, McHugh taught at the Seminary of the Foreign Mission Society of America at Maryknoll and, with C. J. **Callan**, OP, co-edited the *Homiletic and Pastoral Review*; further works followed on theology, sacred Scripture and the liturgy, and he wrote, independently, treatises on Christian doctrine. He became president of the Catholic Biblical Association of America in 1938.

Machutus *see* **Maclovius**

MacIntosh, Douglas Clyde Canadian Baptist theologian, born Breadalbane, Ontario, 18 February 1877, died Chicago, 6 July 1948. Educated at McMaster University, Toronto, and at Chicago, MacIntosh taught systematic theology at Yale University, 1909–42. In his teaching he favoured 'untraditional orthodoxy', by which he meant preaching the Christian message in terms understandable to his age. Among his published writings are *The Problem of Knowledge, Theology as Empirical Science, Social Religion, Personal Religion* and *Thinking about God.*

McIntyre, James Francis Aloysius American archbishop and cardinal, born New York City, 25 June 1886, died Los Angeles, 16 July 1979. In 1948, McIntyre became archbishop of Los Angeles, a diocese that experienced phenomenal growth in the next decades, requiring hundreds of new churches and parochial schools, as well as charitable and social service institutions. He did not shun controversy, defended the rights of Catholics to maintain their own schools, and denounced the federal government in 1951 as 'devoid of principle' in the matter; **Pius XII** made him a cardinal in 1953. He questioned the fitness of Eleanor Roosevelt to chair the UN Human Rights Commission, a post she filled with great distinction, however.

McKay, Claude Roman Catholic Jamaican poet and novelist, born Jamaica, 15 September 1890, died Chicago, 22 May 1948. He was educated in Kansas and settled in New York. In the USA he was shocked by racism. His publications include *Home to Harlem*, the most popular novel by a black American of that time. His was a militant voice in the Harlem Renaissance. He lived in the Soviet Union, France, Spain and Morocco, but returned to the USA. After joining the Catholic Church he worked for a Roman Catholic youth organization. He also he contributed to newspapers and magazines.

McKay, David Oman Mormon leader, born Huntsville, Utah, 8 September 1873, died Salt Lake City, 18 January 1970. He did missionary work in Scotland, but returned to Utah, becoming instructor and principal of what was later to become Webber State College. He became a member of the Quorum of the Twelve Apostles and later its president. He improved relations inside and outside the Church of the Latter Day Saints.

MacKay, John Alexander Presbyterian missionary, educator and ecumenist, born Inverness, Scotland, 7 May 1889, died Princeton, New Jersey, 9 June 1983. He studied at Aberdeen (MA, 1912), Princeton (BD, 1915) and Madrid under the existentialist Miguel de Unamuno, the subject of his Litt.D. (University of San Marcos, Lima, 1925). He married Jane Wells in 1916 and was sent by the Free Church of Scotland to Lima, Peru, 1916–25, as a missionary educator. He was an evangelist with the Latin American Young Men's Christian Association, 1926–32, and attended the Jerusalem meeting of the International Missionary Council in 1928. His classic work *The Other Spanish Christ* appeared in 1932. That year he became a secretary for Africa and Latin America for the Board of Foreign

Missions of the Presbyterian Church in the USA. He was a professor at and then president of Princeton Theological Seminary, 1936–59, and founded *Theology Today* in 1944. He was chairman of the International Missionary Council, 1947–57, and from 1948 a member of the Central Committee of the World Council of Churches. In 1953 his moderatorship of the Presbyterian Church in the USA provided significant leadership against McCarthyite anti-Communist hysteria.

McKenna, Bernard A. American Roman Catholic priest, shrine director, born Philadelphia, Pennsylvania, 8 July 1875, died there, 20 July 1960. Ordained in Philadelphia in 1903, McKenna held at the Catholic University of America the chair of the Immaculate Conception, and became in 1915 the first director of the National Shrine of the Immaculate Conception in Washington, DC. He left the Shrine in 1953 to become pastor of Holy Angels in Philadelphia, and published several books on his work there: *The National Shrine of the Immaculate Conception* and *Memoirs of the First Director of the National Shrine of the Immaculate Conception*.

McKenna, Charles Hyacinth Irish Dominican missionary, born Fillalea, Derry, 8 May 1834, died Jacksonville, Florida, 21 February 1917. Ordained in 1867 and assigned to St Vincent Ferrer Church in New York, McKenna gained a reputation as the best missionary preacher in the USA, according to Cardinal **Gibbons**; he became preacher general of the Order in 1881. He wrote a number of devotional works: *How to Make the Mission*, *The Angelic Guide* and *The Rosary Crown of Mary*. He promoted Catholic societies and popularized the Holy Name Society throughout the country.

McKeon, Richard Peter American philosopher, born Union City, New Jersey, 26 April 1900, died Chicago, Illinois, 31 March 1985. McKeon studied with Etienne **Gilson** in Paris and taught history, Greek and philosophy at the University of Chicago from 1934. His scholarly achievements were many: books on Cicero, the highly regarded *Basic Works of Aristotle* and an important critical edition of Peter **Abelard**'s *Sic et non*. A member of the first three American delegations to UNESCO, he helped prepare the documentation that became the UN

Universal Declaration of Human Rights. McKeon was a founder of the Chicago school of literary critics, or Neo-Aristotelians, and, with *Critics and Criticism*, Chicago successfully challenged other literary endeavours, such as *New Criticism*.

McKeough, Michael American Premonstratensian (Norbertine) priest and educator, born Green Bay, Wisconsin, 1892, died there, 5 June 1960. Ordained a priest in the Order of Prémontré, McKeough made his mark as a professor of education at the Catholic University of America, 1945–54, where he did much to influence the general direction of the educational apostolate of the Church. He was editor of the *National Catholic Educational Review*, 1947–50, and dean of St Norbert College, 1951–60. In his lectures and articles over many years, McKeough insisted on the need for professional training for school administrators.

McKillop, Mary Religious foundress, founded the Sisters of St Joseph of the Sacred Heart ('Josephites'), born Melbourne, 15 January 1842, died Sydney, 8 August 1909. With Father Julian Woods, Mary McKillop established in Adelaide the Sisters of St Joseph of the Sacred Heart, and pronounced her vows in 1866 as Mother Mary of the Cross. She tried to adapt the new community to a colonial environment, but was opposed to such a degree that the local bishops suppressed the community and excommunicated Mother Mary; however, **Pius IX** reinstated the congregation. She founded 160 Josephite houses and 117 schools; at her death the Sisters numbered about 1000, and had spread to New Zealand and Ireland by 1964.

McKinnon, William Daniel American army chaplain, born Melrose, Prince Edward Island, Canada, 1 August 1858, died Manila, Philippines, 25 September 1902. Ordained in 1887, McKinnon campaigned against the bigotry of the American Protective Association, and proved Catholic loyalty in the Spanish–American War by leading 600 coreligionists into the First California Volunteers. As army chaplain at the siege of Manila, he arranged with great risk to his own life the peaceful capitulation of the city, thus saving thousands of lives. Following the peace settlement, he re-established schools, directed relief work for the starving and dispossessed, and ministered to victims of the smallpox and typhoid fever plagues. Exhausted after all these trials, McKinnon did not himself survive an attack of amoebic dysentery.

McLaren, Agnes Scottish Catholic medical missionary, born Edinburgh, 4 July 1837, died Antibes, France, 17 April 1913. Agnes McLaren qualified as a doctor at Montpellier, became a Catholic in 1895 and a Dominican tertiary. She founded a hospital for women in Rawalpindi to be run exclusively by women, since Muslim law prohibits them to have contact with other than men of their own family. She wished to found a religious order to staff the hospital and after five requests to Rome, canon law was amended by decree in 1936 to permit religious women to be engaged in medicine. Her ambition for a community of sisters was realized by Dr Anna **Dengel**, a close associate of Dr McLaren, who founded the Medical Mission Sisters.

Maclaren, Alexander Baptist minister, Bible expositor and twice president of the Baptist Union, born Glasgow, 11 February 1826, died 5 May 1910. Educated at Glasgow University and Stepney College, London (now Regent's Park College, Oxford). Following his ordination as a Baptist minister in 1846 he took charge of Portland Chapel, Southampton. In 1858 he became the minister of Union Chapel, Manchester, a position he held until 1903. President of the Baptist Union of England in 1875 and 1901. Presided over the first Congress of the Baptist World Alliance in 1905. As well as achieving a reputation as a preacher of merit he published numerous devotional books and biblical commentaries.

MacLean, Calum Iain Scottish Roman Catholic Gaelic scholar, born Island of Raasay, Hebrides, 6 September 1915, died Daliburgh, South Uist, 16 August 1960. While furthering his studies in Celtic in Ireland, MacLean became a Catholic and, on his return to Scotland, set out to record, especially in the Catholic districts of the Highlands, the vanishing Gaelic oral tradition. He published *The Highlands* and contributed to learned journals such as *Scottish Studies*, *Scottish Gaelic Studies*, *Bealoideas and Arv*. His great achievement, inspired by his Catholic faith and Highland patriotism, is to have recorded no fewer than 1670 Scottish Gaelic folksongs, 272 Fenian folktales and 4269 other folklore items which, but for his efforts, would have disappeared.

MacLeod, George Fielden Founder of the Iona Community, minister in the Church of Scotland, born Glasgow, 17 June 1895, died Edinburgh, 27 June 1991. He was educated at Winchester, Oxford, Edinburgh and New York and fought in the First World War, subsequently becoming a pacifist. Between 1926 and 1938 he was a minister in Edinburgh and Glasgow. In 1938 he established the Iona Community, rebuilding the ruined abbey on the island as a retreat centre. He was elevated to the peerage in 1967 and the same year became president of the International Fellowship of Reconciliation. His radical politics and his encouragement of ecumenics and liturgical worship made him a controversial figure.

Maclovius (Malo, Machutus, Maclou) Saint, missionary monk to Brittany, born probably in Wales, died near Saintes (Archingeay), between 618 and 640. Maclovius worked in the area around Aleth (Saint-Servan) and the estuary of the Rance, and in the area now bearing his name, St Malo. He was consecrated the first bishop of Aleth, but throughout his life also spent periods as a hermit. Lives from the ninth century paint a picture of a rugged pioneer missionary on horseback, singing and preaching loudly, making both friends and enemies as he travelled. Feast day 15 November.

MacMahon, Ever Irish Roman Catholic bishop and patriot, born Farney, County Monaghan, 1600, executed Enniskillen, County Fermanagh, 17 September 1650. Ordained at the Irish College, Douai, MacMahon returned to Ireland as vicar apostolic of Clogher, where he enlisted troops for Owen Roe **O'Neill**'s regiment in Flanders. Appointed bishop of Down and Connor in 1641, he took part in the insurrection and represented Ulster on the Supreme Council of the Confederation of Kilkenny. He opposed the Ormond Peace of 1646 because it did not provide religious freedom, nor restore confiscated Catholic property. After O'Neill's death he led the Ulster army to defeat at the Battle of Scariffholis; wounded, he was beheaded by Cromwellian troops.

McMahon, Joseph Henry American librarian, born New York City, 18 November 1862, died there, 6 January 1939. A priest of St Patrick's Cathedral, McMahon opened its Free Circulating Library to the general public in 1892, and merged it with other city libraries in 1904 into what became the New York Public Library. McMahon published liturgical works, the best known being *Order of Consecration of a Bishop.* He founded in New York the Catholic Summer School of America, and Our Lady of Lourdes parish.

McMahon, Thomas John American mission director, born Tuxedo Park, New York, 5 April 1909, died New York City, 6 December 1956. Ordained for the Diocese of New York, he became secretary of the Catholic Near East Welfare Association in 1943, and president of the Pontifical Commission for Palestine in 1949, established to assist Palestinian Arab refugees. The rigours of life in the Middle East affected his health, however, and he returned to parish work in New York City in 1954.

McMaster, James Alphonsus American newspaper editor, born Duanesburg, New York, 1 April 1820, died Brooklyn, 21 December 1886. McMaster studied for the Episcopalian ministry at General Theological Seminary, New York; he met a Redemptorist priest, Gabriel Rempler, and became a Catholic in 1845. He joined the New York *Freeman's Journal and Catholic Register*, became the owner in 1848 and fought against Protestantism, free thought and the policies of President Lincoln. Accused of treason and sedition, he was imprisoned in Fort Lafayette in 1861. He championed full canonical rights for pastors in the USA, and thus incurred the opposition of the hierarchy.

McNabb, Vincent Joseph Dominican, popular preacher and theologian, born at Portaferry, Co. Down, 8 July 1868, the tenth of eleven children, died London, 17 June 1943. He was educated at St Malachy's, Belfast, and St Cuthbert's Grammar School, Newcastle upon Tyne. He joined the Dominican novitiate at Woodchester, Gloucestershire and was ordained priest there on 19 September 1891. After higher studies at Louvain he was professor of philosophy at Woodchester from 1897 to 1900 and later professor of theology at Hawkesyard Priory and prior there. In 1913 he preached and lectured in the USA in aid of a new church at

Holy Cross Priory, Leicester, of which he was prior. In December 1916 the Roman authorities of the Dominicans conferred on him the academic distinction of 'Master of Sacred Theology'. McNabb was very active in his work for the Belgian refugees during World War I and in 1919 the Belgian government honoured him with the distinction of Chevalier of the Order of the Crown of Belgium. But it is his London phase of life at St Dominic's Priory, Southampton Road, 1920–43, especially his fervent, and at times eccentric, modes of preaching in the streets of London in his familiar Dominican habit, and patent holiness of life, which is popularly remembered. He wrote a Life of *Francis Thompson and Other Essays* and contributed much to *The Tablet*, *Blackfriars* and the Catholic press in general.

McNeil, Neil   Canadian Roman Catholic archbishop, born Inverness County, Nova Scotia, 23 November 1851, died Toronto, 25 May 1934. McNeil taught, and was later rector, at St Francis Xavier University, Antigonish; he founded the weekly *Aurora* in 1881. He became bishop of St Georges, Newfoundland, in 1904, archbishop of Vancouver in 1910, and archbishop of Toronto in 1912, where he gave strong backing to St Michael's College and to the Pontifical Institute of Medieval Studies in the University.

McNicholas, John Timothy   Irish-American Dominican archbishop, born Kiltimagh, County Mayo, 15 December 1877, died Cincinnati, Ohio, 22 April 1950. Named archbishop of Cincinnati in 1925, McNicholas made special efforts to care for black citizens, to support the labour movement and especially to promote Catholic education at all academic levels. To this last end, he founded the Athenaeum of Ohio to supervise educational institutions, and a teachers' college to train priests, sisters and lay teachers, the Institutum Divi Thomae for the study of philosophy, science and theology. McNicholas was chairman of the commission for the sacred sciences in the Catholic University of America from 1934 until his death.

MacNutt, Francis Augustus   American papal chamberlain, born Richmond, Indiana, 15 February 1863, died Bressanone, Italy, 30 December 1927. From a rich Episcopalian family, MacNutt studied in Europe and in 1883 became a Catholic in Rome, where Pope **Leo XIII** appointed him to his service in the papal court. In 1904, **Pius X** named him a chamberlain, but he resigned his Vatican post in 1905 and settled in Schloss Ratzötz in the Tyrol. His writings include *Letters of Cortes*, *De orbe novo*, *The Eight Decades d' Augbera*, *Bartholomew de las Casas*, and his own memoirs, *A Papal Chamberlain*.

McPherson, Aimee Semple   Pentecostal evangelist and founder of the International Church of the Foursquare Gospel (ICFG), born near Ingersoll, Ontario, 9 October 1890, died Oakland, California, 26 September 1944. Aimee Elizabeth Kennedy first married Robert Semple, who died in 1910 while they were in Hong Kong, and then Harold Stewart McPherson, divorcing him in 1921. After spells ordained in the Assemblies of God and First Baptist Church, San Jose, in 1923 she created Angelus Temple and the ICFG. Despite a period missing in 1926 that led to a court appearance, a breakdown in 1930 and another failed marriage, she preached widely, debated on miracles and evolution, composed a number of hymns and sacred operas, and produced the magazine *The Bridal Call*; 'Foursquare Crusader Books' by her include *This Is That* (1921), *Divine Healing Sermons* (n.d), *In the Service of the King* (1927), and *Give Me my Own God* (1936).

MacPherson, John   Scottish pioneer Roman Catholic religious publisher, born Tomintoul, Banffshire, 29 August 1801, died Dundee, 16 July 1871. From a crofter family, MacPherson studied at Aquhorties College and at Paris, where he was ordained, returning to Scotland in 1827 as professor at Aquhorties. In 1828 he produced on the College's small hand-press, the first issue of *The Catholic Directory for the Clergy and Laity in Scotland*; by mid-century it was being circulated as far away as Tasmania and the West Indies. The *Directory* has continued to appear uninterruptedly ever since, and is an indispensable source for the study of the Catholic Church in Scotland.

McQuaid, Bernard John   American Roman Catholic bishop and educator, born New York City, 15 December 1823, died Rochester, New York, 18 January 1909. Ordained in 1848, McQuaid became rector of Newark Cathedral in 1853, established two orphanages and the cathedral school, founded Seton Hall College and served as chaplain in the Civil War, tending the wounded at Fredericksburg. Named first bishop of Rochester in 1868, McQuaid voted against the definition of papal infallibility at the First Vatican Council; he championed parochial schools and became the constant adversary of Archbishop **Ireland**, whose policies he publicly denounced, and of Cardinal **Gibbons**, whose tolerance of secret societies he opposed. Though a conservative prelate in his policies, he left a strong and well-organized diocese behind him at his death.

Macrae, George Winsor American Jesuit NT scholar, born Lyn, Massachusetts, 27 July 1928, died Boston, 6 September 1985. Following studies at Johns Hopkins and Cambridge, Macrae became a professor at Harvard Divinity School, giving widely popular lectures on John, Paul, Hebrews and Gnosticism. His writings include commentaries on John and Hebrews, and translations and interpretations in *The Nag Hammadi Library*. He edited the *New Testament Abstracts*, served as secretary of the Society of Biblical Literature and was rector of the Ecumenical Institute for Theological Research in Tantur, Jerusalem.

Macrina the Elder Saint, died *c.*340. She lived in Neocaesarea (Pontus, today part of Turkey) and was probably converted to Christianity by **Gregory Thaumaturgus**. During the persecution of Maximinus Daia she survived by hiding with her family for some years in the mountains. She was the grandmother on the paternal side of **Basil the Great**, **Gregory of Nyssa** and **Macrina the Younger**, and a decisive factor in their religious education. Feast day 14 January.

Macrina the Younger Virgin and saint, born Cappadocian Caesarea, *c.*327, died 19 July 379 (or 380). She was the elder sister of **Basil the Great** and **Gregory of Nyssa**. After the death of her fiancé she founded a monastery on a family estate, together with her mother Emmelia and former slaves. Gregory of Nyssa wrote her Life. By attributing to her the role of imaginary teacher in his *On the Soul and Resurrection*, he showed high

esteem for her spiritual influence and learning. Feast day 19 July.

MacRory, Joseph Cardinal archbishop of Armagh, born Ballygawley, County Tyrone, March 1861, died in Armagh, 13 October 1945. MacRory was educated at St Patrick's, Armagh, and St Patrick's, Maynooth, and ordained priest there for Armagh in 1885; his postgraduate studies were at Dunboyne, 1884–6. He joined the staff of Alton Seminary, which moved in 1889 to Oscott, Birmingham, where he was professor of moral theology and sacred Scripture. MacRory became the first principal or president of St Patrick's Academy in Dungannon, County Tyrone, but he was moved again to the chair of sacred Scripture and Oriental languages at Maynooth 1889 and then to NT exegesis in 1905. When he was vice-president of Maynooth he was appointed bishop of Down and Connor in 1915, until he was raised to the primatial see of Armagh as archbishop in 1928. He was named cardinal the following year. His Lenten Pastoral of 1929 commemorating the centenary of Catholic Emancipation and deploring the treatment of Catholics in the Six Counties of Ulster also indicated his continuing ecclesiastical politics as an outspoken Irish nationalist. MacRory was vigorous in promoting the cause of his martyred predecessor in Armagh, Oliver **Plunket**. His Lenten Pastoral of 1941 was impounded by the Northern Ireland censor. He spoke out strongly against the introduction of conscription into the forces from the Six Counties during the Second World War and defended Irish neutrality at the same time. Among his multiple writings, his commentaries on Scripture are outstanding: *St John's Gospel* (1897), *The Epistles of St Paul to the Corinthians* (1935). In 1906 he helped to establish the *Irish Theological Quarterly* and he was a frequent contributor to the *Irish Ecclesiastical Record*.

McSherry, James American Jesuit and author, born Libertytown, Maryland, 29 July 1819, died Frederick City, 13 July 1869. Called to the bar in 1840, McSherry practised in Frederick until his death. As author he contributed to the *United States Magazine* and wrote *History of Maryland*, *Père Jean or the Jesuit Missionary* and *Willitof or the Days of James the First*.

McWilliam, James A.   American Jesuit philosopher, born St Mary's, Kansas, 15 July 1882, died St Louis, Missouri, 20 August 1965. A founding member of the American Catholic Philosophical Association, McWilliams wrote extensively on the relation between modern scientific concepts and the views of Aristotle, **Albert the Great** and **Thomas Aquinas** – see, for example, his monograph on St Thomas's *Commentary on the Physics of Aristotle*. He attended several international philosophy congresses on behalf of the University of St Louis, where he spent a long academic career.

Madeleva, Mary   Sister, American Roman Catholic poet, and educator, born 'Mary Evaline Wolff' at Cumberland, Wisconsin, 24 May 1887, died Boston, 25 July 1964. Sister Madeleva entered the Congregation of the Holy Cross in 1908, and studied at the University of California, where she published *Knights Errant and Other Poems* and *The Pearl: A Study in Spiritual Dryness*; in 1925 also appeared *Chaucer's Nuns and Other Essays*. She became president of St Mary's College, Indiana, in 1934, and opened the School of Sacred Theology in 1943, to which she invited the outstanding thinkers and writers of the day. A true humanist, her prose works covered a wide variety of topics: essays on Coventry **Patmore**, Francis **Thompson**, Edna St Vincent Millay, Hilaire **Belloc** and Alice **Meynell**, whose estimate of Catholic writers, that they should be 'of the centre', appropriately describes her work.

Mader, Andreas Evaristus   German Salvatorian archeologist, born Grosslagheim, Bavaria, 9 January 1881, died Percha, near Munich, 13 March 1949. Mader spent three years in archeological research in Palestine before becoming director of the Oriental Institute of the Görresgesellschaft in Jerusalem, 1926–32. He discovered and excavated the church of the Multiplication of the Loaves at Tabgha, on the western shore of the Sea of Galilee, as well as the famous ancient sanctuary at Mamre, near Hebron, from which came his monumental work *Mambre*.

Maderno, Carlo   Italian architect, born Capolago, Ticino, 1556, died Rome, 20 January 1629. Trained as a sculptor, Maderno worked with his uncle in Rome, and became an architect. Unjustly criticized

for the nave and façade of St Peter's (1607–29) – the plan having been imposed on him by liturgical considerations – he is justly famous for the superb early baroque façade of Santa Susanna (1603), where he successfully combined plastic and structural elements to focus attention on the portal. He also designed the stucco decorations of St Peter's portico, as well as the fountains in the piazza.

Madoz, Joseph   Spanish Jesuit patrologist, born Artajona, Navarre, 27 August 1892, died Oña, Burgos, 15 December 1953. Having completed his studies in Rome, Madoz taught theology at the Jesuit seminary, Oña, then at the Merneffe, Belgium, and again at Oña, until his death. His scholarly work in patrology centred on St Vincent of Lérins and tradition, St **Braulio** of Saragossa, **Albar** of Córdoba, Licinianius of Cartagena and St **Isidore of Seville**, as well as on the figures of Visigothic and Mozarabic Spain.

Madruzzo   A powerful family of Trent in the Italian Tyrol, four of whom were bishops there from 1539 to 1658, without interruption (see below).

Madruzzo, Carlo Emanuele   Born Trent, 1599, died there, 15 December 1658. He succeeded his uncle Carlo Gaudenzio **Madruzzo** as bishop of Trent in 1629 and, frightened by the absence of legitimate heirs, he sought to prevent the extinction of the Madruzzo line by legitimizing his children by his mistress, Claudia Particella.

Madruzzo, Carlo Gaudenzio   Born Issogne, Aosta, 1562, died Rome, 4 August 1629. He succeeded his uncle Lodovico **Mudruzzo** bishop of Trent, and became a cardinal in 1604. He opposed trials for witchcraft, as well as the confessional policy towards Protestants advocated by Cardinal Melchior **Klesl** at the Diet of Regensburg (1613).

Madruzzo, Cristoforo   Born Trent, 8 July 1512, died Tivoli, 5 July 1578. He served in numerous ecclesiastical and diplomatic positions, became prince-bishop of Trent in 1539, prior to his ordination and consecration in 1542, and was named cardinal by Pope **Paul III**. He managed the first convocation of the Council of Trent (1545–7), insisting that Church reform be discussed along with theological debates, being hopeful that such measures would win over the Protestants. He opposed the Council's transfer to Bologna.

Madruzzo, Lodovico Born Trent, 1532, died Rome, 2 April 1600. Nephew of Cristoforo **Mudruzzo**, made cardinal in 1561, he took part in the third session of the Council of Trent 1562–3, at which he advocated the obligation of residency for bishops. He succeeded his uncle at Trent in 1567.

Maes, Boniface Flemish Franciscan spiritual writer, born Ghent, 1627, died there, 3 October 1706. Ordained a Franciscan Recollect, Maes is best known as a writer on mystical and ascetical theology, directed at the less perfect among Christians, while maintaining a high standard of expectation. Among his writings *Consolatorium piorum* asserts that every Christian, and especially every religious, is obliged under pain of mortal sin to strive for perfection, of which there are two degrees: observance of the Commandments, and perfection achieved through continual progress in moral perfection. Every Christian is obliged only by the first degree. Maes is important for the dialectical qualities of his writings, and their charitable and even cheerful spirit.

Maes, Camillus Paul Belgian-born Roman Catholic bishop, born Courtrai, 13 March 1846, died Covington, Kentucky, 11 May 1915. Ordained for the Diocese of Detroit in 1868, Maes became bishop of Covington in 1885, and laboured to bring the inhabitants of Appalachia into the Church, to which end he issued numerous pastoral letters and founded two diocesan papers, *New Catholic Chimes* and the *Christian Year*. He promoted the Catholic University of America, *The Catholic Encyclopedia* and the *Catholic Historical Review*. First president, 1893–1915, of the Priests Eucharistic League, he founded and edited its magazine, *Emmanuel*, and presided over the first five Eucharistic Congresses in the USA.

Maffei A noble Italian family of the Renaissance period. There were two branches: the Verona–Rome, especially notable for its scholars, and the Volterra. Three members of the former, were Can-

ons Regular of the Lateran: **Paolo**, born Verona, died Venice, 1480; superior in Padua and Venice and general of the Order in 1425; **Timoteo**, born c.1400, died Rome, 1470; prior in Fiesole, general three times and bishop of Ragusa; his sermons were very influential on the laity of the day; **Celso** born Verona, c.1425, died Verona, 1508; nephew of Timoteo, general of his Order eight times.

In the sixteenth century. **Bernardino**, born Bergamo, 1514, died Rome, 1553. One of the most learned men of his day. Close to **Paul III**, who appointed him bishop of Mara Marittima in 1547, then archbishop of Chieti and cardinal in 1549. Much esteemed by **Julius III** and legate to Parma. His brother **Marcantonio**, cardinal, born Rome, 1521, died Rome, 1583. He succeeded Bernardino at Chieti, 1566, and served **Pius IV** and **Pius V** in several capacities; the latter appointed him to a commission to prepare written defences against Lutheran teaching. **Giampietro**, born Bergamo, c.1535, died Tivoli, 1603. A political figure in Genoa, 1563–4, he became a Jesuit, wrote a history of Jesuit missions in India and a Life of **Ignatius of Loyola**. For **Francesco Scipione**, born Verona, 1675, died there, 1755, see below.

The Volterran branch. For **Raffaele**, born Volterra, 1451, died there, 1522, see below. His brother **Mario** died Rome, 1537. An intimate of **Leo X**. **Paolo Alessandro**, born Volterra, 1653, died Rome, 1716. Published a biography of Pius V (1712).

Maffei, Francesco Scipione Historian and writer, born Verona, 1 June 1675, died there, 11 February 1755. He was a friend of **Benedict XIV** and wrote extensively on many themes. He was opposed to duelling and magic and actively encouraged the theatre. He attacked the Jansenists in his *De haeresi Semipelagiana* (1744) and published defence of usury. This latter work initially provoked an encyclical by Benedict XIV on 1 November 1745: however, Francesco's work was not condemned. His historical writings include *Hilary of Poitiers* (1730) and *Vita Acephala* (1738), on the life of St **Athanasius**.

Maffei, Raffaele Historian and theologian, born Volterra, 17 February 1451, died there, 25 January 1522. His father was appointed professor of law at Rome's university by **Pius II**, and Raffaele was summoned there. He spent his time in study and in practices of piety, and considered becoming a Franciscan, though he was dissuaded. He married, and returned to Volterra, where he founded a convent. He produced numerous works, among them Lives of contemporary Popes, and encyclopaedic works on philosophy and theology, on geography, on anthropology and other topics.

Magdalen Albrici Blessed, Italian Augustinian abbess, born Como, later fourteenth century, died Brumate (near Como), 13 or 15 May 1465. Orphaned when young, Magdalen entered St Andrew's Convent at Brumate, where her many virtues soon commended her to the office of abbess. Said to have been a visionary, she promoted holiness among her nuns and reputedly worked miracles. She was beatified in 1904. Feast day 13 May.

Mager, Aloysius Austrian Benedictine theologian, born Zimmern, 21 August 1883, died Salzburg, 26 December 1946. A professor of experimental psychology and mystical theology, Mager co-founded in 1931 the Salzburg Hochschulwochen, a Catholic intellectual study group, and became a celebrated authority in the exposition of psychical, and especially of mystical, phenomena. He published several books, among them *Vorlesungen über experimentelle Psychologie* and *Mystik als seelische Wirklichkeit*.

Maginnis, Charles Donagh Irish-born Roman Catholic church architect, born Londonderry, 7 January 1867, died Brookline, Massachusetts, 15 February 1955. Having settled in Boston as a youth, Maginnis, though without formal training, worked in several firms of architects and founded an architectural partnership, Maginnis and Walsh. They designed many structures in the USA and Europe. Among the more notable are the National Shrine of the Immaculate Conception, Washington, the Carmelite Convent, Santa Clara, California, the Cathedral of Mary Our Queen, Baltimore, and some buildings at Notre Dame University, Indiana. He published *Pen Drawing*, a book of self-illustrated essays. He received the Laetare Medal, honorary degrees from several universities and became a Knight of Malta.

Magliabechi, Antonio Florentine librarian, born Florence, 28 October 1633, died there, 27 June 1714. A goldsmith, Magliabechi learned Latin, Greek and Hebrew at the age of 40, became librarian of the Palatine, and a central figure of contemporary literary life. His library of 30,000 volumes he left to 'The poor of Jesus Christ', and it later, in 1861, combined with the Palatine to form the National Library of Italy.

Maglione, Luigi Italian cardinal and diplomat, born Casoria, 2 March 1877, died there, 22 August 1944. Ordained in 1901, Maglione in the 1920s, became nuncio in Switzerland and France, where he supported the ban against *L'Action française*, a cardinal in 1935 and Vatican secretary of state in 1939. He sought in 1939 to arrange a conference with England, France, Germany, Poland and Italy to further **Pius XII**'s attempt to avert the outbreak of war, and in 1940 protested to Joachim von Ribbentrop against German actions inimical to the Church in Poland, as well as in other territories they controlled. He helped to settle many problems that beset the Holy See from the outset of the war.

Maglorius (Maelor) Missionary saint, bishop, abbot, born Glamorgan, Wales, died between 575 and 586. Of Irish origin (son of Umbrafel), Maglorius was educated by **Illtyd** at Llanilltyd Fawr. A disciple of **Samson**, Maglorius travelled with him as a missionary to Brittany, and there founded monasteries under the protection of King Childebert. Eventually, he succeeded Samson as bishop of Dol. In his old age, Maglorius retired to the island of Sark, where he founded a monastery and lived as a hermit. Miracles were attributed to him: the healing of the skin disease of a chieftain in Sark, who gratefully gave him land, the driving out of a dragon in Jersey. Feast day 24 October.

Magnabod of Angers (Maimbeuf) Saint, bishop, born *c*.574, died after 635. As his biographer writes, Magnabod came from a respected family in the Angers region, and was both spiritual and studious. Bishop **Licinius** ordained Magnabod and later gave him charge of the Challonnes-sur-Loire monastery. Magnabod became bishop of Angers *c*.610, attended synods at Paris, 614, and Clichy, 627, wrote a Life of St Maurilius of Angers and built a church dedicated to St Saturinus. Feast day 16 October.

Magnericus Saint and bishop, died 596. Magnericus was raised in Gaul, in the household of Bishop **Nicetius of Trier**, who later ordained him. Bishop Nicetius was exiled by King Clotaire I (the bishop had excommunicated the king for his corruption and licentiousness). Magnericus accompanied him into exile, returning the following year. He was named first Frankish bishop of Trier six years later. In 585, Magnericus gave shelter to another exiled bishop, Theodore of Marseilles, banished by Gunthamnus of Burgundy, even pleading with King Childebert II on his behalf. Feast day 25 July.

Magni, Valeriano Bohemian Capuchin missionary, born Prague, 15 October 1586, died Salzburg, Austria, 29 July 1661. Magni is best known for his role in the religio-political crises that beset the Holy Roman Empire in the seventeenth century: in 1616 he became head of the Capuchin mission to Poland under Sigismund III; in 1627 Emperor **Ferdinand II** commissioned him to implement the Edict of Restitution; **Urban VIII** appointed him apostolic delegate to Bohemia in 1629, and he attended the Diet of Ratisbon (Regensburg) (1630). As a missionary, Magni succeeded in re-establishing the Church in Saxony and Hesse by 1652. Often a controversial figure, from 1635 Magni engaged in disputes with the landgrave of Rheinfels and with the Jesuits, which led to his imprisonment in 1655; however, history attests to his Catholic orthodoxy.

Magnien, Alphonse French-born Sulpician educator, born Bleymard, 9 June 1837, died Baltimore, Maryland, 21 December 1902. Ordained for the Diocese of Orléans, Magnien went to Baltimore in 1869, where he taught philosophy, liturgy and Scripture. He became superior in the USA of the Sulpicians, who took over direction of seminaries in New York, Boston and San Francisco; the Order also established St Austin's College at the Catholic University of America. Magnien became principal adviser to Cardinal James **Gibbons** of Baltimore, and closely involved in national and international ecclesiastical affairs.

Magnus, Johannes Swedish archbishop and historian, born Linköping, 19 March 1488, died Rome, 22 March 1544. Though Magnus was elected archbishop of Uppsala in 1523, Gustavus Vasa, on becoming a Protestant, deprived him of his post. He is the author of *Historia de omnibus Gothorum Sveonumque regibus* and *Historia metropolitanae ecclesiae Upsaliensis*. His brother Olaus **Magnus**, also a historian, went with Johannes into exile after the triumph of the Reformation in Sweden, and succeeded Johannes in the, by then, titular see of Uppsala when he died. He is best known for his contribution to humanistic learning: he published a *Carta Marina* (1539), and a companion volume, *Historia de gentibus septentrionalibus*, some years later, which greatly extended knowledge of Scandinavia and of the peoples of northern Europe.

Magnus, Olaus Swedish historian and geographer, born Skeninge, Sweden, 1490, died Rome, 1 August 1557. He was brother to Johannes **Magnus**, was provost of Strängnäs Cathedral and after John's death succeeded him as archbishop of Uppsala, although he never took up office. He was at the Council of Trent from 1545 to 1549 and lived out his days in Italy. He was one of the most important geographers of his age, had a thorough knowledge of the North and was one of the first to suggest a north-east passage. His map of the North appeared in Venice in 1539. As well as the geography of the northern lands he wrote on their history and natural history. He wrote a Life of **Catherine of Sweden**, daughter of **Bridget of Sweden**, and edited some of his brother's works.

Magnus of Fussen (Magnoaldus, Maginaldus, Mang) Saint, monk, missionary to the Algäu, died *c*.750. Little is reliably known about the life of Magnus. Supposedly he crossed the River Lech at St Manstritt ('footstep of St Magnus') and built a cell, where afterwards the monastery of Fussen was founded, and there he died. In 851, when the relics of Magnus were moved to the new church of Fussen, a manuscript was said to have been found which was the story of the saint's life written by his companion Theodore, but, owing in part to historical inaccuracies, this is now believed to date from the time of the removal of the relics, with even later additions, and to be unreliable. Feast day 6 September.

Maguire, Charles Bonaventure Irish Franciscan missionary, born Dungannon, County Tyrone, 16 December 1765, died Pittsburgh, Pennsylvania, 17 July 1833. Maguire first worked among Germans in The Netherlands, then went to the USA in 1817, in the Pittsburgh area, where he enjoyed great success in pastoral work. He published an apologetic, *A Defense of the Divinity of Jesus Christ and of the Mystery of the Real Presence.*

Maguire, John William Rochefort Irish-born Roman Catholic educator and priest, born County Roscommon, 11 August 1883, died Miami, Florida, 11 February 1940. Maguire emigrated to Canada, then to Spokane, Washington, where he worked as a reporter on the *Spokane Review.* He converted to Catholicism in 1908, joined the Community of Clerics of St Viator, and was ordained in 1914 at the Catholic University of America. He taught at St Viator College and became closely associated with the Social Reform Party, and the Illinois State Federation of Labor; he publicly supported the Bishops' Program of Social Reconstruction after the First World War. A great friend of Labour, he often arbitrated in industrial actions, notably a dispute between five American Federation of Labor unions and the Warner Construction Company, in 1939.

Maher, Michael Irish Jesuit psychologist, born County Carlow, 29 April 1860, died Petworth, England, 3 September 1917. Maher taught at Stonyhurst College and wrote *Psychology: Empirical and Rational*, a standard text in Catholic institutions for 30 years, *Tatian's Diatessaron* and *English Economics and Catholic Ethics*, and contributed to the *Catholic Encyclopedia.*

Mahler, Gustav Austrian composer and conductor, born Kaliste, Bohemia, 7 July 1860, died Vienna, 18 May 1911. He studied at the Vienna Conservatory, attended **Bruckner**'s lectures at Vienna University and greatly admired his works. Mahler's compositions, often concerned with life and death, include nine completed symphonies. His Jewish origins were a barrier to his being appointed to the great conductorship of the Vienna Hofoper, but in 1897 he became a Roman Catholic and secured the appointment. His symphonies, the last of the Viennese school, are regarded as the greatest of their time. His Second Symphony concludes with a setting of the Christian writer **Klopstock**'s poem *Auferstehen* concerning resurrection after death. Mahler's epic Eighth Symphony involved so many performers that it was called the 'Symphony of a Thousand'. It contains choral settings of two striking texts – the ancient Roman Catholic invocation to the Holy Spirit, *Veni Creator Spiritus*, and part of the closing scene from Goethe's *Faust.*

Mai, Angelo Cardinal, philologist and palaeographer, born Schilpario, Italy, 7 March 1782, died Albano, Italy, 9 September 1854. Mai was a Jesuit educated at the Collegium Romanum. He became custodian of the Ambrose Library in Milan and prefect of the Vatican Library. Using manuscripts from the libraries in which he worked he published the following collections of theological and classical works, *Classicorum Auctorum* (1828–38), *Scriptorum Veterum Nova Collectio* (1830–8), *Spicilegium Romanum* (1839–44) and *Nova Patrum Bibliotheca* (1844–71). He was made cardinal in 1838 and became an associate of the French Institute in 1842.

Mai Chaza Prophetess and African Initiated Church leader, Zimbabwe, died *c.*1960. Mai (mother) Chaza was a Methodist before she founded the Guta re Jehovah (City of God) Church in Seke Reserve in 1952 in response to a vision during illness. She encouraged her followers to give up charms and confess to sorcery. She healed the sick using water from her home village, the 'Zion' of the Church movement, and was particularly successful with barren women. Her Christian teaching was infused with elements of traditional religion. The Church grew rapidly and numbered tens of thousands at her death, when Bandal Mapaulos, a Malawian, became the leader.

Maier, Anneliese German historian, born Tübingen, 17 November 1905, died Rome, 2 December 1971. From a Lutheran family, Anneliese Maier studied at Zurich and Berlin, and went to Rome in 1936 to work on the letters of **Leibniz** preserved in the Vatican Library. She lived in Rome during the Second World War, and in 1954 became research professor of the Max-Planck-Gesellschaft; she published work on the history of medieval science under the general title *Studien zur Naturphilosophie der Spätscholastik*. She became a Catholic in 1943 and before her death had begun a project to publish documents concerning the beatific vision controversy involving Pope **John XXII**.

Mailla, Joseph Anne Marie Moyria de French Jesuit missionary, born Maillat (Ain), 16 December 1669, died Peking, 28 June 1748. Mailla went to China in 1701, to Macao in 1703, became proficient in Cantonese and translated the Sunday Gospels, Lives of the saints, the *Spiritual Exercises* of **Ignatius of Loyola** and other religious works into Chinese. He and two other Jesuits mapped a number of provinces at the request of Emperor Khanghi, for which the emperor rewarded him with the rank of mandarin. He mastered the Mandarin language, and translated the history of the empire into French, a work incorporated into Abbé Grosier's *Histoire générale de la Chine* (1777–85). Mailla received a state funeral in Peking.

Maimbourg, Louis French Jesuit and historian, born Nancy, 10 January 1610, died Paris, 13 August 1686. He entered the Society of Jesus in 1626, and became well known as a preacher. He was a vigorous opponent of Jansenism but was sympathetic to Gallicanism. A number of his books were placed on the Index, among them his treatise *On the Establishment and the Prerogatives of the Church of Rome and its Bishops* (1685). By the time it appeared, Pope **Innocent XI** had already ordered his dismissal from the Jesuit Order, 1681. King **Louis XIV**, however, gave him a pension. He was a prolific author, and also wrote against Calvinism and Lutheranism.

Main, John Benedictine, introduced wide range of lay people to Christian meditation, born 1926, died of cancer Montreal, Canada, 30 December 1982. Worked as a civil servant, lawyer and soldier before joining the English Benedictines at Ealing Abbey, London, in 1959. Taught in Benedictine schools in England and the USA and became increasingly aware of his own and others' spiritual need for a form of prayer that was deep but also suited to the situation of ordinary people's lives. He introduced a Christian form of mantra, based partly on the teachings of John **Cassian**. From a small prayer group that began in Ealing in 1975, Main's Christian meditation developed and spread worldwide, especially among lay people. In Montreal in 1977 he also began a mixed monastic community, consisting of religious and lay people. His *Word into Silence* (1981) remains popular.

Maine de Biran, Marie-François-Pierre French statesman, philosopher and writer, born Grateloup, Bergerac, 29 November 1766, died Paris, 20 July 1824. After studies at Périeux he joined the army. He was a member of King Louis XVI's lifeguard and defended his king at Versailles. After the Revolution he retired to the Dordogne and became its administrator. In 1797 he became a member of the Five Hundred, a member and treasurer of the Chamber of Deputies and a councillor of state, but his royalist sympathies made him unpopular and he retired to Grateloup and devoted himself to philosophy, though he reentered politics in the second decade of the nineteenth century. In the final years of his life he was particularly interested in the philosophy of religion. Only one of his works was published in his own lifetime, though soon after his death his reputation as an important metaphysical thinker was rapidly established.

Maintenon, Françoise d'Aubigné de Second wife of **Louis XIV** of France and untitled queen, baptized Niort, Poitou, France, 28 November 1635, died Saint-Cyr, 15 April 1719. She was born in prison and in poor circumstances and baptized as a Roman Catholic. She went to live with a crippled author, Paul Scarron, presided over his literary salon and married him: she was known as 'le Scarron'. After his death she became the governess of the children of the marquise de Montespan by Louis XIV. The king bought Château de Maintenon, granted her the Maintenon title and secretly married her. Her enemies accused her of wielding too much influence over the king, but she played no part in the Revocation of the Edict of Nantes, which denied all rights to Protestants. At Saint-Cyr, near Paris, she founded an institution for the education of young women.

Mair, Martin German humanist statesman, born Wimpfen, *c*.1420, died Landshut, Bavaria, 17 November 1480. Mair studied humanistic disciplines at Heidelberg, and served as counsellor to several German princes in projects to reform and unite Germany. In 1457 he wrote to Aeneas Silvius Piccolomini (the future **Pius II**) listing the German nation's complaints (*gravamina*) against the Roman curia. He tried to make George Podebrad, the Czech Hussite, king of Bohemia and co-ruler with Frederick III, but sided with the Papacy when **Paul II** excommunicated Podebrad for heresy.

Maironis (Jonas Maciulis) Lithuanian Roman Catholic priest and poet, born Pasandravys, Russian Lithuania, 2 November 1862, died Kaunas, 28 June 1932. He studied at Kaunas and at St Petersburg, and later held posts at both places, becoming rector of the Kaunas Seminary and then professor of moral theology at the Lithuanian University. His poetry expresses the desire for Lithuanian independence. All his poetry was published in the collection *Pavasario Balsa*.

Maistre, Joseph Marie de Philosopher and advocate for Christianity as the basis of civilization, born Chambéry (Savoy), 1 April 1754, died Turin, 26 February 1821. Educated first by the Jesuits, he studied law at the University of Turin, then entered the civil service of Savoy. In 1799 he became regent of Sardinia and then, in 1802, ambassador to Russia, for fourteen years. In 1817 he became regent of Savoy, until his death. He was a vigorous opponent of monarchy in government and of religion as the foundation of civilized living. He saw the French Revolution as a divine punishment for the anti-Christianity of France in the age of the Enlightenment. In his treatise *Du Pape* (1819), de Maistre argued that an infallible Papacy was the unique source not only of Christian orthodoxy but also of all legitimate political power and hence essential for all civilized progress. His philosophical reflections *Les Soirées de St-Pétersbourg* (1821) contain much of his thought but he also wrote a polemic against the materialism of Francis **Bacon**'s philosophy – *L'Examen de la philosophie de Bacon* (1826).

Maitani, Lorenzo Sienese architect and sculptor, born Siena, *c.*1270, died Orvieto, 1330. Maitani went to Orvieto in 1308 to work on the cathedral façade and there, as *capomaestro*, he created between 1310 and 1330 the documented bronze

symbol of *St John the Evangelist*, directly influenced by Giovanni Pisano's *Symbols of the Evangelists*, *Scenes from Genesis* and the *Last Judgement*, indirectly influenced by northern Gothic linear sculpture.

Maitland, Frederick William English lawyer and historian of English law, born London, 28 May 1850, died Las Palmas, Canary Islands, Spain, 19 December 1906. He was educated at Eton and Cambridge, studied law at Lincoln's Inn and was called to the bar in 1876. In 1884 he was elected reader in English law at Cambridge and four years later Downing professor of the laws of England. Among his works are *Roman Canon Law in the Church of England* (1898), showing that pre-Reformation canon law in England was that of the Church of Rome, a conclusion which did not go down well with Anglicans, and, with Sir Frederick Pollock, *The History of English Law before the Time of Edward I*.

Majolus of Cluny Saint, monastic reformer and fourth abbot of Cluny, born Avignon(?), between 906 and 915, died Souvigny, 11 May 994. Also known as 'Mayeul'. He studied at Lyons, became archdeacon of Mâcon, and became a Cluniac monk after refusing the bishopric of Besançon. Appointed coadjutor in 954, he became abbot of Cluny in 965. The Cluniac reform spread widely during his reign, and he reformed abbeys in Burgundy, France and Italy. In 974, Emperor **Otto II** offered him the Papacy, which he refused. Hugh Capet asked him to reform Saint-Denis, and he was at the abbey of Souvigny on his way to Paris when he died. Feast day 11 May.

Major, George (Maier) German Lutheran theologian, born Nuremberg, 25 April 1502, died Wittenberg, 28 November 1574. Major studied under Martin **Luther** and Philipp **Melanchthon**, and became professor of theology at Wittenberg; he advanced the thesis, seen as opposed to Luther's justification by faith alone, that good works are necessary for salvation. Major defended himself in what became known as the 'Majoristic controversy', but refrained from using the phrase 'necessary for salvation'; the Formula of Concord (1577) settled the matter by affirming that, though good works are done spontaneously in testimony to the presence of the Holy Spirit, they neither cause nor merit salvation or its preservation, but nor are they detrimental.

Makarios *see* **Macarius.**

Makemie, Francis Regarded as the founder of American Presbyterianism, born in County Donegal, Ireland, 1658, died 1708. After being educated at the University of Glasgow, he was ordained and was sent as a missionary to America in 1683. He worked in North Carolina, Barbados, Maryland and Virginia. He was once arrested for preaching in New York without a licence, but successfully defended himself on the ground of free speech, despite the fact that he was forced to pay legal costs. Makemie contributed to the formation of the Presbytery of Philadelphia in 1706.

Malachy Saint, archbishop of Armagh, born Armagh, 1094, died Clairvaux, while travelling to Rome, 2 November 1148. He was ordained in 1119 and elected abbot of Bangor (County Down) four years later. He became bishop of Connor the following year, and was chosen for Armagh in 1132, though he was only able to take possession of his see two years later. He was very enthusiastic about the monastic system in Gaul and on his journey to Rome in 1139 visited **Bernard of Clairvaux.** On his way back he persuaded five Cistercians to return with him to Ireland, and they established a Cistercian Abbey at Mellifont, County Louth, in 1142. He was making a second visit to Rome, again calling at Clairvaux, when he died. He was canonized in 1199.

Malagrida, Gabriel Italian Jesuit missionary, born Menaggio, 5 December 1689, died Lisbon, 21 September 1761. Malagrida set out from Portugal for Northern Brazil, where he became a celebrated preacher and zealous apostle, acquiring the fame of a saint; in 1751 King John V named him royal councillor for the Portuguese overseas missions. Back in Lisbon, he was jailed in 1758 for plotting against the life of Joseph I, and became mentally deranged as a consequence. On the basis of two books, *Life of St Anne, Mother of Mary* and *Kingdom of the Antichrist*, written while not mentally responsible, the Inquisition condemned him as a heretic, and he died at the stake.

Malaparte, Curzio (Karl Erich Suckert) Italian journalist and writer, born Prato, Italy, 9 June 1898, died Rome, 19 July 1957. He supported Fascism in *La Technique du coup d'état*, but repudiated it in World War II and supported the Allies. He wrote three dramas, and the screenplay for a film, *Il Cristo probito*.

Malaspina, Germanico Italian papal nuncio, died San Severo, 1604. As nuncio to Prague, Malaspina tried to persuade Emperor Rudolph II to carry out Tridentine reforms. In 1592, Pope **Clement VIII** made him nuncio in Poland, where he mediated in the conflict between King Sigismund III and his chancellor, Jan Zamojki. Malaspina accompanied Sigismund to Uppsala in 1593 to claim the crown of Sweden (1593), but his hopes of restoring Catholic supremacy there were dashed when Sigismund's Protestant uncle, Charles, usurped the throne in 1599. Malaspina played a major role in negotiations for the reunion of the Ruthenian Church with Rome.

Malderus, John (Jan van Malderen) Flemish Roman Catholic bishop and theologian, born Leuw-Saint-Pierre, Brussels, 14 August 1563, died Antwerp, 26 July 1633. Professor at Louvain, rector in 1604, bishop of Antwerp in 1611, Malderus held the chair endowed by **Philip II** to explain the texts of St **Thomas Aquinas**, and published commentaries on the *Summa Theologiae*. As a bishop, he showed unusual pastoral zeal, and laboured energetically to prevent the encroachments of Calvinism. To this end, he prepared an excellent catechism in the vernacular, supervised the proper training of his clergy and wrote many letters of pastoral direction.

Maldonatus, Johannes (Juán de Maldonado) Spanish Jesuit exegete, born Casas de la Reina, Estremadura, 1534, died Rome, 5 January 1583. A professor of theology at Paris, he commented on the *Sentences* of **Peter Lombard**, but lost his position in 1574 because of the accusation by some Sorbonne professors that he denied the doctrine of the Immaculate Conception. Although defended at the highest levels in Paris and Rome, he withdrew to Bourges and composed his celebrated commentaries on the four Gospels: *Commentarii in IV Evangelistas*, and other writings on the Scriptures.

Malebranche, Nicolas Oratorian and philosopher, born Paris, 6 August 1638, died there, 13 October 1715. He studied philosophy at the Collège de la Marche and theology at the Sorbonne, entering the Oratory in 1660. He first studied history and then Scripture, but eventually turned to philosophy, inspired by a chance reading of **Descartes**. He was interested in the relationship between faith, reason and empirical observation and sought a midway between Catholicism and Cartesianism. His work includes *De la Recherche de la vérité* (1674) and *Entretiens sur la métaphysique et sur la religion* (1688). His work brought him into contact with **Bossuet** – who was critical – **Leibniz**, Fontenelle and many others. The Jesuits accused him of atheism. His studies also included insects, mathematics and oratory.

Mallinckrodt, Hermann von Political leader, born Minden, Westphalia, 5 February 1821, died Berlin, 26 May 1874. He helped to found the Catholic Centre Party and, as a member of the Reichstag, 1871–4, staunchly opposed **Bismarck**'s Kulturkampf, its violation of constitutional principles and the rights of the Church.

Mallinckrodt, Pauline von Foundress, born Minden, 3 June 1817, died Paderborn, 30 April 1881. She founded the Sisters of Christian Charity, in 1849, a community devoted to teaching in elementary and secondary schools; despite obstacles created by the Kulturkampf, she expanded the membership, moved the motherhouse to Mont-Saint-Guibert, near Brussels, and established houses abroad: in New Orleans, 1873, in Chile, 1879, and in England. Her cause for beatification has been introduced.

Mallon, Alexis French Jesuit philologist, born La Chapelle-Bertin (Haute-Loire), 8 May 1875, died Bethlehem, 7 April 1934. A Coptic philologist, Mallon taught at Cairo, Beirut and the Pontifical Biblical Institute; he established a branch of the Institute at Jerusalem in 1927. He directed excavations at several prehistoric sites in Palestine, and discovered the remnants of a Chalcolithic civilization in the desert at Teleilat-Ghassoul, north-east of the Dead Sea. Mallon published *Grammaire copte*, *Les Hébreux en Egypte*, and many archeological studies in *Biblica*, e.g.: *Mélanges de la Faculté orientale de Beyrouth* and *Dictionnaire d'archéologie chrétienne*.

Malo *see* **Maclovius**

Malone, Sylvester Irish-born social reformer and Roman Catholic priest, born Trim, County Meath, 8 May 1821, died Williamsburg, New York, 29 December 1899. Ordained for the Diocese of New York in 1844, Malone served all his career as pastor at SS Peter and Paul, out of which grew 25 new parishes in his time. He attracted wide public attention as an abolitionist and a liberal, working for the rights of black persons after the Civil War, and as 'the advocate of temperance and of every good cause that works for the public good', as he said of himself. He supported Edward **McGlynn** in the single-tax controversy, and the Irish Land League.

Malory, Thomas Sir, English writer, flourished *c*.1470. His life is shrouded in mystery but he is celebrated as the author of *Le Morte d'Arthur*, the first prose account in English of King Arthur and his Round Table. Malory calls himself 'Syr Thomas Maleore Knight'. He prays for deliverance from prison. He describes himself as: 'The servant of Jesu, both day and night'. He may have been Sir Thomas Malory of Newbold Revel, Warwickshire. Another Thomas Malorie, knight, served Richard Beauchamp, earl of Warwick; he died on 14 March 1471 and was buried in St Francis's at Greyfriars, near Newgate, London.

Malpighi, Marcello Italian physicist and biologist who founded the science of microscopic anatomy, born Crevalcore, near Bologna, 10 March 1628, died Rome, 30 November 1694. He studied at the University of Bologna, became successively professor at Pisa and Messina, and Pope **Innocent XII** made him his personal physician. Malpighi was an honorary member of the Royal Society in London. He made many discoveries resulting from the use of the microscope, including the human taste buds, spinal cord and structure of the brain.

Maltret, Claude (Mailtrait) French Jesuit classical scholar, born La Puy, 3 October 1621, died Toulouse, 3 January 1674. After ordination, Maltret taught classics and sacred Scripture until appointed rector of Montauban in 1662, when he published his critical edition of the Latin translation by Alamannus of the works of Procopius of Caesarea, reprinted several times.

Malula, Joseph   African archbishop and cardinal, born Léopoldville, Belgian Congo, 12 December 1917, died Brussels, 13 June 1989. The first black priest to work in the future capital of Zaire, Malula became archbishop of Léopoldville (Kinshasa) in 1964 and gained stature as a man of integrity in the emerging secular state under President Mobutu, and in his dealings with the conservative orthodoxy of the Vatican. A staunch believer in independence for his country, he worked to prepare future priests and lay preachers for the departure of the Belgians in 1965; for him Christianity meant progress, in particular for African women, to free them from the shackles of domesticity. Opposed to Mobutu's concept of 'Africanization', Malula preached against him before King Baudoin in Kinshasa Cathedral, and wrote a pastoral letter attacking the profanity of the secular authorities. When soldiers sacked his residence in 1972, Malula fled to Louvain University. Having returned to Zaire, Malula introduced African elements into the Mass to an extent that surprised John Paul II on his visit in 1980, and which the Vatican could not accept. Malula had dreamed of a General Council for the African Church, but his death deprived Africa of its foremost representative in Rome.

Malvenda, Tomás   Spanish Dominican exegete, born Játiva, May 1566, died Valencia, 7 May 1628. While still a professor of sacred sciences, Malvenda first made a critique (1600), and then worked with **Baronius** on his revision of the *Annales ecclesiastici*; he revised the Dominican Breviary, Martyrology and Missal; annotated Brasidielli's *Index expurgatorius*, and prepared his *Annales O.P.* His most important work is an uncompleted (up to Ezekiel 16.16) literal translation, with commentary, of the Hebrew OT into Latin – so literal indeed as to be sometimes unintelligible, but of much use in its time.

Maly, Eugene Harry   American Roman Catholic Scripture scholar and priest, born Cincinnati, Ohio, 6 September 1920, died there, 30 July 1980. Ordained for the Diocese of Cincinnati, Maly con-

tributed significantly to biblical studies through his writings and the encouragement of other scholars. He chaired the editorial board of *The Bible Today* from 1962, and regularly wrote the 'Haggadah' column; he published over 90 books and articles for the Jerome Bibilical Commentary and the *New Catholic Encyclopedia*. He was named *peritus* for two sessions of Vatican Council II, and elected president of the Catholic Biblical Association in 1962.

Mamertus   Bishop and saint, died *c*.475. Brother of **Claudianus Mamertus**, he was bishop of Vienne by 463. He earned a rebuke from Pope **Hilary** in 464 for consecrating a bishop of Die and for interfering in an attempted settlement between the Sees of Arles and Vienne. He is famous for introducing the processional litanies on the days prior to Ascension Day as an appeal against natural disasters such as volcanic eruptions and earthquakes; these were the forerunner of the later Rogation Days. Feast day 11 May.

Manasses   Excommunicated archbishop, born Champagne, *c*.1040, died between 1081 and 1100. Elected archbishop of Rheims in 1070, deposed in 1077 and excommunicated in 1080, he cannot be traced after May 1081. He opposed the Gregorian reform and refused to answer charges of uncanonical conduct, hence his deposition and excommunication.

Mance, Jeanne   Religious foundress, founded the first hospital in Quebec, born Langres, Picardy, 1606, died Montreal, 18 June 1673. Following work in hospitals in Champagne, Jeanne Mance joined the first colonists to Montreal in 1641, and founded the Hôtel-Dieu hospital the following year, remaining its director under conditions that constantly demanded heroic acts of all the settlers. She gained a reputation for sanctity that grew after her death, and Catholic nurses of both the USA and Canada asked in 1942 that her cause be introduced. She has a monument to her memory in front of the Hôtel-Dieu, erected in 1909.

Mandonnet, Pierre   French Dominican historian, born Beaumont (Puy-de-Dôme), 26 February 1858, died Le Saulchoir, 4 January 1936. A pioneer in critical historical studies of Thomism and the origins of the Friars Preachers, Mandonnet founded *Le Bulletin thomiste* and *La Revue thomiste*; his bibliography *Des écrits authentiques de St Thomas d'Aquin* became a standard text; his *Siger de Brabant et l'averroïsme latin au XIIIeme siècle*, though a major study in doctrinal history, suffered later under the scholarship of F. van Steenberghen on **Siger**; his *St Dominique: l'idée, l'homme et l'oeuvre* interprets contemporary documentation on St **Dominic**'s intentions for the apostolate of the Friars Preachers.

Manegold of Lautenbach Canon and papal advocate, born Lautenbach, Alsace, *c.*1030, died Marbach, Alsace, *c.*1103. Manegold had been a wandering teacher and for at least some time married before he entered the monastery of Lautenbach around 1084. There he defended the rights of the Pope above the Holy Roman Emperor in his *Manegoldi ad Gebhardum liber*. His enemies forced him to flee in 1086 to Raitenbuch in Bavaria. From there he eventually became prior at Marbach. He was imprisoned by the Emperor in 1098. He also wrote a number of commentaries and a book warning Christians away from pagan writers.

Manetti, Giannozzo Italian statesman and humanist, born Florence, 5 June 1396, died Naples, 26 October 1459. From a noble and wealthy family, Manetti had to defend himself against accusations of treason in 1453 brought by political enemies, and went into exile, where he taught himself Greek and Hebrew. **Nicholas V** gave him a post as apostolic secretary, a large pension and a knighthood; he made translations of the Psalter and the NT, and after Nicholas's death moved to Naples, where King Alfonso held him in similar esteem. Manetti wrote Lives of several classical authors and *Contra Judaeos et Gentes libri X*; his *De dignitate et excellentia hominis*, written for Alfonso to refute *De miseria hominis* of Pope **Innocent III**, was placed on the Spanish Index in 1584.

Manfred King of Sicily from 1258, born *c.*1232, died near Benevenuto, Kingdom of Naples, 26 February 1266. He was involved in disputes between the House of Anjou and imperial claimants. He was a son of the Holy Roman Emperor **Frederick II**. For his half-brother Conrad IV he acted as regent in Italy and later, for his nephew Conrad, he defended the Empire against Pope **Innocent IV**. Manfred fled to the Saracens and with their help he defeated papal troops, and controlled Naples and Sicily. Pope **Alexander IV** excommunicated him. Manfred was killed in the Battle of Benevenuto.

Mangenot, Joseph Eugène French Scripture scholar, born Grémonville (Meuse-et-Moselle), 20 August 1856, died Martrot, 19 March 1922. A professor at the Institut Catholique, Paris, 1903–22, Mangenot collaborated with F. Vigouroux on the *Dictionnaire de la Bible*, became director of the *Dictionnaire de la théologie catholique* and published significant treatises: *L'Authenticité mosaïque du Pentateuque*, *La Résurrection de Jésus* and *Les Évangiles synoptiques*.

Mann, Horace Kinder Roman Catholic priest, educator and historian of the medieval Papacy, born London, 27 September 1859, died Edinburgh, 1 August 1928. He was educated at St Cuthbert's College, Ushaw, Durham and ordained in 1886. After an initial year's teaching at St Cuthbert's he became successively prefect of discipline from 1887 to 1890, and headmaster until 1917, when he was appointed rector of the Beda College in Rome, where he remained until his death. In 1911 Pope **Pius X** had bestowed on Mann the honorary pontifical degree of doctor of divinity, and in 1917 Pope **Benedict XV** gave him the rank of domestic prelate. Mann's major written work is the *Lives of the Popes of the (Early) Middle Ages* (18 vols in 19, London, [1902–32], the last four volumes appearing posthumously, but all now superseded by subsequent research. Also, separately, he wrote a biography of the only English Pope to date, Nicholas Breakspear (**Adrian IV**) (London, 1914).

Manning, Henry Edward Cardinal archbishop of Westminster, born Totteridge, Hertfordshire, 15 July 1808, died London, 14 January 1892. He was educated at Harrow and Oxford, and was elected a fellow of Merton in 1832, was ordained that year, and married shortly after becoming rector of Woolavington in 1833. In 1840, he was appointed archdeacon of Chichester. While at Oxford he had not been associated with the Oxford Movement, and had on the whole adopted an anti-papal attitude, to the distress of John Henry **Newman**. In the 1840s his attitude began to change, especially after a visit to Italy. During the agitation against the restoration of the Roman Catholic hierarchy in 1850 he resigned as archdeacon, travelled to London, and on 6 April 1851 he was received into the Catholic Church: he was ordained priest (his wife had died in 1837) in June that year. He spent three years in Rome before returning to the Diocese of Westminister, where he established a small community in Bayswater, the Oblates of St Charles Borromeo. On the death of **Wiseman** in 1865 he became archbishop of Westminster and then cardinal in 1875. Manning took a leading part in the First Vatican Council and in the debates on papal infallibility. At home he promoted education (in 1874 he even attempted to start a Catholic university in Kensington – it lasted only four years), temperance, assisted in social reform, founded Roman Catholic organizations and helped to resolve the London dock strike of 1889. He was the model for Cardinal Grandison in Disraeli's novel *Lothair*.

Mannix, Daniel Cardinal archbishop of Melbourne, born Charleville in County Cork, 4 March 1864, died Melbourne, Australia, 6 November 1963. He was educated at the Christian Brothers School in Charleville, at St Colman's in Fermoy and St Patrick's, Maynooth, where he was ordained in 1890. For the next three years he lectured in Maynooth on philosophy and theology and was president 1903–12. From 1912 until 1917 he was coadjutor bishop of Melbourne, when he was appointed archbishop. Mannix was an outspoken nationalist, denouncing the extension of conscription to Ireland, and the excesses of the Black and Tans and Auxiliaries. *En route* to Ireland he was arrested by the British on 8 August 1920 and taken to Penzance in Cornwall to prevent his addressing meetings in Ireland and in Britain on nationalist issues. During his 47 years as archbishop of Melbourne he established 108 parishes and nearly 200 schools of all grades. He founded the Newman College for men and St Mary's Hall for women at the University of Melbourne as well as establishing a provincial seminary of Corpus Christi. Mannix was a vigorous promoter of Catholic Action, the Catholic press and the Catholic social movement.

Manogue, Patrick Roman Catholic missionary and bishop, born Desert, Kilkenny, Ireland, 15 March 1831, died Sacramento, California, 27 February 1895. One of seven orphaned children he received his early education at Callan in Ireland, emigrating to the United States in 1848. Studied for the priesthood at the College of St Mary of the Lake in Chicago, Illinois, and later in Paris at the Seminary of Saint-Sulpice, being ordained there on Christmas Day 1861. Returning to the United States, Manogue became responsible for a parish enclosing the whole of northern Nevada, settling in Virginia City. After twenty years of pastoral ministry he was appointed vicar general of the Diocese of Grass Valley, titular bishop of Ceramos in 1881, and bishop in 1884. Following boundary changes authorized by Pope **Leo XIII** the episcopal see was moved to Sacramento, where Manogue built the cathedral of the Blessed Sacrament.

Manríquez y Zárate, José de Jesús Roman Catholic bishop, born León, Guanajuato, Mexico, 7 November 1884, died Mexico City, 28 June 1951. He studied at the seminary in León, and at the South American College in Rome, where he obtained his doctorate in theology, canon law and philosophy, and was ordained in 1907, returning to Mexico two years later. After serving as vicar of the sacristy and prefect of the seminary in León from 1912 to 1922 he was pastor of Guanajuato, where he founded nine parochial schools, two secondary schools and a centre for higher studies for men. He was consecrated as bishop in 1923 and is reported to have evangelized 60,000 Indians. In 1926 he challenged the actions of the President (Calles), who imprisoned him and then exiled him to the United States. He resigned his bishopric in 1934, finally returning to Mexico City in 1944 after seventeen years in exile. In 1949 he was named vicar general of the Archdiocese of Mexico City, and in 1950 he represented his city in Rome at the declaration of the dogma of the Assumption of the Virgin. He died, following a pilgrimage to the Holy Land, on his return. His remains were transferred to the national monument to Christ the King in 1963.

Mantegna, Andrea Italian painter, born Isola di Carturo, 1431, died Mantua, 13 September 1506. His fresco *The Martyrdom of St James and St*

Christopher established him as painter in Padua, and he was invited to Mantua in 1457 by Ludovico Gonzaga: his *Life of Marquess Lodovico Gonzaga* and *Triumph of Caesar* are now in Hampton Court. His earlier altar pictures follow the traditional side-by-side grouping of saints' figures, e.g. *St Luke's Altar* (1453), now in the Brera, Milan. Later altarpieces show Venetian influence, e.g. that of San Zena (1455), in Venice, with a closely knit composition. And his *Adoration of the Magi* (1464), *Madonna della Vittoria* (1495), in the Louvre, and *Madonna and Saints* (1497) show even greater freedom of expression. His *Dead Christ*, in the Brera, Milan, shows a remarkable virtuosity in foreshortening the body.

Manuel II   Patriarch of Constantinople 1244–54, date and place of birth unknown, died Nicaea, *c.* November 1254. Because of the Latin occupation of Constantinople during the years 1204–61, Manuel resided in the temporary Byzantine capital at Nicaea, where he worked with the Emperor **John III**, **Ducas Vatatzes** on a possible union with the Roman Church. Manuel wrote a series of responses to canonical questions, and in 1253 corresponded with Pope **Innocent IV** to discuss the possibility of ecclesiastical union. However, during the same year of 1253–4, he was warned by the regent, Michael VIII Palaeologus, against intrigue as suspect in opposition to the new emperor at Nicaea, Theodore II Lascaris, and Patriarch Manuel II died soon thereafter.

Manuel II Palaeologus   Byzantine emperor, born 1350, died 21 July 1425. He was the son of **John V Palaeologus**. At Constantinople he was besieged by the Turks, but he diplomatically established peaceful relations with the Ottoman Turks, whose advance and conquest of the Byzantine Empire he held back for 50 years. Manuel also pursued religious and literary affairs, and finally retired to a monastery.

Manuel Calecas   *see* **Calecas, Manuel**

Manutius, Aldus   Renaissance printer and publisher, also known as 'Teobaldo Manucci', or 'Aldo Manuzio', born Bassaino, Italy, 1450, died Venice, 6 February 1515. He was a member of a family which became distinguished in the history of early printing and publishing. A publisher in Venice he became noted for edited versions of Greek and Latin classics, especially a five-volume folio edition of Aristotle (1495–8) and 28 *editiones principes* or first printed editions of MSS. He developed an italic type, designed by Francesco Griffo, for useful small octavo volumes. The *Hypernotomachia Poliphili* (1499) by Francesco Colonna is the best example of a fifteenth-century printed illustrated book, and Aldus' printer's mark of a dolphin entwined with an anchor became the hallmark of high quality printing. Aldus helped to make Venice a centre of classical culture and his son, Paulus **Manutius**, and his grandson, Aldus the Second (1547–97), continued the family traditions in the world of printing.

Manutius, Paulus   Renaissance printer and publisher, born Venice, 12 June 1512, died Rome, 6 April 1574. Paulus took over the Aldine press, and restored its reputation for accuracy. He issued accurate editions of Cicero's letters and orations, and treatises on Roman antiquities. Pope **Pius IV** invited Manutius to Rome, where he continued to print books.

Manzoni, Alessandro Francesco Tommaso   Italian poet and novelist, born Milan, 7 March 1785, died Milan, 22 May 1873. Brought up a Catholic, he was linked to the nationalist Risorgimento aiming at Italian unity. He is most famous for his historical novel *I promessi sposi*. He inherited an income and retired to Milan. He wrote a series of religious poems, *Imni sacri*, in honour of Church feasts and the Virgin Mary. Also he wrote a treatise, *Osservazioni sulla orale cattolica*. Manzoni's death gave the occasion to **Verdi** to compose his *Requiem*.

Marbeck, Pilgram   Anabaptist leader, and engineer, born Rottenburg, Tyrol, Austria, *c.*1495, died Augsburg, Germany, 1556. He was educated at the Latin School in Rattenburg to become an engineer, a judge and a city official. In 1527 he lost his position as judge for refusing to prosecute the Anabaptists, instead joining the movement himself. In 1528 he fled to Strasburg, where he continued his work as an engineer, but his leadership in Anabaptist circles led to his imprisonment and then expulsion. From 1544 to 1556 he became Anabaptist leader in Augsburg and, in association with

Hans Denck, became a prolific writer of books and pamphlets which stressed the need for a consecrated and disciplined approach to the Christian way of life but on less stringent lines than that advocated by his counterpart brethren in Switzerland.

Marbod of Rennes   Bishop and poet, born Angers, c.1035, died Angers, 11 September 1123. A pupil at the cathedral school of Angers, he became its master c.1067. He became chancellor of the Diocese of Angers c.1069, and was appointed bishop of Rennes, in Brittany, by Pope **Urban II** in 1096. He resigned at the age of 88, and died shortly thereafter at the abbey of Saint-Aubin in Angers. A skilled poet, he wrote on a variety of subjects, from the lives of the saints and biblical narratives to the qualities and virtues of gemstones and simple lyrics about beautiful girls.

Marc, Clement   Redemptorist priest and moral theologian, born Jouy-sous-les-Côtes, France, 24 July 1831, died Rome, 27 January 1887. He was professed in the Redemptorist novitiate in 1853 and ordained in 1857. He was appointed professor of moral theology at the Redemptorist House of Studies at Teterchen. In 1872 he moved to Rome to complete his *Institutiones morales Alphonsianae*, a work which achieved twenty editions, a complete one being published in 1933–4.

Marca, Pierre de   Archbishop and canonist, born Gan, France, 24 January 1594, died Paris, 29 June 1662. He studied with the Jesuits at Auch, and then law at Toulouse, in 1621 becoming president of the newly established *parlement* at Pau. He was ordained in 1642, after the death of his wife, and made bishop of Conserans in 1647 and archbishop of Toulouse in 1652. Ten years later he was appointed archbishop of Paris, but died before he could take up the post. Throughout this time he was serving in various government roles. He was commissioned by the king to produce his *Dissertationes de concordia sacerdoti et imperii* (1641), a defence of Gallican doctrines, but this was put on the Index of Prohibited Books in 1642. He also wrote against the Jansenists, on the history of his region, Béarn, and on Catalonia, a territory which he had overseen for the French government.

Marcel, Gabriel   French existentialist philosopher,

dramatist and critic, born Paris, 7 December 1889, died Paris, 8 October 1973. He was raised as an agnostic but became a Roman Catholic. His work includes *Journal métaphysique*, *Être et avoir*, *Homo viator* and *Le Mystère d'être*. Also he wrote plays, including *Un Homme de Dieu*, *La Chapelle ardente* and *Rome n'est plus dans Rome*.

Marcella   Saint, born c.325 into Roman aristocratic circles, died after torture during Alaric's sack of Rome, 410. Her father arranged her marriage when she was still very young and, widowed after six months of marriage, she rejected a new offer of marriage from the then consul, despite the pleas of her mother. Having heard about the flowering ascetic movements in Egypt, she started an ascetic community with her mother and many other aristocratic women in her palace on the Aventine. **Jerome** acted as their spiritual guide and master in the Scriptures (382–5). Marcella's monastic settlement was for many decades a centre of intense monastic living. Feast day 31 January.

Marcellinus   Pope, saint, elected 30 June 296, died 25 October 304. Nothing is known of him before his election, but during the persecution of Diocletian, he apparently complied with orders to hand over sacred texts and to offer incense to pagan gods, as did some of his presbyters, who later became Popes. This apostasy was cited by the Donatists as evidence of his moral failure, and was clearly an embarrassment to later churchmen. According to some traditions, he was filled with remorse for his failing, and days later sought execution at the hands of the authorities. He was buried in the cemetery of Priscilla on the Via Salaria. There is in fact no evidence that he was martyred, though he came to be venerated as a saint. His death left the Church of Rome without a leader for more than three years. Feast day 2 June.

Marcellinus and Peter   Saints, Roman martyrs, died 304. Marcellinus was a priest, Peter an exorcist. Evidence of their cult is early and strong: feasts in sacramentaries and calendars, survival of tombs, verses by **Damasus I**. They were buried in the catacomb of Tiburtius, Via Labicana, over which a church was built later. They are also mentioned in the Roman Canon. In 827 Pope

Gregory IV sent their relics to Einhard, former secretary and biographer of Charlemagne, to enrich his monastery at Seligenstadt. Records of miracles are extant. Feast day 2 June.

Marcellinus, Flavius Saint, Roman tribune, notary and a friend of St Augustine of Hippo, date of birth unknown, died Carthage, North Africa, c.413. In 411 during a conference between Catholics and Donatists in Carthage he became acquainted with St Augustine when Marcellinus upheld the Catholic cause. The Donatists accused him and his brother of implication in a revolt at Heraclian, and both were condemned and executed. Augustine visited Marcellinus in prison, praised him in several of his letters and dedicated to him his most famous work, *De civitate Dei*. Marcellinus was subsequently exonerated by the Emperor Honorius, and his name was added to the Roman Martyrology by Cardinal Baronius in the sixteenth century. Feast day 6 April.

Marcello, Benedetto Italian composer and writer, born Venice, 24 July 1686, died Brescia, 24 July 1739. He became a member of the Venetian Council and governor of Pola, Istria, but retired to Brescia. His work includes oratorios, Masses, motets and secular music but he is best known for his Psalm settings. He translated John Dryden's *Timotheus* to provide the libretto for a cantata.

Marcellus I Pope and saint, was bishop of Rome, March 308, only after a difficult succession procedure, died in exile, probably on 16 January 308. While he was Pope he reorganized the city's parishes. With regard to the readmission of the *lapsi* (those who disavowed their faith during Diocletian's persecution), he took a rather firm stance that ultimately led to his removal and exile, probably on the orders of Maxentius. Feast day 16 January.

Marcellus II Pope, born 'Marcello Cervini' at Montepulciano, 6 May 1501, elected to the Papacy 9 April 1555, died 1 May 1555. He studied at Siena and in Rome, was skilled in mathematics and in matters of chronology, and was employed by Paul III as tutor to his nephew, which gave him considerable influence on the Pope himself. He held a succession of bishoprics, before being appointed cardinal in 1539. He was a committed reformer, and served as one of the presidents of the Council of Trent and on Paul III's reform commission. Much was hoped for from his election: he promptly demonstrated his reforming zeal by forbidding his relatives to come to Rome to benefit from the Papacy, and keeping his own name on election, but died of a stroke after only three weeks in office. Palestrina's *Missa Papae Marcelli* was written for him.

Marcellus Akimetes Saint and abbot, also known as 'Marcellus the Righteous', born Apamea in Syria, died near Constantinople, c.485. He became abbot of a monastery near Constantinople. The community were known as 'Akoimetoi', 'sleepless' monks, hence his name. In daily shifts they sang God's praises continuously. Marcellus attended the Council of Chalcedon in 451. Feast day 29 December.

Marcellus of Ancyra Bishop, born c.280, died 374. At the Council of Nicaea (325), as well as in later discussions, Marcellus heavily stressed the hypostatic unity of the Father and the Son, which for too many people in the East smelled of Modalism. He was deposed and fled to Rome, where he found the support of the – also exiled – Athanasius and of Pope Julius I. The Westerners supported him at the Council of Serdica (343), but the Eastern bishops refused to do so and installed Basil (of Ancyra) in his see. In 362 Athanasius, his last supporter, also distanced himself, leaving Marcellus virtually without support.

Marcellus of Chalon-sur-Saône Saint, legendary figure who is supposed to have been martyred in 175 during the reign of the Emperor Marcus Aurelius (161–180). A cult and a church in his honour are mentioned by St Gregory of Tours. Feast day 4 September.

Marcellus of Die Saint, bishop of Die, date of birth not recorded, died Bareuil, Provence, 510. He was consecrated by Maurertus, bishop of Vienne, who was in conflict with the metropolitan city of Arles. Marcellus was temporarily imprisoned and exiled by the Arian king of the Burgundians but eventually returned to his see, where he became distinguished by his piety and zeal as a pastor. His cult at Die was confirmed for the Diocese of Valence by Pope **Pius IX.** Feast day originally 17 January, now 9 April.

Marcellus of Paris Saint, bishop of Paris, fl. early fifth century. The details of his life rely on oral tradition, which depicts him as a zealous pastor and a miracle-worker. St **Germanus of Paris** (c.496–576) requested Venantius **Fortunatus** to compose a *Vita*. Feast day originally 1 November, now 3 November.

Marcellus the Centurion Saint, Roman martyr, his *Acts* place his death in León, Spain, and, more convincingly, in Tingis (Tangier), 298. During the celebrations of the birthday of the Emperors Diocletian and Maximian, Marcellus publicly declared himself a Christian. A centurion, first class, he renounced his military oath, judging it to be incompatible with the practice of the Christian religion. Arrested and condemned to death by the sword. Feast day 30 October.

Marchand, Louis French organist and composer, born Lyons, 2 February 1669, died Paris, 17 February 1732. He became organist at Nevers, Auxerre and Paris, and entered royal service, becoming one of the *organistes du roi*. Daquin was one of his pupils. Admiring crowds in Paris were said to follow Marchand from church to church, to hear him play. He wrote vocal and keyboard compositions, mostly published posthumously.

Marchant, Jacques Pastoral theologian, born Couvin, Namur, France, c.1585, died there, 1648. Following his ordination he taught theology at the abbeys of Floreffe and Lobbes. In 1616 he became pastor in his native village, and in 1630 administrator of the Canton of Chimay. Among his written works his *Hortus pastorum sacrae doctrinae* (3 vols, Mons, 1626–7) was regarded highly, and a thirteen-volume edition of his works was published (Paris, 1865–7), edited by Vivès.

Marchant, Pierre Franciscan and theologian, born Couvin, Liège (Belgium), 1585, died Ghent, 11 November 1661. He was professed in 1601 and taught in the schools of his Order. Soon thereafter he succeeded to high office within the Order, becoming provincial in 1625, and commissary general over the provinces of Germany, Belgium, Holland, England and Ireland in 1639. The last province involved him in Irish politics between the Ormondists who were in opposition to the nuncio, Giovanni **Rinuccini**. Marchant's written justification, *Relatio veridica et sincera status Provinciae Hiberniae*, was condemned in 1661 and ordered to be destroyed by the General Chapter in Rome. Again, his *Santifico S. Joseph Sponsi Virginis in utero asserta* (Bruges, 1630) aroused controversy, and it was placed on the Index in 1633. His principal work, *Tribunal sacramentale* (3 vols, Ghent, 1642), a treatise on moral theology for confessors, adhered to both traditional beliefs and writings of the Doctors of the Church, thus avoiding disputation.

Marchettus of Padua Music theorist and composer, born Padua, Italy, c.1274, fl. 1305–26. He was *maestro di canto* at Padua Cathedral, 1305–7, later residing in Casena and Verona. He composed motets but is chiefly remembered for three treatises: *Lucidarium* (1309–18), *Pomerium* (1318–26) and *Brevis compilacio*, which is largely a summary of *Pomerium*. These treatises provide the most complete explanation of Italian trecento music theory, and plainchant. Marchettus' theories, although respected aroused much controversy, and were never widely accepted.

Marchi, Giuseppe Jesuit and archaeologist, born Tolmezzo, near Undine, Italy, 22 February 1795, died Rome, 10 February 1860. Following his ordination in the Society he taught at Terni, Reggio Emilia, Modena and Rome. His particular interest in Christian archaeology led him to investigate the catacombs and ancient monuments. He became director of the Museum Kircherianum in 1838, *conservatore* of Rome's sacred cemeteries in 1842 and director of the Lateran Museum in 1854. As a member of the Pontificia Academia Romana di Archaeologia he established a corpus of ancient Christian inscriptions and monuments, including *Monumenti della arti christiane primitive* 1: *Architetture cimiterale* (Rome, 1844–7) which gave impetus to the scientific study of Christian archaeology. His outstanding disciple was Giovanni Batista de **Rossi** (1822–94).

Marcian Byzantine emperor, born 396, died 457.

He married **Pulcheria**, sister of the emperor, and succeeded as emperor in 450. Financial reforms made his reign one of considerable prosperity. Theologically, his reign is marked by his successful repression of Monophysitism, Marcian himself attending the sixth session of the Council of Chalcedon (451). But he had to resort to arms to enforce its theological decrees. He enjoyed good relations with Pope **Leo I**, correspondence with whom survives.

Marcion Heretical theologian, died *c.*160. According to anti-Marcionite sources he was born in Sinope, where his father, the local bishop, excommunicated him. He made a fortune as a shipowner and became a member of the Roman Christian community. In 144, however, they too expelled him, returning to him the large sum he had donated. He then founded a very successful Church of his own. The nucleus of Marcion's doctrine is the difference between the loving Father of Jesus Christ and the cruel Judge from the OT. Consequently the God of the NT is not the same as the God of the OT. Therefore, Marcion only acknowledges the NT as the foundation of the Christian faith.

Marcion of Cyr Saint, monk and ascetic, born Cyr, Syria, *c.*300, died in the desert of Chalis, north Syria, *c.*381–91. Son of a patrician family he chose instead the lifestyle of a hermit in fasting and prayer. Two of his disciples, Eusebias and Agapetus, encouraged others to follow the ascetic way of life but Marcion, out of humility, refused either to become their abbot or to be ordained as a priest. He ordered that on his death his body be concealed and his burial place was only discovered 50 years later.

Marco Polo *see* **Polo, Marco**

Marconi, Guglielmo Italian physicist and one of the inventors of wireless telegraphy, born Bologna, 25 April 1874, died Rome, 20 July 1937. He was educated privately, and early on demonstrated an interest in electricity. In England he patented his wireless telegraphy. He sent signals from Cornwall to Newfoundland, proving that the earth's curvature presented no obstacle. He organized a company, The Wireless Telegraph and Signal Company Ltd. He was involved in a legal case regarding patents, but received many honours including the joint Nobel Prize for Physics, his invention having greatly enhanced modern life. He helped in 1930 to establish the first Vatican radio station, at the request of Eugenio Pacelli, the Cardinal Secretary of State and future **Pius XII**. Marconi, who had recently married and had begun once again to practise his Catholic faith, agreed to assist.

Maréchal, Ambrose Archbishop of Baltimore, born Ingres, near Orléans, France, 28 August 1764, died Baltimore, Maryland, 29 January 1828. He began his adult studies in law but soon thereafter entered the seminary in Orléans to study theology. He joined the Sulpician Order and was ordained at Bordeaux in 1792. With two fellow-Sulpicians he arrived in Baltimore the same year, where he served as administrator and pastor in an extensive diocese until 1799. After teaching theology at St Mary's Seminary in Baltimore, and philosophy at Georgetown College, Washington, DC, he was temporarily recalled to France to teach in various diocesan seminaries, returning to the United States in 1812. In 1817 he was consecrated archbishop of Baltimore, where he advanced the building of Baltimore Cathedral, which was dedicated in 1821. On a visit to Rome in the same year he obtained agreement from the Holy See to the nomination of bishops in the United States to come from provincial bishops, a policy still in existence, and he persuaded Pope **Pius VII** to raise the diocesan seminary of St Mary to the rank of a pontifical university from 1822.

Maréchal, Joseph Jesuit philosopher, born Chaleroi, Belgium, 1 July 1878, died Louvain, 11 December 1944. He entered the Society in 1895, obtained a doctorate in biology at the University of Louvain in 1905, and was ordained in 1908. He taught biology, experimental psychology and philosophy at the Jesuit house of studies in Louvain. His principal written work, *Le Point de départ de la métaphysique*, was a vindication of Thomistic realism, published in five volumes, the first four in Bruges–Paris and Brussels–Paris, 1922–4. The fifth and final volume and the most celebrated, published posthumously (Brussels, 1947), was a study of Thomism in the light of contemporary critical philosophy.

Marenzio, Luca Italian composer, born Coccaglio, near Brescia, 1553, died Rome, 22 August 1599. He moved to Rome where he served cardinals and wealthy patrons. He was an unusually prolific publisher of his own music and became known internationally. Though Marenzio is famous for his secular madrigals and villanellas, he also composed Church music, including *c.*75 motets. In England his music was published in Yonge's *Musica transalpina* (1588–97).

Marescotti, Hyacintha Saint, virgin and a member of the Third Order Regular of St Francis, born Vignanello, Papal States, 1585, died Viterbo, 30 January 1640. Unwillingly she entered the convent of St Bernardino in Viterbo and, after ten unhappy and unruly years, was persuaded by her confessor to renounce her behaviour and to follow a stricter regime. Thereafter she devoted her life to devotion to the Passion of Christ with harsh penances, poverty and humility which led to mystical prayer and works of charity. She founded two congregations of Oblates of Mary to care for the sick and for the orphaned and, despite illness, persevered in her reformed way of life. She was beatified by Pope **Benedict XIII** in 1726 and canonized by **Pius VII** in 1807. Her reportedly incorrupt body lay in the convent in Viterbo until the church was destroyed by aerial bombardment. Feast day 30 January.

Maret, Henri Louis Charles Bishop and theologian, born Meyrueis, Lozère, France, 20 April 1805, died Paris, 16 June 1884. He studied at the St Sulpice Seminary in Paris and was ordained in 1830. In 1832 he became chaplain to St Philippe du Roule, and in 1841 professor in the theology faculty at the Sorbonne, dean in 1853, a university whose degrees were not recognized in Rome. In 1860 he was nominated to the See of Vannes but Pope **Pius IX** refused to confirm his appointment on account of his supposed Gallicanism; however, in 1861 he became bishop of Sura. Maret argued that the separation of Church and State could be reconciled with Church traditions, rights and doctrines and in his best-known written work, *Du Concile général et de la paix religieuse* (2 vols, 1869), opposed papal infallibility and stressed the role of bishops in the Church's constitution. In 1871 he was forced by Pius IX publicly to retract his views,

which were deemed to be contrary to the recently proclaimed papal pronouncement *Pastor Aeternus*.

Margaret Clitherow Saint, martyr of York, born York, 1556, died there by crushing, 25 March 1586. She was the daughter of a sheriff of York and converted to Roman Catholicism in 1574. She was charged at York Assizes in 1586 with sheltering Roman Catholic priests. She refused to answer charges, in order to protect her children from having to testify against her. She died by being crushed to death. She was one of the Forty **martyrs of England and Wales** canonized by **Paul VI** in 1970.

Margaret Mary Alacoque Saint, Visitandine, born Lauthecourt, France, 22 July 1647, died Paray-le-Monial, France 17 October 1690. She had an unhappy childhood marked by ill health. In 1671 she entered a convent at Paray-le-Monial. Between 1673 and 1675 she received a number of visions telling her to spread devotion to the Sacred Heart, and to establish a feast in its honour. These were treated as delusions by her superiors but opposition declined with the support of her confessor, Blessed Claude de la Colombière, SJ. She was beatified in 1864 and canonized in 1920. Feast day 16 October.

Margaret of Antioch (Marina) Saint, martyr and patron saint of women in labour. Her dates are unknown. She has been honoured in the Eastern Church since the seventh century but not as a devotion in the West until the twelfth century. She is often depicted with a dragon (symbol of evil). Feast day 20 July, in the East, 17 July.

Margaret of Cortona Penitent, born Laviano, Tuscany, 1247, died Cortona, 22 February 1297. After the murder of her seducer, by whom she had a son, Margaret underwent a conversion, went to Cortona to put herself under the guidance of Franciscans there, and led a life of public penance for 29 years, becoming a Franciscan tertiary. To support herself and her son she nursed elderly women in Cortona, but she gave that up to look after the sick and poor in her own house, and later in the community she founded in Cortona, with the approval of the bishop. She early became the recipient of mystical experiences, and appears to have had the gift of healing. Her holiness was recognized long before her death, and she was proclaimed a saint by the people as soon as she died. Her incorrupt body remains in Cortona. Feast day 22 February.

Margaret of Hungary   Saint, born 1242, died 18 January 1271. The daughter of Bela IV of Hungary, she entered the Dominican convent in Veszprém when only four years old, in fulfilment of a vow made by her parents. Her parents later founded a convent on Hasen Insel, near Buda, where she went in 1252, and where she spent the rest of her life, taking her solemn vows when eighteen and fighting off her father's wish to marry her to the king of Bohemia. The fame of her holiness and of her penitential practices was widespread even during her lifetime. There were frequent attempts to have her canonized, and **Pius VII** permitted her to be venerated as a saint.

Margaret of Lorraine   Blessed, born Vaudemont, Lorraine, France, 1463, died Argentan, 2 November 1521. In 1488 she married René, duke of Alençon, but was widowed with three young children by 1492. During her son's minority she ruled the duchy and, coming under the influence of St **Francis of Assisi**, she adopted an ascetic lifestyle and, when finally free from family responsibilities, joined the Third Order of St Francis of Assisi and withdrew from the court. In 1513 she founded a convent at Argentan where the Rule of St **Clare** was observed. Later she refused the office of abbess for herself. She was buried at Argentan, where her reportedly incorrupt body was venerated until it was profaned by the Jacobins in 1793. Her cult was confirmed by Pope **Benedict XV** in 1921. Feast day 6 November.

Margaret of Metola   Blessed, born Metola, Italy, 1287, died Città di Castello, 13 April 1320. She was of noble birth but suffered from severe disabilities of blindness, dwarfism and a hunchback, and she was kept hidden by her parents from the age of six to sixteen, when they abandoned her. She became a Dominican tertiary and, despite her multiple handicaps, devoted herself to the sick and the dying, and to prisoners in the city's jail. Many miracles were attributed to her after her death, and she was beatified in 1609. Feast day 13 April.

Margaret of Parma   Regent of The Netherlands 1559–67, born Oudenard (Belgium), 28 December 1522, died Ortona, Italy, 18 January 1586. She was the natural daughter of the Emperor **Charles V** and Johanna van der Gheynst, and was educated by the Emperor's aunt and sister. In 1536 Margaret married Duke Alexander de' Medici of Florence but he was assassinated within the year. In 1538 she was married to Ottano Farnese, the thirteen-year-old grandson of Pope **Paul III** and subsequently duke of Parma and Piacenza. Margaret came under the spiritual guidance of St **Ignatius of Loyola**, whom she assisted in the establishment of a house for catechumens in Rome, and of a refuge for fallen women. In 1559 she was appointed regent of The Netherlands by her half-brother, King **Philip II** of Spain, but her regency was marked by political and religious difficulties involving the nobility on one hand and Calvinists on the other. After 1566 she became increasingly isolated when a measure of political and religious independence, the 'Compromise of the Nobles', was passed by the State and King Philip, and she resigned her regency and retired to Parma in the following year.

Margaret of Roskilde   Saint, local Danish saint, date and place of birth unknown, died Ølse, near Køge, Denmark, 25 October 1176. A relative of the archbishop of Lund, Margaret was strangled by her husband, who then attempted to make her death look like a suicide. When they tried to bury her on unhallowed ground, a mysterious light was said to have shone around, causing people to believe in her sanctity. After an investigation, her husband confessed to his crime, and she became the object of local veneration. Feast day 25 October, even though she was never officially canonized.

Margaret of Scotland   Saint, queen of Scotland, born Hungary, c.1045, died Edinburgh Castle, 16 November 1093. She grew up in the fervently Christian Hungarian court until summoned to England in 1057 by **Edward the Confessor**. After his death and the Norman Conquest the family took refuge in Dunfermline, Scotland, with King Malcolm III, whom she married about 1069. She corresponded with Archbishop **Lanfranc** of Canterbury, and is said to have summoned a council for the reform of the practices of the Church in

Scotland, the decisions being known as the 'Five Articles of Margaret'. Her support of the Church included the provision of the Queen's Ferry for pilgrims to St Andrews, and monastic endowments. Her children maintained her strong Christian commitment. She was canonized in 1249.

Margaret of the Blessed Sacrament   Venerable, Discalced Carmelite nun, and promoter of devotion to the Divine Infancy, born Beaune, France, 1619, died there, 26 May 1648. Margaret Parigot is reported to have received her first Holy Communion at the age of eleven; she entered the Discalced Carmelite convent at Beaune in 1631, and was professed with the name Margaret of the Blessed Sacrament, in 1634. Her spiritual progress was directed by the Oratorian Fathers Parisot, 1637–43, and Blaise Chaduc, 1643–8. She was the principal apostle of devotion to the Infancy of Jesus, a cult which spread throughout France. Although she put nothing in writing, her spiritual experiences and confidences were gathered by her prioress and published, and were the sources of Lives, and of translations into the principal European languages. The cause for her beatification was introduced in 1905.

Margil, Antonio   Venerable, Franciscan missionary and promoter of missionary colleges in Spanish America, born Valencia, Spain, 18 August 1657, died Mexico City, 6 August 1726. He entered the Order in 1673 and was ordained in 1682, arriving with 22 fellow friars in Veracruz, Mexico, in 1683. Margil is linked with the institution of missionary colleges under the general title of Propagation of the Faith. He took over the first college, Santa Cruz de Querétaro, in 1684, a year after its foundation, and guided it through its formative years. He developed two more, Cristo Crucificado in Guatemala City in 1701, and Our Lady of Guadalupe in 1708, and his missionary work extended beyond Mexico to Central America, near Panama, and to present-day Louisiana and Texas. A canonical investigation of his life was begun in 1771, and his remains were transferred to the cathedral in Mexico City in 1861.

Margotti, Giacomo   Roman Catholic priest and journalist, born San Remo, Italy, 11 May 1823, died Turin, 6 May 1887. He was ordained in Turin and two years later began working on the first Italian Catholic newspaper, *Armonia della religione con la civilita*, published daily from 1855, Margotti becoming its editor in 1849. The paper strove increasingly to counter the prevalent anticlerical, antipapal and anti-Catholic climate of opinion which was part of the Italian drive towards independence, and Margotti used the paper and other written works to defend suppressed religious foundations and bishops then in exile. Inevitably he came into conflict with governmental authority and his election to the Sub-Alpine Parliament in 1857 was annulled, and the newspaper temporarily suspended in 1859. After a dispute with the owners Margotti left *Armonia* in 1863 and founded *L'Unita cattolica*, in which he continued to attack the State. The *Armonia* ceased publication in 1866, and *L'Unita cattolica*, which had become the property of the Holy See, followed a similar demise in 1929.

Maria (Skobtsova)   Mother, Russian Orthodox nun and martyr, born Riga, 8 December 1891, died Ravensbrück concentration camp, Mecklenburg, 31 March 1945. A daughter of the Russian intelligentsia, she became a nun in Paris in 1932 after a Church divorce from her second husband. The rest of her life was devoted to serving the poor of Paris, especially emigrants. She also assisted George **Florovsky** in his theological research. She was gassed by the Nazis because of her help to escaping French Jews, just before the war's end.

Maria Cristina of Savoy   Venerable, queen, born Cagliari, Sardinia, 14 November 1812, died Naples, 31 January 1836. She was the youngest child of King Victor Emmanuel I (1759–1824), king of Sardinia. Her desire to enter religious life was not granted and she was married to Ferdinand I, king of Naples. Fulfilling her state obligations, nevertheless she maintained her charitable and pious practices and exercised an exemplary influence on the court and upon those around her. Stories about her ill-treatment by her husband may be unfounded but she died giving birth to her only child, who became Francis II, the last Bourbon king of Naples. Her cause for beatification was introduced in 1889, and her heroic virtues approved in 1937.

Marie de l'Incarnation *see* **Mary of the Incarnation**

Marillac, Louise de Saint, foundress, born Ferrières-en-Brie, near Meaux, 12 August 1591, died Paris, 15 March 1660. After the death in 1625 of her husband, Antony Le Gras (they had married in 1613), she supported the work of St **Vincent de Paul**. She established a house in Paris in 1633 for women who might care for the poor – the origins of the Daughters of Charity, for whom she drew up a rule of life. Her congregation grew rapidly and at the time of her death there were over 40 houses of the sisters in France. She was canonized in 1934, and is the patron saint of social workers. Feast day 15 March.

Marín-Sola, Francisco Theologian and Dominican, born Carcar, Navarre, Spain, 22 November 1873, died Manila, Philippines, 5 June 1932. He entered the Dominican Order at Toledo, and was ordained in 1897. On completion of his studies he was sent to Amalung in the Philippines but was imprisoned temporarily during a revolution there. In 1900 he was in Manila at the Colegio de San Juan but ill health, caused by his imprisonment, necessitated his return to Ávila in Spain. Returning to Manila he received a doctorate in theology in 1908. He founded the Dominican College at Rosaryville, Ponchatoula, Louisana, and taught there and at the University of Notre Dame in Indiana. From 1918 to 1927 he was again in Europe, where he held the chair in theology at the Catholic University of Fribourg in Switzerland. He is described as a theologian of vitality and resource, and his best-known publication was *L'Évolution homogène du dogma catholique* (Fribourg, 1924).

Marina *see* **Margaret of Antioch**

Marinho, José Antônio Roman Catholic priest, professor and politician, born Pôrto do Salgado, 7 October 1803, died Rio de Janeiro, 3 March 1853. Although the son of a poor family and a mulatto, seemingly without prospects, a chance encounter with firstly an actor in a travelling company and secondly a rich merchant changed his fortunes and he came to the notice of the bishop of Pernambuco. He embarked on his ecclesiastical studies, temporarily interrupted by a revolution in that city but finally completed in 1829. He obtained the chair of philosophy in Ouro Prêto but became involved in politics when he became substitute deputy in the imperial legislature in Rio de Janeiro in 1839, and a regular deputy in 1842–5. Thereafter he abandoned politics in exchange for pastoral work at Sacramento in Rio de Janeiro and founded a private school, the Colegio Marinho. He was awarded the Order of Christ by Dom Pedro for his services to the Papacy, and for his famous sermons delivered at the imperial chapel on state occasions.

Marinus Tenth-century hermit. After three years at the monastery of Sant'Apollinare-in-Classe, **Romuald of Ravenna** received permission to join the cluster of hermits gathered around the ascetic Marinus in the Veneto. Marinus followed neither Rule nor master in the eremitical life: he sang the whole Psalter every day, 20 under one tree, 30 or 40 under another. Together, Romuald and Marinus spent some four years leading an ascetic life as wandering hermits in central and northern Italy. In 978, at the invitation of Abbot Guarinus of Cuxa, they left Italy for a hermitage in the Pyrenees.

Marinus *see* **Anianus and Marinus**

Marinus I Pope, born Gallese, Tuscany, elected Pope 16 December 882, died Rome, 15 May 884. Marinus was the son of a priest, and had served the papal court from twelve years old, eventually rising to be papal treasurer and bishop of what is now Cerveteri. He was used on several crucial diplomatic missions. When elected, he was the first bishop of Rome to be transferred from one diocese to another, contrary to the ancient canons. He was a conciliator, establishing good relations with the Byzantine emperor, and improving those with the Patriarch **Photius**. He also had a high regard for **Alfred the Great**. His name was sometimes confused with 'Martin', and listed as 'Martin II'.

Marinus II Pope, born Rome, elected to the Papacy 30 October 942, died Rome, May 946. In the mid-tenth century, **Alberic II of Spoleto** was in control of Rome, and of papal elections. Marinus, who was a cardinal-priest and about whose earlier life nothing is known, owed his appointment entirely to Alberic and did nothing without his approval. Little of significance is recorded of his short Papacy. His name was sometimes confused with that of 'Martin', and listed as 'Martin III'.

Marinus and Leo Saints, details of the lives of both are based largely on legends which grew up centuries later and according to which Marinus and Leo were Dalmatian Christians who were condemned to work on repairing the walls of Rimini during the persecution of the Emperor Diocletian, *c.*304. During this time they showed concern for their fellow prisoners and converted some to Christianity. Separately they retired as hermits, Marinus to Mount Titano and Leo to Montefeltro. St Marinus was made a deacon, and St Leo may have been ordained as priest in 359 by Bishop St Gaudentius. The site of Marinus' hermitage is reputed to have become a foundation of a monastery and the tiny republic of San Marino which exists to this day.

Marinus of Anazarbus Saint, according to his (legendary) *Passio*, he was an old man living in Anazarbus (Cilicia). During Diocletian's persecution he was, probably in 285, accused of being a Christian. Brought to Tarsus before the governor of the province he refused, even after torture, to renounce his faith. He was decapitated and his body thrown for the dogs and other wild beasts. Two of the Christians who were in the neighbourhood took advantage of a thunderstorm and succeeded in seizing the relics, which they hid in a cavern and later returned to Anazarbus. Feast day 8 August.

Marion-Brésillac, Melchior Marie Joseph de Founder of the Society of the African Missions, born Castelnaudary, Aude, France, 2 December 1813, died Freetown, Sierre Leone, 28 June 1859. Born into an aristocratic but poor family, he was educated at home to the age of eighteen. He was ordained priest in the Roman Catholic Church in 1838 and worked in a parish until 1841, when he joined the Paris Foreign Missionary Society. As a missionary in India from 1842 to 1854 he advocated an indigenous clergy, and he opposed the caste system to the annoyance of some of his colleagues. He returned to France to take up senior administrative posts, but left to found his own Congregation at Lyons in 1856. In 1858 he was appointed vicar apostolic of Sierra Leone and arrived in Africa in 1859. His mission there was short lived, as he and his companions died of yellow fever within six weeks, but his ideals of a native priesthood and adaptation to local culture became the lynchpins of his foundation.

Maritain, Jacques Roman Catholic philosopher, born Paris, 18 November 1882, died Toulouse, 28 April 1973. Maritain grew up in a liberal Protestant, anticlerical family and studied natural sciences at the Sorbonne. There he met Raïssa Oumansoff (see next entry), a fellow student in the science faculty. They were both unhappy with the materialism of the sciences, and were encouraged by their friend Charles **Péguy** to attend the lectures of Henri **Bergson**, who inspired an interest in philosophy. They were also friendly with Léon **Bloy**, and it was through his influence that both Jacques and Raïssa became Catholics in 1906: they were married two years earlier. Jacques went on to study biology, but became increasingly interested in the philosophy of **Thomas Aquinas**, to which Raïssa had been introduced by her Dominican spiritual director. His conversion and his Thomism ruled out a university career in the France of the period. He built up a close circle of Thomistically minded friends who met at his house at Meudon, some of whom, including Maritain himself, were unusual among Catholics in not supporting the Nationalists during the Spanish Civil War. Maritain taught for many years at the Institut Catholique in Paris, but during the Second World War moved to the United States. He served as French ambassador to the Vatican 1945–8, but then returned to the United States, to a post at Princeton, returning to France only in 1960. In his more than 60 books he demonstrated a particular interest in the theory of knowledge, but also, particularly after his time in the United States, in political theory. His work on human rights is said to have influenced the UN Declaration. His autobiographical reflections, *The Peasant of the Garonne*, first published in French in 1966 during the pontificate of his friend Pope **Paul VI**, appeared to criticize the direction which Catholicism was taking, but he remained a devout Catholic and, after Raïssa's death, he lived with the Little

Brothers of Jesus in Toulouse, becoming a member of the Order in 1970.

Maritain, Raïssa Oumansoff Author, born Rostov on the Don, Russia, 12 September 1883, died Paris, 4 November 1960. She left Russia with her family to escape persecution of the Jews and went on to study at the Sorbonne. In 1904 she married Jacques **Maritain**, the philosopher and writer, and she was converted to Catholicism in 1906. With her husband she played an important part in the French Catholic revival stressing the importance of the philosophy of St **Thomas Aquinas**. She wrote four volumes of poetry, and her personal memoirs in *We Have Been Friends Together* (New York, 1942) and *Adventures in Grace* (New York, 1945). Also she combined in writings with her husband, notably *The Situation of Poetry* (New York, 1955) and, posthumously, *Notes on the Lord's Prayer* (New York, 1964).

Marius of Avenches Saint, chronicler and bishop, born Autun, 530 or 531, died 31 December 594. As bishop of Avenches from 574 until his death, he transferred his episcopal see from Avenches to Lausanne. He compiled a *Chronicle* of the years 455–581, continuing the work of **Prosper of Aquitaine**, recording contemporary events in Italy and the Orient as well as matters in Burgundy. Marius is described as thoroughly Roman in culture and convinced of the permanent survival of the Roman Empire despite surrounding barbarism. He was buried in Lausanne, and his cult was approved in 1605.

Marius Victorinus Philosopher and Christian writer, of African origin, born between c.281 and 291. He taught rhetoric and settled in Rome, where his success gained him a place in the senatorial aristocracy – and a statue on the forum of Trajan. Around 355 he was converted to Christianity. Before his conversion he composed many writings on the liberal arts and on philosophy. His thorough knowledge of Platonic philosophy led his theological activity to a highly original effort to achieve a synthesis between that philosophy and Christian theology. In his many theological writings he defended the equality of the Father and the Son and developed a non-subordinationist view on

the Trinity. His writings exercised great influence on later Latin writers.

Mark Pope and saint, elected 18 January 336, died 7 October 336. Little or nothing else is known of Mark, beyond the fact that he was the son of Priscus, and a Roman. It may have been Mark who laid down that the bishop of Rome should always be consecrated by the bishop of Ostia.

Mark of Arethusa Saint, bishop of Arethusa and confessor, born between 250 and 270, died Arethusa on Mount Lebanon, 28 March 389. He is thought to have been active in the dispute over Arianism and may have joined the Semi-Arians, attending their synods, but he died in the orthodox faith. He was responsible for the destruction of pagan temples, building churches on their sites. Unhappily the reign of the Emperor Julian the Apostate left Mark to the mercy of his fellow townsmen, who exacted their revenge with the most vicious tortures. He survived, even winning the admiration of his tormentors, and eventually was pardoned by the emperor. His cult was approved by Pope **Clement VIII** in 1598. Feast day celebrated by the Greeks on 28 March, or 29 March in some Eastern Churches.

Mark of the Nativity Carmelite of the Touraine Reform, born Cuno, near Samur, France, 9 January 1617, died 23 February 1696. He was educated firstly by the Benedictines, and then the Jesuits at La Flèche, before entering the Carmelite Order at Rennes, where earlier in the century the Touraine reform had been inaugurated. Mark took an active part in furthering the reform, completing and editing directories for novices (1650–1) and directories for external conduct (1677–9). He held the posts of novice master, prior, definitor, visitator and provincial within his Order. Also he served as confessor to the archbishop of Tours, Victor Le Bouteiller. Mark influenced the work of the *Directorium. Carmelitanum, vitae spiritualis* (Vatican, 1940), with an English translation later (Chicago, 1951).

Marley, Marie Hilda Roman Catholic teacher, educator and leader on child guidance, born Durham, England, 13 October 1876, died Glasgow, Scotland, 19 November 1951. She was educated in

Sheffield, studied at Our Lady's Training College for Teachers in Liverpool, and then at London University. She entered the Congregation of the Sisters of Notre Dame of Namur, firstly resident in Teignmouth, Devon, and later at Notre Dame Training College in Glasgow. She emphasized the importance of psychology in the curriculum and prepared a textbook on the subject. She founded the Notre Dame Child Guidance Clinic in Glasgow, becoming the principal pioneer on the subject in Scotland. She retired from teaching in 1941 and was awarded the *Pro Ecclesia et Pontifice* cross by Pope **Pius XII**. In 1951 she was elected vice-president of the International Congress of Catholic Psychologists.

Marmion, Joseph Columba   Benedictine abbot and spiritual writer, born Dublin, 1 April 1858, died Maredsous, 30 January 1923. He studied in Dublin, at Holy Cross, Clonliffe, and in Rome, was ordained and in 1881 returned to pastoral ministry in Ireland, becoming professor of philosophy at Holy Cross. He joined the Benedictines in Belgium in 1886, was made prior of the abbey of Mont César, Louvain, and then, in 1909, abbot of Maredsous. While appreciating Thomist theology, he drew largely on the patristic and liturgical traditions of Benedictine monasticism. After his death his works were published in London as *Christ, the Life of the Soul* (1925), *Christ in the Mysteries* (1925), *Christ, Ideal of the Monk* (1926), *Words of Life on the Margin of the Missal* (1940), *Come to Christ All You who Labour* (1946), *Union with God* (1949) and *Christ, Ideal of the Priest* (1953).

Marnix van St Aldegonde, Philips von   Dutch poet and theologian, born Brussels, 1540, died Leiden, The Netherlands, 15 December 1598. He is best known for his Psalm translations, in which he adhered closely to the original Hebrew, yet wrote with poetic individuality. He was imprisoned by Roman Catholics, and involved extensively in religious and political struggles. In *The Beehive of the Catholic Church*, a prose work, he appeared to defend the Roman Catholic faith, but in reality ridiculed it.

Maro of Cyr   Hermit and saint, died 433. He lived near Cyrrhus in Syria as a hermit with many disciples. St **John Chrysostom** was a friend. Maro

was buried between Apamea and Emesa and a monastery grew up near his grave. In Lebanon the Maronites claim to take their name from this saint. Feast day 14 February.

Marozia   Powerful noblewoman and influential figure in papal politics, born Italy, flourished early 900s. The wife of several important Italian nobles in succession, Marozia was reputedly the mistress of Pope **Sergius III**. For 30 years she exercised profound influence in papal politics, imprisoning **John X** in Castel Sant'Angelo, until his death in 929, and getting her son (presumably by Sergius III) elected Pope **John XI**. Her son by her first marriage, **Alberic II of Spoleto**, captured her during an uprising in 932 and imprisoned her in the same castle she had used. It is not known how she died.

Marquette, Jacques   French Jesuit missionary, born Laon, France, 1 June 1637, died Ludlington, Michigan, 18 May 1675. He joined the Society of Jesus at the age of seventeen and in 1666 was sent to work on the missions to the Indians in Canada. He started work at Three Rivers on the St Lawrence, where he demonstrated a facility for learning the local languages. He set out on his exploration of the Mississippi River in May 1673, drawing maps and keeping a diary as he went. He turned back at the mouth of the Arkansas River, after learning that the Mississippi flowed into the Gulf of Mexico, fearing that were he to go any further he might be captured by Spaniards. He spent the remainder of his life ministering to Indians in the region of what is now Chicago.

Marroquin, Francisco   Bishop of Central America, born probably Santander region, Spain, 1477, died Guatemala City, 18 April 1563. He was ordained by 1528 and arrived in Mexico City with the bishop-elect, **Zumarrága**, who named Marroquin as vicar general. In this role Marroquin acted with firmness and fairness, particularly in his relations with the native Indians, excommunicating those who had treated them cruelly and unjustly. His bishop sent him as provost to Guatemala, Honduras and El Salvador, where he learned the language of the Indians, and in 1537 he was consecrated bishop of Guatemala, the first episcopal consecration in the New World. Marroquin gave a welcome to Dominicans, who were fleeing from Peru, 1535, Mercedarians from Mexico City, 1537, and Franciscans from Spain, 1540, teaching the Indian language to priests and friars. In his endeavours to integrate the Indians into the spiritual, economic and social life of his area of the New World, he constructed churches, a cathedral, schools and orphanages, and, with the Dominicans, founded the Colegio de Santo Tomás.

Marsden, Samuel Anglican chaplain in New South Wales, and missionary to New Zealand, born Bagley, Yorkshire, England, 25 June 1764, died Windsor, New South Wales, 12 May 1838. He studied at Cambridge and was influenced by Charles **Simeon**. Appointed assistant chaplain to the colony of New South Wales, he arrived in Australia in March 1794. In 1804 he became London Missionary Society agent for the South Sea Islands. In 1807 he successfully appealed to the Church Missionary Society to send a civilizing mission to New Zealand, where on Christmas Day 1814 he preached its first Christian sermon. He made seven voyages to New Zealand, but in the first decade supervision from Australia could not compensate for fragile security and weak local leadership. His reputation as a convict settlement 'flogging parson' has balanced more 'romantic views of his stature, but his key role is indisputable.

Marsilius of Padua Italian scholar, author of the controversial *Defensor pacis* (1324), born *c.*1275, died 1342. Studied at Padua, then medicine at Paris, where he became rector, and later at Avignon. He was back in Paris in about 1320 and finished the *Defensor* there in 1324. He sided with the Emperor **Louis IV** of Bavaria against the Papacy: Louis appointed him imperial vicar in Rome, and, when Louis' policy collapsed, he retreated with him to the imperial court in Munich. Marsilius taught that the State, deriving its authority from the people, is what holds society together and that the Church must be subordinate to it. Further, he held that the Church should not own property and that its hierarchy is man-made, not God-given, and ideally the Church should be governed by a General Council, consisting of both clergy and laity. Not surprisingly, the *Defensor* was condemned by **John XXII** in 1327 and Marsilius was excommunicated.

Martí, Mariano Roman Catholic bishop and educator, baptized at Bafrim, Tarragona, Spain, 14 December 1721, died Caracas, 1792. He studied at the provincial seminary and obtained a doctorate in civil and canon law at the University of Cervera (no longer in existence). He was vicar general of the Tarragona diocese in 1761, whence, on the instigation of the king of Spain, he was appointed to the See of Puerto Rico in 1762, being consecrated at La Guaira, Venezuela. In his pastoral work in Puerto Rico he founded twenty schools, and visited his vast diocese in Trinidad, Margarita Island and eastern Venezuela. His arduous journeys impaired his health and on the death of the bishop of Caracas, Martí succeeded him in 1770. During the 21 years of his episcopy he is reported to have ordained 532 priests, and during a pastoral visitation that lasted from 1771 to 1784 he collated geographic, demographic, statistical and artistic data relating to the Venezuelan landscape and lifestyle.

Martiall, John (Marshall) Controversialist, born Daylesford, Worcestershire, 1534, died Lille, France, 3 April 1597. He was educated at Winchester, and at New College, Oxford, graduating in civil law in 1556. He left a teaching post in Winchester in 1560 to join a group of English exiles studying at Louvain. He dedicated his *Treatise on the Cross* (Antwerp 1564) to Queen **Elizabeth I**. In 1568 he received the degree of bachelor of divinity at Douai and eventually was made a canon at Lille, his installation being delayed until 1579 on account of civil unrest there. Little is known thereafter of his final years.

Martin I Saint, Pope, born Todi, elected 5 July 649, deposed 17 June 653, died 16 September 655. Martin had served as apocrisiarius, or papal ambassador, in Constantinople. He accepted election without awaiting imperial approval, and immediately held a synod at the Lateran which condemned monothelitism (the belief that there was only one will in Christ), contrary to the Emperor **Constans II**'s wishes. The emperor had Martin arrested and, although very ill, transferred to Constantinople, where he was tried and condemned to death. The sentence was commuted to banishment to Chersonesus, in the Crimea, where he soon died, though not before the Romans had elected **Eugenius I** to succeed him. He is the last Pope to be venerated as a martyr. He is mentioned by name in the Canon of the Mass in the Bobbio Missal. Feast day 12 November in the West, 13 April in the East.

Martin II   *see* **Marinus I**

Martin III   *see* **Marinus II**

Martin IV   Pope, born 'Simon de Brie' (or 'Brion'), a native of Touraine, between 1210 and 1220, elected 22 February 1281, died 28 March 1285. He had been canon and treasurer at St Martin's, Tours, and then Chancellor of France under **Louis IX** in 1260. He became cardinal-priest of St Cecilia in 1261 and as papal legate he conducted negotiations for the Crown of Sicily with **Charles of Anjou** and presided over several French synods, including that in Bourges in 1276. He was elected Pope against his will, and chose the name 'Martin' in deference to his earlier roles in Tours (there were no Martins II and III, the names being confused with those of **Marinus I** and **II**). He was crowned at Orvieto because of the hostility to a Frenchman among the Roman populace, and mainly lived there. The Romans, to make some sort of relationship with Martin, appointed him a senator for life, a role which he transferred to Charles of Anjou, thus giving Charles an overwhelming authority in the peninsula, and in the Papal States in particular. Charles' attempt to seize Sicily was frustrated by the rising of the people of the island in 1282 (the 'Sicilian Vespers'), but when the rebels offered to become vassals of the Pope, Martin told them to submit to Charles. Instead they offered the crown to Peter of Aragon, who accepted and was excommunicated. Martin also excommunicated Emperor Michael III Palaeologus, despite his attempts to build friendly relations with Rome, thereby destroying a possible union of Latin and Greek Churches. Unpopular with the Roman people, Martin was expelled from Rome and died in Perugia. He was a supporter of the Franciscans, whose privileges he extended by the bull, *Ad Fructus Uberes* in 1281.

Martin V   Pope, born 'Oddone Colonna' at Genazzano, near Rome, *c.*1368, elected 11 November 1417, died Rome, 20 February 1431. He had studied law in Perugia before serving in the papal curia. He was elevated to the papal office by an electoral college drawn from delegates meeting at the Council of Constance. He subsequently complied with the conciliar decree *Frequens* by calling General Councils at Pavia–Siena (1428) and Basel (1431). He entered Rome in September 1420, then set about recovering control of the Papal States, which he did successfully, and improved their administration, thus increasing the Papacy's wealth, as well as that of his Colonna relatives. He sent embassies to the major European powers, and opened negotiations with Constantinople for the reunion of East and West, though nothing came of this. He attempted to suppress the movement in Bohemia started by Jan **Huss**, but also without notable success.

Martin, Clarence Edward   Lawyer, born Martinsburg, West Virginia, 13 April 1880, died there, 24 April 1955. He graduated from West Virginia University in 1899, and the Catholic University of America in Washington, DC, in 1901, and was admitted to the West Virginia Bar. He succeeded to many posts in the legal hierarchy, including that of president of the West Virginia Constitutional Convention which ratified the twenty-first Amendment in 1933, and was president of the American Bar Association from 1932 to 1933. At a meeting of the Bar Association in 1936 he took a leading part in founding the St Thomas More Society of America, and in 1944 he was elected delegate to the Democratic National Convention. In 1929 Pope **Pius XI** had created him a Knight Commander of the Order of St Gregory the Great.

Martin, Gregory   Roman Catholic priest and Bible translator, born Maxfield, Sussex, died Rheims, 28 October 1582. He was educated at St John's College, Oxford, and became a tutor in the household of Thomas **Howard**, duke of Norfolk. When Howard was imprisoned, Martin fled to the English College in Douai and in 1573 he was ordained. He spent some eighteen months in Rome, after taking a group of students to start the new college there. Most of the rest of his life he spent at Rheims, to which the college at Douai had transferred, where he translated the Vulgate into English. The NT was published in the year of his death.

Martin, Konrad Roman Catholic bishop and theologian, born Geismar, Prussia, 18 May 1812, died Mont-Saint-Guibert, Belgium, 16 July 1879. He studied at Munich, Würzburg and Münster, being ordained in 1836. He became professor of moral and pastoral theology at the University of Bonn, writing on dogmatic and pastoral questions. As bishop of Paderborn from 1856 he was noted for his zeal as a leader of the Catholic revival in Germany, and of the cause of Christian unity between Catholics and Protestants. His efforts were undermined by the onset of the Kulturkamp (the struggle between Church and State) which originated in Prussia. Martin was imprisoned between 1874 and 1875 and deprived of his office. On his release he spent his final years in Belgium. Many of his written works were translated into several European languages, including French, Italian and Dutch.

Martin, Paulin Roman Catholic priest, orientalist and biblical scholar, born Lacam (Lot), France, 20 July 1840, died Amelies-les-Bains, 14 January 1890. After reading humanities at the minor seminary in Montfaucon he studied theology at the Sulpician seminary. Following his ordination in 1863 he spent five years in Rome studying the origins of Christianity and, while there, he developed his interest in oriental languages. He returned to Paris in 1868 to serve as priest at St Nicolas-des-Champs and ten years later was appointed professor of Holy Scripture and oriental languages at the Institut Catholique in Paris. He published many articles in historical and scientific reviews, and his best-known books are *La Chaldée, esquisse historique suivie de quelques réflexions sur Orient* (Rome, 1867) and *Grammatica christomatica et glossarium linguae syriacae* (Paris, 1874).

Martin, Raymond Joseph Dominican and theologian, born Neerpelt, Belgium, 27 September 1878, died Etiolles, France, 19 August 1949. He entered the Order in 1896 and was ordained in 1902. From 1906 to 1909 he was master of novices at La Sarte, near Huy in Belgium, and subsequently professor of theology at the Dominican theologate in Louvain, until 1940, where he specialized in the history of medieval theology. His studies produced a new opinion on the essence of original sin, entitled *La Controverse sur le péché originel au début du XIVᵉ*

siècle (Louvain, 1930). In collaboration with J. **Lebon** and J. de **Ghellinck** he instigated a series of patristic and theological studies, Spicilegium Sacrum Lovaniense.

Martin, Victor Canonist and historian, born Saint-Clément, France, 23 May 1886, died Saint-Clément, 7 September 1945. He studied at Moulins from 1899 to 1906 and at the university seminary at Lyons 1906–10, being ordained in his final year. After a curacy in the Diocese of Moulins from 1910 to 1914, he served as chaplain at the church of Saint-Louis des Français in Rome from 1914 to 1919. He gained a degree in canon law in 1919, followed by a doctorate in literature in 1920. In 1921 he went to Strasburg University as professor of canon law, and was dean of the faculty from 1923 to 1945. From 1928 to 1945, Martin was co-director of the 26 volume *Histoire de L'Église depuis les origines jusqu'à nos jours*, founded by Augustin **Fliche**, and his own writings on Gallicanism, such as *Les Origines du gallicanisme* (2 vols, 1939), were highly regarded as an authoritative opinion on that subject.

Martin de Porres Saint, Dominican lay brother, healer, born Lima, Peru, 9 December 1579, died Lima, 3 November 1639. He was of mixed African and Spanish parentage and was apprenticed to a barber-surgeon before becoming a Dominican lay helper at the age of fifteen, and eventually a lay brother. His skills and powers of healing both physical and spiritual suffering became renowned both within and beyond the monastery. He engaged in extreme ascetical practices but was a fount of love and hope for all who encountered him. Feast day 3 November.

Martin of Tours Saint, monk and bishop, born Sabaria, now Szombathely, Hungary, where his father was in the Roman garrison, *c.*316–17, died monastery of Candes, France, which he had founded, 8 November 397. Martin's parents, who were pagan, sent him to Pavia to be educated and there he decided to become a Christian, though only after he had served some three years in the army. He was baptized in 339, but remained in the army until 356, by which time he probably already knew Bishop **Hilary of Poitiers**. He made himself Hilary's disciple and set out on a spiritual pilgrimage, including a return to his family home, where he converted his mother. He was back in Poitiers by 360, and established a hermitage at Ligugé, near the city but in the countryside, where he was joined by many disciples, creating the first monastery in France. He was elected bishop of Tours in July 370, or possibly 371. He continued, however, to live like a monk and continued to found monasteries, of which the first was at Marmoutier: he saw such foundations as a means of evangelizing the countryside, which he considered his major task as bishop. In the controversy over **Priscillian**, 384–6, he defended the Spanish bishop, even though he did not approve of his doctrine, because he did not wish an ecclesiastical matter to be decided by the secular power. His missionary activity spread far outside his own diocese, and he became one of the most popular saints of the Middle Ages, especially in France. The church which **Augustine of Canterbury** took over on his arrival in England, for instance, was dedicated to Martin. A basilica, with a monastery attached, was built at his tomb in Tours, which quickly became an important place of pilgrimage. Feast day 11 November.

Martin of Troppau Dominican chronicler, archbishop, born 1200, died Bologna, 1278. He joined the Dominicans in Prague and was sent to Rome. He became papal chaplain and penitentiary to **Clement IV** and his successors. He was made archbishop of Gnesen (Gniezno) in 1278 and set off for Poland but took ill and died in Bologna. He is the author of *Chronica pontificum et imperatorum*, first published between 1265 and 1268 and later extended to cover the period to 1277. It has a list of Popes on one page of the codex and Emperors on the other, with each page covering a period of about 50 years, but drawing freely and uncritically on fables and legends.

Martindale, Cyril Charles Jesuit, scholar, writer and preacher, born London, 25 May 1879, died there, 18 March 1963. He was educated at Harrow School and on leaving was received into the Catholic Church by the Jesuit fathers in Bournemouth, and entered the Jesuit novitiate soon afterwards. He studied philosophy at St Mary's Hall, Stonyhurst, and matriculated in Oxford in 1901, receiving first-class honours in *Literae Humaniores*. He taught at Stonyhurst College and Manresa House, being ordained in 1911. Despite his scholastic achievements Martindale is remembered for his pastoral apostolate, his exceptional success as a preacher, and for his popular spiritual writings. His influence and enthusiasms radiated into many fields, including the liturgical revival, the Pax Romana (an international movement of Catholic students, and later graduates), which he helped to establish, and the foundation of the Apostleship of the Sea. He was a member of the Permanent Committee of the International Eucharistic Congress, which necessitated worldwide travels and contacts. He was also a popular broadcaster, and the number of converts from all classes of society testified to his contribution to the Church and the Faith. During World War II he was detained in Denmark at the time of its invasion but, at the end of the war, he returned with zeal to his life's work of preaching and the writing of biographies and works on spirituality.

Martínez, Gregorio Dominican theologian, born Segovia, Spain, 12 March 1575, died Valladolid, Spain, 15 May 1637. Although his parents intended a military career for him, Martínez joined the Dominicans in 1591. He became a teacher of philosophy and theology, lecturing at Segovia and Valladolid. He was also a respected preacher and confessor.

Martínez, Juan de Prado Roman Catholic theologian, born Valladolid, Spain, early seventeenth century, died Segovia, Spain, 25 February 1668. Martínez studied theology at Alcalá, where he subsequently became a professor, and in 1662 he was appointed provincial for Spain. A man of genial spirit, his love of learning was infectious. Martínez was also a prolific writer, and was the author of a significant treatise which upheld the Thomist doctrine of the Immaculate Conception.

Martínez, Luis María Roman Catholic archbishop, born Molinos de Cabellero, Mexico, 9 June 1881, died Mexico City, 8 February 1956. He was ordained in 1904, and held a variety of academic posts, in which his learning was much in evidence. In 1923 he became bishop of Anemurio, immediately becoming embroiled in the religious strife of the times which had seen many churches closed.

Martínez was involved in many negotiations whereby this persecution was eased, and in 1937 he became archbishop of Mexico. He continued to work towards reconciliation with the State, and eventually persecution was brought to an end. A gifted preacher and writer, during the course of his long career Martínez earned widespread respect both inside and outside Mexico.

Martínez Compañón y Bujanda, Baltasar   Roman Catholic archbishop, born Cabredo, Spain, 10 January 1737, died Bogotá, Colombia, 17 August 1797. Martínez was ordained in 1761 and went to Peru in 1767 as canon of Lima Cathedral. In 1779 he was made bishop of Trujillo, and as a result of his diverse ministry he came to be recognized as one of the most outstanding bishops of South America. He was the motivator for numerous initiatives which resulted in great improvements in education, agriculture, mining, communications and sanitation, all of which made significant contributions to the general economic development of Peru. He also opened several new seminaries to improve clerical training. In 1788 he was made archbishop of Bogotá, where his ministry proved equally effective.

Martínez de Aldunate, José Antonio   Roman Catholic bishop and scholar, born Santiago, Chile, c.1730, died Santiago, 8 April 1811. Martínez de Aldunate was educated by Jesuits and subsequently studied theology and philosophy. He was ordained in 1756 and for many years served as professor and rector of the University of San Felipe. He also held a variety of ecclesiastical appointments, and in 1804 was made bishop of Guamanga. In 1809 he was named as bishop of Santiago, and the following year became a member of the Chilean ruling council, but a mental illness rendered him unfit to serve in either capacity.

Martínez del Rio, Pablo   Roman Catholic historian and archaeologist, born Mexico City, 10 May 1892, died Mexico City, 26 January 1963. Martínez del Rio was educated by Jesuits at Stonyhurst College in England, subsequently studying at Oxford and the National University of Mexico. In a distinguished academic career he became a respected authority on the pre-Columbian and colonial history of Mexico and Central America. His devout

Catholicism brought a perceptive understanding of the religious dimensions which frequently impinged on political and social issues.

Martini, Giovanni Battista   Italian Roman Catholic priest, music theorist and historian, born Bologna, 24 April 1706, died Bologna, 4 October 1784. He was *maestro di capella* at San Francesco, Bologna. He was in touch with most of the celebrated musicians of his time, including **Mozart**, J. C. **Bach** and Gluck. Martini wrote treatises on music and left a *Storia della musica* incomplete. He composed Church music, including *Litaniae*.

Martini, Martino   Jesuit missionary and scholar, born Trent, Italy, 1614, died Hangchow, China, 6 June 1661. Martini became a Jesuit in 1632 and sailed to China as a missionary in 1640, where he worked for a number of years before returning to take up an appointment in Rome. He urged the establishment of an overland route to China to facilitate communication, and of an education programme for Chinese youth. Martini returned to China in 1656 accompanied by additional missionaries (surviving an attack by pirates *en route*), but was only able to minister for a further two years before succumbing to illness. He also published an important early Western atlas of China, and a contemporary account of the Manchu invasion.

Martini, Simone   Artist, born probably in Siena, Italy, c.1284, died Avignon, France, 1344. Martini studied painting in Siena, possibly under **Duccio**, where he absorbed the Sienese school's Byzantine style. An appointment to the French court at Siena brought him under the influence of the richly colourful and highly decorative French Gothic style, which is reflected in his mature works, such as *The Annunciation* of 1333, and through which he transformed the style of the Sienese school. Martini spent the last years of his career working as a painter at the papal court in Avignon, where he knew **Petrarch**.

Martinus de Fano   Dominican religious and jurist, born Fano, Italy, date unknown, died Bologna, Italy, 1275. Martinus became a professor of law at Fano in 1266, having studied at Bologna. He subsequently held a number of similar appointments in other Italian cities, and was twice mayor of Genoa. He retired from public life in 1264 and entered the Dominican Order. His published works include a number of important volumes on both secular and canon law.

Martinuzzi György Hungarian cardinal who attempted to unify Hungary, born 'György Utjes-enovic' ('Martinuzzi' was his mother's name) at Kamicic, Croatia, 1482, died Alcinc, Transylvania, Hungary, 17 December 1551. He served at the court of John Corvinus, then that of the Duchess Hedwig, before entering in 1504 the monastery of St Lawrence, near Ofen. He became prior of the monastery of Sajolad in northern Hungary. He encountered an acquaintance from the court of the duchess, now a pretender to the throne of Hungary, and entered his service, eventually becoming guardian of his orphaned son. Martinuzzi was made archbishop of Esztergom (Gran) and elevated to the cardinalate. He lived to see Hungary independent from the encroachments both of the empire of the Turks and of the Austrians, but was suspected of secret negotiations with the sultan, and was assassinated.

Marty, Martin Benedictine bishop and missionary, born Schwyz, Switzerland, 12 January 1834, died St Cloud, USA, 19 September 1896. Ordained in 1856, Marty taught at the Benedictine abbey of Einseideln before volunteering to be a missionary among Native Americans in 1860. Initially he worked in Indiana and Dakota, being appointed vicar apostolic of Dakota in 1879. In the following years Marty worked hard at promoting mission work in Dakota, where he had an especial interest in the Sioux tribe, eventually establishing a number of schools and hospitals. In 1889 he became bishop of Sioux Falls, and proceeded to consolidate the infrastructure of the Roman Catholic Church in this new diocese, encouraging Native Americans to take an active role. Shortly before his death he became bishop of St Cloud.

Martyn, Henry East India Company chaplain and translator, born Truro, Cornwall, 18 February 1781, died Tokat, 16 October 1812. A prize-winning student at St John's College, Cambridge (MA, 1804, BD, 1805), he was influenced by Charles **Simeon**. Ordained deacon in 1803 at Ely, family financial obligations prevented him being a mis-sionary, but not from accepting a chaplaincy in India – Dinapore, 1806–9, Cawnpore, 1809–10. There he met with the Baptists at Serampore and translated Scripture into Urdu, Arabic and Persian. In late 1810 he left India for Persia to improve his health and test his Persian translation. The Persian NT was presented to the shah, but Martyn died in north Turkey before he could return to England and his other hope, that of persuading Lydia Grenfell to marry him. He was nursed and buried by the Armenian Church.

Mary (Robinson) Mother of Gethsemane Abbess, Orthodox nun and educator, born Glasgow, 21 July 1896, died Bethany, Jerusalem, 7 November 1969. She was one of two Anglican nuns who converted to Orthodoxy under the influence of Metropolitan **Anastassy** in 1933 in Jerusalem. She became abbess of the Bethany convent, where she opened and financed a school for Arab girls which still continues, despite the major local wars of 1948 and 1967. The convent church of St Mary Magdalene now houses the relics of the new martyr **Elizabeth** (Feodorovna) of Russia.

Mary de Cervelló Saint, Mercedarian religious, born Barcelona, Spain, 1 December 1230, died Barcelona, 19 September 1290. A member of a noble family, Mary was said to have been conceived to her childless parents through the prayers of **Peter Nolasco**, the founder of the Mercedarians. Mary took religious vows at the age of eighteen, and became a Mercedarian herself, under the influence of the Mercadarian priest **Bernardo de Corbera**, establishing a Second Order with a ministry to the sick and poor. She is reputed to have had spiritual gifts of prophecy and discernment – notably in regard to ships in distress, which she is said to have saved through her intercessions. Feast day 19 September.

Mary of Oignies (Marie) Blessed, Flemish mystic and Beguine, born Nivelles, Brabant, 1177, died Oignies, 23 June 1213. She married at fourteen and encouraged her husband to lead a life of poverty and abstinence, nursing lepers in their own home. Her mysticism and miracles attracted attention and she moved to Oignies, where she could live under the spiritual direction of **Jacques de Vitry**. With other Beguines she anticipated the changes in

Catholic devotion to the Passion of Christ and the Holy Eucharist. Feast day 23 June.

Mary of St Joseph Salazar Carmelite religious, born Toledo, Spain, 1548, died Cuerva, Spain, 19 October 1603. From an aristocratic family, Mary at the age of fourteen met **Teresa of Ávila** while in the service of another noble family, and as a result of her example Mary herself took religious vows in 1571. She became one of Teresa's disciples and in the course of the next few years received many letters from her which demonstrate the closeness of their relationship. Following Teresa's death Mary established a Discalced Carmelite house in Lisbon, before moving to Cuerva. Along with the correspondence mentioned above, Mary's own writings, unpublished until 1913, are an important contemporary source of information on St Teresa.

Mary of St Theresa Petijt Carmelite mystic, born Hazebrouck, The Netherlands, 1 January 1628, died Malines (Belgium), 1 November 1677. Also known as 'Sister Mary of St Teresa'. She was a member of a religious community of women in Ghent before taking vows as a Carmelite. She moved to Malines in 1657, where she spent the remainder of her life, living as a recluse. She described her spiritual experiences in an autobiography, in which her particular devotion to the Virgin Mary and its spiritual significance are explored.

Mary of the Incarnation (Mme Acarie) Blessed, married woman and Carmelite nun, born Paris, 1 February 1566, died Pontoise, 18 April 1618. Barbara Avrillot was educated in a convent at Longchamps, and was early noted for her piety. She married, at seventeen, Peter Acarie, a French treasury official and minor noble. After her marriage she became famous for charitable works, chief among which was bringing the Carmelites of the Teresian Reform to Paris in 1604. Although not at this time a nun, she was almost an unofficial novice mistress, guided by her friends Pierre de **Bérulle** and **Francis de Sales.** Her husband died in 1613, and she entered the Carmelites at Amiens the following year. All three of her daughters were Carmelites, and one of her three sons was a priest. She moved to Pontoise in 1616. She was beatified in 1791. Feast day 18 April.

Mary of the Incarnation (Marie Guyard) Venerable, born Tours, 28 October 1599, died Quebec, 30 April 1672. She married, reluctantly, at seventeen, Claude Joseph Martin, a silk manufacturer, and had a son who became a Benedictine, but her husband died two years later. Raising her son prevented her entering the recently established Ursuline convent in Tours until he was twelve years old. Two years later she was appointed mistress of novices. She developed, however, a desire to go on the missions, and was permitted to leave for Quebec in 1639, accompanied by a number of other nuns. Two years later the foundation stone was laid of the first Ursuline convent in North America. She worked among the Iroquois, having set about learning their language as soon as she arrived, until her death. She left a number of spiritual writings.

Mary, Queen of Scots Born Linlithgow Palace, Scotland, 7 December 1542, died Fotheringay Castle, England, 8 February 1587. She was the daughter of James V of Scotland and Mary of Guise, and inherited the Scottish throne when only a week old. In 1547 she was sent to the French court for safety. There she married the Dauphin, the future Francis II, but he died in 1560, leaving her the dowager Queen of France. She returned in 1561 to a Scotland controlled by Protestant lords. In 1565 she married Henry Lord Darnley, who had a claim on the English throne, and in 1566 she gave birth to the future **James VI** of Scotland and **James I** of England. Darnley, from whom she was alienated, was killed in a mysterious explosion in 1566, and married the Earl of Bothwell whom many believed had murdered Darnley. This action so angered the nobility that they rose in arms and defeated Mary's army, she herself being forced to abdicate in favour of her son. She raised another army, and was again defeated, this time fleeing to England, where she was imprisoned by her cousin Queen **Elizabeth I**. English Catholics looked to Mary as someone who would restore Catholicism, and she was implicated in a number of plots, real and imaginary, against the life of Elizabeth. For the Babington Plot of 1586 she was put on trial at Fortheringay in October 1586, and was beheaded there the following year, being refused permission to make her confession and receive communion according to the rite of the Roman Church.

Mary Tudor Roman Catholic queen of England, daughter of **Henry VIII** and **Catherine of Aragon**, born Greenwich, 18 February 1516, died St James's Palace, 17 November 1558. She was well educated and devoted to her mother, and to her mother's Catholic religion. In 1536 she was forced to sign a document acknowledging Henry's religious supremacy and the illegitimacy of her mother's marriage, but none the less in 1553 succeeded to the throne on the death of **Edward VI**. She married **Philip II** of Spain in 1554, an unpopular choice, and he returned to Spain a year later, without Mary having produced an heir. In 1554 Cardinal Reginald **Pole** returned to England and the country was absolved from all papal censure. Persecution of Protestants now began: some 300 died, including **Latimer**, **Ridley** and **Cranmer.**

Masaccio Artist, originally 'Tommaso di Giovanni di Simone Guidi', born San Giovanni Valdarno, Italy, 21 December 1401, died Rome, 1428. Masaccio is thought to have been a pupil of Masolino, with whom he collaborated on a number of commissions, and he spent most of his working life in Florence, where the majority of his paintings are to be found. He was an innovator in using light, space and perspective to bring an added naturalism to his subjects. This is seen in particular in works such as *The Tribute Money* and *The Expulsion from the Garden of Eden*, masterpieces which are regarded as being of primary importance in the history and development of Renaissance art.

Masamune Hakucho (Masamune Tadao) Japanese critic and writer, born Bizen, Japan, 3 March 1879, died Tokyo, 28 October 1962. As a young man, he entered Tokyo Senmon Gakko, later Waseda University. He was baptized a Christian and began writing newspaper criticism. He wrote plays and sombre novels, but is best known as a critic, as in his *Critical Essays on Literary Figures, Thought and Non-thought* and *A Literary Autobiography*.

Masemola, Manche Roman Catholic martyr, born Marishane, South Africa, *c.*1913, died (murdered), near Marishane, *c.*4 February 1928. Manche Masemola was a member of the Pedi tribe of the Transvaal, first coming under the influence of Christianity as a young girl through Roman Catholic missionaries. Christians among the Pedi were widely distrusted for forsaking their traditional religion, and consequently her parents sought to discourage her by all possible means, and with increasing violence. She resisted all their attempts to make her renounce her faith, and eventually they took her to a remote spot and murdered her. Her name was added to the calendar of the Church of the Province of Southern Africa in 1975, and a statue representing her was among those of ten twentieth-century Christian martyrs added to the West front of Westminster Abbey in 1998.

Masias, Juan Blessed, Dominican religious, born Rivera, Spain, 2 March 1585, died Lima, Peru, 26 September 1645. Masias was an illiterate shepherd who used the solitude of his occupation to devote himself to prayer. At the age of 21 he felt called to leave Spain for South America, where he continued to lead a similar lifestyle. In 1622 he was received into the Dominicans, and for the rest of his life served his community as a porter, distributing bread to the poor and continuing his habitual devotion to meditation and prayer when not otherwise occupied. Masias' life of simple piety was recognized by his beatification in 1836.

Masius, Andreas Orientalist, born Lennix-les-Bruxelles, The Netherlands, 30 November 1514, died Zevenaar, The Netherlands, 7 April 1573. Masius studied at Louvain and became secretary to the bishop of Constance. He compiled a grammar and dictionary of Syriac (the first European to do so), and translated a number of Syriac texts. His critical edition of and commentary on the book of Joshua anticipated later scholarship by casting doubts on its authenticity, and also on the Mosaic authorship of other parts of the Pentateuch. Along with the forthright statements concerning Church reform which Masius included in the commentary, this ensured that the work was placed on the Index of Prohibited Books in 1581.

Mason, Charles Harrison Founder of the Church of God in Christ (CGIC), born near Memphis, Tennessee, 8 September 1866, died Detroit, Michigan, 17 November 1961. Born to former slaves, Mason was ordained as a Baptist pastor in 1891, adopting Holiness views in 1893. Because of his views on sanctification, he was expelled from the Baptists and in 1897 set up the CGIC, now one of the largest Pentecostal groups in the world. In 1906 he accepted Pentecostalism after visiting William **Seymour** in Los Angeles. Although especially attractive to blacks, the CGIC had about an equal number of black and white pastors, and in 1914 he was one of only two black pastors to attend E. **Bell**'s convention at Hot Springs. In 1918 he was jailed for allegedly opposing the First World War, although he sold war bonds.

Mason, Lowell Musician, born Medfield, Massachusetts, 8 January 1792, died Orange, New Jersey, 11 August 1872. He became director of music at First Presbyterian Church. His Boston Handel and Haydn Society *Collection of Church Music* went through many editions and had great influence. He organized classes in vocal music and produced many song books. It is estimated that he composed or arranged over 1000 melodies. In London he met **Mendelssohn**. Later he produced many volumes of choir music. Mason adapted the tune 'Mannheim' to the words of the hymn 'Lead Us, Heavenly Father Lead Us'.

Massaja, Guglielmo Cardinal and missionary, born Piova, Italy, 8 June 1809, died Naples, 6 August 1889. Massaja joined the Capuchins in 1826 and following ordination taught philosophy and theology. In 1846 he was sent to Ethiopia as vicar apostolic of Galla, where he made many converts, pioneered medical missions and established churches with indigenous clergy. He travelled widely, gaining an extensive knowledge of the area which included studying the local languages, and producing grammars for the use of other missionaries. Massaja ministered in Ethiopia until 1879, when domestic politics resulted in his being exiled. In 1884 he was created a cardinal by **Leo XIII**, and instructed to write his memoirs for posterity, the twelve volumes of which are still regarded as a work of great significance.

Massignon, Louis French Islamicist, born Nogent-sur-Marne, 25 July 1883, died Paris, 31 October 1962. During a distinguished academic career, Massignon became recognized for his comprehensive knowledge of Islamic civilization. He was particularly interested in Sufism, and especially in the martyred mystic al-Hallaj. Massignon, who later in life became a Catholic priest of the Byzantine rite, was also a provocative commentator on current affairs in the Muslim world.

Massillon, Jean Baptiste French Oratorian bishop and noted preacher, born Hyères, Provence, 24 June 1663, died Beauregard, 10 September 1742. Studied in Hyères and Marseilles and joined the Oratorians in Marseilles in 1681. He taught at Oratorian colleges, and was ordained priest in 1691. He became director of the Seminary of St-Magloire, Paris, in 1696. His reputation as a preacher grew rapidly and he was asked to preach on some of the most prestigious state occasions. Among his most celebrated sermons were the discourse *On the Fewness of the Elect*, 1704, and his Lenten sermons delivered before Louis XV in 1718, published as *Le Petit carême*. He became bishop of Clermont in 1718 and took great pains to care for the physical as well as the spiritual needs of his diocese, including reforming the clergy. In 1719 he was made a member of the French Academy. A collection of his sermons and other writings was published in fifteen volumes by his nephew, Joseph Massillon, in 1745.

Massoulié, Antonin French Dominican theologian, born Toulouse, 28 October 1632, died Rome, 23 January 1706. Massoulié read humanities at Toulouse and Bordeaux, and served as consultor to a papal commission investigating the question of philosophical sin, Quietism and Chinese rites. In a two-volume work he effectively showed that **Báñez** had not invented divine premotion, that it truly represented the thought of St **Thomas Aquinas**, and disproved the accusation that Thomism was Jansenistic. He wrote three treatises against Quietism: *Traité de la véritable oraison*, *Traité de l'amour de Dieu* and *Méditations de St Thomas sur les trois voies*.

Mastrius, Bartholomaeus Italian Franciscan philosopher, born Meldola, Forli, December 1602, died there, 3 January 1673. At Naples, Mastrius came under the influence of Joseph da Trapani, an eminent disciple of **Duns Scotus** and, in collaboration with Bonaventure Bellutus, wrote many works designed to elucidate the Scotist teaching on predestination and divine justice, and its attempt to reconcile human freedom and divine foreknowledge.

Mather, Alexander Methodist preacher and second president of the Methodist Conference, born Brechin, Angus, Scotland, 1733, died York, 22 August 1800. In 1745 he fought at Culloden for the Pretender. Later he worked as a baker, first in Perth, then, from 1752, in London with Thomas Marriott. He underwent an evangelical conversion experience under John **Wesley**'s preaching in 1754. Appointed as an itinerant preacher in 1757 and ordained by Wesley as a superintendent in 1788. Gained a reputation as a preacher of ability and an advocate of the doctrine of Christian perfection. In 1792 he was elected president of the Methodist Conference.

Mather, Cotton New England Puritan and theologian, born Boston, Massachusetts Bay Colony, 12 February 1663, died Boston, 13 February 1728. The son of Increase **Mather**, he entered Harvard at the age of twelve and gained his MA at eighteen. He was ordained in 1685 as a colleague to his father and remained a pastor at the Second Church Boston throughout his life. He published 469 works, including a Church history of America, *Magnalia Christi Americana* (1702), and a handbook for ministerial graduates on doing good, love affairs, poetry and style, *Manuductio ad ministerium* (1726). He defended ministerial leadership in society, despite the social changes which made that difficult, and anticipated later patterns of evangelical activism. He believed in the existence of witchcraft, though he sought to moderate claims of evidence. He was interested in science and medicine and was a strong supporter of smallpox inoculation.

Mather, Increase New England Puritan leader, born Dorchester, Massachusetts Bay Colony, 21 June 1639, died Boston, Massachusetts, 23 August 1723. He entered Harvard at the age of twelve and graduated at seventeen. He studied at Trinity College, Dublin, was ordained teaching pastor of the Second Church Boston, 1664–1723, and became president of Harvard, 1685–1701. A defender of the old Congregational way, he was supported by his son Cotton **Mather**, who was his colleague for 40 years. In 1688 he was sent to England to thank

James II for his declaration of liberty for all faiths and remained long enough to secure the removal of the governor of Massachusetts. Mather's support for the new governor and the charter of 1691 proved unpopular. He was blamed for contributing to the Salem witch trials of 1692, though his cautions about spiritual evidence had been ignored.

Matheson, George Church of Scotland minister and hymn-writer, born Glasgow, 27 March 1842, died North Berwick, 28 August 1906. A brilliant student of philosophy, Matheson was ordained in the Church of Scotland and ministered in Argyllshire and Edinburgh. He was a celebrated preacher and writer, though it is for his hymns that he is now best remembered. He had become blind as a young man, and it has been popularly supposed that the most famous of his hymns, 'O Love that Will Not Let Me Go', was prompted by a broken engagement, terminated on account of his blindness, though in fact Matheson did not write it until much later. His hymns stand out for their poetic quality, written as they were at a period when much hymn-writing tended to be overly sentimental or banal.

Mathew, David James English Roman Catholic cleric, born Lyme Regis, 15 January 1902, died London, 12 December 1975. Brother of Gervase **Mathew**. Ordained at the Beda College, Rome, he served at St Davids Cathedral, Cardiff, and then as chaplain to Catholic students at the University of London. Named apostolic delegate to British Africa in 1946; bishop to the British military forces, 1954–63. He published *Catholicism in England, 1535–1935 – Portrait of a Minority: Its Culture and Tradition*, which helped to provide a new sense of identity to English Roman Catholics.

Mathew, Gervase Dominican scholar, born London, 14 March 1905, died Oxford, 4 April 1976. Brother of David **Mathew**. Gervase (christened 'Anthony') read modern history at Balliol College, joined the Dominicans and spent most of his life at Blackfriars, Oxford, doing pastoral work along with his lecturing and writing. In 1947 he accepted a lectureship in Byzantine studies, and in 1963 published *Byzantine Aesthetics*, his most important work; he is credited with having inaugurated Byzantine studies at Oxford.

Mathew, Theobald Irish Capuchin, the 'Apostle of Temperance', born Thomaston, Tipperary, 10 October 1790, died Cork, 8 December 1856. Great-uncle of David and Gervase **Mathew**. He became Capuchin provincial in 1822. He began his apostolate for temperance as head of the Cork Total Abstinence Society in 1838, and 'gave the pledge' to hundreds of thousands in Ireland, Scotland, England and the USA; the practice often proved ineffective, but he inspired later and more successful movements.

Mathews, Shailer American Baptist theologian, born Portland, Maine, 26 May 1863, died Chicago, Illinois, 23 October 1941. An early proponent of the Social Gospel, Mathews' aim was to apply the teachings of Christ to modern social and economic problems, believing that the ideals and life of Jesus can inspire men to live worthy lives, and that theological thought is meaningful only when it uses social patterns of the times as a vehicle of expression. His theology was presented in numerous books, including *The Social Teachings of Jesus* and *Creative Christianity*, which were widely influential.

Mathieu, François Désiré French archbishop and cardinal, born Einville, Meurthe-et-Moselle, 27 May 1839, died London, 26 October 1908. Named bishop of Angers, then archbishop of Toulouse in 1896 and cardinal in 1899, Mathieu served on the Roman curia as papal envoy. A strong supporter of **Leo XIII**, after whose death he published 'Les derniers jours de Léon XIII et le conclave, par un témoin' *Revue des Deux Mondes*, 1904), he put into effect Leo's policy of *ralliement*, which called for Catholic support of the Third Republic.

Mathis, Michael Ambrose American liturgist, born South Bend, Indiana, 6 October 1885, died University of Notre Dame, Indiana, 10 March 1960. Mathis founded the Bengal (later Holy Cross) Foreign Mission Society in 1917, and a Foreign Mission Seminary in Washington, DC, to train missionaries; he became an authority on India's Catholic missions. He established the Notre Dame School of Liturgical Studies in 1947, the first graduate school of liturgy in North America.

Matignon, Francis Anthony French missionary, born Paris, 10 November 1753, died Boston, Massachusetts, 19 September 1818. Ordained in 1778, Matignon refused to accept the Civil Constitution of the Clergy and left France for the USA; he played an important role in healing the strife between French and Irish Catholics in Boston, and won the respect of the Protestants. With his friend Jean **Cheverus** he laboured in the New England mission field and built the first Catholic church in Boston. He declined to be considered for the post of first bishop of the city, and it went to Cheverus.

Matilda of Germany Saint, born Westphalia, c.895, died Quedlinburg, 14 March 968. She was married to Henry I (the Fowler) of Germany and had a reputation for humility, piety and generosity. On the death of her husband, there was disunity over which son should succeed him, Matilda supporting the loser. Both sons later rejected their mother, accusing her of impoverishing the Crown with her generous almsgiving. She then renounced all her possessions and retired to Westphalia. She was eventually reconciled with her sons, but spent her life in church-building and the building and support of many monasteries. Feast day 14 March.

Matilda of Tuscany (of Canossa) Countess, born 1046, died near Ferrara, 24 July 1114. In childhood she was imprisoned in Germany by **Henry III**. She showed an early interest in religious life and in theological questions. She married in 1069, but separated from her husband, the duke of Lorraine, two years later. She supported Pope **Gregory VII** in the struggles for independence of the Church and the reform of ecclesiastical life. She gave safe conduct and accommodation to the Pope after he excommunicated **Henry IV** following the Synod of Worms (1076). The following year she mediated between Henry and the Pope, but after Henry's breach of faith she dedicated herself to the papal cause of reform. She also supported Gregory's successors, taking an army to Rome to help reinstate Pope **Victor III**. She bequeathed her domains to the Roman Church.

Matos, Gregório de Brazilian poet, born Salvador,

Bahia, 7 April 1633, died Recife, Pernambuco, 1696. Educated by the Jesuits, de Matos studied at Coimbra, Portugal, and settled in Lisbon, where he gained notoriety with his poetry attacking people of rank in politics and society; he returned to Brazil in 1681. The bishop of Bahia appointed him treasurer and vicar general of the cathedral, but de Matos brought disgrace to the position with his scandalous living and obscene writings. Racially prejudiced, he nevertheless exalted negro and mulatto women, and alternately pursued a life of sin and repentance. Exiled to Angola he returned to Brazil later in life and settled in Recife.

Matre, Anthony American Catholic business man, born Cincinnati, Ohio, 16 December 1866, died Elmhurst, Illinois, 16 January 1934. Matre became an organist and choir director, helped to found the National Catholic Welfare Conference and became prominent in business. **Pius X** made him a Knight of St Gregory the Great in 1913, and he served in the Chicago Archdiocesan Holy Name Society, the Catholic Knights of America, the Knights of Columbus and the Third Order of St Francis.

Matthew of Albano Cardinal, legate, and monastic reformer, born Laon, c.1085, died Pisa, 25 December 1135. After studying at Laon under Master **Anselm** (of Laon), he became a priest, and in 1110 entered the Cluniac priory of Saint-Martin-des-Champs at Paris, of which he eventually became prior. He defended his friend **Peter the Venerable** against the deposed Abbot Ponce before Pope **Honorius II**, who created him cardinal-bishop of Albano in 1125, and appointed him legate to France in 1127 and Germany in 1128. After the Council of Pisa (1134), **Bernard of Clairvaux** invited him to restore Milan to papal obedience, and he died shortly after returning to Pisa.

Matthew of Aquasparta Italian cardinal, Franciscan theologian, born Aquasparta, Umbria, c.1238, died Rome, 29 October 1302. Matthew taught at Paris, commented on the *Sapientiae* of **Peter Lombard** and, as minister general 1287–9, strove to settle disputes within the Order; **Nicholas IV** made him a cardinal in 1288. He opposed Thomistic departures from the traditional Augustinianism defended by St **Bonaventure** and the Franciscans.

Matthew of Cracow Polish bishop, theologian, born Cracow, c.1330, died Worms, Germany, 5 March 1410. Matthew taught at Charles University and at Heidelberg, and became confessor to Rupert, king of the Romans; he became bishop of Worms in 1405, and cardinal and papal legate to Germany in 1408. His most important work, *De squaloribus curiae romanae*, advocated supremacy of the Council over the Pope.

Matthew of Vendôme Author, born Vendôme, c.1130, died Vendôme, end of the twelfth century. Educated at Tours, he returned to that city after study at Orléans and Paris; his writings reflect the learning of the cathedral schools. Upon his return to Tours, he was befriended by Archbishop Engelbaud: his most celebrated work, *Tobias*, a version of the book of Tobit in elegiac distichs, completed c.1185, is dedicated to Engelbaud's nephews (one of whom, Bartholomew, had become archbishop of Tours in 1174). His earlier work, *Ars versificatoria*, concentrates on the 'ars poetica'. Another Matthew of Vendôme (d. 1286) was abbot of Saint-Denis and regent of France when **Louis IX** went on Crusade in 1270.

Matthew Paris English Benedictine historian and artist, born c.1200, died in St Albans Monastery, 1259. He became a monk of St Albans, 21 January 1217. He decorated his writings with illustrations from the times and events about which he was writing. He often wrote against what he regarded as the injustices of papal authority and blamed the Papacy for the schism with the Greek Church, and often referred to the 'Beguines', a women's movement centred on Cologne. Matthew wrote with a sense of history rather than merely chronicling its earlier sections. His major work was *Chronica majora*, summarizing the work of **Roger of Wendover** up to 1235; after this he used first-hand accounts, being himself a very close observer of events both political and religious, and apparently quite close to King Henry III. In 1248–9 he was asked to travel to Norway to restore the level of observance in Benedictine houses there.

Matthews, Francis Patrick American Catholic public figure, born Albion, Nebraska, 15 March 1887, died Omaha, 18 October 1952. Matthews supported the New Deal reforms, and President

Roosevelt appointed him to public office; he also devoted much time to charitable and civic affairs, i.e. the National Conference of Catholic Charities and the National Catholic Community Service, for which he was awarded the Grand Cross of the Order of St Gregory in 1902. Vigorously anti-Communist, his remarks as a public servant sometimes lacked judgement, and caused the government to disavow his stance during the Korean War (1950).

Matthews, Mary Bernardina American religious superior, born Charles County, Maryland, 1732, died Port Tobacco, Maryland, 12 June 1800. Mary Matthews entered the Discalced Carmelites in Belgium in 1754, and returned to Maryland in 1782 when **Joseph II** suppressed religious orders in the Low Countries. She established the first American Discalced Carmelite cloister at Port Tobacco in 1790.

Matthews, William American Roman Catholic missionary, born Port Tobacco, Maryland, 16 December 1770, died Washington, DC, 30 April 1854. Scion of one of Maryland's earliest colonial families, and, in 1800, the first native-born American to be ordained to the priesthood, Matthews, though not a Jesuit, served as president of Georgetown College, Washington, founded the first public library there and served as a trustee of the public school system from 1813 to 1844. He established an orphanage for girls, and co-founded the Visitation Girls' School and St Joseph's Orphanage for boys. Because of his family background, he counted as friends some of the great national figures, such as Andrew Jackson, Daniel Webster and Henry Clay. Matthews refused the See of Philadelphia, being reluctant to leave Washington.

Matthopoulos, Eusebius Greek Orthodox priest and missionary, born Melissopetra, Greece, 1849, died Athens, 1929. He became a monk and itinerant missioner, encouraging frequent Communion in his preaching. In 1907 he founded the Zoe ('Life') brotherhood, which aimed to include laity of both sexes, young theologians and teachers. This movement had an enormous impact, both positive and negative, upon the Greek Church and its periodical has a very large circulation.

Mattias, Maria de Blessed, Italian foundress, founded Adorers of the Most Precious Blood, born Vallecorsa, Frosinone, 4 February 1805, died Rome, 20 August 1866. Inspired at an early age to dedicate her life to prayer and good works, Maria founded the Congregation of Sisters Adorers of the Most Precious Blood, dedicated to the education of youth, and opened a school at the request of the bishop of Anagni, 1834; she established some 63 houses in Italy. Feast day 1 October.

Matulaitis (Matulewicz), George Lithuanian apostolic visitor, born Lugine, 13 April 1871, died Vilna, 24 January 1927. Matulaitis taught at the Catholic Academy of St Petersburg, served as bishop of Vilna, 1918–25, and as **Pius XI**'s apostolic visitor to Lithuania, 1925–7. A strong advocate of Catholic–Russian unity, he negotiated a concordat between the Lithuanian government and the Holy See. He undertook a reform of the Congregation of Marian Fathers, in which he had secretly been ordained, and of which he became superior general from 1911 until his death. He founded the Congregation of the Sisters of the Immaculate Conception and, in Byelorussia, the Congregation of the Servants of the Sacred Heart.

Maturin, Basil William Maurice Irish spiritual writer, born Grangegorman, Dublin, February 1847, died at sea, on the *Lusitania*, 7 May 1915. Studied at Trinity College, Dublin, and was ordained deacon in the Anglican Church in 1870. He went to England, was ordained priest at Peterstowe in Herefordshire and in 1873 joined the Society of St John the Evangelist (Cowley Fathers) in Oxford. From 1876 to 1886 he was in Pennsylvania, at the Episcopal church of St Clement in Philadelphia. He returned to England and in 1897 joined the Roman Catholic Church. After two years study in Rome he was ordained and did parish work in London. In 1905 he joined the recently established Society of Westminster Missionaries and took charge of Pimlico parish, and from 1910 spent some time with the Benedictines. In 1914 he became Catholic chaplain at Oxford but died the next year. His writings include *Self-knowledge and Self-discipline* (1905), *Laws of the Spiritual Life* (1907), *Practical Studies on the Parables of Our Lord* (1908), *Some Principles and Practices of the Spiritual Life* (1915 reissue), *Fruits* *of the Life of Prayer* (1916), and *Sermons and Notes* (1916), edited by Wilfrid **Ward**.

Mauriac, François   French Roman Catholic writer, born Bordeaux, 11 October 1885, died Paris, 1 September 1970. He was deeply concerned with the problems of sin and redemption, and the futility of seeking self-fulfilment in wealth, or even in human life. During World War Two he produced many anti-Nazi pamphlets. His novels include *Thérèse Desqueyroux* (1927), perhaps his best-known work, *Viper's Tangle* (1933) and *A Woman of the Pharisees* (1946). He also wrote two studies of Christ, *Vie de Jésus* (1936) and *Le Fils de l'homme* (1958), as well as other religious works, plays and poetry. He was awarded the Nobel Prize for Literature in 1952.

Maurice, Frederick Denison   Anglican theologian and Christian Socialist, born Normanstone, near Lowestoft, Suffolk, 29 August 1805, died London, 1 April 1872. The son of a Unitarian minister and brought up in a home full of religious disputation, he studied at Trinity College, Cambridge, and Exeter College, Oxford. He was ordained in 1834 to the curacy of Bobbenhall, Warwickshire, and became chaplain of Guy's Hospital, London, in 1836, where he lectured on moral philosophy and wrote *The Kingdom of Christ* (1838). In 1840 he was elected professor of english at King's College, London, and in 1846 became professor of theology. With J. M. F. Ludlow and C. **Kingsley** he helped form the Christian Socialist movement. His rejection of the endlessness of the punishments of hell focused opposition to his theology and led to his dismissal from King's College in 1853. He started a Working Men's College in 1854 and was professor of moral philosophy at Cambridge from 1866 until his death.

Maurice of Carnoët   Saint, Cistercian abbot, born Croixanvec, Brittany, *c.*1114, died Carnoët, Brittany, 9 October 1191. Maurice became a monk at the abbey of Langonnet in 1143 and was made abbot in 1147. In 1171, the duke of Brittany asked him to found a monastery in Carnoët, where he was made abbot in 1176. He was known for his miracles, and the abbey was renamed St Maurice after his death. His cultus was eventually approved in 1869. Feast day 5 October in a few local dioceses, 13 October among the Cistercians.

Maurice of Sully   Bishop, builder of Notre Dame in Paris, born Sully, France, *c.*1120, died St-Victor, Paris, 11 September 1196. Of lowly birth, Maurice studied in Paris under Peter **Abelard** and later held low ecclesiatical posts at Notre Dame. As a university professor, he was known as a wonderful preacher. He succeeded **Peter Lombard** as bishop of Paris in 1160. As bishop, he amassed the funds to build the cathedral of Notre Dame, worked to reform his clergy, and published *Sermons on the Gospels* in French (some of the oldest extant French prose). Also a friend of the king and a papal judge, he retired in 1196 to St-Victor, where he died later that year.

Maurin, Aristide Peter   French writer and teacher, born Languedoc, 9 May 1877, died New York City, 15 May 1949. A Christian Brother, Maurin emigrated to Canada and spent fifteen years teaching and working there and in the USA. In 1933 he founded, with Dorothy **Day**, a social movement and a monthly review known as *The Catholic Worker*, in the first issue of which he declared his intention to popularize the papal encyclicals on social justice, and to incite Catholics to assume responsibility for these obligations. In his speeches and writings – many articles and a book, *Easy Essays* – he took his message across the USA. He championed anti-racial action and an intransigent pacifism, maintained even during the Second World War. Despite his anarchist tendencies, Maurin exerted great influence among American Catholics; Dorothy Day gave him credit as 'the man who showed me the way' in her own direction of the Catholic Worker movement.

Maurras, Charles   French political philosopher, born Martigues, Provence, 20 April 1868, died Tours, 15 November 1952. Maurras received a Catholic education and, influenced by **Mistral**, Barrès, **Renan** and Anatole France, expressed in his love for ancient Greece his cult of order and reason. He campaigned for a return of the monarchy to France, supported by the Catholic Church, as the ideal government for France. A prolific journalist, he wrote thousands of articles, and became the driving force of *L'Action française*

(1908–44). With his more than 50 books on politics, philosophy and poetry, Maurras exerted much influence on the conservative bourgoisie until the Holy Office placed his books on the Index, 1914–39. Having supported Mussolini, Franco, and Pétain during the war, he was sentenced to life imprisonment in 1945, and expelled from the Académie Française, but pardoned later. A lapsed Catholic most of his life, he returned to the Church shortly before his death.

Maurus Saint, put into St **Benedict**'s care by his parents when aged twelve, died Glanfeuil, later St-Maur-sur-Loire, 15 January 584. He is said to have founded an abbey at Glanfeuil in France and, after giving up the abbacy, spent the remainder of his life in solitude. But nothing certain is known about Maurus beyond these doubtful details in a Life ascribed to Odo of Glanfeuil. Feast day 15 January.

Maurus, Sylvester Italian Jesuit philosopher, born Spoleto, 31 December 1619, died Rome, 13 January 1687. Maurus earned great renown for his commentaries on Aristotle, which expanded the partial work of earlier commentators to include brief, but pertinent, comments on all his works; it is claimed, indeed, that Maurus makes Aristotle say much that he did not say, but ought to have said. His *Aristotelis opera quae extant omnia brevi paraphras ac perpetuo in haerente explanatione illustrata*, in six volumes, was reprinted in 1885 by Franz **Ehrle**, *et al.*

Maury, Jean Siffrein French cardinal, born Valréas, 26 June 1746, died Rome, 11 May 1817. Maury gained renown as a preacher in Paris, and his *Essai sur l'éloquence de la chaire* earned him fame and membership in the Académie Française. Elected to the Estates-General in 1789, he supported the *ancien régime*, and opposed the nationalization of ecclesiastical properties and the Civil Constitution of the Clergy. He emigrated to Rome in 1792, where **Pius VI** appointed him cardinal, 1794, and nuncio to Emperor Francis II; this animated his zeal for a crusade against the French Revolution. Maury returned to Paris to support Emperor Napoleon, who made him archbishop of Paris in 1810, and he supported Napoleon's policies at the Council of 1811. Returning to Rome, **Pius VII** imprisoned him in the Castel Sant'Angelo, but released him on condition that he resign his post. The fall of Napoleon ruined Maury's career and he spent his last years in obscurity in Rome.

Mausbach, Joseph German Roman Catholic moral theologian, born Wipperfeld, 7 February 1861, died Ahrweiler, 31 January 1931. Ordained at Cologne, Mausbach taught until his death at Münster, where his teaching on St **Augustine** and St **Thomas Aquinas** drew large audiences. His *Die katholische moral* outlines the principles and method of all his work; *Thomas von Aquin als Meister Christlicher Sittenlehrer* contains studies of both Augustine and Aquinas.

Maximilian Bishop and saint, died Cilli, Styria, c.284. Born of a wealthy family, he is said to have given away his wealth and devoted himself to the spiritual life. At Rome, he was sent by Pope **Sixtus II** to Noricum, between Styria and Bavaria, where he became first bishop of Lorch, near Passau. He served for twenty years, and was martyred during Numerian's persecution. Feast day 12 October.

Maximilian Saint, martyred c.295. He is said to have been executed at Theveste in Numidia because he refused military service in the Roman army. Feast day 12 March.

Maximilian I Duke of Bavaria, born Munich, 17 April 1573, died Ingoldstadt, 27 September 1651. He was educated by the Jesuits, of whom he became an important patron, and became Duke on the abdication of his father in 1597. He reformed the finances of the duchy, and its legal code, greatly improved its army, and in 1609 founded the Catholic League. His early victories, in alliance with his cousin the Emperor Ferdinand II, led to the establishment of a permanent Catholic majority in the electors of the Holy Roman Empire. His later campaigns were less successful, but the Treaty of Westphalia, which put an end to the Thirty Years War in 1648, left him in possession of some of the territories he had annexed. He was an active supporter of the Counter Reformation. Among the institutions he endowed was the college of the English Jesuits at Liège, now Heythrop College, University of London.

Maximos III (Mazlum) Melchite patriarch, born Aleppo, Syria, November 1779, died Alexandria, Egypt, 11 August 1855. Ordained in 1806, Michael Mazlum adopted the name 'Maximos' at his election as metropolitan of Aleppo in 1810. The Congregation for the Propagation of the Faith declared the election irregular and he had to reside in Rome, but **Gregory XVI** approved his return to Syria in 1831, where he became patriarch in 1833. He called the Council of Ain-Traz, the only Melchite council approved in *forma generali*, in 1847. He worked to secure autonomy for the Melchites in the Ottoman Empire, and generally advanced the interests of the Melchites in his territory, against the opposition of both Rome and his own bishops.

Maximos IV Sayegh Greek Catholic patriarch, born Aleppo, Syria, 10 April 1878, died Beirut, 5 November 1967. Maximos joined the Missionaries of St Paul at Harissa in 1904, became metropolitan of Tyre in 1919 and, having transferred to Beirut in 1933, patriarch of the Greek Catholic Church in 1947. A strong ecumenist, he spared no effort to reconcile the Churches, while safeguarding the rights of the Eastern Catholics as well as patriarchal prerogatives. A leading personality of Vatican II, his *l'Église grecque melkite au concile* outlines the place that the Christian Orient is called upon to fill in the *aggiornamento* envisaged by the Council and the Holy See. In 1965, **Paul VI** made Maximos a cardinal, a designation not without objection in the Greek Catholic–Melchite Church.

Maximus (the Confessor) Saint, a prolific writer and Greek theologian, born into the Byzantine aristocracy, *c.*580, died Skhemaris, on the Black Sea, *c.*662. Brought up in Constantinople, he became secretary to the Emperor **Heraclius**, but resigned, possibly because of the emperor's doubtful orthodoxy, and became a monk at Chrysopolis (Scutari), where he was eventually elected abbot. He was an active opponent of the Monothelitism embraced by the Emperor **Constans II**. He was imprisoned for six years, then, when *c.*82 years old, was put on trial in Constantinople, had his tongue cut out, his right hand cut off and was sentenced to life imprisonment. He died shortly after his arrival at Skhemaris. He is called 'the Confessor'

because of the sufferings he endured for his faith. Feast day in the West 13 August.

Maximus (Maxim Sandovich) Orthodox saint and martyr, born Zhdenia, Austrian Galicia, 30 September 1886, died (shot) Gorlice, 6 September 1914. He was born a Greek Catholic (Uniate) but studied in Russia and was ordained priest by Metropolitan **Antony** (Khrapovitsky). Thereafter he was an Orthodox missionary in his home region, then part of the Austrian Empire, and converted several villages. He was arrested and when World War I began he was executed, without trial, for treason, as the Orthodox were considered pro-Russian. Canonized by the Orthodox Church of Poland in 1994 at Gorlice. Feast day 6 September.

Maximus of Saragossa Bishop, writer, died *c.*619, presumably in Saragossa. Maximus attended the Councils of Barcelona (599), Toledo (610), and Egara (614) but is principally known as a chronicler of Visigothic history of the period 450–568 and a writer of other works. However, only 33 brief excerpts of his chronicle are extant; they are used and praised by **Isidore of Seville**. Maximus' historical writings parallel those of the other chroniclers Victor of Tunnuna and **John of Biclaro**.

Maximus of Turin Bishop and saint, born *c.*350(?), bishop of Turin in 398, died between 408 and 423. This is all we know for sure about him. His works, mainly some 90 sermons, some of dubious authenticity, reveal him as a pastor genuinely concerned about his flock, rather than as a speculative theologian. His sermons show a marked influence of **Ambrose**. In them he reacts against idolatry, hypocrisy, laxism, corrupt clerics, Arianism and despondency because of the German incursions. Feast day 25 June.

Maxwell, Winifred Countess of Nithsdale, born Scotland, *c.*1678, died Rome, 1749. Lady Nithsdale's husband was captured during the Jacobite rising in 1715, and imprisoned in the Tower of London. Her pleadings to George I to release her husband having gone unheeded, the intrepid woman succeeded in smuggling the count out of prison in female attire, and hid him in London until he could escape to France. She then returned to Scotland to retrieve family papers and joined Lord Nithsdale in exile in Rome, where they ended their days.

Mayer, Rupert Blessed, German Jesuit, born Stuttgart, 23 January 1876, died Munich, 1 November 1945. Mayer became a preacher of parish missions in Germany, Switzerland and The Netherlands, and co-founded the Sisters of the Holy Family, a mission to the very poor; in 1925, he inaugurated the Banhofsmission, a ministry to travellers. One of the first to recognize the incompatibility of Nazism and Christianity, he became an object of police attention when the Nazis came to power in 1933. Mayer regarded Hitler as 'hysterical' and, forbidden to preach, he was arrested in 1939 and sent to Sachsenhausen concentration camp, though he actually spent the war in Ettal Abbey. He returned to Munich in 1945 and resumed preaching, but died six months later. His tomb soon became a place of pilgrimage and John Paul II beatified him in 1987. Feast day 3 May.

Mayne, Cuthbert English Roman Catholic priest, born near Barnstaple, Devon, 1544 (baptized 20 March), executed at Launceston, 30 November 1577. After ordination into the Church of England and education at Oxford, he was appointed chaplain of St John's College. Latterly he was converted to Roman Catholicism and in 1573 moved to an English seminary at Douai. Ordained as priest in 1575, he returned to England in 1576 and settled on the estate of Francis Tregian near Truro in Cornwall. He secretly carried out his work as a priest until his arrest in 1577 and subsequent execution in the market-place at Launceston. Cuthbert was canonized as one of the **Forty Martyrs of England and Wales** in 1970 by Pope **Paul VI**.

Mayol, Joseph French Dominican theologian, born Saint-Maximin, after 1656, died Avignon, 26 September 1709. Mayol taught in various houses of the Order, preached throughout southern France and published two major works: *Abrégé de la dévotion du Rosaire de la mère de Dieu*, and *Summa moralis doctrinae thomisticae circa decem precepta decalogi*.

Mayr, Anton Bavarian Jesuit theologian, born Nesselwang, 24 October 1673, died Ingolstadt, 3 July 1749. Mayr entered the Society in 1689, taught at Freiburg and Ingolstadt and published voluminous treatises covering complete courses in philosophy and theology.

Mazarin, Jules Cardinal and statesman, born Piscina, Abruzzi, 14 July 1602, died Vincennes, France, 9 March 1661. His father was employed by the Colonna family, and Mazarin rose in the papal service through the family's influence, eventually becoming nuncio in Paris in 1634. There he was a supporter of **Richelieu**, so much so that the Spanish complained to **Urban VIII**, who dismissed him in 1636. He was then employed by Richelieu, and became naturalized as French in 1639. On the death of Richelieu he took over the effective government of France during the minority of **Louis XIV**, at least in part because of the closeness of his relationship to Anne of Austria. He was created a cardinal in 1642. His relationship with Rome, which he never again visited, was not cordial even though he left an endowment to the Papacy to prosecute the war against the Turks. He was by title bishop of Metz from 1653 to 1658. Through his skills of negotiation he avoided war between France and Spain. While enriching himself, he also raised France to a powerful position in Europe and after the Treaty of the Pyrenees in 1659, secured marriage between the Infanta Maria Theresa and Louis XIV.

Mazenod, Charles Joseph Eugène de French Roman Catholic bishop and founder, born Aix-en-Provence, 2 August 1782, died Marseilles, 21 May 1861. Ordained in 1811, de Mazenod then began a life-long apostolate to the poor. He succeeded his uncle as bishop of Marseilles in 1837, and founded the Missionary Oblates of Mary Immaculate, whose members he sent to Canada, Ceylon, the USA and South Africa, in all of which the Oblate apostolate achieved remarkable results. An ardent ultramontanist, he nevertheless supported Félicité de **Lamennais** in controversies covering the classics, liturgy and liberalism, though he remained intransigent on educational freedom and the Roman question. His beatification process was introduced in 1936.

Maziel, Juan Baltasar Argentine educator, born Santa Fe, 8 September 1727, died Montevideo, 2 January 1787. Following studies in Spain and Chile, Maziel moved to Buenos Aires, became a member of the Cabildo Ecclesiastico, and adviser to the bishops in various conflicts with royal representatives, with the vicar general of the diocese and with the chancellor of the Real Convictorio de San Carlos. Maziel had a library of over 1000 volumes, which he made available for study, and generally exerted such an influence on the young people of Buenos Aires that they called him *el maestro de la generación de Mayo*.

Mazzarello, Maria Domenica Saint, Italian foundress, founded Daughters of Our Lady Help of Christians (the Salesian Sisters), born Marnese (Piedmont), 9 May 1837, died Nizza Monferrato, 14 May 1881. A dressmaker and member of a local sodality, Maria taught her trade to local girls and so impressed St **John Bosco** during a visit to the village in 1865 that he placed her in charge of a school for girls established by himself. She founded, with ten companions, the Daughters of Our Lady Help of Christians (Salesian Sisters), for the education of poor girls, under a Rule written by John Bosco. The congregation gradually spread to France and Argentina, and had 250 members at her death. **Pius XII** canonized her in 1951. Feast day 14 May.

Mazzella, Camillo Italian cardinal, Italian Jesuit theologian, born Vitulano, 10 February 1833, died Rome, 26 March 1900. Mazzella entered the Society in 1857, and lectured on moral theology at Georgetown University and Woodstock College in the USA, 1867–78; **Leo XIII** then summoned him to a chair at the Gregorian University in Rome to contribute to the Thomistic revival. Made a curial cardinal in 1886, he served in the Congregations of Studies and of Rites. His publications from 1880 include *De Deo creante, De religione et ecclesia, De gratia Christi* and a work against the views of Antonio **Rosmini-Serbati**: *Rosminianarum propositionem . . . trutina theologica*.

Mazzolini, Sylvester Prierias Italian Dominican theologian, born Priero, Piedmont, 1460, died Rome, 1523. A brilliant theologian at Bologna and Pavia, Mazzolini was called to Rome by **Julius II**, and **Leo X** named him master of the sacred palace in 1515. He was instrumental in having the works of the great German humanist Johann **Reuchlin** condemned in 1520, and he initiated opposition to the teachings of Martin **Luther**, vigorously upholding papal supremacy and the view that in matters of faith and doctrine the Pope is infallible. His most complete argument against Luther appeared in *Errata et argumenta M. Lutheri*, as well as in a popular compendium of moral theology, *Summa summarum quae Silvestrina dicitur*.

Mazzuchelli, Samuel Italian Dominican missionary, born Milan, 4 November 1806, died Barton, Wisconsin, 23 February 1864. Following his studies in Rome, Mazzuchelli went to Cincinnati, Ohio, where the bishop assigned him to Mackinac to work among the French Canadians and Indians; he learned the Indian languages and composed a prayer book in the Winnebago tongue. He later became vicar general for the Diocese of Dubuque, received permission in 1844 to establish a Dominican province on the Upper Mississippi, and founded the community of Dominican Sisters of the Most Holy Rosary at Sinsinawa, in 1847, as well as Mound College for boys and Burton Academy.

Meagher, Paul Kevin American Dominican theologian, born Clarion, Pennsylvania, 14 May 1907, died Washington, DC, 2 January 1977. Ordained at Blackfriars, Oxford, in 1931, Meagher came under the influence of Bede **Jarret**, OP, and began a lifelong collaboration with fellow Dominicans Thomas **Gilby**, and Gerald Vann, with whom he co-wrote *The Temptations of Christ*. In 1961 Meagher went to Blackfriars, Cambridge, to join Gilby in launching the 60-volume Latin–English edition of St **Thomas Aquinas'** *Summa Theologiae*; he also edited the moral theology sections of the fifteen-volume *New Catholic Encyclopedia* in Washington, and undertook major work in the *Encyclopedic Dictionary of Religion*. A modern Thomist of wide humanist learning, Meagher adhered closely to the Church's magisterium.

Meagher, Thomas Francis Irish revolutionary and Union officer in the American Civil War, born Waterford Town, Ireland, 23 August 1823, died by drowning near Fort Benton, Montana, 1 July 1867.

He became involved in Irish revolutionary politics and was arrested for treason by the British, transported to Van Diemen's Land (now Tasmania), but escaped to the USA. In New York he studied law, became an American war leader and edited the *Irish News*. In the Civil War, he organized the Irish Brigade and became a brigadier general. In Montana territory he served as acting governor.

Mechitar of Sebaste   Armenian Catholic founder, founded the Order of St Anthony (the 'Mechitarists'), born Sivas, Sebaste, Asia Minor, 7 February 1676, died San Lazzaro, Venice, 27 April 1749. An Armenian priest, Mechitar submitted to Rome in 1696, and formed the Mechitarist community of Uniate monks at Constantinople in 1701, whence they were expelled in 1703 to the Morea and, when the Turks conquered the area, to the island of San Lazzaro, where they settled in 1717. Mechitar built a monastery under the Rule of St **Benedict** complete with church, library and printing press, which published some twenty works, notably a commentary on the Gospel of St Matthew, an Armenian grammar, a dictionary and an Armenian edition of the Bible.

Mechtild of Hackeborn (Mechtilde, Matilda von Hackeborn-Wippra)   Saint, Benedictine, born Eisleben, Saxony, 1240 or 1241, died Helfta, 19 November 1298. Of a noble Thuringian family and sister of Gertrude of Hackeborn. She was born very weak and baptized immediately. The celebrant prophesied that she would lead a saintly and long life. At the age of seven she begged to be allowed to enter the monastery of Rodardsdorf. As a young nun she became known for her humility, fervour and friendliness. Subject to divine revelations she was sought out by those seeking her advice. At the age of 50, two nuns to whom she had confided the revelations wrote a book about them, *The Book of Special Grace*. Feast day 16 November.

Mechtild of Magdeburg   German mystic, writer and Beguine, born into a noble family in Saxony, *c.*1210, died *c.*1280. She became a Beguine at Magdeburg, where she led a contemplative and penitential life. She was subject to visions, which she was instructed to write down by her confessor. She later moved to the Cistercian convent at Helfta, in 1270. Her book *Das fliessende Licht der Gottheit* had great influence in medieval Germany.

Medard of Noyon   Saint, bishop, born Salency (Picardy), *c.*456 or 470, died Noyon, 8 June *c.*545–60. Medard, born of a noble Frankish father and a Gallo-Roman mother, was pious and studious from childhood, leading to his ordination and (despite his objections) consecration as bishop of Vermand. Because of barbarian turmoil, Medard moved his see to Noyon, a more secure location; upon the death of the bishop of Tournai, Medard was asked by King Clotaire, to rule that diocese also. Medard is also known for consecrating **Radegunda** as a deaconess after King Clotaire had murdered her brother. Feast day 8 June.

Medeiros, Humberto Sousa   Portuguese-born American Roman Catholic archbishop, born Arifes, San Miguel, 6 October 1915, died Boston, 17 September 1983. Medeiros emigrated to Fall River as an adolescent, became a priest in 1946, bishop of Brownsville, Texas, in 1966, and archbishop of Boston in 1970, in succession to Cardinal **Cushing**. In 1971 he declared his pastoral agenda in a letter, 'Man's Cities and God's Poor', affirming his commitment to education, racial and ethnic equality and the plight of the poor. His years as leader of the diocese were marked by much unrest and he had to cope with racial tension, the legalization of abortion, human and civic rights and the consequences of a decline in vocations.

Medici, Cosimo de'   Florentine banker and ruler of the Republic of Florence, born Florence, 27 September 1389, died Careggi, near Florence, 1 August 1464. He inherited wealth from his father, the richest banker in the peninsula. He was expelled from Florence but returned for 30 years to be a patron of literature and the arts. Among those he patronized were the sculptors **Ghiberti** and **Donatello** and the painters del **Castagno**, Fra **Angelico** and **Gozzoli**. Cosimo searched out Christian manuscripts and assembled a magnificent library. He was sincerely religious in his later years, and in particular patronized the Dominicans of San Marco. His grandson became Pope **Clement VII**.

Medici, Giovanni dei ('Giovanni delle Bande Nere')

Leading soldier of the illustrious Medici family and supporter of the Papacy, born Forli, Italy, 6 April 1498, died Mantua, 30 November 1526. He was christened 'Lodovico', but, after his father died, took his father's Christian name. Through his mother, he was descended from the Sforza family. Initially he fought for Pope **Leo X**, then served the French. He joined up with the army of the League of Cognac against the Emperor, but was fatally wounded in battle. His son became the first grand duke of Tuscany.

Medina, José Antonio   Peruvian Roman Catholic priest and revolutionary, born Tucumán, Argentina, 1773, died Rio de la Plata, 8 August 1828. Ordained in Chucuisaca, Medina became pastor in Sicasica, not far from La Paz, Bolivia, whose independence from Spain he had long supported, and a leader with Pedro Domingo Murillo of the rebellion of 1809. The revolution failed; Medina opposed the terms of surrender and left with the patriot army to continue the campaign at the Battle of Chacaltaya, where they were defeated. Captured in the mountains of Yungas and imprisoned, he escaped to Chile, where he spent the rest of his life in the Rio de la Plata.

Medina, Juan   Spanish theologian, born Alcalá, 1490, died there, 1546. Medina taught at the University of Alcalá from 1526 until his death, holding the chair, *de los nominales*. He seems to have been a remarkable teacher, but published nothing himself; two works were printed in 1550 on parts of his moral teaching, namely on commutative justice and sacramental penance. Two of Medina's manuscripts have been discovered in the Vatican Library which record the courses he gave on the *Sentences*, based on an exposition by Gabriel **Biel**, the German nominalist.

Medrano, Mariano   Argentine Roman Catholic prelate and philosopher, born Buenos Aires, 1767, died there, 7 April 1851. Medrano became a celebrated teacher at the Colegio de San Carlos in La Plata, where he spread the ideas of Francisco **Suárez**, who greatly influenced the revolution at the close of the eighteenth century. When named bishop of Buenos Aires in 1832 by **Gregory XVI**, the attorney general claimed that the State's right of patronage had been ignored, but a commission

of jurists and theologians resolved the problem of Medrano's acceptance. His tenure of office was notable for the restoration of the hierarchy.

Meehan, Thomas Francis   American historiographer, born Brooklyn, New York, 19 September 1854, died New York City, 7 July 1942. Editor of the *Irish American* and of the *Catholic Encyclopedia*, and on the editorial staff of *America*, Meehan also contributed to the *Catholic World* and to the *Commonweal*. He became editor of *Records and Studies*, journal of the Catholic Historical Society, on the death of Charles Hebermann, and edited *Catholic Builders of the Nation* in 1925.

Mehegan, Mary Xavier   Mother, Irish-born American religious foundress, founded the Sisters of Charity of New Jersey, born Skibereen, 19 February 1825, died Convent Station, New Jersey, 24 June 1915. Baptized 'Catherine Josephine', she went to the USA in 1844, and became one of the first postulants of the Sisters of Charity in New York. When they separated in 1859 from the community in Emmitsburg, Maryland, she and another sister founded a new branch in Newark, New Jersey. The community grew rapidly after the Civil War, new land was purchased, new missions were opened, and the College of St Elizabeth founded at Convent Station, the first college for women in New Jersey. Mary Xavier served as superior of the community for 57 years; the number of sisters grew to 1200, and 100 foundations were made, including schools, hospitals, orphanages and homes for the aged.

Meinrad of Einsiedeln   Saint, died Einsiedeln, 21 January 861. About 836, Meinrad, a monk of Reichenau, came to live in solitude near Lake Zurich (Switzerland), having had to abandon an earlier hermitage beside Lake Zurich because of the number of his visitors. He was murdered by robbers. Later his demesne was occupied by hermits 'Einsiedeln' means hermitage, and a Benedictine monastery was founded there, named after him. Feast day 21 January.

Meinwerk of Paderborn   Blessed, bishop, date and place of birth unknown, died Paderborn, Germany, 5 June 1036. A noble and friend from youth of Emperor **Henry II**, Meinwerk was made bishop of Paderborn by the Emperor in 1009, reputedly so that he could restore it with his own personal wealth. Meinwerk did make his diocese richer, obtained donations from the Emperor himself, and was known as a meticulous, even paternally petty, administrator. He spent much of his time in building and decorating, for both the cathedral and the town. Feast day 5 June.

Melanchthon, Philipp Humanist, educator and Reformer, born 1497, died Wittenberg, 19 April 1560. He studied at Heidelberg, 1509–11 BA and Tübingen, 1512–14, MA, and in 1518 became professor of Greek at Wittenberg. He developed a close friendship with Martin **Luther**, took part in the Leipzig Disputation in 1519, married Katherine Krapp in 1520, and published the first edition of his influential lectures on Romans, *Loci communes*, in 1521. His *Unterricht der visitatoren* (1528) and other writings laid the basis for public education in Germany. He took part in the Diet of Speyer (1529), the Colloquy of Marburg (1529) and the Diet of Augsburg (1530). He was chief architect of the Augsburg Confession. A conciliatory figure, he objected to the overt condemnation of the Papacy in the Schmalkadic Articles of 1537 and was present at Catholic–Protestant colloquies at Worms (1540–1) and Ratisbon (Regensburg) (1541).

Melania the Elder Saint, born Rome, 342, into an aristocratic family, died Jerusalem, *c.*410. When she was 21 she lost her husband and two of her three children. She turned to an ascetic lifestyle, left her eight-year-old son with his inheritance in Rome and travelled with other ascetic women and slaves to Alexandria. Then she lived for a while in the Egyptian desert, from where she travelled to Jerusalem. There she founded a double convent over which she presided for many years. She came in contact with many famous men, including her spiritual master **Rufinus of Aquileia**, **Jerome** and **Augustine**. Feast day 8 June.

Melania the Younger Saint, born Rome, *c.*383, the granddaughter of **Melania the Elder**, died Jerusalem, 31 December 439. After the early death of both their children, she and her husband Pinianus against the will of their family adopted an ascetic lifestyle. With their money they started and kept alive many spiritual communities and charitable institutions. They founded convents in Sicily and Africa and travelled to Egypt and Palestine. On the Mount of Olives they built a convent, where Melania spent the last years of her life after her husband's death. Feast day 31 December.

Melchers, Paulus German archbishop and cardinal, born Münster, 6 January 1813, died Rome, 14 December 1895. Ordained in 1841, Melchers became archbishop of Cologne in 1866 and led the minority group of bishops opposed to the definition of papal infallibility at Vatican Council I, though he subscribed to it readily enough as a conciliar decision, thereby incurring the wrath of the Old Catholics. He sought to avert the Kulturkampf, and after several months imprisonment, in 1874, was obliged to leave Germany and to administer his diocese from Maastricht in The Netherlands. At the request of **Leo XIII**, he resigned his see in 1885 and became a cardinal in the Roman curia.

Meléndez, Juan de Peruvian Dominican chronicler, born Lima, date unknown, died Lima, 1684. Named precentor of the Peruvian province in 1671, Meléndez travelled to Madrid and Rome, where he gathered material for his monumental work *Tesoros verdaderos de las Indias*, wherein is a valuable and detailed description of the city of Lima in the seventeenth century, including an inventory of corporations, churches and convents.

Meletios (Metaxakis) Patriarch of Constantinople, born Lasithi, Crete, 21 September 1871, died Alexandria, Egypt, 27 July 1935. He was, successively, archbishop of Athens, patriarch of Constantinople and patriarch of Alexandria. He also recognized the Orthodox Church in the USA and placed all Greek parishes of the diaspora under Constantinople. He strongly favoured the ecumenical movement and the modernization of Orthodoxy (use of the Gregorian calendar etc.). His influence on the development of modern Greek Orthodoxy is still controversial.

Melito Saint, bishop of Sardis, died 189. In Melito's 'petition to the emperor', dated 175, he writes of the Church and State as works of God for the benefit of all. Another papyrus fragment shows that Melito was concerned about the problem of the dating of Easter. Recovered texts show that the theme of the slain Pascal Lamb was important to him and that his theology is in line with the Logos Christology of the early apologists. He was regarded as the first pilgrim because of his travels to places of Christian origins. Feast day 1 April.

Mellitus Saint, third archbishop of Canterbury, died 24 April 624. He was possibly a Benedictine at St Andrew's monastery in Rome and part of the second cohort of missionaries sent in 601 to help **Augustine** in England. He was consecrated bishop of the East Saxons in 604 with his see in London – St Paul's was built as his cathedral. After a brief banishment to France, he returned to England and became archbishop of Canterbury in 618. Feast day 24 April.

Mello, Anthony de Indian Jesuit, spiritual director and writer, born 1932, died of a heart attack in New York, 2 June 1987. He became director of the Sadhana Institute of Pastoral Counselling in Poona, India, and was mainly only known in India and to those associated with Jesuit institutions until the early 1980s. As soon as his writings, including *The Song of the Bird* (1984), became available in translation in the West, he found himself inundated with invitations to give talks and lead retreats and his reputation and ideas spread worldwide and beyond traditional Christian spirituality circles. His story-telling approach, based on the methods of Zen, Sufi and Jewish spiritual teachers, including Jesus, and his call to people to wake up, live fully and find God in the present, as expressed for instance in his *One Minute Wisdom* (1986), continue to meet the spiritual needs of many people in the modern world.

Melun, Armand de French Catholic social movement leader, born Brumetz, Aisne, 24 September 1807, died Paris, 24 June 1877. Inspired by the work of St **Vincent de Paul**, Melun founded *Annales de la Charité* in 1849, to understand and remedy the plight of indigents. Elected to the legislative assembly in 1849, he laid the foundations of social legislation, and initiated important laws in 1849–51, the most important of which limited the working day of adolescent apprentices, imposed Sunday rest and provided for the instruction of children in reading, writing and religion. Motivated by the social leanings of **Napoleon III**,

Melun influenced the formation of the Sociétés Catholiques de Secours Mutuels, in Paris and in the provinces. During his life he remained at the centre of the Catholic social movement prior to the Third Republic.

Melville, Andrew Scottish Presbyterian leader, born Baldovie, Angus, 1 August 1545, died Sedan, France, 1622. Educated at St Andrews University he went to France, studied at Poitiers and then under **Beza** in Geneva. He returned to Scotland in 1574 and was appointed principal at Glasgow University. He was moderator of the General Assembly in 1578, 1582 (twice), 1587 and 1594. Taking the mantle of Scottish Church leadership after the death of John **Knox** in 1572, he worked to establish Presbyterianism and oppose State interference, and the *Second Book of Discipline* (1578) was largely his work. He was accused of treason in 1584, but became rector at St Andrews, 1590–7, until again in conflict with the king. The English Privy Council confined him to the Tower of London, 1607–11, before he was allowed to go into exile in France, where he taught biblical theology at Sedan.

Melvin, Martin John English Catholic merchant, born Birmingham, 8 June 1879, died Warwickshire, 11 May 1952. Of prosperous Irish parents, Melvin lent his support to the Conservative Party, which earned him honours, and organized charitable activities during the First World War, notably canteens for the Catholic Women's League. In 1917 the hierarchy asked him to help save *The Universe*, the leading Catholic weekly, from financial collapse, which he succeeded in doing, while raising the circulation to nearly 250,000. Named a papal chamberlain, Melvin received the Grand Cross of St Gregory.

Memling, Hans Flemish painter, born Seligenstadt on the Main, *c.*1430, died Bruges, of which he was a citizen by 1465, 11 August 1494. He is regarded as a student of Roger van der Weyden but there is little that is known for sure about him beyond the fact that he was a fairly wealthy man, the owner of three houses in Bruges, and the father of three sons. His first datable painting, a portrait, is of 1467. Much of his work can be seen in St John's Hospital, Bruges, though the claim that he was an inmate there for much of his life has now been disproved. His paintings include the *Shrine of St Ursula*, together with several altarpieces and Madonnas.

Men, Alexander Vladimirovich   Russian Orthodox priest, writer and theologian, born Moscow, 22 January 1935, died (murdered) 9 September 1990. Born of a Jewish family he was secretly baptized, with his mother, as an infant. He became a priest and was a popular and successful speaker and catechist who helped many of the younger generation of the intelligentsia in the later Soviet period to belief and baptism. His writings were equally influential, especially *Christianity for the Twenty-first Century*. His murderers were never found.

Ménard, Léon   French historian, born Tarascon, 12 September 1706, died Paris, 1 October 1767. Educated by the Jesuits in Lyons, Ménard is notable for his *Histoire civile, ecclésiastique et littéraire de la ville de Nîmes, Moeurs et usages des Grecs*, and contributions to the journal of the Académie des Inscriptions.

Menas   Saint, patriarch of Constantinople, participant in the Three Chapters controversy, born Alexandria, *c.*500, died 552. He was ordained to the priesthood in Constantinople. When, in 536, **Anthimus I** was removed from the patriarchate of that city by Pope **Agapetus I** because of the former's Monophysite leanings, Menas was consecrated as the new patriarch by the Pope. Menas opposed the teachings of **Origen** and signed Emperor **Justinian I**'s condemnation of the Three Chapters. This caused Pope **Vigilius**, whose opinion on this issue mirrored his fluctuating relationship with Emperor Justinian, to excommunicate Menas on two separate occasions, only to be reconciled with him later. Menas did not live long enough to witness the Pope's eventual condemnation of the Three Chapters. Feast day 25 August.

Mendel, Gregor Johann   Augustinian priest ('Gregor' is his religious name), biologist and botanist, founder of the science of genetics (Mendelism), born Heinzendorf, Austria, 22 July 1822, died Brünn (Brno, now Czech Republic), 6 January 1884. He entered the Augustinian monastery at Brünn in 1843, and was ordained in 1847. He

taught for a time in the abbey school and was then sent to Vienna, where he studied mathematics, physics and the natural sciences. On his return in in 1853 he returned to teaching until, in 1866, he was elected abbot of his monastery. As abbot he had to engage in a protracted struggle with the government over the taxation of religious houses, which he won – but only after his death. His researches into inheritance in plants began as a novice working in the garden attached to the monastery – his father had been a peasant-farmer – and were inspired by an unease with the theories of **Darwin**.

Mendelssohn, Felix   German composer, pianist and conductor, born Hamburg, 3 February 1809, died Leipzig, 4 November 1847. His father took the extra name 'Bartholdy', hence 'Mendelssohn-Bartholdy', when he became a Lutheran. Felix Mendelssohn was a child prodigy, having at the age of ten his setting of Psalm 19 publicly performed. Mendelssohn helped to revive J. S. **Bach**'s music. At twenty he arranged and conducted a performance of Bach's *St Matthew Passion*, 100 years after it had been first performed, and since when it had largely been forgotten. Mendelssohn held official posts in Germany, travelled widely, and, partly through the patronage of the British royal family, his music became immensely popular in Britain. His oratorios, such as *Elijah*, fell out of popularity in the twentieth century, but his 'Wedding March' from his incidental music to **Shakespeare**'s *A Midsummer Night's Dream* is still popular for weddings.

Mendez, Ramón Ignacio   Venezuelan Roman Catholic archbishop and patriot, born Barinas, 1775, died Bogotá, Colombia, August 1839. Ordained in 1797, Mendez worked for the independence of Venezuela from Spain in 1810; an ally of Simón **Bolívar**, he served as chaplain in the revolutionary armies and signed the Declaration of Independence. Consecrated archbishop of Caracas in 1823, he opposed the new constitution which abridged the rights of the Church, and was exiled in 1830; on his return he refused to accept the government's use of the law of patronage in the matter of the appointment of Church dignitaries, and was again exiled in 1836; he died in exile. A hundred years later his remains were transferred to the National Pantheon in Caracas – a hero, and founder of the nation.

Mendez Plancarte, Gabriel Mexican Roman Catholic priest and humanist writer, born Zamora, 24 January 1905, died Mexico City, 16 December 1949. Ordained in 1927, Mendez Plancarte taught at the Seminario Conciliar de México and the National University, and lectured in the USA and Canada. In 1937 he founded *Ábside*, an imporant cultural review which survived for 29 years without financial support from any public or private institution – unique in the history of Mexico. Among his more notable works are: *Primicias*, and *Nuevos salvos y odas* in poetry; *Hidalgo, reformador intelectual*, a critical assessment; *Humanismo mexicano del siglo XVI*, a critical edition with introduction and notes.

Mendieta, Jerónimo de Spanish Franciscan missionary and author, born Vitoria, 1525, died Mexico, 1604. Mendieta went to Mexico in 1554, and devoted his life to missionary labours among the Indians, whom he defended against the exploitation and avarice of the colonizers, as well as against **Philip II**'s policy of favouring the secular clergy over the friars, which, in his view, destroyed the 'terrestrial paradise' the Franciscans were creating among the Indians. His *Historia eclesiástica indiana* could not, as a consequence of these attitudes, find a publisher until 1870.

Mendo, Andreas Spanish Jesuit theologian, born Logroña, 1608, died Madrid, 11 May 1684. A teacher at the Irish Seminary, Salamanca, and censor for the Spanish Inquisition, Mendo published works on moral theology, e.g. a summary of opinions on moral controversies that was put on the Index in 1678 for laxism, a treatise on morality in contemporary politics and works on ascetical theology, as well as a collection of prayers.

Mendoza, Pedro González de Cardinal archbishop of Toledo, born Guadalajara, 3 May 1428, died there, 11 January 1495. He was the son of the marquis of Santillana. After studying at the University of Salamanca he became bishop of Calahorra in 1453, of Sigüenza in 1467 and Chancellor of Castile, with the title of cardinal, in 1473. He subsequently became archbishop of Seville, in 1474, and of Toledo, in 1482. He helped negotiate the marriage of **Isabella of Castile** with Ferdinand of Aragon (**Ferdinand V** of Castile), and gave encouragement to **Columbus**. He was a humanist, translating the Latin and Greek classics into Spanish, but he also produced a catechism and oversaw the visitation of his dioceses. He left his fortune to an orphanage he had founded in Toledo.

Menéndez Pelayo, Marcelino Spanish Roman Catholic philosopher and historian, born Santander, 3 November 1856, died there, 19 May 1912. A precociously learned youth, he studied at the Universities of Barcelona and Madrid, receiving his doctorate at the latter in 1875. The following year he published *La Ciencia Española*, which defended the Catholic religious tradition of his country. The book brought him considerable fame, and in 1878 he was appointed professor of Spanish literature at the University of Madrid. In 1899 he became director of the National Library. He wrote on literary and philosophical topics, and especially on aesthetics. His best-known work is his *Historia de los heterodoxos Españoles* (1880–2), which argued that the soul of Spain was quintessentially Catholic, and that any display of heterodoxy was a passing whim. He also served as a deputy to the Spanish parliament.

Menéndez, Josefa Sister, Spanish mystic and religious, born Madrid, 4 February 1890, died Poitiers, 29 December 1923. Of humble background, Josefa made a vow of virginity on the day of her First Communion; she became a skilled dressmaker and a Religious of the Sacred Heart in Poitiers in 1910. She led an obscure life in the convent, but the depth of her spiritual life and details of her mystical experiences were revealed in her diaries after her death: temptations by the devil had alternated with visits from the Sacred Heart, the Blessed Virgin and St Madeleine Sophie. Her 'message' appeared posthumously as *Le message du Coeur de Jésus au monde et sa messagère soeur Josefa Menéndez*.

Meneses, Juan Francisco Chilean educator, political figure, born Santiago, 1785, died there, 1860. Loyal to Spain during the independence movement, the victory of José Martin in 1817, forced him into exile in Peru, but he returned in 1821, swore allegiance to the Republican regime, became a Roman Catholic priest, a deputy in the Chilean congress, a senator, and signed the constitution of the Republic in 1833. He served as minister of the interior, of the treasury and of foreign affairs, and became rector of the National Institute, where he introduced sweeping academic reforms.

Menestier, Claude François   French Jesuit heraldist and musicologist, born Lyons, 10 March 1631, died Paris, 21 January 1705. A professor of humanities and librarian, Menestier wrote voluminously in the fields of heraldry and musicology. Among his more than 150 works can be mentioned *Le dessin de la science du blason, La Nouvelle méthode du blason*, which went through many editions, *Des Représentations en musique ancienne et moderne* and *Des Ballets anciens et modernes*.

Mengarini, Gregorio   Italian Jesuit missionary, born Rome, 21 July 1811, died Santa Clara, California, 23 September 1886. Following his ordination, Mengarini went with Pierre **De Smet** to Fort Hall, Idaho, in 1841 to serve the Flathead Indians, and then to the Oregon mission at St Paul. One of the founders of Santa Clara College, he published in 1861 the classic *Salish or Flathead Grammar, Grammatica Linguae Salicae* and *Dictionary of the Kalispel or Flathead India Language*; he also contributed material on Salish dialects for John Wesley Powell's *Contributions to American Ethnology*.

Menno Simons   Anabaptist leader, who gave his name to the Mennonite sect, born Witmarsum, Holland, 1492, died Wustenfelde, in what is now Germany, 15 January 1559. He was ordained in 1515 or 1516, and served first as a curate near his home town and then, from 1532, in Witmarsum as parish priest. He was, however, increasingly drawn towards the doctrine of the Anabaptists, and in 1536 resigned his parish to become an elder. He taught believers' baptism, non-resistance and non-involvement in local government. He also stressed the independence and responsibility of individual congregations. He founded numerous congregations, especially in Holland, though before he died there had been a significant schism among them. His writings were extremely influential on the moderate wing of Mennonites.

Menochio, Giovanni Stefano   Italian Jesuit theologian and exegete, born Pavia, December 1575, died Rome, 4 February 1655. Menochio taught theology and Scripture at Milan, and is deservedly known for his *Brevis explicatio sensus literalis totius Sacrae Scripturae ex optimis quibusque auctoribus per epitomen collecta*, an exegetical study of the whole Bible printed in many editions in every country of Europe.

Merbot   Blessed, martyr, date and place of birth unknown, died Alberschwende, near Bregenz (Austria), 23 March 1120. According to legend, Merbot was the brother of Blessed Diedo of Andelsbuch and Blessed **Ilga**. A Benedictine monk at Mehrerau, he was made pastor of the church in Alberschwende when it was acquired by the abbey. Settlers killed him, but later over his grave a chapel was built that became a pilgrimage site. Feast day 19 March, except in Bregenz, where it is the first Thursday of Lent.

Mercado, Tomás de   Spanish Dominican logician, born Seville, date unknown, died San Juan de Ulúa, Mexico, 1575. Ordained in Mexico, Mercado taught at Seville, where he published his well-known commentary on the principal dialectical work of Peter of Spain (**John XXI**): *Commentarii lucidissimi in textum Petri Hispani*; and a treatise on Aristotle's *Logica major*: *In dialecticam Aristotelis cum opusculo argumentorum*, in which he restores the purity of the Greek in a two-fold commentary.

Mercati, Angelo   Italian Vatican archivist, born Villa Gaida, Reggio Emilia, 10 June 1870, died Rome, 10 March 1955. Mercati served in the Vatican Library as successively *scriptori, primo custode* of the archives, vice-prefect and, from 1925 until his death, prefect; under his direction notable accessions were made, and scholars obtained greater facilities for research. He published nearly 200 works, including translations into Italian of standard works, and miscellaneous essays and articles on the discovery of hitherto unknown documents.

Mercati, Giovanni   Italian Vatican librarian, cardinal, born Villa Gaida, Reggio Emilia, 17 December 1866, died Vatican City, 22 August 1957. Older brother of Angelo **Mercati**. He began his career at the Ambrosian Library, Milan; Franz **Ehrle**, SJ, invited him to the Vatican Library in 1898. Appointed prefect in 1919, he became archivist, librarian in 1936 and a cardinal. One of the most learned scholars of his day, skilled in Greek and Latin patristics, the theology and literature of Byzantium and the Renaissance, he wrote more than 400 works in these various fields, and influenced scholars throughout the world by his publications and scientific research.

Mercator, Gerardus Mathematician, geographer and map-maker, born Rupelmonde, Flanders, 5 March 1512, died Duisburg, Germany, 2 December 1594. Studied at Louvain. He is famous for giving his name to Mercator's projection, and introduced the word 'atlas' to mean a volume of maps – his book of maps had a figure of Atlas on the cover, hence the name. His celebrated projection was to help sailors, and fundamentally is still in use today. His maps include the Holy Land, Europe and the British Isles. Also he devised terrestrial and celestial globes which he presented to **Charles V**, the Holy Roman Emperor. As a Protestant in Catholic Flanders, he decided to settle in Duisburg.

Mercier, Désiré Joseph Belgian cardinal and patriot, born Braine-l'Alleud, 21 November 1851, died Brussels, 23 January 1926. Mercier studied and taught at Louvain, and there founded the chair of Thomistic philosophy at the request of **Leo XIII**, whose encyclical *Aeterni Patris* outlined a programme to extend the philosophy of St **Thomas Aquinas** to the scientific and social disciplines. To this end, Mercier founded the Institut Supérieur de Philosophie and the *Revue philosophique de Louvain*. Made archbishop of Malines and primate of Belgium in 1906, and cardinal in 1907, Mercier demonstrated courage in defending his people during the German occupation in the Great War. Very much aware of social problems, he founded the International Union of Social Studies; a pioneer ecumenist, he welcomed Anglican scholars to the famous Malines Conferences in the 1920s.

Mercier, Louis-Honoré French Canadian statesman who compensated Jesuits for property confiscated by the British, born Athanase, Iberville County, Lower Canada, 15 October 1840, died Montreal, 30 October 1894. Initially he edited a Conservative newspaper, *Le Courier de St-Hyacinthe* and supported Conservatives and Quebec's interests. But he left the party and opposed the Canadian Federation. He abandoned journalism, and, after the Dominion of Canada was formed, he helped establish the Parti National. He was elected a member of the House of Commons. In Quebec he was made solicitor-general and led the Liberal Party, pursuing a pro-French nationalist party policy. Pope **Leo XIII** ennobled him.

Mercori, Giulio (Julius Mercorus) Italian Dominican theologian and polemicist, born Cremona, date unknown, died Milan, 1669. Professor at St Thomas Aquinas College, Naples. Mercori's reputation rests on works written to counteract probabilism, and its openness to laxist moral theories, which **Alexander VII** had directed the Order to counter by promoting the morally sound theology of St **Thomas Aquinas**. He published *Basis totius theologiae moralis . . .* , and, later, *Solutiones trium nodorum* to rebut the criticisms of Pierre **Nicole**, the Jansenist theologian, against the *Basis*.

Mercuriali, Geronimo Italian physician, born Forli, 30 September 1530, died Forli, 13 November 1606. Having studied medicine at Bologna and Padua, Mercuriali did research into little-known ancient medical documents, and produced *De arte gymnastica*, in which he proposed the therapeutic value of physical exercise. He also wrote textbooks on melancholia, diseases of women and children, and practical medicine, all of which enhanced a brilliant reputation, much favoured by Emperor Maximilian II.

Merezhkovsky, Dmitry Sergeyevich Russian writer, born St Petersburg, 14 August 1865, died Paris, 9 December 1941. His books about Christ helped revive interest in religion among educated Russians. Merezhkovsky edited a magazine, and wrote critical studies of Tolstoy, **Dostoevsky** and **Gogol**, and a trilogy, *Christ and Antichrist*. After the Bolshevik Revolution, he left Russia and settled in Paris. He then wrote biographies of Napoleon, **Michelangelo**, Jesus Christ, **Leonardo da Vinci**, St **Augustine**, St Paul, St **Francis of Assisi** and **Joan of Arc**.

Meribanes *see* **Mirian**

Merici, Angela Saint, Italian foundress, founded the Company of St Ursula (the 'Ursulines'), born Desenzano, Lombardy, 21 March 1474, died Brescia, 27 January 1540. In 1533, Angela trained twelve young women to assist her in the teaching of girls, and by 1535 the group had become the Company of St Ursula, dedicated to re-Christianizing family life, and thus society, through the education of future wives and mothers. There were no formal vows, but Angela's Rule prescribed virginity, poverty and obedience; after her death St Charles **Borromeo** adapted the structure to conform to the decisions of the Council of Trent, and **Paul III** formally recognized the Company in 1544. The people of Brescia honoured Angela as a saint when she died, and **Pius VII** canonized her in 1807. Feast day 1 June.

Merk, Augustin German Jesuit exegete, born Achern, Baden, 11 September 1869, died Rome, 3 April 1945. Merk is famous for his small critical edition of the Greek New Testament, with parallel Latin translation, which appeared in 1933 and has since passed through eight editions. Though based on the work of Hermann Von Soden's classic text *Die Schriften des Neuen Testaments* ..., Merk revised more recent editions to accord with his own evaluation of the best MSS, ancient versions and critical studies. His work is almost unique in presenting such a comprehensive rendering of the early sources of the NT within a concise volume.

Merkelbach, Benoît Henri Belgian Dominican theologian, born Tongres, 6 January 1871, died Louvain, 25 July 1942. Merkelbach became a Dominican in 1917, taught at Louvain from 1936 and wrote *Summa Theologiae Moralis*, which followed the order and inspiration of St **Thomas Aquinas**, while departing from the casuistic method in moral theology and returning to that of the Great Doctor. Also a noted Mariologist, he published *Mariologia: Tractatus de Beatissima Virgine Maria Matre Dei*.

Merks, Thomas English bishop, date and place of birth unknown, died 1409. Though usually called 'Merks', the correct name appears to have been 'Merke'. A member of **Richard II**'s entourage,

Merks became a bishop in 1397 and is remembered for his loyalty to Richard in 1399, when Henry Bolingbroke overthrew the monarch; at Henry IV's first parliament he is said to have protested to Henry against the way he treated his predecessor. Perhaps for conspiring against Henry, Merks went to the Tower, was found guilty and deprived of his episcopal post; Henry pardoned him in 1401, however, and had restored him to the hierarchy by 1405.

Merlin, Jacques French theologian, born St-Victurnien, Limousin, *c.*1480, died Paris, 26 September 1541. Educated at Paris, Merlin became a canon of Notre Dame, and grand penitentiary in 1529. He edited the works of **Durandus of Saint-Pourçain** and **Origen**, and a collection of Church Councils, *Conciliorum Generalium*, which helped to prepare for the collections of the seventeenth and eighteenth centuries.

Merlini, Giovanni Italian spiritual director, born Spoleto, 28 August 1795, died Rome, 12 January 1873. Ordained in 1818, Merlini was received by St Gaspare del **Bufalo** into the Society of the Most Precious Blood, becoming moderator general in 1847. He also gave spiritual direction to Blessed Maria de **Mattias** in the foundation of the Sisters Adorers of the Most Precious Blood. His cause of beatification was introduced in 1927.

Mermillod, Gaspard Swiss cardinal, Swiss pioneer in the Catholic social movement, born Carouge, 22 September 1824, died Rome, 23 February 1892. When auxiliary bishop of Lausanne, Mermillod actively promoted Catholic education and founded, with Maria Salesia **Chappuis**, the Sister Oblates of St Francis de Sales at Troyes for the protection of poor working girls. Appointed bishop, and cardinal in 1890, he worked for social reforms and founded, in 1885, the Union Catholique d'Études Sociales et Économiques, which sponsored international conferences on social questions. He wrote the widely circulated *Lettre à un protestant sur l'autorité de l'Église et le schisme*, and another important work: *De la vie surnaturelle dans les âmes*.

Mérode, Frédéric Ghislain de Belgian archbishop, born Brussels, 20 March 1800, died Rome, 10 July

1894. Of an aristocratic family, he distinguished himself as a soldier in Algiers and, ordained at Rome in 1849, **Pius IX** made him his secret chamberlain charged with reform of the Papal States. They became the closest friends, but Mérode's military stance caused a rift with Cardinal **Antonelli**, the secretary of state, who preferred diplomacy to arms, and Mérode resigned in 1865. Named a titular archbishop, at Vatican Council I he opposed the definition of papal infallibility, but remained a faithful friend and supporter of Pius IX.

Merrick, Mary Virginia American Roman Catholic social worker, born Washington, DC, 2 November 1866, died there, 10 January 1955. Crippled as a young girl, Mary Merrick spent her life confined to a bed and wheelchair. Privately educated, she published two books: *Life of Christ* and *The Altar of God*. Her life-long interest in the poor led to the foundation of the Christ Child Society, which provided clothing and gifts for children at Christmas, and she later widened its scope to include a convalescent home, summer camps and other activities; through chapters established across the country she encouraged work in child welfare. She received national and papal recognition for her work.

Merry del Val, Rafael Spanish cardinal and diplomat, born London, 10 October 1865, died Rome, 26 February 1930. Merry del Val joined the papal service, and was secretary to the commission which, in 1896, pronounced against the validity of Anglican ordinations. Named archbishop of Nicaea in 1900, and cardinal and secretary of state by **Pius X** in 1903, he became closely identified, because of his strict doctrinal orthodoxy, with Pius' campaign against Modernism. Made secretary of the Holy Office on the death of Pius, Merry del Val continued to exercise influence as a member of several Roman congregations, and as papal legate to Assisi. He is buried in the crypt of St Peter's near the tomb of Pius X.

Mersch, Emil Belgian Jesuit theologian, born Marche, 30 July 1890, died Lens, France, 23 May 1940. Ordained in 1917, Mersch aimed to construct a theological synthesis in terms of the Mystical Body of Christ: in his *Le Corps mystique du Christ: Études de théologie historique*, he traces the development of the doctrine of the Church; in *La théologie du Corps mystique*, his masterwork, the doctrine is presented as his central theological synthesis. He was killed at Lens in an air attack while on a mission of mercy.

Mersenne, Marin Member of the mendicant Order of Minims, a theologian and mathematician, who discovered what are now called 'Mersenne numbers', born Oizé, Maine, France, 8 September 1588, died Paris, 1 September 1648. Having studied at Le Mans and at the Jesuit College of La Flèche in Paris (where he began a lifelong friendship with **Descartes**), he entered the Minims in 1611. He taught Philosophy at Nevers, 1614–20, and then at Paris. He defended Descartes and **Galileo**, and also counted **Gassendi** among his friends. His earliest works were philosophical or theological, but his later research was in mathematics, physics and astronomy. To the Dutch physicist Christiaan Huygens he proposed the use of the pendulum and thus inspired the pendulum clock. In *Harmonie universelle* Mersenne wrote: 'Music is made particularly and principally to charm the spirit and the ear, and to enable us to pass our lives with a little sweetness.' He left his body to science.

Merton, Thomas American Trappist monk, mystic, poet and spiritual writer, born Prades, France, of a New Zealand mother and American father, 1915, died Bangkok, Thailand, 10 December 1968, the result of an accidental electric shock. A convert to Catholicism in 1938 while studying at Columbia University, where he also taught English, Merton entered the Trappist monastery of Our Lady of Gethsemane at Kentucky in 1941. He was ordained priest in 1949 and though he lived in relative seclusion he participated in civil rights, peace and ecumenical movements. But he is best remembered by his large number of devotional and autobiographical works. Perhaps the one which made the greatest impact on ordinary Christians was his autobiography, *The Seven Storey Mountain* (1948; published in England in a slightly shortened version in 1949 as *Elected Silence*). Other works on spirituality included *Seeds of Contemplation* (1949), *No Man is an Island* (1955) and *Mystics and Zen Masters* (1967). Towards the end of his life he became greatly influenced by Eastern spirituality, especially Zen Buddhism; this aspect of his life is in his *The Asian Journeys of Thomas Merton* (1973). His poetry was published as *The Strange Islands* (1957) and the *Hidden Ground of Love* (1985) contained his correspondence.

Merulo, Claudio Italian composer and organist, born Corregio, 8 April 1533, died Parma, 5 May 1604. He became organist of Brescia Cathedral and later of St Mark's, Venice, and ultimately organist to the Duke of Parma and of Parma Cathedral. He composed music for the Church, including Masses and organ music.

Meschler, Moritz Swiss Jesuit spiritual writer, born Brig, 16 September 1830, died Exaeten, Holland, 3 December 1912. Meschler's spiritual doctrine, developed from personal experience, keen observation and profound reflection, emphasized the following of Christ and liturgical prayer. Among his best-known works in translation are *The Life of Jesus Christ* and *Three Fundamental Principles of the Spiritual Life.*

Meško, Franc Ksaver Slovene priest and author, born Kljucarovci, Lower Styria, 28 October 1874, died Sele, 12 January 1964. Ordained in 1898, Meško settled in the mountain village of Uršlja Sela, which became part of Yugoslavia. His novel *Kaur plavemo* stressed the need for Christian values in contemporary life; he developed a simple and direct style of writing which went well with his depiction of village and peasant life, e.g. in his long novel *Na Poljani*. He also wrote plays, of which *Mati* has enjoyed wide popularity. Meško suffered much persecution as a patriot Slovene during the German occupation in both world wars, and he fled to Bosnia in the second.

Mesrop (Mesrob) Saint, patriarch, an important figure in Armenian culture, born Hassik, province of Taron, *c.*361, died Valarsabad, 441, a year after becoming patriarch. The correct version of his name is probably 'Mashtotz' and his life is told in a biography by his pupil Korium in the middle of the fifth century. Mesrop was skilled in languages, being knowledgeable in Greek, Persian and Syriac, and was secretary to King Chosroes II. In 390 he abandoned this life for first the life of a monk and then that of a missionary, which led to his commissioning a translation of the Bible into Armenian for the use of his converts. There being no Armenian alphabet at the time, he devised one, adopted in 406, from which developed an independent Armenian literature and culture. He created schools across the country to teach the new alphabet, and adapted it for other neighbouring regions he evangelized. He succeeded Sahak III as partriarch in 440.

Messiaen, Olivier Eugène Prosper Charles French composer and organist, born Avignon, 10 December 1908, died Clichy, near Paris, 27 April 1992. His father Pierre was a scholar of English literature, his mother Cécile a poet. He early developed an aptitude for music and when eleven years old entered the Paris Conservatoire, where he was taught by the organist Marcel Dupré and the composer Paul Dukas. In 1931 he became organist at the Church of the Trinity, Paris. At the outbreak of war he joined the army, and was soon captured. On release from the Görlitz internment camp he returned to La Trinité and to teaching at the Conservatoire, where Stockhausen and Boulez were among his pupils. A great deal of his music has a sacred theme, and was inspired by his Roman Catholicism.

Messina, Giuseppe Sicilian Jesuit orientalist, born San Cataldo, 6 January 1893, died Messina, 28 June 1951. An authority on the history, language and religion of Iran, Messina taught on ancient oriental religions, their relation to Christianity and to the post-exilic history of the Jewish people, at the Pontifical Biblical Institute, and directed the series Biblica et Orientalia, in which he edited the text, with a translation and introduction, of the Persian version of **Tatian**'s *Diatessaron* in the Medici Laurentian Library in Florence.

Messmer, Sebastian Gebhard Swiss-born American Roman Catholic archbishop and educator, born Goldach, 29 August 1847, died there, 3 August 1930. Ordained in 1871, Messmer taught at the Catholic University of America before becoming bishop of Green Bay, Wisconsin, where he built schools, asylums and hospitals, promoted rural settlement and sponsored the American Federation of Catholic Societies. He opposed Prohibition, women's suffrage and labour unions, which he regarded as based on socialism. Appointed archbishop of Milwaukee in 1903, he remained there 27 years and gave generous support to Marquette University and St Mary College. Among his published works are *Canonical Procedure in Criminal Cases of Clerics* and *Outlines of Bible Knowledge*.

Meštrović, Ivan Yugoslav sculptor and nationalist, born Vrpolje, Croatia, 15 August 1883, died South Bend, Indiana, 16 January 1962. Inspired by Roman sculpture at Split, and by his studies at Vienna, Meštrovic had a show in Paris in 1910, where **Rodin** referred to him as 'the greatest phenomenon of our day'; he won international fame, a London show in 1915, and became director of Zagreb Academy. Imprisoned briefly during the Second World War, he afterwards taught in the USA at Syracuse and Notre Dame Universities. Religious themes dominate his work: *Mary Magdalen, Gregory, bishop of Nin, Cardinal Stepinac, Christ on the Cross, The Annunciation, Queen of the Universe*. Meštrovic is represented in the great museums of the world, and his work is said to compare in scale and power with that of **Michelangelo**.

Methodia of Kimolos Greek Orthodox saint, recluse and healer, born island of Kimolos, 10 November 1865, died there, 5 October 1908. She was widowed early and took monastic vows but lived entirely alone in a little mountain cell, only leaving it to receive Communion on Sundays. She received large numbers of (only) female visitors and is an example of a 'spiritual mother'. She was never formally canonized but her body was enshrined in a new church, a service was composed in her honour and she was entered into the Greek Church calendar of saints. Feast day 5 October.

Methodius Saint, archbishop, born Thessalonica, *c*.815, died Velehrad (Czech Republic), 6 April 885. He and his brother St **Cyril** were born into a senatorial family and both became priests. They were sent, *c*.863, to Moravia as missionaries at the request of the local ruler, who wanted the liturgy and the Bible in the vernacular. In Moravia they encountered German missionaries, who distrusted them, and they decided to return to Constantino-

ple. They were, however, invited to Rome by Pope **Nicholas I**, though they were received there by his successor, **Adrian II**, who consecrated both of them bishops and created the Archdiocese of Sirmium for Methodius. The Germans continued to oppose him, however, and for a time he was imprisoned and only released on the instruction of Pope **John VIII**. Some claimed that the use of Slavonic in the liturgy was contrary to orthodoxy, but Pope John supported Methodius and confirmed him as archbishop. He and his brother were declared patron saints of Europe, with St **Benedict**, by John Paul II. Feast day 11 May in the East, 14 February in the West.

Methodius of Olympus Bishop(?) and saint: his life is clouded with uncertainty. He may have been bishop of Olympus (Lycia) but Tyre, Patara and Philippi are also associated with his name. He may also have died a martyr's death in 311. He is, we know for sure, the author of *Symposion*, a dialogue in which ten young women praise the virtue of virginity. Several other writings are preserved only in fragments or in a Palaeoslavonic translation. Feast day 18 September.

Metochites, George Byzantine theologian, born, place unknown, *c*.1250, died in exile, *c*.1328. Archdeacon of Hagia Sophia in Constantinople, George Metochites supported the policy of Patriarch **John XI** Beccus and Emperor Michael VIII Palaeologus in their efforts to achieve union with Rome, and participated in the Council of Lyons (1274), where it was concluded. When the union came to an end under Emperor **Andronicus II Palaeologus** in 1282, he was imprisoned and exiled for the rest of his life, despite his son, Theodore, having become first minister of the Byzantine Empire in 1316. George wrote a *Historia dogmatica* on the origin of the schism between Rome and the East after 1274, most valuable for events in his own lifetime.

Metrophanes Critopoulos Patriarch of Alexandria, born Beroea, Macedonia, 1589, died Wallachia, 20 May 1639. As a young monk he was sent to England by **Cyril Lucaris** to study theology and forge links between Anglicanism and Orthodoxy. His theology was eirenic for the period but certainly not Calvinist like his master's. As patriarch of Alexandria he signed the latter's condemnation in 1638. He has been cited as an early ecumenist.

Metrophanes of Smyrna Bishop, born probably in Constantinople, died 887. He was bishop of Smyrna when Patriarch Ignatius was deposed and leader of the bishops who excommunicated **Photius** in 858. He was sent into exile but came back to his see in 867 when Photius was first deposed. He was at the Council in Constantinople in 869 and again condemned Photius. Even after the death of Ignatius in 877, and when appointed by **John VIII**, Metrophanes still refused to recognize Photius and was again banished and in 880 was excommunicated.

Mettenleiter, Johann Georg German musician, born St Ulrich, Württemberg, 6 April 1812, died Regensburg, 6 October 1858. A pioneer of the Church music reform initiated in Regensburg and known as the 'Caecilian' movement, Mettenleiter, with his priest brother, Dominikus, stimulated interest in chant restoration at the Alte Kapelle. Through their collaboration with Karl Proske, the Alte Kapelle also became a centre of activity for the revival of classic polyphony, another of the objectives of Caecilian reform.

Metzger, Max Josef German Roman Catholic priest and peace worker, born Schopfheim, Germany, 3 February 1887, died, by beheading at the hands of the Nazis, in a Berlin prison, 17 April 1944. He was ordained just before World War I, during which he served as an army chaplain, an experience that set him on a life dedicated to promoting peace. He founded the World Peace League and the World Congress of Christ the King and was a founder member of the ecumenical movement Una Sancta. His conflicts with the Nazi regime began in 1934 and he was arrested and imprisoned for the last time in 1943. He was charged with treason and sentenced to death after letters to overseas bishops were intercepted. He had called on them to help in peaceful negotiations to end the war.

Meurin, Sébastien Louis French Jesuit missionary, born Charleville, 26 December 1707, died Prairie du Rocher, Illinois, 23 February 1777. Meurin went to Canada in 1741 and then to the French areas of Illinois near the Mississippi in 1746. A new governor, Philippe d'Abbadie, expelled the Jesuits, and in 1768 when the territory had become English, Meurin offered obedience to Bishop Jean Olivier **Briand** of Quebec, who named him vicar-general of the French settlements; however, the Spanish commandant exiled him and he went to Illinois, where he settled under English rule at Prairie du Rocher. He ministered in the newly founded St Louis, Missouri, and built a log cabin church there in 1770; when the Society were suppressed in 1773, Meurin laboured as a secular priest under the bishop of Quebec.

Mey, Gustav German Roman Catholic theologian, born Neukirch, 2 July 1822, died Schworzkirch, 22 June 1877. Ordained in 1847, Mey took up pastoral work and became an influential pastoral theologian and catechist with writings, such as *Vollständigen Katecheser für die untere Klasse der Katholische Volksschule*, that link catechetics to a living liturgy, and a kerygmatic theology that invites active participation of the young by means of organically structured teaching units. He influenced both the Munich and Viennese schools of catechetics.

Meyendorff, John Orthodox priest, theologian and historian, born Paris, 17 February 1926, died New York, 22 July 1992. Born of Russian *émigré* parents, he taught at the St Sergius Institute, before moving to America in 1959. He was dean of St Vladimir's Seminary, 1984–92, where he taught patristics and Church history. He contributed numerous articles to its learned quarterly as well as writing many important monographs. His chief works include *A Study of Gregory Palamas* (1959), *Christ in Eastern Christian Thought* (1969) and *Byzantine Theology* (1973).

Meyer, Albert Gregory American cardinal and archbishop, born Milwaukee, Wisconsin, 9 March 1903, died Chicago, Illinois, 9 April 1965. Ordained in 1926, trained in biblical studies, Meyer became in 1953 archbishop of Milwaukee, where he embarked on a building programme of schools, churches, convents, hospitals and a new college; he was subsequently equally effective in Chicago, as archbishop and cardinal. A great leader also in the spiritual realm, he fought hard for justice to black persons, and became a chairman of the National Conference on Religion and Race, 1963. At Vatican Council II, Meyer brought his influence to bear on all the major schemas that were produced. Many observers considered him to be the intellectual and moral leader of the USA hierarchy.

Meyer, Conrad Ferdinand Swiss poet and novelist, born Zurich, 11 October 1825, died Kilchberg, near Zurich, 28 November 1898. He studied in France and Italy, and attempted in his writing to create a counterpart to the style of **Michelangelo** in art. Meyer's writings include the prose narratives, *The Saint*, which deals with the conflict between **Thomas Becket** and King Henry II, and *The Monk's Wedding*.

Meynard, André French Dominican theologian, born Lyons, 4 May 1824, died Bourg-en-Bresse, 2 August 1904. The influence of **Lacordaire** led Meynard to the Friars Preachers, and he preached missions until forced by ill health to abandon the pulpit in 1856. He founded the congregation of Third Order Dominican Sisters in 1860 for the care of the sick. As a spiritual theologian he wrote *Traité de la vie intérieure* and *Catéchisme de la vie intérieure et religieuse*, which illustrate his view of the Thomistic tradition that ascetical theology is the study of a soul's progress towards perfection with the ordinary helps of grace, and that mystical theology treats of the extraordinary acts and phenomena of the interior life.

Meynell, Alice Christiana Gertrude English essayist and poet, born Barnes, near London,, 22 September 1847, died London 27 November 1922. The Thompson family spent a great deal of time in Italy and France, and Alice was largely educated by her father, but it was under her mother's influence – her mother became a Roman Catholic in 1870 – that she converted to Catholicism in 1872. She married Wilfrid Meynell in 1877, and together they collaborated on many literary projects, editing *The Weekly Register* and *Merry England*. They were friendly with a wide range of nineteenth-century literary figures, including Coventry **Patmore** and Francis **Thompson**, whom they were the first to publish. She produced several books of essays, mainly from the many periodicals

to which she contributed, but is best known for her poems, which are deeply religious.

Mezger, Franz German Benedictine teacher, born Ingolstadt, 25 October 1632, died Salzburg, 11 December 1701. Brother of Joseph and Paul **Mezger.** He taught philosophy and theology at Salzburg, wrote 10 works on these subjects and made numerous translations from the Maurists, mainly of ascetical treatises.

Mezger, Joseph German Benedictine teacher, born Eichstätt, 5 September 1635, died abbey of St Gallen, Switzerland, 26 October 1683. Brother of Franz and Paul **Mezger.** He taught hermeneutics and polemics at Salzburg and became vice-chancellor and an intimate friend of Jean **Mabillon**, the humanist scholar, who called him 'the most prominent light of the university'.

Mezger, Paul German Benedictine teacher, born Eichstätt, 23 November 1637, died Salzburg, 12 April 1702. Brother of Franz and Joseph **Mezger**. He also taught at Salzburg and succeeded Joseph as vice-chancellor. Of his 33 works, Martin **Grabmann**, the medieval historian, has praised *Theologia scholastica secundus viam et doctrinam d. Thomae* as one of the best presentations of Thomistic theology.

Mezzabarba, Carlo Ambrogio Italian patriarch of Alexandria, born Pavia, c.1685, died Lodi, 7 December 1741. **Clement XI** sent Mezzabarba to the Sino-Manchu emperor in 1719 to seek his support against Jesuit adoption of Chinese rites; K'ang Hsi received him with much honour, but refused absolutely the anti-rites decree and threatened reprisals if it were enforced. Mezzabarba left China in 1721 and his confessor, the Servite Sostegno Viani, wrote a diary of events, *Giornale della Legazione*, which criticized the Peking Jesuits for their part in the affair.

Mezzofanti, Giuseppe Italian cardinal and librarian, born Bologna, 17 September 1774, died Rome, 15 March 1849. A prodigious memory enabled Mezzofanti to master some 40 languages, to have a fair knowledge of 30 more and to have familiarity with some 45 dialects. Ordained in 1797, he taught various languages at Bologna before going to Rome in 1833 as canon of the basilica of St Mary Major, and prefect of the Vatican Library. He contributed much to the science of comparative linguistics.

Michael I (of Antioch) Patriarch and historian, known as 'Michael the Syrian', born Melitene (Malatya, Turkey), 1126, died 1199. Previously a monk and archimandrite at the monastery of Bar-Sauma, Michael became patriarch of Antioch in 1166. As such, he worked to reform the lax ways of the Monophysite Church and struggled with a rival for the patriarchate. He had good relations with the West and was invited to (though he did not attend) the Third Lateran Council. His major work is a history of the world from the Creation until 1199 in Syriac, most useful for its observations on events of Michael's time.

Michael III (of Constantinople) Patriarch from 1170 to 1178, born Anchialos (Bulgaria) and was educated by the archbishop there. After serving in several other ecclesiastical posts, he was named patriarch of Constantinople in late 1169. He dealt with several controversies, saw the condemnation of Constantine of Kerkyra, and opposed the work of Emperor Manuel I Comnenus and Pope **Alexander III** to unify the Orthodox Church with Rome (saying that he would rather be united with the Turks than with Rome). He also worked against the reunification with the Armenian and Jacobite Churches. A number of his letters and synodal acts survive.

Michael Cerularius Patriarch of Constantinople, born Constantinople, c.1005, died the Hellespont, 21 January 1059. He was a member of a senatorial family, and was involved in a coup attempt against the Emperor Michael IV. In an effort to escape punishment he became a monk. He was appointed Patriarch on 25 March 1043 by the Emperor Constantine IX, but he was intransigent over dealings with Rome, which Constantine wished to placate, and his attitude led to the reciprocal excommunication of 1054, which is usually taken as the definitive breach between Constantinople and the papacy (though the papal representative, Humbert, was himself disinclined to negotiate). Michael became increasingly powerful in Constantinople, effectively running the government until he clashed with the Emperor Isaac I Commenus. He

threatened to destroy Isaac, but the Emperor had the support of the liberal intellectuals of the city, as well as the military. He was deposed on 2 November 1058 and arrested. It was too dangerous to put him on trial in the city itself, where he was a popular figure, and he was sent for trial elsewhere, but died on the journey.

Michael de Northburgh English bishop and diplomat, date and place of birth unknown, died Copford, Essex, 9 September 1361. A minister of the king, **Edward III** sent Michael to the Pope in 1345 to obtain a dispensation for the Black Prince to marry a daughter of the duke of Brabant; he did not succeed. He became the king's secretary and Keeper of the Privy Seal, and represented Edward in France, Flanders and Rome. Appointed bishop of London in 1354, and impressed by the French Carthusians, he founded the London Charterhouse, to which he left £2000, as well as £1000 to St Paul's Cathedral. He died of the plague.

Michael de Sanctis Saint, Spanish mystic, born Vich, Catalonia, 1591, died Valladolid, 10 April 1625. Michael made a vow of chasity at the age of eight, joined the Order of Trinitarians at Barcelona and became a priest in Portugal. He displayed extraordinary mystical gifts, such as levitation when rapt in ecstasy; while preaching in Salamanca, he is reported to have been raised into the air in sight of all his audience. A famous preacher, his favourite topic was the ransom of Christian captives of the Moors. **Pius IX** canonized him in 1862. Feast day 10 April.

Michael of Cesena General of the Franciscan Order, born Cesena, Central Italy, 1270, died Munich, 29 November 1342. He studied in Paris and taught in Bologna, before being elected minister general in 1316. He took over the Order at a time when there was division in its ranks. One group (Spirituals) espoused poverty after the way of **Francis**, the other (Community) adhered to a notion of the 'poor use' of possessions as laid down by papal decree. Michael's support of **William of Ockham**, who supported the Spirituals, earned him an excommunication by Pope **John XXII** in 1328. Michael (and Ockham) sided with **Louis** of Bavaria against John XXII, and Michael was replaced as minister general at a General

Chapter of the Order at Paris in 1329, even though only a year before he had been confirmed in office. In 1331 he was expelled from the Franciscans.

Michael Psellus *see* Psellus, Michael.

Michael Scott Scholar, priest, born Scotland *c.*1175, died 1235. Studied mathematics and probably theology at Durham, Oxford and Paris. From Paris he went to Bologna and then, in about 1200, to the court of **Frederick II** in Sicily. In 1209 he went to Toledo, where he met Arabian scholars and learned Arabic, as well as astronomy and alchemy. He returned to Palermo in about 1220 and turned his attention to the study of science and medicine. He was offered, but refused, the See of Cashel in Ireland. He was also offered the See of Canterbury, but local opposition seems to have prevented this appointment. He was at Oxford in 1230, apparently with books on physics and mathematics, as well as copies of works of Aristotle. He acquired a reputation as a magician and appears in several works of literature, including works by **Dante**, **Boccaccio** and Walter Scott, as well as in Italian and Scottish folklore. His writings include *Abbreviato Avicennae* (1210), *Liber physiognomiae. Astronomia, Liber luminis luminum* and *De Alchemia*. He translated the works of Averroes, and Aristotle's *Ethics* from Greek into Latin.

Michaelis, Johann David Protestant biblical critic, born Halle, 27 February 1717, died Göttingen, 22 August 1791. A writer of immense output, he was professor of philosophy, 1746–50, and professor of oriental languages, 1750–91, at the University of Göttingen. His studies concentrated on early versions of the Bible, in particular the Syriac text, the Peshitta. His work on the Mosaic Law (1770–5) was very influential in the development of biblical scholarship in Germany. He also wrote widely in the field of OT studies, on the Messianic Psalms (1759), on Ecclesiastes (1762) and on 1 Maccabees (1776). He also wrote NT and OT introductions. Much of his work was foundational for future critical scholarship

Michaud, Joseph François French editor and historian, born Albens, 19 June 1767, died Passy, 30 September 1839. A historian of the Crusades, Michaud viewed them not merely as religious movements, but as forces with far-reaching consequences in a changing Europe. He wrote several celebrated texts on the subject; his great work is *Recueil des historiens des croisades*, indispensable in situating the Crusades in the historical perspective of European civilization.

Michel, Anton German Roman Catholic cleric and historian, born Ebersberg, Bavaria, 19 December 1884, died Munich, 10 May 1958. Ordained in 1909, Michel taught at Freising Hochschule, where he developed his interest in Byzantine studies, in particular the Byzantine Church and the Eastern Schism. Largely self-taught, his influence in this field, through more than 50 books, and articles in the leading journals, has been profound; though his conclusions have been criticized by some Church historians, his methodology has been widely used, and he contributed greatly to a revival of interest in Byzantine studies.

Michel, Virgil American Benedictine liturgist, born St Paul, Minnesota, 26 June 1890, died Collegeville, 26 November 1938. Ordained in 1916, Michel studied in Europe, where he appreciated the importance of the liturgical movement; upon his return to America he persuaded his superiors of the need for similar studies, and founded the magazine *Orate Fratres* in 1925, and a few years later the Liturgical Press. He contributed greatly to the movement in America, in particular by his insistence on the beneficial consequences of the liturgy in all aspects of human life. A leader in Catholic social action during the Depression years, he spoke out forcefully for a society based on an adequate philosophy of human and spiritual values.

Michelangelo Buonarroti Italian painter, sculptor, architect and poet, born Caprese, 6 March 1475, died Rome, 18 February 1564. He grew up at Settignano, near Florence, among stone carvers. He was educated at Florence, apprenticed to **Ghirlandaio**, who famously said: 'This boy knows more than I do.' Michelangelo travelled to Venice, Bologna, Florence and Rome. In Rome he executed his famous sculpture *Pietà*, and in Florence his masterpiece *David*. At the Vatican he painted the ceiling of the Sistine Chapel, which took him four years to complete, and the *Last Judgement* on the altar wall. He also designed the dome of St Peter's, Rome. He was known to his contemporaries as 'the divine Michelangelo' and he was one of the most influential of artists. He also wrote sonnets, seven of which were set to music by Benjamin **Britten**.

Mickiewicz, Adam   Polish poet and revolutionary, born Zaos'ye, near Novogrudek, Belorussia, then in the Russian Empire, 24 December 1798, died Constantinople, 26 November 1855. He was educated at Vilna, where he studied German and English literature, and in 1819 became a professor at Kovno and shortly afterwards published two volumes of poetry. When in 1824 the student secret society to which he had belonged was suppressed he was banished to Russia. He now began to produce epic, Polish nationalist poems. In 1829 he was allowed to leave Russia and journeyed in Germany, France and Italy, during which time he returned to the fervent practice of Catholicism. He tried to join the Polish insurrection against Russia of 1832 but was turned back at the Prussian frontier. In his poem *Dziady III*, written in 1832 while he was in Paris, he saw Poland as Christ-like, embodying self-sacrifice and redemption. He developed Messianic theories of a new form of faith, which led to his losing his teaching post at the Collège de France. In 1848 he formally abandoned these ideas, and visited Rome, hoping to persuade the Pope to encourage Polish national freedom. When the Crimean War broke out he saw an opportunity to liberate Poland and went to Constantinople in the hope of raising a Polish legion. He contracted cholera, and died there. In 1890 his body was reinterred in Cracow Cathedral and, after Pushkin, he is regarded as the greatest Slav poet.

Middleton, Thomas Cooke   American Augustinian Church historian, born Philadelphia, Pennsylvania, 30 March 1842, died Villanova, Pennsylvania, 19 November 1923. Scion of a Quaker family Middleton entered the Roman Catholic Church in 1854, and was ordained in 1864, spending the rest of his life at Villanova College as teacher, president and secretary to the provincial. He co-founded the American Catholic Historical Society, 1884, and edited the *Records* of the Society from 1899 to 1905. His writings include *Historical Sketch of Villanova* and *Augustinians in the United States*.

Miège, Jean Baptiste   French Jesuit missionary, born La Forêt, Savoie, 18 September 1815, died Woodstock, Maryland, 21 July 1884. After ordination, Miège joined the Missouri province in 1848, and in 1850 was named vicar apostolic of a vast territory east of the Rockies, while living with the Pottawatomi Indians at St Mary's mission. He brought the Benedictines, Carmelites and Sisters of Charity to his vicarate, built an academy, an orphanage, a hospital and a seminary, and completed the cathedral of the Immaculate Conception. He resigned in 1874 and became spiritual director at Woodstock College and first president of Detroit College.

Mier, Servando Teresa de   Dominican friar and activist for Mexican independence, born Monterrey, Mexico, 18 October 1765, died Mexico City, 3 December 1827. During his life, Mier was imprisoned nine times by various ecclesiastical and secular authorities and six times managed to escape. He travelled to France and Spain, was chaplain in the Spanish military during a war against France, and spent the last fifteen years of his life in England, Mexico and the United States, working for Mexican independence. His writings *Historia de la revolución de Nueva España* (1813) and *Carta de un Americano al Español sobre su numero XIX* were written to promote that cause.

Migazzi, Christoph Anton   Roman Catholic prince-archbishop, born Innsbruck, Austria, 23 November 1714, died Vienna, 15 September 1803. Scion of a poor Tyrolese noble family, Migazzi served Empress Maria Theresa as coadjutor to the archbishop of Mechelen (Belgium) and as Austrian ambassador to Spain. Once elected prince-archbishop of Vienna on 18 March 1757, and created cardinal by Pope **Clement XIII** in 1761, he was forced to oppose the empress and her son, **Joseph II**, in their complete subjugation of the church to the Austrian state. His hundreds of petitions and memoranda over 46 years met with no success, and earned him only the contempt of the emperors. He died in Vienna and was buried in St Stephen's Cathedral.

Migne, Jacques Paul French Roman Catholic priest, ecclesiastical publisher and patrologist, born Saint-Flour, near Orléans, 25 October 1800, died Paris, 24 October 1875. Having studied and been ordained in Orléans, Migne moved to Paris in 1833. After three years in ecclesiastical journalism, he began a planned 2000-volume library for the clergy. A genius at organization and inventor in the science of printing, he published 842 volumes in eleven series, before a fire in 1868 destroyed his presses. He rebuilt them, but was suspended by the archbishop of Paris over the use of Mass stipends in financing the work. He is most well-known for his *Series Latina* (221 vols, 1844–64), covering AD 200–1216, and his *Series Graeca*, (162 vols, 1857–66, Greek texts with Latin trans.; 81 vols, 1856–67, Latin trans. only), covering AD 120–1439.

Mignot, Eudoxe Irénée Roman Catholic archbishop, born Brancourt, France, 20 September 1842, died Albi, France, 18 March 1918. Bishop of Fréjus, 1890–9, and archbishop of Albi, 1899–1918, Mignot believed in contact between the Church and modern society. He affirmed the mystery of faith but also believed that reason was not opposed to faith. He promoted **Leo XIII**'s teaching among his clergy in *Lettres sur les études ecclésiastiques* (1900–1). He also wrote against Alfred **Loisy**'s neglect of the validity of oral tradition, in articles eventually published as *L'Église et la critique* (1910), though he sought to protect Loisy from Roman censure and afterwards worked to keep him in the Roman Catholic Church.

Mihan, Charles Venerable, Franciscan priest and martyr, born, place unknown, after 1639, died Ruthin, North Wales, 12 August 1679. Nothing is known of his early life and ordination. In 1672, his provincial approved him as a confessor for the laity. He fled Ireland for Flanders after the edicts of banishment (1673–4). After studies in Bavaria and Rome, he attempted to return to Ireland in 1678. His ship was forced to land in Wales, where he was arrested and imprisoned. His trial occurred the next year, 1679, during the Titus **Oates** scare. When he admitted to being a Catholic priest, he was condemned to death. He was hanged then cut down alive and butchered.

Milanto, Pio Tommaso Dominican theologian and bishop, born Naples, Italy, 12 August 1689, died Castellamare, Italy, 2 April 1748. Milanto became a Dominican in 1704 and taught in the Order schools from 1714. He also taught theology at the University of Naples from 1713 until his election as bishop of Castellamare in 1743. He was accused of rigorism in his moral theological doctrine, though he himself always claimed to be moderate in his opinions. Aside from a number of biographies, he is best known for his *Theses theologico-dogmatico-polemicae* (1734) and his *Vindiciae regularium in causa monasticae paupertatis* (1740), written against the anti-probabilism of Daniello **Concina**.

Milič, Jan The 'father of Czech reform', born 1305, died 1374. Served as a royal official in the court of **Charles IV**. About 1363 he left the imperial service, sold his goods and began to preach against the corruption of the clergy. Succeeding Conrad of Waldhausen as a reformer in Prague, he greatly influenced John **Huss**. In 1367 he was imprisoned by the Inquisition in Rome but was later exonerated by both **Urban V** and **Gregory XI**.

Millais, John Everett Sir, Pre-Raphaelite artist, born Southampton, 8 June 1829, died London, 13 August 1896. He was a leading member of the Pre-Raphaelite group of painters. His work has striking colours and he painted in minute detail. Christian subjects feature in his work, but Dickens attacked Millais' painting *Christ in the House of his Parents*, considering it blasphemous because of its ordinary setting. Other pictures include *The Return of the Dove to the Ark*. His portraits include that of Cardinal **Manning**.

Millar, Moorhouse Ignatius Xavier American Jesuit priest and professor, born Mobile, Alabama, 7 March 1886, died New York City, 14 November 1956. Millar became a Roman Catholic at the age of ten and finished his secondary education at Loyola High School in Baltimore, Maryland. After joining the Society of Jesus in 1903, he held various teaching posts until going to Fordham University in 1920, shortly after his ordination. From 1929 to 1953, he chaired the department of political philosophy and social sciences there. He was an associate editor of the quarterly *Thought* and the author of two books: *Church and State* (1922; with Mgr. John A. **Ryan**) and *Unpopular Essays in the Philosophy of History* (1928).

Millar, Robert Minister of Paisley Abbey, apologist for missions, born Dailly, Ayrshire, 1672, died Paisley, 16 December 1752. He studied at Glasgow University, was ordained at Port Glasgow in 1697 and was minister at Paisley Abbey from 1709 until his death. His two-volume *History of the Propagation of Christianity and Overthrow of Paganism* (Edinburgh, 1723) had 468 subscribers for its first edition and ran to a Dutch translation and two further editions (London, 1726, 1731). His writing predates Mathew **Carey** by 70 years. He advocated a missionary lifestyle of renunciation and his providential view of history and apologetic on the limitations of natural religion provided a measured approach to other religions. He also published a *History of the Church under the Old Testament* (1730).

Miller, Athanasius Benedictine biblical scholar, born Wohlfartsweiler, Germany, 22 September 1881, died Beuron, Germany, 17 April 1963. After joining the Benedictine Order at the age of 21, Miller studied at the International Benedictine College of Sant' Anselmo in Rome and at the University of Strasburg. He taught at Beuron and in 1922 became professor of OT at Sant' Anselmo. In 1940, he was appointed consultor to the Pontifical Biblical Commission, becoming its secretary in 1949. Here he encouraged Catholic biblical scholarship through many significant directives, including the 1950 instruction on teaching the Bible in seminaries. His works include *Introductio specialis in Vetus Testamentum* and a German translation of the Psalms.

Miller, William Founder of the modern Adventist movement, born Pittsfield, Massachusetts, 15 February 1782, died Hampton, New York, 20 December 1849. After being a Deist for most of his life, Miller joined the Baptist Church at the age of 34 and began preaching at the age of 49. His interpretation of Daniel and Revelation led him to predict that Christ would return on 21 March 1843, and he convinced many of the truths of this. The failure of this prediction and two subsequent ones

led to the loss of most of his followers, but one group of them, who combined his prophecies with his doctrinal ideas, eventually founded the Seventh-day Adventist Church.

Millet, Jean François Roman Catholic artist, born Gruchy, France, 4 October 1814, died Barbizon, France, 20 January 1875. Millet first studied painting in Cherbourg, then in Paris under Delaroche in 1837. In 1849, he moved to Barbizon, where he painted 'religious' representations of peasant life in a way that evoked its resignation and hopelessness. His work was not respected, most thinking it designed to incite rebellion, until 1867, when he was awarded a medal of the first class at the Paris Exposition and then the ribbon of the Legion of Honour a year later. His works include *The Sower* (1850), *The Angelus* (1859), *Man with the Hoe* (1863) and *Winter* (1869–74).

Mills, Samuel J. Congregationalist minister and missions activist, born Torrington, Connecticut, 21 April 1783, died at sea, 16 June 1818. In 1801, Mills, the son of a Congregationalist minister, experienced a conversion and call to ministry. Studying at Williams College, he influenced many students later called to mission work. While in Andover Seminary, he and others took the leading steps in founding the American Board of Commissioners for Foreign Missions. In 1816, he helped found the American Bible Society and in 1818 travelled to Africa for the American Colonization Society to buy lands near Cape Mesurado (modern Liberia) for the resettlement of American Negroes. He contracted a fever there and died on the return journey.

Milman, Henry Hart Anglican minister, poet and historian, born London, 10 February 1791, died Ascot, Berkshire, 24 September 1868. Ordained in 1816, Milman held several posts in the Church of England, including dean of St Paul's Cathedral in London, 1849. In his early career, he was noted as a poet (for works like *Fazio* (1815), *The Fall of Jerusalem* (1820) and *Belshazzar* (1822)). Later, he pioneered the translating of Sanskrit poems into English and also helped issue an edition of Horace. He also wrote historical works of varying quality, including *History of the Jews* (1830) and *The History of Latin Christianity down to the Death of Pope*

Nicholas V (1835). As dean of St Paul's, he worked to make the worship there more popular.

Milne, William Pioneer London Missionary Society missionary to Malaya, born Kennethmont, Scotland, April 1785, died Melaka, 2 June 1822. After study at Marischal College, Aberdeen, 1806–7 and at Gosport as a London Missionary Society candidate, in 1812 he was ordained, married Rachel Cowie, and left to join Robert **Morrison** in Canton. He and his family moved to Melaka in May 1815. In 1818 he became the first principal of the Anglo-Chinese College. Others joined the mission, and their material published in English, Chinese, and Malay is part of the early history of printing in the region. Milne edited the *Indo-Chinese Gleaner*, 1817–22 and a monthly magazine in Chinese. His tract *Two Friends* was widely used and he collaborated with Morrison in translating the OT into Chinese. In 1820 Glasgow University awarded him an honorary DD.

Milner, John English Roman Catholic bishop and political activist, born London, 14 October 1752, died Wolverhampton, 19 April 1826. Milner studied theology and was ordained in Douai, France, in 1777. He returned to England, to Winchester, where he pastored and helped English nuns fleeing the French Revolution. As adviser to the English vicars apostolic, he strongly fought any concession by the Catholic Church to the English Crown. In 1803, he was himself appointed vicar apostolic for the Midlands district. As such, he vigorously and controversially defended papal prerogatives, earning both the epithet 'the English Athanasius' and a request from the Congregation for the Propagation of the Faith in Rome to discontinue his writings. His best-known work is *The End of Religious Controversy* (1818).

Miltiades Pope and saint, pontificate *c.*311 to 10 January 314. Elected bishop of Rome shortly after the edict of toleration in 311, Miltiades' role in the legalization of Christianity is not known. He did, however, play a role in the Donatist controversy. At the initiative of Emperor **Constantine I**, he convened a synod in Rome to consider both the election of Caecilian as bishop of Carthage and what the response of the Church should be to those who, like Caecilian, had allegedly apostatized under persecution. At the synod, Miltiades did not endorse the strict stand of the North African bishops and confirmed the election of Caecilian, excommunicating his rival **Donatus of Carthage**. Feast day 10 January.

Miltitz, Karl von German Roman Catholic Church diplomat, born Rabenau, 1490, died near Mainz, 20 November 1529. The posthumous son of a lesser German noble, Miltitz was sent to Rome when he was 24, where, through family influence, he was made a papal notary and titular chamberlain. In September 1518, he was sent to **Frederick III of Saxony** to intervene in the imperial election and persuade Frederick to extradite Martin **Luther.** There and without his superiors' consent, he tried to negotiate with Luther, in hope of resolving the Lutheran crisis. He met Luther several times but achieved no results. He remained in Germany as a cathedral chapter member until his death by drowning in the River Main.

Milton, John English poet, born London, 9 December 1608, died London, 8 November 1674. He was educated at St Paul's School and Cambridge. His early poems include 'On the Morning of Christ's Nativity', 'Upon the Circumcision' and 'The Passion'. He contemplated taking up holy orders but did not do so. In a period of political and religious turmoil, he published a series of pamphlets in defence of civil and religious liberty, and supported the Parliamentary cause and the Commonwealth. He also wrote against episcopacy and, after his wife, the daughter of a royalist, refused to return to him after a visit home, in favour of divorce. He became Latin secretary to the Commonwealth, though he suffered from increasing blindness. At the Restoration he was deprived of office and went into hiding for a time, then devoted himself almost entirely to poetry. His *Paradise Lost*, tracing the fall of Adam and Eve, is regarded as one of the greatest masterpieces of English literature and the greatest religious poem in the English language. Among his other works are *Paradise Regained* and *Samson Agonistes*.

Ming, John Joseph Jesuit priest and sociologist, born Gyswyl, Unterwalden, Switzerland, 20 September 1838, died Parma, Ohio, 17 June 1910. Ming joined the Jesuits just before turning eighteen, studied in Aachen and the abbey of Maria Laach, and was ordained on 13 September 1868. He taught at Görz (Gorizia, Italy) until the expulsion of the Jesuits in 1872, and then went to the United States, where he was eventually assigned to St Louis University, remaining there until his death. He is best known for his contributions to the *American Catholic Quarterly Review* and for his books: *The Data of Modern Ethics Examined* (1894), *The Characteristics and the Religion of Modern Socialism* (1908) and *The Morality of Modern Socialism* (1909), which were among the first scholarly works by a Roman Catholic in sociology.

Minucius Felix Lawyer and Christian apologist, born probably in Africa, late second century, died Rome, *c*.250. Little is known of the life of this early Christian writer, other than that he studied and practised law in Rome and was probably influenced by **Tertullian**. He addressed his *Octavius* to educated pagans. Using the form of a dialogue he lays out the case for paganism in the mouth of one Caecilius and then the case for Christianity in the mouth of Octavius. At the end of the dialogue, Caecilius becomes a Christian. Minucius Felix seems anxious to propagate Christianity without giving offence, and his work contains neither a summary of Christian doctrine nor excessive biblical quotation. His work echoes both that of famous classical authors like Homer and Virgil and that of earlier Christian apologists like **Justin Martyr** and **Athenagoras**.

Miraeus, Aubert Flemish Roman Catholic Church historian, born Brussels, 2 December 1573, died Antwerp, 19 October 1640. Educated in Douai, and at Louvain under Justus **Lipsius**, Miraeus (also called 'Le Mire') spent most of his life in diocesan administration or in the diplomatic service of Albert of Austria, vice-regent of The Netherlands. He served as court chaplain in Brussels, 1615, dean of the cathedral in Antwerp, 1624, and later vicar general, 1635. He wrote voluminously on Church history (39 works), including many works on the history of various monastic orders (most of these date from 1606 to 1622). He also wrote works on the contemporary state of religion in Europe. He was best known, however, for his works (dating from abaout 1622 to 1630) on the history of what is now Belgium.

Mirbt, Carl German Lutheran Church historian, born Gnadenfrei, 21 July 1860, died Göttingen, 27 September 1929. Mirbt served two professorships in Church history: at Marburg from 1889 to 1912 and then in Göttingen from 1921 to 1928. He is best known for his (anti-Catholic) history of the Papacy, *Quellen zur Geschichte des Papsttums und des römischen Katholizismus* (1895), and for his works on 'missiology', which began to be studied as a separate science largely through his work and influence. He was also a member of the Göttingen Society of Sciences and a leading collaborator in the Evangelical Confederation in Germany.

Mirian (Meribanes) First Christian king of Iberia (East Georgia), born Iberia, *c*.282, died Iberia, 361. Mirian was a scion of the House of Mihran, one of the monarchial houses of Iran, and was made king of Iberia by the Iranians to counterbalance the Roman presence in Armenia. He was converted in 334 through the ministry of St Nino and was baptized along with his subjects by priests sent by **Constantine I** in 337. The Georgian Church venerates him as a saint.

Mistral, Frédéric Roman Catholic poet, born Maillane, France, 8 September 1830, died Maillane, 25 March 1914. Mistral was the leading proponent of the movement to restore respect to the Provençal language. His career in this began in boarding school, where his teacher Joseph Roumanille found him translating some Psalms into Provençal verse. After graduating from the University of Aix-en-Provence in law, he, along with Roumanille, founded the Félibrige, an association designed to promote the Provençal language. His works include *Mirèio* (1859), *Lou Pouème dóu Rose* (1897) and a Provençal dictionary, among many others. In 1904, he was awarded the Nobel Prize for Literature, in conjunction with the Spaniard José Echegaray y Eizaguirre.

Mistral, Gabriela (Lucila Godoy y Alcayaga) Roman Catholic poetess and diplomat, born Vicuña, Chile, 6 or 7 April 1889, died Hempstead, New York, 10 January 1957. She began her career as a rural educator. In 1922, she published her first book of poetry, *Desolación*, and thereafter her fame spread. She served Chile as representative to both the League of Nations and the United Nations, and in 1945 became the first Latin American to win the Nobel Prize for Literature. Her poetry, which is profoundly influenced by the Bible, is known for its strong emotional force, for its celebration of womanhood and for its proud connection to the poor and suffering of Latin America.

Mittarelli, Giovanni Benedetto Camaldolese historian and administrator, born Venice, 2 September 1707, died abbey of S. Michele di Murano (near Venice), 14 August 1777. Mittarelli joined the Camaldolese Order (a Benedictine Order) when he was fifteen and served it all his life. In 1747 he was made chancellor of the Order, and in 1760 returned to his home monastery of St Michele di Murano as abbot. From 1765 to 1770, he served in Rome as abbot general of the Order and was highly favoured by Pope **Clement XIII**. Mittarelli's chief work was a history of his Order, *Annales Camaldulenses ordinis S. Benedicti*, (9 vols, 1754–73).

Mitty, John Joseph Roman Catholic archbishop, born New York City, 20 January 1884, died Menlo Park, California, 15 October 1961. Orphaned at an early age, Mitty was educated at Manhattan College, St Joseph's Seminary in Yonkers, the Catholic University of America and the Lateran Seminary in Rome. After serving two pastorates and in the US military as chaplain in World War I, he was appointed ordinary bishop of Salt Lake City in 1926, at the time the youngest Roman Catholic bishop in the country. In 1932, he was appointed coadjutor archbishop of San Francisco and became archbishop in 1935. During his tenure, he was responsible for great growth in the diocese, especially during and following World War II. He is also known for his progressive action on such things as continuing education for parish priests, television ministries and ministries to migrant workers.

Mivart, St George Jackson Roman Catholic biologist, born London, 30 November 1827, died London, 1 April 1900. Though he studied law at Lincoln's Inn, Mivart never practised, preferring instead to concentrate on biology. He made several contributions to the science of anatomy and argued for a theistic form of evolution in his book *On the Genesis of Species* (1871). **Pius IX** awarded

him a doctorate in 1876 for his work in trying to reconcile Church teaching with scientific learning. His understanding of the Church as an evolving institution brought him into conflict with his bishop, and he was refused the sacraments for the two months previous to his death.

Mocquereau, André Roman Catholic musicologist, born Tessoualle, France, 6 June 1849, died Solesmes, France, 18 January 1930. After studying cello at the Paris Conservatory under Charles Dancla, Mocquereau joined the Benedictine abbey of Solesmes in 1875. There, as choirmaster and director of the scriptorium, he worked to restore the classical purity of the Gregorian chant. He developed the Solesmes system of chant notation and helped to publish fifteen volumes of photographic reproductions of old manuscripts under the title *Paléographie musicale grégorienne*.

Modjeska, Helena Roman Catholic actress, born Cracow, Poland, 12 October 1840, died East Newport, California, 8 April 1909. Modjeska began her acting career in the amateur circuits of her native Poland. She soon turned professional and gained renown throughout Europe, particularly for her work in **Shakespeare**, a number of whose plays she translated into Polish. After marrying Count Bozenta Chlapowski, she moved with him to the United States, where she continued to play Shakespearean heroines and established herself as a leading figure on the American stage. Her devout Roman Catholic faith had an influence on many of the entertainers with whom she worked, most notably the Barrymore family.

Moffat, Robert Missionary and linguist in Southern Africa, born Ormiston, East Lothian, 21 December 1795, died Leigh, Kent, 8 August 1883. He moved to Manchester, in 1813 for work and married his employer's daughter, Mary Smith, in 1819. He went to South Africa with the London Missionary Society in 1817 and was famed for converting a notorious group of bandits on the frontier. With Mary he settled among the Tswana at Kuruman. He completed a translation of the NT in Tswana in 1840 and the entire Bible in 1857. His popular *Missionary Labours* was published in 1840. The good relations he established from 1829 with the chief of the Ndebele led to the founding of a London Missionary Society mission near Bulawayo in 1859. He also influenced David Livingstone, who later married his daughter. He returned to Britain in 1871, continuing his speaking engagements until 1878.

Moffatt, James Presbyterian biblical scholar, born Glasgow, Scotland, 4 July 1870, died New York City, 27 June 1944. Moffatt was educated at Glasgow and wrote one of his most important works, *Introduction to the Literature of the New Testament* (1911), while serving as a pastor. In 1911, he began teaching NT at Oxford and in 1915 began teaching Church history at Glasgow and then at Union Theological Seminary in New York City. He is best known for his personal translation of the entire Bible, bringing the fruits of scholarly biblical studies to the general English-reading public. His translation of the NT appeared in 1913, the OT in 1923.

Mogila, Peter Slavic Orthodox metropolitan and theologian, born Moldavia (Moldova), 21 December 1596, died Kiev (Ukraine), 22 December 1646. Mogila and his family moved to Poland after his father died, and, after an unsuccessful attempt to regain his familial possessions in Moldavia, he turned to a religious vocation. In 1627, he became a monk at Pecherskaya Laura (Monastery of the Caves), one of the best-known monasteries in the Eastern Church. He was named archimandrite of the monastery after only three months and in 1633 was appointed metropolitan of Kiev, where he instituted many important reforms. His most important book was *The Orthodox Confession of Faith*, which, in its officially approved form, was considered one of the Symbolic Books of the Orthodox Church for some 200 years.

Mogrovejo, Toribio Alfonso de Roman Catholic archbishop and saint, born Spain, November 1538, died Saña, Peru, 1606. After university studies in Salamanca and Coimbra, Mogrovejo was named Inquisitor of Grenada, an important ecclesiastical post, in 1574. In this work, he gained a reputation for fairness and moderation. Despite the fact that he was not ordained, he was appointed archbishop of Lima in 1579. Through the next year, he received the necessary minor orders, was ordained, and finally consecrated bishop in 1580. In Lima, he instituted a programme of needed reform that

was eventually adopted by most of the Roman Catholic missions in the Western hemisphere. He died from an illness contracted during a pastoral visitation. In 1727, he was canonized by Pope **Benedict XIII**. Feast day 23 March.

Mohlberg, Kunibert Benedictine liturgist, born Efferen, Germany, 17 April 1878, died abbey of Maria Laach, Germany, 21 May 1963. Educated at the abbey of Maria Laach, Beuron and Louvain, Mohlberg early developed an interest in liturgy and its early history, particularly in Germany. His two major works, *Das fränkische Sacramentarium Gelasianum in alamannischer Überlieferung* (1918) and *Ziele und Aufgaben der liturgiegeschichtlichen Forschung* (1919), contributed much to liturgical renewal in Germany. For the last part of his life, he was involved in archival work, mostly in Rome and in Zurich, where he developed a new method of cataloguing old liturgical texts.

Möhler, Johann Adam German Roman Catholic priest and theologian, born Igersheim, 6 May 1796, died Munich, 12 April 1838. Möhler studied at the Catholic Academy of Ellwangen and taught at Tübingen and Munich before his early death from pneumonia, cholera and overwork. He was deeply interested in the unity of the Church, and his early work *Die Einheit in der Kirche* (1825) exhibited great sympathy for the Protestant idea of the invisible Church, for which it received criticism in Roman Catholic circles. Though he seemed to adopt more traditional Roman Catholic ideas later in life, he still serves as an admirable example of the true ecumenical spirit. His other works included *Athanasius der Grosse* (1827), *Symbolik* (1832) and *Neue Untersuchungen der Lehrgegensätze zwischen Katholiken und Protestanten* (1834).

Mohyla, Peter *see* **Peter Mogila**

Moine, Claudine French Roman Catholic mystic, born Scey-sur-Saône, 17 January 1618, died Paris, after 1655. Moine originally came from a well-to-do family, but war destroyed the family fortune, forcing her to seek employment in Paris in 1642. Not long after, she underwent a series of mystical experiences, recorded in her *Relations spirituelles*. In that work, she records and analyses her experiences of both ecstasies and spiritual darkness. Her manuscript was preserved in the Archives of the Foreign Missions in Paris.

Moleyns, Adam Bishop and statesmen, born Sefton, Lancashire (date unkown), died Portsmouth, England, 9 January 1450. Moleyns, son of Sir Richard Moleyns, was educated at Oxford, graduating in law in 1435. At the time, he was already a papal chamberlain and became the King's Proctor in Rome shortly after his graduation. He served in many ecclesiastical posts under **Henry VI**, including Keeper of the Privy Seal, 1444–9 and bishop of Chichester, 1445, making him an important political personage as well. He also studied and fostered humanism in England and maintained a literary correspondence with Aeneas Silvius Piccolomini (who later became Pope **Pius II**).

Molina, Alonso de Franciscan priest, missionary and linguist, born Spain, in Estremadura, 1512/13, died Mexico City, 1585. Molina's family moved to Mexico shortly after its conquest by Spain in 1521, and shortly after that his father died. As a boy, he learned the Nahuatl language of the Aztecs and became a translator for the Franciscan missionaries when they came in 1524. He lived with the Franciscans and joined the Order in 1527. He was known as an impressive preacher and catechist among the indigenous Mexican people. He also pioneered studies in Nahuatl, including producing a dictionary and a grammar and some translations of the Gospels and the Epistles. These translations were not published at the time, owing to the prohibition against printing the Bible in vernacular languages.

Molina, Anthony de Carthusian writer, born Villanueva de los Infantes, Spain, c.1550, died Miraflores, Spain, 21 September 1612. Molina began his religious career in the Order of Augustinian Hermits, in 1589, but eventually joined the Carthusians, seeking more rigid discipline. At the time of his death, he was prior of the Carthusian monastery of Miraflores. He is best known for his many ascetical works, which were originally written in Spanish but soon translated into many other languages. Most of his work was written for priests, but he also adapted his ideas for lay people. His best-known works are his *Instrucción de sacerdotes* (Latin edition, 1618)

and *Exercicios espirituales para personas ocupadas deseosas de su salvación* (1613).

Molina, Juan Ignacio Roman Catholic priest and naturalist, born near Talca, Chile, 20 July 1740, died Imola, Italy, 12 September 1829. Molina joined the Society of Jesus in Santiago in 1755 and was forced to flee the country when Charles III expelled the Jesuits from Chile. He went to Italy, where he continued his study of natural history, eventually teaching the subject in Bologna. The Society of Jesus was suppressed in 1773, and he did not rejoin the Order when it was restored in 1814. He is best known for the great love he bore his native country and for his scientific acumen, both evidenced in his *Saggio sulla storia naturale del Chili* (1782) and *Saggio sulla storia civile del Chili* (1787).

Molina, Luis de Spanish Jesuit theologian, born Cuenca, 1535, died Madrid, 12 October 1600. Molina became a Jesuit in Coimbra, Portugal, in 1553. After studying philosophy at Coimbra for four years and theology at Évora for fifteen, he devoted his full energies to writing. His is best known for his thoughts on the problem of free will, grace and predestination, which incorporate an idea of *scientia media*. These thoughts are contained in his *Concordia liberi arbitrii cum gratiae donis* (1588) and *Appendix ad Concordiam* (1589). His multi-volume work *De justitia et jure* also reveals his insight into problems of ethics and economics. Despite the great controversy originally surrounding his writings, Molina's doctrine of free will is considered acceptable by the Roman Catholic Church.

Molinos, Miguel de Roman Catholic priest and theologian, born Muniesa, Spain, 29 June 1628, died Rome, 28 December 1696. After studies at Valencia and an uneventful early life, Molinos was sent to Rome in 1663. There he remained, gained a reputation as a spiritual director, and wrote *A Spiritual Guide* (1675). He taught that spiritual perfection could be achieved only through contemplation, which would lead to a total abandonment to God, abandonment even of the will to act virtuously and to repel temptation. After years of controversy, in which Molinos seemed to emerge victorious, he was suddenly brought before the

Inquisition in 1685. His doctrine was condemned in 1687, and Molinos admitted his errors and accepted the imposed punishment of penitential imprisonment.

Molloy, Aloysius American Roman Catholic nun, educator, and author, born Sandusky, Ohio, 14 June 1880, died Rochester, Minnesota, 27 September 1954. She was educated at Ohio State University and was the first woman to receive a Ph.D. from Cornell, in 1907. Upon graduation, she became a founding member of the faculty of the College of St Teresa, Winona, Minnesota, of which she later became dean and president, 1928–46. She was a member of the Sisters of St Francis, served on numerous Catholic education councils and committees, and was honoured with the papal cross *Pro Ecclesia et Pontifice*, 1918. Among her numerous books are *The Lay Apostolate* (1915), *A Teresan Ideal in Service and System* (1928) and *Training the Nursing School Faculty* (1930).

Molloy, Francis Irish Franciscan writer, born Diocese of Meath, c.1606, died France, 1677. Molloy (or 'O'Molloy') became a Franciscan in Rome in 1632. He taught both philosophy and theology, the former in Klosterneuburg and Mantua, the latter in Graz and Rome. In Rome he was named procurator of the Irish Franciscans. He is best known for his Gaelic catechism, *Lucerna fidelium, Lochrann na gcreidmheach* (1676) and his Gaelic grammar, *Grammatica latino-hibernica* (1677), though neither is very original, and the grammar is often considered an inferior work.

Molloy, Thomas Edmund American Roman Catholic archbishop, born Nashua, New Hampshire, 4 September 1884, died Brooklyn, New York, 26 November 1956. Educated at St John's Seminary, Brooklyn, and the North American College in Rome, Molloy was ordained in 1908. Except for a brief term in Chicago, he served his entire career in Brooklyn. He served as assistant at St John's Chapel and at Queen of All Saints, secretary to the auxiliary bishop, and later spiritual director of Cathedral College of the Immaculate Conception and president of St Joseph's College for Women. In 1921, he was made bishop by Pope **Benedict XV** and given the personal title archbishop by Pope **Pius XII** in 1951. The diocese prospered under his leadership, and he was known and respected both in and out of the Roman Catholic Church.

Molyneux, Robert English Jesuit missionary and educator, born Lancashire, 24 July 1738, died Washington, DC, 9 December 1808. Molyneux became a Jesuit in 1757, and taught during his novitiate in Bruges (Belgium), where he met John **Carroll**, later Archbishop Carroll, who would be a lifelong supporter and friend. He was sent to America in 1771, where he served as pastor of various churches and then as the second president of Georgetown College in Washington, in 1793. He would become president there again in 1806 after working to secure the restoration of the Society of Jesus in the United States by connecting it to the Jesuits in Russia, one of the few places where the Order was not then suppressed.

Mombaer, John Monk, monastic reformer and writer, born Brussels (Belgium), 1460, died Paris, 29 December 1501. In 1480 John Mombaer (also known as 'Johannes Mauburnus' or 'John of Brussels') entered a monastery of the Congregation of Windesheim, the centre of the Devotio Moderna movement. He was superior of the monastery of Mount St Agnes and was later called to France to institute monastic reform there. Just before his death he was elected abbot of Livry. His works on spirituality, which tend to be rather rigid and mechanical but not wholly devoid of spiritual truth, include *Rosetum exercitiorum spiritualium et sacrarum meditationum* and *Venatorium sanctorum Ordinis Canonicorum Regularium*.

Mombritius, Boninus Itallian humanist, born Milan, c.1424, died before 1502. Not much is known of his life. He came from a poor but noble family, studied in Ferrara and taught at Milan. He had a reputation as a man of both learning and piety. Most of his literary output is dated between 1474 and 1481. In 1481, his professorship was given to another man, and a letter of Alexander Minuziano in 1502 speaks of him as having died. Besides publishing some of his own poetry, such as six books of *De dominica passione libri V*, he worked extensively on editions of authors such as Solon, Hesiod, **Eusebius of Caesarea** and Paul of Venice.

Monaghan, John Patrick Roman Catholic priest and activist, born Dunamore, Ireland, 12 February 1890, died New York City, 26 June 1961. Educated in the diocesan schools of New York City, Monaghan was known as a 'labour priest' for his work among unions and the working class. He helped to found the Catholic Labor Schools in 1935 and the Association of Catholic Trade Unionists (ACTU) in 1937, which organized education for union members, Catholic and non-Catholic, in basic economics, the social teaching of the Church and parliamentary procedure. He also worked for liturgical renewal and conducted a very successful youth programme. For many years he wrote a column in ACTU's organ, the *Labor Leader*, which contains a good record of his thought and activity.

Monceaux, Paul French Roman Catholic historian and archaeologist, born Auxerre, 29 May 1859, died Sceaux, France, 7 February 1941. Monceaux, a noted historian of ancient Greece and Christian North Africa, studied Hellenistic culture at the École française d'Athènes and taught in secondary schools in Algiers and Paris. He spent most of his career as professor of the Collège de France and the École des Hautes Études in Paris. Among many works are *Proxénies grecques* (1884), *La Gréce avant Alexandre* (1892) and his noted, seven-volume *Histoire littéraire de l'Afrique chrétienne depuis les origines jusqu'à l'invasion arabe* (1901–23), which is a meticulous investigation into the writings of Christian North Africa until its fall.

Monchanin, Jules French Roman Catholic diocesan priest and pioneer of inter-faith dialogue, born Fleurie, 10 April 1895, died Paris, 10 October 1957. After his training for the priesthood he seemed destined for a career as a theologian, but chose instead to serve as a chaplain to the poor. In 1939, however, he left for south India, where he was joined, just under a decade later, by Henri **Le Saux**, and together they developed an ashram at Shantivanam in Tamil Nadu. He took the name 'Swami Paramarubyananda'. He was particularly concerned with the inculturation of the Gospel in India, on which he wrote a number of articles. He was taken ill in 1957 and, after being hospitalized for a time in Pondicherry, was moved to a clinic in Paris where he died.

Mone, Franz Joseph German Roman Catholic historian, born Mingolfsheim, Baden, 12 May 1796, died Karlsruhe, 12 March 1871. Mone taught history in Heidelberg and Louvain and was for 43 years director of the General State Archives in Karlsruhe. His work as a historian was driven by his Romantic ideals and mainly focused on the history of culture, primarily German. He worked on German mythology in conjunction with the work of Jacob and Wilhelm Grimm, and his *Lateinische und griechische Messen aus dem II. bis. VI. Jahrhundert* (1850) is an important achievement in the history of Germanic liturgies. He was also responsible for starting the Church–State struggle in Baden with his anonymous *Die katholischen Zustände in Baden* (1841, 1843).

Monica Saint and mother of St **Augustine**, born Thagaste (Numidia), c.331, died Ostia (Italy) autumn, 387. Married to the pagan Patricius, who later under her influence converted to Christianity, she had three children: Navigius, Augustine and a daughter. Monica followed Augustine's spiritual growth closely, including his struggles to free himself from Manichaeism. After a futile attempt to arrange a marriage for him, she attended at Easter 387 his baptism by St **Ambrose**. She died on her way home to Africa. Feast day 27 August.

Monk, William Henry Musician, born London, 16 March 1823, died London, 1 March 1889. He worked as an organist in London in various churches and also at King's College. At Stoke Newington he established daily choral services. He held various teaching posts and was professor of music at Bedford College. He composed hymns and Church music, and was the first music editor of *Hymns, Ancient and Modern*, suggesting its title. Monk wrote music for the popular hymns 'All Things Bright and Beautiful', 'Hark a Herald Voice is Calling' and 'Abide with Me'.

Monroy e Hijar, Antônio Dominican educator and archbishop, born Querétaro, Mexico, c.1632–4, died Santiago de Compostela, 7 November 1715. Born of a highly placed Mexican family, Monroy joined the Dominican Order in 1654 and taught theology in Mexico City, at both the university and the Dominican college there. He travelled to Rome in service to his Order and was there elected master general in 1677. As such, he directed a reform of the Order's constitution. In 1685 he was made archbishop of Santiago de Compostela. He used his episcopal income to build infirmaries and churches, help the poor and amass a significant library, which the Jesuits received after his death.

Monsabré, Jacques Marie French Dominican priest and preacher, born Blois, 12 December 1827, died Le Havre, 22 February 1907. Monsabré joined the Dominican Order in 1855 and soon began to study **Thomas Aquinas**, who was to become his major influence. He began to preach regularly in 1857 and quickly gained a reputation as an outstanding preacher, filling many of the most important pulpits in Europe, including that of Notre Dame. His sermons were known for carrying on the spirit of Thomas Aquinas, addressing themselves not to the emotions but to the intellect in order to give the emotions a proper motivation and grounding. His collected sermons span 35 volumes and went through several editions.

Montaigne, Michel Eyquem de Essayist and moralist, born Périgord, France, 28 February 1533, died Périgord, 13 September 1592. Montaigne was one of the finest representatives of early French humanism. He early made the decision to remain a Roman Catholic, despite the fact that both his brother and his sister became Protestants, and he remained faithful to that Church throughout his life. His father gave him a classical education, and his first love was always reading and learning. He is remembered for his *Essays*, a three-volume work that relates his experiences and moral thought in a way both literary and appealing. Though often accused of being a universal sceptic, Montaigne's writings evince rather a scepticism about what man can do outside the uplifting grace of God.

Montalembert, Charles Forbes René de Roman Catholic historian and liberal activist, born London, 15 April 1810, died Paris, 13 March 1870. Born in England of French parents, Montalembert was raised a Catholic but was deeply influenced by the piety of his Protestant grandfather James Forbes. That piety, combined with the liberal education he received at the Lycée Bourbon and the Collège Ste-Barbe in Paris, combined in his life's work of trying to reconcile Catholicism and the

political ideals of post-revolutionary France. Though he wrote a few works of history (*Histoire de Sainte Elisabeth de Hongrie* (1836) and *Les Moines de L'Occident* (1860–77)), he is best known for his orations and articles in *Le Correspondant* on the role of the Church in a constitutional society and on the necessity of religious freedom.

Montani, Nicola Aloysius Roman Catholic Church music reformer, born Utica, New York, 6 November 1880, died Philadelphia, Pennsylvania, 11 January 1948. After studies in Rome and with Solesmes scholars on the Isle of Wight, Montani was for seventeen years choirmaster at St John the Evangelist Church in Philadelphia. He co-founded the Society of St Gregory of America to further reform of liturgical music and edited the society's publication *The Catholic Choirmaster* for 34 years. He also served as a liturgical editor, diocesan music director and music professor. For his work, he was awarded the first liturgical music award from the Society of St Gregory and an honorary D.Mus. from Seton Hall, both in 1947.

Montanus A second-century prophet, dates and places of birth and death unknown, though his preaching centred on Pepuza in Phrygia (now Turkey) and dated from either 156 or 172. He was probably a recent convert to Christianity: **Jerome** claimed he had been a priest of Cybele. He was associated in his preaching with two prophetesses, Prisca and Maximilla. They believed that the heavenly Jerusalem was shortly to descend on Pepuza, and preached an ascetical doctrine to prepare for it. It had a considerable influence, especially in North Africa.

Montanus, Arias Spanish Roman Catholic exegete and linguist, born Frejenal de la Sierra, Estremadura, 1527, died Seville, 6 July 1598. Montanus studied in Seville and Alcalá and earned distinction for his scholarly help to the Council of Trent. In 1568, he was appointed by **Philip II** to edit the Antwerp Polyglot Bible (1571–80). His critics charged that he tampered with the biblical text, but he was officially cleared of such charges in 1580. After this work, he was put in charge of the Escorial Library and made a professor of oriental languages. Aside from the Polyglot Bible, he also published *Antiquitatum judaicarum libri IX* (1593).

Even today, scholars acknowledge his great learning and contribution to the study of Middle Eastern languages.

Montavon, William F.   American Roman Catholic welfare executive, born Scioto County, Ohio, 14 July 1874, died Washington, DC, 15 February 1959. After studies at Notre Dame University, Indiana, the Institut de Sainte-Croix, Paris, and the Catholic University of America, Montavon served the United States government in Peru as commercial attaché, 1915–18 and representative of the International Petroleum Co., 1918–25. From 1925 to 1951, he was director of the legal department of the National Catholic Welfare Conference, in which capacity he helped with Church–State relations in Mexico, Haiti and Spain, as well as wrote and lectured about health, education and welfare. He was awarded the Catholic Action Medal in 1939 and the Order of St Gregory the Great by Pope **Pius XII** in 1945.

Montcheuil, Yves de   Roman Catholic priest and theologian, born Paimpol, France, 30 January 1900, died Grenoble, France, 10 August 1944. Montcheuil earned his doctorate in theology from the Gregorian University in Rome and taught at the Institut Catholique de Paris from 1935 until his death. He was active in the Catholic Action movement in France and was shot by German soldiers in Grenoble for giving the last rites to members of the French Resistance. His works, all published posthumously, include *Malebranche et le quiétisme*, *Problèmes de vie spirituelle* and *L'Église et le monde actuel*.

Monte, Philippe de   Flemish Roman Catholic composer, born Mechelen (Belgium), 1521, died Prague (Czech Republic), 4 July 1603. Monte began his career as a composer in Italy, but soon joined the court of **Philip II** and travelled with him to both Antwerp and England. In 1568, he was appointed imperial chapelmaster by Maximilian II, a post he held until his death. Monte is best known for his prolific production of madrigals (over 1500 of them) and for his choral Masses and motets. A member of the musical movement of Flemish polyphony, his works are considered conservative and melodic but imbued with a mystical fervour. In his time, his fame was equal to that of

Giovanni da **Palestrina**, though he is less remembered today.

Monteiro da Vide, Sebastião   Roman Catholic archbishop and canon lawyer, born Monforte do Alentejo, Portugal, 19 March 1643, died Salvator, Bahia, Brazil, 7 September 1722. Da Vide was briefly a Jesuit in his youth but left the Order to study canon law in Coimbra. After ordination, he was an ecclesiastical judge and vicar general of Lisbon. In 1701, he was named bishop of Bahia. He was responsible for the first diocesan synod in Portuguese America, but his greatest contribution was to the canonical reform of the Brazilian dioceses with his *Constituições Primeiras do Arcebispado da Bahía*, which he developed for his diocese but which became the model for all Brazilian dioceses into the nineteenth century. His diocese prospered under his leadership, and his application of canon law to the colonial situation was praised by his European counterparts.

Montemayor, Juan Francisco   Roman Catholic priest and lawyer, born Huesca, Spain, 25 August 1620, died Huesca, 1685. Montemayor (also known as 'Montemayor de Cuenca') became a judge in Huesca and judge of the appeals court in Catalonia in 1641. In 1650, he travelled to the Americas as judge for the appeals court of Santo Domingo. In 1653, he became governor of that Spanish territory, as well as captain-general and president of that court of appeals. His performance of these duties led him to be appointed judge to the appeals court of Mexico, and he was ordained during his 22-year tenure there. Known for his juridical skill in maritime law, his most noted work is his *Discurso* on sea warfare and the treatment of naval prisoners of war.

Monterroso, José Benito   Roman Catholic priest and political activist, born Montevideo, Uruguay, 20 June 1780, died Montevideo, 10 March 1838. Monterroso became a Franciscan in 1798. He taught theology for a year, 1810–11, until he left Montevideo to work against the colonial government and for the revolution of Artigas, whom he apparently served as adviser and secretary and upon whom he seemed to have considerable influence. He later supported Francisco Ramírez, and, after Ramírez's overthrow, he left Uruguay to travel in Argentina and Chile. He returned in 1834 but was soon exiled for his political connections. He went to Rome to petition to leave the Franciscan Order and eventually was allowed to return to Montevideo for the last two years of his life.

Montesino, Antonio   Spanish Dominican missionary, born c.1486, died in the West Indies, 1530. Joined the Dominicans in Salamanca. He was one of the first group of Dominicans, under the leadership of Pedro of Córdoba, to land in 1510 in Hispaniola. He was increasingly outraged by the condition and treatment of the native peoples by the Spanish settlers and was one of the first to speak out publicly against it. He was sent back to Spain, where he took his concerns to the king and some steps were taken to rectify the situation. In 1526 he went with Anthony de Cervantes and several hundred colonists to Guandape and onto what is now US territory and it is thought that Mass was said for the first time here. In 1528 he went to Venezuela. He wrote *Informatio juridica in Indorum defensionem.*

Montesinos, Luis de   Spanish Dominican theologian, died 7 October 1621. Entered the Dominicans and studied and later taught philosophy and then theology. He taught Thomistic theology for over 30 years at Alcalá, was exceedingly popular for his teaching and in his person and was referred to as 'Doctor clarus'. He wrote *Commentaria in primum secundae S. Thomae.*

Monteverdi, Claudio   Italian Roman Catholic priest and composer, born Cremona, 15 May 1567, died Venice, 29 November 1643. He studied with **Ingegneri**, served the duke of Mantua and became director of music at St Mark's, Venice. His Church music, which includes three Masses, is often in a mix of new and old styles. The old style is of solemn polyphony; the new style is brilliant and baroque with solos, chorus and instruments. His Church music was inspired by the antiphonal possibilities occasioned by the galleries at St Mark's, Venice. Much of his Church music, such as his *Vespers of the Blessed Virgin* of 1610, was completely forgotten until it was revived only in the twentieth century.

Montfaucon, Bernard de   Maurist patristic scholar, born 1655, died 1741. He was a soldier but joined the Maurist Benedictines in 1676. He is best known for his *Bibliotheca bibliothecarum* (1739), but his writings include an edition of the works of **Athanasius** (1698), *Collectio nova patrum et scriptorum graecorum* (1706), *Palaeographia graeca* (1708), an edition of **Origen**'s *Hexapla* (1713) and a major edition of the works of **John Chrysostom** (13 vols, 1718–38).

Montgomery, Carrie Judd   Minister, writer and social worker, born 1858, died 1946. Montgomery was raised in Buffalo, New York, and in 1880 experienced a healing, described in *The Prayer of Faith* (1880). She was associated with the Holiness movement, the Christian and Missionary Alliance, the Salvation Army and, from 1908, the Pentecostal movement. With her husband she established the Home of Peace in Oakland, California, and developed an orphanage, a training centre for missionaries and a rescue home for girls. She founded *Triumphs of Faith* magazine in 1881, and edited it until 1946. Her books include *Secrets of Victory* (1921), *Heart Melody* (1922) and *Under His Wings* (c.1936).

Montgomery, James   Poet, born Irnine, Ayrshire, 4 November 1771, died Sheffield, 30 April 1854. He was the son of a Moravian minister and educated at the Moravian school at Fulneck, near Leeds. After various unskilled jobs he settled in Sheffield, eventually becoming editor of *Sheffield Iris*. He was twice imprisoned for writing political features. He supported the Bible Society, and denounced social evils such as the slave trade and child chimney sweeps. He supported the Wesleyan Methodists. His political writings are now less known than his hymns, of which he wrote over 400. Montgomery's most popular hymn is the carol 'Angels from the Realms of Glory'.

Moody, Dwight Lyman   Evangelist, born East Northfield, Massachusetts, 5 February 1837, died Northfield, Massachusetts, 22 December 1899. He was converted in Boston and moved to Chicago in 1856, becoming a successful shoe salesman. A Sunday School he started in the slums in 1858 became a church in 1863. He worked under the YMCA, organized Sunday School Teachers' conventions, and visited England in 1867. A preaching tour to Britain, 1872–5, accompanied by the singer Ira **Sankey** brought an enthusiastic response, as did their *Sankey and Moody Hymn Book* (1873). After similar missions in Brooklyn, Philadelphia, New York and Boston, Moody founded the North-field Seminary for Young Women in 1879 and the Mount Hermon School for Young Men in 1881. A second tour to Britain, 1881–4, included universities. In 1889 he helped found what became the Moody Bible Institute.

Moor, Michael   Irish Roman Catholic priest, provost of Trinity College, Dublin, preacher and teacher, born Dublin, 1640, died Paris, 22 August 1726. Studied at Nantes and Paris and taught philosophy and rhetoric. In 1684 he returned to Ireland, was ordained priest and appointed vicar general in the Diocese of Dublin. After the Glorious Revolution of 1688 Moor was appointed provost of Trinity College, Dublin – a post which no Catholic had held – and managed to prevent damage to the library and avoided the looting and burning of its collections. He offended King **James II** and in 1690 retired and went to Paris, and when James went there after the Battle of the Boyne, Moor moved to Rome. He became Censor of the Books and later professor of Greek and philosophy and rector of the college at Montefiascone. In 1701, after the death of James, Moor went back to Paris and became rector of the university, as well as principal of the Collège de Navarre and professor of Hebrew, Greek and philosophy at the Collège de France. With Farrelly he purchased a house near the Irish College for impoverished Irish students. His writings include *De existentia Dei, et humanae mentis immortalite, secundum Cartesii et Aristotelis doctrinum* (1692), *Hortatio ad studium linguae Graecae et Hebraeicae* (1700) and *Vera sciendi methodus* (1716).

Moore, George Foot   Presbyterian biblical scholar and theologian, born West Chester, Pennsylvania, 15 October 1851, died Cambridge, Massachusetts, 16 May 1931. After studying at Yale, Union Theological Seminary and Tübingen, Moore began teaching at Andover Seminary in 1883. He was made president there in 1899. In 1902 he began teaching at Harvard University, and from 1904 to 1928 served as Frothingham professor of history. Noted for his great learning, he wrote many books,

including *Literature of the Old Testament* (1913), *History of Religions* (2 vols, 1913–19) and *Judaism in the First Centuries of the Christian Era* (3 vols, 1927–30).

Moore, Lazarus   Archimandrite, Orthodox priest and writer, born Swindon, England, 1902, died Eagle River, Alaska, 27 November 1992. He became an Anglican missionary in India in 1933. Despite considerable Anglican opposition he was received into Orthodoxy and ordained priest in Yugoslavia in 1934 and 1936 respectively. He worked for fourteen years for the Russian Church in Jerusalem and then as a missionary in India and the USA. He helped many former evangelical groups to become Orthodox. He was a tireless translator of patristic and liturgical texts into English and his *Life of St Seraphim* (1994) has rapidly become a classic.

Moore, Thomas Verner   Roman Catholic priest, monk and psychologist, born Louisville, Kentucky, 22 October 1877, died Mira Flores, Spain, 5 June 1969. Moore began his religious career as a Paulist in 1896 and was ordained in 1901. He studied psychology at the Catholic University of America (Ph.D. 1903) and medicine at Johns Hopkins (MD 1915). After serving as a medical officer in World War I, Moore taught psychology at CUA, became a Benedictine and helped to found, in 1924, St Anselm's Priory (later Abbey), a community for scholar-priests. Upon his retirement from CUA, he moved to Spain, where he became a Carthusian, living in the monastery at Mira Flores until his death. His works include *Principles of Ethics* (1935) and *Driving Forces of Human Nature and their Adjustment* (1948).

Mora, José María Luis   Roman Catholic political theorist, born near Guanajuato, Mexico, 1793, died Paris, 14 July 1850. Mora studied theology, political economy and law and was ordained a priest. However, he gave up the priesthood in 1820 after failing to get a desired ecclesiastical post. From 1821 to 1834, he edited several newspapers and served for one year, 1833–4, as Mexico's minister for education. He was exiled in 1834 and moved to Paris, where he continued to write. He served as ambassador to England 1846–50. His political thought, crucial for understanding political liberalism in Mexico, can be found in his books *Mexico y sus revoluciónes* (1836) and *Obras Sueltas* (1837).

Mora, Miguel de la   Roman Catholic bishop, born Ixtlahuacán del Río, Jalisco, Mexico, 14 August 1874, died San Luis Potosí, 14 July 1930. Mora began his seminary studies in Guadalajara in 1887, was ordained in 1897 and became bishop of Zacatecas in 1911. His diocese was soon embroiled in war as the town was taken by rebels in 1913 and again in 1914. Mora took great care to continue the work of his diocese despite this disruption. He was exiled with the rest of the bishops of Mexico in 1914 but secretly returned two years later and was again expelled. In 1921, he was made bishop of San Luis Potosí. In 1926, when Church activities were made illegal, he managed to stay in the country, in hiding, and worked until the resolution of the Church–State conflict in 1929.

Mora y del Río, José   Roman Catholic archbishop, born Pajacuarán, Michoacán, Mexico, 24 February 1854, died San Antonio, Texas, 22 April 1928. Educated in Mexico and in Rome, Mora y del Río served in several archiepiscopal positions until being appointed first bishop of Tehuantepec in 1893, where he helped improve the social conditions of the people. After serving as bishop of Tulancingo and León, he was appointed archbishop of Mexico in 1908. Soon after this, political upheaval pitted the Church in a struggle with the state of Mexico that was to last twenty years. Through all this, Mora was a strong and uncompromising advocate for the Roman Catholic Church in Mexico. In 1926 he was exiled to the United States, where he died two years later.

Morales, Cristóbal de   Spanish composer, born Seville, *c*.1500, died Málaga(?), September or October 1553. One of the brightest lights in the second generation of sacred composers in Spain, Morales served as director of music in the cathedrals of Ávila and Plasencia and was ten years, 1535–45, a singer in the papal choir in Rome, as well as chapelmaster in numerous locations in Spain. He wrote 21 Masses (his most famous, *Tu es vas electionis*, in honour of Pope **Paul III**) and his work served as a model for Church music throughout the Spanish Empire for up to a century after his death.

Morales, Francisco de   Franciscan missionary, born Soria, Spain, date unknown, died Spain, after 1580. Morales was sent to Peru in 1547 while La Gasca was governor there. From there, he went to Bolivia, where he founded a convent in La Paz and then on to Quito, Ecuador, where he spent six years working to improve the conditions of the indigenous people, including founding the Colegio de San Andrés. He was the Franciscan provincial for Peru from 1559 to 1562, during which time he fought against the system of *encomiendas*, a form of slavery of the indigenous South Americans, and was critical of the colonial government. He returned to Spain in 1568, where he was first responsible for the convent at Valladolid and for the province of Conceptión. In 1579, he was appointed provincial of Castile.

Moran, Patrick Francis   Cardinal archbishop, born Leighlinbridge, Ireland, 16 September 1830, died Sydney, Australia, 16 August 1911. Moran was educated at the Irish College in Rome, ordained there in 1853, and served as its vice-rector, 1856–66. After returning to Ireland, he was made bishop of Ossory in 1872. In 1884 he was named archbishop of Sydney and created cardinal a year later. In Sydney, he worked hard to expand his diocese and publicly supported the movement for Australian nationhood. Moran was an early proponent of the Catholic social movement and an adept historian. His books include *History of the Catholic Archbishops of Dublin* (1864) and *History of the Catholic Church in Australasia* (1895).

Morandus   Benedictine prior and saint, born near Worms, Germany, *c*.1115, died Altkirch, Alsace (France), *c*.1165. Morandus was trained and ordained in Worms and became a monk at the abbey of Cluny upon returning from a pilgrimage to Santiago de Compostela. His exemplary life led him to be named prior first of the monastery of Auvergne and then of Altkirch in Alsace. He was buried in Altkirch, and his tomb soon became a place of pilgrimage. His emblems in art are a bunch of grapes and a pruning knife. Feast day 3 June.

More, Hannah   English playwright, religious writer and philanthropist, born Stapleton, near Bristol, 2 February 1745, the fourth of five remarkably intelligent daughters of a schoolmaster, died Clifton, 7 September 1833. She wrote verses from an early age and in 1773 during a visit to London encountered the actor David Garrick, who encouraged her, as did Samuel **Johnson**, whom she met a year or so later, to write poems and plays. After Garrick's death, however, she withdrew from London society, and committed herself to the education of the poor, to writing edifying books and pamphlets, and to religion. She established schools at Cheddar and in neighbouring villages, set up friendly societies for the relief and education of adults, developed schemes of popular education and combined religious education with training in spinning. She wrote many moral tracts for the poor, two of which led to the foundation of the Religious Tract Society, now the United Society for Christian Literature.

More, Henry Cambridge Platonist theologian, born Grantham, Lincs, 1614, died Cambridge, 1 September 1687. He studied at Eton and Christ's College, Cambridge, where he was elected a fellow in 1639. His parents had been strong Calvinists, and he had always had an interest in religion: the year he was elected fellow of Christ's he was also ordained priest. He stayed at Christ's for the remainder of his life, always rejecting offers of benefices. He had a reputation for great holiness of life and generosity. His first publication, in 1642, was a collection of 'philosophical poems' which revealed his interest in Platonism. He wrote against the materialism of Thomas Hobbes in works such as *An Antidote against Atheism, or an Appeal to the Naturall Faculties of the Minde of Man, whether there be not a God* (1653), *The Immortality of the Soul, so farre forth as it is demonstrable from the Knowledge of Nature and the Light of Reason* (1659) and *Divine Dialogues, containing sundry Disquisitions and Instructions concerning the Attributes of God and His Providence in the World* (1668). He wrote more than a dozen other works in English, and spent the last years of his life translating them into Latin.

More, Thomas Saint, statesman, Roman Catholic martyr, born London, 7 February 1477, died there by beheading, 6 July 1535. More attended school in London and at the age of twelve entered the service of Cardinal John **Morton**, who remained an important influence on his life. He went to Oxford and finished his legal training at Lincoln's Inn: he was called to the bar in 1501, and entered Parliament in 1504. He married in 1505 (and married again, when he was widowed, in 1510), though he had considered entering the Carthusian Order, and had spent some time living in the London Charterhouse. More was noted both for his statecraft, serving **Henry VIII** in many roles, including Speaker of the House of Commons and, after the disgrace of Cardinal **Wolsey**, Lord Chancellor, 1529–32, and for his humanism, best represented by his friendship with **Erasmus** and by his work *Utopia* (1516). He actively opposed Protestantism both as a controversialist (he wrote a book against William **Tyndale**) and as a judge. He was imprisoned in the Tower of London in April 1534, and fifteen months later executed for high treason by Henry VIII for refusing to submit to the Act of Supremacy, which acknowledged the king as head of the newly created Church of England. In the Tower he wrote his *Dialogue of Comfort against Tribulation*, the finest of his spiritual writings. He was canonized in 1935 alongside John **Fisher**. Feast day 9 July.

Moreau, Basil Anthony Roman Catholic priest and founder of religious orders, born Laigné-en-Belin, France, 11 February 1799, died Le Mans, 20 January 1873. Moreau was educated at the seminary in Le Mans and served as professor and assistant superior there after his ordination in 1821. He helped to settle disputes in his diocese between conflicting Orders and in 1837 founded the Holy Cross Congregation. He also founded the Marianites of the Holy Cross in 1841. In addition to his work with religious orders, Moreau also worked to secure a place for Catholic education in post-revolutionary France, founding a number of colleges and publishing works on pedagogy.

Morell de Santa Cruz, Pedro Agustín Roman Catholic priest, bishop and historian, born Santiago de los Caballeros (Dominican Republic), 1694, died Havana, Cuba, 1768. Morell was ordained in Havana in 1718 and was dean of the cathedral of Santiago de Cuba from 1719 to 1750, when he was named bishop of Nicaragua. He returned to Cuba in 1753 and remained there, except for a brief exile in 1762, until his death. He is the first native

Cuban historian whose works have survived and been published. They include *La Relación histórica de los primitivos obispos y gobernadres de Cuba* (1748?) and *Historia de la Isla y Catedral de Cuba* (1760?).

Morelos y Pavón, José María Roman Catholic priest and revolutionary, born Valladolid (modern Morelia, in his honour), Mexico, 30 September 1765, died by firing squad, San Cristóbal Ecatepec, Mexico, 22 December 1815. After being educated in Valladolid, Morelos y Pavón was ordained in 1797. He served as curate of a number of churches, including Nocupétaro, where he built the church building out of his own limited resources. In 1810, he met the revolutionary Hidalgo and agreed to help him, taking on the civil war as a chance for social revolution and a solution to the problems of the poor in Mexico. In 1811, he and his 3000 recruits tried unsuccessfully to take Acapulco. Later campaigns were much more successful. In 1813, he established the Congress of Chilpancingo, but on 6 November 1815 he was overthrown. He was taken prisoner, defrocked by the Inquisition and sentenced to die by a military tribunal.

Moreno, Juan Ignacio Cardinal archbishop, born Guatemala, 24 November 1817, died Madrid, Spain, 24 August 1884. Moreno left the Americas for Spain with his parents in 1834. In Spain he studied law in Valencia and Madrid but then turned to a clerical life. He was ordained in 1849 and served as bishop of Oviedo, 1857, and archbishop of Valladolid, 1864, and Toledo, 1875. He was created cardinal in 1869 by Pope **Pius IX** and was a strong proponent of papal infallibility at the First Vatican Council. He is also well-known for his strong opposition to the Spanish government's restrictions on the Church.

Morfi, Juan Agustín de Franciscan chronicler, born Asturias, Spain, date unknown, died Mexico City, 20 October 1783. Morfi came to the Americas as a layman around 1756 and was professed in what was then New Spain in 1761. Although known in his time as a great speaker and teacher of the arts of speaking, he is best remembered for the chronicles he made when he, against his will, accompanied Teodoro del la Croix on the latter's exploratory trip to Coahuila, Texas. These chron-

icles, with rich ethnographic, historical and geographical material, were incorporated into his *Descripción del Presidio de San Juan Bautista del Río Grande* (written 1778, published 1950) and *Viaje de Indios y Diario del Nuevo México* (published 1935).

Morgan, George Campbell Congregationalist minister, born Tetbury, England, 9 December 1863, died 16 May 1945. The son of a Baptist minister, Morgan began preaching in his teens after being profoundly affected by the preaching of D. L. **Moody**. After some years as a teacher he became a Congregationalist minister, having been rejected by both the Salvation Army and the Methodists. Morgan served as pastor to numerous churches, notably Westminster Chapel in London, where he served twice, from 1904 to 1917, and from 1933 to 1945. One of the finest preachers of his generation, Morgan was much in demand as a guest speaker and travelled widely (he crossed the Atlantic 54 times), attracting large crowds wherever he appeared. His many published sermons, biblical expositions and commentaries are still widely read.

Morgan, Philip Bishop and statesman, born St Davids Diocese, Wales, date unknown, died Hatfield, Hertfordshire, England, 25 October 1435. Morgan studied canon and civil law at Oxford, earning his doctorate in 1404. After serving Archbishop Thomas **Arundel** for a short time, he entered the royal service. Between 1414 and 1417, he served as a diplomat to various European regions and went with Henry V on his invasion of Normandy, of which he was made chancellor in 1418. He was made bishop of Worcester in 1419, but Pope **Martin V** ignored his election as archbishop of York in 1424, transferring him instead to Ely in 1426. From 1422 to 1435 he was a member of the royal Privy Council of England.

Morgan, William Welsh bishop and bible translator, born near Conway, North Wales, 1545, died at St Asaph, 10 September 1604. Educated at St John's College, Cambridge, he was ordained in 1568 but did not take up a full-time parish post until 1578, when he went to Llanrhaeadr-ym-Mochnant. In 1595 he was made bishop of Llandaff and in 1601 of St Asaph. He appears to have had a good command of Semitic languages and his much acclaimed translation of the Bible in Welsh was published in 1588. It has been suggested that it was largely owing to this work that the Welsh language survived.

Morgott, Franz German Roman Catholic priest and theologian, born Mühlheim, 12 June 1829, died Eichstätt, 3 February 1900. Morgott was ordained in 1853 and spent his entire career teaching at Eichstätt Seminary, first in philosophy, 1857–69, then in dogma, 1869–1900. He was an expert in the thought of **Thomas Aquinas** and published several works over specific areas of his thought, including *Geist und Natur im Menschen* (1860), *Die Theorie der Gefühle im System des hl. Thomas* (1864), *Die Mariologie des hl. Thomas* (1878) and *Der Spender der Sacramente nach der Lehre des hl. Thomas* (1886).

Moriarty, Patrick Eugene Augustinian missionary, born Dublin, 4 July 1805, died Villanova, Pennsylvania, 19 July 1875. Moriarty joined the Augustinians in Ireland in 1822 and went to study at the monastery of St Augustine in Rome, where he was ordained. After returning to Ireland and then spending some time in Portugal, he was vicar general of the Madras mission in India from 1835 to 1838, a job that earned him the title of Master of Sacred Theology from Pope **Gregory XVI**. In 1839, he went to the United States, where he lectured extensively, promoted the cause of Catholics and the Irish, became a citizen in 1854, and served three separate terms as commissary general of the Augustine mission. He also laid the foundation for Villanova College (later University), just outside Philadelphia.

Morin, Germain Benedictine scholar, born Caen, France, 6 November 1861, died Orselina-Locarno, Switzerland, 12 February 1946. Morin entered the abbey of Maredsous, Belgium, in 1881, was ordained there in 1886 and embarked on his research career. He moved to Munich in 1907 and remained there, except during the war years, for the rest of his life. He is best known for his erudition in textual scholarship and manuscript research, producing the standard critical edition of the works of **Caesarius of Arles** (2 vols, 1937–42) and recovering lost commentaries and sermons of

Jerome (published in *Anecdota Maredsolana* (1893–1903)) and a number of sermons of **Augustine** not included in the Maurist edition of his works (published in *Miscellanea Agostiniana* (1930)).

Morin, Jean French Roman Catholic theologian and biblical scholar, born Blois, 1591, died Paris, 28 February 1659. Though raised a Protestant and educated at Leiden, The Netherlands, Morin converted to Roman Catholicism in 1618. After his ordination, he began work on the Samaritan Pentateuch. This, and research resulting from it, led him to argue for the superiority of the Greek version of the OT over the Hebrew, which he felt to have been corrupted by the rabbis. In 1639, Morin was called to Rome in order to assist in the reconciliation process with Eastern Churches, a project that led to his work on the sacraments. He was known as a man of great learning and spirit, and his contributions were and are significant for both biblical studies and sacramental theology.

Morone, Giovanni Cardinal, bishop and statesman, born Milan, 25 January 1509, died Rome, 1 December 1580. Morone was the son of the Chancellor of Milan and early entered the papal court of **Clement VII**. Appointed bishop of Modena at the early age of twenty, he served various Popes in diplomatic capacities, particularly in dealings with the Protestant Churches and Germany. He was created cardinal in 1542 and sent to the Council of Trent, then on to Bologna when that council was postponed. He was briefly imprisoned on charges of heresy in 1557, but was later made president of the Council of Trent, in 1563. He worked his entire life for peace and unity in the Church, both with the Eastern Churches and with the new Protestant ones, combining astute statecraft with a very deep spirituality and concern for his Church.

Moroni, Gaetano Papal chamberlain and historian, born Rome, 17 October 1802, died Rome, 3 November 1883. Moroni was originally a barber but when he was quite young was assigned by Cardinal Cappellari to be secretary to the Congregation for the Propagation of the Faith. In 1831, Cappellari became Pope **Gregory XVI** and made Moroni his private chamberlain, where he served as the chief newspaperman of the Curia. He served

Pius IX with the same title but no duties, which allowed him to complete his monumental 103 volume *Dizionario di erudizione storico-ecclesiastica* (1840–61). This work, still consulted, is an important source for much information about the history, people and work of the Roman Church.

Morosini, Gianfrancesco Cardinal and diplomat, born Venice, 1537, died Diocese of Brescia, 1596. A member of the powerful Morosini family of Venice, Gianfrancesco was a friend of St Philip **Neri**. His career was spent in the diplomatic service of the Republic of Venice, serving in Turin, Madrid, Poland and Constantinople. He was also the papal nuncio to Paris. He was created cardinal by Pope **Sixtus V** in 1588, but was probably not favoured by his successor **Clement VIII**, as he finished his career as administrator of the Diocese of Brescia, in mountainous northern Italy from 1590 until his death.

Morosini, Tomaso First Latin patriarch of Constantinople, patriarchate 1205–15. After the conquest of Constantinople by the Latin West, the various parties involved signed a treaty in 1204 stating how they would partition power in the region. As part of the treaty, the Venetians were given power over the Church in Constantinople and elected Tomaso, whose family was one of the most powerful in Venice, as patriarch in 1205. The time was a very turbulent one for the Church in Constantinople, and history has not remembered Morosini favourably, owing in large measure to the partisan history written by **Nicetas Choniates.**

Morris, Martin Ferdinand American Roman Catholic lawyer, born Washington, DC, 3 December 1834, died Washington, 12 September 1909. Morris came from an Irish Catholic family and originally wanted to be a Jesuit, though the death of his father forced him to leave the novitiate to care for his family. He studied law and took a practice in Washington, which flourished and gave him opportunities to take part in many civic and social affairs in that city. In 1871 he helped to found the law school at Georgetown University, and in 1893 he was appointed associated justice of the court of appeals.

Morris, William English poet, socialist and artist, born Walthamstow, 24 March 1834, died London, 3 October 1896. Morris was educated at Marlborough and Oxford, where he indulged far-reaching and diverse interests. An Anglican, he was almost led by his interest in theology to become a Roman Catholic, but he later settled on a career in the arts. He wrote books, studied architecture and interior design, painted, helped publish an edition of **Chaucer** (1896) and translated works from Greek and Icelandic. He was fascinated by a nostalgic view of the medieval time, which influenced much of his art and architecture and led him to mourn the loss of the simple joys of hand crafts brought about by growing industrialization. He founded Morris & Co., with which Dante Gabriel **Rossetti**, **Burne-Jones** and other artists were associated, and the Society for the Protection of Ancient Buildings. On religious themes he produced much literary work, such as *The Life and Death of Jesus*, and artistic work, some for churches, such as windows for Middleton Cheney Parish Church. Burne-Jones designed some windows which Morris executed, as at Jesus College, Cambridge. Morris also designed textiles, wallpaper and carpets.

Morrison, Robert Pioneer Protestant missionary to China, born Morpeth, England, 5 January 1782, died Canton, China, 1 August 1834. Brought up in Newcastle, he joined the Presbyterian Church and in 1802 decided to be a missionary. Appointed by the London Missionary Society to China, he was ordained in January 1807 and arrived in Canton that September. In 1809 he married Mary Morton in Macao and was appointed East India Company translator, which provided support and legitimacy. By 1813 he had translated the NT. Because of the difficulties faced by a Protestant mission based in either China or Macao, he sent his LMS colleague William **Milne** to Melaka, where the Anglo-Chinese College was established in 1818. He visited Britain in 1824–6, after his Chinese–English dictionary and translation of the OT were completed.

Morse, Henry Saint, Jesuit martyr, born Brome, Suffolk, 1595, died Tyburn, 1 February 1645. Morse was converted to Roman Catholicism while studying law in London and left to study theology in Douai, France. After serving four years in an

English prison for his faith, he completed his studies and was ordained in Rome. He returned to England in 1624, was again imprisoned, and completed his Jesuit novitiate while in prison in York. Morse spent the rest of his career working for the Roman Catholic Church and alternately in prison or exile for that work. He was finally executed for subverting the proper loyalties of English subjects in 1645. He was canonized in 1970 as one of the **Forty Martyrs of England and Wales**. Feast day 1 February.

Mortara, Edgar Roman Catholic priest and centre of a Roman Catholic controversy, born Bologna, Italy, 26 August 1851, died Bouhay, Belgium, 11 March 1940. Mortara was born of Jewish parents but was forcibly taken from them to be raised in the papal household because his family's Roman Catholic maid had secretly baptized him when he was a year old. Raised as a ward of Pope **Pius IX**, he became a member of the Canons Regular of the Lateran, took the name 'Pius', was ordained in 1873 and spent the rest of his life working for the conversion of Jewish people. His family tried many times to get him back, but he remained in his new faith. His case was very controversial, instigating the forming of the Alliance Israélite Universelle, a Jewish rights organization, and perhaps even contributing to the downfall of the Papal States.

Morton, John English cardinal archbishop, born either Bere Regis or Milborne St Andrew, Dorset, c.1420, died Knole Manor, Kent, 12 October 1500. Morton studied law at Oxford and was principal of Peckwater Inn there in 1453. His connection with Archbishop Bourgchier of Canterbury got him appointed chancellor to **Henry VI**'s son Edward. He was exiled after the Battle of Towton (1461) but he returned after the Battle of Tewkesbury (1471) and later served Edward IV in diplomatic service. He was made bishop of Ely in 1478, was arrested by Richard III in 1483, and escaped to Flanders. There he served the cause of Henry Tudor, later Henry VII, who made him Chancellor of England in 1487, a post he held until his death.

Moser, Lucas Painter, probably from Rottweil or Weilderstadt, Germany, flourished 1402–34. Moser was the first of a new school of naturalist painters in Germany. Influenced by current artistic trends in France and Flanders, his only undisputedly genuine surviving work is the altarpiece at Tiefenbronn. Depicting scenes from the life of Mary Magdalene as told by **Jacobus de Voragine**, the work apparently did not meet with contemporary favour, as the artist inscribed the following quote on the frame: 'Wail, O Art, wail and lament, for no one cares for thee anymore.'

Moses the Black Saint and monk, born northeast Africa, c.330, died 405. Moses began his life as a servant of an Egyptian official, was dismissed for immoral behaviour, and soon took up the life of an outlaw. The details of his conversion are not recorded, but he next appears at the monastery of Petra in the Desert of Scete. There, through the help of St **Isidore of Pelusium**, he was able to overcome his violent nature and was ordained a priest by Theophilus of Alexandria. He remained at his monastery when it was threatened by the Berbers and perished there with five of his fellow monks.

Mosheim, Johann Lorenz von Lutheran Church historian, born Lübeck, Germany, 9 October 1694, died Göttingen, 9 September 1755. Mosheim began his career teaching philosophy at Kiel and then theology at Helmstedt, 1723. In 1747, he went to Göttingen, where he helped organize the university's structure and served as professor and chancellor until his death. He helped pioneer modern Church history by treating it as a science and not as an apologetical endeavour. His chief works are his historical chronicle *Institutiones historiae ecclesiasticae* (1755), which is essentially a collection of facts from the institutions in the history of the Church, and his six volumes of sermons, *Heilige Reden* (1713–46).

Mosquera, Manuel José Roman Catholic archbishop, born Popayán, Colombia, 1800, died Marseilles, 1853. Mosquera spent his early career in ecclesiastical and educational posts in Popayán and in the University of Cauca. In 1834, he was chosen archbishop of Bogotá by the congress of that year and was confirmed by the Pope the following year. His chief concerns were spiritual reform of his diocesan clergy, for which he reorganized the seminary and provided for his priests to undergo the 'Spiritual Exercises', and the education of youth, for which he adapted the catechism and started many secondary schools. He opposed, with the support of Pope **Pius IX**, the government's interference in ecclesiastical affairs, and was exiled for this in 1852. He died in France on his way to see the Pope in Rome.

Moss, Virginia E. Pentecostal pastor, born Susquehanna, Pennsylvania, 1875, died 1919. Moss experienced a miraculous healing in 1904, and with others started the Door of Hope Mission in Newark in 1906. This became Pentecostal in 1907. In 1910 she opened the Beulah Heights Assembly, and in 1912 the Beulah Heights Bible and Missionary Training School. Several future important Assemblies of God missionaries attended this institution. Her book *Following the Shepherd* was published in 1919.

Mota y Escobar, Alonso de la Roman Catholic bishop, born Mexico City, 1556, died Puebla, Mexico, 15 April 1625. Mota y Escobar was educated in Mexico City and sent by the university there to Spain, where he was tutor to the future Philip III. He took a degree in canon law from Salamanca and then returned to Mexico, where he was dean of several universities, including that of Mexico City. In 1597, he was made bishop of Guadalajara. As such, he helped calm a rebellion by the indigenous Mexicans and won better treatment for them from the colonial government. In 1608 he was transferred to Puebla de los Angeles, where he founded several important institutions, such as hospitals and convents.

Motolinía, Toribio de Benavente Franciscan priest and missionary, born Benavente, León, Spain, *c.*1495, died Mexico City, probably 1565. Father Toribio was one of the 'Twelve Apostles' in Mexico, the first group of Franciscans to establish a mission there, in 1524. He took the Tlaxcalan name 'motolinía', which means 'poverty'. He was head of several parts of the Franciscan mission in Mexico (including provincial from 1548 to 1551) and also worked in Honduras, Nicaragua and Guatemala. His most important work is a history of the indigenous Mexicans in pre-Spanish times entitled *Historia de los indios de Nueva España* (1541).

Mott, John Raleigh American Methodist layman, student leader and international ecumenical statesman, born Livingston Manor, New York State, 25 May 1865, died Orlando, Florida, 31 January 1955. He attended Upper Iowa University and Cornell University, where he was converted. Influenced by D. L. **Moody**, he championed the Student Volunteer Movement's call for 'the evangelization of the world in this generation'. His gifts of leadership were demonstrated in the Young Men's Christian Association (intercollegiate secretary, 1888–1915; general secretary, 1915–31) and in the founding of the World Student Christian Fellowship (general secretary, 1895–1920). A key organizer and the chairman of the 1910 World Missionary Conference in Edinburgh, he was a central figure in the International Missionary Council (chairman, 1928–46) and in the groups which formed the World Council of Churches in 1948. He shared the Nobel Peace Prize in 1946 and is buried in Washington Cathedral.

Mounier, Emmanuel Roman Catholic philosopher, born Grenoble, France, 1 April 1905, died Paris, 22 March 1950. Mounier started his academic career teaching philosophy at St-Omer and is known as the father of personalist philosophy. He was founding editor of the journal *Esprit*, and a member of the French Resistance during World War II. He was imprisoned for this but released on account of a hunger strike, spending the rest of the occupation in Beauvillon and returning to his duties after the war. His philosophy, which focuses on the person as a spiritual being, can be found in his *Personalist Manifesto*, *Personalism* and *Be Not Afraid: Studies in Personalist Sociology*.

Moura, Antônio Maria de Roman Catholic priest and statesman, born Vila Nova da Rainha do Caeté, Minas Gerais, Brazil, 1794, died Rio de Janeiro, 12 March 1842. Moura was abandoned as a child and raised by Captain Caetano José Nascentes, who had his young ward educated in Portugal. When he returned to Brazil, he entered politics and was elected to represent his province. In 1833 he was appointed by the Brazilian government bishop of Rio de Janeiro, but the Pope refused to confirm the appointment because Moura was suspected of siding with the Brazilian government against Rome. The controversy, which almost led to the separation of the Brazilian Church from Rome, lasted six years until Moura withdrew his nomination in 1839.

Mourret, Fernand Sulpician priest and Church historian, born Eygulières (Bouches-du-Rhône), France, 3 December 1854, died Paris, 28 May 1938. Mourret studied in Aix-en-Provence and the seminary of St-Sulpice at Issy. He taught philosophy and some theology until 1902, when he began to teach Church history at the Sulpician school in Paris. Known as both a kind and scholarly professor, he wrote many works, including *Leçons sur l'art de prêcher* (1909), *Précis d'histoire de l'Église* (3 vols 1924) and his best-known, *Histoire générale de l'Église* (9 vols 1914–27), which is still authoritative as a source for contemporary Church history in France.

Mouton, Jean Priest and composer, born Haut-Wignes, near Boulogne, France, *c.*1459, died Saint-Quentin, France, 30 October 1522. Mouton spent his life in music, beginning as a choirboy at the age of seven and serving various Church music posts throughout his life, including choral director at Amiens, 1500 and singer in the chapels of **Louis XII**, 1513 and **Francis I**, from 1515. Even beyond these circles his work was known and appreciated. His compositions, which continue the line of **Josquin des Prez**, are contrapuntal but also clear and calm. They include over 100 motets and about sixteen Masses.

Mowinckel, Sigmund Olaf Plytt Norwegian biblical scholar, born Kjerringøy, 4 August 1884, died Oslo, 4 June 1965. Mowinckel studied in Oslo, Copenhagen, Marburg and Giessen before graduating in 1916 and joining the faculty of Oslo, where he was made full professor in 1922 and where he remained his entire career. He is known especially for his work on the Psalms, originally published as *Psalmenstudien* (6 vols, 1921–4) but popularized in English as *The Psalms in Israel's Worship* (1962). He also made important contributions to prophetic studies in *Prophecy and Tradition* (1946) and to biblical eschatology in *He That Cometh* (1956).

Moyé, John Martin Blessed, Roman Catholic priest, missionary and founder of religious congre-

gations, born Cutting, Lorraine, France, 27 January 1730, died Trier, Germany, 4 May 1793. Educated in Stasburg and Metz, Moyé was ordained in 1754 and spent seventeen years in pastoral work in Metz, founding there the Sisters of Divine Providence in 1762 to help with the education of the poor. He spent the years from 1773 to 1784 as a missionary in China, then returned to pastoral work in France. After the Revolution, he moved the Sisters to Trier in 1791, but the congregation was suppressed by the advancing French army in 1792 (but later restored in 1816). Moyé died in a typhus epidemic the following year. He was beatified by Pope **Pius XII** in 1954.

Mozart, Wolfgang Amadeus Austrian composer, pianist and organist, born Salzburg, 27 January 1756, died Vienna, 5 December 1791. He is regarded as one of the greatest and most versatile of all composers, noted for the joy of his music. He was an infant prodigy and, with his sister, was taken by his father, also an accomplished musician, on tours of Europe. In 1772 he came into the rather stormy service of the archbishop of Salzburg, then, after being called to the coronation of the Emperor **Joseph II** in 1781, settled in Vienna. He married in 1782, and though the marriage was a happy one he was chronically short of money for the later part of his life, despite being a highly prolific composer. His Church music includes Masses noted for their radiant style, a masterly *Requiem* and fine motets, such as *Exsultate Jubilate* and *Ave Verum Corpus*, a miniature instance of his genius. He described the organ as 'the king of instruments', though he wrote very little for it.

Mrak, Ignatius Roman Catholic bishop, born Hotovle, Carniola, Austria, 16 October 1818, died Marquette, Michigan, 1 February 1901. Mrak was ordained in 1837 and went to the United States in 1845 to work with the Native American population in Michigan. He worked in various missions and pastorates among the lakeland peoples until being appointed bishop of Marquette and Sault Ste Marie in 1868. As bishop, he worked for Christian education of the people and the improvement of his clergy. He retired as bishop owing to ill health in 1878, but remained in the area, serving as a hospital chaplain and continuing to work with the people to whom he had dedicated his life.

Muard, Marie Jean Baptiste Roman Catholic priest and founder of the Society of St Edmund, born Vireaux, Yonne, France, 24 April 1809, died La Pierre-qui-Vire, Yonne, 19 June 1854. Muard was educated at the seminary in Sens and ordained in 1834. After six years in parish work, he wanted to become a missionary to China but was denied permission by his bishop. As an alternative, he founded, in 1843, a group of missionary priests called the Society of St Edmund. He spent five years with this community, helping to stabilize its organization, then travelled to Rome and Subiaco, Italy. He returned to France in 1850 and founded the monastery of Sainte Marie de La Pierre-qui-Vire as a Benedictine community of Subiaco. He died from an illness contracted, most, on a preaching mission to Saint-Étienne.

Muench, Aloisius Joseph Cardinal and Church diplomat, born Milwaukee, Wisconsin, 18 February 1889, died Rome, 15 February 1962. The son of German immigrants, Muench studied at St Francis Seminary in Milwaukee and was ordained there. After taking his doctorate in social sciences *summa cum laude* from Fribourg, he began teaching at St Francis in 1922. In 1935, he was appointed bishop of Fargo, North Dakota, a post he held for 23 years, improving the financial condition of the diocese. In 1946, he was named the Pope's representative to postwar Germany, becoming papal nuncio when Germany regained independence in 1951. He was created cardinal in 1959 and was the first American to be active in the Roman curia.

Muhlenberg, Henry Melchior Lutheran Church organizer, born Einbeck, Hanover, Germany, 6 September 1711, died Trappe, Pennsylvania, 7 October 1787. Muhlenberg was sent to America in 1742 after his studies in the Pietist environment of Göttingen. In America, he helped plant new congregations and revitalize old ones as well as secure funds for Lutheran Church expansion in America. Though he was based around Philadelphia, his influence spread to most of the American colonies, and his three sons all achieved prominence in early America, one (Frederick) even becoming the first speaker of the Congress of the United States.

Mulcaster, Richard Anglican educator and author, born Cumberland, c.1531, died Essex, 15 April 1611. Mulcaster studied at Cambridge and Oxford, excelling so well in the classical languages that he was appointed, at 25, as first headmaster of the Merchant Taylors' School in London. From 1596 to 1609 he was headmaster at St Paul's School and finished his career as rector of Stanford Rivers in Essex. Aside from being the tutor of Edmund Spenser, Mulcaster known for his educational theory, which emphasized (interestingly enough) the vernacular over Latin and which also advocated some education for girls and the division of education into elementary and secondary schools.

Muldoon, Peter James American Roman Catholic bishop, born Columbia, California, 10 October 1862, died Rockford, Illinois, 8 October 1927. After his theological training and ordination in 1886, Muldoon was the chancellor and secretary to the archbishop of Chicago from 1888 to 1895. After serving as a pastor in Chicago, he was named titular bishop and vicar general of the diocese in 1901. In 1908, he was named the first bishop of Rockford, where he remained for the rest of his life. As bishop, Muldoon was best remembered for his work in social reform and for his part in the founding of what would later become the National Catholic Welfare Conference. He died after an illness of several months.

Mullanphy, John Roman Catholic philanthropist, born Enniskillen, Fermanagh, Ireland, 1758, died St Louis, Missouri, 29 August 1833. After serving over ten years in the Irish brigade of the French army, Mullanphy married in 1789 and then emigrated to the United States in 1792, where he eventually settled in St Louis. He made a fortune in real estate and cotton and devoted most of it to doing good works. His money helped to found many religious organizations and hospitals, such as the Religious of the Sacred Heart, in 1827, the Sisters of Charity of Emmitsburg, Maryland, 1828, St Ann's Lying-in and Foundling Asylum, 1844–5 and the Society of St Vincent de Paul, 1845. Many of these institutions were the first of their kind in the American West. Mullanphy's one surviving son, Bryan, continued his family's generosity.

Mullany, Azarias of the Cross Roman Catholic educator and author, born near Killenaule, Tipperary, Ireland, 29 June 1847, died Plattsburg, New York, 20 August 1893. Born 'Patrick Francis' Mullany, he went to the United States with his family when he was ten and was professed in the Brothers of the Christian Schools in 1862. He began teaching at Rock Hill College, Maryland, in 1866 and served as president there from 1879 to 1886. In 1888, he moved to the De La Salle Institute in New York City. A well-known lecturer and author, his works include *The Development of Old English Thought* (1879), *Aristotle and the Christian Church* (1888) and *Phases of Thought and Criticism* (1892).

Müller, Adam Heinrich Roman Catholic social philosopher, born Berlin, Germany, 6 June 1779, died Vienna, Austria, 17 January 1829. Though raised a Protestant, Müller became a Roman Catholic in 1805. Serving much of his political career in Austria, he is known for his Romantic economic ideas, which focused on the metaphysical/spiritual side of economics and also promoted tradition, authority, feudalism and a strong national government. His thought is often seen as a precursor to Nazi political thought, and his works include *Elemente der Staatskunst* (1809), *Versuche einer Neuen Theorie des Geldes* (1816) and *Von der Notwendigkeit einer Theologischen Grundlage der Gesamten Staatswissenschaften* (1819).

Mulry, Thomas Maurice American Roman Catholic business man and charity leader, born New York City, 13 February 1855, died New York City, 10 March 1916. The son of a successful New York business man, Mulry continued his father's excavation contractor business, but he is best remembered as leader and representative of the Society of St Vincent de Paul, which he joined at the age of sevnteen. He became president of the Superior Council of the Society in 1915, and under his influence, the Society expanded its work and began co-operating with other charities. Mulry had a lasting influence on the American Catholic Charities movement and worked for national reform in the care of welfare children. His chief work is *The Government in Charity* (1912).

Mun, Albert de French Roman Catholic statesman, born Lumigny, 28 February 1841, died Paris, 6 October 1914. Count de Mun began his life as a military man, serving in both Algeria and France. He served in the Franco-Prussian War and in the Paris Commune of 1871, where his experiences led him to his life's vocation of the re-Christianization of his native land. He organized groups to promote Catholic principles at all levels of society and served in the French parliament from 1881 until his death. Known as 'the worker's deputy', he there championed social legislation and was named to the Académie Française. He also worked for social causes as a journalist in the later part of his life.

Mundelein, George William American cardinal and archbishop, born New York City, 2 July 1872, died Chicago, Illinois, 2 October 1939. Educated at Manhatten College and in Rome, Mundelein was ordained in 1895 and began serving the Diocese of Brooklyn. He served as diocesan chancellor, 1897, domestic prelate, 1906 and member of the Arcadia, 1907, a group of Catholic scholars. He was named titular bishop of Loryma in 1909 and archbishop of Chicago in 1915. In Chicago, he worked to found schools and the Catholic Charities. He was created cardinal in 1924, organized the International Eucharistic Congress in Chicago in 1926, and was a personal friend of Franklin D. Roosevelt. He died suddenly of a coronary thrombosis just months after participating in the election of Pope **Pius XII.**

Mundwiler, Fintan Roman Catholic abbot, born Dietikon, Zurich, Switzerland, 12 July 1835, died St Meinrad, Indiana, USA, 14 February 1898. Mundwiler studied in Einsiedeln, where he was ordained in 1859. That same year he was sent to the newly formed monastery at St Meinrad as rector of the school and he later became prior, 1870. He was elected abbot in 1880 and guided the monastery through many difficulties, including a fire in 1887 and internal dissention. He helped St Meinrad's daughter-house, New Subiaco in Arkansas, to become a full abbey and helped found St Joseph's Abbey in Louisiana, 1889. He also served as first president of the Swiss-American Congregation of Benedictines, 1881.

Muñecas, Ildefonso de las Roman Catholic priest and guerrilla leader, born San Miguel, Tucumán, Peru, date unknown, died near Lake Titicaca, Peru, 1816. Muñecas studied at the University of Córdoba, taking his doctorate in theology around

1800. He studied in Europe for a time, before becoming rector of the parish of Cuzco. In 1814, he joined the rebel movement fighting for independence from Spain, accompanying the rebel leader Pinelo as chaplain and adviser during the latter's march on La Paz. After the rebels defeat, he raised a guerrilla army that plagued the royal troops for two years before he was captured, in 1816. He was shot by one of the soldiers ordered to take him back to Peru.

Mungo *see* **Kentigern**

Munguía, Clemente de Jesús Roman Catholic bishop and scholar, born Los Reyes, Michoacán, Mexico, 21 November 1810, died Rome, 14 December 1868. Munguía studied and practised law before becoming a priest in 1841. He served various posts in the Diocese of Morelia and was elected bishop of Michoacán in 1850. In 1853 he was named president of the Council of State in Mexico but was exiled three years later, after the revolution. He returned, but was exiled again in 1861 and, for the last time, in 1865. He was a noted champion of the rights of the Church and vigorously opposed the intervention of the Liberal Mexican government and of Emperor Maximilian in Church affairs, but he was also known for his scholarly works on the subjects of law and philosophy. He spent his last years in exile in Rome.

Muñoz, Vicente Franciscan architect, born Seville, Spain, 1699, died Salta, Argentina, 8 September 1784. Muñoz became a Franciscan in 1714, after his family had come to Argentina from Spain. He spent most of his career as a builder and architect of churches, and is credited with the building (and perhaps even the design) of some of the most impressive buildings in South America, including the church of San Francisco and the chapel of Terciarios de San Roque in Buenos Aires (1730–54), the dome of the cathedral of Córdoba and the Franciscan church in Salta (begun 1754).

Münster, Sebastian Lutheran Hebraist, geographer and cosmographer, born Nieder-Ingelheim, Germany, 26 January 1488, died Basel, Switzerland, 26 May 1552. Münster began his career as a Franciscan and studied Hebrew at the Franciscan monastery in Ruffnach. Around 1524, he became a Lutheran and professor of Hebrew at Heidelberg. In 1528, he moved to the University of Basel, where he remained for the rest of his life. He edited the *Biblica Hebraica* and its Latin translation (2 vols, 1534–5), and his edition of the book of Tobit can be found in the London Polyglot Bible. He also published well-known and frequently translated illustrated works on geography and cosmology, which were first published in Basel in 1544.

Münzer, Thomas Anabaptist revolutionary, born Stolberg, Germany, before 1490, possibly 1468, died Mühlhausen, Germany, 27 May 1525. Münzer studied in Leipzig and Frankfurt an der Oder and was ordained in the early 1500s. In 1519, he met **Luther**, who recommended him to a church in Zwickau. There he was influenced by Nicholas **Storch** and became enamoured of the idea of direct revelation from God and a theocratic state. After being expelled from Zwickau, he eventually served a church in Allsted in Electoral Saxony, where he produced the first German liturgy. In 1524, after failing to win the support of John of Saxony for his idea of a theocratic state, he encouraged and participated in the peasant uprisings of Mühlhausen and Frankenhausen. He was captured at the latter, tortured and eventually recanted his beliefs before his execution.

Muratori, Lodovico Antonio Roman Catholic priest and historian, born Vignola, Italy, 21 October 1672, died Modena, Italy, 23 January 1750. Muratori started his archival career at the Bibliotheca Ambrosiana in Milan, where he later, in 1740, discovered the famous Muratorian Canon, a second-century list of NT writings. In 1700 he became ducal archivist in Modena. There he wrote *Antichità estensi* (2 vols, 1717, 1740), which established him as a historian. His *Annali d'Italia* (12 vols, 1739–43) was the first attempt at a unified view of Italian history. His work marks Muratori as the father of modern Italian historiography. Though obedient to his superiors in theological matters, Muratori always felt that history should be consulted in the secular phenomena of the Church.

Murialdo, Leonardo Saint and founder of the Pious Congregation of St Joseph, born Turin, Italy,

26 October 1828, died Turin, 30 March 1900. Murialdo studied and was ordained in Turin, 1851, and dedicated himself to educating poor boys in the city. In 1857, he became director of the oratory of San Luigi and in 1866 rector of the Collegio Artigianelli, which aimed at giving youths a Christian education and some trade skills. In 1873, he founded the Pious Congregation of St Joseph, serving as its first superior general. He was a tireless worker for the Catholic worker movement in Italy, serving on many committees and national societies and initiating at least two publications. He was beatified in 1963 by Pope **Paul VI** and canonized by him in 1970. Feast day 30 May.

Muriel, Domingo Jesuit philosopher and canon lawyer, born Tamanes, Spain, 1718, died Faenza, Italy, 23 January 1795. Muriel became a Jesuit in 1734 and, among other jobs, taught philosophy at Córdoba, where he introduced 'Cartesian philosophy'. In 1762 he was chosen as procurator of the courts of Madrid and Rome but was expelled from Spain with the rest of the Jesuits in 1767. He spent his exile in the Papal States, serving as provincial for the Jesuits in Paraguay (headquartered in Faenza, Italy) and writing works on canon law and contemporary history. He was known for both his holy life and his scholarly erudition.

Murillo, Bartolomé Esteban Spanish Roman Catholic painter, born Seville, 1617, died Seville, Spain, 3 April 1682. Murillo early considered an ecclesiastical career, before turning to painting. After study under Velázquez in Madrid, 1642–5, he became well known for his paintings of the Immaculate Conception. A representative of the 'Golden Age' of Spanish baroque, his religious work is colourful and intimate – while his secular paintings foreshadow the trends in painting of the eighteenth century. His other works include *The Angels' Kitchen*, *St Francis with the Crucified Christ* and *The Duenna*.

Murner, Thomas Franciscan poet and satirist, born Oberehnheim, Alsace (France), 24 December 1475, died Oberehnheim, 22 August 1537. Murner became a member of the Order of Friars Minor Conventual at the age of fifteen and was ordained four years later. After studies and travel, he settled in Strasburg in 1502. Four years later he was named poet laureate by Maximilian I. He satirized the abuses of the Church and urged reform, but when **Luther** and **Zwingli** began attacking dogma and traditional authority, Murner turned his pen against them. The Peace of Zurich (1529) required that he stand trial before a Protestant court, but he fled, eventually returning to his native town, where he remained. In his work, Murner embodies many of the contradictory spirits of his time. These works include *Chartiludium logicae* (1507), *Der lutherischen evangelischen Kirchendieb und Ketzerkalander* (1526) and *Causa helvetica orthodoxae fidei* (1528).

Murphy, John Irish Roman Catholic priest and preacher, born Dublin, 29 December 1710, died Dublin, 3 July 1753. The son of a Dublin tallow chandler, Murphy was sent to study in Santiago de Compostela in 1727 and then transferred to Salamanca, where he was known for his intellectual gifts and ascetic spirit. He returned to Ireland for health reasons, was ordained, and served the rest of his life as an assistant priest at St Catherine's, Dublin. His preaching attracted Catholic and Protestants alike, and he had great influence with crowds during turbulent times of riot. He worked ceaselessly to counteract the effects of the Charter Schools in Dublin and was awarded the title of 'Doctor of Divinity' in Rome in 1750. Constant activity and self-mortification undermined his health, and he died young. His funeral was an occasion for a great outpouring of public grief, noted by even the Protestant press of the time.

Murphy, John Joseph Roman Catholic publisher, born County Tyrone, Ireland, 12 March 1812, died Baltimore, Maryland, 27 May 1880. Murphy came to America with his parents when he was 10 and learned the art of printing in Philadelphia. He set up a printer and book store in Baltimore in 1836, and from there his career was set. He published almost 1500 editions of works, the most well known being Cardinal James **Gibbons'** *Faith of Our Fathers*. He was given a papal gold medal for publishing items related to the doctrine of the Immaculate Conception and named 'Typographer of the Holy See' for his issue of *Acta et Decreta of the Second Plenary Council of Baltimore*. He also published numerous Roman Catholic periodicals, speeches by US Congressmen and the work of the Maryland Historical Society.

Murphy, William Martin Irish Roman Catholic newspaper publisher, born Bantry, 21 November 1844, died Dublin, 26 June 1919. The son of a building contractor, Murphy was educated at the Jesuit college in Dublin, Belvedere, and worked in a Dublin architectural firm until his father's death brought him back to Bantry. He took over and expanded his father's business, was elected to the Irish parliament and became president of the Chamber of Commerce. He bought several Dublin newspapers in 1904 and combined them in 1905 to form the *Irish Independent*, to which he later added the *Sunday Independent* and the *Evening Herald*. The papers, while mostly unbiased in their reporting, were nevertheless important media for Catholics and Catholic concerns in Ireland. Murphy also wrote *The Home Rule Act of 1914 Exposed* (1917).

Murray, Anthony Gregory (Dom) Benedictine priest, organist and composer, born London, 27 February 1905, died Downside Abbey, Stratton on the Fosse, Somerset, 19 January 1992. He was educated at Westminster Cathedral Choir School, Ealing Priory School and Cambridge. He assisted Sir Richard **Terry** at Westminster Cathedral and helped to complete the 1940 edition of the highly influential *Westminister Hymnal*. He was mostly associated with Downside Abbey, from which he broadcast a series of highly regarded organ recitals. His 'English Mass', originally in Latin, was the most frequently performed of its kind in Catholic churches in Britain. His book *Gregorian Chant according to the Manuscripts* challenged modern methods of interpretation.

Murray, Daniel Irish Roman Catholic archbishop, born near Arklow, Wicklow, 18 April 1768, died Dublin, 26 February 1852. Murray studied at the Irish College in Salamanca, was ordained, 1792 and returned to Ireland to work as a curate. In 1809, he was appointed coadjutor bishop of Dublin and as such vigorously fought against British governmental vetos of ecclesiastical appointments in Ireland. He was made archbishop of Dublin in 1823. As archbishop, he worked to build schools and hospitals and support new religious communities in his diocese. His political opinions often brought him into conflict with other Irish Catholics, but they also gave him a voice in British policy towards the Roman Catholic Church in Ireland at a critical time.

Murray, Jane Marie American Roman Catholic educator, born Freeport, Michigan, 18 March 1896, died Grand Rapids, Michigan, 22 July 1987. She became a Dominican sister when she was eighteen and studied English at Michigan Central State College, 1925, and the University of Michigan, 1932, and took her licentiate in theology from the Pontifical Institute of Medieval Studies, Toronto, 1950. Her lifelong passion was communicating to young people liturgical truth and its place in life. She wrote many textbooks for use in high schools and colleges, including *The Life of Our Lord* (1942), *Living in Christ* (1946) and *Christ in His Church* (1952).

Murray, John Courtney American Jesuit theologian, born New York City, 12 September 1904, died New York City, 16 August 1967. Murray was educated at Boston College, Woodstock College, and the Gregorian University in Rome. He spent his teaching career, 1937–67 at Woodstock College, during which time he also edited *Theological Studies*, 1941–67. He is best known for his work on Church–State relations, most especially *We Hold these Truths* (1960), in which he argues for the legitimacy of religious freedom. He also wrote a work on the Trinity, *The Problem of God* (1964).

Murray, Patrick Irish Roman Catholic theologian, born Clones, County Monaghan, 18 November 1811, died Maynooth, 15 November 1882. From 1829 until his death, he was first a student and then a professor at Maynooth College. Among his writings, his most important was *De Ecclesia Christi* (3 vols, Dublin 1860–6), for long a leading Roman Catholic source book on the Church, while his work *Essays, Chiefly Theological* (4 vols, Dublin, 1850–3) was for educated laymen.

Murray, Thomas C. Irish playwright, born Macroom, County Cork, 1873, died Dublin, 7 March 1959. He taught at schools in Cork and Dublin, but made his reputation as the writer of plays, almost all of which were produced in the Abbey Theatre, Dublin. Notable among these were *Birth-*

right (1909), *Maurice Harte* (1912) and *Spring* (1918). These depict realistically Irish country characters and deal with the problems of the social system, especially concerning work on the land and rural avarice and rivalry.

Murri, Romolo   Italian Roman Catholic priest and sociologist, born Montesampiebrangeli, 2 August 1870, died Rome, 12 March 1944. Ordained in 1893, he studied at the University of Rome. He founded *Vita Nuova* in 1894 and *Cultura Sociale* in 1898, periodicals advocating the Roman Catholic social movement and Christian democracy. His outspoken approach led to his condemnation by Pope **Pius X** in 1906 and excommunication in 1909. He took to active politics and was elected a parliamentary deputy in 1909. He returned to the Church in 1943.

Musso, Cornelius   Italian Roman Catholic bishop and theologian, born Piacenza, 16 April 1511, died Rome, 9 January 1574. A member of the Conventual Franciscans, he became bishop of Bertinoro in 1541 and transferred to Bitonto in 1544. Giving the inaugural address at the Council of Trent, he actively discussed the sources of revelation, original sin, justification and the sacraments. Afterwards he began to reform his diocese, but opposition from the court of Naples forced his resignation in 1572.

Muste, Abraham Johannes   Pastor and pacifist, born Zierikset, Holland, 8 January 1885, died USA, 11 February 1967. When he was six his family emigrated to the USA. He was ordained minister in the Dutch Reformed Church but when he expressed pacifist views and spoke out against World War I he was expelled from his congregation. He gave up organized religion and directed his energies towards the labour movement and left-wing politics. In 1936 he returned to active ministry in the Christian Church, and became involved in organized pacifism. He became executive secretary of the Fellowship of Reconciliation, a post he held from 1940 to 1953. Then almost 70, he spent the next fourteen years in pacifist activism, directed mainly against nuclear weapons and the Vietnam War. The *Essays of A. J. Muste* are edited by Nat Hentoff (1967).

Musuros, Markos   Greek humanist, born Herak-

lion, Crete, 1470, died Rome, 17 October 1517. After working for a time in Venice with the Aldine Press he taught Greek at Padua, where **Erasmus** attended his lectures. He returned to Venice and worked on the Greek text of Plato. In 1516, he was invited to Rome by **Leo X**, who appointed him archbishop of one see in Greece and bishop of another in Crete, though he never visited either, remaining in Rome to teach Greek.

Muth, Carl   German journalist, born Worms-am-Rhein, 31 January 1867, died Reichenhall, Bavaria, 15 November 1944. Having abandoned his previous plans to take part in mission work, he turned instead to the study of political science and wrote for, and edited, journals in Germany, notably *Hochland*, founded in 1903 as a literary publication, but from 1916 concerned with social and political problems. It appealed to Christians to abandon their anti-socialism and to socialists not to oppose Christianity. It opposed the Nazis and was banned in 1941, but reappeared again in 1946, after Muth's death.

Mutis, José Celestino   Roman Catholic priest, naturalist and scientist, born Cadiz, Spain, 6 April 1732, died Bogotá, Colombia, 2 September 1808. From 1760, while physician to the viceroy of Granada, he researched in natural history, and in 1772 was ordained a priest and became a canon of Bogotá Cathedral. In 1783 he was appointed by King Charles III to lead, with the support of the viceroy and the archbishop Gongora, the Expedición Botánica del Nueva Reino del Granada to investigate the flora and fauna of Colombia, and its natural wealth. Mutis made a particular study of chinchona (quinine).

Muzio, Girolamo   Italian humanist and polemicist, born Padua, 12 March 1496, died near Florence, 1576. He wrote verses and studies of chivalry, but most important were his religious polemics, which included the *Menthe Orchiane* of 1551 against Bernadino **Ochino**, a Franciscan who became a Protestant, and Johann Heinrich **Bullinger**, the Swiss Reformer, and the *Lettre Catholicke* of 1571 on the evils in the Church.

Myconius, Friedrich   German Reformer, born Lichtenfels am Main, 25 December 1490, died

Gotha, 7 April 1546. As a Franciscan he failed to find the assurance of God's grace and turned to **Luther**'s teaching. In 1524 he fled to Electoral Saxony. He became an evangelist and chief preacher of the Reformed Church at Gotha. He was among the divines attending the Marburg Colloquy of 1529, which failed to reach an agreement between Lutherans and Zwinglians. In 1538 he went to England and assisted **Cranmer** in producing the Forty-Two Articles.

Myconius, Oswald Swiss Reformer, born Lucerne, 1488, died Basel, 14 October 1552. His name was originally 'Geisshäusler'; the name 'Myconius' was apparently given him by **Erasmus**. After studying at Basele from 1510 to 1514, he taught at Zurich from 1516 to 1520 and at Lucerne from 1520 to 1522, when his support of the Reformed cause compelled him to leave. In 1523 he returned to Zurich to work with **Zwingli**, until going to Basel in 1532, where he remained until his death. He produced a 'Confession of Faith' at Basel in 1534 and two years later helped to draw up the 'Second Confession of Basel' or First Helvetic Confession, which gained great support. His wish to negotiate with the Lutherans brought him the mistrust of many Zwinglians. His other writings include a Life of Zwingli (1536).

N

Nabuco de Araujo, Joaquim Brazilian abolitionist, born Recife, 19 August 1849, died Washington, DC, 17 January 1910. In 1879 he was elected to the Brazilian Chamber of Deputies, but was unpopular owing to his efforts to abolish slavery. He therefore wrote *O Abolicionem*, which considered the economic problems attached to the abolition of slavery. The support now adopted by the Liberals for abolition secured his return to the Chamber, and he gained the support of Pope **Leo XIII**. On 13 August 1888 slavery was abolished in Brazil. He spent his last years as Brazilian ambassador to the United States of America.

Nacchianti, Giacomo Bishop, Dominican theologian, born Florence, *c*.1500, died Chioggia, 6 March 1569. Becoming a Dominican in 1518, he was made bishop of Chioggia. In 1546 at the Council of Trent, he supported confining the right to vote in the Council to bishops and heads of religious orders. He denied that tradition had equal authority with Scripture, but accepted the final decree upholding this. In 1548 he was the subject of an inquiry in his diocese, but no action was taken. In 1562 he supported the decision that the power of bishops was by papal appointment and not by divine command and that the Mass was a propitiatory sacrifice. He enforced the Council's decrees in his diocese.

Nadal, Geronimo Jesuit theologian, born Palma, Majorca, 11 August 1507, died Rome, 3 April 1580. He had studied with **Ignatius of Loyola** at Alcalá in 1526 and at Paris in 1532–5, but did not follow Ignatius' Spiritual Exercises. He was ordained and taught theology in Majorca from 1538. In 1542 he read a letter by **Francis Xavier** from India, which led him to become a Jesuit at Rome in 1545. He worked closely with Ignatius and became rector of the first Jesuit college (at Messina in Sicily) and adopted the strict *Ratio Studiorum*. In 1554, when Ignatius' health was failing, he became his vicar-general and made visitations in Germany and elsewhere promulgating the Society's constitutions. He attended the Diet of Augsburg and was a papal theologian at the Council of Trent.

Nagai Takashi Japanese Roman Catholic, witness and survivor of the Nagasaki atom bomb, mystic, born 3 January 1908, died Nagasaki, 1 May 1951. He became a doctor, eventually specializing in radiology. Already embarked on a spiritual search, after meeting his future wife he became a Catholic in 1934. His wife was killed by the Nagasaki bomb, though their two children survived. Already ill because of leukaemia, the added effects of radiation left Nagai seriously disabled. He spent the remainder of his days in contemplation and writing in a hut near the former cathedral in Urakami, where the bomb had fallen. His experiences and reflections are recorded in *The Bells of Nagasaki*.

Nagle, Nono Irish educator and foundress, born Ballygriffin, near Mallow, County Cork, *c*.1718, died Cork, 26 April 1784. Hearing that her dead sister Ann had sold dress-lengths of silk for the poor, she resolved to devote herself to the poor. Advised by her Jesuit director, she founded a school in a mud cabin in Cave Lane, Cork, about 1754. Within nine months, although Roman Catholic schools were unlawful, it had 200 girls. Making use of a substantial sum she had inherited, within two years she had five schools for girls and two for boys. In 1771 she brought the Ursuline Nuns into Ireland and in 1775 founded the Society of the Charitable Instruction for the Poor, which after her death became the Presentation Sisters.

Nagle, Urban (Edward J.) American dramatist, born Providence, Rhode Island, 10 September 1905, died Cincinnati, Ohio, 11 March 1965. A Dominican from 1925 and a priest from 1931, he was a professor at Providence College and editor of the *Holy Name Journal*. His main plays were *Barter* (1929), *Catherine the Valiant* (1938), *Lady of Fatima* (1948) and *City of Kings* (1949). He also founded the Blackfriars Guild, in 1937 and co-founded the Catholic Theatre Conference, 1937, and from 1940 to 1951 was moderator of the Blackfriars Guild in New York City.

Nagot, Francis Charles Religious superior, born Tours, France, 19 April 1734, died Emmitsburg, Maryland, 9 April 1816. In 1770 he was superior of the Little Seminary of Saint-Sulpice in Paris and in 1789 vice-rector of the Grand Seminary. In 1790 he was sent to London to arrange for a seminary in the new diocese of Baltimore and the next year went there with three Sulpician priests and five students. They occupied One-Mile Tavern at North Paca Street, to establish St Mary's Seminary, the first such Roman Catholic institute in the United States of America. In 1806 he opened a minor seminary at Pigeon Hill, Pennsylvania, but it closed, and the students moved to Mount St Mary's, Emmitsburg, of which he was the superior.

Nanino, Giovanni Maria Italian composer, born Tivoli, c.1545, died Rome, 11 March 1607. He was apparently a student of **Palestrina**, whom he succeeded as *maestro di cappella* at Santa Maria Maggiore, Rome, in 1571. Then he held the same post at San Luigi de' Francesi from 1575 to 1577 and became a tenor in the papal choir and *maestro* from 1604 to 1606. Famed as a teacher, he was a good composer of the canon under Palestrina's influence. His religious music included Masses and Psalm settings; and he wrote also madrigals and other secular music.

Napoleon III Emperor of the French, born Paris, 20 April 1808, the son of Louis Bonaparte and Hortense de Beauharnais (brother and step-daughter of Napoleon I), died Chislehurst, Kent, 9 January 1873. Louis Napoleon (originally 'Charles Louis Napoleon Bonaparte') became emperor in 1852 and married in 1853 a Spanish countess, Eugenie de Montijo, whose devotion to the cause of the Papacy was believed to have influenced his policies, especially when in 1859 he defeated Austria and made a united Italy possible; he established a French garrison in Rome which kept the city under papal control until the outbreak of the Franco-Prussian War in 1870, when the French troops withdrew from Rome and the city was occupied by the Italian army.

Nary, Cornelius Irish Roman Catholic controversialist and biblical scholar, born near Nuas, County Kildare, c.1660, died Dublin, 3 March 1738. Ordained at Kilkenny in 1634, he went to the Irish College in Paris and graduated as doctor of laws at the University of Paris. After being tutor to the earl of Antrim in London, he became parish priest of St Machan's, Dublin, in about 1700, where he composed a catechism for the parish and translated the NT for liturgical use. He wrote about the Oath of Abjuration, an oath disclaiming any right to the British Crown on the part of the House of Stuart; and he was a renowned controversialist on ecclesiastical topics, his writings including *The Case of the Catholics of Ireland* (1720) and *A Charitable Address to All Who are of the Communion of Rome* (1728).

Natalis, Alexander French Dominican theologian and historian, born Rouen, 19 January 1639, died Paris, 21 August 1724. He became a Dominican 1654 and a doctor of theology at the Sorbonne the next year. He taught philosophy and theology in Paris. His greatest historical work, *Selecta historiae capita et in loca ejusdem insignia dissertiones historicae, chronologicae, criticae, dogmaticae* (1676–86), brought him papal condemnations in 1684, 1685 and 1687, which were withdrawn in 1724 and 1754. He supported the Jansenists, arguing that the bull *Unigenitus* of 1713, which condemned them, was not genuinely the work of the Pope.

Nau, François Nicolas French Roman Catholic priest and orientalist, born Thil, France, 13 May 1864, died Paris, 2 September 1931. Having studied theology and canon law at the Grand Seminary of Saint-Sulpice in Paris, he was ordained in 1887, then studied science at the Sorbonne and from 1890 to 1930 taught mathematics and astronomy at the Institut Catholique. In 1889 he also began to study Syriac and during the rest of his life edited numerous Syriac texts. He was a prolific writer and published numerous studies on the religious literature of the Christian Orient, especially on Syriac thought; he also mastered Greek, Armenian and Arabic. He was a prominent member of the Société Asiatique and was made an honorary *chorepiscopus* by the Marionite patriarch of Antioch. He became professor in oriental languages at the Institut Catholique. He was engaged in the preparation of editions of texts and was, together with Mgr. R. **Graffin**, responsible for the supervision of the *Patrologia Orientalis* series.

Nauclerus, John German humanist and historian, born probably at Württemberg, *c.*1425, died Tübingen, 5 January 1510. From 1450 to 1459 he was tutor and counsellor to the future Duke Eberhard V of Württemberg and also pastor and canon of Brachenheim. He was provost of Stuttgart from 1465 to 1472 and helped to found the University of Tübingen, where he taught canon law and was chancellor and provost from 1483 to 1509. His *Memorabilium omnes aetatis et omnium gentium chronica commentarii* (*c.*1504), a history of the world from the creation, is medieval rather than humanistic but a good source for his period.

Nausea, Friedrich Bishop, born Waischenfeld, Franconia, *c.*1480, died Trent, 6 February 1552. After graduating in law and divinity at Siena, he became secretary to Cardinal Lorenzo **Campeggio**, archbishop of Bologna and papal legate in Germany. Made a canon of Frankfurt-am-Main in 1525, he was soon forced by Lutheran opposition to leave, and was appointed bishop of Vienna in 1541. He sought conciliation with Lutherans and urged the Papacy to permit clerical marriage and the administration of the cup to the laity at Holy Communion.

Navarrete, Domingo Fernández Spanish Dominican missionary and archbishop, born Peñafiel, Old Castile, *c.*1610, died Santo Domingo, 16 February 1689. He became a Dominican *c.*1630 and in 1648 led a mission to the Philippines and founded the University of St Thomas, Manila. In 1657 he went to China, but in 1665 persecution nullified his work. He was appointed in 1673 the Dominican representative in Rome to oppose the Jesuits over the Chinese rites; and in 1677 King Charles II persuaded the Pope to compel him to become archbishop of Santo Domingo. Despite his opposition to the Jesuits' policy in China, he praised them for their help in improving the moral life of his diocese.

Navarro, Juan Spanish musician, born in or near Seville, *c.*1530, died Palencia, 25 September 1580. He sang in the ducal choir at Marchena in 1549 and in Jaén and Málaga in 1553; he was chapelmaster at Ávila Cathedral in 1565 and at Salamanca Cathedral the next year; and he was music master at Ciudad Rodrigo Cathedral, 1574–8 and at Palencia Cathedral, 1578–80. His compositions were especially settings of Psalms and *Magnificats*, which became favourites in Spain, Portugal and Macao.

Nazarius of Lérins Saint, fourteenth abbot of the monastery of Lérins, probably sometime during the reign of the Merovingian Clotaire II (i.e. 584–629), though some put his death *c.*450. He opposed the heathens in France, destroyed a sanctuary of Venus near Cannes and founded on its site a convent for women, which the Saracens destroyed in the eighth century. Feast day 18 November.

Neale, John Mason Anglican priest and editor of early hymns, born London, 24 January 1818, died East Grinstead, Sussex, 6 August 1866. He was educated at Sherborne School and Cambridge, and was instrumental in recovering and editing ancient hymns, in translations from Latin and Greek. He became warden of Sackville College, East Grinstead, an almshouse, and was censored for what were regarded by his bishop as his ritualistic, Catholic views. He edited hymns such as 'O Come, O Come Emmanuel'. However, internationally known to those who are not Christians is his 'Good King Wenceslas'. He wrote the words and adapted them to the music of a 'Spring Carol', slightly incongruously in its last two bars. Many hymns in *Hymns, Ancient and Modern* originate from him.

Neale, Leonard American Roman Catholic archbishop, born Port Tobacco, Maryland, 15 October 1746, died Baltimore, Maryland, 18 June 1817. When a priest and studying theology, he went to England and was then sent as a missionary to British Guiana and in 1783 on to Port Tobacco. In 1793 an outbreak of yellow fever decimated the clergy in Philadelphia, and so he was sent there and became vicar general and helped Miss Alice **Lalor** to found the first community of the Visitation Nuns in America. In 1798 he became president of Georgetown College, Washington, DC, and a coadjutor bishop and in 1815 the second archbishop of Baltimore.

Neander, Joachim Musician, born Bremen, 1650, died there, 31 May 1680. He was educated at Bremen and lived in Frankfurt am Main, Heidelberg and Düsseldorf. He contributed to and helped to compile hymn-books, whose contents were incorporated into the *Marburg Reformed Gesangbuch* and passed into many hymnals in the Reformed Churches. One of his hymns is popular, translated as 'Now Thank We All Our God'. He gave his name to the Neanderthal, a valley near Düsseldorf, and hence, by a curious twist of fate, Neanderthal Man is named after him.

Neander, Johann August Wilhelm German ecclesiastical historian, born 'David Mendel' at Göttingen, 17 January 1789, died Berlin, 14 July 1850. Through F. D. E. **Schleiermacher**'s influence, he was converted from Judaism and was baptized in 1806, changing his name to 'Neander' (i.e. 'New Man'). He taught ecclesiastical history for the rest of his life at Berlin. He wrote a number of works in which he concentrated on persons and sought to discover in history the influence of the divine upon human life. His major work was a six-volume study of the history of the Church until the end of the Middle Ages. A convinced, broad-minded Protestant, he upheld Christian simplicity above the claims of religious rites and the priesthood.

Nectarius (Nektarios) of Aegina Greek Orthodox saint and bishop, born Thrace, 10 October 1846, died Athens, 8 November 1920. He was consecrated metropolitan of Pentapolis in the Alexandrian patriarchate, but was expelled by other bishops, jealous of his rapid promotion. He arrived penniless in Greece, where he directed a small seminary and later, in 1908, became chaplain to a convent on the island of Aegina. He wrote many theological works, but it was as confessor and spiritual adviser that he became revered. After his death huge numbers of miracles were attributed to his intercession and his shrine is one of the most popular in the Orthodox world. He was canonized in 1961. Feast day 9 November.

Needham, John Turberville English Roman Catholic antiquarian and naturalist, born London, 10 September 1713, died Brussels, 30 December 1781. He was educated at the English College, Douai. Ordained in 1738, he was in 1747 the first Roman Catholic cleric to be elected a fellow of the Royal Society of London. From 1743 he wrote scientific papers and books and was elected a fellow of the Society of Antiquaries of London. In 1768 he became director of a literary society in Brussels which became the Imperial Academy in 1773; he was also a canon of Dendermonde Collegiate Church and later of Sorghies in Hainaut.

Neercassel, Johannes van Dutch Roman CAtholic bishop, born Gorcum, 1623, died Zwolle, 6 June 1686. Studied at Cuych, Louvain and Paris, joined the Congregation of the Oratory and was ordained in 1648. He became vicar general of the archbishop of Utrecht in 1653, then bishop of Castoria *in partibus* and the sixth vicar apostolic of the Dutch mission. Of his works, *Amor poentius* (1683) was placed on the Index in 1690, *Tractatus de sanctorum . . . Cultu* (1675) was reproved for disparaging the cult of the saints, and *Tractatus de lectione scripturarum* (1677) was reproved for advocating scriptural readings in the vernacular.

Neill, Stephen Charles Bishop, missionary, scholar, born Edinburgh, 31 December 1900, died 20 July 1984. A brilliant student at Trinity College, Cambridge, in 1924 he went to Dohnavur, India, fell out with Amy **Carmichael**, learnt Tamil and engaged in teaching. He was ordained deacon at Tinnevelly in 1927 and accepted by the Church Missionary Society while in Britain in 1928. He returned to Tinnevelly as a district missionary and was elected bishop in 1939. Forced to resign in 1944 he worked for the World Council of Churches, 1947–54, editing with Ruth **Rouse** the *History of the Ecumenical Movement, 1517–1948* (1954), among other projects. He was professor of mission at the University of Hamburg, 1962–7, and of philosophy and religious studies at Nairobi, 1969–73. He retired to Wycliffe College, Oxford, to travel, write and speak. He was a sensitive scholar, a troubled spirit, a beautiful writer and a great missionary.

Neill, Thomas Patrick   American economist, born Rock Island, Illinois, 12 December 1865, died Washington, DC, 3 October 1942. From 1897 he was professor of economics at the Catholic University of America, Washington, DC, until under Presidents Theodore Roosevelt, William Howard Taft and Woodrow Wilson, he was arbitrator in labour disputes, securing federal inspection for the meat-packing industry, and then dealing with railway problems. He promoted state legislation for industrial safety and workmen's compensation. He was elected president of the American Statistical Association in 1916.

Nellas, Panayiotis   Greek Orthodox lay theologian, born central Greece, 1936, died Athens, 6 April 1986. Typical of many recent Greek theologians, he lived a humble life, as a religious education teacher in a Greek secondary school. His writings were very influential and represent the return of Orthodox theology to its patristic roots. He edited the Greek equivalent to Sources Chrétiennes. His important work on theological anthropology, *Deification in Christ*, has been translated into English (1987).

Nelligan, Emile   French-Canadian poet, born Montreal, 24 December 1879, died Montreal, 18 November 1941. He abandoned his education at the Collège Sainte-Marie, Montreal, to devote himself to poetry. In 1896 he published in a magazine, *Le Samedi*, nine outstanding poems, but his poetic career was short. From 1898 he was in institutions for the mentally ill. His collected poems were published in 1904. His poetry is about the spiritual drama of the effort to escape from human torment into peace and contentment through love, music, religion and even death. He was the first really modern French-Canadian poet.

Nelson, John   English Methodist lay preacher, born Birstall, Yorkshire, 1707, died Leeds, 18 July 1774. While working in London in 1739 he underwent an evangelical conversion. He states in his journal how, on hearing John **Wesley** preach, his 'heart beat like a pendulum of a clock'. Following his return to Yorkshire he began a campaign of aggressive evangelism, working as a stonemason during the day and preaching at night. Working briefly with Benjamin **Ingham**, and then later with John **Bennet** and the other itinerant Methodist preachers, despite occasions of fierce persecution, he established a large number of religious societies throughout the northern counties. In May 1744 he was pressed as a soldier but refused to fight and was finally released on 28 July.

Nemesius of Emesa   Early Christian psychologist, died 400. Except for his work *On the Nature of Man*, nothing is known about him. He may have been bishop of Emesa (now Homs in Syria). He set out to develop the concept of the soul as held by the ancient classical writers so that it coincided with the Christian outlook, and he laid the basis of the Christian philosophy of free will and human action.

Nennius   Welsh historian, died *c*.825. A prologue to an extant medieval manuscript of the Welsh-Latin *Historia Brittonum* attributes the text to the otherwise unknown Nennius. No manuscript is earlier than 1164, and the Harleian recension of the work in the British Library is anonymous. Despite attempts to connect Nennius with the original composition, the date of the prologue has been shown to be *c*.1050.

Neot   Saint, died 877(?). According to tradition he was a Saxon monk of Glastonbury, who was ordained priest by Bishop Aelfheah, visited Rome seven times and preached frequently near Bodmin. He was a kinsman of **Alfred**, king of the West Saxons, whom he is said to have reproved for his harsh rule. He became a hermit in Cornwall and was buried at the place now called St Neot. His relics were brought to Crowland *c*.1003. Feast day 31 July.

Nepos of Arsinoë Millenarianist and bishop of Arsinoë (now Medinet el Faiyum, Egypt), died 120. He wrote liturgical hymns and upheld the Judaizing theology in the Church. He was the leading champion of the Millenarians in Egypt and wrote *A Refutation of the Allegorists* confuting those who gave an allegorical interpretation to the passages in the book of Revelation which seemed to predict a reign by Christ on earth for a thousand years.

Neri, Philip Saint, Italian founder of the Oratorians, born Florence, 1515, died Rome, 26 May 1595. Educated by the Dominicans of San Marco, and attracted to the memory of **Savonarola**, Philip went to Rome in 1533, and co-founded the Confraternity of the Most Holy Trinity, for the care of pilgrims, who in Jubilee Year 1575 numbered 145,000. Following his ordination, the confessional and spiritual conferences at San Girolamo became his apostolate. The growing community became the Congregation of the Oratory, approved by **Gregory XIII** in 1575. Revered as a saint during his lifetime, his gentleness, gaiety and warm personal devotion to Christ made him known as the 'Apostle of Rome'; **Gregory XV** canonized him in 1622. Feast day 26 May.

Nerinckx, Charles Roman Catholic missionary, born Herffelingen (Belgium), 2 October 1761, died Ste Geneviève, Missouri, 12 August 1824. Ordained in 1785, he was parish priest at Mechlin and Merbeck until 1803, when he began covertly to administer the sacraments despite French revolutionary repression. Volunteering to go to America, he ministered to scattered mission stations in Kentucky, which took him six weeks to visit, often in peril, when he spent days on horseback and nights hiding in the woods. He built fourteen churches, organized the first Holy Name Society in Kentucky and founded the Sisters of Loreto, the first American community.

Nerses Saint, Armenian patriarch (*Katholikos*), born Armenia, c.333, died c.373. Educated in Cappadocia and married to a Mamikonian princess, he was the father of St **Isaac the Great**. After his wife's death, he became an ecclesiastic and c.363 was consecrated patriarch of Armenia by force. He set out to reform the Church, which aroused the hostility of King Arshak III, who exiled him. He was recalled in 369 by the dissolute King Pap and poisoned by him at a meal. Feast day 19 November.

Nerses II Patriarch of Armenia (*Katholikos*), possibly born Aschdurag, Bagrevand, died 557. A Jacobite Monophysite, he was Armenian patriarch from 548 to 557, and under him met the Second Council of Tirin or Dovin.

Nerses III Patriarch of Armenia (*Katholikos*), surnamed 'Schinogh' ('the church builder'), died 661. He supported the Greeks against the Arabs and accepted the Council of Chalcedon. Opposition from the Satrap Teodorus led him to withdraw from the administration of the patriarchate from 652 to 658.

Nerses of Lambron Archbishop, born Lambron, Cilicia, 1153, died 17 July 1198. He became a priest in 1169 and archbishop of Tarsus in 1176. He sought to obtain the reunion of the Greek and Armenian Churches. He was a great Armenian writer of commentaries, liturgies and hymns.

Nerses Šnorhali ('the Gracious') Saint and patriarch of Armenia (*Katholikos*), born near the modern Elazig (Turkey), 1102, died Hromkla, the Armenian patriarchal see, 15 August 1173. Catholicos of the Armenians from 1166 in succession to his brother **Gregory III Pahlav**, he opened discussions with the patriarch of Constantinople about reunion of the two Churches, accepting the Byzantine calendar and, more controversially, the doctrine of the Council of Chalcedon on the two natures of Christ. Besides being a significant theologian of the Armenian tradition, he was an outstanding poet of the nation. Feast day 13 August.

Nestlé, Eberhard Lutheran biblical scholar, born Stuttgart, Germany, 1 May 1851, died Stuttgart, 9 March 1913. He held professorships at Ulm and Tübingen from 1883 to 1898, when he became first a professor and then superior at the Evangelical Theological Seminary at Maulbronn. His main work was his edition of the Greek NT text in 1898, which was adopted by the British and Foreign Bible Society in 1904.

Nestor Russian chronicler, born *c.*1056, died *c.*1114. A little-known monk of the Pecherskii Caves Monastery, Kiev, from 1073, he is accepted as the author of Lives of St Theodosius, abbot of the Pecherskii Caves, and the martyrs Princes **Boris** and **Gleb** of Kiev. He is not now believed to be the author of *The Russian Primary Chronicle*, though he may have helped in its production.

Nestorius Patriarch of Constantinople, born Germanikeia (Syria), *c.*381, died Egypt, after 451. Between 10 April 428 and 22 June 431 he was patriarch of Constantinople. His patriarchate was marked by his rigorous moralism, preaching against attendance at games and theatres, and by the controversy he incited by his refusal to call Mary 'Theotokos' ('Mother of God'). He thus clashed with **Cyril of Alexandria** and Pope **Celestine I**. The Council of Ephesus (431), trying in vain to suppress the controversy, only managed to aggravate it. Nestorius was exiled to the monastery in Antioch where he had been a monk before becoming patriarch, then to Petra and finally to the Great Oasis in Upper Egypt. Before his death he accepted the decisions of Chalcedon.

Netter, Thomas Carmelite theologian, born Saffron Walden, Essex, *c.*1370, died Rouen, France, 2 November 1430. His Order having sent him to study at Oxford, he attended the Council of Pisa in 1409 and in England was prominent in persecuting the Wycliffites. He was appointed Henry V's confessor and a representative at Constance in 1415. In 1419 he went to Poland to support the papal army against the Hussites. As spiritual adviser to **Henry VI**, he accompanied him to France in 1430. He wrote to confute the Lollards and Hussites.

Neumann, John Nepomucene Roman Catholic bishop and saint, born Prachatiz, Bohemia, 28 March 1811, died Philadephia, USA (he dropped dead on the street), 5 January 1860. He studied at the diocesan seminary and then at Charles University, Prague. Becoming inspired to be a missionary in America, he was ordained priest in New York in 1836, entered the Redemptorist Congregation in 1842 and was appointed bishop of Philadelphia in 1852. He visited the larger parishes of his diocese annually and the others every two years and once walked 25 miles to confirm an invalid boy. He founded nearly 100 schools, 50 churches and began his cathedral in Philadelphia. He wrote a number of books, including a much-used catechism, and contributed articles to Catholic journals. He was canonized in 1977. Feast day 5 January.

Neumann, Theresa Stigmatized visionary, born Konnersreuth, Bavaria, 9 April 1898, died Konnersreuth, 18 September 1962. Becoming bedridden in 1918 and blind in 1919, she regained her sight in 1923 on the day of the beatification of **Thérèse of Lisieux** and able to walk again in 1925 on the day of the canonization of this saint. During Lent 1926 she had visions of the Passion and received the stigmata, which bled on Fridays. From 1922 she was reputed to eat no solid food and from 1927 no nourishment except daily Holy Communion. After her visions she was credited with unusual insights. No Roman Catholic pronouncement has been made on her case.

Neville, George English archbishop and statesman, born *c.*1433, died Blyth, Nottinghamshire, 8 June 1476. Graduated at Balliol College, Oxford, in 1450 and ordained in 1454, he became an extensive pluralist. He became bishop of Exeter in 1458 and Chancellor in 1460. He succeeded in detaching Louis XI of France from the Lancastrians in 1463 and arranged peace with Scotland the next year. He became archbishop of York in 1465, but Edward IV suspected his loyalty and deprived him of the Chancellorship in 1467. On Edward's flight in 1470 he became Chancellor to **Henry VI**, but on the Yorkist restoration the next year, he was deprived of his posts and imprisoned until 1475. He patronized learning and encouraged Greek studies by collecting Greek manuscripts.

Nevin, John Williamson American Protestant theologian, born Upper Strasburg, Pennsylvania, 20 February 1803, died Lancaster, Pennsylvania, 6 June 1886. He was educated at Union College, Schenectady, New York, and then Princeton Theological Seminary. He went as professor of biblical literature to the Western Theological Seminary in Pittsburgh in 1830. However, although brought up a Presbyterian, he became in 1840 a professor of theology at the Mercersburg Theological Seminary, Pennsylvania, of the more liberal German

Reformed Church and was increasingly influential by originating the 'Mercersburg Theology', which opposed the emotionalism of contemporary American Protestant theology and advocated liturgical renewal and a more sacramental conception of Christianity: his best-known book, *The Mystical Presence* (1846), is on the Lord's Supper. In 1861 he moved to Franklin and Marshall College in Lancaster, Pennsylvania, from 1866 to 1876 serving as its president.

Nevius, John Livingston Presbyterian missionary to China, born Seneca County, New York, 4 March 1829, died Chefoo (Yantai), China, 19 October 1893. After study at Princeton (BD, 1853) in 1854 he arrived in China with his wife Helen Coan. In 1861 they based themselves in Ningpo, Shandong Province. He promoted self-propagating, self-governing and self-supporting Churches using a *Manual for Inquirers* which included instruction on Bible study, prayer, the Apostles' Creed and Scripture passages to be memorized. He was involved in famine relief in 1877 and developed an annual pattern of itineration and the convening of a residential Bible school at their home each June to August. The 'Nevius Plan' was widely followed in Korea after he was invited to explain his methods to Presbyterian missionaries there in 1890.

Newbigin, James Edward Lesslie Bishop, missionary, ecumenist, theologian, born Newcastle upon Tyne, 8 December 1909, died London, 30 January 1998. He was educated at Cambridge, was a Student Christian Movement travelling secretary and in 1936 was ordained by the Church of Scotland to be a missionary in India. He served as a village evangelist, 1936–47, Church of South India bishop in Madurai and Ramnad, 1947–59, secretary of the International Missionary Council, 1959–61, associate general secretary of the World Council of Churches, 1961–5, bishop in Madras, 1965–74, professor of ecumenics and mission, Selly Oak Colleges, 1974–9, and minister, Winson Green United Reformed Church, 1980–8. He received a CBE in 1974 and was moderator of the United Reformed Church, 1978–9. His publications, including *The Other Side of 1984* (1983), *Foolishness to the Greeks* (1986) and *The Gospel in a Pluralist Society* (1989), were a major contribution to the 'Gospel and Culture' movement. His auto-

biography, *Unfinished Agenda*, was published in 1985 and 1995.

Newman, Henry Philanthropist, born Rehoboth, Massachusetts, 10 November 1670, died London, England, 15 June 1743. The son of an American Puritan minister and educated at Harvard College, he became an Anglican and went to England. He was the Secretary of the Society for Promoting Christian Knowledge from 1708 to 1743 and engaged in such philanthropic causes as the charity schools, the dissemination of religious literature, Christian missions in India the relief of foreign religious refugees and the beginnings of prison reform. He was also the colonial agent for New Hampshire and assisted in General Oglethorpe's foundation of the colony of Georgia.

Newman, John Henry Cardinal and writer, born London, 21 February 1801, died Edgbaston, Birmingham, 11 August 1890. He was brought up on the Evangelical wing of the Anglican Church, educated at Oxford, was ordained into the Anglican Church in 1824, and became vicar of the University church of St Mary the Virgin four years later. He became the leading figure in the Oxford Movement and the author of a number of the *Tracts for the Times*, including *Tract no. 90*, which argued that the Thirty-Nine Articles could be understood in a Roman Catholic sense. This appeared in 1841 and caused a considerable controversy. Newman resigned from St Mary's in 1843 and in October 1845 was received into the Roman Catholic Church. Many other notable figures joined him. He went to Rome, and there joined the Oratorians, establishing an Oratory in Birmingham on his return in 1847, which became his home for the rest of his life. He became rector of the Catholic University in Dublin, 1851–8, an appointment which was not a success, but which produced *The Idea of a University* in 1852. He was involved in a controversy with Charles **Kingsley**, who wrote that Newman 'did not consider truth a necessity'. Hence Newman responded with *Apologia pro vita sua* (1864). Exceptionally, in 1879, he was created a cardinal and, though not a diocesan bishop, allowed to remain in Birmingham rather than take up residence in Rome. He was one of the key literary and religious figures of the nineteenth century, and had a genius for writing. His romantic, mystical, imaginative poem *The Dream of Gerontius* drew a correspondingly inspired response from **Elgar** in the form of an oratorio. Excerpts from Newman's poem were published as hymns, perhaps one of the greatest being, Praise to the Holiest in the Height, set to music by various composers. Newman also wrote the still popular 'Lead, Kindly Light'. Works such as *A Grammar of Assent* and *Essay on the Development of Christian Doctrine* remain philosophically and theologically important.

Newton, Isaac   Sir, scientist, born Woolsthorpe, Lincolnshire, 25 December 1642, died Kensington, 20 March 1727. He was a fellow of Trinity College, Cambridge, in 1667 and professor of mathematics in 1669, MP for Cambridge University 1689 and 1701–2 and appointed Master of the Mint in 1699. His chief scientific achievements were the formulation of the law of gravity and the laws of motion, the discovery of the differential calculus and the analysis of white light. Though a practising churchman, he was unorthodox, denying the Trinity as unreasonable, but believing in God as the creator and ruler of the universe.

Newton, John   Minister of religion and hymnwriter, born London, 24 July 1725, died London, 21 December 1807. He went to sea with his father, experienced many maritime adventures, captained a slave ship, and was converted to an evangelical form of Christianity. He became an Anglican priest and curate at Olney. Here he collaborated with William **Cowper** and produced Olney Hymns. He had many friends among the social reformers and produced 280 hymns; 80 were published and many, such as 'Amazing Grace', are still popular.

Nicephorus Blemmydes   Byzantine monk, born Constantinople, 1197, died Emathia, near Ephesus, *c.*1269. He left Constantinople soon after its capture by the Crusaders and joined the clergy of Nicaea. In 1223, 1234 and 1250 he was a theologian-negotiator with the Latin delegates. He educated the future Emperor Theodore II Lascaris and George Akropolites, the founder of the monastery of Emathia in 1248; but he declined Theodore's offer of becoming bishop of Ephesus and patriarch of Nicaea. In 1264 he wrote his autobiography, in which he upheld the Greek ecclesiastical position.

Nicephorus I of Constantinople   Saint, patriarch, born 758, died 2 June 828. As imperial secretary to the court at Constantinople, he zealously opposed the Iconoclasts and attended the Second Council of Nicaea. Though a layman, he was made patriarch of Constantinople in 806, but in 813 Leo the Armenian, who was himself an Iconoclast, became emperor (**Leo V**) and banished him to the monastery of St Theodorus on the Bosporus, which he had founded, and he spent the last years of his life there. In 846 the regent Theodora had his body brought to Constantinople on 13 March, which became his feast day.

Nicetas Choniates   Byzantine historian, born Chonai, near ancient Collosae in Phrygia Pacatiana, *c.*1155, died Nicaea, *c.*1215. Educated at Constantinople, he became secretary to the last of the Comnenian emperors, Andronicu I, and held increasingly important posts under their successors, the Angeli, including that of chamberlain of the public treasury. The usurpation of Alexius V Ducas in 1204 ended his career, and in the same year the city's fall to the Fourth Crusade exiled him. Returning to Constantinople, he finished his history of this Crusade, but failed to gain influence in the newly established empire of Nicaea.

Nicetas David   Religious writer, died 920. His main work was a Life of the Byzantine patriarch Ignatius (*c.*907) supporting him as a saint. He opposed tetragamy (a fourth marriage) and wrote against the emperor and the Patriarch **Euthymius I**. He sought refuge in a hermitage near Media in Bulgaria; he was arrested and taken to Constantinople, but was pardoned and became a monk (taking the name 'David') in the monastery at Agathos until 910. He spent the rest of his life writing homilies and encomia.

Nicetas of Remesiana   Bishop and ecclesiastical author, born *c.*350, died after 414. He was bishop of Remesiana in Dacia (today Bela Palanka, Serbia). Little is known about his life except that he was a friend of **Paulinus** of Nola, whom he visited twice, in 398 and 402. From his works, *Instruction for Baptismal Candidates* (preserved only in fragments) and several other writings (including hymns and liturgical sermons) are important. Of several other works the authenticity is insecure.

Nicetas Stethatos Byzantine mystical writer, born c.1000, died 1050. 'Stethatos' means 'lion-hearted', and he was so called because he rebuked the Emperor **Constantine IX Monomachos** for immorality. When aged fourteen he was a follower of Symeon the New Theologian and already a monk of Studion Monastery, from which he was temporally expelled for believing Symeon to be a saint in his lifetime. He continued to follow Symeon's mysticism, which he expressed in his writings.

Nicetius of Trier Saint, bishop, died Trier, c.566. After entering a monastery at Limoges and becoming its abbot, he was made the twenty-fifth and last of the Gallo-Roman bishops of Trier (by King Theodoric). The barbarous Franks in his diocese were little more than nominal Christians, cruel and violent in behaviour. He excommunicated persistent offenders, including Kings Theudebert I and Clotaire, who exiled him for a time. Personally ascetic and charitable, he restored discipline and orthodoxy among the clergy, founded a school of clerical studies and rebuilt the cathedral. Feast day 5 December.

Nicholas I Pope and saint, born Rome, 820, died Rome, 13 November 867. Made subdeacon by Pope **Sergius II** and deacon by **Leo IV**, he was elected Pope on 24 April 858. In the difficulties after the collapse of **Charlemagne**'s empire, he upheld Christian morality and authority against worldly bishops and ambitious princes, and built and endowed several churches in Rome. He encouraged the Church's missionary activity and secured the position of the Papacy in Western Europe. He was one of the great medieval Popes. Feast day 13 November.

Nicholas I (of Constantinople) Patriarch, saint, born Constantinople, 852, died there, 15 May 925. Born of an Italian slave on an estate of the Patriarch **Photius**, he was a government official, but on Photius' fall in 886 became a monk. Soon after being made patriarch of Constantinople in 901, he was deposed during the dispute over the Emperor **Leo VI**'s tetragamy (fourth marriage). When recalled in 912 he persuaded Pope **John X** to end the schism by allowing the emperor a dispensation

for reasons of state. The Greek Church canonized him. Feast day 15 May.

Nicholas I Pavlovich (of Russia) Emperor, born Tsarskoye Selo, 25 June 1796, died St Petersburg, 2 March 1855. He succeeded to the throne in 1825 and inaugurated a return to national and religious values. He strongly supported Orthodoxy inside Russia and in the Turkish Empire, which contributed to the outbreak of the Crimean War. During his reign several million Uniates (Greek Catholics) in the Ukraine and Belorussia and thousands of Lutherans in the Baltic provinces embraced Orthodoxy. He encouraged the monastic revival which was beginning after the near destruction of monastic life under **Catherine II**.

Nicholas II Pope, born Chevron, Savoy, died Florence, 19 or 27 July 1061. A canon of Liège, he became bishop of Florence in 1046 and was elected Pope in December 1058 in opposition to **Benedict X**. He condemned clerical simony and concubinage, and at Easter 1059 held a synod in the Lateran to remove papal elections from factional and imperial influence. It was decided that these should be held by the cardinal-bishops at Rome subject to imperial confirmation. His pontificate was short, but had important, far-reaching consequences.

Nicholas II (Alexandrovich) Saint, emperor of Russia, born Gatchina, 6 May 1868, died (shot) Ekaterinburg, 17 July 1918. His life inevitably belongs to the political history of Russia but he has been revered as saint and martyr by Russian Orthodox believers from the moment of his death. He was patron and active helper of numerous charities, Orthodox missionary endeavours and other Christian causes (including world peace). Owing to his efforts, St **Seraphim of Sarov** was canonized. His complete lack of resistance to exile, imprisonment and certain death made him a modern example of the ancient Russian 'Passion-bearers', who were martyrs for justice in the face of violence and aggression. He was canonized, together with all the 'New Martyrs', by the Russian Orthodox Church Abroad on 1 November 1982. Feast day 4 July.

Nicholas III Pope, born 'Giovanni Gaetano' at

Rome, *c*.1215, died Soriano, near Viterbo, 22 August 1280. Elected Pope 25 November 1277. A member of the powerful Orsini family, he was chiefly concerned during his pontificate to ensure the independence of the Papacy by restricting the role of other major players on the Italian peninsula, particularly **Charles of Anjou**, king of Sicily but also a Roman senator. He managed to so define the boundaries of the Papal States that they remained thus until they were overrun in the nineteenth-century unification of Italy. In order to prevent disputes over this territory, he arranged an alliance between the Habsburg and Anjou families. The negotiations to this end had not been completed at his death. He improved the efficiency of the papal curia, restored St Peter's, and made the Vatican palace beside St Peter's his normal place of residence – the first Pope who did so. He also entered into negotiations with the Byzantine emperor Michael VIII Palaeologus for a possible reunion of the Churches, and prevented an attack on Constantinople by Charles of Sicily.

Nicholas III Grammaticos (of Constantinople) Patriarch, born Pisidian Antioch(?), died Constantinople, April or May 1111. He possibly left Antioch because of the Turkish incursions *c*.1068. In Constantinople he founded a monastery dedicated to St John, and in August 1084 he was chosen by the emperor to serve as patriarch, and his period of office was marked by intense administrative and canonical activity. He attempted to regulate the difficult questions raised by Leo the Chalcedonian, who opposed the employment of sacred objects for other than religious uses as a form of Iconoclasm, including the use of Church jewels to supplement the needs of the imperial treasury as required by the Emperor **Alexius I Comnenus**. He sought to increase monastic discipline and made efforts to promote bishoprics to the rank of metropolitan sees.

Nicholas IV Pope, born Ascoli, March of Ancona, 1227, died Rome, 4 April 1292. At an early age he entered the Franciscan Order and in 1278, while on a mission to promote peace between France and Castile, was made a cardinal-priest and in 1281 bishop of Palestrina. In 1287 a divided conclave met to elect a Pope, but an outbreak of fever decimated the electors. They met again on 15

February 1288 and unanimously chose Nicholas, but a second election was required to overcome his reluctance. He was the first Franciscan Pope and was subjected to the Angevin influence in Italy.

Nicholas V Pope, born 'Tommaso Parentucelli', the son of a doctor, at Sarzana, 15 November 1397, died Rome, 24 March 1455. A humanist scholar of modest origins, Parentucelli had been a cardinal for only a matter of months before being elected to the papal office on 6 March 1447. His pontificate witnessed the end of the schismatic threat from the Council of Basel, and the fall of Constantinople to the Ottoman Turks, 1453. The New Learning was supported by the Pope's own literary activities, his foundation of the Vatican Library and his patronage of Italian humanists and Greek scholars, including **Bessarion.** His ambitious urban planning in Rome initiated the rebuilding of St Peter's basilica, funding for which came from the Jubilee of 1450.

Nicholas of Aarhus Blessed, born Jutland, *c*.1150, died Aarhus, Denmark, 1180. An illegitimate son of King Canute Magnusson, he spent some time at the Danish court and then went to his estates near Aarhus, where he lived a simple, holy life. He was popularly regarded as a saint, but never recognized by any formal process.

Nicholas of Autrecourt Philosopher and theologian, born Autrecourt, near Verdun, *c*.1300, died *c*.1351. He studied at Paris, and became a prebend at Metz in 1338 while teaching at Paris. Because he attacked the Aristotelian logic incorporated into medieval theology, he was charged at the papal court of Avignon with heresy. **Benedict XII**'s death in April 1342 interrupted the proceedings, which were resumed under **Clement VI**. After condemnation in 1346, he retracted his errors and witnessed the burning of his works in 1347. Taking refuge at **Louis IV** of Bavaria's court, he became dean of Metz Cathedral in 1350, but nothing more is known of him. He represented the growing dissatisfaction with Aristotelian theological thought.

Nicholas of Basel Medieval heretic, died Vienna, *c*.1395. Preaching in the Rhineland near Basel, he proclaimed himself to be inspired and to have episcopal powers. He claimed that submitting to his direction was needed for spiritual perfection, that his followers could not sin and need not obey any other ecclesiastical authority. He escaped the Inquisition for many years, but eventually was burnt at the stake with two supporters at Vienna.

Nicholas of Clamanges Curial official and reformer, born Clamanges, Champagne, c.1360, died 1432. A brilliant student at the University of Paris, he became its rector in 1393. He went to the papal court at Avignon, where he became secretary and librarian to **Benedict XIII** in 1394, remaining faithful to his patron until Benedict's final break with King Charles VI of France in 1408. He was suspected of writing the bull excommunicating the king and was never in office again, spending the rest of his life in his old College of Navarre in Paris. He wrote *In de Ruini Ecclesiae*, attacking religious abuses, such as papal provisions, the sale of benefices and ignorant and immoral clerics, stating 'scarcely a man in a thousand does what his profession requires'.

Nicholas of Cusa Cardinal and philosopher, born Cues, on the Moselle, 1401, died Todi, Umbria, 11 August 1464. Educated at Heidelberg, Padua – where he graduated as a doctor of laws in 1423 – and then in theology at Cologne, he was ordained priest in 1430 and became dean of St Florin's, Coblenz. In 1431 he was at the Council of Basel and secured its reconciliation with the Utraquists, those who believed that Communion should be received under the forms of both bread and wine, a practice which had fallen into disuse. In 1433 he produced *De concordantia catholica*, outlining a reform programme for both Church and Empire. In 1437 he was sent by Pope **Eugenius IV** to Constantinople to try to bring reconciliation with the Orthodox. Originally a conciliarist, he became a supporter of the papal cause and was made a cardinal by **Nicholas V** for his part in securing the Concordat of Vienna (1448). He was appointed bishop of Brixen in the Tyrol in 1450, but was unable to take possession of the see until 1452, from which time he was a conscientious bishop until expelled by Duke Sigismund. He went to Rome, where he was made papal vicar general for the government – and reform – of the city. He

wrote on Church politics, on theology, on science and on philosophy, his best-remembered work being *De docta ignorantia*, on the knowledge of God, which he completed in 1440.

Nicholas of Dinkelsbühl Theologian, born Dinkesbühl, Germany, c.1360, died Vienna, 17 March 1433. He was a canon of St Stephen's Cathedral, Vienna, and in 1425 confessor to Duke Albrecht V, whose ecclesiastical policy he supported. He was the German representative at the assembly which elected Pope **Martin V**, so ending the Western Schism. The Pope commissioned him in 1427 to preach to the Hussites. He was a strong supporter of conciliarism, the doctrine asserting that a General Council constituted the supreme authority in the Church.

Nicholas of Flüe Saint, born near Sachseln, Canton Oberwalden, Switzerland, 21 March 1417, died Sachseln, 21 March 1487. The son of wealthy peasants, he was a soldier, judge and cantonal councillor. In 1467, after a quarter-century of married life, his wife and ten children agreed to his departing to live as a hermit at Ranft, where he lived for nineteen years, reputedly with no food besides Holy Communion. He was esteemed as 'Bruder Klaus' in Switzerland, and his influence with the confederates in 1481 averted a civil war. Feast day 21 March, but in Switzerland, as its patron saint, 25 September.

Nicholas of Gorran Dominican preacher and scriptural commentator, born Gorran, France, 1232, died Paris, c.1295. Entering the order in Gorran, he was educated at St James's Convent, Paris, where he was several times prior. He was confessor and adviser to Philip IV of France and a notable preacher and writer on the Bible.

Nicholas of Hereford Supporter of John **Wycliffe**, born Hereford, died Coventry, 1420. He was a fellow, and sometime bursar, of Queen's College, Oxford, who was ordained priest in 1370. A Lollard who befriended Wycliffe and has been thought to be the translator of the 1380 version of Wycliffe's Bible, he was in 1382 summoned to London to answer for his opinions, and was excommunicated. He set out for Rome to plead his case, but was ordered by the Pope to be imprisoned for life;

he escaped and returned to England in 1391, was imprisoned, recanted, and was made chancellor of Hereford Cathedral, 1397–1417. From 1417 he lived in Coventry as a Carthusian monk.

Nicholas of Hermanssön Saint, bishop, born Skeninge, Sweden, 1331, died Linköping, Sweden, 1391. Educated at Paris and Orléans, he was ordained priest and appointed tutor to the sons of **St Brigid of Sweden**. Eventually he became bishop of Linköping. He is greatly honoured in Sweden as a liturgist and poet. Feast day 24 July.

Nicholas (Kasatkin) of Japan Russian Orthodox saint, bishop and missionary, born near Smolensk, 1 August 1836, died Tokyo, 3 February 1912. He became a missionary in Japan in 1861 and succeeded in founding a fully indigenous local Church entirely staffed by Japanese priests. By 1904 there were 260 congregations, and he was made archbishop of Tokyo in 1906. He also supervised a complete translation of the Orthodox liturgical books and other basic texts. Feast day 3 February.

Nicholas of Lyra Franciscan scholar, born Normandy, c.1270, died Paris, 1340. He became a Franciscan at Verneuil, studied theology in Paris and was a professor at the Sorbonne. He preached and wrote for the conversion of the Jews, but was most important as a biblical exegete, seeking the exact and literal senses of the Scriptures against the allegorical interpretations of the time. His chief work was his *Postillae perpetuae in universam s. Scripturam*, which became a popular biblical commentary. It has been suggested that **Luther** was strongly influenced by him.

Nicholas of Myra Saint, bishop, born, Pararia, Lycia, Asia Minor, died Myra, 6 December 345 or 352. A popular saint in both the Greek and Latin Churches, but little is known about him. He is said during his youth to have made a pilgrimage to Egypt and Palestine. Appointed bishop of Myra, he was imprisoned during the persecution of Diocletian, but released by **Constantine I**. He was said to have been present at the Council of Nicaea, though his name is not on the early lists of names of the bishops at the Council. In 1087 Italian merchants stole his body from Myra and took it to Bari, Italy. Because of the story that he secretly

provided poor young women with money for their dowries he is often depicted carrying three bags of gold, and he is the origin of 'Santa Claus'. Feast day 6 December.

Nicholas of Ochrid and Zhicha (Nikolai Velimirovich) Serbian Orthodox saint, bishop and writer, born Valjevo, Serbia, 23 December 1880, died St Tikhon's monastery, Pennsylvania, 18 March 1956. He studied in Switzerland, Germany, England and Russia. He obtained British support for Serbia during World War I and his whole life was devoted to both his Church and his people. In 1941 he was arrested by the Germans, together with Patriarch Gabriel, and sent to Dachau concentration camp, where he spent two years. Instead of returning to Yugoslavia he went to America, where he continued to lecture and write. His most famous work is *The Prologue of Ochrid* – lives of and meditations on the saints. He was canonized in 1987. Feast day 5 March.

Nicholas of Prussia Saint, born c.1379, died 1456. A native of Prussia, he was one of the original members of the reformed abbey of St Justina at Padua under the Venerable Ludovico Barbo, founder of the Benedictine Cassinese Congregation. He resided successively at Padua, Venice, Padolirone and finally at the abbey of San Niccolò del Boschetto, near Genoa, where he was novice master and prior. Feast day 23 February

Nicholas of Strasburg (Nicholas Kempf) Dominican mystic, born Strasburg, c.1416, died Gamina, 20 November 1497. Educated at Paris and then a lector at the Dominican convent at Cologne, he was made by Pope **John XXII** a canonical visitor of the German Dominican province to resolve the discord there. In 1326 he supported Meister **Eckhart**, whose mystical teaching led to his being tried for heresy before the court of Heinrich, archbishop of Cologne. He was last heard of as vicar of the German Dominicans in 1339 after the settlement of the process against Eckhart. His extant sermons support good works, penitential practices and indulgences, confession and the Eucharist enabling the love of God to convert the sinner.

Nicholas of Tolentino Saint, born Sant' Angelo, March of Ancona, Italy, c.1245, died Tolentino,

Italy, 10 September 1306. He made his profession as an Augustinian friar in 1253 and was ordained priest. He devoted himself to pastoral work among the poor and destitute, preaching almost every day. He is recorded to have achieved remarkable conversions and frequent miracles. He spent his last 30 years at Tolentino, where he was interred, and fragments of his body are said to foretell calamities by bleeding, as in 1452 before the Fall of Constantinople and 1510 before the Reformation. Feast day 10 September.

Nicholas of Verdun Artist, born *c.*1130, died *c.*1205. He is named as the designer in inscriptions attached to two works of art – the ambo formerly attached to the choir screen of the Augustinian abbey of Klosterneuburg and the Shrine of Mary in Notre Dame de Tournai. Other works attributed to him are the Shrine of the Magi in Cologne Cathedral and the Anno Shrine at St Michael's in Siegburg. His style was of immediate influence in the Rhône and Meuse areas and in northern France, as shown by illuminated manuscripts and cathedral sculptures.

Nicholas Oresme Medieval philosopher, born Normandy, *c.*1320, died Lisieux, 11 July 1382. Studying at Paris from 1348 and being a canon of Rouen Cathedral, grand master of the Collège de Navarre and chaplain of King Charles V, he was made bishop of Lisieux in 1377. He considered questions of economics and politics and also natural science. His *De l'origine, nature et mutation des monnaies* was the first scientific investigation of monetary problems, and in *Livre du ciel et du monde* he considered the possibility of many universes and the daily motion of the earth.

Nicholas Paglia Blessed, Dominican administrator and preacher, born Giovinezzo, near Baria, Italy, 1197, died Perugia, 11 February 1255. When studying law at Bologna, he heard St **Dominic** preach in 1218 and joined his Order, founding priories at Trani, Perugia and perhaps Todi, and becoming provincial of the Roman province, 1230–5 and 1255. Pope **Gregory IX** got him to reform the Benedictine monks of St Antonio. He was a good preacher and a charitable administrator. Feast day 14 February.

Nicholas Planas of Athens Orthodox saint and priest, born Naxos, Greece, 1851, died Athens, 2 March 1932. He spent all his adult life ministering in different parish churches in Athens. He is a recent example of 'foolishness for Christ's sake' and was treated with contempt by most of his fellow clergy. His absolute simplicity and gentleness attracted a devoted group of followers, who later wrote down their recollections. Miracles have been continuously claimed at his tomb, and he was eventually canonized under popular pressure. Feast day 18 February.

Nicholas the Studite Saint, born Crete, 793, died Constantinople, 4 February 868. A student at the monastery of the Studion at Constantinople, he went into exile with the abbot during the Iconoclastic persecution and, when able to return, himself became the abbot. Under the Emperor Michael III, he would not recognize the usurper **Photius** and was deposed. When the rightful patriarch, St Ignatius, was restored by the Emperor **Basil I**, Nicholas considered himself too old to become abbot again and remained a simple monk. He was famous as a scribe. Feast day 4 February.

Nicholas Trevet Dominican scholar, born Somerset(?), *c.*1265, the son of Sir Thomas Trent, an itinerant justice, died London(?), *c.*1335. He was a member of the Oxford Dominican priory by November 1297, regent master in the Oxford schools, 1303–7 and 1314–15, and lector at the Dominican London convent, September 1324. He wrote some 30 works, the most important being commentaries on the Bible, **Augustine** and **Boethius**, Livy and Seneca. Later he wrote historical works, particularly his *Annales* from the events immediately after Stephen's accession and ending with a valuable contemporary narrative of the reign of Edward I.

Niclaes, Hendrik Founder of the Family of Love, born Münster, Westphalia(?), 9 or 10 January 1502 or 1501, died Cologne, 1580. He was brought up in a pious Catholic family, and even as a child experienced visions. From 1531 he was in business in Amsterdam, where he gathered followers after believing himself called, in 1540, to become a prophet. He was imprisoned, but escaped and travelled in The Netherlands and to London and

Cologne. He wrote over 50 pamphlets about his prophecies and mystical pantheism. He upheld an actual holiness and righteousness as practised in his 'House of Love'. The greater part of his numerous writings have been lost. He had some supporters in England and The Netherlands, but the 'Nicolaites' died out during the seventeenth century.

Nicodemus of Mammola   Saint, born Cirae, *c.*900, died Mammola, Greece, 25 March 990. When young he became a Basilian monk under St Fatino's spiritual guidance and later went to Mount Cellerano, where his strict form of life drew many followers to his hermitage. In about 975 he established in the woods near Mammola a monastery which after his death was dedicated to him. Feast day 12 March.

Nicodemus of the Holy Mountain (the Hagiorite) Orthodox saint, monk and spiritual writer, born Naxos, Greece, 1749, died Mount Athos, 14 July 1809. After becoming a monk of Athos, he collaborated with St **Macarius of Corinth** in producing anthologies of patristic and spiritual writings which had long been neglected, most famously the *Philokalia* (which was soon translated into Slavonic and Romanian). From this five-volume collection, published in Venice in 1782, can be dated the beginning of the great spiritual and monastic revival of nineteenth-century Orthodoxy. Nicodemus was a strong supporter of frequent Communion. He was proclaimed a saint in the Eastern Church in 1955. Feast day 14 July.

Nicolas, Jean Jacques Auguste   Religious writer, born Bordeaux, 6 January 1807, died Versailles, 17 January 1888. A lawyer and civil servant, he wrote popularly for particular occasions: *Études philosophiques sur le christianisme* (4 vols, 1842–5), for his doubting father-in-law; *Nouvelles Études philosophiques* (1859), after he believed the Virgin Mary had healed his daughter; *L'État sans Dieu* (1872), on republican France; *Rome et la Papauté* (1882), a defence of papal sovereignty after a visit to Rome.

Nicole, Pierre   Theologian, born Chartres, 19 October 1625, died Paris, 16 November 1695. After graduating at the University of Paris in 1649, he taught at Port-Royal, where he became friendly

with Antoine **Arnauld**, with whom he collaborated in many of his writings, and with whom he stayed in Belgium when obliged for a time to leave Paris. His best-known work was his Latin version of **Pascal**'s *Lettres provinciales* (1658). He wrote much defending Jansenists against the Jesuits, but was more moderate in tone than most Jansenist writers: in a posthumous publication, *Traité de la grâce générale* (1715), there is a clear rejection of Jansenism. His *Dix Lettres sur L'hérésie imaginaire* gives an important insight into life at Port-Royal. He also wrote a defence of transubstantiation and wrote against Calvinists and Protestantism in general. His other works include *Traité de l'oraison* (1679) and *Réfutation des principales erreurs des quiétistes* (1695), in which latter book he adopted the stance of **Bossuet**.

Nider, Johann   Dominican writer, born Isny, 1380, died Nuremberg, 13 August 1438. He joined the Order of Preachers at Colmar about 1400 and studied at Vienna and Cologne, where he was ordained. From 1423 as a professor at the University of Vienna and prior of Nuremberg, he supported the reforms of **Raymond of Capua** and Giovanni **Dominici** and in 1429 became prior of the convent of strict observance at Basel and vicar of all the reformed German priories. In 1431 the Council of Basel sent him to try to regain for Catholicism the Hussites in Bohemia. His chief work, *Formicarius* (1437), reveals the contemporary religious and political situation.

Niebuhr, Barthold Georg   Writer and politician, born Copenhagen, Denmark, 27 August 1776, died Bonn, Germany, 2 January 1831. While in the Danish civil service, his hostility to revolutionary and Napoleonic France and support of German nationalism led Baron Heinrich von Stern to get him a position in the Prussian finance administration, where he remained until 1810. As Prussian representative at the Vatican he secured the concordat of 1821. He spent his last years writing on German history, founding the modern empirical science of history in which textual criticism decides the credibility and genuineness of the relevant sources.

Niebuhr, Helmut Richard   American Evangelical theologian, born Wright City, Missouri, 3 September 1894, died New Haven, Connecticut, 5 July 1962. The younger brother of Reinhold **Niebuhr**, he went to the Eden Theological Seminary, Webster Grove, Missouri, and in 1916 was ordained, staying on at the seminary to teach. He went to Yale Divinity School in 1922, taking his doctorate two years later. He returned for a time to his denomination's colleges, but in 1931, after a year in Europe, returned to Yale as professor of Christian ethics and from 1950 until his death as Sterling professor. Under the separate influence of Karl **Barth** and Ernst **Troeltsch**, he accepted the effect of historical revelation in opposition to the ideas of liberal theology. Troeltsch led him to realize that revelations are conditioned by their contemporary historical and cultural expression; and he examined the connection between religious beliefs and social communities in America (*The Social Sources of Denominationalism* (1929)). His best-known work, perhaps, is *Christ and Culture* (1951).

Niebuhr, Reinhold American Evangelical theologian, born Wright City, Missouri, 21 June 1892, died Stockbridge, Massachusetts, 1 June 1971. After Eden Theological Seminary, Webster Grove, Missouri, he went to Yale in 1914; he was ordained in 1915 and pastor of the Bethel Evangelical Church, Detroit, 1915–28. He became professor of ethics and the philosophy of religion at Union Theological Seminary, New York City, 1928–60. He was especially concerned with the relationship between religion and society, and began as an ardent pacifist, but under the influence of the rise of Fascism he left the Fellowship of Reconciliation in 1933 and the Socialist Party in 1940 – he had been the Socialist candidate for the New York Senate in 1930 and for Congress in 1932. In 1941 he founded the journal *Christianity and Crisis*. Influenced by Karl **Barth** and Emil **Brunner**, he revived the doctrine of original sin and expounded a 'vital prophetic Christianity', which had an important effect on contemporary American sociology and politics. Many of his books, which began in 1929 with *Does Civilization Need Religion?*, are concerned with religion and politics.

Nielsen, Laurentius Jesuit missionary to Sweden, born Oslo, Norway, 1538, died Vilna, Lithuania, 5 May 1622. While studying for the Lutheran minis-try at Louvain in 1558, he met the Jesuits, became a Catholic, was admitted to the Society in 1564 and ordained. In 1576 he was sent to Sweden to assist in the conversion of King John III to Roman Catholicism. He taught theology in the new college founded by the converted king. Nielsen then left Sweden, teaching theology elsewhere and founding a college in Denmark in 1606.

Niemöller, Martin Lutheran pastor, German patriot, Nazi opponent and ecumenical leader, born Lippstadt, 4 January 1892, died Wiesbaden, 5 March 1984. Son of a Westphalian Lutheran pastor and a mother of Huguenot ancestry, Niemöller was a decorated submarine commander in World War I and became a Protestant minister in 1924. In 1931 he was appointed pastor at Dahlem in Berlin. Briefly a supporter of Hitler, he was arrested in 1937 for anti-Nazi activities and his commitment to the Confessing Church. He shared in the Stuttgart 'Declaration of Guilt' of 1945, and until 1956 was head of foreign relations for the Evangelical Church in Germany. He was president of the territorial Church of Hesse and Nassau, 1947–64. Widely known for his personal courage and pacifist views, he was a member of the central and executive committees of the World Council of Churches, 1948–61 and president, 1961–8.

Nieuwland, Julius Arthur Scientist and Roman Catholic priest, born Hansbeke, Belgium, 14 February 1878, died Washington, DC, 11 June 1936. Moving with his family to America in 1880, he studied at Notre Dame University and was ordained in 1903. In 1904 he became professor of botany at Notre Dame; he published nearly 100 papers on botanical subjects and gathered a large collection of American plant specimens. In 1918 he became professor of organic chemistry at Notre Dame, and his research led in 1931 to the perfection of a new synthetic rubber, neoprene.

Nifo, Agostino Philosopher, born Sessa, Italy, 1473, died Salerno, *c.*1538. He taught at Naples and then Padua and wrote a number of works, including commentaries on Aristotle, the most important being *Tractatus de immortalitate animae contra Pomponatium*, upholding the immortality of the human soul against **Pomponazzi**, who denied the possibility of the soul existing apart from the body. Nifo was much influenced by Aristotle and, earlier in his career, by the Arab philosopher Averroes.

Nigel Wireker (Nigel of Longchamp)   Satirist; born probably at Longchamp, Normandy, c.1130, died c.1200. Little is known of his life. He quite possibly studied at Paris and was perhaps in **Thomas Becket**'s service. He entered Christ Church, Canterbury, c.1170, and spent the rest of his life as a priest there, perhaps as its precentor. He wrote *Speculum stultorum* ('The Mirror of Fools'), about an ass trying to get a longer tail, be educated in Paris and found a religious order, and *Contra curiales et officiales administratos*, against clerical courtiers and administrators involved in secular politics.

Nightingale, Florence   English nurse and hospital reformer, born Florence, Italy, 12 May 1820, died London, 13 August 1910. Committed to nursing from an early age, she made regular visits to hospitals, studied advances in hygiene and gave practical assistance during an outbreak of cholera. In 1854 she volunteered for duty in the Crimean War and arrived with two friends and 38 nurses, eighteen of whom were nuns (ten Roman Catholic, eight Church of England). She organized the barracks, and cleaned up the hospital and conditions at the front, considerably reducing the mortality rate by firm discipline and sanitation. She returned to England in 1856, where a fund in her honour led to the foundation of the Nightingale School and a Home for Nurses attached to St Thomas's Hospital. Her *Notes on Nursing* (1859) ran to many editions. She continued to take an interest in the state of hospitals both in Britain and in India until the end of her life. She was awarded many decorations, both national and foreign, including in 1907 the Order of Merit, the first time it had been bestowed on a woman. At her death her family was offered a funeral in Westminster Abbey, but, in accordance with Florence Nightingale's instructions, this was refused.

Nikel, Johannes   Roman Catholic biblical scholar, born Sohrau, Upper Silesia, Germany, 18 October 1863, died Breslau, 28 June 1924. After studying theology and oriental languages at Breslau and Würzburg he was ordained in 1886 and was a parish priest until 1890. He taught at a secondary school until 1897 and then lectured on OT exegesis at the University of Breslau, becoming its rector in 1923. In 1907, as consultor of the Pontifical Biblical Commission, he sought to establish agreement between **Pius X**'s conservatism and contemporary biblical criticism. He was more successful in making the OT's teaching popularly understood and applying it to social questions.

Nikon   Patriarch of Moscow, born near Nizhni Novgorod, 1605, died Yaroslavl, 17 August 1681. A vigorous monastic reformer, he was elected patriarch in 1652. Like **Philaret** Romanov he was virtual co-ruler with the Tsar. His clumsy liturgical reforms aimed at conforming Russian usages to contemporary Greek practice gave rise to a major schism (the Old Believers). In 1667 he was deposed, though his reforms were confirmed. Under the next Tsar he was forgiven and reinstated but died before reaching Moscow.

Niles, Daniel Thambyrajah   Sri Lankan evangelist, ecumenical leader and hymn-writer, born Ceylon (Sri-Lanka), 4 May 1908, died Vellore, India, 17 July 1970. 'D. T.' was the son of a lawyer and grandson of a pastor and poet. Educated in Jaffna, he studied at Bangalore, 1929–33 became national secretary of the Student Christian Movement, was ordained to the Methodist ministry in 1936, served as a district evangelist and took part in the International Missionary Council Tambaram Conference, 1938. After being YMCA evangelism secretary in Geneva, 1939–40, he was in pastoral ministry and was general secretary of the National Christian Council of Ceylon, 1941–5. He spoke at the inaugural meeting of the World Council of Churches in 1948, was chairman of the youth department, 1948–52, and evangelism secretary, 1953–9. Instrumental in the founding of the East Asia Christian Conference (EACC) in 1957, he was its first general secretary, and chairman from 1968. He compiled the *EACC Hymnal* and his hymns are found in other collections.

Nilles, Nikolaus   Jesuit liturgist and canon lawyer, born Rippweiler, Luxembourg, 21 June 1828, died Innsbruck, 31 January 1907. Ordained in 1852 and a curate at Amsenberg until 1858, he then became a Jesuit and the next year was professor of canon law at the University of Innsbruck, until 1906. From 1870 to 1896 he was also rector of the seminary there. He wrote a number of works on worship and Church law.

Nilus of Ancyra Saint, known as 'the Wise', died *c*.430. Believed to have been an imperial official at Constantinople; he became a hermit with his son on Mount Sinai. He was a friend of St **John Chrysostom**, was ordained by the bishop of Eleusa in Palestine and became the founder and superior of a monastery near Ancyra. He is now best remembered as an ascetical, theological and biblical writer. Feast day 12 November.

Nilus of Rossano Saint, abbot, died Frascati, near Rome, *c*.1005. A Greek of Italy, he joined the Basilian monks of St Adrian's Abbey, Calabria, and became its abbot. In 981 the Saracens drove the monks to Vellucio, on land given them by the abbey of Monte Cassino. In obedience to his decree shortly before his death at Frascati, his disciple St Bartholomew of Rossano founded there the abbey of Grottaferrata under St **Basil**'s Rule and in the Greek rite. Feast day 26 September.

Nina, Lorenzo Cardinal and Secretary of State under Pope **Leo XIII**, born Recanti (Marches), Italy, 12 May 1812, died Rome, 25 July 1885. After the seminary, he studied law at the University of Rome and was ordained in 1834. He served in the papal curia (with judicial, legislative and executive duties), the Rota (a tribunal of auditors for appeals) and the Congregation of Council (concerned with the discipline of the secular clergy). In 1877 he was made a cardinal and Assessor of the Holy Office, and from 1878 to 1880 he was Secretary of State. He faced the breaking of relations with France in 1880 and the Kulturkampf in Germany from 1871.

Ninguarda, Feliciano Dominican theologian and bishop, born Morbegno, Italy, 1524, died Como, 5 June 1595. He entered the Dominicans in Milan. In 1554 he became vicar general of the Upper German province and later professor of theology at the University of Vienna. Having been procurator for the archbishop of Salzburg at the Council of Trent, he then implemented the Council's reforms for the mendicant orders in Austria, Bohe-

mia and Moravia. Between 1577 and 1595 he was successively bishop of Scala (Salerno), of Santa Agatha dei Goti (Benevento) and of Como, as well as being papal nuncio to Bavaria until 1585. His writings include works on pastoral care.

Ninian Saint, bishop, born *c*.360, died *c*.432. The son of a converted Cumbrian British chieftain, he was said by **Bede** to have been educated at Rome, where he was consecrated bishop in 394 and sent to evangelize Scotland. Travelling through Tours on the way, he met St **Martin**, to whom he later dedicated the church (commonly called 'Candida Casa') he built at Whithorn in Wigtownshire. From here he and his monks evangelized the Britons and Picts; it was long a centre of learning for the Welsh and Irish missionaries and his tomb there was a shrine for medieval pilgrims. Feast day 16 September.

Nithard Soldier, abbot and scholar, born *c*.800, probably killed in the Battle of Angoumois, Aquitaine, 14 June 844. He was the illegitimate son of **Charlemagne**'s daughter, Bertha, and his minister **Angilbert**, and was important through his *Historiarum libri quattuor*, the history of Charles the Bold, 814–43, the chief information about the wars among the sons of **Louis I** the Pious. He was Charles' emissary in 840 to make peace with **Lothair I**, but was relieved of the fief held from Louis the Pious as he refused to defect from Charles. He fought in the Battle of Foulesing, 25 June 841. He was a representative of the western half of the empire to discuss with the representatives of the eastern half dividing the empire between Louis and Charles. He became abbot of Riquier, Centulum, *c*.842.

Nivard Blessed, born *c*.1100, died *c*.1150. The youngest brother of St **Bernard**, whom he joined at Clairvaux later novice master at Vaucelles. Little is known for certain about his subsequent life, and his cult is not confirmed. Feast day 7 February.

Nivard of Ghent Benedictine monk, fl. *c*.1150. Though of German birth, he was influenced by French learning at the monastic schools of Ghent and of Paris. He wrote *Ysengrimus*, an allegory about beasts, satirizing Popes, priests and monks. It opposed papal claims of world-wide authority, and attacked by name bishops and other figures, one of the best works of its genre to that point.

Niza, Marcos de   Franciscan explorer, died Mexico City, 25 March 1558. Probably Italian by birth, he was a priest and member of the Friars Minor of the Regular Observance. In 1531 he left Europe for Hispaniola. Instructed by the commissary general of the Indies, he went to Peru, leading the first Franciscans there. In 1535 he went to Guatemala and in 1537 to Mexico. Between 1540 and 1543, while undertaking further exploration, he served also as provincial in Mexico. Crippled by his expeditions, he was sent to warmer Jalapa (Vera Cruz), but returned to Mexico City to die.

Noailles, Louis Antoine de   Cardinal archbishop, born chateau of Teissîres, near Aurillac, 27 May 1651, died Paris, 4 May 1729. The second son of the duke of Noailles, he became bishop of Cahors in 1679, archbishop of Chalon in 1680, archbishop of Paris in 1695 and a cardinal in 1700. He supported **Clement XI**'s constitution *Vineam Domini Sabaoth* of 1705 condemning the Jansenist clergy, but he forbade the Jesuits to officiate in his diocese in 1713. He opposed the bull *Unigenitus*. Louis XV banished him from the court. He finally accepted the bull in 1728.

Noailles, Pierre Bienvenu   Founder of the Holy Family Sisters of Bordeaux, born Bordeaux, 27 October 1793, died Bordeaux, 8 February 1861. An irreligious youth, he was changed by a visit to the church of Saint-Sulpice in Paris in 1813. Ordained in 1829, he was a curate at Bordeaux and in 1830 founded the Sisters to care for the poor, orphans and the sick.

Nobili, Roberto de   Jesuit missionary, oriental scholar, born Rome, September 1577, died Mylapore, Madras, India, 16 January 1656. He joined the Jesuits in 1597 and went to India in 1605. From 1606 he was based at Madurai, Mysore. He mastered Tamil, Telugu and Sanskrit, familiarized himself with the Hindu Vedas and adopted a sannyasi (holy man) lifestyle to indicate that becoming a Christian did not mean becoming Portuguese. His cultural accommodation methods were attacked as syncretistic in the Malabar rites controversy but gained papal approval from

Gregory XV in the apostolic constitution *Romanae Sedis Antistes*, 31 January 1623. His writings in Tamil and Sanskrit included poems, catechisms and philosophical and theological expositions of the Christian faith.

Nobill, John   Jesuit missionary, born Rome, 8 April 1812, died Santa Clara, California, 1 March 1856. Becoming a Jesuit in 1828, he taught in the Society's colleges in Italy. Ordained in 1843, he volunteered to go to the Oregon region of North America. In 1844 he worked in Fort Vancouver and then among the Indians and settlers of New Caledonia (now British Columbia). He established chapels in the forts and trading posts of the Hudson's Bay Company and went up to the southern boundary of Alaska. In 1849 he was sent to San Francisco and in 1850 founded Santa Clara College, the first Roman Catholic college in California. He was its first president until his death.

Nóbrega, Manuel da   Jesuit missionary, born Portugal, 18 October 1517, died Rio de Janeiro, 18 October 1570. A Jesuit from 1544, he went to Brazil with the first governor-general, Tomé de Sousa, who is said to have landed with a cross, exclaiming, 'This land is our enterprise.' Nóbrega helped to found Salvador in 1550, São Paulo in 1554 and Rio de Janeiro in 1565. He became Brazil's first Jesuit superior and provincial, and in 1567 founded the college of Rio de Janeiro.

Nock, Arthur Darby   English-American historian of religion, born Portsmouth, England, 21 February 1902, died Cambridge, Massachusetts, 11 January 1963. After studies in Cambridge (UK) he became in 1930 professor for the history of religion at Harvard. His area of specialization was the religions of antiquity. Besides editorial work for journals and series he published many books, the most renowned (and criticized) of which is *Conversion . . . from Alexander the Great to Julian*. Together with A. Festugière he also edited the *Corpus Hermeticum*.

Noetus of Smyrna   Heretic, died *c.*200, known chiefly through **Hippolytus**, who stated he was a native of Smyrna. He was probably the first to teach the Patripassian belief that God the Father, through the incarnation, was born, suffered and died. He rejected also the Logos doctrine, accepting only an allegorical interpretation of the Prologue of St John's Gospel. An assembly of presbyters at Smyrna condemned him *c.*200.

Nogaret, Guillaume de Lawyer, born S.-Felix de Caraman, near Toulouse, *c.*1260, died Schönen, 11 April *c.*1313. Professor of law at the University of Montpellier *c.*1292. He was summoned by King Philip IV the Fair to be a member of the royal council and of the *parlement* of Paris. In 1302 he became the king's chief lawyer in his struggle with Pope **Boniface VIII**: his plan to remove Boniface to France for trial for heresy was frustrated by the Pope's death. He probably was prominent in electing the French **Clement V** as Pope and settling the Papacy at Avignon. He was also prominent in confiscating Jewish wealth in 1306 and in the Templars' trial for heresy.

Noldin, Hieronymus Jesuit moral theologian, born Salurn, South Tyrol, Austria, 30 January 1838, died Vienna, 7 November 1922. Ordained in 1861 he became a Jesuit in 1864, and later rector of the Jesuit theological college at Innsbruck. His first book, *Der Andacht zum Heiligen Herzen Jesus* (11th edn, 1923), was about devotion to the Sacred Heart of Jesus. His most important work was the *Summa Theologiae Moralis* (1902), concerning the fundamental principles of the Commandments, morality and the sacraments.

Noll, John Francis Roman Catholic bishop, born Fort Wayne, Indiana, 25 January 1875, died Huntington, Indiana, 31 July 1956. Ordained in 1898, he held various parishes in Fort Wayne Diocese from 1900 to 1925, when he became its bishop, and introduced there the Redemptorists, Capuchins, Slovak Franciscans, Oblates of Mary Immaculate, Society of Priests of the Sacred Heart and Crosier Fathers. He wrote some 150 pamphlets and books on Roman Catholicism, founded magazines and was prominent in the Catholic Press Association, National Organization for Decent Literature and Board of Catholic Missions. He raised a statue of Christ the Light of the World in Washington, DC.

Nonnus of Panopolis Poet, born *c.*400, died *c.*451, the probable author of two Greek poems in hex-

ameters, one an account of the journey of the god Dionysus to India, the other a paraphrase of the Fourth Gospel, of which only a part exists. The latter has some value for what it suggests about the text of the Bible, but otherwise has little importance. Nothing more is known about their author.

Norbert of Xanten Saint, archbishop, born Xanten, Cleves, *c.*1080, died Magdeburg, 6 June 1134. Born of a princely family, he obtained ordination to support his worldly life at the imperial court, but in 1115 an escape from death during a thunderstorm led to his conversion. After failing to reform the canons at Xanten, he gained papal permission to become an itinerant preacher. In 1120 at Prémontré, near Laon, he founded an Order of canons, since called Norbertines or Premonstratensians; and in 1126 he was made archbishop of Magdeburg. Feast day 6 June.

Noris, Henry Theologian and cardinal, born Verona, Italy, 29 August 1631, died Rome, 23 February 1704. Of English descent, after studying with the Jesuits at Rimini, he became an Augustinian. He was in charge of studies in various Augustinian houses in Italy, tutor to the son of the grand duke of Tuscany, and from 1674 to 1692, professor of ecclesiastical history in Pisa, In 1692 **Innocent XII** put him in charge of the Vatican Library and in 1695 made him a cardinal. Most importantly he wrote *Historia Pelagiana et Dissertatio de Synodo V Oecumenica*, about the Pelagian controversy and St **Augustine**'s doctrine of grace. Despite papal approval, this book was denounced by the Holy Office in 1676. Though Noris was acquitted of heresy, in 1744 the Spanish Inquisition placed the book on the Index; in 1748 **Benedict XIV** ordered its removal.

Norwid, Cyprian Kamil Writer and painter, born Laskowo-Gluchy, Poland, 24 September 1821, died Paris, 23 May 1883. He studied painting at Florence in 1844 and then travelled in Italy, Germany, Belgium and Greece until 1848 and, between 1852 and 1854, was in England and America. He spent the last six years of his life in St Cesimir's Asylum for Poor Poles in Paris. His paintings, poems, plays, essays and lectures are based on his philosophic and aesthetic attitude towards the Gospel.

Notburga Saint, born c.1265, died Rattenburg, the Tyrol, 1313 (an alternative account puts her in the ninth or tenth century). She was employed as a maidservant, first in a noble household and then in a peasant family. Though poor herself, she became beloved for the attention she gave to people less fortunate than herself. Her shrine was established at Eben in the Tyrolese Alps. Feast day 14 September.

Notker Balbulus ('the Stammerer') Saint, Benedictine scholar, born Heiligau (now Elgg), Zurich, c.840, died St Gall, 6 April 912. He entered St Gall's Abbey when young and spent his whole life there, becoming librarian, guest-master and precentor. He was famed as a musician, particularly for his liturgical sequences, of which he composed both the words and the music. His biographer, Ekkehart IV, declared him 'weakly in body but not in mind, slow of tongue but not of intellect, pressing forward bodily in things divine, a vessel filled with the Holy Ghost without equal in his time'. Feast day 6 April.

Notker, Labeo Benedictine scholar, called also 'Notker the German', born c.950, died St Gall, 1022. Entered St Gall's Abbey as a child, becoming master of the monastic school for the rest of his life. To introduce Latin literature to his pupils, he pioneered its translation into German. He wrote also several works in Latin and a dissertation on choral music in German. He was distinguished for his ability to develop Old High German into a purposeful language.

Notker of Liège Blessed, born 940, died Liège, 10 April 1008. Of a noble Swabian family, he was made prince-bishop of Liège by his uncle, the Emperor **Otto I**, in 969. As its 'second founder' he improved the moral and intellectual standard of its clergy and built schools and churches. The cathedral school of Saint-Lambert was remarkable in Europe; and he rebuilt the cathedral-like church at Aachen, but it was burnt down in 1185. His relics at Liège are not genuine. Feast day 9 or 10 April.

Notker Physicus Physician and painter, died 12 November 975. He was educated at St Gallen (St Gall), the Benedictine monastery south of Lake Constance, by his uncle, **Ekkhard** II, and became the monastic physician-cellarius about 956 and hospitarius, or guest-master, in 965. A painter of miniatures and composer of hymns, he perhaps helped to paint the monastery's church walls after a fire in 937. He was praised by the Abbot Ekkhard IV. He may be the Notker Notarius who was physician to **Otto I**'s court.

Nouwen, Henri Roman Catholic priest, writer, lecturer and spiritual guide, born Holland, 1932, died of a heart attack there, 21 September 1996. He spent most of his adult life in North America. It was a life marked by a restless searching for a sense of belonging and for an ever deeper spirituality. As part of his journey he spent 1974 with the Trappist community in Genesee, after which he wrote his *Genesee Diary*. In 1981 he spent some time in Bolivia and Peru, living with missionaries there in the poorest communities. Finally, in 1986, he found a home with the L'Arche Daybreak community in Toronto, Canada. His honest recounting of and reflections on this journey in his many books have been a source of help and spiritual fulfilment to many hundreds of thousands of people. His writings include *Reaching Out, Intimacy, The Wounded Healer, The Road to Daybreak: A Spiritual Journey, The Return of the Prodigal Son* and *The Restless Heart*.

Novatian Roman priest, died 258, details of whose life are limited and uncertain. Apparently he joined those who opposed **Cornelius**, elected bishop of Rome in 251, for his indulgence towards those who had lapsed during the Decian persecution and was consecrated a rival bishop of Rome. He suffered martyrdom under Valerian, but his sect survived into the sixth century.

Noyes, Alfred Roman Catholic apologist and poet, born Wolverhampton, 16 September 1880, died Isle of Wight, 20 March 1958. Noyes went to Oxford in 1898, though failed to gain a degree. *The Loom of Years*, his first book, appeared in 1902, and many other publications followed. From 1914 to 1923 he held the chair of modern English literature at Princeton, though he returned to Britain for a time, and worked also in France for the British government: he was made a CBE in 1918. An attempt to reconcile science and Christianity in *The Torch-Bearers* (3 vols, 1922–30) led him to enter the Roman Catholic Church in 1927. He then wrote *The Unknown God* (1934), a work of apologetics, and *Voltaire* (1936). This last work brought him into conflict with Rome, but he was supported by Cardinal **Hinsley**. He moved to the Isle of Wight in 1929, and lived there until his death, though he spent the Second World War in Canada, returning to the Isle of Wight in 1949.

Noyes, John Humphrey Founder of the Oneida Community, born Brattleboro, Vermont, 3 September 1811, died Niagara Falls, Canada, 13 April 1886. He intended a legal career but was converted by the evangelist Charles **Finney**. He first attended the Andover Theological Seminary, moving later to Yale University. He came to believe that it was possible for an individual to free himself from sin in this life, for which perfectionist doctrine he was refused permission to preach, and forced to leave Yale. In 1836 he founded a community in Putney, Vermont, which put into practice Noyes' teaching that all women in the community were the wives of all men, and vice versa. This doctrine of 'complex marriages' led to his arrest, but he jumped bail and in 1848 founded a new community in Oneida, New York State, which also practised complex marriages until 1879, at the same time becoming a highly successful industrial organization. He was once again forced to abandon the community for fear of legal action, and fled to Canada. His books, including *The Berean* and *Bible Communism*, propagated his perfectionist and socialist views, while *American Socialisms* gave an account of Utopian communities in the United States.

Nugent, Francis Franciscan friar, born Ballebranagh, County Meath, Ireland, 1569, died Charleville, France, 18 May 1635. He became a Capuchin at Brussels in 1591 and was prominent in the pre-Quietist movement of The Netherlands, being twice tried and acquitted by the Roman Inquisition. In 1608 he was appointed commissary general to a successful mission to the Rhineland, but disputes among the Capuchins led to his dismissal. He was sent secretly in 1623 to England to negotiate with **James I** for toleration for Roman Catholics, but was unsuccessful. He was deposed in 1632 and spent the rest of his life in retirement.

Nunes Barreto, João Patriarch, born Porto, Portugal, date unknown, died Goa, India, 22 December 1562. As a Jesuit priest he was sent to Morocco, where he rescued and ministered to Christian slaves. In 1554 he was called to Rome and, through the influence of **Ignatius of Loyola** and King John III of Portugal, named patriarch of Abyssinia by Pope **Paul IV** in 1555. With other Jesuits he went to Lisbon that same year and then to Goa. King John wished to form an alliance with the supposed Abyssinian descendants of **Prester John**, the legendary medieval Christian king of Abyssinia, against the Muslims; but after much hardship the Jesuits were expelled from the country in 1633 by its suspicious Emperor Negus.

Nzinga, Doña Ana Queen of Matamba (Angola), born 1582, died 1665. She received baptism in 1622 after being impressed by Christianity during a visit to Luanda as a negotiator in the war between the Portuguese and Matamba. When she became queen in 1627 she abandoned her faith and continued the war with the Portuguese. In 1656 two Capuchins and a cross were brought to her in war booty and under the advice of the spirit of her dead brother she reconverted to Christianity. She encouraged the use of rosaries and changed laws to reflect her Christian conversion, like the outlawing of human burial sacrifices. The construction of Our Lady of Matamba Church was completed in 1665 but conversions waned after her death.

O

Oates, Titus Perjurer, son of an Anabaptist minister who converted to the Church of England, born Oakham, Rutland, 1649, died London, 12 July 1705. Oates studied at Cambridge and was eventually ordained into the ministry of the Church of England. After some years in parish work – during which he and his father were both imprisoned after making false charges against a local schoolmaster – he became a naval chaplain, from which post he was expelled, and then chaplain to the duke of Norfolk's Protestant servants at Arundel. While there he claimed to have been converted to Catholicism, and after studying for a while at Catholic seminaries in Spain, from which he was also expelled, he returned to Britain claiming documented information about an attempt to assassinate **Charles II** and place the Roman Catholic duke of York, his brother **James**, on the throne. This made him a hero for a while; eventually, however, the 'Oates Plot' was disbelieved, though not until a number of eminent Catholics had been executed. Oates was tried and convicted of perjury in 1685.

O'Boyle, Patrick A. Cardinal, first resident archbishop of Washington, titular bishop of St Nicholas in Carcere in Rome, born Scranton, Pennsylvania, 18 July 1896, died Washington, DC, 10 August 1987. After his ordination in 1921, he worked at St Columba's parish in Manhattan and his work with the poor led to senior appointments in Catholic charities and welfare organizations. In 1947, not yet a bishop, he was appointed archbishop of the newly created Archdiocese of Washington, DC. He developed a huge social welfare programme involving the construction of schools, a maternity home for single mothers and housing for the elderly and the mentally handicapped. In 1948, six years before it became law, O'Boyle desegregated Catholic schools and churches in his archdiocese. Outspoken in defence of civil and human rights and racial justice, he made some important interventions on education and against racism and anti-Semitism, during Vatican II. A supporter of *Humanae Vitae*, he upheld official Church teaching on doctrine and morals. Made cardinal in 1967, and became chancellor of the Catholic University of America, where he intervened in several serious disputes.

Obrecht, Jakob Composer of polyphonic Church music, born Bergen-op-Zoom, The Netherlands, 22 November 1452, died Ferrara, Italy, July 1505. He was the first great composer to come from The Netherlands and to write texts in Dutch. He studied at the University of Louvain and was ordained in 1480. He was organist at various religious centres in The Netherlands and at one point, while in Utrecht, **Erasmus** was one of his choirboys. He was invited to Ferrara in 1487, and returned there in 1496, after a period as chaplain at Antwerp Cathedral. He was especially adept at writing music for the Mass, and motets, and was very much a musical experimenter.

O'Brien, John Anthony Roman Catholic priest, author-apologist, Newman club chaplain, founder of the Bureau of Convert Research at the University of Notre Dame, Indiana, born Peoria, Illinois, 20 January 1893, died Notre Dame, 18 April 1980. After pastoral work following his ordination in 1916, he became chaplain to the University of

Illinois, near which he built a chapel and RC student residence, Newman Hall. His life was dedicated to making Christianity accessible and understandable to lay people and to winning converts to Roman Catholicism, and to this end he worked in over 30 dioceses during the middle of the twentieth century. Of his numerous pamphlets and 45 books, *The Faith of Millions* was published in ten languages and eventually appeared in 27 editions.

O'Brien, Terence Albert Dominican priest and bishop, born Limerick, Ireland, 1600, died there, 31 October 1651. After study at Toledo, he returned to Limerick and in 1643 became provincial of his Order in Ireland. He was consecrated bishop in 1647 as coadjutor to the bishop of Emly. He was an opponent of any possible truce in the struggle against the English. When Limerick was besieged in 1651, he was such a strong advocate of resistance that he was not allowed to benefit from any amnesty when the city surrendered. He was court-martialled and executed.

O'Brien, William Vincent Irish-born Dominican, opened the first free, and the first Roman Catholic, school in New York State, born Dublin, c.1740, died New York City, 14 May 1816. Educated in Bologna and Rome, where he entered the Dominican Order, he returned to Dublin in 1770 and was eventually made preacher general. In 1787 he went to Philadelphia, Pennsylvania, and supported John **Carroll** in his efforts to create a bishopric in Baltimore, Maryland. For twenty years he was pastor of St Peter's, Barclay Street, New York, and during this time made a successful fund-raising journey to New Mexico. He opened New York State's first free school in 1800.

O'Callaghan, Edmund Bailey Physician and historian, born Mallow, Cork, Ireland, 29 February 1797, died New York, 29 May 1880. He studied medicine in Paris, then settled in Montreal in 1830. Active in the National Patriotic movement, he played a leading role in the unsuccessful insurrection of 1837. Accused of treason, he fled to the USA, where, in 1846, he published a history of New York State. As keeper of New York's historical manuscripts from 1848, he published eleven volumes of documents from European archives. He was the first to identify the historical importance

of the 'Jesuit Relations', reports written by Jesuit missionaries.

O'Callaghan, Jeremiah Writer and missionary priest, born County Kerry, Ireland, c.1780, died Holyoke, Massachusetts, 23 February 1861. Although ordained for the Diocese of Cloyne, his opposition to usury and the banking system resulted in no diocese in Ireland accepting him for service. In 1830 he was accepted by the Diocese of Boston, Massachusetts, and he spent the rest of his life as a missionary and Roman Catholic apologist in the more remote areas of the diocese. He built several churches, where he refused to accept pew rent, and wrote polemical pamphlets in defence of Catholicism. His well-known *Usury or Interest* (1824) went through many reprints.

O'Callaghan, Roger Jesuit and orientalist, born New York, 13 October 1912, died in a road accident near Baghdad, Iraq, 5 March 1954. After entering the Society of Jesus in 1929, he studied theology and philosophy in Toronto and Rome and later, under W. F. **Albright**, studied Near Eastern history, archeology and languages in Baltimore. He spent a year at the Oriental Institute in Chicago and then taught at the Pontifical Biblical Institute in Rome. He was a member of the American excavations in Nippur (Iraq) in 1953. In his brief life he made several important contributions to his discipline, most importantly his *Aram Naharaim: A Contribution to the History of Upper Mesopotamia in the Second Millennium BC* (Rome, 1948).

O'Callahan, Joseph Timothy Jesuit academic and US Navy chaplain, born Boston, Massachusetts, 14 May 1905, died Worcester, Massachusetts, 18 March 1964. He entered the Society of Jesus in 1922 and studied at Georgetown, Washington, DC. He was ordained in 1934 and taught philosophy and mathematics at Holy Cross College, Worcester. In 1940 he joined the US Navy Chaplain Corps and during World War II served on the aircraft-carrier *Ranger* and later, in the Pacific, on the *Franklin*, which was hit by a Japanese suicide mission. O'Callahan was wounded and later awarded the Congressional Medal of Honor. He retired to Holy Cross, where he wrote his memoirs, published as *I was a Chaplain on the Franklin* (1956).

Ochino, Bernardino Preacher and Protestant reformer, born Sienna, 1487, died Slavkow, Moravia, 1564. He was originally general of the Observantine Franciscans but became a Carthusian and served twice as their vicar general. He was renowned as a preacher. Under the influence of **Peter Martyr Vermigli** he came gradually to accept Protestant doctrines and in 1541 he became a Lutheran, escaping to Geneva to avoid the Inquisition. From 1545 until 1547 he was minister to the Italian Protestants in Augsburg. He went to England at the invitation of Thomas **Cranmer**, where he devoted himself to writing, producing *The Usurped Primacy of the Bishop of Rome* and *The Labyrinth*, which latter book attacked **Calvin**'s doctrine of predestination. He moved, after the accession to the English throne of the Catholic queen **Mary Tudor** in 1553, to Switzerland, whence he was expelled for being unsound on the Trinity and on monogamy, and then to Poland, where he was forbidden to remain, and thence to Slavkow in Moravia, where he died.

Ockeghem, Johannes Composer, born *c.*1410, died Tours, 6 February 1497. Contemporaries had a high regard for this Franco-Flemish musician, the quality of whose Masses, motets and popular chansons puts him in the same league as **Dufay** and **Josquin Des Prez**, the latter of whom may have been Ockeghem's own pupil. He can be traced in Antwerp and in the service of the duke of Bourbon early in his career, and spent the last four decades of his life at the French court, though not without brief spells in Italy and Spain.

O'Clery, Michael Irish Franciscan historian and hagiographer, born Donegal, *c.*1590, died Louvain, 1643. He had an early education in Ireland and then went to the Spanish Netherlands where, in 1622, he joined the Irish Franciscans in Louvain. He returned to Ireland from 1626 to 1637, where he collected valuable material on the lives of Irish saints. He also re-edited early historical documents, compiled genealogies of kings and saints and calendars of saints' feasts. He was a major collaborator in the work on the history of Ireland up to 1616 *The Annals of the Four Masters*

(1632–6) and helped save many Irish historical records from destruction. O'Clery's glossary of obscure Irish Gaelic words, *Foclóir nó Sanasan Nua*, was printed on the St Anthony's College press in Louvain in 1643 and much of the material he collected has been published in recent years.

O'Connell, Anthony Sister of Charity and nurse in the American Civil War, born in Limerick, Ireland, 15 August 1814, died Cincinnati, Ohio, 8 December 1897. Went with her family to the USA as a child. Joined the Sisters of Charity in Emmitsburg, Maryland, in 1835 and two years later was sent to Cincinnati, where she worked in hospitals and children's homes, and founded the first modern medical institution there, the St John's Hotel for Invalids. In 1852 she helped establish the Sisters of Charity of Cincinnati, and in 1861 began work as a nurse in the city and in various military hospitals, her work gaining her the title 'the Florence Nightingale of America'. After the war the congregation took over the former Marine Hospital, renamed it the 'Good Samaritan', and until 1892 Sister Anthony was the administrator of both this and the congregation's newly opened St Joseph's Infant Home, the first institution for unmarried mothers and abandoned infants in the city.

O'Connell, Daniel Irish politician regarded by many as a liberator, born Carhen, County Kerry, 6 August 1775, died Genoa, 15 May 1847. He was sent abroad for his education, but, because of the French Revolution, returned to England, where he studied at Lincoln's Inn and was admitted to the Irish bar in 1798. In 1800 he made his first public appearance, denouncing the union of the Westminster and Dublin parliaments and establishing himself as a major Catholic leader. Though opposed to violence as a means of achieving political ends, he found himself obliged to engage in a duel, in which he shot his opponent dead, something for which he felt remorse for the rest of his life. In 1823 O'Connell formed the Catholic Association, which struggled for Catholic emancipation through legal means. In 1828 he was elected Member of (the Westminster) Parliament for Clare but could not take his seat because of his Catholicism; the next year, however, the Roman Catholic Emancipation Act, giving Catholics equal civic rights (with a small number of exceptions), was passed, thereby allowing O'Connell to take his seat and heading off further agitation. He then fought for repeal of the union. He was imprisoned for a while in 1844 because of these activities, though the judgment of the Irish court was soon overturned in the House of Lords. This had, however, affected his health. Doctors advised a journey to a warmer climate, and it was as he arrived in Italy on this trip that his health at last failed. His heart, at his request, was buried in Rome, but his body was returned to Ireland.

O'Connell, John Patrick US theologian, editor and promoter of the liturgical apostolate, born Chicago, Illinois, 12 January 1918, died there, 20 February 1960. Studied at Quigley Seminary, Chicago, and at St Mary of the Lake Seminary in Mundelein, Illinois, and was ordained in 1943. He worked in a parish and as a teacher and became editor of the Catholic Press Inc. of Chicago, producing the 1950 and subsequent Holy Family editions of the *Holy Bible*, *Sunday Missal*, *Prayer Book* and *The Life of Christ* (1954), *The Bible Story* (1959) and *Christ and the Church* (1960). French and Spanish editions of the Bible were also published under his direction, and he researched the possibility of producing an updated version of the *Catholic Encyclopedia*. He held office in the Liturgical Conference was on the governing body of Liturgical Weeks and was a member of the Catholic Biblical Association and of the Mariological Society.

O'Connell, William Henry First native US cardinal, second archbishop of Boston, born Lowell, Massachusetts, 8 December 1859, died Boston, 22 April 1944. Studied for the priesthood at Charles College, Ellicot City, Maryland, but left and went to read physics and philosophy at Boston College and graduated with first-class honours. He reapplied for the priesthood, was sent to study in Rome and after his ordination worked in parish ministry for ten years in Medland and then in Boston. In 1895 he was made rector of the North American College in Rome, following the resignation of the previous incumbent because of a disagreement with the US hierarchy. In his six years of office he doubled the enrolment, secured the finances and bought a summer residence for the students and faculty at Castel Gandolfo. In 1897 he was made a domestic prelate, in 1901 was made bishop of Portland, Maine, and in 1905 was papal envoy to Japan, to try to establish Catholic missionary possibilities. He was installed as archbishop of Boston in 1907, a post he was to hold for 37 years. Besides being a good pastor he was an efficient administrator and gave his support and encouragement to new home and overseas missionary work, including approving the founding of the Catholic Foreign Missionary Society (Maryknoll missionaries) and the Missionary Servants of the Most Blessed Trinity and Missionary Cenacle Apostolate. He also brought new religious orders to work in the diocese. In 1911 he was made cardinal. There was a doubling and even tripling of the numbers of parishes, schools, colleges, libraries, seminarians, clergy and religious sisters under his administration and many exisiting buildings and institutions were developed and renewed. He spoke out vigorously on matters of the day in both the secular and the ecclesiastical sphere, translated a book of devotions from the Italian and composed motets and the music for *The Holy Cross Hymnal*.

O'Connor, Martin John Archbishop, nuncio, president of the Papal Commission for Social Communications, rector of the North American College in Rome, born Scranton, Pennsylvania, 18 May 1900, died Wilkes-Barre, Pennsylvania, 1 December 1986. Studied in Rome, and gained doctorates in canon law and theology. Ordained in 1924, he held diocesan posts in Scranton and was appointed auxiliary bishop there, before becoming rector of the North American College in 1946, a post he held for eighteen years. From 1948 until his retirement in 1971, O'Connor was president of the various Vatican commissions on the media. During Vatican II he played a major role in seeing the decree *Inter Mirifica* through from preparation to final promulgation, as well as overseeing the press accreditation and coverage of the Council. From 1965 to 1969 he was nuncio to Malta. He returned to Rome and, in 1979, retired to the USA.

O'Connor, Mary Flannery American Catholic novelist writing on spiritual and sacramental themes, born Savannah, Georgia, 25 March 1925, died of lupus, 3 August 1964. Educated at the Georgia State College for Women and the University of Iowa. In her two novels, *Wise Blood* (1952) and *The Violent Bear It Away* (1960), she used Southern fictional characters to discuss redemption, assurance and other theological issues. She also wrote two volumes of short stories, *A Good Man is Hard to Find* (1955) and *Everything that Rises must Converge* (posthumously, 1965).

O'Connor, Michael First bishop of Pittsburgh, Pennsylvania, born Queenstown, Ireland, 27 April 1810, died Woodstock, Maryland, 18 October 1872. He joined the College of Propaganda in Rome in 1824 and after his ordination in 1833 he became vice-rector of the Irish College and professor of Scripture at the Propaganda College. He returned to Ireland in 1834, on the death of his mother, and in 1839 took up the post of rector of St Charles Seminary in Philadelphia. In 1841 he became vicar general of the diocese in Pittsburgh and the first bishop two years later. The next twenty years saw expansions in the diocese in education and church building (including a church for black Americans), and increased numbers of clergy, religious sisters and Catholic laity. O'Connor resigned in 1860 owing to ill health and joined the Jesuits in Germany. He returned to the USA and worked as preacher, retreat master and lecturer in Boston and in Maryland

O'Connor, Thomas Francis US Roman Catholic Church historian and bibliographer, born Syracuse, New York, 14 August 1899, died St Louis, Missouri, 15 September 1950. Studied at Holy Cross College, Worcester, Massachusetts, and Syracuse University, New York. Taught at universities in Arkansas, Missouri and Vermont and worked as historiographer for the Archdiocese of New York. He published many articles on US Church history and was president of the American Catholic Historical Association 1946–7.

O'Connor, Thomas Power Irish journalist and politician, born Athlone, 5 October 1848, died London, 18 November 1929. After graduating in classics from Galway University he worked on the conservative *Saunder's Newsletter* in Dublin and three years later joined the *Daily Telegraph* in London, where he became a subeditor. In 1873 he joined the *New York Herald* and in 1880 was elected to Parliament for Galway. A major figure in the Parnellite group, he was asked to tour the

USA to campaign for Home Rule for Ireland. In 1885 he was elected MP for Liverpool, a constituency with a very large Irish immigrant population, a position he held until his death. He became 'Father of the House of Commons' in 1908. As an MP he worked tirelessly for justice for Catholics, and was a major supporter of Catholic Education. He was interested in promoting a more popular style of writing, and founded and edited several journals and wrote essays, articles and a number of larger political works, including *Gladstone's House of Commons* (1886) and *Memoirs of an Old Parliamentarian* (1929).

O'Cullenan, Gelasius Cistercian, born probably County Donegal, Ireland, date unknown, died a martyr outside Dublin, 21 November 1580. Becoming a monk after study at Salamanca and Paris, he was created abbot of Boyle, County Roscommon, an abbey which had been confiscated. Returning to Ireland, the new abbot is said to have obtained the return of his abbey to the Order. However, he refused to conform and, because of this, he was imprisoned in Dublin, tortured and hanged.

O'Daly, Daniel Dominican priest, diplomat and historian, born County Kerry, Ireland, 1595, died Lisbon, 30 June 1662. After a spell as a priest in Tralee, he taught theology at the Irish Dominican College in Louvain. In 1629, he founded the Irish Dominican College in Lisbon, which eventually became Corpo Santo, and was its first rector; and he established a convent for Irish Dominican nuns at Bom Successo. From 1655, he undertook diplomatic missions on behalf of the Portuguese royal family. He wrote a history of the earls of Munster, from which line he was descended, and of the persecution of Catholics in Ireland.

O'Daniel, Victor Francis American Dominican teacher, historian and archivist, born Cecilville, Kentucky, 15 February 1868, died Washington, DC, 12 June 1960. Studied at St Rose Priory, Springfield, Kentucky and entered the Dominican Order there in 1886. After his ordination in 1891 he studied at Louvain in Belgium and from 1895 to 1913 taught at Dominican institutes in California and Washington DC, during part of which time he was also novice master and then provincial archivist. He was co-founder and, from 1921 to 1927, associate editor of the *Catholic Historical Review*. He wrote a number of books on Dominican history, including *The Dominicans in Early Florida* (1942) and biographies of leading US Dominicans.

Oderic of Pordenone   Franciscan missionary to Asia, born Villanova, near Pordenone, Italy, *c.*1286, died Udine, Italy, 14 January 1331. At some time between 1314 and 1318 he left for Asia, stopping at Trebizon, Erzurum, Tabriz, Shiraz, and at Ormuz, where he embarked for Thana, India. He sailed round the coast of India and visited Sri Lanka, Sumatra, Java, Kalimantan and Vietnam *en route* to Canton and Khanbalik (Peking). After three years he returned to Italy overland and in 1330 dictated the story of his travels, including an account of the work of his Franciscan confrère **John of Monte Corvino** in Peking. He intended to return to China, but died before he could gain papal authority in Avignon. His travels were plagiarized in English by Sir John Mandeville.

Oderisius   Blessed, cardinal and abbot, born Marsi, Italy, date unknown, died Monte Cassino, Italy, 1105. Of noble parentage, Oderisius became a Benedictine at Monte Cassino. He was made cardinal-deacon at St Agatha's and then cardinal-priest at St Cyriacus in Termis, Italy. He was named abbot of Monte Cassino in 1087. He encouraged scholarship in his abbey, wrote poetry himself, and served as a mediator between the Crusaders and the Byzantine Emperor **Alexius I Comnenus**. Feast day 2 December.

O'Devaney, Conor (Cornelius)   Franciscan friar and bishop, born 1533, Ulster, died Dublin, 11 February 1612. He joined the Franciscans in Donegal and worked as a priest in his home region until he was consecrated bishop of Down and Connor at Rome on 27 April 1582. He was imprisoned in Dublin Castle for three years in the 1590s, where he nearly starved to death. He was set at liberty and continued the care of souls in secret, especially in the province of Ulster. He was then re-arrested in June 1611 on a belated charge of aiding Hugh **O'Neill** and the other Ulster lords in their flight to Europe from Lough Swilly in 1607. At a time of a renewed government policy of Protestantization,

O'Devany then, near an octogenarian, was sentenced to death with his friend Patrick Loughran, once O'Neill's chaplain. He was subjected to all the barbarity then attendant on execution for high treason, and serious disorder broke out as the crowd tore at the corpse of the bishop in the search for relics. O'Devaney's execution became critical in the success of the Counter-Reformation in Ireland.

Odilia   Saint, patroness of Alsace died *c.*720. She is thought to have been the daughter of a Frankish lord, Adalricus, to have been born blind and later to have recovered her sight miraculously. She founded a nunnery in a castle granted to her by her father at Obernai in the Vosges Mountains and became abess. This abbey was a famous centre for pilgrims, and was visited by **Charlemagne**, Pope **Leo IX** and possibly **Richard I** of England. The water of the well is said to cure eye disease.

Odilo of Cluny   Saint, fifth abbot of Cluny, born probably in the Auvergne. *c.*962, died at the abbey of Souvigny, 31 December 1048. He became a cleric in St Julien in Brioude, but then entered Cluny in 991, was made within the year assistant to the abbot, and succeeded him as abbot in 994 – which is also when he was ordained. He was a person of great virtue, often hard on himself but gentle with others. He expanded the work of the Cluniac houses, increasing their number from 37 to 65 during his administration. Odilo was a competent administrator, centralizing many of the houses around Cluny itself, and was highly respected by Popes and Emperors. He was responsible for introducing the 'Truce of God' as well as All Souls' Day (2 November), eventually extended from Cluny to the whole Church. He was canonized in 1063. Feast days 1 or 2 January, 29 April, in the Order.

Odin, John Mary   Lazarist priest and archbishop, born Hauteville, Ambierle, France, 25 February 1801, died Hauteville, 25 May 1870. Volunteering for mission work in the USA in 1822, he completed his theological studies there, joined the Lazarists and was ordained 4 May 1824. He became bishop in Texas in 1842 and archbishop of New Orleans in 1861. He was known for his mission work among the American Indians and his efforts to protect his people during the Civil War. He often travelled to Europe to raise recruits and funds and was attending the First Vatican Council at the time of his last illness.

Odo of Bayeux Half-brother of **William I** the Conqueror, born *c.*1036, died Palermo, February 1097. William granted him the See of Bayeux while he was still only about fourteen. He fought personally at Hastings on 14 October 1066, armed with a mace so that he might not, as a cleric, shed blood. He was rewarded with the earldom of Kent and also acquired many ecclesiastical lands, which he distributed among his supporters. After a period of imprisonment he organized a rebellion to put his nephew Robert on the throne. It failed and he fled to Normandy. He later supported the First Crusade and accompanied Robert to Palestine in 1096, but died in Palermo *en route*. It was perhaps Odo who commissioned the Bayeux Tapestry.

Odo of Cambrai Blessed, bishop and theologian, also known as 'Odo of Tournai', born Orléans, France, died Anchin Abbey, near Arras, 19 June 1113. He taught at Toul and Tournai, introduced the Cluniac reform to his monastery, St-Martin of Tournai, and was elected bishop of Cambrai in 1095. Several of his theological works survive. Feast day 20 June.

Odo of Canterbury ('Odo the Good') Saint, archbishop, a Dane from the North of England, date of birth unknown, died Canterbury, 2 June 959. He was rejected by his family when he converted to Christianity, and was adopted by a nobleman in the entourage of King **Alfred.** He took orders, and was appointed to the See of Ramsbury in 927. He at first declined the See of Canterbury offered to him by King Edmund, on the grounds of not being a monk. Nevertheless, the king persisted and he received the Benedictine habit from Fleury and accepted the offer of the see. He was active in renovating buildings and restoring the morals of clergy. Feast day 4 July.

Odo of Châteauroux (de Castro Radulphi) Cardinal, born Champagne, France, 1208, died Orvieto, 26 January 1273. Studied at, taught at and in 1238 became chancellor of the University of Paris. He resigned this post to join the Cistercian Order. He became cardinal of Frascati in 1244 and returned to France as papal legate the following year. He was a friend of King **Louis IX** and went with him to Egypt and Palestine during the Sixth Crusade. He had returned to Italy by 1254, where, apart from a brief spell as legate to Limoges in 1264, he spent the rest of his life.

Odo of Cluny Saint, abbot of Cluny, born Tours, son of a Frankish knight, Abbo, 879, died Cluny, 18 November 942. After study in Paris and returning to the abbey of St Martin at Tours, he was sent to the abbey school at Baume, becoming its abbot in 924, and eventually succeeding St **Berno**, who had also been his predecessor at Baume, as abbot of Cluny in 927. He was largely instrumental in establishing the dominance of this monastery, through the reforms he carried out of other monasteries in France and Italy: he established the monastery of Our Lady on Rome's Aventine. During his abbacy the monastic church of St Peter and St Paul was completed. His writings include three books of moral essays, a work (the *Occupatio*) on the Redemption and some sermons. Feast day 18 November.

Odo of Kent Benedictine abbot and theologian, died 20 January 1200. As prior of Christ Church, Canterbury, he played an important role in the canonical election of Archbishop **Richard of Canterbury** in 1173; he was elected abbot of Battle Abbey in 1175. The authenticity of the theological works ascribed to him is uncertain.

Odo Rigaldus Franciscan theologian and bishop, born near Paris, died Rouen, 2 July 1275. After joining the Franciscans he studied at the University of Paris, where he succeeded **John of La Rochelle** as regent in 1245. He became bishop of Rouen in 1248, and details of his episcopate over the following 21 years can be found in the *Regestrum visitationum*. He aided King **Louis IX** in the treaty with England in 1258. Rigaldus attended the Council of Lyons in 1274, where he worked with **Bonaventure** to try to bring about reunion with the Greek Church. His writings, recently re-assessed as important contributions to thirteenth-century thought, include a commentary on **Peter Lombard**'s *Sentences* and on disputed theological questions of the time. He contributed to the exposition of the Franciscan Rule known as the *Expositio regulae quatuor magistrorum*.

Oecolampadius, John German Reformer, native of Weinsberg, Swabia, born 1482, died Basel, 24 November 1531. He began his academic career studying law at Bologna, but in 1499 moved to Heidelberg to study theology. He later went to Stuttgart and Tübingen, where he encountered **Melanchthon**. He was made cathedral preacher in Basel in 1515, and, after graduating as a doctor in theology, a similar position in Augsburg: it was there that he began to move in the circles of those who sympathized with **Luther**. After a period of two years in a monastery he returned to Basel in 1522 and championed the Reformers cause, publicly defending the Lutheran doctrine of justification by faith alone and the marriage of the clergy, and finally calling for the suppression of Catholic worship in the city. During the Colloquy of Marburg in 1529, he sided with **Zwingli** and his view of the sacraments, and opposed that of the Lutherans. Oecolampadius was noted for his leadership abilities rather than his theological insight.

Oertel, John James Maximilian Journalist, born Auersbach, Bavaria, 27 April 1811, died Jamaica, New York, 21 August 1882. After ordination as a Lutheran minister, he agreed to serve in the USA, arriving in 1837. He was never happy among the German Lutherans there and in 1840 became a Catholic. In 1846 he moved to Baltimore and founded a German Catholic weekly newspaper, the *Kirchenzeitung* (*Church News*). Published in New York from 1851, it became the best-known German Catholic publication in the country. In 1850 he caused a stir with a pamphlet explaining the reasons for his conversion.

Offa King of Mercia and most prominent English monarch before **Alfred the Great**, died 29 July 796. Becoming king in 757, he expanded his kingdom into south-east England, and is famous for the construction of Offa's Dyke, a huge frontier defence on the Welsh border. His relations with Pope **Adrian I** led to a papal delegate's visit to England, the (temporary) establishment of an archbishopric of Lichfield, 787–803, and, on his death, the first anointing of an English monarch, when his son Ecgfrith was consecrated. Despite poor relations with Jaenberht of Canterbury, he contributed generously to the Church, including reputedly founding the abbeys of St Albans and Bath. He corresponded with **Charlemagne**.

O'Fihely, Maurice Franciscan priest and archbishop, born *c.*1460, died Galway, Ireland, 1513. Appointed professor of philosophy at Padua, he wrote a commentary on the works of **Duns Scotus**, published in Venice around 1514. His contemporaries called him *Flos mundi*, 'Flower of the World', in tribute to his great learning and piety. Appointed archbishop of Tuam in 1506, he first remained in Italy, attending the first two sessions of the Lateran Council in 1512. He returned to Ireland in 1513, but fell ill and died in the Franciscan convent in Galway before reaching Tuam.

Ogilvie, John Saint, Jesuit priest, born Drum-na-Keith, Scotland, 1580, died Glasgow, 10 March 1615. He was brought up a Calvinist but was educated in France and was converted to Catholicism at Louvain in 1596. He studied also at Regensburg, entering the Society of Jesus in 1599. For the next decade he worked at Gratz and Vienna but being transferred from the Austrian province to the French he was ordained priest at Paris in 1610. In 1613 he travelled back to Scotland disguised as a horse-dealer and soldier. He found that the Scottish Catholic nobility had conformed to Protestantism at least in appearance and being unable to make much impression on them he travelled to London and then to Paris but was ordered back to Scotland by his superiors. He then ministered to congregations in Edinburgh, Renfew and Glasgow, where he was arrested, tortured and examined. He was sent to Edinburgh, where every effort was made to induce him to conform. At his trial he declared his willingness to shed his blood in defence of the king's temporal power but could not obey in matters of spiritual jurisdiction, which had been unjustly seized. He wrote up an account of his arrest and treatment in prison which was smuggled out by his visitors. He was canonized in 1976. Feast day 10 March.

O'Gorman, Thomas Roman Catholic bishop and professor of ecclesiastical history, born Boston, Maryland, 1 May 1843, died Sioux Falls, South Dakota, 18 September 1921. He studied for the priesthood from the age of ten, when he was sent to France, and was ordained in 1865 for the Diocese of St Paul, Minnesota, though in 1877 he joined the Society of St Paul and worked in New York, until recalled to the diocese by Bishop John **Ireland**, a long-time friend. There he helped to establish a seminary and taught theology as well as English and French. In 1890 he was appointed professor of Church history at the Catholic University, Washington, DC. In 1896 he became bishop of Sioux Falls, a suffragan see to St Paul's, where Ireland was now archbishop. By his death the Catholic population of the diocese had doubled, and the number of clergy more than doubled.

O'Halloran, Maura Christian Zen monk, born Boston, USA, 1955, died in a road accident in Thailand, on her way back to Ireland, 22 October 1982. The family moved to Ireland when she was little. She studied at Trinity College, Dublin, and worked among the poor and outcast in Dublin and in Latin America. She was also on a spiritual quest and this took her to Japan, where she applied to be and was accepted as a member of a Zen monastery in Tokyo. In her *Pure Heart, Enlightened Mind: The Zen Journals of Maura 'Soshin' O'Halloran* we get an insight into the rigorous physical and mental training she underwent, not simply for her own enlightenment but, as her writings make clear, to serve others. There is a statue of her in the grounds of the monastery and she is revered by Christians and Buddhists alike.

O'Hanlon, John Hagiographer of Irish saints, born Stradbally, County Laois, 30 April 1821, died Irishtown, 15 May 1905. He was educated locally and in Carlow. He emigrated with relatives to Quebec in 1842 and from there to America, where he was ordained in Missouri in 1847. He returned to Ireland in 1853 and held various appointments in the Archdiocese of Dublin, notably at St Mary's in Irishtown from 1880 until his death there. A prolific writer, his most outstanding work was *Lives of the Irish Saints* in ten volumes (1875–1903), but he also produced a pastoral work of note: *The Irish Emigrant's Guide to the United States* (1851), and before his death he published *Irish-American History of the United States* (1903). O'Hanlon also wrote fiction, under the pen-name 'Lageniensis'.

O'Hara, Edwin Vincent Roman Catholic bishop, sociologist, born Lanesboro, Minnesota, 6 September 1881, died Milan, Italy, on his way to a Liturgy Congress in Assisi, 11 September 1956. Ordained in 1905 to the Diocese of St Paul, he worked initially as assistant at the cathedral in Portland and set up the Summer Institute for Teachers and the Catholic Education Association of Oregon. He spent a year at the Catholic University of America in Washington, DC, and on his return to Portland became very active in promoting social rights. One of his major concerns was to win the minimum wage, especially for women, and he played a major role in getting this established. He was appointed chairman of the newly formed State Industrial Welfare Commission. He served as a US army chaplain in France and on his return to Oregon in 1918 devoted himself to promoting the welfare and education of Catholics living in rural areas. Two of his publications are *A Program of Catholic Rural Action* (1922) and *The Church and the Country Community* (1927). He was made bishop of Great Falls, Montana, in 1930. He oversaw the establishment of the Confraternity of Christian Doctrine in his own and then in every diocese, set up the Catholic Biblical Association, in 1936 and began publishing the *Catholic Biblical Quarterly* in 1938. In 1939 he became bishop of Kansas City and embarked on a large building programme of churches, convents, schools and colleges.

O'Hara, John Francis Cardinal, president of Notre Dame University, born Ann Arbor, Michigan, 1 May 1888, died Philadelphia, 28 August 1960. He spent his youth in Uruguay, where his father was American consul, and on the family's return to the USA he taught Spanish and studied philosophy at Notre Dame University, Indiana. He joined the Congregation of the Holy Cross in 1912 and was ordained in 1916. After studies in history and commerce he set up a department of commerce at Notre Dame, and was made dean of what then became the College of Commerce. He gave up this post for the more pastoral roles of counsellor and prefect of religion, publishing a student bulletin and allegedly knowing most of the students personally. He became president of Notre Dame in 1935. In 1940 he was consecrated bishop and appointed military delegate to Archbishop **Spellman** of New York, military vicar to the armed forces. O'Hara established and ran headquarters in New York, played an active pastoral role among the military and inaugurated reorganization and reform in the military ordinariate. In 1945 he became bishop of the Diocese of Buffalo, New York, of Philadelphia in 1952 and in 1958 was made cardinal by Pope **John XXIII**.

O'Hely, Patrick   Irish Franciscan, bishop, born Connaught, died by execution in Kilmallock, September 1579. Joined the Franciscans and was sent to study in Alcalá, Spain. He then went to Rome and in 1576 was made bishop of Mayo. He spent some time in Paris on his way back to Ireland and took part in debates on Scholastic philosophy at the university. He sailed from Brittany in 1579 and, with fighting going on throughout Munster, landed at Askeaton, Kerry, and several days later was arrested and sentenced to death by Lord Justice Drury for his unwillingness to renounce his papal affiliation.

O'Hurley, Dermott   Irish archbishop, born 1519, died end of June, 1584. He was educated in Europe and then taught at Louvain, Rheims and then in Rome. In 1581, although not yet ordained priest, he was appointed archbishop of Cashel. He landed in Drogheda, Ireland, in 1583 and was immediately arrested and imprisoned in Dublin Castle. He was tortured and later hanged on St Stephen's Green.

Olaf I Tryggvason   Norwegian king who converted Iceland, Greenland, Orkney and the Faroe Islands to the Christian faith, born 968, died 1000. Raised in Russia at the court of **Vladimir I.** Participated in numerous Viking raids along the North Sea coasts and around the British Isles. During a raid in England in 994 he was converted to Christianity and baptized on the Scilly Isles. In 995 he returned to Norway and, having led a victorious revolt against Earl Hakon, was elected king. He founded the city of Nidaros (modern-day Trondheim). He only partly Christianized Norway but was successful in spreading Christianity in the North Sea and Baltic areas. He was defeated and killed by a joint Swedish and Norwegian force at the naval battle of Svold.

Olaf II Haraldsson   King and patron saint of Norway, helped to establish Christianity in his native country, born 995, died Stiklestad, Norway, 1030. Having spent several years as a Viking raiding the French and English coasts he was converted to Christianity in Rouen, Normandy, in 1013. He returned to Norway in 1015 claiming the throne. Completing the conversion of Norway begun by **Olaf I** he built many churches throughout Norway and introduced clergy into the country. Owing mainly to his severity in eradicating heathenism Norway was invaded in 1028 by **Canute**, king of England and Denmark, and Olaf went into exile at Novgorod. Returning to Norway in 1030 he was killed at the Battle of Stiklestad. He was canonized in 1164. Feast day 29 July.

Oláh, Miklós (Nicolaus)   Archbishop of Gran and primate of Hungary, born Nagyszeben, 10 January 1493, died Nagyszombat, 15 January 1568. He vigorously opposed the Protestant teachings of the Reformation, worked hard to reform the demoralized Catholic clergy and brought the Jesuits to Hungary in 1561. His early career after ordination was largely spent in court circles. He was for many years secretary to Queen Maria and was also chancellor to King **Ferdinand I**. This gave him a political influence he used on behalf of the Catholic religion. He became a bishop in 1543 and was appointed archbishop of Gran in 1553.

Olavide y Jauregui, Pablo de   Scholar of the Enlightenment and Roman Catholic apologist, born Lima, Peru, 1725, died Baeza, Spain, 1803. Went to Spain in 1752 and spent some years in both France and Italy. Appointed chief officer of justice in Seville in 1767 and held other public positions which enabled him to make secularizing educational and economic reforms. In 1776 he fell under the scrutiny of the Inquisition and in 1780 fled to France, where he was welcomed by the Encyclopaedists. During his eighteen years of exile he regained his faith and became an apologist for Catholicism against the secularism of the Enlightenment. In 1798 he went back to Spain, where his semi-autobiographical *El evangelio en triunfo o historia de un filósofo desengañado* was published the same year.

Olazábal, Francisco   Pentecostal evangelist, born Mexico, 1886, died (in a car crash) 1937. Olazábal was converted by George and Carrie **Montgomery**

around 1900, and after working as a Methodist pastor he followed them into Pentecostalism in 1917, joining the Assemblies of God. In 1923 he founded the Latin American Council of Christian Churches, conducting crusades across America and in Puerto Rico.

Oldcastle, John Lord Cobham, Lollard leader, born c.1378, died London, 14 December 1417. The Oldcastles were a Herefordshire family, but nothing is known about this knight's career prior to 1401. His 1408 marriage gave him the title Lord Cobham. In 1413, three decades after **Wycliffe**'s followers were first identified as 'Lollards', Oldcastle appeared before Convocation accused of holding Lollard opinions. During the 40 days he was given to recant, he escaped from the Tower of London and went on to head the Lollard rebellion of 1414. For three years thereafter he lived in hiding. When captured he was executed for treason and heresy.

Oldegar Saint, bishop, political counsellor and Crusader, born Barcelona, 1060, died Barcelona, 1 March 1137. Oldegar held a number of minor ecclesiastical posts in Barcelona before becoming prior of Saint-Adrian in Provence in 1099 and then abbot of Saint-Ruf in Avignon in 1113. He was elected bishop of Barcelona in 1116, and in 1118 was appointed by the Pope and the count of Barcelona-Provence to re-establish the metropolitanate of Tarragona. He attended a number of Councils, including the First Lateran Council in 1123, and helped pave the way politically for the union of Aragon and Catalonia. Feast day 6 March.

Oldham, Hugh Bishop of Exeter, born Lancashire, died 25 June 1519. After going, briefly, to Oxford and then to Cambridge he was ordained and appointed chaplain to the countess of Richmond. He held various positions as dean, archdeacon and prebend and became bishop of Exeter in 1504. He founded Manchester Grammar School and helped found Corpus Christi College, Oxford, for the secular clergy. He was involved in contesting the claims of Archbishop **Warham**, regarding the probate courts, and of the abbot of Tavistock, regarding their respective jurisdictions.

Oldham, Joseph Houldsworth Ecumenical states-man, born Bombay, India, 20 October 1874, died St Leonards-on-Sea, England, 16 May 1969. Educated at Edinburgh and at Trinity College, Oxford, he was secretary of the YMCA in Lahore, 1897–1901, then attended New College, Edinburgh, and Halle under **Warneck**. From 1908 he was organizing secretary of the 1910 World Missionary Conference and in 1912 he became the first editor of the *International Review of Mission*. He was a key figure in the founding of the International Missionary Council in 1921 and the development of the Life and Work movement. An astute lobbyist in regard to German missions during and after World War I and African affairs in the twenties and thirties, he wrote *Christianity and the Race Problem* (1924) and edited the *Christian News Letter* during World War II. Though licensed by the United Free Presbyterian Church, he remained a layman and later became an Anglican.

Oldmeadow, Ernest James Journalist and novelist, born in Chester, England, 31 October 1867, died London, 11 September 1949. Raised as a Wesleyan, he became a Roman Catholic in 1897. A man of wide interests and vivacious character, he edited the *Musical Times*, wrote biographical studies and novels and set up his own wine business. He edited the Roman Catholic weekly *The Tablet* from 1923 until 1936. His writings include *Francis, Cardinal Bourne*, 2 vols, 1940–4, studies of Chopin, **Mozart** and Schumann, and among his better-known novels are *Lady Lohengrin* (1896), *Susan* (1907), *The Scoundrel* (1907) and *Antonio* (1909).

Oldoini, Agostino Jesuit historian and bibliographer, born La Spezzia, Italy, 6 January 1612, died Perugia, 23 March 1683. He entered the Society of Jesus in 1628 and after his studies taught classics at Perugia, where he later became professor of moral theology. His first book was on Latin grammar, but his later works were on history, mainly of the Papacy and of cardinals, and bibliography. He is best known for a re-edition and continuation, down to the pontificate of **Clement IX**, of Cicacconio's *Vitae et res gestae pontificum romanorum*, which he published in four volumes between 1670 and 1677.

Olga (Helga) Saint, born Pskov, Prussia, c.890, died Kiev, 11 July 969. Of royal birth she revenged herself for her husband's death and this event is described with approval by **Nestor** in the *Primary Chronicle*. He also paints a picture of a highly competent ruler. At some later date she was baptized and attempted to gain autonomy for the Russian Church, negotiating both with Rome and with Byzantium, visiting **Constantine VII** Porphyrogenitus at Constantinople. She also wrote to the Emperor **Otto I** asking for missionaries, because her own conversion had not been followed by her people at that time. She was given a Christian burial and recognized as a saint. Feast day 11 July.

Olier, Jean-Jacques Founder of the Society and Seminary of Saint-Sulpice, born Paris, 20 September 1608, died there, 2 April 1657. He studied with the Jesuits in Lyons, where his father was a civil servant, and was encouraged in his priestly vocation by **Francis de Sales.** He went to Paris to study theology at the Sorbonne. He undertook a pilgrimage to Loreto to seek a cure for his failing sight – a cure which, he believed, was granted him. He was ordained in 1633. He thought of becoming a Carthusian, and toured monasteries, but returned to Paris on his father's death. He there came under the influence of de **Condren**, the superior of the Oratory, and of St **Vincent de Paul.** Both encouraged him in his work of reviving religious life in France. One means to this was a seminary to prepare priests for the work. In 1641 he took over the parish of St-Sulpice, one of the most difficult in the country. He established a community of priests to assist him in looking after the poor, in providing education and in setting up homes for orphans and for prostitutes. His seminary first began in his own house, but then he set it up in a separate building. The society he founded to continue these efforts was different from other religious orders in that it was a community of secular priests dedicated to a common life and became a model for other dioceses. He conducted missions to the Auvergne and Brittany during his lifetime and established centres to combat Calvinism and Jansenism as well as educate the ignorant.

Oliger, Livarius Francisan historian, born Schorbach (then Germany now France), 17 February 1875, died Rome, 29 January 1951. He held university posts in Italy and Germany and was co-founder, in 1926, of the Franciscan Journal *Antonianum*. His writings include works of biography and hagiography as well as on most aspects of Franciscan history. His most famous is his *Expositio quattuor magistrorum super regulam fratrum minorum, 1241–1242* (Rome, 1950).

Olivaint, Pierre French Jesuit, born Paris, 22 February 1816, murdered there, 26 May 1871. He entered the Jesuits in 1845 and was ordained in 1850. He taught history at, and then became rector of, the Collège de Vaugirard, and was Jesuit superior in Paris. During the revolt of the Commune against Versailles in 1871 he was arrested and was one of 47 people massacred by the mob in Belleville.

Olivetan, Pierre Robert Biblical scholar and Reformer, born Noyon, France, c.1506, died Ferarra, Italy, 1538. Co-operated with his relative Jean **Calvin** in publishing the latter's French translation of the Bible. Fled from Paris to Orléans and in 1528 was studying Greek and Hebrew in Strasburg. He prepared a French Bible translation, *La Bible qui est toute la Sainte criture*, for the Waldensian sect, published at Neuchâtel in June 1535 with a preface by Calvin.

Ollé-Laprune, Léon French philosopher, born 1839, died Paris, 10 February 1898. In 1875 he became professor of philosophy at the École Normale Supérieure, Paris, where he had studied between 1858 and 1861. He was a leading Catholic figure in philosophy, recognizing the limits of a purely intellectual approach to his subject. And wishing to emphasize the part played by the heart in philosophical concerns. He laid the foundations for the work of later philosophers such as M. **Blondel** and H. **Bergson**, and also of the Modernist movement. His works include *La Philosophie de Malebranche* (1870) and *La Philosophie et le temps présent* (1890). In later life he became an acknowledged lay Catholic leader.

Olmos, Andrés de Franciscan missionary and linguist, born near Oña, Burgos, Spain, c.1491, died Tampico, Mexico, August 1570. He went to New Spain (as Mexico was then) in 1528 with his superior, Juan de **Zumarrága**. He spent some time in Guatemala and was superior in Tecamachalco in 1543. He travelled widely around the region as a missionary among the Indian peoples, penetrating far into the interior. He wrote an *Arte de la lengua mexicana* and prepared grammars in two Indian languages, Totonac and Huastec, to help him in his work.

Olsson, Erik (Olai) Swedish historian, hymnwriter and theologian, born *c.*1422, died Uppsala, Sweden, 24 December 1486. He was a canon at Uppsala, *magister* of sacred theology at Siena in 1475 and then professor of theology at the newly founded University of Uppsala from 1477 until his death. His major work is his patriotic *Chronica regni Gothorum* (*Chronica Erici Olai*), written in the late 1460s and early 1470s.

Olympias Saint, born between 361 and 368 into a rich, influential family in Constantinople, died between 408 and 410. After the early death of her husband, a high official, she refused a second marriage. Because of her ascetic lifestyle and her many donations to the Church, she became at the age of 30 a deaconess in the Church of Constantinople. She started an ascetic community, which shared her life of service and soon counted 250 adherents. Very close to several bishops, especially **John Chrysostom**, she fell into disgrace together with him and was exiled. Seventeen letters from this period, written by Chrysostom to her, have been preserved. Feast day 24/26 July in Orthodox Churches; 17 December in the Martyrology Roman.

Oman, John Wood Presbyterian theologian, born Stenness, Orkney, 23 July 1860, died Cambridge, England, 17 May 1939. He was privately tutored in Orkney, attended Edinburgh University, 1877–82, and the United Presbyterian Theological Hall, 1882–5, spending summer semesters at Erlangen, 1883 and Heidelberg, 1885. He was minister at Clayport Street Presbyterian Church, Alnwick, Northumberland, 1889–1907, and from 1907 professor of theology and from 1922 principal of Westminster College, Cambridge. He retired in 1935. He translated and introduced **Schleiermacher**'s *Speeches on Religion* (1893). His writing combined a passion for truth with pastoral awareness and included *Vision and Authority* (1902), *Grace and Personality* (1917) and *The Natural and the Supernatural* (1931).

Omer of Thérouanne Saint, bishop, died *c.*670. Upon the death of his mother, Omer and his father entered the monastery of Luxeuil (*c.*615). There, under **Eustace**, Omer became proficient in the study of the Scriptures. In 637, when King Dagobert sought a bishop for Thérouanne, the capital of the Morini in Belgic Gaul, Omer was consecrated. At one time the city had been Christianized but had later relapsed into paganism. Omer succeeded in restoring true faith and practice. Along with monks of Luxeuil (**Bertinus**, Mommolin and Ebertan) he founded Sithiu Abbey, which became an important spiritual centre, and also the church of Our Lady of Sithiu, with a small monastery. Feast day 9 September.

Omnibonus Bishop and canon lawyer, date and place of birth unknown, died Verona, Italy, 22 October 1185. A student of **Gratian**, Omnibonus (or 'Omnebene') taught canon law at Bologna and Verona. He was made bishop of Verona in 1157. An early commentator on Gratian's *Decretum*, he is probably the author of the *Abbreviatio Decreti*, which is essentially a reordering of the *Decretum*. He also seems to have written a theological treatise that seems influenced by the thought of **Abelard** and **Hugh of Saint-Victor**.

Onahan, William James Leading Irish-American Roman Catholic layman, business man and civic leader, born County Carlow, Ireland, 24 November 1836, died Chicago, Illinois, 12 January 1919. He emigrated to the USA in 1851, started his working life as an office boy, but quickly rose to occupy more-powerful positions in the business world. He became involved in the peace movement and in Democratic politics as well as working actively on behalf of the Diocese of Chicago and several religious orders. He occupied various civic positions in Chicago, and campaigned on behalf of Irish immigrants and to promote temperance. He wrote pamphlets and contributed to many Catholic journals, mainly on aspects of Catholic history and citizenship. He was honoured in 1895 by **Leo XIII**.

O'Neill, Hugh Leader of the final Irish rebellion in **Elizabeth** I's reign, the Nine Years' War, born Dungannon, County Tyrone, *c.*1550, died Rome, 20 July 1616 (his tomb is in St Peter's). After the murder of his father Matthew in 1558, Hugh was raised in the Pale and in England by his English patrons, made 3rd Baron Dungannon and created 2nd Earl of Tyrone as a bulwark against the pretensions of Turlough O'Neill. In 1592 his ally and son-in-law Red Hugh O'Donnell helped him to achieve supremacy in Ulster. But O'Neill calculated that he had more to gain, possibly control of all Ireland, as the Gaelic O'Neill, and he was the last O'Neill to be so inaugurated at the traditional crowning place of Tullahogue. With his allies O'Donnell and Maguire, they sought Spanish aid and presented their struggle against the English Protestant Crown as a religious crusade for faith and fatherland, but not many of the Old English Catholics in Ireland joined him. The allied defeat at Kinsale in 1601, O'Neill's submission at Mellifont in 1603 and the celebrated 'Flight of the Earls' to the Continent in 1607 marked the end of the Gaelic order and prepared the way for the Plantations under King **James I** and VI.

O'Neill, Owen Roe The Catholic Confederacy's most successful general in the Civil War and nephew of Hugh **O'Neill**, born North Armagh, *c.*1582, died Cloughoughter Castle, County Cavan, 6 November 1649. In 1605 he joined the Irish regiments in Spanish Flanders, where he became an outstanding military general, serving with especial distinction in the siege of Arras against the French in 1640. While based at Louvain he made many friends among the Irish Franciscan exiles, who shaped his political views and his loyalty to Counter-Reformation Catholicism. Following the rising of 1641 he returned to Ireland aiming to reverse the Ulster Plantation and to achieve full religious liberty for Catholics. The Confederation at Kilkenny, with Giovanni Battista **Rinuccini** as its uneasy papal legate, found in O'Neill a willing and charismatic leader. His victory at Benburb, County Tyrone, on 5 June 1646 over the Scots Parliamentarians under General Munro was his highest achievement in the Civil War. His fellow Old English generals Preston and Castlehaven did not trust him and his support for the papal nuncio alienated him from the Confederation when he refused to support the peace efforts of Ormond in 1646 and 1648. In February 1649 Rinuccini left Ireland. In May that year the Confederation made a truce with Inchiquin and in August Oliver **Cromwell** arrived in Ringsend, Dublin. O'Neill

belatedly made alliance with Ormond but he died the following month at Cavan. There is little evidence to support the tradition that Owen Roe was poisoned by an enemy agent.

O'Neill, Sara Benedicta Foundress of the St Benedict Library, Chicago, Illinois, born Chicago, 17 March 1869, died there, 11 January 1954. Studied at Northwestern University, Evanston, Illinois, and later at the University of Chicago, and taught for 35 years at the Tilden Public High School in Chicago. She was impressed by the contribution to learning the Benedictines had made through their libraries and made several visits to the Benedictine Monastery in Monte Cassino, Italy, where, in 1902, she became an Oblate of St Benedict. It was here that she had the idea of opening a library in Chicago, and her efforts to win encouragement and support bore fruit when the St Benedict Library, which became a meeting-place for intellectuals, opened in 1931.

Optatus Saint, bishop of Milevis, North Africa, fl. *c.*370. Little is known for sure about him except his treatise against the Donatists, produced 367 to 385. Book I argues against the foundations of Donatism, books II–VI argue that there is no catholicity among them, book VII claims that repentant Donatists can be readmitted to the Church. **Augustine**'s refutation of Donatism was influenced by Optatus' work. Feast day 4 June.

Optina Elders Russian Orthodox saints, this group of monks is generally reckoned to number fourteen – the earliest, Moses, born 15 January 1782, and the last Isaachius, martyred in 1937. They all belonged to the Optina Hermitage in the Kaluga district, which was a centre of spiritual direction and renewal inspired by the Hesychast tradition, brought to Russia by disciples of St **Paisius Velichkovsky**. Most of the elders made themselves available to visitors, who came from all over the Russian Empire. Several gave counsel also by correspondence. Optina was closed by the Soviet authorities in the 1920s and the last elders all suffered varying degrees of persecution. See separate entries for **Macarius of Optima** and **Ambrose of Optina**. Canonized 1990. Collective feast day 11 October.

Ordericus Vitalis Benedictine and historian, born near Shrewsbury, England, the son of a French priest and an English mother, 1075, died St-Évroul, Normandy, c.1142. He joined the Benedictines at St-Évroul in 1085. His writings include a thirteen-volume *Ecclesiastical History*, which provides some interesting insights into the Norman conquest of England in 1066 and the political and ecclesiastical politics of northern France at that time.

Oré, Luis Gerónimo de Bishop, linguist, member of the Franciscan Order, born Ayacucho, Peru, 1554, died Concepción, Chile, 30 January 1630. Ordained in Lima at the end of 1582 and worked as a missionary in Southern Peru. In 1598 he became vicar of the convent in Lima, where he taught courses in the Quechua and Aymara languages, and was engaged to supervise the catechetical work among the Indians in surrounding dioceses. From 1604 to 1613 he lived in Italy and Spain, and wrote and published works on music and liturgy, catechetics and the sacraments. Much of this was translated into Indian languages for missionary use. He also wrote a Life of **Francis Solanus**. From 1614 he worked in Florida and Cuba, and in 1618 was appointed to the See of Concepción. Although Oré visited the diocese only three times he made major improvements there, including opening a seminary and protecting the rights of the Indians.

O'Reilly, Bernard Roman Catholic pastor and biographer of Popes, born near Westport, County Mayo, 29 September 1820, died in the Academy of Mount St Vincent, New York, 26 April 1907. His father, Patrick, was an officer in the French army and was active in the French landings in Mayo during the 1798 rising. He sent Bernard to Laval University in Quebec, where he was ordained in 1843. His care for the sick and dying in the fever ships arriving in the St Lawerence River from the Irish famine became legendary. In a life of 64 years of priestly ministrations he worked in Canada, Britain, France, Italy and America. During the American Civil War he was chaplain to the 69th Regiment of the Irish Brigade under General Thomas Francis **Meagher**. After the war he joined the Jesuits and lectured at Fordham. He wrote a major biography of **Pius IX** and became an intimate of Pope **Leo XIII**, who appointed him to write his official biography. Besides biography he wrote many novels, and articles of Catholic interest for the *American Encyclopaedia*.

O'Reilly, Edmund Ecclesiastical statesman, born Diocese of Dublin, c.1598, died Saumur on the Loire, spring 1669. He studied at Douai, Antwerp and Louvain, returning to Ireland in 1641 and espousing the cause of Owen Roe **O'Neill** in the Civil War. He was made vicar general of Dublin but was dismissed under suspicion of betraying Ormond's forces to Michael Jones in 1649. Peter **Walsh**, the Franciscan, was his lifelong enemy and was responsible for O'Reilly's dismissal and indeed an attempt on his life. In 1650 Archbishop Thomas **Fleming** restored O'Reilly as vicar-general and held a synod in the secrecy of the Glenmalure woods in Wicklow, during which he had Peter Walsh excommunicated. O'Reilly was imprisoned for a time under an unproven charge of murder. Under **Cromwell**'s banishment of priests he fled to Lille in Flanders, but returned to Ireland as archbishop of Armagh in 1657. During 1659–61 he reorganized the Church in Ulster, but yet again the hostility of Peter Walsh made it impossible for O'Reilly to continue in Armagh during the Restoration. He returned to the Irish Colleges in Belgium and France, ordaining many priests for the Irish mission.

O'Reilly, Hugh Archbishop of Armagh, born Ballintemple, Clanmahon, c.1580, died 1651 or 1653. He was a member of the ruling family of Breifne, County Cavan, and was educated there by the Franciscans. He studied philosophy at Rouen, but the date of his ordination is unknown. In 1618 he was appointed bishop of Kilmore and was raised to the primatial see of Armagh by **Urban VIII** in 1625 and consecrated in St Peter's, Drogheda, in July 1626 (he did not receive his pallium from Rome until c.1630). One of his aims was to restore confiscated churches and their lands, but he had little success. He was an ardent reformer of his clergy, depriving many for concubinage and exercising strict control over admissions to the priesthood, as well as holding regular synods despite the attentions of the government. He was arrested and imprisoned for a year. His famous Synod of Kells held in 1642 laid the foundations for the Confederation of Kilkenny. As a patron of learning he helped Fr John **Colgan** in collecting manuscripts and paid for the publication of the monumental *Acta Sanctorum Hiberniae*, Colgan's monument to Irish hagiography.

Origen Theologian, born into a Christian, Alexandrian family *c.*184, died from the consequences of tortures undergone during Decius' persecution, 254. After a career as teacher of grammar and catechism, he started following the courses of Ammonius Saccas, the leading Neoplatonist. Gradually Origen developed, while teaching in Alexandria, his own systematic theology out of the synthesis between Neoplatonism and Christianity. Origen was in the first place an exegete, and many of his writings are commentaries and homilies on the Scriptures. Alongside his exegetical writings he also produced the first systematic theology (*De Principiis*). He also took seriously the dialogue with pagans (cf. the *Contra Celsum*). On one of his many travels, Origen was ordained priest in Palestinian Caesarea. **Demetrius of Alexandria**, who had already protested that Origen, despite being a layman, preached, convened on his return a synod in Alexandria that exiled him from Egypt. Origen returned to Palestine and had there, until his death, a third teaching career. He is one of the greatest theologians of the early Church.

Orione, Luigi Roman Catholic priest and founder of the Little Work of Divine Providence (Piccola Opera della Divina Providenza), born Pontecurone, Italy, 23 June 1872, died San Remo, Italy, 12 March 1940. After spending some time as a Franciscan and then a Salesian he eventually became a secular priest and was ordained in Tortona in 1895. He opened a lodging house which eventually welcomed the needy in general. From the original foundation, designed to serve the poor, developed the Little Sisters of Charity, the Sons, Brothers and Hermits of Divine Providence and, especially for blind women who wanted to devote themselves to a life of prayer, the Sacramentine Sisters. Within 50 years there were nearly 4000 members of these five related institutes, and they were to be found throughout the world.

Orlando de' Medici Saint, hermit, born probably in Milan, died Borgone Monastery in Salsmaggiore, near Parma, 15 September 1386. Lived as a solitary in Borgone for about 26 years. His bones were taken to St Bartholomeo's Church in Busseto, Cremona, and since the end of the fourteenth century many miracles have been attributed to him and his cult has flourished. Feast day 15 September.

Orléans-Longueville Antoinette d' Foundress of the Congregation of Our Lady of Calvary, born Trie, near Rouen, 1572, died Poitiers, 25 April 1618. Widowed in 1596, she entered the convent of the Feuillantines (Toulouse) in 1599. After her profession she was ordered by the Pope to act as coadjutrix to her aunt, Eleanor de Bourbon, abbess of Fontevrault, and to aid her in the reform of her monastery. In 1614 Antoinette founded a new monastery in Poitiers, dedicated to Our Lady of Calvary: she and her followers desired to lead a strictly cloistered life of contemplation. Originally the Congregation of Our Lady of Calvary was a small observant congregation cut off from the rest of the Order; it was promoted to the status of an independent Order after Antoinette's death.

Orosius Fifth-century historian, born Braga, *c.*390, died *c.*418. He moved to Africa where he became acquainted with **Augustine**, who in 414 sent him to Palestine to recruit St **Jerome** in the fight against Pelagianism. After the Council of Diospolis (415) upheld Pelagianism, Orosius wrote a *Liber apologeticus* defending his standpoint. He returned to Africa in the spring of 416. He later wrote *Historia adversus Paganos*, which attacked the notion that Rome's problems were due to her turning from the gods to Christianity.

O'Rourke, John Joseph Jesuit Scripture scholar, rector of the Pontifical Biblical Institute, born New York, 16 June 1875, died there, 27 March 1958. Entered the Society of Jesus in 1895 and studied at Stonyhurst and Oxford in England, and at St Louis in the USA. He was ordained in 1910, and sent to Rome in 1913 to teach at the Biblical Institute. From 1924 to 1930 he was rector and expanded the curriculum to include Egyptian, Georgian, Iranian and Sanskrit. In 1927 he founded a subsidiary house in Jerusalem and the following year obtained for the Institute the ability to confer doctoral degrees in sacred Scripture. In 1930 he arranged for the excavations at Teleilat Ghassul to be undertaken. He returned to New York to teach in 1937; he was superior of the house in Jerusalem from 1947 until 1949, when he returned to New York as spiritual director.

Orozco, Alfonso de Blessed, Augustinian writer, born Oropesa, Toledo, Spain, 17 October 1500, died Madrid, 19 September 1591. He joined the Augustinians in 1521 and from 1530 to 1554 was superior of several of their houses in succession. In 1554, he became court preacher and counsellor to the king, **Charles V**, and remained as adviser to his son, **Philip II**. He wrote and edited a number of spiritual and apologetical works, most notably *Vergel de oración y monte de contemplación* in 1544. He was beatified on 1 October 1881.

Orozco y Jiménez, Francisco Roman Catholic archbishop and educator, born Zamora, Michoacán, Mexico, 19 November 1864, died Guadalajara, 18 February 1936. As a seminarian, he studied in Rome and then taught in several colleges and seminaries in Mexico. He became bishop of Chiapas in 1902 and archbishop of Guadalajara in 1913. During the following years of upheaval, he went into hiding and exile several times. In both dioceses he improved material and social conditions, notably founding several schools. He supported the Jesuits, helping them financially and in other ways. He arranged the publication of several collections of documents on local Church history.

Orsi, Giuseppe Agostino Dominican Church historian, theologian and cardinal, born Florence, 9 May 1692, died Rome, 12 June 1761. Joined the Dominicans in 1708. He was master of studies in Florence, and in 1732 became professor of theology, prior at the college of St Thomas in Rome and theologian to Cardinal Neri **Corsini** and, in 1749, to **Benedict XIV**. He was made a cardinal by **Clement XIII** in 1759. He held senior positions in several of the Congregations. A prolific writer, his chief work, the *Storia ecclesiastica*, published in twenty volumes in Rome between 1747 and 1761, went up only to the sixth century. He also wrote on doctrine and morals, the sacraments, and against Gallicanism.

Orsini, Giordano Cardinal, died 29 May 1438. Created a cardinal in 1405, this Roman patrician

was among the conciliarists who met at Pisa in 1409, but he later enjoyed the favour of **Martin V** and **Eugenius IV**, whose primacy he supported against the Council of Basel. He was bishop of Albano from 1412 and of Sabina from 1431. Cardinals Orsini and Niccolò **Albergati** were significant patrons of humanism while the Popes were distracted by political affairs. Orsini took part in the hunt for manuscripts which characterized early fifteenth-century humanism and collected an extensive library. **Nicholas of Cusa** was one of his secretaries.

Orsini, Latino Cardinal, died 11 August 1477. The career of Latino Orsini illustrates both the clerical dynasticism of his age and the transfer of traditional hostility between the Roman baronial clans of Orsini and Colonna into the Sacred College of Cardinals. Archbishop of Trani from 1439, Latino was succeeded there by two of his kinsmen. Cardinal from 1448 and archbishop of Tusculum from 1468, he became a key, if shadowy, political player and power behind the papal throne during the early years of **Sixtus IV**'s pontificate, not least as uncle by marriage of Lorenzo de' Medici, *de facto* ruler of Florence.

Ortigue, Joseph Louis d' Music scholar, born Cavaillon, France, 22 May 1802, died Paris, 20 November 1866. Educated in both law and music, he served as a judge as well as working as a music teacher and critic, contributing to several newspapers and periodicals. From 1840, he concentrated on his efforts to revitalize Church music, especially to revive Gregorian chant. He founded a specialist periodical, *La Maîtrise*, with L. de Niedermeyer, specifically for the improvement of Church music. He was the author of several publications on the subject, notably a *Dictionnaire de plain-chant* in 1853.

Ortíz, Diego Composer and teacher, born Toledo, Spain, around 1510, died Naples(?), 1570. He was music master at the viceroy's chapel in Naples. While there, he published in Rome in 1553 a pioneering treatise in Italian and Spanish on how to ornament cadences and other passages in viol music. Entitled in Spanish *Trattado de Glosas sobre Clausulas y otros generos de puntos en la Musica de Violones*, it was a ground-breaking work on the art of variation for bowed instruments. He composed several works of sacred music, contained in his *Musices liber primus* of 1565, but is best known for his attractive arrangements.

Ortíz de Zárate, Pedro Venerable, Roman Catholic priest and martyr, born Jujuy, Argentina, 1622, died in the Chaco, 27 October 1683. He was a rich and devout landowner who, after the death of his wife in 1653, studied with the Jesuits and was ordained in 1659. He organized and funded a missionary expedition, leaving Jujuy with two Jesuits on 18 October 1682. They founded two settlements in the forests of the Chaco, among apparently friendly Indian people. But he was killed the following year, together with one of his companions, the Jesuit Father Salinas.

Ortolana (Hortulana) Blessed, mother of St **Clare** and St **Agnes of Assisi**, died Italy, before 1238. Always very devout, she travelled as a pilgrim to the Holy Land around 1192, before marrying Count Favarone di Offreduccio of Assisi. She had four children. After the death of her husband, she joined her third daughter, Beatrice, at the convent of the Poor Clares at San Damiano, near Florence. She was buried near her daughters in the church of St Clare in Assisi. Feast day 2 January.

Osanna of Mantua Blessed, mystic, born 1449, died 20 June 1505. She had a visionary experience when she was a small child and became a Dominican tertiary. She lived at home and followed a life of prayer, helped the poor and the sick and interceded on behalf of victims of injustice. Her own model was the Dominican **Savonarola** of Florence, and like him she was critical of the Pope, **Alexander VI**.

Osbald of Northumbria King, abbot, died 799. Osbald, a warlike Northumbrian nobleman, supported King Ethelred against the rival king Aelfwald, burning the house of the latter's son Bearn. **Alcuin** wrote to him urging him, King Ethelred and others to abandon violence and behave as Christians. King Ethelred was murdered on 20 April 796, and Osbald succeeded him to the throne; however, after 27 days he lost the support of his followers and fled to Lindisfarne. Alcuin persuaded Osbald to become a monk to redeem his soul. Shortly after this Osbald took ship north to the land of the Picts, becoming an abbot there.

Osbern of Gloucester Benedictine lexicographer and exegete, born probably Pinnock, Gloucestershire, flourished c.1150. Very little is known of Osbern's life, except that he was a Benedictine in Gloucester and had some connection to Bishop Gilbert **Foliot** of Hereford. He wrote a large number of commentaries, which were never published, but is best known for his *Liber derivationum* (or *Panormia*), a dictionary of word derivations which soon became well known in Europe and was **Huguccio** of Pisa's main source for his own *Liber derivationum*.

Osbert of Clare Prior of Westminster and poet, fl. 1136–60. A strong promoter of the Feast of the Immaculate Conception, he was prior of Westminster from c.1136. Author of two hymns on St Anne, and Latin poems addressed to Abbot Geoffrey of St Albans (**Geoffrey of Dunstable**) and to Prince Henry (the future Henry II), the last work comparing the prince to Augustus and himself to Virgil. Although not a major medieval literary figure, he was well regarded by his contemporaries; his letter collection is particularly valuable for understanding the twelfth century.

Osiander, Andreas Reformation theologian, born c.1498, died 1552. He was ordained priest in 1520 and became a Lutheran some four years later. He took part in the Marburg Colloquy in 1529 and in the Augsburg Diet the following year. He helped put together the Ansbach–Kulmbach–Nuremberg Church Order, and in 1533 published his *Kinderpredigten* on the Catechism. In 1548 he became professor at Königsberg and two years later published his *De justificatione*, which reveals his divergence from **Luther**'s interpretation of justification by faith. He also wrote the first 'Harmony' of the Gospels and brought out a revised edition of the Vulgate.

Osmund of Salisbury Saint, bishop, died 3 December 1099. He was a Norman and followed **William I** to England, possibly as a chaplain, and as William's chancellor assisted with the compilation of the Domesday Book. He became bishop of Salisbury in 1078 and built a cathedral at Sarum (not the present one, which dates from 1225), which he consecrated in April 1092. He also organized the cathedral chapter, which was a model for others. Feast day 4 December.

Ossat, Arnaud d'   Diplomat and cardinal, born Laroque-en-Magnac, France, c.1537, died Rome, 1604. He served in Church diplomatic circles and, in 1589, became the representative in Rome of the widow of King Henry III. When **Henry IV** converted to Catholicism on succeeding to the throne, d'Ossat negotiated with Pope **Clement VIII** on his behalf. He persuaded the Pope to accept this conversion and grant absolution. His diplomatic correspondence was seen as a model of the genre. He stayed in Rome, but was made bishop of Rennes in 1596 and of Bayeux in 1600. He became a cardinal in 1599.

O'Sullivan Beare, Philip   Catholic historian, poet and polemicist, born County Cork, 1590s, of a family of seventeen, only four of whom survived the close of the Elizabethan war and their family exile to Spain; there is no solid information as to the date or place of his death. Smith's *History of Cork* (1750) claims that Philip returned to Ireland and entered the Franciscans. His major work, *Historiae Catholicae Hiberniae compendium* (1621), is an important reflection of Irish Counter-Reformation mentality. In his patriotism he gives pride of place to the O'Sullivans, especially to his uncle Donal's heroic defence of Dunboy Castle and epic winter march to Leitrim after the Hiberno-Spanish defeat at Kinsale. His *Cambrensis eversus* contains a scathing attack on the slanders of **Giraldus Cambrensis** on Ireland and the Irish, and he throws in those of Richard **Stanyhurst** and James **Ussher** as well. He also wrote hagiographies of St **Patrick** and of St Mochua and included an early account of Irish flora and fauna in his *Zoilimastix* – or whip for liars. (1625).

Oswald of Northumbria   Saint, king, born c.605, killed in battle, 5 August 642, possibly at Oswestrey ('Oswald's Tree'?). When Oswald's father Ethelfrith died, **Edwin** seized the throne, forcing him into exile on Iona. Here he was converted to the Christian faith. Returning to Northumbria after Edwin's death, he set about spreading the Christian faith through the help of **Aidan**, sent from Iona

for this purpose to the See of Lindisfarne. Oswald was killed by Penda of Mercia in the seventh year of his reign. Feast day 5 August, or 8 or 9 August in some places.

Oswald of York   Saint, archbishop, born probably Denmark, c.925, died Worcester, England, 29 February 992. Oswald was educated by the archbishop of Canterbury and ordained at the monastery of Fleury, which he had entered. He served as bishop of Worcester, 961 and archbishop of York from 972. During his episcopal tenure, he worked to found and reform religious houses and was one of the primary promoters of the Anglo-Saxon monastic revival of the 900s. His methods were peaceful and by example. Along with **Dunstan**, another monastic reformer, he crowned Kings Edgar, **Edward** the Martyr and Ethelred II. Feast day 28 February.

Othlo of Sankt Emmeram   Benedictine scholar, born near Freising, Germany, c.1010, died Sankt Emmeram Abbey, Regensburg, Germany, 23 November, c.1070. Othlo was educated at Tegernsee and Hersfeld Abbeys before entering Sankt Emmeram in 1032. A gifted young man, Othlo studied classical literature and wrote *De doctrina spirituali*, which is partially a critique of pagan authors. He left Sankt Emmeram around 1062 because of a disagreement with the local bishop and travelled to other monasteries to write and study before returning around 1068. Other works include *Proverbia* and *De cursu spirituali*. He also seems to have written some counterfeit charters for the benefit of his abbey.

Othmar (Otmar, Audemar, Audomar)   Abbot and saint, born c.689, died Werd, near Stein-am-Rhein, Switzerland, 16 November 759. Educated for the priesthood at the imperial court, in 719 he was invited to direct a colony of monks who had settled near the grave of St **Gall**; he built them a monastery and gave them a Rule. For defending the autonomy of the house, he was imprisoned and exiled, and established the first house for lepers in Switzerland. In 769 his remains were returned to the abbey of St Gallen (St Gall), and in 867 they were buried in a church named for him. Feast day 16 November.

O'Toole, George Barry Roman Catholic priest, educationist and philosopher, co-founder of the Catholic University in Peking (Beijing), China, born Ohio, USA, 11 December 1886, died Washington, DC, 26 March 1944. Studied philosophy and theology in Ohio and Rome, and was ordained in Rome in 1911. After five years diocesan and parish work he taught philosophy, theology and animal biology at universities in Pennsylvania. With the Benedictine Archabbot Aurelius Stehle, he founded the Catholic (Fu Jen) University of Peking and was rector there from 1925 to 1933. He was professor of philosophy at Duquesne University, 1934–7, and at the Catholic University of America, Washington, DC, 1937–44. During this time he was also editor-in-chief of *China Monthly*.

Ott, Michael Benedictine abbot, born Neustadt am Main, Bavaria, 18 March 1870, died Crookston, Minnesota, 15 February 1948. After studying at St John's University, Collegeville, Minnesota, he joined the Benedictines in 1889. He then studied in Rome, where he was ordained on 29 June 1894. He returned to his old university until elected abbot of St Peter's Abbey, Muenster, Saskatchewan, Canada, where his abbatial blessing took place on 28 October 1919. In 1921, St Peter's became an abbey *nullius*, directly subject to the Holy See. He founded a school in Muenster which became a junior college affiliated to the University of Saskatchewan.

Ottaviani, Alfredo Cardinal, founder of the 'Oasis of St Rita' orphanage in Frascati, born into a poor family in Trastavere, Rome, one of six children, 29 October 1890, died in the Vatican, 3 August 1979. After his ordination in 1916 he went on to take doctorates in philosophy and theology, and in canon and Roman law. He taught philosophy and law and helped found the canon law journal *Apollinari*. He held important positions in what are now the Council for Public Affairs and the Congregation for the Doctrine of the Faith. He was made a cardinal by **Pius XII** in 1953. In his capacity as president of the Commission for Theology he was responsible for the drafting of the decree on the Church *Lumen Gentium*, and the decree on revelation *Dei Verbum*. His writings include works on canon law and on the encyclicals of **Leo XIII** and **Pius XI**.

Otterbein, Philip William Co-founder and first bishop of the Church of the United Brethren in Christ, born Dillenburg, Germany, 3 June 1726, died Baltimore, Maryland, 17 November 1813. He was ordained a minister of the German Reformed Church in 1749. In 1753, he emigrated to America, where he was pastor to several communities before settling in Baltimore in 1744. He founded the United Brethren with Martin **Boehm** after meeting the Mennonite preacher in 1767. He continued to maintain close ties with the Reformed Church as well as with early Methodist leaders.

Otto I (the Great) German king and Holy Roman Emperor, born 23 October 912, died Memleben, 7 May 973. Elected king of Germany in 936. Despite serious internal feuds and problems, Otto extended his territories, entering Lombardy and Burgundy, and continued the Christian mission into Denmark. He also won victories over the Slavs and Magyars. In 962 he was crowned as Holy Roman Emperor by Pope **John XII.** By the treaty of *Privilegium Ottonianum* the temporal power of the Papacy was extended. He is remembered as the founder of the first Reich, bringing together Germany and much of Italy as one empire. He established a strong German (Ottonian) Church.

Otto II German king and Holy Roman Emperor, born 955, died Rome, 7 December 983. Became king of Germany in 961 and Holy Roman Emperor in 967, ruling solely in 973. In 978 he drove the French out of Lorraine and unsuccessfully besieged Paris. He invaded Italy, capturing Naples, Salerno and Taranto, but was defeated at the Battle of Cotrone in 982. He did much to enhance papal authority, restoring **Benedict VII** to the papal throne and holding an influential synod in 981.

Otto III Holy Roman Emperor, born near Cleves, June 980, died Paterno, near Rome, 23–4 January 1002. The son of Emperor **Otto II** and the Byzantine princess Theophano, he was elected king of Germany and Italy in June 983, and crowned Emperor on 21 May 996 (by his kinsman **Gregory V**, whom he appointed to the Papacy), although his succession was by no means automatic or without difficulty. The profound piety of Gerbert of Aurillac (whom he later appointed to the Papacy as **Sylvester II**) and Bishop **Adalbert of Prague**

(who was later martyred in Poland) greatly impressed him; **Romuald of Ravenna** wanted him to become a monk. Otto used German missionary zeal to promote a strictly Christian *Renovatio imperii Romanorum*, in which Emperor and Pope would jointly rule; his attempts to convert Poland and Hungary were for the most part successful, and he was crowned king of Hungary in 1001. He died of malaria after an uprising in Rome forced him to retreat to Ravenna.

Otto IV (Otto of Brunswick) German king and Holy Roman Emperor, born 1175, died 1218. German king from 1198 (crowned on 12 July) and Holy Roman Emperor from 1209. Raised at the court of his uncle **Richard I** of England. On becoming Holy Roman Emperor a feud developed between himself and Pope **Innocent III**. Otto annexed certain areas of papal territory, including Southern Italy, resulting in his excommunication in 1210. Defeated in battle at Bouvines in 1214 he spent the remainder of his life in retirement on his estate at Brunswick.

Otto, Rudolf German Protestant philosopher and theologian, born Peine, Hanover, 25 September 1869, died Marburg, 7 March 1937. Educated at the gymnasium in Hildesheim and the Universities of Erlangen and Göttingen. He taught theology at Göttingen from 1897 to 1904, Breslau from 1904 to 1917 and Marburg from 1917 to 1929. Famous for his book *Das Heilige* (*The Idea of the Holy*, 1917), in which, in discussing how 'the Holy' can be known, he put forward the idea of the 'numinous'. His other works include *Mysticism: East and West* (1926).

Otto of Bamberg Bishop of Bamberg, missionary and saint, born Swabia, 1060, died Bamberg, 30 June 1139. Having worked as a teacher and priest in Poland he was appointed chancellor for **Henry IV**, Holy Roman Emperor, in 1101. Became bishop of Bamberg in 1106. In this office he carried out a reform of his diocese, creating over twenty monasteries and completing the cathedral. Otto did much to heal the breach between Pope and Emperor in the celebrated 'investiture contest' in **Henry V**'s time and to bring about the Concordat at Worms in 1122. In 1124 he undertook the first of two missionary journeys to Pomerania (Poland),

successfully converting many of the inhabitants. He was canonized in 1189. Feast day 30 September.

Otto of Freising Monk, bishop and historian, born *c.*1111, died Morimond, Champagne, 22 September 1158. St **Leopold of Austria** was his father and he was the uncle of **Frederick I Barbarossa**. Otto studied under **Abelard** in Paris and entered the Cistercian abbey of Morimond, apparently on a sudden impulse while on his return home. He was elected abbot some three years later, around 1136, but became bishop of Freising in 1138 and was involved in the Second Crusade (1147–8). He was one of the first scholars to introduce the study of Aristotle into Germany. His main writings are the *Chronicon seu historia de duabus civitatibus* (1143–6) and *Gesta Friderici* (1156–8), both important historical commentaries on the events of his own times – and of his own relatives.

Ouen Statesman, archbishop of Rouen, born Sancy, near Soissons, *c.*609, died Clichy-la-Garenne, near Paris, 24 August 683 or 684. Ouen was educated at St Medard Abbey and served in the courts of Clotaire II and Dagobert I (as chancellor to the latter). He founded the abbey of Rebais in 634 or 636, was ordained, and then consecrated archbishop of Rouen in 640 or 641. Ouen fought pockets of paganism in his diocese, wrote the Life of his friend St Eligius which is an important historical/ecclesiological source, and continued as a statesman, upholding Ebroin, the mayor of the palace, against the aristocracy, and negotiating peace between Neustria and Austrasia in Cologne at the invitation of Thierry I. His fatal illness struck as he returned from Cologne.

Ovalle, Alonso de Jesuit priest and historian, born Santiago, Chile, 1601, died Lima, Peru, 16 March 1651. He joined the Jesuits in 1618, and became a well-known preacher in Chile. Elected procurator for Rome and Madrid in 1640, he travelled to Europe, reaching Spain in 1642 and Rome the following year. He wrote a history of Chile, *Histórica relación del reino de Chile*, published in Italian and Spanish in Rome in 1646. Regarded as a reliable historical account written in an elegant style, it is considered the best literary work of Chile's colonial period and has been translated into several European languages.

Overberg, Bernard Heinrich German Catholic priest and educator, born near Osnabrück, 1 May 1754, died Münster, 9 November 1826. Studied at Rheine and then Münster and was ordained in 1779. Became assistant to the vicar general, Franz Friedrich Wilhelm von **Fürstenberg**, and helped reform and reorganize educational theory and the schooling system, especially the training of teachers. He can be credited with introducing the profession of female lay teacher. He gave a weekly public lecture, well attended by all classes of people, summarizing all he had taught the trainee teachers that week, and taught catechism in a local convent. He became confessor to Princess **Galitzin**, influenced the conversion to Catholicsm of, among others, Count Friedrich Leopold von **Stolberg** and was confessor and guide to several founders of religious orders of women. His most important work, *Answeisung zum zweckmässigen Schulunterricht für die Schullehrer im Fürstentum Münster* (latest edition 1957), is on educational theory.

Owen, Nicholas Saint, English Jesuit lay brother, martyr, died by torture, 1606. He joined the Jesuits before 1580 and was probably a carpenter or builder. He protested the innocence of Edmund **Campion** and was himself imprisoned. He was released or escaped and worked for some eighteen years with Fathers John **Gerard** and Henry **Garnett**, devising and constructing ingenious hiding places. He was again arrested and imprisoned in the Tower but escaped and possibly helped Gerard escape. He was finally arrested at Hindlip Hall in Worcestershire, again sent to the Tower, tortured on the rack and by other means which eventually killed him. He was canonized in 1970 as one of the **Forty Martyrs of England and Wales**.

Ozanam, Antoine Frederic Catholic writer, lecturer and founder of the Society of St Vincent de Paul, born Milan, 23 April 1813, died of tuberculosis and exhaustion at Marseilles, 8 September 1853. Studied law and literature at Paris. A leader in the nineteenth-century Roman Catholic revival in France. His society, formed in 1833, consisted of laymen with an apostolate of carrying out spiritual and charitable work among the poor. In 1844 he was appointed professor in foreign literature at the Sorbonne. In 1848 he co-edited the *Ère nouvelle*, a periodical expressing Catholic Socialism. His writings include *La Civilisation chrétienne chez les Francs* (1849).

Ozman, Agnes Pentecostal evangelist, born Albany, Wisconsin, 15 September 1870, died Los Angeles, 29 November 1937. Raised a Methodist, she attended training schools in Minnesota and New York before entering Charles **Parham**'s Bethel Bible College in Topeka, Kansas in 1900. There, in 1901, she became the first modern Christian known to have experienced glossolalia, which Parham saw as evidence for Spirit baptism and which led to the first Pentecostal revival. Agnes worked as a city evangelist, and in 1906 she identified with Pentecostalism, marrying a Pentecostal preacher who later became affiliated with the Assemblies of God.

Oznam, Garfield Bromley US Methodist bishop, born Sonora, California, 14 August 1891, died White Plains, New York, 12 March 1963. He studied at the University of Southern California, Los Angeles, and at Boston University. After his ordination in 1916, he worked as a pastor and as a teacher and became president of De Pauw University, Greencastle, Indiana. He was elected bishop in 1936 and served as bishop in Nebraska, Massachusetts, New York and Washington, DC. He was president of the World Council of Churches from 1948 to 1954. A liberal, he was accused, but cleared, of Un-American Activities. His writings include *Labor and Tomorrow's World* (1945) and *The Church and Contemporary Change* (1950).

P

Pacca, Bartolommeo Cardinal and diplomat, born Benevento, Italy, 25 December 1756, died Rome, 19 April 1844. From a noble family, Pacca served as nuncio in Cologne and at Lisbon during the closing years of the eighteenth century, and in both places ecclesiastical politics made his task difficult. In 1801 he became a cardinal, and as a firm supporter of the *ancien régime* opposed the French Concordat of 1801. During the turbulent relationship between Napoleonic France and the Vatican in the early nineteenth century, Pacca suffered periods of imprisonment or exile at the hands of the French as a result of his sympathies. After the fall of Napoleon, Pacca strove to restore as much of the old order as possible, and resisted any attempts at liberalizing the Church. Later in his career he served as bishop for a number of Italian dioceses.

Pace, Edward Aloysius Roman Catholic priest, psychologist and educationalist, born Starke, USA, 3 July 1861, died Washington DC, 26 April 1938. Ordained in 1885 following study in Rome, Pace served as rector of St Augustine's Cathedral in Florida before being selected to become a founder member of faculty for the Catholic University of America in 1888. After further studies in Europe he eventually joined the University in 1891, as professor of psychology. Thereafter he served the University in a number of capacities, during the course of which he gained an international reputation as an experimental and educational psychologist, recognized by numerous awards and honours.

Pace, Richard English humanist scholar and diplomat, born Winchester, c.1482, died London, July 1536. Following study at Oxford, and ordination, Pace became secretary to **Henry VIII** and also undertook diplomatic missions in Europe on behalf of Thomas **Wolsey**. In 1519 he succeeded John **Colet** as dean of St Paul's, followed by a series of further honours and benefices as a result of the king's favouritism. Pace also continued his diplomatic activities, and was involved in academic affairs at both Oxford and Cambridge, where he promoted the cause of humanist scholarship. He eventually suffered a nervous breakdown which led to his withdrawal from public life.

Pachelbel, Johann German composer and organist, baptized Nuremberg, 1 September 1653, died there, 3 March 1706. He studied music at Altdorf and Regensburg, and held a variety of posts as organist before being appointed organist at the St Sebalduskirche in Nuremberg, in 1695, a post he held for the rest of his life. He also taught organ, and one of his pupils was Johann Christoph Bach, who in turn taught his younger brother Johann Sebastian **Bach**. His chorale preludes were influential in spreading the appreciation of Lutheran melodies.

Pachomius Saint, founder of coenobitic monasticism, born Esneh, Egypt, c.290, died Egypt, 346. One of the great monastic fathers, Pachomius became a hermit at Schenesit under Palemon; dissatisfied with eremitic life, he settled in Tabennisi and developed the first *coenobium*, a monastery based on the full communal life. His second foundation, at Pabau, became the motherhouse in a federation of nine monasteries and two convents over which he presided. The Rules of Pachomius were composed in Coptic, and translated into Latin (by **Jerome** in 404), Greek and Ethiopian; they influenced in some degree all subsequent monastic Rules, e.g. that of St **Benedict** *c.*540, and thus the form of monasticism that prevails today. Feast day 14 May (Western calendar), 15 May (Orthodox calendar), 9 May (Coptic calendar).

Pacian of Barcelona Saint, bishop, born Spain, *c.*310, died Barcelona, before 392. The main source of information about Pacian is **Jerome**'s *De viris illustribus*, a book dedicated to his son, Dexter, the praetorian prefect, in which Pacian is praised for his learning, sanctity and pastoral zeal. His extant writings are *De Baptismo*, a sermon on baptism and original sin; *Contra Novatianos*, three letters to Sympronian on the Novatian heresy; and *Paraenesis sive exhortatensis libellus*, on the forgiveness of sins. The first letter to Sympronian contains the famous line: 'My name is Christian, my surname, Catholic.' Feast day 9 March.

Pacioli, Luca Franciscan mathematician, born Borgo San Sepulchro, Italy, 1445, died *c.*1515. Pacioli was educated by Franciscan friars and became deeply influenced by humanist scholarship. In his later mathematical researches this led him to study the work of earlier mathematicians, which he then synthesized with the discoveries of more recent times. As a result of Pacioli's contacts with artists and architects, mathematics ceased to be a purely academic study and came to be applied more practically in art and design, as demonstrated in his treatise *Divina proportione*, written in collaboration with **Leonardo da Vinci**.

Padilla, Diego Francisco Augustinian priest and Colombian patriot, born Bogotá, Colombia, *c.*1754, died Bojacá, Colombia, 9 April 1829. Padilla joined the Augustinians *c.*1770, one of ten brothers and sisters to join a religious order. A gifted writer, he published a series of anonymous pamphlets which defended religious beliefs and argued the case for Colombian independence, of which he was an ardent supporter. By 1810 he had become a leading figure in the independence movement, and in 1816 he was exiled by the Spanish authorities. He was pardoned in 1820 and allowed to return, and for the rest of his life lived in the town where he had once served as priest.

Padilla y Estrada, Ignacio de Augustinian bishop, born Mexico City, 1695, died Mérida, Mexico, 20 July 1760. Padilla y Estrada was of the nobility but dedicated himself to study and the ascetic life after joining the Augustinians. He became a doctor of theology of the University of Mexico, then taught theology and philosophy at the Colegio de San Pablo, where he became rector. He also held a number of ecclesiastical appointments, and in 1745 was made archbishop of Santo Domingo. In this office he encouraged clerical reforms and the restoration of churches. In 1753 he was made bishop of Mérida, reforming and enlarging the seminary there and endowing scholarships for children of the poor. He also took a keen interest in the welfare of the Indians, supporting hospitals and providing schools for them, often at his own expense.

Paget, Francis Anglican bishop, born London, 24 May 1851; died Elford, 4 August 1911. He was educated at Shrewsbury and Christ Church, Oxford, where he was awarded a DD in 1885. He was ordained in 1877, and was a disciple of **Pusey**. In 1885 he became Regius professor of pastoral theology and a canon of Christ Church, being promoted to dean in 1892 and chaplain to the bishop of Oxford: he himself succeeded to the bishopric in 1901. As bishop of Oxford, Paget warmly supported the Oxford Movement, and the reintroduction of Tractarian principles by the *Lux Mundi* group, and himself contributed the essay on 'Sacraments'. His *Spirit of Discipline* contains a notable essay on 'Accidie', having studied the term (meaning negligence or indifference) in a number of ancient authors, as well as in its modern significance. He was an influential member of the Royal Commission on Ecclesiastical Discipline, 1904–6.

Pagi, Antoine French Franciscan historian, born Rognes, 31 March 1624, died Aix, 5 June 1699. He studied with the Jesuits at Aix, entered the Franciscans at Arles and wrote historical treatises on the Roman consuls, on St **Martin of Tours** and on St **Anthony of Padua**. His main work is a massive critical gloss on the *Annales ecclesiastici* of Cardinal **Baronius**.

Pagi, François French Franciscan historian, nephew of Antoine **Pagi**, born Lambesc, Provence, 7 September 1654, died Orange, 21 January 1721. He studied with the Oratorians at Toulon, joined the Franciscans, and became provincial three times. He edited and published his uncle's work under the title *Critica historico-chronologica*, and is best known for *Pontificum Romanorum gesta*, a history of the Popes up to 1447.

Pagnini, Santes (Pagninus, Pagnino) Italian Dominican philologist, born Lucca, Tuscany, 18 October 1470, died Lyons, 24 August 1536. Pagnini's translation of the Hebrew Bible into Latin, the first since **Jerome**, introduced the numbering of verses, chapter by chapter, still in use in modern Bibles; this influenced English versions of the OT. He went to Lyons in 1524, where he successfully preached against both Waldensians and Lutherans.

Paine, John Saint, Roman Catholic priest and martyr, date and place of birth unknown, died (executed) Chelmsford, England, 2 April 1582. Paine is thought to have come from a Protestant background, but the date and circumstances of his conversion to Catholicism are unknown. He studied at Douai and was ordained in 1576, after which he returned to England. He ministered in secret as chaplain to Lady Petre, a staunch Catholic, but was eventually betrayed and arrested. He was interrogated and tortured in the Tower of London before being tried, and was condemned for treason, on the strength of his Catholic priesthood, and put to death. He was beatified by **Leo XIII** in 1886 and was one of the **Forby Martyrs of England and Wales** in 1970.

Paisius (Paissy) Velichkovsky Orthodox saint and abbot, born Poltava, 21 December 1722, died Niamets Monastery, Romania, 15 November 1794. He rejected the Latinized theology of the Kiev Academy and travelled to Mount Athos to become a monk. He founded several monasteries on Hesychast principles in Moldavia, as the Russia of **Catherine II** was anti-monastic. The houses used both Slavonic and Romanian, and from there the Slavonic *Philokalia*, which he translated (see St **Nicodemus of the Holy Mountain**), was disseminated. Paisius thus began the monastic revival of nineteenth-century Russia. Feast day 15 November.

Palacios, Manuel Antonio Roman Catholic bishop, born Luque, Paraguay, July 1824, died (executed) Lomas Valentinas, Paraguay, 21 December 1868. Palacios was ordained in 1848 and became bishop of Asunción in 1865. During the Paraguayan War of 1864–70 he served as first chaplain of the army. By 1868 it had become apparent that Paraguay's defeat was inevitable, and to avoid further unnecessary bloodshed Palacios counselled surrender. For this he was accused of treason and arrested, along with a group of other prominent Paraguayans who held the same view. They were all then summarily tried and executed, having first been tortured to extract spurious confessions.

Palafox y Mendoza, Juan de Roman Catholic bishop, born Fitero, Spain, 1600, died Osma, Spain, 1659. The illegitimate son of a nobleman, Palafox was ordained following study at Salamanca, and in 1610 went to Mexico as bishop of Puebla de los Angeles. His ecclesiastical policies brought him into conflict with several religious orders, especially the Jesuits, whose activities he sought to restrict. He also supported education and opened numerous schools and academies, but a new constitution he drafted for the University of Mexico also proved contentious. In 1649 Palafox returned to Spain and subsequently became bishop of Osma. He was regarded as a pious and learned man, and in the eighteenth century was nominated for beatification; this did not proceed, but his reputation for sanctity was given papal confirmation in 1767.

Palamas, Gregory *see* **Gregory Palamas**

Palestrina, Giovanni Pierluigi da Italian composer, born Palestrina, *c*.1525, died Rome, 2 February 1594. He was a choirboy in Palestrina and Rome, and educated in Rome. He returned to Palestrina in 1544, and married. When his bishop became Pope **Julius III**, he brought Palestrina to Rome, in 1551, as master of the Julian, and then of the pontifical, choirs. Besides being married, he also composed madrigals, both of which were against the rules for Church musicians, and he was dismissed – though with a pension – from his office. He managed, however, to obtain other posts in churches in Rome. Roman plagues killed his wife and two of his children, and he decided to become a priest – but then married again. He was a remarkably prolific composer, and the Council of Trent regarded Palestrina's austere Church music, exemplified in his *Missa Papae Marcelli*, as the pure style to which other composers must aspire.

Paley, William Anglican theologian, born Peterborough, July 1743, died Lincoln 25 May 1805. Paley was educated at Cambridge, where he subsequently pursued an academic career with great success. He tutored in London before being elected fellow of his college, Christ's, in 1766, he was ordained the following year. He left Cambridge in 1776, on his marriage, and held various benefices in Cumberland before becoming a prebend of Carlisle in 1780, archdeacon two years later and chancellor of the diocese in 1785. He was made sub-dean of Lincoln in 1795, and in the same year rector of Bishop-Wearmouth, near Durham, where he lived for the rest of his life, except for his three-month annual residence at Lincoln. It was during one such residence that he died. He had won recognition with his clear and forceful lectures at Cambridge on ethics, metaphysics and the NT. His first book, *The Principles of Moral and Political Philosophy*, outlined the Utilitarian doctrine of the time and became a standard text. His fame rests on *A View of the Evidences of Christianity* and *Natural Theology*, which argued from the evidences of design in the universe for the existence of God. Paley's rational approach guided the 'evidential school' of theologians in the Church of England during its latitudinarian heyday, but could not match the ideas of the Oxford Movement or withstand the development of higher criticism.

Palladius Saint, Irish bishop, died in Brittany after 432. According to the *Chronicon* of **Prosper of Aquitaine**, **Celestine I** sent Palladius, a Roman deacon, 'ad Scotos in Christum credentes', to the Irish Christians, as their first bishop, to combat Pelagianism. He is recorded as being an associate of St **Germanus**, bishop of Auxerre, a delegate to the British Church. Early lives of St **Patrick** portray Palladius as an unsuccessful missionary who abandoned his task, or died, leaving the way open for

Patrick, then in Gaul, who is supposed to have received permission from Germanus to continue the work of Palladius in Ireland. Feast day 7 July.

Palladius of Helenopolis Bishop, born Galatia, *c*.363, died probably Asperna, 430. A disciple of **Evagrius Ponticus**, Palladius spent many years with the monks of Egypt and Palestine before being consecrated by St **John Chrysostom** as bishop of Helenopolis. When the Synod of the Oak condemned John in 403, on charges brought by some Egyptian monks, Palladius pleaded his case in Rome, but this led to his own exile in Egypt, where he wrote a Life of the saint. Palladius returned in 412 and became bishop of Asperna, where he wrote his *Lausiac History*; it portrays the desirable monastic life, and the work is considered of the highest importance for the history of early monasticism.

Pallavicino, Pietro Sforza Jesuit theologian, historian and cardinal, born Rome, 28 November 1607, died Rome, 5 June 1667. In order to enter the Church, Pallavicino renounced his rights to his family inheritance, and following study became a Jesuit in 1637. He eventually became a professor at the Roman College and was created cardinal in 1659. Although he wrote a number of theological treatises, Pallavicino's reputation rests on his historical works, principally his monumental history of the Council of Trent, begun in 1652. He also wrote an important Life of Pope **Alexander VII**, which remained in manuscript form until 1839.

Palmer, Phoebe Worrall Methodist revivalist and editor, born New York City, 18 December 1807, died New York City, 2 November 1874. A confidante of several Methodist bishops and educators, she led the Tuesday Meeting for the Promotion of Holiness that stimulated the Holiness Movement's international rise. She was a much-sought revivalist in the US, Canada and Britain. Circulation of the *Guide to Holiness* exceeded 37,000 while she was its editor, making it by far the most widely read Methodist paper of its day. Her dozen books include *Promise of the Father* (1859), an early defence of a woman's right to preach, and *Way of Holiness* (1843), a study in spiritual life that has had over 50 editions.

Palmer, William Irish Tractarian theologian, born Dublin, 14 February 1803, died London, 1885. He graduated from Trinity College, Dublin, in 1824, was ordained, and moved to Oxford, where he eventually became a member of Worcester College. Palmer's *Origines liturgicae* brought him into contact with John Henry **Newman**, and others of the party afterwards known as 'Tractarian'. He knew well the controversy with Rome, gained by a study of Cardinal **Bellarmine** and other eminent Roman Catholic apologists. Strongly opposed both to Popery and to Dissent, he expounded what he conceived to be Anglican doctrine in an ingenious *Treatise on the Church of Christ*, designed to prove that the Church of England is a branch of the Catholic Church, co-ordinate with the Roman and Greek Churches. He became rector of Whitchurch Canonicorum in Devon in 1846, and a baronet in 1865 on the death of his father.

Pammachius Saint, Roman Christian, born Rome, *c.*340, died there, 410. A senator of the Furian family and a friend of St **Jerome**, who dedicated to Pammachius several works, including commentaries on the Minor Prophets and on Daniel. After the death of his wife Paulina, daughter of St **Paula**, he took the monastic habit and used his wealth for charitable causes, among them the famous hospital for pilgrims at Portus and the church of SS Giovanni e Paolo in Rome. A peaceful man, he disapproved of Jerome's lack of moderation in the controversy between him and **Rufinus** on the subject of **Origen**. St **Augustine** addressed his *Epistola 58* to Pammachius. Feast day 30 August.

Pamphilus Saint, born Berytus (Beirut), *c.*240, died Caesarea, Palestine, 16 February 310. A pupil of Pierius at Alexandria, he had a deep veneration for the teaching of **Origen**, and wrote an *Apology for Origen* with the help of **Eusebius of Caesarea**, who in turn held Pamphilus in great esteem. **Jerome** testifies to Pamphilus' authorship of the first five books, but when he became an anti-Origenist, Jerome discredited the work and attributed it to Eusebius, who added a sixth book after Pamphilus' martyrdom, and took for himself the name 'Eusebius of Pamphilus'. Feast day 1 June.

Pancras Saint, boy martyr. There are no reliable historical data about him, but it seems certain that a martyr of this name existed in the early fourth century; Pope **Symmachus** built a church over his tomb in the Via Aurelia at the spot where he suffered decapitation a month after his conversion, when not yet fourteen. The first church built at Canterbury bore his name and contained a portion of his relics; the railway station in London is so called from its location in the parish which held the old cemetery of St Pancras. Feast day 12 May.

Pantaleon Saint, martyred in Rome, *c.*305. Nothing is known for certain about him, but legend would have Pantaleon a physician in the court of Emperor Galerius at Nicomedia who, though brought up a Christian, fell into apostasy because of the evil example of the palace; a Christian called Hermolaus led him back to the faith. He suffered martyrdom when Diocletian gave orders to purge the court of Christians. He is honoured as one of the patron saints of physicians, second only to St Luke. Feast day 27 July.

Papasarantopoulos, Chrysostom Greek Orthodox missionary priest, born Vasilitsion, Greece, 1903, died Kananga, Zaire, 29 December 1972. He became a monk at the age of fifteen but did not study theology until he was 50. In 1960 he went to Uganda and then Kenya to help the struggling indigenous Orthodox. He translated liturgical books and prepared many Africans for the priesthood. He was much loved and made known the African local Church to the Orthodox world. Late in life and in poor health, he moved to Zaire, where he died, an active missionary minister to the end.

Papenbroeck, Daniel van Jesuit, hagiographer and writer, born Antwerp, 17 March 1628, died there, 2 June 1714. From 1659 he became assistant to Jean **Bolland**, working on the *Acta Sanctorum*, his name appearing on eighteen volumes. In 1675 he published his *Propylaeum antiquarium circa veri ac falsi discrimen in vetustis membranis*, in which he rejected the authenticity of the Merovingian diplomas. This called forth a reply by Jean **Mabillon** in his *De re diplomatica* (1681), the arguments of which Papenbroeck later accepted. In 1675 he caused a controversy with the Carmelites by rejecting as fable their belief that the OT prophet Elijah had been a monk and the founder of monasticism.

Paphnutius Saint, an Egyptian anchorite who suffered martyrdom in 305 under Diocletian, according to the Roman Martyrology. Feast day 24 September.

Paphnutius (the Buffalo) Egyptian anchorite and priest of the desert of Scete, died date unknown, but when John **Cassian** visited him in 395, he is reported to have been 90 years old. In 397 he held a public reading of the letter of the Patriarch Theophilus of Alexandria condemning anthropomorphism as contrary to the Christian doctrine that God is strictly incomparable, and incomprehensible.

Paphnutius Saint, Egyptian monk, a disciple of St **Anthony of Egypt** and bishop of Upper Thebaid, died *c.*360. In the persecution under Maximin Daia he suffered such great hardship and cruelty that the assembled bishops at the Council of Nicaea, which he attended, were amazed at his fortitude. He apparently dissuaded the Council from ordering all clergy to put away their wives. Feast day 11 September.

Papias of Hierapolis One of the Apostolic Fathers, from Hierapolis in Phrygia, born *c.*60; died *c.*135. What is known of Papias' early life comes from St **Irenaeus**, who referred to him as 'a man of the old time' and a companion of St **Polycarp**. His great five-volume work *Expositions of the Oracles of the Lord* is the prime early authority for the Gospels of Matthew and Mark, and survives only in fragments in later writers, chiefly **Eusebius of Caesarea**. Eusebius calls him 'bishop' of Hierapolis, but whether with good ground is uncertain.

Papini, Giovanni Italian author, born Florence, 9 January 1881, died there, 8 July 1956. Largely self-taught, a militant atheist and nationalist, Papini made a spectacular conversion to Catholicism, and thereafter put the impetuosity of his authorial style at the service of religion. His *Storia di Cristo* gained international notoriety, *Les Ouvriers de la Vigne*, *St Augustin* and *Gog* followed, and *Diavolo* (1953), source of much controversy, was censured by the Holy See. He published also lyrical works, *Cento*

Pagine di poesia and especially *Un Uomo finito*, being a sincere reflection of his interior struggles and a desire for faith.

Paramarubyananda, Swami *see* **Monchanin, Jules**

Paredi, Angelo Giovanni Roman Catholic priest, librarian and patristic scholar, born Canzo, Como, Italy, 7 August 1908, died Milan, in the diocesan priests' house, to which he had retired in 1995, 7 April 1997. He was educated in seminaries in the Archdiocese of Milan, and ordained in the cathedral of Milan on 30 May 1931. He was sent to teach at the archdiocesan school at Seregno, where he stayed until 1937, while studying at Milan's Catholic University of the Sacred Heart: his thesis *I prefazione ambrosiani* was published by the University in 1937 and awarded the prize of the Reale Accademia d'Italia. That same year he went to teach Latin and Greek at the College of St Charles. In 1957 he joined the staff of the Biblioteca Ambrosiana, and was elected its prefect on 12 May 1967, having effectively performed that task for the previous three years. He was highly successful in attracting funds to improve the Library, and linked up with the Medieval Institute of the University of Notre Dame in the United States to microfilm its archives: he was awarded an honorary doctorate by Notre Dame in 1971. He retired in 1984, but continued his scholarly publishing until a couple of years before his death. His main interests lay in the Library and in St **Ambrose** himself and his contemporaries, but he also published a number of works on St Thomas **More**.

Parham, Charles American Pentecostal author and educator, born Muscatine, Iowa, 4 June 1873, died Baxter Springs, Kansas, 29 January 1929. In 1898 Parham was an independent minister in Topeka, Kansas, and following a tour of Holiness centres he founded a Bible school where Pentecostal theology was first formulated in 1901 after the first experience of glossolalia. William **Seymour** attended his second Bible school, in Houston, and took his theology to Azusa Street. In 1907 Parham was arrested for sodomy. Although the charges were dropped, the scandal ruined him. He produced the journal *Apostolic Faith*, and wrote *Kol Kare Bomidbar: A Voice Crying in the Wilderness* (1902) and *The Everlasting Gospel* (*c.*1919).

Park, Edward Amasa American Congregationalist theologian, born Providence, Rhode Island, 29 December 1808, died Andover, 4 June 1900. Park was professor of Christian theology at Andover Theological Seminary, where he was one of the founders of the journal *Bibliotheca Sacra*. He sought to combine the Calvinism of Jonathan **Edwards** with the humanistic spirit of nineteenth-century America, and his views are regarded by some as having made the reductionism of theological liberalism more easily accepted.

Parker, Matthew Archbishop of Canterbury, born Norwich, 6 August 1504, died London, 17 May 1575. He entered the University of Cambridge in 1522, and was ordained five years later, being elected a fellow of Corpus Christi College in 1528. Although invited to be a founding student of Cardinal's College (later Christ Church), Oxford, by Cardinal **Wolsey**, he turned down the offer. Appointed chaplain to Anne Boleyn in 1535, and to **Henry VIII** two years later, Parker identified himself with the moderate reformers. Under **Mary** he was deprived, and lived in obscurity until 1559, when **Elizabeth I** appointed him to Canterbury, where he represented a *via media* in the issue of the Thirty-Nine Articles, while firmly adhering to the Book of Common Prayer, with its ceremonies and vestments. His chief scholarly contribution is the preservation of hundreds of ancient MSS in the library of Corpus Christi College.

Parker, Theodore American Unitarian minister, born Lexington, Massachusetts, 24 August 1810, died Boston, 10 May 1860. A graduate of Harvard Divinity School, Parker became a Unitarian minister on whom the Transcendentalism of Ralph Waldo **Emerson**, **Kant** and **Schleiermacher** exercised much influence. His sermon 'The Transient and the Permanent in Christianity', and publication of *Discourse on Matters Pertaining to Religion*, aroused the hostility of the Boston clergy against views which conflicted with Unitarian orthodoxy. A scholar and firm advocate of Temperance, prison reform and education for women, and in the forefront of the Anti-Slavery Crusade, he ranks with William Ellery **Channing** as one of the two great leaders of American Unitarianism.

Parry, Hubert Sir, English composer, born Bournemouth, Dorset, 27 February 1848, died Worthing, Sussex, 7 October 1918. He was educated at Eton and Oxford. He helped to raise the status of music and musicians in Britain, and became a professor at the Royal College of Music and professor of music at Oxford. He was a prolific composer and wrote many religious works. Three of his works are especially popular: *And Did Those Feet (Jerusalem)*, the Coronation anthem *I Was Glad*, and the hymn 'Dear Lord and Father of Mankind.'

Parsons, Robert (also Persons), Jesuit missionary, born Nether Stowey, Somersetshire, 24 June 1546, died Rome, 15 April 1610. Educated at Oxford, Parsons became a Catholic and a Jesuit at Louvain, and returned to England with Edmund **Campion** to work as a missionary, until forced to flee to France after Campion's arrest, where he organised priests for the English mission. His most enduring achievement is his work for education, notably as rector (1597–1610) of the English College, Rome, and his major part in the foundation of the English Colleges at Valladolid, Seville and St Omer.

Parsons, Wilfred American Jesuit editor, born Philadelphia, Pennsylvania, 17 March 1887, died Washington, DC, 28 October 1958. Following studies in Louvain and Rome, Parsons became professor of theology at Woodstock, Maryland. Appointed editor of *America* in 1925, he took strong positions on economic and moral issues, and gave moderate support to the New Deal reforms; he sharply criticized Father Charles **Coughlin**, founder of the National Union for Social Justice, for his eccentric and anti-Semitic social doctrines. Parsons founded the cultural review *Thought*, and taught political science at Georgetown University, where he published *Early Catholic Americana*, and at the Catholic University.

Pascal, Blaise French scientist and Christian apologist, born Clermont-en-Auvergne, 19 June 1623, died Paris, 19 August, 1662. A precocious youth, Pascal engaged in various mathematical and physical experiments from an early age; he became famous for inventing the first known calculating machine, and proving the existence of a vacuum and the weight of air. He made contact with the Jansenists at Port-Royal and, in 1654, made his 'definitive conversion', when he discovered the 'God of Abraham, the God of Isaac, the God of Jacob, not that of the philosophers and men of science'. In 1656, the condemnation of Antoine **Arnauld** by the Sorbonne prompted his *Lettres écrites à un provincial* – eighteen in all, six of which identified the issue as being a purely personal quarrel, while the remaining twelve attacked the Jesuit theories of grace (Molinism) and moral theology (probabilism), exposing the immoral character of their casuistry ('slippery equivocations'), and opposing to it the rigorist morality of the Jansenists. Condemned by the Congregation of the Index in 1657, the work continued to provoke violent controversy. The *Pensées*, greatly influenced by Michel de **Montaigne**, are fragments of material for *Apologie de la religion chrétienne* gathered together after Pascal's death. The work originated in 1657 in his desire to convert, through reason, the free-thinking and the incredulous. It seeks to persuade of the unique applicability of Christianity to the human condition, and to assist the reader gradually to accept the light of revelation; he opposed any compromise between humanism and Christianity. The wealth of profound insight and the brilliant style of this moving mystical work received only moderate acclaim in the seventeenth century, and condemnation by the philosophers of the eighteenth, before the acclaim of **Chateaubriand** and the Romantics.

Paschal I Pope, saint, born Rome, elected 24 January 817, died Rome, 11 February 824. He studied in the school attached to the Lateran, joined the papal civil service and, when elected, was abbot of the monastery of St Stephen. Relations between Pope and Emperor (**Louis I the Pious**) were good, until Louis' son **Lothair I** came to Rome to be crowned co-emperor (for the second time) in 823. Lothair appeared to usurp some papal authority while in the city, something welcomed by Paschal's enemies. Two of them were executed, much to the anger of Louis, though Paschal disclaimed responsibility. Paschal protested against the revival of Iconoclasm in the East, and provided refuge for Greek monks driven out by the Iconoclasts. He also built several splendidly decorated churches. He was, however, unpopular in Rome itself for his dictatorial manner, and an unruly crowd interrupted his funeral. His claims to sainthood were not recognized before the sixteenth century, and his feast day (11 February) is no longer celebrated.

Paschal II Pope, born 'Rainerius' at Bieda di Galatea, in the Romagna, date unknown, elected to the Papacy 13 August 1099, died Rome, January, 1118. Paschal entered a monastery as a boy, became cardinal-priest of San Clemente under **Gregory VII** and served as legate in Spain under **Urban II**. He succeeded Urban and renewed the papal decrees against lay investiture, excommunicating Emperor **Henry IV** of Germany in 1102. In August 1110, **Henry V** marched on Rome determined to obtain an imperial coronation and the right of investiture. In a compromise of February 1111 Henry agreed to renounce investiture (bestowal of ring and crozier), and the Church to forgo the *regalia*, and bishops and abbots were to retain tithes and offerings. The agreements were soon repudiated by both sides, and Paschal condemned lay investiture again in 1116.

Paschal Baylon Saint, Spanish Franciscan lay brother, born Torre-Hermosa, Aragon, 24 May 1540, died Villareal, Castellon, 15 May 1592. A shepherd until the age of 24, Paschal lived a life of austerity and prayer; he entered the convent of Franciscans of the Alcantarine Reform, where he practised extreme mortification; he continued throughout his life to be particularly devoted to the cult of the Blessed Sacrament. On a mission to France, he defended the doctrine of the Real Presence, at risk to his life from the Calvinists. He was canonized in 1690, **Leo XIII** designated him patron of all Eucharistic congresses and societies. Feast day 17 May.

Paschasius Radbertus Saint, Carolingian theologian, born Soissons, *c*.785, died Corbie, *c*.860. Paschasius entered the Benedictine abbey of Corbie under **Adalard** (a cousin of **Charlemagne**), whom he accompanied into Saxony in 822. Elected abbot, he attended the Council of Paris in 847, but resigned in 849 and devoted himself to study. He wrote a Life of Adalard, a *Commentary on the Book of Lamentations*, a *Commentary on St Matthew*, and his most famous work, *De corpore et sanguine Domini*, composed for the monks of Corvey in

Saxony, and the first doctrinal monograph on the Eucharist. Feast day 26 April.

Pastor, Ludwig von German ecclesiastical historin, born Aachen, 31 January, 1854, died Innsbruck, 30 September 1928. Pastor taught at Innsbruck, became director of the Austrian Historical Institute in Rome, and ambassador to the Holy See. A convert to Catholicism and the first historian to be given access to the secret archives of the Vatican, he compiled biographies of Catholic figures: Johannes **Janssen**, August **Reichensperger**, Max von Gagau, and others of the Reformation period. His principal work, the monumental *History of the Popes since the Close of the Middle Ages*, in sixteen volumes, is an indispensable study of the Papacy.

Patmore, Coventry Kersey Dighton English poet and essayist, born Woodford, Essex, 23 July 1823, died Lymington, Hampshire, 26 November 1896. He was educated privately, though in 1839 he spent some months at a school in France. He considered taking orders in the Anglican Church, but hesitated to do so because his father, upon whom he might have to depend, was a freethinker. In 1845, however, his father suffered a substantial financial loss, and Patmore had to find a post. He worked for twenty years as an assistant in the printed books department of the British Museum. His *Poems* met with success, and brought him to the attention of Dante Gabriel **Rossetti** and others of the Pre-Raphaelite movement. In 1854 appeared his long 'verse novel', *The Angel in the House*; it was hugely successful, selling almost 250,000 copies. He had, in 1847, married the daughter of a Congregationalist minister. She died in 1862, and in 1864 he converted to Catholicism in Rome, married a wealthy and devout Catholic and retired to Sussex; he read St **Thomas Aquinas** and St **John of the Cross**, and produced his finest work, *The Unknown Eros*, reflecting the spiritual change effected by his conversion.

Paton, John Gibson Scottish missionary, born Kirkmanhoe, near Dumfries, 24 May 1824, died Melbourne, Australia, 28 January 1907. His parents belonged to the Reformed Presbyterian Church of Scotland, and Paton worked for six years for the Glasgow City Mission before being appointed a missionary to the New Hebrides (Vanuatu), in 1858. Following the death of his wife and child in 1862, he went to Australia, where he promoted interest in missionary work on Vanuatu, and settled in Melbourne as mission organizer and publicist for the Church. His autobiography, reluctantly written, played a great part in spreading Paton's influence and in stimulating support for his missionary cause.

Paton, William Mission strategist and ecumenical leader, born London, 13 November 1886, died Kendal, England, 21 August 1943. He studied at Pembroke College, Oxford, and Westminster College, Cambridge. Following a conversion experience in 1905, he rebuilt the Cambridge Student Christian Movement and became men's candidates' secretary of the Student Volunteer Missionary Union. He was ordained as a Presbyterian, sent to India, 1916–19, and published *Jesus Christ and the World's Religions* (1916). He returned to India, 1922–6, as first secretary of the National Christian Council of India and then succeeded **Oldham** as secretary of the International Missionary Council (IMC) and editor of the *International Review of Mission*, 1927–43. He organized the IMC meetings at Jerusalem in 1928 and Tambaram in 1938, and in 1942 was involved in establishing the British Council of Churches. He died unexpectedly and his breadth of vision was lost at a critical time. Among his many published works are *Social Ideas in India*, *The Faiths of Mankind* and *The Message of the World Wide Church*.

Patrick Saint, 'Apostle of the Irish', born in Britain near the village of Bannavem Taburniae (exact location unknown, but somewhere along the north-west coast), c.386(?), died Ireland, c.460(?). Brought up a Christian, the son of a Roman official who was also a deacon (Patrick's grandfather was a priest), he was captured by pirates and taken to Ireland at the age of sixteen. He made his way back to Britain and trained for the ministry. At some point he went as 'Bishop in Ireland' (his own phrase), and there spent his life evangelizing, ordaining clergy and instituting monks and nuns. In addition to the *Epistola* to Coroticus (a chieftain in Britain), his other work to have survived, the *Confession*, is a moving personal account of his spiritual pilgrimage. Feast day 17 March.

Patrick, Simon Bishop of Ely, born Gainsborough, Lincolnshire, 8 September 1626, died Ely, 31 May 1707. After schooling in Gainsborough he entered Queens' College, Cambridge, and was first ordained as a Presbyterian but became convinced that episcopal ordination was essential. He was ordained again in 1654. He became rector of St Paul's Church in Covent Garden, London, in 1662. In 1689 he became bishop of Chichester, and two years later of Ely. A prominent Latitudinarian, Patrick wrote *A Brief Account of the new Sect of Latitude-Men*. As bishop of Ely he helped to found the Society for Promoting Christian Knowledge (SPCK), and promoted the work of the Society for the Propagation of the Gospel in foreign parts, founded by Thomas **Bray** in 1701 to assist in the missionary work initiated by the SPCK. He wrote many controversial treatises in defence of the Church of England against the Roman Catholics, including *A Full View of the Doctrines and Practices of the Ancient Church relating to the Eucharist*, and *Texts Examined which Papists cite out of the Bible to prove the Supremacy of St Peter and the Pope over the whole Church*, both reprinted in Bishop Gibson's *Preservative against Popery* (1738).

Patteson, John Coleridge English missionary bishop, born Feniton Court, 1827; died Nukapu, Melanesia, 16 September 1871. He was educated at Eton and Balliol and in 1852 became a fellow of Merton College. Ordained in the Church of England the following year, Patteson accompanied George **Selwyn**, bishop of New Zealand, to the Melanesian Mission (founded by Selwyn to extend the Anglican Church to the islands northwards). He toured the islands, learnt some 23 of the languages, and founded a college on Norfolk Island for the training of boys. He was consecrated first bishop of Melanesia in 1861. In 1871 he landed alone on the island of Nukapu, where the natives killed him in revenge for an outrage committed on its inhabitants by some Englishmen a few months before. His death roused the English conscience and the mission gained new ground in the hearts of the Melanesians.

Pattison, Andrew Seth Pringle Scottish philosopher, original name 'Andrew Seth', born Edinburgh, 20 December 1856, died Haining, 1 September 1931. Educated at Berlin, Jena and Göttingen, Seth taught at Edinburgh from 1891 and showed much sympathy with German Idealism; he held that 'God or the Absolute', though not Himself an individual among others, was the source of individuation. To the end a liberal traditionalist in the **Kant**–Hegel tradition, he inclined away from Hegel by reason of his own moralistic individualism. His most important work, *The Idea of God in the Light of Recent Philosophy*, is an elaboration of his Gifford Lectures; and *Studies in the Philosophy of Religion* were originally lectures delivered at Aberdeen.

Pattison, Mark English author, born Hornby, North Riding, 10 October 1813, died Harrogate, 30 July 1884. At Oriel College, Oxford, Pattison came under the influence of John Henry **Newman**, recently removed from his tutorship, and contributed to some of the translations for *Library of the Fathers*, becoming a keen Tractarian; his enthusiasm for the Oxford Movement declined, however, and with it his faith in institutional Christianity. Essentially a man of learning, his personality is revealed in his *Essays*, and his most important work is the biography of *Isaac Casaubon*, an enduring contribution to the history of modern scholarship.

Paul   *see* **John and Paul**

Paul I Saint, elected Pope, born Rome, date unknown, elected 29 May 757, died Rome, 28 June 767. Paul succeeded his brother **Stephen III**, and his pontificate is chiefly remembered for his close alliance with **Pepin III** of the Franks. He reorganized the temporal power of the Papacy, and tried unsuccessfully to effect a reconciliation with the Iconoclastic Byzantine emperor **Constantine V** Copronymus. He has been considered a firm, even harsh, ruler but the times were disorderly, and his biographer rather shifts the blame for his behaviour onto tyrannical subordinates. Feast day 28 June.

Paul II Pope, born 'Pietro Barbo' at Venice, 23 February 1417, elected to the Papacy 30 August 1464, died Rome, 26 July 1471. A Venetian patrician who belonged to an extensive clerical dynasty and whose early career was determined by the patronage of his uncle **Eugenius IV**, he continued the work of previous fifteenth-century Popes with regard to imposing central authority on the Papal States. He attempted to reform the Curia, abolished the College of Abbreviators, 1466, and suffered being called an illiterate persecutor of learning for having suppressed in 1468 the Roman Academy on religious grounds. He was, however, friendly to Christian scholars. He began negotiations with Ivan III for the union of the Russian Church with the Roman See; he carried on fruitless negotiations in 1469 with Emperor Frederick III for a crusade against the Turks. Though not a man for radical reforms or unusual views, Paul had an attractive personality, and has never been accused of promoting nephews or favourites. Much of his wealth went into building the Palazzo di S. Marco (now Palazzo Venezia) in Rome.

Paul III   Pope, born 'Alessandro Farnese' at Camino, 29 February 1468, elected 13 October 1534, died Rome, 10 November 1549. A cardinal at 26, and given to a life of luxury in the circle of Lorenzo de' Medici, Farnese was also patron of the Catholic Reform; he appointed as cardinals men of virtue and scholarship, favoured the new Orders, e.g. the Ursulines and the Barnabites, and approved the Society of Jesus in 1540. In 1542 he restored the Inquisition, but procrastinated in the matter of a reform council, which finally opened at Trent in 1545. Less successful in political matters, he further alienated England with his bull against **Henry VIII** in 1538, and had no success in checking the spread of Protestantism in Europe. A lover and patron of art and scholarship, he commissioned **Michelangelo** to paint the *Last Judgement*, and to resume work on St Peter's.

Paul IV   Pope, born 'Gian Pietro Carafa' near Avellino, 28 June 1476, elected 13 May 1555, died Rome 18 August, 1559. A member of the circle of reform cardinals favoured by **Paul III**, in 1524 Carafa had founded, with St **Cajetan**, the Theatine Order, aimed at reform of the Church from its grave abuses and scandals. As archbishop of Naples from 1536, he reorganized the Inquisition, which earned him great unpopularity. A severe and reforming Pope, he mistrusted the Council of Trent, which he would not allow to re-open. Hostile to Spanish domination of the Kingdom of Naples, he had to sue for peace after the defeat of his nephew Carlo Carafa and the invasion of the Papal States by the duke of Alba. The Romans rioted when he died, displaying relief that his harsh rule had ended.

Paul V   Pope, born 'Camillo Borghese' at Rome, 17 September 1552, elected 16 May 1605, died Rome, 28 January 1621. Borghese had studied law at Perugia and Padua, had joined the papal curia and risen through its ranks to become cardinal in 1596 and inquisitor in 1603. He succeeded **Leo XI**, and his extreme conception of papal prerogative made strife inevitable. He provoked disputes with the Italian states over ecclesiastical rights; others yielded, but Venice resisted, determined to be supreme in her own territory, despite excommunication and interdict. Paul condemned the oath that **James I** of England demanded of Catholics following the Gunpowder Plot. He censured **Galileo Galilei**, in 1616, for teaching the Copernican theory of the solar system, and suspended **Copernicus**' treatise 'until corrected'. He approved the Congregation of the Oratory, the French Oratory of Pierre de **Bérulle**; he canonized Charles **Borromeo** and **Frances of Rome**, beatified **Ignatius of Loyola**, **Francis Xavier**, Philip **Neri** and **Teresa of Ávila**. He completed St Peter's and extended the Vatican Library.

Paul VI   Pope, born 'Giovanni Battista Montini' at Concesio, Lombardy, 26 September 1897, elected to the Papacy 12 June 1963, died Castel Gandolfo, 6 August 1978. His father had been a politician, and Montini displayed a keen interest in Italian politics. He was ordained in 1920, went to Rome to study, then joined the Secretariat of State. While in the Secretariat he served also as chaplain to Catholic students, by that means becoming friendly with many who would become prominent in the post-war years, including Aldo Moro, murdered during Montini's pontificate. His liberal sympathies were an irritation to Mussolini. He was appointed archbishop of Milan in 1954, and a cardinal four years later. Montini succeeded **John XXIII**, having played a major role in preparing Vatican Council II (1962–5). His attitude to the first session, at which he spoke only twice, was cool, not to say critical. However, following his election, Paul opened the second session in September 1963, and promulgated its decrees. A progressive in social and political matters, and very much aware of the Third World, Paul issued *Progressio populorum* (1967), a call for social justice in the evolution of developing lands, visited South America, Africa, India and the Holy Land, and pleaded for peace at the UN General Assembly in 1965. His ecumenical gestures included reconciliation with Orthodox Patriarch **Athenagoras** in Istanbul, and meeting with Michael **Ramsey**, archbishop of Canterbury, with whom he established the Anglican–Roman Catholic International Commission; he met with heads of the Armenian and Jacobite Churches and the World Council of Churches. Despite his reform of the Curia, which diminished Italian influence and reduced the pomp and circumstance of the Papacy, in theology Paul was a conservative: his encyclical *Mysterium fidei* reasserted traditional Eucharistic doctrine, while paving the way for liturgical reform *Humanae vitae* condemned artificial methods of birth control and *Sacerdotalis coelibatus* insisted on the necessity of priestly celibacy in the Latin Rite and approved the 1977 declaration by the Congregation for the Doctrine of the Faith against the ordination of women to the priesthood. He was very well read, and numbered scholars such as Jacques **Maritain** among his friends.

Paul of Constantinople   Saint, date of birth unknown, died Armenia, *c.*350. Paul succeeded Alexander as patriarch in 337, only to be displaced in 341 by the Arian **Eusebius of Nicomedia**, upon whose death the orthodox Christians recalled him, but the Arians elected Macedonius, who had the support of **Constantius II**, and Paul again went into exile in the West. Under pressure from **Constans I**, Paul regained his see in 346; on Constans' death, in 351, the Arians again drove Paul into exile, where they killed him. A close friend of St **Athanasius** and Pope (St) **Julius I**, he zealously upheld orthodoxy. Feast day 7 June.

Paul of Samosata   Patriarch of Antioch from 260 to 268, born Samosata on the Euphrates, date unknown, died perhaps Antioch, 272. In his *History*, **Eusebius** (of Caesarea) reports that Paul became suspected of 'low and mean views as to Christ, namely that he was in his nature an ordinary man'; this in contrast with the rising orthodoxy which merged Jesus' human consciousness in

the divine Logos. From other sources we infer that Paul regarded the baptism of Jesus as a great stage in his moral advance, he being a man who came to be God, rather than God become man. His teaching having been condemned by the Synod of Antioch, Paul was deposed in 268 but refused to give up the church.

Paul of the Cross   Saint, religious founder, born Ovada, Italy, 3 January 1694, died Rome, 18 October 1775. Paul led a life of prayer and great austerity until, in 1720, mystical experiences inspired him to found a congregation of men totally dedicated to the Passion of Our Lord. Ordained in 1727, he drew up a Rule and retired to Monte Argentario, where the first Passionist 'Retreat' opened in 1737; **Benedict XIV** approved the Rule in 1741. He also founded a contemplative community of women Passionists. One of the most celebrated preachers of his age, especially on the Passion, he became famous as a miracle worker and spiritual director. Feast day 28 April.

Paul the Deacon (Paul Warnefried)   Carolingian historian, born in the Frioul, *c.*720, died Monte Cassino, *c.*799. Exceptionally well educated, probably at Pavia, Paul became a monk at Monte Cassino; about 781 he visited **Charlemagne**, who honourably received him because of his learning and culture. On his return to Monte Cassino, he began his chief work, *Historia gentis Langobardorum*, in six volumes, an account of the Lombards from legendary times to the death of Liutprand in 744; it is a vivid picture of life at the time, based on documents not available to subsequent historians.

Paul the Hermit (of Thebes)   Saint, traditionally the first Christian hermit, born in the Thebaid, date unknown, died in the desert, *c.*340. According to St **Jerome**'s *Vita Pauli*, the only authority, Paul suffered in the Decian persecution of 249–51 and fled to the desert, where he lived for some 100 years a life of prayer and penitence in a cave. St **Anthony** is said to have visited him when he was 113 years old and later to have buried him, wrapped in a mantle which he had himself received from St **Athanasius**. In later art, Paul is commonly shown with a palm tree or two lions. Feast day 15 January.

Paul the Silentiary   *see* **Paulus Silentiarius**

Paula   Saint, Roman matron and foundress, born Rome, 5 May 347, died Bethlehem, 26 January 404. Of noble birth and a widow at 31 with five children (among them St **Eustochium**), Paula became a disciple of St **Jerome** and, with Eustochium, followed him to Palestine in 385, and then to Bethlehem, where she used her wealth to found a monastery for monks, a convent for nuns and a guest house for pilgrims. She studied the Scriptures under Jerome, who wrote her eulogy in *Epistola 108*. Her granddaughter cared for Jerome in his old age. Feast day 26 January.

Paulinus   Saint, bishop of Trier, date and place of birth unknown, died Phrygia, 358. A disciple of St Maximin, he succeeded him in the See of Trier and, a strong opponent of Arianism, was banished to Phrygia after the Synod of Arles (353). His relics were brought back to Trier in 396. Feast day 31 August.

Paulinus   Biographer of St **Ambrose**, born Milan, fourth century, died *c*.422. Paulinus became Ambrose's secretary, and was with him when he died in 397. A deacon, he travelled to North Africa on behalf of the Church of Milan, where at the request of St **Augustine**, he wrote the *Life of St Ambrose*, *c*.422, a work that is strong on miraculous events, but which ignores factual evidence. Paulinus supported Augustine during the Pelagian controversy, and may have composed the *libellus* listing charges against Celestius which was sent to Pope **Zosimus**.

Paulinus   Saint, bishop of Nola, born Bordeaux, *c*.353, died Nola, 22 June 431. From a prominent family and well educated, Paulinus qualified for the senate and served as governor of Campania. He married Therasia and went to live in Spain, whence, after the death of their only child, they returned to Campania to lead a monastic life near the tomb of **St Felix of Nola**; he became bishop of Nola, *c*.409. Acquainted with many notable Christians of his time, he corresponded with SS **Sulpicius Severus**, **Augustine**, **Jerome** and **Martin of Tours**, among others. Some 50 of his *Epistolae* are extant. Feast day 22 June.

Paulinus   Saint, first bishop of the Northumbrians and bishop of York, date and place of birth unknown, died Rochester, 10 October 644. **Gregory I** sent Paulinus to England in 601 to assist **Augustine of Canterbury** in his mission. He was ordained bishop in 625. He escorted **Ethelburga**, a Christian, to be the bride of **Edwin**, king of Northumbria, whom he converted to the faith two years later; Edwin assigned York to Paulinus as his see. **Honorius I** sent the pallium to Paulinus, as a sign of his status as a metropolitan at York, but he never wore it in his cathedral, because after Edwin was slain at Hatfield Chase in 633, Paulinus retired to Kent, where he became bishop of Rochester. Feast day 10 October.

Paulinus   Saint, Italian patriarch of Aquileia, born Friuli, *c*.750, died Aquileia, 11 January 802. A noted grammarian and scholar, Paulinus was appointed by **Charlemagne** a master in the Palace School and in 787 patriarch of Aquileia, one of his main concerns being to suppress Adoptionism, taught by **Elipandus of Toledo** and Felix of Urgel, at the Councils of Regensburg, Frankfurt and Cividale. His writings include two anti-Adoptionist works: *Libellus Sacrosyllabus contra Elipandum* and *Libri iii contra Felicem*. Feast day 28 January.

Paulus Diaconus   *see* **Paul the Deacon**

Paulus Silentiarius   Christian poet, born and died in the sixth century. A high official under **Justinian** (the 'silentiary' being an usher appointed to keep silence in the imperial palace), Paulus' principal extant work is a hymn to mark the consecration of Sancta Sophia, and of its pulpit, in all some 1300 hexameters after the style of **Nonnus**, with short iambic dedications to Justinian. The poem was recited at the second dedication of the church, 562, in the episcopal hall of the patriarchate. The work is of importance for the history of Byzantine art in the sixth century.

Pavan, Pietro   Cardinal, born Treviso, near Venice, 30 August 1903, died Rome, 26 December 1994. Pavan, who came from a politically active Roman Catholic family, was educated in local seminaries, and sent for further studies to the Jesuit-run Gregorian University in Rome, and made a special study of the social teaching of

Catholicism. He was ordained priest in 1928 and returned to Treviso to teach in the seminary while studying economics and sociology at the University of Padua: *The Teaching of the Church in the Temporal Order* was published in 1936 and *Christian Democracy* appeared in 1953. He was called to Rome in 1946 to advise the anti-Communist Association of Italian Christian Workers, and two years later became professor of social thought at the Lateran University. He advised Pope **John XXIII** on the writing of his encyclical *Mater et Magistra* of 1961, and was responsible for drafting the text of *Pacem in Terris* (1963). At the Second Vatican Council he was particularly active in conciliar committees dealing with human rights. After the Council he taught at a number of Roman universities, and from 1969 to 1975 was the rector of the Lateran University. He was created a cardinal in 1985.

Payne, Ernest Alexander Baptist historian, administrator and ecumenical leader, born London, 19 February 1902, died London, 14 January 1980. He studied in London, Oxford and Marburg and was ordained in 1928. Family circumstances prevented his going as a missionary to India, and in 1932 he became young people's secretary of the Baptist Missionary Society. He taught at Regent's Park College, 1940–51, was general secretary of the Baptist Union of Great Britain and Ireland, 1951–67, chairman of the British Council of Churches, 1962–71, a member of the central committee of the World Council of Churches, 1954–75, and president, 1968–75. His publications include *The Free Church Tradition in the Life of England* (1944, 1951), *Baptist Thought and Practice* (1952) and a facsimile edition (1961) of William **Carey**'s *An Enquiry into the Oligations of Christians to use means for the Conversion of the Heathens* (1961).

Peake, Arthur Samuel English biblical scholar, born Leek, Staffordshire, 24 November 1865, died Manchester, 19 August 1929. Son of a Primitive Methodist (Wesleyan Methodist), he was educated at various schools and then at St John's College, Oxford. He had considered ordination into the Church of England, but in the end remained all his life a Methodist layman. In 1889 he was elected a fellow of Merton College, and began to teach at Mansfield College, the recently established training college at Oxford for Free Church ministers. In 1892 he became tutor at the newly founded Hartley Primitive College, Manchester, and is credited with having raised during his lifetime the whole standard of ministry in the Methodist Church. In 1904, when it was decided to set up a theological faculty in Manchester University, he took a major part in devising the course, and was appointed Rylands professor of biblical criticism. Peake edited the *Holborn Review* from 1919, and achieved widespread renown with books such as *The Bible: its Origin, its Significance, and its Abiding Worth*, *The Problems of Suffering in the Old Testament*; and especially his *Commentary on the Bible*, which had wide circulation and great influence.

Pearson, John Anglican bishop of Chester, born Great Snoring, Norfolk, 28 February 1612, died Chester, 16 July 1686. He went to Eton and was admitted to Queens' College, Cambridge, his father's former college, in 1631, but moved to King's, graduating MA in 1639, in which year he was ordained. Pearson supported the Royalist cause during the Civil War, and after the Restoration became professor of divinity at Cambridge, 1660–2. In 1662 he became master of Trinity College and in 1670 bishop of Chester. His reputation rests mainly on the *Exposition of the Creed*; it has been a standard text in English divinity, and the notes reflect a rich mine of patristic and general learning. His other great work, the *Vindiciae Epistolarum S. Ignatii*, is an elaborate response to Jean **Daillé**'s attack on the authenticity of the letters ascribed to **Ignatius of Antioch**.

Peckham, John Archbishop of Canterbury, born Patcham, Sussex, 1225, died Mortlake, 8 December 1292. Educated at Lewes and the Universities of Paris and Oxford. He joined the Franciscans in about 1250. From 1269 to 1271 he lectured at Paris. In 1277 he was appointed *lector sacri palatii* at Rome. Appointed archbishop of Canterbury in 1279. He carried out various ecclesiastical reforms, including the passing of legislation against pluralities and absenteeism, and to improve attendance at the Eucharist and raise the standard of the clergy. As a writer he produced works on theology, science and philosophy, including *Perspectiva communis* and *De sphaera*.

Pecock, Reginald Welsh bishop of Chichester, born St Davids Diocese, c.1393, died Thorney Abbey, Cambridge, c.1461. He was elected a fellow of Oriel College, Oxford, in 1417, and ordained priest in 1421. Shortly afterwards he moved to London, and engaged in polemic against the Lollards. He became bishop of St Asaph in 1444 and in 1450 was transferred to Chichester. Deposed from his bishopric in 1457, because, it was claimed, he had, among other things, rejected the authenticity of the Apostles' Creed and exalted the light of reason as a rule of faith. The charges were, however, motivated by political hostility. He recanted, but remained confined to Thorney Abbey. His best-known work, *The Repressor of Overmuch Wijting* [i.e. *Blaming*] *of the Clergy*, written to convert the Lollards, is a critical summation and rebuttal of their teaching, and a landmark in English literature.

Peebles, Bernard Mann American classical scholar, born Norfolk, Virginia, 1 January 1906, died Washington, DC, 22 November 1976. Educated in the USA and at Rome, where he became a Catholic, Peebles served in World War II, returned to St John's College, Annapolis, in 1945, then went to the Catholic University in 1948, as professor of Latin and Greek. A member of several classical associations, he published papers on the poet Prudentius, on classical and medieval Latin and on patristics. He edited the journal *Traditio*, and the series Fathers of the Church, his translation for which of **Sulpicius Severus'** Life of St **Martin of Tours** is considered to be outstanding. A retiring, gentle man, Peebles was murdered by a street assailant while working on a definitive edition of Sulpicius Severus for the Corpus Christianorum.

Peeters, Flor Belgian organist, composer and writer, born Tielen, 4 July 1903, died Antwerp, 4 July 1986. He was a pupil of Dupré and Tournemire and became director of the Antwerp Conservatoire. He wrote many organ works and much Church music.

Pegis, Anton Charles American philosopher, born Milwaukee, 24 August 1905, died Toronto, 13 May 1978. Pegis studied under Etienne **Gilson** at the Medieval Institute in Toronto, and lectured at Marquette and Fordham Universities, 1931–44; he then returned to Toronto as professor of the history of philosophy. Pegis considered Thomism as the finest Christian example of a theology which employed philosophy as its handmaiden; he defended the rationality of Christian philosophy outlined by **Leo XIII** in *Aeterni Patris*, and thought that Christian revelation, far from destroying that rationality, strengthened and deepened it in the way of the Augustinian themes of God and the soul.

Péguy, Charles Pierre French poet and philosopher, born Orléans, 7 August 1873, died Villeroy, on the eve of the Battle of the Marne, 5 September 1914. Proud of his peasant heritage, Péguy studied at the École Normale Supérieure, notably under Henri **Bergson**. He left the Church, became a socialist, married and opened a bookshop in Paris, which became a meeting-place for intellectuals. He was a major supporter of Alfred Dreyfus, a Jewish army officer falsely accused of treason and espionage. (It was later shown that the French establishment, including many in the Roman Catholic establishment associated with it, was prepared to sacrifice this innocent man to save its own honour.) A fervent humanitarian, he believed in the establishment of a 'universal socialist Republic, the only remedy for universal wrong'. His patriotism had found early expression in the person of **Joan of Arc**, and she inspired *La Mystère de la Charité de Jeanne d'Arc*, a meditation on love, and *Le Porche du mystère de la deuxième vertu*, which celebrates hope; *La Tapisserie de sainte Geneviève et de Jeanne d'Arc*, *La Tapisserie de Notre-Dame* and *Ève* are vast litanies in which poetry is transmuted into prayer. Péguy founded *Cahiers de la Quinzaine* (motto: the social revolution will be moral or nothing), which published his own works. He early professed himself an atheist, but returned to the Catholic faith c.1907, though not to the Church; he remained estranged from his Catholic contemporaries, and republicans and socialists distrusted him because of his attacks on the modern world and its belief in progress, recalling those of Léon **Bloy** and Georges **Bernanos**. His literary reputation has continued to grow since his death.

Pelagia Saint, virgin and martyr, died c.311. Pelagia's name occurs in the Canon of the Ambrosian

Mass of Milan, and her fate is known from praise of her by SS **Ambrose** and **John Chrysostom**. Only fifteen years of age when Roman soldiers surrounded her house during a persecution by Diocletian, she threw herself from a window into the sea to preserve her chastity. Five other saints of the name are mentioned in the Roman Martyrology. Feast day 9 June.

Pelagia of Antioch Saint, died c.457. A celebrated dancer and courtesan, who, converted by St Nonnus, bishop of Edessa, went to Jerusalem disguised as a man and lived a life of penance in the Garden of Olives. Feast day 8 October.

Pelagia of Tarsus Saint, died c.302. She is said to have become a Christian after refusing to marry the son of Diocletian; the emperor then wanted her to be his mistress, but she refused and he ordered her to be burned to death. Feast day 8 October.

Pelagia Ivanovna of Diveyevo (Serebrenikova) Russian Orthodox 'fool for Christ's sake', born Arzamas, Russia, October 1809, died Diveyevo Convent, 30 January 1884. Her unconventional behaviour led to her being disowned by her family and she eventually went to live at the Diveyevo Convent, which had been founded by St **Seraphim**. The saint blessed her life there before he died. She seems to have been mentally afflicted and not just to have been assuming foolishness, though she was extremely sharp-witted and observant. She was believed by the nuns and by pilgrims to have the gifts of prophecy and of healing and she certainly foresaw the destruction of Diveyevo. Her canonization is expected soon.

Pelagius British monk, described by St **Augustine** as a 'saintly man', but eventually condemned as a heretic, born possibly in Ireland, c.350, died after 418. He arrived in Rome in about 380 and just before 410 went to Africa and thence to Palestine, where he lived until about 418. In Rome he lived an exemplary ascetic life and although not ordained became spiritual director to both clergy and laity. He taught that the human will is completely free and equally able to choose good or evil. Grace he saw as being external, its function being to help in the action that the will could achieve by

itself. Death he regarded as an integral part of the human condition, not a consequence of original sin, which he also denied and consequently saw no need for infant baptism. Jesus' life, death and resurrection provide a good example rather than bring about any kind of new life, and prayer for the conversion of others is futile. It was not until Pelagius had left Rome that his ideas began to become known and controversial, mainly through the preaching of his friend Coelestius. The debate raged for many years. Both Pelagius and Coelestius were excommunicated in 417 but both protested their faith and were restored to communion. Coelestius however proved too combative in trying to explain his views and was expelled from Rome. Soon afterwards Pelagius was expelled from Palestine, after which time there is no record of him. The controversy was continued by Coelestius, **Julian of Eclanum** and others. It gave rise to important writings by **Jerome** and Augustine and was finally condemned at the Council of Ephesus in 431. Pelagius' works include *De fide Trinitatis*, no longer extant, and *Expositiones XIII Epistularum Pauli* (before 405), *Epistola ad Demetriadem* (414) and *Libellus fidei* (to Pope **Innocent I**, 417). All the last three are extant, as are fragments of letters, and of *De natura* (414), *De libero arbitrio* (416) and *Liber testimoniorum*, and other anonymous works are possibly by Pelagius.

Pelagius I Pope, scholar and aristocrat, died 3 March 561. He was a deacon and went with Pope **Agapetus I** to Constantinople, succeeded **Vigilius** as apocrisiarius, or papal ambassador, in 537 and as Pope in 555. He had been opposed to the condemnation, by the Emperor **Justinian**, of the Antiochenes, **Theodore of Mopsuestia**, **Theodoret** of Cyrrhus and Ibas of Edessa – known as the condemnation of the 'Three Chapters' – and wrote eloquently against the condemnation. He had a change of heart later, however, when it became clear that the emperor wanted him for Pope. He was unwelcome in Rome, and when after several months he still could not find three bishops to officiate at his consecration, the ceremony had to be performed with two bishops and a presbyter representing the bishop of Ostia. He sought to establish his orthodoxy with both Church and political leaders, and set about restoring the physical, social and political structures of Rome after the devastation caused by the Gothic wars. He reorganized the papal finances, relieved the situation of those reduced to poverty and generally began to bring Rome back to a feeling of normality. In so doing he won over many of his earlier opponents, but not the Northern Italian bishops, who were not to be in communion with Rome again for another 150 years.

Pelagius II Pope, born Rome, died there of the plague, 7 February 590. He became Pope in 579 and tried to gain the assistance of both Constantinople and the Frankish king against the Lombard threat, but secured the support of neither. He eventually enjoyed a truce with the Lombards, though only for a few years. He continued much of the rebuilding work on the physical and social fabric in Rome, turned his family house into an almshouse and was probably responsible for moving the high altar in St Peter's to the position immediately above the relics of the saint. He tried, without success, to heal the breaches with the Northern Italian bishops caused by the Three Chapters controversy, and came into dispute with the patriarch of Constantinople over the meaning and use by the latter of the term 'ecumenical patriarch', which appeared to suggest primacy.

Penington, Isaac English Puritan and Quaker, born London, 1616, died Goodnestone Court, 8 October 1679. Son of the Lord Mayor of London, Penington became a Quaker with his wife in 1658, after hearing George **Fox**, founder of the Society of Friends, preach in Bedfordshire. A person of station, noble character and an able writer, his position made him a valuable acquisition to the Society. Imprisoned in 1661 for refusing to take the Oath of Allegiance, and on several subsequent occasions, his house and other property confiscated, his health weakened, Penington's modesty and gentleness shone through in his many religious works and a political treatise in defence of democratic principles. His writings were of great assistance in the building up of the new Quaker Society.

Penn, William English Quaker and founder of Pennsylvania, born London, 14 October 1644, died Ruscombe, Berkshire, 30 July 1718. Sent down from Oxford in 1661 for refusal to conform to the restored Anglicanism, Penn attached himself to the Quakers in 1667, and published *The Sandy Foundation Shaken*, against belief in the Trinity and Christ's Atonement, which led to his imprisonment in the Tower in 1668. While there he wrote *No Cross, no Crown*, a treasured Quaker classic. He obtained from **Charles II** a grant of land in North America, and founded in 1682 a colony, which took the name 'Pennsylvania', and the city of Philadelphia, formulating a constitution and laws incorporating the most enlightened liberal ideas, including religious and political equality, even for Catholics; he secured final approval for his 'holy experiment', or 'Frame of Government,' in 1701. Back in England, he published *An Essay towards the Present and Future Peace of Europe*, advocating a European parliament, and *Primitive Christianity*, upholding the identity of Quaker principles with those of the early Church.

Pennefather, William Irish Evangelical divine, born Merrion Square, Dublin, 5 February 1816, died London, 30 April 1873. He was educated at Trinity College, Dublin, ordained in 1842, and appointed pastor in Mellifont, near Drogheda, in 1844, staying there throughout the famine. In 1848 he moved to England, to incumbencies in Buckinghamshire and Hertfordshire, before in 1864 moving to St Jude's, Mildmay Park, Islington. Pennefather founded what became the Mildmay Deaconess Institution (subsequently St Catherine's Deaconess House, Highbury), devoted to care of the sick and education of neglected children, and the only training institution in the Evangelical tradition. As a mission preacher, he was known all over England and was one of the few clergy who have been equally active, and equally successful, in both evangelistic and pastoral work.

Pepin III (the Short) King of the Franks, born Paris, 714, died Saint-Denis, near Paris, 24 September 768. Son of **Charles Martel**, Pepin and his brother Carloman succeeded to the office of mayor of the palace; in 747, Carloman retired to a monastery, leaving Pepin as sole ruler. Elected king in 751, he was anointed by St **Boniface** in 752, and by Pope **Stephen II (III)** in 754. Throughout his reign he furthered the ecclesiastical reforms begun by St Boniface, thereby increasing the prestige of the Church among his people. His donation to the Papacy of lands conquered from the Lombards laid the foundations for the Papal States. His achievements paved the way for his illustrious son **Charlemagne**.

Peradze, Grigol Georgian Orthodox theologian, ecumenist and saint, born Bakusiche, Kakhetai, 13 September 1899, died Auschwitz, Poland, 6 December 1942. Himself the son of a priest, Peradze entered the local seminary in 1913, but in 1921 was sent by the Georgian patriarch to study in Berlin and then in Bonn. He spent a year working with the Bollandists in Brussels, and was appointed a lecturer in the Institute of Oriental Studies in Bonn. By 1929 it was clear, after the Soviet occupation of his homeland, that he could not return. He established the first Georgian Orthodox congregation outside Georgia and in 1931 was ordained to serve as its priest. In 1934 he went to the Orthodox theological faculty in Warsaw, and was interned by the Nazis in May 1942 for assisting persecuted Jews.

Perceval, Arthur Philip English Tractarian theologian, born 22 November 1799, died London, 11 June 1853. Educated at Oriel College, Perceval warmly approved of the Tractarian movement at Oxford, and in 1841 published a *Vindication of the Authors of the Tracts for the Times*, principally defending John Henry **Newman** against attacks made on his *Tract no. 90*. In *A Collection of Papers Connected with the Theological Movement of 1833*, he had himself been the author of *Tracts* nos 33, 35 and 36. Queen Victoria deprived him of his royal chaplaincy in 1850 because of his opposition to the Gorham judgement of 1847, in the matter of baptismal regeneration (which prompted Henry **Manning** and Robert **Wilberforce** to secede to Rome).

Pergolesi, Giovanni Battista Italian baroque composer, born Jesi, 4 January 1710, died Pozzuoli, near Naples, 17 March 1736. In collaboration with Leonardo **Leo**, another Neapolitan, Pergolesi worked out the classic formula for comic opera – *opera buffa*; his works include, notably, *La serva padrona*, an example of his lightness and delicacy of style. A prolific artist, he composed much sacred music, his best known being the very popular *Stabat Mater* for two solo voices and strings, and the *Salve Regina*, in C minor, for soprano and strings, outstanding in the sentimental style of Catholic sacred music.

Perkin, Noel Pentecostal missions executive, born England, 1893, died 1979. Perkin made contact with the Christian and Missionary Society in Toronto while working for the Bank of Montreal, and following ordination, he worked for them for three years in Argentina. In 1926 he joined the Assemblies of God, acting as mission secretary from 1927 to 1959. He oversaw a vast expansion in missionary activity, produced the *Missionary Manual* (1931) and supported the establishment of indigenous Churches. In 1959 he became the first Pentecostal president of the Evangelical Foreign Missions Association. With John Garlock he wrote *Our World Witness* (1963).

Perkins, William English Puritan theologian, born Marston Jabbett, Warwickshire, 1558, died Cambridge, 22 October 1602. A student of Christ's College, Cambridge, he was elected fellow of the College in 1584. He had a great reputation both as a teacher and as a preacher. Perkins became prominent as a vigorous anti-Roman theologian and a supporter of Puritan principles. His *Reformed Catholike*, against the Catholic Church, sought to draw the line between Protestant and Roman beliefs, beyond which it seemed to him concessions and conciliation on the part of the Reformed Churches could not go. William Bishop, titular bishop of Chalcedon, assailed the book in his *Reformation of a Catholic Deformed by W. Perkins*, but praised the quality of Perkins' writing. His works were held in high repute in the seventeenth century by theologians with Calvinist sympathies.

Perpetua and Felicity Saints. *The Acts of Perpetua and Felicity* tells how Perpetua and her slave, with other catechumens in Carthage, were imprisoned and after their baptism condemned to execution in the arena. The document, perhaps written by Perpetua herself in Latin, later translated into Greek, and possibly edited by **Tertullian**, also tells of the interesting visions of Perpetua and the priest Saturus, also martyred, who had instructed the women in the faith. Beautifully written, the text is a precious record because contemporary with the events. Perpetua and Felicity are mentioned in the Roman calendar of 354; the basilica dedicated to them was among the most important in Carthage. Feast day 6 March.

Perrin, Henri French pioneer worker-priest, born 13 April 1914, died in a road accident, 25 October 1954. He went with French workers conscripted to work in German factories in World War II and, during the brief time before his identity was discovered and he was sent back to France, discovered how alien and irrelevant to the working classes the Catholic Church had become. This led to a new form of ministry after the war in which priests took their place alongside workers in ordinary jobs, often becoming active in the unions, winning the respect of the workers and gradually revealing their own beliefs and identities. The role of Perrin and others in supposedly Communist-dominated unions brought condemnation from Rome and in 1954 the French bishops stopped the experiment. Many priests returned to their parishes but others continued in the factories and gave up their priesthood. Perrin was spared the decision by his accidental death that year. His story is told in *Priest and Worker: The Autobiography of Henri Perrin*.

Perrone, Giovanni Italian Jesuit theologian, born Chieri (Turin), 2 March 1794, died Castel Gandolfo, 28 August 1876. Perrone taught in the Roman College; he played a principal role in the struggle against Georg **Hermes**' attempt to adjust the principles of Catholic theology to the philosophy of Immanuel **Kant**, and in the preparation for the definition of the dogmas of papal infallibility and the Immaculate Conception, which he defended in his work *De immaculato B. Mariae conceptu*. In general he contributed notably to the revival of ecclesiastical studies, and his *Praelectiones theologiae dogmaticae* went to 34 editions.

Perroton, Marie Françoise French Roman Catholic missionary, born Lyons, 1796, died 1873. As a tertiary of the Society of Mary she went to Ouvia, Fiji, in 1843 as a lay missionary. She was a pioneer in taking seriously the advancement of women in the Oceania region and of retaining important aspects of local culture rather than imposing non-essential elements of Western Christianity. In 1869 she was professed as a sister of the Institute of Our Lady of the Missions.

Pétau, Denis French Jesuit theologian, born Orléans, 21 August 1583, died Paris, 11 December 1652. Pétau studied at Paris, where Isaac **Casaubon** aroused his interest in the Fathers of the Church. One of the most erudite men of the age, he carried on and improved the chronological labours of J. J. **Scaliger**, and published an *Opus de doctrina temporum*, which has often been reprinted. His eminence chiefly rests on his vast, but unfinished, *De theologicis dogmatibus*, the first systematic attempt ever made to treat the development of Christian doctrine from the historical point of view; the work greatly influenced John Henry **Newman**.

Peter *see* **Marcellinus and Peter**

Peter Astralabe (Astrolabius) Son of **Abelard** and **Héloïse**, born Paris, *c*.1118, died 29 or 30 October year unknown. Little is known about him: Abelard's didactic poem *Carmen ad Astralabium* is dedicated to him, and he is briefly mentioned in the *Historia calamitatum*. **Peter the Venerable** wrote to Héloïse that he would attempt to find a prebend for him, but it is unknown whether he was successful, for although an 'Astralabe' appears as a canon of Nantes Cathedral in 1150 and as abbot of a Cistercian monastery at Hauterive (Switzerland), it is uncertain if either refers to the son of Abelard and Héloïse.

Peter Claver Saint, Spanish Jesuit missionary, known as 'Apostle of the Negroes', born Verdu, Catalonia, *c*.1580, died Cartagena, Colombia, 8 September 1654. He studied at the University of Barcelona and joined the Society of Jesus when he was twenty. He was sent to the Jesuit College in Majorca, returned to Barcelona to study theology, and in April 1610 was sent at his own request to Cartagena. He at once began ministering to the slaves who arrived from Africa in terrible conditions. Following ordination in 1615, he declared himself 'the slave of the negroes for ever', and championed their cause against the slave owners. He devoted himself to their temporal and spiritual welfare, and is said to have baptized some 300,000 people. **Leo XIII** canonized him in 1888. Feast day 9 September.

Peter Comestor French theologian, born Troyes, *c*.1100, died Paris, *c*.1180. While chancellor of

Notre Dame cathedral school, and a Canon Regular of Saint-Victor, from 1169, he wrote *Historia scholastica*, which became the accepted Bible history for the Middle Ages. His other writings include commentaries on the Gospels, on **Peter Lombard**'s *Commentary on the Psalms*, and a treatise on the sacraments.

Peter Damian Saint, Italian Benedictine, born Ravenna, 1007, died Faenza, 23 February 1072. An uncompromising prelate against the evils of the day, Peter upheld clerical celibacy and struggled against the simoniacal practices of the clergy. Made Cardinal Bishop of Ostia in 1057, he enjoyed great authority in the Church for his learning, zeal and integrity. His *Liber gratissimus* defended the validity of orders conferred by simonists, against the rigorist views of Cardinal **Humbert**; his *Liber Gomorrhianus* attacked the moral decadence of the clergy. Never formally canonized, his cult began after his death, and in 1828 **Leo XII** proclaimed him a 'Doctor of the Church'. Feast day 23 February.

Peter de Bruys French priest and heretic, date and place of birth unknown, died St-Gilles, Languedoc, after 1130. Known through the writings of **Peter the Venerable** and **Abelard**, it seems that Peter, deprived of his office of priest, began to preach in Dauphiné and Provence; he rejected infant baptism, the Mass, church buildings, prayers for the dead, the veneration of the cross, large parts of the Scriptures and the authority of the Church. He founded the sect of the Petrobrusians, who ill-treated priests and incited monks to marry; a French mob killed him for desecrating crosses. The Second Lateran Council condemned his teaching in 1139.

Peter Fourier Saint and co-founder (with Alix Le Clerq) of the Canonesses Regular of Our Lady, born Lorraine, France, 1565, died 9 December 1640. Joined the Canons Regular of St Augustine in 1585. After his ordination in 1589 he pursued his doctoral studies before taking charge of the abbey parish at Chaumousey, and later the parish at Mattaincourt. When his efforts to reform practices, and then to provide free education for boys, had failed, he enlisted the support of Alix Le Clerq and three other women, the nucleus of the new religious order, to set about providing for the education of girls. His later reforming efforts met with greater success, and in 1632 Peter became superior general of the reformed Congregation of Our Saviour. The Congregation successfully established the provision of boys' education. Feast day 9 December.

Peter John Olivi Franciscan philosopher and theologian, born Sérignan, near Béziers, France, 1248, died Narbonne, 14 March 1298. He entered the Franciscans at the age of twelve, at Béziers, and was sent to study in Paris under **Bonaventure**. He was an adherent of the strict interpretation of the Franciscan rule about poverty, and wrote a treatise on it in Rome in 1279, on the instructions of the minister general. In 1282 a chapter at Strasburg declared some of his views heretical. His writings were ordered to be seized, but he was rehabilitated by the minister general **Matthew of Aquasparta**, who sent him to teach in Florence, and later in Montpellier. He had moved to Narbonne by 1295, and died there. He wrote a great deal, on philosophy, Scripture and theology, but it was his work on asceticism in the Franciscan tradition, and on mysticism, which had the most enduring influence. He was venerated as a saint soon after his death.

Peter Lombard Italian theologian, born near Novara, Lombardy, *c.*1095, died Paris, 21 August 1160. Following studies in Italy, Peter taught at the cathedral school of Notre Dame from 1143; his commentaries on the Psalms and on the Pauline Epistles were written before and after 1148, respectively. His chief treatise, the *Sententiarum libri quattuor* (*c.*1155–8; generally referred to as the *Sentences*, meaning 'opinions'), is arranged in four books, on 'The Trinity', 'The Creation and Sin', 'The Incarnation and the Virtues', and 'The Sacraments and the Four Last Things'. An immediate success, the work received commentaries from most theologians and philosophers of the time, e.g. SS **Bonaventure**, **Albert the Great** and **Thomas Aquinas**. Though attacked after Peter's death by **Walter of Saint-Victor** and others, the *Sentences* were pronounced orthodox by the Fourth Lateran Council, and became obligatory in the academic curriculum after 1222; the English Franciscan **Alexander of Hales** adopted the work, instead of the Bible, as the textbook for his lectures in theology at the University of Paris.

Peter Martyr Saint, Italian Dominican inquisitor, born Verona, c.1205, died near Milan, 6 April 1252. Though born into a predominantly Cathar (Albigensian) family, Peter grew up a Catholic. He attended the University of Bologna and, after deciding to enter the Dominicans, received the habit from **Dominic** himself, and became a renowned preacher and dedicated controversialist against the Cathars. In 1251, **Innocent IV** appointed him inquisitor in Milan and Como, and he and his companion were assassinated by the Cathars near Milan. Fra **Angelico** depicted him in a famous fresco in the convent of San Marco, Florence, with a wounded head, his finger to his lips. Feast day 29 April.

Peter Martyr Vermigli Italian Protestant divine, born Florence, 8 September, 1499, died Zurich, 12 November 1562. Peter's name derives from his father's vow to dedicate his surviving children to **Peter Martyr**. He became abbot of the Augustinians at Spoleto and studied the works of Reformers, such as Martin **Bucer** and Ulrich **Zwingli**; this led him to be prohibited from preaching, in 1542, so he went to Zurich and Basel, and then to Strasburg, where he taught philosophy and married a nun. Thomas **Cranmer** invited him to England and he there received a pension, becoming Regius professor of divinity at Oxford in 1548. With the accession of **Mary Tudor** he returned to Strasburg, but his theology influenced the English Reformation during the reign of **Elizabeth I**.

Peter Nolasco Saint, Spanish founder of the Order of Our Lady of Ransom (Mercedarians), born Barcelona, c.1182, died Barcelona, 25 December c.1256. Little is known of Peter's early life; by the mid-1220s he was engaged in his life's work of ransoming the Christian slaves of Muslim masters in Catalonia. When others associated themselves with his activities, the Mercedarian Order began to take shape, and **Gregory IX** approved it in 1235. **Urban VIII** canonized Peter in 1628. Feast day 28 January.

Peter of Alcántara Saint, Spanish Franciscan mystic and reformer, born Garavita, Alcántara, 1499, died Arenas, 18 October 1562. Peter entered the Franciscans in 1515 after studies at Salamanca, joining the stricter branch, the Observatines, in 1517. He was ordained in 1524. Peter fostered the discalced reform, a controversial movement within the Friars Minor, the adherents being known as 'Alcantarines', who continued to exist as one of the four branches of the Observants until all were united in 1897. A man of the greatest austerity and mortification, a renowned mission preacher and spiritual director, he advised **Teresa of Ávila** in her reform of the Carmelites. He was canonized in 1669, and the Sacred Congregation of Rites made him patron saint of Brazil in 1826. Feast day 19 October.

Peter of Alexandria Saint, bishop and martyr, died Alexandria, 25 November 311. **Eusebius** describes him as 'a model bishop, remarkable alike for his virtuous life and for his keen study of the Scriptures'. He survived the persecution of Diocletian, and followed a policy of leniency towards those who had apostatized through fear or torture. While himself in hiding, another bishop, Melitius of Lycopolis, who favoured a more stringent policy towards the lapsed, usurped Peter's authority at Alexandria. Peter returned to his see in 311, but was beheaded by Maximin Daia shortly afterwards. A little of his work survives in fragments, from which it appears that he opposed Origenism. Feast day 26 November.

Peter of Candia *see* **Alexander V**

Peter (Polyansky) of Krutitsa Russian Orthodox saint, martyr and bishop, born Voronezh province, Russia, 1863, died (shot) Verkhne-Ural prison, Chelyabinsk, 10 October 1937. After the death of Patriarch **Tikhon** in 1925 he was one of the three successors nominated in the patriarch's will. As the other two bishops were in exile, he administered the Church amid the persecution and confusion caused by the Soviet government. His refusal completely to capitulate to the Communists led to his confinement and eventually exile to Tobolsk. Thereafter his sentences were constantly renewed and increased to keep him from contact with other bishops, but he was commemorated as head of the Russian Church everywhere until his death was confirmed.

Peter of Laodicea Greek patristic writer, flourished in the seventh or eighth century. What is known of Peter derives from an eleventh-century MS of Gospel catenae (i.e. 'chains' of quotations from previous commentators), wherein he is credited with a commentary on St Matthew's Gospel. The only undoubted work of Peter's to survive is a short *Exposition of the Lord's Prayer*.

Peter of Spain *see* John XXI

Peter of Tarentaise Saint, French archbishop, born near Vienne, 1102; died Bellevau, 14 September 1174. Peter joined the Cistercians at Bonnevaux, became first abbot of Taruivé in Savoy and archbishop of Tarentaise; with great difficulty he reformed his diocese, founding many hospitals. He supported **Alexander III** against Emperor **Frederick I Barbarossa**, and undertook a mission from him to reconcile Henry II of England and **Louis VII** of France. Venerated as a saint even in his lifetime; **Celestine III** canonized him in 1191. Feast day 8 May.

Peter Orseolo Saint, Venetian doge and hermit, born Venice, 928, died Cuxa, 10 January 984. Under the influence of Abbot Guarinus of Cuxa, he resigned as doge of Venice – during his reign he used his own money to rebuild St Mark's Cathedral and the Doge's Palace – to enter the religious life. **Peter Damian** claimed that he entered Cuxa as reparation for his role in the murder of his predecessor as doge. He accompanied **Romuald of Ravenna** to Cuxa in 978, and initially led a coenobitic life there, but soon joined Romuald's hermitage in the Pyrenees, staying behind when Romuald returned to Italy some ten years later. Feast day 10 or 14 January.

Peter the Aleut Orthodox saint and martyr, date of birth unknown, died (martyred) San Francisco, 8 September 1815. He was a young Alaskan (Aleutian) Indian of the Orthodox faith who, on a trading expedition down the Pacific coast, was captured by Spaniards in California. He was tortured to make him change his faith but he refused. He died after his hands and feet were cut off. Not officially canonized but venerated as a martyr by all the American Orthodox. Feast day (with St **Herman of Alaska**) 12 December.

Peter the Cantor French theologian, born probably in Rheims, date unknown, died Cistercian abbey, Longpont, 22 September 1197. A professor in Paris, Peter held the office of cantor in the cathedral from 1184, whence his name. Elected dean of the Rheims cathedral chapter in 1196. His works include treatises on dogmatic, moral and canonical subjects, and biblical glosses, of which one was published, *Verbum abbreviatum*, also called *Summa de virtutibus*.

Peter the Fuller Monophysite patriarch, born Constantinople, date unknown, died Antioch, 488. Tradition has it that Peter had been expelled from the convent of Acoemetae at Constantinople for his Monophysite leanings and opposition to Chalcedon. He then had himself consecrated bishop of Antioch in 470, under the patronage of Emperor **Zeno** the Isaurian, in opposition to the rightful patriarch Martyrius, a supporter of the Chalcedonian definition. Deposed, Peter regained his position in 475; again ousted in 477, he recovered it in 482, giving his assent to Zeno's Henoticon. To further the Monophysite cause, Peter inserted into the Trisagion the clause 'who was crucified for us', which, despite its innocent sound, was intended to express one nature in Christ. **Theodore Lector** recounts that he also introduced the recitation of the Nicene Creed at the Eucharist, as a proclamation of Monophysite adherence to Nicaea.

Peter the Hermit French religious, born Amiens, *c.*1050, died Neufmoustier, near Huy, 8 July 1115. Before the Council of Clermont (1095), Peter had tried, unsuccessfully, to make a pilgrimage to Jerusalem; following **Urban II**'s proclamation of the First Crusade, he travelled to Cologne, from where he led the 'People's Crusade' of 20,000 in 1096. At Civetot, ahead of the main force, most of Peter's followers were killed by the Turks on entering Anatolia, but he gathered the survivors and joined **Godfrey of Bouillon**'s army. During the siege of Antioch he apparently tried to escape, but survived this dishonour and helped to found the Belgian monastery at Neufmoustier, where he died.

Peter the Venerable French abbot of Cluny, born Montboissier, Auvergne, *c.*1092, died Cluny, 25 December 1156. Peter made his profession at Cluny under St **Hugh**, and became abbot in 1122, ruling 200 to 300 monks at Cluny and 2000 in dependent houses throughout Western Europe. An able administrator, he held that monastic life should include humane studies, and promoted the first translation of the Koran into Latin (1143). He came into conflict with his great friend St **Bernard** over the nature of monasticism, gave shelter to **Abelard** at Cluny, wrote against the Muslims, against **Peter de Bruys** and against the Jews (1144–7); his writings show little acquaintance with the Fathers, but profound knowledge of the Scriptures.

Peter Waldo *see* **Waldo, Peter**

Petersen, Theodore C. German Coptic scholar. born Madras, India, 1 February 1883, died Washington, DC, 14 March 1966. Petersen studied at the Lutheran Foreign Missionary Seminary in Hermannsburg, became a Roman Catholic in 1907, went to the USA and received ordination as a Paulist Father in Washington in 1912. He taught Hebrew, Arabic and Coptic at the Catholic University, and founded the Institute of Christian Oriental Research, which gained an international reputation in early Coptic scholarship. His cultural attainments – he had considerable ability in wood carving and sculpture – were broad, and he served on the iconography committee for the National Shrine of the Immaculate Conception in Washington.

Pethrus, Petrus Lewi Pentecostal leader, born Sweden, 1884, died Stockholm, 1974. Pethrus was a Baptist minister who embraced Pentecostalism in Oslo in 1907. In 1913 he and his congregation were expelled from the Swedish Baptist Convention, and Pethrus went on to create the largest Pentecostal congregation in the world. In 1939 he hosted the World Pentecostal Conference. Pethrus founded a rescue mission, a publishing house, a Bible school, a secondary school, a bank and a world-wide radio network, as well as the periodical *Evangelii Harold* from 1916 and the daily newspaper *Dagen* from 1945. He wrote many books, the earliest of which is *Jesus Kommer* (1912).

Petrarch, Francesco Italian poet and humanist, born Arezzo, 20 July 1304, died Arquà, 19 July 1374. Petrarch followed his family, exiled by the Black Guelphs, to Avignon in 1312 and studied at Montpellier and Bologna. On his return from exile in 1327, he met 'Laura' (possibly Laure de Noves), for whom he felt a great passion, and she became the inspiration for poems collected in the *Canzoniere*: *Rime (Sparse)*, sonnets glorifying her physical and spiritual beauty; and *I Trionfi (The Triumphs)*, strongly influenced by **Dante**'s *Divina Commedia*, which celebrates the triumph of the Divine over all things, and the ultimate redemption of man from the dominion of the senses. These, and his epic *Africa* on Scipio Africanus' war between Rome and Carthage, won him the poet's crown in 1341. His *Secretum* consists of three dialogues between himself and St **Augustine**, who seeks to turn the poet's mind from the transitory things of this world to thoughts of eternal life. His religious nature, often at odds with a passion for pagan culture, expressed itself also in the treatises *De otio religioso*, dedicated to the Carthusians, *De vita solitaria*, in praise of solitude, and *De remediis utriusque fortunae*, on the transitoriness of human life.

Petre, Maude Dominica British Catholic Modernist theologian, born Margaretting, Essex, 4 August 1863, died London, 16 December 1942. After some years as a religious, she studied theology in Rome, becoming one of the first modern Catholic women theologians. In July 1890 she became a nun, a member of the Filles de Marie, a congregation she left in 1907. From 1900, when she met George **Tyrrell**, who was giving a retreat to her community, she was a supporter of what later became Modernism. Her own emphasis was always on defending the freedom to raise questions inside the Church. She became Tyrrell's literary executor, and after refusing to swear the 'anti-Modernist' oath imposed on all Catholics, was excommunicated by her bishop. She moved to London, where she was able to continue as a Catholic, although she never compromised on her principles.

Petri, Olaus Swedish Reformer, born Örebro, Diocese of Strängnäs, 6 January 1493, died Stockholm, 19 April 1552. Educated by the Carmelites and then at Wittenberg, where he witnessed **Luther**'s revolt, Petri, ordained a deacon in 1520, devoted himself to spreading Reform teaching. King Gustavus Vasa allowed him to preach the Reformation in Stockholm Cathedral, and in 1527 the Diet of Västerås officially broke with Rome. By 1552 Sweden had become definitively Lutheran and both Olaus and his brother Lorenz, bishop of Uppsala, opposed any efforts at reconciliation with Rome during the early years of the Council of Trent.

Petrock Saint, lived in the sixth century. Probably the son of a Welsh chieftain and, as recounted in the ancient Latin Life of St Cadoo, from the royal family of Gwent. After studies in Ireland (where he perhaps instructed St Kevin), he made his way to Cornwall and founded monasteries at Padstow (i.e., Petrockstowe) and Bodmin. In the late twelfth century, a Breton religious canon stole his body from Bodmin and took it to St Méen in Brittany, where he is venerated as 'St Perreux', and whence originated the Latin *Vita Petroci*. Feast day 4 June.

Petronilla of Chemillé First abbess of Fontevrault, died Fontevrault, 1149. She was a cousin of **Geoffrey of Vendôme**. **Robert of Arbrissel** appointed her the first abbess of Fontevrault on his deathbed; his decision to place the double monastery that he had founded under the authority of an abbess was not without criticism, but it did allow Fontevrault to maintain its unique character. During her more than 30 years as abbess, the double monastery of Fontevrault expanded dramatically, and some 44 Fontevrist houses were established during her reign.

Petronius Saint, bishop of Bologna c.432–50, details of his birth and death unknown. Petronius' *Vita* describes him as the son of the *praetorium* of Gaul, and he himself may have held civil office before becoming bishop. He erected a church and monastery dedicated to St Stephen and modelled on the church of the Holy Sepulchre in Jerusalem, which he had visited. His relics were discovered in Bologna in 1141, and the *Vita*, written 1162/80, is highly controversial. In any case he is now commemorated in the church of San Petronio, a vast gothic structure in Bologna. Feast day 4 October.

Pfander, Karl Gottlieb Lutheran missionary and Islamic scholar, born Weiblingen, 3 November 1803, died Richmond, 1 December 1865. Through his missionary work among Muslims, Pfander gained a comprehensive knowledge of Islam and its literature. This was evident in his famous Christian apologetic entitled *Balance of Truth*, aimed at Muslim readers and published in 1829. It drew extensively on the Koran and other Islamic sources in an attempt to establish common ground between the two religions, though proceeding to argue that Christianity was superior. Pfander also participated with both skill and politeness in public debates with Islamic theologians.

Pflug, Julius von German theologian and bishop, born Eyra, near Leipzig, 1499; died Zeitz, 3 September 1546. Of Saxon descent and educated at Leipzig, Bologna and Padua, his humanistic ideals made him eager for peace with the Protestants; to this end he participated in conferences at Leipzig (1534) and Ratisbon (1541), indicating his willingness to tolerate even a married clergy and Communion under both species. Elected the last Catholic bishop of Naumburg, he had to wait a year for recognition by Elector Johann Friedrich, who meanwhile put in an avowed Lutheran, **Nikolaus von Amsdorf**.

Philaret (Drozdov) of Moscow Russian Orthodox saint, bishop and writer, born Kolomna, 26 December 1782, died Moscow, 19 November 1867. Appointed metropolitan of Moscow in 1826, he dominated the Russian Church until his death. He was a prolific writer of theological, spiritual and pastoral works, and supervised the first Russian-language Bible. His *Christian Catechism* was very influential and was translated into many of the languages of the Russian Empire. He helped to draft the decree of Alexander II emancipating the serfs. Feast day 19 November.

Philaret (Romanov) of Moscow Patriarch, born 1553, died Moscow, 12 October 1633. He was of noble Russian birth and was made a monk probably against his will. After the victory over the Poles in 1613, his son Michael was elected first tsar of the Romanov dynasty. Philaret became patriarch in the same year and held the title 'Great Lord' with his son. He was virtual ruler of Russia until his death and encouraged the study of theology throughout Russia. He was strongly anti-Western in both religion and politics.

Philaster Saint, bishop and anti-heretical writer,

died *c*.397. Philaster became bishop of Brescia and took part in the Council of Aquileia (381); about 385 he wrote a treatise refuting 28 Jewish and 128 Christian heresies. The material, largely drawn from **Irenaeus** and **Epiphanius**, includes among those condemned the notable heretic Simon Magus, as well as persons who believed only that the stars occupied a fixed place in the heavens, rather than being set in place each evening by God. Despite this lack of perspective, however, the book filled a need and St **Augustine** made use of it. Feast day 18 July.

Phileas of Thmuis   Saint, martyr, born date and place unknown; died Alexandria, 4 February 306. Of noble birth and great wealth, Phileas became bishop of Thmuis in the Nile Delta. He and three other bishops protested to Melitius, bishop of Lycopolis, that his adherents had invaded their dioceses, thus beginning the Melitian Schism. Imprisoned during the Diocletian persecution and tried by Culcianus, governor of Egypt, he was beheaded along with Philoromus, a Roman official. A letter to his people in Thmuis from his dungeon is preserved by **Eusebius** in his *Ecclesiastical History*; the *Acta* of his martyrdom are considered authentic. Feast day 4 February.

Philibert of Rebais   Saint, French Benedictine abbot, born Eauze, *c*.618, died abbey of Noirmoutier, 20 August 684. Of a noble family in Gascony, Philibert took the monastic habit in 636 at Rebais under St **Ouen**; he later founded the monastery of Jumièges and a convent for women at Pavilly, on land given him by Clovis II. For denouncing the injustice of Ebroin, mayor of the palace in 674, he lost his post and retired to the island of Her, where he established the monastery of Noirmoutier. Feast day 20 August.

Philip   Chancellor of the Diocese of Paris, born Paris, between 1160 and 1185, died there, 23 December 1236. Little is known of his early life, but he appears as chancellor in 1218. His period of office coincided with many disputes within the University of Paris, between the University and the Pope, and between the Orders. He fell out with the Dominicans, but remained friendly with the Franciscans, in whose church he was buried.

Philip II   King of Spain from 1556, born Valladolid, 21 May 1527, died the Escorial, 13 September 1598. From his father **Charles V**, Philip inherited Spain, The Netherlands, the Italian territories and the New World; as husband of **Mary Tudor**, he was also king of England, though not crowned. Fanatically religious, he had an overwhelming fear of heresy and attacked it vigorously wherever found. Yet he managed usually to be at odds with the Papacy over such issues as the Tridentine reforms and control of Spanish bishoprics. Politically, he ruled his dominions as an absolute monarch, and tried constantly to impose his will upon Europe: against France and Italy, against the Turks in the Mediterranean and against enemies of the Catholic religion in all his dominions. Though seen as a stubborn, arrogant, unreasonable tyrant, he also impressed as a devout Catholic motivated by the best interests of Church and State.

Philip, John   Superintendent of the London Missionary Society (LMS) in southern Africa, born Kirkaldy, Scotland, 14 April 1777, died Hankey, Cape Colony, 27 August 1851. He studied for the Congregational ministry at Hoxton and was called to Belmont, Aberdeen, in 1804. There he married Jane Ross in 1809. He went to southern Africa in 1819 to investigate criticisms of the LMS work by the British authorities. From 1823 he campaigned for civil rights for Khoi and mixed-race people and won recognition for them in the UK parliament in 1828, the year his book, *Researches in Africa*, was published. He persuaded the Paris Evangelical Mission Society, the Rhenish Missionary Society and the American Board of Commissions for Foreign Missions to begin work in South Africa, but also believed that only Africans could convert Africa. His stands on social issues made him unpopular with the colonial authorities, as with Afrikaans and English settlers, but were appreciated by Coloureds. After the Xhosa War he gave evidence of the colonists' responsibility for the war.

Philip Neri   *see* **Neri, Philip**

Philip of Hesse   Promoter of the Reformation, born Marburg, 13 November 1504, died Kassel, 31 March 1567. Philip met Martin **Luther** at the Diet of Worms (1521) and, though there does not seem to have been any popular desire for it, he determined to introduce the Reformation into Hesse. He founded a university at Marburg for Protestant theologians in 1527, and presided at the Conference of Marburg in 1529, to attempt an understanding between **Zwingli** and Luther on the subject of the Real Presence in the Eucharist. He also organized the Protestant princes, in 1530, in the Schmalkaldic League, but dissension between the parties impaired its effectiveness and it as well as the whole cause of Protestantism, was further weakened by Philip's bigamous marriage in 1540, which had been approved by Luther. However, he continued to work for reunion between Catholics and Protestants.

Philip Sidetes Church historian, fl. early fifth century. A native of Side in Pamphylia, Philip removed to Constantinople, where St **John Chrysostom** ordained him deacon; he tried three times to become patriarch. He wrote a 36-volume *Christian History*, a hotch-potch of miscellaneous learning dealing with the whole period from the beginning of the world to 430; only small fragments of the work remain. An apology against Julian the Apostate has been lost.

Philippa of Hainaut Queen consort of **Edward III**, born Holland, c.1314, died York, 15 August 1369. Daughter of William the Good, count of Holland and Hainaut, and Jeanne de Valois, granddaughter of Philip III of France, Philippa married Edward in 1326, at York. The alliance ensured for Edward in his French wars the support, along with their own troops, of Philippa's influential kindred. She encouraged the weaving trade at Norwich and coal mining on her estates at Tynedale. Her popularity is attested to by the many anecdotes of her piety and generosity, among which is that of her intervention on a famous occasion to save the citizens of Calais from Edward's vengeance after the Battle of Crécy (1346). The patroness of Jean Froissart, she assisted his travels in England, Scotland, Aquitaine and Italy to compose his four books of *Chroniques*. She exercised considerable influence over her husband and her death was a misfortune for the kingdom at large, since Edward then came under the domination of Alice Perrers, a mistress who interfered to pervert the course of justice to the advantage of her friends.

Phillip, Robert Oratorian and court chaplain, born Scotland, c.1580, died Paris, 4 January 1647. The first known dates in his early life are his ordination at the Scots College, Rome, in 1612, and his arrest, in 1613, in Edinburgh as a traitor; sent into exile, he joined the Oratory of Cardinal **Bérulle**, who sent him to England as confessor to Queen Henrietta Maria, 1628. When he obtained from Rome financial aid for **Charles I** at the time of the Long Parliament, its leaders denounced him as a papal spy. Imprisoned, but released, he left with the queen for Paris in 1642, and remained her chaplain there.

Phillips, George German historian and scholar, born Königsberg, 6 January 1804, died Aigen, 6 September 1872. The son of Anglo-Scottish parents who had settled in East Prussia, Phillips taught at Berlin, Munich and Vienna; he became a Catholic in 1828 and played an active part in the revival of Catholic life and culture in the German-speaking countries. A champion of ultramontanism, he contributed particularly to the doctrines of papal primacy and infallibility which carried the day at the First Vatican Council.

Philotheus Coccinus Byzantine theologian, born Thessalonica, c.1300, died Constantinople, 1379. Born of a Jewish mother, Philotheus became a monk on Sinai and later abbot of Grand Laura on Mount Athos; he defended the Hesychastic docrine (inner mystical prayer associated with the monks of Mount Athos) of **Gregory Palamas**. Named bishop of Heraclia in Thrace in 1347, and patriarch of Constantinople in 1353, he was deposed as patriarch the following year, but reappointed in 1364. He asserted Constantinople's independence from Rome, even under pressure to seek help from the Latin Church to ward off Ottoman advances. He canonized Gregory Palamas and declared him a Doctor of the Church. His writings on Hesychasm, *Antirhetica* and the *Hagioritic Tome*, are especially important.

Philoxenus Syrian bishop, born Tahal, Persia, c.450, died Philippopolis, Thrace, 523. Appointed bishop of Mabbug (Hierapolis) in 485 by **Peter the Fuller**, he and his contemporary, Severus, were among the leading thinkers and writers of the nascent Syrian Orthodox Church. Excommunicated and banished in 499 for his vehement defence of Monophysite doctrine, and his refusal to accept the definitions of the Council of Chalcedon, he is honoured as a Doctor of the Church by the Monophysites, and his writings in Syriac are considered classics; they include a set of thirteen *Discourses on the Christian Life*, and several works on the Incarnation.

Photius Patriarch of Constantinople, born there, c.820, died monastery of Armeniaki, 6 February 891. Photius seems to have belonged to a distinguished family, to have received a good education and to have preferred a secular career as scholar and statesman to becoming a monk. He became first imperial secretary, and Emperor Michael III chose him, while still a layman, to succeed Ignatius as patriarch in 858, in the hope that he would be acceptable to the conservative and moderate factions of the Byzantine Church. Photius was consecrated, but Ignatius refused to abdicate, and the emperor called on the Pope to take part in the synod of 861. Pope **Nicholas I** sent legates, who approved the deposition and approved Photius' appointment, but the Pope himself later said that they had exceeded their powers, reinstated Ignatius and not only deposed Photius but nullified all his acts. This degree of interference by the Pope was deeply resented in Constantinople. Photius accused Rome of intruding into Constantinople's sphere of influence in Bulgaria, and also of upholding erroneous doctrine, namely the inclusion of the Filioque clause in the Creed. Ignatius was brought back by a new emperor in 867, and remained as patriarch until his death in 877, when Photius again took charge. He resigned in 886 at the accession of the Emperor **Leo VI**. Photius had excommunicated the Pope in 867, and the 'Photian schism' highlighted the tensions between the Eastern and Western Churches. Photius himself was a very learned man. He wrote a treatise on the Holy Spirit which provided the rationale for his, and subsequent Greek, objections to the Filioque clause. His *Myriobiblion* summarizes the content of some hundreds of books he had read, many of which have since been lost.

Piccolomini, Aeneas Silvius *see* Pius II

Piccolomini, Francesco *see* Pius III

Piccolomini A noble family of Siena, granted the title Counts Palatine by Emperor Frederick III. Among the more illustrious were the Popes, **Aeneas Silvius** (**Pius II**), and his nephew, **Francesco** (**Pius III**). Also, Cardinal **Jacopo Ammanati de' Piccolomini**, adopted by Pius II; Blessed **Ambrogio**, died 1348, founded the Olivetan Benedictines; **Alessandro**, humanist, born Siena, 13 June 1508, died Siena, 12 March 1578. His works include translations of Ovid, Virgil, Aristotle's *Poetics* and *Rhetoric*; made bishop of Patras, 1574 and coadjutor of Siena until his death. **Francesco**, born Siena, 1582, died Rome, 1651, general of the Society of Jesus from 1649. **Celio**, cardinal archbishop of Siena from 1671, died 1681. **Octavio**, born Florence, 1599, died Vienna, 1656, duke of Amalfi, Austrian general during the Thirty Years' War, he fought in the Battle of Lützen under Wallenstein, whom he betrayed, provoking his own assassination; he is one of the heroes of Schiller's tragedy *Wallenstein*.

Pico della Mirandola, Giovanni Italian humanist, born Mirandola, 24 February 1463, died Florence, 17 November 1494. Son of the ruling family of Mirandola, Pico learned Hebrew, Aramaic and Arabic, and was the first to seek in the Kabbala proof of the Christian mysteries. He compiled a set of 900 *Conclusiones* (1486) in all branches of philosophy and theology, with a preface called *Oratio de Hominis dignitate*, asserting the unique position of man outside the Neoplatonic hierarchy; he proposed to defend the work in Rome, but **Innocent VIII** found some of it heretical, so Pico abandoned the project. He later presented to Lorenzo de' Medici the *Heptaplus*, a mystical exposition of the Creation, and also composed *De ente et uno*, an attempt to reconcile Plato and Aristotle. On his deathbed Girolamo **Savonarola**, whose disciple he had become, clothed him in the Dominican habit.

Pierleoni An influential Roman family associated with the Papacy during the Gregorian reform. Its first known member, **Baruch**, was a converted Roman Jew called 'Benedictus Christianus', who died before 1051; his son **Leo** (last mentioned 1062) consistently favoured Hildebrand (**Gregory VII**), as did his son **Petrus Leonis** (died 1128), who gave the family its name. Their closeness to

Hildebrand, from a notice in the *Annales Pegavienses* and other evidence, gave rise to the controversial theory that they were related to **Gregory VI** and Gregory VII. His son, also **Petrus Leonis**, a monk at Cluny, whom **Paschal II** made cardinal, became the Antipope Anacletus II; a schism involving Pope **Innocent II**, who had the powerful help of **Bernard of Clairvaux**, came to an end with the death of Anacletus in 1138.

Piero della Francesca   Italian Renaissance painter, born Borgo Sansepolcro, Republic of Florence, *c.*1420, died Borgo Sansepolcro, 12 October 1492. His father was Benedetto de' Franceschi, an apparently prosperous tanner and shoemaker. By 1439 Piero was in Florence, working with Domenico Veneziano, but in 1442 he became a member of the council of his home town, and from then on continued to divide his time between Sansepolcro and wherever his commissions took him – Arezzo, Ferrara, Rimini, Rome (where he painted frescoes, now disappeared, for Pope **Pius II**) and Urbino, whose duke became the painter's chief patron. Among his best-known works are *Resurrection* painted *c.*1463 for the Palazzo Comunale at Sansepolcro, and portraits of his patron Federico da Montefeltro, duke of Urbino, and of his wife, Battista Sforza, painted in 1465 and now in the Uffizi in Florence. For the last two decades or so of his life he retired to Sansepolcro, where he wrote on the theory of perspective and, in 1480, became prior of the Confraternity of St Bartholomew.

Pierre d'Ailly (Petrus de Alliaco)   Cardinal, theologian, philosopher and Church reformer, born Compiègne, 1350, died Avignon, 9 August 1420. In 1372 he entered the college of Navarre in Paris, and became professor of theology there eight years later. In 1384 he became rector, and in 1389 chaplain to Charles VI of France as well as Chancellor of the University of Paris. His chief concern, however, was with the Great Western Schism. In 1409 he attended the Council of Pisa, and at the Synod of Rome three years later he proposed a programme of reform. He attended the Council of Constance from 1414 to 1418, supporting the belief of the supremacy of the Council over the Pope. In the course of the Council he published a work on the reformation of the Church, part of a

much larger work on the Council itself: it had a considerable impact upon the Reformers a century later, and on the Council of Trent. He was an opponent of the notion of the infallibility of the Church, and taught that the spiritual authority of priests and bishops comes directly from God. He was a major figure in his time, and apart from his university offices he held a number of benefices, including that of the bishopric of Cambrai, where he had formerly been archdeacon. He was made a cardinal in 1412. As a philosopher, he was much influenced by the English scholars Roger **Bacon** and **William of Ockham**. He wrote on many topics, including astrology and mysticism. He was also interested in geography, and his *Imago Mundi* helped inspire Christopher Columbus to sail west in the hope of finding the Indies.

Pierre de la Ramée   *see* **Ramus, Peter**

Pigge, Albert (Pighius)   Dutch theologian, born Kampen, *c.*1490, died Utrecht, 29 December 1542. Following studies at Louvain, Pigge served in Rome under **Adrian VI**, his former teacher, and wrote a treatise, *Admenses Graecorum errores*, to pave the way for reunion with the Orthodox Church. His principal work is *Hierarchiae Ecclesiasticae assertio*, an elaborate defence of tradition and papal infallibility. In opposition to Martin **Luther** and Jean **Calvin**, he taught that original sin is not an inherent fault, but an extrinsic imputation, thus minimizing its effects, but under the influence of Johann Gropper he adopted the doctrine of double justice which the Council of Trent declined to support.

Pignatelli, Joseph Mary   Saint, Spanish Jesuit, born Saragossa, 27 December 1737, died San Pantaleone, 11 November 1811. Joseph led the Society after its expulsion from Spain in 1767, and went to Bologna when **Clement XIV** suppressed the entire Order in 1773. He could not join the remnant in White Russia, because of ill health, but worked to establish a vice-province in Parma; the general in St Petersburg named him provincial of Italy in 1803. From Rome, Joseph directed the re-establishment of the Society in Sardinia in 1807, and opened colleges at Rome, Orvieto and Tivoli. He greatly facilitated the full restoration of the

Society in 1814. **Pius XII** canonized him in 1954. Feast day 28 November.

Pike, James Albert American bishop, born Oklahoma City, 14 February 1913, died near the Dead Sea, 3 September 1969. Raised a Roman Catholic, Pike studied for the priesthood but turned agnostic, became a lawyer and served in World War II. His faith renewed, he received ordination in the Episcopalian Church in 1946, and became bishop of California in 1958. Charges of heresy were brought against him for his theories on the Trinity and the divinity of Jesus; his fellow bishops censured him in 1966, and he resigned his post as bishop, giving up formal Church membership in 1969. He went to Israel to research a new book, and died in a wilderness area, having lost his way after his car broke down.

Pimenta, Silvério Gomes Brazilian Roman Catholic archbishop, born Congoulias do Campo, Minas Gerais, 12 January 1840, died Mariana, 30 August 1922. Son of a humble black family, Pimenta taught Latin in the seminary, acquiring a masterly proficiency; he worked as journalist for four years and became vicar general of Mariana in 1877, despite objections as to his colour. He succeeded to the See of Mariana in 1896, amid acclaim by his people, and was the first archbishop in 1906. He displayed great zeal in leading his diocese, and in 1920 became the first clergyman to be elected to the Brazilian Academy of Letters.

Pinson, Mack M. Pentecostal evangelist, born Georgia, USA, 1873, died 1953. Pinson became a Baptist in 1893, joined the Holiness movement, and was ordained in 1903. In 1907 he had a Pentecostal experience which led to his leaving the Baptists and organizing Pentecostal Churches in the American South. He helped to organise the Assemblies of God and pastored along the Mexican border. He founded a periodical, *Word and Witness*, in which he put forward his 'finished work' position. Pinson also helped to slow the rebaptizing of believers during the Oneness controversy.

Pio, Padre Italian Capuchin, born Pietrelcina, 25 May 1887, died San Giovanni Rotondo, 23 September 1968. Ordained in 1910, having nurtured since the age of five a desire to consecrate himself

to God for ever, Francesco Forgione lived an uneventful life until assigned to the friary of San Giovanni Rotondo, where in 1918 he received the visible signs of the stigmata. Known as 'Padre Pio', he had to cope with suspicion, embarrassment and disciplinary action as a consequence of this phenomenon; the Vatican, cautious in its deliberations, forbade him to say Mass publicly and restricted his activities for thirteen years, until **Pius XI** lifted the ban in 1933. He remained at San Giovanni for 50 years, yet attracted people from all over the world who came for spiritual favour, intercession and direction. His one monument is the hospital he founded, Casa Sollievo della Sofferenza. John Paul II visited his tomb in 1987.

Pionius Saint, martyr, executed at Smyrna during the Decian persecution, *c.*250, having been arrested while celebrating the anniversary of the martyrdom of St **Polycarp**. Pionius' death is described in *Acta Pionii*, allegedly recorded by eyewitnesses, and known to **Eusebius** as a reliable document. Though not to be identified as the author of the legendary Life of St Polycarp (400), he may well be the Pionius mentioned at the end of the *Martyrdom of St Polycarp*. Feast day 1 February.

Piper, William Hamner American Pentecostal pastor and editor, born Lydia, Maryland, 8 June 1868, died 29 December 1911. Piper was ordained in the Brethren Church in 1893, but came to identify with the Christian Catholic Church of John Alexander **Dowie** two years after an experience of healing. Piper joined Dowie's Zion City, but left, disillusioned, in 1906. In 1907 he founded the Stone Church in Chicago, which at first excluded Pentecostalism but later embraced it. Piper experienced Spirit baptism in 1908. From that year he produced *The Latter Rain Evangel* magazine.

Pirckheimer, Charitas Abbess, born Nuremberg, 21 March 1466, died Convent of St Clara, 19 August 1532. Abbess of the Poor Clares, widely read in the classics and the Fathers, Charitas, sister of Willibald **Pirckheimer**, corresponded with Albrecht **Dürer** and Desiderius **Erasmus**, and lived a peaceful life for twenty years. When Lutheranism reached Nuremberg, life changed dramatically; the convent became a target of the governor, who assigned the nuns Lutheran preachers, harassed and persecuted them, but they remained firmly anti-Lutheran.

Pirkheimer, Willibald Humanist scholar, born Eichstät, 5 December 1470, died Nuremberg, 22 December 1530. Willibald favoured **Martin Luther** and attacked Johann **Eck**, his chief opponent, in a bitter satire, *Eccius dedolatus*. Excommunicated in 1520, but absolved in 1521, he denounced Luther's teaching and attacked the Protestants with force when he learned of the persecutions to which his sister Charitas (see above) was being subjected, especially as his two daughters were nuns at her convent.

Pirminius Saint, German Benedictine abbot, died *c*.753. A Visigoth refugee from Aquitaine or Spain during the Moorish invasions, according to a ninth-century *vita*, Pirminius founded Reichenau in *c*.724, and other monasteries among the Alemanni in Baden and Alsace, which became important centres of religious and cultural development. He is regarded as the author of *Dicta Pirminii*, or *Scarapsus*, a brief account of salvation history which circulated widely in Carolingian times; it contains the earliest commentary on the present form of the Apostles' Creed. Feast day 3 November.

Pitra, Jean Baptiste French Benedictine patristic scholar, born Champforgeuil, 1 August 1812, died Rome, 9 February 1889. Pitra gained a reputation as an archeologist when in 1839 he deciphered the 'Inscription of Autun' on a third-century grave. Ordained at Solesmes in 1843, he travelled widely and found MSS which he published in *Spicilegium Solesmense*; he had unrivalled knowledge of many branches of patristic and Byzantine literature. **Pius IX** made him cardinal and librarian of the Vatican; **Leo XIII** employed him to catalogue the Palatine Greek codices there. He died at work, alone and poor, as he had lived.

Pius I Saint, Pope from *c*.140. Both **Eusebius** and **Jerome** place his accession in the fifth year of Antonius Pius, i.e. 142, and his reign at fifteen years, dying at Rome, *c*.154. A native of Aquileia, and according to the 'Muratorian Fragment' a brother of Hermas, author of the *Shepherd*, an account of a series of revelations made to Hermas

by different heavenly visitors. There is no evidence for the tradition that Pius died a martyr. Feast day 11 July.

Pius II Pope from 1458, born 'Enea Silvio (Latin: Aeneas Silvius) Piccolomini' at Corsignano (subsequently Pienza), near Siena, 1405, died Ancona, 15 August 1464. From a leading Sienese family, Piccolomini was a prolific writer of history, poetry, biography and autobiography. He was a secretary of the Council of Basel, and opposed **Eugenius IV**. He subsequently negotiated the return of Germany to Eugenius's obedience 1445, became bishop of Trieste, and of Siena, 1449, and cardinal, 1456, served the Council of Basel and Emperor Frederick III, before taking holy orders. Upon election to the Papacy, he rejected the worldliness of his previous life and championed the cause of papal primacy, a particular triumph being the 1462 revocation of the Pragmatic Sanction of Bourges. Pius called the Congress of Mantua (1459) to co-ordinate a Crusade against the Ottomans and died at Ancona after vainly waiting for military support from the Christian powers.

Pius III Pope for 26 days, from September to October 1503, born 'Francesco Todeschini-Piccolomini' at Siena, 9 May 1439, died Rome, 18 October 1503. Appointed archbishop of Siena, aged 22, by his uncle **Pius II**, who sent him on a legation to Regensburg, and later sent by **Sixtus IV** to secure the restoration of ecclesiastical authority in Umbria. He opposed the policy of **Alexander VI**, and was elected Pope amid the upheavals following upon the death of the latter, through the interested influence of Cardinal della Rovere, afterwards **Julius II**. He permitted Cesare **Borgia** to return to Rome, and took in hand the reform of the Curia. A man of blameless life, he could have accomplished much had he lived.

Pius IV Pope from 1559, born 'Gian Angelo Medici' at Milan, 31 March 1499, died Rome, 9 December 1565. Not related to the Florentine Medicis, he held several offices at the Curia, became archbishop of Ragusa in 1545, and was made cardinal by **Paul III** and papal legate by **Julius III** in Romagna. He succeeded **Paul IV**, reversed his imperial policy and brought his relatives to trial; Pius' own nepotism had a happy result for the Church in the cardinalate of his nephew Charles **Borromeo**. His greatest achievement was the Council of Trent, which he successfully concluded in 1563, and whose decrees he executed, namely: a new Index of Prohibited Books, the Roman Catechism, the imposition of the Professio Fidei Tridentina on all holders of ecclesiastical office and reformation of the Sacred College.

Pius V Saint, Pope from 1566, born 'Michele Ghislieri' at Bosco Marengo, Lombardy, 17 January 1504, died Rome, 1 May 1572. Ordained a Dominican in 1528, Ghislieri made a career in the Inquisition, which led to his becoming a cardinal and Inquisitor General of Christendom, 1558; Charles **Borromeo** helped him to be elected **Pius IV**'s successor. He worked zealously for the reform of the Church and compelled bishops and clergy to accept the recommendations of the Council of Trent. He struggled against the spread of the Reformation, encouraged the Spanish invasion of England, and famously excommunicated **Elizabeth I**, in 1570, when she imprisoned Mary Stuart. He succeeded in forming the alliance of Spain and Venice which defeated the Ottoman Turks at Lepanto in 1571. Feast day 5 May.

Pius VI Pope from 1775, born 'Giovanni Angelico Braschi' at Cesena, 25 December 1717, died Valence, France, 29 August 1799. **Clement XIV** created Braschi cardinal in 1773, and he succeeded Clement in 1775. His rule was marked by virulent anticlericalism, secularism and atheism – with all of which he lacked the judgement and strength to deal effectively. He dealt ineptly with Febronianism in Germany and Josephinism in Austria, but did finally condemn all Febronian teaching in the bull *Auctorem Fidei* (1794). The French Revolution brought great problems; Pius condemned the Civil Constitution of the Clergy of 1791, but also denounced the Declaration of the Rights of Man, and all the libertarian political ideals that inspired the Revolution. Bonaparte occupied the States of the Church, and in 1797 the Vatican had to surrender Ferrara, Bologna and the Romagna. General Berthier occupied Rome in 1798 and declared it a republic; he took Pius prisoner and, despite his age and infirmity, drove him out of

Italy across the Alps, until he finally died, still a prisoner, in south-east France.

Pius VII Pope from 1800, born 'Luigi Barnaba Chiaramonti' at Cesena, 14 August 1742; died Rome, 20 August 1823. Chiaramonti joined the Benedictines, **Pius VI** appointed him bishop of Tivoli and a cardinal, and he succeeded Pius in a conclave at Venice. His main problem being relations with France, Pius proved conciliatory in his dealings with Napoleon, with whom he concluded a Concordat which restored religion in France; in 1804 Pius accepted Napoleon's invitation to consecrate him emperor in Paris. In 1805, Bonaparte occupied Ancona, despite Pius' protests, in 1808 a French army entered Rome and Pius refused to negotiate, upon which the Papal States were incorporated into the French Empire. When Pius excommunicated those responsible (*Quum memoranda*), he was deported to Grenoble, imprisoned at Savona and then at Fontainebleau in 1812. Released in 1814, following French defeats in Russia and Germany, Pius returned to Rome and, among his more notable acts, re-established the Jesuits, suppressed by **Clement XIV** in 1773; the Congress of Vienna restored the States of the Church.

Pius VIII Pope from 1829, born 'Francesco Saverio Castiglioni', at Cingoli, 20 November 1761, died Rome, 30 November 1830. Appointed bishop of Montalto in 1800, Castiglioni's refusal to take an oath of allegiance to Bonaparte caused him to be imprisoned in 1808; he had the support of the conservative faction at his election to succeed **Leo XII**. Beset by chronic ill health, he none the less asserted his authority, and his first encyclical, *Traditi humilitati nostrae*, announced this intention, as well as his intention to combat indifferentism, maintain marriage laws and promote Christian education; he opposed secret societies, notably Freemasonry, in the subsequent *Litteris altero*.

Pius IX Pope from 1846, born 'Giovanni Maria Mastaï Ferretti', at Senigallia, 13 May 1792, died Rome, 7 February 1878. **Gregory XVI**'s reactionary policies had alienated the Italian people, and Ferretti began well by granting a general amnesty of political prisoners and exiles, showing himself favourable to the movement of national unity; but his concessions came too late to satisfy the revolutionaries. He appealed to the Catholic European powers, and a French army occupied Rome in 1849. Pius then abandoned his liberal attitude in politics, but his power decreased until, with the seizure of Rome by Victor Emmanuel in 1870, he lost temporal sovereignty. Other endeavours on the other hand had merit: he erected many new dioceses and missionary centres, he restored the hierarchy in England, in 1850, and in The Netherlands, in 1853, and his definition of the Immaculate Conception in 1854 stimulated Catholic devotion. His *Syllabus errorum*, and the encyclical *Quanta Cura*, supported the traditional beliefs of Catholicism by condemning various forms of Modernism. The definition of papal infallibility by the First Vatican Council increased the authority of the Papacy, and more than compensated for the loss in temporal dominion that marked his pontificate.

Pius X   Saint, Pope from 1903, born 'Giuseppe Melchior Sarto' at Riese, near Treviso, 1835, died Rome, 20 August 1914. Sarto succeeded **Leo XIII** and signified that his rule should be pastoral rather than political, as stated in his first encyclical, *E supremi Apostolatus*. However, political considerations forced themselves upon him, and he condemned the French proposal of 1905 that, in separating Church and State, the latter should control Church property; he thus secured independence from State interference. In the field of social policy, Pius laid down the principles of Catholic Action in *Il fermo proposito*, with the aim of restoring Christ to His rightful place within the home, the schools and society in general; social action and the labour question were integral to the total programme. He gave a lasting stimulus to the spiritual life of the faithful, and laid the foundations of the modern liturgical movement in his reform of the Breviary, and in his *motu proprio*, which restored Gregorian chant to its traditional place in the liturgy. Venerated as a saint in his lifetime, he was canonized by **Pius XII** in 1954. Feast day 3 September.

Pius XI   Pope from 1922, born 'Ambrogio Damiano Achille Ratti' at Desio, 31 May 1857, died Rome, 10 February 1939. Ratti succeeded **Benedict**

XV, and declared the chief objective of his pontificate to be the restoration of all things in Christ, symbolized in the institution of the Feast of Christ the King. His great encyclicals have the same direction and are landmarks in moral theology: *Divini illius magistri* deals with education; *Casti connubii* condemns contraception and seeks to restore a proper respect for married life, and the best-known, *Quadragesimo anno*, extends the social teaching of **Leo XIII**. He supported Catholic Action in the encyclical *Ubi arcano* (1922). He settled the Roman Question with the Lateran Treaty (1929); he condemned the excesses of Fascism (1931), Nazism (1937) and Bolshevism (1937). He encouraged the foreign missions, the need for native episcopates and respect for the rites of Eastern Churches; all such initiatives stemmed from his progressive approach to the Church's mission in modern times.

Pius XII   Pope from February, 1939, born 'Eugenio Maria Giuseppe Pacelli' at Rome, 2 March 1876, died Rome, 9 October 1958. Chief collaborator of **Pius XI**, whom he succeeded, Pius' first encyclical, that year, *Summi Pontificatus*, set out the principles that were to guide his pontificate: to restore to God His due place in the life of the world, and unity in the defence of Natural Law; while his 'Christmas Allocution' enunciated the principles of a lasting peace in 'Five Peace Points'. From the outbreak of World War II, he increased Catholic humanitarian aid, and intervened, without success, for peace among nations; he condemned Fascism and Nazism. In like manner he protested, in vain, against the fate of Catholics in Communist countries after the war. Wishing to identify Christian doctrine in the modern world, he multiplied his speeches, media-diffused messages and encyclicals; he formalized the dogma of the Assumption of Mary in *Munificentissimus Deus*, condemned Marxism, atheistic existentialism and Freudianism; he increased the number of native bishops in mission countries. Pius has been reproached for his alleged 'silence' in the face of Nazi atrocities, in particular involving the Jews. However it was, these accusations developed only after his death. At the end of the war, as commentators agreed at the time, the Papacy had not enjoyed such a good press in the world since 1848. Public opinion had been struck by Pius' repeated appeals in favour of the rights of the human person and respect for Natural Law, by his many attempts to humanize the conflict and by the aid, discreet but efficacious, brought by the Vatican to the victims of Nazi persecution.

Plantier, Claude Henri French Roman Catholic bishop, born Ain, Ceyzériat, 2 March 1813, died Nîmes, 25 May 1875. Plantier had an early reputation as preacher of the Lent and Advent courses at Notre Dame de Paris, notably on the Church's doctrinal authority; as bishop of Nîmes, 1855–75, and a forceful apologist, he attacked Ernest **Renan**'s *Vie de Jésus*, the Reformed Church of France and liberalism. An ardent upholder of papal temporal power, he supported ultramontanism and strongly favoured the definition of papal infallibility at Vatican Council I. He denounced Scholasticism for its pernicious sophisms.

Plantin, Christophe French bookbinder and printer, born near Tours, *c.*1520, died Antwerp (Belgium), 1 July 1589. Plantin's works reflected fine craftsmanship, and among his numerous publications noted for both accuracy and beauty is the famous *Biblia Regis*, an eight-volume polyglot with Hebrew, Aramaic, Greek, Syriac and Latin texts. He was granted a monopoly of liturgical books within the Spanish dominions, which greatly strengthened his business. He was himself, however, associated with the Family of Love, an association which brought him considerable difficulty in his early years in Antwerp. His original workshop and equipment are preserved as the Plantin-Moretus Museum.

Planudes, Maximus Byzantine humanist and theologian, born Nicomedia, *c.*1260, died Constantinople, *c.*1310. Planudes possessed a knowledge of Latin remarkable at a time when Rome and Italy were regarded with hatred and contempt by the Byzantines. We owe to him a prose version of Aesop's *Fables* and a Life of the author; he translated St **Augustine**'s *De Trinitate* into Greek, as well as works of classical authors, and an enconium of SS Peter and Paul. Planudes, especially by his translations, paved the way for the introduction of the Greek language and literature into the West.

Plasden, Polydore Saint, English martyr, born London, 1563, executed there, 10 December 1591. Ordained at the English College, Rheims in 1586, Plasden returned to the English mission and laboured in Sussex; he went to London and, with Edmund **Gennings**, was arrested while saying Mass in the house of Swithun **Wells**. Condemned for high treason, he protested his loyalty to Queen **Elizabeth I**, while remaining faithful to his religious convictions. Sir Walter Raleigh, who supervised the execution, ordered leniency, directing that Polydore be hanged until dead before dismembering began. He was canonized in 1970 as one of the **Forty Martyrs of England and Wales**. Feast day 10 December.

Plater, Charles Dominic English Jesuit, born London, 2 September 1875, died Malta, 21 January 1921. Educated at Stonyhurst College, he entered the Society of Jesus in 1894 and while still a seminarian, began his commitment to the Catholic social movement with a conference paper on retreats for working men (1906), which resulted in a series of retreat houses. He was ordained in 1910 and in 1916 was appointed rector of the Jesuit house at Oxford, where had himself studied. He achieved its recognition as a permanent private hall of the university, giving it the name 'Campion Hall'. He is best known for founding the Catholic Social Guild, which encouraged working people to study social subjects in study circles as a way to social justice. The Catholic Workers' College (now Plater College) at Oxford, founded after his death, grew out of his effectiveness and interest in worker education. He was sent to Malta after his health suddenly broke down, and died there.

Platina, Bartolomeo (Bartolomeo Sacchi) Italian humanist, born Piadena, 1421, died Rome, 21 September 1481. A soldier under Francesco Sforza and Piccinino, Platina became a tutor, studied Greek at Florence and went to Rome in 1462, where **Pius II** was his patron; he joined the humanistic Roman Academy of Pomponius Laetus, but when **Paul II** succeeded in 1464, he lost his job, and his insolent protests caused his imprisonment. He returned to favour under **Sixtus IV**, who made him Vatican librarian, and to whom he dedicated a history of the Popes, *Liber de vita Christi ac de vitis summorum pontificum omnium*; he used the book to denigrate Paul II, but the work is valuable for its treatment of contemporary events.

Plessington, John Saint, English martyr, born Dimples Hall, Lancashire, *c*.1637, died Chester, 19 July 1679. Ordained at the English College, Valladolid, in 1662, he returned to the English mission and ministered at Holywell, the shrine of St **Winefride**; he then became tutor in the Massey household at Puddington, while being in reality a missionary. He objected firmly to the marriage of a prominent Catholic heiress to a Protestant, which caused his betrayal and arrest at the time of the Titus **Oates** conspiracy. Though the authorities were unable to involve him in the plot, they charged him with being a priest and executed him. His canonization occurred in 1970, as one of the **Forty Martyrs of England and Wales**. Feast day 20 June.

Plowden, Charles English Jesuit, from a distinguished Catholic family that gave ten of its members to the Society of Jesus, born Plowden Hall, Shropshire, 19 August 1743, died Jougne, France, 13 June 1821. Ordained at Rome in 1770, he taught at Bruges with John **Carroll**, future American bishop, and both were imprisoned in 1773 when the Jesuits were suppressed. In 1784 he became chaplain to Thomas **Weld** at Lulworth Castle in Dorset, and in 1790 the two founded Stonyhurst College; with the restoration of the Society in 1814 Charles became rector, and provincial of the English province.

Plowden, Francis English Jesuit, brother of Charles **Plowden**, born Plowden Hall, 28 June 1749, died Paris, 4 January 1819. A seminarian at Bruges when the Society was suppressed, he returned to England, studied law and received an honorary degree from Oxford for his *Jura Anglorum*, a commentary on English law; his best work, *An Historical Review of the State of Ireland*, written for the British government, and *Ireland since the Union*, caused a libel action to be decided against him, and forced him to flee to France to avoid paying a fine of £5000; he died in obscurity and poverty.

Plowden, Edmund Recusant jurist, forebear of Charles and Francis **Plowden**, born Plowden Hall, Shropshire, 1518, died London, 6 February 1585. Admitted to the bar at the Middle Temple in 1538, Powden served as a Member of Parliament in the reigns of **Mary** and **Elizabeth I**. His career as a lawyer brought him frequently into opposition with the government; the Privy Council regarded him with suspicion and he often acted as defence counsel for prominent Catholics. A staunch and courageous Catholic, regarded by contemporaries as one of the most gifted lawyers of his age, Plowden refused the position of Lord Chancellor offered him by Elizabeth, the price being renunciation of the old faith.

Plumpe, Joseph Conrad American patristic scholar, born Cloverdale, Ohio, 12 April 1901, died Worthington, 8 December 1957. Plumpe studied classics at Münster and Berlin, taught classics at the Josephinum in Ohio, and Latin and Greek at the Catholic University of America; he co-founded the patristic series Ancient Christian Writers, and his chief individual work is *Mater ecclesia: An Inquiry into the Concept of the Church as Mother in Early Christianity*.

Plunket, Oliver Saint, martyr, archbishop of Armagh and the first Irishman to be canonized since **Lawrence O'Toole** in the thirteenth century, born Loughcrew, County Meath, 1 November 1629, into an Old English family, executed at Tyburn, 1 July 1681, the last of the Irish bishops to die a martyr's death. After early education in Dublin he was sent to the Irish College in Rome under the care of the papal legate. He was ordained for the Irish mission in 1654 but because of the penal laws his return to Ireland was much delayed; he remained in Rome until 1669 and was a professor in the College of the Propaganda Fidei, where he also acted as agent for the Irish clergy, but he also served much among the poor and infirm in the hospital of Santo Spirito. He was appointed archbishop of Armagh in 1669 and duly consecrated at Ghent in November of that year. During his ten-year episcopate he was unceasing in his efforts to build up the Church in Ireland, holding synods, confirming, ordaining, and travelling incessantly throughout the country. Catholicism was given only occasional tolerance in this period so that in effect he administered much in secret or in remote forests and hillsides. Plunket was a thoroughly conscientious archbishop in also rooting out clerical abuses; he established the Jesuits at Drogheda, where they opened a school and a seminary. He was forced into hiding in 1673, and from then until his arrest in 1679 his life was one of danger and physical hardship. He was charged with implication in the Titus **Oates** Plot, i.e. conspiring to bring about an armed rebellion. On the evidence of an apostate priest, he was first imprisoned in Dublin Castle, then removed to Newgate in London. In a travesty of a trial Plunket was found guilty of high treason; he was hanged, drawn and quartered at Tyburn, the last Catholic to be martyred there. He was canonized on 12 October 1975. Feast day 1 July.

Pococke, Edward English orientalist, born Oxford, November 1604, died there, 10 September 1691. After studies at Magdalen and Corpus Christi Colleges, Pococke went to Aleppo in 1630 as a chaplain, and on his return to Oxford in 1635, became professor of Arabic and succeeded to the chair of Hebrew. He had immense erudition and helped to prepare Brian **Walton**'s Polyglot Bible (1657), and published an Arabic edition of Hugo **Grotius**' *De veritate christianae religionis*, for the diffusion of Christianity among Muslims; he issued in 1663 an Arabic text, with Latin translation, of the *Historia compendiosa dynastiarum* of Bar Hebraeus, the Jewish/Christian Syrian bishop **Abu 'l-Faraj**.

Poiret, Pierre French Protestant spiritual writer, born Metz, 15 April 1646, died Rijnsburg, Holland, 21 May 1719. When Poiret began to equate Christianity with mysticism, he went to live with the Flemish enthusiast and mystical writer Antoinette Bourignon, until her death in 1680; his *L'Économie divine* interpreted her ideas and he edited her writings. He studied the mysticism of **Jakob Böhme**, Mme **Guyon** and earlier writers, such as **Thomas à Kempis** and **Johann Tauler**. His masterwork, *Bibliotheca mysticorum selecta*, is an extensive collection of information on minor writers; through his disciple Gerhard Tersteegen, he exercised much influence on German Pietism.

Pole, Reginald Archbishop of Canterbury, born Stourton Castle, Staffordshire, 3 March 1500, died Lambeth Palace, London, 17 November 1558. He was educated at the Sheen Charterhouse, then with the Carmelites at Oxford, before entering Magdalen College, Oxford, where he was taught by **Linacre** and **Latimer**. He became a member of the reforming circle of devout humanists, including Thomas **More** and **Erasmus**. In 1522 he went abroad, including to Rome, where he was kindly received, and on his return in 1527 he went back to the Sheen Charterhouse. He refused **Henry VIII**'s offer of the See of York or Winchester, and went abroad again, to avoid the developing troubles in England. He wrote in 1534–6 *Pro Ecclesiasticae unitatis defensione*, censuring the king's conduct in the matter of his divorce from **Catherine of Aragon**. An Act of Attainder was passed against his family in 1539, and his mother executed in 1541. **Paul III** put him on a commission for the reform of the Church, created him cardinal in 1536, and named him one of the three legates appointed to preside at the Council of Trent. At Paul's death in 1549 he was very nearly elected to the Papacy. **Julius III** appointed him legate in England under **Mary Tudor**, and he went to Canterbury as archbishop in 1556: though a cardinal, he was not ordained priest until March 1556, and was consecrated archbishop two days afterwards. Pole fell out with **Paul IV**, the queen became the Pope's enemy, and he cancelled Pole's legation, accusing him also of doctrinal unsoundness. Pole died twelve hours after Mary and is buried near the site of **Thomas Becket's** shrine at Canterbury.

Poling, Daniel Alfred American Protestant clergyman, born Portland, 30 November 1884, died Philadelphia, 7 February 1968. Reared in the Evangelical Church, Poling became head, in 1927, of Christian Endeavour, an interdenominational youth movement; as editor of *Christian Herald*, 1927–65, he spoke prominently in support of conservative causes, both political and theological; he wrote many popular works of devotion and counsel. He served as minister at New York City's Marble Collegiate Church, and of the Baptist Temple in Philadelphia.

Polo, Marco Merchant, adventurer, traveller, born Venice (or Korcula, Croatia), *c.*1254, died Venice, 8 January 1324. His father Niccolò and uncle Maffeo traded with the Middle East, and Marco first met his father in 1269 when he returned with letters from Kublai Khan. Marco then accompanied his father and uncle in 1271, travelling through Palestine, Turkey and Afghanistan to join the Silk Road, reaching the Mongol capital Shang-tu probably in 1274. After many adventures Marco returned by sea, touching at Champa (Vietnam), Sumatra, Sri Lanka and India *en route* to Hormuz and then Venice which he reached in 1295. Marco was captured by the Genoese during a sea-fight, and while in prison dictated his memoirs. *Il milione* was widely copied, amended and translated. Although it appeared then (and in different ways since) to be fantastic, in medieval Europe it opened a rare window of awareness of the lands, peoples, and Christians, in Asia.

Polsky, Michael Russian Orthodox priest and Church historian, born in a Kuban Cossak village, 6 November 1891, died San Francisco, 21 May 1960. He was ordained priest in 1920, imprisoned by the Bolsheviks several times and came to know many of the Russian bishops, being entrusted with secret missions by Patriarch **Tikhon**. He was one of the few to escape the Soviet Union in the 1930s, crossing the border into Iran in 1935. He served as priest in various places, including London, and wrote *The New Martyrs of Russia* (1949, 1957) – still one of the most complete accounts of the communist persecution. He drew on the memories of dozens of survivors.

Polycarp Saint, Apostolic Father and martyr, born *c.*70, died Smyrna, 23 February *c.*155. One of the Apostolic Fathers, Polycarp links together the apostolic age and that of nascent Catholicism. St **Irenaeus** says in a letter to Florinus that Polycarp 'had intercourse with John [the Apostle or Elder], and with the rest of those who had seen the Lord'; John later made him bishop of Smyrna. Other sources fot his life are the Epistle of Polycarp to the Church at Philippi, wherein he describes his visit to the bishop of Rome **Anicetus**, and their discussions with regard to Quartodeciman celebration of the festival of Easter; the Epistle of **Ignatius of Antioch** to Polycarp; and the Epistle of the Church at Smyrna to the Church at Philomelium, one of the most precious texts of the second century, which gives an account of the martyrdom of Polycarp on a burning pyre. Feast day 23 February.

Polychromius Bishop of Apamaea in Syria, died *c.*430. Lauded by **Theodoret** in his history as the 'best of shepherds', Polychronius, a biblical exegete of the Antiochene school, wrote commentaries on Job, Daniel and Ezekiel, of which only fragments survive, chiefly in catenae. He expressly condemned the Alexandrian tradition of allegorical exegesis, but seems to have died before the decisions of the Council of Ephesus on the union of the divine and human natures.

Polycrates Bishop of Ephesus, flourished second century. The leading Quartodeciman of Asia Minor, who, after convening a synod (*c.*190), sturdily opposed Pope (St) **Victor I** in his wish to settle the controversy, to which end he threatened to excommunicate Polycrates and other Asia Minor bishops if they refused to give up their practice of keeping Easter on 14 Nisan, instead of on the following Sunday. The two ceased to be in communication over the incident, an important illustration of the early claims of the Roman see.

Pomponazzi, Pietro Italian philosopher, born Mantua, 16 September 1462, died Bologna, 18 May 1525. Pomponazzi separated philosophical reflection from dogmas of the faith, returning thereby to the doctrine of 'double truth' attributed to Averroes. He claimed the right to study Aristotle, and especially *De anima*, for himself, and held that **Thomas Aquinas** had entirely misconceived the Aristotelian theory of the active and the passive intellect. In his great work *Tractatus de immortalitate animiae*, he called into question the immortality of the soul: that, as the soul is the form of the body (as Aquinas also asserted), it must, by hypothesis, perish with the body; form apart from matter being unthinkable. The work was burned at Venice and condemned by Rome, but Pomponazzi declared his adherence to the Catholic faith.

Pomposa   *see* **Columba and Pomposa**

Pontianus Saint, Pope, elected 21 July 230, died 28 September 235. The *Liber Pontificalis* refers to him as a Roman, son of Calpurnius; **Eusebius** says he reigned six years. Little else is known of his origins, or activities, except that he must have presided at the Roman synod which approved the condemnation of **Origen** by **Demetrius**, bishop of

Alexandria, in 230. Exiled to the mines of Sardinia by Maximinian Thrax in 235, along with Antipope **Hippolytus**, he died the same year of harsh treatment in the 'island of death'. The bodies of both were returned to Rome and buried by Pope **Fabian** in the catacombs of St **Callistus**. Feast day 19 November.

Pontius Saint, biographer of St **Cyprian**, died *c*.260. A North African, and Cyprian's deacon at Carthage, Pontius followed him into exile at Curubis. According to St **Jerome**, Pontius wrote *Vita et Passio Cypriani*, the latter's earliest biography. Feast day 8 March.

Pope, Hugh English Scripture scholar and preacher, born Kenilworth, Warwickshire, 5 August 1869, died Edinburgh, 22 November 1946. Educated at the Oratory School under Cardinal **Newman**, Henry Vincent Pope became a Dominican, adopting the name 'Hugh'. Following his studies in Rome he began a course of open-air lectures on Christian doctrine that helped to develop the future nationwide Catholic Evidence Guild. Always in demand as a preacher and writer, he published mostly scriptural works: *The Date of Deuteronomy, Catholic Aids to the Bible*; *The Layman's New Testament, The Church and the Bible, The Life and Times of St Augustine of Hippo*.

Poppo of Stavelot Saint, Belgian abbot, born Deinze, 978, died Marchienne-au-Pont, 25 January 1048. After a career in the army and pilgrimages to the Holy Land, Poppo became a monk at the monastery of St-Thierry, near Rheims. He was invited to join the abbey of Saint-Vanne and to undertake the reform of several abbeys in Flanders and Lorraine. He succeeded to the abbatial see of Stavelot-Malmédy in 1020. He was admired by the Emperor **Henry II**, and served him as a political adviser. Feast day 25 June.

Porete, Marguerite Beguine martyr, author and preacher, died Paris, 1 June 1310. What little is known of her is preserved in the proceedings of the inquisitorial court which condemned her as a heretic. She appears to have been a religious woman, identified with the Beguiness, who normally lived quiet lives of devotion in communities of Christian laywomen, based largely in the Low Countries. Her mystical spirituality was published in *A Mirror for Simple Souls*. She was arrested because of her persistence in preaching the ideas in this book, was condemned on 11 April and burnt at the stake as an unrepentant heretic on 1 June 1310.

Porphyry of Gaza Saint, ascetic and bishop, born Thessalonica, *c*.347, died Gaza, 26 February 420. Porphyry had been a monk in Egypt for ten years, according to Mark the Deacon, and in Palestine before being ordained in 392, and named bishop of Gaza, a hotbed of paganism. He tirelessly instructed his people, won many converts and succeeded, with help from Empress Eudoxia, in repressing the persecutions in his diocese. Feast day 26 February.

Porras y Ayllón, Rafaela Saint, Spanish foundress, born Pecho Abad, Córdoba, 1 March 1850, died Rome, 6 January 1925. The youngest of thirteen children, Rafaela and her sister Dolores were, in 1875, the first novices of the Society of Mary Reparatrix. They remained in Córdoba when the Society moved to Seville, and founded the Handmaids of the Sacred Heart of Jesus, dedicated to perpetual adoration, teaching and catechetics; Rome approved the Society in 1886, and Rafaela became first superior general. By 1961 the Handmaids had 61 houses and more than 2700 members. She was canonized in 1977. Feast day 18 May.

Portal, Étienne Fernand French Vincentian priest and ecumenist, born Laroque, l'Hérault, 1855, died Javel, 19 June 1926. Quite by chance Portal met Lord **Halifax** on Madeira in 1890, and this led him to campaign for dialogue between Rome and Canterbury, and to publish *Les Ordinations anglicanes* in 1894, promoted in England by Halifax. Though **Leo XIII** declared Anglican orders to be null and void in *Apostolicae Curae* (1896) Portal was not discouraged, and launched *Revue catholique des Églises* in 1904, to help Catholics discover Christians of other confessions – Orthodox and Protestant. A tireless and gifted promoter of the cause of ecumenism, Portal had his most tangible success in the Malines Conversations of 1921–5, which he and Halifax originated and sustained.

Portalié, Eugène French Jesuit theologian, born

Mende, Lozère, 3 January 1852, died Arnélie-les-Bains, 20 April 1909. As a professor at the Institut Catholique de Toulouse, Portalié's chief interest centred on the history of the development of dogma, and St **Augustine**'s teaching on grace; he had a penetrating faculty of analysis which always sought out the essential. He joined vigorously in the anti-Modernist controversies around the 'philosophy of action' of Maurice **Blondel**, and the 'moral dogmatism' of Lucien **Laberthonnière**. He contributed scholarly articles to the *Bulletin de littérature ecclésiastique* and the *Dictionnaire de théologie catholique.*

Possidius Saint, African bishop, born *c.*370, died *c.*440, places unknown. One of **Augustine**'s first disciples at Hippo, Possidius became bishop of Calama in Numidia *c.*400, and helped Augustine in his struggles against Donatism and Pelagianism. They were lifelong friends; Possidius attended Augustine when he died at Hippo in 430, and wrote a short but valuable sketch of the great bishop. Feast day 16 May.

Postel, Marie Madeleine Saint, French religious foundress, born La Bretonne, Normandy, 28 November 1756, died Saint-Sauveur-le-Vicomte, 16 July 1846. She opened a school for poor children and maintained their religious instruction during the French Revolution. In 1807 she and three others took vows of religion in a new community, the Sisters of the Christian Schools of Mercy, for the education of girls, with a Rule from John Baptist de **La Salle** for the Brothers of the Christian Schools. An imaginative educator, the congregation flourished under her leadership; she received canonization in 1925. Feast day 16 July.

Potamius Earliest known bishop of Lisbon, died after 359. A leading churchman of the West, Potamius originally professed the orthodox Nicene position, but for a time aligned himself with the Arianizing policy of Emperor **Constantius II**; he at least accepted, if he did not help to compose, the Second Creed of Sirmium (357), which suppressed the term 'substance' in Trinitarian speculation, asserting the subordination of the Son to the Father. Four short orthodox works of colourful and assertive language survive, as well as a fragment of a letter written during his heretical period.

Pothinus Saint, bishop and martyr, born Asia Minor, *c.*87, died Lyons, 177. The first bishop of Lyons, Pothinus is said to have been a disciple of St **Polycarp**, who sent him to Gaul in mid-second century. Taken in the persecution under Marcus Aurelius, he died in prison aged 90, after being maltreated and stoned. Feast day 2 June.

Potter, Mary English religious foundress, born London, 22 November 1849, died Rome, 9 April 1913. At the age of twenty, Mary became convinced of a call to a life dedicated to the comfort of the sick and dying. Though engaged to be married at the time, she renounced her betrothed, and founded the Little Company of Mary at Hyson Green in 1877. Her cause for beatification has been introduced.

Pouget, François Aimé French Oratorian catechist, born Montpellier, 28 August 1666, died Paris, 4 April 1723. A *curé* at Saint-Roch, Paris, Pouget joined the Congregation of the Oratory in 1696, and became rector of its seminary at Montpellier. His fame rests on the popular, but controversial, Montpellier Catechism, which, under the patronage of archbishops de **Noailles** of Paris and **Colbert** of Montpellier, had 30 editions from 1702 to 1710. However, the Congregation of the Index condemned the work for its Jansenist doctrines, the French edition in 1710 and the English version in 1725.

Poulain, Augustin French Jesuit mystical theologian, born Cherbourg, 15 December 1836, died Paris, 19 July 1919. While spiritual director and retreat master in Paris, Poulain wrote *Des Grâces d'oraison*, a work which surprised his associates, who had not suspected his mystical orientation. An immediate success, much reprinted and translated, the work, though not the result of any direct experience on his part, presented a complex subject in a clear didactic treatise, drawing a clear distinction between the ascetical and mystical states, which aroused much controversy.

Poulenc, Francis French composer, born Paris, 7 January 1899, died there, 30 January 1963. A member of the anti-Romantic 'Groupe des Six', under the leadership of Eric Satie and Jean Cocteau, they opposed the refinement and elegance of

Debussy and Ravel. Poulenc rediscovered Roman Catholicism in 1935 and this inspired his greatest choral compositions, including his Mass, the *Exultate Deo* and *Salve Regina*. His clarity, spontaneity and melodic gifts are also evident in his Organ Concerto, and his operas, e.g., *Les Dialogues des Carmélites*. One of his most successful works is his *Gloria*, a cantata rather than a Mass-setting.

Pounde, Thomas Jesuit Recusant, born Belmont, Lancashire, 29 May 1539, died there, 5 March 1615. A scion of the landed aristocracy, a lawyer and courtier under **Elizabeth I**, and outwardly a Protestant, Pounde retired from court in 1569, professed his Catholicism and became reconciled to the Church. He planned to go to Rome, but was arrested in 1574, the first of fifteen such occasions during his life. While in the Tower in 1579, he received a letter affiliating him officially to the Society of Jesus. He obtained from **James I** a final release from prison in 1604. He circulated in manuscript among Catholics a treatise, *The Six Reasons*, an attack on the Protestant *scriptura sola* principle.

Pourrat, Pierre French theologian, born Millery, Rhône, 7 February, 1871; died Lyons, 12 March 1957. Ordained a Sulpician in 1896, Pourrat served from 1926 to 1945 as superior of La Solitude, the formation house of Saint-Sulpice at Issy-les-Moulineaux, during which time he composed *La Spiritualité chrétienne*, a concise and critically sound history of spirituality from biblical to modern times.

Powderly, Terence Vincent American labour leader, born Carbondale, Pennsylvania, 22 January 1849, died Washington, DC, 24 June 1924. Having risen through the ranks of labour from the age of thirteen, Powderly became a lawyer, a government official and grand master of the Knights of Labour, which, though a secret society, he endeavoured to make acceptable to the Church by modifying the religious trappings and the secrecy. His patience in explaining the need for trade unions, and his co-operation with Cardinal James **Gibbons**, brought around a reactionary hierarchy, and paved the way for positive recognition of the rights of workers expressed in **Leo XIII**'s *Rerum novarum*. His principal published work is *Thirty Years of Labour* (1899).

Power, Emily Mother, Irish-born American educator, born County Waterford, 12 January 1844, died Sinsinawa, Wisconsin, 16 October 1909. Emily Power joined the community of Dominican Sisters in Benton, became its head in 1867, and moved the motherhouse back to its original foundation site at Sinsinawa. She is credited with planning the community's educational apostolate that includes schools at every level, two colleges, and centres for European studies at Fribourg and Florence. She championed the cause of miners in Minnesota and Montana, of workers in' the Chicago stockyards, and brought them material assistance during their strikes and lock-outs.

Poynter, William English Roman Catholic bishop, born Petersfield, Hampshire, 20 May 1762, died London, 26 November 1827. Ordained at the English College, Douai, Poynter spent time in prison during the French Revolution, but returned to England, became president of St Edmund's College, Old Hall Green, in 1801, asssistant to the vicar apostolic of the London district with the rank of bishop in 1803 and himself vicar apostolic of the London district in 1812. He led the group of Catholics who had been dissatisfied with the position of the bishops on the Relief Act (1791), which freed from the Statutes of Recusancy and the Oath of Supremacy those who took a prescribed oath.

Praetorius, Michael (Michael Hieronymus Schultheiss) German composer, born Kreuzberg, 15 February 1571, died Wolfenbüttel, 15 February 1621. Praetorius is the most celebrated of a distinguished family of musicians; he served as *kapellmeister* at Gröningen while still a student, before serving the court at Wolfenbüttel and at Dresden and Halle. In the spirit of Lutheran reform, he composed a large *œuvre*, in twenty volumes, of motets, hymns, spiritual canticles and dances. His theoretical work *Syntagma musicum* is a valuable source for the history of ancient and ecclesiastical music. His charming 'Away in a Manger', is still one of our most popular Christmas hymns.

Prandota Blessed, bishop of Cracow, born

Beałaczóv, Poland, early thirteenth century, died Cracow, 21 September 1266. Little is known of his early life, except that he seems to have studied abroad and on his return to have become a canon of Sandomierz. As bishop of Cracow from 1242, he did much to secure the canonization of St Stanislas in 1253, an event which bolstered national unity and put an end to in-fighting among the princes. He was also eager to encourage missionary activity, though in this he had, for political reasons, less success. He also encouraged the growth of religious orders in his vast diocese, and was renowned for his generosity to the needy. His tomb in the cathedral at Cracow quickly became, and long remained, a centre of pilgrimage. Feast day 21 September.

Praxeas   Heretic, flourished *c.*200. For what little is known of him, we are indebted to **Tertullian**'s *Adversus Praxean* (*c.*213); he is said to have arrived in Rome from Asia and to have turned Pope **Zephyrinus**, or **Victor I**, against the Montanists. He proclaimed himself a leader of the Patripassian Monarchians, who held that God the Father suffered as the Son, thus maintaining the unity of the Godhead. As Tertullian put it, 'he crucified the Father' (*Patrem crucifixit*), since he conceived of the Godhead as emptied into the person of Christ in order to assume the temporary role of Redeemer.

Praxeda (Prassede)   Saint, virgin and martyr. Her spurious *Acta* has it that Praxeda sheltered Christians during the persecution of Marcus Aurelius, and that she and St **Pudentiana** were sisters, since she is buried next to her in the catacomb of Priscilla; it is a recorded fact that her remains were transferred to the church of S. Prassede built by **Paschal I**. Feast day 21 July.

Prester John   Legendary Christian king of Asia. The name 'Prester [priest] John' first appears in **Otto of Freising**'s *Chronicle*, as that of a priest-king reigning in the Far East, beyond Persia and Armenia, who had defeated the Muslims and would lead the Crusades. Another tradition identifies him with the emperor of Ethiopia (commonly confused with India in the Middle Ages); when Western Christendom came into direct contact with this emperor in the fourteenth century,

he seemed willing to attack the Muslim states and support the Crusades. A third theory, implied in an account by **William of Rubrouck**, a Franciscan missionary, identifies Prester John with a Chinese prince, Gor Khan, who defeated the sultan of Persia in 1141 and founded an empire wherein lived a number of Nestorian Christians – Marco **Polo** mentions him in the account of his journey. The story of Prester John no doubt originally gathered round some nucleus of fact, but the nature of it has been difficult to determine.

Price, Charles Sydney   Pentecostal evangelist, born UK, 1887, died Canada 1947. Price emigrated to Canada as a young man and became a Methodist and later Congregational pastor with Modernist views. These views, however, were changed by attendance at a meeting led by Aimee Semple **McPherson**, and he started an independent Pentecostal Church in Lodi, California. Price preached widely in North America, Europe and the Middle East, his meetings marked by experiences of miraculous healings. In 1926 he began a periodical, *Golden Grain*, and he wrote *The Story of My Life* and *The Real Faith*.

Price, Richard   Welsh Nonconformist minister and philosopher, born Tynton, Glamorgan, 23 February 1723, died Bunhill Fields, London, 19 April 1791. He was educated at various schools, then at a dissenting academy in London. He remained in London as a chaplain to Mr Streatfield in Stoke Newington, ministering as well to various congregations in the area. In an early publication, *Review of the Principal Questions in Morals*, Price defended a view of ethics, similar to the later one of Immanuel **Kant**, which held that the rightness and wrongness of an action belonged to it intrinsically; he criticized the 'moral sense' view of ethics, which had secured popularity through such writers as Lord Shaftesbury. In the field of politics and economics, he entered the controversy over population growth with *An Essay on the Population of England, from the Revolution to the Present Time*; he strongly supported the American and French Revolutions, as 'both glorious'. He joined with Dr Joseph **Priestley** in becoming an original member of the Unitarian Society.

Prierias, Sylvestro Mazzolini   Italian Dominican,

born Prierio, Piedmont, 1456, died Rome, 1523. Prierias entered the Dominicans at the age of sixteen, and **Leo X** appointed him 'Master of the Sacred Palace' in 1515. His celebrity comes principally from his polemics with Martin **Luther**. He attacked Luther's theses on indulgences, became involved in the juridical process against Luther and Johann **Reuchlin**, and in the cases of Pietro **Pomponazzi** and **Erasmus**. After the bull *Exsurge*, he collected his criticisms in the *Errata et argumenta Martini Luteris recitata, detecta, repulsa et copiosissime trita*. He played an important role in the development of the Church's position against Luther. He died during the sack of Rome.

Priestley, Joseph English chemist and theologian, born Fieldhead, near Leeds, 13 March 1733, died Northumberland, Pennsylvania, 6 February 1804. Ordained in the Presbyterian ministry, Priestley came to hold Arian views on the person of Christ, rejected the doctrine of the Atonement and the inspiration of the Bible, which views he shared with other Arians and determinists at Warrington Academy. As pastor of the Mill Hill Chapel, Leeds, he embraced Socianianism, and brought out the *Theological Repository*, a critical periodical that favoured complete toleration for Roman Catholics and the abolition of a traditional Church. He denied the impeccability and infallibility of Christ in his *History of Early Opinion Concerning Jesus Christ*, became one of the founders of the Unitarian Society in 1791, and defended the French Revolution in *Letters to Burke*. Following *The History and Present State of Electricity*, the Royal Society awarded him the Copely Medal for his discovery of oxygen in 1774, and of other gases, discoveries which made him a founder of chemistry.

Primasius North African bishop of Hadrumetum, flourished sixth century. Primasius' commentary on Revelation drew extensively on Tyconius and **Augustine**, and throws valuable light on the history of the Old Latin version of the NT. **Justinian** summoned him to Constantinople in 551 and, because of his association with **Theodore of Mopsuestia**, involved him in the controversy of the Three Chapters – three subjects condemned by Justinian, i.e. (1) the person and works of Theodore of Mopsuestia, (2) the writings of **Theodoret**

against **Cyril of Alexandria**, (3) the letter of Ibas of Edessa to Maris – in the hope of conciliating the Monophysites by a display of anti-Nestorian zeal. In the event, Primasius strongly supported Pope **Vigilius** in 553 in his eventual acceptance of the edict against the Chapters.

Priscillian The first person known to have been executed for heresy, born Spain, *c.*340, died Trier, 384. He was a wealthy layman who began preaching an ascetical doctrine in the early 370s. He attracted the hostility of some bishops, and a Council was called at Saragossa, in 380, which condemned his teachings but not his person. He was then consecrated bishop of Ávila by some sympathetic bishops who felt he needed more authority. He travelled to Gaul, where he converted a wealthy woman, Eucrotia, to his beliefs. They went to Italy to win support, but then travelled to Trier to plead their case before the emperor. Their opponents won the day, however, and Priscillian and Eucrotia were executed, despite the efforts of **Martin of Tours** to prevent it.

Probst, Ferdinand German liturgical scholar, born Ehingen, 28 March 1816, died Breslau, 26 December 1899. Ordained priest in 1840, Probst became a professor at Breslau in 1864 and dean of the cathedral in 1896. A scholar of great erudition, his works concentrate on liturgical development during the early centuries, but his interpretations of the material are regarded as being marked by excessive conservatism, and his conclusions are criticized as being overly speculative, not to say fanciful.

Proclus Saint, patriarch of Constantinople, died 24 July 447. Consecrated bishop of Cyzicus in 426, Proclus could not occupy his See and remained in Constantinople as a popular preacher; he delivered a famous sermon on the 'Theotokos' (the one who gave birth to God, i.e., the Virgin Mary), a term which **Nestorius** said did not accord with the full humanity of Christ, and himself proposed 'Christotokos' in its place. Elected patriarch in 434, Proclus gained popular support by his moderate view of orthodoxy, though he attacked the beliefs and morals of the Jews in classical fashion. He is said to have introduced the Trisagion: 'Holy God, Holy and strong, Holy and immortal, have mercy on us', as a feature of Orthodox worship. Feast day 24 October.

Procopius of Gaza Christian rhetorician and biblical exegete, born Gaza, c.475, died Gaza, c.528. A leading figure in the 'school of Gaza', little of his writing survives, and that consists mostly of extensive extracts from Philo, **Origen**, **Basil**, **Theodoret** and **Cyril of Alexandria**. His commentaries on the Octateuch and other books of the OT, e.g. Samuel, Kings, Chronicles, form a continuous explanation of the biblical text, by indicating the commonality of exegetical opinion among the Church Fathers.

Prosper of Aquitaine Saint, theologian, born Aquitaine, c.390, died Rome, after 463. At Marseilles, Prosper defended **Augustine** against the Pelagians, and the opposition to his teachings on grace and predestination current among the disciples of John **Cassian**. In reply, Augustine wrote *De praedestinatione sanctorum* and *De dono perseverantiae*. In 431 after Augustine's death, he sought **Celestine I**'s support for Augustinian doctrines, in defence of which, as well as against Vincent of Lérins and Cassian, he published a number of works. After the latter's death, c.435, he modified his strict Augustinianism, rejected predestination to damnation, and affirmed the will of God to save all men, though he believed in fact that a great number could not attain salvation. Feast day 25 June.

Protase *see* **Gervase and Protase**

Prudentius (Aurelius Prudentius Clemens) Poet, born 348 at, possibly, Saragossa (or possibly Calahorra or Tarragona), died Spain, perhaps at Calahorra, c.410. Born into a Christian family, he pursued a career in law, then in the imperial civil service, twice being city prefect. Towards the end of the fourth century he abandoned his career for one of asceticism and the writing of poetry, an art form still treated with suspicion by Christians. His many poems and hymns – meant for congregational singing, some of which have since entered the liturgy – display a thorough knowledge of the pagan classics. His *Contra Symmachum* argues that Christians may be as patriotic as the pagan senator who clashed with **Ambrose** over the Altar of Vic-

tory in Rome. Some poems/hymns are on theological topics; others recount the lives of saints.

Prudentius Galindo Spanish bishop, born Spain, died Troyes, 6 April 861. Prudentius became chaplain at the court of **Louis I** the Pious, and bishop of Troyes c.843. In the controversy on predestination, he defended the monk **Gottschalk of Orbais** against **Hincmar**, with *Epistola ad Hincmarum*; he taught the 'Augustinian' doctrine of double predestination, and wrote a treatise *De Praedestinatione contra Joannem Scotum*, i.e. **Eriugena**, whom Hincmar had called to his aid. He also wrote a continuation of the *Annales Bertiniani* for the years 835–61, valuable for the history of the Frankish Empire.

Prynne, William Puritan pamphleteer, born Swainswick, Somerset, 1600, died Lincoln's Inn, London, 24 October 1669. Educated at Oxford and called to the bar, Prynne, a Puritan to the core, lacked sympathy with human nature, and attacked prevailing fashions without any sense of proportion; *Histriomastix* (1633) condemned stage plays in general and contained veiled references to **Charles I** and Henrietta Maria which led to a sentence of imprisonment for life, a fine, expulsion from Lincoln's Inn and the pillory; he escaped the first two. However, throughout his life in over 200 pamphlets and monographs, he published attacks on the royal family, Anglican ritual and policy, the Independents, the Levellers, the Quakers and the papists; he defended Presbyterianism and subjection of the clergy to the Crown. After the Restoration, **Charles II** made him Keeper of the Tower Records, but he soon attacked Anglicanism in a series of publications, among them *A Short, Sober, Pacific Examination of Exuberances in the Common Prayer* and *A Moderate, Seasonable Apology for Tender Consciences Touching not Bowing at the Name of Jesus*.

Psellus, Michael Politician, monk and chronicler, born Constantinople 1018, died probably after 1081, though where is uncertain. He was a civil servant in the administration of Constantinople until his liberal views clashed with those of **Michael Cerularius**, and in 1054 he was forced to become a monk. He returned to the city, however, and later became one of those who helped bring about Cerularius' downfall. Little else is heard of him, though he wrote a complex and informative history of the period 967–1078, the *Chronography*, based very largely on his own observations. He also wrote on philosophy, theology and law.

Psellus, Michael (Constantine) Byzantine scholar and statesman, born Constantinople, 1018, died *c.*1078. Under **Constantine IX Monomachos** (1042–55), Psellus became one of the most influential men in the empire. As professor of philosophy at the newly founded Academy of Constantinople from 1045, he revived the cult of Plato at a time when Aristotle held the field; this, together with his admiration for the old pagan glories of Hellas, aroused suspicions as to his orthodoxy. Under Isaac I Comnenus and Constantine X Ducas he continued to exercise great influence. His writings include commentaries on Plato, Aristotle and the Bible; his *Chronographia* is an important source for the years 976–1077, and was used by historians such as **Anna Comnena** and **Zonaras**.

Pudentiana Saint, virgin, martyr. According to the Roman Martyrology, a Roman virgin of the early Church, a daughter of St Pudens and the sister of St **Praxeda**. The cult seems to rest on a mistaken interpretation of 'Pudentiana' as a noun, rather than an adjective attributing the foundering of *ecclesia Pudentiana* in Rome to St Pudens. The *Acta* of SS Pudentiana and Praxedis, printed by the Bollandists, are not earlier than the eighth century. Feast day 19 May.

Puerto, Nicolás del Mexican Roman Catholic bishop, born Santa Catalina Minas, date unknown, died Oaxaca, 1681. A Mexican Indian, Puerto studied with the Jesuits at Oaxaca and was ordained a diocesan priest; he became a teacher at, and later rector and chancellor of, the Colegio Mayor de Santos in Mexico City, consultor to the Inquisition in 1657 and bishop of Oaxaca in 1679; he established a seminary before his death two years later.

Pugin, Augustus Welby Architect, born London 1 March 1812, died Ramsgate, Kent, 14 September 1852. He was educated at Christ's Hospital and then, professionally, by his father. He became a

Roman Catholic in 1834, and then wrote *Contrasts* (1836), which traced the decline in architectural style back to the Reformation. He designed many Roman Catholic churches, including St George's Cathedral, Southwark. He pioneered the revival of Gothic architecture in the nineteenth century, so was responsible for many notable Victorian buildings, especially churches in a Victorian, neo-Gothic style. However, many of his designs were not fully carried out, and thus his genius is often more fairly displayed in the drawings than by the buildings themselves. Among his numerous churches, only St Augustine's in Ramsgate followed his complete design, and this because he paid for it himself. He assisted Sir Charles Barry in working out the details of the designs for the new Houses of Parliament at Westminster. To support his architectural views he wrote *Contrasts*, mentioned above, and *The True Principles of Christian Architecture* (1841), as well as more than twenty other books. A skilful etcher, he illustrated a number of his works, written with much eloquence, great antiquarian knowledge and considerable humour.

Pulcheria Saint, Byzantine empress, born Constantinople, 19 January 399, died there, July 453. The daughter of Emperor Arcadius, elder sister of Theodosius II and a woman of uncommon ability and deep piety, Pulcheria had made a vow of virginity, and led a secluded life away from the court. A strong defender of orthodoxy, she induced her brother, Theodosius, to condemn Nestorianism (two separate persons in the incarnate Christ), and received a letter of gratitude from **Cyril of Alexandria**. On the death of her brother in 450, she became empress, took the aged senator **Marcian** as her consort, and forthwith organized a General Council to meet at Chalcedon in 451; she attended the sixth session in person. She has been venerated as a saint since the Middle Ages. Feast day 10 September.

Pullen, Robert English theologian, date and place of birth unknown, died probably Rome, 1147. Pullen is said to have come from Exeter to the schools of Oxford, where he began to teach the Scriptures in 1133, 'the study of which had become obsolete in England'; by 1139 he had moved to Paris, where St **Bernard** esteemed 'the wholesome doctrine that is in him'. Pullen went to Rome and

Celestine II created him cardinal in 1143; **Lucius II** made him chancellor of the Holy Roman Church in 1144, an office he continued to hold under **Eugenius III**, St Bernard's friend and pupil. His main surviving work is *Sententiarum theologicarum libri viii*, a theological compilation with a wide range, but soon supplanted by the treatise of **Peter Lombard**, 'Master of the Sentences'.

Purcell, Henry British composer, born probably in London, *c.*1659, died there, 21 November 1695. His father was a musician in the royal household and he was a chorister at the Chapel Royal and later organist at Westminster Abbey and the Chapel Royal. He was responsible for music at the coronations of 1685 and 1689. He wrote much Church music, notably *Rejoice in the Lord*, *Te Deum* and magnificent funeral music for Queen Mary. The *Trumpet Voluntary*, once ascribed to him, was later shown to have been composed by Jeremiah Clarke.

Purvey, John English Wycliffite preacher, born Lathbury, Buckinghamshire, *c.*1353, died *c.*1428. Ordained in 1377, possibly after spending some time at the University of Oxford, Purvey became a dedicated companion of John **Wycliffe** after the latter's withdrawal to Lutterworth in 1382. He is presumed to be the translator, revisor and popularizer of Wycliffe's works among the Lollards, including a revision of his Bible from its early literal version to a more idiomatic edition. Purvey was brought to trial for these activities in 1401; he recanted, but subsequently reverted to Lollardy, and continued to disseminate Lollard doctrine.

Pusey, Edward Bouverie English Tractarian leader, born Pusey, Berkshire, 22 August 1800, died Ascot Priory, 16 September 1882. From a Huguenot family of Flemish origin, he was educated at Eton and at Christ Church, Oxford, and elected to a fellowship at Oriel in 1823, where he became familiar with John **Keble** and John Henry **Newman**; he studied at Göttingen and in 1828 the Duke of Wellington appointed him to the Regius professorship of Hebrew, with the attached canonry of Christ Church. In 1833 he joined Newman, Keble and Richard Hurrell **Froude** in their effort to revive the Catholic tradition in the Church of England; his essay 'Scriptural views of Holy Baptism' changed the character of the *Tracts for the Times* from pamphlets to learned studies. Oxford authorities condemned his moderate Catholic sermon on 'The Presence of Christ in the Holy Eucharist' (1843), the doctrine round which almost all the subsequent theology of his followers revolved, and which revolutionized the practices of Anglican worship. Of his larger works on the Eucharist, the *Eirenicon* endeavoured to find a basis of union between the Church of England and the Church of Rome, emphasizing that Anglicanism retained the sacraments (the Real Presence) and apostolic succession; but his hopes were dashed by Newman's discouraging response, and by the definition of papal infallibility at Vatican Council I. He fought to retain the High Church tradition within the Church of England, and in 1845 was instrumental in the establishment of the first of the Anglican sisterhoods.

Putzer, Joseph Austrian-born Redemptorist priest, born Rodenek, Tyrol, 4 March 1836, died Ilchester, Maryland, 15 May 1904. Putzer went to the USA in 1876, engaged in pastoral work and taught in the seminary at Ilchester. He published *Commentarium in facultates apostolicas*, a work that so revised and enlarged an earlier work by a colleague, Anthony **Konings**, that writers on both sides of the Atlantic hailed it for clearness, depth and accurate scholarship. He also published 'Instructio de confessariis', and many other articles in Catholic periodicals and newspapers, always to wide acclaim.

Q

Quadrupani, Carlo Giuseppe Italian Barnabite preacher, born Induno, Lombardy, 1740, died Induno, 14 July 1806. Superior of St Alessandro's, Milan, and provincial of the Barnabites of Lombardy. Celebrated as a spiritual writer, and especially as a preacher, throughout Italy, he conducted retreats for the clergy and laity in the major cities, hearing confessions and ministering to the sick. His writings went through many editions, were immensely popular and were still being published in this century, the most significant of which were gathered in *Documenti di vita spirituale*.

Quaque, Philip First African Anglican clergyman, born 1741, son of a Fanti chief from Ghana, died Ghana, 1816. Thomas Thompson of the Society for the Propagation of the Gospel (SPG) asked Quaque's father for three boys to educate in England. Quaque was among the three and spent eleven years there, being baptized in 1759, ordained in 1765 and marrying an English woman. In 1795 he returned to Ghana with SPG as a missionary and teacher and worked with the Bible Band. Later his son, Samuel, took up the work and after Philip's death the Bible Band invited the Methodist Mission to work in Ghana.

Quarles, Francis English religious poet, born Romford, Essex, 1592 (baptized 8 May), died London, 8 September 1644. Educated at Christ's College, Cambridge, he went to Heidelberg in 1613, returned to England two years later, and began to publish biblical paraphrases: *Job Militant* (1624) and *Divine Poems* (1630); *Divine Fancies* (1632) was a small volume of epigrams and meditations in verse. His popular *Emblems* appeared in 1635, partly derived from two Jesuit manuals, *Pia desideria* (1624) and *Typus mundi* (1627). He took the Royalist side in the Civil War, and wrote a pamphlet, *The Loyall Convert* (1644), defending the cause. After his death, *The Shepherd's Oracles* was published, a satire in verse on the contemporary religious disputes. His poetry revealed deep religious feeling, coloured by an acute sense of sin, and influenced the imagery of **Donne**, **Herbert** and **Crashaw**.

Quasten, Johannes German patristic scholar, born Homberg, 3 May 1900, died Freiburg im Breisgau, 10 March 1987. Educated at Münster, where F. J. **Dölger** determined his orientation towards the study of Christian antiquity and literature. Ordained in 1926, he specialized in Christian archaeology during a stay in Rome, and participated in explorations at Monastir (then in Yugoslavia). His second doctoral thesis, on the Good Shepherd in early Christian art (1931), enabled him to teach as a *Privat-docent* in Münster. However, his career became increasingly difficult under the Nazis and he went to Rome, where Cardinal Pacelli (the future **Pius XII**), who was looking for a professor for the chair of patristics and archaeology at the Catholic University of America, suggested he take it up. Though knowing little English, he accepted, and was highly appreciated for his competence and culture. He published many studies in the area of patristics, especially liturgy, but the work that made his name is *Patrology*, a standard reference work which details the lives, writings and theological teaching of post-biblical authors of the early Church. His writings made a significant contribution to the liturgical movement preceding Vatican II, and he was a member of the Council's preparatory commission for the liturgy. Quasten formed a generation of patristic scholars for North America.

Quelen, Hyacinthe Louis de Archbishop of Paris, born Paris, 8 October 1778, died there, 31 December 1839. He attended St-Sulpice, was ordained in 1807 and was assigned to La Grande Aumônerie, of which he became vicar-general in 1814. Named bishop of Paris in 1817, then coadjutor, he succeeded Cardinal **Talleyrand-Périgord** in 1821 as archbishop. An able and pastorally committed prelate, he reorganized the seminaries, initiated ecclesiastical retreats and ordered the preaching of missions in parishes. He opposed the revolution of 1830, and the subsequent rule of Louis-Philippe, which inhibited his negotiations for a new concordat with the Holy See. He is remembered for his conferences at Notre Dame Cathedral, proposed by students who wanted teaching outside the normal tone of sermons; they were an immediate success, conducted by distinguished prelates, and Quelen had the brilliant idea, in 1835, of enlisting **Lacordaire**, and then **Ravignan**, of more sober eloquence. The conferences were one of the great acts of his episcopate, and are still very popular after 150 years.

Quesnel, Pasquier French Oratorian and scholar, born Paris, 14 July 1634, died Amsterdam, 2 December 1719. A student of the Jesuits and at the Sorbonne, ordained in the Congregation of the Oratory in 1659, he was given the direction of students, and wrote spiritual books, among which was *Réflexions morales*, which emphasized the value of the Scriptures in increasing true devotion. In 1675 he published a scholarly edition of the works of **Leo I**, placed on the Index because of the Gallician tendencies developed in the notes. Accused of Jansenism in 1681, he refused to subscribe to an anti-Jansenist formula imposed by his superiors in 1684. He went to Brussels and lived with Antoine **Arnauld**, until the latter's death in 1694. Imprisoned by the bishop of Malines in 1703, he escaped and fled to Holland. He spent the rest of his life defending his *Réflexions*, which, though commended by Cardinal de **Noailles** of Paris, was condemned by **Clement XI** in the bull *Unigenitus* (1713). Among the 101 propositions condemned were the theses that no grace is given outside the Church, that grace is irresistible, that without grace man is incapable of any good and that all acts of a sinner, even prayer and attendance at Mass, are sins. Quesnel never accepted the condemnation, protested the profound orthodoxy of his thought and appealed to a future General Council for his vindication; he asked for and received the last sacraments.

Quevedo, Juan de Spanish Franciscan missionary bishop, born Bejori, Old Castile, died Barcelona, 24 December 1519. In 1513 he was appointed bishop of Santa Maria de la Antigua and was the first bishop on the mainland of America.

Quiñones, Francisco de Spanish cardinal and reformer. Born León, 1480, died Veroli, 27 October 1540. He joined the Franciscans in 1498, was minister general, 1523–8, was created cardinal in 1527 and became bishop of Coria in 1531. In 1529 he took part in negotiations over **Henry VIII**'s divorce, defending the interests of **Catherine of Aragon**. He felt a strong vocation to missionary work and in 1523 sent 'Twelve Apostles' to New Spain, with a mandate, contained in what has been called the 'Magna Carta of Mexican civilization', in which he stressed the qualities of the missionary, and the standards of missionary methods. However, his name is chiefly associated with a reform of the Roman Breviary, at the request of **Clement VII**, published in 1535, and known as the 'Breviary of the Holy Cross'. It became very popular, though intended for private use, and more than 100 editions were made between 1536 and 1566. Attacked in some quarters, it was suppressed by the Council of Trent. Quiñones was inhumed in the basilica of the Holy Cross in Jerusalem, where he had commissioned Sansovino to erect his sepulchral monument.

Quiroga, Vasco de Spanish bishop and social reformer, born Madrigal de las Altas Torres, *c.*1470, died Pátzcuaro, Mexico, 14 March 1565. Little is known of his early life except that he remained a layman and became a canon lawyer. A member of the five-man governing 'audiencia' of New Spain, sent there to maintain royal authority, he exerted all his efforts to ensure relations with the native inhabitants were tempered with legal justice and charity. He was particularly concerned to promote the cause of the slaves, and often judged in their favour. He established near Mexico City a hospital-town called Santa Fe, patterned after the social plan of **More**'s *Utopia*, to care for the sick and needy, and to provide instruction in the Catholic faith. In 1533 he went to Michoacán, where he made a similar foundation of the same name; this became a diocese in 1536, and Quiroga its first bishop, passing through all the orders and consecrated in 1538. He founded the Colegio de San Nicolas, the first New World institution to train priests to be proficient in native languages.

R

Rabanus Maurus Blessed, archbishop, German Benedictine theologian, born Mainz, *c.*780, died Winkel (Rhine), 4 February 856. Rabanus went to Tours *c.*802, to study with **Alcuin**. His literary output began in 810 with the poem 'De laudibus sanctae crucis'; there followed *De institutione clericorum*, a manual for the use of priests, relying heavily on St **Augustine**, St **Gregory** the Great and **Isidore**; *De computo*, on the division of time and the date of Easter. He also wrote extensive commentaries on the Bible (Pentateuch, Ruth, Proverbs, Jeremiah, Ezekiel, Wisdom, Matthew, the Pauline Epistles). Rabanus compiled his writings, as did Alcuin, with the help of pupils, and they are important for their role in the Carolingian renaissance.

Rabbula Syrian bishop of Edessa, born Kenneshnu, near Aleppo, *c.*350, died Edessa, 435. Rabbula converted to Christianity and threw himself into Christian ascetic practices, sold his possessions and separated from his wife and kinsfolk. He lived for a time in a monastery, then as a hermit. Chosen to succeed Diogenes as bishop of Edessa on the latter's death in 411, he readily accepted without any of the customary show of reluctance. He ruled his diocese with extraordinary energy, insisted on discipline among the clergy and monks under his authority, and combated with fierce determination all heresies. A friend of **Cyril of Alexandria**, he translated his treatise *De recta fide* into Syriac. He died after 24 years of episcopal life, immensely lamented by his people.

Rabelais, François French humorist, born Chinon, *c.*1483, died Paris, April 1553. Rabelais joined the Franciscans in 1511, became a literary monk, a professor of anatomy, and in 1523 joined the Benedictines. He is the author of *Pantagruel* (1532) and *Gargantua* (1534), novels which continue their themes in *Tiers Livre* (1546), *Quart Livre* (1552) and *Cinquième Livre* (1564). In these satirical works, Pantagruel and Gargantua are presented as giants, symbols of the new faith in the moral and physical powers of man, king of the universe, in which Panurge makes his burlesque voyage through society and its institutions. Rabelais mocks the monastic ideal, the superstitious veneration of saints, old-fashioned education and university theology. A powerfully original writer, influenced by **Erasmus** and **Luther**, he ridicules both Catholics and Protestants, and defends liberal humanism and Gallicanism. Above all Rabelais was intoxicated with life and learning, and his work is foremost a paean to language, the inventiveness and richness of his vocabulary seemingly unequalled.

Rachis King of the Lombards, 744–9 and 756–7, died Monte Cassino, date unknown. As duke of Friuli, Rachis succeeded Liutprand in a kingdom centred in northern and central Italy, with outposts at Spoleto and Benevento. He favoured a policy of peace with the Papacy, and promoted its interests, in opposition to many Lombard nobles, who allied themselves with his brother **Aistulf**. They deposed Rachis in 749 in Aistulf's favour, and he retired to Monte Cassino; he regained the throne on his brother's death for a brief period.

Racine, Jean Baptiste French tragic dramatist, born La Ferté-Milon, baptized 22 December 1639, died Paris, 21 April 1699. Educated at the Jansenist schools of Port-Royal and Beauvais, Racine launched his theatrical career in Paris with *La Thébaïde*, presented by Molière's troupe, followed by *Alexandre*, both acclaimed by the public, but condemned by his former masters at Port-Royal. Racine responded to their criticisms with, from 1667 to 1677: *Andromaque, Les Plaideurs, Britannicus, Bérénice, Bajazet, Mithridate, Iphigénie* and *Phèdre*, in all of which he showed that tragedy could be a school of virtue, as it had been for the Greeks. He goes further than the heroic drama of **Corneille**, and presents passion as a truly tragic, blinding, uncontrollable, destructive force, associated with hatred, in the desire to possess the beloved. This original approach conformed to a pessimistic Jansenist outlook on the human condition, and it helped to reconcile him with Port-Royal. Faithful to his former masters with *Cantiques spirituels* (1694) and *Abrégé de l'histoire de Port-Royal*, Racine appears not only as the best disciple of Port-Royal, but as the veritable creator of French tragedy.

Raclot, Mathilde French missionary and educator, born Surauville (Vosges), 1814, died Tokyo, 1911. Mathilde joined the Sisters of the Holy Infant Jesus (Ladies of St Maur) at the age of eighteen, and distinguished herself as a teacher, before leaving with a group of the Sisters for Malaysia, where they devoted themselves, at Penang, to founding orphanages, nurseries and schools for the poor. She answered the call of the vicar apostolic and went to Japan in 1872, where she established houses at Tokyo in 1875 and Shizuoka in 1903.

Rad, Gerhard von German Old Testament scholar, born Nuremberg, the son of a distinguished psychiatrist, 21 October 1901, died Heidelberg, 31 October 1971. After studies at Erlangen and Tübingen he became a Lutheran pastor but, in reaction to the growing anti-Semitism in Germany, which was coupled with a rejection of the Old Testament, he decided to undertake further Scripture studies and took up teaching posts at Erlangen in 1929 and in 1930 at Leipzig. In 1934 he became a professor at Jena, although the majority of the faculty were sympathetic to the Nazis. He associated himself with the Confessing Church. He served in the German army during World War II, and was captured by US troops. After the war he became a professor at Göttingen in 1945 and at Heidelberg in 1949, where he remained for the rest of his life. As an exegete he was a proponent of historical criticism of the Old Testament, because he believed that this would help to reveal the underlying faith of the Israelite people. Among many other works he produced major commentaries on the books of Genesis (1949) and Deuteronomy (1964), and an enormously influential *Theology of the Old Testament*, volume 1, on the theology of the historical tradition, in 1957, and volume 2, on the prophetic tradition, three years later.

Radbod of Utrecht Saint, Frankish monk and bishop, born Namur, *c.*850, died Low Countries, 29 November 917. Educated at the court of **Charles II** the Bald, Radbod became a monk, taught the famous Abbot Hugo and, in 900, became bishop of Utrecht; the Normans drove him out the following year and he went to nearby Deventer, from where he carried on his diocesan duties. He furthered the Utrecht tradition for learning, wrote poetry, history and a work on St **Martin of Tours**; the Catholic University of Nijmegen bore his name until 1923. Renowned for charity and pastoral rule, Radbod tried to eradicate the traces of the Frisian pagans, of whom his great-grandfather had been the last king. Feast day 29 November.

Radegunda Saint, queen of the Franks (518–87), born Erfurt, date unknown, died Poitiers, 13 August 587. Born a Thuringian princess, Radegunda fell as booty, aged twelve, to Theodoric, king of Austrasia, and Clotaire I, king of Neustria, whom she married after six years of prayer in retirement. Clotaire led a dissolute life, and Radegunda left him in 555 after he murdered her brother, and founded with his help a convent at Poitiers, where she had gathered some 200 high-born converts by 587. Radegunda collected relics, notably one of the True Cross, which gave the name 'Holy Cross' to the convent; and, having installed an abbess, she lived as a simple nun in her community. She is said to have cured a blind man who attended her funeral, and her cult began immediately afterwards, bringing about her popular canonization. Feast day 13 August.

Raffeiner, John Stephen Austrian Roman Catholic missionary, born Mals (Tyrol), 26 December 1785, died Brooklyn, New York, 16 July 1861. Raffeiner abandoned the study of medicine for the priesthood, and went to New York in 1833 to establish German centres and churches throughout New York State. He founded some 30 churches, and became vicar general for the German population; he was much revered, and regarded as an apostle to the Germans.

Rahewin of Freising Frisian historian, date and place of birth unknown, died Freising(?) c.1170. Rahewin served as assistant, chaplain and notary to Bishop **Otto of Freising**, c.1144, and later became provost there of St Vitus. He is remembered for adding books 3 and 4 to Otto's *Gesta Frederici imperatoris*, taking forward the account to 1160. His *Dialogus de pontificatu sancte Romane ecclesie* served the political and ecclesiastical interests of **Alexander III**, and he wrote the highly regarded poems 'Theophilus' and 'De Deo et angelis'.

Rahlfs, Alfred German Lutheran scriptural scholar, born Linden, 29 May 1865, died Göttingen, 8 April 1935. Rahlfs spent most of his academic career at the University of Göttingen, where he devoted himself to editing a critical text of the Septuagint for the Akademie der Wissenschaft. Three volumes appeared: *Ruth*, *Genesis* and *Psalmis cum Odis*, as well as a two-volume edition for students using only the three basic codices (Vaticanus, Sinaiticus and Alexandrinus). His classification of the books of the Greek Septuagint was used in the 1955 edition of the Bible prepared by L'École Biblique de Jérusalem.

Rahmani (Ignatius Ephrem II) Patriarch of Antioch for Syrian Catholics, born Mossoul, 12 October 1848, died Cairo, 7 May 1929. Rahmani studied at the Syro-Chaldean Seminary under the Dominicans at Mossoul and, ordained in 1873, became patriarch in 1898. Though he kept good relations with the Holy See, France and Austria, he also came to terms with the Ottoman powers, and governed his community in the spirit of their decrees, while remaining faithful to Catholicism. Rahmani built churches, orphanages, seminaries and schools, and founded in 1901, at Harissa-Daroun, the Congregation of Ephremite Sisters. He set up a printing press with Arabic and Syriac characters at Charfeh, from where his linguistic and liturgical works made him widely known in the academic world.

Rahner, Hugo German Jesuit theologian, born Pfullendorf, 3 May 1900, died Munich, 21 December 1968. Older brother of Karl **Rahner**. He was professor of Church history and patrology at the University of Innsbruck from 1937 until his death. Rahner emphasizes the positive contribution to Christianity of the culture of Greece and Rome, while showing how the piety of the ancient world has been incorporated and sanctified in the Church (*Greek Myths and Christian Mystery*). This effort of synthesis aims to reach what he calls the theology of the heart (*theologia cordis*), as in *Our Lady and the Church*, where he develops the theme of Mary as a symbol of the Church. However, Rahner's theology of the heart is also pastoral: his view of the chief role of the priestly vocation (*Theology of Proclamation*) is that it is 'the reconstruction of our traditional knowledge, fashioning out of our dogmatic theology what can be of immediate use in performing the great work to which we are called – preaching'. As an historian, Rahner was concerned especially to throw light on the real **Ignatius of Loyola** and his spirituality, to which end he published authoritative works: *Ignatius Loyola and the Historical Consequence of his Piety* and *Ignatius Loyola, the Man and the Theologian*.

Rahner, Karl German Jesuit theologian, born Freiburg im Breisgau, 5 March 1904, died Innsbruck, 30 March 1984. Younger brother of Hugo **Rahner** joined the theological faculty of Innsbruck in 1936, and was later professor at Munich and at Münster. His thought largely developed from Joseph **Maréchal**'s *Le Point de départ de la métaphysique*, and he expounded his basic position in *Geist in Welt* (1939), in which man, as incarnate spirit, can come explicitly to accept Christ, since he is necessarily open to the presence of God, whom he implicitly discovers in his acts of knowing, willing and loving. Indeed, all men are 'anonymously Christian', a concept which defends the uniqueness and necessity of Christ, while admitting, with Vatican II, the real possibility of salvation for non-Christians in their freely given response to the grace communicated by God, through Christ; since these persons do not recognize the character of the grace received, it can be called 'anonymous'. Rahner's theory is developed also to cover the situation of those who have no real contact with religion; they can have anonymous faith arising out of love, and so come to salvation. Named a *peritus* at the Second Vatican Council, Rahner was hugely influential in all areas, and the council documents contain many Rahnerian themes. He is considered one of the major theologians of the twentieth century; he marked in a decisive way most of the questions debated in the Catholic Church during the period of Vatican II, in that which preceded and prepared it, as well as in that which followed and exploited it.

Raikes, Robert English founder of Sunday Schools, born Gloucester, 14 September 1735, died Gloucester, 5 April 1811. Raikes succeeded his father as owner and printer of the *Gloucester Journal* and, having become aware of the lack of any religious training for poor children, he started a Sunday School at Gloucester in 1780. He gave the enterprise publicity in his journal and in the London papers, which awakened considerable interest. For nearly 30 years he continued actively to promote this undertaking, and lived to witness its wide extension throughout England. His statue stands on the Thames Embankment.

Raimondi, Luigi Italian cardinal and theologian, born Lussito d'Acqui, 25 October 1912, died Rome, 24 June 1975. Ordained in 1936, Raimondi was named by **Paul VI** as apostolic delegate in Washington, where he ordained 22 bishops, and oversaw the creation of twelve new dioceses and three archdioceses. His tenure found him dealing with the tensions confronting the Roman Catholic Church as it sought its way through the immediate post-conciliar era. Paul made him a cardinal and appointed him prefect of the Sacred Congregation for Saints' Causes.

Raimondi, Pietro Italian composer, Vatican musician, born Rome, 20 December 1786, died Rome, 30 October 1853. Raimondi presented his opera buffa *Le Bizzarie d'amore* in 1807; this was followed by 60 operas and 21 ballets. In 1852 he succeeded Basili as *maestro di capella* at St Peter's,

where he composed many works for massed choirs. His music, however, has not survived the decline of the Romantic influence.

Rainald of Bar Blessed, abbot of Cîteaux, date and place of birth unknown, died Provence, 1150. From the family of the counts of Bar-sur-Seine, Rainald joined the Cistercians at Clairvaux, and St **Bernard** nominated him abbot of Cîteaux in 1133. Rainald helped to repair the rift that had developed between Bernard and **Abelard**. His only extant work is part of the *Instituta generalis capituli*, a collection of statutes published by his successor, Goswin, about 1150. Feast day 16 December.

Rainald of Dassel archbishop of Cologne (1159–67), born *c.*1118, died 14 August 1167. The younger son of the Saxon count Rainald I, Rainald showed himself an ardent supporter of imperial power, particularly of **Frederick I Barbarossa**, at the expense of the Papacy. He became Chancellor in 1156 and remained a militant statesman, supporting the Antipopes Victor IV and Paschal III against **Alexander III**, a mistake that resulted in his excommunication in 1163. He died on a campaign in Italy.

Rainald of Ravenna Blessed, Italian archbishop, born Milan, *c.*1250, died Ravenna, 18 August 1321. **Boniface VIII** entrusted Rainald with several important missions: bishop of Vicenza; legate on a peace mission to England and France, 1299; director of spiritual affairs in the Romagna, and archbishop of Ravenna, 1302; papal commissioner for the investigation of the Knights Templar in central and northern Italy. **Pius IX** beatified him in 1852. Feast day 18 August.

Rainaldi, Carlo Italian architect of the baroque period, born Rome, 5 May 1611, died Rome, 8 February 1691. Rainaldi collaborated with his father, Girolamo, also an architect of renown, on the design of S. Agnese at the Piazza Navona. After Girolamo's death, he worked in the high baroque style, and created the brilliant church of Santa Maria in Campitelli, noted for its original use of space and light effects; the façade of Sant Andrea della Valle; and the twin churches at the Piazza del Popolo, which served as the monumental north gateway to Rome.

Rainerius of Pomposa Italian Benedictine monk at the beginning of the thirteenth century. Nothing is known of his life. Rainerius dedicated to one John, a member of the papal household (*capellans papae*), a collection of decretals of **Innocent III**, compiled in 1201 from papal registers and comprising 123 decretal letters, most of them dating from the first three years of Innocent's pontificate; the only extant manuscript is in the abbey of St-Thierry, near Rheims.

Rale, Sebastian French Jesuit missionary, born Pontarlier, 4 January 1657, died Norridgewok, Maine, 23 August 1724. Rale went to the Abenaki Indian village near Quebec in 1689 and, in 1694, to the Abenakis in Maine on the Kennebec River, where he remained 30 years. He became involved, however, in the Anglo-French conflict for control of Maine, his sympathies being with the French. Rale was blamed for the failure of conferences and treaties to settle the conflict, and English soldiers, contrary to orders, killed Rale in a raid at Norridgewok. A monument to him stands in Boston.

Ralph de Turbine (Ralph d'Escures) French archbishop of Canterbury, date and place of birth unknown, died 20 October 1122. Ralph became abbot of St-Martin at Séez in 1089, and in 1100 fled to England, where he passed some time with St **Anselm** and Gundulf, whom he succeeded in 1108 as bishop of Rochester. Ralph succeeded to Canterbury in 1114, after Anselm died. He claimed authority in Wales and Scotland, and refused to consecrate **Thurston** at York because the latter declined to profess obedience to Canterbury. This involved him in a quarrel with **Paschal II** and his successors, **Gelasius II** and **Calixtus II**, but Ralph still refused to consecrate Thurston, and the dispute was unsettled when he died.

Ralph (Ranulf) Higden English Benedictine chronicler, born West Country, *c.*1280, died 12 March 1364. A monk of St Werbergh's Abbey, Chester, from 1292, Ralph travelled much in England and is remembered for his *Polychronicon*, a universal history of knowledge, geography and science, in which he cites some 40 authorities, divided into seven books, after the seven days of the Creation. More than 100 MSS survive, and it was enormously popular, considered a standard work for more than 200 years.

Ralph of Caen French historian of the Crusades, born Caen, *c.*1080, died after 1131. Educated under Arnulf of Rohez, Ralph is best known for his original and lively *Gesta Tancredi*, an account of the Norman contributions to the Crusades, much influenced by Virgil, Homer, Caesar and Cicero, in a mixture of prose and verse. Ralph had served with Bohemund of Tarentum and with Tancred, and the narration bears the stamp of authenticity, as coming from the pen of an eyewitness.

Ralph of Coggeshall English Cistercian abbot, born Bernewell, Cambridgeshire, date unknown, died Coggeshall, *c.*1227. Ralph became abbot of Coggeshall in 1207. After his resignation in 1218, he continued a *Chronicon Anglicanum* begun at the monastery in 1066; his own part covers the period 1187 to 1224, and is a valuable source for King **Richard I** (the Lionheart) and the Crusades, and the last years of King John. Ralph also continued the Chronicle of Ralph Niger, extending it from 1162 to 1178, and wrote short annals for 1066 to 1223.

Ralph of Diceto Angevin historian and theologian, born *c.*1120, died 22 November 1202. Ralph became archdeacon of London in 1152, and dean of St Paul's Cathedral in 1180. One of the outstanding personalities of the late twelfth century, he completely overhauled the administration of the chapter's churches and manors, reformed the statutes and undertook a rigorous building programme. He wrote historical works: *Abbreviationes chronicorum* and *Yruagines historiarum*, a contemporary chronicle of great value for its political insights and careful choice of documents.

Ralph of Selkirk Second abbot of Tiron, died 1118. A monk of the reformed Benedictine Order of Tiron; a marginal note in the Melrose Chronicle records, 'Ralph, sent from Tiron, became the first abbot of Selkirk' (Selkirk was the first daughter-house of the Order of Tiron). After the death of **Bernard of Tiron**, the founder of the Order, Ralph – perhaps because of the influence of King **David I** of Scotland – was elected to succeed him, but he served for only two years.

Ralph Strode English Scholastic philosopher and logician, dates of birth and death unknown. A contemporary of John **Wycliffe**, from whose *Responsiones ad Rodolphum Strodum*, Strode appears to have argued against predestination, and to have supported the endowments of the Church. Only two of his works survive: *Consequentiae*, on the syllogism, and *Obligations*, on Scholastic dialectic, which were both published in Italy. **Chaucer** dedicated his *Troilus and Criseyde* jointly to the poet **Gower** and to 'the philosophical Strode'.

Ralph Tortarius French Latin poet, born Gien-sur-Loire, *c.*1063, died after 1117. Ralph joined the Benedicines at Saint-Benoît-sur-Loire, and is known as the author of the section 1031 to 1114 of the *History of the Miracles of St Benedict*, a work begun in the ninth century. He also wrote poetry filled with vivid accounts of social life and descriptions of the countryside. Raby considered him one of the best twelfth-century poets, interested, like the others, in the secular themes that flourished in that century, even the gross and the obscene.

Ram, Pierre François Xavier de Belgian churchman and historian, born Louvain, 2 September 1804, died Louvain, 14 May 1865. Professor at Malines immediately before the revolution of 1830, and much influenced by Félicité de **Lamennais**, Ram tried to bring about a coalition of Liberals and Catholics against the Dutch government established by the Great Powers on the fall of Napoleon Bonaparte, and to give a democratic character to the policy of the Church. While at Malines, he succeeded in bringing about the foundation of the Catholic University, transferred to Louvain in 1834.

Ramabai, Pandita Indian poet, scholar and reformer, born Karnataka, 1858, died 5 April 1922. She was born into a wealthy Brahmin family and her father ensured that his wife and daughters were educated in the classic works in Sanskrit. Her family perished in the famine of the 1870s and Pandita, still in her teens, fended for herself, travelling across India to the sacred shrines and sites and reciting Sanskrit poetry to the gathered crowds. She married but was soon widowed and left with a young child and no status. She embarked on her life's work, opening welfare and education centres and campaigning to improve the political situation of widows and of women in general. She was invited to England by a congregation of Anglican nuns and while there she converted to Christianity. She returned to India and continued her work, extending it to unmarried mothers and young girls. She was criticized by Hindus for denying her roots and by Christians because she did not have the conversion of the people she worked with as a major priority. She had little time for the denominational infighting between Christians and centred her life on the Jesus of the Bible rather than on ecclesiastical dogmas.

Rambert of Bologna Italian Dominican theologian and bishop, born Bologna, 1250, died Venice, 8 November 1308. Rambert studied at Paris during St **Thomas Aquinas**' second term in the university, 1269–72. He himself taught there from 1290 to 1299, when he returned to Bologna and became bishop of Castello, until his death. An early defender of Thomas's teaching, in his *Apologeticum veritatis contra corruptorium* he refuted the charges brought by William de la Mare's *Correctorium fratis Thomae* and, though incomplete, it is evidence of early Dominican allegiance to St Thomas's teachings.

Ramírez, Santiago Spanish Dominican, born Sauriano, 25 July 1891, died Salamanca, 18 December 1967. For 22 years Ramírez taught moral theology at Fribourg, and is regarded as among the great commentators on St **Thomas Aquinas**' works; during 1933–5, he opposed Jacques **Maritain** on the status of Christian Scholastic philosophy. Deeply involved in contemporary issues, he wrote a renowned work on Ortega y Gasset: *La filiosofia de Ortega y Gasset*. Ramirez served as a *peritus* at Vatican II, during which he wrote *De episcopatu*, on the bishop's place in the Church, and on collegiality.

Ramírez de Fuenleal, Sebastián Spanish Jesuit, bishop, born Cuenca, date unknown, died Valladolid, 22 January 1547. Ramírez went to Santo Domingo in 1527 as bishop elect, and governed with great prudence and integrity, highly regarded by his contemporaries. In 1531, **Charles V** appointed him president of the second 'audiencia' in Mexico, then in a chaotic state as a result of the arbitrary actions of his predecessors on that tribunal. He returned to Spain about 1535 as bishop of Twy, then of León in 1539 and Cuenca in 1542.

Ramos Arizpe, Miguel Mexican Roman Catholic priest and politician, born Coahuila, 15 February 1775, died Mexico City, 28 April 1843. Ordained in 1803, Ramos Arizpe represented Coahuila in the Spanish Cortes, became a Mason in Cadiz, and adopted liberalism. He was accused of conspiracy and arrested on the order of Ferdinand VII, but the successful Liberal revolution of 1820 gave him his freedom; in 1821, he arrived in Tampico and engaged in Masonic propaganda, as well as in conspiracy against Iturbide. When the latter was overthrown and the Republic established, Ramos Arizpe became a leader of the federalist party and a major contributor to the constitution.

Rampolla del Tindaro, Mariano Sicilian cardinal, born Polizzi, 17 August 1843, died Rome, 16 December 1913. **Leo XIII** made Rampolla, ordained in 1866, cardinal and secretary of state in 1887, and he oriented papal diplomacy towards an understanding with France and Russia, in opposition to the Triple Alliance (Italy, Germany, Austria-Hungary). This policy, and his support for democratic and social aspirations, attracted the hostility of Austria, manifest during the conclave following Leo's death. Rampolla obtained 29 of 62 votes; however, the Polish cardinal, Puzyna, declared that Emperor Franz Joseph would veto his election. The intervention caused a scandal, and on the next vote Rampolla obtained 30 votes, but his election could not go forward, because of determined opposition; a majority of cardinals formed around Guiseppe Sarto, who became **Pius X**.

Ramsey, Arthur Michael Archbishop of Canterbury, born Cambridge, 14 November 1904, died Oxford, 23 April 1988. Ramsey became the one hundredth archbishop of Canterbury, in 1961. He wished to be an apostle for the unity of Christians, to improve relations between Church and State, and to lead the Church to an engagement in the world as one that listens and teaches. In 1966, **Paul VI** received him warmly and, in a highly symbolic gesture for relations between the two Churches,

slipped his own episcopal ring on Ramsey's finger. From this meeting was born the Anglican–Roman Catholic International Commission (ARCIC), charged with studying the points of convergence, as well as discord, between the Churches, with a view to coming together in stages. The Commission reached 'substantial agreement' in its reports in 1982 on the Eucharist and on Ministry and Ordination, but only 'convergence' on Authority. A second commission, ARCIC II, submitted a report in 1999 that tackled the thorny issues of papal primacy and the infallibility of the college of bishops. The foundation of Ramsey's ecumenical ecclesiology was laid in his *The Gospel and the Catholic Church* (1936), and his many subsequent books each took up and developed one or other aspect. Ramsey envisaged the Anglican Church as a stage towards the universal Church to which all Churches must belong, a return to the source of unity which is the Gospel.

Ramus, Peter (Pierre de la Ramée) French humanist, born Cuts (Oise), 1515, died Paris, 26 August 1572. Ramus studied at Paris, where he joined in the reaction against Scholasticism, going so far as to write for a master's thesis 'Everything that Aristotle taught is false.' He followed this up by the publication of *Aristotelicae animadversiones* and *Dialecticae partitiones*, the former a criticism of the old logic, and the latter a new textbook of the science, proposed by himself. In 1551 Henry II appointed him a professor at the Collège de France, where he was hugely popular. In 1561 he became a Calvinist and had to leave France, returning only to fall victim to his opponents in the Massacre of St Bartholomew's Day.

Rancé, Armand Jean Le Bouthillier de Abbot, founder of the Trappist Cistercians, born Paris, 9 January 1626, died La Trappe, 27 October 1700. At the age of ten Rance became commendatory abbot of La Trappe, and a canon of Notre Dame, Paris; at twelve he published a translation of Anacreon. He studied theology with great distinction, defeating **Bossuet** at the baccalaureat. Ordained in 1651, he embarked on a worldly career at the court of **Louis XIV**. After a few years, however, he underwent a complete change of life, retired to his abbey of La Trappe in 1662, and there introduced the most austere reforms. He denied that monks should devote themselves to study and maintained, instead, that they should consider themselves criminals doomed to a life of severity, subject to humiliations created by the abbot, and practise austerity even at the cost of ruined health. He resigned his abbacy in 1695, because of his own declining health.

Ranke, Leopold von German historian, born Wiehe, 21 December 1795, died Berlin, 23 May 1886. A Lutheran, a student of theology and classical philology, Ranke turned to history, and by 1818 had moved to a synthesis of Lutheran mysticism, Neoplatonism and humanism (Goethe and **Herder**). He set a pattern for the importance of the study of original sources, by a fundamentally objective attitude to history, history 'as it actually happened'. He was the most influential and widely read historian of his century, the 'Columbus of modern history', as Lord **Acton** termed him. His most famous work, *History of the Popes during the Sixteenth and Seventeenth Centuries*, removed the Papacy from denominational polemics, and showed the development of papal power, stressing its political rather than religious significance; it was placed on the Index in 1841.

Ranson, Charles Wesley General secretary of the International Missionary Council, born Ballyclare, Ireland, 15 June 1903, died Lakeville, Connecticut, 13 January 1988. He studied at Edgehill Theological College, Queen's University, Belfast, and Oriel College, Oxford, before being ordained in 1929 and sent as a Methodist missionary to India. He was secretary of the National Christian Council of India, Burma and Ceylon, 1943–5, and published *The Christian Minister in India* (1945). He became research secretary of the International Missionary Council in 1946, and then general secretary. He was founding director of the Theological Education Fund, 1958–63, and president of the Irish Methodist Conference, 1961–2. He taught at Drew University, 1962–8, and at Hartford Seminary, 1968–72, and then pastored the Congregational Church, Salisbury, Connecticut, until he retired in 1975. His autobiography, *A Missionary Pilgrimage*, was published in 1988.

Raphael (Hawaweeny) Orthodox missionary bishop, born Damascus, Syria, 8 November 1860,

died New York, 27 February 1915. Educated at Constantinople and Kiev, he was sent to care for Arabic-speaking Orthodox of the Russian diocese. He established many parishes and was eventually consecrated assistant bishop for Brooklyn. He is regarded by 'Antiochian' Americans as their founding father. His canonization is now being prepared.

Raphael (Raffaello Sanzio) Most famous of the Renaissance painters, born Urbino, 16 April 1483, died Rome, 6 April 1520. Raphael first studied with his father, Giovanni Santi, worked under Perugino at Perugia and painted the *Crucifixion* (National Gallery, London), then moved to Florence in 1505, where he quickly absorbed the influence of **Leonardo**, **Michelangelo** and Fra **Bartolommeo**, and painted the *Madonna del Granduca* (Pitti, Florence) and the *Ansidei Madonna* (National Gallery). **Julius II** summoned him to Rome in 1508 to decorate the Vatican 'Stanze'. **Leo X** commissioned him to design a set of ten tapestries for the Sistine Chapel (Raphael Tapestries), of which seven cartoons are in the Victoria and Albert Museum, London; also the *Disputa* and *St Peter Released from Prison*, the celebrated *Sistine Madonna* (Dresden), and *Madonna della Sedia* (Pitti). In 1514 Leo appointed him to succeed **Bramante** as chief architect of St Peter's.

Rapin, René French Jesuit theologian, born Tours, 3 November 1621, died Paris, 27 October 1687. Rapin wrote many theological and ascetical works, such as *L'Esprit du christianisme*, *La Perfection du christianisme* and *La Foi des derniers siècles*. He is remembered especially, however, for the strong stand he took against Jansenism; his *Histoire du Jansenisme*, and *Mémoires sur l'Église, la société, la cour, la ville et le Jansenisme* are important for the information they provide regarding the early phase of the Jansenist crisis in France.

Rapp, Johann Georg German founder of the Harmony Society, born Iplinger, 1 November 1757, died Economy, USA, 7 August 1847. Deeply influenced by J. **Böhme**, P. J. **Spener** and other German mystical theologians, Rapp gathered some followers into a spiritual family and founded the Harmony Society at Harmony, Butler County,

Pennsylvania. All goods were held in common, and celibacy enforced. The community moved to New Harmony in 1814, and to Economy, near Pittsburgh, in 1825. Rapp's eclectic theology was expounded in his *Thoughts on the Destiny of Man* (1824).

Rasputin, Grigori Efimovich Russian religious figure, born Pokrovskoe, Siberia, *c.*1871, died Petrograd, 16 December 1916. Of little education, Rasputin left his wife and children in 1904 to become a religious pilgrim. He joined the Khlysty sect (People of God), which combined emotional religion with sexual licence, and the name 'Rasputin' (debauched) began to be applied to him at this time, but he also gained credence as a faith healer. Introduced to the royal family in 1907, he seemed at first to be able to cure the Tsarevitch Alexis of haemophilia. Both **Nicholas II** and Empress Alexandra regarded him as a friend and saviour of the dynasty, even accepting his advice on matters of state, which favouritism only widened the gap between them and the people. A group of nobles assassinated Rasputin in an effort to save the monarchy. He was interred with solemnity on Alexandra's orders, but a mob dug up his cadaver after the Revolution and burned it.

Rassler, Christoph German Jesuit theologian, born Constance, 12 August 1654, died Rome, 16 July 1723. Rassler taught at Ingolstadt and Dillingen for 30 years from 1685, before going to Rome as revisor general. Deeply engaged in the theological disputes of his day, he adopted a moderate position in the controversy over the rectitude of following a merely probable moral opinion, against the extremes of rigorism and laxism; in *Norma recti* (1713), he proposed what became termed 'equiprobabilism', a theory which apparently influenced Eusebius **Amort**, to whom St **Alphonsus Liguori** acknowledged indebtedness in his later development of the theory.

Rastell, John English printer, brother-in-law of St Thomas **More**, born Coventry, 1475, died London, 1536. Rastell entered the Middle Temple before 1500, married Elizabeth More, and settled in London, where he added printing to his legal work; his printed books include More's *Pico* and **Linacre**'s *Latin Grammar*. John **Frith** influenced him

to adopt Lutheran ideas, and he campaigned against tithes. In spite of his friendship with Thomas **Cromwell**, he died in prison.

Rastell, William Nephew of Thomas **More**, born London, 1508, died Louvain, 1565. A printer like his father, John **Rastell**, he published his uncle's controversial writings. William studied law at Lincoln's Inn, became a judge of the Queen's Bench in 1558 under **Mary Tudor**, and published More's 'English Works'. Exiled by **Elizabeth I** to Louvain, he wrote a Life of Thomas More and published his Latin works.

Ratherius of Verona Belgian Benedictine bishop, born near Liège, *c.*890, died Namur, 25 April 974. A man of fractious and ambitious character, well read in the classics, Ratherius played a prominent part in the ecclesiastical life of the century. In 926 he accompanied his abbot, Hilduin, to Italy, where the king, Hugo of Provence, Hilduin's cousin, made him bishop of Verona, but he antagonized Hugo and had to vacate his see. Made bishop of Liège in 953, he had to resign in 955, but regained the See of Verona in 962, until 968. A writer and theologian, his most important work is *Praeliquia*, a guide to right living, and his other writings, often full of invective, throw meaningful light on his age.

Ratichius *see* **Ratke, Wolfgang.**

Ratisbonne, Marie Alphonse Religious founder, born Strasburg, 1 May 1814, died Ain Karim, 6 May 1884. From a Jewish family, he became a Catholic in 1827, and joined the Society of Jesus, which he left after ordination, and went to Palestine in 1855, where he laboured among both Jews and Muslims. To further this work of conversion, he and his brother (see below) founded the Congregation of Notre Dame de Sion for women in 1843, and the Fathers of Sion in 1852; he also founded, for the Sisters of Sion, the Ecce Homo Monastery in Palestine, and later opened two orphanages. Since the Second Vatican Council, the role of the Order has shifted from conversion of Jews to world-wide dialogue with the Jewish faith.

Ratisbonne, Marie Theodore Co-founder of the Congregation of Notre Dame de Sion and the Fathers of Sion, born Strasburg, 28 December

1802, died Paris, 10 January 1884. Brother of Marie Alphonse **Ratisbonne**. Converted to Catholicism from Judaism in 1827 after studying the Bible and Church history, ordained in 1830, Théodore sought to promote understanding between Christians and Jews, and to bring about the conversion of Jews. Among his numerous writings are *Histoire de St Bernard et de son siècle, La question Juive* and *Manuel de la mère chrétienne*.

Ratke, Wolfgang (Ratichius)   German educationist, born Wilster, Schleswig-Holstein, 18 October 1571, died Erfurt, 27 April 1635. Educated at Rostock for the Lutheran ministry, Ratke turned to education and developed a system based upon Francis **Bacon**'s principles of induction, the premiss being that of 'proceeding from things to names', from the particular to the general, and from the mother tongue to foreign languages. In 1618 he opened schools at Augsburg and elsewhere, but they had failed by 1620 and he became a wanderer until his death. His ideas were far in advance of his time, and he lacked executive ability to implement them.

Ratramnus of Corbie   French theological controversialist, date and place of birth unknown, died Corbie, *c*.825. Ratramnus entered the Benedictine abbey of Corbie, near Amiens, but otherwise little is known of his life. His best-known writing is a treatise on the Eucharist, *De corpore et sanguine Domini liber*, in which, seeking to reconcile science and religion, he controverts the doctrine of transubstantiation as taught by his contemporary **Paschasius Radbertus**. Ratramnus' views failed to find acceptance, their author was soon forgotten, and the work was condemned at the Synod of Vercelli in 1050. He perhaps won most fame in his own day for *Contra Graecorum opposita*, a valued contribution to the controversy between the Eastern and Western Churches that had been raised by the publication of the encyclical letter of **Photius** in 867.

Rattigan, Bernard T.   American Roman Catholic priest and educator, born Boston, 3 November 1908, died Brighton, Massachusetts, 11 October 1963. Ordained in 1933, Rattigan studied at the Catholic University of America and taught there until 1962, when he became director of the Confraternity of Christian Doctrine in the Archdiocese of Boston. His special field was the philosophy of education, in which he expressed a strongly Thomistic viewpoint.

Rausch, James   American Roman Catholic bishop, born Albany, Minnesota, 4 September 1928, died Phoenix, Arizona, 18 May 1981. Ordained in the Diocese of St Cloud, Minnesota, in 1956, Rausch became involved in the Justice and Peace Commission of the United States Catholic Conference, before being made an auxiliary bishop of St Cloud. He spoke extensively on the role of the Church in the areas of civil and human rights, political involvement in moral concerns, and the role of the laity in both political and ecclesiastical life. A leading figure in the 'Call to Action' convention of the Catholic laity in Detroit in 1979, he met opposition from the conservative wing of the Church. As bishop of Phoenix from 1977, he championed the cause of the underprivileged, again alienating the conservative and affluent faction. Recognized as prophetic in the diocese, he was ahead of his time in the exercise of the episcopal office.

Rauschen, Gerhard   German patrologist and Church historian, born Heinsberg, 13 October 1854, died Bonn, 12 April 1917. Rauschen studied theology and classical philology at Bonn and Freiburg and became professor of Church history at Bonn in 1902, where he published a manual of patrology, and studies on the Eucharist and penance in the early Church. In 1904 he began the series Florilegium Patristicum, for which he edited eleven works, among them works on Vincent of Lérins, **Justin Martyr** and **Tertullian**.

Rauschenbusch, Walter   American Baptist theologian and chief exponent of the 'Social Gospel', born Rochester, New York, 4 October 1861, died Rochester, 25 July 1918. Rauschenbusch served as pastor of the Second German Baptist Church, New York, where he became deeply concerned with urban problems. From this experience and his reading of Henry George, Tolstoy, Marx, Bellamy and Beatrice and Sydney Webb, came *Christianity and the Social Crisis*, which established him as leader of the Social Gospel movement, challenging the individualism and pietism of nineteenth-century American Protestantism. He preached the

'Kingdom of God', a theme which emphasized social transformation and economic betterment as the purpose for which the Church exists, and rejected un-Christian elements, e.g. competition, monopoly, the concentration of economic power, and the profit motive.

Rauscher, Joseph Othman von Austrian cardinal, born Vienna, 6 October 1797, died there, 24 November 1875. Rauscher studied at Vienna, became professor of theology at Salzburg in 1832, director of the Oriental Academy and adviser for religious affairs to the government, in which capacity he negotiated the terms under which the Jesuits were permitted to work in Austria-Hungary. As bishop of Seckau in 1849, he played an important role in the agreement abolishing Josephinism, and the Emperor Franz Joseph's concordat of 1855. Rauscher opposed the definition of papal infallibility, as well as its presentation, at Vatican Council I. When he could not prevent the definition, he left Rome before the final vote on the decree, though he allowed its publication in his diocese in 1870.

Rautenstrauch, Franz Stephan Hungarian Benedictine, a central figure in Josephinism, born Blottendorf, 26 July 1734, died Erlaw, 30 September 1785. Rautenstrauch joined the Benedictines in 1750, became abbot at Braunau in 1773, and a favourite of Empress Maria Theresa, who obliged the archbishop of Prague to accept Rautenstrauch's *Prolegomenain jus ecclesiasticum*, a work the prelate had already condemned for its teaching that Church was subordinate to State. In 1776, **Joseph II** decreed that only theological matters contained in Rautenstrauch's *Synopsis juris ecclesiastici publici et privati* might be taught; as this book had suppressed fundamental truths such as papal infallibility and primacy, as well as the Immaculate Conception of Mary, they could no longer be taught.

Ravalli, Antonio Italian Jesuit missionary, born Ferrara, 16 May 1812, died Stevensville, Montana, 2 October 1884. Ravalli studied medicine and acquired mechanical skills as preparation for the missions; in 1843 he accompanied Pierre **De Smet** to the Kalispel Indian and St Mary's Mission territories in Montana, and then among the Coeur

d'Atenes of Idaho. He worked among the Indians for almost 40 years, using his medical skills and building a flour mill, sawmill and a church, which he adorned with his own wood carvings. He was held in great esteem, rivalled only by De Smet's, and the Indians at St Mary's buried him in their own cemetery there. He is commemorated in Montana by a station bearing his name on the Northern Pacific Railroad near Missoula.

Ravanello, Oreste Italian composer and organ virtuoso, born Venice, 25 August 1871, died Padua, 1 July 1938. Appointed organist at St Mark's, Venice, in 1893, Ravanello, together with Lorenzo Perosi, furthered the reforms of Patriarch Sarto (St **Pius X**); he succeeded Tebaldini at St Anthony's, Padua, in 1898, and became director of the Instituto Musicale in 1914. His compositions numbered 225, including 32 Masses, the popular *St Calasanctus*, a Requiem, motets and various string and piano works. He was much influenced by **Palestrina**, J. S. **Bach** and Debussy.

Ravaschieri, Balthasar Blessed, Italian Franciscan, born Chiaveri, 1419, died Briasco, 17 October 1492. Of a noble family, Ravaschieri's aunts, both Franciscan tertiaries, provided a sense of piety and morality in his life after his father's death. He entered a friary of Franciscan Observants, and in 1478 met Bernardine of Feltre, whose friend and associate he became. Until afflicted with a crippling case of gout, which he saw as a means of drawing closer to God, he continued to preach and hear confessions. A cult, begun at his death, was confirmed in 1930, for the Franciscans, Pavia and Genoa. Feast day 17 October.

Ravignan, Gustave François Xavier de French Jesuit, born Bayonne, 1 December 1795, died Paris, 26 February 1858. Ravignan gained an impressive reputation as a preacher of missions and retreats, and fame for his Lenten sermons at Amiens and St Thomas d'Aquin in Paris. In 1836, he succeeded **Lacordaire** at Notre-Dame de Paris, where he attracted immense congregations by his oratory and commanding presence, winning many converts from the intelligentsia. Much sought after as a spiritual guide, he became known as 'the spiritual father of his generation'. He also wrote in defence of the Society: *De l'existence et de l'institut des*

Jésuites, a study which brought to light the anti-Jesuit bias which had led to their suppression. in the eighteenth century.

Ravoux, Augustin French Roman Catholic priest and missionary, born Langeac, 11 January 1815, died St Paul, Minnesota, 17 January 1906. Ravoux volunteered for missionary work in the Upper Mississippi in 1838; the first priest to serve the area in 100 years, he learned the language of the Dakotas, wrote *The Path to the House of God*, a devotional work in their tongue, and became pastor, 1844–51, of that extensive territory. After the Sioux uprising, he helped in setting up the Diocese of St Paul in 1851, and became vicar general, 1857–9. In retirement in St Paul, he wrote several works on his life and times as a missionary.

Raymond Martini Spanish Dominican theologian and orientalist, born Subirats, Catalonia, *c.*1220, died Barcelona, 1285. Raymond taught in the Dominican schools of Hebrew studies at Barcelona, and of Arabic studies at Tunis, founded to Christianize North African Muslims and Spanish Jews. An adviser to **Louis IX** of France on his crusade against Tunis, Raymond also acted as censor of books for Aragon under **James I**. His best-known work, *Pugio fidei* (1278), is based on Islamic and Hebrew works and the *Summa contra Gentiles* of St **Thomas Aquinas**.

Raymond Nonnatus Saint, Spanish Mercedarian, born Portello, *c.*1204, died Cardona, 31 August 1240. Raymond's surname derives from his reputed birth by Caesarean section after his mother's death. He joined the Mercedarian Order *c.*1224, and is credited with noteworthy activity in ransoming captives in Moorish North Africa and in Spain. The details of Raymond's life are not well authenticated, the earliest Life written long after his death. He is the patron of midwives, of mothers in labour and of the innocent charged with crime. A painting of him preaching, by Carlo Saraceni (1585–1625), is in St Adrian's Church, Rome. Feast day 31 August.

Raymond of Agiles French historian, flourished late eleventh century. He wrote *Historia Francorum qui ceperunt Jerusalem*, a major chronicle of the First Crusade, on which he accompanied his bishop, **Adhemar of Puy**. He became chaplain to Count **Raymond IV of Toulouse**, and recounts details concerning the visions of Peter Bartholomew and the finding of the Holy Lance, the authenticity of which Raymond defends, even claiming to have touched it before it was removed from the ground where it had been buried, a narrative that has been questioned.

Raymond of Capua Blessed, Italian Dominican, born Capua, *c.*1330, died Nuremberg, Germany, 5 October 1399. Raymond became a Dominican and spiritual director of St **Catherine of Siena**, together with whom he tried to reconcile Florence and the Tuscan League with the Papacy; he also worked with Catherine at Avignon in 1376 to return **Gregory XI** to Rome and end the schism. His *Legenda* (1477) is important on Catherine's life and spirituality; he wrote a Life of St Agnes of Montepulciano, whom he knew in 1363, and a treatise on the *Magnificat*. **Leo XIII** confirmed his cult in 1899. Feast day 5 October.

Raymond of Fitero Saint, Spanish Cistercian abbot, died probably before 1161. Known in Spain as 'Raimondo Serra'. He entered the Cistercian Order in France, but soon participated in the foundation at Fitero in 1140, where he became abbot. King Sancho III of Castile accepted Raymond's offer to defend Calatrava against the Moors in 1158, and granted the fortress to him. Raymond made it into a monastery, to where he transferred his monks, welcoming warriors who offered their help, or who wished to take the habit; thus was created the Order of Calatrava, which received papal approval in 1164. He was never formally canonized; his remains are in the cathedral of Toledo. Feast day 15 March.

Raymond of Peñafort Saint, Spanish Dominican canonist, born Vilafranca del Penedès, *c.*1175, died Barcelona, 6 January 1275. Raymond joined the Dominicans in 1221, and wrote his most influential work, *Summa de casibus*, a systematic treatment of doctrinal and canonical questions for confessors; **Gregory IX** then called him to Rome as his confessor. Elected third master general in 1238, he resigned in 1240 to return to Spain and an apostolate to the Jews and Moors, writing, preaching and working against heresy and Islam. Feast day 23 January.

Raymond of Roda-Barbastro Saint, Spanish monk, died Huesca, 21 June 1126. Prior of the monastery of St Saturninus in Toulouse, Raymond became bishop of Roda, and of Barbastro, in northern Aragon. Famed as a zealous bishop of outstanding personal virtue, he was driven from his see in the political turmoil of the time, despite the intervention of **Paschal II**. Raymond accompanied Alfonse I of Castile on his Cutanda campaign, and his expedition to Malaga; on his return journey he fell ill and died. Alfonso later restored Barbastro to the jurisdiction of Roda. Feast day 21 June.

Raymond of Sebonde Spanish philosopher, born Barcelona, date unknown, died Toulouse, 29 April 1436. Raymond's only work, *Liber naturae sive creaturarum* (1484), later printed as *Theologia naturalis*, written originally in Spanish, achieved great fame in the sixteenth century through M. de **Montaigne**, who translated it into French and defended it. It was a work of Neoplatonic inspiration, and the Council of Trent put the prologue on the Index, because it over-emphasized the authority of the 'Book or Law of Nature' at the expense of Scripture and tradition, maintaining that it is possible for human reason to discover the contents of Christian revelation in nature alone.

Raymond of Toulouse Saint, patron of Toulouse, died Toulouse, 3 July 1118. Dedicated by his parents to St Saturninus, Raymond abandoned the religious life, married and, after the death of his spouse, devoted himself to charitable works. He was generous to the poor, built and endowed a hospital for poor clerics and rebuilt the church of St Saturninus. His cult dates from 1652, following the ending of an epidemic, attributed to his intercession. Feast day 3 July.

Raymond IV of Toulouse (Raymond de Saint-Gilles) Count of Toulouse, a leader of the First Crusade, born *c.*1042, died Tripoli, 28 February 1105. Count from 1093, Raymond participated in the battles at Nicaea, Antioch and Jerusalem. He twice refused the crown of Jerusalem, alleging his reluctance to rule in the city where Christ had suffered. He died before the capture of Tripoli, but left his mark upon history in the account of its foundation.

Raymond V of Toulouse Count of Toulouse from 1148, grandson of **Raymond IV**, born 1148, died 1194. He fought victoriously against King Henry II of England and King Alfonse II of Aragon.

Raymond VI of Toulouse Son and heir of **Raymond V**, born Toulouse, October 1156, died there, August 1222. Count of Toulouse from 1194, and tolerant, Raymond did nothing against the Albigensian heresy, for which **Innocent III** excommunicated him and launched a Crusade against him and the heretics in 1208. Raymond took the side of the Papacy, but changed camps in 1209 only to be vanquished with his ally Peter II of Aragon at the Battle of Muret, and again in 1215 by Simon de Montfort, after which he implored the pardon of the Pope. By 1217, he had reconquered Toulouse and, by his death, most of his estates.

Raymond VII of Toulouse Last count of Toulouse, born Beaucaire, July 1197, died Millau, September 1249. Raymond continued to fight the Albigensian Crusade and the de Montfort family, reconquered Carcassonne in 1224, but could not prevail against the Crusade of **Louis VIII**, to whose widow he was obliged to cede his domains in 1229, and accept the foundation of the University of Toulouse, destined to fight the Albigensian heresy.

Raynaldus *see* **Rinaldi, Odorio**

Raynauld, Théophile French Jesuit theologian, born Sospello, near Nice, 15 November 1583, died Lyons, 31 October 1663. He was regarded as the most learned theologian of his time; Cardinal **Richelieu** sought Raynauld's assistance when the Spanish Jesuit Hurtado de Mendoza attacked the cardinal's political alliance with the Huguenots. Vociferous in his criticism of the Inquisition, he violently attacked the Dominicans both for their directing role and on their doctrine of grace. An anti-Dominican diatribe of 1662 caused the Jesuit general, J. P. Oliva, to disown the work; it was put on the Index and publicly burned at Aix and Toulouse.

Rea, Alonso de (Fray Alonso de Larrea) Mexican Franciscan chronicler, born Querétaro, 1606, died place unknown, 1660. Rea became definitor, chronicler and first Creole provincial at Michoacán in 1649. A truthful and precise historian, he described the artistry of Tarascan featherwork mosaics, the paintings of indigenous lacquer, the famous 'Christs of Michoacán' sculpture and the skill of the Indians as metalworkers. A witness of the plague that devastated the region, he recounted the zeal of the Franciscans in curing and in burying the thousands of Tarascans who died.

Read, James English missionary, born Abridge, Essex, 3 December 1777, died Eland's Post, Cape Colony, 8 May 1852. Originally a carpenter, he worked with **Van der Kemp** from 1800 among the Khoikhoi and mixed race (Cape coloured) at Bethelsdorp, a village established to allow them freedom in the racially divided Cape. From 1829 he ministered to the Kat River settlement of coloured people and established good relations with the Xhosa. He was ostracized by the white community for supporting legal redress and equality for the Cape coloured and marrying a Khoi woman, Sara. His son, James, was to continue his father's ministry, while his daughters became teachers.

Realino, Bernardino Saint, Italian Jesuit and humanist, born Carpi, 1 December 1530, died Lecce, 2 July 1616. Realino was named master of novices by Francis Borgia, the general. Assigned to Lecce in Apulia, he remained there 42 years, founding a college, building a baroque church and gaining a reputation for sanctity in the direction of souls. Numerous miraculous cures and prophecies were attributed to him, as well as several visions of Our Lady and the crucified Jesus. He agreed on his deathbed to be the protector of Lecce in heaven. **Pius XII** canonized him in 1947. Feast day 4 July.

Rebora, Clemente Italian poet, born Milan, 6 January 1885, died Stresa, 1 November 1957. His family of Milanese intellectuals imbued Rebora with the political anticlericalism and idealism that were the hallmarks of the Risorgimento. He fought in the Great War, which made him abhor violence in all forms, and induced him to work for peace in society. He re-entered the Church in 1929, and

became a priest of the Institute of Charity – the Rosmini Fathers – at Domodossola. In 1955, after nearly 30 years of silence, he received the 'Cittadella' award for his poem 'Curriculum vitae', a long autobiographical work reflecting the contrasts in his life.

Rebuffi, Pierre French priest and lawyer, born Baillargues, near Montpellier, 1487, died Paris, 2 November 1557. Rebuffi taught at Toulouse, Poitiers, Bourges and, from 1534, Paris, earning such a reputation that **Paul III** wished him to become an auditor of the Rota. The most important of his learned works were published after his death, and include the *Praxis beneficiorum* (1664).

Reding, Augustine Swiss abbot and theologian, born Lichtensteig, 10 August 1625, died Einsiedeln, 13 March 1692. Reding joined the Benedictines at the age of sixteen, and became professor of theology at Salzburg in 1654. Elected prince-abbot in 1670, he presided over a period of great intellectual and spiritual growth at the monastery; the number of monks doubled, some of them becoming eminent professors at universities. He wrote *Theologica scholastica universa*, a commentary (13 vols) on the *Summa Theologiae* of St **Thomas Aquinas**, and his most important work.

Rees, Thomas Welsh religious historian, born Pen Pontbren, Carmarthenshire, 13 December 1815, died Swansea, 29 April 1885. With almost no formal education, Rees became a coal miner at Aberdare while still very young, but gave it up and opened a school. Virtually self-taught and ordained in the Congregational Church, he held pastorates at Aberdare, Llanelly, Cendl and Swansea. His *History of Protestant Non-conformity in Wales* is a sound piece of work and his preaching was much appreciated. He became chairman of the Congregational Union of England and Wales.

Rees, William (Gwilym Hiraethog) Welsh Congregational minister, social leader, born Llansannan, Denbighshire, 8 November 1802, died Liverpool, 8 November 1883. Rees spent his early years as a shepherd, but acquired considerable literary culture in the Welsh language. He became a Congregational minister, a powerful preacher and a good theologian. As editor of *The Times* (Wales) from

1843, he introduced radical politics and championed modern Welsh nationalism. He corresponded with Giuseppe Mazzini, the Italian patriot and revolutionary, and was a key figure in linking the evangelical churches in Wales with what later became Liberalism.

Regan, Agnes Gertrude American Roman Catholic lay leader, born San Francisco, 26 March 1869, died Washington, DC, 30 September 1943. A teacher, Mrs Regan's chief contribution lay in promoting the role of the laity, especially of Catholic women, in active work for Church and country. Freedom having increased their obligation to society, she encouraged Catholic women to organize at the parish, diocesan and national levels so that they could contribute to social betterment. She worked for closer relations with the people of Latin America, and brought young women from these countries to study at the National School of Social Service.

Reginald, Valerius (Regnault, Raynauld) French Jesuit moral theologian, born Usie, Besançon, c.1544, died Dole, 15 March 1623. Reginald completed his ecclesiastical studies at Paris, entered the Society, and proceeded on a long and brilliant teaching career in Jesuit colleges, notably at Dole. His *Praxis fori paenitentialis* (1616) ranks among the classics of casuistry.

Reginald of Orléans Blessed, French Dominican preacher, born Orléans, 1183, died Paris, 1 February 1220. Reginald studied at Paris and became dean of the Canons of Saint-Aignan, Orléans. St **Dominic** received him into his Order in 1218, following a near fatal illness during which, in a vision, Our Lady is said to have shown Reginald the Dominican habit. He went to Paris in 1219 to help the young Dominican foundation at the university, where he died. Acclaimed for his preaching and holy life, he was beatified by **Pius IX** in 1875. Feast day 12 February.

Reginald of Priverno Italian Dominican theologian, born Priverno, c.1230, died Anagni, c.1295. Reginald met **Thomas Aquinas** around 1260, and became his confessor, secretary and constant companion; he accompanied Thomas on all his journeys and gave his funeral oration at Fossanova. He

succeeded St Thomas in the chair of philosophy at Naples, and finished his commentaries on St Paul's Epistles, St John's Gospel and Aristotle's *De anima*. Reginald collected St Thomas's works, including the four *Opuscula*, which he recorded from the master's lectures.

Regino of Prum German abbot, born Altrip, near Speyer, 840, died Trier, 915. Regino became abbot of Prum in 892, and abbot of St Martin's, Trier, in 899. His chief work is the *Libri duo de synodalibus causis et disciplinis ecclesiasticis*, which begins with 96 questions as guidelines for the bishop on parochial visitations, and then 89 questions concerning procedural regulations relating to the laity. The work had only limited success until **Burchard of Worms** used it in the eleventh century, since when it has enjoyed great and lasting influence.

Regiomontanus (Johannes Müller) German astronomer, born Königsberg, 6 June 1436, died Rome, 1476. Known as the greatest predecessor of **Copernicus**, Regiomontanus observed what became known as Halley's Comet in 1472 and, considering comets as stars and not as meteors, was one of the founders of scientific cometography. His major treatise *De triangulis libri omnimodus* is the earliest work treating of trigonometry as a substantive science. Pope **Sixtus IV** summoned Regiomontanus to Rome in 1472, to aid in the reform of the calendar; he died there, most likely of the plague.

Regis, Jean-François Saint, French Jesuit missionary, born Fontcouverte, Narbonne, 31 January 1597, died Lalouvesc, Ardèche, 31 December 1640. Regis devoted his life to converting the Huguenots; his influence reached all classes and brought about a lasting spiritual revival throughout France. Miraculous cures were attributed to him, and thousands immediately venerated him as a saint at his death. St Jean-Baptiste Marie **Vianney** ascribed his own vocation and his accomplishments to Regis. **Clement XII** declared him a saint in 1737. His legacy includes the Sisters of St Francis Regis, known as the 'Religious of the Cenacle', founded in 1830. Feast day 16 June.

Regis, Pierre Sylvain French Cartesian philosopher, born La Salvetat, Agenais, 1632, died Paris, 1 November 1707. Regis defended **Descartes**

against the criticisms of the 'Système' by P. D. **Huet** and J. B. du Hamel and Nicolas **Malebranche**. Named to the Academy of Sciences in 1699, Regis influenced Cartesian dualism in the direction of empiricism, and defended the real union of body and soul. He taught a moral philosophy based on self-love, and a political science based on absolute power, in the tradition of Thomas Hobbes.

Reguera, Emmanuel de la Spanish Jesuit mystical theologian, born Burgos, 1668, died Rome, 1747. Reguera became revisor general of the Society in Rome, where he translated into Latin Godinez' *Practica de la theologica mystica* (1681), under the title *Praxis theologiae mysticae . . .*, considered one of the finest *summae* of mystical theology in the eighteenth century, though the work became influential only through a resumé (1774) by Dominikus Schramm, OSB.

Reichelt, Karl Ludvig Pioneer of missionary understanding of Buddhism, born Barbu, Arendal, Norway, 1 September 1877, died Hong Kong, 13 March 1952. He trained for the Norwegian Missionary Society in Stavanger and reached China in October 1903. He developed an interest in mission towards Buddhist monks and in 1920 formed what became the Christian Mission to Buddhists in Nanking. It was relocated to Tao Fong Shan, Hong Kong, in 1931. He combined a Pietist background with theological liberalism, and saw the Johannine *logos* as the key to understanding Chinese spirituality. He was a critic of **Kraemer** at the 1938 International Missionary Council conference. Most of his writings were in Norwegian and Chinese, but include *Religion in a Chinese Garment* (1951). He was under house arrest during World War II, returned to Norway and in 1951 went back to Tao Fong Shan, where he is buried.

Reichensperger, August German Catholic politician, born Koblenz, 22 March 1808, died Cologne, 16 July 1895. Reichensperger's interest in the Church and in politics began with the persecution of Archbishop Droste of Cologne, and his admiration of the French and Belgian constitutional systems, which combined monarchical authority with civil liberties and freedom for the Church. Originally of liberal tendencies, he developed ultramontane opinions and, in 1852, founded, with his brother Peter (see below), the Prussian Catholic Party, to recover freedom for the Church and parity for the Catholic minority.

Reichensperger, Peter German Catholic politician, younger brother of August Reichensperger, born Koblenz, 28 May 1810, died Berlin, 31 December 1892. Though elected a member of the Liberal opposition, he wrote against the democrats during the Prussian revolution of 1848–9, and joined the Prussian Catholic Party, opposing government restrictions against his Church and fellow Catholics; however, he supported the monarchy against the Liberal majority on any reform. With August, he promoted the Centre Party, and took an active part on the ultramontane side.

Reid, Richard American newspaper editor, born Winchester, Massachusetts, 21 January 1896, died New Rochelle, New York, 24 January 1961. As secretary of the Georgia Catholic Laymen's Association, Reid played a prominent role in developing the Roman Catholic Church's position on public questions, and in promoting interracial justice. He wrote *The Morality of the Newspaper*, lectures given at Notre Dame, and *Three Days to Eternity*, with Edward Moffatt. He received the Laetare Medal in 1936, and the Hoey Interracial Justice Medal in 1946.

Reid, Thomas Scottish philosopher, born Strachan, 26 April 1710, died Glasgow, 7 October 1796. Reid succeeded Adam Smith in the chair of moral philosophy at Glasgow. Against the idealism of George **Berkeley** and the sceptical conclusions of David Hume, he rehabilitated the immediate perception of external objects, and the truths of sensible knowledge. Among the names Reid gave to the principles which lift us out of subjectivity into perception is 'principles of common sense', an unfortunate term since it conveyed to many the false impression of Scottish philosophy, that he had merely appealed from the reasoned conclusions of philosophers to the unreasoned beliefs of common life; he thus became known as the founder of the Scottish School of Common Sense.

Reiffenstuel, Amaletus (Johann Georg) German Franciscan theologian, born Tegernsee, Bavaria, 2

July 1642, died Freising, 10 May 1703. Reiffenstuel wrote the important *Theologia moralis* prior to his major work *Ius canonicum universum*, which, based on the decretals of **Gregory IX**, provides, in a series of questions, an exposition of canon law, from the Council of Trent, the subsequent papal contributions and the practice of the Roman curia; it became a standard work of reference for later scholars and assured for Reiffenstuel his high place among canonists.

Reilly, Wendell Canadian Sulpician and biblical scholar, born North Hatley, Quebec, 25 March 1875, died Baltimore, Maryland, 7 October 1950. Reilly studied at the Grand Séminaire, Montreal, and the Institut Catholique, Paris, and undertook scriptural studies at the École Biblique in Jerusalem, completing them in Rome at the Pontifical Biblical Commission. He worked on the Westminster revision of the Bible, translating and commenting on St John's Gospel; he translated the Epistle to the Ephesians for the Confraternity of Christian Doctrine NT, and was first editor, 1939–47, of the *Catholic Biblical Quarterly*.

Reimarus, Hermann Samuel German philosopher, born Hamburg, 22 December 1694, died there, 1 March 1768. Reimarus is known for an historical critique of the Gospels in which, calling into question revelation, the divinity of Christ and the Trinity, he developed a rationalist conception of religion, a pure naturalistic Deism, the essential truths of which are the existence of a wise and good creator, and the immortality of the soul. These truths are discoverable by reason, and are such as can constitute the basis of a universal religion, contrary to one revealed, which could never be intelligible and credible to all men. The Bible does not in any case present such revelation; it abounds in error as to matters of fact, contradicts human experience, reason and morals, and is one tissue of folly, deceit, enthusiasm, selfishness and crime. Reimarus, however, attacked atheism with equal effect and sincerity, being a man of high moral character, respected and esteemed by his contemporaries.

Reinach, Salomon French scholar, born Saint-Germain-en-Laye, 29 August 1855, died Boulogne-sur-Mer, 4 November 1932. Reinach joined the French School at Athens, and made valuable archaeological discoveries in Smyrna, Thasos, Lesbos, Carthage, Odessa and elsewhere, 1880–93, which occasioned major publications on Roman and Greek sculpture and painting, as well as on artists of the Middle Ages and the Renaissance. His best-known work is *Orpheus, histoire générale des religions*, considered a rather superior work marked by hostility to Christianity and overtaken by later and more solid investigation in the history of religion.

Reinhold, Hans Anscar German Roman Catholic liturgist, born Hamburg, 1897, died Pittsburgh, Pennsylvania, 1968. Reinhold joined the Benedictines, but left them to become a diocesan priest and to organize an apostolate to seamen at Bremmerhaven and Hamburg, where he introduced such liturgical novelties as the dialogue Mass, Mass facing the people and the nocturnal celebration of the Easter Vigil. He went to New York in 1935, where his liturgical innovations and suspected Communist sympathies did not endear him to conservative ecclesiastical circles, but he persuaded them of the benefits participation of the laity could have for the renewal of the life of the Church in all its social aspects. He served as director of the Liturgical Conference, helped to organize the Vernacular Society of America and attended conferences of scholars in Europe, where the reforms adopted by Vatican II were first proposed.

Reinkens, Joseph Hubert German Old Catholic bishop, born Burtscheid, near Aix-la-Chapelle, 1 March 1821, died Bonn, 4 January 1896. Reinkens took holy orders, and became professor of ecclesiastical history at Breslau in 1853. He opposed the proclamation of papal infallibility and joined **Döllinger** and other influential theologians in organizing resistance to the decree, signing the Declaration of Nuremberg in 1871. The Old Catholics having decided to separate from Rome, Reinkens was chosen as their bishop in Germany, and through his efforts the Old Catholic movement crystallized into an organized Church with a definite status in the German states. In 1881, Reinkens visited England and received Holy Communion with bishops of the Church of England; he defended the validity of Anglican orders against his co-religionists in Holland.

Reisach, Karl August von   German cardinal archbishop, born Roth, 6 July 1800, died Contamine, France, 16 December 1869. As archbishop of Munich from 1846, a confidant of the Pope and the kings of Bavaria and Prussia, Reisach upheld the Church's freedom in conflicts with the government and, as a consequence, Maximilian requested his transfer to Rome, where **Pius IX** made him a cardinal. He negotiated the concordat with Wüttemberg in 1857 and Baden in 1859, became president of the preparatory commission for Vatican Council I, and in 1867 president of the commission for Church–State questions.

Reisch, Gregor   German humanist, born Balingen, *c*.1467, died Freiburg, 9 May 1525. Reisch entered the Carthusians and embarked on his *magnum opus*, the *Margarita philosophica*, which became an indispensable encyclopaedia and is still considered a major document of the popular science of that time. Reisch acted as consultant to Johann **Froben** at Basel on his press's great edition of St **Jerome**; **Erasmus** acknowledged Reisch's role, though he took over the direction himself so as to ensure the required standard of textual criticism.

Reitzenstein, Richard   German historian of religion, born Breslau, 2 April 1861, died Göttingen, 3 March 1931. Reitzenstein developed an interest in ancient religions, especially the origins of Christianity, which he attempted to show, in *Poimandres*, had been influenced by the religions of Hermes Trismegistus. In his more famous work *Die hellenistischen Mysterien-religionen*, he tried, again unconvincingly, to show that Gnosticism and Greek mystery religions had influenced early Christianity.

Reland, Hadrian   Dutch orientalist, born Ryp, near Alkmaar, 16 July 1676, died Utrecht, 5 January 1718. Reland became professor of rabbinism and Semitic languages at Harderwijk in 1699 and at Utrecht in 1701. His most important works are: *Palaestina ex noteribus monumentis illustrata*, a classic work based on data gathered in the course of centuries by pilgrims, travellers and cartographers of the Holy Land, the value of which was barely recognized before the nineteenth century; *Antiquitates sacrae veterum Hebraeorum*; and *De Religione Mohammedica*, considered a defence of Islam and placed on the Index.

Rembert of Bremen-Hamburg   Saint, archbishop, died Bremen, 11 June 888. Rembert became a monk at Turnholt, near Bruges, where he met St **Ansgar**, whom he succeeded as archbishop of Hamburg, and whose Life he wrote. He is reported to have evangelized parts of Scandinavia, but that is doubtful. He is buried near the cathedral church in Bremen. Feast day 4 February.

Rembrandt Harmensz van Rijn   Dutch painter, etcher and draftsman, born Leiden, 15 July 1606, died Amsterdam, 4 October 1669. He studied at Amsterdam under Pieter Lastman. His work includes *The Bride of Tobias*, *The Angel Leaving Tobias*, *The Marriage of Samson*, *The Return of the Prodigal Son* and *The Adoration of the Magi*. He became bankrupt and died in poverty. His many etchings on biblical themes tend to display, especially in his later years, a rather dark Calvinism.

Remesal, Antonio de   Spanish Dominican chronicler, born Galicia, date unknown, died Zacatecas, Mexico, 1627. Remesal studied at Salamanca, where he was in 1594, became a noted linguist, went to Guatemala in 1613 and settled there and in Mexico. He wrote *Historia de la Provincia de San Vincente de Chiapa y Guatemala*, a valuable history of missionary activity beginning with the conquest of Mexico and Central America. The work was denounced to the Inquisition as branding all priests as bastards and all nobles as adulterous traitors to the king, but the Holy Office vindicated him and the work was published, after which he returned to the missions for the remainder of his life.

Remigio de Girolami (Remi of Florence)   Dominican theologian, born Florence, 1235, died there, 1319. Remigio studied at Paris, entered the Dominicans, knew St **Thomas Aquinas** and later followed his doctrine. He taught at Santa Maria Novella in Florence, where his lectures were open to Florentine citizens, among whom may well have been **Dante Alighieri**, whose *Convivio* seems to have been inspired by Remigio.

Remigius of Auxerre Carolingian humanist and theologian, born *c.*841, died Paris, 908. A Benedictine monk and teacher at St-Germain, Rheims, 862, and Paris, where he had **Odo of Cluny** as his pupil, Remigius is important in the evolution of Scholasticism in that he continued the earlier Carolingian learning in reviving the work of **Alcuin**, Dundrad and John Scotus **Eriugena**; he glossated and commented on the works of Cato, Terence, Virgil, Juvenal and **Bede**, as well as on the theological work of **Boethius** and his *De consolatione philosophiae*.

Remigius of Lyons Saint, archbishop, died Lyons, 28 October 875. Chaplain of **Lothair I** and **Charles II** the Bald, Remigius succeeded Amulo in the See of Lyons, in the midst of the predestination controversy. Though disapproving of **Gottschalk**'s views, he was no partisan of his adversary, Archbishop **Hincmar** of Rheims, as he considered neither to have done justice to the thought of St **Augustine** on the subject. He took part in the Councils of Langres (859) and Toucy (860), and attempted to regain confiscated Church property. Feast day 29 October.

Remigius of Rheims Saint, bishop, 'Apostle of the Franks', also known as 'Remi', born Laon, *c.*437, died Rheims, 13 January *c.*533. Scion of an influential family: his father Aemitius, count of Laon, his mother St Cilinia, his younger brother St Principius, Remigius became bishop at the age of 22. A great friend of **Clovis**, he converted the king to Christianity and baptized him, along with 3000 Franks (according to **Gregory of Tours**), on Christmas Day 496, following Clovis's defeat of the Alemanni at the Battle of Tolbiac. Clovis became known as the eldest son of the Church, whose influence in the subsequent history of Christianity in the West has been inestimable. Remigius' relics have lain in the abbey of Saint-Rémi since 1049. Feast day 1 October.

Remigius of Rouen Saint, Frankish archbishop, died Rouen, *c.*772. An illegitimate son of **Charles Martel** and brother of **Pepin III**, he succeeded Rainfroi as archbishop of Rouen in 755. While on a mission in 760 to **Paul I** and **Desiderius**, king of the Lombards, Remigius was impressed by the chant of the monks, and brought some back to introduce Gregorian chant and Roman liturgical practice in the Frankish kingdom. His name has figured in the Rouen Breviary since 1627. Feast day 19 January.

Remy, Arthur Frank Joseph German philologist, born Elberfeld, 26 June 1871, died White Plains, New York, 24 October 1954. Educated in the USA, Remy taught Germanic philology at Columbia University from 1899 for 42 years. He served as president of the US Catholic Historical Society, and wrote *The Influence of India and Persia on the Poetry of Germany* and major articles in the *Catholic Encyclopedia* and the *Germanic Review*.

Renan, Joseph Ernest French philosopher and orientalist, born Tréguier, 27 February 1823, died Paris, 2 October 1892. Renan studied at the seminary of Issy, where his reading of Hegel brought on a serious religious crisis (*Souvenirs d'enfance et de jeunesse*). From his search for certainty in life came *L'Avenir de la science*, in which he affirmed that religion must be replaced by a science of humanity: philology. He went to Palestine in 1860, and this inspired him to write *L'Histoire des origines du Christianisme* (7 vols), intended to be the foundation of 'a rational and ethical Christianity'. The first volume, *La Vie de Jésus*, which cost him his chair of Hebrew at the Collège de France, had a considerable impact as much for its poetical style as for the rationalist interpretation of Jesus, to whom he had already referred as merely 'this incomparable man'. Conscious of being a 'tissue of contradictions', he celebrated ancient Greece which seemed to have attained perfect harmony between beauty, reason and a sense of the divine (*La Prière sur l'Acropole*).

Renaudot, Eusèbe French theologian and orientalist, born Paris, 20 July 1648, died Paris, 1 September 1720. Renaudot acquired an unusual learning in Eastern tongues and, having been elected to the Académie Française, began at the age of 62 to publish works, in Latin translations from the original sources, on the liturgy and ritual of the Oriental Church, a history of the Coptic Church of Alexandria and accounts in Arabic of seafarers' journeys to India and China. He also published *Perpétuité de la foi catholique de l'Église*, designed to supply proofs of the 'perpetuity of the faith' of the Church on the subject of the sacraments, then a burning topic between French Catholics and Protestants.

Reni, Guido Italian painter, born Bologna, 4 November 1575, died Bologna, 18 August 1642. Influenced by **Caravaggio**, Reni became a dominant force in Italian art; under the patronage of **Paul V** and Cardinal **Caffarelli Borghese**, he worked on the frescoes in the chapel of the Quirinal palace, and at S. Maria Maggiore. He settled at Bologna, *c.*1614, where he painted *Apotheosis of St Dominic*. In his many religious works, the cult of the human body and idealized beauty expresses itself particularly in his mythological paintings of elegant, sensual figures (*Labours of Hercules*). He enjoyed an immense reputation in Europe, being considered the most brilliant representative of the Bolognese school.

Renier of Huy Italian sculptor and goldsmith, flourished *c.*1110 to *c.*1150. The earliest known sculptor of the Meuse River region, Flanders, Renier's masterpiece is the bronze baptismal font of St Bartélemy, Liège, commissioned by Abbot Hellinus. The font is in the shape of a cylinder supported by twelve oxen, decorated with four relief panels of biblical scenes of baptisms in which is evident the influence of Ottonian and Byzantine art.

Repington, Philip (Repyngdon) English bishop and cardinal, date and place of birth unknown, died Lincoln, July(?)1424. Repington joined the Augustinian Canons at Leicester before 1382, and came to the fore as a defender of the doctrines of John **Wycliffe**, for which he was excommunicated, but he was soon pardoned, when he abandoned his unorthodox opinions. He became chaplain and confessor to Henry IV in 1399, being described as 'clericus specialissimus domini Regis Henrici'. He was chosen bishop of Lincoln in 1404, and in 1408 **Gregory XII** made him a cardinal.

Repplier, Agnes American essayist and biographer, born Philadelphia, 1 April 1855, died there, 16 December 1950. Dismissed from school as a rebel, Agnes Repplier began writing short stories at the age of sixteen and published a story in *Catholic World*, the editor of which, Isaac Hecher, suggested she write essays, which she did to some advantage. Her collections include *Books and Men*, *A Happy Half-Century*, *To Think of Tea* and *Eight Decades*, all personal and literary pieces; and her other works include three excellent biographies: *Père Marquette*, *Mère Marie of the Ursulines* and *Junipero Serra*, all of which have earned her a lasting place in American literature.

Resch, Peter American author, born Chicago, 27 February 1895, died Kirkwood, Montana, 29 April 1956. Ordained in the Brothers of Mary, of which he became provincial of St Louis province, Resch wrote extensively for Catholic periodicals, and wrote numerous tracts. Among his publications are several related to the objectives of his congregation: *Marianist Meditations*, *Our Blessed Mother*, *A Life of Mary*, *Co-Redemptorix*. He translated Henri Lebon's *The Marianist Way* and Emil Newbert's *Our Mother*.

Respighi, Ottorino Italian composer, born Bologna, 9 July 1879, died Rome, 18 April 1936. Respighi studied music at the Liceo Musicale of Bologna, and composition under Rimsky-Korsakov at St Petersburg and under Max Bruch at Berlin. He became director of the Rome Conservatory in 1923. His work is characterized by impressionism (*Fountains of Rome* (1916), *Pines of Rome* (1924)) and by a return to the modal melodies of plainchant (*Gregorian Concerto* for violin (1922)). He composed operas, such as *Maria Egiziaca*, first produced at the Carnegie Hall in 1931, chamber music and melodies.

Retief, Pieter Voortrekker leader, born Cape Colony, 1780, killed in Zululand, 6 February 1838. He left Cape Colony aged 57, leading a group of Afrikaners on their trek to find new lands and establish a new state away from British rule. A symbolic figure in Afrikaner folk history, he died at the hands of a Zulu king, Dingane, while trying to negotiate a land deal with him. His death led to a war in which the Afrikaners beat the Zulus. This victory encouraged the Afrikaners to consider themselves God's chosen people and Retief a martyr.

Retz, Jean François Paul de Gondi Cardinal, French prelate and agitator, born Montmirail, 20

September 1613, died Paris, 24 August 1679. Tutored by St **Vincent de Paul**, Retz at eighteen demonstrated audacious revolutionary principles, and acquired status among the people of Paris through his influence in the Fronde in 1648, which he turned against Cardinal **Mazarin**. However, devoid of political principle, with the break-up of the Fronde, he was left in the lurch. He recovered through a stroke of luck when **Innocent X**, by inadvertence, made him a cardinal in 1650, and this brought about a temporary alliance with Mazarin in opposition to the Fronde engaged in a final test of strength against the Crown. He retired to the rich abbacy of St-Denis in 1662, becoming a loyal servant of Louis **XIV**, especially in his relations with the Holy See.

Reuchlin, Johann   German humanist and Hebraist, born Pforzheim, 22 February 1455, died Bad Liebenzell, 30 June 1522. Reuchlin firmly established Hebrew studies in Germany; he immersed himself in the Kabbala, defending it and the Talmud against attacks by the Dominicans of Cologne and the converted Jew Johannes Pfefferkorn, who had urged the destruction of all Hebrew books. Pfefferkorn denounced him in *Handspiegel*, and Reuchlin replied bitterly in *Augenspiegel*, which **Leo X** condemned in 1520. The protagonists in this increasingly bitter struggle represented, on the one hand, conservative Scholastic theologians and, on the other, champions of the new humanistic studies. Ever the humanist himself, Reuchlin's name is second only to that of his younger contemporary, **Erasmus**.

Reumont, Alfred von   German scholar and diplomatist, born Aachen, 15 August 1808, died Aachen, 27 April 1887. Named after **Alfred the Great**, the English king, Reumont studied at Bonn and Heidelberg, entered the Prussian diplomatic service, one of the few Catholics then allowed such a career, and combined loyalty to the king and to the Holy See; he was the friend and adviser of Frederick William IV. Reumont published a history of Rome, *Geschichte der Stadt Rom*.

Reusch, Franz Heinrich   German Old Catholic theologian, born Brilou, Westphalia, 4 December 1825, died Bonn, 3 March 1900. Reusch became editor of *Bonner Theologisches Literaturblatt*, to which he contributed translations of works by John Henry **Newman** and Cardinal **Wiseman**. Reusch opposed the decree on the infallibility of the Pope; the archbishop of Cologne forbade him to lecture, and in 1872 he was excommunicated. He joined the Old Catholics, took charge of their parish in Bonn and served as vicar general to the Old Catholic bishop Joseph **Reinkens**, but left them when they abolished clerical celibacy in 1878. Reusch's fame rests on his edition of the *Autobiography* of Cardinal **Bellarmine**, and a two-volume outline of disputes among Catholics concerning moral theology, which has not been superseded.

Reuss, Edouard Guillaume Eugène   Lutheran biblical scholar, born Strasburg, 18 July 1804, died there 18 April 1891. Reuss is important for his investigations into the sources and authorship of the Pentateuch. He set out to show that its traditional unity of authorship could no longer be held, that the work was a compilation of documents: the Yahwist (J) of the ninth century BC, the Elohist (E) somewhat later, the Deuteronomic Code (D) of prophetic origin, and the Priestly Code (P) post-prophetic. His student Karl Heinrich Graf subsequently proved the post-exilic origin of (P).

Rey, Anthony   French Jesuit educator, born Lyons, 19 March 1807, died Ceralvo, Mexico, 19 January 1847. Rey went to Georgetown College, Washington, DC, as professor of metaphysics and ethics. During the Mexican War he served as army chaplain at the siege of Monterey, exposing himself frequently to enemy fire in ministering to wounded and dying soldiers. He appears to have been ambushed and slain by guerrillas near Ceralvo while on a mission to Matamoras.

Reyes, Alfonso   Mexican writer, poet, critic, born Monterey, 17 May 1889, died Mexico City, 27 December 1959. Reyes' abundant literary work tends to highlight the renewal of aesthetic national traditions, wherein lies the importance of his intellectual influence in Mexico. He contributed to the study of **Góngora**, Ruiz de Alarcon and others, and published 'Vision de Anahuac', a prose poem on a native Mexican theme; his *Homélie pour la culture*, *L'Expérience littéraire* and other works showed him to be the 'universal Mexican'.

Reymont, Władysław Stanisław Polish novelist, born Kobiele Wielkie, 7 May 1867, died Warsaw, 5 December 1925. Following some works on peasant life and religious events, *Pilgrimage to Jasna Gora*, for example, Reymont wrote a series of novels: *Komediantka* (The Comedienne) and *Fermenty* (The Ferments), on the world of the theatre; *Ziernia Obiecana* (The Promised Land), on the industrialization of Lodz; *Rok 1794* (The Year 1794), an historical trilogy in which he relived the epoch of Koscinszko; *Za fronten* (Behind the Front). In 1924 he won the Nobel Prize for Literature for his master-work *Chiopi* (The Peasants), a great poetical novel in four volumes, each of which depicts a season, illustrating the life of a village of Mazovie with its rude and simple inhabitants.

Reynold, Frédéric Gonzague de French-Swiss historian and critic, born Cressier, comté de Fribourg, 1880, died Cressier, 9 April 1970. Reynold studied at the Institut Catholique, Paris, received a doctorate in letters from the Sorbonne and held professorships at Geneva, Berne and Fribourg. He served on a diplomatic mission to the Vatican in 1923 and with the League of Nations Committee on Intellectual Co-operation, 1923–38. Catholic functions included membership of the International Committee for Eucharistic Congresses, 1925, and presidency of the Catholic Union for International Studies, 1926. In his writings he sought to develop a European-oriented philosophy of history, and a Christian-centred theology of the historical process. His chief work is the seven-volume *La Formation d'Europe*, in which he maintains that the concept of European unity derives from a Christian ideal.

Reynolds, Hiram F. Nazarene general superintendent and missions executive, born Lyons, Illinois, 12 May 1854, died Haverhill, Massachusetts, 13 July 1938. A Methodist pastor in New England, he became president and later full-time revivalist for the Vermont Holiness Association. He was a general superintendent of the Church of the Nazarene from 1907 to 1932 and, simultaneously, the missions executive for twelve years. He tirelessly advocated cross-cultural missions, effectively publicized the cause, and was the first general superintendent to visit Nazarene churches and missions outside North America, stamping the denomination with a global vision.

Reynolds, Richard Saint, English martyr, born Devon, *c.*1487, died Tyburn, London, 4 May 1535. Richard became a Benedictine monk at Syon Abey, Isleworth, where he achieved prominence as a preacher and spiritual adviser. **Henry VIII** sought the backing of Syon in his divorce proceedings, but failed. Reynolds was arrested and sent to the Tower, where he stoutly disputed with Thomas **Cromwell** Henry's claim to lead the English Church. Condemned for treason, Richard was executed at Tyburn. He was canonized in 1970 as one of the **Forty Martyrs of England and Wales**. Feast day 11 May.

Rheinberger, Josef German composer, born Vaduz, Lichtenstein, 17 March 1839, died Munich, 25 November 1901. Rheinberger's musical talents were evident early and earned him the position of organist at the parish church at the age of seven; he composed a three-part Mass the following year. He studied at the Munich Conservatory, and gave his attention largely to sacred music from 1877. He composed important works in every form, including twenty organ sonatas, which influenced many young composers, among them George Chadwick and Horatio Parker, distinguished members of the Boston group of composers.

Rhenanus, Beatus German humanist, born Schlettstadt, Alsace, 22 August 1485, died Strasburg, 20 July 1547. Educated at the Latin school of Schlettstadt, Rhenanus went to Paris in 1503, where he came under the influence of Aristotle's writings. In 1511 he went to Basel, where he met Desiderius **Erasmus** and took an active share in the publishing enterprise of Johannes **Froben**. Like Erasmus, Rhenanus had welcomed **Luther**'s protests against indulgences and other abuses in the Church, but also withdrew his support when an open break occurred. He returned to Schlettstadt in 1536, and personally superintended the printing of Erasmus' more important works.

Rho, Giacomo Italian Jesuit mathematician and missionary, born Milan, 29 January 1592, died Peking, 27 April 1638. Rho went to Macao in 1620, entered China in 1624 and was appointed to the

Imperial Bureau of Astronomy in Peking in 1631, where he worked with Johann Schall von Bell on reform of the Chinese calendar, in the tradition of Matteo **Ricci**, SJ, who sought to convert the Chinese by means of science.

Rhodes, Alexandre de Jesuit missionary to Vietnam, born Avignon, France, 15 March 1593, died Isfahan, Persia, 5 November 1660. He entered the Jesuit novitiate in Rome in 1612 and was ordained in 1618. He travelled to Lisbon that year, to Goa, 1619–22, and Melaka, reaching Macao in May 1623. He did language study in Thanh Chiem (Quang Nam) from 1624 and laboured in Tonkin, 1627–30, until expelled. He was professor of theology at the Jesuit College in Macao, 1630–40, before his second mission to Vietnam, 1640–45. He was in Rome, 1649–52 and France, 1652–4 and became Jesuit superior in Persia in November 1655. He devised the Vietnamese script and wrote the first books in that alphabet. He was imprisoned several times, established a Vietnamese catechumenate, worked for a Vietnamese clergy and the inculturation of Asian Christianity, and by 1640 had seen the baptism of some 100,000 Vietnamese.

Riario, Girolamo Italian instigator of the infamous Pazzi conspiracy against the Medicis, born 1443, died Forli, 14 April 1488. In the ensuing war, Girolamo took Forli from Hercules I, duke of Ferrara, and made himself lord of the city. He was assassinated by conspirators.

Riario, Pietro Italian prelate, born 1445, died Rome, 5 January 1474. Nephew of **Sixtus IV**, Riario joined the Franciscans, became a cardinal at the age of 25 and lived a life of lavish ostentation and notorious immorality. He purchased the town of Imola, which he gave to his brother, Girolamo **Riario**.

Ribadeneira, Pedro de Spanish Jesuit hagiologist, born Toledo, 1 November 1526, died Madrid, 22 September 1611. Received into the Society by **Ignatius of Loyola** at the age of thirteen, Ribadeneira's most important work is the *Life of Loyola*, the first to be written, in which he affirmed that Ignatius had wrought no miracle except the foundation of his Society (thus drawing a parallel with Muhammad, whose only miracle, originally, was

the Koran). He showed himself an able, though credulous, writer in his Lives of Loyola's successors **Lainez** and St **Francis Borgia**.

Ribera, Francisco de Spanish Jesuit exegete, born Villacastin, 1537, died Salamanca, 24 November 1591. Ribera taught Scripture at Salamanca and wrote commentaries notable for their wide erudition, use of patristic sources and attention to the literal sense of scriptural passages. He was confessor to St **Teresa of Ávila**, and his Life of her, *La vida de la Madre Teresa de Jesús*, has gone through many editions.

Ribera, Jusepe de (José de) Spanish painter, born Xativa, near Valencia, 12 January 1591, died Naples, 5 September 1652. Influenced by the works of Michelangelo **Caravaggio** and his disciples, Ribera's paintings represent realistic scenes of martyrs, as well as isolated figures of saints, anchorites and philosophers (*Aesop*, *Archimedes*). Towards 1635, he developed a more vibrant style, warmer colours (*Immaculate Conception*). Among Ribera's principal works are *St Januarius emerging from the Furnace* (cathedral of Naples) and *Descent from the Cross* (Neapolitan Cortosa), generally regarded as his masterpiece.

Ribet, Jerome French Sulpician mystical theologian, born Aspet, Haute-Garonne, 16 January 1837, died Algiers, 29 May 1909. Ordained in 1863, Ribet left the Sulpicians in 1855 and became parish priest at Sauran. His principal work is *La Mystique divine distinguée des contrefaçons diaboliques et des analogies humaines*, in which he distinguishes mystical stages, contrasts them with totally natural phenomena, and examines their causes. He died in Algiers in the house of the White Fathers at Notre-Dame d'Afrique.

Ribot, Théodule Armand French philosopher and psychologist, born Guingamp, 18 December 1839, died Paris, 9 December 1916. Ribot was one of the first to make of psychology a science independent of metaphysics, both experimental and founded on biology. In his best-known book, *Heredité: étude psychologique*, he brings together a large number of instances of inherited peculiarities, and pays particular attention to the physical element of mental life, ignoring all non-material factors. In *La Psy-*

chologie anglaise contemporaine, he shows his sympathy with the sensationalist school, and again in his translation of Herbert **Spencer**'s *Principles of Psychology*.

Ricardus Anglicus   *see* **Richard de Mores**

Ricardus de Senis Italian cardinal, born Siena, mid-thirteenth century, died near Genoa, February 1314. Ricardus served in the papal curia under **Nicholas IV** and **Boniface VIII**, who entrusted him and two French canonists with the task of codifying the two pontiffs' laws in the *Liber Sextus*. He also served in **Clement V**'s curia in Vienne and Avignon.

Riccardi, Niccolò Italian Dominican theologian, born Genoa, 1585, died Rome, 1639. Professor of theology at and regent of the Collegio San Tomaso at the Minerva, Rome, 1621. **Urban VIII** made Riccardi 'Master of the Sacred Palace' in 1629. His literary works include the noteworthy *Historiae Concilii Tridenti emaculatae synopsis*, as well as theological treatises, commentaries and apologetics.

Ricci, Lorenzo Italian Jesuit, born Florence, 2 August 1703, died Castel Sant'Angelo, Rome, 24 November 1775. General from 1758, Ricci had worked closely with **Clement XIII** to protect the Church and the Society from their common enemies; the Pope, in the brief *Apostolicum Pascendi*, served notice to European rulers that he would not be forced into action against the Society. However, **Clement XIV** was more pliant, and to appease the clamorous Bourbon governments, he issued the brief *Dominus ac Redemptor*, suppressing the Society in 1773. Ricci and his assistants were imprisoned in Castel Sant'Angelo, where he died.

Ricci, Matteo Jesuit missionary in China, born Macerata, Italy, 1552, died, Peking, 1610. Trained in natural sciences in Rome. He went to Goa in 1578, Macao in 1582, Chao-ch'ing (Zhaoqing) in 1583, Shao-chou (Shaozhou) in 1589, Nanking (Nanjing) in 1599 and Peking (Beijing) in 1601. Respected by the Chinese for demonstrating European technology to them, he gained converts in the highest circles by explaining Christianity in

Confucian terms. He translated the Ten Commandments and wrote a catechism and *The True Doctrine of God* (1595) in Chinese. His method of evangelism caused controversy and was finally forbidden by the Roman Catholic Church in 1742.

Ricci, Scipione de' Italian bishop, ecclesiastical reformer, born Florence, 9 January 1741, died Rignana, 27 December 1809. When he became bishop of Pistoia, Ricci promoted Josephinist doctrines and a higher standard of morals, to which end he founded a theological academy at Prato and appointed professors in sympathy with his views; he was especially opposed, as he saw it, to excessive devotions to the Sacred Heart. He carried through a plan of reform at the Synod of Pistoia (1786), seeking to create a schismatic Church, but the bishops disavowed the decrees, and **Pius VI** condemned the Synod in *Auctorem Fidei*. He resigned his see, but later became reconciled to the Church.

Ricci, Vittorio Italian Dominican missionary, born Fiesole, 18 January 1621, died Parran, Philippines, 17 February 1685. While a student at Rome, Ricci met Juan Battista Morales, who influenced him to undertake mission work, and he began his apostolate among the Chinese of Parran; in 1655 he moved to Fukien, China, as vicar provincial for South China and Formosa. He wrote *Istoria della missione de FF Predicatori nel regno di Cina*, an account of the Dominican missions, especially of the province of the Holy Rosary of the Philippines.

Riccioli, Giovanni Battista Italian Jesuit astronomer and geographer, born Ferrara, 17 April 1598, died Bologna, 25 June 1671. Riccioli discovered the 'aschen light' around Venus in 1643, which gives the planet the appearance of the 'old moon in the new moon's arms' and, in 1650, the duplicity of Nizar, the first recognized double star. He made, with Grimaldi, a map of the moon in 1651.

Ricciotti, Giuseppe Biblical scholar and orientalist, born Rome, 27 February 1890, died there, 22 January 1964. Ordained in 1913, Ricciotti taught Hebrew and comparative Semitics at Genoa, and Oriental Church history at Rome and Bari; he published works on Syriac literature and scholarly commentaries on books of the Bible. He popularized the study of Scripture in Italy, and several of his works have been translated into English: *The Life of Christ*, *Paul the Apostle*, *The Acts of the Apostles* and *The History of Israel*.

Rice, Edmund Ignatius   Founder of the Irish Christian Brothers and the Presentation Brothers, born near Callan, Kilkenny, 1 June 1762, died Waterford, 29 August 1844. Rice sought permission from **Pius VI** to establish a society to provide free education to poor boys; he opened a school in Waterford in 1803, forming a religious society in the Rule of the Presentation Sisters of Cork. Rice later asked **Pius VII** for permission to adopt the Rule of the Christian Brothers, founded by St John Baptist de **La Salle**, himself becoming 'Brother Ignatius' in 1821, and superior general until he retired in 1838. At his death the Brothers had some 100 houses in Ireland with 300 attached schools and over 30,000 pupils; and branches in Australia, Canada, India and Gibraltar.

Rice, Luther   American Baptist missionary, born Northboro, Massachusetts, 25 March 1783, died Edgefield, South Carolina, 25 September 1836. Ordained in 1812, he went to India with the first group of American missionaries, and was rebaptized at Calcutta by English Baptist missionaries. He returned to America in 1813 to campaign for the support of Baptist foreign missions, and founded Columbian College (now George Washington University), in Washington, DC. His activities in this regard helped to consolidate Baptist missionary objectives, but some adherents opposed educated ministers as well as missionary organizations.

Rich, Richard   First Baron Rich, born St Lawrence Jewry, London, *c.*1490, died Rochford, Essex, 12 June 1567. Rich knew Sir Thomas **More**, who assessed Rich as being 'not of any commendable fame'. In 1533 he became Solicitor-General under Thomas **Cromwell**, acting as a 'lesser hammer' for the operation of **Henry VIII**'s Act of Supremacy. He played an odious role in the trials of More and Bishop John **Fisher**, his evidence being instrumental in securing their convictions; More accused Rich of perjury, a charge history has sustained. In spite of this, and sharing in the spoils

from the monasteries, Rich remained a Roman Catholic; his testimony helped to convict Cromwell, and he was a willing agent in the Catholic reaction which followed. Created a baron and Lord Chancellor in 1548, he survived several changes of regime, and swore his allegiance to **Elizabeth I** at her accession.

Richard I (Coeur de Lion)   King of England, born Oxford, 8 September 1157, died at the siege of Chalûs Castle near Limoges, 6 April 1199. Richard succeeded his father Henry II in 1189. The greatest warrior in Europe, he organized the Third Crusade on learning that Saladin had captured Jerusalem. On his way to the Holy Land he stormed Messina, conquered Cyprus and married Berengaria of Navarre. He conquered Acre in 1191, but, though he defeated Saladin, could not take Jerusalem. He concluded a truce with him, and returned to England to confront his brother John and Philip II of France, who were intriguing against him in Normandy. Captured by Leopold, duke of Austria, who handed him over to the Holy Roman Emperor **Henry VI**, Richard paid a ransom and was back in England by 1194, where he crushed John's rebellion and spent his last five years in warfare with Philip in Normandy.

Richard II   King of England, born Bordeaux, 6 January 1367, died Pontefract Castle, Yorkshire, 14 February 1400. Son of Edward the Black Prince, Richard inherited from his grandfather, **Edward III**, a kingdom suffering from war with France, plague, taxation and a decadent and privileged nobility. Heavy taxation provoked the revolt of Wat Tyler in 1381, and the popular rebellion of the Lollards. Richard subdued Ireland in 1394, and seized control of government in 1397 after a long struggle with the English nobles. However, his rapprochement with Charles VI of France, and his authoritarian rule resulted in a revolt by his cousin, Henry Bolingbroke (Henry IV), who overthrew him, and he died a prisoner. Religiously orthodox, he patronized Benedictines, Carthusians, Dominicans and Franciscans. **Shakespeare** evoked his life in *Richard II*.

Richard, François Marie Benjamin   French prelate, born Nantes, 1 March 1819, died Paris, 29 January 1908. A Sulpician, Richard became archbishop of

Paris in 1886 and a cardinal. When the Assumptionist Fathers were dissolved as an illegal association in 1900, he paid them an official visit, for which he was censured by the government. In general a moderate man, he did not hold with the extremist policy of the ultramontanes, and maintained a reasonable stance in the struggle over the Law of Associations and the Law of Separations. In September 1906 he presided at an assembly of bishops and archbishops at his palace in rue de Grenelle, contrary to papal instructions, and in December had to give up his palace to state authorities, 'evicted' as it was seen by many in sympathy with him.

Richard, Gabriel French Sulpician missionary, born Saintes, 15 October 1767, died Detroit, 13 October 1832. Richard fled the Revolution to Detroit, where he worked among the Indians with such success that in only three years he had prepared more than 500 persons for confirmation. Richard became famous for leading the relief work when Detroit was destroyed by fire in 1805. He founded a printing press and published a Bible for Indians. When he was imprisoned by the British during the War of 1812, Chief Tecumseh obtained his release. He died ministering to victims in a cholera epidemic in Detroit.

Richard de la Vigne, François Marie Archbishop of Paris, born Nantes, 1 March 1819, died Paris, 28 January 1908. Richard instituted the petition for the beatification of (Jean-Baptiste **Vianney**) while bishop of Belley, 1872–75. He defended the Church against the hostility of the Third Republic at the time of the law separating Church and State (1905). Richard could not abide **Leo XIII**'s policy of Catholic co-operation in civil matters, and was expelled from his see because he supported **Pius X**'s rejection of the status given the Church in France. He resisted Alfred **Loisy** and Modernism and supported the formation of the Institut Catholique de Paris.

Richard de Mores (Ricardus Anglicus) Augustinian canon, born Lincolnshire, date unknown, died Dunstable, 9 April 1242. The first English canonist to teach at Bologna, Richard there completed, 1196–8, several works important to canon law, the *Summa Brevis*, for example, an elementary intro-

duction to **Gratian**'s *Decretum: Distinctiones decretorum*; *Summa de ordine indiciario*, a treatise on canonical procedure; *Casus decretalium*, a summary of Bernard of Pavia's *Breviarum extravagantium*; *Apparatus decretalium*, one of the first and most influential commentaries on the new compilation, and an important source for Tancred's *Glossa ordinaria*.

Richard Fishacre English theologian, born Diocese of Exeter, died Oxford, 1248. The first Dominican to study at Oxford, he belonged to the Augustinian school, but sought to incorporate the writings of Aristotle into his theology. His principal sources were St **Bernard of Clairvaux**, **Alexander of Hales**, **Hugh of Saint-Cher** and **Robert Grosseteste.** He wrote the first commentary at Oxford on the *Sentences* of **Peter Lombard**. His influence was great at Oxford and at Paris, notably on Simon Hinton, St **Bonaventure** and, indirectly, on St **Albert the Great**.

Richard Fitzralph Irish archbishop, born Dundalk, c.1300, died Avignon, 10 November 1360. Richard held benefices in various English dioceses before becoming archbishop of Armagh in 1346. Well known at Avignon, he preached before the papal court and took part in current controversies about the beatific vision and the Armenians, and wrote many treatises against the mendicant orders and their privileges, notably *De pauperie salvatoris*. He quarrelled with the friars in London in 1356–7, but died before the case was decided. Attempts were made in the fourteenth century to canonize him, but these had to be dropped.

Richard Grant of Canterbury (Le Grand) Archbishop, place and date of birth unknown, died Italy, 3 August 1231. **Gregory IX** appointed him to Canterbury in 1229, where he engaged in sharp jurisdictional disputes with Henry III and the justiciar Hubert de Burgh. He went to Rome to plead his case but died on the return journey, and is buried in the house of the Friars Minor at St Gemini Umbria.

Richard of Bury English Benedictine, bishop, born near Bury St Edmunds, Suffolk, 28 January 1286, died Auckland, Durham, 24 April 1345. Studied at Oxford and joined the Benedictines. He was tutor to the future King **Edward III** and on the latter's accession to the throne became bishop of Durham in 1333, then High Chancellor in 1334 and in 1336 Treasurer of England. He founded Durham College at Oxford. He was an avid collector of books and is the author of *Philobiblon*.

Richard of Campsall   English secular theologian, born Oxford, *c.*1285, died there, *c.*1350. A fellow of Balliol and Merton, Richard became regent master at Oxford from 1322. An opponent of **Duns Scotus** and **William of Ockham**'s nominalism, he wrote *Logica Campsale valde utilistis et realis contra Ockham*, and remained an independent thinker. He is buried in the choir of Merton College Chapel, Oxford.

Richard of Canterbury   Benedictine archbishop, also known as 'Richard of Dover', died 16 February 1184. Richard became a monk and chaplain to **Theobald of Canterbury**. He succeeded **Thomas Becket** at Canterbury, consecrated by **Alexander III** in 1174. He resolutely upheld the rights of his see, but was never extreme in his defence of the liberties of the Church. Richard is important in the development of canon law in England, and he presided over one of the earliest provincial councils in English ecclesiastical history.

Richard of Chichester   Saint, English bishop, born Wyche (Droitwich), *c.*1198, died Dover, 3 April 1253. Richard became chancellor of Canterbury under St **Edmund of Abingdon**, whom he accompanied in his exile, and whom he was with at his death. In 1244 he was elected bishop of Chichester (where he instituted the offering for the cathedral at Chichester later known as 'St Richard's pence'); Henry III at first refused Richard, and only gave way under threat of excommunication by **Innocent IV**. A man of deep spirituality and an excellent administrator, Richard preached Crusades and showed much eagerness to reform the manners and morals of the clergy, and to introduce greater reverence into the services of the Church. Miracles were reportedly wrought at his tomb in Chichester. He was canonized by **Urban IV** in 1262; his shrine in Chichester Cathedral was destroyed by order of **Henry VIII** in 1538. Feast day 3 April.

Richard of Connington   English Franciscan theologian, died Cambridge, 1330. Sixteenth provincial minister of the English province, Richard joined the poverty debate and wrote *Beatus qui intelligit*, a treatise on evangelical poverty; also *Responsiones ad conclusiones domini papae*, a dialogue between a friar and the Pope relative to problems of the papal bull *Ad Conditorem Canonum*. Richard's doctrine reflects Augustinian and Aristotelian thinking. He is buried at Cambridge.

Richard of Devizes   English Benedictine monk and chronicler, born Devizes, twelfth century. He spent his life in St Swithun's monastery at Winchester, and wrote the historically valuable *Chronicon de rebus gestis Ricardi primi*, a major source of information about **Richard I**'s reign, covering the Third Crusade, containing witty criticism of secular clergy and evincing animosity towards religious communities, especially the Carthusians, whom he detested.

Richard of Gravesend   English bishop, died 13 December 1279. Held the See of Lincoln from 1258. He assisted Simon de Montfort in negotiations for Anglo-French peace and sided with him against Henry III. Suspended by the papal legate Ottobono Fieschi (later **Adrian V**), Richard became reconciled with Henry, received absolution from **Clement IV** in Rome, and returned to England to administer his diocese. He is buried in Lincoln cathedral.

Richard of Gravesend   English bishop, died 9 December 1303. Nephew of **Richard of Gravesend**, bishop of Lincoln. Became bishop of London in 1280. He opposed the metropolitan claims of John **Peckham** of Canterbury, and aligned himself with the other suffragan bishops. He undertook missions to Philip IV of France on behalf of Edward I. His extensive library figures in the earliest known priced book catalogue.

Richard of Kilvington   English philosopher and controversialist, born Diocese of York, died London, before 1362. Educated at Oxford, Richard held many benefices, including the deanship of St Paul's. He strongly supported **Richard Fitzralph** in the anti-mendicant controversy, in particular with the Franciscan Roger Conway on evangelical poverty.

Richard of Knapwell (Clapwell) English Dominican, born Knapwell, Cambridgeshire, date unknown, died Bologna, c.1288. A master of theology at Oxford, he defended the orthodoxy of St **Thomas Aquinas**, proving that the Franciscan 'correction' stemmed from a failure to grasp the Thomist doctrine, which, correctly understood, is philosophically and theologically sound.

Richard of Middleton (Mediavilla) Franciscan theologian, born c.1249, died Rheims, 30 March 1302. Of English or French birth, Richard was *magister regius* (nicknamed the 'Doctor solidus') of the Franciscan studium in Paris from 1284, and his principal work is a commentary on **Peter Lombard**'s *Sentences*, which, though generally in the Augustinian tradition, tends towards the position of St **Thomas Aquinas** on some points.

Richard of Saint-Victor Victorine mystical theologian, born Scotland, died Paris, 10 March 1173. Richard became prior of the abbey of Saint-Victor in 1162, and died in office. The first writer to systematize mystical theology, Richard insisted on the importance of demonstration and argument in matters of theology, it is not enough merely to parade an array of authorities. His most important theological treatise, *De Trinitate*, presented a complex argument, based on the nature of love, of necessary reason for a triune deity. His spiritual teaching greatly influenced the Franciscan school, especially St **Bonaventure**.

Richard of Swyneshed (Swineshead, Suisseth) Oxford philosopher, fl. 1340–5. His fame rests on the *Liber calculationum*, from which he is known as 'the Calculator', a work among his others that prepared the way for infinitesimal calculus. **Leibniz** said in 1696 that Richard had introduced mathematics into Scholastic philosophy.

Richard of Wallingford English Benedictine, born Wallingford, c.1292, died 23 May 1336. He joined the Benedictines at St Albans, c.1315, became abbot and wrote on mathematics, astronomy and the general statutes of the Benedictines. He is famous for inventing a great astronomical clock, 'Albion', which indicated the times and seasons, as well as movements of the sun, moon and other planets. He died of leprosy.

Richard Rufus of Cornwall Franciscan theologian, born England, died Oxford, c.1260. Richard commented on the *Sentences* of **Peter Lombard**, having to hand the previous works of **Alexander of Hales**, **Hugh of Saint-Cher** and **Richard Fishacre**. A student of Aristotle, he anticipated Johannes **Duns Scotus** in appreciating the value of the universal; for him all creation demonstrates the existence of the Creator, and he denies the validity of the ontological argument, but admits that, from the possibility of *ens a se*, one can conclude to its existence.

Riche, Jodoco Flemish Franciscan, born Ghent, 1495, died Popayan, New Granada, 1575. He went to Peru while Pizarro was still at Tumbes waiting to meet the Inca at Cajamarca. A large area of land was assigned to the Franciscans, property formerly occupied by the palace of the Inca, on which to build a church, monastery and garden. Riche designed the buildings and directed construction; he founded the Colegio de San Andreas to train Indians in crafts and trades, how to plough with oxen, to make yokes and carts, and he taught them to read and write and to play musical instruments.

Richelieu, Armand Jean du Plessis de French cardinal and politician, born Paris, 9 September 1585, died Paris, 4 December 1642. Richelieu succeeded his brother in the family bishopric of Luçon in 1607. He gained the patronage of Marie de Médicis and became secretary of state, but when she fell from power in 1617 he was dismissed and exiled to Avignon, where he wrote *Les principaux points de la foi de l'Église catholique*, and *Instruction du chrétien*, a famous catechism written for his diocese. Made cardinal in 1623 by **Gregory XV**, he was appointed Louis XIII's principal minister in 1624, and from that date he dominated French political life. He aimed to establish an absolutist state and to raise France to the leading European power; by the time of his death he had succeeded in both these objectives. He kept his political and religious commitments separate; as in the controversy over Gallicanism, when he attempted to hold the balance between acceptance of the Pope's spiritual authority and rejection of his interference in French temporal affairs. A patron of art and literature, he founded the Académie Française in 1635.

Richer, Edmond French cleric and theorist of Gallicanism, born Chesley, Langres, 15 September 1559, died Paris, 29 November 1631. As syndic in 1602, Richer defended the Sorbonne against the religious orders, especially the Jesuits, and this controversy led him to develop an intransigent Gallicanism in opposition to their ultramontanism – *De ecclesiastica et politica potestate*. The book was condemned, he lost his post as syndic, and Cardinal **Richelieu** forced him to issue a partial retraction in 1629. Richer claimed superiority of the Councils over the Popes, and the competence of all the faithful as well as the hierarchy to preserve divine revelation. The Jansenists adopted these ideas in the eighteenth century.

Richey, Raymond American healing evangelist, born Illinois, 1893, died Houston(?), 1968. Although a minister's son, Richey led a non-religious life until he experienced healing of his eyes in 1911. He later became his father's assistant in Houston, and experienced a further healing, from tuberculosis, in 1919. His first meeting as a healing evangelist was in Hattiesburg, Mississippi. He travelled widely across the Americas, and visited Europe, Japan and Korea, achieving world fame. At a 1923 meeting in Tulsa he paraded healed individuals through the streets, and claimed 11,000 conversions in one day.

Richter, Franz Xaver Moravian composer, conductor and violinist, born Holleschau, 1 December 1709, died Strasburg, 12 September 1789. Composer at the Mannheim court, appointed kapellmeister at Strasburg Cathedral, Richter, with other composers of the Mannheim orchestra, contributed much to early symphonic history, creating a sacred style similar in form, texture and sonority to the Bohemian. In this fusing of the Bohemian–Mannheim and traditional Viennese baroque, he composed over 40 Masses, as well as Passions, Requiems, motets, Psalm settings and other Church music.

Rickaby, Joseph English Jesuit, born Yorkshire, 20 November 1845, died North Wales, 18 December 1932. Professor of philosophy at Stonyhurst and of theology at Campion Hall, Oxford, Rickaby's chief work is an annotated edition of St **Thomas Aquinas'** *Summa contra Gentiles*, entitled *God and his Creatures*. He also wrote more than 30 books, and 60 articles for *The Month*, that contributed significantly to the new Scholastic revival.

Ricoldus de Monte Croce Italian missionary, born Florence, *c*.1243, died there, 31 October 1320. Ricoldus entered the Dominicans in 1267 and travelled to the East by way of Palestine, to Baghdad, returning *c*.1301. The fall of Acre in 1291 occasioned the *Epistolae ad ecclasiam triumphantem*, a lamentation addressed to Our Lord and Our Lady. On his return to Florence he published *Impregnatio Alcorani*, a widely used apology against the errors of Islam, printed often in the fifteenth and sixteenth centuries.

Ridder, Charles American journalist, born New York City, 11 June 1888, died Poughkeepsie, New York, 10 October 1964. Ridder joined the *Catholic News* in 1900, became president of the Catholic Press Association, helped to found the National Catholic Welfare Conference News Service and the Catholic Youth Organization. **Pius XII** created him Knight of Malta in 1950 and Knight of the Holy Sepulchre in 1952, to which honour **John XXIII** added a star in 1959.

Ridley, Nicholas English bishop, born Northumberland, *c*.1500, died Oxford, 16 October 1555. Chaplain to Thomas **Cranmer** in 1537, Ridley, a Reformist, influenced his eucharistic leanings away from Real Presence doctrine; as master of Pembroke College, he helped to establish Protestantism at Cambridge. On becoming bishop of London, Ridley denied the doctrine of transubstantiation; he supported Lady Jane Grey's claim to the crown, and on **Mary Tudor**'s accession in 1553 was deprived of his see and excommunicated. When heresy became a capital offence, he and Hugh **Latimer** were burned at the stake before Balliol Hall.

Riemenschneider, Tilman German woodcarver and sculptor, born Franconia, *c*.1460, died Würzburg, 7 July 1531. Riemenschneider took a prominent part on the peasants' side in the Peasants' War of 1525; sent to prison and almost executed, he was saved by his reputation for work of deeply religious feeling. He is now, after three centuries of neglect, considered among the best artists in the late Gothic style. Among his most notable pieces are the Altar of the Blessed Sacrament in St Jacobus, Rothenburg ob der Tauber, as well as carvings in the Lady Chapel and on the high altar in Würzburg Cathedral.

Rienzo, Cola di   Italian nationalist agitator, born Rome, c.1313, died Rome, 8 October 1354. His fertile imagination and intensive study of classical authors together persuaded Rienzo of his divinely inspired mission to bring about a rebirth of the Roman Empire. In May 1347 he stirred up a popular revolution and, appointed 'Tribune of the People', restored order and chased the patrician families from the city. However, he became increasingly autocratic, lost the favour of the Pope and crippled the people with taxes to pay for his extravagances; he had to flee in December 1347 to the protection of the Spiritual Franciscans at Monte Marella. **Innocent VI** sent him back to Rome, which he entered triumphantly in 1354, but his behaviour offended the noble families and the people, who killed him. A colourful figure, his story inspired an opera by Richard Wagner.

Riganti, Giovanni Battista   Italian canonist, born Amalfi, 1661, died Rome, 17 January 1735. Riganti became auditor of the Congregation of Bishops and Regulars, a position he held for 35 years, after which the notes he had gathered were published (1744) by his nephews at the command of **Benedict XIV** under the title *Commentaria in regulas, constitutiones et ordinationes Concillariae Apostolicae*, notes which make plain his attempt to resolve the problems that arose under concordat law.

Rigby, John   Saint, English martyr, born Lancashire, c.1570, died London, 21 June 1600. Of little formal education, Rigby had left the Church but later became reconciled; while at the Old Bailey to plead the case of his master's daughter for non-appearance on a recusant charge, he admitted his own reconciliation to Catholicism, a capital offence. In Newgate Prison, he rejected any compromise with the queen's Church, and went to a barbaric death, saying distinctly on the scaffold: 'God forgive you. Jesus receive my soul.' He was canonized in 1970 as one of the **Forty Martyrs of England and Wales**. Feast day 21 June.

Riggs, Thomas Lawrason   American Roman Catholic chaplain, born Connecticut, 28 June 1888, died New Haven, 26 April 1943. Ordained for the Diocese of Hartford in 1922, Riggs entered on his career as first Catholic chaplain at Yale University, in which post he remained until his death. He built the striking St Thomas More Chapel at Yale, was a founder of the *Commonweal*, the Catholic weekly, and a participant in the National Conference of Christians and Jews.

Rigord of Saint-Denis   French chronicler, born Languedoc, c.1150, died 17 November 1208. Rigord devoted ten years to composing for Philip II the *Gesta Philippi Augusti*, at first a wholly laudatory account of his reign, but following the king's divorce, his affair with Agnes de Meramie and his appropriation of Church property it becomes severely critical of Philip's reign.

Rilke, Rainer Maria   Austrian poet, born Prague, 4 December 1875, died Montreux, 29 December 1926. After a misspent youth, Rilke led an errant existence in Europe, living in Paris on several occasions, North Africa, Egypt, and at Meudon, where Auguste **Rodin** influenced him as an artist; he became one of the most influential modern lyricists, his work being a peculiar blend of impressionism and mysticism. Dedicated to his poetry, he yet often despaired of his task, until in 1922, partly under Paul Valéry's influence, his genius was recognized in *Duineser Elegien*, *55 Sonette* and *Orpheus*, the culmination of his work.

Rimbaud, Jean Nicholas Arthur   French poet, born Charleville, 20 October 1854, died Marseilles, 10 November 1891. At the age of sixteen, Rimbaud embarked on a literary career marked by rebellion against authority and bourgeois mores, a turbulent life with Paul Verlaine, and the composition of his three groups of writings: poems in verse form, such as *Voyelles*, *Le Bateau ivre*, *Poètes de sept ans*; the metaphysical autobiography *Une Saison en enfer*; and the prose poems of *Les Illuminations*. Catholic critics like Paul **Claudel** found in the last a revelation of the supernatural, interpreting his poetry as translating a religious experience of

Being. His writing is such that atheists and Catholics, mystics and surrealists, can find in it confirmation of their own beliefs.

Rinaldi, Odorico (Raynaldus) Italian Church historian, born Treviso, June 1594, died Rome, 22 January 1671. Ordained an Oratorian, Rinaldi served twice as superior general and, at the request of **Innocent X**, succeeded Cardinal **Baronius** as director of *Annales Ecclesiae*, extending that chronicle in defence of Roman Catholicism from 1198 to 1565. His work is distinguished by its use of original sources, and though both men had made numerous chronological errors, the documents have proved themselves invaluable to succeeding scholars, such as the Bollandists.

Ring, Thomas Francis American lay leader, born Boston, c.1841, died there, 16 September 1898. Ring founded the first central council of the St Vincent de Paul Society, initiated formal co-operation with non-Catholic charitable agencies and became the first Catholic officer of the National Conference of Charities and Corrections. He spoke as a Catholic layman at the Chicago World Fair in 1893, and was seen by some Catholic leaders as the American **Ozanam**.

Rinuccini, Giovanni Battista Italian prelate, born Rome, 15 September 1592, died Fermo, 13 December 1653. Rinuccini entered the papal service, and in 1645 **Innocent X** named him nuncio to Ireland. In the crisis that had arisen over the response of the Anglo-Irish leaders to the grant by **Charles I** of only minimal tolerance to the Catholic religion, Rinuccini and the Irish bishops declared all supporters of such an agreement to be excommunicated, and they were imprisoned. The Anglo-Irish leaders did not accept this position and, though they were excommunicated again in 1648, the public did not support the action. Rinuccini thus failed in his mission to obtain equal status for the Catholic religion under Protestant rule.

Riordan, Patrick American Roman Catholic archbishop, born New Brunswick, Canada, 27 August 1841, died San Francisco, 27 December 1914. Riordan became archbishop of San Francisco in 1883, and founded the parochial school system. A delegate to The Hague Tribunal of 1910, Riordan won the case of the Pious Fund against Mexico, obliging them to pay indemnities to the Church in California; the Mexicans have ignored the ruling ever since. A leader in the restoration of public facilities after the earthquake in 1906, he quickly revived parish life, which exceeded its former levels. Fluent in six languages, Riordan was highly popular among the immigrants working in California.

Ripa, Matteo Italian missionary, born Salerno, 29 March 1682, died Naples, 29 March 1746. Ordained in 1705, Ripa went to China as a member of a papal delegation in 1710, studied Chinese in Canton and went to Peking, where he worked as court painter in the reign of Emperor Kang-hi, who also permitted him to do missionary work. When the emperor died, Ripa returned to Italy and opened the Chinese College at Naples for the training of missionaries. **Clement XII** approved the school in 1732, which continued until 1860 to prepare priests for the Chinese mission.

Ripalda, Juan Martínez de Spanish Jesuit theologian, born Pamplona, 1594, died Madrid, 26 April 1648. Ripalda entered the Society in 1609 and spent most of his career at Salamanca, becoming one of the best theologians in Spain, if not in Europe. He took up distinctive positions on grace and faith, his most important work being *De ente supernaturali*, which includes many questions not treated in standard texts; other works are preserved in manuscript at Salamanca and at the Biblioteca Nacional.

Rist, Valerius Bavarian Franciscan missionary and bishop, born Neuberg, 6 January 1696, died Nhatrang, Cochin China, 15 September 1737. He joined the Reformed Franciscans in 1712 and went to Cambodia, where he became pro-vicar, as well as of Laos, in 1730, and bishop of Cambodia, Vietnam and Cochin China in 1737. His missionary journeys were most successful; he converted many pagans, and wrote an unfinished catechism in Cambodian and a valuable itinerary of his travels in Indo-China.

Rita of Cascia Saint, Italian Augustinian nun, born Roccaporena, 1377, died May 1447. After the death of her tyrannical husband, she joined the Augustinians, owing, it is related, to supernatural intervention after they had refused her, and lived a life of heroic penance that won the admiration of all her contemporaries. Through her own austerity and sufferings, including a painful wound on her forehead, she became known as the 'Saint of Desperate Cases'. Her symbol is roses, which are blessed in commemoration on her feast day, in Augustinian churches. Feast day 22 May.

Ritschl, Albrecht German theologian, born Berlin, 25 March 1822, died Göttingen, 20 March 1889. Relying on the critical philosophy of **Kant**, Ritschl sought a middle way between an ontological and metaphysical articulation of Christian truths and a theology which conforms merely with a subjective piety. Thus Jesus Christ reveals God's intention for man's moral perfection; his divinity is to be understood not as an historical statement of fact, but as an expression of the revelational-value (*offenbarungswert*) of Christ for the community which trusts in him as God. The Gospel has been, and still is, committed to a community, not to individuals. Ritschl's teachings exercised an immense influence on the theology of Germany in the latter half of the nineteenth century.

Riva Aguero, José de la Peruvian historian, born Lima, 26 February 1885, died there, 21 October 1944. A professor at San Marcos University, Riva became mayor of Lima and minister of state, a post he gave up in disgust at the law permitting divorce. This action marked his return to the Church after a period of religious scepticism, and he spent his last years in historical research, in defence of the Hispanic-mestizo aspects of Peruvian culture, and the rights of the Church. His chief works include *La historia del Peru* and *El caracter de la literatura del Peru independiente*.

Rivadavia, Bernardino Argentinian politician, born Buenos Aires, 20 May 1780, died Cadiz, 2 September 1845. Rivadavia joined the revolution of 1810, became president of the republic, and promoted reforms that ensure his place among the founders of modern Argentina. However, in his efforts to reform the Church, he sought to subject it to the State, so as to be able to gain recognition from the Holy See of its legislation on religious matters. He had not wanted to create a schismatic Church, but the suppression of monasteries and confiscation of their properties led the country to the brink of separation from Rome.

Rivière, Jean French Roman Catholic theologian, born Montcabrier, 12 November 1878, died Bourg-Saint-Bernard, 3 May 1946. After ordination, Rivière taught dogma at Albi, but the Holy Office censured his teaching on Christ's knowledge and he lost his post; he then taught fundamental theology at Strasburg, 1919–46. He acquired a reputation as an authority on the history and theology of the dogma of Redemption, and his doctoral dissertation, *Le Dogme de la Redemption: Étude historique*, followed by *Étude théologique*, have ensured his lasting influence in this field.

Robert II King of France, born Orléans, *c.*970, died Melun, 30 July 1031. Robert spent much time conquering the Duchy of Burgundy and in settling disputes caused by Constance of Arles, his third wife. **Gregory V** anathematized him in 998 until he renounced his second wife Bertha of Burgundy. The first king to claim thaumaturgic powers, Robert favoured primogeniture in the royal succession, and sponsored the Peace of God. He enjoyed singing hymns in the company of clerks and advocated monastic reform, hence the surname, Robert 'the Pious'.

Robert, André French OT scholar, born Courseulles-sur-Mer, 9 November 1883, died Paris, 28 May 1955. Ordained a Sulpician in 1909, he taught at the seminary in Issy-les-Mouleneaux and at the Institut Catholique in Paris. He published numerous works on the OT, and was director of the *Supplément du dictionnaire de la Bible*, and associate editor of the *Bible de Jérusalem* and of the *Initiation biblique*.

Robert Bacon Dominican theologian, born after 1150, died Oxford, 1248. The first Dominican master of theology at Oxford, Robert joined the Order in 1234, and became a close associate of St **Edmund of Abingdon** and **Richard Fishacre.** He is noteworthy for his public denunciation of Peter des Roches before Henry III at the Parliament of 1233. A theologian in the Augustinian tradition; a few of his works survive, but only in fragments.

Robert Cowton (Cotton, Conton) English Franciscan theologian, flourished 1300–13. He became a disciple of Johannes **Duns Scotus** in Oxford, and succeeded him as lecturer on the *Sentences* of **Peter Lombard**, on which he wrote a commentary based on the master's notes, showing that on certain problems he could surpass him. The Dominican Thomas Sutton defended St **Thomas Aquinas** against Cowton in three books of his questions on the *Sentences*, and attacked Scotus in the fourth book.

Robert de Baldock English churchman, born Middlesex, died London, 28 May 1327. A man of great ability, Robert became Chancellor of England in 1323, and remained loyal to King Edward II when captured with him at Neath Abbey in 1326. Put on trial at Hereford, Robert was confined by the bishop, **Adam of Orleton**, in the episcopal prison. When he was transferred to London, the mob seized Robert and threw him into Newgate Prison, where he died of his wounds. Though three times recommended for bishoprics by Edward, he had failed to win appointment.

Robert de Bruges Blessed, Belgian abbot, born Bruges, eleventh century, died Clairvaux, 29 April 1157. Persuaded by **Bernard of Clairvaux** to accept the monastic vocation in 1131, Robert became in 1139 first Cistercian abbot at Our Lady of Dunes Abbey in Flanders. He succeeded Bernard as second abbot of Clairvaux in 1153. He is mentioned in the Cistercian Martyrology of 1491, as well as in the Missal of 1526. Feast day 29 April.

Robert de Courçon English theologian, born Keddleston, *c.*1159, died Damietta, Egypt, February 1219. Robert taught at Paris and wrote a *Summa theologica* (*c.*1204), as well as a commentary on **Peter Lombard**'s *Sentences*. **Innocent III** appointed him cardinal legate to France in 1212, and mandated him to promulgate what became the charter of the University of Paris, *Universitas magistrorum et scholarium Paristis studentium*, which confirmed the prohibition of the teaching of Aristotle's philosophical works. He went to Egypt as a preacher with the Crusades and died during the siege of Damietta.

Robert de Cricklade (Canutus) English Augustinian writer, born Cricklade, died Oxford, *c.*1174.

Robert became a Canon Regular of St Augustine at St Mary's in Cirencester, and became prior of St Frideswide's, Oxford, in 1141. He wrote a Life of **Thomas Becket**, who Robert says cured him of an illness; also an abridgement of the 37 books of Pliny's *Natural History*, which he dedicated to Henry II, and a *De connubio Jacobi*; he also studied the Hebrew texts of Josephus.

Robert de Sorbon French theologian, born 1201, died Paris, 1274. Ordained *c.*1226, Robert taught at Paris and through the influence of the comte d'Artois, became confessor to **Louis IX**, who encouraged him to found a theological college for needy lay students at the university, opened in 1257 and later known as the Sorbonne.

Robert Grosseteste English bishop, born Stradbroke, Suffolk, *c.*1168, died Buckden, near Huntingdon, 9 October 1253. One of the most learned men of the thirteenth century, Robert studied at Paris and Oxford, introduced the new Aristotelian learning, commented on Greek texts of the NT and edited many early Christian writings. A firm supporter of the English Franciscans, he profoundly influenced the Grey Friars through his theology and scholarship. Elected bishop of Lincoln in 1235, Robert proved himself a zealous, if rigorist, administrator; he denounced ignorance among the clergy and did what he could to improve the state of learning. He was critical of the Roman curia, especially of the appointment of Italian prelates, ignorant of the language and country, to wealthy English benefices. He did not however deny the doctrine of papal supremacy. He has always been highly regarded in England for his scholarship and his episcopal dedication. He is buried in Lincoln Cathedral.

Robert Guiscard Norman conqueror of Southern Italy, born Normandy, *c.*1015, died Cephalonia, 17 July 1085. Son of Tancred de Hauteville, he joined his brothers in Italy *c.*1047, and began a systematic conquest of the country, gaining recognition from **Nicholas II** in 1059 as duke of Apulia, Calabria and Sicily. By 1071 Robert had completed his Italian conquests and later allied himself with **Gregory VII**, becoming his dubious ally against **Henry IV** in 1084. He died in a great expedition against the Byzantine Empire.

Robert Holcot English Dominican theologian, born Northamptonshire, c.1290, died Northampton, 1349. Robert studied and taught at both Oxford and Cambridge and he claimed to be a Thomist, though he often disagreed with St **Thomas Aquinas** and there were nominalist elements in his teaching, derived from the new ideas of **William of Ockham**. Robert rejected the power of reason to attain to any knowledge of God, stressing His total freedom and absolute power (*potentia Dei absoluta*) to the point where He could even dispense with grace, and accept man's natural actions as meritorious for salvation. He died during the Black Death.

Robert Kilwardby English Dominican archbishop, born Leicestershire, c.1215, died Viterbo, Italy, 10 September 1279. Appointed to the See of Canterbury in 1272, Robert carefully avoided politics, called frequent synods, insisted upon monastic discipline and promoted charitable works. He is best known for his condemnation of certain doctrines, some of which had been held by **Thomas Aquinas**, notably his teaching regarding the unicity of substantial form, which he believed to be, in its implications, repugnant to the Catholic faith.

Robert of Arbrissel Blessed, hermit, wandering preacher and founder of the Order of Fontevrault, born Arbrissel, Brittany, c. 1055, died Orsan, France, 25 February 1116 or 1117. After studying at Paris, he was archpriest at Rennes, 1085–90, taught briefly at Angers, and then lived as a hermit in the forest of Craon, where he established a house of canons at La Roë to house his followers. Given a papal licence to preach by Pope **Urban II**, he resigned the abbacy of La Roë and began a career as a wandering preacher. He converted many to the religious life, and to house his many followers he was forced to build a double monastery at Fontevrault c.1100. He placed the Order under the control of an abbess, **Petronilla**, shortly before his death; he was buried at Fontevrault. The several attempts to canonize him all failed. Feast day 25 February.

Robert of Flamborough English canon penitentiary at Saint-Victor, Paris, born Flamborough, c. 1135, died Paris, between 1219 and 1233. Robert wrote *Liber poenitentialis*, a small book of instruc-

tions for confessors, based on canonically obsolete penitential discipline the use of which resulted in excessive legalism in moral guidance. Though he was criticized by his contemporaries, the book was yet copied and annotated for practical use over a century later.

Robert of Jumièges French archbishop, born Normandy, died Jumièges, Normandy, 26 May 1055. Elected abbot of Jumièges he there became a friend of the future **Edward the Confessor**, an exile at the time, who chose him in 1044 as bishop of London and, in 1051, for the See of Canterbury. The most important of several Norman and French prelates in the late Old English Church, he opposed the ambitions of Earl Godwin and influenced his banishment in 1050, but was deposed and banished in his turn in 1052 when Godwin returned.

Robert of Melun English Scholastic theologian and bishop, born c.1100, died Hereford, 27 February 1167. Robert taught theology in Melun, where he criticized the teaching of Peter **Abelard** on original sin, and **Peter Lombard**'s claim that the power to sin is a true power coming from God. His *Liber sententiarum* is important in the evolution of medieval theological doctrines.

Robert of Molesme Saint, founder of the monastery at Cîteaux, born Troyes, c.1027, died Molesme, 21 March 1110. While prior of the Benedictines at Molesme, Robert, together with other monks, was permitted to leave and to organize a new monastery at Cîteaux based on the original interpretation of the Benedictine Rule. Some eighteen months later he was ordered to return as abbot to his former monastery at Molesme. The Cistercian movement introduced a wave of reform and Cîteaux continued to prosper under Alberic, **Stephen Harding** and St **Bernard**. Feast day 29 April.

Robert of Newminster Saint, English abbot, born Yorkshire, died Newminster, 7 June 1159. Educated in Paris, Robert joined the Cistercians, helped to found Fountain Abbey, and founded the abbey of Newminster in 1139. The abbey grew rapidly, establishing three daughter-houses in less than ten years. Robert's tomb at Newminster became the scene of numerous miracles and of popular pilgrimage until the Reformation. Though he was never officially canonized, the Cistercians approved his cult in 1656. Feast day 7 June.

Robert of Orford (De Colletorto) English Dominican theologian, flourished in the late thirteenth century. Almost nothing is known of his life, but his works are profound, and in them he presents a strong defence, with only mild polemic, of the teachings of St **Thomas Aquinas** against **Henry of Ghent**, **Giles of Rome** and William de la Mare.

Robert of Rheims (Robert the Monk) French chronicler of the First Crusade, flourished early in the twelfth century. He can probably be identified with Robert of Saint-Denis, later of Marmoutier. He is thought to have visited the Holy Land at the beginning of the twelfth century, and on his return wrote a popular account, *Hierosolymitana expeditio*, which embellished previous Frankish reports.

Robert of Soleto (Robert of Sala, Salle) Blessed, Italian Celestine monk, born Sala, 1273, died Morrone, 18 July 1341. Received into his Order by Peter of Morrone (later **Celestine V**) in 1289, Robert founded monasteries and hospices for the sick and orphans. Contemporaries revered him for his spirit of penance and devotion to the Sacred Passion. Feast day 18 July.

Robert of Torigny (Robertus de Monte) Abbot and chronicler, died 24 June 1186. A monk of the Benedictine abbey of Bec, Robert became the most celebrated abbot of Mont-Saint-Michel, where he promoted discipline, learning and physical expansion. A man of deep learning and high culture, he was invited by **Alexander III** to participate in the Synod of Tours (1163). He revised the *Gesta Normanorum ducum* of **William of Jumièges**, and continued the chronicle of Sigebert of Gembloux, an important source of Anglo-French history; he translated the works of Aristotle and drew up a catalogue of the episcopal sees of France.

Robert of Winchelsea English archbishop, born Winchelsea, c.1240, died Otford, 11 May 1313. Having served as rector of the University of Paris, where he may have studied under **Thomas Aquinas**, Robert became archbishop of Canterbury in

1293. He upheld **Boniface VIII**'s bull *Clericis Laicos* and resisted Edward I's demands for clerical subsidies in the war with France. **Clement V** suspended Robert in 1305 at Edward's behest, but he resumed his see on Edward II's accession in 1307. He upheld his prerogatives against ecclesiastical as well as royal encroachment.

Robert Pullen (Pullus, Pellamus, Pullin) English theologian and cardinal, born c.1080, died Viterbo, September 1146. St **Bernard of Clairvaux** advised Robert to teach at Paris because of the sound doctrine he acknowledged him to possess. **Lucius II** called him to Rome in 1144 and made him the first English cardinal. Bernard further advised him to counsel and support **Eugene III**, the new Cistercian Pope.

Robert Stratford English bishop, born c.1290, died Aldingbourne, 9 April 1362. Educated at Oxford, chancellor of the university from 1335, he held many Church and State offices, including Chancellor of England, and bishop of Chichester from 1337. Himself honest, but undistinguished, Robert owed much to his older brother, John **Stratford**, in whose fortunes he shared.

Robert Waldby of York English friar and archbishop, born Yorkshire, died York(?), 1398. An opponent of John **Wycliffe**, he had been in Aquitaine with the Black Prince around 1363–7, and became bishop of Aire in 1386, archbishop of Dublin in 1390, bishop of Chichester and archbishop of York in 1396. As a loyal supporter of **Richard II** and of his policy in Ireland, he was buried by the king's command in Westminster Abbey.

Roberts, John Saint, Welsh martyr, born Trawgynod, c.1576, died Tyburn, London, 10 December 1610. Ordained a Benedictine in Spain in 1602, Roberts returned to England in 1603; arrested and exiled, he returned the same year, and laboured for seven years in the English mission. Arrested four times and banished twice, he was finally brought to trial in London in 1610, condemned and executed. He was cannonized in 1970 as one of the **Forty Martyrs of England and Wales**. Feast day 10 December.

Roberts, Thomas d'Esterre English Jesuit archbishop, born Le Havre, 7 March 1893, died London, 28 February 1976. Roberts became archbishop of Bombay in 1937, and very quickly proposed that, at a time of growing aspiration for national independence, the see should be led by an Indian archbishop, which resulted in the appointment of Valerian Gracias in 1950. Back in England, Roberts campaigned for causes such as disarmament, world peace, ban-the-bomb and a rethink of Church teaching on artificial contraception, which issue brought him into conflict with Cardinal **Heenan** of Westminster in 1964. Known as the 'Rogue bishop' for his non-conformist views, he was a pastor of warmth and sensitivity to the sufferings of others, many of whom found in him a great source of faith.

Robertson, James Canadian Presbyterian ecclesiastic, born Perthshire, 24 April 1839, died Toronto, 4 January 1902. Robertson emigrated to Canada in 1855 and, ordained in the Presbyterian Church at Toronto, he became a most effective administrator of the missions in Western Canada, and in 1895 moderator of the Church in Canada. He has been honoured by the annual Robertson Memorial Lectureship of the Presbyterian Church.

Robespierre, Maximilien François de Leader in the French Revolution, born Arras, 6 May 1758, died Paris, 28 July 1794. Elected to the Estates-General and to the National Assembly, Robespierre won election to the Convention of 1792, where he dominated the Committee of Public Safety during the Reign of Terror. An intellectual disciple of J. J. **Rousseau**, he denounced anti-Christian radicals, instituted the Republic of Virtue in 1794, and the cult of the Supreme Being as an alternative to Catholicism; however, popular enthusiasm was slight, indeed a reaction took place among the deputies that ended with Robespierre's downfall and execution by guillotine.

Robinson, Edward American biblical scholar, born Southington, Connecticut, 10 April 1794, died New York City, 27 January 1863. Robinson taught Scripture at Andover Seminary, Massachusetts, founded the American Biblical Repository, edited **Gesenius**' *A Hebrew and English Lexicon of the Old Testament*, and taught at Union Theologi-cal Seminary. He travelled in the Holy Land in 1837–9, identifying more Palestinian archaeological sites than had been discovered since the time of **Eusebius of Caesarea**, and published his findings in the highly reputed *Biblical Researches in Palestine, Mount Sinai and Arabia Petraea*.

Robinson, Henry Wheeler English Baptist theologian, born Northampton, 7 February 1872, died Oxford, 12 May 1945. Robinson became a teacher at Rawdon Baptist College, and then principal of Regent's Park College, London, an institution which he transferred to Oxford. In 1934 he was appointed reader in biblical criticism at Oxford University and three years later chairman of the Board of the Faculty of Theology, the first Free-churchman to hold this position. He retired from his post as principal of Regent's Park College in 1942: he regarded the move of the College from London to Oxford as his most significant achievement. He made his mark in the fields of OT theology and the doctrines of the Holy Spirit and redemption. Among his major works are: *Deuteronomy and Joshua*, *The Christian Doctrine of Man*, *Redemption and Revelation* and *Inspiration and Revelation in the Old Testament*.

Robinson, John English pastor of the Pilgrim Fathers, born Lincolnshire or possibly Nottinghamshire, *c.*1575, died Leiden, 1 March 1625. Little is known of his early life, though towards the end of the sixteenth century he may have studied at Cambridge. He became a minister, perhaps in Norwich, and separated from the Established Church to join a band of Congregationalists, with whom he migrated to Amsterdam in 1608 and then to Leiden. The community, declaring fealty to the British Crown and to the Anglican bishops, decided to found a colony along the Hudson River. Though prevented from joining them, Robinson encouraged and assisted their enterprise, and they in turn recognized him as pastor of the Pilgrims who landed in 1620 at Plymouth Rock in the *Mayflower*. He was a member of Leiden University and defended Counter-Remonstrant interests there and at the Synod of Dort; cf. *A Defence of the Doctrine Propounded by the Synod of Dort* (1624). He defended Separatism in *Justification of Separation from the Church* (1610), but the scope of his work is seen in his essays *Observations Divine and Moral* (1625).

Robinson, John Arthur Thomas Anglican theologian, Scripture scholar and bishop, born Canterbury, 15 June 1919, died Arncliffe, Yorkshire, 5 December 1983. Named suffragan bishop of Woolwich in 1959, he first came to prominence the following year when he was cited to appear for the defence in the case over the publication of *Lady Chatterley's Lover*. Robinson published *Honest to God* in 1963, sparking a heated debate about a modern, more secular, interpretation of traditional Christianity. Stimulated by the writings of Paul **Tillich**, Rudolph **Bultmann** and Dietrich **Bonhoeffer**, Robinson's highly original treatise proved a best-seller: he rejected the image of God as an old man in the sky, rather is he in depth – within each of us. He himself, however, regarded *Redating the New Testament* (1976) as his *magnum opus*. In *Can We Trust the New Testament?*, written shortly afterwards, Robinson showed himself as a defender of the historicity of Christianity.

Robinson, Paschal Irish Franciscan prelate, born Dublin, 26 April 1870, died Dublin, 26 August 1948. After ordination in Rome in 1900, Robinson spent ten years teaching and writing – *The Real St Francis*, *The Writings of St Francis*, *The Life of St Clare* – and being editor of *Archivum Franciscorum historicum*. He served on the American delegation to the Paris Peace Conference in 1919, and as apostolic visitor to Palestine, and to the Latin and Uniate Churches there and in Transjordan and Cyprus. From 1930 until his death he served as the first papal nuncio to Ireland since the time of **Cromwell**.

Robinson, William US lawyer and educationist, born Norwich, Connecticut, 26 July 1834, died Washington, DC, 6 November 1911. He studied at Willistan Seminary, Wesleyan University and Dartmouth College and Theological Seminary, and was ordained in the Episcopalian Church. He was a minister in Pittston, Pennsylvania, from 1857 to 1858 and at Scranton, Pennsylvania, from 1859 to 1862. The following year he joined the Roman Catholic Church, and he was professor of law at Yale from 1869 to 1895. During this time he also served as a judge and on the legislature. In 1895

he became a professor at the Catholic University of America, where he developed the School of Social Sciences and became dean of the School of Law. He wrote widely on the law and jurisprudence.

Robot, Isidore French missionary, abbot, born Tharoiseau, 18 July 1837, died Dallas, Texas, 15 February 1887. Ordained a Benedictine in 1862, Robot served as military chaplain in the Franco-Prussian War, and then volunteered for the New Orleans mission in 1871. He founded a Benedictine monastery in Oklahoma, which ministered to the Potawatomi and Chocktaw Indians, building schools for boys and girls, and centres to train Indians in trades and skills.

Roca y Corney, Joaquín Spanish journalist and librarian, born Barcelona, 1804, died there, 1873. He began his journalistic career as editor of *Diairo de Barcelona* in 1831; he created the Catholic periodical press in Spain, with the foundation in 1837 of *La Religion* and, with Jaime **Balmes** in 1842, of *La Civilicación*. Head of the Barcelona Public Library and of the university library there, and a member of the Real Academia de Buemas Letras, he wrote *Nujeres de la Biblia*, *La esperanza del Cristiano* and *La religion y la politica*.

Rocafuerte, Vincente Ecuadorean revolutionary, born Guayaquil, 3 May 1783, died Lima, 16 May 1847. Rocafuerte met Simón **Bolívar** in Paris, and this fuelled his sympathy for the liberators of Quito. He succeeded Flores as president of Ecuador and demonstrated liberal principles; he respected official religion, though he opposed excesses of the clergy, and brought in a foreign Protestant to direct his educational system. Dictatorial in his manner, Rocafuerte squashed any opposition, and helped to prepare the uprising of 1845 against Flores, who had succeeded him as president.

Rocca, Angelo Italian Augustinian humanist, bishop, born Rocca Contrada, 1545, died Rome, 7 April 1620. Rocca became editor of the Vatican Press for the Bible, General Councils and patristic works in 1585, and bishop of Tagaste in 1605. He participated in the edition of the Vulgate under **Sixtus V** and **Gregory XIV**, and wrote two volumes on St **Augustine** and free will. With his private book collection, he founded the Biblioteca Angelica, Rome's first public library.

Rocco da Cesinale   Italian Capuchin, born Cesinale, 30 April 1830, died Chieti, 19 December 1900. Rocco served as theologian at Vatican Council I, and apostolic delegate to Santo Domingo, where he discovered and authenticated the remains of Christopher **Columbus** in the cathedral there. His *Storia delle missioni* traces the history of the Capuchin missions from their beginning to 1700.

Roch   Saint, French healer of the plague-stricken, born Montpellier, *c.*1350, died Angera, *c.*1378. Little is known of Roch's life; the *Vita* by Francis Diedo, chronologically impossible and of doubtful value, credits him with curing many victims of the plague in the town of Aquapendente, and in other cities. His cult first appeared in Montpellier in 1410, and he was invoked against the plague in an outbreak in 1414 during the Council of Constance. His relics are venerated in Venice. Feast day 16 August.

Rodat, Emilie de   Saint, French foundresss, born Druelle, near Rodez, 6 April 1787, died Villefranche-de-Rouergue, 19 December 1852. Always concerned for the needs of the poor, Emilie tried her vocation in various religious congregations before opening a school for poor girls in Villefranche, where she founded, with Abbé Antoine Marty, the Sisters of the Holy Family of Villefranche, dedicated to educational and charitable works among the poor. Her own sanctification included many spiritual trials against the temptation to abandon her faith. **Pius XII** canonized her in 1950. Feast day 19 September.

Rodin, Auguste   French sculptor, born Paris, 12 November 1840, died Meudon, 17 November 1917. Rodin entered the School of Decorative Arts at the age of fourteen, and went on to become the greatest sculptor since **Michelangelo** and **Bernini**. His cast of *The Age of Bronze* (1877) was considered remarkable; with *St John the Baptist* (1879), his talent received unanimous recognition. Inspired by the masters of the Italian Renaissance, he drew from **Dante** the theme for *The Gate of Hell*, and its dominating figure of *The Thinker*

(reminiscent of Michelangelo's *Jeremiah* and *Lorenzo de' Medici*), later recast, along with other figures, as single statues. Among his most famous official and public works are the tragic *Burghers of Calais*, *Victor Hugo*, *Balzac*, *Clemenceau* and *The Kiss* – provocative expressions all, which exerted an extraordinary force upon contemporary sculpture.

Rodrigues Tcuzu João   Portuguese Jesuit, born Laurego, *c.*1562, died Macao, 1 August 1633. Rodrigues went to Japan as a youth, entered the Society there, and distinguished himself as a missionary in Japan and China from 1613, as well as as an author and interpreter at the Japanese court, where he was considered the highest European authority on the Japanese language and culture. He wrote a history of Japan and a Portuguese–Japanese dictionary and grammar.

Rodrigues Zorrilla, José Santiago   Chilean Roman Catholic bishop, born Santiago, 1752, died Madrid, 1832. Ordained in 1775, Rodrigues taught at the University of San Felipe, and refused to recognize the junta at independence, or the constitution of 1812; he became bishop during the Spanish restoration, but the patriots exiled him in 1821. He returned to his see in 1822, but a government suspicious of his loyalty exiled him to Spain in 1825. His involvement in politics had deprived his diocese of guidance during a crucial period of Chilean history.

Rodriguez, Alfonso   Spanish Jesuit writer, born Valladolid, April 1538, died Seville, 21 February 1616. Rodriguez filled the post of novice master for most of his life, becoming famous for the collection of his spiritual conferences, *The Practice of Perfection and of Christian Virtues*, given to novices.

Rodríguez, Alphonsus   Saint, Spanish Jesuit mystic, born Segovia, 25 July 1532, died Majorca, 31 October 1617. Rodríguez married, but on the death of his wife and family sought admission to the Society; accepted in 1571 as a lay brother and sent to the college of Montesione, he served as house porter for 46 years, being remembered for his humility, obedience, patience and mystical absorption in prayer. **Leo XIII** canonized him in 1888. Feast day 30 October.

Rodriguez, Cayetano José Argentine Franciscan patriot, born Buenos Aires, 1761, died there, 1823. Rodriguez joined the Franciscans at the age of sixteen, and became a professor of philosophy and theology. A member of the first national assembly, he opposed anti-Catholic and Masonic influences in the government, to which end he founded two newspapers, *El Centinela* and *El Official del Dia*.

Rodriguez de Mendoza Peruvian Roman Catholic priest and educator, born San Juan de la Frontera, 15 April 1750, died Lima, 10 June 1825. Ordained in 1778, Rodriguez worked in pastoral ministry among the Indians at Marcaval, a lowly and isolated town, and then became rector of San Carlos in Lima, where he remained for 30 years. He made the institution into an effective educational centre, for which he is famous, producing many intellectual and patriotic leaders, prominent in religion and politics.

Rodulphus Glaber Burgundian Benedictine chronicler, born Burgundy, *c.*985, died Auxerre, *c.*1047. Received as an oblate at Saint-Germain d'Auxerre, Rodulphus lived an unstable monastic life at several Cluniac residences. However, Abbot (St) William of Saint-Benigne and Abbot **Odilo of Cluny** both recognized his literary and artistic talents, which produced two works: *Historium libri quinque*, a handbook of history (900–1046), dedicated to Odilo, and the *Vita* of St William, his revered abbot. As a dedicated chronicler, Rodulphus remains our only source for many events of the Cluniac age.

Roe, Alban (Bartholomew) Saint, English martyr, born Suffolk, 1583, died London, 21 January 1642. A Protestant, Roe converted to Catholicism and enrolled at the English College, Douai, in 1608, but was dismissed for insubordination. Undaunted, he joined the Benedictines at Dieulouard (later Ampleforth), and after ordination in 1615, went to Paris to help found the community of St Edmund. He returned to the English mission in 1618, was caught the same year and imprisoned in New Prison, Maiden Lane, until 1623. Banished to Douai (later Downside), he returned after two years, was again apprehended, imprisoned in St Albans, and subsequently in the Fleet Prison, London, where he ministered to fellow Catholics. Transferred to Newgate Prison in 1642, but this time tried as a priest and seducer of the people, Roe was condemned to be hanged, drawn and quartered at Tyburn. He was canonized in 1970 as one of the **Forty Martyrs of England and Wales**. Feast day 15 December.

Roelas, Juan de las Spanish priest-painter, born Seville, *c.*1558, died Olivares, 23 April 1625. His Venetian style earned Roelas the title the 'Spanish Tintoretto', and he worked exclusively in the decoration of churches, specializing in altarpieces with life-size figures backed by angelic choirs in heavenly glory. The *Death of St Isidore* in the church of St Isidore, Seville, is considered his masterpiece.

Roemer, Theodore American Capuchin historian, born Appleton, Wisconsin, 19 January 1889, died Mount Calvary, 7 January 1953. Prominent in the field of Franciscan education, Roemer specialized in historical research of the missions. Among his works in this area, *The Ludwig-Missionsverein* and *The Church in the United States* traced the historical contribution of the sect from Munich, and *Ten Decades of Alms* outlined the impact of mission-aid.

Roger I (of Sicily) Great count of Sicily and Calabria from 1072, born 1031, died Mileto, 1101. Youngest son of the Norman Tancred, Roger and his brother, **Robert Guiscard**, systematically overthrew Muslim and Byzantine elements in Southern Italy, becoming organizers of the new 'Sicilian' state, and granting religious freedom to Greeks, Christians, Jews and Muslims.

Roger II (of Sicily) King, son of **Roger I**, born 1095, died 1154. He conquered Apulia and Salerno, effectively uniting Sicily and the southern part of the peninsula, and was crowned king of this new 'Kingdom of Sicily' by Antipope **Anacletus II** (and recognized later by **Innocent II**). He is credited with the fusion of Western, Byzantine and Arabic cultures in southern Italy and Sicily.

Roger de Pont l'Évêque Norman archbishop of York, died York, 21 November 1181. A contemporary of **Thomas Becket** in the household of **Theobald**, archbishop of Canterbury, Roger supported Henry II in his great quarrel with Becket, towards whom he was personally antipathetic. For having crowned Henry in 1170, Becket secured from **Alexander III** a bull suspending Roger from office, but he was reinstated after Becket's death, from complicity in whose murder Roger was absolved. He pressed, unsuccessfully, for recognition of the primacy of York over the Church in Scotland.

Roger le Fort Blessed, French bishop and confessor, born Ternes, Limousin, died Bourges, 1 March 1367 or 1368. Professor at Orléans, Roger became bishop there in 1321, and of Limoges in 1343. Dedicated to the apostolate, austere in his personal life and noted for his charity, he founded the Celestine priory at Ternes. He was venerated during his lifetime, and his tomb became a place of pilgrimage. Feast day 1 March.

Roger Marston English Franciscan theologian, born c.1245, died c.1303. Roger studied at Paris and witnessed the vehement theological disputations between St **Thomas Aquinas** and his own professor, John **Peckham**, at the inception of the precentor of Peronne; he became as a consequence a determined opponent of Thomist departures from traditional Augustinianism. Roger was thirteenth minister of the English Franciscan province, and his writings are important in understanding the system of **Duns Scotus**.

Roger of Elan Blessed, English Cistercian, died 4 January, after 1162. Roger joined the Cistercians at Lorroy-en-Berry, Bourges, and became first abbot of Elan, in the Champagne, in 1148. His *Vita*, considered unreliable, records that Archbishop Henry of Rheims, brother of King **Louis VII**, did not like the bread offered to him by the monks, and granted to the monastery as much land in Attigny as could be ploughed by five yoke of oxen in a year, to provide better grain. Feast day 4 January.

Roger of Hoveden (Howden) English chronicler, born Yorkshire, died c.1201–2. A priest, Roger first appeared in the service of Henry II, as his representative in Scotland in 1174; he acted as clerk and itinerant justice of the forest for him and for **Richard I**, whose Third Crusade he joined in 1191, and was present at the siege of Acre. He wrote a chronicle covering the period 649–1201, being something of a revision of the contemporary *Gesta Regis Henrici Benedicti Abbatis* (probably also by Roger).

Roger of Nottingham English Franciscan theologian, a member of the Oxford Friary, Roger flourished 1343–58. His only extant works are an *Insolubilia*, according to which all truly insoluble propositions are false, although many propositions are only mistakenly considered to be insoluble; and an *Introitus*, or introduction, to the second book of the *Sentences*. He seems to have been faithful to the older Franciscan theology of **Bonaventure**, **Richard Rufus** and **Duns Scotus**.

Roger of Salisbury Norman bishop, died Salisbury, December 1139. An obscure priest of Caen, Roger attached himself to the Conqueror's son, Henry I, who appointed him Chancellor of England, then bishop of Salisbury in 1101. Though held in low esteem by contemporary monastic chroniclers, he pleased Henry, who regarded him as second only to the king. He pledged to support Matilda as heir to England's crown, and helped Stephen de Blois seize the throne in 1135. Having become powerful and wealthy, Stephen dismissed Roger, and he returned to Salisbury, a broken man, having erred in using his priestly position as a buttress for political power.

Roger of Swyneshed English Benedictine logician, died Glastonbury Abbey, Somerset, shortly before 12 May 1365. Roger wrote *De obligationibus et insolubilibus*, two treatises on logic used as textbooks at some continental universities in the Middle Ages, and *De motibus naturalibus*, a treatise on physics, in part concerned with the possible proportions of velocities in moving bodies, considered important in medieval science, but as yet to be fully appreciated.

Roger of Todi Blessed, Italian Franciscan, born Todi, Umbria, died 5 January 1237. Received into the Order by St **Francis** himself, who referred to Roger as an exemplar of charity, in his *Speculum perfectionis*, and appointed him spiritual director at the convent of Poor Clares in Rieti. His friend **Gregory IX** called him a saint and approved his cult for the city of Todi, where he is buried. Thomas of Pavia in his dialogues credited him with sixteen miracles, and **Benedict XIV** approved his feast. Feast day 5 January.

Roger of Wendover English chronicler, died 6 May 1236. Roger joined the Benedictines and founded the historical school at St Albans, as well as being prior of the dependent house of Belvoir. His chief work, *Chronica sine Flores historiarum*, largely derived from other writers, is nevertheless a valuable source for English history from 1201 to 1235.

Roger of Worcester English bishop, born *c.*1133, died Tours, France, 9 August 1179. Grandson of Henry I and a friend of **Thomas Becket**, Roger retained the favour of his cousin Henry II. Moderate in his stance and concerned for the authority of the king, he nevertheless upheld the principles for which Becket contended. As a judge-delegate, he is important for the decretal collections of his judicial activities from the mid-1170s. Both **Giraldus Cambrensis** and **Alexander III** considered him one of the outstanding and exemplary English prelates of the time.

Rogers, John English Protestant martyr, born Deritend, near Birmingham, *c.*1500, died London, 4 February 1555. Rogers became chaplain to the English merchants at Antwerp, where he met William **Tyndale**, turned to Protestantism and married. He returned to London and denounced the greed of the court of **Edward VI**. Arrested in 1554, under **Mary Tudor**, he and other prisoners confessed their faith in extreme Calvinistic doctrines, which brought about their condemnation. Rogers refused to recant his beliefs and died at the stake in Smithfield – the first martyr in the Marian persecution – 'as if he had been led to a wedding' said Noailles, the French ambassador.

Rogers, Mary American foundress of the Maryknoll Sisters, born Boston, 27 October 1882, died New York City, 9 October 1955. She had assisted Bishop James **Walsh** to found the Catholic Foreign Mission Society of America (Maryknoll), and in 1912, with five other women, she founded the Maryknoll Sisters of the Third Order of St Dominic, which she headed for 35 years. By the 1950s, there were 1000 Sisters in more than 80 missions in Latin America and elsewhere.

Rogue, Pierre René Blessed, French martyr, born Vannes, 11 June 1758, died there, 1 March 1796. Rogue joined the Vincentians, and refused to subscribe to the Civil Constitution of the Clergy during the Revolution. Forbidden to exercise his priestly functions, he continued to do so in secret until apprehended in 1795. He ministered to his fellow prisoners until he was guillotined. **Pius XI** beatified him in 1934. Feast day 1 March.

Rohrbacher, René François French Church historian, born Langette, Moselle, 27 September 1789, died Paris, 1856. After ordination, Rohrbacher joined with Félicité de **Lamennais** in the Congregation of St Peter, but broke with him when he refused to submit to Rome. He taught history at Nancy and wrote *Catéchisme du sens commun* and *Histoire universelle de l'Église catholique*, in which he attempted to rectify some of the unacceptable ideas of Lamennais, especially that the Church had become decadent. As an ultramontane, Rohrbacher sought to glorify the Papacy's role in history and to influence the growth of ultramontanism among the clergy.

Rojas, José Guatemalan Franciscan missionary, born Quezaltenango, 31 August 1775, died Ica, Peru, 23 July 1839. During the independence movement in Central America, Rojas strongly opposed attempts by the civil authorities to control the Church in Guatemala and Honduras, especially a plan to place a priest, José **Delgado**, as bishop of León without the consent of Rome. For his pains, Rojas was once condemned to death and twice sent into exile, the last time in Peru in 1831, where his solicitude for the poor earned him the name 'Padre Guatemala'.

Roland of Cremona Italian Dominican theologian, born Italy, died Bologna, 1259. Roland founded the priory at Cremona in 1226, and taught at Paris from 1229 as the first religious to occupy the chair of theology. He is important in the development of the Dominicans' devotion to sacred learning that set the scene for the emergence of St **Thomas Aquinas**.

Rolendis Saint, Frankish princess and virgin, flourished seventh or eighth century. A thirteenth-century *Vita* describes Rolendis as the daughter of a king in Gaul, probably the Lombard **Desiderius**. To avoid marriage she fled to the convent of St Ursula in Cologne, but died *en route* in Villers-Poterie (Belgium). Her cult developed early around the relics contained in her eighth-century sarcophagus.

Rolevinck, Werner German Catholic theologian, born Laer bei Horstman, Westphalia, 1425, died Cologne, 26 August 1502. A renowned figure in the Charterhouse of St Barbara, Cologne, he wrote more than 50 exegetical, ascetic and theological works (some still unpublished), including his best-known, *Fasciculus temporum*, a universal history from the coming of Christ to his own day; and *De laude veteris Saxoniae nunc Westphaliae dictae*, a lively account of the manners and customs of his homeland.

Rolle de Hampole, Richard English hermit, born Thornton, Yorkshire, *c.*1290, died Hampole, near Doncaster, 29 September 1349. Richard early felt a call to the solitary, but not enclosed, life and settled at Hampole, where he died of the plague. The most widely read English mystical writer of his time, his poetry and prose have survived in some 400 manuscripts, of which the more imporant are: *De incendio amoris*, in defence of the contemplative and ecstatic life, and how he reached the highest point of divine rapture; and, despite his anti-feminist leanings, his writings for Margaret Kirkby and other holy women at Yedingham: *Ego dormio*, *On the Love of God*, *The Form of Perfect Living* and their attainment through contemplation.

Romagne, James René French Roman Catholic priest and missionary, born Mayenne, 10 July 1762, died Sace, 19 November 1836. Romagne refused to take the oath required by the Civil Constitution of the Clergy during the Revolution, and fled to England in 1792, then went to America in 1799; there he worked among the Abenaki Indians and white Catholics in Maine, and secured a land grant for the Indians of Passamaquoddy Bay

in 1801. Romagne composed the *Indian Prayer Book*, and taught the women spinning and weaving and the men agriculture. He returned to France in 1818 as parish priest of Sace, where he died.

Romaine, William Evangelical clergyman and theologian, born Hartlepool, 25 September 1714, died London, 26 July 1795. Educated at Hertford College (Hart Hall) and Christ Church, Oxford. Ordained deacon in 1736 and priest two years later. In 1749 he was appointed lecturer at St Dunstan's-in-the-West and in 1750 at St George's, Hanover Square. Owing to the influence of George **Whitefield** he became an extreme Calvinist. In 1751 he briefly held the professorship of astronomy at Gresham College. In 1766 he became the incumbent of St Anne's, Blackfriars. His writings include the *Hebrew Concordance of Marius de Calasio* (1748) and his trilogy on *The Life, Walk and Triumph of Faith*.

Romano of Rome Dominican theologian, died before 28 May 1273. A scion of the noble Orsini family, he went to Paris in 1266, where he studied under St **Thomas Aquinas**, who directed him in reading the *Sentences*, and whom he succeeded in 1272. Influenced by St **Bonaventure**, **Hannibaldus de Hannibaldis** and **Robert Kilwardby**, he did not follow St Thomas in doctrine, e.g. in repudiating the Augustinian thesis of divine illumination.

Romanus Pope (August to November 897), cardinal-priest of St Peter in Chains. Romanus replaced the murdered **Stephen VI** following the latter's 'Council of the Cadaver' on the corpse of his predecessor, **Formosus**, which had been rescued from the Tiber and given decent burial in St Peter's. Nothing is known of the circumstances of his election, nor of his short reign, and his successor **Theodore II** lasted only two weeks.

Romanus I Lecapenus Byzantine emperor, 920–44, born Lakape, Armenia, *c.*870, died Prote, 15 June 948. Emperor **Leo VI** befriended Romanus, who became emperor himself in 920. He saved Byzantium from disaster at the hands of the Bulgarian king Symeon, restrained Arab depredations in Southern Italy and protected the peasantry, who alone, not the nobles, furnished both taxes and soldiers. Romanus strove to maintain friendly relations with Rome. Deposed by his son-in-law **Constantine VII**, the joint emperor, he died in exile.

Romanus Melodus Saint, religious poet of the Byzantine Church, born Emesa, Syria, *c.*490, died Constantinople, *c.*555–65. Perhaps of Jewish extraction, Romanus came to Constantinople during the reign of **Anastasius I**. His Akathistos Hymn, *Kontakia* (on the Nativity), 24 alphabetically arranged stanzas in praise of the Virgin Mary, composed after she appeared to him in a vision on Christmas Eve, is still one of the most widely known and best-loved liturgical texts of the Byzantine Church, and is rated as a masterpiece of world literature. Feast day 1 October.

Romero, Juan Spanish Jesuit missionary, born Marchena, Seville, 1559, died Santiago, Chile, 31 March 1630. Romero went to Lima in 1589, trained in Peru for the missions, which he served until 1597, became superior of the Argentina mission and, later, first vice-provincial of Chile, 1625. As a theologian he published a two-volume *De praedestinatione.*

Romero, Oscar Arnulfo Salvadorian Roman Catholic archbishop, born Ciudad Barros, 15 August 1917, died San Salvador, 24 March 1980. Ordained in Rome in 1942, Romero returned to El Salvador and, influenced by Opus Dei, attacked Liberation Theology as expounded by Jon Sobrino, SJ. Thus a noted conservative when he became archbishop of San Salvador in 1977, he subsequently espoused the principles of Liberation Theology and, supported by all but one of his fellow bishops, endorsed, in a pastoral letter, proportionate counter-violence to the oppressive policies of the dictatorial regime. He tried to negotiate between the three main factions in the country, but was assassinated while celebrating Mass at the Divine Providence Hospital.

Rommen, Heinrich A. German scholar and lawyer, born Cologne, 21 February 1897, died Arlington, Virginia, 19 February 1967. As head of the Social Action department, Office of the Volksverein at Mönchengladbach, Rommen suffered persecution and imprisonment by the Nazis, but fled to England in 1938, and then went to the USA. He is chiefly noted for his contribution to the revival of

interest in natural law, his principal works being *The State in Catholic Thought* and *The Natural Law*, in which he shows the difference between the State of Nature theories of Hobbes and **Rousseau** and the Aristotelian-Thomistic Scholastic tradition as outlined in Catholic social thought, in **John XXIII**'s *Pacem in Terris*, for example, and the pastoral constitution on 'The Church in the Modern World' (*Gaudium et Spes*) of Vatican II.

Romuald II of Salerno Italian archbishop, born Salerno, died there, 1182 or 1183. Born into the Gearna family of Salerno, Romuald is renowned as the typical medieval churchman, politician and scholar: elected to the See of Salerno in 1153, an intimate friend of King William I of Sicily, much esteemed in Rome and entrusted by the Holy See to arrange a treaty of peace between **Alexander III** and Emperor **Frederick I Barbarossa**. He is remembered for his *Chronicon universale*, a history of events from the creation of the world to his own time.

Romuald of Ravenna Saint, founder of the Camaldolese, born Ravenna, Italy, *c.*952, died Val di Castro, near Fabriano, Italy, 19 June 1027. His father having killed a kinsman, Romuald entered the monastery of Sant'Apollinare-in-Classe to do penance on his behalf. After three years as a monk, he received permission to join the cluster of hermits gathered around the ascetic **Marinus** in the Veneto. Together, Romuald and Marinus spent some four years leading an ascetic life as wandering hermits in Central and Northern Italy; in 978, at the invitation of Abbot Guarinus of Cuxa, they left Italy for a hermitage in the Pyrenees. Romuald returned to Italy some ten years later in order to strengthen his father's monastic vocation. Emperor **Otto III** greatly admired Romuald, and appointed him abbot of his old monastery of Sant'Apollinare-in-Classe: his reign was not a success, and after about a year he resigned in order to return to the eremitic life. His most important eremitical foundations were Camaldoli and Vallombrosa. Feast day 7 February.

Ronan Saint, missionary bishop of the seventh century. Ronan is venerated in Brittany and may have been Irish, though several saints of that name are venerated in Ireland, such as SS Ronan of

Lough Derg, of Lismore, of Down, of Meath; the most famous is Ronan Find, son of Berach of Louth, who died *c*.664, and whose cult spread abroad perhaps as far as Brittany. Feast day 1 June.

Ronge, Johann German Roman Catholic priest, born Bischofswalde, 16 October 1813, died Vienna, 26 October 1887. Ronge founded the German Catholics movement (Deutschkatholizismus) as a reaction against veneration of the relic of the Holy Coat, fostered by the bishop of Trier. Excommunicated and degraded from the priesthood, Ronge organized a schismatic Church which abandoned its Catholic foundations and veered toward rationalism. More an agitator than a reformer, Ronge enjoyed a few years of notoriety and then sank into obscurity.

Ronsard, Pierre de French humanist and poet, born La Poissonnière, Vendôme, 11 September 1524, died Saint-Cosme-lès-Tours, 27 December 1585. Ronsard studied the classics and, with Joachim du Bellay, headed a new school of French Renaissance poetry, the Pléiade (his use of the term dates from 1556), to enrich its themes and, through imitation of Pindar and Horace, and a closer alliance to music, to elevate it from a craft to an inspired art. He became a poet in the court of Charles IX, and sided with the Crown during the religious wars. He condemned the Huguenots as false reformers and traitors, but dedicated works to **Elizabeth I** of England, while his sympathy for Mary Queen of Scots led him to condemn Elizabeth's counsellors. The Calvinists accused him of paganism, sycophancy and immorality. His *Hercule Chrétien* is a fine example of the fusion of classical and Christian themes, and attests to his later orthodoxy.

Roothaan, Johann Philipp Dutch Jesuit, born Amsterdam, 23 November 1785, died Rome, 8 May 1853. From a Calvinist background, Roothaan contributed significantly to the re-emergence of the Jesuits after **Pius VII** restored them throughout the world in 1814. He became general in 1829, worked to regain the old prestige and efficiency and imposed a revised interpretation of Ignatian spirituality, the 'Ratio Studiorum', and Thomism. He encouraged European Jesuits to work in the USA, built up the Maryland province into a viable

unit and provided for the founding of Marquette University.

Roper, William Son-in-law of St Thomas **More**, born, *c*.1495, died 4 January 1578. Roper married More's daughter, Margaret, and his account of the last meeting between her and her father, written after the latter's execution, with a picture so vivid as to suggest his presence there, is the chief source of information regarding More's personal life. A Lutheran for a time, he returned to the Catholic faith, gave generous financial support to Catholics in England, assisted in the publication of books in defence of the faith and aided in the foundation of the English College at Douai.

Rosa y Figueroa, Francisco de la Mexican Franciscan historian, born 1697, died Mexico City, late eighteenth century. Of noble Creole lineage, Rosa held several important posts within the Order in the province of the Holy Evangelist in New Spain. As provincial archivist he classified and catalogued the rich archives relating to the early Spanish presence in the area. In 1773 he wrote *Discursos humildes* against a decree of Charles III that only Spanish be spoken in New Spain; Rosa defended the Indian languages and insisted on the necessity of teaching them.

Rosalia Saint, Italian recluse, died 1160. A Basilian, or possibly a Benedictine nun. Information before the seventeenth century concerning Rosalia's life is unreliable. She is the patroness of Palermo, where, during a plague that raged there in 1624, a vision granted to one of the stricken led to a search for her remains, which were found in a grotto on Monte Pellegrino. The plague abated when they were brought to Palermo; a supposedly autographic inscription on the wall of the cave identified her, and confirmed her having chosen to live there for the love of Jesus Christ. **Urban VIII** added her name to the Roman Martyrology in 1630. Feast day 15 July.

Rosas, Juan Manuel Argentine dictator, born Buenos Aires, 30 March 1793, died Southampton, England, 14 March 1877. A big-scale rancher, he organized his gauchos into an informal militia, which he used in support of conservatism and federalism; this identified him to Federalists as the man to maintain peace and order, and they elected him governor of the province. He had excellent relations with the Church and the Jesuits until 1842, when he expelled the Society. Rosas represented the reactionary, agrarian interests of the interior; tyrannical, unenlightened and undemocratic, he did unify the country. He died in exile.

Rosati, Joseph Italian Roman Catholic bishop, born Sora, Naples, 12 January 1789, died Rome, 25 September 1843. Rosati joined the Congregation of the Missions and volunteered for the USA mission, becoming bishop of St Louis, Missouri, in 1824. A strong administrator, he built a cathedral and many churches, brought the Religious of the Sacred Heart of Jesus from France to St Louis, opened St Louis Hospital with the Daughters of Charity, and fostered the founding of St Louis University by the Jesuits. **Gregory XVI** sent him to Haiti as apostolic delegate in 1840, where he reconciled Church–State difficulties in a concordat.

Rose of Lima Saint, first saint of the New World, born Lima, 20 April 1586, died there, 24 August 1617. Baptized 'Isabel de Flores', Rose became a Dominican tertiary, and took St **Catherine of Siena** as her model, living a life of remarkable austerity and penance in a cell she had built in the garden of the family home. In a room of the house she set up an infirmary, where she cared for destitute children and infirm elderly people. The Inquisition pronounced her great mystical gifts and social activities as directed by impulses of grace. **Clement X** canonized her in 1671, and proclaimed her patron of Peru, the Americas, the Indies and the Philippines. Feast day 12 April.

Rose of Viterbo Saint, Italian Third Order Franciscan, born Viterbo, 1235, died there, 6 March 1252. Having reputedly received an apparition from Our Lady that cured her, Rose joined the Third Order Secular of St Francis, and championed the cause of the Papacy against Emperor **Frederick II**. At the age of fifteen she tried to enter the Convent of St Mary, but was refused admission and retired to a cell in her father's house. She died at the age of seventeen and her body remains incorrupt after seven and a half centuries. **Calixtus III** canonized her in 1457. Feast day 4 September.

Roseline Saint, French Carthusian, born Château d'Arcs (Fréjus), 1263, died Celle-Roubaud (Provence), 17 January 1329. Roseline entered the Carthusians at the age of fifteen, practised severe penances and worked miracles, becoming prioress at Celle-Roubaud, c.1300. She is venerated throughout France and is pictured as a Carthusian nun with maniple and stole. Feast day 17 January.

Roselli, Salvatore Maria Italian Dominican theologian, born Naples, died Rome, 3 October 1784. Roselli taught at the College of St Thomas, Rome, where, reacting against the philosophy of René **Descartes**, he promoted that of St **Thomas Aquinas**. In his *Summa philosophia* he presented authentic Scholastic philosophy according to the mind of St Thomas, comparing classical Thomistic philosophy with modern systems of empiricism, rationalism, Cambridge Platonism and naturalism; in general his work can be said to inaugurate the neo-Thomist movement.

Roskovanyi, Augustus Hungarian Roman Catholic bishop, born Szama, 7 December 1807, died 24 February 1892. Ordained in 1831, Roskovanyi received the abbey of Saar as a benefice, and became bishop of Waitsen in 1851, and of Neutra in 1859. His many works on the primacy of the Church, on the sacraments and on Our Lady are important for the documents they contain.

Rosmini-Serbati, Antonio Italian philosopher, born Rovereto, 24 March 1797, died Stresa, 1 July 1855. Rosmini studied at Pavia and Padua, and, following ordination in 1821, founded the Institute of the Brethren of Charity, known as 'Rosminians', priests or laymen who devote themselves to preaching, the education of youth, and works of charity. His works *The Five Wounds of the Holy Church* and *The Constitution of Social Justice* aroused great opposition, especially among the Jesuits, and were placed on the Index in 1849; they were proclaimed free from censure by the Congregation of the Index before his death. **Leo XIII**, however, condemned 40 of his propositions in 1887, and forbade their being taught. Rosmini's fame rests on his stature as a speculative thinker and writer in the fields of moral philosophy, theology and educational theory. He sought to develop out of the thought of **Augustine** and

Thomas **Aquinas** an objective and unifying base for all human knowledge and action, as a counterweight to **Kant**'s subjectivism. His insights into the thought of the great Doctors were genuine and profound, but were not appreciated by the Scholastics of the nineteenth century. However, there has been a revival of interest in Rosmini since 1955, and John Paul II, in 1988, spoke of 'the growing admiration and interest for the person of Antonio Rosmini and for his thought'.

Rossello, Maria Giuseppa Saint, Italian foundress, born Albisola Marina, 27 May 1811, died Savana, 7 December 1880. Maria became a Franciscan tertiary in 1827 and worked among the poor in Savoy; in 1837 she founded the Congregation of the Daughters of Our Lady of Mercy, of which she became superior general, and expanded its mission to the education of girls and the care of the sick. **Pius XII** canonized Maria in 1949, by which time the Daughters numbered some 3000 in 263 houses throughout Italy and Latin America. Feast day 7 December.

Rossetti, Carlo Italian cardinal, born Ferrara, 1614, died Faenza, 23 November 1681. Rossetti came to the attention of Cardinal Barberini, who in 1639 sent him to the English court, where he tried to help English Catholics and to convert **Charles I**. When he tried to negotiate a loan to assist the king against the Parliamentarians, however, the Puritans became hostile and Rossetti fled to Flanders in 1641. Appointed bishop of Faenza in 1643, and later cardinal, he devoted himself with great zeal to his diocese.

Rossetti, Christina Georgina Poetess and writer, born London, 5 December 1830, died London, 29 December 1894. She was the sister of Dante Gabriel **Rossetti**. She wrote poetry most of her life and published devotional books. She became engaged to the artist James Collinson, but broke it off when he became a Roman Catholic. Her Christmas carol 'In the Bleak Midwinter', sung to the tune 'Cranham' by **Holst**, is well known.

Rossetti, Dante Gabriel Poet and Pre-Raphaelite artist, born London, 12 May 1828, died Birchington-on-Sea, Kent, 9 April 1882. He was the brother of Christina **Rossetti**. He was educated at King's College School, London, and the Royal Academy of Art. His poetry includes 'The Blessed Damozel' and sonnets. He formed the Pre-Raphaelite Brotherhood with Holman Hunt and **Millais**, and aimed to present 'truth to nature'. He executed his paintings in minute detail and painted outdoors. Famous paintings of his are *The Girlhood of the Virgin Mary* and *Ecce Ancilla Domini*, depicting the Annunciation.

Rossi, Giovanni Batista de Italian archaeologist of Christian Rome, born Rome, 22 February 1822, died Castelgandolfo, 20 September 1894. Influenced by G. **Marchi**, SJ, Rossi used documentary evidence in the Vatican Library to explore the ancient catacombs and thus to map out and interpret the inscriptions. His work became the foundation for all subsequent Christian archaeology. His masterwork is *Roma sotterranea cristiana*, and he contributed much to specialist journals and *Corpus inscriptionum latinarum*.

Rossi, Jean Baptiste Saint, Roman Catholic priest, born Voltaggio (Genoa), 22 February 1698, died Rome, 23 May 1764. From an impoverished family and of a sickly constitution, Jean Baptiste needed a special dispensation to be ordained, in 1721, but proved himself an outstanding and popular priest, concerned for the temporal and spiritual welfare of the poor, preaching in market-places, hospitals, prisons and at any gathering of the poorer classes. **Leo XIII** canonized him in 1881. Feast day 23 May.

Rostock, Sebastian Venerable, German Roman Catholic bishop, born Grottkau, Silesia, 24 August 1607, died Breslau, 9 June 1671. A member of the cathedral chapter of Breslau during the Thirty Years' War, Rostock was engaged principally in providing spiritually and materially for some 600 parishes of the diocese restored to Catholicism at the command of Ferdinand III. It fell to Rostock to renew religious practices in these churches and to staff them with clergy.

Rosweyde, Heribert Founder of modern hagiography, born Utrecht, 29 January 1568, died Antwerp, 5 October 1629. He went to the university at Douai, but in 1588, after two years at Douai, he joined the Society of Jesus. After his noviceship, however, he returned to the university to study philosophy, then he went to Louvain for theological studies. He taught philosophy at Douai from 1597 to 1600, and then 'controversy' (questions disputed with Protestantism) at St-Omer and Antwerp until 1607. In that year, however, he conceived a plan for a scientific study of the lives of the saints. He himself had such a variety of tasks in his life that he was never able to realize the plan he had drawn up, though he left some studies of saints' lives, a martyrology and a history of the Church in Flanders. The project was launched by Jean **Bolland** some years after his death.

Roswitha of Gandersheim (Hrotsvitha) German canoness and poetess, born *c.*935, died after 1000. Exceptionally well-read for her time in classical as well as Christian literature, Roswitha wrote poetry on German historical themes, though is best known for her plays, which she modelled on the work of Terence, seeking, however, to illustrate Christian virtue, rather than human frailty as he had done. Her writings do not seem to have been much read in the Middle Ages; they were discovered and printed in 1501, since when they have been translated and adapted to suit a revival of interest.

Roth, Heinrich German Jesuit missionary, born Augsburg, 18 December 1620, died Agra, India, 20 June 1668. Roth went to Ethiopia, and in 1651 arrived in Goa; he reached the empire of the Great Mogul in 1653 and became rector of the Jesuit residence in Agra in 1659. He learned Urdu, Persian and Sanskrit and, having studied Indian philosophy and religion, compiled a Sanskrit grammar.

Rother, Stanley American Roman Catholic priest and missionary, born Okarche, Oklahoma, 27 March 1935, died Guatemala, 28 July 1981. Following his ordination in 1963, Rother volunteered for the Guatemala mission, where in the most adverse circumstances he sought to sow the seeds of an indigenous Church. By 1979, the Tzutuhil Indians and Ladinos of his area of Santiago Atitlan were oppressed by increasing violence and kidnapping; priests, nuns, catechists and lay readers were victims of torture, and Rother himself was murdered in his rectory, believing that his refusal to flee had averted the execution of Indian residents in the house.

Rouault, Georges Henri French painter and printmaker, born Belleville, 27 May 1871, died Paris, 13 February 1958. A pupil of Gustave Moreau at the École des Beaux-Arts from 1890, Rouault studied with Matisse and others who came to be known as 'Les Fauves'. He depicted in a uniquely expressionist style the vices of his age, painting corrupt judges, clowns and prostitutes, albeit with a truly Christian compassion and gentleness. He won the Prix Chenevard in 1893 with *The Child Jesus among the Doctors*. He turned to printmaking and executed the famous *Miserere* series of 60 etchings and aquatints, considered the finest graphic art of the twentieth century. Diaghilev commissioned him to design settings and costumes for *The Prodigal Son*, and he designed stained-glass windows for the church at Assy. **Pius XII** named Rouault a papal knight in 1953; he was given a state funeral, the first accorded an artist by the French government.

Rougemont, François Flemish Jesuit missionary, born Maastricht, 2 April 1624, died Tai Tsang, China, 4 November 1676. Rougemont left for China in 1656, travelled on foot through India, arriving in the area of Shanghai in 1659. Exiled in Canton, 1665–71, he wrote *Historia Tartaro-Simica nova*, relating the takeover of China by the Manchu dynasty, and the persecution of missionaries. He urged the need for a native clergy, and the use of Chinese in the liturgy, and collaborated on a Chinese–Latin edition of a Life of Confucius, influential in introducing Confucian ethical theories to the West.

Rouleau, Felix Raymond Marie Canadian cardinal archbishop, born Île-Verte, Quebec, 6 April 1866, died Quebec City, 31 May 1931. Ordained a Dominican in 1892, Rouleau became provincial in 1919, bishop of Valleyfield in 1923 and archbishop of Quebec in 1926, and was made cardinal the following year. Known as a mystic and theologian, he presided at the founding of the Academy of St Thomas Aquinas at Laval University.

Rouquette, Adrien Emmanuel American Roman Catholic priest and missionary, born New Orleans,

13 February 1813, died there, 15 July 1887. Ordained in 1845, Rouquette set up mission chapels among the Choctaw Indians along the bayous in St Tamany Parish, where he lived and worked from 1859 until the end of his life. He published a poetic essay, 'Les Savannes', and became editor of *Le Propagateur catholique* of Louisiana.

Rouse, Clara Ruth English missionary and ecumenical leader, born Clapham, South London, 17 September 1872, died 29 September 1956. She studied at Girton College, Cambridge, from where she joined the Student Volunteer Movement. She became editor of the *British Student Volunteer* and a travelling secretary among women students, visited North America and was a missionary in India, 1899–1901. John R. **Mott** asked her to visit Europe and she became a secretary of the World Student Christian Fellowship, 1905–24. An effective organizer, speaker, leader, fund-raiser and traveller, she maintained a strong commitment to evangelism. After World War I she helped launch European Student Relief. She was educational secretary of the Missionary Council of the National Assembly of the Church of England, 1925–39, and for decades one of the most influential women in the international Christian community. She was a member of the World's Young Women's Christian Association Executive Committee, 1906–46, and president 1938–46. She was widely published and shared with Stephen **Neill** in editing *A History of the Ecumenical Movement* (1954).

Rousseau, Jean Jacques French-Swiss writer and philosopher, born Geneva, 28 June 1712, died Ermenonville, 2 July 1778. Raised a Calvinist, Rousseau converted to Catholicism and went to Paris in 1742, where he collaborated with Denis Diderot on the *Encyclopédie*. Literary celebrity came in 1750 with *Discours sur les sciences et les arts*; and *Discours sur l'origine de l'inégalité* (1754) had considerable influence on modern political thought. Having returned to Calvinism, Rousseau composed three of the century's most influential books: *Julie ou la Nouvelle Héloïse*, a passionate love story propounding a return to the natural life; *Emile*, a treatise on education, in parallel with *The Social Contract*, Rousseau's concept of a just state in which the free man voluntarily submits to the general will of the people. His religious ideas were condemned in 1762, and, wanting to justify himself before posterity, he wrote the *Confessions*, a curious mixture of vanity and self-accusation. Though he can be seen as the forerunner of both Romanticism and modern totalitarianism, his elevation of the individual above society contributed to democratic thought. By substituting a sentimental faith for revealed religion, and by removing Christian doctrine from its supernatural context, he paved the way for humanistic liberalism.

Rousselot, Pierre French Jesuit theologian, born Nantes, 29 December 1878, died Western Front, 25 April 1915. Rousselot greatly influenced the revival and the interpretation of the doctrine of St **Thomas Aquinas**. Both in his doctoral thesis and in *Pour l'histoire du problème de l'amour au Moyen-Âge*, he examined the Thomistic theory of participation: the validity of knowledge to which the human intellect is naturally directed; the natural love of man for God and the effects upon it of original sin, preferring a Graeco-Thomistic conception of love which reconciles the love of God and that of self.

Routley, Erik Congregational minister and hymn authority, born Brighton, Sussex, 31 October 1917, died Nashville, Tennessee, 8 October 1982. Educated at Lancing College, Sussex, and Magdalen and Mansfield Colleges, Oxford, he served the Church in various appointments in England and Edinburgh, and became professor of Church music at Westminster Choir College, Princeton, New Jersey, in 1975. He had an inspiring genius for the pastoral use of hymns, a scholarly knowledge of hymnody, and assisted in the compilation of many hymn-books, from *Congregational Praise* (1951) onwards, including *Hymns for Celebration* (1974). He was the foremost British hymnologist of his generation.

Rovenius, Philippus Dutch Roman Catholic archbishop, born Deventer, 1 January 1574, died Utrecht, 10 October 1651. Appointed titular archbishop of Philippi in 1620, Rovenius endured conflict with the religious orders, especially the Jesuits, who refused to accept his jurisdiction. During the anti-Catholic period of the revolution against Spain, he ministered to the spiritual needs of Dutch Catholics; condemned by a civil court in

1646, he was forced to live in hiding to escape punishment. His major writings include *Tractatus de missionibus*, which established him as an eminent missiologist.

Rowland, Daniel Revivalist preacher and pioneer of the Welsh Calvinistic Methodist Church, born Nantcmnlle, Wales, 1711, died Llangeitho, 16 October 1790. Ordained deacon in the Church of England in 1734 and priest in 1735. Following his evangelical conversion under the preaching of Griffith **Jones**, he carried out extensive evangelism in various parts of Wales, giving rise to revivals, particularly at Llangeitho in 1762. From 1737 he worked with Howell **Harris** and from 1743 with William **Williams**. He was dispossessed of his church in 1763, and a 'New Church' was built for him at Llangeitho. He wrote several hymns and sermons and published a Welsh translation of John **Bunyan**'s *Holy War*.

Rowley, Harold Henry English biblical scholar, born Leicester, 24 March 1890, died Manchester, 4 October 1969. Rowley became a minister in the United Church, professor in Shantung Christian University, China, and lecturer in Hebrew at University College, Wales, and at Manchester University. He published much on OT criticism and commentary, and one of his last books of essays, *From Moses to Qumran*, indicates the great range of his scholarship. He played a leading role in bringing together the divided world of OT scholarship after the Second World War, and gained world-wide esteem as foreign secretary of the (British) Society for Old Testament Study in the post-war years.

Roy, Camille Canadian Roman Catholic priest and literary critic, born Berthier-en-Bas, Quebec, 22 October 1870, died Quebec City, 24 June 1943. After ordination, Roy studied at the Sorbonne and the Institut Catholique de Paris, before being associated with Université Laval as a teacher and administrator for more than 40 years. Roy contributed literary criticism to the periodical *La Nouvelle France*, and numerous studies in historical criticism gathered in collections published in 1909 and 1943.

Roy, Maurice Canadian Roman Catholic bishop and primate, born Quebec City, 5 January 1905, died there, 1985. Roy taught at Université Laval, and enlisted as a military chaplain in 1939, being mentioned in despatches. Named archbishop of Quebec, and cardinal in 1965, Roy became a leader in the 'Quiet Revolution' in Quebec society, and oversaw the pacific transfer into State hands of schools, orphanages, hospitals and other such institutions. He served on the preparatory commission on church doctrine for the Second Vatican Council, and as president of the Justice and Peace Commission, being the author of *Message on the Second Development Decade*, and *Reflections on the Tenth Anniversary of Pacem in Terris*, of **John XXIII**. It was to Roy that **Paul VI** addressed *Octagesimo adveniens*, the letter, drafted by Roy himself, to mark the eightieth anniversary of **Leo XIII**'s encyclical *Rerum Novarum*.

Royce, Josiah American philosopher, born Grass Valley, California, 20 November 1855, died Cambridge, Massachusetts, 14 September 1916. The teaching of Le Conte and Sill, and his reading of Herbert **Spencer** and J. S. Mill, formed the empirical basis of Royce's philosophy. He studied at Leipzig and Göttingen, went to Johns Hopkins in 1876 and met William James, whose influence got him invited to Harvard, where he remained until his death. Influenced by Hegelian idealism, his philosophy tries to reconcile the exigencies of theoretical thought and those of the practical life, to affirm the Absolute without denying the concept of the individual. (See: *The Spirit of Modern Philosophy* and *The World and the Individual*.)

Rozanov, Vasili Russian philosopher, born Vietluga, 2 May 1856, died Sergiev Posad, 4 February 1919. Rozanov taught history in provincial secondary schools, and published excellent studies of **Dostoevsky**, notably *The Grand Inquisitor*, in which the problem of spiritual freedom is shown as fundamental to his religious ideology. Though a Christian himself, Rozanov rejected the Church's attitude to sex as too ascetic: he understood sex to be a mystical experience that yearned to be blessed and sanctified; he sought to establish a naturalistic cult with procreation as its central rite.

Rubbra, Edmund English Roman Catholic composer, pianist and author, born Northampton, 23

May 1901, died Gerrards Cross, Buckinghamshire, 13 February 1986. As a boy he attended the Congregational Church. He studied under **Holst** at the Royal College of Music, and at Reading University. During the Second World War he served first as a gunner, but then formed a string trio (which continued for a time after the war) to entertain the troops. Although attracted to Buddhism, he became a Roman Catholic in 1947, the same year that he became a lecturer in music at Oxford University. He remained at Oxford until 1968, and from 1961 to 1974 he also taught at the Guildhall School of Music. He wrote many religious works, often settings of metaphysical poetry, ancient hymns of the Roman Catholic Church, themes associated with the Virgin Mary and a symphony in tribute to **Teilhard de Chardin**. Rubbra's last, unfinished symphony was adapted as a Symphonic Prelude for organ by his pupil Michael Dawney.

Rubeis, Leonardo de Italian Franciscan theologian, born Giffoni, near Salerno, died Avignon, after 17 March 1407. **Urban VI** deposed Rubeis as master general at the beginning of the Western Schism, though the Antipope **Clement VII** made him a cardinal. Rubeis severely criticized Antipope **Benedict XIII** for not trying to heal the Schism, and returned to the papal side in 1403. His most important theological works are a commentary on the Song of Songs, two works on the Schism, and a commentary on the four books of *Sentences*.

Rubens, Peter Paul Flemish artist, born Siegen, 28 June 1577, died Antwerp, 30 May 1640. A true man of the Renaissance, brilliant painter and engraver of religious, mythological and historical portraits and landscapes, Rubens is the apotheosis of Flemish expression, as were **Michelangelo**, **Titian** and **Rembrandt** in their respective schools. Rubens developed his mannerist style in Italy, 1600–8 and, where earlier Flemish artists had reacted with formalism, Rubens found both sensual and spiritual vitality. Among his important works, *St Helena*, *Christ Crowned with Thorns* (influenced by Annibale **Carracci** and **Caravaggio**) and the famous *Elevation of the Cross* in Antwerp Cathedral, show the influence of Michelangelo and Tintoretto. In 1620–30, he produced his great cycle of the *Life of Marie de Médicis*; in 1628 he painted the king and queen of England, and did

the preliminary work for the ceiling of the Banqueting Hall in Whitehall (completed 1634). Rubens was mourned by the whole of Europe when he died.

Rubino, Antonio Italian Jesuit missionary, born Strambino, 1 March 1578, died Nagasaki, 22 March 1643. Rubino went to India in 1602 and laboured there for 36 years; he composed a seven-volume *Catena evangelica*, a guide for preachers. He learned the languages of China and Japan while a visitor there, and proposed, in *Metodo della doctrina . . .*, adapting some Roman rituals to the Far Eastern religions; the treatise was placed on the Index in 1660. Rubino and his companions were seized in Gatauma and died in prison at Nagasaki.

Rubio, Antonio Mexican Jesuit philosopher, born Villa de Rueda, Spain, 1548, died Alcalá, 1615. Rubio went to Rome as Jesuit procurator in 1601, and thereafter taught at Alcalá. Though he followed **Thomas Aquinas**, he was critical of the Angelic Doctor, and departed from him on certain issues, notably the distinction between essence and existence. His excellent grasp of Aristotle and his respectful commentaries on St Thomas place him with the best of his contemporaries, Toletus, **Fonseca**, **Suárez** and Vázquez.

Rublev, Andrei Russian icon painter and monk, born *c*.1360, died Spasso-Andronikov Monastery, Moscow, 29 January 1430, having become a monk, it is thought, fairly late in life. Otherwise little is known of his life except that he worked as an assistant to the Greek painter Theothanes of Constantinople, while Theothanes was in Moscow in the early years of the fifteenth century. Rublev inherited the spiritual legacy of St **Sergius** through his successor, St Nikon, as can be seen in his work on the cathedral of the Annunciation, Moscow, and in his most famous painting, the *Old Testament Trinity* in the Tretiakov Gallery. With others of his peers, he represents the culmination of Orthodox Church art in the fourteenth and fifteenth cenuries; they greatly influenced the development of Russian icon painting.

Rubrouck *see* **William of Rubruk**

Rucellai, Bernardo Historian and antiquarian,

born Florence, 11 August 1448, died Florence, 7 October 1514. As cultural patrons and as men of letters, the Rucellai family feature heavily in histories of Renaissance Florence. Bernardo was the son of Giovanni Rucellai (1403–81), for whom Leon Battista Alberti designed the Palazzo Rucellai and the façade of the Dominican church of S. Maria Novella. His *De bello italico* documents the opening phase of the Italian Wars after the French invasion of 1494. The gardens he laid out, known as the Orti Oricellari, later became a meeting-place for early sixteenth-century Florentine intellectuals.

Ruch, Charles French Roman Catholic theologian, born Nancy, 28 September 1873, died Strasburg, 29 August 1945. Ordained in 1897, Ruch became bishop of Nancy in 1918, and of Strasburg in 1919. He engaged in two bitter controversies: in defence of the Church against the concordat of 1801, which suppressed religious instruction in primary schools; and in support of the French position in Alsace-Lorraine, which caused a split among the French- and German-speaking Catholics in his diocese. He made various contributions on the sacraments and the Mass to the *Dictionnaire de théologie catholique*.

Rudigier, Franz-Josef Venerable, Austrian Roman Catholic bishop, born Partheneu, 7 April 1811, died Linz, 29 November 1884. In 1845 Rudigier became court chaplain and tutor to Franz Josef and to Maximilian, later emperors of Austria and Mexico respectively. As bishop of Linz he zealously defended the Church's rights, and opposed Josephinism and secular liberalism; he promoted Catholic association, the Catholic press and Catholic social action. His cause for canonization was introduced in 1905.

Rudolph I German king, born Aargau, 1 May 1218, died Germersheim, 15 July 1291. Head of the Habsburg house, elected king in 1273, in preference to **Alfonso X** of Castile, or Ottocar II of Bohemia, Rudolph had the support of **Gregory X**, who wished to oppose French–Angevin interests. When Rudolph demanded that all illegally acquired Crown lands be surrendered, Ottocar refused to do so and Rudolph crushed him and his Slav allies, the Poles and Silesians, at the Battle of Marchfield (1278); he thus secured

the base of power and control for the House of Habsburg, in the person of his son Albert.

Ruffini, Ernesto Italian cardinal archbishop, born San Benedetto, Po, 19 January 1888, died Palermo, 11 June 1968. Ordained in 1910, Ruffini studied at the Pontifical Biblical Institute, and taught sacred Scripture at the Lateran Seminary. Appointed archbishop of Palermo by **Pius XII**, and a cardinal in 1946, Ruffini attacked Pierre **Teilhard de Chardin**'s evolutionary theories in his own *Theory of Evolution judged by Reason and Faith*. He is considered one of the leading theologians of the Second Vatican Council.

Ruffo, Fabrizio Italian cardinal, born Sanlucido, 16 September 1744, died Naples, 13 December 1827. Of noble birth, Ruffo worked within the Roman curia, where his reforms in the States of the Church aroused so much opposition that he retired to Naples and attached himself to the Bourbon court. When the French attacked Naples, Ruffo raised an army (the Sanfedists), and regained the city for the Bourbons by promises of easy peace terms for the French and Italian Jacobins. He returned to Rome in 1814, where he finally accepted the changes of the Napoleonic period.

Ruffo, Vicenzo Italian Church musician, born Verona, c.1505, died Sacile, 9 February 1587. Ruffo served as *maestro di capella* at Verona, Milan and Pistoia, 1554–79, and when again at Milan Cathedral, came under the influence of Archbishop (later Saint) Charles **Borromeo**, who, concerned to implement reforms of the Council of Trent, persuaded Ruffo to revise and clarify his musical style, noticeable in work including Masses, motets, Psalm settings and settings of the *Magnificat*.

Rufina and Justa Saints, virgin martyrs, probably martyred in Spain in 287 for refusing to sell, as vessels for pagan worship, the earthenware they had made. Feast day 19 July.

Rufina and Secunda Saints, sisters, virgin martyrs, died c.257. They are recorded as having been martyred in the Valerian persecution, and buried on the Via Cornelia at the ninth milestone. Feast day 10 July.

Rufinus   Italian archbishop and theologian, born perhaps near Assisi, first half of the twelfth century, died before 1192. archbishop of Sorrento, Rufinus wrote a *Summa decretorum*, and introduced for the first time a systematic exposition of **Gratian**'s *Decretum*; also, *De bonis pacis*, an exposition of St **Augustine**'s *De Civitate Dei*, asserting that the spiritual and temporal orders are, each in its own sphere, independent of each other.

Rufinus of Aquileia   Italian monk and writer, born Concordia, near Aquileia, 345, died Messina, 410. Rufinus became a close friend of St **Jerome**, studied Scripture and **Origen** under **Didymus the Blind** and **Gregory of Nazianzus**, at Alexandria in 371, and finally settled in Jerusalem in 381. He translated Greek theological works into Latin, including St **Basil**'s Rule for the monks at Pinetum; also Gregory of Nazianzus and **Eusebius**, as well as his own commentary on the Apostles' Creed. His translation of Origen's *De Principiis* (398), in the preface of which he mentioned Jerome's alleged admiration of Origen, led to a permanent breach in their friendship, and to Jerome's calling him 'Tyrannius'.

Ruinart, Thierry   French Benedictine scholar, born Rheims, 10 June 1657, died Auberge de Hautvillers, 29 September 1709. Ruinart entered the abbey of St-Remi in 1674, and then the monastery of Saint-Germain-des-Prés, the great centre of Maurist learning, where he became a friend of Jean Mabillon, with whom he published volumes VIII and IX of the *Acta sanctorum ordinis Sancti Benedicti*. He wrote a daily journal in 1698 and 1699, at the height of the disputes between the Jesuits and Maurists. His correspondence has been kept in the Bibliothèque Nationale in Paris.

Ruiz, Peter of the Visitation   Spanish priest and liturgist, born Toledo, died 1601. Dubbed 'prince of the rubricists', Ruiz took part in the reform of the Roman calendar under **Gregory XIII**, and that of the Breviary and the Roman Missal under **Clement VIII**. He spent 26 years editing and revising the rubrics in *De ceremoniis ecclesiasticis*, only to have it ignored by the Congregation of Rites, through the petty intrigue of a curial cardinal.

Ruiz Blanco, Matias   Spanish Franciscan mission-ary, born Estepa, 1645, died *c.*1708. Ruiz Blanco volunteered for the Piritu missions in Venezuela in 1672, and promoted the welfare of the Indians there for 30 years. He prepared grammars and dictionaries in the Cumanagoto language, so that it could serve as the common tongue of the various tribes in the Piritu area.

Ruiz de Montoya, Antonio   Peruvian Jesuit missionary, born Lima, 11 November 1583, died there, 11 April 1653. Ruiz studied at Córdoba, and began his missionary work in Paraguay, where he was superior of the Paraguayan Reductions, 1623–37. He founded a number of missions and defended the rights of the Indians against attacks of the Paulistas, and also in Spain before the Council of the Indies, where he sought royal protection for them. He wrote *Tesoro de la lingua Guarani* and *Arte y vocabulario de la lingua Guarani*, works of lasting linguistic value.

Ruiz y Flora, Leopoldo   Mexican Roman Catholic archbishop, born Amealco, Querétaro, 12 November 1865, died Morelia, 12 December 1941. Ruiz became bishop of León, Linares and Monterey, and in 1912 archbishop of Morelia. He founded eight schools within his dioceses, created many new parishes and directed his social apostolate to industrial and agricultural workers. A long-time friend of President Porfirio Diaz, he was exiled by the victorious rebels in 1914, and again in 1925 during the Mexican persecution of the Church. **Pius XI** named him apostolic delegate and he achieved a *modus vivendi* with President Portes Gil, who, however, exiled him when the Holy See condemned violations of their agreement.

Rummel, Joseph Francis   American Roman Catholic archbishop, born Steinmauern, Germany, 1 October 1876, died New Orleans, 8 November 1964. Rummel went to New York as a child, and served in Harlem, where he witnessed racial conflict. As archbishop of New Orleans, he championed racial integration, coming to prominence in 1949, when he refused to sanction an outdoor celebration where whites and blacks could not participate together. In 1953 he ruled that blacks would no longer be required to give way to whites in receiving Holy Communion, nor be excluded from parish organizations. Clergy and laity were bitterly hostile, and when he ordered the integration of parochial schools, state and city officials, many of them Catholics, appealed to Rome against him, to no avail. Rummel threatened with excommunication any Catholic legislator who worked for segregation, and closed a parish that refused to accept a black priest.

Runcie, Robert Alexander Kennedy   Archbishop of Canterbury, born Crosby, near Liverpool, 2 October 1921, died St Albans, Hertfordshire, 11 July 2000. He was drawn to Anglo-Catholicism both by his sister and by the headmaster of Merchant Taylors' School, Crosby, which he attended. He went from there to Oxford University in 1941, but joined the Scots Guards, and won the Military Cross, before returning to the University after the war. He studied for the priesthood at Wescott House, Cambridge. He was ordained a deacon in 1950 and a priest the following year, taking up a curacy at Gosforth on Tyneside. In 1952 he returned to Wescott House, of which he became vice-principal, before becoming dean of Trinity Hall, Cambridge in 1956, and principal of the theological college at Cuddesdon in 1960. He became bishop of St Albans in 1970, and in 1979 (a reluctant) archbishop of Canterbury. He was much committed to ecumenism, receiving Pope John Paul II at Canterbury in May 1982, but his commitment to the ordination of women in 1987 made relations with the Roman Catholic and Orthodox Churches more difficult. In the aftermath of the riots in Brixton, London, he set up a commission, whose report, *Faith in the City* (1985), was regarded as very left-wing. He also provoked the anger of the Conservative prime minister of the day when, in 1982 in a service for the dead in the Falklands War he prayed for the Argentinian, as well as the British, soldiers who had lost their lives. He retired as archbishop in 1991, and returned to live in St Albans. He was created a life peer on his retirement.

Rupert of Deutz   German Benedictine abbot, born Liège, *c*.1075, died Deutz, 4 March 1129. A strong supporter of the Gregorian reform, Rupert refused ordination until his simoniacal bishop had been reconciled with Rome, in 1106. He defended the mystical theology traditionally held by the Benedictines, especially against the dialectical methods of **Anselm of Laon** and **William of Champeaux**. A noted scriptural exegete, he gained little attention until the Reformation, when his imprecise language led to conflicting interpretations of his doctrine of the Eucharist, in particular his use of 'impanation' rather than 'transubstantiation'.

Rupert of Ottobeuren   Blessed, German Benedictine abbot, died Ottobeuren, 1145. Abbot of Ottobeuren from 1102, Rupert introduced the Cluniac reforms as elaborated in the constitutions of Abbot **William of Hirsau**, whose monastery had contributed to the cause of ecclesiastical reform in Germany. Feast day 14 or 15 August.

Rupert of Salzburg   Saint, founder and first bishop of Salzburg, died 27 March 718. A descendant of the Frankish Merovingian royal line, Rupert founded Sankt Peter (*c*.700), the oldest monastery in Austria, on the ruins of ancient Juvavum, with a community of Irish-Celtic monks, and also the convent of Nonnberg, entrusted to his niece Erentrude as first superior; both these communities later became Benedictine. With his companions, Rupert evangelized the country around about, built churches, civilized the people, developed the local economy by opening the saltmines, and (thus) gave Juvavum its modern name of 'Salzburg'. Feast day 27 March.

Ruskin, John   English art critic and social philosopher, born London, 8 February 1819, died Coniston, 20 January 1900. Born into a wealthy Evangelical family, Ruskin devoted the first period of his career to art criticism, establishing a reputation with *Modern Painters*, *The Seven Lamps of Architecture* and *The Stones of Venice*. In these works love is the root of all good art, pride the source of all bad art, Gothic architecture expresses the harmony between medieval cathedrals and the culture from which they sprang; the Gothic architecture of Venice reflects national and domestic virtue, whereas the Venetian Renaissance mirrors corruption. Ruskin's views of art and morality were the object of some ridicule, but basically he was attacking the vulgar and sensational. He renounced his Evangelical heritage in 1855, and could then dismiss anti-Catholic notes to his earlier works as pieces of rabid and utterly false Protestantism. He was a close friend of Cardinal

Manning, so some had expected his conversion to Roman Catholicism, but he does not seem to have considered such a step. Ruskin was the most influential art critic of the nineteenth century, and greatly influenced Marcel Proust, William **Morris** and George Bernard Shaw, among many others.

Russell, Charles Taze   American founder of the Jehovah's Witnesses, born Pittsburgh, Pennsylvania, 16 February 1852, died Pampa, Texas, 31 October 1916. Russell reacted against doctrines of hell and fixed the date for the Second Coming, first as 1874, then as 1914. He caricatured the Christian doctrine of the Trinity as Three Gods in one person, and held that Christ was not God, but the first created being. He organized Bible study groups, and in 1879 began publication of the magazine *Zion's Watch Tower and Herald of Christ's Presence.*

Russell, John   English bishop, born Winchester, died Lincolnshire, 30 December 1494. Russell entered the royal service, became archdeacon of Berkshire in 1466, bishop of Rochester and then of Lincoln, 1480. He was named Chancellor of England in 1483, but Richard III dismissed him in 1485 on suspicion of disloyalty. He served five kings, amassed a considerable library, and Thomas **More** praised him as 'a wyse manne and a good . . . one of the beste learned menne . . . England hadde in hys time'.

Russell, Mary Baptist   Mother, Irish foundress of the Sisters of Mercy in California, born Killowen, 18 April 1829, died San Francisco, 6 August 1898. She responded to a request by Archbishop **Alemany** of San Francisco for a Mercy Foundation, going there as superior of eight volunteers in 1854, to service the needs of victims of poverty, disease and immorality in a decade of physical and moral disorder in the city. In the cholera epidemic of 1855, they were given charge of the county hospital, which she turned into St Mary's Hospital. She made several other charitable foundations in California, including five schools.

Russell, Odo   British diplomat, born Florence, 20 February 1829, died Potsdam, 25 August 1884. A Protestant, Russell succeeded Lord Lyons as envoy to the Holy See in 1858, becoming friendly with

Pius IX, Cardinal **Antonelli** and Cardinal **Manning**. He remained neutral on the question of papal infallibility during Vatican I, believing that his intervention would prejudice his influence in Rome.

Russell, Richard   English Roman Catholic bishop in Portugal, born Berkshire, 1630, died Vizen, 15 November 1693. As a young man, Russell worked at the English College in Lisbon, and became a priest and chaplain to the Portuguese ambassador to England. He was made a canon of the English Chapter in 1661 and bishop of Portalegre in 1671, then the Chapter wanted him to resign his see and, as a validly ordained bishop of the jurisdiction in England, to exercise those functions there; but Russell refused, regarding the plan as schismatic. He later became bishop of Vizen in Portugal.

Russell, William Thomas   American Roman Catholic bishop, born Baltimore, 20 October 1863, died Charleston, South Carolina, 18 March 1927. Appointed secretary to Cardinal **Gibbons** in 1894, Russell became bishop of Charleston in 1916. He had a successful episcopate, and joined three other bishops named to the board of the National Catholic War Council during the Great War; he continued to serve on the executive of its successor, the National Catholic Welfare Council. He opened many new parishes and welcomed the Holy Ghost Fathers and the Oblate Sisters of Providence into the diocese.

Rutherford, Joseph Franklin   American president of the Watch Tower Bible and Tract Society, born Morgan County, Missouri, 8 November 1869, died San Diego, California, 8 January 1942. Rutherford succeeded Charles Taze **Russell**, the founder, as president of the Society, coining the name 'Jehovah's Witnesses' for the movement in 1931. He wrote twenty books attacking all Christian Churches, especially Roman Catholics, and greatly increased the membership to over 100,000.

Ruysbroeck, Jan van (Ruusbroec)   Blessed, Flemish mystic, born Ruysbroeck, near Brussels, 1293, died Groenendaal, 2 December 1381. He left home at the age of eleven, and went to live with an uncle, a canon of St-Gudule. His training was for the priesthood, and he was ordained *c.*1317. They continued to live together until they retired to a hermitage in 1343 to live a more devout life, establishing a community which later evolved into a community of canons regular. He became prior. His writings, notably *The Spiritual Espousals*, were influential at the time. His works show influences from **Augustine** to **Eckhart**, having a strong flavour of Pseudo-Dionysus the Areopagite. His work has been the subject of criticism but like the other Rhineland Mystics he is again becoming noticed. He was beatified in 1908. Feast day 2 December.

Ryan, Abram Joseph American poet, born Hagerstown, Maryland, 5 February 1838, died Louisville, Kentucky, 22 April 1886. Ordained a Vincentian priest just prior to the Civil War, Ryan served as chaplain in the Confederate army. He commemorated their defeat in his poignant poem 'The Conquered Banner', which became the lament of the entire South. He went on to journalism in Louisiana, Georgia and Alabama, and edited two weekly newspapers, and a variety of religious tracts.

Ryan, Dermot Irish Roman Catholic archbishop, born Dublin, 27 June 1924, died Rome, 21 February 1985. Appointed archbishop of Dublin in 1972, Ryan renewed initiatives with regard to the poor, the illiterate and the unemployed; he faced new challenges, resulting from unprecedented population growth, in healthcare and education, marriage, sexual relations and protection of the unborn. Named a cardinal of the Roman curia, he died following his appointment as pro-prefect of the Sacred Congregation for the Evangelization of Peoples.

Ryan, James Hugh American Roman Catholic bishop, born Indianapolis, 15 December 1886, died Omaha, Nebraska, 23 November 1947. Ryan taught at the Catholic University of America, and served as secretary of the National Catholic Welfare Conference. Named bishop of Omaha in 1935, and to the bishops' committee of **Pius XII**'s *Peace Points*, he spoke out on controversial subjects, opposed Nazism and condemned the American Medical Association's recognition of birth control. He wrote the *Peace Points* of Pope Pius XII, among his other publications.

Ryan, John Augustine American Roman Catholic social philosopher, born Dakota County, Minnesota, 25 May 1869, died Washington, DC, 16 September 1945. The definition of society's obligations in **Leo XIII**'s *Rerum Novarum* captured Ryan's imagination, and his lifelong task became the awakening of American Catholics to the realities of the social order. His *Socialism: Promise or Menace?* and *Distributive Justice*, classic statements, became his most important contributions to Catholic social thought. His *Bishops' Program for Social Reconstruction* (1919) proposed social reforms now taken for granted in the USA. He became director of the Social Action Department of the National Catholic Welfare Conference in 1920, and an adviser to President Roosevelt in his New Deal programme.

Ryan, Patrick John Irish-American Roman Catholic archbishop, born Thurles, Ireland, 20 February 1831, died Philadelphia, 11 February 1911. Ryan emigrated to St Louis, Missouri, in 1852 and, following ordination, gained recognition as an orator; **Pius IX** invited him to Rome to preach the English Lenten sermons in 1868. Named archbishop of Philadelphia in 1884, he made his mark as an administrator, greatly increasing the number of churches, schools, training institutions and charitable organizations. An amiable and witty man, he succeeded in breaking down the anti-Catholic feeling that had existed in Philadelphia, and enjoyed the esteem of the entire city.

Ryder, Sue English philanthropist, born Yorkshire, 3 July 1923, died Sudbury, Suffolk, 2 November 2000. She was brought up a devout Anglican, and was sent away to school at Benenden. At the outbreak of war in 1939 she volunteered to serve as a nurse, but was drafted into the Special Operations Executive to help prepare secret agents for return – in her case – to occupied Poland. Her experience of working with Poles attracted her into the Roman Catholic Church. After the war she worked in Germany with former prisoners. In 1952 she founded a home for ex-prisoners of war at Celle and the following year turned her mother's house at Cavendish, near Sudbury, into a home for the sick and disabled. In 1959 she married Leonard **Cheshire**, who was engaged in similar work. By the time of her death there were 28 such homes in Poland alone, and many others elsewhere. She was much decorated by Britain (including being made a life peer with the title 'Baroness Ryder of Warsaw' in 1979), Poland and Yugoslavia.

Ryken, Francis Xavier Dutch religious, born Elshout, 30 August 1797, died Bruges, Belgium, 26 November 1871. Feeling called to the religious life, but unable to enter a monastery, Ryken formed a community, with the convert and editor Joachim Le Sage ten Broeck, in 1823. Having sought, but not obtained, Rome's approval for a community of brothers devoted to education, he went to the USA in 1832, where he worked among the Potawatomi Indians in Michigan. Determined to found a brotherhood, he finally established at Bruges, in 1839, the Brothers of St Francis Xavier (Xaverians). The congregation opened a home in England in 1848, and a school in Louisville, Kentucky, in 1854.

S

Sá, Manoel de Jesuit theologian, born Villa de Condé, Portugal, 1530, died Arona, Piedmont, 30 December 1596. Joined the Jesuits in 1545, became professor of philosophy at Alcalá in 1551 and in 1557 went to teach theology in Rome. He was appointed to the Septuagint Commission by **Pius V**. Publications include several Scripture commentaries and a dictionary of casuistry, *Aphorismi Confessariorum*, which was initially placed on the Index as it allowed confession and absolution by letter. This was corrected in 1608, removed from the Index and was much used by moral theologians. De Sá spent the latter part of his life in pastoral work in Genoa and Loreto.

Sabas Saint, monk, born Mutalaska, Cappadocia, 439, died Marsaba, 5 December 532. After several years of life as a solitary, he founded, to the south of Jerusalem, the Mar Saba lavra, which still exists. Unusually for a monk of that period and with some reluctance, he was ordained to the priesthood in 490, and soon after was created superior of all the hermits in Palestine by the patriarch of Jerusalem. Strongly orthodox in his theology, he played a leading role in the struggle against the Monophysites and the Origenists. A typicon of the Eastern church bears his name. Feast day 5 December.

Sabatier, Louis-Auguste French Protestant theologian, born Vallon, 22 October 1839, died Paris, 12 April 1901. Professor of Reformed dogmatics at Strasburg University between 1868 and 1873, and at the new Protestant faculty in Paris from 1877. Much influenced by **Schleiermacher** and **Ritschl**, he applied the methods of historical criticism to the NT. Exercised great influence in both Protestant and Catholic theology by his interpretation of Christian dogma as the symbolism of religious feelings. In Catholic circles this influence paved the way for Modernism. Publications include *The Apostle Paul* (1870, ET 1891), *La Vie intime des dogmes* (1890), *Sketch of a Philosophy of Religion* (1897, ET 1897) *Religions d'autorité et la religion de l'esprit* (1903, ET 1904).

Sabatier, Paul Calvinist pastor and Franciscan scholar, born St Michel-de-Chabrillanoux, 3 August 1858, died Strasburg, 4 March 1928. Studied theology at Paris, where his teachers included A. **Sabatier** and E. **Renan**. Ill-health forced him to give up his pastoral posts and he dedicated the rest of his life to research. Spent much time in Italy, at Assisi. The liberal outlook of his *Life of St Francis* (1893, ET 1894) condemned it to the Index in 1894. He was the director of two series of publications, *Collection de documents pour l'histoire religieuse et littéraire du moyen âge* (1898–1909) and *Opuscules de critique historique* (1901–19). He founded societies of Franciscan studies at Assisi and in London. He gave the Jowett Lectures in London in 1908 on the Roman Catholic Modernist Movement, with which he was an active sympathizer.

Sabatier, Pierre Maurist scholar, born Poitiers, 1682, died Rheims, 24 March 1742, and joined the Benedictines in 1700 at Rheims. Was later a student of T. Ruinart at St-Germain-des-Prés, and was sent back to Rheims in 1727 because of his alleged Jansenist tendencies. His magnum opus, *Bibliorum Sacrorum Latinae Versiones Antiquae*, an almost complete collection of all the then available material for the Old Latin text of the Bible, was published in Rheims in 1743, just after his death.

Sabellius Christian teacher at Rome, early third century, fl. *c.*220. Very little is known of his life; he may have come to Rome from Libya. He was excommunicated by pope **Calixtus** in 217, apparently for teaching that God was revealed in three different modes at different times, rather than being essentially triune. This modalist monarchianism, as it was later called, proved influential in the West, especially among those who resisted talk of a subordination of Christ to God, but it was deemed heretical by the Roman church leaders.

Sabigotona *see* **Aurelius and Sabigotona**.

Sabina Martyr and saint of the early second century, Italy. Her *acta*, written much later, say she was a widow from Umbria who was converted by her servant, Serapia – who came from Antioch in Syria. The *acta* states that in the persecution under Hadrian both were arrested, but while Serapia was killed Sabina was initially released, only to be rearrested and put to death the following year. The church of St Sabina on the Aventine Hill is believed to contain her relics. Feast day 29 August.

Sabinian Pope, born Volterra, Tuscany, consecrated 13 September 604, died 22 February 606. He had served as papal representative in Constantinople under **Gregory I**, though Gregory thought him insufficiently firm on the issue of the controversial title 'ecumenical patriarch'. He then acted as a papal representative in Gaul. Little is known about his pontificate, though he incurred the anger of the people of Rome for selling grain in time of famine, rather than giving it away as Gregory had done.

Sacheverell, Henry High Anglican divine and pamphleteer, born Marlborough, 1674, died Highgate, in what is now London, 5 June 1724. He championed the cause of the High Church and the Tories in their opposition to the Whig government's policy of toleration and Occasional Conformity, and during his time as chaplain at St Saviour's, Southwark (now Southwark Cathedral), he wrote and preached against it. His views were condemned by the Commons in 1709 as seditious, and Sacheverell was charged with high crimes and misdemeanours. His light sentence reflected the opposition among the Tories and many Whigs, to his condemnation. The fall of the Whigs in 1710 is seen as largely due to the action taken againt Sacheverell.

Sadoleto, Jacopo Born Modena 1477, died Rome, 18 October 1547. Cardinal, philosopher and classics scholar, he became secretary to **Leo X** in 1513, bishop in 1517 and was made cardinal by **Paul III** in 1536. He remained throughout his later years a trusted and respected adviser to Paul. Among Sadoleto's concerns was the reconciliation of the Protestants, but many of his efforts in this regard, notably toward **Melanchthon** and the city of Geneva, were without success. He was a constant advocate of reform and in 1537 was appointed to the commission for the reform of the Church and the preparation of a general council. Among his writings are works on original sin and a commentary on Romans. The latter was thought, in its original and uncorrected edition, to have Semipelagian tendencies.

Sahdona Early seventh-century Persian spiritual writer and monk. He became bishop of Mahoze in the Church of the East in about 640, but was excommunicated because of his teaching on the person of Christ. He fled to Edessa, and it is most likely there that he wrote his *Book of Perfection*, which remains a masterpiece of Syriac spiritual writing.

Saint-Cyran, Abbé de (Jean Duvengier de Hauranne) One of the authors of Jansenism. Born Bayonne, 1581, died Paris, 11 October 1643. Studied at the Jesuit College in Louvain and later at Paris and Bayonne, where he became a close friend of Jansen, from whom he received much correspondence between 1617 and 1635. He preferred the theology of **Augustine** to the Scholasticism of his time, and after he was appointed Abbé, in 1620, set about trying to reform Catholicism along Augustinian lines, hoping to be able to defeat Protestantism with its own weapons. His power and influence led to his five-year imprisonment at Vincennes, at the instigation of Cardinal **Richelieu**. His writings include tracts against the Jesuits and a defence of the rights of the episcopate against the Papacy.

Saint-Simon, Claude Henri de Rouvroy Socialist thinker, born Paris, 17 October 1760 into a noble family, died Paris, 19 May 1825. One of the earliest French socialists, he fought on the American side in the War of Independence, and in the 1789 French Revolution he gave up his titles and changed his name. In his earlier writings he developed his thesis that the industrial classes should take precedence, as they were the only ones who worked for the temporal and moral good of all. In later years he developed his ideas, notably in his *Nouveau Christianisme* (1825), on the role religion should play in bringing about a more just society. Followers of Sainte-Simon set up a religiously based communitarian group, but one of them, Enfantin, was arrested in 1832 and condemned for preaching free love.

Salama Abuna, or bishop, of Ethiopia from 1348 until his death in 1388. Like all Ethiopian abuna he was an Egyptian and a monk. He translated religious books from Arabic into Amharic, greatly increasing the amount of Ethiopian literature available. His aim was to improve the biblical and theological knowledge of the Ethiopian church, and he developed the monasteries as places of learning. During his episcopacy he largely ignored the growing Ewostathian, or sabbatarian, movement which was to cause problems for his successors. He is regarded by many Ethiopians as their greatest abuna.

Salmasius, Claudius French classical scholar, born Semur-en-Auxois, 1588, died Spa, 3 September 1653. He studied at Paris, became a friend of I. Casaubon and was converted to Calvinism. In 1632 he became professor at Leiden, where he wrote *De usuris liber* (1638) and *De modo usurarum* (1639), arguing that usuary and Christianity are compatible. He also wrote his *Defensio pro Carolo I* (1649), accusing the English of regicide, in response to which **Milton** wrote his acclaimed *Pro populo anglicano defensio* (1651)

Salmon, George Priest, theologian and mathematician, born Cork, Ireland, 25 September 1819, died Dublin, 22 January 1904. He spent most of his life at Trinity College, Dublin, first as a student then as a fellow, from 1841, as Regius Professor of divinity, from 1866, and as provost, from 1888. He was ordained priest in the Church of Ireland in 1845 and played a leading role after 1870 in the reconstruction of the church. He lectured and wrote against the tenets of the Roman Catholic Church and in defence of Protestantism in his *Infallibilty of the Church.*

Saltmarsh, John Controversial English preacher, writer and pamphleteer, born Yorkshire, about 1612, died Ilford, Essex, 11 December 1647. Strongly supported episcopacy and conformity when first appointed rector of Heslerton, North Yorkshire, in about 1639, but eventually became a campaigner for complete religious liberty. Was appointed to Brasted in Kent in 1644 and became chaplain in Fairfax's army in 1646. His best known works are *Holy Discoveries* (1640) and *Sparkles of Glory* (1647).

Salvatierra, Juan Maria Jesuit missionary to Mexico, born Milan, 15 November 1648, died 17 July 1717, Guadalajara. He joined the Jesuits in Genoa and in 1675 went to Mexico, where he continued his theological studies and eventually became professor at the college in Puebla. In 1680 he was given permission to devote his life to the conversion of the Indians, and set off for the mountain region of Tarumari in south-western Chihuahua. In 1690 he was appointed inspector of the Jesuit missions in the north-western region. In 1697 Salvatierra was sent, at his own request and funded by the newly established and controversial 'Pious Fund', to proselytize Lower California. Within the first few years, though not without difficulty, he founded six missions – to which he returned after a short period as provincial. He remained in this work until 1717, when he died, in Guadalajara, en route to a meeting to which he had been summoned with the new viceroy in Mexico. That almost the whole city turned out for his funeral is a mark of the affection and respect he commanded.

Salvianus Latin writer, lived and worked in Gaul in the fifth century. **Gennadius**, the historian from the same place and time, describes him as a priest of the church of Marseilles. He travelled in Gaul and Africa. In his writings, somewhat rhetorical in style, he advocates continence for married couples and suggests people make the Church their heirs. Like other Latin moralists he contrasted Roman corruption with Germanic virtue.

Sambuga, Joseph Anton Roman Catholic theologian of Italian origin, born near Heidelberg, 9 June 1752, died near Salzburg, either 5 January or 5 June 1815. He went to school at Mannheim and Wiesloch and to the University of Heidelberg to begin theological studies which, for family reasons, he finished in Italy. He was ordained priest in 1774 at Como, worked briefly there as hospital chaplain and returned to Germany to take up posts as chaplain, court preacher and parish priest. In 1797 he returned to the court at Mannheim as teacher of religion to the future King Louis I of Bavaria, and moved with the court to Munich.

Sampson, Richard English bishop, doctor of canon law, born towards the end of the fifteenth century, died 25 September 1554, Staffordshire. Was educated at Cambridge, Paris and Lens and was appointed by **Wolsey** as chancellor and vicar general in the Diocese of Tournay. He also held the positions of dean of St Stephen's, Westminster, and of the Chapel Royal in 1516, archdeacon of Cornwall in 1517 and prebendary of Newbold in 1519. He was ambassador to **Charles V** for three years from 1522, and also held positions as dean of Windsor in 1523, vicar of Stepney in 1526, prebendary of St Paul's and Lichfield, archdeacon of Suffolk in 1529, dean of Lichfield in 1533, rector of Hackney in 1534 and treasurer of Salisbury in 1535. He was one of **Henry VIII**'s chief agents in the divorce proceedings, and in June 1536 was elected bishop of Chichester. On royal authority alone he was translated to Coventry and Lichfield in 1543, a post he held throughout the reign of **Edward VI** but lost when he confessed his allegiance to the Pope.

Samson Saint, bishop of Dol in Brittany, born about 486 in South Wales, died sometime after 557, probably in Brittany. He was ordained by St Dubric and became a monk, and later abbot, of the monastic community on Caldey Island. He is thought to have visited Ireland and to have lived for a while in a cave near the River Severn. He was made a bishop and, following a vision, went to Cornwall and then on to Brittany, where he founded the monastery which was to be at the hub of much missionary activity. He was present at the Councils of Paris in 553 and 557. Feast day 28 July.

Samuel Bishop and interpreter of the Coptic churches to the West. Born December 1920 in Cairo, assassinated 6 October 1981. Leading figure in bringing theological reconciliation in the different Orthodox churches, and in promoting Orthodox–Roman Catholic dialogue. Educated in Cairo and later at Princeton, he became a member of the Makary El Souriany monastic order in 1949. Attended Evanston in 1954 and later became a member of the World Council of Churches central committee. Was consecrated bishop in 1962, established the rural diakonia and promoted Coptic education in Egyptian villages. Became director of the churches' department of social studies and was appointed by President Anwar Al-Sadat to lead the church in its relations with the state.

Sánchez, Alonso Coello Court and ecclesiastical painter, born Valencia, Spain, about 1514, died Madrid, 1590. He was a great admirer of **Titian**, whose ideas on colouring he employs, and the pupil of Sir Antonio Mor. He went with Mor to Portugal in 1552 and entered the service of Don Juan, son-in-law of **Charles V** of Spain and brother-in-law of **Philip II** – whose service he later entered. He painted the portraits of several leading churchmen, including Popes **Gregory XIII** and **Sixtus V**, but one of his most famous is that of St **Ignatius of Loyola** – working from casts and sketches made some years earlier. The portrait of his friend, Padre Siguenza, which hangs in the Escorial, is judged his greatest work.

Sánchez, Antonio Jesuit writer and diplomat, born Guadalajara, Spain, 1547, died Alcalá, 27 May 1593. He joined the Society of Jesus on 27 May 1565. Sánchez was one of the first Jesuits in the Philippines when he accompanied Bishop Salazar on his mission there in 1581. He became counsellor to the bishop and wrote the Acts of the Synod of Manila. During this same period he was twice sent on official business to China and later wrote an account of Christianity in the country at that time. In 1586 he successfully accomplished two ambassadorial missions for the Philippines: first to Philip II in Madrid, and then to Pope **Sixtus V** in Rome. He expelled several problematic Spanish Jesuits, and his diplomatic skills ensured that both the king and the Inquisition were better disposed towards the Society.

Sánchez, José Bernardo Franciscan, born Old Castile, Spain, 7 September 1778, died California, 15 January 1833. He joined the Franciscans in October 1794, went to the missionary college in San Fernando, Mexico, in 1803 and then to California the following year. He spent sixteen years at the San Diego Mission before moving to the Mission Purisma and then to San Gabriel. Between 1827 and 1831 he was superior or *presidente* of the missions, a job he did not enjoy, and spent much of his time vigorously opposing the secularization scheme of Governor Echeandia. He was allowed to return to regular missionary work in 1831, two years before his death.

Sánchez, Tomás Moral theologian and Spanish Jesuit, born Cordova, 1550, died Granada, 19 May 1610. He joined the Society of Jesus in 1567, having initially been refused entry because of a speech impediment, and was master of novices and teacher of moral theology and canon law at Granada. The work for which Sanchez is most famous is his *Disputationes de sancti matrimonii sacramento*, which first appeared in 1602. A volume of a later edition, which appeared in Venice in 1614, was placed on the Index. This edition left out a passage which defended the Pope's right to legitimize the children of a non-canonical but otherwise valid marriage, without state interference. Although he completed the first volume, the second volume in his *Opus Morale in Praecepta Decalogi*, along with the *Consilia Morale*, was the work of editors using Sanchez' notes and did not appear until after his death.

Sancroft, William Archbishop of Canterbury, born Fressingfield, Suffolk, 30 January 1617, died there, November 1693. Educated and then a fellow at Emmanuel College, Cambridge, until he was thrown out by the Puritans in 1651. He later became chaplain to Charles II, prebendary of Durham, then master of Emmanuel College in 1662

and dean of York, then of St Paul's in 1664. At Durham he had been involved in the 1662 edition of the Book of Common Prayer, and at St Paul's he co-operated with **Wren** over the rebuilding of the cathedral after the fire of 1666. He went to Canterbury in 1678 and did much to strengthen the Anglican Church. With the accession of **James II**, Sancroft found himself in opposition to the royal policies which led to his eventual imprisonment in the Tower, though he was soon acquitted. He was suspended from office on 1 August 1689, when he refused to recognize William of Orange as rightful king, and he lived out his retirement in Suffolk.

Sander, Anton Historian, born Antwerp, 1586, died Afflighem, Belgium, 10 January 1664. Studied at Douai and Louvain and, after ordination, became a leading opponent of the Anabaptist movement in Flanders. He worked as cardinal's secretary and later as penitentiary at Ypres. From 1657 he devoted his life to historical studies and soon moved to the Benedictine abbey at Afflighem. He left about 40 published works and as many unpublished.

Sanders, Nicholas Priest and theologian, born at Charlwood, Surrey, 1530, died Ireland, 1581. Educated at Winchester and Oxford, he had to flee England under **Elizabeth** and was ordained and continued his doctoral studies in Rome. He attended the Council of Trent as theologian to Cardinal **Hosius**, and later accompanied him on diplomatic visits to Poland, Prussia and Lithuania. In Louvain from about 1565 he came to be regarded as one of the leaders of the English Catholic exiles. He went to Spain in 1573 to try to raise money for the exiles and, as papal agent, sailed from there with James Fitzgerald to carry arms to Ireland in 1578. His *De schismate Anglicano*, published shortly after his death, provides a popular Catholic account of the period.

Sanderson, Robert Bishop of Lincoln, born Sheffield, 1587, died Buckden, 29 January 1663. Educated at Lincoln College, Oxford, where he became a fellow in 1606. He was ordained in 1611 and became royal chaplain in 1631 and Regius Professor of divinity at Oxford the following year. He was imprisoned briefly during the Civil War but was reinstated to his professorship in 1660 and soon after became bishop of Lincoln. In 1661 he made a significant contribution to the Savoy Conference, and the following year wrote the draft preface to the new Prayer Book. His *Nine Cases of Conscience Occasionally Determined*, published in 1678, was an important contribution to the moral theology of the time.

Sandford, Frank Evangelist and author, born Bowdomham, Maine, 1862, died 1948. Sandford began as a Free Baptist pastor, and became influenced by the Holiness Movement and the Christian Alliance. He travelled widely as an independent evangelist, and he founded an authoritarian community, Shiloh, near Durham, Maine. In 1905 he bought two boats to evangelize the world, but after a journey to Africa in 1911, in which several crewmembers died from starvation, he served a term in prison for manslaughter. He wrote *Seven Years with God* (1900) and *The Art of War for the Christian Soldier* (1904).

Sandys, Edwin Archbishop of York, born Hawkshead, Lancashire, 1516, died Southwell, 10 July 1588. After graduating from St John's College, Cambridge, he became master of St Catharine's Hall and vice-chancellor of the university in 1553. He was sent to the Tower in 1553 for supporting Lady Jane Grey, but eventually escaped to the Continent. He came back to England when **Elizabeth** came to the throne, and occupied the sees of Worcester, London, and then York from 1577. He helped translate the Bishops' Bible. He was strongly anti-Roman, and his Puritan leanings brought him into occasional clashes with his clergy.

Sanford, Agnes Mary American healing pioneer, born 1897, died 1982. Sanford entered the healing ministry after experiencing healing from depression, producing *The Healing Light* in 1947. In 1955 with her husband she founded the School of Pastoral Care, in which clergy and medical practitioners could meet. An Episcopalian, she had the Pentecostal experience in 1953–4, although she continued to see healing in terms of natural processes. Other books she wrote include *Behold Your God* (1958), *The Healing Gifts of the Spirit* (1966), *The Healing Power of the Bible* (1969) and *Sealed Orders* (1972).

Sangnier, Marc French Roman Catholic, founder of *The Sillon* movement, born Paris, 3 April 1873, died there, 28 March 1950. From his youth he was involved in efforts to bring those aspects of Roman Catholic teaching that supported democracy and social justice to the fore, and to the attention of those people whose lives it might most affect: the working classes. His efforts were encouraged in 1891 by Pope **Leo XIII**'s encyclical *Rerum Novarum*. In 1894 he founded *The Sillon (Furrow)* newspaper which gave rise to the Sillon movement, consisting mainly of young French Roman Catholics committed to democracy and social justice. After being initially encouraged by the hierarchy the Sillonists began to widen their appeal and aroused fears in the more conservative 'integralists'. Following his earlier condemnation of 'modernism', and fearing the application of democratic ideals to the Church itself, **Pius X** condemned the Sillon movement in 1910. Many of the original Sillonists went on to found and develop other Catholic social action movements.

Sangster, William Edwin Robert Methodist minister and president of the Methodist Conference, born London, 5 June 1900, died of muscular atrophy, 24 May 1960. Following a period in the army, he studied at Handsworth College, Birmingham, in 1920, later Richmond College, Surrey. Ordained in 1926, he itinerated in North Wales, Liverpool, Scarborough, Leeds and, in 1939, at Westminster Central Hall. Awarded a doctorate by the University of London in 1942. Having gained an international reputation as a preacher, he was elected president of the Conference in 1950. In 1953 his published sermon 'What would a revival of religion do for Britain?' made headline news. In 1955 he served as general secretary of the Methodist Home Mission Department. His numerous books include *The Path to Perfection* (1943), *The Craft of Sermon Illustration* (1946) and *The Craft of Sermon Construction* (1949).

Sankey, Ira Born Edinburgh, Pennysylvania, USA, 28 August 1840, died Brooklyn, New York, 13 August 1908. He collaborated with D. L. **Moody**, whom he met at a convention of the Young Men's Christian Association in 1870, in evangelistic meetings in the USA and Britain. They published *Sacred Songs* with great success over 30 years. The popular style of these songs became that for evangelistic song books to the present day. Neither he nor Moody benefited from the sale of their hymn-books: all the money was turned over to trustees for a school Moody had established.

Saravia, Hadrian à   Protestant divine, born Hesden, Artois, 1532, died Kent, 1613. Joined the Franciscans at St Omer, but left when he joined the Dutch Reformed Church in 1557. He lived at Austin Friars in London, England, from 1559 to 1562 and helped to draft the Belgic Confession. When he went to Antwerp as minister to the Walloon congregation he recommended this to William of Orange. In 1568 he became an English national and was master of King Edward VI School in Southampton from 1572 to 1578. He returned to The Netherlands and served as a minister, and then as professor of theology at Leiden from 1584. Because of his support for the earl of Leicester he was forced to flee back to England, where he eventually held canonries at Canterbury and Westminster, and in 1610 the living of Great Chart. Of his many writings the most important is his *De Diversis Ministrorum Evangelii Gradibus* (1590), apparently directed against Theodore Beza, in which he demonstrates his sympathy for episcopacy and argues his position by an appeal, unusual for a Protestant theologian, to divine law.

Sarpi, Paolo   Venetian, anti-papal Servite priest, historian and politician, born Venice, 14 August 1552, died there, mid-January 1623. Joined the Servite Order in his early teens and was teaching theology, canon law and philosophy by his early twenties. Ordained in 1574, he was appointed provincial in 1579, then procurator general, based in Rome, from 1585 to 1588. On his return to Venice his earlier sympathy for and friendships with those opposed to Rome became manifest, and he was watched by the inquisition in Venice. Rome also stepped in to block his appointment to several episcopal sees in the Venetian Republic, but these actions only served to drive him to closer association with, and put him under the protection of, the Venetian senate. This alliance weakened, however, when peace between the Pope and Venice was restored, and the latter distanced themselves from Sarpi's increasingly bitter anti-papal invec-

tives, especially as found in his best-known work, *Istoria del Concilio Tridentino* (London, 1619).

Sava   Saint, first archbishop of the Serbian Orthodox Church, born Ras (Serbia) between 1170 and 1175, died Turnovo, Bulgaria, 12 or 14 January 1236. Son of Serbian ruler Stefan Nemanja, at seventeen he ran away to become a monk on Mount Athos, where he and his father founded Hilandar Monastery. Later as abbot of Studenica in Serbia, he preached, taught and interceded in political crises. In 1219 Sava went to Nicaea, to Patriarch Manuel I Sarantenos and Emperor Theodore I Lascaris, in exile from Constantinople and the Crusaders' Latin Kingdom, to present Serbia's request for its own archbishop; Sava himself was consecrated (Easter, 1219 or 1220), which enabled the Serbian church to be autocephalous and self-perpetuating. Due to Sava's work, Serbia, on the border between Rome and Constantinople, lies in the Orthodox world. Feast day 14 January by the Eastern calendar (27 January).

Savile, Henry   Scholar, warden of Merton College, Oxford, and provost of Eton, born Bradley, near Halifax, 30 November 1549, died Eton, 19 February 1622. Studied at Brazenose College, Oxford, and in 1565 became a fellow of Merton, becoming warden in 1585. Although not ordained he became provost of Eton in 1596 and from 1604 worked on preparing the Authorized Version of the Bible. Between 1610 and 1613 he brought out his eight-volume edition of the works of **John Chrystostom**.

Savonarola, Girolamo   Italian Dominican reformer, born Ferrara, 21 September 1452, died by execution, Florence, 23 May 1498. He was destined, like his father, to be a physician, but instead suddenly joined the Dominicans in Bologna in 1475 and taught there and at San Marco in Florence, which was a centre for the leading humanist scholars of the region. From 1491 when he was appointed prior at San Marco his preaching became increasingly critical of both Church and State and apocalyptic in tone. He eventually separated the Dominicans of San Marco from the congregations of the Lombardy Reform and set about trying to implement political, religious and moral reform in Florence based on biblical and Christian principles and in opposition to the humanists. When he did not accede to a request from **Alexander VI** to visit Rome and explain his actions, he was forbidden to preach and in 1497 was excommunicated. In the following year he was condemned as a heretic, hanged and burned. His *Triumphus crucis* is a spirited exposition of his understanding of orthodox Catholicism.

Sawtrey, William Lollard priest, date of birth unknown, died (burnt as a heretic), London, 26 February 1401. A Norfolk priest, Sawtrey was first interrogated for suspected heresy in 1399, but he successfully repudiated the charges. Two years later he was arrested on further charges of heresy for his doubts concerning transubstantiation and the propriety of some traditional rituals. This time he was condemned, on the grounds that he had relapsed into the heresies of which he had previously recanted.

Sawyer, Harry Alphonso Ebun West African theologian and Anglican clergyman, born Bona Sakrim, Sierra Leone, 1909, died 1986. He was educated at Fourah Bay College and Durham University. Ordained in 1943, he ministered in Freetown for most of his life, becoming a canon of St George's Cathedral. He was on the staff of Fourah Bay College from 1948, becoming its principal from 1962 to 1974 and vice-chancellor of the University of Sierra Leone from 1970 to 1972. In 1968 he published *Creative Evangelism*, which outlined his respect for African language, religion and culture and explained his belief that Christianity should transcend all cultural forms. He saw in the OT parallels with African traditional religion and emphasized the importance of liturgical rite in worship. He brought an African outlook to both the Anglican Communion and the World Council of Churches.

Sayers, Dorothy Leigh Writer and Christian apologist, born Oxford, England, 13 June 1893, died London, England, 17 December 1957. A graduate of Oxford University, Dorothy L. Sayers worked as a teacher and in advertising before becoming a writer, first becoming famous for her detective novels. A member of the circle of Christian scholars which included C. S. **Lewis** and J. R. R. **Tolkien**, she shared their concern to defend traditional Christianity, writing a number of apolo-

getic works and a famous serialized radio play entitled *The Man Born to Be King*, concerning the events surrounding the crucifixion. In contrast to the literary genres which made her famous, Sayers' first love was medieval literature, and towards the end of her life she produced a highly regarded English translation of **Dante**'s *Divine Comedy*.

Scaliger, Joseph Justus Reformed historian and philologist, born Agen, France, 4 August 1540, died Leiden, The Netherlands, 21 January 1609. Scaliger was educated in Paris, where he studied Greek and oriental languages. He was converted to Calvinism in his twenties, and travelled widely in the course of his academic career, during which he gained a reputation as an erudite philologist for his scholarly editions of classical writings. He is also regarded as the founder of the science of chronology. Scaliger's Calvinism was of a tolerant and liberal kind, and he was unusual in his time for the high regard in which he held the Jews.

Scaramelli, Giovanni Battista Jesuit writer and missionary, born Rome, Italy, 23 November 1687, died Macerata, Spain, 11 January 1752. Scaramelli became a Jesuit in 1707 and was ordained in 1717. For most of his life he ministered as a home missionary, and his florid preaching style attracted large crowds. He also wrote a considerable number of devotional writings, and it is for these that he is best remembered. The most significant of these is usually regarded as *Direttorio Mistico*, in essence a handbook for spiritual directors, which is recognized as a classic in its field.

Scarlatti, Pietro Alessandro Gaspare Italian composer mainly of well over 100 operas and many religious works, born 2 May 1660, Palermo, Sicily, died Naples, 24 October 1725. His first opera was commissioned by a religious confraternity in Rome where he had gone to study when some twelve years old. Queen **Christina of Sweden** became his patron for several years before, in 1684, he entered the service of the king of Naples. In 1702 he went to Florence, in 1707 back to Rome, and two years later back again to Naples. He wrote a Mass for Pope **Clement XI** in 1716.

Schaff, Philip Reformed theologian and church historian, born Chur, Switzerland, 1819, died New

York City, 25 October 1893. Educated at Tübingen, Halle and Berlin, Schaff's career was mostly spent in America, where he moved in 1844 at the invitation of J. W. **Nevin**, with whom he shared a theological outlook which became known as the 'Mercersburg Theology'. This regarded traditional Reformed doctrines and liturgical practices as the key to renewal in the Church. During his long academic career Schaff published a large number of works, including his twelve-volume *History of the Christian Church*, and new editions or translations of early Christian literature, the most notable being the sets of patristic writings entitled Nicene and Post-Nicene Fathers. Schaff also presided over the American committee jointly responsible with British counterparts for the Revised Version translation of the Bible.

Scharper, Philip J. US publisher, writer, lecturer and ecumenist, born Baltimore, Maryland, 15 September 1919, died North Tarrytown, NY, 5 May 1985. He was a Jesuit from 1937 to 1948 and studied at Georgetown and Fordham Universities. He left the Society and married in 1949. He taught at Xavier University in Cincinnati from 1948 to 1950 and at Fordham from 1951 to 1955. He edited *Commonweal* for two years and from 1957 to 1970 was editor-in-chief at Sheed and Ward in New York, publishing leading US and European theologians. He was the first Catholic president and chairman of the Religious Education Association of the USA and Canada. He helped in the preparation of the Document *Gaudium et Spes* of Vatican Council II and in 1967 worked as advisor to the Vatican Secretariat for Promoting Christian Unity. He was opposed to US involvement in Vietnam and worked towards greater justice in the world. In 1970 he became founding editor of the Maryknoll Fathers' Orbis Books, and was a major publisher of liberation theology. Together with his wife, Sarah, he wrote award-winning religious programme TV scripts. He wrote articles, edited and contributed to sixteen books and was the author of *Meet the American Catholic* (1968).

Scheeben, Matthias Joseph Roman Catholic theologian, born Meckenheim, Germany, 1 March 1835, died Cologne, Germany, 21 July 1888. Following education at the Gregorian University in Rome and ordination in 1858, Scheeben was appointed professor at the Catholic seminary in Cologne in 1860, a post he held until the end of his life. During his career he wrote a large number of theological treatises, and took an active part at the First Vatican Council, where he upheld the doctrine of papal infallibility. The crowning point of Scheeben's considerable literary output was his *Handbuch der katholischen Dogmatik*, published in three volumes between 1873 and 1887. In addition to the Fathers and traditional Thomism this also drew on the insights of modern theologians, though without concessions to the rationalist and naturalist ideas typical of German theology in the nineteenth century.

Schelling, Friedrich Wilhelm Joseph von Philosopher, born Leonberg, Germany, 27 January 1775, died Ragaz, Switzerland, 20 August 1854. Following education at Tübingen, Schelling began his career as a teacher at Jena, where he first came into contact with the Romantic movement. He subsequently held a number of academic positions, notably at Munich and Berlin. Although Schelling exercised a profound influence on the development of nineteenth-century German philosophy through his principal thesis of a transcendental Absolute in which all opposites are ultimately resolved, the detail of this was constantly evolving and cannot be systematized. He moved through various phases of pantheism and nature religion, with borrowings from Neoplatonism and Gnosticism, though towards the end of his career he attempted to reconcile his ideas with more traditional Christian theism.

Schleiermacher, Friedrich Daniel Ernst German theologian and preacher, born Breslau, 21 November 1768, died Berlin, 12 February 1834. His pious parents – his father was a military chaplain – sent him to a Moravian school and seminary, but he left in 1787 to attend the University of Halle, where his mother's brother was a professor of theology. He spent two years studying Kant, but when his uncle moved to become a pastor near Frankfurt an der Oder he followed him, and studied theology under him. In 1794 he became an assistant pastor, and two years later took up a post as pastor at a hospital near Berlin. *On Religion*, written in response to the rationalism of many of his friends, argued that the religious sentiment was prior in each Christian to any dogmatic formulation. It was published in 1799 and made a considerable impression. After a number of minor appointments he returned to Halle as professor of theology, and university preacher. In 1807 he moved to Berlin, where he became pastor at the Trinity Church and, in 1810, professor of theology at the new university there, which he had helped to found. His most important work, *The Christian Faith*, published in 1821–2 was a major systematic treatise on Christian dogmatics, and made him a major force in Protestant theology.

Schmemann, Alexander   Born 13 September 1921, Revel, Estonia, professor of church history and liturgical theology from 1951, and also dean from 1962 until his death, 13 December 1983, St Vladimir's Orthodox Theological Seminary, Crestwood, New York. He studied theology in Paris, influenced there by **Afanasiev**, and in 1945 went on to become professor of Byzantine church history at the St Sergius Orthodox Institute in Paris. He lectured as adjunct professor at Union Theological Seminary, General Seminary and Columbia University. He was chairman of the World Council of Churches Youth department and a member of the Faith and Order commission. He was in favour of Orthodox unity and promoted the establishment of the autocephalous Orthodox Church in America in 1970. Under his leadership St Vladimir's became a centre of academic excellence and liturgical revival. Schmemann was editor of St Vladimir's *Theological Quarterly*. His publications include *The Historical Road of Eastern Orthodoxy* (1963) *Church, World, Mission: Reflections on Orthodoxy in the West* (1979) and *The Eucharist, Sacrament of the Kingdom* (1988).

Schmidlin, Joseph   Father of Catholic missiology, born Kleinlandau, Sundgau, Alsace, 29 May 1876, tortured and died at Schirmeck concentration camp, Alsace, 10 January 1944. He gained his doctorate at Strasbourg in 1906, was professor of theology and patrology in Münster, and was given a lectureship in missiology in 1910. This was raised to a chair in 1914, the first missiology chair in any Catholic university. His prodigious writing included *Katholische Missionsgeschichte* (1925) and the editing of *Zeitschrift für Missionswissenschaft* for 25 years from 1911. He developed ideas from

Gustav Warneck and was the inspiration behind the 'Münster school' of Catholic missiology which emphasized proclamation and salvation over church planting. He was tireless in stimulating students, including many studying for doctorates, in speaking, and in establishing mission groups. His pugnacity often led to conflict. He was forcibly retired by the Nazis in 1934 and later imprisoned.

Schmidt, Wilhelm   Ethnologist, born Hörde, Germany, 16 February 1868, died Fribourg, Switzerland, 10 February 1954. At fifteen he attended St Michael's Mission House, Steyl, The Netherlands, and was ordained priest of the Society of the Divine Word (SVD) in 1892. He studied Middle Eastern languages in Berlin in 1893–5, and taught in Mödling, Vienna, in 1896–1938, at the University of Vienna in 1921–38 and at Fribourg in 1942–51, where he moved in 1938 to escape the Nazis. Largely self-educated, he gained international recognition for disentangling the relationships between Southeast Asian and Oceanic languages. A gifted and enthusiastic teacher, he wrote in longhand some 650 publications including *Der Ursprung der Gottesidee* (12 vols, 1912–55) and *Sprachfamilien und Sprachkreisen der Erde* (1926). He founded the *Anthropos International Review of Ethnology and Linguistics* (1906), the Anthropos Institute (Mödling, 1932, Fribourg, 1938) and the papal ethnological museum in Rome.

Schorsch, Dolores   Born Morris, Illinois, 16 June 1896, died 17 June 1984. She became a Benedictine in Chicago. She taught in Canon City, Colorado, and became principal of St Scholastica High School, Chicago. With the collaboration of her brother, the reverend Alexander Schorsch, CM, she wrote and edited *A Course in Religion for Elementary Schools*, later known as the *Jesu Maria Course in Religion*. This innovative course included poetry, stories of the lives of the saints, church history and music. It was used, not only in the USA, but in other English-speaking countries, and was adapted in China.

Schriech, Louise Van de   Belgian/American pioneer educator. Born Bergen-Op-Zoom, 14 November 1813, died Cincinnati, 3 December 1886. Educated in Belgium, she entered the Sisters of

Notre Dame de Namur, and in 1840 was one of eight religious to take the community to Ohio. From 1848 she was superior of all Notre Dame houses east of the Rockies. An able administrator, she added 25 foundations, including academies, and some 50 elementary schools were staffed by her sisters; as early as 1867 the sisters directed a school in Cincinnati for black girls and did the same in Philadelphia in 1877; she opened night schools for Catholic adult immigrants. As a religious and as an educator, her policy was one of austerity, respect for the individual and good sense, which, combined with freedom from sentimental religious attitudes, has characterized the Notre Dame educational tradition.

Schubert, Franz Austrian composer, born Vienna, 31 January 1797, died there, 19 November 1828. With the encouragement of his father, he joined the choir school of the Imperial Chapel in Vienna, and studied under Salieri. After his studies he worked for his father, a schoolmaster, for three years, and then lived by his composing, though he died before he had heard any of his major works performed. In his genial Masses the texts of the *Gloria* and *Credo* are often truncated, not for theological reasons but to make the settings shorter. His celebrated *Ave Maria* is a setting of Sir Walter Scott.

Schumacher, Ernst Friedrich Roman Catholic economist and author, born Bonn, Germany, 16 August 1911, died Switzerland, 4 September 1977. He was educated at Berlin and Bonn, in both of which institutions his father was professor of economics. He won a Rhodes scholarship to New College, Oxford, and then went to the school of banking at Columbia University, New York. He returned to Germany but, ill at ease with the Nazi regime. During the war he worked as an agricultural labourer, but also as an adviser to the government and became, after the war, a member of the Control Commission in Germany, a post which required him to take out British nationality. In 1950 he became economic adviser to the National Coal Board and its chief statistician for the latter part of his time. After the death of his first wife in 1960 – they had married in 1936 – he began to question the economic system of the West. He became economic adviser to the Burmese government, and his experience there led him towards Buddhism. Instead, however, he became a Roman Catholic, together with his second wife, whom he married in 1962, and one of his daughters from his first marriage. He developed his theories of intermediate technology as a means for helping poorer countries on the way to development and set up, in 1966, the Intermediate Technology Development Group – he held the post of chairman until his death, which occurred on a railway train while he was on his way to a conference in Switzerland. His book of essays, *Small is Beautiful: Economics as if People Mattered* was published in 1973 and became a best-seller. The following year he was appointed a CBE.

Schütz, Heinrich German Lutheran composer, born Köstritz, now Bad Köstritz, near Gera, 8 October 1585, died Dresden, 6 November 1672. He was a chorister at Cassel, studied at Marburg University and with Giovanni **Gabrieli** in Venice, and settled in Dresden. He wrote many works for the Lutheran Church: *Psalms of David, Resurrection Story, Cantiones Sacrae, Symphoniae Sacrae* and *Kleine Geistliche Konzerte*. He was influenced by Gabrieli's style. He wrote settings of the passion according to *St Matthew, St Luke* and *St John*.

Schwartz, Christian Friedrich Lutheran missionary to South India, born Sonnenburg, Neumark, Prussia (now Stonsk, Gorzow, Poland), 22 October 1726, died Thanjavur, India, 13 February 1798. Showing early gifts as a linguist and an interest in missions, he trained at Halle, then was ordained in Copenhagen in 1749 and sent to India. He arrived at Tranquebar in June 1750 to build on the work of **Ziegenbalg** and Plütschau begun in 1706. In 1760 he visited Jaffna, and in 1764 moved to Tiruchirapalli, ministering to English and Indians in local conflicts. In 1768 he became an East India chaplain. He maintained his missionary role and trained helpers to work in villages. In 1778 he moved to Thanjavur. His outstanding integrity, teaching and missionary gifts were widely applauded.

Schweitzer, Albert Lutheran theologian, born Kayserberg, Alsace, 14 January 1875, died Lambaréné, Gabon, 4 September 1965. His father was a Lutheran pastor, and he studied theology in Strasburg (while also studying the organ in Paris), then philosophy and theology in Paris and Berlin, gaining doctorates in both disciplines. He became a Lutheran minister at Strasburg, 1899, a lecturer, 1902, and principal of a theological college, 1903. He wrote *The Mystery of the Kingdom of God* (1901, ET 1925) and *The Quest of the Historical Jesus* (1906, ET 1910), arguing in this latter book that Jesus expected an imminent end of the world. This thesis marked a new era in theological thought whilst arousing opposition from all quarters. He had, however, begun in 1905 to study medicine. In 1912 he took his medical degree and the following year started a hospital to fight leprosy at Lambaréné, in what was then French Equatorial Africa, where he worked for most of the rest of his life, placing great emphasis on 'reverence for life', expounded in his *Kulturphilosophie* (1923). He returned to Germany in 1917, and was interned, but in 1918 went back to Strasburg until his return to Lambaréné in 1924. In 1953 he was awarded the Nobel Peace Prize.

Scory, John Bishop of Chichester and then Hereford, born in Norfolk, died Whitbourne, 26 June 1585. He became a Dominican in Cambridge *c*.1530, but after the suppression of the religious houses he became a preacher at Canterbury and a chaplain to Thomas **Cranmer**, and later to Nicholas **Ridley**, the bishop of London. He was appointed bishop of Rochester in 1551, then of Chichester the following year. At **Mary**'s accession he renounced his wife, but soon left England, going eventually to Geneva, and returning to England on **Elizabeth**'s accession. In 1559 he became bishop of Hereford, and assisted at the consecration of Matthew **Parker**.

Scott, Douglas R. Pentecostal evangelist, born Ilford, Essex, 1900, died France, 1967. Scott experienced baptism in the Spirit and healing of a speech impediment in 1925, when George **Jeffreys** laid hands on him. He travelled to Le Havre to learn French as a preparation for evangelistic work in Africa. Through his preaching at the Ruban Bleu mission, which was attended with healings, he established Pentecostalism in France before going on to Congo and French North Africa.

Scott, Giles Gilbert British Roman Catholic architect, born London, 9 November 1880, died there 8 February 1960. Educated at Beaumont College. An early success was his competition-winning design for Liverpool's Anglican Cathedral. It is built on a monumental scale, one of the largest churches in Christendom. He went on to design many ecclesiastical buildings: the nave at Downside Abbey, and chapels at Ampleforth Abbey and Charterhouse School. For London, he designed both Battersea Power Station and the Bankside Power Station, now the new Tate Modern gallery, as well as the new Waterloo Bridge. He is known for his vivid verticals. His commissions also include small churches such as the Annunciation Church in Bournemouth.

Scott, Thomas Evangelical clergyman and Bible commentator, born Braytoft, Lincolnshire, 4 February 1747, died Aston Sandford, 16 April 1821. Having been dismissed as a trainee surgeon due to misconduct, he worked as a farmhand. Ordained priest in 1773, he held curacies at Stoke Goldington and Gayhurst in Buckinghamshire, and nearby Ravenstone from 1775 to 1786. In 1781 he succeeded John **Newton** as curate of Olney. In 1785 he became chaplain of the Lock Hospital, London, and in 1801, vicar of Aston Sanford. He was influential in forming the Church Missionary Society, acting as its first secretary. His publications include his autobiography, *The Force of Truth* (1779) and his *Commentary on the Bible* published as weekly periodicals between 1788 and 1792.

Seabury, Samuel First bishop of the US Protestant Episcopal Church, born Groton, Connecticut, 30 November 1729, died New London, Connecticut, 25 February 1796. He was educated at Yale and at Edinburgh. His first career was in medicine, but in 1753 he became a priest, serving in New Jersey and in New York as a member of the Society for the Propagation of the Gospel. He was also a chaplain to the British, and campaigned against the declaration of independence. He was elected bishop of Connecticut and Rhode Island in 1783, but could not obtain consecration as such from England – he received it in Edinburgh from Scottish bishops. When he returned to the USA in 1785 as bishop he became rector of St James' Church in New London, where he died.

Segundo, Juan Luis Jesuit priest and theologian, born Montevideo, Uruguay, 31 October 1925, died there, 17 January 1996. Segundo entered the Society of Jesus in 1941, studied philosophy in Argentina and theology in Louvain before his ordination in 1955, and then went on to study at Paris. He returned to Uruguay in 1959, where he founded the Centro Peter Faber for the study of social and theological issues. He never held any academic post in his own country, but was regularly invited to lecture abroad. His five-volume *Theology for the Artisans of a New Humanity* (New York, 1974; original Spanish, Buenos Aires 1972) remains one of the few systematic theologies in the liberation theology tradition, of which he was one of the founders.

Selwyn, Arthur George Primate of New Zealand and bishop of Lichfield, and revered in some parts of the Anglican Communion as a saint, born London, 5 April 1809, died Lichfield, 11 April 1878. He attended the same preparatory school as John Henry **Newman**, before going on to Eton and Cambridge. He was ordained in 1833 and made bishop for New Zealand in 1841, learning Maori on his way to his post. His was the first such appointment in Britain's colonial territories, and – by mistake – the Pacific islands were included under his charge. In 1854 he returned to England to seek permission to divide up his diocese, and for the structure which he had evolved to govern it. In the Maori war the following year he attempted to serve both sides, and was critical of the policies of the British companies in New Zealand which had occasioned the uprising. He returned to Britain in 1867 for the first Lambeth Conference of the world-wide Anglican hierarchy, and while in England he accepted the see of Lichfield, becoming its bishop the following January. He governed the diocese until his death. Selwyn College, Cambridge, was founded in his memory, and one of his sons became its first principal.

Semple, Robert James Pentecostal evangelist and missionary, born Northern Ireland, 1881, died Hong Kong, 19 August 1910. Semple's career as an evangelist began in Toronto in 1907, following several years of menial work in New York and Chicago, where he was converted. In 1908 he married Aimee Elizabeth Kennedy, and he was ordained by William Durham the following year. Durham's mission provided funds for the couple to go to China. In Hong Kong, Semple engaged in literature distribution and preached through an interpreter while he and his wife learnt Cantonese. Within a few months, however, he died of malaria.

Seraphim (Rose) Orthodox priest, monk and writer, born San Diego, 13 August 1934, died Platina, California, 2 September 1982. He was a student of Zen Buddhism when he converted to Orthodoxy. He became a monk and founded an influential journal, encouraged by St John Maximovich, specializing in the translation of Russian spiritual writing and saints' lives. He wrote a number of conservative but original works such as *Orthodoxy and the Religion of the Future* (1983) which are strongly apocalyptic.

Seraphim of Sarov Russian Orthodox saint and monk, born Kursk, 19 July 1759, died Sarov monastery, 2 January 1833. With the blessing of **Dosithea** of Kiev he became a monk at Sarov in 1780. In 1794 he entered total seclusion in the nearby forest for sixteen years, followed by another fifteen years in silent prayer in the monastery. In 1825 he opened his room to all visitors, and his fame as healer and spiritual adviser spread throughout Russia. He left no writings, but his famous *Conversation with Motovilov* on the acquisition of the Holy Spirit has been constantly reprinted. He was canonized at the insistence of the Imperial Family in 1903. Feast day 2 January.

Sergius (Sergei Stragorodsky) Patriarch of Moscow, born Arzamas, Russia, 11 January 1867, died Moscow, 15 May 1944. He had a brilliant academic and ecclesiastical career and after the revolution became deputy to Patriarch **Tikhon**'s successor (Metropolitan **Peter Polyansky**). In 1927 he issued his famous declaration of loyalty to the Soviet State, to obtain relief for the Orthodox Church from persecution. His policy was criticized inside and outside Russia and bought the Church few benefits. It remained, however, the basis of the Moscow patriarchate's dealings with the communists until the collapse of the Soviet Union.

Sergius I Pope, saint, born Palermo of a Syrian

family, consecrated 15 December 687, died 9 September 701. He studied in Rome, and became priest in charge of the church of St Susanna and was elected on **Conon**'s death after two other candidates disputed the election between them. Sergius was the popular choice, and had the backing of the imperial representative. Sergius nonetheless soon clashed with the Emperor Justinian II, who called a council in 692 without inviting any Western bishops. It was concerned chiefly with disciplinary matters, but its decisions cut across Western practice. Justinian persuaded the papal representative in Constantinople to sign the acts of the council, but Sergius himself refused to do so, and when an imperial representative was sent either to extract a signature or to arrest the Pope, the imperial troops supported Sergius, and turned on the imperial official, who had to seek refuge from Sergius. He showed considerable interest in the church in England, and in the missionary work of **Willibrord**, making him archbishop of the Frisians. Sergius also concerned himself with the liturgy, improving the churches of Rome, adding the *Agnus Dei* to the liturgy, introducing processions for certain feasts, and began the celebration of the feast of the Exaltation of the Cross.

Sergius II   Pope, consecrated January 844, died 27 January 847. Sergius, an old man at his election, was the choice of the noble families at Rome after the people of the city had chosen someone else. He was consecrated without waiting for imperial approval, which angered the Emperor Lothair, whose son Louis promptly came to Rome, devastating papal estates as he marched through them. At a synod in St Peter's the Pope had to agree that in future no Pope might be consecrated without imperial approval, and the presence of an imperial representative. In August 846 Muslim invaders ransacked St Peter's and St Paul's and this, combined with the open bribery and simony practised by the Pope's brother, made him unpopular.

Sergius III   Pope, born Rome, consecrated 29 January 904, died Rome, 14 April 911. He was consecrated bishop of Caere by Pope **Formosus**, against his will, he claimed, and was happy to be reduced back to the rank of deacon when Formosus' ordinations were declared invalid. He was ambitious to be Pope himself, and already having a diocese was,

as in the case of Formosus himself, technically a barrier to this. He was elected to the Papacy in 898 but was promptly deposed and driven into exile. Seven years later, in 904, when there was again a conflict over the succession, he marched on Rome, threw the Antipope Christopher in gaol, and had him murdered, and was re-elected by acclaim. He dated his pontificate, however, from 898. Sergius was backed by Roman nobles, including the influential Theophylact: it was later claimed that he had a child, the future **John XI**, by Marozia, the daughter of Theophylact. He once more nullified all the doings of Formosus and, in the East, approved of the fourth marriage of the Emperor **Leo VI**, disregarding the canon law of the Eastern Church, and the patriarch of Constantinople's own opposition to the marriage.

Sergius IV   Pope, born Peter, at Rome, elected 31 July 1009, died 12 May 1012. The son of a shoemaker, he changed his name so as not to be Pope Peter II. Otherwise, very little of note occurred during his pontificate, apart from the destruction of the Holy Sepulchre in Jerusalem in October 1009 by Caliph al-Hakim.

Sergius of Radonezh   Saint and monastic founder, born Rostov, 3 May 1314, died monastery of Zagorsk, near Moscow, 25 September 1392. Baptized Bartholomew, Sergius was born into a noble and pious family at Rostov, but when the principality was annexed to Moscow, the family moved there. Bartholomew's mother and father decided to enter religious life, and after their deaths in 1334, Bartholomew determined to do likewise, and formally became a monk in 1337, taking the name Sergius. At the beginning he lived alone, in a hermitage in the forest at Radonhezh, but a community grew around him, all living as hermits until an emissary of the patriarch of Constantinople suggested they form a community. They did so, after consulting the metropolitan of Moscow, and elected Sergius as abbot. They called it the Monastery of the Holy Trinity. Further foundations followed, and Sergius is regarded as the founder of Russian monasticism. He was canonized in 1448. Feast day 25 September.

Sergius of the Baltic (Sergei Voskresensky)   Russian Orthodox bishop and missionary, born c.1898, died (assassinated) near Riga, Latvia, 28 April 1944. Of obscure background, he was used by **Sergius** of Moscow in negotiations with the Soviet, becoming bishop in 1930, though he was without formal education. He was in Riga when the Germans occupied the Baltic States and Pskov, and with their support became metropolitan for the newly conquered territories. He was an energetic missionary responsible for the staffing of hundreds of reopened churches. His success made him enemies and he was shot by persons unknown in his car. The church revival he encouraged was never entirely extinguished in this area.

Serra, Junipero   Spanish Franciscan missionary to Central and North America, born Petra, Majorca, 24 November 1713, died Monterey, California, 28 August 1784. He joined the Franciscans in September 1730 and was educated at the university in Palma, Majorca, where he became professor of philosophy. In 1749 he was sent to the college in San Fernando, Mexico, but undertook missionary work among the indigenous population in the Sierra Gorda mission. After serving there for nine years he was recalled to Mexico and in 1767 was appointed superior of a group of Franciscan missionaries which made their way northward along the coast of California. He founded 21 missions in upper California, the first being at San Diego on 16 July 1769. He was a remarkable preacher and was given the right to confirm his converts, even though he was not a bishop (then an unusual privilege). He was beatified in 1987.

Severinus   Pope, born Rome, consecrated 28 May 640, died there 2 August 640. There was an almost two-year delay between Severinus' election and his consecration, because of his refusal to sign an imperial document endorsing the Monothelite heresy. While he waited, the papal treasury was plundered by the imperial representative in Italy, in order to pay his troops.

Severinus of Noricum   Saint, monk and apostle of Noricum (Austria), died there, 8 January c.480. His life was written some 30 years after his death by a disciple. He seems to have been from Italy, possibly Rome itself, but spent his early years in the desert in the east. Some time in the middle of the fifth century he moved to Noricum, where he founded a number of monasteries, though he himself lived in a hermitage. Feast day 8 January.

Severus   Patriarch of Antioch, born Sozopolis in Psidia, c.465, died Xoïs, Egypt, 538. After studying at Alexandria and Beirut he became a Christian in 488, being baptized at Leontinum in Libya, and a monk in Palestine: he founded his own monastery near Gaza. He went to Constantinople to defend Monophysite monks, and became friendly with the Emperor Anastasius to such an extent that he was proposed as patriarch of Constantinople. There proved to be too much opposition to this, however, and he became patriarch of Antioch, being consecrated on 6 November 512. Six years later he had to flee to Egypt where he became leader of the Monophysites in opposition to the Emperor Justinian I, though later, in 535, he was able to return to Constantinople under the patronage of the Empress Theodora. Justinian I condemned him again in August 536, and he returned to Egypt. His Monophysitism was moderate, and he had a reputation not only for his learning – he produced a great number of writings, preserved mainly in Syriac, including homilies, letters and a collection of prayers – but also for the holiness of his life.

Seymour, William Joseph   Pentecostal leader and bishop, born Centerville, Louisiana, 2 May 1870, died Los Angeles 28 September 1922. Raised a Baptist, Seymour entered the Holiness movement around 1900, and in 1903 was attending Lucy **Farrow**'s Holiness church in Houston. Farrow became influenced by Charles **Parham**, and Seymour attended Parham's school in Houston, accepting Pentecostalism. In 1906 Seymour became a pastor in Los Angeles, acquiring a building at 312 Azusa Street and incorporating his ministry as the Pacific Apostolic Faith Movement. Large numbers came to Azusa Street from across America and beyond, seeking the Pentecostal experience. In 1906 Seymour split with Parham, and in 1908 Seymour's influence decreased when the mailing list for his *Apostolic Faith* magazine was taken away by helpers who disapproved of his marrying. He became a bishop in 1915.

Shaftesbury, Anthony Ashley Cooper (seventh earl of)   Evangelical philanthropist, social reformer, born London, 28 April 1801, died Folkestone, 1

October 1885. Educated at Harrow and Christ Church, Oxford. Became Tory MP for Woodstock in 1826. The main figure behind the reform of the Lunacy Acts, the passing of the Ten Hours Bill 1847 and the Factory Act 1874. Campaigned for the improvement of working conditions for women and children in mines, and for chimney sweeps. Chairman of the Ragged School Union and for many years president of the British and Foreign Bible Society. The first president of the Church Pastoral Aid Society and actively involved in the National Society for the Prevention of Cruelty to Children.

Shakespeare, William English dramatist and poet, born Stratford-upon-Avon, baptized in the parish church, 26 April 1564, died Stratford-upon-Avon, 23 April 1616. Surprisingly little incontrovertible information is available on the life of one so universally renowned. He probably went to Stratford Grammar School and there is evidence to suggest that his family was Roman Catholic. He worked as an actor-dramatist in London and was one of the four founders of London's Globe Theatre. Christian themes recur in his writings. He is buried in Stratford parish church. Generations of critics worldwide have praised his works which cover all aspects of human life. Many studies of Shakespeare and Christianity have been published, including Ivor Morris, *Shakespeare's God: The Role of Religion in the Tragedies* (London, 1972), and Shakespeare's Roman Catholic background is explored in Anthony Holden's *William Shakespeare* (London, 1999).

Shanahan, Joseph Roman Catholic missionary bishop in eastern Nigeria, born Glankeen, Ireland, 1871, died Nairobi, Kenya, 1943. Trained by the Holy Ghost Fathers in Ireland and France, he went to Nigeria in 1902. When he took over leadership of the mission in 1906 he changed its direction from liberating slaves to using schools as the prime means for rural evangelism. He travelled widely in Igboland persuading local chiefs of the benefits of schools and worked on the school commission of the colonial government. In 1924 he founded the Sisters of the Holy Rosary to train missionaries for the education of girls. Ill-health forced him to retire in 1931. A popular figure, largely responsible

for the success of the Catholic Church in eastern Nigeria, he was reburied in Onitsha in 1955.

Shaxton, Nicholas Bishop of Salisbury, born probably in Norfolk, *c.*1485, died Cambridge, 5 August 1556. He studied at Cambridge, being elected a fellow of Gonville Hall. In discussing the divorce of **Henry VIII** he showed himself to be on the king's side. In 1533 he was presented to a living in Wiltshire by the king, and shortly afterwards was made treasurer of Salisbury Cathedral. Anne Boleyn made him her almoner. He was appointed to the bishopric of Salisbury in 1535, Thomas **Cranmer** being one of the consecrating bishops. In the religious controversies of the age he followed a Protestant line, and resigned his bishopric in 1539 over the Six Articles. He was later arraigned for heresy on the Eucharist, but recanted, and maintained his more Catholic views throughout the reign of **Edward VI**, even separating from his wife and living in celibacy. Under **Mary Tudor** he became suffragan to the bishop of Ely. He asked to be buried in the Gonville chapel.

Sheed, Francis Joseph Born Sydney, Australia, 20 March 1897, died Jersey City, New Jersey, 20 November 1981. In Sydney, he studied law, then in London he joined the Catholic Evidence Guild and spoke at Hyde Park Corner. He displayed knowledge, clarity and humour. He married Maisie **Ward** and they founded the publishing company of Sheed & Ward. Initially they published Hilaire **Belloc**, G. K. **Chesterton**, Christopher **Hollis** and Ronald **Knox**. They also published many translations. In 1933 they opened a New York office, publishing more controversial writers, such as Hans Küng and Charles Davis. Sheed wrote or translated books on St **Bonaventure**, St **Augustine** and Pope **Alexander VI**. Sheed's own books included *Nullity of Marriage, Communism and Man* and *To Know Jesus Christ*. In 1973 Sheed & Ward was sold to the Universal Press Syndicate. Francis Sheed was the first layman to receive an honorary doctorate in sacred theology from Rome.

Sheen, Fulton J. Roman Catholic bishop, radio and television preacher, born El Paso, Illinois, 8 May 1895, died New York City, 9 December 1979. After ordination in 1919, Sheen studied in Washington, DC, Louvain and Rome. He taught at the

Catholic University of America in Washington from 1926 until 1950 when he was appointed the national director of the Society for the Propagation of the Faith. In this position he quarrelled with Cardinal Francis **Spellman**, archbishop of New York, over control of funds. In 1951, he was appointed auxiliary bishop of the Archdiocese of New York. A gifted preacher, he gained a national reputation for his television broadcasts of *Life is Worth Living* (1952–5). In 1966, he became bishop of Rochester, New York, where he tried to implement the decrees of Vatican Council II.

Shehan, Lawrence J. Born Baltimore, Maryland, 18 March 1898, died there, 26 August 1984. He was educated in Baltimore, Maryland, and Rome, where he was ordained. He worked in the Archdiocese of Baltimore, and was appointed auxiliary bishop of Baltimore and Washington. When in 1947 Washington and Baltimore dioceses were separated, he was made bishop of Bridgeport, Connecticut. He was active in many organizations, including the Episcopal Committee on Motion Pictures, Radio and Television. He was appointed archbishop of Baltimore and made a cardinal, being active in the Second Vatican Council. One of his main interests was ecumenism. He promoted racial justice and took part in the funeral ceremonies of Dr Martin Luther **King** Junior.

Sheil, Bernard J. Born Chicago, 18 February 1886, died Tucson, Arizona, 13 September 1969. He studied in Illinois, was an outstanding basketball player, but chose to become a priest. He worked in Chicago, and in World War I served as a naval chaplain. In 1928 he was appointed auxiliary bishop of Chicago. Pope **John XXIII** named him a titular archbishop. Sheil established the Catholic Youth Organization, offering sports, theatre workshops and free medical and dental services. The CYO spread nationwide. In 1930 Sheil founded what is now Lewis College. The CYO Educational Department included theology, philosophy, social studies and liberal studies. His work extended to the blind, and to scouts, and he established the WFJL Roman Catholic broadcasting station. Sheil supported unions, and hence became known as 'labour's bishop', attended interfaith meetings and condemned McCarthyism.

Shembe, Isaiah Mdliwamafa Founder of the Nazareth Baptist Church, born 1869, Ntabamhlophe, KwaZulu-Natal, South Africa, died 1935. He was introduced to Christianity by the Wesleyans but was baptized by the Baptists in July 1906. He worked as an itinerant evangelist, developing a healing ministry in 1910. In 1911 he established his church with a holy city at Ekuphakameni and an annual pilgrimage to a holy mountain. He wrote hymns and liturgy which echoed Zulu traditions. Suspicions that his followers thought him divine and that the rites were too close to traditional religion brought criticism from outside the church, but its membership grew to about one million. After his death his son and then his grandson took over the leadership.

Sheppard, Hugh Richard Lawrie ('Dick') Born Windsor, England, 2 September 1880, died London, England, 31 October 1937. Anglican minister, pacifist and broadcaster. During the 1920s and 1930s 'Dick' Sheppard was probably the best-known churchman in Britain. Ordained in 1907, he served in several curacies before being appointed vicar of St Martin-in-the-Fields in London in 1914. His concern to communicate Christianity without stuffiness and through practical social action made both the church and Sheppard famous, especially when he became the first churchman to exploit the potential of broadcasting. Sheppard was impatient with ecclesiastical cant and was a determined advocate of church reform. This, along with his ability to relate to people of all kinds, made him a popular figure. In the last few years of his life Sheppard also played a prominent role in the pacifist movement, and in 1936 founded the Peace Pledge Union.

Sheridan, Terence James Born Dublin, Ireland, 16 September 1908, died Manila, Philippines, 11 December 1970. He studied in Dublin and became a Jesuit. He wrote plays and sketches. In 1934 he moved to Hong Kong, wrote for *The Rock*, a magazine, and taught at Wah Yan College, Hong Kong. He mounted productions of Cantonese operas in English, and launched two magazines, as well as writing religious plays and film scripts. He worked in Singapore and Manila, where he joined the staff of the East Asian Pastoral Institute, teaching communication and film. He travelled widely.

His death took place at the time of Pope **Paul VI**'s visit to Manila.

Shuster, George N. Born Lancaster, Wisconsin, 1894, died South Bend, Indiana, 25 January 1977. He was educated at the universities of Notre Dame, Indiana, and of Poitiers, Berlin and Columbia. He taught English at Notre Dame and Brooklyn Polytechnic Institute, and was president of Hunter College. He was interested in Catholic English literature, on which he wrote extensively. In the 1930s his books also reflect his concern at the rise of Hitler. Shuster helped to create UNESCO and was concerned about the Communist regimes in eastern Europe, as in his account of Cardinal Mindszenty in *In Silence I Speak*. Shuster also wrote extensively on Catholic Education in *In A Changing World* and other studies. He chaired a group of scholars conducting the first population-control research under Catholic auspices.

Siegman, Edward Ferdinand Born Cleveland, Ohio, 4 June 1908, died at Notre Dame University, Indiana, 2 February 1967. He joined the Society of the Precious Blood, was ordained in Ohio and attended the Catholic University of America. He became professor of sacred Scripture at St Charles Seminary, Ohio. He helped to found the Catholic Biblical Association of America, and became editor of *Catholic Biblical Quarterly*. Later he became associate professor at the Catholic University and in 1966 professor of sacred Scripture at Notre Dame University. With C. E. Elwell, he wrote *Christ in Promise, in Person, in His Church*. He helped to translate *The New American Bible*.

Siger of Brabant Priest and philosopher, born Brabant, *c.*1240, died Orvieto, between 1281 and 1284. He studied at Paris, and stayed there to teach in the university, where he was much influenced by the thought of the Arab philosopher Averroës. This was considered by many to be heterodox, and over 200 propositions drawn from his writings were condemned by the bishop of Paris in 1277. He took refuge in the papal court, then at Orvieto, but was stabbed to death by a madman. His writings had a considerable influence in his time, particularly his belief, contradicted by **Thomas Aquinas**, that the role of a philosopher was to discover not so much the truth as what others had said before. He also believed it a philosopher's duty to follow reason wherever it might lead, regardless of whether it contradicted Christian doctrine.

Siloan the Athonite Orthodox saint and monk, born Tambov Province, Russia 1866, died Mount Athos, 11 September 1938. He lived in quiet obscurity at the Russian monastery on Mount Athos. His teaching on prayer and his luminous love for all revealed by his disciple **Sophronius** (**Sophrony Sakharov**) have made his name famous and Father Sophrony's writings have been translated into many languages. Canonized in Constantinople, 1989. Feast day 11 September.

Silverius Pope, saint, born at Frosinone, the son of Pope **Hormisdas**, consecrated 8 June 536, deposed 11 November 537, died Palmaria, 2 December 537. He was forced upon a reluctant Rome by the last Ostrogothic king of Italy, and had strong Ostrogothic sympathies. He was stripped of his office in March 537 by the Byzantine general Belisarius – who accused him of plotting with the Goths – so that the way would be open for the appointment of **Vigilius**, the Empress **Theodora**'s candidate. He was deported, but the emperor ordered him to be taken back to Rome to stand trial. Vigilius, now in office, had him deported again, and this time got from him a statement of his abdication. He died shortly afterwards, and is venerated for his sufferings for the orthodox faith – Theodora being a Monophysite. Feast day 20 June.

Simeon, Charles Anglican evangelical leader, born Reading, 24 September 1759, died Cambridge, England, 12 November 1836. He was educated at Eton and King's College, Cambridge, where he experienced an evangelical conversion in 1779. He was minister of Trinity Church, Cambridge, from 1782 to his death, despite intense opposition in the early years. In 1799 he helped found what became the Church Missionary Society. He was scrupulous in his churchmanship, coached evangelical students, established a trust to purchase advowsons which still bears his name, and provided some notable chaplains for the East India Company. He had an extensive correspondence and his sermons were widely circulated, including in North America. His biblical focus, moderate Calvinism and model of church loyalty remain important influences. An enthusiastic supporter of the British and Foreign Bible Society. His written works include the *Horae Homiletica*.

Simon Stock Saint, Carmelite, born *c*.1165, died Bordeaux, France, 16 May 1265. It is thought that Simon Stock was originally so named because of a legend that as a young man he lived as a hermit inside a tree trunk, though the story has no historical basis. Evidence suggests he was English, and he is known to have become general of the Carmelites, probably *c*.1254, and to have had a reputation for piety among his contemporaries. He is principally remembered for his 'vision of the scapular', in which the Virgin Mary appeared to him holding a Carmelite scapular and declaring that whoever died in it would be saved. This gave rise to the belief that whoever lived and died as a Carmelite could not be eternally damned. Feast day 16 May.

Simon Stylites (the Elder) First and most famous of the 'pillar saints', born *c*.388 at Sisan, Northern Syria, died Telanissos, near Antioch, 2 September 459. He worked as a shepherd before joining a monastery. The excesses of his penances and fasting were such that he was soon forced to remove himself from the community into a hut, where he continued his life of prayer and austerity. Three years later he moved onto a rock in the desert, but his fame had spread and he was besieged by pilgrims seeking his wisdom and blessings. He had a small pillar erected with a platform at the top on which he lived. It was replaced with increasingly higher pillars over the years. He wrote letters, including one to the Emperor Leo in support of the Council of Chalcedon, from his pillar, addressed those assembled below and, by means of a ladder, pilgrims and others were able to speak with him personally. The remains of the pillar, on which Simon spent 36 years in all, and of the four basilicas built in his honour, survive at Qal 'at Sim 'ân. Feast day 1 September.

Simplicius Pope, saint, born Tivoli, consecrated 3 March 468, died 10 March 483. His pontificate was largely concerned with an attempt to keep the Eastern Empire loyal to the decisions of the Coun-

cil of Chalcedon of 451, under Pope **Leo**, about the nature of Christ. The Emperor Zeno and his patriarch Acacius were attempting, without technically breaching Chalcedon, to re-unite the monophysite (i.e. 'one nature') protagonists with the Chalcedonians. In Rome itself Simplicius converted a public building for use as a church, the first known example of this. Feast day 10 March.

Simpson, Albert Benjamin Founder of the Christian and Missionary Alliance, born Bayview, Prince Edward Island, 1843, died New York, 1919. Simpson received Spirit baptism while a Presbyterian minister in Kentucky. He became an independent pastor in 1881, founding the Gospel Tabernacle in New York. Simpson proclaimed the 'Fourfold Gospel' of Christ as Saviour, Sanctifier, Healer and Coming King. Although open to Pentecostalism, he was critical of its obsession with supernaturalism. For *Living Truths* magazine he wrote 'The Baptism of the Holy Spirit: A Crisis or an Evolution' (1905), 'The Ministry of the Spirit' (1907), and 'A Story of Providence' (1907).

Simpson, William Wallace Pentecostal missionary to Central Asia, born White County, Tennessee, 1869, died USA, 1949. Wallace began as a Congregational minister, and in 1892 travelled to Tibet with the Christian and Missionary Alliance. However, he left the CMA in 1912 following a Pentecostal experience and joined the Assemblies of God. He became well known as he evangelized widely in China, Manchuria, Tibet and Mongolia, and taught indigenous clergy at a number of Bible institutions.

Singh, Sundar Indian Christian and mystic or holy man ('Sadhu'), born 3 September 1889, Rampur, North India, into a wealthy Sikh family, died India, *c*.1929. He inherited his piety from his mother who always hoped he would become a holy man, but his father was determined he should enter his business and sent him to a Christian missionary school. He left the school, in 1904, because they made him read the Christian Scriptures, and he publicly burned a copy of the Gospels, but repented after three days, had a vision, became a Christian and was turned out of his family. He was baptized on his sixteenth birthday and at one point became a Franciscan but refused ordination. Proud of his Sikh ancestry, he never adopted European dress, being committed to presenting Christianity 'in an Eastern Bowl rather than a European Vessel'. Disappointed not to die at the age of 33, he was last heard of in April 1929 when he set off on another journey to Tibet despite his failing health.

Siricius Pope, saint, born Rome, consecrated December 384, died 26 November 399. A deacon under Pope **Damasus**, he was a popular choice as bishop of Rome, both among the people and with the emperor. He was firm and direct in government, issuing his decrees in the manner of an imperial official, to be binding in local churches in the West. Although he was a vigorous defender of orthodox doctrine, he criticized bishops who had condemned the heretic Priscillian to death. Feast day 26 November.

Sisinnius Pope, a Syrian by birth, consecrated 15 January 708, died 4 February 708. Nothing of significance occurred during the elderly Pope's brief pontificate, except that he took steps, not followed up after his death, to rebuild the walls of Rome.

Sixtus (Xystus) I Pope, saint, consecrated *c.*116, died 125. Nothing is known about him. It is unclear whether he died as a martyr, as tradition suggests he did. Feast day 3 April.

Sixtus (Xystus) II Pope, saint and martyr, consecrated August 257, died 6 August 258. He was probably of Greek origin, and little is known of his pontificate except that he restored good relations with the Church in Africa, damaged by **Stephen I**. He did this without sacrificing his principles, for a letter has survived from Sixtus to **Dionysius** of Alexandria defending the validity of baptism administered by heretics. On the day of his death he was dragged from the chair where he was sitting teaching, in the cemetery of Praetextatus, and beheaded on the spot, together with some of his attendant deacons. Feast day 7 August.

Sixtus (Xystus) III Pope, saint, born at Rome, consecrated 31 July 432, died 19 August 440. Sixtus' chief concern, in the aftermath of the Council of Ephesus in 431, was to reconcile war-ring factions without betraying the decrees of the council. In this he was largely successful, as he was in maintaining for the most part good relations with the patriarch of Constantinople, without giving up papal claims, for example, to have jurisdiction over the disputed area of Illyricum. He built Rome's first recorded monastery, and rebuilt the Liberian basilica as Santa Maria Maggiore, to celebrate the Council of Ephesus and, in its iconography, to proclaim papal authority. Feast day 19 August.

Sixtus IV Pope, born Francesco della Rovere, Celle, near Savona, 21 July 1414, elected to the Papacy 12 August 1471, died Rome, 12 August 1484. A Franciscan theologian who taught at a number of Italian universities prior to his election to the papal office. In spite of this he played an active part in Italian inter-state relations, most notably in the war which followed the anti-Medicean Pazzi Conspiracy of 1478, in Florence, and in the War of Ferrara of 1482–4. One of the most notorious of Renaissance nepotists, he raised six of his nephews to the Sacred College of Cardinals. In the cultural sphere, he refounded the Vatican Library and is remembered as the builder of the Sistine Chapel.

Sixtus V Pope, born Felice Peretti, a farm labourer's son, at Grottammare, Ancona, 15 December 1520, elected 24 April 1585, died 27 August 1590. He was educated by the Franciscans and, at twelve, joined the Order. He was ordained in 1547, and graduated a doctor of theology at Fermo the following year. He was brought to Rome by the cardinal protector of the Franciscans largely because of his preaching ability, and came to the notice of **Paul IV**. He was put on several commissions for the reform of the Church, and was made an Inquisitor, then in 1566 bishop of Sant'Agata dei Goti. He became a cardinal in 1570 and bishop of Fermo in 1571. As Pope he was eager to press ahead with reform – too eager in one respect: thinking that the reform of the Vulgate was going ahead too slowly he produced his own version, which had to be withdrawn. More importantly he reorganized the papal curia, setting up the system of 'Congregations' which still survives. This had the added bonus that it did away with the need for consistories, and possible challenges to papal authority. He also insisted that bishops should regularly report to Rome on the state of their sees, the *ad limina* visits. Politically he backed Catholic princes in their attempt to push back Lutheranism, but he was astute enough to recognize that Henry of Navarre was likely to win control of France, and therefore in his last years did not support Philip of Spain against him. He spent a great deal of money beautifying Rome, and constructing new aqueducts, as well as establishing the Vatican Library and the Vatican printing press. The money for all this he raised out of taxes and other sources in the Papal States, which he ruthlessly reduced to order soon after his election, executing thousands of brigands, and then by introducing financial reforms. None of this made him popular among the people of Rome, and a mob destroyed his statue on hearing of his death.

Skehan, Patrick William Roman Catholic priest and biblical scholar, born New York, 30 September 1909, died Washington, DC, 9 September 1980. He studied at Fordham University, and at St Joseph's Seminary, Yonkers, New York. At the Catholic University of America, he studied Scripture and Semitic languages, and later taught Semitic languages. Admired for his scholarship, integrity and teaching, he was visiting professor to the Pontifical Biblical Institute, Rome, and was consultor to the Pontifical Biblical Commission. He was one of the editors of the Dead Sea Scrolls and contributed to the *New American Bible*. In the Catholic Biblical Association, he was president and later treasurer. He was associate editor of the *Catholic Biblical Quarterly* and *Old Testament Abstracts*.

Skydsgaard, Kristen Ejner Member of the WCC Faith and Order commission, 1952–68, and of the commission of ecumenical research of the Lutheran World Federation. Born in Fünen, Denmark, 15 November 1902, he went on to become active in establishing and developing the Institute for Ecumenical Research at Strasburg, where he was board president from 1964 to 1974. He was an observer at the Second Vatican Council for the Lutheran World Federation and spoke on the need to study Christian doctrine in its historical perspectives. He took part in the lengthy ecumenical debate on the relation between Scripture and Tradition, and in Roman Catholic–Protestant theological and ecclesial dialogue. He published *One in Christ* (Philadelphia, Muhlenberg, 1957) and edited *Konzil und Evangelium* (Göttingen, Vandenhoeck & Ruprecht, 1962).

Slessor, Mary Mitchell United Presbyterian missionary to eastern Nigeria, born Aberdeen, Scotland, 2 December 1848, died, Itu, Nigeria, 13 January 1915. She worked in the linen mills of Dundee from the age of eleven. In 1876 the United Presbyterian Church Mission Committee agreed to send her to Calabar as a teacher. An able and independent woman, in 1888 she went to live alone among the Okoyong, establishing a household of outcast women and twins she saved from death. She followed the colonial administration east in order to help those affected by creating new stations and spreading the Gospel. She had a different approach to mission from many of her contemporaries, adapting thoroughly to the culture of the people with whom she worked.

Slipyj, Josef Ukrainian Uniate, cardinal, born Zazdrist, Ukraine, 17 February 1892, died Rome, 7 September 1984. The Austro-Hungarian empire extended to the western Ukraine when he was born. He studied at Lvov, Innsbruck and Rome, and was ordained a priest, teaching at Lvov. He founded a theological quarterly, *Bohoslovia*. He was coadjutor to the metropolitan Szeptyckyj of Lvov, whom he succeeded as head of the Uniate Ukrainian Church. He suffered at the hands of the Nazis and the Communists, and spent eighteen years in prison and labour camps and in exile in Siberia. In 1963 he returned to Rome and Pope **Paul VI** gave him the title Major Archbishop of the Ukrainian Church, a title newly created by the Second Vatican Council. In 1965 he became a cardinal. He visited exiled Ukrainians in Europe and America. In Rome, he built a Ukrainian Catholic Cathedral.

Smales, Joseph Pentecostal pastor, born England, 1867, died South Pasadena, 16 September 1926. Smale began his Baptist pastorate in Ryde, Isle of Wight, and in 1895 became pastor of the First Baptist Church in Los Angeles. He visited the Welsh Revival and sought a similar experience for his church, but following disagreements with church leaders set up his own First New Testament

Church in 1906. This church featured Pentecostal experiences, although Smale did not experience glossolalia personally. He wrote *A Tract for the Times* (no date) defending Pentecostalism, although he became disillusioned in 1907 and founded a separate Grace Baptist Church.

Smith, John *see* **Smyth, John**

Smith, Wilfred Cantwell Presbyterian theologian and Islamicist, born Toronto, 21 July 1916, died there, 7 February 2000. After studying at Upper Canada College he spent a year travelling in Europe and Egypt before taking a degree in oriental studies at Toronto in 1938, where he was an active member of the Student Christian Movement, becoming its president in 1937. He then studied theology and oriental languages at Cambridge before going to Lahore, in what is now Pakistan, in 1940 to work among Muslims, and in 1943 he was appointed to an Interdenominational Mission in India as presbyterian: he had more sympathy with the United Church of Canada, and joined that denomination in 1960. In 1943 he published *Modern Islam in India*, which reflected his Marxist sympathies, and his antipathy to British rule in India, an antipathy which prevented his return to Cambridge. Instead he studied for his doctorate at Princeton. He then taught at McGill University as professor of comparative religion and, from 1951, director of the Institute of Islamic Studies. In 1964 he moved to Harvard's Centre for the Study of World Religions as director, before returning to Canada, to Dalhousie University, in 1973. In 1978 he went back to Harvard as professor of comparative religion, retiring, and returning finally to Toronto, in 1984. His major works include *The Meaning and End of Religion* (1963, and often reprinted) and *Towards a World Theology* (1981, 1989).

Smith, William Robinson Theologian and Semitic scholar, born Keig, Aberdeenshire, 8 November 1846, died Cambridge, 31 March 1894. He was educated at home by his father before entering the University of Aberdeen in November 1861, and then, in November 1866, New College, Edinburgh, to study for the Free Church of Scotland ministry. He was proficient in German, and spent some time in Germany, being particularly influenced by

Ritschl. In 1870 he was appointed professor of oriental languages and Old Testament exegesis at the Free Church College in Aberdeen. His contributions to the ninth edition of the *Encyclopedia Britannica* aroused so much controversy that he had to demand a trial for heresy to clear his name. He was, however, removed from his chair in 1881. He then accepted a post as assistant editor of the *Encyclopedia Britannica*, and moved to Edinburgh. He completed the task by 1888, by which time he had moved to Cambridge as professor of Arabic in 1883, chief librarian in 1886 and Adams Professor of Arabic in 1889. His best-known work, *Religion of the Semites: Fundamental Institutions*, the text of lectures he had delivered in Aberdeen, appeared that year. It represented only the first of the three sets of lectures: the others remained unpublished. He died in his Cambridge college, but was buried in his home parish of Keig.

Smyth (Smith), John English Nonconformist minister and 'father' of Baptist churches, born *c.*1554, died at Amsterdam towards the end of August 1612. He may have studied at Christ's College, Cambridge, 1571 to 1576, though the identification is uncertain. He was ordained into the Church of England and was city preacher at Lincoln, 1600–5. He renounced the Church of England in 1606, and became minister to a group of Separatists at Gainsborough, Lincolnshire. In 1608 he went with John Robinson to Amsterdam, and accepted the newly-emerging 'Baptist' principle of believers' baptism, earning himself the title, 'Se-baptist' (self-baptizer) because he first baptized himself and then the rest, including **Thomas Helwys**, founder of the first Baptist Church on British soil. He wrote *The Differences of the Churches of the Separation* (*c.*1608).

Socinus (Sozzini), Fausto Paolo Unitarian theologian, born Siena, 5 December 1539, died Lucławice, Poland, 3 March 1604. He came from an important legal family in Siena, but his parents having died while he was young, he had only a rudimentary education. He began the study of law, but under the influence of his uncle **Lelio Socinus** moved to theology. He went to Lyons in 1561, where he published a study of St John's Gospel which denied the divinity of Christ. He went on to Zürich, where his uncle had just died. He then worked in Florence, as a secretary in the court of the Grand Duke Cosimo I, but on the death of Cosimo went to Basel (1574–8), where he published his major works *De Christo Servatore* and *De statu primi hominis ante lapsum*, then to Klausenburg – now Cluj in Romania – and in 1579 to Cracow. From 1583–8 he lived in Pawlikowice, and from 1588–98 back in Cracow. He was, however, forced to flee Cracow when he was attacked by students who opposed his anti-Trinitarian doctrines. He spent the remainder of his life in Lusclawice

Socinus (Sozini), Lelio Francesco Maria Anti-Trinitarian theologian, born Siena 1525, died Zürich 4 May 1562. He came from a family of distinguished jurists, and himself began the study of law at Bologna, but became increasingly interested in philosophy and theology. He went to Venice, and then travelled in Switzerland, England, France and the Netherlands. He settled for a time in Switzerland where he debated the resurrection of the body with **Calvin**, and then went on to Wittenberg, to study under **Melanchthon**, but returned to Italy in 1552, where he influenced his nephew **Fausto Socinus** (or Sozzini: uncle and nephew spelt their names differently). From 1551 he made his home mainly in Switzerland, finally (in 1559) settling in Zürich, but he continued to travel in Germany and Poland. The main theological influence on his thought was, however, not the Swiss reformers but the Italian Protestant Camillo Renato.

Socrates Historian, born Constantinople at the end of the fourth century and spent much of his life there. Possibly trained in law and seems to have travelled to other countries in the East. His *Church History*, dedicated to a Theodorus, his patron, who encouraged him to continue the work of **Eusebius**, begins in 306 and continues to 439. It is divided into seven sections, corresponding to the imperial succession in the East. Though opposed to the heresies of the period, his tone and approach is moderate and respectful, an approach that led some to suspect his orthodoxy. A layman, he was totally committed and submissive to the Church, and had the highest respect for the clergy and especially for the monks, but this did not prevent him advocating the value of reading pagan

writers. He drew on a wide variety of sources, but he has been criticized for giving too little attention to events in the West – he never mentions Augustine, for instance – and for being too credulous of miracles and other portents.

Söderblom, Nathan Archbishop of Sweden from 1914, historian of religions, ecumenical movement pioneer, Nobel peace prize winner in 1930. Born 15 January 1866, Trönö, Sweden, died 12 July 1931. Studied theology at Uppsala and served as chaplain to the Swedish legation in Paris from 1894 to 1901. After receiving his Ph.D. in ancient Persian religion he became professor of the history of religion at Uppsala from 1901 to 1914, and latterly also lectured at Leipzig. From his student days he encouraged the churches to unite, despite their doctrinal differences, to bring Christian principles to bear on society and promote world peace. He saw some success in the Universal Conference on Life and Work held in Stockholm in 1925, and in the first world conference in 1927 of the Faith and Order movement.

Soloviev, Vladimir Ecumenist, journalist, mystic, philosopher, poet, theologian. Born 16 January 1853, Moscow, died 31 July 1900. He came to believe strongly in the continuing mystical union of the Orthodox and Roman Catholic churches and hence the need for their external unity. Early on he thought this could serve as a focus of religious unity for all humanity, but later became more pessimistic about this. He was strongly influenced by **Böhme**, **Schelling** and Hegel and in his work tried to combine the Christian theology of the incarnation with the pantheism of these philosophers. The character Alyosha in **Dostoevsky**'s *Brothers Karamazov* is modelled on Soloviev. Among his translated works are *Russia and the Universal Church* (London, Bles, 1948) and *God, Man and the Church* (Cambridge, James Clarke, 1937).

Soper, Donald Methodist minister, president of the Conference, and Labour life peer, born London, 1903, died 26 December 1998. Educated at Haberdashers' Aske's school, St Catharine's College, Cambridge, and the London School of Economics, where he gained a doctorate. Following his ordination in 1926 he worked at the South

London Mission and began an open-air preaching ministry at Tower Hill and Hyde Park which lasted over seventy years. From 1936 to 1978 he served as superintendent of the West London Mission. In 1960 he was co-founder (with R. H. Tawney) of the Christian Socialist Movement and a regular contributor to *Tribune*. Elected president of Conference in 1953 and later appointed as a Labour life peer. An active member of the Methodist Peace Fellowship, the League Against Cruel Sports, the Voluntary Euthanasia Society and other causes.

Sophronius Saint, patriarch of Jerusalem from 634, and usually identified as 'the Sophist'. Born *c.*560, probably in Egypt, where he lived as a monk from about 580, before moving near to the Jordan, and in 619 to Jerusalem, where he died in 638, shortly after negotiating the surrender of Jerusalem to the Arabs. He was the chief opponent of Monothelitism in his later years. His writings include Lives of the Alexandrians Cyrus and John, sermons and poems.

Sophronius (Sophrony Sakharov) Archimandrite, Orthodox monk and writer, born Moscow, 22 September 1896, died Essex, England, 11 July 1993. A talented Russian émigré artist who became a monk on Mount Athos, where he was a disciple of St **Siloan**. He later founded the well-known Orthodox monastery at Tolleshunt Knights, Essex, which has published and translated his writings on St Siloan. Feast day 11 March.

Sophronius of Bulgaria Orthodox saint and bishop, born Kotelin, Bulgaria, 1739, died Bucharest, 22 September 1813. Consecrated bishop of Vratsa, he laboured to protect his flock from arbitrary mistreatment by the Turkish authorities and also translated spiritual literature into colloquial Bulgarian. He was forced out of Bulgaria and went to Bucharest, where he continued to write for his people. There he also wrote his own *Life and Sufferings*. Canonized by the Bulgarian church 1964. Feast day 22 September.

Soter Pope, saint, consecrated *c.*166, died *c.*174. Born in the Campania, we know he sent a gift to the church at Corinth, because a letter of thanks has survived. It was during his pontificate that Easter became an annual feast of the Church. It is common to celebrate Soter as a martyr, but there is no evidence that he was one. Feast day 22 April.

Soto, Domingo de Dominican theologian, born Segovia, 1495, died Salamanca, 15 November 1560. He studied at Alcalá and Paris, and entered the Dominicans at Burgos in 1524 and taught there until 1532, when he took up a chair of theology at Salamanca University. In 1545 he was chosen by **Charles V** as Imperial Theologian at the Council of Trent. He became confessor to Charles and lived for a time in Germany. He returned to Salamanca in 1550 and was shortly after elected to the principal chair in theology there. His main writings are *De Natura et de Gratia* and *De Justitia et Jure*.

Soubirous, Bernardette Saint and visionary, born Lourdes, 7 January 1844, died Nevers 16 April 1879. She was born into a very poor family, and was uneducated. While gathering wood beside the River Gave on 11 February 1858 she had the first of eighteen visions of the Virgin Mary, who identified herself, in the local patois, under the recently declared title of 'The Immaculate Conception'. Though she was not at first believed, the visions came eventually to be accepted, and Lourdes became a major shrine. Bernardette was then accepted into the school of the Sisters of Charity of Nevers, who had a house in Lourdes, and in 1866 joined the order at Nevers. She was canonized in 1933.

Souter, Alexander NT and patristic scholar, born 1873 in the UK, died there, 1949. Educated at Aberdeen and Cambridge, he was professor of NT Greek at Oxford from 1903 to 1911, and Regius Professor of humanity at Aberdeen from 1911 to 1937.

South, Robert Anglican theologian, born Hackney, near London, 4 September 1634, died Westminster, 8 July 1716. South was ordained in 1658, in secret, having at one time been sympathetic to Presbyterianism. Over the next twenty years he held a wide variety of ecclesiastical appointments, during which he gained great popularity for his abilities as a preacher. His sermons were frequently outspoken, and may have contributed to his failure to achieve high office, though he is thought at one time to have declined an offer of a bishopric. South also published a number of theological works, most of which are contributions to the occasionally controversial theological debates of the period.

Southcott, Joanna Religious fanatic, born Gittisham, Devon, May 1750, died London, 27 December 1814. A domestic servant, Joanna Southcott became a Methodist in 1791, and the following year became convinced she was a prophetess. In the course of the next few years until her death she wrote and published a series of tracts through which she claimed to convey various apocalyptic prophecies. A box she had sealed up, and which she claimed also held important prophecies, was opened in 1927 and found to contain items such as a nightcap and a lottery ticket. It is likely that her obvious delusions and eccentricities were attributable to the brain disease from which she eventually died.

Southern, Richard historian, born Jarrow, 8 February 1912, died Oxford, 6 February 2001. He was educated at the Royal Grammar School, Newcastle-on-Tyne, and at Balliol College, Oxford, where he won the Alexander Prize of the Royal Historical Society. He went on to Exeter College as a fellow, and then back to Balliol. In 1961 he became Chichele Professor and a fellow of All Souls, moving to St John's College as president in 1969, a post from which he retired in 1981. His writings concentrated on the history of the – mainly, but not only – English medieval church and some of its most significant figures such as saint **Anselm** and **Robert Grosseteste**. His final works were on the medieval universities. He was made a knight in 1974, and awarded a prize in 1987 by the Fondazione Internazionale Balzan as the 'greatest historian of medieval Europe'. He was a lifelong member of the Church of England, and, though a layman, an occasional preacher both in his parish churches and on university occasions.

Southwell, Robert Saint, Jesuit poet and martyr, born Horsham St Faith, England, 1561, died (executed) London, England, 21 February 1595. A member of a predominantly Catholic family, Southwell was educated by Jesuits in Douai and Paris, becoming a Jesuit himself in 1578 in Rome. He was ordained in 1584 and taught at the English College before returning to England in 1587 to work clandestinely for the cause of English Catholicism. His secret presses published several works of experimental poetry, which influenced **Shakespeare** and are today highly regarded by literary scholars. Southwell was eventually betrayed, and was captured and imprisoned in 1592. Following prolonged torture, Southwell's priesthood finally condemned him, and he was put to death at Tyburn in 1595. He was beatified by **Pius XI** in 1929 and canonized as one of the **Forty Martyrs**.

Sozomen (Salmaninius Hermias Sozomenus) Church historian of the early fifth century. He was born into a Christian family in Bethelia, near Gaza in Palestine and settled in Constantinople in the early part of the fifth century. His major work is his nine-volume *History of the Church*, which takes up where **Eusebius of Caesarea**'s work ends, in 323, and takes the story up to 425. He gives a good account of the rise of monasticism and of the spread of Christianity to the Armenians, Saracens and Goths but does not go into any detail about the theological controversies of the time.

Spagnoletto, Il *see* Ribera, Jusepe de

Spalatin, Georg (Burkhardt) Lutheran reformer and scholar, born Spalt, Germany, 17 January 1484, died Altenburg, Germany, 26 January 1545. Spalatin studied at Erfurt, and in 1509 was appointed tutor to the sons of Frederick III (the Wise) of Saxony, subsequently becoming Frederick's secretary and librarian. In 1511 Frederick sent Spalatin to study in Wittenberg, where he was taught by Martin **Luther** and became one of his followers. Spalatin's counsel was much valued by Frederick, who was won over to Luther's ideas mainly as a result of Spalatin's influence. Spalatin was also responsible for introducing Lutheran reforms to Altenburg in 1525, and continued to work in the Lutheran cause until his death, although his later years were troubled by depression.

Sparrow, Anthony Anglican bishop, born Depden, near Bury St Edmunds, 1612, died Norwich, 19 May 1685. A fellow of Queens' College, Cambridge, as a High-Churchman Sparrow incurred the opposition of the Puritans, who had him expelled from his position in 1633. He became archdeacon of Sudbury at the Restoration, and contributed to the revision of the Prayer Book. In a book published in 1657 he defended this revision, arguing that it contained neither Roman Catholic 'superstitions' nor divisive doctrinal innovations. He was made bishop of Exeter in 1667, and of Norwich in 1676.

Spartas, Christopher (Reuben Mukasa) Ugandan Orthodox bishop and missionary, born near Kampala c.1900, died 1982. Son of a minor Bugandan chief, he was early attracted to pan-Africanism and rejected the paternalism of the (Anglican) Church Missionary Society. He founded his own 'African Orthodox Church' which was eventually recognized by the Greek patriarch of Alexandria in 1946. Much later he was consecrated bishop. He is the founding father of Orthodoxy in East Africa.

Spellman, Francis Cardinal archbishop of New York, born Whitman, Massachusetts, 4 May 1889, died New York City, 2 December 1967. He received his seminary education in Rome, where he studied for the Archdiocese of Boston. After pastoral work in Boston and an assignment in Rome, **Pius XI** named Spellman as auxilary bishop of Boston in 1932. In 1939, **Pius XII**, whose friendship he always enjoyed, appointed him archbishop of New York. A capable administrator, he was named Military Vicar for the Armed Forces in 1939, and in 1946 he became a cardinal. He was strongly anti-Communist, and recognized the Church's responsibility to the poor and the immigrants in New York. At Vatican Council II, Spellman defended the Latin Mass. He supported the civil rights movement, but also defended the involvement of America in Vietnam.

Spencer, Ivan Quay President of Elim Bible Institute and founder of the Elim Fellowship, born 1888, died 1970. Raised in Pennsylvania, Spencer experienced a healing from typhoid fever, and while working in Macedon, New York, he joined the Elim Tabernacle in Rochester. He received the Pentecostal experience in 1912, and after a time with the Methodists joined the Assemblies of God in 1920. In 1924 he opened the Elim Bible Institute, and in 1928 the Elim Ministerial Fellowship to confer ministerial credentials. In 1943 he became a founding delegate of the Evangelical

Association. From 1931 he edited the *Elim Pentecostal Herald*.

Spencer, John Semitic scholar and dean of Ely Cathedral, born Bocton, Kent, 30? October 1630, died Cambridge, 27 May 1693. Spencer spent his entire academic career at Corpus Christi College, Cambridge, and was master from 1667. He made a detailed study of the laws and rites of the Jews, which he compared with those of neighbouring Semitic nations, as a result of which he is regarded as a pioneer in the study now termed comparative religion. Considerably in advance of its time, his work was not taken further until the nineteenth century.

Spener, Philipp Jakob Lutheran pastor and founder of Pietism, born Rappoltsweiler, then in Germany but now in France, 23 January 1635, died Berlin, Germany, 5 February 1705. Spener was brought up as a devout Lutheran, and while studying in Switzerland his faith was enriched by an exposure to both Reformed theology and the writings of Richard **Baxter** and other English Puritans. In 1666 he became chief pastor in Frankfurt, and in seeking to deepen the devotional life of his congregation began to hold prayer and Bible study meetings in his house. Similar housegroups quickly sprang up, and were known as the 'Guilds of Piety', hence 'Pietism'. Pietism soon became a widespread movement within Lutheranism, and helped to restore its original personal spirituality and devotional warmth, characteristics which over time had been gradually lost.

Speyr, Adrienne von Medical doctor, spiritual writer and stigmatic, born in La Chaux-de-Fonds, Switzerland, 10 September 1902, died Basel, Switzerland, 17 September 1967. She married in 1927 and qualified as a doctor the following year. In 1934 she was devastated by the death of her husband but remarried two years later and maintained a busy medical practice. She had had spiritual experiences since childhood and pursued an undirected spiritual search. In 1940 she met Hans Urs von Balthasar, who became her confessor, spiritual director and a lifelong friend, and she converted to Roman Catholicism. Her religious experiences intensified, resulting, in 1942, in her displaying the stigmata. Von Balthasar left the

Jesuits and was co-founder with her of a secular institute. He wrote down von Speyr's experiences and insights and was instrumental in having these works, often composed when she was in a state of intense mystical experience, published. They run to many dozen volumes, and consist mainly in meditations on biblical texts, but she also writes on the mystical experience itself and on the works of others, including **Teresa of Ávila** and **John of the Cross**, deriving from this state. They include *Apokalypse* (1950), *Das Wort und die Mystik* (1970) and *The Gates of Eternal Life* (English translation 1983). The English translation of von Balthasar's own book, *A First Glance at Adrienne von Speyr*, was published in 1981.

Spinckes, Nathaniel Anglican non-juror, born near Northampton, England, 1653, died London, 28 July 1727. Spinkes was ordained in the Church of England in 1678 following study at Cambridge. He held a series of clerical appointments before becoming prebendary and rector of St Martin's Church, Salisbury, in 1687. In 1690 he refused to take the oath of allegiance to William and Mary and was consequently deprived of his living. He was made a bishop in 1713 by George Hickes, the acknowledged head of the Nonjuror party, though never subsequently holding any appointment at this level. Spinckes was known as a man of considerable learning, and was much respected for his personal piety. He wrote a number of studies concerning the ecclesiastical politics of his day, and several collections of highly regarded devotional works.

Spitta, Friedrich Lutheran church historian, NT scholar and hymnologist, born Wittingen, Germany, 11 January 1852, died Göttingen, Germany, 7 June 1924. He was ordained in 1879, taking up a parish and a teaching career (in Bonn) both in 1881. Spitta held academic appointments at a number of German universities, culminating in professorships at Strasburg in 1887, and at Göttingen in 1918. During his career he published a large number of scholarly works on the history of the early Church, NT theology and studies of church music and liturgy.

Spitta, Karl Johann Philipp Hymn-writer, born Hanover, Germany, 1 August 1801, died Burgdorf,

28 September 1859. His family were originally French Huguenots. He was educated at Göttingen University, 1821–4, and eventually became a Lutheran pastor, though originally not attracted to a career in the Church, preferring rather to pursue poetry. He held a variety of positions in the Lutheran Church, and wrote many hymns. They were published in *Psalter Und Harfe*.

Spottiswode, John Scottish Episcopalian bishop, born 1565, died 26 November 1639. Spottiswode was originally a Presbyterian but later came to support the episcopacy favoured by **Charles I**, who appointed him archbishop of Glasgow in 1603. Spottiswode strove to establish episcopacy throughout the Scottish church, strengthening his ability to do so by unilaterally declaring himself moderator of the General Assembly in 1618. When the strength of the opposition to episcopacy was demonstrated by the signing of the National Covenant in 1637, Spottiswode fled to England, and was deposed by the Assembly shortly afterwards.

Spurgeon, Charles Haddon Baptist minister, born 19 June 1834, Kelvedon, Essex, died 31 January 1892, Mentone, France. His father and grandfather were Independent ministers but Spurgeon was baptized as a believer and joined the church at Isleham, Cambridgeshire, in 1850. In 1852 he was appointed pastor at Waterbeach, Cambridgeshire, and in 1856 to the pastorate of New Park Street church, Southwark, in London. Calvinist in theology, he was a powerful orator and the most popular preacher of his day, drawing crowds of thousands to his services, and as a prolific author his influence extended throughout England and beyond. Increasingly concerned about the influence of the criticial method in theology amongst Baptists, he resigned from the Baptist Union in 1887, the so-called Downgrade Controversy. Spurgeon established a training college for pastors, almshouses and an orphanage, and an association of colporteurs to distribute religious tracts.

Spyridon Saint, bishop, died about 348. He was bishop of Tremithus in Cyprus and was probably one of the bishops at the Council of Nicaea in 325, and definitely at the Council of Sardica in 343. Feast day in the East, 12 December; in the West, 14 December.

Stafford, Anthony   English devotional writer, born Eaton, Socon, Bedfordshire, 1587, died in or soon after 1645. He studied at Oriel College, Oxford, and wrote several theological treatises which apparently gave offence to the Puritans. In 1612 he published *Meditations and Resolutions, Moral, Divine and Political* and in 1615 a book on Diogenes, but he was notorious among the Puritans for his *The Female Glory; or the Life and Death of the Virgin Mary*, which was published in 1635. It was edited and reprinted in 1860 as *Life of the Blessed Virgin*.

Stainer, John, Sir   Musician, born Southwark, Surrey, 6 June 1840, died Verona, Italy, 31 March 1901. He was a chorister at St Paul's Cathedral, and was only fourteen when he obtained his first post as a church organist. He subsequently held appointments as an organist at Oxford, where he studied, being awarded a doctor of music degree in 1865, and St Paul's Cathedral. He was an excellent choir trainer and made the cathedral's choir the best in England. He became professor of music at Oxford, 1889–99. He wrote much church music, including a once popular oratorio *The Crucifixion*. He helped to compile hymn-books and choir music collections. Also he helped to raise standards of musical taste in the Anglican Church. Stainer's hymn tunes include *Love Divine*.

Stamp, William Wood   Methodist minister and president of the Methodist Conference, born Bradford, Yorkshire, 1801, died Liverpool, 1877. Following his conversion in 1822 he ended his apprenticeship as a surgeon and became a Methodist itinerant. He served as a minister in several Circuits including Newcastle, Bradford and London. In 1860 he was elected president of Conference. For many years he was editor of the Wesleyan Year Book and was the author of several works, including *The History of Wesleyan Methodism in Bradford* (1841) and *The Orphan House of Wesley* (1863).

Stanford, Charles Villiers   Composer, born Dublin, 30 September 1852, died London, 29 March 1924. He was educated at Cambridge, where he became organ scholar at Trinity College, and in Germany. From 1896 he settled in London. As a composer he was influenced by the idiom of Schumann and Brahms. He became director professor of music at Cambridge. He wrote much church music, notably a *Service in B Flat* and hymn tunes, though purists have complained that his religious music, much used in church services, is not very devout in style.

Staniloae, Dumitru   Romanian Orthodox priest and theologian, born Vladeni, Transylvania, 16 November 1903, died Bucharest, 4 October 1993. He lectured in theology in Sibiu and Bucharest from 1929 to 1973, except for a five-year period, 1959–64, when he was imprisoned by the government, who also stopped his work on the Romanian edition of the *Philokalia*. This, together with his *Dogmatic Theology* (1978, translated into English as *The Experience of God* 1994) is his most important work.

Stanislaus   Saint, bishop of Cracow and patron of Poland, born into a noble family at Szczepanów in 1030, murdered in the Church of St Michael in Cracow, 11 April 1079. He was educated in Gniezno, and, possibly, in Paris, then became a canon of Cracow, being appointed its bishop in 1072. While King Boleslaus was campaigning against the Duchy of Kiev, Stanislaus appears to have joined the opposition led by the King's brother: Boleslaus himself is said to have assassinated him, while he was saying mass. His body was later buried in the cathedral at Cracow, and he was canonized at Assisi in 1253. Feast day 11 April.

Stanley, Arthur Penrhyn   Broad Church Anglican divine, born 1813, died 1881. Studied at Rugby under T. Arnold and at Balliol College, Oxford, and in 1838 became a fellow of University College. He was tolerant of both Tractarian and liberal extremes. In 1851 he was canon of Canterbury and was professor of ecclesiastical history at Oxford from 1856 until 1864, when he became dean of Westminster. At Westminster he was determined to make the Abbey a national shrine for all, irrespective of their denominational adherence, and upset conservative churchmen by his invitation to all the scholars who had produced the Revised Version of the Bible, among them a Unitarian, to receive Holy Communion in the Abbey. He was strongly opposed to disciplinary action against

Colenso, and appeared in many ways unorthodox, but was very influential, and more widely read than were most divines. His publications include *Life and Correspondence of Thomas Arnold* (1844), *Memorials of Canterbury* (1854), *Sinai and Palestine* (1856), *Lectures on the History of the Eastern Church* (1861), *Lectures on the History of the Jewish Church* (3 parts, 1863–76) and volumes of sermons.

Stanley, Henry Morton (John Rowlands)   Explorer, administrator, writer, born 1842, died 1904. He took the name Henry Morton Stanley after his adoptive father. In 1868 he was foreign correspondent to the *New York Herald*, and in March 1871 left Zanzibar to seek Livingstone. They met the following November. Between 1873 and 1889 he made other journeys of exploration, and discovered and reported on over 2 million square miles of the interior of Africa. His communications with the CMS during his crossing of Africa from east to west in 1874–7 led to the beginning of mission work in Uganda, and Christian missionary work in much of Central Africa was only possible because of his discoveries.

Stanton, Arthur Henry   Anglo-Catholic priest, born Stroud, Gloucestershire, 21 June 1839, died there, 28 March 1913. He studied at Rugby and Trinity College, Oxford, and then prepared for the ministry at Cuddesdon, was ordained in 1862 and went to St Alban's parish in Holborn, then a poor area of London, where he remained for the next 50 years. Though not always supported by the official Church of England – he was accused of Romish tendencies – he attracted a large following by his powerful preaching and the sincerity and devotion with which he served the people of his parish. His work went largely unrecognized by the official church, however, and it was only in the last month of his life that he was offered any advancement – a prebendary at St Paul's – which he courteously refused. His funeral was attended by vast crowds.

Stanyhurst, or Stanihurst, Richard   Priest, author and translator, born Dublin, *c.*1545, died probably at Brussels, 1618. His father James Stanyhurst was the author of devotional works and Recorder of Dublin and Speaker of the Irish House of Commons, and Richard was the uncle of Archbishop James **Ussher**. He was educated at University College, Oxford, which he entered in 1563, and Lincoln's Inn. On his return to Ireland he married, and it may be at this point that he became a Catholic, probably under the influence of Edmund **Campion**, whom he had known at Oxford, and with whom he had collaborated in Ireland. With the tightening up of the recusancy laws he went to The Netherlands. On the death of his wife in 1579 he went to The Netherlands and married again, but on the death of his second wife in 1602 he became a priest, and chaplain to the archduke. Stanyhurst is remembered as an eminent author of several theological treatises and translations, for example the first four books of Virgil's *Aeneid* into heroic verse (1582) – but his chief politico-ecclesiastical work was *De Rebus in Hibernia Gestis* with multiple extracts from the works of the twelfth-century **Giraldus Cambrensis** and with additional notes published at Antwerp in 1584. Geoffrey Keating, a near contemporary historian, was exceptionally critical of every word written by Stanyhurst as being full of errors and of malicious anti-Gaelic representations of the Irish church, people and society. Stanyhurst apparently promised a public recantation of his more extreme views. His translations from Virgil were generally condemned by the classicists. Both his sons became Jesuits, one dying young but the other, William, being a noted Latin writer also.

Stapledon, Walter de   Bishop, born 1261, died at the hands of the London mob, 1326. He came from a prosperous Devon family, became professor of canon law at Oxford and chaplain to **Clement V**. In 1308 he was made bishop of Exeter. From 1320 he was Lord Treasurer and reformed the royal exchequer and helped to rebuild Exeter Cathedral. He founded Stapledon Hall, which became Exeter College, Oxford. His association with the misgovernment of Edward II led to his murder.

Stapleton, Thomas   English Roman Catholic theologian and writer, born Henfield, West Sussex 1535, died Louvain, 12 October 1598. He was educated at Winchester and New College, Oxford, where he became a fellow. He became a prebendary of Chichester, but on **Elizabeth**'s accession fled to Louvain, where he studied theology. He returned to England, but because he was not willing to renounce the authority of the Pope, was deprived of his prebend and in 1563 went back to Louvain. From 1569 he was teaching at Douai, in the university faculty of theology and from 1585 in the Jesuit college as well. In 1590 **Philip II** made him professor of Scripture at Louvain, where he succeeded Michael **Bay.** He became dean of Hilverenbeck, and although he ascribed more limited rights to the Pope than many RC writers, **Clement XIII** made him protonotary apostolic in 1597. His writings include the *Principiorum Fidei Doctrinalium Demonstratio* (1578), *Tres Thomae* (1588), namely, the Apostle, St **Thomas Becket**, and St Thomas **More**), and *Auctoritatis Ecclesiasticae Defensio* (1592), directed against W. Whitaker.

Stein, Edith (Teresia Benedicta of the Cross) Saint, Carmelite nun, philosopher and contemplative, born into a devout Jewish family in Wroclaw (Breslau), Poland, 12 October 1891, died Auschwitz, Poland, 10 August 1942. She lost her faith in her youth and became interested in philosophy. She went to the University of Göttingen, where she studied under, and became assistant to, Husserl, the father of phenomenology. She also came into contact with Catholicism there, through Max Scheler, and became interested in the answers it provided. She was finally converted through reading the autobiography of **Teresa of Ávila**, and was baptized on 1 January 1922. She left the university and went to teach at a girls' school at Speyer in the Rhineland, run by Third Order Dominican sisters. Here she translated the treatise *On Truth* by **Thomas Aquinas**. In 1932 she was appointed lecturer at the Education Institute at Münster in Westphalia, but had to leave this post because of Nazi anti-Semitic legislation. She joined the Carmelite sisters at Cologne, and took the name Teresa Benedicta of the Cross. At Cologne she completed *Finite and Eternal Being*, in which she attempted to synthesize the philosophy of St Thomas with modern thought, especially with phenomenology. When, at the end of 1938, the Nazi persecution of the Jews became increasingly intense, she went into the Carmel at Echt, Holland, and it was here that she wrote *The Science of the Cross*, a presentation of the life and teaching of St John of the Cross. When the Dutch bishops condemned Hitler's anti-Semitic excesses she was one of a number of priests and other religious of Jewish origin who were arrested as a reprisal. She was taken to the concentration camp at Auschwitz, where she died in the gas chamber. She was beatified in 1987.

Steiner, Rudolf Founder of Anthroposophy, born into a Roman Catholic family in Kraljevic, then in Austria, 27 February 1861, died Basel, 30 March 1925. Studied natural sciences at the University of Vienna and spent seven years, from 1890, editing Goethe's scientific and general works. His work led him increasingly to attempt to provide an adequate explanation of the world of Spirit and into a Christocentric mysticism. He became leader of a branch of the Theosophists in 1902, and among his writings of the next decade was his *Spiritual Hierarchies*, in which he developed his views on the centrality of Christ and which marked his move away from the Theosophists and their preoccupations with Eastern mysticism and the occult. Steiner's approach was more world-affirming, and he saw his task as trying to reveal the spiritual elements in the material world. In 1912, taking 55 of the 65 lodges of the German Theosophical Society with him, he formed the Anthroposophical Society. Many Anthroposophical organizations, including the Steiner/Waldorf schools, continue to flourish as does the associated but more overtly liturgical Christian Community.

Stephen Saint, first king of Hungary, born Gran, 975, died 15 August 1038. He became a Christian, with his father, Geza, and was baptized by **Adalbert of Prague** in 985. As king from 997 he set out to Christianize his country. He was a supporter of the Papacy and asked the Pope if he could establish epicopal sees throughout Hungary. This was granted and he received a royal crown from the Pope with which he was crowned in 1001. He founded a monastery in Jerusalem and pilgrims' refuges in Rome, Ravenna and Constantinople. He was distraught when his son **Emeric** was killed and there would be no devout Christian to succeed him. He was canonized in 1083, together with Emeric. Feast day 16 August (in Hungary 20 August, the day of the translation of his relics to Buda).

Stephen I Saint, pope, born Rome, died 2 August 257. He became Pope on 12 May 254 and was immediately called upon by the bishop of Lyons, Faustinus, to take action against **Marcion**, the bishop of Arles who had become a follower of the schismatic Novatus. He took no action, and help was sought from **Cyprian** of Carthage, who in turn appealed to the Pope, and it seems he complied. Stephen was also called on to intervene in another dispute arising from the Decian persecution, this time in Spain, where he declared two of those apparently guilty of apostasy to be restored to the Church. In a later dispute with Cyprian he maintained, against Cyprian, that those baptized in schismatic sects need not be rebaptized when they join the 'true Church'. The *Liber Pontificalis* cites Stephen as suggesting that clergy should wear special clothes when engaged in liturgical celebrations. Feast day 2 August.

Stephen II Pope, elected 22 or 23 March 752, died 25 or 26 March 752. He had a stroke almost immediately after his election, and died shortly after that. As consecration, rather than election, was considered the beginning of a pontificate in the early Middle Ages, he was not regarded as a Pope properly constituted. Hence the dual system of numbering of subsequent Stephens.

Stephen II (III) Pope, he was an orphan and had been brought up in the Lateran, died 26 April 757. He became Pope on 26 March 752, following the death of the original **Stephen II** only four days after his election and before his consecration. Because of the Lombard threat, under his pontificate ever closer alliances were forged between the Papacy and the Carolingian dynasty: a fact that would influence the relations between the Church and the kingdoms of western Europe for several centuries. Ravenna had already fallen to the Lombards, and when the Lombard king Aistulf besieged Rome, Stephen, having exhausted all other methods, crossed the Alps to ask the assistance of the Frankish king, Pepin. This was agreed in early 754, and later that year Stephen crowned Pepin, forbade the French from choosing a king from any other family, and gave him the title 'Patrician of the Romans'. In 755 the Lombards were defeated and Stephen returned to Rome. But on new year's day 756 Aistulf attacked Rome, Pepin and his armies

returned and Rome was finally delivered from the Lombard threat. Stephen supported Aistulf's successor, Desiderius, in return for the restoration of certain cities, but these promises were not kept. Stephen corresponded with the Emperor Constantine over the restoration of sacred images; he restored many of the ancient churches and built a hospital for the poor near St Peter's.

Stephen III (IV) Pope, Benedictine monk, born about 720, died 1 or 3 August 772. He was elected Pope on 7 August 768, after the expulsion of the usurper Constantine. He held a synod at the Lateran in 769 to ensure that laymen would no longer be eligible to elect or to be elected Pope. This was to be reserved to cardinals. The same synod confirmed the veneration of images, and anathematized the iconoclastic synod of 754. Through Stephen's support Leo was able to hold the see of Ravenna against a lay contender, and with the help of the Frankish kings some of the land taken by the Lombards was recovered. In the following years the Pope was unable to prevent a marriage between **Charlemagne** and the daughter of Desiderius, the Lombard king. Stephen then unwisely allied himself with the Lombards, because before his death the Franks and Lombards were once again enemies.

Stephen IV (V) Pope, consecrated 22 June 816, died 24 January 817. On his election he made the people of Rome swear fealty to **Charlemagne**'s successor **Louis** the Pious, and went to Rheims in October to meet him. In the cathedral at Rheims he anointed (the first time this had been done) and crowned Louis, thus reinforcing papal claims to intervene in the succession to the imperial title. Pope and Emperor had long discussions, apparently strengthening the bonds between the Papacy and the Franks. Stephen died a few months after returning to Rome.

Stephen V (VI) Pope, born into a noble family in Rome, consecrated September 885, died 14 September 891. He served in the Lateran and became a cardinal priest before his election by acclamation. He upset the Emperor **Charles** the Fat by not awaiting his approval, but invited him to come to Rome, where Stephen was threatened both by internal squabbles and by threats from Saracen invaders. When Charles was overthrown, Stephen treated with contenders for the legacy of **Charlemagne**, but eventually threw in his lot with Guido, Count of Spoleto, whom he crowned emperor in 891. He also felt it necessary to maintain good relations with Constantinople, hoping for military assistance from the Byzantine emperor. In Moravia, where **Methodius** had died just at the time of his election, Stephen forbade the Slavonic liturgy, and the Moravian church was reorganized along German lines, driving Methodius' immediate disciples to Bulgaria, where they continued to develop the Slavonic liturgy. It was from here that Christianity penetrated Russia: Stephen's decision over Moravia, therefore, fundamentally affected the future development of Christianity in the East.

Stephen VI (VII)   Pope, born Rome, the son of a priest, consecrated May 896, deposed and died August 897. He had been created bishop of Anagni by Pope **Formosus**. As already a bishop, he was not supposed to accept the see of Rome. One way round this was to nullify Formosus' acts, which was done at the 'Synod of the Cadaver', when Formosus' dead body was put on trial, dressed in papal vestments and seated on a throne and, when found guilty, stripped and his body thrown into the Tiber. This macabre event so alienated the Roman people that Stephen was also soon after attacked, stripped of his insignia of office, and thrown into gaol, where he was strangled.

Stephen VII (VIII)   Pope, born Rome, priest of the church of St Anastasia, consecrated December 928, died February 931. Nothing of significance is recorded of his pontificate.

Stephen VIII (IX)   Pope, born Rome, consecrated 14 July 939, died October 942. He had very little independence of movement, being dominated entirely by Alberic II, the effective ruler of Rome, who had put him on the papal throne. They shared, however, a desire for monastic renewal, and an interest in the Cluniacs as the means thereto. It seems likely that Stephen conspired against Alberic: he was put in prison, mutilated and died there of his injuries.

Stephen IX (X)   Pope, born Frederick, son of the duke of Lorraine, elected 2 August 1057, died

Florence, 29 March 1058. Educated at Liège, he became a canon, then archdeacon there before coming to Rome in the entourage of **Leo IX.** He was one of the members of the fateful embassy to Constantinople in 1054, which resulted in the mutual excommunication of Pope and Patriarch. He entered the monastery of Monte Cassino in 1055, becoming abbot there in 1057, and being appointed a cardinal. He was consulted about the choice of a successor to **Victor II** – and was eventually chosen himself, though he remained abbot. As Pope he was deeply concerned about improving the standards of clerical observance, bringing into the papal entourage others, such as **Peter Damian**, whom he made a cardinal despite Peter's protests, who shared his views. In politics, he was determined to contain the Normans in Southern Italy, and thought of employing his brother Godfrey, duke of Lorraine, for this purpose, creating him emperor. It was when he went to Florence to discuss these plans with Godfrey that he died.

Stephen de Lexinton   Cistercian reformer, abbot and founder of the Cistercian college in Paris, born Lexinton, Nottinghamshire, between 1190 and 1196, died Ourscamp Abbey, Oise, France, 21 March 1260. After studying at Paris and Oxford, he was appointed to a canonry at Southwell, Nottinghamshire, by King John in 1215, and in 1221 became a Cistercian monk at Quarr on the Isle of Wight. Made abbot of Stanley (Wiltshire) in 1223, he was sent to reform the Irish Cistercian houses in 1227, and in 1229 was appointed abbot of Savigny. In 1243 he was elected abbot of Clairvaux, and he founded the Cistercian house of studies at Paris, the College St Bernard, in 1245, for which he was deposed the next year by the abbot of Cîteaux. Pope **Alexander IV** ordered that he be reinstated, but he instead retired to Clairvaux's daughter-house of Ourscamp, where he died.

Stephen Harding   Saint, abbot, born Sherborne, Dorset, England, about 1050, died 28 March 1134. He was educated at the monastery of Sherborne and later studied in Paris and Rome. On his way back from Rome he passed through Burgundy, stopped at the Abbey of Molesme and in 1098, under the guidance of the abbot, **Robert**, decided to join the community. He went with Robert and others to Cîteaux, to establish a reformed foundation there, and became prior under the second abbot, **Alberic**, and then abbot in 1100. The abbey had become impoverished and few people had come to join them, until in 1112 **Bernard** along with thirty of his confreres joined the community, and from there it began to flourish. Stephen was an excellent organizer and thirteen new foundations had been established from Cîteaux before his death, with an administrative and pastoral system to match, the 'Charter of Charity'. This was approved by **Callistus II** in 1119. Feast day 17 April in the Roman Calendar; the Cistercians keep it on 15 July.

Stephen of Obazine Blessed, monastic reformer, founder and first abbot of Obazine, born Vierjo, near Limoges, c.1085, died Bonaigue, 8 March 1159. A secular priest, he became a hermit under the influence of one of **Robert of Arbrissel**'s disciples. His eremitical community became an abbey in 1142 and, with its daughter-houses, merged with the Order of Cîteaux in 1147. Although never officially canonized, his cult was approved by Pope **Clement XI** in 1701. Feast day 11 March.

Stevenson, Robert Louis Novelist, essayist and poet, born Edinburgh, 13 November 1850, died Valima, Samoa, 3 December 1894. He was educated at Edinburgh Academy, Edinburgh University, and studied law. He is one of the few writers whose novels, especially *Treasure Island* and *Dr Jekyll and Mr Hyde*, have remained continually popular. Though he is best known as a novelist, he also wrote prayers. He originated the phrase 'To travel hopefully is better than to arrive.' He struggled with ill-health all his life. His prayers are little known. One morning prayer opens 'The day returns and brings us the petty round of irritating concerns and duties. Help us to play the man.'

Stigand Archbishop of Canterbury, born East Anglia, died Winchester about 1072. A king's priest under **Canute**, he was made bishop of Elmham, East Anglia, in 1043, of Winchester in 1047, and in 1052, whilst retaining the see of Winchester, was appointed archbishop of Canterbury, thus combining the two richest bishoprics in England. He eventually secured papal recognition in 1058, but it was from **Benedict X**, a schismatic Pope deposed the following year. Stigand was a patron of the arts but, in his eagerness to gain land and monasteries, displayed the weaknesses of the English church before 1066. He was not a good leader and this, combined with the questions over his status at Canterbury, provided a pretext for **William I**'s invasion in 1066. He was honoured by William until the throne was secure, but in 1070 was deposed, and he died in custody at Winchester.

Stillingfleet, Edward Bishop of Worcester, theologian, born Cranborne, Dorset, 17 April 1635, died Westminster, 27 March 1699. He was educated at Cranborne School and at St John's College, Cambridge, where in 1653 he became a fellow. He was vicar of Sutton in Bedfordshire, chaplain to Charles II, dean of St Paul's and later bishop of Worcester. His writings include *Irenicum* (1659), *Origines Sacrae* (1662), *Rational Account of the Grounds of the Protestant Religion* (1664). He also published three pamphlets in 1696-7 on the Trinity in response to Locke's *Essay Concerning Human Understanding*.

Stolberg, Friedrich Leopold, Graf zu Roman Catholic convert, diplomat, poet and historian, born into an eclectic Christian family in Brammstedt, Holstein (then part of Denmark), 7 November 1750, died Sondermuhlen, near Osnabruck, 5 December 1819. Studied law at the University of Halle, and in Göttingen joined the German poets' circle. He held various posts, including that of envoy of the Protestant prince-bishop of Lübeck to the Danish court in 1777, was a magistrate in Neuenberg in 1785 and Danish envoy to Berlin in 1789. In 1791 he was made president of the board of ecclesiastical administration of the prince-bishop of Lübeck, and in 1797 was ambassador to Russia. In 1800 he was received into the RC Church and resigned all his positions and many of his friends deserted or attacked him. Remaining friends included Goethe and Lavater. He continued to enjoy Protestant hymns and prayers, and the work of Protestant poets. His writings include translations of the Greek classics, but after his conversion he devoted himself to writing the fifteen-volume *Geschichte der Religion Jesu Christi* (1806–18) a not always scholarly, though very influential, history of Christianity from OT times to the death of St **Augustine**. He also wrote a life of *Alfred the Great* (1817), one of **Vincent de Paul** and devotional works such as *Bucblein von der Liebe* (1819).

Stone, Darwell Anglo-Catholic theologian, born 1859, died 1941. Studied at Merton College, Oxford, was ordained priest and in 1885 became vice-principal, and in 1888 principal of Dorchester (Oxon) Missionary College. In 1909 he became principal of Pusey House, Oxford, a post he held until 1934. He strenuously upheld High Church principles, and defended the more traditional theology against that of the Lux Mundi School. Later he became increasingly the leader of the Anglo-Catholic Movement in the Church of England. His writings include *Holy Baptism* (1899), *Outlines of Christian Dogma* (1900), *The Christian Church* (1905).

Storch, Nicholas Died after 1536, Anabaptist, leader of the Zwickau Prophets during Thomas **Münzer's** time in the city, from 1520 to 1551. This group was forced to leave Zwickau in 1521 and went to Wittenberg, where their knowledge of the Bible impressed teachers like P. **Melanchthon** and N. von **Amsdorf**. His teaching was spiritualist and millenarianist. Storch stayed in West Thuringia in 1523, and after the defeat of the rebels in the Peasants' War in central Germany he emerged as the leader of an Anabaptist sect in northern Franconia. It is possible that he returned to Zwickau.

Stowe, Harriet Elizabeth Beecher American author of *Uncle Tom's Cabin*, among other works, born 14 June 1811, Litchfield, Connecticut, died Hartford, Connecticut, 1 July 1896. Her father was a Congregationalist minister, and her husband, Calvin Stowe, whom she married in 1836, was also a minister and a biblical scholar. Before her marriage she taught in her sister's school, first in Hartford and afterwards in Cincinnati. After her marriage she turned to writing, living in Cincinnati until 1850 when her husband took up a professorial post in Brunswick, Maine. It was there that she wrote *Uncle Tom's Cabin; or, Life Among the Lowly*, which first appeared in serial form in an anti-slavery paper. She continued her campaign against slavery in *The Key to Uncle Tom's Cabin*, which appeared in 1853. She spent the remainder of her life writing, including a volume of religious verse and many articles for magazines.

Stratford, John Archbishop of Canterbury, born Stratford-upon-Avon, date of birth unknown, died Mayfield, Sussex, 23 August 1348. By 1322 he had become archdeacon of Lincoln and dean of the Court of Arches. Appointed bishop of Winchester in 1323. Influential in the abdication of Edward II, and chancellor under Edward III. In 1333 became archbishop of Canterbury and a firm opponent of the monarch on certain political issues.

Stratford, Robert *see* **Robert Stratford**.

Strauss, David Friedrich German theologian, born Ludwigsberg, 29 January 1808, died there, 8 February 1874. He was a pupil of Baur at the seminary at Blaubeuren, and in 1825 went to the Tübingen Stift, where he came under the influence of **Schleiermacher** and Hegel. He did further studies in Berlin, and in 1832 became 'Repetent' at the Stift and lecturer on Hegelian philosophy at Tübingen. He wrote *Leben Jesu* (1835), in which he applied the 'myth theory' to the life of Christ, which denied the historical foundation of all supernatural elements in the Gospels. These were assigned to an unintentionally creative legend (the 'myth'), which developed between the death of Christ and the writing of the Gospels. The work led to Strauss's dismissal from his post at Tübingen. His two-volume *Die christliche Glaubenslehre* (1840–1) is a polemical history of Christian doctrine down to its alleged dissolution in Hegelian philosophy. His other works include *Leben Jesu fur das deutsche Volk* (1864), a more positive version of his first work, *Der Christus des Glaubens und der Jesus der Geschichte* (1865), an attack on Schleiermacher's attempt to combine the 'historical Jesus' with the 'Christ' of dogma, and *Der alte und der neue Glaube* (1872), which rejects human immortality and negates Christianity in favour of scientific materialism.

Stravinsky, Igor Feodorovich Russian Orthodox composer, born Oranienbaum, now Lomonosov, near St Petersburg, Russia, 17 June 1882, died New York, 6 April 1971. He studied under Rimsky Korsakov. He was a strikingly original genius, usually receiving both critical acclaim and commercial success; his work went through unpredictable phases, entering into different styles. Among his masterly religious work are his *Symphony of Psalms*, and *Mass*. He settled in the USA and in his old age wrote several religious works: *Canticum Sacrum; Threni; A Sermon, a Narrative and a Prayer; Abraham and Isaac;* and *Requiem Canticles*.

Streeter, Burnett Hillman   Theologian and NT scholar, born Croydon, 17 November 1874, died in a plane crash near Basel, 10 September 1937. Studied at Queen's College, Oxford, was a fellow from 1905 to 1933 and provost from 1933 to 1937. From 1915 to 1934 he was also a canon of Hereford Cathedral. He contributed to *Oxford Studies in the Synoptic Problem* (ed. W. Sanday, 1911), which helped to establish belief in the priority of St Mark and the existence of 'Q'. His other writings include *The Four Gospels* (1924), *Reality* (1926), an attempt at a correlation between science and theology, *The Primitive Church* (1929) and essays in a series of books beginning with *Foundations* (1912) and ending with *Adventure* (1926), all of which he edited. In 1932 he delivered the Bampton Lectures on *The Buddha and the Christ*. He was an active supporter of the Student Christian Movement, the Modern Churchmen's Union and, later, of the Oxford Group movement.

Strigel, Victorinus   Reformation theologian, born Kaufbeuren, Swabia, 26 December 1526, died Heidelburg, 26 June 1569. Studied in Freiburg im Breisgau and from 1542 at Wittenberg under **Melanchthon.** Taught at Erfurt, and in 1548 became first professor and rector of the new school at Jena. In opposition to strict Lutheranism he taught more moderate and conciliatory doctrines and defended a form of synergism. He was involved in a dispute at Weimar in 1560 on the relation of the human will to divine grace in the work of conversion. In 1563 he was appointed professor as Leipzig but had to resign, because of opposition to the Calvinistic tendencies of his Eucharistic doctrine, and became a professor at Heidelberg. He wrote a commentary on most of the Bible, and as well as theology wrote on philology and history.

Stringfellow, William   US Episcopal church theologian and social activist, born 26 April 1928, died 2 March 1985. He was a committed Christian but decided against ordination and became active in the international Student Christian Movement. He served in the army, trained as a lawyer at Harvard and went to practise among the poor in Harlem. He came into conflict with the Episcopal Church for supporting the case for the ordination of women. He was opposed to the Vietnam war and became a friend of Daniel Berrigan, who was later arrested by the FBI at Stringfellow's home, and who spoke for many when he described Stringfellow at his funeral as an 'honoured keeper and guardian of the Word of God'.

Strossmayer, Joseph Georg   Croatian Roman Catholic bishop, born 1815 in Osijek into a family of Austrian descent, died 1905. Was ordained priest in 1838 and in 1847 became chaplain at the imperial court in Vienna. In 1850 he was made bishop of Djakovo in Croatia, promoted the cause of pan-Slavism, worked for reunion with the Orthodox Church of Serbia and Russia (negotiating with V. **Solovie V**), and contributed financially to develop education for all, regardless of denominational allegiance. He was at the First Vatican Council in 1869–70, where he was a leading opponent of the pronouncement on papal infallibility, and created a stir by his defence of Protestantism.

Stubbs, John (Stubbe)   Puritan writer, born Norfolk about 1543, died France, 1590. Studied at Trinity College, Cambridge, where he joined the Puritans, and at Lincoln's Inn. In 1579 he published an attack on **Elizabeth I**'s proposed marriage to the Catholic Francis, duke of Anjou, *The Discovery of a Gaping Gulf whereinto England is like to be swallowed by another French marriage*. Stubbs was arrested in 1579 and along with his publisher had his right hand cut off and was imprisoned in the Tower. He was released eighteen months later and was commissioned by Lord Burghley to write a reply (1587, now apparently lost) to W. Allen's *Defence of the English Catholics* (1584). He produced an English version of some of T. **Beza**'s *Meditations on the Psalms* (1582). In 1589 he became MP for Great Yarmouth, but died shortly afterwards.

Stubbs, William   Anglican bishop, church historian, born Knaresborough, Yorkshire 21 June 1825, died Cuddesdon, 22 April 1901. He was educated at Ripon Grammar School, was nominated a servitor at Christ Church, Oxford, and in 1848 became a fellow of Trinity College. He was rector of Navestock from 1850 to 1866 and Regius Professor of modern history at Oxford from 1866 to 1884. From 1879 he was also a canon of St Paul's and was made bishop of Chester in 1884, and of Oxford in 1889. He contributed nineteen volumes to the Rolls Series of *Chronicles and Memorials*, and his other works include *Registrum Sacrum Anglicanum* (1858), lists of the English bishops, and, with A. W Haddon, the three-volume *Councils and Ecclesiastical Documents relating to Great Britain and Ireland* (1869–73).

Studd, Charles Thomas Missionary, born Spratton, Northants, 2 December 1860, died Imbi, Belgian Congo, 16 July 1931. Studied at Eton and Trinity College, Cambridge. He volunteered for missionary work in China and laid the foundations for the Student Volunteer Movement. He went to China with the China Inland Mission in 1885 and lived like one of the Chinese, a practice early advocated by CIM, but had to return to England in 1894 because of ill-health. He went to India in 1900 and became pastor of a non-denominational church at Ootacamund, but was again taken ill and had to retire back to England. Despite his poor health he again set sail, in 1910, this time for Central Africa and stayed there for the remainder of his life. In 1912, he founded the Heart of Africa Mission and later the World Evangelization Crusade, whose activities spread to South America and beyond.

Studdert Kennedy, Geoffrey Anketell Anglican priest, born into an Irish family in Leeds, 27 June 1883 and died in Liverpool, 8 March 1929. Educated at Leeds Grammar School, at Trinity College, Dublin, and at Ripon Clergy College. He was vicar of St Paul's, Worcester, from 1914 to 1921, and chaplain to the forces from 1916 to 1919. From the men in the trenches he won the affectionate title of 'Woodbine Willie', from a brand of cigarettes he distributed. He was unconventional in his theological views, believing in God's passibility and desiring a more enlightened Christian moral code. In 1922 he was appointed rector of St Edmund, King and Martyr, Lombard Street, London. He continued to travel and preach missions and worked in association with the Industrial Christian Fellowship. His books, popular in form, include *Rough Rhymes* (1918), *The Hardest Pan* (1918), *The Wicket Gate* (1923), and *The Word and the Work* (1925).

Stumpf, Johannes Swiss Protestant theologian and historian. Born Bruchsal, 23 April 1500, died Zurich, *c.*1578. He studied at Heidelberg and Strasburg and entered the Order of St John in 1521. The following year he became prior of his Order and people's priest in Bubikon. The date of his conversion to Lutheranism is not known; but he continued as Protestant pastor at Bubikon until 1543, when he took a church in Stammheim. Though usually conciliatory, he resolutely defended **Zwingli**'s view of the Eucharist. He wrote numerous historical, geographical and theological works, and his Swiss chronicle 1548 remained authoritative into the eighteenth century. Another of his treatises, *Reformationschronik*, contains the first biography of Zwingli.

Sturm, Johannes German humanist and educator, founder of the German Gymnasium, born Schleiden 1 October 1507, died Strasburg 3 March 1589. Educated at Schleiden in the palace school of the Earl of Manderschied, and from 1522 to 1524 he studied under the Brethren of the Common Life at Liège, Belgium. He left to go to the University of Louvain, and thence to the College de France, Paris, where he studied medicine for two years and remained until 1529 as a lecturer. In 1537 the magistrates of Strasburg invited him to organize a classical Latin school in the city and the following year his plans were approved and Strasburg Gymnasium opened on 22 March, with Sturm as headmaster, a chair he held for 43 years. In 1567, it became the College of Strasburg and Sturm was appointed rector in perpetuo. Sturm's Gymnasium was primarily for the sons of nobles and gentlemen and had a threefold aim: piety, knowledge and eloquence. He permitted his students to speak only Latin and confined the use of the vernacular to catechism instruction in the first year. During the Reformation, Sturm adopted the Lutheran cause but was unsympathetic to the policies of the dominant faction of the Lutheran Church in Strasburg, and in 1583 he was dismissed from his post. Sturm was a prolific writer, his works included *De Litterarum Ludis Recte Aperiendis* (The Correct Way of Opening Schools of Literature), and a series of letters containing instructions to his teachers and often referred to as 'Epistolae Cicero-Sturmantanae' because of frequent excerpts from Cicero (1565). He also wrote a life of B. Rhenanus. Sturm's humanistic theories of education influenced the curriculum of European and English schools for over 300 years.

Sturzo, Luigi Catholic priest, political leader, social theorist, born Caltagirone, Sicily, 1871, died 1959. He was ordained in 1894 and later taught in his native town and served as mayor. In 1919 he was a founding member of the Catholic Partito Popolare, which in 1923 the Vatican, under pressure from Mussolini, effectively suppressed. Sturzo went into exile in England in 1924, studying, writing and serving as a convent chaplain, though he was also active in pan-European Catholic movements opposed to Franco and the growing threat of Fascism in general. He started a journal, *People and Freedom*. In 1940 Sturzo went to the United States, where he remained until after the war. He was made a senator for life by the president of Italy in 1952. His writings include *International Community and the Right of War* (1930); *Church and State* (1939); *True Life* (1943); and *Inner Laws of Society* (1944). Always a devout man despite the treatment of him by his Church, he has been proposed as a candidate for canonization.

Suárez, Francisco Jesuit philosopher and theologian, born Granada, 5 January 1548, died Lisbon, 25 September 1617. He entered the Society of Jesus in Salamanca in 1564, studied at Salamanca University and was ordained in 1572. He taught at various Jesuit colleges in Spain, in Rome in 1580–5, and finally at Coimbra in 1597–1615. A personally devout and modest man, he was widely recognized as the leading theologian of his day. He was a prolific writer. His scholarly influence was enormous both during his lifetime and after his death: the Society of Jesus for the most part followed Suárez' particular brand of Thomistic philosophy and theology – which was distinct in several aspects from that of **Thomas Aquinas** himself – down to the twentieth century. He also wrote on issues of the day, including the ethics of the conquest of the Americas, and was a significant thinker in the philosophy of law. His *De defensione fidei* was written in response to Pope **Paul V**'s request to refute the errors of King **James I** of England.

Suenens, Leon-Jozef Belgian cardinal and ecumenist, born Brussels, 16 July 1904, died there, 6 May 1996. He studied at the Gregorian University in Rome from 1921, was ordained a priest of the (Mechelen) Malines archdiocese in 1927 and continued his studies for a further two years. In 1930 he became professor of philosophy at the Mechelen seminary and in 1940 was made vice-rector of the Catholic University of Louvain. He became auxiliary bishop to Cardinal Van Roey in 1945, and in 1961 succeeded him as archbishop of Malines-Brussels and primate of Belgium. He was made cardinal the following year. He was a major influence in the preparations for, proceedings of, and the follow-up to the Second Vatican Council, notably in the creation of the permanent diaconate, the setting of an age limit of 75 for bishops and promoting the increased role of the laity in ministry. Following the council he became a leading figure of the ecumenical movement, suggested the establishment of an International Theological Commission and was active in promoting collegiality among the bishops and collaborative ministry between laity and clergy. At the third Synod of Bishops in 1971 he proposed that in certain regions and circumstances married men should be considered for ordination. He gave his support to lay movements such as the Legion of Mary, Marriage Encounter and was especially active in guiding Charismatic renewal through some of its more turbulent times. His writings include *Theology of the Legion of Mary* (1954) and other books on Mary and the Gospels in everyday life, *Co-responsibility in the Church* (1968), *The Future of the Christian Church* (1970), *A New Pentecost* (1975), *Ecumenism and Charismatic Renewal* (1978), *Conflict and Repentance: Charismatic Renewal and Social Action* (with Dom Helder **Camara**, 1979) and *Renewal and the Powers of Darkness* (1982), the first part of his memoirs, *Memories* (1991), *God's Unexpected Ways* (1993) and, on a friend of 33 years, *King Baudouin: The Testimony of a Life* (1995). Just before his death he published a short book entitled *Life after Life* (1996).

Suger Abbot of St-Denis near Paris. Of humble origin, he was probably born near St Denis, *c.*1081, and died there, 13 January 1151. About 1091 he entered the abbey of St-Denis, where he was a fellow-student of King **Louis VI**. From 1106 onwards, he was active in the affairs of his own and other abbeys, and was used by the French king as an ambassador to the papal curia. He was elected abbot of St-Denis in 1122. He was an influential adviser of the French Crown, and a reformer in both Church and State. He built a new church for his abbey, one of particular importance for the history of the development of Gothic architecture, and he left a detailed account of its consecration. His *Vita Ludovici Grossi* is a primary source for his age.

Suicer, Johann Kaspar Author of the *Thesaurus Ecclesiasticus*, born Fraenfeld, Switzerland, 26 June, 1620, died Zurich, 8 November 1684. He was educated at the French academies of Montauban and Saumur (1640–3), taught Latin, Greek and Hebrew at Zurich from 1644 and was professor of Greek at the Collegium Carolinum from 1660 to 1683. His still indispensable *Thesaurus Ecclesiasticus e Patribus Graecis Ordine Alphabetico* appeared in 1682. He wrote other works on Greek linguistics, and had a part in drawing up the common statement of faith, the *Consensus Helveticus*, of the Swiss Protestant churches in 1675.

Sullivan, (Sir) Arthur Composer, organist and conductor, born Lambeth, London, 13 May 1842, died London, 22 November 1900. He was a chorister at the Chapel Royal, and studied at the Royal Academy of Music and under Sterndale Bennett at Leipzig. Though chiefly known for his comic operas composed in collaboration with W. S. Gilbert, Sullivan composed hymns, church music, sacred songs and other religious pieces. He wrote oratorios including *The Light of the World* and *The Golden Legend*. His song *The Lost Chord*, and hymn *Onward Christian Soldiers* remain popular.

Sulpicius Severus Historian and hagiographer, born *c.*360 of wealthy parents in Aquitaine, died 420–30. Sulpicius studied law, had a highly successful practice and a wife, but his wife's death occasioned a conversion to asceticism *c.*394. He established his own community on his estate of Primuliacum and was ordained, though it is not clear when or by whom. The style of his *Life of Martin of Tours* (396) was highly influential for later hagiography, portraying him as a man of God, whose holiness was attested by miracles: Martin was still alive at this point. He wrote further on Martin, particularly on his powers of healing, and composed a Chronicle from the creation to AD 400, citing both Christian and pagan sources.

Sumner, Mary Elizabeth Founder of the Mothers' Union, born Mary Heywood, 31 December 1828, Swinton, Manchester, died Winchester, 11 August 1921. She was educated by her parents, who had moved, a few years after her birth, to Hope End, Hereford. She married George Sumner, whom she had met while on holiday in Rome in July 1848, and they went to live in Crawley, where her husband served as chaplain to his uncle, the archbishop of Canterbury. In 1851 they moved to Old Alresford, Hampshire, where George Sumner was rector. In 1876 she started to hold meetings for mothers, but it was not until 1885 that she made a speech at a conference in Portsmouth which gave rise to the Mothers' Union, both in England and worldwide. Under her leadership it enjoyed rapid and remarkable growth. She continued to promote it until shortly before her death.

Sundkler, Bengt (Gustav Malcolm) Lutheran missionary, historian and missiologist, born Degefors, Sweden, 7 May 1909, died Uppsala, Sweden, 1995. He studied at the University of Uppsala, was ordained in 1936 and completed his doctorate in 1937. He was a missionary in South Africa in 1937–42 and in Tanganyika in 1942–45. After returning to Sweden he became research secretary of the International Missionary Council in London, 1948–9, then professor of church history and the history of mission in 1949–74 at Uppsala. He was Lutheran bishop in Bukoba, Tanzania, 1961–4 and a member of the Theological Education Fund Committee in 1958–63 and of the Central Committee of the WCC in 1961–5. His publications include *Bantu Prophets in South Africa* (1948, 1961), *The Church of South India: The Movement Towards Union, 1900–1947* (1954), *The Christian Ministry in Africa* (1960), and (with Christopher Steed), *History of Christianity in Africa* (2000).

Sung, John Shang-chieh   Chinese evangelist, born Hong Chek, Hinghwa, Fujian, China, 27 September 1901, died near Beijing, China, 18 August 1944. He was converted in 1909 in Hinghwa, where his father pastored a Methodist church. He left for study in the United States in 1920 and graduated from Ohio Wesleyan University (B.Sc., 1923) and Ohio State University (M.Sc., 1924; Ph.D., 1926). He experienced a spiritual crisis while at Union Seminary, New York, spent six months in a mental hospital, and returned to Hinghwa in 1927. In 1928 he married Yu Chin Hua, taught at Hinghwa Memorial School and became involved with the revival ministry of the Bethel Band. He was appointed Hinghwa Methodist Conference evangelist in 1930 and began conducting missions in many parts of China. The impact of his ministry in Southeast Asia in 1935–9 remains widely felt, and some of the evangelistic groups he started were in operation 50 years later.

Surin, Jean Joseph   French Jesuit, mystic and spiritual writer, born Bordeaux, 9 February 1600, died there, 22 April 1665. He was educated by the Jesuits in Bordeaux, and joined them in 1616, completing his formation in 1630. Four years later he was sent, at the request of Cardinal **Richelieu**, to Loudun to exorcise some Ursuline nuns who were allegedly possessed by the devil. Whether it was associated with his experiences there or not he endured some twenty years of psychological and emotional disturbance, during which time he appears to have had some genuine mystical experiences. He eventually regained some stability and seems to have emerged as a good spiritual director and writer. His main writings are *Catéchisme spirituel* (1657), *Les Fondements de la vie spirituelle* (1667) and *Dialogues spirituelles*, published after his death. An 'adaptation' of his *Fondements*, for Church of England readers, was made in 1844.

Suso, Henry   *see* **Henry Suso**

Sutton, Christopher   English devotional writer, born Hampshire *c.*1565, died London, May or June 1629. He was educated at Oxford, was made a canon of Westminster in 1605 and of Lincoln in 1618. His *Godly Meditations upon the Most Holy Sacrament of the Lord's Supper* (1601) was perhaps the most popular and well known of his writings.

In it he defends a doctrine of Christ's presence in the Eucharist which is midway between transubstantiation and **Zwingli**'s teaching on a merely symbolic change, arguing that while consecration causes no change in the substance of the bread and wine it radically alters their use. When J. H. **Newman** reissued the book in 1838, with a new preface, it became popular for a while with the Tractarians.

Swainson, Charles Anthony   English theologian, born Liverpool 29 May 1820, died Cambridge, 15 September 1887. Cambridge educated, he became a fellow of Christ's College in 1841. After his ordination in 1844 he became principal of Chichester Theological College, moving on to become Norris professor of divinity at Cambridge in 1864, was elected master of Christ's College in 1881 and became vice-chancellor of the university in 1885. His main publications include *The Creeds of the Church* (1858) and *The Nicene and Apostles' Creeds* (1875).

Swedenborg, Emmanuel   Swedish scientist and mystical thinker, born Stockholm, 29 January 1688, died London, 29 March 1772. He studied at Uppsala and travelled widely, including to England, where he was much influenced by Henry More, John **Locke** and Isaac **Newton**. He had a great influence on William **Blake**, but was much criticized by Immanuel **Kant** in the latter's *Träume eines Geistersehers* (1766). A great mathematician with an inventive mind, he was appointed in 1716 by Charles XII to the Swedish Board of Mines, a position he held for thirty years. He believed strongly that the universe has a fundamentally spiritual structure and his *Prodromus Philosophiae Racionatis de Infinito et Causa Finali* (1734) argues the case, using purely physical scientific analysis. In the mid-1740s he had a series of deeply religious experiences, which led him to set up the New Church, a sort of spiritual fraternity consisting of those of any denomination who accepted his 'doctrine of correspondence', between the physical and spiritual world. He viewed Christ as the greatest manifestation of humanity, but rejected the doctrine of the Atonement. There was no separate 'ecclesial' body until 1787, when five ex-Wesleyan preachers established it as the New Jerusalem Church in London. The first congregation in the

USA was set up in Baltimore in 1792. Numerous offshoots have emerged, but there are currently some 65,000 mainstream Swedenborgians worldwide. Of his many publications, *Arcana Coeleste* (1756), in eight volumes, is the most comprehensive and his *Divine Love and Wisdom* (1763) perhaps best epitomizes his doctrines.

Swete, Henry Barclay Biblical and patristic scholar, born Bristol, 14 March 1835, died Cambridge, 10 May 1917. Professor at King's College, London, from 1882 to 1890, and Regius professor at Cambridge from 1890 to 1915. He was involved in several co-operative publishing projects to encourage the study of theology, including the *Journal of Theological Studies*, the series of Cambridge Patristic Texts and the Cambridge Handbooks of Liturgical Study. His own writings include a two-volume history of the doctrine of the Holy Spirit (1909 and 1912), Scripture commentaries and works on the early Church Fathers.

Swift, Jonathan An Englishman, he was ordained Anglican priest in Ireland in 1695 and was dean of St Patrick's, Dublin, from 1713. Born Dublin, 30 November 1667, died there 19 October 1745. Satirist, poet, pamphleteer and novelist, mostly remembered for his *Gulliver's Travels*, published in 1726. Religiously, he opposed both the Northern Irish and Scottish Presbyterians and the English Dissenters. Politically, though a Whig, he wrote against the Occasional Conformity Act of 1708, was uneasy with his party's leanings towards Nonconformists and spoke out against the English misgovernment of Ireland. His concern for justice won him the confidence and acclaim of the ordinary people.

Swithin Saint, died 2 July 862. Bishop of Winchester from 852. Originally buried outside the walls of the minster, but in 971 his body was moved to a shrine inside the newly rebuilt cathedral. His relics disappeared when his shrine was destroyed in 1538, in the Reformation. It is unclear why the belief arose that the weather on his feast day, 15 July, would be the weather of the following forty days. One theory is that a similar belief is associated with SS Processus and Martinian, on whose feast day St Swithin died.

Sylvester I Saint, pope, consecrated 31 January 314, died Rome, 31 December 335. Legend asserts that he baptized the emperor **Constantine** and that he was the recipient of the Donation of Constantine, an eighth-century document purporting to be a record of the emperor's conversion and profession of faith, and which allegedly granted wide temporal rights to Sylvester and his successors. Little is known of his life, but recognition of the primacy of the See of Rome increased during his period of office. He did not attend the Council of Nicaea in 325 but was represented by two legates. Feast day in the West, 31 December; in the East, 2 January.

Sylvester II Pope and scholar, born in the Auvergne about 940, elected 2 April 999, died Rome, 12 May 1003. Gerbert of Aurillac was educated by the Benedictines at Aurillac and later was a student then master at the cathedral school in Rheims. He became archbishop of Rheims in 991 and of Ravenna in 998, a year before becoming Pope. He was highly regarded by the emperors **Otto II** and **III**. He chose the name Sylvester in full awareness that his predecessor of that name had long been regarded as the model of papal co-operation with the emperor. While the emperor would attempt to restore the Empire itself, the Pope would endeavour to restore the sanctity of the Church. In fact Sylvester did much to realize this ideal, opposing simony and upholding clerical celibacy, and strengthening the Church in Eastern Europe. The Romans, however, were unhappy under the governance of a Frenchman, and for a year the Pope had to live outside the city.

Sylvester III Pope, born John, a Roman, elected 20 January 1045, deposed 10 March 1045, died mid-year, 1063. He was made Pope when **Benedict** was deposed, but when Benedict made a come-back he, in his turn, was deposed, and returned to functioning, until his death, as bishop of Sabina.

Symmachus Probably late second century. His was one of the Greek translations of the OT for **Origen**'s Hexapla. His style is more readable though less accurate than that of his fellow contributors. Little is known about his life. **Jerome** and **Eusebius** both state that he was an Ebionite, one of the early sects of Jewish Christians, but Epiphanius believed him to be a Samaritan who became a Jewish proselyte.

Symmachus Saint, Pope from 22 November 498 until his death, 19 July 514. A Sardinian convert from paganism who strictly upheld Roman doctrine and papal claims. He was the successful papal candidate – supported by the clergy and the majority of the laity in opposition to the archpriest Laurence, who was favoured by the aristocratic laity – following the death of Pope **Anastasius II.** After a bloody struggle between the factions in Rome the candidacy of Symmachus was endorsed by the Arian King Theodoric. Later in his reign he opposed the Henoticon, supported by the emperor **Zeno**, as being contrary to the Catholic faith and expelled the Manichaeans from Rome. He sent the pallium to Bishop **Caesarius** in Arles (the first bishopric outside Italy to receive the honour) and confirmed its primacy over the Gallican and Spanish churches. He introduced the singing of the Gloria (by bishops only) on Sundays and feast days, helped the poor, including those persecuted by the Arians, and embellished St Peter's and other churches in Rome. Feast day 19 July.

Synesius Bishop of Ptolemais, born Cyrene (Libya) *c*.370 into an ancient family which had possibly converted to Christianity, died Ptolemais 413. Married a Christian in *c*.404 and studied at Alexandria under the Neo-platonist philosopher Hypatia. Wrote a number of treatises, none of which are on particularly Christian themes, and a series of hymns which express Trinitarian and Incarnational theologies strongly influenced by Neoplatonisn. His surviving correspondence provides important insights into the life of the provincial church. Synesius was consecrated bishop in 410 by Theophilus, patriarch of Alexandria.

T

Tache, Alexandre Antonin Canadian archbishop, born Fraserville, Quebec, 23 July 1823, died St Boniface, Manitoba, 22 June 1894. He studied at the Grand Seminaire, Montreal, became an Oblate of Mary Immaculate and was ordained in St Boniface Cathedral. A missionary to the Indian nations, he was named co-adjutor at St Boniface, and consecrated bishop at Marseilles by Eugène de **Mazenod**, founder of the Oblates, for whom the evangelization of the Indians in western Canada was a special vocation. Tache succeeded to the see in 1853, but continued to travel widely in his territory, as far north as Great Slave Lake. Disregard by the government of the rights of the people of the Northwest Territories resulted in an insurrection in 1869, led by Louis Riel, and Tache worked hard to obtain safeguards for the national and religious rights of the population. Made archbishop in 1871, he championed the rights of the indigenous population, founded a French-language newspaper and played an important role in solving the controversy over Catholic schools, which, though guaranteed in the Manitoba constitution, were suppressed by an unjust law in 1890.

Talantov, Boris Russian Orthodox lay writer and dissident, born Kostroma, Russia, 1903, died Viatka prison, 4 January 1971. Despite constant police harassment he protested against the renewed persecution of the Church in Russia during and after the Khrushchev period. He recognized the destruction of hundreds of church buildings and condemned the silence of the senior bishops. In 1969 he was arrested for 'anti-Soviet activity' and died serving a prison sentence.

Talbot, Francis Xavier Jesuit author and editor, born Philadelphia, 25 January 1889, died, 3 December 1953. He entered the Society of Jesus and was ordained at Woodstock in 1921. He taught at Loyola School, NY, and Boston College, Massachusetts, became literary editor, and editor in chief, of the Jesuit weekly *America* in 1936. He was president of Loyola College, Baltimore, 1947–50, archivist at Georgetown University, parish priest at St Aloysius Church, Washington, and engaged in retreat work at Manresa-on-the-Severn, Annapolis. Talbot contributed significantly to the cultural and intellectual life of Catholicism in the USA through his association with founding organizations and activities, such as the Catholic Book Club, 1928; the Catholic Poetry Society, 1930; the Spiritual Book Associates, 1932 and, when editor of *America*, the journal *Theological Studies*. He was active in the Catholic Theatre Conference, the Catholic Library Association, the National Motion Picture Bureau. He wrote *Jesuit Education in Philadelphia* (1927) *Saint among the Hurons* (1949), and *Saint among the Savages* (1935). He contributed frequently to the *Encyclopaedia Britannica* and to the *Britannia Yearbook*.

Talbot, Matthew Venerable, Irish reformed alcoholic, born Dublin, 2 May 1856, died there, 7 June 1925. He first worked as a messenger with a wine merchant and then with the Port and Docks Board. He later became a builder's labourer, spending all his money on drink until, in 1884, he 'took the pledge' and became a total abstainer from alcohol. He became increasingly devout, attending Mass daily, which, with the demands of his job, meant rising at 4.00 a.m. He adopted other ascetic practices, including sleep on a wooden bed, and fasting. He gave most of his earnings to charity. His final job was in a timber yard, where he worked until the day before he died. He died on his way to Mass. It was then discovered that he had bound his body with chains as a form of mortification.

Talbot, Peter   Irish archbishop, born Malahide, Dublin, 1620, died in prison, early November 1680. He joined the Jesuits and studied in Portugal, was ordained in Rome and taught theology at Antwerp. Along with his brothers he served at the court of **Charles II**, in exile in Cologne, acting as ambassador on several occasions to Spain and France. He served briefly in England after the Restoration but had to flee to Europe because of intrigues at court. In 1669 he was made archbishop of Dublin and in 1670 held the first diocesan synod in Dublin. It began with High Mass which had not been publicly celebrated for some forty years. Talbot was engaged in bitter debate with Oliver **Plunket** for some years over the wording of an Oath of Allegiance. His efforts to win relief from some of the injustices endured by Catholics led to allegations of treason and fresh efforts to suppress all Roman Catholic institutions, and in 1673 renewed persecution began. Talbot fled to Paris, but in 1675 returned to England and eventually sought and in 1677 received permission to return to Ireland. Despite his enfeebled state of health he was implicated in a conspiracy and in 1678 was arrested near Maynooth and imprisoned in Dublin Castle, where he suffered for two years. Before his death he was reconciled with Plunket, a fellow prisoner, who also gave him the last sacraments.

Talleyrand-Périgord, Charles Maurice de   French bishop, prince and statesman, born Paris, the eldest son of the Comte Daniel de Talleyrand, 13 February 1754, died there, May 1838. Studied at St Sulpice and became an abbé. Although not really committed to his apparent calling he was ordained in 1789 and became bishop of Autun in 1789. He joined the revolutionary cause, became a member of the Constitutional Committee that passed the Declaration of the Rights of Man and was one of only four bishops to take the oath on the Civil Constitution of the Clergy. In 1791 he resigned his see and he was excommunicated. He travelled to London and to the USA and on his return to France in 1796 was made minister of foreign affairs. He welcomed Napoleon Bonaparte and assisted in drafting the Concordat. He was released from his clerical vows, reinstated to communion with Rome and married. As Napoleon's chief aide he was made grand chamberlain, vice-elector of the Empire and prince of Benevenuto. He fell out of favour when he opposed the Franco-Russian and the Spanish Wars. He returned to power in 1814, was active at the Congress of Vienna and helped prevent the break-up of France. In 1830 he went as ambassador to England until, in 1834, he had concluded the *entente cordiale*. He retired to Valençay, where he wrote his *Memoirs* and just before his death repented and repudiated any harm he had done the Catholic Church.

Tallis, Thomas   'The father of English cathedral music', born *c.*1505, died Greenwich, Kent, 23 November 1585. He was possibly a chorister of the Chapel Royal, and then organist at Waltham Abbey. He was then a lay clerk at Canterbury Cathedral and a gentleman of the Chapel Royal. He served Catholic and Protestant monarchs. He was a close associate of William **Byrd**'s, being granted with him a 25-year monopoly of music printing in 1575. His church music is often on a grand scale, as shown in his motet *Spem In Alium* for eight five-part choirs. To Matthew Parker's *The Whole Psalter*, Tallis contributed nine tunes. The eighth tune, since the early eighteenth century, has been sung to Thomas **Ken**'s words *Glory To Thee My God This Night*.

Tamburini, Michelangelo   Italian Jesuit, born Modena, 27 September 1648, died Rome, 28 February 1730. He was admitted to the Society of Jesus in 1665. An admirer of **Ignatius of Loyola** and his ideas of Catholic reform, he taught philosophy at Bologna and theology at Mantua. He was named theologian to Cardinal Rainaud d'Este, whose influential support helped him in his being named rector, then provincial, and finally general of the Society in 1706, in succession to Thyrsus Gonzalez. He promoted the full flourishing of Jesuit missionary activity, such as the Reductions in Paraguay, new missions in the Levant and the continuance of Roberto de **Nobili**'s 'Brahman Christianity' in India. However, Tamburini was obliged to defend the Society against mounting opposition, from the Jansenists especially, to its methods of evangelization, which **Clement XI**, already unfavourably disposed, considered, in the case of China in particular, too permissive vis-à-vis indigenous customs, and he renewed the interdict against Christians there. The Jesuits were also accused of disobeying the pontiff, which Tamburini rejected, but **Innocent III** aggravated the situation by requiring a copy of all Tamburini's instructions. During the whole of his generalate Tamburini was opposed to a Roman curia in part won over by Jansenism, and though matters improved under **Benedict XIII** in 1724, the situation remained difficult in the missions.

Tanqueray, Adolf Alfred Sulpician priest, theologian, born Blainville, Normandy, 1 May 1854, died Aix-en-Provence, 21 February 1932. Studied at Saint-Lô, Coutances, Saint-Sulpice and Rome. He was ordained in 1878 and joined the Society of St Sulpice. He taught in Rodez, France, in Baltimore, USA and in Saint-Sulpice, Paris, and was superior for twelve years at the Solitude novitiate at Issy. He retired to Aix. His writings include *Synopsis Theologiae Dogmaticae* (1894–6) and *Synopsis Theologiae Moralis et Pastoralis* (1902–5) – both in three volumes, both issued later in condensed versions, and both for a time much used by students for the Roman Catholic priesthood. He also wrote on mystical and ascetical theology and contributed to Catholic periodicals.

Tapiedi, Lucien One of 333 Christians killed in New Guinea in World War II, and one of those recently commemorated by the erection of a statue in Westminster Abbey, London. Born about 1922, Taupota village in the north of Papua, died, at the hands of a member of the Orokaiva tribe, near Kurumbo, 1942. He was educated at mission schools and in 1939 became a student at St Aidan's teacher training college. Joined the staff of Sangara as an evangelist and teacher in 1941. Japanese forces invaded the island in July 1942 and Tapiedi was killed while trying, along with other missionaries, to escape capture.

Tappouni, Ignatius Gabriel Cardinal, Catholic patriarch of Antioch of the Syrians. Born Mosul, Iraq, 3 November 1879, died Beirut, 29 January 1968. Of a Syrian family that converted to Cathol-

icism in mid-eighteenth century, he studied at the Syro-Chaldean seminary of Mosul, directed by French Dominicans, and was ordained in 1902. Named bishop of Danaba in 1912, and auxiliary of the patriarch of Antioch of the Syrians, he exercised jurisdiction in dioceses of the Syrian and Armenian rites in south-east Turkey and northeast Syria, among oriental Christians of Jacobite, Orthodox and Catholic confessions. The Christians in that part of the Ottoman empire were gravely inhibited in the practice of their faith, and Tappouni himself was arrested by the Turks, accused of treason and condemned to death at Aleppo. Only the intervention of **Benedict XV**, and of Empress Zita of Austria and her government, released him in 1918. Named archbishop of Aleppo in 1921 and patriarch of Antioch of the Syrians in 1929, he was responsible for regrouping and rehabilitating survivors of the massacres and, with the end of the French mandate in Syria and Lebanon, of negotiating assurances for the rights of the Christian minorities in predominantly Muslim Syria. He worked to establish sound ecumenical relations with the Syrian church. He was a member of the Congregation for the Evangelisation of Peoples for the oriental churches, and, at the height of his influence, the only oriental member of the Council of Presidents of Vatican II.

Tarasius Saint, patriarch of Constantinople, died 25 February 806. His father was the prefect of Constantinople and he entered state service, becoming secretary to the Empress Irene II. Though not in orders he became patriarch by popular acclaim in 784, but only with the agreement of the empress to the suggestion that he would try to restore church unity. **Hadrian I** gave reluctant approval and agreed to participate in the Second Council of Nicaea, 787, which rejected Iconoclasm and restored unity between Rome and Constantinople. Tarasius was involved in several controversies after this but eventually became venerated as a saint. Feast day 25 February in the West.

Tasso, Torquato Italian poet, born 11 March 1544, Sorrento, died 25 April 1595, Rome. His father, Bernardo, was also a poet. He was educated with the son of the duke of Urbino. In 1559, while in Venice, he began to write *Gerusalemme Liberata*,

'Jerusalem Liberated' an epic poem about the capture of Jerusalem during the first Crusade, but decided he was not yet mature enough for this task. The following year he went to Padua to study law. He did not complete his major work until 1575, by which time he was in the service of Cardinal Luigi d'Este. Much of his other poetry in these years was of courtly love. He began to worry about his religious convictions, so much so that he was thought mentally unstable and was locked up in an asylum from 1579 to 1586. After his release he moved around Italy, writing religious poetry in particular at this time. In 1592 he gained a patron in Rome, Cardinal Cinzio Aldobrandini, a nephew of Pope **Clement VIII**, and wrote a new version of *Gerusalemme Liberata*, *Gerusalemme Conquistata*, published in 1593. Late the following year, on Tasso's return to Rome from Venice, the Pope bestowed a pension on him, but he fell ill soon afterwards, and died in the convent of San Onofrio.

Tatian Christian apologist, a native of the Euphrates Valley, born *c.*110, died Syria, *c.*180. He was educated in Greek rhetoric and philosophy, a convert to Christianity, *c.*150–65, living in Rome and a pupil of **Justin Martyr**. Became estranged from the Catholic Church *c.*172 because of his rigorist views, and returned to Syria, where he founded an ascetic religious community of Encratites, embracing a mixture of Christianity and Stoicism. His *Diatessaron*, a version of the four Gospels as a continuous narrative, was used in the Syrian church until the fifth century and persisted among Christians as a life of Jesus in various western languages up to the Middle Ages.

Tauler, Johann German Dominican mystic, born Strasburg, 1300, died there, 16 June 1361. He entered the Order in 1315 at Strasburg and was sent to Cologne, where **Eckhart** was teaching, just at the time that he was condemned. He was highly thought of as a preacher, but also as a spiritual director of nuns. His teaching reflects some of the Platonism, inherited by the Dominicans from **Albert** the Great, which brought condemnation on Eckhardt. His life was an exemplar of practical expression of mystical insight, notably his complete devotion to those suffering from the Black Death in 1348. He wrote nothing. His sermons were taken down, seemingly by his confreres, and collected in *Die Predigten Taulers*. They are best known in translation as 'The Spiritual Conferences'.

Tausen, Hans 'The Danish Luther', born Birkende, Fyn Island, 1494, died Ribe, 11 November 1561. Of peasant stock, he entered the Order of St John of Jerusalem, studied at Rostock, Copenhagen, Louvain and Wittemberg, 1523–4, where he encountered the theses of Martin **Luther.** In 1526, he resigned from the Order and became the principal advocate of the Reform in his country. Appointed pastor at Viborg, Tausen took the initiative of breaking with the rule of the apostolic succession, and himself consecrated his colleagues so as to create a Reformed Church. Becoming chaplain to **Frederick I**, Tausen persuaded the crown to proclaim an independent national church. The Diet of 1526, in decreeing that bishops would henceforth be named by the king and consecrated by the archbishop of Lund, without reference to the Pope, effectively ensured a rupture with Rome. The assembly of the nobles at Copenhagen could not restore unity in the Danish church, and the city adopted the 43 evangelical articles of 'Confessio Hofniensis', the work of Tausen. Frederick's son, Christian III, established Lutheranism as the state church in 1536, arrested all opposing bishops and confiscated church property. Tausen co-operated and, as a final triumph, was appointed bishop of Ribe in 1542, an office he held with great zeal and ability for twenty years.

Taverner, John English composer, born South Lincolnshire, *c.*1490, died Boston, Lincolnshire, 18 October 1545. He worked in London and Tattershall, Lincolnshire, and was master of the choristers at Cardinal College, later Christ Church, Oxford. He composed Masses, Magnificats and other church music. His Mass based on the tune *The Western Wynde* is well known. Taverner, in the *Benedictus* of his Mass *Gloria Tibi Trinitas* incorporated a plainsong theme originally sung to the words *Gloria Tibi Trinitas* and adapted to the words *In Nomine Domini*. A large number of composers up to the time of Purcell wrote instrumental pieces called *In Nomine* based on this theme.

Tawil, Joseph Melkite archbishop, born Damascus, 25 December 1913, died Boston, 17 February 1999. He studied in both Damascus and Jerusalem, before being ordained priest in Jerusalem on 20 July 1936. He became president of the Patriarchal College, Cairo, and then patriarchal vicar of Damascus in 1959, being consecrated bishop, with the personal title of archbishop, in Alexandria on 1 January 1960. He was appointed apostolic exarch for Melkite Greek Catholics in the United States in October 1969. The exarchate became a full diocese, or eparchy (of Newton) in 1976. In opposition to the Vatican he supported the traditional right of Eastern Catholics to ordain married men. He retired from the exarchate in December 1989.

Taylor, Frances Margaret English religious foundress. Born Stoke Rochford, Lincolnshire, 20 January 1832, died London, 9 June 1900. Daughter of an Anglican minister, she first entered the Anglican sisterhood but left and, in 1853, joined Florence **Nightingale**'s lady volunteers and went to the Crimea in 1854. She met Mother Mary Bridgeman and the Sisters of Mercy, was received into the Catholic Church and entered the French Sisters of Charity, rue de Bac, Paris; her superiors and Cardinal **Manning** urged her to return to London, where she founded the Poor Servants of the Mother of God in 1869, which she also directed until her death. She was also editor of *The Lamp*, and collaborated in launching *The Messenger of the Sacred Heart*, and *The Month*, periodicals which have become firmly established in the cultural and intellectual life of the Church.

Taylor, George Floyd Pentecostal leader, born Duplin County, North Carolina, 1881, died Franklin County, GA, 1934. Taylor joined the Holiness Church of North Carolina in 1903, becoming a preacher that year. He founded two Holiness schools in North Carolina. In 1907 he experienced glossolalia and wrote *The Spirit and the Bride*, defending Pentecostalism. In 1908 his church became the Pentecostal Holiness Church, and Taylor was superintendent from 1913 to 1915. From 1919 he edited the *Pentecostal Holiness Advocate* and was founding president of the Franklin Springs Institute. He also produced Sunday school literature and after a 1929 trip to the Middle East published *A Tour of Bible Lands*.

Taylor, Hugh English Roman Catholic priest, martyr, born Durham, died by hanging, York, 25 November 1585. In 1582 he went to Rheims, was ordained and in March 1585 was sent back to England. He was arrested later that year and was the first person to die under the new Statute of **Elizabeth.** The following day Marmaduke Bowes, a layman, was also hanged for having harboured Taylor.

Taylor, James Hudson Founder of the China Inland Mission, born Barnsley, Yorkshire, 1832, died Changsha, China, 1 June 1905. Brought up a Methodist, at the age of eighteen he felt called to preach the Gospel in China. After studying medicine he arrived in Shanghai in 1856, under the auspices of the China Evangelization Society, and in 1862 abandoned European dress and life-style. He ran the Christian hospital in Ning-po, worked on a revision of the NT in the Ning-po dialect and launched the China Inland Mission on a visit to England in 1865, returning with sixteen missionaries. By 1871 he had 30 European missionaries and 50 Chinese working from thirteen central stations. The Boxer Rising of 1900 took place whilst he was in England and killed 58 of his missionaries and 21 of their children. His broken spirit and failing health prevented his return to China, but he managed a visit in 1905 and died there.

Taylor, William Methodist missionary and bishop, born Rockbridge County, Virginia, 2 May 1821, died Palo Alto, California, 18 May 1902. He was a Methodist home missionary in frontier California and a National Holiness Association revivalist before turning to cross-cultural missions. In India and South America, he implemented a self-supporting missions strategy ('the Pauline method') independent of the Methodist missions board. In 1884 the Methodist Episcopal Church elected him bishop for Africa, and he employed his controversial strategies there. Taylor's methods bred mixed results, including creation of an entire Methodist conference in South India and an indigenous Pentecostal denomination in Chile.

Teilhard de Chardin, Pierre French theologian and scientist, born Chateau de Sarcenat, Puy-de-Dome, 1 May 1881, died New York, 10 April 1955 (on Easter Sunday, as he had wished). He was ordained in the Society of Jesus in 1911. As well as his theological training, he was strongly attracted to the natural sciences, studied geology and palaeontology at the Musée de Paris under M. Boule, and was professor at the Catholic University of Paris from 1920 to 1928. For many years he had pursued a philosophical and religious quest into the origins of man, and revealed in his writings originality, and an aptitude for the grand design: a new phenomenology, a synthesis of science and religion in which (*The Phenomenon of Man*, 1959), under the continual creative action of God, the world develops according to a law of increasing complexity and consciousness until the appearance of man (cosmogenesis); and the process converges in a rhythm of hypersocialization toward an Omega point (Christogenesis). In *Le Milieu Divin*, Teilhard sketches a mystical spirituality in which, by activity and trial, man can become one with the unifying action of Christ, the Alpha and Omega of the universe, a transformation centred on the Eucharist and the building of the Mystical Body. He was not allowed by the Society to publish most of his writings, nor to accept a chair at the College de France, because of his radical evolutionism and language that sometimes gives the impression of confusion between the natural and supernatural designs. Nevertheless, Teilhard's attempt to relate the Christian concept of creation to the contemporary scientific understanding of nature was remarkable.

Tekakwitha, Kateri   Born probably at what is now Auriesville, New York State, 1656, died Cauyghnawaga, Canada, 17 April 1680. She was brought up by an anti-Christian uncle after surviving an outbreak of smallpox which killed the rest of her family. After encountering a group of Jesuit missionaries when she was eleven, she began to live an ascetic form of life, and at the age of twenty was baptized. Because she was persecuted for her beliefs, she fled to the St **Francis Xavier** mission at Sault Saint-Louis, near Montreal, where she took a vow of virginity and lived an exemplary life, becoming known as 'the lily of the Mohawks'. She was beatified on 22 June 1980. Feast day 17 April.

Telesphorus   Pope, saint, elected *c.*125, died *c.*136. The name suggests that he was Greek, but little else is known about him, though it is probable that he died a martyr. Feast day 5 January in the West, 22 February in the East.

Temple, William   Archbishop of Canterbury, ecumenical leader. Born Exeter, 15 October 1881, died Canterbury, 26 October 1944. He was successively exhibitioner at Balliol College, headmaster of Repton, rector of St James, Piccadilly, canon of Westminster, bishop of Manchester, archbishop of York, and of Canterbury, 1942. He developed forceful ideas of pastoral work: to demonstrate on the basis of philosophical reflection the creditability of Christianity; to infuse the Anglican Church with a new energy in the development of ecumenism and political engagement. He also proposed a modernization of the Church so that the nation could be united on a common basis of ethical and religious values. To survive, the Church must acquire greater autonomy in the matter of doctrine and liturgy. From the 1930s, Temple campaigned for an international union of churches, and inaugurated an ecumenical council in 1944 at St Paul's. Without having specifically elaborated a doctrinal synthesis, Temple from his early days professed a Christian socialism in the light of political movements of the time. In 1941 he presided at the 'Malvern Conference', having inspired the Conference on Politics, Economics and Citizenship (COPEC), on the role of Christians in a society of unemployment and poverty. In two works: *Men without Work* and *Christianity and Social Order*, he maintained that even though the Church has not the necessary competence to dictate to the state what it should do, she can and ought 'collectively' to use her moral influence to create a climate favourable to structural reforms. By his political and intellectual stature, Temple dominated the Anglican Church in the first half of this century, and by his battle for greater autonomy and openness on the world, he was a prophet of modern times.

Teresa of Ávila (Teresa of Jesus)   Saint, Spanish mystic, Carmelite reformer, born Ávila, 28 March 1515, died Alba de Tormes, 4 October 1582. Initially educated at home, she spent just over a year in her mid-teens at the Augustinian school in Ávila but had to leave because of ill-health, which she suffered throughout her life. In 1535 she left her family and joined the Carmelites in Ávila. Although disapproving this move, her father eventually gave his blessing. Teresa, intent on pursuing a life of religious perfection, entered more and more deeply into prayer and began to experience a series of visions and ecstasies. So that she and others could lead a life of greater mortification she determined to open a house where the primitive rule of the Carmelites would be observed. The Convent of St Joseph was opened, against much opposition, in 1562, and this was followed, against similar opposition, by several more Discalced houses both for women and, with the aid of **John of the Cross**, for men. On the instructions of her spiritual advisers she wrote her *Life*, and also began a book for the sisters, *The Way of Perfection*. These and her other writings, including *Foundations* and *The Interior Castle*, are all regarded as classics of the spiritual life. Teresa was declared a Doctor of the Church in 1970. Feast day 15 October.

Teresa of Calcutta (Agnes Gonxha Bojaxhiu) Mother, religious founder, born into an Albanian family in Skopje, Macedonia, 27 August 1910, died Calcutta, 5 September 1997. She joined the Sisters of Loreto at Rathfarnham, Ireland, in 1928, expressed what she understood as her call to work in India and was sent as a novice to study and work in Darjeeling, and in 1929 went to work in the Loreto school in Calcutta. In 1946 she became convinced that God wanted more from her, and felt increasingly called to serve the very poor. In 1948 with her superior's permission she left the Loreto convent, took the name Teresa and, dressed in a simple blue and white sari, went to live in a Calcutta slum area, where she cared for the destitute and the dying, and taught the children of the very poorest. She was soon joined by others, among them those she had taught, and in 1950 the Missionaries of Charity was approved as a new religious order. In 1963 the Missionary Brothers of Charity was established and in 1969 the International Co-Workers of Mother Teresa. Mother Teresa established the work of the Order worldwide, including the cities of the supposedly privileged West, where many of the destitute, desperate and dying have benefited from the acceptance and care of the sisters. In 1979 she was awarded the Nobel Peace Prize.

Terry, (Sir) Richard Roman Catholic music editor, conductor, organist and composer, born Ellington, Northumberland, 3 January 1865, died Kensington, London, 18 April 1938. He studied at Oxford and Cambridge and held various organist and teaching posts. He became organist at Downside Abbey and Director of Music at Westminster Cathedral. Through his editing of the *Westminster Hymnal*, he helped to raise standards of taste in music in the Roman Catholic Church in Britain. He edited and published editions of **Calvin**'s *Psalter* and the *Scottish Psalter*, and wrote a book on *Catholic Church Music*. His hymn tunes are extremely effective, such as Billing sung to the words *Praise To The Holiest* and Highwood to *O Perfect Love*.

Tertullian, Quintus Septimius Florens Apologist and theologian, born Carthage, *c*.155, died there, *c*.220. He is the earliest and the greatest of the early church writers of the West prior to **Augustine**. Harnach said that Tertullian in fact created Christian Latin literature: 'one might almost say that literature sprang from him full-grown, alike in form and substance as Athena from the head of Zeus'. **Cyprian** depended on Tertullian, and called him his master, as did Augustine on both; the three North Africans are fathers of the Western churches. He converted to Christianity *c*.195, and put his whole culture at the service of the faith, attacking without mercy his adversaries: pagans, Jews, heretics; multiplying his sermons and treatises for the instruction of the faithful, and pursuing with mordant irony all those who contradicted him. However, he who had strengthened the Church against Gnosticism could not abide its tendency to a political organization and, being unable to reconcile incompatibilities, he broke with the Church around 213; he then became the most powerful leader of Montanism in the West, and leader of a party known as the Tertullians, who remained faithful to his memory until Augustine brought them back to the fold in 428.

Tetzel, Johann German preacher and seller of indulgences. Born Pirna, near Meissen, 1465, died Leipzig, 11 August 1519. He entered the Dominican Order at Leipzig, was prior at Glogau, and appointed Inquisitor for Poland in 1509. He was known as a preacher of indulgences, combining the elocutionary gifts of a revivalist orator with the shrewdness of an auctioneer. He painted in lurid colours the terrors of purgatory, while dwelling on the cheapness of the indulgence which would purchase remission, and his prices were lowered as each sale approached its end. In 1516, Tetzel was appointed sub-commissioner in Meissen for the indulgence granted to those who contributed to the rebuilding of St Peters, and his efforts irretrievably damaged the complicated and abstruse Catholic doctrine on the subject; 'as soon as the coin clinks in the chest', he cried, 'the soul is freed from purgatory'. His preaching took him near Wittenberg and **Luther**, already hostile to indulgences, was roused to publish his 95 theses in 1517, attacking the whole system, to which he riposted with 106 theses in defence of his actions. However, sober Catholics felt that Tetzel's vulgar extravagances had prejudiced Catholic doctrine, and he hid in the Dominican convent at Leipzig in fear of popular violence. He was, however, grossly calumniated. His teaching on indulgences for the living was orthodox; on those for the dead he followed the teaching of the Mainz Instruction, that they were gained independently of dispositions of contrition in the person seeking the indulgence, who also had the right to apply them absolutely to a specific soul in purgatory. This was of course erroneous, and **Cajetan** condemned the teaching at Rome.

Tewodros II (Theodore) Emperor of Ethiopia, born c.1818 and named Kassa. Shot himself on Good Friday 1868 after defeat by the British. He fought his way to power in 1855, reunifying the country and restoring an effective royal rule. He identified himself with a prophecy of a king who would follow Christ and bring peace. His personal life of monogamy despite childlessness, concern for the poor, a desire to improve the justice system and the army and to rebuild churches suggests a genuine faith. However, he became increasingly ruthless in implementing reforms. Whilst supporting the ancient Ethiopian church he attacked the Roman Catholic Church and tortured some of its leaders. He welcomed Protestant missionaries for their technical skills and connections with Europe but forbade any attempts at evangelism.

Thaddeus *see* **Addai**

Thaisia (Taisia) of Lenshino Russian Orthodox abbess and spiritual writer, born near Novgorod, 1840, died Leushino Convent, 2 January 1915. Against her mother's wishes she became a nun. She was a founder of convents and reformer of women's monastic life and had the strong support of St **John of Kronstadt**. She wrote a vivid spiritual autobiography and was a prominent poet.

Theissen, Jerome Abbot primate of the Benedictine Confederation, born in Loyal, Wisconsin, USA, 30 December 1930, died Rome, 11 September 1995. He entered St John's Abbey, Collegeville, Minnesota, in 1951 and was ordained priest in 1957. He studied theology at Sant'Anselmo in Rome before ordination, and returned there for doctoral studies, which he completed in 1966. He returned to teach theology at St John's, and became co-director of its Institute of Ecumenical and Cultural Studies. In 1979 he was elected abbot of St John's, and abbot primate of the Benedictine Confederation in September 1992, a title which carried with it the abbacy of Sant'Anselmo, and chancellor of the Athenaeum attached to it. As abbot primate he travelled widely visiting monasteries, especially in developing countries.

Theobald of Canterbury Archbishop, born near the abbey of Bec, Normandy, date unknown, died 18 April 1161. The son of a knight, he became a monk at Bec, prior in 1127, abbot in 1137 and, the choice of King Stephen, archbishop of Canterbury in 1138. In the disturbed political times of Stephen's reign, he attempted to maintain a neutral position, in contrast to the conduct of his rival, **Henry of Blois**, bishop of Winchester, who fought for the privileges of the Church; Theobald made it his rule to support the de facto sovereign. However, a serious matter arose when Theobald refused, on papal orders, to crown Count Eustace, Stephen's eldest son, and he was banished from the kingdom, but Pope **Eugenius** terrified Stephen into a reversal of the decision. In 1153, Theobald succeeded in reconciling Stephen with Henri d'Anjou, and in securing for the latter the succession to the throne. Theobald's main political ideal was cooperation between Church and State, recognizing that if they clashed, the vigour of the secular power would be impaired no less than the ecclesiastical. With his defeat of the schemes of

Henry of Blois, in his attempts to assert the supremacy of the king, in his championship of episcopal authority over monasteries, his attempts to withstand royal 'tyranny', his success in choosing subordinates, among whom **Thomas Becket**, the humanist **John of Salisbury** and the canon lawyer Vacarius, he did much to give the English church a new identity and purpose.

Theodora I Byzantine empress, born Constantinople, *c.*495, died there, 548. She was the wife of **Justinian I**, who married her in 523, having amended the law that forbade marriage of a patrician to a woman of servile origin, shortly before his accession, at which he made her an independent and equal co-ruler, inserting her name with his own in the oath of allegiance. In the religious strife which distracted the empire, Theodora took part with the Monophysites, while Justinian was a warm upholder of the decrees of Chalcedon, and she was influential in having Justinian adopt his reactionary policy which, especially in the dispute over the 'Three Chapters', sought to reconcile the Monophysites and the Chalcedonians, even at the expense of the decrees of Chalcedon. Although she had, according to Precopius, lived a dissolute early life, she was a woman of outstanding intellect and learning and, as empress, shrewd, courageous in the Nika riots of 532, when she rallied the emperor and court, a moral reformer and an example of true Christian piety, observing the feasts and fasts punctiliously. She did not suffer any affront, and had a reputation for severity. Though condemned by **Baronius** as 'civis inferni', Paul Silentiarius called her St Theodora, two years after her death.

Theodore I Pope, born Jerusalem (the son of a bishop), consecrated 24 November 642, died 14 May 649. He had possibly come to Rome as a refugee after the Arab invasions of Palestine and, as a Greek, was well versed in the theological controversies of the time. The chief matter at issue was the number of wills in Christ – not an arcane argument because the belief that there was only one ('monothelitism') would imply that Christ was not fully human. The deposed patriarch of Constantinople, Pyrrhus, travelled to Rome to recant his belief in monothelitism, and Theodore promptly recognized him as the lawful patriarch. But when he found that his recantation did not

regain him his see, he withdrew it, and went off to the imperial court at Ravenna. Theodore excommunicated him. When the emperor tried to bring peace among the warring parties by producing a document which simply insisted on the definitions of the first five Councils and forbidding any further discussion, the papal representative at Constantinople refused to sign, was exiled, and the office of the papal ambassador was closed. Theodore himself died before being presented with this document, the Typos as it was called.

Theodore II Pope, elected and died November 897. He was a Roman, and eager to bring back some stability to the Roman see. He recovered the body of Pope **Formosus** from the Tiber, and buried it with honour, and annulled the decisions of the 'synod of the cadaver' which had condemned the late Pope.

Theodore II Emperor, *see* **Tewodros II**

Theodore Lector Ecclesiastical historian of sixth-century Constantinople. Mainly known for two works: the *Tripartite History*, which gives extracts from the histories of the Church written by **Socrates, Sozomen** and **Theodoret**, and another which he wrote to continue the story down to the time of Justin I, who died in 527.

Theodore of Canterbury (of Tarsus) Saint, archbishop of Canterbury, first metropolitan of all England, born Tarsus, Cilicia, about 602, died Canterbury, 19 September 690. The candidate, Wighard, whom Kings Oswy and Egbert had sent to be consecrated to the See of Canterbury after the death of Deusdedit in 664, died on his way to Rome. Pope **Vitalian** chose Hadrian, abbot of a monastery near Naples, but he was reluctant to take the post and suggested the 66-year-old Theodore, a holy and learned monk. Vitalian accepted this nomination but insisted that Hadrian, as well as **Benedict Biscop**, go with Theodore to ensure his orthodoxy. Theodore was consecrated in Rome in 668. His journey to Canterbury took a year, during which time he learned English and familiarized himself with the situation of the Church in England. He took possession of his see on 27 May 669. He did much to unify the Church in England: he visited all the churches, endorsed the good teaching and morals he found, reformed abuses, introduced the Roman chant in the divine office and reformed the government of the Church by reorganizing dioceses and confirming new bishops. He resolved two disputes at York in favour of **Wilfrid**. He held two important synods of the whole Church, one at Hertford in 672 and another at Hatfield in 679. Theodore and Hadrian attracted many pupils eager to learn Greek and Latin, astronomy and mathematics as well as theology and doctrine, and this learning spread throughout the country. His writings include *Iudicia*, *Laterculus Malalianus*, a Latin translation of the *Passio S. Anastassi* and a Penitential. Feast day 19 September.

Theodore of Mopsuestia Bishop and theologian, born Antioch, *c.*350, died Mopsuestia, 428. The most eminent representative of the so-called school of Antioch, and a friend of **John Chrysostom**. He attached himself to the school of the great exegete and ascetic **Diodore**, under whom he became most skilful, ultimately outstripping his master in biblical learning. Around 392 he became bishop of Mopsuestia, in Cilicia, was held in much respect and took part in several synods with a great reputation for orthodoxy. His doctrine concerning the Incarnation was condemned at the Council of Ephesus in 431, and in *Contra Diodorum et Theodorum*, **Cyril of Alexandria** accused Theodore of having taught the same 'impiety' for which **Nestorius** had been condemned. At the second Council of Constantinople in 553, his writings were the first of the Three Chapters to be condemned, and he himself was anathematized as heretical. However, some of his works were translated into Syrian, a heritage of the Nestorian Church, and these show that he may sometimes have been judged unjustly, since his terminology, writing as he did before Chalcedon, could not always be precise on questions of Christology. His insistence on the human soul of Christ, and on the significance of his free moral activity in the work of redemption, are among his positive contributions to the development of Christology.

Theodoret Bishop of Cyrrhus and controversial Church Father, born Antioch, *c.*393, died around 466. He was an important writer in the domains of exegesis, dogmatic theology, church history and ascetic theology. As an exegete Theodoret belongs to the Antiochene school, of which **Diodore** of Tarsus and **Theodore** of Mopsuestia were the heads. As a dogmatic theologian, he took part in the Nestorian controversy and opposed, for more than twenty years, the views of **Cyril** and **Dioscorus** of Alexandria; he taught that in the person of Christ we must strictly distinguish two natures (hypostases), which are united indeed in one person (prosopon), but are not amalgamated in essence. He became bishop of Cyrrhus, a small city in a wild district between Antioch and the Euphrates, where he spent the remainder of his life. Though uncertain, the date of his death must have been some six or seven years later than the Council of Chalcedon in 451. He was diligent in the cure of souls, labouring hard and successfully for the conversion of the numerous Gnostic communities and other heretical sects, which still existed in his diocese. He himself claims to have brought more than a thousand Marcionites within the pale of the Church, and to have destroyed many copies of the *Diatessaron* of **Tatian**, which were still in ecclesiastical use. A century after his death, his writings against Cyril became the subject of the 'Three Chapters' controversy, and were condemned by the Council of Constantinople.

Theodosius I (the Great) Roman Emperor 379–95, dates of birth and death unknown. Shortly after his baptism in 380, he ordered all Christians to profess the faith of the bishops of Rome and Alexandria, that is to say the Nicene Creed. Totally unsympathetic to Arianism, he deposed Demophilus of Constantinople, the Arian bishop, and installed **Gregory of Nazianzus**. Arianism and other heresies became legal offences, sacrifice was forbidden, paganism outlawed, and all church buildings returned to Catholics. The Council of Constantinople abolished Arian claims and its acts were ratified by Theodosius, who published a decree establishing Catholicism as the religion of the Empire. Theodosius showed a willingness, in his relations with St **Ambrose** of Milan, to recognize the limitations of the state in regulating ecclesiastical affairs and, in 390, after the massacre at Thessalonika, accepted Ambrose's dictum that, even in political matters, the emperor was subject to the Church's moral judgements.

Theodulf of Orléans A Visigoth from the Islamic invasion of Spain. Born *c.*750, died 821. He was an important figure at **Charlemagne**'s court; by 798 he was bishop of Orléans and abbot of Fleury, and present at Charlemagne's coronation at Rome in 800. An intimate of the court circle at Aachen, he is a witness to its life and intellectual concerns, and his 79 poems, epigrams and hymns include verses referring to **Alcuin**, Einhard and Charlemagne himself. By his own literary achievements he showed himself a worthy member of the learned circle which graced the Carolingian court. His hymn 'All glory, laud and honour' became the Palm Sunday processional of the western church; six contemporary manuscripts of Theodulf's edition of the Bible survive, two with sumptuous decoration. His most distinctive achievement is his scholarly revision of the Vulgate, which, with its variant readings, even referring back to the original Hebrew, is the most scholarly of the age. Theodulf maintained his influence for a short time after the death of Charlemagne, but he was later accused of having taken part in the conspiracy of Bernard of Italy against Louis I, the Pious, and was exiled, in 818, to a monastery in Angers. He asserted his innocence to the end and, as no proof of his guilt has come down to us, we should presuppose his innocence from what we know of his life and political principles.

Theophan the Recluse (Feofan Govorov) Russian Orthodox saint, bishop and spiritual writer, born Orel district, 10 January 1815, died Vyshi monastery, 6 January 1894. He rose to become bishop of Vladimir but in 1866 retired to become a recluse at a small monastery. There he wrote many letters of spiritual direction, produced Russian versions of the *Philokalia* and composed his own spiritual works on the Jesus Prayer and other topics. His *Path to Salvation* is available in English (1996). Feast day 10 January.

Theophanes the Confessor Saint, historian, born Constantinople, *c.*760, died Samothrace, 12 March 817. He was a court official, and married, but he and his wife both entered monasteries – more correctly, Theophanes founded one himself on Mt Sigriane, but was exiled to Samothrace because he rejected iconoclasm. In his *Chronographia*, which follows a strict chronological narrative, he has

hardly a good word to say for any emperor after **Constantine I**. Feast day 12 March.

Theophilus of Kiev Caves (Feofil) Orthodox saint, monk and 'Fool for Christ's sake', born near Kiev, October 1788, died 28 October 1853. He became a monk but soon began to act in a strange manner, dressing and talking in a way which shocked many. Others began to visit him for help and advice, though he often threw wealthy people out. He was said to have predicted the disasters of the Crimean War to Emperor Nicholas I. Long venerated locally, he was canonized in Ukraine in 1994. Feast day 28 October.

Thérèse of Lisieux Saint, French Carmelite nun, born Alençon, 2 January 1873, died Lisieux, 30 September 1897. Drawn to religious perfection early in life, she entered the Carmelite convent at Lisieux at fifteen, and was professed in 1890. In 1895, on the feast of the Trinity, Thérèse conceived the wish to offer herself as a holocaust victim to the merciful love of the Lord. A few days later, praying the Way of the Cross, a shaft of fire penetrated her: God had ratified her request. In April 1896, Thérèse haemorrhaged for the first time and she was happy to be going soon to heaven. However, her faith in another world was severely tested in the following weeks, made the more burdensome by her growing desire 'to pass her heaven doing good in the world'. Fortified by Our Lord's promise: 'There where I am, you will be also', Thérèse reacted to this temptation by multiplying her acts of faith, and offering her sufferings for the unbelieving. A year after her death appeared *Histoire d'une âme*, her autobiography, to which the superior, Agnes, her older sister, had appended fragments of letters, poems, prayers and souvenirs. Thérèse is known and invoked throughout the world; miracles and conversions multiply. She was canonized in 1925 by **Pius XI**, who declared her 'the star of his pontificate'. In 1927, he named her patron of the missions, the equal of **Francis Xavier** and, in 1944, she joined **Joan of Arc** as patroness of France. Feast day 1 October.

Therry, John Joseph Irish pioneer priest in Australia, born Cork, 1790, died Sydney, 25 May 1864. Educated at St Patrick's College, Carlow, and ordained in 1815, he went to New South Wales in 1820 as official chaplain to the British convict colony. For ten years he fought alone for religious liberty and equal status for Catholics against the dominance of an Anglican-oriented administration. A forthright, uncompromising and rugged character, he protested unceasingly against the abuses of the convict system and the treatment of his people. He built the first Catholic churches and schools, and restored among convicts, mostly from Ireland, the self-respect, faith and hope they had lost under a harsh penal system. His charity was in the tradition of St **Vincent de Paul**, undiscriminating, available to all, and he went out of his way for prisoners and road gangs. He laid the groundwork for the acceptance of religious equality in New South Wales, once Catholic Emancipation was achieved in England. He became a parish priest near Sydney in 1835, when the first bishop was appointed; later at Hobart in Tasmania and Melbourne, and again in Sydney in 1847. He is buried in the crypt of St Mary's Cathedral, which he founded.

Thierry of Chartres Scholar, archdeacon, born Brittany, about 1100, died Chartres, c.1155. He was present at the Council of Soissons of 1121, taught in Paris between 1125 and 1141 and was made archdeacon of Dreux in 1137. He taught the liberal arts, which included logic and rhetoric, and Greek philosophy, in terms of which he sought to explain aspects of Christian doctrine. Highly thought of in his day as a philosopher, he bequeathed his library to the cathedral, and retired to a monastery.

Thomas, Ronald Stuart Anglican clergyman and poet, born Cardiff, 29 March 1913, died near Holyhead, 25 September 2000. He was born in Cardiff but the family settled in Holyhead in 1918. He read classics at University College, Bangor, and trained for ministry in the Church in Wales at St Michael's College, Llandaf. He was ordained in 1936 and served in Chirk, Denbighshire, and then Hammer in Flintshire. He became rector of Manafon, Monmouth, in 1942, and began to learn Welsh, and to publish poetry: his first volume appeared in 1946. In 1954 he moved to Eglwysfach, Cardiganshire, in order to be in closer contact with Welsh-speakers. In 1967 he moved to a largely Welsh-speaking parish at Aberdaron in Caerna-

vonshire. He retired from the ministry in 1978, going to live at Y Rhiw, near Aberdaron. His poetry – he published more than twenty volumes – reflected the Welsh countryside and its people and, particularly, a grimly austere view of religion. He became an ardent Welsh nationalist, even speaking, in the 1990s, in defence of those setting fire to English-owned holiday homes. In 1993 he moved back to Holyhead, and remained there until his death. He was several times nominated for, but never awarded, the Nobel Prize for Literature.

Thomas à Kempis Ascetical writer, born Kempsen, the Rhineland, c.1380, died Zwolle, The Netherlands, 8 August 1471. He went to school in Kempsen, studied at Deventer and entered the Mount St Agnes monastery of the Canons of St Augustine, where he was ordained in 1413, and remained until his death, preaching, writing, copying MSS and widely sought after as a spiritual adviser. His writings ranged in ascetics, homiletics, poetry, biography, etc., all of which are pervaded by the devotional spirit which finds its expression in the *De Imitatione Christi*. He is considered the most complete and outstanding representative of the 'Devotio Moderna', as articulated in his treatises on the life of the soul and in his conferences, *Orationes et Meditationes de Vita Christi*, and *Soliloquium Animae*.

Thomas Aquinas Saint, philosopher and theologian, born Roccasecca, near Monte Casino, c.1225, died Fossanuova, near Maenza, 7 March 1274. Eminent in the history of European thought, he is its most important and influential Scholastic theologian and philosopher, of whom **Pius XI** said that the Church had made him 'her very own'. He joined the Dominicans in 1244; kidnapped by his shocked and disapproving family and shut up for a year, he would not change his mind. On his release he went to study at Cologne, where **Albert the Great** soon recognized his genius, and the two were in profound intellectual sympathy; he became master in theology in 1256. The rest of Thomas' life was spent between Paris and Italy, studying, lecturing, preaching and, above all, writing incessantly. During his first teaching appointment at Paris he wrote a defence of the mendicant orders against **William of St Amour**, a commentary on the *Sentences* of **Peter Lombard**, *De Ente et Essen-*

tia, and works on Isaiah and Matthew. In 1259, he began *Summa contra Gentiles*, a treatise on God and his creation argued partly by the use of pure reason, without faith, against Islam, Jewry, heretics and pagans. Islam had produced famous Aristotelian thinkers, and Thomas' aim was to answer them from Aristotle himself. In 1266 he started his *Summa Theologiae*, a great theological synthesis of theology and a comprehensive statement of his mature thought on all the Christian mysteries; it proceeds through objections and authoritative replies in each article to a concise summary of his views on the matter under discussion, after which the various objections are answered. The work is organized in three parts which treat respectively of God and creation, of the human person as a free moral agent, and of Christ as the way of man to God. He treated sacred doctrine as a single discipline embracing the whole life of the Church, including worship, morals and spiritual practice. Various of his teachings were attacked during his life and after his death, but from 1278, general chapters insisted that his writings be respected and defended within the Order. He was canonized in 1323 by **John XXII**. Thomism was revived in the sixteenth century, and by the time of the Council of Trent, the Church had accepted the substance of his teaching as an authentic expression of doctrine. In 1567, **Pius V** declared him Doctor of the Church; in 1879, **Leo XIII**'s bull, *Aeterni Patris*, enjoined the study of Aquinas on all theological students as a clear, systematic philosophy capable of defending Christian tradition from contemporary attack. In 1880 Thomas was declared patron of all Catholic universities and, in 1923, **Pius XI** reiterated his authority as a teacher. In 1974, **Paul VI** proposed Thomas as a model for theologians, not only for his doctrinal positions, but also for his openness to the world of his day. Since Vatican II, there has been another revival of Thomistic studies and renewed interest in his teaching, not limited within confessional boundaries, notably on the value of his thought on moral development. Feast day 28 January.

Thomas Becket Saint, archbishop and martyr, born London, 1118, murdered in Canterbury cathedral, England, 29 December 1170. He was educated at Merton Priory and in Paris. He worked as a merchant in London before joining the household of the archbishop of Canterbury, who made him archdeacon, and recommended him to King Henry II, whom he subsequently, from 1154, served well as chancellor. The king appointed him archbishop of Canterbury in 1162, seeing this as a way of imposing royal authority over the Church. But Becket opposed the king's attempts and, after several years of conflict and attempts at reconciliation, the king declared he wanted rid of him. Four knights murdered the archbishop as he prepared for vespers. The people acclaimed him a saint and the king had to acknowledge his crime by fasting, walking barefoot to Canterbury and submitting to scourging. Becket was canonized in 1173. Feast day 29 December.

Thompson, Francis English poet and critic. Born Preston, Lancashire, 18 December 1859, died London, 13 November 1907. His father converted to Catholicism; Francis was educated at Ushaw College, and determined on a literary life. A period of friendlessness and failure followed, in which he became a solitary figure, addicted to opium, living as a derelict in the streets and alleys, who yet turned his visions of beauty into verse. In 1893 he sent a poem to the magazine *Merrie England*, which was published by Wilfrid Meynell, and he and his wife sought out Francis and rescued him from starvation and self-destruction. Critics were sympathetic to a volume of his verse, *Poems*, and Coventry **Patmore** wrote a eulogistic notice in the *Fortnightly Review*, in 1894. The beauty and strange inventiveness of his diction gave him a place by himself among contemporary poets, more akin to Keats and Shelley than any of his own day. *Sister Songs* (1895), and *New Poems* (1897) confirmed the opinion formed of his remarkable gifts. He wrote nearly 500 reviews and critical essays during his last ten years; a life of St **Ignatius of Loyola** (1909), and of St **John Baptist de la Salle** (1911). Among his work there is a certain amount that can be called eccentric, but the beautiful *The Daisy*, his intimate and reverent poems about children, and his magnificent 'The Hound of Heaven', are unsurpassed for inspiration and utterance, making him unique among the poets of his time.

Thompson, Frank Charles Methodist minister and creator of *Thompson's Chain Reference Bible*, born Elmira, New York, 1858, died 1940. Thompson became a minister in 1879, and while pastoring at Genesee, New York, church members offered to pay for publication of the marginal notes in his Bible. The first edition of his Bible appeared in 1908, and it became popular from 1915, since when around 3 million copies have been sold. The Bible was endorsed by Aimee Semple **McPherson**, and is popular among Pentecostal Christians. Thompson also wrote *Barriers to Eden* (c.1939) and *Bob's Hike to the Holy City* (n.d.).

Thurston, Herbert Henry Charles   Jesuit priest and historian, born London, 15 November 1856, died London, 3 November 1939. He was educated at Jesuit schools in England and joined the English Jesuits in 1874. Four years later he was awarded his BA at the University of London, and then followed the usual course of studies, interrupted by a lengthy period of teaching at Beaumont College, Old Windsor, from 1880 to 1887. He was ordained priest in September 1890, and worked in the Jesuit school in Wimbledon before going to the Jesuit community in Mayfair in 1894, where he stayed until his death. He published nearly 800 articles in a range of Catholic periodicals, mainly on historical topics. His scholarship was impeccable, and he did not let his own undoubted piety get in the way of his researches. He wrote some 150 articles for *The Catholic Encyclopedia*, and between 1926 and 1938 helped to revise Butler's *Lives of the Saints*, producing an edition which remained the standard for over half a century. He published a number of books, some of them on psychic phenomena, in which he had a particular interest. Three books were published long after his death by his biographer, Joseph Crehan, SJ.

Tikhon of Moscow (Bellavin)   Saint and patriarch of Moscow, born Pskov Province, Russia, 19 January 1865, died Moscow, 7 April 1925. Appointed bishop for North America in 1898, he greatly extended the Russian diocese there, accepting dozens of former uniate parishes and encouraging the liturgical use of English. In 1917 he was elected the first Russian patriarch since the seventeenth century. He led the Church against the Bolshevik persecution and protested against the laws from the beginning; he was imprisoned, abused, threatened and finally probably poisoned. He was buried in his beloved Donskoy Monastery. Canonized 1989. Feast day 7 April.

Tikhon of Zadonsk   Russian Orthodox saint, bishop and spiritual writer, born near Novgorod, 1724, died Zadonsk monastery, 13 August 1783. In 1763 he was appointed to the important Voronezh diocese, but he resigned in 1767 and from 1769 until his death lived in seclusion at Zadonsk. His spiritual writings have always been popular in Russia and include *Journey to Heaven* and *Instructions to the Clergy*. Canonized 1861. Feast day 13 August.

Tile, Nehemiah   Founder of the first African Initiated Church in South Africa, born c.1850 from southern Nguni, died 1891. During the 1870s he was an evangelist for the Wesleyan Methodist Mission in the Eastern Cape and became a minister in 1879. In 1883 he was denied full minister status because the mission disapproved of his attempts to prevent the government imposing their administration on the Thembu people. From this dispute the Thembu National Church was born in 1884. Although its connection with Thembu politics faded it remained a strong independent church.

Tillich, Paul   German-American theologian and philosopher of religion. Born Starzeddel, Brandenberg, 20 August 1886, died Chicago, Illinois, 22 October 1965. Son of a Lutheran pastor, he studied at Berlin, Tübingen and Halle, and became a minister and chaplain in the Great War. Compelled by his connection with the Religious Socialists to leave Germany in 1933, he went to the USA and a professorship at Union Theological Seminary, NY, at the invitation of **Reinhold Niebuhr**. He was professor at Harvard in 1955, and Nuveen professor of theology at the Divinity School, Chicago, in 1962. Tillich was very influential in his aim to bridge the gap between Christian faith and modern culture, in making it intelligible to secular man while preserving its unique substance. His 'method of correlation' aimed to illustrate that the content of Christian revelation answers the questions arising out of the cultural situation; each age finds the particular aspect of the Gospel most relevant to its problems. The problem of today arises from man's estrangement, his anxiety at the threat of 'non-being' but, through participation in

God, he can acquire the courage to exist even in the face of anxiety. His most important work is probably *Systematic Theology* (3 vols, 1951–64), in which he discusses the value of symbolic statements about God and how they can be interpreted as identifying God as 'being-itself'.

Timothy Ailouros Saint (in the Coptic Church), bishop of Alexandria, date of birth unknown, died Alexandria, 31 July 477. His nickname means 'the cat', or 'the weasel'. As a priest, he opposed the Council of Chalcedon, and organized Monophysite resistance to it in Egypt. He was exiled by the Emperor Leo I, acting under pressure from Pope **Leo I**, when he had become bishop of Alexandria after the assassination of his orthodox rival. He regained the bishopric briefly, after being recalled from exile in 475.

Tippett, (Sir) Michael English composer and conductor, born London, 2 January 1905, died London, 10 January 1998. He studied at the Royal College of Music and became director of music at Morley College. He was brought up in the Anglican Church. His music shows great humanistic compassion for mankind, as expressed in *A Child of Our Time*, in which the negro spirituals fulfilled the same role as the Lutheran chorales in J. S. **Bach**'s *St Matthew Passion*. Tippett was influenced by English sixteenth-century composers, American blues and **Beethoven**. His works inspired by religious themes include *The Vision of St Augustine*, a *Magnificat* and *Nunc Dimittis* and, for organ, *Preludio al Vespro di Monteverdi*.

Tischendorf, Kobegott Friedrich Konstantin Von German biblical critic, born Legenfeld, Saxony, 18 January 1815, died Leipzig, 7 December 1874. He studied at Leipzig and was influenced by J. B. Winer to take a special interest in NT criticism. In 1840 he qualified as lecturer in theology with a dissertation on the recensions of the NT text, becoming convinced of the need for new and exacter collations of MSS. The great triumph of the next laborious years was the decipherment of the palimpsest 'Codex Ephraemi Syri Rescriptus', of which both the OT and the NT were printed before 1845. From a trip to Sinai he brought a great treasure, 43 leaves of the OT book of what is now known as the 'Codex Sinaiticus', published in 1846 as the 'Codex Frederico-Augustanus'. In 1853 and 1859, he made two more voyages, during the last of which, financed by the Russian government, he at length got access to the remainder of the precious Sinaitic codex, and persuaded the monks to present it to the Tsar, at whose cost it was published in 1862, in four folio volumes, as 'Bibliorum Codex Sinaiticus'. Among his other important work were eight editions of the Greek NT, the last of which (1869) remains a standard work of reference for the NT.

Tisserant, Eugène Gabriel French cardinal and scholar. Born Nancy, 24 March 1884, died Albano, Italy, 21 February 1972. He studied at the Ecole Biblique in Jerusalem; Ecole des Hautes Etudes, Ecole des Langues Orientales and Institut Catholique, Paris. Ordained in 1907, he began his career as a 'scriptor orientalis' in the Vatican Library. He served in the Great War and returned to the Vatican, where as assistant prefect of the library from 1919 to 1930, he searched out rare books and manuscripts in Eastern Europe and the Near East. He became prefect of the library, and a bishop in 1937. Known in the curia as 'Il Francese', he played an important role in church affairs for more than half a century. By his own admission, he took issue in 1940 with **Pius XII** for his 'apostolic silence', in the knowledge of the crimes of the belligerents; and he berated the Ustasi representative for the crimes of Croatian Catholics. As prefect for the Congregation for the Oriental Churches, he attempted to steer the Vatican through the innumerable difficulties of the Eastern churches during and after World War II. He was a traditionalist and an influential head of the Board of Presidents at Vatican II. He supported **Paul VI**'s policies in the post-conciliar period, and was seen by many of the laity as adopting a less than progressive stance in the controversy surrounding the encyclical letter *Humanae Vitae* of 1968.

Titian Anglicized form of the name Tiziano Vecelli, Italian painter, born at Pieve, in Cadore, Republic of Venice, c.1488/90, died Venice, 27 August 1576. He studied in Venice under Gentile **Bellini**, then with **Giorgione**, where he became well known. He became the council of Venice's official painter. In Rome, Pope **Paul III** commissioned work from him. He painted portraits of the Pope and met **Michelangelo**. He is regarded as one of the greatest of all portrait painters. His work includes *The Assumption of the Virgin* and *Christ and the Tribute Money*.

Tolkien, John Ronald Reuel English writer, born Bloemfontein, Orange Free State, South Africa, 3 January 1892, died Bournemouth, England, 22 September 1973. At the age of three he came to Britain on holiday with his mother, but his father died while they were away, and his mother made their home near Birmingham. He attended St Edward's Grammar School, where he was an outstanding pupil, and Exeter College, Oxford. His mother, who had become a Roman Catholic, had died when he was twelve, and he was made a ward of one of the Fathers of the Birmingham Oratory: his deep religious faith greatly influenced his writings. He was in the Battle of the Somme, and though he escaped without wound, his health suffered greatly, and he was spared further war service. He returned to Oxford and in 1925 became professor of Anglo-Saxon and English literature. He wrote many scholarly essays and also poems and plays but he is certainly most famous for his books *The Hobbit* (1937) and *The Lord of the Rings* (1954–5), the latter concerning a series of myths created by Tolkien himself and describing the struggle between good and evil.

Tolstoi, Leo Nikolaevich Russian author, born Yasnaya Polyana, Tula Province, 9 September 1828, died, of pneumonia, on Astapovo railway station, 20 November 1910. He was born into an aristocratic family and, as a boy, inherited his father's huge estate. He went to Kazan University to study oriental languages, but returned to his estates without taking a degree. He then led a somewhat dissolute life, which he quickly found unsatisfactory, and in 1851 joined an artillery regiment in the Caucasus – the experience inspired his first writings. He was in command of a battery at the siege of Sebastopol during the Crimean War. After the war he travelled for a time in western Europe and then returned to his estate as a progressive-minded landlord. He married in 1862, and had thirteen children. He had written a number of stories born of his war experiences and his travels, but his greatest novel, *War and Peace* (1865–9) reflects a philosophical theory of the meaning of

historical events. *Anna Karenina* was published 1873–7. He had given up the Orthodox Faith at the age of sixteen, believing that the essence of Christianity was love of neighbour and non-resistance to evil. Despite being excommunicated by the Orthodox Church in 1910, he was much visited by people who admired his belief in the simple goodness of the Russian peasant – a type of life he attempted to live under his own roof. His wife refused to conform to his new asceticism, and it was in flight from his house and family that he died, accompanied by his youngest daughter.

Tomlinson, Ambrose Jessup Pentecostal leader, born near Westfield, Indiana, 22 September 1865, died 2 October 1943. Tomlinson joined a Holiness group in 1903, soon becoming pastor of several affiliated churches. In 1907 the churches adopted the name Church of God (a term in use elsewhere), and Tomlinson became permanent overseer in 1914. In 1907 he had a Pentecostal experience. He travelled widely and supported racially integrated churches. He produced the magazines *Samson's Foxes* (1901–2), *The Evening Light* and *Church of God Evangel* (from 1910) and *Faithful Standard*, as well as articles and a book, *Last Great Conflict* (1913).

Tomlinson, Homer General overseer of the Church of God (Queens, New York), born 1892, died 4 December 1968. The eldest son of Ambrose **Tomlinson**, Homer pursued a career in advertising while helping his father. When he did not succeed to his father's position, he founded his own denomination. He performed a coronation service for himself in 101 capital cities, claiming that his presence brought prosperity and stopped conflict. He also ran for president for the Theocratic Party, promising to end the Church–State division. In *Shout of the King* he claimed to be friends with Eisenhower, Roosevelt and the Wright brothers.

Toplady, Augustus Montague Calvinistic Anglican clergyman and hymnwriter, born Farnham, Surrey, 4 November 1740, died of tuberculosis, London, 11 August 1778. Educated at Westminster School and Trinity College, Dublin. Converted in 1755 and ordained as priest in 1764. Served as minister in several locations, including Broad Hembury, Devon. In 1775 he became minister of the French

Calvinist Reformed Church in London. A bitter opponent of John **Wesley**'s Arminianism, the two men exchanged pamphlets critical of the other. He wrote several hymns, the most famous being 'Rock of Ages'. His published works include a translation of Jerome Zanchius' *Absolute Predestination* (1769).

Torquemada, Tomás de Spanish inquisitor general, born Valladolid, 1420; died Ávila, 16 September 1498. He joined the Dominicans at Valladolid at an early age, and his biographers state that his modesty was so great that he refused to accept the doctor's degree in theology, the Order's most prized honour. In 1842 he was appointed an inquisitor in the newly established Spanish Inquisition, and first inquisitor general in 1483. The political and social confusion of Spain he attributed to the lax toleration of religious differences he thought he saw among Christians, Jews, Saracens, heretics and apostates, and persuaded **Isabella** and Ferdinand V to reorganize the Inquisition, established in Spain since 1236. For their part the monarchs saw in this a means of overcoming the independence of the nobility and clergy, by which the royal power had been obstructed, and thereby to unite the kingdoms of Spain. A papal bull was issued by **Sixtus IV** in 1479 authorizing a new form of Inquisition and, in 1483, the whole Inquisition for Castile and Aragon was unified under Torquemada's control. During the eighteen years of his absolute authority, it is said that he burnt some 2000 persons, and otherwise punished vast numbers. He was bent on ridding the country of the hated Moors, and by 1490 they had been vanquished. It was then the turn of the Jews, and the sovereigns issued a decree ordering every Jew to either embrace Christianity or leave the country within four months. But Torquemada forbade Christians any contact with Jews, so they could not sell their goods, which fell to the Inquisition. Nearly one million Jewish families were thus driven out of the country by Torquemada; the loss to Spain was enormous, and led to the commercial decay of the country. The name of Torquemada stands in history for all that is intolerant and narrow, despotic and cruel. He was no real statesman or minister of the Gospel, but a blind fanatic, who failed to see that faith cannot be imposed by force.

Torres, Camilo Colombian priest, sociologist, revolutionary. Born Bogotá, 3 February 1927, died 16 February 1966. Born into a ruling family, he was ordained at the diocesan seminary in Bogotá in 1953, and studied at the Catholic University, Louvain, where he was rector of the Latin American College. He returned to Bogotá as chaplain of the university, and began actively to criticize and to propose rectification of the social inequalities which, though he initially thought they could be achieved within existing social and political structures, he soon saw would require radical change in the structures themselves. To this end, he founded the United Front, in 1964, into which he attempted to recruit people of widely divergent political views. However, the radical solutions he proposed evoked strong opposition from the government and the Catholic hierarchy; he called for revolution, and a break became inevitable. He was granted laicization in June 1965, and the same year he joined a guerilla movement of the left; in the following February, he was killed in an ambush on a military patrol. Torres never abandoned his claim to be a Catholic, a priest and a revolutionary. He persuaded many to follow him, and even those who could not subscribe to his ideals respected his integrity and dedication. His call to revolutionary action against entrenched injustice has made him an inspiration and a legend.

Torres, Francisco Jesuit theologian and controversialist, born Herrera, Palencia, *c*.1504, died Rome, 21 November 1584. He studied at Salamanca and then came to Rome. He attended the Council of Trent in 1562–3 as a papal theologian. In 1567 he joined the Jesuits and became professor of the Roman College, where he assisted in the revision of the Vulgate. He defended the authenticity of many controversial documents, including Apostolic canons and the Nicene canons, and upheld controverted doctrines such as the Immaculate Conception, the superiority of Pope over councils, Communion under one kind, and the divine origin of episcopal authority. He was very anti-Protestant in his stance.

Traherne, Thomas Mystical writer and metaphysical poet, born Hereford, 1637, died Teddington, 27 September 1674. He was educated at Oxford, was ordained and lived in Credenhill, Herefordshire, and London. He wrote *Roman Forgeries* (1673), which claimed, as the title suggests, that significant Roman Catholic documents were forgeries. His *Christian Ethics*, was published the year after his death, but he is most highly regarded for his poetical *Centuries of Meditation*, not published until 1903. He also wrote the poems *The Rapture* and *An Hymn upon St Bartholomew's Day*.

Tregelles, Samuel Prideaux　Biblical textual critic, born Falmouth, 30 January 1813, died Plymouth, 24 April 1875. Tregelles learned Hebrew, Aramaic, Greek and Welsh while working at Neath Abbey Ironworks in South Wales. From 1838 he was engaged in the production of a new critical Greek text for the NT to replace the *Textus Receptus*. He travelled widely, collating hundreds of MSS, giving an interim report in *An Account of the Printed Text of the Greek NT* (1854) and publishing the text intermittently, book-by-book between 1857 and 1870.

Trembelas, Panagiotis　Greek Orthodox lay theologian, born 1886, died Athens, 18 November 1977. He was professor of dogmatics at Athens from 1939 to 1957 and the author of 78 theological works. He was a founder-member of the Zoe Brotherhood and of a new spiritual movement 'Sotir' in 1960. His principle work is *Dogmatics of the Orthodox Catholic Church* (3 vols, 1961), which has been translated into French.

Troeltsch, Ernst　German theologian and philosopher, born near Augsburg, 17 February 1865, died Berlin, 1 February 1923. The son of a doctor, a Lutheran in a Catholic part of Germany, he studied partly in a Catholic school, then at the Universities of Erlangen and Göttingen. He was ordained in 1889, and worked for a year in his home parish before returning to Göttingen, where, in 1891, he was appointed to teach theology. He moved to Bonn in 1829 and Heidelberg in 1894 and was professor of philosophy and civilization at Berlin from 1915 until his death. He was among the earliest scholars to apply sociological theories to theology and to be open to serious dialogue with other religions. His writings include *Die Absolutheit des Christentums und die Religionsgeschichte* (1902), *Die Soziallehren der christlichen Kirchen und Gruppen* (1912), *Der Historismus und seine Probleme* (1922) and *Christian Thought: Its History and Application* (1923).

Troy, John Thomas　Irish Dominican, archbishop, born Blanchardstown, Dublin, 10 May 1739, died Dublin, 11 May 1823. Studied in Dublin, joined the Dominicans there and was sent to Rome. Taught philosophy, theology and canon law and in 1772 became prior. In 1776 he was named bishop of Ossary, Ireland. He was not popular with the clergy nor with the people, whose violent efforts to overcome injustices he denounced, but his legalistic approach did result in improvements in education and in reform among the clergy. In 1781 he was appointed adminstrator of Armagh, and in 1786 archbishop of Dublin. In 1798 he threatened excommunication to those who joined the rebellion. He was greatly in support of the Union and in 1799 accepted the government veto on the appointment of Irish bishops.

Truth, Sojourner　Abolitionist and preacher, born as Isabella, a slave in Hurley, New York, about 1797, died 26 November 1883. At her mother's knee she developed a deep faith in the loving and strong God who would one day help her to be free. She married and had five children and one day simply walked away from her master's farm, taking her youngest child with her, and went to New York. She felt called to spread what she understood as God's will for freedom and equality for black people and, having changed her name, she became an itinerant preacher. She called for repentance of sins, the results of which she saw as embracing the liberation of women and of all black people. In 1847 the autobiography which she had dictated, *The Narrative of Sojourner Truth*, was published. She supported the Union Army in the Civil War, and in 1864 she met Abraham Lincoln and stayed on in Washington to work among the former slaves in the refugee camps. Although she witnessed the formal abolition of slavery in 1865, she spent the remainder of her life working towards winning real freedom and equality for black people.

Tubman, Harriet　Abolitionist, born a slave on a plantation in Maryland, USA, about 1820, died a free woman in Auburn, New York, 10 March 1913. From a very young age she had experienced visions and had resisted internalizing her oppression and, putting her faith in the God of Moses rather than the slave owners, vowed to be free one day. Eventually she escaped from the plantation and got to Pennsylvania, a free state, where she set about arranging the liberation of other slaves. She worked for the Union Army in the Civil War, as a nurse and also as a spy and scout. She remained poor, and gained little public recognition and acclaim, but continued to work with and for those weaker and poorer than herself.

Tucker, Alfred Robert Anglican bishop of Uganda, born 1849, Woolwich, England, died London, 15 June 1914. Supported by the Church Missionary Society (CMS) he arrived in Uganda in December 1890 to work with a rapidly expanding church. He upheld **Venn**'s principle of self-government for the 'native' church, ordaining the first six deacons in 1893. By 1908 the Ugandan church had greater autonomy than most other churches in Africa but his missionary colleagues refused to be under the local church. He was instrumental in Uganda becoming a British Protectorate, first by raising funds to enable the East Africa Company to remain in Uganda, 1891, and then encouraging the British government to take over. In this he argued that the civilizing effects of Christianity would prevent further civil war.

Turibius of Lima *see* **Mogrovejo, Toribio Alfonso de**

Turner, Cuthbert Hamilton Church historian and NT scholar, born London, 12 July 1860, died Oxford, 10 October 1930. He was educated at Winchester and at New College, Oxford, where he first studied classics and then theology. He became an assistant lecturer at St John's College, in 1888 assistant lecturer to the Regius Professor of ecclesiastical history and the following year a fellow of Magdalen College. He was Dean Ireland professor of exegesis from 1920 till 1930. He was the first editor, in 1899, of the *Journal of Theological Studies* and wrote extensively throughout his career, being mainly concerned with issues around chronology and textual criticism, though in later life he made a particular study of the Gospel of Mark. His major work was as editor of the massive *Ecclesiae Occidentalis Monumenta Juris Antiquis-*

sima (1899–1930), which includes documents relating to Western canon law. He produced a great number of short studies, including a classic study of the 'Chronology of the NT' in Hasting's *Dictionary of the Bible.*

Tyndale, William (or Tindale) English biblical translator and Protestant martyr. Born Monmouthshire, *c*.1491, died Vilvorde, Belgium, 6 October 1536. He studied at Oxford and removed to Cambridge, where **Erasmus** had helped to establish a reputation for Greek and theology. He was ordained in 1521, and began his translation of the NT. Unable to get support in England, and suspected of heresy, he went to Germany and settled in Hamburg, never to return to England. He met **Luther**, many of whose views he shared, and began to print his translation at Cologne in 1525, but this was interrupted by the magistrates and completed at Worms that year. On its arrival in England in 1526, it was bitterly attacked by Archbishop **Warham** of Canterbury, Bishop Tunstall of London and Thomas **More**; two editions were published at Worms, and he revised it in 1535. He also translated the Pentateuch (1530), and Jonah (1531). Tyndale's translations, direct from the Greek and Hebrew into straightforward, vigorous English, remain the basis of both the Authorized and the Revised versions. Like Luther, he insisted on the authority of Scripture in he Church, but he moved away from Luther's teaching on justification by faith alone towards the idea of double justification by faith and works. He wrote against Thomas **Wolsey** and the 'Divorce' (*Practice of Prelates*, 1530), and against More, his ablest opponent, who defended the Church and its authority against his bitter attack upon it. He was arrested for heresy through treachery, in 1535, imprisoned, strangled and burnt at the stake.

Tyrrell, George Jesuit and Modernist theologian, born Dublin, Ireland, 6 February 1861, died Storrington, 15 July 1909. An Anglican, he became a Catholic in 1879 and joined the Jesuits, being ordained in 1891. He taught moral philosophy for two years before being assigned, in 1896, to the staff of the Jesuit journal *The Month*, for which he wrote a large number of articles, some of which were reprinted in book form. Much of his published writings were on spirituality, and were much admired. They did, however, attract the criticism of ecclesiastical censors, and he was withdrawn from *The Month* in 1900 and sent to a parish in Richmond, Yorkshire. He continued to publish privately, however, in contravention of the rule of the Jesuits, and he was dismissed in 1906. In 1907,

Pope **Pius IX** condemned Tyrrell and other 'Modernists', such as Maude **Petre**, in whose house he was now staying, in the encyclical *Pascendi*. He was excommunicated, though he continued to assert he was a loyal Catholic. He was forbidden a Catholic funeral, but Henri **Bremond** presided at the service, for which he, too, was punished.

U

Ullathorne, William Bernard English monk and archbishop, born Pocklington, Yorkshire, 7 May 1806, died Oscott, Warwickshire, 21 March 1889. Of an old English family and descendant of Thomas **More**, he was ordained a Benedictine in 1530. He served as vicar general of Australia, where he organized the Church, working especially among the convicts, whose cause he exposed in *Horrors of Transportation*, an attack on British policy and the convict system. He returned to England in 1840, and an appointment as vicar apostolic for the Western and Central Districts, in 1848. He played a leading role in the restoration of the English hierarchy, in 1850, when he was appointed bishop of Birmingham. He worked closely with Cardinal **Wiseman** to reconcile the old Catholics with the recent Oxford converts and the Italian priests of the modern congregations, taking up an intermediate position, and forming a firm friendship with J. H. **Newman**. During his 38-year tenure of the see, 67 new churches, 32 convents and nearly 200 mission schools were built. He resigned in 1888, having been a moving force in the nineteenth-century revival of Catholicism in England.

Underhill, Evelyn Anglican exponent of the mystical life. Born Wolverhampton, 6 December 1875, died London, 15 June 1941. The only daughter of a distinguished agnostic of a tolerant disposition, she was educated at King's College, London. At the age of 32, she became convinced, while on a retreat at a convent, of the truth of Catholicism. She deferred conversion to Rome, however, because of her engagement to Stuart Moore, whom she later married, but then resolved not to enter the Church at all after the papal encyclical *Pascendi* condemned modernism, with which she sympathized. In her spiritual struggles she turned to study of the mystics; in 1911 she published *Mysticism*, which has become a standard work on the subject, covering a range from **Teresa of Ávila** to J. **Böhme**, and from Christian mystical experience to Neoplatonist speculations. In 1911 she came to know Baron **von Hügel**, who became her spiritual director in 1921, and led her to communicant membership in the Church of England. She was the first woman invited to give a series of theological lectures at Oxford University in 1921. A prolific writer of smaller books blending scholarship and devotion, the most important work of her later years was *Worship* (1936), which embodied her general outlook in a broad review of the subject. In her last years, just prior to the war, she became an ardent pacifist.

Urban I Saint, Pope 222 to 230. Little is known of his pontificate. He is sometimes said to have been a martyr, but there was no persecution in Rome during his time in office. Feast day 25 May.

Urban II Blessed, Pope March 1088 to July 1099. Born Chatillon-sur-Marne, *c.*1042, died Rome, 1099. Odon de Chatillon studied at Rheims, under St **Bruno**, who afterwards became his most trusted adviser, and in 1070 entered the monastery of Cluny. He was called to Rome, where **Gregory VII** made him cardinal bishop of Ostia in 1080. He was elected to the Papacy in 1088, adhered to the Gregorian reform and sought ways to restore relations with the Byzantine church. He presided at the Council of Melfi in 1089, which renewed the prohibitions against simony, lay investiture and the marriage of priests; at Piacenza in 1095, he declared the ordinations of **Clement III**, the Anti-pope, and his adherents, void and, in response to an appeal from the Byzantine emperor, Alexis I Comnenus, called on Christian warriors to defend the Eastern church. At Clermont, in the same year, Urban preached the first Crusade, the most memorable achievement of his pontificate. However, if his success in preaching the Crusade illustrated the remarkable recovery of the Papacy, his vision of 'rapprochement' with Byzantium, and church unity, was doomed to failure. The division was only reinforced with a stronger, more centralized government in the emergence of the Roman curia, and a growth in the influence of the college of cardinals. Urban died before the news of the capture of Jerusalem by the Crusaders could reach him. Feast day 29 July.

Urban III Pope, born Umberto Crivelli into a noble family in Milan, elected 25 November 1185, died Ferrara, 19 October 1187. He had been archdeacon of Bourges, then of Milan, before being made a cardinal in 1182 and archbishop of Milan (an office he retained during his pontificate) in January 1185. He was elected Pope at Verona, and stayed there because of Roman hostility. He was antagonistic towards the Emperor **Frederick Barbarossa** for largely family reasons, and refused to crown Frederick's son Henry as co-emperor. When this coronation was performed by the patriarch of Aquileia, he suspended him from office. He also refused to accept the common practice that, during a vacancy, the proceeds of a benefice should go to the crown. The final break came over his refusal to accept Frederick's candidate for the bishopric of Trier and appointed his own. Frederick sent his son to invade the Papal States and managed to unite the majority of the German bishops behind his policy. Urban at first gave in, then changed his mind and proposed excommunicating Frederick, but the city of Verona decided they no longer wanted the Pope on their territory. He was on his way to Ferrara when he died.

Urban IV Pope, born Jacques Pantaléon at Troyes, France, c.1200, elected 29 August 1261, died Perugia, 2 October 1264. The son of a shoemaker, he studied in Paris, became archdeacon of Liège and came to the notice of **Innocent IV** at the Council of Lyons in 1245, who used him as a diplomat. In

1252 he became bishop of Verdun and three years later patriarch of Jerusalem. He was not a cardinal when elected Pope: there were only eight cardinals at the time and they could not choose one from among themselves. One of his first acts, therefore, was to create fourteen more cardinals. He had to try to establish his authority in Rome. He managed to set up a government there, but it was too insecure for him to move back to the city. His next concern was to regain control of the Papal States, and to prevent Sicily falling into the hands of Manfred, the son of the emperor Frederick II. Urban's proposal was to offer Sicily to Charles of Anjou, who accepted. Manfred took up arms against the Pope, who had to retreat into Orvieto, and then to Perugia, where he died. At the time of his death he was in discussions with the Byzantine emperor, Michael Palaeologus, who was anxious to prevent any renewed Crusade against Constantinople and was prepared to recognize papal authority to this end.

Urban V Blessed, Pope from 28 September 1362, died Avignon, 19 December 1370. He was born Guillaume de Grimoard at Grisac in France in 1310, studied at Montpelier, became a Benedictine in Marseilles and then returned to Montpelier to teach canon law before becoming abbot of St-Germain at Auxerre in 1352 and of St Victor at Marseilles in 1361. He was elected Pope as a compromise candidate in a much-disputed election, the first choice having turned down the office, and as a moderate reformer lived a monastic lifestyle in the papal palace. In 1367 he returned the papal curia to Rome, taking up residence in the Vatican, the papal palace of the Lateran being uninhabitable. He was eager to forward the reunion of the churches of East and West, and was visited in Rome by the Byzantine emperor, though nothing further was achieved. He made efforts to rebuild Rome, including the Lateran, but unrest in Italy, and renewal of the war between England and France in 1370, forced his return to Avignon, where he died a couple of months after his arrival. Feast day 19 December.

Urban VI Pope from 8 April 1378, born Bartolomeo Prignano in 1318 and was a native of Naples, died, possibly of poisoning, Rome, 15 October 1389. Bartolomeo, a canon lawyer, had been archbishop of, successively, Acerenza and, from 1377, Bari. He was a highly efficient, much-admired, papal civil servant first at Avignon and then at Rome. He was hurriedly elected Pope, however, under pressure from the people of Rome for an Italian. However, in August of 1378, French cardinals revolted, declaring the election was void because carried out under duress, and in September that year they elected **Clement VII**, thus beginning the 39-year 'Great Schism', during which there were two, and sometimes three, rival claimants to the Papacy. Urban VI's pontificate was marred by his undoubted instability of temperament, and by violence.

Urban VII   Pope, born Giambattista Castagna at Rome, 4 August 1521, elected 15 September, died 27 September 1596. A doctor of law, he had studied at Perugia, Padua and Bologna, entered the papal civil service as a lawyer and was named archbishop of Rossano in 1553. He attended the final session of the Council of Trent, served in the papal diplomatic service, and became governor of Bologna and an adviser to the Inquisition. He caught malaria the night after his election, and died before he was crowned.

Urban VIII   Pope, August 1623 to July 1644. Born Maffeo Barberini, Florence, 5 April 1568, died Rome, 29 July 1644. Of an old Florentine family, he early entered the papal service, became cardinal in 1606, and finally, after a long, sweltering, contentious conclave, he was elected, by 50 out of 55 possible votes, to succeed **Gregory XV**. Urban was vain, self-willed and extremely conscious of his position; he saw the Papacy chiefly as a temporal principality, and made it his first care to render it formidable. He fortified the port of Città Vecchia and strengthened the Castel Sant' Angelo, equipping it with cannon made from the bronze of the Pantheon, an act of vandalism to which the Romans attributed the epigram 'Quod non fecerunt barbari, fecerunt Barberini'. Among his ecclesiastical activities, he revised the breviary, rewriting many of the hymns himself, and the church calendar; he canonized many saints, including **Ignatius of Loyola**, **Elizabeth of Portugal**, **Francis Borgia**. In 1627, he founded the College of the Propaganda for the education of missionaries. Under him **Galileo Galilei**, whose genius he acknowledged and whose per-

sonal friend he had been for years, was condemned for the second time, in 1633, and compelled to abjure. Urban was the last Pope to practise nepotism on a grand scale. He failed to found a princely house, but he enriched his family to an extent that astonished even the Romans. He made a brother and two nephews cardinals, advanced other brothers and enriched them all so exorbitantly that in old age he felt conscience-stricken. In his closing years, he allowed himself to be involved in a war over the papal fief of Castro, the result of which was a humiliating defeat and crippled finances for the Papal State. The Roman populace, already cruelly oppressed by his prodigal extravagance, broke into riotous jubilation at the news of his death.

Uspensky, Leonid (Leonide Ouspensky)   Orthodox iconographer and lay theologian, born near Voronezh, Russia, died Paris, 12 December 1987. After the revolution he studied art in Paris and became an icon painter. He also collaborated with Vladimir **Lossky** in developing a modern theology of iconography. His main work is *Theology of the Icon* (2 vols, 1992).

Ussher, James   Irish archbishop and scholar, born Dublin, 4 January 1580, died Reigate, 21 March 1656, and on his death was given a state funeral in Westminster Abbey by **Cromwell**, despite his associations with **Charles I**. He was one of the very first students of Trinity College, Dublin, where he studied theology, despite his father's wish that he should travel to London to study law. He became a fellow of the college, and his first visit to England was to buy books for the nascent library of Trinity. He was ordained in 1601, became professor of divinity in 1607, and was twice elected vice-chancellor. In 1621 he became bishop of Meath and in 1625 archbishop of Armagh. He set himself the task of reading through all the Fathers of the Church, and his knowledge was considerable: his works include *Discourse of the Religion currently Professed by the Irish and British* (1622), and the *Annales Veteris et Novi Testamenti* (1650–4), which includes his famous biblical chronology. Starting from the biblical genealogies he calculated that the world was created in 4004 BC. Although a discredited scheme, it ranks as a first attempt at a biblical chronology. After the Irish rebellion of 1641 he spent the remainder of his life in England.

Vagnozzi, Egidio Roman Catholic cardinal and papal diplomat, born Rome, Italy, 2 February 1906, died Rome, 26 December 1986. After training at the Lateran Pontifical Seminary and obtaining three doctorates from the Roman Seminary, Vagnozzi was ordained and served in the Vatican's Secretariat of State, 1930–2, before being transferred to the office of the Apostolic Delegate to the United States, where he served until 1942. After terms in Lisbon, Paris and India, Vagnozzi was made titular archbishop of Myra in 1949 and served as apostolic delegate in 1949–51, and later papal nuncio in 1951–8, in Manila. He became apostolic delegate to the United States in 1958 and in 1967 was created cardinal by Pope **Paul VI**. A year later he was made prefect of economic affairs of the Vatican, where he served until his death.

Valdés, Alfonso de Spanish writer, born Cuenca, 1490, died Vienna, 1532. He was the older of twin brothers, the other being Juan, who are among the most representative figures of the Spanish Renaissance. Alfonso was a noted humanist and admirer of **Erasmus.** After the sack of Rome in 1527, he wrote *Dialogo de Lactantio y un Arcadiano* to justify the event; it vigorously attacks the Papacy for its part in contemporary international politics, and for the corrupt state of the Church over which it presided, especially the curia, setting in contrast the fundamentals of NT Christianity as Erasmus interpreted them. He repeats the same themes in *Dialogo de Mercurio y Caron* (1529), where he attacks religion that has become a matter of outward empty forms, devotion to inanimate objects, and good works undertaken on a quid pro quo basis. Both works incurred the hostility of the

Spanish Inquisition, but had a considerable popular reputation.

Valdés, Juan de Spanish religious writer, born Cuenca, *c.*1490, died Naples, 1541. The younger twin of Alfonso, he studied at Alcala, and fled from the Inquisition in 1531 on publication of his *Dialogo de Doctrina Cristiana*, in 1529, which provoked strong reactions for its Erasmian tendencies. Though he never intended to start a religious movement, he found himself the centre and inspirer of a devoted group of followers anxious for reforms and spiritual revival of the Church, among whom were Giulia Gonzaga and Vittoria **Colonna**. Although he never repudiated the Church or the sacraments, his conception of personal religion and interiority was largely Protestant in character, subordinating ceremony and forms to personal experience of sin and guilt, faith and repentance, and works of love as the fruits of the indwelling Holy Spirit; and this had a wide appeal for the Reformed traditions, after the posthumous publication of his works. The influence of **Erasmus** can be seen in his tendency to go back to the sources of Christianity; his Evangelism and Paulinism; the spiritual interpretation of the Credo, commandments and sacraments, as well as his belief in justification by faith. He wrote a number of other religious works expounding Christian doctrine and the Scriptures, among which *Alfabeto Cristiano* (1536); also, he translated the Hebrew Psalter into Castilian.

Valentine Saint, martyred in the second half of the third century in Rome. Two Valentines are mentioned in early martyrologies as having feast days on 14 February. One was a Roman priest and the other bishop of Interamna, modern-day Terni, and both appear to have been buried on the Flaminian Way. The current Porto del Popolo, previously the Flaminian Gate, was also known as the Gate of St Valentine. It is not clear whether there really were two people or whether there was just one who became the protagonist of two different legends. The association of Valentine with lovers appears to be due to the belief that his feast day was the day on which the birds began to pair.

Valentine (Valentinus)　Pope, elected August 827, died September 827. The son of Leontius, and a career papal civil servant, he was archdeacon of Rome at his unanimous election, but died shortly afterwards.

Valerian　Saint, bishop of Cemele in southern Gaul, died *c.*460. Not much is known about him, but he was present at the Councils of Riez (439) and Viason (442). He defended the jurisdictional rights of Arles against Pope **Leo the Great** and was reputed to be semi-Pelagian in his theological outlook. His writings include *Epistola ad Monachos de Virtutibus et Ordine Doctrinae Apostolicae* and twenty homilies found in the seventeenth century, their subject matter being largely moral and ascetic. Feast day 23 July.

Valerian (Trifa)　Romanian Orthodox bishop and missionary, born Campeni, Romania, 28 June 1914, died Portugal, 27 January 1987. As a young priest he was a successful university chaplain before World War II. He emigrated to America in 1950 and in 1960 was ordained bishop of the majority of Romanian parishes and did much to establish a local church. Deeply hated by the Romanian Communist government, he was accused of anti-Semitic activities because of disinformation planted by Romania among Jewish organizations in the USA in 1974. As a result he was exiled to Portugal, where he died.

Valignano, Alessandro　Italian Jesuit missionary, born Chieti, Abruzzi, February 1539; died Macao, 20 January 1606. He is recognized as the greatest organizer and superior of the Jesuit mission in the Far East since **Francis Xavier**. Born into an influential family, and a doctor of law from Padua in

1557, he expected preferment at Rome from **Paul IV**, but the latter having died in 1559, he returned to Padua, became involved in a lawsuit, and was imprisoned and expelled from the territory of the Venetian Republic. He later underwent an unspecified religious experience, entered the Society of Jesus at Rome in 1566, and was ordained in 1570. In 1573 he was appointed visitator to supervise the growth of the Jesuit mission in Asia and was provincial of India, during which time he gave a strong impetus to the missions and to the Church in general in many Asian countries, but nowhere was his influence greater than in Japan. His missionary policy there was based on a far-reaching adaptation of national customs to Christian precepts; he drew up a plan for the development of self-supporting missions, and composed a booklet of ceremonies for Japan (produced in Bungo, Valignano's headquarters, in 1581). A native clergy was being trained, and the appointment of native bishops anticipated; a catechism for Japan was printed during his lifetime, as well as a report about the martyrdom of Rudolph **Acquaviva** and companions. His success there is attested by his having organized the first diplomatic missions from Japan to Europe, and by his legacy of some 300,000 baptisms at the time of his death.

Van der Kemp, Johannes Theodorus　Pioneer missionary with the London Missionary Society (LMS), born Rotterdam, The Netherlands, 17 May 1747, died Capetown, Cape Colony, 15 December 1811. Originally a soldier, he went to the Cape Colony (South Africa) in 1798 after studying medicine in Scotland. He was the first missionary to the Xhosa and also worked with slaves in Capetown and the Khoikhoi at Bethelsdorp. Outspoken in his defence of equality for these people he was disliked by most of the whites. This was exacerbated by his marriage to a Malagasy ex-slave. A linguist, he wrote a simple grammar and vocabulary of the Xhosa language and a catechism in the Khoi language.

Van der Veldt, James H.　Franciscan psychologist, born Sloten, The Netherlands, 15 March 1893, died Washington, DC, USA, 18 August 1977. Van der Veldt joined the Order of Friars Minor in Amsterdam in 1912, was ordained in 1919, and studied in Nijmegen, The Netherlands, and Milan,

Italy, before receiving his doctorate from Louvain, Belgium. He went to Rome in 1928, where he taught philosophy and psychology. He moved to the diocesan seminary of New York (St Joseph's) in 1940 and in 1945 joined the psychology department at the Catholic University of America, Washington, DC. Known for his integration of psychological insights with philosophy, his many works include *Psychiatry and Catholicism* (1952, with Robert Odenwald), *Psychology for Counselors* (1971) and *The Ecclesiastical Orders of Knighthood* (1956), often considered a definitive work on the subject.

Van Gogh, Vincent Dutch painter, born Groot Zundert, 30 March 1853, died Auvers-sur-Oise, 29 July 1890. Worked for art dealers in The Hague, London and Paris, as a teacher and preacher in London and as a bookseller in Dordrecht. He trained briefly as an evangelist in Brussels in 1878, and then went as a missionary among the miners of Borinage, but was dismissed for giving away all his goods to the needy. Extremely depressed, he began to draw and paint. Always poor, and suffering continually from ill-health, he sold only one of his paintings during his lifetime. On Christmas Eve 1888, frustrated and disillusioned, he mutilated his left ear. In April 1889 he voluntarily entered an asylum. On being released he attempted suicide on 27 July 1890 and died two days later. His most famous works include *The Starry Night* and *Sunflowers*.

Vaughan, Henry Welsh poet, born Llansaintffraed, Brecknock, 17 April 1622, died Llansaintffraed, Brecknock, 23 April 1695. He studied in Oxford and London, and worked as a physician at Breton and Newton-by-Usk. After an illness during which he read 'the blessed man, Mr George **Herbert**', his poetry became mainly religious.

Vaughan, Herbert Alfred Cardinal archbishop of Westminster, born Gloucester, 15 April 1832, died Mill Hill, London, 19 June 1903. Of an old Herefordshire family of landed gentry, remarkable for their faithfulness to the old religion, he was the eldest of six sons and five daughters given to the Church. Herbert was educated at Stonyhurst and Downside, in Belgium and Rome; ordained at Lucca in 1854, he became vice-president of St

Edmund's College, Ware, and joined the Oblates of St Charles. He left St Edmund's in 1861 and set about establishing a college to train missionaries; in 1866 he founded the Mill Hill missionaries, whose members were commissioned to work among the black population of the USA; also, the Josephite Fathers and the Franciscan Missionary Sisters of St Joseph. He was the intimate of and successor to Cardinal Henry **Manning**, whose ultramontanism he continued, and he bought *The Tablet* in 1869 to champion the ultramontane cause. He founded Westminster Cathedral, designed by J. F. Bentley, became archbishop in 1892 and cardinal in 1893. The most notable events of his tenure were obtaining permission from Rome for Catholics to attend Oxford and Cambridge; the building of Westminster Cathedral (begun 1895); the discussion regarding Anglican ordinations, which ended in their condemnation by **Leo XIII** in 1896, and recognition, in the Education Act of 1902, of his fundamental principle that denominational schools merited government support.

Vaughan Williams, Ralph Composer, folk music collector and conductor, born Down Ampney, Gloucestershire, 12 October 1872, died London, 26 August 1958. He studied at Cambridge and the Royal College of Music and became a friend of Gustav **Holst**. He was a prolific composer and wrote music of all kinds, often inspired by Tudor polyphony and English folk music. His *Mass in G Minor* was written for Westminster Cathedral. He edited the *English Hymnal*, music from which was widely reprinted in other hymnals. He also wrote *Sancta Civitas* and several hymn tunes, e.g. *Come Down O Love Divine*, to the tune Down Ampney. He founded a trust to support later composers.

Vaux, Roland Guérin de Dominican biblical scholar, born Paris, France, 17 December 1903, died Jerusalem, Israel, 10 September 1971. After studies at the Sorbonne in Paris and ordination in 1929, de Vaux joined the Order of Preachers in Amiens, France, in 1930. In 1933, he joined the faculty of the Ecole Biblique in Jerusalem, where he would spend the rest of his career, teaching ancient Near Eastern history, Akkadian and OT. He also edited *Revue Biblique* in 1938–53, directed the Ecole Biblique in 1945–65 and served as prior of St Stephen in 1949–52. He was heavily involved in the development of the *Jerusalem Bible* and was the author of many works, including *Les Institutions de L'Ancien Testament* (1958, 1960), *Les sacrifices de L'Ancien Testament* (1964) and *Archaeology and the Dead Sea Scrolls* (English, 1973). His work also garnered him numerous international awards and honorary doctorates.

Vawter, Bruce Vincentian biblical scholar, born Fort Worth, Texas, USA, 11 August 1921, died Chicago, Illinois, USA, 1 December 1986. Originally from the Church of Christ and later an Episcopalian, Vawter became a Roman Catholic in 1937, attended the seminary in Denver, Colorado, and joined the Vincentian Order in Perryville, Missouri, in 1942. After studies in Rome, he taught at several seminaries in the United States until going to DePaul University in Chicago in 1968, where he remained until his death. As well as serving as editor of the *Catholic Biblical Quarterly* and authoring numerous scholarly articles, Vawter contributed greatly to the popularization of the new methods of biblical studies endorsed by papal encyclical *Divino afflante Spiritu* through works such as *A Path Through Genesis* and *The Conscience of Israel*.

Vaz, Joseph Apostle of Ceylon, born Goa, 21 April 1651, died Kandy, 16 January 1711. Ordained in 1676, Vaz laboured in Goa until he was able to found a group of Oratorians in 1685 to go to Ceylon, where the Dutch denied religious freedom to Catholics. He arrived there in 1686, disguised as a beggar to avoid persecution. Notwithstanding many hardships, he had success and won the confidence of the king of Kandy, who restored religious liberty. Other Oratorians joined him, and the territory was geographically divided so as to assign responsibility among them. The faith spread rapidly and Vaz, who was revered for the holiness of his life, resisted with difficulty the conferment of ecclesiastical honours. By the time of his death, more than 70,000 persons openly professed the faith in Ceylon.

Venantius Fortunatus *see* **Fortunatus, Venantius**

Venn, Henry Church Missionary Society secretary, champion of indigenous church principles,

born Clapham, London, 10 February 1796, died London, 13 January 1873. His grandfather and father were leading Anglican evangelicals associated with the 'Clapham Sect'. He was educated at Queens' College, Cambridge (BA, 1818; MA, 1821; BD, 1828), and ordained deacon in 1819 and priest in 1821. He served parishes in Hull and London and in 1841 became CMS clerical secretary. Over 32 years he developed mission theories which looked to local leadership to take over from expatriate missionaries. His concepts of the 'euthanasia of the mission', 'native pastorate' and 'self-propagating, self-financing and self-governing' churches (the latter also formulated by Rufus Anderson in North America) proved significant and enduring, though they were out of fashion for a period in the face of late Victorian visions of imperial duty.

Verbiest, Ferdinand Flemish Jesuit missionary and astronomer. Born Courtrai, 9 October 1623, died Peking, 28 January 1688. He entered the Society of Jesus in 1641, and succeeded Adam Schall von Bell in 1666 as president of the Imperial Board of Astronomy in Peking. In 1665, anti-Christian unrest had developed and a young Muhammadan was appointed instead. Both priests were imprisoned and saved from execution only by the occurrence of two earthquakes. In working on the reform of the Chinese calendar, Verbiest was able successfully to demonstrate the superiority of their own proposals, and the observatory was returned to the Jesuits. He rebuilt the observatory along the lines of Tycho Brahe's, i.e. observation through mathematical calculations rather than the use of telescopes. His knowledge in various fields made him influential with the Chinese government and he was instrumental in determining the Russo-Chinese boundary. He published astronomical observations dealing with Chinese calendar reform, a 32-volume complete handbook of astronomy, and a systematic treatise on European astronomy.

Verbist, Théophile Belgian missionary, founder of the Scheut Fathers. Born Antwerp, 12 June 1823, died Inner Mongolia, 23 February 1868. Ordained in 1846, he requested permission to establish a Belgian mission in China, and was encouraged by Rome to found a mission congregation at Scheut near Brussels, which became, in 1862, the Congregation of the Immaculate Heart of Mary, of which he was superior general. Named pro vicar apostolic of Mongolia, he arrived in China in 1865 with a number of his colleagues, and during the next two and a half years established orphanages, gave instruction to Christians and trained a native clergy. He did not attempt to convert the non-Christians of the vicariate because of the missioners' unfamiliarity with the local language and customs, which he lamented. During an inspection tour of his vicariate, Verbist was taken ill and died, probably of typhus, at Lao-Hu-Kou.

Verdi, Giuseppe Italian composer, born Le Roncole, near Busetto, 10 October 1813, died Milan, 27 January 1901. He began his career playing the organ in a village church. He studied at Milan, and his first success was the opera *Nabucco*, famous for its chorus of the Hebrew slaves. Verdi was not a churchgoer, but he celebrated the memory of the poet **Manzoni** in his imaginative and profound *Requiem*, for soloists, chorus and orchestra. In his later years he wrote several original religious works: *Pater Noster, Ave Maria, Stabat Mater, Te Deum* and *Lauda al Virgine Maria*. At Milan he endowed a home for musicians.

Vermeersch, Arthur Belgian Jesuit, moral theologian and canonist. Born Ertvelde, 26 August 1858, died Louvain, 12 July 1936. Educated at Louvain before becoming a Jesuit in 1879, he taught moral theology and canon law there from 1893 to 1918. Apart from his teaching, his interest in social justice and papal social teaching occasioned several books and articles on social legislation in Belgium, particularly in reference to the Belgian Congo, which he visited. His views anticipated the unrest in Africa which erupted after the Second World War, and stressed the need for racial justice based on Christian principles of the Gospels and encyclicals. He contributed much to the *Catholic Encyclopaedia* on moral theology and canon law, published several works on social questions in Belgium: *Manuel Social* (1900); *La Question congolaise* (1906); *Guide social belge* (1911); and *Tolerance* (1912), an analysis of the problem of religious freedom in civil society, and of the relation between Church and State. In addition to his theological and canonical writings he published, during the last decade of his life, articles on the

Lambeth Conference of the Anglican Church, the notion of social justice in the encyclical *Rerum Novarum*, Christian marriage in connection with *Casti Connubii* and social legislation in connection with the encyclical *Quadragesimo Anno* (1931) of **Pius XI.**

Vermigli, Peter Martyr *see* **Peter Martyr Vermigli**

Verot, Jean-Pierre Augustin Marelin French bishop, born Le Puy, 23 May 1805, died St Augustine, Florida, 10 June 1876. Ordained a French Sulpician in 1828, he went to Baltimore in 1830, taught at St Mary's College and did pastoral work, showing deep concern for the slaves and the poor. Named vicar apostolic of Florida in 1858, he found it a wretched area with three priests, two churches and seven mission chapels. He worked heroically to build up the church in his vicariate; brought in priests, nuns and Christian Brothers from Europe, and appealed to Catholics in Europe and America to migrate to Florida. He was a Southern sympathizer in the Civil War and, though he attacked the slave trade and outlined a code of rights and duties of masters, he defended their property rights in *A Tract for the Times: Slavery and Abolitionism* (1861). He ministered to Union prisoners at Andersonville, provided sisters and nurses in military hospitals, and invited blacks to share the benefits of Catholic education. He was a stormy petrel at Vatican I, *l'enfant terrible*, who scolded the council, condemned the theory that blacks have no souls, opposed the definition of papal infallibility and absented himself from the final public vote on the dogma. Back in the USA, he continued his efforts on behalf of the blacks, the Seminole Indians and the progress of the Church. He relinquished the more important see of Savannah to become first bishop of St Augustine in 1870.

Veuillot, Louis François French Catholic writer and journalist, born Boynes (Loiret), 11 October 1813, died Paris, 7 April 1883. He was the leading lay apologist for ultramontanism, and editor of *l'Univers*, of little importance at that time, but which acquired international significance through his defence of the Church. Belligerent, satirical, imprecatory and often intemperate in style, the violence of his views led to his imprisonment in 1844, but he authored a prodigious literary output to defend the temporal power of the Papacy, to fight against Gallicanism and Liberalism, and to secure the Church's hegemony in the educational structure of France. When *l'Univers* was suspended by the government, Veuillot continued to advocate his views: *The Perfume of Rome* (1861) attested his attachment to the Holy See; *The Smells of Paris* (1866) his repulsions, including the liberal Catholicism of **Montalembert** and **Dupanloup**. During the First Vatican Council, he was so closely in the confidence of **Leo XIII** that *l'Univers* became an almost official organ, and he lobbied for an extreme position for infallibility. His brilliant and incisive style and single-minded devotion to Catholicism made him one of the foremost defenders of the Church in nineteenth-century France and earned him wide respect, though dislike in many quarters for his manners. His brother, Eugène, rallied *l'Univers* to the conciliatory policies of **Leo XIII**, but after his death, his sister Elise founded *La Verité française*, to continue his tradition of intransigence.

Vialar, Emilie de Saint, French religious foundress, born Gaillac (Tarn), 12 September 1797, died Marseilles, 24 August 1856. Of the minor nobility, she refused to marry, took a private vow of chastity and devoted herself to the sick and the poor. In 1832, with an inheritance, she established a house in Gaillac and founded the Sisters of St Joseph of the Apparition, which received episcopal approval in 1835. The sisters were devoted to educating children and caring for the sick, and were distinguished in Algeria for their heroic care of the afflicted during a cholera epidemic. When, in 1840, Bishop Dupuch of Algiers tried to submit the congregation totally to his aims, Emilie opposed him, and the sisters were excommunicated and dismissed from the diocese. The sisters encountered many obstacles in France in pursuit of their apostolate, and finally settled the mother house in Marseilles. By Emilie's own vigorous leadership, the congregation grew by the time of her death to more than 40 houses in France, the Near East and also Burma and Australia. She was canonized in 1951. Feast day 24 August.

Vianney, Jean-Baptiste Marie Saint, French patron of parish priests, born Dardilly, near Lyons, 8 May 1786, died Ars, 4 August 1859. He had little formal education, and his youth was spent herding cattle. At eighteen, he began to study privately for the priesthood, with Abbé Balley. He was called up for military service, but deserted, and remained in hiding until a general amnesty was declared in 1810. He returned to his studies, but was dismissed because of his inability to learn Latin. Abbé Balley again resumed his private tutoring, winning Jean-Baptiste two special examinations, and he was finally ordained in 1815. He was assigned to the remote village of Ars-en-Dombe, which was seriously lacking in a true sense of religion, where he lived a most ascetical life, existing for years on little more than potatoes. Jean-Baptiste restored the church, visited every family and taught catechism; from the pulpit he chided his flock for drunkenness, blasphemy, profanity, obscenity, dancing and working on Sunday. In eight years he transformed the religious life of Ars, and achieved almost worldwide fame, with tens of thousands of visitors coming every year to seek his counsel. He was credited with an ability to read hearts; many miracles and wonders were attributed to him. During his last years, he regularly spent up to eighteen hours a day in the confessional. He was canonized in 1925, and declared patron of parish clergy by **Pius XI** in 1929. Feast day 4 August.

Victor I Saint, Pope from 189, born, place unknown, died 198, Rome. According to the *Liber Pontificalis*, he was an African by birth. The principal event of his pontificate, and an important step in the history of the papal supremacy, was the 'Quarto deciman' controversy, for the settlement of which he ordered synods to be held throughout Christendom. He himself assembled a council at Rome, where he insisted that Polycrates of Ephesus, and other Eastern bishops, conform to the Roman practice of keeping Easter only on Sunday, rather than on 14 Nisan, whatever the day of the week; though he threatened them with excommunication otherwise, it seems he was dissuaded from such severity by St **Irenaeus** and other bishops. Among other incidents of his pontificate, Victor deposed the presbyter Florinus for defending Valentinian doctrines, and excommunicated Theodotus, the founder of Dynamic Monarchianism. According to St **Jerome**, Victor was the first ecclesiastical authority to write in Latin, but it seems he wrote nothing but his encyclicals, which would have been published in both Latin and Greek, so this claim is doubtful. He was venerated as a martyr, but there is no evidence that he died of violence, nor is there any to confirm the *Liber Pontificalis* report that he was buried near St Peter in the Vatican. Feast day 28 July.

Victor II Pope, born Gebhard of Dollnstein-Hirschberg in Swabia, *c*.1018, enthroned 13 August 1055, died Arezzo, 28 July 1057. From 1042 a very able bishop of Eichstätt, he was named Pope by the Emperor **Henry III** but only agreed to accept a year later, when at Regensburg, and even then never gave up his bishopric of Eichstätt. He immediately set about a programme of reform: the choice of name indicated a break with the recent past and a return to the purity of the early Church. Apart from reform, he was also preoccupied with the Norman presence in southern Italy, and went to Germany to seek the emperor's assistance. While he was there Henry died, leaving his infant son in the care of the Pope. Victor had the boy's mother Agnes recognized as regent, and negotiated peace between Henry's family and potential threats to **Henry IV**. To strengthen his hold over central Italy Victor made his brother abbot of Monte Cassino and a cardinal, but died shortly afterwards of fever.

Victor III Blessed, Pope, born Daufer, and related to the Lombard dukes of Benevento, *c*.1027, elected 24 May 1086, died Monte Cassino, 16 September 1087. He was a pious man, had been a hermit, a monk at Benevento (taking the name Desiderius), at Monte Cassino, where he became abbot, rebuilt the monastery, expanded its library and generally encouraged scholarship, and then in 1059 a cardinal with responsibility for the monasteries in southern Italy. In his position as cardinal he undertook several diplomatic missions on behalf of the Papacy, and was with **Gregory VII** on his deathbed. He did not accept the Papacy when elected, but retired to Monte Cassino and was only persuaded to take up the office a year later. Although consecrated in Rome, he was never able fully to establish control over the city. He held an important council at Benevento, which reiterated the main themes of the reforms of Gregory VII. Feast day 16 September.

Vigilius Pope, consecrated 29 March 537, died Syracuse, Sicily, 7 June 555. He was born into the Roman nobility, became a deacon and was named as his successor by **Boniface II** – an uncanonical procedure which brought a storm of protest. He was sent instead as the papal representative to Constantinople, and while there secretly agreed with the Empress **Theodora** that, in return for a guarantee of the Papacy, he would reject the decision on the nature of Christ as agreed at the Council of Chalcedon. The Byzantine general Belisarius, possibly on the orders of Theodora, deposed Pope **Silverius** and had Vigilius elected in his place. Vigilius, however, was not in a position to deliver his promises to Theodora, though he assured her, and the anti-Chalcedonian patriarch, that he shared their beliefs. He told the emperor **Justinian** the contrary, however. When Justinian wanted him to sign a condemnation of the Three Chapters, selections from the writings of three theologians Justinian judged to be Nestorian heretics opposed to Chalcedon, in the hope that this would encourage the Monophysites to accept the council, Vigilius hesitated. Justinian had him seized while saying Mass in November 545, and taken to Sicily and then to Constantinople, where he arrived in January 547. In April the following year he agreed to condemn the Three Chapters, and was himself excommunicated by some Western bishops for doing so. When, however, Justinian re-issued his condemnation of the Three Chapters in 551, Vigilius, still in Constantinople, protested. He was arrested, and fled across the Bosphorus to Chalcedon itself. Justinian now called a council in Constantinople which condemned the Three Chapters and excommunicated Vigilius personally. Vigilius gave in, issued his own, required, condemnation, and after spending another year in the Eastern capital, set out to return to Rome, but died on the way.

Villeneuve-Bargemont, Jean-Paul Alban de French political economist. Born St Aubain (Var), 8 August 1784, died Paris, 8 June 1850. Of a leading noble family of Provence, the vicomte entered the civil service of the French empire and held several posts in the prefectorial administration during the Napoleonic and Restoration periods. He sat as a deputy between 1830 and 1848, but spent most of his time on studies of political economy and poverty; his *Economie Politique Chretienne* (1834) has been described as anticipating Christian socialist views in France. He opposed the ideas of Saint-Simon on inheritance, of Malthus on population, and of the entire Manchester School on *laissez-faire* economics. Instead, as a consequence of a visit to Lille, where nearly half the population were paupers, he sought such direct action as the extension of charitable relief, workers' savings associations, compulsory free education and the provision of a 'sufficient wage' before profits. He was an author of the law of 1841 limiting child labour, and of an amendment to the fiscal law of 1847 dispensing from stamp tax and registration fees, the marriage of the poor and the legitimation of their children. As an economist, he stood apart from Adam Smith and Jean-Baptiste Say, whose doctrines he considered materialistic, but showed a certain naivety in ignoring the economic forces stimulating industrialization. He believed that the state ought to intervene to protect the weak against the 'new feudalism of patrons'.

Villot, Jean Roman Catholic cardinal and Vatican secretary of state, born Clermont-Ferrand, France, c.1905, died Rome, Italy, 9 March 1979. After teaching in Clermont-Ferrand and Lyons, Villot became secretary to the French episcopal conference in 1950, and was named French-language secretary at the Second Vatican Council in 1962. In 1967 Pope **Paul VI** made him prefect of the Congregation of the Clergy. Two years later, he was appointed the first non-Italian Vatican secretary of state at a time when the Roman Catholic Church was dealing with the implementation of curial reform and the storm of controversy surrounding the papal encyclical *Humanae Vitae*. Villot modernized the curial bureaucracy and set an example for the priestly function of the bureaucrats by his own preaching and hearing of confessions. He also presided over the Conclaves that elected Popes **John Paul I** and **John Paul II**, though he died only a few months after the latter took office.

Vincent de Paul Saint, French apostle of charity, born Pouy (Landes), April 1581, died Paris, 27 September 1660. Son of a peasant family, he became a priest in 1606 and, according to his own account, was captured by pirates and made a slave

in Tunisia before returning to Avignon with his former master, whom he converted. In 1608 he went to Paris, where he met Pierre **Bérulle**, who profoundly influenced his life, and engaged him as tutor to the family of P.-E. de Gondi, general of the galleys, and this gave Vincent the opportunity of compassionate work among the unfortunate galley slaves and convicts. His gradual conversion to God's work had begun, and he was to embrace a life of heroic charity. St **Francis de Sales** gave him charge of the convents of the Visitation Order in Paris and, with St **Jane Frances de Chantal**, he founded the Visitandines, whose superior he was from 1622. In 1625 he founded the Congregation of the Missions (Lazarists, or Vincentians) to give missions to country people and train priests. With Louise de **Marillac**, he founded the Sisters of Charity, who are entirely devoted to the care of the sick and the poor; in 1638 he created the first viable home for foundlings. Vincent sent his missionaries abroad to North Africa for the relief of Christian slaves, and into heretic countries to win them to Catholicism. In France he founded a hospice for men; another, La Salpetriere, for the indigent poor and yet another for foundling children. Vincent de Paul was not a profound, nor an original, thinker, but his success was a result of natural talents and a tremendous amount of work, sincere dedication over many years and, above all, a profound spiritual life. The piety that he practised and that he taught was simple, non-mystical, Christocentric, oriented towards action, and few have accomplished as much. He was canonized in 1885. In 1883 the Society of St Vincent de Paul (a lay association for personal service to the poor) was founded by Frederic **Ozanam**. Feast day 27 September.

Vincent Ferrer Dominican saint, born Valencia, c.1350, the son of an Englishman who had settled in Spain, died Vannes, France, 5 April 1419. He received the Dominican habit in Valencia in 1367, taught philosophy at Lerida and was sent as a deacon to preach in Barcelona. He was sent to Toulouse for a year after being accused of prophesying, but later returned to Spain, where he converted the rabbi Paul of Burgos, who became bishop of Cartagena. In the Great Schism he sided with **Clement VII** and his successor, Pedro de Luna, who took the name **Benedict XIII**. Vincent went to Avignon and attempted to persuade Benedict to reach an agreement with his Roman rival. When he failed in this, Vincent set off on preaching tours of southern France, Switzerland and northern Italy. In 1405 he went to Flanders, returning to Spain in 1407, where he preached even in the Islamic areas of the region. In 1414 he went to Perpignan to try once again to persuade Benedict to resign, but again failed. He told King Ferdinand of Castile and Aragon that he would be justified in withdrawing support from Benedict, thereby assisting in the ending of the schism. His final years were spent preaching in northern France. He was canonized in 1455. Feast day 5 April.

Vincent of Lérins   Saint and theologian, born at Toul into an aristocratic family, died at the monastery of Lérins, c.435. Little is known of his life, though a contemporary says that he had been a soldier before being attracted (with his brother Loup) to the monastic life, entering Lérins c.425. His fame rests particularly on his *Commonitorium*, and also on a collection of excerpts he made from the writings of St Augustine. Both books were written under the pseudonym of 'Pilgrim' (*Peregrinus*). The *Commonitorium* enunciates the principle that to distinguish orthodoxy from heresy it is necessary to accept 'quod ubique, quod semper, quod ab omnibus' ('what everywhere, always and by everybody') has been believed. The greater part of the text of the *Commonitorium* is an historical study demonstrating this principle. The first printed edition of the book appeared in 1528, and had an impact on Reformation debates; the 'Vincentian' or 'Lerinian' canon also deeply influenced John Henry **Newman**. Feast day 24 May.

Vingren, Adolf Gunnar   Swedish Pentecostal missionary, born Sweden, 1879, died 1932. Vingren went to the USA in 1903, becoming a Baptist pastor in 1909. Soon after, however, he had a Pentecostal experience, and as a result of a prophecy travelled to Brazil in 1910. Here he was asked to leave a local Baptist church because of his Pentecostalism. With eighteen others he founded a church called the Assembly of God, now the largest Pentecostal group in Brazil.

Visser't Hooft, Willem Adolf   Dutch ecumenical

leader and first general secretary of the World Council of Churches (WCC), born Harlem, Netherlands, 20 September 1900, died Geneva, 4 July 1985. His doctoral thesis at Leiden, where he joined the Student Christian Movement, was on 'The Background of the Social Gospel in America'. That marked his ecumenical interest, which was at the forefront of his activities from then on. John R. **Mott** stimulated his vision for world mission, and from 1922 Karl **Barth** undergirded his theology. In 1924 he became secretary of the Young Men's Christian Association in Geneva; in 1925 he participated at the Stockholm Conference on Life and Work, where he was the youngest delegate; in 1931 he was elected general secretary of the World Student Christian Federation. At Utrecht in 1938 he was elected general secretary of the Provisional Committee for the World Council of Churches, and in 1948 assumed the same post when the WCC was formally inaugurated, retiring in 1966. During the Second World War, Visser't Hooft remained in Geneva to assist refugees from Nazi Germany, and to act as a link between churches in occupied territories and the rest of the world. He was internationally recognized as the leader of the modern ecumenical movement, and was greatly honoured on his retirement for his long and distinguished ecumenical career. Cardinal Willebrands, president of the Vatican Secretariat for Promoting Christian Unity, said of Visser't Hooft at the time of his death that 'his perceptive mind made him aware of the importance of the participation of the Catholic church in the ecumenical movement, and the problems it created'. His major works include *Has the Ecumenical Movement a Future?* (1974); *The Fatherhood of God in an Age of Emancipation* (1982).

Vitalian   Pope, born Segni, consecrated 30 July 657, died Rome, 27 January 672. Upon his election Vitalian set about establishing good relations with Constantinople, trying to do so by evading the doctrinal issues which separated the two capitals and their bishops. The Emperor **Constans II** was ready to respond, and even came to Rome in July 663. He did, however, also allow Ravenna to be a see independent of Rome. When Constans was murdered in 668, Vitalian gave his endorsement to **Constantine V**, the late emperor's heir, rather than to a usurper, a gesture the new emperor did not forget, backing Vitalian's doctrinal position against his patriarch. It was Vitalian who sent the Greek monk **Theodore of Tarsus** to England as archbishop of Canterbury, and who backed the effort in Northumbria to have the Roman, rather than the Celtic, method of calculating the date of Easter accepted in the church in England.

Vitalis of Savigny Blessed, hermit, wandering preacher, and founder of the congregation of Savigny, born Tierceville, near Bayeux, France, 160–5, died Savigny, 16 September 1122. A chaplain to Count Robert of Mortain, he left *c*.1095 in order to become a wandering preacher and hermit in the forests of Craon. The abbey of Savigny was established around 1115; the congregation of Savigny greatly influenced English and Norman monasticism, but was torn apart by dissent among the English houses and merged with the order of Cîteaux in 1147. Feast days 16 September and 7 January.

Vitaly (Maximenko) Russian Orthodox bishop and missionary, born Taganrog, southern Russia, 8 August 1873, died Jordanville Monastery, New York, 21 March 1960. He became a monk of Pochaev Monastery in 1902 and was in charge of its printing and publications. In exile in Czechoslovakia he established a new monastery and newspaper to encourage the return of the Uniates (Greek Catholics) to Orthodoxy. As bishop in the USA, from 1933 until his death, he again founded a monastery with a printing press. His autobiography *Motives From My Life* (1955) surveys his tireless work.

Vitoria, Francisco de Spanish Dominican theologian and international jurist. Born Vitoria, old Castile, *c*.1483, died Salamanca, 12 August 1546. He was a student and professor for eighteen years in Paris, where he became acquainted with **Erasmus**, Juan Luis **Vives** and other leading humanists. Appointed professor at Salamanca, he introduced the *Summa Theologiae* of **Thomas Aquinas** as a classroom text, supplanting the *Sententiae* of **Peter Lombard**. In the international sphere, Vitoria, a staunch advocate of the rights of Indians, who he maintained had been in peaceful possession of their property, and the true owners, unless otherwise evident, questioned, in *De Indis*, the right of

Spain to bring them under her domination; what right Spanish sovereigns had over them in temporal and civil matters; and what rights civil or church authorities had over them in spiritual matters. Vitoria admitted that enlightened states (Spain) might take over backward ones (Indians), if it was in the interests of the latter and not merely for the profit of the former, thus laying down the principle of the system of mandates established after the Great War. In his 'relectio', Vitoria first defined international law and the way in which, in a changing world, it bound all states of the international community and the individuals who, taken together, composed the states of the world. He maintained that the rights of Spain in the New World derived from the 'Law of Nations that is derived from natural law', the 'natural reason established among all nations'. Vitoria also stated the relationship of states to one another. He applied the principles of Aquinas to sovereign states within an international society; he built his theory on Thomistic political and social principals by preserving the thoroughly objective and theological character of society, authority and law. He thus outlined a world organization based on the equality of states. Vitoria is often regarded today as 'the father of international law', the first to define it as derived from an international morality. In *De Postestate Civilii*, Vitoria elaborated on his belief that humanity constitutes a universal society and it needs a law by which to be governed – the Law of Nations. He held that the world could set up an authority to govern the international community and to create laws that are just and fitting for all persons. To this end, Vitoria visualized an international society constituting one integral, political order, which would be endowed with greater power and authority than that of the League of Nations, or the United Nations of our own day.

Vivaldi, Antonio Italian priest, composer and violinist, born Venice, 4 March 1678, died Vienna, 28 July 1741. He was a pupil of his father and of Legrenzi and was popularly known as 'Il Prete Rosso', the red-haired priest. In Venice he worked in the service of the Conservatorio dell' Ospedale della Pietà, a music school for girls. He travelled extensively, was highly prolific, and was admired by J. S. **Bach**. His church music comprises many distinguished works such as his psalm *Dixit Dominus*, *Magnificat*, *Stabat Mater* and brilliant *Gloria*.

Vives, Juan Luis Spanish humanist and social reformer. Born Valencia, 6 March 1492, died Bruges, 6 May 1540. A refugee from the Inquisition, he studied at Paris and was appointed professor of humanities at Louvain. He became a close friend of **Erasmus**, with whose encouragement he published his commentary on St **Augustine**'s *De Civitate Dei* in 1522, dedicated to **Henry VIII**. He was invited to lecture on philosophy at Oxford and became a good friend of Thomas **More**. He returned to Bruges in 1524, married and devoted himself to writing. Vives opposed the philosophy of the schoolmen, in particular a reliance on the interpretation of Aristotle that ignored the latter's own reliance on experience and observation. Like Erasmus, he expounded the 'Devotio Moderna', being intent on the moral implications of philosophy; he appealed to 'common sense' as verification of religious and moral truth. He denounced poverty as a disgrace, a danger to the state, and advocated relief for the poor; he championed the education of women, maintaining the object of which to be, not preparation for a career but, rather, an increase in practical wisdom leading to moral excellence. He has been acclaimed as the father of moral psychology and his *De Anima et Vita* (1538) was one of the first modern volumes on psychology. Among his more significant works: *De Concordia et discordia* (1509), in the cause of pacificism; *De Prima Filosofia*, on Christian philosophy; *Jesu Cristi Triumphus* (1514), on ascetical work, and *De Institutione Femine Cristianae* (1523), on a feminist Christianity.

Vladimir of Kiev Saint, known as Vladimir the Great, the first Christian ruler of what is now Russia, died 1015. His date of birth is uncertain, but he was about 32 when he married the daughter of Basil II of Constantinople, and became a Christian. This event seems to have marked a considerable conversion of heart, as well as of religion, and he became an active protagonist for Christianity, converting, with the aid of Byzantine missionaries, at least the nobility and richer merchants of Kiev. His sons **Boris and Gleb** are revered as martyrs. Feast day 15 July.

Vladimir of Kiev (Bogoyavensky) Russian Orthodox saint, metropolitan and martyr, born Tambov Province, Russia, 1 January 1848, died Kiev, 25 January 1918. He was, uniquely, metropolitan successively of Moscow, St Petersburg and Kiev. As senior bishop he presided over the church council of Moscow (1917–18). He was tortured and murdered by Bolshevik irregulars at the Kiev Caves monastery – the first of very many bishops of the Russian church to be martyred. Feast day 25 January, the nearest Sunday to which is dedicated to all the 'new martyrs' of Russia.

Vogelsang, Karl von Prussian leader for social reform. Born Liegnitz, 3 September 1818, died Vienna, 8 November 1890. After legal studies and a career in the civil service, he became a Catholic in 1850 and actively interested in socio-economic problems. He moved to Austria in 1864 as editor of *Das Vaterland*, a journal hostile to industrial capitalism, and though a conservative, he saw with a clear eye, in the realities of the new industrial order, a division of social classes in which a large segment of the population was being exploited, and became zealous for social justice. He attacked capitalism because it subordinated the economy to profit, exploited most social strata, promoted egoism and disrupted society. Only Christian social ethics could link the old and new orders in a way that would be meaningful, and he developed a complete social theory, creating an employer–employee relationship which could lead to the sharing of profit and ownership. Though idealistic, his ideas spread and influenced a number of industrialists to initiate reforms to improve the lot of the labourers, reforms taken up and developed in succeeding generations.

Von Hügel, Friedrich Baron, English Roman Catholic theologian and philosopher, born Florence, 8 May 1852, died London, 27 January 1925. His father was Austrian, his mother English, a convert to Catholicism from Presbyterianism. He was educated by a variety of tutors, among them Anglicans and Lutherans as well as Catholics. He made his home in England after his marriage in 1873, though he did not become a British subject until 1914. He was a liberal who sympathized with the historical critical approach to OT studies and was part of a growing movement to this end within the Roman Catholic Church. Many of his friends were among the modernists condemned by the Catholic Church, such as **Loisy** and **Tyrrell**, but he himself escaped censure. Von Hügel constantly struggled with the relationship of Christianity to history and was sympathetic with **Troeltsch**'s views. He founded the London Society for the Study of Religion in 1905, which included a diverse group of scholars. His publications included *The Mystical Element of Religion as Studied in St Catherine of Genoa and her Friends* (1908) and *Eternal Life* (1912).

Wadding, Luke Irish theologian, born Waterford, 16 October 1588, died Rome, 18 November 1657. Son of a profoundly Catholic family, prolific in vocations, he was forced to leave Ireland, went to Lisbon, then became a Franciscan in 1607 and president of the Irish college at Salamanca. He accompanied a Spanish mission to Rome requesting definition of the Immaculate Conception, and stayed there until his death. He founded the college of St Isidore for the education of Irish Franciscans, of which he was rector for fifteen years, the Ludovisian College for Irish secular clergy, and a novitiate at Capranica. He was vice procurator-general of the Order and vice commissary, a consultor for the Congregation of Propaganda, Holy Office, Index and Sacred Rites. Wadding always kept the feast of St Patrick with great solemnity at St Isidore's, and it is due to his influence, as a member of the commission for the reform of the breviary, that the feast has been celebrated by the universal Church. A voluminous writer, he published the first collection of the writings of St **Francis**, the first edition of the works of **Duns Scotus**, and a *Biblioteca* of Franciscan writers. His fame as a writer and critic, however, rests above all on the *Annales Ordinis Minorum*, a history of the Order from the time of St Francis until 1540, subsequently continued to 1622. Wadding declined ecclesiastical honours; his piety was equal to his learning and he died the death of a saint.

Wade, John Francis French composer, known above all as the originator and probably the composer of *Adeste Fideles*, born 1710 or 1711, died Douai, France, 16 August 1786. Little is known of his life. He worked as a music copyist at Douai,

when it was populated by English Catholics seeking education and fleeing religious persecution. The cheerful and original *O Come All Ye Faithful* is one of the most popular of all carols.

Waffalaert, Gustave Joseph Belgian moral and spiritual theologian, born Rollegern, 27 August 1847, died Bruges, 16 December 1931. He taught theology at the major seminary, Bruges, and became bishop of Bruges in 1894. He was the author of *Tractatus theologici de virtutibus cardinalibus* (1895), *De la science morale* (1894) and *Sur l'obilgation en conscience des lois civiles* (1884). He founded the magazine *Collationes Brugaises* in 1896 and, as bishop, a series, *Meditationes theologicae* (1896–1905). His mystical and ascetical doctrine reveals the influence of Blessed Jan van **Ruysbroeck** and St **John of the Cross**.

Wagner, Liborius German priest and martyr, born Mulhausen, 1593, died Schonemgar, 9 December 1631. Converted to Catholicism by the Jesuits, he was ordained in 1625 and worked, during his first pastorate at Altenmunster, to reclaim Catholics from Protestantism. Betrayed when the Swedes invaded Germany during the Thirty Years War, Liborius refused to recant his faith and was imprisoned, tortured and killed. His body was thrown into the Main, but recovered, and has been in Klosterheidenfeld since 1803. The process for his beatification was begun in 1931.

Walafrid Strabo (or Strabus, i.e. 'squint-eyed') German monk and theological writer, born in Swabia, c.808, died, drowned in the Loire, 18 August 849. Educated at Reichenau under Tatto,

Grimaldus and Wettin, to whose visions he devotes one of his poems, he was for a decade, from 829, tutor of **Charles the Bald**, and rewarded by being made abbot of Reichenau in 838. He was expelled from his house and fled to Spires for the reason that, from his own verses, notwithstanding his having been tutor to Charles, he had espoused the side of his elder brother, **Lothair**, on the death of **Louis the Pious** in 840. He was, however, restored to his monastery in 842. His *De exordiis* is a valuable source of information on the liturgical and religious customs of his time. He advocated a moderate veneration of images and favoured the daily celebration of Mass by priests. Walafrid is best remembered for his poetry, and his *Visio Wettinis*, composed at eighteen, records visions of hell, purgatory and paradise that anticipate those of **Dante**. His most famous poem, *Hortulus*, is a collection of verses on the 23 herbs and flowers in his monastery garden, their mythological or Christian associations and their healing properties. He was considered a worthy successor to **Alcuin** in Latin lyric.

Walburga of Heidenheim Saint, Benedictine abbess, born England, *c.*710, died Heidenheim, 25 February 779. She was raised and educated at Wimborne in Dorsetshire, went as a missionary to Germany at the request of St **Boniface**, entered the double monastery of Heidenheim, founded by her brothers according to Anglo-Saxon models, and succeeded her sister St Winnebald as abbess. She was one of the most popular medieval saints; she especially favoured the education of German women and, unlike the cult of other women saints of the time, she was venerated as a patroness against hunger and disease in an area exceeding by far the radius of her activities. Each year from October to February, it is said, oil (Walburga's oil) flows from a stone slab near her relics at Eichstätt, and is collected into small bottles for use with prayers of healing for the sick. Feast day 25 February.

Waldenström, Paul Peter Swedish theologian and churchman, born Lulea, 20 July 1838, died Ludingo, 14 July 1917. Ordained to the Lutheran ministry, he found its theological outlook depressing, preferring the revivalist emphasis on Scripture rather than creeds, and insisted that salvation came through a personal commitment to Christ. He held the Fall to have alienated man, not God, and that a reconciliation is required which takes away the sin of the world, this having been given in Christ. He resigned his ministry in 1882 and converted to a north-Swedish pietist movement, the Evangelical National Association, similar to the Moravian Brethren, founded in 1856 for the reform of religion in Sweden; he became its leader and editor of the movement's publication, *Pietisten*. He was also a member of the Swedish Ricksdag. He wrote much of a devotional and inspirational nature which was widely regarded as the best reading after the Bible.

Waldo, Peter (Valdes, Valdesius) Founder of the Poor Men of Lyons, or Waldenses, born Lyons, *c.*1140, died *c.*1215. The Waldenses were a heretical sect which appeared in the second half of the twelfth century and, in a much modified form, has survived to the present day. Valdes was a wealthy merchant who, having read translations of the Gospels in Provençal, experienced a spiritual conversion in 1176. In imitation of St Alexis, he left his family, gave his goods to the poor and took a vow of poverty. His example created a great stir in Lyons and soon found imitators, particularly among the lower and uneducated classes. He became an itinerant preacher and waged a vigorous campaign against worldliness in the Church, organizing his followers into two classes: the Perfect (*perfecti*), and the Friends, or Believers (*amici* or *credentes*). Valdes' way of life was approved by **Alexander III** in 1179, but he was forbidden to preach, which prohibition he ignored, and he was condemned as a heretic by **Lucius** in 1184. Nothing is known of him thereafter. Through emigration the Waldenses have survived in Europe and in North and South America, with congregations in Germany, France, Uruguay, Argentina and the USA. The Waldensian church has an aggregate membership of about 35,000; it receives financial support from the 'American Waldensian Aid Society', founded in 1926, and from a similar foundation in Britain.

Walker, Samuel Evangelical clergyman, associate of John **Wesley** and George **Whitefield**, born Exeter, Devon, 16 December 1714, died Blackheath, 19 July 1761. Educated at Exeter College, Oxford.

Appointed curate of Doddiscombsleigh in 1737. He went as tutor to Lord Rolle's youngest son on a grand tour in the following year. After a brief period as curate of Lanlivery he became vicar of Truro in 1746 and Talland in 1747. He underwent a religious conversion in about 1747 due mainly to the influence of George Conon, a Scottish school teacher. Disagreeing with pluralism, he shortly after resigned the latter living. At Truro his evangelical preaching brought about a revival. Retired to Bristol and then Blackheath in 1760. His publications include *The Christian* (1755) a collection of his sermons.

Wall, John Saint, English martyr, born Chingle Hall, Lancashire, 1620, died Worcester, 22 August 1679. He was sent to Douai at the age of thirteen, entered the English College, Rome, was ordained in 1645, and 'sent to the Mission' in 1648. In 1651, he was professed at St Bonaventure's Friary, Douai, as Joachim of St Anne. He returned to England in 1656 and laboured with great zeal for twenty years in Warwickshire. During the turbulence caused by the **Oates** Plot in 1678, Wall was apprehended at Rushoch Court, near Bromsgrove, and confined to Worcester Gaol for refusing, his priestly status having been declared, the Oath of Supremacy. He was sent to London to be questioned concerning the Oates Plot, and, though proved innocent of conspiracy, condemned for his priesthood in 1679, and executed. His head, recovered after his execution, was preserved at Douai until the French Revolution, when it was lost. He was canonized in 1970. Feast day 26 August.

Walpole, Henry Saint, English martyr, born Docking, Norfolk, 1558, died York, 7 April 1595. He was converted to the faith by the execution of Edmund **Campion**, in whose honour he wrote a long narrative poem, secretly printed, and offensive to the government. He went to Rheims in 1582, by way of Rouen and Paris, was admitted to the English College, Rome, and became a Jesuit priest at Paris in 1588. A chaplain to the Spanish forces in Holland, he was imprisoned by the English at Flushing in 1589 and 'sent to the Mission' in 1593. He was arrested two days after landing in Yorkshire and imprisoned, then sent to the Tower in London, where he was repeatedly tortured, before being returned to Yorkshire for trial and execution,

under the Act that made it high treason for a native Englishman ordained abroad to minister as a priest in England. Feast day 7 April.

Walsh, James Anthony American missionary, born Boston, 24 February 1867, died Maryknoll, New York, 14 April 1936. He graduated from Harvard University, entered St John's Seminary, Brighton, and was ordained in 1892 for the diocese of Boston. He had an abiding interest in the foreign missions, which he was able to further in 1903, when he became director of the diocesan branch of the Society for the Preservation of the Faith, and began publishing a mission magazine in 1907. With Reverend Thomas Price he achieved his hope for an American congregation for the missions when they founded the Catholic Foreign Mission Society of America, approved by Rome in 1911, and soon to be known as the Maryknoll Fathers, of which the mother house was situated near New York City. The first missionaries went to Yeungkong, China, in 1918, under the leadership of Thomas Price, who died there the following year. The Society grew rapidly, with missions in Korea, Japan, Manchuria, the Philippines and Hawaii. Elected superior general in 1929, Walsh was made a bishop in 1933 and continued until his death to influence the growth of Maryknoll and of mission consciousness in the USA. Among his written works are: *A Modern Martyr*; *Thoughts from Modern Martyrs*; and *Observations in the Orient*, the fruit of two tours there in 1926 and 1931.

Walsh, Peter Irish Franciscan, politician and controversialist, born Moortown, Co. Kildare, c.1615, died London, 15 March 1688. He studied at Louvain, where he joined the Franciscans and acquired Jansenist tendencies. In 1639 he returned to teach philosophy and theology at Kilkenny, then in the hands of the rebel 'Catholic Confederation', but was suspended in 1647, and disciplined, for the opponents of the papal nuncio **Rinuccini**. In 1648, after the Inchiquin Truce, he sided openly with those bishops and priests who resisted Rinuccini's censure, and in 1649 helped to secure peace with the viceroy Ormonde. At the Restoration, he urged Ormonde to support the Irish Roman Catholics as the natural friends of royalty, and tried to mitigate their lot, and efface the impression made by their successive rebellions, by a loyal remonstrance to **Charles II**, formulated in Dublin in 1661 by a group of Anglo-Irish Catholics, mostly laymen, boldly repudiating papal infallibility and interference in public affairs, and affirming undivided allegiance to the Crown. He was excommunicated by the Franciscan chapter-general in 1670, but remained a Catholic, keeping good relations with the Anglicans. He apparently signed a recantation and submission to the Holy See before his death, though this has been questioned. His writings are egotistical, his pride and stubbornness explain his insubordination, and he consistently upheld the doctrine of civil liberty against the pretensions of the Papacy.

Walsh, William Irish bishop, born Dunboyne, Co. Meath, 1512, died Alcala de Henares, Spain, 4 January 1577. He joined the Cistercians at Bectine, received a doctorate of divinity at Oxford, and was forced to flee Ireland when Thomas **Cromwell** suppressed Bectine in 1537. The tumult of the Reformation in England and Ireland is reflected in Walsh's career. In Rome he was chaplain to Cardinal **Pole**; he transferred to the Augustinians, was named bishop of Meath in 1554, when Catholicism was restored under **Mary I**, and served on several ecclesiastical commissions during her reign. At **Elizabeth**'s succession in 1558, he refused the Oath of Supremacy, and opposed the introduction of Elizabethan liturgy and the Book of Common Prayer. His episcopal status was challenged, and Rome declared void Pole's use of legative power to appoint bishops, but **Pius IV** reappointed him in 1564. Walsh was imprisoned in Dublin Castle, but escaped to France and then to Spain, where he was suffragan to the archbishop of Toledo.

Walsh, William Joseph Archbishop of Dublin, patriot and theologian, born Dublin, 30 January 1841, died Dublin, April 1921. He attended the Catholic University when **Newman** was rector, entered St Patrick's College, Maynooth, in 1858, was ordained in 1867, and became president. He was drawn into the agitation for land tenure reform, intervened decisively by exposing, before the Bessborough Commission appointed by **Gladstone**, the flagrant abuses of the landlords, and influenced the drafting of the Land Act of 1881. As archbishop of Dublin from 1881, despite strong opposition by the British government, he firmly supported Home Rule, and demanded that training colleges and universities for Catholics be supported with public funds. He was elected first chancellor of the National University of Ireland. He tried, with success, to interpret Irish matters to Roman officials, who had been inclined to take the view of the British ruling class on Ireland's social problems. Walsh was a champion of Irish peasants, an advocate of trade unions and of women's suffrage, and their admission to the university and to the professions. He opposed the Irish Government Bill of 1912, publicly denounced the partition of Ireland and supported Sinn Fein during the 1919 elections, though he participated in efforts to bring them and Lloyd Geroge's government together for negotiations.

Walsingham, Thomas English Benedictine and chronicler, died about 1422. He is supposed to have been a native of Walsingham in Norfolk and was probably educated at the abbey of St Alban's, where he appears to have passed the whole of his monastic life, except the six years between 1394 and 1400, during which he was prior at another Benedictine house at Wymondham, Norfolk. He produced a series of voluminous chronicles, of which the chief work is *Historia Anglicana*, covering the periods 1272 and 1422, a most important source for English history, though only the period from 1376 to 1422 is Walsingham's work. He was a collector of facts rather than an historian in the modern sense, painstaking and trustworthy, and to him we are indebted for knowledge of many historical incidents not mentioned by other writers. He is, for instance, our chief authority for the reigns of Richard II, and Henry IV and V, for the particulars of Wat Tyler's insurrection of 1381, and for much that is known about **Wycliffe** and the Lollards.

Walter of Merton English bishop, born Merton, Surrey, died Rochester, 27 October 1277. A graduate of Manger Hall, Oxford, where he became the friend of **Adam Marsh** and **Robert Grosseteste**. He was protonotary of the royal chancery in 1258, and took part in the negotiations for the grant of Sicily to Edmund Crouchback. For this and other services, Henry III made him chancellor in place of Nicholas of Ely, and bishop of Rochester in

1274. In 1264 Walter drew up statutes for a 'house of the scholars of Merton', at Malden in Surrey, and ten years later they were transferred to a permanent house at Oxford. Thus founded and endowed by Walter, Merton College is the earliest example of collegiate life at Oxford, providing as it did for a common corporate life under the rule of a warden, and has served as a model for universities ever since. He is buried in Rochester Cathedral and is described in the 'Annales monastici' as a man of liberality and great worldly learning.

Walter of Saint-Victor French mystic philosopher and theologian. He was prior of the Parisian abbey of Saint-Victor between 1173 and his death, *c.*1190, having succeeded **Richard of Saint-Victor**. About the time of the Third Lateran Council (1179), he wrote his notorious polemic, *Contra Quatuor Labyrinthos Franciae*, the four labyrinths being **Abelard**, **Gilbert de la Porrée**, **Peter Lombard** and Peter of Poitiers. The work is a bitter attack on their dialectical method in theology, condemning the use of logic in the elucidation of the mysteries of the faith; he was indignant at the thought of treating the mysteries of the Trinity and the Incarnation 'with scholastic levity', and poured abuse on philosophers, theologians and even grammarians. His anti-intellectual stance expressed with such violence, under the pretext of defending orthodoxy, was self-defeating; his contemporaries were not convinced, and he probably hastened the triumph of the method he attacked. In any event, Peter Lombard was recognized as an authority in theology, his method was adopted in the schools, and his famous *Books of Sentences* used as a text and commented on by all the great teachers, a distinction it retained throughout the thirteenth century.

Walther, Carl Ferdinand William German Lutheran theologian, born Langenchursdorf, 25 October 1811, died St Louis, Missouri, 7 May 1887. He attended the University of Leipzig, was ordained a Lutheran minister in 1837, and made pastor in Braemsdorf. He had come under Pietistic influences at Leipzig, was profoundly influenced by Martin Stephan, pastor in Dresden, and joined the newly awakened Lutheran confessional movement. His convictions about pure doctrine, and a vital personal faith, inhibited his acceptance of the growing rationalism of the state church, and in 1839 he migrated with a large number of Saxon Lutherans to America, rather than accept a union with the Reformed Church. He settled in Perry county, where he became a pastor, established what became Concordia Seminary, and was professor of theology when Concordia moved to St Louis in 1850–87. He published *Der Lutheraner* in 1844, intended to bring together Lutheran conservatives, and, in 1855, *Lehre hud Wehre*, in which most of his theological writings appeared. He advocated traditional Lutheran doctrine, with emphasis on the binding force of Lutheran confessions and divine predilection as the cause of faith; man was unconditionally dependent on grace for salvation. Walther played a leading role in what is now the Lutheran Church–Missouri Synod, of which he was president in 1847–50 and 1864–78. He is generally regarded as the outstanding Lutheran theologian in America in the nineteenth century.

Walton, Brian English biblical scholar and bishop, born Seymour, near York, *c.*1600, died London, 29 November 1661. He was educated at Cambridge, ordained in 1623 and named rector of St Martin's in London, where, having become involved in the troubles of the times, he was accused of 'subtile tricks and popish innovations', deprived of his rectory and imprisoned in 1642. He then went to Oxford and there planned the great Polyglot Bible, which was to be 'completer, cheaper and provided with a better critical apparatus than any previous work of its kind'. It came out in six great folios in 1657; nine languages were used and his collaborators were among the best scholars of the day. The Polyglot Bible is a great monument of industry and of capacity for directing a vast undertaking, making his name familiar to every student of the Scriptures, and it has not been superseded. His scholarship was rewarded at the Restoration, when he was made bishop of Chester in 1660.

Walton, William British composer, born Oldham, 29 March 1902, died Ischia, Italy, 8 March 1983. He was a chorister at Christ Church, Oxford. His choral music, such as his brilliantly resounding oratorio *Belshazzar's Feast*, is noted for its inspiration. Walton wrote carols, and choral music including the *Cantico del sole*, a setting of St **Francis of Assisi**.

Wang, Zhiming Chinese Christian killed in the Cultural Revolution, and one of the ten martyrs recently commemorated by the erection of a statue in Westminster Abbey, London, born 1907, probably in the Yunnan region of China, died there, by execution, 29 December 1973. He went to mission schools and in 1944 was chairman of the Sapushan Church Council in Wuding, Yunnan. He worked as a teacher and, after his ordination in 1951, as a pastor. He was arrested along with other members of his family in 1969, and imprisoned until his death. There is a memorial to him in Wuding.

Ward, Barbara (Lady Jackson) Economist and environmentalist, born York, 23 May 1914, died Lodsworth, Sussex, 31 May 1981. She was educated at the Convent of Jesus and Mary, Felixstowe, at the Sorbonne and Somerville College, Oxford, where she read for the (then recently instituted) degree of politics, philosophy and economics. From 1940 to 1950 she was an assistant editor on the *Economist*. During the war years she – with Christopher **Dawson** in particular – edited the Catholic quarterly *The Dublin Review* and ran the Sword of the Spirit, an organization, originally ecumenical in intent, started by Cardinal **Hinsley** to bring the churches behind the war effort. She was a regular and very popular broadcaster on the BBC, and was made a governor. After her marriage to Robert Jackson in 1950 she moved to what is now Ghana, where he was responsible for the Volta River project. She became increasingly interested in issues of development economics. She began to lecture around the world, but particularly in the United States, where from 1959 to 1968 she was a Carnegie fellow at Harvard. From 1967 to 1973 she was Einstein Professor at Columbia University, then she moved back to England to become president of the International Institute for Environment and Development. She was a devout Catholic, as much at home raising money for Padre **Pio**'s hospital as in spurring on the Vatican on matters of aid and, later, the environment. She was a member of the Pontifical Commission for Justice and Peace. She was made a life peer in 1976. She wrote many books, some of them for the United Nations, others the compilation of lectures she had given. Her first major publication, on colonialism, was *The International Share-Out* (1938); other titles include *Five Ideas that Change the World* (1959) and *Spaceship Earth* (1966).

Ward, Hugh Irish Franciscan, historian and hagiographer, born Donegal, about 1590, died 8 November 1635. In 1607 he went to study in Salamanca, Spain, and in 1616 joined the Franciscans. He was sent to teach philosophy in Paris, and became professor of divinity at St Anthony's College, Louvain, and rector in 1626. His great interest was in Irish history. He helped found the school of Irish Archaeology at Louvain and conceived the idea of writing a history of Ireland and the lives of the Irish saints. Patrick **Fleming** worked in libraries on the continent, Michael **O'Clery** went to collect and study the manuscripts in Ireland and Ward worked on those which had been transcribed from or sent from numerous locations. By the time of Ward's death there were several manuscripts ready for publication, including *De nomenclatura hiberniae, De statu et processu veteris in Hibernia reipublicae, Martyrologium ex multis vetustis Latino-Hibernicum, Anagraphen magnalium S. Patricii, Investigatio Ursulanae expeditionis* and *S. Ramuldo Acta.*

Ward, Maisie English author and publisher, born Shanklin, Isle of Wight, 4 January 1889, died New York City, 28 January 1975. She was the daughter of Wilfrid **Ward**, historian of the nineteenth-century English Catholic revival, and Josephine Ward, novelist. She grew up in a literary and religious tradition that prepared her for life as an intellectual lay apostle, in a family which counted among its eminent friends **Chesterton, Belloc**, George Windham and Baron **Von Hügel**. She served as a Red Cross nurse during the Great War, after which she became a charter member of the Catholic Evidence Guild. She married Frank **Sheed** in 1926, another active worker, and they founded Sheed and Ward in London, and in New York in 1933. They brought a new dimension to Catholic publishing, aiming to lift the awareness of Catholic readers 'just above the middle of the brow', to include new works in English as well as European writers such as **Claudel**, Karl **Adam**, Henri **Ghéon**, François **Mauriac**, Hans Küng. Sheed and Ward was considered by many Catholics in both Europe and America as their mentor during the middle years of the twentieth century. For Christopher **Dawson**

its foundation marked an epoch in the history of English Catholicism which 'changed the whole climate'. Of the number of her books, Ward's *The Wilfred Wards and the Transition* (1934) and *Insurrection versus Resurrection* (1937) together formed a history of the evolution of Catholic thought from 1870 to 1920. She wrote perhaps the definitive life of G. K. Chesterton, was an active supporter of The Grail, and of Dorothy **Day** and the Catholic Worker movement. She was a woman of remarkable humanity, wit and intellectual vigour.

Ward, Margaret Saint, English martyr, born Congleton, Cheshire, died Tyburn, 30 August 1588. She was in service with the Whittles, a London Catholic family, when arrested for helping a secular priest, William Watson, to escape from Bridewell prison. She smuggled a rope into his cell which, left dangling from a cornice of the roof after his escape, was traced to Margaret. Robert **Southwell** described her torture to the Jesuit General, Claudius **Acquaviva**: 'she was flogged and hung up by the wrists, the tips of her toes just touching the ground so that she was crippled and paralysed'. She refused to reveal Watson's whereabouts, nor would she accept freedom if she attended at a Protestant service. She was executed at Tyburn and canonized in 1970. Feast day 20 August.

Ward, Mary Lay apostle, foundress of the Institute of the Blessed Virgin Mary, born Mulwith, Yorkshire, 2 February 1586, died Hewarth, Yorkshire, 30 January 1646. Of a wealthy Catholic family, her early life was uneventful. On advice from Jesuits in St Omer, she entered a Belgian convent of Poor Clares in 1606, but left only a year later to found another convent at Gravelines, which she also left, after giving it most of her fortune. Soon afterwards she established another convent – although the members of its community did not bind themselves to the seclusion then usual among nuns – in St Omer, opening a school for English girls there, with a modified Poor Clare rule; however, she then, in 1611, adopted the Jesuit rule. Her ideas were regarded as dangerously novel, arousing the opposition of those English clergy opposed to the Jesuits. Mary obtained approbation none the less from the local bishop, and sent the 'Scheme of the Institute' to **Paul V** in 1616, which was favourably received, but not approved. She

went to Rome, and was well received by **Gregory XV**, but **Urban VIII** was much less sympathetic. She left Rome and travelled to Germany, visiting on the way Federigo **Borromeo**, the cardinal archbishop of Milan, and a supporter of her enterprise. New houses were opened but, in 1629, despite her pleadings before a special congregation of cardinals in Rome, Urban suppressed the Institute. Mary travelled to Vienna, where she was imprisoned as a heretic, though the emperor had her released. She travelled on to Munich, where she was again imprisoned, this time for some three months before being released on the instructions of Pope Urban, who was impressed by her patience under trial and by the support shown her by the emperor and by Maximilian I of Bavaria. She returned to Rome and obtained permission for some sisters to continue their apostolate while living in community under private vows. She was also permitted to establish a house in Rome itself. She returned to England in 1639, first to a house in London, then, with the onset of the Civil War, to Hutton Rudby and finally to Hewarth, near York, where she died. Mary Ward's Institute received approval from **Clement XI** in 1703, and final approbation in 1877, but other modern congregations had meanwhile patterned their rule upon hers. **Pius XII** spoke of Mary Ward to the First International Congress of the Lay Apostolate in 1951 as 'cette femme incomparable', and ranked her with St **Vincent de Paul** as promoter of the lay apostolate.

Ward, Wilfrid Philip British author, Catholic apologist, born Ware, Hertfordshire, 2 January 1856, died London, 9 April 1916. Son of William George **Ward**, attended Ushaw College and the Gregorian University, lectured in philosophy at Ushaw, was a member of the royal commission on Irish university education in 1901 and, in 1906, editor of the *Dublin Review*, through which he influenced discussion of Catholic ideas and national events. He gave the Lowell Lectures in Boston and toured the USA, lecturing on John Henry **Newman**, Cardinal **Vaughan** and Alfred Tennyson. He was most noted for his biographical studies: *William George Ward and the Oxford Movement* (2 vols, 1889); *William George Ward and the Catholic Revival* (1893); *Life and Times of Cardinal Wiseman* (1897); and the monumental two-volume *Life of Newman* (1912). Ward sought in his writings to temper the effects of modernism, relying on New-man's theory of development to progress from the 'state of siege' that had prevailed in the English church since the Reformation, to an alternative that would prove attractive even to non-Catholics, and thus to promote dialogue among Catholics, Anglicans and Nonconformists.

Ward, William George English Catholic theolo-gian, a leader of the Oxford Movement, born London, 21 March 1812, died there, 6 July 1882. He took Anglican orders at Balliol College, Oxford, in 1840, but his pamphlets in support of John Henry **Newman** cost him his lectureship and tuto-rial position there the following year. From then on Ward and his associates worked undisguisedly for union with the Church of Rome, and in 1844 he published his *Ideal of a Christian Church*, in which he openly contended that the only hope for the Church of England lay in submission to Rome. When he refused to disavow the work, the univer-sity authorities censured the book and degraded Ward from his degrees. Ward left the Church of England in September 1845, and others followed, including Newman himself. He gave himself up to ethics, metaphysics and moral philosophy, carried on a controversial correspondence with John Stu-art Mill, and took a leading part in discussions of the Metaphysical Society founded by James Know-les, of which Tennyson, Huxley and Martineau were also prominent members. He was a vehement opponent of liberal Catholicism, espoused an extreme ultramontanism, congenial to his friend and protector Archbishop **Manning**, and gave vig-orous support to the promulgation of the dogma of papal infallibility in 1870. He was with Manning against Newman in holding that Catholicism should not be exposed to the 'corrupting influ-ences' of Oxford and Cambridge. He was buried in the Isle of Wight, where the family had been landed gentry.

Warde, M. Francis Xavier Foundress of the Sisters of Mercy in the USA, born Mountrath, Ireland, 1810, died Manchester, New Hampshire, 17 Sep-tember 1884. Frances was the first postulant, in 1831, of the just-founded Sisters of Mercy, and was indispensable in consolidating the community under Mother McAuley. In 1843 she went with six companions to the Diocese of Pittsburgh, where, in spite of attacks of typhus and tuberculosis, which at first decimated the community, she estab-lished parish schools, academies, a House of Mercy for young women, an orphanage and the first hospital in western Pennsylvania. Mother Warde also made foundations in Chicago, Loretto and Providence, Rhode Island, where her courage and commanding presence saved the convent from destruction by the 'Know Nothings', in 1850. A woman of astounding energy, she opened schools, hospitals, homes and other insttutions in Maine, Philadelphia, Nebraska, New Jersey, California and Manchester, New Hampshire, where she was superior for 26 years, promoting night schools for young mill hands.

Wardlaw, Henry Scottish prelate, born Wilton, c.1365, died St Andrews, 6 April 1440. He was educated at Oxford and Paris and, while residing at the papal court, Avignon, was chosen bishop of St Andrews, being consecrated in 1403, owing his ecclesiastical preferment to the schismatic Anti-popes. Returning to Scotland, he was tutor to the future **James I** and, having helped to secure his release from captivity in England, crowned him in May 1424. Henry clearly understood the needs of his war-torn and impoverished country, and strove for political stability, the encouragement of learn-ing, peace with England and clerical reform. He appears to have been an excellent bishop, although he tried to suppress the teaching of John **Wycliffe** by burning his adherents. Wardlaw's chief title to fame is as founder of the university of St Andrews, the first Scottish university, the privileges of which were confirmed in a bull of **Benedict XIII** in 1413. The university was to be 'an impregnable rampart of doctors and masters to resist heresy'.

Warham, William Archbishop of Canterbury, lord chancellor of England, born Church Oakley, Hampshire, 1450, died Hackington, 22 August 1532. Educated at Winchester and New College, Oxford, he was appointed bishop of London in 1501, and archbishop of Canterbury in 1504. In 1506 he was principal negotiator in Henry VII's marriage to Margaret of Savoy; he crowned **Henry VIII** and **Catherine of Aragon** in 1509. In 1515 he was replaced as chancellor by Cardinal **Wolsey**, adversary throughout his career. Involved early on, in 1527, in the inquiry into Henry's marriage to

Catherine, he prudently avoided public participation; initially he supported Henry because, for
reasons unknown, he had always been uneasy
about the legitimacy of the king's marriage, and
Henry now pinned much hope on him. In 1530 he
too signed the letter to the Pope seeking consent
to Henry's divorce. But with remarkable courage,
Warham, after the divorce, rebelled in 1532, formally protested all acts undermining the Pope's
authority and the prerogatives of his see of Canterbury, urging Magna Carta in defence of the liberties of the Church. In reply Henry alleged abuses
in William's jurisdiction; the latter braced himself
to fight, but suddenly, it seems, he capitulated and
accepted the famous 'capitulation of the clergy', in
May 1532. He was a generous friend to **Erasmus**,
whom he had wanted to settle in England, and
remarkably devoted to St **Thomas Becket**.

Warneck, Gustav Adolf Founder of modern missiology, born Naumburg near Halle, 6 March 1834,
died Halle, 25 December 1910. He entered Halle
University in 1855. In 1862 he became assistant
pastor in Roitzsch, Saxony, and the following year
pastor in Dommitzsch, Leipzig. He obtained a
doctorate in Jena, 1871, and spent three years
working with the Rheinish Mission Society in
Barmen, 1871–4, realizing that his health did not
permit him to serve overseas. In 1873 he founded
Allgemeine Missions-Zeitschrift, which he edited till
his death. In 1874 he moved to Rothenschirmbach
near Eisleben, and pastored there for 22 years
before accepting the first chair of mission studies
in Germany, at Halle, 1897–1908. His publications
include *Missionsstunden* (3 vols, 1883–99) and
Evangelische Missionslehre (5 vols, 1887–1905).

Warren, Max Anglican missionary and writer,
born Dun Laoghaire, Ireland, 13 August 1904, died
Sussex, 23 August 1977. His parents were Church
Missionary Society missionaries in India, where he
spent the first eight years of his life before going to
Marlborough and Jesus College, Cambridge. He
then studied at Ridley Hall, Cambridge, and went
as a missionary to Nigeria in 1927. He stayed less
than a year because of ill-health, and in 1932 was
ordained. He served on a parish in Boscombe and
in 1936 became vicar of Holy Trinity, Cambridge.
In 1942 he was appointed general secretary of the
CMS. From then until 1963, when he resigned

from the CMS, he became one of the most important figures in the missionary movement, lecturing
and writing on missionary themes. He was both
supporter, and critic, of the World Council of
Churches, being an opponent of over-centraliza-
tion. He encouraged scholarship within the evangelical tradition of the Church of England, and
also the creation of religious communities in that
tradition. After his retirement from the CMS he
served for a decade as a canon of Westminster
Abbey, eventually becoming sub-dean. He retired
from the abbey in 1973.

Watson, David C. K. Anglican evangelical priest
and writer, born 1933, died York, 1984. Watson
experienced a baptism in the Spirit in the early
1960s while serving in Cambridge. Through team
ministry and teaching he built a large congregation
in York, and he led a number of missions, making
an important contribution to British Christian life.
He was also an ecumenist. His books include *My
God is Real* (1970), *One in the Spirit* (1973), *I
Believe in Evangelism* (1976), *You are My God*
(1983) and a posthumously published description
of his terminal cancer, *Fear No Evil*.

Watts, Isaac Hymn-writer, born Southampton,
17 July 1674, died Stoke Newington, London, 25
November 1748. He was educated at Southampton
and at a Dissenting Academy in Stoke Newington.
He wrote theological works and poems, but is best
known for his hymns, of which he wrote over five
hundred. Many are widely used, such as *O God
Our Help In Ages Past* and *When I Survey The
Wondrous Cross*. He has been called 'The father of
English hymnody'.

Wattson, Paul James Francis American ecumenist,
founder of the Society of the Atonement, born
Millington, Maryland, 16 January 1863, died Garrison, NY, 8 February 1940. He studied at General
Theological Seminary, NY, was ordained in the
Episcopal Church in 1886, and founded at Graymoor, with Mother Lurana White, an Episcopal
nun, the Society of the Atonement, a group of
Franciscan friars and sisters dedicated to unity with
Rome. In 1903 he began publishing *The Lamp*, in
which he defended papal infallibility and urged all
Anglicans to return to Rome. To this end, he
inaugurated in 1909 a period of prayer called the

Church Unity Octave, which became the Chair of Unity Octave, and observed by other churches as the Universal Week of Prayer for Christian Unity. The Graymoor community of seventeen friars, sisters and laymen was received corporately into the Catholic Church in 1909, and Watson was re-ordained a priest in 1910. He founded St Christopher's Inn, a refuge for homeless men, organized the Graymoor Press, and the *Ave Maria Hour*, on radio; he established a major seminary in Washington, DC, and played a crucial role in the formation of the Catholic Near East Welfare Association.

Waugh, Evelyn English Roman Catholic writer, born London, 28 October 1903, died Combe Florey, near Taunton, Somerset, 10 April 1966. He was educated at Lancing and Oxford, and became a schoolmaster – a profession which he hated, and later lampooned in *Decline and Fall*. He was received into the Roman Catholic Church in 1930 by Martin **D'Arcy** and wrote a life of Edmund **Campion** (1935), which won the Hawthornden Prize, as something of a thank-offering, donating the royalties to Campion Hall, the Jesuit Oxford College of which at the time D'Arcy was master. His novel *Brideshead Revisited* chronicles an upper-class, English Roman Catholic family. Waugh described it humorously as 'an attempt to trace the workings of the divine purpose in a pagan world'. During the war he served in the Royal Marines, and he drew upon those experiences for the *Sword of Honour* trilogy. Apart from a number of comic novels and the semi-autobiographical *The Ordeal of Gilbert Pinfold*, Waugh also wrote travel books, including *The Holy Places*, and a biography of Ronald **Knox**.

Weatherhead, Leslie Dixon Methodist minister and psychologist, born London, 14 October 1893, died Bexhill, 3 January 1976. He studied theology at Richmond theological college and Manchester University. He began his ministry in Farnham, but in 1915 joined the Indian army and served as chaplain to the forces before becoming a minister in Madras in 1919 then subsequently in Manchester, 1922–5, Leeds, 1925–36, and in London at the City Temple, 1936–60 (a Congregational Church in London, though he remained a Methodist); and he was twice elected president of the Methodist Conference. He became a recognized authority on pastoral psychology and a pioneer in establishing a partnership between religion and psychiatry. In 1966–7 he was president of the Institute of Religion and Medicine. He was made a Freeman of the City of London and Commander of the Order of the British Empire in 1959. He was the author of some 40 books, including *The Transforming Friendship* (1928), and *Psychology, Religion and Healing* (1951) – for which last he was awarded a doctorate by the University of London.

Webbe, Samuel (Senior) English Roman Catholic musician, born London, 1740, died there, 25 May 1816. He was organist of various Roman Catholic embassy chapels in London, at a time when Roman Catholics had to practise their faith almost in secrecy. He composed music for the Roman Catholic Church and is almost certainly the author of the popular hymn tunes *Melcombe* and *Tantum Ergo*, which have been adopted also in Protestant churches.

Webbe, Samuel (Junior) English Roman Catholic musician, son of Samuel **Webbe** (Senior), born London, 15 October 1768, died Hammersmith, Middlesex, 25 November 1843. He studied with his father and with Clementi. He was organist of Paradise Street Unitarian Church, Liverpool, and of Roman Catholic churches in Liverpool and London. His career was a continuation of his father's and he compiled collections of church music. From Thomas Haweis, Webbe adapted the tune *Richmond*, which became popular sung to *Praise to the Holiest in the Height* and other words.

Wedel, Cynthia Clark Ecumenist, born 26 August 1908, Dearborn, Michigan, USA, died 24 August 1986, Alexandria, Virginia, USA. She was president of the World Council of Churches in 1975–83, associate general secretary of the US National Council of Churches of Christ in 1960–9 and president in 1969–72. She led other Christian organizations and specialist committees, including those on women, the family and media. She was an observer at the Second Vatican Council.

Weekes, Thomas English composer, baptized Elsted, Sussex, 25 October 1576, buried London, 1 December 1623. He was successively organist of Winchester College and of Chichester Cathedral.

He is notable for his madrigals and church music. His church compositions include anthems, a *Gloria in Excelsis Deo*, and *Hosanna to the Son of David*.

Weigel, Gustave American theologian and ecumenist, born Buffalo, NY, 15 January 1906, died New York City, 3 January 1964. He entered the Society of Jesus in 1922, and was ordained at Woodstock College in 1933; he studied theology at the Gregorian, Rome, and was professor of theology at Woodstock from 1948 until his death. Weigel travelled widely, wrote numerous books and articles in journals, lectured incessantly at universities in the USA, Germany, Chile and Colombia, and was a Catholic consultant for the *Encyclopaedia Britannica*. He had contact and dialogue with many Protestant theologians, including Paul **Tillich**, and collaborated with his colleague, John Courtney Murray, in studies of the Church–State problem. His theological activity focused on the ecumenical movement; he became its most prominent American theologian and attended meetings of the World Council of Churches. As consulting member of the Secretariate for Promoting Christian Unity, he went to Rome to help prepare the Vatican Council's Decree on Ecumenism, and during the Council itself he acted as liaison and interpreter for non-Catholic observers.

Weil, Simone French Jewish writer, religious seeker drawn to the Church, born Paris, 1909, died Ashford, Kent, 24 August 1943. She graduated from the École Normale Supérieure, a student of Alain; a teacher, she joined the working classes to implement her political ideals. She had, from an early age, been attracted to bolshevism, became an anarchist, and helped Trotsky. She joined the International Brigade against Franco in the Spanish Civil War. She was agnostic and anticlerical when, in 1938, on a visit to Solesmes, 'Christ took hold of her'; from then on she became convinced of his love and divinity, and discovered the meaning of the Passion. She had an ardent compassion for the unfortunate, a great desire for the truth and an eagerness to search out the will of God. Until her death, however, she was torn between the conflicting positions of a sincere attraction to Christ, and the social, historical and philosophical objections that oppressed her, remaining in the position of 'waiting for God'.

Weisheipl, James Athanasius US Dominican, philosopher, writer and editor, born Oshkosh, Wisconsin, 3 July 1923, died Saskatoon, Saskatchewan, 3 December 1985. Studied in Oshkosh, joined the Dominicans and studied in Illinois and in Rome. He was ordained in 1949, taught in England for a time and from 1957 until 1965 taught the history of medieval philosophy at the Dominican House of Studies in River Forest, Illinois. He taught at the Pontifical Institute of Medieval Studies and at the University of Toronto. In 1965 he established the American section of the Leonine Commission, which is responsible for producing the definitive critical edition of the works of **Thomas Aquinas**. He was a contributing editor to the multi-volume *New Catholic Encyclopedia*, a visiting fellow at Oxford and for 1963–4 president of the American Catholic Philosophical Association. In 1978 he was given the rare honour of receiving the Dominican title of Master of Sacred Theology. His writings include *Nature and Gravitation, The Development of Physical Theory on the Middle Ages* and *Friar Thomas d'Aquino*.

Weld, Thomas English Catholic layman, born Lulworth, Dorsetshire, 1750, died Stonyhurst, 1810. Of an ancient English family conspicuous for its zeal for the Church, Thomas distinguished himself in relieving the misfortunes of the refugees of the French Revolution. He gave Stonyhurst College, with 30 acres of land, to the exiled Jesuits; he entirely supported the English Poor Clares, who had fled from Gravelines, and he founded and supported a Trappist monastery at Lulworth, since removed to Mount Melleray, Ireland. He is said to have given half his income to charity. Besides his conspicuous piety and great hospitality (one of the first English Catholics to entertain the king in 1789 and 1791), he was also from the first a steady supporter of Bishop **Milner**. He had a large family, six daughters and nine sons, two of whom also died at Stonyhurst, one of them, John, being its rector. His eldest son, Thomas (born London, 22 January 1773, died Rome, 19 April 1837), continued his father's liberalities, earning praise from Cardinal **Wiseman** for his generosity to all the religious establishments in the west of England. He also befriended Milner and stood by him almost alone in 1813, when the Catholic Committee turned against the intrepid bishop. Thomas junior was created a cardinal in 1830.

Wellesz, Egon Austrian, later British, Roman Catholic composer and musicologist responsible for the modern decoding of Byzantine chant, born Vienna, 21 October 1885, died Oxford, 9 November 1974. He was Schoenberg's first pupil, and was appointed a professor of music at Vienna University. He moved to Britain in 1938 and became a music fellow at Lincoln College, Oxford, later reader in Byzantine music. He was a versatile and prolific composer, his church music including a *Mass* and *Alleluia*. Created a Knight of St Gregory.

Wellhausen, Julius German Old Testament scholar, born Hameln an der Weser, where his father was a Lutheran pastor, 17 May 1844, died Göttingen, 7 January 1918. He studied first in Hanover, and then theology in Göttingen, where he came under the influence of Heinrich **Ewald**, who encouraged him in the study of Semitic languages. He started teaching in Göttingen in 1870, became a professor at Greifswald two years later, and ten years after that moved to Halle as professor of Semitic languages (it was complained at Greifswald that his teaching did not adequately prepare students for the ministry) and in 1885 to Marburg and finally in 1892 back to Göttingen, where he retired in 1913. Although in the last decade or so of his working life he turned his attention to the New Testament, publishing commentaries on each of the four Gospels, his fame rests on his Old Testament criticism, helping to establish, in books such as his *Prolegomena to the History of Israel* (1883) and *The Composition of the Hexateuch* (1885) the now generally accepted theory of the distinct sources of the biblical text.

Wells, Swithun Saint, English martyr, born Bambridge, near Winchester, *c.*1536, died London, 10 December 1591. Son of a country gentleman, well educated, travelled abroad, a linguist, musician, poet and sportsman. He was a tutor in the household of the earl of Southampton, set up his own school near Bath and conformed to the Anglican Communion. In 1582 he came under suspicion for popish tendencies, abandoned teaching and actively supported the Roman church, devoting himself to the service of seminary priests. In 1586,

Wells and his wife took a house at Gray's Inn Fields, London, to further his missionary endeavour; he was twice arrested and interrogated, but released for lack of evidence. However, in 1591, while he was absent, his wife offered hospitality to two priests and they, and six worshippers, were apprehended at Mass in the house. The priests were charged with high treason and Swithun, arrested later, his wife and the worshippers were tried and condemned to death. Alice Wells was reprieved and died in prison; Swithun went to his death with tranquillity and fortitude, forgiving his executioners. Feast day 10 December.

Wenceslas Saint, patron of the Czech Republic, royal duke of Bohemia, born *c.*907, murdered by his pagan brother, Boleslav, at Alt-Bunzlau, 28 September 929 or 935. His grandmother, St Ludmilla, raised him as a Christian until she was killed by his pagan mother, who ruled as regent until 934, when Wenceslas came of age. He put his duchy under the protection of King Henry the Fowler of Germany and invited German Christian missionaries into Bohemia. He is the 'Good King' of the Christmas carol. His remains are in St Vitus Cathedral in Prague. Feast day 28 September.

Wesley, Charles A founder of Methodism, born Epworth, Lincolnshire, 18 December 1707, died London, 29 March 1788. He was the eighteenth child of Susanna and Samuel Wesley, rector of Epworth, and younger brother of John. Educated at Westminster School and Christ Church, Oxford. Although he lost his first twelve months at Oxford in 'diversions', he 'awoke out of his lethargy' and, in 1729, became part of the 'Holy Club', which led a fellow student to exclaim in ridicule: 'Here is a new set of methodists sprung up.' The name stuck, and Oxford Methodism began its course. He was ordained in 1735 and went to Georgia, with John, as secretary to the governor. He returned the following year and on Whit Sunday, 1738, experienced an evangelical conversion, which satisfied his longing for a personal saving faith in Christ. He now became the poet of the Evangelical Revival, and wrote more than 6500 hymns, varying in merit, but some of the highest order, which made him one of the great hymn-writers of all ages. He began his work of evangelism in the houses of friends, visited the prisons, and preached in the churches until the doors were closed against him; he became one of the most powerful preachers in the Revival. Charles disapproved of John's ordinations, and generally showed a fiercer, though not stronger, devotion to the established church. He married Sarah (Sally) Gwynne in 1749, who bore him eight children.

Wesley, John Founder of Methodism, born Epworth Rectory, Lincolnshire, 27 June 1703, died City Road, London, 2 March 1791. He was the fifteenth child of Susanna and Samuel Wesley, rector of Epworth, and older brother of Charles. He studied at Charterhouse school and Christ Church, Oxford, where a friend spoke of him as 'a young fellow of the finest classical taste and the most liberal and manly sentiments'. His reading of **Thomas à Kempis** and others gave him 'a settled conviction to became a real Christian'; he took holy orders in 1728. He joined a society for spiritual improvement, founded by Charles and a few others, and the scope of this 'Holy Club' was widened when John joined it and became its leader. The members met for prayer, study of the Greek NT, self-examination and works of charitable relief. Returning from a journey to Georgia, with Charles, for the Society for the Propagation of the Gospel, during which he was much influenced by the Georgia Moravians, he met a disciple of Count Nikolaus von **Zinzendorf**, Peter **Böhler**, who convinced him that Christ had died for him. Wesley adhered to a Moravian-inspired society in Fetter Lane and, on 24 May 1738, 'at a quarter to nine', experienced 'conversion', and his 'heart strangely warmed' by a reading from **Luther**'s preface to Romans. This experience made him an evangelist, and it pleased God, he declared, 'to kindle a fire which I trust shall never be extinguished'. Wesley embarked on his life work, the objective of which was 'the reform of the nation, particularly the church, and to spread Scriptural holiness over the land'. For 52 years, the Methodist movement became the creation of his mind and spirit; his travels throughout the land were unceasing, and his influence spread widely. He hoped the Methodists would never leave the Church of England, but some of his actions, particularly the ordinations he himself performed from 1784, broke ecclesiastical law and forced a separation; his lay preachers, appeal to Noncon-

formists, and distrust of the parish system also contributed. In time, active opposition to the Methodists lessened, and mob violence, so common earlier, disappeared. He died 'England's Grand Old Man', an Anglican priest to the last, and is buried behind the Methodist City Road chapel. Wesley's fame rests in part on his extraordinary preaching and missionary tours, in the fields or wherever he might assemble an audience; his message was simple: 'salvation is through Jesus Christ. A new life awaits every man who loves Jesus, believes in the Atonement, repents his sins, and lives according to the law'.

Wesley, Samuel Sebastian Organist and composer, born London, 14 August 1810, died Gloucester, 19 April 1876. He was a chorister of the Chapel Royal, organist of various chapels and cathedrals, finally of Gloucester Cathedral. He helped to reform cathedral music, to compile various collections of hymns and psalms, and composed tunes of his own.

Westcott, Brook Foss Bishop of Durham, born Birmingham, 12 January 1825, died 27 July 1901, Auckland Castle, the palace of the bishops of Durham. He went to King Edward VI's School, Birmingham, then Trinity College, Cambridge, where he was elected a fellow in 1849. He was ordained in 1851, and the following year moved to Harrow. It was there that he started to produce his works on the New Testament, beginning with, in 1855, a *General Survey of the History of the Canon of the New Testament during the First Four Centuries*. Books appeared at regular intervals, and in 1870 he became Regius professor of divinity at Cambridge. He was much in demand for spiritual and vocational advice, and became president of the Cambridge Clergy Training School, now Westcott House. He had at the same time a canonry at Peterborough, and when he resigned that post in 1883 was appointed to a canonry at Westminster Abbey. In 1881, in conjunction with F. J. Hort, he published a two-volume critical text of the New Testament in Greek. This was followed by other New Testament commentaries and other scriptural and patristic studies. In 1890 he was offered, and accepted, the bishopric of Durham. In that post he interested himself in social issues, especially the problems of the miners. He continued to publish as bishop, including his major doctrinal work, *The Gospel of Life* (1892).

Weston, Frank Anglican missionary bishop of Zanzibar, born London, 13 September 1871, died Tanzania, 2 November 1924. He joined the Universities' Mission to Central Africa (UMCA) in 1898 after working in slum parishes in England. In 1901 he became principal of St Andrew's Training College at Kiungani, and he was consecrated bishop of Zanzibar in 1908. His Anglo-Catholic views led him to oppose a federation of Protestant churches in East Africa proposed at the Kikuyu Conference of 1913, but at the Lambeth Conference of 1920 he encouraged debate on ecumenism. He also condemned the appointment of the liberal theologian B. H. **Streeter** to a canonry at Hereford in 1915. He chaired the second Anglo-Catholic Congress in 1923. His writings include *The One Christ* (1907) and *Serfs of Great Britain* (1920), which spoke out against forced labour in Africa.

Wheaton, Elizabeth Ryder Evangelist and social reformer, born Wayne County, Ohio, 1844, died Tabor, Iowa, 28 July 1923. Wheaton joined a Holiness group in the early 1880s following the deaths of her husband and son. She worked as a prison evangelist, visiting nearly every state in the USA, Canada and Mexico, and as a street evangelist outside bars and brothels, being herself imprisoned in Edinburgh for holding a street meeting. In 1906 Frank **Bartleman** took her to the Apostolic Faith Mission in Azusa Street, and she had a Pentecostal experience the following year.

Whitefield, George Anglican clergyman, born Gloucester, 16 December 1714, died Newburyport, Massachusetts, USA, 30 September 1770. His parents were innkeepers and he worked as a domestic at Pembroke College, Oxford, to pay his lecture fees. He became acquainted with John and Charles **Wesley**, and in 1735 experienced a religious conversion. Having been ordained deacon in 1736, he began an evangelizing tour in Bath, Bristol and other towns, his eloquence at once attracting immense crowds. As the clergy did not welcome him to their pulpits, he began to preach in the open air, and his voice was so clear and powerful that it could reach 20,000 folk. His fervour and dramatic action held them spell-bound,

and his homely pathos soon broke down all barriers. Back in America, 1739–40, he was one of the leading figures in the 'Great Awakening', and preached in all the principal towns of the Atlantic seaboard. He helped organize the Calvinistic Methodists in Wales in 1743. He made seven American preaching tours, but is not considered a founder of Methodism there, since he disregarded denominational lines. On his last voyage in 1769, he arranged for the conversion of his orphanage into Bethesda College. He was by now affected by a severe asthmatic complaint, but to those who advised him to take some rest, he replied: 'I had rather wear out than rust out.' It was said that 'in the compass of a single week, and that for years, he spoke in general forty hours, and in many sixty, and that to thousands'. He was one of the greatest pulpit orators of the eighteenth century, the impact of his preaching coming not from its content, but from his personality.

Whiting, Richard Blessed, last abbot of Glastonbury, martyr, born unknown, died Tor Hill, Glastonbury, 15 November 1539. Educated at the abbey, under Richard Bere, he was ordained in Wells Cathedral in 1501. He was nominated by Cardinal **Wolsey** to succeed Bere on his death in 1525, a selection formally witnessed by Thomas **More**. As a member of the House of Lords, he was immediately involved in **Henry VIII**'s divorce, but prudently took no stand on the matter, though privately unsympathetic. In 1534, he and his 51 monks took the Oath of Royal Supremacy. Glastonbury was the greatest of the great monasteries, a target for suppression and destruction and a source of great wealth for the king. **Cromwell**'s visitor, Robert Layton, found such good order in 1535, however, that the monastery was left unmolested. Cromwell continued to assure Whiting that there would be no suppression, but in 1539 Layton and the royal commission arrived without warning, interrogated the weak and sickly old abbot, perceived his 'cankered and traitorous heart', and took him to the Tower for examination by Cromwell himself. They searched the monastery and found valuable articles hidden away, which enabled them to change treason to robbery as a basis for arresting Whiting. He remained adamant in the faith, and was secretly and without trial condemned to death; he was taken back to Glastonbury, laid on a trundel and dragged through the town to be hanged, drawn and quartered. Feast day 1 December.

Wigram, George Vicessimus Biblical lexicographer, born 28 March 1805, died 1 January 1879. He declined to follow his brother, Joseph Wigram, later bishop of Rochester, into holy orders and attached himself to the Plymouth Brethren instead. In 1839 he produced *The Englishman's Greek Concordance to the NT* followed by *The Englishman's Hebrew and Chaldee Concordance to the OT* (1843). Both of these publications provide a concordance of each word in the original text cross-referenced with an English word list. In 1867 he published *The Hebraist's Vade Mecum*, the first systematic attempt to give a complete verbal index to the Hebrew and Aramaic biblical texts.

Wilberforce, William English anti-slavery leader, born Hull, 24 August 1759, died London, 29 July 1833. At the age of fourteen he wrote a letter to a York paper about the evils of the slave trade. He studied at St John's College, Cambridge, was elected to the House of Commons in 1780, renewing a friendship with William Pitt, and, in 1784, was elected for both Hull and Yorkshire. He became a convert to evangelical Christianity, and associated with the Clapham Sect, a group of evangelicals active in public life. Pitt suggested he become leader of the anti-slavery campaign. The intellectual climate of the time was favourable to ideas of human liberty and happiness, and he continued to champion the cause, in and out of Parliament, until slavery was abolished in the British Empire in 1833, only a few weeks before his death. Wilberforce also had profound religious influence; his *Practical View of the Prevailing Religious System of Professed Christians* (1797), a bestseller for forty years, argued convincingly that reform of society must begin with individual sanctification; with great skill he had used evangelization to help with the anti-slavery campaign. He played a leading role in the formation of the British and Foreign Bible Society in 1804, and the Church Missionary Society in 1799. During the Oxford Movement a generation later, three of his four sons were among the many followers of John Henry **Newman** who entered the Catholic Church. The third, Samuel, 'Soapy Sam', who broke with

Newman and Henry **Manning** on their conversion to Rome, became a high church bishop of Oxford and Winchester. He is remembered for the 1859 debate at Oxford on **Darwin**'s theory of evolution, at which his intervention precipitated the later nineteenth-century conflict between science and religion.

Wiley, H. Orton Nazarene theologian, born Marquette, Nebraska, 15 November 1877, died Pasadena, California, 22 August 1961. He was a pastor, college president (notably Pasadena College), editor of his denominational paper, and a strategist for the Church of the Nazarene's system of Christian colleges and universities. Trained in biblical theology at Pacific School of Religion, he wrote several commentaries, but his chief contribution was in systematic theology. His three-volume *Christian Theology* (1940–3) established him as the primary spokesman of the Wesleyan-Arminian perspective in his lifetime and was a widely used text in evangelical Wesleyan denominations until the 1980s.

Wilfrid Saint, bishop and monastic founder, born possibly at Ripon, Yorkshire, c.634, died near Oundle, Northamptonshire, 709. He was educated at Lindisfarne, Rome and Lyons, and on his return became abbot of Ripon. He was a major protagonist of Roman, rather than Celtic, practices, a view which triumphed at the Synod of Whitby. He was chosen to be bishop of York, but when he returned in 666 from France, where he had gone to be consecrated, he discovered that **Chad** had been installed in his place. He was however granted the see by Archbishop **Theodore (of Canterbury)** three years later. When Theodore a decade later divided his enormous diocese without consulting him, Wilfrid appealed to Rome. Rome granted his appeal, but the king of Northumbria would not accept the decision, and imprisoned and then exiled Wilfrid, who went to Sussex to preach Christianity, and to found a monastery at Selsey. He was reinstated in 686, but with limited jurisdiction. In 703 a synod deprived him yet again of the see of York, and of his monasteries. Again he appealed to Rome and was vindicated, but in 705 a compromise was reached by which he was left with the diocese of Hexham and his monasteries, but not the see of York. Feast day 12 October.

William I King of England, born Falaise, *c.*1028, died Rouen, 1087. Duke of Normandy in 1035, Lord of Maine in 1062 and Brittany in 1064, William was designated by his kinsman, **Edward the Confessor**, in 1051, as heir to the English kingdom; he defeated Harold II at Battle, near Hastings, in 1066, and, by five years of intermittent campaign, subjected the kingdom to his will. William was master of the Norman church, and it attained a distinguished reputation under his guidance, with a monastic revival achieving its best expression at Bec, and canonical reform made effective through conciliar legislation; but nowhere reflected the reforming spirit of the time more closely, or more justly enjoyed papal favour than Britain. **Nicholas II** legalized William's irregular marriage in 1059; **Alexander II** and Hildebrand (Pope **Gregory VII**) supported William's invasion of England. William championed secular control in church affairs: a barrier was erected to the traffic between the English church and the Roman curia; papal claims to feudal overlordship were decisively rejected; the Investiture struggle found no expression in England in William's reign. Gregory recognized the merits and strengths of William's policies and acted with prudence and circumspection; greater vitality and power of direction increased the monarchy's strength and resources. In a profligate age, William was distinguished by the purity of his married life, by temperate habits and by a sincere piety; he was averse to unnecessary bloodshed or cruelty. He was avaricious, but his church policy shows a disinterestedness as rare as it was honourable. William's reign was a watershed in English history and, by his influence, helped to shape the history of the Western church.

William of Aebelholt Saint, Danish abbot, born Paris, *c.*1127, died Aebelholt, 6 April 1203. Son of a noble family, William became a canon regular of Sainte-Geneviève-de-Paris. **Absalon of Lund**, bishop of Roskilde, called him to Denmark to reform the house of canons on Eskilsø. As first abbot of Aebelholt in 1175, he exerted great influence as a writer and teacher and acted as an intermediary in Franco-Scandinavian controversies; he worked for peace, and for freedom of the Church. His cult began with numerous miracles shortly after his death, and he was canonized in 1224. Feast day 6 April.

William of Alnwick English Franciscan Scholastic, bishop, born Alnwick, Northumberland, date unknown, died Avignon, March 1333. William studied under **Duns Scotus** at Paris and taught at Oxford, Montpellier, Bologna and Naples. In the Franciscan general chapter at Perugia, he signed the document *De paupertate Christi* (1322), a protest against **John XXII**; the bishops of Bologna and Ferrara were ordered by the Pope to proceed against 'William the Englishman'. He became bishop of Giovinazzo in 1330 through his friendship with Robert of Sicily. He left a commentary on **Peter Lombard**'s *Sentences*, and many *quaestiones disputate*.

William of Aquitaine Saint, monastic founder, born *c.*755, died Gellone Abbey, 28 May 812. A cousin of **Charlemagne**, who appointed William count of Toulouse and protector of his son **Louis** the Pious, king of Aquitaine. William recaptured Barcelona from the Moors in 803, and founded a monastery at Gellone, where he was professed in 806. He appears in several *Chansons de geste* as William *au court-nez*; his biographical material is contained in the eleventh-century *Ardonis vita Benedicti abbatis Anianensis*. Feast day 28 May.

William of Arnaud Blessed, French Dominican martyr, born Montpellier, date unknown, died Avignonet, near Toulouse, 29 May 1242. Little is known of William's life until 1234, when **Gregory IX** appointed him Inquisitor for four dioceses in Provence; his zeal in rooting out heresy was such as to have him banished from Toulouse, though he is said to have converted many by his 'sweetness and charity'. Lured to a castle at Avignonet by the bailiff of Count Raymond VII of Toulouse, William and his companions were murdered, giving rise to reports of miracles and cures, and confirmation of a cult by **Pius IX** in 1866. Feast day 29 May.

William of Auvergne (Paris) French Scholastic philosopher, born Aurillac (Cantal), shortly before 1190, died Paris, 30 March 1249. A professor at Paris, William became archbishop in 1228; he protected the mendicant orders, opposed pluralism and had influence at the court of St **Louis**. He compiled a vast philosophico-theological encyclopaedia, *Magisterium Divinale ac Sapientiale*, relying on the works of Aristotle, Maimonides and Avicenna, their language and their commentaries, but he did not entirely succeed in synthesizing new terms with traditional ideas.

William of Auxerre Philosopher and theologian, born Auxerre, c.1150, died Rome, 3 November 1231. Renowned in Paris as a theologian, he was appointed in 1230 by **Gregory IX** member of a commission of three to correct the physical treatises of Aristotle to bring him into line with Christian thought, and to make him acceptable to the university of Paris. He died, however, before he could complete his part of this important assignment. He was largely influenced by **Augustine** and **Anselm of Canterbury** in his theology, and to some degree by **Hugh** and **Richard of Saint-Victor**, and Avicenna. His fame rests largely on the *Summa aurea*, inspired by the *Sentences* of **Peter Lombard**, but covering some issues not treated by him. It is divided into four books: 1. The One and Triune God; 2. Creation, Angels and Man; 3. Christ and the virtues; 4. Sacraments and the four last things. The work had extraordinary influence on contemporary authors, and on later Scholastics such as **Albert the Great**, St **Thomas Aquinas** and St **Bonaventure**. He is considered the first medieval theologian to develop a systematic treatise on free will, the virtues and the natural law.

William of Bourges Saint, archbishop of Bourges, born Arthel, 1150, died Bourges, 10 January 1209. William became abbot of the Cistercian monastery at Fontaine Saint-Jean in 1184, then of Châlis in 1187; named archbishop of Bourges in 1200, he lived a life of strict observance, and died while preparing a Crusade against the Albigenses; he is buried in his cathedral. **Honorius III** canonized him in 1218. Feast day 10 January.

William of Champeaux French Scholastic philosopher, bishop, born Champeaux, near Melun, c.1070, died Châlons-sur-Marne, 1122. A student of Roscelin and **Anselm of Laon**, he became master of the cathedral school of Paris, where he had Peter **Abelard** as a disciple. In the controversy over universals, he supported the realist position criticized by Abelard, whose ridicule drove him from his post. He modified his extreme doctrines in retirement, and abandoned the distinctive tenets of realism altogether in his later years as bishop of Châlons.

William of Conches French philosopher, born Normandy, c.1090, died Chartres, c.1160. A disciple of Bernard of Chartres, he sought to further the study of profane sciences and literature in the interests of Christian humanism. Of his writings, the *Philosophia Mundi* was attacked by **William of Saint-Thierry**, who considered it a modalistic view of the Trinity. He also wrote *Dragmaticon*, which posited 'nature' as the formal cause of the world; glosses on Priscian's *Institutiones Grammaticae*, Plato's *Timaeus*, and **Boethius'** *De Consolatione Philosophiae*, on the meaning of philosophy, God and spiritual beings, the material universe, the creation of man.

William of Corbeil Archbishop of Canterbury, the first after the Norman Conquest not to have been a monk, born Corbeil, near Paris, c.1070, died Canterbury, 21 November 1136. William studied under **Anselm of Laon** and apparently was afterwards a clerk in the household of Ranulph Flambard, bishop of Durham, but in mid-career he became a canon of Dover. Seeking a more rigorous religious life he became an Augustinian canon of St Osyth's in Essex, where he was also elected as prior. As archbishop, to which post he was appointed in 1123, he proved himself a vigorous reformer at three important councils at Westminster, in 1125, 1127 and 1129 – outlawing clerical marriage and fornication and prohibiting the inheritance of benefices. He did much to resolve the ancient disputes between York and Canterbury, but in the latter's favour and, as is now known, by conveniently forged documentary evidence on the part of the Canterbury chapter. He was instrumental in crowning King Stephen in contravention of the oath he and other bishops had sworn to Matilda in 1128. Because of this **Henry of Huntingdon** gave William a bad press, writing that ' he could not be praised because there is nothing to praise'. However, his spiritual and religious commitment is above suspicion.

William of Dijon *see* **William of Volpiano**

William of Firmatus Saint, French hermit, perhaps bishop, born Tours, date unknown, died Mantilly,

24 April c.1095. Educated at Tours, a canon of St Venantius, William became a soldier and physician. He retired to the wilderness with his mother, and lived as a hermit after her death. Renowned for his sanctity, miracles were credited to him, including the freeing from prison of Count **Baldwin** of Boulogne, later king of Jerusalem. Stephen of Fougères, bishop of Rennes, wrote his life. Feast day 24 April.

William of Hirsau   Blessed, abbot, born 1026, died at the abbey of Hirsau, 4 July 1091. He entered the monastery of St Emmeran in Regensburg as a child oblate, and in 1069 was named second abbot of Hirsau. He was a supporter of the reforms of **Gregory VII**, and eventually adopted a form of the Cluniac observance for his monastery, and for those founded from Hirsau. He wrote treatises on music and on astronomy. Feast day 5 July.

William of Jumièges (William Calculus)   French Benedictine chronicler, flourished c.1070. Little is known of his life, but he is famous for *Gesta Historia Normannorum ducum*, in eight books, an authoritative account of the Norman people from 851 to 1137. The first four volumes are a revision of the work of Dudo of Saint-Quentin, and the work was very successful in its day; about 40 MSS survive.

William of Malmesbury   English Benedictine monk, born south-west England, c.1090, died Malmesbury, 1143. William spent most of his life at Malmesbury, became librarian, read very widely and wrote *Gesta Regum Anglorum*, a history of England from early times, completed by *Historia Novella* to his own day, including the civil war of King Stephen; also *Gesta pontificum Anglorum*, which deals with English bishops, sees and monasteries of the same period. He was the best English chronicler of the twelfth century.

William of Moerbeke   Dominican archbishop and translator, born Moerbeke, Belgium, c.1215, died Corinth, 1286. He studied at Cologne under **Albert the Great**. By 1260 he had served in Thebes and Nicaea and, urged by **Thomas Aquinas**, he began to edit and translate ancient Greek authors, and became the most eminent and prolific translator of the thirteenth century. He gave Latin scholars a

careful, literal version of Aristotle, Archimedes and books of Ptolemy, Hero, Galen and Hippocrates, which remained standard until the sixteenth century. Roger Bacon said these literal translations were 'barbaric', but their fidelity allowed Aquinas to grasp Aristotle's exact meaning, and generally gave Western scholars a much more accurate text of Aristotle than had been available, enabling the Scholastics to distinguish between authentic Aristotelian positions and the Neoplatonic interpretations that had been added to them; and they enable modern scholars to reconstruct Greek originals, many of which are lost.

William of Newburgh   English Augustinian canon, born near Bridlington, Yorkshire, 1136, died Newburgh, c.1200. Educated by the canons of Newburgh, where he spent his life, William became the finest English historian of his age. His *Historia rerum Anglicarum*, composed at the request of Ernald, abbot of Rievaulx, covering the years 1066 to 1198, is remarkable for an unusually (for the times) keen sense of historical criticism, and its dismissal of commonly held, but unsubstantiated, fables of the famous; it is an important source for the reign of Henry II.

William of Norwich   Saint, English alleged child-martyr, born near Norwich, 1132, died there, 22 March 1144. A tanner's apprentice aged twelve, William is said to have been enticed from his home on Tuesday of Holy Week into the house of a Jew in Norwich; his mutilated body was found in Mousehold Wood on Holy Saturday. According to Thomas of Monmouth, a monk and the only authority for the legend, William had been crucified by the Jews during Passover. This earliest known example of blood accusation against the Jews was investigated in 1759 by Cardinal Lorenzo Ganganelli (**Clement XIV**), who refuted the legend absolutely. The cult of William dates from 1151, when many visions and miracles were reported at his tomb. Feast day 25/6 March.

William of Notre Dame de L'Olive   Saint, Flemish hermit, born Brabant, date unknown, died Mariemont, 10 February 1240. A baker early in life, William became a canon of St Norbert (Premonstratensian) at Aisne, but soon left to live as a hermit at Mariemont in Belgium. He founded

Notre Dame de L'Olive, an abbey for women that became affiliated with Cîteaux; the first nuns came from Fontenelle and from Moustier-sur-Sambre. Feast day 10 February.

William of Ockham English Franciscan philosopher, theologian and political writer, born Ockham, Surrey, c.1285, died Munich, 10 April 1347. He became a Franciscan, studied and taught at Oxford. One of the most influential philosophers of the fourteenth century, he represented the 'via moderna', as opposed to the 'via antiqua', of **Thomas Aquinas**, who, with the Schoolmen in the previous century, had tried to achieve an accord between faith and reason by reinterpreting Aristotle. Other Franciscan scholars from **Bonaventure** to **Duns Scotus** had argued for the faith by rejecting Aristotle, but these systems depended on the doctrine of Realism, which Ockham rejected, advocating, rather, a radical empiricism in which the basis of knowledge is direct experience of individual things, Nominalism, hence 'Ockhams Razor', the view that 'what can be done with fewer assumptions, is done in vain with more'. This Nominalism was of great significance for science, since it suggested that natural phenomena could be investigated rationally. God to Ockham, however, was above all knowledge; He cannot be apprehended by reason, as the Thomists taught, nor by illumination as the Augustinians believed, but only by faith. The Scholastics, who did not always appreciate the precise meaning of the terms he used, accused him of paving the way for Martin **Luther**, who professed himself an Ockhamist. As a Franciscan, Ockham sided with the 'Spirituals', who embraced a strict theory of poverty, and he accused Pope **John XXII** of heresy in this matter. His stance led to his excommunication in 1328, and expulsion from his Order in 1331. He then sought the protection of **Louis of Bavaria**. He argued that it was the emperor's duty to depose a heretical Pope, and that the Pope had no jurisdiction over an imperial election. His views provided theoretical backing for the conciliar movement of the fifteenth century.

William of Paris *see* **William of Auvergne**

William of Poitiers Norman historian, born Preaux, Eure, c.1020, died c.1087, place unknown.

Educated at Poitiers, William lived the life of a knight until he became chaplain to **William** the Conqueror, and accompanied him on his military expeditions, though not at the battle of Hastings (1066). The best informed man of his age, William knew the Greek and Latin authors and wrote a life of the Conqueror. *Gesta Guielmi II, ducis Normannorum Regis Anglorum I* is contemporary and based on direct testimonies; only a fragment remains of the one extant MS.

William of Rubruk Franciscan missionary and travel writer, born Rubrouc, France, about 1200, died after 1256. Went with **Louis IX** of France on a Crusade to Tripoli and Acre. In 1253 he was sent on a mission from Constantinople throughout China, the Crimea and Asia Minor, and he arrived back in Tripoli in 1255. He wrote an account of this journey which is regarded as a masterpiece of its time and genre, providing valuable information and insights. He proved that the Caspian was an inland sea, pointed out the relationships between certain languages and races and threw light on some of the religions of the East. The account of the journey appears in English, translated by Rockhill, as *The Journey of William of Rubruk to the Eastern Parts* (London, 1900).

William of Saint-Amour Born Saint-Amour, Jura, c.1200, died there, 13 September 1272. William studied theology at Paris, where he took a violent dislike to the mendicant orders and their academic privileges; he led opposition in the university against their masters, **Bonaventure** and **Thomas Aquinas**, who were suspended in 1254. **Innocent IV** issued a bull *Quociens pro comunni*, rescinding their privileges to hear confessions, administer the sacraments and bury the faithful; **Alexander IV** abrogated these restrictions in 1255. William, for his part, was forbidden to teach and exiled from France, though his disciples revived the anti-mendicant polemic before his death.

William of Saint-Thierry Monk, spiritual writer and theologian, friend of **Bernard of Clairvaux**, born Liège, the end of the 1070s, died Signy, 8 September 1148. Joined the Benedictines in 1100 and became abbot at St-Thierry, near Rheims, in 1120. Bernard discouraged William from joining him at Clairvaux but instead in 1135 he resigned as abbot and joined the Cistercians at their newly established house at Signy in the Ardennes. His writings include discussions on the relation between knowledge and love, and between the body and soul, the question of grace, and the presence of God in the Eucharist. The latter work was dedicated to St Bernard, and William's *Epistula ad Fratres de Monte Dei de Vita Solitaria* (the 'Golden Letter') was occasionally and mistakenly attributed to Bernard.

William of Toulouse   Saint, French theologian and mystic, born Toulouse, 1297, died Paris, 18 May 1369. William entered the Augustinian Order at nineteen, and lectured at Paris. He had a special devotion to the souls in purgatory, read the lives of the saints often and sought to model his life on theirs; he overcame many temptations in his struggle for perfection. Miracles accumulated after his death; his cult was approved 50 days later, and confirmed in 1893. Feast day 18 May.

William of Tripoli   Dominican missionary, born Tripoli, Lebanon, *c.*1220, died after 1273, place unknown. Ordained at Acre, William represented **Urban IV** at the court of **Louis IX**, bishop of Tyre and count of Haifa. **Gregory X** named him his representative with **Marco Polo** on his journey to China in 1271–95, but he left the embassy in Cilicia. He then composed, at Gregory's request, the *Tractatus de statu Saracenorum et de Muhammadi pseudopropheta*, which relied on his personal experiences, and deals with Muhammad, the spread of Islam, and the Islamic doctrine and law as expounded in the Qur'an.

William of Tyre   Palestinian historian, born Palestine, *c.*1130, died there, October 1186. The son of a merchant family, he studied theology in France under **Peter Lombard** and law at Bologna under Hugh de Porta Ravennata. Ordained before 1161, he returned to Tyre, where Amalric, king of Jerusalem, appointed him archbishop. After 1169 he began his *Historia rerum in partibus transmarinis gestarum*, comprising the *Gesta Regum* and *Gesta Almarici*, and covering events from 1095, the preaching of the First Crusade, to 1184. The work is a primary authority from 1127 to his own day, and is marked by insight and careful sifting of evidence from a wide range of sources.

William of Vercelli   Saint, Italian abbot, born Vercelli, Piedmont, 1085, died monastery of San Salvatore at Goleto, near Nusca, 25 June 1142. As a youth William became a hermit and built a monastery at Monte Vergine, near Avellino, and a celebrated shrine there to Our Lady in 1124. When disagreements arose with other monks, William moved to Serra Cognata and founded other monasteries, including the one near Nusca where he died. He also founded in 1119 the now extinct congregation of Benedictine monks called Williamites. Feast day 25 June.

William of Volpiano   Saint, reforming abbot, born 962 in the castle on Isola S. Giulio, on Lake Orta, Italy, died abbey of Fécamp, 1 January 1031. He was the son of the count of Volpiano, and entered as a child oblate the monastery of San Genuario, near Vercelli. In 987 he met Abbot Majolus of Cluny, and returned with him to Cluny. Majolus entrusted him with the reform of a number of monasteries, one of which, Saint Bénigne at Dijon, elected him abbot in 990, at which point he was ordained priest. A large number of monasteries followed the reforms he instituted, and by the time of his death he ruled some 40 houses. A small number of his letters and sermons, and a single treatise, survive. Feast day 1 January.

William of Waynfiete   Bishop of Winchester, born Wainfleet, Lincs, *c.*1395, died South Waltham, Hants, 2 August 1486. Ordained in 1420, William became master of St Mary Magdalen Hospital, near Winchester, and provost of Eton College in 1440. He succeeded, on Henry VI's recommendation, Cardinal **Beaufort** at Winchester in 1447, and founded a Hall at Oxford that became Magdalen College, for the study of theology and philosophy. Henry appointed him chancellor in 1456, and he acquiesced in the accession of Edward IV. He left Magdalen the largest and best endowed of any Oxford college.

William of Wykeham   Bishop of Winchester, chancellor of England and founder of Winchester College and New College, Oxford, born into a poor family in Wickham, Hampshire, England, in mid-1324, died South Waltham, 27 September 1404. Having served in public office, including as clerk of the royal works at Henley and surveyor of the royal works at Windsor, he was made Keeper of the Privy Seal in 1364 and elected bishop of Winchester in 1366. He was consecrated the following year and was also made chancellor, a post he was forced to resign in 1371, following the losses sustained in the war with France. He then concentrated on reforms within his diocese and began plans for his educational foundations. In 1376 he lost the financial control of his diocese following accusations by John of Gaunt. He was restored to favour and full episcopal control under Richard II and served a second time as chancellor from 1389 to 1391 and on royal commissions and other committees until 1399. He spent his remaining years in retirement.

William of York (Fitzherbert, also known as William of Thwayt)   Saint, archbishop of York, died, possibly of poisoning, 8 June 1154. About the year 1130, he was canon and treasurer of York Minster. On the death of the previous archbishop in 1140, William was proposed for the see of York. He was supported by the king and in Rome by Henry of Blois, but stood in opposition to Henry Murdac, a Cistercian monk who enjoyed wide ecclesiastical support, including that of **Theobald**, the archbishop of Canterbury and, in Rome, that of **Bernard of Clairvaux**. William was suspected of simony, and it was alleged that there was undue royal pressure in his nomination. He was, however, able to clear his name and in 1143 was consecrated archbishop by the papal legate. He reformed the diocese and won the affection of the people. William had never collected the pallium sent in 1146 by Pope **Lucius II**, and when Lucius died his successor, **Eugenius III**, a Cistercian, took up the cause of Murdac and William was deposed. He travelled to Rome and later took refuge with Henry of Blois in Winchester. Both Eugenius and Murdac died in 1153, and the incoming Pope, **Anastasius IV**, restored William to the see of York and gave him the pallium. He returned to York to popular acclaim, and when everyone escaped unharmed when a bridge over the Ouse collapsed, the supposed miracle was attributed to him. He died suddenly within a month of his return. Feast day 8 June.

Williams, Charles Walter Stansby   Poet, novelist, biographer and lay theologian, born London, 20

September 1886, died Oxford, 15 May 1945. He was educated at St Albans School and University College, London. He joined Oxford University Press as a reader in 1908 on graduation, and remained on its staff until his death, largely serving as a book editor, and in charge of the series The World's Classics. His first book of poetry, *The Silver Stair*, was published in 1912 with the backing of Alice and Wilfred **Meynell**, and its success persuaded Oxford to publish in all a dozen of his books. Shortly after the outbreak of World War II the press moved its offices from London to Oxford, where Williams became a regular member of the Inklings, and was invited both to tutor and to lecture: the university awarded him an honorary MA in 1943. Like many of the Inklings he was a devout member of the Church of England. In 1917 he married Florence Conway, and they had one son.

Williams, Henry   Anglican missionary to New Zealand, born Nottingham, 11 February 1792, died Pakaraka, New Zealand, 16 July 1867. He served in the navy during the Napoleonic War, and retired from active service in 1815. He married in 1818 and entered the ministry, being ordained in 1822, after which he sailed for New Zealand and served on the Church Missionary Society's mission at Paihia, where, in 1826, he was joined by his brother William Williams, who was later to become a bishop. After a slow start they had considerable success among the Maori population: he played an important role in persuading the Maoris to accept a British protectorate by the Treaty of Waitangi of 1840. In subsequent conflicts between the Maoris and the British governor, his sympathies lay with the Maoris to the extent that he was called a traitor, and the Church Missionary Society expelled him, though he was later reinstated. In 1876 the Maoris erected a cross in his memory at Paihia.

Williams, Ralph Darby   Assemblies of God missionary to Latin America, born Sudbrook, England, 1902, died 1982. Williams was ordained in 1925, six years after having a Pentecostal experience. On the advice of Alice Luce, Williams and his brother Richard became missionaries in Latin America, arriving in El Salvador in 1929. He established Bible institutes in 1931 and 1937, and became field superintendent for Central America in 1940, the number of churches in the region increasing from four to 400. Williams used indigenous church principles, and from 1976 worked in a US institute for training clergy in Latin America. His *Memoirs* are unpublished.

Williams, Roger Founder of the colony of Rhode Island, born London, c.1603, died Providence, Rhode Island, March 1683. He graduated from Cambridge in 1627, acknowledged his belief in the 'thirty-nine articles and the Book of Common Prayer', was ordained in the Church of England, and emigrated to Massachusetts in 1631. He was a centre of controversy for his extreme 'separatist' views: his insistence that only purchase from the Indians, not royal grants, conferred title to colonial lands, and his denial that civil magistrates had any authority in religious matters. He was formally tried for his opinions and banished from Massachusetts in 1636. With four companions, he founded the same year the first settlement in Rhode Island, which he named 'Providence Plantations', in remembrance of 'God's merciful providence to him in his distress'. He learned the language of the Indians in the vicinity, bought the land upon which he had settled, a foundation on the basis of complete religious toleration. Settlers joined the colony, some Anabaptists by whom Williams himself was baptized, and others by him in turn, thus establishing the first Baptist church in America. However, he soon became a 'Seeker', or Independent, but continued to preach, believing that while direct apostolic succession is necessary to a true church, none had existed since the early centuries, and therefore there is no true church on earth. In 1642 he secured a charter for the colony and became president of Rhode Island until 1657. His view that Church and State must be separate, and that the state must not coerce the conscience of the individual, are a treasured part of the Baptist heritage in America.

Williams, William Welsh poet and hymn-writer, born Cefn-y-Coed, near Llandovery, 1717, died nearby at Pant-y-Celyn, 11 January 1791. His father had been a Presbyterian, but founded an independent church. William, however, was ordained deacon in the Church of Wales in 1740 and became a curate. His sympathies grew closer to Methodism, and he was never ordained priest. He resigned his curacy, but continued to regard himself as an Anglican minister, even though he and his family were members of a Methodist congregation. After his marriage in 1749 he settled near Pant-y-Celyn, whence he continued his preaching tours of Wales until his death. He had considerable gifts as a hymn-writer, more than 800 hymns being ascribed to him. His first volume of hymns was published in 1744. His best known hymn, 'Guide me, O Thou great Jehovah', originally written in Welsh, appeared in 1772.

Willibrord English missionary and patron saint of The Netherlands and Luxemburg, born Northumbria, 658, died Echternach, Luxemburg, 7 November 739. He studied under St **Wilfrid** at Ripon, became a monk and at the age of twenty joined a community in Ireland, where he was ordained. In 690 he went with a group of confreres on a mission to Frisia and was welcomed to the court of Pepin of Herstal. He quickly secured papal support for his mission, and in Rome in 695 Pope **Sergius I** consecrated him archbishop of the Frisians. He established a cathedral in Utrecht and in 698 founded the monastery of Echternach, from which he made missionary journeys as far as Denmark, Heligoland and Thuringia. He encountered opposition from the pagan Duke Ragbod, but after his death was able to return to Frisia, where he enjoyed the ecclesiastical support of St **Boniface** in repairing the damages wrought by Ragbod. He was buried in the abbey at Echternach, where his shrine has become a centre of pilgrimage.

Wilson, John Leonard Anglican bishop of Singapore, born Witton Gilbert, Durham, 23 November 1897, died Wensleydale, Yorkshire, 18 August 1970. He was educated at Knutsford and Queen's College, Oxford, and trained for the priesthood at Wycliffe Hall. He was at Coventry Cathedral in 1924–6, where he was ordained, and in Cairo in 1927–9 with the Church Missionary Society, though his modernist theology proved controversial. He was in parish work in the north of England when in 1938 he was invited by R. O. Hall to be dean of St John's Cathedral, Hong Kong, where he was consecrated bishop of Singapore, 22 July 1941. Despite the surrender of Singapore on 15 February 1942, he was allowed to visit prisoners and take confirmations until interned in March 1943. He barely survived interrogation on 17–19 October 1943, and in 1947 he confirmed one of his torturers. He was dean of Manchester, 1949–53, and bishop of Birmingham, 1953–69. He was awarded a CMG in 1946 and a KCMG in 1968.

Wilson, Thomas Bishop of Sodor and Man, British Isles, born Burton, Cheshire, 20 December 1663, died Bishops' Court, Isle of Man, 7 March 1755. Trained as a medical doctor at Trinity College, Dublin, but then went into the Church. Was consecrated bishop of Sodor and Man in 1698 and moved to Kirkmichael, Isle of Man, where he lived for his remaining 57 years. He set about raising moral, spiritual, educational and ecclesiastical standards as well as building churches and public libraries. He was frequently engaged in controversy, but he was himself a tolerant man, and had good relations with Christians of other denominations. His *Principles and Duties of Christianity* (1707) also referred to as the 'Manx Catechism' was the first book to be printed in the Manx language.

Wimmer, Boniface Archabbot, founder of Benedictine monasticism in North America, born Thalmassing, Bavaria, 14 January 1809, died Latrobe, Pennsylvania, 8 December 1887. He was ordained a diocesan priest in 1831, and entered the Benedictine monastery of St Michael's, Metten, in 1832. Wimmer arrived in America with candidates for the Benedictine Order on 15 September 1846 to minister to German immigrants. On 18 October, he settled near Latrobe, Pennsylvania, and established a monastic community, which later became St Vincent Archabbey. Wimmer's monastery prospered, and he established others in Minnesota, Kansas, New Jersey and North Carolina. In 1855, the Holy See appointed Wimmer abbot. He was elected abbot in 1858, and Rome designated him abbot for life in 1866. Wimmer attended Vatican Council I as a Council Father. In 1883, **Leo XIII** gave Wimmer the title of archabbot.

Winefride (Welsh, Gwenfrewi) Patron saint of North Wales, daughter of a nobleman, who appears to have flourished in the middle of the seventh century. Tradition has it that her head was cut off by a chieftain, Caradoc ap Alaric or Alan,

because she refused to marry him. According to legend a well (St Winefride's Well at Holywell, Flint – still a place of pilgrimage) sprang up where her head touched the ground; her uncle and mentor, St Beuno, reunited her severed head to its body and Winefride was restored to life. She established a convent and became abbess. Her relics were re-buried in Shrewsbury, England, in 1138. Feast day 3 November.

Wiseman, Nicholas Cardinal, born Seville, Spain, of Irish parents, 2 August 1802, died London, 15 February 1865. He was educated at Ushaw College, County Durham, and at the English College in Rome, of which he was later rector. He became doctor of divinity in 1824 and was ordained the following year. His particular expertise was in Syriac studies: his *Horae Syriacae* appeared in 1828 to European-wide acclaim. From 1835 to 1836 he was lecturing in England, and in June 1840 he was consecrated as a bishop, appointed coadjutor for the Midland District, and rector of Oscott College. He helped to found the *Dublin Review*, and it was an article by him in that journal on Donatism which made **Newman** question his position as an Anglican. When Pope **Pius IX** restored the English hierarchy in 1850, Wiseman was translated from the London District, where in 1848 he had become vicar apostolic, to Westminster as the first archbishop and cardinal. This restoration was denounced by some of the public as 'papal aggression', and effigies of the Pope and of Wiseman were burned on Guy Fawkes' Day. He wrote a number of books and articles and a highly successful historical novel *Fabiola*. He was responsible for the words of the once very popular Roman Catholic hymn *Full in the Panting Heart of Rome*.

Wishart, George Scottish Reformer and martyr, born c.1510, died St Andrews, 28 March 1546. He graduated from Aberdeen, and taught NT Greek as a schoolmaster in Montrose. Charged with heretical tendencies, he fled first to England and then to the continent. He returned to England in 1543, taught at Cambridge for a year and went back to Scotland to preach the Gospel, particularly in Angus, as a fervent and vigorous Calvinist preacher; his words moved his hearers to destroy churches. Wishart eventually became involved in political intrigues concerned with a plot to assassinate Cardinal David Beaton. In 1546 he was arrested in East Lothian, tried, convicted and burned for heresy in front of the archiepiscopal castle of St Andrews, against the will of regent and people, but at the instigation of Beaton. Within three months, partly in revenge for Wishart and partly for political reasons, the cardinal was assassinated and the castle occupied by his murderers.

Wolsey, Thomas Archbishop of York, cardinal, papal legate, born Ipswich, *c.*1473, died Leicester Abbey, 29 November 1530. Educated at Magdalen College, Oxford, and ordained priest in 1498, he showed little ability for either theology or scholarship, and being of the view that the Church was primarily a source of employment and secular advancement, he pursued wealth and fame. He was chaplain to both Henry VII and **Henry VIII**; royal service led quickly to ecclesiastical preferment and in six years he became archbishop of Canterbury and chancellor. In 1515 he was made cardinal by the Pope, in 1518 papal legate, and thus supreme in both Church and State under the king. He was, however, an orthodox Catholic in his outlook, his religion 'probably highly conventional, but not purely formal'. Wolsey's policy was to serve the Pope and king, and for most of his career the two were in harmony. When Wolsey failed to secure the king's divorce, his career was shattered; his monopoly of power and haughty ways had long been resented, he had no defenders, and his great house, Hampton Court, and his appointments were confiscated in 1530. Stripped of his office, he attempted to fulfil his duties as archbishop of York for the first time, but none of this saved him, and he was suspected of trying to regain power. He was arrested that year, and only his death on the way to London saved him from execution.

Woodworth-Etter, Maria Beulah Holiness-Pentecostal evangelist, born near Lisbon, Ohio, 22 July 1844, died Indianapolis, 16 September 1924. Woodworth-Etter began preaching around 1880 and was a member of the Churches of God (Winebrenner) from 1884 to 1904. From 1885 she began large meetings, attracting more than 8000 people, and marked by healings, trances and people being 'slain in the Spirit'. In 1912 she was invited to conduct a meeting in Dallas by F. F. Bosworth,

marking the start of her association with the Pentecostal movement. In 1918 she founded a church in Indianapolis, now the Lakeview Christian Centre. She wrote *Signs and Wonders* (1916, reprinted 1980).

Woolman, John US Quaker preacher, anti-slavery campaigner, born Northampton, near Burlington, New Jersey, August 1720, died of smallpox, York, England, 7 October 1772. He was by trade a baker, but from 1743 until his death he campaigned tirelessly, moving from one Quaker community to another across the USA, in favour of rights for Negroes and against slavery. His campaigning took him to England, but within a few weeks of his arrival he had died. His best known work is his *Journal* (Philadelphia, 1774), which he started in 1756, and this and his other writings are thought to be among the finest expressions of Quaker belief.

Wrede, William German NT scholar, born Bücken-bei-Hanover, 10 May 1859, died Breslau, 23 November 1906. The son of a Lutheran pastor, he studied theology at Leipzig, 1877–9, and Göttingen, 1879–81, then worked in various posts, including as a pastor, while he completed his studies of **Clement** of Rome. His first academic post was in Marburg, and he then became professor of NT studies at Breslau from 1895 until his death. He was a founder member of the history of religions school, and the title of one of his publications, *Das Messiasgeheimnis in den Evangelien* (1901), gave the name to the subsequent discussion of the 'messianic secret'. He challenged the idea that Mark's Gospel was an accurate historical account of Jesus' life and argued that Jesus did not claim to be the Messiah. In *Paulus* (1905), he posited that it was Paul who really gave Christian teaching its subsequent shape.

Wren, Christopher (Sir) Architect of St Paul's Cathedral, London, England, born into an Anglican clergy family in East Knoyle, near Tisbury, Wiltshire, 20 October 1632, died London, 25 February 1723. Educated at Westminster School and at Wadham College, Oxford, he became a fellow of All Souls in 1653 and was appointed professor of astronomy at Gresham College, London, in 1657. In 1660 he returned to Oxford. He helped found and, from 1680 to 1682, was president of the Royal Society. After the Great Fire in 1666 Wren was responsible for redesigning many of the buildings in London, including over 50 churches, the most famous of which is St Paul's. These were designed specifically with the Anglican liturgy in mind, and so that worshippers could see and hear clearly what was being said and done.

Wright, John Joseph US cardinal and theologian, born Boston, Massachusetts, 18 July 1909, died August 1979. Studied at Boston College, the Gregorian University and North American College, Rome. He was ordained in 1935 and went to teach at St John's seminary, Boston. In 1945 he became secretary and in 1947 auxiliary to Cardinal **O'Connell**. In 1950 he was made first bishop of Worcester, Massachusetts, became bishop of Pittsburgh in 1959 and in 1969 was made cardinal. He was a member of the Theological Commission preparing for Vatican Council II and had a major hand in the preparation and subsequent *Constitution on the Church in the Modern World* and in the *Dogmatic Constitution on the Church*. He was instrumental in follow-up episcopal letters and was at four of the synods of bishops in the late 1960s and 1970s. From 1969 he was prefect of the Congregation for the Clergy and was responsible for innovating priest councils, the *General Catechetical Directory* and diocesan pastoral councils involving lay people. He was a member of several Roman congregations and commissions, including that for the revision of the Code of Canon Law. He was a leading exponent of Catholic social teaching and urged the participation of Catholics in justice and peace issues, and in ecumenism. *Resonare Christum* is a three-volume collection of his talks from 1950 on.

Wroth, William First Welsh Nonconformist pastor, Puritan preacher, born near Abergavenny in the mid-1570s, died Monmouthshire, 1641. Studied at New Inn Hall, Christ Church and Jesus College, Oxford, graduating MA in 1605, and became rector at Llanfaches, Monmouthshire, between 1611 and 1617. Having undergone a dramatic conversion in 1620, following the death of a friend, he made his name as a Puritan preacher. In 1639, at Llanfaches, he set up the first separatist church in Wales.

Wulfstan Saint, bishop of Worcester, and last of the Anglo-Saxon bishops, born Little Itchington, near Warwick, c.1008, died 18 January 1095. Educated by Benedictines at Evesham and Peterborough, he became a monk at Worcester, and schoolmaster and prior in the cathedral monastery there. In 1062 he accepted with some reluctance to be bishop of Worcester. He became famous for his continued monastic asceticism and personal sanctity. He had earlier been on friendly terms with Harold; he submitted to **William I**, the Conqueror, in 1066, and was very useful in checking the rebellious barons during the revolt of 1075. He was equally loyal to William II in his struggle with the Welsh. Wulfstan's relations with his superiors were not so harmonious, and both **Lanfranc** of Canterbury and Bayeux of York at one time unsuccessfully demanded his removal. By his preaching at Bristol, Wulfstan is said to have put an end to the kidnapping of English men and women and selling them as slaves. He wrote numerous homilies in Old English, including the famous *Lupi Sermo ad Anglos*, as well as works of politic theory, notably his *Institutes of Polity, Civil and Ecclesiastical*. He also drafted a number of laws, including most of those promulgated by Ethelred II and Canute. He was canonized by **Innocent III**. Feast day 19 January.

Wycliffe, John English Reformer and translator, born near Richmond, Yorkshire, about 1329, died Lutterworth, Leicestershire, 31 December 1384. He was educated at Balliol College, Oxford, of which he became master. He was ordained, became a doctor of theology and a canon of Lincoln and later rector of Lutterworth. He was sent to Bruges in 1374 to represent the government in discussions with papal representatives. In his *De Dominio Domino*, on divine authority, he believed all authority should be based on grace, and maintained that the secular authorities had the power to control the clergy. This led to a trial for heresy in 1378, which ended in confusion. It was at this point that the Great Schism began, which added weight to his criticism of the Papacy. His opposition to the authority of the Pope is expressed in his *De Potestate Papae*. He now began to write in English and began to arrange for the Scriptures to be translated into English and his enthusiasm led to the first entire translation, completed with the assistance of **Nicholas de Hereford** and John **Purvey**. He arranged for travelling preachers to spread his doctrines and rejected the doctrine of transubstantiation, of priestly absolution in the confessional, and of indulgences. In 1382 his opinions were condemned by the archbishop of Canterbury, and many of his followers ('Lollards') arrested. He himself was not touched, however, and he withdrew from Oxford to spend the rest of his life at Lutterworth.

Wynkoop, Mildred Bangs Nazarene theologian, born Seattle, Washington, 9 September 1905, died Lenexa, Kansas, 21 May 1997. The first woman elected president of the Wesleyan Theological Society, she was a pastor's wife, then herself a pastor and evangelist before embarking at mid-life on an academic career. She was founding president of Japan Nazarene Theological Seminary and taught systematic theology at three American colleges and seminaries. *A Theology of Love* (1972), her reinterpretation of Wesleyan theology, was her primary publication. Other writings include *Foundations of Wesleyan-Arminian Theology* (1967) and *John Wesley: Christian Revolutionary* (1970).

Wyszyński, Stefan Primate of Poland, cardinal, born Zuzela, Russian Poland, 3 August 1901, died of stomach cancer, 28 May 1981. After his initial seminary studies he was ordained in 1924 and did further studies at the Catholic University of Lublin, receiving his doctorate in canon law in 1929. He became bishop of Lublin in 1946 and in 1949 was named archbishop of Gniezno/Warsaw and primate of Poland. He was made cardinal in 1953 and for the next years was a government internee. As well as being Poland's spiritual leader he was effectively its national leader, negotiating a role for the Church that maintained its independence but did not threaten its existence. He promoted devotion to Mary and traditional piety and morality. At the same time he stood up for the rights of all the Polish people and his country's independence.

Wyttenbach, Thomas Swiss Reformer, born in Biel (Bienne), Switzerland, 1472, died there, 1526. Educated at Tübingen and then became lecturer in biblical studies at Basel, where one of his students was **Zwingli**. He held pastoral ministries: first as priest in Biel, from 1507 to 1515, and then as canon at Berne to 1519, when he returned to Biel to support the Reformation. He married in 1524 and was forced to retire from office.

X

Xaintonge, Anne de Venerable, French foundress, born Dijon, 21 November 1567, died Dole, 8 June 1621. Anne received an education normally reserved for the son of a renowned lawyer. She yearned to provide education for girls similar to that at the Jesuit college of Gochan, near her home, and saw it as her vocation to establish a religious community of women dedicated to the apostolate of education 'embracing rich and poor with the same love', and non-cloistered, a project opposed by family, friends and clergy. However, she persevered, and in 1606, with three companions, founded in Dole the Society of St Ursula, a teaching community for women which, at her death, counted six foundations in eastern France and Switzerland; the congregation now conducts schools in Europe, Africa and America. She was declared Venerable in 1900.

Xavier, Francis *see* **Francis Xavier**

Xenia the Blessed of St Petersburg Russian Orthodox saint and 'Fool for Christ's Sake', born 1732, died St Petersburg, 1803. She was married to an officer, who died suddenly. Afterwards she took his name, dressed in his uniform and wandered the capital. She was revered as a healer and prophetess. She worked at night in all weathers helping to build the Smolenskoye Cemetery Church near which she was buried. Her grave was a place of pilgrimage even in the Soviet period. She was canonized in the emigration in 1978 and in Russia in 1988 and her shrine is now restored. Feast day 24 January.

Ximénez de Cisneros, Francisco Cardinal archbishop of Toledo, inquisitor general, born Terralaguna, Castile, 1436, died Roa, near Valladolid, 8 November 1517. Educated at Salamanca, he became a Franciscan in 1484. Chosen by Queen **Isabella** as her confessor, his grand career began; appointed vicar provincial of the Franciscans in Castile in 1494, and archbishop of Toledo and primate of Spain in 1495. He was one of the great reformers and renewers of Christian life in Spain in the era before Trent: he furthered the reformation of the religious orders, especially the conventual Franciscans; and the renewal of ecclesiastical and Christian life in his archdiocese, holding synods, rigorously administering the revenues, visiting the suffragan dioceses, and printing liturgical and devotional books. He revived the Mozarabic rite, and though he ordered the burning of thousands of Qur'ans, he preserved the Moorish books of medicine, philosophy and history. He was virtual ruler of Castile on the death of Philip in 1506, and personally directed the conquest of Oran in Algeria. He held together the realms of Ferdinand and Isabella, suppressed factions, improved agriculture, lowered taxes, supported the humane policies of **Las Casas** in the Indies. Made a cardinal in 1507, he was a zealous patron of learning and founded, in 1508, out of his private income, the Univerity of Alcala, to which he brought distinguished scholars from Paris, Bologna and Salamanca. Ximénez' austerity and love of poverty were proverbial, and though accused of excessive severity, he was one of the nation's great political geniuses, a glory of the golden age of Spain.

Xintomane, Lois Evangelist to Tsonga at Rikatla, Mozambique, from April 1882, died March 1894.

A Tsonga from Transvaal who, with her husband and daughter, established a rapidly growing church characterized by ecstatic worship, the casting out of evil spirits, emphasis on literacy and Sunday observance. Lois' preaching attracted people and her agricultural skills facilitated prolonged hospitality for new converts. Her toleration of polygamy and dowry drew criticism from the Swiss Free Evangelical Church missionaries at Spelonken, Tranvaal, from where she had come. In 1887 she was joined by Paul Berthoud, whose control diminished the number of church attenders. Despite this Lois avoided a split in the church and remained loyal to the mission.

Xystus   *see* **Sixtus I, II, III**

Y

Yai'qob Abuna (bishop) of Ethiopia between 1337 and *c.*1345. Like all Ethiopian abunas he came from the Coptic Church of Egypt. An effective leader of the Church at a time of expansion. Organized the many Ethiopian monks to reform the Church and evangelize, particularly in the Shoan highlands. He attacked the tradition of royal polygamy, which led eventually to his enforced return to Egypt. As a result of his ministry the Church spread to new areas and the importance of monogamy was stressed. Although the king continued to have three wives, clergy were monogamous and polygamous people were excluded from Communion.

Yonge, Charlotte Mary Novelist, born Otterbourne near Winchester, 11 August 1823, died in the neighbouring village of Elderfield, 24 March 1901. She was largely educated by her father, and encouraged in her early career by **Keble**, a major influence on her life, who became her vicar in 1835. She taught as a Sunday School teacher for 71 years. She devoted much of her literary work to advancing the Christian faith through fiction. Her work included *The Heir of Redclyffe* (1853), *Heartsease* (1854), *The Daisy Chain* (1856), *The Trial* (1864), *The Pillars of the House* (1873) and *Magnum Bonum* (1879). In all she published around 160 books. For well over 40 years she edited the *Monthly Packet*, a magazine aimed at children.

Yorke, Peter Christopher Journalist, civic leader, born Galway, Ireland, 15 August 1864, died San Francisco, 5 April 1925. Educated at Maynooth, he was ordained in Baltimore in 1887. He volunteered for the Diocese of San Francisco and, an able theologian, orator and pastor, as well as a fiery polemicist, he was soon involved in controversy. As editor of the *Monitor*, official paper of the archdiocese, he fought bigotry on the west coast instigated by the American Protective Association and, against them, formed the American Women's Liberal League, and the Catholic Truth Society of San Francisco, to defend religious liberty. He was a friend of Labour and mediated several strikes, notably that of the Teamsters in 1901, where his emphasis on the principles of *Rerum Novarum* (1891), and the right to collective bargaining, helped to turn public opinion in favour of the workers, whose union was ultimately recognized by the employers. He founded the *Leader* in 1902, and through it supported the cause of Irish nationalism, becoming vice president of Sinn Fein, and collected money for Dr Hyde's Gaelic League. Among his wide-ranging activities, he founded Innesfael, a home for working girls; he was an advocate of temperance, a regent of the University of California, and vice-president of the National Catholic Educational Association. His *Textbooks of Religion* (1901) became standard texts in schools; he was the author of *Lectures on Ghosts* (1897); *Roman Liturgy* (1903); *Altar and Priest* (1913); and *The Mass* (1921).

Young, Brigham President of the Mormon Church, colonizer of Utah, born Whitingham, Vermont, 1 June 1801, died Salt Lake City, Utah, 29 August 1877. Too poor to be given an education (he had only eleven days of formal training), he joined the Church of Jesus Christ of Latter Day Saints in 1832, rose steadily as an official, did missionary work in the east and organized the exodus of the oppressed faithful from Missouri when they were driven out in 1838–9. When the Mormon prophet, Joseph Smith, was murdered in 1844, Young assumed leadership of most of the stricken faithful, led the epic march westward to the Valley of the Great Salt Lake and started a settlement based on agriculture and embodying Mormon economic and family ideals. He established the Mormon theocracy in Utah, and was appointed governor of the territory in 1850, but aroused the hostility of the federal government and many non-Mormons when he openly advocated plural marriage, after 1852. Young's superb administrative ability enabled the Mormons to survive and prosper, becoming a cohesive community of 140,000 by the time of his death. He married 27 wives, who bore him 56 children; the last filed for divorce and toured the country denouncing polygamy. He is venerated by his followers as a prophet, but many do not share his views on polygamy, plurality of gods, blood atonement and other doctrines.

Young, Patrick Royal librarian and scholar, born Seaton, Scotland, 29 August 1584, died Bromfield, Essex, 7 September 1652. Educated first at St Andrews then, when his father and he came to London in the retinue of King **James I and VI**, at Oxford, and was ordained there in 1605 before being appointed chaplain at All Souls College. He had moved to London within a couple of years and became Royal Librarian. It is thought that he worked with James I on the Latin edition of his Works, published in 1619. In 1628 the Patriarch **Cyril Lucaris** sent the library the Codex Alexandrinus, and among Young's many publications is the *editio princeps* of **Clement** of Rome's *First Letter to the Corinthians*, taken from the Codex.

Young, Robert Scottish printer and orientalist, born Haddingtonshire, 10 September 1822, died Edinburgh, 14 October 1888. He was apprenticed to a printer when he was sixteen, a job which he later combined with bookselling and studying languages. He went to India as a literary missionary in 1856 and became superintendent of the mission press at Surat in 1861. A Calvinist in theology, he believed in literal inspiration. He had an insatiable appetite for Eastern languages, ancient and modern, and is best known for his *Analytical Concordance to the Bible* (1879), which contains 118,000 references with each English word arranged under its own Hebrew or Greek original.

Youville, Marie Marguerite d' Blessed, Canadian foundress of the Grey Nuns, born Varennes, 15 October 1701, died Montreal, 23 December 1771. She was the niece of Pierre de la Verendrye, pioneer explorer of the Canadian Northwest, and great granddaughter of Pierre Boucher, the father of Canada. She married at twenty, and though operating a family business, devoted much time to charity. She was widowed in 1730, after eight years of unhappy marriage to a man despised in Canada and in France for defrauding Indians and merchants by illegal trade. She was left with four sons, who became priests. In 1737, she and three companions formed a small community and began caring in their home for the destitute. Despite misunderstanding, open hostility and even violence from the people of Montreal, they persevered in their good work, and the authorities asked Marguerite in 1749 to administer the General Hospital, then in ruins. This led, with the sanction of Louis XV, to the founding of the Grey Nuns in 1753, for whom she organized a religious life, inaugurated closed retreats for women, began the first home for foundlings in North America and opened hospital wards for soldiers. She was beatified in 1959. Feast day 3 May.

Z

Zabarella, Francesco Italian canonist and ecclesiastical diplomat, cardinal, born Padua, 10 August 1360, died Constance, 26 September 1417. He studied jurisprudence at Bologna, then taught from 1385 to 1410 canon law at Florence and at Padua while a member of the Paduan and Venetian diplomatic services. Invited by **Boniface IX**, he attended the Council of Pisa in 1409 as an adviser in the matter of the Great Schism. He was appointed bishop of Florence in 1410 by the Antipope **John XXIII**, and a cardinal the following year. He supported John at the Council of Rome in 1412–13, and conducted negotiations with Emperor Sigismund for the Council of Constance, where his courageous conduct, even after John had fled in 1415, contributed largely to the eventual resolution of the schism. Though a staunch supporter of John, he advised him to abdicate, while opposing the Avignon Antipope **Benedict XIII**, and continued until his death to bring about the election of a new Pope. His proposals in 1403–8 for ending the schism were collected in *De schismate* (Strasburg, 1545), but were placed on the Index, because it asserted the supremacy of the general council over the Pope. His writings on canon law, the *Lectura super Clementinis* (1402), and the *Commentaria in libros Decretalium* (1396–1404), long remained standard works.

Zabarella, Jacopo Italian Renaissance philosopher, born Padua, 7 September 1533, died there, 25 October 1589. He was professor of logic and natural philosophy at Padua from 1564 until his death. A most lucid exponent of Renaissance Aristotelianism, especially in logic, his commentaries on Aristotle's texts, partly influenced by humanism and by Averroes' Latin texts of the *Posterior Analytics*, *Physics* and *De Anima*, have been used by modern classicists, e.g. W. D. Ross, in their interpretations and editions. Zabarella's own theories of logic and method are considered of permanent systematic importance, and made an impact beyond Italy. **Galileo** cites him twice, once in general approval, once to oppose him on primary matter. An edition of his logic was made in Lyons in 1587, but it was without influence in France. In Germany, where Reforming theologians had been students of his at Padua, he was considered among the moderns as of at least equal authority with P. **Melanchthon**, and rivalled only by the Portuguese, P. da **Fonseca**, SJ. He influenced **Leibniz**' professor of logic and was avidly studied by Leibniz himself.

Zaccaria, Anthony Saint, Italian founder of the Barnabite Order and the Angelicals of St Paul, born Cremona, 1502, died there, 5 July 1539. He studied medicine at Padua and practised among the poor in his home town, where he began teaching catechism in the church of St Vitale, and became a priest in 1528, having felt called to exercise spiritual as well as physical compassion. At his first Mass, angels are reported to have appeared at the altar. In 1530, he was transferred to Milan, where he, with two friends, founded the Congregation of Clerks Regular of St Paul, known generally as Barnabites, approved by **Clement VII** in 1533. They were bound by vows 'to regenerate and revive the love of divine worship and a properly Christian way of life, by frequent preaching and faithful ministry of the sacraments'. The teaching of St Paul and emphasis on the Eucharist were two characteristic devotions. He also instituted, with Countess Ludovica Torelli, the Angelicals of St Paul for religious women. Their joint ambition was to reform the decadent society of the sixteenth century, beginning with the clergy, and including a renewal of spiritual life in monasteries of women and men in Italy at a time of notorious abuses. He was canonized by **Leo XIII** in 1897 and his body rests at Milan in the crypt of St Barnabas. Feast day 5 July.

Zaccaria, Francesco Antonio Theologian, historian and prolific writer, born Venice, 27 March 1714, died Rome, 10 October 1795. He was educated by the Jesuits, and entered the Society in 1731. He was appointed prefect of the library of the Roman College in 1742, and began to preach in northern and central Italy, where his eloquence gained him great renown. In 1751 he was transferred to the Roman province, as archivist and librarian for Francis III, duke of Modena. In 1767, the superior general, Lorenzo **Ricci**, recalled him to Rome to reorganize the library of the Gesu. **Clement XIII** granted him a pension for his defence of the Papacy, but this was stopped and his manuscripts confiscated when the Society was suppressed in 1773. He was imprisoned for a time in the Castel San Angelo, where he endured much suffering, but **Pius VI** restored his pension and named him professor of church history at Sapienza, and director of the Academia de Nobili Ecclesiastici. His numerous works – some 160 publications, not to mention a great number in manuscript – included theological treatises, church history and canon law, and annotated editions of **Menochio**, **Dante**, **Tamburini** and others.

Zachariae, Johann Theologian, opponent of John **Huss**, born Erfurt, c.1362, died there, 25 July 1428. He was a lector at Oxford in 1389–91; member of the University of Erfurt 1410, which delegate he was to the Council of Constance. His sermons there were memorable and he is said to have convicted the great heretic, John Huss, whence his title, 'Hussomastix'. He was provincial of the Saxon province of Augustinians and, in 1419, presided at the general chapter of Asti which ended the division within the Order caused by the Western Schism; he cast the deciding vote in favour of Augustine Favaroni of Rome as general. Zachariae

wrote extensive commentaries on Matthew, Mark, Luke and the Apocalypse.

Zacharias Patriarch of Jerusalem, born Constantinople, died Jerusalem, 21 February 631. He was a priest, and guardian of the sacred vessels in the Hagia Sophia at Constantinople, and patriarch of Jerusalem in 609, succeeding Isaac. He tried to prevent the capture of Jerusalem and massacre of the inhabitants during the Persian invasion of 614, but was captured and sent into exile in Persia. While there, he remained in touch with his people by encyclical letter and exhorted the church in Jerusalem to penance and patience; Jerusalem was liberated by Heraclius in 628, and Zacharias re-entered the city with a relic of the true cross. While in exile, restoration of the sacred monuments had been begun by Abbot Modestus, superior of the monastery of St Theodosius, who succeeded Zacharias as patriarch in 631.

Zacharias Saint, Pope 741–52. Nothing is known of his early life other than that he was a Greek by birth in Calabria. He was the last Greek Pope and appears to have been on intimate terms with **Gregory III**, whom he succeeded. A cultivated man, he translated Gregory's *Dialogues* into Greek, and was noted for his political adroitness and great personal persuasiveness. He reversed his predecessor's policy toward the Lombards, who were threatening Rome with invasion, and prevailed upon King Liutbrand and his successor, Rachis, to make peace with Rome and to restore four captured cities. It was largely through his tact in dealing with these princes in a variety of emergencies that the exarchate of Ravenna was rescued from becoming part of the Lombard kingdom. In 751 he sanctioned the deposition of the last Merovingian, Childeric III, in Pepin III's favour. He held synods at Rome in 743 and 745; the latter confirmed the condemnation of two heretics, Adalbert and Clement, by St **Boniface**. He sought to persuade the emperor in Byzantium to abandon his policy of supporting iconoclasm. Zacharias was an energetic and efficient administrator who, as well as controlling the militia and civil government of Rome, took an active interest in the papal patrimonies. Feast day 5 March.

Zacharias Scholasticus (also Zacharias of Mitylene

and Zacharias Rhetor) Metropolitan of Mitylene, church historian, born Mairema, Palestine, *c.*465, died Constantinople, after 536. Educated at the famous school of Gaza, he was known, with Procopius and Aeneas of Gaza, as one of the 'Gaza Triad'; he studied philosophy at Alexandria and law at Beirut. About 492 he became a lawyer at Constantinople, took part in the cultural life of the court and was later selected as metropolitan of Mitylene, island of Lesbos. He attended the Synod of Constantinople in 536, which condemned the deposed patriarch Anthinus Severus of Antioch; despite his original acceptance of the Henoticon, Zacharias adhered to the court theology and rallied to the Catholic position. His most important work was a church history, valuable for the years 450–91, which survives in Syriac embedded in a later compilation. He also wrote a biography of Severus of Antioch, a dialogue, *De Opificio Mundi*, against the Neoplatonists, and anathemas against the Manichees, known as the *Seven Chapters*.

Zahm, John Augustine Educator, apologist and author of important studies on the relation between science and religion, particularly on the question of evolution. Born New Lexington, Ohio, 14 June 1851, died Munich, 11 November 1921. After graduation from the University of Notre Dame, he joined the Holy Cross Congregation and was ordained in 1875. He was professor of physics at Notre Dame, but in 1892 he began writing on the relationship of Catholic dogma to modern science, since he believed that theistic evolution, i.e. that God created the universe 'in potentia', rather than 'in actu', was a distinct possibility. Zahm lectured on the theme of science and religion in the USA and at International Scientific Congresses in Brussels and Fribourg; he wrote essays and books, notably *Bible, Science and Faith* (1894), *Evolution and Dogma* (1896), on the theme that no conflict should exist between science and Catholicism. He was provincial of the Congregation of the Holy Cross in the USA, 1896 to 1906.

Zahn, Theodor von German Protestant NT and patristic scholar, born Moers, near Essen, 10 October 1838, died Erlangen, 15 March 1933. He was Privatdozent and extraordinary professor at Göttingen, and professor successively at Kiel, Erlangen and Leipzig between 1868 and 1900. His work was characterized by vast erudition and great thoroughness; he wrote extensively on all fields of NT criticism, and his contribution as editor of the *Kommentar zam Neuen Testament* (18 vols, Leipzig, 1903, and following), and author of commentaries on Matthew, Luke, John, Acts, Romans, Galatians and the Apocalypse, established him as a leading conservative in exegesis. His studies in the field of patristics were no less productive and contained much pioneer work. With A. von **Harnack** and O. von Gebhardt, he edited *Patrum Apostolicorum Opera* (1875–8).

Zahur, Raphael Priest, and one of the leaders of the modern renaissance in Egypt, born Cairo, 7 March 1759, died there, 13 October 1831. He studied at the Franciscan school in Cairo and at universities in Rome, was ordained a Salvatorian and, upon Napoleon's conquest, was named to the Egyptian Institute; in 1803 he was also named, by Bonaparte, to the Institut de Langues Orientales as professor of Arabic. Sylvestres de Soucy and Champollion (of Rosetta Stone renown) were among his students. He translated from the Italian four books on spirituality by Pinamonti, composed a text for retreats, edited a unique eighth-century liturgical manuscript. He wrote books on a wide variety of subjects, notably an Arabic–Italian dictionary, and a *Chronology* from Adam to Jesus Christ, with comparison to Roman, Greek and Persian sources. One of his finest works is a book of Arabic music. Most of his original manuscripts have been preserved in Paris, Cairo, Beirut and Istanbul.

Zamometić, Andrea Croatian archbishop, reform agitator, date and place of birth unknown, died Basel, 13 November 1484. Became a Dominican at Udine, then taught at Padua, where he was a friend of Francesco della Rovere, future Pope **Sixtus IV**. Having been made archbishop of Krajina, Albania, Emperor Frederich III sent him to Rome in 1478, and in 1480, where he openly attacked the venality, rapacity and nepotism of the Rovere family, and was imprisoned in Sant'Angelo. Released after intervention by the emperor, but still smarting from the humiliation, he attempted to rally the Pope's enemies, such as **Lorenzo de' Medici, Louis XI** of France, the universities of Paris, Louvain and Cologne. In the cathedral of Basel in 1482, he called for the reconvention of the reforming Council of Basel, and demanded that the Pope cease all exercise of power until the council should pronounce judgement on him. His supporters would not go along with such extreme action, and the city fathers, who had at first welcomed the project as good for the economy, became alarmed at the consequences of an interdict. Andrea became more insulting and vituperative, but the emperor had had enough and ordered him back to court. Basel put him in chains, and he hanged himself in his cell, two years later. **Botticelli** commemorated the story in the Sistine Chapel by depicting justice being executed on Korah for his rebellion against Moses.

Zamora, Alfonso de Spanish Hebraist, born Zamora, c.1474, died place unknown, c.1531. He was born a Jew, and converted to Catholicism in 1506, taking the name Alfonso. Professor of Hebrew at Salamanca, he contributed extensively to the complutensian Polyglot Bible, editing the Hebrew text of the OT and its Aramaic Targum; he wrote a Hebrew grammar and dictionary, and a Christian apologetic addressed to Roman Jews, to prove that Jesus of Nazareth was the promised Messiah.

Zamora, Alonso de Colombian Dominican historian, born Bogotá, 24 May 1635, died there, c.1717. Ordained in Panama about 1659, he was made provincial chronicler in 1688, and provincial in 1698. His major work of civil and ecclesiastical history, *Historia de la provincia de San Antonio del Nuevo Reyno de Granada del Orden de predicadores*, was begun by José de Caldas and completed by Zamora in 1696, in five volumes. The first is devoted to the flora and fauna; books II–V are chronicles covering 1528 to 1696. Zamora's style is simple and often dull; he thought the written word should be used for moral purposes, not for literary beauty. Three editions of the chronicle have been published, the latest in Bogotá, in 1945.

Zanchi, Girolamo Calvinist, theologian, born 2 February 1516 near Bergamo, Italy, died Heidelberg, 9 November 1590. Joined the Augustinian Canons in 1531 and studied at Lucca, where he came under Calvinist influences. These were strengthened when he met **Calvin** in 1551. Two years later he became professor of OT studies at Strasburg, where he found himself entangled in disputes concerning both predestination and the Lord's Supper. He resigned his post in 1563 and moved back to Northern Italy, where he worked as preacher for the Reformed church. He left Italy again in 1567 to take up the post of professor of dogmatics at Heidelberg, until the arrival of Lutheranism in 1576, when he moved to Neustadt. His writings include a preparatory Confession (with Z. Ursinus), later part of the *Harmonia Confessionum* (Geneva, 1581) and *De Religione Christiana* (Neustadt, 1585).

Zanella, Giacomo Italian poet, born Chiampo, near Vicenza, 9 September 1820, died Astichello, 17 May 1888. After ordination to the priesthood, he taught at the lyceum in Chiampo, but his patriotic sympathies excited the jealousy of the Austrian authorities and he was forced to resign in 1853. After the liberation of Venetia, he became professor at Padua, and a distinguished poet. His last published volume contains a series of sonnets of great beauty addressed to the river at Astichello, resembling Wordsworth's 'Sonnets to the Duddon', and a blank verse idyll 'Il Pettirosso', bearing a strong, though accidental, resemblance to similar compositions of **Coleridge**. Deeply impressed by the problems of the day, he sought to reconile science and religion, especially in the fine dialogue between **Milton** and **Galileo**, where the former, impressed by Galileo's predictions of the intellectual consequences of scientific progress, resolves 'to justify the ways of God to man'. Zanella was regarded as a broad-minded and patriotic ecclesiastic, a poet of elegance and finish, with a place of his own in modern Italian literature.

Zapata de Cardenas, Luis Spanish Franciscan, archbishop of Bogotá, born Llerena, c.1515, died Bogotá, 24 January 1590. Of a noble family, he fought in the Spanish regiment. He entered the Franciscan Order about 1542, was commissary general in Peru in 1561, and provincial of San Miguel in 1566; named bishop of Cartegena de Indias in 1569, archbishop of Bogotá in 1570, entering the diocese in 1573. His primary effort was to make missionary work effective, and to this end he sought native Creole and Mestizo clergy. He ordered canon Miguel de Espejo to write a catechism as a practical guide to pastors, which included important guides on native culture and social customs. He ordained more than 100 Creole and Mestizo priests, and this substitution for religious from Spain caused disputes with Franciscans, Dominicans and Augustinians. Zapata redistributed the Indian doctrinas, and established the first seminary in Colombia in 1583, where he himself taught the Muysca language to future pastors of the indigenous population.

Zapata y Sandoval, Juan   Mexican bishop of Guatemala, born Mexico City, date unknown, died Guatemala City, 9 January 1630. (His surname is more properly written Sandoval y Zapata, thus avoiding confusion with his uncle Juan Zapata, OSA, died 1607.) Of the aristocracy, Juan was ordained an Augustinian priest, taught at Mexico City and, from 1602 to 1613, at Valladolid, Spain. Named bishop of Chiapa, New Spain, in 1613, he was consecrated at Puebla de los Angeles, and promoted to the see of Guatemala in 1621. In his treatise *De justitia distributiva*, Juan strongly urged that the civil and ecclesiastical offices of the overseas empire should be entrusted to native-born colonials, rather than to persons from Spain. He is thus credited with having opened the door to Creole advancement in New Spain.

Zarlino, Gioseffo   Italian Renaissance music theorist, born Chioggia, 22 March 1517, died Venice, 14 February 1590. A Franciscan theologian of great promise at 24, he soon devoted himself to the study of music under the guidance of Adrian Willaert, then choirmaster at St Mark's. Willaert died in 1562, and Zarlino succeeded him in 1565. He is now remembered chiefly for valuable contributions to the theory of music: the most comprehensive exposition of contrapuntal principles produced up to that time; rules for the proper placement of text that are still a model for editors of late sixteenth-century vocal music. He was also famous as a practical musician and as a composer, though the number of his printed works is limited to a volume, *Modulationes Sex Vocum* (Venice, 1566), and to a few motets and madrigals. Among these was music written to celebrate the battle of Lepanto (7 October 1571) and a solemn Mass on the occasion of the founding in 1577 of the church of Santa Maria della Salute, to commemorate the plague.

Zatvornik, Theophan   Russian orthodox bishop and spiritual writer, born Cernavsk, 10 January 1815, died Pushkin, 1894. He was born George Vasilievic Govorov, son of a priest. Ordained at Kiev, 1841, he became a monk taking the name Theophan. He taught at Kiev, Novgorod and St Petersburg. He went to Palestine in 1847 to found a Russian centre and remained seven years, studying Greek and the Fathers. He returned to Russia, was named bishop of Tambov in 1857, and transferred to Vladimir in 1863. He retired to a monastery in 1866, devoting his time to prayer and writing, becoming a complete recluse, refusing to see anyone, for the last 22 years of his life. In his works, Zatvornik approached the Catholic doctrine on frequent Communion, which was contrary to the ordinary teaching of the Orthodox Church at the time. Indeed, these writings, apart from doctrinal errors inherited from his Protestant-tinged professors, reflect a mind and spirit steeped in patristic thought and the teachings of St **Thomas Aquinas**. His doctrine is thus in the genuine Catholic tradition, although he was no partisan of the church of Rome; for him, the Catholic Church was just another sect terrorized by the Inquisition and a despotic Pope, who attributed to himself divine qualities.

Zegada, Escolástico   Argentine priest and educator, born Juguy, 10 February 1813, died there, 1871. Of noble birth, a nephew of **Gorriti**, he was ordained in 1836. Greatly concerned for the education of youth of both sexes, he founded and supported the Collegio de Educandos, a normal school for the training of teachers. He brought Vincentian sisters from France in 1864 to educate the girls, and Lazarist priests for the boys. In 1850 he built and endowed the San Roque hospital. Zegada introduced the first printing press in Juguy, rebuilt the ruined churches of San Francisco and la Merced, and founded the 'Recoba', a society with social and economic goals. He was named provincial governor of Juguy, and took part later in the constituent parliament of 1855. He wrote a work of much importance, *Instrucciones Cristianas*, which was used as a text in the schools of Argentina.

Zeno East Roman emperor, 474–91. He was an Isaurian of noble birth and married Ariadne, daughter of **Leo I**, in 468. Nothing is known of his early life, but after his marriage, he became patrician and commander of the imperial guard and of the armies of the East. In 474 Leo died after appointing Zeno's son, Leo, to succeed him, but Zeno, with the help of his mother-in-law, Verina, got himself crowned as well and became sole emperor within the year, on the death of his son. The patriarchs, Peter Mongus of Alexandria and Acacius of Constantinople, influenced Zeno to move against the Catholic John Talaia and the Isaurian rebel Illus, who was championing Catholicism in Antioch. Zeno's name is associated with the Henoticon, or instrument of union, signed by all the Eastern bishops, designed to terminate the Monophysite controversy by compromising the doctrine of the Council of Chalcedon. The result was a 35-year Acacian schism with Rome, during which the See of Constantinople became paramount in the East, but Antioch, Palestine and Alexandria were rent permanently by Monophysitism, and gradually the national churches of Armenia, Persia and Ehiopia were cut off from Rome.

Zeno of Verona Saint, bishop, died *c.*375. An African by birth, but little else is known of him. He seems to have flourished during the decade before his death, according to St **Ambrose** (397), and his own anti-Arian writings, which have affinities with African writers such as **Tertullian** and **Cyprian**, but, as they did not come into circulation until the earlier Middle Ages, were unknown to St **Jerome**, *De Viris Illustribus*, and to **Gennadius**. The sermons, *Tractatus*, reveal a pastoral-minded bishop intent on instilling a liturgical and sacramental life in his flock, insisting on liberality, hospitality and care for the poor. Ninety three of his sermons survive; his teaching on the Trinity and the Incarnation reveals the undeveloped status of theology in the West, but he insists on the absolute virginity of Mary, before, in, and after giving birth to Our Lord. The miraculous preservation of Verona from flood in 598, attributed to Zeno's intercession, greatly increased his cult. Feast day 12 April.

Zenzelinus de Casanis French canonist and civil lawyer, born south-west France, date unknown, died Avignon, 1334. He taught civil and then canon law at Montpellier until 1318, after when he occupied several curial posts at the Avignon papal court, notably that of chaplain, in 1327, and auditor of the Rota. Zenzelinus was an important author whose writings are essentially canonical, viz, a commentary on 21 decretals of **John XXII** (Paris, 1510). He was a defender of papal authority during the political and religious controversies preceding the Great Schism. Indeed, he contributed, from a fine acquaintance with the doctrinal tradition, to a clearer understanding of the legal foundations of papal authority from which his conclusions are, in effect, a defence of pontifical rights, so much attacked in his day.

Zephyrinus Saint, Pope 199–217. He was born the son of a Roman, Halrundius (*Liber pontificalis*), and **Eusebius** records that he reigned for eighteen or nineteen years, succeeding **Victor I**. According to **Hippolytus**, who became an Antipope, Zephyrinus had little intelligence (*aner idiotes kai agrammatos*), or strength of character, and the somewhat important controversies on doctrine and discipline that marked his pontificate are more appropriately associated with himself, and **Calixtus**, his principle adviser, and his successor. Zephyrinus would not condemn Monarchianism and Patripassianism, as Hippolytus wished him to do. The statements Hippolytus attributes to him form, according to **Harnack**, the oldest recorded, dogmatic definition of a Roman bishop. There is no proof of his alleged martyrdom in the martyrology of St **Jerome**, and his place of burial in the cemetery of Callistus is uncertain. Feast day 26 August.

Zernov, Nicholas Russian Orthodox ecumenist and scholar, founder of the House of St Gregory and Macrina in Oxford, born Moscow, 9 October 1898, died Oxford, England, 25 August 1980. Left Russia in 1921 and went to study theology in Belgrade and later at Oxford, where he settled in 1934. For the following thirteen years he was secretary of the Fellowship of St Alban and St Sergius, and in 1947 became the first Spalding lecturer in Eastern Orthodox culture at the university. The House of St Gregory and Macrina, which he founded in 1959, became a focal point for dialogue, study and socializing, and for worship for the Orthodox community. His writings include

Eastern Christendom (1961) and *The Russian Religious Renaissance of the Twentieth Century* (1963).

Ziegelbauer, Magnoald Swabian historian, born Ellwangen, 5 October 1689, died Olmutz, 14 January 1750. After his ordination as a Benedictine in 1713, he taught theology and moved to Reichenau in 1726. He represented the monastery at the court in Vienna in 1730, taught moral theology at Gottweig and, from 1747, resided at Olmutz as secretary to the quietly effective learned society, 'Societas Icognitorum'. He published *Historia rei Litterariae OSB*, in four volumes (Augsburg, 1746), a history of Benedictine letters, and still a respected historical source.

Ziegenbalg, Batholomäus Pioneer Lutheran missionary to South India, born Pulsnitz, Saxony, 1682, died Tranquebar, 23 February 1719. He studied at Halle and along with his fellow student Heinrich Plütschau responded to a call to India from King Frederick IV of Denmark. They were ordained in Copenhagen and arrived in Tranquebar, in July 1706, to hostility from Hindu and Danish authorities. Ziegenbalg set up a printing press supported by the Society for the Propagation of Christian Knowledge in London, and published a Tamil grammar, hymn-books, catechisms and the NT. He completed the OT up to Ruth and established elementary schools and a seminary for Tamil clergy. He researched Indian religion and culture, but his *Genealogie der Malabarischen Götter* was not published until 1867 (ET, 1869).

Zierikzee, Cornelius of *see* **Cornelius of Zierikzee**

Zigabenus, Euthymius *see* **Euthymius Zigabenus**.

Zigliara, Tommaso Dominican cardinal, philosopher and theologian, born Bonifacio, Corsica, 29 October 1833, died Rome, 10 May 1893. Having studied at Rome and Perugia, he was professor at Viterbo and at the Collegium Divi Thomae, becoming regent in 1873. He was a friend and trusted adviser to **Leo XIII**, who made him a cardinal, and director of the critical edition of the works of St **Thomas Aquinas**, of which he wrote the notes in vol. 1; he was also president of the Roman Academy of St Thomas Aquinas, and prefect of the Congregation of Studies. Consulted on the question of **Rosmini-Serbati**, and though deeply involved in disputes about the alleged ontologism of Rosmini, he was untouched by controversial odium. He helped to prepare important encyclicals, including *Aeterni Patris* and *Rerum Novarum*. He effectively fostered the growth of Thomistic studies through his influential position in the Roman curia and his *Summa philosophica* (3 vols, Rome, 1876), widely used, and for some decades a standard text. He helped to esablish modern fundamental theology through his exploration of its philosophical grounds.

Zilboorg, Gregory Psychiatrist, medical historian and criminologist. Born Kiev, 25 December 1890, died New York City, 17 September 1959. Son of orthodox Jewish parents, he qualified in medicine at St Petersburg, served in the Russian army and participated in the February Revolution. Forced to leave Russia in 1919, he went to New York, qualified MD again at Columbia University, practised psychiatry, and wrote, lectured widely and taught at the Catholic University of America, at Fordham and in workshops, on pastoral care and psychotherapy. He became a Roman Catholic in 1954 and, against Freud, defended the validity of a religious point of view, in papers on the relationship of religion to psychiatry and psychoanalysis.

Zimara, Marco Antonio Renaissance philosopher of the Paduan Averroist school. Born San Pietro di Galatina (Lecce), *c*.1470, died Padua, 1532. Of humble origins, he nevertheless received a remarkably wide-ranging education, and a doctorate in arts. He edited the works of the most discussed philosophers of the time, including Averroes and St **Albert the Great**. Leaving Padua in 1509, because of the war with Venice, he taught at Lecce, Salerno and the Conventual Studium in Naples, before being recalled to Padua in 1525 by the Venetian Senate. He was an expert on the entire Corpus Aristotelium and Averroes commentaries, which he defended against the errors of the Bolognese school, who espoused the position of Siger of Brabant, and later against that of the Simplicians, who followed the interpretation of the *De Anima* of Simplicius. The importance of his exposition is confirmed in *Solutiones contradictionum in dictis Averrois* (Venice, 1508), and the *Tabula et* *dilucidationes in dicta Aristotelis et Averrois* (Venice, 1537).

Zimmer, Patrick   German philosopher and theologian, born Wurttemburg, 22 February 1752, died Landshut, 16 October 1820. He studied at Ellwangen and Dillingen, was ordained a priest in 1775, and became professor of dogmatic theology there until 1791, when he was named pastor at Steinheim. Though this appointment was given as the reason for his removal from Dillingen, it seems more likely to have been opposition to his philosophical ideas. His many volumes of treatises reflect a persistent anti-Kantian polemic, and a certain affinity for the pantheistic notions of F. Schelling, although, personally, he was said to be always sincerely orthodox in his belief, and generous both to his doctrinal adversaries and to the poor. He was rector of the University of Landshut and a deputy to the Bavarian parliament when he died. His principal works were *Theologiae Christianae theoreticae systema* (Dillingen, 1787) and *Theologia Christiana specialis* (4 vols, Landshut, 1802–6).

Zimmerman, Otto   Jesuit theologian and spiritual writer, born Dottingen, Switzerland, 24 May 1873, died Lucerne, 13 January 1932. He entered the upper German province of the Society in 1890, was a collaborator of the review *Stimmen der Zeit* from 1905, and wrote much on asceticism, including his chief work, *Lehrbuch der Aszetik* (Freiburg, 1930), which quickly became the leading book of its kind in German, on account of the richness of its bibliography, balance of judgement and breadth of treatment; its reputation as a solid guide in the ascetical field has been maintained.

Zingarelli, Nicola Antonio   Italian composer and violinist, born Naples, 4 April 1752, died Torre del Greco (Naples), 5 May 1837. Eldest son of the singer Riccardo Zingarelli, he studied at Naples, held court posts because of his operas, of which he was a prolific composer – 37, many produced at La Scala, and Haydn produced two at Eszterhaza; the best known, *Giuletta e Romeo* (1796), a favourite with Malibran – a number of oratorios, including *Isaiah*, written for the Birmingham Festival in 1829. He was 'maestro di capella' at Milan in 1792, then at Santa Casa di Loreto in 1794–1804, and

succeeded Guglielmo at the Sistine Chapel. Napoleon had him arrested in 1811 for refusing to conduct a Te Deum at St Peters in honour of his being named king of Rome. Afterwards he concentrated on church music, composing 28 Masses, many motets, magnificats, credos, stabat maters and hymns, among some 541 items in the Loreto archives.

Zingerle, Pius   Syrian scholar, born Meran, Tyrol, 17 March 1801, died Mals, Tyrol, 10 January 1881. He taught theology at the Benedictine abbey of Marienberg, was professor of Arabic at the Sapienza in Rome, 1862–5, a consultor of the Congregatio de Propaganda Fide, and 'scriptor' at the Vatican Library. He published numerous volumes of Syriac texts in German translation and is especially noted for his translations of St **Ephrem**, i.e. *Ausgewahlte Schriften des hl.Ephrem* (6 vols, Innsbruck, 1830–7).

Zinzendorf, Nicolaus Ludwig   Count of Zinzendorf and Pottendorf, religious reformer, born Dresden, 26 May 1700, died Herrnhut, 6 May 1760. One of the most striking and influential leaders of the Protestant world in the eighteenth century, he founded the Herrnhuter 'Brudergemeine', or Moravian Brethren. Son of an aristocratic Austrian Lutheran family with Pietist leanings, he studied at the Halle School of Lutheran Pietism, and at Utrecht, where he made Calvinist contacts, and at Wittenberg University in 1716. Evangelization was his chief interest: he organized religious assemblies in his home and was host to Protestant emigrants from Austria, many of them descendants of the Bohemian Brethren, bringing with them the heritage of the suppressed Hussite Unity of the Brethren (Unitas Fratrum). With German Pietists, they formed the nucleus of the new town of Herrnhut, and were first members of the Moravian church, which emerged as a separate denomination in the 1740s. His evangelical mission in Europe, the West Indies and North America aroused controversy, and he was attacked as an innovator by Lutheran orthodoxy, but his beliefs were examined and approved in 1734. Many of his followers worked as missionaries, especially among 'despised' races and peoples. He was influential with evangelicals, especially John **Wesley**, but his teaching on the relation between justification and sanctification, and the emotionalism of his 'religion of the heart', was found by some to be objectionable. His chief contribution to missiology was his awakening within Protestantism of an awarenes of cross-cultural mission as a fundamental task of the Church.

Zita Virgin, saint, born Monsagrati, Tuscany, 1218, died Lucca, 27 April 1278. Patroness of domestic servants, at the age of twelve she entered the service of the Fratenelli family at Lucca and remained there until her death. Misunderstood and even maltreated at first, her piety, humility and exactitude in performing her domestic duties, in which she regarded herself, rather, as the servant of God, won the love and respect of her employers and fellow servants. She is especially venerated in Lucca, which **Dante** and Fazio degli Uberti called 'Santa Zita'. Her coffin was opened in 1446, 1581 and 1652, revealing her body intact, and she was canonized by **Innocent XII** in 1696. Her relics lie in St Frigidian's church, Lucca. Feast day 27 April.

Zizka, John Bohemian general and Hussite leader, born Trocnov, c.1358, died Pribyslav, 11 October 1424. Of a family who belonged to the gentry, he was a Bohemian patriot and took part in the civil wars during the reign of Wenceslaus IV, as leader of the Taborites in the Hussite movement. When in 1419 a Hussite procession in Prague was stoned from the town hall, Zizka headed those who threw the town councillors from its windows. He led the people of Prague in their victories during the wars of 1420–3 against Emperor Sigismund, and the Crusades authorized by Pope **Martin V**. He saw himself as 'Zelator praecipus' of the law of Christ, and considered as his enemies 'those who did not take the Body and Blood of Christ in both kinds', which included Sigismund, Germans, Catholics and compromising Utraquists. As commander-in-chief of all Hussite forces, he was often victorious against the emperor and his other perceived enemies, which he always regarded as a militant defence of the 'cause of the Chalice'. Recent research regards him not merely as a radical adventurer, but as a leader fully conscious of the religious, national and social issues at stake.

Zoega, Jorgen Danish archaeologist and numismatist, born Daler, 20 December 1755, died Rome, 10 February 1809. He studied at Altona, Göttingen and Leipzig, and numismatics at Vienna. His work on Egyptian monuments in Rome greatly advanced knowledge of ancient Egypt, and he wrote on the pharaohs, obelisks, hieroglyphs and the more recent Coptic periods. He became a Catholic in 1783 and married the daughter of a Roman painter, Maria Pietrucioli. Through his patron Stefano Borgia, later cardinal, he was named interpreter of modern languages at the Propaganda. Appointed Danish consul-general at Rome in 1798, professor at Kiel in 1802, and elected to the acadamies of science of Rome and Vienna. He was commissioned by the Danish government to work on a study of medals and ancient coins at Copenhagen, Munich and other cities. He collaborated on the first modern Icelandic–Danish dictionary.

Zoerardus and Benedict Saints, Slovak hermits of Zobor in late tenth-early eleventh centuries. Born in Silesia, Zoerardus came to Slovakia from Poland during the reign of King (St) **Stephen** of Hungary (1002–3). He was also known as Andrew (Slovak name Svorad), and with his disciple, Benedict (Stojislav), lived an eremitico-cenobitical life, combining aspects of the Camaldolese and the Benedictine traditions, in the cave of Shalka, Diocese of Nitra. He excelled in mortification and penance; chains embedded in his flesh witnessed to his self-inflicted chastisement. The master died in 1009, and the disciple was martyred three years later by robbers and thrown into the river Vak in 1012. The relics of both are in the cathedral of Nitra; their cult was approved in 1083. St Svorad-Andrew is patron of some well-known Slovak institutions, e.g. St Andrew's Benedictine Abbey in Cleveland, Ohio, spritual centre of the Slovaks in North America. Feast day 17 July.

Zoilo, Annibale Renaissance church musician of the Roman school, born Rome, c.1537, died Loreto, 1592. He was 'maestro di capella' at St John Lateran and at the papal chapel in 1568–70, and then at Santa Casa in Loreto until 1592. He collaborated with **Palestrina** on a revision of the Roman Gradual, but the work was not completed, and the official 'Editio Medicea' was the work of others. He was a member of the Compagnia dei Musici di Roma, antecedent of the present Academia di

Santa Cecilia. His extant works number three Masses, a 'Second Book of Madrigals' (Rome, 1563), several motets, including a 12-voice Salve Regina, and a 16-voice Tenebrae, and other madrigals and songs.

Zoilus of Alexandria Chalcedonian patriarch (540–51), date and place of birth and death unknown. A Palestinian monk, he was named patriarch of Alexandria by the Apocrisiarius Pelagius (later Pope), after the deposition of Paul of Tabennisi at the Council of Gaza, in 540. Though not learned, he was a staunch follower of the Council of Chalcedon against the Monophysites, as was his predecessor, and was compelled to sign the Edict of **Justinian I** opposing the 'Three Chapters', in 544. However, he sent messengers to Pope Vigilius in 546 to protest that he had complied only under duress, and to excuse his weakness. He was forced to flee Alexandria, during a local revolt, to refuge in Constantinople, and Justinian deposed him in 551 because he refused to condemn the 'Three Chapters'.

Zola, Emile Edward Charles Antoine Novelist, born Paris, 2 April 1840, died there, 29 September 1902. He distinguished himself in his twenties, while a clerk at the publishing house Hachette, as a vigorous and aggressive critic in articles on literature and art in the paper *L'Evenement*. His gruesome and powerful novel, *Therese Raquin* (1867), also created a good deal of interest. Like that of Balzac's 'Comedie humaine', Zola set out to create a world of his own in his major work, *Rougon-Macquart* (20 vols), the 'naturalistic and social history of a family during the Second Empire'. He was an apostle of the realistic school, and his view of man's greed, lust and gluttony was presented with great power. Indeed, his style was notorious for crude descriptions and lewd imagery, as well as intemperate and overt anti-clericalism, viz, his trilogy, *Trois Villes: Lourdes, Rome, Paris*, the likely reasons for his works being placed on the Index. Zola owed his fame to political posture as much as to talent. He was able to stir public emotions, and played an important part in the Dreyfus affair. He wrote his famous letter 'J'accuse' (January, 1898, in *L'Aurore*), condemning the judgement of the General Staff that Captain Dreyfus, a Jew, was a traitor. It denounced all who had

a hand in hounding down that unfortunate officer, but the public outcry forced him to seek refuge in England. Whatever the effectiveness of his action, Zola displayed great courage and disinterestedness. When he died, asphyxiated in his flat by a defective fireplace, perhaps set deliberately by a workman disgusted by Zola's anti-militarism, he received a public funeral, at which Dreyfus was present. Zola had just finished *Verite* (*Quatre Evangiles*) dealing with the proceedings of the trial. The sensational close to Zola's career was the signal for a burst of eulogy; Anatole France delivered an impassioned oration at the grave.

Zola, Giuseppe Italian Jansenist theologian, born Concessio, near Brescia, 1739, died there, 5 November 1806. Professor of moral theology at the University of Brescia, he led an agitated life as a follower of the politico-religious movements of the time, and he and his friend **Tamburini** championed the ideas of C. O. **Jansen** and **Richer** in north Italy; both were relieved of their teaching duties by the bishop, because of their Jansenistic rigorism. Zola later taught church history at Pavia, where he was also director of the German College. When the emperor Joseph II died, the Lombard bishops re-established their episcopal seminaries, and Zola was again dismissed along with Tamburini. After Bonaparte's annexation of the Cisalpine Republic in 1796–9, Zola occupied the chair of diplomatic law at Pavia, a position he was able to keep after Napoleon's victory at Marengo, and the formation of the kingdom of Italy.

Zolli, Eugenio Semitic scholar and convert to Catholicism. Born Israel Zoller at Brody, Austrian Galicia, 17 September 1881, died Rome, 2 March 1956. He became Chief Rabbi of Trieste in 1914, where he changed his name to Zolli. He taught Hebrew at Padua, and in 1940 went to Rome as Chief Rabbi. When the Germans invaded Rome, Zolli tried to get the Jewish community to disperse, and himself went into hiding, though continuing to exercise leadership and paying, with financial help from the Vatican, the ransom that the Nazis demanded from Roman Jews. In 1945, he became a Catholic and, although some Jews attributed it to base motives, his conversion was clearly the ultimate result of a life-long interest, evident in his earlier writings, in the person of Christ, and the strong influence of the charity of **Pius XII**, whose baptismal name he chose. He taught Semitics at the University of Rome and the Pontifical Biblical Institute from then almost until his death.

Zonaras, John Byzantine chronicler and theologian at Constantinople, born late eleventh century, died after 1160. Under **Alexis I Comnenus**, he was commander of the bodyguard and private secretary to the emperor, but in the succeeding reign, he retired to a monastery on Hagia Glykeria (one of the prince's islands), where he spent the rest of his life writing books. His most important work, *Epitome Historon*, a compendium of history in Greek in eighteen volumes, extends from the creation of the world to the death of Alexius in 1118. The earlier part is largely drawn from Josephus; for the Roman history he followed Dio Cassius, whose first twenty books are not otherwise known to us. The work was much read, excerpted and translated, e.g. into Old Slavonic, in the later Middle Ages. His massive commentary on the canons of the apostles, the councils and synods, and the fathers, is perhaps the greatest achievement of Byzantine canon law. Other works attributed to Zonaras include commentaries on the poems of **Gregory of Nazianzus**, a hymn to the Blessed Virgin, and lives of the saints, of which there is no reason to doubt the genuineness.

Zorell, Franz German Jesuit, biblical scholar, orientalist and lexicographer, born Rosenburg, 29 September 1863, died Rome, 14 December 1947. He is best known for his immensely erudite Bible lexicons. He was deeply immersed in humanistic studies at Feldkirch, and in Semitic languages at Tübingen, before entering the Society of Jesus in 1884. After studies in England and The Netherlands, he went to Baku in 1897 for special studies in Greek and began his first monumental work, a Greek lexicon of the NT, which he published twelve years later. He began work on a Hebrew and Aramaic lexicon of the OT in 1911; its final fascicule was readied for publication just before his death and published in 1954. He also taught Armenian and Georgian at the Pontifical Biblical Institute.

Zorilla de San Martín, Juan National poet of Uruguay, born Montevideo, 28 December 1855, died there, 3 November 1931. He was also a journalist, legislator, professor, diplomat, orator and historian. He published his first book of lyric poetry, *Notas de un Himno*, at Santiago de Chile. On his return to Uruguay, he served as a judge. In 1879, he so dramatically recited his poem, *La Leyenda Patria*, at the foot of the statue erected in honour of the liberators in 1825 that it became a symbol of nationhood, and he was considered thereafter the national poet. He founded and edited the Catholic periodical *El Bien Publico*. His poem 'Tabare' (1889) was acclaimed by critics, such as the Spaniard Juan Valera, as a poetic evocation of the native races and of the development of the Spanish Christian civilization. While ambassador in France, he sought from the Holy See the establishment of a Uruguyan archbishopric.

Zosimus Saint, Pope (18 March 417 to 26 December 418). His pontificate was short and stormy. The *Liber Pontificalis* describes him as 'of Greek origin, his father was Abram'; this seems to indicate Jewish ancestry, though nothing else is known of his origins. He succeeded **Innocent I**, to whom he may have been recommended by St **John Chrysostom**, and his election seems to have affronted a part of the Roman clergy. He figured in two incidents of note: (1) He granted to Patrocles, bishop of Arles, who voted for his election, the title of papal vicar in Gaul, and made him metropolitan of the provinces of Vienne and Narbonne. The bishops of Gaul resented this disturbance of their status quo. (2) In the Pelagian affair, **Augustine** had no sooner uttered at Carthage his famous words 'Causa finita est', approved by Innocent I, than **Pelagius** and Caelestius appealed to Zosimus, who absolved them as falsely accused. The African bishops were outraged, and so informed the Pope, who was compelled to reverse his stand. He informed the Africans that he had not yet made up his mind but that, meanwhile, the decision of his predecessor was to stand. He took the occasion to read the Africans a lecture on the Roman primacy reaffirming the tradition that the judgement of the Apostolic See must not be disputed. In the event, the Africans appealed to Emperor Honorius, who condemned Pelagius, and Zosimus was obliged to issue at Carthage, in 418, his *Epistola Tractoria* condemning Pelagianism. Zosimus' fractious temper coloured all the controversies in which he took part, in Gaul, Africa and Italy, including Rome, where part of the clergy appealed to the court at Ravenna against him. He excommunicated them and would have gone further, had he not died of a serious illness. The ninth-century Martyrology of Ado was the first to list him as a saint. Feast day 26 December.

Zrínyi, Miklós   Count, Hungarian warrior, statesman and poet, born Ozaly (Csakvar), Croatia, died Kursanec Forest, 18 November 1664. At the court of cardinal Peter Pasmany, SJ, he conceived a great enthusiasm for his native language and literature, although he always placed arms before arts. He learnt the art of war in defending the Croatian frontier against the Turks, proved himself one of the first captains of the age, and was acknowledged at his death as the national leader of the Hungarians. In 1645, he acted against the Swedes in Moravia; at Szkallc he scattered a Swedish division and took 2000 prisoners; at Eger he saved the emperor, who had been surprised in his camp at Wrangel; he routed the army of Rakoczy on the Upper Theiss. In 1646, he distinguished himself in the Turkish war. He always defended the political rights of the Croats and maintained that, as regarded Hungary, they were to be looked upon not as 'partes annexiae', but as 'regnum'. He applied St Ignatius' teaching on the 'Two Standards' both to Christian welfare in his military sorties against the Turks, and to his literary works. In his writings, he stressed unceasingly the absolute need for a Crusade against the Turks. His long epic poem *Szigeti Veszedelem* (*Siege of Sziget*, 1651) was written to commemorate his great grandfather, Nicholas Zrinyi, who had been killed opposing the forces of Suleiman I, and also to inspire all Hungarians to free the country from Turkish rule. He was killed by a wild boar in the forest of Csaktornya.

Zumarrága, Juan de   Spanish missionary in Mexico, born Tavira de Durango, Vizcaya, c.1468, died Mexico City, 3 June 1548. A Franciscan, he was provincial of Concepción, and appointed first bishop of Mexico in 1527, his diocese extending to the southern limit of Guatemala. He verified and approved the apparition of Our Lady of Guadalupe, Tepeyac, in honour of which he erected the first hermitage in 1531. Zumarraga was appointed

protector and defender of the Indians, but was opposed by the civil authorities in the exercise of his office. He excommunicated them, and was called to Spain where the king accepted his defence. Returning to Mexico, Juan promoted church discipline, and founded schools and colleges for Indian children of both sexes. With Viceroy Mendoza, he built the first seminary and secondary school in America in 1536, laid the groundwork of the University of Mexico in 1553, and established the first printing press in the New World, in 1539. He published a number of books in Mexican and Castilian, and wrote several himself, e.g. *Regla Christiana* (1544). Appointed inquisitor, he was removed because of his rigorous procedure, though he had acted from high motives of ecclesiastical discipline. Out of misplaced zeal, he permitted the destruction of ancient temples and writings. Zumarraga is one of the great figures of Spanish colonial history and the dominant one of the early church in Mexico. His excesses as an administrator do not outweigh his great merits as protector of the Indians, and promoter of the Christian and cultural life of Mexico.

Zurbarán, Francisco de   Spanish baroque artist, born Fuente de Cantos, Estremadura, 7 November 1598, died Madrid, 27 August 1664. With his contemporaries Velasquez and Alonso Cano, he stands among the great masters of the Seville school, known for his paintings of monks, and works of deep spiritual feeling. His style was characterized by a dramatic tenebrism merged with extreme realism (*Christ on the cross*, 1627; *St Serapion*, 1628). He is famed for his white-robed monks in monastic cycles – life of S. Pedro Nolasco, 1628, and life of S. Buenaventura, 1629 – remarkable for large areas of dark colour and brilliantly lighted simple forms. His style became somewhat softer and lighter in Madrid, 1634–9, but he returned to his earlier tenebrist style in the 1640s, influenced by Ribera, reverting to a softening of expression derived from Murillo in his last years.

Zwierlein, Frederick James   American church historian, born Rochester, NY, 16 November 1881, died there, 5 October 1960. Ordained a priest in 1904, he studied at Louvain and Rome, and taught church history and art at St Bernard's seminary,

Rochester. He wrote a three-volume *Life and Letters of Bishop McQuaid* (1927), which was highly informative and a pioneering work in the field of American church history. Another study concentrated on American–Filipino Church–State relations after the Spanish–American war, *Theodore Roosevelt and Catholics, 1888–1919* (1956).

Zwimba, Matthew Chigaga   Founder of the first African Initiated Church among the Shona, born in Eastern Rhodesia *c.*1880, died *c.*1930. A catechist in the Wesleyan Methodist Missionary Society, he established the first mission school in the area but was dismissed by the missionaries in 1907. He founded his own church, the Shivi Chena Church, in 1915, which combined Christian and traditional elements in its worship. The movement was suppressed when he declared to be saints those Shona killed by the settlers in the Uprisings. The numbers of adherents dwindled because of the suppression, but the church remains significant as the first independent Shona movement of its kind. Zwimba also became the spokesperson for the Zimba reserve area.

Zwingli, Huldrych (Ulrich)   Founder of the Reformation in Switzerland, contemporary of **Erasmus** and Martin **Luther**. Born Wildhaus, Toggenburg Valley, St Gall, 1 January 1484, died Kappel, 11 October 1531. Of peasant stock, an uncle was abbot of Fischinger, and another, parish priest of Wildhaus. After studies in theology at Berne, Vienna and Basel, he was made pastor of Glarus in 1506–16. He read widely and deeply in the Fathers, Greek and Latin, especially **Origen**, **Jerome**, **Augustine** (*Enchiridion*), and acquired a command of patristic literature greater than that of Luther or Calvin. He was a humanist of the type abhorred by Luther, more interested in secular disputes than doctrinal innovations, and thus free from the spiritual experiences which drove Luther into a cloister and a feverish 'searching of the scriptures'. In 1515, Zwingli met Erasmus, and from then until 1522 the works of the great humanist were decisive in his intellectual and religious development as a Reformer. Like Erasmus, Zwingli concluded that man cannot overcome sin in this life, but must consider his entire life as a penance, a battle against sin, and a challenge to follow Christ's example. In thus stressing sanctification and responsibility, Zwingli owes a significant debt to the notion of 'Militia', as developed by Erasmus in his own *Enchiridion*: Christ is our 'captain', who sacrifices himself for his troops, an example to his men, who opposes the corrupted doctrine of the Church and has come not only to save the world, but also to change it. In the year he met Erasmus, Zwingli attacked the ecclesiastical law of fasting and asserted that the Bible was the sole rule of faith. His innovations were accepted by the town council of Zurich in 1523, after he presented his 67 theses; the next year church property was seized by the state, and abolition of the sacraments, celibacy, indulgences, veneration of images, and good works was begun. In 1525, the Mass was replaced by the memorial service of the Last Supper. The Catholic cantons united against him, and in a public disputation held at Baden in 1525, Johann **Eck** of Ingolstadt won a complete victory for the Old Faith. In 1528, Berne adopted the heresy as completely as Zurich, and, to force the new doctrines on the Catholic cantons, Zwingli urged civil war. His insolences as ecclesiastical and political leader of Zurich forced the Catholics to arms in 1531. They were victorious, while Zwingli fell in battle. His doctrine was developed by Heinrich **Bullinger**, whose attempt at union with Luther on the question of the Lord's Supper failed, though he reached an agreement with Calvin at Geneva in 1545.

INDEX OF DATES OF DEATH

91	Anacletus
100	Abdias of Babylon
	Addai
	Flavia Domitilla
107	Ignatius of Antioch
109	Evaristus
112	Beatus of Lungern
116	Alexander I
120	Nepos of Arsinoë
125	Sixtus I
135	Papias of Hierapolis
136	Telesphorus
142	Hyginus
154	Pius I
155	Polycarp
160	Marcion
165	Justin Martyr
166	Soter
168	Anicetus
170	Benignus of Dijon
175	Lucius
	Marcellus of Chalon-sur-Saône
177	Blandina
	Pothinus
180	Claudius Apollinaris
	Aristides
	Dionysius of Corinth
	Symmachus
	Tatian
189	Melito
190	Athenagoras
192	Eleutherius
198	Victor I
200	Noetus of Smyrna
202	Irenaeus of Lyons
	Leonides of Alexandria
215	Clement of Alexandria
220	Quintus Septimius Florens
	Tertullian
222	Bardesanes
	Calixtus
232	Demetrius of Alexandria
235	Hippolytus of Rome
	Pontianus
236	Anterus
240	Sextus Julius Africanus

245	Beryllus
250	Agatha
	Alban
	Alexander of Jerusalem
	Barbara
	Denis
	Epimarchus
	Fabian
	Minucius Felix
	Pionius
253	Cornelius
254	Lucius I
	Origen
255	Apollonia of Alexandria
256	Dionysius of Alexandria
257	Rufina and Secunda
	Stephen I
258	Cyprian
	Felicissimus and Agapitus
	Lawrence
	Novatian
	Sixtus II
259	Fructuosus
260	Felix of Nola
	Pontius
268	Dionysius
	Firmilian
270	Gregory Thaumaturgus
272	Domnus of Antioch
	Paul of Samosata
274	Felix I
282	Anatolius of Laodicea
283	Eutychian
284	Maximilian
285	Claudius
	Crispin and Crispinian
287	Rufina and Justa
295	Maximilian
296	Gaius
298	Marcellus the Centurion
300	Chrysanthus and Daria
302	Afra
	Agnes
	Anastasia
	Anthimus
	Cosmas and Damian

	Pelagia of Tarsus
303	Anthimus
	Elmo
	Emygdius of Ancona
	Euphemia of Chalcedon
	Firmin of Amiens
	Foy
	Genesius of Arles
	Genesius the Comedian
	George
	Lucy
304	Chrysogonus
	Crispina
	Demetrius of Sirmium
	Marcellinus and Peter
	Marcellinus
305	Dorotheus of Antioch
	Dorothy
	Pantaleon
	Paphnutius
306	Phileas of Thmuis
309	Marcellus I
310	Pamphilus
311	Eusebius
	Methodius of Olympus
	Pelagia
	Peter of Alexandria
312	Lucian of Antioch
316	Blaise
327	Arnobius the Elder
328	Alexander
	Gregory the Illuminator
329	Agricius of Trier
330	Helena
	Lactantius
333	Macarius of Jerusalem
335	Sylvester I
336	Arius
	Eustathius of Antioch
	Mark
337	Constantine the Great
340	Eusebius of Caesarea
	Macrina the Elder
	Paul the Hermit
341	Asterius of Cappadocia
342	Eusebius of Nicomedia

345 Aphraates
     Nicholas of Myra
346 Pachomius
348 Spyridon
350 Constans I
     Paul of Constantinople
351 Julius Firmicus Maternus
352 Julius I
355 Donatus of Carthage
356 Anthony of Egypt
358 Hosius
     Paulinus
359 Eusebius of Emesa
     Potamius
360 Paphnutius
361 Constantius II
     John and Paul
     Mirian
364 Basil of Ancyra
366 Acacius of Caesarea
     Liberius
367 Hilary of Poitiers
369 Caesarius of Nazianzus
370 Gorgonia
     Lucifer of Cagliari
     Optatus
371 Eusebius of Vercelli
     Hilarion of Gaza
373 Athanasius
     Ephrem the Syrian
     Nerses
374 Marcellus of Ancyra
375 Zeno of Verona
377 Eustathius of Sebaste
     Julian of Saba
379 Basil the Great
     Macrina the Younger
380 Eusebius of Samosata
     Frumentius
     Innocent
381 Marcion of Cyr
384 Damasus I
     Priscillian
386 Cyril of Jerusalem
387 Monica
389 Mark of Arethusa
390 Apollinaris of Laodicea
     Gregory of Nazianzus
     Macarius of Egypt
392 Pacian of Barcelona
393 Diodore of Tarsus
394 Decimus Magnus Ausonius
     Amphilochius of Iconium
     Eunomius of Constantinople
     Gregory of Nyssa
     John of Egypt
     Macarius of Alexandria
395 Gelasius of Caesarea
397 Ambrose
     Martin of Tours
     Philaster
398 Didymus the Blind
399 Evagrius of Pontus
     Fabiola

     Siricius
400 Anthemius of Poitiers
     Julian of Le Mans
     Nemesius of Emesa
401 Anastasius I
402 Epiphanius of Constantia
403 Gregory of Elvira
404 Paula
405 Moses the Black
406 Auraeus
407 Desiderius of Langres
408 Olympias
410 Bachiarius
     Asterius of Amasea
     Euphrasia
     Exuperius of Toulouse
     Marcella
     Melania the Elder
     Pammachius
     Rufinus of Aquileia
413 Flavius Marcellinus
     Synesius
414 Nicetas of Remesiana
417 Innocent I
     John of Jerusalem
418 Orosius
     Pelagius
419 Julia Eustochium
420 Jerome
     Porphyry of Gaza
     Sulpicius Severus
422 Boniface I
     Paulinus
425 Atticus of Constantinople
     Bessarion of Egypt
     Macarius Magnes
429 Alipius
     Aurelius of Carthage
430 Augustine
     Honoratus of Arles
     Nilus of Ancyra
     Palladius of Helenopolis
     Polychronius
431 Paulinus
432 Celestine
     Ninian
     Palladius
433 Leontius of Fréjus
     Maro of Cyr
434 Acacius of Beroea
435 John Cassian
     Isidore of Pelusium
     Rabbula
439 Isaac the Great
     Melania the Younger
440 Possidius
441 John of Antioch
     Mesrop
444 Brice
     Cyril of Alexandria
447 Proclus
448 Germanus of Auxerre
449 Domnus of Antioch
     Flavian of Constantinople

     Hilary of Arles
     Sixtus III
450 Anianus of Chartres
451 Auctor of Metz
     Livarius of Metz
     Nestorius
     Nonnus of Panopolis
452 Bassianus of Ephesus
453 Anianus of Orleans
     Pulcheria
454 Dioscorus of Alexandria
     Eutyches
455 Arnobius the Younger
     Julian of Eclanum
457 Cyril of Panopolis
     Marcian
     Pelagia of Antioch
458 Anatolius of Constantinople
459 Simon Stylites
460 Adelphus of Metz
     Patrick
     Valerian
461 Leo the Great
463 Prosper of Aquitaine
465 Anthimus
466 Theodoret
468 Hilary
     Hyacinth
     Hydatius
471 Gennadius I of Constantinople
473 Euthymius the Great
474 Mamertus Claudianus
     Diadochus of Photike
     Leo I
475 Aurelius of Armenia
     Annabilis
     Gerasimus
     Mamertus
477 Basiliscus
480 Severinus of Noricum
483 Simplicius
484 Laetus
485 Marcellus Akimetes
488 Peter the Fuller
490 Anthemius of Constantia
     Faustus of Riez
492 Felix III
496 Epiphanius of Pavia
     Gelasius I
498 Anastasius II
500 Aeonius of Arles
     Geneviève
     Zacharias Scholasticus
505 Blossius Aemilius Dracontius
     Gennadius of Marseilles
507 Aper of Toul
510 Eugendus of Condat
     Marcellus of Die
511 Clovis
514 Symmachus
518 Anastasius I
     Elias of Jerusalem
519 Avitus of Vienne
520 Apollinaris of Valence

521 Magnus Felix Ennodius
523 Hormisdas
     Philoxenus
524 Anicius Manlius Severinus
     Boethius
525 John I
527 Julian of Halicarnassus
528 Brigid
     Procopius of Gaza
529 Jacob of Serugh
530 Adrianus
     Caesaria
     Avitus
     Dioscorus
     Felix IV
531 Eleutherius of Tournai
532 Boniface II
     Sabas
533 Fulgentius of Ruspe
     Remigius of Rheims
535 Epiphanius of Constantinople
     John II
536 Agapetus I
537 Silverius
538 Bar-Cursus
     Severus
540 Carileffus
     Hilarius of Mende
542 Innocent of Le Mans
543 Caesarius of Arles
     Leontius of Byzantium
544 John of Réomé
545 Clotilde
548 Ferrandus
     Theodora I
549 Cyprian of Toulon
     Finnian of Clonard
550 Anthimus I
     Benedict
     Brieuc
     Arator
     Cosmas Indicopleustes
     Desideratus of Bourges
     Dionysius Exiguus
     Domitian of Ancyra
     Dorotheus of Gaza
     Dubricius
     Eptadius
     Innocent of Maronia
     Isaac of Monte Luco
     Junilius Africanus
551 Aurelian of Arles
     Gall of Clermont
552 Menas
555 Romanus Melodus
     Vigilius
557 Cyril of Scythopolis
     Nerses II
     Samson
558 John the Silent
     Leobin
560 Cloud
     Domitian of Maastricht
     Jordanis

561 Pelagius I
565 Justinian I
566 Nicetius of Trier
567 Liberatus of Carthage
568 Laudus
570 Gildas
     Goar of Trier
     Imma
     Ita of Killeedy
571 Facundus of Hermiane
574 John III
575 Abraham Kidunia
     John Philoponus
     Maglorius
576 Germanus of Paris
577 John III Scholasticus
     John Malalas
578 Jacob Baradai
     Brendan of Clonfert
579 Benedict I
     Finnian of Moville
580 Brendan of Birr
     Cassiodorus
     Cerbonius
581 Domnolus of Le Mans
     Eparchius
582 Eutychius of Constantinople
584 Maurus
585 Hermenegild
586 John of Ephesus
587 Daig
     Radegunda
588 Agnes of Poitiers
     Frigidian of Lucca
590 Laudomar
     Pelagius II
591 Aredius
593 Leobard
594 Gregory of Tours
     Marius of Avenches
595 John IV
596 Magnericus
597 Columba
599 Anastasius I
     Kenneth
600 Evagrius Scholasticus
     Evroul of Saint-Fuschien-au-Bois
     Glodesindis
     Honoratus of Amiens
     Leander of Seville
601 Aunarius of Auxerre
     David of Wales
602 Comgall
603 Fintan of Clonenagh
604 Augustine of Canterbury
     Gregory the Great
     Gregory of Agrigentum
605 Ingenuin
606 Colman of Cloyne
     Desiderius of Vienne
     Sabinian
607 Boniface III
     Eulogius of Alexandria
609 Anastasius II

610 Cyrion
     Venantius Honorius Clementianus
        Fortunatus
     Henana
611 Colman of Lynally
612 Kentigern
614 Landulf of Evreux
615 Boniface IV
     Columbanus
616 Ethelbert of Kent
     Licinius
618 Deusdedit I
619 Fulgentius of Ecija
     John the Almsgiver
     Lawrence of Canterbury
     Maximus of Saragossa
622 John of Biclaro
623 Bertrand of Le Mans
     Lupus of Sens
624 Austregisilus
     Mellitus
625 Boniface V
     Deicolus of Lure
     Gery of Cambrai
627 Athala of Bobbio
     Justus of Canterbury
629 Eustace of Luxeuil
631 Zacharias
633 Edwin
635 Fintan of Taghmon
     Magnabod of Angers
636 Isidore of Seville
638 Honorius I
     Sophronius
640 Bertulf of Bobbio
     Gall
     Gudwal
     Severinus
641 Arnulf of Metz
     Heraclius
642 John IV
     Oswald of Northumbria
644 Ethelburga
     Paulinus
647 Abbo of Metz
     Judicael of Quimper
649 John Climacus
     Theodore I
650 Agil
     Alopen
     Birinus
     Fursey
651 Aidan of Lindisfarne
     Braulio
652 Adalbald
     Iduberga
653 Bavo
     Hadoindus
     Honorius of Canterbury
     Irene of Portugal
655 Desiderius of Cahors
     Martin I
657 Eugenius I
     Eugenius of Toledo

Fara
658 Aunemund of Lyons
659 Gertrude of Nivelles
660 Donatus of Besançon
Eligius of Noyon
Emmerham
Germerius
Landry
661 Finan of Lindisfarne
Nerses III
662 Genesius of Clermont
Maximus
663 Chlodulf of Metz
Cunibert of Cologne
664 Cedda
665 Fructuosus of Braga
Leobard
666 Jonas of Bobbio
667 Ildefonsus of Toledo
668 Constans II Pogonatus
670 Gangolf
Kilian of Aubigny
Omer of Thérouanne
671 Cataldus of Rachau
672 Chad
Vitalian
673 Bova
674 Aigulf of Lerins
675 Amandus
Anianus and Marinus
Faro of Meaux
Germanus of Münster-Granfelden
676 Adeodatus II
Colman of Lindisfarne
Ethelburga
678 Donus
Genesius of Lyons
679 Deodatus of Nevers
Etheldreda of Northumbria
Leodegar
680 Arbogast of Strasburg
Bathilde
Botulf
Caedmon
Cyneburg
Eusebia of Hamay
Hilda of Whitby
Humbert of Maroilles
681 Agatho
Gislenus
682 Barbatus
683 Ebbe
Leo II
Ouen
684 Philibert of Rebais
685 Benedict II
Constantine IV Pogonatus
686 John V
Landelin
687 Conon
Cuthbert of Lindisfarne
688 Anstrudis
Landoald
689 Caedwalla

Kilian of Würzburg
690 Amalberga
Benedict Biscop
Bertha of Val d'Or
Desiderius Rhodonensis
Godo
Hadalinus
Hunegundis
Julian of Toledo
Theodore of Canterbury
691 Jonatus
693 Ansbert of Rouen
Claudius of Condat
Erconwald of London
695 Barontius
Ermenburga
Ethelburga
Ewald the Black
698 Lambert of Maastricht
700 Anastasius Sinaita
701 Sergius I
704 Adamnan of Iona
Austreberta
705 Adalbert the Deacon
Bertila of Chelles
Bertulf of Renty
Hedda
John VI
706 Bonitus of Clermont
Evroul
707 Hidulf
Hidulf of Lobbes
John VII
708 Sisinnius
709 Aldhelm
Bertinus
Hadrian of Canterbury
Wilfrid
710 Irmina
712 Gudula
714 Elfleda
Guthlac
715 Constantine
Damian
John VI
716 Ceolfrid of Wearmouth
717 Hildelide
Liutwin of Trier
718 Rupert of Salzburg
720 Giles
Odilia
721 John of Beverley
725 Aubert of Avranches
Bertha of Blangy
Corbinian of Freising
Cuthburga
726 Ine
729 Egbert
John of Otzun
730 Landry
731 Brithwald
Gregory II
732 Gerald of Mayo
734 Adela

Erkembodo
735 Bede
Eugenia
Frideswide
738 Eucherius of Orléans
Leutred
739 Willibrord
740 Andrew of Crete
741 Charles Martel
Gregory III
742 Acca
Germanus I
750 Agilulf of Cologne
Bilhild
Ebbo
Gerulf
Hadeloga
Magnus of Fussen
752 Stephen II
753 Pirminius
754 Adalar
Anastasius
Boniface
Burchard of Würzburg
Eoban
John Damascene
756 Aistulf
757 Stephen II
758 Cuthbert of Canterbury
759 Othmar
760 Cosmas the Melodian
766 Chrodegang of Metz
Egbert
767 Paul I
768 Pepin III
770 Ambrose of Cahors
Cuthbert of Wearmouth
772 Amalberga
Remigius of Rouen
Stephen III
775 Constantine V
Gummar
776 Gregory of Utrecht
779 Walburga of Heidenheim
780 Ethelbert of York
Lebuinus
Lioba
783 Hildegard of Kempten
784 Alberic of Utrecht
785 Leo Thaumaturgus
787 Lull
790 Gumbert of Ansbach
Leontius Armenius
791 Angilramnus of Metz
795 Adrian I
796 Offa
798 Beatus of Liebana
799 Judith of Niederaltaich
Osbald of Northumbria
Paul the Deacon
802 Paulinus
803 Anselm of Nonantola
Irene
804 Alcuin

805	Ethelhard of Canterbury	
806	Tarasius	
807	Elipandus of Toledo	
809	Ludger of Münster	
812	William of Aquitaine	
814	Angilbert	
	Charlemagne	
815	George Syncellus	
816	Leo III	
817	Leidradus of Lyons	
	Stephen IV	
	Theophanes the Confessor	
820	Leo V	
821	Benedict of Aniane	
	Theodulf of Orléans	
824	Paschal I	
825	Ratramnus of Corbie	
	Ida of Herzfeld	
	Nennius	
827	Adalard	
	Claudius of Turin	
	Eugenius II	
	Hildigrim	
	Valentine	
828	Apollinaris of Monte Cassino	
	Clement of Ireland	
	Nicephorus I of Constantinople	
829	Macarius of Pelecete	
832	Deochar	
833	Ansegis	
834	Aelfryth	
	Deusdedit of Monte Cassino	
836	Hatto of Reichenau	
837	Anthony I	
838	Eusebia of Saint-Cyr	
840	Agobard of Lyons	
	Einhard	
	Eldrad	
	Louis I	
842	Barnard of Vienne	
	Gregory Dekapolites	
843	Jonas of Orléans	
844	Gregory IV	
	Nithard	
847	Sergius II	
849	Walafrid Strabo	
850	Adalgis of Novara	
	Amalarius of Metz	
	Aurelian of Réomé	
	Benedict the Levite	
851	Ebbo of Rheims	
852	Aurelius and Sabigotona	
853	Columba and Pomposa	
	Haymo of Halberstadt	
854	Indrechtach	
855	Folcwin	
	Haimo of Auxerre	
	Hilduin of Saint-Denis	
	Leo IV	
	Lothair I	
856	Argimir	
	Aurea of Cordoba	
	Jieron	
	Rabanus Maurus	
858	Benedict III	
859	Eulogius of Córdoba	
860	Florus of Lyons	
	Paschasius Radbertus	
861	Albar	
	Meinrad of Einsiedeln	
	Prudentius Galindo	
862	Servatus Lupus	
	Swithin	
863	John VII	
864	John of Ravenna	
865	Ansgar	
	Bardas	
866	Irmengard	
867	Nicholas I	
868	Gottschalk of Orbais	
	Guntbert of Saint-Bertin	
	Nicholas the Studite	
869	Cyril	
	Edmund the Martyr	
	Lothair II	
870	Ebbe the Younger	
	Hunfried	
872	Adrian II	
	Athanasius of Naples	
873	Johannitius	
874	Ermenrich of Passau	
875	Ado of Vienne	
	Adrian	
	George Hamartolus	
	Louis II	
	Remigius of Lyons	
876	Andrew of Fiesole	
	Heiric of Auxerre	
	Hemma	
877	Charles the Bald	
	John Scotus Eriugena	
	Neot	
878	Anastasius the Librarian	
879	Fintan of Rheinau	
	Hincmar of Laon	
880	Christian of Stablo	
	Isaac of Langres	
	Liutbirg	
881	John the Deacon of Rome	
882	Hincmar	
	John VIII	
884	Bertharius	
	Marinus I	
885	Adrian III	
	Methodius	
886	Ansbald	
	Basil I	
887	Metrophanes of Smyrna	
888	Charles the Fat	
	Rembert of Bremen-Hamburg	
891	Photius	
	Stephen V	
894	Flodoard of Rheims	
896	Boniface VI	
	Formosus	
	Gauderich of Velletri	
897	Stephen VI	
	Theodore II	
898	Lambert of Spoleto	
899	Alfred the Great	
900	John IX	
901	Anthony II	
	Grimbald	
903	Benedict IV	
	Elias of Thessalonika	
904	Leo V	
905	Auxilius of Naples	
	Froilan	
907	Boris I of Bulgaria	
908	Remigius of Auxerre	
909	Adalbero of Augsburg	
	Adalgar of Bremen	
	John Asser	
	Gerald of Aurillac	
911	Sergius III	
912	Demetrian of Khytri	
	Leo VI	
	Notker Balbulus	
913	Anastasius III	
914	Lando	
915	Regino of Prum	
916	Attilanus	
	Clement the Bulgarian	
	Hoger of Bremen-Hamburg	
917	Euthymius I	
920	Nicetas David	
921	Ludmila	
923	Costa ben Luca	
924	Edward the Elder	
925	Alberic I of Spoleto	
	Nicholas I	
927	Berno	
928	Leo VI	
929	John X	
930	Hucbald of Saint-Amand	
931	Stephen VII	
932	Wenceslas	
935	John XI	
936	Gennadius of Astorga	
939	Leo VII	
940	Eutychius of Alexandria	
941	Agapios of Hierapolis	
942	Odo of Cluny	
	Stephen VIII	
944	Arethas of Caesarea	
946	Marinus II	
948	Romanus I Lecapenus	
950	Helentrudis	
954	Alberic II of Spoleto	
	Frederick of Mainz	
955	Agapetus II	
	Lantbert of Freising	
958	Eberhard of Einsiedeln	
959	Constantine VII	
	Gerard of Brogne	
	Odo of Canterbury	
960	Elias of Reggio	
961	Atto of Vercelli	
962	Adalbero I	
	Gauzelin of Toul	
964	John XII	
965	Aymard	

	Benedict V		Zoerardus
	Bruno of Cologne	1010	Ansfrid
	Leo VIII	1012	Alphege of Canterbury
968	Matilda of Germany		Coloman
969	Olga		Guido of Anderlecht
972	John XIII		John Vincentius
	Liutprand of Cremona		Sergius IV
973	Ekkehard of Sankt Gallen	1014	Brian Boru
	Otto the Great	1015	Adelaide of Vilich
974	Benedict VI		Boris and Gleb
	John of Gorze		Aquilinas
	Ratherius of Verona		Vladimir of Kiev
975	Conrad of Constance	1019	Heimerad
	Notker Physicus	1020	Aelfric Grammaticus
976	Gero of Cologne	1021	Heribert of Cologne
978	Edward	1022	Labeo Notker
	Gerold	1023	Hartwich of Salzburg
980	Leo Luke	1024	Benedict VIII
983	Anthony III		Henry II
	Benedict VII	1025	Basil II
	Ludolf of Corvey		Burchard of Worms
	Otto II	1026	Bononius
984	Ethelwold of Winchester		Leo of Vercelli
	John XIV	1027	Romuald of Ravenna
	Peter Orseolo	1028	Fulbert of Chartres
985	Boniface VII	1030	Olaf II
988	Adalbero of Rheims	1031	Adalgott I
	Adaldag		Aribo of Mainz
	Dunstan		Dominic of Sora
990	Ekkehard of Sankt Gallen		Emeric of Hungary
	Folcwin of Lobbes		Robert II
	Nicodemus of Mammola		William of Volpiano
992	Adso of Montier-en-Der	1032	John XIX
	Leo Diaconus	1033	Kunigunde
	Oswald of York	1034	Adhemar of Chabannes
993	Luke of Armento	1035	Canute
994	Gerard of Toul	1036	Anastasius
	Majolus of Cluny		Meinwerk of Paderborn
995	Gebhard II of Constance		Odo of Bayeux
996	Gregory of Einsiedeln	1038	Ethelnoth of Canterbury
	John XV		Stephen
997	Adalbert of Prague	1043	Abu'l-Faraj'Abdallah ibn at-Tayyib
999	Gregory V		Alexius the Studite
1000	Olaf I		Hallvard Vebjörnsson
	Roswitha of Gandersheim	1044	Gregory of Ostia
1001	Gregory Narek	1045	Angelram
	John XVI		Brithwald of Wilton
1002	Gregory of Cerchiara		Bruno of Würzburg
	Otto III		Günther of Niederaltaich
1003	John XVII	1046	Druthmar
	Sylvester II		Gerard of Csanad
1004	Abbo of Fleury		Guido of Pomposa
1005	Adalbero II	1047	Clement II
	Aelfric of Canterbury		Gregory VI
	Benedict of Benevento		Rodulphus Glaber
	Nilus of Rossano	1048	Berno of Reichenau
1006	Fulcran of Lodeve		Damasus II
	Gaudentius of Gniezno		Odilo of Cluny
1007	Heriger of Lobbes		Poppo of Stavelot
1008	Froumund of Tegernsee	1049	Elias bar Shinaya
	Notker of Liège	1050	Guido of Arezzo
1009	Bruno of Querfurt		Nicetas Stethatos
	John the Deacon of Venice	1051	Bardo of Oppershofen
	John XVIII		Gerard of Cambrai
			Baruch Pierleoni
1052	Halinard of Lyons		
1054	Hermannus Contractus		
	Lazarus the Confessor		
	Leo IX		
1055	Constantine IX Monomachos		
	Robert of Jumièges		
1056	Anselm of Liège		
	Benedict IX		
	Henry III		
1057	Victor II		
1058	Gregory Magistros		
	Stephen IX		
1060	Dominic Loricatus		
	Ekkehard of Sankt Gallen		
	Gisela		
1061	Adelmannus		
	Humbert of Silva Candida		
	Nicholas II		
1062	Leo Pierleoni		
1063	Constantine III Leichudes		
	Sylvester III		
1066	Ansuerus		
	Edward the Confessor		
	Gottschalk		
1067	Gervase of Rheims		
1068	Marianus Argyrus		
1069	Ealdred of York		
1070	Othlo of Sankt Emmeram		
1072	Adalbert of Hamburg-Bremen		
	Peter Damian		
	Stigand		
1073	Alexander II		
	Benedict X		
	John Gualbert		
1075	Anno of Cologne		
	Erlembald		
	Gundecar		
	John VIII		
1076	Beatrice of Tuscany		
	Dominic of Silos		
	Lietbert of Cambrai-Arras		
1077	Arnulf of Milan		
1078	Gebizo		
	Herluin of Bec		
	John of Fécamp		
	Michael Psellus		
1079	Arnulf of Gap		
	Leo of Cava		
	Stanislaus		
1080	David of Vastmanland		
	Eskil		
1081	Adam of Bremen		
	Bernard of Aosta		
	Lambert of Hersfeld		
	Michael Psellus		
1082	John Italus		
1084	Bartholomew of Marmoutier		
	Bruno of Magdeburg		
1085	Alphanus of Salerno		
	Atto of Milan		
	Gregory VII		
	Irmgardis of Cologne		
	Robert Guiscard		

1086 Anselm of Lucca
     Canute IV
     Victor III
1087 Arnulf of Soissons
     Constantine the African
     William I
     William of Poitiers
1088 Berengarius of Tours
     Bernard of Constance
     Berthold of Reichenau
     Durandus of Troarn
     Gebhard of Salzburg
1089 Lanfranc
1090 Adalbero of Würzburg
     Aimeric of Angoulème
     Benzo of Alba
     Bonizo of Sutri
     Guitmond of Aversa
1091 Adelaide of Turin
     Altmann of Passau
     Benedict II of Cluse
     William of Hirsau
1093 Margaret of Scotland
1095 Gerard of Sauve-Majeure
     Gilbert of Saint-Amand
     Ladislaus of Hungary
     William of Firmatus
     Wulfstan
1097 Adelelm of Burgos
     Andrew of Strumi
1098 Adhemar of Puy
     Gottschalk of Limburg
     Hugh of Remiremont
1099 Osmund of Salisbury
     Urban II
1100 Bernold of Constance
     Godfrey of Bouillon
     Guibert of Ravenna
1101 Bruno
     Roger I
1103 Frutolf of Michelsberg
     Manegold of Lautenbach
1105 Alberic of Monte Cassino
     Gregory II Vkajaser
     Joan of Santa Lucia
     John of Lodi
     Oderisius
     Raymond of Toulouse IV
1106 Henry IV
     Hugh of Die
1108 Gerald of Braga
     Gerard of York
1109 Anselm of Canterbury
     Dominic of the Causeway
     Edigna
     Hugh of Cluny
1110 Gebhard III of Constance
     George Cedrenus
     Robert of Molesme
1111 Nicholas III Grammaticos
1112 Hersende of Montsoreau
1113 Ida of Boulogne
     Odo of Cambrai
1114 Matilda of Tuscany

     Nestor
1115 Godfrey of Amiens
     Hugh of Flavigny
     Ilga
     Ivo of Chartres
     Leo Marsicanus
     Peter the Hermit
1116 Robert of Arbrissel
1117 Anselm of Laon
     Bernard of Tiron
     Gervin of Oudenburg
     Gilbert Crispin
     Ralph Tortarius
1118 Alexius I Comnenos
     Baldwin I of Jerusalem
     Florence of Worcester
     Hugh of Fleury
     Lidanus
     Paschal II
     Ralph of Selkirk
     Raymond of Toulouse
1119 Gelasius II
1120 Botvid
     Egino
     Euthymius Zigabenus
     Merbot
1121 Erminold of Prüfening
     Jon Ogmundsson
1122 Daniel Palomnik
     Ralph de Turbine
     Vitalis of Savigny
     William of Champeaux
1123 Bertrand of Comminges
     Bruno of Segni
     Marbod of Rennes
1124 Calixtus II
     Constabilis
     Guibert of Nogent
1125 Cosmas of Prague
     Henry V
     Lambert of Saint-Bertin
     Lambert of Saint-Omer
1126 Raymond of Roda-Barbastro
1127 Arnold of Hiltensweiler
     Fulcher of Chartres
     Herluka of Bernried
1128 Eadmer
     Petrus Leonis Pierleoni
1129 Rupert of Deutz
1130 Bartholomew of Simeri
     Baudry of Bourgueil
     Honorius II
     Irnerius
     Isidore the Farmer
     Peter de Bruys
1131 Adelhelm
     Adjutor
     Baldwin II of Jerusalem
     Canute Lavard
     Ralph of Caen
1132 Geoffrey of Vendôme
     Gregory of Catina
     Hugh of Grenoble
1133 Hildebert of Lavardin

1134 Norbert of Xanten
     Stephen Harding
1135 Matthew of Albano
1136 Guigo I
     Humbeline
     Jutta
     Leopold of Austria
     William of Corbeil
1137 Lothair III
     Louis VI
     Oldegar
1138 Geoffrey of Bayeux
     Gerard of Clairvaux
     Gezzelinus
     Heimo of Michelsberg
1139 John of Matera
     Otto of Bamberg
     Roger of Salisbury
1140 Gaucherius
1141 Aimeric of Santa Maria Nuova
     Garembert
     Hugh of Saint-Victor
1142 Peter Abelard
     Berthold of Garsten
     Ordericus Vitalis
     William of Vercelli
1143 Innocent II
     William of Malmesbury
1144 Celestine II
     William of Norwich
1145 Conrad Bosinlother
     John of Valence
     Lucius II
     Rupert of Ottobeuren
1146 Adelard of Bath
     Geoffrey of Dunstable
     Gregory of Bergamo
     Robert Pullen
1147 Henry of Bonn
     Robert Pullen
1148 Alberic of Ostia
     Anna Comnena
     Eon of Stella
     Ernest of Zwiefalten
     Malachy
     William of Saint-Thierry
1149 Petronilla of Chemillé
1150 Neilos Doxopatres
     Famian
     Guarinus of Sion
     Guido the Lombard
     Kjeld
     Nivard
     Rainald of Bar
1151 Suger
1152 Chelidonia
     Gilbert of Neuffontaines
1153 Bernard of Clairvaux
     David I
     Eugenius III
     Henry Murdac
     Macarius Scottus
1154 Anastasius IV
     Conrad of Bavaria

Gilbert de la Porrée
Lawrence of Durham
Roger II
William of York
1155 Arnold of Brescia
Christina of Markyate
Geoffrey of Monmouth
Henry of Huntingdon
Thierry of Chartres
1156 Arnold of Bonneval
Henry of Uppsala
Honorius of Autun
Peter the Venerable
1157 Guerric of Igny
John of Seville
Rober of Bruges
1158 Anselm of Havelberg
Otto of Freising
1159 Adrian IV
Amadeus of Lausanne
Guarinus of Palestrina
Robert of Newminster
Stephen of Obazine
1160 Adalgott II
Gratian
Peter Lombard
Rosalia
William of Conches
Zonoras
1161 Eric of Sweden
Raymond of Fitero
Theobald of Canterbury
1162 Roger of Elan
1163 Baldwin III of Jerusalem
Henricus Aristippus
John of Châtillon
Joscio
Leonius
1164 Fastred de Cavamiez
Hartmann of Brixen
Héloïse
Hugh of Amiens
Hugh of Fosses
1165 Elizabeth of Schönau
Goswin
Morandus
1166 Adam of Ebrach
Aelred
Gregory III Pahlav
John of Spain
1167 Gilbert
Rainald of Dassel
Robert of Melun
1169 Gerhoh of Reichersberg
Hilary of Chichester
Isaac of Stella
1170 Dominic Gundisalvi
Herman of Scheda
John the Deacon of Rome
Rahewin of Freising
Thomas Becket
1171 Henry of Blois
1172 Achard of Saint-Victor
Gilbert of Holland

Hugh of Fouilloy
1173 Haimo of Landecop
Nerses Šnorhali
Richard of Saint-Victor
1174 Peter of Tarentaise
Robert de Cricklade
1175 Andrew of Saint-Victor
1176 Galdinus
Margaret of Roskilde
1177 Gerlach
Helmond
1178 Anthelm of Chignin
Boso
John of Montfort
1179 David of Himmerod
Hildegarde of Bingen
Roger of Worcester
1180 Adam of Saint-Victor
Andreas Capellanus
Clarenbaud of Arras
Eskil of Lund
John of Salisbury
Lawrence O'Toole
Louis VII
Nicholas of Aarhus
Peter Comestor
1181 Alexander III
Roger de Pont l'Évêque
1182 Bogomilyof of Gniezno
Cyril of Turov
Hugh Etherian
John Beleth
Leo Tuscus
Romuald II of Salerno
1183 Hildegunde of Meer
1184 Arnulf of Lisieux
Bartholomew of Exeter
Benezet
Eckbert of Schönau
1185 Baldwin IV of Jerusalem
Louis of Arnstein
Lucius III
Omnibonus
William of Tyre
1186 Robert of Torigny
1187 Gilbert Foliot
Gerard of Cremona
Gregory VIII
John Faventius
Urban III
1188 Geoffrey of Clairvaux
Guigo II
Hildegunde of Schönau
1189 Gilbert of Sempringham
1190 Baldwin of Canterbury
Frederick I Barbarossa
Joseph of Exeter
Laborans
Walter of Saint-Victor
1191 Clement III
Maurice of Carnoët
1192 Rufinus
1193 Amatus of Nusco
Benedict of Peterborough

Gregory IV Tegha
1194 Godfrey of Saint-Victor
Henry of Settimello
Hugh of Bonnevaux
Raymond of Toulouse V
1195 Theodore Balsamon
Henry the Lion
Herrad of Landsberg
1196 Maurice of Sully
1197 Henry VI
Peter the Cantor
1198 Celestine III
Henry of Clairvaux
Nerses of Lambron
1199 Everard of Ypres
Jocelin of Glasgow
John of Cornwall
Michael I
Richard I
1200 Fulcoius of Beauvais
Michael Glycas
Hadewych
Hugh of Lincoln
John of Oxford
Nigel Wireker
Odo of Kent
William of Newburgh
1201 Absalon of Lund
Fulk of Neuilly
Roger of Hoveden
1202 Alan of Tewkesbury
Conrad of Querfurt
Haymarus Monachus
Joachim de Flore
Ralph of Diceto
1203 Alan of Lille
Guy of Bazoches
William of Aebelholt
1204 Isfried
1205 Damasus
Hubert Walter
Nicholas of Verdun
1206 Amalric of Bene
John X
1207 Bona
Didacus of Azevedo
1208 Guy de Montpellier
Julian of Cuenca
Rigord of Saint-Denis
1209 William of Bourges
1210 Gervase of Canterbury
Honorius Magister
Huguccio
1212 Adam of Dryburgh
Felix of Valois
Geoffrey of York
1213 Everard of Bethune
John of Matha
Mary of Oignies
1214 Arnold of Lübeck
John de Grey
1215 Charles of Villers
David of Dinant
Nicetas Choniates

Peter Waldo
1216 Innocent III
Jocelin of Brakelond
1217 Hroznata
John of Montmirail
1218 Franca Vitalta
Otto IV
1219 Leo II
Robert de Courçon
1220 Alanus Anglicus
Berard of Carbio
Bernard of Compostela I
Geoffrey of Vinsauf
Gunther of Pairis
John of Wales
Reginald of Orléans
1221 Abraham of Smolensk
Adam of Perseigne
Dominic
1222 Raymond of Toulouse VI
1223 Giraldus Cambrensis
1224 Giles of Corbeil
1225 Arnaldus Amalrici
Engelbert of Cologne
Garnerius of Rochefort
Gilbertus Anglicus
1226 Beatrice d'Este
Francis of Assisi
Louis VIII
1227 Conrad of Ottobeuren
Daniel of Belvedere
Honorius III
Ralph of Coggeshall
1228 Stephen Langton
1229 Helinand of Froidmont
1230 Benedetto Antelami
Bertrand of Garriga
Everard the German
1231 Anthony of Padua
Dodo of Asch
Elizabeth of Hungary
Ida of Nivelles
Richard Grant of Canterbury
Richard of Canterbury
William of Auxerre
1232 Agnellus of Pisa
1234 Cyril of Constantinople
Gervase of Tilbury
1235 John Parenti
Michael Scott
1236 Philip
Roger of Wendover
Sava
1237 Jordan of Saxony
Roger of Todi
1238 Ortolana
1239 Caesarius of Speyer
Herman of Salza
1240 Ambrose of Massa
Caesarius of Heisterbach
Thomas de Chabham
Edmund of Abingdon
Germanus II
Jacques de Vitry

Raymond Nonnatus
William of Notre Dame de l'Olive
1241 Celestine IV
Gervase of Melcheley
Gregory IX
Herman Joseph
1242 Ceslaus of Silesia
Jocelin of Wells
John of Salerno
Richard de Mores
William of Arnaud
1243 Hedwig
Innocent IV
1244 Guala of Bergamo
Haymo of Faversham
Henry of Heisterbach
1245 Alexander of Hales
Christian of Prussia
Eberhard of Rohrdorf
Gerard of Villamagna
John of La Rochelle
1246 Peter González Elmo
Humiliana de Circulis
John Teutonicus
Lutgardis
1247 Benedict the Pole
Conrad of Mazovia
Guido of Cortona
1248 John le Blund
Jordan Forzate
Lawrence of Spain
Richard Fishacre
Robert Bacon
1249 Raymond of Toulouse VII
William of Auvergne
1250 Adam Mulieris Pulchrae
Ascellino
Bartholomaeus Anglicus
Frederick II
Gerard of Brussels
John Canonicus
John de Sacobosco
Jordanus de Nemore
Julian of Speyer
Jutta of Fuchsstadt
Ludolph of Ratzeburg
1251 Bartholomew of Trent
1252 Blanche of Castile
Ferdinand III (of Castile)
John da Pian del Carpine
Peter Martyr
Rose of Viterbo
1253 Agnes of Assisi
Clare
Elias of Cortona
Richard of Chichester
Robert Grosseteste
1254 Andrew Caccioli
John III Ducas Vatatzes
Manuel II
1255 Hugh of Lincoln
Nicholas Paglia
1256 William of Rubruk
Peter Nolasco

1257 Hugh of Digne
1258 Adam Marsh
Bartholomew of Brescia
Juliana of Liège
1259 Bronislawa
Henry of Livonia
Matthew Paris
Roland of Cremona
Rolendis
1260 Alfred of Sareshel
Aymer of Lusignan
Gandolf of Binasco
Hugolino of Gualdo Cattaneo
Jutta of Sanferhausen
Luchesius of Poggibonsi
Richard Rufus of Cornwall
Stephen de Lexinton
1261 Alexander IV
1262 Beatrice d'Este
Giles of Assisi
Henry of Zwiefalten
Jordan of Giano
1263 Alexander Nevsky
Hugh of Saint-Cher
1264 John Lobedau
Urban IV
1265 Eve of Liège
Giles of Santarem
Simon Stock
1266 Manfred
Prandota
1267 Bernard of Compostela II
John de Deo
1268 Beatrice of Nazareth
Henry de Bracton
Clement IV
1269 Nicephorus Blemmydes
1270 Andrew of Longjumeau
Bartholomew of Vicenza
Bombolognus of Bologna
Boniface of Savoy
Isabelle of France
Louis IX
1271 Elizabeth of Portugal
Hostiensis
Leo of Assisi
Margaret of Hungary
1272 Berthold of Regensburg
Christopher of Romandiola
David of Augsburg
Gerard of Abbeville
Hannibaldus de Hannibaldis
John of Garland
William of Saint-Amour
1273 Arsenius Autorianos
Odo of Châteauroux
Romano of Rome
William of Tripoli
1274 Bonaventure
Robert de Sorbon
Thomas Aquinas
1275 Baldwin of Brandenburg
Boethius of Sweden
John of Hoveden

Martinus de Fano
Odo Rigaldus
Raymond of Peñafort
1276 Adrian V
Gregory X
Henry of Merseburg
Innocent V
James I
1277 Humbert of Romans
John XXI
Walter of Merton
1278 Martin of Troppau
Zita
1279 Richard of Gravesend
Robert Kilwardby
1280 Albert the Great
Mechtild of Magdeburg
Nicholas III
1281 Siger of Brabant
1282 Agnes of Bohemia
Ingrid Elovsdotter
1283 Bernard of Besse
John of Vercelli
Joseph I
1284 Alfonso X
Guibert of Tournai
Jordan of Osnabrück
1285 Charles of Anjou
John of Wales
Luke Belludi
Martin IV
Raymond Martini
1286 Bar-Hebraeus
William of Moerbeke
1287 Honorius IV
1288 Richard of Knapwell
1289 Adenulf of Anagni
Giles of Foscarari
John of Parma
1290 Cecilia Romana
Gregory II
John de Seccheville
John Garsias
John of Bastone
Mary de Cervelló
1291 Franco Lippi
Rudolph I
1292 Bernard of Trille
James of Certaldo
Kunigunde
Nicholas IV
John Peckham
1293 Henry of Ghent
1294 Adam of Buckfield
Roger Bacon
1295 Leo of Cava
Nicholas of Gorran
Reginald of Priverno
1296 Bernard of Montmirat
Celestine V
William Durandus
1297 Guigo de Ponte
John XI
Margaret of Cortona

1298 Emmanuel
Jacobus de Voragine
Mechtild of Hackeborn
Peter John Olivi
1299 Henry of Newark
Jolenta of Hungary
1300 Dinus Mugellanus
Ida of Louvain
1301 James de Blanconibus
1302 Andrew de Comitibus
Arnolfo di Cambio
Pierre Flotte
Gertrude the Great
Matthew of Aquasparta
Richard of Middleton
1303 Boniface VIII
Ivo of Helory
Roger Marston
1304 Benedict XI
Giles of Lessines
John de Ponteys
John Pelingotto
1305 Godfrey of Fontaines
1306 Angelus de Scarpetis
Conrad of Offida
Jacopone da Todi
Joan of Orvieto
John of Paris
Nicholas of Tolentino
1307 Fra Dolcino
Joan of Signa
1308 Clare of Montefalco
Johannes Duns Scotus
James of Viterbo
Rambert of Bologna
1309 Angela of Foligno
Augustine Novellus
1310 Athanasius I
Christiana of Lucca
Alexius Falconieri
John de Grocheo
Maximus Planudes
Marguerite Porete
1311 Arnold of Villanova
Anthony Bek
Bernard of Saisset
Henry of Mechelen
1312 Christina of Stommeln
1313 Gonsalvus Hispanus
Guido de Baysio
Henry VII
Guillaume de Nogaret
Notburga
Richard of Gravesend
Robert of Winchelsea
1314 Clement V
Hugh of Trimberg
Jacques de Molay
John of Freiburg
Ricardus de Senis
1315 Andrew Dotti
Henry of Bolzano
John le Moine
Raymond Lull

1316 Giles of Rome
1317 Henry of Harclay
Jehan de Joinville
1318 'Abdisho bar Berika
Duccio di Buoninsegna
1319 John XIII
Remigio de Girolami
1320 Antonius Andreas
John of Lichtenberg
Margaret of Metola
Ricoldus de Monte Croce
1321 Dante Alighieri
Pierre Dubois
Rainald of Ravenna
1322 John of La Verna
1323 Augustine Kazotoic
Berenger Fredoli
Nedellic Harvey
1324 Abu'l-Barakat
Marco Polo
1325 Elzéar of Sabran
1326 John Walwayn
Walter de Stapledon
1327 Aimeric of Piacenza
Bartholomew of Lucca
Meister Eckhart
James II
Robert de Baldock
1328 Augustine of Ancona
Francis of Meyronnes
John of Jandun
John of Monte Corvino
John of Sterngassen
George Metochites
1329 Roseline
1330 Anfredus Gonteri
William Duranti
Lorenzo Maitani
Richard of Connington
1331 Bernard Gui
Engelbert
Oderic of Pordenone
1332 Andronicus II Palaeologus
1333 Bernard Lombardi
Imelda
William of Alnwick
1334 Pietro Cavallini
Durandus of Saint-Pourçain
John XXII
Zenzelinus de Casanis
1335 John Lutterell
Nicholas Trevet
1336 Giotto di Bondone
Richard of Wallingford
1337 John of Langton
1339 John of Caramola
1340 Andras Báthory
Matthew Blastares
Henry of Friemar
John of Naples
Nicholas of Lyra
1341 Andronicus III Palaeologus
William Courtenay
Julia Falconieri

Robert of Soleto
1342   Benedict XII
       Marsilius of Padua
       Michael of Cesena
1344   Francis of Marchia
       Simone Martini
1345   Adam of Orleton
       John de Ridevall
       John of Viktring
       Richard of Bury
1346   Gregory Sinaites
       John Bacanthorpe
       John of Reading
1347   Bartholomew of San Concordio
       Gasbert de Laval
       John XIV
       William of Ockham
1348   Pierre Bertrand
       Claritus
       Andreae Johannes
       John de Offord
       John of Rodington
       Louis IV
       Ambrogio Piccolomini
       John Stratford
1349   Gregory Akindynos
       John Discalceatus
       John of Acton
       John of Dumbleton
       Robert Holcot
       Richard de Hampole Rolle
1350   Armand de Belvezer
       Barlaam of Calabria
       Bartholomew of Urbino
       Bertrand of Aquileia
       John of Mirecourt
       Richard of Campsall
1351   Henri Bohic
       Landolf Caracciolo
       John de Muris
       Nicholas of Autrecourt
1352   John of Bromyard
       Clement VI
       Ewostatewos
1353   David Dishypatos
1354   Cola di Rienzo
       Cola di Rienzo
1357   Bartolo of Sassoferrato
       Herman of Schildesche
1358   Adam Wodham
       Delphina of Signe
       Gregory of Rimini
1359   Gregory Palamas
1360   Alberic of Rosate
       John Crathorn
       Theodore Dexios
       Öser Irmhart
       Richard Fitzralph
1361   Michael de Northburgh
       Johann Tauler
1362   Innocent VI
       John de Saint-Pol
       John Lathbury
       Richard of Kilvington

Robert Stratford
1363   Nilus Cabasilas
       Callistus I
       Giovanni da Lecceto Chigi
       Lupold of Bebenburg
1364   Alan of Walsingham
       Charles of Blois
       Ernest of Pardubice
       Ralph Higden
1365   John Calderini
       Roger of Swynesched
1366   Henry Suso
1367   Gil Álvarez de Albornoz
       John Colombini
       Roger le Fort
1369   John Grandison
       Philippa of Hainaut
       William of Toulouse
1370   Eberhard of Tüntenhausen
       Henry of Herford
       John Buridan
       John of Ripa
       Urban V
1373   Andrew Corsini
       Bridget of Sweden
       John of Thoresby
       John of Waldby
1374   Anthony Pavonius
       Conrad of Megenburg
       John Klenkok
       Jan Milíc
       Francesco Petrarch
1375   Isaac Argyros
       Giovanni Boccaccio
1376   Henry of Diessenhofen
1377   Edward III
       Guillaume de Machaut
1378   Charles IV
       Gregory XI
       Ludolph of Saxony
       Roch
1379   John of Bridlington
       Philotheus Coccinus
1380   Catherine of Siena
       John of Wales
       Jordan of Quedlingburg
1381   John Ball
       Catherine of Sweden
       John Lapus Castilioneus
       Jan van Ruysbroeck
1382   Macarius Chrysocephalos
       Nicholas Oresme
1383   William Flete
       John de Lignano
1384   Gerardus Magnus Groote
       John Wycliffe
1385   Gabriele Ferretti
       Geoffrey Hardeby
1386   Orlando de' Medici
1388   John Welles
       Salama
1389   Adam of Houghton
       John of Appleby
       Urban VI

1390   Nicholas Cabasilas
       Conrad of Gelnhausen
1391   Guido Marramaldi
       John de Fantutiis
       John V Palaeologus
       Nicholas of Hermanssön
1392   Sergius of Radonezh
1393   John of Nepomuk
1394   Clement VII
1395   Walter Hilton
       Nicholas of Basle
1397   Adam Easton
       Anthony IV
       Henry of Oyta
       John Gilbert
       Francesco Landini
       Laurentius de Piv
1398   Robert Waldby of York
1399   John Kynyngham
       Raymond of Capua
1400   Michele Aiguani
       Baldus de Ubaldis
       Geoffrey Chaucer
       Giuliana Chigi
       Florentius Radewijns
       William Langland
       Richard II
1401   Andrew Franchi
       William Sawtrey
1404   Boniface IX
       William of Wykeham
1405   Pietro Corsini
1406   Henry Despenser
       Innocent VII
1407   Johannes Brammart
       Leonardo de Rubeis
1408   Angelo Acciaioli
       Antonio de Butrio
       John Gower
       Henry of Kalkar
1409   Melchior Broederlam
       Thomas Merks
1410   Alexander V
       Bartolo di Fredi
       Manuel Calecas
       Matthew of Cracow
1411   Thomas Chillenden
       Johannes Ciconia
       John Parvus
1413   Julian of Norwich
1414   Thomas Arundel
       Jeanne Marie de Maille
1415   Manuel Chrysoloras
       Richard Courtenay
       John Huss
1416   Jerome of Prague
1417   Gregory XII
       Robert Hallum
       John Oldcastle
       Francesco Zabarella
1418   Dietrich of Nieheim
1419   Lucrezia Borgia
       John Catrik
       Clare Gambacorta

Giovanni Dominici
John XXIII
Vincent Ferrer
1420 Nicholas Hereford
Nicholas of Hereford
1421 Richard Clifford
1422 Thomas Walsingham
1423 Benedict XIII
Henry Bowet
Brevicoxa
1424 Nicholas Bubwith
Philip Repington
John Zizka
1425 Piero di Giovanni Lorenzo Monaco
Manuel II Palaeologus
1426 Hubert van Eyck
John Benincasa
1427 Gentile da Fabriano
1428 Guillaume Fillastre
Masaccio
John Purvey
Johann Zachariae
1429 Jean le Charlier de Gerson
1430 Álvarez of Cordoba
Bartholomew of Rome
Christina of Pisan
Thomas Netter
Andrei Rublev
1431 Henry of Gorkum
Joan of Arc
Martin V
1432 Nicholas of Clamanges
1433 Margery Kempe
Nicholas of Dinkelsbühl
1434 Jagiello
John Langdon
1435 Angelina of Marsciano
Peter Gambacorta
John of Falkenberg
Philip Morgan
1436 Raymond of Sebonde
1438 Joseph Bryennios
Johann Nider
Giordano Orsini
1439 Ambrose Traversari
1440 Andrés de Escobar
Frances of Rome
Henry Wardlaw
1441 Jan van Eyck
1443 Niccolò Albergati
Henry Chichele
Ferdinand
John of Ragusa
1444 Bernardine of Siena
Leonardo Aretino Bruni
John Capreolus
Giuliano Cesarini
Mark Eugenicus
1445 Thomas Brouns
John Bassandus
1446 Filippo Brunelleschi
William Lyndwood
1447 Henry Beaufort
Colette

Eugenius IV
Rita of Cascia
1448 Robert Gilbert
John VIII Palaeologus
1450 Andrew Abellon
Leonello d'Este
Louis d'Aleman
Adam Moleyns
1451 Amadeus VIII of Savoy
Andrew Chrysoberges
Giovanni Contarini
Stefan Lochner
1453 Constantine XI Palaeologus
John Dunstable
1454 John Kemp
1455 Fra Angelico
Lorenzo Ghiberti
Edmund Lacy
Nicholas V
1456 Christina of Spoleto
John Capistran
Lawrence Justinian
Lawrence of Ripafratta
Lorenzo Giustiniani
Nicholas of Prussia
1457 Andrea del Castagno
1458 Calixtus III
Domenico Capranica
Thomas Gascoigne
Helen of Udine
1459 Antoninus
Giovanni Aurispa
Gregory III
Giannozzo Manetti
1460 Anthony Neyrot
Archangelo of Calatafimi
Gilles Binchois
Henry the Navigator
1461 Anthony of Stroncone
Charles VII
Reginald Pecock
1462 Andrew of Rinn
1463 Flavio Biondo
Catherine of Bologna
Prospero Colonna
Didacus of Alcalá
1464 William Booth
John Capgrave
Thomas Ebendorfer
Isidore of Kiev
Cosimo de' Medici
Nicholas of Cusa
Pius II
1465 Thomas Bekynton
Richard Caunton
John Free
Magdalen Albrici
Hans Memling
1466 Enguerrand Charonton
Donatello
1467 John Lowe
1468 Eustochia Calafato
1469 Juan de Carvajal
Eustochium of Padua

Fra Filippo Lippi
1470 Rodrigo Sanchez de Arevalo
Jacopo Bellini
Cornelius of Zierikzee
Andrew Holes
Timoteo Maffei
1471 Denis the Carthusian
Gennadius II of Constantinople
Henry VI
Isaias Boner
Thomas Malory
Paul II
Thomas à Kempis
1472 Amadeus IX of Savoy
Antonia of Florence
Bessarion
1473 James Beaton
Guillaume Fillastre
John Cantius
Jean Jouffroy
1474 Guillaume Dufay
Pietro Riario
1475 Alan de la Roche
Dirk Bouts
John Macrory Macgrath
1476 Hans Böhm
James of the Marches
George Neville
Regiomontanus
1477 Richard Andrewe
John Arundel
Bernard of Kraiburg
Marie de Bretagne
Henry of Herp
Latino Orsini
1478 William Grey
Walter Hunt
1479 Jacopo Ammanati de' Piccolomini
Antonello da Messina
Andreas de Barbatia
Robert Briçonnet
Cherubino of Avigliana
1480 Lawrence Booth
Jan Dlugosz
Paolo Maffei
Martin Mair
1481 Richard Beauchamp
Constantius of Fabriano
Francesco Filelfo
Bartolomeo Platina
1482 Anthony Bonfadini
Luca Della Robbia
Hugo van der Goes
1483 Guillaume d' Estouteville
Robert Flemming
1484 László Báthory
Elias de Bourdeille
Casimir
John of Dukla
Sixtus IV
Andrea Zamonetic
1485 Rudolphus Frisius Agricola
Andrew of Peschiera
John Blackman

Christopher Maccassoli
Frances d'Amboise
Franciscus de Accoltis
1486 Thomas Bourchier
João Consobrino
George of Trebizond
Erik Olsson
William of Waynflete
1487 John Argyropoulos
Nicholas of Flüe
1488 Pere-Luís Borgia
Girolamo Riario
1489 Wessel Gansfort
Thomas Kemp
1490 Thomas Chaundler
Christina of Hamm
Joan of Portugal
1491 William Caxton
Antonio Grassi
1492 Antoine Busnois
Peter Courtenay
Innocent VIII
Piero della Francesca
Balthasar Ravaschieri
1494 Archangela Girlani
Domenico Ghirlandaio
Giovanni Pico della Mirandola
John Russell
1495 Angelo Carletti di Chivasso
Gabriel Biel
Roberto Caracciolo
Pedro González de Mendoza
1496 Filippo Buonaccorsi
1497 Juan Borgia
Benozzo Gozzoli
Nicholas of Strasburg
Johannes Ockeghem
1498 Charles VIII
Giovanni Gigli
Alexander Hegius
Girolamo Savonarola
Tomás de Torquemada
1499 Arnold Bostius
Marsilio Ficino
James Goldwell
1500 Stefano Infessura
Joseph of Methone
John Morton
1501 Columba of Rieti
Robert Gaguin
Francesco di Giorgio
Constantine Lascaris
John Mombaer
1502 Johannes Annius
Andreas Lang
Francesco Laurana
Boninus Mombritius
Werner Rolevinck
1503 Alexander VI
Pierre d'Aubusson
Johann von Dalberg
Henry Deane
Louise of Savoy
Pius III

1504 John Holt
Isabella of Castile
1505 Adam of Fulda
Joan of France
Ladislaus of Gielniow
Jakob Obrecht
Osanna of Mantua
1506 Alexander Agricola
Christopher Columbus
Andrea Mantegna
1507 Gentile Bellini
Cesare Borgia
Petrus Burrus
Francis of Paola
1508 Giovanni Colonna
Ludovicus Bologninus
Celso Maffei
1509 Margaret Beaufort
1510 Sandro Botticelli
Angelina
Catherine of Genoa
Garcia de Cisneros
Johannes Geiler von Kaysersberg
Giorgione da Castelfranco
John Nauclerus
1511 Amrogio Calepino
Oliviero Carafa
Antoine de Févin
John Liccio
1512 Sigismondo de' Conti
1513 Johann Amerbach
Alonso de Espinar
Julius II
Geremia Lambertenghi of Como
Maurice O'Fihely
1514 Christopher Bainbridge
Donato Bramante
Guillaume Briçonnet
William Elphinstone
Bernardo Rucellai
1515 Jacques Almain
Bernal Buyl
Giovanni Giocondo
Pietro Lombard
Louis XII
Aldus Manutius
Luca Pacioli
1516 Baptist of Mantua
Giovanni Bellini
Ferdinand IV
1517 Andreas Ammonius
Fra Bartolomeo
Jofré Borgia
Heinrich Isaac
Markos Musurus
Francisco Ximénez de Cisneros
1518 Publio Fausto Andrelini
Loyset Compère
1519 John Colet
William Grocyn
Leonardo da Vinci
Hugh Oldham
Juan de Quevedo
Johann Tetzel

1520 Agostino Chigi
Fabrizio Colonna
Helena Duglioli
Ippolito d'Este
Raphael
1521 Adrian of Castello
Alfonso of Madrid
Bernard Andre
William Atwater
Tamás Bakócz
Sebastian Brant
Pedro de Córdoba
Josquin des Prez
Leo X
Margaret of Lorraine
1522 Franchino Gaforio
William Lily
Raffaele Maffei
Jean Mouton
Johann Reuchlin
1523 Adrian VI
Bernardino López de Carvajal
Prospero Colonna
Domenico Grimani
Ulrich von Hutten
Sylvester Prierias Mazzolini
1524 Zacharias Calliergis
Zaccaria Ferreri
Alejandro Geraldini
Thomas Linacre
1525 Johannes Altenstaig
Antoine Brumel
Pietro Dolfin
Frederick III of Saxony
Jakob Fugger
Thomas Münzer
Pietro Pomponazzi
Gregor Reisch
1526 Vittore Carpaccio
Conrad Grebel
Giovanni dei Medici
Thomas Wyttenbach
1527 Demetrius Ducas
Hieronymus Emser
Johann Froben
Domenico Jacobazzi
Niccolò Machiavelli
1528 Albrecht Dürer
Richard Foxe
Matthias Grünewald
Patrick Hamilton
Balthasar Hubmaier
Thomas Illyricus
Lukáš of Prague
1529 Baldassare Castiglione
Johannes Cuspinian
Juan del Encina
Karl von Miltitz
1530 Andrea del Sarto
Mercurino Arborio di Gattinara
Henry
Antonio Montesino
Willibald Pirkcheimer
Thomas Wolsey

1531 Alfonso de Zamora
Johann Augustanus Faber
Richard Kedermynster
Jan Laski
John Oecolampadius
Tilman Riemenschneider
William Warham
Huldrych Zwingli
1532 Pietro Accolti
Bartholomaeus Arnoldi
Pompeo Colonna
Giles of Viterbo
Charitas Pirckheimer
Alfonso de Valdés
Marco Antonio Zimara
1533 Lodovico Ariosto
Johannes Eberlin
John Frith
1534 John Alen
Aventinus
Elizabeth Barton
Edward Bocking
Guillaume Briçonnet
Tommaso de Vio Cajetan
Clement VII
Correggio
John Lascaris
1535 Heinrich Cornelius Agrippa von
Nettesheim
Girolamo Balbi
John Fisher
Poul Helgesen
John Houghton
Lawrence of Villamagna
Robert Lawrence
Thomas More
Richard Reynolds
1536 Arnold Badet
Hector Boece
Catherine of Aragon
Philippus Decius
Desiderius Erasmus
Agostino Giustiniani
Jakob Hutter
Conrad Köllin
Jacques Lefèvre d'Étaples
Richard Pace
Santes Pagnini
John Rastell
Nicholas Storch
William Tyndale
1537 Robert Aske
Thomas Bedyll
John Claymond
Jerome Emiliani
Mario Maffei
Thomas Murner
1538 Agostino Nifo
Pierre Robert Olivetan
1539 John Beche
Hans Brask
Lorenzo Campeggio
Francesco Chiericati
Adrian Fortescue

George of Saxony
Johannes Justus Lanspergius
Richard Whiting
Anthony Zaccaria
1540 Thomas Abell
Francisco Alvares
Guillaume Budé
Thomas Cromwell
Francesco Guicciardini
Matthäus Lang
Angela Merici
Francisco de Quiñones
Juan Luis Vives
1541 Wolfgang Capito
Carlstadt
John Clerk
Johannes Faber
Andreas Rudolf Bodenstein von
Karlstadt
Jacques Merlin
Juan de Valdés
1542 Girolamo Aleandro
Alessandro Cesarini
Gasparo Contarini
Francis of Osuna
Sebastian Franck
Julian Garces
Ortwin Gratius
Leo Jud
Maria Laurentia Longo
Albert Pigge
1543 Afonso I
Berthold of Chiemsee
Josse Clichtove
Nicolaus Copernicus
Johann Eck
Nikolaus Ellenbog
Gian Matteo Giberti
Melchior Hoffman
1544 Ludwig Blarer
Bartolomeo Ferrari
Jacobus Latomus
Edward Lee
Johannes Magnus
1545 Pietro Aaron
Johannes Crotus Rhubianus
Costanza Festa
Bartolommeo Fumo
Antonio de Guevara
Georg Spalatin
John Taverner
1546 Thomas Elyot
Peter Faber
Martin Luther
Juan Medina
Friedrich Myconius
Julius von Pflug
Francisco de Vitoria
George Wishart
1547 Tommaso Badia
Pietro Bembo
Johannes de Buys
Cajetan
Catherine of Racconigi

Vittoria Colonna
Francis I
Henry VIII
William Knight
John Longland
Sebastián Ramírez de Fuenleal
Beatus Rhenanus
Jacopo Sadoleto
1548 Carpentras
Gregorio Cortese
Juan Diego
Juan de Zumarrága
1549 Benedetto Accolti
Domingo Betanzos
Daniel Bomberg
Antonio Criminali
Paul III
1550 John of God
Simon Lemnius
1551 Martin Bucer
James MacGregor
György Martinuzzi
1552 Francis Amelry
Lars Anderson
Matteo Serafini da Bascio
Joannes Cochlaeus
Francis Xavier
Moritz von Hutten
Paulus Jovius
Claude Le Jay
Sebastian Münster
Oswald Myconius
Friedrich Nausea
Andreas Osiander
Olaus Petri
1553 Ambrosius Catharinus
Charles de Bouelles
Lucas Cranach
Edward VI
Bernardino Maffei
Cristóbal de Morales
François Rabelais
1554 Thomas Howard
Richard Sampson
1555 Georgius Agricola
Giovanniangelo Arcimboldi
John Bradford
Jacobus Clemens non Papa
Stephen Gardiner
Justus Jonas
Julius III
Hugh Latimer
Marcellus II
Nicholas Ridley
John Rogers
1556 Pietro Aretino
Giovanni della Casa
Thomas Cranmer
George Day
Ignatius of Loyola
David Joris
Lorenzo Lotto
Pilgram Marbeck
Nicholas Shaxton

1557 Veit Amerbach
     Eberhard Billick
     Jan Bunderius
     Ascanio Colonna
     Olaus Magnus
     Pierre Rebuffi
1558 Silvestro Aldobrandini
     Alfonso de Castro
     Johann Bugenhagen
     Charles V
     George Dowdall
     Clément Janequin
     Mary Tudor
     Marcos de Niza
     Reginald Pole
1559 Robert Estienne
     Luigi Lippomano
     Menno Simons
     Paul IV
1560 James Brooks
     Melchior Cano
     Andrea Doria
     Jean Du Bellay
     Guillaume Duprat
     Nicolas Gombert
     Jan Laski
     Philipp Melanchthon
     Domingo de Soto
1561 Louis Bourgeois
     Carlo Carafa
     Hans Tausen
1562 Bonifacius Amerbach
     Adrianus Petit Coclico
     João Nunes Barreto
     Peter Martyr Vermigili
     Peter of Alcántara
     Lelio Francesco Maria Socinus
1563 Sebastian Castellio
     Henricus Glareanus
     Ercole Gonzaga
     Francisco Marroquin
     Polydore Plasden
1564 Ambrosius Blarer
     Diethelm Blarer
     Jean Calvin
     Ferdinand I
     Michelangelo Buonarroti
     Bernardino Ochino
1565 Nikolaus von Amsdorf
     Alfonso Carafa
     Guillaume Farel
     Ranuccio Farnese
     Diego Lainez
     Toribio de Benavente Motolinía
     Pius IV
     Vasco de Quiroga
     William Rastell
1566 Francis Blosius
     Bonsignore Cacciaguerra
     George Cassander
     Castellino da Castelli
     Bartolomé de Las Casas
1567 Abdisho IV
     Jakob Arcadelt

     Gerwig Blarer
     Thomas Blarer
     Pietro Carnesecchi
     Juan de la Cruz
     Guido De Brès
     Philip of Hesse
     Richard Rich
1568 Roger Ascham
     William Barlow
     Stanislaus Kostka
     Jean Parisot de La Valette
     Miklós Oláh
1569 Edmund Bonner
     Gilbert Bourne
     Pieter (the Elder) Brueghel
     Camillo Campeggi
     Miles Coverdale
     John of Ávila
     Giacomo Nacchianti
     Victorinus Strigel
1570 Ignacio de Azevedo
     Pedro de Betanzos
     Johann Brenz
     Marco Antonio Cavazzoni
     Gaspar da Cruz
     John Felton
     Leonhard Haller
     Bartholomaeus Latomus
     Manuel da Nóbrega
     Andrés de Olmos
     Diego Ortíz
1571 Giovanni Animucia
     Benvenuto Cellini
     Claude Togniel de Espence
     Jean Garet
     John Jewel
1572 Tommaso Aldobrandini
     Francis Borgia
     Angelo Bronzino
     Pierre Certon
     John Clement
     Gaspard II de Coligny
     Ippolito d'Este
     Juan Focher
     Francis Borgia
     Pedro de Gante
     Claude Goudimel
     Thomas Howard
     John Knox
     Denis Lambin
     Pius V
     Peter Ramus
1573 Giovanni Aldobrandini
     Michel de L'Hôpital
     Andreas Masius
1574 Giulio Acquaviva
     François Baudouin
     Joachim Camerarius
     Catherine Tomas
     Demochares
     Bartolomeo Eustachio
     Damião de Góis
     Charles de Lorraine de Guise
     George Major

     Paulus Manutius
     Cornelius Musso
1575 Marcin Bielski
     Anna Bijns
     Johann Heinrich Bullinger
     Jean Dumoulin
     Matthias Flacius Illyricus
     Jerónimo de Loaysa
     Tomás de Mercado
     Matthew Parker
     Jodoco Riche
1576 Geronimo Cardano
     Bartolomé de Carranza
     Pedro de Espinareda
     Cornelius Jansen
     Girolamo Muzio
     Titian
1577 Girolamo Cavazzoni
     Diego de Covarrubias y Leyva
     Antoine Le Conte
     Cuthbert Mayne
     William Walsh
1578 Antonio de Córdoba
     Diego of Estella
     Martin Eisengrein
     Nicholas van Esch
     Nicholas Heath
     Pierre Lescot
     Cristoforo Madruzzo
     Alessandro Piccolomini
     William Roper
     Johannes Stumpf
1579 Pietro Camaiani
     Henry Cole
     Franz David
     Henry Fitzalan
     Stanislaus Hosius
     Juan de Juanes
     Diego de Landa
     Patrick O'Hely
1580 Baltasar Álvarez
     Maurice Clenock
     Francisco de Morales
     Giovanni Morone
     Geronimo Nadal
     Juan Navarro
     Hendrik Niclaes
     Gelasius O'Cullenan
1581 Louis Bertrand
     Jacques de Billy
     Alexander Briant
     Richard Bristow
     Edward Campion
     Maurice Eustace
     Francisco Foreiro
     Nicholas Sanders
1582 Duke of Alva
     George Buchanan
     Thomas Cottam
     Luke Kirby
     Gregory Martin
     John Paine
     Teresa of Ávila
1583 Rudolf Acquaviva

Edward Arden
John Bodey
William Carter
Zaccaria Dolfin
Erastus
Marcantonio Maffei
Johannes Maldonatus
1584 Charles Borromeo
Gaspar de Carvajal
Giovanni Francesco Commendone
Wilhelm Eisengrein
Felix Figliucci
Richard Gwyn
Melchior Hittorf
John de Feckenham
Dermot O'Hurley
Francisco Torres
1585 Georges d'Armagnac
Jerome Hermes Bolsec
Richard Creagh
Hernando Franco
Andrea Gabrieli
Thomas Goldwell
Gregory XIII
Maurice Kenraghty
Alonso de Molina
Edmund Plowden
Pierre de Ronsard
John Scory
Thomas Tallis
Hugh Taylor
1586 Martin Aspilcueta
Antonio Augustin
Istvan Báthory
Martin Chemnitz
Margaret Clitherow
Louis d'Este
Antoine Perrenot de Granvelle
Clitherow Margare
Margaret of Parma
1587 Pietro Aldobrandini
Petrus de Buys
Felix of Cantalice
John Foxe
Vincenzo Ruffo
1588 Diego Durán
Louis of Granada
Edwin Sandys
Margaret Ward
1589 Benedict the Moor
Catherine de' Medici
Alessandro Farnese
Ivan Gundulic
Martin Kromer
Marguérin de La Bigne
Christophe Plantin
Johannes Sturm
Jacopo Zabarella
1590 Bartholomew of Braga
Giorgio Blandrata
Nicolás Alfonso de Bobadilla
Stephen Brinkley
Catherine de' Ricci
Giovanni Paolo Lancelotti

Alonso Coello Sánchez
Sixtus V
Girolamo Zanchi
Luis Zapata de Cardenas
Gioseffo Zarlino
1591 Aloysius Gonzaga
Domingo de la Anunciación
Mattia dei Gibboni Aquarius
Edmond Auger
Antonio Carafa
Edmund Gennings
Gregory XIV
Innocent IX
John of the Cross
Jacobus de Kerle
Luis de León
Alfonso de Orozco
Francisco de Ribera
John Stubbs
Swithun Wells
1592 Bartolomeo Ammanati
Juan de Atienza
Marc'Antonio Ingegneri
Michel Eyquem de Montaigne
Paschal Baylon
Annibale Zoilo
1593 Jacques Amyot
Henry Barrow
William Davies
Scipione Gonzaga
John Greenwood
Antonio Sánchez
1594 William Allen
Bálint Balassa
John Boste
Orlando di Lasso
Gerardus Mercator
Giovanni Pierluigi da Palestrina
1595 Christophe de Cheffontaines
Philip Howard
Cornelius Loos
Ludovico López
Philip Neri
Feliciano Ninguarda
Robert Southwell
Henry Walpole
1596 Jean Bodin
John Bridgewater
Gianfrancesco Morosini
Manoel de Sá
Urban VII
1597 José de Anchieta
Peter Canisius
Felipe de Jesús Casas Martinez
Gilbert Generbrard
John Martiall
1598 Michel de Bay
John Jones
Philips von Marnix van St
  Aldegonde
Arias Montanus
Philip II
Thomas Stapleton
1599 Andras Báthory

Peter da Fonseca
Francisco Guerrero
Luca Marenzio
1600 José de Acosta
Sebastian de Aparicio
Martinus Balticus
Jean de la Barrière
Giordano Bruno
David Chrytraeus
James Dowdall
Niels Hemmingsen
Richard Hooker
Lodovico Madruzzo
Luis de Molina
John Rigby
1601 Gian Francesco Aldobrandini
Tycho Brahe
Wolfgang von Dalberg
Germaine of Pibrac
Anne Line
Peter Ruiz of the Visitation
1602 Agostino Carracci
Francisco Cepeda
William Perkins
1603 Francisco de Alvarado
Juan Azor
James Beaton
Jakob Christoph Blarer
Thomas Cartwright
Andrea Cesalpino
Pierre Charron
Elizabeth I
Joseph of Cupertino
Stanislaw Karnkowski
Giampietro Maffei
Mary of St Joseph Salazar
Philippe de Monte
1604 Domingo Bañez
Agustín Dávila y Padilla
Germanico Malaspina
Jerónimo de Mendieta
Claudio Merulo
William Morgan
Arnaud d'Ossat
Fausto Paolo Socinus
1605 Ippolito Aldobrandini
Francis Arias
Martin del Barco Centenera
Theodore Beza
Clement VIII
Leo XI
1606 Renard de Beaume
Giovanni Baptista Corrado
Everard Digby
John Forbes
Henry Garnett
Justus Lipsius
Melchior Lussy
Geronimo Mercuriali
Toribio Alfonso de Mogrovejo
Nicholas Owen
Alessandro Valignano
1607 Caesar Baronius
Cesar de Bus

Juan de Castellanos
Achille Gagliardi
Giovanni Maria Nanino
1608 Andrew Avellino
Miguel Cabello de Balboa
William Barclay
Giovanni Bologna
Jeanne-Baptiste de Bourbon
Francis Caracciolo
Martin Antoine Del Rio
Thomas Garnett
Henri duc de Joyeuse
1609 Pedro de Aguado
Jacobus Arminius
Giovanni Matteo Asola
Annibale Carracci
Giovanni dalla Croce
Giovanni Gastoldi
Juan de los Angeles
John Leonardi
Reginaldo de Lizárraga
Joseph Justus Scaliger
1610 Cinzio Passeri Aldobrandini
Bernardo Bitti
Henricus Canisius
Michelangelo Merisi da
  Caravaggio
Pierre Victor Cayet
Francis Solanus
Henry IV
Robert Parsons
Matteo Ricci
John Roberts
Tomás Sánchez
1611 Mattia da Salò Bellintani
William Benedict Fitch
Richard Mulcaster
Pedro de Ribadeneira
1612 Ottavio Acquaviva (the elder)
Silvestro Aldobrandini
John Almond
George Blackwell
Christopher Clavius
Giovanni Gabrieli
Hans Leo von Hassler
Joseph of Leonessa
Anthony de Molina
Conor O'Devaney
John Smyth
1613 Robert Abercromby
Giovanni Maria Artusi
Gulielmus Estius
Carlo Gesualdo
John Baptist of the Conception
Hadrian à Saravia
1614 Felice Anerio
Camillus of Lellis
Luisa de Carvajal
Isaac Casaubon
Luis de Cerqueira
Jerome Gratian
El Greco
1615 Claudius Acquaviva
John of Jesus Mary

John Ogilvie
Thomas Pounde
Antonio Rubio
1616 Claude d' Abbeville
Miguel de Cervantes Saavedra
Thomas Helwys
Pedro de Ledesma
Hugh O'Neill
Bernardino Realino
Alfonso Rodriguez
William Shakespeare
1617 Christoph Brouwer
Jean Chapeauville
Julius Echter von Mespelbrunn
Maria Victoria Fornari-Strata
Diego Gonzalez Holguín
Alphonsus Rodríguez
Rose of Lima
Francisco Suárez
1618 Jacques Davy Duperron
Francis Johnson
Mary of the Incarnation
Antoinette d' Orléans-Longueville
Richard Stanyhurst
1619 Anne of Denmark
Antoine Arnauld
Ludovico Carracci
Hippolytus Galantini
Achille Harlay
Joseph de Jouvancy
Lawrence of Brindisi
1620 Diego Álvarez de Paz
Laurent Benard
Juan Pablo Bonet
Angelo Rocca
1621 Pietro Aldobrandini
Anne of Jesus
Johann Arndt
John Barclay
Pedro Bedon
Robert Bellarmine
John Berchmans
Luis de Montesinos
Paul V
Michael Praetorius
Anne de Xaintonge
1622 Pablo José de Arriaga
Francis de Sales
Anthony Le Gaudier
Johann Lohelius
Andrew Melville
Laurentius Nielsen
Henry Savile
1623 Henry Ainsworth
William Byrd
Nicolas Coeffeteau
Philippe Du Plessis-Mornay
Gregory XV
Josaphat Kuncevyc
Leonardus Lessius
Valerius Reginald
Paolo Sarpi
Thomas Weekes
1624 Martin Becanus

Isabella Cristina Bellinzaga
Jakob Böhme
Alessandro d'Este
Ketevan of Georgia
Luis de La Puente
1625 Domingo Lazaro de Arregui
Christopher Bagshaw
Ludovico Bertonio
John Cameron
Domenico Pietro Cerone
Thomas Dempster
Michael de la Fuente
Orlando Gibbons
James I
Michael de Sanctis
Alonso de la Mota y Escobar
John Robinson
Juan de las Roelas
1626 Lancelot Andrewes
Anne of St Bartholomew
Agustin Antolinez
Francis Bacon
Caesar Clement
Paolo Comitoli
Pierre Coton
John Dowland
Christopher Holywood
1627 Laurent Lawrence Beyerlink
Giacinto da Casale
Bartolomé Díez Laurel
Luis de Góngora y Argote
Andrea del Guasto
Antonio de Remesal
1628 Gregor Aichinger
Anthimus II
Edmund Arrowsmith
Avvakum Petrovich
Roque González
Tomás Malvenda
1629 Paolo Agostini
Pierre de Bérulle
Luis de Bolanos
Johannes Buxtorf (the Elder)
William Gifford
Tomás de Lemos
Carlo Maderno
Carlo Gaudenzio Madruzzo
Heribert Rosweyde
Christopher Sutton
1630 Giovanni Francesco Anerio
Théodore Agrippa d'Aubigné
Filippo Fabri
Melchior Klesl
Luis Gerónimo de Oré
Juan Romero
Juan Zapata y Sandoval
1631 Diego Álvarez
Lewis Bayly
Federigo Borromeo
Constantine of Barbanson
John Donne
Patrick Fleming
Edmond Richer
Liborius Wagner

1632 Antonio de Araujo
      Archangel of Pembroke
      George Calvert
      Rodriguez Bartolomeo Gutiérrez
1633 Robert Browne
      Scipione Caffarelli Borghese
      Carlo Carafa
      Marina de Escobar
      George Herbert
      John Malderus
      Philaret of Moscow
      Rodrigues Tcuzu João
1634 Cosmo Alamanni
      Antonio de Andrade
      Luiz de Azevedo
1635 Luis Juárez
      Louis Lallemant
      Paulus Laymann
      Francis Nugent
      Wolfgang Ratke
      Philipp Jakob Spener
      Hugh Ward
1636 Diego Francisco Aduarte
      Jean Arnoux
      Alonzo de Benavides
      Justus de Harduwijn
      John of Saint-Samson
1637 Ferdinand II
      John Gerard
      Johann Gerhard
      Peter Huyssens
      Cornelius a Lapide
      Gregorio Martínez
1638 Ippolito Aldobrandini
      Christof Besold
      Cassian of Nantes
      Cyril Lucaris
      Dionysius of the Nativity
      Cornelius Otto Jansen
      François Le Clerc du Tremblay
      Cyril Lucaris
      Giacomo Rho
1639 Thomas Arundell
      Etienne Binet
      Tommaso Campanella
      Martin de Porres
      Metrophanes Critopoulos
      Niccolò Riccardi
      John Spottiswode
1640 Agostino Agazzari
      Roger Anderton
      Lazzaro Cattaneo
      Francesco Collius
      George Con
      André Duchesne
      Jeanne de Lestonnac
      Hyacintha Marescotti
      Aubert Miraeus
      Peter Fourier
      Jean-François Regis
      Peter Paul Rubens
1641 David Augustine Baker
      Ambrose Barlow
      Severin Binius

      Jane Frances Fremiot de Chantal
      Charles de Condren
      Franciscus Gomarus
      Antony Hickey
      William Wroth
1642 Jacques Bonfrère
      Marco da Gagliano
      Galilei Galileo
      Guido Reni
      Armand Jean du Plessis de
        Richelieu
      Alban Roe
1643 Lawrence Anderton
      Nicholas Bonet
      Benedetto Castelli
      Jean Duvergier de Hauranne
      Henry Fitzsimon
      Girolamo Frescobaldi
      Anne Hutchinson
      Claudio Monteverdi
      Michael O'Clery
      Antonio Rubino
      Abbé de Saint-Cyran
1644 Carlo Carafa
      Alfonso d' Este
      John of Saint Thomas
      Geoffrey Keating
      Francis Quarles
      Urban VIII
1645 Walter Coleman
      Hugo Grotius
      François de La Rochefoucauld
      William Laud
      Juan Masias
      Henry Morse
      Anthony Stafford
1646 Charles François d' Abra de
        Raconis
      Cecilia of the Nativity
      Achille Harlay
      Isaac Jogues
      John Chrysostom of Saint-Lô
      Duarte Lobo
      Peter Mogila
      Mary Ward
1647 Thomas Abington
      Francisco de Avila
      Pietro Casani
      Francesco Bonaventura Cavalieri
      Bernabé Cobo
      Thomas Hooker
      Caspar Hurtado
      Robert Phillip
      John Saltmarsh
1648 Athanasius of Brest
      Francis de Capillas
      Lelio Falconieri
      Gabriel Sionita
      Edward Herbert
      Joseph Calasanctius
      Wilhelm Lamormaini
      Jacques Marchant
      Margaret of the Blessed Sacrament
      Marin Mersenne

      Juan Martínez de Ripalda
1649 Giulio Aleni
      Agostino Barbosa
      Etienne Bauny
      Vincenzo Carafa
      Charles I
      Richard Crashaw
      Elizabeth of Ranfaing
      John Floyd
      Christopher Justel
      Owen Roe O'Neill
1650 Philippus Aquinas
      Constantino Cajetan
      David Calderwood
      Manoel Cardoso
      René Descartes
      François Florent
      Guillaume Gibieuf
      Ever MacMahon
1651 Diego Basalenque
      Nicholas Caussin
      Louis Chardon
      Juan Coronel
      Job of Pochaev
      Terence Albert O'Brien
      Hugh O'Reilly
      Alonso de Ovalle
      Francesco Piccolomini
      Philippus Rovenius
1652 Michael Alford
      Gregorio Allegri
      John Cotton
      Nicholas Lancicius
      Cristovão de Lisboa
      Francisco de Lugo
      Denis Pétau
      Jusepe de Ribera
      Patrick Young
1653 Raymond Bonal
      Henri Calénus
      José Cataldino
      Jacques Goar
      François de Harlay
      Giovanni Battista Rinuccini
      Antonio Ruiz de Montoya
      Claudius Salmasius
1654 Jean Louis Guez de Balzac
      Antonio de la Calancha
      Vincenzo Candido
      Peter Claver
      Diego de Córdova y Salinas
      Peter Claver
1655 Jacques Boonen
      Pierluigi Carafa
      Thomas Fleming
      Pierre Gassendi
      Innocent X
      Giovanni Stefano Menochio
      Claudine Moine
1656 William Rudesind Barlow
      Georg Calixtus
      Thomas Gage
      Godfrey Goodman
      Roberto de Nobili

Octavio Piccolomini
James Ussher
1657 Raphael Aversa
Andrew Bobola
William Bradford
Jean-Jacques Olier
Luke Wadding
1658 John Colgan
Oliver Cromwell
Gil Gonzalez Davile
Bartholomew Holzhauser
Carlo Emanuele Madruzzo
1659 Jean de Bernières-Louvigny
Manuel Díaz
Juan Bautista de Lezana
Jean Morin
Juan de Palafox y Mendoza
1660 Domingo Chimalpain
John Gennings
José Juárez
Juan de Lugo
Louise de Marillac
Alonso de Rea
Alexandre de Rhodes
Vincent de Paul
1661 Jacqueline Marie Angélique
Arnauld
Jean de La Haye
Valeriano Magni
Pierre Marchant
Martino Martini
Jules Mazarin
Brian Walton
1662 John Biddle
François Bourgoing
Horacio Carocci
Johann Cruger
Gaspar Druzbicki
Henry Holden
Pierre de Marca
Daniel O'Daly
Blaise Pascal
1663 Antonino Diana
Théophile Raynaul
Robert Sanderson
1664 Abraham Ecchellensis
Moïse Amyraut
Francisco de Araujo
Johannes Buxtorf 62e Younger)
Juan Gutiérrez de Padilla
Anton Sander
Miklós Zrinyi
Francisco de Zurbarán
1665 María Fernández Coronel Agreda
Jean Bolland
Kenelm Digby
Johannes Grueber
Doña Ana Nzinga
Jean Joseph Surin
1666 Redmond Caron
Benedikt Carpzov
Clemente Galano
Guercino
1667 Alexander VII

Pedro de Alva y Astorga
Rodrigo de Arriaga
Pedro de San José Betancur
Francesco Borromini
Alonso Cano
Johann Jakob Froberger
Philippe Labbe
Pietro Sforza Pallavicino
1668 Jakob Balde
Alonso Briceno
Hermann Busenbaum
Bernardino de Cárdenas
Mateo de Castro
Jehudah Jonah ben Jishaq
Juan de Prado Martínez
Heinrich Roth
1669 Charles d'Aremberg
John Austin
Antonio Caballero
Clement IX
Pietro Berrettini da Cortona
Jean Duval
Arnold Geulincx
Giulio Mercori
Edmund O'Reilly
William Prynne
Rembrandt Harmensz van Rijn
1670 Cristobal de Acuña
Charles of Sezze
Jeanne Marie Chezard de Matel
Johannes Amos Comenius
Jean Daillé
1671 Francesco Bordoni
Joseph de Gibalin
Anthony Grassi
Leo of St John
Giovanni Battista Riccioli
Odorio Rinaldi
Sebastian Rostock
1672 Robert Arnauld d'Andilly
Jeanne Catherine Agnès Arnauld
Rinaldo d'Este
Jean Lejeune
Mary of the Incarnation
Heinrich Schütz
1673 Balthasar of St Catherine of Siena
Giovanna Maria of the Cross
Francisco López Capillas
John Lynch
Jeanne Mance
Bartholomaeus Mastrius
1674 Ottavio Acquaviva (the younger)
Anthony of the Holy Ghost
Vincent Baron
Giovanni Bona
Guillaume Vincent de Contenson
Hans Ludwig Engel
Robert Herrick
Joseph of the Holy Spirit
Jean de Labadie
Claude Maltret
John Milton
Thomas Traherne
1675 Cecilius Calvert

Stanislaw Lubieniecki
Jacques Marquette
1676 Pier Francesco Cavalli
Clement X
Thomas Cornwallis
Daniel Garakonthie
François Rougemont
1677 Angelus Silesius
Isaac Barrow
Richard Bellings
George Digby
Jeanne Du Houx
Mary of St Theresa Petijt
Francis Molloy
1678 William Chalmers
Sigismondo Chigi
Miguel de Elizalde
Prospero Fagnani
William Herincx
John Kemble
Jéronimo Lobo
1679 Philip Evans
Pierre Lambert de la Motte
David Lewis
Alfonso Litta
John Lloyd
Ivan Lucic
Charles Mihan
Isaac Penington
John Plessington
Jean François Paul de Gondi Retz
John Wall
1680 Antonio Maria Abbatini
Giovanni Lorenzo Bernini
Bedrich Bridel
Richard Cameron
Carlo Carafa
François Etienne Caulet
John Eudes
Richard Gerard
Athanasius Kircher
Peter Lambeck
Joachim Neander
Peter Talbot
Kateri Tekakwitha
1681 Gabriel Bucelin
Francisco de Burgoa
Pedro Calderón de la Barca
Jean Baptiste Gonet
Godfrey Henschenius
Nikon
Celio Piccolomini
Oliver Plunket
Nicolás del Puerto
Carlo Rossetti
1682 Ludovico Buglio
Juan Lobkowitz Caramuel
Franz Egon von Fürstenberg
Antoine Dadin de Hauteserre
Claude de La Colombière
Bartolomé Esteban Murillo
1683 Juraj Krizanic
Jean Le Vacher
Joseph Mezger

Agostino Oldoini
Pedro Ortíz de Zárate
Roger Williams

1684 Juan de Cárdenas
Elena Lucrezia Piscopia Cornaro
Pierre Corneille
Henri Dumont
Isaac Le Maistre
Juan de Meléndez
Andreas Mendo
Johann Kaspar Suicer

1685 Jean Luc d'Achery
Daniello Bartoli
Jean Cabassut
Charles II
Francis Harold
Juan Francisco Montemayor
Vittorio Ricci
Anthony Sparrow

1686 Nicolas Barré
Abraham Calov
Charles of the Assumptiom
William Dugdale
Louis Maimbourg
Johannes van Neercassel
John Pearson

1687 Giulio Bartolucci
Constantijn Huygens
Sylvester Maurus
René Rapin

1688 Diego de Avendano
Bohuslav Balbin
John Bunyan
Charles Dufresne Du Cange
Lucas Fernández de Piedrahita
Francesco Foggia
Isaac Habert
Ferdinand Verbiest
Peter Walsh

1689 Claude Jean Allouez
John Belasyse
Gilbert de Choiseul du Plessis
    Praslin
Christina of Sweden
Innocent XI
Domingo Fernández Navarrete

1690 Marguerite Marie Alacocque
Angela Maria of the Immaculate
    Conception
Robert Barclay
Domenico de Gubernatis
Margaret Mary Alacoque

1691 Louis Abelly
Alexander VIII
Richard Baxter
George Fox
Lawrence of the Resurrection
Gregory Lopez
Edward Pococke
Carlo Rainaldi

1692 Henri Arnauld
Jean Michel d'Astorg d' Aubarède
Robert Boyle
Jean Crasset

Alessandro Francesco Saverio
    Filippucci
Augustine Reding

1693 Thomas Codrington
Lorenzo Brancati
Flavio Chigi
Claudio Coello
John de Britto
Johann Kaspar von Kerll
Richard Russell
William Sancroft
John Spencer

1694 Antoine Arnauld
José de Carabantes
Juan de Santiago y León Garabito
Philip Thomas Howard
Marcello Malpighi

1695 Dionigi da Piacenza
Antoine Goudin
Juana Inés de la Cruz
Jean de La Fontaine
Pierre Nicole
Henry Purcell
Henry Vaughan

1696 François de Harlay-Chanvallon
Prospero Intorcetta
John III Sobieski
Mark of the Nativity
Gregório de Matos
Miguel de Molinos

1697 Joseph Anthelmi
Gregory Barbarigo
Claude Dablon

1698 Francisco Aguiar y Seixas
Philippe Avril
Catherine de Bar
Basil of Soissons
John Huddleston

1699 Johann Benedikt Carpzov
Antoine Pagi
Jean Baptiste Racine
Edward Stillingfleet

1700 Marguerite Bourgeoys
Girolamo Casava
John Dryden
Innocent XII
Armand Jean Le Bouthillier de
    Rancé

1701 Louis Hennepin
James II
Franz Mezger

1702 Henri Marie Boudon
Michel Colbert
Oliver Heywood
Paul Mezger

1703 Innocent Le Masson
Anacletus Reiffenstuel

1704 Frances Bedingfield
Heinrich Johann Franz von Biber
Jacques Bénigne Bossuet
Louis Bourdaloue
Basilio Brollo
Marc Antoine Charpentier
Wilhelm Egon von Fürstenberg

John Locke
Henry Noris

1705 Francesco Antonio Febei
Tirso González de Santalla
Claude François Menestier
Titus Oates

1706 Giuseppe Agnelli
Marc' Antonio Barbarigo
Jean-Baptiste Duhamel
Fortunatus Hueber
George Joseph Kamel
Beatrice Kimpa Vita
Boniface Maes
Antonin Massoulié
Johann Pachelbel

1707 Samuel Benedikt Carpzov
Jacques-Nicolas Colbert
Dositheus
Jean François Gerbillon
Étienne Le Camus
Jean Mabillon
Simon Patrick
Pierre Sylvain Regis

1708 François de Montmorency Laval
Charles Le Gobien
Francis Makemie
Matias Ruiz Blanco

1709 Abraham of Sancta Clara
Pierre Cally
Gaspar Castner
Demetrius of Rostov
François de La Chaize
Joseph Mayol
Thierry Ruinart

1710 Pieter Codde
Charles Maurice Le Tellier

1711 Nicolas Boileau-Despréaux
Claude Frassen
Gabriel Gerberon
Thomas Ken
Eusebio Francisco Kino
François Lamy
Joseph Vaz

1712 Juan Bautista José Cabanilles

1713 William Cave
Arcangelo Corelli
David Hollaz
Pierre Jurieu
Bryan McGurk

1714 Gottfried Arnold
Carlo Fontana
Matthew Henry
Claude Lacroix
Antonio Magliabechi
Daniel van Papenbroeck

1715 Diego Francisco de Altamirano
Emmanuel Théodore Bouillon de
    la Tour d'Auvergne
Charles Calvert
James Maurus Corker
Felix of Nicosia
François de Salignac de la Mothe
    Fénelon
John of Tobolsk

Bernard Lamy
Louis XIV
Nicolas Malebranche
Antônio Monroy e Hijar
1716 Andre João Antonā
Francis of Geronimo
Louis-Marie Grignion de Montfort
Hippolyte Helyot
Gottfried Wilhelm Leibniz
Paolo Alessandro Maffei
Robert South
1717 Antonio Baldinucci
Alonso de Zamora
Jeanne-Marie Guyon
Juan Maria Salvatierra
1718 Etienne Baluze
William Penn
Hadrian Reland
1719 Niccolò Acciaioli
Louis Ellies Dupin
Henry of Saint Ignatius
John Baptiste de la Salle
Michel Le Tellier
Françoise d'Aubigné de
  Maintenon
Pierre Poiret
Pasquier Quesnel
Bartholomäus Ziegenbalg
1720 Eusèbe Renaudot
1721 Clement XI
Pierre Coustant
Bernardino Della Chiesa
Charles Eyston
Pierre-Daniel Huet
François Pagi
1722 Henri de Boulainvilliers
Sebastião Monteiro da Vide
1723 Joseph Bingham
Andrés de Borda
Mary Joseph Butler
Edmund Byrne
Guillaume Dubois
Johann Bernhard Fischer von
  Erlach
Claude Fleury
Francisco Larraga
Peter Leuren
Increase Mather
François Aimé Pouget
Christoph Rassler
(Sir) Christopher Wren
1724 Jacques Echard
Melchior Pérez Holguín
Innocent XIII
Alexander Natalis
Sebastian Rale
Henry Sacheverell
1725 Samuel Fritz
Alessandro Scarlatti
1726 Antonio Arbol y Díez
Philip Michael Ellis
Michel Richard de Lalande
Antonio Margil
Michael Moor

1727 August Hermann Francke
Isaac Newton
Nathaniel Spinckes
1728 Gabriel Daniel
Zeger Bernard van Espen
Polycarp Leyser
Cotton Mather
1729 Matthew Atkinson
Francesco Bianchini
Samuel Clarke
Jean Hardouin
Christoph Franz von Hutten
Pierre Le Brun
Louis Antoine de Noailles
1730 Giovanni Francesco Barbarigo
Benedict XIII
Thomas Bray
Johann Georg von Eckhart
Michelangelo Tamburini
1731 Innocent of Irkutsk
1732 François Vachon de Belmont
Joachim Bouvet
Lucy Filippini
Johann Ernst Hanxleden
Louis Marchand
1733 Juan Ignacio de Castorena y Ursua
François Couperin
1734 Alessandro Falconieri
Bonaventure Giffard
1735 Claude Judde
Giovanni Battista Riganti
1736 Jacques Charles de Brisacier
Antonio Caldara
Jeanne Delanoue
Johannes Albert Fabricius
Jean Leclerc
Giovanni Battista Pergolesi
1737 Mariano Armellini
Claude Buffier
François Catrou
Adolf von Dalberg
Rinaldo d'Este
Valerius Rist
1738 Charles-Joachim Colbert
Jean François Dandrieu
Jean Baptiste Labat
Cornelius Nary
1739 Angelo of Acri
Alvaro Cienfuegos
Charles Hyacinth Hugo
John Joseph of the Cross
Benedetto Marcello
1740 Charles du Plessis d' Argentre
Benedict XIV
Andres Blanqui
Clement XII
Hyacinthe René Drouin
Antonio Lotti
1741 Johann Joseph Fux
Carlo Ambrogio Mezzabarba
Bernard de Montfaucon
Antonio Vivaldi
1742 Richard Bentley

Francisca Josefa del Castillo y
  Guevara
Vincenzo Lodovico Gotti
Pierre de Lauzon
Jean Baptiste Massillon
Pierre Sabatier
1743 Paul Gabriel Antoine
André-Hercule de Fleury
Xaver Ehrenbert Fridelli
Henry Newman
1744 Leopold Anton Eleutherius
  Firmian
Roman Hinderer
Crescentia Hoss
Thomas Innes
Leonardo Leo
1745 Jonathan Swift
1746 Costanzo Giuseppe Beschi
Johann Kaspar Ferdinand Fischer
Hermann von der Hardt
Joseph François Lafitau
Matteo Ripa
1747 Trojano Acquaviva
David Brainerd
Theodore Jacobus Frelinghuysen
Emmanuel de la Reguera
1748 'Abdallah Zahir
Jacques Philippe Lallemant
Joseph Anne Marie Moyria de
  Mailla
Pio Tommaso Milanto
Isaac Watts
1749 Gottfried von Bessel
Justus Henning Boehmer
John Phillip Böhm
Lorenzo Boturini Benaducci
Jean Olivier Briand
Louis Nicolas Clérambault
Joseph François de Gallifet
Winifred Maxwell
Anton Mayr
Mechitar of Sebaste
1750 José Arlegui
Johann Sebastian Bach
Crispin of Viterbo
Lodovico Antonio Muratori
Magnbald Ziegelbauer
1751 Henri François d' Aguesseau
Annibale Albani
Jean Pierre de Caussade
Phillip Doddridge
François Armand Gervaise
Andrew Gordon
Leonard of Port Maurice
1752 Giulio Alberoni
Domenico Blasucci
Placidus Bocken
Joseph Butler
Edward Dicconson
José Ribeiro da Fonseca
Pedro Lozano
Robert Millar
Giovanni Battista Scaramelli
1753 George Berkeley

John Murphy
1754 Fortunato of Brescia
James Gibbs
Chrysostomus Hanthaler
Joasaph of Belgorod
1755 Henri François Xavier de Belsunce
de Castelmoron
John Cennick
Francesco Durante
Isidro Félix de Espinosa
Francesco Scipione Maffei
Johann Lorenz von Mosheim
Thomas Wilson
1756 Concina Daniello
Benjamin Elbel
1757 Eustratios Argenti
Charles-René Billuart
Augustin Calmet
Andreas Faulhaber
1758 Jonathan Edwards
1759 John Bennet
Apolinário da Conceicáo
Fulgenzio Cunialati
Bernardo Gaetano Guadagni
George Frideric Handel
1760 Bessarion of Romania
Claudio Casciolini
Andrija Kacic-Miošic
Ignacio de Padilla y Estrada
Nicolaus Ludwig Zinzendorf
1761 Rémi Ceillier
Pierre François Xavier de
Charlevoix
Francesco Feo
Stephen Hales
Griffin Jones
William Law
Gabriel Malagrida
Giuseppe Agostino Orsi
Samuel Walker
1762 Jean Calas
Marquard Herrgott
1763 Lucio Ferraris
William Grimshaw
1764 Jean Baptiste Rossi
1766 Filippo Acciaioli
Jean Astruc
Giovanni Lorenzo Berti
Giuseppe Castiglione
Markus Hansiz
1767 Johann Gottlob Carpzov
Léon Ménard
1768 Joseph Simon Assemani
Miguel Cabrera
Egidio Forcellini
Nathaniel Lardner
Pedro Agustín Morell de Santa
Cruz
Hermann Samuel Reimarus
1769 Girolamo Ballerini
Pietro Ballerini
Clement XIII
Marc Antoine Laugier

1770 Francisco del Andraca y Tamayo
Castillo
Neri Corsini
Alexander Cruden
Alexander MacDonald
George Whitefield
1771 Matthias Charles Chardon
Marie Marguerite d'Youville
1772 Arsenius
Sigismundo Asperger
Joseph Hartzheim
Benjamin Ingham
Jean Louis Leloutre
Emmanuel Swedenborg
John Woolman
1773 Alban Butler
Philip Embury
Daniele Farlati
Enrique Florez
Howell Harris
Michel Le Quien
1774 Michel Benoît
Clement XIV
Oliver Goldsmith
Augustin von Hallerstein
Niccolò Jommelli
John Nelson
1775 Eusebius Amort
Peter Böhler
Pierre Dens
Paul of the Cross
Lorenzo Ricci
1776 Dosithea of the Kiev Caves
1777 Sébastien Louis Meurin
Giovanni Benedetto Mittarelli
1778 Carolus Linnaeus
Jean Jacques Rousseau
Augustus Montague Toplady
1779 Diego José Abad y Sánchez
Alessandro Albani
François Bedos de Celles
William Boyce
Cosmas of Aitolia
Giovanni Battista Faure
Andrea Gallandi
1780 Pierre Martial Cibot
Johann Valentin Haydt
1781 José Cardiel
Richard Challoner
José Climent
Francisco Tomás Hermenegildo
Garces
Ignatius of Laconi
John Turberville Needham
1782 Joseph Aloysius Assemani
Stephen Erodius Assemani
Johann Christian Bach
Guillaume François Berthier
Maria Theresia Haze
1783 Leopold Ernst Firmian
Johann Adolph Hasse
Charles François Houbigant
Benjamin Kennicott
Benedict Joseph Labré

Juan Agustín de Morfi
1784 Thomas Falkner
Samuel Johnson
Ann Lee
François Louis Chartier de
Lotbinière
Giovanni Battista Martini
Vicente Muñoz
Nono Nagle
Salvatore Maria Roselli
Junipero Serra
1785 Joseph Allegranza
Jean Lévesque de Burigny
Etienne François de Choiseul
John William Fletcher
Franz Stephan Rautenstrauch
1786 Carlo Sebastiano Berardi
Ferdinand Farmer
Benjamin La Trobe
John Francis Wade
1787 Alphonsus Liguori
Ruggiero Giuseppe Boscovich
Francisco Javier Clavigero
Philippe André Grandidier
Louise of France
Juan Baltasar Maziel
Henry Melchior Muhlenberg
1788 Louis-Philippe Mariauchau d'
Esglis
Johann Ignaz von Felbiger
Johann Georg Hamann
Charles Wesley
1789 Gabriel Du Pac de Bellegrade
Filippo Salvatore Gilij
Franz Xaver Richter
1790 Johann Bernhard Basedow
Nicolas-Sylvestre Bergier
Augustin Pablo Castro
Johann Nikolaus von Hontheim
Joseph II
Daniel Rowland
1791 Cassiano da Macerata
Charles Cordell
Martin Dobrizhoffer
Maria Francesca Gallo of the Five
Wounds
Martin Gerbert von Hornau
Selina Hastings
Johann David Michaelis
Wolfgang Amadeus Mozart
Richard Price
John Wesley
William Williams
1792 Ignacio de Castro
Armand Chapt de Rastignac
Giuseppe Garampi
François Joseph La
Rochefoucauld-Bayers
Mariano Martí
1793 Jean Joseph Marie Amiot
Nicolas Jean Hugou de Bassville
Lorenz Grassell
Rafael Landívar
John Martin Moyé

1794   Juan Domingo Arricivita
        Antoine Henri Bérault-Bercastel
        Andrès Cavo
        Edward Gibbon
        Etienne-Charles de Lomenie de
            Brienne
        Paisius Velichkovsky
        Maximilien François de
            Robespierre
1795   James Boswell
        Franz Ludwig von Erthal
        Moritz Hohenbaum van der Meer
        Domingo Muriel
        William Romaine
        Francesco Antonio Zaccaria
1796   Antonio Caballero y Góngora
        Daniel Carroll
        Catherine II
        Thomas Reid
        Pierre René Rogue
        Samuel Seabury
1797   Melchiore Carpani
        Olaudah Equiano
        Jean François Hubert
        Baltasar Martínez Compañón y
            Bujanda
1798   John Barclay
        Charles Berington
        Joseph Hilarius von Eckhel
        Alexander Kilham
        Christian Friedrich Schwartz
1799   Maria Gaetana Agnesi
        Mateo Aimerich
        José Antonio Alzate
        Jozsef Batthyány
        John Fitzgerald
        Joasaph
        Gaspar Juárez
        Pius VI
1800   Francisco Antonio Barbastro
        William Cowper
        Alexander Mather
        Mary Bernardina Matthews
1801   Augustine Chong Yak-Jong
        Diego of Cadiz
        Manuel de Lacunza y Dias
        Johann Kaspar Lavater
1802   Friedrich Karl Joseph von Erthal
        Alexander Geddes
        Pierre Gibault
        Christopher Hopper
1803   Giovanni Francesco Albani
        Johann Gottfried von Herder
        Friedrich Gottlieb Klopstock
        Fermind Francisco de Lasuen
        Christoph Anton Migazzi
        Pablo de Olavide y Jauregui
        Xenia the Blessed
1804   Jean de Dieu Raymond de
            Boisgelin de Cuce
        Johann Heinrich Frankenberg
        Immanuel Kant
        Francisco Antonio de Lorenzana
        Joseph Priestley

1805   Manuel José de Ayala
        Luigi Boccherini
        Matthias Dannenmeyer
        Macarius of Corinth
        William Paley
1806   Isaac Backus
        Eugenius Bulgaris
        Amalia Gallitzin
        Michael Haydn
        Carlo Giuseppe Quadrupani
        Giuseppe Zola
1807   Henry Essex Edgeworth de
            Firmont
        John Newton
1808   Jacob Albright
        Louis Pierre Anquetil
        Jean Baptiste de Belloy
        Robert Molyneux
        José Celestino Mutis
1809   Anselm von Eckhart
        Franz Joseph Haydn
        Nicodemus of the Holy Mountain
        Scipione de' Ricci
        Jorgen Zoega
1810   Pedro Nolasco Barrientos
        Giovanni Battista Caprara
        Thomas Eyre
        Franz Friedrich Wilhelm von
            Fürstenberg
        Le Plat
        Thomas Weld
1811   Filippo Casoni
        Jacques-André Emery
        George Hay
        Miguel Hidalgo y Costilla
        Engelbert Klupfel
        John MacDonald
        José Antonio Martínez de
            Aldunate
        Joseph Mary Pignatelli
        Robert Raikes
        Johannes Theodorus Van der
            Kemp
1812   Martin Boehm
        Wenzeslaus Clemens
        Hieronymus Colloredo
        Johann Friedrich Hugo Nepomuk
            Eckenbrecht von Dalberg
        Egidio Maria of St Joseph
        Johann Michael Feneberg
        Johann Jakob Griesbach
        Henry Martyn
1813   André Ernest Modeste Grétry
        Philip William Otterbein
        Sophronius of Bulgaria
1814   Thomas Coke
        Pierre Toussaint Durand de
            Maillane
        Michael Egan
        José Antonio Liendo y Goicoechea
        Antonio Francisco Lisboa
        Joanna Southcott
1815   Francesco Saverio Maria Bianchi
        Claudius Buchanan

        John Carroll
        José de Cuero y Caicedo
        Andrew Fuller
        Leopold of Gaiche
        Michael Levadoux
        José María Morelos y Pavón
        Peter the Aleut
        Joseph Anton Sambuga
1816   Francis Ashbury
        Marie Rose Julie Billiart
        Charles Inglis
        Giovanni Lantrua
        Ildefonso de las Muñecas
        Francis Charles Nagot
        William Vincent O'Brien
        Philip Quaque
        Samuel senior Webbe
1817   Karl Theodor von Dalberg
        Timothy Dwight
        John Fawcett
        Jean Siffrein Maury
        Leonard Neale
1818   Nicolas Aguilar
        Joseph Ludwig Colmar
        Jan Antonin Kozeluh
        Francis Anthony Matignon
        Samuel J. Mills
1819   Frances Margaret Allen
        Friedrich Leopold, Graf zu
            Stolberg
1820   Simon Assemani
        Augustin de Barruel
        Thomas Matthew Carr
        Clement Hofbauer
        Lorenzo Litta
        Patrick Zimmer
1821   Joseph Benson
        Maurice Jean de Brogue
        Pedro José Chávez de la Rosa
        Gregory V
        Joseph Marie de Maistre
        Charles Plowden
        Thomas Scott
1822   Ignacio Andia y Varela
        Antonio Canova
        Narciso Coll y Prat
        René Just Haüy
        Joanna Angelica de Jesus
        Pal Krishna
        William Milne
1823   Juan Antonio Llorente
        Pius VII
        Cayetano José Rodriguez
        John Thomas Troy
1824   Ercole Consalvi
        Anna Katharina Emmerich
        Hans Nielsen Hauge
        Marie-François-Pierre Maine de
            Biran
        Charles Nerinckx
1825   Alexander I
        David Bogue
        Dmitri Stepanovich Bortniansky
        John Connolly

Simon Felix Gallagher
Nicolás García Xerez
Dominick Lynch
Rodriguez de Mendoza
Claude Henri de Rouvroy Saint-
   Simon

1826 Moses Baker
Joseph Pierre Picot de Clorivière
Reginald Heber
John Milner
Bernard Heinrich Overberg

1827 Ludwig van Beethoven
Luis Beltran
William Blake
Kasimir von Haffelin
Servando Teresa de Mier
William Poynter
Fabrizio Ruffo

1828 Matias de Córdova
John Lanigan
Ambrose Maréchal
José Antonio Medina
Franz Schubert

1829 Placidus Braun
Dean Gregorio Funes
François-Joseph Gossec
Leo XII
Juan Ignacio Molina
Adam Heinrich Müller
Diego Francisco Padilla

1830 Simón Bolívar
Anne-Antonine Jules de
   Clermont-Tonnerre
Giulio Maria Della Somaglia
Elias Hicks
John Henry Hobart
Pio Brunone Lanteri
Pius VIII

1831 Leopold Max Firmian
Henri Baptiste Grégoire
Georg Hermes
Rafael Lasso de la Vega
Barthold Georg Niebuhr
Raphael Zahur

1832 Charles Butler
Charles Carroll
Francisco de Paula Castaneda
José Matías Delgado
Juan José Díaz de Espada y Landa
Edward Dominic Fenwick
Hannah Kilham
Joseph Kinghorn
Gabriel Richard
José Santiago Rodrigues Zorrilla

1833 José Cecilio Avila
William Byrne
Bartolomea Capitanio
Samuel Drew
Louis William Valentine Dubourg
Pierre-André Latreille
Charles Bonaventure Maguire
Hannah More
John Mullanphy
José Bernardo Sánchez

Seraphim of Sarov
William Wilberforce

1834 Giuseppe Albani
Henriette Aymer de la Chevalerie
Daniel Barber
William Black
William Carey
Alexandre Etienne Choron
Samuel Taylor Coleridge
Lorenzo Dow
James Warren Doyle
André Hubert Fournet
Edward Irving
Johann Theodor Hermann
   Katerkamp
George Lacombe
Robert Morrison
Freidrich Daniel Ernst
   Schleiermacher

1835 Samuel Bagster (son)
Louis Marie Baudouin
Maddalena Gabriella Canossa

1836 Jean-Louis Lefebvre Cheverus
Richard Hurrell Froude
Herman of Alaska
Anthony Kohlmann
Karel Hynek Mácha
Maria Cristina of Savoy
Luther Rice
James René Romagne
Charles Simeon

1837 Thomas Babington
Gaspare del Bufalo
Pierre Marie Joseph Coudrin
Johann Nepomuk Hummel
Michael Hurley
Giacomo Leopardi
Nicola Antonio Zingarelli

1838 Thomas Attwood
Jeanne Elisabeth Bichier des Ages
George Elder
Christmas Evans
Ivan Petrovich Kotliarevskyi
Samuel Marsden
Johann Adam Möhler
José Benito Monterroso
Pieter Retief
John Thomas Talleyrand-Périgord

1839 Simon Bruté de Rémur
Mathew Carey
Joseph Fesch
Pedro José Fonte
Ramón Ignacio Mendez
Joseph François Michaud
Hyacinthe Louis de Quelen
José Rojas

1840 Stefano Bellesini
Louis Gabriel Ambroise de Bonald
Marcellin Joseph Benoit
   Champagnat
Nathaniel Emmons
José Gaspar de Francia
Demetrius Augustine Gallitzin
Joseph Javier Guzmán y Lecaros

Heinrich Klee
Alexander MacDonnell

1841 Franz Xaver von Baader
Joseph Charles Benziger
Peter Chanel
John Baptist Mary David
Gabriel Deshayes
Denis Frayssinous
Catherine McAuley

1842 Anthimus III
Anthimus V
Thomas Arnold
Peter Augustine Baines
Francisco Balmaceda
Clemens Maria Brentano
William Ellery Channing
Luigi Cherubini
Giuseppe Benedetto Cottolengo
John Dubois
Martin von Dunin
John England
Heinrich Friedrich Wilhelm
   Gesenius
Juan Ignacio de Gorriti
John Ireland
Antônio Maria de Moura

1843 Francisco Sales de Arrieta
Samuel Dyer
Diogo Antônio Feijó
Elizabeth Galitzin
Francis Scott Key
Hryhorii Federovych Kvitka
Miguel Ramos Arizpe
Joseph Rosati
Samuel junior Webbe

1844 Giuseppe Baini
Thomas Fowell Buxton
José Bento Leite Ferreira de Melo
Charles de Forbin-Janson
Johann Gänsbacher
William Joseph Gaston
Edward Kavanagh
Bartolommeo Pacca
Edmund Ignatius Rice

1845 José de la Canal
Francesco Capaccini
José Ignacio Cienfuegos
Elizabeth Fry
Bernardino Rivadavia

1846 Januário da Cunha Barbosa
Mariano Egaña
Joseph von Eybler
Benedict Joseph Fenwick
Francisco García Diego y Moreno
Anthony Gianelli
Gregory XVI
Johann Leonard Hug
Andrew Kim
Teresa Lalor
Marie Madeleine Postel

1847 Charles Januarius Acton
Virgil Horace Barber
Thomas Chalmers
William Crotch

Kaspar Ett
Vincenza Gerosa
Thomas Griffiths
Henry Francis Lyte
Macarius of Altai
Felix Mendelssohn
Daniel O'Connell
Johann Georg Rapp
Anthony Rey
Vincente Rocafuerte
1848 Denis Auguste Affre
Manuel Andrade y Pastor
Edward Baines
Jaime Luciano Balmes
John Stephen Bazin
Johann Wilhelm Bickell
Bernhard Bolzano
Emily Jane Brontë
Carlos Maria Bustamante
François Auguste René, Vicomte
 de Chateaubriand
Annette Elisabeth von Droste-
 Hülshoff
Johann Joseph von Görres
Cornelius Heeney
William Hogan
Damas Antonio Larrañaga
1849 Jean Alexis François. Artaud de
 Montor
Dominic Barberi
Wilhelm De Wette
Marie Rose Durocher
Peter Gratz
Ján Hollý
Evan MacEachen
Giuseppe Mezzofanti
William Miller
1850 Honoré de Balzac
Bashir II al-Shihabi
Edward Bickersteth
Guillaume Joseph Chaminade
José Alejo Eyzaguirre
Jean Baptiste Girard
Giuseppe Giusti
Adoniram Judson
José María Luis Mora
Johann August Wilhelm1 Neander
Jean-Paul Alban de Villeneuve-
 Bargemont
1851 Archibald Alexander
Paul Thérèse David d' Astros
Samuel Basgster (father)
Samuel Eccleston
Anne-Marie Javouhey
John Lingard
Mariano Medrano
John Philip
1852 Rose Philipine Duchesne
Ludger Duvernay
Vincenzo Gioberti
Nikolai Vasilevich Gogol
Jan Kollár
Francis Mary Libermann
Daniel Murray

Augustus Welby Pugin
James Read
Emilie de Rodat
1853 Stephen Theodore Badin
Cesare Balbo
Sebastian Brunner
Melchior von Diepenbrock
Anthony Norris Groves
José Antônio Marinho
Manuel José Mosquera
Antoine Frederic Ozanam
Arthur Philip Perceval
Pietro Raimondi
Johann Philip Roothaan
Theophilus of Kiev Caves
1854 Edward Barron
Jean Baptiste Bouvier
Karl Ludwig von Haller
Luigi Lambruschini
Félicité Robert de Lamennais
Fielding Lucas
Angelo Mai
William Matthews
James Montgomery
Marie Jean Baptiste Muard
Friedrich Wilhelm Joseph von
 Schelling
1855 Charlotte Brontë
Maria Crocifissa Di Rosa
Michael Ghebre
Thomas Kelly
Søren Aabye Kierkegaard
Frederick Lucas
Francisco Javier de Luna Pizarro
Maximos III
Adam Mickiewicz
Nicholas I Pavlovich
Antonio Rosmini-Serbati
1856 Theodore Guerin
William Vincent Harold
Theobald Mathew
John Nobill
René François Rohrbacher
Emilie de Vialar
1857 Lucien Bonaparte
Ferdinand Toussaint Chatel
Joseph Crétin
José Benito Lamas
1858 Mary Aikenhead
Jabez Bunting
Jeanne Marie Chavoin
John Larkin
Jean Mathias Pierre Loras
Johann Georg Mettenleiter
Gustave François Xavier de
 Ravignan
1859 John Barry
Francis de Sales Brunner
Zygmunt Krasinski
Alphonse François Lacroix
Charles Lenormant
Melchior Marie Joseph de
 Marion-Brésillac
Karl Johann Philipp Spitta

Jean-Baptiste Marie Vianney
1860 Ernst Moritz Arndt
Jerusha Barber
Ferdinand Christian Baur
Anthony Blanc
Christian Carl Josias von Bunsen
Joseph Cafasso
Gabriele Ferretti
Henry Granville Fitzalan-Howard
Evariste Régis Huc
Giustino de Jacobis
Aleksei Stepanovich Khomiakov
Jean-Marie-Robert de Lamennais
Anna Maria Lapini
Macarius of Optina
Giuseppe Marchi
Juan Francisco Meneses
John Nepomucene Neumann
Theodore Parker
1861 Frances Mary Teresa Ball
Friedrich August Biener
Henry De Courcy
August Friedrich Gfrörer
Jean Baptiste Henri Lacordaire
Charles Joseph Eugène de
 Mazenod
Pierre Bienvenu Noailles
Jeremiah O'Callaghan
John Stephen Raffeiner
Richard Reitzenstein
1862 Ignaz Assmayer
Andrew Byrne
Julius Peter Garesché
Patrick Raymond Griffith
Pauline-Marie Jaricot
Juste Adrien Lenoir de La Fage
Maironis
1863 Pietro Alfieri
Lyman Beecher
John Elmsley
Frederick William Faber
Andrés María Gallo
Michael Garicoïts
Anton Günther
Francis Patrick Kenrick
Albert Knoll
Edward Robinson
1864 Gaetano Bedini
Andrew Carney
Joseph Carrière
Charles de Coux
Johannes von Geissel
Olympe Philippe Gerbet
John Joseph Hughes
James Netsetov of Alaska
Samuel Mazzuchelli
John Joseph Therry
1865 Francis Asbury Baker
Madeleine Sophie Barat
Philippe Joseph Benjamin Buchez
George Bull
Constanza Cerioli
María Miguela Desmaisières of the
 Blessed Sacrament

Johann Hirscher
Adolf Kolping
Benjamin Kurtz
Louis Christophe Léon La
  Moricière
Karl Gottlieb Pfander
Pierre François Xavier de Ram
Nicholas Wiseman

1866 Massimo Taparelli d'Azeglio
Gaetano Baluffi
Alexander Campbell
Jeremiah Williams Cummings
Francesco Maria of Camporosso
Thomas Marie Joseph Gousset
Jean Pierre Gury
Angela Hughes
John Keble
John Kenedy
Maria de Mattias
John Mason Neale
Joseph Louis d' Ortigue

1867 Johann Kaspar Aiblinger
Basilio Arrillaga
Louis-Eugène-Marie Bautain
Elizabeth Eppinger
Filaret
Ignatius
Thomas Francis Meagher
Philaret of Moscow
Henry Williams

1868 Frederic Baraga
William Chalmers Burns
Pierre Julien Eymard
Giuseppe Frassinetti
Margaret Mary Hallahan
Arthur Marie Le Hir
Thomas D'Arcy McGee
Henry Hart Milman
Clemente de Jesús Munguía
Manuel Antonio Palacios
Théophile Verbist

1869 Felix Joseph Barbelin
Alois Buchner
William Carleton
Charles De la Croix
Alphonse Marie Louis de Prat de
  Lamartine
Peter Paul Lefèvre
James McSherry
Karl August von Reisach
John Augustine Ryan

1870 Anthony Mary Claret
Karel Jaromír Erben
Lars Paul Esbjörn
Thomas Grant
James Keogh
Charles Forbes René de
  Montalembert
John Mary Odin

1871 James Burns
Kuriakos Elias Chavara
Hermann Cohen
Georges Darboy
Joseph Deharbe

Thomas Ewing
François Joseph Fetis
John MacPherson
Franz Joseph Mone
Pierre Olivaint
John Coleridge Patteson
Francis Xavier Ryken
Escolástico Zegada

1872 Jean Henri Merle d'Aubigné
John McLeod Campbell
Henry Coskery
Joseph Fessler
José Sebastián de Goyeneche y
  Barreda
Auguste Joseph Alphonse Gratry
Nikolai Frederik Severin
  Grundtvig
Johannes Konrad William Löhe
Lowell Mason
Frederick Denison Maurice
Michael O'Connor
George Phillips

1873 Robert Abell
Jean Louis Rodolphe Agassiz
Augustine de Bacher
Pierre Jean De Smet
Peter Kindekens
Alessandro Francesco Tommaso
  Manzoni
Giovanni Merlini
Basil Anthony Moreau
Napoleon III
William Pennefather
Marie Françoise Perroton
Joaquín Roca y Corney
Henry Venn

1874 David William Bacon
George Anthony Belcourt
Thomas Binney
Charles Etienne Brasseur de
  Bourbourg
Auguste Carayon
Joseph Casavant
Edward Creighton
François-Pierre-Guillaume Guizot
Hermann von Mallinckrodt
Francis Patrick McFarland
Phoebe Worrall Palmer
David Friedrich Strauss
Lobegott Friedrich Konstantin von
  Tischendorf

1875 Henry James Anderson
Maria Salesia Chappuis
Jean-Claude Colin
Jacques Augustin Marie
  Crétineau-Joly
Georg Heinrich August Ewald
José Ignacio Víctor de Eyzaguirre
Charles Grandison Finney
Alexander Penrose Forbes
St John Fournier
Thomas Furlong
Gabriel García Moreno
Jacques Marie Achille Ginoulhiac

Prosper-Louis-Pascal Guranger
Benjamin Peach Keasberry
Charles Kingsley
Jacques Paul Migne
Jean François Millet
Patrick Eugene Moriarty
Claude Henri Plantier
Joseph Othman von Rauscher
Samuel Prideaux Tregelles
Jean-Pierre Augustin Marelin
  Verot

1876 Giacomo Antonelli
Orestes Augustus Brownson
Horace Bushnell
Gino Capponi
Thomas Louis Connolly
Edmond Henri de Coussemaker
George David Cummins
John Dobree Dalgairns
Franz Xavier Dieringer
John Dykes
Henry Gauntlett
Daniel Bonifatius Haneberg
Catherine Labouré
Giovanni Perrone
Samuel Sebastian Wesley

1877 Johann Heinrich Achterfeldt
Sir Henry Baker
Pierre Marie Bataillon
José Ignacio de Checa y Barba
Caroline Chisholm
Toru Dutt
Alexandre Herculano de Carvalho
  e Araújo
Johann Christian Konrad von
  Hoffman
Wilhelm Emmanuel von Ketteler
Armand de Melun
Gustav Mey
Juan Manuel Rosas
William Wood Stamp
Brigham Young

1878 Michele Accolti
Johann Baptist Alzog
Thaddeus Amat
Anthimus IV
Anthimus VI
Franz Joseph Ritter von Buss
Edward Caswall
Paul Cullen
Ambrose Lisle March Phillipps De
  Lisle
Alexander Duff
Félix Antoine Philibert Dupanloup
Alessandro Franchi
Thomas Galberry
Charles Hodge
John Dunmore Lang
Pius IX
Arthur George Selwyn

1879 Augustin Bonnetty
Cornelia Connelly
Joseph Mary Finotti
Vinzenz Ferrer Gasser

Jean Joseph Gaume
Karolina Gerhardinger
Gottlieb Christoph Adolph von
   Harless
Frances Ridley Havergal
Innocent of Alaska
Jeanne Jugan
Robert Francis Kilvert
Martin Kundig
Konrad Martin
George Vicessimus Wigram
1880   Emmanuel d'Alzon
Johann Christoph Blumhart
Joseph Ripley Chandler
Kenelm Henry Digby
Sarah Kirkland
Luis Alves Lima e Silva
John Joseph Murphy
Edmund Bailey O'Callaghan
Maria Giuseppa Rossello
1881   Antonio Ballerini
Anton Berlage
Thomas Carlyle
Daniel Comboni
Feodor Mikhailovich Dostoevsky
Johann Ludwig Krapf
Johann Rudolph Kutschker
Jacques Nicolas Lemmens
Klemens Löffler
John MacHale
Pauline von Mallinckrodt
Maria Domenica Mazzarello
John Henry McCaffrey
Arthur Penrhyn Stanley
Pius Zingerle
1882   Bruno Bauer
Moses Michael Coady
John Nelson Darby
Charles Robert Darwin
Ralph Waldo Emerson
Paola Frassinetti
Ivan Sergeevich Gagarin
Hugh Patrick Gallagher
Silvestre Guevara y Lira
Mary Haughery
Peter Henry Lemke
Patrick Nelson Lynch
Patrick Murray
John James Maximilian Oertel
Edward Bouverie Pusey
Dante Gabriel Rossetti
William George Ward
1883   Thomas Rawson Birks
Francis Norbert Blanchet
Henri Marie Gaston de
   Bonnechose
Thomas Nicholas Burke
John Colenso
Victor Auguste Dechamps
Heinrich Joseph Denzinger
Mamerto Esquiú
Charles Ewing
Joseph Kleutgen
Charles Porterfield Krauth

Louise Lateau
Robert Moffat
Gaetano Moroni
Cyprian Kamil Norwid
William Rees
Sojourner Truth
Louis François Veuillot
1884   Jan Theodoor Beelen
Luigi Billio
Marie de Jésus Deluil-Martiny
Anthony Konings
Henri Louis Charles Maret
Gregor Johann Mendel
Jean Baptiste Miège
Juan Ignacio Moreno
Mark Pattison
Pelagia Ivanovna of Diveyevo
Marie Alphonse Ratisbonne
Marie Théodore Ratisbonne
Antonio Ravalli
Franz-Josef Rudigier
Odo Russell
M. Francis Xavier Warde
1885   Ignace Bourget
Marie Victoire Thérèse Couderc
Joseph Jungmann
Louis of Casoria
John McCloskey
Lorenzo Nina
William Palmer
Thomas Rees
Anthony Ashley Cooper
   Shaftesbury
1886   Blas Cañas y Calvo
Emily Elizabeth Dickinson
Johannes Baptist Franzelin
Mary Aloysia Hardey
Anastasius Hartmann
William Koyi
Eugène Lachat
Franz Liszt
Charles Lwanga
Francis Thompson McDougall
James Alphonsus McMaster
Gregorio Mengarini
John Williamson Nevin
John Humphrey Noyes
Leopold von Ranke
Abram Joseph Ryan
Louise Van de Schriech
1887   John Bapst
Henry Ward Beecher
Catherine Blenkinsop
Moritz Brosig
Jakob Burckhardt
Mary Frances Clarke
Elisha John Durbin
Angela Gillespie
Johannes Kuhn
Baptista Lynch
Clement Marc
Giacomo Margotti
Alfred von Reumont
Isidore Robot

Johann Ronge
Adrien Emmanuel Rouquette
Charles Anthony Swainson
Carl Ferdinand William Walther
Boniface Wimmer
1888   Joseph Sadoc Alemany
Matthew Arnold
John Bosco
John William Burgon
John Christopher Drumgoole
John Rose Greene Hassard
Isaac Thomas Hecker
Henri Friedrich Hémy
Benjamin Herder
John Bosco
Robert Kalley
John Baptist Lamy
John Joseph Lynch
Jean Jacques Auguste Nicolas
Matthias Joseph Scheeben
Robert Young
Giacomo Zanella
1889   Josephus Albertus Alberdingk
   Thijm
Horatius Bonar
James Bouchard
John Bright
Robert Browning
James Andrew Corcoran
James Curley
Damien of Molokai
Mary Teresa Dease
Charles Joseph de Harlez
Gerard Manley Hopkins
Joseph Barber Lightfoot
Joseph Projectus Machebeuf
Guglielmo Massaja
William Henry Monk
Jean Baptiste Pitra
Albrecht Ritschl
William Bernard Ullathorne
1890   Antonio Maria Adragna
Sir Edward Baines
Catherine Booth
Casper Henry Borgess
Rosa di Traetto Carafa
Franz Julius Delitzsch
Johann Joseph Ignaz von
   Döllinger
César Auguste Franck
Pierre Jean Antoine Gailhac
Pedro Gual
Karl August von Hase
Michael Heiss
Josef Hergenröther
Franz Hettinger
Innocenzo of Berzo
Vicenta María López y Vicuña
Paulin Martin
Michael Joseph McGivney
John Henry Newman
Vincent Van Gogh
Karl von Vogelsang
1891   Ambrose of Optina

Armand François Marie de
    Charbonnel
Samuel Adjai Crowther
Carlo Mari Curci
Thomas Valpy French
Charles Emile Freppel
Richard Gilmour
Ferdinand Gregorovius
Ludwig Haynald
Johann Baptist Heinrich
Johannes Janssen
Pelagio Antonio de Labastida y
    Dàvalos
Paul Anton Lagarde
John Loughlin
Antonio de Macedo Costa
Edouard Guillaume Eugène Reuss
Jean Nicholas Arthur Rimbaud
Nehemiah Tile

1892 Giuseppe d'Annibale
William A. Blenkinsop
Jeronimo Emiliano Clara
Thomas Cook
Pius Bonifatius Gams
Charles Louis Gay
Fenton John Anthony Hort
Charles Martial Allemand
    Lavigerie
Matteo Liberatore
Richard Adelbert Lipsius
Enoch Louis Lowe
Henry Edward Manning
Gaspard Mermillod
Peter Reichensperger
Joseph Ernest Renan
Augustus Roskovanyi
Charles Haddon Spurgeon

1893 Georgianna Emma Drew
    Barrymore
Phillips Brooks
Henry James Coleridge
Johann Czerski
Joseph Gerhard Dwenger
Jakob Frohschammer
Charles François Gounod
Karl Joseph von Hefele
Magnus Jocham
Azarias Mullany of the Cross
John Livingston Nevius
Philip Schaff
Tommaso Zigliara

1894 Leon Federico Aneiros
Suitbert Bäumer
William Maziere Brady
Conrad of Parzham
Patrick Corrigan
Joseph Theodore Crampon
Joseph Epping
Clara Fey
James Anthony Froude
Ceferino González y Díaz Tuñón
George Peter Alexander Healy
Joaquín García Icazbalceta
Eugene Kelly

Louis Honoré Mercier
Frédéric Ghislain de Mérode
Christina Rossetti
Giovanni Batista de Rossi
William Robinson Smith
Robert Louis Stevenson
Alexandre Antonin Tache
Theophan the Recluse
Lois Xintomane
Theophan Zatvornik

1895 Cecil Frances Alexander
Johann Bollig
Peter Hardeman Burnett
Cesare Cantù
Johannes Gottlieb Christaller
Robert William Dale
André Garin
Bernard Jungmann
Patrick Manogue
Paulus Melchers
August Reichensperger

1896 Timothy Warren Anglin
Eugenio Biffi
Peter J. Blenkinsop
Anton Bruckner
Henri Chaumont
Mary Irene Fitzgibbon
Jean Barthélémy Hauréau
Maurice d' Hulst
Patrick Charles Keely
Peter Richard Kenrick
Martin Marty
Sir John Everett Millais
William Morris
Coventry Kersey Dighton Patmore
Joseph Hubert Reinkens
Harriet Beecher Stowe

1897 Johannes Brahms
Ricardo Cappa y Manescau
José Manuel Estrada
Augustine Francis Hewit
Juan Ambrosio Huerta
Teresa Jornet e Ibars
Gandarillas Joaquin Lárrain
James Legge
Anthony O'Connell
Thérèse of Lisieux

1898 Otto von Bismarck
Thomas Bracken
Sir Edward Burne-Jones
John Caird
Januarius Vincent De Concilio
John De Neve
Achille Desurmont
William Dix
William Ewart Gladstone
Paul Hinschius
Katharina Kasper
Louis François Richer Laflèche
James McGrath
Conrad Ferdinand Meyer
Fintan Mundwiler
Léon Ollé-Laprune
Thomas Francis Ring

Mary Baptist Russell

1899 Aemilio de Augustinis
Vincent Barzynski
Francisco Bauza
Thomas Edward Bridgett
Jean Baptiste Carnoy
Charles Pascal Chiniquy
Edouard Paul Dhorme
Hilarius of Sexten
James Kennedy
Sylvester Malone
Dwight Lyman Moody
Ferdinand Probst

1900 Samuel Berger
Cyprien Marie Boutrais
John Patrick Crichton-Stuart
Armand David
Edouard Genicot
Gregorio Grassi
James Augustine Healy
Friedrich Bernhard Maasen
Camillo Mazzella
Edward McGlynn
St George Jackson Mivart
Franz Morgott
Leonardo Murialdo
Edward Amasa Park
Franz Heinrich Reusch
Rocco da Cesinale
John Ruskin
Vladimir Soloviev
(Sir) Arthur Sullivan
Frances Margaret Taylor

1901 Joseph Bach
Albert de Broglie
James Chalmers
Mandell Creighton
James Fitton
John Baptist Hogan
Josef Edmund Jorg
Franz Xaver Kraus
Julia McGroarty
Ignatius Mrak
Josef Rheinberger
Auguste Sabatier
Sir John Stainer
William Stubbs
Giuseppe Verdi
Brook Foss Westcott
Charlotte Mary Yonge

1902 John Emerich Edward Dalberg
    Acton
Antanas Baranzauskas
Thomas Joseph Bouquillon
Agostino Ciasca
Frederick Louis Colin
Michael Augustine Corrigan
Thomas William Croke
Patrick Augustine Feehan
Contardo Ferrini
Maria Teresa Goretti
Theodor Granderath
Vital Grandin
Hugh Price Hughes

Lionel Pigot Johnson
Miescylaw Halka Ledóchowski
Alphonse Magnien
William Daniel McKinnon
Arthur Darby Nock
James Robertson
William Taylor
Emile Edouard Charles Antoine
   Zola

1903   Thomas William Allies
Denis Mary Bradley
Heinrich Brück
Marie Joseph Cassant
Joseph Dabrowski
George Deshon
Charles Gavan Duffy
Frank J. Ewart
Frederic William Farrar
Henri Constant Fouard
Gemma Galgani
Frederick Francis Xavier Katzer
Leo XIII
Damian Litz
Alfred Herbert Vaughan

1904   John Baptist Brondel
Henri Raymond Casgrain
Hélène de Chappotin de Neuville
Antonín Dvořák
William Henry Elder
Louis Mary Fink
William Russell Grace
James Hunnewell Kekela
André Meynard
Joseph Putzer
George Salmon
Henry Morton Stanley

1905   Hans Urs von Balthasar
Thomas John Barnardo
Maria Theresia Bonzel
Placide Louis Chapelle
Heinrich Seuse Denifle
George Hobart Doane
Alphonse Favier
Benjamin Hardin Irwin
Anthony M. Keiley
Allan McDonald
John O'Hanlon
Joseph Georg Strossmayer
James Hudson Taylor

1906   Gustav Bickell
Josephine Elizabeth Butler
Carlos Calvo
Shchetkovsky Chrysanthu
Marcellino da Civezza
Henry Cosgrove
Charles Stanton Devas
Elizabeth of the Trinity
Emrys ap Iwan
Rosa Flesch
Pierre Lambert Goossens
Simon Gregorcic
René Holaind
Émile-Paul-Constant-Ange Le
   Camus

Frederick William Maitland
George Matheson
Augustin Ravoux
William Wrede

1907   Jules Chevalier
John Creighton
John Alexander Dowie
Edward Fitzgerald
Franz Xaver von Funk
Sir William Hales Hingston
Joris-Karl Huysmans
Franz Philipp Kaulen
Baron Kelvin of Largs (William
   Thomson)
Utto Kornmüller
Thomas Joseph Lamy
Jacques Marie Monsabré
Nikolaus Nilles
Bernard O'Reilly
John Gibson Paton
Francis Thompson
George Tyrrell

1908   Jean Baptiste Berthier
Louis Alexandre Brisson
Edward Caird
Rudolph Cornely
Alfred Allen Curtis
Charles Antoine Federer
François Auguste Gevaert
Leo Heirich
John of Kronstadt
Lucie-Christine
François Désiré Mathieu
Methodia of Kimolos
François Marie Richard de la
   Vigne
François Marie Benjamin Richard
Ira Sankey

1909   Alexis
Nicolas Armentia
Jeanne Henriette Cécile Bruyère
Mary Gwendoline Caldwell
Miguel Antonio Caro
Peter Fenelon Collier
William Harris
Henry Charles Lea
William George McCloskey
Mary McKillop
Bernard John McQuaid
Helena Modjeska
Martin Ferdinand Morris
Eugène Portalié
Emily Power
Jerome Ribet

1910   Pierre Aubry
Alexander Baumgartner
John Cameron
Mary Baker Eddy
Emil Albert Friedberg
Franz Xaver Haberl
Heinrich Julius Holtzmann
Henri Huvelin
Emil Friedrich Kautzch
John La Farge

Louis Aloysius Lambert
Louis of Besse
Karl Lueger
Alexander Maclaren
John Joseph Ming
Joaquim Nabuco de Araujo
Florence Nightingale
Robert James Semple
Gustav Adolf Warneck

1911   Thomas Dwight
Antonio Fogazzaro
Joseph Knabenbauer
James F. Loughlin
Gustav Mahler
Patrick Francis Moran
Francis Paget
William Hamner Piper
Mathilde Raclot
William Robinson
Patrick John Ryan

1912   Vincent de Paul Bailly
Alfons Bellesheim
William Booth
Richard Lalor Burtsell
William Byrne
Alfonso Capecelatro
William Newton Clarke
Antoine Dechevrens
Victor Frins
James Gairdner
Henry George Ganss
Augustus Henry Keane
Charles Loyson
Marcelino Menéndez Pelayo
Moritz Meschler
Nicholas of Japan

1913   Anthimus VII
John B. Bannon
Samuel Barnett
Charles Augustus Briggs
Patrick Ford
Franz Adam Göpfert
John Joseph Hogan
Mykhailo Kotsiubyns'kyi
Franz Xavier Laurin
Agnes McLaren
Eberhard Nestlé
Mary Potter
Mariano Rampolla del Tindaro
Arthur Henry Stanton
Harriet Tubman

1914   Robert Hugh Benson
Geremia Bonomelli
Samuel Rolles Driver
Marius Férotin
Domenico Ferrata
Alexander Campbell Fraser
Elena Guerra
Franz von Hummelauer
Hugo von Hurter
Johannes Katschthaler
Elisabeth Lesueur
Maximus
Frédéric Mistral

Albert de Mun
Charles Pierre Péguy
Pius X
Patrick Riordan
Alfred Robert Tucker
1915 Jozef Aertnys
Elizabeth V. Baker
Phineas Franklin Bresee
Edith Louisa Cavell
John Chilembwe
Louise Claret de la Touche
Thomas James Conaty
Luigi Guanella
Michael Haller
Léon Harmel
John Cuthbert Hedley
Heinrich Kellner
Camillus Paul Maes
Basil William Maurice Maturin
Mary Xavier Mehegan
Raphael
Pierre Rousselot
Mary Mitchell Slessor
Thaisia of Leushino
1916 Paul Allard
Leopold Beaudenom
Gaston Cashwell
Adam Chmielowski
Hyacinth Marie Cormier
John Costigan
Pierre Maurice Marie Duhem
Ella B. Edes
Charles Eugène de Foucauld
Ivan Franko
Marcel Hebert
George Francis Houck
Timothy Edward Howard
Godefroid Kurth
Albert Lacombe
Thomas Maurice Mulry
Grigori Efimovich Rasputin
Théodule Armand Ribot
Josiah Royce
Charles Taze Russell
Wilfrid Philip Ward
1917 Peter Abbelen
Edmund Bishop
Léon Henri Marc Bloy
Franz Brentano
John Daniel Crimmins
Josefa Díaz y Clusellas
William Joseph Gabriel Doyle
Henry Fitzalan-Howard
Frances Xavier Cabrini
Johann Friedrich
Federico González Suárez
Ramón Ibarra y González
John Kochurov
James Johnson
Michael Maher
Charles Hyacinth McKenna
Gerhard Rauschen
Auguste Rodin
Henry Barclay Swete

Paul Peter Waldenström
1918 Henry Brooks Adams
Julius Bachem
Philotheus Bryennios
Gennaro Bucceroni
Francis Silas Chatard
Charles Warren Currier
Thomas Francis Cusack
Norbert Del Prado
Elizabeth Feodorovna
John Murphy Farley
John E. Garvin
Albert Hauck
John Healy
John Ireland
Francis Mary Jordan of the Cross
John Joseph Keane
Alfred Joyce Kilmer
Jules Lachelier
Andrew Arnold Lambing
August Lehmkuh
Eudoxe Irénée Mignot
Nicholas II
Sir Hubert Parry
Walter Rauschenbusch
Vladimir of Kiev
Julius Wellhausen
1919 Henry Marriott Bannister
Louis Pierre Baunard
Arthur Devine
Frank Duverneck
Cyril Sigourney Webster Fay
Thomas Bernard Fitzpatrick
John Campbell Gibson
Georg von Hertling
Edgar Loening
Virginia E. Moss
William Martin Murphy
Augustin Poulain
Vasili Rozanov
Albert Benjamin Simpson
1920 Léon Adolphe Amette
Paul Bedjan
Wilhelm Bousset
Sir Malachy Bowes Daly
François Ernest Gigot
Louise Imogen Guiney
Abraham Kuyper
Paul Lejay
Eugene Harry Maly
Nectarius of Aegina
1921 Charles Antoine
Charles Joseph Bonaparte
Etienne Emile Marie Boutroux
Henry Athanasius Brann
Max Dvorák
Peter Taylor Forsyth
James Gibbons
Franz Hitze
William Ambrose Jones
William Henry Ketcham
Alois Knöpfler
Joseph Maria Koudelka
Frank McGloin

Thomas O'Gorman
Charles Dominic Plater
Mary Elizabeth Sumner
William Joseph Walsh
John Augustine Zahm
1922 Lyman Abbott
Benedict XV
Maria Bertilla Boscardin
Alfred Henri Joseph Cauchie
Friedrich Delitzsch
Louis Duchesne
Eulogio Gregorio Gillow y Zavalza
James Hastings
Alberto Lepidi
Joseph Eugène Mangenot
Alice Christiana Gertrude Meynell
Hieronymus Noldin
Silvério Gomes Pimenta
Pandita Ramabai
William Joseph Seymour
1923 Arishima Takeo
Rui Barbosa
Eudorus Bell
Henry Bewerunge
Paul Bureau
Peter Paul Cahensly
Ulysse Chevalier
John Clifford
William Bourke Cochran
Konrad Eubel
Adrian Fortescue
Paul von Hoensbroech
Joseph Columba Marmion
Josefa Menéndez
Thomas Cooke Middleton
Ernst Troeltsch
Elizabeth Ryder Wheaton
1924 Herman Joseph Alerding
Sabine Baring-Gould
Sir Frederick Bridge
Théodore Dubois
Maurice Francis Egan
Gabriel Urbain Fauré
Nikolaus Gihr
Leo Michael Haid
Gottfried Hoberg
Charles Humbert René La Tour
du Pin
William McGarvey
Johannes Nikel
Terence Vincent Powderly
Friedrich Spitta
Charles Villiers Stanford
Frank Weston
Maria Beulah Woodworth-Etter
1925 Louis Nazaire Bégin
Marco Enrico Bossi
Thomas Joseph Campbell
John Patrick Carroll
Leon Gustave Dehon
Jonah of Manchuria
Rafaela Porras y Ayllón
Wladyslaw Stanislaw Reymont
Rudolf Steiner

Matthew Talbot
Tikhon of Moscow
Friedrich Von Hügl
Christopher Peter Yorke
1926 Giuseppe Allamano
Suzanne Aubert
Wolf Wilhelm Baudissin
Juan Cagliero
Jan Cieplak
J.A. Bethune Cook
Louis Couppé
Charles William Eliot
Albert Farges
Antonio Gaudí y Cornet
Anacleto González Flores
Paul Haupt
Rose Hawthorne
Karl Holl
Josef Hollweck
Albert Houtin
Anton Huonder
Jan Kasprowicz
Joseph Kirlin
Alphonsa Lathrop
Désiré Joseph Mercier
Étienne Fernand Portal
Rainer Maria Rilke
Joseph Smales
1927 Reginald Buckler
Gyula Fényi
Louis Claude Fillion
Léonce de Grandmaison
Hugo Gressmann
Étienne Harent
Jeremiah James Harty
Frederick Holweck
Carlos Maximiano Pimenta de
  Laet
Francis Augustus MacNutt
George Matulaitis
Peter James Muldoon
William Thomas Russell
1928 Juan González Arintero
Antonio Astrain
Joseph Mary Cataldo
Theophilus Parsons Chandler
Ernst Commer
Marie Louise De Meester
Hermann Dieckmann
Alfred Durand
Heinrich Federer
Jackson de Figueiredo
Francis James Finn
William Henry Temple Gairdner
Michael Hetzenauer
Leoš Janácek
Martin Kukucín
Jules Lemire
Peter Lenz
Friedrich Loofs
Horace Kinder Mann
Manche Masemola
José Mora y del Río
Ludwig von Pastor

Paul Sabatier
1929 Pierre Batiffol
Benjamin of Petrograd
Charles Henry Brent
Otokar Brezina
Lucy Broadway
Enrico Buonpensiere
Louis Ernest Dubois
John Nicol Farquhar
Francis Neil Aidan Gasquet
William Wadé Harris
Edouard Hugon
Rudolf Kittel
Ignaz Klug
Franz Xaver Kugler
Leonhard Lemmens
Eusebius Matthopoulos
Barnabas Edward McDonald
Carl Mirbt
Thomas Power O'Connor
Charles Parham
Arthur Samuel Peake
Rahmani
Sundar Singh
Geoffrey Anketell Studdert
  Kennedy
George Floyd Taylor
1930 Joaquim Arcoverde de
  Albuquerque Cavalcanti
Nicholas Frederic Brady
Robert Bridges
Alvarez Felix Alejandro Cepeda
Joseph Dahlmann
Randall Thomas Davidson
Bernard Duhr
Leopold Fonck
Adolf von Harnack
Seraphine Ireland
Rafael Merry del Val
Sebastian Gebhard Messmer
André Mocquereau
Miguel de la Mora
Cuthbert Hamilton Tucker
Matthew Chigaga Zwimba
1931 Louis Billot
Viktor Cathrein
Guido Maria Conforti
Joseph Dutton
George Logan Duval
Crescento Errázuriz y Valdivieso
Michael Francis Fallon
Ambroise Gardeil
Vincent d' Indy
Bruno Katterbach
Joseph Mausbach
George Foot Moore
François Nicolas Nau
Andrew Seth Pringle Pattison
Felix Raymond Marie Rouleau
Nathan Söderblom
Charles Thomas Studd
Gustave Joseph Waffalaert
Juan Zorilla de San Martin
1932 Horace Newton Allen

Ursmer Berlière
Paul Billerbeck
Clemens Blume
Joseph Booth
Wilhelm Brambach
Christopher John Brennan
Francis Patrick Duffy
Frederick Willem van Eeden
Francisco Elguero
James Thomas Foley
Charles Gore
Hartmann Grisar
Hermann Gunkel
Johannes Hehn
Beda Kleinschmidt
Lucien Laberthonnière
Francisco Marín-Sola
Nicholas Planas of Athens
Salomon Reinach
Joseph Rickaby
Adolf Alfred Tanqueray
Adolf Gunnar Vingren
Otto Zimmerman
1933 Francis Alexander Anglin
Henri Bremond
Joseph Bruneau
Karl Ferdinand Reinhardt Budde
John Chapman
Maurice De La Taille
Jerman Joseph Heuser
Albin van Hoonacker
Thomas Augustine Judge
Apolo Kivebulaya
Theodor von Zahn
1934 Cicero Romão Batista
Umberto Benigni
Edward Cuthbert Butler
Franz Ehrle
Edward Elgar
Zephyrind Engelhardt
Pietro Gasparri
Charles Lindley Wood Halifax
Gustav Holst
Daniel Eldred Hudson
Bede Jarret
John of Latvia
Alexis Mallon
Anthony Matre
Neil McNeil
1935 Eberhard Arnold
Otto Bardenhewer
Francis Crawford Burkitt
Erich Caspar
Jean Baptiste Chautard
John Patrick Chidwick
Peter Dahmen
Donatien De Bruyne
Selden Peabody Delany
Leonid Feodorov
Paul Fournier
Ignazio Guidi
François Marie Kersuzan
Meletios
Alfred Rahlfs

Isaiah Mdliwamafa Shembe
1936 Antony
Nelson Henry Baker
Frank Bartleman
Hermann Bäuerle
Pablo Cabrera
Gilbert Keith Chesterton
John Joseph Curran
Timothy Dempsey
Pascual Díaz y Barreto
Finley Peter Dunne
Zacarías García Villada
Willis Hoover
Montague Rhodes James
Blasio Kigosi
Frederick Charles Kolbe
Eduard König
Alexis Lépicier
Pierre Mandonnet
Julius Arthur Nieuwland
Francisco Orozco y Jiménez
Ottorino Respighi
Arthur Vermeersch
James Anthony Walsh
1937 Jean Vincent Bainvel
Christopher Edmund Becker
Romanus Butin
Fernand Cabrol
Francis Patrick Garvan
Patrick Joseph Healy
James Heerinckx
Hermann Herder
Edmund Arbuthnott Knox
Ludwig Lercher
John Gresham Machen
Guglielmo Marconi
Francisco Olazábal
Rudolf Otto
Agnes Ozman
Peter of Krutitsa
Hugh Richard Lawrie Sheppard
Burnett Hillmann Streeter
1938 Adhémar d'Alès
Ernst Barlach
Bernhard Bartmann
Eric Norman Bromley Burrows
Edmond Dublanchy
Paolo Maria Ferretti
Lawrence Francis Flick
Rudolph Walter Howard Frere
Rafael Guajázar Valencia
Patrick Joseph Hayes
Adolf Julicher
Marie Joseph La Grange
Genevieve Garvan Brady McAuley
Virgil Michel
Fernand Mourret
Edward Aloysius Pace
Oreste Ravanello
Hiram F. Reynolds
Siloan the Athonite
(Sir) Richard Terry
1939 Ludwig Bonvin
Heinrich Brauns

Matthew Heywood Campbell
Broun
Louis Joseph Paul Napoléon
Bruchési
Emilio Campana
Ch'eng Ching-Yi
Mary Joseph Dempsey
Charles Du Bos
Lorenz Dürr
Ford Madox Ford
Johann Baptist Frey
Alban Goodier
Georges Goyau
Thomas Hughes
Michael Joseph Lavelle
Johannes Lindworsky
Joseph Ma Liang
Joseph Henry McMahon
George William Mundelein
John Wood Oman
Pius XI
Herbert Henry Charles Thurston
1940 Fabijan Abrantovic
Charles F. Andrews
Thomas Ball Barratt
Edouard Branly
James Aloysius Burns
Marie Joseph Butler
Patrick Henry Callahan
Carl Clemens
Franz Josef Dölger
Albert Ehrhard
Gjergj Fishta
John Clement Fitzpatrick
Eric Gill
Joseph August Gredt
Paul Jouon
Joseph Kramp
Pierre de Labriolle
Paulin Ladeuze
Lars Peter Larsen
Frédéric Vincent Lebbe
Alfred Firmin Loisy
John William Rochefort Maguire
Emil Mersch
Edgar Mortara
Luigi Orione
Frank Charles Thompson
Paul James Francis Wattson
1941 Mihaly Babits
Marie Vincent Bernadot
Edward Alfred D'alton
Walford Davies
Hippolyte Delehaye
Velimir Dezelic
Ludwig Eisenhofer
Paul Joseph Foik
Franz Gillmann
René Graffin
Henri Hyvernat
Johann Peter Kirsch
Maximilian Maria Kolbe
Louis Laurand
Bodhan Lepkyi

Shailer Mathews
William James McGarry
Dmitry Sergeyevich Merezhkovsky
Paul Monceaux
Emile Nelligan
Leopoldo Ruiz y Flora
Darwell Stone
Evelyn Underhill
1942 Antonio María Arregui
Henri Marie Alfred Baudrillart
Karl Bihlmeyer
Titus Brandsma
Theodor Brauer
Josephine van Dyke Brownson
Ralph Adams Cram
Filippo Crispolti
Léon Daudet
Gilbert Joseph Garraghan
Gorazd of Prague
Joseph de Guibert
Michael Vincent Kelly
Wladimir Ledóchowski
Cintra Sebastião Leme da Silveir
Hans Lietzmann
Thomas Francis Meehan
Benoît Henri Merkelbach
Thomas Patrick Neill
Grigol Peradze
Maude Dominica Petre
Joseph Franklin Rutherford
Edith Stein
Lucien Tapiedi
1943 Paul Lendrum Blakely
Pietro Bondolfi
William Adams Brown
Camille Callewaert
William Raymond Corrigan
Maurice Denis
Franz Diekamp
Edward Aloysius Duff
John F. Fenlon
Paul Florensky
Amédée Gastoué
Arthur Hinsley
Franz Jägerstätter
Stephen Jeffreys
Vincent Joseph McNabb
William Paton
Agnes Gertrude Regan
Thomas Lawrason Riggs
Camille Roy
Joseph Shanahan
Ambrose Jessup Tomlinson
Simone Weil
1944 Miguel Asín Palacios
Joseph Bonnet
Sergei Nikolaevich Bulgakov
James Cannon
Alexis Carrel
Franz Feldmann
Alfred Goodrich Garr
Michael Gatterer
Henri Ghéon
Edward Joseph Hanna

Francis William Howard
George Johnson
Paul Fridolin Kehr
Edward Leen
Luigi Maglione
Joseph Maréchal
Antonia McHugh
Aimee Semple McPherson
Max Josef Metzger
James Moffatt
Yves de Montcheuil
Romolo Murri
Carl Muth
William Henry O'Connell
George Barry O'Toole
José de la Riva Aguero
Joseph Schmidlin
Sergius
Sergius of the Baltic
John Shang-chieh Sung
William Temple

1945 Ernest Bernard Allo
Vendanayagam Samuel Azariah
Maurice Baring
Béla Bartók
Dietrich Bonhoeffer
Alexandre Cingria
Crisogóno de Jésus Sacramentado
Alfred Delp
Francis Patrick Havey
Robert Alexander Jaffray
Käthe Kollwitz
Henri Leclercq
Eric Liddell
Andrew George Little
Joseph MacRory
Maria
Victor Martin
Rupert Mayer
Augustin Merk
George Campbell Morgan
Henry Wheeler Robinson
Charles Ruch
Charles Walter Stansby Williams

1946 (Sir) Hugh Allen
Ernesto Buonaiuti
David Smith Cairns
Victor Day
Eulogius
Clemens Augustinus von Galen
John Joseph Glennon
Maximilian Joseph Heimbucher
Samuel Edward Keeble
James Francis Kenney
Joseph Hillery King
Kirsopp Lake
Francis Xavier Lasance
Victor Martial Leroquais
Ernst Lohmeyer
Aloysius Mager
Carrie Judd Montgomery
Germain Morin
Hugh Pope
Jean Rivière

1947 Roland Allen
Josephine Bakhita
Joseph Braun
Alexandre Brou
Jean Calès
John Joseph Cantwell
George Gordon Coulton
Franz Cumont
Michael Joseph Curley
Maurice De Wulf
Martin Dibelius
Peter Ernest Dietz
Jorge Dintilhac
Joseph Frobes
Peter Guilday
Johannes Haller
Robert Fulton Keegan
Charles Sydney Price
James Hugh Ryan
Franz Zorell

1948 Emile Amann
Constantine Bacha
Anton Baumstark
Nikolai Aleksandrovich Berdiaev
Georges Bernanos
Odo Casel
Jean Baptiste Chabot
Joseph Chaine
Hugh Connolly
M. Frederic Dunne
Edward Joseph Flanagan
Leonel Franca
Augustyn Hlond
Edgar Hocedez
Joseph Huby
Nelson Hume
Rufus Matthew Jones
Francis Clement Kelley
Gerhard Kittel
Vital Lehodey
Douglas Clyde MacIntosh
Claude McKay
Nicola Aloysius Montani
Michael Ott
Paschal Robinson
Frank Sandford

1949 Maurice Blondel
Juan Sinforiano Bogárin
Peter Browe
William George Bruce
John Montgomery Cooper
Mariano Cuevas
Werner Goossens
Martin Grabmann
John Bernard Kevenhoerster
James Kleist
Andreas Evaristus Mader
Raymond Joseph Martin
Aristide Peter Maurin
Gabriel Mendez Plancarte
Ernest James Oldmeadow
William Wallace Simpson
Alexander Souter

1950 Michael Bihl

Patrick James Byrne
Martin Henry Carmody
Walter Sharp Carroll
Agneta Chang
Georges Desvallières
Joseph de Ghellinck
Albert Gille
Samuel Gosling
Fritz Kern
Gerardus van der Leeuw
John Ambrose McHugh
John Timothy McNicholas
Emmanuel Mounier
Thomas Francis O'Connor
Wendell Reilly
Agnes Repplier
Marc Sangnier

1951 John Louis Belford
Alfred Bertholet
Louis Brehier
Amy Carmichael
Marcellino de Castellvi
Thomas Francis Coakley
Joseph Dunn
Walter Farrell
George Fedotov
Augustin Fliche
Martin Stanislaus Gillet
Edward Benedict Jordan
Simon Kimbangu
Louis Lavelle
José de Jesús Manríquez y Zárate
Marie Hilda Marley
William Hildrup McClellan
Giuseppe Messina
Nagai Takashi
Livarius Oliger

1952 Henri Bourassa
Emma L. Cotton
Ambrose Blackman Crumpler
Henry Davis
Gregory Dix
Michael von Faulhaber
Francis Xavier Ford
Ernest Reginald Hull
Joseph Caspar Husslein
Ludwig Kaas
Joseph Lilly
Francis Patrick Matthews
Charles Maurras
Martin John Melvin
Karl Ludvig Reichelt

1953 Felix Marie Abel
Joseph Hilaire Pierre Belloc
Ugo Betti
William Bishop
Edward Sheffield Brightman
Frank M. Bruce
Warren Fay Carothers
Paul Irénée Couturier
Patrick Edward Crowley
Gabriel of St Mary Magdalen
Jean Guiraud
Francis Joseph Haas

Johannes Hatzfeld
Mar Ivanios
Félix Klein
Albert Cornelius Knudson
John Scott Lidgett
Joseph Madoz
Mack M. Pinson
Theodore Roemer
Francis Xavier Talbot

1954 William Albers
Donald McPherson Baillie
John B. Brunini
Ferdinand Cavallera
Pierre Marie Alain Couturier
Anton Deimel
Alcide de Gasperi
Hugh Simons Gibson
Waldemar Gurian
Alfred George Hogg
Frances Caryll Houselander
William Ralph Inge
Martin Jugie
Kenneth Escott Kirk
Elizabeth Sarah Kite
Cuthbert Charles Lattey
Eduoard Le Roy
René Le Senne
Francis Peter Lebuff
Robert Howard Lord
Elizabeth Mary Lynskey
Aloysius Molloy
Roger O'Callaghan
Sara Benedicta O'Neill
Henri Perrin
Arthur Frank Joseph Remy
Wilhelm Schmidt

1955 Gustave Bardy
August Benziger
Philotheus Heinrich Boehner
Dominikus Böhm
Aelred Carlyle
Paul Louis Charles Marie Claudel
Martin Patrick Durkin
Valère Fallon
Georg Graf
Edward Hawks
Joseph Loysius Hickey
Theodor Innitzer
Johannes de Jong
Edward Kissane
Daniel Aloysius Lord
Alice Eveline Luce
Charles Donagh Maginnis
Clarence Edward Martin
Angelo Mercati
Mary Virginia Merrick
John Raleigh Mott
André Robert
Mary Rogers
Pierre Teilhard de Chardin

1956 Michel Andrieu
Sir Frank Brangwyn
Hans Carossa
Mathias Constantine Faust

René Follet
Edward J. Galvin
John Garstang
Aleksandr Tikhonovich
    Grechaninov
Paul Heinsich
Georg Hofmann
Jens Johannes Jørgensen
James Bernard MacElwane
Luis María Martínez
Thomas John McMahon
Moorhouse Ignatius Xavier Millar
Thomas Edmund Molloy
Nicholas of Ochrid and Zhicha
John Francis Noll
Edwin Vincent O'Hara
Giovanni Papini
Peter Resch
Clara Ruth Rouse
Eugenio Zolli

1957 Valentin Marie Breton
Royston Dunnachie Ignatius
    Campbell
Francis Ceuppens
Alexander Joseph Denomy
Peter Masten Dunne
Gustavo Juan Franceschi
James Martin Gillis
James Leo Hagerty
Michel d' Herbigny
Ronald Arbuthnott Knox
Joseph-Marie Lebon
Curzio Malaparte
Joseph Raymond McCarthy
Giovanni Mercati
Gabriela Mistral
Jules Monchanin
Joseph Conrad Plumpe
Pierre Pourrat
Clemente Rebora
Dorothy Leigh Sayers

1958 George Allen Kennedy Bell
Jean-François Bonnefoy
Joseph Bonsirven
Fred Francis Bosworth
José Maria Caro Rodríguez
Carlos Eduardo Castaneda
Jeremiah Denis Mathias Ford
Karl Heim
Artur Michel Landgraf
Vladimir Nikolaevich Lossky
Anton Michel
Alfred Noyes
John Joseph O'Rourke
Wilfred Parsons
Pius XII
Georges Henri Rouault
Ralph Vaughan Williams

1959 Matthew Francis Brady
Joseph Charbonneau
Nicholas Charnetsky
Mary Samuel Coughlin
Sir Jacob Epstein
Walter Freytag

Francis Friedel
Friedrich Funder
Agostino Gemelli
Charles Aloysius Hart
Matthew Hoehn
Louis-Théophile Le Fort
Edwin Lewis
Crisanto Luque
William F. Montavon
Thomas C. Murray
Alfonso Reyes
Luigi Sturzo
Gregory Zilboorg

1960 John Baillie
Walter Bauer
Lambert Beauduin
Howard Joseph Carroll
Mateo Crawley Boevey
Miguel De Andrea
Bernard William Dempsey
Esther John
Edward Augustus Fitzpatrick
Pio Franci de' Cavalieri
William Leland Galvin
Edward Francis Garesché
Albert Gélin
Armstrong Gibbs
Bernard William Griffin
Lajos Harsányi
Jozef Cíger Hronský
Duane Garrison Hunt
Kagawa Toyohiko
John Keogh
Frank J. Lewis
Calum Iain MacLean
Mai Chaza
Raïssa Oumansoff Maritain
Michael Ambrose Mathis
Bernard A. McKenna
Michael McKeough
John Patrick O'Connell
Victor Francis O'Daniel
John Francis O'Hara
Michael Polsky
William Edwin Robert Sangster
Giles Gilbert Scott
Vitaly
Frederick James Zwierlein

1961 Mother Gerald Barry
Henry Edouard Prosper Breuil
Frank Nathan Daniel Buchman
Bernard Capelle
Thomas Anthony Dooley
Andrés Fernández Truyos
Paul Galtier
Francis Patrick Keough
Wilhelm Koppers
Henry S. Lucas
Charles Harrison Mason
Thomas John McDonnell
John Joseph Mitty
John Patrick Monaghan
Richard Reid
H. Orton Wiley

1962 Niels Bohr
    Bruno de Jésus Marie
    Charles Jerome Callan
    Louis Capéran
    Alberto Maria Carreño
    Acacius Coussa
    George Dandoy
    Giuseppe De Luca
    Paul David Devanandan
    Jaroslav Durych
    Franc Saleski Finzgar
    Edgar Johnson Goodspeed
    John Ireland
    George Jeffreys
    Joseph Löw
    Masamune Hakucho
    Louis Massignon
    Raymond Augustine McGowan
    Ivan Meštrovic
    Aloisius Joseph Muench
    Theresa Neumann
    Helmut Richard Niebuhr
1963 Maria Atkinson
    Henry Carr
    Pasquale D'Elia
    Gerald Ellard
    John Farrow
    Nicholas Sydney Gibbes
    William Godfrey
    Gustav Gundlach
    Paul Hindemith
    Walther Holtzmann
    John XXIII
    John Fitzgerald Kennedy
    John La Farge
    Clive Staples Lewis
    Daniel Mannix
    Cyril Charles Martindale
    Pablo Martínez del Rio
    Athanasius Miller
    Kunibert Mohlberg
    Garfield Bromley Oznam
    Francis Poulenc
    Bernard T. Rattigan
1964 Berthold Altaner
    Johan Herman Bavinck
    Hermann Joseph Bückers
    Harry James Carman
    Marie Alphonse Dain
    Alfred Leo Duggan
    Réginald Garrigou-Lagrange
    Henri Grégoire
    Denis John Bernard Hawkins
    Carlton Joseph Huntley Hayes
    Douglas Francis Jerrold
    Paul Ernst Kahle
    Gerald Andrew Kelly
    Paul Lehmann
    Mary Madeleva
    Franc Ksaver Meško
    Joseph Timothy O'Callahan
    Mary Flannery O'Connor
    Giuseppe Ricciotti
    Charles Ridder

    Joseph Francis Rummel
    Gustave Weigel
1965 Anastassy
    Donato Baldi
    William Branham
    Daniel Angelo Philip Callus
    Jean Calvet
    Francis Xavier Connolly
    Henri Daniel-Rops
    Charles De Koninck
    Thomas Stearns Eliot
    Fan Noli
    Ernest Frederick Kevan
    Photios Kontonglu
    Hendrick Kraemer
    Nikolai Onufrievich Lossky
    Roderick A. MacEachen
    James A. McWilliam
    Albert Gregory Meyer
    Sigmund Olaf Plytt Mowinckel
    Urban Nagle
    Albert Schweitzer
    Paul Tillich
1966 Karl Adam
    Nicholas Afanasiev
    Heinrich Emil Brunner
    Donald Gee
    Joseph Gorham
    Fredrick G. Hochwalt
    John of San Francisco
    Régis Jolivet
    Joseph Kiwanuka
    Carl Kraeling
    Theodore C. Petersen
    Camilo Torres
    Evelyn Waugh
1967 Konrad Adenauer
    Edward Philip Arbez
    Harold Idris Bell
    Alexander Birkenmajer
    Sebastian Bullough
    Joseph-Leon Cardijn
    Francis J. Connell
    John D. Conway
    Friedrich Gogarten
    Friedrich Heiler
    Philip Hughes
    George K. Hunton
    Albert Luthuli
    Maximos IV Sayegh
    John Courtney Murray
    Abraham Johannes Muste
    Santiago Ramírez
    Heinrich A. Rommen
    Douglas R. Scott
    Edward Ferdinand Siegman
    Francis Spellman
    Adrienne von Speyr
1968 Karl Barth
    Augustin Bea
    Francis Brennan
    Lucien Cerfaux
    Ignatius T. Eschmann
    Austin Marsden Farrer

    Franklin Clark Fry
    Romano Guardini
    Paul Hallinan
    Samuel Henry Hooke
    Douglas Horton
    Martin Luther King
    Kenneth Scott Latourette
    Bryan J. McEntegart
    Thomas Merton
    Padre Pio
    Daniel Alfred Poling
    Hugo Rahner
    Hans Anscar Reinhold
    Raymond Richey
    Ernesto Ruffini
    Ignatius Gabriel Tappouni
    Homer Tomlinson
1969 Higini Angles
    Rudolf G. Bandas
    Walter Baumgartner
    Josef Beran
    Roy J. Deferrari
    Hilaire Duesberg
    Harry Emerson Fosdick
    Harold Charles Gardiner
    Mary (Robinson) Mother of
        Gethsemane
    Thomas McAvoy
    Martin R.P. McGuire
    Thomas Verner Moore
    Joseph Houldsworth Oldham
    James Albert Pike
    Harold Henry Rowley
    Bernard J. Sheil
1970 Alexis I of Moscow
    Asa Alonso Allen
    Geoffrey Beaumont
    Heinrich Brüning
    Richard Cushing
    Christopher Dawson
    Paul Nikolaevich Evdokimov
    Joseph Roswell Flower
    Charles de Gaulle
    William Humbert Kane
    Evgrav Evgrafovich Kovalevsky
    François Mauriac
    David Oman McKay
    Daniel Thambyrajah Niles
    Frédéric Gonzague de Reynold
    Terence James Sheridan
    Ivan Quay Spencer
    John Leonard Wilson
1971 Gregory Peter Agagianian
    William Foxwell Albright
    H.A. Baker
    Timothy Bouscaren
    Michael Browne
    William Carlo
    Cyril
    Hubert Junker
    Baroness Gertrud von Le Fort
    Anneliese Maier
    Reinhold Niebuhr
    Gerhard von Rad

Igor Feodorovich Stravinsky
Boris Talantov
Roland Guérin de Vaux
1972 Athenagoras of Constantinople
Henry Wolfe Baines
Louis F. Budenz
Thomas F. Carey
Padraic Colum
Geoffrey Francis Fisher
George P. Klubertanz
Chrysostom Papasarantopoulos
Eugène Gabriel Tisserant
1973 Wystan Hugh Auden
Amleto Giovanni Cicognani
Charles Harold Dodd
Clarence Elwell
Kent Sigvart Knutson
Henri Le Saux
Achille Liénart
Gordan Lindsay
Gabriel Marcel
Jacques Maritain
Zhiming Wang
1974 Henry Joel Cadbury
Jean Daniélou
David Jones
David Knowles
(Sir) Arnold Lunn
Petrus Lewi Pethrus
Egon Wellesz
1975 Peter Anson
Joseph Burns Collins
Eamon De Valera
Godfrey Rolles Driver
José María Escriva de Balaguer y
    Albas
Bernard Marmaduke Fitzalan-
    Howard
Thomas Gilby
Ronald Owen Hall
John Carmel Heenan
Lorenz Jaeger
Charles Journet
Josef Andreas Jungmann
David James Mathew
Luigi Raimondi
Maisie Ward
1976 Benjamin Britten
Rudolph Karl Bultmann
John Cogley
Thomas Corbishley
Martin Cyril D'Arcy
Kathryn Kuhlman
Giacomo Lercaro
Pierre-André Liégé
Gervase Mathew
Bernard Mann Peebles
Thomas d'Esterre Roberts
Leslie Dixon Weatherhead
1977 Donald Attwater
James Marshall Campbell
Alphonse Henry Clemens
William Conway
Rutilio Grande

Fannie Lou Hamer
James Edward Hayden
Dietrich von Hildebrand
Christopher Hollis
James G. Keller
Giorgio La Pira
Janani Luwum
Macarius III
Paul Kevin Meagher
Ernst Friedrich Schumacher
George N. Shuster
Panagiotis Trembelas
James H. Van der Veldt
Max Warren
1978 Leo Cyril Brown
Leonard Feeney
Étienne Henri Gilson
John Paul I
Mulenga Alice Lenshina
Paul VI
Anton Charles Pegis
1979 John Joseph Cavanaugh
Chao Tzu Ch'en
Luke Connaughton
Charles Edward Coughlin
George Vasilievich Florovsky
James Francis Aloysius McIntyre
Alfredo Ottaviani
Noel Perkin
Fulton J. Sheen
Jean Villot
John Joseph Wright
1980 Maura Clarke
Dorothy Day
Anna Dengel
Albert-Louis Descamps
Ita Ford
Hubert Jedin
Dorothy Kazel
John Anthony O'Brien
Ernest Alexander Payne
Oscar Arnulfo Romero
Patrick William Skehan
Nicholas Zernov
1981 David Martyn Lloyd-Jones
James Rausch
Stanley Rother
Samuel
Francis Joseph Sheed
Barbara Ward
Stefan Wyszynski
1982 Giovanni Benelli
Annibale Bugnini
John Patrick Cody
John J. Considine
Mitchell J. Dahood
Pericle Felici
John Main
Maura O'Halloran
Erik Routley
Agnes Mary Sanford
Seraphim
Christopher Spartas
Ralph Darby Williams

1983 Terence Cooke
Pieter Frans Fransen
Herbert Howells
James Robert Knox
Stephen A. Leven
John Alexander MacKay
Humberto Sousa Medeiros
John Arthur Thomas Robinson
Alexander Schmemann
William Walton
1984 Albert Bayly
Hobart Freeman
Johannes Hofinger
Luigi G. Ligutti
Bernard John Francis Lonergan
Stephen Charles Neill
Martin Niemöller
Karl Rahner
Dolores Schorsch
Lawrence J. Shehan
Josef Slipyj
David C.K. Watson
1985 Basil (Krivocheine) of Brussels
Eugene Carson Blake
Catherine De Hueck Doherty
George Winsor Macrae
Richard Peter McKeon
Maurice Roy
Dermot Ryan
Philip J. Scharper
William Stringfellow
Willem Adolf Visser't Hooft
James Athanasius Weisheipl
1986 Nicholas Bhengu
Ivan Dujcev
Maurice Duruflé
Eugene R. Kennedy
Corita Kent
Geoffrey Laycock
Stanislaus Lyonsnet
Panayiotis Nellas
Martin John O'Connor
Flor Peeters
Edmund Rubbra
Harry Alphonso Ebun Sawyer
Egidio Vagnozzi
Bruce Vawter
Cynthia Clark Wedel
1987 Robert Pierce Beaver
Pierre Benoît
John Richard Connery
Finis Jennings Dake
John Dodd
David Johannes Du Plessis
Clare Boothe Luce
Anthony de Mello
Jane Marie Murray
Patrick A. O'Boyle
Johannes Quasten
Leonid Uspensky
Valerian
1988 Melvin Lyle Hodges
Festo Kivengere
Arthur Michael Ramsey

Charles Wesley Ranson
1989 Henry Cleophas Ball
Don Wilson Basham
Lennox Berkeley
Kathleen Bliss
Ignacio Ellacuría
Madeleine Hutin
Joseph Malula
1990 Serge Nikolaevich Bolshakoff
Thea Bowman
Frederick Fyvie Bruce
Marie Dominique Chenu
Fritz Eichenberg
Donald Anderson McGavran
Alexander Vladimirovich Men
1991 Mother Alexandra
Pedro Arrupe
David Hynd
Jean Langlais
Henri de Lubac
George Fielden MacLeod
1992 David Bosch
Leonard Cheshire

John Tracy Ellis
Donald Guthrie
Olivier Messiaen
John Meyendorff
Lazarus Moore
Anthony Gregory Murray
1993 Sophronius
Dumitru Staniloae
1994 Jacques Ellul
Bede Griffiths
Pietro Pavan
1995 Madeleine Barot
Yves Marie-Joseph Congar
Bengt Sundkler
Jerome Theisen
1996 Joseph Bernardin
Henri Nouwen
Juan Luis Segundo
Leon-Jozef Suenens
1997 Nicholas Arseniev
Angelo Giovanni Paredi
Teresa of Calcutta
Mildred Bangs Wynkoop

1998 Raymond E. Brown
Philip Caraman
Eligius Dekkers
Jane E. Ellis
Alois Grillmeier
Trevor Huddleston
James Edward Lesslie Newbigin
Donald Soper
(Sir) Michael Tippett
1999 Helder Passoa Câmara
Oscar Cullmann
Basil Hume
Joseph Tawil
2000 George Raymond Beasley-Murray
Eberhard Bethge
Peter Chad Tigar Levi
Richard McCormick
William Duff McHardy
Robert Alexander Kennedy Runcie
Sue Ryder
Wilfred Cantwell Smith
Ronald Stuart Thomas
Richard Southern

INDEX OF PLACES OF DEATH

ALASKA
Joasaph, 1799
Herman of Alaska, 1836
Lazarus Moore, 1992

ALBANIA
Berat   Cosmas of Aitolia, 1779
Shkoder   Gjergj Fishta, 1940
Tamanrasset   Charles Eugène de Foucauld, 1916

ANGOLA
Anthony of the Holy Ghost, 1674

ARGENTINA
Buenos Aires   Luis de Bolanos, 1629
Pedro Nolasco Barrientos, 1810
Cayetano José Rodriguez, 1823
Luis Beltran, 1827
Gregorio Funes, 1829
Mariano Medrano, 1851
Leon Federico Aneiros, 1894
Miguel De Andrea, 1960
Charco   Pedro Ortíz de Zárate, 1683
Córdoba   Andres Blanqui, 1740
Mamerto Esquiú, 1883
Humahuaca   Pedro Lozano, 1752
Juguy   Escolástico Zegada, 1871
Lujan   Jozef Cíger Hronský, 1960
Mendoza   Diego Gonzalez Holguín, c.1617
Parana   Francisco de Paula Castaneda, 1832
Salta   Vicente Muñoz, 1784

ARMENIA
Nerses Šnorhali, 1173
Gregory of Nyssa, c.394
Paul of Constantinople, c.350
Costa ben Luca, c.923
Leo II, 1219

AUSTRALIA
Douglas Park   Louis Couppé, 1926
Melbourne   John Gibson Paton, 1907
Daniel Mannix, 1963
Sydney   John Joseph Therry, 1864
John Dunmore Lang, 1878
Mary McKillop, 1909
Patrick Francis Moran, 1911
Christopher John Brennan, 1932
Windsor   Samuel Marsden, 1838

AUSTRIA
Bregenz   Merbot, 1120
Breitenwang   Lothair III, 1137
Cilli   Maximilian, c.284
Göttweig   Gottfried von Bessel, 1749
Graz   Ernst Commer, 1928
Innsbruck   Andrew of Rinn, 1462
Mercurino Arborio di Gattinara, 1530
Jakob Hutter, 1536
Joseph Jungmann, 1885
Nikolaus Nilles, 1907
Hugo von Hurter, 1914
Ludwig von Pastor, 1928
Hartmann Grisar, 1932
Ludwig Lercher, 1937
Michael Gatterer, 1944
Josef Andreas Jungmann, 1975
Karl Rahner, 1984
Lambach   Adalbero of Würzburg, 1090
Linz   Franz-Josef Rudigier, 1884
Noricum   Severinus of Noricum, c.480
Persenberg   Bruno of Würzburg, 1045
St Pölten   Joseph Fessler, 1872
Salzburg   Hartwich of Salzburg, 1023
Gebhard of Salzburg, 1088
Matthäus Lang, 1540
Valeriano Magni, 1661
Franz Mezger, 1701
Paul Mezger, 1702
Heinrich Johann Franz von Biber, 1704
Leopold Anton Eleutherius Firmian, 1744
Placidus Bocken, 1752
Michael Haydn, 1806
Joseph Anton Sambuga, 1815
Johannes Katschthaler, 1914
Aloysius Mager, 1946
Paul Heinsich, 1956
Vienna   Coloman, 1012
Altmann of Passau, 1091
Gregory of Rimini, 1358
Jordan of Quedlinburg, c.1380
Nicholas of Basle, 1395
Henry of Oyta, 1397
Nicholas of Dinkelsbühl, 1433
Thomas Ebendorfer, 1464
Balthasar Hubmaier, 1528

Vienna	Johannes Cuspinian, 1529
	Alfonso de Valdés, 1532
	Johannes Faber, 1541
	Claude Le Jay, 1552
	Ferdinand I, 1564
	Petrus de Buys, 1587
	Martin Becanus, 1624
	Ferdinand II, 1637
	Wilhelm Lamormaini, 1648
	Octavio Piccolomini, 1656
	Peter Lambeck, 1680
	Juraj Krizanic, 1683
	Abraham of Sancta Clara, 1709
	Johann Bernhard Fischer von Erlach, 1723
	Antonio Caldara, 1736
	Johann Joseph Fux, 1741
	Antonio Vivaldi, 1741
	Markus Hansiz, 1766
	Joseph II, 1790
	Martin Dobrizhoffer, 1791
	Wolfgang Amadeus Mozart, 1791
	Joseph Hilarius von Eckhel, 1798
	Christoph Anton Migazzi, 1803
	Matthias Dannenmeyer, 1805
	Franz Joseph Haydn, 1809
	Hieronymus Colloredo, 1812
	Jan Antonin Kozeluh, 1818
	Clement Hofbauer, 1820
	Ludwig van Beethoven, 1827
	Franz Schubert, 1828
	Adam Heinrich Müller, 1829
	Leopold Max Firmian, 1831
	Johann Gänsbacher, 1844
	Joseph von Eybler, 1846
	Jan Kollár, 1852
	Sebastian Brunner, 1853
	Ignaz Assmayer, 1862
	Anton Günther, 1863
	Joseph Othman von Rauscher, 1875
	Johann Rudolph Kutschker, 1881
	Johann Ronge, 1887
	Karl von Vogelgesang, 1890
	Anton Bruckner, 1896
	Johannes Brahms, 1897
	Gustav Bickell, 1906
	Karl Lueger, 1910
	Gustav Mahler, 1911
	Hieronymus Noldin, 1922
	Leopold Fonck, 1930
	Theodor Innitzer, 1955
	Friedrich Funder, 1959
	Wilhelm Koppers, 1961
	Wystan Hugh Auden, 1973
Viktring	John of Viktring, c.1345
Villach	John Capistran, 1456
Wiener Neustadt	Melchior Klesl, 1630
AZERBAIJAN	Bar-Hebraeus, 1286
BAHAMAS	John Bernard Kevenhoerster, 1949
BARBADOS	James F. Loughlin, 1911
BELARUS	
Grodno	Casimir, 1484
Pinsk	Andrew Bobola, 1657
Vitebsk	Josaphat Kuncevyc, 1623
BELGIUM	
Afflighem	Anton Sander, 1664
Antwerp	Cornelius of Zierikzee, c.1470
	Anna Bijns, 1575
	Christophe Plantin, 1589
	Anne of St Bartholomew, 1626
	Laurent Lawrence Beyerlink, 1627
	Heribert Rosweyde, 1629
	John Malderus, 1633
	Aubert Miraeus, 1640
	Peter Paul Rubens, 1640
	Jean Bolland, 1665
	Godfrey Henschenius, 1681
	Daniel van Papenbroeck, 1714
	Flor Peeters, 1986
Aywières	Lutgardis, 1246
Bois d'Haine	Louise Lateau, 1883
Bouhay	Edgar Mortara, 1940
Brogne	Gerard of Brogne, 959
Bruges	Jan van Eyck, 1441
	Hans Memling, c.1465
	Antoine Busnois, 1492
	Juan Luis Vives, 1540
	Peter Huyssens, 1637
	Francis Xavier Ryken, 1871
	Gustave Joseph Waffalaert, 1931
	Albin van Hoonacker, 1933
	Donatien De Bruyne, 1935
	Camille Callewaert, 1943
Brussels	Hugo van der Goes, 1482
	Alfonso de Castro, 1558
	Pieter (the Elder) Brueghel, 1569
	Cornelius Loos, 1595
	Jerome Gratian, 1614
	Richard Stanyhurst, 1618
	Anne of Jesus, 1621
	Caesar Clement, 1626
	Henri Calénus, 1653
	Jacques Boonen, 1655
	Charles d' Aremberg, 1669
	Antoine (The Great) Arnauld, 1694
	John Turberville Needham, 1781
	François Joseph Fetis, 1871
	Thomas Joseph Bouquillon, 1902
	François Auguste Gevaert, 1908
	Edith Louisa Cavell, 1915
	Godefroid Kurth, 1916
	Leon Gustave Dehon, 1925
	Désiré Joseph Mercier, 1926
	Hippolyte Delehaye, 1941
	Franz Cumont, 1947
	Francis Ceuppens, 1957
	Joseph Malula, 1989
	Leon-Jozef Suenens, 1996
Cosfort Forest	Gervin of Oudenburg, 1117
Fayt-le-Manage	Edgar Hocedez, 1948
Ghent	Bavo, 653
	Gerulf, 750
	Hubert van Eyck, 1426

Colette, 1447
Guillaume Fillastre, 1473
Arnold Bostius, 1499
Jan Bunderius, 1557
Cornelius Jansen, 1576
Pierre Marchant, 1661
Boniface Maes, 1706
Heiligen   Ansfrid, 1010
Heverlee   Marie Louise De Meester, 1928
Huy   Domitian of Maastricht, 560
Liège   Lambert of Maastricht, c.698
Notker of Liège, 1008
Anselm of Liège, 1056
Henry IV, 1106
Henry of Mechelen, 1311
Jean Chapeauville, 1617
Henry of Saint Ignatius, 1719
Maria Theresia Haze, 1782
Augustine de Backer, 1873
Lierre   Beatrice of Nazareth, 1268
John De Neve, 1898
Lobbes   Hidulf of Lobbes, 707
Heriger of Lobbes, 1007
Louvain   Dirk Bouts, 1475
Jacobus Latomus, 1544
William Rastell, 1565
Jean Garet, 1571
Jean Dumoulin, 1575
Michel de Bay, 1598
Thomas Stapleton, 1598
Justus Lipsius, 1606
Martin Antoine Del Rio, 1608
Leonardus Lessius, 1623
Michael O'Clery, 1643
John Colgan, 1658
Pierre François Xavier de Ram, 1865
Jan Theodoor Beelen, 1884
Bernard Jungmann, 1895
Edouard Genicot, 1900
Thomas Joseph Lamy, 1907
Arthur Vermeersch, 1936
Paulin Ladeuze, 1940
Benoît Henri Merkelbach, 1942
Joseph Maréchal, 1944
Valère Fallon, 1955
Bernard Capelle, 1961
Pieter Frans Fransen, 1983
Malines   Mary of St Theresa Petijt, 1677
Pierre Dens, 1775
see also Mechelen
Maredsous   Ursmer Berlière, 1932
Mariemont   William of Notre Dame de l'Olive, 1240
Mechelen   Ida of Louvain, c.1300
Pierre Lambert Goossens, 1906
see also Malines
Mechlin   Victor Auguste Dechamps, 1883
Mont-Saint-Guibert   Konrad Martin, 1879
Namur   Juliana of Liège, 1258
Marie Rose Julie Billiart, 1816
Joseph-Marie Lebon, 1957
Nivelles   Iduberga, 652
Ottignies   Albert-Louis Descamps, 1980
Oudenbourg   Arnulf of Soissons, 1087
Poperinge   Maurice De Wulf, 1947

Rosières   Henri Grégoire, 1964
Saint-Trond   Adalbero I, 962
Signy   William of Saint-Thierry, 1148
Sint-Niklaas-Waas   Werner Goossens, 1949
Soignies   Gilles Binchois, 1460
Spa   Claudius Salmasius, 1653
Steenbrugge   Eligius Dekkers, 1998
Tournai   Eleutherius of Tournai, 531
Guibert of Tournai, 1284
Henry of Ghent, 1293
Jacques Bonfrère, 1642
Vilvorde   William Tyndale, 1536
Ypres   Cornelius Otto Jansen, 1638
Mary Joseph Butler, 1723

BOHEMIA
Alt-Bunzlau   Wenceslas, c.932
Benesabe   Patrick Fleming, 1631
Brno   Gregor Johann Mendel, 1884
Hartmanice   Günther of Niederaltaich, 1045
Jaromerice   Otokar Brezina, 1929
Kutná Hora   Bedrich Bridel, 1680
Litomerice   Karel Hynek Mácha, 1836
Mladá   Lukáš of Prague, 1528
Ostrava   Leoš Janácek, 1928
Prague   Cosmas of Prague, 1125
Agnes of Bohemia, 1282
Charles IV, 1378
John of Nepomuk, 1393
Jacobus de Kerle, 1591
Tycho Brahe, 1601
Philippe de Monte, 1603
Johann Lohelius, 1622
Rodrigo de Arriaga, 1667
Bohuslav Balbin, 1688
Bernhard Bolzano, 1848
Karel Jaromír Erben, 1870
Antonín Dvorák, 1904
Jaroslav Durych, 1962
Pribyslav   John Zizka, 1424
Roudnice   Ernest of Pardubice, 1364
Slavkow   Bernardino Ochino, 1564
Velehrad   Methodius, 885

BOLIVIA
La Paz   Nicolas Armentia, 1909
Potosí   Melchior Pérez Holguín, c.1724
Santa Cruz de la
   Sierra   Bernardino de Cárdenas, 1668
Sucre   Juan Ignacio de Gorriti, 1842

BRAZIL
Bahia   Andre João Antonã, 1716
Barbacena   Antonio de Macedo Costa, 1891
Espiritu Santo   Antonio de Araujo, 1632
Olinda   Helder Passoa Câmara, 1999
Pouso Alegre   José Bento Leite Ferreira de Melo, 1844
Recife   Gregório de Matos, 1696
Reritiba   José de Anchieta, 1597
Rio de Janeiro   Manuel da Nóbrega, 1570
Antônio Maria de Moura, 1842
Januário da Cunha Barbosa, 1846
José Antônio Marinho, 1853
Luis Alves Lima e Silva, 1880

Rui Barbosa, 1923
Carlos Maximiano Pimenta de Laet, 1927
Jackson de Figueiredo, 1928
Joaquim Arcoverde de Albuquerque
    Cavalcanti, 1930
Leme da Silveira Cintra Sebastião, 1942
Leonel Franca, 1948
Rio Grande do Sul Roque González, 1628
Salvador Joanna Angelica de Jesus, 1822
  Sebastião Monteiro da Vide, 1722
São Paolo Antônio Feijó, 1843

BULGARIA
Didymotoch John X, 1206
Sofia Cyril, 1971
  Ivan Dujcev, 1986
Strongylon Constantine V, 775
Turnovo Sava, 1236

CANADA
Antigonish John Cameron, 1910
Auriesville Isaac Jogues, 1646
Cauyghnawaga Kateri Tekakwitha, 1680
Combermere Catherine De Hueck Doherty, 1985
East Margaree Moses Michael Coady, 1882
Halifax Charles Inglis, 1816
  William Black, 1834
  Thomas Louis Connolly, 1876
  Sir Malachy B0owes Daly, 1920
London Michael Francis Fallon, 1931
  James Thomas Foley, 1932
Longueuil Marie Rose Durocher, 1849
Montreal Jeanne Mance, 1673
  Marguerite Bourgeoys, 1700
  François Vachon de Belmont, 1732
  Marie Marguerite d'Youville, 1771
  Ludger Duvernay, 1852
  Ignace Bourget, 1885
  Louis Honoré Mercier, 1894
  Charles Pascal Chiniquy, 1899
  Frederick Louis Colin, 1902
  Sir William Hales Hingston, 1907
  Louis Joseph Paul Napoléon Bruchési,
    1939
  Emile Nelligan, 1941
  John Main, 1982
New Brunswick George Anthony Belcourt, 1874
Niagara Falls John Humphrey Noyes, 1886
Ottawa Thomas D'Arcy McGee, 1868
  John Costigan, 1916
  Francis Alexander Anglin, 1933
  James Francis Kenney, 1946
  William Carlo, 1971
Outremont Henri Bourassa, 1952
Quebec Mary of the Incarnation, 1672
  Claude Dablon, 1697
  François de Montmorency Laval, 1708
  Pierre de Lauzon, 1742
  Jean Olivier Briand, 1749
  Jean François Hubert, 1797
  Frances Margaret Allen, 1819
  Henri Raymond Casgrain, 1904
  Louis Nazaire Bégin, 1925
  Felix Raymond Marie Rouleau, 1931

  Camille Roy, 1943
  Maurice Roy, 1985
St Albert Vital Grandin, 1902
St Boniface Alexandre Antonin Tache, 1894
St Hyacinthe Joseph Casavant, 1874
Sainte-Luce-sur-Mer Joseph Bonnet, 1944
Saskatoon James Athanasius Weisheipl, 1985
Three Rivers Louis François Richer Laflèche, 1898
Toronto John Elmsley, 1863
  John Joseph Lynch, 1888
  Mary Teresa Dease, 1889
  Timothy Warren Anglin, 1896
  James Robertson, 1902
  Neil McNeil, 1934
  Michael Vincent Kelly, 1942
  Ignatius T. Eschmann, 1968
  Anton Charles Pegis, 1978
  Wilfred Cantwell Smith, 2000
Tracalie John MacDonald, 1811
Vancouver Henry Carr, 1963
Victoria Joseph Charbonneau, 1959

CANARY ISLANDS Ignacio de Azevedo, 1570
  Frederick William Maitland, 1906

CEYLON Joseph Vaz, 1711

CHILE
Concepción Luis Gerónimo de Oré, 1630
Rio de la Plata José Antonio Medina, 1828
Santiago Juan Romero, 1630
  José Antonio Martínez de Aldunate, 1811
  Ignacio Andia y Varela, 1822
  Joseph Javier Guzmán y Lecaros, 1840
  Francisco Balmaceda, 1842
  Mariano Egaña, 1846
  José Alejo Eyzaguirre, 1830
  Juan Francisco Meneses, 1860
  Blas Cañas y Calvo, 1886
  Crescento Errázuriz y Valdivieso, 1931
  José Maria Caro Rodríguez, 1958
Talca José Ignacio Cienfuegos, 1845
Valparaiso Mateo Crawley Boevey, 1960

CHINA
Beijing Chao Tzu Ch'en, 1979
  see also Peking
Canton Robert Morrison, 1834
  Francis Xavier Ford, 1952
Changsha Giovanni Lantrua, 1816
  James Hudson Taylor, 1905
Chefoo John Livingston Nevius, 1893
Chongqing Frédéric Vincent Lebbe, 1940
Fuchow Giulio Aleni, 1649
Fukien Francis de Capillas, 1648
Hangchow Lazzaro Cattaneo, 1640
  Manuel Díaz, 1659
  Martino Martini, 1661
  Prospero Intorcetta, 1696
Kuang-chou Antonio Caballero, 1669
Lin-ch'ing Bernardino Della Chiesa, 1721
Macao Alessandro Valignano, 1606
  Rodrigues Tcuzu João, 1633

Alessandro Francesco Saverio Filippucci, 1692

Samuel Dyer, 1843

Manchuria   Jonah of Manchuria, 1925

Nhatrang   Valerius Rist, 1737

Peking   John of Monte Corvino, 1328

Matteo Ricci, 1610

Giacomo Rho, 1638

Ludovico Buglio, 1682

Ferdinand Verbiest, 1688

Jean François Gerbillon, 1707

Gaspar Castner, 1709

Joachim Bouvet, 1732

Xaver Ehrenbert Fridelli, 1743

Joseph Anne Marie Moyria de Mailla, 1748

Giuseppe Castiglione, 1766

Michel Benoît, 1774

Augustin von Hallerstein, 1774

Pierre Martial Cibot, 1780

Jean Joseph Marie Amiot, 1793

Alphonse Favier, 1905

John Shang-chieh Sung, 1944

see also Beijing

San-yuan   Basilio Brollo, 1704

Shangchuan Dao   Francis Xavier, 1552

Shanghai   Joseph Ma Liang, 1939

Shansi   Gregorio Grassi, 1900

Tai Tsang   François Rougemont, 1676

Weihsien   Eric Liddell, 1945

Wutsin   Roman Hinderer, 1744

Yingkou   William Chalmers Burns, 1868

Yunnan   Zhiming Wang, 1973

see also Taiwan

COLOMBIA

Barranquilla   Eugenio Biffi, 1896

Bogotá   Luis Zapata de Cardenas, 1590

Pedro de Aguado, 1609

Alonso de Zamora, *c.*1717

Baltasar Martínez Compañón y Bujanda, 1797

José Celestino Mutis, 1808

Ramón Ignacio Mendez, 1839

Andrés María Gallo, 1863

Miguel Antonio Caro, 1909

Marcellino de Castellvi, 1951

Crisanto Luque, 1959

Bojacá   Diego Francisco Padilla, 1829

Cartagena   Peter Claver, 1654

Popoyan   Jodoco Riche, 1575

Tunja   Juan de Castellanos, 1607

Francisca Josefa del Castillo y Guevara, 1742

CONGO

Elizabethville   Simon Kimbangu, 1951

Imbi   Charles Thomas Studd, 1931

Mboga   Apolo Kivebulaya, 1933

CRETE

Andrew of Crete, 740

Bardas, 865

Joseph Bryennios, 1438

Demetrius Ducas, *c.*1527

CROATIA   Velimir Dezelic, 1941

CUBA   Pablo José de Arriaga, 1622

Pedro Agustín Morell de Santa Cruz, 1768

Juan José Díaz de Espada y Landa, 1832

CYPRUS   Hilarion of Gaza, 371

John of Montfort, *c.*1177

William Duranti, 1330

Andrew Chrysoberges, 1451

Felix of Nicosia, 1715

Macarius III, 1977

CZECH REPUBLIC *see* Bohemia

DENMARK

Aarhus   Nicholas of Aarhus, 1180

Aebelholt   William of Aebelholt, 1203

Copenhagen   Adrianus Petit Coclico, 1562

Niels Hemmingsen, 1600

Søren Aabye Kierkegaard, 1855

Nikolai Frederik Severin Grundtvig, 1872

Niels Bohr, 1962

Haraldsted   Canute Lavard, 1131

Odense   Canute IV, 1086

Ølse   Margaret of Roskilde, 1176

Ribe   Hans Tausen, 1561

Svendborg   Jens Johannes Jørgensen, 1956

EAST INDIES   Robert Alexander Jaffray, 1945

ECUADOR

Jéveros   Samuel Fritz, *c.*1725

Quito   Pedro Bedon, 1621

Rafael Lasso de la Vega, 1831

Gabriel García Moreno, 1875

José Ignacio de Checa y Barba, 1877

Federico González Suárez, 1917

EGYPT

Alexandria   Demetrius of Alexandria, 232

Apollonia of Alexandria, 255

Dionysius of Alexandria, 256

Anatolius of Laodicea, *c.*282

Dorothy, *c.*305

Phileas of Thmuis, 306

Peter of Alexandria, 311

Alexander, 328

Athanasius, 373

Didymus the Blind, 398

Isidore of Pelusium, *c.*435

Cyril of Alexandria, 444

John Philoponus, 575

Eulogius of Alexandria, 607

Maximos III, 1855

Meletios, 1935

Cairo   Abu 'l-Barakat, 1324

Raphael Zahur, 1831

William Henry Temple Gairdner, 1928

Rahmani, 1929

Damietta   Robert de Courçon, 1219

Gaza   Porphyry of Gaza, 420

Procopius of Gaza, *c.*528

	Dorotheus of Gaza, c.550
Heliopolis	Barbara, 250
Kaison	Jacob Baradai, 578
Mount Sinai	Anastasius Sinaita, 700
Pispir	Anthony of Egypt, 356
Xoïs	Severus, 538

EL SALVADOR	Nicolas Aguilar, 1818
	José Matías Delgado, 1832
	Rutilio Grande, 1977
	Maura Clarke, 1980
	Ita Ford, 1980
	Dorothy Kazel, 1980
	Oscar Arnulfo Romero, 1980
	Ignacio Ellacuría, 1989

ENGLAND	
Aldeburgh	Benjamin Britten, 1976
Andover	John Bodey, 1583
Arundel	Henry Granville Fitzalan-Howard, 1860
	Bernard Marmaduke Fitzalan-Howard, 1975
Bath	Joseph Butler, 1752
	Peter Augustine Baines, 1842
	Aelred Carlyle, 1955
Bedford	John of Rodington, 1348
Bedfordshire	Anthony Stafford, 1645
Berkshire	William Penn, 1718
	Henry Hart Milman, 1868
	William Ralph Inge, 1954
Birmingham	Edward Caswall, 1878
	John Henry Newman, 1890
	Robert William Dale, 1895
Bolton	Christopher Hopper, 1802
Bournemouth	John Keble, 1866
	John Nelson Darby, 1882
	Joseph Barber Lightfoot, 1889
Bradford	Charles Antoine Federer, 1908
Brighton	David Bogue, 1825
Bristol	Hannah More, 1833
	Anthony Norris Groves, 1853
	Hugh Connolly, 1948
Buckinghamshire	Gilbert Keith Chesterton, 1936
	Edmund Rubbra, 1986
Bury St Edmunds	Jocelin of Brakelond, 1216
Buxton	Frederick Fyvie Bruce, 1990
Cambridge	Richard of Connington, 1330
	Thomas Elyot, 1546
	Martin Bucer, 1551
	Nicholas Shaxton, 1556
	John de Feckenham, 1584
	William Perkins, 1602
	John Spencer, 1693
	Richard Bentley, 1742
	Charles Simeon, 1836
	Thomas Rawson Birks, 1883
	Charles Anthony Swainson, 1887
	Fenton John Anthony Hort, 1892
	William Robinson Smith, 1894
	Henry Barclay Swete, 1917
	Francis Crawford Burkitt, 1935
	John Wood Oman, 1939
	George Gordon Coulton, 1947
	Thomas Gilby, 1975

Canterbury	Augustine of Canterbury, 604
	Ethelbert of Kent, 616
	Justus of Canterbury, 627
	Theodore of Canterbury, 690
	Hadrian of Canterbury, 709
	Brithwald, 731
	Ethelhard of Canterbury, 805
	Odo of Canterbury, 959
	Dunstan, 988
	Aelfric of Canterbury, 1005
	Ethelnoth of Canterbury, 1038
	Anselm of Canterbury, 1109
	Eadmer, 1128
	William of Corbeil, 1136
	Thomas Becket, 1170
	Hubert Walter, 1205
	Gervase of Canterbury, c.1210
	Thomas Arundel, 1414
	Richard Hooker, 1600
	Orlando Gibbons, 1625
	Frederic William Farrar, 1903
	Lucy Broadway, 1929
	William Temple, 1944
	George Allen Kennedy Bell, 1958
Carlisle	David I, 1153
Chelmsford	Armstrong Gibbs, 1960
Cheshire	John Bennet, 1759
Chester	John Plessington, 1679
	John Pearson, 1686
Chichester	Hilary of Chichester, 1169
	John of Langton, 1337
	John Arundel, 1477
	William Barlow, 1568
	John William Burgon, 1888
	Albert Bayly, 1984
Colchester	John Beche, 1539
Coniston	John Ruskin, 1900
Cornwall	Cuthbert Mayne, 1577
	Samuel Drew, 1833
	Bernard William Griffin, 1960
Coventry	Nicholas of Hereford, 1420
Derbyshire	Sarah Kirkland, 1880
Devon	John Grandison, 1369
	Edmund Lacy, 1455
	Robert Herrick, 1674
	Richard Hurrell Froude, 1836
	Alexander Duff, 1878
	James Anthony Froude, 1894
	Edmund Bishop, 1917
	Sabine Baring-Gould, 1924
	Alban Goodier, 1939
	Christopher Dawson, 1970
	Philip Caraman, 1998
Dorchester	Birinus, 650
Dorset	Edward, 978
Dunstable	Richard de Mores, 1242
Durham	Richard of Bury, 1345
	John Boste, 1594
	Thomas Eyre, 1810
	Brook Foss Westcott, 1901
Ely	Etheldreda of Northumbria, 679
	Alan of Walsingham, 1364
	William Grey, 1478
	Simon Patrick, 1707

Essex	Michael de Northburgh, 1361
	Richard Rich, 1567
	John Paine, 1582
	Richard Mulcaster, 1611
	William Byrd, 1623
	John Saltmarsh, 1647
	Patrick Young, 1652
	John Locke, 1704
	Catherine Booth, 1890
	Sophronius, 1993
Eton	Henry Savile, 1622
	Montague Rhodes James, 1936
Exeter	Henry de Bracton, 1268
	William Courtenay, c.1341
	James Dowdall, 1600
Farnborough	Marius Férotin, 1914
Farne Islands	Cuthbert of Lindisfarne, 687
Glastonbury	Brithwald of Wilton, 1045
	Richard Whiting, 1539
Gloucester	James Brooks, 1560
	Robert Raikes, 1811
	Samuel Sebastian Wesley, 1876
Gloucestershire	Arthur Henry Stanton, 1913
	Louise Imogen Guiney, 1920
Guildford	Joseph Hilaire Pierre Belloc, 1953
Hampshire	Adam of Orleton, 1345
	William of Wykeham, 1404
	William of Waynflete, 1486
	Joseph Bingham, 1723
	Matthew Atkinson, 1729
	Charles Kingsley, 1875
	Sir Edward Baines, 1890
	Coventry Kersey Dighton Patmore, 1896
	Charlotte Mary Yonge, 1901
	Fernand Cabrol, 1937
	Leonard Cheshire, 1992
Harrogate	Mark Pattison, 1884
Hartlepool	Henri Friedrich Hémy, 1888
Haworth	Emily Jane Brontë, 1848
	Charlotte Brontë, 1855
Hereford	Robert of Melun, 1167
	John Kemble, 1678
	Robert Francis Kilvert, 1879
Herefordshire	Andrew of Saint-Victor, 1175
	John of Bromyard, 1352
	Alfred Leo Duggan, 1964
Hertfordshire	Philip Morgan, 1435
	Claudius Buchanan, 1815
	Edward Bickersteth, 1850
	George Bull, 1865
	Arthur Hinsley, 1943
Huntingdon	Henry of Huntingdon, 1155
	Robert Grosseteste, 1253
	Catherine of Aragon, 1536
Iona	Egbert , 729
Isle of Man	Thomas Wilson, 1755
Isle of Wight	Jeanne Henriette Cécile Bruyère, 1909
	Alfred Noyes, 1958
Jarrow	Bede, 735
Kendal	William Paton, 1943
Kent	Ermenburga, c.695
	Richard of Chichester, 1253
	Richard of Gravesend, 1313
	Robert of Winchelsea, 1313

	Thomas Bourchier, 1486
	John Morton, 1500
	Hadrian à Saravia, 1613
	Nathaniel Lardner, 1768
	Augustus Welby Pugin, 1852
	Napoleon III, 1873
	Charles Robert Darwin, 1882
	Dante Gabriel Rossetti, 1882
	Robert Moffat, 1883
	Anthony Ashley Cooper Shaftesbury, 1885
	Edmund Arbuthnott Knox, 1937
	Simone Weil, 1943
	Andrew George Little, 1945
Lancashire	Roger Anderton, c.1640
	Lawrence Anderton, 1643
	John Lingard, 1851
Lancaster	Edmund Arrowsmith, 1628
	Ambrose Barlow, 1641
Leeds	John Nelson, 1774
Leicester	Thomas Wolsey, 1530
Leicestershire	John Wycliffe, 1384
	Ambrose Lisle March Phillipps De Lisle, 1878
Lichfield	Arthur George Selwyn, 1878
Lincoln	Hugh of Lincoln, 1255
	Adam Marsh, 1258
	Philip Repington, 1424
	Robert Flemming, 1483
	William Atwater, 1521
	William Paley, 1805
Lincolnshire	Botulf, 680
	Guthlac, 714
	Gilbert of Sempringham, 1189
	John Russell, 1494
	John Taverner, 1545
Liverpool	William Wood Stamp, 1877
	William Rees, 1883
	Matthew Arnold, 1888
	Geoffrey Anketell Studdert Kennedy, 1929
London	Erconwald of London, c.693
	Hildelide, 717
	Alphege of Canterbury, 1012
	Edward the Confessor, 1066
	Bartholomew of Exeter, 1184
	Hugh of Lincoln, 1200
	Honorius Magister, c.1210
	John Peckham, 1292
	Walter de Stapledon, 1326
	Robert de Baldock, 1327
	Nicholas Trevet, 1335
	John Bacanthorpe, c.1346
	Richard of Kilvington, c.1362
	Geoffrey Hardeby, 1385
	John Gilbert, 1397
	Geoffrey Chaucer, 1400
	William Sawtrey, 1401
	John Gower, 1408
	John Oldcastle, 1417
	Richard Clifford, 1421
	William Lyndwood, 1446
	Robert Gilbert, 1448
	John Dunstable, 1453
	Henry VI, 1471
	William Caxton, 1491

Henry Deane, 1503
Andreas Ammonius, 1517
Bernard Andre, 1521
William Lily, 1522
Thomas Linacre, 1524
John Frith, 1533
Elizabeth Barton, 1534
Edward Bocking, 1534
John Fisher, 1535
John Houghton, 1535
Robert Lawrence, 1535
Thomas More, 1535
Richard Reynolds, 1535
Richard Pace, 1536
John Rastell, 1536
Adrian Fortescue,1539
Thomas Abell, 1540
Thomas Cromwell, 1540
John Clerk, 1541
Edward VI, 1553
John Bradford, 1555
Stephen Gardiner, 1555
John Rogers, 1555
George Day, 1556
George Dowdall, 1558
Reginald Pole, 1558
Mary Tudor, 1558
Polydore Plasden, 1563
Roger Ascham, 1568
Edmund Bonner, 1569
Miles Coverdale, 1569
John Felton, 1570
Thomas Howard, 1572
Matthew Parker, 1575
Nicholas Heath, 1578
Henry Cole, c.1579
Henry Fitzalan, 1579
Alexander Briant, 1581
Richard Bristow, 1581
Edward Campion, 1581
Thomas Cottam, 1582
Luke Kirby, 1582
Edward Arden, 1583
William Carter, 1583
Richard Creagh, 1585
Edmund Plowden, 1585
Thomas Tallis, 1585
John Foxe, 1587
Margaret Ward, 1588
Edmund Gennings, 1591
Swithun Wells, 1591
Henry Barrow, 1593
John Greenwood, 1593
Robert Southwell, 1595
John Jones, 1598
John Rigby, 1600
Anne Line, 1601
Elizabeth I, 1603
Everard Digby, 1606
Henry Garnett, 1606
Thomas Garnett, 1608
John Roberts, 1610
John Almond, 1612
George Blackwell, 1612

Luisa de Carvajal, 1614
Isaac Casaubon, 1614
Thomas Helwys, 1616
Anne of Denmark, 1619
Thomas Weekes, 1623
James I, 1625
Lancelot Andrewes, 1626
Francis Bacon, 1626
Christopher Sutton, 1629
John Donne, 1631
George Calvert, 1632
David Augustine Baker, 1641
Alban Roe, 1642
Francis Quarles, 1644
Walter Coleman, 1645
William Laud, 1645
Henry Morse, 1645
Edward Herbert, 1648
Charles I, 1649
Godfrey Goodman, 1656
Oliver Cromwell, 1658
Brian Walton, 1661
John Biddle, 1662
Kenelm Digby, 1665
John Austin, 1669
William Prynne, 1669
John Milton, 1674
Thomas Traherne, 1674
Cecilius Calvert, 1675
Isaac Barrow, 1677
George Digby, 1677
Richard Gerard, 1680
Oliver Plunket, 1681
Charles II, 1685
John Bunyan, 1688
Peter Walsh, 1688
John Belasyse, 1689
Richard Baxter, 1691
George Fox, 1691
Robert Boyle, 1692
Henry Purcell, 1695
Edward Stillingfleet, 1699
John Dryden, 1700
Titus Oates, 1705
James Maurus Corker, 1715
Robert South, 1716
(Sir) Christopher Wren, 1723
Henry Sacheverell, 1724
Isaac Newton, 1727
Nathaniel Spinckes, 1727
Samuel Clarke, 1729
Thomas Bray, 1730
Bonaventure Giffard, 1734
Henry Newman, 1743
Isaac Watts, 1748
James Gibbs, 1754
John Cennick, 1755
George Frideric Handel, 1759
Stephen Hales, 1761
Samuel Walker, 1761
Alexander Cruden, 1770
Emmanuel Swedenborg, 1772
Oliver Goldsmith, 1774
Peter Böhler, 1775

London Augustus Montague Toplady, 1778
William Boyce, 1779
Richard Challoner, 1781
Johann Christian Bach, 1782
Samuel Johnson, 1784
Benjamin La Trobe, 1786
Charles Wesley, 1788
Selina Hastings, 1791
Richard Price, 1791
John Wesley, 1791
Edward Gibbon, 1794
James Boswell, 1795
William Romaine, 1795
Alexander Geddes, 1802
John Newton, 1807
Joanna Southcott, 1814
Samuel Webbe senior, 1816
Joseph Benson, 1821
William Blake, 1827
William Poynter, 1827
Charles Butler, 1832
William Wilberforce, 1833
Samuel Taylor Coleridge, 1834
Samuel Bagster (son), 1835
Thomas Attwood, 1838
John Ireland, 1842
Samuel Webbe junior, 1843
Thomas Griffiths, 1847
Edward Baines, 1848
Arthur Philip Perceval, 1853
Frederick Lucas, 1855
Jabez Bunting, 1858
Frederick William Faber, 1863
Nicholas Wiseman, 1865
James Burns, 1871
Frederick Denison Maurice, 1872
William Pennefather, 1873
Henry Venn, 1873
Thomas Binney, 1874
Henry Gauntlett, 1876
Caroline Chisholm, 1877
Kenelm Henry Digby, 1880
Thomas Carlyle, 1881
William George Ward, 1882
William Palmer, 1885
William Henry Monk, 1889
Henry Edward Manning, 1892
Christina Rossetti, 1894
Sir John Everett Millais, 1896
William Morris, 1896
Sir Edward Burne-Jones, 1898
Thomas Edward Bridgett, 1899
St George Jackson Mivart, 1900
(Sir) Arthur Sullivan, 1900
Frances Margaret Taylor, 1900
Mandell Creighton, 1901
Hugh Price Hughes, 1902
Lionel Pigot Johnson, 1902
Thomas William Allies, 1903
Alfred Herbert Vaughan, 1903
Thomas John Barnardo, 1905
Francis Thompson, 1907
François Désiré Mathieu, 1908
Florence Nightingale, 1910

William Booth, 1912
James Gairdner, 1912
Augustus Henry Keane, 1912
Alfred Robert Tucker, 1914
Wilfrid Philip Ward, 1916
Henry Fitzalan-Howard, 1917
Peter Taylor Forsyth, 1921
Alice Christiana Gertrude Meynell, 1922
John Clifford, 1923
Adrian Fortescue, 1923
Sir Frederick Bridge, 1924
Charles Villiers Stanford, 1924
Friedrich Von Hügel, 1925
Thomas Power O'Connor, 1929
Randall Thomas Davidson, 1930
Charles Gore, 1932
John Chapman, 1933
Edward Cuthbert Butler, 1934
Gustav Holst, 1934
Bede Jarret, 1934
Hugh Richard Lawrie Sheppard, 1937
(Sir) Richard Terry, 1938
Herbert Henry Charles Thurston, 1939
Evelyn Underhill, 1941
Maude Dominica Petre, 1942
Vincent Joseph McNabb, 1943
Henri Leclercq, 1945
Samuel Edward Keeble, 1946
Ernest James Oldmeadow, 1949
Ernest Reginald Hull, 1952
John Scott Lidgett, 1953
Frances Caryll Houselander, 1954
Dorothy Leigh Sayers, 1957
Ralph Vaughan Williams, 1958
Sir Jacob Epstein, 1959
Giles Gilbert Scott, 1960
George Jeffreys, 1962
Nicholas Sydney Gibbes, 1963
Cyril Charles Martindale, 1963
Douglas Francis Jerrold, 1964
Thomas Stearns Eliot, 1965
Ernest Frederick Kevan, 1965
Donald Gee, 1966
David Jones, 1974
(Sir) Arnold Lunn, 1974
John Carmel Heenan, 1975
David James Mathew, 1975
Martin Cyril D'Arcy, 1976
Thomas Corbishley, 1976
Thomas d'Esterre Roberts, 1976
Ernest Alexander Payne, 1980
David Martyn Lloyd-Jones, 1981
Herbert Howells, 1983
Lennox Berkeley, 1989
Donald Guthrie, 1992
James Edward Lesslie Newbigin, 1998
(Sir) Michael Tippett, 1998
Basil Hume, 1999
Peter Chad Tigar Levi, 2000
Maidstone William Grocyn, 1519
Manchester John Nicol Farquhar, 1929
Arthur Samuel Peake, 1929
Harold Henry Rowley, 1969
Middlesex Olaudah Equiano, 1797

Eric Gill, 1940

Newcastle upon Tyne — Charles Cordell, 1791
Norfolk — Edmund the Martyr, 869
Margery Kempe, c.1433
John Capgrave, 1464
Thomas Howard, 1554
William Cowper, 1800
Thomas Fowell Buxton, 1844
Northampton — Robert Holcot, 1349
Robert Browne, 1633
Northamptonshire — Cyneburg, c.680
Wilfrid, 709
William Law, 1761
Andrew Fuller, 1815
Northumberland — Aidan of Lindisfarne, 651
Acca, 742
Josephine Elizabeth Butler, 1906
Norwich — William of Norwich, 1144
John of Oxford, 1200
Henry Despenser, 1406
Julian of Norwich, 1413
Anthony Sparrow, 1685
Joseph Kinghorn, 1832
Heinrich Brüning, 1970
Geoffrey Laycock, 1986
Nottingham — Alexander Kilham, 1798
Nottinghamshire — Walter Hilton, 1395
George Neville, 1476
Oxford — Frideswide, 735
Robert de Cricklade, c.1174
Agnellus of Pisa, 1232
Robert Bacon, 1248
Richard Fishacre, 1248
Richard Rufus of Cornwall, c.1260
Roger Bacon, 1294
Richard of Campsall, c.1350
Thomas Gascoigne, 1458
Walter Hunt, 1478
Hugh Latimer, 1555
Nicholas Ridley, 1555
Thomas Cranmer, 1556
Edward Pococke, 1691
George Berkeley, 1753
Benjamin Kennicott, 1783
James Legge, 1897
Edward Caird, 1908
Samuel Rolles Driver, 1914
Henry Marriott Bannister, 1919
Robert Bridges, 1930
Cuthbert Hamilton Tucker, 1930
Eric Norman Bromley Burrows, 1938
Henry Wheeler Robinson, 1945
Charles Walter Stansby Williams, 1945
(Sir) Hugh Allen, 1946
Kenneth Escott Kirk, 1954
Clive Staples Lewis, 1963
Austin Marsden Farrer, 1968
Egon Wellesz, 1974
Godfrey Rolles Driver, 1975
Ronald Owen Hall, 1975
Gervase Mathew, 1976
Nicholas Zernov, 1980
Jane E. Ellis, 1998

Arthur Michael Ramsey, 1988
Richard Southern, 2001
Oxfordshire — Aelfric Grammaticus, 1020
Charles Eyston, 1721
illiam Stubbs, 1901
Henry Davis, 1952
Cuthbert Charles Lattey, 1954
Charles Harold Dodd, 1973
Peterborough — Benedict of Peterborough, 1193
Plymouth — Samuel Prideaux Tregelles, 1875
Pontefract — Richard II, 1400
Portsmouth — Adam Moleyns, 1450
Arthur Darby Nock, 1902
Ramsgate — Elizabeth Fry, 1845
Reading — John Lathbury, 1362
Dominic Barberi, 1849
Reigate — James Ussher, 1656
Rochester — Paulinus, 644
Walter of Merton, 1277
John Lowe, 1467
Rugby — Thomas Arnold, 1842
St Albans — Alban, 250
Geoffrey of Dunstable, 1146
Matthew Paris, 1259
John Ball, 1381
Robert Alexander Kennedy Runcie, 2000
Salford — Robert Hugh Benson, 1914
Salisbury — Roger of Salisbury, 1139
Andrew Holes, 1470
George Herbert, 1633
Sheffield — James Montgomery, 1854
Sherborne — Henry Murdac, 1153
Geoffrey Francis Fisher, 1972
Shropshire — Thomas Falkner, 1784
Somerset — Aldhelm, 709
Adam of Dryburgh, 1212
Nicholas Bubwith, 1424
John Blackman, 1485
William Knight, 1547
William Crotch, 1847
William Dix, 1898
Walford Davies, 1941
Ronald Arbuthnott Knox, 1957
Evelyn Waugh, 1966
Christopher Hollis, 1977
Anthony Gregory Murray, 1992
Southampton — Juan Manuel Rosas, 1877
Southwell — Gerard of York, 1108
Lawrence Booth, 1480
Staffordshire — Richard Sampson, 1554
John William Fletcher, 1785
Margaret Mary Hallahan, 1868
Sebastian Bullough, 1967
Luke Connaughton, 1979
Stoke-on-Trent — Samuel Gosling, 1950
Stratford-upon-Avon — William Shakespeare, 1616
Suffolk — Thoms Brouns, 1445
William Sancroft, 1693
Sue Ryder, 2000
Surrey — Ethelwold of Winchester, 984
Edward III, 1377
Charles Calvert, 1715
Henry James Coleridge, 1893

	Denis John Bernard Hawkins, 1964		Richard Andrewe, 1477
Sussex	John Stratford, 1348		Robert Aske, 1537
	Robert Stratford, 1362		Edward Lee, 1544
	John Mason Neale, 1866		Hugh Taylor, 1585
	John Dobree Dalgairns, 1876		Margaret Clitherow, 1586
	John Dykes, 1876		Henry Walpole, 1595
	Cornelia Connelly, 1879		John Woolman, 1772
	George Tyrrell, 1907		Alexander Mather, 1800
	Samuel Barnett, 1913	Yorkshire	Cedda, 664
	Michael Maher, 1917		Aelred, 1166
	Sir Hubert Parry, 1918		John of Hoveden, c.1275
	Sir Frank Brangwyn, 1956		Richard de Hampole Rolle, 1349
	John Ireland, 1962		John of Thoresby, 1373
	Joseph Houldsworth Oldham, 1969		Henry Bowet, 1423
	David Knowles, 1974		Mary Ward, 1646
	Leslie Dixon Weatherhead, 1976		Oliver Heywood, 1702
	Donald Attwater, 1977		William Grimshaw, 1763
	Max Warren, 1977		John Fawcett, 1817
	Barbara Ward, 1981		Charles Lindley Wood Halifax, 1934
	Kathleen Bliss, 1989		Rudolph Walter Howard Frere, 1938
	George Raymond Beasley-Murray, 2000		John Leonard Wilson, 1970
Tewkesbury	Alan of Tewkesbury, 1202		John Arthur Thomas Robinson, 1983
Warwick	Thomas Cartwright, 1603		
Warwickshire	William Dugdale, 1686	ERITREA	Giustino de Jacobis, 1860
	William Bernard Ullathorne, 1889		
	Martin John Melvin, 1952	ETHIOPIA	Frumentius, 380
Watford	Albert Gille, 1950		Luiz de Azevedo, 1634
Wearmouth	Benedict Biscop, 690		Cassian of Nantes, 1638
Wells	Jocelin of Wells, 1242		Michael Ghebre, 1855
	Thomas Bekynton, 1465		
Weston-Super-Mare	Joseph Booth, 1932	FINLAND	Henry of Uppsala, c.1156
Whitby	Hilda of Whitby, 680		
	Elfleda, 714	FRANCE	
Wiltshire	William of Malmesbury, 1143	Agdle	Raymond Bonal, 1653
	John Jewel, 1571	Aix-en-Provence	Andrew Abellon, 1450
	Thomas Ken, 1711		Antoine Pagi, 1699
Wimborne	Cuthburga, c.725		Pierre Toussaint Durand de Maillane, 1814
Winchester	Swithin, 862		Adolf Alfred Tanqueray, 1932
	Alfred the Great, 899		Maurice Blondel, 1949
	Grimbald, 901		Michel d'Herbigny, 1957
	Stigand, c.1072	Albi	Eudoxe Irénée Mignot, 1918
	Henry Beaufort, 1447	Altkirch	Morandus, c.1165
	Peter Courtenay, 1492	Amboise	Charles VIII, 1498
	Richard Foxe, 1528	Amiens	Honoratus of Amiens, c.600
	Mary Elizabeth Sumner, 1921		Angilbert, 814
Windsor	Richard Beauchamp, 1481		Petrus Burrus, 1507
	Henry VIII, 1547		Louis Christophe Léon La Moricière, 1865
	William Cave, 1713	Angers	Marbod of Rennes, 1123
	Samuel Bagster (father), 1851		Geoffrey of Vendôme, 1132
Wolverhampton	Charles Berington, 1798		William Barclay, 1608
	John Milner, 1826		Henri Arnauld, 1692
Worcester	Oswald of York, 992		Charles Emile Freppel, 1891
	Florence of Worcester, 1118	Angoulême	Eparchius, 581
	John Wall, 1679		Jean Louis Guez de Balzac, 1654
	Edward Elgar, 1934	Angoumois	Nithard, 844
York	Egbert, 766	Antibes	Agnes McLaren, 1913
	Ethelbert of York, 780	Antony	Léon Adolphe Amette, 1920
	Ealdred of York, 1069	Apt	Delphina of Signe, c.1358
	William of York, 1154	Arce	Ebbo, c.750
	Roger de Pont l'Évêque, 1181	Arles	Genesius of Arles, c.303
	Henry of Newark, 1299		Hilary of Arles, 449
	John Kynyngham, 1399		Aeonius of Arles, 500
	Philippa of Hainaut, 1369		Caesaria, c.530
	William Booth, 1464		

| | | Caesarius of Arles, 543 | Bordeaux | Decimus Magnus Ausonius, 394 |

Caesarius of Arles, 543
Louis d'Aleman, 1450
Arras — Odo of Cambrai, 1113
John Buridan, 1370
Ars — Jean-Baptiste Marie Vianney, 1859
Arthez d'Asson — Henri Bremond, 1933
Aulps — Guarinus of Sion, 1150
Auray — Charles of Blois, 1364
Aurillac — Gerald of Aurillac, 909
Autrecourt — Nicholas of Autrecourt,
Auvers-sur-Oise — Van Gogh, Vincent, 1890
Auxerre — Aunarius of Auxerre, 601
Haimo of Auxerre, 855
Heiric of Auxerre, 876
Rodulphus Glaber, c.1047
Jacques Amyot, 1593
Étienne Henri Gilson, 1978
Avignon — Benezet, 1184
Bernard of Trille, 1292
Guido de Baysio, 1313
John le Moine, 1315
Giles of Rome, 1316
Henry of Harclay, 1317
Berenger Fredoli, 1323
Bernard Lombardi, 1333
William of Alnwick, 1333
John XXII, 1334
Zenzelinus de Casanis, 1334
John Lutterell, 1335
Benedict XII, 1342
Simone Martini, 1344
John of Reading, 1346
Pierre Bertrand, c.1348
Clement VI, 1352
Richard Fitzralph, 1360
Innocent VI, 1362
Urban V, 1370
John Klenkok, 1374
Clement VII, 1394
Pietro Corsini, 1405
Leonardo de Rubeis, 1407
Carpentras, 1548
Charles de Lorraine de Guise, 1574
Georges d' Armagnac, 1585
Cesar de Bus, 1607
Joseph Mayol, 1709
Avignoult — William of Arnaud, 1242
Avranches — Aubert of Avranches, 725
Achard of Saint-Victor, 1172
Barbizon — Jean François Millet, 1875
Bareuil — Marcellus of Die, 510
Bayeaux — Jean Michel d'Astorg d' Aubarède, 1692
Beaulieu — Albert Farges, 1926
Bec — Herluin of Bec, 1078
Bernay — Georges Goyau, 1939
Besançon — Donatus of Besançon, 660
Louis William Valentine Dubourg, 1833
Michael Garicoïts, 1863
Béziers — Jean Baptiste Gonet, 1681
Pierre Jean Antoine Gailhac, 1890
Blois — Antoine de Févin, 1511
Catherine de' Medici, 1589
Jeanne-Marie Guyon, 1717
Bony — Garembert, 1141

Bordeaux — Decimus Magnus Ausonius, 394
Gerard of Sauve-Majeure, 1095
Simon Stock, 1265
John of Paris, 1306
Jeanne de Lestonnac, 1640
Jean Joseph Surin, 1665
Joseph François Lafitau, 1746
Jean-Louis Lefebvre Cheverus, 1836
Guillaume Joseph Chaminade, 1850
Pierre Bienvenu Noailles, 1861
Jacques Ellul, 1994
Boulogne-sur-Mer — Salomon Reinach, 1932
Bourg-en-Bresse — André Meynard, 1904
Bourges — Austregisilus, 624
Desideratus of Bourges, 550
Ambrose of Cahors, 770
William of Bourges, 1209
Roger le Fort, 1367
Joan of France, 1505
Antoine Le Conte, 1577
, Louis Lallemant, 1635
Guillaume François Berthier, 1782
Caen — Jean de Bernières-Louvigny, 1659
John Eudes, 1680
Pierre Cally, 1709
Cahors — Desiderius of Cahors, c.655
Christopher of Romandiola, 1272
Cambrai — Gery of Cambrai, 625
Gerard of Cambrai, 1051
Lietbert of Cambrai-Arras, 1076
Guillaume Dufay, 1474
François de Salignac de la Mothe Fénelon, 1715
Candes — Martin of Tours, 397
Carnoët — Maurice of Carnoët, 1191
Celle-Roubaud — Roseline, 1329
Cerfroid — Felix of Valois, 1212
Châlon-sur-Marne — William of Champeaux, 1122
Chalon-sur-Saône — Peter Abelard, 1142
Chambary — Henri Daniel-Rops, 1965
Chamonix — Oscar Cullmann, 1999
Charleville — Francis Nugent, 1635
Chartres — Anianus of Chartres, 450
Laudomar, c.590
Fulbert of Chartres, 1028
Thierry of Chartres, 1155
William of Conches, c.1160
John of Salisbury, 1180
Clairvaux — Gerard of Clairvaux, 1138
Bernard of Clairvaux, 1153
Rober of Bruges, 1157
Eskil of Lund, 1182
Everard of Ypres, c.1199
Clamart — Amédée Gastoué, 1943
Nikolai Aleksandrovich Berdiaev, 1948
Clermont — Gall of Clermont, 551
Genesius of Clermont, 662
Cloux — Leonardo da Vinci, 1519
Comminges — Bertrand of Comminges, 1123
Contamine — Karl August von Reisach, 1869
Corbie — Ratramnus of Corbie, 825
Adalard, 827
Courtrai — Pierre Flotte, 1302
Creil-sur-Oise — Guillaume Vincent de Contenson, 1674

Deauville	Ford Madox Ford, 1939		Alexandre Brou, 1947
Dieppe	Pierre Aubry, 1910	Le Havre	Jacques Marie Monsabré, 1907
Dijon	Benignus of Dijon, 170	Le Mans	Innocent of Le Mans, c.542
	Elizabeth of the Trinity, 1906		Domnolus of Le Mans, 581
	Gustave Bardy, 1955		Bertrand of Le Mans, 623
Dole	Anne de Xaintonge, 1621		Basil Anthony Moreau, 1873
	Valerius Reginald, 1623	Lens	Emil Mersch, 1940
	Étienne Harent, 1927	Lille	John Martiall, 1597
Le Dorat	Charles Antoine, 1921		Edmond Henri de Coussemaker, 1876
Douai	Goswin, c.1165		Louis Pierre Baunard, 1919
	Gulielmus Estius, 1613		Achille Liénart, 1973
	William Rudesind Barlow, 1656	Limoges	Eligius of Noyon, 660
	John Gennings, 1660		Gaucherius, 1140
	Charles of the Assumptiom, 1686		Richard I, 1199
	John Francis Wade, 1786		Bernard of Besse, 1283
Ekelsbecke	Folcwin, 855		Jean Lejeune, 1672
Elbeuf	Henri Constant Fouard, 1903	Lisieux	Nicholas Oresme, 1382
Epernay	Hincmar, 882		Thérèse of Lisieux, 1897
Etiolles	Raymond Joseph Martin, 1949	Lobbes	Folcwin of Lobbes, 990
Eu	Lawrence O'Toole, 1180	Lodeve	Fulcran of Lodeve, 1006
Evreux	Henri Marie Boudon, 1702	Lorgues	Martin Jugie, 1954
Fécamp	William of Volpiano, 1031	Lourdes	Lucien Cerfaux, 1968
	John of Fécamp, 1078	Luxeuil	Eustace of Luxeuil, 629
Flavigny	Rémi Ceillier, 1761	Lyons	Blandina, 177
Fleury-sur-Loire	Hugh of Fleury, 1118		Pothinus, 177
Fontainebleau	Jules Lachelier, 1918		Irenaeus of Lyons, c.202
Fontenelle	Ansegis, 833		Aurelian of Arles, 551
Fontroide	Arnaldus Amalrici, 1225		Genesius of Lyons, 678
La Fôrete-sur-Sèvre	Philippe Du Plessis-Mornay, 1623		Bonitus of Clermont, 706
Fréjus	Joseph Anthelmi, 1697		Agobard of Lyons, 840
Gellone	William of Aquitaine, 812		Florus of Lyons, c.860
Glanfeuil	Maurus, 584		Remigius of Lyons, 875
Grandmont	Geoffrey of York, 1212		Benedict the Pole, 1247
Grenoble	Hugh of Grenoble, 1132		Hostiensis, 1271
	Heinrich Cornelius Agrippa von Nettesheim, 1535		Bonaventure, 1274
			Jean le Charlier de Gerson, 1429
	Étienne Le Camus, 1707		Santes Pagnini, 1536
	Yves de Montcheuil, 1944		Claude Goudimel, 1572
Hainault	Josquin des Prez, 1521		Jerome Hermes Bolsec, 1585
Hannecourt	Félix Klein, 1953		Francis de Sales, 1622
Harfleur	Richard Courtenay, 1415		Théophile Raynaul, 1663
Hautecombe	Geoffrey of Clairvaux, 1188		Joseph de Gibalin, 1671
Hauteville	John Mary Odin, 1870		Joseph François de Gallifet, 1749
Hautmont	Ansbert of Rouen, 693		Pauline-Marie Jaricot, 1862
Hazebrouck	Jules Lemire, 1928		Joseph Carrière, 1864
Héricourt	Johann Jakob Froberger, 1667		Marie Victoire Thérèse Couderc, 1885
Hesdin	John Parvus, 1411		Joseph Chaine, 1948
Hohenburg	Eugenia, 735		Paul Irénée Couturier, 1953
Houat	Gildas, 570		Pierre Pourrat, 1957
Igny	Guerric of Igny, 1157		Albert Gélin, 1960
Induno	Carlo Giuseppe Quadrupani, 1806		Régis Jolivet, 1966
L'Isle d'Adam	Henry Edouard Prosper Breuil, 196	Macon	Aunemund of Lyons, 658
Issy	Louis Claude Fillion, 1927	Maillane	Frédéric Mistral, 1914
Jougne	Charles Plowden, 1821	Malvisade	Émile-Paul-Constant-Ange Le Camus,
La Pierre-qui-Vire	Marie Jean Baptiste Muard, 1854		1906
Lalouvesc	Jean-François Regis, 1640	Mantilly	William of Firmatus, c.1095
Langres	Desiderius of Langres, c.407	Marbach	Manegold of Lautenbach, c.1103
	Ceolfrid of Wearmouth, 716	Marmoutier	Bartholomew of Marmoutier, 1084
	Isaac of Langres, 880	Marseilles	John Cassian, 435
Laniscat	Joseph Huby, 1948		Gennadius of Marseilles, 505
Laon	Anstrudis, 688		Eusebia of Saint-Cyr, 838
	Anselm of Laon, 1117		Francesco Laurana, c.1502
	Jean Bodin, 1596		Henri François Xavier de Belsunce de
Laval	Louis Laurand, 1941		Castelmoron, 1755

	Charles de Forbin-Janson, 1844
	Manuel José Mosquera, 1853
	Antoine Frederic Ozanam, 1853
	Emilie de Vialar, 1856
	Charles Joseph Eugène de Mazenod, 1861
	Marie de Jésus Deluil-Martiny, 1884
	Jean Nicholas Arthur Rimbaud, 1891
Maubuisson	Blanche of Castile, 1252
Meaux	Fara, 657
	Faro of Meaux, c.675
	Fulcoius of Beauvais, c.1200
	Durandus of Saint-Pourçain, 1334
Melun	Robert II, 1031
Mentone	Thomas Illyricus, 1528
	Charles Haddon Spurgeon, 1892
Metz	Auctor of Metz, 451
	Livarius of Metz, 451
	Adelphus of Metz, 460
	Glodesindis, 600
	Abbo of Metz, 647
	Chrodegang of Metz, 766
	Angilramnus of Metz, 791
	Amalarius of Metz, 850
	Adalbero II, 1005
	Matthias Charles Chardon, 1771
	Michael Bihl, 1950
Meudon	Auguste Rodin, 1917
	Paul Nikolaevich Evdokimov, 1970
Mezerolles	Fursey, c.650
Millau	Raymond of Toulouse VII, 1249
Montauban	John Cameron, 1625
Montelon	Eptadius, 550
Montereau	Guillaume Briçonnet, 1534
Montpellier	John of Vercelli, 1283
	Jacques Marie Achille Ginoulhiac, 1875
	Augustin Fliche, 1951
Morimond	Otto of Freising, 1158
Moulins	Robert Briçonnet, 1479
	Jean Baptiste Chautard, 1935
Mure d'Isère	Pierre Julien Eymard, 1868
Nancy	Elizabeth of Ranfaing, 1649
	Louis Alexandre Brisson, 1908
Nantes	Frances d'Amboise, 1485
	Jean Louis Leloutre, 1772
	Paul Jouon, 1940
	Pierre de Labriolle, 1940
Narbonne	Peter John Olivi, 1298
	Nedellic Harvey, 1323
	Gasbert de Laval, 1347
	Guillaume Briçonnet, 1514
	Anthony Mary Claret, 1870
Neuffontaines	Gilbert of Neuffontaines, 1152
Neuilly	Fulk of Neuilly, 1201
	Georges Bernanos, 1948
Nice	Henry Francis Lyte, 1847
	Charles Etienne Brasseur de Bourbourg, 1874
	Charles Gavan Duffy, 1903
	Léon Harmel, 1915
Niederbronn	Elizabeth Eppinger, 1867
Nîmes	Claude Henri Plantier, 1875
	Emmanuel d' Alzon, 1880
Nogent	Cloud, c.560
	Héloïse, 1164

Notre Dame de L'Hermitage	Marcellin Joseph Benoit Champagnat, 1840
Notre Dame de la Neyliere	Jean-Claude Colin, 1875
Noyon	Charles de Bouelles, 1553
Oberehnheim	Thomas Murner, 1537
Oise	Stephen de Lexinton, 1260
Orange	François Pagi, 1721
Orléans	Anianus of Orleans, c.453
	Jonas of Orléans, 843
	François Florent, 1650
Oroër	Evroul of Saint-Fuschien-au-Bois, c.600
Orsan	Robert of Arbrissel, c.1116
Pairis	Gunther of Pairis, c.1220
Paray-le-Monial	Margaret Mary Alacoque, 1690
Paris	Denis, c.250
	Geneviève, c.500
	Clovis, 511
	Germanus of Paris, 576
	Bathilde, 680
	Ouen, 683
	Pepin III, 768
	Remigius of Auxerre, 908
	Adhemar of Puy, 1098
	Louis VI, 1137
	Hugh of Saint-Victor, 1141
	Suger, 1151
	Peter Lombard, 1160
	Fastred de Cavamiez, 1164
	Richard of Saint-Victor, 1173
	Adam of Saint-Victor, 1180
	Louis VII, 1180
	Peter Comestor, c.1180
	Arnulf of Lisieux, 1184
	Godfrey of Saint-Victor, c.1194
	Maurice of Sully, 1196
	Amalric of Bene, 1206
	Reginald of Orléans, 1220
	Giles of Corbeil, 1224
	Philip, 1236
	Alexander of Hales, 1245
	John of La Rochelle, 1245
	William of Auvergne, 1249
	Adam Mulieris Pulchrae, 1250
	John de Sacobosco, c.1250
	Julian of Speyer, 1250
	Aymer of Lusignan, 1260
	Isabelle of France, 1270
	Gerard of Abbeville, 1272
	John of Garland, c.1272
	Robert de Sorbon, 1274
	Boethius of Sweden, 1275
	John of Wales, 1285
	Adenulf of Anagni, 1289
	Nicholas of Gorran, c.1295
	Godfrey of Fontaines, c.1305
	Marguerite Porete, 1310
	Gonsalvus Hispanus, 1313
	Jacques de Molay, 1314
	Elzéar of Sabran, 1325
	Anfredus Gonteri, 1330
	Nicholas of Lyra, 1340
	Henri Bohic, 1351

Paris

William of Toulouse, 1369
Robert Gaguin, 1501
John Mombaer, 1501
Jacques Almain, 1515
Louis XII, 1515
Publio Fausto Andrelini, 1518
Antoine Brumel, 1525
Guillaume Budé, 1540
Jacques Merlin, 1541
François Rabelais, 1553
Pierre Rebuffi, 1557
Clément Janequin, 1558
Louis Bourgeois, 1561
Jakob Arcadelt, c.1567
Claude Togniel de Espence, 1571
Pierre Certon, 1572
Gaspard II de Coligny, 1572
Denis Lambin, 1572
Peter Ramus, 1572
Demochares, 1574
François Baudouin, 1574
Pierre Lescot, 1578
Jacques de Billy, 1581
Marguérin de La Bigne, 1589
James Beaton, 1603
Pierre Charron, 1603
Renard de Beaume, 1606
Henry IV, 1610
Pierre Victor Cayet, 1610
William Benedict Fitch, 1611
Jacques Davy Duperron, 1618
Antoine Arnauld, 1619
Laurent Benard, 1620
Anthony Le Gaudier, 1622
Nicolas Coeffeteau, 1623
Christopher Bagshaw, 1625
Pierre Coton, 1626
Pierre de Bérulle, 1629
Edmond Richer, 1631
Archangel of Pembroke, 1632
François Le Clerc du Tremblay, 1638
Etienne Binet, 1639
Tommaso Campanella, 1639
André Duchesne, 1640
Charles de Condren, 1641
Armand Jean du Plessis de Richelieu,
   1642
Jean Duvergier de Hauranne, 1643
Abbé de Saint-Cyran, 1643
Charles François d'Abra de Raconis, 1646
John Chrysostom of Saint-Lô, 1646
Achille Harlay, 1646
Robert Phillip, 1647
Marin Mersenne, 1648
Gabriel Sionita, 1648
Christopher Justel, 1649
Philippus Aquinas, 1650
Guillaume Gibieuf, 1650
Nicholas Caussin, 1651
Louis Chardon, 1651
Denis Pétau, 1652
Jacques Goar, 1653
Pierre Gassendi, 1655
Claudine Moine, c.1655

Jean-Jacques Olier, 1657
Jean Morin, 1659
Louise de Marillac, 1660
Vincent de Paul, 1660
Jean de La Haye, 1661
François Bourgoing, 1662
Henry Holden, 1662
Pierre de Marca, 1662
Blaise Pascal, 1662
Philippe Labbe, 1667
Jean Duval, 1669
Jeanne Marie Chezard de Matel, 1670
Leo of St John, 1671
Robert Arnauld d'Andilly, 1674
Vincent Baron, 1674
William Chalmers, 1678
Jean François Paul de Gondi Retz, 1679
Pierre Corneille, 1684
Henri Dumont, 1684
Jean Luc d' Achery, 1685
Nicolas Barré, 1686
Louis Maimbourg, 1686
René Rapin, 1687
Charles Dufresne Du Cange, 1688
Gilbert de Choiseul du Plessis Praslin,
   1689
Louis Abelly, 1691
Lawrence of the Resurrection, 1691
Jean Crasset, 1692
Antoine Goudin, 1695
Jean de La Fontaine, 1695
Pierre Nicole, 1695
Basil of Soissons, 1698
Catherine de Bar, 1698
Jean Baptiste Racine, 1699
Michel Colbert, 1702
Jacques Bénigne Bossuet, 1704
Louis Bourdaloue, 1704
Marc Antoine Charpentier, 1704
Wilhelm Egon von Fürstenberg, 1704
Claude François Menestier, 1705
Jean-Baptiste Duhamel, 1706
Jean Mabillon, 1707
Pierre Sylvain Regis, 1707
Charles Le Gobien, 1708
François de La Chaize, 1709
Nicolas Boileau-Despréaux, 1711
Claude Frassen, 1711
Gabriel Gerberon, 1711
Nicolas Malebranche, 1715
Hippolyte Helyot, 1716
Etienne Baluze, 1718
Louis Ellies Dupin, 1719
Eusèbe Renaudot, 1720
Pierre Coustant, 1721
Pierre-Daniel Huet, 1721
Henri de Boulainvilliers, 1722
Guillaume Dubois, 1723
Claude Fleury, 1723
François Aimé Pouget, 1723
Jacques Echard, 1724
Alexander Natalis, 1724
Michael Moor, 1726
Gabriel Daniel, 1728

Pierre Le Brun, 1729
Jean Hardouin, 1729
Louis Antoine de Noailles, 1729
Louis Marchand, 1732
François Couperin, 1733
Claude Judde, 1735
Jacques Charles de Brisacier, 1736
Claude Buffier, 1737
François Catrou, 1737
Charles-Joachim Colbert, 1738
Jean François Dandrieu, 1738
Jean Baptiste Labat, 1738
André-Hercule de Fleury, 1743
Thomas Innes, 1744
Jacques Philippe Lallemant, 1748
Louis Nicolas Clérambault, 1749
Henri François d' Aguesseau, 1751
Jean Astruc, 1766
Léon Ménard, 1767
Marc Antoine Laugier, 1769
Michel Le Quien, 1773
Charles François Houbigant, 1783
Jean Lévesque de Burigny, 1785
Etienne François de Choiseul, 1785
Nicolas-Sylvestre Bergier, 1790
Armand Chapt de Rastignac, 1792
François Joseph La Rochefoucauld-Bayers,
    1792
Maximilien François de Robespierre, 1794
Louis Pierre Anquetil, 1808
Jean Baptiste de Belloy, 1808
Giovanni Battista Caprara, 1810
Jacques-André Emery, 1811
André Ernest Modeste Grétry, 1813
Augustin de Barruel, 1820
Maurice Jean de Brogue, 1821
René Just Haüy, 1822
Marie-François-Pierre Maine de Biran,
    1824
Claude Henri de Rouvroy Saint-Simon,
    1825
François-Joseph Gossec, 1829
Henri Baptiste Grégoire, 1831
Pierre-André Latreille, 1833
Henriette Aymer de la Chevalerie, 1834
Alexandre Etienne Choron, 1834
George Lacombe, 1834
Pierre Marie Joseph Coudrin, 1837
Jeanne Elisabeth Bichier des Ages, 1838
Charles Maurice de Talleyrand-Périgord,
    1838
Hyacinthe Louis de Quelen, 1839
Louis Gabriel Ambroise de Bonald, 1840
Luigi Cherubini, 1842
Denis Auguste Affre, 1848
François Auguste René, Vicomte de
    Chateaubriand, 1848
Jean Alexis François Artaud de Montor,
    1849
Honoré de Balzac, 1850
José María Luis Mora, 1850
Jean-Paul Alban de Villeneuve-
    Bargemont, 1850
Anne-Marie Javouhey, 1851

Vincenzo Gioberti, 1852
Francis Mary Libermann, 1852
Félicité Robert de Lamennais, 1854
René François Rohrbacher, 1856
Lucien Bonaparte, 1857
Ferdinand Toussaint Chatel, 1857
Gustave François Xavier de Ravignan,
    1858
John Barry, 1859
Zygmunt Krasinski, 1859
Evariste Régis Huc, 1860
Madeleine Sophie Barat, 1865
Joseph Louis d'Ortigue, 1866
Louis-Eugène-Marie Bautain, 1867
Arthur Marie Le Hir, 1868
Alphonse Marie Louis de Prat de
    Lamartine, 1869
Charles Forbes René de Montalembert,
    1870
Georges Darboy, 1871
Pierre Olivaint, 1871
Jacques Paul Migne, 1875
Catherine Labouré, 1876
Armand de Melun, 1877
Augustin Bonnetty, 1879
Jean Joseph Gaume, 1879
Ivan Sergeevich Gagarin, 1882
Cyprian Kamil Norwid, 1883
Louis François Veuillot, 1883
Henri Louis Charles Maret, 1884
Marie Théodore Ratisbonne, 1884
Mary Aloysia Hardey, 1886
César Franck, 1890
Charles Louis Gay, 1892
Joseph Ernest Renan, 1892
Joseph Theodore Crampon, 1894
Henri Chaumont, 1896
Jean Barthélémy Hauréau, 1896
Maurice d'Hulst, 1896
Léon Ollé-Laprune, 1898
Edouard Paul Dhorme, 1899
Armand David, 1900
Albert de Broglie, 1901
John Baptist Hogan, 1901
Auguste Sabatier, 1901
Emile Edouard Charles Antoine Zola,
    1902
Anthony M. Keiley, 1905
Carlos Calvo, 1906
Joris-Karl Huysmans, 1907
François Marie Benjamin Richard, 1908
François Marie Richard de la Vigne, 1908
Henri Huvelin, 1910
Vincent de Paul Bailly, 1912
Charles Loyson, 1912
Albert de Mun, 1914
Marcel Hebert, 1916
Théodule Armand Ribot, 1916
Augustin Poulain, 1919
Paul Lejay, 1920
Etienne Emile Marie Boutroux, 1921
Paul Bureau, 1923
Théodore Dubois, 1924
Gabriel Urbain Fauré, 1924

Paris	Albert Houtin, 1926
	Léonce de Grandmaison, 1927
	Pierre Batiffol, 1929
	Louis Ernest Dubois, 1929
	Ambroise Gardeil, 1931
	Vincent d' Indy, 1931
	François Nicolas Nau, 1931
	Lucien Laberthonnière, 1932
	Maurice De La Taille, 1933
	Paul Fournier, 1935
	Jean Vincent Bainvel, 1937
	Adhémar d'Alès, 1938
	Fernand Mourret, 1938
	Edouard Branly, 1940
	Alfred Firmin Loisy, 1940
	Dmitry Sergeyevich Merezhkovsky, 1941
	Henri Marie Alfred Baudrillart, 1942
	Maurice Denis, 1943
	Sergei Nikolaevich Bulgakov, 1944
	Alexis Carrel, 1944
	Henri Ghéon, 1944
	Ernest Bernard Allo, 1945
	Eulogius, 1946
	Victor Martial Leroquais, 1946
	Jean Baptiste Chabot, 1948
	Georges Desvallières, 1950
	Emmanuel Mounier, 1950
	Marc Sangnier, 1950
	Jean Guiraud, 1953
	Eduoard Le Roy, 1954
	René Le Senne, 1954
	André Robert, 1955
	Paul Louis Charles Marie Claudel, 1955
	Valentin Marie Breton, 1957
	Jules Monchanin, 1957
	Vladimir Nikolaevich Lossky, 1958
	Georges Henri Rouault, 1958
	Raïssa Oumansoff Maritain, 1960
	Bruno de Jésus Marie, 1962
	Louis Massignon, 1962
	Francis Poulenc, 1963
	Marie Alphonse Dain, 1964
	Nikolai Onufrievich Lossky, 1965
	Nicholas Afanasiev, 1966
	Evgrav Evgrafovich Kovalevsky, 1970
	François Mauriac, 1970
	Gabriel Marcel, 1973
	Jean Daniélou, 1974
	Pierre-André Liégé, 1976
	Maurice Duruflé, 1986
	Leonid Uspensky, 1987
	Marie Dominique Chenu, 1990
	Jean Langlais, 1991
	Henri de Lubac, 1991
	Olivier Messiaen, 1992
	Madeleine Barot, 1995
	Yves Marie-Joseph Congar, 1995
Passy	Joseph François Michaud, 1839
Périgord	Michel Eyquem de Montaigne, 1592
Perigueux	Adalbald, 652
Pern	Jeanne Jugan, 1879
Perpignan	Olympe Philippe Gerbet, 1864
Perseigne	Adam of Perseigne, 1221
Pibrac	Germaine of Pibrac, 1601
Ploërmel	Jean-Marie-Robert de Lamennais, 1860
Poitiers	Hilary of Poitiers, 367
	Anthemius of Poitiers, 400
	Radegunda, 587
	Agnes of Poitiers, 588
	Gilbert de la Porrée, 1154
	John de Grey, 1214
	Antoinette d'Orléans-Longueville, 1618
	André Hubert Fournet, 1834
	Auguste Carayon, 1874
	Josefa Menéndez, 1923
Pont-à-Mousson	Paul Gabriel Antoine, 1743
Port-Royal	Jacqueline Marie Angélique Arnauld, 1661
	Jeanne Catherine Agnès Arnauld, 1672
Puteaux	Leopold Beaudenom, 1916
Quimper	John Discalceatus, 1349
Rambouillet	Francis I, 1547
Le Reclus	François Armand Gervaise, 1751
Remiremont	Arnulf of Metz, c.641
Rennes	John of Saint-Samson, 1636
Rheims	Remigius of Rheims, c.533
	Bova, 673
	Liutwin of Trier, c.717
	Flodoard of Rheims, 894
	Bruno of Cologne, 965
	Adalbero of Rheims, 988
	Gervase of Rheims, 1067
	Eon of Stella, c.1148
	Richard of Middleton, 1302
	Guillaume de Machaut, 1377
	Gregory Martin, 1582
	William Gifford, 1629
	Pierre Sabatier, 1742
	Thomas Marie Joseph Gousset, 1866
	Louis Brehier, 1951
Rodez	John Capreolus, 1444
	Isaac Habert, 1688
	Philippe Joseph Benjamin Buchez, 1865
Rouen	Remigius of Rouen, c.772
	William I, 1087
	Hugh of Amiens, 1164
	Odo Rigaldus, 1275
	Thomas Netter, 1430
	Joan of Arc, 1431
	Stephen Brinkley, 1590
	Bernard Lamy, 1715
	John Baptiste de La Salle, 1719
	Henri Marie Gaston de Bonnechose, 1883
Rully	Jean Jouffroy, 1473
Saint-Amand	Hucbald of Saint-Amand, 930
	Gilbert of Saint-Amand, 1095
Saint-Amour	William of Saint-Amour, 1272
Saint-Bertin	Joscio, 1163
Saint-Brieuc	Brieuc, 550
Saint-Clément	Victor Martin, 1945
St Cloud	Charles François Gounod, 1893
Saint-Cyr	Françoise d'Aubigné de Maintenon, 1719
St Denis	François Lamy, 1711
	François Bedos de Celles, 1779
	Louise of France, 1787
St Évroul	Ordericus Vitalis, c.1142
St Géniez	Denis Frayssinous, 1841
St Germain	Thomas Codrington, c.1693
	James II, 1701

Saint-Germer-de-
    Flay   Germerius, 660
Saint-Gilles   Giles, c.720
                       Peter de Bruys, 1130
St Laurent-sur-Sèvre   Louis-Marie Grignion de Montfort, 1716
                       Gabriel Deshayes, 1841
St Malo   John Lynch, c.1673
St Maximin   Marie Joseph La Grange, 1938
St Omer   John Floyd, 1649
                       Michael Alford, 1652
                       Alban Butler, 1773
St Quentin   Jean Mouton, 1522
                       1518, Loyset Compère, 1518
Sainte-Radegond   René Graffin, 1941
Saint-Remy-de-
    Provence   Léon Daudet, 1942
Saumur   Gilbert Generbrard, 1597
                       Moïse Amyraut, 1664
                       Edmund O'Reilly, 1669
                       Jeanne Delanoue, 1736
Savigny   Vitalis of Savigny, 1122
                       Haimo of Landecop, 1173
Sceaux   Paul Monceaux, 1941
Schirmeck   Joseph Schmidlin, 1944
Sedan   Andrew Melville, 1622
Senones   Augustin Calmet, 1757
Sens   Lupus of Sens, 623
                       Etienne-Charles de Lomenie de Brienne,
                          1794
Seringes   Alfred Joyce Kilmer, 1918
Sèvres   Samuel Berger, 1900
                       Jean Calvet, 1965
Sithiu   Bertinus, 709
Soissons   Leidradus of Lyons, 817
                       Godfrey of Amiens, 1115
Solesmes   André Mocquereau, 1930
Strasburg   Arbogast of Strasburg, 680
                       Tauler, Johann, 1361
                       Ludolph of Saxony, 1378
                       Johannes Geiler von Kaysersberg, 1510
                       Sebastian Brant, 1521
                       Wolfgang Capito, 1541
                       Beatus Rhenanus, 1547
                       Johannes Sturm, 1589
                       Philippe André Grandidier, 1787
                       Franz Xaver Richter, 1789
                       Edouard Guillaume Eugène Reuss, 1891
                       Paul Sabatier, 1928
                       Charles Ruch, 1945
                       Emile Amann, 1948
                       Michel Andrieu, 1956
                       Hilaire Duesberg, 1969
Thérouanne   Hunfried, 870
Thionville   Hildegard of Kempten, 783
Thury-en-Valois   Achille Desurmont, 1898
Tiron   Adjutor, 1131
Toul   Aper of Toul, 507
                       Gauzelin of Toul, 962
                       Gerard of Toul, 994
Toulouse   Raymond of Toulouse, 1118
                       Gilbert, c.1167
                       Raymond of Toulouse VI, 1222
                       Bertrand of Garriga, 1230
                       William of Arnaud, 1242

                       Raymond of Sebonde, 1436
                       Arnold Badet, 1536
                       Jean Arnoux, 1636
                       Claude Maltret, 1674
                       Antoine Dadin de Hautesserre, 1682
                       Jean Pierre de Caussade, 1751
                       Jean Calas, 1762
                       Anne-Antonine Jules de Clermont-
                          Tonnerre, 1830
                       Paul Thérèse David d' Astros, 1851
                       Ferdinand Cavallera, 1954
                       Joseph Bonsirven, 1958
                       Louis Capéran, 1962
                       Jacques Maritain, 1973
Tours   Brice, 444
                       Clotilde, 545
                       Gregory of Tours, 594
                       Alcuin, 804
                       Berengarius of Tours, 1088
                       Hildebert of Lavardin, 1133
                       Roger of Worcester, 1179
                       Jean Marie de Maille, 1414
                       Elias de Bourdeille, 1484
                       Johannes Ockeghem, 1497
                       Francis of Paola, 1507
                       Charles Maurras, 1952
Trédez   Ivo of Helory, 1303
Trèves   John Bridgewater, 1596
Troyes   Prudentius Galindo, 861
                       Gilbert of Holland, 1172
Troyes   Maria Salesia Chappuis, 1875
Tulle   Charles du Plessis d'Argentre, 1740
Val-près-Le-Puy   Jean Calès, 1947
Valence   Apollinaris of Valence, c.520
                       Barnard of Vienne, 842
                       Humbert of Romans, 1277
                       Pius VI, 1799
Valenciennes   Guido De Brès, 1567
Vannes   Vincent Ferrer, 1419
                       Pierre René Rogue, 1796
Vendeé   Louis Marie Baudouin, 1835
Verdun   Alberic of Ostia, 1148
Versailles   Louis XIV, 1715
                       Michel Richard de Lalande, 1726
                       Jean Jacques Auguste Nicolas, 1888
Vienne   Avitus of Vienne, c.519
                       Desiderius of Vienne, c.606
                       Ado of Vienne, 875
Villéreal   Louis Lavelle, 1951
Vincennes   Jules Mazarin, 1661
                       Jacques Augustin Marie Crétineau-Joly,
                          1875
Vinsauf   Geoffrey of Vinsauf, 1220

GABON   Albert Schweitzer, 1965

GERMANY
Aachen   Benedict of Aniane, 821
                       Alfred von Reumont, 1887
                       Alfons Bellesheim, 1912
                       Viktor Cathrein, 1931
Altenburg   Georg Spalatin, 1545
Ansbach   Gumbert of Ansbach, c.0790
Aschaffenburg   Wolfgang von Dalberg, 1601

Friedrich Karl Joseph von Erthal, 1802
Johann Friedrich Hugo Nepomuk
  Eckenbrecht von Dalberg, 1812
Clemens Maria Brentano, 1842

Augsburg
Afra, 302
Adalbero of Augsburg, 909
Egino, 1120
Herluka of Bernried, 1127
David of Augsburg, 1272
Öser Irmhart, c.1360
Jakob Fugger, 1525
Pilgram Marbeck, 1556
Gregor Aichinger, 1628
Placidus Braun, 1829

Bad Boll Johann Christoph Blumhart, 1880
Bad Kissinger Berthold Altaner, 1964
Bad Kreuth Jakob Frohschammer, 1893
Baden Baden Heinrich Julius Holtzmann, 1910
Peter Browe, 1949

Bamberg
Frutolf of Michelsberg, 1103
Heimo of Michelsberg, 1138
Otto of Bamberg, 1139
Hugh of Trimberg, c.1314
Lupold of Bebenburg, 1363
Artur Michael Landgraf, 1958

Bayreuth Franz Liszt, 1886
Berlin
Johann Cruger, 1662
Freidrich Daniel Ernst Schleiermacher,
  1834
Johann August Wilhelm Neander, 1850
Hermann von Mallinckrodt, 1874
Leopold von Ranke, 1886
Peter Reichensperger, 1892
Paul Hinschius, 1898
Paul von Hoensbroech, 1923
Ernst Troeltsch, 1923
Wolf Wilhelm Baudissin, 1926
Karl Holl, 1926
Erich Caspar, 1935
Hans Lietzmann, 1942
Franz Jägerstätter, 1943
Max Josef Metzger, 1944
Käthe Kollwitz, 1945
Edward Joseph Flanagan, 1948

Beuron Athanasius Miller, 1963
Bingen Hildegarde of Bingen, 1179
Bartholomew Holzhauser, 1658

Bonn
Constantine of Barbanson, 1631
Georg Hermes, 1831
Barthold Georg Niebuhr, 1831
Ernst Moritz Arndt, 1860
Christian Carl Josias von Bunsen, 1860
Johann Heinrich Achterfeldt, 1877
Joseph Hubert Reinkens, 1896
Franz Heinrich Reusch, 1900
Franz Philipp Kaulen, 1907
Victor Frins, 1912
Heinrich Kellner, 1915
Gerhard Rauschen, 1917
Anton Huonder, 1926
Eduard König, 1936
Carl Clemens, 1940
Albert Ehrhard, 1940
Franz Feldmann, 1944

Anton Baumstark, 1948
Walther Holtzmann, 1963
Hubert Jedin, 1980
Bosau Helmond, c.1177
Braunsberg Robert Abercromby, 1613
Bremen
Ansgar, 865
Rembert of Bremen-Hamburg, 888
Adalgar of Bremen, 909
Adaldag, 988
Adam of Bremen, 1081
Joachim Neander, 1680

Breslau
Ceslaus of Silesia, 1242
Joannes Cochlaeus, 1552
Sebastian Rostock, 1671
Angelus Silesius, 1677
Richard Reitzenstein, 1861
Moritz Brosig, 1887
Ferdinand Probst, 1899
William Wrede, 1906
Johannes Nikel, 1924

Brunswick Martin Chemnitz, 1586
Burghausen Wilhelm Emmanuel von Ketteler, 1877
Burtscheid Gregory of Cerchiara, 1002
Cassel Heimerad, 1019
Celle Hadalinus, c.690
Johann Arndt, 1621

Chemnitz Georgius Agricola, 1555
Cologne
Agilulf of Cologne, 750
Adelaide of Vilich, 1015
Heribert of Cologne, 1021
Gregory VI, 1047
Caesarius of Heisterbach, 1240
Herman Joseph, c.1241
Albert the Great, 1280
Johannes Duns Scotus, 1308
Christina of Stommeln, 1312
Meister Eckhart, 1327
Johannes Brammart, 1407
Henry of Kalkar, 1408
Henry of Gorkum, 1431
Stefan Lochner, 1451
Werner Rolevinck, 1502
Conrad Köllin, 1536
Johannes Justus Lanspergius, 1539
Ortwin Gratius, 1542
Eberhard Billick, 1557
George Cassander, 1566
Hendrik Niclaes, 1580
Melchior Hittorf, 1584
Severin Binius, 1641
Franz Egon von Fürstenberg, 1682
Claude Lacroix, 1714
Joseph Hartzheim, 1772
Johannes von Geissel, 1864
Adolf Kolping, 1865
Matthias Joseph Scheeben, 1888
August Reichensperger, 1895
Julius Bachem, 1918
Paul Bedjan, 1920
Joseph Frobes, 1947
Dominikus Böhm, 1955
Constance Conrad of Constance, 975
Gebhard II of Constance, 995
Gebhard III of Constance, 1110

John Huss, 1415
Manuel Chrysoloras, 1415
Jerome of Prague, 1416
Francesco Zabarella, 1417
Robert Hallum, 1417
Paulus Laymann, 1635
Vital Lehodey, 1948

Corvey — Ludolf of Corvey, 983
Druthmar, 1046

Dachau — Titus Brandsma, 1942
Darmstadt — Peter Gratz, 1849
Eberhard Arnold, 1935

Dernbach — Katharina Kasper, 1898
Dillingen — Georg Graf, 1955
Dresden — Hieronymus Emser, 1527
George of Saxony, 1539
Heinrich Schütz, 1672
Samuel Benedikt Carpzov, 1707
Friedrich August Biener, 1861

Duisberg — Gerardus, 1594
Düsseldorf — Paul Ernst Kahle, 1964
Eichstätt — Moritz von Hutten, 1552
Franz Morgott, 1900
Josef Hollweck, 1926

Einsiedeln — Gregory of Einsiedeln, 996
Eisenach — Nikolaus von Amsdorf, 1565
Eisleben — Martin Luther, 1546
Erfurt — Henry of Friemar, 1340
Johann Zachariae, 1428
Wolfgang Ratke, 1635
Andrew Gordon, 1751

Erlangen — Johann Christian Konrad von Hoffman, 1877
Theodor von Zahn, 1933
Johannes Lindworsky, 1939

Essen — John of Falkenberg, 1435
Falkenberg — John of Falkenberg, 1435
Flossenburg — Dietrich Bonhoeffer, 1945
Frankfurt am Main — Matthias Flacius Illyricus, 1575
Hans Leo von Hassler, 1612
Johannes Janssen, 1891
Joseph Kramp, 1940
Paul Hindemith, 1963

Frankfurt an den Oder — Paul Billerbeck, 1932
Freiburg — John of Freiburg, 1314
Gregor Reisch, 1525
Marquard Herrgott, 1762
Engelbert Klupfel, 1811
Johann Leonard Hug, 1846
Johann Hirscher, 1865
Johann Baptist Alzog, 1878
Franz Joseph Ritter von Buss, 1878
Suitbert Bäumer, 1894
Gottfried Hoberg, 1924
Johannes Quasten, 1987

Freising — Rahewin of Freising, 1170
Anacletus Reiffenstuel, 1703
Magnus Jocham, 1893

Freudenstadt — Frank Nathan Daniel Buchman, 1961
Gaming — Nicholas of Strasburg, 1497
Giessen — Wilhelm Bousset, 1920
Görlitz — Jakob Böhme, 1624
Goslar — Adalbert of Hamburg-Bremen, 1072
Gotha — Friedrich Myconius, 1546

Göttingen — Henry II, 1024
Johann Lorenz von Mosheim, 1755
Johann David Michaelis, 1791
Georg Heinrich August Ewald, 1875
Albrecht Ritschl, 1889
Paul Anton Lagarde, 1891
Julius Wellhausen, 1918
Friedrich Spitta, 1924
Carl Mirbt, 1929
Alfred Rahlfs, 1935
Walter Bauer, 1960
Friedrich Gogarten, 1967

Gummersheim — Louis of Arnstein, 1185
Halberstadt — Hildigrim, 827
Haymo of Halberstadt, 853
John Teutonicus, 1246

Halle — Matthias Grünewald, 1528
August Hermann Francke, 1727
Justus Henning Boehmer, 1749
Heinrich Friedrich Wilhelm Gesenius, 1842
Emil Friedrich Kautzch, 1910
Gustav Adolf Warneck, 1910
Edgar Loening, 1919
Friedrich Loofs, 1928
Hermann Gunkel, 1932

Hamburg — Benedict V, 965
Stanislaw Lubieniecki, 1675
Johannes Albert Fabricius, 1736
Hermann Samuel Reimarus, 1768
Friedrich Gottlieb Klopstock, 1803

Hanover — Gottfried Wilhelm Leibniz, 1716
Heidelberg — Conrad of Gelnhausen, 1390
Rudolphus Frisius Agricola, 1485
Johann von Dalberg, 1503
Victorinus Strigel, 1569
Girolamo Zanchi, 1590
Adolf von Harnack, 1930
Martin Dibelius, 1947
Walter Freytag, 1959
Gerhard von Rad, 1971

Heidenheim — Walburga of Heidenheim, 779
Heilsberg — Martin Kromer, 1589
Helfta — Gertrude the Great, 1302
Helmstedt — Georg Calixtus, 1656
Polycarp Leyser, 1728
Hermann von der Hardt, 1746

Henef — Hermann Joseph Bückers, 1964
Herrnhut — Nicolaus Ludwig Zinzendorf, 1760
Herzfeld — Ida of Herzfeld, 825
Hesse — Kunigunde, c.1033
Hildesheim — Ebbo of Rheims, 851
Himmerod Eifel — David of Himmerod, 1179
Hohenberg — Herrad of Landsberg, 1195
Ingolstadt — Johann Eck, 1543
Veit Amerbach, 1557
Martin Eisengrein, 1578
Henricus Canisius, 1610
Christof Besold, 1638
Anton Mayr, 1749

Jena — Johann Gerhard, 1637
Johann Jakob Griesbach, 1812
Richard Adelbert Lipsius, 1892

Karlsbad — August Friedrich Gfrörer, 1861

Karlsruhe	Franz Joseph Mone, 1871
	Wilhelm Brambach, 1932
Kassel	Philip of Hesse, 1567
	Johann Wilhelm Bickell, 1848
Kaufburen	Crescentia Hoss, 1744
Kitzingen	Hadeloga, 750c
Koblenz	Bartholomaeus Latomus, 1570
	Le Plat, 1810
Königsberg	Immanuel Kant, 1804
Königstein	Clemens Blume, 1932
Konnersreuth	Theresa Neumann, 1962
Kornthal	Johann Ludwig Krapf, 1881
Kulmsee	Jutta of Sangerhausen, 1260
Landshut	Martin Mair, 1480
	Patrick Zimmer, 1820
	Josef Edmund Jorg, 1901
Landstuhl	Franz Gillmann, 1941
Leipzig	Johann Tetzel, 1519
	Joachim Camerarius, 1574
	Benedikt Carpzov, 1666
	Johann Benedikt Carpzov, 1699
	Johann Sebastian Bach, 1750
	Felix Mendelssohn, 1847
	Kobegott Friedrich Konstantin von Tischendorf, 1874
	Franz Julius Delitzsch, 1890
	Emil Albert Friedberg, 1910
	Albert Hauck, 1918
	Rudolf Kittel, 1929
Lenzen	Gottschalk, 1066
Lindenburg	Heinrich Brauns, 1939
Lochau	Frederick III of Saxony, 1525
Lübeck	Arnold of Lübeck, 1214
	Johann Gottlob Carpzov, 1767
Ludwigsberg	David Friedrich Strauss, 1874
Magdeburg	Bruno of Magdeburg, 1084
	Norbert of Xanten, 1134
	Bartholomaeus Anglicus, 1250
	Jordan of Giano, 1262
	Henry of Merseburg, c.1276
	Johann Bernhard Basedow, 1790
Mainz	Auraeus, 406
	Bilhild, 750
	Lioba, 780
	Frederick of Mainz, 954
	Ekkehard of Sankt Gallen, 990
	Karl von Miltitz, 1529
	Johannes de Buys, 1547
	Joseph Ludwig Colmar, 1818
	Johann Baptist Heinrich, 1891
	Heinrich Brück, 1903
	Fritz Kern, 1950
Marburg	Elizabeth of Hungary, 1231
	Karl Ferdinand Reinhardt Budde, 1933
	Rudolf Otto, 1937
	Adolf Julicher, 1938
	Rudolph Karl Bultmann, 1976
Metten	Utto Kornmüller, 1907
Miesbach	Maximilian Joseph Heimbucher, 1946
Mindelheim	Johannes Altenstaig, 1525
Minden	Henry of Herford, 1370
Mönchengladbach	Gustav Gundlach, 1963
Mülhausen	Thomas Münzer, 1525
Munich	Michael of Cesena, 1342
	William of Ockham, 1347
	Orlando di Lasso, 1594
	Johann Kaspar von Kerll, 1693
	Frances Bedingfield, 1704
	Fortunatus Hueber, 1706
	Johann Georg Hamann, 1788
	Johann Adam Möhler, 1838
	Heinrich Klee, 1840
	Franz Xaver von Baader, 1841
	Kaspar Ett, 1847
	Johann Joseph von Görres, 1848
	Johann Kaspar Aiblinger, 1867
	Karolina Gerhardinger, 1879
	Gottlieb Christoph Adolph von Harless, 1879
	Johann Joseph Ignaz von Döllinger, 1890
	Ferdinand Gregorovius, 1891
	Pius Bonifatius Gams, 1892
	Joseph Bach, 1901
	Josef Rheinberger, 1901
	Heinrich Seuse Denifle, 1905
	Johann Friedrich, 1917
	John Augustine Zahm, 1921
	Bernard Duhr, 1930
	Otto Bardenhewer, 1935
	Rupert Mayer, 1945
	Andreas Evaristus Mader, 1949
	Michael von Faulhaber, 1952
	Anton Michel, 1958
	Paul Lehmann, 1964
	Friedrich Heiler, 1967
	Romano Guardini, 1968
	Hugo Rahner, 1968
	Alois Grillmeier, 1998
Münster	Ludger of Münster, 809
	Hermann Busenbaum, 1668
	Amalia Gallitzin, 1806
	Franz Friedrich Wilhelm von Fürstenberg, 1810
	Bernard Heinrich Overberg, 1826
	Johann Theodor Hermann Katerkamp, 1834
	Anton Berlage, 1881
	Franz Diekamp, 1943
	Clemens Augustinus von Galen, 1946
Neuenheerse	Helentrudis, c.950
Nuremberg	Raymond of Capua, 1399
	Johann Nider, 1438
	Albrecht Dürer, 1528
	Willibald Pirkcheimer, 1530
	Johann Pachelbel, 1706
Ochsenhausen	Henry of Zwiefalten, 1262
Olpe	Maria Theresia Bonzel, 1905
Osnabruck	Friedrich Leopold, Graf zu Stolberg, 1819
Ottobeuren	Nikolaus Ellenbog, 1543
Paderborn	Meinwerk of Paderborn, 1036
	Herman of Scheda, 1170
	Pauline von Mallinckrodt, 1881
	Beda Kleinschmidt, 1932
	Bernhard Bartmann, 1938
	Johannes Hatzfeld, 1953
	Lorenz Jaeger, 1975
Passau	Ermenrich of Passau, 874
	Leopold Ernst Firmian, 1783

	Alois Buchner, 1869		Karl Heim, 1958
	Ignaz Klug, 1929		Karl Adam, 1966
Perlebey	Gottfried Arnold, 1714	Ulm	Henry Suso, 1366
Potsdam	Odo Russell, 1884		Martinus Balticus, 1600
Prüm	Hilduin of Saint-Denis, c.855		Hermann Bäuerle, 1936
	Ansbald, 886	Vöhringen	Johann Michael Feneberg, 1812
Puch	Edigna, 1109	Waldbreitbach	Rosa Flesch, 1906
Pullach	Joseph Braun, 1947	Weimar	Lucas Cranach, 1553
Quedlinburg	Matilda of Germany, 968		Johann Gottfried von Herder, 1803
Rappoltsweiler	Philipp Jakob Spener, 1635		Johann Nepomuk Hummel, 1837
Rastatt	Johann Kaspar Ferdinand Fischer, 1746	Weingarten	Gerwig Blarer, 1567
Ratzeburg	Ansuerus, 1066		Gabriel Bucelin, 1681
Regensburg	Hemma, 876	Wiesbaden	Martin Niemöller, 1984
	Othlo of Sankt Emmeram, c.1070	Wilparting	Anianus and Marinus, 675
	William of Hirsau, 1091	Wiltern	Friedrich Bernhard Maasen, 1900
	Berthold of Regensburg, 1272	Wismar	Ludolph of Ratzeburg, 1250
	Conrad of Megenburg, 1374	Wittenberg	Adam of Fulda, 1505
	Aventinus, 1534		Johann Bugenhagen, 1558
	Karl Theodor von Dalberg, 1817		Philipp Melanchthon, 1560
	Johann Georg Mettenleiter, 1858		George Major, 1574
	Franz Xaver Haberl, 1910		Abraham Calov, 1686
	Michael Haller, 1915	Wolfenbüttel	Michael Praetorius, 1621
	Lorenz Dürr, 1939	Worms	Burchard of Worms, 1025
Reichenau	Hermannus Contractus, 1054		Matthew of Cracow, 1410
Reichenhall	Carl Muth, 1944	Würzburg	Conrad of Querfurt, 1202
Rengsdorf	Eberhard Bethge, 2000		Herman of Schildesche, 1357
Rostock	David Chrytraeus, 1600		Hans Böhm, 1476
	Hugo Grotius, 1645		Tilman Riemenschneider, 1531
	Ernst Barlach, 1938		Bartholomaeus Arnoldi, 1532
Ruhlpolding	Georg von Hertling, 1919		Julius Echter von Mespelbrunn, 1617
St-Peter-im-			Christoph Franz von Hutten, 1729
Schwarzwald	Nikolaus Gihr, 1924		Johann Georg von Eckhart, 1730
Sankt-Gerold	Gerold, 978		Franz Ludwig von Erthal, 1795
Schneidemühl	Johann Czerski, 1893		Heinrich Joseph Denzinger, 1883
Schomberg	Alois Knöpfler, 1921		Franz Hettinger, 1890
Schonemgar	Liborius Wagner, 1631		Franz Adam Göpfert, 1913
Schweinfurt	Franz Josef Dölger, 1940		Konrad Eubel, 1923
Schwelm	Engelbert of Cologne, 1225		Johannes Hehn, 1932
Siegberg	Anno of Cologne, 1075		Christopher Edmund Becker, 1937
Spandau	Hermann Cohen, 1871		Paul Fridolin Kehr, 1944
Speyer	Daniel Bonifatius Haneberg, 1876	Wustenfelde	Menno Simons, 1559
Stuttgart	Johann Brenz, 1570	Zeitz	Julius von Pflug, 1546
	Johannes Gottlieb Christaller, 1895		
	Eberhard Nestlé, 1913	GREECE	
Tegernsee	Froumund of Tegernsee, c.1008	Athens	Aristides, 180
	John Emerich Edward Dalberg Acton, 1902		Athenagoras, 190
			Charles Lenormant, 1859
Trier	Agricius of Trier, 329		Nectarius of Aegina, 1920
	Priscillian, 384		Eusebius Matthopoulos, 1929
	Irmina, 710		Nicholas Planas of Athens, 1932
	Adela, 734		Photios Kontonglu, 1965
	Regino of Prum, 915		Panagiotis Trembelas, 1977
	Christoph Brouwer, 1617		Panayiotis Nellas, 1986
	John Martin Moyé, 1793	Chios	Macarius of Corinth, 1805
	Rudolph Cornely, 1908	Constantia	Anthemius of Constantia, 490
	Hubert Junker, 1971	Corinth	Dionysius of Corinth, 180
Tübingen	Gabriel Biel, 1495		William of Moerbeke, 1286
	John Nauclerus, 1510	Edessa	Ephrem the Syrian, c.373
	Ferdinand Christian Baur, 1860		Rabbula, 435
	Johannes Kuhn, 1887	Lesbos	Irene, 803
	Franz Xaver von Funk, 1907		Manuel Calecas, 1410
	Karl Bihlmeyer, 1942	Mammola	Nicodemus of Mammola, 990
	Johannes Haller, 1947	Mount Athos	Anthony III, 983
	Gerhard Kittel, 1948		Anthimus II , 1628

	Nicodemus of the Holy Mountain, 1809
	Siloan the Athonite, 1938
Paroria	Gregory Sinaites, 1346
Philippopolis	Philoxenus, 523
Rhodes	Pierre d'Aubusson, 1503
Samothrace	Theophanes the Confessor, 817
Thessalonika	Elias of Thessalonika, 903
	Matthew Blastares, 1340
	Gregory Palamas, 1359
	Theodore Dexios, c.1360
GRENADA	Reginald Buckler, 1927
GUATEMALA	Francisco Marroquin, 1563
	Francisco Cepeda, 1602
	Juan Zapata y Sandoval, 1630
	Pedro de San José Betancur, 1667
	José Antonio Liendo y Goicoechea, 1814
	Nicolás García Xerez, 1825
	Stanley Rother, 1981
HAITI	François Marie Kersuzan, 1935
HAWAII	Damien of Molokai, 1889
	James Hunnewell Kekela, 1904
	Joseph Dutton, 1931
HONG KONG	Robert James Semple, 1910
	Karl Ludvig Reichelt, 1952
HUNGARY	
Alcinc	György Martinuzzi, 1551
Alt-Kinsburg	Hroznata, 1217
Buda	Gerard of Csanad, 1046
Budapest	Mihaly Babits, 1941
Esztergom	Bálint Balassa, 1594
Kalocsa	Gyula Fényi, 1927
Kursanec Forest	Miklós Zrinyi, 1664
Nagyvárad	Andras Báthory, 1340
Varadin	Gian Francesco Aldobrandini, 1601
INDIA	
Agra	Heinrich Roth, 1668
Calcutta	Alphonse François Lacroix, 1859
	George Dandoy, 1962
	Teresa of Calcutta, 1997
Chichawatni	Esther John, 1960
Dehra Dun	Paul David Devanandan, 1962
Dohnavur	
Tirunelveli	Amy Carmichael, 1951
Dornakal	Vendanayagam Samuel Azariah, 1945
Goa	João Nunes Barreto, 1562
	Rudolf Acquaviva, 1583
	Antonio de Andrade, 1634
Indore	Henri Le Saux, 1973
Kerala	Kuriakos Elias Chavara, 1871
Lahore	Henry James Anderson, 1875
Madras	Roberto de Nobili, 1656
Manapar	Costanzo Giuseppe Beschi, 1746
Oreiour	John de Britto, 1693
Palur	Johann Ernst Hanxleden, 1732
Patna	Anastasius Hartmann, 1886
Punnaikayel	Antonio Criminali, 1549
Serampore	William Carey, 1834

Shantivanam	Bede Griffiths, 1994
Sylhet	Pal Krishna, 1822
Thanjavur	Christian Friedrich Schwartz, 1798
Trichinopoly	Reginald Heber, 1826
Trivandrum	Mar Ivanios, 1953
Vellore	Daniel Thambyrajah Niles, 1970
INDONESIA	Dionysius of the Nativity, 1638
INNER	
MONGOLIA	Théophile Verbist, 1868
IRELAND	
Armagh	Bryan McGurk, 1713
	Joseph MacRory, 1945
	William Conway, 1977
Artane	John Alen, 1534
Ballinrobe	Edward Alfred D'alton, 1941
Bangor	Comgall, 602
Birr	Brendan of Birr, 580
Carlow	James Warren Doyle, 1834
Clonard	Finnian of Clonard, c.549
Clonfert	Brendan of Clonfert, 578
Clonmel	Maurice Kenraghty, 1585
	Geoffrey Keating, c.1644
Clontarf	Brian Boru, 1014
Cork	Nono Nagle, 1784
	Theobald Mathew, 1856
Dublin	John de Saint-Pol, 1362
	Gelasius O'Cullenan, 1580
	Maurice Eustace, 1581
	Conor O'Devaney, 1612
	Christopher Holywood, 1626
	Redmond Caron, 1666
	Richard Bellings, 1677
	Peter Talbot, 1680
	Edmund Byrne, 1723
	Cornelius Nary, 1738
	Jonathan Swift, 1745
	John Murphy, 1753
	John Thomas Troy, 1823
	John Lanigan, 1828
	Catherine McAuley, 1841
	Daniel Murray, 1852
	Thomas Kelly, 1855
	William Vincent Harold, 1856
	Mary Aikenhead, 1858
	Frances Mary Teresa Ball, 1861
	William Carleton, 1869
	Paul Cullen, 1878
	Gerard Manley Hopkins, 1889
	George Salmon, 1904
	John B. Bannon, 1913
	Arthur Devine, 1919
	William Martin Murphy, 1919
	William Joseph Walsh, 1921
	Matthew Talbot, 1925
	Edward Leen, 1944
	John Joseph Glennon, 1946
	Paschal Robinson, 1948
	Thomas C. Murray, 1959
	Eamon De Valera, 1975
Enniskillen	Ever MacMahon, 1650
Galway	Maurice O'Fihely, 1513

Irishtown   John O'Hanlon, 1905
Kildare   Brigid, 528
Kilkenny   Henry Fitzsimon, 1643
Limerick   Terence Albert O'Brien, 1651
Londonderry   Cecil Frances Alexander, 1895
Maynooth   Patrick Murray, 1882
                   Henry Bewerunge, 1923
Mayo   Gerald of Mayo, 732
Navan   Edward J. Galvin, 1956
Taghmon   Fintan of Taghmon, 635
Thurles   Thomas William Croke, 1902
Tuam   John MacHale, 1881
                   John Healy, 1918
Waterford   Edmund Ignatius Rice, 1844
Wexford   Thomas Furlong, 1875

IRAQ
Baghdad   Abu 'l-Faraj 'Abdallah ibn at-Tayyib, 1043
                   Roger O'Callaghan, 1954
                   Johannitius, 873

ITALY
Acri   Angelo of Acri, 1739
Agnone   Francis Caracciolo, 1608
Albano   Angelo Mai, 1854
                   Eugène Gabriel Tisserant, 1972
Amalfi   Landolf Caracciolo, 1351
Amatrice   Joseph of Leonessa, 1612
Anagni   Haymo of Faversham, 1244
Ancona   Emygdius of Ancona, c.303
                   Pius II, 1464
                   Filippo Acciaioli, 1766
Anzio   Ercole Consalvi, 1824
Apulia   Frederick II, 1250
                   Augustine Kazotoic, 1323
Aquila   Bernardine of Siena, 1444
                   Antonia of Florence, 1472
Arcella   Anthony of Padua, 1231
Arezzo   Victor II, 1057
                   Gregory X, 1276
Armento   Luke of Armento, 993
Arno   Christiana of Lucca, 1310
Arona   Manoel de Sá, 1596
Ascoli   Constantius of Fabriano, 1481
                   Pietro Camaiani, 1579
Assisi   Francis of Assisi, 1226
                   Agnes of Assisi, 1253
                   Clare, 1253
                   Leo of Assisi, 1271
                   Anthony of Stroncone, 1461
Astichello   Giacomo Zanella, 1888
Aversa   Guitmond of Aversa, c.1090
                   Fabrizio Colonna, 1520
                   Carlo Carafa, 1644
Bari   Marianus Argyrus, c.1068
Bastia   Conrad of Offida, 1306
Benevento   Barbatus, 0682
Bergamo   Alberic of Rosate, 1360
                   Innocenzo of Berzo, 1890
Bevagna   James de Blanconibus, 1301
Bobbio   Columbanus, 615
                   Bertulf of Bobbio, 640
Bologna   Irnerius, c.1130
                   Gratian, c.1160

                   Dominic, 1221
                   Bartholomew of Brescia, 1258
                   Rolendis, 1259
                   Bombolognus of Bologna, 1270
                   Martinus de Fano, 1275
                   Martin of Troppau, 1278
                   Richard of Knapwell, c.1288
                   Giles of Foscarari, 1289
                   John Garsias, 1290
                   Cecilia Romana, c.1290
                   Dinus Mugellanus, c.1300
                   Aimeric of Piacenza, 1327
                   Andreae Johannes, 1348
                   John Calderini, 1365
                   John de Fantutiis, 1391
                   Laurentius de Piv, 1397
                   Michele Aiguani, 1400
                   Antonio de Butrio, 1408
                   Alexander V, 1410
                   Catherine of Bologna, 1463
                   Andreas de Barbatia, 1479
                   Helena Duglioli, 1520
                   Pietro Pomponazzi, 1525
                   Francesco Chiericati, 1539
                   Gasparo Contarini, 1542
                   Giovanni Maria Artusi, 1613
                   Ludovico Carracci, 1619
                   Thomas Dempster, 1625
                   Guido Reni, 1642
                   Francesco Bonaventura Cavalieri, 1647
                   Guercino, 1666
                   Giovanni Battista Riccioli, 1671
                   Balthasar of St Catherine of Siena, 1673
                   Diego José Abad y Sánchez, 1779
                   Giovanni Battista Martini, 1784
                   Francisco Javier Clavigero, 1787
                   Augustin Pablo Castro, 1790
                   Rafael Landívar, 1793
                   Paolo Maria Ferretti, 1938
                   Giacomo Lercaro, 1976
Bolzano   Albert Knoll, 1863
Brescia   Louis II, 875
                   Adelmannus, 1061
                   Angela Merici, 1540
                   Gianfrancesco Morosini, 1596
                   Mattia da Salò Bellintani, 1611
                   Benedetto Marcello, 1739
                   Giuseppe Zola, 1806
                   Maria Crocifissa Di Rosa, 1855
                   Geremia Bonomelli, 1914
Bressanone   Francis Augustus MacNutt, 1927
Bricherasio   Anthony Pavonius, 1374
Brixen   Hartmann of Brixen, 1164
Brumate   Albrici Magdale, 1465
Cagliari   Ignatius of Laconi, 1781
Camerino   John of Parma, 1289
Canischio   Adelaide of Turin, 1091
Caposele   Domenico Blasucci, 1752
Capranica   Stanislaus Hosius, 1579
Capri   Aigulf of Lerins, 674
Capua   Alfonso Capecelatro, 1912
Caramagna   Catherine of Racconigi, 1547
Castel Gandolfo   Giovanni Perrone, 1876
                   Giovanni Batista de Rossi, 1894

Paul VI, 1978

Castellamare | Pio Tommaso Milanto, 1748
Catania | Agatha, 250
Certaldo | Giovanni Boccaccio, 1375
Chieti | Rocco da Cesinale, 1900
Chioggia | Gioseffo Zarlino, 1517
Giacomo Nacchianti, 1569
Cluse | Benedict II of Cluse, 1091
Como | Aribo of Mainz, 1031
Edmond Auger, 1591
Feliciano Ninguarda, 1595
Luigi Guanella, 1915
Cortona | Guido of Cortona, 1247
Elias of Cortona, 1253
Margaret of Cortona, 1297
Cotignola | Anthony Bonfadini, 1482
Cremona | Bonizo of Sutri, 1090
Roland of Cremona, 1259
Anthony Zaccaria, 1539
Marc'Antonio Ingegneri, 1592
Elba | Cerbonius, c.580
Fabriano | Romuald of Ravenna, 1027
John of Bastone, 1290
Faenza | Peter Damian, 1072
John Faventius, 1187
Carlo Rossetti, 1681
José Cardiel, 1781
Domingo Muriel, 1795
Fermo | Anthony Grassi, 1671
Ferrara | Matilda of Tuscany, 1114
Urban III, 1187
Huguccio, 1210
Beatrice d'Este, 1262
Lucrezia Borgia, 1419
Leonello d'Este, 1450
Giovanni Aurispa, 1459
Jakob Obrecht, 1505
Ippolito d'Este, 1520
Lodovico Ariosto, 1533
Pierre Robert Olivetan, 1538
Mateo Aimerich, 1799
Fiesole | Andrew of Fiesole, c.876
Andrew Corsini, 1373
Florence | Stephen IX, 1058
Nicholas II, 1061
John of Salerno, 1242
Humiliana de Circulis, 1246
Arnolfo di Cambio, c.1302
Alexius Falconieri, 1310
Remigio de Girolami, 1319
Ricoldus de Monte Croce, 1320
Giotto di Bondone, 1336
Julia Falconieri, 1341
Claritus, 1348
Francesco Landini, 1397
John XXIII, 1419
John Catrik, 1419
Piero di Giovani Lorenzo Monaco, 1425
Andrés de Escobar, c.1440
Leonardo Aretino Bruni, 1444
Filippo Brunelleschi, 1446
Lorenzo Ghiberti, 1455
Andrea del Castagno, 1457
Antoninus, 1459

Cosimo de' Medici, 1464
Donatello, 1466
Francesco Fielelfo, 1481
Luca Della Robbia, 1482
Piero della Francesca, 1492
Domenico Ghirlandaio, 1494
Giovanni Pico della Mirandola, 1494
Girolamo Savonarola, 1498
Marsilio Ficino, 1499
Ludovicus Bologninus, 1508
Sandro Botticelli, 1510
Bernardo Rucellai, 1514
Fra Bartolomeo, 1517
Heinrich Isaac, 1517
Niccolò Machiavelli, 1527
Andrea del Sarto, 1530
Francesco Guicciardini, 1540
Benedetto Accolti, 1549
Paulus Jovius, 1552
Benvenuto Cellini, 1571
Angelo Bronzino, 1572
Girolamo Muzio, 1576
Bartolomeo Ammanati, 1592
Giovanni Bologna, 1608
Hippolytus Galantini, 1619
Marco da Gagliano, 1642
Galilei Galileo, 1642
Antonio Magliabechi, 1714
Giovanni Lorenzo Berti, 1766
Giuseppe Giusti, 1850
Anna Maria Lapini, 1860
Carlo Mari Curci, 1891
Giovanni Papini, 1956
Giorgio La Pira, 1977
Giovanni Benelli, 1982
Foggia | Charles of Anjou, 1285
Pericle Felici, 1982
Foligno | Angela of Foligno, 1309
Angelina of Marsciano, 1435
Mariano Armellini, 1737
Forli | Girolamo Riario, 1488
Geronimo Mercuriali, 1606
Fossanuova | Thomas Aquinas, 1274
Frascati | Benedict IX, 1056
Galese | Famian, 1150
Gemolo | Beatrice d'Este, 1226
Genoa | Jacobus de Voragine, 1298
Arnold of Villanova, 1311
Ricardus de Senis, 1314
Catherine of Genoa, 1510
Andrea Doria, 1560
Maria Victoria Fornari-Strata, 1617
Daniel O'Connell, 1847
Francesco Maria of Camporosso, 1866
Giuseppe Frassinetti, 1868
Gerace | Barlaam of Calabria, 1350
Goleto | William of Vercelli, 1142
Golloro | Louis Billot, 1931
Grottaferrata | Jean-François Bonnefoy, 1958
Gualdo Cattaneo | Hugolino of Gualdo Cattaneo, 1260
Imola | Manuel de Lacunza y Diaz, 1801
Juan Ignacio Molina, 1829
Gaetano Baluffi, 1866
Ischia | William Walton, 1983

Lecce	Bernardino Realino, 1616		Victor III, 1086
Leghorn	Marcellino da Civezza, 1906		Constantine the African, 1087
Lodi	Carlo Ambrogio Mezzabarba, 1741		Oderisius, 1105
	Melchiore Carpani, 1797		Bernard of Montmirat, 1296
Loreto	Nicolás Alfonso de Bobadilla, 1590	Montefalco	Clare of Montefalco, 1308
	Annibale Zoilo, 1592	Montefiascone	Lucy Filippini, 1732
	Richard Crashaw, 1649	Monteleone	Leo Luke, c.980
Lovere	Bartolomea Capitanio, 1833	Naples	Innocent IV, 1243
Lucca	Frigidian of Lucca, c.588		Augustine of Ancona, 1328
	Zita, 1278		John of Naples, 1340
	Gemma Galgani, 1903		Guido Marramaldi, c.1391
	Elena Guerra, 1914		Giannozzo Manetti, 1459
Lucedio	Bononius, 1026		James of the Marches, 1476
Macerata	Cassiano da Macerata, 1791		Pompeo Colonna, 1532
Mals	Pius Zingerle, 1881		Juan de Valdés, 1541
Mantua	Anselm of Lucca, 1086		Maria Laurentia Longo, 1542
	Bartholomew of Rome, 1430		Cajetan, 1547
	Archangela Girlani, 1494		Ambrosius Catharinus, 1553
	Andrea Mantegna, 1506		Ascanio Colonna, c.1557
	Baptist of Mantua, 1516		Alfonso Carafa, 1565
	Giovanni dei Medici, 1526		Diego Ortíz, 1570
Marengo	Lambert of Spoleto, 898		Mattia dei Gibboni Aquarius, 1591
Meluccà	Elias of Reggio, c.960		Andrew Avellino, 1608
Merano	Hilarius of Sexten, 1899		Carlo Gesualdo, 1613
Messina	Rufinus of Aquileia, 410		Domenico Pietro Cerone, 1625
	Eustochia Calafato, 1468		Jusepe de Ribera, 1652
	Constantine Lascaris, 1501		Francis of Geronimo, 1716
Milan	Ambrose, 397		Alessandro Scarlatti, 1725
	Aurelius of Armenia, 475		Giovanni Battista Pergolesi, 1736
	Aquilinas, c.1015		Leonardo Leo, 1744
	Erlembald, 1075		Matteo Ripa, 1746
	Arnulf of Milan, 1077		Francesco Durante, 1755
	Anselm of Havelberg, 1158		Niccolò Jommelli, 1774
	Galdinus, 1176		Maria Francesca Gallo, 1791
	Peter Martyr, 1252		Egidio Maria of St Joseph, 1812
	Franchino Gaforio, 1522		Francesco Saverio Maria Bianchi, 1815
	Prospero Colonna, 1523		Fabrizio Ruffo, 1827
	Bartolomeo Ferrari, 1544		Maria Cristina of Savoy, 1836
	Giovanniangelo Arcimboldi, 1555		Giacomo Leopardi, 1837
	Castellino da Castelli, 1566		Nicola Antonio Zingarelli, 1837
	Charles Borromeo, 1584		Charles Januarius Acton, 1847
	Giovanni Gastoldi, 1609		Guglielmo Massaja, 1889
	Isabella Cristina Bellinzaga, 1624		Rosa di Traetto Carafa, 1890
	Federigo Borromeo, 1631	Nola	Felix of Nola, 260
	Cosmo Alamanni, 1634		Paulinus, 431
	Francesco Collius, 1640	Novara	Adalgis of Novara, 850
	Giulio Mercori, 1669		Bernard of Aosta, 1081
	Joseph Allegranza, 1785	Ortona	Margaret of Parma, 1586
	Ruggiero Giuseppe Boscovich, 1787	Orvieto	Ambrose of Massa, 1240
	Maria Gaetana Agnesi, 1799		Hugh of Saint-Cher, 1263
	Alessandro Francesco Tommaso Manzoni, 1873		Hannibaldus de Hannibaldis, 1272
			Odo of Châteauroux, 1273
	Cesare Cantù, 1895		Siger of Brabant, c.1281
	Giuseppe Verdi, 1901		Joan of Orvieto, 1306
	Edwin Vincent O'Hara, 1956		Lorenzo Maitani, 1330
	Agostino Gemelli, 1959	Ostia	Monica, 387
	Angelo Giovanni Paredi, 1997	Padua	Luke Belludi, c.1285
Modena	Adrian III, 885		Johannes Ciconia, 1411
	Correggio, 1534		Eustochium of Padua, 1469
	Achille Gagliardi, 1607		Marco Antonio Zimara, 1532
	Lodovico Antonio Muratori, 1750		Giovanni Francesco Commendone, 1584
Monte Cassino	Benedict, 550		Jacopo Zabarella, 1589
	Paul the Deacon, c.799		Filippo Fabri, 1630
	Apollinaris of Monte Cassino, 828		Elena Lucrezia Piscopia Cornaro, 1684

Gregory Barbarigo, 1697
Giovanni Francesco Barbarigo, 1730
Egidio Forcellini, 1768
Daniele Farlati, 1773
Simon Assemani, 1820
Oreste Ravanello, 1938

Palestrina — Guarinus of Palestrina, 1159

Parma — Guido of Pomposa, 1046
Andrew of Strumi, 1097
Orlando de' Medici, 1386
Ranuccio Farnese, 1565
Agostino Carracci, 1602
Claudio Merulo, 1604
Francesco Bordoni, 1671
Guido Maria Conforti, 1931

Passignano — John Gualbert, 1073

Pavia — Epiphanius of Pavia, 496
Magnus Felix Ennodius, 521
Anicius Manlius Severinus Boethius, 524
Damian, 715
Baldus de Ubaldis, 1400

Perugia — Urban IV, 1264
Innocent III, 1216
Nicholas Paglia, 1255
Giles of Assisi, 1262
Benedict XI, 1304
Bartolo of Sassoferrato, 1357
John Welles, 1388
Columba of Rieti, 1501
Giovanni Paolo Lancelotti, 1590
Giovanni Baptista Corrado, 1606
Paolo Comitoli, 1626
Agostino Oldoini, 1683

Pesaro — Clement II, 1047

Pescina — Ella B. Edes, 1916

Piacenza — Lothair II, 869
Francis of Meyronnes, c.1328
Giulio Alberoni, 1752
Anthony Gianelli, 1846

Pisa — Beatrice of Tuscany, 1076
Matthew of Albano, 1135
Bona, 1207
Bartholomew of San Concordio, 1347
Angelo Acciaioli, 1408
Franciscus de Accoltis, 1485

Pistoia — Barontius, 695
Andrew Franchi, 1401
Lawrence of Ripafratta, 1456
Benozzo Gozzoli, 1497

Pittoli — Franca Vitalta, 1218

Poggibonsi — Luchesius of Poggibonsi, 1260

Prato — Catherine de' Ricci, 1590

Ravenna — Germanus of Auxerre, 448
John I, 525
Alighieri Dant, 1321
Bessarion, 1472

Riveti — Giuseppe d' Annibale, 1892

Rome — Anacletus, 91
Ignatius of Antioch, 107
Evaristus, c.109
Alexander I, 116
Pius I, c.154
Justin Martyr, c.165
Anicetus, 168

Eleutherius, 192
Victor I, 198
Anterus, 236
Fabian, 250
Minucius Felix, 250
Felicissimus and Agapitus, 258
Lawrence, 258
Dionysius, 268
Eutychian, 283
Gaius, 296
Agnes, 302
Anthimus, c.302
Genesius the Comedian, 303
Pantaleon, c.305
Eusebius, 311
Sylvester I, 335
Damasus I, 384
Fabiola, 399
Anastasius I, 401
Marcella, 410
Pammachius, 410
Innocent I, 417
Boniface I, 422
Celestine, 432
Arnobius the Younger, 455
Prosper of Aquitaine, c.463
Hilary, 468
Gelasius I, 496
Anastasius II, 498
Symmachus, 514
Hormisdas, 523
Dioscorus, 530
Boniface II, 532
John II, 535
Arator, c.550
Dionysius Exiguus, 550
John III, 574
Benedict I, 579
Pelagius II, 590
Gregory the Great, 604
Boniface III, 607
Boniface IV, 615
Deusdedit I, 618
Boniface V, 625
Honorius I, 638
Severinus, 640
John IV, 642
Eugenius I, 657
Vitalian, 672
Adeodatus II, 676
Donus, 678
Agatho, 681
Leo II, 683
Benedict II, 685
John V, 686
Conon, 687
Caedwalla, 689
John VI, 705
Pope Constantine, 715
Ine, 726
Gregory II, 731
Gregory III, 741
Paul I, 767
Adrian I, 795

Leo III, 816
Paschal I, 824
Eugenius II, 827
Gregory IV, 844
Leo IV, 855
Benedict III, 858
Nicholas I, 867
Cyril, 869
Adrian II, 872
Anastasius the Librarian, 878
Marinus I, 884
Boniface VI, 896
Formosus, 896
Benedict IV, 903
Leo V, 904
Auxilius of Naples, 905
Sergius III, 911
Anastasius III, 913
John XI, 935
Leo VII, 939
Marinus II, 946
Alberic II of Spoleto, 954
Agapetus II, 955
Leo VIII, 965
Benedict VI, 974
Benedict VII, 983
Otto II, 983
John XIV, 984
Boniface VII, 985
Gregory V, 999
Otto III, 1002
John XVII, 1003
Sylvester II, 1003
Nilus of Rossano, c.1005
Benedict VIII, 1024
Halinard of Lyons, 1052
Leo IX, 1054
Humbert of Silva Candida, 1061
Sylvester III, 1063
Alexander II, 1073
Benedict X, 1073
Atto of Milan, 1085
Urban II, 1099
Paschal II, 1118
Calixtus II, 1124
Honorius II, 1130
Gregory of Catina, c.1132
Innocent II, 1143
Lucius II, 1145
Robert Pullen, 1147
Anastasius IV, 1154
Arnold of Brescia, 1155
Adrian IV, 1159
Boso, 1178
Gregory VIII, 1187
Laborans, c.1190
Clement III, 1191
Guy de Montpellier, 1208
John of Matha, 1213
William of Auxerre, 1231
Jacques de Vitry, 1240
Gregory IX, 1241
Bernard of Compostela II, 1267
Innocent V, 1276

Honorius IV, 1287
Nicholas IV, 1292
William Durandus, 1296
Matthew of Aquasparta, 1302
Boniface VIII, 1303
Cola di Rienzo, 1354
Bridget of Sweden, 1373
Gregory XI, 1378
Catherine of Siena, 1380
Urban VI, 1389
Adam Easton, 1397
Boniface IX, 1404
Innocent VII, 1406
Gentile da Fabriano, 1427
Guillaume Fillastre, 1428
Masaccio, 1428
Martin V, 1431
Frances of Rome, 1440
Eugenius IV, 1447
Fra Angelico, 1455
Nicholas V, 1455
Calixtus III, 1458
Domenico Capranica, 1458
Gregory III, 1459
Flavio Biondo, 1463
Prospero Colonna, 1463
Isidore of Kiev, 1464
John Free, 1465
Juan de Carvajal, 1469
Rodrigo Sanchez de Arevalo, 1470
Timoteo Maffei, 1470
Paul II, 1471
Pietro Riario, 1474
Regiomontanus, 1476
Bartolomeo Platina, 1481
Guillaume d' Estouteville, 1483
Sixtus IV, 1484
George of Trebizond, 1486
John Argyropoulos, 1487
Pere-Luís Borgia, 1488
Innocent VIII, 1492
Juan Borgia, 1497
Giovanni Gigli, 1498
Stefano Infessura, c.1500
Johannes Annius, 1502
Alexander VI, 1503
Pius III, 1503
Giovanni Colonna, 1508
Oliviero Carafa, 1511
Sigismondo de' Conti, 1512
Julius II, 1513
Christopher Bainbridge, 1514
Donato Bramante, 1514
Giovanni Giocondo, 1515
Markos Musurus, 1517
Agostino Chigi, 1520
Raphael, 1520
Leo X, 1521
Adrian VI, 1523
Bernardino López de Carvajal, 1523
Domenico Grimani, 1523
Sylvester Prierias Mazzolini, 1523
Zaccaria Ferreri, c.1524
Giles of Viterbo, 1532

Rome

Pietro Accolti, 1532
Clement VII, 1534
John Lascaris, 1534
Tommaso de Vio Cajetan, 1534
Mario Maffei, 1537
Lorenzo Campeggio, 1539
Girolamo Aleandro, 1542
Johannes Magnus, 1544
Costanza Festa, 1545
Peter Faber, 1546
Tommaso Badia, 1547
Pietro Bembo, 1547
Vittoria Colonna, 1547
Jacopo Sadoleto, 1547
Gregorio Cortese, 1548
Paul III, 1549
Bernardino Maffei, 1553
Julius III, 1555
Ignatius of Loyola, 1556
Olaus Magnus, 1557
Silvestro Aldobrandini, 1558
Luigi Lippomano, 1559
Paul IV, 1559
Jean Du Bellay, 1560
Carlo Carafa, 1561
Michelangelo Buonarroti, 1564
Diego Lainez, 1565
Pius IV, 1565
Bonsignore Cacciaguerra, 1566
Pietro Carnesecchi, 1567
Stanislaus Kostka, 1568
Giovanni Animucia, 1571
Francis Borgia, 1572
Ippolito d'Este, 1572
Pius V, 1572
Giovanni Aldobrandini, 1573
Giulio Acquaviva, 1574
Bartolomeo Eustachio, 1574
Paulus Manutius, 1574
Cornelius Musso, 1574
Geronimo Cardano, 1576
Bartolomé de Carranza, 1576
Giovanni Morone, 1580
Geronimo Nadal, 1580
Zaccaria Dolfin, 1583
Marcantonio Maffei, 1583
Johannes Maldonatus, 1583
Wilhelm Eisengrein, 1584
Francisco Torres, 1584
Thomas Goldwell, 1585
Gregory XIII, 1585
Martin Aspilcueta, 1586
Felix of Cantalice, 1587
Alessandro Farnese, 1589
Antonio Carafa, 1591
Aloysius Gonzaga, 1591
Gregory XIV, 1591
Innocent IX, 1591
William Allen, 1594
Giovanni Pierluigi da Palestrina, 1594
Christophe de Cheffontaines, 1595
Philip Neri, 1595
Torquato Tasso, 1595
Urban VII, 1596

Luca Marenzio, 1599
Jean de la Barrière, 1600
Giordano Bruno, 1600
Lodovico Madruzzo, 1600
Juan Azor, 1603
Andrea Cesalpino, 1603
Arnaud d' Ossat, 1604
Ippolito Aldobrandini, 1605
Clement VIII, 1605
Leo XI, 1605
Caesar Baronius, 1607
Giovanni Maria Nanino, 1607
Annibale Carracci, 1609
John Leonardi, 1609
Cinzio Passeri Aldobrandini, 1610
Robert Parsons, 1610
Ottavio Acquaviva (the elder), 1612
Silvestro Aldobrandini, 1612
Christopher Clavius, 1612
Felice Anerio, 1614
Camillus of Lellis, 1614
Claudius Acquaviva, 1615
Hugh O'Neill, 1616
Joseph de Jouvancy, 1619
Angelo Rocca, 1620
Pietro Aldobrandini, 1621
John Barclay, 1621
Robert Bellarmine, 1621
John Berchmans, 1621
Paul V, 1621
Gregory XV, 1623
Alessandro d'Este, 1624
Paolo Agostini, 1629
Tomás de Lemos, 1629
Carlo Maderno, 1629
Carlo Gaudenzio Madruzzo, 1629
Cornelius a Lapide, 1637
John Gerard, 1637
Ippolito Aldobrandini, 1638
Niccolò Riccardi, 1639
George Con, 1640
Antony Hickey, 1641
Benedetto Castelli, 1643
Girolamo Frescobaldi, 1643
Urban VIII, 1644
Pietro Casani, 1647
Joseph Calasanctius, 1648
Agostino Barbosa, 1649
Vincenzo Carafa, 1649
Constantino Cajetan, 1650
Francesco Piccolomini, 1651
Gregorio Allegri, 1652
Vincenzo Candido, 1654
Pierluigi Carafa, 1655
Innocent X, 1655
Giovanni Stefano Menochio, 1655
Raphael Aversa, 1657
Luke Wadding, 1657
Juan Bautista de Lezana, 1659
Juan de Lugo, 1660
Antonino Diana, 1663
Abraham Ecchellensis, 1664
Alexander VII, 1667
Francesco Borromini, 1667

Pietro Sforza Pallavicino, 1667
Jehudah Jonah ben Jishaq, 1668
Mateo de Castro, c.1668
Clement IX, 1669
Pietro Berrettini da Cortona, 1669
Charles of Sezze, 1670
Odorio Rinaldi, 1671
Rinaldo d'Este, 1672
Ottavio Acquaviva (the younger), 1674
Giovanni Bona, 1674
Clement X, 1676
Prospero Fagnani, 1678
Alfonso Litta, 1679
Ivan Lucic, 1679
Giovanni Lorenzo Bernini, 1680
Carlo Carafa, 1680
Athanasius Kircher, 1680
Daniello Bartoli, 1685
Francis Harold, 1685
Giulio Bartolucci, 1687
Sylvester Maurus, 1687
Francesco Foggia, 1688
Christina of Sweden, 1689
Innocent XI, 1689
Alexander VIII, 1691
Carlo Rainaldi, 1691
Lorenzo Brancati, 1693
Flavio Chigi, 1693
Philip Thomas Howard, 1694
Marcello Malpighi, 1694
Miguel de Molinos, 1696
Girolamo Casava, 1700
Innocent XII, 1700
Louis Hennepin, 1701
Henry Noris, 1704
Francesco Antonio Febei, 1705
Tirso González de Santalla, 1705
Giuseppe Agnelli, 1706
Antonin Massoulié, 1706
Arcangelo Corelli, 1713
Carlo Fontana, 1714
Emmanuel Théodore de la Tour
    d'Auvergne Bouillon, 1715
Paolo Alessandro Maffei, 1716
Niccolò Acciaioli, 1719
Clement XI, 1721
Christoph Rassler, 1723
Innocent XIII, 1724
Francesco Bianchini, 1729
Benedict XIII, 1730
Michelangelo Tamburini, 1730
Alessandro Falconieri, 1734
Giovanni Battista Riganti, 1735
Alvaro Cienfuegos, 1739
Benedict XIV, 1740
Clement XII, 1740
Vincenzo Lodovico Gotti, 1742
Trojano Acquaviva, 1747
Emmanuel de la Reguera, 1747
Winifred Maxwell, 1749
Crispin of Viterbo, 1750
Annibale Albani, 1751
Leonard of Port Maurice, 1751
Bernardo Gaetano Guadagni, 1759

Claudio Casciolini, 1760
Giuseppe Agostino Orsi, 1761
Jean Baptiste Rossi, 1764
Joseph Simon Assemani, 1768
Clement XIII, 1769
Neri Corsini, 1770
Clement XIV, 1774
Paul of the Cross, 1775
Lorenzo Ricci, 1775
Alessandro Albani, 1779
Joseph Aloysius Assemani, 1782
Stephen Erodius Assemani, 1782
Benedict Joseph Labré, 1783
Salvatore Maria Roselli, 1784
Filippo Salvatore Gilij, 1789
Giuseppe Garampi, 1792
Nicolas Jean Hugou de Bassville, 1793
Andrès Cavo, c.1794
Francesco Antonio Zaccaria, 1795
Gaspar Juárez, 1799
Giovanni Francesco Albani, 1803
Francisco Antonio de Lorenzana, 1804
Jorgen Zoega, 1809
Filippo Casoni, 1811
Jean Siffrein Maury, 1817
Pius VII, 1823
Kasimir von Haffelin, 1827
Leo XII, 1829
Giulio Maria Della Somaglia, 1830
Pius VIII, 1830
Giuseppe Albani, 1834
Anthony Kohlmann, 1836
Gaspare del Bufalo, 1837
Joseph Fesch, 1839
Joseph Rosati, 1843
Giuseppe Baini, 1844
Bartolommeo Pacca, 1844
Francesco Capaccini, 1845
Gregory XVI, 1846
Giuseppe Mezzofanti, 1849
Pietro Raimondi, 1853
Johann Philip Roothaan, 1853
Jean Baptiste Bouvier, 1854
Luigi Lambruschini, 1854
Gabriele Ferretti, 1860
Giuseppe Marchi, 1860
Pietro Alfieri, 1863
Maria de Mattias, 1866
Clemente de Jesús Munguía, 1868
Thomas Grant, 1870
Giovanni Merlini, 1873
Giacomo Antonelli, 1876
Alessandro Franchi, 1878
Pius IX, 1878
Antonio Ballerini, 1881
Paola Frassinetti, 1882
Gaetano Moroni, 1883
Luigi Billio, 1884
Lorenzo Nina, 1885
Johannes Baptist Franzelin, 1886
Clement Marc, 1887
Jean Baptiste Pitra, 1889
Antonio Maria Adragna, 1890
Matteo Liberatore, 1892

Rome

Gaspard Mermillod, 1892
Tommaso Zigliara, 1893
William Maziere Brady, 1894
Frédéric Ghislain de Mérode, 1894
Johann Bollig, 1895
Paulus Melchers, 1895
Aemilio de Augustinis, 1899
Camillo Mazzella, 1900
Agostino Ciasca, 1902
Miescylaw Halka Ledóchowski, 1902
Leo XIII, 1903
Mary Potter, 1913
Mariano Rampolla del Tindaro, 1913
Domenico Ferrata, 1914
Pius X, 1914
Hyacinth Marie Cormier, 1916
Gennaro Bucceroni, 1918
Benedict XV, 1922
Alfred Henri Joseph Cauchie, 1922
Louis Duchesne, 1922
Alberto Lepidi, 1922
Rafaela Porras y Ayllón, 1925
Juan Cagliero, 1926
Michael Hetzenauer, 1928
Enrico Buonpensiere, 1929
Francis Neil Aidan Gasquet, 1929
Edouard Hugon, 1929
Leonhard Lemmens, 1929
Rafael Merry del Val, 1930
Bruno Katterbach, 1931
Cicero Romão Batista, 1934
Umberto Benigni, 1934
Franz Ehrle, 1934
Pietro Gasparri, 1934
Ignazio Guidi, 1935
Alexis Lépicier, 1936
Ottorino Respighi, 1936
James Heerinckx, 1937
Guglielmo Marconi, 1937
Genevieve Garvan Brady McAuley, 1938
Johann Baptist Frey, 1939
Thomas Hughes, 1939
Pius XI, 1939
Joseph August Gredt, 1940
Johann Peter Kirsch, 1941
Filippo Crispolti, 1942
Joseph de Guibert, 1942
Wladimir Ledóchowski, 1942
Edward Joseph Hanna, 1944
Romolo Murri, 1944
Augustin Merk, 1945
Ernesto Buonaiuti, 1946
Franz Zorell, 1947
Martin Stanislaus Gillet, 1951
Livarius Oliger, 1951
Ludwig Kaas, 1952
Ugo Betti, 1953
Gabriel of St Mary Magdalen, 1953
Anton Deimel, 1954
Angelo Mercati, 1955
René Follet, 1956
Georg Hofmann, 1956
Eugenio Zolli, 1956
Curzio Malaparte, 1957

Giovanni Mercati, 1957
Pius XII, 1958
Pio Franci de' Cavalieri, 1960
Paul Galtier, 1961
Acacius Coussa, 1962
Giuseppe De Luca, 1962
Joseph Löw, 1962
Aloisius Joseph Muench, 1962
Pasquale D'Elia, 1963
Réginald Garrigou-Lagrange, 1964
Giuseppe Ricciotti, 1964
Charles De Koninck, 1965
Augustin Bea, 1968
Higini Angles, 1969
Josef Beran, 1969
Gregory Peter Agagianian, 1971
Michael Browne, 1971
Anneliese Maier, 1971
Amleto Giovanni Cicognani, 1973
José María Escriva de Balaguer y Albas, 1975
Luigi Raimondi, 1975
Alfredo Ottaviani, 1979
Jean Villot, 1979
Anna Dengel, 1980
Annibale Bugnini, 1982
Mitchell J. Dahood, 1982
Luigi G. Ligutti, 1984
Josef Slipyj, 1984
Dermot Ryan, 1985
Stanislaus Lyonnet, 1986
Egidio Vagnozzi, 1986
Madeleine Hutin, 1989
Pedro Arrupe, 1991
Pietro Pavan, 1994
Jerome Thessen, 1995

Roverto   Giovanna Maria of the Cross, 1673
Salerno   Alphanus of Salerno, 1085
                 Gregory VII, 1085
                 Herman of Salza, 1239
                 Agostino Nifo, 1538
                 Alphonsus Liguori, 1787
San Martino   Scipione Gonzaga, 1593
San Remo   Franz Xaver Kraus, 1901
                 Hélène de Chappotin de Neuville, 1904
                 Louis of Besse, 1910
                 Luigi Orione, 1940
San Sepolcro   Angelus de Scarpetis, c.1306
San Severo   Germanico Malaspina, 1604
Schio   Josephine Bakhita, 1947
Sele   Franc Ksaver Meško, 1964
Selia   Alcide de Gasperi, 1954
Sezze   Lidanus, 1118
Siena   Franco Lippi, 1291
                 Augustine Novellus, 1309
                 Duccio di Buoninsegna, c.1318
                 Giovanni da Lecceto Chigi, 1363
                 Giuliana Chigi, 1400
                 Bartolo di Fredi, 1410
                 Niccolò Albergati, 1443
                 Francesco di Giorgio, 1501
                 Philippus Decius, 1536
                 Alessandro Piccolomini, 1578
                 Felix Figliucci, 1584

	Agostino Agazzari, 1640		Pietro Aaron, 1545
Spello	Andrew Caccioli, 1254		Daniel Bomberg, 1549
Spilimbergo	Bertrand of Aquileia, 1350		Matteo Serafini da Bascio, 1552
Spoleto	Christina of Spoleto, 1456		Pietro Aretino, 1556
	Fra Filippo Lippi, 1469		Marco Antonio Cavazzoni, c.1570
Squillace	Jofré Borgia, 1517		Titian, 1576
Subiaco	Chelidonia, 1152		Girolamo Cavazzoni, 1577
Suna	Contardo Ferrini, 1902		Andrea Gabrieli, 1585
Susa	Hugh of Die, 1106		Ivan Gundulic, 1589
Taranto	Cataldus of Rachau, c.671		Gioseffo Zarlino, 1590
Teano	Bertharius, 884		Giovanni Matteo Asola, 1609
Tiferno	Antonio Maria Abbatini, 1680		Giovanni dalla Croce, 1609
Tivoli	Eugenius III, 1153		Giovanni Gabrieli, 1612
	Grassi, Antoni, 1491		Paolo Sarpi, 1623
	Cristoforo Madruzzo, 1578		Claudio Monteverdi, 1643
	Louis d'Este, 1586		Pier Francesco Cavalli, 1676
	Giampietro Maffei, 1603		Dionigi da Piacenza, 1695
Todi	Nicholas of Cusa, 1464		Antonio Lotti, 1740
Tolentino	Nicholas of Tolentino, 1306		Mechitar of Sebaste, 1749
Torcello	Bartholomew of Lucca, 1327		Concina Daniello, 1756
La Torre	Bruno, 1101		Fulgenzio Cunialati, 1759
Trani	Diego Álvarez, 1631		Giovanni Benedetto Mittarelli, 1777
Trent	Bartholomew of Trent, 1251		Andrea Gallandi, 1779
	Friedrich Nausea, 1552		Johann Adolph Hasse, 1783
	Ercole Gonzaga, 1563		Antonio Canova, 1822
	Carlo Emanuele Madruzzo, 1658		Robert Browning, 1889
Treviso	Henry of Bolzano, 1315	Vercelli	Eusebius of Vercelli, 371
	Maria Bertilla Boscardin, 1922		Atto of Vercelli, 961
Turin	Eldrad, c.840		Leo of Vercelli, 1026
	Domenico de Gubernatis, 1690		Fra Dolcino, 1307
	Carlo Sebastiano Berardi, 1786		Amadeus IX of Savoy, 1472
	Joseph Marie de Maistre, 1821	Veroli	Athanasius of Naples, 872
	Pio Brunone Lanteri, 1830	Verona	Lucius III, 1185
	Cesare Balbo, 1853		Omnibonus, 1185
	Joseph Cafasso, 1860		Celso Maffei, 1508
	Massimo Taparelli d' Azeglio, 1866		Gian Matteo Giberti, 1543
	Giacomo Margotti, 1887		Francesco Scipione Maffei, 1755
	John Bosco, 1888		Girolamo Ballerini, 1769
	Leonardo Murialdo, 1900		Pietro Ballerini, 1769
	Giuseppe Allamano, 1926		Maddalena Gabriella Canossa, 1835
Udine	Oderic of Pordenone, 1331		Sir John Stainer, 1901
	Helen of Udine, 1458	Vicenza	Bartholomew of Vicenza, 1270
Urbino	John Pelingotto, 1304		Antonio Fogazzaro, 1911
	Bartholomew of Urbino, 1350	Vigevano	Christopher Maccassoli, 1485
Vallucola	Andrew Dotti, 1315		Juan Lobkowitz Caramuel, 1682
Vedana	Cyprien Marie Boutrais, 1900	Villamagna	Gerard of Villamagna, 1245
Velletri	Gauderich of Velletri, c.896	Viterbo	Robert Pullen, 1146
	Hugh Etherian, 1182		Rose of Viterbo, 1252
Venafro	Gebizo, c.1078		Alexander IV, 1261
Venice	Jordan Forzate, 1248		Clement IV, 1268
	Rambert of Bologna, 1308		Adrian V, 1276
	Marco Polo, 1324		John XXI, 1277
	Peter Gambacorta, 1435		Robert Kilwardby, 1279
	Giovanni Contarini, 1451		Nicholas III, 1280
	Lawrence Justinian, 1456		Gil Álvarez de Albornoz, 1367
	Jacopo Bellini, 1470		Hyacintha Marescotti, 1640
	Antonello da Messina, 1479		Lelio Falconieri, 1648
	Paolo Maffei, 1480		Giovanni Battista Faure, 1779
	Gentile Bellini, 1507		Gaetano Bedini, 1864
	Giorgione da Castelfranco, 1510	Vivarium	Cassiodorus, 580
	Pietro Lombaro, 1515		
	Aldus Manutius, 1515		
	Giovanni Bellini, 1516	JAMAICA	Thomas Gage, 1656
	Pietro Dolfin, 1525		Moses Baker, 1826

JAPAN
Karuizawa — Arishima Takeo, 1923
Nagasaki — Felipe de Jesús Casas Martinez, 1597
Luis de Cerqueira, 1614
Bartolomé Díez Laurel, 1627
Rodriguez Bartolomeo Gutiérrez, 1632
Antonio Rubino, 1643
Takashi Naga, 1951
Tokyo — Mathilde Raclot, 1911
Nicholas of Japan, 1912
Joseph Dahlmann, 1930
Kagawa Toyohiko, 1960
Masamune Hakucho, 1962

KENYA
Joseph Shanahan, 1943
Roland Allen, 1947

KOREA
Patrick James Byrne, 1950
Agneta Chang, 1950

LATVIA
Mitau — Henry Essex Edgeworth de Firmont, 1807
Riga — John of Latvia, 1934
Sergius of the Baltic, 1944

LEBANON
Arethusa — Mark of Arethusa, 389
Beirut — Baldwin III of Jerusalem, 1163
John Garstang, 1956
Maximos IV Sayegh, 1967
Ignatius Gabriel Tappouni, 1968
Saida — Constantine Bacha, 1948
Shuwair — 'Abdallah Zahir, 1748
Tripoli — Raymond of Toulouse IV, 1105

LITHUANIA
Pasandravys — Maironis, 1862
Vilna — Laurentius Nielsen, 1622

LUXEMBURG
Willibrord, 739
Gezzelinus, 1138
Garnerius of Rochefort, c.1225
Johann Nikolaus von Hontheim, 1790
Alexander Baumgartner, 1910
Edmond Dublanchy, 1938

MALTA
Jean Parisot de La Vallette, 1568
Nicholas Bonet, 1643
Charles Dominic Plater, 1921
Daniel Angelo Philip Callus, 1965

MEXICO
Ceralvo — Anthony Rey, 1847
Charo — Diego Basalenque, 1651
Chiapas — Matias de Córdova, 1828
Coacaleco — Pelagio Antonio de Labastida y Dàvalos, 1891
Cuauhtitlan — Juan Diego, 1548
Ejutla — Eulogio Gregorio Gillow y Zavalza, 1922
Guadalajara — Juan de Santiago y León Garabito, 1694
Anacleto González Flores, 1926
Magdalena — Eusebio Francisco Kino, 1711
Mérida — Diego de Landa, 1579
Juan Coronel, 1651

Mexico City — Juan Ignacio de Castorena y Ursua, 1733
Ignacio de Padilla y Estrada, 1760
Juan de Zumarrága, 1548
Marcos de Niza, 1558
Toribio de Benavente Motolinía, 1565
Juan Focher, 1572
Pedro de Gante, 1572
Hernando Franco, 1585
Alonso de Molina, 1585
Domingo de la Anunciación, 1591
Domingo Chimalpain, 1660
Francisco López Capillas, 1673
Juana Iñés de la Cruz, 1695
Francisco Aguiar y Seixas, 1698
Andrés de Borda, 1723
Antonio Margil, 1726
Miguel Cabrera, 1768
Juan Agustín de Morfi, 1783
José Antonio Alzate, 1799
Servando Teresa de Mier, 1827
Miguel Ramos Arizpe, 1843
Carlos Maria Bustamante, 1848
Manuel Andrade y Pastor, 1848
Basilio Arrillaga, 1867
Ramón Ibarra y González, 1917
Pascual Díaz y Barreto, 1936
Rafael Guajázar Valencia, 1938
Mariano Cuevas, 1949
Gabriel Mendez Plancarte, 1949
José de Jesús Manríquez y Zárate, 1951
Luis María Martínez, 1956
Alfonso Reyes, 1959
Alberto Maria Carreño, 1962
Pablo Martínez del Rio, 1963
Morelia — Francisco Elguero, 1932
Leopoldo Ruiz y Flora, 1941
Oaxaca — Nicolás del Puerto, 1681
Pátzcuaro — Vasco de Quiroga, 1565
Puebla — Julian Garces, 1542
Sebastian de Aparicio, 1600
Alonso de la Mota y Escobar, 1625
Querétaro — Isidro Félix de Espinosa, 1755
Juan Domingo Arricivita, 1794
San Cristóbal
Ecatepec — José María Morelos y Pavón, 1815
San Juan de Ulúa — Tomás de Mercado, 1575
San Luis Potosí — Miguel de la Mora, 1930
Sonora — Francisco Antonio Barbastro, 1800
Tampico — Andrés de Olmos, 1570
Teozapotlán — Francisco de Burgoa, 1681
Tepotzotlán — Horacio Carocci, 1662
Zacatecas — Pedro de Espinareda, 1576
Antonio de Remesal, 1627

THE NETHERLANDS
Adwert — Emmanuel, 1298
Amersfoort — Zeger Bernard van Espen, 1728
Johannes de Jong, 1955
Amsterdam — John Smyth, 1612
Francis Johnson, 1618
Henry Ainsworth, 1623
Rembrandt Harmensz van Rijn, 1669
Johannes Amos Comenius, 1670
Pasquier Quesnel, 1719

Jean Leclerc, 1736
Josephus Albertus Alberdingk Thijm, 1889
Johan Herman Bavinck, 1964
Asch   Dodo of Asch, 1231
Breda   Johann Heinrich Frankenberg, 1804
Deventer   Lebuinus, c.780
Gerardus Magnus Groote, 1384
Florentius Radewijns, 1400
Alexander Hegius, 1498
Dokkum   Adalar, 754
Egmond   Adalbert the Deacon, 705
Exaeten   Joseph Epping, 1894
Moritz Meschler, 1912
Grave   Jean Baptiste Berthier, 1908
Groningen   Wessel Gansfort, 1489
Franciscus Gomarus, 1641
The Hague   Constantijn Huygens, 1687
Abraham Kuyper, 1920
Heerenberg   Franz von Hummelauer, 1914
Hocht   Charles of Villers, c.1215
Houthem   Gerlach, 1177
Leiden   Philips von Marnix van St Aldegonde, 1598
Jacobus Arminius, 1609
Joseph Justus Scaliger, 1609
John Robinson, 1625
Arnold Geulincx, 1669
Maastricht   Dietrich of Nieheim, 1418
Joseph Knabenbauer, 1911
Rijnsburg   Pierre Poiret, 1719
Roermond   Denis the Carthusian, 1471
Rotterdam   Pierre Jurieu, 1713
Simpelveld   Clara Fey, 1894
Utrecht   Gregory of Utrecht, 776
Alberic of Utrecht, 784
Henry V, 1125
Albert Pigge, 1542
Philippus Rovenius, 1651
Pieter Codde, 1710
Hadrian Reland, 1718
Gabriel Du Pac de Bellegrade, 1789
Gerardus van der Leeuw, 1950
Valenkenburg   Theodor Granderath, 1902
August Lehmkuh, 1918
Hermann Dieckmann, 1928
Witten   Jozef Aertnys, 1915
Zevenaar   Andreas Masius, 1573
Zwolle   Thomas à Kempis, 1471
Alan de la Roche, 1475
Johannes van Neercassel, 1686

NEW ZEALAND   Dunedin, 1898
Thomas Bracken, 1898
Pakaraka   Henry Williams, 1867
Wellington   Suzanne Aubert, 1926
Henry Wolfe Baines, 1972

NICARAGUA   Pedro de Betanzos, 1570

NORTH AFRICA
Algiers   Raymond Lull, 1315
Jean Le Vacher, 1683
Charles Martial Allemand Lavigerie, 1892

Jerome Ribet, 1909
Carthage   Quintus Septimius Florens Tertullian, c.220
Cyprian, 258
Flavius Marcellinus, c.413
Aurelius of Carthage, 429
Blossius Aemilius Dracontius, c.505
Ferrandus, c.548
Fez   Ferdinand, 1443
Hippo   Augustine, 430
Ruspe   Fulgentius of Ruspe, 533
Sicca   Arnobius the Elder, 327
Tagaste   Alipius, 429
Tangier   Marcellus the Centurion, 298
Tunis   Louis IX, 1270
Anthony Neyrot, 1460

NORWAY
Bredcedt   Hans Nielsen Hauge, 1824
Drammen   Hallvard Vebjörnsson, 1043
Oslo   Sigmund Olaf Plytt Mowinckel, 1965
Stiklestad   Olaf II, 1030

PALESTINE
Acre   Baldwin of Canterbury, 1190
Aila   Elias of Jerusalem, 518
Bethelehem   Jerome, 420
Paula, 404
Julia Eustochium, c.419
Alexis Mallon, 1934
Caesarea   Alexander of Jerusalem, 250
Pamphilus, 310
Eusebius of Caesarea, c.340
Acacius of Caesarea, 366
Basil the Great, 379
Gelasius of Caesarea, c.395
Arethas of Caesarea, 944
Jerusalem   Cyril of Jerusalem, 386
Melania the Elder, c.410
Melania the Younger, 439
Domnus of Antioch , 449
Sabas, 532
Zacharias (Patriarch of Jerusalem), 631
John Damascene, c.754
1034, Adhemar of Chabannes, 1034
Godfrey of Bouillon, 1100
Baldwin II of Jerusalem, 1131
Felix Marie Abel, 1953
Donato Baldi, 1965
Mary (Robinson) Mother of Gethsemane, 1969
Roland Guérin de Vaux, 1971
Pierre Benoît, 1987
Lydda   George, 303

PANAMA   Lucas Fernández de Piedrahita, 1688

PAPUA   James Chalmers, 1901
Lucien Tapiedi, 1942

PARAGUAY   Reginaldo de Lizárraga, 1609
José Cataldino, 1653
Sigismundo Asperger, 1772
José Gaspar de Francia, 1840

Manuel Antonio Palacio, 1868
José Manuel Estrada, 1897
Juan Sinforiano Bogárin, 1949

PERU
Cuzco — Ignacio de Castro, 1792
Ica — José Rojas, 1839
Lake Titicaca — Ildefonso de las Muñecas, 1816
Lima — Jerónimo de Loaysa, 1575
Gaspar de Carvajal, 1584
Juan de Atienza, 1592
Bernardo Bitti, 1610
Francis Solanus, 1610
Rose of Lima, 1617
Martin de Porres, 1639
Juan Masias, 1645
Francisco de Avila, 1647
Bernabé Cobo, 1647
Alonso de Ovalle, 1651
Antonio Ruiz de Montoya, 1653
Diego de Córdova y Salinas, 1654
Cristobal de Acuña, 1670
Juan de Meléndez, 1684
Diego de Avendano, 1688
Diego Francisco de Altamirano, 1715
Francisco del Andraca y Tamayo Castillo, 1770
José de Cuero y Caicedo, 1815
Rodriguez de Mendoza, 1825
Francisco Sales de Arrieta, 1843
Vincente Rocafuerte, 1847
Francisco Javier de Luna Pizarro, 1855
José Sebastián de Goyeneche y Barreda, 1872
Pedro Gual, 1890
Juan Ambrosio Huerta, 1897
José de la Riva Aguero, 1944
Jorge Dintilhac, 1947
Potosi — Diego Álvarez de Paz, 1620
Saña — Toribio Alfonso de Mogrovejo, 1606

THE PHILIPPINES
Manila — George Joseph Kamel, 1706
William Daniel McKinnon, 1902
Francisco Marín-Sola, 1932
Terence James Sheridan, 1970
Nueva Segovia — Diego Francisco Aduarte, 1636
Parran — Vittorio Ricci, 1685

POLAND
Auschwitz — Maximilian Maria Kolbe, 1941
Grigol Peradze, 1942
Edith Stein, 1942
Biala — Marcin Bielski, 1575
Breslau — see Germany: Breslau
Chelmo — John Lobedau, 1264
Cracow — Stanislaus, 1079
Bronislawa, 1259
Prandota, 1266
Isaias Boner, 1471
John Cantius, 1473
Jan Dlugosz, 1480
Filippo Buonaccorsi, 1496
Adam Chmielowski, 1916

Bodhan Lepkyi, 1941
Frauenberg — Nicolaus Copernicus, 1543
Gdansk — Adalbert of Prague, 997
Hans Brask, 1539
Glatz — Andreas Faulhaber, 1757
Gniezno — Gaudentius of Gniezno, c.1006
Jolenta of Hungary, 1299
Jakobshagen — David Hollaz, 1713
Kalisz — Jan Laski, 1531
Leopolis — Clemente Galano, 1666
Lowicz — Stanislaw Karnkowski, 1603
Lucawice — Socinus, Fausto Paolo, 1604
Miedzyrzec — Benedict of Benevento, 1005
Posen — Gaspar Druzbicki, 1662
Poznán — Martin von Dunin, 1842
Stary Sacz — Kunigunde, 1292
Uniejow — Bogomilyof of Gniezno, 1182
Warsaw — John III Sobieski, 1696
Wladyslaw Stanislaw Reymont, 1925
Augustyn Hlond, 1948
Alexander Birkenmajer, 1967
Wroclaw — see Germany: Breslau
Zakopane — Jan Kasprowicz, 1926

PORTUGAL
Aveiro — Joan of Portugal, 1490
Braga — Fructuosus of Braga, 665
Estremoz — Elizabeth of Portugal, 1271
Lisbon — Potamius, 359
Henry of Bonn, 1147
John de Deo, 1267
João Consobrino, 1486
Francisco Foreiro, 1581
Duke of Alva, 1582
Louis of Granada, 1588
Peter da Fonseca, 1599
Francisco Suárez, 1617
Lawrence of Brindisi, 1619
Duarte Lobo, 1646
Manoel Cardoso, 1650
Daniel O'Daly, 1662
Phillip Doddridge, 1751
Gabriel Malagrida, 1761
Porto — José Ribeiro da Fonseca, 1752
Santarem — Irene of Portugal, 653
Alexandre Herculano de Carvalho e Araújo, 1877
Setubal — Royston Dunnachie Ignatius Campbell, 1957
Gaspar da Cruz, 1570

ROMANIA
Bucharest — Sophronius of Bulgaria, 1813
Dumitru Staniloae, 1993
Deva — Franz David, 1579
Gyulafehérvár — Giorgio Blandrata, 1590
Niamets — Paisius Velichkovsky, 1794

RUSSIA
Alapaevsk — Elizabeth Feodorovna, 1918
Chelyabinsk — Peter of Krutitsa, 1937
Irkutsk — Innocent of Irkutsk, 1731
Leningrad — Basil (Krivocheine) of Brussels, 1985
see also St Petersburg